Webster's New
DICTIONARY
and
Roget's
THESAURUS

THOMAS NELSON PUBLISHERS

NASHVILLE · CAMDEN · NEW YORK

Manufactured in the United States of America.

Library of Congress Cataloging in Publication Data

Webster's new dictionary
  Webster's new dictionary. And, Roget's thesaurus.

  1. English language—Dictionaries. 2. English language
—Synonyms and antonyms. I. Roget's thesaurus. 1984.
PE1628.W55686 1984   423   84-4751
ISBN 0-8407-4115-4

2 3 4 5 6 7 8 9 10 11 12 13 14 15 16 17 18 19 20 — 88 87 86

PREFACE

The American Heritage Dictionary of the English Language, edited by William Morris, presented several innovations in lexicography, principally in the areas of design and illustrations, guidance on matters of usage, and etymology. This edition of *Webster's New Dictionary,* although prepared by the staff of the American Heritage Dictionary, is an independent reference work embodying in smaller form the innovations of the parent book. It is also available in paperback form published by Dell Publishing Co., Inc. The design of this edition is adapted to present fine illustrations, maps, and charts in full-column or full-page width throughout the Dictionary. Usage notes derived from the deliberations of the American Heritage Panel on English Usage over a period of four years are included in the text. Etymologies are given throughout, and many of the words of the native Old English vocabulary are traced to their prehistoric origins in a short Appendix of Indo-European roots following the main body of the Dictionary. Above all, the definitions have been selected, and rewritten or edited, to be as accurately lucid and useful as possible.

Guide to the Dictionary

The Main Entry

The main entry is the word or phrase one looks up in the Dictionary. It is printed in boldface type a little to the left of the rest of the type.

Two or more entries that are identical in spelling but have different etymologies are entered separately; each entry bears a superscript number.

baste[1]

baste[2]

baste[3]

The entry word, whether a solid word, syllabicated word, hyphenated compound, or phrase, is alphabetized as if it were written solid.

wa·ter

Water Bearer

wa·ter·borne

water buffalo

Abbreviations are alphabetized in the same sequence as words.

Syllabication

An entry word is divided into syllables by centered dots.

rep·re·sen·ta·tion

In a phrasal entry, words that appear as separate entries are not syllabicated.

die·sel engine

Engine is a separate entry, **diesel** is not.

However, when principal parts of regular verbs appear as parts of phrasal entries, they are *not* syllabicated.

Variants

If two or more different spellings of a single word are entered, they are set in boldface type and are treated in two ways:

(1) A variant may follow the main entry, separated from it only by a comma. This indicates that the two forms are used almost equally frequently.

ax, axe

(2) When one spelling is distinctly preferred, the variant is introduced by the word "Also."

me·di·e·val . . . Also **me·di·ae·val**.

A large class of variants consists of spellings preferred in British English and sometimes used in American English. Such variants as **colour** and **centre** are labeled *Chiefly Brit.* The variant **-ise**, which occurs in many British spellings where American has **-ize** (for example, **realize, realise**), is not given unless it is also a common American variant.

When a word that has a variant occurs in a compound, the variant is not repeated at the compound; for example, the variant **colour** is given at **color**, but it is not repeated at **colorblind** and other compounds.

A variant spelling that would, if entered, fall within five entries of the preferred spelling is not entered separately.

Apart from variant spellings, which are given at the beginning of an entry, there are often two or more distinct words or phrases that have identical meaning. These alternate names for the same thing are treated as follows:

(1) The alternate name is a main entry, and the preferred form is given in the definition.

ad·ju·tant . . . *n.* **1.** . . . **2.** A stork, the marabou.

darning needle. 1. . . . **2.** A dragonfly.

bi·car·bon·ate of soda. Sodium bicarbonate.

In the last case, because the main entry is a phrasal compound, it is set in boldface type; this indicates that the entry for the preferred form is to be found in its proper alphabetical order in the letter *s*.

(2) The main entry is fully defined; if the alternate name is mentioned, it is treated as a regular synonym, i.e., it appears in lightface roman type.

Sodium bicarbonate. A white . . . ; bicarbonate of soda.

(3) If the alternate name applies only to a single sense of the definition, it is entered just after the proper part-of-speech label or definition number.

mu·si·cal . . . *adj.* . . . —*n.* musical comedy. A play . . .

an·ise . . . *n.* **1.** A plant having aromatic licorice-flavored seeds. **2.** Also **an·i·seed** . . . The seeds, used as a flavoring.

In these particular cases, **musical comedy** and **aniseed** will not be entered separately because they would fall within five entries of the main entry.

Inflected Forms

Inflected forms regarded as being irregular or offering possible spelling problems are entered in boldface type, usually in shortened form, immediately following the part-of-speech label or the numbered sense of the definition to which they apply.

base . . . **baser, basest.**

well . . . **better, best.**

fly . . . **flew, flown, flying.**

Regular inflections are normally not entered. For the purposes of this Dictionary, regular inflections include:

1. Plurals formed by suffixing *-s* or *-es*. The regular plural is shown, however, when there is an irregular variant plural or when the spell-

ing of the regular plural might present difficulty, as with words ending in -*o*.

cac·tus . . . *pl.* **-ti** (-ti′) or **-tuses**

to·ma·to . . . *pl.* **-toes.**

pi·an·o . . . *pl.* **-os.**

2. Past tenses and past participles formed by suffixing -*ed* with no other change in the verb form, as **marked, parked,** etc.
3. Present participles formed by suffixing -*ing* with no other change in the verb form, as **marking, parking,** etc.
4. Present-tense forms, with the exception of such highly irregular forms as **is, has,** etc.
5. Comparatives and superlatives formed by suffixing -*er* and -*est* with no other change in the positive form of the adjective and adverb, as **taller, tallest,** etc.

The inflected forms of verbs are given in the following order: past tense, past participle (if it differs from the past tense), and present participle.

fly . . . **flew, flown, flying.**

Alternate inflected forms are given and labeled.

Irregular inflected forms that would fall within five entries of the main entry are not entered separately; in such cases they are pronounced at the main entry. If, however, they fall more than five entries from the main entry (i.e., the infinitive form of a verb, the singular of a noun, etc.), they are separately entered, pronounced, and identified by italicized abbreviations as a part or parts of a verb, comparative of an adjective, plural of a noun, etc.

Order of Definitions

When an entry has multiple numbered definitions, these are ordered by a method of synchronic semantic analysis intended to serve the convenience of the general user of the Dictionary. The numerical order does not indicate the historical sequence in which the senses developed. The first definition, then, is not necessarily the earliest sense of the word, though it may be. Rather, the first definition is the central meaning about which the other senses can most logically be organized. The organization seeks to clarify the fact that, despite its various meanings, the entry is a single "word" and not a number of separate words that happen to be spelled the same way.

Numbers and Letters

When an entry has more than one definition, these are numbered in sequence. In a *combined entry* (one in which the entry word belongs to more than one part of speech), the definitions are numbered in separate sequences beginning with **1.** after each part of speech.

be·hind . . . *adv.* **1.** In, to, or toward the rear . . . **2.** In a place . . . **3.** In arrears; late. —*prep.* **1.** At the back of . . . **2.** On the further side of . . .

When a numbered definition has two or more closely related senses, these are marked **a., b.,** etc.

lat·i·tude . . . *n.* **1.** . . . **2.** . . . **3. a.** The angular distance N or S of the equator, measured in degrees along a meridian. **b.** A region considered in relation to this distance.

When a general definition is further qualified by several specific meanings, the letters **a., b.,** etc., are used.

card[1] . . . *n.* **1.** A small, flat piece of stiff paper or thin pasteboard with numerous uses: **a.** One of a set . . . **b.** A post card. **c.** One bearing . . .

Numbered Boldface Definitions Plurals

If a noun has, in addition to its ordinary sense, a sense or senses in which it often appears in the plural, this fact is indicated as follows:

ground . . . *n.* **1.** . . . **4.** Often **grounds.** The foundation or basis . . .

If a noun is *always* used in the plural or if the plural form takes a singular verb, the plural form appears in boldface before the definition and the parenthetical grammatical note.

com·mon . . . *adj.* **1.** Belonging equally to all; joint . . . —*n.* **1.** A tract of land . . . **2. Commons.** The lower house of Parliament . . .

gut . . . *n.* **1.** . . . **4. guts.** *Slang.* Courage; fortitude.

a·cous·tic . . . *adj.* Also **a·cous·ti·cal.** Pertaining to sound . . . —*n.* **acoustics. 1.** (*takes sing. v.*). The scientific study of sound. **2.** (*takes pl. v.*). The total effect . . .

Combined Upper-case and Lower-case Forms

When upper-case and lower-case words of the same spelling have the same etymology, both forms are usually included in the same entry.

If the lower-case form is a common word with a specific upper-case sense, the lower-case form is the main entry. Most upper-case and lower-case combinations are of this sort.

sav·ior . . . *n.* Also **sav·iour. 1.** One who . . . **2. the Savior.** Christ.

If, on the other hand, the upper-case form is the original sense and is still current, it is the main entry.

A·pol·lo . . . *n.* **1.** Greek sun god, patron of . . . **2. apollo.** Any young man . . .

The word "Often" immediately following a boldface number indicates that a word is often or usually upper-case (or lower-case) in that sense.

cock·ney . . . *n.* **1.** Often **Cockney.** A native of . . . **2.** The dialect . . .

Part-of-Speech Labels

The italicized labels below, which follow the pronunciation of the entry word, are used to indicate parts of speech.

n.	noun
adj.	adjective
adv.	adverb
pron.	pronoun
conj.	conjunction
prep.	preposition
v.	verb
interj.	interjection
comb. form.	combining form

The following additional italicized labels are used to indicate inflected forms:

fem.n.	feminine noun
pl.	plural
sing.	singular
pres.p.	present participle
p.t.	past tense
p.p.	past participle
compar.	comparative
superl.	superlative

Part-of-Speech Labels in Combined Entries

In combined entries, the part-of-speech labels that follow the first one are preceded by a dash. Such labels precede all elements that apply to that part of speech, and may be followed by any elements (pronunciation, other labels, etc.) that can appear immediately following the main-entry word, its pronunciation, etc.

ad·lib . . . *v.* **-libbed, -libbing.** To improvise . . . —*n.* Something ad-libbed . . .

If, however, a language, status, or field label applies to a whole entry, the label precedes all part-of-speech labels.

mug² . . . *Slang. n.* **1.** The face . . . **2.** . . . —*v.* **mugged, mugging. 1.** . . .

Verbs

Parentheses are used to indicate a direct object or an intransitive sense in which the object of the verb is included.

ad·min·is·ter . . . *v.* **1.** To manage. **2. a.** To give (a drug) remedially. **b.** To dispense (a sacrament) . . .

Parentheses are also used around a final preposition to indicate that a verb can be used either transitively or intransitively in that sense, i.e., that it can be followed by a direct object or that its object may be omitted entirely.

kink . . . *n.* **1.** A small, tight . . . —*v.* To form kinks (in).

Idioms

Many entry words are commonly used in phrases the meaning of which is not clear from the meanings of the separate words. Except as noted, such phrases are defined at the entry for the most significant word in the phrase. The phrase is introduced by a boldface dash and is set in boldface type. Phrases such as **water buffalo**, made up of an attributive

(adjective or noun) plus a noun, are separate main entries. Verb phrases that form nouns are also separate main entries; for example, **make up** is a separate entry because of the noun **make-up**.

Main Entry Words Having Meaning Only in a Phrase

A certain small class of words has current meaning only in phrasal combinations and is so treated.

a·back . . . *adv.* —**take aback.** To startle; confuse.

re·ly . . . *v.* **-lied, -lying.** —**rely on** (or **upon**). **1.** To depend. **2.** To trust confidently.

Usage Labels

Usage labels are restrictive labels that serve to warn the reader that a term is not properly available for use in all contexts. A usage label applies only to the definition or definitions that follow it. A single entry may have standard (unlabeled) definitions and any combination of labeled definitions.

Informal signifies "cultivated colloquial," that is, the speech of educated persons when they are more interested in what they are saying than in how they are saying it. *Informal* terms are also used in writing that seeks the effect of speech, but they are not used in formal writing.

Slang does not define a level of speech, as does *Informal,* but a style having features that are usually not hard to identify. Slang may occur in all but the most formal language and remain slang. A primary rule to distinguish it from nonstandard speech is that a slang term may not be used merely to indicate the meaning of a word; it always carries some deliberately informal connotation in addition and suggests some intention—however dully conceived—of rhetorical effect, such as incongruity, hyberbole, irreverence, etc.

Nonstandard, unlike *Informal* and *Slang,* indicates usages that are widespread but not acceptable. It includes forms such as "irregardless" and "ain't."

Obsolete (Obs.) is for obsolete words, few of which are entered; in order to be entered an obsolete term must have appeared in standard literature either frequently or prominently. (A distinction must be made between a term for an obsolete thing and a term that is itself obsolete. The former is not labeled, but the historical situation is explained in the definition, e.g., "An 18th-century hat . . .")

Archaic is used for terms that were once common and continue to have some use, but are now used only to suggest an earlier style. The label does not suggest a date beyond which a word cannot be found, merely that when it is found in a contemporary context, it is readily identifiable as belonging to a style of language no longer in general use.

Rare terms were never common. The label does not imply *Archaic;* a rare term may be of recent coinage. The label is not used for terms whose use is rare because of the limitation of their application, such as abstruse technical terms; it is confined to general terms for which more common synonyms are available.

Poetic is used for such locutions as a shortening (*o'er*) that is or was common in poetry but was never common in prose.

Regional is used for terms that are not common to American speech in general but exist in more than one locality.

Other Labels

Important words belonging to major English dialectal areas of the U.S. or outside the U.S. are so labeled.

Etymologies

Etymologies appear in square brackets following the definitions. [?] indicates "of obscure origin." The symbol < is used to mean "from" and is often an indication that transitional stages have been omitted in order to give a concise history of the word. The etymologies of most basic words are given, with particular emphasis on native words (i.e., words derived from Old English) having their origins in Indo-European. Many of these cross-refer to the Appendix, which begins on page 807.

The abbreviations used in etymologies usually appear as main entries in their proper alphabetical order; they are all listed in "Abbreviations and Symbols used in Etymologies," on page XII.

Field Labels

An italicized word or abbreviation denoting a specific subject and preceding a definition indicates a specialized sense not identical with any other sense the word may have apart from the labeled field.

Abbreviations

Abbreviations are included as main entries in the vocabulary.

Pronunciation

Pronunciation is given for all main entries and for other forms as needed. It is indicated in parentheses following the form to which it applies.

The set of symbols used is designed to enable the reader to reproduce a satisfactory pronunciation with no more than quick reference to the key. All pronunciations given are acceptable in all circumstances. When more than one is given, the first is assumed to be the most common, but the difference in frequency may be insignificant.

It is obvious that Americans do not all speak alike. It is equally obvious, nevertheless, that Americans can understand one another, at least on the level of speech sounds. In fact, the differences among the major regional varieties of American speech are such that for most words a single set of symbols can represent the pronunciation found in each

regional variety, provided the symbols are planned for the purpose stated above: to enable the reader to reproduce a satisfactory pronunciation. When a single pronunciation is offered in this Dictionary, the reader will supply those features of his own regional speech that are called forth by his reading of the key. Apart from regional variations in pronunciation, there are variations among social groups. The pronunciations recorded in this Dictionary are exclusively those of educated speech. In every community, educated speech is accepted and understood by everyone, including those who do not themselves use it.

Pronunciation Key

A shorter form of this key appears across the bottom of each pair of facing pages. The symbols marked with an asterisk are discussed in this guide.

spellings	AHD
pat	ă
pay	ā
care	*âr
father	ä
bib	b
church	ch
deed, milled	d
pet	ĕ
bee	ē
fife, phase	f
gag	g
hat	h
which	hw
pit	*ĭ
pie, by	ī
pier	*îr
judge	j
kick, cat, pique	k
lid, needle	*l (nēd′l)
mum	m
no, sudden	*n (sŭd′n)
thing	ng
pot, *horrid	ŏ
toe, *hoarse	ō
caught, paw, *for	ô
noise	oi
took	o͝o
boot	o͞o
out	ou
pop	p
roar	*r
sauce	s
ship, dish	sh
tight, stopped	t
thin	th
this	*th*
cut	ŭ
urge, term, firm, word, heard	*ûr
valve	v
with	w
yes	y
zebra, xylem	z
vision, pleasure, garage	zh
about, item, edible, gallop, circus	*ə
butter	*ər

FOREIGN

French **a**mi	à
French **f**eu,	œ
German sch**ö**n	
French t**u**,	ü
German **ü**ber	
German i**ch**,	KH
Scottish lo**ch**	
French bo**n**	N̈
French compiè**gne**	y' (kôN-pyĕn′y')

STRESS

Primary stress **′**	**bi·ol′o·gy** (bī-ŏl′ə-jē)
Secondary stress **′**	**bi′o·log′i·cal** (bī′ə-lŏj′ĭ-kəl)

Explanatory Notes

ə: This nonalphabetical symbol is called a *schwa*. The symbol is used in the Dictionary to represent only a reduced vowel, i.e., a vowel that receives the weakest level of stress (which can be thought of as no stress) within a word and therefore nearly always exhibits a change in quality from the quality it would have if it were stressed, as in *telegraph* (tĕl′ə-grăf′) and *telegraphy* (tə-lĕg′rə-fē). Vowels are never reduced to a single exact vowel; the schwa sound will vary, sometimes according to the "full" vowel it is representing and often according to its phonetic environment.

ĭ: This symbol is used to represent the second vowel in **artist** (är′tĭst), a vowel that has been only partially reduced and therefore cannot be represented by the schwa. The choice between schwa (ə) and "breve i" (ĭ) to represent reduced vowels is arrived at through a complex set of considerations. In nearly every case in which (ĭ) appears, there is also a variant pronunciation closer to (ə). As long as reduced vowels receive no stress, the surrounding sounds will lead the reader to produce either (ə) or (ĭ), according to his regional speech pattern.

/y/: The *y* between virgules indicates that the sound is present in the pronunciation of some speakers and absent from the pronunciation of others, as in the word *duty*, where two pronunciations may occur, (dōō′tē) and (dyōō′tē). In this Dictionary both pronunciations are represented in (d/y/ōō′tē).

âr These symbols represent vowels that
îr have been altered by a following *r*. This
ûr situation is traditionally exemplified by
ər the words *Mary, merry,* and *marry*. In some regional varieties all three are pronounced alike: (mĕr′ē). However, in a broad range of individual American speech patterns cutting across regional boundaries, the three words are distinguished. It is this pattern that the Dictionary represents, thus: *Mary* (mâr′ē), *merry* (mĕr′ē), *marry* (măr′ē). Some words, however, are heard in all three

pronunciations, indistinctly grading one into another. For these words the Dictionary represents only (âr), for example, *care* (kâr), *dairy* (dâr′ē).

In words such as *hear, beer,* and *dear,* the vowel could be represented by (ē) were it not for the effect of the following *r*, which makes it approach (ĭ) in sound. In this Dictionary a special symbol (îr) is used for this combination, as in *beer* (bîr).

There are regional differences in the distinctions among various pronunciations of the syllable *-or.* In pairs such as *for, four; horse, hoarse;* and *morning, mourning,* the vowel varies between (ô) and (ō). In this Dictionary these vowels are represented as follows: *for* (fôr), *four* (fôr, fōr); *horse* (hôrs), *hoarse* (hôrs, hōrs). Other words for which both forms are shown include those such as *more* (môr, mōr) and *glory* (glôr′ē, glōr′-).

Another group of words with variations for the *-or* syllable includes words such as *forest* and *horrid,* in which the pronunciation of *o* before *r* varies between (ô) and (ŏ). In these words the (ôr) pronunciation is given first: *forest* (fôr′ĭst, fŏr′-).

The symbol (ûr) used in *her* (hûr), *fur* (fûr), etc., has a regular regional variant that is not separately recorded. In one pattern the effect of the *r* is heard simultaneously with the vowel; in the other some, but not all, such syllables are heard with a vowel like ŭ or ə before the onset of the *r*.

Syllabic Consonants

There are two consonants that are represented as complete syllables. These are *l* and *n* (called *syllabics*) following stressed syllables ending in *d* or *t* in such words as *bottle* (bŏt′l), *fatal* (fāt′l), *button* (bŭt′n), *ladle* (lād′l), and *hidden* (hĭd′n). Syllabic *n* is not shown after a syllable ending in *-nd* or *-nt: abandon* (ə-băn′dən), *mountain* (moun′tən); but syllabic *l* is shown in that position: *spindle* (spĭnd′l).

Stress

In this Dictionary, stress, the relative degree of loudness with which the syllables of a word (or phrase) are spoken, is indicated in three different ways. An unmarked syllable has the weakest stress in the word. The strongest stress is marked with a bold mark (′). An intermediate level of stress, here called *secondary,* is marked with a similar but lighter mark (′).

Words of one syllable show no stress mark, since there is no other stress level to which the syllable is compared.

The pronunciations are syllabicated for clarity. Syllabication of the pronunciation does not necessarily match the syllabication of the entry word being pronounced. The former follows strict, though not obvious, phonological rules; the latter represents the established practice of printers and editors.

ABBREVIATIONS AND SYMBOLS
USED IN ETYMOLOGIES

abbr, abbreviation
abl, ablative
acc, accusative
Afr, African
Afrik, Afrikaans
Algon, Algonquian
aor, aorist
Ar, Arabic
Aram, Aramaic
Assyr, Assyrian
aug, augmentative
Av, Avestan
Brit, British
Bulg, Bulgarian
Cant, Cantonese
Celt, Celtic
Chin, Chinese
Corn, Cornish
CRom, Common Romance
Dan, Danish
dat, dative
dial, dialectal
dim, diminutive
Dravid, Dravidian
Du, Dutch
Egypt, Egyptian
Eng, English
Esk, Eskimo
etym, etymology
expr, expressive
F, French
fem, feminine
Frank, Frankish
freq, frequentative
Fris, Frisian
fut, future
G, German
gen, genitive
Gk, Greek
Gmc, Germanic
Goth, Gothic
Heb, Hebrew
Hitt, Hittite
Hung, Hungarian

Icel, Icelandic
IE, Indo-European
imit, imitative
Ind, Indic
Ir, Irish
Iran, Iranian
It, Italian
Ital, Italic
Jap, Japanese
L, Latin
Latv, Latvian
LG, Low German
LGk, Late Greek
Lith, Lithuanian
LL, Late Latin
Mand, Mandarin
masc, masculine
MDu, Middle Dutch
ME, Middle English
Medit, Mediterranean
Mex, Mexican
MGk, Medieval Greek
MHG, Middle High
  German
ML, Medieval Latin
MLG, Middle Low German
Nah, Nahuatl
neut, neuter
NF, Norman French
NL, New Latin
nom, nominative
Norw, Norwegian
OCS, Old Church Slavonic
OE, Old English
OF, Old French
OHG, Old High German
OIr, Old Irish
OIt, Old Italian
ON, Old Norse
ONF, Old North French
OP, Old Persian
OProv, Old Provençal
orig, originally
OS, Old Saxon

OSpan, Old Spanish
OSwed, Old Swedish
part, participle
perf, perfect
perh, perhaps
Pers, Persian
Phoen, Phoenician
pl, plural
Pol, Polish
Port, Portuguese
poss, possibly
pp, past participle
pres, present
prob, probably
pron, pronoun
Prov, Provençal
prp, present participle
pt, past tense
redupl, reduplicated
refl, reflexive
Rum, Rumanian
Russ, Russian
Scand, Scandinavian
Scot, Scottish
Sem, Semitic
sing, singular
Sk, Sanskrit
Slav, Slavic
Span, Spanish
superl, superlative
Sw, Swedish
Tag, Tagalog
Tam, Tamil
Tokh, Tokharian
trans, translation
Turk, Turkish
var, variant
VL, Vulgar Latin
W, Welsh
Yidd, Yiddish
< from
[?] Of obscure origin
* unattested

Aa

a, A (ā) *n.* **1.** The 1st letter of the English alphabet. **2.** The 1st in a series. **3.** The highest grade in quality.

a **1.** are (measurement). **2.** *Phys.* atto-.

A **1.** acre. **2.** ammeter. **3.** ampere. **4.** area. **5.** The 6th tone in the scale of C major.

a. **1.** acceleration. **2.** acre. **3.** acreage. **4.** adjective. **5.** anonymous. **6.** answer. **7.** are (measurement).

A. **1.** acre. **2.** alto. **3.** America; American. **4.** answer.

a (ə; *emphatic* ā) *indef. art.* **1. a.** —Used before a noun to indicate nonspecific membership in a class or category: *a generous man.* **b.** —Used before a plural noun with an intervening adjective: *a few phrases.* **2. a.** Similar; like: *birds of a feather.* **b.** Any: *not a drop left.* **3.** —Used prepositionally to indicate *in* or *for each*: *take one a day.* **4.** —Used before nouns that begin with a consonant sound: *a book.* [< OE *ān,* one. See oino-.]

a-¹. *comb. form.* Without, not, or opposite to: **amoral.** [< Gk *an,* not.]

a-². *comb. form.* **1.** On or in: **aboard.** **2.** In the act of: *a-fishing.* **3.** In the direction of, situated at, or toward: **astern.** [< OE *an, on,* ON.]

a-³. *comb. form.* **1.** Up, out, or away: **awake.** **2.** Intensified action: **amaze.** [< OE *ā-.*]

a-⁴. *comb. form.* Of or from: **anew.** [< OE *of,* OF.]

AA Alcoholics Anonymous.

A.A. Associate in Arts.

AAA **1.** American Automobile Association. **2.** antiaircraft artillery.

aard·vark (ärd'värk') *n.* A burrowing African mammal having large ears and a long snout. [Obs Afrik, "earth-pig."]

ab. about.

A.B. Bachelor of Arts.

a·back (ə-băk') *adv.* —**take aback.** To startle; confuse.

ab·a·cus (ăb'ə-kəs) *n., pl.* **-cuses** or **-ci** (-sī'). A manual computing device consisting of a

abacus

frame holding parallel rods strung with movable counters. [< Gk *abax,* slab.]

a·baft (ə-băft', ə-bäft') *adv.* Toward the stern. —*prep.* Toward the stern from. [< ON + OE *beæftan,* behind.]

ab·a·lo·ne (ăb'ə-lō'nē) *n.* A marine mollusk having a large, ear-shaped shell. [Amer Span *abulón.*]

a·ban·don (ə-băn'dən) *v.* **1.** To give up; forsake. **2.** To desert. **3.** To desist from. —*n.* A complete surrender of inhibitions. [< OF *(metre) a bandon,* "(to put) in ɔne's power."] —**a·ban'don·er** *n.* —**a·ban'don·ment** *n.*

a·ban·doned (ə-băn'dənd) *adj.* Shameless; immoral. —**a·ban'doned·ly** *adv.*

a·base (ə-bās') *v.* **abased, abasing.** To humble; humiliate. —**a·base'ment** *n.* —**a·bas'er** *n.*

a·bash (ə-băsh') *v.* To make ashamed or uneasy; embarrass; disconcert. [< OF *esbahir,* to gape at.] —**a·bash'ment** *n.*

a·bate (ə-bāt') *v.* **abated, abating.** **1.** To reduce in amount, degree, or intensity; lessen. **2.** To put an end to. [< OF *abattre,* to beat down.] —**a·bat'a·ble** *adj.* —**a·bat'er** *n.*

a·bate·ment (ə-bāt'mənt) *n.* **1.** Diminution in degree or intensity. **2.** The amount abated; reduction.

ab·bé (ăb'ā, ă-bā') *n.* In France, a title given to a priest.

ab·bess (ăb'ĭs) *n.* The female superior of a convent of nuns.

ab·bey (ăb'ē) *n., pl.* **-beys.** **1.** A monastery or convent. **2.** An abbey church. [< LL *abbātia* < *abbās,* ABBOT.]

ab·bot (ăb'ət) *n.* The superior of a monastery. [< OE *abbod* < LL *abbās* < Aram *abbā,* father.] —**ab'bot·ship'** *n.*

abbr. abbreviation.

ab·bre·vi·ate (ə-brē'vē-āt') *v.* **-ated, -ating.** To make shorter, esp. to reduce to an abbreviation. [< LL *abbreviāre,* to shorten.] —**ab·bre'vi·a'tor** (-ā'tər) *n.*

ab·bre·vi·a·tion (ə-brē'vē-ā'shən) *n.* **1.** The act or product of abbreviating. **2.** A shortened form of a word or phrase, as *Mass.* for *Massachusetts.*

ab·di·cate (ăb'dĭ-kāt') *v.* **-cated, -cating.** To relinquish (power or responsibility) formally. [L *abdicāre,* to disclaim.] —**ab'di·ca'tion** *n.*

ab·do·men (ăb'də-mən, ăb-dō'mən) *n.* The part of the mammalian body between the thorax and the pelvis. [L *abdōmen,* belly.] —**ab·dom'i·nal** (-dŏm'ə-nəl) *adj.*

ab·duct (ăb-dŭkt') *v.* To carry off by force; kidnap. [L *abdūcere.*] —**ab·duc'tion** *n.* —**ab·duc'tor** *n.*

a•beam (ə-bēm') *adv.* At right angles to the keel of a ship.

a•bed (ə-bĕd') *adv.* In bed.

ab•er•ra•tion (ăb'ə-rā'shən) *n.* 1. Deviation or departure from the normal, the typical, or the expected. 2. a. Blurring or distortion of an image. b. A defect, as in a mirror or lens, causing such distortion. [< L *aberrāre*, to go astray.] —**ab•er'rant** *adj.*

a•bet (ə-bĕt') *v.* abetted, abetting. 1. To encourage; incite. 2. To assist. [< OF *abeter*, to entice.] —**a•bet'ment** *n.* —**a•bet'tor, a•bet'ter** *n.*

a•bey•ance (ə-bā'əns) *n.* The condition of being temporarily set aside; suspension. [< OF *abeance*, desire < *abaer*, "to gape at."]

ab•hor (ăb-hôr') *v.* -horred, -horring. To dislike intensely; loathe. [< L *abhorrēre*, to shrink from.] —**ab•hor'rence** (-hôr'əns, -hŏr'əns) *n.*

ab•hor•rent (ăb-hôr'ənt, -hŏr'ənt) *adj.* Disgusting; loathsome. —**ab•hor'rent•ly** *adv.*

a•bide (ə-bīd') *v.* abode or abided, abiding. 1. To be in store for; await. 2. To tolerate; bear. 3. To remain; last. —**abide by.** To conform to; comply with. [< OE *ābīdan.*]

Ab•i•djan (ăb'ĭ-jän'). The capital of the Ivory Coast. Pop. 258,000.

a•bil•i•ty (ə-bĭl'ə-tē) *n., pl.* -ties. 1. The quality of being able to do something; power to perform. 2. A skill or talent. [< L *habilitās* < *habilis,* ABLE.]

ab•ject (ăb'jĕkt', ăb-jĕkt') *adj.* 1. Contemptible; mean; base. 2. Miserable; wretched. [< L *abjicere,* to cast away.] —**ab'jec'tion** *n.* —**ab'ject'ly** *adv.* —**ab'ject'ness** *n.*

ab•jure (ăb-jŏŏr') *v.* -jured, -juring. 1. To recant solemnly. 2. To renounce under oath; forswear. [< L *abjūrāre.*] —**ab•jur'er** *n.*

abl. ablative.

ab•la•tion (ă-blā'shən) *n.* A wearing away; erosion. [< L *ablātus,* "removed."]

ab•la•tive (ăb'lə-tĭv) *adj.* Designating a grammatical case indicating separation, direction away from, and sometimes manner or agency, found in some Indo-European languages. [< L *ablātivus,* "expressing removal."] —**ab'la•ti'val** (ăb'lə-tī'vəl) *adj.* —**ab'la•tive** *n.*

a•blaze (ə-blāz') *adj.* 1. On fire. 2. Radiant with bright color.

a•ble (ā'bəl) *adj.* abler, ablest. 1. Having sufficient ability. 2. Capable or talented. [< L *habilis,* manageable < *habēre,* to handle.] —**a'bly** *adv.*

–able, –ible. *comb. form.* 1. Susceptible, capable, or worthy of (the action of a verb or implied verb): **debatable.** 2. Inclined to (the nature of a noun or implied noun): **knowledgeable.**

a•ble-bod•ied (ā'bəl-bŏd'ēd) *adj.* Physically strong and healthy.

able-bodied seaman. A merchant seaman certified for all seaman's duties.

ab•lu•tion (ă-blōō'shən) *n.* A washing of the body, esp. with religious connotation. [< L *abluere,* to wash away.]

ab•ne•gate (ăb'nĭ-gāt') *v.* -gated, -gating. To deny to oneself; renounce. [L *abnegāre,* to refuse.] —**ab'ne•ga'tion** *n.*

ab•nor•mal (ăb-nôr'məl) *adj.* Not normal; deviant. —**ab•nor'mal•ly** *adv.*

ab•nor•mal•i•ty (ăb'nôr-măl'ə-tē) *n., pl.* -ties. 1. An abnormal state or condition. 2. An abnormal phenomenon.

a•board (ə-bôrd', ə-bōrd') *adv.* On board a ship or other vehicle. —*prep.* On board of.

a•bode (ə-bōd'). *p.t.* & *p.p.* of **abide.** —*n.* A dwelling place; home.

a•bol•ish (ə-bŏl'ĭsh) *v.* To put an end to; annul. [< L *abolēre,* to destroy.]

ab•o•li•tion (ăb'ə-lĭsh'ən) *n.* 1. An act of abolishing or the state of being abolished; annulment. 2. **Abolition.** The termination of slavery in the U.S. —**ab'o•li'tion•ar'y** *adj.*

ab•o•li•tion•ism (ăb'ə-lĭsh'ən-ĭz'əm) *n.* Advocacy of the abolition of slavery in the U.S. —**ab'o•li'tion•ist** *n.*

A-bomb (ā'bŏm') *n.* An atomic bomb.

a•bom•i•na•ble (ə-bŏm'ə-nə-bəl) *adj.* Detestable; loathsome. —**a•bom'i•na•bly** *adv.*

a•bom•i•nate (ə-bŏm'ə-nāt') *v.* -nated, -nating. To detest; abhor. [L *abōmināri,* "to shun as a bad omen."] —**a•bom'i•na'tor** *n.*

a•bom•i•na•tion (ə-bŏm'ə-nā'shən) *n.* 1. A great dislike; loathing. 2. Something that elicits great dislike.

ab•o•rig•i•nal (ăb'ə-rĭj'ə-nəl) *adj.* Native; indigenous. —*n.* An aborigine.

ab•o•rig•i•ne (ăb'ə-rĭj'ə-nē') *n.* One of the original inhabitants of a region. [< L *Aborigines,* name of a pre-Roman people.]

a•bort (ə-bôrt') *v.* To terminate pregnancy or full development prematurely. [L *abortāre,* freq of *aborīrī,* to die, disappear.] —**a•bor'tive** *adj.* —**a•bor'tive•ly** *adv.*

a•bor•tion (ə-bôr'shən) *n.* 1. Induced premature termination of pregnancy or development. 2. Something malformed or incompletely developed. —**a•bor'tion•al** *adj.*

a•bor•tion•ist (ə-bôr'shən-ĭst) *n.* One who performs illegal abortions.

a•bound (ə-bound') *v.* 1. To be great in number or amount. 2. To be fully supplied; teem. [< L *abundāre,* to overflow.]

a•bout (ə-bout') *adv.* 1. Approximately; nearly. 2. Toward a reverse direction. 3. Aimlessly: *wander about.* 4. In the vicinity. —*prep.* 1. On all sides of. 2. Near to. 3. Here and there; in or on: *strolled about the grounds.* 4. Concerning. 5. Ready to commence: *about to leave.* —*adj.* Astir: *up and about.* [< OE *būtan.* See **ud-.**]

a•bout-face (ə-bout'fās') *n.* A reversal of orientation or attitude.

a•bove (ə-bŭv') *adv.* 1. Overhead: *the sky above.* 2. In heaven. 3. Upstairs. 4. In a higher place. 5. In an earlier part of a text. 6. In a higher rank or position. —*prep.* 1. Over. 2. Superior to: *Principles are above expediency.* 3. Beyond the level or reach of. 4. In preference to. —*n.* Something that is above. —*adj.* Appearing earlier in the same text. [< OE *abufan.* See **upo.**]

a•bove•board (ə-bŭv'bôrd', -bōrd') *adv.* Without deceit. —**a•bove'board'** *adj.*

abr. abridged; abridgment.

ab•ra•ca•dab•ra (ăb'rə-kə-dăb'rə) *n.* 1. A word held to possess supernatural powers to ward off disaster. **2.** Jargon; gibberish. [< LGk *abrasadabra*, a magic word.]

a·brade (ə-brād′) *v.* **abraded, abrading.** To wear away by friction. [L *abrādere*, to scrape off.] —**a·brad′er** *n.*

A·bra·ham (ā′brə-hăm′). The 1st patriarch and progenitor of the Hebrew people.

ab·ra·sion (ə-brā′zhən) *n.* **1.** A wearing away by friction. **2.** A scraped or worn area.

ab·ra·sive (ə-brā′sĭv, -zĭv) *adj.* Causing abrasion. —*n.* An abrasive substance.

a·breast (ə-brĕst′) *adv.* Side by side. —**abreast of** (or **with**). Keeping up with.

a·bridge (ə-brĭj′) *v.* **abridged, abridging.** To reduce the length of; condense; shorten. [< LL *abbreviāre,* ABBREVIATE.] —**a·brid′ger** *n.* —**a·bridg′ment, a·bridge′ment** *n.*

a·broad (ə-brôd′) *adv.* **1.** Out of one's own country. **2.** Out of doors. **3.** Broadly; widely. [ME *abro(o)d,* "broadly, widely scattered."]

ab·ro·gate (ăb′rō-gāt′) *v.* **-gated, -gating.** To put an end to; abolish; annul. [L *abrogāre.*] —**ab′ro·ga′tion** *n.* —**ab′ro·ga′tor** *n.*

a·brupt (ə-brŭpt′) *adj.* **1.** Unexpectedly sudden. **2.** Curt; brusque. **3.** Jerky; disconnected: *abrupt, nervous prose.* **4.** Steeply inclined. [< L *abrumpere,* to break off.] —**a·brupt′ly** *adv.* —**a·brupt′ness** *n.*

abs **1.** absolute; absolutely. **2.** absolute temperature.

ab·scess (ăb′sĕs′) *n.* A localized collection of pus surrounded by inflamed tissue. [L *abscēssus,* "a going away."]

ab·scise (ăb-sīz′) *v.* **-scised, -scising.** To cut off; remove. [L *abscindere.*] —**ab·scis′sion** (-sĭzh′ən) *n.*

ab·scis·sa (ăb-sĭs′ə) *n., pl.* **-sas** or **-scissae** (-sĭs′ē′). *Math.* The coordinate representing the distance of a point from the *y*-axis in a plane Cartesian coordinate system, measured along a line parallel to the *x*-axis. [< L *abscindere,* ABSCISE.]

ab·scond (ăb-skŏnd′) *v.* To leave quickly and secretly and hide oneself. [L *abscondere.*] —**ab·scond′er** *n.*

ab·sence (ăb′səns) *n.* **1.** The state of being away. **2.** The time during which one is away. **3.** Lack: *an absence of curiosity.*

ab·sent (ăb′sənt) *adj.* **1.** Not present. **2.** Not existent; lacking. **3.** Inattentive. —*v.* (ăb-sĕnt′). To keep (oneself) away. [< L *abesse,* to be away.] —**ab′sent·ly** *adv.*

ab·sen·tee (ăb′sən-tē′) *n.* One who is absent. —*adj.* Of or pertaining to one who is absent.

ab·sen·tee·ism (ăb′sən-tē′ĭz′əm) *n.* Habitual failure to appear, esp. for work.

ab·sent-mind·ed (ăb′sənt-mīn′dĭd) *adj.* Heedless of one's surroundings; preoccupied. —**ab′-sent-mind′ed·ly** *adv.*

ab·sinthe (ăb′sĭnth) *n.* A strong green liqueur made from wormwood. [< L *absinthium,* wormwood.] —**ab·sin′thi·an** *adj.*

ab·so·lute (ăb′sə-lōōt′) *adj.* **1.** Perfect in quality or nature; complete. **2.** Not mixed; pure. **3. a.** Not limited by restrictions or exceptions; unconditional. **b.** Unqualified in extent or degree; total. **4.** Not to be doubted or questioned; positive. **5.** Lacking a particular gram-

matical connection with other words in a sentence: *an absolute phrase.* [< L *absolvere,* to free from, complete.] —**ab′so·lute′ly** *adv.* —**ab′-so·lute′ness** *n.*

absolute value. The numerical value of a quantity without regard to its sign.

absolute zero. The temperature at which substances possess minimal energy, equal to –273.15°C or –459.67°F.

ab·so·lu·tion (ăb′sə-lōō′shən) *n. R.C.Ch.* The formal remission of sin imparted by a priest as part of the sacrament of penance.

ab·so·lut·ism (ăb′sə-lōō′tĭz′əm) *n.* **1.** Government in which all power is vested in the ruler. **2.** The political theory reflecting this. —**ab′so·lut′ist** *n.* & *adj.* —**ab′so·lu·tis′tic** *adj.*

ab·solve (ăb-zŏlv′, -sŏlv′) *v.* **-solved, -solving. 1.** To set free from guilt, an obligation, etc.; acquit. **2. a.** To grant a remission of sin to. **b.** To remit (a sin). [< L *absolvere,* to free from.] —**ab·solv′a·ble** *adj.*

ab·sorb (ăb-sôrb′, -zôrb′) *v.* **1.** To take in through or as through pores or interstices; soak in or up. **2.** To occupy the full attention of; engross. [< L *absorbēre.*]

ab·sorb·ent (ăb-sôr′bənt, ăb-zôr′-) *adj.* Capable of absorbing something. —*n.* A substance that absorbs. —**ab·sorb′en·cy** *n.*

ab·stain (ăb-stān′) *v.* To refrain from; forbear. [< L *abstinēre,* to hold (oneself) back.] —**ab·stain′er** *n.*

ab·ste·mi·ous (ăb-stē′mē-əs) *adj.* Eating and drinking in moderation. [L *abstēmius.*]

ab·sti·nence (ăb′stə-nəns) *n.* **1.** Restraint of one's desires. **2.** A refraining from drinking alcoholic beverages or from eating certain foods. —**ab′sti·nent** *adj.*

ab·stract (ăb-străkt′, ăb′străkt′) *adj.* **1.** Considered apart from concrete existence or a specification thereof. **2.** Theoretical; not applied or practical. **3.** Thought of or stated without reference to a specific instance. **4.** *Fine Arts.* Having nonobjective design, form, or content. —*n.* (ăb′străkt′). **1.** A summary. **2.** Something abstract, as a term. —*v.* (ăb-străkt′). **1.** To take away; remove. **2.** To filch; steal. **3.** (ăb′străkt′). To summarize. [< L *abstractus,* "removed from (concrete reality)."]

ab·strac·tion (ăb-străk′shən) *n.* **1.** The act or process of abstracting. **2.** A product of this process; a general idea or word representing a physical concept. **3.** Preoccupation. **4.** An abstract work of art.

ab·struse (ăb-strōōs′) *adj.* Difficult to understand; recondite. [< L *abstrūdere,* to hide.] —**ab·struse′ly** *adv.* —**ab·struse′ness** *n.*

ab·surd (ăb-sûrd′, -zûrd′) *adj.* Ridiculously incongruous or unreasonable. [< L *absurdus.*] —**ab·surd′i·ty, ab·surd′ness** *n.* —**ab·surd′ly** *adv.*

A·bu Dha·bi (ä′bōō dä′bē). A sheikdom in E Arabia and capital of the United Arab Emirates. Pop. 46,400.

a·bun·dance (ə-bŭn′dəns) *n.* Also **a·bun·dan·cy** (-dən-sē). A great quantity; plentiful amount. [< L *abundāre,* ABOUND.] —**a·bun′dant** *adj.* —**a·bun′dant·ly** *adv.*

a·buse (ə-byōōz′) *v.* **abused, abusing. 1.** To use wrongly or improperly. **2.** To maltreat. **3.** To

---

ô paw, for/oi boy/ou out/ŏŏ took/ōō coo/p pop/r run/s sauce/sh shy/t to/th thin/*th* the/
ŭ cut/ûr fur/v van/w wag/y yes/z size/zh vision/ə ago, item, edible, gallop, circus/

berate; insult. —*n.* (ə-byōōs'). **1.** Misuse. **2.** A corrupt practice or custom. **3.** Maltreatment. **4.** Insulting language. [< L *abūsus,* a using up.] —**a•bu′sive** *adj.* —**a•bu′sive•ly** *adv.*

a•but (ə-bŭt') *v.* **abutted, abutting.** To lie adjacent; border upon. [< OF *abuter,* to buttress, put an end to.] —**a•but′ter** *n.*

a•but•ment (ə-bŭt′mənt) *n.* **1.** The act or process of abutting. **2.** A structure that receives the thrust of an arch or bridge.

a•bysm (ə-bĭz′əm) *n.* An abyss. [< LL *abyssus,* ABYSS.]

a•bys•mal (ə-bĭz′məl) *adj.* **1.** Unfathomable; extreme. **2.** Of or resembling an abyss. —**a•bys′mal•ly** *adv.*

a•byss (ə-bĭs') *n.* **1. a.** The primeval chaos. **b.** The bottomless pit; hell. **2.** Any immeasurably profound depth or void. [LL *abyssus.*]

a•byss•al (ə-bĭs′əl) *adj.* **1.** Abysmal. **2.** Of or pertaining to the great depths of the oceans.

Ab•ys•sin•i•a (ăb′ə-sĭn′ē-ə). Ethiopia. —**Ab′-ys•sin′i•an** *adj.* & *n.*

ac alternating current.

Ac actinium.

a.c. before meals (NL *ante cibum*).

A.C. **1.** alternating current. **2.** before Christ (NL *ante Christum*).

a/c account; account current.

a•ca•cia (ə-kā′shə) *n.* **1.** Any of various trees having tight clusters of small yellow or white flowers. **2.** Any of several related trees. [L.]

acad. academic; academy.

ac•a•dem•ic (ăk′ə-dĕm′ĭk) *adj.* **1.** Of or characteristic of a school. **2.** Liberal or classical rather than technical or vocational, as studies. **3.** Formalistic; conventional. **4.** Theoretical; speculative. —**ac′a•dem′i•cal•ly** *adv.*

ac•a•de•mi•cian (ăk′ə-də-mĭsh′ən) *n.* A member of an association of scholars, artists, etc.

ac•a•dem•i•cism (ăk′ə-dĕm′ə-sĭz′əm) *n.* Also **a•cad•e•mism** (ə-kăd′ə-mĭz′əm). Traditional formalism, especially in art.

a•cad•e•my (ə-kăd′ə-mē) *n., pl.* **-mies. 1.** An association of scholars. **2.** A school for special instruction. **3.** A private secondary or college-preparatory school. [< Gk *Akadēmia,* name of the place where Plato taught.]

A•ca•di•a (ə-kā′dē-ə). **1.** A French colony of E Canada that included Nova Scotia and New Brunswick. **2.** A parish in S Louisiana settled by Acadian exiles. —**A•ca′di•an** *n.* & *adj.*

a•can•thus (ə-kăn′thəs) *n., pl.* **-thuses** or **-thi** (-thī'). **1.** A plant of the Mediterranean region having large, thistlelike leaves. **2.** An architectural ornament representing these leaves. [< Gk *akantha,* thorn.]

a cap•pel•la (ä kə-pĕl′ə). Without instrumental accompaniment. [It, "in the manner of the chapel (or choir)."]

acc. **1.** acceleration. **2.** account; accountant. **3.** accusative.

ac•cede (ăk-sēd') *v.* **-ceded, -ceding. 1.** To give consent; agree. **2.** To come into an office or dignity. [< L *accēdere,* to approach, agree.] —**ac•ced′ence** (-sēd′əns) *n.* —**ac•ced′er** *n.*

ac•cel•er•ate (ăk-sĕl′ə-rāt') *v.* **-ated, -ating.** To move or cause to move faster. [L *accelerāre.*] —**ac•cel′er•a•ble** *adj.* —**ac•cel′er•a′tive** *adj.*

ac•cel•er•a•tion (ăk-sĕl′ə-rā′shən) *n.* **1.** The act of accelerating. **2.** The rate of change of velocity with respect to time.

ac•cel•er•a•tor (ăk-sĕl′ə-rā′tər) *n.* Something that causes acceleration: **a.** The gas pedal of an automobile. **b.** A research device that accelerates charged particles.

ac•cel•er•om•e•ter (ăk-sĕl′ə-rŏm′ə-tər) *n.* Any of various devices used to measure acceleration.

ac•cent (ăk′sĕnt) *n.* **1.** *Ling.* The relative prominence of a syllable of a word by greater intensity, **stress accent,** or by modulation of pitch or tone, **pitch accent. 2.** Vocal emphasis given to a syllable, word, or phrase. **3.** A characteristic pronunciation: *a Southern accent.* **4.** A mark or symbol used to indicate the vocal quality of a particular letter: *an acute accent.* **5.** A mark or symbol used to indicate the stressed syllables of a spoken word. **6.** Rhythmical stress in verse or music. —*v.* (ăk′sĕnt', ăk-sĕnt'). **1.** To stress the pronunciation of. **2.** To mark with a printed accent. **3.** To call attention to. [< L *accentus,* accentuation, "song added to (speech)."] —**ac•cen′tu•al** *adj.* —**ac•cen′tu•al•ly** *adv.*

ac•cen•tu•ate (ăk-sĕn′chōō-āt') *v.* **-ated, -ating. 1.** To pronounce or mark with an accent. **2.** To stress; emphasize. —**ac•cen′tu•a′tion** *n.*

ac•cept (ăk-sĕpt') *v.* **1.** To receive (something offered) willingly or gladly. **2.** To admit to a group or place. **3.** To answer affirmatively. **4.** *Comm.* To consent to pay, as by a signed agreement. [< L *acceptāre,* freq of *accipere,* to receive, "take to oneself."]

ac•cept•a•ble (ăk-sĕp′tə-bəl) *adj.* Satisfactory. —**ac•cept′a•bil′i•ty** *n.* —**ac•cept′a•bly** *adv.*

ac•cep•tance (ăk-sĕp′təns) *n.* **1.** The act of accepting or state of being accepted or acceptable. **2.** An accepted time draft or bill of exchange.

ac•cep•ta•tion (ăk′sĕp-tā′shən) *n.* The usual or accepted meaning, as of a word.

ac•cess (ăk′sĕs) *n.* **1.** The act or means of approaching. **2.** The right to enter or use. **3.** A sudden outburst. [< L *accēdere,* to near, approach.]

ac•ces•si•ble (ăk-sĕs′ə-bəl) *adj.* **1.** Easily approached or entered. **2.** Easily obtained. —**ac•ces′si•bil′i•ty** *n.*

ac•ces•sion (ăk-sĕsh′ən) *n.* **1.** The attainment of rank or dignity. **2.** An increase by means of something added. **3.** Agreement; assent.

ac•ces•so•ry (ăk-sĕs′ər-ē) *n., pl.* **-ries.** Also **ac•ces•sa•ry. 1.** Something supplementary. **2.** Something nonessential but useful. **3.** One who though absent aids in or contributes to the commission of a crime. [< ML *accessor,* helper, accessory.] —**ac•ces′so•ri•ly** *adv.* —**ac•ces′so•ri•ness** *n.* —**ac•ces′so•ry** *adj.*

ac•ci•dence (ăk′sə-dəns, -dĕns') *n.* The area of grammar that deals with word inflections.

ac•ci•dent (ăk′sə-dənt, -dĕnt') *n.* **1.** An unexpected and undesirable event. **2.** Fortune; chance. [< L (*rēs*) *accidēns,* "(a thing) happening."]

ac•ci•den•tal (ăk′sə-dĕn′təl) *adj.* Occurring unexpectedly or unintentionally. —*n. Mus.* A chromatically altered note not belonging to the key signature. —**ac′ci•den′tal•ly** *adv.*

ac•claim (ə-klām′) *v.* **1.** To applaud. **2.** To salute or hail. —*n.* Enthusiastic applause. [L *acclāmāre*, to shout at.] —**ac•claim′er** *n.*

ac•cla•ma•tion (ăk′lə-mā′shən) *n.* **1.** An enthusiastic oral vote of approval without formal ballot. **2.** Applause of acceptance or welcome.

ac•cli•mate (ə-klī′mĭt, ăk′lə-māt′) *v.* **-mated, -mating.** Also **ac•cli•ma•tize** (ə-klī′mə-tīz′) **-tized, -tizing.** To accustom or become accustomed to a new environment or situation; adapt. —**ac′-cli•ma′tion, ac•cli′ma•ti•za′tion** *n.*

ac•cliv•i•ty (ə-klĭv′ə-tē) *n., pl.* **-ties.** An upward slope, as of ground. [< L *acclīvis*, uphill.] —**ac•cliv′i•tous** *adj.*

ac•co•lade (ăk′ə-lād′, ăk′ə-läd′) *n.* **1.** An embrace of greeting or salutation. **2.** Praise; approval: *critics′ accolades.* [< Prov *acolada*, an embrace.]

ac•com•mo•date (ə-kŏm′ə-dāt′) *v.* **-dated, -dating. 1.** To do a favor for; oblige. **2.** To supply with. **3.** To contain comfortably or have space for. **4.** To adapt; adjust. **5.** To settle; reconcile. [L *accommodāre*, to make fit.] —**ac•com′mo•da′tive** *adj.*

ac•com•mo•dat•ing (ə-kŏm′ə-dā′tĭng) *adj.* Helpful and obliging. —**ac•com′mo•dat′ing•ly** *adv.*

ac•com•mo•da•tion (ə-kŏm′ə-dā′shən) *n.* **1.** The act or state of accommodating or being accommodated; adaptation. **2.** Anything that meets a need; convenience. **3. accommodations. a.** Lodgings. **b.** A seat, compartment, or room on a public vehicle. **4.** *Comm.* A loan or other financial favor.

ac•com•pa•ni•ment (ə-kŭm′pə-nē-mənt, ə-kŭmp′nē-) *n.* **1.** Something that accompanies; concomitant. **2.** A vocal or instrumental part that supports a solo part.

ac•com•pa•nist (ə-kŭm′pə-nĭst, ə-kŭmp′nĭst) *n.* One who plays an accompaniment.

ac•com•pa•ny (ə-kŭm′pə-nē, ə-kŭmp′nē) *v.* **-nied, -nying. 1.** To go along or occur with. **2.** To perform an accompaniment to. [< OF *accompagner*.] —**ac•com′pa•ni•er** *n.*

ac•com•plice (ə-kŏm′plĭs) *n.* One who aids or abets a lawbreaker in a criminal act. [< ME *a complice*, a COMPLICE.]

ac•com•plish (ə-kŏm′plĭsh) *v.* To succeed in doing; bring to pass. [< OF *accomplir*, to complete.] —**ac•com′plish•er** *n.*

ac•com•plished (ə-kŏm′plĭsht) *adj.* **1.** Completed; done; finished. **2.** Skilled; expert. **3.** Sophisticated.

ac•com•plish•ment (ə-kŏm′plĭsh-mənt) *n.* **1.** The act of accomplishing or of being accomplished; completion. **2.** Something completed successfully. **3.** Social poise.

ac•cord (ə-kôrd′) *v.* To agree or be in agreement. —*n.* **1.** Agreement; harmony. **2.** A settlement, esp. of conflicting opinions between nations. [< VL *accordāre*, "to be heart-to-heart with."] —**ac•cord′a•ble** *adj.*

ac•cord•ance (ə-kôr′dəns) *n.* Agreement; conformity. —**ac•cord′ant** *adj.*

ac•cord•ing•ly (ə-kôr′dĭng-lē) *adv.* **1.** Correspondingly. **2.** Consequently.

ac•cor•di•on (ə-kôr′dē-ən) *n.* A portable, bellows-operated musical instrument with a keyboard and metal reeds. [< G *Akkord*, agreement, "harmony."] —**ac•cor′di•on•ist** *n.*

ac•cost (ə-kôst′, ə-kŏst′) *v.* To approach and speak to first. [< VL **accostāre*, to come alongside someone.] —**ac•cost′a•ble** *adj.*

ac•count (ə-kount′) *n.* **1. a.** A narrative of events. **b.** A written or oral explanation, as of blame. **2. a.** A precise list of monetary transactions. **b.** Any detailed list. **3.** A business relationship involving the exchange of money or credit. **4.** Importance: *a man of some account.* —**on account.** In part payment of. —**on account of.** Because of. —**on no account.** Under no circumstances. —**take into account.** To take into consideration. —*v.* To consider or esteem. —**account for. 1.** To make or render a reckoning, as of funds received. **2.** To be the explanation or cause of. **3.** To be answerable for. [< OF *acompter*, "to count up to," reckon.]

ac•count•a•ble (ə-koun′tə-bəl) *adj.* Answerable. —**ac•count′a•bil′i•ty** *n.* —**ac•count′a•bly** *adv.*

ac•count•ant (ə-koun′tənt) *n.* An expert in accounting. —**ac•count′ant•ship′** *n.*

ac•count•ing (ə-koun′tĭng) *n.* The bookkeeping methods involved in recording the business transactions and preparing the financial statements of a business.

ac•cou•ter (ə-kōō′tər) *v.* Also **ac•cou•tre.** To outfit and equip, as for military duty. [F *accoutrer*.]

ac•cou•ter•ment (ə-kōō′tər-mənt) *n.* Also **ac•cou•tre•ment. 1.** The act of accoutering. **2.** accouterments. Extra equipment, as of a soldier; trappings.

Ac•cra (ə-krä′, ăk′rə). The capital of Ghana. Pop. 338,000.

ac•cred•it (ə-krĕd′ĭt) *v.* **1.** To attribute to. **2.** To authorize. **3.** To certify as meeting a prescribed standard. **4.** To believe. —**ac•cred′i•ta′tion** *n.*

ac•cre•tion (ə-krē′shən) *n.* **1.** Any growth or increase in size, esp. by gradual external addition. **2.** Something added to promote such growth. [< L *accrēscere*, ACCRUE.]

ac•crue (ə-krōō′) *v.* **-crued, -cruing. 1.** To come to someone or something as a gain or increment. **2.** To increase by regular growth, as interest on capital. [< L *accrēscere*, to increase.] —**ac•cru′al** *n.* —**ac•crue′ment** *n.*

acct. account.

ac•cul•tur•a•tion (ə-kŭl′chə-rā′shən) *n.* Modification of a primitive culture by contact with an advanced culture.

ac•cu•mu•late (ə-kyōōm′yə-lāt′) *v.* **-lated, -lating.** To amass or gather; mount up; collect. [L *accumulāre*.] —**ac•cu′mu•la′tion** *n.*

ac•cu•mu•la•tor (ə-kyōōm′yə-lā′tər) *n.* **1.** One that accumulates. **2.** A register or electric circuit that stores figures for computation.

ac•cu•ra•cy (ăk′yər-ə-sē) *n.* Exactness; correctness.

ac•cu•rate (ăk′yər-ĭt) *adj.* Having no errors; correct. [< L *accūrāre*, to attend to carefully.] —**ac′cu•rate•ly** *adv.* —**ac′cu•rate•ness** *n.*

ac•curs•ed (ə-kûr′sĭd, ə-kûrst′) *adj.* Also **ac•**

ô paw, for/oi boy/ou out/ŏŏ took/ōō coo/p pop/r run/s sauce/sh shy/t to/th thin/*th* the/ ŭ cut/ûr fur/v van/w wag/y yes/z size/zh vision/ə ago, item, edible, gallop, circus/

accusative / acquiesce

curst. 1. Under a curse. 2. Abominable. —ac·curs'ed·ly adv.

ac·cu·sa·tive (ə-kyōō'zə-tĭv) adj. Of or pertaining to a grammatical case that indicates the direct object of a verb or the object of certain prepositions. [< L (cāsus) accūsātīvus, "(case) indicating accusation."] —ac·cu'sa·tive n. —ac·cu'sa·tive·ly adv.

ac·cuse (ə-kyōōz') v. -cused, -cusing. 1. To charge (someone) with an error. 2. Law. To bring charges against (someone) for a misdeed. [< L accūsāre, to accuse, "call to account."] —ac'cu·sa'tion n. —ac·cus'er n.

ac·cus·tom (ə-kŭs'təm) v. To familiarize or become familiarized, as by constant practice.

ac·cus·tomed (ə-kŭs'təmd) adj. 1. Usual; normal. 2. In the habit of.

ace (ās) n. 1. A playing card, die, or domino having one spot. 2. In racket games, a point scored by the failure of one's opponent to return a serve. 3. A fighter pilot who has shot down five or more enemy planes. 4. Informal. An expert in any field. —adj. Informal. First-rate; expert. [< L ās, unit.]

ace in the hole. A hidden advantage.

-aceous. comb. form. Of, pertaining to, or of the nature of: farinaceous. [< L -āceus, "of a specific kind or group."]

a·cerb (ə-sûrb') adj. 1. Sour; bitter; astringent. 2. Acid; sharp. [L acerbus, sharp, bitter.] —a·cer'bi·ty n.

ac·er·bate (ăs'ər-bāt') v. -bated, -bating. To vex; annoy. [< L acerbus, ACERB.]

ac·e·tate (ăs'ə-tāt') n. 1. A durable transparent film derived from cellulose and used esp. in packaging and photography. 2. Fibers or fabric derived from cellulose acetate.

a·ce·tic acid (ə-sē'tĭk). A clear, colorless, pungent organic acid, $C_2H_4O_2$, used in chemical synthesis and photography. [< L acētum, vinegar.]

a·cet·i·fy (ə-sĕt'ə-fī') v. -fied, -fying. To convert to acetic acid or vinegar.

ac·e·tone (ăs'ə-tōn') n. A colorless, extremely flammable liquid, C_3H_6O, used as a solvent.

ac·e·tyl·cho·line (ăs'ə-tĭl-kō'lēn', ə-sĕt'l-) n. A white crystalline compound, $C_7H_{17}NO_3$, that transmits nerve impulses across intercellular gaps.

a·cet·y·lene (ə-sĕt'l-ēn', -ən) n. A colorless, highly flammable gas, C_2H_2, used for metal welding and cutting.

a·ce·tyl·sal·i·cyl·ic acid (ə-sĕt'l-săl'ə-sĭl'ĭk). Aspirin.

ache (āk) v. ached, aching. 1. To suffer a dull, sustained pain. 2. Informal. To yearn. —n. A dull, steady pain. [< OE ācan.]

a·chieve (ə-chēv') v. achieved, achieving. 1. To accomplish successfully. 2. To attain with effort. [< OF achever, "to bring to a head."] —a·chieve'ment n. —a·chiev'er n.

A·chil·les (ə-kĭl'ēz) The hero of Homer's Iliad.

Achilles' heel. A small but mortal weakness.

Achilles' tendon. The large tendon running from the heel bone to the calf muscle.

ach·ro·mat·ic (ăk'rə-măt'ĭk) adj. 1. Free of color. 2. Refracting light without spectral color separation. —ach'ro·mat'i·cal·ly adv.

ac·id (ăs'ĭd) n. 1. a. Any of a large class of substances in aqueous solution capable of turning litmus indicators red, dissolving certain metals to form salts, reacting with bases or alkalis to form salts, or having a sour taste. b. A substance that ionizes in solution to give the positive ion of the solvent. c. A substance capable of giving up a proton. 2. Slang. A hallucinogen, LSD. —adj. Biting; ill-tempered: an acid wit. [L acidus, sharp, sour < acēre, to be sour.] —a·cid'i·ty n.

a·cid·i·fy (ə-sĭd'ə-fī') v. -fied, -fying. To convert to acid. —a·cid'i·fi'a·ble adj. —a·cid'i·fi·ca'tion n. —a·cid'i·fi'er n.

ac·i·do·sis (ăs'ĭ-dō'sĭs) n. Pathologically high blood acidity.

acid test. A decisive, critical test of worth.

a·cid·u·lous (ə-sĭj'ōō-ləs) adj. Sour in feeling or manner. [< L acidus, ACID.]

-acious. comb. form. A tendency toward or abundance of something: fallacious.

-acity. comb. form. A quality or state of being: tenacity.

ack. acknowledgment.

ack-ack (ăk'ăk') n. Mil. Slang. 1. Antiaircraft fire. 2. An antiaircraft gun.

ac·knowl·edge (ăk-nŏl'ĭj) v. -edged, -edging. 1. To recognize the existence or truth of. 2. To express gratitude for. 3. To report the receipt of. 4. Law. To accept or certify as legally binding. —ac·knowl'edg·er n. —ac·knowl'edg·ment, ac·knowl'edge·ment n.

ac·me (ăk'mē) n. The point of utmost attainment. [Gk akmē, point.]

ac·ne (ăk'nē) n. An inflammatory disease of the oil glands, characterized by pimples. [< Gk akmē, eruption on the face, ACME.]

ac·o·lyte (ăk'ə-līt') n. 1. One who assists a priest at Mass. 2. An attendant or follower. [< Gk akolouthos, follower, following.]

A·con·ca·gua (ä'kōn-kä'gwä) The highest mountain (22,835 ft.) in the W Hemisphere, in Argentina.

ac·o·nite (ăk'ə-nīt') n. 1. A poisonous plant, the monkshood. 2. A medicinal preparation made from its roots. [< Gk akoniton.]

a·corn (ā'kôrn', ā'kərn) n. The nut of the oak tree, having a cuplike base. [< OE æcern. See ōg-.]

a·cous·tic (ə-kōō'stĭk) adj. Also a·cous·ti·cal (-stĭ-kəl). Pertaining to sound, the sense of hearing, or the science of sound. —n. acoustics (ə-kōō'stĭks). 1. (takes sing. v.). The scientific study of sound. 2. (takes pl. v.). The total effect of sound, esp. in an enclosed space. [Gk akoustikos.] —a·cous'ti·cal·ly adv.

acpt. acceptance.

ac·quaint (ə-kwānt') v. 1. To make familiar. 2. To inform. [< L accognōscere, to know perfectly.] —ac·quaint'ed adj.

ac·quain·tance (ə-kwān'təns) n. 1. Knowledge about someone or something. 2. A person or persons whom one knows.

ac·qui·esce (ăk'wē-ĕs') v. -esced, -escing. To consent or comply passively. [L acquiēscere, to agree tacitly.] —ac'qui·es'cence n. —ac'qui·es'cent adj. —ac'qui·es'cent·ly adv.

ă pat/ā ate/âr care/ä bar/b bib/ch chew/d deed/ĕ pet/ē be/f fit/g gag/h hat/hw what/ ĭ pit/ī pie/îr pier/j judge/k kick/l lid, fatal/m mum/n no, sudden/ng sing/ŏ pot/ō go/

ac•quire (ə-kwĭr′) v. -quired, -quiring. To gain possession of. [< L acquīrere, to add to, get.] —ac•quire′ment n.

ac•qui•si•tion (ăk′wə-zĭsh′ən) n. 1. The act of acquiring. 2. Something acquired, esp. as an addition to an established group.

ac•quis•i•tive (ə-kwĭz′ə-tĭv) adj. Tending to acquire. —ac•quis′i•tive•ness n.

ac•quit (ə-kwĭt′) v. -quitted, -quitting. 1. To clear of a charge. 2. To release from obligation. 3. To conduct (oneself). [< VL *acquītāre, "to bring to rest," set free.]

ac•quit•tal (ə-kwĭt′l) n. Law. The judgment that a person is not guilty of a crime as charged.

ac•quit•tance (ə-kwĭt′əns) n. A release from an obligation.

a•cre (ā′kər) n. 1. A unit of area equal to 4,840 square yards. 2. acres. Property in the form of land. [< OE æcer. See agro-.] —a′cre•age (ā′kər-ĭj, ā′krĭj) n.

ac•rid (ăk′rĭd) adj. 1. Harsh in taste or smell. 2. Caustic in language. [< L ācer, sharp, bitter.] —a•crid′i•ty (ə-krĭd′ə-tē) n.

ac•ri•mo•ny (ăk′rə-mō′nē) n. Animosity in speech or manner. [L ācrimōnia, sharpness < ācer, sharp.] —ac′ri•mo′ni•ous adj. —ac′ri•mo′-ni•ous•ness n.

acro-. comb. form. A height, tip, or point. [< Gk akros, topmost.]

ac•ro•bat (ăk′rə-băt′) n. One skilled in feats of agility and balance. [< Gk akrobatēs, "one who walks on tiptoe."] —ac′ro•bat′ic adj.

ac•ro•bat•ics (ăk′rə-băt′ĭks) n. (takes sing. v.). 1. The art of an acrobat. 2. Any manifestation of spectacular agility.

ac•ro•nym (ăk′rə-nĭm′) n. A word formed from the initial letters of a name, as WAC for Women's Army Corps, or by combining initial letters or parts of a series of words, as radar for radio detecting and ranging.

ac•ro•pho•bi•a (ăk′rə-fō′bē-ə) n. Abnormal fear of high places.

a•crop•o•lis (ə-krŏp′ə-lĭs) n. 1. The fortified height or citadel of an ancient Greek city. 2. Acropolis. The citadel of Athens. [Gk akropolis, "upper city."]

a•cross (ə-krôs′, ə-krŏs′) prep. 1. On, at, or from the other side of: across the road. 2. So as to cross; through: draw lines across the paper. 3. From one side of to the other: a bridge across a river. —adv. 1. From one side to the other: The bridge swayed when he ran across. 2. On or to the opposite side: We came across by ferry. [< OF a croix, "in the form of a cross."]

a•cross-the-board (ə-krôs′thə-bôrd′, -bōrd′, ə-krŏs′-) adj. Including all categories or members.

a•cros•tic (ə-krôs′tĭk, ə-krŏs′-) n. 1. A poem or series of lines in which certain letters, usually the first in each line, form a name or message. 2. A word square. [Gk akrostikhis, "end-line."]

a•cryl•ic resin (ə-krĭl′ĭk). Any of numerous polymers used to produce synthetic rubbers and lightweight plastics.

act (ăkt) n. 1. The process of doing something. 2. Something that is done. 3. An enactment, as of a legislative body. 4. A major division of a play or opera. 5. A performance that forms part of a longer presentation, as in vaudeville. 6. Informal. A pose: put on an act. —v. 1. To perform the part of, as in a play. 2. To behave or comport oneself: She acts like a lady. 3. To be an actor. 4. To appear to be: The dog acts friendly. 5. To do something. 6. To function in a specific way. —act up. Informal. To misbehave or malfunction. [< L āctus, pp of agere, to drive, do.]

ACTH A pituitary hormone used to stimulate cortisone secretion. [A(DRENO)C(ORTICO)-T(ROPIC) H(ORMONE).]

ac•tin (ăk′tĭn) n. A muscle protein, active with myosin in muscular contraction. [< L āctus, an ACT.]

act•ing (ăk′tĭng) adj. Temporarily assuming the duties of another. —n. The occupation or performance of an actor.

ac•ti•nide (ăk′tĭ-nīd′) n. Any of a series of chemically similar, mostly synthetic, radio-active metallic elements with atomic numbers ranging from 89 (actinium) through 103 (lawrencium).

ac•tin•i•um (ăk-tĭn′ē-əm) n. Symbol Ac A radioactive metallic element found in uranium ores and used as a source of alpha rays. Atomic number 89, longest-lived isotope Ac 227. [< Gk aktis, ray.]

ac•tion (ăk′shən) n. 1. The state or process of doing. 2. An act or deed. 3. A movement or manner of movement. 4. actions. Behavior or conduct. 5. The operating parts of a mechanism: the action of a gun. 6. The plot of a story or play. 7. A lawsuit. 8. Combat.

ac•ti•vate (ăk′tə-vāt′) v. -vated, -vating. 1. To set in motion. 2. To organize (a military unit). 3. To make active, reactive, or radioactive.

ac•tive (ăk′tĭv) adj. 1. In action; moving. 2. Capable of functioning. 3. Causing action or change. 4. Participating: an active member of a club. 5. Not passive or quiescent. 6. Characterized by energetic action. 7. Denoting that the subject of a sentence is performing or causing the action expressed by the verb: active voice. 8. Producing profit: active accounts. 9. Mil. On full duty and full pay. [L āctivus < āctus, ACT.]

ac•tiv•ism (ăk′tĭv-ĭz′əm) n. A theory or practice based on militant action. —ac′tiv•ist n.

ac•tiv•i•ty (ăk-tĭv′ə-tē) n., pl. -ties. 1. The state of being active. 2. Energetic action. 3. A specified form of action, esp. one in the area of recreation. 4. The intensity of a radioactive source.

act of God. Law. An unforeseeable or inevitable occurrence, such as a tornado, caused by nature.

ac•to•my•o•sin (ăk′tō-mī′ə-sĭn) n. A system of actin and myosin that with other substances constitutes muscle fiber.

ac•tor (ăk′tər) n. A theatrical performer. —ac′-tress (-trĭs) fem.n.

Acts of the Apostles. Also Acts. The 5th book of the New Testament.

ac•tu•al (ăk′chōō-əl) adj. 1. In existence; real. 2. Existing or acting at the present. [< LL *àctuális,* "pertaining to acts."] —**ac'tu•al•ly** *adv.*

ac•tu•al•i•ty (ăk'chōō-ăl'ə-tē) *n., pl.* **-ties.** **1.** The state of being actual. **2. actualities.** Actual conditions or facts.

ac•tu•ar•y (ăk'chōō-ĕr'ē) *n., pl.* **-ies.** A statistician who computes insurance risks and premiums. [L *àctuárius,* secretary of accounts.] —**ac'tu•ar'i•al** (-âr'ē-əl) *adj.*

ac•tu•ate (ăk'chōō-āt') *v.* **-ated, -ating.** **1.** To put into action. **2.** To stimulate; motivate. —**ac'-tu•a'tion** *n.*

a•cu•i•ty (ə-kyōō'ə-tē) *n.* Keenness; acuteness. [< L *acuere,* to sharpen.]

a•cu•men (ə-kyōō'mən) *n.* Keenness of insight. [L *acúmen,* (mental) sharpness.]

a•cute (ə-kyōōt') *adj.* **1.** Having a sharp point. **2.** Keenly perceptive. **3.** Sensitive. **4.** Extremely severe or sharp. **5.** *Med.* Reaching a crisis rapidly, as a disease. **6.** Designating angles less than 90°. [L *acútus,* sharp, pp of *acuere,* to sharpen.] —**a•cute'ness** *n.*

ad (ăd) *n.* An advertisement.

A.D. **1.** active duty. **2.** anno Domini.

A.D.A. Americans for Democratic Action.

ad•age (ăd'ĭj) *n.* A short maxim or proverb. [< L *adagium,* proverb.]

a•da•gio (ə-dä'jō, -jē-ō') *adv. Mus.* Slowly. [It *adagio,* "at ease."] —**a•da'gio** *adj.*

Ad•am (ăd'əm). The first man and progenitor of mankind. Genesis 2:7.

ad•a•mant (ăd'ə-mənt, -mănt') *n.* A stone believed to be impenetrable. —*adj.* Unyielding. [< Gk *adamas,* hard metal, diamond, poss "unbreakable."]

Ad•ams (ăd'əmz). **1. John.** 1735–1826. 2nd President of the U.S. (1797–1801). **2. John Quincy.** 1767–1848. 6th President of the U.S. (1825–29).

John Adams

Adam's apple. The projection of the largest laryngeal cartilage at the front of the throat, esp. in men.

a•dapt (ə-dăpt') *v.* To adjust or become adjusted to new or different conditions. [L *adaptáre,* to fit to.] —**a•dapt'a•bil'i•ty, a•dapt'a•ble•ness** *n.* —**a•dapt'a•ble** *adj.*

ad•ap•ta•tion (ăd'ăp-tā'shən) *n.* **1.** The act or process of adapting. **2.** Adjustment or change.

a•dap•tive (ə-dăp'tĭv) *adj.* Tending to adapt. —**a•dap'tive•ly** *adv.*

add (ăd) *v.* **1.** To join or unite so as to increase in size, quantity, or scope. **2.** To combine to form a sum. **3.** To say or write further. [< L *addere,* to add, "to put to."]

add. **1.** addendum. **2.** addition.

ad•den•dum (ə-děn'dəm) *n., pl.* **-da** (-də). Something added; a supplement.

ad•der (ăd'ər) *n.* **1.** Any of various venomous Old World snakes. **2.** Any of several nonvenomous snakes popularly believed to be harmful. [< OE *nædre,* snake. See **nĕtr-.**]

ad•dict (ə-dĭkt') *v.* To devote or give (oneself) habitually or compulsively to. —*n.* (ăd'ĭkt). A person who is addicted, esp. to narcotics. [< L *addícere,* to award to.] —**ad•dic'tion** *n.* —**ad•dic'tive** *adj.*

Ad•dis Ab•a•ba (ăd'ĭs ăb'ə-bə). The capital of Ethiopia. Pop. 505,000.

Ad•di•son's disease (ăd'ə-sənz). A usually fatal disease caused by failure of the adrenal cortex.

ad•di•tion (ə-dĭsh'ən) *n.* **1.** The act, process, or result of adding. **2.** Something added; a supplement or annex. —**ad•di'tion•al** *adj.* —**ad•di'tion•al•ly** *adv.*

ad•di•tive (ăd'ə-tĭv) *adj.* Involving addition. —*n.* A substance added in small amounts to something else to alter it.

ad•dle (ăd'l) *v.* **-dled, -dling.** **1.** To make or become confused. **2.** To spoil, as an egg. [< OE *adela,* filth, urine.]

ad•dress (ə-drěs') *v.* **1.** To speak to. **2.** To mark with a destination. **3.** To direct one's efforts or attention to. —*n.* (ə-drěs'). **1.** A formal spoken or written communication. **2.** (*also* ăd'rěs). The indication of destination on mail. **3.** (*also* ăd'rěs). The location at which an organization or person can be reached. **4.** Skillfulness. [< VL **addrictiáre,* to direct oneself toward.]

ad•dress•ee (ăd'rěs-ē', ə-drěs'ē') *n.* One to whom something is addressed.

ad•duce (ə-d/y/ōōs') *v.* **-duced, -ducing.** To cite

John Quincy Adams

---

as an example or means of proof. [L *addūcere*, to bring to (someone).]

Ad·e·laide (ăd′l-ād′). A city of S Australia. Pop. 640,000.

A·den (äd′n, ād′n). The capital of Southern Yemen, on the Gulf of Aden in the SE part of the country. Pop. 264,300.

Aden, Gulf of. An arm of the Arabian Sea between Somalia and Southern Yemen.

ad·e·nine (ăd′n-ēn′, -ĭn) *n.* A constituent of nucleic acid, $C_5H_5N_5$.

ad·e·noids (ăd′n-oidz′) *pl.n.* Lymphoid tissue growths above the throat in the nose. [< Gk *adēn*, gland.] —**ad′e·noid′** *adj.*

a·den·o·sine triphosphate (ə-dĕn′ə-sēn′). An organic compound, $C_{10}H_{16}N_5O_{13}P_3$, that provides energy for metabolic reactions.

a·dept (ə-dĕpt′) *adj.* Highly skilled. [L *adeptus*, "having attained (knowledge or skill)."] —**ad′ept′** (ăd′ĕpt′) *n.* —**a·dept′ly** *adv.* —**a·dept′ness** *n.*

ad·e·quate (ăd′ĭ-kwĭt) *adj.* **1.** Able to satisfy a requirement. **2.** Barely satisfactory or sufficient. [< L *adaequāre*, to make equal to.] —**ad′e·qua·cy** (-kwə-sē) *n.* —**ad′e·quate·ly** *adv.*

ad·here (ăd-hîr′) *v.* -hered, -hering. **1.** To stick to as if glued. **2.** To maintain loyalty, as to a person. **3.** To follow without deviation. [L *adhaerēre*, to stick to.] —**ad·her′ence** *n.* —**ad·her′ent** *adj.* & *n.* —**ad·her′er** *n.*

ad·he·sion (ăd-hē′zhən) *n.* The act or state of adhering.

ad·he·sive (ăd-hē′sĭv) *adj.* **1.** Tending to adhere; sticky. **2.** Gummed so as to adhere. —*n.* An adhesive substance.

ad hoc (ăd hŏk′). For a specific purpose, case, or situation. [L, "toward this."]

ad ho·mi·nem (ăd hŏm′ĭ-nĕm′). Appealing to prejudice rather than reason. [L, "to the man."]

a·dieu (ə-d/y/ōō′) *interj.* Farewell. —*n.* A farewell. [OF *a dieu*, "(I commend you) to God."]

ad in·fi·ni·tum (ăd ĭn′fə-nī′təm). Endlessly. [L, "to infinity."]

ad·i·pose (ăd′ə-pōs′) *adj.* Fatty: *adipose tissue.* [< L *adeps*, fat.]

Ad·i·ron·dacks (ăd′ə-rŏn′dăks′). A mountain range in NE New York.

adj. **1.** adjacent. **2.** adjective. **3.** adjutant.

ad·ja·cent (ə-jā′sənt) *adj.* Next to; adjoining. [< L *adjacēre*, to lie near.]

ad·jec·tive (ăj′ĭk-tĭv) *n.* Any of a class of words used to modify a noun or other substantive by limiting, qualifying, or specifying. [< L *adjectivus*, "attributive."] —**ad′jec·ti′val** (-tĭ′vəl) *adj.* —**ad′jec·ti′val·ly** *adv.*

ad·join (ə-join′) *v.* **1.** To be next to. **2.** To unite. [< L *adjungere*, to join to.] —**ad·join′ing** *adj.*

ad·journ (ə-jûrn′) *v.* **1.** To suspend until a later stated time. **2.** To move from one place to another. [< OF *ajourner*, "to put off to an appointed day."] —**ad·journ′ment** *n.*

ad·judge (ə-jŭj′) *v.* -judged, -judging. **1.** To determine, rule, or award by judicial procedure. **2.** To judge or deem.

ad·ju·di·cate (ə-jōō′dĭ-kāt′) *v.* -cated, -cating.

To settle by judicial procedure. —**ad·ju′di·ca′tion** *n.* —**ad·ju′di·ca′tive** *adj.* —**ad·ju′di·ca′tor** (-kā′tər) *n.*

ad·junct (ăj′ŭngkt′) *n.* One attached to another in a subordinate relationship. [< L *adjungere*, ADJOIN.] —**ad·junc′tive** *adj.*

ad·ju·ra·tion (ăj′ŏō-rā′shən) *n.* An earnest appeal: *"the tenderest adjurations of a dying friend"* (De Quincey).

ad·jure (ə-jŏōr′) *v.* -jured, -juring. **1.** To enjoin solemnly, as under oath or penalty: *"and adjuring her in the name of God to declare the truth"* (Increase Mather). **2.** To entreat. [< L *adjūrāre*, to swear to.]

ad·just (ə-jŭst′) *v.* **1.** To regulate or adapt. **2.** To settle (a debt or claim). [< VL **adjuxtāre*, to put close to.] —**ad·just′a·ble** *adj.* —**ad·just′er** *n.* —**ad·just′ment** *n.*

ad·ju·tant (ăj′ŏō-tənt) *n.* **1.** A military officer who is an administrative assistant to a commander. **2.** A stork, the marabou. [< L *adjūtāre*, to aid.]

ad lib (ăd lĭb′). Extemporaneously.

ad-lib (ăd-lĭb′) *v.* -libbed, -libbing. To improvise or extemporize. —*n.* Something ad-libbed. [< L *ad libitum*, "to (one's) liking."] —**ad-lib′ber** *n.*

Adm. admiral.

ad·man (ăd′măn′) *n.* One employed in advertising.

ad·min·is·ter (ăd-mĭn′ĭs-tər) *v.* **1.** To manage. **2. a.** To give (a drug) remedially. **b.** To dispense (a sacrament). **3.** To mete out. **4.** To tender (an oath). **5.** To manage or dispose of (an estate). —**ad·min′is·trant** (-trənt) *n.*

ad·min·is·tra·tion (ăd-mĭn′ĭs-trā′shən) *n.* **1.** The act of administering. **2.** Management. **3. a.** The executive body of a government. **b.** Its term of office. **4.** The management and disposal of an estate. —**ad·min′is·tra′tive** *adj.*

ad·min·is·tra·tor (ăd-mĭn′ĭs-trā′tər) *n.* **1.** A business or government executive. **2.** One appointed to administer an estate.

ad·mi·ra·ble (ăd′mər-ə-bəl) *adj.* Deserving admiration; excellent. —**ad′mir·a·bly** *adv.*

ad·mi·ral (ăd′mər-əl) *n.* **1.** The commander in chief of a navy or fleet. **2.** A naval officer of the next-to-the-highest rank. [< Ar *'amīr-al-*, "commander of."]

ad·mi·ral·ty (ăd′mər-əl-tē) *n., pl.* -ties. **1.** A court exercising jurisdiction over all maritime causes. **2. Admiralty.** The British navy department.

ad·mire (ăd-mīr′) *v.* -mired, -miring. **1.** To regard with wonder and approval. **2.** To esteem; respect. [L *admīrārī*, to wonder at.] —**ad′mi·ra′tion** (-mə-rā′shən) *n.* —**ad·mir′er** *n.* —**ad·mir′ing·ly** *adv.*

ad·mis·si·ble (ăd-mĭs′ə-bəl) *adj.* Allowable. —**ad·mis′si·bil′i·ty** *n.* —**ad·mis′si·bly** *adv.*

ad·mis·sion (ăd-mĭsh′ən) *n.* **1.** The act or procedure of admitting. **2.** Something admitted, as an acknowledgment or confession. **3.** Appointment to a position or situation. **4.** The right to enter; access. **5.** An entrance fee.

ad·mit (ăd-mĭt′) *v.* -mitted, -mitting. **1.** To permit to enter or serve as a means of entrance. **2.** To have room for. **3.** To afford possibility; allow;

permit (with *of*). **4. a.** To acknowledge; confess. **b.** To concede. [< L *admittere*, to send in to.]

ad·mit·tance (ăd-mĭt'əns) *n.* Right of entrance.

ad·mit·ted·ly (ăd-mĭt'ĭd-lē) *adv.* By general admission.

ad·mix (ăd-mĭks') *v.* To mix or become mixed. —**ad·mix'ture** *n.*

ad·mon·ish (ăd-mŏn'ĭsh) *v.* **1.** To reprove mildly but seriously. **2.** To counsel against. [< VL *admonestāre*, var of L *admonēre*, to bring to (someone's) mind.] —**ad'mo·ni'tion** (-mə-nĭsh'ən), **ad·mon'ish·ment** *n.* —**ad·mon'i·to'ry** (-ə-tôr'ē, -tōr'ē) *adj.*

ad·nate (ăd'nāt') *adj. Biol.* Joined to or fused with another part or organ. Said of parts not usually united. [< L *adnāscī*, to be born in addition to.] —**ad·na'tion** *n.*

ad nau·se·am (ăd nô'zē-əm). To a disgusting degree. [L.]

a·do (ə-dōō') *n.* Bustle; bother. [ME < *at do*, "to do."]

a·do·be (ə-dō'bē) *n.* **1.** A sun-dried brick of clay and straw. **2.** Clay from which such bricks are made. **3.** A structure built with such bricks. [< Ar *al-ṭōba*, "the brick."] —**a·do'be** *adj.*

ad·o·les·cence (ăd'l-ĕs'əns) *n.* The period or state of development from the onset of puberty to maturity. [< L *adolēscere*, to grow up.] —**ad'o·les'cent** *adj. & n.*

Ad·o·nai (ăd'ō-nī'). Lord (spoken substitute for the ineffable name of God). [Heb *adōnāi* < Phoen *adōn*, lord.]

A·don·is (ə-dŏn'ĭs, ə-dō'nĭs) *n.* A beautiful youth. [Gk *Adōnis* (a lover of Aphrodite) < Phoen *adōn*, lord.]

a·dopt (ə-dŏpt') *v.* **1.** To take (a child) into one's family legally and raise as one's own. **2.** To take and follow by choice or assent. **3.** To take up and use as one's own. [L *adoptāre*, to choose for oneself.] —**a·dopt'er** *n.* —**a·dop'tion** *n.* —**a·dop'tive** *adj.*

a·dor·a·ble (ə-dôr'ə-bəl, ə-dōr'-) *adj. Informal.* Delightful; lovable. —**a·dor'a·bly** *adv.*

a·dore (ə-dôr', ə-dōr') *v.* adored, adoring. **1.** To worship with divine honors. **2.** To love deeply. **3.** *Informal.* To like very much. [< L *adōrāre*, to pray to.] —**ad'o·ra'tion** (ăd'ə-rā'shən) *n.* —**a·dor'er** *n.*

a·dorn (ə-dôrn') *v.* **1.** To be a decoration to; enhance. **2.** To decorate with or as with ornaments. [< L *adornāre*, to put ornaments on.] —**a·dorn'er** *n.* —**a·dorn'ment** *n.*

ad·re·nal (ə-drē'nəl) *adj.* **1.** At, near, or on the kidneys. **2.** Pertaining to the adrenal glands or their secretions.

adrenal gland. Either of two small endocrine glands, one located above each kidney.

ad·ren·a·lin (ə-drĕn'əl-ĭn) *n.* Also **a·dren·a·line.** Epinephrine.

ad·re·no·cor·ti·co·trop·ic hormone (ə-drē'nō-kôr'tĭ-kō-trŏp'ĭk, -trō'pĭk). A hormone, ACTH.

A·dri·at·ic Sea (ā'drē-ăt'ĭk). An arm of the Mediterranean between Italy and the Balkan Peninsula.

a·drift (ə-drĭft') *adv.* Without anchor or direction. —**a·drift'** *adj.*

a·droit (ə-droit') *adj.* **1.** Dexterous. **2.** Skillful under pressing conditions. [F < *a droit*, "rightly."] —**a·droit'ly** *adv.* —**a·droit'ness** *n.*

ad·sorb (ăd-sôrb', -zôrb') *v.* To take in (liquid or gas) on the surface of a solid. —**ad·sorp'tion** (-sôrp'shən, -zôrp'-) *n.* —**ad·sorp'tive** *adj.*

ad·u·late (ăj'ōō-lāt') *v.* -lated, -lating. To praise excessively or fawningly. [< L *adulārī*, to flatter.] —**ad'u·la'tion** *n.* —**ad'u·la'tor** *n.* —**ad'u·la·to'ry** (-lə-tôr'ē, -tōr'ē) *adj.*

a·dult (ə-dŭlt', ăd'ŭlt') *n.* One who has attained maturity or legal age. —*adj.* **1.** Fully developed and mature. **2.** Intended for mature persons. [L *adultus*, pp of *adolescēre*, to grow up.] —**a·dult'hood'** *n.*

a·dul·ter·ate (ə-dŭl'tə-rāt') *v.* -ated, -ating. To make impure or inferior by adding extraneous or improper ingredients. [L *adulterāre*, to pollute, commit adultery.] —**a·dul'ter·ant** *n. & adj.*

a·dul·ter·y (ə-dŭl'tər-ē, -trē) *n., pl.* -ies. Sexual intercourse between a married person and one other than the lawful spouse. —**a·dul'ter·er** *n.* —**a·dul'ter·ess** (-trĭs, -tər-ĭs) *fem.n.* —**a·dul'ter·ous** *adj.* —**a·dul'ter·ous·ly** *adv.*

ad·um·brate (ăd-ŭm'brāt', ăd'əm-brāt') *v.* -brated, -brating. **1.** To give a sketchy outline. **2.** To foreshadow. [L *adumbrāre*, overshadow.] —**ad'um·bra'tion** *n.*

adv. adverb.

ad·vance (ăd-văns', -väns') *v.* -vanced, -vancing. **1.** To move or bring forward or onward. **2.** To propose. **3.** To aid the growth or progress of. **4.** To make progress. **5.** To raise or rise in rank, amount, or value. **6.** To cause to occur sooner; hasten. **7.** To pay (money) before legally due. —*n.* **1.** The act of moving or going forward. **2.** Improvement; progress. **3.** A rise in price or value. **4. advances.** Personal approaches to secure acquaintance, favor, or agreement. **5.** Payment of money before legally due. —**in advance. 1.** In front. **2.** Ahead of time. —*adj.* **1.** Prior. **2.** Going before. [< L *abante*, "from before."] —**ad·vance'ment** *n.* —**ad·vanc'er** *n.*

ad·van·tage (ăd-văn'tĭj, ăd-vän'-) *n.* **1.** A favorable position or factor. **2.** Benefit or profit; gain. **3.** *Tennis.* The first point scored after deuce. [< OF *avantage*, "the condition of being ahead."] —**ad'van·ta'geous** (ăd'văn-tā'jəs) *adj.* —**ad'van·ta'geous·ly** *adv.*

Ad·vent (ăd'vĕnt') *n.* **1.** The coming of Christ. **2.** The period including four Sundays before Christmas. **3. advent.** A coming or arrival. [< L *advenīre*, to come to.]

ad·ven·ti·tious (ăd'vĕn-tĭsh'əs) *adj.* Not inherent; accidental. [L *adventīcius*, "arriving (from outside)."] —**ad'ven·ti'tious·ly** *adv.*

ad·ven·ture (ăd-vĕn'chər) *n.* **1.** A risky undertaking. **2.** An unusual or suspenseful experience. **3.** A business venture. [< L *adventūrus*, fut part of *advenīre*, to arrive.] —**ad·ven'tur·ous** *adj.* —**ad·ven'tur·ous·ness** *n.*

ad·ven·tur·er (ăd-vĕn'chər-ər) *n.* **1.** One who undertakes risky ventures. **2.** A soldier of fortune. **3.** One who unscrupulously seeks wealth and social position.

ă pat/ā ate/âr care/ä bar/b bib/ch chew/d deed/ĕ pet/ē be/f fit/g gag/h hat/hw what/ ĭ pit/ī pie/îr pier/j judge/k kick/l lid, fatal/m mum/n no, sudden/ng sing/ŏ pot/ō go/

ad·verb (ăd'vûrb') *n.* **1.** A part of speech comprising a class of words that modify a verb, adjective, or other adverb. **2.** A word belonging to this class, as *rapidly* in *He runs rapidly.* [< L *adverbium,* "added word."] —**ad·ver'bi·al** *adj.* —**ad·ver'bi·al·ly** *adv.*

ad·ver·sar·y (ăd'vər-sĕr'ē) *n., pl.* **-ies.** An opponent; enemy. [< L *adversus,* ADVERSE.]

ad·verse (ăd-vûrs', ăd'vûrs') *adj.* **1.** Actively opposed; hostile. **2.** Unfavorable. [< L *adversus,* pp of *advertere,* to turn toward (with hostility).] —**ad·verse'ly** *adv.*

ad·ver·si·ty (ăd-vûr'sə-tē) *n., pl.* **-ties.** Hardship; misfortune.

ad·vert (ăd-vûrt') *v.* To allude; refer. [< L *advertere,* to turn toward.]

ad·ver·tise (ăd'vər-tīz') *v.* **-tised, -tising.** **1.** To call attention to a product or business so as to promote sales. **2.** To notify. [< OF *a(d)vertir,* to advert.] —**ad'ver·tis'er** *n.*

ad·ver·tise·ment (ăd'vər-tīz'mənt, ăd-vûr'tĭs-mənt, -tĭz-mənt) *n.* A notice designed to attract public attention.

ad·ver·tis·ing (ăd'vər-tī'zĭng) *n.* **1.** The business of preparing and distributing advertisements. **2.** Advertisements collectively.

ad·vice (ăd-vīs') *n.* Opinion about a course of action; counsel. [< VL *advīsum,* opinion.]

ad·vis·a·ble (ăd-vī'zə-bəl) *adj.* Prudent; expedient. —**ad·vis'a·bil'i·ty** *n.*

ad·vise (ăd-vīz') *v.* **-vised, -vising.** **1.** To offer advice to. **2.** To recommend. **3.** To inform. [< VL *advīsāre,* to observe.] —**ad·vi'ser, ad·vi'sor** *n.* —**ad·vi'so·ry** *adj.*

ad·vise·ment (ăd-vīz'mənt) *n.* Careful consideration.

ad·vo·cate (ăd'və-kāt') *v.* **-cated, -cating.** To speak in favor of; recommend. —*n.* (ăd'və-kĭt, -kāt'). **1.** One who argues for a cause or person; a supporter or defender. **2.** A lawyer. [< L *advocāre,* to summon to (give evidence).] —**ad'vo·ca·cy** *n.*

adz, adze (ădz) *n.* A tool with an arched blade at right angles to the handle, used for shaping wood. [< OE *adesa.*]

A.E.A. Actors' Equity Association.

AEC Atomic Energy Commission.

Ae·ge·an Sea (ĭ-jē'ən). An arm of the Mediterranean between Greece and Turkey.

ae·gis (ē'jĭs) *n.* **1.** Protection. **2.** Patronage. [< Gk *aigis,* the shield of Zeus.]

Ae·ne·as (ĭ-nē'əs). Trojan hero, reputed ancestor of the Romans.

ae·on. Variant of eon.

aer·ate (âr'āt') *v.* **-ated, -ating.** **1.** To supply with or expose to gas. **2.** To supply (blood) with oxygen. —**aer·a'tion** *n.*

aer·i·al (âr'ē-əl) *adj.* **1.** Of, in, inhabiting, or caused by the air. **2.** Lofty. **3.** Airy. **4.** Of, for, or by aircraft. —*n.* An antenna. [< Gk *aēr,* air.] —**aer'i·al·ly** *adv.*

aer·i·al·ist (âr'ē-əl-ĭst) *n.* An acrobat who performs on a tightrope, trapeze, or similar apparatus.

aer·ie (âr'ē, îr'ē) *n.* A high nest, as of an eagle. [< L *ārea,* open field, AREA.]

aero-. *comb. form.* **1.** Air, gas, or the atmosphere. **2.** Aircraft. [< Gk *aēr,* air.]

aer·o·dy·nam·ics (âr'ō-dī-năm'ĭks) *n. (takes sing. v.).* The dynamics of gases, esp. of atmospheric interactions with moving objects. —**aer'o·dy·nam'ic** *adj.*

aer·o·em·bo·lism (âr'ō-ĕm'bə-lĭz'əm) *n.* **1.** The presence of air bubbles in the heart or blood vessels. **2. Caisson disease.**

aer·o·naut (âr'ə-nôt') *n.* A pilot or navigator of a balloon or lighter-than-air craft.

aer·o·nau·tics (âr'ə-nô'tĭks) *n. (takes sing. v.).* **1.** The design and construction of aircraft. **2.** Aircraft navigation. —**aer'o·nau'tic, aer'o·nau'ti·cal** *adj.*

aer·o·plane (âr'ə-plān') *n. Chiefly Brit.* An airplane.

aer·o·sol (âr'ə-sôl', -sŏl', -sōl') *n.* **1.** A gaseous suspension of fine particles. **2.** Detergent, insecticide, or paint packaged under pressure in a dispenser.

aer·o·space (âr'ō-spās') *adj.* **1.** Pertaining to the earth's atmosphere and the space beyond. **2.** Pertaining to the science or technology of flight. —**aer'o·space'** *n.*

Aes·chy·lus (ĕs'kə-ləs, ēs'-). 525–456 B.C. Greek tragic poet.

Aes·cu·la·pi·us (ĕs'kyōō-lā'pē-əs). Roman god of medicine.

Ae·sop (ē'sŏp', ē'səp). Greek fabulist of the late sixth century B.C. —**Ae·so'pi·an** (-sō'pē-ən) *adj.*

aes·thete, es·thete (ĕs'thēt') *n.* One who cultivates or affects a superior appreciation of the beautiful.

aes·thet·ic, es·thet·ic (ĕs-thĕt'ĭk) *adj.* **1.** Of or pertaining to aesthetics. **2.** Of, pertaining to, or sensitive to the beautiful; artistic. —*n.* **aesthetics, esthetics.** *(takes sing. v.).* The branch of philosophy that provides a theory of the beautiful and of the fine arts. [< Gk *aisthētikos,* pertaining to sense perception.] —**aes·thet'i·cal·ly** *adv.*

ae·ther. Variant of ether.

AF **1.** air force. **2.** audio frequency.

a.f. audio frequency.

A.F. air force.

a·far (ə-fär') *adv.* From, at, or to a distance; far away.

af·fa·ble (ăf'ə-bəl) *adj.* **1.** Amiable. **2.** Mild; gentle. [< L *affābilis* < *affāri,* to speak to.] —**af'fa·bil'i·ty** *n.* —**af'fa·bly** *adv.*

af·fair (ə-fâr') *n.* **1.** Anything done or to be done; concern. **2. affairs.** Business matters. **3.** A short romantic or sexual involvement. [< OF *a faire,* "to do."]

af·fect¹ (ə-fĕkt') *v.* **1.** To bring about a change in. **2.** To touch the emotions of. [L *afficere* (pp *affectus*), to do something to.]

Usage: Affect and *effect* are never interchangeable. *Affect* is now used principally in the senses of influence *(smoking affects health)* and pretense or imitation *(affecting nonchalance to hide fear); effect* refers only to accomplishment or execution *(reductions designed to effect economy).*

af·fect² (ə-fĕkt') *v.* **1.** To simulate or imitate so as to impress; feign. **2.** To fancy: *affect big hats.* [< L *affectāre,* to strive after, freq of *afficere,* to AFFECT.] —**af·fect'er** *n.*

af•fec•ta•tion (ăf'ĕk-tā'shən) *n.* Artificial behavior designed to impress others.

af•fect•ed (ə-fĕk'tĭd) *adj.* Assumed or simulated to impress others. —**af•fect'ed•ly** *adv.*

af•fect•ing (ə-fĕk'tĭng) *adj.* Full of pathos; touching; moving.

af•fec•tion (ə-fĕk'shən) *n.* A tender feeling toward another. [< L *affectiō*, (friendly) disposition < *afficere*, to AFFECT.] —**af•fec'tion•ate** *adj.* —**af•fec'tion•ate•ly** *adv.*

af•fer•ent (ăf'ər-ənt) *adj.* Directed toward a central organ or section. [< L *afferre*, to bring toward.]

af•fi•ance (ə-fī'əns) *v.* -anced, -ancing. To betroth. [< OF *affier*, to trust to.]

af•fi•da•vit (ăf'ə-dā'vĭt) *n. Law.* A written declaration made under oath. [ML, "he has pledged" < *affidāre*, to trust to.]

af•fil•i•ate (ə-fĭl'ē-āt') *v.* -ated, -ating. 1. To adopt as a subordinate associate. 2. To associate (with). —*n.* (ə-fĭl'ē-ĭt). An associate or subordinate. [ML *affiliāre*, "to take to oneself as a son."] —**af•fil'i•a'tion** *n.*

af•fin•i•ty (ə-fĭn'ə-tē) *n., pl.* -ties. 1. An attraction or attractive force. 2. Relationship; kinship. [< L *affinis*, neighboring.]
Usage: Affinity may be followed by *of, between,* or *with.* Thus, *affinity of* persons (or things), *between* two persons (or things), *with* another person (or thing).

af•firm (ə-fûrm') *v.* 1. To declare or maintain to be true. 2. To confirm. —**af•firm'a•ble** *adj.* —**af'fir•ma'tion** (ăf'ər-mā'shən) *n.*

af•firm•a•tive (ə-fûr'mə-tĭv) *adj.* 1. Giving assent; responding in a positive manner. 2. Confirming. —*n.* 1. A word or phrase signifying assent. 2. The side in a debate that upholds a proposition.

affirmative action. Action taken to provide equal opportunity, as in hiring, for members of previously disadvantaged groups, such as women and minorities.

af•fix (ə-fĭks') *v.* 1. To attach: *affix a label to a package.* 2. To append: *affix a postscript.* —*n.* (ăf'ĭks'). 1. Something attached or added. 2. A word element that is attached to a base, stem, or root.

af•fla•tus (ə-flā'təs) *n.* A creative impulse; an inspiration. [< L *afflāre*, to breathe on.]

af•flict (ə-flĭkt') *v.* To inflict suffering upon; cause distress to. [< L *affligere*, to dash against.] —**af•flic'tion** *n.* —**af•flic'tive** *adj.*

af•flu•ence (ăf'lōō-əns) *n.* Wealth; abundance. [< L *affluere*, to flow to.] —**af'flu•ent** *adj.* —**af'flu•ent•ly** *adv.*

af•ford (ə-fôrd', ə-fōrd') *v.* 1. To have the financial means for. 2. To be able to spare or give up. 3. To provide. [< OE *geforthian*, to further.] —**af•ford'a•ble** *adj.*

af•fray (ə-frā') *n.* A quarrel or noisy brawl. [< OF *affreer*, to fight in public.]

af•front (ə-frŭnt') *v.* 1. To offend. 2. To confront. —*n.* An insult. [< VL **affrontāre.*]

Af•ghan (ăf'găn', -gən) *n.* 1. A native of Afghanistan. 2. Pashto. 3. **afghan.** A coverlet knitted or crocheted in colorful geometric designs. —*adj.* Of or pertaining to Afghanistan, its people, or their language.

af•ghan•i (ăf-găn'ē) *n.* The basic monetary unit of Afghanistan.

Af•ghan•i•stan (ăf-găn'ə-stăn'). A kingdom of SW Asia. Pop. 13,800,000. Cap. Kabul.

Afghanistan

a•fi•ci•o•na•do (ə-fē'sē-ə-nä'dō, ə-fĭs'ē-ə-) *n., pl.* -dos. A devotee. [Span, pp of *aficionar,* to inspire affection.]

a•field (ə-fēld') *adv.* 1. Off the usual track. 2. Away from one's home. 3. To or on a field.

a•fire (ə-fīr') *adj. & adv.* 1. On fire. 2. Intensely interested.

a•flame (ə-flām') *adj. & adv.* 1. On fire. 2. Keenly interested.

AFL-CIO The American Federation of Labor and Congress of Industrial Organizations.

a•float (ə-flōt') *adj. & adv.* 1. Floating. 2. At sea. 3. Flooded.

a•flut•ter (ə-flŭt'ər) *adj.* Nervous and excited.

a•foot (ə-fŏŏt') *adj. & adv.* 1. Walking; on foot. 2. In progress.

a•fore•said (ə-fôr'sĕd', ə-fōr'-) *adj.* Spoken of earlier.

a•fore•thought (ə-fôr'thôt', ə-fōr'-) *adj.* Premeditated: *malice aforethought.*

a•foul (ə-foul') *adv. & adj.* In an entanglement or collision.

Afr. Africa; African.

a•fraid (ə-frād') *adj.* 1. Filled with fear. 2. Reluctant; averse: *afraid of work.* [< OF *affreer,* to AFFRAY.]

a•fresh (ə-frĕsh') *adv.* Anew; again.

Af•ri•ca (ăf'rĭ-kə). A continent in the E Hemisphere, S of Europe and between the Atlantic and Indian oceans. —**Af'ri•can** *adj. & n.*

Af•ri•kaans (ăf'rĭ-käns', -känz') *n.* The language of the Republic of South Africa, developed from 17th-century Dutch.

Af•ri•kan•er (ăf'rĭ-kä'nər) *n.* An Afrikaans-speaking descendant of the Dutch settlers of South Africa.

Af•ro (ăf'rō) *n.* A hair style characterized by dense frizzy hair worn naturally. —*adj.* African in manner or style.

Af•ro-A•mer•i•can (ăf'rō-ə-mĕr'ə-kən) *adj.* Of or pertaining to American Negroes of African ancestry. —*n.* An American Negro of African ancestry.

Af•ro-A•si•at•ic (ăf'rō-ā'zhē-ăt'ĭk) *n.* A lan-

guage family of SW Asia and N Africa. **—Af′-ro-A′si•at′ic** *adj.*
aft (ăft, äft) *Naut. adv.* At, in, toward, or near the stern of a vessel. *—adj.* Situated near or at the stern; after. [Prob short for ABAFT.]
aft. afternoon.
af•ter (ăf′tər, äf′-) *prep.* **1.** Behind in place or order. **2.** In pursuit of: *He runs after girls.* **3.** Concerning: *asked after you.* **4.** At a later time than. **5.** In the style of: *satires after Horace.* **6.** With the same name as: *named after her mother.* **7.** In conformity to: *a man after my own heart.* **8.** Past the hour of: *five minutes after three. —adv.* **1.** Behind; in the rear. **2.** At a subsequent time. *—adj.* **1.** Later; following: *afterglow.* **2.** *Naut.* Nearer the stern of a vessel. *—conj.* Subsequent to the time that. [< OE *æfter.* See apo-.]
af•ter•birth (ăf′tər-bûrth′, äf′-) *n.* The placenta and fetal membranes expelled from the uterus after childbirth.
af•ter•burn•er (ăf′tər-bûr′nər, äf′-) *n.* A device for augmenting the thrust of a jet engine.
af•ter•care (ăf′tər-kâr′, äf′-) *n.* Treatment or special care given to convalescent patients.
af•ter•ef•fect (ăf′tər-ə-fĕkt′, äf′-) *n.* A delayed or prolonged response to a stimulus.
af•ter•glow (ăf′tər-glō′, äf′-) *n.* **1.** Light emitted or remaining after removal of a source of illumination. **2.** A comfortable feeling following a pleasant experience.
af•ter•im•age (ăf′tər-ĭm′ĭj, äf′-) *n.* A visual image that persists after a visual stimulus ceases.
af•ter•life (ăf′tər-līf′, äf′-) *n.* A life believed to follow death.
af•ter•math (ăf′tər-măth′, äf′-) *n.* **1.** A consequence or result. **2.** A second crop of grass in the same season. [< AFTER + OE *mǣth,* a mowing.]
af•ter•most (ăf′tər-mōst′, äf′-) *adj.* Nearest the end or rear; hindmost; last.
af•ter•noon (ăf′tər-nōōn′, äf′-) *n.* The day from noon until sunset.
af•ter•taste (ăf′tər-tāst′, äf′-) *n.* A taste or feeling persisting after the stimulus causing it is no longer present.
af•ter•thought (ăf′tər-thôt′, äf′-) *n.* An idea, response, or explanation that occurs to one after an event or decision.
af•ter•ward (ăf′tər-wərd, äf′-) *adv.* Also **af•ter•wards** (-wərdz). In or at a later time; subsequently.
Ag silver (L *argentum*).
A.G. **1.** adjutant general. **2.** attorney general.
a•gain (ə-gĕn′) *adv.* **1.** Once more; anew. **2.** To a previous place, position, or state. **3.** Furthermore. **4.** On the other hand: *He might go, and again he might not.* **5.** In return; in response. [< OE *ongeagn,* in return, against < Gmc *gagina.*]
a•gainst (ə-gĕnst′) *prep.* **1.** In a direction or course opposite to. **2.** So as to come into contact with: *waves dashing against the shore.* **3.** In hostile opposition or resistance to: *struggle against fate.* **4.** Contrary to; opposed to: *against my better judgment.* **5.** In contrast: *dark colors against a fair skin.* **6.** As a defense

or safeguard from. **7.** To the account or debt of. [ME < AGAIN.]
a•gape¹ (ə-gāp′, ə-găp′) *adv. & adj.* In a state of wonder or amazement.
a•ga•pe² (ä′gə-pā′) *n., pl.* **-pae** (-pē′). The love feast accompanied by Eucharistic celebration in the early Christian church. [Gk *agapē,* love.]
a•gar (ä′gär, ä′gär) *n.* Also **a•gar-a•gar** (ä′-gär′ä′gär′, ä′gär′ä′-). A mucilaginous material prepared from certain seaweeds. [Malay, "jelly, gelatin."]
ag•ate (ăg′ĭt) *n.* **1.** A variety of chalcedony with color banding or irregular clouding. **2.** A child's marble made of this or similar material. **3.** A printer's type size, approx. $5^1/_2$ points. [< Gk *akhátēs.*]
a•ga•ve (ə-gā′vē, ə-gä′-) *n.* Any of various fleshy-leaved tropical American plants. [< Gk *agauos,* noble.]
age (āj) *n.* **1.** The period or amount of time during which someone or something exists. **2.** The time in life when one officially assumes certain rights or responsibilities. **3.** A distinctive period or stage. **4.** The state of being old. **5.** A long time. *—v.* **aged, aging** or **ageing.** To grow or cause to grow old or older. [< L *aetās,* age.] **—ag′er** *n.*
–age. *comb. form.* **1.** Collectively: **leafage. 2.** Relation to or connection with: **parentage. 3.** Condition or position: **marriage. 4.** Charge or fee: **postage. 5.** Residence or place: **orphanage.** [< LL *-āticus.*]
a•ged (ä′jĭd) *adj.* **1.** Old; advanced in years. **2.** (äjd). Of the age of: *aged three.*
age•ism (ä′jĭz′əm) *n.* Discrimination based on age, as against middle-aged and elderly people. **—age′ist** *n. & adj.*
age•less (āj′lĭs) *adj.* **1.** Never seeming to grow old. **2.** Existing forever; eternal.
a•gen•cy (ä′jən-sē) *n., pl.* **-cies. 1.** Action; operation; power. **2.** A mode of action; means. **3.** A business or service acting for others.
a•gen•da (ə-jĕn′də) *pl.n. (takes sing. v.).* Sing. **-dum** (-dəm). A list or program of things to be done. [L, pl of *agendum* < *agere,* to ACT.]
a•gent (ä′jənt) *n.* **1.** One that acts or has power to act. **2.** One that acts as the representative of another. **3.** A means of doing something; instrument. [< L *agere,* to ACT.]
ag•glom•er•ate (ə-glŏm′ə-rāt′) *v.* **-ated, -ating.** To form into a rounded mass. [L *agglomerāre.*] **—ag•glom′er•a′tion** *n.*
ag•glu•ti•nate (ə-glōōt′n-āt′) *v.* **-nated, -nating. 1.** To join by adhesion. **2.** To cause (red blood cells or microorganisms) to clump together. [L *agglūtināre.*] **—ag•glu′ti•na′tion** *n.* **—ag•glu′ti•na′tive** *adj.*
ag•glu•ti•nin (ə-glōōt′n-ĭn) *n.* A substance that induces agglutination.
ag•gran•dize (ə-grăn′dīz′, ăg′rən-dīz′) *v.* **-dized, -dizing. 1.** To increase; enlarge; extend. **—ag•gran′dize•ment** (ə-grăn′dĭz-mənt, ə-grăn′dīz′-) *n.* **—ag•gran′diz′er** *n.*
ag•gra•vate (ăg′rə-vāt′) *v.* **-vated, -vating. 1.** To make worse. **2.** To annoy; vex. [L *aggravāre,* to make heavier.] **—ag′gra•va′tion** *n.*

ŏ paw, for/oi boy/ou out/ŏŏ took/ōō coo/p pop/r run/s sauce/sh shy/t to/th thin/*th* the/
ŭ cut/ûr fur/v van/w wag/y yes/z size/zh vision/ə ago, item, edible, gallop, circus/

ag·gre·gate (ăg′rə-gĭt′) *adj.* Gathered togethei into a mass constituting a whole. —*n.* (ăg′rə-gĭt). A collective mass or sum; total. —*v.* (ăg′rə-gāt′) **-gated, -gating.** To gather into a mass, sum, or whole. [< L *aggregāre,* to add to (the flock).] —**ag′gre·ga′tion** *n.*

ag·gres·sion (ə-grĕsh′ən) *n.* **1.** The commencing of hostilities; an assault. **2.** Hostile action or behavior. [< L *aggredī,* to attack.] —**ag·gres′sor** (-grĕs′ər) *n.*

ag·gres·sive (ə-grĕs′ĭv) *adj.* **1.** Actively hostile. **2.** Assertive; bold. —**ag·gres′sive·ly** *adv.* —**ag·gres′sive·ness** *n.*

ag·grieve (ə-grēv′) *v.* **-grieved, -grieving. 1.** To distress; afflict. **2.** To injure unjustly; offend. [< L *aggravāre,* to AGGRAVATE.]

a·ghast (ə-găst′, ə-gäst′) *adj.* Horror-stricken; appalled. [< OE *gæstan* < *gāst,* GHOST.]

ag·ile (ăj′əl, ăj′īl) *adj.* Moving quickly and easily; nimble. [< L *agilis,* easily moved < *agere,* to ACT.] —**ag′ile·ly** *adv.* —**a·gil′i·ty** (ə-jĭl′ə-tē), **ag′ile·ness** *n.*

ag·i·tate (ăj′ə-tāt′) *v.* **-tated, -tating. 1.** To stir or move violently. **2.** To upset; disturb. **3.** To arouse or try to arouse public interest. [L *agitāre,* freq of *agere,* to ACT.] —**ag′i·tat′ed·ly** *adv.* —**ag′i·ta′tion** *n.* —**ag′i·ta′tor** *n.*

a·gleam (ə-glēm′) *adj. & adv.* Gleaming.

a·glim·mer (ə-glĭm′ər) *adj. & adv.* Glimmering.

a·glit·ter (ə-glĭt′ər) *adj. & adv.* Glittering.

a·glow (ə-glō′) *adj. & adv.* Glowing.

ag·nos·tic (ăg-nŏs′tĭk) *n.* One who doubts the possibility of knowing the existence of God or absolute truth. —**ag·nos′tic** *adj.* —**ag·nos′ti·cism′** *n.*

Ag·nus De·i (ăg′nəs dē′ī, äg′nōōs dā′ē). **1.** The Lamb of God (emblem of Christ). John 1:29; Isaiah 53:7. **2.** A liturgical prayer to Christ.

a·go (ə-gō′) *adj. & adv.* Gone by; in the past. [< OE *āgān,* to go away.]

a·gog (ə-gŏg′) *adj.* Eagerly expectant; excited. [< OF *en gogues,* "in merriments."] —**a·gog′** *adv.*

–agogue, –agog. *comb. form.* A leader or inciter: **demagogue.** [< Gk *agōgos,* leading, drawing forth.]

ag·o·nize (ăg′ə-nīz′) *v.* **-nized, -nizing.** To suffer or afflict with great anguish. [< Gk *agōnizesthai,* to contend for a prize < *agōnia,* AGONY.] —**ag′o·niz′ing·ly** *adv.*

ag·o·ny (ăg′ə-nē) *n., pl.* **-nies.** Intense physical pain or mental distress. [< Gk *agōnia,* contest, anguish < *agein,* to drive.]

ag·o·ra·pho·bi·a (ăg′ə-rə-fō′bē-ə) *n.* Abnormal fear of open spaces. —**ag′o·ra·pho′bic** (-fō′bĭk, -fŏb′ĭk) *adj.*

agr., agric. agricultural; agriculture.

a·grar·i·an (ə-grâr′ē-ən) *adj.* **1.** Of or pertaining to land and its ownership. **2.** Pertaining to farming; agricultural. [< L *ager,* land, field.]

a·gree (ə-grē′) *v.* agreed, agreeing. **1.** To consent; give assent. **2.** To be in accord. **3.** To share an opinion or understanding. **4.** To be suitable or beneficial. **5.** To correspond, as in grammatical case or number. [< VL **aggrātāre,* to be pleasing to.]

a·gree·a·ble (ə-grē′ə-bəl) *adj.* **1.** Pleasing; pleasant. **2.** Ready to consent; willing. —**a·gree′a·ble·ness** *n.* —**a·gree′a·bly** *adv.*

a·gree·ment (ə-grē′mənt) *n.* **1.** The act or state of agreeing. **2.** Concord; harmony. **3.** An arrangement between parties; covenant.

ag·ri·busi·ness (ăg′rĭ-bĭz′nĭs) *n.* Farming engaged in as big business, embracing the production, processing, and distribution of farm products and the manufacture of farm equipment. [AGRI(CULTURE) + BUSINESS.]

ag·ri·cul·ture (ăg′rĭ-kŭl′chər) *n.* Cultivation of crops and the raising of livestock; farming. [< L *agrī cultūra,* "cultivation of land."] —**ag′ri·cul′tur·al** *adj.* —**ag′ri·cul′tur·ist** *n.*

a·ground (ə-ground′) *adv. & adj.* Against the ground, as in shallow water: *The ship ran aground.*

a·gue (ā′gyōō) *n.* An attack of fever accompanied by chills or shivering. [< ML *(febris) acūta,* "sharp (fever)."]

ah (ä) *interj.* Expressive of surprise, pain, satisfaction, etc.

a·ha (ä-hä′) *interj.* Expressive of surprise or triumph.

a·head (ə-hĕd′) *adv.* **1.** At or to the front. **2.** Before; in advance. **3.** Onward; forward. —**get** (or **be**) **ahead.** To near or attain success.

a·hoy (ə-hoi′) *interj.* Used as a nautical call or greeting.

aid (ād) *v.* To help; assist. —*n.* **1.** The giving of assistance. **2.** One who or that which provides assistance. [< L *adjuvāre,* to give aid to.] —**aid′er** *n.*

aide (ād) *n.* An assistant.

aide-de-camp (ād′də-kămp′) *n., pl.* **aides-de-camp.** A military officer acting as assistant to a superior officer.

ai·grette, ai·gret (ā-grĕt′, ā′grĕt) *n.* An ornamental tuft of plumes. [F *aigrette,* "egret."]

ail (āl) *v.* **1.** To feel ill. **2.** To make ill or uneasy. [< OE *eglan.* See agh-1.]

ai·lan·thus (ā-lăn′thəs) *n.* A weedy tree with numerous pointed leaflets. [< NL.]

ai·le·ron (ā′lə-rŏn′) *n.* A movable control surface on the trailing edge of an airplane wing. [F, "little wing."]

ail·ment (āl′mənt) *n.* A mild illness.

aim (ām) *v.* **1.** To direct (a weapon, blow, etc.). **2.** To direct one's efforts or purpose. —*n.* **1.** The act of aiming. **2.** The direction of something aimed. **3.** Purpose; intention. [< OF *aesmer,* to guess at < L *aestimāre,* to ESTIMATE.]

aim·less (ām′lĭs) *adj.* Without direction or purpose. —**aim′less·ly** *adv.*

a·in. Variant of **ayin.**

ain't (ānt). *Nonstandard.* Contraction of *am not, are not, is not, has not,* and *have not.* *Usage: Ain't* is acceptable only when used knowingly to provide humor or shock or to reproduce certain speech patterns. Informally, the interrogative construction *aren't I* has somewhat more acceptance as an alternative to *ain't I.*

air (âr) *n.* **1. a.** A colorless, odorless, tasteless gaseous mixture, chiefly nitrogen (78%) and oxygen (21%). **b.** The earth's atmosphere. **2.** A

ă pat/ā ate/âr care/ä bar/b bib/ch chew/d deed/ĕ pet/ē be/f fit/g gag/h hat/hw what/ ĭ pit/ī pie/îr pier/j judge/k kick/l lid, fatal/m mum/n no, sudden/ng sing/ŏ pot/ō go/

breeze; wind. **3.** An impression; appearance: *an air of fear.* **4. airs.** Affectation. **5.** A melody or tune. **—on the air.** Broadcast; being broadcast. *—v.* **1.** To expose to air. **2.** To give public utterance to. [Blend of senses of several origins: 1. Atmosphere: < Gk *aēr*, breath; 2. Manner: < OF *aire*, "place of origin" < L *ager*, place, field, and L *ārea*, open space, AREA; 3. Melody: It *aria*, ARIA.]

air·borne (âr'bôrn', -bōrn') *adj.* Carried by or through the air.

air·brush (âr'brŭsh') *n.* An atomizer using compressed air to spray paint.

air·burst (âr'bûrst') *n.* An explosion in the atmosphere.

air·con·di·tion (âr'kən-dĭsh'ən) *v.* To control, esp. lower, the temperature and humidity of (an enclosure). **—air conditioner. —air conditioning.**

air·craft (âr'krăft', -kräft') *n., pl.* **-craft.** Any machine or device, including airplanes, helicopters, etc., capable of atmospheric flight.

aircraft carrier. A warship carrying aircraft.

air·drome (âr'drōm') *n.* An airport.

air·drop (âr'drŏp') *n.* A delivery, as of supplies or troops, by parachute from aircraft in flight.

Aire·dale (âr'dāl') *n.* A large terrier with a wiry tan and black coat.

air embolism. Aeroembolism.

air·field (âr'fēld') *n.* **1.** An airport having hard-surfaced runways. **2.** A landing strip.

air·foil (âr'foil') *n.* An aircraft control part or surface, such as a wing, propeller blade, or rudder.

air force. The aviation branch of a country's armed forces.

air gun. A gun discharged by compressed air.

air lane. A regular route of travel for aircraft; an airway.

air·lift (âr'lĭft') *n.* A system of transporting troops or supplies by air when surface routes are blocked. **—air'lift'** *v.*

air·line (âr'līn') *n.* **1.** A system for transport of passengers and freight by air. **2.** A business organization providing such a system. **3.** The shortest, most direct distance between two points.

air·lin·er (âr'lī'nər) *n.* A large passenger airplane.

air lock. An airtight chamber between regions of unequal pressure.

air mail. Also **air·mail** (âr'māl'). **1.** The system of conveying mail by aircraft. **2.** Mail thus conveyed. **—air'-mail'** *v.*

air·man (âr'mən) *n.* **1.** An enlisted man in the air force. **2.** An aviator.

air mile. A nautical mile.

air·plane (âr'plān') *n.* A winged vehicle capable of flight, heavier than air and propelled by jet engines or propellers.

air·port (âr'pôrt', -pōrt') *n.* A tract of leveled land with cargo and passenger facilities where aircraft take off and land.

air raid. A bombing attack by military aircraft. **—air'-raid'** *adj.*

air·ship (âr'shĭp') *n.* A self-propelled lighter-than-air craft with directional control surfaces; dirigible.

air·sick·ness (âr'sĭk'nĭs) *n.* Nausea resulting from flight in an aircraft. **—air'sick'** *adj.*

air·speed (âr'spēd') *n.* Speed, esp. of an aircraft, relative to the air.

air·strip (âr'strĭp') *n.* A minimally equipped airfield.

air·tight (âr'tīt') *adj.* **1.** Impermeable by air or gas. **2.** Unassailable: *an airtight excuse.*

air·way (âr'wā') *n.* An air lane.

air·wor·thy (âr'wûr'thē) *adj.* Fit to fly: *an airworthy old plane.* **—air'wor'thi·ness** *n.*

air·y (âr'ē) *adj.* **-ier, -iest. 1.** Of or like air. **2.** Open to the air; breezy. **3.** Light as air; graceful or delicate. **4.** Insubstantial; unreal. **5.** Nonchalant; carefree. **—air'i·ly** *adv.* **—air'i·ness** *n.*

aisle (īl) *n.* A passageway between rows of seats, as in a church or auditorium. [< OF *aile*, wing of a building.]

a·jar (ə-jär') *adv. & adj.* Partially opened, as a door. [ME *on char*, "in the act of turning."]

a·kim·bo (ə-kĭm'bō) *adj. & adv.* With the hands on the hips and the elbows bowed outward. [ME *in kenebowe*, "in keen bow."]

a·kin (ə-kĭn') *adj.* **1.** Of the same kin; related. **2.** Similar in quality or character.

Ak·ka·di·an (ə-kā'dē-ən) *n.* A Semitic language of a region of ancient Mesopotamia. **—Ak·ka'di·an** *adj.*

Ak·ron (ăk'rən). A city of Ohio. Pop. 290,000.

-al[1]. *comb. form.* A pertinence to or connection with: **adjectival.**

-al[2]. *comb. form.* The act or process of doing or experiencing the action indicated by the verb stem: **denial.**

Al aluminum.

A.L. American Legion.

à la (ä'lä, ä'lə, ăl'ə). In the style or manner of.

ALA American Library Association.

Ala. Alabama.

Al·a·bam·a (ăl'ə-băm'ə). A S state of the U.S. Pop. 3,444,000. Cap. Montgomery. **—Al'a·bam'i·an** (-ē-ən), **Al'a·bam'an** *adj. & n.*

al·a·bas·ter (ăl'ə-băs'tər, -bäs'tər) *n.* A dense, translucent, white or tinted fine-grained gypsum. [< Egypt *'a-la-Baste*, "vessel of (the goddess) *Baste.*"]

à la carte (ä' lä kärt', ăl'ə). With a separate price for each item on the menu. [F, "by the menu."]

a·lac·ri·ty (ə-lăk'rə-tē) *n.* Cheerful eagerness; sprightliness. [< L *alacer*, eager.]

à la king (ä' lə kĭng', ăl'ə). In cream sauce, often with pimiento and mushrooms.

Al·a·mo, the (ăl'ə-mō'). A mission in San Antonio, Texas, site of a defeat of Texans by Mexican forces (1836).

à la mode (ä' lə mōd', ăl'ə). **1.** Fashionable. **2.** Served with ice cream, as pie. [F, "in the fashion."]

a·larm (ə-lärm') *n.* **1.** A sudden feeling of fear. **2.** A warning of danger. **3.** A device that sounds a warning. **4.** The bell or buzzer of a clock. **5.** A call to arms. *—v.* To frighten or warn by an alarm. [< OIt *all'arme*, "to arms!"] **—a·larm'ing·ly** *adv.*

a·larm·ist (ə-lär'mĭst) *n.* A person who needlessly alarms others. **—a·larm'ism'** *n.*

---

a·las (ə-lăs′, ə-läs′) *interj.* Expressive of regret or anxiety.

A·las·ka (ə-lăs′kə). The largest state of the U.S., in extreme NW North America. Pop. 302,000. Cap. Juneau. —**A·las′kan** *adj. & n.*

alb (ălb) *n.* A white linen robe worn by the celebrant of a Mass. [< L *albus,* white.]

al·ba·core (ăl′bə-kôr′, -kōr′) *n.* A large marine fish that is a major source of canned tuna. [< Ar *al-bakrah,* "the young camel."]

Al·ba·ni·a (ăl-bā′nē-ə, -bān′yə, ôl-). A socialist country on the Adriatic. Pop. 2,000,000. Cap. Tirana.

Albania

Al·ba·ni·an (ăl-bā′nē-ən, -bān′yən, ôl-) *n.* **1.** A native or inhabitant of Albania. **2.** The Indo-European language of the Albanians. —**Al·ba′ni·an** *adj.*

Al·ba·ny (ôl′bə-nē). The capital of New York State. Pop. 115,000.

al·ba·tross (ăl′bə-trôs′, -trŏs′) *n.* Any of various large, web-footed, long-winged sea birds. [Port *alcatraz,* pelican.]

al·be·it (ôl-bē′ĭt, ăl-) *conj.* Although. [ME *al be it,* "let it be entirely (that)."]

Al·ber·ta (ăl-bûr′tə). A province of W Canada. Pop. 1,332,000. Cap. Edmonton. —**Al·ber′tan** *n. & adj.*

al·bi·no (ăl-bī′nō) *n., pl.* **-nos.** A person or animal having abnormally pale skin, very light hair, and lacking normal eye coloring. [< L *albus,* white.] —**al′bin·ism′** (ăl′bə-nĭz′əm) *n.*

al·bum (ăl′bəm) *n.* **1.** A book with blank pages for stamps, photographs, etc. **2.** One or more phonograph records in one binding. [L, blank tablet, neut of *albus,* white.]

al·bu·men (ăl-byōō′mən) *n.* **1.** The white of an egg. **2.** Albumin. [L *albūmen* < *albus,* white.]

al·bu·min (ăl-byōō′mən) *n.* Any of several proteins found in egg white, blood serum, milk, and plant and animal tissue.

Al·bu·quer·que (ăl′bə-kûr′kē). A city of New Mexico. Pop. 244,000.

al·caz·ar (ăl-kăz′ər, ăl′kə-zär′) *n.* A Spanish palace or fortress.

al·che·my (ăl′kə-mē) *n.* **1.** A traditional chemical philosophy concerned primarily with changing base metals into gold. **2.** Any seemingly magical power. [< Ar *al-kīmiyā′,* "the art of transmutation."] —**al·chem′i·cal** (-ĭ-kəl) *adj.* —**al′che·mist** *n.*

Al·ci·bi·a·des (ăl′sĭ-bī′ə-dēz′). 450?–404 B.C. Athenian statesman and general.

al·co·hol (ăl′kə-hôl′) *n.* **1.** Any of a series of related organic compounds having the general formula $C_nH_{2n+1}OH$. **2.** Ethanol. **3.** Intoxicating liquor containing alcohol. [< ML, fine powder of antimony used to tint the eyelids.]

al·co·hol·ic (ăl′kə-hôl′ĭk, -hŏl′ĭk) *adj.* **1.** Of or resulting from alcohol. **2.** Containing or preserved in alcohol. **3.** Suffering from alcoholism. —*n.* One who suffers from alcoholism.

al·co·hol·ism (ăl′kə-hôl-ĭz′əm) *n.* Habitual excessive alcoholic consumption.

al·cove (ăl′kōv′) *n.* A recess or partly enclosed extension of a room. [< Ar *al-qubbah,* "the vault."]

al·de·hyde (ăl′də-hīd′) *n.* Any of a class of highly reactive compounds obtained by oxidation of alcohols. [< NL *al(cohol) dehyd(rogenatum),* "dehydrogenized alcohol."]

al·der (ăl′dər) *n.* Any of various shrubs or trees growing in cool, moist places. [< OE *aler.* See el-².]

al·der·man (ôl′dər-mən) *n.* A member of a municipal legislative body. [< OE *(e)aldormann,* viceroy.] —**al′der·man·cy** *n.*

Al·der·ney (ôl′dər-nē) *n., pl.* **-neys.** One of a breed of dairy cattle. [< *Alderney,* island in the English Channel.]

ale (āl) *n.* An alcoholic beverage similar to but more bitter than beer. [< OE *ealu.* See alu-.]

a·le·a·to·ry (ā′lē-ə-tôr′ē, -tōr′ē) *adj.* Dependent upon chance. [< L *ālea,* dice.]

a·lee (ə-lē′) *adv. Naut.* At, on, or to the leeward side.

a·lem·bic (ə-lĕm′bĭk) *n.* An apparatus formerly used for distilling. [< Ar *al-anbīg.*]

a·leph (ä′lĭf) *n.* Also **a·lef.** The 1st letter of the Hebrew alphabet, representing a glottal stop.

a·lert (ə-lûrt′) *adj.* **1.** Vigilantly attentive; watchful. **2.** Mentally responsive; quick. **3.** Brisk; lively. —*n.* **1.** A signal warning of danger. **2.** The period during which such a warning is in effect. —*v.* To warn. [< It *all'erta,* "on the watch."] —**a·lert′ness** *n.*

Al·e·ut (ăl′ē-ōōt′) *n., pl.* **-ut** or **-uts.** Also **A·leu·tian** (ə-lōō′shən). An Eskimo native of the Aleutian Islands. —**A·leu′tian** *adj.*

Aleutian Islands. An island chain extending in a westward arc from Alaska.

Al·ex·an·der the Great (ăl′ĭg-zăn′dər, -zăn′dər). 356–323 B.C. King of Macedonia; conqueror of Greece, Persia, and Egypt.

Al·ex·an·dri·a (ăl′ĭg-zăn′drē-ə, -zăn′drē-ə). A city of Egypt. Pop. 1,513,000.

al·ex·an·drine (ăl′ĭg-zăn′drĭn, -zăn′drĭn) *n.* A line of English verse in iambic hexameter.

al·fal·fa (ăl-făl′fə) *n.* A cloverlike plant with purple flowers, widely cultivated for forage. [< Ar *al-faşfaşah.*]

Al·fred the Great (ăl′frĭd). A.D. 849–899. King of England (A.D. 871–899).

al·fres·co (ăl-frĕs′kō) *adv. & adj.* In the fresh air; outdoors. [It, "in the fresh (air)."]

al·gae (ăl′jē) *pl.n. Sing.* **-ga** (-gə). Any of various primitive, chiefly aquatic, one-celled or multicellular plants, as the seaweeds. [< L *alga,* seaweed.] —**al′gal** (-gəl) *adj.*

ă pat/ā ate/âr care/ä bar/b bib/ch chew/d deed/ĕ pet/ē be/f fit/g gag/h hat/hw what/ ĭ pit/ī pie/îr pier/j judge/k kick/l lid, fatal/m mum/n no, sudden/ng sing/ŏ pot/ō go/

al·ge·bra (ăl′jə-brə) *n.* A generalization of arithmetic in which symbols represent members of a specified set of numbers and are related by operations that hold for all numbers in the set. [< Ar *al-jebr, al-jabr,* "the (science of) reuniting."] —**al′ge·bra′ic** (-brā′ĭk) *adj.*

algebraic sum. The sum of algebraic quantities produced by arithmetic addition, in which negative quantities are added by the subtraction of corresponding positive quantities.

Al·ge·ri·a (ăl-jĭr′ē-ə). A republic of NW Africa. Pop. 10,454,000. Cap. Algiers. —**Al·ge′ri·an** *adj. & n.*

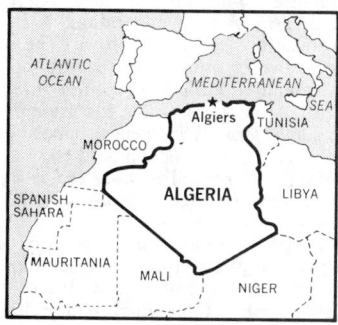

Algeria

–algia. *comb. form.* Pain or disease of: neuralgia. [< Gk *algos,* pain.]

Al·giers (ăl-jĭrz′). The capital of Algeria. Pop. 884,000.

Al·gon·qui·an (ăl-gŏng′kwē-ən, -kē-ən) *n., pl.* -an or -ans. Also **Al·gon·ki·an** (-kē-ən). 1. A family of North American Indian languages spoken in an area from the Atlantic seaboard W to the Rocky Mountains, and from Labrador S to North Carolina and Tennessee. 2. A member of a tribe using a language of this family. —**Al·gon′qui·an** *adj.*

Al·gon·quin (ăl-gŏng′kwĭn, -kĭn) *n., pl.* -quin or -quins. Also **Al·gon·kin** (-kĭn). 1. A member of any of several Algonquian-speaking North American Indian tribes formerly inhabiting a region N of the St. Lawrence River. 2. The language of these tribes. 3. Any Indian of these tribes.

al·go·rithm (ăl′gə-rĭth′əm) *n.* Any mechanical or repetitive computational procedure. [< Muhammad ibn-Musa al-Khwarizmi (A.D. 780–850?), Arab mathematician.]

a·li·as (ā′lē-əs, āl′yəs) *n.* An assumed name. —*adv.* Otherwise named: *Johnson, alias Rogers.* [L *aliās,* otherwise < *alius,* other.]

al·i·bi (ăl′ə-bī′) *n.* 1. A form of defense in which a defendant tries to prove he was elsewhere when a crime was committed. 2. An excuse. [L *alibī,* elsewhere.]

a·li·en (ā′lē-ən, āl′yən) *adj.* 1. Owing allegiance to another country or government. 2. Not one's own; unfamiliar: *an alien culture.* 3. Repugnant; adverse: *Lying is alien to his nature.* —*n.* 1. An unnaturalized resident of a

country. 2. A member of another people, region, etc. 3. One excluded from some group; an outsider. [< L *alius,* other.]

al·ien·a·ble (ăl′yən-ə-bəl, ā′lē-ən-) *adj. Law.* Able to be transferred to the ownership of another. —**al′ien·a·bil′i·ty** *n.*

al·ien·ate (āl′yən-āt′, ā′lē-ən-) *v.* -ated, -ating. To cause to become unfriendly or indifferent. [< L *aliēnus,* ALIEN.] —**al′ien·a′tion** *n.*

al·ien·ist (āl′yən-ĭst, ā′lē-ən-) *n.* A physician accepted by a court as an expert on the mental competence of principals or witnesses appearing before it.

a·light¹ (ə-līt′) *v.* alighted or alit, alighting. 1. To come down and settle, as after flight. 2. To dismount. [< OE *ālīhtan,* to lighten < *līht,* LIGHT (adjective).]

a·light² (ə-līt′) *adj. & adv.* Burning; lighted.

a·lign (ə-līn′) *v.* Also **a·line, alined, alining.** 1. To arrange in a line. 2. To ally oneself with one side of an argument, cause, etc.

a·lign·ment (ə-līn′mənt) *n.* Also **a·line·ment.** Arrangement or position in a straight line.

a·like (ə-līk′) *adj.* Having close resemblance; similar. —*adv.* In the same way, manner, or degree. —**a·like′ness** *n.*

al·i·ment (ăl′ə-mənt) *n.* Food; nourishment. [< L *alimentum* < *alere,* to nourish.]

al·i·men·ta·ry (ăl′ə-měn′trē, -tər-ē) *adj.* Pertaining to food or nutrition.

alimentary canal. The mucous-membrane-lined tube of the digestive system, extending from the mouth to the anus and including the pharynx, esophagus, stomach, and intestines.

al·i·mo·ny (ăl′ə-mō′nē) *n., pl.* -nies. An allowance for support paid to a divorced person by his former spouse. [L *alimōnia,* support < *alere,* to nourish.]

al·i·phat·ic (ăl′ə-făt′ĭk) *adj.* Pertaining to organic compounds in which the carbon atoms are linked in open chains rather than rings. [< Gk *aleiphar,* oil.]

a·lit (ə-līt′). *p.t. & p.p.* of alight.

a·live (ə-līv′) *adj.* 1. Having life; living. 2. Not extinct or inactive. 3. Full of life; lively. 4. Sensitive. 5. Teeming. —**a·live′ness** *n.*

al·ka·li (ăl′kə-lī′) *n., pl.* -lis or -lies. 1. A hydroxide or carbonate of an alkali metal, the aqueous solution of which is bitter, slippery, caustic, and basic. 2. Any of various soluble mineral salts found in natural water and arid soils. [< Ar *al-qalīy,* the ashes (of saltwort, a plant).]

alkali metal. Any of a group of highly reactive metallic elements, including lithium, sodium, potassium, rubidium, cesium, and francium.

al·ka·line (ăl′kə-līn, -lĭn′) *adj.* 1. Relating to or containing an alkali. 2. Basic. —**al′ka·lin′i·ty** (-lĭn′ə-tē) *n.*

alkaline-earth metal. Any of a group of metallic elements, especially calcium, strontium, and barium, but generally including beryllium, magnesium, and radium.

al·ka·lize (ăl′kə-līz′) *v.* -lized, -lizing. Also **al·ka·lin·ize** (-lĭn-īz′) -ized, -izing. To make alkaline or become an alkali. —**al′ka·li·za′tion, al′-ka·lin′i·za′tion** *n.*

al·ka·loid (ăl′kə-loid′) *n.* Any of various physiologically active nitrogen-containing organic bases derived from plants, including nicotine, quinine, cocaine, atropine, and morphine.

al·ka·lo·sis (ăl′kə-lō′sĭs) *n.* Pathologically high alkali content in the blood and tissues.

al·kyd resin (ăl′kĭd). A widely used durable synthetic resin.

all (ôl) *adj.* **1.** The total extent of: *all Christendom.* **2.** The entire number or quantity of: *all men.* **3.** The utmost of: *in all truth.* **4.** Every: *all kinds.* **5.** Any: *beyond all doubt.* **6.** Nothing but: *all skin and bones.* —*pron.* Each and every one: *All were drowned.* —*n.* **1.** Everything one has: *He gave his all.* **2.** The whole number; totality. —*adv.* **1.** Wholly: *all wrong.* **2.** Each: *a score of five all.* **3.** Exclusively: *The cake is all for him.* —**all but.** Nearly. [< OE *eall* < Gmc *allaz.*]

Al·lah (ăl′ə, ä′lə) *n.* The name of the Deity in Islam.

all-a·round. Variant of **all-round.**

al·lay (ə-lā′) *v.* **1.** To lessen; relieve. **2.** To calm; pacify. [< OE *ālecgan.*] —**al·lay′er** *n.*

al·le·ga·tion (ăl′ĭ-gā′shən) *n.* **1.** The act or result of alleging. **2.** An assertion requiring substantiation.

al·lege (ə-lĕj′) *v.* **-leged, -leging. 1.** To assert to be true; affirm. **2.** To assert without proof. [< L *allēgāre,* to dispatch, cite.] —**al·leg′ed·ly** (-ĭd-lē) *adv.* —**al·leg′er** *n.*

Al·le·ghe·ny Mountains (ăl′ə-gā′nē). A section of the Appalachians extending from Pennsylvania to Virginia.

al·le·giance (ə-lē′jəns) *n.* **1.** Loyalty owed to a nation, sovereign, or cause. **2.** The obligations of a vassal to an overlord. [< OF *ligeance* < LIEGE.] —**al·le′giant** *adj.*

al·le·go·ry (ăl′ə-gôr′ē, -gōr′ē) *n., pl.* **-ries.** The symbolic embodiment of generalizations intended to reflect a given aspect of experience. [< Gk *allēgorein,* "to speak in other terms."] —**al′le·gor′ic, al′le·gor′ic·al** *adj.*

al·le·gret·to (ăl′ə-grĕt′ō, ä′lə-) *adv. Mus.* Slower than allegro. —**al′le·gret′to** *adj.*

al·le·gro (ə-lĕg′rō, ə-lā′grō) *adv. Mus.* At a fast tempo. [It, "lively."] —**al·le′gro** *adj.*

al·lele (ə-lēl′) *n.* Any of a group of possible mutational forms of a gene. —**al·le′lic** (ə-lē′lĭk, ə-lĕl′ĭk) *adj.*

al·le·lu·ia (ăl′ə-lōō′yə) *interj.* Expressive of praise to God or of thanksgiving.

Al·len·town (ăl′ən-toun′). A city of Pennsylvania. Pop. 108,000.

al·ler·gen (ăl′ər-jən) *n.* A substance that causes an allergy. —**al′ler·gen′ic** (-jĕn′ĭk) *adj.*

al·ler·gist (ăl′ər-jĭst) *n.* A physician specializing in allergies.

al·ler·gy (ăl′ər-jē) *n., pl.* **-gies. 1.** Hypersensitive or pathological reaction to environmental factors or substances in amounts that do not affect most people. **2.** An adverse sentiment; dislike. [G *Allergie,* "altered reaction."] —**al·ler′gic** (ə-lûr′jĭk) *adj.*

al·le·vi·ate (ə-lē′vē-āt′) *v.* **-ated, -ating.** To make more bearable. [LL *alleviāre,* to lighten.] —**al·le′vi·a′tion** *n.* —**al·le′vi·a′tor** *n.*

al·ley (ăl′ē) *n., pl.* **-leys. 1.** A narrow passageway between or behind buildings. **2.** A bowl-ing alley. —**up one's alley.** *Slang.* Compatible with one's interests or qualifications. [< OF *alee,* fem pp of *aler,* to go.]

al·li·ance (ə-lī′əns) *n.* **1. a.** A pact of union or confederation between nations. **b.** The nations so conjoined. **2.** A union, relationship, or connection by kinship, marriage, or common interest. **3.** An affinity.

al·li·ga·tor (ăl′ə-gā′tər) *n.* **1.** A large amphibious reptile with sharp teeth, powerful jaws, and a shorter snout than the related crocodiles. **2.** Leather made from alligator hide. [< Span *el lagarto,* the lizard.]

alligator pear. An avocado. [Folk etym, var of AVOCADO.]

al·lit·er·ate (ə-lĭt′ə-rāt′) *v.* **-ated, -ating.** To form or arrange with alliteration.

al·lit·er·a·tion (ə-lĭt′ə-rā′shən) *n.* The occurrence of two or more words having the same initial sound, as *wailing in the winter wind.* [< AD- (to) + LETTER.] —**al·lit′er·a′tive** *adj.*

allo-. *comb. form.* Divergence, opposition, or difference. [< Gk *allos,* other.]

al·lo·cate (ăl′ō-kāt′, ăl′ə-) *v.* **-cated, -cating.** To allot; assign. [< ML *allocāre,* to place to.] —**al′lo·ca′tion** *n.*

al·lo·morph (ăl′ə-môrf′) *n. Ling.* Any of the variant forms of a morpheme; for example, the phonetic *s* of *cats, z* of *dogs,* and *iz* of *horses* are allomorphs of the English morpheme *s.* —**al′lo·mor′phic** (-môr′fĭk) *adj.*

al·lo·nym (ăl′ə-nĭm′) *n.* The name of one person assumed by another.

al·lo·phone (ăl′ə-fōn′) *n. Ling.* Any of the variant forms of a phoneme; for example, the *p* of *pit* and the *p* of *spit* are allophones of the English phoneme *p.* —**al′lo·phon′ic** (-fŏn′ĭk) *adj.*

al·lot (ə-lŏt′) *v.* **-lotted, -lotting. 1.** To distribute by lot. **2.** To give or assign. —**al·lot′ment** *n.*

al·lot·ro·py (ə-lŏt′rə-pē) *n.* The existence of two or more crystalline or molecular structural forms of an element. —**al′lo·trope** (ăl′ə-trōp′) *n.* —**al′lo·trop′ic** (ăl′ə-trŏp′ĭk) *adj.*

all-out (ôl′out′) *adj.* Wholehearted: *all-out effort.*

al·low (ə-lou′) *v.* **1.** To let happen; permit. **2.** To acknowledge or admit. **3.** To permit to have. **4.** To make provision for. **5.** To provide: *allow funds in case of emergency.* **6.** To admit: *allow that to be true.* [< OF *allouer,* to permit, approve.] —**al·low′a·ble** *adj.*

al·low·ance (ə-lou′əns) *n.* **1.** The act of allowing. **2.** A regular provision of money, food, etc. **3.** A price discount.

al·low·ed·ly (ə-lou′ĭd-lē) *adv.* By general admission; admittedly.

al·loy (ăl′oi′, ə-loi′) *n.* **1.** A macroscopically homogeneous mixture or solid solution, usually of two or more metals. **2.** Anything added that lowers value or purity. [< L *alligāre,* to bind to, ALLY.] —**al′loy′** (ə-loi′, ăl′oi′) *v.*

all right. 1. Satisfactory; average. **2.** Correct. **3.** Uninjured. **4.** Very well; yes. **5.** Without a doubt: *He's a fool, all right!*

all-round (ôl′round′) *adj.* Also **all-a·round** (ôl′ə-round′). **1.** Comprehensive in extent. **2.** Versatile.

All Saints' Day. November 1, a church festival in honor of all saints.

All Souls' Day. November 2, observed by the Roman Catholic Church as a day of prayer for souls in purgatory.

all•spice (ôl'spīs') *n.* The aromatic berries of a tropical American tree, used as a spice.

all-star (ôl'stär') *adj.* Made up of star performers.

al•lude (ə-lōōd') *v.* **-luded, -luding.** To refer to indirectly. [L *allūdere,* to play with.] —**al•lu'sion** *n.* —**al•lu'sive** *adj.*

al•lure (ə-lōōr') *v.* **-lured, -luring.** To entice with somethin' desirable; tempt. —*n.* The power to entice. [< OF *aleurrer.*] —**al•lure'ment** *n.* —**al•lur'ing•ly** *adv.*

al•lu•vi•um (ə-lōō'vē-əm) *n., pl.* **-viums** or **-via** (-vē-ə). Sediment deposited by flowing water, as in a river bed. [L < *alluere,* to wash against.] —**al•lu'vi•al** *adj.*

al•ly (ə-lī', ăl'ī') *v.* **-lied, -lying.** To unite or connect in a formal or close relationship or bond. —*n.* (ăl'ī', ə-lī') *pl.* **-lies.** One united with another in a formal or personal relationship. [< L *alligāre,* to bind to.]

al•ma ma•ter (ăl'mə mä'tər, ăl'mə). **1.** The school, college, or university one has attended. **2.** The anthem of a school, college, or university. [L, "cherishing or fostering mother."]

al•ma•nac (ôl'mə-năk', ăl'-) *n.* An annual publication having calendars with weather forecasts, astronomical information, and often other useful facts. [< ML *almanachus.*]

Al Ma•nam•ah (ăl mə-năm'ə). The capital of Bahrain. Pop. 89,000.

al•might•y (ôl-mī'tē) *adj.* **1.** Omnipotent. **2.** *Informal.* Great: *an almighty din.* —*n.* —**the Almighty.** God.

al•mond (ä'mənd, ăm'ənd) *n.* **1.** An oval, edible nut with a soft, light-brown shell. **2.** A tree bearing such nuts. [< LL *amandula* < L *amygdala.*]

al•most (ôl'mōst', ôl-mōst') *adv.* Slightly short of; not quite. [< OE *ealmǣst,* for the most part.]

alms (ämz) *pl.n.* Money or goods given to the poor in charity. [< OE *ælmesse* < Gmc **alemosina* < LL *eleēmosyna.*]

alms•house (ämz'hous') *n.* A poorhouse.

al•oe (ăl'ō) *n.* **1.** Any of various chiefly African plants having fleshy, spiny-toothed leaves. **2.** aloes *(takes sing. v.).* A cathartic drug made from the juice of the leaves of such a plant. [< OE *aluwe* < L *aloē.*] —**al'o•et'ic** (ăl'ō-ĕt'ĭk) *adj.*

a•loft (ə-lôft', ə-lŏft') *adv.* **1.** In or into a high place. **2.** Toward the upper rigging of a ship. [< ON *ā lopt,* "in the sky."]

a•lo•ha (ä-lō'hä') *interj. Hawaiian.* Expressive of greeting or farewell.

a•lone (ə-lōn') *adj.* **1.** Apart from other people; single; solitary. **2.** Excluding anything or anyone else; with nothing further; sole; only. [< ME *al one,* "all one."] —**a•lone'** *adv.*

a•long (ə-lông', ə-lŏng') *prep.* **1.** In a line with; following the length or path of. **2.** With a progressive motion. **3.** In association; together. **4.** As a companion: *Bring your son*

along. **5.** Advanced: *The evening was well along.* **6.** Approaching: *along about midnight.* —*prep.* Over, through, or by the length of. [< OE *andlang,* "extending opposite."]

a•long•shore (ə-lông'shôr', -shôr', ə-lŏng'-) *adv.* Along, near, or by the shore, either on land or in the water.

a•long•side (ə-lông'sīd', ə-lŏng'-) *adv.* Along, near, at, or to the side of anything. —*prep.* By the side of; side by side with.

a•loof (ə-lōōf') *adj.* Distant; indifferent. [< obs *aloufe!,* "(steer the ship) up into the wind!"] —**a•loof'ness** *n.*

a•loud (ə-loud') *adv.* **1.** Audibly: *afraid to say it aloud.* **2.** Orally: *Read this passage aloud.*

alp (ălp) *n.* A high mountain.

al•pac•a (ăl-păk'ə) *n.* **1.** A South American mammal related to the llama. **2. a.** The fine, soft wool of this animal. **b.** Cloth made from it. [Span.]

al•pen•horn (ăl'pən-hôrn') *n.* A long, curved horn used to call cows to pasture.

al•pen•stock (ăl'pən-stŏk') *n.* A long staff with an iron point, used by mountain climbers.

al•pha (ăl'fə) *n.* The 1st letter of the Greek alphabet, representing *a.*

al•pha•bet (ăl'fə-bĕt', -bĭt) *n.* **1.** The letters of a language, arranged in an order fixed by custom. See *Table of Alphabets* on following pages. **2.** Elementary principles; rudiments. [< Gk *alphabētos* : ALPHA + BETA.]

al•pha•bet•i•cal (ăl'fə-bĕt'ĭ-kəl) *adj.* Also **al•pha•bet•ic** (-bĕt'ĭk). **1.** Arranged in the customary order of the letters of a language. **2.** Expressed by an alphabet. —**al'pha•bet'i•cal•ly** *adv.*

al•pha•bet•ize (ăl'fə-bə-tīz') *v.* **-ized, -izing.** To arrange in alphabetical order.

Alpha Cen•tau•ri (sĕn-tôr'ē). A double star in Centaurus, 4.4 light-years from Earth.

alpha particle. *Symbol* α A positively charged composite particle, indistinguishable from a helium atom nucleus and consisting of two protons and two neutrons.

alpha ray. A stream of alpha particles.

alpha rhythm. Also **alpha wave.** The most common waveform found in electroencephalograms of the adult cerebral cortex, 8–12 smooth, regular oscillations/second in subjects at rest.

Alps (ălps). The major mountain system of south-central Europe, forming an arc from S France to Albania. —**Al'pine'** (ăl'pīn') *adj.*

al•read•y (ôl-rĕd'ē) *adv.* By this or a specified time. [ME *al redy,* "all ready."]

al•right (ôl-rīt') *adv. Nonstandard.* All right.

al•so (ôl'sō) *adv.* Besides; in addition; likewise; too. [< OE *ealswā,* even so.]

al•so-ran (ôl'sō-răn') *n.* One defeated in a competition.

alt. 1. alteration. **2.** alternate. **3.** altitude.

Alta. Alberta.

Al•ta•ic (ăl-tā'ĭk) *n.* A language family of Europe and Asia. —**Al•ta'ic** *adj.*

Al•ta•ir (ăl-tä'ĭr, ăl-târ') *n.* A very bright, double, variable star in the constellation Aquila, approx. 15.7 light-years from Earth.

al•tar (ôl'tər) *n.* Any elevated structure on

ô paw, for/oi boy/ou out/ōō took/ōō coo/p pop/r run/s sauce/sh shy/t to/th thin/*th* the/
ŭ cut/ûr fur/v van/w wag/y yes/z size/zh vision/ə ago, item, edible, gallop, circus/

TABLE OF ALPHABETS

The transliterations shown are those used in the etymologies of this Dictionary.

Arabic

The different forms in the four numbered columns are used when the letters are (1) in isolation; (2) in juncture with a previous letter; (3) in juncture with the letters on both sides; (4) in juncture with a following letter.

Long vowels are represented by the consonant signs 'alif (for ā), wāw (for ū), and yā (for ī). Short vowels are not usually written.

Transliterations with subscript dots represent "emphatic" or pharyngeal consonants, which are pronounced in the usual way except that the pharynx is tightly narrowed during articulation.

Hebrew

Vowels are not represented in normal Hebrew writing, but for educational purposes they are indicated by a system of subscript and superscript dots.

The transliterations shown in parentheses apply when the letter falls at the end of a word. The transliterations with subscript dots are pharyngeal consonants, as in Arabic.

The second forms shown are used when the letter falls at the end of a word.

Greek

The superscript ' on an initial vowel or rhō, called the "rough breathing," represents an aspirate. Lack of aspiration on an initial vowel is indicated by the superscript ', called the "smooth breathing."

When gamma precedes kappa, xi, khi, or another gamma, it has the value n and is so transliterated. The second lower-case form of sigma is used only in final position.

Russian

[1]This letter, called tvordiĭ znak, "hard sign," is very rare in modern Russian. It indicates that the previous consonant remains hard even though followed by a front vowel.

[2]This letter, called myakiĭ znak, "soft sign," indicates that the previous consonant is palatalized even when a front vowel does not follow.

	Forms				
1	2	3	4	Name	Sound
ا	ا			'alif	'
ب	ب	ـبـ	بـ	bā	b
ت	ت	ـتـ	تـ	tā	t
ث	ث	ـثـ	ثـ	thā	th
ج	ج	ـجـ	جـ	jīm	j
ح	ح	ـحـ	حـ	ḥā	ḥ
خ	خ	ـخـ	خـ	khā	kh
د	د			dāl	d
ذ	ذ			dhāl	dh
ر	ر			rā	r
ز	ز			zāy	z
س	س	ـسـ	سـ	sīn	s
ش	ش	ـشـ	شـ	shīn	sh
ص	ص	ـصـ	صـ	ṣād	ṣ
ض	ض	ـضـ	ضـ	ḍād	ḍ
ط	ط	ـطـ	طـ	ṭā	ṭ
ظ	ظ	ـظـ	ظـ	ẓā	ẓ
ع	ع	ـعـ	عـ	'ayn	
غ	غ	ـغـ	غـ	ghayn	gh
ف	ف	ـفـ	فـ	fā	f
ق	ق	ـقـ	قـ	qāf	q
ك	ك	ـكـ	كـ	kāf	k
ل	ل	ـلـ	لـ	lām	l
م	م	ـمـ	مـ	mīm	m
ن	ن	ـنـ	نـ	nūn	n
ه	ه	ـهـ	هـ	hā	h
و	و			wāw	w
ى	ى	ـىـ	ىـ	yā	y

HEBREW

Forms	Name	Sound
א	'aleph	
ב	bēth	b (bh)
ג	gimel	g (gh)
ד	dāleth	d (dh)
ה	hē	h
ו	waw	w
ז	zayin	z
ח	ḥeth	ḥ
ט	ṭeth	ṭ
י	yodh	y
כ ך	kāph	k (kh)
ל	lāmedh	l
מ ם	mēm	m
נ ן	nūn	n
ס	samekh	s
ע	'ayin	'
פ ף	pē	p (ph)
צ ץ	ṣadhe	ṣ
ק	qōph	q
ר	rēsh	r
שׂ	sin	s
שׁ	shin	sh
ת	tāw	t (th)

GREEK

Forms	Name	Sound
A α	alpha	a.
B β	beta	b
Γ γ	gamma	g (n)
Δ δ	delta	d
E ε	epsilon	e
Z ζ	zēta	z
H η	ēta	ē
Θ θ	thēta	th
I ι	iota	i
K κ	kappa	k
Λ λ	lambda	l
M μ	mu	m
N ν	nu	n
Ξ ξ	xi	x
O o	omicron	o
Π π	pi	p
P ρ	rhō	r (rh)
Σ σ ς	sigma	s
T τ	tau	t
Υ υ	upsilon	u
Φ φ	phi	ph
X χ	khi	kh
Ψ ψ	psi	ps
Ω ω	ōmega	ō

RUSSIAN

Forms	Sound
А а	a
Б б	b
В в	v
Г г	g
Д д	d
Е е	e
Ж ж	zh
З з	z
И и Й й	i, ĭ
К к	k
Л л	l
М м	m
Н н	n
О о	o
П п	p
Р р	r
С с	s
Т т	t
У у	u
Ф ф	f
Х х	kh
Ц ц	ts
Ч ч	ch
Ш ш	sh
Щ щ	shch
Ъ ъ	"1
Ы ы	y
Ь ь	'2
Э э	e
Ю ю	yu
Я я	ya

which sacrifices may be offered or incense burned or before which religious ceremonies may be enacted. [< OE < L *altāre*.]

al·tar·piece (ôl'tər-pēs') *n.* A painting, carving, etc., placed above and behind an altar.

al·ter (ôl'tər) *v.* **1.** To change; make or become different; modify. **2.** To castrate or spay. [< ML *alterāre* < L *alter*, other.] —**al'ter·a'tion** *n.*

al·ter·a·tive (ôl'tə-rā'tĭv) *adj.* **1.** Tending to alter or produce alteration. **2.** *Med.* Tending to restore normal health. —*n.* Also **al·ter·ant** (ôl'tər-ənt). *Med.* An alterative treatment or medication.

al·ter·ca·tion (ôl'tər-kā'shən) *n.* A heated and noisy quarrel. [< L *altercāri* < *alter*, another.]

al·ter e·go (ôl'tər ē'gō). **1.** Another aspect of oneself. **2.** An intimate friend. [L, "other I."]

al·ter·nate (ôl'tər-nāt', ăl'-) *v.* **-nated, -nating.** **1.** To occur in successive turns. **2.** To pass from one state, action, or place to a second and back indefinitely. —*adj.* (ôl'tər-nĭt, ăl'-). **1.** Happening or following in turns. **2.** Designating or pertaining to every other one of a series. **3.** Substitute: *an alternate plan.* —*n.* (ôl'tər-nĭt, ăl'-). A person acting in place of another. [L *alternāre* < *alter*, other.] —**al'ter·nate·ly** *adv.* —**al'ter·na'tion** *n.*

alternating current. Electric current that reverses direction at regular intervals.

al·ter·na·tive (ôl-tûr'nə-tĭv, ăl-) *n.* **1.** A choice between two or more than two possibilities. **2.** One of the things to be chosen. —*adj.* Allowing or necessitating a choice. —**al·ter'na·tive·ly** *adv.*

al·though (ôl-thō') *conj.* Also **al·tho.** Regardless of the fact that; even though.

al·tim·e·ter (ăl-tĭm'ə-tər) *n.* An instrument for determining altitude.

al·ti·tude (ăl'tə-t/yōōd') *n.* **1.** The height of a thing above a reference level, esp. above the earth's surface. **2.** The angular distance of a celestial object above the horizon. **3.** The perpendicular distance from the base of a geometric figure to the opposite vertex, parallel side, or parallel surface. [< L *altitūdō* < *altus*, high.] —**al'ti·tu'di·nal** *adj.*

al·to (ăl'tō) *n., pl.* **-tos. 1.** A low female singing voice. **2.** The range between soprano and tenor. [It, "high."]

al·to·geth·er (ôl'tə-gĕth'ər, ôl'tə-gĕth'ər) *adv.* **1.** Entirely. **2.** With all included or counted: *Altogether 100 people were there.*

al·tru·ism (ăl'trōō-ĭz'əm) *n.* Selfless concern for the welfare of others. [F *altruisme* < *autrui*, other.] —**al'tru·ist** *n.* —**al'tru·is'tic** *adj.* —**al'tru·is'ti·cal·ly** *adv.*

al·um (ăl'əm) *n.* Any of several similar double sulfates, esp. AlK(SO$_4$)$_2$•12H$_2$O, used medicinally as topical astringents and styptics. [< L *alūmen*.]

a·lu·mi·na (ə-lōō'mə-nə) *n.* Any of several forms of aluminum oxide, Al$_2$O$_3$, used in aluminum production and in abrasives, refractories, and ceramics. [< L *alūmen*, ALUM.]

a·lu·mi·num (ə-lōō'mə-nəm) *n.* Also chiefly *Brit.* **a·lu·min·i·um** (ăl'yə-mĭn'ē-əm). *Symbol* **Al** A silvery-white, ductile metallic element used to form many hard, light, corrosion-resistant

alloys. Atomic number 13, atomic weight 26.98. [< ALUMINA + -IUM.]

a·lum·na (ə-lŭm'nə) *n., pl.* **-nae** (-nē'). A female graduate or former student of a school, college, or university.

a·lum·nus (ə-lŭm'nəs) *n., pl.* **-ni** (-nī'). A male graduate or former student of a school, college, or university. [L, a pupil, foster son.]

al·ways (ôl'wāz, -wĭz) *adv.* **1.** On every occasion. **2.** Continuously; forever. [< OE *ealne weg*, "(along) all the way."]

am (ăm; *unstressed* əm). 1st person sing. present indicative of **be.** [< OE *eam*. See **es-**.]

am amplitude modulation.

Am americium.

AM amplitude modulation.

Am. America; American.

a.m. ante meridiem.

A.M. **1.** ante meridiem. **2.** Master of Arts.

AMA American Medical Association.

a·main (ə-mān') *adv.* With full force.

a·mal·gam (ə-măl'gəm) *n.* **1.** An alloy of mercury with other metals, as with tin or silver. **2.** A blend of diverse elements. [< ML *amalgama*.]

a·mal·ga·mate (ə-măl'gə-māt') *v.* **-mated, -mating.** To form an amalgam. —**a·mal'ga·ma'tion** *n.* —**a·mal'ga·ma'tor** *n.*

a·man·u·en·sis (ə-măn'yōō-ĕn'sĭs) *n., pl.* **-ses** (-sēz). A secretary. [< L *(servus) ā manū*, "(slave) at hand(writing)."]

am·a·ranth (ăm'ə-rănth') *n.* **1.** Any of various often weedy plants with greenish or purplish flowers. **2.** An imaginary flower that never fades. [< Gk *amarantos*, unfading.] —**am'a·ran'thine** *adj.*

Am·a·ril·lo (ăm'ə-rĭl'ō). A city of Texas. Pop. 138,000.

am·a·ryl·lis (ăm'ə-rĭl'ĭs) *n.* A bulbous plant having large, lilylike reddish or white flowers. [< L, girl's name.]

a·mass (ə-măs') *v.* To accumulate. [< OF *amasser*.] —**a·mass'ment** *n.*

am·a·teur (ăm'ə-chōōr', -ə-tər, -ə-tyōōr') *n.* **1.** One who engages in an activity as a pastime rather than as a profession. **2.** One lacking expertise. [< L *amātōr*, a lover.] —**am'a·teur'ish** *adj.* —**am'a·teur·ism'** *n.*

am·a·to·ry (ăm'ə-tôr'ē, -tōr'ē) *adj.* Of or expressive of sexual love.

a·maze (ə-māz') *v.* **amazed, amazing.** To affect with surprise or wonder; astound. [< OE *āmasian*, to bewilder.] —**a·maz'ed·ly** (ə-mā'zĭd-lē) *adv.* —**a·maze'ment** *n.*

Am·a·zon[1] (ăm'ə-zŏn', -zən) *n.* **1.** *Gk.Myth.* A member of a nation of female warriors in a region near the Black Sea. **2. amazon.** A tall, vigorous, aggressive woman. [< Gk.] —**Am'a·zo'ni·an** (-zō'nē-ən) *adj.*

Am·a·zon[2] (ăm'ə-zŏn', -zən). A river of South America rising in the Andes and flowing through N Brazil to the Atlantic. —**Am'a·zo'ni·an** (-zō'nē-ən) *adj.*

amb. ambassador.

am·bas·sa·dor (ăm-băs'ə-dər, -dôr') *n.* An official representative of the highest rank, accredited by one government to another. [< Gmc *ambakhtaz < L *ambactus*, vassal.]

ă pat/ā ate/âr care/ä bar/b bib/ch chew/d deed/ĕ pet/ē be/f fit/g gag/h hat/hw what/ ĭ pit/ī pie/îr pier/j judge/k kick/l lid, fatal/m mum/n no, sudden/ng sing/ŏ pot/ō go/

—am•bas′sa•do′ri•al (ăm-băs′ə-dôr′ē-əl, -dôr′ē-əl) *adj.* —am•bas′sa•dor•ship′ *n.*

am•ber (ăm′bər) *n.* **1.** A hard, translucent yellow, orange, or brownish-yellow fossil resin, used for jewelry and ornaments. **2.** Medium to dark orange yellow. [< Ar *'anbar,* ambergris, amber.] —am′ber *adj.*

am•ber•gris (ăm′bər-grĭs′, -grēs′) *n.* A waxy, grayish substance produced by sperm whales and used in making perfumes. [< OF *ambre gris,* "amber gray."]

ambi-. *comb. form.* Both. [< L.]

am•bi•ance (ăm′bē-əns) *n.* Environment; atmosphere. [< L *ambiēns,* AMBIENT.]

am•bi•dex•trous (ăm′bĭ-dĕk′strəs) *adj.* Able to use both hands with equal facility.

am•bi•ent (ăm′bē-ənt) *adj.* Surrounding. [< L *ambīre,* to go around.]

am•big•u•ous (ăm-bĭg′yōō-əs) *adj.* **1.** Susceptible of multiple interpretation. **2.** Doubtful; uncertain. [L *ambiguus,* uncertain < *ambigere,* to wander about.] —am′bi•gu′i•ty (-gyōō′ə-tē), am•big′u•ous•ness *n.*

am•bi•tion (ăm-bĭsh′ən) *n.* **1.** A strong desire to achieve something; will to succeed. **2.** The object or goal desired. [< L *ambitiō,* a going around (for votes).]

am•bi•tious (ăm-bĭsh′əs) *adj.* **1.** Characterized by ambition. **2.** Challenging: *an ambitious plan.* —am•bi′tious•ly *adv.*

am•biv•a•lence (ăm-bĭv′ə-ləns) *n.* The existence of mutually conflicting feelings about a person or thing. [Gm *Ambivalenz* (coined by Freud).] —am•biv′a•lent *adj.*

am•ble (ăm′bəl) *v.* -bled, -bling. To move at an easy gait; saunter. [< L *ambulāre.*] —am′ble *n.* —am′bler *n.*

am•bro•sia (ăm-brō′zhə, -zhē-ə) *n.* **1.** The food of the Greek gods and immortals. **2.** Something of exquisite flavor or fragrance. [< Gk, "immortality."] —am•bro′sial *adj.*

am•bu•lance (ăm′byə-ləns) *n.* A vehicle equipped to transport the sick or wounded. [< F *(hôpital) ambulant,* itinerant (hospital).]

am•bu•la•to•ry (ăm′byə-lə-tôr′ē, -tōr′ē) *adj.* **1.** Of or involving walking. **2.** Capable of walking. **3.** Moving about; movable. [< L *ambulāre,* to go about, walk.]

am•bus•cade (ăm′bə-skād′) *n.* An ambush.

am•bush (ăm′boŏosh′) *n.* **1.** Concealment from which a surprise attack is launched: *lie in ambush.* **2.** A surprise attack made from a concealed position. [< VL **imboscāre,* "to hide in the bushes."] —am′bush′ *v.*

a•me•ba. Variant of amoeba.

a•me•lio•rate (ə-mēl′yə-rāt′) *v.* -rated, -rating. To make or become better; improve. [< F *améliorer,* to improve.] —a•me′lio•ra′tion *n.*

a•men (ä-mĕn′, ā-) *interj.* Used at the end of prayers to express solemn concurrence. [< Heb *āmēn,* certainly, verily.]

a•me•na•ble (ə-mē′nə-bəl, ə-mĕn′ə-) *adj.* **1.** Tractable; responsive: *amenable to reason.* **2.** Responsible; accountable. [< F *amener,* to lead, bring.] —a•me′na•bil′i•ty *n.*

a•mend (ə-mĕnd′) *v.* **1.** To improve. **2.** To correct; rectify. **3.** To alter (a law) formally. [< L *ēmendāre,* to free from faults.]

a•mend•ment (ə-mĕnd′mənt) *n.* **1.** Improvement, correction, or reformation. **2. a.** A formal alteration of a law. **b.** The parliamentary process whereby such alteration is made.

a•mends (ə-mĕndz′) *pl.n.* Reparation for insult or injury.

a•men•i•ty (ə-mĕn′ə-tē, ə-mē′nə-) *n., pl.* -ties. **1.** Pleasantness; agreeableness. **2.** A means of comfort or convenience. **3. amenities.** Social courtesies; civilities. [< L *amoenus,* pleasant, delightful.]

Amer. America; American.

a•merce (ə-mûrs′) *v.* amerced, amercing. **1.** To penalize by an arbitrary fine. **2.** To punish. [< NF *a merci,* at the mercy of.]

A•mer•i•ca (ə-mĕr′ə-kə). **1.** The United States of America. **2.** North America. **3.** South America. **4.** Often **the Americas.** North America, Central America, and South America together. [< *Americus* Vespucius (Latinized form of Amerigo VESPUCCI).]

A•mer•i•can (ə-mĕr′ə-kən) *n.* A native of one of the Americas or a U.S. citizen. —**A•mer′i•can** *adj.*

A•mer•i•ca•na (ə-mĕr′ə-kä′nə, -kăn′ə, -kā′nə) *pl.n.* A collection of things relating to American history, folklore, or geography.

American English. English as spoken in the U.S.

American Indian. A member of any of the aboriginal peoples of North America (except the Eskimos), South America, and the West Indies.

A•mer•i•can•ism (ə-mĕr′ə-kən-ĭz′əm) *n.* **1.** A custom, trait, or tradition originating in the U.S. **2.** A language usage characteristic of American English.

A•mer•i•can•ize (ə-mĕr′ə-kən-īz′) *v.* To make or become American in spirit or methods. —**A•mer′i•can•i•za′tion** *n.*

American Legion. An organization of U.S. veterans of World War I, World War II, and the Korean War, founded in 1919.

American Library Association. An organization of libraries and librarians, founded in 1876.

American Revolution. The war fought between Great Britain and her colonies in North America (1775–83) by which the colonies won independence; Revolutionary War.

American Samoa. A group of U.S. islands in the South Pacific. Pop. 20,000.

American Spanish. The Spanish language of the W Hemisphere.

am•er•ic•i•um (ăm′ə-rĭsh′ē-əm) *n. Symbol* **Am** A white metallic radioactive element used as a radiation source in research. Atomic number 95, longest-lived isotope Am 243.

Am•er•ind (ăm′ə-rĭnd′) *n.* An American Indian or an Eskimo. —**Am′er•in′di•an** *adj. & n.*

am•e•thyst (ăm′ə-thĭst) *n.* A purple or violet form of transparent quartz or a purple variety of corundum, used as a gemstone. [< Gk *amethustos,* amethyst, "anti-intoxicant."]

a•mi•a•ble (ā′mē-ə-bəl) *adj.* **1.** Good-natured; agreeable. **2.** Cordial; friendly. [< LL *amīcābilis,* AMICABLE.] —**a′mi•a•bil′i•ty, a′mi•a•ble•ness** *n.* —**a′mi•a•bly** *adv.*

ô paw, for/oi boy/ou out/ŏŏ took/ōō coo/p pop/r run/s sauce/sh shy/t to/th thin/*th* the/
ŭ cut/ûr fur/v van/w wag/y yes/z size/zh vision/ə ago, item, edible, gallop, circus/

am•i•ca•ble (ăm'ĭ-kə-bəl) *adj.* Friendly; peaceable. [< LL *amicābilis* < L *amicus*, friend.] —**am'i•ca•bil'i•ty, am'i•ca•ble•ness** *n.* —**am'i•ca•bly** *adv.*

a•mid (ə-mĭd') *prep.* Also **a•midst** (ə-mĭdst'). In the middle of; among.

a•mid•ships (ə-mĭd'shĭps') *adv.* Midway between the bow and the stern of a ship.

a•mi•no acid (ə-mē'nō, ăm'ə-nō'). **1.** Any organic compound containing both an amino group (NH₂) and a carboxylic acid group (COOH). **2.** A compound of the form NH₂CHRCOOH, found as an essential component of the protein molecule. [< AM(MO-NIUM) + -INE.]

A•mish (ä'mĭsh, ăm'ĭsh) *pl.n.* Mennonites of a sect founded in the 17th century by Jacob Amman, Swiss religious reformer. —**A'mish** *adj.*

a•miss (ə-mĭs') *adj.* Out of proper order; wrong. —*adv.* In an improper or faulty way. —**take amiss.** To misunderstand or feel offended by. [< ME *a mis.*]

am•i•ty (ăm'ə-tē) *n.* Friendly relations, as between states. [< L *amicus*, friend.]

Am•man (ä-mǎn'). The capital of Jordan. Pop. 296,000.

am•me•ter (ăm'mē'tər) *n.* An instrument that measures electric current.

am•mo (ăm'ō) *n. Mil.* Ammunition.

am•mo•nia (ə-mōn'yə) *n.* **1.** A colorless, pungent gas, NH₃, extensively used to manufacture fertilizers and a wide variety of nitrogen-containing organic and inorganic chemicals. **2.** Ammonium hydroxide. [< L (*sal*) *ammōniācus*, "(salt) of *Amen*" (Egyptian god of life).]

ammonia water. Ammonium hydroxide.

am•mo•ni•um (ə-mō'nē-əm) *n.* The ion NH₄⁺. [< AMMON(IA).]

ammonium hydroxide. A colorless basic aqueous solution of ammonia, NH₄OH.

am•mu•ni•tion (ăm'yə-nĭsh'ən) *n.* **1. a.** Projectiles, along with their fuzes and primers, that can be fired from guns. **b.** Explosive materials used in war. **2.** Any means of offense or defense. [< OF *la munition*, the munition.]

am•ne•sia (ăm-nē'zhə) *n.* Loss of memory. [< Gk *amnēsia.*] —**am•ne'si•ac'** (ăm-nē'zē-ăk', -zhē-ăk') *n. & adj.*

am•nes•ty (ăm'nəs-tē) *n., pl.* **-ties.** A general pardon, esp. for political offenders. [< Gk *amnēstia*, "forgetfulness."]

a•moe•ba, a•me•ba (ə-mē'bə) *n., pl.* **-bas** or **-bae** (-bē). Any of various minute one-celled organisms having an indefinite, changeable form. [< Gk *amoibē*, change.] —**a•moe'bic** (-bĭk) *adj.*

a•mok. Variant of **amuck.**

a•mong (ə-mŭng') *prep.* Also **a•mongst** (ə-mŭngst'). **1.** In or through the midst of. **2.** In the group, number, or company of. **3.** By the joint action of. **4.** With portions to each of. **5.** Between one another. See **mag-.** [< OE *gemang*, a crowd. See **mag-.**]

a•mon•til•la•do (ə-mŏn'tə-lä'dō) *n., pl.* **-dos.** A pale dry sherry. [Span.]

a•mor•al (ā-môr'əl, ā-mŏr'əl) *adj.* Neither

moral nor immoral. —**a'mo•ral'i•ty** (ā'mô-rǎl'ə-tē) *n.* —**a•mor'al•ly** *adv.*

am•o•rous (ăm'ər-əs) *adj.* Of, inclined to, or indicative of sexual love. [< L *amor*, love < *amāre*, to love.] —**am'or•ous•ness** *n.*

a•mor•phous (ə-môr'fəs) *adj.* **1.** Lacking definite form. **2.** Lacking distinct crystalline structure. [< Gk *amorphos.*] —**a•mor'phous•ly** *adv.* —**a•mor'phous•ness** *n.*

am•or•tize (ăm'ər-tīz', ə-môr'tīz') *v.* **-tized, -tizing.** To liquidate (as a debt) by installment payments. [< VL *admortīre*, to deaden.] —**am'or•ti•za'tion** *n.*

a•mount (ə-mount') *n.* **1.** A total, aggregate, or sum. **2.** Principal plus its interest. **3.** Quantity. —*v.* **1.** To reach as a total. **2.** To be equivalent or tantamount. [< OF *amont*, upward, "to the mountain."]

a•mour (ə-mōōr') *n.* An illicit love affair. [< L *amor*, love.]

a•mour-pro•pre (ə-mōōr'prôp'r') *n.* Self-respect.

am•per•age (ăm'pər-ĭj, ăm'pîr'ĭj) *n.* The strength of an electric current expressed in amperes.

am•pere (ăm'pîr') *n.* A unit of electric current: the steady current that when flowing in straight parallel wires of infinite length, separated by a distance of one meter in free space, produces a force between the wires of 2×10^{-7} newtons per meter of length. [< A.M. *Ampère* (1775–1836), French mathematician.]

am•per•sand (ăm'pər-sănd') *n.* The character (&) representing *and*. [Contraction of "*and per se and*," "& (the sign) by itself (equals) *and*."]

am•phet•a•mine (ăm-fĕt'ə-mēn', -mĭn) *n.* **1.** A colorless volatile liquid, C₉H₁₃N, used primarily as a central nervous system stimulant. **2.** A phosphate or sulfate of amphetamine, similarly used.

amphi–. *comb. form.* **1.** On both sides or ends or on all sides. **2.** Around. [< Gk *amphi*, on both sides.]

am•phib•i•an (ăm-fĭb'ē-ən) *n.* **1.** An organism, as a frog or toad, having an aquatic early stage and developing air-breathing lungs as an adult. **2.** An aircraft that can take off and land on either land or water. **3.** A vehicle that can move over land and on water. —*adj.* Amphibious.

am•phib•i•ous (ăm-fĭb'ē-əs) *adj.* **1.** Able to live both on land and in water. **2.** Able to operate on land and water. [Gk *amphibios*, "living a double life."]

am•phi•the•a•ter (ăm'fə-thē'ə-tər) *n.* An oval or round building having tiers of seats rising around an arena.

am•pho•ra (ăm'fə-rə) *n., pl.* **-rae** (-rē') or **-ras.** An ancient Greek jar with two handles and a narrow neck, used to carry wine or oil. [L.]

am•ple (ăm'pəl) *adj.* **-pler, -plest. 1.** Large; capacious. **2.** Sufficient; abundant. [< L *amplus.*] —**am'ple•ness** *n.* —**am'ply** *adv.*

am•pli•fy (ăm'plə-fī') *v.* **-fied, -fying. 1.** To enlarge, extend, or increase. **2.** To make louder. —**am'pli•fi•ca'tion** (-fə-kā'shən) *n.* —**am'pli•fi•ca'tive** (-fĭ-kā'tĭv) *adj.* —**am'pli•fi'er** *n.*

am•pli•tude (ăm'plə-t/y/ōōd') *n.* **1.** Fullness;

ă pat/ā ate/âr care/ä bar/b bib/ch chew/d deed/ĕ pet/ē be/f fit/g gag/h hat/hw what/
ĭ pit/ī pie/îr pier/j judge/k kick/l lid, fatal/m mum/n no, sudden/ng sing/ŏ pot/ō go/

copiousness. **2.** Breadth, as of mind. **3.** The maximum value of a periodically varying quantity.

amplitude modulation. The encoding of a carrier wave by variation of its amplitude in accordance with an input signal.

am•poule, am•pule (ăm′p/y/ōōl) *n.* A small sealed vial used as a container for a hypodermic injection solution. [< L *ampulla.*]

am•pu•tate (ăm′pyōō-tāt′) *v.* **-tated, -tating.** To cut off, as a limb. [L *amputāre,* to cut around.] —**am′pu•ta′tion** *n.*

am•pu•tee (ăm′pyōō-tē′) *n.* A person who has had one or more limbs amputated.

Am•ster•dam (ăm′stər-dăm′). The constitutional capital of the Netherlands. Pop. 868,000.

amt. amount.

amu *Phys.* atomic mass unit.

a•muck (ə-mŭk′) *adv.* Also **a•mok** (ə-mŭk′, ə-mŏk′). In a murderous frenzy or in a fit of wildness: *run amuck.* [Malay *amok,* furious attack.]

am•u•let (ăm′yə-lĭt) *n.* Something worn as a charm against evil or injury. [L *amulētum.*]

A•mur (ä-mōōr′). A river of E Asia.

a•muse (ə-myōōz′) *v.* **amused, amusing.** To entertain; divert. [< OF *amuser,* "to cause to idle away time."] —**a•muse′ment** *n.*

a•myg•da•lin (ə-mĭg′də-lĭn) *n.* *Chem.* Laetrile.

an (ăn, ən). *indef. art.* A form of *a* used before words beginning with a vowel or with an unpronounced *h: an elephant; an hour.* [< OE *ān,* one. See o**ino**-.]

an–. *comb. form.* Not; without. [Gk *an-,* not.]

–an, –n. *comb. form.* **1.** Pertaining to, belonging to, or resembling: **Mexican. 2.** Believing in or adhering to: *Mohammedan.*

ana–. *comb. form.* **1.** Upward progression. **2.** Reversion. **3.** Renewal or intensification. [< Gk *ana,* up.]

a•nach•ro•nism (ə-năk′rə-nĭz′əm) *n.* **1.** The error of placing persons, things, or events in an inappropriate historical period. **2.** One that is chronologically out of place, esp. one that is behind the times. [< Gk *anakhronismos.*] —**a•nach′ro•nis′tic, a•nach′ro•nis′ti•cal** *adj.* —**a•nach′ro•nis′ti•cal•ly** *adv.*

an•a•con•da (ăn′ə-kŏn′də) *n.* A large tropical American snake that constricts its prey in its coils. [Perh < Dravid.]

a•nae•mi•a. Variant of **anemia.**

an•aes•the•sia. Variant of **anesthesia.**

an•a•gram (ăn′ə-grăm′) *n.* A word formed by transposing the letters of another word. [< ANA- + -GRAM.]

An•a•heim (ăn′ə-hīm′). A city in SW California. Pop. 104,000.

a•nal (ā′nəl) *adj.* Of or near the anus.

anal. 1. analogous; analogy. **2.** analysis; analytic.

an•al•ge•si•a (ăn′əl-jē′zē-ə, -zhə) *n.* Inability to feel pain while conscious. [< Gk *analgēsia,* want of feeling.] —**an′al•ge′sic** *adj. & n.*

analog computer. A computer in which numerical data are represented by analogous physical magnitudes or electrical signals.

a•nal•o•gous (ə-năl′ə-gəs) *adj.* Similar in a

way that permits the drawing of an analogy. [< Gk *analogos,* proportionate.]

an•a•logue (ăn′ə-lôg′, -lŏg′) *n.* Also **an•a•log. 1.** Something that bears an analogy to something else. **2.** *Biol.* An organ or structure that is similar in function to one in another kind of organism but is of dissimilar evolutionary origin.

a•nal•o•gy (ə-năl′ə-jē) *n., pl.* **-gies. 1.** Correspondence in some respects between things otherwise dissimilar. **2.** An inference that if two things are alike in some respects they must be alike in others.

a•nal•y•sis (ə-năl′ə-sĭs) *n., pl.* **-ses** (-sēz′). **1.** The separation of a whole into constituents with a view to its examination and interpretation. **2.** A statement of the results of such a study. **3.** Psychoanalysis. [< Gk *analusis,* a releasing.] —**an′a•lyst** *n.* —**an′a•lyt′ic** (-ə-lĭt′ĭk), **an′a•lyt′i•cal** *adj.*

an•a•lyze (ăn′ə-līz′) *v.* **-lyzed, -lyzing.** To make an analysis of.

an•a•pest (ăn′ə-pĕst′) *n.* A metrical foot composed of two short syllables followed by one long one. [< Gk *anapaistos,* "struck back."]

an•ar•chic (ăn-är′kĭk) *adj.* Also **an•ar•chi•cal** (-kĭ-kəl). Lacking order or control; lawless. —**an•ar′chi•cal•ly** *adv.*

an•ar•chism (ăn′ər-kĭz′əm) *n.* The theory that all forms of government are oppressive and should be abolished. —**an′ar•chist** *n.* —**an′ar•chis′tic** *adj.*

an•ar•chy (ăn′ər-kē) *n., pl.* **-chies. 1.** Absence of any form of political authority. **2.** Disorder and confusion. [Gk *anarkhia.*]

anat. anatomical; anatomist; anatomy.

a•nath•e•ma (ə-năth′ə-mə) *n., pl.* **-mas. 1.** A formal ban or curse, as an excommunication. **2.** Someone or something cursed or shunned. [LL, a curse, a person cursed, an offering.] —**a•nath′e•ma•tize′** *v.* **(-tized, -tizing).**

An•a•to•li•a (ăn′ə-tō′lē-ə). Asia Minor.

An•a•to•li•an (ăn′ə-tō′lē-ən) *n.* An extinct group of Indo-European languages of ancient Anatolia, including Hittite. —**An′a•to′li•an** *adj.*

a•nat•o•my (ə-năt′ə-mē) *n., pl.* **-mies. 1.** The structure of an organism or organ. **2.** The science of the structure of organisms and their parts. **3.** A detailed analysis. [< Gk *anatomē,* dissection.] —**an′a•tom′i•cal** (-ə-tŏm′ĭ-kəl), **an′a•tom′ic** *adj.*

anc. ancient.

–ance, –ancy. *comb. form.* An action, quality, or condition: **riddance, compliancy.**

an•ces•tor (ăn′sĕs′tər) *n.* A person or organism from which another or others have descended. [< L *antecessor,* "one that goes before" < *antecēdere,* to go before.]

an•ces•try (ăn′sĕs′trē) *n., pl.* **-tries. 1.** Line of descent; lineage. **2.** Ancestors collectively. —**an•ces′tral** (ăn-sĕs′trəl) *adj.*

an•chor (ăng′kər) *n.* A heavy metal device attached to a vessel and cast overboard to keep the vessel in place. —**at anchor.** Anchored. —*v.* To hold or be held with or as with an anchor. [< OE *ancor* < L *anc(h)ora.*]

an•chor•age (ăng′kər-ĭj) *n.* A place for anchoring a ship.

ô paw, for/oi boy/ou out/ōō took/ōō coo/p pop/r run/s sauce/sh shy/t to/th thin/*th* the/
ŭ cut/ûr fur/v van/w wag/y yes/z size/zh vision/ə ago, item, edible, gallop, circus/

An•chor•age (ăng'kər-ĭj). A city of Alaska. Pop. 44,000.

an•cho•rite (ăng'kə-rīt') *n.* A religious hermit. [< LGk *anakhōrêtês,* "one who withdraws."] —**an'cho•rit'ic** (-rĭt'ĭk) *adj.*

an•cho•vy (ăn'chō'vē, ăn-chō'vē) *n.* Any of various small, edible, herringlike marine fishes. [Span *anchova.*]

an•cien ré•gime (äN-syăN' rā-zhēm'). 1. The political and social system in France before the revolution of 1789. 2. Any former system. [F, "former regime."]

an•cient (ān'shənt) *adj.* 1. Very old. 2. Belonging to times long past, esp. to the period before the fall of the Western Roman Empire (A.D. 476). —*n.* 1. A very old person. 2. ancients. The ancient Greeks and Romans. [< OF < VL *anteānus,* "going before" < L *ante,* before.] —**an'cient•ness** *n.*

Ancient Chinese. The language of ancient China.

Ancient Greek. See Greek.

an•cil•lar•y (ăn'sə-lĕr'ē) *adj.* 1. Subordinate. 2. Auxiliary; accessory: *ancillary functions.* [L *ancillāris,* servile.]

–ancy. Variant of -ance.

and (ənd, ən; *stressed* ănd) *conj.* 1. Together with or along with; as well as. 2. Added to; plus: *Two and two makes four.* 3. As a result: *Seek, and ye shall find.* 4. *Informal.* To. Used between finite verbs: *try and find it.* [< OE < Gmc *anda.*]

an•dan•te (än-dän'tā, ăn-dăn'tē) *adv. Mus.* Moderately slow in tempo. [It, "walking."] —**an•dan'te** *adj.*

an•dan•ti•no (än'dän-tē'nō, ăn'dăn-tē'nō) *adv. Mus.* Slightly faster in tempo than andante. [It, dim of ANDANTE.] —**an'dan•ti'no** *adj.*

An•des (ăn'dēz). A mountain system stretching the length of W South America from Venezuela to Tierra del Fuego. Highest elevation, Aconcagua (22,835 ft.). —**An'de•an** *adj.*

and•i•ron (ănd'ī'ərn) *n.* One of a pair of metal supports for logs in a fireplace. [< OF *andier,* firedog.]

and/or. Used to indicate that either *and* or *or* may be used to connect words, phrases, or clauses depending upon what meaning is intended.

An•dor•ra (ăn-dôr'ə, -dŏr'ə). A republic in the

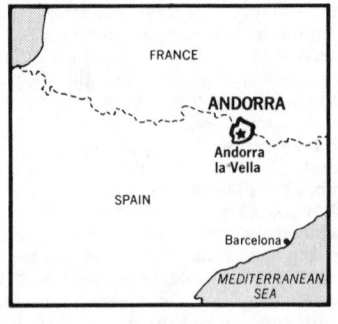

Andorra

E Pyrenees. Pop. 13,000. Cap. Andorra la Vella.

andro–. *comb. form.* The male sex or masculine. [< Gk *anēr (andr-),* man.]

an•dro•gen (ăn'drə-jən) *n.* A hormone that develops and maintains masculine characteristics. —**an'dro•gen'ic** (-jĕn'ĭk) *adj.*

an•drog•e•nous (ăn-drŏj'ə-nəs) *adj.* Pertaining to production of male offspring.

an•drog•y•nous (ăn-drŏj'ə-nəs) *adj.* Having female and male characteristics in one. —**an•drog'y•ny** *n.*

an•droid (ăn'droid') *n.* A synthetic man created from biological materials; a humanoid.

An•drom•e•da (ăn-drŏm'ə-də) *n.* A constellation in the N Hemisphere.

–andry. *comb. form.* Number of husbands: monandry.

–ane. *comb. form. Chem.* A saturated hydrocarbon: propane.

an•ec•dote (ăn'ĭk-dōt') *n.* A short account of an interesting or humorous incident. [< Gk *anekdota,* "things unpublished."] —**an'ec•do'tal** *adj.* —**an'ec•dot'ic** (ăn'ĭk-dŏt'ĭk) *adj.* —**an'ec•dot'ist** (-dō'tĭst) *n.*

an•e•cho•ic (ăn'ĕ-kō'ĭk) *adj.* Neither having nor producing echoes.

a•ne•mi•a (ə-nē'mē-ə) *n.* Also **a•nae•mi•a.** Pathological deficiency in the oxygen-carrying material of the blood. [< Gk *anaimia.*] —**a•ne'mic** *adj.*

an•e•mom•e•ter (ăn'ə-mŏm'ə-tər) *n.* An instrument for measuring wind force and speed. [< Gk *anemos,* wind.]

a•nem•o•ne (ə-nĕm'ə-nē) *n.* 1. Any of various plants having white, purple, or red cup-shaped flowers. 2. See sea anemone. [< Gk *anemōnē.*]

a•nent (ə-nĕnt') *prep.* Regarding; concerning. [< OE *on efen,* alongside.]

an•es•the•sia (ăn'ĭs-thē'zhə) *n.* Also **an•aes•the•sia.** Total or partial loss of sensation. [< Gk *anaisthēsia,* lack of sensation.]

an•es•the•si•ol•o•gy (ăn'ĭs-thē'zē-ŏl'ə-jē) *n.* Also **an•aes•the•si•ol•o•gy.** The medical study and application of anesthetics. —**an'es•the'si•ol'o•gist** *n.*

an•es•thet•ic (ăn'ĭs-thĕt'ĭk) *adj.* Also **an•aes•thet•ic.** Causing anesthesia. —*n.* An anesthetic agent.

an•es•the•tize (ə-nĕs'thə-tīz') *v.* -tized, -tizing. Also **an•aes•the•tize.** To induce anesthesia in. —**an•es'the•tist** *n.* —**an•es'the•ti•za'tion** *n.*

a•new (ə-n/y/ōō') *adv.* 1. Again. 2. In a new way.

an•gel (ān'jəl) *n.* 1. One of the immortal beings attendant upon God. 2. A kind and lovable person. 3. A financial backer of an enterprise, esp. a dramatic production. [< Gk *angelos,* messenger.] —**an•gel'ic** (-jĕl'ĭk), **an•gel'i•cal** *adj.* —**an•gel'i•cal•ly** *adv.*

an•gel•fish (ān'jəl-fĭsh') *n.* Any of several tropical fishes having a flattened body.

an•gel•i•ca (ăn-jĕl'ĭ-kə) *n.* A plant having aromatic seeds, leaves, stems, and roots used as flavoring.

an•ger (ăng'gər) *n.* A feeling of extreme hostility, indignation, or exasperation; wrath;

---

rage; ire. —*v.* To make or become angry. [< ON *angr,* grief.]

an•gi•na (ăn-jī′nə) *n.* 1. Any disease in which spasmodic and painful suffocation or spasms occur. 2. **Angina pectoris.** [L, quinsy.]

angina pec•to•ris (pĕk′tə-rĭs). Severe paroxysmal pain in the chest, associated with feelings of suffocation and apprehension. [NL, "angina of the chest."]

Angl. Anglican.

an•gle¹ (ăng′gəl) *v.* **-gled, -gling.** To fish with a hook and line. **—angle for.** To try to get something by using schemes. —*n. Slang.* A scheme. [< OE *angul,* fishhook. See ank-.] **—an′gler** *n.*

an•gle² (ăng′gəl) *n.* 1. a. The figure formed by two lines diverging from a common point. b. The rotation required to superimpose either of two such lines or angles on the other. 2. a. The position or direction from which an object is viewed. b. A point of view. —*v.* **-gled, -gling.** 1. To move or turn at an angle or by angles. 2. To hit (a ball) at an angle. [< L *angulus,* angle, corner.]

An•gles (ăng′gəlz) *pl.n.* A Germanic people that migrated to England in the 5th century A.D. and with the Jutes and Saxons formed the Anglo-Saxon peoples. [L *Anglī, Anglii* (pl) < Gmc.] **—An′gli•an** *adj. & n.*

an•gle•worm (ăng′gəl-wûrm′) *n.* An earthworm, used as fishing bait.

An•gli•can (ăng′glĭ-kən) *n.* A member of the Church of England or of any of its related churches, esp. the Protestant Episcopal Church. [< ML *Anglicus,* English.] **—An′gli•can** *adj.* **—An′gli•can•ism′** *n.*

An•gli•cism (ăng′glə-sĭz′əm) *n.* Also **an•gli•cism.** An idiom peculiar to the English language, esp. as spoken in England; Briticism.

An•gli•cize (ăng′glə-sīz′) *v.* **-cized, -cizing.** Also **an•gli•cize.** To make or become English in form, idiom, or character. **—An′gli•ci•za′tion** *n.*

Anglo–. *comb. form.* English or England.

An•glo•phile (ăng′glə-fīl′) *n.* Also **an•glo•phile.** An admirer of England. **—An′glo•phile′** *adj.* **—An′glo•phil′i•a** *n.*

An•glo•phobe (ăng′glə-fōb′) *n.* Also **an•glo•phobe.** One who has an aversion to England. **—An′glo•phobe′** *adj.* **—An′glo•pho′bi•a** *n.*

An•glo-Sax•on (ăng′glō-săk′sən) *n.* 1. A member of one of the Germanic peoples who settled in Britain in the 5th and 6th centuries A.D. 2. Any of the descendants of these peoples. 3. See **Old English.** 4. Any person of English ancestry. **—An′glo-Sax′on** *adj.*

An•go•la (ăng-gō′lə). An independent country occupying 481,351 square miles in SW Africa. Pop. 5,790,000. Cap. Luanda.

An•go•ra (ăng-gôr′ə, -gōr′ə) *n.* 1. A goat, rabbit, or cat with long, silky hair. 2. **angora.** Yarn or fabric made from the hair of an Angora goat or rabbit. [< *Angora,* former name for *Ankara.*]

an•gry (ăng′grē) *adj.* **-grier, -griest.** 1. Feeling, showing, or resulting from anger. 2. Having a menacing aspect: *angry clouds.* 3. Inflamed: *an angry sore.* **—an′gri•ly** (-grə-lē) *adv.*

angst (ängkst) *n.* A feeling of anxiety. [G.]

Ang•ström (ăng′strəm) *n. Symbol* **A** A unit of length equal to one hundred-millionth (10⁻⁸) of a centimeter. [< A.J. *Ångström* (1814–1874), Swedish physicist.]

an•guish (ăng′gwĭsh) *n.* An agonizing physical or mental pain. —*v.* To feel or cause to feel anguish. [< L *angustia,* narrowness.] **—an′-guished** *adj.*

an•gu•lar (ăng′gyə-lər) *adj.* 1. Having an angle or angles. 2. Measured by an angle or degrees of an arc. 3. Bony and lean. 4. Awkward: *an angular gait.* **—an′gu•lar′i•ty, an′gu•lar•ness** *n.* **—an′gu•lar•ly** *adv.*

an•hy•dride (ăn-hī′drīd′) *n.* A chemical compound formed from another by the removal of water.

an•hy•drous (ăn-hī′drəs) *adj.* Without water. [Gk *anudros,* waterless.]

an•i•line (ăn′ə-lĭn) *n.* Also **an•i•lin.** A colorless, oily, poisonous liquid, $C_6H_5NH_2$, used to manufacture rubber, dyes, resins, pharmaceuticals, and varnishes.

an•i•mad•vert (ăn′ə-măd-vûrt′) *v.* To comment critically, usually with disapproval. [L *animadvertere,* to direct the mind to.] **—an′i•mad•ver′sion** *n.*

an•i•mal (ăn′ə-məl) *n.* 1. An organism distinguished from a plant by structural and functional characteristics, such as the ability to move. 2. A nonhuman organism of this kind. 3. A bestial person; brute. —*adj.* 1. Of or relating to animals. 2. Sensual or physical as distinguished from spiritual. [< L *animālis,* living < *animus,* breath, soul.]

an•i•mal•cule (ăn′ə-măl′kyōōl) *n.* A microscopic or minute animal. [NL *animalculum,* dim of ANIMAL.]

animal starch. Glycogen.

an•i•mate (ăn′ə-māt′) *v.* **-mated, -mating.** 1. To give life to. 2. To impart interest to. 3. To inspire to action. 4. To make or produce (a cartoon) so as to convey the illusion of motion. —*adj.* (ăn′ə-mĭt). 1. Possessing life; living. 2. Of or relating to animal life. 3. Lively; vivacious. [L *animāre,* to fill with breath.] **—an′i•mat′ed•ly** *adv.* **—an′i•ma′tion** *n.*

a•ni•ma•to (ä′nē-mä′tō) *adv. Mus.* In an animated or lively manner. [It.] **—a′ni•ma′to** *adj.*

an•i•ma•tor (ăn′ə-mā′tər) *n.* One that animates, esp. an artist or technician who produces an animated cartoon.

an•i•mism (ăn′ə-mĭz′əm) *n.* Attribution of an innate soul to natural phenomena and objects. **—an′i•mist** *n.* **—an′i•mis′tic** *adj.*

an•i•mos•i•ty (ăn′ə-mŏs′ə-tē) *n., pl.* **-ties.** Bitter hostility or hatred. [< LL *animōsitās,* vehemence, spirit.]

an•i•mus (ăn′ə-məs) *n.* A feeling of animosity.

an•i•on (ăn′ī′ən) *n.* A negatively charged ion that migrates to an anode, as in electrolysis. [Gk, "that which goes up."] **—an′i•on′ic** (-ŏn′ĭk) *adj.*

an•ise (ăn′ĭs) *n.* 1. A plant having aromatic licorice-flavored seeds. 2. Also **an•i•seed** (ăn′ĭ-sēd′). The seeds, used as flavoring. [< Gk *anison.*]

an•i•sette (ăn′ə-sĕt′, -zĕt′) *n.* An anise-flavored liqueur.

ō paw, for/oi boy/ou out/ŏŏ took/ōō coo/p pop/r run/s sauce/sh shy/t to/th thin/*th* the/
ŭ cut/ûr fur/v van/w wag/y yes/z size/zh vision/ə ago, item, edible, gallop, circus/

An•ka•ra (ăng′kə-rə, äng′-). The capital of Turkey. Pop. 650,000.

an•kle (ăng′kəl) n. 1. The joint, consisting of the bones and related structure, that connects the foot with the leg. 2. The slender section of the leg immediately above the foot. [< ON *ankula* and OE *ancleow*. See ank-.]

an•klet (ăng′klĭt) n. 1. An ornament worn around the ankle. 2. A short sock covering the ankle.

ann. 1. annals. 2. annual. 3. annuity.

an•nals (ăn′əlz) pl.n. 1. A chronological record of the events of successive years. 2. Any descriptive record; history. [L *(librī) annālēs*, "yearly (books)."] —**an′nal•ist** n.

An•nap•o•lis (ə-năp′ə-lĭs). The capital of Maryland. Pop. 30,000.

an•neal (ə-nēl′) v. 1. To heat and slowly cool (glass or metal) to toughen and reduce brittleness. 2. To temper. [< OE *onǣlan.*]

an•nex (ə-nĕks′, ăn′ĕks) v. 1. To add or join to, esp. to a larger thing. 2. To incorporate (territory) into an existing country or state. —n. (ăn′ĕks′, ăn′ĭks). A building added on to a larger one or situated near the main one. [< L *annectere* (pp *annexus*), to bind to.] —**an′nex•a′tion** n.

an•ni•hi•late (ə-nī′ə-lāt′) v. -lated, -lating. To destroy completely. [< LL *annihilāre*, to reduce to nothing.] —**an•ni′hi•la′tor** n.

an•ni•hi•la•tion (ə-nī′ə-lā′shən) n. 1. An annihilating or being annihilated. 2. The phenomenon in which a particle and an antiparticle, such as an electron and a positron, disappear with a resultant release of energy approximately equivalent to the sum of their masses.

an•ni•ver•sa•ry (ăn′ə-vûr′sər-ē) n., pl. -ries. The annual recurrence of an event that took place in some preceding year or its commemorative celebration on this date. [< L *anniversārius*, "returning yearly."]

an•no Dom•i•ni (ăn′ō dŏm′ə-nī′, dŏm′ə-nē). In a specified year of the Christian era. [L, "in the year of the Lord."]

an•no•tate (ăn′ō-tāt′) v. -tated, -tating. To furnish (a literary work) with critical or explanatory notes. [L *annotāre*, to note down.] —**an′no•ta′tion** n. —**an′no•ta′tive** adj. —**an′no•ta′tor** n.

an•nounce (ə-nouns′) v. -nounced, -nouncing. 1. To bring to public notice. 2. To proclaim the arrival of. 3. To serve as an announcer. [< L *annuntiāre.*] —**an•nounce′ment** n.

an•nounc•er (ə-noun′sər) n. A radio or television performer who provides program continuity and gives commercial and other announcements.

an•noy (ə-noi′) v. 1. To bother or irritate. 2. To injure or harm; molest. [< LL *inodiāre*, to make odious.] —**an•noy′ing•ly** adv.

an•noy•ance (ə-noi′əns) n. 1. The act of annoying. 2. A nuisance. 3. Vexation; irritation.

an•nu•al (ăn′yōō-əl) adj. 1. Recurring or done every year; yearly. 2. Of or pertaining to a year: *an annual income.* 3. Living and growing for only one year or season: *annual plants.* —n. 1. A periodical published yearly; yearbook.

2. An annual plant. [< L *annus*, year.] —**an′nu•al•ly** adv.

an•nu•i•tant (ə-n/y/ōō′ə-tənt) n. A person who receives an annuity.

an•nu•i•ty (ə-n/y/ōō′ə-tē) n., pl. -ties. 1. The annual payment of an allowance or income. 2. a. The interest or dividends paid annually on an investment of money. b. The investment made.

an•nul (ə-nŭl′) v. -nulled, -nulling. To nullify or cancel, as a marriage or a law. [< LL *annullāre*, to make into nothing.] —**an•nul′la•ble** adj. —**an•nul′ment** n.

an•nu•lar (ăn′yə-lər) adj. Forming or shaped like a ring. [< L *annulus*, ring.] —**an′nu•lar•ly** adv.

an•nu•lus (ăn′yə-ləs) n., pl. -luses or -li (-lī′). A ringlike figure, part, structure, or marking. [L *annulus*, ring.]

an•nun•ci•ate (ə-nŭn′sē-āt′) v. -ated, -ating. To announce; proclaim. [L *annuntiāre*, to AN-NOUNCE.]

an•nun•ci•a•tion (ə-nŭn′sē-ā′shən) n. 1. The act of announcing. 2. Annunciation. a. The angel Gabriel's announcement of the Incarnation. Luke 1:26-38. b. The festival, on March 25, celebrating this.

an•ode (ăn′ōd′) n. A positively charged electrode. [Gk *anodos*, a way up.] —**an•o′dal** (-ō′-dəl), **an•od′ic** (-ŏd′ĭk) adj.

an•o•dize (ăn′ə-dīz′) v. -dized, -dizing. To coat (a metallic surface) by electrolysis with a protective oxide.

an•o•dyne (ăn′ə-dīn′) n. A soothing or pain-relieving agent. [< Gk *anōdunos*, free from pain.]

a•noint (ə-noint′) v. To apply oil to, esp. in a religious ceremony. [< L *inunguere.*] —**a•noint′er** n. —**a•noint′ment** n.

a•nom•a•ly (ə-nŏm′ə-lē) n., pl. -lies. 1. Deviation from the normal order, form, or rule; abnormality. 2. Anything irregular or abnormal. [< Gk *anōmalos*, uneven.] —**a•nom′a•lis′-tic** (-lĭs′tĭk) adj. —**a•nom′a•lous** adj.

a•non (ə-nŏn′) adv. In a short time; soon. [< OE *on ān*, "into one," at once.]

anon. anonymous.

a•non•y•mous (ə-nŏn′ə-məs) adj. Having an unknown or withheld name, authorship, or agency. [< Gk *anōnumos*, nameless.] —**an′o•nym′i•ty** (-ə-nĭm′ə-tē), **a•non′y•mous•ness** n. —**a•non′y•mous•ly** adv.

an•oth•er (ə-nŭth′ər) adj. 1. Additional; one more. 2. Distinctly different; some other. 3. Different but of the same character. —pron. 1. An additional or different one. 2. One of the same kind. [ME *an other.*]

ans. answer.

an•swer (ăn′sər, än′-) n. 1. A spoken or written reply, as to a question. 2. A solution or result, as to a problem. —v. 1. To reply to. 2. To respond correctly to. 3. To serve (a purpose). 4. To be responsible for. [< OE *andswaru.* See swer-¹.] —**an′swer•a•ble** adj. —**an′swer•er** n.

ant (ănt) n. Any of various usually wingless insects that live in complexly organized colonies. [< OE *ǣmette.* See mai-¹.]

–ant. *comb. form.* Performing, promoting, or causing an action: **deodorant.**

ant. **1.** antenna. **2.** antonym.

ant•ac•id (ănt-ăs′ĭd) *n.* A substance that neutralizes acid.

an•tag•o•nism (ăn-tăg′ə-nĭz′əm) *n.* Opposition; hostility. —**an•tag′o•nist** *n.* —**an•tag′o•nis′tic** *adj.* —**an•tag′o•nis′ti•cal•ly** *adv.*

an•tag•o•nize (ăn-tăg′ə-nīz′) *v.* **-nized, -nizing.** To arouse the hostility of. [Gk *antagōnizesthai,* to struggle against.]

Ant•arc•tic (ănt-ärk′tĭk, -är′tĭk) *adj.* Of or pertaining to the regions surrounding the South Pole. —*n.* **the Antarctic.** Antarctica and its surrounding waters. [< L *antarcticus,* southern.]

Ant•arc•ti•ca (ănt-ärk′tĭ-kə, -är′tĭ-kə). A continent largely contained within the Antarctic Circle, and almost entirely covered by a sheet of ice.

Antarctic Circle. A parallel of latitude, 66° 33′ S, marking the limit of the S Frigid Zone.

Antarctic Ocean. The waters surrounding Antarctica.

An•tar•es (ăn-târ′ēz) *n.* The brightest star in the southern sky, in the constellation Scorpius. [Gk *antarēs,* "opposite Mars."]

an•te (ăn′tē) *n. Poker.* The stake each player must put up before receiving his hand or new cards. —*v.* **-ted** or **-teed, -teing.** **1.** *Poker.* To put up (an ante). **2.** *Slang.* To pay (one's share). [< L *ante,* before.]

ante–. *comb. form.* **1.** In front of. **2.** Previous to. [< L *ante,* before, in front of.]

ant•eat•er (ănt′ē′tər) *n.* Any of various long-snouted animals that feed primarily on ants.

an•te-bel•lum (ăn′tē-běl′əm) *adj.* Of the period before the Civil War. [L *ante bellum,* before the war.]

an•te•ce•dent (ăn′tə-sēd′ənt) *adj.* Going before; preceding. —*n.* **1.** One that precedes. **2.** An event preceding another. **3. antecedents.** One's ancestry. **4.** The word, phrase, or clause to which a relative pronoun refers. —**an′te•ce′dence** *n.* —**an′te•ce′dent•ly** *adv.*

an•te•cham•ber (ăn′tĭ-chăm′bər) *n.* A smaller room leading into a larger one.

an•te•date (ăn′tĭ-dāt′) *v.* **-dated, -dating. 1.** To precede in time. **2.** To give a date earlier than the actual date.

an•te•di•lu•vi•an (ăn′tĭ-də-lōō′vē-ən) *adj.* **1.** Of the era before the Flood. **2.** Very old; antiquated.

an•te•lope (ăn′tə-lōp′) *n.* Any of various slender, swift-running, long-horned hoofed mammals. [< OF *antelop,* a mythical oriental beast.]

an•te me•rid•i•em (ăn′tē mə-rĭd′ē-əm). Before noon. [L.]

an•ten•na (ăn-těn′ə) *n.* **1.** *pl.* **-nae** (-nē). One of the paired, flexible, sensory organs on the head of an insect, crustacean, etc. **2.** *pl.* **-nas.** A metallic apparatus for sending and receiving electromagnetic waves; aerial. [L, sail yard.] —**an•ten′nal** *adj.*

an•te•pe•nult (ăn′tĭ-pē′nŭlt′, -pĭ-nŭlt′) *n.* The 3rd syllable from the end of a word. —**an′te•pe•nul′ti•mate** (-pĭ-nŭl′tə-mĭt) *adj. & n.*

an•te•ri•or (ăn-tîr′ē-ər) *adj.* **1.** Located in front. **2.** Prior in time. [< L *ante,* before.]

an•te•room (ăn′tĭ-rōōm′, -rŏŏm′) *n.* A waiting room.

an•them (ăn′thəm) *n.* **1.** A hymn of praise or loyalty. **2.** A sacred choral composition. [< OE *antefn,* antiphonal song < ML *antiphōna.*]

an•ther (ăn′thər) *n.* The pollen-bearing organ at the end of a stamen. [< ML *anthēra,* pollen.]

an•thol•o•gy (ăn-thŏl′ə-jē) *n., pl.* **-gies.** A collection of literary pieces. [< Gk *anthologia,* "flower gathering," a collection.] —**an•thol′o•gist** *n.*

an•thra•cite (ăn′thrə-sīt′) *n.* Coal having a high carbon content and little volatile matter; hard coal. [< ANTHRAX.]

an•thrax (ăn′thrăks′) *n.* An infectious, usually fatal disease of animals, esp. of cattle and sheep, that is transmissible to man. [< Gk, charcoal, carbuncle, pustule.]

anthrop. anthropological; anthropology.

anthropo–. *comb. form.* Man or human. [< Gk *anthrōpos,* man.]

an•thro•po•cen•tric (ăn′thrə-pō-sěn′trĭk) *adj.* Interpreting reality in terms of human values and experience.

an•thro•poid (ăn′thrə-poid′) *adj.* Resembling man, as certain apes. —*n.* An anthropoid ape, such as a gorilla or chimpanzee.

an•thro•pol•o•gy (ăn′thrə-pŏl′ə-jē) *n.* The scientific study of the origin, culture, and development of man. —**an′thro•po•log′ic** (-pə-lŏj′ĭk), **an′thro•po•log′i•cal** *adj.* —**an′thro•po•log′i•cal•ly** *adv.* —**an′thro•pol′o•gist** *n.*

an•thro•po•mor•phism (ăn′thrə-pō-môr′fĭz′əm) *n.* The attribution of human characteristics to nonhuman beings or things. —**an′thro•po•mor′phic** *adj.*

an•ti (ăn′tī′, ăn′tē) *n. Informal.* A person who is opposed to a group, policy, proposal, or practice. [< ANTI-.]

anti–. *comb. form.* **1.** Opposition to, effectiveness against, or counteraction. **2.** Reciprocal correspondence to. [< Gk *anti,* opposite, against.]

an•ti•bal•lis•tic missile (ăn′tĭ-bə-lĭs′tĭk, ăn′tī-). A defensive missile designed to intercept and destroy a ballistic missile in flight.

an•ti•bi•ot•ic (ăn′tĭ-bī-ŏt′ĭk, ăn′tī-) *n.* Any of various substances, such as penicillin and streptomycin, produced by certain fungi, bacteria, and other organisms, that inhibit the growth of or destroy microorganisms, and are widely used to prevent or treat diseases.

an•ti•bod•y (ăn′tĭ-bŏd′ē) *n., pl.* **-ies. 1.** Any of various proteins in the blood that are generated in reaction to foreign proteins or carbohydrates of certain types, neutralize them, and thus produce immunity against certain microorganisms or their toxins. **2.** An object composed of antimatter.

an•tic (ăn′tĭk) *n.* Often **antics.** A ludicrous act or gesture; a caper. [It *antico,* "ancient," "grotesque."] —**an′tic** *adj.*

an•ti•christ (ăn′tĭ-krĭst′) *n.* **1.** A great enemy of Christ. **2. Antichrist.** Title of Christ's personal antagonist. I John 2:18.

---

an•tic•i•pate (ăn-tĭs'ə-pāt') *v.* -pated, -pating. **1.** To realize beforehand; foresee. **2.** To look forward to. **3.** To act in advance to prevent; forestall. [L *anticipāre*, to take before.] —**an•tic'i•pa'tion** *n.* —**an•tic'i•pa'tor** *n.* —**an•tic'i•pa•to'ry** (-pə-tôr'ē, -tōr'ē) *adj.*

an•ti•cli•max (ăn'tĭ-klī'măks') *n.* **1.** A decline in disappointing contrast with a previous rise. **2.** Something commonplace concluding a series of significant events. —**an'ti•cli•mac'tic** *adj.* —**an'ti•cli•mac'ti•cal•ly** *adv.*

an•ti•dote (ăn'tĭ-dōt') *n.* Something that counteracts a poison or injury. [< Gk *antidoton.*] —**an'ti•dot'al** (ăn'tĭ-dōt'l) *adj.*

an•ti•freeze (ăn'tĭ-frēz') *n.* A substance, such as alcohol, mixed with a liquid to lower the freezing point of the latter.

an•ti•gen (ăn'tĭ-jən) *n.* Also **an•ti•gene** (-jēn). Any substance that when introduced into the body stimulates antibody production. —**an'ti•gen'ic** (-jĕn'ĭk) *adj.* —**an'ti•gen'i•cal•ly** *adv.* —**an'ti•ge•nic'i•ty** (-jə-nĭs'ə-tē) *n.*

An•ti•gua (ăn-tē'gwə, -gə). A self-governing island of the West Indies; a former British colony. Pop. 62,000. Cap. Saint Johns.

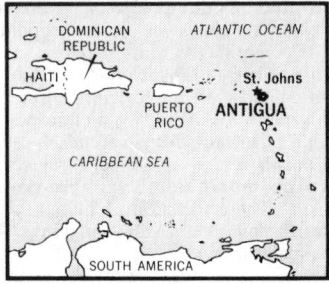

Antigua

an•ti•his•ta•mine (ăn'tĭ-hĭs'tə-mēn', -mĭn) *n.* Any of various drugs used to reduce physiological effects associated with histamine production in allergies and colds.

an•ti•knock (ăn'tĭ-nŏk') *n.* A substance added to gasoline to reduce engine knock.

An•til•les (ăn-tĭl'ēz). The main island group of the West Indies, forming a chain that separates the Caribbean from the Atlantic.

an•ti•log•a•rithm (ăn'tĭ-lôg'ə-rĭth'əm, ăn'tĭ-lŏg'-, ăn'tĭ-) *n.* The number for which a given logarithm stands; for example, where log *x* equals *y*, the *x* is the antilogarithm of *y*.

an•ti•ma•cas•sar (ăn'tĭ-mə-kăs'ər) *n.* A protective covering for the backs of chairs and sofas.

an•ti•mat•ter (ăn'tĭ-măt'ər) *n.* A hypothetical form of matter consisting of antiparticles and having positron-surrounded nuclei composed of antiprotons and antineutrons.

an•ti•mo•ny (ăn'tə-mō'nē) *n. Symbol* **Sb** A metallic element used in a wide variety of alloys, esp. with lead in battery plates, and in paints, semiconductor devices, and ceramic

products. Atomic number 51, atomic weight 121.75. [< ML *antimonium.*]

an•ti•neu•tri•no (ăn'tĭ-n/y/ōō-trē'nō, ăn'tĭ-) *n., pl.* -nos. The antiparticle of the neutrino.

an•ti•neu•tron (ăn'tĭ-n/y/ōō'trŏn', ăn'tĭ-) *n. Symbol* **n** The antiparticle of the neutron.

an•ti•nu•cle•on (ăn'tĭ-n/y/ōō'klē-ŏn', ăn'tĭ-) *n.* The antiparticle of a nucleon.

an•ti•ox•i•dant (ăn'tĭ-ŏk'sə-dənt, ăn'tĭ-) *n.* A chemical compound or substance that inhibits oxidation.

an•ti•par•ti•cle (ăn'tĭ-pär'tĭ-kəl, ăn'tĭ-) *n.* A subatomic particle, such as a positron or antineutron, having the same mass, average lifetime, magnitude of electric charge, and other properties as the particle to which it corresponds, but having the opposite electric charge, opposite intrinsic parity, and opposite magnetic characteristics.

an•ti•pas•to (ăn'tē-päs'tō) *n., pl.* -tos. An assortment of appetizers often served as a main course. [It.]

an•tip•a•thy (ăn-tĭp'ə-thē) *n., pl.* -thies. **1.** A feeling of aversion. **2.** The object of aversion. [< Gk *antipāthēs*, of opposite feelings.] —**an•tip'a•thet'ic** (-thĕt'ĭk) *adj.*

an•ti•per•son•nel (ăn'tĭ-pûr'sə-nĕl', ăn'tĭ-) *adj. Mil.* Designed to inflict casualties on personnel.

an•ti•phon (ăn'tə-fŏn', -fən) *n.* **1.** A devotional composition sung responsively as part of a liturgy. **2.** A response: *a resounding antiphon of dissent.* [< Gk *antiphōna*, sung responses.] —**an•tiph'o•nal** (-tĭf'ə-nəl) *adj.*

an•tiph•o•ny (ăn-tĭf'ə-nē) *n., pl.* -nies. **1.** Antiphonal singing. **2.** A sound or other effect that echoes or answers another.

an•ti•pode (ăn'tĭ-pōd') *n.* A direct or diametrical opposite. [< Gk *antipous*, with the feet opposite.] —**an•tip'o•dal** *adj.*

an•ti•pro•ton (ăn'tĭ-prō'tŏn', ăn'tĭ-) *n.* The antiparticle of the proton.

an•ti•py•ret•ic (ăn'tĭ-pī-rĕt'ĭk) *adj.* Reducing or tending to reduce fever. —*n.* An antipyretic medicine. —**an'ti•py•re'sis** (-rē'sĭs) *n.*

an•ti•quar•y (ăn'tə-kwĕr'ē) *n., pl.* -ies. A student of or dealer in antiquities. —**an'ti•quar'i•an** (ăn'tĭ-kwâr'ē-ən) *adj. & n.*

an•ti•quate (ăn'tə-kwāt') *v.* -quated, -quating. To make obsolete. —**an'ti•qua'tion** *n.*

an•tique (ăn-tēk') *adj.* **1.** Of or belonging to ancient times, esp. of ancient Greece or Rome. **2.** Belonging to or typical of an earlier period. —*n.* An object having special value because of its age, esp. a work of art or handicraft that is over 100 years old. —*v.* -tiqued, -tiquing. To give the appearance of an antique to. [< L *antiquus*, ancient, former.]

an•tiq•ui•ty (ăn-tĭk'wə-tē) *n., pl.* -ties. **1.** Ancient times, esp. the times preceding the Middle Ages. **2.** The quality of being old or ancient: *a carving of great antiquity.*

an•ti•Sem•ite (ăn'tĭ-sĕm'īt', ăn'tĭ-) *n.* A person hostile toward Jews. —**an'ti•Se•mit'ic** (-sə-mĭt'ĭk) *adj.* —**an'ti•Sem'i•tism** *n.*

an•ti•sep•sis (ăn'tə-sĕp'sĭs) *n.* The destruction of microorganisms that cause disease, fermentation, or putrefaction.

---

an·ti·sep·tic (ăn′tə-sĕp′tĭk) *adj.* **1.** Pertaining to or capable of producing antisepsis. **2.** Thoroughly clean. **3.** Austere; drab. *—n.* An antiseptic drug or agent. **—an′ti·sep′ti·cal·ly** *adj.*

an·ti·so·cial (ăn′tĭ-sō′shəl, ăn′tĭ-) *adj.* **1.** Unsociable. **2.** Interfering with the social order. **—an′ti·so′cial·ly** *adv.*

an·tith·e·sis (ăn-tĭth′ə-sĭs) *n., pl.* **-ses** (-sēz′). **1.** Direct contrast; opposition. **2.** The direct opposite. **3.** *Rhet.* The juxtaposition of sharply contrasting ideas. [< Gk.] **—an′ti·thet′i·cal** (-tə-thĕt′ĭ-kəl), **an′ti·thet′ic** *adj.*

an·ti·tox·in (ăn′tĭ-tŏk′sĭn) *n.* **1.** An antibody formed in response to, and capable of neutralizing, a poison of biological origin. **2.** An animal serum containing such antibodies.

an·ti·trust (ăn′tĭ-trŭst′, ăn′tĭ-) *adj.* Concerned with the regulation of trusts or similar monopolies.

ant·ler (ănt′lər) *n.* One of the paired, often branched bony growths on the head of a deer. [< VL *anteoculāris.*] **—ant′lered** (-lərd) *adj.*

Ant·li·a (ănt′lē-ə) *n.* A constellation in the S Hemisphere.

an·to·nym (ăn′tə-nĭm′) *n.* A word having a sense opposite to that of another word. [ANT(I)- + -ONYM.] **—an·ton′y·mous** (ăn-tŏn′ə-məs) *adj.*

Ant·werp (ănt′wûrp). A city of Belgium. Pop. 253,000.

an·u·re·sis (ăn′yŏo-rē′sĭs) *n.* Inability to urinate. **—an′u·ret′ic** (-rĕt′ĭk) *adj.*

a·nus (ā′nəs) *n., pl.* **anuses.** The excretory opening of the alimentary canal. [L *ānus.*]

an·vil (ăn′vĭl) *n.* A block of iron or steel with a flat top on which metals are shaped by hammering. [< OE *anfealt.* See pel-¹.]

anx·i·e·ty (ăng-zī′ə-tē) *n., pl.* **-ties.** A state of uneasiness; apprehension; worry. [L *anxietās* < *anxius,* ANXIOUS.]

anx·ious (ăngk′shəs, ăng′shəs) *adj.* **1.** Worried about some uncertain event or matter. **2.** Eagerly or earnestly desirous. [L *anxius* < *angere,* to torment.] **—anx′ious·ly** *adv.* **—anx′ious·ness** *n.*

an·y (ĕn′ē) *adj.* **1.** One, no matter which, from three or more. **2.** Some, regardless of quantity. *—pron.* **1.** Any one or ones among three or more. **2.** Any quantity or part. [< OE *ǽnig.* See oino-.]

an·y·bod·y (ĕn′ē-bŏd′ē, -bəd-ē) *pron.* Anyone. *—n.* A person of some consequence: *everybody who is anybody.*

an·y·how (ĕn′ē-hou′) *adv.* **1.** In any way or by any means whatever. **2.** In any case.

an·y·more (ĕn′ē-môr′, -mōr′) *adv.* From now on.

an·y·one (ĕn′ē-wŭn′, -wən) *pron.* Anybody; any person.

an·y·place (ĕn′ē-plās′) *adv.* To, in, or at any place; anywhere.

an·y·thing (ĕn′ē-thĭng) *pron.* Any object, occurrence, or matter whatever.

an·y·way (ĕn′ē-wā′) *adv.* **1.** In any manner whatever. **2.** Nevertheless.

an·y·where (ĕn′ē-hwâr′) *adv.* **1.** To, in, or at any place. **2.** To any extent or degree.

a·or·ta (ā-ôr′tə) *n., pl.* **-tas** or **-tae** (-tē′). The main trunk of the systemic arteries, carrying blood away from the heart. [< Gk *aortē,* aorta, "appendixes (of the heart)."] **—a·or′tic** *adj.*

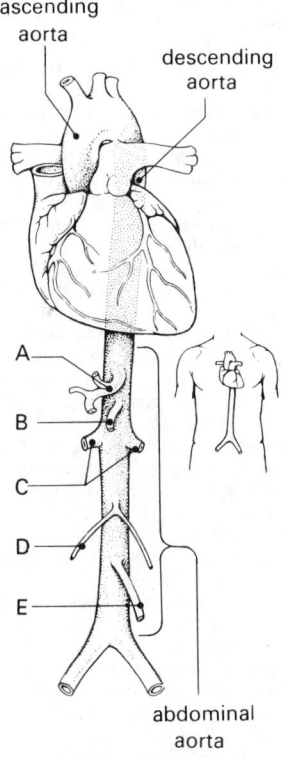

ascending aorta
descending aorta

A
B
C
D
E

abdominal aorta

aorta
A. Celiac artery
B. Superior mesenteric artery
C. Renal arteries
D. Spermatic artery
E. Inferior mesenteric artery

a·ou·dad (ä′ŏo-dăd′) *n.* A wild sheep of N Africa with long, curved horns and a beardlike growth of hair on the neck and chest. [F.]

Ap. **1.** Apostle. **2.** April.

AP **1.** Associated Press. **2.** additional premium. **3.** antipersonnel.

ap. apothecary.

a.p. additional premium.

A.P. Associated Press.

A/P **1.** account paid. **2.** accounts payable.

A.P.A. **1.** American Philological Association. **2.** American Psychiatric Association.

a·pace (ə-pās′) *adv.* At a rapid pace; quickly; swiftly.

A·pach·e (ə-păch′ē) *n., pl.* **Apache** or **-es.** **1.** A member of an Athapascan-speaking tribe of North American Indians inhabiting the SW

U.S. and N Mexico. **2.** Their languages. [Span.]

ap•a•nage. Variant of **appanage.**

a•part (ə-pärt′) *adv.* **1. a.** In pieces. **b.** To pieces. **2. a.** Separately or at a distance in time, place, or position. **b.** To one side; aside. [< OF *a part*, to the side.]

a•part•heid (ə-pärt′hīt′, -hāt′) *n.* An official policy of racial segregation promulgated in the Republic of South Africa. [Afrik, "apartness."]

a•part•ment (ə-pärt′mənt) *n.* A room or suite of rooms designed for dwelling. [< It *appartare*, to separate.]

ap•a•thy (ăp′ə-thē) *n.* **1.** Lack of emotion or feeling. **2.** Lack of interest in things; indifference. [Gk *apatheia*.] —**ap′a•thet′ic** *adj.* —**ap′a•thet′i•cal•ly** *adv.*

ap•a•tite (ăp′ə-tīt′) *n.* A mineral, $Ca_5F(PO_4)_3$, used as a source of phosphorus compounds. [G *Apatit*.]

ape (āp) *n.* **1.** A large primate such as a chimpanzee, gorilla, gibbon, or orang-utan. **2.** Any monkey. **3.** A mimic or imitator. **4.** A clumsy, coarse person. —*v.* **aped, aping.** To mimic. [< OE *apa* < Gmc *apan-*.]

Ap•en•nines (ăp′ə-nīnz′). A mountain range of Italy, extending the length of the peninsula.

a•pé•ri•tif (ä-pĕr′ə-tēf′) *n.* A drink of alcoholic liquor taken before a meal. [F.]

ap•er•ture (ăp′ər-chŏŏr′, -chər) *n.* An opening; orifice. [< L *apertus*, pp of *aperire*, to open.] —**ap′er•tur′al** *adj.*

a•pex (ā′pĕks′) *n., pl.* **apexes** or **apices** (ā′pə-sēz′, ăp′ə-). The highest point of anything; culmination; peak. [L, point, summit, top.]

a•pha•sia (ə-fā′zhə) *n.* Loss of the ability to articulate ideas in any form, resulting from brain damage. —**a•pha′si•ac′** (-zē-ăk′) *n.* —**a•pha′sic** *adj. & n.*

a•phe•li•on (ə-fē′lē-ən, ə-fēl′yən) *n., pl.* **-lia** (-lē-ə). The orbital point on a planetary orbit farthest from the sun.

a•phid (ā′fĭd, ăf′ĭd) *n.* Any of various small insects that suck sap from plants.

aph•o•rism (ăf′ə-rĭz′əm) *n.* **1.** A brief statement of a principle. **2.** A maxim; an adage. [< Gk *aphorismos*, a distinction.] —**aph′o•ris′tic** *adj.* —**aph′o•ris′ti•cal•ly** *adv.*

a•pho•tic (ā-fō′tĭk) *adj.* Without light.

aph•ro•dis•i•ac (ăf′rə-dĭz′ē-ăk′) *adj.* Stimulating or intensifying sexual desire. —*n.* An aphrodisiac drug or food. [< Gk *aphrodisios*, of Aphrodite.]

Aph•ro•di•te (ăf′rə-dī′tē). Greek goddess of love and beauty.

A•pi•a (ä-pē′ä). The capital of Western Samoa. Pop. 22,000.

a•pi•ar•y (ā′pē-ĕr′ē) *n., pl.* **-ies.** A place where bees are raised for their honey. [< L *apis*, bee.] —**a′pi•a•rist** (-ə-rĭst) *n.*

a•pi•ces. Alternate *pl.* of **apex.**

a•piece (ə-pēs′) *adv.* To or for each one: *Give them an apple apiece.*

a•plomb (ə-plŏm′, ə-plŭm′) *n.* Self-confidence; poise. [F, uprightness.]

apmt. appointment.

apo-. *comb. form.* **1.** Being away from. **2.** Lack

of. **3.** Separation of. [< Gk *apo*, away from, off.]

APO Army Post Office.

Apoc. **1.** Apocalypse. **2.** Apocrypha; Apocryphal.

A•poc•a•lypse (ə-pŏk′ə-lĭps′) *n.* **1.** The last book of the New Testament, Revelation. **2.** **apocalypse.** A prophetic revelation. [< Gk *apokalupsis*, revelation.]

a•poc•a•lyp•tic (ə-pŏk′ə-lĭp′tĭk) *adj.* Also **a•poc•a•lyp•ti•cal** (-tĭ-kəl). Of or pertaining to a prophetic revelation or disclosure. —**a•poc′a•lyp′ti•cal•ly** *adv.*

A•poc•ry•pha (ə-pŏk′rə-fə) *pl.n. (takes sing. v.).* **1.** The 14 books of the Septuagint considered uncanonical by Protestants because they are not part of the Hebrew Scriptures. Eleven of these books are accepted in the Roman Catholic canon. **2. apocrypha.** Writings of questionable authorship or authenticity. [< ML *(scripta) apocrypha*, hidden (writings).]

a•poc•ry•phal (ə-pŏk′rə-fəl) *adj.* **1.** Of questionable authorship or authenticity. **2.** False; counterfeit. **3. Apocryphal.** Of or having to do with the Apocrypha. —**a•poc′ry•phal•ly** *adv.* —**a•poc′ry•phal•ness** *n.*

ap•o•gee (ăp′ə-jē) *n.* **1.** The point in the orbit of the moon or of an artificial satellite most distant from the earth. **2.** The farthest or highest point; apex. [< Gk *apogaios*, "away from the earth."] —**ap′o•ge′an** (-jē′ən), **ap′o•ge′ic** (-jē′ĭk) *adj.*

A•pol•lo (ə-pŏl′ō) *n.* **1.** Greek sun god, patron of prophecy, music, and medicine. **2. apollo.** A young man of great physical beauty.

Apollo

a•pol•o•get•ic (ə-pŏl′ə-jĕt′ĭk) *adj.* Making an apology. —*n.* A formal defense or apology. —**a•pol′o•get′i•cal•ly** *adv.*

ap•o•lo•gi•a (ăp′ə-lō′jē-ə, -jə) *n.* A formal defense or justification.

a·pol·o·gist (ə-pŏl′ə-jĭst) *n.* A person who argues in defense or justification of another person or cause.

a·pol·o·gize (ə-pŏl′ə-jīz′) *v.* **-gized, gizing.** To make an apology. —**a·pol′o·giz′er** *n.*

a·pol·o·gy (ə-pŏl′ə-jē) *n., pl.* **-gies. 1.** A statement expressing regret for a fault or offense. **2.** A formal justification or defense. **3.** An inferior substitute. [< Gk *apologia*, speech in defense.]

ap·o·phthegm. Variant of apothegm.

ap·o·plex·y (ăp′ə-plĕk′sē) *n.* Sudden loss of muscular control, sensation, and consciousness, resulting from rupture or blocking of a blood vessel in the brain. [< Gk *apoplēxia*.] —**ap′o·plec′tic** *adj.*

a·port (ə-pôrt′, ə-pōrt′) *adj. Naut.* On or toward the port, or left, side.

a·pos·ta·sy (ə-pŏs′tə-sē) *n., pl.* **-sies.** An abandonment of one's religious faith, political party, or cause. [< Gk *apostasia*, desertion, revolt.]

a·pos·tate (ə-pŏs′tāt′, -tĭt) *n.* One who forsakes his faith or principles.

a pos·te·ri·o·ri (ä pŏs-tîr′ē-ôr′ē, -ōr′ē, ā pŏs-tîr′ē-ôr′ī′, -ōr′ī′). *Logic.* Denoting reasoning from facts or particulars to general principles, or from effects to causes; inductive; empirical. [L, "from the subsequent."]

a·pos·tle (ə-pŏs′əl) *n.* **1. Apostle.** One of a group of disciples chosen by Christ to preach his gospel, esp. one of the original twelve. **2.** One who leads a new cause. [< OE *apostol* < Gk *apostolos*, messenger.]

ap·os·tol·ic (ăp′ə-stŏl′ĭk) *adj.* **1.** Of or pertaining to the Apostles, their faith, teachings, etc. **2.** Of or pertaining to the pope as successor of Saint Peter.

a·pos·tro·phe[1] (ə-pŏs′trə-fē) *n.* The superscript sign (′) used to indicate the omission of a letter or letters from a word, the possessive case, and certain plurals. [< Gk *(prosōidia) apostrophos*, "(accent of) turning away."]

a·pos·tro·phe[2] (ə-pŏs′trə-fē) *n.* A digression in discourse, esp. a turning away from an audience to address an absent or imaginary person.

apothecaries' measure. A system of liquid volume measure used in pharmacy.

apothecaries' weight. A system of weights used in pharmacy and based on an ounce equal to 480 grains and a pound equal to 12 ounces.

a·poth·e·car·y (ə-pŏth′ə-kĕr′ē) *n., pl.* **-ies.** A druggist; pharmacist. [< LL *apothecārius*, warehouse man.]

ap·o·thegm (ăp′ə-thĕm′) *n.* Also **ap·o·phthegm.** A maxim; proverb. [Gk *apophthegma*, a pointed saying.]

ap·o·them (ăp′ə-thĕm′) *n.* In a regular polygon, the perpendicular distance from the center to any of the sides. [< APO- + THEME.]

a·poth·e·o·sis (ə-pŏth′ē-ō′sĭs, ăp′ə-thē′ə-sĭs) *n., pl.* **-ses** (-sēz′). **1.** Exaltation to divine rank; deification. **2.** An exalted or glorified ideal. [< Gk *apotheōsis.*]

app. 1. apparatus. **2.** *Lib.Serv.* appendix. **3.** apprentice.

Ap·pa·la·chians (ăp′ə-lā′chənz, -lā′chē-ənz, -lăch′ənz). The major mountain system of E North America, extending from Quebec to Alabama.

ap·pall (ə-pôl′) *v.* To fill with consternation or dismay. [< OF *apalir*, to grow pale.] —**ap·pall′ing** *adj.*

ap·pan·age (ăp′ə-nĭj) *n.* Also **ap·a·nage. 1.** A source of revenue, as land, given by a king for the maintenance of a member of the ruling family. **2.** A natural adjunct.

ap·pa·ra·tus (ăp′ə-rā′təs, -răt′əs) *n., pl.* **-tus** or **-tuses. 1.** The totality of means by which a designated function is performed or a specific task executed. **2.** A machine or group of machines. **3.** A political organization. [L *apparātus*, pp of *apparāre*, to prepare.]

ap·par·el (ə-păr′əl) *n.* Clothing, esp. outer garments. —*v.* **-eled** or **-elled, -eling** or **-elling.** To clothe; dress. [< OF *apareil*, preparation, apparatus.]

ap·par·ent (ə-păr′ənt, ə-pâr′-) *adj.* **1.** Readily seen; visible. **2.** Readily understood or perceived. [< OF *aparoir*, to appear.] —**ap·par′ent·ly** *adv.*

ap·pa·ri·tion (ăp′ə-rĭsh′ən) *n.* **1.** A ghost; specter. **2.** A sudden or unusual sight. [< LL *apparitiō*, appearance.]

ap·peal (ə-pēl′) *n.* **1.** An earnest request. **2.** An application to some higher authority, as for corroboration. **3.** The power of arousing interest. **4.** *Law.* **a.** The transfer of a case from a lower to a higher court for a new hearing. **b.** A request for a new hearing. —*v.* **1.** To make an earnest request, as for help, corroboration, etc. **2.** To be attractive or interesting. **3.** To transfer or apply to transfer (a case) to a higher court for rehearing. [< L *appellāre*, to apply to, entreat.] —**ap·peal′ing·ly** *adv.*

ap·pear (ə-pîr′) *v.* **1.** To become visible. **2.** To come into existence. **3.** To seem or look. **4.** To come before the public. **5.** *Law.* To present oneself formally before a court. [< L *appārēre.*]

ap·pear·ance (ə-pîr′əns) *n.* **1.** The act or an instance of appearing. **2.** The outward aspect of something. **3.** Something that appears; phenomenon. **4.** A pretense; false show. **5. appearances.** Circumstances; outward indications.

ap·pease (ə-pēz′) *v.* **-peased, -peasing.** To bring peace to or placate, esp. by granting concessions. [< OF *apaisier.*] —**ap·pease′ment** *n.* —**ap·peas′er** *n.*

ap·pel·lant (ə-pĕl′ənt) *n.* One who appeals a court decision.

ap·pel·late (ə-pĕl′ĭt) *adj.* Having the power to hear appeals and to reverse court decisions. [< L *appellāre*, to APPEAL.]

ap·pel·la·tion (ăp′ə-lā′shən) *n.* **1.** A name or title. **2.** The act of naming. [< L *appellāre*, to APPEAL.]

ap·pel·lee (ăp′ə-lē′) *n.* One against whom an appeal is taken.

ap·pend (ə-pĕnd′) *v.* To attach; add as a supplement. [L *appendere.*]

ap·pend·age (ə-pĕn′dĭj) *n.* Something appended, as an attached organ or part.

ap·pen·dec·to·my (ăp′ən-děk′tə-mē) *n., pl.*
-mies. *Surg.* Removal of the vermiform appendix.

ap·pen·di·ci·tis (ə-pěn′də-sī′tĭs) *n.* Inflammation of the vermiform appendix.

ap·pen·dix (ə-pěn′dĭks) *n., pl.* **-dixes** or **-dices** (-də-sēz′). **1.** A collection of supplementary material at the end of a book. **2.** The **vermiform appendix.** [L < *appendere*, APPEND.]

ap·per·tain (ăp′ər-tān′) *v.* To belong as a function or part.

ap·pe·tite (ăp′ə-tīt′) *n.* **1.** A desire for food or drink. **2.** Any physical craving or desire. [< L *appetitus* < *appetere*, to strive after.] **—ap′pe·ti′tive** (ap′ə-tī′tĭv, ə-pĕt′ə-tĭv) *adj.*

ap·pe·tiz·er (ăp′ə-tī′zər) *n.* A food or drink served before a meal to stimulate the appetite.

ap·pe·tiz·ing (ăp′ə-tī′zĭng) *adj.* Stimulating the appetite. **—ap′pe·tiz′ing·ly** *adv.*

appl. applied.

ap·plaud (ə-plôd′) *v.* To express approval (of) by clapping the hands. [L *applaudere*, to clap at.] **—ap·plaud′er** *n.*

ap·plause (ə-plôz′) *n.* Approval, esp. when shown by the clapping of hands.

ap·ple (ăp′əl) *n.* **1.** A firm, rounded, often red-skinned edible fruit. **2.** A tree bearing such fruit. [< OE *æppel*. See abel-.]

ap·ple·jack (ăp′əl-jăk′) *n.* Brandy distilled from fermented cider.

ap·ple-pol·ish (ăp′əl-pŏl′ĭsh) *v. Informal.* To seek favor by toadying. **—apple polisher.**

ap·ple·sauce (ăp′əl-sôs′) *n.* **1.** Stewed, sweetened apple pulp. **2.** *Slang.* Nonsense; foolishness; rubbish.

ap·pli·ance (ə-plī′əns) *n.* A device or instrument, esp. one operated by electricity and designed for household use. [< APPLY.]

ap·pli·ca·ble (ăp′lĭ-kə-bəl, ə-plĭk′ə-) *adj.* Capable of being applied; appropriate. **—ap′pli·ca·bil′i·ty** *n.* **—ap′pli·ca·bly** *adv.*

ap·pli·cant (ăp′lĭ-kənt) *n.* One who applies, as for a job.

ap·pli·ca·tion (ăp′lĭ-kā′shən) *n.* **1.** The act of applying. **2.** Anything that is applied, such as a cosmetic. **3. a.** A method of applying or using; specific use. **b.** The capacity of being usable; relevance. **4.** Close attention; diligence. **5. a.** A request, as for a job. **b.** The printed form upon which such a request is often made.

ap·pli·ca·tor (ăp′lĭ-kā′tər) *n.* An instrument for applying something, such as medicine.

ap·plied (ə-plīd′) *adj.* Put in practice; used: *applied physics.*

ap·pli·qué (ăp′lĭ-kā′) *n.* Decoration made by sewing or applying cut pieces of material to the surface of another. [F, pp of *appliquer*, to put on, apply.] **—ap′pli·qué′** *v.* (**-quéd, -quéing**).

ap·ply (ə-plī′) *v.* **-plied, -plying. 1.** To bring into contact with something; put on or upon. **2.** To adapt for a special use. **3.** To devote (oneself or one's efforts) to something. **4.** To be pertinent. **5.** To make a request, as for a job. [< OF *aplier* < L *applicāre*, to join to, apply.] **—ap·pli′er** *n.*

ap·pog·gia·tu·ra (ə-pŏj′ə-tŏōr′ə) *n. Mus.* An embellishing note, usually one step above or

below the note it precedes and indicated by a small note or special sign. [It.]

ap·point (ə-point′) *v.* **1.** To name for an office or position. **2.** To fix or set by authority. **3.** To furnish; equip: *a well-appointed room.* [< OF *(rendre) à point,* "(to bring) to a point."]

ap·point·ee (ə-poin′tē′) *n.* A person who is appointed to an office or position.

ap·point·ive (ə-poin′tĭv) *adj.* Pertaining to or filled by appointment: *an appointive office.*

ap·point·ment (ə-point′mənt) *n.* **1.** The act of appointing. **2.** The office or position to which a person has been appointed. **3.** An arrangement to do something or meet someone. **4. appointments.** Fittings or equipment.

Ap·po·mat·tox (ăp′ə-măt′əks). The town in Virginia where Lee surrendered to Grant (April 9, 1865).

ap·por·tion (ə-pôr′shən, ə-pōr′-) *v.* To divide and assign according to some plan or proportion; allot. [OF *apportionner.*] **—ap·por′tion·ment** *n.*

ap·pose (ă-pōz′) *v.* **-posed, -posing. 1.** To apply (one thing) to another. **2.** To arrange (things) near to each other or side by side. [Back-formation < APPOSITION.]

ap·po·site (ăp′ə-zĭt) *adj.* Suitable; appropriate. **—ap′po·site·ly** *adv.* **—ap′po·site·ness** *n.*

ap·po·si·tion (ăp′ə-zĭsh′ən) *n.* **1.** *Gram.* A construction in which a noun or noun phrase is placed with another as an explanatory equivalent, as in *Copley, the famous painter, was born in Boston.* **2.** A placing side by side or next to each other. [< L *appōnere* (pp *appositus*), to place near to.] **—ap·pos′i·tive** *adj. & n.*

ap·praise (ə-prāz′) *v.* **-praised, -praising.** To evaluate, esp. in an official capacity. [< LL *appretiāre,* to set a value on.] **—ap·prais′al** *n.* **—ap·prais′er** *n.*

ap·pre·cia·ble (ə-prē′shə-bəl) *adj.* Capable of being noticed or measured; noticeable. **—ap·pre′cia·bly** *adv.*

ap·pre·ci·ate (ə-prē′shē-āt′) *v.* **-ated, -ating. 1.** To estimate the quality or value of. **2.** To value highly. **3.** To be fully aware of; realize. **4.** To be thankful for. **5.** To raise or go up in value or price. [LL *appretiāre,* to set a value on] **—ap·pre′ci·a·tor** (-ā′tər) *n.*

ap·pre·ci·a·tion (ə-prē′shē-ā′shən) *n.* **1.** Gratefulness; gratitude. **2.** Awareness or delicate perception, esp. of aesthetic qualities.

ap·pre·cia·tive (ə-prē′shə-tĭv, -shē-ā′tĭv) *adj.* Capable of or showing appreciation.

ap·pre·hend (ăp′rĭ-hěnd′) *v.* **1.** To arrest. **2.** To grasp mentally; understand. **3.** To anticipate with anxiety. [< L *apprehendere,* to seize.]

ap·pre·hen·sion (ăp′rĭ-hěn′shən) *n.* **1.** An uneasy anticipation of the future; dread. **2.** An arrest. **3.** The ability to understand.

ap·pre·hen·sive (ăp′rĭ-hěn′sĭv) *adj.* Anxious about the future; uneasy. **—ap′pre·hen′sive·ly** *adv.* **—ap′pre·hen′sive·ness** *n.*

ap·pren·tice (ə-prěn′tĭs) *n.* **1.** One who is learning a trade under a skilled craftsman. **2.** Any beginner. **—v. -ticed, -ticing.** To place or take on as an apprentice. [< OF *aprendre,* to learn.] **—ap·pren′tice·ship′** *n.*

ap•prise (ə-prīz') *v.* **-prised, -prising.** Also **ap•prize.** To cause to know; inform. [< F *apprendre,* to cause to learn.]

ap•proach (ə-prōch') *v.* **1.** To come near or nearer (to). **2.** To come close to in appearance; approximate. **3.** To make a proposal to; make overtures to. —*n.* **1.** The act of coming near. **2.** A fairly close resemblance; an approximation. **3.** A way of reaching; an access. **4.** Often **approaches.** An advance or overture made by one person to another. [< LL *appropiāre,* to go nearer to.] —**ap•proach'a•bil'i•ty** *n.* —**ap•proach'a•ble** *adj.*

ap•pro•ba•tion (ăp'rə-bā'shən) *n.* Approval; sanction.

ap•pro•pri•ate (ə-prō'prē-ĭt) *adj.* Suitable; proper. —*v.* (ə-prō'prē-āt') **-ated, -ating. 1.** To set apart for a specific use. **2.** To take possession of. [< LL *appropriāre,* to make one's own.] —**ap•pro'pri•ate•ly** *adv.* —**ap•pro'pri•ate•ness** *n.* —**ap•pro'pri•a'tor** *n.*

ap•pro•pri•a•tion (ə-prō'prē-ā'shən) *n.* **1.** The act of appropriating to oneself or to a specific use. **2.** Public funds set aside for a specific purpose.

ap•prov•al (ə-prōō'vəl) *n.* **1.** The act of approving. **2.** An official approbation; a sanction. —**on approval.** For examination by a potential customer without obligation to buy.

ap•prove (ə-prōōv') *v.* **-proved, -proving. 1.** To have a favorable opinion (of); regard favorably. **2.** To consent to. [< L *approbāre,* to make good.] —**ap•prov'ing•ly** *adv.*

approx. approximate; approximately.

ap•prox•i•mate (ə-prŏk'sə-mĭt) *adj.* **1.** Almost exact or correct. **2.** Very similar. **3.** Close together. —*v.* (ə-prŏk'sə-māt') **-mated, -mating.** To come close to; be nearly the same as. [< LL *approximāre,* to come near to.] —**ap•prox'i•mate•ly** *adv.* —**ap•prox'i•ma'tion** *n.*

appt. appoint; appointed; appointment.

ap•pur•te•nance (ə-pûrt'n-əns) *n.* Something added to another, more important thing; an accessory. [< LL *appertinēre,* appertain.]

Apr. April.

a•pri•cot (ā'prĭ-kŏt', ăp'rĭ-) *n.* **1.** A yelloworange peachlike fruit. **2.** A tree bearing such fruit. [< Ar *al-birqūq,* "the apricot" < LGk *praikokion.*]

A•pril (ā'prəl) *n.* The 4th month of the year. April has 30 days. [< L *aprīlis,* perh "month of Venus."]

a pri•o•ri (ä prē-ôr'ē, ā prī-ôr'ī'). **1.** From a known or assumed cause to a necessarily related effect; deductive. **2.** Based on theory rather than on experience. [L, "from the previous (causes or hypotheses)."]

a•pron (ā'prən, ā'pərn) *n.* **1.** A garment worn over the front of the body to protect one's clothes. **2.** Anything resembling an apron in appearance or function. **3.** The paved strip around airport hangars and terminal buildings. **4.** The part of a stage in a theater extending in front of the curtain. **5.** A continuous conveyor belt. [ME *(an) apron,* orig *(a) napron.*]

ap•ro•pos (ăp'rə-pō') *adj.* Pertinent; opportune. —*adv.* Pertinently. —**apropos of.** With

reference to. [F *à propos,* "to the purpose."]

apse (ăps) *n.* A semicircular or polygonal, usually domed, projection of a church. [ML *apsis.*]

apt (ăpt) *adj.* **1.** Exactly suitable; appropriate. **2.** Likely. **3.** Inclined; given. **4.** Quick to learn or understand. [< L *aptus,* pp of *apere,* to fasten.] —**apt'ly** *adv.* —**apt'ness** *n.*

apt. apartment.

ap•ti•tude (ăp'tə-t/y/ōōd') *n.* **1.** A natural talent; inclination. **2.** Quickness in learning. [< LL *aptitūdō,* fitness < *aptus,* APT.]

aq•ua (ăk'wə, ä'kwə) *n., pl.* **aquae** (ăk'wē, ä'-kwī') or **-uas. 1.** Water. **2.** Light bluish green. [L, water.] —**aq'ua** *adj.*

aq•ua•ma•rine (ăk'wə-mə-rēn', ä'kwə-) *n.* **1.** A transparent blue-green variety of beryl, used as a gemstone. **2.** Pale blue to light greenish blue.

aq•ua•naut (ăk'wə-nôt', ä'kwə-) *n.* A person trained to live in underwater installations and participate in scientific research.

aq•ua•plane (ăk'wə-plān', ä'kwə-) *n.* A board on which one rides in a standing position while it is towed by a motorboat. —**aq'ua•plane'** *v.* **(-planed, -planing).**

aqua re•gi•a (rē'jē-ə). A corrosive, fuming mixture of hydrochloric and nitric acids, capable of dissolving platinum and gold.

a•quar•i•um (ə-kwâr'ē-əm) *n., pl.* **-ums** or **-ia** (-ē-ə). **1.** A water-filled enclosure in which living aquatic animals and plants are kept. **2.** A place for exhibiting such animals and plants. [< L *aquārius,* of water.]

A•quar•i•us (ə-kwâr'ē-əs) *n.* **1.** A constellation in the equatorial region of the S Hemisphere. **2.** The 11th sign of the zodiac.

a•quat•ic (ə-kwŏt'ĭk, ə-kwăt'-) *adj.* **1.** Living or growing in or on water. **2.** Taking place in or on water.

aqua vi•tae (vī'tē). **1.** Alcohol. **2.** Whiskey, brandy, or other strong liquor.

aq•ue•duct (ăk'wə-dŭkt') *n.* **1.** A conduit designed to transport water from a remote source, usually by gravity. **2.** An elevated structure supporting a conduit or canal passing over a river or low ground. [L *aquae ductus.*]

a•que•ous (ā'kwē-əs, ăk'wē-) *adj.* Of, similar to, containing, or dissolved in water; watery. [< L *aqua,* AQUA.]

aqueous humor. A clear, lymphlike fluid in the chamber of the eye between the cornea and the lens.

Aq•ui•la (ăk'wə-lə) *n.* A constellation in the N Hemisphere and the Milky Way. [L *aquila,* EAGLE.]

aq•ui•line (ăk'wə-līn', -lĭn) *adj.* **1.** Of or similar to an eagle. **2.** Resembling an eagle's beak: *an aquiline nose.* [< L *aquila,* eagle.]

A•qui•nas (ə-kwī'nəs), **Saint Thomas.** 1225–1274. Italian philosopher and theologian.

ar. Variant of are[2].

-ar. *comb. form.* Like, pertaining to, or of the nature of: **titular.**

Ar argon.

ar. arrival; arrive.

A/R account receivable.

Ar•ab (ăr′əb) *n.* **1.** A native of Arabia. **2.** Any of a Semitic people of the Near East and North Africa. [< Ar *'arab.*] —**Ar′ab** *adj.*

ar•a•besque (ăr′ə-běsk′) *n.* An ornate design of intertwined floral, foliate, and geometric figures. [< It *arabesco,* "done in the Arabic fashion."]

A•ra•bi•a (ə-rā′bē-ə). A peninsula of SW Asia between the Red Sea and the Persian Gulf. —**A•ra′bi•an** *adj. & n.*

Arabian Sea. The part of the Indian Ocean bounded by E Africa, Arabia, and W India.

Ar•a•bic (ăr′ə-bĭk) *adj.* Of or pertaining to Arabia, the Arabs, their language, or their culture. —*n.* **1.** The SW Semitic language of the Arabs. **2.** The literary language of the Koran, as employed in most formal usage in Arabic-speaking countries.

Arabic numerals. The numerical symbols 1,2,3,4,5,6,7,8,9, and 0.

ar•a•ble (ăr′ə-bəl) *adj.* Fit for cultivation. [< L *arāre,* to plow.]

a•rach•nid (ə-răk′nĭd) *n.* One of a group of eight-legged organisms including the spiders, scorpions, ticks, and mites. [< Gk *arakhnē,* spider.]

Ar•a•ma•ic (ăr′ə-mā′ĭk) *n.* A NW Semitic language. —**Ar′a•ma′ic** *adj.*

Ar•a•wak (ăr′ə-wäk′) *n., pl.* **-wak** or **-waks. 1.** A member of an Arawakan-speaking Indian people now living chiefly in certain regions of the Guianas. **2.** Their language.

Ar•a•wa•kan (ăr′ə-wä′kən) *n., pl.* **-kan** or **-kans. 1.** A South American Indian language family spoken in a wide area comprising the Amazon basin in Brazil, Venezuela, Colombia, the Guianas, Peru, Bolivia, and Paraguay. **2.** An Indian or an Indian people of this linguistic stock. —**Ar′a•wa′kan** *adj.*

ar•ba•lest (är′bə-lĭst) *n.* Also **ar•be•list.** A medieval missile launcher designed on the crossbow principle. [< L *arcus,* bow + BALLISTA.]

ar•bi•ter (är′bə-tər) *n.* One who has the power to judge or decide. [< L *arbiter,* judge.]

ar•bit•ra•ment (är-bĭt′rə-mənt) *n.* **1.** The act of arbitrating. **2.** The judgment of an arbiter.

ar•bi•trar•y (är′bĭ-trĕr′ē) *adj.* **1.** Determined by whim or caprice. **2.** Based on individual judgment. **3.** Not limited by law; despotic. [< L *arbiter,* ARBITER.] —**ar′bi•trar′i•ly** (-ə-lē) *adv.* —**ar′bi•trar′i•ness** *n.*

ar•bi•trate (är′bə-trāt′) *v.* **-trated, -trating. 1.** To judge or decide as an arbitrator. **2.** To submit (a dispute) to settlement by an arbitrator. **3.** To serve as an arbitrator or arbiter. —**ar′bi•tra′tion** *n.*

ar•bi•tra•tor (är′bə-trā′tər) *n.* A person chosen to settle the issue between parties engaged in a dispute.

ar•bor¹ (är′bər) *n.* Also *chiefly Brit.* **ar•bour.** A shady garden shelter or bower. [< OF *(h)erbier,* herbage, plot of grass.]

ar•bor² (är′bər) *n.* **1.** An axis or shaft supporting a rotating part on a lathe. **2.** A bar for supporting cutting tools. **3.** A spindle of a wheel, as in watches and clocks. [L *arbor,* tree.]

ar•bo•re•al (är-bôr′ē-əl, är-bōr′-) *adj.* **1.** Per-

taining to or resembling a tree. **2.** Living in trees.

ar•bo•re•tum (är′bə-rē′təm) *n., pl.* **-tums** or **-ta** (-tə). A place for the study and exhibition of trees.

ar•bor•vi•tae (är′bər-vī′tē) *n.* **1.** Any of several evergreen trees with small, scalelike leaves. **2.** *Anat.* The white matter of the cerebellum, in cross section having the appearance of a tree.

ar•bu•tus (är-byōō′təs) *n.* A trailing plant with evergreen leaves and pink or white flowers. [< L *arbūtus,* strawberry tree.]

arc (ärk) *n.* **1.** Anything shaped like a bow, curve, or arch. **2.** A segment of a curve. **3.** A luminous discharge of electric current crossing a gap between two electrodes. —*v.* **arced** or **arcked, arcing** or **arcking.** To form an arc. [< L *arcus,* bow, arc.]

A.R.C. American Red Cross.

ar•cade (är-kād′) *n.* **1.** A series of arches supported by columns. **2.** A roofed passageway, esp. one with shops on either side. [< It *arcata < arco,* arch.]

ar•cane (är-kān′) *adj.* Known only by those having secret knowledge; esoteric. [L *arcānus,* closed, secret.]

arch¹ (ärch) *n.* **1.** A curved structural device, esp. of masonry, forming the upper edge of an opening or a support, as in a bridge or doorway. **2.** Any similar structure, as a monument. **3.** Anything curved like an arch. —*v.* **1.** To supply with an arch. **2.** To form or cause to form an arch. [< L *arcus,* arc.] —**arched** (ärcht) *adj.*

arch² (ärch) *adj.* **1.** Chief; principal. **2.** Mischievous; roguish: *an arch glance.* —**arch′ly** *adv.* —**arch′ness** *n.*

arch-. *comb. form.* **1.** Highest rank or chief status. **2.** Ultimate of a kind. [< Gk *arkhos,* chief, ruler.]

–arch. *comb. form.* A ruler: **matriarch.** [< Gk *arkhos,* ruler.]

arch. architect; architectural; architecture.

archaeol. archaeology.

ar•chae•ol•o•gy, ar•che•ol•o•gy (är′kē-ŏl′ə-jē) *n.* The systematic recovery and scientific study of material evidence of human life and culture in past ages. [< LL *archaeologia,* "the study of antiquity."] —**ar′chae•o•log′i•cal** (-ə-lŏj′i-kəl), **ar′chae•o•log′ic** *adj.* —**ar′chae•o•log′i•cal•ly** *adv.* —**ar′chae•ol′o•gist** *n.*

Ar•che•o•zo•ic. Variant of Archeozoic.

ar•cha•ic (är-kā′ĭk) *adj.* Also **ar•cha•i•cal** (-ĭ-kəl). **1.** Belonging to a much earlier time. **2.** No longer current or applicable. **3.** Designating words and language that were once common, but are now used chiefly to suggest an earlier style or period. [< Gk *arkhaios,* ancient < *arkhē,* beginning.] —**ar•cha′i•cal•ly** *adv.*

ar•cha•ism (är′kē-ĭz′əm, är′kā-) *n.* An archaic word, phrase, idiom, or expression. —**ar′cha•ist** *n.* —**ar′cha•is′tic** (-ĭs′tĭk) *adj.*

arch•an•gel (ärk′ān′jəl) *n.* A celestial being next in rank above an angel.

arch•bish•op (ärch-bĭsh′əp) *n.* A bishop of the highest rank.

arch•dea•con (ärch-dē′kən) *n.* A church offi-

ă pat/ā ate/âr care/ä bar/b bib/ch chew/d deed/ĕ pet/ē be/f fit/g gag/h hat/hw what/ ĭ pit/ī pie/îr pier/j judge/k kick/l lid, fatal/m mum/n no, sudden/ng sing/ŏ pot/ō go/

cial, chiefly in the Anglican Church, in charge of temporal and other affairs in a diocese.
arch·di·o·cese (ärch-dī′ə-sĭs, -sēs′, -sēz′) *n.* A diocese under an archbishop's jurisdiction.
arch·duke (ärch-d/y/oōk′) *n.* In certain royal families, esp. that of imperial Austria, a prince. —**arch·duch′ess** *fem.n.*
arch·en·e·my (ärch-ĕn′ə-mē) *n., pl.* -**mies.** 1. A chief enemy. 2. Satan.
ar·che·ol·o·gy. Variant of **archaeology.**
Ar·che·o·zo·ic (är′kē-ə-zō′ĭk) *adj.* Also **Ar·chae·o·zo·ic.** Pertaining to the earlier of two generally arbitrary divisions of the Precambrian era. —*n.* The Archeozoic era.
arch·er (är′chər) *n.* 1. One who shoots with a bow and arrow. 2. **Archer.** Sagittarius. [< LL *arcuarius,* "of a bow."]
arch·er·y (är′chər-ē) *n.* The art, sport, or skill of shooting with a bow and arrows.
ar·che·type (är′kə-tīp′) *n.* An original model after which other similar things are patterned. [< Gk *arkhetupos,* first molded as a pattern, exemplary.] —**ar′che·typ′al** (-tī′pəl), **ar′che·typ′ic** (-tīp′ĭk), **ar′che·typ′i·cal** *adj.*
arch·fiend (ärch-fēnd′) *n.* 1. A chief fiend. 2. Satan.
ar·chi·e·pis·co·pal (är′kē-ĭ-pĭs′kə-pəl) *adj.* Of or pertaining to an archbishop.
ar·chi·man·drite (är′kə-măn′drīt′) *n. E.O.Ch.* 1. A cleric ranking below a bishop. 2. The head of a monastery and the equivalent of a Western abbot.
Ar·chi·me·des (är′kə-mē′dēz). 287?–212 B.C. Greek mathematician. —**Ar′chi·me′de·an** (är′-kə-mē′dē-ən, -mĭ-) *adj.*
ar·chi·pel·a·go (är′kə-pĕl′ə-gō′) *n., pl.* -**goes** or -**gos.** 1. A large group of islands. 2. A sea containing a large group of islands. [< It *Arcipelago,* "the Chief Sea."]
archit. architecture.
ar·chi·tect (är′kə-tĕkt′) *n.* 1. One who designs and supervises the construction of buildings or other large structures. 2. Any planner. [< Gk *arkhitektōn,* master builder.]
ar·chi·tec·ton·ics (är′kə-tĕk-tŏn′ĭks) *n. (takes sing. v.).* 1. The science of architecture. 2. Structural design, as in a musical work. —**ar′·chi·tec·ton′ic** *adj.*
ar·chi·tec·ture (är′kə-tĕk′chər) *n.* 1. The art and science of designing and erecting buildings. 2. A style and method of design and construction: *Byzantine architecture.* —**ar′chi·tec′tur·al** *adj.* —**ar′chi·tec′tur·al·ly** *adv.*
ar·chi·trave (är′kə-trāv′) *n.* The lowermost part of an entablature, resting directly on top of a column in classical architecture. [< OIt, "chief beam."]
ar·chives (är′kīvz′) *pl.n.* 1. Public records pertaining to an organization or institution. 2. A place in which such records are preserved. [< Gk *arkheia,* public records, archives.]
ar·chi·vist (är′kə-vĭst, är′kī′-) *n.* One in charge of archives.
ar·chon (är′kŏn′, -kən) *n.* One of the 9 principal magistrates of ancient Athens. [< Gk *arkhōn,* "ruler."] —**ar′chon·ship′** *n.*
arch·way (ärch′wā′) *n.* 1. A passageway under an arch. 2. An arch covering a passageway.

–archy. *comb. form.* Rule or government: *oligarchy.*
arcked (ärkt). Alternate *p.t.* & *p.p.* of **arc.**
arcking (är′kĭng). Alternate *pres.p.* of **arc.**
arc lamp. An electric lamp in which a current traverses a gas between two incandescent electrodes.
arc·tic (ärk′tĭk, är′tĭk) *adj.* 1. Of, near, or characteristic of the North Pole or polar regions; frigid. 2. **Arctic.** Of or relating to a geographic area extending from the North Pole to the northern timberline. —*n.* A warm, waterproof overshoe. [< Gk *arktikos.*]
Arctic Circle. A parallel of latitude at 66° 33′ N, marking the limit of the N Frigid Zone.
Arctic Ocean. The polar ocean between North America and Eurasia.
Arc·tu·rus (ärk-t/y/oōr′əs) *n.* The brightest star in the constellation Boötes.
ar·cu·ate (är′kyoō-ĭt, -āt′) *adj.* Also **ar·cu·at·ed** (-ā′tĭd). Having the form of a bow; curved; arched. [< L *arcus,* ARC.]
–ard, –art. *comb. form.* One who does something to excess: *drunkard.*
ar·den·cy (är′dən-sē) *n.* Strength or intensity of feeling; ardor.
ar·dent (är′dənt) *adj.* 1. a. Characterized by warmth of passion or desire. b. Characterized by strong enthusiasm; zealous. 2. Glowing; flashing: *ardent eyes.* 3. Hot as fire; burning. [< L *ardēre,* to burn.] —**ar′dent·ly** *adv.*
ar·dor (är′dər) *n.* Also *Brit.* **ar·dour.** 1. a. Great intensity, as of passion or desire. b. Strong enthusiasm; zeal. 2. Intense heat, as of fire. [< L *ardēre,* to burn.]
ar·du·ous (är′joō-əs) *adj.* Demanding great effort or labor; strenuous; difficult. [L *arduus,* high, steep.] —**ar′du·ous·ly** *adv.* —**ar′du·ous·ness** *n.*
are¹ (är). 2nd person sing. and present tense indicative pl. of **be.** [< OE *earon.*]
are² (âr, är) *n.* Also **ar** (är). A metric unit of area equal to 100 square meters.
ar·e·a (âr′ē-ə) *n.* 1. A flat, open surface or space. 2. Any specific region, as of a building, city, or geographic entity. 3. The range or scope of anything. 4. The measure of a planar region or of the surface of a solid. [L *ārea,* open field.]
Area Code. Also **area code.** A number, often with three digits, assigned to a telephone area, as in the U.S. and Canada, used in calling from one area to another.
ar·e·a·way (âr′ē-ə-wā′) *n.* A small sunken area allowing access or light and air to a basement.
a·re·na (ə-rē′nə) *n.* 1. The area in the center of an ancient Roman amphitheater where contests were held. 2. A sphere of conflict, activity, etc. [L *(h)arēna,* sand, arena covered with sand.]
aren't (ärnt, är′ənt). Contraction of *are not.* See Usage note at **ain't.**
Ar·e·op·a·gus (är′ē-ŏp′ə-gəs) *n.* The highest council of ancient Athens.
Ar·es (âr′ēz). Greek god of war.
ar·gent (är′jənt) *n.* Silver. [< L *argentum.*] —**ar′gent** *adj.*

Ar·gen·ti·na (är'jən-tē'nə). A republic of SE South America. Pop. 22,252,000. Cap. Buenos Aires. —**Ar'gen·tine'**, **Ar·gen·tin'e·an** *adj. & n.*

Argentina

Ar·go (är'gō) *n.* A constellation in the S Hemisphere.

ar·gon (är'gŏn') *n. Symbol* **Ar** A colorless, odorless, inert gaseous element constituting approx. 1% of the earth's atmosphere, used in electric lamps, fluorescent tubes, and radio vacuum tubes. Atomic number 18, atomic weight 39.94. [< Gk *argos*, inert, idle.]

ar·go·sy (är'gə-sē) *n., pl.* **-sies.** **1.** A large merchant ship. **2.** A fleet of such ships. [< It *Ragusa*, former name of Dubrovnik, Yugoslavia.]

ar·got (är'gō, -gət) *n.* A specialized vocabulary used by a particular group, esp. the jargon of the underworld. [F.]

ar·gue (är'gyōō) *v.* **-gued, -guing.** **1.** To put forth reasons for or against something. **2.** To maintain in argument; contend. **3.** To dispute; quarrel. **4.** To persuade or influence, as by presenting reasons. [< L *arguere*, to make clear, assert.] —**ar'gu·a·ble** *adj.*

ar·gu·ment (är'gyə-mənt) *n.* **1. a.** A discussion in which disagreement is expressed; debate. **b.** A quarrel. **2.** A course of reasoning aimed at demonstrating the truth or falsehood of something. [< L *argūmentum* < *arguere*, ARGUE.]

ar·gu·men·ta·tion (är'gyə-měn-tā'shən) *n.* The presentation and elaboration of an argument; debate.

ar·gu·men·ta·tive (är'gyə-měn'tə-tĭv) *adj.* Given to arguing; disputatious.

ar·gyle (är'gīl') *n.* A knitted design of varicolored diamonds crossed by contrasting diagonal lines. [< the Scottish clan Campbell of *Argyle.*]

a·ri·a (ä'rē-ə) *n.* A solo vocal piece with instrumental accompaniment, as in an opera. [It, melody, "air."]

-arian. *comb. form.* **1.** Sect: Unitarian. **2.** A belief: vegetarian.

ar·id (är'ĭd) *adj.* **1.** Lacking moisture; parched; barren. **2.** Lacking interest; dull. [< L *āridus.*] —**a·rid'i·ty** (ə-rĭd'ə-tē) *n.*

Ar·ies (âr'ēz, âr'ē-ēz') *n.* **1.** A constellation in the N Hemisphere. **2.** The 1st sign of the zodiac. [L *ariēs*, ram.]

a·right (ə-rīt') *adv.* Properly; correctly.

a·rise (ə-rīz') *v.* **arose, arisen** (ə-rĭz'ən), **arising.** **1.** To get up, as from a chair. **2.** To move upward. **3.** To come into being. **4.** To result or issue (with *from*). [< OE *ārīsan.*]

ar·is·toc·ra·cy (är'ĭs-tŏk'rə-sē) *n., pl.* **-cies.** **1.** A hereditary ruling class or nobility. **2.** Government by such a class. **3.** Any group or class considered to be superior. [< Gk *aristokratia*, "rule by the best (citizens)."] —**a·ris'to·crat'** (ə-rĭs'tə-krăt', är'ĭs-tə-) *n.* —**a·ris'to·crat'ic** *adj.* —**a·ris'to·crat'i·cal·ly** *adv.*

Ar·is·toph·a·nes (är'ĭs-tŏf'ə-nēz'). 448?–380? B.C. Athenian comic poet.

Ar·is·tot·le (är'ĭs-tŏt'l). 384–322 B.C. Greek philosopher.

a·rith·me·tic (ə-rĭth'mə-tĭk) *n.* **1.** The mathematics of integers under addition, subtraction, multiplication, division, involution, and evolution. **2.** Computation or problem solving involving real numbers and the arithmetic operations. [< Gk *arithmētikē (tekhnē)*, "(the art) of counting."] —**ar'ith·met'ic** (är'ĭth-mět'-ĭk), **ar'ith·met'i·cal** (-ĭ-kəl) *adj.* —**ar'ith·met'i·cal·ly** *adv.*

arithmetic mean. The number obtained by dividing the sum of a set of quantities by the number of quantities in the set; average.

-arium. *comb. form.* A place or housing for: planetarium.

Ar·i·zo·na (är'ə-zō'nə). A SW state of the U.S. Pop. 1,772,000. Cap. Phoenix. —**Ar'i·zo'nan** *adj. & n.*

ark (ärk) *n.* **1.** Often **Ark.** The ancient Hebrew chest containing the Ten Commandments on tablets. **2.** The boat built by Noah for the Flood. [< Gmc **ark-* < L *arca*, chest.]

Ar·kan·sas (är'kən-sô'). A S state of the U.S. Pop. 1,923,000. Cap. Little Rock. —**Ar·kan'san** (-kăn'zən) *adj. & n.*

Ar·kan·sas River (är'kən-sô', är-kăn'zəs). A river of the south-central U.S.

arm¹ (ärm) *n.* **1.** An upper limb of the human body. **2.** A part similar to an arm. **3.** A projecting support on a chair or sofa. **4.** Power; authority: *the arm of the law.* —**with open arms.** Cordially. [< OE *earm* < Gmc **armaz.*]

arm² (ärm) *n.* **1.** A weapon. **2.** A branch of a military force, such as the infantry. —*v.* **1.** To equip with weapons. **2.** To prepare for or as if for war. [< ARMS.] —**armed** *adj.*

ar·ma·da (är-mä'də, -mā'də) *n.* A fleet of warships. [Span < L *armāta*, army, fleet.]

ar·ma·dil·lo (är'mə-dĭl'ō) *n., pl.* **-los.** A burrowing tropical American mammal having a covering of armorlike bony plates. [Span, dim of *armado*, armored.]

Ar·ma·ged·don (är'mə-gĕd'n) *n.* In the Bible, the scene of a final battle between the forces of good and evil, to occur at the end of the world. [< Heb *har megiddōn*, the mountain region of *Megiddo.*]

ar·ma·ment (är'mə-mənt) *n.* **1.** The weapons and supplies of a military unit. **2.** Often **ar-**

ă pat/ā ate/âr care/ä bar/b bib/ch chew/d deed/ĕ pet/ē be/f fit/g gag/h hat/hw what/ ĭ pit/ī pie/îr pier/j judge/k kick/l lid, fatal/m mum/n no, sudden/ng sing/ŏ pot/ō go/

maments. All the military forces and war equipment of a country. **3.** The process of arming for war. [< L *armāmenta,* implements < *arma,* ARMS.]

ar•ma•ture (är'mə-chŏŏr') *n.* **1. a.** The rotating part of a dynamo, consisting of copper wire wound around an iron core. **b.** The moving part of a device such as a relay, buzzer, or loud-speaker. **c.** A piece of soft iron connecting the poles of a magnet. **2.** A protective covering; armor. [L *armātūra,* equipment.]

arm•chair (ärm'châr') *n.* A chair with sides for supporting the arms.

armed forces. The military forces of a country.

Ar•me•ni•a (är-mē'nē-ə, -mēn'yə). An ancient country of W Asia, now divided among the Soviet Union, Turkey, and Iran.

Ar•me•ni•an (är-mē'nē-ən, -mēn'yən) *n.* **1.** A native or inhabitant of Armenia. **2.** The Indo-European language of the Armenians. —**Ar•me'ni•an** *adj.*

Armenian Soviet Socialist Republic. A republic of the Soviet Union. Pop. 2,493,000. Cap. Yerevan.

ar•mi•stice (är'mə-stĭs) *n.* A temporary cessation of hostilities by mutual consent; truce. [F.]

arm•let (ärm'lĭt) *n.* A band worn on the arm for ornament or identification.

ar•mor (är'mər) *n.* Also *Brit.* **ar•mour.** **1.** A defensive covering, such as chain mail, worn to protect the body against weapons. **2.** Any tough protective covering, such as the metallic plates on tanks. **3.** Any safeguard. **4.** The armored vehicles of an army. [< L *armāre,* to arm.] —**ar'mored** *adj.*

ar•mo•ri•al (är-môr'ē-əl, är-mōr'-) *adj.* Of or pertaining to heraldic arms.

ar•mor•y (är'mər-ē) *n., pl.* **-ies.** **1.** An arsenal. **2.** An arms factory.

arm•pit (ärm'pĭt') *n.* The hollow under the arm at the shoulder.

arm•rest (ärm'rĕst') *n.* A support for the arm, as on a car door.

arms (ärmz) *pl.n.* **1.** Weapons. **2.** Warfare. **3.** Heraldic bearings. [< L *arma,* weapons, tools.]

ar•my (är'mē) *n., pl.* **-mies.** **1.** A large body of men organized for warfare. **2.** The entire military land forces of a country. **3.** Any large group of people organized for a specific cause. **4.** A multitude, as of people or animals. [< L *armāre,* to arm.]

ar•ni•ca (är'nĭ-kə) *n.* **1.** A plant having yellow, daisylike flowers. **2.** A tincture of these flowers. [ML.]

Ar•nold (är'nəld). **1. Benedict.** 1741–1801. American general; attempted to surrender West Point to the British (1780). **2. Matthew.** 1822–1888. English poet and critic.

a•ro•ma (ə-rō'mə) *n.* A pleasant, often spicy, characteristic odor. [< Gk *arōma,* aromatic spice.] —**ar'o•mat'ic** (ăr'ə-măt'ĭk) *adj.*

a•rose (ə-rōz'). *p.t.* of **arise.**

a•round (ə-round') *adv.* **1.** On or to all sides or in all directions. **2.** In a circle or circular motion. **3.** In or toward the opposite direction.

4. From one place to another: *wander around.* **5.** Close at hand; nearby. —*prep.* **1.** On all sides of. **2.** So as to enclose, surround, or envelop. **3.** About the circumference of; encircling. **4.** About the central point of. **5.** In or to various places within or near. **6.** On or to the farther side of: *the house around the corner.* **7.** *Informal.* Approximately at. [< A- (on) + ROUND (noun).]

a•rouse (ə-rouz') *v.* **aroused, arousing.** **1.** To awaken from or as if from sleep. **2.** To stir up; excite; stimulate. —**a•rous'al** *n.*

ar•peg•gi•o (är-pĕj'ē-ō', -pĕj'ō) *n., pl.* **-os.** The playing of the notes of a chord in rapid succession rather than simultaneously. [It, "chord played as on a harp."]

arr. arrival; arrive; arrived.

ar•raign (ə-rān') *v.* **1.** To call before a court to answer to an indictment. **2.** To call to account; accuse. [< VL *adrationāre,* "to call to account."] —**ar•raign'ment** *n.*

ar•range (ə-rānj') *v.* **-ranged, -ranging.** **1.** To put into a deliberate order or relation. **2.** To agree about; settle. **3.** To reset (music) for other instruments or voices. [< OF *arangier.*] —**ar•range'ment** *n.* —**ar•rang'er** *n.*

ar•rant (ăr'ənt) *adj.* Unmitigated: *an arrant thief.*

ar•ras (ăr'əs) *n.* **1.** A tapestry. **2.** A wall hanging, esp. of tapestry. [< NF *Arras,* city in N France.]

ar•ray (ə-rā') *v.* **1.** To arrange or draw up, as troops. **2.** To deck in finery; adorn. —*n.* **1.** An orderly arrangement of objects, troops, etc. **2.** An impressive collection. **3.** Splendid attire; finery. [< VL *arrēdāre,* to arrange.]

ar•rear (ə-rîr') *n.* **1.** Often **arrears.** An overdue debt or unfulfilled obligation. **2.** Often **arrears.** The state of being behind in fulfilling obligations or payments: *in arrears.* [< OF *arriere,* behind.]

ar•rest (ə-rĕst') *v.* **1.** To stop or check. **2.** To seize and hold by legal authority. —*n.* The act of arresting or state of being arrested. —**under arrest.** Detained in legal custody. [< VL *arrestāre,* to cause to stop.] —**ar•rest'er** *n.*

ar•rest•ing (ə-rĕs'tĭng) *adj.* Attracting and holding the attention.

ar•ri•val (ə-rī'vəl) *n.* **1.** The act of arriving. **2.** A person or thing that arrives or has arrived.

ar•rive (ə-rīv') *v.* **-rived, -riving.** **1.** To reach a destination. **2.** To come at last: *The day of crisis has arrived.* **3.** To achieve success or recognition. [< VL *arripāre,* to land, come to shore.] —**ar•riv'er** *n.*

ar•ro•gant (ăr'ə-gənt) *adj.* Overbearingly proud; haughty. [< L *arrogāre,* ARROGATE.] —**ar'ro•gance** *n.* —**ar'ro•gant•ly** *adv.*

ar•ro•gate (ăr'ə-gāt') *v.* **-gated, -gating.** To appropriate or claim without right. [L *arrogāre,* to claim for oneself.] —**ar'ro•ga'tion** *n.* —**ar'ro•ga'tive** (-gā'tĭv) *adj.*

ar•row (ăr'ō) *n.* **1.** A straight, thin shaft, shot from a bow and usually having a pointed head and flight-stabilizing feathers at the end. **2.** A symbol shaped like an arrow, used to indicate direction. [< OE *arwe, earh.* See arkw-.]

ar•row•head (ăr'ō-hĕd') *n.* **1.** The striking tip

of an arrow. **2.** A marsh plant having arrowhead-shaped leaves.

ar·row·root (ăr'ō-rōōt', -rŏŏt') *n.* An edible starch made from the root of a tropical American plant.

ar·roy·o (ə-roi'ō) *n., pl.* **-os.** A deep gully cut by an intermittent stream; a dry gulch. [< L *arrugia,* mine shaft.]

ar·se·nal (är'sə-nəl) *n.* **1.** A place for the storing, making, or repairing of munitions. **2.** A stock of weapons. [It *arsenale,* orig naval dockyard.]

ar·se·nate (är'sə-nĭt, -nāt') *n.* A salt or ester of arsenic acid.

ar·se·nic (är'sə-nĭk) *n.* **1.** *Symbol* **As** A highly poisonous metallic element used in insecticides, weed killers, solid-state devices, and various alloys. Atomic number 33, atomic weight 74.922. **2.** **Arsenic trioxide.** *—adj.* **ar·sen·ic** (är-sĕn'ĭk). Of or containing arsenic. [< Gk *arsenikon,* yellow orpiment.]

arsenic trioxide. A poisonous white compound, As_2O_3, used in insecticides, rat poison, and weed killers.

ar·son (är'sən) *n.* The crime of burning buildings or other property. [< ML *arsiō,* act of burning.] —**ar'son·ist** *n.*

art¹ (ärt) *n.* **1. a.** The activity of creating beautiful things. **b.** Works, such as paintings or poetry, resulting from such activity. **2.** A branch of artistic activity, as musical composition, using a special medium and technique. **3.** The aesthetic values of an artist as expressed in his works. **4.** Any of various disciplines, as the humanities, that do not rely exclusively on the scientific method. **5.** A craft or trade and its methods. **6.** Any practical skill: *the art of letter writing.* **7.** Cunning; contrivance. **8.** Printed graphic material as distinguished from text. [< L *ars.*]

art² (ärt, ərt). *Archaic.* 2nd person sing. present indicative of **be.** [< OE *eart.*]

–art. Variant of **-ard.**

art. **1.** article. **2.** artificial. **3.** artillery.

Ar·te·mis (är'tə-mĭs). Greek goddess; patroness of women and wild animals.

ar·te·ri·o·scle·ro·sis (är-tîr'ē-ō-sklə-rō'sĭs) *n.* A chronic disease in which thickening and hardening of arterial walls interfere with blood circulation. —**ar·te'ri·o·scle·rot'ic** (-rŏt'ĭk) *adj.*

ar·ter·y (är'tər-ē) *n., pl.* **-ies.** **1.** Any of a branching system of muscular tubes that carry blood away from the heart. **2.** A major transport route into which local routes flow. [< Gk *artēria.*] —**ar·te'ri·al** (-tîr'ē-əl) *adj.*

ar·te·sian well (är-tē'zhən). A drilled well in which water is forced up by internal hydrostatic pressure. [F *(puit) artésien,* (well) of *Artois,* region of France.]

art·ful (ärt'fəl) *adj.* **1.** Skillful; clever. **2.** Cunning; crafty; deceitful. —**art'ful·ly** *adv.* —**art'ful·ness** *n.*

ar·thri·tis (är-thrī'tĭs) *n.* Inflammation of a joint or joints. —**ar·thrit'ic** (-thrĭt'ĭk) *adj. & n.*

arthro–. *comb. form.* Joint. [< Gk *arthron,* joint.]

ar·thro·pod (är'thrə-pŏd') *n.* Any of a large group of invertebrates, including the insects and crustaceans, having a segmented body and jointed legs.

Ar·thur (är'thər). **1.** Reputed king of the Britons of the 6th century A.D. **2. Chester Alan.** 1830–1886. 21st President of the U.S. (1881–85).

Chester A. Arthur

ar·ti·choke (är'tə-chōk') *n.* **1.** The unopened flower head of a thistlelike plant, covered with thick, leaflike scales and eaten as a vegetable. **2.** The plant itself. [It *articiocco.*]

ar·ti·cle (är'tĭ-kəl) *n.* **1.** An individual thing in a class, esp. a commodity. **2.** A particular section of a series in a formal document. **3.** A nonfictional composition that forms an independent section of a publication. **4.** Any of a class of words used to signal nouns and specify their application. In English, the articles are *a* and *an* (indefinite articles) and *the* (definite article). [< L *articulus,* small joint, division, dim of *artus,* joint.]

ar·tic·u·lar (är-tĭk'yə-lər) *adj.* Pertaining to a joint or joints. [< L *articulus,* small joint.]

ar·tic·u·late (är-tĭk'yə-lĭt) *adj.* **1.** Having the power of speech. **2.** Able to speak clearly and skillfully. **3.** *Biol.* Jointed. —*v.* (är-tĭk'yə-lāt') **-lated, -lating. 1.** To utter (speech sounds). **2.** To pronounce distinctly. **3.** To give voice to, as an emotion. **4.** To unite by or form a joint. [< L *articulāre,* to divide into joints, utter distinctly.] —**ar·tic'u·late·ly** *adv.* —**ar·tic'u·la'tion** *n.* —**ar·tic'u·late·ness** *n.*

ar·ti·fact (är'tə-făkt') *n.* Also **ar·te·fact.** An object produced or shaped by human workmanship, esp. a simple tool of archaeological interest. [< L *ars,* ART + *factum,* something made.]

ar·ti·fice (är'tə-fĭs) *n.* **1.** A crafty expedient. **2.** Subtle deception. **3.** Ingenuity; skill. [< L *artificium < artifex,* craftsman.]

ar·ti·fi·cial (är'tə-fĭsh'əl) *adj.* **1.** Made by man rather than natural forces. **2.** Made in imitation of something natural. **3.** Feigned; pretended. [< L *artificiālis < artificium,* ARTI-

FICE.] —**ar'ti·fi'ci·al'i·ty** (-ē-ăl'ə-tē) *n.* —**ar'ti·fi'- cial·ly** *adv.*

artificial respiration. The restoring of normal breathing in an asphyxiated but living person, usually by forcing air into and out of the lungs.

ar·til·ler·y (är-tĭl'ər-ē) *n.* 1. Large-caliber mounted guns. 2. The branch of an armed force that specializes in the use of such guns. [< OF *atilier*, to fortify, arm.] —**ar·til'ler·y·man** *n.*

ar·ti·san (är'tə-zən, -sən) *n.* One skilled in making a particular commodity; craftsman. [< L *artītus*, skilled in arts.]

art·ist (är'tĭst) *n.* 1. One who creates works of art, esp. a painter or sculptor. 2. A public entertainer. 3. A practitioner of printed graphics.

ar·tis·tic (är-tĭs'tĭk) *adj.* 1. Of art or artists. 2. Skilled. 3. Appreciative of the fine arts. —**ar·tis'ti·cal·ly** *adv.*

art·ist·ry (är'tĭs-trē) *n.* Artistic ability or quality.

art·less (ärt'lĭs) *adj.* 1. Without guile; ingenuous. 2. Natural; simple. 3. Lacking art; crude. —**art'less·ly** *adv.* —**art'less·ness** *n.*

art·y (är'tē) *adj.* -ier, -iest. Affecting artistry. —**art'i·ly** *adv.* —**art'i·ness** *n.*

ar·um (âr'əm) *n.* Any of various plants having small flowers on a clublike spike surrounded by a leaflike part. [< L.]

-ary. *comb. form.* Of, engaged in, or connected with: **reactionary.**

Ar·y·an (âr'ē-ən) *n.* 1. A member or descendant of the prehistoric people that spoke Proto-Indo-European. 2. Proto-Indo-European or a language or language group descended from it. 3. In Nazi ideology, a Caucasian gentile. —**Ar'y·an** *adj.*

as (ăz, əz) *adv.* 1. To the same extent or degree; equally. 2. For instance: *large carnivores, as bears.* —*conj.* 1. To the same degree or quantity that: *as sweet as sugar.* 2. In the same way that: *Think as I think.* 3. At the same time that; while. 4. Since; because. 5. For the reason that: *Study so as to learn.* 6. Though: *Pretty as it is, it's worthless.* 7. That: *I don't know as I can.* —**as for** (or **to**). With regard to; concerning. —**as if** (or **though**). In the same way that it would be if. —**as is.** Just the way it is or appears. —*pron.* 1. That; which; who: *I received the same grade as you.* 2. A fact that: *The sun is hot, as everyone knows.* —*prep.* In the role, capacity, or function of: *acting as a mediator.* [< OE *alswā, ealswā,* just as, ALSO.]

As arsenic.

AS antisubmarine.

as·a·fet·i·da (ăs'ə-fĕt'ə-də) *n.* An offensive-smelling plant resin, formerly used in medicine. [< ML *asafoetida.*]

as·bes·tos (ăs-bĕs'təs, ăz-) *n.* Either of two incombustible fibrous mineral forms of impure magnesium silicate, used for fireproofing, building materials, and brake linings. [L, an incombustible fiber.]

as·cend (ə-sĕnd') *v.* 1. To move upward; rise. 2. To climb (a slope). [< L *ascendere.*]

as·cen·dan·cy (ə-sĕn'dən-sē) *n.* Also **as·cen· den·cy.** The state of being dominant.

as·cen·dant (ə-sĕn'dənt) *adj.* Also **as·cen·dent.** 1. Inclining or moving upward; rising. 2. Dominant; superior. —*n.* The state of being dominant or in power: *in the ascendant.*

as·cen·sion (ə-sĕn'shən) *n.* 1. The act or process of ascending. 2. **the Ascension.** The ascent of Christ into heaven, celebrated on the 40th day after Easter.

as·cent (ə-sĕnt') *n.* 1. The act of ascending. 2. An upward slope.

as·cer·tain (ăs'ər-tān') *v.* To discover through investigation; find out. [< OF *acertainer.*]

as·cet·ic (ə-sĕt'ĭk) *adj.* Practicing austere self-discipline, esp. from religious motives. [< Gk *askētēs,* hermit.] —**as·cet'ic** *n.* —**as·cet'i·cism'** *n.*

a·scor·bic acid (ə-skôr'bĭk). A vitamin, $C_6H_8O_6$, found in citrus fruits, tomatoes, potatoes, and leafy green vegetables, used to prevent scurvy; vitamin C.

as·cot (ăs'kət, -kŏt') *n.* A scarf or broad necktie loosely knotted with overlapping ends. [< *Ascot,* a village of S England, site of a famous annual horse race.]

as·cribe (ə-skrīb') *v.* -cribed, -cribing. 1. To attribute to a specified cause or source. 2. To assign as an attribute. [< L *ascribere,* to add to in writing.] —**as·crip'tion** (ə-skrĭp'shən) *n.*

a·sep·sis (ā-sĕp'sĭs) *n.* The state of being free of pathogenic organisms. —**a·sep'tic** (-sĕp'tĭk) *adj.*

a·sex·u·al (ā-sĕk'shōō-əl) *adj.* 1. Having no evident sex or sex organs. 2. Pertaining to reproduction without male or female gametes, as in binary fission or budding.

ash[1] (ăsh) *n.* 1. The grayish-white to black, soft solid residue of combustion. 2. Pulverized particulate matter ejected by volcanic eruption. 3. **ashes.** Human remains, esp. after cremation. [< OE *asce, æsce.* See as-.]

ash[2] (ăsh) *n.* 1. Any of various trees having compound leaves and strong, durable wood. 2. The wood of such a tree. [< OE *æsc.*]

a·shamed (ə-shāmd') *adj.* 1. Feeling shame. 2. Reluctant through fear of shame. —**a·sham'ed·ly** (ə-shā'mĭd-lē) *adv.*

ash·en (ăsh'ən) *adj.* 1. Of or resembling ashes. 2. Deathly pale.

a·shore (ə-shôr', ə-shōr') *adv.* Toward or on the shore.

Ash Wednesday. The 7th Wednesday before Easter and the 1st day of Lent.

A·sia (ā'zhə, ā'shə). The largest of the earth's continents, occupying the E part of the Eurasian land mass and adjacent islands and separated from Europe by the Ural Mountains. Pop. 1,852,946,000. —**A'sian, A'si·at'ic** *adj. & n.*

Asia Minor. The W peninsula of Asia, between the Black Sea and the Mediterranean.

a·side (ə-sīd') *adv.* 1. On or to one side. 2. Apart; dispensed with: *all joking aside.* —**aside from.** Excluding; excepting. —*n.* 1. A piece of dialogue that other actors on stage are supposed not to hear. 2. A digression.

as·i·nine (ăs'ə-nīn') *adj.* Stupid or silly. [< L *asinus,* ass.] —**as'i·nin'i·ty** (-nĭn'ə-tē) *n.*

ask (ăsk, äsk) *v.* 1. To put a question to. 2. To

inquire (about). **3.** To request (of or for).
4. a. To require or call for. **b.** To expect or
demand. **5.** To invite. [< OE *āscian, ācsian.*
See **ais-**.]

a·skance (ə-skăns') *adv.* **1.** With a side glance.
2. With disapproval or distrust. [< ME
ascaunce, "as if to say," "so to speak."]

a·skew (ə-skyōō') *adj.* Crooked. —*adv.* To
one side; awry. [A- (on) + SKEW.]

a·slant (ə-slănt', ə-slänt') *adj.* Slanting. —*adv.*
At a slant. —*prep.* Obliquely over or across.

a·sleep (ə-slēp') *adj.* **1.** Sleeping. **2.** Inactive.
3. Numb. —*adv.* Into a condition of sleep.

a·so·cial (ā-sō'shəl) *adj.* **1.** Avoiding the society of others. **2.** Inconsiderate; self-centered.

asp (ăsp) *n.* Any of several venomous Old
World snakes. [< Gk *aspis.*]

as·par·a·gus (ə-spăr'ə-gəs) *n.* **1.** The young,
edible stalks of a widely cultivated plant. **2.**
The plant itself. [< Gk *asparagos.*]

A.S.P.C.A. American Society for the Prevention of Cruelty to Animals.

as·pect (ăs'pĕkt') *n.* **1.** A particular facial expression. **2.** Appearance to the eye, esp. from
a specific view. **3.** A particular phase in which
something, as an idea, appears as viewed by
the mind. **4.** A side facing in a particular
direction. [< L *aspicere,* look at.]

as·pen (ăs'pən) *n.* Any of several poplar trees
having leaves that flutter readily in the wind.
[< OE *æspe,* an aspen. See **apsā.**]

as·per·i·ty (ăs-pĕr'ə-tē) *n.* **1.** Roughness or
harshness. **2.** Ill temper. [< L *asper,* rough.]

as·perse (ə-spûrs', ă-) *v.* **-persed, -persing.** To
defame; slander. [L *aspergere,* to sprinkle on.]
—**as·per'sion** (-spûr'zhən, -shən) *n.*

as·phalt (ăs'fôlt') *n.* **1.** A brownish-black solid
or semisolid mixture of bitumens used in paving, roofing, and waterproofing. **2.** Mixed asphalt and crushed stone gravel or sand, used
for paving or roofing. [< Gk *asphaltos,* bitumen, pitch, asphalt.]

as·pho·del (ăs'fə-dəl') *n.* Any of several Old
World plants having white or yellow flowers.
[< Gk *asphodelos.*]

as·phyx·i·ate (ăs-fĭk'sē-āt') *v.* **-ated, -ating.** To
cause or undergo unconsciousness or death
from lack of oxygen. [< Gk *asphuxia,* stopping of the pulse.] —**as·phyx'i·a'tion** *n.*

as·pic (ăs'pĭk) *n.* A jelly made from chilled
meat or vegetable juices. [F *(sauce) à l'aspic.*]

as·pi·dis·tra (ăs'pə-dĭs'trə) *n.* A widely grown
house plant having long, tough evergreen
leaves. [< Gk *aspis,* shield.]

as·pi·ra·tion (ăs'pə-rā'shən) *n.* **1.** Expulsion of
breath in speech. **2. a.** A strong desire for high
achievement. **b.** An object of such desire.

as·pire (ə-spīr') *v.* **-pired, -piring.** To have a
great ambition; strive toward an end. [< L
aspīrāre, to breathe upon, favor.] —**as'pi·rant**
(ăs'pər-ənt, ə-spīr'-) *n. & adj.*

as·pi·rin (ăs'pər-ĭn, -prĭn) *n.* A white crystalline compound of acetylsalicylic acid, $C_9H_8O_4$,
used to relieve pain and fever. [AC(ETYL) +
spir(aeic acid), old name for salicylic acid +
-IN.]

ass (ăs) *n.* **1.** A hoofed animal, such as the
donkey, related to and resembling the horse.

2. A silly or stupid person. [< OE *assa* < OIr
asan < L *asinus.*]

as·sail (ə-sāl') *v.* **1.** To attack with violent
blows. **2.** To attack verbally. [< VL **assalī-
re.*] —**as·sail'a·ble** *adj.* —**as·sail'ant** *n.*

as·sas·sin (ə-săs'ĭn) *n.* A murderer, esp. one
who carries out a plot to kill a public official
or other prominent person. [< Ar *ḥashshāsh,*
"hashish addict."]

as·sas·si·nate (ə-săs'ə-nāt') *v.* **-nated, -nating.**
To murder (a prominent person). —**as·sas'si·
na'tion** *n.*

as·sault (ə-sôlt') *n.* **1.** A violent physical or
verbal attack. **2.** An unlawful attempt or
threat to injure another physically. **3.** Rape.
—*v.* To attack violently. [< VL **assaltus.*]

assault and battery. *Law.* An executed threat
to use force upon another.

as·say (ăs'ā', ă-sā') *n.* **1.** Qualitative or quantitative analysis of a substance, esp. of an ore
or drug. **2.** The result of such analysis. —*v.*
(ă-sā', ăs'ā'). **1.** To subject to or undergo an
assay. **2.** To evaluate; assess. **3.** To attempt.
[< OF *assai, essai,* trial, ESSAY.]

as·sem·blage (ə-sĕm'blĭj) *n.* **1.** The act or
product of assembling. **2.** A collection of people or things. **3.** A fitting together of parts, as
of a machine.

as·sem·ble (ə-sĕm'bəl) *v.* **-bled, -bling.** **1.** To
bring or gather together into a group; congregate. **2.** To fit or join together the parts of. [<
VL **assimulāre,* to bring together.]

as·sem·bly (ə-sĕm'blē) *n., pl.* **-blies.** **1.** A
group of persons gathered for a common
purpose. **2. Assembly.** The lower house of a
legislature. **3. a.** The putting together of parts
to make a completed product. **b.** A set of
parts so assembled. **4.** A signal calling troops
to assemble.

as·sem·bly·man (ə-sĕm'blē-mən) *n.* A member of a legislative assembly.

as·sent (ə-sĕnt') *v.* To express agreement (with
to). —*n.* **1.** Agreement. **2.** Consent. [< L, "to
join in feeling."]

as·sert (ə-sûrt') *v.* **1.** To state or express positively. **2.** To defend or maintain, as one's
rights. [L *asserere,* "to join to oneself," claim.]
—**as·ser'tive** *adj.*

as·ser·tion (ə-sûr'shən) *n.* A positive statement without support of proof.

as·sess (ə-sĕs') *v.* **1.** To estimate the value of
(property) for taxation. **2.** To charge with a
tax, fine, or other special payment. **3.** To evaluate. [< L *assidēre,* "to sit beside," be an
assistant judge.] —**as·sess'a·ble** *adj.* —**as·sess'-
ment** *n.* —**as·ses'sor** *n.*

as·set (ăs'ĕt') *n.* **1.** A useful or valuable quality
or possession. **2. assets.** All of a person's or
business' properties and claims against others
that can be applied to cover liabilities. [< OF
asez, "enough (to satisfy creditors)."]

as·sid·u·ous (ə-sĭj'ōō-əs) *adj.* Constant in application or attention; diligent. [L *assiduus <
assidēre,* to sit beside, attend to.] —**as'si·du'i·ty**
(ăs'ə-d/y/ōō'ə-tē), **as·sid'u·ous·ness** *n.*

as·sign (ə-sīn') *v.* **1.** To set apart for a particular purpose. **2.** To appoint. **3.** To give out
as a task. **4.** To ascribe; attribute. **5.** *Law.* To

transfer (property, rights, or interests). [< L *assignāre*, to mark out.]

as•sig•na•tion (ăs′ĭg-nā′shən) *n.* An appointment for a meeting between lovers.

as•sign•ment (ə-sīn′mənt) *n.* 1. The act of assigning. 2. Something assigned. 3. *Law.* The transfer of a claim, right, interest, or property.

as•sim•i•late (ə-sĭm′ə-lāt′) *v.* -lated, -lating. 1. To consume and incorporate into the body. 2. To absorb or become absorbed, as knowledge. 3. To make or become similar. [< L *assimilāre*, to make similar to.] —as•sim′i•la•ble *adj.* —as•sim′i•la′tion *n.*

as•sist (ə-sĭst′) *v.* To aid; help. —*n.* 1. An act of giving aid. 2. a. *Baseball.* A handling of the ball that enables a runner to be put out. b. A pass that enables a teammate to score, as in basketball or ice hockey. [< L *assistere*, to stand beside, help.] —as•sist′er *n.*

as•sis•tance (ə-sĭs′təns) *n.* Help; aid.

as•sis•tant (ə-sĭs′tənt) *n.* One that assists; a helper.

as•size (ə-sīz′) *n.* 1. A judicial inquest. 2. **as•sizes.** One of the periodic court sessions held in the counties of England and Wales. [< OF *assis*, pp of *asseior*, to seat.]

assn. association.

assoc. associate; association.

as•so•ci•ate (ə-sō′shē-āt′, -sē-āt′) *v.* -ated, -ating. 1. To join in a relationship. 2. To connect or join together. 3. To connect in the mind. —*n.* (ə-sō′shē-ĭt, -sē-ĭt, -shē-āt′, -sē-āt′). 1. A partner; colleague. 2. A companion. —*adj.* (ə-sō′shē-ĭt, -sē-ĭt, -shē-āt′, -sē-āt′). Joined with others and having equal or nearly equal status. [< L *associāre*, to join to.]

as•so•ci•a•tion (ə-sō′sē-ā′shən, -shē-ā′shən) *n.* 1. The act of associating. 2. An organized body of people; a society.

as•so•ci•a•tive (ə-sō′shē-ā′tĭv, -sē-ā′tĭv, -shə-tĭv) *adj.* 1. Characterized by association. 2. Mathematically independent of the grouping of elements: *If a + (b + c) = (a + b) + c, the operation indicated by + is associative.*

as•so•nance (ăs′ə-nəns) *n.* Resemblance in sound, esp. in the vowel sounds of words. [< L *assonāre*, to sound in response to.]

as•sort (ə-sôrt′) *v.* To separate into groups according to kinds; classify. [OF *assorter*.]

as•sort•ed (ə-sôr′tĭd) *adj.* Of different kinds; various.

as•sort•ment (ə-sôrt′mənt) *n.* 1. The act of assorting. 2. A variety.

asst. assistant.

as•suage (ə-swāj′) *v.* -suaged, -suaging. 1. To make less severe. 2. To satisfy; appease. [< VL *assuāviāre*, to add sweetness to, sweeten.]

as•sume (ə-sōōm′) *v.* -sumed, -suming. 1. To undertake. 2. To take on; adopt. 3. To feign; affect. 4. To take for granted; suppose. [< L *assūmere*, to take to oneself.]

as•sump•tion (ə-sŭmp′shən) *n.* 1. The act of assuming. 2. A statement accepted as true without proof. 3. **Assumption. a.** The bodily taking up of the Virgin Mary into heaven after her death. **b.** A church feast on August 15 celebrating this event.

as•sur•ance (ə-shōōr′əns) *n.* 1. The act of as-

suring. 2. A statement or indication that inspires confidence. 3. a. Freedom from doubt. b. Self-confidence.

as•sure (ə-shōōr′) *v.* -sured, -suring. 1. To inform confidently. 2. To make certain. 3. To insure, as against loss. [< ML *assecūrāre*, to make sure.]

as•sured (ə-shōōrd′) *adj.* 1. Undoubted; guaranteed. 2. Confident. 3. Insured. —as•sur′ed•ly (-ĭd-lē) *adv.*

As•syr•i•a (ə-sîr′ē-ə). An ancient empire of W Asia. —**As•syr′i•an** *adj.* & *n.*

as•ta•tine (ăs′tə-tēn′) *n. Symbol* **At** A highly unstable radioactive element, used in medicine as a radioactive tracer. Atomic number 85, longest-lived isotope At 210. [< Gk *astatos*, unstable.]

as•ter (ăs′tər) *n.* Any of various plants having daisylike, variously colored flowers. [< Gk *astēr*, star.]

as•ter•isk (ăs′tə-rĭsk′) *n.* A star-shaped figure (*) used in printing to indicate a reference to a footnote or an omission. [< Gk *asteriskos*, little star.]

as•ter•ism (ăs′tə-rĭz′əm) *n.* 1. a. A cluster of stars. b. A constellation. 2. A six-rayed starlike figure optically produced in some minerals. [< Gk *astēr*, star.]

a•stern (ə-stûrn′) *adv. Naut.* 1. Behind a vessel. 2. Toward the rear of a vessel.

as•ter•oid (ăs′tə-roid′) *n.* 1. Any of numerous celestial bodies with characteristic diameters between one and several hundred miles and orbits lying chiefly between Mars and Jupiter; planetoid. 2. A starfish. [< Gk *astēr*, star.]

asth•ma (ăz′mə) *n.* A chronic respiratory disease marked by labored breathing, chest constriction, and coughing. [< Gk.] —asth•mat′ic (-măt′ĭk) *adj.*

a•stig•ma•tism (ə-stĭg′mə-tĭz′əm) *n.* 1. A refractive defect of a lens that prevents focusing of sharp, distinct images. 2. Faulty vision caused by such a defect in the lens of the eye. [A- + Gk *stigma*, spot, "focus."] —as′tig•mat′ic (ăs′tĭg-măt′ĭk) *adj.*

a•stir (ə-stûr′) *adj.* Moving about.

a•ston•ish (ə-stŏn′ĭsh) *v.* To fill with sudden wonder or amazement. [< VL *extonāre*, to strike with thunder, stun.] —a•ston′ish•ment *n.*

As•tor (ăs′tər), **John Jacob.** 1763–1848. American capitalist.

a•stound (ə-stound′) *v.* To strike with sudden wonder. [< ME *astonen*, astonish.]

a•strad•dle (ə-străd′l) *adv.* & *prep.* Astride.

as•tra•khan (ăs′trə-kăn′, -kən) *n.* Curly fur made from the skins of young lambs from the region of Astrakhan, on the Volga delta in the U.S.S.R.

as•tral (ăs′trəl) *adj.* Of or resembling the stars. [< L *astron*, star.]

a•stray (ə-strā′) *adv.* 1. Away from the correct direction. 2. Away from right or good.

a•stride (ə-strīd′) *adv.* With the legs separated so that one is on each side of something. —*prep.* Upon or over and with a leg on each side of.

as•trin•gent (ə-strĭn′jənt) *adj.* 1. Tending to draw together or constrict tissue. 2. Harsh.

ô paw, for/oi boy/ou out/ŏŏ took/ōō coo/p pop/r run/s sauce/sh shy/t to/th thin/*th* the/
ŭ cut/ûr fur/v van/w wag/y yes/z size/zh vision/ə ago, item, edible, gallop, circus/

—n. An astringent substance or drug. [< L *astringere,* to bind together.] —as•trin′gen•cy *n.*

astro–. *comb. form.* **1.** Star or star-shaped. **2.** Outer space. [< Gk *astron,* star.]

astrol. astrologer; astrological; astrology.

as•tro•labe (ăs′trə-lāb′) *n.* A medieval instrument used to determine the altitudes of celestial bodies. [< Gk *(organon) astrolabon,* "(instrument) for taking the stars."]

as•trol•o•gy (ə-strŏl′ə-jē) *n.* The study of the positions and aspects of heavenly bodies with a view to predicting their influence on human affairs. —as•trol′o•ger *n.* —as′tro•log′ic (ăs′-trə-lŏj′ĭk), as′tro•log′i•cal *adj.*

astron. astronomer; astronomical; astronomy.

as•tro•naut (ăs′trə-nôt′) *n.* A person trained to pilot, navigate, or otherwise participate in the flight of a spacecraft; cosmonaut.

as•tro•nau•tics (ăs′trə-nô′tĭks) *n. (takes sing. v.).* The science and technology of space flight. —as′tro•nau′tic, as′tro•nau′ti•cal *adj.*

as•tro•nom•i•cal (ăs′trə-nŏm′ĭ-kəl) *adj.* Also **as•tro•nom•ic** (-nŏm′ĭk). **1.** Of or pertaining to astronomy. **2.** Inconceivably large; immense.

astronomical unit. A unit of length equal to the mean distance of the earth from the sun, approx. 93 million miles.

as•tron•o•my (ə-strŏn′ə-mē) *n.* The scientific study of the universe beyond the earth. [< Gk *astronomos,* "star-arranger."] —as•tron′o•mer *n.*

as•tro•phys•ics (ăs′trō-fĭz′ĭks) *n. (takes sing. v.).* The physics of stellar phenomena. —as′-tro•phys′i•cal *adj.*

as•tute (ə-st/y/ōōt′) *adj.* Keen in judgment. [< L *astus,* craft.] —as•tute′ness *n.*

A•sun•ción (ä′sōōn-syôn′). The capital of Paraguay. Pop. 305,000.

a•sun•der (ə-sŭn′dər) *adv.* **1.** Into separate parts. **2.** Apart in position or direction. [< OE *onsundran* < ON + *sunder,* apart, separate (see **sen-**).]

a•sy•lum (ə-sī′ləm) *n.* **1.** An institution for the mentally ill or aged. **2.** A place offering safety. **3.** The protection afforded by a sanctuary. [< Gk *asulon,* sanctuary.]

a•sym•met•ric (ā′sĭ-mĕt′rĭk) *adj.* Also **a•sym•met•ri•cal** (-rĭ-kəl). Not symmetrical. —a′sym•met′ri•cal•ly *adv.* —a•sym′me•try *n.*

as•ymp•tote (ăs′ĭm-tōt′, -ĭmp-tōt′) *n. Math.* A line considered a limit to a curve in the sense that the perpendicular distance from a moving point on the curve to the line approaches zero as the point moves an infinite distance from the origin. [< Gk *(grammē) asumptōtos,* "(a line) not falling together."] —as′ymp•tot′ic (-tŏt′ĭk), as′ymp•tot′i•cal (-ĭ-kəl) *adj.* —as′ymp•tot′i•cal•ly *adv.*

at (ăt, ət) *prep.* **1.** —Used to indicate position, location, or state: *at home; at rest.* **2.** —Used to indicate a direction or goal: *look at us; jump at the chance.* **3.** —Used to indicate location in time: *at noon.* **4.** —Used to indicate manner, means, or cause: *get there at top speed.* [< OE *æt.* See **ad-**.]

At astatine.

at•a•vism (ăt′ə-vĭz′əm) *n.* The reappearance of a characteristic in an organism after several generations of absence. [< L *atavus,* ancestor,

great-great-great-grandfather.] —at′a•vis′tic *adj.* —at′a•vis′ti•cal•ly *adv.*

ate (āt; *Brit.* ĕt). *p.t.* of **eat.**

–ate¹. *comb. form.* **1. a.** Possessing: **affectionate.** **b.** Shaped like or having the general characteristics of: *Latinate.* **2.** A substance derived from or a salt or ester of an acid: **sulfate.** **3.** Used to form certain verbs: **pollinate.** [< L *-ātus.*]

–ate². *comb. form.* Rank; office: **rabbinate.** [< L *-āt(us)* + *-us,* 4th declension ending.]

at•el•ier (ăt′l-yā′) *n.* A workshop or studio, esp. an artist's studio. [< OF *astelier,* woodpile, hence carpenter's shop.]

a tem•po (ä tĕm′pō). *Mus.* In normal time; resuming the original tempo. [It, "in time."]

Ath•a•pas•can (ăth′ə-păs′kən) *n.* Also **Ath•a•bas•can** (-băs′kən). **1.** A language family of North American Indians, including languages of Alaska, the Pacific coast of North America, and the Navaho and Apache languages of the SW U.S. **2.** A member of an Athapascan-speaking tribe. —*adj.* Of or pertaining to this language family.

a•the•ism (ā′thē-ĭz′əm) *n.* Disbelief in or denial of the existence of God. [< Gk *atheos,* godless.] —a′the•is′tic, a′the•is′ti•cal *adj.* —a′-the•is′ti•cal•ly *adv.*

a•the•ist (ā′thē-ĭst) *n.* One who denies the existence of God.

A•the•na (ə-thē′nə). Greek goddess of wisdom and the arts.

Athena

ath•e•ne•um (ăth′ə-nē′əm) *n.* Also **ath•e•nae•um.** **1.** An institution for the promotion of learning. **2.** A library. [< Gk *Athēnaion,* Athena's temple, where philosophy was taught.]

Ath•ens (ăth′ənz). The capital of Greece. Pop.

1,853,000. —**A•the′ni•an** (ə-thē′nē-ən) *n.* & *adj.*

a•thirst (ə-thûrst′) *adj.* Eager (for).

ath•lete (ăth′lēt′) *n.* One who takes part in competitive sports. [< Gk *athlētēs,* contestant.]

athlete's foot. A contagious skin infection caused by parasitic fungi, usually affecting the feet, causing itching, cracking, and scaling.

ath•let•ic (ăth-lĕt′ĭk) *adj.* **1.** Of or pertaining to athletics or athletes. **2.** Physically strong; vigorous. —*n.* **athletics.** *(takes pl. v.).* Athletic activities, as competitive sports.

a•thwart (ə-thwôrt′) *adv.* Crosswise. —*prep.* **1.** Across. **2.** Contrary to.

a•tilt (ə-tĭlt′) *adj.* & *adv.* Tilted; inclined upward.

–ation. *comb. form.* **1.** Action or process of: **pollination.** **2.** State, condition, or quality of: **discoloration.** **3.** Result or product of: **civilization.** [< L *-ātus,* -ATE.]

–ative. *comb. form.* Relation, nature, or tendency: **illustrative.** [< L *-ātus,* -ATE.]

At•lan•ta (ăt-lăn′tə). The capital of Georgia. Pop. 497,000.

At•lan•tic Ocean (ăt-lăn′tĭk). The second largest of the earth's oceans, lying between the Americas in the W and Europe and Africa in the E.

at•las (ăt′ləs) *n.* **1.** A bound collection of maps. **2.** *Anat.* The top or first cervical vertebra of the neck, which supports the head. [< the Titan ATLAS.]

At•las (ăt′ləs). *Gk.Myth.* A Titan condemned to support the heavens on his shoulders.

Atlas Mountains. A mountain system in NW Africa.

at•mos•phere (ăt′mə-sfîr′) *n.* **1.** The gaseous mass or envelope surrounding a celestial body, esp. that surrounding the earth, and retained by the body's gravitational field. **2.** A unit of pressure equal to 1.01325 x 10⁵ newtons per square meter. **3.** A psychological environment or effect. [NL *atmosphaera,* "sphere of vapor."] —**at′mos•pher′ic** (-sfîr′ĭk, -sfĕr′ĭk) *adj.*

a•toll (ă′tôl′, ă′tŏl′, ă′-) *n.* A ringlike coral island that encloses a lagoon. [Malayalam *atoḷu,* "reef."]

at•om (ăt′əm) *n.* **1.** Anything considered an irreducible constituent of a specified system. **2.** The irreducible, indestructible material unit of ancient atomism. **3.** A unit of matter, the smallest unit of an element, consisting of a dense central positively charged nucleus surrounded by a system of electrons, the entire structure characteristically remaining undivided in chemical reactions except for limited removal, transfer, or exchange of certain electrons. **4.** This unit regarded as a source of nuclear energy. [< Gk *atomos,* indivisible.]

a•tom•ic (ə-tŏm′ĭk) *adj.* **1.** Of or relating to an atom or atoms. **2.** Of or employing atomic energy. **3.** Very small.

atomic bomb. **1.** An explosive weapon of great destructive power derived from the rapid release of energy in the fission of heavy atomic nuclei, as of uranium 235. **2.** Any bomb deriving its destructive power from the release of nuclear energy.

atomic clock. An extremely precise timekeeping device regulated in correspondence with a characteristic invariant frequency of an atomic or molecular system.

atomic energy. **1.** The energy released from an atomic nucleus in fission or fusion. **2.** This energy regarded as a source of practical power.

atomic mass unit. A unit of mass equal to $\frac{1}{12}$ the mass of the carbon isotope with mass number 12, approx. 1.6604 x 10⁻²⁴ gram.

atomic number. *Symbol* **Z** The number of protons in an atomic nucleus.

atomic pile. A nuclear reactor.

atomic reactor. A nuclear reactor.

atomic weight. The average weight of an atom of an element, usually expressed relative to 1 atom of the carbon isotope taken to have a standard weight of 12.

at•om•ism (ăt′əm-ĭz′əm) *n.* A Greek philosophical theory of the late 5th century B.C., according to which simple, indivisible, and indestructible atoms are the basic components of the entire universe.

at•om•ize (ăt′əm-īz′) *v.* **-ized, -izing. 1.** To reduce or separate into atoms. **2. a.** To reduce (a liquid) to a spray. **b.** To spray (a liquid) in this form. —**at′om•i•za′tion** *n.*

at•om•iz•er (ăt′əm-ī′zər) *n.* A device for producing a fine spray.

atom smasher. An atomic particle accelerator.

a•to•nal•i•ty (ā′tō-năl′ə-tē) *n.* *Mus.* A style of composition in which tonal center or key is disregarded. —**a•to′nal** (ā-tō′nəl) *adj.*

a•tone (ə-tōn′) *v.* **atoned, atoning.** To make amends (for). [< ME *at one,* of one mind, in accord.] —**a•ton′er** *n.*

a•tone•ment (ə-tōn′mənt) *n.* **1.** Amends or reparation made for an injury or wrong. **2.** Often **Atonement.** The reconciliation of God and man.

a•top (ə-tŏp′) *prep.* On top of.

–ator. *comb. form.* One who or that which acts or does: **radiator.**

–atory. *comb. form.* Pertinence to, characteristic of, result or effect of: **perspiratory.**

ATP adenosine triphosphate.

a•tri•um (ā′trē-əm) *n., pl.* **atria** (ā′trē-ə) or **-ums.** A bodily cavity or chamber, as in the heart; auricle. [L *ātrium.*] —**a′tri•al** *adj.*

a•tro•cious (ə-trō′shəs) *adj.* **1.** Extremely evil or cruel. **2.** Exceptionally bad. [< L *ātrōx,* "dark-looking," horrible.]

a•troc•i•ty (ə-trŏs′ə-tē) *n., pl.* **-ties.** An atrocious action, condition, or object.

at•ro•phy (ăt′rə-fē) *n., pl.* **-phies.** Emaciation or wasting of tissues, organs, or the entire body. —*v.* **-phied, -phying.** To cause or undergo atrophy. [< Gk *atrophos,* ill-nourished.]

at•ro•pine (ăt′rə-pēn′, -pĭn) *n.* Also **at•ro•pin** (-pĭn). An extremely poisonous alkaloid, $C_{17}H_{23}NO_3$, obtained from belladonna and related plants, used to dilate the pupil of the eye. [G *Atropin.*]

att. attorney.

at•tach (ə-tăch′) *v.* **1.** To fasten on or affix; connect. **2.** To adhere. **3.** To affix or append.

4. To ascribe or assign. **5.** To bind by ties of affection or loyalty. **6.** To seize (persons or property) by legal writ. [< OF *attacher*, to fasten (with a stake).] —**at•tach′er** *n.*

at•ta•ché (ăt′ə-shā′, ă-tă′shā′) *n.* A person assigned to a diplomatic mission in a particular capacity. [F, "one attached."]

at•tach•ment (ə-tăch′mənt) *n.* **1.** The act of attaching or condition of being attached. **2.** Something that serves to attach one thing to another. **3.** Fond regard. **4.** A supplementary part. **5.** The legal seizure of property.

at•tack (ə-tăk′) *v.* **1.** To set upon with force. **2.** To bombard with hostile criticism. **3.** To start work on. **4.** To begin to affect harmfully. —*n.* **1.** An assault. **2.** Seizure by a disease. **3.** The manner in which a musical passage or phrase is begun. [< OIt *attaccare*.]

at•tain (ə-tān′) *v.* **1.** To gain or accomplish. **2.** To arrive at. [< OF *ataindre*, to reach to.] —**at•tain′a•ble** *adj.*

at•tain•der (ə-tān′dər) *n.* The loss of civil rights legally consequent to a capital offense. [< OF *ataindre*, to affect, infect, ATTAIN.]

at•tain•ment (ə-tān′mənt) *n.* **1.** The act of attaining. **2.** An acquirement or acquisition.

at•taint (ə-tānt′) *v.* To condemn by a sentence of attainder.

at•tar (ăt′ər) *n.* A fragrant oil obtained from flower petals. [Pers *'aṭir*, perfumed.]

at•tempt (ə-tĕmpt′) *v.* To try. —*n.* **1.** An effort. **2.** An attack: *an attempt on his life.* [< L *attemptāre.*] —**at•tempt′er** *n.*

at•tend (ə-tĕnd′) *v.* **1.** To be present (at). **2.** To accompany. **3.** To take care of. **4.** To heed. [< L *attendere*, to stretch toward, direct attention to.] —**at•tend′er** *n.*

at•ten•dance (ə-tĕn′dəns) *n.* **1.** The act of attending. **2.** The persons or number of persons present, as at a class.

at•ten•dant (ə-tĕn′dənt) *n.* **1.** One who attends or waits on another. **2.** One who is present. **3.** An accompanying circumstance; consequence. —*adj.* Accompanying or consequent. —**at•ten′dant•ly** *adv.*

at•ten•tion (ə-tĕn′shən) *n.* **1.** Concentration of one's mental powers upon an object. **2.** Observant consideration; notice. **3.** Consideration or courtesy. **4.** An erect posture assumed on command by a soldier. —**at•ten′tive** *adj.*

at•ten•u•ate (ə-tĕn′yōō-āt′) *v.* -**ated,** -**ating. 1.** To make or become slender, fine, or small. **2.** To weaken. **3.** To lessen in density; dilute or rarefy (a liquid or gas). **4.** To make (a pathogenic microorganism) less virulent. [L *attenuāre*, to make thin.]

at•test (ə-tĕst′) *v.* **1.** To affirm to be correct, true, or genuine. **2.** To provide evidence of. —**attest to.** To bear witness. [< L *attestārī.*]

Att. Gen. attorney general.

at•tic (ăt′ĭk) *n.* A story or room directly below the roof of a house. [< *Attic story*, a top story having square columns in the ATTIC style.]

At•tic (ăt′ĭk) *adj.* Of or pertaining to ancient Attica, Athens, or the Athenians. —*n.* The Ancient Greek dialect of Athens.

At•ti•ca (ăt′ĭ-kə). The hinterland of ancient Athens.

At•ti•la (ăt′ə-lə, ə-tĭl′ə). A.D. 406?–453. King of the Huns.

at•tire (ə-tīr′) *v.* -**tired,** -**tiring.** To dress; clothe; deck. —*n.* Clothing; array. [< OF *atirier*, to arrange into ranks.]

at•ti•tude (ăt′ə-t/y/ōōd′) *n.* **1.** A posture or manner of carrying oneself, indicative of a mood or condition. **2.** A state of mind or feeling. **3.** The orientation of an aircraft's or spacecraft's axes relative to a reference line, plane, or direction of motion. [< L *aptitūdō*, faculty, fitness.] —**at′ti•tu′di•nal** *adj.*

attn. attention.

atto-. *comb. form.* One quintillionth of (a specified unit). [< Norw *atten*, eighteen.]

at•tor•ney (ə-tûr′nē) *n., pl.* -**neys.** A person, esp. a lawyer, legally appointed or empowered to act for another. [< OF *atorner*, to appoint.]

attorney general *pl.* **attorneys general.** The chief law officer and legal counsel of the government of a state or the U.S.

at•tract (ə-trăkt′) *v.* **1.** To cause to draw near or adhere. **2.** To draw or direct to oneself by some quality or action. **3.** To allure or be alluring. [< L *attrahere.*]

at•trac•tion (ə-trăk′shən) *n.* **1.** The act or quality of attracting. **2.** A feature that attracts. **3.** A public spectacle or entertainment.

at•trac•tive (ə-trăk′tĭv) *adj.* **1.** Having the power to attract. **2.** Appealing; charming. —**at•trac′tive•ly** *adv.*

at•trib•ute (ə-trĭb′yōōt) *v.* -**uted,** -**uting.** To regard or assign as belonging to or resulting from someone or something; ascribe. —*n.* (ăt′rə-byōōt′). **1.** A distinctive feature of or object associated with a person or thing. **2.** An adjective. [L *attribuēre.*] —**at•trib′ut•a•ble** *adj.* —**at′tri•bu′tion** *n.*

at•trib•u•tive (ə-trĭb′yə-tĭv) *n.* A word, such as an adjective, or word group that is placed adjacent to the noun it modifies without a linking verb. —*adj.* **1.** Of or functioning as an attributive. **2.** Of or having the nature of an attribute. —**at•trib′u•tive•ly** *adv.*

at•tri•tion (ə-trĭsh′ən) *n.* **1.** A rubbing away or wearing down by friction. **2.** A gradual, natural reduction in membership or personnel, as through retirement, resignation, or death. [< L *atterere*, to rub against.]

at•tune (ə-t/y/ōōn′) *v.* -**tuned,** -**tuning. 1.** To tune. **2.** To bring into harmony.

atty. attorney.

Atty. Gen. attorney general.

at wt atomic weight.

a•typ•i•cal (ā-tĭp′ĭ-kəl) *adj.* Not typical.

Au gold (L *aurum*).

au•burn (ô′bərn) *n.* A reddish brown. [< ML *alburnus*, whitish.] —**au′burn** *adj.*

Auck•land (ôk′lənd). A city of New Zealand, on North Island. Pop. 515,100.

au cou•rant (ō kōō-rän′). Informed on current affairs. [F, "in the current."]

auc•tion (ôk′shən) *n.* A public sale in which items are sold to the highest bidder. —*v.* —**auction off.** To sell at or by an auction. [L *auctiō*, (a sale by) increase (of bids).]

auc•tion•eer (ôk′shə-nîr′) *n.* One who conducts an auction.

ă pat/ā ate/âr care/ä bar/b bib/ch chew/d deed/ĕ pet/ē be/f fit/g gag/h hat/hw what/ ĭ pit/ī pie/îr pier/j judge/k kick/l lid, fatal/m mum/n no, sudden/ng sing/ŏ pot/ō go/

auc•to•ri•al (ôk-tôr′ē-əl, ôk-tôr′-) *adj.* Of or pertaining to an author.

aud. audit; auditor.

au•da•cious (ô-dā′shəs) *adj.* **1.** Fearlessly daring; reckless. **2.** Arrogantly insolent. [< L *audāx*, bold.] **—au•da′cious•ly** *adv.* **—au•dac′i•ty** (ô-dăs′ə-tē) *n.*

au•di•ble (ô′də-bəl) *adj.* Capable of being heard. [< L *audīre*, to hear.] **—au′di•bil′i•ty** (ô′də-bil′ə-tē) *n.*

au•di•ence (ô′dē-əns) *n.* **1.** A gathering of spectators or listeners. **2.** Those reached by a book, radio broadcast, or television program. **3.** A formal hearing or conference. **4.** An opportunity to be heard. [< L *audīre*, to hear.]

au•di•o (ô′dē-ō′) *adj.* **1.** Pertaining to audible sound or to the broadcasting of sound. **2.** Pertaining to the high-fidelity reproduction of sound. —*n.* **1.** The audio part of television equipment. **2.** Audio broadcasting or reception. **3.** Audible sound.

audio frequency. A range of frequencies usually from 15 cycles per second to 20,000 cycles per second, characteristic of signals audible to the normal human ear.

au•di•o•phile (ô′dē-ō-fīl′) *n.* A high-fidelity audio hobbyist.

au•di•o•vis•u•al (ô′dē-ō-vĭzh′ōō-əl) *adj.* **1.** Both audible and visible. **2.** Pertaining to educational materials, such as filmed or televised lectures, that present information in both audible and visible form.

au•dit (ô′dĭt) *n.* **1.** An examination, adjustment, or correction of records or accounts. **2.** An examined and verified account. —*v.* **1.** To examine, verify, or correct (accounts, records, or claims). **2.** To attend (a college course) without receiving academic credit. [< L *audītus*, a hearing.]

au•di•tion (ô-dĭsh′ən) *n.* **1.** The act or sense of hearing. **2.** A presentation of something heard; a hearing. **3.** A trial hearing, as of a performer. —*v.* To give or be tested in an audition. [< L *audīre*, to hear.]

au•di•tor (ô′də-tər) *n.* **1.** A listener. **2.** One who audits.

au•di•to•ri•um (ô′də-tôr′ē-əm, -tōr′ē-əm) *n., pl.* **-ums** or **-toria** (-tôr′ē-ə, -tōr′ē-ə). A room or building to accommodate an audience. [< L *audīre*, to hear.]

au•di•to•ry (ô′də-tôr′ē, -tōr′ē) *adj.* Pertaining to the sense, the organs, or the experience of hearing. [< L *audīre*, to hear.]

aug. augmentative.

Aug. August.

au•ger (ô′gər) *n.* A tool for boring. [< OE *nafogār*, "tool for piercing wheel hubs."]

aught (ôt) *n.* Also **ought.** A cipher; the symbol 0; zero. [< *an aught*, orig, a NAUGHT.]

aug•ment (ôg-měnt′) *v.* To make or become greater; enlarge; increase. [< LL *augmentāre* < L *augēre*, to increase.] **—aug′men•ta′tion** *n.*

au gra•tin (ō grät′n, grăt′n, ō). Topped with crumbs and/or grated cheese and browned. [F.]

au•gur (ô′gər) *n.* A seer or prophet; soothsayer. —*v.* **1.** To predict, prognosticate, or foretell. **2.** To betoken. [L.]

au•gu•ry (ô′gyə-rē) *n., pl.* **-ries.** **1.** The art, ability, or practice of auguring; divination. **2.** The rite performed by an augur. **3.** A sign or omen.

au•gust (ô-gŭst′) *adj.* Inspiring awe or admiration; majestic; venerable. [L *augustus,* venerable.] **—au•gust′ly** *adv.*

Au•gust (ô′gəst) *n.* The 8th month of the year. August has 31 days. [< AUGUSTUS.]

Au•gus•ta (ô-gŭs′tə). The capital of Maine. Pop. 22,000.

Au•gus•tan (ô-gŭs′tən) *adj.* Of, belonging to, or characteristic of the reign or times of Augustus Caesar.

Au•gus•tine (ô′gə-stēn′, ô-gŭs′tĭn), **Saint.** A.D. 354–430. Latin church father and philosopher. **—Au′gus•tin′i•an** (ô′gə-stĭn′ē-ən) *adj.*

Augustus

Au•gus•tus (ô-gŭs′təs). 63 B.C.–A.D. 14. Founder of the imperial Roman government.

auk (ôk) *n.* A chunky, short-winged sea bird of northern regions. [< ON *ālka*.]

auld (ōld) *adj. Scot.* Old.

aunt (ănt, änt) *n.* **1.** The sister of one's father or mother. **2.** The wife of one's uncle. [< L *amita,* paternal aunt.]

au•ra (ôr′ə) *n., pl.* **-ras** or **aurae** (ôr′ē). **1.** An invisible breath or emanation. **2.** A distinctive air or quality that characterizes a person or thing. [< L, breeze.]

au•ral (ôr′əl) *adj.* Of, pertaining to, or perceived by the ear. [< L *auris,* ear.] **—au′ral•ly** *adv.*

au•re•ate (ôr′ē-ĭt) *adj.* Of a golden color; gilded; ornate. [< L *aureus,* golden.] **—au′re•ate•ly** *adv.* **—au′re•ate•ness** *n.*

au•re•ole (ôr′ē-ōl′) *n.* Also **au•re•o•la** (ô-rē′ə-lə). A halo. [< L *aureolus,* golden.]

Au•re•o•my•cin (ôr′ē-ō-mī′sĭn) *n.* A trademark for an antibiotic.

au•ri•cle (ôr′ĭ-kəl) *n.* Also **au•ric•u•la** (ô-rĭk′yə-lə) *pl.* **-lae** (-lē′) or **-las. 1. a.** The external part of the ear. **b.** An atrium of the heart. **2.** An earlike part or appendage. [< L *auris,* ear.] **—au′ri•cled** (-kəld) *adj.*

au•ric•u•lar (ô-rĭk′yə-lər) *adj.* **1.** Aural. **2.** Perceived by or spoken into the ear. **3.** Having the shape of an ear. **4.** Of or pertaining to an auricle of the heart. **—au•ric′u•lar•ly** *adv.*

au·rif·er·ous (ô-rĭf'ər-əs) *adj.* Containing gold; gold-bearing.

Au·ri·ga (ô-rī'gə) *n.* A constellation in the N Hemisphere. [L *aurīga*, charioteer.]

au·ro·ra (ô-rôr'ə, ô-rōr'ə, ə-) *n.* High-altitude, many-colored, flashing luminosity, visible in night skies of polar and sometimes temperate zones. [L *aurōra*, dawn.]

aurora aus·tra·lis (ô-strā'lĭs). Aurora occurring in southern regions; southern lights.

aurora bo·re·al·is (bôr'ē-ăl'ĭs, bōr'-). Aurora occurring in northern regions; northern lights.

au·ro·ral (ô-rôr'əl, ô-rōr'-, ə-) *adj.* Of or like an aurora.

aus·cul·ta·tion (ô'skəl-tā'shən) *n.* Diagnostic monitoring of the sounds made by internal organs. [< L *auscultāre*, to listen to.]

aus·pice (ô'spĭs) *n., pl.* **auspices** (ô'spə-sēz'). **1. auspices.** Protection or support; patronage. **2.** A portent or omen. [L *auspicium*, bird divination.]

aus·pi·cious (ô-spĭsh'əs) *adj.* Propitious; fortunate; prosperous. **—aus·pi'cious·ly** *adv.* **—aus·pi'cious·ness** *n.*

Aust. Austria; Austria-Hungary.

aus·tere (ô-stîr') *adj.* **1.** Severe; stern; somber; grave. **2.** Ascetic; simple; bare. [< Gk *austēros*, harsh, rough, severe.] **—aus·ter'i·ty** (ô-stĕr'ə-tē), **aus·tere'ness** *n.*

Aus·tin (ôs'tən). The capital of Texas. Pop. 252,000.

aus·tral (ôs'trəl) *adj.* Southern. [< L *auster*, south.]

Aus·tra·lia (ô-strāl'yə). **1.** A continent, lying SE of Asia between the Pacific and Indian oceans. **2.** A country comprising this continent and the island of Tasmania. Pop. 11,360,000. Cap. Canberra.

Australia

Aus·tra·lian (ô-strāl'yən) *n.* **1.** A native or citizen of Australia. **2.** An aborigine of Australia. **—Aus·tra'lian** *adj.*

Aus·tri·a (ôs'trē-ə). A republic in C Europe. Pop. 7,074,000. Cap. Vienna. **—Aus'tri·an** *adj. & n.*

Aus·tri·a-Hun·ga·ry (ôs'trē-ə-hŭng'gə-rē). A former dual monarchy of C Europe.

Aus·tro-A·si·at·ic (ôs'trō-ā'zhē-ăt'ĭk) *n.* A language family of SE Asia. **—Aus'tro-A'si·at'ic** *adj.*

auth. 1. authentic. **2.** author. **3.** authority. **4.** authorized.

au·then·tic (ô-thĕn'tĭk) *adj.* **1.** Worthy of trust, reliance, or belief. **2.** Genuine; real. [< Gk *authentikos*, genuine, authoritative.] **—au'then·tic'i·ty** (-tĭs'ə-tē) *n.*

au·then·ti·cate (ô-thĕn'tĭ-kāt') *v.* **-cated, -cating.** To establish or confirm as authentic. **—au·then'ti·ca'tion** *n.*

au·thor (ô'thər) *n.* **1.** The writer of a literary work; a writer. **2.** The beginner, originator, or creator of anything. [< L *auctor*, creator.]

au·thor·i·tar·i·an (ə-thôr'ə-târ'ē-ən, ə-thŏr'-, ô-) *adj.* Characterized by or favoring absolute obedience to authority. **—n.** One who believes in or practices authoritarian policies. **—au·thor'i·tar'i·an·ism'** *n.*

au·thor·i·ta·tive (ə-thôr'ə-tā'tĭv, ə-thŏr'-, ô-) *adj.* **1.** Having or arising from proper authority. **2.** Wielding authority.

au·thor·i·ty (ə-thôr'ə-tē, ə-thŏr'-, ô-) *n., pl.* **-ties. 1.** The right and power to command, enforce laws, exact obedience, determine, influence, or judge. **2. a.** A person or group invested with this right and power. **b. authorities.** Government officials having this right and power. **3.** Authorization. **4. a.** An accepted source of expert information. **b.** A citation from such a source. **5.** An expert in a given field: *an authority on plants.* [< L *auctōritās* < *auctor*, AUTHOR.]

au·thor·ize (ô'thə-rīz') *v.* **-ized, -izing. 1.** To grant authority or power to. **2.** To sanction. **3.** To justify. **—au'thor·i·za'tion** *n.*

Authorized Version. The King James Bible.

au·thor·ship (ô'thər-shĭp') *n.* **1.** The profession or occupation of writing. **2.** A source or origin, as of a book or idea.

au·tism (ô'tĭz'əm) *n.* **1.** Abnormal subjectivity; acceptance of fantasy rather than reality. **2.** A form of childhood schizophrenia characterized by acting out and withdrawal; infantile autism. [< AUT(O)- + -ISM.]

au·to (ô'tō) *n., pl.* **-tos.** An automobile.

auto-. *comb. form.* Acting or directed from within; self; same. [< Gk *autos*, self.]

auto. automatic.

au·to·bahn (ou'tō-bän') *n., pl.* **-bahns.** A German superhighway.

au·to·bi·og·ra·phy (ô'tō-bī-ŏg'rə-fē, -bē-ŏg'-rə-fē) *n., pl.* **-phies.** The story of a person's life written by himself; memoirs.

Austria

ă pat/ā ate/âr care/ä bar/b **bib**/ch **chew**/d **deed**/ĕ pet/ē be/f fit/g **gag**/h **hat**/hw **what**/
ĭ pit/ī pie/îr **pier**/j **judge**/k **kick**/l lid, fatal/m **mum**/n no, sudden/ng **sing**/ŏ pot/ō go/

au•toch•tho•nous (ô-tŏk'thə-nəs) *adj.* Indigenous; aboriginal.

au•toc•ra•cy (ô-tŏk'rə-sē) *n., pl.* **-cies.** 1. Government by a single person having unlimited power. 2. A country or state having this form of government. —**au'to•crat'** (ô'tə-krăt') *n.* —**au'to•crat'ic** *adj.*

au•to•graph (ô'tə-grăf', -gräf') *n.* 1. A person's own signature or handwriting. 2. A manuscript in the author's handwriting. —*v.* 1. To sign. 2. To write in one's own handwriting.

au•to•mat (ô'tə-măt') *n.* A self-service restaurant in which food is obtained from coin-operated machines.

au•to•mate (ô'tə-māt') *v.* **-mated, -mating.** To convert to, control, or operate by automation.

au•to•mat•ic (ô'tə-măt'ĭk) *adj.* 1. a. Acting or operating in a manner essentially independent of external influence or control. b. Self-regulating. 2. Involuntary; reflex. 3. Capable of firing continuously until ammunition is exhausted. —*n.* An automatic firearm or device [Gk *automatos*, acting by itself.]

au•to•ma•tion (ô'tə-mā'shən) *n.* 1. The automatic operation or control of a process, equipment, or a system. 2. The totality of mechanical and electronic techniques and equipment used to achieve such operation or control. 3. The condition of being automatically controlled or operated. —**au'to•ma'tive** *adj.*

au•tom•a•ton (ô-tŏm'ə-tən, -tŏn') *n., pl.* **-tons** or **-ta** (-tə). 1. A robot. 2. One that behaves in an automatic or mechanical fashion.

au•to•mo•bile (ô'tə-mō-bēl', -mō'bēl', ô'-tə-mō-bēl') *n.* A self-propelled land vehicle, esp. a four-wheeled passenger vehicle propelled by an internal-combustion engine. —*adj.* Automotive. —**au'to•mo•bil'ist** *n.*

au•to•mo•tive (ô'tə-mō'tĭv) *adj.* 1. Self-moving; self-propelling. 2. Of or pertaining to automobiles.

au•to•nom•ic nervous system (ô'tə-nŏm'ĭk). The division of the vertebrate nervous system that regulates involuntary action, as of the intestines, heart, and glands, and comprises the sympathetic nervous system and the parasympathetic nervous system.

au•ton•o•mous (ô-tŏn'ə-məs) *adj.* 1. Independent; self-contained. 2. Self-governing. [Gk *autonomos*, self-ruling.] —**au•ton'o•my** *n.*

au•top•sy (ô'tŏp'sē, ô'təp-) *n., pl.* **-sies.** The examination of a dead body to determine the cause of death; post-mortem. [< Gk *autopsia*, a seeing for oneself.]

au•to•sug•ges•tion (ô'tō-səg-jĕs'chən) *n.* The process by which a person induces self-acceptance of an opinion, belief, or plan of action.

au•tumn (ô'təm) *n.* 1. The season of the year between summer and winter. 2. A time or period of maturity verging on decline. [< L *autumnus*.] —**au•tum'nal** (-tŭm'nəl) *adj.*

autumnal equinox. The equinox of September 22 or 23, marking the start of autumn.

aux. auxiliary.

aux•il•ia•ry (ôg-zĭl'yər-ē, -zĭl'ər-ē) *adj.* 1. Giving assistance or support; aiding; helping. 2. Subsidiary; supplementary. —*n., pl.* **-ries.** 1.

One that acts in an auxiliary capacity. 2. Also **auxiliary verb.** A verb that accompanies certain verb forms to express tense, mood, voice, or aspect. [< L *auxilium*, help.]

av. 1. avenue. 2. average. 3. avoirdupois.

a•vail (ə-vāl') *v.* To be of use or advantage (to); assist; help. —*n.* Use, benefit: *to* (or *of*) *no avail.* [< L *valēre*, to be strong, be worth.]

a•vail•a•ble (ə-vā'lə-bəl) *adj.* Accessible for use; at hand; usable.

av•a•lanche (ăv'ə-lănch', -länch') *n.* A fall or slide of a large mass of snow, rock, or other material down a mountainside. [F.]

a•vant-garde (ä'vänt-gärd') *n.* 1. A group, as of writers or artists, regarded as the vanguard of a given field. 2. The admirers of such a group and critics acting as its spokesmen —*adj.* 1. Of or belonging to the vanguard, as in the arts. 2. Ahead of the times. [F, vanguard.]

av•a•rice (ăv'ə-rĭs) *n.* Greed for wealth; cupidity. [< L *avēre*, to desire.] —**av'a•ri'cious** (ăv'ə-rĭsh'əs) *adj.*

av•a•tar (ăv'ə-tär') *n.* One regarded as an incarnation. [Sk *avatāra*, descent.]

a•vaunt (ə-vônt', ə-vänt') *interj. Archaic.* Used as a command to be gone. [< OF *avant*, "forward," "go away!"]

avdp. avoirdupois.

ave., Ave. avenue.

A•ve Ma•ri•a (ä'vā mə-rē'ə). Also **A•ve Mar•y** (ä'vē mâr'ē). 1. A Roman Catholic prayer; Hail Mary. Luke 1:28, 42. 2. a. A recitation of this prayer. b. The hour, as at dawn and sunset, when it is customarily said. 3. One of the small beads on a rosary used to count recitations of this prayer. [< ML, "Hail Mary!"]

a•venge (ə-vĕnj') *v.* **avenged, avenging.** 1. To take revenge for (a wrong, injury, etc.). 2. To take vengeance (on behalf of). [< L *vindicāre*, to VINDICATE.] —**a•veng'er** *n.* —**a•veng'ing•ly** *adv.*

av•e•nue (ăv'ə-n/y/oo') *n.* 1. A wide street, thoroughfare, or path. 2. A means of approach to a given place, activity, or goal. [< L *advenīre*, to come to.]

a•ver (ə-vûr') *v.* **averred, averring.** To declare in a positive, dogmatic, or formal manner. [< ML *avērāre*, to assert as true.]

av•er•age (ăv'rĭj, ăv'ər-ĭj) *n.* 1. A number that typifies a set of numbers of which it is a function; the arithmetic mean. 2. A relative proportion or degree indicating position or achievement; a representative type. —*adj.* 1. Of, pertaining to, or constituting a mathematical average. 2. Typical; usual. —*v.* **-aged, -aging.** 1. To calculate, obtain, or amount to an average of. 2. To distribute proportionately. [Earlier *averie*, loss on damaged shipping, hence loss shared equitably among investors.]

a•verse (ə-vûrs') *adj.* —**averse to.** Opposed; reluctant. [< L *āvertere*, AVERT.]

a•vert (ə-vûrt') *v.* 1. To turn away. 2. To ward off or prevent. [< VL *āvertīre*.]

A•ves•ta (ə-vĕs'tə) *n.* The sacred writings of the ancient Persians.

A·ves·tan (ə-vĕs'tən) *n.* The eastern dialect of Old Iranian, which is the oldest attested group in the Indo-Iranian branch of Indo-European.

a·vi·an (ā'vē-ən) *adj.* Of or pertaining to birds. [< L *avis*, bird.]

a·vi·ar·y (ā'vē-ĕr'ē) *n., pl.* **-ies.** A large enclosure for birds, as in a zoo. [< L *avis*, bird.] **—a'vi·a·rist** (ā'vē-ə-rĭst, -ĕr'ĭst) *n.*

a·vi·a·tion (ā'vē-ā'shən, ăv'ē-) *n.* **1.** The operation of aircraft. **2.** The production of aircraft. **3.** Military aircraft. [< L *avis*, bird.]

a·vi·a·tor (ā'vē-ā'tər, ăv'ē-) *n.* A pilot.

av·id (ăv'ĭd) *adj.* **1.** Eager; greedy. **2.** Enthusiastic; ardent. [< L *avidus* < *avēre*, to long for.] **—av'id·ly** *adv.*

a·vid·i·ty (ə-vĭd'ə-tē) *n.* Eagerness; greed.

a·vi·on·ics (ā'vē-ŏn'ĭks, ăv'ē-) *n. (takes sing. v.).* The science and technology of electronics applied to aeronautics and astronautics. **—a'·vi·on'ic** *adj.*

av·o·ca·do (ăv'ə-kä'dō) *n., pl.* **-dos. 1.** A tropical fruit with leathery skin and bland, yellow-green pulp. **2.** A tree bearing such fruit. [< Nah *ahuacatl*, "testicle" (< the shape of the fruit).]

av·o·ca·tion (ăv'ō-kā'shən) *n.* An activity engaged in, in addition to one's regular work or profession; hobby. [< L *āvocāre*, to call away.]

av·o·cet (ăv'ə-sĕt') *n.* A long-legged shore bird with a long, slender beak. [< It *avocetta*.]

A·vo·ga·dro number (ä'və-gä'drō, ăv'ə-). Also **Avogadro's number, Avogadro constant.** The number of molecules in a mole of a substance, approx. 6.0225 x 10^{23}.

a·void (ə-void') *v.* To keep away from; shun. [< OF *esvuidier*, "to empty out," to leave.] **—a·void'ance** *n.* **—a·void'er** *n.*

av·oir·du·pois (ăv'ər-də-poiz') *n.* **1.** Avoirdupois weight. **2.** Weight; heaviness. [ME *avoir de pois*, "commodities sold by weight."]

avoirdupois weight. A system of weights and measures, used in most English-speaking countries, based on a pound containing 16 ounces or 7,000 grains and equal to 453.59 grams.

a·vouch (ə-vouch') *v.* **1.** To guarantee. **2.** To affirm. [< L *advocāre*, to call on (as adviser).]

a·vow (ə-vou') *v.* To acknowledge openly; confess. [< L *advocāre*, to call on (as adviser), appeal to.] **—a·vow'al** *n.*

a·vun·cu·lar (ə-vŭng'kyə-lər) *adj.* Of, pertaining to, or resembling an uncle. [< L *avunculus,* maternal uncle.]

A/W actual weight.

a·wait (ə-wāt') *v.* **1.** To wait (for). **2.** To be in store for. [< ONF *awaitier,* watch for, wait on.]

a·wake (ə-wāk') *v.* **awoke** or *rare* **awaked, awaked** or *rare* **awoke, awaking. 1.** To rouse from sleep; wake up. **2.** To excite. **3.** To stir up. —See Usage note at **wake.** *—adj.* **1.** Not asleep. **2.** Alert; vigilant; watchful. [< OE *awacian.*]

a·wak·en (ə-wā'kən) *v.* To wake up; awake. —See Usage note at **wake.** **—a·wak'en·ing** *adj. & n.*

a·ward (ə-wôrd') *v.* **1.** To grant or declare as

merited or due. **2.** To bestow for performance or quality. *—n.* **1.** A decision, as one made by a judge or arbitrator. **2.** Something awarded. [< ONF *eswarder,* to judge after careful observation.]

a·ware (ə-wâr') *adj.* Conscious; cognizant; alert: *aware of the consequences.* [< OE *gewær.* See wer-[4].] **—a·ware'ness** *n.*

a·wash (ə-wŏsh', ə-wôsh') *adj. & adv.* **1.** Level with and washed by waves. **2.** Flooded.

a·way (ə-wā') *adv.* **1.** At or to a distance. **2.** In or to a different place or direction. **3.** From one's presence or possession. **4.** Out of existence: *dwindling away.* **5.** Continuously: *working away.* **6.** Immediately: *Fire away!* *—adj.* **1.** Absent: *while he's away.* **2.** At a distance: *He is miles away.* [< OE *aweg, onweg,* "on the way (from)."]

awe (ô) *n.* **1.** An emotion of mingled reverence, dread, and wonder. **2.** Respect tinged with fear. *—v.* **awed, awing** or **aweing.** To inspire with awe. [< ON *agi.*]

a·wea·ry (ə-wîr'ē) *adj.* Tired; weary.

a·weigh (ə-wā') *adj. Naut.* Hanging just clear of the bottom, as an anchor. [A- (on) + WEIGH.]

awe·some (ô'səm) *adj.* Inspiring awe.

awe-strick·en (ô'strĭk'ən) *adj.* Also **awe-struck** (-strŭk'). Full of awe.

aw·ful (ô'fəl) *adj.* **1.** Extremely bad or unpleasant. **2.** Dreadful; appalling. **3.** Great: *an awful fool.* [ME *aweful* < AWE + -FUL.]

aw·ful·ly (ô'fə-lē, ôf'lē) *adv.* **1.** In an awful manner. **2.** Very.

a·while (ə-hwīl') *adv.* For a short time.

awk·ward (ôk'wərd) *adj.* **1.** Lacking grace or dexterity; clumsy. **2.** Hard to handle; unwieldy. **3.** Uncomfortable; inconvenient. **4.** Embarrassing; trying. [ME *awkeward,* "in the wrong direction," awry.] **—awk'ward·ly** *adv.* **—awk'ward·ness** *n.*

awl (ôl) *n.* A pointed tool for making holes, as in wood or leather. [< OE *eal* < Gmc **āl-.*]

awn (ôn) *n.* One of the bristles on a grass spike. [< ON *ögn.*]

awn·ing (ô'nĭng) *n.* A structure, as of canvas, stretched over a frame as a shelter from weather. [?]

a·woke (ə-wōk'). *p.t. & rare p.p.* of **awake.**

A.W.O.L., awol (ā'wôl') *Mil.* Absent (or absence) without leave.

a·wry (ə-rī') *adv.* **1.** Twisted toward one side; askew. **2.** Amiss; wrong. [ME *awrie, on wry* : ON + WRY.] **—a·wry'** *adj.*

ax, axe (ăks) *n., pl.* **axes.** A chopping or cutting tool with a bladed head mounted on a handle. [< OE *æx.* See agwesı.] **—ax, axe** *v.* **(axed, axing).**

ax. axiom.

ax·i·al (ăk'sē-əl) *adj.* Of, on, around, or along an axis. **—ax'i·al·ly** *adv.*

ax·i·om (ăk'sē-əm) *n.* **1.** An undemonstrated proposition concerning an undefined set of elements, properties, functions, and relationships; postulate. **2.** A self-evident or accepted principle. [< Gk *axiōma,* "that which is thought fitting or worthy."] **—ax'i·o·mat'ic** *adj.* **—ax'i·o·mat'i·cal·ly** *adv.*

ă pat/ā ate/âr care/ä bar/b bib/ch chew/d deed/ĕ pet/ē be/f fit/g gag/h hat/hw what/
ĭ pit/ī pie/îr pier/j judge/k kick/l lid, fatal/m mum/n no, sudden/ng sing/ŏ pot/ō go/

ax•is (ăk′sĭs) *n., pl.* **axes** (ăk′sēz′). **1.** A straight line about which an object rotates or may be conceived to rotate. **2.** An unlimited line, half-line, or line segment serving to orient a space or a geometrical object, esp. a line about which the object is symmetrical. **3.** A center line or linear part along which parts of a structure or body are arranged. **4.** *Fine Arts.* An imaginary line to which elements of the work are referred for measurement or symmetry. **5. the Axis.** The alliance of Germany and Italy (1936), later including Japan and other nations, that opposed the Allies in World War II. [L, hub, axis.]

ax•le (ăk′səl) *n.* A supporting shaft on which a wheel turns. [< ON *ōxull.*]

ax•o•lotl (ăk′sə-lŏt′l) *n.* Any of several western North American and Mexican salamanders that retain their external gills when mature. [Nah.]

ax•on (ăk′sŏn′) *n.* Also **ax•one** (ăk′sōn′). The core of a nerve fiber that generally conducts impulses away from the nerve cell. [< Gk *axōn,* axis.]

aye¹ (ī). Also **ay.** *n.* An affirmative vote. —*adv.* Yes. [Earlier *ay, ei,* orig., *I.*]

aye² (ā) *adv.* Also **ay.** *Poetic.* Always; ever. [< ON *ei.*]

a•yin (ä′yĭn) *n.* Also **a•in.** The 16th letter of the Hebrew alphabet, representing a glottal stop.

Ay•ma•ra (ī′mä-rä′) *n., pl.* **-ra** or **-ras.** **1.** A member of an Indian people inhabiting Bolivia and Peru. **2.** Their language or language family. —**Ay′ma•ran′** *adj.* & *n.*

AZ Arizona (with Zip Code).

az. azimuth.

a•zal•ea (ə-zāl′yə) *n.* Any of several shrubs often cultivated for their showy, variously colored flowers. [NL, "the dry plant" (growing in dry soil).]

A•zer•bai•jan Soviet Socialist Republic (ä′zər-bī-jän′, ăz′ər-). A constituent republic of the Soviet Union on the Caspian Sea. Pop. 5,111,000. Cap. Baku.

az•i•muth (ăz′ə-məth) *n.* **1.** The horizontal angular distance from a fixed reference direction to a position, object, or object referent, as to a great circle intersecting a celestial body, usually measured clockwise in degrees along the horizon from a point due south. **2.** *Mil.* The lateral deviation of a projectile or bomb. [< Ar *as-sumūt,* pl of *as-samt,* "the way," compass bearing.]

A•zores (ā′zôrz, ə-zôrz′). An island group belonging to Portugal in the N Atlantic.

Az•tec (ăz′tĕk′) *n.* **1.** A member of an Indian people of Mexico noted for their advanced civilization before the Spanish conquest. **2.** Their language, Nahuatl. —*adj.* Also **Az•tec•an** (-ən). Of the Aztecs, their language, culture, or empire.

az•ure (ăzh′ər) *n.* The blue of the clear daytime sky. [< Ar *allāzaward,* lapis lazuli.] —**az′ure** *adj.*

Bb

b, B (bē) *n.* **1.** The 2nd letter of the English alphabet. **2.** The 2nd in a series. **3.** The 2nd highest grade in quality.

b *Phys.* barn.

B **1.** boron. **2.** The 7th tone in the scale of C major.

b. **1.** base. **2.** *Mus.* basso. **3.** breadth.

B. **1.** bachelor. **2.** bacillus. **3.** Bible. **4.** British.

Ba barium.

B.A. **1.** Bachelor of Arts. **2.** British Academy. **3.** British Association (for the Advancement of Science).

baa (bă, bä) *n.* The bleat of a sheep. [Imit.] —**baa** *v.*

Ba•al (bā′əl) *n., pl.* **-alim** (-ə-lĭm). **1.** Any of various local fertility and nature gods of the ancient Semitic peoples. **2.** Any false god or idol.

Bab•bitt (băb′ĭt) *n.* A smug, provincial member of the American middle class. [< the main character in the novel *Babbitt* by Sinclair Lewis (1885–1951).]

bab•ble (băb′əl) *v.* **-bled, -bling. 1.** To utter incoherent, meaningless sound. **2.** To talk foolishly; chatter. —*n.* The sound or act of babbling. [ME *babelen.*] —**bab′bler** *n.*

babe (bāb) *n.* **1.** A baby. **2.** *Slang.* A girl or young woman. [ME *babe.*]

ba•bel (bā′bəl, băb′əl) *n.* Also **Ba•bel. 1.** A confused sound of voices. **2.** A scene of noise and confusion. [< the city of *Babel* (thought to be Babylon), where construction of a tower was interrupted by the confusion of tongues.]

bab•ka (băb′kə) *n.* A yeast-leavened cake made with raisins and almonds. [Pol, "little old woman."]

ba•boon (bă-bōōn′) *n.* A large African monkey with a prominent muzzle. [< OF *babuin,* gaping figure, baboon.]

ba•bush•ka (bə-bōōsh′kə) *n.* A head scarf folded triangularly and tied under the chin. [Russ, "grandmother."]

ba•by (bā′bē) *n., pl.* **-bies. 1.** A very young child; infant. **2.** The youngest member of a family or group. **3.** One who acts like an infant. **4.** *Slang.* A girl or young woman. —*v.* **-bied, -bying.** To pamper; coddle. [ME *babie.*] —**ba′by•hood′** *n.* —**ba′by•ish** *adj.*

ô paw, for/oi boy/ou out/ŏŏ took/ōō coo/p pop/r run/s sauce/sh shy/t to/th thin/*th* the/
ŭ cut/ûr fur/v van/w wag/y yes/z size/zh vision/ə ago, item, edible, gallop, circus/

Bab·y·lon (băb′ə-lən, -lŏn′). The capital of ancient Babylonia.

Bab·y·lo·ni·a (băb′ə-lō′nē-ə). An ancient empire in Mesopotamia.

Bab·y·lo·ni·an (băb′ə-lō′nē-ən) *adj.* Of or pertaining to Babylonia. —*n.* **1.** A native or inhabitant of Babylonia. **2.** The Semitic language of the Babylonians, a form of Akkadian.

ba·by′s-breath (bā′bēz-brĕth′) *n.* A plant with numerous small white flowers.

ba·by-sit (bā′bē-sĭt′) *v.* To care for children when the parents are not at home. —**baby sitter.**

bac·ca·lau·re·ate (băk′ə-lôr′ē-ĭt) *n.* **1.** The degree of bachelor, conferred upon graduates of colleges and universities. **2.** A farewell address delivered to a graduating class, as of a college. [< ML *baccalaureātus,* var of *baccalārius,* BACHELOR.]

bac·cha·nal (băk′ə-năl′, -näl′, băk′ə-nəl) *n.* **1.** A drunken or riotous celebration, originally in honor of Bacchus. **2.** A participant in such a celebration.

Bac·chus (băk′əs). Greco-Roman god of wine. —**Bac′chic** *adj.*

Bach (bäKH), **Johann Sebastian.** 1685–1750. German composer and organist.

bach·e·lor (băch′ə-lər, băch′lər) *n.* **1.** An unmarried man. **2. a.** A college or university degree signifying completion of the undergraduate curriculum. **b.** A person holding such a degree. [< ML *baccalārius.*] —**bach′e·lor·hood′** *n.* —**bach′e·lor·ship′** *n.*

bach·e·lor′s-but·ton (băch′ə-lərz-bŭt′n, băch′lərz-) *n.* The cornflower.

ba·cil·lus (bə-sĭl′əs) *n., pl.* **-cilli** (-sĭl′ī′). Any of various rod-shaped bacteria. [< LL dim of L *baculum,* rod, stick.]

back (băk) *n.* **1. a.** The region of the vertebrate body nearest the spine. **b.** The upper part of the body in invertebrates. **2.** The part farthest from or behind the front; the rear. **3.** The reverse side. **4.** A football player positioned in the backfield. —*v.* **1.** To move backward or in a reverse direction. **2.** To support; strengthen. **3.** To bet on. **4.** To form the back of. —**back down.** To withdraw from a former stand. —*adj.* **1.** At the rear. **2.** Distant; remote. **3.** Of or for a past date or time. **4.** Backward. —*adv.* **1.** To or toward the rear. **2.** To or toward a former place, state, or time. **3.** In reserve, concealment, or check. **4.** In return. [< OE *bæc* < Gmc **bakam.*]

back·bite (băk′bīt′) *v.* To speak spitefully or slanderously of a person who is not present. —**back′bit′er** *n.*

back·bone (băk′bōn′) *n.* **1.** The vertebrate spine. **2.** A main support. **3.** Strength of character.

back·er (băk′ər) *n.* One who supports or gives aid.

back·field (băk′fēld′) *n. Football.* **1.** The players stationed behind the line of scrimmage. **2.** The area occupied by these players.

back·fire (băk′fīr′) *n.* An explosion of prematurely ignited fuel or of unburned exhaust. —*v.* **1.** To explode in a backfire. **2.** To produce an unexpected, unwanted result.

back·for·ma·tion (băk′fôr-mā′shən) *n.* The creation of a new word by deletion of what is construed to be an affix from an existing word, as *laze* from *lazy.*

back·gam·mon (băk′găm′ən) *n.* A board game for two, with moves determined by throws of dice. [Prob < BACK + GAME.]

back·ground (băk′ground′) *n.* **1.** The area, space, or surface against which objects are seen or represented. **2.** Conditions or events forming a setting. **3.** A place or state of relative obscurity. **4.** One′s experience or training.

back·hand (băk′hănd′) *n.* **1.** A motion, as of a tennis racket, made with the back of the hand facing outward and moving forward. **2.** Handwriting with letters that slant to the left.

back·hand·ed (băk′hăn′dĭd) *adj.* **1.** With the motion or direction of a backhand. **2.** Containing a disguised insult or rebuke.

back·ing (băk′ĭng) *n.* **1.** Something that supports from the back. **2.** Support or aid. **3.** Supporters; endorsers.

back·lash (băk′lăsh′) *n.* **1.** A sudden backward whipping motion. **2.** An antagonistic reaction, as in socio-economic relations.

back·log (băk′lŏg′, -lôg′) *n.* A reserve supply or accumulation.

back·pack (băk′păck′) *n.* A kind of knapsack, often mounted on a lightweight frame. —*v.* **1.** To hike while carrying a backpack. **2.** To carry in a backpack. —**back′pack′er** *n.*

back·side (băk′sīd′) *n.* The buttocks; rump.

back·slide (băk′slīd′) *v.* To revert to wrongdoing. —**back′slid′er** *n.*

back·spin (băk′spĭn′) *n.* A spin that tends to retard, arrest, or reverse the linear motion of an object, esp. of a ball.

back·stop (băk′stŏp′) *n.* A screen or fence to prevent a ball from being thrown or hit far out of a playing area.

back·stretch (băk′strĕch′) *n.* The part of a racecourse farthest from the spectators and opposite the homestretch.

back·stroke (băk′strōk′) *n.* **1.** A backhanded stroke. **2.** A swimming stroke executed with the swimmer on his back and moving the arms upward and backward.

back talk. An insolent retort.

back·track (băk′trăk′) *v.* **1.** To retrace one′s route. **2.** To reverse one′s stand; retreat.

back·ward (băk′wərd) *adv.* Also **back·wards** (-wərdz). **1.** Toward the back. **2.** With the back leading. **3.** In reverse. **4.** Toward a former, often worse, condition. —*adj.* **1.** Reversed. **2.** Reluctant; unwilling. **3.** Retarded in development. —**back′ward·ness** *n.*

back·wash (băk′wŏsh′, -wôsh′) *n.* A backward flow or motion, as of water or air.

back·wa·ter (băk′wô′tər, -wŏt′ər) *n.* A place of stagnation or arrested progress.

back·woods (băk′wŏŏdz′, -wŏŏdz′) *pl.n.* Heavily wooded, thinly settled areas.

ba·con (bā′kən) *n.* Salted and smoked meat from the back and sides of a pig. —**bring home the bacon.** *Informal.* **1.** To provide food and other necessities. **2.** To make good; succeed. [< Frank **bako,* ham.]

Ba·con (bā′kən). **1. Francis.** 1561–1626. Eng-

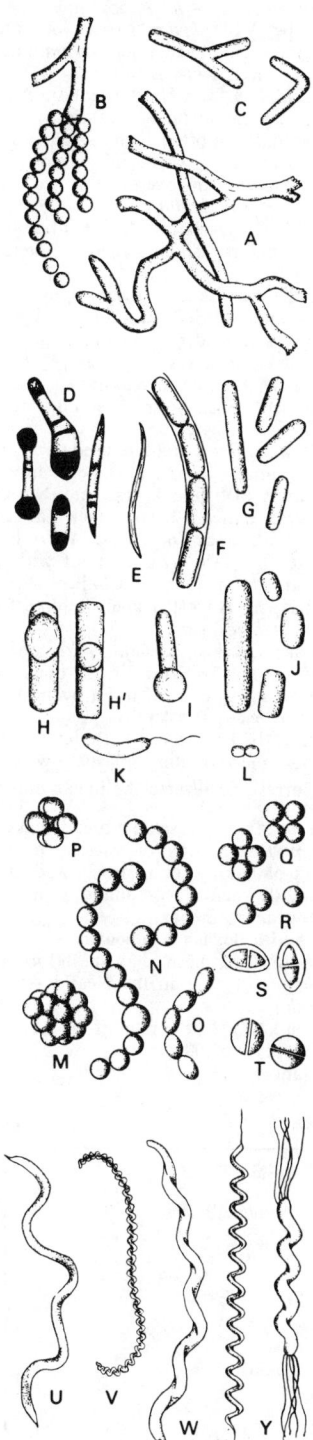

lish essayist and statesman. **2. Roger.** 1214?–1294. English philosopher and scientist.

bac·te·ri·a (băk-tîr′ē-ə) *pl.n. Sing.* **-terium** (-tîr′ē-əm). Any of numerous sometimes parasitic unicellular organisms having various forms and often causing disease. [< Gk *baktērion*, dim of *baktron*, rod.] —**bac·te′ri·al** *adj.* —**bac·te′ri·al·ly** *adv.*

bac·te·ri·cide (băk-tîr′ə-sīd′) *n.* A substance that destroys bacteria. —**bac·te′ri·ci′dal** *adj.*

bac·te·ri·ol·o·gy (băk-tîr′ē-ŏl′ə-jē) *n.* The scientific study of bacteria. —**bac·te′ri·o·log′ic** (-ə-lŏj′ĭk), **bac·te′ri·o·log′i·cal** *adj.* —**bac·te′ri·o·log′i·cal·ly** *adv.* —**bac·te′ri·ol′o·gist** *n.*

bad (băd) *adj.* **worse, worst. 1.** Having undesirable qualities; not good. **2.** Inferior; poor. **3.** Unfavorable. **4.** Rotten; spoiled. **5.** Severe; intense: *a bad cold.* **6.** Sorry; regretful. [Perh < OE *bædan*, to compel, afflict. See **bheidh-**.] —**bad′ly** *adv.* —**bad′ness** *n.*

Usage: Bad (adj.), not *badly,* is the proper form following linking verbs such as *feel* and *look* when the desired sense is *ill* or *regretful.*

bade (băd). A *p.t.* of **bid.**

badge (băj) *n.* An emblem worn as a sign of rank, membership, or honor. [< NF *bage.*]

badg·er (băj′ər) *n.* **1.** A burrowing animal with a thick, grizzled coat. **2.** The fur of a badger. —*v.* To harry; pester. [< BADGE.]

bad·i·nage (băd′ə-näzh′) *n.* Light, playful banter. [< VL *bātāre*, to gape.]

bad·min·ton (băd′mĭn′tən) *n.* A net game

bacteria

A. *Actinomyces bovis*
B. *Streptomyces* species
C. *Mycobacterium tuberculosis*
D. *Corynebacterium diphtheriae*
E. *Fusobacterium fusiforme*
F. *Sphaerotilus natans*
G. *Salmonella typhosa*
H, H′. *Bacillus* species
I. *Clostridium tetani*
J. *Bacillus megaterium*
K. *Vibrio comma*
L. *Brucella abortus*
M. *Staphylococcus aureus*
N. *Streptococcus pyogenes*
O. *Streptococcus lactis*
P. *Sarcina homarus*
Q. *Gaffkya tetragena*
R. Single cocci in fission
S. *Diplococcus pneumoniae*
T. *Neisseria gonorrhoeae*
U. *Borrelia recurrentis*
V. *Leptospira icterohaemorrhagae*
W. *Spirochaeta plicatilis*
X. *Treponema pallidum*
Y. *Spirillum minus*

played with a shuttlecock and long-handled rackets. [< *Badminton,* England.]

baf·fle (băf'əl) *v.* **-fled, -fling. 1.** To foil; thwart. **2.** To make helplessly puzzled. —*n.* Any structure used to impede, regulate, or alter flow direction, as of a gas, of sound, or of a liquid. [?] —**baf'fle·ment** *n.* —**baf'fler** *n.*

bag (băg) *n.* **1.** A nonrigid container, as of cloth or paper. **2.** A suitcase or purse. **3.** An amount of game taken at a time. —*v.* **bagged, bagging. 1.** To hang or bulge loosely. **2.** To capture or kill, as game. [< ON *baggi.*]

bag·a·telle (băg'ə-tĕl') *n.* A trifle. [< L *băca, bacca,* berry.]

ba·gel (bā'gəl) *n.* A tough, chewy ring-shaped roll. [< OHG *boug,* ring.]

bag·gage (băg'ĭj) *n.* **1.** The bags and belongings carried while traveling; luggage. **2.** A wanton or impudent woman. [< OF *bague,* bundle, pack.]

bag·gy (băg'ē) *adj.* **-gier, -giest.** Bulging or hanging loosely. —**bag'gi·ness** *n.*

Bagh·dad (băg'dăd'). Also **Bag·dad.** The capital of Iraq. Pop. 2,124,000.

bag·pipe (băg'pīp') *n.* Often **bagpipes.** A wind instrument with an inflatable bag that produces the different tones.

ba·guette (bă-gĕt') *n.* A gem cut into a narrow rectangle. [F, "small rod."]

Ba·ha·ma Islands (bə-hä'mə). Also **Ba·ha·mas** (-mæz). An independent country of over 700 islands SW of Florida in the Atlantic. Pop. 190,000. Cap. Nassau. —**Ba·ha'mi·an** (bə-hä'mē-ən, -hä'mē-ən) *adj. & n.*

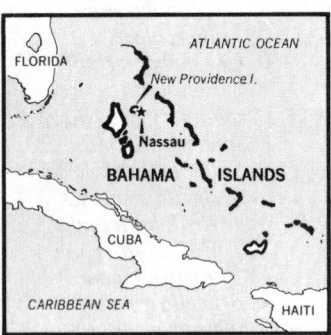

Bahama Islands

Bah·rain (bä-rān'). An independent sheikdom comprising an archipelago in the Persian Gulf. Pop. 300,000. Cap. Al Manamah.

baht (bät) *n., pl.* **bahts** or **baht.** The basic monetary unit of Thailand.

bail¹ (bāl) *n.* **1.** Money supplied as a guarantee that an arrested person will appear for trial. **2.** Release obtained by such security. **3.** One providing such security. —*v.* To release by providing or taking such security. [< OF *baillier,* to take charge of, carry.] —**bail'er** *n.*

bail² (bāl) *v.* To empty a boat of water by scooping or dipping. —**bail out.** To parachute from an aircraft. —*n.* A container used for bailing. [< VL **bājula,* "carrier (of water)."]

bail³ (bāl) *n.* An arched, hooplike handle, as of a pail. [< ME *baile,* handle.]

bail·iff (bā'lĭf) *n.* **1.** A court attendant who has custody of prisoners and maintains order in a courtroom. **2.** An official who assists a British sheriff by executing writs and making arrests. **3.** *Chiefly Brit.* An overseer of an estate; steward. [< OF *baillif.*]

bail·i·wick (bā'lĭ-wĭk') *n.* **1.** The office or district of a bailiff. **2.** One's field of interest or authority.

Bai·ly's beads (bā'lēz). Bright spots of sunlight that appear briefly around the edge of the moon's disk immediately before and after the central phase in a solar eclipse. [< F. *Baily* (1774–1844), British astronomer.]

bairn (bârn) *n. Scot.* A child; son or daughter. [< OE *bearn.*]

bait (bāt) *n.* **1.** Food or a lure used to catch fish or trap animals. **2.** An enticement; lure. —*v.* **1.** To supply (a fishhook, trap, etc.) with bait. **2.** To lure; entice. **3.** To attack (a captive animal) with dogs for sport. **4.** To harass; persecute. [< ON *beita,* to hunt with dogs, harass, and *beita,* food, fish bait.] —**bait'er** *n.*

baize (bāz) *n.* An often green feltlike fabric. [F *baie* (pl *baies*).]

bake (bāk) *v.* **baked, baking. 1.** To cook with continuous dry heat, esp. in an oven. **2.** To harden or dry in or as if in an oven. [< OE *bacan.* See **bhē-.**] —**bak'er** *n.*

Ba·ke·lite (bā'kə-līt') *n.* A trademark for a group of thermosetting plastics with high chemical and electrical resistance.

bak·er·y (bā'kə-rē) *n., pl.* **-ies.** An establishment for baking or selling bread, cake, etc.

baking powder. Any of various powdered mixtures of baking soda, starch, and at least one slightly acidic compound, used as a leavening agent in baking.

baking soda. Sodium bicarbonate.

bak·sheesh (băk'shēsh', băk-shēsh') *n.* A gratuity or gift of alms in the Near East. [Pers *bakhshish.*]

Ba·ku (bä-kōō'). The capital of the Azerbaijan S.S.R. Pop. 1,261,000.

bal. balance.

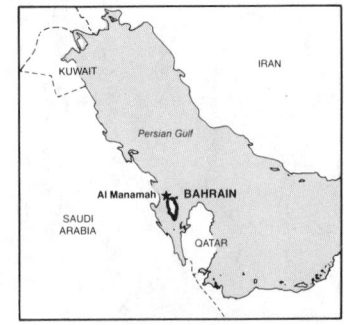

Bahrain

bal·a·lai·ka (băl'ə-lī'kə) *n.* A Russian musical instrument with a triangular body and three strings.
bal·ance (băl'əns) *n.* **1.** A weighing device consisting essentially of a lever that is brought into equilibrium by adding known weights to one end while the unknown weight hangs from the other. **2.** Equilibrium. **3.** An influence or force tending to produce equilibrium. **4. a.** Equality of totals in the debit and credit sides of an account. **b.** A difference between such totals. **5.** Anything that remains or is left over. **6.** Equality of symbolic value on each side of an equation. **7.** A balance wheel. —*v.* -anced, -ancing. **1.** To weigh or poise in or as if in a balance. **2.** To bring into or be maintained in equilibrium. **3.** To counterbalance. **4.** To compute the difference between the debits and credits of (an account). [< LL *(lībra) bilanx,* (a balance) having two scales.]
balance of payments. A systematic recording of a nation's total payments to foreign countries, including its total receipts from abroad.
balance wheel. A wheel that regulates rate of movement in machine parts, as in a watch.
bal·bo·a (băl-bō'ə) *n.* The basic monetary unit of Panama. [< Vasco de *Balboa* (1475–1517), Spanish explorer.]
bal·brig·gan (băl-brĭg'ən) *n.* A knitted cotton fabric. [< *Balbriggan,* Irish seaport where it was first manufactured.]
bal·co·ny (băl'kə-nē) *n., pl.* -nies. **1.** A platform projec'ing from the wall of a building and surrounded by a railing. **2.** A gallery projecting over the main floor in a theater or auditorium. [It *balcone.*]
bald (bôld) *adj.* **1.** Lacking hair on the top of the head. **2.** Lacking natural or usual covering. **3.** Having a white head: *bald eagle.* **4.** Unadorned. [ME *ballede.*] —**bald'ly** *adv.* —**bald'ness** *n.*
bal·da·chin (bôl'də-kĭn, băl'-) *n.* Also **bal·da·quin, bal·da·chi·no** (băl'də-kē'nō). A canopy over an altar, throne, etc. [< OIt *Baldacco,* BAGHDAD.]
bal·der·dash (bôl'dər-dăsh') *n.* Words without sense; nonsense. [?]
bald·ing (bôld'ĭng) *adj.* Gradually losing one's hair.
bal·dric (bôl'drĭk) *n.* A leather belt worn across the chest to support a sword or bugle. [< OF *baldrei.*]
bale (bāl) *n.* A large bound package of raw or finished material. —*v.* **baled, baling.** To wrap in bales. [ME.] —**bal'er** *n.*
Bal·e·ar·ic Islands (băl'ē-ăr'ĭk, bə-lîr'ĭk). A Spanish island group in the Mediterranean. Pop. 443,000.
ba·leen (bə-lēn') *n.* Whalebone. [< L *balaena,* whale.]
bale·ful (bāl'fəl) *adj.* **1.** Malignant in intent or effect. **2.** Ominous. —**bale'ful·ly** *adv.* —**bale'ful·ness** *n.*
Ba·li (bä'lē). An island of Indonesia, off the E end of Java. Pop. 2,196,000. Cap. Denpasar. —**Ba'li·nese'** *adj. & n.*
balk (bôk) *v.* **1.** To stop short and refuse to go on. **2.** To thwart; check. —*n.* A hindrance;

setback. [< OE *balc, balca,* bank, ridge in plowing.] —**balk'er** *n.* —**balk'y** *adj.*
Bal·kan (bôl'kən) *adj.* **1.** Of the Balkan Peninsula of SE Europe. **2.** Of the Balkans or their inhabitants. —**the Balkans.** The states that occupy the Balkan Peninsula.
Balkan Peninsula. A peninsula in SE Europe, E of Italy.
ball¹ (bôl) *n.* **1.** A spherical or almost spherical body or entity. **2. a.** Any of various more or less rounded objects used in games. **b.** A game played with such an object. **3.** A pitched baseball that does not pass through the strike zone and is not swung at by the batter. **4.** A rounded part or protuberance: *the ball of the foot.* —*v.* To form or become formed into a ball. [< ON *bŏllr.*]
ball² (bôl) *n.* **1.** A large formal gathering for social dancing. **2.** *Slang.* An enjoyable time. [< OF *baller,* to dance.]
bal·lad (băl'əd) *n.* **1.** A narrative poem, often of folk origin and intended to be sung, consisting of simple stanzas and usually having a recurrent refrain. **2.** A slow, romantic popular song. [< Prov *balada,* piece to be accompanied by dancing.] —**bal'lad·eer'** (-ə-dîr') *n.* —**bal'lad·ry** *n.*
bal·last (băl'əst) *n.* **1.** Any heavy material placed in the hold of a ship or the gondola of a balloon to enhance stability. **2.** Coarse gravel or crushed rock laid to form a roadbed. —*v.* To stabilize or provide with ballast. [Perh < OSw *barlast,* "bare load" (cargo carried for its weight).]
ball bearing. 1. A friction-reducing bearing, consisting essentially of a ring-shaped track containing freely revolving hard metal balls. **2.** A hard ball used in such a bearing.
bal·le·ri·na (băl'ə-rē'nə) *n.* A female ballet dancer. [< It *ballare,* to dance.]
bal·let (bă-lā', băl'ā') *n.* **1.** A dance genre characterized chiefly by a highly formalized technique. **2.** A choreographic presentation, usually with music, on a narrative or abstract theme. [< It *ballare,* to dance.]
ballistic missile. A projectile that assumes a free-falling trajectory after an internally guided, self-powered ascent.
bal·lis·tics (bə-lĭs'tĭks) *n. (takes sing. v.).* **1. a.** The study of the dynamics of projectiles. **b.** The study of the flight characteristics of projectiles. **2. a.** The study of the functioning of firearms. **b.** The study of the firing, flight, and effect of ammunition. [< Gk *ballein,* to throw.] —**bal·lis'tic** *adj.* —**bal'lis·ti'cian** (băl'ĭ-stĭsh'ən) *n.*
bal·loon (bə-lōōn') *n.* **1.** A flexible bag inflated with a gas such as helium that causes it to rise in the atmosphere, esp. such a bag with sufficient capacity to lift a suspended gondola. **2.** An inflatable toy rubber bag. —*v.* To expand or cause to expand like a balloon. [F *ballon* < It *palla,* ball.]
bal·lot (băl'ət) *n.* **1.** A paper or ticket used to cast or register a vote. **2.** The act, process, or method of voting. **3.** A list of candidates for office. **4.** The total of all votes cast in an election. **5.** The right to vote; franchise. —*v.*

ô paw, for/oi boy/ou out/ŏŏ took/ōō coo/p pop/r run/s sauce/sh shy/t to/th thin/*th* the/
ŭ cut/ûr fur/v van/w wag/y yes/z size/zh vision/ə ago, item, edible, gallop, circus/

To cast a ballot. [It *ballotta,* small ball or pebble used for voting.]

ball•room (bôl'rōōm', -rōōm') *n.* A large room for dancing.

bal•ly•hoo (băl'ē-hōō') *n.* Sensational advertising. *—v.* To promote with ballyhoo. [?]

balm (bäm) *n.* **1.** An aromatic resin, oil, or ointment used medicinally. **2.** Any of various aromatic plants. **3.** Something that soothes or comforts. [< L *balsamum,* BALSAM.]

balm•y (bä'mē) *adj.* -ier, -iest. **1.** Having the quality or fragrance of balm. **2.** Mild and pleasant: *a balmy breeze.*

ba•lo•ney (bə-lō'nē) *n. Slang.* Nonsense.

bal•sa (bôl'sə) *n.* **1.** A tropical American tree with very light, buoyant wood. **2.** The wood of this tree. [Span.]

bal•sam (bôl'səm) *n.* **1.** An aromatic resin or ointment obtained from various trees or plants. **2.** A tree yielding balsam. **3.** A plant cultivated for its colorful flowers. [L *balsamum.*]

Balt (bôlt) *n.* A member of one of the Baltic-speaking peoples.

Bal•tic (bôl'tĭk) *adj.* **1.** Pertaining to the Baltic Sea or to the countries on its E coast. **2.** Of or designating an Indo-European group of languages consisting of Lithuanian, Latvian, and Old Prussian. *—n.* The Baltic language group.

Baltic Sea. A long arm of the Atlantic Ocean in N Europe, NE of Germany.

Bal•ti•more (bôl'tə-môr', -mōr'). The largest city of Maryland. Pop. 906,000. **—Bal'ti•mo're•an** *adj. & n.*

Bal•to-Sla•vic (bôl'tō-slä'vĭk, -slăv'ĭk) *n.* A subfamily of the Indo-European language family, composed of Baltic and Slavic.

bal•us•ter (băl'ə-stər) *n.* One of the upright supports of a handrail. [< It *balaustro.*]

bal•us•trade (băl'ə-strād') *n.* A rail and the row of posts that support it. [< It *balaustrata* < *balaustro,* BALUSTER.]

Ba•ma•ko (bäm'ə-kō'). The capital of the Republic of Mali. Pop. 120,000.

bam•boo (băm-bōō') *n.* A tall tropical grass with hollow, woody stems having a wide variety of uses. [Prob < Malay *bambū.*]

bam•boo•zle (băm-bōō'zəl) *v.* -zled, -zling. To trick; deceive. [Perh < a cant var of *bumbazzle.*] **—bam•boo'zler** *n.*

ban (băn) *v.* banned, banning. To prohibit, esp. officially. *—n.* A prohibition imposed by law or official decree. [< OE *bannan,* to summon, proclaim, and < ON *banna,* to prohibit, curse. See bhā-2.]

ba•nal (bə-näl', -năl', bā'nəl) *adj.* Completely ordinary. [F, commonplace.] **—ba•nal'i•ty** (bə-năl'ə-tē, bā-) *n.*

ba•nan•a (bə-năn'ə) *n.* **1.** The crescent-shaped fruit of a treelike tropical plant, having pulpy flesh and yellow or reddish skin. **2.** A plant bearing such fruit. [< native W Afr name.]

band[1] (bănd) *n.* **1.** A thin strip of flexible material used to encircle and bind together. **2.** A range of numerical values. *—v.* To bind or identify with a band. [< OF *bande,* bond, tie.]

band[2] (bănd) *n.* **1.** A group of people or an-

imals. **2.** A group of musicians who play together. *—v.* To assemble or unite in a group. [OF *bande,* a troop.]

band•age (băn'dĭj) *n.* A strip of material used to protect a wound or other injury. *—v.* -aged, -aging. To apply such a covering to. [F < *bande,* BAND (strip).]

Band-Aid (bănd'ād') *n.* **1.** A trademark for an adhesive bandage. **2.** Any temporary or superficial remedy or solution.

ban•dan•na, ban•dan•a (băn-dăn'ə) *n.* A large scarf for the head. [< Port.]

Ban•dar Se•ri Be•ga•wan (băn'där sĕr'ē bə-gä'wən). The capital of Brunei. Pop. 36,500.

ban•di•coot (băn'dĭ-kōōt') *n.* A ratlike Australian marsupial with a long snout. [Telegu *pandikokku.*]

ban•dit (băn'dĭt) *n.* A robber; gangster. [It *bandito.*] **—ban'dit•ry** *n.*

ban•do•leer, ban•do•lier (băn'də-lîr') *n.* A belt with pockets for cartridges, worn across the chest. [F *bandoulière.*]

band saw. A power saw consisting essentially of a continuous, toothed metal band.

band•wag•on (bănd'wăg'ən) *n.* **1.** A decorated wagon carrying musicians in a parade. **2.** An apparently ascendant cause that attracts often cynically opportunistic followers.

ban•dy (băn'dē) *v.* -died, -dying. **1.** To toss back and forth. **2.** To discuss or exchange in a casual or frivolous manner. *—adj.* Bent in an outward curve: *bandy legs.* [Perh < OF *bander,* to bandy at tennis.]

bane (bān) *n.* **1.** A cause of death or ruin. **2.** A deadly poison. [< OE *bana,* slayer, ruin. See bhen-.] **—bane'ful** *adj.*

bang[1] (băng) *n.* **1.** A sudden loud noise or thump. **2.** *Slang.* A sense of excitement; thrill. *—v.* **1.** To hit noisily. **2.** To close or handle noisily or violently. *—adv.* Exactly; precisely. [< Scand.]

bang[2] (băng) *n.* Often bangs. Hair cut straight across the forehead. [Perh < ON *banga,* to cut off.]

Bang•kok (băng'kŏk', băng-kŏk'). The capital of Thailand. Pop. 1,669,000.

Ban•gla•desh (băng'glə-dĕsh'). An independent nation bordering on India and Burma. Pop. 50,844,000. Cap. Dacca.

ban•gle (băng'gəl) *n.* **1.** A rigid bracelet or anklet. **2.** A pendent ornament.

Ban•gui (bäng-gē'). The capital of the Central African Republic. Pop. 187,000.

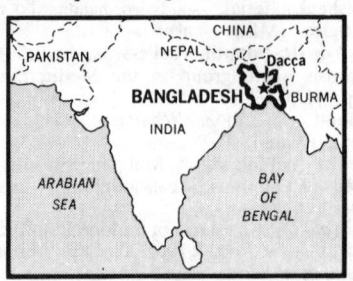

Bangladesh

ban•ish (băn′ĭsh) v. 1. To force to leave a country by official decree; exile. 2. To drive away; expel. [< OF *banir.*] —**ban′ish•ment** n.

ban•is•ter (băn′ĭ-stər) n. Also **ban•nis•ter.** 1. A baluster. 2. The balustrade of a staircase. [Var of BALUSTER.]

ban•jo (băn′jō) n., pl. **-jos** or **-joes.** A fretted stringed instrument having a hollow circular body with a stretched diaphragm of vellum. [< L *pandoura*, three-stringed lute.]

Ban•jul (bän-jōōl′). The capital of Gambia. Pop. 40,000.

bank¹ (băngk) n. 1. Any piled-up mass, as of snow or clouds. 2. A steep natural incline. 3. An artificial embankment. 4. The slope of land adjoining a lake, river, or sea. 5. An elevated area of a sea floor. 6. Lateral tilting of an aircraft in a turn. —v. 1. To border or protect with a bank. 2. To pile up; amass. 3. To cover (a fire) with ashes or fuel for low burning. 4. To construct with a slope rising to the outside edge. 5. To tilt (an aircraft) laterally in flight. [ME *banke.*]

bank² (băngk) n. 1. A business establishment authorized to perform financial transactions, such as receiving and lending money. 2. The building in which such an establishment is located. 3. The funds owned by a gambling establishment. 4. A supply or stock for use in emergencies: *a blood bank.* —v. 1. To deposit (money) in a bank. 2. To transact business with a bank. 3. To operate a bank. —**bank on.** To have confidence in. [< It *banca*, bench, moneychanger's table.] —**bank′er** n.

bank³ (băngk) n. 1. A set of similar entities arranged in a row: *a bank of elevators.* 2. A row of oars in a galley. —v. To arrange or set up in a row. [< OF *banc.*]

bank•book (băngk′bŏok′) n. A book held by a depositor in which his deposits and withdrawals are recorded by his bank.

bank•ing (băng′kĭng) n. The business of a bank or occupation of a banker.

bank note. A note issued by an authorized bank payable to the bearer on demand and acceptable as money.

bank•roll (băngk′rōl′) n. 1. A roll of paper money. 2. A person's ready cash. —v. To underwrite the expense of.

bank•rupt (băngk′rŭpt′, -rəpt) n. 1. A debtor who is judged insolvent and whose remaining property is administered for his creditors. 2. One depleted of some resource or quality. —adj. 1. Legally declared a bankrupt. 2. Financially ruined. 3. Depleted; destitute. —v. To cause to become bankrupt. [< It *banca rotta*, "broken counter."] —**bank′rupt•cy** n.

ban•ner (băn′ər) n. 1. A piece of cloth attached to a staff and used as a standard by a monarch, military commander, etc. 2. The flag of a nation, state, army, or sovereign. 3. A headline spanning the width of a newspaper page. —adj. Outstanding; superior. [< VL *bandāria.*]

ban•nis•ter (băn′ĭs-tər) n. Variant of **banister.**

banns (bănz) pl.n. Also **bans.** Announcement in a church of an intended marriage. [ME *banes*, pl of *bane*, ban, proclamation.]

ban•quet (băng′kwĭt) n. 1. An elaborate feast. 2. A ceremonial dinner honoring a guest or occasion. [OF, dim of *banc*, bench.] —**ban′quet•er** n.

ban•quette (băng-kĕt′) n. 1. A platform lining a trench or parapet wall where soldiers may stand when firing. 2. A long upholstered bench, either placed against or built into a wall. [< Prov *banqueta*, dim of *banca*, bench.]

ban•shee (băn′shē) n. A female spirit in Gaelic folklore believed to presage a death in a family by wailing. [Ir Gael *bean sidhe*, "woman of the fairies."]

ban•tam (băn′təm) n. 1. One of a breed of small domestic fowl. 2. A small aggressive person. [< *Bantam*, town in Java.]

ban•ter (băn′tər) n. Good-humored teasing. —v. To tease or mock gently. [?]

Ban•tu (băn′tōō) n., pl. **-tu** or **-tus.** 1. A member of any of several Negroid peoples of C and S Africa. 2. A language family, including Swahili and Zulu. [Bantu *Ba-ntu*, "people."] —**Ban′tu** adj.

ban•yan (băn′yən) n. A tropical tree having many aerial roots that develop into additional trunks. [< Port *banian*, a Hindu merchant.]

Bap., Bapt. Baptist.

bap•tism (băp′tĭz′əm) n. 1. A Christian sacrament of spiritual rebirth by which the recipient is cleansed of original sin through the symbolic application of water. 2. An ordeal of initiation. [< LL *baptisma.*] —**bap•tis′mal** (-məl) adj. —**bap•tis′mal•ly** adv.

Bap•tist (băp′tĭst) n. A member of any of various Protestant denominations practicing baptism by immersion. —**Bap′tist** adj.

bap•tize (băp-tīz′, băp′tīz′) v. **-tized, -tizing.** 1. To dip or immerse in water in a baptismal ceremony. 2. To cleanse; purify. 3. To initiate. 4. To give a first or Christian name to. [< LL *baptizāre.*] —**bap•tiz′er** n.

bar (bär) n. 1. A relatively long, rigid piece of solid material. 2. a. A solid oblong block of a substance, as soap. b. A unit of quantity based on such a block. 3. An obstacle. 4. A band, as one formed by light. 5. The nullifying of a claim or action. 6. The railing in a courtroom enclosing the part of the room where the judges and lawyers sit, witnesses are heard, and prisoners are tried. 7. A particular system of law courts. 8. The profession of law. 9. A vertical line dividing a musical staff into measures. 10. A counter at which drinks are served. —v. **barred, barring.** To fasten or obstruct with or as if with bars. —prep. Excluding. [< VL *barra.*]

bar. barometer; barometric.

barb (bärb) n. 1. A sharp backward-pointing projection, as on a weapon or fishhook. 2. A cutting remark. —v. To provide with barbs. [< L *barba*, beard.] —**barbed** adj.

Bar•ba•dos (bär-bā′dōs, -dəs). The easternmost island of the West Indies, a former British colony independent since 1966. Pop. 254,000. Cap. Bridgetown.

bar•bar•i•an (bär-bâr′ē-ən) n. 1. One belonging to a people of relatively uncivilized culture and typically destructive tendencies. 2. A fierce or coarse person. [< L *barbarus*, BAR-BAROUS.] —**bar·bar'i·an** *adj.*

bar·bar·ic (bär-băr'ĭk) *adj.* Of, pertaining to, or characteristic of a barbarian.

bar·ba·rism (bär'bə-rĭz'əm) *n.* 1. An act, trait, or custom characterized by brutality or coarseness. 2. The use of words or forms considered nonstandard in a language.

bar·bar·i·ty (bär-băr'ə-tē) *n., pl.* -**ties.** 1. Harsh or cruel conduct. 2. An inhuman, brutal act. 3. Crudity; coarseness.

bar·ba·rous (bär'bər-əs) *adj.* 1. Uncivilized. 2. Characterized by savagery or coarseness. [L *barbarus* < Gk *barbaros*, non-Greek, foreign, rude.] —**bar'ba·rous·ly** *adv.*

bar·be·cue (bär'bĭ-kyōō') *n.* 1. A grill, pit, or outdoor fireplace for roasting meat. 2. Meat roasted over an open fire or on a spit. —*v.* -**cued, -cuing.** To cook (meat) over live coals or an open fire. [Amer Span *barbacoa*.]

barbed wire. Twisted strands of fence wire with barbs at regular intervals.

bar·bell (bär'bĕl') *n.* A bar with adjustable weights at each end, lifted for sport or exercise.

bar·ber (bär'bər) *n.* One whose business is to cut or trim hair or beards. —*v.* To cut the hair or beard of. [< L *barba*, beard.]

bar·ber·ry (bär'bĕr'ē) *n.* Any of various often spiny shrubs with small reddish berries. [< Ar *barbārīs*.]

bar·ber·shop (bär'bər-shŏp') *n.* The place of business of a barber.

bar·bi·can (bär'bĭ-kən) *n.* A tower or other fortification on the approach to a castle or town. [< ML *barbacana*.]

bar·bi·tu·rate (bär-bĭch'ər-ĭt, -ə-rāt', bär'bə-t/y/ōōr'ĭt, -āt') *n.* Any of a group of derivatives of **bar·bi·tu·ric acid** (bär'bə-t/y/ōōr'ĭk), C₄H₄N₂O₃, used as sedatives or hypnotics.

barb·wire (bärb'wïr') *n.* Barbed wire.

bar·ca·role (bär'kə-rōl') *n.* Also **bar·ca·rolle.** A Venetian gondolier's song with a rhythmic pulse suggestive of rowing. [< It *barcaruolo*, gondolier.]

Bar·ce·lo·na (bär'sə-lō'nə). A city of NE Spain. Pop. 1,696,000.

bar chart. A bar graph.

bard (bärd) *n.* 1. One of an ancient Celtic order of singing, narrative poets. 2. A poet. [< Ir *bárd* and W *bardd*.] —**bard'ic** *adj.*

bare (bâr) *adj.* **barer, barest.** 1. Without the usual or appropriate covering. 2. Exposed to view; undisguised. 3. Lacking the usual equipment or decoration. 4. Without addition or qualification. 5. Just sufficient: *bare necessities.* —*v.* **bared, baring.** To make bare. [< OE *bær.* See bhoso-.]

bare·back (bâr'băk') *adj.* Also **bare·backed** (bâr'băkt'). Using no saddle: *a bareback rider.* —**bare'back'** *adv.*

bare·faced (bâr'fāst') *adj.* 1. Without covering or beard on the face. 2. Without disguise; brazen: *a barefaced lie.*

bare·foot (bâr'fōōt') *adj.* Also **bare·foot·ed** (-fōōt'ĭd). Wearing nothing on the feet. —**bare'foot'** *adv.*

bare·hand·ed (bâr'hăn'dĭd) *adj.* 1. Having no

covering on the hands. 2. Unaided by tools or weapons.

bare·head·ed (bâr'hĕd'ĭd) *adj.* Having no head covering.

bare·leg·ged (bâr'lĕg'ĭd, -lĕgd') *adj.* Having the legs uncovered. —**bare'leg'ged** *adv.*

bare·ly (bâr'lē) *adv.* 1. By a very little; hardly. 2. Without disguise; openly.

bar·gain (bär'gĭn) *n.* 1. a. An agreement or contract, esp. one involving the sale and purchase of goods or services. b. The terms or conditions of such an agreement. c. The property acquired or services rendered as a result of such an agreement. 2. Something offered or acquired at a price advantageous to the buyer. —*v.* 1. To negotiate the terms of a sale, exchange, or other agreement. 2. To arrive at an agreement. [< OF *bargaignier,* to haggle.] —**bar'gain·er** *n.*

barge (bärj) *n.* 1. A long, usually flat-bottomed freight boat. 2. A large pleasure boat used for parties. —*v.* **barged, barging.** 1. To move about clumsily. 2. To collide (with). 3. To intrude (with *in* or *into*). [< OF.]

bar graph. A graph consisting of parallel, usually vertical, bars or rectangles with lengths proportional to specified quantities.

bar·ite (bâr'īt') *n.* A colorless crystalline mineral of barium sulfate that is the chief source of barium chemicals. [< Gk *barus,* heavy.]

bar·i·tone (bär'ə-tōn') *n.* A male voice having a range higher than a bass and lower than a tenor. [< Gk *barutonos,* deep-sounding.]

bar·i·um (bâr'ē-əm, băr'-) *n. Symbol* **Ba** A soft, silvery-white metal, used to deoxidize copper, in various alloys, and in rat poison. Atomic number 56, atomic weight 137.34. [< earlier form of BARITE.] —**bar'ic** *adj.*

bark¹ (bärk) *n.* The short, harsh sound characteristically made by a dog. —*v.* 1. To utter or produce such a sound. 2. To speak sharply; snap. [< OE *beorcan,* to bark. See bherg-.]

bark² (bärk) *n.* The often rough outer covering of the stems and roots of trees and other woody plants. —*v.* 1. To remove bark from. 2. To scrape skin from: *bark one's shins.* [< ON *bǫrkr.*]

bark³ (bärk) *n.* Also **barque.** 1. A sailing ship with from three to five masts. 2. Any boat, esp. a small sailing vessel. [< OF *barque,* prob < Gk *baris,* Egyptian barge.]

bar·keep·er (bär'kē'pər) *n.* One who owns or runs a bar selling alcoholic beverages.

bar·ken·tine (bär'kən-tēn') *n.* Also **bar·quen·tine.** A sailing ship with from three to five masts.

bark·er (bär'kər) *n.* One who stands at the entrance to a show and solicits customers with a loud sales pitch.

bar·ley (bär'lē) *n.* 1. A cereal grass bearing grain used as food and in making beer and whiskey. 2. The grain itself. [< OE *bære, bere,* barley. See bhares-.]

bar·maid (bär'mād') *n.* A woman who serves drinks in a bar.

bar·man (bär'mən) *n.* A bartender.

bar mitz·vah (bär mĭts'və). Also **bar miz·vah.** 1. A thirteen-year-old Jewish male who ceremonially assumes the religious responsibilities of an adult. **2.** The ceremony confirming a bar mitzvah. [Heb *bar mitzvāh,* "son of command."]

barn (bärn) *n.* **1.** A large farm building used for storing produce and for sheltering livestock. **2.** A large shed for the housing of vehicles. [< OE *bern, berern,* "barley house."]

bar·na·cle (bär'nə-kəl) *n.* A small, hard-shelled marine crustacean that attaches itself to submerged surfaces. [< ML *bernaca.*] —**bar'na·cled** *adj.*

barn·storm (bärn'stôrm') *v.* To travel about the countryside presenting plays, lecturing, or making political speeches. —**barn'storm'er** *n.*

barn·yard (bärn'yärd') *n.* The often enclosed yard adjacent to a barn.

ba·rom·e·ter (bə-rŏm'ə-tər) *n.* **1.** An instrument for measuring atmospheric pressure, used in weather forecasting and in determining elevation. **2.** An indicator of change. [< Gk *baros,* weight.] —**bar'o·met'ric** (băr'ə-mĕt'-rĭk), **bar'o·met'ri·cal** *adj.* —**bar'o·met'ri·cal·ly** *adv.* —**ba·rom'e·try** *n.*

bar·on (băr'ən) *n.* **1.** A male member of the lowest rank of nobility in Great Britain, certain European countries, and Japan. **2.** A man with great power in a particular field. [< ML *barō,* man, warrior.] —**bar'on·ess** *fem.n.*

bar·on·et (băr'ə-nĭt, băr'ə-nĕt') *n.* An Englishman holding a hereditary title of honor next below a baron. —**bar'on·et·cy** *n.*

ba·ro·ni·al (bə-rō'nē-əl) *adj.* **1.** Of or pertaining to a baron. **2.** Stately; imposing.

ba·roque (bə-rōk') *adj.* **1.** Characteristic of an artistic style current in Europe about 1550–1700 and marked by massive forms and elaborate decoration. **2.** Characteristic of a contrapuntal musical style of composition current in Europe about 1600–1750. **3.** Flamboyant in style. [< It *barocco,* after the founder of the style, Federigo *Barocci* (1528–1612).]

barque. Variant of **bark³**.

bar·quen·tine. Variant of **barkentine**.

bar·racks (băr'ĭks) *n. (takes sing. v.).* A building or group of buildings used esp. to house soldiers. [< It *baracca,* soldier's tent.]

bar·ra·cu·da (băr'ə-kōō'də) *n.* A narrow-bodied, chiefly tropical marine fish with very sharp teeth. [Span.]

bar·rage¹ (băr'ĭj) *n.* An artificial obstruction in a watercourse. [< F *barrer,* to bar.]

bar·rage² (bə-räzh') *n.* **1.** A heavy curtain of artillery fire directed so as to screen friendly troops. **2.** A rapid outpouring: *a barrage of questions.* [< F *(tir de) barrage,* barrier (fire).] —**bar·rage'** *v.* (**-raged, -raging**).

bar·ra·try (băr'ə-trē) *n., pl.* **-tries. 1.** The offense of exciting quarrels or groundless lawsuits. **2.** An unlawful breach of duty on the part of a ship's master or crew, resulting in injury to the ship's owner. **3.** The sale or purchase of positions in the church or state. [< OF *baraterie,* deception.] —**bar'ra·trous** *adj.*

bar·rel (băr'əl) *n.* **1.** A large cask usually made of curved wooden staves and having a flat top and bottom. **2.** The quantity that a barrel will hold. **3.** A unit of volume or capacity, varying in the U.S. from 31 to 42 gallons as established by law or usage. **4.** The metal, cylindrical part of a firearm through which the bullet travels. **5.** The cylindrical part or hollow shaft of various instruments and mechanisms. —*v.* **-reled** or **-relled, -reling** or **-relling. 1.** To pack in a barrel. **2.** *Slang.* To move at a high speed. [< OF *baril.*]

bar·ren (băr'ən) *adj.* **1. a.** Not producing offspring. **b.** Infertile; sterile. **2.** Lacking vegetation. **3.** Unproductive; unprofitable. **4.** Devoid; lacking: *writing barren of insight.* **5.** Dull. —*n.* A tract of barren land. [< OF *baraigne.*] —**bar'ren·ness** *n.*

bar·rette (bə-rĕt', bä-) *n.* A small clasp used to hold the hair in place. [F, dim of *barre,* bar.]

bar·ri·cade (băr'ə-kād', băr'ə-kād') *n.* A makeshift barrier or fortification set up across a route of access. —*v.* **-caded, -cading.** To block or confine with a barricade. [< OF *barrique,* barrel.] —**bar'ri·cad'er** *n.*

bar·ri·er (băr'ē-ər) *n.* **1.** A fence, wall, or other structure built to bar passage. **2.** Something that restricts or prevents free interchange or movement. **3.** A boundary or limit: *the sound barrier.* [< OF *barriere.*]

bar·ri·o (bä'ryō) *n., pl.* **-os.** A chiefly Spanish-speaking community or neighborhood in a U.S. city. [Ar *barri,* of an open area.]

bar·ris·ter (băr'ĭ-stər) *n. Chiefly Brit.* A lawyer admitted to plead at the bar in the superior courts. [< BAR (railing).]

bar·room (bär'rōōm', -rōōm') *n.* A room or building in which alcoholic beverages are sold at a bar.

bar·row (băr'ō) *n.* **1. a.** A flat, rectangular tray or cart having handles at each end. **b.** The load carried on such a tray. **2.** A wheelbarrow. [< OE *bearwe,* basket, wheelbarrow. See **bher-¹.**]

Bart. baronet.

bar·tend·er (bär'tĕn'dər) *n.* One who mixes and serves alcoholic drinks at a bar.

bar·ter (bär'tər) *v.* To exchange (goods or services) without using money. —*n.* The practice of bartering. [< OF *barater,* to barter, cheat.] —**bar'ter·er** *n.*

bas·al (bā'səl, -zəl) *adj.* **1.** Pertaining to, located at, or forming a base. **2.** Of primary importance; basic. —**bas'al·ly** *adv.*

basal metabolism. The least amount of energy required to maintain vital functions in an organism at complete rest.

ba·salt (bə-sôlt', bā'sôlt') *n.* A hard, dense, dark volcanic rock. [< L *basaltēs.*] —**ba·sal'tic** (bə-sôl'tĭk) *adj.*

base¹ (bās) *n.* **1.** The lowest or supporting part or layer; bottom. **2.** The fundamental principle or underlying concept of a system or theory. **3.** A chief constituent. **4.** The fact, observation, or premise from which a measurement or reasoning process is begun. **5.** *Sports.* A goal, starting point, or safety area. **6.** A center of organization, supply, or activity. **7. a.** A fortified center of operations. **b.** A supply center for a large force. **8.** *Ling.* A morpheme or morphemes regarded as a form to which affixes or other bases may be added.

ô **paw,** for/oi **boy**/ou **out**/ōō **took**/ōō **coo**/p **pop**/r **run**/s **sauce**/sh **shy**/t **to**/th **thin**/*th* **the**/
ŭ **cut**/ûr **fur**/v **van**/w **wag**/y **yes**/z **size**/zh **vision**/ə **ago, item, edible, gallop, circus**/

9. A line used as a reference for measurement or computations. **10. a.** Any of a large class of compounds, including the hydroxides and oxides of metals, having a bitter taste, a slippery solution, the ability to turn litmus blue, and the ability to react with acids to form salts. **b.** A molecular or ionic substance capable of combining with a proton to form a new substance. **11.** *Math.* The number that is raised to various powers to generate the principal counting units of a number system. **—off base. 1.** *Baseball.* Not touching the base occupied. **2.** Badly mistaken, inaccurate, or unprepared. **—***adj.* Forming or serving as a base. **—***v.* **based, basing. 1.** To form or make a base for. **2.** To find a basis for; establish. [< Gk *basis*, pedestal, base.]

base² (bās) *adj.* **baser, basest. 1.** *Archaic.* Of low birth, rank, or position. **2.** Servile; menial. **3.** Treacherous; contemptible. **4.** Inferior in quality or value. **5.** Containing inferior substances: *a base metal.* [< LL *bassus*, fat, low.] **—base′ly** *adv.* **—base′ness** *n.*

base•ball (bās′bôl′) *n.* **1.** A game played with a wooden bat and hard ball by two opposing teams of nine players, each team playing alternately in the field and at bat, the players at bat having to run a course of four bases laid out in a diamond pattern in order to score. **2.** The ball used in this game.

base•board (bās′bôrd′, -bōrd′) *n.* A molding that conceals the joint between an interior wall and a floor.

base•born (bās′bôrn′) *adj.* **1.** Of humble birth. **2.** Born of unwed parents; illegitimate. **3.** Ignoble; contemptible.

base•less (bās′lĭs) *adj.* Having no basis or foundation.

base•ment (bās′mənt) *n.* **1.** The substructure or foundation of a building. **2.** The lowest habitable story of a building.

ba•ses. *pl.* of **basis.**

bash (băsh) *v.* To strike with a heavy and crushing blow. **—***n.* **1.** A heavy, crushing blow. **2.** *Slang.* A celebration; party. [?]

bash•ful (băsh′fəl) *adj.* **1.** Shy; retiring. **2.** Hesitant; unsure. [< ME *baschen*, to abash.] **—bash′ful•ly** *adv.* **—bash′ful•ness** *n.*

ba•sic (bā′sĭk) *adj.* **1.** Of, pertaining to, or constituting a basis. **2.** *Chem.* **a.** Producing or resulting from a base. **b.** Containing a base, esp. in excess of acid. **—***n.* Something that is basic. **—ba′si•cal•ly** *adv.*

bas•il (băz′əl, bāz′əl) *n.* An aromatic herb, with leaves used as seasoning. [< Gk *basilikon,* "royal," king.]

bas•i•lar (băs′ə-lər) *adj.* Also **bas•i•lar•y** (-lĕr′ē). Pertaining to or located at or near the base, esp. the base of the skull.

ba•sil•i•ca (bə-sĭl′ĭ-kə) *n.* **1.** An oblong building of ancient Rome used as a court or place of assembly. **2.** Such a building used as a Christian church. **3.** A church accorded certain ceremonial rights by the pope. [< Gk *basilikē (stoa),* "royal (portico, court)."]

bas•i•lisk (băs′ə-lĭsk′, băz′-) *n.* A legendary dragon with lethal breath and glance. [< Gk *basiliskos,* "little king."]

ba•sin (bā′sən) *n.* **1.** An open, rounded vessel used esp. for holding liquids. **2.** The amount contained in such a vessel. **3.** A washbowl; a sink. **4.** An artificially enclosed area of a river or harbor. **5.** A small enclosed or partly enclosed body of water. **6.** Any bowl-shaped depression in a land or ocean-floor surface. [< VL *bacca,* water vessel.]

ba•sis (bā′sĭs) *n., pl.* **-ses** (-sēz′). **1.** A foundation upon which something rests. **2.** The chief component of anything. **3.** Principle; criterion. [< Gk, base.]

bask (băsk, bäsk) *v.* **1.** To expose oneself pleasantly to warmth. **2.** To thrive in the presence of an advantageous influence. [ME *basken.*]

bas•ket (băs′kĭt) *n.* **1. a.** A container made of interwoven material. **b.** The amount a basket will hold. **2.** Either of two metal hoops with suspended nets that serve as goals in basketball. [< NF.]

bas•ket•ball (băs′kĭt-bôl′) *n.* **1.** A game played between two teams of five players each, the object being to throw the ball through an elevated basket on the opponent's side of the rectangular court. **2.** The ball used in this game.

Basque (băsk) *n.* **1.** One of a people inhabiting the W Pyrenees in France and Spain. **2.** The language of the Basques, having no known linguistic affinities. **—Basque** *adj.*

bas-re•lief (bä′rĭ-lēf′) *n.* Low relief.

bass¹ (băs) *n., pl.* **bass** or **basses.** Any of several freshwater or marine food fishes. [< OE *bærs.* See **bhar-.**]

bass² (bās) *n.* **1.** A low-pitched tone. **2.** The tones in the lowest register of a musical instrument. **3.** The lowest part in vocal or instrumental part music. **4.** A male singing voice of the lowest range. [ME *bas,* low, base.] **—bass** *adj.*

bass drum (bās). A large cylindrical drum having a low, resonant sound when struck.

bas•set (băs′ĭt) *n.* Also **basset hound.** A dog with short legs and long, drooping ears. [< OF, short and low < *bas,* low, base.]

bas•si•net (băs′ə-nĕt′) *n.* An oblong basket resting on legs, used as a crib for an infant. [< OF *bacin,* basin.]

bas•so (băs′ō, bä′sō) *n.* A singer with a bass voice. [It.]

bas•soon (bə-sōōn′, bă-) *n.* A low-pitched woodwind instrument with a double reed and a long wooden body. [< It *bassone,* aug of BASSO.] **—bas•soon′ist** *n.*

bass viol (bās). A double bass.

bass•wood (băs′wŏŏd′) *n.* A North American linden tree.

bast (băst) *n.* Fibrous plant material. [< OE *bæst* < Gmc *bastaz.*]

bas•tard (băs′tərd) *n.* **1.** An illegitimate child. **2.** Any product of irregular or dubious origin. **3.** *Slang.* An obnoxious or nasty person. **4.** *Slang.* An unfortunate fellow. **—***adj.* **1.** Born of unwed parents; illegitimate. **2.** Not genuine. **3.** Of inferior breed or kind. [Perh < OF *(fils de) bast,* "packsaddle (son)."] **—bas′tard•y** *adj.* **—bas′tard•y** *n.*

ă pat/ā ate/âr care/ä bar/b bib/ch chew/d deed/ĕ pet/ē be/f fit/g gag/h hat/hw what/
ĭ pit/ī pie/îr pier/j judge/k kick/l lid, fatal/m mum/n no, sudden/ng sing/ŏ pot/ō go/

bas•tard•ize (băs′tər-dīz′) *v.* **-ized, -izing.** To debase; corrupt.

baste¹ (bāst) *v.* **basted, basting.** To sew loosely with large, running, temporary stitches. [< OF *bastir,* to build, prepare, baste.]

baste² (bāst) *v.* **basted, basting.** To pour liquid over (meat) while cooking. [?]

baste³ (bāst) *v.* **basted, basting. 1.** To beat vigorously. **2.** To berate. [Perh < ON *beysta,* to thrash, strike.]

bas•tion (băs′chən, băs′tē-ən) *n.* **1.** A projecting part of a rampart or other fortification. **2.** Any well-fortified position. [< OF *bastille,* a jail.]

bat¹ (băt) *n.* **1.** A stout wooden stick or club; cudgel. **2.** A sharp blow. **3. a.** A rounded, tapered, wooden club used to strike a baseball or softball. **b.** A flat-surfaced wooden club used in cricket. **4.** *Slang.* A binge; spree. —*v.* **batted, batting.** To hit with or as if with a bat. [< OE *batt,* cudgel, club.]

bat² (băt) *n.* A mouselike flying mammal with membranous wings. [< Scand.]

bat³ (băt) *v.* **batted, batting.** To flutter: *bat one's eyelashes.* [Prob < OF *batre,* to beat.]

batch (băch) *n.* **1.** An amount produced or needed for one operation, as baking. **2.** The quantity produced as the result of one operation: *a batch of cement.* **3.** A group of persons or things. [< OE *bæcce* < *bacan,* to BAKE.]

bate (bāt) *v.* **bated, bating. 1.** To lessen the force of: *bate one's breath.* **2.** To take away; subtract. [< ME *abaten,* to abate.]

ba•teau (bă-tō′) *n., pl.* **-teaux** (-tōz′). A light, flat-bottomed boat. [< F.]

bath (băth, bäth) *n., pl.* **baths** (bă*th*z, bäths, bă*th*s, bäths). **1.** The act of washing or immersing the body in water. **2.** The water used for bathing. **3.** A bathtub. **4.** A liquid or a liquid and its container, used to regulate the temperature of, soak, or otherwise act upon an immersed object. **5.** A bathroom. **6.** Often **baths.** Rooms or a building equipped for bathing. [< OE *bæth.* See **bhē-.**]

bathe (bā*th*) *v.* **bathed, bathing. 1.** To take a bath. **2.** To go swimming. **3.** To immerse in or become immersed in or as if in liquid. **4.** To suffuse. [< OE *bathian.*] —**bath′er** *n.*

ba•thet•ic (bə-thĕt′ĭk) *adj.* Characterized by bathos.

bath•house (băth′hous′, bäth′-) *n.* **1.** A building equipped for bathing. **2.** A building with dressing rooms for swimmers.

ba•thos (bā′thŏs′) *n.* **1.** A ludicrously abrupt transition from an elevated to a commonplace style. **2.** Insincere or grossly sentimental pathos. [Gk, depth.]

bath•robe (băth′rōb′, bäth′-) *n.* A loose-fitting robe worn before and after bathing and for lounging.

bath•room (băth′rōōm′, -rŏŏm′, bäth′-) *n.* A room with a bath or shower and usually a sink and toilet.

bath•tub (băth′tŭb′, bäth′-) *n.* A usually oblong tub for bathing.

Bath•urst (băth′ərst). The former name for Banjul.

bath•y•sphere (băth′ĭ-sfîr′) *n.* A reinforced,

spherical deep-diving chamber, manned, and lowered by cable.

ba•tik (bə-tēk′, băt′ĭk) *n.* **1.** A dyeing method in which designs are made by covering fabric parts with removable wax. **2.** Cloth thus dyed. [Malay.] —**ba•tik′** *adj.*

ba•tiste (bə-tēst′, bă-) *n.* A fine light fabric of cotton, linen, etc. [Earlier *baptist* cloth, first made in the 13th century by *Baptiste* of Cambrai, France.]

ba•ton (bə-tŏn′, băt′n) *n.* A stick, esp. the slender rod used by a conductor to direct an orchestra. [< LL *bastum,* stick.]

Bat•on Rouge (băt′n rōōzh′). The capital of Louisiana. Pop. 166,000.

bats (băts) *adj. Slang.* Crazy.

bats•man (băts′mən) *n. Cricket.* A player at bat.

bat•tal•ion (bə-tăl′yən) *n.* **1.** A tactical military unit, consisting of a headquarters company and four infantry companies or a headquarters battery and four artillery batteries. **2.** An indefinite number of military troops. [< OIt *battaglione,* aug of *battaglia,* troop.]

bat•ten (băt′n) *n.* A flexible wooden strip for covering, fastening, or flattening parts. —*v.* To secure with battens: *batten down the hatches.* [< F *bâton,* baton.]

bat•ter¹ (băt′ər) *v.* To pound or damage with heavy blows. [< OF *battre,* to beat.]

bat•ter² (băt′ər) *n. Baseball.* The player whose turn it is to bat.

bat•ter³ (băt′ər) *n.* A thick, beaten mixture, as of flour and liquid, used in cooking. [ME *bater.*]

bat•ter•ing-ram (băt′ər-ĭng-răm′) *n.* A siege engine used to batter down walls and gates.

bat•ter•y (băt′ə-rē) *n., pl.* **-ies. 1.** The unlawful beating of a person. **2. a.** An artillery emplacement. **b.** A set of artillery pieces, as on a warship. **3.** An array: *a battery of lawyers.* **4.** The pitcher and catcher on a baseball team. **5.** The percussion section of an orchestra. **6.** A device for generating an electric current. [< OF *battre,* to BATTER.]

bat•ting (băt′ĭng) *n.* Cotton or wool fiber wadded into a flat mass.

bat•tle (băt′l) *n.* **1.** A large-scale combat between two armed forces. **2.** Any intense or extended struggle. —*v.* **-tled, -tling.** To engage in battle. [< VL *battâlia.*]

bat•tle-ax, bat•tle-axe (băt′l-ăks′) *n., pl.* **-axes. 1.** An ax formerly used as a weapon. **2.** *Slang.* An overbearing woman.

battle cry. 1. A shout uttered by troops in battle. **2.** A militant slogan.

bat•tle•dore (băt′l-dôr′, -dōr′) *n.* A flat wooden paddle used in batting a shuttlecock. [ME *batildore.*]

bat•tle•field (băt′l-fēld′) *n.* A place where a battle is fought.

bat•tle•ment (băt′l-mənt) *n.* An indented parapet on top of a wall.

bat•tle•ship (băt′l-shĭp′) *n.* Any of the most heavily armed and armored class of modern warships.

bat•ty (băt′ē) *adj.* **-tier, -tiest.** *Slang.* Crazy; eccentric.

ô paw, for/oi boy/ou out/ōō took/ōō coo/p pop/r run/s sauce/sh shy/t to/th thin/*th* the/
ŭ cut/ûr fur/v van/w wag/y yes/z size/zh vision/ə ago, item, edible, gallop, circus/

bau·ble (bô′bəl) *n.* A trinket. [< OF *baubel*, plaything.]

Bau·de·laire (bōd-lâr′), **Charles.** 1821–1867. French poet.

baux·ite (bôk′sīt′) *n.* The principal ore of aluminum, 30–75% $Al_2O_3 \cdot nH_2O$, with iron oxide and silica as impurities. [< *Les Baux,* S France.]

bawd (bôd) *n.* A woman of ill repute; a prostitute. [ME *bawde.*]

bawd·y (bô′dē) *adj.* **-ier, -iest.** Humorously coarse; vulgar; lewd. —**bawd′i·ly** *adv.* —**bawd′-i·ness** *n.*

bawl (bôl) *v.* To cry out loudly; bellow. —**bawl out.** To scold or reprimand in a loud voice. —*n.* A loud, extended outcry; a wail. [ME *baulen.*] —**bawl′er** *n.*

bay[1] (bā) *n.* A body of water partly enclosed by land, but having a wide outlet to the sea. [< OF *baie.*]

bay[2] (bā) *n.* **1.** A compartment set off from other compartments making up a given structure. **2.** A projecting compartment containing a window. **3.** Any opening or recess in a wall. [< OF *baee,* an opening.]

bay[3] (bā) *adj.* Reddish-brown. —*n.* **1.** A reddish brown. **2.** A reddish-brown animal, esp. a horse. [< L *badius.*]

bay[4] (bā) *v.* To bark with long, deep, howling cries. —*n.* **1.** The position of one cornered by pursuers. **2.** A long, howling bark. [< VL **abbaiāre.*]

bay[5] (bā) *n.* **1.** A laurel. **2.** A similar tree or shrub. **3. bays.** A crown of laurel leaves, given as a sign of honor. **4. bays.** Honor; renown. [ME *baye,* laurel berry.]

bay·ber·ry (bā′běr′ē) *n.* **1.** An aromatic shrub bearing waxy berries. **2.** The fruit of such a shrub.

bay leaf. The aromatic leaf of a laurel, used as seasoning.

bay·o·net (bā′ə-nĭt, -nět′, bā′ə-nět′) *n.* A sword or knife adapted to be fixed near the muzzle end of a rifle. —*v.* **-neted** or **-netted, -neting** or **-netting.** To stab with a bayonet. [< *Bayonne,* France.]

bay·ou (bī′ōō, bī′ō) *n., pl.* **-ous.** A marshy, sluggish body of water tributary to a lake or river. [< Choctaw *bayuk.*]

bay rum. An aromatic liquid originally distilled from the leaves of a tropical American tree.

ba·zaar (bə-zär′) *n.* Also **ba·zar. 1.** An Oriental market consisting of a street lined with shops and stalls. **2.** A fair for charity. [< Pers *bāzăr.*]

ba·zoo·ka (bə-zōō′kə) *n.* A rocket launcher consisting of a portable smoothbore tube. [< the *bazooka,* a crude wind instrument made of pipes.]

bb ball bearing.

BB (bē′bē′) *n.* A standard size of lead shot that measures 0.18 inch in diameter.

BBB Better Business Bureau.

BBC British Broadcasting Corporation.

BB gun. A small air rifle for firing BB shot.

bbl barrel.

B.C. 1. before Christ. **2.** British Columbia.

bd. 1. board. **2.** bond. **3.** *Bookbinding.* bound.

B.D. 1. bank draft. **2.** bills discounted.

be (bē) *v.*

	1st person	2nd person	3rd person
Present Tense			
singular	am	are †	is
plural	are	are	are
†Archaic 2nd person singular **art**			
Past Tense			
singular	was	were ‡	was
plural	were	were	were
‡Archaic 2nd person singular **wast** *or* **wert**			
Present Participle: **being**		Present Subjunctive: **be**	
Past Participle: **been**		Past Subjunctive: **were**	

1. To exist in actuality; have reality or life: *I think, therefore I am.* **2.** To exist in a specified place: *"Oh, to be in England,/Now that April's there"* (Robert Browning). **3.** To occupy a specified position: *The food is on the table.* **4.** To take place; occur. **5.** To go. Used chiefly in the past and perfect tenses: *Have you ever been to Italy?* **6.** *Archaic.* To belong; befall. Used in the subjunctive: *Peace be unto you.* **7.** —Used as a copula linking a subject and a predicate nominative, adjective, or pronoun, in such senses as: **a.** To equal in meaning or identity: *"To be a Christian was to be a Roman."* (James Bryce). **b.** To signify; symbolize: *A is excellent, C is passing.* **c.** To belong to a specified class or group: *Man is a primate.* **d.** To have or show a specified quality or characteristic: *She is lovely. All men are mortal.* **8.** —Used as an auxiliary verb in certain constructions, as: **a.** With the past participle of a transitive verb to form the passive voice: *The election is held annually.* **b.** With the present participle of a verb to express a continuing action: *We are working to improve housing conditions.* **c.** With the present participle or the infinitive of a verb to express intention, obligation, or future action: *She is to eat her dinner before she may play. He is leaving next month.* **d.** With the past participle of certain intransitive verbs of motion to form the perfect tense: *"Where be those roses gone which sweetened so our eyes?"* (Philip Sidney). [< OE *bēon,* to come to be. See **bheu-.**]

be-. *comb. form.* **1.** A complete or profuse covering or affecting. **2.** A thorough or excessive degree. **3.** An action that causes a condition to exist. [< OE *be-, bi-,* about, over, on all sides, away, away from.]

Be beryllium.

B.E. Board of Education.

B/E bill of exchange.

beach (bēch) *n.* The shore of a body of water. [Earlier *baich.*]

beach·comb·er (bēch′kō′mər) *n.* One who lives on what he can salvage or earn along the beach.

beach·head (bēch′hěd′) *n.* A position on an enemy shoreline captured by advance troops of an invading force.

bea·con (bē′kən) *n.* **1.** A signal fire. **2.** A lighthouse. **3.** A radio transmitter that emits a

---

ă pat/ā ate/âr care/ä bar/b bib/ch chew/d deed/ě pet/ē be/f fit/g gag/h hat/hw what/
ĭ pit/ī pie/îr pier/j judge/k kick/l lid, fatal/m mum/n no, sudden/ng sing/ŏ pot/ō go/

signal to guide aircraft. [< OE *bēacen.* See **bhā-¹.**]

bead (bēd) *n.* **1.** A small piece of material pierced for stringing. **2. beads. a.** A necklace made of such pieces. **b.** A rosary. **3.** Any small, round object. **4.** A narrow projecting strip. [< OE *gebed,* prayer (bead). See **bhedh-².**] —**bead'y** *adj.*

bea·dle (bēd'l) *n.* A minor parish official in England. [< OE *bydel.* See **bheudh-.**]

bea·gle (bē'gəl) *n.* A small, smooth-coated hound with drooping ears. [Perh < OF *be-egueule,* noisy person.]

beak (bēk) *n.* **1.** The horny, projecting mouth parts of a bird; bill. **2.** A similar part or structure. [< L *beccus.*]

beak·er (bē'kər) *n.* **1.** A large drinking cup with a wide mouth. **2.** An open glass cylinder with a pouring lip, used as a laboratory vessel. [< ON *bikarr.*]

beam (bēm) *n.* **1.** A length of timber forming a supporting member in construction. **2.** A ship's maximum breadth. **3.** A constant directional radio signal for navigational guidance. **4. a.** A ray of light. **b.** A group of particles traveling together in close parallel trajectories. —**on the beam.** On the right track. —*v.* **1.** To emit or transmit. **2.** To radiate. **3.** To smile radiantly. [< OE *bēam* < Gmc *baumaz.*]

bean (bēn) *n.* **1.** The often edible seed or seed pod of any of various plants. **2.** A plant bearing such seeds or pods. **3.** *Slang.* The head. —*v. Slang.* To hit on the head. [< OE *bēan.* See **bha-bhā-.**]

bear¹ (bâr) *v.* **bore, borne** or **born, bearing. 1.** To carry; support. **2.** To endure. **3.** To conduct (oneself). **4.** To have; show; exhibit. **5.** To transmit: *bear good tidings.* **6.** To render; give: *bear witness.* **7.** *p.p.* **born.** To give birth to. **8.** To yield; produce. **9. a.** To permit of or be liable to: *This will bear investigation.* **b.** To have relevance; apply. **10.** To exert pressure. **11.** To proceed (in a specified direction): *bear right.* —**bear out.** To prove right; confirm. —**bear with.** To be patient with; tolerate. [< OE *beran.* See **bher-¹.**] —**bear'a·ble** *adj.* —**bear'-er** *n.*

bear² (bâr) *n.* **1.** Any of various usually large mammals having a shaggy coat and a short tail. **2.** A clumsy or ill-mannered person. **3.** *Stock Market.* An investor or concern that sells shares in the expectation that prices will fall. [< OE *bera.* See **bher-³.**]

beard (bîrd) *n.* **1.** The hair on the chin and cheeks of a man. **2.** Any similar hairy or hairlike growth, as on an animal or plant. —*v.* To confront boldly. [< OE. See **bhardhā.**]

bear·ing (bâr'ĭng) *n.* **1.** Deportment; mien. **2.** A device that supports, guides, and reduces friction between fixed and moving machine parts. **3.** A supportive element. **4.** Relationship or relevance. **5. a.** Direction measured relative to geographic or celestial reference lines. **b.** A navigational determination of position. **6. bearings.** Grasp of one's situation: *get one's bearings.* **7.** A heraldic emblem.

beast (bēst) *n.* **1.** An animal, esp. a large four-footed animal. **2.** A brutal person. [< L *bēstia.*]

beat (bēt) *v.* **beat, beaten** (bēt'n) or **beat, beating. 1.** To strike repeatedly. **2.** To forge. **3.** To flatten by trampling; tread. **4.** To defeat. **5.** To excel; surpass. **6.** *Slang.* To baffle. **7.** To pulsate; throb. **8.** To mix rapidly: *beat eggs.* **9.** To flap, as wings. —*n.* **1.** A stroke; blow. **2.** A pulsation; throb. **3.** A rhythmic stress. **4.** A regular round: *the night beat.* —*adj.* Tired; exhausted. [< OE *bēatan.* See **bhau-.**] —**beat'er** *n.* —**beat'ing** *n.*

be·a·tif·ic (bē'ə-tĭf'ĭk) *adj.* Showing or producing exalted joy or bliss. [< LL *beātificus.*] —**be'a·tif'i·cal·ly** *adv.*

be·at·i·fy (bē-ăt'ə-fī') *v.* **-fied, -fying. 1.** To make blessedly happy. **2.** To proclaim to be one of the blessed. —**be·at'i·fi·ca'tion** (-fĭ-kā'shən) *n.*

be·at·i·tude (bē-ăt'ə-t/y/ōōd') *n.* Supreme blessedness; exalted joy or happiness. [< L *beātus,* blessed.]

beat·nik (bēt'nĭk) *n.* A young person of the 1950's whose rejection of American mores and dress was associated with a quest for spiritual illumination.

beau (bō) *n., pl.* **beaus** or **beaux** (bōz). **1.** A suitor. **2.** A dandy. [< L *bellus,* handsome, fine.]

Beau Brum·mell (bō brŭm'əl). A dandy; fop. [< *"Beau"* Brummell (1778–1840), British dandy.]

Beau·mont (bō'mŏnt). A city of Texas. Pop. 119,000.

beaut (byōōt) *n. Slang.* Something outstanding of its kind: *"When I make a mistake, it's a beaut."* (Fiorello H. La Guardia). [Short for BEAUTY.]

beau·te·ous (byōō'tē-əs, -tyəs) *adj.* Beautiful, esp. to the sight.

beau·ti·cian (byōō-tĭsh'ən) *n.* A cosmetologist.

beau·ti·ful (byōō'tə-fəl) *adj.* Having beauty. —**beau'ti·ful·ly** *adv.*

beau·ti·fy (byōō'tə-fī') *v.* **-fied, -fying.** To make beautiful. —**beau'ti·fi·ca'tion** *n.*

beau·ty (byōō'tē) *n., pl.* **-ties. 1.** A quality that delights the senses or exalts the mind; loveliness. **2.** One possessing this quality. [< VL *bellitās* < L *bellus,* pretty, handsome, fine.]

beaux. Alternate *pl.* of **beau.**

bea·ver (bē'vər) *n.* **1.** A large aquatic rodent with thick fur, a paddlelike tail, and sharp front teeth with which it fells trees to build dams. **2.** The fur of a beaver. [< OE *beofor.* See **bher-³.**]

be·calm (bĭ-käm') *v.* To render motionless for lack of wind.

be·came (bĭ-kām'). *p.t.* of **become.**

be·cause (bĭ-kôz', -kŭz') *conj.* For the reason that; since. —**because of.** By reason of; on account of. [ME *bi cause* : BY + CAUSE.]

beck (bĕk) *n.* A summons. —**at one's beck and call.** Very willingly obedient. [< ME *becken,* to beckon.]

beck·on (bĕk'ən) *v.* **1.** To summon, as by nodding or waving. **2.** To attract. [< OE *bēcnan.* See **bhā-¹.**] —**beck'on·er** *n.* —**beck'on·ing·ly** *adv.*

be·cloud (bĭ-kloud') *v.* To obscure.

ô paw, for/oi boy/ou out/ŏŏ took/ōō coo/p pop/r run/s sauce/sh shy/t to/th thin/*th* the/
ŭ cut/ûr fur/v van/w wag/y yes/z size/zh vision/ə ago, item, edible, gallop, circus/

be•come (bĭ-kŭm′) *v.* -came, -come, -coming.
1. To grow or come to be. 2. To be appropriate or suitable to. —**become of.** To be the fate of.

be•com•ing (bĭ-kŭm′ĭng) *adj.* 1. Appropriate; suitable. 2. Attractive. —**be•com′ing•ly** *adv.*

bed (bĕd) *n.* 1. A piece of furniture for reclining and sleeping. 2. A small plot of cultivated ground: *flower bed.* 3. **a.** The surface at the bottom of a body of water. **b.** A horizontally extending layer of earth or rock. 4. A foundation. —*v.* **bedded, bedding.** 1. To furnish with a bed. 2. To put to bed. 3. **a.** To prepare (soil) for planting. **b.** To plant in a prepared bed of soil. 5. To lay flat or arrange in layers. 6. To embed. [< OE *bedd.* See **bhedh-¹.**]

be•daub (bĭ-dôb′) *v.* To smear.

be•daz•zle (bĭ-dăz′əl) *v.* -zled, -zling. To dazzle so completely as to confuse or blind. —**be• daz′zle•ment** *n.*

bed•bug (bĕd′bŭg′) *n.* A wingless, bloodsucking insect that often infests human dwellings.

bed•clothes (bĕd′klōz′, -klōthz′) *pl.n.* Coverings for a bed.

bed•ding (bĕd′ĭng) *n.* 1. Bedclothes. 2. A foundation.

be•deck (bĭ-dĕk′) *v.* To adorn.

be•dev•il (bĭ-dĕv′əl) *v.* To plague; harass.

be•dew (bĭ-d/y/ōō′) *v.* To wet with or as if with dew.

bed•fel•low (bĕd′fĕl′ō) *n.* 1. One with whom a bed is shared. 2. A temporary associate.

be•di•zen (bĭ-dī′zən, -dĭz′ən) *v.* To dress or ornament gaudily.

bed•lam (bĕd′ləm) *n.* 1. Any place of noisy confusion. 2. A madhouse. [ME *Bedlem, Bethlem,* Hospital of St. Mary of *Bethlehem.*]

Bed•ling•ton terrier (bĕd′lĭng-tən). A dog of a breed developed in England, having a woolly grayish or brownish coat.

Bed•ou•in (bĕd′ōō-ĭn) *n.* An Arab of any of the nomadic tribes of the deserts of North Africa, Arabia, and Syria. [< Ar *badāwin.*]

be•drag•gle (bĭ-drăg′əl) *v.* -gled, -gling. To make wet and limp.

bed•rid•den (bĕd′rĭd′n) *adj.* Confined to one's bed because of illness or infirmity. [< OE *bedrida,* "one who is bedridden" : BED + *rīdan,* to RIDE.]

bed•rock (bĕd′rŏk′) *n.* Solid rock that underlies the earth's surface.

bed•roll (bĕd′rōl′) *n.* A portable roll of bedding.

bed•room (bĕd′rōōm′, -rŏŏm′) *n.* A room for sleeping.

bed•side (bĕd′sīd′) *n.* The space alongside a bed, esp. the bed of a sick person. —**bed′side′** *adj.*

bed•sore (bĕd′sôr′, -sōr′) *n.* A pressure-induced skin ulceration occurring during long confinement to bed.

bed•spread (bĕd′sprĕd′) *n.* A decorative bed covering.

bed•stead (bĕd′stĕd′) *n.* The frame supporting a bed.

bed•time (bĕd′tīm′) *n.* The time when one goes to bed.

bee (bē) *n.* 1. Any of various winged, often stinging insects that gather nectar and pollen from flowers and in some species produce honey. 2. A gathering where people work together or compete. [< OE *bēo.* See **bhei-¹.**]

beech (bēch) *n.* A tree having light-colored bark, small, edible nuts, and strong, heavy wood. [< OE *bēce.* See **bhāgo-.**]

beech•nut (bēch′nŭt′) *n.* The nut of the beech tree.

beef (bēf) *n.* 1. The flesh of a full-grown steer, bull, ox, or cow. 2. *pl.* **beeves** (bēvz). Such an animal raised for meat. 3. Human strength; brawn. 4. *pl.* **beefs.** *Slang.* A complaint. —*v. Slang.* To complain. —**beef up.** *Slang.* To reinforce; build up. [< L *bōs (bov-),* ox.] —**beef′i•ness** *n.* —**beef′y** *adj.*

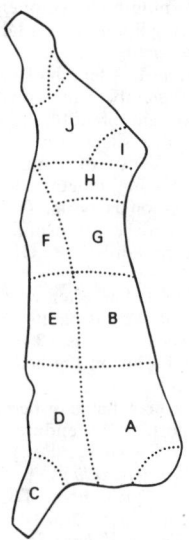

beef
A. Chuck
B. Ribs
C. Shank
D. Brisket
E. Plate
F. Flank
G. Loin (tenderloin and porterhouse)
H. Sirloin
I. Rump
J. Round

bee•hive (bē′hīv′) *n.* 1. A hive for bees. 2. A very busy place.

bee•keep•er (bē′kē′pər) *n.* One who keeps bees; an apiarist.

bee•line (bē′līn′) *n.* A fast, straight course.

Be•el•ze•bub (bē-ĕl′zĭ-bŭb′) *n.* The Devil.

been (bĭn). *p.p.* of **be.**

beer (bĭr) *n.* 1. An alcoholic beverage brewed from malt and hops. 2. Any of various carbonated soft drinks. [< OE *bēor.*]

ă pat/ā ate/âr care/ä bar/b bib/ch chew/d deed/ĕ pet/ē be/f fit/g gag/h hat/hw what/
ĭ pit/ī pie/îr pier/j judge/k kick/l lid, fatal/m mum/n no, sudden/ng sing/ŏ pot/ō go/

bees•wax (bēz'wăks') *n.* The wax secreted by bees for making honeycombs and having a variety of commercial uses.

beet (bēt) *n.* **1.** A cultivated plant with a fleshy dark-red or whitish root used as a vegetable or as a source of sugar. **2.** The root of such a plant. [< OE *bēte.*]

Bee•tho•ven (bā'tō-vən), **Ludwig van.** 1770–1827. German composer.

bee•tle[1] (bēt'l) *n.* An insect with horny front wings that cover the hind wings when not in flight. [< OE *bitela.*]

bee•tle[2] (bēt'l) *adj.* Jutting: *beetle brows.* —*v.* -tled, -tling. To project. [< ME *bitel-brouwed,* having shaggy eyebrows.]

bee•tle[3] (bēt'l) *n.* A heavy mallet or similar tool. [< OE *bīetel.*]

beeves. A *pl.* of **beef.**

bef. before.

be•fall (bǐ-fôl') *v.* -fell, -fallen, -falling. **1.** To come to pass. **2.** To happen to: *"There shall no evil befall thee."* (Psalms 91:10).

be•fit (bǐ-fǐt') *v.* -fitted, -fitting. To be suitable to or appropriate for.

be•fog (bǐ-fôg', -fŏg') *v.* -fogged, -fogging. To obscure.

be•fore (bǐ-fôr', -fōr') *adv.* **1.** In front; ahead; in advance. **2.** In the past; previously. —*prep.* **1.** In front of. **2.** Prior to. **3.** Awaiting. **4.** In the presence of. **5.** Under the consideration of: *the case before the court.* **6.** In preference to; sooner than. **7.** In advance of or in precedence of, as in rank, condition, or development. —*conj.* **1.** In advance of the time when: *before he went.* **2.** Rather than; sooner than: *He would die before he would betray his country.* [< OE *beforan.* See **per¹.**]

be•fore•hand (bǐ-fôr'hǎnd', bǐ-fôr'-) *adv.* In advance; early. —**be•fore'hand'** *adj.*

be•foul (bǐ-foul') *v.* To sully.

be•friend (bǐ-frěnd') *v.* To act as a friend to.

be•fud•dle (bǐ-fŭd'l) *v.* -dled, -dling. To confuse. —**be•fud'dle•ment** *n.*

beg (běg) *v.* begged, begging. **1.** To ask for as charity. **2.** To entreat. **3.** To evade: *beg the question.* [ME *beggen.*]

be•gan (bǐ-găn'). *p.t.* of **begin.**

be•get (bǐ-gět') *v.* -got *or rare* -gat (-găt') -gotten *or* -got, -getting. To father; sire. [< OE *begietan.* See **ghend-.**] —**be•get'ter** *n.*

beg•gar (běg'ər) *n.* One who solicits alms for a living. —*v.* **1.** To impoverish. **2.** To render impotent.

beg•gar•ly (běg'ər-lē) *adj.* Of a beggar; very poor. —**beg'gar•li•ness** *n.*

beg•gar•y (běg'ə-rē) *n.* Extreme poverty; penury.

be•gin (bǐ-gǐn') *v.* -gan, -gun, -ginning. **1.** To commence. **2.** To come into being. [< OE *beginnan* < Gmc **bi-ginnan.*] —**be•gin'ner** *n.*

be•gin•ning (bǐ-gǐn'ǐng) *n.* Commencement, origin, or genesis.

be•gone (bǐ-gôn', -gŏn') *interj.* Expressive of dismissal.

be•go•nia (bǐ-gôn'yə) *n.* Any of various plants cultivated for their showy leaves or flowers. [< M. *Bégon* (1638–1710), governor of Santo Domingo.]

be•got (bǐ-gŏt'). *p.t.* and alternate *p.p.* of **beget.**

be•got•ten (bǐ-gŏt'n). *p.p.* of **beget.**

be•grime (bǐ-grīm') *v.* -grimed, -griming. To soil, as with dirt or grime.

be•grudge (bǐ-grŭj') *v.* -grudged, -grudging. **1.** To envy. **2.** To give with reluctance.

be•guile (bǐ-gīl') *v.* -guiled, -guiling. **1.** To deceive; cheat. **2.** To divert. **3.** To cause to vanish. —**be•guile'ment** *n.* —**be•guil'er** *n.*

be•gum (bē'gəm, bā'-) *n.* A Moslem lady of rank. [Urdu *begam.*]

be•gun (bǐ-gŭn'). *p.p.* of **begin.**

be•half (bǐ-hǎf', -hǎf') *n.* Interest, support, or benefit: *on his behalf.* [ME *(on min) behalfe,* "on my side."]

be•have (bǐ-hāv') *v.* -haved, -having. **1.** To act, react, or function in a particular way. **2. a.** To conduct oneself in a specified way. **b.** To conduct oneself in a proper way. [ME *behaven,* "to hold oneself."]

be•hav•ior (bǐ-hāv'yər) *n.* Also *chiefly Brit.* **be•hav•iour.** **1.** Deportment; demeanor. **2.** Action, reaction, or function under specified circumstances. —**be•hav'ior•al** *adj.*

be•head (bǐ-hěd') *v.* To separate the head from; decapitate.

be•he•moth (bǐ-hē'məth, bē'ə-mŏth') *n.* A huge animal mentioned in the Old Testament. [< Heb *bəhēmāh,* beast.]

be•hest (bǐ-hěst') *n.* An order or authoritative command. [< OE *behǣs.*]

be•hind (bǐ-hīnd') *adv.* **1.** In, to, or toward the rear: *He walked behind.* **2.** In a place or condition that has been passed or left: *He left his gloves behind.* **3.** In arrears; late. **4.** Slow: *His watch is running behind.* —*prep.* **1.** At the back of or in the rear of. **2.** On the farther side of. **3.** In a former place, time, or situation. **4.** After (a set time): *behind schedule.* **5.** Below, as in rank. **6.** In support of. [< OE *behindan.*]

be•hind•hand (bǐ-hīnd'hǎnd') *adv.* **1.** In arrears. **2.** Behind the times. —**be•hind'hand'** *adj.*

be•hold (bǐ-hōld') *v.* -held (-hěld'), -holding. To gaze at; look upon. —*interj.* Expressive of amazement. [< OE *behealdan,* to possess, hold, observe.] —**be•hold'er** *n.*

be•hold•en (bǐ-hōl'dən) *adj.* Obliged; indebted.

be•hoove (bǐ-hōōv') *v.* -hooved, -hooving. To be necessary or proper for: *It behooves us to take warning.* [< OE *behōfian,* to require.]

beige (bāzh) *n.* Light grayish brown. [F.] —**beige** *adj.*

be•ing (bē'ǐng) *n.* **1.** Existence. **2.** One that exists. **3.** One's inward nature.

Bei•rut (bā-rōōt'). The capital of Lebanon. Pop. 500,000.

be•la•bor (bǐ-lā'bər) *v.* **1.** To beat; thrash. **2.** To insist repeatedly or harp upon: *belabor a point.*

be•lat•ed (bǐ-lā'tǐd) *adj.* Tardy. [BE- + obs *lated* < LATE.] —**be•lat'ed•ly** *adv.*

be•lay (bǐ-lā') *v.* **1.** To make fast; secure. **2.** *Naut.* To stop: *Belay there!* —*n.* A hold in mountain climbing. [< OE *belecgan,* to cover, surround.]

belaying pin. A pin used on shipboard for securing running gear.

ô paw, for/oi boy/ou out/ŏŏ took/ōō coo/p pop/r run/s sauce/sh shy/t to/th thin/*th* the/
ŭ cut/ûr fur/v van/w wag/y yes/z size/zh vision/ə ago, item, edible, gallop, circus/

belch (bĕlch) v. **1.** To expel gas from the stomach through the mouth; eruct. **2.** To gush forth; erupt. [ME *belchen*.] —**belch** n.

be·lea·guer (bĭ-lē′gər) v. **1.** To besiege. **2.** To harass; beset. [Du *belegeren*.]

Bel·fast (bĕl′făst′, -fäst′, bĕl-făst′, -fäst′). The capital of Northern Ireland. Pop. 410,000.

bel·fry (bĕl′frē) n., pl. **-fries. 1.** A church bell tower. **2.** The part of a steeple in which the bells are hung. [ME *berfrey*, siege tower, bell tower.] —**bel′fried** adj.

Bel·gium (bĕl′jəm). A kingdom of NW Europe. Pop. 9,428,000. Cap. Brussels. —**Bel′gian** (bĕl′jən) adj. & n.

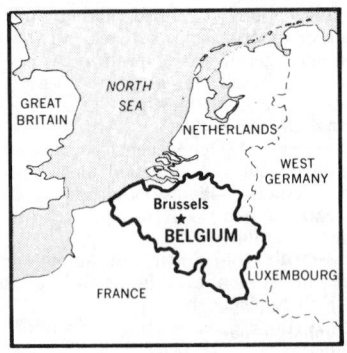

Belgium

Bel·grade (bĕl′grăd′, bĕl-grăd′). The capital of Yugoslavia. Pop. 598,000.

be·lie (bĭ-lī′) v. **-lied, -lying. 1.** To misrepresent or disguise. **2.** To show to be false. **3.** To frustrate or disappoint. —**be·li′er** n.

be·lief (bĭ-lēf′) n. **1.** Trust; confidence. **2.** A conviction or opinion. **3.** A tenet or body of tenets; creed.

be·lieve (bĭ-lēv′) v. **-lieved, -lieving. 1.** To accept as true or real. **2.** To credit with veracity; have confidence in; trust. **3.** To expect or suppose; think. **4.** To hold a religious belief. [< OE *belēfan, gelēfan*. See **leubh-**.] —**be·liev′a·ble** adj. —**be·liev′er** n.

be·lit·tle (bĭ-lĭt′l) v. **-tled, -tling. 1.** To represent or speak of as small or unimportant; depreciate; disparage. **2.** To cause to seem less or little. —**be·lit′tle·ment** n. —**be·lit′tler** n.

Be·lize (bə-lēz′). A country in Central America. Pop. 122,000. Cap. Belmopan.

bell (bĕl) n. **1.** A hollow metal instrument that emits a metallic tone when struck. **2.** Something shaped like a bell. **3.** A stroke on a bell to mark the hour on shipboard. —v. To furnish with a bell. [< OE *belle*. See **bhel-⁴**.]

bel·la·don·na (bĕl′ə-dŏn′ə) n. **1.** A poisonous plant having small black berries. **2.** A medicine derived from this plant, used to treat asthma. [It, "fair lady."]

bell·hop (bĕl′hŏp′) n. A hotel porter.

bel·li·cose (bĕl′ĭ-kōs′) adj. Warlike; pugnacious. [< L *bellicus*, of war.] —**bel′li·cos′i·ty** (-kŏs′ə-tē) n. **bel′li·cose′ness** n.

bel·lig·er·ent (bə-lĭj′ər-ənt) adj. **1.** Aggressively hostile; truculent. **2.** Waging war. —n. A war-

ring state. [< L *belligerāre*, to wage war.] —**bel·lig′er·ence, bel·lig′er·en·cy** n.

bel·low (bĕl′ō) v. **1.** To roar in the manner of a bull. **2.** To shout in a deep loud voice. [< OE **belgan*. See **bhel-⁴**.] —**bel′low** n.

bel·lows (bĕl′ōz, -əz) n. (takes pl. v.). A hand-operated device for directing a strong current of air, as to increase the draft of a fire. [< OE *belig*, bag, bellows. See **belly**.]

bell·weth·er (bĕl′wĕth′ər) n. **1.** A male sheep that wears a bell and leads a flock. **2.** One followed as a leader.

bel·ly (bĕl′ē) n., pl. **-lies. 1.** The part of the body that contains the intestines; the abdomen. **2.** The underside of the body of an animal. **3.** The stomach. [< OE *belig*, bag, purse, bellows. See **bheigh-**.]

bel·ly·ache (bĕl′ē-āk′) n. A stomach ache.

bel·ly·but·ton (bĕl′ē-bŭt′n) n. Informal. The navel.

Bel·mo·pan (bĕl′mə-păn′). The capital of Belize. Pop. 2,000.

be·long (bĭ-lông′, -lŏng′) v. **1.** To be the property or concern of. **2.** To be part of or in natural association with something. **3.** To be a member of an organization. **4.** To have a proper or suitable place. [ME *belongen*.]

be·long·ing (bĭ-lông′ĭng, bĭ-lŏng′-) n. **1.** belongings. Personal possessions. **2.** Close and secure relationship.

be·loved (bĭ-lŭv′ĭd, -lŭvd′) adj. Greatly loved. —**be·lov′ed** n.

be·low (bĭ-lō′) adv. **1.** In or to a lower place or level. **2.** On earth: *creatures here below.* —prep. **1.** Lower than; under. **2.** Inferior to.

belt (bĕlt) n. **1.** A supportive or ornamental band of leather worn around the waist. **2.** A continuous moving band used as a machine element. **3.** A geographic region that is distinctive in some specific way. **4.** Slang. A powerful blow. —v. **1.** To encircle; gird. **2.** To attach with a belt. **3.** To strike with or as if with a belt. [< OE < Gmc **baltjaz*.]

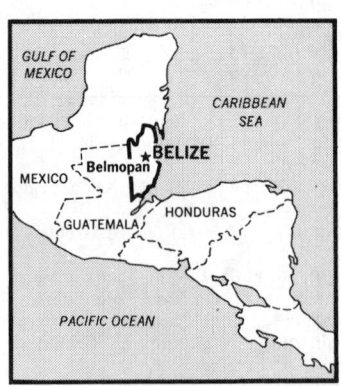

Belize

be·ma (bē′mə) n., pl. **-mata** (-mə-tə). **1.** Also **bi·mah** (bē′mə). The platform from which services are conducted in a synagogue. **2.** The sanctuary of an Eastern Orthodox church. [< Gk *bēma*, platform.]

be•moan (bǐ-mōn') *v.* To lament.

be•muse (bǐ-myōōz') *v.* -mused, -musing. To preoccupy; bewilder.

bench (běnch) *n.* **1.** A long seat for two or more persons. **2. a.** The judge's seat in court. **b.** The office or position of a judge. **3.** The court or judges. **4.** A craftsman's worktable. [< OE *benc.*]

bend (běnd) *v.* bent, bending. **1.** To tighten (a bow). **2.** To curve. **3.** To turn or deflect. **4.** To coerce or subdue. **5.** To concentrate; apply. **6.** To fasten. **7.** To yield; submit. —*n.* **1.** The action of bending. **2.** Something bent; a curve; crook. **3.** A knot that joins one rope to another or to some object. **4.** bends. Caisson disease. [< OE *bendan.* See bhendh-.]

be•neath (bǐ-nēth') *adv.* **1.** In a lower place; below. **2.** Underneath. —*prep.* **1.** Below; under. **2.** Unworthy of. [< OE *binithan* : *bi*, BY + *nithan*, (from) below (see ni).]

ben•e•dic•tion (běn'ə-dǐk'shən) *n.* The invocation of blessing, esp. at the end of a worship service. [< L *benedīcere*, to bless, speak well of.]

ben•e•fac•tor (běn'ə-fǎk'tər) *n.* One who gives financial or other aid. —**ben'e•fac'tress** *fem.n.*

be•nef•i•cence (bə-něf'ə-səns) *n.* The quality of charity or kindness. [< L *beneficus,* generous.] —**be•nef'i•cent** *adj.*

ben•e•fi•cial (běn'ə-fǐsh'əl) *adj.* Helpful; advantageous. [< BENEFICE.] —**ben'e•fi'cial•ly** *adv.* —**ben'e•fi'cial•ness** *n.*

ben•e•fi•ci•ar•y (běn'ə-fǐsh'ē-ĕr-ē, -fǐsh'ə-rē) *n., pl.* -ies. The recipient of a benefit, as from an insurance policy, will, or trust fund.

ben•e•fit (běn'ə-fǐt) *n.* **1.** An advantage. **2.** An aid; help. **3.** A payment or series of payments to one in need. **4.** A fund-raising public entertainment. —*v.* **1.** To be helpful or advantageous to. **2.** To derive advantage; profit. [< L *bene facere,* to do well.]

be•nev•o•lence (bə-něv'ə-ləns) *n.* **1.** Charitable good nature. **2.** An act of charity. [< L *benevolēns,* "wishing well."] —**be•nev'o•lent** *adj.*

Ben•gal (běn-gôl', běng-gôl'). A region of NE India, divided in 1947 into East Bengal, now in Bangladesh, and West Bengal, Republic of India.

Ben•ga•li (běn-gô'lē, běng-gô'-) *n., pl.* -li or -lis. **1.** An inhabitant of Bengal. **2.** The Indic language of Bengal. —**Ben•ga'li** *adj.*

Ben•ga•si (běn-gä'zē). Also **Ben•gha•zi.** A city of NE Libya. Pop. 170,000.

be•night•ed (bǐ-nī'tǐd) *adj.* Ignorant.

be•nign (bǐ-nīn') *adj.* **1.** Of a kindly disposition; gracious. **2.** Not malignant: *a benign tumor.* [< L *benignus,* "good-natured."]

Be•nin (bě-nēn'). A republic of W Africa. Pop. 2,700,000. Cap. Porto-Novo.

bent (běnt) *p.t.* & *p.p.* of **bend.** —*adj.* **1.** Deviating from a straight line; crooked. **2.** Determined. **3.** Headed toward. —*n.* **1.** An individual tendency, disposition, or inclination. **2.** A transverse framework used for strengthening a bridge.

be•numb (bǐ-nǔm') *v.* **1.** To make numb, esp. by cold. **2.** To make inactive; stupefy.

Ben•ze•drine (běn'zə-drēn') *n.* A trademark for an amphetamine.

ben•zene (běn'zēn', běn-zēn') *n.* A clear, colorless, flammable liquid, C_6H_6, derived from petroleum and used to manufacture DDT, detergents, insecticides, and motor fuels. [BENZ(OIN) + -ENE.]

benzene ring. The hexagonal ring structure in the benzene molecule, each vertex of which is occupied by a carbon atom.

ben•zine (běn'zēn', běn-zēn') *n.* Also **ben•zin** (běn'zǐn). Ligroin.

ben•zol (běn'zôl', -zōl') *n.* Benzene. Not in technical use.

be•queath (bǐ-kwēth', -kwēth') *v.* **1.** To leave by will. **2.** To pass on or hand down. [< OE *becwethan,* to say, bequeath. See gwet-.]

be•quest (bǐ-kwěst') *n.* **1.** The act of bequeathing. **2.** Something left by will.

be•rate (bǐ-rāt') *v.* -rating, -rates. To rebuke harshly.

Ber•ber (bûr'bər) *n., pl.* -ber or -bers. **1.** A member of one of several Moslem tribes of North Africa. **2.** The Afro-Asiatic languages of these tribes. —**Ber'ber** *adj.*

be•reave (bǐ-rēv') *v.* -reaved or -reft (-rěft'), -reaving. To deprive of, as by death. [< OE *berēafian.*] —**be•reave'ment** *n.*

be•ret (bə-rā') *n.* A round, soft, visorless cloth cap. [< LL *birrus,* hooded cape.]

ber•i•ber•i (běr'ē-běr'ē) *n.* A thiamine deficiency disease characterized by partial paralysis, emaciation, and anemia. [Singhalese.]

Be•ring Sea (bîr'ǐng, bâr'-). The part of the N Pacific between Alaska and Siberia.

Bering time. The time in W Alaska and the Aleutian Islands in the 11th time zone west of Greenwich.

Berke•ley (bûrk'lē). A city of California. Pop. 111,000.

berke•li•um (bûrk'lē-əm) *n. Symbol* **Bk** A synthetic radioactive element. Atomic number 97, longest-lived isotope Bk 247. [< BERKELEY.]

Ber•lin (bĕr-lĭn'). The former capital of Germany, now surrounded by East Germany and

Benin

divided into **East Berlin** and **West Berlin.** —**Ber·lin′er** *n.*

Ber·mu·da (bər-myōō′də). A British colony in the Atlantic Ocean. Pop. 48,000. Cap. Hamilton. —**Ber·mu′di·an** (-dē-ən) *adj.* & *n.*

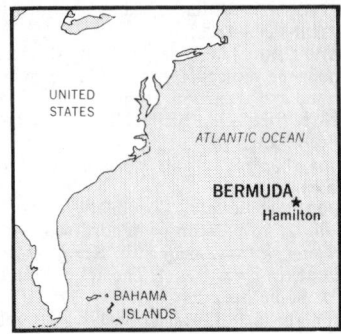

Bermuda

Bern (bûrn, bĕrn). Also **Berne.** The capital of Switzerland. Pop. 167,000.

Ber·noul·li effect (bər-nōō′lē). The reduction of internal fluid pressure with increased stream velocity. [After D. *Bernoulli* (1700–1782), Swiss mathematician.]

ber·ry (bĕr′ē) *n., pl.* **-ries.** **1.** A usually small, fleshy, many-seeded fruit. **2.** A seed or dried kernel, as of coffee. [< OE *berige.*]

ber·serk (bər-sûrk′, -zûrk′) *adj.* **1.** Destructively violent. **2.** Deranged. [ON *berserkr,* "bear's skin."] —**ber·serk′** *adv.*

berth (bûrth) *n.* **1.** A built-in bed on a ship or vehicle. **2. a.** A space for a ship to dock or anchor. **b.** Enough space for a ship to maneuver. **3.** A job, esp. on a ship. —*v.* **1.** To bring (a ship) to a berth; dock. **2.** To provide (a ship) with a berth. [Prob < BEAR, "to proceed."]

Ber·til·lon system (bûr′tə-lŏn). A former system for identifying persons by means of a record of various body measurements, coloring, and markings. [< A. *Bertillon* (1853–1914), French criminologist.]

ber·yl (bĕr′əl) *n.* A mineral, essentially $Be_3Al_2Si_6O_{18}$, the chief source of beryllium and used as a gem. [< Gk *bērullos.*] —**ber′yl·line** (-ə-lĭn, -līn′) *adj.*

be·ryl·li·um (bə-rĭl′ē-əm) *n.* Symbol **Be** A high-melting, lightweight, corrosion-resistant, rigid, steel-gray metallic element used as an aerospace structural material, as a moderator and reflector in nuclear reactors, and in a copper alloy used for springs, electrical contacts, and nonsparking tools. Atomic number 4, atomic weight 9.0122. [< BERYL.]

be·seech (bĭ-sēch′) *v.* **-sought** or **-seeched, -seeching.** To request earnestly; implore. [ME *besechen,* to seek.] —**be·seech′er** *n.*

be·seem (bĭ-sēm′) *v. Archaic.* To be appropriate for; befit.

be·set (bĭ-sĕt′) *v.* **-set, -setting. 1.** To attack from all sides. **2.** To trouble persistently; harass. —**be·set′ment** *n.*

be·side (bĭ-sīd′) *prep.* **1.** Next to. **2.** In comparison with. **3.** Except for. **4.** Apart from. —**beside oneself.** Extremely agitated. —*adv.* In addition to.

be·sides (bĭ-sīdz′) *adv.* **1.** In addition; also. **2.** Moreover; furthermore. **3.** Otherwise; else. —*prep.* **1.** In addition to. **2.** Except for.

be·siege (bĭ-sēj′) *v.* **-sieged, -sieging. 1.** To lay siege to. **2.** To crowd around. **3.** To harass or importune, as with requests. —**be·siege′ment** *n.* —**be·sieg′er** *n.*

be·smear (bĭ-smîr′) *v.* To smear over.

be·smirch (bĭ-smûrch′) *v.* **1.** To soil; sully. **2.** To dishonor; tarnish. —**be·smirch′er** *n.* —**be·smirch′ment** *n.*

be·sot (bĭ-sŏt′) *v.* **-sotted, -sotting.** To muddle or stupefy, esp. with liquor.

be·sought (bĭ-sôt′). *p.t.* & *p.p.* of **beseech.**

be·span·gle (bĭ-spăng′gəl) *v.* **-gled, -gling.** To ornament with spangles.

be·spat·ter (bĭ-spăt′ər) *v.* **1.** To soil, as with mud. **2.** To defame.

be·speak (bĭ-spēk′) *v.* **-spoke, -spoken** or **-spoke, -speaking. 1.** To be or give a sign of; indicate. **2.** To reserve. **3.** To foretell.

be·spread (bĭ-sprĕd′) *v.* **-spread, -spreading.** To spread over, usually thickly.

be·sprin·kle (bĭ-sprĭng′kəl) *v.* **-kled, -kling.** To sprinkle over, as with water.

Bes·se·mer converter (bĕs′ə-mər). A large pear-shaped container used in the Bessemer process. [< Sir Henry *Bessemer* (1813–1898), British metallurgist.]

Bessemer process. A method for making steel by blasting compressed air through molten iron to burn out excess carbon and other impurities.

best (bĕst) *adj. superl.* of **good. 1.** Surpassing all others in quality. **2.** Most satisfactory or desirable: *the best solution.* **3.** Greatest: *the best part of a week.* —*adv. superl.* of **well. 1.** Most advantageously. **2.** To the greatest extent; most. —**had best.** Should. —*n.* **1.** The best among several. **2.** The best person or persons. **3.** The best condition: *look your best.* **4.** One's best clothing. **5.** The best effort one can make. **6.** One's regards: *Give them my best.* —**at best.** Under the most favorable conditions. —**for the best.** For the ultimate good. —**get** (or **have) the best of.** To defeat or outwit. —**make the best of.** To do as well as possible under unfavorable conditions. —*v.* To surpass; defeat. [< OE *betest.*]

bes·tial (bĕs′chəl, bĕst′yəl) *adj.* Having the qualities of, or behaving in the manner of, a beast or brute; savage. [< L *bēstia,* BEAST.] —**bes′ti·al′i·ty** *n.* —**bes′tial·ly** *adv.*

be·stir (bĭ-stûr′) *v.* **-stirred, -stirring.** To make active; rouse.

best man. A bridegroom's chief attendant.

be·stow (bĭ-stō′) *v.* To present as a gift or honor; confer. —**be·stow′al** *n.*

be·strew (bĭ-strōō′) *v.* **-strewed, -strewed** or **-strewn, -strewing.** To strew or scatter things profusely.

be·stride (bĭ-strīd′) *v.* **-strode, -stridden, -striding.**

1. To sit or stand on with the legs widely spread; straddle. 2. To step over.

bet (bĕt) *n*. 1. A wager. 2. The event on which a wager is made. 3. The amount risked in a wager. —*v*. **bet, betting.** 1. To make or place a bet (with). 2. To make a bet on (a contestant or an outcome). [Perh short for ABET.] —**bet′tor, bet′ter** *n*.

bet. between.

be•ta (bā′tə, bē′-) *n*. The 2nd letter of the Greek alphabet, representing *b*.

be•ta•ine (bē′tə-ēn′) *n*. A sweet, crystalline alkaloid, $C_5H_{11}NO_2$, occurring in sugar beets and other plants and used in treatment of muscular degeneration. [< L *bēta*, beet.]

be•take (bĭ-tāk′) *v*. **-took, -taken, -taking.** To cause (oneself) to go or move.

beta particle. A high-speed electron or positron.

beta ray. A stream of beta particles, esp. of electrons.

beta rhythm. Also **beta wave.** The second most common waveform occurring in electroencephalograms of the adult brain, having a frequency of 18–30 cycles/second and associated with an alert waking state.

be•tel (bēt′l) *n*. An Asiatic plant, whose leaves are chewed with the **betel nut,** the seed of a palm tree, as a stimulant and narcotic. [Port *betel, betle.*]

bête noire (bĕt nwär′). Someone or something that one esp. dislikes. [F, "black beast."]

beth (bĕt) *n*. The 2nd letter of the Hebrew alphabet, representing *b(bh).*

be•think (bĭ-thĭngk′) *v*. **-thought, -thinking.** To remind (oneself).

Beth•le•hem (bĕth′lĭ-hĕm, bĕth′lē-əm). The Palestinian town where David lived and Jesus was born.

be•tide (bĭ-tīd′) *v*. **-tided, -tiding.** To happen (to); befall. [< OE *tīdan,* to happen. See dā-.]

be•times (bĭ-tīmz′) *adv*. In good time; early.

be•to•ken (bĭ-tō′kən) *v*. To give a sign or portent of. [< OE *bitācnian.*]

be•took (bĭ-tŏŏk′). *p.t.* of betake.

be•tray (bĭ-trā′) *v*. 1. To commit treason against or be a traitor to. 2. To be disloyal or faithless to. 3. To show, reveal, or indicate, esp. unintentionally. 4. To seduce and forsake (a woman). [< ME *trayen,* to betray.] —**be•tray′al** *n*. —**be•tray′er** *n*.

be•troth (bĭ-trōth′, bĭ-trôth′) *v*. To promise to marry. —**be•troth′al** *n*.

be•trothed (bĭ-trōthd′, bĭ-trôtht′) *n*. A person who is engaged to be married.

bet•ter (bĕt′ər) *adj. compar.* of **good.** 1. Greater in excellence or higher in quality. 2. More useful. 3. Larger; greater: *the better part of a summer.* 4. Healthier. —**better off.** In a better condition. —*adv. compar.* of **well.** 1. In a more useful way. 2. To a greater or higher extent. 3. More: *better than a year.* —**go (someone) one better.** To outdo. —**had better.** Ought to. —**think better of.** To change one's mind. —*n*. 1. Something more useful or suitable. 2. Often **betters.** One's superiors, esp. in social standing or intelligence. —**for the better.** Resulting in an improvement. —**get (or have) the better of.** To

gain an advantage over. —*v*. 1. To make or become better. 2. To surpass or exceed. [< OE *betera.* See bhad-.]

bet•ter•ment (bĕt′ər-mənt) *n*. 1. An improvement. 2. Often **betterments.** Any improvement that adds to the value of real property.

be•tween (bĭ-twēn′) *prep*. 1. In the space, time, quantity, or degree of comparison separating. 2. In interaction or interrelation of. —**between you and me.** In confidence. —*adv*. In an intermediate space, position, or time; in the interim. —**in between.** In an intermediate situation. [< OE *betwēonum.*]

Usage: Between (prep.) is always followed by words in the objective case: *between you and me* (not *you and I*).

be•twixt (bĭ-twĭkst′) *adv. & prep. Archaic.* Between. [< OE *betwēohs, betwihs.*]

BeV Billion (10^9) electron volts.

bev•el (bĕv′əl) *n*. 1. The angle or inclination of a line or surface that meets another at any angle but 90°. 2. A rule with an adjustable arm, used to measure or draw angles. —*adj*. Inclined at an angle. —*v*. **-eled** or **-elled, -eling** or **-elling.** 1. To cut at an inclination that forms an angle other than a right angle. 2. To be inclined; slope. [OF *bevel.*]

bev•er•age (bĕv′rĭj, bĕv′ə-rĭj) *n*. A liquid refreshment, usually excluding water. [< OF *bevrage.*]

bev•y (bĕv′ē) *n., pl.* **-ies.** A group, esp. of quail or girls.

be•wail (bĭ-wāl′) *v*. To express sorrow or regret (over); lament. —**be•wail′er** *n*.

be•ware (bĭ-wâr′) *v*. **-wared, -waring.** To be on guard (against); be cautious (of). Used chiefly in the imperative or infinitive.

be•wil•der (bĭ-wĭl′dər) *v*. To confuse or befuddle, esp. with numerous conflicting situations, objects, or statements. [BE- + archaic *wilder,* to stray.] —**be•wil′der•ment** *n*.

be•witch (bĭ-wĭch′) *v*. 1. To place under one's power by magic. 2. To fascinate; charm. [< OE *wiccian,* to bewitch.]

bey (bā) *n*. 1. A provincial governor in the Ottoman Empire. 2. A native ruler of the former kingdom of Tunis. [Turk.]

be•yond (bē-ŏnd′) *prep*. 1. Farther away than; on the far side of. 2. After (a specified time). 3. Outside the limits, reach, or scope of. —*adv*. Farther along. [OE *begeondan.*]

bez•el (bĕz′əl) *n*. 1. A slanting surface on the edge of various cutting tools. 2. The upper, faceted portion of a cut gem. 3. A groove or flange designed to hold the beveled edge of a watch crystal or a gem. [?]

bf, bf., b.f. boldface.

B/F *Accounting.* brought forward.

B.G. brigadier general.

bhang (băng) *n*. A narcotic made from hemp. [< Sk *bhangā,* hemp.]

bhp, b.hp. brake horsepower.

Bhu•tan (bōō-tăn′, -tän′). Also **Bho•tan** (bō-). A kingdom in the Himalayas. Pop. 800,000. Cap. Thimphu. —**Bhu′tan•ese′** *n. & adj.*

bi–, bin–. *comb. form.* 1. Two. 2. **a.** Occurrence in intervals of two. **b.** Occurrence twice during. 3. Occurrence on both sides or di-

---

ô paw, for/oi boy/ou out/ŏŏ took/ōō coo/p pop/r run/s sauce/sh shy/t to/th thin/*th* the/
ŭ cut/ûr fur/v van/w wag/y yes/z size/zh vision/ə ago, item, edible, gallop, circus/

rections. **4.** *Chem.* **a.** An element or group in twice the proportion necessary for stability. **b.** Of organic compounds, a double radical. [< L *bis*, twice.]
Bi bismuth.
bi•a•ly (bē-ä′lē) *n., pl.* **-lys.** A flat roll topped with onion flakes. [< *Bialystok,* Poland.]
bi•an•nu•al (bī-ăn′yōō-əl) *adj.* Happening twice each year; semiannual. See Usage note at **bimonthly.** —**bi•an′nu•al•ly** *adv.*
bi•as (bī′əs) *n.* **1.** A line cutting diagonally across the grain of fabric. **2. a.** Prejudice. **b.** An instance of this. **3.** The fixed voltage applied to an electrode. —*v.* **-ased** or **-assed,** **-asing** or **-assing.** **1.** To prejudice or influence. **2.** To apply a small voltage to (a grid). [< OF *biais,* oblique.] —**bi′as** *adj. & adv.*
bib (bĭb) *n.* **1.** A cloth worn by children to protect clothing during meals. **2.** The part of an apron or overalls covering the chest. —*v.* **bibbed, bibbing.** To drink. [< ME *bibben,* to tipple, drink.] —**bib′ber** *n.*
Bib. Bible; Biblical.
bi•be•lot (bĭb′lō) *n.* A trinket. [< OF *beubelet.*]
bibl., Bibl. Biblical.
Bi•ble (bī′bəl) *n.* **1.** The sacred book of Christianity, a collection of ancient writings including the books of both the Old Testament and the New Testament. **2.** The Old Testament, the sacred book of Judaism; Hebrew Scriptures. [< Gk *(ta) biblia,* "(the) books."] —**Bib′li•cal** (bĭb′lĭ-kəl) *adj.*
biblio–. *comb. form.* Books. [< Gk *biblion,* book.]
bibliog. bibliographer; bibliography.
bib•li•og•ra•phy (bĭb′lē-ŏg′rə-fē) *n., pl.* **-phies.** **1.** A list of the works of an author or publisher or of sources of information in print on a specific subject. **2. a.** The description and identification of the editions, dates of issue, authorship, and typography of books, or other written material. **b.** A compilation of such information. —**bib′li•og′ra•pher** *n.* —**bib′li•o•graph′i•cal** (-lē-ə-grăf′ĭ-kəl), **bib′li•o•graph′ic** *adj.* —**bib′li•o•graph′i•cal•ly** *adv.*
bib•li•o•phile (bĭb′lē-ə-fīl′) *n.* A connoisseur of books.
bib•u•lous (bĭb′yə-ləs) *adj.* Given to convivial drinking. [< L *bibere,* to drink.]
bi•cam•er•al (bī-kăm′ər-əl) *adj.* Composed of two branches: *a bicameral legislature.* [BI- + LL *camera,* room, CHAMBER.]
bi•car•bon•ate of soda (bī-kär′bə-nāt′, -nĭt). Sodium bicarbonate.
bi•cen•ten•ni•al (bī′sĕn-tĕn′ē-əl) *adj.* **1.** Happening once every 200 years. **2.** Lasting for 200 years. **3.** Pertaining to a 200th anniversary. —*n.* A 200th anniversary.
bi•ceps (bī′sĕps′) *n., pl.* **-ceps** or **-cepses** (-sĕp′sĭz). A muscle having two points of origin, esp. the large muscle at the front of the upper arm that flexes the elbow joint. [< L, "two-headed."]
bick•er (bĭk′ər) *v.* To engage in a petty quarrel. —*n.* A petty quarrel. [ME *bikeren,* to attack.]
bi•col•or (bī′kŭl′ər) *adj.* Also **bi•col•ored** (-ərd). Having two colors.

bi•cor•po•ral (bī-kôr′pər-əl) *adj.* Also **bi•cor•po•re•al** (bī′kôr-pôr′ē-əl, -pōr′ē-əl). Having two distinct bodies or main parts.
bi•cus•pid (bī-kŭs′pĭd) *adj.* One of the two-pointed teeth located between the canines and molars.
bi•cy•cle (bī′sĭk′əl, -sĭ-kəl) *n.* A vehicle consisting of a metal frame mounted upon two wire-spoked wheels with rubber tires, a seat, handlebars for steering, and two pedals or a small motor by which it is driven. [F.] —**bi′cy′cle** *v.* (-cled, -cling). —**bi′cy•clist** *n.*
bid (bĭd) *v.* **I. bade, bidden** (bĭd′n) or **bid, bidding.** **1.** To direct; command. **2.** To utter (a greeting). **3.** To invite to attend. **II. bid, bid, bidding.** **1.** To seek to win or attain something; strive. **2.** *Card Games.* To state one's intention to take (tricks of a certain number or suit): *bid four hearts.* **3.** To offer (an amount) as a price. —*n.* **1. a.** An offer of a price, as for a contract. **b.** The amount offered. **2.** An invitation. **3.** *Card Games.* **a.** The act of bidding. **b.** The number of tricks or points declared. **c.** The trump declared. **d.** A player's turn to bid. **4.** An earnest effort; a striving. [< OE *biddan* (see bhedh-²) and < OE *bēodan,* to proclaim, command (see bheudh-).] —**bid′der** *n.*
b.i.d. *Med.* twice a day (L *bis in die*).
bide (bīd) *v.* **bided** or **bode, bided, biding.** **1.** To remain the same. **2.** To stay: *bide at home.* —**bide one's time.** To await. [< OE *bīdan.* See bheidh-.]
bi•en•ni•al (bī-ĕn′ē-əl) *adj.* **1.** Lasting or living for two years. **2.** Happening every second year. —See Usage note at **bimonthly.** —*n.* **1.** An event that occurs once every two years. **2.** A plant that completes its life cycle and dies in its second year. —**bi•en′ni•al•ly** *adv.*
bier (bîr) *n.* A stand on which a coffin is placed to lie in state. [< OE *bēr, bǣr.* See bher-¹.]
bi•fo•cal (bī-fō′kəl) *adj.* **1.** Having two different focal lengths. **2.** Correcting for both near and distant vision. —*n.* **bifocals.** Eyeglasses with bifocal lenses.
bi•fur•cate (bī′fər-kāt′, bī-fûr′kāt′) *v.* **-cated, -cating.** To divide into two parts or branches. [< L *bifurcus,* two-forked.] —**bi′fur•ca′tion** *n.*
big (bĭg) *adj.* **bigger, biggest. 1.** Of considerable size, number, quantity, magnitude, or extent; large. **2.** Grown-up. **3.** Pregnant. **4.** Important. —*adv.* **1.** Boastfully. **2.** Successfully. [ME, strong, stout, full-grown.] —**big′gish** *adj.* —**big′ness** *n.*
big•a•my (bĭg′ə-mē) *n., pl.* **-mies.** The crime of marrying one person while still married to another. [< OF *bigame,* bigamous.] —**big′a•mist** *n.* —**big′a•mous** *adj.*
Big Dipper. An asterism in Ursa Major, consisting of seven stars forming a dipper-shaped configuration.
big•horn (bĭg′hôrn′) *n.* A wild mountain sheep of W North America, having large, curved horns.
bight (bīt) *n.* **1.** A loop in a rope. **2.** A curve in a shoreline. **3.** A bay. [< OE *byht,* bend, angle.]
big•ot (bĭg′ət) *n.* An intolerant person, esp. in

BOOKS OF THE BIBLE

Bible translation is one of the world's oldest scholarly activities; the tradition runs back to the 3rd century B.C. As of the present date, at least some book of the Bible has been translated into more than 1,400 languages. Since there are more than 3,000 languages in the world, it is reasonable to assume that the field will continue to expand. English has an uncommonly rich heritage in this respect; since the metrical paraphrases and Gospels of Anglo-Saxon times, the entire book has been translated again and again. The Jewish Publication Society *Holy Scriptures According to the Masoretic Text*, issued in 1916 by a committee of Jewish scholars, is accepted as standard in American Judaism, and its contents are listed here. For Roman Catholics, both the Douay Version (1582–1610) and the almost completed Confraternity Old and New Testaments have been officially approved for teaching and Church use. The new Revised Standard Version, Catholic Edition (1946–54), is also approved but has as yet gained universal acceptance only among scholars. Protestants may use either the King James Bible (or Authorized Version, as it is often called, especially in Great Britain), which appeared in 1611 under the patronage of James I; or they may use the Revised Standard Version (1946-52). The following table presents the contents as listed in the Douay and King James Versions because they have the longest tradition of general acceptance and the widest range of distribution.

HEBREW SCRIPTURES

Genesis	Micah	II Kings	Song of Songs
Exodus	Nahum	Isaiah	Ruth
Leviticus	Habakkuk	Jeremiah	Lamentations
Numbers	Zephaniah	Ezekiel	Ecclesiastes
Deuteronomy	Haggai	THE TWELVE	Esther
Joshua	Zechariah	Hosea	Daniel
Judges	Malachi	Joel	Ezra
I Samuel	Psalms	Amos	Nehemiah
II Samuel	Proverbs	Obadiah	I Chronicles
I Kings	Job	Jonah	II Chronicles

OLD TESTAMENT

DOUAY VERSION	KING JAMES VERSION	DOUAY VERSION	KING JAMES VERSION
Genesis	Genesis	Canticle of Canticles	Song of Solomon
Exodus	Exodus	Wisdom	
Leviticus	Leviticus	Ecclesiasticus	
Numbers	Numbers	Isaias	Isaiah
Deuteronomy	Deuteronomy	Jeremias	Jeremiah
Josue	Joshua	Lamentations	Lamentations
Judges	Judges	Baruch	
Ruth	Ruth	Ezechiel	Ezekiel
I Kings	I Samuel	Daniel	Daniel
II Kings	II Samuel	Osee	Hosea
III Kings	I Kings	Joel	Joel
IV Kings	II Kings	Amos	Amos
I Paralipomenon	I Chronicles	Abdias	Obadiah
II Paralipomenon	II Chronicles	Jonas	Jonah
I Esdras	Ezra	Micheas	Micah
II Esdras, alias Nehemias	Nehemiah	Nahum	Nahum
Tobias		Habacuc	Habakkuk
Judith		Sophonias	Zephaniah
Esther	Esther	Aggeus	Haggai
Job	Job	Zacharias	Zechariah
Psalms	Psalms	Malachias	Malachi
Proverbs	Proverbs	I Machabees	
Ecclesiastes	Ecclesiastes	II Machabees	

NEW TESTAMENT

Matthew.	Matthew	I Timothy	I Timothy
Mark	Mark	II Timothy	II Timothy
Luke	Luke	Titus	Titus
John	John	Philemon	Philemon
The Acts of the Apostles	Acts	To the Hebrews	Hebrews
THE EPISTLES		The Epistle of James	James
Paul to the Romans	Romans	I Peter	I Peter
I Corinthians	I Corinthians	II Peter	II Peter
II Corinthians	II Corinthians	I John	I John
Galatians	Galatians	II John	II John
Ephesians	Ephesians	III John	III John
Philippians	Philippians	Jude	Jude
Colossians	Colossians	The Apocalypse of	Revelation
I Thessalonians	I Thessalonians	St. John the Apostle	
II Thessalonians	II Thessalonians		

Part of a page from a Spanish Hebrew Bible, 1479

matters of religion, race, or politics. [< OF, a pejorative term for the Normans.] —**big'ot·ed** *adj.* —**big'ot·ry** *n.*

big·wig (bĭg'wĭg') *n. Informal.* An important person; dignitary.

bike (bīk) *n. Informal.* A bicycle. —**bike** *v.* (**biked, biking**).

bi·ki·ni (bĭ-kē'nē) *n.* A woman's brief two-piece bathing suit. [< *Bikini,* an atoll in the Pacific Ocean.]

bi·lat·er·al (bī-lăt'ər-əl) *adj.* **1.** Of or having two sides. **2.** Affecting two sides or parties equally. —**bi·lat'er·al·ly** *adv.*

bile (bīl) *n.* **1.** A bitter, alkaline, brownish-yellow or greenish-yellow liquid that is secreted by the liver and aids in the digestion of fats. **2.** Irascibility; ill humor. [< L *bīlis.*]

bilge (bĭlj) *n.* **1.** The lowest inner part of a ship's hull. **2.** Water that collects in this part. **3.** *Slang.* Stupid talk; nonsense. [Prob var of BULGE.]

bi·lin·gual (bī-lĭng'gwəl) *adj.* Expressed in or able to speak two languages. [L *bilinguis.*]

bil·ious (bĭl'yəs) *adj.* **1.** Of, pertaining to, or containing bile. **2.** Pertaining to gastric distress caused by sluggishness of the liver or gall bladder. **3.** Irascible.

bil·i·ru·bin (bĭl'ə-rōō'bĭn, bī'lə-) *n.* A red-

dish-yellow organic compound, $C_{33}H_{36}O_6N_4$, derived from hemoglobin during normal and pathological destruction of erythrocytes. [< L *bīlis,* BILE + *ruber,* red.]

bilk (bĭlk) *v.* To defraud, cheat, or swindle. [?]

bill¹ (bĭl) *n.* **1.** A statement of charges. **2.** A list of particulars, as a playbill or menu. **3.** An advertising poster or similar public notice. **4.** A piece of paper money. **5.** A bill of exchange. **6.** A draft of a law presented for approval to a legislature. **7.** *Law.* A document containing a formal statement of a case or complaint. —*v.* **1.** To present a statement of costs to. **2.** To enter on a bill. **3.** To advertise by public notice. [< ML *billa.*]

bill² (bĭl) *n.* **1.** The beak of a bird. **2.** A beak-like part. —*v.* To touch beaks together. —**bill and coo.** To kiss and murmur amorously. [< OE *bile.* See *bhei-².*]

bill·board (bĭl'bôrd', -bōrd') *n.* A structure for the display of advertising posters.

bil·let (bĭl'ĭt) *n.* **1.** A lodging for troops. **2.** A written order directing that such quarters be provided. **3.** A position of employment. —*v.* To assign quarters to by billet. [ME *bylett.*]

bil·let-doux (bĭl'ā-dōō', bĭl'ē-) *n., pl.* **billets-doux** (bĭl'ā-dōō/z/', bĭl'ē-). A love letter. [F.]

bill·fold (bĭl'fōld') *n.* A wallet.

ă pat/ā ate/âr care/ä bar/b bib/ch chew/d deed/ĕ pet/ē be/f fit/g gag/h hat/hw what/
ĭ pit/ī pie/îr pier/j judge/k kick/l lid, fatal/m mum/n no, sudden/ng sing/ŏ pot/ō go/

bil•liards (bĭl'yərdz) *n. (takes sing. v.).* A game in which a cue is used to hit three balls against one another or the side cushions of a rectangular table. [< F *billard*, bent stick, billiard cue.] —**bil'liard** *adj.*

bil•lings•gate (bĭl'ĭngz-gāt') *n.* Foul-mouthed abuse. [< *Billingsgate*, fishmarket of London.]

bil•lion (bĭl'yən) *n.* **1.** The cardinal number represented by 1 followed by 9 zeros. **2.** *Brit.* The cardinal number represented by 1 followed by 12 zeros. [< BI- + (M)ILLION.] —**bil'lion** *adj.*

bil•lionth (bĭl'yənth) *n.* **1.** The ordinal number one billion in a series. **2.** One of a billion equal parts. —**bil'lionth** *adj. & adv.*

bill of exchange. A written order directing that a specified sum of money be paid to a specified person.

bill of fare. A menu.

bill of lading. A document listing and acknowledging receipt of goods for shipment.

Bill of Rights. The first ten amendments to the Constitution of the United States.

bil•low (bĭl'ō) *n.* **1.** A large wave. **2.** A great swell or surge, as of smoke. —*v.* To surge, roll, or rise in billows. [< ON *bylgja*.]

bil•ly (bĭl'ē) *n., pl.* **-lies.** *Informal.* A short wooden club. [Prob < the name *Billy.*]

billy goat. A male goat.

bi•mah. Variant of bema.

bi•met•al•lism (bī-mĕt'l-ĭz'əm) *n.* The policy of using gold and silver as the monetary standard of currency and value. —**bi•met'al•list** *n.*

bi•month•ly (bī-mŭnth'lē) *adj.* Happening every two months. —*adv.* Once every two months. —*n., pl.* **-lies.** A publication issued bimonthly.

Usage: Bimonthly, in careful usage, means "once in two months"; *biweekly,* "once in two weeks"; and *biyearly,* "once in two years." They are not interchangeable with *semimonthly, semiweekly,* and *semiyearly,* which refer to occurrence twice a month, week, and year, respectively. A similar distinction exists between *biennial* (once in two years, lasting two years) and *biannual* (twice a year).

bin (bĭn) *n.* A storage receptacle or container. [< OE *binne,* basket, crib. See bhendh-.]

bin—. Variant of bi-.

bi•na•ry (bī'nə-rē) *adj.* **1.** Having two distinct parts. **2.** Having a numerical base of 2. [< L *bīnī,* two by two.]

bin•au•ral (bī-nôr'əl, bĭn-ôr'əl) *adj.* **1.** Hearing with or related to two ears. **2.** Pertaining to sound transmission from two sources.

bind (bīnd) *v.* **bound, binding. 1.** To tie or encircle, as with a rope. **2.** To bandage. **3.** To hold or restrain. **4.** To compel, as with a sense of duty. **5.** To place under legal obligation. **6.** To make or become solid. **7.** To enclose and fasten (a book) between covers. **8.** To reinforce with an edge or border. **9.** To constipate. [< OE *bindan.* See bhendh-.] —**bind'a•ble** *adj.* —**bind'er** *n.*

bind•er•y (bīn'də-rē) *n., pl.* **-ies.** A shop where books are bound.

binge (bĭnj) *n. Slang.* A carousal. [Brit dial *binge,* to fill a boat with water, to drink.]

bin•oc•u•lar (bə-nŏk'yə-lər, bī-) *adj.* **1.** Involving both eyes. **2.** Having two eyes arranged to produce stereoscopic vision. —*n.* Often **binoculars.** An optical device, such as field glasses, designed for use by both eyes at once.

bi•no•mi•al (bī-nō'mē-əl) *adj.* Consisting of or pertaining to two names or terms. —*n.* A mathematical expression consisting of two terms connected by a plus or minus sign. [BI- + Gk *nomos,* portion, part.]

bio—. *comb. form.* Life or living organisms. [< Gk *bios,* life.]

bi•o•chem•is•try (bī'ō-kĕm'ĭs-trē) *n.* The chemistry of biological substances and processes. —**bi'o•chem'i•cal** *adj.* —**bi'o•chem'i•cal•ly** *adv.* —**bi'o•chem'ist** *n.*

biog. biographer; biographical; biography.

bi•og•ra•phy (bī-ŏg'rə-fē, bē-) *n., pl.* **-phies.** A written account of a person's life; a life history. —**bi•og'ra•pher** *n.* —**bi'o•graph'ic** (-ə-grăf'-ĭk), **bi'o•graph'i•cal** *adj.*

bi•o•de•grad•a•ble (bī'ō-dī-grā'də-bəl) *adj.* Capable of being decomposed by natural biological processes: *a biodegradable detergent.*

bi•o•feed•back (bī'ō-fēd'băk') *n.* A technique whereby one seeks to consciously regulate a bodily function thought to be involuntary, as heartbeat, by using an instrument to monitor the function.

biol. biological; biologist; biology.

bi•ol•o•gy (bī-ŏl'ə-jē) *n.* **1.** The science of life processes and living organisms. **2.** The life processes of any category of living organisms. —**bi'o•log'i•cal** (-lŏj'ĭ-kəl) *adj.* —**bi•ol'o•gist** *n.*

bi•on•ic (bī-ŏn'ĭk) *adj.* Using or containing mechanical equipment to strengthen or replace part of a living creature. [BI(O-) + (ELECTR-) ONIC.]

bi•o•phys•ics (bī'ō-fĭz'ĭks) *n. (takes sing. v.).* The physics of biological processes. —**bi'o•phys'i•cist** *n.*

bi•op•sy (bī'ŏp'sē) *n., pl.* **-sies.** Examination of tissues removed from the body as an aid to medical diagnosis. —**bi•op'sic** (bī-ŏp'sĭk) *adj.*

bi•par•ti•san (bī-pär'tə-zən) *adj.* Consisting of or supported by members of two parties. —**bi•par'ti•san•ship'** *n.*

bi•par•tite (bī-pär'tīt') *adj.* **1.** Having two parts. **2.** Having two parts, one for each party: *a bipartite treaty.* [< L *bipartīre,* to divide into two parts.] —**bi'par•ti'tion** (-tĭsh'ən) *n.*

bi•ped (bī'pĕd') *n.* A two-footed animal.

bi•plane (bī'plān') *n.* An airplane with single or paired wings at two different levels.

bi•po•lar (bī-pō'lər) *adj.* **1.** Pertaining to or having two poles. **2.** Relating to or involving both of the earth's poles.

bi•ra•cial (bī-rā'shəl) *adj.* Involving members of two races. —**bi•ra'cial•ism'** *n.*

birch (bûrch) *n.* **1.** Any of several trees with papery, easily peeled bark. **2.** The hard wood of such a tree. **3.** A birch rod used for whipping. —*v.* To whip (someone) with a birch rod. [< OE *birce, beorce.* See bherəg-.]

bird (bûrd) *n.* A warm-blooded, egg-laying, feathered vertebrate with forelimbs modified to form wings. [< OE *brid.*]

ô paw, for/oi boy/ou out/ŏŏ took/ōō coo/p pop/r run/s sauce/sh shy/t to/th thin/*th* the/ ŭ cut/ûr fur/v van/w wag/y yes/z size/zh vision/ə ago, item, edible, gallop, circus/

bird•ie (bûr′dē) *n. Golf.* One stroke under par for any hole.

bird•lime (bûrd′līm′) *n.* A sticky substance smeared on twigs to capture small birds.

bird of paradise. Any of various birds of New Guinea and Australia with characteristically showy plumage.

bird's-eye (bûrdz′ī′) *adj.* 1. Patterned with small spots: *bird's-eye maple.* 2. Seen from high above: *a bird's-eye view.*

bi•ret•ta (bə-rĕt′ə) *n.* A square cap worn esp. by Roman Catholic clergymen. [< ML *birretum,* cap.]

Bir•ming•ham (bûr′mĭng-hăm′). 1. A city in N Alabama. Pop. 301,000. 2. (bûr′mĭng-əm). The second-largest city in England. Pop. 1,103,000.

birth (bûrth) *n.* 1. a. The act or condition of being born. b. The act or process of bearing young. 2. Origin; ancestry. 3. A beginning. [< ON *burdhr.*]

birth•day (bûrth′dā′) *n.* The day or anniversary of one's birth.

birth•mark (bûrth′märk′) *n.* A mark present on the body from birth.

birth•place (bûrth′plās′) *n.* The place where someone is born or where something originates.

birth•rate (bûrth′rāt′) *n.* The number of births in a specified population per unit time, esp. per year.

birth•right (bûrth′rīt′) *n.* Any privilege to which a person is entitled by birth.

birth•stone (bûrth′stōn′) *n.* A jewel associated with the month of one's birth, thought to bring him good luck.

bis•cuit (bĭs′kĭt) *n.* 1. A small cake of bread leavened with baking powder or soda. 2. *Chiefly Brit.* A cracker or cooky. [< ML **biscoctus (panis),* "twice-cooked (bread)."]

bi•sect (bī′sĕkt′, bī-sĕkt′) *v.* 1. To divide or cut into two equal parts. 2. To split; fork. [BI- + -SECT.] **—bi′sec′tion** *n.* **—bi′sec′tion•al** *adj.* **—bi′sec′tion•al•ly** *adv.*

bi•sec•tor (bī′sĕk′tər, bī-sĕk′-) *n.* A straight line that bisects an angle.

bi•sex•u•al (bī-sĕk′shōō-əl) *adj.* 1. Pertaining to both sexes. 2. Having both male and female organs. 3. Sexually attracted to members of both sexes.

bish•op (bĭsh′əp) *n.* 1. A high-ranking Christian clergyman, usually in charge of a diocese. 2. A chessman that can move diagonally across any number of unoccupied spaces of the same color. [< VL **biscopus.*]

bish•op•ric (bĭsh′əp-rĭk) *n.* 1. The office of a bishop. 2. The diocese of a bishop.

Bis•marck (bĭz′märk). The capital of North Dakota. Pop. 35,000.

Bis•marck (bĭz′märk), **Otto von.** 1815–1898. First chancellor of the German Empire.

bis•muth (bĭz′məth) *n. Symbol* **Bi** A white, crystalline, brittle, metallic element used in alloys to form sharp castings for objects sensitive to high temperatures and in various low-melting alloys for fire-safety devices. Atomic number 83, atomic weight 208.980. [NL *bisemutum.*] **—bis′muth•al** *adj.*

bi•son (bī′sən, -zən) *n.* A shaggy-maned, short-horned bovine mammal of W North America. [L *bisōn.*]

bisque¹ (bĭsk) *n.* 1. A thick cream soup usually made with shellfish. 2. Any thick cream soup. 3. Ice cream mixed with crushed macaroons or nuts. [F.]

bisque² (bĭsk) *n.* Fired unglazed pottery. [< BISCUIT.]

bis•tro (bē′strō, bĭs′trō) *n., pl.* **-tros.** A small bar or restaurant. [F.]

bit¹ (bĭt) *n.* 1. A small piece or amount. 2. A moment. 3. a. An entertainment routine. b. A short scene or episode in a play or movie. 4. *Informal.* A particular kind of activity. 5. *Informal.* An amount equal to ⅛ of a dollar: *two bits a head.* **—do one's bit.** To make one's contribution. [< OE *bita,* piece bitten off. See **bheid-.**]

bit² (bĭt) *n.* 1. A pointed and threaded tool for drilling and boring. 2. The metal mouthpiece of a bridle. [< OE *bite,* a sting, bite. See **bheid-.**]

bit³ (bĭt) *n.* 1. A single character of a computer language having just two characters, such as either of the binary digits 0 or 1. 2. A unit of information storage capacity, as of a computer memory. [BI(NARY) (DIGI)T.]

bitch (bĭch) *n.* 1. A female dog. 2. *Slang.* A spiteful woman. 3. *Slang.* A complaint. 4. *Slang.* A confounding problem. *—v. Slang.* To complain. [< OE *bicce,* female dog < Gmc **bekjōn-.*]

bitch•y (bĭch′ē) *adj.* **-ier, -iest.** *Slang.* Spiteful, malicious, or ill-tempered.

bite (bīt) *v.* **bit, bitten** or **bit** (bĭt′n) or **bit** (bĭt) (see Usage note below), **biting.** 1. To cut or tear (something) with or as if with the teeth. 2. To sting, as does a mosquito. 3. To corrode. 4. To cause or have a stinging effect or a sharp taste. 5. To take bait. **—bite the dust.** To fall dead. *—n.* 1. The act of biting. 2. An injury resulting from biting. 3. a. A stinging or smarting sensation. b. An incisive, penetrating quality. 4. A mouthful. 5. A light meal or snack. 6. The angle at which the upper and lower teeth meet. [< OE *bītan.* See **bheid-.**]

Usage: Of the two participles *bitten* and *bit,* only *bitten* is now standard in the passive. *The boy was bitten* (not *bit*) *by the dog.*

bit•ter (bĭt′ər) *adj.* 1. Having a taste that is sharp and unpleasant. 2. Causing sharp pain to the body or discomfort to the mind. 3. Exhibiting strong animosity. 4. Marked by resentfulness. [< OE *biter.* See **bheid-.**] **—bit′ter•ly** *adv.* **—bit′ter•ness** *n.*

bit•tern (bĭt′ərn) *n.* A long-necked, brownish wading bird with a resonant cry. [< VL **būtitaurus,* "bird that bellows like an ox."]

bit•ter•root (bĭt′ər-rōōt′, -rŏŏt′) *n.* A plant of W North America with showy pink or white flowers.

bit•ters (bĭt′ərz) *pl.n.* A bitter, usually alcoholic liquid made with herbs or roots and used in cocktails or as a tonic.

bit•ter•sweet (bĭt′ər-swēt′) *n.* 1. A woody vine having yellowish fruits that split open to expose seeds with fleshy red coverings. 2. A

ă pat/ā ate/âr care/ä bar/b bib/ch chew/d deed/ĕ pet/ē be/f fit/g gag/h hat/hw what/
ĭ pit/ī pie/îr pier/j judge/k kick/l lid, fatal/m mum/n no, sudden/ng sing/ŏ pot/ō go/

species of nightshade with purple flowers and poisonous red berries. —*adj.* Bitter and sweet at the same time.

bi·tu·men (bĭ-t/y/o͞o′mən) *n.* Any of various mixtures of hydrocarbons found in asphalt and tar and used for surfacing roads and waterproofing. [< L *bitūmen.*]

bi·tu·mi·nous (bĭ-t/y/o͞o′mə-nəs, bī-) *adj.* 1. Like or containing bitumen. 2. Pertaining to a mineral coal that burns with a smoky, yellow flame.

bi·va·lent (bī-vā′lənt) *adj.* Having valence 2.

bi·valve (bī′vălv′) *n.* A mollusk, as an oyster or clam, with a shell having two hinged parts. —**bi′valve′** *adj.*

biv·ou·ac (bĭv′o͞o-ăk, bĭv′wăk) *n.* A temporary encampment made by soldiers in the field. —*v.* -acked, -acking. To encamp in a bivouac. [F.]

bi·week·ly (bī-wēk′lē) *adj.* Happening every two weeks. See Usage note at **bimonthly.** —*n., pl.* -lies. A publication issued every two weeks. —**bi·week′ly** *adv.*

bi·year·ly (bī-yîr′lē) *adj.* Happening every two years. See Usage note at **bimonthly.** —**bi·year′ly** *adv.*

bi·zarre (bĭ-zär′) *adj.* Strikingly unconventional; odd. [F, orig "handsome," "brave."]

Bi·zet (bē-zā′), **Georges.** 1838–1875. French composer.

Bk berkelium.

bk. 1. bank. 2. book.

bkg. banking.

bkpg. bookkeeping.

bl. 1. black. 2. blue.

B/L bill of lading.

blab (blăb) *v.* **blabbed, blabbing.** 1. To reveal (a secret), esp. through unreserved talk. 2. To chatter indiscreetly. [ME *blabben.*] —**blab′ber** *n.* —**blab′by** *adj.*

blab·ber (blăb′ər) *v.* To chatter. [ME *blabberen.*]

black (blăk) *adj.* 1. Being of the darkest achromatic visual value; producing or reflecting comparatively little light and having no predominant hue. 2. Having no light whatsoever. 3. Negroid. 4. Dark in color. 5. Evil. 6. Cheerless. 7. Sullen. 8. Calamitous. —*n.* 1. An achromatic color value of minimum lightness or maximum darkness; one extreme of the neutral gray series of colors, the opposite being white. 2. A Negro. —**in the black.** Solvent. —*v.* To make black. [< OE *blæc.* See bhel-¹.] —**black′ish** *adj.* —**black′ness** *n.*

black-and-blue (blăk′ən-blo͞o′) *adj.* Discolored from a bruise.

black·ball (blăk′bôl′) *n.* 1. A small black ball used as a negative ballot. 2. A vote against admission of an applicant. —**black′ball′** *v.* —**black′ball′er** *n.*

black·ber·ry (blăk′běr′ē, -bər-ē) *n.* 1. The blackish, glossy, edible berry of a thorny plant. 2. The plant itself.

black·bird (blăk′bûrd′) *n.* Any of various birds having black or predominantly black plumage.

black·board (blăk′bôrd′, -bōrd′) *n.* A surface for writing on with chalk.

black·en (blăk′ən) *v.* 1. To make or become black. 2. To defame. —**black′en·er** *n.*

black eye. A bruised discoloration of the flesh surrounding the eye.

black-eyed Susan. A plant having daisylike flowers with orange-yellow rays and dark-brown centers.

black·guard (blăg′ərd, -ärd) *n.* A scoundrel. [Orig, the menials of a noble household.]

black·head (blăk′hĕd′) *n.* A plug of dried fatty matter capped with blackened dust and epithelial debris that clogs a skin pore.

black·jack¹ (blăk′jăk′) *n.* A small leather-covered bludgeon with a flexible handle.

black·jack² (blăk′jăk′) *n.* A card game in which the object is to accumulate cards with a total count nearer to 21 than that of the dealer.

black light. Invisible ultraviolet or infrared radiation.

black·list (blăk′lĭst′) *n.* A list of disapproved persons. —*v.* To place (a name) on a blacklist.

black magic. Magic as practiced in league with the Devil; witchcraft.

black·mail (blăk′māl′) *n.* Extortion by threat of exposure. [BLACK + ME *maill,* tribute.] —**black′mail′** *v.* —**black′mail′er** *n.*

black market. A market in which goods are sold in violation of restrictions. —**black marketer.** —**black marketeer.**

Black Muslim. A member of the **Nation of Islam.**

black·out (blăk′out′) *n.* 1. The extinguishing or concealing of lights that might be visible to enemy aircraft during an air raid. 2. A temporary loss of consciousness. 3. A stoppage, as of news.

Black Power. A movement among American Negroes to achieve political power without integration.

Black Sea. A large inland sea between Europe and Asia Minor.

black sheep. A person considered disgraceful by his family.

black·smith (blăk′smĭth′) *n.* One who forges and shapes iron with an anvil and hammer. [ME *blaksmith,* "a worker in black metal" (iron).]

black·thorn (blăk′thôrn′) *n.* A thorny shrub with white flowers and bluish-black, plumlike fruit.

black·top (blăk′tŏp′) *n.* A bituminous material, such as asphalt, used to pave roads. —**black′top′** *v.*

black widow. A black and red spider of which the female is extremely venomous.

blad·der (blăd′ər) *n.* 1. Any of various distensible membranous sacs found in most animals, esp. the urinary bladder. 2. Anything resembling a sac. 3. *Pathol.* A blister, pustule, or cyst filled with fluid or air. [< OE *blædre.* See bhlē-².]

blade (blād) *n.* 1. The flat-edged cutting part of a sharpened tool or weapon. 2. A similar flat, thin part or structure. 3. A dashing young man. [< OE *blæd,* leaf, blade. See bhel-³.] —**blad′ed** *adj.*

blain (blān) *n.* A skin sore; blister; blotch. [< OE *blegen,* a swelling.]

ŏ paw, for/oi boy/ou out/o͞o took/o͞o coo/p pop/r run/s sauce/sh shy/t to/th thin/*th* the/ ŭ cut/ûr fur/v van/w wag/y yes/z size/zh vision/ə ago, item, edible, gallop, circus/

Blake (blāk), **William.** 1757–1827. English poet and engraver.

blame (blām) v. blamed, blaming. 1. To hold responsible. 2. To censure. —n. 1. Responsibility for a fault or error. 2. Censure. [< OF blamer, blasmer.] —blam′er n.

blame·wor·thy (blām′wûr′thē) adj. Deserving of blame. —blame′wor′thi·ness n.

blanch (blănch, blänch) v. 1. To make or become pale or white. 2. To remove the skin from by immersing in hot water: blanch almonds. [< OF blanc, white.]

blanc·mange (blə-mänj′) n. A flavored and sweetened milk pudding, thickened with cornstarch. [< OF blancmanger, "white food."]

bland (blănd) adj. 1. Characterized by a moderate or tranquil quality. 2. Lacking a distinctive character. [L blandus, flattering, "soft-spoken."] —bland′ly adv. —bland′ness n.

blan·dish (blăn′dĭsh) v. To coax by flattery; cajole. [< L blandīrī < blandus, BLAND.] —blan′dish·er n. —blan′dish·ment n.

blank (blăngk) adj. 1. Bearing no writing or marking of any kind. 2. Not filled in: a blank questionnaire. 3. Having no finishing grooves: a blank key. 4. Expressing nothing; vacant. 5. Devoid of activity. 6. Complete: a blank refusal. —n. 1. An empty space. 2. a. A space to be filled in on a document. b. A document having one or more such spaces. 3. An unfinished article, such as a key form. 4. A gun cartridge with a charge of powder but no bullet. 5. A dash indicating omission of a word or letter. 6. The center white circle of a target. —draw a blank. Informal. To fail utterly. —v. 1. To remove from view. 2. To prevent (an opponent in a game or sport) from scoring. [ME blaunk, white, not written on.] —blank′ly adv. —blank′ness n.

blan·ket (blăng′kĭt) n. 1. A piece of wool or other thick cloth used as a covering for warmth, esp. on a bed. 2. A thick layer that covers. —adj. Covering a wide range of conditions. —v. To cover with or as if with a blanket. [ME, orig, a white woolen material.]

blank verse. Verse consisting of unrhymed iambic lines.

blare (blâr) v. blared, blaring. To sound or utter loudly. [ME bleren, to bellow.]

blar·ney (blär′nē) n. Smooth, flattering talk. [< the Blarney Stone, in Blarney, Ireland which is said to impart certain skills to those who kiss it.]

bla·sé (blä-zā′, blä′zā) adj. Having a cynically jaded manner. [< F blaser, to blunt, surfeit.]

blas·pheme (blăs-fēm′) v. -phemed, -pheming. To speak of (God or something sacred) in an irreverent or forbidden manner. [< Gk blasphēmein, to reproach.] —blas·phem′er n. —blas′phe·mous (blăs′fə-məs) adj. —blas′phe·mous·ly adv. —blas′phe·my n.

blast (blăst, bläst) n. 1. A strong gust of wind. 2. A forcible stream of air from an opening, esp. one in a blast furnace to aid combustion. 3. The sound produced by the blowing of a whistle. 4. An explosion. 5. A verbal assault. 6. Slang. A big or wild party. —(at) full blast. At full capacity. —v. 1. To explode. 2. To

blight; wither. 3. To criticize vigorously. 4. Slang. To damn. [< OE blæst. See bhlē-².]

blas·te·ma (blă-stē′mə) n., pl. -mas or -mata (-mə-tə). A segregated region of embryonic cells from which a specific organ develops. [< Gk blastēma, offspring, offshoot.]

blast off. To commence flight, as a rocket or space vehicle.

blast-off (blăst′ôf′, bläst′-) n. Also blast-off. The launching of a rocket or space vehicle.

bla·tant (blā′tənt) adj. 1. Unpleasantly loud. 2. Offensively conspicuous; obvious. [< L blatīre, to blab, gossip.] —bla′tant·ly adv.

blath·er (blăth′ər) v. To speak foolishly or nonsensically. [< ON bladhra, to prattle.] —blath′er n. —blath′er·er n.

blaze¹ (blāz) n. 1. A burst of fire. 2. Any bright, hot light. 3. A destructive fire, esp. one that spreads rapidly. 4. A sudden outburst, as of emotion. —v. blazed, blazing. 1. To burn with a bright flame. 2. To shine brightly. 3. To be deeply excited, as by emotion. [< OE blæse, torch, bright fire. See bhel-¹.]

blaze² (blāz) n. 1. A white spot, as on the face of a horse. 2. A mark cut on a tree to indicate a trail. —v. blazed, blazing. To indicate (a trail) by marking trees with cuts. [Prob < MLG bles.]

blaz·er (blā′zər) n. An informal sport jacket.

bla·zon (blā′zən) n. 1. A coat of arms. 2. A splendid display. —v. To adorn with or as if with blazons. [< ME blasoun, shield, coat of arms.]

bldg. building.

bleach (blēch) v. To make or become white or colorless. —n. A chemical agent used for bleaching. [< OE blǣcan. See bhel-¹.]

bleach·ers (blē′chərz) pl.n. An unroofed outdoor grandstand.

bleak (blēk) adj. 1. Exposed to the elements; barren. 2. Cold and cutting. 3. Gloomy and somber. [< ON bleikr, shining, white.]

blear (blîr) v. 1. To blur (the eyes) with or as with tears. 2. To blur; dim. [ME bleren.] —blear′i·ness n. —blear′y adj.

bleat (blēt) n. The characteristic cry of a goat, sheep, or calf. —v. To utter such a sound. [< OE blǣtan. See bhlē-¹.]

bleed (blēd) v. bled (blĕd), bleeding. 1. To lose or extract blood. 2. To feel sympathetic grief: My heart bleeds for you. 3. To exude or extract sap. 4. Slang. To pay out or extort money, esp. an exorbitant amount. 5. To become mixed or run, as dyes in wet cloth. 6. To draw a fluid from; drain. [< OE blēdan < Gmc *blōthjan.]

bleed·er (blē′dər) n. A hemophiliac.

bleed·ing-heart (blē′dĭng-härt′) n. A garden plant with nodding, pink flowers.

blem·ish (blĕm′ĭsh) n. A flaw or disfigurement. [< OF blemir, blesmir, to make pale.]

blench¹ (blĕnch) v. To draw back or shy away, as from fear; flinch. [< OE blencan, to deceive.]

blench² (blĕnch) v. To turn pale; blanch.

blend (blĕnd) v. 1. To make into or become a uniform mixture. 2. To become merged into one. —n. 1. That which is blended. 2. Ling. A word produced from parts of other words, as

---

smog from *smoke* and *fog.* [< ON *blanda.*] —blend'er *n.*

bleph•a•ri•tis (blĕf'ə-rī'tĭs) *n.* Inflammation of the eyelid. [< Gk *blepharon,* eyelid.]

bless (blĕs) *v.* **blessed** or **blest** (blĕst), **blessing.** 1. To make holy; sanctify. 2. To make the sign of the cross over. 3. To invoke divine favor upon. 4. To honor as holy; glorify. 5. To confer well-being upon. 6. To favor, as with talent. [< OE *blētsian* < Gmc *blōthisōjan,* "to hallow with blood."] —**bless'ed** (blĕs'ĭd) *adj.* —**bless'ed•ly** *adv.*

Blessed Sacrament. *R.C.Ch.* The consecrated Host.

Blessed Virgin. The Virgin Mary.

bless•ing (blĕs'ĭng) *n.* 1. The act or words of one who blesses. 2. An expression of good wishes. 3. A special favor granted by God. 4. Anything contributing to happiness. 5. Approbation. 6. A short prayer at mealtime.

blew (blōō). *p.t.* of **blow.**

blight (blīt) *n.* 1. A destructive plant disease. 2. An injurious environmental condition. 3. One that withers hopes or impairs growth. [?] —**blight** *v.*

blimp (blĭmp) *n.* A buoyant aircraft. [Prob (type) B + LIMP.]

blind (blīnd) *adj.* 1. Without the sense or use of sight. 2. Of or for sightless persons. 3. Performed without preparation: *a blind attempt.* 4. Not based on reason or evidence: *blind faith.* 5. Acting without human control: *blind fate.* 6. Hidden from sight. 7. Closed at one end. —*n.* 1. Something that shuts out light. 2. A shelter for concealing hunters. —*v.* 1. To deprive of sight. 2. To dazzle. 3. To deprive (a person) of his mental powers. [< OE, blind, obscure. See bhel-¹.] —**blind'ness** *n.*

blind date. *Informal.* A social engagement between a man and a woman who have not previously met.

blind•ers (blīn'dərs) *pl.n.* A pair of leather flaps attached to a horse's bridle to curtail side vision.

blind•fold (blīnd'fōld') *v.* 1. To cover the eyes with or as if with a bandage. 2. To hamper the sight or comprehension of. —*n.* A bandage over the eyes. —*adj.* 1. With eyes covered. 2. Reckless. [< OE *geblindfellian,* "to strike blind."]

blind•man's buff (blīnd'mănz'). A game in which one person, blindfolded, tries to catch and identify one of the other players. [*Buff,* short for BUFFET (a blow).]

blink (blĭngk) *v.* 1. To close and open (one or both eyes) rapidly. 2. To flash on and off. 3. To close the eyes to. —*n.* 1. The act or an instance of blinking. 2. A glimpse. 3. A flash of light; a glimmer. —**on the blink.** *Slang.* Not in working condition. [ME *blinken.*]

blintz (blĭnts) *n.* Also **blin•tze** (blĭn'tsə). A thin, rolled pancake stuffed with various fillings. [Yidd *blintse.*]

blip (blĭp) *n.* A spot of light on a radar screen. [Imit.]

bliss (blĭs) *n.* 1. Serene happiness. 2. The ecstasy of salvation. [< OE *bliss, blīths* < Gmc *blithsjo* < *blīthiz,* BLITHE.] —**bliss'ful** *adj.*

blis•ter (blĭs'tər) *n.* 1. A thin swelling of the skin, containing watery matter, caused by irritation. 2. Something resembling a blister. [ME *blester, blister.*] —**blis'ter** *v.*

blithe (blīth, blĭth) *adj.* Cheerful; carefree. [< OE *blīthe* < *blīthiz,* gentle, mild.]

blithe•some (blīth'səm, blĭth'-) *adj.* Cheerful; merry.

blitz (blĭts) *n.* 1. A blitzkrieg. 2. An intensive air raid. 3. Any intense campaign. —**blitz** *v.* [< BLITZKRIEG.]

blitz•krieg (blĭts'krēg') *n.* A swift, sudden military offensive. [G, "lightning war."]

bliz•zard (blĭz'ərd) *n.* A heavy snowstorm with high winds. [?]

blk. 1. black. 2. block. 3. bulk.

bloat (blōt) *v.* To make or become swollen. [< earlier *blowt,* soft, flabby.]

blob (blŏb) *n.* 1. A soft, amorphous mass. 2. A splotch of color. [ME.]

bloc (blŏk) *n.* A group of persons or nations united for common action. [< OF, BLOCK.]

block (blŏk) *n.* 1. A solid piece of wood or other hard substance having one or more flat sides. 2. A stand from which articles are displayed at an auction. 3. A pulley or a system of pulleys set in a casing. 4. A set of like items. 5. a. A section of a town bounded on each side by consecutive streets. b. A segment of a street bounded by successive cross streets. 6. An act of obstructing. 7. An obstacle. 8. *Med.* An obstruction of a neural, digestive, or other physiological process. 9. *Psychol.* Sudden cessation of a thought process without an immediate observable cause. 10. *Slang.* A person's head. —*v.* 1. To stop or impede the passage of. 2. *Med.* To interrupt the proper functioning of (a physiological process). —**block out.** 1. To plan with few details. 2. To obscure from view. [< OF *bloc.*] —**block** *adj.* —**block'age** (blŏk'ĭj) *n.* —**block'er** *n.*

block•ade (blŏ-kād') *n.* The closing off of a city or other area to traffic and communication. [< BLOCK.] —**block•ade'** *v.* (-aded, -ading). —**block•ad'er** *n.*

block and tackle. An apparatus of pulley blocks and cables for hauling.

block•bust•er (blŏk'bŭs'tər) *n.* *Informal.* 1. A bomb capable of destroying a city block. 2. Anything of devastating effect.

block•head (blŏk'hĕd') *n.* A dolt.

bloke (blōk) *n.* *Brit. Slang.* A man. [?]

blond (blŏnd) *adj.* 1. Also *fem.* **blonde.** Having fair hair. 2. Pale or yellowish, as hair. 3. Light-colored. —*n.* Also *fem.* **blonde.** A blond person. [OF.]

blood (blŭd) *n.* 1. The red fluid circulated by the heart through the vertebrate vascular system, carrying oxygen and nutrients throughout the body and waste materials to excretory channels. 2. Loosely, life. 3. Bloodshed. 4. Temperament. 5. Kinship. 6. Racial or national ancestry. 7. Personnel. 8. A dashing young man. [< OE *blōd* < Gmc *blōtham.*]

blood bath. A massacre.

blood•cur•dling (blŭd'kûrd'lĭng) *adj.* Terrifying. —**blood'cur'dling•ly** *adv.*

blood•hound (blŭd'hound') *n.* A hound with

drooping ears, sagging jowls, and a keen sense of smell.

blood·less (blŭd′lĭs) *adj.* **1.** Having no blood. **2.** Achieved without bloodshed.

blood·let·ting (blŭd′lĕt′ĭng) *n.* **1.** The bleeding of a vein as a therapeutic measure. **2.** Bloodshed.

blood·line (blŭd′līn′) *n.* Direct line of descent.

blood poisoning. 1. Toxemia. **2.** Septicemia.

blood pressure. The pressure of the blood within the arteries.

blood relation. Also **blood relative.** A person who is related by birth.

blood·shed (blŭd′shĕd′) *n.* **1.** The shedding of blood. **2.** Carnage.

blood·shot (blŭd′shŏt′) *adj.* Red and irritated: *bloodshot eyes.*

blood stream. The stream of blood flowing through the circulatory system of a living body.

blood·suck·er (blŭd′sŭk′ər) *n.* An animal that sucks blood, as a leech. —**blood′suck′ing** *adj.*

blood·thirst·y (blŭd′thûr′stē) *adj.* Thirsting for bloodshed; murderous; cruel.

blood vessel. Any elastic, tubular canal, such as an artery, vein, or capillary, through which blood circulates.

blood·y (blŭd′ē) *adj.* **-ier, -iest. 1.** Of, containing, or stained with blood. **2.** Giving rise to bloodshed: *a bloody fight.* **3.** Bloodthirsty; cruel. **4.** *Brit. Vulgar.* Used as an intensive: *bloody fool.* —*adv. Brit. Vulgar.* Used as an intensive: *bloody well right.* —*v.* **-ied, -ying.** To stain with or as if with blood. —**blood′i·ly** *adv.* —**blood′i·ness** *n.*

bloody mary. Also **Bloody Mary.** A drink made with vodka and tomato juice.

bloom (bloom) *n.* **1.** The flower or blossoms of a plant. **2. a.** The condition or time of flowering. **b.** A condition or time of vigor and beauty; prime. **3.** A fresh, rosy complexion. **4.** A thin, powdery coating on some fruits, leaves, or stems. —*v.* **1.** To bear flowers. **2.** To shine with health and vigor; to glow. **3.** To grow or flourish. [< ON *blōm.*]

bloom·er (bloo′mər) *n.* One that blooms.

bloom·ers (bloo′mərz) *pl.n.* Women's wide, loose pants or underpants, gathered at or above the knee. [< Amelia *Bloomer* (1818–1894), American social reformer.]

bloom·ing (bloo′mĭng) *adj.* **1.** Flowering; blossoming. **2.** Flourishing. **3.** *Slang.* Utter. Used as an intensive: *a blooming idiot.*

bloop·er (bloo′pər) *n.* **1.** *Baseball.* A weakly hit fly ball that carries just beyond the infield. **2.** *Informal.* A faux pas. [< *bloop,* sound of such a hit.]

blos·som (blŏs′əm) *n.* **1.** A flower or flowers, esp. of a plant yielding edible fruit. **2.** The condition or time of flowering: *peach trees in blossom.* —*v.* **1.** To flower; bloom. **2.** To develop; flourish. [< OE *blōstma.* See **bhel-³.**] —**blos′som·y** *adj.*

blot (blŏt) *n.* **1.** A spot; a stain: *a blot of ink.* **2.** A moral blemish; a disgrace. —*v.* **blotted, blotting. 1.** To spot or stain. **2.** To bring moral disgrace to. **3.** To erase; cancel (with *out*). **4.** To darken; hide. **5.** To dry with absorbent

material. **6.** To make a blot. **7.** To become blotted. [ME.]

blotch (blŏch) *n.* **1.** A spot or blot; a splotch. **2.** A discoloration on the skin; blemish. **3.** Any of various plant diseases caused by fungi and resulting in brown or black dead areas on leaves or fruit. [Prob a blend of BLOT and BOTCH.] —**blotch** *v.*

blot·ter (blŏt′ər) *n.* **1.** A piece of blotting paper. **2.** A book containing daily records, as of occurrences or transactions.

blotting paper. Absorbent paper used to blot a surface by soaking up excess ink.

blouse (blous, blouz) *n.* **1.** A loosely fitting shirtlike garment. **2.** The service coat or tunic worn by members of the U.S. Army. —*v.* **bloused, blousing.** To hang or drape loosely around the waist.

blow¹ (blō) *v.* **blew, blown** (blōn), **blowing. 1.** To be in a state of motion, as the wind. **2. a.** To be carried by or as if by the wind. **b.** To cause to move by means of a current of air. **3.** To drive a current of air upon, in, or through. **4.** To expel a current of air, as from a bellows. **5.** To sound or cause to sound by expelling a current of air: *blow a trumpet.* **6.** To pant. **7.** To cause to explode. **8.** To melt (a fuse). **9.** To spout water and air, as a whale. **10.** To shape by forcing air or gas through at the end of a pipe: *blow glass.* **11.** *Slang.* To depart. **12.** *Slang.* To spend (money) freely. —**blow over.** To subside. —*n.* **1. a.** A blast of air or wind. **b.** A storm. **2.** The act of blowing. [< OE *blāwan.* See **bhlē-².**] —**blow′er** *n.*

blow² (blō) *n.* **1.** A sudden hard stroke, as with the fist. **2.** A sudden shock or calamity. **3.** A sudden attack. —**come to blows.** To begin to fight. [ME *blaw.*]

blow³ (blō) *v.* **blew, blown** (blōn), **blowing.** To bloom or cause to bloom. [< OE *blōwan,* to blossom.]

blow·gun (blō′gŭn′) *n.* A long narrow pipe through which darts or pellets may be blown.

blow out. 1. To extinguish or be extinguished by blowing, as a candle. **2.** To burst suddenly, as a tire. **3.** To melt, as a fuse. **4.** To fail, as an electrical apparatus.

blow·out (blō′out′) *n.* **1. a.** A sudden bursting, as of an automobile tire. **b.** The hole so made. **c.** The ruptured object. **2.** A sudden escape of a confined gas. **3.** The burning out of a fuse. **4.** *Slang.* A large party or social affair.

blow·pipe (blō′pīp′) *n.* **1.** A metal tube in which a flow of gas is mixed with a controlled flow of air to concentrate the heat of a flame. **2.** A long iron pipe used to blow molten glass.

blow·torch (blō′tôrch′) *n.* A gas burner that produces a flame hot enough to melt soft metals.

blow up. 1. To explode. **2.** To lose one's temper. **3.** To enlarge the size of (a photographic print). **4.** To fill with air.

blow·up (blō′ŭp′) *n.* **1.** An explosion. **2.** A violent outburst of temper. **3.** A photographic enlargement.

blub·ber¹ (blŭb′ər) *v.* To weep noisily. [ME *blubren,* to bubble, foam.] —**blub′ber** *n.*

blub·ber² (blŭb′ər) *n.* **1.** The fat of whales and

ă pat/ā ate/âr care/ä bar/b bib/ch chew/d deed/ĕ pet/ē be/f fit/g gag/h hat/hw what/ ĭ pit/ī pie/îr pier/j judge/k kick/l lid, fatal/m mum/n no, sudden/ng sing/ŏ pot/ō go/

other marine mammals. **2.** Excessive body fat. [ME *bluber*, bubble, èntrails, fish or whale oil.]

blu•cher (bloo'chər, -kər) *n.* A laced shoe having the vamp and tongue made of one piece. [< G.L. von *Blücher* (1742–1819), Prussian field marshal.]

bludg•eon (blŭj'ən) *n.* A short club having one end thicker than the other. —*v.* **-eoned, -eoning.** **1.** To hit with or as if with a bludgeon. **2.** To threaten or bully. [?]

blue (bloo) *n.* **1.** Any of a group of colors whose hue is that of a clear sky. **2.** Anything of this color. —**out of the blue.** Unexpected; unforeseen. —**the blue. 1.** The sea. **2.** The sky. —**the blues. 1.** A state of melancholy. **2.** A style of jazz evolved from Negro folk songs having usually a slow tempo. —*adj.* **bluer, bluest. 1.** Of the color blue. **2.** Having a gray or purplish color, as from cold or contusion. **3.** Gloomy; dreary. **4.** Puritanical; strict. **5.** Aristocratic. —**once in a blue moon.** Rarely. —*v.* **blued, bluing. 1.** To make or become blue. **2.** To use bluing on. [< OF *bleu* < CRom *blāvus.*] —**blu'ish** *adj.*

blue baby. An infant born with bluish skin caused by inadequate oxygenation of the blood.

blue•bell (bloo'bĕl') *n.* Any of various plants having blue, bell-shaped flowers.

blue•ber•ry (bloo'bĕr'ē, -bər-ē) *n.* **1.** A juicy, edible, blue, or purplish berry. **2.** A shrub bearing such berries.

blue•bird (bloo'bûrd') *n.* A North American bird with blue plumage and usually a rust-colored breast.

blue blood. 1. Noble descent. **2.** A member of the aristocracy.

blue•bon•net (bloo'bŏn'ĭt) *n.* A plant with compound leaves and clusters of blue flowers.

blue book. Also **blue•book** (bloo'book'). **1.** A book listing socially prominent people. **2.** A blank notebook with blue covers in which to write college examinations.

blue•bot•tle (bloo'bŏt'l) *n.* A fly with a bright metallic-blue body.

blue chip. A stock highly valuable because of public confidence in its long record of steady earnings. —**blue'-chip'** *adj.*

blue-col•lar (bloo'kŏl'ər) *adj.* Pertaining to wage earners in jobs involving manual labor.

blue•fish (bloo'fĭsh') *n.* A marine food and game fish.

blue•grass (bloo'grăs', -gräs') *n.* **1.** A grass with bluish or grayish leaves. **2.** A type of folk music of the southern U.S., marked by fast tempos and the use of banjos and guitars.

blue•ing. Variant of **bluing.**

blue jay. A bird with a crested head and predominantly blue plumage.

blue•nose (bloo'nōz') *n.* A puritanical person.

blue•pen•cil (bloo'pĕn'səl) *v.* **-ciled, -ciling.** To edit with or as with a blue pencil.

blue point. An edible oyster found chiefly off Blue Point, Long Island, N.Y.

blue•print (bloo'prĭnt') *n.* **1.** A photographic reproduction, as of architectural plans, rendered as white lines on a blue background. **2.** Any carefully designed plan.

blue•stock•ing (bloo'stŏk'ĭng) *n.* A pedantic or scholarly woman.

bluff¹ (blŭf) *v.* To mislead or intimidate by a false display of confidence —*n.* **1.** The act or practice of bluffing. **2.** One who bluffs. [Du *bluffen*, to boast.] —**bluff'er** *n.*

bluff² (blŭf) *n.* A steep headland or bank; cliff. —*adj.* **1.** Presenting a broad, steep front. **2.** Brusque; blunt. [?]

blu•ing (bloo'ĭng) *n.* Also **blue•ing.** A rinsing agent used to counteract the yellowing of laundered fabrics.

blun•der (blŭn'dər) *n.* A stupid and grave mistake. —*v.* **1.** To move awkwardly or clumsily. **2.** To make a stupid mistake. [ME *blunderen*, to proceed blindly, bungle.]

blun•der•buss (blŭn'dər-bŭs') *n.* **1.** A short musket of wide bore and flaring muzzle. **2.** A stupid, clumsy person. [Var of Du *donderbus*, "thunder gun."]

blunt (blŭnt) *adj.* **1.** Having a thick, dull edge or end. **2.** Outspoken; brusque. **3.** Slow to understand; dull. —*v.* To make or become blunt. [ME, dull, blunt, stupid.] —**blunt'ly** *adv.*

blur (blûr) *v.* **blurred, blurring. 1.** To make or become indistinct; obscure. **2.** To smear or stain. **3.** To lessen the perception of; dim. —*n.* **1.** A smear; a smudge. **2.** Anything hazy and indistinct. [?] —**blur'ry** *adj.*

blurb (blûrb) *n.* A brief commendatory publicity notice, as on a book jacket.

blurt (blûrt) *v.* To utter impulsively. [Prob imit.]

blush (blŭsh) *n.* A sudden reddening of the face from modesty, embarrassment, or shame. [< OE *blyscan*. See bhel-¹.] —**blush** *v.*

blus•ter (blŭs'tər) *v.* **1.** To blow in loud, violent gusts, as wind in a storm. **2.** To speak noisily and boastfully. [ME *blusteren.*] —**blus'ter** *n.* —**blus'ter•er** *n.*

blvd. boulevard.

b.m. bowel movement.

bo•a (bō'ə) *n.* **1.** A large, nonvenomous tropical snake, such as the **boa constrictor,** that coils around and crushes its prey. **2.** A long scarf of feathers, fur, etc. [< L *boa*, a large water snake.]

boar (bôr, bōr) *n.* **1.** An uncastrated male pig. **2.** A wild pig with dense, dark bristles. [< OE *bār* < Gmc **bairoz.*]

board (bôrd, bōrd) *n.* **1.** A long, flat slab of sawed lumber. **2.** A flat piece of wood or similarly rigid material, adapted for a special use. **3.** A table, esp. one for serving food. **4.** Meals collectively: *board and lodging.* **5.** A table at which official meetings are held. **6.** A body of administrators. **7.** An electrical-equipment panel. **8.** A border or edge. **9.** The side of a ship. —**on board.** Aboard. —**the boards.** A theater stage. —*v.* **1.** To cover or close with boards: *board up a door.* **2.** To furnish with or receive meals in return for pay. **3.** To enter or go aboard (a vehicle or ship). [< OE *bord*, plank, border. See bherdh-.]

board•er (bôr'dər, bōr'-) *n.* One who pays a homeowner for regular meals or meals and lodging.

boarding house. Also **board•ing•house** (bôr'-

ding-hous', bōr'-). A private home that takes in paying guests and provides meals or meals and lodging.

board·walk (bôrd'wôk', bōrd'-) *n.* A promenade, esp. of planks, along a beach or waterfront.

boast (bōst) *v.* **1.** To talk about or speak with excessive pride. **2.** To take pride in, or be enhanced by, the possession of. —*n.* **1.** An instance of bragging. **2.** That which one brags about. [ME *bosten.*] —**boast'er** *n.*

boast·ful (bōst'fəl) *adj.* Tending to boast. —**boast'ful·ly** *adv.* —**boast'ful·ness** *n.*

boat (bōt) *n.* **1.** A relatively small, usually open water craft. **2.** A ship. Not in nautical usage. **3.** A dish shaped like a boat: *a gravy boat.* —**in the same boat.** In the same situation. [< OE *bāt* and ON *bātr.* See **bheid-.**] —**boat'ing** *n.*

boat·man (bōt'mən) *n.* One who works on, deals with, or operates boats.

boat·swain (bō'sən) *n.* A warrant officer or petty officer in charge of a ship's deck crew, rigging, anchors, and cables.

bob¹ (bŏb) *n.* **1.** A short jerking movement. **2.** Any small knoblike pendent object. **3.** A fishing float. **4.** A short haircut on a woman or child. —*v.* **bobbed, bobbing. 1.** To move or jerk up and down. **2.** To cut (hair) short. —**bob up.** To appear suddenly. [< ME *bobbe,* cluster of flowers and *bobben,* to move up and down.] —**bob'ber** *n.*

bob² (bŏb) *n., pl.* **bob.** *Brit. Slang.* A shilling. [?]

bob·bin (bŏb'ĭn) *n.* A spool or reel for thread, as on a sewing machine. [F *bobine.*]

bob·by (bŏb'ē) *n., pl.* **-bies.** *Brit. Slang.* A policeman. [After Sir Robert Peel, who was Home Secretary of England when the Metropolitan Police Force was created (1828).]

bobby pin. A ridged, tight metal hair clip. [< BOB (lock of hair).]

bobby socks. Girls' ankle socks.

bob·cat (bŏb'kăt') *n.* A North American wild cat with spotted fur and a short tail.

bob·o·link (bŏb'ə-lĭngk') *n.* An American songbird. [Imit of its call.]

bob·sled (bŏb'slĕd') *n.* A long racing sled typically made of two shorter sleds joined in tandem. [< BOB (short).] —**bob'sled'** *v.* (-sledded, -sledding).

bob·tail (bŏb'tāl') *n.* **1.** A shortened tail. **2.** An animal having such a tail. —**bob'tail', bob'tailed'** *adj.*

bob·white (bŏb-hwīt') *n.* A small North American quail. [Imit of its call.]

Boc·cac·cio (bə-kä'chē-ō'), **Giovanni.** 1313–1375. Italian author.

bock beer (bŏk). A dark spring beer. [G < *Eimbeck,* city in Hanover.]

bode¹ (bōd) *v.* **boded, boding.** To be an omen of: *His ill will bodes no good.* [< OE *boda,* messenger. See **bheudh-.**]

bode² (bōd). Alternate *p.t.* of **bide.**

bod·ice (bŏd'ĭs) *n.* The fitted part of a woman's dress that extends from the waist to the shoulder. [Orig *bodies,* pl of BODY.]

bod·i·ly (bŏd'ə-lē) *adj.* **1.** Of or pertaining to the body. **2.** Physical: *bodily welfare.* —*adv.*

1. In person. **2.** As a complete physical entity: *He carried her bodily from the room.*

bod·kin (bŏd'kĭn) *n.* **1.** A small pointed instrument for making holes in fabric or leather. **2.** A blunt needle for pulling tape or ribbon through a series of loops or a hem. **3.** *Obs.* A dagger. [ME *boidekyn.*]

bod·y (bŏd'ē) *n., pl.* **-ies. 1. a.** The physical structure of an organism, esp. a human being or animal. **b.** A corpse. **2.** The trunk or torso of a human being or animal. **3.** *Law.* **a.** A person. **b.** A group of individuals regarded as an entity; corporation. **4.** A number of persons or things; a group. **5.** The main or central part of something. **6.** Any bounded aggregate of matter: *a body of water.* **7.** Consistency of substance, as in textiles, wine, etc. [< OE *bodig* < Gmc **bot-,* container.]

bod·y·guard (bŏd'ē-gärd') *n.* A person or persons, usually armed, responsible for the physical safety of someone.

body politic. Collectively, the people of a politically organized nation or state.

Boer (bôr, bōr, bōōr) *n.* A Dutch colonist or a descendant of a Dutch colonist in South Africa. [Du, "peasant," "farmer."] —**Boer** *adj.*

bog (bôg, bŏg) *n.* Soft, water-logged ground; a marsh. —*v.* **bogged, bogging.** To hinder or be hindered; slow; impede (with *down*). [Scot Gael *bogach.*]

bo·gey (bō'gē) *n., pl.* **-geys. 1.** Also **bo·gie, bo·gy** *pl.* **-gies.** An evil or mischievous spirit. **2.** *Golf.* One stroke over par on a hole.

Bo·go·tá (bō'gə-tä'). The capital of Colombia. Pop. 1,697,000.

bo·gus (bō'gəs) *adj.* Counterfeit; fake.

Bo·he·mi·an (bō-hē'mē-ən) *n.* Also **bo·he·mi·an.** A writer or artist who disregards conventional standards of behavior. —**Bo·he'·mi·an** *adj.*

boil¹ (boil) *v.* **1.** To vaporize a liquid by applying heat. **2.** To cook by boiling. **3.** To be in a state of agitation, as boiling water. **4.** To be greatly excited, as with rage. **5.** To heat to the boiling point. **6.** To separate by evaporation as a result of boiling. —**boil down. 1.** To reduce in bulk or size by boiling. **2.** To summarize. —*n.* The state, condition, or act of boiling. [< OF *bouillir.*]

boil² (boil) *n.* A painful, pus-filled swelling of the skin and subcutaneous tissue caused by bacterial infection. [< OE *bȳle.* See **beu-.**]

boil·er (boi'lər) *n.* A vessel in which water is heated and circulated, either as hot water or as steam, for heating or power.

boil·er·mak·er (boi'lər-mā'kər) *n. Slang.* A drink of whiskey with beer as a chaser.

Boi·se (boi'zē, -sē). The capital of Idaho. Pop. 75,000.

bois·ter·ous (boi'stər-əs, -strəs) *adj.* **1.** Violent and turbulent. **2.** Noisy and unrestrained. [< ME *boistous,* rude, fierce, stout.] —**bois'ter·ous·ly** *adv.* —**bois'ter·ous·ness** *n.*

Bol. Bolivia.

bold (bōld) *adj.* **1.** Fearless; courageous. **2.** Unduly forward; brazen; impudent. **3.** Clear and distinct to the eye: *a bold handwriting.* **4.** Steep, as a cliff. —**make bold.** To take the liberty; dare. [< OE *beald.*] —**bold'ly** *adv.* —**bold'ness** *n.*

bold•face (bōld'fās') *n.* A typeface that produces a conspicuous black impression. —*v.* -**faced, -facing. 1.** To mark (copy) for printing in boldface. **2.** To print or set in boldface.

bold-faced (bōld'fāst') *adj.* **1.** Impudent. **2.** Set or marked for printing in boldface.

bole (bōl) *n.* The trunk of a tree. [< ON *bolr.*]

bo•le•ro (bō-lâr'ō) *n., pl.* -**ros. 1.** A short jacket, usually with no front fastening. **2. a.** A Spanish dance in triple meter. **b.** The music for this dance. [Span.]

bol•i•var (bŏl'ə-vər) *n.* The basic monetary unit of Venezuela. [< Simón BOLÍVAR.]

Bo•lí•var (bō-lē'vär), **Simón.** 1783–1830. Venezuelan leader in South American struggles for national independence.

Simón Bolívar

Bo•liv•i•a (bə-lĭv'ē-ə). A republic of west-central South America. Pop. 3,520,000. Caps. La Paz and Sucre. —**Bo•liv'i•an** *adj. & n.*

boll (bōl) *n.* A rounded seed pod, as of cotton. [ME *bolle.*]

Bolivia

boll weevil. A long-snouted beetle, having larvae that damage cotton bolls.

bo•lo•gna (bə-lō'nə, -nē, -nyə) *n.* A large sausage made of mixed meats. [< BOLOGNA.]

Bo•lo•gna (bō-lō'nyä). A city of N Italy. Pop. 482,000.

Bol•she•vik (bōl'shə-vĭk', bŏl'-) *n.* A member of the party that seized power and set up a proletarian dictatorship in Russia (1917–22). [Russ *Bol'shevik,* "one of the majority."] —**Bol'she•vik'** *adj.* —**Bol'she•vism'** *n.*

bol•ster (bōl'stər) *n.* A long, narrow pillow or cushion. —*v.* To prop up with or as if with a bolster. [< OE, cushion. See **bhelgh-.**] —**bol'ster•er** *n.*

bolt¹ (bōlt) *n.* **1.** A sliding bar that is used to fasten doors and gates. **2.** A metal bar in a lock thrown or withdrawn by turning the key. **3.** A threaded metal pin used with a nut to hold parts together. **4.** A short, heavy arrow used with a crossbow. **5.** A flash of lightning or a thunderbolt. **6.** A sudden movement; dash. **7.** A large roll of cloth. —*v.* **1.** To secure or lock with a bolt. **2.** To eat hurriedly; gulp. **3.** To desert or withdraw support from (a political party). **4.** To utter impulsively. **5.** To move or spring suddenly; dash. **6.** To flower or produce seeds prematurely. [< OE, heavy arrow. See **bheld-.**]

bolt² (bōlt) *v.* To sift. [< OF *buleter.*]

bo•lus (bō'ləs) *n., pl.* -**luses. 1.** A small round mass. **2.** *Pharm.* A large pill or tablet. [< Gk *bōlos,* lump, clod.]

bomb (bŏm) *n.* **1.** An explosive weapon dropped on or thrown at a target. **2.** A portable, manually operated container that ejects a spray, foam, or gas under pressure. —*v.* To attack or destroy with bombs. [< It *bomba.*]

bom•bard (bŏm-bärd') *v.* **1.** To attack with bombs or missiles. **2.** To attack persistently. **3.** To irradiate (an atom). [< OF *bombarde,* cannon.] —**bom•bard'ment** *n.*

bom•bar•dier (bŏm'bər-dîr') *n.* The member of an aircraft crew who operates the bombing equipment. [< OF *bombarde,* BOMBARD.]

bom•bast (bŏm'băst') *n.* Grandiloquent and pompous speech or writing. [Earlier *bombace,* cotton padding.] —**bom•bas'tic** *adj.*

Bom•bay (bŏm-bā'). A seaport of the W Republic of India. Pop. 2,772,000.

bom•ba•zine (bŏm'bə-zēn') *n.* A fine twilled fabric often dyed black. [< L *bombyx,* silk.]

bomb•er (bŏm'ər) *n.* An aircraft designed to carry and drop bombs.

bomb•shell (bŏm'shĕl') *n.* **1.** A bomb. **2.** A shocking surprise.

bomb•sight (bŏm'sīt') *n.* A device in aircraft for aiming bombs.

bo•na fide (bō'nə fīd', fī'dē, bŏn'ə). **1.** Done or made in good faith: *a bona fide offer.* **2.** Authentic: *a bona fide Rembrandt.* [L, "in good faith."]

bo•nan•za (bə-năn'zə) *n.* **1.** A rich mine or vein of ore. **2.** Any source of great wealth. [Span, fair weather, prosperity.]

bon•bon (bŏn'bŏn') *n.* A candy having a creamy center and often coated with chocolate. [F.]

---

bond (bŏnd) *n.* **1.** Anything that binds, ties, or fastens together. **2. bonds.** Shackles. **3.** Often **bonds.** A uniting force or tie; a link. **4.** A binding agreement. **5.** The promise or obligation by which one is bound. **6.** A union or cohesion between parts. **7.** *Chem.* A chemical **bond.** **8.** A sum of money paid as bail or surety. **9.** One who acts as bail; bondsman. **10.** A certificate of debt issued by a government or corporation, guaranteeing payment of the original investment plus interest by a specified future date. **11.** The state of storing goods in a warehouse until the taxes or duties due on them are paid. **12.** Surety against losses, theft, etc. **13.** Also **bond paper.** A superior grade of white paper. *—v.* **1.** To mortgage or place a guaranteed bond on. **2.** To furnish bond or surety for. **3.** To place (an employee or merchandise) under bond or guarantee. **4.** To join securely, as with glue. [< ON *band.*]
bond•age (bŏn′dĭj) *n.* The condition of a slave or serf; serfdom. [< OE *bônda,* householder.]
bonds•man (bŏndz′mən) *n.* **1.** Also **bond•man** (bŏnd′mən). A slave; serf. **2.** One who provides bond or surety for another.
bone (bōn) *n.* **l. a.** The dense, semirigid, porous, calcified connective tissue of the skeleton of most vertebrates. **b.** A skeletal structure made of this material. **2.** A similar material resembling bone, such as ivory. **3.** Something made of bone or similar material. **—have a bone to pick with.** To have grounds for a dispute with. **—make no bones about.** To be frank and candid about. *—v.* **boned, boning.** To remove the bones from. **—bone up on.** To study intensively, usually at the last minute. [< OE *bān* < Gmc **baina-.*]
bone-dry (bōn′drī′) *adj.* Very dry.
bone•fish (bōn′fĭsh′) *n.* A chiefly tropical marine game fish.
bone meal. Bones crushed and ground to a coarse powder, used as plant fertilizer and animal feed.
bon•er (bō′nər) *n. Slang.* A blunder.
bon•fire (bŏn′fīr′) *n.* A large outdoor fire. [ME *banefyre,* a fire in which bones were burned.]
bon•go drum (bŏng′gō). One of a pair of connected and tuned drums. [Amer Span *bongó.*]
bo•ni•to (bə-nē′tō) *n., pl.* **-to** or **-tos.** Also **bo•ni•ta** (-tə). A food and game fish related to the tuna. [Span, "beautiful."]
bon mot (bôN′ mō′) *pl.* **bons mots** (bôN′ mōz′). A clever saying. [F, "good word."]
Bonn (bŏn). The capital of the German Federal Republic. Pop. 142,000.
bon•net (bŏn′ĭt) *n.* **1.** A hat that is held in place by ribbons tied under the chin. **2.** A feather headdress worn by some American Indians. **3.** A removable metal plate over a valve or other machinery part. **4.** *Brit.* An automobile hood. *—v.* To put a bonnet on. [< OF *bonet.*]
bon•nock. Variant of **bannock.**
bon•ny (bŏn′ē) *adj.* **-nier, -niest.** Also **bon•nie.** *Chiefly Brit.* Cheerful; pleasant. [Perh < OF *bon,* good.] **—bon′ni•ness** *n.*

bon•sai (bōn-sī′) *n., pl.* **-sai.** **1.** The growing of dwarfed, ornamental trees in small pots. **2.** A tree thus grown. [Jap, "potted plant."]
bo•nus (bō′nəs) *n., pl.* **-nuses.** Something given or paid in addition to the usual or expected amount. [< L *bonus,* good.]
bon vi•vant (bôN vē-väN′) *pl.* **bons vivants** (bôN vē-väN′). A person who enjoys life fully.
bon voy•age (bôN vwä-yäzh′). A wish for a pleasant journey extended to a departing traveler. [F, "good trip."]
bon•y (bō′nē) *adj.* **-ier, -iest.** **1.** Of, resembling, or made of bone. **2.** Having many bones. **3.** Very thin. **—bon′i•ness** *n.*
boo (bōō) *n., pl.* **boos.** A shout expressing contempt or disapproval. [Imit.] **—boo** *v.*
boo•by (bōō′bē) *n., pl.* **-bies.** Also **boob** (bōōb). A stupid person. [< L *balbus,* stammering.]
booby prize. An insignificant or comical award.
booby trap. A device or situation that catches a person off guard.
boo•dle (bōōd′l) *n. Slang.* **1.** Money accepted as a bribe. **2.** Stolen goods. [< Du *boedel,* estate, effects.]
book (bōōk) *n.* **1.** A volume made up of pages fastened along one side and encased between protective covers. **2.** A written or printed literary work. **3.** A volume in which financial transactions are recorded. **4.** A main division of a larger written or printed work. **5.** A libretto. **6. the Book.** The Bible. **7.** A record of bets placed on a race. *—v.* To list, reserve, or schedule by writing in or as if in a book. [< OE *bōc,* written document, composition. See **bhāgo-.**]
book•case (bōōk′kās′) *n.* A piece of furniture with shelves for holding books.
book end. A prop for keeping a row of books upright.
book•ie (bōōk′ē) *n. Slang.* A bookmaker.
book•ing (bōōk′ĭng) *n.* A scheduled engagement, as for a performance.
book•ish (bōōk′ĭsh) *adj.* **1.** Fond of books; studious. **2.** Relying on book learning.
book•keep•ing (bōōk′kē′pĭng) *n.* The recording of the accounts and transactions of a business. **—book′keep′er** *n.*
book learning. Knowledge gained from books rather than from practical experience.
book•let (bōōk′lĭt) *n.* A small bound book.
book•mak•er (bōōk′mā′kər) *n.* One who accepts and pays off bets.
book•mark (bōōk′märk′) *n.* A marker, such as a ribbon, placed between the pages of a book.
book•mo•bile (bōōk′mō-bēl′) *n.* A truck equipped for use as a mobile lending library.
book•plate (bōōk′plāt′) *n.* A label pasted inside a book and bearing the owner's name.
book•worm (bōōk′wûrm′) *n.* One who spends much time reading or studying.
boom¹ (bōōm) *v.* **1.** To make a deep, resonant sound. **2.** To flourish or cause to flourish swiftly or vigorously. *—n.* **1.** A booming sound. **2.** A sudden increase, as in growth, wealth, or popularity. [ME *bomben, bummen* (imit).]
boom² (bōōm) *n.* **1.** A long spar extending

from a mast to hold a sail. **2.** A long pole extending upward from the mast of a derrick to support or guide objects lifted. **3.** A chain of floating logs enclosing other free-floating logs. **4.** A long, movable arm used to maneuver a microphone. [Du, tree, pole.]

boo•mer•ang (bōō′mə-răng′) *n.* **1.** A flat, curved missile that can be hurled so that it returns to the thrower. **2.** An action that rebounds detrimentally. *—v.* To act as a boomerang. [Native Australian word.]

boom town. A town showing sudden growth and prosperity.

boon¹ (bōōn) *n.* **1.** Something beneficial or pleasant; a blessing. **2.** A favor or request. [< ON *bōn*, prayer, request.]

boon² (bōōn) *adj.* Jolly; convivial: *a boon companion.* [ME *bone,* "good."]

boon•docks (bōōn′dŏks′) *pl.n.* —**the boondocks.** *Slang.* Back country; hinterland. [Tag *bundok,* mountain.]

boon•dog•gle (bōōn′dôg′əl, -dŏg′əl) *v.* **-gled, -gling.** To waste time on pointless and unnecessary work. *—n.* Time-wasting work. —**boon′dog′gler** *n.*

Boone (bōōn), **Daniel.** 1734–1820. American pioneer; explored and settled Kentucky.

boor (bōōr) *n.* A person with rude, clumsy manners and little refinement. [Du *boer,* farmer.]

boor•ish (bōōr′ĭsh) *adj.* Like a boor; rude; ill-mannered. —**boor′ish•ly** *adv.*

boost (bōōst) *v.* **1.** To raise or lift by or as if by pushing up from below. **2.** To increase; raise. **3.** To promote vigorously. *—n.* **1.** A lift or help. **2.** An increase. [?]

boost•er (bōō′stər) *n.* **1.** A device for increasing power or effectiveness. **2.** A promoter. **3.** A rocket used to launch a missile or space vehicle. **4.** A supplementary dose of a vaccine.

booster cable. An electric cable used to connect an automobile battery to a power source for charging.

boot¹ (bōōt) *n.* **1.** A protective piece of footwear covering the foot and part or all of the leg. **2.** Any protective covering or sheath. **3.** *Brit.* An automobile trunk. **4.** A kick. —**the boot.** *Slang.* A discharge from employment. *—v.* **1.** To put boots on. **2.** To kick. [< OF *bote.*]

boot² (bōōt) *v. Archaic.* To be of help; avail. *—n.* —**to boot.** In addition. [< OE *bōt,* advantage, addition.]

boot•black (bōōt′blăk′) *n.* A person who cleans and polishes shoes for a living.

boot camp. A military training camp for recruits.

boo•tee (bōō′tē) *n.* Also **boo•tie.** A soft, usually knitted, sock for a baby.

Bo•ö•tes (bō-ō′tēz) *n.* A constellation in the N Hemisphere.

booth (bōōth) *n., pl.* **booths** (bōō*th*z, bōōths). **1.** A small enclosed compartment. **2.** An area in a restaurant with a table and seats whose backs serve as partitions. **3.** A small stall for the display of wares. [ME *bouth.*]

boot•leg (bōōt′lĕg′) *v.* **-legged, -legging.** To make, sell, or transport illegally, as liquor.

—adj. Made, sold, or transported illegally. —**boot′leg′ger** *n.*

boot•less (bōōt′lĭs) *adj.* Giving no advantage or benefit. —**boot′less•ly** *adv.*

boot•lick (bōōt′lĭk′) *v.* To behave in a servile manner.

boot tree. A shoetree.

boo•ty (bōō′tē) *n., pl.* **-ties.** **1.** Plunder taken from an enemy. **2.** Any seized or stolen goods. [< OF *butin.*]

booze (bōōz) *n. Informal.* Intoxicating liquor. *—v.* **boozed, boozing.** *Informal.* To drink intoxicating liquor to excess. [ME *bousen,* to carouse.] —**booz′er** *n.* —**booz′y** *adj.*

bor. borough.

bo•rax (bôr′ăks′, -əks, bōr′-) *n.* A crystalline compound, **sodium borate,** Na₂B₄O₇, used in manufacturing glass, detergents, and pharmaceuticals. [< Ar *būraq.*]

bor•del•lo (bôr-dĕl′ō) *n., pl.* **-los.** A brothel. [< OF *bordel,* "small house," brothel.]

bor•der (bôr′dər) *n.* **1.** A surrounding margin or rim. **2.** A geographic or political boundary. *—v.* **1.** To provide with a border. **2.** To lie on the border of. **3.** To verge; approach. [< OF *border,* to border.]

bor•der•land (bôr′dər-lănd′) *n.* **1.** Land on or near a border. **2.** An uncertain area or situation.

bor•der•line (bôr′dər-līn′) *n.* **1.** A line that marks a border. **2.** An indefinite line between two qualities or conditions. *—adj.* Marginally certain.

bore¹ (bôr, bōr) *v.* **bored, boring.** **1.** To make a hole in or through, as with a drill. **2.** To make by drilling or digging, as a tunnel. *—n.* **1.** A hole made by or as if by drilling. **2.** The interior diameter of a hole, tube, cylinder, etc. **3.** The caliber of a firearm. [< OE *borian.* See **bher-².**] —**bor′er** *n.*

bore² (bôr, bōr) *v.* **bored, boring.** To tire with repetition or tediousness. *—n.* One arousing boredom. [?]

bore³ (bôr, bōr). *p.t.* of **bear¹.**

bo•re•al (bôr′ē-əl, bōr′-) *adj.* Pertaining to or located in the north; northern. [< Gk *Boreās,* the north wind.]

bore•dom (bôr′dəm, bōr′-) *n.* The condition of being bored.

bo•ric acid (bôr′ĭk, bōr′-). A white or colorless compound, H₃BO₃, used as an antiseptic and preservative. [< BORON.]

bor•ing¹ (bôr′ĭng, bōr′-) *n.* **1.** The making of a hole by or as if by drilling. **2.** A hole made in this way. **3.** The material produced by such drilling.

bor•ing² (bôr′ĭng, bōr′-) *adj.* Uninteresting and tiresome; dull.

born (bôrn) A *p.p.* of **bear¹.** *—adj.* **1.** Brought into life. **2.** Having an innate talent: *a born artist.*

borne (bôrn, bōrn). A *p.p.* of **bear¹.**

Bor•ne•o (bôr′nē-ō′). An island of the W Pacific Ocean, divided between Indonesia, Malaysia, and Brunei.

bo•ron (bôr′ŏn′, bōr′-) *n. Symbol* **B** A soft, brown, amorphous or crystalline, nonmetallic element used in flares, nuclear reactor control

---

ô paw, for/oi boy/ou out/ōō took/ōō coo/p pop/r run/s sauce/sh shy/t to/th thin/*th* the/ ŭ cut/ûr fur/v van/w wag/y yes/z size/zh vision/ə ago, item, edible, gallop, circus/

elements, abrasives, and hard metallic alloys. Atomic number 5, atomic weight 10.811. [BO-R(AX) + (CARB)ON.]

bor•ough (bûr′ō, bûr′ə) *n.* **1.** A self-governing incorporated town, as in certain U.S. states. **2.** One of the five administrative units of New York City. [< OE *burg, burh,* fortress, fortified town. See **bhergh-²**.]

bor•row (bŏr′ō, bôr′ō) *v.* **1.** To obtain or receive (something) on loan with intent to return. **2.** To adopt or use as one's own: *They borrowed his ideas.* [< OE *borgian.* See **bhergh-¹**.] —**bor′row•er** *n.*

borscht (bôrsht) *n.* Also **borsht, borsch** (bôrsh). A hot or cold beet soup. [Russ *borshch,* "cow parsnip."]

bort (bôrt) *n.* Poorly crystallized diamonds used for industrial cutting and abrasion. [Prob < Du *boort.*]

Bosch (bŏs, bôs), **Hieronymus.** 1450?–1516. Dutch painter.

bos•ky (bŏs′kē) *adj.* Covered with shrubs or trees; wooded. [< ME *bosk, bush,* bush.]

bos•om (bōōz′əm, bōō′zəm) *n.* **1.** The human chest or breasts. **2.** The center or heart: *in the bosom of one's family.* —*adj.* Intimate: *a bosom friend.* [< OE *bōsm.* See **beu-**.]

Bos•po•rus (bŏs′pər-əs). A strait between European and Asian Turkey.

boss¹ (bôs, bŏs) *n.* **1.** An employer or supervisor. **2.** One who controls a political party or machine. —*v.* **1.** To supervise. **2.** To command in a domineering manner. [Du *baas,* master.]

boss² (bôs, bŏs) *n.* A knoblike protuberance or ornament. —*v.* To decorate with bosses. [< OF *boce.*]

boss•y (bô′sē, bŏs′ē) *adj.* **-ier, -iest.** Commanding, domineering, or overbearing. —**boss′i•ly** *adv.* —**boss′i•ness** *n.*

Bos•ton (bô′stən, bŏs′tən). The capital of Massachusetts. Pop. 641,000. —**Bos•to′ni•an** (bô-stō′nē-ən, bŏs-) *adj. & n.*

Bos•well (bŏz′wĕl′, -wəl), **James.** 1740–1795. Scottish lawyer; biographer of Samuel Johnson.

bot. **1.** botanical; botanist; botany. **2.** bottle.

bot•a•ny (bŏt′n-ē) *n.* The biological science of plants. [< Gk *botanē,* pasture, herb, plant.] —**bo•tan′i•cal** (bə-tăn′ĭ-kəl), **bo•tan′ic** *adj.* —**bot′a•nist** *n.*

botch (bŏch) *v.* **1.** To ruin through clumsiness; bungle. **2.** To repair clumsily. [ME *bocchen,* to patch up.] —**botch** *n.* —**botch′er** *n.*

botch•y (bŏch′ē) *adj.* **-ier, -iest.** Carelessly or clumsily done. —**botch′i•ly** *adv.*

both (bōth) *adj.* Two or two in conjunction: *Both boys arrived.* —*pron.* The one and the other: *Both are patriots.* —*conj.* As well; together; equally: *both Keats and Shelley.* [< ON *bāthir.*]

both•er (bŏth′ər) *v.* **1.** To irritate, particularly by small annoyances; pester; harass. **2.** To trouble or concern oneself. —*n.* A cause or state of disturbance. [Perh < Ir *buaidhrim,* I vex.] —**both′er•some** (-səm) *adj.*

Bot•swa•na (bŏt-swä′nə). A republic in S Africa. Pop. 670,000. Cap. Gaborone.

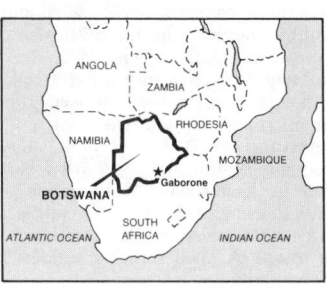

Botswana

Bot•ti•cel•li (bŏt′ĭ-chĕl′ē), **Sandro.** 1444?–1510. Italian painter.

bot•tle (bŏt′l) *n.* **1.** A receptacle, usually glass, having a narrow neck and a mouth that can be corked or capped. **2.** The quantity a bottle contains. —**the bottle.** **1.** Intoxicating drink: *addicted to the bottle.* **2.** Milk or formula fed to a baby from a bottle: *brought up on the bottle.* —*v.* **-tled, -tling.** To place in a bottle or bottles. —**bottle up.** To confine as if in a bottle: *bottle up one's emotions.* [< OF *botele, botaille.*] —**bot′tler** *n.*

bot•tle•neck (bŏt′l-nĕk′) *n.* **1.** A narrow passage, road, etc. **2.** Any hindrance to production or progress.

bot•tom (bŏt′əm) *n.* **1.** The lowest or deepest part of anything. **2.** The underside. **3.** The supporting part of something; base. **4.** The basic underlying quality; essence. **5.** The land below a body of water: *a river bottom.* **6.** *Informal.* The buttocks. —*adj.* Lowest; undermost; fundamental. [< OE *botm.* See **bhudh-**.] —**bot′tom•less** *adj.*

bottom line. 1. The lowest line in a financial statement, showing net income or loss. **2.** The end result of anything.

bot•u•lism (bŏch′ŏō-lĭz′əm) *n.* An often fatal food poisoning caused by bacteria and characterized by vomiting, abdominal pain, coughing, muscular weakness, and visual disturbance. [G *Botulismus,* "sausage-poisoning."]

bou•doir (bōō′dwär′, -dwôr′) *n.* A woman's private room. [F, "place for pouting."]

bouf•fant (bōō-fänt′) *adj.* Puffed-out; full: *a bouffant hair style.* [< F *bouffer,* to swell, puff up (the cheeks).]

bough (bou) *n.* A large branch of a tree. [< OE *bōg, bōh.* See **bhāghu-**.]

bought (bôt). *p.t. & p.p.* of **buy.**

bouil•lon (bōō′yŏn′, bōōl′yōn′, -yən) *n.* A clear meat broth. [< OF *bouilir,* to boil.]

boul•der (bōl′dər) *n.* A large rounded stone block. [< Scand.]

boul•e•vard (bōōl′ə-värd′, bōō′lə-) *n.* A broad city street, often tree-lined. [< OF *boloart,* rampart.]

bounce (bouns) *v.* **bounced, bouncing. 1.** To rebound elastically from a collision. **2.** To cause to collide and rebound. **3.** To bound in a lively and energetic manner. —*n.* **1.** A bound or rebound. **2.** A spring or leap. **3.**

ă pat/ā ate/âr care/ä bar/b bib/ch chew/d deed/ĕ pet/ē be/f fit/g gag/h hat/hw what/ ĭ pit/ī pie/îr pier/j judge/k kick/l lid, fatal/m mum/n no, sudden/ng sing/ŏ pot/ō go/

Capacity to bounce. **4.** Spirit; vigor. [ME *bunsen,* to beat, thrust.] **—bounc'y** *adj.*

bounc•er (boun'sər) *n.* A person employed to expel disorderly persons from a public place.

bounc•ing (boun'sĭng) *adj.* Vigorous; healthy: *a bouncing baby.* **—bounc'ing•ly** *adv.*

bound¹ (bound) *v.* **1.** To leap or spring. **2.** To progress by bounds. *—n.* **1.** A leap. **2.** A bounce. [F *bondir,* to bounce, orig "to rebound."]

bound² (bound) *n.* **1.** Often **bounds.** A boundary. **2. bounds.** The territory on, within, or near limiting lines. **—out of bounds. 1.** Beyond boundaries. **2.** Transgressing conventional limits. *—v.* **1.** To limit. **2.** To constitute the limit of. **3.** To demarcate. [< OF *bunde, bodne.*]

bound³ (bound). *p.t.* & *p.p.* of **bind.** *—adj.* **1.** Confined by bonds; tied: *muscle-bound.* **2.** Under obligation. **3.** Equipped with a cover or binding. **4.** Predetermined; certain.

bound⁴ (bound) *adj.* Headed for: *bound for home.* [ME *boun,* prepared, ready to go.]

bound•a•ry (boun'drē, -də-rē) *n., pl.* **-ries.** A border or limit. [< BOUND (limit).]

bound•en (boun'dən) *adj.* **1.** Under obligation. **2.** Obligatory: *his bounden duty.*

bound•er (boun'dər) *n. Chiefly Brit.* A vulgar man.

bound•less (bound'lĭs) *adj.* Without limit; infinite. **—bound'less•ly** *adv.*

boun•te•ous (boun'tē-əs) *adj.* **1.** Generous. **2.** Plentiful. [< OF *bonte,* bounty.] **—boun'te•ous•ly** *adv.* **—boun'te•ous•ness** *n.*

boun•ti•ful (boun'tĭ-fəl) *adj.* Bounteous. **—boun'ti•ful•ly** *adv.*

boun•ty (boun'tē) *n., pl.* **-ties. 1.** Liberality in giving. **2.** Something that is given liberally. **3.** A reward or inducement, esp. one given by a government. [< L *bonitās,* goodness.]

bou•quet (bō-kā', boō-) *n.* **1.** A bunch of flowers. **2.** (boō-kā'). An aroma, esp. of a wine. [< ONF *bosquet,* clump.]

bour•bon (bûr'bən) *n.* A whiskey distilled from fermented corn mash. [< *Bourbon* County, Ky.]

bour•geois (boōr-zhwä', boōr'zhwä') *n., pl.* **-geois. 1.** One belonging to the middle class. **2.** *(takes pl. v.).* The bourgeoisie. **3.** In Marxist theory, a capitalist. *—adj.* Of, pertaining to, or typical of the middle class. [< OF *bourg,* fortified town.]

bour•geoi•sie (boōr'zhwä-zē') *n.* **1.** The middle class. **2.** In Marxist theory, the capitalist class.

bout (bout) *n.* **1.** A contest; match. **2.** A period of time spent in a particular way: *a drinking bout.* [ME *bought,* bend, turn.]

bou•tique (boō-tēk') *n.* A small retail shop that specializes in gifts, fashionable clothes, and accessories. [F.]

bou•ton•niere (boō'tə-nîr', -tən-yâr') *n.* Also **bou•ton•nière.** A flower or small bunch of flowers worn in a buttonhole. [< OF *bouton,* button.]

bo•vine (bō'vĭn', -vēn') *adj.* **1.** Of, related to, or resembling a cow or cattle. **2.** Dull; stolid. [< L *bōs* (bov-), ox, cow.] **—bo'vine** *n.*

bow¹ (bou) *n.* The front section of a ship or boat. [< MLG *boog.*]

bow² (bou) *v.* **1.** To bend (the head, knee, or body) in order to express greeting, consent, courtesy, submission, or veneration. **2.** To acquiesce; submit. *—n.* An inclination of the head or body, as in greeting, consent, etc. **—take a bow.** To accept applause. [< OE *būgan.* See bheug-.]

bow³ (bō) *n.* **1.** Something that is bent, curved, or arched. **2.** A weapon consisting of a curved stave, strung taut, and used to launch arrows. **3.** A rod strung with horsehair, used in playing violins, violas, etc. **4.** A knot usually having two loops and two ends. *—v.* **1.** To bend into a bow. **2.** To play a stringed instrument with a bow. [< OE *boga,* bow, arch. See bheug-.]

bowd•ler•ize (bōd'lə-rīz', boud'-) *v.* **-ized, -izing.** To expurgate prudishly. [< T. *Bowdler* (1754–1825), English editor who published an expurgated edition of Shakespeare's works.] **—bowd'ler•i•za'tion** *n.*

bow•el (bou'əl, boul) *n.* **1.** An intestine, esp. in man. **2.** Often **bowels.** The digestive tract below the stomach. **3. bowels.** The interior of anything. [< OF *bouel.*]

bow•er (bou'ər) *n.* A shaded, leafy recess; arbor. [< OE *būr,* a dwelling. See bheu-.]

bowl¹ (bōl) *n.* **1.** A hemispherical vessel for food or fluids. **2.** A bowl-shaped part, as of a spoon. **3.** A bowl-shaped edifice such as a football stadium. [< OE *bolla.* See bhel-².]

bowl² (bōl) *n.* **1.** A heavy ball rolled in certain games. **2.** A throw of such a ball. *—v.* To throw or roll a ball in bowling. **—bowl along.** To move smoothly and rapidly. **—bowl over. 1.** To knock over with something rolled. **2.** To overwhelm. [< L *bulla,* ball.]

bow•leg•ged (bō'lĕg'ĭd, -lĕgd') *adj.* Having legs that curve outward at the knee.

bowl•er¹ (bō'lər) *n.* One that bowls.

bowl•er² (bō'lər) *n. Chiefly Brit.* A derby hat. [< J. *Bowler,* 19th-century London hatmaker.]

bowl•ing (bō'lĭng) *n.* A game played by rolling a ball down a wooden alley in order to knock down a triangular group of ten pins.

bowling alley. 1. An alley used in bowling. **2.** A building containing such alleys.

bow•sprit (bou'sprĭt', bō'-) *n.* A spar extending forward from the bow of a ship. [< MLG *bōchsprēt.*]

box¹ (bŏks) *n.* **1.** A rectangular container, often with a lid. **2.** The amount such a container can hold. **3.** A separated compartment for a small group, as in a theater. **4.** A booth. **5.** An awkward situation. *—v.* To place in or as if in a box. [< OE.]

box² (bŏks) *n.* A blow or cuff. *—v.* **1.** To hit with the hand. **2.** To engage in a boxing match with. [ME.]

box³ (bŏks) *n.* **1.** A shrub with small evergreen leaves and hard, yellowish wood. **2.** Also **box•wood** (bŏks'woōd'). The wood of this shrub. [< OE < L *buxus.*]

box•car (bŏks'kär') *n.* An enclosed and covered railway car for the transportation of freight.

box•er¹ (bŏk'sər) *n.* A pugilist.

ô paw, for/oi boy/ou out/oō took/oō coo/p pop/r run/s sauce/sh shy/t to/th thin/*th* the/
ŭ cut/ûr fur/v van/w wag/y yes/z size/zh vision/ə ago, item, edible, gallop, circus/

box·er² (bŏk'sər) *n.* A short-haired dog with a brownish coat and a square-jawed muzzle.
box·ing (bŏk'sĭng) *n.* The sport of fighting with the fists.
box office. A ticket office, as of a theater.
boy (boi) *n.* A male child or youth. —*interj.* Used as a mild exclamation. [ME *boye,* orig "male servant," "knave."] —**boy'hood'** *n.*
boy·cott (boi'kŏt') *v.* To abstain from using, buying, or dealing with, as a means of protest. [< C. *Boycott* (1832–1897), Irish land agent.] —**boy'cott'** *n.*
boy·sen·ber·ry (boi'zən-bĕr'ē) *n.* A large, edible berry hybridized from the loganberry, blackberry, and raspberry. [< R. *Boysen,* 20th-century American horticulturist.]
bp boiling point.
bp. bishop.
B.P. bills payable.
B.P.O.E. Benevolent and Protective Order of Elks.
Br bromine.
Br. 1. Britain; British. 2. Brother (religious).
B/R bills receivable.
bra (brä) *n.* A brassiere.
brace (brās) *n.* 1. A clamp. 2. Any device that steadies or supports something. 3. **braces.** A pair of suspenders. 4. An appliance used to support a bodily part. 5. Often **braces.** An arrangement of bands and wires fixed to the teeth to correct irregular alignment. 6. A cranklike device for securing and turning a bit. 7. One of two symbols, { }, used to connect written or printed lines. 8. *pl.* **brace.** A pair of like things. —*v.* **braced, bracing.** 1. To support with or as if with a brace. 2. To prepare so as to be ready for an impact or danger. 3. To invigorate. —**brace up.** To summon one's strength or endurance. [ME, arm guard, support.]
brace·let (brās'lĭt) *n.* An ornamental band or chain for the wrist. [< OF *bracel,* "little arm," armlet.]
brack·en (brăk'ən) *n.* A large fern with tough stems and branching, finely divided fronds. [ME *braken.*]
brack·et (brăk'ĭt) *n.* 1. A simple rigid structure fixed to a vertical surface and projecting to support a shelf or other weight. 2. A shelf supported by brackets. 3. a. Either of a pair of symbols, [ ], used to enclose written or printed material. b. Either of a pair of symbols, < >, similarly used. 4. A classification, esp. according to income. —*v.* 1. To support with brackets. 2. To place within brackets. 3. To classify or group together. [< OF *braguette,* a pouch.]
brack·ish (brăk'ĭsh) *adj.* Containing some salt; briny. [< Du *brak,* salty.]
bract (brăkt) *n.* A leaflike plant part below a flower or flower cluster. [< L *bractea, brattea,* metal plate or leaf.]
brad (brăd) *n.* A tapered nail with a small head or a side projection instead of a head. [< ON *broddr,* spike.]
brae (brā) *n. Scot.* A hillside. [ME *bra.*]
brag (brăg) *v.* **bragged, bragging.** To talk boastfully. [ME *braggen.*] —**brag'ger** *n.*

brag·ga·do·ci·o (brăg'ə-dō'shē-ō) *n., pl.* -os. 1. A braggart. 2. a. Empty bragging. b. Swaggering manner. [< *Braggadocchio,* name coined by Edmund Spenser (1552?–1599), British poet.]
brag·gart (brăg'ərt) *n.* One given to bragging. [< F *braguer,* to brag.]
Brah·ma (brä'mə) *n. Hinduism.* The personification of divine reality in its creative aspect.

Brahma

Brah·man (brä'mən) *n.* Also **Brah·min** (-mĭn). 1. The single principle comprising all reality, goal of Vedantic mysticism. 2. A member of the highest Hindu caste, originally composed of priests. [< Sk *brahmán-,* priest.]
Brah·man·ism (brä'mən-ĭz'əm) *n.* Also **Brah·min·ism** (brä'mĭn-). 1. The religious practices and beliefs of ancient India. 2. The social caste system of the Brahmans of India. —**Brah'man·ist** *n.*
Brah·ma·pu·tra (brä'mə-pōō'trə). A river of NE India and East Pakistan.
Brahms (brämz), **Johannes.** 1833–1897. German composer.
braid (brād) *v.* 1. To interweave three or more strands of; plait. 2. To decorate with an ornamental trim. —*n.* 1. A narrow length of braided fabric, hair, etc. 2. An ornamental trim. [< OE *bregdan.* See **bherək-.**] —**braid'er** *n.*
Braille (brāl) *n.* Also **braille.** A system of writing and printing for the blind, in which raised dots represent letters and numerals. [< L. *Braille* (1809–1852), French musician and inventor.]
brain (brān) *n.* 1. The portion of the central nervous system in the vertebrate cranium that is responsible for the interpretation of sensory impulses, the coordination and control of bodily activities, and the exercise of emotion and thought. 2. *Informal.* Often **brains.** Intellectual

---

ă pat/ā ate/âr care/ä bar/b bib/ch chew/d deed/ĕ pet/ē be/f fĭt/g gag/h hat/hw what/
ĭ pit/ī pie/îr pier/j judge/k kick/l lid, fatal/m mum/n no, sudden/ng sing/ŏ pot/ō go/

a,1	b,2	c,3	d,4	e,5	f,6	g,7	h,8	i,9
j,0	k	l	m	n	o	p	q	r
s	t	u	v	w	x	y	z	&

punctuation

,	;	:	.	!	(	)	" ?	"

apostrophe	numeral	hyphen	capital	numerical positions in the cell
				1 ● ● 4
				2 ● ● 5
				3 ● ● 6

Braille alphabet

capacity. —*v.* To smash in the skull of. [< OE *brægen.* See **mregh-mo.**]

brain child. *Informal.* An original idea or plan.

brain•less (brăn'lĭs) *adj.* Stupid.

brain•storm (brăn'stôrm') *n.* A sudden inspiration.

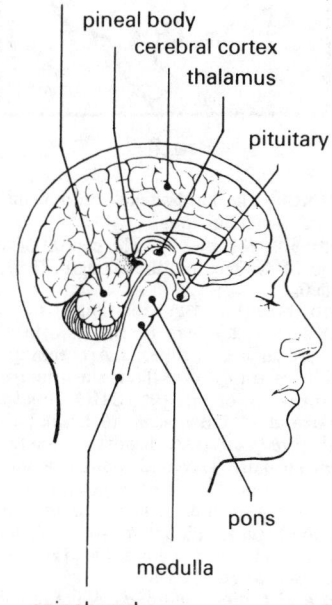

cerebellum
pineal body
cerebral cortex
thalamus
pituitary
pons
medulla
spinal cord

brain

brain•wash (brăn'wŏsh', -wôsh') *v.* To subject to brainwashing.

brain•wash•ing (brăn'wŏsh'ĭng, -wôsh'ĭng) *n.* Intensive indoctrination to change a person's convictions radically.

brain wave. 1. A rhythmic fluctuation of electric potential between parts of the brain. **2.** A sudden inspiration.

brain•y (brā'nē) *adj.* **-ier, -iest.** *Informal.* Intelligent; learned; smart. —**brain'i•ly** *adv.* —**brain'-i•ness** *n.*

braise (brāz) *v.* **braised, braising.** To cook by browning and then simmering in a covered container. [< F *braise,* hot charcoal.]

brake[1] (brāk) *n.* A device for slowing or stopping motion, as of a vehicle or machine. —*v.* **braked, braking.** To reduce the speed of with or as if with a brake. [< ME, crushing instrument.]

brake[2] (brāk) *n.* A fern such as bracken. [ME, var of BRACKEN.]

brake[3] (brāk) *n.* A densely overgrown area; thicket. [< OE *(fearn)braca,* bed of (fern).]

brake•age (brā'kĭj) *n.* The action or capacity of a brake.

brake fluid. The liquid used in a hydraulic brake cylinder.

brake horsepower. The actual or useful horsepower of an engine.

brake•man (brāk'mən) *n.* A railroad employee who assists the conductor and checks on the operation of the train's brakes.

brake shoe. A curved metal block that presses against and thereby arrests the rotation of a wheel.

bram•ble (brăm'bəl) *n.* A prickly plant or shrub such as the blackberry or the raspberry. [< OE *brǽmbel.* See **bhrem-.**] —**bram'bly** *adj.*

bran (brăn) *n.* The outer husks of cereal grains separated from the flour by sifting. [< OF.]

ô paw, for/oi boy/ou out/ŏŏ took/ōō coo/p pop/r run/s sauce/sh shy/t to/th thin/*th* the/
ŭ cut/ûr fur/v van/w wag/y yes/z size/zh vision/ə ago, item, edible, gallop, circus/

branch (brănch, bränch) *n.* **1.** An extension dividing off from the trunk, main stem, or a limb of a tree or plant. **2.** A similar structure or part. **3.** A limited part of a larger or more complex body. —*v.* **1.** To put forth; spread out in branches. **2.** To separate into subdivisions; diverge. —**branch out.** To enlarge the scope of one's interest or activities. [< LL *branca,* foot, paw.]

brand (brănd) *n.* **1.** A trademark or label. **2.** The make of a product thus marked: *a popular brand of soap.* **3.** A mark indicating ownership, burned on the hide of an animal. **4.** A mark formerly burned into the flesh of criminals. **5.** Any mark of disgrace; stigma. **6.** A piece of burning or charred wood. —*v.* **1.** To mark with or as if with a brand. **2.** To stigmatize. [< OE, piece of burning wood. See **bhreu-²**.]

bran·dish (brăn'dĭsh) *v.* **1.** To flourish menacingly, as a weapon. **2.** To display ostentatiously. [< OF *brand,* sword, blade.]

brand-new (brănd'n/y/ōō') *adj.* In fresh and unused condition.

bran·dy (brăn'dē) *n., pl.* **-dies.** An alcoholic liquor distilled from wine or fermented fruit juice. —*v.* **-died, -dying.** To flavor or preserve with brandy. [< Du *brandewijn,* "distilled wine."]

brash (brăsh) *adj.* **1.** Hasty and unthinking; rash. **2.** Impudent; saucy. [Perh imit.] —**brash'ly** *adv.* —**brash'ness** *n.*

Bra·sí·lia (brə-zē'lyə). The capital of Brazil. Pop. 141,000.

brass (brăs, bräs) *n.* **1.** An alloy of copper and zinc with other metals in varying lesser amounts. **2.** Objects made of brass. **3. brasses.** *Mus.* Wind instruments made of brass. **4.** *Informal.* Blatant self-assurance; effrontery. **5.** *Slang.* High-ranking military officers. [< OE *bræs.*] —**brass** *adj.*

bras·siere, bras·sière (brə-zîr') *n.* A woman's undergarment worn to support and shape the breasts. [F *brassière.*]

brass tacks. *Informal.* Essential facts.

brat (brăt) *n.* A child, esp. an unruly one. [Prob < dial *brat,* coarse garment.] —**brat'ti·ness** *n.* —**brat'ty** *adj.*

bra·va·do (brə-vä'dō) *n., pl.* **-does** or **-dos.** **1.** Defiant or swaggering show of courage; false bravery. **2.** An instance of such behavior. [< Span *bravo,* brave.]

brave (brāv) *adj.* **braver, bravest.** **1.** Displaying courage. **2.** Making a fine display; splendid. —*n.* A North American Indian warrior. —*v.* **braved, braving.** **1.** To undergo or face courageously. **2.** To defy; challenge. [< VL *brabus,* wild, savage.] —**brave'ly** *adv.* —**brave'ness** *n.*

brav·er·y (brā'və-rē, brāv'rē) *n., pl.* **-ies.** The state or quality of being brave; courage.

bra·vo (brä'vō, brä-vō') *interj.* Expressive of approval. —*n., pl.* **-vos.** A shout or cry of "bravo." [It, fine, brave.]

bra·vu·ra (brə-vyōōr'ə) *n.* **1.** Brilliant musical technique or style. **2.** A showy manner or display. [It, "bravery," spirit.]

brawl (brôl) *n.* A noisy quarrel or fight. —*v.* To quarrel noisily. [ME *brawlen.*]

brawn (brôn) *n.* **1.** Solid and well-developed muscles. **2.** Muscular power. [< OF *braon,* flesh, muscle.] —**brawn'i·ly** *adv.* —**brawn'i·ness** *n.* —**brawn'y** *adj.*

bray (brā) *v.* To utter a loud, harsh cry, as a donkey. —*n.* **1.** The cry of a donkey. **2.** Any sound resembling this. [ME *brayen,* to make noise.]

braze (brāz) *v.* **brazed, brazing.** To solder together using a solder with a high melting point. [Prob < F *braser.*]

bra·zen (brā'zən) *adj.* **1.** Made of brass. **2.** Resembling brass in color, quality, or hardness. **3.** Having a loud, resonant sound. **4.** Impudent; bold. [< OE *bræsen* < *bræs,* BRASS.] —**bra'zen·ly** *adv.* —**bra'zen·ness** *n.*

bra·zier¹ (brā'zhər) *n.* One who works in brass.

bra·zier² (brā'zhər) *n.* A metal pan for holding burning coals or charcoal. [< F *braise,* burning coals.]

Bra·zil (brə-zĭl'). A republic of South America. Pop. 70,967,000. Cap. Brasília. —**Bra·zil'ian** *adj. & n.*

Brazil

Brazil nut. The hard-shelled, edible nut of a tropical American tree.

Braz·za·ville (brăz'ə-vĭl). The capital of the Republic of Congo, on the Congo River. Pop. 200,000.

breach (brēch) *n.* **1.** A violation or infraction, as of a law. **2.** A gap or rift, esp. in a solid structure such as a dike. **3.** A breaking up of friendly relations. —*v.* To make a hole or gap in; break through. [< OHG *brehhan,* to break, and < OE *brecan,* to break.]

bread (brĕd) *n.* **1.** A foodstuff made from baked, usually leavened dough made with moistened flour. **2.** Food in general, regarded as necessary for life. **3.** The necessities of life; livelihood: *earn one's bread.* —*v.* To coat with bread crumbs, esp. before cooking. [< OE *brēad.* See **bhreu-².**]

bread and butter. *Informal.* A means of support.

bread·bas·ket (brĕd'băs'kĭt, -bäs'kĭt) *n.* A region serving as a principal source of grain supply.

bread•fruit (brĕd'frōōt') *n.* The large, round, edible fruit of a tropical tree.
bread•stuff (brĕd'stŭf') *n.* **1.** Bread. **2.** Flour or grain used in making bread.
breadth (brĕdth) *n.* **1.** The measure or dimension of something from side to side. **2.** Wide extent or scope. **3.** Liberality of views. [< OE *brǣdu* < Gmc **braithaz,* BROAD.]
bread•win•ner (brĕd'wĭn'ər) *n.* One who supports a family by his earnings.
break (brāk) *v.* **broke, broken, breaking. 1. a.** To separate into or reduce to pieces by sudden force; come apart. **b.** To crack without separating into pieces. **2. a.** To render or become unusable by or as if by breaking. **b.** To give way; collapse. **3.** To force or make a way into, through, or out of. **4.** To pierce the surface of. **5.** To disrupt the continuity or unity of: *break ranks.* **6.** To come into being or notice, esp. suddenly: *The news broke.* **7.** To begin suddenly: *breaks into bloom.* **8.** To change suddenly: *His voice broke.* **9.** To overcome or surpass. **10. a.** To ruin or destroy: *"For a hero loves the world till it breaks him"* (Yeats). **b.** To demote. **c.** To train to obey. **11.** To lessen in force: *break a fall.* **12.** To collapse or crash into surf or spray, as waves. **13.** *Informal.* To occur. **—break in. 1.** To train. **2.** To enter forcibly. **3.** To interrupt. **—break off. 1.** To stop suddenly. **2.** To discontinue a relationship. **—break out. 1.** To erupt. **2.** To escape, as from prison. **—***n.* **1.** The act of breaking. **2.** The result of breaking; a fracture or crack. **3.** A disruption of continuity. **4.** An emergence: *the break of day.* **5.** *Informal.* A stroke of luck. [< OE *brecan.* See **bhreg-**.]
break•age (brā'kĭj) *n.* **1.** The act or process of breaking. **2.** A quantity broken. **3. a.** Loss as a result of breaking. **b.** An allowance for such a loss.
break•down (brāk'doun') *n.* **1.** The act or process of breaking down and failing to function or the condition resulting from this. **2.** A collapse in physical or mental health. **3.** An analysis, outline, or summary consisting of itemized data or essentials. **4.** Disintegration or decomposition into parts or elements.
break•er (brā'kər) *n.* **1.** One that breaks. **2.** A wave that breaks into foam.
break•fast (brĕk'fəst) *n.* The first meal of the day. [< ME *breken faste,* to break (one's) fasting.] **—break'fast** *v.*
break•neck (brāk'nĕk') *adj.* Heedless of safety.
break•through (brāk'thrōō') *n.* **1.** An act of breaking through an obstacle or restriction. **2.** A major achievement that permits further progress, as in technology.
break•wa•ter (brāk'wô'tər, -wŏt'ər) *n.* A barrier that protects a harbor or shore from the impact of waves.
breast (brĕst) *n.* **1.** A mammary gland, esp. the human mammary gland. **2.** The surface of the body extending from the neck to the abdomen. **—make a clean breast of.** To make a full confession of. **—***v.* To confront boldly. [< OE *brēost.* See **bhreus-**.]
breast•bone (brĕst'bōn') *n.* The sternum.

breast•plate (brĕst'plāt') *n.* Armor plate that covers the breast.
breast stroke. A swimming stroke in which one lies face down and extends the arms in front of the head, then sweeps them back laterally while kicking the legs.
breast•work (brĕst'wûrk') *n.* A temporary fortification, usually breast-high.
breath (brĕth) *n.* **1.** The air inhaled and exhaled in respiration. **2.** Respiration. **3.** The capacity to breathe. **4.** A single respiration. **5.** A momentary stirring of air. **6.** A trace. **7.** A soft-spoken sound. [< OE *brǣth,* odor, exhalation. See **bhreu-**.] **—breath'less** *adj.*
breathe (brēth) *v.* **breathed, breathing. 1.** To inhale and exhale. **2.** To live. **3.** To pause to rest. **4.** To utter, esp. quietly. **—breath'a•ble** *adj.*
breath•er (brē'thər) *n.* **1.** One who breathes in a specified manner. **2.** *Informal.* A strenuous or exhausting task. **3.** *Informal.* A short rest period.
breath•tak•ing (brĕth'tā'kĭng) *adj.* Inspiring awe. **—breath'tak'ing•ly** *adv.*
breech (brēch) *n.* **1.** The buttocks. **2.** The part of a firearm behind the barrel or, in a cannon, behind the bore. [< OE *brēc,* breeches.]
breech•es (brĭch'ĭz) *pl.n.* **1.** Knee-length trousers. **2.** Any trousers. [Pl of BREECH.]
breed (brēd) *v.* **bred** (brĕd), **breeding. 1.** To produce (offspring); reproduce. **2.** To bring about; engender. **3.** To raise (animals). **4.** To rear; bring up. **—***n.* **1.** A genetic strain, esp. of a domestic animal developed and maintained by man. **2.** A kind; sort. [< OE *brēdan.* See **bhreu-**.]
breed•ing (brē'dĭng) *n.* **1.** One's line of descent. **2.** Training in the proper forms of social and personal conduct.
breeze (brēz) *n.* **1.** A gentle wind. **2.** A wind from 4 to 31 miles per hour. [Perh < OSpan *briza,* northeast wind.] **—breez'i•ly** *adv.* **—breez'y** *adj.*
Bre•men (brĕm'ən). A city in West Germany. Pop. 588,000.
Bret•on (brĕt'n) *n.* **1.** A native or inhabitant of Brittany. **2.** The Celtic language of Brittany. **—Bret'on** *adj.*
breve (brēv, brĕv) *n.* **1.** A symbol (˘) placed over a vowel to show that it has a short sound. **2.** A single musical note equivalent to two whole notes. [< ME *bref,* brief.]
bre•vi•ar•y (brē'vē-ĕr-ē, brĕv'-ē-) *n., pl.* **-ies.** A book containing the hymns, offices, and prayers for the canonical hours. [L *breviārium,* abridgment.]
brev•i•ty (brĕv'ə-tē) *n.* **1.** Briefness of duration. **2.** Concise expression; terseness. [< L *brevis,* BRIEF.]
brew (brōō) *v.* **1.** To make (ale or beer) from malt and hops by infusion, boiling, and fermentation. **2.** To make (a beverage) by boiling or steeping. **3.** To be imminent; impend. **—***n.* A beverage made by brewing. [< OE *brēowan.* See **bhreu-**.] **—brew'er** *n.*
brew•er•y (brōō'ər-ē) *n., pl.* **-ies.** A place where beer or ale is brewed.

ô paw, for/oi boy/ou out/ōō took/ō̄o coo/p pop/r run/s sauce/sh shy/t to/th thin/*th* the/
ŭ cut/ûr fur/v van/w wag/y yes/z size/zh vision/ə ago, item, edible, gallop, circus/

Brezh·nev (brězh′něf), **Leonid Ilyich.** Born 1906. Soviet statesman; general secretary of the Communist Party (since 1966).

Leonid Brezhnev

bri·ar¹ (brī′ər) *n.* Also **bri·er.** A shrub with a hard, woody root used to make tobacco pipes. [F *bruyère,* heath.]

bri·ar². Variant of **brier.**

bribe (brīb) *n.* Anything offered or given to someone in a position of trust to induce him to act dishonestly. —*v.* **bribed, bribing.** To give or offer a bribe (to). [< OF *briber,* to beg.] —**brib′er** *n.* —**brib′er·y** *n.*

bric-a-brac (brĭk′ə-brăk′) *n.* Objects collectively, usually small, displayed as ornaments. [F *bric-à-brac.*]

brick (brĭk) *n.* A molded rectangular block of clay, baked until hard and used as a construction material. —*v.* To construct or cover with brick. [ME *brike.*]

brick·bat (brĭk′băt′) *n.* **1.** A piece of brick, esp. one used as a weapon. **2.** A blunt criticism or remark.

brick·lay·er (brĭk′lā′ər) *n.* A person skilled in building with bricks. —**brick′lay′ing** *n.*

bri·dal (brīd′l) *n.* A wedding. —*adj.* Of or pertaining to a bride or a wedding. [< OE *brȳdealu,* "bride ale."]

bride (brīd) *n.* A woman recently married or about to be married. [< OE *brȳd* < Gmc *brūdhiz.*]

bride·groom (brīd′grōōm′, -grōōm′) *n.* A man recently married or about to be married. [< OE *brȳdguma,* "bride's man."]

brides·maid (brīdz′mād′) *n.* A woman who attends the bride at a wedding.

bridge¹ (brĭj) *n.* **1.** A structure spanning and providing passage over a waterway or other obstacle. **2.** Anything structurally or functionally analogous to a bridge. **3.** The upper bony ridge of the human nose. **4.** *Mus.* **a.** A thin, upright piece of wood in some stringed instruments that supports the strings above the

sounding board. **b.** A transitional passage connecting two subjects or movements. **5.** *Dent.* A fixed or removable replacement for one or several, but not all, of the natural teeth, usually anchored at each end to a natural tooth. **6.** A crosswise platform above the main deck of a ship from which the ship is controlled. —*v.* **bridged, bridging. 1.** To build a bridge over. **2.** To cross by or as if by a bridge. [< OE *brycg.*] —**bridge′a·ble** *adj.*

bridge² (brĭj) *n.* Any of several card games for four players, derived from whist. [Earlier *biritch.*]

bridge·head (brĭj′hĕd′) *n.* A military position established by advance troops in enemy territory to afford protection for the main attacking force.

Bridge·port (brĭj′pôrt′, -pōrt′). A city of Connecticut. Pop. 155,000.

Bridge·town (brĭj′toun′). The capital of Barbados. Pop. 94,000.

bridge·work (brĭj′wûrk′) *n.* *Dent.* **1.** A bridge. **2.** Prosthetics involving bridges.

bri·dle (brīd′l) *n.* **1.** The harness fitted about a horse's head, used to restrain or guide. **2.** Any restraint. —*v.* **-dled, -dling. 1.** To put a bridle on. **2.** To control or restrain. **3.** To display scorn or resentment. [< OE *brīdel.* See **bherək-.**] —**bri′dler** *n.*

brief (brēf) *adj.* **1.** Short in time or extent. **2.** Condensed in expression. —*n.* **1.** A short or condensed statement or summary. **2.** A summary of a legal case or argument. —*v.* **1.** To summarize. **2.** To give concise information or instructions to. [< L *brevis,* short.] —**brief′ly** *adv.* —**brief′ness** *n.*

brief·case (brēf′kās′) *n.* A portable rectangular case.

bri·er¹ (brī′ər) *n.* Also **bri·ar.** A thorny plant, such as a rosebush. [< OE *brǣr, brēr.*]

bri·er². Variant of **briar¹.**

brig¹ (brĭg) *n.* A two-masted sailing ship, square-rigged on both masts. [Short for BRIGANTINE.]

brig² (brĭg) *n.* A ship's prison. [Prob < BRIG¹.]

bri·gade (brĭ-gād′) *n.* **1.** A military unit consisting of a variable number of combat battalions, with supporting services. **2.** Any group of persons organized for a specific purpose. [< OIt *brigata,* troop, company.]

brig·a·dier general (brĭg′ə-dir′) *pl.* **brigadier generals.** An officer ranking above a colonel in the U.S. Army, Air Force, and Marine Corps. [F < BRIGADE.]

brig·and (brĭg′ənd) *n.* A robber, esp. one of a band. [ME *brigaunt,* foot soldier, bandit.]

brig·an·tine (brĭg′ən-tēn′) *n.* A two-masted, square-rigged sailing ship having a fore-and-aft mainsail. [< It *brigantino,* "pirate ship."]

Brig. Gen. brigadier general.

bright (brīt) *adj.* **1.** Emitting or reflecting light; shining. **2.** Brilliant in color; vivid. **3.** Glorious; splendid. **4.** Auspicious. **5.** Happy; cheerful. **6.** Intelligent. [< OE *beorht.* See **bherəg-.**] —**bright′ly** *adv.* —**bright′ness** *n.*

bright·en (brīt′n) *v.* **1.** To make or become bright or brighter. **2.** To make or become more cheerful.

ă pat/ā ate/âr care/ä bar/b bib/ch chew/d deed/ĕ pet/ē be/f fit/g gag/h hat/hw what/ ĭ pit/ī pie/îr pier/j judge/k kick/l lid, fatal/m mum/n no, sudden/ng sing/ŏ pot/ō go/

bril•liant (brĭl'yənt) *adj.* **1.** Shining. **2.** Brightly vivid in color. **3.** Glorious; splendid. **4.** Marked by extraordinary intellect. [< F *briller*, to shine.] —**bril'liance, bril'lian•cy** *n.* —**bril'liant•ly** *adv.*

bril•lian•tine (brĭl'yən-tēn') *n.* An oily, perfumed hairdressing. [< F *brillant*, brilliant.]

brim (brĭm) *n.* **1.** The rim or uppermost edge of a cup or other vessel. **2.** A projecting rim or edge. [ME *brimme.*]

brim•ful (brĭm'fŏŏl') *adj.* Also **brim•full.** Completely full.

brim•stone (brĭm'stōn') *n. Obs.* Sulfur. [< OE *brynstān.*]

brin•dle (brĭnd'l) *adj.* Also **brin•dled** (brĭnd'əld). Tawny or grayish with darker streaks or spots, as an animal's coat. [ME *brende.*]

brine (brīn) *n.* **1.** Water containing large amounts of a salt, esp. of sodium chloride. **2.** The ocean. [< OE *brȳne.*]

bring (brĭng) *v.* **brought, bringing. 1.** To take with oneself to a place. **2.** To carry as an attribute. **3.** To lead into a specified state or situation. **4.** To induce. **5.** To cause to occur. **6.** To sell for. —**bring about.** To cause to happen. —**bring forth.** To produce. —**bring off.** To accomplish successfully. —**bring out. 1.** To reveal. **2.** To produce. —**bring up. 1.** To rear (a child). **2.** To mention. [< OE *bringan.* See bher-¹.]

brin (brĭn) *n.* One of the ribs of a fan. [Fr *brin.*]

bring•ing-up (brĭng'ĭng-ŭp') *n.* The care, training, and education of a child.

brink (brĭngk) *n.* **1.** The upper edge of a steep or vertical declivity. **2.** The verge of something. [ME *brinke.*]

brin•y (brī'nē) *adj.* **-ier, -iest.** Of, pertaining to, or resembling brine; salty. —*n. Slang.* The sea. —**brin'i•ness** *n.*

bri•o (brē'ō) *n.* Vigor; vivacity. [It, "vivacity."]

bri•oche (brē-ōsh', -ōsh') *n.* A rich, rounded, soft roll or bun. [< OF.]

bri•quette, bri•quet (brĭ-kĕt') *n.* A block of compressed coal dust or charcoal. [< F *brique*, brick.]

Bris•bane (brĭz'bən, -bān). A city of SE Australia. Pop. 664,000.

brisk (brĭsk) *adj.* **1.** Moving or acting quickly. **2.** Keen or sharp. **3.** Invigorating. [Prob var of BRUSQUE.] —**brisk'ly** *adv.* —**brisk'ness** *n.*

bris•ket (brĭs'kĭt) *n.* **1.** The chest of an animal. **2.** Meat from this part. [ME *brusket.*]

bris•ling (brĭz'lĭng, brĭs'-) *n.* A small sardine. [Norw.]

bris•tle (brĭs'əl) *n.* A short, stiff hair. —*v.* **-tled, -tling. 1.** To erect the bristles, as an animal. **2.** To react with agitation. **3.** To stand out stiffly. **4.** To be covered with bristlelike growth. [< OE *byrst*, bristle. See bhar-.] —**bris'tly** *adj.*

Bris•tol (brĭs'təl). A port in SW England. Pop. 431,000.

Brit. Britain; British.

Brit•ain (brĭt'n). Great Britain.

britch•es (brĭch'ĭz) *pl.n. Informal.* Breeches.

Brit•i•cism (brĭt'ə-sĭz'əm) *n.* A word or phrase peculiar to English as spoken in Great Britain.

Brit•ish (brĭt'ĭsh) *adj.* Of or pertaining to Great Britain, the United Kingdom, or its people. —*n.* **1.** The people of Great Britain. **2.** The language spoken in Great Britain; British English. **3.** The language spoken by the ancient Britons.

British Co•lum•bi•a (kə-lŭm'bē-ə). The westernmost province of Canada. Pop. 1,789,000. Cap. Victoria.

British Commonwealth of Nations. The former name for the **Commonwealth of Nations.**

British Empire. The former British Commonwealth of Nations and all British colonies, dependencies, etc.

British English. The English language as spoken, pronounced, and written in England.

Brit•ish•er (brĭt'ĭ-shər) *n. Informal.* A native of Great Britain.

British Guiana. The former name for Guyana.

British Hon•du•ras (hŏn-d/y/ŏŏr'əs). The former name for Belize.

British Isles. A group of islands off the coast of Europe, comprising Great Britain, Ireland, and adjacent smaller islands.

British thermal unit. The quantity of heat required to raise the temperature of 1 pound of water by 1°F.

British warm. A short, double-breasted overcoat originally worn by British army officers.

Brit•on (brĭt'n) *n.* **1.** A native of Britain. **2.** One of a Celtic people who inhabited ancient Britain.

brit•tle (brĭt'l) *adj.* Likely to break; fragile: *brittle porcelain.* [< OE *brytel.* See bhreu-¹.] —**brit'tle•ness** *n.*

bro. brother.

broach (brōch) *n.* **1.** A tapered, serrated tool used to shape or enlarge a hole. **2.** A gimlet for tapping casks. **3.** Variant of **brooch.** —*v.* **1.** To begin to talk about. **2.** To pierce in order to draw off liquid. [< OF *broche*, a spit.] —**broach'er** *n.*

broad (brôd) *adj.* **1.** Wide from side to side. **2.** Spacious. **3.** Widely diffused. **4.** Covering a wide scope. **5.** Liberal; tolerant. **6.** Plain and clear; not subtle. **7.** Indicating a vowel that is pronounced as it is when the *a* in *bath* is pronounced like the *a* in *bard.* [< OE *brād* < Gmc *braithaz.*] —**broad'ly** *adv.*

broad arrow. 1. An arrow with a wide, barbed head. **2.** A wide arrowhead mark identifying British government property.

broad•ax, broad•axe (brôd'ăks') *n., pl.* **-axes.** An ax with a wide, flat head and a short handle; a battle-ax.

broad•bill (brôd'bĭl') *n.* Any of various birds having a short, wide bill and brightly colored plumage.

broad•brim (brôd'brĭm') *n.* A hat with a broad, flat brim, as those worn by Quakers.

broad•cast (brôd'kăst', -käst') *v.* **-cast** or **-casted, -casting. 1.** To transmit (a program) by radio or television. **2.** To make known widely. **3.** To sow (seed). —*n.* **1.** Transmission of a radio or television program or signal. **2.** A radio or television program. —*adj.* **1.** Of or pertaining to transmission by radio or television. **2.** Scattered over a wide area. —*adv.*

ô **paw,** for/oi **boy**/ou **out**/ŏŏ **took**/ōō **coo**/p **pop**/r **run**/s **sauce**/sh **shy**/t **to**/th **thin**/*th* **the**/
ŭ **cut**/ûr **fur**/v **van**/w **wag**/y **yes**/z **size**/zh **vision**/ə **ago, item, edible, gallop, circus**/

In a scattered manner; far and wide. —**broad'-cast'er** *n.*

broad•cloth (brôd'klôth', -klŏth') *n.* **1.** A thickly textured woolen cloth. **2.** A fine, closely woven cotton, silk, or synthetic fabric.

broad•en (brôd'n) *v.* To make or become broad or broader.

broad jump. In track events, a jump made for distance rather than height.

broad•loom (brôd'lōōm') *n.* Carpet woven on a loom from 4½ feet to 18 feet wide. —**broad'loom'** *adj.*

broad-mind•ed (brôd'mīn'dĭd) *adj.* Liberal; tolerant. —**broad'-mind'ed•ness** *n.*

broad•side (brôd'sīd') *n.* **1.** The side of a ship above the water line. **2.** Simultaneous discharge of all the guns on one side of a warship. **3.** An explosive verbal attack.

broad•sword (brôd'sôrd', -sōrd') *n.* A sword with a wide blade.

broad•tail (brôd'tāl') *n.* The flat, rippled fur of a prematurely born Asian sheep.

bro•cade (brō-kād') *n.* A fabric with a raised interwoven design. [< It *broccato*, embossed fabric.] —**bro•cad'ed** *adj.*

broc•co•li (brŏk'ə-lē) *n.* A plant with a green, densely clustered flower head eaten as a vegetable before the buds open. [< It *broccolo*, cabbage sprout.]

bro•chure (brō-shōōr') *n.* A pamphlet or booklet. [F, "a stitching."]

bro•gan (brō'gən) *n.* A heavy, ankle-high shoe. [< Ir Gael *brōg*, BROGUE².]

brogue¹ (brōg) *n.* A strong dialectal accent, esp. an Irish accent. [< BROGUE².]

brogue² (brōg) *n.* A sturdy oxford shoe. [Ir Gael *brōg*.]

broil (broil) *v.* To cook by direct radiant heat. [< OF *bruller, brusler*, to burn.]

broil•er (broi'lər) *n.* **1.** A device or compartment used for broiling. **2.** A young chicken suitable for broiling.

broke (brōk) *p.t.* of **break**. —*adj. Informal.* Lacking funds.

bro•ken (brō'kən) *p.p.* of **break**. —*adj.* **1.** Fractured; shattered. **2.** Violated, as promises. **3.** Discontinuous. **4.** Spoken imperfectly. **5.** Defeated; humbled. **6.** Tamed. **7.** Not functioning.

bro•ken•heart•ed (brō'kən-här'tĭd) *adj.* Grievously sad.

bro•ker (brō'kər) *n.* One who acts as an agent in negotiating contracts, purchases, or sales in return for a fee. [ME, peddler, go-between.]

bro•ker•age (brō'kər-ĭj) *n.* **1.** The business of a broker. **2.** A fee or commission paid to a broker.

bro•mide (brō'mīd') *n.* **1.** A binary compound of bromine. **2.** A sedative, **potassium bromide. 3.** A commonplace remark or notion. —**bro•mid'ic** (-mĭd'ĭk) *adj.*

bro•mine (brō'mēn') *n. Symbol* **Br** A heavy, corrosive, reddish-brown, nonmetallic liquid element used in producing gasoline antiknock mixtures, fumigants, and photographic chemicals. Atomic weight 79.904, atomic number 35. [< Gk *brōmos*, stench.]

bron•chi•al (brŏng'kē-əl) *adj.* Of or pertaining to the bronchi or any of their extensions. —**bron'chi•al•ly** *adv.*

bron•chi•tis (brŏng-kī'tĭs) *n.* Chronic or acute inflammation of the mucous membrane of the bronchial tubes.

broncho–. *comb. form.* Bronchi.

bron•chus (brŏng'kəs) *n., pl.* **-chi** (-kī', -kē'). Either of two main branches of the trachea, leading directly to the lungs. [< Gk *bronkhos*, trachea, windpipe, throat.]

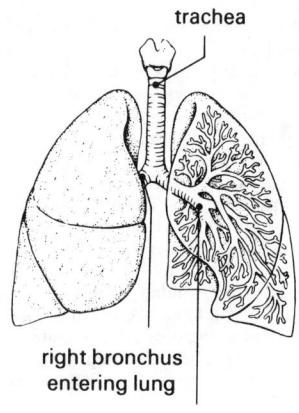

trachea

right bronchus
entering lung

bronchial tree

bronchus

bron•co (brŏng'kō) *n., pl.* **-cos.** A wild or semiwild horse of W North America. [< Span, rough, wild.]

bron•to•saur (brŏn'tə-sôr') *n.* Also **bron•to•sau•rus** (brŏn'tə-sôr'əs). A very large, herbivorous dinosaur. [< Gk *brontē*, thunder.]

Bronx, the (brŏngks). A borough of New York City. Pop. 1,425,000.

bronze (brŏnz) *n.* **1.** Any of various alloys principally of copper and tin. **2.** A work of art made of bronze. **3.** Moderate yellowish or olive brown. —*v.* **bronzed, bronzing.** To give the appearance of bronze to. [< It *bronzo*.] —**bronze** *adj.*

Bronze Age. A period of human culture between the Stone Age and the Iron Age, characterized by weapons and implements made of bronze.

brooch (brōch, brōōch) *n.* Also **broach.** A large decorative pin or clasp. [ME *broche*, brooch, broach (tool).]

brood (brōōd) *n.* A group of young animals, esp. of young birds hatched at one time. —*v.* **1.** To sit on or cover (eggs or newly hatched young). **2.** To ponder moodily. —*adj.* Kept for breeding: *a brood mare.* [< OE *brōd.* See bhreu-².]

brood•er (brōō'dər) *n.* **1.** One that broods. **2.** A heated enclosure for raising young chickens.

brood•y (brōō'dē) *adj.* **-ier, -iest.** Inclined to brood; moody; meditative.

ă pat/ā ate/âr care/ä bar/b bib/ch chew/d deed/ĕ pet/ē be/f fit/g gag/h hat/hw what/
ĭ pit/ī pie/îr pier/j judge/k kick/l lid, fatal/m mum/n no, sudden/ng sing/ŏ pot/ō go/

brook¹ (brŏŏk) *n.* A small freshwater stream. [< OE *brōc* < Gmc *brōka.*]
brook² (brŏŏk) *v.* To put up with. [< OE *brūcan*, to enjoy.]
Brook•lyn (brŏŏk'lĭn). A borough of New York City. Pop. 2,627,000.
broom (brŏŏm, brŏŏm) *n.* 1. A long-handled brushlike implement used for sweeping. 2. A shrub with yellow flowers and small leaves. [< OE *brŏm*, broom plant. See bhrem-.] —**broom'y** *adj.*
bros. brothers.
broth (brôth, brŏth) *n.* Soup consisting of the water in which meat, fish, or vegetables have been boiled. [< OE. See bhreu-².]
broth•el (brŏth'əl, brô*th*'-, brô'thəl, -*th*əl) *n.* A house of prostitution. [< OE *brēothan*, to deteriorate. See bhreu-¹.]
broth•er (brŭ*th*'ər) *n.* 1. A male having the same mother and father as another, **full brother**, or one parent in common with another, **half brother.** 2. One who has a close bond with another or others. 3. A member of a men's religious order who is not in holy orders. [< OE *brōthor*. See bhrāter-.] —**broth'er•ly** *adj.* —**broth'er•li•ness** *n.*
broth•er•hood (brŭ*th*'ər-hŏŏd') *n.* 1. The state of being a brother or brothers. 2. An association of men united for common purposes. 3. All the members of a specific profession or trade.
broth•er-in-law (brŭ*th*'ər-ĭn-lô') *n.*, *pl.* **brothers-in-law.** 1. The brother of one's spouse. 2. The husband of one's sister. 3. The husband of the sister of one's spouse.
brougham (brŏŏm, brŏŏ'əm, brô'əm) *n.* 1. A closed carriage with an open driver's seat in front. 2. An automobile with an open driver's seat. [< H.P. *Brougham* (1778–1868), Scottish jurist.]
brought (brôt). *p.t.* & *p.p.* of **bring.**
brou•ha•ha (brŏŏ'hä-hä') *n.* An uproar. [F.]
brow (brou) *n.* 1. a. The ridge over the eyes. b. An eyebrow. c. The forehead. 2. The edge of a steep place. [< OE *brū*, eyelash, eyelid, eyebrow. See bhrū-.]
brow•beat (brou'bēt') *v.* To intimidate; domineer; bully.
brown (broun) *n.* Any of a group of colors between red and yellow in hue. —*adj.* 1. Of the color brown. 2. Deeply suntanned. —*v.* To make or become brown, esp. to cook until brown. [< OE *brūn.* See bher-³.] —**brown'ish** *adj.*
brown•ie (brou'nē) *n.* 1. A small, helpful elf of folklore. 2. A square of flat, moist chocolate cake.
Brown•ing (brou'nĭng), **Robert.** 1812–1889. English poet.
brown•stone (broun'stōn') *n.* 1. A brownish-red sandstone. 2. A house built or faced with such stone.
browse (brouz) *v.* **browsed, browsing.** 1. To inspect in a leisurely and casual way. 2. To feed on leaves, young shoots, and other vegetation; graze (on). [< OF *broust*, shoot, twig.]
Brue•ghel (brœ'gəl), **Pieter.** 1525?–1569. Flemish painter.

bru•in (brŏŏ'ĭn) *n.* A bear. [Du, BRUIN, "brown."]
bruise (brŏŏz) *v.* **bruised, bruising.** 1. a. To injure the skin without rupture. b. To suffer such injury. 2. To dent or mar. 3. To pound into fragments. —*n.* An injury in which the skin is not broken; contusion. [< OE *brȳsan*, to crush (see bhreus-²) and OF *bruisier*, to break, crush.]
bruit (brŏŏt) *v.* To spread news of; repeat. [< OF, noise.]
brunch (brŭnch) *n.* A combination of breakfast and lunch. [BR(EAKFAST) + (L)UNCH.]
Bru•nei (brŏŏ-nī'). A British-protected sultanate of NW Borneo, on the South China Sea. Pop. 135,600. Cap. Bandar Seri Begawan.

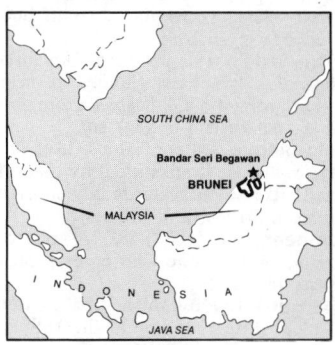

Brunei

bru•net (brŏŏ-nĕt'). Also *fem.* **brunette.** *adj.* Dark or brown in color, as hair. —*n.* A person with brown hair. [< OF *brun*, brown.]
brunt (brŭnt) *n.* The main impact, force, or burden, as of a blow. [ME *brunt.*]
brush¹ (brŭsh) *n.* 1. A device consisting of bristles or other flexible material fastened into a handle, for scrubbing, applying paint, grooming the hair, etc. 2. A light touch in passing. 3. A brief encounter. 4. The bushy tail of a fox or other animal. 5. A sliding connection completing a circuit between a fixed and a moving conductor. —*v.* 1. To use a brush (on). 2. To apply or remove with or as if with motions of a brush. 3. To touch lightly in passing; graze against. [< OF *broisse.*]
brush² (brŭsh) *n.* Also **brush•wood** (brŭsh'-wŏŏd'). 1. A dense growth of bushes. 2. Cut or broken branches. [< OF *broce.*]
brush-off (brŭsh'ôf', -ŏf') *n.* Slang. An abrupt dismissal.
brusque (brŭsk) *adj.* Also **brusk.** Abrupt and curt; discourteously blunt. [< It *brusco*, sour, sharp.] —**brusque'ness** *n.*
Brus•sels (brŭs'əlz). The capital of Belgium. Pop. 1,066,000.
Brussels sprouts. The small, budlike heads of a variety of cabbage, eaten as a vegetable.
bru•tal (brŏŏt'l) *adj.* Characteristic of a brute; cruel; harsh; crude. —**bru•tal'i•ty** (brŏŏ-tăl'ə-tē) *n.* —**bru'tal•ly** *adv.*

ô paw, for/oi boy/ou out/ŏŏ took/ŏŏ coo/p pop/r run/s sauce/sh shy/t to/th thin/*th* the/
ŭ cut/ûr fur/v van/w wag/y yes/z size/zh vision/ə ago, item, edible, gallop, circus/

bru•tal•ize (brōōt'l-īz') v. -ized, -izing. 1. To render brutal. 2. To treat in a brutal manner.
brute (brōōt) n. 1. An animal; beast. 2. A brutal person. —adj. 1. Of or relating to beasts. 2. Characterized by physical power or instinct rather than intelligence: brute force. [< L brūtus, heavy.] —brut'ish adj.
B.S. 1. Bachelor of Science. 2. balance sheet. 3. bill of sale.
B.S.A. Boy Scouts of America.
bsh. bushel.
bsk. basket.
Bt. baronet.
Btu British thermal unit.
bu. 1. bureau. 2. bushel.
bub•ble (bŭb'əl) n. A rounded, generally spherical, hollow, or sometimes solid, object, esp. a small globule of gas trapped in a liquid. —v. -bled, -bling. To form or give off bubbles. [ME bobelen.] —bub'bly adj.
bu•bo (b/y/ōō'bō) n., pl. -boes. An inflamed swelling of a lymphatic gland, esp. near the armpit or groin. [< Gk boubōn, groin, swollen gland.] —bu•bon'ic (-bŏn'ĭk) adj.
bubonic plague. A contagious, usually fatal epidemic disease transmitted by fleas from infected rats and characterized by chills, fever, vomiting, diarrhea, and buboes.
buc•ca•neer (bŭk'ə-nîr') n. A pirate. [F boucanier, pirate, "one who cures meat on a barbecue frame."]
Bu•chan•an (byōō-kăn'ən, bə-), James. 1791–1868. 15th President of the U.S. (1857–61).

James Buchanan

Bu•cha•rest (b/y/ōō'kə-rěst'). The capital of Rumania. Pop. 1,372,000.
buck¹ (bŭk) n. 1. An adult male animal, as the deer. 2. A spirited or dandified young man. —adj. Lowest in rank: buck private. [< OE buc, stag, and bucca, he-goat. See bhugo-.]
buck² (bŭk) v. 1. To leap forward and upward suddenly; rear up. 2. To butt (against). 3. To jolt. 4. To throw (a rider or burden) by bucking. 5. To oppose directly and stubbornly. [< BUCK¹.] —buck n. —buck'er n.

buck³ (bŭk) n. Slang. A dollar. [Short for BUCKSKIN.]
buck•board (bŭk'bôrd', -bōrd') n. A four-wheeled open carriage with the seat attached to a flexible board. [< obs buck, body of a wagon.]
buck•et (bŭk'ĭt) n. 1. A cylindrical vessel used for holding or carrying liquids or solids; pail. 2. Any of various machine compartments that receive and convey material, as the scoop of a steam shovel. 3. The amount that a bucket will hold. [< NF buket, bucket, tub.]
bucket seat. A seat with a rounded or molded back, as in sports cars.
buck•eye (bŭk'ī') n. 1. A North American tree with upright flower clusters and glossy brown nuts. 2. The nut of this tree.
buck fever. Informal. Nervous excitement felt by a novice hunter at the first sight of game.
buck•hound (bŭk'hound') n. A hound used for hunting deer.
buck•ish (bŭk'ĭsh) adj. 1. Characteristic of a fop; dandified. 2. Impetuous; dashing. —buck'ish•ly adv.
buck•le¹ (bŭk'əl) n. 1. A clasp, esp. a frame with movable tongues for fastening two strap or belt ends. 2. An ornament resembling such a clasp. —v. -led, -ling. To fasten or secure with a buckle. [< OF boucle, metal ring, buckle.]
buck•le² (bŭk'əl) v. -led, -ling. 1. To bend, warp, or crumple under pressure or heat. 2. To collapse or yield. —n. A bend, bulge, or other distortion. [< OF boucler, "to fasten with a buckle."]
buck•ler (bŭk'lər) n. A small round shield carried or worn on the arm. [< OF boucle, boss on a shield.]
buck•ram (bŭk'rəm) n. A coarse cotton fabric, heavily sized with glue, used for stiffening garments and in bookbinding. [ME bokram, a fine linen.]
buck•saw (bŭk'sô') n. A wood-cutting saw, usually set in an H-shaped frame. [< SAW-BUCK.]
buck•shot (bŭk'shŏt') n. A large lead shot for shotgun shells.
buck•skin (bŭk'skĭn') n. Strong, soft leather originally made from deerskin.
buck•tooth (bŭk'tōōth') n. A prominent, projecting upper front tooth. [< BUCK¹.] —buck'-toothed' (bŭk'tōōtht') adj.
buck•wheat (bŭk'hwēt') n. 1. A plant having small, edible triangular seeds often ground into flour. 2. The seeds of this plant. [Partial trans of MDu boecweite, "beech wheat."]
bu•col•ic (byōō-kŏl'ĭk) adj. Pastoral; rustic. [< Gk boukolos, cattle herder.]
bud (bŭd) n. 1. A small, protuberant plant structure containing undeveloped flowers, leaves, etc. 2. A budlike part, as an asexually produced reproductive structure. 3. An undeveloped or incipient stage. —v. budded, budding. 1. To form or produce a bud or buds. 2. To develop as from a bud. [ME budde.] —bud'der n.
Bu•da•pest (bōō'də-pěst'). The capital of Hungary. Pop. 1,900,000.

ă pat/ā ate/âr care/ä bar/b bib/ch chew/d deed/ě pet/ē be/f fit/g gag/h hat/hw what/
ĭ pit/ī pie/îr pier/j judge/k kick/l lid, fatal/m mum/n no, sudden/ng sing/ŏ pot/ō go/

Bud·dha (bŏŏ′də, bŏŏd′ə). Title of Gautama Siddhartha. 563?–483? B.C. Indian philosopher; founder of Buddhism. [Sk, "awakened."]

Buddha

Bud·dhism (bŏŏ′dĭz′əm, bŏŏd′ĭz′-) *n.* Buddha's doctrine that suffering is inseparable from existence but that inward extinction of the self and the senses culminates in a state of illumination beyond both suffering and existence. —**Bud′dhist** *n. & adj.*
bud·dy (bŭd′ē) *n., pl.* **-dies.** A good friend; comrade; pal; chum. [Prob a baby-talk var of BROTHER.]
budge (bŭj) *v.* **budged, budging. 1.** To move or cause to move slightly. **2.** To alter or cause to alter a position or attitude. [< OF *bouger.*]
budg·er·i·gar (bŭj′ə-rē-gär′) *n.* Also **budg·ie** (bŭj′ē). A small, colorful parakeet popular as a cage bird. [Native Australian name.]
budg·et (bŭj′ĭt) *n.* **1.** An itemized summary of probable expenditures and income for a given period, usually with a plan for meeting expenses. **2.** The total sum of money allocated for a particular purpose or time period. —*v.* **1.** To make a budget. **2.** To enter or plan for in a budget. [ME *bouget,* wallet.]
Bue·nos Ai·res (bwā′nəs âr′ēz, ir′ēz, bō′nəs). The capital of Argentina. Pop. 3,876,000.
buff¹ (bŭf) *n.* **1.** A soft, thick, undyed leather made chiefly from the skins of buffalo, elk, or oxen. **2.** The color of this leather; light yellowish brown. —*adj.* Made of or the color of buff. —*v.* To polish or shine with a soft cloth. [Orig, "buffalo."]
buff² (bŭf) *n.* One who is enthusiastic and knowledgeable about a given subject. [Orig a New York volunteer fireman < their buff uniforms.]
buf·fa·lo (bŭf′ə-lō′) *n., pl.* **-loes** or **-los** or **buffalo.** **1.** Any of several oxlike African or Asian mammals. **2.** The American bison. —*v. Slang.* To intimidate. [< Gk *boubalos,* African antelope, buffalo.]
Buf·fa·lo (bŭf′ə-lō′). A city of New York State. Pop. 463,000.
buff·er¹ (bŭf′ər) *n.* An implement used to shine or polish, as a soft cloth.
buff·er² (bŭf′ər) *n.* **1.** One that lessens, absorbs, or protects against the shock of an impact. **2.** A substance capable of maintaining the relative acid-base concentration in a solution by neutralizing, within limits, added acids or bases. [Prob < ME *buffe,* a blow.]
buf·fet¹ (bə-fā′, bŏŏ-) *n.* **1.** A sideboard. **2.** A counter for meals or refreshments. **3.** A meal at which guests serve themselves from dishes displayed on a table or sideboard. [F.]
buf·fet² (bŭf′ĭt) *n.* A blow or cuff with or as if with the hand. —*v.* **1.** To hit or strike against repeatedly. **2.** To force (one's way). [< OF.] —**buf′fet·er** *n.*
buf·foon (bə-fŏŏn′) *n.* A clown; jester; fool. [< It *buffare,* to puff.] —**buf·foon′er·y** *n.*
bug (bŭg) *n.* **1.** Any of various often harmful insects. **2.** Any insect, spider, etc. **3.** *Informal.* A disease-producing microorganism. **4.** A mechanical, electrical, or other systemic defect or difficulty. **5.** *Slang.* An enthusiast; buff. **6.** A small hidden microphone or other device used for eavesdropping. —*v.* **bugged, bugging. 1.** *Slang.* To annoy; pester. **2.** To eavesdrop on, esp. with electronic devices. [?]
bug·a·boo (bŭg′ə-bŏŏ′) *n., pl.* **-boos.** A steady source of annoyance or concern. [Perh < Celt.]
bug·bear (bŭg′bâr′) *n.* An object of obsessive dread. [< ME *bugge* + BEAR.]
bug-eyed (bŭg′īd′) *adj. Slang.* Agog.
bug·gy (bŭg′ē) *n., pl.* **-gies.** A small light carriage. [?]
bu·gle (byŏŏ′gəl) *n.* A trumpetlike instrument without keys or valves. [ME, buffalo, horn, bugle.] —**bu′gle** *v.* **(-gled, -gling).** —**bu′gler** *n.*
build (bĭld) *v.* **built** (bĭlt) or *archaic* **builded, building. 1.** To erect; construct. **2.** To fashion; create. **3.** To add to; develop. **4.** To establish a basis for. —**build up.** To construct or develop in stages. —*n.* The physical make-up of a person or thing. [< OE *byldan* < *bold,* a dwelling. See bheu-.] —**build′er** *n.*
build·ing (bĭl′dĭng) *n.* **1.** A structure; edifice. **2.** The act, process, or occupation of constructing.
built-in (bĭlt′ĭn′) *adj.* Constructed as part of a larger unit; not detachable; permanent: *a built-in cabinet.*
Bu·jum·bu·ra (bŏŏ′jəm-bŏŏr′ə, bŏŏ-jŏŏm′-bŏŏr′ə). The capital of Burundi. Pop. 47,000.
bulb (bŭlb) *n.* **1.** A rounded underground plant part, as of a tulip or onion, from which a new plant develops. **2.** A rounded object, projection, or part. **3.** An incandescent lamp or its glass housing. [L *bulbus,* bulb, onion.] —**bul′bar** *adj.*
bul·bous (bŭl′bəs) *adj.* **1.** Bulb-shaped. **2.** Growing from a bulb, as a tulip.
Bulg. Bulgaria; Bulgarian.

ô paw, for/oi boy/ou out/ŏŏ took/ōō coo/p pop/r run/s sauce/sh shy/t to/th thin/*th* the/
ŭ cut/ûr fur/v van/w wag/y yes/z size/zh vision/ə ago, item, edible, gallop, circus/

Bul·gar·i·a (bŭl-gâr′ē-ə, bōōl-). A Balkan republic on the Black Sea. Pop. 8,211,000. Cap. Sofia.

Bulgaria

Bul·gar·i·an (bŭl-gâr′ē-ən, bōōl-) *adj.* Of or pertaining to Bulgaria, its people, or their language. —*n.* **1.** Also **Bulgar** (bŭl′gər, bōōl′-gär′). A native of Bulgaria. **2.** The Slavic language spoken by Bulgarians.

bulge (bŭlj) *n.* A protruding part; an outward curve or a swelling. —*v.* **bulged, bulging.** To cause to curve outward; swell up. [< L *bulga*, leather bag.] —**bulg′y** *adj.*

bulk (bŭlk) *n.* **1.** Great size, mass, or volume. **2.** The major portion of something. —*v.* To be or appear to be massive in size; loom. [< ON *bulki*, cargo.] —**bulk′y** *adj.*

bulk·age (bŭl′kij) *n.* Any substance that stimulates peristalsis by increasing the bulk of material in the intestine.

bulk·head (bŭlk′hěd′) *n.* **1.** An upright partition dividing a ship into compartments. **2.** A wall or embankment constructed in a mine or tunnel. [< BULK.]

bull¹ (bōōl) *n.* **1. a.** The adult male of cattle or certain other large mammals. **b.** The uncastrated adult male of domestic cattle. **2.** One who buys commodities or securities in anticipation of a rise in prices. **3. Bull.** Taurus. **4.** *Slang.* Empty talk; nonsense. —*adj.* **1.** Male. **2.** Larger than others. **3.** Characterized by rising prices: *a bull market.* [< OE *bula* < ON *boli.*]

bull² (bōōl) *n.* A papal document. [< L *bulla,* bubble, seal.]

bull. bulletin.

bull·dog (bōōl′dôg′, -dŏg′) *n.* A stocky, short-haired dog with a large, square-jawed head. —*v.* -**dogged, -dogging.** To throw (a steer) by seizing its horns and twisting its neck.

bull·doze (bōōl′dōz′) *v.* -**dozed, -dozing. 1.** To dig up or move with a bulldozer. **2.** *Slang.* To bully.

bull·doz·er (bōōl′dō′zər) *n.* A tractor having a metal scoop in front for moving earth and rocks.

bul·let (bōōl′ĭt) *n.* A cylindrical metallic projectile that is fired from a gun. [< L *bulla,* bubble, ball.]

bul·le·tin (bōōl′ə-tən, -tĭn) *n.* **1.** A printed or broadcast statement on a matter of public interest. **2.** A periodical published by an organization or society.

bull·fight (bōōl′fit′) *n.* A public spectacle, esp. in Spain and Mexico, in which a matador engages and usually executes a fighting bull. —**bull′fight′er** *n.* —**bull′fight′ing** *n.*

bull·finch (bōōl′finch′) *n.* A European bird with a short, thick bill and a red breast.

bull·frog (bōōl′frôg′, -frŏg′) *n.* A large frog with a deep, resonant croak.

bull·head (bōōl′hěd′) *n.* A North American freshwater catfish.

bull·head·ed (bōōl′hěd′ĭd) *adj.* Stubborn; headstrong. —**bull′head′ed·ness** *n.*

bul·lion (bōōl′yən) *n.* Gold or silver metal. [< NF, "mint."]

bull·ish (bōōl′ĭsh) *adj.* **1.** Like a bull. **2.** Stubborn. **3.** Expecting a rise in stock-market prices. —**bull′ish·ness** *n.*

bul·lock (bōōl′ək) *n.* A steer or young bull. [< OE *bulluc,* dim of *bula,* BULL.]

bull·pen (bōōl′pĕn′) *n.* **1.** A pen for confining bulls. **2.** An area where relief pitchers warm up during a baseball game.

bull's eye. Also **bull's-eye** (bōōlz′i′). The small central circle on a target or a shot that hits this circle.

bul·ly (bōōl′ē) *n., pl.* -**lies.** One who is habitually cruel to smaller or weaker people. —*v.* -**lied, -lying.** To behave like a bully. —*adj.* Excellent; splendid. [Orig "sweetheart."]

bul·rush (bōōl′rŭsh′) *n.* Any of various tall grasslike sedges or similar marsh plants. [ME *bulrish.*]

bul·wark (bōōl′wərk, bŭl′-, -wôrk′) *n.* **1.** A wall or wall-like structure for defense; rampart. **2.** Anything serving as a defense against attack or encroachment. [< MHG *bolwerc.*]

bum (bŭm) *n.* **1.** A tramp; hobo. **2.** One who seeks to live off others. —*v.* **bummed, bumming.** *Informal.* **1.** To live or acquire by begging and scavenging. **2.** To loaf. —*adj.* *Slang.* **1.** Of poor quality. **2.** Disabled; malfunctioning. [< earlier *bummer,* a loafer.]

bum·ble·bee (bŭm′bəl-bē′) *n.* Any of various large, hairy bees.

bump (bŭmp) *v.* **1.** To strike or collide with. **2.** To knock. **3.** To displace; oust. —*n.* **1.** A light blow, collision, or jolt. **2.** A slight swelling or lump. [Imit.]

bump·er¹ (bŭm′pər) *n.* A device used to absorb the impact of a collision, esp. a horizontal metal bar attached to the front or rear of an automobile.

bump·er² (bŭm′pər) *n.* **1.** A drinking vessel filled to the brim. **2.** Something unusually large or full. —*adj.* Unusually abundant: *a bumper crop.* [Perh < BUMP.]

bump·kin (bŭmp′kĭn, bŭm′-) *n.* An awkward, untutored rustic. [Perh orig "Dutchman."]

bump·tious (bŭmp′shəs) *adj.* Crudely forward and self-assertive in behavior; pushy. [Perh a blend of BUMP and FRACTIOUS.]

bun (bŭn) *n.* **1.** A rounded, often sweetened roll. **2.** A tight roll of hair resembling this. [ME *bunne.*]

bunch (bŭnch) *n.* A group, cluster, or tuft.

ă pat/ā ate/âr care/ä bar/b bib/ch chew/d deed/ĕ pet/ē be/f fit/g gag/h hat/hw what/
ĭ pit/ī pie/îr pier/j judge/k kick/l lid, fatal/m mum/n no, sudden/ng sing/ŏ pot/ō go/

bunco / burly

[ME *bunche.*] —**bunch** *v.* —**bunch'y** *adj.*

bun•co (bŭng'kō) *n., pl.* **-cos.** A swindle; confidence game. [Span *banca,* name of a card game, "bank."]

bun•dle (bŭnd'l) *n.* **1.** Anything bound, wrapped, or otherwise held together; package. **2.** *Slang.* A large sum of money. —*v.* **-dled, -dling.** To tie, wrap, fold, or otherwise secure together. —**bundle up.** To dress warmly. [ME *bundel.*] —**bun'dler** *n.*

bung (bŭng) *n.* A stopper for a bunghole. [< MDu *bonghe.*]

bun•ga•low (bŭng'gə-lō') *n.* A small cottage, usually of one story. [Perh < Hindi *bangla,* "of Bengal."]

bung•hole (bŭng'hōl') *n.* The hole in a cask, keg, or barrel through which liquid is poured in or drained out.

bun•gle (bŭng'gəl) *v.* **-gled, -gling.** To work, manage, or act ineptly or inefficiently. [Perh < Scand.] —**bun'gler** *n.*

bun•ion (bŭn'yən) *n.* A painful, inflamed swelling at the bursa of the big toe. [Prob < earlier dial *bunny, bony,* swelling.]

bunk[1] (bŭngk) *n.* A narrow bed attached like a shelf against a wall. [Poss short for BUNKER.]

bunk[2] (bŭngk) *n. Slang.* Bunkum.

bun•ker (bŭng'kər) *n.* **1.** A bin or tank for fuel storage, as on a ship. **2.** A sand trap serving as an obstacle on a golf course. **3.** A fortified earthwork. [Earlier Scot *bonker.*]

bun•kum (bŭng'kəm) *n.* Empty or meaningless talk. [< *Buncombe* County, North Carolina.]

bun•ny (bŭn'ē) *n., pl.* **-nies.** *Informal.* A rabbit. [< dial *bun,* squirrel.]

Bun•sen burner (bŭn'sən). A small, adjustable gas-burning laboratory burner. [< R.W. *Bunsen* (1811–1899), German chemist.]

bunt (bŭnt) *v.* **1.** To butt (something) with the head. **2.** *Baseball.* To tap (a pitched ball) with a half swing so that the ball rolls slowly in front of the infielders. —*n.* **1.** A butt. **2.** *Baseball.* **a.** The act of bunting. **b.** A bunted ball. [Prob < Celt.]

bunt•ing[1] (bŭn'tĭng) *n.* **1.** A light cloth used for making flags. **2.** Flags collectively. [?]

bunt•ing[2] (bŭn'tĭng) *n.* Any of various birds with short, cone-shaped bills. [ME *buntynge.*]

bunt•ing[3] (bŭn'tĭng) *n.* A hooded sleeping bag for infants. [?]

buoy (boo'ē, boi) *n.* **1.** A float moored in water as a warning of danger or as a marker for a channel. **2.** A device made of buoyant material for keeping a person afloat. —*v.* **1.** To mark (a water hazard or a channel) with a buoy. **2.** To keep afloat. **3.** To uplift the spirits of. [ME *boye.*]

buoy•an•cy (boi'ən-sē, boo'yən-) *n.* **1.** The tendency to remain afloat in a liquid or to rise in air or gas. **2.** The upward force of a fluid. **3.** The ability to recover quickly from setbacks. **4.** Cheerfulness. —**buoy'ant** *adj.*

bur[1] (bûr) *n.* Also **burr. 1.** A seed, fruit, etc., encased in a rough, prickly covering. **2.** Any of various rotary cutting tools designed to be attached to a drill. [ME *burre.*]

bur[2]. Variant of **burr.**

Bur. 1. bureau. **2.** Burma.

bur•den (bûrd'n) *n.* **1. a.** Something that is carried. **b.** Something that is difficult to bear. **2.** A responsibility or duty. **3.** The amount of cargo a vessel can carry. —*v.* To load or overload; weigh down; oppress. [< OE *byrthen.* See bher-[1].] —**bur'den•some** *adj.*

bur•dock (bûr'dŏk') *n.* A coarse, weedy plant with bristly purplish flowers.

bu•reau (byŏor'ō) *n., pl.* **-reaus** or **bureaux** (byŏor'ōz). **1.** A chest of drawers. **2.** A government department or subdivision of a department. **3.** An office or business that performs a specific duty. [F.]

bu•reauc•ra•cy (byŏo-rŏk'rə-sē) *n., pl.* **-cies. 1. a.** Administration of a government chiefly through bureaus. **b.** The nonelective officials staffing such bureaus. **2.** Government marked by diffusion of authority among numerous offices and adherence to inflexible rules of operation. **3.** Any unwieldy administration. [BUREAU + -CRACY.] —**bu'reau•crat'** (byŏor'ə-krăt') *n.* —**bu'reau•crat'ic** *adj.*

burg (bûrg) *n.* A city or town. [< OE. See bhergh-[2].]

bur•geon (bûr'jən) *v.* **1.** To put forth new buds, leaves, etc.; begin to sprout or grow. **2.** To develop rapidly; flourish. [< ME *burjon,* a bud.]

burg•er (bûr'gər) *n. Informal.* A hamburger.

bur•gess (bûr'jĭs) *n.* A freeman, citizen, or representative of an English borough. [< OF *burgeis.*]

burgh (bûrg) *n.* A chartered town in Scotland. [Scot, var of BOROUGH.]

burgh•er (bûr'gər) *n.* A solid citizen; bourgeois. [G *Bürger* or Du *burger.*]

bur•glar (bûr'glər) *n.* One who commits burglary; housebreaker. [< ML *burgulator.*]

bur•glar•i•ous (bər-glâr'ē-əs) *adj.* Of or pertaining to burglary.

bur•glar•ize (bûr'glə-rīz') *v.* **-ized, -izing.** To commit burglary on.

bur•glar•proof (bûr'glər-proof') *adj.* Secure against burglary.

bur•gla•ry (bûr'glə-rē) *n., pl.* **-ries.** The crime of breaking into and entering a house with intent to commit a felony.

bur•go•mas•ter (bûr'gə-măs'tər, -mäs'tər) *n.* The principal magistrate of some European cities, comparable to a mayor. [Partial trans of Du *burgemeester.*]

Bur•gun•dy (bûr'gən-dē) *n., pl.* **-dies. 1.** A red or white wine produced in Burgundy, a region of SE France. **2. burgundy.** Dark red.

bur•i•al (bĕr'ē-əl) *n.* The interment of a dead body. [< OE *byrgels* (pl). See bhergh-[1].]

burl (bûrl) *n.* **1.** A rounded excrescence on a tree trunk or branch. **2.** The wood from such an excrescence. [< OF *bourle.*]

bur•lap (bûr'lăp') *n.* A coarsely woven cloth of jute, hemp, etc. [?]

bur•lesque (bər-lĕsk') *n.* **1.** Any ludicrous or mocking imitation. **2.** Vaudeville entertainment characterized by ribald comedy and display of nudity. —*v.* **-lesqued, -lesquing.** To imitate mockingly. [< It *burlesco.*]

bur•ly (bûr'lē) *adj.* **-lier, -liest.** Heavy and strong. [ME *burli, borlich,* stately, big.]

ô paw, for/oi boy/ou out/oō took/ōō coo/p pop/r run/s sauce/sh shy/t to/th thin/*th* the/ ŭ cut/ûr fur/v van/w wag/y yes/z size/zh vision/ə ago, item, edible, gallop, circus/

Bur·ma (bûr′mə). A republic of SE Asia. Pop. 24,229,000. Cap. Rangoon.

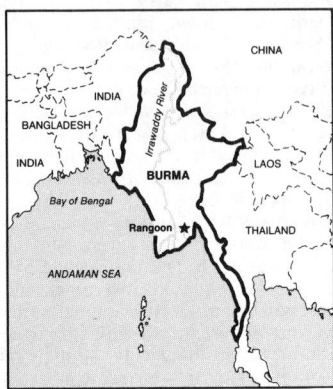

Burma

Bur·mese (bər-mēz′, -mēs′) *adj.* Of or pertaining to Burma, its people, or their language. —*n., pl.* **-mese.** **1.** A native of Burma. **2.** The Sino-Tibetan language of Burma.

burn (bûrn) *v.* **burned** or **burnt, burning.** **1.** To undergo or cause to undergo combustion. **a.** To destroy or be destroyed by fire. **b.** To damage or be damaged by fire or heat. **3.** To produce by fire or heat: *burn a clearing in the brush.* **4.** To use as a fuel. **5.** To impart a sensation of intense heat to: *The chili burned his mouth.* **6.** To emit heat or light by or as if by means of fire. **7.** To feel or look hot. **8.** To be consumed with strong emotion. —*n.* **1.** An injury produced by fire, heat, or a heat-producing agent. **2.** *Aerospace.* One firing of a rocket. [< OE *beornan, byrnan* and *bærnan.* See **bhreu-².**]

burn·er (bûr′nər) *n.* **1.** The part of a stove that produces heat. **2.** A device in which something is burned: *an oil burner.*

bur·nish (bûr′nĭsh) *v.* To polish or become polished by or as if by rubbing. [< OF *burnir, brunir,* "to make brown."] —**bur′nish** *n.*

bur·noose (bər-nōōs′) *n.* A hooded cloak worn by Arabs. [< Ar *bournous.*]

Burns (bûrnz), **Robert.** 1759–1796. Scottish poet.

burnt (bûrnt). Alternate *p.t.* & *p.p.* of **burn.** —*adj.* Affected by or as if by burning.

burp (bûrp) *n.* A belch. [Imit.] —**burp** *v.*

burr¹ (bûr) *n.* Also **bur.** **1.** A rough trilling of the letter *r,* as in Scottish pronunciation. **2.** A whirring sound.

burr². Variant of **bur.**

bur·ro (bûr′ō, bŏŏr′ō) *n., pl.* **-ros.** A small donkey. [Span.]

bur·row (bûr′ō) *n.* A hole or tunnel dug in the ground by an animal, such as a rabbit or mole. —*v.* **1.** To dig a burrow. **2.** To move or form by or as if by tunneling. [ME *borow.*]

bur·sa (bûr′sə) *n., pl.* **-sae** (-sē) or **-sas.** A saclike bodily cavity, esp. one located between joints. [< Gk, bag, purse.]

bur·sar (bûr′sər, -sär′) *n.* An official in charge of funds, as at a college. [< Gk *bursa,* purse.]

bur·si·tis (bər-sī′tĭs) *n.* Inflammation of a bursa, esp. of the shoulder, elbow, or knee joints.

burst (bûrst) *v.* **burst, bursting.** **1.** To force open or fly apart suddenly, esp. from internal pressure. **2.** To be full to the breaking point. **3.** To emerge suddenly and in full force. **4.** To become audible or visible suddenly. **5.** To give sudden utterance or expression: *burst into song.* —*n.* **1.** The act or result of bursting; a rupture or explosion. **2.** A sudden outbreak. [< OE *berstan.* See **bhres-.**]

Bu·run·di (bōō-rōōn′dē). A country of C Africa. Pop. 3,274,000. Cap. Bujumbura.

Burundi

bur·y (bĕr′ē) *v.* **-ied, -ying.** **1.** To place in the ground and cover with earth. **2.** To place (a dead body) in a grave or tomb. **3.** To hide; conceal. [< OE *byrgan.* See **bhergh-¹.**]

bus (bŭs) *n., pl.* **buses** or **busses.** A large motor vehicle for carrying passengers. —*v.* **bused** or **bussed, busing** or **bussing.** *Informal.* To transport in a bus. [Short for OMNIBUS.]

bus. business.

bus boy A waiter's assistant.

bus·by (bŭz′bē) *n., pl.* **-bies.** A tall fur hat worn in certain regiments of the British Army. [?]

bush (bŏŏsh) *n.* **1.** A low, branching, woody plant; shrub. **2.** Land covered with dense shrubby growth. **3.** A dense growth or tuft. —*v.* To form a dense, tufted growth. [ME *busshe.*] —**bush′y** *adj.*

bushed (bŏŏsht) *adj. Informal.* Extremely tired; exhausted.

bush·el (bŏŏsh′əl) *n.* **1.** A U.S. Customary System unit of volume or capacity, used in dry measure and equal to 4 pecks or 2,150.42 cubic inches. **2.** A corresponding British Imperial System unit, used in dry and liquid measure, equal to 2,219.36 cubic inches. [< OF *boissiel.*]

bush·ing (bŏŏsh′ĭng) *n.* A fixed or removable metal lining used to constrain, guide, or reduce friction. [< earlier *bush.*]

Bush·man (bŏŏsh′mən) *n.* A member of a nomadic Negroid people of SW Africa.

bush·mas·ter (bŏŏsh′măs′tər, -mäs′tər) *n.* A large, venomous tropical American snake.

bush·whack (bŏŏsh′hwăk′) *v.* **1.** To make

---

one's way through thick woods by cutting away bushes and branches. 2. To ambush. —**bush'whack'er** n.

busi•ness (bĭz'nĭs) n. 1. The occupation in which a person is engaged. 2. Commercial, industrial, or professional dealings. 3. Any commercial establishment. 4. Volume of commercial trade. 5. Commercial policy or practice. 6. One's concern or interest: *"The business of America is business."* (Calvin Coolidge). 7. An affair or matter: *a peculiar business.* —**mean business.** To be in earnest. [< OE *bisignis,* care, solicitude < *bisig,* BUSY.]

busi•ness•like (bĭz'nĭs-līk') adj. Methodical; efficient.

bus•kin (bŭs'kĭn) n. 1. A laced half boot worn by actors of Greek and Roman tragedies. 2. Tragedy. [< OF *bouzequin.*]

bus•ses. Alternate pl. of **bus.**

bust¹ (bŭst) n. 1. A woman's bosom. 2. A piece of sculpture representing a person's head, shoulders, and upper chest. [< It *busto,* piece of sculpture.]

bust² (bŭst). *Slang.* v. 1. To burst or break. 2. To make or become short of money. 3. To demote. 4. To punch. 5. To place under arrest. —n. 1. A failure. 2. A time of widespread financial depression. 3. An arrest. [Var of BURST.]

bus•tle¹ (bŭs'əl) v. -tled, -tling. To move energetically and busily. [Prob < dial *busk,* to prepare.] —**bus'tle** n. —**bus'tler** n.

bus•tle² (bŭs'əl) n. A frame or pad giving extra fullness at the upper back of a woman's skirt. [Perh < G *Buschel,* a bunch, pad.]

bus•y (bĭz'ē) adj. -ier, -iest. 1. Actively engaged in some form of work. 2. Crowded with activity. 3. Temporarily in use, as a telephone line. —v. -ied, -ying. To make busy. [< OE *bysig, bisig.*] —**bus'i•ly** (bĭz'ə-lē) adv. —**bus'y•ness** n.

bus•y•bod•y (bĭz'ē-bŏd'ē) n. One who pries into the affairs of others.

but (bŭt; *unstressed* bət) conj. 1. On the contrary. 2. Contrary to expectation; however. 3. Except; save. 4. Except that: *They should have resisted but that they lacked courage.* 5. Without the result that: *It never rains but it pours.* 6. Other than: *I have no goal but to end war.* 7. That. Often used after a negative. 8. That . . . not. Used after a negative or question: *There never is a tax law presented but someone will oppose it.* 9. Who . . . not; which . . . not: *None came to him but were treated well.* —prep. With the exception of; barring; save. —**but for.** Were it not for. —adv. No more than; only; just. —**all but.** Nearly; almost: *His poem is all but finished.* —n. An objection, restriction, or exception: *no ifs, ands, or buts.* [< OE *būtan.* See ud-.]

bu•tane (byōō'tān') n. Either of two isomers of a gaseous hydrocarbon, C_4H_{10}, produced synthetically from petroleum and used as a household fuel, refrigerant, and aerosol propellant.

butch•er (bŏŏch'ər) n. 1. One who slaughters and dresses animals for food. 2. One who sells meat. 3. A cruel or wanton killer. —v. 1. To slaughter or dress (animals). 2. To kill cruelly

or wantonly. 3. To botch; bungle. [< OF *bouchier.*]

but•ler (bŭt'lər) n. A chief male servant in a household. [< OF *bouteillier,* a bottle bearer.]

butt¹ (bŭt) v. To hit with the head or horns. —**butt in** (or into). *Informal.* To meddle. [< NF *buter, boter.*]

butt² (bŭt) n. A person or thing serving as an object of ridicule. [ME *butte,* target.]

butt³ (bŭt) n. 1. The larger end of something: *the butt of a rifle.* 2. A short or broken remnant. [ME *butte,* thicker end.]

butte (byōōt) n. A hill rising abruptly above the surrounding area and having sloping sides and a flat top. [F.]

but•ter (bŭt'ər) n. 1. A soft, yellowish, fatty substance churned from milk or cream and used as a food. 2. A similar substance. —v. 1. To put butter on. 2. *Informal.* To flatter. [< OE *butere* < Gmc < Gk *bouturon,* "cow cheese."]

but•ter•cup (bŭt'ər-kŭp') n. A plant with glossy yellow flowers.

but•ter•fat (bŭt'ər-făt') n. The oily content of milk, from which butter is made.

but•ter•fin•gers (bŭt'ər-fĭng'gərz) n. (*takes sing. v.*). A clumsy or awkward person who drops things. —**but'ter•fin'gered** adj.

but•ter•fly (bŭt'ər-flī') n., pl. -flies. Any of various narrow-bodied insects with four broad, usually colorful wings.

but•ter•milk (bŭt'ər-mĭlk') n. The sour liquid that remains after the butter has been churned from milk.

but•ter•nut (bŭt'ər-nŭt') n. 1. The oily, edible nut of a North American tree. 2. A tree bearing such nuts.

but•ter•scotch (bŭt'ər-skŏch') n. A candy or flavoring made from melted butter and brown sugar. [Perh orig made in Scotland.]

butt joint. A joint formed by two abutting surfaces.

but•tocks (bŭt'əks) pl.n. The two rounded parts of the lower back. [ME.]

but•ton (bŭt'n) n. 1. A small knob, disk, etc., esp. one sewn on a garment as a fastener or trimming. 2. Any of various objects of similar appearance. —**on the button.** *Informal.* Exactly. —v. To fasten with a button or buttons. [< OF *bouton,* bud, button.]

but•ton•hole (bŭt'n-hōl') n. A slit or loop through which a button is inserted. —v. -holed, -holing. To accost and detain in conversation.

but•tress (bŭt'rĭs) n. 1. A structure, usually brick or stone, built against a wall for support. 2. Anything that serves to support. [< OF *(ars) bouterez,* thrusting (arch).] —**but'tress** v.

bux•om (bŭk'səm) adj. Ample of figure: *a buxom woman.* [Earlier flexible, gay < OE *būgan,* to bend. See bheug-.]

buy (bī) v. bought, buying. 1. To acquire in exchange for money; purchase. 2. To be capable of purchasing. 3. To acquire by sacrifice or exchange. 4. To bribe. —n. 1. Anything bought. 2. *Informal.* A bargain. [< OE *bycgan* < Gmc **bugjan.*]

buy•er (bī'ər) n. 1. One who buys; a customer. 2. One who buys for a retail store.

buzz (bŭz) *v.* **1.** To make a low droning or vibrating sound like that of a bee. **2.** To talk excitedly in low tones. [ME *bussen,* to drone (imit).] —**buzz** *n.*

buz·zard (bŭz′ərd) *n.* **1.** Any of various North American vultures. **2.** *Chiefly* ¹ *Brit.* Any of various broad-winged hawks. [< OF *busard.*]

buzz·er (bŭz′ər) *n.* Any of various electric signaling devices that make a buzzing sound.

B.V. Blessed Virgin.

bx. box.

by (bī) *prep.* **1.** Next to. **2.** With the use of; through. **3.** Up to and beyond; past. **4.** In the period of; during: *sleeping by day.* **5.** Not later than: *by 5:00 P.M.* **6.** In the amount of: *letters by the thousands.* **7.** To the extent of: *shorter by two inches.* **8.** According to: *by his own account.* **9.** In the presence or name of. **10.** Through the agency or action of: *killed by a bullet.* **11.** In succession to; after: *day by day.* **12.** In behalf of; for: *He does well by his employees.* **13.** —Used to link certain expressions to be taken together and indicating: **a.** multiplication of quantities. **b.** coordination of measurements: *a room 12 by 18 feet.* —*adv.* **1.** On hand; nearby: *stand by.* **2.** Aside; away: *He put it by for later.* **3.** Up to, alongside, and past: *The car raced by.* **4.** Into the past: *as years go by.* —**by and large.** On the whole; for the most part. [OE *bī, bi, be.* See **ambhi.**]

bye (bī) *n.* The position of one who draws no opponent for a round in a tournament and so advances to the next round. [< BY (aside, hence "secondary").]

Bye·lo·rus·sian (byĕl′ō-rŭsh′ən) *n.* **1.** A native of the Byelorussian S.S.R. **2.** The language of the Byelorussians. —**Bye′lo·rus′sian** *adj.*

Byelorussian Soviet Socialist Republic. Also

Bye·lo·rus·sia (byĕl′ō-rŭsh′ə). A constituent republic of the Soviet Union, in the W, in Europe. Pop. 9,003,000. Cap. Minsk.

by·gone (bī′gôn′, -gŏn′) *adj.* Past: *bygone days.* —*n.* —**let bygones be bygones.** To let past differences be forgotten.

by·law (bī′lô′) *n.* A law or rule governing the internal affairs of an organization. [ME *bilawe, bylawe,* "village law."]

by-line (bī′līn′) *n.* A line at the head of a newspaper or magazine article with the author's name. —**by′-lin′er** *n.*

by-pass (bī′păs′, -päs′) *n.* **1.** A road or highway that passes around or to one side of an obstructed area. **2.** *Elec.* A shunt. —*v.* To go around instead of through.

by-path (bī′păth′, -päth′) *n.* An indirect or little-used path.

by-prod·uct (bī′prŏd′əkt) *n.* Something produced in the making of something else.

By·ron (bī′rən), **George Gordon, Lord.** 1788–1824. English poet. —**By·ron′ic** *adj.*

by·stand·er (bī′stăn′dər) *n.* One who is present at some event without participating in it.

by·street (bī′strēt′) *n.* A side street.

by·way (bī′wā′) *n.* **1.** A side road. **2.** A secondary or overlooked field of study.

by·word (bī′wûrd′) *n.* **1.** A proverb. **2.** One that proverbially represents a type, class, or quality. [< OE *biword* : BY + WORD.]

Byz·an·tine Empire (bĭz′ən-tēn′, -tīn′, bĭ-zăn′-tĭn). The eastern part of the later Roman Empire, continuing after the fall of Rome as its successor until 1453.

By·zan·ti·um (bĭ-zăn′shē-əm, -tē-əm). **1.** A Greek city on the site of which the city of Constantinople (now Istanbul) was founded in A.D. 330. **2.** The Byzantine Empire and its culture.

Cc

c, C (sē) *n.* **1.** The 3rd letter of the English alphabet. **2.** The 3rd in a series. **3.** The 3rd highest in quality.

c **1.** carat. **2.** centi-. **3.** cubic.

C **1.** *Elec.* capacitance. **2.** carbon. **3.** centigrade. **4.** coulomb. **5.** *Mus.* The 1st tone in the scale of C major. **6.** The Roman numeral for 100 (L *centum*).

c. **1.** cape. **2.** cent. **3.** century. **4.** chapter. **5.** circa. **6.** copy. **7.** copyright. **8.** cup.

C. **1.** cape. **2.** Catholic. **3.** cent. **4.** century. **5.** chapter. **6.** church. **7.** circa. **8.** city. **9.** copyright. **10.** corps. **11.** court.

ca circa.

Ca calcium.

CAA Civil Aeronautics Authority.

cab (kăb) *n.* **1.** A taxicab. **2.** The compartment

of a heavy vehicle, in which the operator sits. [Short for TAXICAB and CABIN.]

ca·bal (kə-băl′) *n.* **1.** A conspiratorial group. **2.** A conspiracy. [F *cabale.*]

ca·ban·a (kə-băn′ə, -băn′yə) *n.* A shelter on a beach used as a bathhouse. [Span *cabaña.*]

cab·a·ret (kăb′ə-rā′) *n.* A restaurant providing short programs of live entertainment. [F.]

cab·bage (kăb′ĭj) *n.* A plant having a compact, rounded head of leaves eaten as a vegetable. [< ONF *caboche.*]

cab·in (kăb′ĭn) *n.* **1.** A small, roughly built house. **2. a.** Living quarters on a ship. **b.** An enclosed compartment on a boat or airplane. [< LL *capanna,* hut, cabin.]

cab·i·net (kăb′ə-nĭt) *n.* **1.** A cupboardlike repository with shelves, drawers, or compart-

---

ă pat/ā ate/âr care/ä bar/b bib/ch chew/d deed/ĕ pet/ē be/f fit/g gag/h hat/hw what/
ĭ pit/ī pie/îr pier/j judge/k kick/l lid, fatal/m mum/n no, sudden/ng sing/ŏ pot/ō go/

ments for the safekeeping or display of objects. **2.** Often **Cabinet.** The body of persons appointed by a chief of state or prime minister to head departments of the government and act as his advisers. [< ONF *cabine*, a gambling house.] —**cab'i•net** *adj.*

ca•ble (kā'bəl) *n.* **1.** A large-diameter steel or fiber rope. **2.** A bound or sheathed group of mutually insulated conductors. **3.** A cablegram. —*v.* **-bled, -bling.** To send a cablegram to. [< ML *capulum*, rope for fastening cattle.]

ca•ble•gram (kā'bəl-grăm') *n.* A telegram sent by submarine cable.

ca•boose (kə-bōōs') *n.* The last car on a freight train, having kitchen and sleeping facilities for the crew. [Prob < Du *kabuis*.]

ca•ca•o (kə-kā'ō, -kä'ō) *n.* **1.** The seed of a tropical American tree, used in making chocolate and cocoa. **2.** The tree itself. [< Nah *cacahuatl*, cacao beans.]

cache (kăsh) *n.* **1.** A hiding place used for storage. **2.** A place for concealment and safekeeping. **3.** A store of goods hidden in a cache. [< F *cacher*, to hide.] —**cache** *v.* **(cached, caching).**

ca•chet (kă-shā') *n.* **1.** A seal on a letter or document. **2.** A mark of distinction, individuality, or authenticity. [< OF *cacher*, to hide, press together.]

cack•le (kăk'əl) *v.* **-led, -ling. 1.** To make the shrill cry characteristic of a hen after laying an egg. **2.** To laugh or talk in a similar manner. —*n.* The act or sound of cackling. [ME *cakelen*.] —**cack'ler** *n.*

ca•coph•o•ny (kə-kŏf'ə-nē) *n., pl.* **-nies.** Jarring, discordant sound. [< Gk *kakophōnos*, having a bad sound.] —**ca•coph'o•nous** *adj.* —**ca•coph'o•nous•ly** *adv.*

cac•tus (kăk'təs) *n., pl.* **-ti** (-tī') or **-tuses.** Any of various leafless, fleshy-stemmed, often spiny plants of arid regions. [< Gk *kaktos*, the *cardoon* (a thistlelike plant).]

cad (kăd) *n.* An ungentlemanly man. [Short for CADDIE.] —**cad'dish** *adj.*

ca•dav•er (kə-dăv'ər) *n.* A dead body. [L.] —**ca•dav'er•ic** *adj.*

ca•dav•er•ous (kə-dăv'ər-əs) *adj.* Corpselike; gaunt or pallid.

cad•dle (kăd'ē). Also **cad•dy** *n., pl.* **-dies.** One hired to assist a golfer, esp. by carrying his clubs. —*v.* **-died, -dying.** To serve as a caddie. [F *cadet*, CADET.]

Cad•do•an (kăd'ō-ən) *n.* A family of North American Indian languages formerly spoken in areas W of the Mississippi.

cad•dy (kăd'ē) *n., pl.* **-dies.** A small boxlike container, esp. for tea. [< Malay *kati*, a unit of weight.]

–cade. *comb. form.* Procession or parade: **motorcade.**

ca•dence (kād'əns) *n.* **1.** Rhythmic flow or movement. **2.** Vocal inflection or modulation. **3.** A progression of chords moving to a harmonic close. [< OIt *cadenza*.] —**ca'denced** *adj.*

ca•den•za (kə-dĕn'zə) *n.* An ornamental flourish or section, as near the end of a movement of a concerto. [< OIt, CADENCE.]

ca•det (kə-dĕt') *n.* **1.** A student training to be a military officer. **2.** A younger son or brother. [F.] —**ca•det'ship** *n.*

cadge (kăj) *v.* **cadged, cadging.** To get by begging; mooch. [< ME *cadgear*, carrier.] —**cadg'er** *n.*

cad•mi•um (kăd'mē-əm) *n. Symbol* **Cd** A soft, bluish-white metallic element used in low-friction alloys, solders, dental amalgams, and nickel-cadmium storage batteries. Atomic number 48, atomic weight 112.40. [< L *cadmia*, zinc ore.] —**cad'mic** (-mĭk) *adj.*

cad•re (kăd'rē) *n.* A group of trained personnel forming the nucleus of an organization. [< L *quādrum*, a square.]

ca•du•ce•us (kə-d/y/ōō'sē-əs) *n., pl.* **-cei** (-sē-ī'). The winged, snake-entwined staff of Hermes, used as the symbol of the medical profession. [L *cādūceus*.]

cae•cum. Variant of cecum.

Cae•sar (sē'zər), **Gaius Julius.** 100–44 B.C. Roman statesman and general.

Julius Caesar

Cae•sar•e•an (sĭ-zâr'ē-ən). Also **Cae•sar•i•an, Ce•sar•e•an, Ce•sar•i•an.** *adj.* Pertaining to Caesar. —*n.* A Caesarean section.

Caesarean section. Also **caesarean section.** A surgical incision through the abdominal wall and uterus, performed to extract a fetus. [< a tradition that Julius *Caesar* was born by this operation and named *ā caesō mātris ūterē*, "from the *incised* womb of his mother."]

Cae•sar•ism (sē'zə-rĭz'əm) *n.* Military dictatorship or absolute government. —**Cae'sar•ist** *n.* —**Cae'sar•is'tic** *adj.*

cae•si•um. Variant of cesium.

cae•su•ra (sĭ-zhōōr'ə, -z/y/ōōr'ə) *n.* A pause in phrasing a metrical line. [L, "a cutting off."] —**cae•su'ral, cae•su'ric** *adj.*

C.A.F. cost and freight.

ca•fé (kă-fā', kə-) *n.* A restaurant, bar, etc. [F, coffee.]

ca•fé au lait (kă-fā' ō lā'). **1.** Coffee diluted with hot milk. **2.** A light coffee color. [F, "coffee with milk."]

caf•e•te•ri•a (kăf'ə-tîr'ē-ə) *n.* A restaurant in

which customers carry their meals from a service counter to tables. [< Span *cafetero,* coffee maker or seller.]

caf•feine (kă-fēn', kăf'ē-ĭn) *n.* Also **caf•fein.** A bitter white alkaloid, $C_8H_{10}N_4O_2 \cdot H_2O$, derived from coffee, tea, and cola nuts, and used as a stimulant and diuretic. [< G *Kaffee,* coffee.]

caf•tan (kăf'tən, kăf-tăn') *n.* A long, coatlike garment worn in the Near East. [Russ *kaftan.*]

cage (kāj) *n.* **1.** A barred or grated enclosure for confining birds or animals. **2.** A similar enclosure or structure. —*v.* **caged, caging.** To confine in or as in a cage. [< L *cavea,* a hollow, enclosure.]

cag•ey (kā'jē) *adj.* **-ier, -iest.** Also **cag•y.** Wary; shrewd; careful; cautious. [?] —**cag'i•ly** *adv.* —**cag'i•ness** *n.*

ca•hoots (kə-hōōts') *pl.n.* —**in cahoots.** In questionable collaboration. [Perh < F *cahute,* cabin, hut.]

Cain (kān) Eldest son of Adam and Eve, who killed his brother Abel. Genesis 4. —**raise Cain.** To create a disturbance; make trouble.

cairn (kârn) *n.* A mound of stones erected as a landmark or memorial. [ME *carne.*]

Cai•ro (kī'rō). The capital of Egypt. Pop. 3,346,000.

cais•son (kā'sŏn', -sən) *n.* **1.** A watertight structure within which construction work is carried on. **2. a.** A large box used to hold ammunition. **b.** A horse-drawn vehicle, usually two-wheeled, once used to carry ammunition. [< OF *casson.*]

caisson disease. A disorder caused by too rapid return from high pressure to atmospheric pressure, characterized by cramps, paralysis, and eventual death unless treated by gradual decompression.

cai•tiff (kā'tĭf) *n.* A base coward; wretch. [< L *captivus,* CAPTIVE.]

ca•jole (kə-jōl') *v.* **-joled, -joling.** To coax; wheedle. [F *cajoler,* "to chatter like a caged jay."] —**ca•jol'er** *n.* —**ca•jol'er•y** *n.*

Ca•jun (kā'jən) *n.* A native of Louisiana descended from French exiles from Acadia.

cake (kāk) *n.* **1.** A sweet food made from baked batter or dough. **2.** A thin baked or fried portion of batter or other food. **3.** A shaped mass, as of soap. —*v.* **caked, caking.** To make or become a hard or compact mass. [< ON *kaka.*]

cal calorie.

cal. **1.** calendar. **2.** caliber.

Cal. California (unofficial).

cal•a•bash (kăl'ə-băsh') *n.* A large, hard-shelled gourd often used as a utensil. [< Span *calabaza.*]

cal•a•boose (kăl'ə-bōōs') *n.* *Slang.* A jail. [< Span *calabozo,* a dungeon.]

cal•a•mine (kăl'ə-mīn', -mĭn) *n.* A pink powder of zinc oxide with a small amount of ferric oxide, dissolved in mineral oils and used in skin lotions. [< ML *calamīna.*]

ca•lam•i•ty (kə-lăm'ə-tē) *n., pl.* **-ties.** A cause of great distress; disaster. [< L *calamitās.*] —**ca•lam'i•tous** *adj.* —**ca•lam'i•tous•ly** *adv.* —**ca•lam'i•tous•ness** *n.*

cal•car•e•ous (kăl-kâr'ē-əs) *adj.* Of or con-

taining calcium carbonate, calcium, or limestone; chalky.

calci-. *comb. form.* Lime or calcium. [< L *calx,* lime, limestone.]

cal•cif•er•ous (kăl-sĭf'ər-əs) *adj.* Of or containing calcium or calcium carbonate.

cal•ci•fy (kăl'sə-fī') *v.* **-fied, -fying.** To make or become stony or chalky by deposition of calcium salts. —**cal'ci•fi•ca'tion** *n.*

cal•ci•mine (kăl'sə-mīn') *n.* A white or tinted liquid containing zinc oxide, water, glue, and coloring matter, used as a wash for walls and ceilings.

cal•cine (kăl'sīn', kăl-sīn') *v.* **-cined, -cining.** To heat to a high temperature but below the melting or fusing point, causing loss of moisture, reduction, or oxidation. [< L *calx,* lime.] —**cal'ci•na'tion** *n.*

cal•cite (kăl'sīt') *n.* A common crystalline form of natural calcium carbonate. —**cal•cit'ic** (-sĭt'ĭk) *adj.*

cal•ci•um (kăl'sē-əm) *n.* *Symbol* Ca A silvery metallic element that occurs in bone, shells, limestone, and gypsum, and forms compounds used to make plaster, quicklime, cement, and metallurgic and electronic materials. Atomic number 20, atomic weight 40.08. [< L *calx,* lime, limestone < Gk *khalix,* pebble.]

calcium carbonate. A colorless or white crystalline compound, $CaCO_3$, occurring naturally in chalk, limestone, and marble, and used in manufactured products including commercial chalk, medicines, and dentifrices.

calcium chloride. A white deliquescent compound, $CaCl_2$, used chiefly as a drying agent, refrigerant, and preservative.

calcium hydroxide. A soft white powder, $Ca(OH)_2$, used in making cements, paints, hard rubber products, and petrochemicals.

calcium oxide. A white, caustic, lumpy powder, CaO, used in manufacturing steel, glassmaking, waste treatment, and insecticides.

cal•cu•late (kăl'kyə-lāt') *v.* **-lated, -lating.** **1.** To compute mathematically. **2.** To estimate; reckon. **3.** To intend; plan. [< L *calculus,* small stone (used in reckoning).] —**cal'cu•la•ble** *adj.* —**cal'cu•la•bly** *adv.*

cal•cu•lat•ed (kăl'kyə-lā'tĭd) *adj.* Estimated with forethought: *a calculated risk.* —**cal'cu•lat'ed•ly** *adv.*

cal•cu•lat•ing (kăl'kyə-lā'tĭng) *adj.* Shrewd; scheming; conniving.

cal•cu•la•tion (kăl'kyə-lā'shən) *n.* **1.** The act, process, or result of calculating. **2.** Deliberation; foresight.

cal•cu•la•tor (kăl'kyə-lā'tər) *n.* A keyboard machine for the automatic performance of arithmetic operations.

cal•cu•lus (kăl'kyə-ləs) *n., pl.* **-li** (-lī') or **-luses.** **1.** An abnormal mineral concretion in the body, such as a stone in the gallbladder or kidney. **2.** The combined mathematics of differential and integral calculus. [L, small stone used in reckoning.]

Cal•cut•ta (kăl-kŭt'ə). A city of NE India. Pop. 2,927,000.

cal•dron (kôl'drən) *n.* Also **caul•dron.** A large kettle or vat. [< L *caldāria,* warm bath.]

ă pat/ā ate/âr care/ä bar/b bib/ch chew/d deed/ĕ pet/ē be/f fit/g gag/h hat/hw what/ ĭ pit/ī pie/îr pier/j judge/k kick/l lid, fatal/m mum/n no, sudden/ng sing/ŏ pot/ō go/

MONTHS OF THREE PRINCIPAL CALENDARS

GREGORIAN		HEBREW		MOSLEM	
		Months correspond approximately to those in parentheses		Beginning of year retrogresses through the solar year of the Gregorian calendar	
name	number of days	name	number of days	name	number of days
January	31	Tishri (September–October)	30	Muharram	30
February in leap year	28 29	Heshvan in some years (October–November)	29 30	Safar	29
March	31	Kislev in some years (November–December)	29 30	Rabi I	30
April	30	Tevet (December–January)	29	Rabi II	29
May	31	Shevat (January–February)	30	Jumada I	30
June	30	Adar* in leap year (February–March)	29 30	Jumada II	29
July	31	Nisan (March–April)	30	Rajab	30
August	31	Iyar (April–May)	29	Sha'ban	29
September	30	Sivan (May–June)	30	Ramadan	30
October	31	Tammuz (June–July)	29	Shawwal	29
November	30	Av (July–August)	30	Dhu'l-Qa dah	30
December	31	Elul (August–September)	29	Dhu'l-Hijja in leap year	29 30

*Adar is followed in leap year by the intercalary month Veadar, or Adar Sheni, having 29 days.

cal·en·dar (kăl′ən-dər) *n.* **1.** A system of reckoning time divisions, esp. in years, months, weeks, and days. **2.** A table showing such divisions, usually for a year. **3.** A chronological list or schedule. —*v.* To enter on a calendar; schedule. [< L *kalendārium*, a moneylender's account book.]
cal·ends (kăl′əndz) *n., pl.* **-ends.** The first day of the month in the ancient Roman calendar. [< L *kalendae*.]
calf¹ (kăf, käf) *n., pl.* **calves** (kăvz, kävz). **1.** The young of cattle or certain other large mammals, as the elephant. **2.** Also **calf·skin** (kăf′skĭn′, käf′-). **a.** The hide of a calf. **b.** Fine leather made from it. [< OE *cealf* < Gmc *kalbam.*]
calf² (kăf, käf) *n., pl.* **calves** (kăvz, kävz). The fleshy back part of the leg, between the knee and ankle. [< ON *kalfi.*]
Cal·ga·ry (kăl′gə-rē). A city of SW Alberta, Canada. Pop. 311,000.
cal·i·ber (kăl′ə-bər) *n.* Also *chiefly Brit.* **cal·i·bre. 1.** The diameter of the inside of a tube, as the bore of a gun. **2.** The diameter of a bullet or shell. **3.** Quality; worth. [< Ar *qālib*, shoemaker's last.]
cal·i·brate (kăl′ə-brāt′) *v.* **-brated, -brating. 1.** To check or adjust the graduations of a quan-

ô paw, for/oi boy/ou out/o͞o took/o͞o coo/p pop/r run/s sauce/sh shy/t tò/th thin/*th* the/
ŭ cut/ûr fur/v van/w wag/y yes/z size/zh vision/ə ago, item, edible, gallop, circus/

titative measuring instrument. **2.** To measure the caliber of. —**cal'i•bra'tion** n. —**cal'i•bra'tor** (-brā'tər) n.

cal•i•co (kăl'ĭ-kō) n., pl. **-coes** or **-cos.** A cotton cloth printed with an all-over pattern. [< *Calicut*, former name for Kozhikode, India.]

Calif. California.

Cal•i•for•nia (kăl'ə-fôrn'yə, -fôr'nē-ə). A W state of the U.S. Pop. 19,953,000. Cap. Sacramento. —**Cal'i•for'nian** adj. & n.

cal•i•for•ni•um (kăl'ə-fôr'nē-əm) n. *Symbol* **Cf** A synthetic radioactive element produced in trace quantities by helium isotope bombardment of curium. Atomic number 98, longest-lived isotope Cf 251.

cal•i•per (kăl'ə-pər) n. **1.** Often **calipers.** An instrument having two curved hinged legs used to measure internal and external dimensions. **2.** A vernier caliper. [Var. of CALIBER.]

ca•liph (kā'lĭf, kăl'ĭf) n. Also **ca•lif.** A. Moslem chief of state regarded as a successor to Mohammed. [< Ar *khalīfa*, "successor."] —**ca'-liph•ate'** n.

cal•is•then•ics (kăl'əs-thĕn'ĭks) pl.n. Simple gymnastic exercises to promote physical well-being. [CAL(L)I- + Gk *sthenos*, strength.] —**cal'is•then'ic** adj.

calk. Variant of **caulk.**

call (kôl) v. **1.** To cry or utter loudly or clearly. **2.** To summon. **3.** To telephone. **4.** To name; designate. **5.** To consider; estimate. **6.** To pay a brief visit. **7.** To demand payment of (a loan or bond issue). **8.** To stop (a baseball game) officially. **9.** *Poker.* To demand that an opponent show his cards. —**call down.** To rebuke; scold. —**call for. 1.** To require or demand. **2.** To come and get. —**call off.** To cancel or postpone. —n. **1. a.** A shout or loud cry. **b.** A characteristic cry, esp. of a bird. **2.** A summons or invitation. **3.** Demand; need. **4.** A short visit. **5.** A communication by telephone. [< OE *ceallian*, to call, shout < ON *kalla*.] —**call'er** n.

cal•la (kăl'ə) n. Also **calla lily.** A plant with a showy, usually white petallike leaf enclosing a clublike flower stalk. [< Gk *kallaia*, wattle of a cock.]

calli–. *comb. form.* Beauty. [< Gk *kallos*, beauty.]

cal•lig•ra•phy (kə-lĭg'rə-fē) n. **1.** The art of fine handwriting. **2.** Penmanship; handwriting. —**cal•lig'ra•pher** n. —**cal'li•graph'ic** (kăl'ə-grăf'ĭk) adj.

call•ing (kô'lĭng) n. **1.** A vocation, occupation, or profession. **2.** An inner urge; strong impulse.

cal•li•o•pe (kăl'ē-ōp', kə-lī'ə-pē') n. An organlike musical instrument fitted with steam whistles. [< *Calliope*, Gk muse of epic poetry.]

Cal•lis•to (kə-lĭs'tō) n. One of the 12 moons of Jupiter, the largest known moon of any planet.

cal•lous (kăl'əs) adj. **1.** Having calluses; toughened. **2.** Emotionally hardened; unfeeling. —v. To make or become callous. —**cal'-lous•ly** adv. —**cal'lous•ness** n.

cal•low (kăl'ō) adj. Immature; inexperienced: *a callow youth.* [< OE *calu*, bald. See gal-¹.] —**cal'low•ness** n.

cal•lus (kăl'əs) n., pl. **-luses.** A localized thickening and enlargement of the horny layer of the skin. —v. To form or develop a callus. [L.]

calm (käm) adj. Not agitated or tumultuous; quiet; serene. —n. **1.** Absence of motion or turmoil; serenity. **2.** A condition of little or no wind. —v. To make or become calm. [< OIt *calma*.] —**calm'ly** adv. —**calm'ness** n.

cal•o•mel (kăl'ə-mĕl', -məl) n. A white, tasteless compound, Hg₂Cl₂, used as a purgative. [< NL *calomelas*, "beautiful black."]

ca•lor•ic (kə-lôr'ĭk, -lŏr'ĭk) adj. Pertaining to heat or calories. —n. A hypothetically indestructible all-pervading fluid, formerly postulated to explain the properties of heat.

cal•o•rie (kăl'ər-ē) n. **1.** The amount of heat required to raise the temperature of 1 gram of water by 1°C at 1 atmosphere pressure; small calorie. **2.** The amount of heat required to raise the temperature of 1 kilogram of water by 1°C at 1 atmosphere pressure; large calorie. [< L *calor*, heat.]

cal•o•rif•ic (kăl'ə-rĭf'ĭk) adj. Pertaining to or generating heat.

cal•o•rim•e•ter (kăl'ə-rĭm'ə-tər) n. An apparatus for measuring heat.

cal•u•met (kăl'yə-mĕt', -mət, kăl'yə-mĕt') n. A long-stemmed pipe used by North American Indians for ceremonial purposes. [< F *chalumeau*, a straw.]

ca•lum•ni•ate (kə-lŭm'nē-āt') v. **-ated, -ating.** To speak falsely and maliciously of; slander. [< L *calumnia*, CALUMNY.] —**ca•lum'ni•a'tion** n. —**ca•lum'ni•a'tor** n.

cal•um•ny (kăl'əm-nē) n., pl. **-nies.** A maliciously false and injurious statement; slander. [< L *calumnia*, "trickery," "deception."] —**ca•lum'ni•ous** (kə-lŭm'nē-əs) adj.

Cal•va•ry (kăl'vər-ē). The hill near Jerusalem where Jesus was crucified. [< LL *Calvāria*.]

calve (kăv, käv) v. **calved, calving.** To give birth to a calf.

calves. pl. of **calf.**

Cal•vin (kăl'vĭn), **John.** 1509–1564. French theologian.

Cal•vin•ism (kăl'vĭn-ĭz'əm) n. The doctrine of Calvin, esp. his affirmation of predestination and redemption by grace alone. —**Cal'vin•ist** n. & adj. —**Cal'vin•is'tic** adj.

ca•lyp•so (kə-lĭp'sō) n. A type of West Indian music with improvised lyrics on topical or humorous subjects.

ca•lyx (kā'lĭks, kăl'ĭks) n., pl. **-lyxes** or **calyces** (kā'lə-sēz', kăl'ə-). The usually green segmented outer envelope of a flower. [L.]

cam (kăm) n. A multiply curved wheel mounted on a rotating shaft and used to produce reciprocating motion. [Perh < G *Kamm*, "comb."]

ca•ma•ra•de•rie (kä'mə-rä'də-rē, kăm'ə-) n. Comradely good will among friends. [< F *camarade*, comrade.]

cam•ber (kăm'bər) n. **1.** A slight arching, as of a road surface. **2.** A setting of automobile wheels closer together at the bottom than at the top. [< L *camurus*, bent or curved inward.]

ă pat/ā ate/âr care/ä bar/b bib/ch chew/d deed/ĕ pet/ē be/f fit/g gag/h hat/hw what/
ĭ pit/ī pie/îr pier/j judge/k kick/l lid, fatal/m mum/n no, sudden/ng sing/ŏ pot/ō go/

Cam·bo·di·a (kăm-bō'dē-ə). A country of SE Asia. Pop. 8,110,000. Cap. Phnom Penh. —**Cam·bo'di·an** n. & adj.

Cam·bri·an (kăm'brē-ən) adj. Of or belonging to the geologic time, rock system, or sedimentary deposits of the first period of the Palcozoic era. —n. The Cambrian period. [< Cambria, Wales.]

cam·bric (kăm'brĭk) n. A fine white linen or cotton fabric.

Cam·bridge (kăm'brĭj). 1. A city in E England; site of Cambridge Univ. Pop. 167,000. 2. A city in E Massachusetts; site of Harvard Univ. Pop. 108,000.

Cam·den (kăm'dən). A city in SW New Jersey. Pop. 117,000.

came¹ (kăm) n. A slender, grooved lead bar used to hold together the panes in stained glass or latticework windows.

came² (kăm). p.t. of come.

cam·el (kăm'əl) n. A humped, long-necked animal used in Old World desert regions as a beast of burden. [< Gk kamēlos < Sem.]

ca·mel·lia (kə-mēl'yə) n. 1. The showy, many-petaled flower of an evergreen shrub. 2. The shrub itself. [< G.J. Kamel (1661–1706), Czech Jesuit missionary.]

ca·mel·o·pard (kə-mēl'ə-pärd') n. Archaic. A giraffe. [< Gk kamēlopardalis.]

Cam·em·bert (kăm'əm-bâr') n. A creamy, mold-ripened cheese that softens on the inside as it matures. [< Camembert, village in Normandy.]

cam·e·o (kăm'ē-ō') n., pl. -os. A gem, medallion, etc., with a design cut in raised relief, usually of a contrasting color. [ME cameu.]

cam·er·a (kăm'ər-ə, kăm'rə) n. 1. An apparatus consisting of a lightproof enclosure having an aperture with a shuttered lens through which the image of an object is focused and recorded on a photosensitive film or plate. 2. The part of a television transmitting apparatus that receives the primary image and transforms it into electrical impulses. [LL, room.]

Cam·e·roon (kăm'ə-rōōn'). Also **Cam·e·roun**. A republic of C Africa. Pop. 6,575,000. Cap. Yaoundé.

cam·i·sole (kăm'ə-sōl') n. A woman's short sleeveless undergarment. [< OProv camisa, shirt.]

cam·o·mile. Variant of chamomile.

cam·ou·flage (kăm'ə-fläzh', -fläj') n. A means of concealment that creates the effect of being part of the natural surroundings. —v. -flaged, -flaging. To conceal by such means. [F.] —**cam'ou·flag'er** n.

camp¹ (kămp) n. 1. a. A place where a group of people is temporarily lodged in makeshift shelters. b. The shelters in such a place or the persons using them. 2. A place consisting of more or less permanent vacation cabins. 3. A group favorable to a common cause, doctrine, or political system. —v. To shelter or lodge in a camp; encamp. [< L campus, open field.]

camp² (kămp) n. Something, as a form of decorative art, felt to be so banal or dated as to be intrinsically entertaining. [?] —**camp'y**

adj.

cam·paign (kăm-pān') n. 1. A series of military operations undertaken as one stage in a war. 2. An operation undertaken to attain some political, social, or commercial goal. —v. To engage in a campaign. [< LL campānia, countryside.] —**cam·paign'er** n.

cam·pa·ni·le (kăm'pə-nē'lē) n., pl. -les (-lēz) or -li (-lē). A bell tower, esp. one freestanding but associated with a church. [< LL campāna, bell.]

camp·er (kăm'pər) n. 1. A person who camps outdoors or who attends a camp for recreation. 2. a. A compact, vanlike vehicle resembling an automobile-and-trailer combination, designed to serve as a dwelling and used for camping or on long motor trips. b. A portable shelter resembling the top part of a trailer, made to be mounted on a pickup truck to form such a vehicle.

camp·fire (kămp'fīr') n. 1. An outdoor fire in a camp, used for warmth or cooking. 2. A meeting held around such a fire.

camp·ground (kămp'ground') n. An area used for setting up a camp.

cam·phor (kăm'fər) n. A volatile crystalline compound, $C_{10}H_{16}O$, used as an insect repellent. [< ML camphora.] —**cam'phor·at'ed** (-āt'ĭd) adj. —**cam·phor'ic** adj.

camp·site (kămp'sīt') n. An area used or suitable for camping.

cam·pus (kăm'pəs) n., pl. -puses. The grounds of a school, college, or university. [L campus, field, plain.]

cam·shaft (kăm'shăft', -shäft') n. An engine shaft fitted with a cam or cams.

can¹ (kăn; unstressed kən) v. Past tense could, present tense can. —Used as an auxiliary indicating ability, power or prerogative, capacity, or possible contingency. [< OE cunnan, to know how. See gnō-.]

can² (kăn) n. 1. A metal container. 2. a. An airtight storage container usually made of tin-coated iron. b. The contents of such a container. —v. canned, canning. 1. To seal in a can or jar. 2. Slang. a. To dismiss; fire. b. To dispense with: can the chatter. [< OE canne < Gmc *kannōn-.] —**can'ner** n.

can. 1. canceled. 2. canon. 3. canto.

Can. Canada; Canadian.

Ca·naan (kā'nən). In Biblical times, Palestine

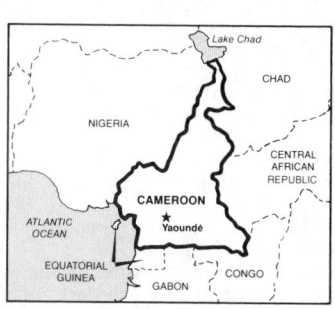

Cameroon

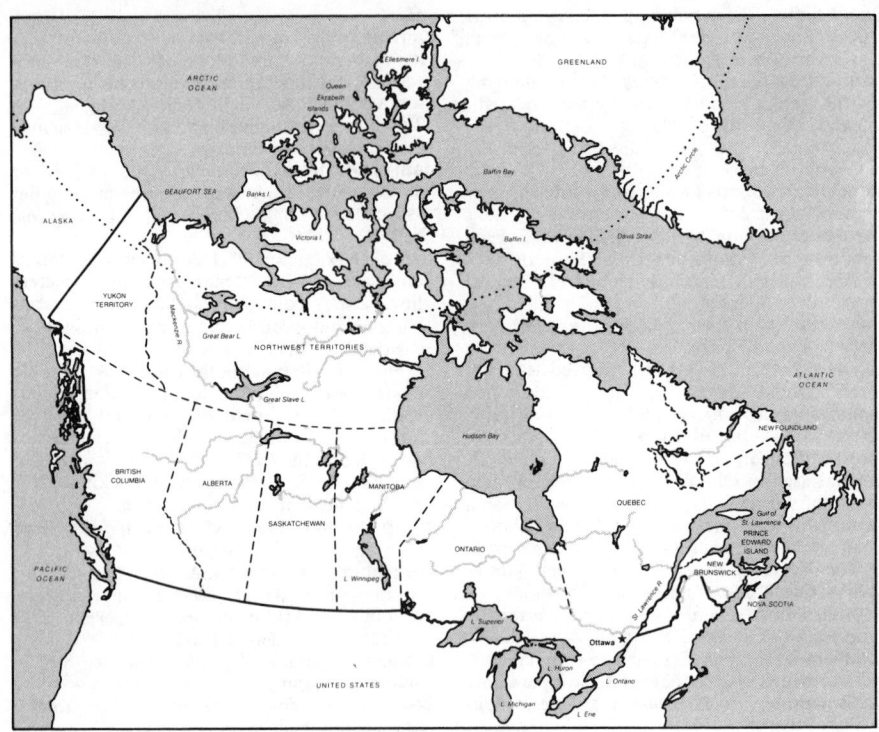

Canada

between the Jordan and the Mediterranean; the Promised Land. —Ca′naan•ite′ *n.*

Can•a•da (kăn′ə-də). A Commonwealth nation occupying the N half of North America. Pop. 19,785,000. Cap. Ottawa. —Ca•na′di•an (kə-nā′dē-ən) *adj. & n.*

Canadian French. French as used in Canada.

ca•naille (kə-nī′, -nāl′) *n.* The masses; mob. [< It *canaglia,* "pack of dogs."]

ca•nal (kə-năl′) *n.* **1.** A man-made channel filled with water. **2.** *Anat.* A tube or duct. [< L *canālis,* channel.]

ca•nal•ize (kə-năl′īz′, kăn′əl-) *v.* -ized, -izing. **1.** To furnish with or convert into canals. **2.** To provide an outlet for. —ca•nal′i•za′tion *n.*

Canal Zone. A strip of territory across the Isthmus of Panama, under lease to the U.S. for the Panama Canal.

can•a•pé (kăn′ə-pā′, -pē) *n.* A cracker, piece of toast, etc., topped with a spread or tidbit. [F, "couch" ("seat" for the relish).]

ca•nard (kə-närd′) *n.* A false or unfounded story. [F, "duck."]

ca•nar•y (kə-nâr′ē) *n., pl.* -ies. A usually yellow songbird popular as a cage bird. [< the CANARY ISLANDS.]

Canary Islands. An island group of Spain off the NW coast of Africa.

ca•nas•ta (kə-năs′tə) *n.* A card game related to rummy and requiring two decks of cards. [Span, "basket" (< the use of two decks, or a "basketful," of cards).]

Can•ber•ra (kăn′bĕr′ə, -bər-ə). The capital of Australia. Pop. 89,000.

can•can (kăn′kăn′) *n.* An exuberant exhibition dance characterized by high kicking. [F.]

can•cel (kăn′səl) *v.* **1.** To cross out with lines or other markings. **2.** To annul or invalidate. **3.** To mark or perforate (a postage stamp, check, etc.) to insure against its further use. **4.** To neutralize; offset. **5. a.** To remove a common factor from the numerator and denominator of a fraction. **b.** To remove a common factor or term from both members of an equation or inequality. [< L *cancellāre,* to make like a lattice, cross out.] —can′cel•a•ble *adj.* —can′cel•er *n.* —can′cel•la′tion *n.*

can•cer (kăn′sər) *n.* **1. a.** A malignant tumor that tends to invade healthy tissue and spread to new sites. **b.** The pathological condition characterized by such growths. **2.** A pernicious, spreading evil. [L, crab, creeping ulcer.] —can′cer•ous *adj.*

Can•cer (kăn′sər) *n.* **1.** A constellation in the N Hemisphere. **2.** The 4th sign of the zodiac.

can•de•la•brum (kăn′də-lä′brəm, -lăb′rəm, -lä′brəm) *n., pl.* -bra (-brə) or -brums. Also **can•de•la•bra** *pl.* -bras. A decorative candlestick with several branches. [< L *candēla,* CANDLE.]

can•did (kăn′dĭd) *adj.* **1.** Impartial; fair. **2.** Straightforward; open. **3.** Not posed: *a candid picture.* [< L *candidus,* glowing, white, pure.] —can′did•ly *adv.* —can′did•ness *n.*

ă pat/ā ate/âr care/ä bar/b bib/ch chew/d deed/ĕ pet/ē be/f fit/g gag/h hat/hw what/ ĭ pit/ī pie/îr pier/j judge/k kick/l lid, fatal/m mum/n no, sudden/ng sing/ŏ pot/ō go/

can·di·date (kăn′də-dāt′, -dĭt) *n.* A person who seeks or is nominated for an office, prize, honor, or the like. [L *candidātus*, "(Roman candidate) clothed in a white toga."] —**can′di·da·cy** (-də-sē), **can′di·da·ture′** (-də-chŏŏr′, -chər) *n.*

can·dle (kăn′dəl) *n.* A solid, usually cylindrical mass of tallow, wax, or other fatty substance with an axially embedded wick that is burned to provide light. [< L *candēla.*]

can·dle·light (kăn′dəl-līt′) *n.* Also **can·dle·light·ing** (-ĭng). 1. Illumination from a candle or candles. 2. Dusk; twilight.

can·dle·pin (kăn′dəl-pĭn′) *n.* A slender bowling pin used in a variation of the game of tenpins.

can·dle·stick (kăn′dəl-stĭk′) *n.* A holder for a candle.

can·dor (kăn′dər) *n.* Also *chiefly Brit.* **can·dour.** Frankness of expression; sincerity; straightforwardness. [L, whiteness, purity.]

can·dy (kăn′dē) *n., pl.* **-dies.** A sweet confection made with sugar and a variety of other ingredients. —*v.* **-died, -dying.** To cook or coat with sugar or syrup. [Short for sugar candy < Ar *qandi*, candied.]

cane (kān) *n.* 1. A slender, often hollow or flexible woody or pithy stem. 2. A plant with such stems. 3. Interwoven strips of such stems, esp. rattan. 4. A walking stick or similar rod. —*v.* **caned, caning.** 1. To beat with a cane. 2. To weave with cane. [< Gk *kanna*, reed, cane.] —**can′er** *n.*

cane·brake (kān′brāk′) *n.* A dense thicket of cane.

cane sugar. Sugar obtained from sugar cane.

ca·nine (kā′nīn′) *adj.* Of or pertaining to dogs or related animals; doglike. —*n.* 1. One of the conical teeth between the incisors and the bicuspids. 2. A canine animal. [< L *canis*, dog.]

Ca·nis Ma·jor (kā′nĭs mā′jər). A constellation in the S Hemisphere.

Canis Mi·nor (mī′nər). A constellation in the equatorial region of the S Hemisphere.

can·is·ter (kăn′ĭs-tər) *n.* 1. A container, usually of thin metal, for holding dry foods. 2. A metallic cylinder that, when fired from a gun, bursts and scatters the shot packed inside it. 3. The part of a gas mask containing a filter for poison gas. [L *canistrum*, reed basket.]

can·ker (kăng′kər) *n.* An ulcerous sore of the mouth and lips. [< L *cancer*, CANCER.] —**can′ker·ous** *adj.*

canned (kănd) *adj.* 1. Preserved and sealed in a can or jar. 2. Recorded or taped.

can·ner·y (kăn′ər-ē) *n., pl.* **-ies.** An establishment where meat, vegetables, and other foods are canned.

can·ni·bal (kăn′ə-bəl) *n.* 1. A person who eats the flesh of human beings. 2. Any animal that feeds on others of its own kind. [< Span *Canibalis, Caribales*, name (recorded by Columbus) of the man-eating Caribs of Cuba and Haiti.] —**can′ni·bal·ism′** *n.* —**can′ni·bal·is′tic** *adj.*

can·ni·bal·ize (kăn′ə-bə-līz′) *v.* **-ized, -izing.** To remove serviceable parts from (damaged airplanes, tanks, etc.) for use in the repair of other equipment. —**can′ni·bal·i·za′tion** *n.*

can·non (kăn′ən) *n., pl.* **-non** or **-nons.** 1. A weapon for firing projectiles, consisting of a heavy metal tube mounted on a carriage. 2. Any heavy firearm larger than 0.60 caliber. 3. *Brit.* A carom made in billiards. [< It *cannone*, "large tube, barrel."]

can·non·ade (kăn′ə-nād′) *v.* **-aded, -ading.** To bombard with cannon fire. —*n.* An extended discharge of artillery.

can·non·ball (kăn′ən-bôl′) *n.* A round projectile fired from a cannon. —*v.* To travel rapidly in the manner of a cannonball.

can·non·eer (kăn′ə-nîr′) *n.* A gunner or artilleryman.

can·not (kăn′ŏt, kă-nŏt′) *v.* The negative form of **can.**

can·ny (kăn′ē) *adj.* **-nier, -niest.** 1. Skillful; competent. 2. Shrewd; prudent. [< CAN¹.] —**can′ni·ly** *adv.* —**can′ni·ness** *n.*

ca·noe (kə-nōō′) *n.* A light, slender boat with pointed ends, propelled by paddles. —*v.* **-noed, -noeing.** To carry or travel by canoe. [< Span *canoa.*] —**ca·noe′ist** *n.*

can·on¹ (kăn′ən) *n.* 1. A law or code of laws established by a church council. 2. A secular code of law. 3. A basis for judgment; standard. 4. a. The books of the Bible officially recognized by the Church. b. The calendar of saints accepted by the Roman Catholic Church. 5. *Mus.* A round. [< L *canōn*, measuring line, rule.]

can·on² (kăn′ən) *n.* One of a chapter of priests serving in a cathedral or collegiate church. [< LL *canōnicus*, one living under a rule.]

ca·non·i·cal (kə-nŏn′ĭ-kəl) *adj.* Also **ca·non·ic** (-ĭk). 1. Pertaining to, required by, or abiding by canon law. 2. Authoritative; orthodox. —**ca·non′i·cal·ly** *adv.* —**can′on·ic′i·ty** (kăn′ə-nĭs′ə-tē) *n.*

canonical hours. A form of prayer, prescribed by canon law, normally to be recited at specified times of the day.

can·on·ize (kăn′ə-nīz′) *v.* **-ized, -izing.** 1. To declare officially (a deceased person) to be a saint. 2. To glorify; exalt. —**can′on·i·za′tion** *n.*

can·o·py (kăn′ə-pē) *n., pl.* **-pies.** 1. A covering fastened or held horizontally above a person or an object for protection or ornamentation. 2. An ornamental, rooflike structure. —*v.* **-pied, -pying.** To form or place a canopy over. [< ML *canapeum, canopeum*, (couch with a) mosquito net.]

canst (kănst). *Archaic.* 2nd person sing. present tense of **can.** Used with *thou.*

cant¹ (kănt) *n.* 1. Angular deviation from a vertical or horizontal plane or surface. 2. The tilt caused by such a motion. 3. A slanted edge or surface. —*v.* To cause to slant or tilt. [< L *canthus*, iron tire, rim of a wheel.]

cant² (kănt) *n.* 1. Wheedling speech. 2. Discourse recited mechanically. 3. Hypocritically pious language. 4. The special vocabulary peculiar to the members of a group. —*v.* 1. To speak in a whining, pleading tone. 2. To speak sententiously; moralize. [Prob < NF, singing, jargon.] —**cant′ing·ly** *adv.*

ŏ paw, for/oi boy/ou out/ŏŏ took/ōō coo/p pop/r run/s sauce/sh shy/t to/th thin/*th* the/
ŭ cut/ûr fur/v van/w wag/y yes/z size/zh vision/ə ago, item, edible, gallop, circus/

can't (kănt, känt). Contraction of *cannot*.

Cant. Cantonese.

can·ta·bi·le (kän-tä'bē-lā') *adj. Mus.* In a smooth, lyrical, flowing style. [< LL *cantābilis,* singable.] —**can·ta'bi·le'** *adv.*

can·ta·loupe (kăn'tə-lōp') *n.* A melon with a ribbed, rough rind and orange flesh. [< *Cantalupo,* a papal villa near Rome.]

can·tank·er·ous (kăn-tăng'kər-əs) *adj.* Illtempered and quarrelsome. [Prob < ME *contekour,* rioter, brawler.]

can·ta·ta (kən-tä'tə) *n.* A vocal and instrumental composition comprising choruses, solos, and recitatives. [It *(aria) cantata,* "sung (aria)."]

can·teen (kăn-tēn') *n.* 1. a. A store for on-base military personnel. b. *Brit.* A club for soldiers. 2. An institutional recreation hall or cafeteria. [< It *cantina,* a wine cellar.]

can·ter (kăn'tər) *n.* A gait slower than the gallop but faster than the trot. [Short for *Canterbury gallop.*] —**can'ter** *v.*

Can·ter·bur·y (kăn'tər-běr'ē). A cathedral city of SE England. Pop. 33,000.

can·thus (kăn'thəs) *n., pl.* **-thi** (-thī'). The corner at either side of the eye, formed by the meeting of the upper and lower eyelids. [< Gk *kanthos.*]

can·ti·cle (kăn'tĭ-kəl) *n.* A liturgical chant. [< L *cantus,* song.]

can·ti·le·ver (kăn'tə-lē'vər, -lěv'ər) *n.* A projecting beam or other structure supported only at one end. [Poss CANT¹ + LEVER.]

can·tle (kăn'təl) *n.* The rear part of a saddle. [< NF *cantel.*]

can·to (kăn'tō) *n., pl.* **-tos.** A principal division of a long poem. [< L *cantus,* song.]

can·ton (kăn'tən, -tŏn') *n.* A small territorial division of a country, esp. one of the states of Switzerland. —*v.* 1. (kăn'tən, -tŏn'). To divide into parts. 2. (kăn-tŏn', -tŏn'). To assign quarters to. [F, corner, subdivision.] —**can'ton·al** *adj.*

Can·ton (kăn'tŏn', kăn-tŏn'). 1. A port in SE China. Pop. 1,840,000. 2. A city in NE Ohio. Pop. 114,000.

Can·ton·ese (kăn'tə-nēz', -nēs') *n., pl.* **-ese.** 1. The Chinese dialect spoken in S China. 2. A native or inhabitant of the Canton region. —**Can'ton·ese'** *adj.*

can·ton·ment (kăn-tŏn'mənt, kăn-tŏn'-) *n.* 1. The assignment of troops to temporary quarters. 2. The quarters assigned.

can·tor (kăn'tər) *n.* The official soloist or chief singer of the liturgy in a synagogue. [L, singer.]

can·vas (kăn'vəs) *n.* 1. A heavy, closely woven fabric of cotton, hemp, etc., used for making tents and sails. 2. A piece of such material used as the surface for a painting. 3. Sailcloth. 4. Sails. 5. The floor of a boxing or wrestling ring. [< VL *cannabāceus,* "made of hemp."]

can·vas·back (kăn'vəs-băk') *n.* A North American duck with a reddish head and neck and a whitish back.

can·vass (kăn'vəs) *v.* 1. To scrutinize. 2. a. To go through or to solicit votes, orders, subscriptions, etc. b. To conduct a survey. —*n.*

1. An examination or discussion. 2. A solicitation of votes, sales orders, or opinions. [< CANVAS.] —**can'vass·er** *n.*

can·yon (kăn'yən) *n.* A narrow chasm with steep cliff walls eroded by running water. [< Span *cañon,* pipe, tube, conduit.]

cap (kăp) *n.* 1. A usually close-fitting covering for the head, with or without a visor. 2. Any of numerous objects similar to a head covering in form, use, or position: *a bottle cap.* —*v.* **capped, capping.** 1. To put a cap on. 2. To lie over or on top of: *Snow capped the hills.* [< LL *cappa,* hood.]

cap. 1. capacity. 2. capital (city). 3. capital letter.

C.A.P. Civil Air Patrol.

ca·pa·ble (kā'pə-bəl) *adj.* Having capacity or ability; competent. —**capable of.** 1. Qualified for. 2. Open to: *an error capable of remedy.* [< LL *capābilis,* "able to hold."] —**ca'pa·bil'i·ty** *n.* —**ca'pa·ble·ness** *n.* —**ca'pa·bly** *adv.*

ca·pa·cious (kə-pā'shəs) *adj.* Able to contain a large quantity; spacious; roomy. [< L *capāx,* able to hold.] —**ca·pa'cious·ly** *adv.* —**ca·pa'cious·ness** *n.*

ca·pac·i·tance (kə-păs'ə-təns) *n.* 1. The ratio of charge to potential on an electrically charged, isolated conductor. 2. The ratio of the electric charge transferred from one to the other of a pair of conductors to the resulting potential difference between them. —**ca·pac'i·tive** *adj.* —**ca·pac'i·tive·ly** *adv.*

ca·pac·i·tate (kə-păs'ə-tāt') *v.* **-tated, -tating.** To render fit; make qualified; enable. —**ca·pac'i·ta'tion** *n.*

ca·pac·i·tor (kə-păs'ə-tər) *n.* An electric circuit element used to store charge temporarily, consisting in general of two metallic plates separated by a dielectric.

ca·pac·i·ty (kə-păs'ə-tē) *n., pl.* **-ties.** 1. The ability to receive, hold, or absorb. 2. A measure of this ability; volume. 3. The maximum amount that can be contained. 4. The maximum amount of production: *factories operating below capacity.* 5. The ability to learn or retain knowledge. 6. The quality of being suitable for or receptive to specified treatment: *the capacity of elastic to be stretched.* 7. The position in which one functions; role: *his capacity as host.* 8. *Elec.* a. *Obs.* Capacitance. b. A measure of the output of a generator. —*adj.* As numerous as possible: *a capacity crowd.* [< L *capāx,* CAPACIOUS.]

ca·par·i·son (kə-păr'ə-sən) *n.* An ornamental covering for a horse's saddle or harness. [OF *caparaĉon.*]

cape¹ (kāp) *n.* A sleeveless garment worn hanging over the shoulders. [< LL *cappa,* hood, cloak.]

cape² (kāp) *n.* A point or head of land projecting into a sea or other body of water; promontory. [< L *caput,* head.]

ca·per¹ (kā'pər) *n.* 1. A playful leap or hop. 2. A wild escapade. —*v.* To leap or frisk about. [Short for CAPRIOLE.]

ca·per² (kā'pər) *n.* A pickled flower bud of a Mediterranean shrub, used as a condiment. [< L *capparis.*]

ă pat/ā ate/âr care/ä bar/b bib/ch chew/d deed/ě pet/ē be/f fit/g gag/h hat/hw what/
ĭ pit/ī pie/îr pier/j judge/k kick/l lid, fatal/m mum/n no, sudden/ng sing/ŏ pot/ō go/

cape•skin (kăp'skĭn') *n.* Soft leather made from sheepskin.
Cape Town. Also **Cape•town** (kăp'toun'). The legislative capital of the Republic of South Africa. Pop. 508,000.
caph. Variant of **kaph.**
cap•il•lar•i•ty (kăp'ə-lăr'ə-tē) *n., pl.* **-ties.** The interaction between contacting surfaces of a liquid and a solid that distorts the liquid surface from a planar shape.
cap•il•lar•y (kăp'ə-lĕr'ē) *adj.* **1.** Pertaining to or resembling a hair; fine and slender. **2.** Having a very small internal diameter, as a tube. **3.** In or pertaining to the capillaries. **4.** Pertaining to capillarity. *—n., pl.* **-ies. 1.** One of the minute blood vessels that connect the arteries and veins. **2.** Any tube with a small internal diameter. [< L *capillus*, hair.]
capillary attraction. The force that causes a liquid to be raised against a vertical surface, as is water in a clean glass tube.
cap•i•tal¹ (kăp'ə-təl) *n.* **1.** A town or city that is the official seat of government in a political entity. **2.** Wealth in the form of money or property. **3. a.** The net worth of a business. **b.** The funds invested in a business by the owners or stockholders. **4.** Capitalists considered as a class. **5.** Any asset or advantage. **6.** A capital letter. *—adj.* **1.** First and foremost; chief. **2.** Pertaining to a political capital. **3.** First-rate; excellent: *a capital fellow.* **4.** Extremely serious: *a capital blunder.* **5.** Punishable by or involving death: *capital punishment.* **6.** Pertaining to capital. [< L *capitālis*, "of the head," important.]
cap•i•tal² (kăp'ə-təl) *n.* The top of a column. [< LL *capitellum*, "small head."]
capital goods. Goods used in the production of commodities.
cap•i•tal•ism (kăp'ə-təl-ĭz'əm) *n.* An economic system characterized by freedom of the market with private and corporate ownership of the means of production and distribution that are operated for profit.
cap•i•tal•ist (kăp'ə-təl-ĭst) *n.* **1.** An investor of capital in business. **2.** Any person of great wealth. *—adj.* Of or pertaining to capitalism or capitalists. *—***cap'i•tal•is'tic** *adj.* *—***cap'i•tal•is'ti•cal•ly** *adv.*
cap•i•tal•i•za•tion (kăp'ə-təl-ə-zā'shən) *n.* **1.** The act, practice, or result of capitalizing. **2.** The total investment of owners in a business.
cap•i•tal•ize (kăp'ə-təl-īz') *v.* **-ized, -izing. 1.** To utilize as or convert into capital. **2.** To supply with capital. **3.** To begin a word with an upper-case letter. **4.** To turn to advantage; profit by; exploit: *capitalize on an opponent's error.*
capital letter. A letter of a size larger than and often in a form differing from its corresponding smaller letter; an upper-case letter.
capital punishment. The death penalty.
capital stock. The total amount of stock authorized for issue by a corporation.
cap•i•ta•tion (kăp'ə-tā'shən) *n.* A tax fixed at an equal sum per person; a per capita tax. [< LL *caput*, head, person.]

cap•i•tol (kăp'ə-təl) *n.* A building in which a legislature assembles.
ca•pit•u•late (kə-pĭch'ōō-lāt') *v.* **-lated, -lating. 1.** To surrender under specified conditions. **2.** To give up all resistance; acquiesce. [< ML *capitulāre*, to draw up under heads or chapters.] *—***ca•pit'u•la'tion** *n.*
ca•pon (kā'pŏn', -pən) *n.* A castrated rooster raised for eating. [< L *capō.*]
ca•pric•cio (kə-prē'chō, -chē-ō') *n., pl.* **-cios.** An instrumental work with a whimsical style and a free form. [It, caprice.]
ca•price (kə-prēs') *n.* **1.** An impulsive change of mind. **2.** An inclination to make such a change. [< It *capriccio*, "head with hair standing on end."]
ca•pri•cious (kə-prĭsh'əs, -prē'shəs) *adj.* Characterized by or subject to whim; fickle.
Cap•ri•corn (kăp'rĭ-kôrn') *n.* **1.** Capricornus. **2. Tropic of Capricorn.**
Cap•ri•cor•nus (kăp'rĭ-kôr'nəs) *n.* Also **Cap•ri•corn. 1.** A constellation in the equatorial region of the S Hemisphere. **2.** The 10th sign of the zodiac. [L, "goat-horned."]
cap•ri•ole (kăp'rē-ōl') *n.* **1.** An upward leap made by a trained horse without going forward. **2.** A leap or jump. [< It *capriola*, "leap of a goat."]
caps. capsule.
cap•size (kăp'sīz', kăp-sīz') *v.* **-sized, -sizing.** To overturn or cause to turn over. [?]
cap•stan (kăp'stən) *n.* **1.** A vertical revolving cylinder for hoisting weights by winding in a cable. **2.** A small cylindrical pulley used to regulate the speed of magnetic tape in a tape recorder. [< L *capistrum*, halter.]
cap•su•lar (kăp'sə-lər, -syōō-lər) *adj.* Of or like a capsule.
cap•su•late (kăp'sə-lāt', -syōō-lāt', -lĭt) *adj.* In or formed into a capsule.
cap•sule (kăp'səl, -syōōl) *n.* **1.** A soluble gelatinous sheath enclosing a dose of an oral medicine. **2.** A fibrous, membranous, or fatty envelope enclosing an organ or part. **3.** A seed case that dries and spilts open. **4.** A pressurized modular compartment of an aircraft or spacecraft. [< L *capsula*, dim of *capsa*, box.]
cap•tain (kăp'tən) *n.* **1.** One who commands, leads, or guides. **2.** The officer in command of a ship. **3.** A commissioned officer, as in the army, who ranks above a first lieutenant. **4.** A commissioned officer in the navy who ranks above a commander. *—v.* To command or direct. [< LL *capitāneus*, chief.] *—***cap'tain•cy** *n.* *—***cap'tain•ship** *n.*
cap•tion (kăp'shən) *n.* **1.** A short legend or description, as of an illustration or photograph. **2.** A subtitle in a motion picture. **3.** A title, as of a document or chapter. [Orig "arrest," record of execution of a commission < L *capere*, to seize.]
cap•tious (kăp'shəs) *adj.* **1.** Marked by a disposition to find fault. **2.** Intended to entrap or confuse. [< L *captiōsus*, "ensnaring."]
cap•ti•vate (kăp'tə-vāt') *v.* **-vated, -vating.** To fascinate by special charm or beauty. [LL *captīvāre*, to capture.] *—***cap'ti•va'tion** *n.*
cap•tive (kăp'tĭv) *n.* **1.** A prisoner. **2.** One who

ô paw, for/oi boy/ou out/ōō took/ōō coo/p pop/r run/s sauce/sh shy/t to/th thin/*th* the/
ŭ cut/ûr fur/v van/w wag/y yes/z size/zh vision/ə ago, item, edible, gallop, circus/

is enslaved by a strong emotion or passion. —*adj.* **1.** Held as prisoner. **2.** Obliged to be present: *a captive audience.* [< L *captīvus* < *capere,* to seize.] —**cap•tiv′i•ty** *n.*

cap•tor (kăp′tər, -tôr′) *n.* One who captures. [< L *capere,* to seize.]

cap•ture (kăp′chər) *v.* **-tured, -turing. 1.** To take captive. **2.** To win possession or control of. —*n.* **1.** The act of capturing; seizure. **2.** One that is seized, caught, or won. [< L *capere,* to seize.]

car (kär) *n.* **1.** An automobile. **2.** A conveyance with wheels that runs along tracks, as a streetcar or railroad car. [< L *carrus,* two-wheeled wagon.]

car. carat.

Ca•ra•cas (kə-rä′kəs, -răk′əs). The capital of Venezuela. Pop. 1,639,000.

car•a•cul. Variant of **karakul.**

ca•rafe (kə-răf′) *n.* A glass bottle for serving water or wine at the table; decanter. [< Ar *gharrāf.*]

car•a•mel (kăr′ə-məl, kär′məl) *n.* **1.** A chewy candy made with sugar, butter, cream or milk, and flavoring. **2.** Burnt sugar, used for coloring and sweetening. [F.]

car•a•pace (kăr′ə-pās′) *n.* A hard outer covering, as the upper shell of a turtle. [< Span *carapacho.*]

car•at (kăr′ət) *n.* **1.** A unit of weight for precious stones, equal to 200 milligrams. **2.** Variant of **karat.** [< Ar *qīrāt,* small weight, carat.]

car•a•van (kăr′ə-văn′) *n.* **1.** A company of travelers journeying together, esp. across a desert. **2.** A single file of vehicles or pack animals. **3.** A large covered vehicle; van. [< Pers *kārwān.*]

car•a•van•sa•ry (kăr′ə-văn′sə-rē) *n., pl.* **-ries.** Also **car•a•van•se•rai** (-rī′). **1.** In the Near or Far East, an inn for caravans. **2.** Any large inn.

car•a•vel (kăr′ə-věl′) *n.* A small, light sailing ship of the kind used by the Spanish and Portuguese in the 15th and 16th centuries. [< OF *caravelle.*]

car•a•way (kăr′ə-wā′) *n.* **1.** A plant with pungent, aromatic seeds used in cooking. **2.** The seeds of this plant. [ME.]

car•bide (kär′bīd′) *n.* A binary compound of carbon with a more electropositive element.

car•bine (kär′bīn′, -bēn′) *n.* A light shoulder rifle with a short barrel. [F *carabine.*]

carbo-. *comb. form.* Carbon. [< CARBON.]

car•bo•hy•drate (kär′bō-hī′drāt′) *n.* Any of a group of chemical compounds, including sugars, starches, and cellulose, containing carbon, hydrogen, and oxygen only, with the ratio of hydrogen to oxygen atoms usually 2:1.

car•bol•ic acid (kär-bŏl′ĭk). Phenol.

car•bon (kär′bən) *n. Symbol* **C 1.** A naturally abundant nonmetallic element that occurs in many inorganic and in all organic compounds, exists in amorphous, graphitic, and diamond allotropes, and is capable of chemical self-bonding to form an enormous number of chemically, biologically, and commercially important long-chain molecules. Atomic number 6, atomic weight 12.01115. **2. a.** A sheet of carbon paper. **b.** A copy made by using carbon paper. [< L *carbō,* charcoal.]

carbon 14. A naturally radioactive carbon isotope with atomic mass 14 and half-life 5,700 years, used in dating ancient carbon-containing objects.

car•bon•ate (kär′bə-nāt′) *v.* **-ated, -ating.** To charge with carbon dioxide gas. —**car′bon•a′tion** *n.* —**car′bon•a′tor** *n.*

carbon dioxide. A colorless, odorless, incombustible gas, CO_2, formed during respiration, combustion, and organic decomposition.

car•bon•ic acid (kär-bŏn′ĭk). A weak, unstable acid, H_2CO_3, present in solutions of carbon dioxide in water.

car•bon•if•er•ous (kär′bə-nĭf′ər-əs) *adj.* Producing, containing, or pertaining to carbon or coal.

Car•bon•if•er•ous (kär′bə-nĭf′ər-əs) *adj.* Of, designating, or belonging to a division of the Paleozoic era including the Mississippian and Pennsylvanian periods, characterized by swamp formation and deposition of plant remains later hardened into coal. —*n.* The Carboniferous period.

carbon monoxide. A colorless, odorless, highly poisonous gas, CO, formed by the incomplete combustion of carbon or carbon compounds.

carbon paper. A lightweight paper faced on one side with a dark pigment that is transferred by the impact of typewriter keys or by writing pressure to a copying surface.

carbon tetrachloride. A poisonous, nonflammable, colorless liquid, CCl_4, used in fire extinguishers and as a solvent.

Car•bo•run•dum (kär′bə-rŭn′dəm) *n.* A trademark for a silicon carbide abrasive.

car•boy (kär′boi′) *n.* A large container usually encased in a protective covering and often used to hold corrosive liquids. [< Ar *qarrābah.*]

car•bun•cle (kär′bŭng′kəl) *n.* A painful, localized, pus-producing, sometimes fatal infection of the skin. [< L *carbunculus,* small glowing ember, tumor.] —**car•bun′cu•lar** (-kyə-lər) *adj.*

car•bu•re•tor (kär′bə-rā′tər, kär′byə-) *n.* A device used in gasoline engines to produce an efficient explosive vapor of fuel and air. [< F *carbure,* carbide.]

car•cass (kär′kəs) *n.* A dead body, esp. of an animal. [F *carcasse.*]

car•cin•o•gen (kär-sĭn′ə-jən, kär′sĭn-ə-jĕn′) *n.* A cancer-causing substance. [<Gk *karkinos,* cancer, crab.] —**car′cin•o•gen′ic** *adj.*

card¹ (kärd) *n.* **1.** A small, flat piece of stiff paper or thin pasteboard with numerous uses: **a.** One of a set of playing cards. **b.** A post card. **c.** One bearing a greeting or a person's name and other information, as a Christmas or business card. **2.** A program of events, as at horse races. **3.** *Informal.* An amusing or eccentric person. [< L *charta,* leaf of papyrus.]

card² (kärd) *n.* A wire-toothed brush used to disentangle textile fibers or raise the nap on a fabric. [< L *cārere,* to card.] —**card** *v.* —**card′er** *n.*

ă pat/ā ate/âr care/ä bar/b bib/ch chew/d deed/ĕ pet/ē be/f fit/g gag/h hat/hw what/
ĭ pit/ī pie/îr pier/j judge/k kick/l lid, fatal/m mum/n no, sudden/ng sing/ŏ pot/ō go/

card•board (kärd′bôrd′, -bōrd′) *n.* A stiff pasteboard made of paper pulp.

car•di•ac (kär′dē-ăk′) *adj.* Of or near the heart.

Car•diff (kär′dĭf). The major city of Wales. Pop. 260,000.

car•di•gan (kär′dĭ-gən) *n.* A sweater or collarless jacket opening down the front. [< J.T. Brudenell, 7th Earl of *Cardigan* (1797–1868), British army officer.]

car•di•nal (kärd′n-əl, kärd′nəl) *adj.* 1. Of foremost importance. 2. Of a dark to vivid red color. —*n.* 1. *R.C.Ch.* One of the highest-ranking dignitaries, below papal rank, appointed by the pope to assist him in governing the church. 2. Dark to vivid red. 3. A crested, bright-red North American bird. [< LL *cardinālis,* principal, of a hinge.]

car•di•nal•ate (kärd′n-əl-ĭt, kärd′nəl-, -āt′) *n. R.C.Ch.* 1. The body comprising all the cardinals. 2. The rank, dignity, or term of a cardinal.

cardinal number. A number, such as 3 or 11 or 412, used to indicate quantity but not order.

cardio–. *comb. form.* The heart. [< Gk *kardia,* heart.]

car•di•o•gram (kär′dē-ə-grăm′) *n.* The curve traced by a cardiograph, used to diagnose heart defects.

car•di•o•graph (kär′dē-ə-grăf′, -gräf′) *n.* An instrument used to record the movements of the heart.

car•di•ol•o•gy (kär′dē-ŏl′ə-jē) *n.* The medical study of the diseases and functioning of the heart. —**car′di•ol′o•gist** *n.*

car•di•o•vas•cu•lar (kär′dē-ō-văs′kyə-lər) *adj.* Involving the heart and the blood vessels.

cards (kärdz) *pl.n. (Often takes sing. v.).* A game played usually with a deck of 52 cards.

care (kâr) *n.* 1. Mental distress and grief. 2. An object or source of attention or solicitude. 3. Caution: *handle with care.* 4. Supervision; charge: *in the care of a nurse.* —**(in) care of.** At the address of. —*v.* **cared, caring.** 1. To be concerned or interested. 2. To object; mind. [< OE *caru, cearu.*]

ca•reen (kə-rēn′) *v.* 1. To move rapidly and in an uncontrolled manner. 2. To cause (a ship) to lean to one side; tilt. [< F *(en) carène,* "(on) the keel."] —**ca•reen′er** *n.*

ca•reer (kə-rîr′) *n.* 1. A chosen pursuit; lifework. 2. A person's progress in his occupation. —*v.* To move or run at full speed. [F *carrière,* racecourse, course, career.]

care•free (kâr′frē′) *adj.* Free of worries and responsibilities.

care•ful (kâr′fəl) *adj.* 1. Cautious in thought, speech, or action. 2. Thorough; painstaking. —**care′ful•ly** *adv.* —**care′ful•ness** *n.*

care•less (kâr′lĭs) *adj.* 1. Inattentive; negligent. 2. Marked by or resulting from lack of thought. 3. Inconsiderate: *a careless remark.* 4. Free from cares; cheerful. —**care′less•ly** *adv.* —**care′less•ness** *n.*

ca•ress (kə-rĕs′) *n.* A gentle touch or gesture of fondness. —*v.* To touch or treat in an affectionate or loving manner. [< It *carezza,* endearment.] —**ca•ress′er** *n.*

car•et (kăr′ĭt) *n.* A proofreading symbol used to indicate where something is to be inserted in a line of printed or written matter. [L, "there is lacking."]

care•tak•er (kâr′tā′kər) *n.* One employed to look after or take charge of goods, property, or a person; custodian.

care•worn (kâr′wôrn′, -wōrn′) *adj.* Showing the effects of worry or grief.

car•fare (kär′fâr′) *n.* Fare charged a passenger.

car•go (kär′gō) *n., pl.* **-goes** or **-gos.** The freight carried by a ship, airplane, or other vehicle. [Span, load, cargo.]

car•hop (kär′hŏp′) *n.* A waiter at a drive-in restaurant.

Car•ib (kăr′ĭb) *n., pl.* **-ib** or **-ibs.** 1. Also **Car•i•ban** (-ə-bən, kə-rē′-). a. A member of a group of American Indian peoples of N South America and the Lesser Antilles. b. A member of one of these peoples. 2. Any of the languages of these peoples. —**Car′ib** *adj.*

Car•i•ban (kăr′ə-bən, kə-rē′bən) *n., pl.* **-ban** or **-bans.** 1. Carib. 2. A language family of the Lesser Antilles and N South America, comprising the languages spoken by the Caribs. —**Car′i•ban** *adj.*

Car•ib•be•an Sea (kăr′ə-bē′ən, kə-rĭb′ē-ən). An extension of the Atlantic bounded by Central and South America and the West Indies. —**Car′ib•be′an** *adj.*

car•i•bou (kăr′ə-bōō′) *n., pl.* **-bou** or **-bous.** A New World arctic deer, considered identical to the reindeer. [< Algon.]

car•i•ca•ture (kăr′ĭ-kə-chŏŏr′) *n.* 1. A representation, esp. pictorial, in which a subject's distinctive features or peculiarities are exaggerated for comic or grotesque effect. 2. An imitation so inferior as to be absurd. —*v.* **-tured, -turing.** To represent or imitate in or as in a caricature. [< It *caricatura,* caricature, "exaggeration."] —**car′i•ca•tur′ist** *n.*

car•ies (kâr′ēz) *n.* Decay of a bone or tooth. [L *cariēs,* caries, decay.]

car•il•lon (kăr′ə-lŏn′, kə-rĭl′yən) *n.* A set of bells played chiefly on a keyboard. [F.]

ca•ri•na (kə-rī′nə) *n., pl.* **-nae** (-nē′). *Biol.* A keel-shaped ridge, such as that on the breastbone of a bird or in the petals of certain flowers. [< L *carīna,* keel.]

Ca•ri•na (kə-rī′nə) *n.* A constellation in the S Hemisphere.

car•load (kär′lōd′) *n.* The amount a car carries or is able to carry.

car•mine (kär′mĭn, -mīn′) *n.* A strong to vivid red color. [< ML *carminium.*] —**car′mine** *adj.*

car•nage (kär′nĭj) *n.* Massive slaughter, as in war. [< ML *carnāticum,* slaughter of animals.]

car•nal (kär′nəl) *adj.* 1. Relating to the desires of the flesh; sensual. 2. Not spiritual. [< L *carō,* flesh.] —**car•nal′i•ty** (kär-năl′ə-tē) *n.*

car•na•tion (kär-nā′shən) *n.* 1. A plant cultivated for its fragrant many-petaled flowers. 2. A flower of this plant. [< OF, flesh-colored, carnation.]

car•nel•ian (kär-nēl′yən) *n.* A pale to deep red or reddish-brown variety of clear chalcedony, used in jewelry. [< OF *corneline.*]

car•ni•val (kär′nə-vəl) n. 1. The season just before Lent, marked by merrymaking and feasting. 2. A traveling amusement show. [OIt carnelevare, "the putting away of flesh," Shrovetide.]

car•ni•vore (kär′nə-vôr′, -vōr′) n. A flesh-eating animal, esp. one of a group including dogs, cats, bears, and weasels.

car•niv•o•rous (kär-nĭv′ər-əs) adj. Flesh-eating or predatory. [L carnivorus.] —car•niv′-o•rous•ly adv.

car•ol (kär′əl) v. -oled or -olled, -oling or -olling. 1. To celebrate or praise in song. 2. To sing joyously. —n. A song or hymn of praise or joy, esp. for Christmas. [< OF carole, a carol.] —car′ol•er n.

car•om (kär′əm) n. 1. A billiards shot in which the cue ball successively strikes two other balls. 2. A collision followed by a rebound. —v. 1. To collide with and rebound. 2. To make a carom in billiards. [< Span carambola, a kind of fruit.]

car•o•tene (kär′ə-tēn′) n. An orange-yellow to red hydrocarbon, $C_{40}H_{56}$, occurring in many plants and converted to vitamin A in the animal liver. [< L carôta, carrot.]

ca•rot•id (kə-rŏt′ĭd) n. Either of the two major arteries in the neck that carry blood to the head. [< Gk karoun, to stupefy.] —ca•rot′id•al adj.

ca•rous•al (kə-rou′zəl) n. A jovial, riotous drinking party.

ca•rouse (kə-rouz′) n. Boisterous, drunken merrymaking; a carousal. —v. -roused, -rous-ing. To go on a drinking spree. [< OF (boire) carous, (to drink) all out.] —ca•rous′er n.

car•ou•sel, car•rou•sel (kär′ə-sĕl′, -zĕl′) n. A merry-go-round. [F carrousel.]

carp¹ (kärp) v. To find fault and complain constantly; nag or fuss. [< ON karpa, to boast.] —carp′er n.

carp² (kärp) n., pl. carp or carps. An edible freshwater fish of ponds and lakes. [< LL carpa.]

car•pal (kär′pəl) adj. Anat. Of, pertaining to, or near the carpus: the carpal joint. —n. Any bone of the carpus.

Car•pa•thi•an Mountains (kär-pā′thē-ən). Also Car•pa•thi•ans (-ənz). A mountain system of E Europe.

car•pen•ter (kär′pən-tər) n. One whose occupation is constructing, finishing, and repairing wooden objects and structures. [< L carpen-tãrius (artifex), carriage(-maker).] —car′pen•ter v. —car′pen•try n.

car•pet (kär′pĭt) n. 1. A thick, heavy covering for a floor, usually made of wool or synthetic fibers. 2. The fabric used for this. —v. To cover with or as with a carpet. [< OIt carpita.]

car•pet•bag (kär′pĭt-băg′) n. A traveling bag made of carpet fabric.

car•pet•bag•ger (kär′pĭt-băg′ər) n. A Northerner who went to the South after the Civil War for political or financial advantage. —car′pet•bag′ger•y n.

car•port (kär′pôrt′, -pōrt′) n. A roof projecting from the side of a building, used as a shelter for an automobile.

car•pus (kär′pəs) n., pl. -pi (-pī′). 1. a. The wrist. b. The bones of the wrist. 2. Any joint corresponding to the wrist in quadrupeds. [< Gk karpos, wrist.]

car•rel (kär′əl) n. A nook in the stacks of a library, designed for individual use. [Perh < OF carole, CAROL.]

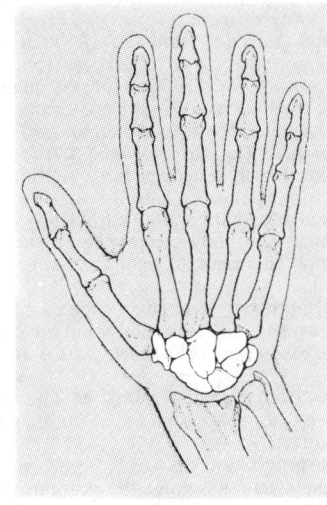

carpus

car•riage (kăr′ĭj) n. 1. A four-wheeled, horse-drawn passenger vehicle. 2. A movable machine part for holding or shifting another part. 3. Conveyance of goods; transport. 4. Manner of carrying oneself; bearing. [< ONF carier, to transport in a vehicle, carry.]

car•ri•er (kăr′ē-ər) n. 1. One that carries or conveys. 2. A person or corporation engaged in transporting passengers or goods. 3. An immune organism that transmits a pathogen to others. 4. An aircraft carrier.

carrier wave. An electromagnetic wave that can be modulated to transmit sound or images.

car•ri•on (kăr′ē-ən) n. Dead and decaying flesh. —adj. 1. Of or similar to carrion. 2. Carrion-eating. [< L carô, flesh.]

car•rot (kăr′ət) n. The edible, yellow-orange root of a widely cultivated plant. [< Gk karôton.]

car•rou•sel. Variant of carousel.

car•ry (kăr′ē) v. -ried, -rying. 1. To bear; convey; transport. 2. To win over. 3. To take; seize; capture. 4. To keep or have on one's person. 5. To involve; imply. 6. To conduct (oneself) in a specified manner. 7. To sustain; support. 8. To offer for sale or keep in stock. 9. To cover a range; reach. 10. To secure the adoption of. 11. To win most of the votes of. 12. To keep in one's accounts. —carry away. To excite greatly; transport. —carry on. 1. To manage; conduct. 2. To continue despite hindrance. 3. To act in a foolish or overwrought manner. —carry out. 1. To put into practice. 2. To obey. —carry through. 1. To complete. 2. To sustain. —n., pl. -ries. 1. An act or manner of carrying. 2. A portage, as between two navigable rivers. 3. The range of a gun or projectile. [< ONF carier, to transport in a vehicle.]

Car•son City (kär'sən). The capital of Nevada. Pop. 15,000.

cart (kärt) n. 1. A two-wheeled vehicle. 2. Any small vehicle. —v. 1. a. To convey in a cart. b. To convey laboriously; lug. 2. To remove or transport unceremoniously: He was carted off to jail. [< OE cræt and ON kartr.] —cart'a•ble adj. —cart'er n.

carte blanche (kärt bläNsh'). Unrestricted discretion. [F, "blank card."]

car•tel (kär-tĕl') n. A monopolistic combination of independent business enterprises. [< Olt carta, card.]

Car•ter (kär'tər), James Earl ("Jimmy"). Born 1924. 39th President of the U.S. (since 1977).

Car•te•sian (kär-tē'zhən) adj. Belonging to the system of Descartes. —Car•te'sian•ism' n.

Cartesian coordinate. A coordinate in a Cartesian coordinate system.

Cartesian coordinate system. 1. A two-dimensional coordinate system in which the co-ordinates of a point are its distances from two intersecting, often perpendicular, straight lines, the distance from each being measured along a straight line parallel to the other. 2. A three-dimensional coordinate system in which the coordinates of a point are its distances from each of three intersecting, often mutually perpendicular, planes along lines parallel to the intersection of the other two.

Car•thage (kär'thĭj). An ancient city on the N coast of Africa. —Car'tha•gin'i•an (kär'thə-jĭn'ē-ən) adj. & n.

car•ti•lage (kär'tə-lĭj) n. A tough white fibrous connective tissue attached to the articular surfaces of bones. [L cartilāgo.] —car'ti•lag'i•nous (-lăj'ə-nəs) adj.

car•tog•ra•phy (kär-tŏg'rə-fē) n. The making of maps. [< F carte, map, card + -GRAPHY.] —car•tog'ra•pher n. —car'to•graph'ic (kär'tə-grăf'ĭk) adj.

car•ton (kärt'n) n. A cardboard box or container. [< It cartone, pasteboard.]

car•toon (kär-tōōn') n. 1. A satirical drawing or caricature. 2. A painter's preliminary sketch. 3. A comic strip. [It cartone, pasteboard, CARTON.] —car•toon'ist n.

car•tridge (kär'trĭj) n. 1. A tubular case containing the propellant powder and primer of small arms ammunition or shotgun shells. 2. A small modular unit of a larger apparatus containing such equipment as a phonograph stylus, photographic film, magnetic tape, or writing ink. [< F cartouche, cartridge.]

cart•wheel (kärt'hwēl') n. 1. The wheel of a cart. 2. A somersault or handspring with the arms and legs extended. 3. Slang. A silver dollar.

carve (kärv) v. carved, carving. 1. To divide into pieces by cutting; slice. 2. To cut and serve meat at table. 3. To fashion by cutting. [<

OE ceorfan. See gerebh-.] —carv'er n.

car•y•at•id (kăr'ē-ăt'ĭd) n., pl. -ids or -atides (-ăt'ə-dēz'). A supporting column sculptured in the form of a woman.

ca•sa•ba (kə-sä'bə) n. A melon with a yellow rind and sweet, whitish flesh. [< Kassaba, former name of Turgutlu, Turkey.]

Cas•a•blan•ca (kăs'ə-blăng'kə, kä'sə-bläng'-kə). A seaport of Morocco. Pop. 1,085,000.

Cas•a•no•va (kăs'ə-nō'və, kăz'-) n. A philanderer. [< G.J. Casanova de Seingalt (1725–1798), Italian adventurer.]

cas•cade (kăs-kād') n. 1. A waterfall or a series of small waterfalls. 2. An analogous structure or phenomenon. —v. -caded, -cading. To fall in or as a cascade. [< It cascare, to fall.]

Cascade Range. The N section of the Sierra Nevada Mountains.

cas•car•a (kăs-kăr'ə) n. Also cas•car•a sa•gra•da (sə-grä'də). The dried bark of a tree of NW North America, used as a laxative. [Span cáscara, bark.]

case[1] (kās) n. 1. A specified instance; example. 2. A question or problem; matter. 3. A persuasive argument, demonstration, or justification. 4. An inflectional pattern or form, esp. of a noun or pronoun, expressing syntactic function or relation. 5. An action or suit in law. 6. a. An instance of sickness or injury. b. A patient. —v. cased, casing. Slang. To inspect (premises), as with intent to rob. [< L cāsus, fall, event, occurrence.]

case[2] (kās) n. 1. A container or receptacle. 2. A covering. 3. A set or pair. 4. The frame of a window or door. 5. A tray with compartments for storing printing type. —v. cased, casing. To put into or cover with a case. [< L capsa, chest, case.]

case•hard•en (kās'härd'n) v. To harden the surface of (iron or steel) by high-temperature shallow infusion of carbon followed by quenching. [< CASE (covering).]

case history. The facts relevant to the development of an individual or group condition under study or treatment.

ca•se•in (kā'sē-ĭn, kā'sēn') n. A white, tasteless, odorless milk and cheese protein, used to make plastics, adhesives, paints, and foods. [< L cāseus, cheese.]

case•ment (kās'mənt) n. 1. A window sash that opens outward by means of hinges. 2. A window with such sashes. 3. A case or covering. [ME.] —case'ment•ed adj.

case study. A detailed analysis of an individual or group.

cash (kăsh) n. 1. Ready money. 2. Immediate money payment for goods or services. —v. To exchange for or convert into ready money. [OF casse, money box.]

cash•ew (kăsh'ōō, kə-shōō') n. 1. A tropical American tree bearing kidney-shaped nuts. 2. The nut of this tree. [< Tupi acajú.]

cash•ier[1] (kă-shîr') n. 1. The officer of a bank or business concern in charge of paying and receiving money. 2. A business employee responsible for cash transactions. [< F caisse, money box.]

cash•ier² (kă-shîr') *v.* To dismiss in disgrace from a position of responsibility. [Du *casseren.*]

cash•mere (kăzh'mîr', kăsh'-) *n.* 1. Fine wool from an Asian goat. 2. A soft fabric made from this wool. [< *Kashmir*, India.]

cas•ing (kā'sĭng) *n.* An outer cover; case.

ca•si•no (kə-sē'nō) *n., pl.* **-nos.** A gambling house. [It, dim of *casa*, house.]

cask (kăsk, käsk) *n.* A barrel for holding liquids. [Span *casco*, helmet, cask.]

cas•ket (kăs'kĭt, käs'-) *n.* 1. A small case for jewels or other valuables. 2. A coffin. [< OF *cassette.*]

Cas•pi•an Sea (kăs'pē-ən). The largest inland body of water in the world, in SW Asia.

casque (kăsk) *n.* A helmet. [< Span *casco*, CASK.]

Cas•san•dra (kə-săn'drə) *n.* One who utters unheeded prophecies. [< *Cassandra*, Trojan prophetess.]

cas•sa•va (kə-sä'və) *n.* A tropical American plant with a starchy root from which tapioca is derived. [Span *cazabe*, cassava bread.]

cas•se•role (kăs'ə-rōl') *n.* 1. A baking dish in which food is cooked and served. 2. Food served in such a dish. [< OF, saucepan.]

cas•sette (kă-sĕt') *n.* A cartridge for film or magnetic tape. [F, small box.]

cas•sia (kăsh'ə) *n.* 1. a. A tropical Asian tree with cinnamonlike bark. b. The bark, used as a spice. 2. Any of various related trees and plants, some of which yield senna. [< Gk *kassia*, a kind of plant.]

Cas•si•o•pe•ia (kăs'ē-ə-pē'ə) *n.* A W-shaped constellation in the N Hemisphere.

cas•sock (kăs'ək) *n.* A long garment worn by clergymen. [< Pers *kazagand*, padded jacket.]

cast (kăst, käst) *v.* **cast, casting.** 1. To throw; hurl; fling. 2. To turn; direct; aim: *cast an eye.* 3. To give or deposit (a ballot). 4. To shed; discard. 5. To add up (a column of figures); compute. 6. To assign, as an actor's part. 7. To form by molding. —*n.* 1. A throw. 2. A throw of the dice. 3. a. A mold. b. A rigid plaster dressing, as for immobilizing and protecting a broken bone. 4. Type; stamp; hue. 5. A twist, warp, or squint. 6. Something thrown off or shed. 7. The actors in a play. [< ON *kasta*, to throw.]

cas•ta•nets (kăs'tə-nĕts') *pl.n.* A pair of concave shells of ivory or hardwood held in the hand and clicked in accompaniment to music and dancing. [< Span *castaña*, chestnut.]

cast•a•way (kăst'ə-wā', käst'-) *adj.* 1. Shipwrecked; cast adrift or ashore. 2. Discarded; thrown away. —**cast'a•way'** *n.*

caste (kăst, käst) *n.* 1. One of the four major hereditary classes into which Hindu society is divided. 2. a. Any rigidly exclusive social class. b. A social system based on such exclusivity. 3. Social status: *lose caste.* [Port *casta*, caste, race, breed.]

cas•tel•lan (kăs'tə-lən) *n.* The governor of a castle. [< L *castellum*, CASTLE.]

cas•tel•lat•ed (kăs'tə-lā'tĭd) *adj.* Furnished with battlements like a castle.

cast•er (kăs'tər, käs'-) *n.* Also **cas•tor.** 1. A small wheel on a swivel under a piece of furniture or other heavy object, to make it easier to move. 2. A small bottle or cruet for condiments.

cas•ti•gate (kăs'tə-gāt') *v.* **-gated, -gating.** To punish or criticize severely. [L *castigāre*, to correct, punish.] —**cas'ti•ga'tion** *n.*

Cas•tile (kăs-tēl'). A region and former kingdom of Spain.

Cas•til•ian (kăs-tĭl'yən) *n.* 1. Originally, the dialect of Castile, now the standard form of Spanish as spoken in Spain. 2. A native or inhabitant of Castile. —**Cas•til'ian** *adj.*

cast•ing (kăs'tĭng, käs'-) *n.* 1. Something cast off or out. 2. Something cast in a mold. 3. The selection of actors or performers.

cast iron. A hard, brittle nonmalleable iron-carbon alloy containing 2.0–4.5% carbon and 0.5–3% silicon.

cas•tle (kăs'əl, käs'-) *n.* 1. A fortified group of buildings. 2. The rook in chess. —*v.* **-tled, -tling.** *Chess.* To move the king from his own square two squares to one side and then, in the same move, bring the rook from that side to the square immediately past the new position of the king. [< L *castellum*, castle.]

cast off. 1. To discard or reject. 2. To let go; set loose. 3. To estimate the space a manuscript will occupy when set into type.

cast-off (kăst'ôf', -ŏf', käst'-) *adj.* Discarded.

cast•off (kăst'ôf', -ŏf', käst'-) *n.* Someone or something that has been discarded.

cas•tor. Variant of **caster.**

cas•tor oil (kăs'tər). A colorless or yellowish oil extracted from the seeds of a tropical plant and used as a cathartic and a fine lubricant.

cas•trate (kăs'trāt') *v.* **-trated, -trating.** To remove the testicles of; geld. [L *castrāre.*] —**cas'tra'tion** *n.*

cas•u•al (kăzh'ōō-əl) *adj.* 1. Occurring by chance. 2. Occasional. 3. a. Informal. b. Designed for informal wear. 4. Careless; negligent. [< L *cāsus*, fall, chance.] —**cas'u•al•ly** *adv.* —**cas'u•al•ness** *n.*

cas•u•al•ty (kăzh'ōō-əl-tē) *n., pl.* **-ties.** 1. One injured or killed in an accident. 2. One injured, killed, captured, or missing in action against an enemy. 3. A disastrous accident. [< CASUAL.]

cas•u•ist (kăzh'ōō-ĭst) *n.* One given to adroit rationalization. [< L *cāsus*, chance, case.] —**cas'u•is'tic** *adj.* —**cas'u•is'ti•cal•ly** *adv.* —**cas'u•ist•ry** *n.*

ca•sus bel•li (kā'səs bĕl'ī', kä'səs bĕl'ē'). An act that justifies a declaration of war. [L, "occasion of war."]

cat (kăt) *n.* 1. A carnivorous mammal domesticated as a catcher of rats and mice and as a pet. 2. A related animal, as the lion, tiger, or leopard. [< OE *catt* < Gmc **kattuz.*]

cat. catalogue.

cata-. *comb. form.* 1. Reversing of a process. 2. Lower in position or down from. [< Gk *kata*, down, down from, according to.]

cat•a•clysm (kăt'ə-klĭz'əm) *n.* A violent and sudden upheaval. [< Gk *katakluzein*, to deluge, inundate.] —**cat'a•clys'mic** (-klĭz'mĭk) —**cat'a•clys'mal** (-klĭz'məl) *adj.*

---

cat•a•combs (kăt′ə-kōmz′) *pl.n.* A series of underground tunnels with recesses for graves. [< OF *catacombe,* a subterranean chamber.]

cat•a•falque (kăt′ə-fălk′, -fôlk′, -fôk′) *n.* The platform on which a coffin rests during a state funeral. [< VL *catafalicum,* scaffold.]

Cat•a•lan (kăt′l-ăn′, -ən) *n.* **1.** A native of Catalonia. **2.** The Romance language of Catalonia. —**Cat′a•lan′** *adj.*

cat•a•lep•sy (kăt′l-ĕp′sē) *n.* Muscular rigidity, lack of awareness of environment, and lack of response to external stimuli. [< Gk *katalēpsis,* "a seizing."] —**cat′a•lep′tic** *adj.*

cat•a•logue (kăt′l-ôg′). Also **cat•a•log.** *n.* An itemized, sometimes descriptive list. —*v.* **-logued, -loguing. 1.** To make a catalogue of. **2.** To list in a catalogue. [< Gk *katalegein,* to recount, enumerate.] —**cat′a•logu′er** *n.*

Cat•a•lo•ni•a (kăt′l-ō′nē-ə, -nyə). A region and former republic of NE Spain.

ca•tal•pa (kə-tăl′pə, -tôl′pə) *n.* A tree with large leaves, showy flower clusters, and long, slender pods. [< Muskhogean.]

cat•a•lyst (kăt′l-ĭst) *n.* A substance that modifies, esp. increases, the rate of a chemical reaction without being consumed in the process. [< Gk *katalusis,* dissolution.] —**ca•tal′y•sis** (kə-tăl′ə-sĭs) *n.* —**cat′a•lyt′ic** *adj.*

cat•a•lyze (kăt′l-īz′) *v.* **-lyzed, -lyzing.** To act on (a reaction) as a catalyst.

cat•a•ma•ran (kăt′ə-mə-răn′) *n.* A boat with two parallel hulls. [Tamil *kaṭṭumaram.*]

cat•a•mount (kăt′ə-mount′) *n.* A mountain lion or lynx. [Short for catamountain, var of earlier *cat of the mountain.*]

cat•a•pult (kăt′ə-pŭlt′) *n.* **1.** An ancient military engine for hurling large missiles. **2.** A mechanism for launching aircraft from the deck of a ship. —*v.* To hurl or spring up, as from a catapult. [< Gk *katapaltēs.*]

cat•a•ract (kăt′ə-răkt′) *n.* **1.** A great waterfall or downpour. **2.** Opacity of the lens or capsule of the eye, causing partial or total blindness. [< Gk *katar(rh)aktēs,* "a down-swooping."]

ca•tarrh (kə-tär′) *n.* Inflammation of mucous membranes, esp. of the nose and throat. [< Gk *katarrhous,* a flowing down.] —**ca•tarrh′al, ca•tarrh′ous** *adj.*

ca•tas•tro•phe (kə-tăs′trə-fē) *n.* A great and sudden calamity; disaster. [< Gk *katastrephein,* to turn down.] —**cat′a•stroph′ic** (kăt′ə-strŏf′ĭk) *adj.* —**cat′a•stroph′i•cal•ly** *adv.*

cat•a•to•ni•a (kăt′ə-tō′nē-ə) *n.* A schizophrenic disorder characterized by immobility, stupor, negativism, and silence. —**cat′a•ton′ic** (-tŏn′ĭk) *adj.* & *n.*

cat•bird (kăt′bûrd′) *n.* A dark-gray North American songbird with a call like the mewing of a cat.

cat•boat (kăt′bōt′) *n.* A broad-beamed sailboat carrying a single sail on a mast stepped well forward.

cat•call (kăt′kôl′) *n.* A shrill cry of derision. —**cat′call′** *v.*

catch (kăch) *v.* **caught, catching. 1.** To capture, esp. after a chase. **2.** To snare or trap. **3.** To surprise. **4.** To take or apprehend suddenly. **5.** To grasp. **6.** To snatch; grab. **7.** To inter-

cept. **8.** To become ensnared. **9.** To become subject to; contract, as by contagion. **10.** To fasten. **11.** To take in and retain. **12.** To get to in time: *catch the plane.* **13.** To watch: *catch a late movie.* —*n.* **1. a.** The act of catching, as a ball. **b.** A game of throwing and catching a ball. **2.** A fastening or checking device. **3.** Something caught. **4.** One worth catching. **5.** A snatch or fragment. **6.** An unsuspected drawback. [< L *captāre,* to chase, strive to seize.]

catch•all (kăch′ôl′) *n.* A receptacle for odds and ends. —**catch′all′** *adj.*

catch•er (kăch′ər) *n.* **1.** One that catches. **2.** The baseball player whose position is behind home plate.

catch•ing (kăch′ĭng) *adj.* **1.** Infectious. **2.** Attractive; alluring.

catch•up. A variant of ketchup.

catch•y (kăch′ē) *adj.* **-ier, -iest. 1.** Easily remembered: *a catchy melody.* **2.** Tricky; deceptive: *a catchy question.*

cat•e•chism (kăt′ə-kĭz′əm) *n.* An instructional summary of the basic principles of a religion in question-and-answer form. [< LGk *katēkhizein,* to teach orally.] —**cat′e•chist** *n.* —**cat′e•chize′** *v.* (**-chized, -chizing).**

cat•e•chu•men (kăt′ə-kyōō′mən) *n.* A convert receiving religious instruction before baptism. [< LGk *katēkhein,* to teach orally.]

cat•e•gor•i•cal (kăt′ə-gôr′ĭ-kəl, -gŏr′ĭ-kəl) *adj.* Also **cat•e•gor•ic.** Absolute; certain. —**cat′e•gor′i•cal•ly** *adv.* —**cat′e•gor′i•cal•ness** *n.*

cat•e•go•rize (kăt′ə-gə-rīz′) *v.* **-rized, -rizing.** To put into categories; classify. —**cat′e•go•ri•za′tion** *n.*

cat•e•go•ry (kăt′ə-gôr′ē, -gōr′ē) *n., pl.* **-ries.** A specifically defined division in a system of classification; a class. [< LL *categoria,* accusation, predicament, category of predicables.]

cat•e•nar•y (kăt′ə-něr′ē, kə-tē′nər-ē) *n., pl.* **-ies.** The curve theoretically formed by a perfectly flexible, uniform, inextensible cable suspended from two points. [< L *catēna,* chain.]

cat•e•nate (kăt′ə-nāt′) *v.* **-nated, -nating.** To connect in a series of ties or links; form into a chain. —**cat′e•na′tion** *n.*

ca•ter (kā′tər) *v.* **1.** To provide food or entertainment. **2.** To provide anything wished for or needed. [< ME *catour,* a caterer.] —**ca′ter•er** *n.*

cat•er-cor•nered (kăt′ər-kôr′nərd, kăt′ē-). Also **cat•er-cor•ner** (-nər), **cat•ty-cor•nered** (kăt′ē-kôr′nərd). *adj.* Diagonal. —*adv.* Diagonally. [< obs *cater,* four at dice.]

cat•er•pil•lar (kăt′ər-pĭl′ər, kăt′ə-) *n.* The wormlike, often hairy larva of a butterfly or moth. [< OF *catepeiose,* "hairy cat."]

cat•er•waul (kăt′ər-wôl′) *v.* To make a discordant sound or shriek. [< ME *caterwrawen.*] —**cat′er•waul′** *n.*

cat•fish (kăt′fĭsh′) *n.* Any of various scaleless fishes with whiskerlike feelers near the mouth.

cat•gut (kăt′gŭt′) *n.* A tough cord made from the dried intestines of certain animals.

ca•thar•sis (kə-thär′sĭs) *n., pl.* **-ses** (-sēz′). **1.** Purgation, esp. for the digestive system. **2.** A

ŏ paw, for/oi boy/ou out/o͞o took/o͞o coo/p pop/r run/s sauce/sh shy/t to/th thin/*th* the/
ŭ cut/ûr fur/v van/w wag/y yes/z size/zh vision/ə ago, item, edible, gallop, circus/

purifying or figurative cleansing of the emotions. [< Gk *katharsis*.]

ca·thar·tic (kə-thär'tĭk) *adj.* Purgative; cleansing. —*n.* A cathartic agent, as a laxative. —**ca·thar'ti·cal·ly** *adv.*

ca·the·dral (kə-thē'drəl) *n.* The principal church of a bishop's see. [< LL *cathedrālis.*]

cath·e·ter (kăth'ə-tər) *n.* A slender, flexible tube inserted into a body channel to distend or maintain an opening to an internal cavity. [< Gk *kathetēr*, something inserted.]

cath·ode (kăth'ōd') *n.* A negatively charged electrode. [Gk *kathodos*, way down, descent.]

cath·ode-ray tube (kăth'ōd-rā'). A vacuum tube in which a hot cathode emits electrons that are accelerated as a beam, further focused, and allowed to fall on a fluorescent screen.

cath·o·lic (kăth'lĭk, kăth'ə-lĭk) *adj.* 1. Universal; comprehensive. 2. **Catholic.** Of or pertaining to Catholics or to the Roman Catholic Church. —*n.* **Catholic.** A member of the Roman Catholic Church. [< Gk *katholou*, in general.] —**ca·thol'i·cal·ly** (kə-thŏl'ĭk-lē) *adv.*

Ca·thol·i·cism (kə-*th*ŏl'ə-sĭz'əm) *n.* The faith, doctrine, system, and practice of the Roman Catholic Church.

cath·o·lic·i·ty (kăth'ə-lĭs'ə-tē) *n.* 1. Broadmindedness. 2. Comprehensiveness; universality. 3. **Catholicity.** Roman Catholicism.

cat·i·on (kăt'ī'ən) *n.* An ion having a positive charge and, in electrolytes, characteristically moving toward a negative electrode. [< Gk *katienai*, to go down.] —**cat'i·on'ic** (-ŏn'ĭk) *adj.*

cat·kin (kăt'kĭn') *n. Bot.* A dense cluster of scalelike flowers, as of a birch.

cat nap. A short nap.

cat·nip (kăt'nĭp') *n.* An aromatic plant to which cats are strongly attracted.

cat-o'-nine-tails (kăt'ə-nīn'tālz') *n.* A whip consisting of nine knotted cords fastened to a handle.

cat's cradle. A game in which an intricately looped string is transferred from the hands of one player to another.

Cats·kills (kăts'kĭlz'). A mountain range in SE New York State.

cat's-paw (kăts'pô') *n.* Also **cats·paw.** A dupe or tool.

cat·sup. A variant of **ketchup.**

cat·tail (kăt'tāl') *n.* A tall-stemmed, long-leaved marsh plant with a dense, brown, cylindrical flower head.

cat·tle (kăt'l) *pl.n.* Horned, hoofed mammals, as cows, bulls, and oxen, esp. those domesticated for beef, dairy products, etc. [ME *catel*, personal property, livestock < ML *capitāle*, property.]

cat·ty (kăt'ē) *adj.* **-tier, -tiest.** Malicious; spiteful. —**cat'ti·ly** *adv.* —**cat'ti·ness** *n.*

cat·ty-cor·nered. Variant of **cater-cornered.**

cat·walk (kăt'wôk') *n.* A narrow walk, as on the sides of a bridge.

Cau·ca·sian (kô-kā'zhən, -kăzh'ən, -kā'shən, -kăsh'ən) *n.* 1. A native of the Caucasus. 2. A member of the Caucasoid ethnic division. 3. The group of languages spoken in the area of the Caucasus that are neither Indo-European

nor Altaic. [< the CAUCASUS.] —**Cau·ca'sian** *adj.*

Cau·ca·soid (kô'kə-soid') *adj.* Pertaining to a major ethnic division of the human species having skin color varying from very light to brown. —*n.* A Caucasoid individual.

Cau·ca·sus (kô'kə-səs). A region and range of mountains in the SW Soviet Union.

cau·cus (kô'kəs) *n., pl.* **-cuses** or **-cusses.** A meeting of the members of a political party to decide upon questions of policy and the selection of candidates for office. [Prob < Algon.] —**cau'cus** *v.* (**-cused** or **-cussed, -cusing** or **-cussing**)

cau·dal (kôd'l) *adj.* Of the tail or hind parts. [< L *cauda*, tail.] —**cau'dal·ly** *adv.*

caught (kôt). *p.t. & p.p.* of **catch.**

caul·dron. Variant of **caldron.**

cau·li·flow·er (kô'lĭ-flou'ər, kŏl'ĭ-) *n.* 1. A cabbagelike plant with a large, compact, whitish flower head, eaten as a vegetable. 2. The head itself. [Prob < It *cavolofiore*, "flowered cabbage."]

cauliflower ear. An ear deformed by repeated blows.

caulk (kôk) *v.* Also **calk.** 1. To make (a boat) watertight by packing seams with oakum or tar. 2. To make (pipes) tight against leakage by sealing. [< ONF *cauquer*, to trample, tread.] —**caulk'er** *n.*

caus·al (kô'zəl) *adj.* 1. Pertaining to or involving a cause. 2. Constituting or expressing a cause. —**cau·sal'i·ty** (-zăl'ə-tē) *n.* —**caus'al·ly** *adv.*

cau·sa·tion (kô-zā'shən) *n.* 1. The act or process of causing. 2. A causal agency.

cause (kôz) *n.* 1. A person or thing responsible for an action or result. 2. A reason; motive. 3. Good or sufficient reason. 4. A goal or principle. 5. *Law.* **a.** The ground for legal action. **b.** A lawsuit. —*v.* **caused, causing.** To make happen; bring about. [< L *causa*, reason, purpose, motive.] —**caus'er** *n.*

cause cé·lè·bre (kôz sā-lĕb'r'). *French.* 1. A celebrated legal case. 2. An issue arousing heated debate.

cause·way (kôz'wā') *n.* A raised roadway across water or marshland. [< VL *calciāta*, paved + WAY.]

caus·tic (kôs'tĭk) *adj.* 1. Able to burn, corrode, or dissolve. 2. Biting or cutting: *caustic comment.* [< Gk *kaustikos*.]

cau·ter·ize (kô'tə-rīz') *v.* **-ized, -izing.** To burn or sear so as to destroy aberrant tissue. [< Gk *kautēriazein*, to brand.] —**cau'ter·i·za'tion** *n.*

cau·tion (kô'shən) *n.* 1. Forethought to avoid danger or harm. 2. A warning. 3. *Informal.* Someone or something that is striking. —*v.* To warn against danger; put on guard. [< L *cautiō*, a guarding.] —**cau'tion·ar'y** *adj.*

cau·tious (kô'shəs) *adj.* Practicing caution; wary; careful. —**cau'tious·ly** *adv.*

cav·al·cade (kăv'əl-kād', kăv'əl-kād') *n.* 1. A ceremonial procession, esp. of horsemen. 2. A colorful procession or pageant. [< OIt *cavalcare*, to ride on horseback.]

cav·a·lier (kăv'ə-lîr') *n.* 1. A gentleman accomplished in arms. 2. A gallant. 3. A lady's

---

ă pat/ā ate/âr care/ä bar/b bib/ch chew/d deed/ĕ pet/ē be/f fit/g gag/h hat/hw what/
ĭ pit/ī pie/îr pier/j judge/k kick/l lid, fatal/m mum/n no, sudden/ng sing/ŏ pot/ō go/

dancing partner. —*adj.* **1.** Haughty; arrogant. **2.** Carefree and gay; offhand. [< LL *caballārius*, horseman.] —**cav·a·lier'ly** *adv.*

cav·al·ry (kăv'əl-rē) *n., pl.* **-ries.** Troops mounted on horseback or riding in armored vehicles. [< OIt *cavaliere*, cavalier.] —**cav·al·ry·man** *n.*

cave (kāv) *n.* A hollow beneath the earth's surface, often having an opening in the side of a hill or cliff. [< L *cavus*, hollow.]

ca·ve·at (kā've-ăt', kăv'ē-, kä'vē-) *n.* A warning. [L, let him beware.]

cave in. To collapse.

cave-in (kāv'ĭn') *n.* **1.** An action of caving in. **2.** A place where the ground has caved in.

cave man. **1.** A prehistoric man who lived in caves. **2.** One who is crude or brutal, esp. toward women.

cav·ern (kăv'ərn) *n.* A large cave. [< L *cavus*, hollow.] —**cav'ern·ous** *adj.*

cav·i·ar (kăv'ē-är') *n.* Also **cav·i·are.** The salted roe of a sturgeon or other large fish, eaten as a relish. [Prob < Turk *havyār*.]

cav·il (kăv'əl) *v.* **-iled** or **-illed, -iling** or **-illing.** To quibble or carp. —*n.* A trivial objection. [< L *cavillāri*, to satirize, criticize.]

cav·i·ty (kăv'ə-tē) *n., pl.* **-ties.** **1.** A hollow or hole. **2.** A pitted area in a tooth, caused by caries. [< LL *cavitās*, hollowness.]

ca·vort (kə-vôrt') *v.* To prance; caper; frolic.

caw (kô) *n.* The hoarse, raucous call of a crow or similar bird. [Imit.] —**caw** *v.*

cay (kē, kā) *n.* An islet of coral or sand; key. [Prob < OF *quai*, quay.]

cay·enne pepper (kī-ĕn', kā-). Also **cay·enne.** A very pungent condiment made from the fruit of a variety of the pepper plant. [< Tupi *kyinha*.]

Cb columbium.

C.B.D. cash before delivery.

cc cubic centimeter.

cc. chapters.

c.c. carbon copy.

CCC Civilian Conservation Corps.

Cd cadmium.

c.d. cash discount.

Cdr. commander.

Ce cerium.

C.E. **1.** chemical engineer. **2.** civil engineer.

cease (sēs) *v.* **ceased, ceasing.** **1.** To discontinue; stop. —*n.* Cessation. [< L *cessāre*, to delay, stop.] —**cease'less** *adj.* —**cease'less·ly** *adv.*

cease-fire (sēs'fīr') *n.* A suspension of active hostilities; truce.

ce·cum (sē'kəm) *n., pl.* **-ca** (-kə). Also **cae·cum.** **1.** A cavity with only one opening. **2.** The large pouch forming the beginning of the large intestine. [< L (*intestinum*) *caecum*, blind (intestine).] —**ce'cal** (sē'kəl) *adj.*

ce·dar (sē'dər) *n.* **1.** Any of various evergreen trees with durable, aromatic, often reddish wood. **2.** The wood of such a tree. [< L *cedrus*, cedar, juniper.]

cede (sēd) *v.* **ceded, ceding.** **1.** To relinquish, as by treaty. **2.** To transfer; assign. [< L *cēdere*, withdraw.]

ceil·ing (sē'lĭng) *n.* **1.** The interior upper surface of a room. **2.** A maximum limit. **3.** A

vertical boundary, as of operable aircraft altitude. [ME *celing*.]

cel·a·don (sĕl'ə-dŏn') *n.* **1.** Pale to very pale green. **2.** Pale to very pale blue. [< *Céladon*, wan character in d'Urfé's "*Astrée*" (1610).] —**cel'a·don'** *adj.*

cel·e·brant (sĕl'ə-brənt) *n.* **1.** The priest officiating at the celebration of the Eucharist. **2.** One who participates in a celebration.

cel·e·brate (sĕl'ə-brāt') *v.* **-brated, -brating.** **1.** To observe (a day or event) with ceremonies of respect or festivity. **2.** To perform (a religious ceremony). **3.** To extol; praise. [L *celebrāre*, to frequent, fill, celebrate.] —**cel'e·bra'tion** *n.* —**cel'e·bra'tor** *n.*

cel·e·brat·ed (sĕl'ə-brā'tĭd) *adj.* Famous.

ce·leb·ri·ty (sə-lĕb'rə-tē) *n., pl.* **-ties.** **1.** A famous person. **2.** Renown; fame. [L *celebritās*.]

ce·ler·i·ty (sə-lĕr'ə-tē) *n.* Swiftness; speed. [< L *celer*, swift.]

cel·er·y (sĕl'ər-ē) *n.* A plant cultivated for its succulent, edible stalks and its small seeds, used as seasoning. [< Gk *selinon*.]

ce·les·tial (sə-lĕs'chəl) *adj.* **1.** Pertaining to sky or the heavens. **2.** Heavenly; divine. [< L *caelestis* < *caelum*, sky, heaven.]

celestial equator. A great circle on the celestial sphere in the same plane as the earth's equator.

celestial navigation. Ship or aircraft navigation based on the positions of celestial bodies.

celestial pole. Either of two points at which the earth's axis intersects the celestial sphere.

celestial sphere. An imaginary sphere of infinite extent with the earth at its center.

ce·li·ac (sē'lē-ăk') *adj.* Of or relating to the abdomen.

cel·i·ba·cy (sĕl'ə-bə-sē) *n.* The condition of being unmarried, esp. because of religious vows. [< L *caelebs*, unmarried.]

cel·i·bate (sĕl'ə-bĭt) *n.* One who remains unmarried. —*adj.* Unmarried.

cell (sĕl) *n.* **1.** A narrow, confining room, as in a prison or convent. **2.** The basic organizational unit of some revolutionary parties. **3.** *Biol.* The smallest structural unit of an organism that is capable of independent functioning, consisting of nuclei, cytoplasm, various organelles, and inanimate matter, all surrounded by a membrane. **4.** A small enclosed cavity or space, as in a honeycomb. **5.** *Elec.* **a.** A single unit for electrolysis or for conversion of chemical into electric energy, usually consisting of a container with electrodes and an electrolyte. **b.** A single unit that converts radiant energy into electric energy. [< L *cella*, storeroom, chamber.]

cel·lar (sĕl'ər) *n.* **1.** An underground storage room. **2.** A stock of wines. [< L *cella*, storeroom, CELL.]

cel·lo (chĕl'ō) *n., pl.* **-los.** Also **'cel·lo.** An instrument of the violin family, pitched lower than the viola but higher than the double bass. [Short for VIOLONCELLO.] —**cel'list** *n.*

cel·lo·phane (sĕl'ə-fān') *n.* A thin, flexible, transparent cellulose material used as a moistureproof wrapping. [< CELLULOSE.]

ô paw, for/oi boy/ou out/ŏŏ took/ōō coo/p pop/r run/s sauce/sh shy/t to/th thin/*th* the/
ŭ cut/ûr fur/v van/w wag/y yes/z size/zh vision/ə ago, item, edible, gallop, circus/

cel·lu·lar (sĕl′yə-lər) *adj.* **1.** Of or resembling a cell. **2.** Consisting of cells.

Cel·lu·loid (sĕl′yə-loid′) *n.* A trademark for a colorless, flammable material used for toys, toilet articles, and photographic film.

cel·lu·lose (sĕl′yə-lōs′, -lōz′) *n.* An amorphous polymer, $(C_6H_{10}O_5)_x$, the main constituent of all plant tissues and fibers, used in the manufacture of paper, textiles, and explosives. [< F *cellule*, biological cell.]

Cel·o·tex (sĕl′ə-tĕks) *n.* A trademark for a building board used for insulation and soundproofing.

Cel·si·us (sĕl′sē-əs, -shəs) *adj.* Pertaining to a temperature scale that registers the freezing point of water as 0°C and the boiling point as 100°C under normal atmospheric pressure; centigrade. [< A. *Celsius* (1701–1744), Swedish astronomer.]

Celt (kĕlt, sĕlt) *n.* Also **Kelt** (kĕlt). **1.** One of an ancient people of W and C Europe, including the Britons and the Gauls. **2.** A speaker of a Celtic language.

Celt·ic (kĕl′tĭk, sĕl′-). Also **Kelt·ic** (kĕl′tĭk) *n.* A subfamily of the Indo-European family of languages, including Welsh, Irish Gaelic, and Scottish Gaelic. —**Celt′ic** *adj.*

cem·ba·lo (chĕm′bə-lō′) *n., pl.* **-los.** A harpsichord. [It.]

ce·ment (sĭ-mĕnt′) *n.* **1.** A construction adhesive, essentially powdered, calcined rock and clay materials that form a paste with water and set as a solid mass. **2.** Any adhesive; glue. **3.** Also **ce·ment·um** (sĭ-mĕn′təm). A bony substance covering the roots of teeth. —*v.* To bind with or as if with cement. [< L *caementum*, rough quarried stone.] —**ce·ment′er** *n.*

cem·e·ter·y (sĕm′ə-tĕr′ē) *n., pl.* **-ies.** A graveyard. [< Gk *koimētērion*, sleeping room, burial place.]

cen. **1.** central. **2.** century.

–cene. *comb. form.* A recent geologic period: Eocene. [< Gk *kainos*, new, fresh.]

cen·o·bite (sĕn′ə-bīt′, sē′nə-) *n.* A member of a religious convent or community. [< Gk *koinobion*, life in community.] —**cen′o·bit′ic** (-bĭt′ĭk), **cen′o·bit′i·cal** *adj.*

cen·o·taph (sĕn′ə-tăf′, -täf′) *n.* A monument erected in honor of a dead person whose remains lie elsewhere. [< Gk *kenotaphion*, empty tomb.] —**cen′o·taph′ic** *adj.*

Ce·no·zo·ic (sē′nə-zō′ĭk, sĕn′ə-) *adj.* Pertaining to the most recent era of geologic time, which includes the Tertiary and Quaternary periods and is characterized by the evolution of mammals, birds, plants, modern continents, and glaciation. —*n.* The Cenozoic era.

cen·sor (sĕn′sər) *n.* **1.** An official examiner of printed or other materials, who may prohibit what he considers objectionable. **2.** One of two Roman magistrates responsible for supervising the census. —*v.* To examine and expurgate. [< L *cēnsēre*, to assess, estimate, judge.] —**cen·so′ri·al** (sĕn-sôr′ē-əl, sĕn-sōr′-) *adj.*

cen·so·ri·ous (sĕn-sôr′ē-əs, sĕn-sōr′-) *adj.* Faultfinding or critical. —**cen·so′ri·ous·ly** *adv.*

cen·sor·ship (sĕn′sər-shĭp′) *n.* **1.** The action or a policy of censoring. **2.** The office of a Roman censor.

cen·sure (sĕn′shər) *n.* An expression of blame or disapproval. —*v.* **-sured, -suring.** To criticize severely; blame. [< L *cēnsor*, censor.] —**cen′sur·a·ble** *adj.* —**cen′sur·er** *n.*

cen·sus (sĕn′səs) *n., pl.* **-suses.** A periodic official enumeration of population. [< L *cēnsēre*, to assess, tax.]

cent (sĕnt) *n.* **1.** A subdivision of the dollar of the U.S. **2.** A subdivision of the dollar of Australia, Canada, Ethiopia, Guyana, Jamaica, Liberia, Malaysia, New Zealand, Trinidad and Tobago, Western Samoa, Hong Kong, and Singapore. **3.** A subdivision of the guilder of the Netherlands, Surinam, and the Netherland Antilles, the leone of Sierra Leone, the piaster of South Vietnam, the rand of the Republic of South Africa, the rupee of Ceylon and Mauritius, and the yuan of the Republic of China. **4.** A subdivision of the shilling of Kenya, Tanzania, Uganda, and the Somali Republic. [OF, "hundred."]

cent. **1.** central. **2.** century.

cen·taur (sĕn′tôr′) *n.* One of a race of mythological monsters having the head, arms, and trunk of a man and the body and legs of a horse.

Cen·tau·rus (sĕn-tôr′əs) *n.* Also **Cen·taur** (sĕn′-tôr′). A constellation in the S Hemisphere.

cen·ta·vo (sĕn-tä′vō) *n., pl.* **-vos.** A monetary unit equal to $^1/_{100}$ of the colon of El Salvador, the cordoba of Nicaragua, the escudo of Portugal, the lempira of Honduras, the cruzeiro of Brazil, the peso of Argentina, Bolivia, Colombia, Cuba, the Dominican Republic, Mexico, and the Philippines, the quetzal of Guatemala, the sol of Peru, and the sucre of Ecuador. [Span, "a hundredth."]

cen·te·nar·i·an (sĕn′tə-nâr′ē-ən) *n.* A person one hundred years old or older. —**cen′te·nar′i·an** *adj.*

cen·ten·a·ry (sĕn-tĕn′ə-rē, sĕn′tə-nĕr′ē) *adj. & n.* Centennial. [L *centēnārius*, of a hundred.]

cen·ten·ni·al (sĕn-tĕn′ē-əl) *adj.* **1.** Of or pertaining to an age or period of 100 years. **2.** Of or pertaining to a 100th anniversary. —*n.* A 100th anniversary or its celebration. [L *centum*, hundred + (BI)ENNIAL.] —**cen·ten′ni·al·ly** *adv.*

cen·ter (sĕn′tər). Also *chiefly Brit.* **cen·tre.** *n.* **1.** A point equidistant or at the average distance from all points on the sides or outer boundaries of anything; middle. **2. a.** A point equidistant from the vertexes of a regular polygon. **b.** A point equidistant from all points on the circumference of a circle or on the surface of a sphere. **3.** A point around which something revolves; axis. **4.** A part of an object that is surrounded by the rest; core. **5.** A place of concentrated activity or influence. **6.** A group whose political views and practice are midway between liberal and conservative positions. **7.** A player who holds a middle position. —*v.* **1.** To place in or on a center. **2.** To concentrate or cluster. **3.** To have a center. [< L *centrum*.]

ă pat/ā ate/âr care/ä bar/b bib/ch chew/d deed/ĕ pet/ē be/f fit/g gag/h hat/hw what/ ĭ pit/ī pie/îr pier/j judge/k kick/l lid, fatal/m mum/n no, sudden/ng sing/ŏ pot/ō go/

cen·ter·board (sĕn'tər-bôrd', -bōrd') n. A flat board or metal plate that can be lowered through the bottom of a sailboat as a keel.
cen·ter·piece (sĕn'tər-pēs') n. A decorative object or arrangement placed at the center of a dining table.
centi-. comb. form. A hundredth. [< L centum, hundred.]
cen·ti·grade (sĕn'tĭ-grād') adj. 1. Divided into 100°. 2. Celsius.
cen·ti·gram (sĕn'tĭ-grăm) n. One hundredth of a gram.
cen·ti·li·ter (sĕn'tə-lē'tər) n. One hundredth of a liter.
cen·time (sän'tĕm') n. 1. A subdivision of the franc of France, Belgium, Burundi, Cameroun, Central African Republic, Chad, Congo (Brazzaville), Dahomey, Gabon, Guinea, Ivory Coast, Luxembourg, Malagasy Republic, Mali, Mauritania, Niger, Rwanda, Senegal, Switzerland, Togo, Upper Volta, and of various overseas departments and territories of France. 2. a. A subdivision of the dinar of Algeria. b. A subdivision of the gourde of Haiti.
cen·ti·me·ter (sĕn'tə-mē'tər, sän'-) n. Also **cen·ti·me·tre**. A unit of length equal to ¹⁄₁₀₀ of a meter or 0.3937 inch.
cen·ti·pede (sĕn'tə-pēd') n. A wormlike arthropod with many legs and body segments.
cen·tral (sĕn'trəl) adj. 1. At, near, or being the center. 2. Principal; essential. —n. 1. A telephone exchange. 2. A telephone-exchange operator. —**cen'tral·ly** adv.
Central African Republic. A country of C Africa. Pop. 1,800,000. Cap. Bangui.

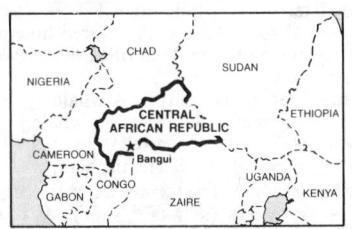

Central African Republic

Central America. The region extending from the S border of Mexico to the N border of Colombia. —**Central American.**
cen·tral·ism (sĕn'trəl-ĭz'əm) n. The assignment of authority to a central leadership, as in an organization. —**cen'tral·ist** n. & adj. —**cen'tral·is'tic** (sĕn'trəl-ĭs'tĭk) adj.
cen·tral·i·ty (sĕn-trăl'ə-tē) n. The state or quality of being central.
cen·tral·ize (sĕn'trəl-īz') v. -ized, -izing. To draw toward the center or under central authority. —**cen'tral·i·za'tion** n.
central nervous system. The portion of the vertebrate nervous system consisting of the brain and spinal cord.
Central Standard Time. The local civil time of the 90th meridian W of Greenwich, Eng-

land, six hours earlier than Greenwich time, observed in the C United States.
cen·tre. Chiefly Brit. Variant of **center**.
cen·trif·u·gal (sĕn-trĭf'yə-gəl, -trĭf'ə-gəl) adj. 1. Moving or directed away from a center or axis. 2. Operated by means of centrifugal force. —**cen·trif'u·gal·ly** adv.
centrifugal force. The component of apparent force on a body in nonlinear motion, as observed from that body, that is directed away from the center of curvature or axis of rotation.
cen·tri·fuge (sĕn'trə-fyōōj') n. A compartment spun about a central axis to separate contained materials of different density or to simulate gravity with centrifugal force. —**cen·trif'u·ga'tion** (sĕn-trĭf'yə-gā'shən, sĕn-trĭf'ə-) n.
cen·trip·e·tal (sĕn-trĭp'ə-təl) adj. Directed or moving toward a center or axis. —**cen·trip'e·tal·ly** adv.
cen·trist (sĕn'trĭst) n. One taking a position in the political center.
cen·tro·some (sĕn'trə-sōm') n. A small mass of differentiated cytoplasm.
cen·tu·ri·on (sĕn-t/y/ōōr'ē-ən) n. An officer commanding a century in the Roman army. [< L centuriō.]
cen·tu·ry (sĕn'chə-rē) n., pl. -ries. 1. A period of 100 years. 2. A unit of the Roman army. [L centuria, a group of a hundred.]
ce·phal·ic (sə-făl'ĭk) adj. In, on, or relating to the head or skull. [< Gk kephalē, head.] —**cephalic.** comb. form. Head or skull: orthocephalic.
cephalic index. The ratio of the maximum width of the head to its maximum length, multiplied by 100.
ceph·a·li·za·tion (sĕf'ə-lə-zā'shən) n. Zool. The gradually increasing concentration of the brain and sensory organs in the head during animal evolution.
—**cephalus.** comb. form. A head: hydrocephalous.
ce·ram·ic (sə-răm'ĭk) n. 1. Any of various hard, brittle, heat-resistant and corrosion-resistant materials made by firing clay or other minerals. 2. ceramics. (takes sing. v.). a. Objects made of such materials. b. The art or technique of making objects of such materials, esp. from fired clay or porcelain. [< Gk keramos, potter's clay, earthenware.] —**ce·ram'ic** adj. —**ce·ram'ist** n.
ce·re·al (sîr'ē-əl) n. 1. An edible grain, as wheat or corn. 2. A food prepared from such grain. [L cereālis, of grain.] —**ce're·al** adj.
cer·e·bel·lum (sĕr'ə-bĕl'əm) n., pl. -lums or -bella (-bĕl'ə). The structure of the brain responsible for regulation of complex voluntary muscular movement. [< L cerebrum, brain.] —**cer'e·bel'lar** (-bĕl'ər) adj.
ce·re·bral (sə-rē'brəl, sĕr'ə-brəl) adj. 1. Of or pertaining to the brain or cerebrum. 2. Appealing to or marked by the intellect. —**ce·re'bral·ly** adv.
cerebral cortex. The extensive outer layer of gray tissue of the cerebral hemispheres, largely responsible for higher nervous functions.
cerebral palsy. Impaired muscular power and

coordination from brain damage usually occurring at or before birth.

ce•re•bro•spi•nal (sə-rē′brō-spī′nəl, sĕr′ə-brō-) *adj.* Pertaining to the brain and spinal cord.

cerebrospinal fluid. The serumlike fluid that bathes the lateral ventricles of the brain and the cavity.of the spinal cord.

cerebrospinal meningitis. An acute, infectious, often fatal epidemic meningitis.

ce•re•brum (sə-rē′brəm, sĕr′ə-brəm) *n., pl.* -brums or -bra (-brə). The large rounded structure of the brain occupying most of the cranial cavity, divided into two cerebral hemispheres. [L, brain.]

cere•cloth (sîr′klôth′, -klŏth′) *n.* Cloth coated with wax, formerly used for wrapping the dead.

cere•ment (sîr′mənt) *n.* A shroud.

cer•e•mo•ni•al (sĕr′ə-mō′nē-əl) *adj.* Characterized by ceremony; formal. —*n.* A set of ceremonies for an occasion; a rite. —**cer′e•mo′ni•al•ist** *n.* —**cer′e•mo′ni•al•ly** *adv.*

cer•e•mo•ni•ous (sĕr′ə-mō′nē-əs) *adj.* 1. Fond of ceremony. 2. Rigidly formal. —**cer′e•mo′ni•ous•ly** *adv.* —**cer′e•mo′ni•ous•ness** *n.*

cer•e•mo•ny (sĕr′ə-mō′nē) *n., pl.* -nies. 1. A formal act or set of acts as prescribed by ritual, custom, or etiquette. 2. Strict observance of formalities or etiquette. [< L caerimōnia, sacredness, religious rite.]

ce•re•us (sîr′ē-əs) *n.* Any of several tall tropical American cacti. [< L cēra, wax.]

cer•iph. Chiefly Brit. Variant of serif.

ce•rise (sə-rēs′, -rēz′) *n.* Purplish red. [< OF, cherry.]

ce•ri•um (sîr′ē-əm) *n.* Symbol Ce A lustrous, iron-gray, malleable metallic element, used in various metallurgic and nuclear applications. Atomic number 58, atomic weight 140.12. [< Ceres, an asteroid between Mars and Saturn.]

ce•rous (sîr′əs) *adj.* Of, pertaining to, or containing cerium. [CER(IUM) + -OUS.]

cert. certificate; certification; certified.

cer•tain (sûrt′n) *adj.* 1. Definite. 2. Inevitable. 3. Indisputable. 4. Dependable. 5. Not identified but assumed to be known: *a certain woman.* 6. Limited: *to a certain degree.* —*pron.* An indefinite but limited number; some. —**for certain.** Surely. [< VL *certānus.*] —**cer′tain•ly** *adv.*

cer•tain•ty (sûrt′n-tē) *n., pl.* -ties. 1. The state of being certain. 2. An established fact.

certif. certificate.

cer•tif•i•cate (sər-tĭf′ĭ-kĭt) *n.* 1. A document testifying to a fact, qualification, or promise. 2. A written statement legally authenticated. —*v.* (sər-tĭf′ə-kāt′) -cated, -cating. To authorize by a certificate. [< LL certificāre, CERTIFY.] —**cer′ti•fi•ca′tion** *n.*

cer•ti•fied (sûr′tə-fīd′) *adj.* 1. Guaranteed in writing. 2. Holding a certificate. 3. Committed to a mental institution.

certified check. A check guaranteed by a bank.

certified mail. Uninsured first-class mail whose delivery is recorded by having the addressee sign for it.

certified public accountant. An accountant who has met a state's legal requirements.

cer•ti•fy (sûr′tə-fī′) *v.* -fied, -fying. 1. To confirm formally as true, accurate, or genuine. 2. To acknowledge on (a check) that the depositor has funds for its payment. 3. To declare legally insane. [< LL certificāre, to make certain.] —**cer′ti•fi′a•ble** *adj.* —**cer′ti•fi′a•bly** *adv.* —**cer′ti•fi′er** *n.*

cer•ti•tude (sûr′tə-t/y/ōōd′) *n.* Complete assurance.

ce•ru•le•an (sə-rōō′lē-ən) *adj.* Sky-blue; azure. [< L caeruleus, dark-blue, azure.]

ce•ru•men (sə-rōō′mən) *n.* A yellowish, waxy secretion of the external ear; earwax. [< L cēra, wax.]

Cer•van•tes Sa•a•ve•dra (sər-văn′tēz sä′ä-vě′drä), **Miguel de.** 1547–1616. Spanish author.

cer•vi•cal (sûr′vĭ-kəl) *adj.* Pertaining to a neck or a cervix.

cer•vine (sûr′vīn′) *adj.* Pertaining to, resembling, or characteristic of a deer. [< L cervus, deer. See ker-1.]

cer•vix (sûr′vĭks) *n., pl.* -vixes or -vices (-və-sēz′, -vī′sēz). A neck-shaped anatomical structure, as the narrow outer end of the uterus. [L cervīx, neck.]

Ce•sar•e•an, Ce•sar•i•an. Variants of Caesarean.

ce•si•um (sē′zē-əm) *n.* Also cae•si•um. Symbol Cs A soft, silvery-white ductile metal, liquid at room temperature, used in photoelectric cells. Atomic number 55, atomic weight 132.905. [< L caesius, bluish-gray.]

ces•sa•tion (sĕ-sā′shən) *n.* A ceasing; a temporary or complete halt.

ces•sion (sĕsh′ən) *n.* 1. A surrendering, as of territory to another country by treaty. 2. A ceded territory. [< L cessiō.]

cess•pool (sĕs′pōōl′) *n.* A covered hole or pit for receiving sewage. [Var of earlier cesperalle, drainpipe.]

ce•ta•ce•an (sĭ-tā′shən) *n.* A whale or related aquatic mammal. [< L cētus, whale.]

Ce•tus (sē′təs) *n.* A constellation in the equatorial region of the S Hemisphere.

Cey•lon (sĭ-lŏn′). The former name for Sri Lanka. —**Cey′lo•nese′** (sē′lə-nēz′, -nēs′) *adj. & n.*

Ceylon lily. A large, bulbous plant of the amaryllis family, native to S Asia, having red-striped white flowers.

Cf californium.

cf. compare (L confer).

c.f. cost and freight.

C.F. cost and freight.

C/F Acct. carried forward.

c.f.i. cost, freight, and insurance.

cg centigram.

c.g. center of gravity.

C.G. 1. coast guard. 2. commanding general. 3. consul general.

ch chain (measurement).

ch. 1. chaplain. 2. chapter. 3. check. 4. chief. 5. child; children. 6. church.

C.H. 1. clearing-house. 2. courthouse. 3. customhouse.

Cha•blis (shă-blē′) *n.* A dry white wine made in Chablis. France.

ă pat/ā ate/âr care/ä bar/b bib/ch chew/d deed/ĕ pet/ē be/f fit/g gag/h hat/hw what/ ĭ pit/ī pie/îr pier/j judge/k kick/l lid, fatal/m mum/n no, sudden/ng sing/ŏ pot/ō go/

Chad (chăd). A republic in north-central Africa. Pop. 3,800,000. Cap. N'Djamena.

Chad

chafe (chāf) v. **chafed, chafing.** 1. To make or become worn or sore from rubbing. 2. To make or become annoyed. 3. To warm by rubbing. [< OF *chauffer,* to warm (by rubbing).]

chaff¹ (chăf) n. 1. Grain husks separated from the seed, as by threshing. 2. Trivial or worthless matter. 3. Strips of metal foil released in the atmosphere to inhibit radar. [< OE *ceaf.*]

chaff² (chăf) v. To make fun of good-naturedly; tease. —n. Good-natured teasing; banter. [Prob a blend of CHAFF and CHAFE.] —**chaff'er** n.

chaf·fer (chăf'ər) v. To bargain or haggle. [ME *cheapfare,* trade, merchandise.] —**chaf'fer·er** n.

chaf·finch (chăf'ĭnch) n. A small European songbird with reddish-brown plumage. [< CHAFF¹ + FINCH.]

chafing dish. A dish or pan heated from below, used to cook food at the table.

cha·grin (shə-grĭn') n. Embarrassment or humiliation. —v. To humiliate. [F, sadness.]

chain (chān) n. 1. A connected, flexible series of links, usually of metal, used for binding or connecting. 2. Anything that restrains. 3. **chains.** Bonds, fetters, or shackles. 4. Any series of related things. 5. A number of commercial establishments, under common ownership. 6. a. A measuring instrument for surveying, consisting of 100 linked pieces of iron or steel. b. A unit of length, equal to 100 links or 66 feet. 7. a. A similar instrument used in engineering. b. A unit of length equal to 100 feet. —v. 1. To bind or make fast with a chain or chains. 2. To confine. [< L *catēna.*]

chain gang. A group of convicts chained together to labor outdoors.

chain mail. Flexible armor of joined metal links or scales.

chain·man (chān'mən) n. *Surveying.* Either of the two persons who hold the measuring chain.

chain-re·act (chān'rē-ăkt') v. To undergo a chain reaction.

chain reaction. 1. A series of events, each of which induces or otherwise influences its successor. 2. A multistage nuclear reaction so constituted, esp. a self-sustaining series of fissions in which the average number of neutrons produced per unit of time exceeds the number absorbed or lost. 3. A series of chemical reactions in which one product of a reacting set is a reactant in the following set.

chain saw. A power saw with teeth linked in an endless chain.

chair (châr) n. 1. A piece of furniture consisting of a seat, legs, and back, and often arms, designed for one person. 2. a. A seat of office, authority, or dignity, as that of a bishop, judge, or chairman. b. One who holds such an office. 3. *Slang.* The electric chair. [< L *cathedra,* chair.]

chair lift. A cable-suspended, power-driven chair assembly used to transport people up or down mountains.

chair·man (châr'mən) n. One who presides over an assembly, meeting, etc. —**chair'man·ship'** n. —**chair'wom'an** *fem.n.*

chaise longue (shāz' lông') pl. **chaise longues** or **chaises longues** (shāz' lông'). A chair with a seat long enough to support the sitter's outstretched legs. [F, "long chair."]

chal·ced·o·ny (kăl-sĕd'n-ē) n., pl. **-nies.** A translucent to transparent milky or grayish quartz. [< Gk *khalkēdōn,* a mystical stone.] —**chal'ce·don'ic** adj.

cha·let (shă-lā') n. 1. A house with an overhanging roof, common in Switzerland. 2. The hut of a herdsman in the Alps. [F.]

chal·ice (chăl'ĭs) n. 1. A goblet. 2. A cup for the consecrated wine of the Eucharist. [< L *calix,* cup, goblet.]

chalk (chôk) n. 1. A soft, compact calcium carbonate with varying amounts of silica, quartz, feldspar, or other mineral impurities. 2. A piece of chalk used for marking on a blackboard. —v. 1. To mark, draw, or write with chalk. 2. To treat (soil) with chalk. —**chalk up.** To earn, score, or credit. —adj. Made with chalk. [< L *calx,* stone, pebble.] —**chalk'i·ness** n. —**chalk'y** adj.

chalk·board (chôk'bôrd', -bôrd') n. A blackboard.

chal·lah (кнä'lə) n. Also **hal·lah** (кнä'lə, hä'lə). A usually braided loaf of white egg bread traditionally eaten by Jews on the Sabbath. [Heb *ḥalláh.*]

chal·lenge (chăl'ənj) n. 1. A call to engage in a contest. 2. A demand for an explanation. 3. A sentry's call for identification. 4. The quality of requiring full use of one's abilities: *a career that offers a challenge.* 5. A formal objection, esp. to the qualifications of a juror or voter. —v. **-lenged, -lenging.** 1. To call to engage in a contest. 2. To dispute. 3. To order to halt and be identified. 4. To object formally to (a juror or voter). 5. To have due claim to; call for. 6. To stimulate. [< L *calumnia,* trickery, false accusation.] —**chal'lenge·a·ble** adj. —**chal'leng·er** n.

chal·lis (shăl'ē) n. A light, usually printed fabric of wool, cotton, etc. [Poss < the English surname *Challis.*]

cham·ber (chām′bər) *n.* **1.** A room, esp. a bedroom. **2.** A judge's office. **3.** A hall, esp. for the meeting of a legislative assembly. **4.** A legislative, judicial, or deliberative assembly. **5.** Any enclosed space; cavity. **6.** An enclosed space at the bore of a gun that holds the charge. [< LL *camera.*]

cham·ber·lain (chām′bər-lĭn) *n.* **1.** An official who manages a sovereign's household. **2.** A high-ranking officer in a royal court. **3.** A treasurer. [< Frank *kamerling,* bedchamber servant.]

cham·ber·maid (chām′bər-mād′) *n.* A servant who cleans bedrooms, esp. in hotels.

chamber music. Music composed for trios, quartets, etc., and appropriate for performance in a small concert hall.

chamber of commerce. An association of businessmen for the promotion of their interests in the community.

cham·bray (shăm′brā′) *n.* A lightweight usually cotton fabric woven with white threads across a colored warp. [< *Cambrai,* France.]

cha·me·leon (kə-mēl′yən, -mē′lē-ən) *n.* **1.** Any of various lizards capable of changing color. **2.** A changeable person. [< Gk *khamaileōn,* "ground lion."]

cham·ois (shăm′ē) *n., pl.* **chamois** (shăm′ēz). **1.** A goatlike mammal of mountainous regions of Europe. **2.** Also **cham·my, sham·my** *pl.* **-mies.** Soft leather made originally from the hide of this animal. [OF.]

cham·o·mile, cam·o·mile (kăm′ə-mīl′) *n.* An aromatic plant with daisylike white flowers. [< Gk *khamaemēlon,* "earth-apple."]

champ¹ (chămp) *v.* To chew upon noisily. [Poss imit.]

champ² (chămp) *n. Informal.* A champion.

cham·pagne (shăm-pān′) *n.* **1.** A sparkling white wine originally produced in Champagne, France. **2.** Pale yellow.

cham·paign (shăm-pān′) *n.* Level and open country. [< LL *campānia.*]

cham·pi·on (chăm′pē-ən) *n.* **1.** One that holds first place or wins first prize in a contest, esp. in sports. **2.** One who defends a cause or another person. **3.** One who fights; a warrior. *—v.* To fight as champion of; support. *—adj.* Holding first place or prize; superior to all others. [< LL *campiō.*]

cham·pi·on·ship (chăm′pē-ən-shĭp′) *n.* **1.** The position of a champion. **2.** Defense or support. **3.** A competition held to determine a winner.

Chanc. **1.** chancellor. **2.** chancery.

chance (chăns, chäns) *n.* **1. a.** The abstract nature shared by unexpected, random, or unpredictable events. **b.** This quality regarded as a cause of such events; luck. **2.** The likelihood of occurrence of an event; probability. **3.** An opportunity. **4.** A risk. **5.** A raffle ticket. **6.** An unexpected or fortuitous event. *—v.* **chanced, chancing.** **1.** To happen by chance. **2.** To risk. **—chance on** (or **upon**). To find or meet accidentally. [< VL *cadentia,* "a fall," happening.] **—chance** *adj.*

chan·cel (chăn′səl, chän′-) *n.* The space around the altar of a church for the clergy and choir. [< LL *cancellus,* altar.]

chan·cel·ler·y (chăn′səl-ər-ē, -slər-ē, chän′-) *n., pl.* **-ies.** **1.** The position or office of a chancellor. **2.** The office of an embassy, consulate, or legation.

chan·cel·lor (chăn′səl-ər, -slər, chän′-) *n.* **1.** A state official of high rank. **2.** The chief minister of state in some countries. **3.** The head of certain universities. **4.** The judge of a chancery court in some U.S. states. [< LL *cancellārius,* secretary, doorkeeper.] **—chan′cel·lor·ship′** *n.*

chan·cer·y (chăn′sər-ē, chän′-) *n., pl.* **-ies.** **1.** A court with jurisdiction in equity. **2.** An office of archives. **3.** A chancellery. [< ME *chancelerie,* chancellery.]

chan·cre (shăng′kər) *n.* A dull-red, hard, insensitive lesion that is the first manifestation of syphilis. [< L *cancer,* ulcer, CANCER.]

chanc·y (chăn′sē, chän′-) *adj.* **-ier, -iest.** Uncertain or hazardous.

chan·de·lier (shăn′də-lîr′) *n.* A branched fixture for lights, usually suspended from a ceiling. [< L *candēlābrum,* candelabrum.]

chan·dler (chăn′dlər, chän′-) *n.* **1.** One who makes or sells candles. **2.** A dealer in specified goods or equipment. **—chan′dler·y** *n.*

change (chānj) *v.* **changed, changing.** **1.** To be or cause to become different; alter. **2.** To exchange for or replace by another. **3.** To give or receive an equivalent sum of money in lower denominations or foreign currency. **4.** To put fresh clothes or coverings on. *—n.* **1.** The process or condition of changing. **2.** Money given in exchange for money of higher denomination. **3.** Any small coins. **4.** A fresh set of clothing. [< LL *cambiāre.*] **—change′a·ble** *adj.* **—chang′er** *n.*

change·less (chānj′lĭs) *adj.* Enduring; unchanging. **—change′less·ly** *adv.*

change·ling (chānj′lĭng) *n.* A child secretly exchanged for another.

change of life. The menopause.

chan·nel (chăn′əl) *n.* **1.** The bed of a stream. **2.** The deeper part of a river or harbor. **3.** A strait. **4.** A tubular passage. **5.** A means of passage. **6. channels.** Official routes of communication. **7.** A specified frequency band for the transmission and reception of electromagnetic signals. **8.** A trench, furrow, or groove. *—v.* **1.** To make or form channels in. **2.** To direct or guide along a channel. [< L *canālis,* CANAL.]

Channel Islands. A group of nine British islands in the English Channel.

chan·son (shän′sən) *n.* A song. [F.]

chant (chănt, chänt) *n.* **1.** A melody in which a number of words are sung on each note. **2.** A canticle sung thus. **3.** A monotonous rhythmic voice. *—v.* **1.** To sing (a chant). **2.** To say or sing in the manner of a chant. **3.** To celebrate in song. [Prob < OF *chanter,* to sing.] **—chant′er** *n.*

chan·teuse (shäN-tœz′) *n.* A woman singer, esp. a nightclub singer.

chant·ey (shăn′tē, chăn′-) *n., pl.* **-eys.** A song sailors sing in rhythm with their work. [Prob < F *chanter,* to sing, CHANT.]

chan·ti·cleer (chăn′tə-klîr′, shăn′-) *n.* A

rooster. [< OF *chanter*, to CHANT + *cler*, clear.]

chan•try (chăn′trē, chän′-) *n., pl.* -tries. 1. An endowment for the saying of masses and prayers. 2. An altar or chapel endowed for this purpose. [< OF *chanter*, to CHANT.]

Cha•nu•kah (KHä′nŌŌ-kə) *n.* Also **Ha•nuk•kah, Ha•nu•kah.** An eight-day Jewish festival commemorating a victory over the Syrians and the rededication of the Temple at Jerusalem. [Heb *ḥanukkâh*, "dedication."]

cha•os (kā′ŏs′) *n.* 1. Total disorder or confusion. 2. Often **Chaos.** The amorphous void supposed to have existed before the Creation. [< Gk *khaos*, empty space, chaos.] —**cha•ot′ic** (kā-ŏt′ĭk) *adj.* —**cha•ot′i•cal•ly** *adv.*

chap¹ (chăp) *v.* **chapped, chapping.** To split or roughen, esp. from cold or exposure. [ME *chappen.*]

chap² (chăp) *n. Informal.* A man; fellow. [Short for CHAPMAN.]

chap. chapter.

chap•ar•ral (shăp′ə-răl′) *n. Southwestern U.S.* A dense thicket of shrubs. [< Span *chaparro*, evergreen oak.]

cha•peau (shă-pō′) *n., pl.* -peaux (-pōz′) or -peaus. A hat. [F.]

chap•el (chăp′əl) *n.* 1. A place of worship subordinate to a church, esp. in a college, hospital, etc. 2. The services held at a chapel. [< OF *chapele.*]

chap•er•on (shăp′ə-rōn′) *n.* Also **chap•er•one.** One, esp. an older woman, who for propriety accompanies young unmarried people in public. —*v.* To act as chaperon to or for. [F, "hood," protection.]

chap•lain (chăp′lĭn) *n.* A clergyman attached to a chapel, military unit, or other organization. [< ML *capella*, chapel.]

chap•let (chăp′lĭt) *n.* 1. A wreath for the head. 2. *R.C.Ch.* **a.** A string of prayer beads having one third the number of a rosary's beads. **b.** The prayers counted on such beads. 3. Any string of beads. [< OF *chapelet.*]

Chap•lin (chăp′lĭn), **Charles ("Charlie").** 1889-1977. British motion-picture actor.

chap•man (chăp′mən) *n. Brit.* A peddler; hawker. [< OE *cēapman* : *cēap*, trade (see cheap) + MAN.]

chaps (chăps, shăps) *pl.n.* Trouserlike leather leg coverings worn by cowboys. [Short for Mexican Span *chaparreras.*]

chap•ter (chăp′tər) *n.* 1. A main division of a book. 2. A local branch of a club, fraternity, etc. 3. An assembly of members, as of a religious order. [< L *capitulum*, "small head."]

char¹ (chär) *v.* **charred, charring.** 1. To scorch or become scorched. 2. To reduce or be reduced to charcoal by incomplete combustion. [Back-formation < CHARCOAL.]

char² (chär) *n.* Any of several fishes related to the trout. [?]

char•ac•ter (kăr′ĭk-tər) *n.* 1. A distinguishing feature or attribute; a characteristic. 2. The moral or ethical structure of a person or group. 3. Moral strength; integrity. 4. Reputation. 5. *Informal.* An eccentric person. 6. A person portrayed in a drama, novel, etc. 7. A symbol

in a writing system. 8. Any structure, function, or attribute determined by a gene or group of genes. [< Gk *kharaktēr*, engraved mark, brand.]

char•ac•ter•is•tic (kăr′ĭk-tə-rĭs′tĭk) *adj.* Distinctive; typical. —*n.* A distinguishing feature or attribute. —**char′ac•ter•is′ti•cal•ly** *adv.*

char•ac•ter•ize (kăr′ĭk-tə-rīz′) *v.* -ized, -izing. 1. To describe the qualities of. 2. To be a distinguishing trait of. 3. To give character to, as on the stage. —**char′ac•ter•i•za′tion** *n.*

cha•rades (shə-rādz′) *pl.n.* A game in which words are represented in pantomime until guessed by the other players. [< Prov *charra*, to chat.]

char•coal (chär′kōl′) *n.* 1. A black, porous carbon-containing material, produced by the destructive distillation of wood and used as a fuel, filter, and absorbent. 2. A drawing pencil made from this substance. 3. Dark gray. [Perh < L *carbo*, CARBON + COAL.]

chard (chärd) *n.* A variety of beet with large, succulent leaves used as a vegetable. [F *carde.*]

charge (chärj) *v.* **charged, charging.** 1. To entrust with a duty, responsibility, etc. 2. To command. 3. To blame or accuse. 4. To set as a price. 5. To demand payment from. 6. To record as a debt. 7. To attack violently. 8. To load or fill with; impregnate. 9. **a.** To cause formation of a net electric charge on or in (a conductor). **b.** To energize (a storage battery). —*n.* 1. Care, custody, or responsibility. 2. A person or thing entrusted to one's care. 3. A command or injunction. 4. An accusation or indictment. 5. Cost; price. 6. A debit in an account. 7. An attack. 8. A load; burden. 9. The quantity needed to fill an apparatus or container. 10. **a.** The intrinsic property of matter responsible for all electric phenomena, occurring in two forms arbitrarily designated *negative* and *positive.* **b.** A measure of this property. [< LL *carricāre*, to load.]

char•gé d'af•faires (shär-zhä′ də-fâr′) *pl.* **chargés d'affaires** (shär-zhä′, shär-zhäz′). An official temporarily in charge of an embassy or legation.

charg•er (chär′jər) *n.* 1. One that charges. 2. A cavalry horse.

Cha•ri-Nile (shä′rē-nīl′) *n.* A family of languages spoken in E and C Africa.

char•i•ot (chăr′ē-ət) *n.* An ancient two-wheeled vehicle used in war, races, and processions. [< L *carrus*, vehicle.] —**char′i•o•teer′** *n.*

cha•ris•ma (kə-rĭz′mə) *n.* A quality attributed to those with exceptional ability to secure the devotion of large numbers of people. [Gk *kharisma*, favor, divine gift.] —**char′is•mat′ic** (kăr′ĭz-măt′ĭk) *adj.*

char•i•ta•ble (chăr′ə-tə-bəl) *adj.* 1. Generous to the needy. 2. Tolerant in judging others. 3. Of or for charity. —**char′i•ta•bly** *adv.*

char•i•ty (chăr′ə-tē) *n., pl.* -ties. 1. Help or alms given to the poor. 2. An organization or fund that helps the poor. 3. An act or feeling of benevolence. 4. Forbearance in judging others. 5. *Theol.* **a.** The benevolence of God toward man. **b.** The love of man for his fellow men. [< L *cāritās*, love, regard.]

char·la·tan (shär'lə-tən) *n.* One claiming knowledge or skill that he does not have. [< It *cerretano,* inhabitant of *Cerreto,* village near Spoleto, Italy.] —**char'la·tan·ism'** *n.*

Char·le·magne (shär'lə-mān'). A.D. 742–814. King of the Franks; first Holy Roman Emperor.

Charles·ton (chärl'stən). 1. A seaport of South Carolina. Pop. 67,000. 2. The capital of West Virginia. Pop. 72,000.

char·ley horse (chär'lē). *Informal.* A muscular cramp or stiffness, esp. of the leg or arm, caused by excessive exertion. [Prob < the use of *Charley* as a name for lame horses.]

Char·lotte (shär'lət). A city of SW North Carolina. Pop. 202,000.

Char·lotte·town (shär'lət-toun'). The capital of Prince Edward Island Province, Canada. Pop. 19,000.

charm (chärm) *n.* 1. The power or quality of pleasing or attracting. 2. A small ornament worn on a bracelet. 3. Anything worn for its supposed magical effect; an amulet. 4. Any action or formula thought to have magical power. —*v.* 1. To attract; be alluring or pleasing. 2. To act upon as if with magic; bewitch. [< L *carmen,* song, incantation.] —**charm'er** *n.* —**charm'ing** *adj.*

char·nel (chär'nəl) *n.* Also **char·nel house.** A building or room in which bones or bodies are placed. [< LL *carnālis,* carnal.]

Char·on (kâr'ən). *Gk.Myth.* The ferryman of Hades.

chart (chärt) *n.* 1. A map. 2. A sheet with information in the form of graphs or tables. —*v.* 1. To make a chart of. 2. To plan. [< L *charta,* papyrus leaf, paper.]

char·ter (chär'tər) *n.* 1. A document issued by a governmental authority, creating a corporation and defining its rights and privileges. 2. A document outlining the organization of a corporate body. 3. An authorization from an organization to establish a local chapter. 4. The hiring or leasing of an aircraft, vessel, etc. —*v.* 1. To grant a charter to. 2. To hire or lease by charter. [< L *charta,* papyrus leaf.]

charter member. An original member of an organization.

char·treuse (shär-trōōz', -trōōs') *n.* 1. A yellow or pale-green liqueur. 2. Brilliant yellowish green. [< *la Grande Chartreuse,* Carthusian monastery near Grenoble, France.]

char·wom·an (chär'wŏŏm'ən) *n. Brit.* A woman hired to do cleaning.

char·y (châr'ē) *adj.* **-ier, -iest.** 1. Careful; wary. 2. Sparing. [< OE *cearig,* sorrowful.] —**char'i·ly** *adv.* —**char'i·ness** *n.*

chase¹ (chās) *v.* **chased, chasing.** 1. To pursue; follow. 2. To hunt. 3. To put to flight; drive away. 4. *Informal.* To rush. —*n.* 1. The act of chasing. 2. **the chase.** The sport of hunting. 3. That which is hunted. [< L *captāre,* to seize.]

chase² (chās) *n.* A groove cut in an object; a slot. —*v.* **chased, chasing.** To decorate (metal) by engraving or embossing. [< OF *chas,* "enclosure."]

chas·er (chā'sər) *n.* 1. One that chases. 2.

Informal. A drink of water, beer, etc., taken after hard liquor.

chasm (kăz'əm) *n.* 1. A deep cleft in the earth's surface; a narrow gorge. 2. A gap; hiatus. [< Gk *khasma.*] —**chas'mal** *adj.*

Chas·si·dim (KHä-sē'dĭm) *pl.n. Sing.* **Chas·sid** (KHä'sĭd). Also **Has·si·dim, Ha·si·dim.** A sect of orthodox Jewish mystics founded in Poland (about 1750). [Heb *hasīdhīm,* "pious ones."] —**Chas·si'dic** *adj.*

chas·sis (shăs'ē, chăs'ē) *n., pl.* **-sis** (shăs'ēz, chăs'ēz). 1. The rectangular steel frame that holds the body and motor of an automotive vehicle. 2. The landing gear of an aircraft, including the wheels, floats, and other structures. 3. The framework that holds the functioning parts of a radio, television set, etc. [< L *capsa,* box.]

chaste (chāst) *adj.* 1. Morally pure; modest. 2. Abstaining from unlawful sexual intercourse. 3. Celibate. 4. Simple in style; not ornate. [< L *castus,* morally pure.] —**chaste'ly** *adv.* —**chaste'ness** *n.*

chas·ten (chā'sən) *v.* 1. To punish; discipline. 2. To restrain; moderate. 3. To purify: *chasten one's style.* [< L *castigāre,* to CASTIGATE.]

chas·tise (chăs-tīz') *v.* **-tised, -tising.** 1. To punish, usually by beating. 2. To criticize severely. [< ME *chastien,* chasten.] —**chas·tise'ment** (chăs-tīz'mənt, chăs'tĭz-mənt) *n.*

chas·ti·ty (chăs'tə-tē) *n.* The state or quality of being chaste.

chat (chăt) *v.* **chatted, chatting.** To converse in an easy or informal manner. —*n.* An informal conversation. [< ME *chatteren,* to chatter.]

cha·teau, châ·teau (shă-tō') *n., pl.* **-teaux** (chă-tōz'). 1. A French castle. 2. A large country house.

chat·e·laine (shăt'ə-lān') *n.* 1. The mistress of a chateau. 2. A clasp or chain worn at a woman's waist to hold keys, a watch, etc.

Chat·ta·noo·ga (chăt'ə-nōō'gə). A city of SE Tennessee. Pop. 130,000.

chat·tel (chăt'l) *n.* 1. An article of movable property. 2. A slave. [ME *chatel,* property, goods.]

chat·ter (chăt'ər) *v.* 1. To utter inarticulate speechlike sounds. 2. To talk rapidly, incessantly, and inanely. 3. To click together quickly, as the teeth from cold. [ME *chatteren.*] —**chat'ter** *n.* —**chat'ter·er** *n.*

chat·ter·box (chăt'ər-bŏks') *n.* An extremely talkative person.

chat·ty (chăt'ē) *adj.* **-tier, -tiest.** Given to informal conversation. —**chat'ti·ly** *adv.* —**chat'ti·ness** *n.*

Chau·cer (chô'sər), **Geoffrey.** 1340?–1400. English poet.

chauf·feur (shō'fər, shō-fûr') *n.* One employed to drive a private automobile. [F, stoker.] —**chauf'feur** *v.*

chau·vin·ism (shō'vən-ĭz'əm) *n.* 1. Fanatical patriotism. 2. Prejudiced belief in the superiority of one's own group: *male chauvinism.* [< N. *Chauvin,* legendary French soldier extremely devoted to Napoleon.] —**chau'vin·ist** *n.* —**chau'vin·is'tic** *adj.*

cheap (chēp) *adj.* 1. Inexpensive. 2. Charging

low prices. **3.** Costing little effort: *a cheap victory.* **4.** Of low value or quality. **5.** Not worthy of respect. **6.** Stingy. —*adv.* Inexpensively. [< OE *cēap*, purchase, bargain < Gmc **kaupaz*, trader.] —**cheap′ly** *adv.* —**cheap′ness** *n.*
cheap•en (chē′pən) *v.* To make or become cheap or cheaper. —**cheap′en•er** *n.*
cheap•skate (chēp′skāt′) *n. Slang.* A stingy person.
cheat (chēt) *v.* **1.** To deceive by trickery; swindle. **2.** To act dishonestly. —*n.* **1.** A fraud or swindle. **2.** One guilty of swindle or dishonesty. [ME *cheten,* to revert.] —**cheat′er** *n.* —**cheat′ing•ly** *adv.*
check (chĕk) *n.* **1.** An abrupt halt or stop. **2.** A restraint. **3.** A standard of comparison to verify accuracy. **4.** A mark to show verification. **5.** A slip for identification: *a baggage check.* **6.** A bill at a restaurant. **7.** Also *chiefly Brit.* **cheque.** A written order to a bank to pay an amount from funds on deposit. **8. a.** A pattern of small squares. **b.** A fabric with such a pattern. **9.** *Chess.* A move in which an opponent's king is attacked. —*v.* **1.** To arrest the motion of abruptly. **2.** To hold in restraint. **3.** To examine, as for accuracy. **4.** To make a check mark on. **5.** To deposit for temporary safekeeping: *check one's hat.* **6.** To have item-for-item correspondence. —**check in.** To register, as at a hotel. —**check out. 1.** To pay one's bill and leave, as from a hotel. **2.** To investigate; confirm. **3.** To correspond to what is expected. [< Ar *shāh,* king, check at chess.] —**check′a•ble** *adj.*
check•er (chĕk′ər) *n.* **1.** One of the disks used in the game of checkers. **2.** One who checks. —*v.* To mark with a checked pattern. [< ME *cheker,* chessboard.]
check•er•board (chĕk′ər-bôrd′, -bōrd′) *n.* A game board divided into 64 squares of two alternating colors on which chess and checkers are played.
check•ered (chĕk′ərd) *adj.* **1.** Divided into squares. **2.** Marked by light and dark patches. **3.** Marked by changes in fortune: *a checkered career.*
check•ers (chĕk′ərz) *n. (takes sing. v.).* A game played on a checkerboard by two persons, each with 12 disks.
check•mate (chĕk′māt′) *v.* -**mated,** -**mating. 1.** *Chess.* To attack (an opponent's king) so that no escape or defense is possible, thus ending the game. **2.** To defeat completely. [< Ar *shāh māt,* the king is perplexed or dead.] —**check′mate′** *n.*
check•room (chĕk′rōōm′, -rŏŏm′) *n.* A place where hats, coats, etc., may be stored temporarily.
check•up (chĕk′ŭp′) *n.* **1.** A thorough examination, as for accuracy. **2.** A physical examination.
Ched•dar (chĕd′ər) *n.* Also **ched•dar.** Any of several types of smooth, hard cheese. [< *Cheddar,* village in Somerset, England.]
cheek (chēk) *n.* **1.** The fleshy part of either side of the face below the eye and between the nose and ear. **2.** Something resembling this. **3.** Im-

pudence; sauciness. [< OE *cēace* < Gmc **kēkōn.*]
cheek•bone (chēk′bōn′) *n.* A bone in the upper cheek, the zygomatic bone.
cheek•y (chē′kē) *adj.* -**ier,** -**iest.** Impudent. —**cheek′i•ly** *adv.* —**cheek′i•ness** *n.*
cheep (chēp) *n.* A faint, shrill chirp, as of a young bird. [Imit.] —**cheep** *v.*
cheer (chîr) *n.* **1.** Gaiety; happiness. **2.** Anything that gives happiness or comfort. **3.** A shout of encouragement or congratulation. —*v.* **1.** To fill with happiness. **2. a.** To encourage or acclaim with cheers. **b.** To shout cheers. [ME *chere,* cheer, disposition, face.]
cheer•ful (chîr′fəl) *adj.* **1.** In good spirits. **2.** Promoting cheer. —**cheer′ful•ly** *adv.* —**cheer′ful•ness** *n.*
cheers (chîrz) *interj.* Used as a toast.
cheer•y (chîr′ē) *adj.* -**ier,** -**iest.** Cheerful. —**cheer′i•ly** *adv.* —**cheer′i•ness** *n.*
cheese (chēz) *n.* A solid food prepared from the pressed curd of milk. [< OE *cēse* < Gmc **kasjus* < L *cāseus.*]
cheese•cloth (chēz′klôth′, -klŏth′) *n.* A coarse, loosely woven cotton gauze.
chee•tah (chē′tə) *n.* A spotted, swift-running wild cat of Africa and SW Asia. [Hindi *cītā.*]
chef (shĕf) *n.* A cook, esp. a chief cook. [< OF *chief, chef,* chief.]
Che•khov (chĕk′ôf′), **Anton Pavlovich.** 1860–1904. Russian author.
chem. chemical; chemist; chemistry.
chem•i•cal (kĕm′ĭ-kəl) *adj.* **1.** Pertaining to chemistry. **2.** Involving or produced by chemicals. —*n.* A substance produced by or used in a chemical process. [< ML *alchimia,* alchemy.] —**chem′i•cal•ly** *adv.*
chemical bond. Any of several forces or mechanisms, esp. the ionic bond, covalent bond, and metallic bond, by which atoms or ions are bound in a molecule or crystal.
chemical engineering. The technology of large-scale chemical production. —**chemical engineer.**
Chemical Mace. A trademark for a mixture of organic chemicals used in aerosol form as a disabling weapon.
chemical warfare. Warfare using chemicals other than explosives as weapons.
chem•i•lu•mi•nes•cence (kĕm′ĭ-lōō′mə-nĕs′-əns) *n.* The emission of light as a result of a chemical reaction at environmental temperatures.
che•mise (shə-mēz′) *n.* **1.** A woman's loose, shirtlike undergarment. **2.** A dress that hangs straight from the shoulders. [< LL *camīsia,* linen shirt, nightgown.]
chem•ist (kĕm′ĭst) *n.* **1.** A scientist specializing in chemistry. **2.** *Chiefly Brit.* A pharmacist.
chem•is•try (kĕm′ĭs-trē) *n., pl.* -**tries. 1.** The science of the composition, structure, properties, and reactions of matter, esp. of atomic and molecular systems. **2.** The composition, structure, properties, and reactions of a substance.
chemo–. *comb. form.* Chemicals or chemical reactions.
chem•o•ther•a•py (kĕm′ō-thĕr′ə-pē, kē′mō-)

---

n. The treatment of disease with chemicals.
chem·ur·gy (kĕm′ər-jē, kĕ-mûr′-) *n.* The development of new industrial chemical products from organic raw materials, esp. from those of agricultural origin.

che·nille (shə-nēl′) *n.* 1. A soft, tufted cord of silk, cotton, or worsted. 2. Fabric made of this cord. [F, "caterpillar."]

cheque. *Chiefly Brit.* Variant of **check.**

cher·ish (chĕr′ĭsh) *v.* To hold dear. [< OF *cher*, dear.] —**cher′ish·er** *n.*

Cher·o·kee (chĕr′ə-kē′, chĕr′ə-kē′) *n., pl.* -**kee** or -**kees.** 1. A member of an Iroquoian-speaking tribe of North American Indians, formerly inhabiting SE North America. 2. The language of this tribe.

cher·ry (chĕr′ē) *n., pl.* -**ries.** 1. A small, fleshy, rounded fruit with a hard stone. 2. A tree bearing such fruit. 3. The wood of such a tree. 4. Deep or purplish red. [< VL *ceresia.*]

cher·ub (chĕr′əb) *n.* 1. *pl.* -**ubim** (-/y/ə-bĭm′). A winged celestial being. 2. *pl.* -**ubs.** A representation of such an angel as a winged child with a chubby, rosy face. [Heb *kərŭbh.*] —**che·ru′bic** (chə-rōō′bĭk) *adj.*

Ches·a·peake Bay (chĕs′ə-pēk′). An inlet of the Atlantic Ocean, in Virginia and Maryland.

chess (chĕs) *n.* A board game for two players, each possessing an initial force of a king, a queen, two bishops, two knights, two rooks, and eight pawns, all maneuvered following individual rules of movement with the objective of checkmating the opposite king. [< OF *eschec*, check.]

chess·board (chĕs′bôrd′, -bōrd′) *n.* A checkerboard.

chess·man (chĕs′măn′, -mən) *n.* A piece used in playing chess.

chest (chĕst) *n.* 1. The part of the body between the neck and abdomen. 2. A sturdy box with a lid, used for storage. 3. A bureau or dresser. [< OE *cest*, box < Gmc *kistā* < L *cista.*] —**chest′ed** *adj.*

ches·ter·field (chĕs′tər-fēld′) *n.* An overcoat with a velvet collar. [< an Earl of *Chesterfield* of the 19th century.]

chest·nut (chĕs′nŭt′, -nət) *n.* 1. An edible nut enclosed in a prickly bur. 2. A tree bearing such nuts. 3. The wood of such a tree. 4. Reddish brown. 5. An old, stale joke, story, etc. [< Gk *kastenea* + NUT.] —**chest′nut** *adj.*

cheth. Variant of **heth.**

chev·a·lier (shĕv′ə-lîr′) *n.* A member of certain orders of knighthood or merit. [< LL *caballārius*, horseman.]

chev·i·ot (shĕv′ē-ət) *n.* A heavy, twilled woolen fabric used chiefly for suits and overcoats.

chev·ron (shĕv′rən) *n.* An insignia consisting of stripes meeting at an angle, worn on the sleeve of a uniform to indicate rank or length of service.

chew (chōō) *v.* To grind (something) with the teeth. —**chew out.** *Slang.* To scold or reprimand. —**chew the rag.** *Slang.* To chat. [< OE *cēowan.* See gyeu-.] —**chew′er** *n.*

Chey·enne¹ (shī-ăn′, -ĕn′) *n., pl.* -**enne** or -**ennes.** 1. A member of a tribe of Algonquian-speaking North American Indians, formerly inhabiting C Minnesota and the Dakotas. 2. The language of this tribe.

Chey·enne² (shī-ăn′, -ĕn′). The capital of Wyoming. Pop. 41,000.

chi (kī) *n.* Also **khi.** The 22nd letter of the Greek alphabet, representing *kh* or *ch.*.

Chiang Kai-shek (jyäng′ kī′shĕk′, chyäng′, chăng′). Born 1887. Chinese statesman and general.

chi·a·ro·scu·ro (kē-är′′ə-sk/y/ōōr′ō) *n., pl.* -**ros.** The technique of using light and shade in pictorial representation.

chic (shēk) *adj.* Sophisticated; elegant; modish. [< G *Schick*, skill.] —**chic** *n.* —**chic′ly** *adv.*

Chi·ca·go (shə-kä′gō, -kô′gō, -kä′gə). A city in NE Illinois, second-largest in the U.S. Pop. 3,367,000. —**Chi·ca′go·an** *n.*

chi·can·er·y (shĭ-kā′nər-ē) *n., pl.* -**ies.** Deception by trickery. [< OF *chicaner*, to quibble.]

Chi·ca·no (shĭ-kä′nō, chĭ-) *n. pl.* -**nos.** A Mexican-American. —*adj.* Of or pertaining to Mexican-Americans. [< American Span *Chicano* < Span *Mejicano*, a Mexican.]

chick (chĭk) *n.* 1. A young bird, esp. a chicken. 2. *Slang.* A girl; young woman.

chick·a·dee (chĭk′ə-dē′) *n.* A small, gray, dark-crowned North American bird. [Imit.]

chick·en (chĭk′ən) *n.* 1. The common domestic fowl or its young. 2. The edible flesh of a chicken. —*adj. Slang.* Afraid. —*v.* —**chicken out.** To lose one's nerve. [< OE *cicen.*]

chicken feed. *Slang.* A trifling amount of money.

chick·en-heart·ed (chĭk′ən-här′tĭd) *adj.* Cowardly; timid.

chick·en-liv·ered (chĭk′ən-lĭv′ərd) *adj.* Cowardly; timid.

chicken pox. A viral disease, usually of young children, characterized by skin eruption and slight fever.

chick·pea (chĭk′pē′) *n.* The edible, pealike seed of a bushy Old World plant. [< L *cicer* + PEA.]

chick·weed (chĭk′wēd′) *n.* A low, weedy plant with small white flowers.

chic·le (chĭk′əl) *n.* The coagulated milky juice of a tropical American tree, used in making chewing gum. [< Nah *chictli.*]

chic·o·ry (chĭk′ər-ē) *n.* 1. A plant with blue, daisylike flowers and leaves used as salad. 2. The ground, roasted root of this plant, used as a coffee admixture or substitute. [< Gk *kikhora.*]

chide (chīd) *v.* **chided** or **chid** (chĭd), **chided** or **chid** or **chidden** (chĭd′n), **chiding.** To scold; reprimand. [< OE *cīd*, strife.] —**chid′er** *n.*

chief (chēf) *n.* One who is highest in rank or authority. —*adj.* 1. Highest in rank, authority, or office. 2. Principal; most important. [< L *caput*, head.] —**chief′ly** *adv.*

chief·tain (chēf′tən) *n.* The leader of a clan or tribe.

chif·fon (shĭ-fŏn′, shĭf′ŏn′) *n.* A fabric of sheer silk or rayon. —*adj.* 1. Of or relating to chiffon. 2. *Cooking.* Having a light and fluffy consistency. [F, "rag."]

chig·ger (chĭg′ər) *n.* 1. A mite that lodges on the skin and causes intense itching. 2. Also

---

ă pat/ā ate/âr care/ä bar/b bib/ch chew/d deed/ĕ pet/ē be/f fit/g gag/h hat/hw what/
ĭ pit/ī pie/îr pier/j judge/k kick/l lid, fatal/m mum/n no, sudden/ng sing/ŏ pot/ō go/

chig•oe (chĭg'ō, chē'gō). A tropical flea that causes similar itching. [< Cariban.]
chi•gnon (shēn-yŏn', shēn'yŏn') n. A knot of hair worn at the back of the head. [< OF *chaignon*, chain.]
Chi•hua•hua (chĭ-wä'wä, -wə) n. A very small smooth-coated dog. [< *Chihuahua*, Mexico.]
chil•blain (chĭl'blān') n. An inflammation followed by itchy irritation on the hands, feet, or ears, resulting from exposure to moist cold. [CHIL(L) + BLAIN.]
child (chīld) n., pl. **children** (chĭl'drən). 1. Any person between birth and puberty. 2. One who is childish or immature. 3. A son or daughter; an offspring. —**with child.** Pregnant. [< OE *cild* < Gmc *kiltham*.] —**child'hood'** n. —**child'less** adj.
child•birth (chīld'bûrth') n. Parturition.
child•ish (chīl'dĭsh) adj. 1. Of, similar to, or suitable for a child. 2. Immature in behavior. —**child'ish•ly** adv. —**child'ish•ness** n.
child•like (chīld'līk') adj. Like or befitting a child, as in innocence.
chil•dren. pl. of child.
Chil•e (chĭl'ē). A republic of W South America. Pop. 8,515,000. Cap. Santiago. —**Chil'e•an** (chĭl'ē-ən) adj. & n.

Chile

chil•e con car•ne (chĭl'ē kŏn kär'nē). A highly spiced dish of red peppers, meat, and sometimes beans. [Span, "chili with meat."]
chil•i (chĭl'ē) n., pl. **-ies.** 1. The very pungent pod of a variety of red pepper. 2. Chile con carne. [< Nah *chilli*.]
chill (chĭl) n. 1. A moderate but penetrating coldness. 2. A sensation of coldness or a similar feeling, as from fever or fear. 3. A dampening of enthusiasm or spirit. —adj. chilly. —v. 1. To make or become cold. 2. To dispirit. [< OE *ciele*. See gel-³.]
chill•y (chĭl'ē) adj. **-ier, -iest.** 1. Cold enough to cause shivering. 2. Seized with cold. 3. Unfriendly. —**chill'i•ly** adv. —**chill'i•ness** n.
chime (chĭm) n. 1. Often **chimes.** A set of bells tuned to the musical scale. 2. The musical sound produced by a bell or bells. —v. **chimed,**

chiming. 1. To sound with a harmonious ring when struck. 2. To agree; harmonize. 3. To make (the hour) known by ringing bells. —**chime in.** 1. To interrupt, as a conversation. 2. To join in harmoniously. [ME, cymbal, chime.] —**chim'er** n.
chi•me•ra (kĭ-mîr'ə, kə-) n. 1. **Chimera.** *Gk.Myth.* A fire-breathing monster with the head of a lion, the body of a goat, and the tail of a serpent. 2. An impossible or foolish fancy. [< Gk *khimaira*, chimera, "she-goat."]
chi•mer•i•cal (kĭ-mĕr'ĭ-kəl, -mîr'ĭ-kəl, kə-) adj. Unrealistic; fantastic.
chim•ney (chĭm'nē) n. 1. A usually vertical passage through which smoke and gases escape from a fire or furnace. 2. A glass tube for enclosing the flame of a lamp. [< L *camīnus*, furnace.]
chim•pan•zee (chĭm'păn-zē', chĭm-păn'zē) n. A dark-haired, gregarious African ape. [Native African name.]
chin (chĭn) n. The central forward portion of the lower jaw. —v. **chinned, chinning.** 1. To grasp an overhead horizontal bar and pull oneself up until one's chin is level with it. 2. *Informal.* To chat. [< OE *cinn.* See genu-².]
Chin. China; Chinese.
chi•na (chī'nə) n. Pottery, esp. high-quality porcelain.
Chi•na (chī'nə). 1. Officially, People's Republic of China. A republic in east-central Asia, occupying the territory of China proper. Pop. 800,000,000. Cap. Peking. 2. Officially, Republic of China. A republic occupying Taiwan and nearby smaller islands. Pop. 12,429,000. Cap. Taipei.

China

China Sea. A portion of the Pacific Ocean along the E coast of Asia.
chinch bug (chĭnch). A small black and white insect very destructive to grains and grasses.
chin•chil•la (chĭn-chĭl'ə) n. 1. A squirrellike South American rodent with soft pale-gray fur. 2. The fur of this animal. 3. A thick wool cloth used for overcoats. [Span.]
chin•cough (chĭn'kôf', -kŏf') n. **Whooping cough.**
Chi•nese (chī-nēz', -nēs') adj. Of or pertaining to China, its people, or its languages. —n., pl.

-nese. 1. A native of China or one of Chinese ancestry. **2.** One of a group of Sino-Tibetan languages and dialects spoken in China. **3.** Mandarin, the standard language of China.

chink¹ (chĭngk) *n.* A crack or narrow fissure. [Perh < OE *cinu*, crack.] —**chink'y** *adj.*

chink² (chĭngk) *n.* A short, metallic sound. —*v.* To make this sound. [Imit.]

chi•no (chē'nō, shē'-) *n., pl.* **-nos. 1.** A twilled cotton fabric. **2. chinos.** Trousers made of this material. [Amer Span *chino*, "toasted."]

Chi•nook (shə-nŏok', chə-) *n., pl.* **-nook** or **-nooks. 1.** A member of a tribe of North American Indians formerly inhabiting Oregon. **2.** The language of this tribe.

Chi•nook•an (shə-nŏok'ən, chə-) *n.* A North American Indian language family of Washington and Oregon. —*adj.* Of or pertaining to the Chinook.

chintz (chĭnts) *n.* A printed, usually glazed cotton fabric. [< Hindi *chīnṭ.*]

chintz•y (chĭnt'sē) *adj.* **-ier, -iest. 1.** Of or decorated with chintz. **2.** Gaudy; trashy; cheap.

chip (chĭp) *n.* **1.** A small piece broken or cut off. **2.** A mark made by the breaking of such a piece. **3.** A coinlike disk used as a counter, as in poker. **4.** A thin, crisp piece of food. —*v.* **chipped, chipping.** To break or cut so as to form a chip or chips. —**chip in.** To contribute, as money or a comment. [< OE *cipp*, beam, piece cut off a beam.]

chip•munk (chĭp'mŭngk') *n.* A small squirrel-like rodent with a striped back. [< Algon.]

chipped beef. Dried beef sliced very thin.

chip•per (chĭp'ər) *adj.* Cheerful; brisk. [?]

Chip•pe•wa (chĭp'ə-wô', -wä', -wä') *n., pl.* **-wa** or **-was.** Also **Chip•pe•way** (-wä'). Ojibwa.

chip•py (chĭp'ē) *n., pl.* **-pies.** *Slang.* A prostitute.

chiro—. *comb. form.* Hand. [< Gk *kheir.*]

chi•rop•o•dy (kə-rŏp'ə-dē, shə-) *n.* Podiatry. —**chi•rop'o•dist** *n.*

chi•ro•prac•tic (kīr'ə-prăk'tĭk) *n.* A system of therapy in which manipulation of the spinal column and other bodily structures is the preferred method of treatment. —**chi'ro•prac'-tor** *n.*

chirp (chûrp) *v.* To utter a short, high-pitched sound, as of a small bird. [ME *chirpen.*] —**chirp** *n.*

chir•rup (chûr'əp, chĭr'-) *v.* To utter a series of chirps or similar sounds.

chis•el (chĭz'əl) *n.* A metallic cutting and shaping tool with a sharp, beveled edge. —*v.* **-eled** or **-elled, -eling** or **-elling. 1.** To shape or cut with a chisel. **2.** *Slang.* To swindle or obtain by swindling. [< VL *caesellus.*] —**chis'el•er** *n.*

chit¹ (chĭt) *n.* **1.** A voucher for an amount owed for food and drink. **2.** *Chiefly Brit.* A note; memo. [< Hindi *ciṭṭha*, note, pass.]

chit² (chĭt) *n.* A pert girl. [ME *chitte*, young animal.]

chit•chat (chĭt'chăt') *n.* Casual conversation or gossip. [Redupl of CHAT.]

chit•ter•lings (chĭt'lĭnz) *pl.n.* Also **chit•lins, chit•lings.** The intestines of pigs, prepared as food. [ME *chiterling.*]

chiv•al•rous (shĭv'əl-rəs) *adj.* Also **chiv•al•ric** (shĭ-văl'rĭk, shĭv'əl-). **1.** Having the qualities attributed to an ideal knight. **2.** Of or pertaining to chivalry. —**chiv'al•rous•ly** *adv.*

chiv•al•ry (shĭv'əl-rē) *n., pl.* **-ries. 1.** The medieval institution of knighthood. **2.** The qualities, as bravery and courtesy, idealized by knighthood. **3.** A chivalrous act. [< LL *caballārius*, horseman, cavalier.]

chive (chīv) *n.* A plant with grasslike, onion-flavored leaves used as seasoning. [< L *cēpa*, onion.]

chiv•vy (chĭv'ē) *v.* **-vied, -vying.** Also **chiv•y.** *Brit.* To chase or harass. [< dial *chevy chase*, pursuit.]

chlo•ral (klôr'əl, klōr'-) *n.* A colorless, mobile oily liquid, CCl_3CHO, used to manufacture DDT and chloral hydrate.

chloral hydrate. A colorless crystalline compound, $CCl_3CH(OH)_2$, used as a sedative.

chlo•ride (klôr'īd', klōr'-) *n.* Any binary compound of chlorine. [CHLOR(O)- + -IDE.]

chlo•rin•ate (klôr'ə-nāt', klōr'-) *v.* **-ated, -ating.** To treat or combine with chlorine or a chlorine compound. —**chlo'ri•na'tion** *n.*

chlo•rine (klôr'ēn', klōr'-, -ĭn) *n. Symbol* **Cl** A highly irritating, greenish-yellow gaseous element, used to purify water, as a disinfectant, a bleaching agent, and in the manufacture of chloroform and carbon tetrachloride. Atomic number 17, atomic weight 35.45. [CHLOR(O)- + -INE.]

chloro—. *comb. form.* **1.** The color green. **2.** The presence of chlorine. [< Gk *khlōros*, greenish yellow.]

chlo•ro•form (klôr'ə-fôrm', klōr'-) *n.* A clear, colorless liquid, $CHCl_3$, used in refrigerants and propellants and as an anesthetic. —*v.* **1.** To anesthetize or kill with chloroform. **2.** To apply chloroform to.

chlo•ro•phyll (klôr'ə-fĭl, klōr'-) *n.* A green plant pigment essential in photosynthesis.

chock (chŏk) *n.* A block or wedge placed under a boat, barrel, or wheel to keep it from moving. —*v.* To secure by a chock or chocks. —*adv.* Completely; fully. [?]

chock-a-block (chŏk'ə-blŏk') *adj.* Squeezed or crowded together.

chock-full (chŏk'fŏŏl', chŭk'-) *adj.* Completely filled.

choc•o•late (chôk'lĭt, chô'kə-lĭt, chŏk'-) *n.* **1.** Husked, roasted, and ground cacao seeds. **2.** A candy or beverage made from this. **3.** Deep reddish or grayish brown. [Span.] —**choc'o•late** *adj.*

choice (chois) *n.* **1.** The act of choosing; selection. **2.** The power or right to choose; option. **3.** Something chosen. **4.** A number or variety from which to choose. **5.** The best part. —*adj.* **choicer, choicest. 1.** Of fine quality. **2.** Selected with care. [< OF *choisir*, to choose.]

choir (kwīr) *n.* **1.** An organized group of singers, esp. one singing in a church. **2.** The part of a church used by such singers. **3.** A group or section of orchestral instruments. [< L *chorus*, dance, chorus.]

choke (chōk) *v.* **choked, choking. 1.** To terminate, interfere with, or have difficulty in breathing, as by constricting the windpipe; suffocate. **2.** To repress or check forcefully. **3.** To block up; obstruct; clog. **4.** To reduce the air intake of (a carburetor), thereby enriching the fuel mixture. —*n.* **1.** The act or sound of choking. **2.** A device used to choke an internal-combustion engine. [< OE ăcē-ocian < Gmc *kēkŏn-.]

chok•er (chō′kər) *n.* A short, close-fitting necklace.

chol•er•a (kŏl′ər-ə) *n.* An acute, infectious, often fatal epidemic disease characterized by watery diarrhea, vomiting, cramps, suppression of urine, and collapse. [L, bilious diarrhea.]

chol•er•ic (kŏl′ə-rĭk, kə-lĕr′ĭk) *adj.* Bad-tempered; irritable.

cho•les•ter•ol (kə-lĕs′tə-rôl′, -rōl′) *n.* A glistening white soapy crystalline substance, $C_{27}H_{45}OH$, occurring notably in bile, gallstones, the brain, blood cells, plasma, egg yolk, and seeds. [< Gk kholē, bile + stereos, hard, solid.]

choose (chōōz) *v.* **chose, chosen, choosing.** **1.** To decide upon and pick out; select. **2.** To prefer; desire: *choose to go.* [< OE cēosan. See geus-.] —**choos′er** *n.*

choos•y (chōō′zē) *adj.* **-ier, -iest.** Also **choos•ey.** Fastidious in choosing; particular. —**choos′i• ness** *n.*

chop (chŏp) *v.* **chopped, chopping. 1.** To cut by striking with a heavy, sharp tool. **2.** To cut into bits; mince. **3.** To hit with a short downward stroke. —*n.* **1.** A swift, short blow or stroke. **2.** A small cut of meat, usually from the rib, shoulder, or loin and containing a bone. **3.** A short, irregular motion of waves. [ME *choppen.*] —**chop′per** *n.*

Cho•pin (shō′păn′), **Frédéric.** 1810–1849. Polish composer.

chop•py (chŏp′ē) *adj.* **-pier, -piest.** Shifting abruptly, as waves. —**chop′pi•ness** *n.*

chops (chŏps) *pl.n.* The jaws, cheeks, or jowls. [?]

chop•stick (chŏp′stĭk′) *n.* One of a pair of slender sticks used as eating implements in China and Japan. [< Pidgin English *chop.*]

chop su•ey (chŏp sōō′ē). A Chinese-American dish made with small pieces of meat, bean sprouts, and other vegetables, served with rice. [Cant *tsap sui.*]

cho•ral (kôr′əl, kōr′-) *adj.* Of or for a chorus or choir. —**cho′ral•ly** *adv.*

cho•rale (kə-răl′, -räl′) *n.* Also **cho•ral. 1.** A hymn, esp. one harmonized for four voices. **2.** A chorus or choir. [G *Choral(gesang),* "choral (song)."]

chord¹ (kôrd, kōrd) *n.* A combination of three or more usually concordant tones sounded simultaneously. [< ME *cord,* agreement, harmony, short for ACCORD.]

chord² (kôrd, kōrd) *n.* **1.** A line segment that joins two points on a curve. **2.** A string or cord, esp. a cordlike anatomical structure. [< CORD.]

chore (chôr, chōr) *n.* A task, esp. a routine or troublesome one. [< OE *cierr,* piece of work < Gmc *karzi.*]

cho•re•a (kô-rē′ə, kō-) *n.* A nervous disorder, esp. of children, marked by uncontrollable movements of the arms, legs, and face; St. Vitus' dance. [< Gk *khoreia,* choral dance.]

cho•re•og•ra•phy (kôr′ē-ŏg′rə-fē, kōr′-) *n.* Also **cho•reg•ra•phy** (kə-rĕg′rə-fē). The creation or arrangement of ballets or dances. [< Gk *khoros,* dance + -GRAPHY.] —**cho′re•o•graph′** (kôr′-ē-ə-grăf′, -gräf′, kōr′-) *v.* —**cho′-re•og′ra•pher** *n.* —**cho′re•o•graph′ic** *adj.*

cho•rine (kôr′ēn′, kōr′-) *n. Slang.* A chorus girl; a show girl.

chor•is•ter (kôr′ĭs-tər, kŏr′-, kōr′-) *n.* A singer in a choir.

cho•roid (kôr′oid′, kōr′-) *n.* Also **cho•roi•de•a** (kô-roi′dē-ə, kō-). The dark-brown vascular coat of the eye between the sclera and the retina.

chor•tle (chôrt′l) *v.* **-tled, -tling.** To chuckle loudly and throatily. [Blend of CHUCKLE and SNORT, coined by Lewis Carroll.] —**chor′tle** *n.*

cho•rus (kôr′əs, kōr′-) *n., pl.* **-ruses. 1.** A group of singers who perform together. **2.** Music for such a group. **3.** A group of dancers in a musical comedy, revue, etc. **4.** A group speaking or reciting together. **5.** The simultaneous utterance of several voices. **6.** A repeated refrain or melodic section of a song. —*v.* **-rused** or **-russed, -rusing** or **-russing.** To sing or utter in chorus. [< Gk *khoros,* dance, chorus.]

chose (chōz). *p.t.* of **choose.**

cho•sen (chō′zən). *p.p.* of **choose.** —*adj.* Selected from or preferred above others. —*n., pl.* **chosen. 1.** One of the elect. **2.** The elect collectively.

chow¹ (chou) *n.* A dog with a long, dense reddish-brown or black coat. [Perh < Pidgin English < Cant *kao.*]

chow² (chou) *n. Slang.* Food; victuals. [Pidgin English.]

chow•der (chou′dər) *n.* A thick seafood soup, often in a milk base. [F *chaudière,* stew pot.]

chow mein (chou′ mān′). A Chinese-American dish of stewed vegetables and meat served over fried noodles. [< Mand *ch'ao³ mien⁴,* "fried noodles."]

Chr. Christ; Christian.

chres•ard (krĕs′ärd) *n.* Water present in soil and available for plant absorption. [Gk *khrēsis,* use + *ardein,* to water.]

Christ (krīst) *n.* The title given to Jesus of Nazareth. [< Gk *Khristos,* "the anointed (one)."]

chris•ten (krĭs′ən) *v.* **1.** To baptize. **2.** To give a name to at baptism. **3.** To name and dedicate ceremonially: *christen a ship.* [< CHRISTIAN.] —**chris′ten•er** *n.*

Chris•ten•dom (krĭs′ən-dəm) *n.* **1.** Christians collectively. **2.** The Christian world.

chris•ten•ing (krĭs′ə-nĭng) *n.* The Christian sacrament of baptism.

Chris•tian (krĭs′chən) *adj.* **1.** Professing belief in Christianity. **2.** Pertaining to Jesus or his teachings. **3.** Pertaining to Christianity or its adherents. —*n.* One who professes belief in Christianity.

Chris•ti•an•i•ty (krĭs′chē-ăn′ə-tē) *n.* **1.** The Christian religion, founded on the teachings of

Jesus. 2. Christendom. 3. The state or fact of being a Christian.

Christian Science. A church and religious system emphasizing healing through spiritual means. Officially, Church of Christ, Scientist. —**Christian Scientist.**

Christ•mas (krĭs'məs) n. December 25, a holiday celebrated by Christians as the anniversary of the birth of Jesus.

chro•mat•ic (krō-măt'ĭk) adj. 1. Pertaining to colors or color. 2. Mus. Proceeding by half tones: a chromatic scale. [< Gk khrōma, color, modification of musical tone.] —**chro•mat'i•cal•ly** adv. —**chro•mat'i•cism'** n.

chrome (krōm) n. 1. Chromium. 2. Anything plated with a chromium alloy. [< Gk khrōma, color.]

chro•mi•um (krō'mē-əm) n. Symbol **Cr** A lustrous, hard, steel-gray metallic element used to harden steel alloys, to produce stainless steels, and in corrosion-resistant decorative platings. Atomic number 24, atomic weight 51.996. [< CHROME.]

chro•mo•some (krō'mə-sōm') n. A DNA-containing linear body of the cell nuclei of plants and animals, responsible for the determination and transmission of hereditary characteristics. [Gk khrōma, color + -SOME[2].] —**chro'mo•so'mal** (-sō'məl).

chron. chronological; chronology.

Chron. Chronicles (Old Testament).

chron•ic (krŏn'ĭk) adj. Of long duration; prolonged; lingering. [< Gk khronos, time.] —**chron'i•cal•ly** adv.

chron•i•cle (krŏn'ĭ-kəl) n. A chronological record of historical events. —v. -cled, -cling. To record in or as if in a chronicle. [< Gk (biblia) khronika, "chronological (books)."] —**chron'i•cler** (-klər) n.

chrono-. comb. form. Time. [< Gk khronos, time.]

chron•o•graph (krŏn'ə-grăf', -gräf', krō'nə-) n. An instrument that records time intervals.

chronc'. chronological; chronology.

chron•o•log•i•cal (krŏn'ə-lŏj'ĭ-kəl, krō'nə-) adj. Also **chron•o•log•ic** (-lŏj'ĭk). Arranged in order of occurrence. —**chron'o•log'i•cal•ly** adv.

chro•nol•o•gy (krə-nŏl'ə-jē) n., pl. -gies. 1. The determination of dates and sequences of events. 2. The arrangement of events in time. 3. A chronological list or table. —**chro•nol'o•gist** n.

chro•nom•e•ter (krə-nŏm'ə-tər) n. An exceptionally precise timepiece.

chrys•a•lis (krĭs'ə-lĭs) n. 1. The pupa of an insect, esp. a moth or butterfly, enclosed in a firm case or cocoon. 2. Anything still in the process of development. [< Gk khrusallis, golden pupa of a butterfly.]

chry•san•the•mum (krĭ-săn'thə-məm) n. A plant cultivated in various forms for its showy flowers. [< Gk khrusanthemon, "gold flower."]

chub•by (chŭb'ē) adj. -bier, -biest. Rounded and plump. [Prob < Scand.] —**chub'bi•ly** adv. —**chub'bi•ness** n.

chuck¹ (chŭk) v. 1. To pat or squeeze playfully, esp. under the chin. 2. To toss. 3. Infor-

mal. To throw out. —n. 1. An affectionate pat or squeeze under the chin. 2. A toss. [Perh < OF choquer, to strike, shock.]

chuck² (chŭk) n. 1. A cut of beef extending from the neck to the ribs. 2. A clamp that holds a tool, or the material being worked, in a machine such as a drill or lathe. [Var of CHOCK.]

chuck•le (chŭk'əl) v. -led, -ling. To laugh quietly. —**chuck'le** n. —**chuck'ler** n.

chuck wagon. A wagon equipped with food and cooking utensils, as in a lumber camp.

chug (chŭg) n. A brief dull, explosive sound made by or as if by a laboring engine. —v. chugged, chugging. 1. To make such sounds. 2. To move while making such sounds: a train chugging along. [Imit.]

chuk•ka (chŭk'ə) n. A short, ankle-length boot with two pairs of eyelets.

chum (chŭm) n. A close friend. —v. chummed, chumming. 1. To be a close friend. 2. To share a room. [Oxford University slang, said to be < chamber fellow, "roommate."]

chum•my (chŭm'ē) adj. -mier, -miest. Informal. Intimate; friendly. —**chum'mi•ly** adv. —**chum'mi•ness** n.

chump (chŭmp) n. A blockhead; dolt. [Prob a blend of CHUNK and LUMP or STUMP.]

Chung•king (chŏŏng'kĭng'). A city in south-central China. Pop. 2,121,000.

chunk (chŭngk) n. 1. A thick piece of something. 2. A substantial amount. [Prob a var of CHOCK.]

chunk•y (chŭng'kē) adj. -ier, -iest. Short and thick; stocky; thickset. —**chunk'i•ly** adv. —**chunk'i•ness** n.

church (chûrch) n. 1. All Christians regarded as a spiritual body. 2. A building for public worship. 3. A congregation. 4. A religious service. 5. Often **Church.** Any Christian denomination. 6. Ecclesiastical power as distinguished from the secular: the separation of church and state. [< LGk (dōma) kuriakon, the Lord's (house).]

church•go•er (chûrch'gō'ər) n. One who attends church regularly.

Church•ill (chûr'chĭl). A river in north-central Canada.

Church•ill (chûr'chĭl), Sir **Winston.** 1874–1965. British statesman.

Winston Churchill

church•man (chûrch′mən) *n.* 1. A clergyman. 2. A member of a church. **Church of Christ, Scientist.** See Christian Science.

Church of England. The episcopal and liturgical national church of England.

church•war•den (chûrch′wôrd′n) *n. Ang.& Epis.Ch.* A lay officer who handles the secular affairs of a church.

church•yard (chûrch′yärd′) *n.* A yard adjacent to a church, often used as a burial ground.

churl (chûrl) *n.* 1. A rude, boorish person. 2. A medieval English peasant. [< OE *ceorl,* man, freeman of the lowest rank < Gmc **karlaz.*] —**churl′ish** *adj.* —**churl′ish•ly** *adv.*

churn (chûrn) *n.* A vessel in which cream or milk is agitated to make butter. —*v.* 1. To stir or agitate (milk or cream) in a churn. 2. To make (butter) by churning. 3. To move or be moved with great agitation. [< OE *cyrin* < Gmc **kernjōn.*] —**churn′er** *n.*

chute (shōōt) *n.* 1. An inclined trough or passage down which things can pass. 2. *Informal.* A parachute. [< OF *cheoir,* to fall.]

chut•ney (chŭt′nē) *n.* Also **chut•nee.** A pungent relish made of fruits, spices, and herbs. [Hindi *caṭni.*]

chutz•pah (кнōōts′pə) *n. Slang.* Brazenness; gall. [Yidd.]

Chu•vash (chōō-väsh′) *n., pl.* -**vash** or -**vashes.** 1. One of a Tatar people living chiefly in east-central Soviet Russia, in Europe. 2. The Turkic language of these people.

Ci curie.

CIA Central Intelligence Agency.

ci•ca•da (sĭ-kā′də, -kä′də) *n.* A large insect with membranous wings and specialized organs producing a shrill, droning sound. [L *cicāda.*]

cic•a•trix (sĭk′ə-trĭks′, sĭ-kā′trĭks) *n., pl.* -**trices** (sĭk′ə-trī′sēz, sĭ-kā′trə-sēz′). Recently formed connective tissue on a healing wound. [< L *cicātrix.*]

Cic•e•ro (sĭs′ə-rō′), **Marcus Tullius.** 106–43 B.C. Roman statesman and orator.

–cide. *comb. form.* 1. Killer of: **insecticide.** 2. Murder or killing of: **genocide.** [< LL *caedere,* to kill.]

ci•der (sī′dər) *n.* The juice pressed from apples, used to produce vinegar or as a beverage. [< Gk *sikera,* strong drink.]

ci•gar (sĭ-gär′) *n.* Tobacco leaves rolled into a cylinder for smoking. [Span *cigarro.*]

cig•a•rette (sĭg′ə-rĕt′, sĭg′ə-rĕt′) *n.* Also **cig•a•ret.** A small roll of finely cut tobacco enclosed in paper for smoking. [< F *cigare,* cigar.]

cig•a•ril•lo (sĭg′ə-rĭl′ō) *n., pl.* -**los.** A small, narrow cigar.

cil•i•a (sĭl′ē-ə) *pl.n. Sing.* -**ium** (-ē-əm). *Biol.* Microscopic hairlike processes. [< L *cilium,* the lower eyelid.] —**cil′i•ate** (sĭl′ē-ĭt, -āt′) *adj.*

cil•i•ar•y (sĭl′ē-ĕr′ē) *adj.* 1. Of or like cilia. 2. Of or pertaining to the ciliary body.

ciliary body. The thickened part of the vascular tunic of the eye that connects the choroid with the iris.

cinch (sĭnch) *n.* 1. A strap that holds a pack or saddle in place. 2. *Slang.* Something easy to accomplish —*v.* 1. To tighten a saddle girth on. 2. *Slang.* To make certain of: *cinch a victory.* [< L *cingere,* to gird.]

cin•cho•na (sĭng-kō′nə, sĭn-chō′nə) *n.* 1. A South American tree whose bark yields quinine and other medicinal alkaloids. 2. The dried bark of such a tree. [< F. H. de Ribera, countess of *Cinchón* (1576–1639).]

Cin•cin•nat•i (sĭn′sə-năt′ē, -năt′ə). A city of SW Ohio. Pop. 453,000.

cinc•ture (sĭngk′chər) *n.* A belt; girdle. [L *cinctūra,* girdle.] —**cinc′ture** *v.* (-**tured, -turing**).

cin•der (sĭn′dər) *n.* 1. A burned substance that is not reduced to ashes, but is incapable of further combustion. 2. A partly charred substance that can burn further, but without flame. 3. cinders. Ashes. [< OE *sinder,* (iron) slag, dross. See **sendhro-.**]

cin•e•ma (sĭn′ə-mə) *n.* 1. A motion picture. 2. A motion-picture theater. 3. **the cinema. a.** Motion pictures collectively. **b.** The motion-picture industry. **c.** The art of making motion pictures. [< Gk *kinēma,* motion.] —**cin′e•mat′ic** (sĭn′ə-măt′ĭk) *adj.* —**cin′e•mat′i•cal•ly** *adv.*

cin•e•ma•tog•ra•phy (sĭn′ə-mə-tŏg′rə-fē) *n.* The technique of making motion pictures.

cin•na•bar (sĭn′ə-bär′) *n.* A heavy reddish compound, HgS, that is the principal ore of mercury. [< L *cinnābaris.*]

cin•na•mon (sĭn′ə-mən) *n.* 1. The aromatic reddish or yellowish-brown bark of a tropical Asian tree, dried and often ground for use as a spice. 2. Reddish or light yellowish brown. [< Heb *qinnāmown.*]

CIO, C.I.O. Congress of Industrial Organizations.

ci•pher (sī′fər) *n.* 1. The mathematical symbol (0) denoting absence of quantity; zero. 2. Any Arabic numeral or figure. 3. **a.** Any system of secret writing in which units of plain text are substituted according to a predetermined key. **b.** The key to such a system. **c.** A message in cipher. —*v.* To compute arithmetically. [< Ar *ṣifr.*]

cir., circ. 1. circular. 2. circumference.

cir•ca (sûr′kə) *prep.* About. Used before approximate dates or figures. [< L *circum,* round about.]

cir•cle (sûr′kəl) *n.* 1. A plane curve everywhere equidistant from a given fixed point, the center. 2. A planar region bounded by such a curve. 3. Anything shaped like a circle. 4. A group of people sharing an interest, activity, or achievement. —*v.* -**cled, -cling.** 1. To make a circle around. 2. To move in a circle or circles. [< L *circus,* ring.] —**cir′cler** *n.*

cir•clet (sûr′klĭt) *n.* A small circle, esp. a circular ornament.

cir•cuit (sûr′kĭt) *n.* 1. **a.** A closed, usually circular, curve. **b.** The region enclosed by such a curve. 2. Any closed path or route. 3. **a.** A closed path followed by an electric current. **b.** A configuration of electrically or electromagnetically connected components or devices. 4. A territory under the jurisdiction of a

judge, in which he holds periodic court sessions. [< L *circuire*, *circumire*, to go around.]
circuit breaker. An automatic switch that stops the flow of current in an overloaded electric circuit.
cir·cu·i·tous (sər-kyōō'ə-təs) *adj.* Being or taking a roundabout, lengthy course.
cir·cuit·ry (sûr'kə-trē) *n.* 1. The plan for an electric circuit. 2. Electric circuits collectively.
cir·cu·lar (sûr'kyə-lər) *adj.* 1. Pertaining to a circle. 2. a. Having the shape of a circle. b. Round. 3. Moving in or forming a circle. —*n.* A printed notice intended for mass distribution. —**cir'cu·lar'i·ty** *n.*
cir·cu·lar·ize (sûr'kyə-lə-rīz') *v.* -ized, -izing. To publicize with circulars.
circular saw. An electric saw consisting of a toothed disk rotated at high speed.
cir·cu·late (sûr'kyə-lāt') *v.* -lated, -lating. 1. To move in or flow through a circle or circuit. 2. To move around, as from person to person or place to place. 3. To move or cause to move, as air. —**cir'cu·la'tor** *n.*
cir·cu·la·tion (sûr'kyə-lā'shən) *n.* 1. Movement in a circle or circuit. 2. The movement of blood through bodily vessels as a result of the heart's pumping action. 3. a. The distribution of a periodical publication. b. The number of copies sold or distributed.
cir·cu·la·tor·y system (sûr'kyə-lə-tôr'ē, -tôr'ē). The system of structures by which blood and lymph are circulated throughout the body.
circum-. *comb. form.* Around or on all sides. [< L *circum*, around.]
circum. circumference.
cir·cum·cise (sûr'kəm-sīz') *v.* -cised, -cising. 1. To remove the prepuce of (a male). 2. To remove the clitoris of (a female). [< L *circumcidere*, "to cut around."] —**cir'cum·ci'sion** (-sĭzh'ən) *n.*
cir·cum·fer·ence (sər-kŭm'fər-əns) *n.* 1. a. The boundary line of a circle. b. Any perimeter. 2. The length of such a boundary or perimeter. [< L *circumferre*, to carry around.]
cir·cum·flex (sûr'kəm-flĕks') *n.* A mark (ˆ) used over a vowel to indicate quality of pronunciation. [L *circumflexus*, "a bending around."]
cir·cum·lo·cu·tion (sûr'kəm-lō-kyōō'shən) *n.* A roundabout expression, as in speech or writing. [< L *circumloqui*, "to speak in a roundabout way."] —**cir'cum·loc'u·to'ry** (-lŏk'yə-tôr'ē, -tôr'ē) *adj.*
cir·cum·lu·nar (sûr'kəm-lōō'nər) *adj.* Around the moon.
cir·cum·nav·i·gate (sûr'kəm-năv'ĭ-gāt') *v.* -gated, -gating. To sail completely around.
cir·cum·scribe (sûr'kəm-skrīb') *v.* -scribed, -scribing. 1. To draw a line around. 2. To confine within bounds; restrict. —**cir'cum·scrip'tion** (-skrĭp'shən) *n.*
cir·cum·so·lar (sûr'kəm-sō'lər) *adj.* Around the sun.
cir·cum·spect (sûr'kəm-spĕkt') *adj.* Heedful of consequences. [< L *circumspicere*, to look around, take heed.] —**cir'cum·spec'tion** *n.*
cir·cum·stance (sûr'kəm-stăns') *n.* 1. One of the conditions or facts attending an event and

having some bearing upon it. 2. The sum of determining factors beyond willful control. 3. Often **circumstances.** Financial status or means. 4. Formal display; ceremony: *pomp and circumstance.* —**under no circumstances.** Never. —**under** (or **in**) **the circumstances.** Given these conditions. [< L *circumstāre*, to stand around.]
cir·cum·stan·tial (sûr'kəm-stăn'shəl) *adj.* 1. Of or dependent upon circumstances. 2. Of no primary significance; incidental. 3. Complete and full of detail.
cir·cum·stan·ti·ate (sûr'kəm-stăn'shē-āt') *v.* -ated, -ating. To give detailed proof or description of. —**cir'cum·stan'ti·a'tion** *n.*
cir·cum·vent (sûr'kəm-vĕnt') *v.* To entrap or overcome by craft. [L *circumvenīre*, to come around.] —**cir'cum·ven'tion** *n.*
cir·cus (sûr'kəs) *n.* 1. A traveling show of acrobats, clowns, trained animals, etc., often performing under a tent. 2. *Informal.* Any humorous or rowdy occurrence. [L *circus*, ring, CIRCLE.]
cirque (sûrk) *n.* A steep hollow, often containing a small lake, at the upper end of a mountain valley. [< L *circus*, ring, CIRCLE.]
cir·rho·sis (sĭ-rō'sĭs) *n.* A chronic disease of the liver that ultimately results in liver failure and death. [< NL, "orange-colored disease."] —**cir·rhot'ic** (sĭ-rŏt'ĭk) *adj.*
cir·ro·cu·mu·lus (sĭr'ō-kyōōm'yə-ləs) *n.* A high-altitude cloud composed of a series of small, regularly arranged cloudlets in the form of ripples or grains.
cir·ro·stra·tus (sĭr'ō-strā'təs, -străt'əs) *n.* A high-altitude, thin hazy cloud, usually covering the sky and often producing a halo effect.
cir·rus (sĭr'əs) *n., pl.* **cirri** (sĭr'ī'). A high-altitude cloud composed of narrow bands or patches of thin, generally white, fleecy parts. [< L *cirrus*, curl, filament, tuft.]
cis·tern (sĭs'tərn) *n.* A receptacle for holding water, esp. rainwater. [< L *cisterna*, water tank.] —**cis·ter'nal** *adj.*
cit. 1. citation; cited. 2. citizen.
cit·a·del (sĭt'ə-dəl, -dĕl') *n.* 1. A fortress in a commanding position in or near a city. 2. Any stronghold. [< L *civitās*, CITY.]
cite (sīt) *v.* **cited, citing.** 1. To quote as an authority or example. 2. To mention as support, illustration, or proof. 3. To commend for meritorious action, esp. in military service. 4. To summon before a court of law. [< L *citāre*, freq of *ciēre*, to set in motion, summon.] —**ci·ta'tion** *n.*
cit·i·fy (sĭt'ĭ-fī') *v.* -fied, -fying. 1. To make urban. 2. To mark with the styles and manners of the city. —**cit'i·fi·ca'tion** *n.* —**cit'i·fied'** *adj.*
cit·i·zen (sĭt'ə-zən) *n.* 1. A person owing loyalty to and entitled by birth or naturalization to the protection of a given state. 2. An inhabitant of a city or town. [< OF *cite*, city.]
cit·i·zen·ry (sĭt'ə-zən-rē) *n., pl.* -ries. Citizens collectively.
cit·i·zen·ship (sĭt'ə-zən-shĭp') *n.* The status of a citizen with its attendant duties, rights, and privileges.

ă pat/ā ate/âr care/ä bar/b bib/ch chew/d deed/ĕ pet/ē be/f fit/g gag/h hat/hw what/ ĭ pit/ī pie/îr pier/j judge/k kick/l lid, fatal/m mum/n no, sudden/ng sing/ŏ pot/ō go/

cit•rate (sĭt'rāt') *n.* A salt or ester of citric acid.

cit•ric acid (sĭt'rĭk). A colorless acid, $C_6H_8O_7 \cdot H_2O$, occurring in lemon, lime, and pineapple juices.

cit•ron (sĭt'rən) *n.* **1.** The aromatic, thick-skinned, lemonlike fruit of an Asiatic tree. **2.** A melon with a thick, hard rind. **3.** The preserved rind of either of these fruits, used in cooking. [< L *citrus,* citron tree.]

cit•ron•el•la (sĭt'rə-nĕl'ə) *n.* A light-yellow, aromatic oil obtained from a tropical grass and used in insect repellents and perfumery. [< F *citron,* citron.]

cit•rus (sĭt'rəs) *adj.* Also **cit•rous.** Of or pertaining to related trees or fruit such as the orange, lemon, lime, and grapefruit. —*n., pl.* **-ruses.** A citrus tree. [< L, citron tree, citrus tree.]

cit•y (sĭt'ē) *n., pl.* **-ies. 1.** A town of significant size. **2.** An incorporated municipality with definite boundaries and legal powers set forth in a state charter. **3.** The inhabitants of a city as a group. —*adj.* Of or in a city. [< L *cīvitās,* citizenry, state, (later) city.]

city hall. 1. The building housing the offices of a municipal government. **2.** The municipal government itself.

cit•y-state (sĭt'ē-stāt') *n.* A sovereign state consisting of a city and its surrounding territory.

civ. civil; civilian.

civ•et (sĭv'ĭt) *n.* **1.** Also **civet cat.** A catlike African mammal that secretes a musky fluid. **2.** This fluid, used in making perfumes. [< Ar *zabād.*]

civ•ic (sĭv'ĭk) *adj.* Of a city, citizens, or citizenship. —*n.* **civics** *(takes sing. v.).* The study of civic affairs, esp. the rights and duties of citizenship. [< L *cīvis,* citizen.]

civ•ies. Variant of **civvies.**

civ•il (sĭv'əl) *adj.* **1.** Of a citizen or citizens. **2.** Of ordinary community life, as distinct from the military or ecclesiastical. **3.** Civilized. **4.** Polite. [< L *cīvis,* citizen.] —**civ'il•ly** *adv.* —**civ'il•ness** *n.*

civil engineer. An engineer trained in the design and construction of public works.

ci•vil•ian (sə-vĭl'yən) *n.* A person in civil life, as distinguished from one in the armed forces.

ci•vil•i•ty (sə-vĭl'ə-tē) *n., pl.* **-ties. 1.** Politeness. **2.** A courteous act or utterance.

civ•i•li•za•tion (sĭv'ə-lə-zā'shən) *n.* **1.** Any human society having an advanced stage of development in the arts and sciences and social, political, and cultural complexity. **2.** The type of culture developed by a particular people or epoch.

civ•i•lize (sĭv'ə-līz') *v.* **-lized, -lizing.** To bring out of a primitive or savage state. —**civ'i•liz'a•ble** *adj.* —**civ'i•liz'er** *n.*

civ•i•lized (sĭv'ə-līzd') *adj.* **1.** Having a highly developed society. **2.** Of a people or nation so developed. **3.** Cultured; refined.

civil law. The body of law dealing with the rights of private citizens.

civil liberty. Legal guarantees of an individual's right to free speech, thought, and action.

civil rights. Rights belonging to a person by virtue of his status as a citizen or as a member of civil society.

civil service. All branches of public service that are not legislative, judicial, or military.

civil war. 1. A war between factions or regions of one country. **2. Civil War.** The war between the Union and the Confederacy (1861–65); War Between the States.

civ•vies (sĭv'ēz) *pl.n.* Also **civ•ies.** *Slang.* Civilian clothes.

ck. 1. cask. **2.** check. **3.** cook.

cl centiliter.

Cl chlorine.

cl. 1. class; classification. **2.** clause. **3.** clearance. **4.** clerk.

c.l. 1. carload. **2.** *Sports.* center line. **3.** common law.

clab•ber (klăb'ər) *n.* Sour, curdled milk. —*v.* To curdle. [< *clabair,* thick sour milk.]

clack (klăk) *v.* **1.** To make or cause to make an abrupt, dry sound, as by the collision of hard surfaces. **2.** To chatter. —*n.* A clacking sound. [< ON *klaka.*] —**clack'er** *n.*

clad (klăd). Alternate *p.t.* & *p.p.* of **clothe.**

claim (klām) *v.* **1.** To demand as one's due. **2.** To state to be true. **3.** To call for; require. —*n.* **1.** A demand for something as one's rightful due. **2.** Title or right. **3.** Something claimed. **4.** A statement of something as a fact. [< L *clāmāre,* to call.]

claim•ant (klā'mənt) *n.* A person making a claim.

clair•voy•ance (klâr-voi'əns) *n.* The supposed power to perceive things that are out of the natural range of human senses. [F, "clear-seeing."] —**clair•voy'ant** *n. & adj.*

clam (klăm) *n.* Any of various bivalve mollusks, many of which are edible. —*v.* **clammed, clamming.** To hunt for clams. —**clam up.** To refuse to talk. [Short for *clamshell,* "bivalve that shuts tight like a clamp."]

clam•bake (klăm'bāk') *n.* A picnic where clams and other foods are baked.

clam•ber (klăm'ər, klăm'bər) *v.* To climb with difficulty. [< ON *klembra,* orig "to grip."]

clam•my (klăm'ē) *adj.* **-mier, -miest.** Disagreeably moist and cold. [< OE *clǣman,* to stick, smear.] —**clam'mi•ly** *adv.* —**clam'mi•ness** *n.*

clam•or (klăm'ər). Also *chiefly Brit.* **clam•our.** *n.* **1.** A loud outcry; hubbub. **2.** A vehement expression of protest. —*v.* To make a clamor. [< L *clāmāre,* to cry out.] —**clam'or•ous** *adj.*

clamp (klămp) *n.* A device used to join, grip, support, or compress mechanical parts. —*v.* To fasten or support with or as if with a clamp. [< MDu *clampe.*] —**clamp'er** *n.*

clan (klăn) *n.* **1.** A number of families, as in the Scottish Highlands, claiming a common ancestor. **2.** Any group of numerous relatives or associates. [< Scot Gael *clann,* children, family.] —**clan'nish** *adj.* —**clan'nish•ly** *adv.* —**clans'man** (klănz'mən) *n.*

clan•des•tine (klăn-dĕs'tən) *adj.* Concealed; secret. [< L *clandestīnus.*]

clang (klăng) *v.* To make or cause to make a loud, metallic sound. —*n.* A clanging sound. [L *clangere,* to sound.]

clan•gor (klăng′ər, klăng′gər) n. Also *chiefly Brit.* **clan•gour.** A clang or repeated clanging.

clank (klăngk) n. A metallic sound, sharp but not as resonant as a clang. —v. To make this sound. [Imit.]

clap (klăp) v. **clapped, clapping. 1.** To strike (the palms of the hands) together, as in applauding. **2.** To come together with a sharp noise. **3.** To tap with the open hand, as in greeting. **4.** To put or send suddenly: *clap in jail.* —n. **1.** The act or sound of clapping the hands. **2.** A loud or explosive noise. **3.** A slap. [< OE *clappian,* to throb, beat.]

clap•board (klăb′ərd, klăp′bôrd′, -bôrd′) n. A board with one edge thicker than the other, overlapped to cover the outer walls of frame houses.

clap•per (klăp′ər) n. A person or thing that claps, esp., the tongue of a bell.

clap•trap (klăp′trăp′) n. Pretentious, insincere, or empty language.

claque (klăk) n. A group of persons hired to applaud at a performance. [< F *claquer,* to clap.]

clar•et (klăr′ət) n. A dry red table wine. [< ML *(vīnum) clārātum,* "clarified (wine)."]

clar•i•fy (klăr′ə-fī′) v. **-fied, -fying.** To make or become clear. —**clar′i•fi•ca′tion** n.

clar•i•net (klăr′ə-nĕt′) n. A woodwind instrument having a straight, cylindrical tube with a flaring bell and a single-reed mouthpiece, played by means of finger holes and keys. [< L *clārus,* CLEAR.] —**clar′i•net′ist** n.

clar•i•on (klăr′ē-ən) adj. Shrill and clear. [< L *clārus,* CLEAR.]

clar•i•ty (klăr′ə-tē) n. Clearness; lucidity.

clash (klăsh) v. **1.** To collide or strike together with a loud, harsh noise. **2.** To conflict; disagree. —n. **1.** A loud metallic noise. **2.** A conflict. [Imit.]

clasp (klăsp, kläsp) n. **1.** A fastening, such as a hook, used to hold two objects or parts together. **2. a.** An embrace. **b.** A grip of the hand. —v. **1.** To fasten with or as if with a clasp. **2.** To hold in a tight grasp. [< ME *claspen,* to grip, grasp.] —**clasp′er** n.

class (klăs, kläs) n. **1.** A group whose members have at least one attribute in common; kind; sort. **2.** Any division by quality or grade. **3.** A social stratum whose members share similar characteristics. **4. a.** A group of students graduated in the same year. **b.** A group of students meeting to study the same subject. **5.** *Slang.* High style in manner or dress. —v. To classify. [< L *classis,* one of the six divisions of the Roman people, army, fleet.]

class action. A lawsuit in which the plaintiff or plaintiffs bring suit both on their own behalf and on behalf of many others who have the same claim against the defendant.

clas•sic (klăs′ĭk) adj. **1.** Of the highest rank. **2.** Serving as a model of its kind. **3.** Pertaining to ancient Greek or Roman literature or art. **4.** In accordance with established principles and methods. —n. **1.** An artist, author, or work of the highest rank. **2. classics.** The literature of ancient Greece and Rome.

clas•si•cal (klăs′ĭ-kəl) adj. **1.** Often **Classical.**
Of, pertaining to, or in accordance with the precedents of ancient Greek and Roman art and literature. **2.** Pertaining to or versed in studies of antiquity. **3.** *Mus.* **a.** Pertaining to or designating the European music of the latter half of the 18th century. **b.** Designating any music in the educated European tradition, distinguished from popular or folk music. **4.** Standard and authoritative. [< CLASSIC.]

clas•si•cism (klăs′ə-sĭz′əm) n. **1.** Aesthetic principles based on the culture, art, and literature of ancient Greece and Rome and characterized by emphasis on form, simplicity, proportion, and restrained emotion. **2.** Classical scholarship. —**clas′si•cist** n.

clas•si•fy (klăs′ə-fī′) v. **-fied, -fying. 1.** To arrange according to class or category. **2.** To designate as secret or restricted, as a document. —**clas′si•fi•ca′tion** (-fĭ-kā′shən) n. —**clas′si•fi′er** n.

class•mate (klăs′māt′, kläs′-) n. A member of the same academic class.

class•room (klăs′rōōm′, -rŏŏm′, kläs′-) n. A room in which academic classes are conducted.

class•y (klăs′ē, kläs′ē) adj. **-ier, -iest.** *Slang.* Stylish; elegant.

clat•ter (klăt′ər) v. To make or cause to make a rattling sound. —n. **1.** A rattling sound. **2.** A loud disturbance. [< OE *clatrian.* See **gal-².**]

clause (klôz) n. **1.** A group of words containing a subject and a predicate that forms part of a compound or complex sentence. **2.** A distinct article or provision in a document. [< ML *clausa,* close of a rhetorical period.]

claus•tro•pho•bi•a (klôs′trə-fō′bē-ə) n. Pathological fear of confined spaces. [< L *claustrum,* enclosed place + -PHOBIA.] —**claus′tro•pho′bic** adj.

clav•i•chord (klăv′ĭ-kôrd′) n. An early musical keyboard instrument. [< L *clāvis,* key + CHORD.]

clav•i•cle (klăv′ĭ-kəl) n. A bone that links the sternum and the scapula. [< L *clāvis,* key.] —**cla•vic′u•lar** (klă-vĭk′yə-lər) adj.

cla•vier (klə-vîr′, klā′vē-ər, klăv′ē-ər) n. **1.** A keyboard. **2.** Any stringed keyboard instrument. [< F *clavier,* keyboard.]

claw (klô) n. **1.** A sharp, often curved nail on the toe of an animal. **2.** A pincerlike part, as of a lobster. **3.** Anything resembling a claw, as the cleft end of the head of a hammer. —v. To scratch or dig with or as if with claws. [< OE *clawu.*]

clay (klā) n. **1.** A fine-grained, firm natural material, plastic when wet, that is used in making bricks, tiles, and pottery. **2.** Moist earth; mud. [< OE *clǣg.*] —**clay′ey** (klā′ē), **clay′ish** adj.

clean (klēn) adj. **1.** Free from impurities; unsoiled. **2.** Thorough; complete. **3.** Morally pure. —adv. **1.** In a clean manner. **2.** *Informal.* Entirely. —**come clean.** *Slang.* To admit the truth. —v. To rid of dirt or other impurities. —**clean up. 1.** To rid of dirt. **2.** *Informal.* To make a large profit. [< OE *clǣne.* See **gel-².**] —**clean′ness** n.

---

clean-cut (klēn′kŭt′) *adj.* 1. Clearly defined.
2. Wholesome; neat.

clean·ly (klĕn′lē) *adj.* -lier, -liest. Habitually
neat and clean. —*adv.* (klēn′lē). In a clean
manner. —**clean′li·ness** (klĕn′lē-nĭs) *n.*

cleanse (klĕnz) *v.* cleansed, cleansing. To free
from dirt, defilement, or guilt. [< OE
clǣnsian.] —**cleans′er** *n.*

clear (klîr) *adj.* 1. Free from anything that
dims or obscures. 2. Free from impediment;
open. 3. Easily perceptible; distinct. 4. Discerning or perceiving easily: *a clear mind.*
5. Free from doubt or confusion. 6. Free from
qualification or limitation. 7. Freed from contact or connection; disengaged: *clear of danger.* 8. Freed from burden or obligation.
—*adv.* 1. Distinctly. 2. *Informal.* Entirely. —*v.*
1. To make or become clear, light, or bright.
2. To rid of impurities or blemishes. 3. To rid
of obstructions. 4. To free from a charge of
guilt. 5. To pass by, under, or over without
contact. 6. To gain as net profit or earnings.
7. To pass through a clearing-house, as a
check. 8. To free (the throat) of phlegm.
—**clear out.** *Informal.* To go away. —**clear up.**
1. To make or become understandable. 2. To
become fair, as the weather. —*n.* A clear or
open space. [< L *clārus,* bright, clear.]
—**clear′a·ble** *adj.* —**clear′er** *n.* —**clear′ly** *adv.*
—**clear′ness** *n.*

clear·ance (klîr′əns) *n.* 1. The act of clearing.
2. The amount by which a moving object
clears something. 3. Permission to proceed.

clear-cut (klîr′kŭt′) *adj.* 1. Distinctly defined.
2. Evident.

clear·ing (klîr′ĭng) *n.* A tract of land from
which trees have been removed.

clear·ing-house (klîr′ĭng-hous′) *n.* Also **clear·
ing·house.** An office where banks exchange
checks and drafts and settle accounts.

cleat (klēt) *n.* A wooden or metallic projection
used to grip, provide support, or prevent slipping. [< OE **clēat,* lump, wedge.]

cleav·age (klē′vĭj) *n.* 1. The act, process, or
result of splitting. 2. A fissure or division.

cleave¹ (klēv) *v.* cleft or cleaved or clove, cleft or
cleaved or cloven, cleaving. 1. To split or
separate. 2. To pierce or penetrate. [< OE
clēofan. See gleubh-.]

cleave² (klēv) *v.* cleaved or clove, cleaved,
cleaving. To adhere or cling (to). [< OE
cleofian.]

cleav·er (klē′vər) *n.* A heavy knife or hatchet
used by butchers.

clef (klĕf) *n.* A symbol on a musical staff,
indicating the pitch of the notes. [F, key,
musical key.]

cleft (klĕft). A *p.t.* & *p.p.* of **cleave¹.** —*adj.*
Divided; split. —*n.* A crack; crevice.

clem·a·tis (klĕm′ə-tĭs) *n.* Any of various vines
with white or purplish flowers and plumelike
seeds. [< L *clēmatis.*]

clem·en·cy (klĕm′ən-sē) *n.* 1. Mercy; leniency. 2. Mildness of weather.

Clem·ens (klĕm′ənz), **Samuel Langhorne.**
Pen name, Mark Twain. 1835–1910. American
novelist and essayist.

clem·ent (klĕm′ənt) *adj.* 1. Lenient or mer-

ciful. 2. Mild, as the weather. [< L *clēmēns,*
mild, gentle.] —**clem′ent·ly** *adv.*

clench (klĕnch) *v.* 1. To bring together (hands
or teeth) tightly. 2. To grasp or grip tightly.
3. To clinch. —*n.* 1. A tight grip or grasp.
2. Anything that clenches. [< OE *beclencan.*]

Cle·o·pat·ra (klē′ə-pătˈrə, -pāˈtrə, -päˈtrə).
69–30 B.C. Queen of Egypt.

cler·gy (klûr′jē) *n., pl.* -gies. The body of men
ordained for religious service. [< OF *clerc,*
ecclesiastic, clerk.]

cler·gy·man (klûr′jē-mən) *n.* A member of the
clergy.

cler·ic (klĕr′ĭk) *n.* A member of the clergy.

cler·i·cal (klĕr′ĭ-kəl) *adj.* 1. Of or pertaining to
clerks or office workers. 2. Of, relating to, or
characteristic of the clergy or a clergyman.

cler·i·cal·ism (klĕr′ĭ-kəl-ĭz′əm) *n.* A policy of
supporting the influence of the clergy in political or secular matters.

clerk (klûrk) *n.* 1. A person who performs such
business functions as keeping records and attending to correspondence. 2. A salesman in a
store. —*v.* To work as a clerk. [< LL *clēricus,*
a cleric.] —**clerk′ship′** *n.*

Cleve·land (klēv′lənd). A city of NE Ohio.
Pop. 751,000.

Cleve·land (klēv′lənd), **(Stephen) Grover.**
1837–1908. 22nd and 24th President of the
U.S. (1885–89; 1893–97).

Grover Cleveland

clev·er (klĕv′ər) *adj.* 1. Showing mental quickness and originality. 2. Dexterous. [Prob <
ME *cliver,* expert to seize, dexterous.] —**clev′-
er·ly** *adv.* —**clev′er·ness** *n.*

clew. Variant of **clue.**

cli·ché (klē-shā′) *n.* A trite expression or idea.
[F, "stereotyped."]

click (klĭk) *n.* A brief, sharp, nonresonant
sound. —*v.* 1. To make or cause to make one
or a series of clicks. 2. *Slang.* **a.** To become a
success. **b.** To function well together. [Imit.]
—**click′er** *n.*

cli·ent (klī′ənt) *n.* 1. One for whom professional services are rendered. 2. A customer or

patron. [< L *cliēns,* dependent, follower.]

cli•en•tele (klī'ən-tĕl') *n.* 1. The clients of a professional person. 2. A body of customers or patrons.

cliff (klĭf) *n.* A high, steep, or overhanging face of rock. [< OE *clif* < Gmc **klibam.*]

cli•mac•ter•ic (klī-măk'tər-ĭk, klī'măk-tĕr'ĭk) *n.* 1. A period or year of major physiological changes. 2. Menopause. [< Gk *klimaktēr,* rung of a ladder, crisis.]

cli•mac•tic (klī-măk'tĭk) *adj.* Pertaining to or constituting a climax.

cli•mate (klī'mĭt) *n.* 1. The prevailing weather in a particular region. 2. A region manifesting particular meteorological conditions. 3. A prevailing condition in human affairs. [< LL *clīma,* climate, zone of latitude.] —cli•mat'ic (klī-măt'ĭk), cli•mat'i•cal, cli'ma•tal (-mə-təl) *adj.* —cli•mat'i•cal•ly *adv.*

cli•max (klī'măks') *n.* 1. The point of greatest intensity in a series or progression of events or statements; culmination. 2. Orgasm. —*v.* To reach or bring to a climax. [L, rhetorical climax.]

climb (klīm) *v.* 1. To move up or ascend, esp. by using the hands and feet. 2. To rise in rank or fortune. 3. To slope upward. 4. To grow upward. —climb down. To move downward; descend. —*n.* 1. The act of climbing; ascent. 2. A place to be climbed. [< OE *climban.*] —climb'a•ble *adj.* —climb'er *n.*

clime (klīm) *n. Poetic.* Climate.

clinch (klĭnch) *v.* 1. To fasten securely, as with a nail or bolt. 2. To settle decisively. 3. To embrace so as to immobilize an opponent's arms. —*n.* 1. The act, process, or result of clinching. 2. *Slang.* An amorous embrace. [Var of CLENCH.]

clinch•er (klĭn'chər) *n.* One that clinches, esp. a decisive point, fact, or remark.

-cline. *comb. form.* Slope: syncline. [< Gk *klinein,* to lean.]

cling (klĭng) *v.* clung, clinging. To hold fast or adhere to something physically or emotionally. [< OE *clingan.*] —cling'er *n.*

clin•ic (klĭn'ĭk) *n.* 1. A medical lecture in which patients are examined and treated in the presence of students. 2. An institution associated with a hospital and dealing chiefly with outpatients. 3. A center that offers counsel or instruction. [< Gk *klinikē,* medical treatment at sickbed.]

clin•i•cal (klĭn'ĭ-kəl) *adj.* 1. Pertaining to a clinic. 2. Pertaining to direct observation and treatment of patients. 3. Analytical; highly objective. —clin'i•cal•ly *adv..*

clink[1] (klĭngk) *v.* To make or cause to make a soft, sharp, ringing sound. —*n.* Such a sound.

clink[2] (klĭngk) *n. Slang.* A prison. [< The Clink, a prison in London.]

clink•er (klĭng'kər) *n.* The incombustible, fused residue that remains after the combustion of certain coal. [< obs Du *klinckaerd,* "one that clinks."]

clip[1] (klĭp) *v.* 1. To cut off or out with shears. 2. To cut short; curtail. 3. *Informal.* To hit with a sharp blow. 4. *Slang.* To cheat or over-

charge. —*n. Informal.* A brisk pace. [< ON *klippa,* to cut short.]

clip[2] (klĭp) *n.* 1. A device for fastening; clasp. 2. A container for holding cartridges. —*v.* 1. To grip securely; fasten. 2. *Football.* To block (an opponent not carrying the ball) illegally from the rear. [< OE *clyppan.*]

clip•per (klĭp'ər) *n.* 1. Often clippers. An instrument for cutting, clipping, or shearing. 2. A sailing vessel built for great speed.

clip•ping (klĭp'ĭng) *n.* Something cut off or out, esp. an item from a newspaper.

clique (klēk, klĭk) *n.* An exclusive group of people. [F.]

clit•o•ris (klĭt'ə-rĭs, klī'tə-) *n.* A small erectile organ at the upper end of the vulva. [< Gk *kleitoris,* "small hill."] —clit'o•ral (-rəl) *adj.*

clk. clerk.

cloak (klōk) *n.* 1. A loose outer garment. 2. Anything that covers or conceals. —*v.* 1. To cover with a cloak. 2. To conceal. [ME *cloke.*]

clob•ber (klŏb'ər) *v. Slang.* To batter; defeat completely. [?]

cloche (klōsh) *n.* A close-fitting woman's hat. [F, bell.]

clock[1] (klŏk) *n.* Any instrument for measuring or indicating time. —*v.* To record the time or speed of. [< MDu *clocke,* bell, clock.]

clock[2] (klŏk) *n.* An embroidered or woven decoration on a stocking or sock.

clock•wise (klŏk'wīz') *adv.* In the same direction as the rotating hands of a clock. —clock'-wise' *adj.*

clock•work (klŏk'wûrk') *n.* The mechanism of a clock or similar mechanism.

clod (klŏd) *n.* 1. A lump, esp. of earth or clay. 2. An ignorant or stupid person. [< OE *clott,* lump, CLOT.] —clod'dish *adj.*

clod•hop•per (klŏd'hŏp'ər) *n.* 1. A clumsy, coarse person. 2. clodhoppers. Big, heavy shoes.

clog (klŏg) *n.* 1. An obstacle. 2. A weight attached to an animal's leg to hinder movement. 3. A heavy, usually wooden-soled shoe. —*v.* 1. To impede or encumber. 2. To make or become obstructed. [ME *clogge,* block of wood.] —clog'gy *adj.*

cloi•son•né (kloi'zə-nā') *n.* Enamelware in which the surface decoration is formed by different colors of enamel separated by thin strips of metal. [< F *cloisonner,* to partition.]

clois•ter (klois'tər) *n.* 1. A covered walk with an open colonnade on one side, running along the inside wall of a building. 2. A place of religious seclusion, esp. a monastery or convent. —*v.* To confine in or as if in a cloister; seclude. [< L *claustrum,* enclosed place.]

clop (klŏp) *v.* clopped, clopping. To make the sound of a horse's hoofs against pavement. —*n.* Such a sound. [Imit.]

close (klōs) *adj.* closer, closest. 1. Proximate in time, space, or relation; near. 2. Compact: *a close weave.* 3. Near a surface, as of the skin: *a close shave.* 4. Nearly equivalent or even, as a contest. 5. Fitting tightly. 6. Not deviating from an original: *a close copy.* 7. Precise. 8. Complete; thorough: *close attention.* 9. Bound by mutual interests or affections; intimate.

ă pat/ā ate/âr care/ä bar/b bib/ch chew/d deed/ĕ pet/ē be/f fit/g gag/h hat/hw what/ ĭ pit/ī pie/îr pier/j judge/k kick/l lid, fatal/m mum/n no, sudden/ng sing/ŏ pot/ō go/

10. Shut or shut in. **11.** Confined in space. **12.** Confined to specific persons; restricted. **13.** Hidden; secluded. **14.** Secretive. **15.** Miserly. **16.** Lacking fresh or circulating air. —*v.* (klōz) **closed, closing. 1.** To shut or become shut. **2.** To fill up. **3.** To end; finish. **4.** To join or unite; bring into contact. **5.** To enclose; shut in. **6.** To reach an agreement. —**close down** (or **up**). To stop or cease entirely. —**close in.** To surround and advance upon. —*n.* (klōz). A conclusion. —*adv.* (klōs). In a close manner. [< L *clausus,* pp of *claudere,* to close.] —**close′ly** (klōs′lē) *adv.* —**close′ness** (klōs′nĭs) *n.*

closed circuit. A television transmission circuit with a limited number of reception stations and no broadcasting facilities.

closed shop. A union shop.

close-fist•ed (klōs′fĭs′tĭd) *adj.* Stingy; miserly; penurious.

close-mouthed (klōs′mouthd′, -moutht′) *adj.* Not disposed to talking; reticent.

clos•et (klŏz′ĭt,. klŏ′zĭt) *n.* **1.** A small room or compartment for storage of supplies and clothes. **2.** A small private chamber. —*v.* To shut up in a private room, as for discussion. [< OF *clos,* enclosure.]

close-up (klōs′ŭp′) *n.* A picture taken at close range.

clo•sure (klō′zhər) *n.* **1.** The act of closing or condition of being closed. **2.** Something that closes. **3.** Cloture.

clot (klŏt) *n.* A thick, viscous, or coagulated mass. [< OE *clott,* lump. See gel-¹.] —**clot** *v.* **(clotted, clotting).**

cloth (klôth, klŏth) *n., pl.* **cloths** (klôths, klŏ*th*z, klôths, klŏ*th*z). **1.** Fabric formed by weaving, knitting, or pressing natural or synthetic fibers. **2.** A piece of fabric used for a specific purpose, as a tablecloth. **3.** Professional mode of dress. **4. the cloth.** The clergy. [< OE *clāth.*]

clothe (klō*th*) *v.* **clothed** or **clad, clothing. 1.** To put clothes on; dress. **2.** To cover as with clothes; invest. [< OE *clāthian* < *clāth,* CLOTH.]

clothes (klōz, klō*th*z) *pl.n.* Articles of dress; wearing apparel.

clothes•horse (klōz′hôrs′, klō*th*z′-) *n.* **1.** A frame on which clothes are hung. **2.** A person considered excessively concerned with dress.

clothes•pin (klōz′pĭn, klō*th*z′-) *n.* A clip of wood or plastic for fastening clothes to a line, as for drying.

cloth•ier (klō*th*′yər, klō′*th*ē-ər) *n.* One who makes or sells clothing or cloth.

cloth•ing (klō′*th*ĭng) *n.* Clothes collectively.

clo•ture (klō′chər) *n.* Also **clo•sure** (-zhər). A parliamentary procedure by which debate is ended and an immediate vote taken. [< OF *closure,* closure.]

cloud (kloud) *n.* **1.** A visible body of fine water droplets or ice particles in the earth's atmosphere. **2.** Any visible mass in the air, as of dust. **3.** A swarm. **4.** Anything that darkens or fills with gloom. —**under a cloud.** Under suspicion. —*v.* **1.** To cover with or as if with clouds. **2.** To become overcast. **3.** To make or become gloomy or troubled. **4.** To cast aspersions on. [< OE *clūd,* rock, hill. See gel-¹.] —**cloud′less** *adj.*

cloud•burst (kloud′bûrst′) *n.* A sudden rainstorm; downpour.

cloud seeding. The distributing of dry ice crystals or silver iodide smoke through clouds to stimulate rainfall.

cloud•y (klou′dē) *adj.* **-ier, -iest. 1.** Full of or covered with clouds. **2.** Of or like clouds. **3.** Not transparent. **4.** Obscure; vague. —**cloud′i•ly** *adv.* —**cloud′i•ness** *n.*

clout (klout) *n.* A blow, esp. with the fist. —*v.* To hit with the fist. [< OE *clūt,* patch.]

clove¹ (klōv) *n.* The dried aromatic flower bud of a tropical Asian tree, used as a spice. [ME *clowe (of gilofre),* "nail-shaped bud (of clove).")]

clove² (klōv) *n.* A separable section of a bulb, as of garlic. [< OE *clufu.* See gleubh-.]

clove³ (klōv). Alternate *p.t.* of **cleave¹** and **cleave².**

clo•ven (klō′vən). Alternate *p.p.* of **cleave¹.** —*adj.* Split; divided.

clo•ver (klō′vər) *n.* Any of various plants having compound leaves with three leaflets and tight heads of small flowers. [< OE *clǣfre* < Gmc *klaibrōn.*]

clown (kloun) *n.* **1.** A buffoon or jester who entertains in a circus or other presentation. **2.** A rude, vulgar person; boor. —*v.* To behave like a clown. [Prob < Scand.] —**clown′-ish** *adj.* —**clown′ish•ly** *adv.*

cloy (kloi) *v.* To surfeit, esp. with something too rich or sweet. [Short for obs *accloy,* to nail, hence to clog, satiate.]

C.L.U. chartered life underwriter.

club¹ (klŭb) *n.* **1.** A heavy stick suitable for use as a weapon; cudgel. **2.** A stick used in certain games, such as golf and hockey, to drive a ball. **3.** Any of a suit of playing cards marked with a black symbol shaped like a cloverleaf. —*v.* **clubbed, clubbing.** To strike or beat with or as with a club. [< ON *klubba,* club.]

club² (klŭb) *n.* **1.** A group of people organized for a common purpose. **2.** The meeting place of such a group. —*v.* **clubbed, clubbing.** To contribute or combine for a common purpose. [Prob archaic *club,* to gather into a mass.]

club•foot (klŭb′fŏŏt′) *n.* **1.** Congenital deformity of the foot, marked by a misshapen appearance. **2.** A foot so deformed. —**club′-foot′ed** *adj.*

club sandwich. A sandwich, usually of three slices of toast with various fillings.

cluck (klŭk) *v.* To utter a sound characteristic of a brooding hen. —*n.* **1.** Such a sound. **2.** A stupid or foolish person. [Imit.]

clue (klōō) *n.* Also **clew.** Anything that guides or directs in the solution of a problem or mystery. —*v.* **clued, clueing** or **cluing.** To give (someone) guiding information. [< OE *cliewen,* ball of yarn.]

clump (klŭmp) *n.* **1.** A clustered mass or thick grouping; lump. **2.** A heavy dull sound. —*v.* **1.** To walk with a heavy tread. **2.** To form clumps (of). [< MLG *klumpe.*]

clum•sy (klŭm′zē) *adj.* **-sier, -siest. 1.** Lacking physical coordination, skill, or grace; awkward; unwieldy. **2.** Gauche; inept. [< obs

---

clumse, to be numb with cold.] —**clum'si•ly** *adv.*
—**clum'si•ness** *n.*

clung (klŭng). *p.t.* & *p.p.* of **cling.**

clus•ter (klŭs'tər) *n.* Any configuration of elements occurring close together; group; bunch. —*v.* To gather, grow, or form into clusters. [< OE.]

clutch¹ (klŭch) *v.* To grasp or attempt to grasp and hold tightly. —*n.* **1.** A tight grasp or a device for grasping. **2. clutches.** Control or power. **3.** A device for engaging and disengaging two working parts of a shaft or of a shaft and a driving mechanism. [< OE *clyccan* < Gmc **klukjan.*]

clutch² (klŭch) *n.* The eggs or chicks produced or hatched at one time. [< ON *klekja,* to hatch.]

clut•ter (klŭt'ər) *n.* A confused or disordered state; litter; jumble. —*v.* To litter or pile in a disordered state. [< ME *clot,* lump, clot.]

clys•ter (klĭs'tər) *n. Rare.* An enema. [< Gk *klustēr,* "liquid for washing out."]

cm centimeter.

Cm curium.

Cmdr. commander.

cml. commercial.

C/N credit note.

co-. *comb. form.* **1.** Joint, together, or mutually. **2.** Same, similar. **3.** Complement of an angle. [< L.]

Co cobalt.

CO conscientious objector.

co. **1.** company. **2.** county.

Co. company.

c.o. **1.** care of. **2.** *Accounting.* carried over. **3.** cash order.

C.O. **1.** commanding officer. **2.** conscientious objector.

c/o care of.

coach (kōch) *n.* **1.** A closed carriage with four wheels. **2.** A bus. **3.** A railroad passenger car. **4.** One who trains athletes or athletic teams. **5.** A private tutor who prepares a student for an examination. —*v.* To teach or train; tutor. [< *Kocs,* town in Györ, Hungary, where such carriages originated.] —**coach'er** *n.*

coach•man (kōch'mən) *n.* One who drives a coach.

co•ad•ju•tor (kō'ə-jōō'tər, kō-ăj'ə-tər) *n.* A coworker; assistant, esp. to a bishop. [< L *coadjūtor.*]

co•ag•u•lant (kō-ăg'yə-lənt) *n.* An agent that causes coagulation. —**co•ag'u•lant** *adj.*

co•ag•u•late (kō-ăg'yə-lāt') *v.* **-lated, -lating.** To form a soft, semisolid, or solid mass. [< L *coāgulāre,* to curdle.] —**co•ag'u•la'tion** *n.*

coal (kōl) *n.* A natural dark-brown to black, carbon-containing solid used as a fuel. [< OE *col.* See **geulo-.**]

co•a•lesce (kō'ə-lĕs') *v.* **-lesced, -lescing.** To grow or come together; fuse; unite. [L *coalēscere,* to grow together.] —**co'a•les'cence** *n.* —**co'a•les'cent** *adj.*

co•a•li•tion (kō'ə-lĭsh'ən) *n.* An alliance or union, esp. a temporary one. [< L *coalēscere,* COALESCE.] —**co'a•li'tion•ist** *n.*

coal oil. Kerosene.

coal tar. A viscous black liquid obtained by the destructive distillation of coal, used in paints, roofing, and insulation materials.

coarse (kôrs, kōrs) *adj.* **coarser, coarsest.** **1.** Of inferior quality. **2.** Lacking in delicacy or refinement. **3.** Not fine in texture; rough. [ME *coars,* ordinary, coarse.] —**coarse'ly** *adv.* —**coarse'ness** *n.*

coars•en (kôr'sən, kōr'-) *v.* To make or become coarse. —**coars'en•er** *n.*

coast (kōst) *n.* **1.** The seashore. **2.** A slope down which one may coast, as on a sled. **3.** The act of sliding or coasting. —*v.* **1.** To slide down an inclined slope. **2.** To move without further acceleration. **3.** To sail near or along a coast. **4.** To move aimlessly. [< L *costa,* rib, side.] —**coast'al** (kōs'təl) *adj.*

coast•er (kōs'tər) *n.* **1.** One that coasts. **2.** A disk placed under a drinking glass to protect a surface beneath.

coast guard. Also **Coast Guard.** The military coastal patrol of a nation.

coast•line (kōst'līn') *n.* The shape or boundary of a coast.

coat (kōt) *n.* **1.** An outer garment covering the body from the shoulders to the waist or below. **2.** A natural outer covering, as the fur of an animal. **3.** Also **coating.** A layer of some material covering something else. —*v.* To provide or cover with a coat or layer. [< Frank **kotta.*] —**coat'ed** *adj.*

coat of arms. A shield blazoned with heraldic bearings or the insignia itself.

coat of mail *pl.* **coats of mail.** An armored coat made of chain mail.

co•au•thor (kō-ô'thər) *n.* A collaborating or joint author.

coax (kōks) *v.* To urge, persuade, or try to persuade by pleading or flattery; wheedle. [Earlier *coaks, cokes,* to fool.] —**coax'er** *n.* —**coax'ing•ly** *adv.*

co•ax•i•al (kō-ăk'sē-əl) *adj.* Having a common axis.

coaxial cable. A transmission cable consisting of a conducting outer metal tube enclosing and insulated from a central conducting core.

cob (kŏb) *n.* **1.** The central core of an ear of corn. **2.** A male swan. **3.** A stocky, short-legged horse. [ME *cobbe,* lump, round object.]

co•balt (kō'bôlt') *n. Symbol* **Co** A hard, brittle metallic element, used for magnetic alloys, high-temperature alloys, and glass and ceramic pigments. Atomic number 27, atomic weight 58.9332. [G *Kobalt, Kobold.*]

cob•ble (kŏb'əl) *v.* **-bled, -bling.** **1.** To mend (boots or shoes). **2.** To put together clumsily. [Prob < COBBLER¹.]

cob•bler¹ (kŏb'lər) *n.* One who mends boots and shoes. [ME *cobelere.*]

cob•bler² (kŏb'lər) *n.* A fruit pie having only a thick top crust.

cob•ble•stone (kŏb'əl-stōn') *n.* A naturally rounded stone, formerly used for paving streets. [Perh < ME *cobbe,* lump, COB + STONE.]

co•bra (kō'brə) *n.* A venomous Asian or African snake that expands the skin of the neck to form a flattened hood. [< Port *cobra (de capello),* "snake (with a hood)."]

cob•web (kŏb'wĕb') *n.* 1. The web spun by a spider or a strand of such a web. 2. Something resembling a cobweb in gauziness or flimsiness. [< OE *āttorcoppe,* spider + WEB.]

co•caine (kō-kān', kō'kān') *n.* Also **co•cain.** A narcotic alkaloid, $C_{17}H_{21}NO_4$, extracted from the leaves of a South American tree and used as a surface anesthetic. [Span *coca,* the tree + -INE.]

coc•cus (kŏk'əs) *n., pl.* **-ci** (-sī', kŏk'ī'). A bacterium with a spherical shape. [< Gk *kokkos,* pit.]

coc•cyx (kŏk'sĭks) *n., pl.* **coccyges** (kŏk-sī'jēz, kŏk'sə-jēz'). A small bone at the base of the spinal column. [< Gk *kokkux,* cuckoo, coccyx.] **—coc•cyg′e•al** (kŏk-sĭj'ē-əl) *adj.*

coch•i•neal (kŏch'ə-nēl', kŏch'ə-nēl') *n.* 1. A brilliant red dye. 2. Vivid red. [< L *coccinus,* scarlet.]

coch•le•a (kŏk'lē-ə) *n., pl.* **-leae** (-lē-ē'). A spiral tube of the inner ear containing nerve endings essential for hearing. [< Gk *kokhlos,* land snail.] **—coch′le•ar** *adj.*

cock¹ (kŏk) *n.* 1. A male bird, esp. the adult male of the domestic fowl. 2. A faucet or valve. 3. **a.** The hammer in a firearm. **b.** Its position when ready for firing. *—v.* 1. To set the hammer of (a firearm) in position for firing. 2. To tilt or turn up or to one side. [< LL *coccus.*]

cock² (kŏk) *n.* A cone-shaped pile of straw or hay. [ME *cok.*]

cock•ade (kŏk-ād') *n.* A rosette or knot of ribbon worn esp. on the hat as a badge. [< F *cocarde,* jauntily tilted hat.]

cock•a•ma•mie (kŏk'ə-mā'mē) *adj.* Also **cock•a•ma•my.** *Slang.* 1. Trifling; second-rate. 2. Ludicrous; nonsensical.

cock•a•too (kŏk'ə-tōō') *n.* A crested Australian parrot. [< Malay *kakatua.*]

cock•a•trice (kŏk'ə-trĭs, -trīs') *n.* A mythical serpent with the power to kill with its glance. [< LL *calcātrix,* "the tracker."]

cock•crow (kŏk'krō') *n.* The time of day when the cock crows; dawn.

cock•er•el (kŏk'ər-əl) *n.* A young rooster. [< COCK¹.]

cock•er spaniel (kŏk'ər). A dog with long, drooping ears and a silky coat. [Orig used for hunting woodcocks.]

cock•eye (kŏk'ī') *n.* A squinting eye.

cock-eyed (kŏk'īd') *adj.* 1. Cross-eyed. 2. Crooked; askew.

cock•fight (kŏk'fīt') *n.* A fight between gamecocks that are often fitted with metal spurs.

cock•horse (kŏk'hôrs') *n.* A wooden toy horse.

cock•le¹ (kŏk'əl) *n.* A bivalve mollusk with a ribbed, heart-shaped shell. [< OF *coquille,* shell.]

cock•le² (kŏk'əl) *n.* Any of several weedy plants growing in grain fields. [< L *coccus,* a kind of berry.]

cock•ney (kŏk'nē) *n., pl.* **-neys.** 1. Often **Cockney.** A native of the East End, a section of London. 2. The dialect or accent of cockneys. [ME *cokeney,* "cock's egg," pampered brat.] **—cock′ney** *adj.*

cock•pit (kŏk'pĭt') *n.* 1. A pit or enclosed space for cockfights. 2. The space in an airplane for the pilot and crew.

cock•roach (kŏk'rōch') *n.* A flat-bodied brownish insect common as a household pest. [< Span *cucaracha.*]

cocks•comb (kŏks'kōm') *n.* 1. The comb of a rooster. 2. The cap of a jester, decorated to resemble a rooster's comb. 3. Also **coxcomb.** A pretentious fop.

cock•sure (kŏk'shŏŏr') *adj.* Completely sure; overconfident. **—cock′sure′ly** *adv.*

cock•tail (kŏk'tāl') *n.* 1. A mixed alcoholic drink. 2. An appetizer, as of seafood. *—adj.* 1. Of or pertaining to cocktails. 2. Suitable for wear on semiformal occasions. [?]

cock•y (kŏk'ē) *adj.* **-ier, -iest.** *Informal.* Cheerfully self-confident; conceited.

co•co (kō'kō) *n., pl.* **-cos.** The coconut or the coconut palm. [< Port *coco,* "goblin," coconut shell.]

co•coa (kō'kō) *n.* 1. Roasted powdered cacao seeds with most of the fat removed. 2. A beverage made from this powder and milk or water. [Var of CACAO.]

co•co•nut (kō'kə-nŭt', -nət) *n.* Also **co•coa•nut.** The large, hard-shelled, edible nut of a tropical palm tree, the **coconut palm,** having a hollow center filled with milky fluid. [COCO + NUT.]

co•coon (kə-kōōn') *n.* 1. The silky or fibrous pupal case spun by the larva of a moth or other insect. 2. A similar protective covering or structure. [< Prov *coco,* eggshell, hence cocoon.]

cod (kŏd) *n., pl.* **cod** or **cods.** Also **cod•fish** (kŏd'fĭsh'). A commercially important food fish of N Atlantic waters. [ME.]

COD 1. cash on delivery. 2. collect on delivery.

co•da (kō'də) *n. Mus.* The final passage of a movement or composition. [It, "tail."]

cod•dle (kŏd'l) *v.* **-dled, -dling.** 1. To cook in water just below the boiling point. 2. To treat indulgently; baby. **—cod′dler** *n.*

code (kōd) *n.* 1. A systematically arranged and comprehensive collection of laws or rules and regulations. 2. A system of signals used in transmitting messages. 3. An arbitrary system of symbols, letters, or words used for transmitting brief or secret messages. *—v.* **coded, coding.** To systematize, arrange, or convert into a code. [< L *cōdex,* CODEX.]

co•deine (kō'dēn', kō'dē-ĭn) *n.* A narcotic alkaloid, $C_{18}H_{21}NO_3$, derived from opium or morphine. [< Gk *kōdeia,* capsule of the poppy.]

co•dex (kō'dĕks') *n., pl.* **codices** (kō'də-sēz', kŏd'ə-). A manuscript volume, esp. of a classic work or of the Scriptures. [L *cōdex,* tree trunk, board, writing tablet, book (of laws).]

codg•er (kŏj'ər) *n.* An old man. [Poss < earlier *cadger,* carrier, peddler.]

cod•i•cil (kŏd'ə-sĭl) *n.* A supplement or appendix to a will. [< L *cōdex,* CODEX.]

cod•i•fy (kŏd'ə-fī', kō'də-) *v.* **-fied, -fying.** 1. To arrange or systematize. 2. To code. **—cod′i•fi•ca′tion** *n.* **—cod′i•fi′er** *n.*

co-ed, co•ed (kō'ĕd') *n.* A female college

student. —*adj.* Co-educational. [Short for *co-educational student.*]
co•ed•u•ca•tion (kō'ĕj-ŏo-kā'shən) *n.* The education of both men and women at the same institution. —**co'-ed•u•ca'tion•al** *adj.*
co•ef•fi•cient (kō'ə-físh'ənt) *n.* **1. a.** A numerical factor of an elementary algebraic term, as 4 in the term 4x. **b.** The product of all but one of the factors of a mathematical expression. **2.** A numerical measure of a physical or chemical property that is constant for a specified system. [< CO- + EFFICIENT.]
co•en•zyme (kō-ĕn'zīm') *n.* A heat-stable organic molecule that must be loosely associated with an enzyme for the enzyme to function.
co•e•qual (kō-ē'kwəl) *adj.* Equal with one another. —*n.* An equal. —**co'e•qual'i•ty** (-kwŏl'ə-tē) *n.* —**co•e'qual•ly** *adv.*
co•erce (kō-ûrs') *v.* **-erced, -ercing. 1.** To compel to act or think in a given manner. **2.** To dominate; restrain. [< L *coercēre,* to enclose together, constrain.] —**co•erc'er** *n.* —**co•er'cion** *n.* —**co•er'cive** *adj.*
co•e•val (kō-ē'vəl) *adj.* Of the same period of time. [L *coaevus.*] —**co•e'val•ly** *adv.*
co•ex•ist (kō'ĭg-zĭst') *v.* To exist together, at the same time, or in the same place. —**co'ex•is'tence** *n.*
co•ex•tend (kō'ĭk-stĕnd') *v.* To extend through the same space or duration. —**co'ex•ten'sive** *adj.*
cof•fee (kô'fē, kŏf'ē) *n.* **1.** An aromatic brown beverage prepared from the beanlike seeds of a tropical tree. **2.** The seeds of this tree. **3.** The tree itself. [< Ar *qahwah.*]
coffee house. Also **cof•fee•house** (kô'fē-hous', kŏf'ē-). A restaurant where coffee and other refreshments are served.
cof•fee•pot (kô'fē-pŏt', kŏf'ē-) *n.* A pot for brewing or serving coffee.
coffee shop. A small restaurant in which light meals are served.
coffee table. A long, low table, often placed before a sofa.
cof•fer (kô'fər, kŏf'ər) *n.* **1.** A strongbox. **2.** **coffers.** Funds; treasury. [< L *cophinus,* basket.]
cof•fer•dam (kô'fər-dăm', kŏf'ər-) *n.* A temporary watertight enclosure built in the water and pumped dry so that construction, as of piers, can be undertaken.
cof•fin (kô'fən, kŏf'ən) *n.* A box in which a corpse is buried. [< Gk *kophinus,* basket, measure of capacity.]
C. of S. chief of staff.
cog (kŏg) *n.* **1.** A tooth on the rim of a wheel. **2.** A subordinate member of an organization. [ME *cogge.*]
cog. cognate.
co•gent (kō'jənt) *adj.* Forcibly convincing. [< L *cōgere,* to force, drive together.] —**co'gen•cy** (-jən-sē) *n.* —**co'gent•ly** *adv.*
cog•i•tate (kŏj'ə-tāt') *v.* **-tated, -tating. 1.** To meditate; ponder. **2.** To think carefully about. [L *cōgitāre.*] —**cog'i•ta'tion** *n.*
co•gnac (kōn'yăk', kŏn'-, kôn'-) *n.* A fine French brandy. [< *Cognac,* France.]
cog•nate (kŏg'nāt') *adj.* **1.** Having a common

ancestor or origin, esp. culturally or linguistically akin. **2.** Analogous in nature. —*n.* One that is cognate with another. [L *cōgnātus.*]
cog•ni•tion (kŏg-nĭsh'ən) *n.* **1.** The mental process or faculty by which knowledge is acquired. **2.** Knowledge. [< L *cognōscere* (pp *cognitus*), to get to know, learn.] —**cog'ni•tive** (kŏg'nə-tĭv) *adj.*
cog•ni•zance (kŏg'nə-zəns) *n.* Conscious knowledge or recognition; awareness. [< L *cognōscere,* to learn.] —**cog'ni•zant** *adj.*
cog•no•men (kŏg-nō'mən) *n., pl.* **-mens** or **-nomina** (-nŏm'ə-nə). **1.** A family name; surname. **2.** Any name, esp. a descriptive nickname. [L *cōgnōmen,* "additional name."]
co•hab•it (kō-hăb'ĭt) *v.* To live together in a sexual relationship when not legally married. [LL *cohabitāre.*] —**co•hab'i•ta'tion** *n.*
co•heir (kō-âr') *n.* A joint heir.
co•here (kō-hîr') *v.* **-hered, -hering. 1.** To stick or hold together. **2.** To be logically connected. [L *cohaerēre.*]
co•her•ent (kō-hîr'ənt, kō-hĕr'-) *adj.* **1.** Sticking together; cohering. **2.** Orderly or logical. —**co•her'ence, co•her'en•cy** *n.*
co•he•sion (kō-hē'zhən) *n.* **1.** The process or condition of cohering. **2.** The mutual attraction by which the elements of a body are held together. —**co•he'sive** (-sĭv) *adj.* —**co•he'sive•ly** *adv.* —**co•he'sive•ness** *n.*
co•hort (kō'hôrt') *n.* **1.** A group or band united in some struggle. **2.** A companion or associate. [< L *cohors,* enclosed yard, company of soldiers.]
coif (koif) *n.* A tight-fitting cap. [< LL *cofia.*]
coif•feur (kwä-fœr') *n. Fem.* **coif•feuse** (kwä-fœz'). A hairdresser. [F.]
coif•fure (kwä-fyŏor') *n.* A style of arranging the hair. [F.]
coil (koil) *n.* **1.** A series of connected spirals or concentric rings formed by gathering or winding. **2.** A spiral or ring. **3.** *Elec.* **a.** A wound spiral of insulated wire. **b.** Any device of which such a spiral is the major component. —*v.* To wind in coils. [< L *colligere,* to collect.] —**coil'er** *n.*
coin (koin) *n.* **1.** A piece of metal issued and authorized by a government for use as money. **2.** Metal money collectively. —*v.* **1.** To make (coins) from metal. **2.** To invent (a word or phrase). [< L *cuneus,* wedge.]
coin•age (koi'nĭj) *n.* **1.** The process of coining. **2.** Coins collectively.
co•in•cide (kō'ĭn-sīd') *v.* **-cided, -ciding. 1.** To occupy the same position simultaneously. **2.** To happen at the same time. **3.** To correspond exactly. [ML *coincidere.*]
co•in•ci•dence (kō-ĭn'sə-dəns, -dĕns') *n.* The state or fact of coinciding. —**co•in'ci•den'tal, co•in'ci•dent** *adj.* —**co•in'ci•den'tal•ly** *adv.*
co•i•tus (kō'ə-təs) *n.* Also **co•i•tion** (kō-ĭsh'ən). Sexual intercourse. [L, "meeting."]
coke¹ (kōk) *n.* The solid residue of coal after removal of volatile material, used as fuel. [ME *coke.*]
coke² (kōk) *n. Slang.* Cocaine.
Coke (kōk) *n.* A trademark for Coca-Cola, a soft drink.

ă pat/ā ate/âr care/ä bar/b bib/ch chew/d deed/ĕ pet/ē be/f fit/g gag/h hat/hw what/
ĭ pit/ī pie/îr pier/j judge/k kick/l lid, fatal/m mum/n no, sudden/ng sing/ŏ pot/ō go/

col. 1. collect. 2. college; collegiate. 3. colony. 4. column.

Col. 1. colonel. 2. Colorado (unofficial). 3. Colossians (New Testament).

co•la¹ (kō′lə) *n.* 1. A carbonated drink made with an extract from the nuts of a tropical tree. 2. Also **ko•la.** A tree bearing such nuts.

co•la². Alternate *pl.* of colon.

col•an•der (kŭl′ən-dər, kŏl′-) *n.* A perforated bowl-shaped kitchen utensil used for draining. [< L *cōlāre,* to strain.]

cold (kōld) *adj.* 1. Having a low temperature. 2. Uncomfortably chilled. 3. Unconscious; insensible: *knocked cold.* 4. Not affected by emotion; objective. 5. Sexually frigid. —*n.* 1. Relative lack of warmth. 2. A chilly sensation. 3. A viral infection of the mucous membranes of the respiratory passages. [< OE *ceald.* See **gel-³.**] —**cold′ly** *adv.* —**cold′ness** *n.*

cold-blood•ed (kōld′blŭd′ĭd) *adj.* 1. Ruthless; heartless. 2. Having a body temperature that varies with the environment, as a fish or reptile. —**cold′-blood′ed•ness** *n.*

cold cream. An emulsion for cleansing and softening the skin.

cold cuts. Slices of assorted cold meats.

cold feet. *Slang.* Failure of nerve.

cold front. The leading portion of a cold atmospheric air mass moving against, and eventually replacing, a warm air mass.

cold sore. A small sore on the lips that often accompanies a fever or cold.

Cole•ridge (kōl′rĭj), **Samuel Taylor.** 1772–1834. English poet and critic.

cole•slaw (kōl′slô′) *n.* Also **cole slaw.** A salad of shredded raw cabbage. [Du *koolsla.*]

co•le•us (kō′lē-əs) *n., pl.* **-uses.** A plant cultivated for its showy, varicolored leaves. [< Gk *koleos, koleon,* sheath.]

col•ic (kŏl′ĭk) *n.* Acute paroxysmal pain in the abdomen. [< Gk *kōlikos,* suffering in the colon.] —**col′ick•y** *adj.*

col•i•se•um (kŏl′ə-sē′əm) *n.* A large public amphitheater. [< the *Colosseum* at Rome.]

co•li•tis (kō-lī′tĭs) *n.* Inflammation of the mucous membrane of the colon.

coll. college; collegiate.

col•lab•o•rate (kə-lăb′ə-rāt′) *v.* **-rated, -rating.** 1. To work together, esp. in a joint intellectual effort. 2. To cooperate treasonably. [< LL *collabōrāre.*] —**col•lab′o•ra′tion** *n.* —**col•lab′o•ra′tive** *adj.* —**col•lab′o•ra′tor** *n.*

col•lage (kō-läzh′) *n.* An artistic composition of materials and objects pasted on a surface. [< F *coller,* to glue, paste.]

col•lapse (kə-lăps′) *v.* **-lapsed, -lapsing.** 1. To fall down or inward suddenly; cave in. 2. To cease to function; break down suddenly. 3. To fold compactly. [< L *collāpsus,* pp of *collābī,* to fall together.] —**col•lapse′** *n.* —**col•laps′i•ble** *adj.*

col•lar (kŏl′ər) *n.* 1. The part of a garment that encircles the neck. 2. An encircling bandlike part or structure suggestive of a collar. 3. A ringlike device used to limit, guide, or secure a part. —*v.* To seize or detain. [< L *collāre,* necklace, collar.]

col•lar•bone (kŏl′ər-bōn′) *n.* The clavicle.

col•lard (kŏl′ərd) *n.* Often **collards.** A leafy, cabbagelike vegetable.

col•late (kə-lāt′, kŏl′āt′, kō′lāt′) *v.* **-lated, -lating.** 1. To examine and compare (texts) carefully. 2. To assemble in proper numerical sequence. [L *collātus.*] —**col•la′tor** *n.*

col•lat•er•al (kə-lăt′ər-əl) *adj.* 1. Situated or running side by side. 2. Serving to corroborate. 3. Of a secondary nature. 4. Of, designating, or guaranteed by property acceptable as security for a loan or other obligation. 5. Having an ancestor in common but descended from a different line. —*n.* A collateral security. [< ML *collaterālis.*]

col•la•tion (kə-lā′shən, kŏ-, kō-) *n.* 1. The act or process of collating. 2. A light meal.

col•league (kŏl′ēg′) *n.* A fellow member; associate, esp. in a profession. [< L *collēga,* one chosen to serve with another.]

col•lect (kə-lĕkt′) *v.* 1. To bring together in a group; assemble; accumulate. 2. To call for and obtain payment of: *collect taxes.* —*adj.* With payment to be made by the receiver. —*adv.* So that the receiver is charged. [< L *colligere,* to gather together.] —**col•lec′tion** *n.* —**col•lec′tor** *n.*

col•lect•ed (kə-lĕk′tĭd) *adj.* Self-possessed; composed. —**col•lect′ed•ly** *adv.*

col•lect•i•bles (kə-lĕk′tə-bəlz) *pl.n.* Objects that are collected because they are novel, rare, or bizarre.

col•lec•tive (kə-lĕk′tĭv) *adj.* 1. Formed by collecting. 2. Of, pertaining to, or made by a number of individuals acting as a group: *a collective decision.* —*n.* A collective enterprise or those working in it. —**col•lec′tive•ly** *adv.*

col•lec•tiv•ism (kə-lĕk′tə-vĭz′əm) *n.* The principle or system of collective ownership and control of the means of production and distribution.

col•lege (kŏl′ĭj) *n.* 1. A school of higher learning that grants a bachelor's degree. 2. Any of the undergraduate divisions or schools of a university. 3. A technical or professional school, often affiliated with a university. 4. A body of persons having a common purpose or common duties. [< L *collēga,* COLLEAGUE.] —**col•le′giate** (kə-lē′jĭt, -jē-ĭt) *adj.*

col•le•gian (kə-lē′jən, -jē-ən) *n.* A college student.

col•lide (kə-līd′) *v.* **-lided, -liding.** 1. To come together with violent, direct impact. 2. To meet in opposition. [L *collīdere.*] —**col•li′sion** (kə-lĭzh′ən) *n.*

col•lie (kŏl′ē) *n.* A large, long-haired dog originally used to herd sheep. [Scot.]

col•lier (kŏl′yər) *n. Brit.* 1. A coal miner. 2. A coal ship.

col•lier•y (kŏl′yər-ē) *n., pl.* **-ies.** *Brit.* A coal mine.

col•lin•e•ar (kō-lĭn′ē-ər, kə-) *adj.* 1. Lying on the same line. 2. Containing a common line.

col•lo•di•on (kə-lō′dē-ən) *n.* Also **col•lo•di•um** (-dē-əm). A highly flammable colorless or yellowish syrupy solution, used to hold surgical dressings and for making photographic plates. [< Gk *kolla,* glue.]

col•loid (kŏl′oid′, kō′loid′) *n.* 1. A suspension

of finely divided particles that do not settle out of, and cannot be readily filtered from, the uniform medium in which they are suspended. **2.** The particulate matter so suspended. —*adj.* Also **col•loi•dal** (kə-loid'l, kō-). Of, relating to, or having the nature of a colloid. [< Gk *kolla*, glue.]

col•lo•qui•al (kə-lō'kwē-əl) *adj.* Characteristic of or appropriate to conversation but not formal writing. [< COLLOQUY.] —**col•lo'qui•al•ism'** *n.* —**col•lo'qui•al•ly** *adv.*

col•lo•qui•um (kə-lō'kwē-əm) *n., pl.* **-ums** or **-quia** (-kwē-ə). A seminar, usually led by a different lecturer at each meeting.

col•lo•quy (kŏl'ə-kwē) *n., pl.* **-quies.** A conversation, esp. a formal one. [< L *colloquium*, conversation.]

col•lu•sion (kə-lōō'zhən) *n.* A secret agreement for a deceitful or fraudulent purpose. [< L *collūdere*, to play together.] —**col•lu'sive** *adj.*

Colo. Colorado.

co•logne (kə-lōn') *n.* A liquid made of alcohol and fragrant oils. [F *eau de cologne*, "water of COLOGNE."]

Co•logne (kə-lōn'). A city of west-central West Germany. Pop. 848,000.

Co•lom•bi•a (kə-lŭm'bē-ə). A republic of NW South America. Pop. 17,432,000. Cap. Bogotá. —**Co•lom'bi•an** *adj. & n.*

Colombia

Co•lom•bo (kə-lŭm'bō). The capital of Sri Lanka. Pop. 561,000.

co•lon¹ (kō'lən) *n.* A punctuation mark (:) used to introduce a quotation, explanation, example, etc. [L *colon*, unit of verses.]

co•lon² (kō'lən) *n., pl.* **-lons** or **-la** (-lə). The section of the large intestine from the cecum to the rectum. [< Gk *kolon*, large intestine.] —**co•lon'ic** (kə-lŏn'ĭk) *adj.*

co•lon³ (kō-lōn') *n., pl.* **-lons** (-lōnz'). **1.** The basic monetary unit of Costa Rica. **2.** The basic monetary unit of El Salvador. [Span *colón.*]

colo•nel (kûr'nəl) *n.* An officer, as in the army, ranking immediately above a lieutenant colonel. [< OIt *colonnello*, "commander of a column."] —**colo'nel•cy, colo'nel•ship'** *n.*

co•lo•ni•al (kə-lō'nē-əl) *adj.* **1.** Of or pertaining to a colony or colonies. **2.** Often **Colonial.**

a. Of or relating to the 13 British colonies that became the original United States of America. **b.** Of or relating to the colonial period in the U.S. —*n.* An inhabitant of a colony.

co•lo•ni•al•ism (kə-lō'nē-ə-lĭz'əm) *n.* A policy by which a nation maintains or extends its control over foreign dependencies. —**co•lo'ni•al•ist** *n. & adj.*

col•o•nist (kŏl'ə-nĭst) *n.* **1.** An original settler of a colony. **2.** An inhabitant of a colony.

col•o•nize (kŏl'ə-nīz') *v.* **-nized, -nizing. 1.** To establish a colony in. **2.** To settle in a colony. —**col'o•ni•za'tion** (kŏl'ə-nə-zā'shən) *n.* —**col'o•niz'er** *n.*

col•on•nade (kŏl'ə-nād') *n. Archit.* A series of regularly spaced columns. [< L *columna*, column.] —**col'on•nad'ed** *adj.*

col•o•ny (kŏl'ə-nē) *n., pl.* **-nies. 1.** A group of emigrants settled in a distant land but subject to a parent country. **2.** A territory thus settled. **3.** Any region politically controlled by another country. **4. Colony.** Any of the 13 British colonies that became the original United States of America. **5.** A group with the same interests, concentrated in a particular area. **6.** A group of the same kind of animals or plants living or growing together. [< L *colōnia*, farm, settlement.]

col•or (kŭl'ər). Also *chiefly Brit.* **col•our.** *n.* **1.** That aspect of things that is caused by differing qualities of the light reflected or emitted by them. **2.** A dye, paint, etc., that imparts color. **3.** Skin tone. **4. colors.** A flag or banner, as of a country or military unit. **5.** Outward, often deceptive, appearance. **6.** Vividness or picturesqueness. —**with flying colors.** With great success. —*v.* **1.** To impart color to; change the color of. **2.** To give a distinctive character to; influence. **3.** To misrepresent. **4.** To blush. [< L.]

Col•o•ra•do (kŏl'ə-rä'dō, -răd'ə). A state of the W U.S. Pop. 2,207,000. Cap. Denver. —**Col'o•ra'dan** *adj. & n.*

Colorado River. A river of the W U.S.

col•or•a•tion (kŭl'ə-rä'shən) *n.* Arrangement of colors.

col•or•a•tu•ra (kŭl'ər-ə-t/y/ŏor'ə) *n.* **1.** Florid ornamentation in vocal music. **2.** A singer specializing in this.

col•or•blind (kŭl'ər-blīnd') *adj.* Unable to distinguish certain colors. —**col'or•blind'ness** *n.*

col•ored (kŭl'ərd) *adj.* **1.** Having color. **2.** Often **Colored.** Designating a dark-skinned people, esp. Negroes. **3.** Distorted or biased.

col•or•fast (kŭl'ər-făst', -fäst') *adj.* Having color that will not run or fade, as fabrics. —**col'or•fast'ness** *n.*

col•or•ful (kŭl'ər-fəl) *adj.* **1.** Abounding in colors. **2.** Vivid. —**col'or•ful•ly** *adv.*

col•or•less (kŭl'ər-lĭs) *adj.* **1.** Without color. **2.** Weak in color; pallid. **3.** Lacking vividness. —**col'or•less•ly** *adv.* —**col'or•less•ness** *n.*

co•los•sal (kə-lŏs'əl) *adj.* Enormous; gigantic. [< L *colossus*, COLOSSUS.] —**co•los'sal•ly** *adv.*

co•los•sus (kə-lŏs'əs) *n., pl.* **-lossi** (-lŏs'ī') or **-suses.** Anything of enormous size or importance. [L.]

col•our. *Chiefly Brit.* Variant of **color.**

ă pat/ā ate/âr care/ä bar/b bib/ch chew/d deed/ě pet/ē be/f fit/g gag/h hat/hw what/
ĭ pit/ī pie/îr pier/j judge/k kick/l lid, fatal/m mum/n no, sudden/ng sing/ŏ pot/ō go/

colt (kōlt) *n.* A young male horse, zebra, etc. [< OE, young ass or camel.]

Co·lum·bi·a (kə-lŭm'bē-ə). 1. The capital of South Carolina. Pop. 114,000. 2. A river of the NW U.S.

col·um·bine (kŏl'əm-bīn') *n.* Any of several plants with variously colored, conspicuously spurred flowers.

co·lum·bi·um (kə-lŭm'bē-əm) *n. Symbol* Cb Niobium. —co·lum'bic *adj.*

Co·lum·bus (kə-lŭm'bəs). 1. The capital of Ohio. Pop. 540,000. 2. A city of W Georgia. Pop. 154,000.

Co·lum·bus (kə-lŭm'bəs), Christopher. 1451–1506. Italian navigator.

col·umn (kŏl'əm) *n.* 1. A supporting pillar consisting of a base, shaft, and capital. 2. Anything resembling a column. 3. One of two or more vertical sections of printed lines on a page. 4. A feature article that appears regularly in a periodical. 5. A long row, as of troops. [< L *columna.*] —co·lum'nar (kə-lŭm'-nər), col'umned *adj.*

col·um·nist (kŏl'əm-nĭst, -ə-mĭst) *n.* A writer of a newspaper column.

com–. *comb. form.* Together; jointly. [< L *cum,* with.]

com. 1. comma. 2. commerce; commercial. 3. commissioner. 4. committee. 5. common.

co·ma (kō'mə) *n., pl.* -mas. A deep, prolonged unconsciousness. [< Gk *kōma,* deep sleep, lethargy.]

Co·man·che (kə-măn'chē) *n., pl.* -che or -ches. 1. A member of a tribe of Uto-Aztecan-speaking North American Indians, formerly ranging over the W plains. 2. The language of this tribe. —Co·man'che *adj.*

co·ma·tose (kō'mə-tōs', kŏm'ə-) *adj.* 1. Unconscious. 2. Lethargic; torpid.

comb (kōm) *n.* 1. A thin, toothed strip of plastic or other material, used to arrange the hair. 2. Something resembling a comb, as a card for processing wool. 3. A fleshy crest on the crown of the head of domestic fowl and other birds. 4. A honeycomb. —*v.* 1. To arrange with or as if with a comb. 2. To card (wool or other fiber). 3. To search thoroughly. [< OE *camb.* See gembh–.]

comb. 1. combination. 2. combining.

com·bat (kəm-băt', kŏm'băt') *v.* 1. To fight against; contend. 2. To oppose vigorously. —*n.* (kŏm'băt'). Fighting, esp. armed battle. [< VL *combattere,* to fight with.] —com·bat'ive *adj.*

com·bat·ant (kəm-băt'ənt, kŏm'bə-tənt) *n.* One taking part in armed combat.

combat fatigue. A nervous disorder involving anxiety, depression, and irritability, induced by combat.

comb·er (kō'mər) *n.* A long, cresting wave of the sea.

com·bi·na·tion (kŏm'bə-nă'shən) *n.* 1. The act of combining or state of being combined. 2. Something resulting from combining; an aggregate. 3. A sequence of numbers or letters used to open certain locks.

com·bine (kəm-bīn') *v.* -bined, -bining. 1. To make or become united; merge; blend. 2. To form a chemical compound. —*n.* (kŏm'bīn'). 1. A machine that harvests and threshes grain. 2. A group of persons united for commercial or political advantage. [< LL *combināre.*] —com·bin'er *n.*

combining form. *Gram.* A word element that combines with other word forms to create compounds.

com·bo (kŏm'bō) *n., pl.* -bos. *Informal.* A small band, usually of jazz musicians. [Short for COMBINATION.]

com·bus·ti·ble (kəm-bŭs'tə-bəl) *adj.* Capable of burning. —*n.* A combustible substance. [< L *combūrere,* to burn up.] —com·bus'ti·bil'i·ty *n.* —com·bus'ti·bly *adv.*

com·bus·tion (kəm-bŭs'chən) *n.* 1. A burning. 2. A chemical change, esp. oxidation, accompanied by the production of heat and light. —com·bus'tive *adj.*

comd. commanding.

comdg. commanding.

Comdr. commander.

Comdt. commandant.

come (kŭm) *v.* came, coming. 1. To advance; approach. 2. To arrive. 3. To reach a particular result, state, or position. 4. To move into view. 5. To exist at a particular point or place: *The letter* T *comes before* U. 6. To happen: *How did you come to know that?* 7. To issue from; originate. 8. To be obtainable: *It comes in two sizes.* —come about. To occur. —come across. To meet by chance. —come around (or round). 1. To recover. 2. To change opinion. —come between. To cause estrangement. —come by. To acquire. —come down with. To become ill. —come off. 1. To become detached. 2. To occur. —come out. 1. To be disclosed. 2. To make a formal social debut. —come through. To succeed. —come to. To recover consciousness. —come up with. *Informal.* To propose; produce. —how come? *Informal.* Why? —*interj.* Expressive of anger or impatience: *Come now, that's enough.* [< OE *cuman.* See gwā-.]

come·back (kŭm'băk') *n.* 1. A return to a former position or status. 2. A retort; repartee.

co·me·di·an (kə-mē'dē-ən) *n.* 1. A professional entertainer who performs various comic acts. 2. An actor in comedy. —co·me'di·enne' (-mē'dē-ĕn') *fem.n.*

com·e·do (kŏm'ə-dō') *n., pl.* -dos or comedones (kŏm'ə-dō'nēz). A blackhead. [< L *comedere,* to eat up.]

come·down (kŭm'doun') *n.* A decline in status.

com·e·dy (kŏm'ə-dē) *n., pl.* -dies. 1. a. A play, motion picture, etc., that is humorous in its treatment of theme and character. b. A comic element in such a work. 2. A comic occurrence or situation in life. [< Gk *kōmōidia.*] —co·me'dic (kə-mē'dĭk) *adj.*

come·ly (kŭm'lē) *adj.* -lier, -liest. Having a pleasing appearance; attractive; handsome; graceful. [< OE *cўmlic,* lovely, splendid.] —come'li·ness *n.*

co·mes·ti·ble (kə-mĕs'tə-bəl) *adj.* Edible. —*n.* Anything edible. [< L *comedere,* to eat up.]

com•et (kŏm'ĭt) *n.* A celestial body having a solid head surrounded by a nebulous luminescent cloud and an elongated curved vapor tail arising when the head approaches the sun. [< Gk *(astēr) komētēs,* "long-haired (star)."]

comet
Comet Alcock, photographed
September 1, 1959

come•up•pance (kŭm'ŭp'əns) *n. Informal.* Punishment that one deserves.

com•fort (kŭm'fərt) *v.* To soothe in time of grief or fear; console. —*n.* **1.** A state of ease or well-being. **2.** Consolation; solace. **3.** One that brings ease. **4.** Capacity to give physical ease: *the comfort of his favorite chair.* [< LL *confortāre,* to strengthen.]

com•fort•a•ble (kŭm'fər-tə-bəl, kŭmf'tər-bəl) *adj.* **1.** Providing comfort. **2.** Being in a state of comfort. **3.** *Informal.* Adequate: *comfortable earnings.* —**com'fort•a•ble•ness** *n.* —**com'fort•a•bly** *adv.*

com•fort•er (kŭm'fər-tər) *n.* **1.** One that comforts. **2.** A quilt.

com•ic (kŏm'ĭk) *adj.* Also **com•i•cal.** **1.** Of or pertaining to comedy. **2.** Amusing; humorous. —*n.* **1.** One who is comical. **2. comics.** *Informal.* Comic strips. [< Gk *kōmos,* revel, merrymaking.] —**com'i•cal•ly** *adv.*

comic strip. A narrative series of cartoons, as in Sunday newspapers.

com•ing (kŭm'ĭng) *adj.* **1.** Approaching next. **2.** Showing promise of success.

Com•in•tern (kŏm'ĭn-tûrn) *n.* The Third International, esp. its Moscow executive committee. [Communist International.]

comm. 1. commission; commissioner. **2.** commonwealth.

com•ma (kŏm'ə) *n.* A punctuation mark (,) used to indicate a separation of ideas or elements within the structure of a sentence. [< Gk *komma,* a cut, section, clause.]

com•mand (kə-mănd', -mänd') *v.* **1.** To give orders (to). **2.** To exercise authority (over); rule. **3.** To dominate by location; overlook. —*n.* **1. a.** The act of giving orders. **b.** An order so given. **2.** The authority to command. **3.** Ability to control; mastery. **4.** A unit or post under the command of one officer. [< VL **commandāre.*]

com•man•dant (kŏm'ən-dănt', -dänt') *n.* A commanding officer.

com•man•deer (kŏm'ən-dîr') *v.* To seize arbitrarily, esp. for public use.

com•mand•er (kə-măn'dər, kə-män'-) *n.* **1.** One who commands. **2.** An officer in the navy who ranks next above a lieutenant commander.

commander in chief *pl.* **commanders in chief.** The supreme commander of all the armed forces of a nation.

com•mand•ing (kə-măn'dĭng, kə-män'-) *adj.* **1.** In command. **2.** Impressive. **3.** Dominating. —**com•mand'ing•ly** *adv.*

commanding officer. An officer in charge of a military unit.

com•mand•ment (kə-mănd'mənt, kə-mänd'-) *n.* **1.** A command; edict. **2.** Often **Commandment.** Any of the Ten Commandments.

com•man•do (kə-măn'dō, kə-män'-) *n., pl.* **-dos** or **-does.** A member of a small military unit trained to make quick raids.

com•mem•o•rate (kə-mĕm'ə-rāt') *v.* **-rated, -rating. 1.** To honor the memory of. **2.** To serve as a memorial to. [L *commemorāre,* to call to mind clearly.] —**com•mem'o•ra'tion** *n.* —**com•mem'o•ra•tive** (-ər-ə-tĭv) *adj.*

com•mence (kə-mĕns') *v.* **-menced, -mencing.** To begin; start. [< VL **cominitiāre.*]

com•mence•ment (kə-mĕns'mənt) *n.* **1.** A beginning; start. **2.** A graduation ceremony, as in a college.

com•mend (kə-mĕnd') *v.* **1.** To represent as worthy; recommend. **2.** To praise. **3.** To commit to the care of another. [< L *commendāre,* to commit to one's charge, commend.] —**com•mend'a•ble** *adj.* —**com•mend'a•bly** *adv.* —**com'men•da'tion** (kŏm'ən-dā'shən) *n.*

com•men•su•ra•ble (kə-mĕn'sər-ə-bəl, -shər-ə-bəl) *adj.* Able to be measured by a common standard. [< LL *commēnsūrābilis.*]

com•men•su•rate (kə-mĕn'sə-rĭt, -shə-rĭt) *adj.* **1.** Of the same size, extent, or duration. **2.** Corresponding in scale; proportionate. **3.** Commensurable. [LL *commēnsūrātus.*]

com•ment (kŏm'ĕnt') *n.* **1.** An expression of criticism, analysis, or observation. **2.** A statement of opinion. —*v.* To make a comment or comments (on). [< L *commentum,* contrivance, interpretation.]

com•men•tar•y (kŏm'ən-tĕr'ē) *n., pl.* **-ies.** A series of explanations or interpretations.

com•men•ta•tor (kŏm'ən-tā'tər) *n.* A radio or television reporter.

com•merce (kŏm′ərs) *n.* **1.** The buying and selling of goods; trade. **2.** Social intercourse. [< L *commercium.*]
com•mer•cial (kə-mûr′shəl) *adj.* **1.** Of, pertaining to, or engaged in commerce. **2.** Having profit as a major aim. —*n.* An advertisement on radio or television.
com•mer•cial•ism (kə-mûr′shə-lĭz′əm) *n.* Commercial practices, aims, and attitudes.
com•mer•cial•ize (kə-mûr′shə-līz′) *v.* **-ized, -izing.** To make commercial, esp. for financial gain. —**com•mer′cial•i•za′tion** *n.*
com•min•gle (kə-mĭng′gəl) *v.* **-gled, -gling.** To mix.
com•mis•er•ate (kə-mĭz′ə-rāt′) *v.* **-ated, -ating.** To feel or express sorrow or pity; sympathize. [L *commiserāri.*] —**com•mis′er•a′tion** *n.*
com•mis•sar (kŏm′ə-sär′) *n.* A Communist Party official in charge of political indoctrination and enforcement of party loyalty. [Russ *komissar.*]
com•mis•sar•i•at (kŏm′ə-sâr′ē-ĭt) *n.* An army department in charge of food and supplies.
com•mis•sar•y (kŏm′ə-sĕr′ē, -sâr′ē) *n., pl.* **-ies.** A store where food or equipment is sold, esp. one on a military post. [< ML *commissārius,* commissioner, agent.]
com•mis•sion (kə-mĭsh′ən) *n.* **1. a.** Authorization to carry out a task. **b.** The authority so granted. **c.** The task so entrusted. **d.** A document conferring such authorization. **2.** A group authorized to perform certain duties or functions. **3.** A committing; perpetration: *commission of a crime.* **4.** An allowance to a salesman or agent for his services. **5.** A document conferring the rank of a military officer. —*v.* **1.** To grant a commission to. **2.** To place an order for. [< L *committere,* COMMIT.]
commissioned officer. Any officer who holds a commission and ranks above an enlisted man or warrant officer.
com•mis•sion•er (kə-mĭsh′ən-ər) *n.* **1.** A member of a commission. **2.** A departmental official in charge of a public service.
com•mit (kə-mĭt′) *v.* **-mitted, -mitting.** **1.** To do, perform, or perpetrate: *commit a murder.* **2.** To consign; entrust. **3.** To place in confinement or custody. **4.** To pledge (oneself) to a position on some issue. [< L *committere,* to join, connect, entrust.] —**com•mit′ment** *n.*
com•mit•tee (kə-mĭt′ē) *n.* A group officially delegated to perform a function, as reporting or acting on a matter. [ME *committe,* trustee.] —**com•mit′tee•man** *n.*
com•mode (kə-mōd′) *n.* **1.** A low cabinet or chest of drawers. **2.** A movable cupboard containing a washbowl. **3.** A toilet. [F, "convenient."]
com•mo•di•ous (kə-mō′dē-əs) *adj.* Spacious; roomy. [< L *commodus,* convenient.]
com•mod•i•ty (kə-mŏd′ə-tē) *n., pl.* **-ties.** Anything useful, esp. a transportable agricultural or mining product. [< L *commoditās,* advantage, convenience.]
com•mo•dore (kŏm′ə-dôr′, -dōr′) *n.* **1.** A naval officer ranking below a rear admiral. **2. a.** The senior captain of a naval squadron or merchant fleet. **b.** The presiding officer of a

yacht club. [< Du *komandeur,* commander.]
com•mon (kŏm′ən) *adj.* **1.** Belonging equally to all; joint. **2.** Pertaining to the whole community; public: *the common good.* **3.** Widespread; prevalent; general. **4.** Usual; ordinary. **5.** Most widely known; occurring most frequently. **6.** Without special characteristics; average; standard. **7.** Unrefined; coarse. —*n.* **1.** A tract of land belonging to a whole community. **2. Commons.** The lower house of Parliament in Great Britain and Canada. —**in common.** Equally; jointly. [< L *commūnis.*] —**com′mon•ly** *adv.* —**com′mon•ness** *n.*
Common Celtic. The vocabulary of the reconstructed ancestor of the Celtic languages that is attested in the major Celtic subdivisions.
common denominator. A quantity into which all the denominators of a set of fractions can be evenly divided.
com•mon•er (kŏm′ə-nər) *n.* A person without noble rank.
common fraction. A fraction having an integer as a numerator and an integer as a denominator.
Common Germanic. The vocabulary of the prehistoric ancestor of the Germanic languages that is attested in all its major subdivisions.
common law. Any unwritten, generally applied system of law based on court decisions, usages, and customs. —**com′mon-law′** *adj.*
common logarithm. A logarithm to the base 10.
common market. 1. Any customs union. **2. Common Market.** An economic union established in 1958, originally including Belgium, France, Italy, Luxembourg, the Netherlands, and West Germany.
com•mon•place (kŏm′ən-plās′) *adj.* Ordinary; common. —*n.* Something ordinary or common, esp. a trite or obvious remark.
Common Romance. The vocabulary of the reconstructed ancestor of the Romance languages that is attested in all the major Romance subdivisions and that developed from Vulgar Latin in the first century A.D.
common sense. Native good judgment.
com•mon•weal (kŏm′ən-wēl′) *n.* **1.** The public good. **2.** *Archaic.* A commonwealth.
com•mon•wealth (kŏm′ən-wĕlth′) *n.* **1.** The people of a nation or state. **2.** A nation or state governed by the people; republic. **3.** A union or federation of self-governing states. [ME *commun welthe,* "public welfare."]
Commonwealth of Nations. Formerly **British Commonwealth of Nations.** The political community constituted by the former British Empire.
com•mo•tion (kə-mō′shən) *n.* Violent or turbulent motion; agitation. [< L *commovēre,* to move violently.]
com•mu•nal (kə-myōōn′əl, kŏm′yə-nəl) *adj.* **1.** Of or pertaining to a commune or community. **2.** Public. —**com′mu•nal′i•ty** *n.* —**com•mu′nal•ly** *adv.*
com•mune¹ (kə-myōōn′) *v.* **-muned, -muning.** To converse intimately. —*n.* (kŏm′yōōn′). In-

timate conversation. [< OF *comun, commun,* common.]

com•mune² (kŏm'yŏŏn') *n.* 1. The smallest local political division of various European countries. 2. A place used for group living. 3. The group of people engaged in such living. [< L *commūnis,* public, COMMON.]

com•mu•ni•ca•ble (kə-myōō'nĭ-kə-bəl) *adj.* 1. Able to be communicated or transmitted. 2. Talkative. —**com•mu'ni•ca•bil'i•ty, com•mu'ni•ca•ble•ness** *n.* —**com•mu'ni•ca•bly** *adv.*

com•mu•ni•cant (kə-myōō'nĭ-kənt) *n.* 1. One who receives Communion. 2. One who communicates.

com•mu•ni•cate (kə-myōō'nə-kāt') *v.* -cated, -cating. 1. To make known; impart. 2. To transmit, as a disease. 3. To receive Communion. [L . *commūnicāre,* "to make common."] —**com•mu'ni•ca'tor** *n.*

com•mu•ni•ca•tion (kə-myōō'nə-kā'shən) *n.* 1. The act of communicating; transmission. 2. The exchange of thoughts, messages, etc. 3. Something communicated. 4. **communications.** A means of communicating.

communications satellite. An artificial satellite used to aid communications, as by reflecting or relaying a radio signal.

com•mu•ni•ca•tive (kə-myōō'nə-kā'tĭv, -nĭ-kə-tĭv) *adj.* 1. Talkative. 2. Pertaining to communication. —**com•mu'ni•ca'tive•ness** *n.*

com•mun•ion (kə-myōōn'yən) *n.* 1. A sharing, as of thoughts or feelings. 2. a. A religious or spiritual fellowship. b. A Christian denomination. 3. **Communion.** a. The Eucharist. b. The consecrated elements of the Eucharist. [< L *commūniō,* participation by all.]

com•mu•ni•qué (kə-myōō'nə-kā', kə-myōō'-nə-kā') *n.* An official communication. [< L *commūnicāre,* COMMUNICATE.]

com•mu•nism (kŏm'yə-nĭz'əm) *n.* 1. A system characterized by the absence of social classes and by common ownership of production means. 2. **Communism.** a. The theory of revolutionary struggle toward this system. b. Socialism as exemplified in countries ruled by Communist parties. [< OF *commun,* common.] —**com'mu•nist** *n.* & *adj.* —**com'mu•nis'tic** *adj.* —**com'mu•nis'ti•cal•ly** *adv.*

com•mu•ni•ty (kə-myōō'nə-tē) *n., pl.* -ties. 1. a. A group of people living in the same locality and under the same government. b. The locality in which they live. 2. A social group or class. 3. Similarity: *a community of interests.* 4. Society as a whole. [< L *commūnis,* COMMON.]

com•mu•ta•tion (kŏm'yə-tā'shən) *n.* 1. A substitution, exchange, or interchange. 2. The travel of a commuter. 3. *Law.* A reduction of a penalty to a less severe one. [< L *commutāre,* COMMUTE.]

com•mu•ta•tive (kŏm'yə-tā'tĭv, kə-myōō'-tə-tĭv) *adj.* 1. Pertaining to, involving, or characterized by substitution, interchange, or exchange. 2. Logically or mathematically independent of order.

com•mu•ta•tor (kŏm'yə-tā'tər) *n.* A device connected to the coils of an electric motor or generator to provide a unidirectional current

from the generator or a reversal of current into the coils of the motor.

com•mute (kə-myōōt') *v.* -muted, -muting. 1. To substitute; interchange. 2. To change (a penalty or payment) to a less severe one. 3. To travel as a commuter. —*n. Informal.* The distance traveled by a commuter. [<L *commutāre,* to exchange.]

com•mut•er (kə-myōō'tər) *n.* One who travels regularly between his home in one community and his work in another.

comp. 1. comparative. 2. compilation. 3. complete. 4. composition; compositor.

com•pact¹ (kəm-păkt', kŏm-, kŏm'păkt') *adj.* 1. Closely and firmly united or packed. 2. Expressed briefly. —*v.* (kəm-păkt'). To press, join, or pack firmly together. —*n.* (kŏm'păkt'). 1. A small cosmetic case. 2. A relatively small automobile. [< L *compactus,* pp of *compingere,* to join together.] —**com•pact'ly** *adv.* —**com•pact'ness** *n.*

com•pact² (kŏm'păkt') *n.* An agreement or covenant. [< L *compactus,* pp of *compaciscī,* to agree together.]

com•pac•ter (kəm-păk'tər, kŏm'păk'-) *n.* An apparatus that compresses refuse into relatively small packs for handy disposal.

com•pan•ion (kəm-păn'yən) *n.* 1. A comrade; associate. 2. A person employed to live or travel with another. 3. One of a pair or set of things. [< VL **compāniō,* "one who eats bread with another."] —**com•pan'ion•ship'** *n.*

com•pan•ion•a•ble (kəm-păn'yə-nə-bəl) *adj.* Sociable; friendly. —**com•pan'ion•a•bly** *adv.*

com•pa•ny (kŭm'pə-nē) *n., pl.* -nies. 1. A group of people. 2. People assembled for a social purpose. 3. A guest or guests. 4. Companionship; fellowship. 5. A business enterprise; firm. 6. A troupe of dramatic or musical performers: *a repertory company.* 7. A subdivision of a regiment or battalion. [< VL **compāniō,* COMPANION.]

compar. comparative.

com•pa•ra•ble (kŏm'pər-ə-bəl) *adj.* 1. Able to be compared. 2. Worthy of comparison. —**com'pa•ra•bly** *adv.*

com•par•a•tive (kəm-păr'ə-tĭv) *adj.* 1. Pertaining to or involving comparison. 2. Relative. 3. Designating a degree of comparison of adjectives and adverbs higher than positive and lower than superlative. —*n.* The comparative degree or an adjective or adverb expressing the comparative degree. —**com•par'a•tive•ly** *adv.*

com•pare (kəm-pâr') *v.* -pared, -paring. 1. To represent as similar, equal, or analogous (with *to*). 2. To examine in order to note the similarities or differences of (with *with*). 3. To form the positive, comparative, or superlative degree of (an adjective or adverb). —*n.* —**beyond** (or **without**) **compare.** Without comparison; unequaled. [< L *comparāre,* to pair, match.] —**com•par'er** *n.*

com•par•i•son (kəm-păr'ə-sən) *n.* 1. The act of comparing. 2. Similarity. 3. The modification or inflection of an adjective or adverb to denote the positive, comparative, or superlative degree.

com•part•ment (kəm-pärt'mənt) *n.* One of the

ă pat/ā ate/âr care/ä bar/b bib/ch chew/d deed/ĕ pet/ē be/f fit/g gag/h hat/hw what/
ĭ pit/ī pie/îr pier/j judge/k kick/l lid, fatal/m mum/n no, sudden/ng sing/ŏ pot/ō go/

parts or spaces into which an area is subdivided.
com·part·men·tal·ize (kŏm'pärt-mĕn'təl-iz', kəm-pärt'-) v. **-ized, -izing.** To divide into compartments.
com·pass (kŭm'pəs, kŏm'-) n. **1.** A device used to determine geographical direction, esp. a magnetic needle horizontally mounted and free to pivot until aligned with the magnetic field of the earth. **2.** Often **compasses.** A V-shaped device for drawing circles or circular arcs. **3.** An enclosing line or boundary. **4.** An enclosed space or area. **5.** A range or scope; extent. —v. **1.** To make a circuit of; circle. **2.** To surround. **3.** To accomplish. **4.** To scheme; plot. [< VL *compassāre, "to measure off by steps."]

compass
Compass card

com·pas·sion (kəm-păsh'ən) n. A deep feeling of sharing the suffering of another; mercy. [< LL compatī (pp compassus), to sympathize with.] —**com·pas'sion·ate** adj.
com·pat·i·ble (kəm-păt'ə-bəl) adj. **1.** Capable of living or performing in harmonious combination with others. **2.** Capable of orderly, efficient integration and operation with other elements in a system. [< LL compatī, to sympathize with.] —**com·pat'i·bil'i·ty, com·pat'-i·ble·ness** n. —**com·pat'i·bly** adv.
com·pa·tri·ot (kəm-pā'trē-ət, -ŏt') n. A fellow countryman.
com·peer (kəm-pîr', kŏm'pîr') n. **1.** A peer; equal. **2.** A comrade.
com·pel (kəm-pĕl') v. **-pelled, -pelling. 1.** To force; constrain. **2.** To obtain by force. [< L compellere, "to drive (cattle) together," force.]
com·pen·di·um (kəm-pĕn'dē-əm) n., pl. **-ums** or **-dia** (-dē-ə). A short, complete summary. [L, "that which is weighed together," gain.]
com·pen·sate (kŏm'pən-sāt') v. **-sated, -sating. 1.** To make up for or offset. **2.** To recompense or reimburse. [L compensāre, to weigh one thing against another, counterbalance.] —**com·pen·sa'tion** n. —**com·pen'sa·to'ry** (kəm-pĕn'sə-tôr'ē, -tōr'ē) adj.
com·pete (kəm-pēt') v. **-peted, -peting.** To con-

tend with another; vie. [L competere, "to strive together."]
com·pe·tence (kŏm'pə-təns) n. Also **com·pe·ten·cy** (-tən-sē). **1.** The state or quality of being competent. **2.** Sufficient means for a comfortable existence.
com·pe·tent (kŏm'pə-tənt) adj. **1.** Properly qualified; capable. **2.** Adequate for a purpose. [< L competere, to be competent, COMPETE.] —**com'pe·tent·ly** adv.
com·pe·ti·tion (kŏm'pə-tĭsh'ən) n. **1.** A vying with others for profit, prize, or position. **2.** A contest of skill. —**com·pet'i·tive** (kəm-pĕt'ə-tĭv) adj. —**com·pet'i·tive·ness** n.
com·pet·i·tor (kəm-pĕt'ə-tər) n. One who competes, as in sports or business; rival.
com·pile (kəm-pīl') v. **-piled, -piling. 1.** To gather into one book or corpus. **2.** To compose from materials gathered from several sources. [< L compīlāre; "to heap together," plunder.] —**com'pi·la'tion** (kŏm'pə-lā'shən) n. —**com·pil'er** n.
com·pla·cen·cy (kəm-plā'sən-sē) n. Also **com·pla·cence** (-səns). **1.** A feeling of contentment. **2.** Smugness. [< L complacēre, to please.] —**com·pla'cent** adj. —**com·pla'cent·ly** adv.
com·plain (kəm-plān') v. **1.** To express feelings of pain, dissatisfaction, or resentment. **2.** To make a formal accusation or bring a formal charge. [< OF complaindre.] —**com·plain'er** n.
com·plain·ant (kəm-plā'nənt) n. One who makes a complaint, as in a court of law; plaintiff.
com·plaint (kəm-plānt') n. **1.** An expression of pain, dissatisfaction, or resentment. **2.** A reason for complaining; grievance. **3.** A cause of physical pain. **4.** Law. A formal accusation or charge.
com·plai·sance (kəm-plā'səns, -zəns) n. Willing compliance.
com·plai·sant (kəm-plā'sənt, -zənt, kŏm'-plā-zănt') adj. Cheerfully obliging. [< L complacēre, to please.] —**com·plai'sant·ly** adv.
com·ple·ment (kŏm'plə-mənt) n. **1.** Something that completes, perfects, or makes up a whole. **2.** The quantity or number needed to make up a whole. **3.** Full quantity, allowance, or amount. **4.** An angle related to another so that the sum of their measures is 90°. **5.** A word or words used after a verb to complete a predicate. —v. (kŏm'plə-mĕnt'). To add or serve as a complement to. [< L complēre, to COMPLETE.] —**com'ple·men'ta·ry** (-mĕn'tə-rē, -mĕn'trē) adj.
com·plete (kəm-plēt') adj. **1.** Having all necessary or normal parts. **2.** Concluded; ended. **3.** Thorough; perfect. —v. **-pleted, -pleting. 1.** To make whole. **2.** To finish; end. [< L complēre, to fill up.] —**com·plete'ly** adv. —**com·ple'tion** (-plē'shən) n.
com·plex (kəm-plĕks', kŏm'plĕks') adj. **1.** Consisting of interconnected parts. **2.** Intricate; complicated. —n. (kŏm'plĕks'). **1.** A whole composed of interconnected parts. **2.** A connected group of repressed ideas that compel characteristic or habitual patterns of thought, feeling, and action. [L complexus, pp

---

ô paw, for/oi boy/ou out/ŏŏ took/ōō coo/p pop/r run/s sauce/sh shy/t to/th thin/*th* the/
ŭ cut/ûr fur/v van/w wag/y yes/z size/zh vision/ə ago, item, edible, gallop, circus/

of *complectere*, to entwine.] —com•plex'i•ty *n*.
com•plex•ion (kəm-plĕk'shən) *n*. 1. The natural hue, texture, and appearance of the skin. 2. General character or appearance. [< ML *complexiō*, "combination of corporeal humors."] —com•plex'ion•al *adj*.
complex number. A number of the form *a* + *bi*, where *a* and *b* are real numbers and *i*² = −1.
com•pli•ance (kəm-plī'əns) *n*. Also **com•pli•an•cy** (-ən-sē). 1. A yielding to a wish or demand. 2. A disposition to yield to others. —com•pli'ant *adj*. —com•pli'ant•ly *adv*.
com•pli•cate (kŏm'plĭ-kāt') *v*. -cated, -cating. To make or become complex, intricate, or perplexing. [L *complicāre*, to fold together.] —com'pli•ca'tion *n*.
com•plic•i•ty (kəm-plĭs'ə-tē) *n*. The state of being an accomplice, as in wrongdoing.
com•pli•ment (kŏm'plə-mənt) *n*. 1. An expression of praise or admiration. 2. A formal act of civility, courtesy, or respect. —*v*. To pay a compliment to. [< L *complēre*, to fill up.]
com•pli•men•ta•ry (kŏm'plə-mĕn'tər-ē, -trē) *adj*. 1. Expressing a compliment. 2. Given free as a courtesy.
com•ply (kəm-plī') *v*. -plied, -plying. To agree; acquiesce, as to a command. [< L *complēre*, to fill up.]
com•po•nent (kəm-pō'nənt) *n*. A relatively simple part of a complex entity; element; constituent. [< L *compōnere*, to place together.] —com•po'nent *adj*.
com•port (kəm-pôrt') *v*. 1. To conduct oneself in a particular manner. 2. To agree; harmonize. [< L *comportāre*, to bring together, support.]
com•port•ment (kəm-pôrt'mənt) *n*. Bearing; deportment.
com•pose (kəm-pōz') *v*. -posed, -posing. 1. To make up the constituent parts of. See Usage note at comprise. 2. To make by putting together parts or elements. 3. To create, as a piece of music. 4. To make calm or tranquil. 5. To arrange or set (type or matter to be printed). [< OF *composer*.]
com•posed (kəm-pōzd') *adj*. Calm; serene. —com•pos'ed•ly (-pō'zĭd-lē) *adv*.
com•pos•er (kəm-pō'zər) *n*. One who composes music.
com•pos•ite (kəm-pŏz'ĭt) *adj*. 1. Made up of distinct components; compound. 2. Of or belonging to a large plant family with flower heads consisting of small, densely clustered flowers, often of different kinds, as the daisy. —*n*. 1. A composite structure or entity. 2. A composite plant. [L *compositus*, pp of *compōnere*, to put together.] —com•pos'ite•ly *adv*.
com•po•si•tion (kŏm'pə-zĭsh'ən) *n*. 1. The act or result of composing. 2. The arrangement of parts composed. 3. Process or technique in structuring music or art. 4. A short school essay. 5. Typesetting. [< L *compōnere*, to put together, arrange.]
com•pos•i•tor (kəm-pŏz'ə-tər) *n*. A typesetter.
com•post (kŏm'pōst) *n*. A mixture of decaying organic matter used as fertilizer. [< L *compositus*, put together, COMPOSITE.]

com•po•sure (kəm-pō'zhər) *n*. Self-possession; calm. [< COMPOSE.]
com•pote (kŏm'pōt) *n*. 1. Fruit stewed in syrup. 2. A long-stemmed dish for fruit or nuts. [< OF *composte*, stewed fruit.]
com•pound¹ (kŏm-pound', kəm-) *v*. 1. To combine; mix. 2. To produce by combining. 3. To compute (interest) on principal and accrued interest. 4. To make greater; increase. —*adj*. (kŏm'pound, kŏm-pound'). Consisting of two or more parts. —*n*. (kŏm'pound). 1. A compound entity. 2. A combination of words or word elements regarded as a unit. 3. A pure, macroscopically homogeneous substance consisting of atoms or ions of different elements in definite proportions, usually having properties unlike those of its constituent elements. [< L *compōnere*, to put together.]
com•pound² (kŏm'pound) *n*. A group of residences enclosed by a barrier. [< Malay *kampong*, village, cluster of buildings.]
compound eye. An eye, as of insects, composed of many light-sensitive elements.
compound flower. A flower head of a composite plant, consisting of numerous small flowers appearing as a single bloom.
compound fracture. A fracture in which broken bone lacerates soft tissue.
com•pre•hend (kŏm'prĭ-hĕnd') *v*. 1. To understand. 2. To include; comprise. [< L *comprehendere*, to grasp mentally.] —com'pre•hen'sion (-shən) *n*.
com•pre•hen•si•ble (kŏm'prĭ-hĕn'sə-bəl) *adj*. Also **com•pre•hend•i•ble** (-hĕn'də-bəl). Capable of being comprehended. —com'pre•hen'si•bil'i•ty *n*. —com'pre•hen'si•bly *adv*.
com•pre•hen•sive (kŏm'prĭ-hĕn'sĭv) *adj*. 1. Totally inclusive. 2. Comprehensible. —com'pre•hen'sive•ly *adv*.
com•press (kəm-prĕs') *v*. To press together or force into a smaller space; condense. —*n*. (kŏm'prĕs'). A pad applied to control bleeding or reduce pain or infection. [< L *comprimere* (pp *compressus*), to press together.] —com•press'i•bil'i•ty *n*. —com•press'i•ble *adj*. —com•pres'sion *n*. —com•pres'sive *adj*.
com•pres•sor (kəm-prĕs'ər) *n*. A machine that compresses gases.
com•prise (kəm-prīz') *v*. -prised, -prising. 1. To consist of. 2. To include; contain. [< OF *comprendre* (pp *compris*), to comprehend.]
Usage: By definition, the whole *comprises* the parts or *is composed of* them; the parts *compose* or *make up* the whole: The Union *comprises (is composed of) 50 states. Fifty states compose the Union.*
com•pro•mise (kŏm'prə-mīz') *n*. 1. a. A settlement of differences by mutual concessions. b. The result of such a settlement. 2. Something combining the qualities of different things. —*v*. -mised, -mising. 1. To settle by or agree to concessions. 2. To expose to suspicion or disrepute. [< L *comprōmittere*, to promise mutually.] —com'pro•mis'er *n*.
comp•trol•ler. Variant of controller.
com•pul•sion (kəm-pŭl'shən) *n*. 1. The act of compelling or forcing. 2. The state of being compelled. 3. An irresistible impulse to act.

ă pat/ā ate/âr care/ä bar/b bib/ch chew/d deed/ĕ pet/ē be/f fit/g gag/h hat/hw what/
ĭ pit/ī pie/îr pier/j judge/k kick/l lid, fatal/m mum/n no, sudden/ng sing/ŏ pot/ō go/

[< L *compellere* (pp *compulsus*), COMPEL.]
—**com•pul′sive** *adj.* —**com•pul′sive•ly** *adv.*
com•pul•so•ry (kəm-pŭl′sə-rē) *adj.* 1. Employing or exerting compulsion; coercive. 2. Obligatory; required. —**com•pul′so•ri•ly** *adv.*
com•punc•tion (kəm-pŭngk′shən) *n.* Uneasiness caused by guilt; remorse. [< LL *compunctiō*, "prick of conscience."]
com•pute (kəm-pyōōt′) *v.* -puted, -puting. To determine by mathematics, esp. by numerical methods. [L *computāre*, to reckon together.] —**com•put′a•ble** *adj.* —**com′pu•ta′tion** *n.*
com•put•er (kəm-pyōō′tər) *n.* 1. A person who computes. 2. A device that computes, esp. an electronic machine that performs high-speed mathematical or logical calculations or assembles, stores, correlates, or otherwise processes and prints information derived from coded data in accordance with a predetermined program.
com•put•er•ize (kəm-pyōō′tə-rīz′) *v.* -ized, -izing. 1. To process or store (information) with or in an electronic computer or system of computers. 2. To furnish with a computer or computer system.
com•rade (kŏm′răd, -rĭd, kŭm′-) *n.* A friend or associate. [< OF *camarade*, roommate, soldier sharing the same room.] —**com′rade•ship′** *n.*
con¹ (kŏn) *adv.* Against; in opposition to. —*n.* That which weighs against, as evidence. [< L *contrā*, against.]
con² (kŏn) *v.* conned, conning. To study, peruse, or examine carefully. [< OE *cunnan*, to know how. See gnō-.] —**con′ner** *n.*
con³ (kŏn) *Slang.* *v.* conned, conning. To swindle or defraud. —*n.* A swindle. [Short for CONFIDENCE.]
con⁴ (kŏn) *n.* *Slang.* A convict.
Con•a•kry (kän′ə-krē). The capital of the Republic of Guinea. Pop. 112,000.
con•cat•e•nate (kŏn-kăt′ə-nāt′) *v.* -nated, -nating. To connect in a series. [< LL *catēnāre*.] —**con•cat′e•nate** (-nĭt, -nāt′) *adj.* —**con•cat′e•na′tion** *n.*
con•cave (kŏn-kāv′) *adj.* Curved like the inner surface of a sphere. [< L *concavus*, vaulted, hollow.] —**con•cav′i•ty** (-kăv′ə-tē) *n.*
con•ceal (kən-sēl′) *v.* To keep from observation, discovery, or understanding. [< L *concēlāre*.] —**con•ceal′er** *n.* —**con•ceal′ment** *n.*
con•cede (kən-sēd′) *v.* -ceded, -ceding. 1. To acknowledge as true, just, or proper. 2. To yield, as a right. [< L *concēdere*, to yield.]
con•ceit (kən-sēt′) *n.* 1. Too high an opinion of one's abilities or worth. 2. An ingenious or witty thought. 3. An elaborate or exaggerated metaphor. [< CONCEIVE.]
con•ceit•ed (kən-sē′tĭd) *adj.* Vain.
con•ceive (kən-sēv′) *v.* -ceived, -ceiving. 1. To become pregnant (with). 2. To imagine; understand. 3. To express in particular words. [< L *concipere*, to take to oneself, be impregnated.] —**con•ceiv′a•bil′i•ty** *n.* —**con•ceiv′a•ble** *adj.* —**con•ceiv′a•bly** *adv.* —**con•ceiv′er** *n.*
con•cen•trate (kŏn′sən-trāt′) *v.* -trated, -trating. 1. To direct or draw toward a common center; focus. 2. *Chem.* To increase the concentration

of. —*n.* *Chem.* A product of concentration. [Prob < L *com-*, same + CENTER.] —**con′cen•tra′tive** *adj.* —**con′cen•tra′tor** *n.*
con•cen•tra•tion (kŏn′sən-trā′shən) *n.* 1. The act of concentrating or state of being concentrated. 2. Something concentrated. 3. The amount of a specified substance in a unit amount of another substance.
concentration camp. A camp where prisoners of war, enemy aliens, or political prisoners are confined.
con•cen•tric (kən-sĕn′trĭk) *adj.* Having a common center. —**con•cen′tri•cal•ly** *adv.* —**con′cen•tric′i•ty** *n.*
con•cept (kŏn′sĕpt) *n.* An idea, esp. an abstraction drawn from the specific. [< LL *conceptus*, a thing conceived, thought.]
con•cep•tion (kən-sĕp′shən) *n.* 1. The formation of a zygote capable of survival and maturation in normal conditions. 2. A beginning; start. 3. The ability to form mental concepts; invention. 4. A concept, plan, or thought. [< L *concipere*, to take to oneself, CONCEIVE.]
con•cep•tu•al•ize (kən-sĕp′chōō-əl-īz′) *v.* -ized, -izing. To form concepts.
con•cern (kən-sûrn′) *v.* 1. To pertain or relate to; affect. 2. To engage the interests of. 3. To cause anxiety or uneasiness in. —*n.* 1. Something of interest or importance. 2. Earnest regard: *concern for one's well-being.* 3. Relation; reference. 4. Anxiety; worry. 5. A business establishment. [< ML *concernere*, to relate to, involve with.]
con•cerned (kən-sûrnd′) *adj.* Anxious; disturbed.
con•cern•ing (kən-sûr′nĭng) *prep.* In reference to.
con•cert (kŏn′sûrt) *n.* 1. A public musical performance. 2. Agreement in purpose, feeling, or action. —**in concert.** All together; in agreement. —*v.* (kən-sûrt′). 1. To plan or arrange by mutual agreement. 2. To contrive or devise. [< OIt *concertare*, to bring into agreement, harmonize.]
con•cert•ed (kən-sûr′tĭd) *adj.* Planned or accomplished together; combined.
con•cer•ti•na (kŏn′sər-tē′nə) *n.* A small, hexagonal accordion with buttons for keys.
con•cer•tize (kŏn′sər-tīz′) *v.* -tized, -tizing. To perform in concerts.
con•cert•mas•ter (kŏn′sərt-măs′tər, -mäs′tər) *n.* The first violinist and assistant conductor in a symphony orchestra.
con•cer•to (kən-chĕr′tō) *n.*, *pl.* -tos. A composition for an orchestra and one or more solo instruments. [It, concert.]
con•ces•sion (kən-sĕsh′ən) *n.* 1. The act of conceding. 2. Something conceded. 3. Something granted by a government to be used for a specific purpose. 4. The privilege of maintaining a subsidiary business within certain premises.
con•ces•sion•aire (kən-sĕsh′ən-âr′) *n.* The holder of a concession.
con•ces•sive (kən-sĕs′ĭv) *adj.* Tending to concede.
conch (kŏngk, kŏnch) *n.*, *pl.* **conchs** or **conches**

ô paw, for/oi boy/ou out/ŏŏ took/ōō coo/p pop/r run/s sauce/sh shy/t to/th thin/*th* the/
ŭ cut/ûr fur/v van/w wag/y yes/z size/zh vision/ə ago, item, edible, gallop, circus/

(kŏn′chĭz). A tropical marine mollusk with a large, often brightly colored spiral shell. [< Gk konkhē.]

con•cil•i•ate (kən-sĭl′ē-āt′) v. -ated, -ating. 1. To overcome the animosity of. 2. To win, as favor. [L conciliāre, to bring together, unite.] —con•cil′i•a′tion n. —con•cil′i•a′tor n. —con•cil′i•a•to′ry (-ə-tôr′ē, -tōr′ē) adj.

con•cise (kən-sīs′) adj. Expressing much in few words; succinct. [< L concīdere, to cut up.] —con•cise′ly adv. —con•cise′ness n.

con•clave (kŏn′klāv, kŏng′-) n. A secret meeting. [< L conclāve, "room locked with a key."]

con•clude (kən-klōōd′) v. -cluded, -cluding. 1. To bring to an end. 2. To agree. 3. To reach a decision about. 4. To determine; decide; resolve. [< L conclūdere, to shut up closely.] —con•clu′sion n.

con•clu•sive (kən-klōō′sĭv) adj. Decisive; final.

con•coct (kən-kŏkt′) v. 1. To prepare by mixing ingredients. 2. To invent; contrive. [L concoquere, to cook together.] —con•coc′tion n.

con•com•i•tant (kən-kŏm′ə-tənt) adj. Existing or occurring concurrently. —n. An accompanying state or thing. [< L concomitārī, to accompany.]

con•cord (kŏn′kôrd, kŏng′-) n. Harmony; accord; concurrence. [< L concors, "of the same mind."]

Con•cord (kŏng′kərd). 1. A town in Massachusetts; site of a battle (April 19, 1775) of the Revolutionary War. Pop. 13,000. 2. The capital of New Hampshire. Pop. 30,000.

con•cor•dance (kən-kôr′dəns) n. 1. A state of agreement. 2. An alphabetical index of the words in a book with their contextual occurrence.

con•cor•dant (kən-kôr′dənt) adj. Harmonious; agreeing.

con•cor•dat (kən-kôr′dăt′) n. A formal agreement; compact.

con•course (kŏn′kôrs, -kōrs, kŏng′-) n. 1. A crowd; throng. 2. A moving or flowing together. 3. A large open space for the gathering or passage of crowds. [< L concurrere, to run together.]

con•cres•cence (kən-krĕs′əns) n. The uniting, esp. the growing together, of related parts, as of physical particles or anatomical structures. [< L concrēscere, to grow together.]

con•crete (kŏn-krēt′, kŏn′krēt) adj. 1. Relating to an actual, specific thing or instance; not general; particular. 2. Existing in reality or in real experience. 3. Formed by the coalescence of separate particles or parts into one mass; solid. 4. Made of concrete. —n. (kŏn′krēt, kŏn-krēt′). 1. A construction material consisting of conglomerate gravel, pebbles, broken stone, or slag in a mortar or cement matrix. 2. A mass formed by the coalescence of particles. —v. (kŏn′krēt, kŏn-krēt′) -creted, -creting. 1. To form into a mass by coalescence or cohesion of particles. 2. To build, treat, or cover with concrete. [< L concrētus, pp of concrēscere, to grow together, harden.]

con•cre•tion (kən-krē′shən) n. 1. A hard, solid mass. 2. The process of forming such a mass.

con•cu•bine (kŏng′kyə-bīn′, kŏn′-) n. A woman who cohabits with a man without being married to him. [< L concubīna, "one to sleep with."]

con•cu•pis•cence (kŏn-kyōō′pə-səns) n. Sexual desire; lust; sensuality. [< L concupere, to have a strong desire for.]

con•cur (kən-kûr′) v. -curred, -curring. 1. To have the same opinion; agree. 2. To act together. 3. To coincide. [< L concurrere, to run together.] —con•cur′rence n.

con•cur•rent (kən-kûr′ənt) adj. 1. Happening at the same time or place. 2. Operating in conjunction. 3. Meeting or tending to meet at the same point. —con•cur′rent•ly adv.

con•cus•sion (kən-kŭsh′ən) n. 1. A violent jarring; shock. 2. An injury of a soft structure, esp. of the brain, resulting from a violent blow.

con•demn (kən-dĕm′) v. 1. To express disapproval of; censure; criticize. 2. To pronounce judgment against; sentence. [< L condemnāre.] —con′dem•na′tion (kŏn′dĕm-nā′shən) n.

con•dense (kən-dĕns′) v. -densed, -densing. 1. To compress. 2. To abridge. 3. To form a liquid from a vapor. [< L condēnsāre.] —con•den′sa•ble adj. —con′den•sa′tion (kŏn′dən-sā′shən) n. —con•den′ser n.

con•de•scend (kŏn′dĭ-sĕnd′) v. To deal with others in a patronizing manner. [< ML condēscendere, to stoop to.] —con′de•scen′sion n.

con•dign (kən-dīn′) adj. Deserved; adequate: condign censure. [< L condignus, wholly worthy.] —con•dign′ly adv.

con•di•ment (kŏn′də-mənt) n. A seasoning for food, such as mustard. [< L condīre, to season, preserve by pickling.]

con•di•tion (kən-dĭsh′ən) n. 1. The particular state of being of a person or thing. 2. State of health. 3. A disease or ailment: a heart condition. 4. A prerequisite. 5. A qualification. 6. Often conditions. The existing circumstances: poor driving conditions. 7. Gram. The dependent clause of a conditional sentence. —v. 1. To make conditional. 2. To put into a proper condition. [< L conditio, condicio, agreement, stipulation.]

con•di•tion•al (kən-dĭsh′ən-əl) adj. 1. Imposing, depending on, or containing a condition or conditions. 2. Not certain; tentative. 3. Gram. Stating or implying a condition or prerequisite. —n. Gram. A mood, tense, clause, or word expressing a condition.

con•di•tioned (kən-dĭsh′ənd) adj. 1. Subject to stipulations. 2. Prepared for a specific action. 3. Exhibiting or trained to exhibit a new or modified response.

con•di•tion•ing (kən-dĭsh′ən-ĭng) n. The process or result of inducing new or modified behavioral responses.

con•dole (kən-dōl′) v. -doled, -doling. To express sympathy to one in pain, grief, or misfortune. [< LL condolēre, to feel another's pain.] —con•do′lence n. —con•dol′er n.

con•dom (kŏn′dəm) n. Also cun•dum (kŭn′dəm). A rubber sheath for covering the penis to prevent disease or conception. [Said to have been invented by Dr. Condom, 18th-century English physician.]

con•do•min•i•um (kŏn′də-mĭn′ē-əm) *n.* **1. a.** Joint sovereignty, esp. joint rule of a territory by two or more states. **b.** The territory so governed. **2.** An apartment building in which the apartments are owned individually.

con•done (kən-dōn′) *v.* **-doned, -doning.** To forgive or disregard (an offense) without protest or censure. [L *condōnāre,* to give up, forgive.] **—con′do•na′tion** (kŏn′dō-nā′shən) *n.*

con•dor (kŏn′dôr, -dər) *n.* A very large vulture of the Andes or the mountains of California. [Span *cóndor.*]

con•duce (kən-d/y/ōōs′) *v.* **-duced, -ducing.** To contribute or lead to. [< L *condūcere,* to lead together, contribute.] **—con•du′cive** *adj.*

con•duct (kən-dŭkt′) *v.* **1.** To direct the course of; manage. **2.** To lead or guide. **3.** To serve as a medium or channel for conveying; transmit. **4.** To behave oneself. *—n.* (kŏn′dŭkt). **1.** The way a person acts. **2.** Management; administration. **3.** The act of leading or guiding. [< L *condūcere,* to lead together.] **—con•duc′tion** *n.* **—con•duc′tive** *adj.*

con•duc•tor (kən-dŭk′tər) *n.* **1.** One who conducts or leads. **2.** The person in charge of a train, bus, etc. **3.** The director of a musical ensemble. **4.** A substance or medium that conducts heat, light, sound, or esp., an electric charge.

con•duit (kŏn′dĭt, -dōō-ĭt) *n.* **1.** A channel or pipe for conveying fluids. **2.** A tube or duct for enclosing electric wires or cable. [< L *condūcere,* to lead together, CONDUCT.]

cone (kōn) *n.* **1.** A surface generated by a straight line passing through a fixed point and moving along the intersection with a fixed curve. **2.** The figure formed by such a surface bound by its vertex and an intersecting plane. **3.** A scaly, rounded or cylindrical seed-bearing structure, as of a pine. **4.** A photoreceptor in the retina of the eye. [< Gk *kōnos.*]

Con•el•rad (kŏn′əl-rǎd) *n.* A U.S. defense system requiring termination of all broadcasting except for official emergency messages, to prevent enemy navigation with commercial signals.

Con•es•to•ga wagon (kŏn′ĭs-tō′gə). A covered wagon with broad wheels, used by American pioneers. [< *Conestoga,* Pennsylvania.]

co•ney. Variant of cony.

conf. conference.

con•fab•u•late (kən-fǎb′yə-lāt′) *v.* **-lated, -lating.** **1.** To talk informally; chat. **2.** To replace fact with fantasy in memory. [L *confābulāri.*] **—con•fab′u•la′tion** *n.*

con•fec•tion (kən-fěk′shən) *n.* A sweet preparation, such as candy or preserves. [< L *conficere* (pp *confectus*), to prepare.]

con•fec•tion•er (kən-fěk′shən-ər) *n.* One who makes or sells confections.

con•fec•tion•er•y (kən-fěk′shən-ĕr′ē) *n., pl.* **-ies.** **1.** Confections collectively. **2.** A confectioner's shop.

confed. confederation.

con•fed•er•a•cy (kən-fěd′ər-ə-sē) *n., pl.* **-cies.** An alliance; league. [< L *confoederāre,* to unite.]

con•fed•er•ate (kən-fěd′ər-ĭt) *n.* **1.** An ally.

2. An accomplice. **3. Confederate.** A supporter of the Confederate States of America. *—adj.* **1.** United in a confederacy; allied. **2. Confederate.** Of or pertaining to the Confederate States of America. *—v.* (kən-fěd′ə-rāt′) **-ated, -ating.** To form into or become part of a confederacy. [< L *confoederāre,* to unite in a league.] **—con•fed′er•a′tive** *adj.*

Confederate States of America. The confederation of 11 Southern states that seceded from the U.S. in 1860 and 1861.

con•fed•er•a•tion (kən-fěd′ə-rā′shən) *n.* **1.** An act of confederating. **2.** An alliance, esp. of states and nations.

con•fer (kən-fûr′) *v.* **-ferred, -ferring.** **1.** To bestow, as an honor. **2.** To hold a conference. [L *conferre,* to bring together, contribute.]

con•fer•ence (kŏn′fə-rəns, -frəns) *n.* **1.** A meeting for consultation or discussion. **2.** An association, as of schools, for mutual benefit; league. [< L *conferre,* CONFER.]

con•fess (kən-fěs′) *v.* **1.** To disclose or acknowledge one's misdeed or fault. **2.** To concede the truth or validity of. **3. a.** To make known (one's sins), esp. to a priest for absolution. **b.** To hear the confession of. [< LL *confitēri* (pp *confessus*), to acknowledge.] **—con•fess′ed•ly** (-ĭd-lē) *adv.*

con•fes•sion (kən-fěsh′ən) *n.* **1.** An act of confessing. **2.** Something confessed. **3.** A formal declaration of guilt. **4.** The disclosure of sins to a priest for absolution. **5.** A Christian denomination.

con•fes•sion•al (kən-fěsh′ən-əl) *n.* An enclosure in which a priest hears confessions.

con•fes•sor (kən-fěs′ər) *n.* **1.** A priest who hears confession. **2.** One who confesses.

con•fet•ti (kən-fět′ē) *n. (takes sing. v.).* Bits of colored paper scattered at festive celebrations. [< It *confetto,* confection, candy.]

con•fi•dant (kŏn′fə-dǎnt′, -dänt′, kŏn′fə-dǎnt, -dänt) *n.* One to whom secrets are confided.

con•fide (kən-fīd′) *v.* **-fided, -fiding.** **1.** To tell in confidence. **2.** To put into another's keeping. [< L *confidere.*] **—con•fid′er** *n.*

con•fi•dence (kŏn′fə-dəns) *n.* **1.** Trust in a person or thing. **2.** An intimate and trusting relationship. **3.** Something confided. **4.** A feeling of assurance or certainty. **—con′fi•dent** *adj.* **—con′fi•dent•ly** *adv.*

con•fi•den•tial (kŏn′fə-děn′shəl) *adj.* **1.** Done or communicated in confidence. **2.** Entrusted with the confidence of another. **—con′fi•den′tial•ly** *adv.*

con•fig•u•ra•tion (kən-fĭg′yə-rā′shən) *n.* The arrangement of the parts or elements of something. [< L *configūrāre,* "to form together."] **—con•fig′u•ra′tive, con•fig′u•ra′tion•al** *adj.*

con•fine (kən-fīn′) *v.* **-fined, -fining.** **1.** To keep within bounds; restrict. **2.** To imprison. [< L *confinis,* having the same border.] **—con•fine′ment** *n.* **—con•fin′er** *n.*

con•firm (kən-fûrm′) *v.* **1.** To corroborate; verify. **2.** To strengthen; establish. **3.** To ratify. **4.** To administer the religious rite of confirmation. [< L *confirmāre.*]

con•fir•ma•tion (kŏn′fər-mā′shən) *n.* **1.** An act of confirming. **2.** A verification. **3.** A rite admitting a baptized person to full membership in a church.

con•firmed (kən-fûrmd') *adj.* **1.** Verified. **2.** Inveterate: *a confirmed bachelor.* **3.** Having received the rite of confirmation.

con•fis•cate (kŏn'fĭs-kāt') *v.* -cated, -cating. **1.** To seize (private property) for a public treasury. **2.** To seize by or as by authority. [L *confiscāre,* to lay up in a chest, confiscate.] —**con'fis•ca'tion** *n.* —**con'fis•ca'tor** *n.*

con•flict (kŏn'flĭkt) *n.* **1.** A prolonged battle. **2.** A controversy; disagreement. **3.** The opposition of mutually exclusive impulses, desires, or tendencies. —*v.* (kən-flĭkt'). To còme into opposition; collide; differ. [< L *conflīctus,* pp of *conflīgere,* to clash together, contend.] —**con•flic'tive** *adj.*

con•flu•ence (kŏn'floo-əns) *n.* Also **con•flux** (-flŭks). **1.** A flowing together of two or more streams. **2.** The point of juncture of such streams. **3.** A gathering together. [< L *confluere,* to flow together.] —**con'flu•ent** *adj.*

con•form (kən-fôrm') *v.* **1.** To make or become similar. **2.** To act or be in agreement; comply. **3.** To act in accordance with customs or rules. [< L *conformāre,* "to have the same form," shape after.] —**con•form'er** *n.*

con•for•ma•tion (kŏn'fər-mā'shən) *n.* **1.** The structure of something as determined by the arrangement of its parts. **2.** A symmetrical arrangement of the parts of a thing.

con•form•ist (kən-fôr'mĭst) *n.* One who conforms to current usages.

con•form•i•ty (kən-fôr'mə-tē) *n.* Also **con•for•mance** (-fôr'məns). **1.** Similarity in form or character; correspondence. **2.** Action or behavior in correspondence with current customs, rules, or styles.

con•found (kən-found', kŏn-) *v.* **1.** To confuse or cause to become confused. **2.** To fail to distinguish. [< L *confundere,* to pour together, mix up.] —**con•found'er** *n.*

con•front (kən-frŭnt') *v.* **1.** To come face to face with. **2.** To face with hostility; oppose. [< ML *confrontāre,* to have a common border.] —**con'fron•ta'tion** *n.*

Con•fu•cian•ism (kən-fyoo'shən-ĭz'əm) *n.* The ethical system based on the teachings of Confucius. —**Con•fu'cian** *adj. & n.*

Con•fu•cius (kən-fyoo'shəs). 551–479 B.C. Chinese philosopher.

con•fuse (kən-fyooz') *v.* -fused, -fusing. **1.** To perplex or bewilder. **2.** To assemble without order or sense. **3.** To mistake one thing for another. [< L *confusus,* pp of *confundere,* to pour together, mix, confound.] —**con•fus'ed•ly** (-fyoo'zĭd-lē) *adv.* —**con•fus'ing•ly** *adv.*

con•fu•sion (kən-fyoo'zhən) *n.* **1.** The act of confusing or state of being confused. **2.** Disorder; jumble.

con•fute (kən-fyoot') *v.* -futed, -futing. To prove to be wrong or in error. [L *confutāre,* to check, suppress, restrain.] —**con'fu•ta'tion** *n.*

Cong. Congress; Congressional.

con•geal (kən-jēl') *v.* **1.** To solidify or cause to solidify, as by freezing. **2.** To coagulate; jell. [< L *congelāre,* to freeze solid.]

con•gen•ial (kən-jēn'yəl) *adj.* **1.** Having the

same tastes or temperament; sympathetic. **2.** Suited to one's needs; agreeable. [CON- + GENIAL.] —**con•ge'ni•al'i•ty** (-jē'nē-ăl'ə-tē) *n.* —**con•gen'ial•ly** *adv.*

con•gen•i•tal (kən-jĕn'ə-təl) *adj.* **1.** Existing at birth but not hereditary. **2.** Characteristic, as if by nature: *a congenital liar.* [< L *congenitus,* born together with.] —**con•gen'i•tal•ly** *adv.*

con•ger (kŏng'gər) *n.* Also **conger eel.** A large, scaleless marine eel. [< Gk *gongros.*]

con•ge•ries (kən-jîr'ēz) *n. (takes sing. v.)* A collection of things heaped together; an aggregate. [< L *congeriēs,* heap, pile.]

con•gest (kən-jĕst') *v.* **1.** To overfill. **2.** To accumulate excessive blood in (a vessel or organ). [L *congerere* (pp *congestus*), to bring together, heap ˌup.] —**con•ges'tion** *n.* —**con•ges'tive** *adj.*

con•glo•bate (kŏn-glō'bāt', kŏng'glō-) *v.* -bated, -bating. To gather into or become a globe or ball. —*adj.* Shaped like or formed into a ball. [< L *conglobāre,* to make into a globe.] —**con'glo•ba'tion** *n.*

con•glom•er•ate (kən-glŏm'ə-rāt') *v.* -ated, -ating. To form or collect into an adhering or rounded mass. —*n.* (kən-glŏm'ə-rĭt). **1.** A collected heterogeneous mass; a cluster. **2.** *Geol.* A rock consisting of pebbles and gravel embedded in a loosely cementing material. **3.** A business corporation made up of a number of different companies that operate in widely diversified fields. —*adj.* (kən-glŏm'-ə-rĭt). **1.** Gathered into a mass; clustered. **2.** *Geol.* Made up of loosely cemented heterogeneous material. [< L *conglomerāre,* to roll together.]

con•glom•er•a•tion (kən-glŏm'ə-rā'shən) *n.* **1.** The process of conglomerating or state of being conglomerated. **2.** A collection or mass of miscellaneous things; a cluster. **3.** A coherent mass.

Con•go (kŏng'gō). A river of C Africa.

Congo, Democratic Republic of the. A former name for Zaire. —**Con•go•lese'** *adj. & n.*

Congo, Republic of. A republic and former French colony in west-central Africa. Pop. 915,000. Cap. Brazzaville. —**Con'go•lese'** (kŏng'gə-lēz', -lēs') *adj. & n.*

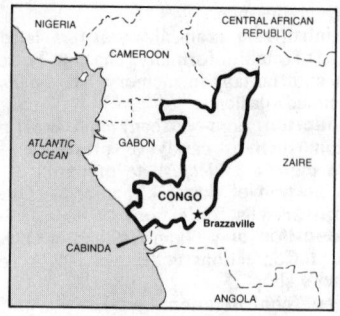

Republic of Congo

con•grat•u•late (kən-grăch′ōō-lāt′) v. -lated,
-lating. To express pleasure at the achievement
or good fortune of. [L *congrātulārī*, to rejoice
with someone.] **—con•grat′u•la′tion** n. **—con•**
grat′u•la•to′ry (-lə-tôr′ē, -tôr′ē) adj.
con•gre•gate (kŏng′grə-gāt′) v. -gated, -gating.
To come together in a crowd; assemble. [< L
congregāre, to assemble.]
con•gre•ga•tion (kŏng′grə-gā′shən) n. 1. An
act of congregating. 2. An assemblage;
gathering. 3. A group of people gathered for
religious worship.
con•gre•ga•tion•al (kŏng′grə-gā′shən-əl) adj.
1. Of or pertaining to a congregation. 2. **Con•**
gregational. Of or pertaining to a Protestant
denomination in which each member church is
self-governing.
Con•gre•ga•tion•al•ist (kŏng′grə-gā′shən-əl-
ĭst) n. A member of a Congregational Christian church. **—Con′gre•ga′tion•al•ism′** n.
con•gress (kŏng′grĭs) n. 1. A formal assembly
or meeting for the discussion of problems.
2. A national legislature, esp. of a republic.
3. **Congress.** The legislature of the U.S., consisting of the Senate and the House of
Representatives. [< L *congressus* < *congredī*,
to come together.]
con•gres•sion•al (kən-grĕsh′ən-əl) adj. 1. Of
or pertaining to a congress. 2. **Congressional.**
Of or pertaining to the Congress of the U.S.
con•gress•man (kŏng′grĭs-mən) n. Also **Con•**
gress•man. A member of the U.S. Congress.
con•gress•wom•an (kŏng′grĭs-wōōm′ən) n.
Also **Con•gress•wom•an.** A female member of
the U.S. Congress.
con•gru•ent (kŏng′grōō-ənt, kən-grōō′ənt) adj.
1. Corresponding; congruous. 2. Coinciding
exactly when superimposed: *congruent trian-*
gles. [< L *congruere*, to meet together, agree.]
—con′gru•ence n. **—con′gru•ent•ly** adv.
con•gru•ous (kŏng′grōō-əs) adj. 1. Corresponding in character or kind; harmonious.
2. Congruent. **—con•gru′i•ty** (kən-grōō′ə-tē) n.
—con′gru•ous•ly adv.
con•ic (kŏn′ĭk) adj. Also **con•i•cal** (-ĭ-kəl). Of
or shaped like a cone.
con•i•fer (kŏn′ə-fər, kō′nə-) n. A cone-bearing
tree, as a pine or hemlock. **—co•nif′er•ous**
(kō-nĭf′ər-əs) adj.
conj. 1. conjugation. 2. conjunction.
con•jec•ture (kən-jĕk′chər) v. -tured, -turing.
To infer from inconclusive evidence; guess.
—n. Inference based on inconclusive evidence; guesswork. [< L *conjicere*, "to throw
together," put together mentally.] **—con•jec′-**
tur•a•ble adj. **—con•jec′tur•al** adj.
con•join (kən-join′) v. To join together; connect; unite. **—con•join′er** n. **—con•joint′**
(-joint′) adj. **—con•joint′ly** adv.
con•ju•gal (kŏn′jōō-gəl, -jə-gəl) adj. Of marriage or the marital relationship. [< L *con-*
jungere, to join together (in marriage).] **—con′•**
ju•gal•ly adv.
con•ju•gate (kŏn′jōō-gāt′, -jə-gāt′) v. -gated,
-gating. To inflect (a verb). —adj. (kŏn′-
jōō-gĭt). 1. Joined together, esp. in pairs. 2.
Inversely or oppositely related with respect to
one of a group of otherwise identical prop-

erties. —n. (kŏn′jōō-gĭt). Either of a pair of
conjugate quantities. [< L *conjugāre*, to yoke
or join together.] **—con′ju•ga′tor** n.
con•ju•ga•tion (kŏn′jōō-gā′shən, kŏn′jə-) n.
1. The act of conjugating or state of being
conjugated. 2. The inflection of a verb. 3. An
act or process of sexual joining in reproduction. **—con′ju•ga′tion•al** adj.
con•junct (kən-jŭngkt′, kŏn′jŭngkt) adj.
Joined together; united. [< L *conjunctus*, pp
of *conjungere*, to join together.]
con•junc•tion (kən-jŭngk′shən) n. 1. A joining
together; combination. 2. Simultaneous occurrence. 3. A word connecting other words,
phrases, clauses, or sentences.
con•junc•ti•va (kŏn′jŭngk-tī′və, kən-jŭngk′tī-
və) n., pl. -vas or -vae (-vē). The mucous
membrane that lines the inner surface of the
eyelid and the exposed surface of the eyeball.
[< ML *(membrāna) conjunctīva*, "the connective (membrane)."] **—con′junc•ti′val** adj.
con•junc•tive (kən-jŭngk′tĭv) adj. 1. Connective. 2. Combined; conjunct. 3. *Gram.* Used
as a conjunction. [< L *conjunctus*, CONJUNCT.]
con•junc•ti•vi•tis (kən-jŭngk′tə-vī′tĭs) n. Inflammation of the conjunctiva.
con•junc•ture (kən-jŭngk′chər) n. 1. A combination of circumstances or events. 2. A critical set of circumstances.
con•jure (kŏn′jər, kən-jōōr′) v. -jured, -juring.
1. To entreat solemnly, esp. by an oath. 2. To
summon (a devil) by sorcery. 3. To effect by
magic or legerdemain. **—conjure up.** To contrive, imagine, or evoke. [< L *conjūrāre*, to
swear together, conspire.] **—con′ju•ra′tion**
(-rā′shən) n. **—con′jur•er** n.
conk (kŏngk) v. *Slang.* To hit, esp. on the head.
—conk out. To fail suddenly. [Prob var of
CONCH.]
Conn. Connecticut.
con•nect (kə-nĕkt′) v. 1. To join; link; unite.
2. To associate or consider as related. [< L
connectere.] **—con•nect′ed•ly** adv.
Con•nect•i•cut (kə-nĕt′ə-kət). A state of the
NE U.S. Pop. 3,032,000. Cap. Hartford.
con•nec•tion (kə-nĕk′shən) n. 1. Union; junction. 2. A bond; link. 3. An association or
relation. 4. Logical ordering of words or
ideas; coherence. 5. The relation of a word to
its context. 6. **connections.** People with whom
one is associated.
con•nec•tive (kə-nĕk′tĭv) adj. Serving or tending to connect. —n. A connecting word, such
as a conjunction.
con•nip•tion (kə-nĭp′shən) n. *Informal.* A fit of
violent emotion. [?]
con•nive (kə-nīv′) v. -nived, -niving. 1. To feign
ignorance of a wrong, thus implying consent.
2. To cooperate secretly; conspire. [< L *con-*
nivēre, to close the eyes, be indulgent.] **—con•**
niv′ance n. **—con•niv′er** n.
con•nois•seur (kŏn′ə-sûr′) n. An informed
and astute judge in matters of taste. [< L
cognōscere, to get acquainted with.]
con•no•ta•tion (kŏn′ə-tā′shən) n. The configuration of associative implications constituting
the general sense of an abstract expression
beyond its explicit sense. **—con′no•ta′tive** adj.

ô paw, for/oi boy/ou out/ōō took/ōō coo/p pop/r run/s sauce/sh shy/t to/th thin/*th* the/
ŭ cut/ûr fur/v van/w wag/y yes/z size/zh vision/ə ago, item, edible, gallop, circus/

con•note (kə-nōt') v. -noted, -noting. 1. To suggest or imply in addition to literal meaning. 2. To involve as a condition or consequence. [ML *connotāre*, "to mark in addition."]

con•nu•bi•al (kə-nōō'bē-əl) adj. Of marriage or the married state; conjugal. [L *connūbiālis.*]

con•quer (kŏng'kər) v. 1. To defeat or subdue, as by force of arms. 2. To overcome. [< L *conquīrere*, to search for, procure, win.] —con'quer•a•ble adj. —con'quer•or n.

con•quest (kŏn'kwĕst, kŏng'-) n. 1. The act or process of conquering. 2. Something acquired by conquering.

con•quis•ta•dor (kŏn-kwĭs'tə-dôr) n. One of the Spanish conquerors of Mexico and Peru in the 16th century.

Cons. 1. constable. 2. consul.

con•san•guin•e•ous (kŏn'săng-gwĭn'ē-əs) adj. Related by blood. [L *consanguineus.*]

con•san•guin•i•ty (kŏn'săng-gwĭn'ə-tē) n. 1. Blood relationship. 2. Close affinity.

con•science (kŏn'shəns) n. 1. The faculty of recognizing the distinction between right and wrong in regard to one's own conduct. 2. Conformity to one's own sense of right conduct. [<L *conscīre*, to be conscious.]

con•sci•en•tious (kŏn'shē-ĕn'shəs) adj. 1. Scrupulous; honest. 2. Painstaking and thorough; careful. —con'sci•en'tious•ly adv. —con'sci•en'tious•ness n.

conscientious objector. One who on the basis of religious and moral principles refuses to bear arms or participate in military service.

con•scious (kŏn'shəs) adj. 1. a. Having an awareness of one's own existence and environment. b. Capable of complex response to environment. c. Not asleep; awake. 2. Subjectively known: *conscious remorse.* 3. Intentional; deliberate: *a conscious insult.* [L *conscius*, knowing with others, aware of.] —con'scious•ly adv. —con'scious•ness n.

con•scious•ness-rais•ing (kŏn'shəs-nĭs-rā'zĭng) n. 1. A technique whereby one learns to analyze one's own life situation and then to transform it so as to achieve liberation from oppression. 2. A technique whereby one is made aware of discrimination against a particular class of people who have been oppressed. —con'scious•ness-rais'er n.

con•script (kŏn'skrĭpt) n. One who is compulsorily enrolled for military service. —v. (kən-skrĭpt'). To draft for military service. [< L *conscriptus*, pp of *conscrībere*, to write together.] —con•scrip'tion n.

con•se•crate (kŏn'sə-krāt') v. -crated, -crating. 1. To make or declare sacred; hallow. 2. R.C.Ch. To change (the elements of bread and wine) into the body and blood of Christ. 3. To initiate (a priest) into the order of bishops. 4. To dedicate to some service or goal. [< L *consecrāre.*] —con'se•cra'tion n.

con•sec•u•tive (kən-sĕk'yə-tĭv) adj. Following successively without interruption. [< L *consequī*, to follow up.] —con•sec'u•tive•ly adv.

con•sen•sus (kən-sĕn'səs) n. Collective opinion or agreement. [< L *consentīre*, to agree, CONSENT.]

Usage: Consensus is preferable to the stock expression *consensus of opinion*, which is redundant.

con•sent (kən-sĕnt') v. To give assent; accede; agree. —n. Acceptance, agreement, or approval. [< L *consentīre*, to feel together, agree.] —con•sent'er n.

con•se•quence (kŏn'sə-kwĕns) n. 1. An effect; result. 2. Importance or significance.

con•se•quent (kŏn'sə-kwĕnt, -kwənt) adj. Following as a result. [< L *consequī*, to follow up, accompany.] —con'se•quent'ly adv.

con•se•quen•tial (kŏn'sə-kwĕn'shəl) adj. 1. Having important consequences. 2. Conceited; pompous. —con'se•quen'tial•ly adv.

con•ser•va•tion (kŏn'sûr-vā'shən) n. Preservation from loss, waste, or harm, esp. the official preservation of natural resources. —con'ser•va'tion•al adj. —con'ser•va'tion•ist n.

con•ser•va•tism (kən-sûr'və-tĭz'əm) n. Disposition to maintain existing order.

con•ser•va•tive (kən-sûr'və-tĭv) adj. 1. Favoring preservation of the existing order. 2. Moderate; prudent; cautious. 3. Traditional in manner or style. 4. Tending to conserve; preservative. —n. A conservative person.

con•ser•va•tor (kən-sûr'və-tər) n. 1. A protector. 2. *Law.* A guardian.

con•ser•va•to•ry (kən-sûr'və-tôr'ē, -tōr'ē) n., pl. -ries. 1. A glass-enclosed room or greenhouse in which plants are grown. 2. A school of music or dramatic art.

con•serve (kən-sûrv') v. -served, -serving. 1. To protect from loss or depletion; preserve. 2. To preserve (fruits). —n. (kŏn'sûrv). A jam made of two or more fruits stewed in sugar. [< L *conservāre.*] —con•serv'a•ble adj.

con•sid•er (kən-sĭd'ər) v. 1. To deliberate upon; examine. 2. To think or deem. 3. To believe; judge. [< L *consīderāre*, to observe.]

con•sid•er•a•ble (kən-sĭd'ər-ə-bəl) adj. 1. Fairly large in amount, extent, or degree. 2. Worthy of consideration; important; significant. —con•sid'er•a•bly adv.

con•sid•er•ate (kən-sĭd'ər-ĭt) adj. Having regard for the needs or feelings of others. [< L *consīderāre*, to be considerate, CONSIDER.]

con•sid•er•a•tion (kən-sĭd'ə-rā'shən) n. 1. Deliberation. 2. A factor in forming a judgment. 3. Thoughtfulness; solicitude. 4. Recompense.

con•sid•ered (kən-sĭd'ərd) adj. 1. Reached after deliberation. 2. Esteemed.

con•sid•er•ing (kən-sĭd'ər-ĭng) prep. In view of. —adv. *Informal.* All things considered.

con•sign (kən-sīn') v. 1. To give over to the care of another; entrust. 2. To turn over formally to another's charge. 3. To deliver for custody or sale, as merchandise. 4. To allot or assign. [< L *consignāre*, to seal, sign.] —con'sign•ee' n. —con•sign'or n.

con•sign•ment (kən-sīn'mənt) n. A shipment of goods or a cargo to an agent for sale or custody.

con•sist (kən-sĭst') v. 1. To be made up or composed (with *of*). 2. To be inherent; lie. [< L *consistere*, to stand still, exist.]

con•sis•ten•cy (kən-sĭs'tən-sē) n., pl. -cies. Also **con•sis•tence** (-təns). 1. Agreement or compatibility among things or parts. 2. Uni-

formity. **3.** Degree of texture or firmness.
—**con•sis'tent** adj. —**con•sis'tent•ly** adv.
con•sis•to•ry (kən-sĭs'tər-ē) n., pl. -ries. A gathering of Roman Catholic cardinals presided over by the pope. [< L consistere, to take one's place (at a meeting), stand, CONSIST.] —**con'sis•to'ri•al** (kŏn'sĭs-tôr'ē-əl, -tôr'ē-əl) adj.
consol. consolidated.
con•sole¹ (kən-sōl') v. -soled, -soling. To comfort; solace. [< L consōlārī.] —**con'so•la'tion** (kŏn'sə-lā'shən) n. —**con•sol'er** n.
con•sole² (kŏn'sōl) n. **1.** The desklike part of an organ that contains the keyboard, stops, and pedals. **2.** A cabinet for a radio, television set, or phonograph, designed to stand on the floor. **3.** A control panel. [< L consōlārī, CONSOLE.]
con•sol•i•date (kən-sŏl'ə-dāt') v. -dated, -dating. **1.** To form into a compact mass; solidify. **2.** To unite into one system or body; combine. [L consolidāre.] —**con•sol'i•da'tion** n. —**con•sol'i•da'tor** n.
con•som•mé (kŏn'sə-mā') n. A clear soup made of meat or vegetable stock or both. [F, "concentrate."]
con•so•nance (kŏn'sə-nəns) n. **1.** Agreement; harmony. **2.** Repetition of terminal consonants as an alternative to full rhyme.
con•so•nant (kŏn'sə-nənt) adj. In agreement or accord. —n. **1.** A speech sound produced by a partial or complete obstruction of the air stream. **2.** A letter or character representing such a sound. [< L (littera) consonāns, "(letter) sounded with (a vowel)."]
con•so•nan•tal (kŏn'sə-nǎn'təl) adj. Of, relating to, or being a consonant. —**con'so•nan'tal•ly** adv.
con•sort (kŏn'sôrt) n. A husband or wife, esp. the spouse of a monarch. —v. (kən-sôrt'). **1.** To keep company; associate. **2.** To be in agreement. [< L consors, "one who shares the same fate."]
con•sor•ti•um (kən-sôr'shē-əm) n., pl. -tia (-shē-ə). An international combination of capitalists and financiers. [< L consors, companion, CONSORT.]
con•spic•u•ous (kən-spĭk'yōō-əs) adj. Prominent; remarkable. [< L conspicere, to look at closely, observe.] —**con•spic'u•ous•ly** adv. —**con•spic'u•ous•ness** n.
con•spir•a•cy (kən-spĭr'ə-sē) n., pl. -cies. A plot, esp. an illegal one. [< L conspīrāre, CONSPIRE.]
con•spire (kən-spīr') v. -spired, -spiring. **1.** To plan secretly, esp. to commit an illegal act; plot. **2.** To combine or act together. [< L conspīrāre, "to breathe together," agree, unite.] —**con•spir'a•tor** (-spîr'ə-tər) n. —**con•spir'a•to'ri•al** adj. —**con•spir'er** n.
const. 1. constable. **2.** constant. **3.** constitution.
Const. 1. constable. **2.** constitution.
con•sta•ble (kŏn'stə-bəl, kŭn'-) n. A peace officer or policeman. [< LL comes stabulī, "count of the stable."]
con•stab•u•lar•y (kən-stǎb'yə-lěr'ē) n., pl. -ies. **1.** The body of constables of a district or city.

2. An armed police force organized like a military unit.
con•stan•cy (kŏn'stən-sē) n. **1.** Steadfastness; loyalty. **2.** Stability.
con•stant (kŏn'stənt) adj. **1.** Continually recurring; persistent. **2.** Unchanging; invariable. **3.** Steadfast. —n. **1.** A thing that is unchanging or invariable. **2.** A condition, factor, or quantity that is invariant in specified circumstances. [< L constāre, to stand together, remain steadfast.] —**con'stant•ly** adv.
Con•stan•ti•no•ple (kŏn'stăn-tə-nō'pəl). The former name for Istanbul.
con•stel•la•tion (kŏn'stə-lā'shən) n. **1.** Any of various stellar groups considered to resemble and named after various mythological characters, inanimate objects, and animals. **2.** A position of the stars at the time of one's birth, regarded as determining one's character or fate. **3.** A grouping or configuration. [< LL constellātiō, group of stars.]
con•ster•na•tion (kŏn'stər-nā'shən) n. Sudden confusion or dismay.
con•sti•pa•tion (kŏn'stə-pā'shən) n. Difficult, incomplete, or infrequent evacuation of the bowels. [< L constīpāre, to press together.]
con•stit•u•en•cy (kən-stĭch'ōō-ən-sē) n., pl. -cies. **1.** The body of voters represented by an elected legislator. **2.** An electoral district.
con•stit•u•ent (kən-stĭch'ōō-ənt) adj. **1.** Serving as part of a whole; component. **2.** Empowered to elect. **3.** Authorized to make or amend a constitution. —n. **1.** One represented by an elected official. **2.** A component. [< L constituere, CONSTITUTE.]
con•sti•tute (kŏn'stə-t/yōōt') v. -tuted, -tuting. **1.** To make up; compose. **2.** To establish formally. **3.** To appoint to an office; designate. [< L constituere, to cause to stand, set, fix.]
con•sti•tu•tion (kŏn'stə-t/yōō'shən) n. **1.** The act or process of constituting. **2.** The composition of something; make-up. **3.** A person's prevailing state of health. **4. a.** The basic law of a politically organized body. **b.** The document setting forth such law. **5. the Constitution.** The Constitution of the U.S., adopted in 1787 and put into effect in 1789.
con•sti•tu•tion•al (kŏn'stə-t/yōō'shən-əl) adj. **1.** Basic; essential. **2.** Contained in, consistent with, or operating under a constitution. —n. A walk taken regularly for one's health. —**con'sti•tu•tion•al'i•ty** n.
constr. construction.
con•strain (kən-strān') v. **1.** To compel; oblige. **2.** To confine. **3.** To restrain. [< L constringere, to draw or bind tightly together.] —**con•strain'a•ble** adj. —**con•strain'er** n.
con•strained (kən-strānd') adj. **1.** Resulting from constraint; restrained. **2.** Forced; unnatural. —**con•strain'ed•ly** (-strān'ĭd-lē) adv.
con•straint (kən-strānt') n. **1.** Compulsion; restraint. **2.** Lack of ease; embarrassment.
con•strict (kən-strĭkt') v. **1.** To compress, contract, or squeeze. [L constringere (pp constrictus), to CONSTRAIN.] —**con•stric'tion** n. —**con•stric'tive** adj. —**con•stric'tor** n.
con•struct (kən-strŭkt') v. To make or build.

[L *construere* (pp *constructus*), to pile up together, build.] —con•struc'tor *n.*
con•struc•tion (kən-strŭk'shən) *n.* 1. The action or business of building. 2. A structure. 3. An interpretation. 4. A meaningful syntax-bound string of words in a sentence.
con•struc•tive (kən-strŭk'tĭv) *adj.* 1. Useful; helpful. 2. Structural. —con•struc'tive•ly *adv.*
con•strue (kən-strōō') *v.* -strued, -struing. 1. To explain syntactic relations within a sentence. 2. To interpret. 3. To translate. [< L *construere*, to CONSTRUCT.] —con•stru'er *n.*
con•sul (kŏn'səl) *n.* 1. Either of the two chief magistrates of the Roman Republic, elected for a term of one year. 2. An official appointed by a government to reside in a foreign city and represent its citizens there. [< L.] —con'su•lar *adj.*
con•su•late (kŏn'sə-lĭt) *n.* The premises occupied by a consul.
con•sult (kən-sŭlt') *v.* 1. To seek the advice of. 2. To exchange views; confer. [< L *consulere*, to take counsel.] —con•sult'ant *n.* —con'sul•ta'tion *n.* —con•sult'a•tive (-sŭl'tə-tĭv) *adj.*
con•sume (kən-s/y/ōōm') *v.* -sumed, -suming. 1. To eat up; devour. 2. To use up; expend. 3. To waste; squander. 4. To destroy. 5. To absorb; engross. [< L *consūmere*, to take completely.] —con•sum'a•ble *adj.*
con•sum•er (kən-s/y/ōō'mər) *n.* 1. One that consumes. 2. A buyer.
con•sum•er•ism (kən-sōō'mə-rĭz'əm) *n.* The movement seeking to protect the rights of consumers, as by requiring honest advertising and improved safety standards.
con•sum•mate (kŏn'sə-māt') *v.* -mated, -mating. 1. To complete; achieve. 2. To fulfill (a marriage) with the first act of sexual intercourse. —*adj.* (kən-sŭm'ĭt). 1. Perfect.. 2. Complete; utter. [< L *consummāre*, to bring together, sum up.] —con•sum'mate•ly *adv.*
con•sump•tion (kən-sŭmp'shən) *n.* 1. The act or process of consuming. 2. The amount consumed. 3. The use of consumer goods. 4. a. A wasting of tissue. b. Tuberculosis. [< L *consūmere*, CONSUME.]
con•sump•tive (kən-sŭmp'tĭv) *adj.* 1. Wasteful; destructive. 2. Of or afflicted with consumption. —con•sump'tive•ly *adv.*
cont. 1. containing. 2. contents. 3. continent. 4. continue; continued. 5. contract. 6. contraction. 7. control.
con•tact (kŏn'tăkt') *n.* 1. A coming together or touching of objects or surfaces. 2. A relationship; association. 3. Connection. 4. A conducting connection between two electric conductors. —*v.* (kŏn'tăkt, kən-tăkt'). 1. To come or put into contact. 2. To get in touch with. —*adj.* (kŏn'tăkt'). 1. Of or making contact. 2. Caused or transmitted by touching. [L *contāctus*, pp of *contingere*, to touch, border upon.]
contact lens. A thin corrective lens fitted over the cornea.
con•ta•gion (kən-tā'jən) *n.* 1. a. Disease transmission by contact. b. A disease so transmitted. c. The causative agent of such a disease. 2. Transmission of an influence or emotional state. [< L *contingere*, to touch, CONTACT.]
con•ta•gious (kən-tā'jəs) *adj.* 1. Transmissible by contact. 2. Carrying or capable of carrying disease. 3. Tending to spread; catching.
con•tain (kən-tān') *v.* 1. To enclose. 2. To comprise; include. 3. To be able to hold. 4. To restrict. [< L *continēre*, to hold together, enclose.] —con•tain'ment *n.*
con•tain•er (kən-tā'nər) *n.* A receptacle.
con•tam•i•nant (kən-tăm'ə-nənt) *n.* Something that contaminates.
con•tam•i•nate (kən-tăm'ə-nāt') *v.* -nated, -nating. To make impure by contact or mixture. [< L *contāmināre*.] —con•tam'i•na'tion *n.* —con•tam'i•na'tive *adj.*
contd. continued.
con•temn (kən-tĕm') *v.* To view with contempt; despise. [< L *contemnere*.]
contemp. contemporary.
con•tem•plate (kŏn'təm-plāt') *v.* -plated, -plating. 1. To ponder or consider. 2. To intend; expect. [L *contemplārī*, to observe carefully.] —con'tem•pla'tion *n.* —con•tem'pla•tive (kən-tĕm'plə-tĭv) *adj.* —con'tem•pla'tor *n.*
con•tem•po•ra•ne•ous (kən-tĕm'pə-rā'nē-əs) *adj.* Contemporary. [L *contemporāneus*.]
con•tem•po•rar•y (kən-tĕm'pə-rĕr'ē) *adj.* 1. Belonging to the same period of time. 2. Of about the same age. 3. Current; modern. —*n.*, *pl.* -ies. 1. One of the same time or age. 2. A person of the present time. [ML *contemporārius*.] —con•tem'po•rar'i•ly *adv.*
con•tempt (kən-tĕmpt') *n.* 1. Bitter scorn; as for something vile; disdain. 2. Open disrespect or willful disobedience to a court, legislature, etc. [< L *contemptus*, pp of *contemnere*, CONTEMN.]
con•tempt•i•ble (kən-tĕmp'tə-bəl) *adj.* Deserving contempt; despicable.
con•temp•tu•ous (kən-tĕmp'chōō-əs) *adj.* Manifesting contempt; scornful. —con•temp'tu•ous•ly *adv.* —con•temp'tu•ous•ness *n.*
con•tend (kən-tĕnd') *v.* 1. To strive, vie, or dispute. 2. To maintain or assert. [< L *contendere*, to strain, strive with.] —con•tend'er *n.*
con•tent¹ (kŏn'tĕnt) *n.* 1. Often contents. That which is contained in something. 2. Often contents. Subject matter, as of a book. 3. Meaning or significance. 4. The proportion of a specified substance. [< L *contentus*, pp of *continēre*, CONTAIN.]
con•tent² (kən-tĕnt') *adj.* Satisfied. —*v.* To satisfy. —*n.* Satisfaction; contentment. [< L *contentus*, pp of *continēre*, to restrain, CONTAIN.]
con•tent•ed (kən-tĕn'tĭd) *adj.* Satisfied. —con•tent'ed•ly *adv.* —con•tent'ed•ness *n.*
con•ten•tion (kən-tĕn'shən) *n.* Dispute; controversy. [< L *contendere*, CONTEND.] —con•ten'tious *adj.* —con•ten'tious•ness *n.*
con•tent•ment (kən-tĕnt'mənt) *n.* The state of being contented.
con•ter•mi•nous (kən-tûr'mə-nəs) *adj.* Having a boundary in common; contiguous. [L *conterminus*.] —con•ter'mi•nous•ness *n.*
con•test (kŏn'tĕst') *n.* 1. A struggle; fight. 2. A competition. —*v.* (kən-tĕst', kŏn'tĕst'). 1. To

compete or strive for. 2. To dispute; challenge. [< L *contestārī*, bring in (a lawsuit) by calling witnesses.] —con•test′a•ble *adj.*

con•test•ant (kən-těs′tənt, kŏn′těs′tənt) *n.* A competitor or challenger.

con•text (kŏn′těkst) *n.* 1. The verbal or written environment in which a word or group of words occurs. 2. The overall situation in which an event occurs. [< L *contextus*, coherence, sequence of words.] —con•tex′tu•al (kən-těks′chōō-əl) *adj.* —con•tex′tu•al•ly *adv.*

con•tig•u•ous (kən-tĭg′yōō-əs) *adj.* 1. Touching. 2. Next or adjacent to. [< L *contingere*, to touch on all sides, CONTACT.] —con′ti•gu′i•ty (kŏn′tə-gyōō′ə-tē) *n.*

con•ti•nence (kŏn′tə-nəns) *n.* 1. Self-restraint. 2. Abstention from sexual activity. 3. Ability to control bladder or bowel functions. [< L *continēre*, to contain.] —con′ti•nent *adj.*

con•ti•nent (kŏn′tə-nənt) *n.* 1. One of the principal land masses of the earth. 2. the Continent. The mainland of Europe. [L *(terra) continēns,* "continuous (land)."]

con•ti•nen•tal (kŏn′tə-něn′təl) *adj.* 1. Of or like a continent. 2. Often Continental. European. 3. Continental. Of or pertaining to the American colonies during the Revolutionary War. —*n.* Continental. A soldier in the Continental Army. —con′ti•nen′tal•ly *adv.*

continental shelf. A generally shallow, flat submerged portion of a continent.

con•tin•gen•cy (kən-tĭn′jən-sē) *n., pl.* -cies. A fortuitous or possible event.

con•tin•gent (kən-tĭn′jənt) *adj.* 1. Possible. 2. Conditional. 3. Fortuitous. —*n.* 1. A quota, as of troops. 2. A representative group. [< L *contingere*, to touch on all sides, CONTACT.]

con•tin•u•al (kən-tĭn′yōō-əl) *adj.* 1. Recurring often. 2. Continuous; incessant. —con•tin′u•al•ly *adv.*

con•tin•u•ance (kən-tĭn′yōō-əns) *n.* 1. The act or fact of continuing. 2. Duration. 3. Unbroken sequence. 4. Postponement or adjournment of legal proceedings.

con•tin•u•a•tion (kən-tĭn′yōō-ā′shən) *n.* 1. The act or fact of continuing or state of being continued. 2. A supplement; sequel.

con•tin•ue (kən-tĭn′yōō) *v.* -ued, -uing. 1. To persist. 2. To endure; last. 3. To remain in a state, capacity, or place; abide. 4. To go on after an interruption; resume. 5. To extend. 6. To retain. 7. *Law.* To postpone or adjourn. [< L *continēre*, to hold together, be continuous, CONTAIN.] —con•tin′u•er *n.*

con•ti•nu•i•ty (kŏn′tə-n/yōō′ə-tē) *n., pl.* -ties. 1. The state or quality of being continuous. 2. An uninterrupted succession.

con•tin•u•ous (kən-tĭn′yōō-əs) *adj.* Extending or prolonged without interruption; unbroken. —con•tin′u•ous•ly *adv.* —con•tin′u•ous•ness *n.*

con•tin•u•um (kən-tĭn′yōō-əm) *n., pl.* -tinua (-tĭn′yōō-ə) or -ums. Something in which no part can be distinguished from neighboring parts except by arbitrary division.

con•tort (kən-tôrt′) *v.* To twist or wrench out of shape. [L *contorquēre* (pp *contortus*), to twist together.] —con•tor′tion *n.* —con•tor′tive *adj.*

con•tor•tion•ist (kən-tôr′shən-ĭst) *n.* An acro-

bat who can twist his body into extraordinary postures. —con•tor′tion•is′tic *adj.*

con•tour (kŏn′tōōr) *n.* 1. The outline of a figure, body, or mass. 2. contours. A surface, esp. of a curving form. —*adj.* Following the contour lines of uneven terrain to limit erosion of topsoil. [< It *contornare*, to go around.]

contour line. A line, as on a map, joining points of equal elevation.

contour map. A map showing elevations and surface configuration by means of contour lines.

contr. 1. contract. 2. contraction.

contra-. *comb. form.* Against, opposing, or contrary. [< L *contrā*, against.]

con•tra•band (kŏn′trə-bănd′) *n.* 1. Goods prohibited in trade. 2. Smuggled goods. 3. Smuggling. [< It *contrabbando.*]

con•tra•cep•tion (kŏn′trə-sĕp′shən) *n.* Prevention of conception. —con′tra•cep′tive (-sĕp′tĭv) *adj. & n.*

con•tract (kŏn′trăkt′) *n.* An enforceable agreement; covenant. —*v.* (kən-trăkt′, kŏn′trăkt′). 1. To enter into or establish by contract. 2. To catch (a disease). 3. To shrink by drawing together. 4. To shorten (a word or words) by omitting or combining some of the letters. [< L *contractus*, pp of *contrahere*, to draw together, bring about.] —con•tract′i•ble *adj.* —con•trac′tion *n.* —con′trac′tor *n.*

con•trac•tile (kən-trăk′təl) *adj.* Capable of contracting.

con•tra•dict (kŏn′trə-dĭkt′) *v.* 1. To assert the opposite of. 2. To deny the statement of. 3. To be contrary to or inconsistent with. [L *contrādīcere*, to speak against.] —con′tra•dic′tion *n.* —con′tra•dic′to•ry *adj.*

con•tra•dis•tinc•tion (kŏn′trə-dĭ-stĭngk′shən) *n.* Distinction by contrast.

con•trail (kŏn′trāl′) *n.* A visible trail of water droplets or ice crystals formed in the wake of an aircraft. [CON(DENSATION) + TRAIL.]

con•tra•in•di•cate (kŏn′trə-ĭn′də-kāt′) *v.* -cated, -cating. To indicate the inadvisability of. —con′tra•in′di•ca′tion *n.*

con•tral•to (kən-trăl′tō) *n., pl.* -tos. 1. The lowest female voice or voice part. 2. A singer having such a voice. [It.]

con•trap•tion (kən-trăp′shən) *n.* An elaborate device. [< CONTRIVE and TRAP + -TION.]

con•tra•pun•tal (kŏn′trə-pŭnt′l) *adj.* Of or incorporating counterpoint.

con•tra•ri•e•ty (kŏn′trə-rī′ə-tē) *n., pl.* -ties. The condition of being contrary.

con•trar•i•wise (kŏn′trěr′ē-wīz′) *adv.* 1. Oppositely. 2. On the contrary.

con•tra•ry (kŏn′trěr′ē) *adj.* 1. Opposite, as in character or direction. 2. Adverse; unfavorable. 3. Perverse; willful. 4. Opposed; counter. —*n., pl.* -ries. That which is contrary; the opposite. —*adv.* In opposition; contrariwise. [< L *contrā*, against.] —con′tra′ri•ly *adv.*

con•trast (kən-trăst′) *v.* 1. To set in opposition in order to show differences. 2. To show differences when compared. —*n.* (kŏn′trăst′). 1. Dissimilarity between things compared. 2. Something showing such dissimilarity. [< ML *contrāstāre.*] —con•trast′ing•ly *adv.*

ŏ paw, for/oi boy/ou out/ōō took/ōō coo/p pop/r run/s sauce/sh shy/t to/th thin/*th* the/
ŭ cut/ûr fur/v van/w wag/y yes/z size/zh vision/ə ago, item, edible, gallop, circus/

con·tra·vene (kŏn'trə-vēn') v. -vened, -vening.
1. To act or go contrary to. 2. To contradict.
[< LL *contrāvenīre*, to come against, oppose.]
con·tre·temps (kŏn'trə-täN') n. An inopportune or embarrassing occurrence. [F.]
contrib. contribution; contributor.
con·trib·ute (kən-trĭb'yōōt) v. -uted, -uting. To
give a share to or participate in. [L *contribuere*, to bring together, unite, collect.]
—**con'tri·bu'tion** n. —**con·trib'u·tor** n. —**con·trib'u·to'ry** (-tôr'ē, -tōr'ē) adj.
con·trite (kən-trīt') adj. Repentant. [< ML
contrītus, "broken in spirit," repentant.]
—**con·trite'ly** adv. —**con·tri'tion** (-trĭsh'ən) n.
con·tri·vance (kən-trī'vəns) n. 1. A scheme;
plan. 2. A mechanical device.
con·trive (kən-trīv') v. -trived, -triving. 1. To
plan; devise. 2. To make or fabricate. 3. To
manage or effect. [< LL *contropāre*, to represent figuratively, compare.] —**con·triv'ed·ly**
adv. —**con·triv'er** n.
con·trol (kən-trōl') v. -trolled, -trolling. 1. To
exercise a regulating influence over; direct.
2. To verify or regulate by systematic comparison. —n. 1. Power to regulate, direct, or
dominate. 2. Restraint; reserve. 3. A standard
of comparison for verifying the results of an
experiment. 4. Often **controls.** A set of
instruments for regulating a machine. [< ML
contrārotulāre, to check by a counter roll or
duplicate register.] —**con·trol'la·ble** adj.
con·trol·ler (kən-trō'lər) n. 1. One who controls. 2. Also **comp·trol·ler.** The chief accountant of a corporation.
con·tro·ver·sy (kŏn'trə-vûr'sē) n., pl. -sies. A
protracted public dispute. [< L *contrōversus*,
turned against, disputed.] —**con'tro·ver'sial**
(-vûr'shəl) adj. —**con'tro·ver'sial·ly** adv.
con·tro·vert (kŏn'trə-vûrt') v. To deny. [<
CONTROVERSY.] —**con'tro·vert'i·ble** adj.
con·tu·ma·cious (kŏn't/y/ōō-mā'shəs) adj.
Obstinately rebellious; insubordinate. —**con'-
tu·ma·cy** (kŏn't/y/ōō-mə-sē) n.
con·tu·me·ly (kŏn't/y/ōō-mə-lē) n. Insulting
treatment. [< L *contumēlia*, insult, reproach.]
—**con'tu·me'li·ous** (-mē'lē-əs) adj.
con·tuse (kən-t/y/ōōz') v. -tused, -tusing. To
injure without breaking the skin; bruise. [< L
contundere (pp *contūsus*), to beat, pound.]
—**con·tu'sion** n.
co·nun·drum (kə-nŭn'drəm) n. A riddle.
con·va·lesce (kŏn'və-lĕs') v. -lesced, -lescing.
To recuperate from an illness. [L *convalēscere*.] —**con'va·les'cence** n. —**con'va·les'cent**
adj. & n.
con·vec·tion (kən-vĕk'shən) n. Heat transfer
by fluid motion between regions of unequal
density that result from nonuniform heating.
[< L *convehere*, to carry together, bring along.]
con·vene (kən-vēn') v. -vened, -vening. To
assemble, meet, or convoke. [< L *convenīre*.]
con·ven·ience (kən-vēn'yəns) n. 1. Suitability. 2. Personal comfort. 3. Anything that
increases comfort or makes work easier.
con·ven·ient (kən-vēn'yənt) adj. 1. Suited to
one's comfort or needs. 2. Easy to reach;
accessible. [< L *convenīre*, to be suitable,
CONVENE.] —**con·ven'lent·ly** adv.

con·vent (kŏn'vənt, -vĕnt') n. A monastic
community or house, esp. of nuns. [< L
conventus, a coming together, assembly.]
—**con·ven·tu·al** (kən-vĕn'chōō-əl) adj.
con·ven·tion (kən-vĕn'shən) n. 1. a. A formal
assembly, as of a political party. b. The delegates attending such an assembly. 2. An international agreement or compact. 3. General
usage or custom. 4. An accepted or prescribed
practice. [< L *convenīre*, to come together,
CONVENE.]
con·ven·tion·al (kən-vĕn'shən-əl) adj. 1. Approved by or following general usage; customary. 2. Commonplace or ordinary. —**con·
ven'tion·al·ism'** n. —**con·ven'tion·al'i·ty** n.
—**con·ven'tion·al·ly** adv.
con·verge (kən-vûrj') v. -verged, -verging. 1. To
tend toward a common point or result. 2.
Math. To approach a limit. [< LL *convergere*,
to incline together.] —**con·ver'gence, con·ver'-
gen·cy** n. —**con·ver'gent** adj.
con·ver·sant (kŏn'vər-sənt, kən-vûr'-) adj.
Familiar, as by experience. [< L *conversārī*, to
associate with, CONVERSE.]
con·ver·sa·tion (kŏn'vər-sā'shən) n. An informal spoken exchange; a familiar talk.
—**con'ver·sa'tion·al** adj. —**con'ver·sa'tion·al·ly**
adv.
con·ver·sa·tion·al·ist (kŏn'vər-sā'shən-əl-ĭst)
n. One given to or skilled at conversation.
con·verse¹ (kən-vûrs') v. -versed, -versing. To
engage in conversation; talk informally. —n.
(kŏn'vûrs'). Conversation. [< L *conversārī*, to
associate with.]
con·verse² (kən-vûrs', kŏn'vûrs') adj. Reversed, as in relation or order. —n. (kŏn'-
vûrs'). Something that has been reversed; the
opposite. [L *conversus*, pp of *convertere*, to
turn around.] —**con·verse'ly** adv.
con·ver·sion (kən-vûr'zhən, -shən) n. 1. The
act of converting or state of being converted.
2. A change in which one adopts a new religion. 3. The unlawful appropriation of another's property. 4. The exchange of one type
of security or currency for another.
con·vert (kən-vûrt') v. 1. To change into another form, substance, etc.; transform. 2. To
persuade or be persuaded to adopt a given
religion or belief. 3. To adapt to a new or
different purpose. 4. To exchange for something of equal value. 5. To misappropriate.
—n. (kŏn'vûrt'). One who has accepted religious conversion. [< L *convertere*, to turn
around, transform.] —**con·vert'er, con·ver'tor** n.
con·vert·i·ble (kən-vûr'tə-bəl) adj. Capable of
being converted. —n. An automobile with a
top that can be folded back or taken off.
con·vex (kŏn'vĕks, kən-vĕks') adj. Curved
outward, as the exterior of a sphere. [L *convexus*, arched, convex.] —**con·vex'i·ty** n.
con·vey (kən-vā') v. 1. To carry; transport.
2. To transmit. 3. To communicate; impart.
[< ML *conviāre*, to go with, escort.] —**con·
vey'er, con·vey'or** n.
con·vey·ance (kən-vā'əns) n. 1. The act of
transporting. 2. A vehicle. 3. A legal document effecting the transfer of title to property.
con·vict (kən-vĭkt') v. To find or prove guilty

of an offense. —*n.* (kŏn'vĭkt'). A person found guilty of a crime, esp. one serving a prison sentence. [< L *convincere* (pp *convictus*), to prove guilty, CONVINCE.]
con·vic·tion (kən-vĭk'shən) *n.* **1.** The act of convicting or state of being convicted. **2.** A fixed or strong belief.
con·vince (kən-vĭns') *v.* **-vinced, -vincing.** To bring to belief by argument and evidence; persuade. [L *convincere,* to overcome, refute, prove guilty.] —**con·vinc'er** *n.* —**con·vinc'ing** *adj.* —**con·vinc'ing·ly** *adv.*
Usage: Convince is regularly followed by *of* or a clause introduced by *that,* but not by an infinitive with *to. Persuade,* however, can be used with all three constructions. Thus: *He convinced me* (or *I was convinced*) *of his good intentions. He convinced me* (or *I was convinced*) *that I should go. He persuaded* (not *convinced*) *me to go.*
con·viv·i·al (kən-vĭv'ē-əl) *adj.* Sociable; jovial. [< L *convivium,* "a living together," banquet.] —**con·viv'i·al'i·ty** *n.* —**con·viv'i·al·ly** *adv.*
con·vo·ca·tion (kŏn'vō-kā'shən) *n.* **1.** The act of convoking. **2.** A formal assembly.
con·voke (kən-vōk') *v.* **-voked, -voking.** To cause to assemble; convene. [< L *convocāre,* to call together, summon.]
con·vo·lut·ed (kŏn'və-lōō'tĭd) *adj.* **1.** Coiled; twisted. **2.** Intricate; complicated. [< L *convolvere,* to interweave.]
con·vo·lu·tion (kŏn'və-lōō'shən) *n.* **1.** A coiling or twisting together. **2.** An intricacy. **3.** One of the convex folds of the surface of the brain.
con·voy (kŏn'voi', kən-voi') *v.* To escort for protection. —*n.* (kŏn'voi'). An accompanying and protecting force. [< OF *convoier, conveier,* convey.]
con·vulse (kən-vŭls') *v.* **-vulsed, -vulsing. 1.** To shake or agitate violently. **2.** To cause irregular and involuntary muscular contractions. [L *convellere* (pp *convulsus*), to pull violently, wrest.]
con·vul·sion (kən-vŭl'shən) *n.* **1.** An intense paroxysmal involuntary muscular contraction. **2.** A violent disturbance. —**con·vul'sive** *adj.* —**con·vul'sive·ly** *adv.*
co·ny (kō'nē, kŭn'ē) *n., pl.* **-nies.** Also **co·ney** *pl.* **-neys. 1.** A rabbit or similar animal. **2.** The fur of a rabbit. [< L *cunīculus.*]
coo (kōō) *v.* To utter the murmuring sound of a dove or pigeon. —*n.* The murmuring call of a dove or a similar sound. [Imit.]
cook (kōōk) *v.* **1.** To prepare food for eating by applying heat. **2.** To prepare or treat by heating. —*n.* One who prepares food for eating. [< L *coquere,* to cook.]
cook·book (kōōk'bōōk') *n.* A book of cooking recipes.
cook·er·y (kōōk'ər-ē) *n.* The art or practice of cooking.
cook·out (kōōk'out') *n.* A meal cooked and served outdoors.
cook·y, cook·ie (kōōk'ē) *n., pl.* **-ies.** Also **cook·ey** *pl.* **-eys.** A small, sweet, usually flat cake. [< Du *koek,* cake.]
cool (kōōl) *adj.* **1.** Moderately cold. **2.** Reduc-

ing discomfort in hot weather: *a cool blouse.* **3.** Calm; controlled. **4.** Showing dislike or indifference. **5.** Impudent. **6.** *Slang.* Excellent. —*v.* **1.** To make or become less warm. **2.** To make or become less intense. —*n.* **1.** Moderate cold. **2.** *Slang.* Composure. [< OE *cōl.* See **gel-³.**] —**cool'ly** *adv.* —**cool'ness** *n.*
cool·ant (kōō'lənt) *n.* A fluid that draws off heat by circulating through a machine or bathing a mechanical part.
cool·er (kōō'lər) *n.* **1.** A refrigerator. **2.** *Slang.* Jail.
Coo·lidge (kōō'lĭj), **(John) Calvin.** 1872–1933. 30th President of the U.S. (1923–29).

Calvin Coolidge

coo·lie (kōō'lē) *n.* Also **coo·ly** *pl.* **-lies.** An unskilled Oriental laborer. [Hindi *kulī, qulī.*]
coon (kōōn) *n.* A raccoon. [Short for RACCOON.]
coon·hound (kōōn'hound') *n.* A smooth-coated black and tan hound of a breed developed in the SE U.S. to hunt raccoons.
coon's age. *Slang.* A long time.
coon·skin (kōōn'skĭn') *n.* **1.** The pelt of the raccoon. **2.** An article made of coonskin, such as a hat. —**coon'skin'** *adj.*
coop (kōōp) *n.* A cage, as for poultry. —*v.* To confine in or as in a coop. [ME *coupe,* wicker basket, chicken coop.]
co-op (kō-ŏp', kō'ŏp') *n.* A cooperative.
coop. cooperative.
coop·er (kōō'pər) *n.* One who makes wooden tubs and casks. [ME *couper.*]
Coop·er (kōō'pər), **James Fenimore.** 1789–1851. American novelist.
coop·er·age (kōō'pər-ĭj) *n.* **1.** A cooper's work or products. **2.** A cooper's workshop.
co·op·er·ate (kō-ŏp'ər-āt') *v.* **-ated, -ating.** To work together toward a common end. [L *cooperārī.*] —**co·op'er·a'tion** (kō-ŏp'ər-ā'shən) *n.*
co·op·er·a·tive (kō-ŏp'rə-tĭv, -ə-rā'tĭv) *adj.* **1.** Willing to cooperate. **2.** Engaged in joint economic activity. —*n.* An enterprise collec-

tively owned and operated for mutual benefit: *a farmers' cooperative.* —co•op'er•a•tive•ly *adv.* —co•op'er•a•tive•ness *n.*

co-opt (kō-ŏpt') *v.* To elect as a fellow member or colleague. [L *cooptāre.*]

co•or•di•nate (kō-ôr'də-nāt', -nĭt) *n.* **1.** One equal in rank or order. **2.** One of a set of numbers that determines the location of a point in a space of a given dimension. —*adj.* (kō-ôr'də-nĭt, -nāt'). **1.** Of equal rank or order. **2.** Of or involving coordination. **3.** Of or based on coordinates. —*v.* (kō-ôr'də-nāt') -nated, -nating. **1.** To place in the same rank or order. **2.** To arrange in proper relative position. **3.** To harmonize in a common action. [Back-formation < COORDINATION.] —co•or'di•nate•ly *adv.* —co•or'di•na'tor *n.*

co•or•di•na•tion (kō-ôr'də-nā'shən) *n.* **1.** The act of coordinating or state of being coordinate. **2.** The coordinated functioning of muscles in the execution of a complex task. [< LL *coōrdinātiō,* arrangement in the same order.]

coot (kōōt) *n.* **1.** A short-billed dark-gray water bird. **2.** *Informal.* A foolish old man. [ME *cote.*]

cop (kŏp) *n. Informal.* A policeman. —*v.* copped, copping. *Slang.* To steal or take. [Short for *copper,* policeman, "catcher."]

cop. copyright.

cope¹ (kŏp) *v.* coped, coping. To contend, esp. on even terms or with success. [< OF *couper,* to strike.]

cope² (kŏp) *n.* A long ecclesiastical vestment. [< LL *cappa,* cloak, hood.]

Co•pen•ha•gen (kō'pən-hā'gən). The capital of Denmark. Pop. 924,000.

Co•per•ni•cus (kō-pûr'nə-kəs), **Nicolaus.** 1473–1543. Polish astronomer.

co•pi•lot (kō'pī'lət) *n.* The second or relief pilot of an aircraft.

cop•ing (kō'pĭng) *n.* The top part of a wall. [< COPE².]

co•pi•ous (kō'pē-əs) *adj.* Ample; abundant. [< L *cōpia,* abundance.] —co'pi•ous•ly *adv.* —co'pi•ous•ness *n.*

co•pla•nar (kō-plā'nər) *adj.* Lying or occurring in the same plane.

co•pol•y•mer (kō-pŏl'ə-mər) *n.* A polymer of two or more different monomers.

cop•per¹ (kŏp'ər) *n.* **1.** *Symbol* **Cu** A ductile, malleable, reddish-brown metallic element that is an excellent conductor of heat and electricity and is used for electrical wiring, water piping, and corrosion-resistant parts. Atomic number 29, atomic weight 63.54. **2.** A copper object or coin. [< L *Cyprium (aes),* "(copper) of Cyprus."]

cop•per² (kŏp'ər) *n. Slang.* A policeman. [< COP.]

cop•per•as (kŏp'ər-əs) *n.* A greenish crystalline compound, FeSO₄•7H₂O, used in fertilizers and inks and in water purification. [< ML *cup(e)rosa.*]

cop•per•head (kŏp'ər-hĕd') *n.* A venomous reddish-brown snake of E U.S.

cop•pice (kŏp'ĭs) *n. Chiefly Brit.* A thicket. [< OF *coupeiz,* "thicket for cutting."]

cop•ra (kŏp'rə) *n.* Dried coconut meat from which coconut oil is extracted. [Port.]

copse (kŏps) *n.* A thicket. [Short for COPPICE.]

Copt (kŏpt) *n.* A native of Egypt descended from ancient Egyptian stock, esp. one belonging to the Christian church.

Cop•tic (kŏp'tĭk) *n.* The Afro-Asiatic language of the Copts. —Cop'tic *adj.*

cop•u•la (kŏp'yə-lə) *n.* A verb, usually a form of *be,* that identifies the predicate of a sentence with the subject. [L *cōpula,* link, bond.] —cop'u•lar *adj.*

cop•u•late (kŏp'yə-lāt') *v.* -lated, -lating. To engage in coitus. [< L *cōpula,* link, bond.] —cop'u•la'tion *n.*

cop•u•la•tive (kŏp'yə-lā'tĭv, -lə-tĭv) *adj.* **1.** Joining or uniting. **2.** Serving to connect coordinate words or clauses, as the conjunction *and.*

cop•y (kŏp'ē) *n., pl.* -ies. **1.** An imitation or reproduction of something original; duplicate. **2.** One specimen of a printed text or picture. **3.** A manuscript or other material to be set in type. —*v.* -ied, -ying. **1.** To make a copy of. **2.** To follow as a model; imitate. [< ML *cōpia,* transcript, right of reproduction.]

cop•y•book (kŏp'ē-bōōk') *n.* A book of models of penmanship for imitation.

copy boy. A boy in a newspaper office who carries copy and runs errands.

cop•y•cat (kŏp'ē-kăt') *n.* An imitator.

copy desk. The desk in a newspaper office where copy is edited and prepared for typesetting.

cop•y•ist (kŏp'ē-ĭst) *n.* One who makes written copies.

cop•y•read•er (kŏp'ē-rē'dər) *n.* One who edits and corrects newspaper copy for publication.

cop•y•right (kŏp'ē-rīt') *n.* The exclusive right granted by law to publish, sell, or distribute a literary or artistic work. —*adj.* Also **cop•y•right•ed** (-rī'tĭd). Protected by copyright. —cop'y•right' *v.*

cop•y•writ•er (kŏp'ē-rī'tər) *n.* One who writes advertising copy.

co•quette (kō-kĕt') *n.* A woman who flirts. [< F *coquet,* flirtatious man.] —co•quet'tish *adj.*

cor. **1.** corner. **2.** corpus.

Cor. Corinthians (New Testament).

cor•a•cle (kôr'ə-kəl, kŏr'-) *n.* A boat made of waterproof material stretched over wicker or wooden hoops. [< W *corwgl, cwrwgl.*]

cor•al (kôr'əl, kŏr'əl) *n.* **1.** A hard, stony substance, often used for jewelry, formed from the massed skeletons of minute marine organisms. **2.** Such an organism or a structure formed by such organisms. **3.** Yellowish red or pink. [< Gk *korallion.*] —cor'al *adj.*

Coral Sea. A portion of the SW Pacific Ocean, NE of Australia.

cor•bel (kôr'bəl, -bĕl) *n.* A bracket of stone or other building material, projecting from a wall and used to support a cornice or an arch. [< OF.]

cord (kôrd) *n.* **1.** A string or small rope of twisted strands or fibers. **2.** An insulated, flexible electric wire fitted with a plug. **3. a.** A raised rib on the surface of a cloth. **b.** A fabric

---

ă pat/ā ate/âr care/ä bar/b bib/ch chew/d deed/ĕ pet/ē be/f fit/g gag/h hat/hw what/ ĭ pit/ī pie/îr pier/j judge/k kick/l lid, fatal/m mum/n no, sudden/ng sing/ŏ pot/ō go/

or cloth with such ribs. **4.** A unit of cut fuel wood, equal to 128 cubic feet in a stack measuring 4 by 4 by 8 feet. —*v.* **1.** To fasten with a cord. **2.** To pile (wood) in cords. [< L *chorda*, catgut, cord.] —**cord′er** *n.*

cor•dial (kôr′jəl) *adj.* Hearty; warm; sincere. —*n.* **1.** A stimulant. **2.** A liqueur. [< L *cor (cord-)*, heart.] —**cor′dial′i•ty** (kôr′jăl′ə-tē, -jē-ăl′-, -dē-ăl′-) *n.* —**cor′dial•ly** *adv.*

cor•dil•le•ra (kôr′dĭl-yâr′ə, kôr-dĭl′ər-ə) *n.* A chain of mountains. [< Span *cuerda*, cord, chain.] —**cor′dil•ler′an** *adj.*

cord•ite (kôr′dīt′) *n.* A smokeless explosive powder dissolved in acetone, dried, and extruded in cords. [< CORD.]

cor•do•ba (kôr′də-bə) *n.* The basic monetary unit of Nicaragua. [< F. de *Córdoba* (1475–1526), Spanish explorer.]

cor•don (kôr′dən) *n.* **1.** A line of people, military posts, ships, etc., stationed around an area to enclose or guard it. **2.** A cord or ribbon worn as an ornament or decoration. [< OF *corde*, cord.]

cor•do•van (kôr′də-vən) *n.* A fine leather made originally at Córdoba, Spain. [Span *cordobán.*]

cor•du•roy (kôr′də-roi, kôr′də-roi′) *n.* **1.** A durable, ribbed cotton fabric. **2. corduroys.** Corduroy trousers. [Prob < CORD + obs *deroy*, a coarse woolen fabric.]

core (kôr, kōr) *n.* **1.** The hard or fibrous central part of certain fruits, as an apple. **2.** The most important part of anything. —*v.* **cored, coring.** To remove the core of: *core apples.* [ME.] —**cor′er** *n.*

CORE (kôr, kōr) Congress of Racial Equality.

co•re•spon•dent (kō′rĭ-spŏn′dənt) *n.* A person charged with having committed adultery with the defendant in a suit for divorce. [CO- + RESPONDENT.]

Cor•fam (kôr′făm) *n.* A trademark for a synthetic leather.

co•ri•an•der (kôr′ē-ăn′dər, kōr′ē-) *n.* An herb with aromatic seeds used as a condiment. [< Gk *koriandron.*]

Co•rin•thi•an order (kə-rĭn′thē-ən). One of the three classical orders of architecture, characterized by a fluted column having a capital decorated with acanthus leaves.

co•ri•um (kôr′ē-əm, kōr′-) *n., pl.* **coria** (kôr′ē-ə, kōr′-).** The skin layer beneath the epithelium, containing nerve endings, sweat glands, and blood and lymph vessels. [< L, skin, hide.]

cork (kôrk) *n.* **1.** The light, porous outer bark of a Mediterranean tree, the **cork oak. 2.** A bottle stopper or other object made from this. —*v.* To stop or seal with or as with a cork. [< Span *alcorque*, cork sole or shoe.]

cork•er (kôr′kər) *n. Slang.* Someone or something that is remarkable.

cork•screw (kôrk′skrōō′) *n.* A spiral-shaped device for drawing corks from bottles. —*adj.* Like a corkscrew in shape; spiral.

corm (kôrm) *n.* An underground plant stem similar to a bulb. [< Gk *kormos*, a trimmed tree trunk.]

cor•mo•rant (kôr′mər-ənt) *n.* A water bird with dark plumage, webbed feet, and a hooked

bill. —*adj.* Greedy; gluttonous; rapacious. [< OF *cormoran.*]

corn¹ (kôrn) *n.* **1.** A tall, widely cultivated cereal grass bearing seeds on large ears; maize. **2.** The seeds or ears of this plant. **3.** *Brit.* Any of various widely grown cereal plants or their grain. **4.** *Slang.* Something trite or dated. —*v.* **1.** To preserve in brine: *corned beef.* **2.** To feed (animals) with corn or grain. [< OE *corn.* See grə-no-.]

corn² (kôrn) *n.* A horny thickening of the skin, usually on or near a toe, resulting from pressure or friction. [< L *cornū*, horn.]

corn•cob (kôrn′kŏb′) *n.* The woody core of an ear of corn.

cor•ne•a (kôr′nē-ə) *n.* A uniformly thick, transparent, nearly circular convex structure covering the lens of the eye. [ML *cornea (tēla)*, "horny (tissue)."] —**cor′ne•al** *adj.*

cor•ne•ous (kôr′nē-əs) *adj.* Made of horn or a hornlike substance; horny. [< L *cornū*, horn.]

cor•ner (kôr′nər) *n.* **1. a.** The position at which two lines or surfaces meet. **b.** The immediate interior or exterior region of the angle formed at this position, bounded by the two lines or surfaces. **2.** The place where two streets meet. **3.** A position from which escape is difficult. **4.** Any part or region. **5.** A remote or secret place or area. **6.** Speculation in a stock or commodity by controlling the available supply so as to raise its price. —**cut corners.** *Informal.* To reduce expenses, care in execution, etc. —*v.* **1.** To place or drive into a corner. **2.** To form a corner in (a stock or commodity). —*adj.* On, at, or used in a corner. [< L *cornū*, horn, extremity.]

cor•ner•stone (kôr′nər-stōn′) *n.* **1.** A stone at the corner of a building uniting two intersecting walls; quoin. **2.** Such a stone laid at a ceremony. **3.** The essential or main basis of something.

cor•net (kôr-nĕt′) *n.* A three-valved instrument of the trumpet class. [< L *cornū*, horn.] —**cor•net′ist** *n.*

corn•flow•er (kôrn′flou′ər) *n.* A garden plant with usually deep-blue flowers.

cor•nice (kôr′nĭs) *n.* A horizontal molded projection that crowns or completes a building or wall. [< It.]

Cor•nish (kôr′nĭsh) *n.* The Celtic language formerly spoken in Cornwall. —**Cor′nish** *adj.*

corn•meal (kôrn′mēl′) *n.* Meal made from corn.

corn•stalk (kôrn′stôk′) *n.* Also **corn stalk.** A stalk or stem of corn, esp. maize.

corn•starch (kôrn′stärch′) *n.* A purified starchy flour made from corn, used as a thickener in cooking.

corn sugar. A sugar, dextrose.

corn syrup. A syrup prepared from corn and containing glucose.

cor•nu•co•pi•a (kôr′nə-kō′pē-ə) *n.* A cone-shaped horn overflowing with fruit, flowers, and corn, signifying prosperity. [L *cornūcōpia*, horn of plenty.] —**cor′nu•co′pi•an, cor′nu•co′pi•ate′** *adj.*

Corn•wall (kôrn′wôl). A region in the extreme SW of England.

ō paw, for/oi boy/ou out/ŏŏ took/ōō coo/p pop/r run/s sauce/sh shy/t to/th thin/*th* the/ ŭ cut/ûr fur/v van/w wag/y yes/z size/zh vision/ə ago, item, edible, gallop, circus/

corn•y (kôr'nē) *adj.* **-ier, -iest.** *Slang.* Trite, dated, or mawkishly sentimental.

co•rol•la (kə-rŏl'ə) *n.* The structure formed by the petals of a flower. [< L *corōna,* garland, CORONA.]

cor•ol•lar•y (kôr'ə-lĕr-ē, kŏr'-) *n., pl.* **-ies. 1.** A proposition that follows with little or no proof from one already proven. **2.** A natural consequence; result. [< L *corolla,* small garland.]

co•ro•na (kə-rō'nə) *n., pl.* **-nas** or **-nae** (-nē). A faintly colored luminous ring around a celestial body visible through a haze or thin cloud. [L *corōna,* garland, crown.]

Co•ro•na•do (kôr'ä-nä'dō), **Francisco Vásquez de.** 1510–1554. Spanish explorer.

cor•o•nar•y (kôr'ə-nĕr-ē, kŏr'-) *adj.* **1.** Pertaining to either of two arteries that originate in the aorta and supply blood directly to the heart tissues. **2.** Pertaining to the heart. *—n., pl.* **-ies.** A coronary thrombosis. [< L *corōna,* garland, crown, CORONA.]

coronary thrombosis. The occlusion of a coronary artery by a blood clot, often leading to destruction of heart muscle.

cor•o•na•tion (kôr'ə-nā'shən, kŏr'-) *n.* The act or ceremony of crowning a sovereign or his consort. [< L *corōna,* crown, CORONA.]

cor•o•ner (kôr'ə-nər, kŏr'-) *n.* A public officer whose function is to investigate any death thought to be of other than natural causes. [ME, officer charged with maintaining the record of the crown's pleas.]

cor•o•net (kôr'ə-nĕt', -nīt', kŏr'-) *n.* **1.** A small crown worn by nobles below the rank of sovereign. **2.** A jeweled chaplet or headband. [< L *corōna,* crown, CORONA.]

corp. corporation.

cor•po•ra. *pl.* of **corpus.**

cor•po•ral[1] (kôr'pə-rəl) *adj.* Of the body; bodily. [< L *corpus (corpor-),* body.]

cor•po•ral[2] (kôr'pə-rəl, -prəl) *n.* A noncommissioned officer of the lowest rank, as in the army. [Obs F.]

cor•po•rate (kôr'pə-rĭt) *adj.* **1.** Formed into a corporation; incorporated. **2.** Of a corporation. **3.** United or combined into one body; collective. [< L *corporāre,* to make into a body.]

cor•po•ra•tion (kôr'pə-rā'shən) *n.* **1.** A body of persons granted a charter legally recognizing them as a separate entity having its own rights, privileges, and liabilities. **2.** Such a body created for purposes of government.

cor•po•re•al (kôr-pôr'ē-əl, -pō'rē-əl) *adj.* **1.** Characteristic of the body. **2.** Of a material nature; tangible. [< L *corpus,* CORPUS.]

corps (kôr, kŏr) *n., pl.* **corps** (kōrz, kôrz). **1.** A specialized branch or department of the armed forces. **2.** A tactical unit of ground combat forces between a division and an army. **3.** A body of persons under common direction. [< L *corpus,* body, CORPUS.]

corpse (kôrps) *n.* A dead body, esp. of a human being. [< L *corpus,* body, CORPUS.]

cor•pu•lence (kôr'pyə-ləns) *n.* Fatness; obesity. [< L *corpulentus* < *corpus,* CORPUS.] —**cor'pu•lent** *adj.* —**cor'pu•lent•ly** *adv.*

cor•pus (kôr'pəs) *n., pl.* **-pora** (-pə-rə). **1.** A

human or animal body, esp. when dead. **2.** A structure constituting the main part of an organ. **3.** A large collection of writings. [L, body, substance.]

Cor•pus Chris•ti (kôr'pəs krĭs'tē). A city of SW Texas. Pop. 168,000.

cor•pus•cle (kôr'pəs-əl, -pŭs-əl) *n.* Also **cor•pus•cule** (kôr-pŭs'kyōōl). **1.** A cell capable of free movement in a fluid or matrix as distinguished from a cell fixed in tissue. **2.** A small, discrete particle. [< L *corpus,* CORPUS.] —**cor•pus'cu•lar** (-kyə-lər) *adj.*

corpus de•lic•ti (dĭl-ĭk'tī). **1.** *Law.* The material evidence of the fact that a crime has been committed. **2.** Loosely, the victim's corpse in a murder case. [NL, "body of the crime."]

corr. 1. correction. **2.** correspondence; correspondent.

cor•ral (kə-răl') *n.* An enclosure for confining livestock. *—v.* **-ralled, -ralling. 1.** To drive into and hold in a corral. **2.** *Informal.* To seize; capture. [Span.]

cor•rect (kə-rĕkt') *v.* **1.** To remove the errors or mistakes from. **2.** To mark the errors in. **3.** To admonish or punish. **4.** To remove or counteract, as a malfunction. *—adj.* **1.** Accurate or true. **2.** Conforming to standards; proper. [< L *corrigere* (pp *correctus*), to make straight, correct.] —**cor•rect'ive** *adj. & n.* —**cor•rect'ly** *adv.* —**cor•rect'ness** *n.*

cor•rec•tion (kə-rĕk'shən) *n.* **1.** The act or process of correcting. **2.** That which is substituted for a mistake or fault. **3.** Punishment. **4.** A quantity added or subtracted to improve accuracy. —**cor•rec'tion•al** *adj.*

correl. correlative.

cor•re•la•tion (kôr'ə-lā'shən, kŏr'-) *n.* A causal, complementary, parallel, or reciprocal relationship, esp. a structural, functional, or qualitative correspondence between two comparable entities. [ML *correlātiō.*] —**cor're•late'** *v.* **(-lated, -lating).** —**cor're•late'** *adj.*

cor•rel•a•tive (kə-rĕl'ə-tĭv) *adj.* **1.** Reciprocally related. **2.** Indicating a reciprocal or complementary grammatical relation, as the conjunctions *neither* and *nor.* *—n.* **1.** Either of two correlative entities. **2.** *Gram.* A correlative word or expression.

cor•re•spond (kôr'ə-spŏnd', kŏr'-) *v.* **1.** To be in agreement, harmony, or conformity. **2.** To be similar or equal (with *to*). **3.** To communicate by letter.

cor•re•spon•dence (kôr'ə-spŏn'dəns, kŏr'-) *n.* **1.** The act, fact, or state of agreeing or conforming. **2.** Similarity or analogy. **3. a.** Communication by the exchange of letters. **b.** The letters written or received.

cor•re•spon•dent (kôr'ə-spŏn'dənt, kŏr'-) *n.* **1.** One who communicates by means of letters. **2.** One employed, as by a newspaper, to supply news from a distant place. **3.** A thing that corresponds; a correlative. *—adj.* Corresponding; consistent.

cor•ri•dor (kôr'ĭ-dər, -dôr, kŏr'-) *n.* **1.** A narrow passageway, generally with rooms or apartments opening onto it. **2.** A tract of land forming a passageway. [< OIt *corridore,* "a run."]

ă pat/ā ate/âr care/ä bar/b bib/ch chew/d deed/ĕ pet/ē be/f fit/g gag/h hat/hw what/ ĭ pit/ī pie/îr pier/j judge/k kick/l lid, fatal/m mum/n no, sudden/ng sing/ŏ pot/ō go/

cor•ri•gen•dum (kôr'ə-jĕn'dəm, kŏr'-) *n., pl.* **-da** (-də). **1.** An error in a book. **2.** **corrigenda.** A list of errors with their corrections, in a book. [< L *corrigere*, to CORRECT.]

cor•rob•o•rate (kə-rŏb'ə-rāt') *v.* **-rated, -rating.** To strengthen or support (other evidence). [L *corrōborāre.*] —**cor•rob'o•ra'tion** *n.* —**cor•rob'o•ra'tive** *adj.* —**cor•rob'o•ra'tor** *n.* —**cor•rob'o•ra•to'ry** (-ər-ə-tôr'ē, -tôr'ē) *adj.*

cor•rode (kə-rōd') *v.* **-roded, -roding.** To wear away gradually, esp. by chemical action. [< L *corrōdere*, to gnaw to pieces.] —**cor•ro'sion** *n.* —**cor•ro'sive** *adj.* —**cor•ro'sive•ly** *adv.*

cor•ru•gate (kôr'ə-gāt', kôr'yə-, kŏr'-) *v.* **-gated, -gating.** To make folds or parallel and alternating ridges and grooves (in). [L *corrūgāre*, to make full of wrinkles.] —**cor'ru•gate', cor'ru•gat'ed** (-gā'tĭd) *adj.* —**cor'ru•ga'tion** *n.* —**cor'ru•ga'tor** *n.*

corrugated iron. A structural sheet iron, usually galvanized, shaped in parallel furrows and ridges for rigidity.

cor•rupt (kə-rŭpt') *adj.* **1.** Immoral; perverted. **2.** Marked by venality. **3.** Decaying; putrid. —*v.* To make or become corrupt. [< L *corruptus*, pp of *corrumpere*, break to pieces, destroy.] —**cor•rupt'i•ble** *adj.* —**cor•rup'tion** *n.* —**cor•rup'tive** *adj.* —**cor•rupt'ly** *adv.*

cor•sage (kôr-säzh') *n.* A small bouquet worn by a woman, as at the shoulder. [OF, torso, bust.]

cor•sair (kôr'sâr) *n.* **1.** A pirate. **2.** A swift pirate ship. [< ML *cursus*, plunder.]

cor•set (kôr'sĭt) *n.* A close-fitting undergarment, often reinforced by stays, worn to support and shape the waistline, hips, and breasts. [< OF.]

Cor•si•ca (kôr'sĭ-kə). An island of France, in the Mediterranean. —**Cor'si•can** *adj. & n.*

cor•tege (kôr-tĕzh', -tāzh') *n.* **1.** A train of attendants; retinue. **2.** A ceremonial procession. [< It *corteggiare*, to pay honor, court.]

Cor•tés (kôr-tĕz'), **Hernando.** 1485-1547. Spanish explorer, conqueror of the Aztecs.

cor•tex (kôr'tĕks) *n., pl.* **-tices** (-tə-sēz') or **-texes.** **1.** The outer layer of an organ or part. **2.** *Bot.* **a.** A layer of tissue in roots and stems lying between the epidermis and vascular tissue. **b.** An external layer such as bark or rind. [L, bark, shell, rind.] —**cor'ti•cal** *adj.* —**cor'ti•cal•ly** *adv.*

cor•ti•sone (kôr'tə-sōn, -zōn) *n.* An adrenal hormone, $C_{21}H_{28}O_5$, active in carbohydrate metabolism and used to treat rheumatoid arthritis, adrenal insufficiency, and gout.

co•run•dum (kə-rŭn'dəm) *n.* An extremely hard aluminum oxide mineral, occurring in gem varieties and in a common form used chiefly in abrasives. [Tamil *kuruntam.*]

cor•us•cate (kôr'əs-kāt', kŏr'-) *v.* **-cated, -cating.** To sparkle; glitter; scintillate. [L *coruscāre*, to thrust, vibrate, glitter.] —**cor'us•ca'tion** *n.*

cor•vette (kôr-vĕt') *n.* **1.** A lightly armed warship, smaller than a destroyer. **2.** An armed sailing vessel smaller than a frigate. [< OF.]

co•ry•za (kə-rī'zə) *n.* An acute inflammation of the nasal mucous membrane, marked by discharge of mucus, sneezing, and watering of the eyes. [< Gk *koruza*, catarrh.]

cos•met•ic (kŏz-mĕt'ĭk) *n.* A preparation, such as face powder or skin cream, designed to beautify the body. [< Gk *kosmein*, to arrange, order.] —**cos•met'ic** *adj.*

cos•mic (kŏz'mĭk) *adj.* Also **cos•mi•cal** (-mĭ-kəl). **1.** Pertaining to the universe, esp. as distinct from the earth or, sometimes, from the solar system. **2.** Vast. [Gk *kosmikos*, of the universe.] —**cos'mi•cal•ly** *adv.*

cosmic ray. A stream of ionizing radiation of extraterrestrial origin, chiefly of protons, alpha particles, and other atomic nuclei but including some high-energy electrons and photons.

cosmo–. *comb. form.* World or universe. [< COSMOS.]

cos•mog•o•ny (kŏz-mŏg'ə-nē) *n., pl.* **-nies.** The astrophysical study of the evolution of the universe.

cos•mol•o•gy (kŏz-mŏl'ə-jē) *n.* **1.** A branch of philosophy dealing with the origin, processes, and structure of the universe. **2.** The astrophysical study of the structure and constituent dynamics of the universe. —**cos'mo•log'i•cal** (-mə-lŏg'ĭ-kəl) *adj.* —**cos•mol'o•gist** *n.*

cos•mo•naut (kŏz'mə-nôt) *n.* An astronaut.

cos•mo•pol•i•tan (kŏz'mə-pŏl'ə-tən) *adj.* **1.** Common to the whole world. **2.** At home in all places or in many spheres of interest. —*n.* A cosmopolitan person. [< Gk *kosmopolitēs*, citizen of the world.]

cos•mos (kŏz'məs, -mŏs) *n.* **1.** The universe regarded as an orderly, harmonious whole. **2.** Any system regarded as ordered, harmonious, and whole. **3.** Harmony and order as distinct from chaos. **4.** A garden plant with variously colored, daisylike flowers. [Gk *kosmos*, order, the universe, the world.]

Cos•sack (kŏs'ăk) *n.* A member of a people of the S Soviet Union, noted as cavalrymen. [Russ *kazak.*] —**Cos'sack** *adj.*

cost (kôst) *n.* **1.** An amount paid or required in payment for a purchase. **2.** A loss or penalty; detriment. —*v.* To require a specified payment, expenditure, effort, or loss. [< L *constāre*, to stand firm, cost at a particular price.]

Cos•ta Ri•ca (kŏs'tə rē'kə, kôs'-). A republic of Central America, between Panama and Nicaragua. Pop. 1,414,000. Cap. San José. —**Costa Rican.**

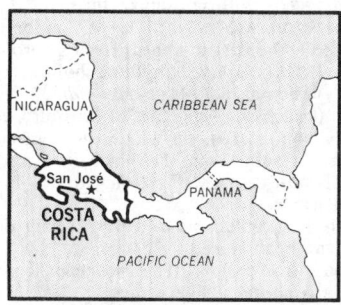

Costa Rica

cost·ly (kôst′lē) *adj.* -lier, -liest. 1. Of high price or value; expensive. 2. Entailing loss or sacrifice. —cost′li·ness *n.*

cost-plus (kôst′plŭs′, kŏst′-) *n.* Cost of production plus a fixed rate of profit. Often used as a basis for government contracts.

cos·tume (kŏs′t/y/ōōm, kŏs-t/y/ōōm′) *n.* 1. A style of dress, esp. one characteristic of a particular country or period. 2. A set of clothes for a particular occasion or season. [< L *consuētūdō*, CUSTOM.]

co·sy. Variant of cozy.

cot (kŏt) *n.* A narrow bed, esp. one made of canvas stretched on a collapsible frame. [Hindi *khāṭ*, bedstead, couch.]

cote (kōt) *n.* A small shed or shelter for sheep or birds. [< OE.]

co·te·rie (kō′tə-rē) *n.* A small group of persons who associate frequently. [< OF, an association of peasant tenants.]

co·til·lion (kō-til′yən, kə-) *n.* 1. A lively dance of the 18th century, with intricate patterns and steps. 2. A formal debutante ball. [F *cotillon*, peasant dress, country dance.]

cot·tage (kŏt′ĭj) *n.* 1. A small, single-storied country house. 2. A small summer house. [< OE *cot*, cottage.]

cottage cheese. An extremely soft, mild white cheese made of strained and seasoned curds of skim milk.

cot·ter (kŏt′ər) *n.* A bolt, wedge, key, or pin inserted through a slot in order to hold parts together. [< dial *cotterel*.]

cotter pin. A split cotter inserted through holes in two or more pieces and bent at the ends to fasten them together.

cot·ton (kŏt′n) *n.* 1. The downy white fiber surrounding the seeds of a plant cultivated in warm regions. 2. The plant itself. 3. Thread or cloth made from cotton fiber. —*v.* To take a liking to; become friendly. [< Ar *quṭn*.] —cot′ton·y *adj.*

cotton gin. See gin[2].

cot·ton·mouth (kŏt′n-mouth′) *n.* A snake, the water moccasin.

cot·ton·seed (kŏt′n-sēd′) *n.* The seed of cotton, used as a source of an oil used in cooking and in the manufacture of paints, soaps, and other products.

cot·ton·tail (kŏt′n-tāl′) *n.* A New World rabbit having a tail with a white underside.

cot·ton·wood (kŏt′n-wōōd′) *n.* A poplar tree having seeds with cottonlike tufts.

cot·y·le·don (kŏt′ə-lēd′n) *n.* An embryonic plant leaf, the first to appear from a sprouting seed. [< Gk *kotulē*, anything hollow, cup.] —cot′y·le′don·al, cot′y·le′do·nous *adj.*

couch (kouch) *n.* An article of furniture, commonly upholstered, on which one can sit or recline; a sofa. —*v.* To place in a certain verbal context. [< OF *coucher*, to lay down.] —couch′er *n.*

couch·ant (kou′chənt) *adj. Her.* Lying down with the head raised.

cou·gar (kōō′gər) *n.* The mountain lion. [< Tupi *suasuarana*, "like a deer."]

cough (kôf, kŏf) *v.* 1. To expel air from the lungs suddenly and noisily. 2. To expel by coughing (with *up* or *out*). [< OE *cohhian*.] —cough *n.*

could (kōōd). *p.t.* of can.

could·n't (kōōd′ənt). Contraction of could not.

cou·lomb (kōō′lŏm′, -lŏm′) *n.* A unit of electrical charge equal to the quantity of charge transferred in one second by a steady current of one ampere. [< C.A. de *Coulomb* (1736–1806), French physicist.]

coun·cil (koun′səl) *n.* 1. An assembly called together for consultation, deliberation, etc. 2. An administrative, legislative, or advisory body. [< L *concilium*, meeting, assembly.]

coun·cil·man (koun′səl-mən) *n.* A member of a council, esp. of a city council.

coun·cil·or (koun′sə-lər) *n.* Also coun·cil·lor. A member of a council.

coun·sel (koun′səl) *n.* 1. An exchanging of opinions and ideas; discussion. 2. Advice or guidance. 3. A deliberate resolution; plan. 4. *pl.* counsel. A lawyer or group of lawyers. —*v.* -seled or -selled, -seling or -selling. 1. To give counsel to; advise. 2. To urge the adoption of; recommend. [< L *consilium*, deliberation, consultation.]

coun·sel·or (koun′sə-lər) *n.* Also coun·sel·lor. 1. An adviser. 2. An attorney, esp. a trial lawyer.

count[1] (kount) *v.* 1. To name or list one by one in order to determine a total. 2. To recite numerals in ascending order. 3. To include in a reckoning: *ten dogs, counting the puppies.* 4. To believe or consider to be. 5. To merit consideration. 6. To be of value or importance: *His opinions count for little.* —count on. To rely. —*n.* 1. The act of counting. 2. A number reached by counting. 3. A reckoning. 4. *Law.* Any of the charges in an indictment. [< L *computāre*, to sum up, reckon.] —count′a·ble *adj.*

count[2] (kount) *n.* In some European countries, a nobleman whose rank corresponds to that of an English earl. [< LL *comes (comit-)*, occupant of any state office.]

count·down (kount′doun′) *n.* The act of counting backward aloud to indicate the time elapsing before an event or operation.

coun·te·nance (koun′tə-nəns) *n.* 1. Appearance, esp. the expression of the face. 2. The face. 3. Support or approval. —*v.* -nanced, -nancing. To approve; condone. [< OF *contenir*, to behave, contain.]

count·er[1] (koun′tər) *adj.* Contrary; opposing. —*n.* One that is counter; an opposite. —*v.* To move, do, or act in opposition to. —*adv.* In a contrary manner or direction. [< L *contrā*, contrary to, against.]

count·er[2] (koun′tər) *n.* 1. A table or similar flat surface on which money is counted, business transacted, or food served. 2. A piece, as of wood or ivory, used for keeping a count or a place in games. [< L *computāre*, to COUNT.]

count·er[3] (koun′tər) *n.* A person or device that counts.

counter-. *comb. form.* 1. Opposition, as in direction or purpose. 2. Reciprocation. [< L *contrā*, opposite to, COUNTER.]

coun·ter·act (koun′tər-ăkt′) *v.* To oppose and

mitigate the effects of by contrary action. —**coun'ter·ac'tion** n.

coun·ter·at·tack (koun'tər-ə-tăk') n. A return attack. —**coun'ter·at·tack'** v.

coun·ter·bal·ance (koun'tər-băl'əns, koun'-tər-băl'əns) n. 1. Any force or influence equally counteracting another. 2. A weight that balances another. —**coun'ter·bal'ance** v. (-anced, -ancing).

coun·ter·clock·wise (koun'tər-klŏk'wīz') adv. In a direction opposite to that of the movement of the hands of a clock. —**coun'ter·clock'wise'** adj.

coun·ter·cul·ture (koun'tər-kŭl'chər) n. A culture created by or for the alienated young in opposition to traditional values.

coun·ter·feit (koun'tər-fĭt) v. 1. To make a copy of, usually with intent to defraud; forge. 2. To feign; pretend. —adj. 1. Made in imitation of what is genuine with intent to defraud. 2. Feigned; pretended; simulated. —n. A fraudulent imitation or facsimile. [< ML contrāfacere, to make in contrast to.] —**coun'ter·feit·er** n.

coun·ter·in·tel·li·gence (koun'tər-ĭn-tĕl'ə-jəns) n. The branch of an intelligence service charged with keeping information from an enemy and preventing subversion and sabotage.

coun·ter·mand (koun'tər-mănd', -mänd') v. 1. To reverse (a command or order). 2. To recall by a contrary order. [< COUNTER- + OF mander, to command.]

coun·ter·mea·sure (koun'tər-mĕzh'ər) n. A measure or action taken in opposition to another.

coun·ter·of·fen·sive (koun'tər-ə-fĕn'sĭv) n. A large-scale attack by an army, designed to stop the offensive of an enemy.

coun·ter·pane (koun'tər-pān') n. A bedspread. [< ML culcita puncta, "stitched quilt."]

coun·ter·part (koun'tər-pärt') n. One that closely or exactly resembles another, as in function or relation.

coun·ter·point (koun'tər-point') n. 1. The technique of combining two or more melodic lines so that they establish a harmonic relationship while retaining their linear individuality. 2. A contrasting but parallel theme.

coun·ter·poise (koun'tər-poiz') n. 1. A counterbalancing weight. 2. A force or influence that balances or counteracts another. 3. The state of being balanced or in equilibrium. —v. (koun'tər-poiz') -poised, -poising. To oppose with an equal weight.

coun·ter·rev·o·lu·tion (koun'tər-rĕv'ə-lōo'shən) n. A movement arising in opposition to a revolution.

coun·ter·sign (koun'tər-sīn') v. To sign (a previously signed document), as for authentication. —n. A second or confirming signature, as on a previously signed document.

coun·ter·sink (koun'tər-sĭngk') v. -sunk, -sinking. 1. To enlarge the top part of (a drilled hole) so that a screw or bolthead will lie flush with or below the surface. 2. To drive a screw or bolt into (such a hole). —n. 1. A tool for

making such a hole. 2. A hole so made.

coun·ter·ten·or (koun'tər-tĕn'ər) n. A male singer with a range above that of tenor.

coun·ter·weight (koun'tər-wāt') n. A weight used as a counterbalance.

count·ess (koun'tĭs) n. 1. The wife or widow of a count or earl. 2. A woman holding the title of count or earl in her own right.

count·less (kount'lĭs) adj. Innumerable.

coun·try (kŭn'trē) n., pl. -tries. 1. A large tract of land distinguishable by features of topography, biology, or culture. 2. A rural area. 3. The territory of a nation or state. 4. The land of a person's birth or citizenship or to which a person owes allegiance. —adj. Of or pertaining to rural areas. [< ML (terra) contrāta, "(land) lying opposite or before one."]

country club. A suburban club with facilities for golf, other outdoor sports, and social activities.

coun·try·man (kŭn'trē-mən) n. 1. A man from one's own country. 2. A rustic.

coun·try·side (kŭn'trē-sīd') n. 1. A rural region. 2. Its inhabitants.

coun·ty (koun'tē) n., pl. -ties. An administrative subdivision of a state or country. [< ML comitātus, territory of a count.]

coup (kōo) n. 1. A brilliantly executed stratagem. 2. A coup d'état. [< L colaphus, blow.]

coup de grâce (kōo' də gräs'). 1. The finishing stroke, as given to someone mortally wounded. 2. Any decisive or finishing stroke. [F, "stroke of mercy."]

coup d'é·tat (kōo' dā-tä'). A sudden, deliberate violation of constitutional forms by a group of persons in authority. [F, "stroke of state."]

cou·pé (kōo-pā') n. Also coupe (kōop). A closed two-door automobile. [< F (carrosse) coupé, "cut-off (carriage)."]

coup·le (kŭp'əl) n. 1. Two items of the same kind. 2. Something that joins two things. 3. A man and woman united in some way, as by marriage. 4. Informal. A few; several: a couple of days. —v. -led, -ling. 1. To link together. 2. To form pairs. 3. To marry. 4. To copulate. [< L cōpula, bond, link.]

coup·let (kŭp'lĭt) n. Two successive lines of verse with the same rhyme scheme and meter.

cou·pon (k/y/ōo'pŏn') n. 1. A certificate attached to a bond that represents a sum of interest due at a stated maturity. 2. A certificate entitling the bearer to certain benefits, such as a cash refund. [< OF colpon, "a piece cut off."]

cour·age (kûr'ĭj) n. The quality of mind that enables one to face danger with self-possession or confidence; bravery. [ME corage, heart as the seat of feeling, courage < L cor, heart.] —**cou·ra'geous** (kə-rā'jəs) adj. —**cou·ra'geous·ly** adv. —**cou·ra'geous·ness** n.

cou·ri·er (kōor'ē-ər, kûr'-) n. A messenger, esp. one on urgent or official business. [< L currere, to run.]

course (kôrs, kōrs, kōors) n. 1. Onward movement in a particular direction. 2. The route taken by something that moves, as a stream. 3. Duration: in the course of a year. 4. A mode of action or behavior. **5.** Regular development: *The fad ran its course.* **6.** *Ed.* **a.** A complete body of prescribed studies. **b.** A unit of such studies. **7.** A part of a meal served as a unit at one time. —**in due course.** At the right time. —**of course.** Without any doubt; certainly. —*v.* **coursed, coursing. 1.** To move swiftly (through or over); traverse. **2.** To hunt (game) with hounds. **3.** To follow a direction. **4.** To flow. [< L *cursus,* pp of *currere,* to run.]

cours·er (kôr′sər, kōr′-, kōōr′-) *n. Poetic.* A swift horse.

court (kôrt, kōrt) *n.* **1.** A courtyard. **2.** A short street. **3.** A royal mansion or palace. **4.** The retinue of a sovereign. **5.** A sovereign's governing body, including ministers and state advisers. **6. a.** A person or body of persons appointed to hear and submit a decision on legal cases. **b.** The room in which such cases are heard. **c.** The regular session of a judicial assembly. **7.** An open, level area, marked with lines, upon which tennis, handball, basketball, etc., are played. —**out of court.** Without a trial. —*v.* **1.** To attempt to gain the favor of by flattery or attention. **2.** To attempt to gain the love of; woo. **3.** To invite, often unwittingly or foolishly: *court disaster.* [< L *cohors (cohort-),* enclosure, court, cohort.] —**court′li·ness** *n.* —**court′ly** *adj. & adv.*

cour·te·ous (kûr′tē-əs) *adj.* Considerate toward others. [< OF *cort,* court.] —**cour′te·ous·ly** *adv.* —**cour′te·ous·ness** *n.*

cour·te·san (kôr′tə-zən, kōr′-) *n.* Also **cour·te·zan.** A prostitute, esp. one associating with men of rank. [< L *cohors,* COURT.]

cour·te·sy (kûr′tə-sē) *n., pl.* **-sies. 1.** Gracious manner or manners. **2.** A polite gesture or remark.

court·house (kôrt′hous′, kōrt′-) *n.* A building housing judicial courts.

court·i·er (kôr′tē-ər, kōr′-, -tyər) *n.* An attendant at a sovereign's court.

court·mar·tial (kôrt′mär′shəl, kōrt′-) *n., pl.* **courts-martial. 1.** A military court of officers to try persons for offenses under military law. **2.** A trial by court-martial. —*v.* **-tialed** or **-tialled, -tialing** or **-tialling.** To try by court-martial.

court·room (kôrt′rōōm′, kōrt′-, -rōōm′) *n.* A room for court proceedings.

court·ship (kôrt′shĭp′, kōrt′-) *n.* The act or period of wooing a woman.

court·yard (kôrt′yärd′, kōrt′-) *n.* An open space surrounded by walls or buildings.

cous·in (kŭz′ən) *n.* **1.** A child of one's aunt or uncle. **2.** A relative descended from a common ancestor. [< L *consōbrīnus,* maternal first cousin.]

co·va·lent bond (kō-vā′lənt). A chemical bond formed by the sharing of one or more electrons, esp. pairs of electrons, between atoms.

cove (kōv) *n.* A small, sheltered bay. [< OE *cofa,* chamber, cave.]

cov·en (kŭv′ən, kō′vən) *n.* An assembly of witches. [< ME *covent,* a gathering, convent.]

cov·e·nant (kŭv′ə-nənt) *n.* **1.** A binding agreement; contract. **2.** God's promises to man, as recorded in the Old and New Testaments. —*v.* To promise by or enter into a covenant. [< OF *co(n)venir,* to agree, convene.]

cov·er (kŭv′ər) *v.* **1.** To place upon, over, or in front of (something) so as to protect, shut in, or conceal. **2.** To clothe. **3.** To occupy the surface of: *Dust covered the table.* **4.** To extend over: *a farm covering 100 acres.* **5.** To hide or conceal, as a fact or crime. **6.** To protect by insurance. **7.** To defray (an expense). **8.** To deal with; treat of. **9.** To travel or pass over. **10.** To hold within the range and aim of a firearm. **11.** *Jour.* To report the details of (an event or situation). **12.** *Informal.* To act as a substitute during someone's absence. —*n.* **1.** Something that covers. **2.** Shelter of any kind. **3.** Something that conceals or disguises. **4.** A table setting for one person. **5.** An envelope or wrapper for mail. —**take cover.** To seek protection, as from enemy fire. —**under cover.** Operating secretly. [< L *cooperīre,* to cover completely.] —**cov′er·er** *n.*

cov·er·age (kŭv′ər-ĭj) *n.* **1.** *Jour.* The extent to which something is reported. **2.** The protection afforded by insurance.

cov·er·alls (kŭv′ər-ôlz′) *pl.n.* A loose-fitting one-piece garment worn by workmen to protect their clothes.

covered wagon. A wagon with an arched canvas top, used by American pioneers.

cov·er·let (kŭv′ər-lĭt) *n.* A bedspread.

cov·ert (kŭv′ərt, kō′vərt) *adj.* **1.** Sheltered. **2.** Concealed; hidden; secret. —*n.* **1.** A covering or cover. **2.** A shelter or hiding place. **3.** Thick underbrush affording cover for game. **4.** Also **covert cloth.** A sturdy twilled woolen cloth. [< OF *covrir,* to cover.] —**cov′ert·ly** *adv.* —**cov′ert·ness** *n.*

cov·er·up (kŭv′ər-ŭp′) *n.* Also **Also cov·er·up. 1.** An effort or strategy designed to conceal something, such as a crime or scandal. **2.** An enveloping garment. —**cov′er-up′** *adj.*

cov·et (kŭv′ĭt) *v.* To desire (that which is another's); crave. [< L *cupiditās,* desire.] —**cov′et·er** *n.*

cov·et·ous (kŭv′ə-təs) *adj.* Excessively desirous; avaricious; greedy: *covetous of learning.* —**cov′et·ous·ly** *adv.* —**cov′et·ous·ness** *n.*

cov·ey (kŭv′ē) *n., pl.* **-eys.** A small flock or group, as of partridges. [< OF *covee,* a brood.]

cow¹ (kou) *n.* **1.** The mature female of cattle or of other animals such as the whale or elephant. **2.** Broadly, any domesticated bovine. [< OE *cū.* See **gwou-**.]

cow² (kou) *v.* To frighten with threats or a show of force. [Perh < ON *kūga,* to oppress.]

cow·ard (kou′ərd) *n.* One who lacks courage in the face of danger or pain. [< OF *couard.*] —**cow′ard·ly** *adj. & adv.*

cow·ard·ice (kou′ər-dĭs) *n.* Lack of courage in the face of danger, pain, etc.

cow·bird (kou′bûrd′) *n.* A blackbird of a species that lays its eggs in the nests of other birds.

cow·boy (kou′boi′) *n.* **1.** A hired man, esp. in the U.S., who tends cattle and performs many of his duties on horseback. **2.** A performer of feats of horsemanship, calf roping, etc., at a rodeo.

cow•catch•er (kou′kăch′ər) *n.* An iron frame on the front of a locomotive or streetcar that clears the track.

cow•er (kou′ər) *v.* To cringe or shrink away in fear. [Prob < Scand.]

cow•hide (kou′hīd′) *n.* 1. The hide of a cow or leather made from it. 2. A strong, heavy, flexible whip, usually made of braided leather. —*v.* -hided, -hiding. To whip with a cowhide.

cowl (koul) *n.* 1. The hood worn by monks. 2. A hood-shaped covering used to increase the draft of a chimney. 3. The top portion of the front part of an automobile body, supporting the windshield and dashboard. 4. Also **cowl•ing** (kou′lĭng). A removable metal covering for an aircraft engine. [< L *cucullus,* hood.]

cow•lick (kou′lĭk′) *n.* A projecting tuft of hair on the head that will not lie flat.

co•work•er (kō′wûrk′ər) *n.* A fellow worker.

cow•poke (kou′pōk′) *n. Informal.* A cowboy, as at a cattle ranch.

cow•pox (kou′pŏks′) *n.* A contagious skin disease of cattle, caused by a virus that is isolated and used to vaccinate humans against smallpox.

cow•punch•er (kou′pŭn′chər) *n. Informal.* A cowboy.

cow•ry (kou′rē) *n., pl.* -ries. Also **cow•rie.** Any of various tropical marine mollusks with glossy, often brightly marked shells. [Hindi *kaurī.*]

cow•slip (kou′slĭp′) *n.* 1. An Old World primrose with yellow flowers. 2. The **marsh marigold.** [< OE *cūslyppe,* "cow dung."]

cox•comb. Variant of **cockscomb.**

cox•swain (kŏk′sən, kŏk′swān′) *n.* A person who steers a boat or racing shell.

coy (koi) *adj.* Affectedly shy or devious. [< L *quiētus,* quiet.] —**coy′ly** *adv.* —**coy′ness** *n.*

coy•o•te (kī-ō′tē, kī′ō-tē′) *n.* A wolflike animal, common in W North America. [< Nah *coyotl.*]

coz•en (kŭz′ən) *v.* To deceive; cheat. [Poss < obs It *cozzonare,* "to be a horse trader," cheat.] —**coz′en•er** *n.*

co•zy (kō′zē) *adj.* -zier, -ziest. Also **co•sy.** Snug and comfortable. —*n., pl.* -zies. A padded covering to keep a teapot hot. [Scot *cosie.*] —**co′zi•ly** *adv.* —**co′zi•ness** *n.*

cp. compare.

C.P. Communist Party.

C.P.A. certified public accountant.

cpd. compound.

Cpl. corporal.

C.P.O. chief petty officer.

cps cycles per second.

Cr chromium.

cr. 1. credit; creditor. 2. crown.

crab[1] (krăb) *n.* 1. Any of various chiefly marine crustaceans having a broad body with a shell-like covering. 2. **Crab.** The constellation and sign of the zodiac Cancer. [< OE *crabba.* See gerebh-.]

crab[2] (krăb) *n.* 1. A crab apple. 2. A quarrelsome, ill-tempered person. —*v.* crabbed

(krăbd), **crabbing.** *Informal.* To criticize. [Prob < Scand.]

crab apple. 1. A small, tart applelike fruit. 2. A tree bearing such fruit.

crab•bed (krăb′ĭd) *adj.* 1. Ill-tempered. 2. Difficult to read: *crabbed handwriting.*

crab•by (krăb′ē) *adj.* -bier, -biest. Grouchy; ill-tempered.

crab•grass (krăb′grăs′, -grăs′) *n.* A coarse grass that spreads and displaces other grasses in lawns.

crack (krăk) *v.* 1. To break or cause to break with a sharp sound; snap. 2. To break or cause to break without dividing into parts. 3. To change sharply in pitch or timbre, as the voice from emotion. 4. To strike. 5. To break open or into. 6. To discover the solution to, esp. after considerable effort. 7. *Informal.* To tell (a joke). 8. To decompose (petroleum) into simpler compounds by cracking. —*n.* 1. A sharp, snapping sound, such as gunfire. 2. A partial split or break; flaw; fissure. 3. A narrow space: *The window was open a crack.* 4. A sharp, resounding blow. 5. A cracking vocal tone or sound. 6. A chance: *gave him a crack at the job.* 7. A sarcastic remark. 8. *adj.* moment; instant: *at the crack of dawn.* —*adj.* Superior; first-rate: *a crack marksman.* [< OE *cracian.* See ger-2.]

crack down. To become demanding, severe, or strict: *crack down on student absences.*

crack•down (krăk′doun′) *n.* Sudden punitive action.

crack•er (krăk′ər) *n.* 1. A thin, crisp wafer or biscuit, usually made of unleavened, unsweetened dough. 2. A firecracker. 3. A poor white person of the rural SE U.S. Used disparagingly.

crack•er•jack (krăk′ər-jăk′) *adj. Slang.* Of excellent quality or ability; remarkably fine. —**crack′er•jack′** *n.*

crack•ing (krăk′ĭng) *n.* Thermal decomposition, sometimes with catalysis, of a complex substance, esp. of petroleum.

crack•le (krăk′əl) *v.* -led, -ling. 1. To make or cause to make a succession of sharp, snapping noises. 2. To cause (china) to become covered with a network of fine cracks. [Freq of CRACK.] —**crack′le** *n.*

crack•pot (krăk′pŏt′) *n.* An eccentric person. —**crack′pot′** *adj.*

crack up. *Informal.* 1. To crash; collide. 2. To have a mental breakdown. 3. To laugh or cause to laugh boisterously.

crack•up (krăk′ŭp′) *n. Informal.* 1. A collision, as of an airplane or automobile. 2. A mental breakdown.

–cracy. *comb. form.* Government or rule: *bureaucracy.* [< Gk *kratos,* power.]

cra•dle (krād′l) *n.* 1. An infant's low bed with rockers. 2. A place of origin. 3. A framework of wood or metal used to support something, such as a ship on land. —*v.* -dled, -dling. To place into, rock, hold, or lie in or as if in a cradle. [< OE *cradol, cradel.*]

cra•dle•song (krād′l-sông′, -sŏng′) *n.* A lullaby.

craft (krăft, kräft) *n.* 1. Skill or ability, esp. in

handwork or the arts. **2.** Skill in evasion or deception. **3. a.** A trade, esp. one requiring manual dexterity. **b.** The membership of such a trade; a guild. **4.** *pl.* **craft.** A boat, ship, or aircraft. [< OE *cræft* < Gmc **kraftaz*, **krab-taz*, strength.]
crafts•man (krăfts'mən, krăfts'-) *n.* **1.** A skilled worker in a craft. **2.** An artist as considered with regard to technique. —**crafts'-man•ly** *adj.* —**crafts'man•ship'** *n.*
craft•y (krăf'tē, krăf'-) *adj.* -ier, -iest. Skilled in deception; shrewd; cunning. —**craft'i•ly** *adv.* —**craft'i•ness** *n.*
crag (krăg) *n.* A steeply projecting rock mass. [< Celt.]
crag•gy (krăg'ē) *adj.* -gier, -giest. Having crags; steep and rugged. —**crag'gi•ness** *n.*
cram (krăm) *v.* **crammed, cramming. 1.** To squeeze into an insufficient space; stuff. **2.** To fill too tightly. **3.** To gorge (oneself) with food. **4.** *Informal.* To make a concentrated last-minute review of a subject in studying for an examination. [< OE *crammian.* See ger-¹.] —**cram'mer** *n.*
cramp¹ (krămp) *n.* **1.** A sudden, involuntary, severely painful muscular contraction, the result of strain or chill. **2.** A temporary partial paralysis of habitually or excessively used muscles: *writer's cramp.* **3. cramps.** Sharp, persistent pains in the abdomen. —*v.* To cause or have a cramp. [< OF *crampe.*]
cramp² (krămp) *v.* To confine; restrict; hamper. [MDu *crampe*, hook.]
cran•ber•ry (krăn'bĕr'ē, -bər-ē) *n.* **1.** The tart red, edible berry of a trailing North American plant. **2.** The plant itself. [Part trans of LG *kraanbere*, "cranberry."]
crane (krān) *n.* **1.** A large wading bird with a long neck, long legs, and a long bill. **2.** A machine for hoisting heavy objects. —*v.* **craned, craning.** To stretch one's neck for a better view. [< OE *cran.* See ger-².]
cra•ni•um (krā'nē-əm) *n.*, *pl.* -ums or -nia (-nē-ə). **1.** The skull of a vertebrate. **2.** The portion of the skull enclosing the brain. [< Gk *kranion.*] —**cra'ni•al** *adj.*
crank (krăngk) *n.* **1.** A device for transmitting rotary motion, consisting of a handle attached at right angles to a shaft. **2.** *Informal.* An eccentric idea or person. —*v.* To start or operate (an engine) by turning a crank. [< OE *cranc.*]
crank•case (krăngk'kās') *n.* The metal case enclosing the crankshaft and associated parts in a reciprocating engine.
crank•shaft (krăngk'shăft', -shäft') *n.* A shaft that turns or is turned by a crank.
crank•y (krăng'kē) *adj.* -ier, -iest. **1.** Ill-tempered; peevish. **2.** Odd; eccentric. —**crank'i•ly** *adv.* —**crank'i•ness** *n.*
cran•ny (krăn'ē) *n.*, *pl.* -nies. A small crevice; fissure. [< OF *cran, cren,* notch.]
craps (krăps) *n.* *(takes sing. v.).* A gambling game played by throwing two dice. [< F *crabs, craps.*]
crap•shoot•er (krăp'shōō'tər) *n.* One who plays craps.
crash¹ (krăsh) *v.* **1.** To fall, break, or collide

noisily. **2.** To make a sudden loud noise. **3.** To fail suddenly, as a business. —*n.* **1.** A sudden loud noise. **2.** A collision. **3.** A sudden business failure. [< ME *crasen*, to shatter, craze, and *dashen*, to dash.]
crash² (krăsh) *n.* A coarse cotton or linen fabric used for towels and curtains. [Russ *krashenina*, a kind of colored linen.]
crass (krăs) *adj.* Grossly ignorant; coarse; stupid. [L *crassus*, fat, gross, dense.] —**crass'ly** *adv.* —**crass'ness** *n.*
-crat *comb. form.* A member or supporter of a class or form of government: **bureaucrat.**
crate (krāt) *n.* A slatted wooden container for storing or shipping things. —*v.* **crated, crating.** To pack into a crate. [L *cratis*, wickerwork.]
cra•ter (krā'tər) *n.* **1.** A bowl-shaped depression at the mouth of a volcano. **2.** A similar depression or pit. [L *crātēr*, bowl, crater.]
cra•vat (krə-văt') *n.* A necktie. [F *cravate.*]
crave (krāv) *v.* **craved, craving. 1.** To have an intense desire for. **2.** To beg earnestly for. [< OE *crafian*, to beg, demand < Gmc **krab-jan.*] —**crav'er** *n.* —**crav'ing•ly** *adv.*
cra•ven (krā'vən) *adj.* Cowardly. —*n.* A coward. [ME *cravant.*] —**cra'ven•ly** *adv.*
crav•ing (krā'vĭng) *n.* A consuming desire; yearning.
craw (krô) *n.* The crop of a bird or the stomach of an animal. [< OE *craga.*]
craw•fish (krô'fĭsh') *n.* A crayfish.
crawl (krôl) *v.* **1.** To move slowly by dragging the body along the ground; creep. **2.** To advance slowly. **3.** To be or feel as if covered with crawling things. **4.** To swim the crawl. —*n.* **1.** The act of crawling. **2.** A rapid swimming stroke. [< ON *krafla*, to crawl, creep.]
cray•fish (krā'fĭsh') *n.* A small, lobsterlike freshwater crustacean. [< OF *crevise.*]
cray•on (krā'ən, -ŏn') *n.* A stick of colored wax, charcoal, or chalk, used for drawing. [< L *crēta*, chalk.]
craze (krāz) *v.* **crazed, crazing.** To be or cause to become insane. —*n.* A short-lived fashion; fad. [< ON **krasa*, to shatter.]
cra•zy (krā'zē) *adj.* -zier, -ziest. **1.** Unbalanced mentally; insane. **2.** *Informal.* Immoderately fond. **3.** *Informal.* Impractical. —**cra'zi•ly** *adv.* —**cra'zi•ness** *n.*
creak (krēk) *v.* To make or move with a grating or squeaking sound. —*n.* A grating or squeaking sound. [ME *creken* (imit.).]
cream (krēm) *n.* **1.** The fatty component of milk. **2.** Yellowish white. **3.** A substance resembling cream, as certain foods or cosmetics. **4.** The choicest part. —*v.* **1.** To beat (butter) to a creamy consistency. **2.** To prepare in a cream sauce. [< LL *chrisma*, ointment, and *crāmum*, cream.] —**cream** *adj.* —**cream'y** *adj.*
cream cheese. A soft white cheese made of cream and milk.
cream•er•y (krē'mə-rē) *n.*, *pl.* -ies. An establishment where dairy products are prepared or sold.
crease (krēs) *n.* A line made by pressing, folding, or wrinkling. —*v.* **creased, creasing.** To fold; be or become wrinkled. [< ME *crest*, ridge, crest.] —**creas'er** *n.*

---

cre•ate (krē-āt') v. -ated, -ating. 1. To cause to exist; originate. 2. To bring about; produce. [< L creāre.]

cre•a•tion (krē-ā'shən) n. 1. The act of creating. 2. The world and all things in it. 3. A product of human invention. 4. **the Creation.** God's primal act of bringing the world into existence.

cre•a•tive (krē-ā'tĭv) adj. Characterized by originality; imaginative. —**cre'a•tiv'i•ty** n.

cre•a•tor (krē-ā'tər) n. 1. One that creates. 2. **Creator.** God.

crea•ture (krē'chər) n. 1. An animal. 2. A person, esp. one regarded with pity or contempt. 3. One subservient to another.

crèche (krĕsh) n. A representation of the Nativity scene. [< OF creche, manger, crib.]

cre•dence (krē'dəns) n. 1. Acceptance as true; belief. 2. The quality of being trustworthy. [< L crēdere, to believe.]

cre•den•tial (krĭ-dĕn'shəl) n. 1. That which entitles one to credit or authority. 2. Often **credentials.** Written evidence of qualification.

cred•i•ble (krĕd'ə-bəl) adj. 1. Believable; plausible. 2. Reliable. [< L crēdere, to believe, entrust.] —**cred'i•bil'i•ty, cred'i•ble•ness** n. —**cred'i•bly** adv.

cred•it (krĕd'ĭt) n. 1. Belief; trust. 2. The quality of being trustworthy. 3. A good reputation. 4. A source of honor: a credit to his family. 5. Approval; respect. 6. Certification of completion of a course of study. 7. Reputation for financial solvency and integrity. 8. Time allowed for payment for anything sold on trust. 9. Entry in an account of payment received. 10. The balance in a person's bank account. —v. 1. To believe; trust. 2. To give credit to. [< L crēdere, to believe, entrust.]

cred•it•a•ble (krĕd'ĭ-tə-bəl) adj. Deserving commendation. —**cred'it•a•bil'i•ty, cred'it•a•ble•ness** n. —**cred'it•a•bly** adv.

cred•i•tor (krĕd'ə-tər) n. A person or firm to whom money is owed.

cre•do (krē'dō, krā'-) n., pl. -dos. A statement of belief; creed. [L crēdo, "I believe."]

cred•u•lous (krĕj'ŏŏ-ləs, krĕd'yŏŏ-) adj. Disposed to believe too readily; gullible. [< L crēdere, to believe.] —**cre•du'li•ty** (krĭ-d/y/ŏŏ'-lə-tē) n. —**cred'u•lous•ly** adv.

Cree (krē) n., pl. **Cree** or **Crees.** 1. A member of a tribe of Algonquian-speaking Indians formerly living in C Canada. 2. The language of this tribe.

creed (krēd) n. 1. A statement of the essential articles of a religious belief. 2. Any statement of conviction, principles, etc. [< L crēdo, "I believe."]

creek (krēk, krĭk) n. A small stream, often a tributary to a river. [ME creke, crike.]

Creek (krēk) n., pl. **Creek** or **Creeks.** 1. A member of a confederacy of several Muskhogean-speaking Indian tribes, formerly inhabiting the SE U.S. 2. The language of these tribes.

creel (krēl) n. A wicker basket, esp. one used for carrying fish. [ME (Scot) crel, crelle.]

creep (krēp) v. **crept, creeping.** 1. To move on hands and knees with the body close to the ground. 2. To move furtively or slowly. 3. To grow along the ground or other surface, as a vine. 4. To have a tingling sensation. [< OE crēopan.] —**creep'er** n.

creep•y (krē'pē) adj. -ier, -iest. Informal. Causing or having a sensation of repugnance or fear. —**creep'i•ness** n.

cre•mate (krē'māt', krĭ-māt') v. -mated, -mating. To incinerate (a corpse). [L cremāre, to burn, consume by fire.] —**cre•ma'tion** (krĭ-mā'shən) n. —**cre'ma'tor** n.

cre•ma•to•ry (krē'mə-tôr'ē, -tōr'ē, krĕm'ə-) n., pl. -ries. A furnace or place for cremating corpses.

cren•e•lat•ed (krĕn'ə-lā'tĭd) adj. Having battlements. [< OF crenel, a crenelation.] —**cren'e•la'tion** n.

Cre•ole (krē'ōl') n. 1. Any person of European descent born in the West Indies or Spanish America. 2. A person descended from the original French settlers of Louisiana. 3. The French patois spoken by these people. 4. Any person of mixed European and Negro ancestry. [< Port crioulo, Negro born in his master's house.] —**Cre'ole** adj.

cre•o•sote (krē'ə-sōt') n. 1. A colorless to yellowish oily liquid, obtained by the destructive distillation of wood tar and formerly used to treat tuberculosis and chronic bronchitis. 2. A yellowish to greenish-brown oily liquid obtained from coal tar and used as a wood preservative and disinfectant. [G Kreosot, "flesh preserver."]

crepe (krāp) n. A thin, crinkled fabric of silk, wool, etc. [< OF crespe, crisp, curly.]

crept (krĕpt). p.t. & p.p. of **creep.**

cre•pus•cu•lar (krē-pŭs'kyə-lər) adj. Of or like twilight; dim. [< L crepusculum, twilight.]

cres•cen•do (krə-shĕn'dō, -sĕn'dō) n., pl. -dos. 1. A gradual increase in the volume or intensity of sound. 2. A musical passage played in a crescendo. —adj. Gradually increasing in volume or intensity. [It, "increasing."] —**cres•cen'do** adv.

cres•cent (krĕs'ənt) n. 1. The figure of the moon in its first quarter, with concave and convex edges ending in points. 2. Something shaped like this. [< L crēscere, to increase, grow.]

cress (krĕs) n. Any of various related plants with pungent leaves often used in salads. [< OE cresse, cærse. See gras-.]

crest (krĕst) n. 1. A tuft or similar projection on the head of a bird or other animal. 2. A heraldic device used on seals, stationery, etc. 3. The top of something, as a wave; summit. —v. 1. To reach the crest of (a hill). 2. To form into a crest, as a wave. [< L crista, crest, plume.]

crest•fall•en (krĕst'fô'lən) adj. Dejected; dispirited. —**crest'fall'en•ly** adv.

Cre•ta•ceous (krĭ-tā'shəs) adj. Of or belonging to the geologic time, system of rocks, or sedimentary deposits of the most recent period of the Mesozoic era, characterized by the development of flowering plants and the disappearance of dinosaurs. —n. The Cretaceous period. [< L crēta, chalk, white earth, clay + -ACEOUS.]

ô paw, for/oi boy/ou out/ŏŏ took/ōō coo/p pop/r run/s sauce/sh shy/t to/th thin/th the/
ŭ cut/ûr fur/v van/w wag/y yes/z size/zh vision/ə ago, item, edible, gallop, circus/

Crete (krēt). A Greek island in the Mediterranean. —**Cre′tan** (krē′tən) *adj.* & *n.*

cre·tin·ism (krē′tĭn-ĭz′əm) *n.* A thyroid deficiency causing arrested mental and physical development. [< F *crétin*, idiot.] —**cre′tin** *n.*

cre·tonne (krĭ-tŏn′, krē′tŏn′) *n.* A heavy unglazed cotton or linen fabric used for draperies and slipcovers. [< *Creton*, village in Normandy.]

cre·vasse (krə-văs′) *n.* A deep fissure, as in a glacier. [< OF *crevace*, crevice.]

crev·ice (krĕv′ĭs) *n.* A narrow crack; fissure. [< L *crepāre*, to rattle, crack.]

crew¹ (krōō) *n.* **1.** A group of people working together. **2.** The personnel manning a ship or an aircraft. [ME *creue*, military reinforcement.]

crew² (krōō). A *p.t.* of **crow²**.

crib (krĭb) *n.* **1.** A child's bed with high sides. **2.** A small building for storing corn. **3.** A rack or trough for fodder. **4.** *Informal.* A translation or synopsis used dishonestly as an aid in doing schoolwork. —*v.* **cribbed, cribbing. 1.** To confine in or as in a crib. **2.** *Informal.* To use a crib in examinations; cheat. [< OE *cribb*, manger.] —**crib′ber** *n.*

crib·bage (krĭb′ĭj) *n.* A card game scored by inserting pegs into holes on a board. [Poss < CRIB.]

crick (krĭk) *n.* A painful cramp, as in the back or neck. [ME *crike*.]

crick·et¹ (krĭk′ĭt) *n.* A leaping insect of which the male produces a shrill, chirping sound. [< OE *criquer*, to click, creak.]

crick·et² (krĭk′ĭt) *n.* A game played with bats, a ball, and wickets by two teams of 11 players each. [Prob < OF *criquet*, wicket or bat in a ball game.]

cri·er (krī′ər) *n.* One who shouts out public announcements.

crime (krīm) *n.* An act committed or omitted in violation of the law. [< L *crimen*, verdict, judgment, crime.]

Cri·me·a (krī-mē′ə). A peninsula of the Soviet Union, extending into the Black Sea. —**Cri·me′an** *adj.*

crim·i·nal (krĭm′ə-nəl) *adj.* **1.** Of or pertaining to crime. **2.** Guilty of crime. —*n.* One who has committed a crime. —**crim′i·nal′i·ty** *n.* —**crim′i·nal·ly** *adv.*

crim·i·nol·o·gy (krĭm′ə-nŏl′ə-jē) *n.* The study of crime and criminals. —**crim′i·nol′o·gist** *n.*

crimp (krĭmp) *v.* **1.** To press into small folds or ridges; corrugate. **2.** To curl (hair). —*n.* **1.** The act of crimping. **2.** Something that has been crimped. [< OE *gecrympan*, to curl.] —**crimp′er** *n.*

crim·son (krĭm′zən) *n.* A deep red. —*v.* To make or become crimson. [< Ar *qirmizi*.]

cringe (krĭnj) *v.* **cringed, cringing.** To shrink back, as with fear; cower. [ME *crengen*.]

crin·kle (krĭng′kəl) *v.* **-kled, -kling.** To wrinkle; ripple. —*n.* A wrinkle or ripple. [ME *crinkelen*.] —**crin′kly** *adj.*

crin·o·line (krĭn′ə-lĭn) *n.* **1.** A fabric used to line and stiffen garments. **2.** A hoop skirt. [< It *crinolino*.] —**crin′o·line** *adj.*

crip·ple (krĭp′əl) *n.* One who is partly disabled, lame, or otherwise deficient. —*v.* **-pled, -pling.** To disable or damage. [< OE *crypel*.]

cri·sis (krī′sĭs) *n., pl.* **-ses** (-sēz′). A crucial situation; turning point. [< Gk *krisis*, turning point.]

crisp (krĭsp) *adj.* **1.** Firm but easily broken; brittle. **2.** Firm and fresh: *crisp celery.* **3.** Brisk; invigorating. **4.** Having small curls or waves. —*v.* To make or become crisp. [< OE < L *crispus*, crisped, curly.] —**crisp′i·ness** *n.* —**crisp′ly** *adv.* —**crisp′y** *adj.*

criss·cross (krĭs′krôs′, -krŏs′) *v.* **1.** To mark with crossing lines. **2.** To move crosswise through or over. —*n.* A pattern made of crossing lines. [Var of *christcross*.]

crit. critic; critical; criticism.

cri·te·ri·on (krī-tîr′ē-ən) *n., pl.* **-teria** (-tîr′ē-ə) or **-ons.** A standard on which a judgment can be based. [Gk *kritērion*, a means for judging, standard.]

crit·ic (krĭt′ĭk) *n.* **1.** One who judges anything, esp. literary or artistic works. **2.** One who finds fault. [< Gk *kritikos*, able to discern, critical.]

crit·i·cal (krĭt′ĭ-kəl) *adj.* **1.** Tending to criticize. **2.** Characterized by careful evaluation. **3.** Pertaining to critics or criticism. **4.** Forming or of the nature of a crisis. —**crit′i·cal·ly** *adv.* —**crit′i·cal·ness** *n.*

critical mass. The smallest mass of a fissionable material that will sustain a nuclear chain reaction.

crit·i·cism (krĭt′ə-sĭz′əm) *n.* **1.** The act of making judgments or evaluations. **2.** A review or article expressing the judgments of a critic. **3.** Censure; disapproval.

crit·i·cize (krĭt′ə-sīz′) *v.* **-cized, -cizing. 1.** To judge the merits and faults of; analyze and evaluate. **2.** To find fault with.

cri·tique (krĭ-tēk′) *n.* A critical review or commentary.

crit·ter (krĭt′ər) *n.* *Regional.* A creature, esp. a domestic animal. [Var of CREATURE.]

croak (krōk) *v.* **1.** To utter a low, hoarse sound, as a frog or crow. **2.** To speak with a low, hoarse voice. **3.** *Slang.* To die. —*n.* A croaking sound. [ME *croken* (imit).] —**croak′er** *n.* —**croak′i·ly** *adv.* —**croak′y** *adj.*

cro·chet (krō-shā′) *v.* **-cheted** (-shād′), **-cheting** (-shā′ĭng). To make (a piece of needlework) by looping thread with a hooked needle. —*n.* Needlework made by crocheting. [< OF *croc(he)*, a hook.]

crock (krŏk) *n.* An earthenware vessel. [< OE *crocca*.]

crock·er·y (krŏk′ə-rē) *n.* Earthenware.

croc·o·dile (krŏk′ə-dīl′) *n.* A large tropical aquatic reptile with armorlike skin, sharp teeth, and long, narrow jaws. [< Gk *krokodilos*, "worm of the pebbles."]

cro·cus (krō′kəs) *n., pl.* **-cuses** or **-ci** (-sī′). A garden plant with showy, variously colored early-blooming flowers. [< Gk *krokos*, saffron.]

crois·sant (krwä-säɴ′) *n.* A rich crescent-shaped roll. [< OF, crescent.]

Crom·well (krŏm′wĕl′, -wəl, krŭm′-), **Oliver.** 1599–1658. English statesman and general;

Lord Protector of the Commonwealth (1653–58).

crone (krōn) *n.* A withered old woman. [< MDu *caroonje*, old ewe, dead body.]

cro•ny (krō'nē) *n., pl.* **-nies.** A close friend or companion. [Earlier *chrony*, "old companion."]

crook (krŏŏk) *n.* **1.** Something bent or curved; a hooked part. **2.** A bent or curved implement. **3.** A swindler; thief. —*v.* To curve; bend. [< ON *krōkr*, a hook.]

crook•ed (krŏŏk'ĭd) *adj.* **1.** Having bends or curves. **2.** Dishonest; fraudulent. **3.** Misshapen. —**crook'ed•ly** *adv.*

croon (krōōn) *v.* To sing or hum (a song) softly. —*n.* A crooning sound. [< MDu *krōnen*, to groan, lament.] —**croon'er** *n.*

crop (krŏp) *n.* **1. a.** Agricultural produce. **b.** A specific yield of such produce. **2.** A short haircut. **3.** A short riding whip. **4.** A pouchlike enlargement of a bird's esophagus, in which food is partially digested. —*v.* **cropped, cropping. 1.** To cut off the ends of. **2.** To cut very short. **3.** To reap; harvest. —**crop up** (or **out**). To appear unexpectedly. [< OE *cropp*, cluster, bunch, ear of corn.]

cro•quet (krō-kā') *n.* An outdoor game in which wooden balls are driven through a series of wickets. [Perh < F *crochet*, a hook.]

cro•quette (krō-kĕt') *n.* A small cake of minced food fried in deep fat. [< F *croquer*, to crunch, crack (imit).]

cro•sier (krō'zhər) *n.* Also **cro•zier.** A bishop's staff. [< OF *crosse*, bishop's staff.]

cross (krôs, krŏs) *n.* **1.** An upright post with a transverse piece near the top. **2.** A symbolic representation of the cross on which Jesus was crucified. **3.** A trial or affliction. **4.** A pattern formed by two intersecting lines. **5. a.** A hybrid plant or animal. **b.** The process of hybridization. —*v.* **1.** To go or extend across. **2.** To intersect. **3.** To draw a line across. **4.** To place crosswise. **5.** To thwart or obstruct. **6.** To breed by hybridizing. —*adj.* **1.** Lying crosswise. **2.** Contrary or opposing. **3.** Irritable; annoyed. **4.** Crossbred; hybrid. [< L *crux (cruc-).*] —**cross'ness** *n.*

cross•bar (krôs'bär', krŏs'-) *n.* A horizontal bar or line.

cross•beam (krôs'bēm', krŏs'-) *n.* A transverse beam, as a joist.

cross•bones (krôs'bōnz', krŏs'-) *n.* A representation of two bones placed crosswise, usually under a skull.

cross•bow (krôs'bō', krŏs'-) *n.* A medieval weapon consisting of a bow fixed crosswise on a stock.

cross•breed (krôs'brēd', krŏs'-) *v.* To hybridize. —*n.* A hybrid.

cross-coun•try (krôs'kŭn'trē, krŏs'-) *adj.* **1.** Moving across open country rather than roads. **2.** From one side of a country to the opposite side.

cross•cur•rent (krôs'kûr'ənt, krŏs'-) *n.* **1.** A current flowing across another. **2.** A conflicting tendency.

cross•cut (krôs'kŭt', krŏs'-) *v.* To cut or run crosswise. —*adj.* **1.** Used for cutting cross-

wise: *a crosscut saw.* **2.** Cut across the grain. —*n.* A transverse course or cut.

cross-ex•am•ine (krôs'ĭg-zăm'ĭn, krŏs'-) *v.* To question (someone) closely, esp. to compare the resulting answers with previous responses. —**cross'-ex•am'i•na'tion** *n.*

cross-eye (krôs'ī', krŏs'ī') *n.* A form of strabismus in which one or both eyes deviate toward the nose. —**cross'-eyed'** *adj.*

cross•hatch (krôs'hăch', krŏs'-) *v.* To shade with sets of intersecting parallel lines.

cross•ing (krôs'ĭng, krŏs'-) *n.* **1.** An intersection, as of roads. **2.** The place at which something, as a river, can be crossed.

cross•piece (krôs'pēs', krŏs'-) *n.* A transverse piece, as of a structure.

cross-pol•li•nate (krôs'pŏl'ə-nāt', krŏs'-) *v.* To fertilize (a plant or flower) with pollen from another. —**cross'-pol'li•na'tion** *n.*

cross-re•fer (krôs'rĭ-fûr', krŏs'-) *v.* To refer from one part of a book, index, etc., to another. —**cross'-ref'er•ence** *n.*

cross•road (krôs'rōd', krŏs'-) *n.* **1.** A road that intersects another. **2. crossroads.** A place where roads meet.

cross section. 1. A section formed by a plane cutting through an object, usually at right angles to an axis. **2.** A piece so cut or a graphic representation of it. **3.** A representative sample. —**cross'-sec'tion•al** *adj.*

cross•talk (krôs'tôk', krŏs'-) *n.* Interference noise on a telephone or other electronic receiver.

cross•walk (krôs'wôk', krŏs'-) *n.* A street crossing marked for pedestrians.

cross•wise (krôs'wīz', krŏs'-) *adv.* Also **cross•ways** (-wāz'). Across; running transversely.

crotch (krŏch) *n.* The angle or fork formed by the junction of parts, as by two branches or legs. [Poss a var of CRUTCH.] —**crotched** (krŏcht) *adj.*

crotch•et (krŏch'ĭt) *n.* An odd or whimsical notion. [< OF *crochet*, small hook.] —**crotch'et•i•ness** *n.* —**crotch'et•y** *adj.*

crouch (krouch) *v.* **1.** To stoop with the limbs close to the body. **2.** To cringe. [< OF *crochir*, to be bent.] —**crouch** *n.*

croup (krōōp) *n.* A pathological condition affecting the larynx in children, characterized by respiratory difficulty and a harsh cough. [Prob imit of coughing.]

crou•pi•er (krōō'pē-ər, -pē-ā') *n.* An attendant at a gaming table who collects and pays bets. [F, orig "rider on the rump (behind another rider)."]

crou•ton (krōō'tŏn', krōō-tŏn') *n.* A cube of toasted bread. [< L *crusta*, CRUST.]

crow¹ (krō) *n.* A large, glossy black bird with a raucous call. [< OE *crāwe*. See ger-².]

crow² (krō) *v.* **1.** crowed or crew. To utter the shrill cry of a rooster. **2.** To boast; exult. **3.** To make a sound expressive of pleasure. —*n.* **1.** The cry of a rooster. **2.** An inarticulate sound expressive of pleasure or delight. [< OE *crāwan*. See ger-².]

Crow (krō) *n., pl.* **Crow** or **Crows.** **1.** A member of a tribe of Siouan-speaking Indians of SE Montana. **2.** The language of this tribe.

ô paw, for/oi boy/ou out/ōō took/ōō coo/p pop/r run/s sauce/sh shy/t to/th thin/*th* the/
ŭ cut/ûr fur/v van/w wag/y yes/z size/zh vision/ə ago, item, edible, gallop, circus/

crow•bar (krō′bär′) *n.* A metal bar used as a lever.

crowd (kroud) *n.* 1. A large number of persons or things gathered together; throng. 2. A clique. —*v.* 1. To gather in numbers. 2. To press or shove; push. 3. To cram tightly together. [< OE *crūdan*, to hasten. See greut-.] —**crowd′er** *n.*

crow•foot (krō′fo͞ot′) *n., pl.* -foots. Any of various plants of the family that includes the buttercups.

crown (kroun) *n.* 1. A head covering worn as a symbol of sovereignty. 2. The power of a monarch. 3. A wreath worn on the head as a symbol of victory. 4. Anything resembling a crown in shape or position. 5. The top of the head. 6. A former British coin. 7. The highest point of anything. 8. The part of a tooth that is covered by enamel and projects beyond the gum line. —*v.* 1. To put a crown upon. 2. To invest with regal power. 3. To confer honor upon. 4. To surmount or be the highest part of. [< L *corōna*, garland, wreath.]

crown colony. A British colony, usually having an appointed governor, in which the sovereign has complete control of legislation.

crown prince. The heir apparent to a throne.

crow's-nest (krōz′nĕst′) *n.* A lookout platform near the top of a ship's mast.

cro•zier. Variant of **crosier.**

cru•ces. Alternate *pl.* of **crux.**

cru•cial (kro͞o′shəl) *adj.* 1. Of decisive importance. 2. Difficult; trying. [< L *crux (cruc-)*, CROSS.] —**cru′cial•ly** *adv.*

cru•ci•ble (kro͞o′sə-bəl) *n.* A vessel made of a refractory substance, used for melting materials at high temperatures. [ME *crusible.*]

cru•ci•fix (kro͞o′sə-fĭks′) *n.* An image of Christ on the cross. [< LL *crucifigere*, CRUCIFY.]

cru•ci•fix•ion (kro͞o′sə-fĭk′shən) *n.* 1. The act of crucifying. 2. A representation of Christ on the cross. 3. **the Crucifixion.** The crucifying of Christ.

cru•ci•form (kro͞o′sə-fôrm′) *adj.* Cross-shaped.

cru•ci•fy (kro͞o′sə-fī′) *v.* -fied, -fying. 1. To put to death by nailing or binding to a cross. 2. To torment; torture. [< L *crucifigere.*]

crude (kro͞od) *adj.* cruder, crudest. 1. In an unrefined or natural state; raw. 2. Lacking finish, tact, or taste. 3. Roughly made. [< L *crūdus*, bloody, raw.] —**crude′ly** *adv.* —**cru′di•ty, crude′ness** *n.*

crude oil. Petroleum.

cru•el (kro͞o′əl) *adj.* Causing pain or suffering; merciless. [< L *crūdēlis*, morally unfeeling, cruel.] —**cru′el•ly** *adv.* —**cru′el•ty** *n.*

cru•et (kro͞o′ĭt) *n.* A glass bottle for holding vinegar or oil at the table. [< OF *crue*, flask.]

cruise (kro͞oz) *v.* cruised, cruising. 1. To sail or travel over or about, as for pleasure. 2. To travel at a speed providing maximum operating efficiency. —*n.* A sea voyage for pleasure. [Perh < Du *kruisen*, to sail to and fro.]

cruis•er (kro͞o′zər) *n.* 1. One of a class of fast warships of medium tonnage. 2. A large motorboat whose cabin has living facilities. 3. A police squad car.

crul•ler (krŭl′ər) *n.* A small cake of twisted sweet dough fried in deep fat. [< Du *krullen*, to curl.]

crumb (krŭm) *n.* 1. A small piece broken or fallen, as from bread. 2. Any fragment or scrap. —*v.* 1. To break into crumbs. 2. To cover with bread crumbs. [< OE *cruma.*]

crum•ble (krŭm′bəl) *v.* -bled, -bling. To break or fall into small parts or crumbs.

crum•pet (krŭm′pĭt) *n. Chiefly Brit.* A soft, muffinlike bread baked on a griddle. [Prob < ME *crompid (cake)*, "curled cake."]

crum•ple (krŭm′pəl) *v.* -pled, -pling. 1. To crush together into wrinkles. 2. To collapse.

crunch (krŭnch) *v.* 1. To chew with a noisy, grinding sound. 2. To crush noisily. [Imit.] —**crunch** *n.*

cru•sade (kro͞o-sād′) *n.* 1. Often **Crusade.** Any of the Christian military expeditions in the 11th, 12th, and 13th centuries to recover the Holy Land. 2. Any zealous movement for a cause. —*v.* -saded, -sading. To engage in a crusade. [< L *crux*, CROSS.] —**cru•sad′er** *n.*

crush (krŭsh) *v.* 1. To mash or squeeze so as to break or injure. 2. To break, pound, or grind. 3. To extract or obtain by pressure. 4. To shove or crowd. 5. To overwhelm; subdue. —*n.* 1. The act of crushing. 2. A great crowd. 3. *Informal.* An infatuation. [< OF *croissir.*]

crust (krŭst) *n.* 1. The hard outer part of bread. 2. A piece of bread consisting mostly of this part. 3. Any hard, crisp covering or surface. —*v.* To cover or become covered with a crust. [< L *crusta*, shell.] —**crust′y** *adj.*

crus•ta•cean (krŭ-stā′shən) *n.* Any of various chiefly aquatic arthropods having a segmented body with a hard outer covering, as a lobster, crab, or shrimp. [< NL *crustacea*, "the shelled ones."]

crutch (krŭch) *n.* 1. A support used as an aid in walking, usually having a crosspiece to fit under the armpit. 2. Anything depended upon for support. [< OE *crycc.*]

crux (krŭks, kro͞oks) *n., pl.* **cruxes** or **cruces** (kro͞o′sēz). 1. A critical or crucial point. 2. A puzzling problem. [L, CROSS.]

Crux (krŭks) *n.* A constellation in the S Hemisphere; Southern Cross.

cru•zei•ro (kro͞o-zā′rō, -rō) *n., pl.* -ros. The basic monetary unit of Brazil.

cry (krī) *v.* cried, crying. 1. To make inarticulate sobbing sounds; weep. 2. To utter loudly; shout. 3. To utter a characteristic sound or call, as an animal does. 4. To proclaim in public. —*n., pl.* **cries.** 1. A loud utterance of emotion. 2. Any loud utterance; shout. 3. A fit of weeping. 4. An urgent appeal. 5. The characteristic call of an animal. —**a far cry.** A long way. [< OF *crier.*]

cry•ba•by (krī′bā′bē) *n.* One who cries or complains frequently with little cause.

cry•ing (krī′ĭng) *adj.* Demanding immediate action: *a crying need.*

cry•o•gen•ics (krī′ō-jĕn′ĭks) *n.* (takes sing. v.). The science of low-temperature phenomena. [< Gk *kruos*, frost.] —**cry′o•gen′ic** *adj.*

crypt (krĭpt) *n.* 1. An underground chamber, esp. one used as a burial place. 2. *Anat.* Any of various small pits, recesses, glandular cav-

---

ă pat/ā ate/âr care/ä bar/b bib/ch chew/d deed/ĕ pet/ē be/f fit/g gag/h hat/hw what/ ĭ pit/ī pie/îr pier/j judge/k kick/l lid, fatal/m mum/n no, sudden/ng sing/ŏ pot/ō go/

ities, or follicles in the body. [< Gk *kruptos,* hidden.]

cryp·tic (krĭp'tĭk) *adj.* Secret; enigmatic; mystifying. [< Gk *kruptos,* hidden.]

crypto-. *comb. form.* Hidden or secret. [< Gk *kruptos,* hidden.]

cryp·to·gram (krĭp'tə-grăm') *n.* Something written in code or cipher.

cryp·tog·ra·phy (krĭp-tŏg'rə-fē) *n.* The art of writing in or deciphering secret code. —**cryp·tog'ra·pher** *n.*

crys·tal (krĭs'təl) *n.* **1. a.** A three-dimensional atomic, ionic, or molecular structure of periodically repeated, identically constituted, congruent unit cells. **b.** The unit cell of such a structure. **2.** A body, as a piece of quartz, having such a structure. **3.** Anything similar to crystal, as in transparency. [< Gk *krustallos.*] —**crys'tal·line** *adj.*

crys·tal·lize (krĭs'tə-līz') *v.* **-lized, -lizing. 1.** To form or cause to form a crystalline structure. **2.** To assume or cause to assume a definite and permanent form. —**crys'tal·li·za'tion** *n.*

crys·tal·log·ra·phy (krĭs'tə-lŏg'rə-fē) *n.* The science of crystal structure and phenomena. —**crys'tal·log'ra·pher** *n.*

Cs cesium.

C.S. **1.** chief of staff. **2.** Christian Science; Christian Scientist. **3.** civil service.

CST, C.S.T. Central Standard Time.

C.T. Central Time.

ct. **1.** cent. **2.** court.

ctf. certificate.

ctn. carton.

ctr. center.

Cu copper (L *cuprum*).

cu. cubic.

cub (kŭb) *n.* **1.** A young bear, wolf, lion, etc. **2.** A novice, as in newspaper reporting. [?]

Cu·ba (kyōō'bə). An island republic in the Caribbean. Pop. 7,256,000. Cap. Havana. —**Cu'ban** *adj. & n.*

Cuba

cub·by·hole (kŭb'ē-hōl') *n.* A small compartment. [< Du *kubbe,* basket.]

cube (kyōōb) *n.* **1.** A regular solid having six congruent square faces. **2.** The third power of a number or quantity. —*v.* **cubed, cubing. 1.** To raise to the third power, as a number or quantity. **2.** To form or cut into cubes or the shape of a cube. [< L *cubus* < Gk *kubos.*]

cu·bic (kyōō'bĭk) *adj.* **1.** Having the shape of a cube. **2. a.** Having three dimensions. **b.** Hav-

ing volume equal to a cube whose edge is of a stated length. **3.** Of the third power, order, or degree.

cu·bi·cle (kyōō'bĭ-kəl) *n.* A small compartment. [L *cubiculum,* sleeping chamber.]

cub·ism (kyōō'bĭz'əm) *n.* An early 20th-century school of painting and sculpture tending through geometrical reduction of natural forms to establish independence of all imitative intention. —**cub'ist** *adj. & n.*

cu·bit (kyōō'bĭt) *n.* An ancient unit of linear measure, approx. 17 to 22 inches. [< L *cubitum,* cubit, elbow.]

cuck·old (kŭk'əld) *n.* A man whose wife has committed adultery. —*v.* To make a cuckold of. [< OF *cucu,* cuckoo.]

cuck·oo (kōō'kōō, kŏŏk'ōō) *n.* **1.** An Old World bird with grayish plumage and a characteristic two-note call. **2.** Any of various related birds. —*adj. Slang.* Demented; foolish. [ME *cuccu* (imit.).]

cu·cum·ber (kyōō'kŭm'bər) *n.* The long, green-skinned, white-fleshed fruit of a sprawling vine, used in salads and for pickling. [< L *cucumis.*]

cud (kŭd) *n.* Food regurgitated from the first stomach to the mouth of a ruminant and chewed again. [< OE *cwudu, cudu.*]

cud·dle (kŭd'l) *v.* **-dled, -dling. 1.** To fondle; hug. **2.** To nestle; snuggle. [?]

cudg·el (kŭj'əl) *n.* A short, heavy club. —*v.* To beat with a cudgel. [< OE *cycgel.*]

cue¹ (kyōō) *n.* The long, tapered rod used to propel a billiard ball. [F *queue,* "tail."]

cue² (kyōō) *n.* **1.** A signal to begin or enter, as in a play. **2.** A reminder. [?] —**cue** *v.* (**cued, cuing**).

cuff¹ (kŭf) *n.* **1.** A fold at the bottom of a sleeve. **2.** The turned-up fold at the bottom of a trouser leg. —**off the cuff.** *Informal.* Extemporaneously. [ME *cuffe,* glove, mitten.]

cuff² (kŭf) *v.* To strike with the hand; slap. [?] —**cuff** *n.*

cuff links. A pair of linked buttons used to fasten shirt cuffs.

cui·rass (kwĭ-răs') *n.* A piece of armor for the breast and back. [< VL **coriāca,* "leather buckler."]

cui·sine (kwĭ-zēn') *n.* A characteristic style of preparing food. [< LL *coquīna,* a kitchen, cookery.]

cul-de-sac (kŭl'dĭ-săk', kōōl'-) *n., pl.* **cul-de-sacs. 1.** A dead-end street. **2.** An impasse. [F, "bottom of the sack," blind alley.]

–cule. *comb. form.* Smallness: **molecule.** [< L *-culus, -cula, -culum.*]

cu·li·nar·y (kyōō'lə-nĕr'ē, kŭl'ə-) *adj.* Of kitchens or cookery. [< L *culīna,* kitchen.]

cull (kŭl) *v.* **1.** To pick out from others; select. **2.** To gather; collect. [< L *colligere,* to COL-LECT.] —**cull'er** *n.*

cul·mi·nate (kŭl'mə-nāt') *v.* **-nated, -nating.** To reach the highest point or degree; climax. [< L *culmen (culmin-),* top, summit.] —**cul'mi·na'tion** *n.*

cul·pa·ble (kŭl'pə-bəl) *adj.* Responsible for wrong or error; blameworthy. [< L *culpāre,* to blame.] —**cul'pa·bil'i·ty** *n.* —**cul'pa·bly** *adv.*

cul•prit (kŭl'prĭt) *n.* A person charged with or found guilty of a crime. [< the 17th-century legal phrase *"Culprit,* how will you be tryed?"]

cult (kŭlt) *n.* **1.** A system or community of religious worship. **2.** Obsessive devotion to a person or. ideal. [< L *cultus,* cultivation, a laboring, worship.] —**cul'tic** *adj.*

cul•ti•vate (kŭl'tə-vāt') *v.* -**vated,** -**vating.** **1.** To improve and prepare (land) for raising crops. **2.** To grow or tend, as a plant or crop. **3.** To form and refine, as by education. **4.** To seek the acquaintance or good will of. [< L *cultus,* pp of *colere,* to till, cultivate.] —**cul'ti•va'tion** *n.* —**cul'ti•va'tor** *n.*

cul•ture (kŭl'chər) *n.* **1.** Cultivation of the soil. **2.** The raising of animals or growing of plants, esp. to improve stock. **3.** A growth or colony of microorganisms in a nutrient medium. **4.** The totality of socially transmitted behavior patterns characteristic of a people. **5.** A style of social and artistic expression peculiar to a society or class. **6.** Intellectual and artistic activity. —*v.* -**tured,** -**turing.** **1.** To cultivate. **2.** To develop in a culture medium, as microorganisms or tissues. [< L *cultus,* cultivation.] —**cul'tur•al** *adj.* —**cul'tur•al•ly** *adv.*

cul•vert (kŭl'vərt) *n.* A drain crossing under a road or embankment. [?]

cum•ber (kŭm'bər) *v.* To weigh down; hamper. [Perh < OF *combre,* hindrance.]

cum•ber•some (kŭm'bər-səm) *adj.* Unwieldy; burdensome. —**cum'ber•some•ness** *n.*

cum•in (kŭm'ĭn) *n.* **1.** The aromatic seeds of an Old World plant, used as a condiment. **2.** The plant itself. [< Gk *kuminon.*]

cum lau•de (kōōm lou'də, lou'dĕ, kŭm lô'dĕ). With honor. [NL, "with praise."]

cum•mer•bund (kŭm'ər-bŭnd') *n.* A broad, pleated sash worn as a waistband, esp. by men. [Hindi *kamarband.*]

cu•mu•la•tive (kyōōm'yə-lā'tĭv, -yə-lə-tĭv) *adj.* Increasing by successive addition. [< L *cumulus,* heap.] —**cu'mu•la'tive•ly** *adv.*

cu•mu•lo•nim•bus (kyōōm'yə-lō-nĭm'bəs) *n., pl.* -**buses** or -**bi** (-bī'). An extremely dense, vertically developed cumulus with a relatively hazy outline and a glaciated top, usually producing heavy rains, thunderstorms, or hailstorms.

cu•mu•lus (kyōōm'yə-ləs) *n., pl.* -**li** (-lī'). A dense white, fluffy, flat-based cloud with a multiple rounded top and a well-defined outline. [< L, heap, mass.]

cun•dum. Variant of **condom.**

cu•ne•i•form (kyōō'nē-ə-fôrm', kyōō-nē'-) *adj.* Wedge-shaped, as the characters used in ancient Mesopotamian writings. —*n.* Cuneiform writing. [< L *cuneus,* wedge + -FORM.]

cun•ning (kŭn'ĭng) *adj.* **1.** Shrewd; crafty. **2.** Exhibiting ingenuity. —*n.* **1.** Skill in deception. **2.** Expertness; dexterity. [Perh < OE *cunnan,* to know. See **gnō-.**] —**cun'ning•ly** *adv.*

cup (kŭp) *n.* **1.** A small, open container used for drinking. **2.** A measure of capacity equal to ½ pint, 8 ounces, or 16 tablespoons. **3.** Anything resembling a cup. —*v.* **cupped, cupping.** To shape like a cup: *cup one's hand.* [< OE *cuppe* < LL *cuppa,* drinking vessel.]

cup•board (kŭb'ərd) *n.* A closet or cabinet, usually with shelves for storing food, crockery, etc.

cup•cake (kŭp'kāk') *n.* A small, cup-shaped cake.

cu•pid•i•ty (kyōō-pĭd'ə-tē) *n.* Avarice; greed. [< L *cupere,* to desire.]

cu•po•la (kyōō'pə-lə) *n.* A small, usually domed structure surmounting a roof. [< L *cūpa,* tub, vat.]

cur (kûr) *n.* **1.** A mongrel dog. **2.** A base person. [Perh < ON *kurra,* to growl.]

cur. **1.** currency. **2.** current.

cu•ra•çao (kyōōr'ə-sō') *n.* A liqueur flavored with orange peel. [< *Curaçao,* island in the Caribbean.]

cu•ra•re (kōō-rär'ē, kyōō-) *n.* Also **cu•ra•ri, u•ra•ri** (ōō-rär'ē, yōō-). A resinous extract obtained from various South American trees, used medicinally as a muscle relaxant and by some South American Indians as an arrow poison. [< Cariban *kurari.*]

cu•rate (kyōōr'ĭt) *n.* **1.** A clergyman who has charge of a parish. **2.** A clergyman who assists a rector or vicar. [< ML *cūrātus,* "one having a (spiritual) cure."]

cur•a•tive (kyōōr'ə-tĭv) *adj.* Serving or tending to cure. —*n.* A remedy.

cu•ra•tor (kyōō-rā'tər, kyōōr'ə-tər) *n.* The director of a museum, library, or similar institution. [< L *cūrāre,* to take care of.]

curb (kûrb) *n.* **1.** Anything that checks or restrains. **2.** Also *Brit.* **kerb.** A concrete or stone edging along a sidewalk. **3.** A chain or strap serving in conjunction with the bit to restrain a horse. —*v.* **1.** To check or restrain. **2.** To furnish with a curb. [< OF *courbe,* a curved object, horse's bit.] —**curb'er** *n.*

curb•stone (kûrb'stōn') *n.* A row of stones that constitutes a curb.

curd (kûrd) *n.* Often **curds.** The coagulated part of milk, used to make cheese. [ME *curd, crudde.*]

cur•dle (kûrd'l) *v.* -**dled,** -**dling.** To become or cause to become curd; coagulate; thicken. [Freq of CURD.]

cure (kyōōr) *n.* **1.** Restoration of health. **2.** A medical treatment or drug used to restore health. —*v.* **cured, curing.** **1.** To restore to health. **2.** To rid of (disease). **3.** To process so as to prepare, preserve, or finish (a substance). [< L *cūra,* care, charge, healing.] —**cur'a•ble** *adj.* —**cure'less** *adj.* —**cur'er** *n.*

cure-all (kyōōr'ôl') *n.* Something that cures all diseases or evils; panacea.

cu•ret•tage (kyōōr'ə-täzh', kyōō-rĕt'ĭj) *n.* Surgical scraping of a bodily cavity. [< F *curer,* to cure.]

cur•few (kûr'fyōō) *n.* A regulation enjoining specified classes of the population to retire from the streets at a prescribed hour. [< OF *cuevrefeu,* "a covering of the fire."]

cu•ri•a (kyōōr'ē-ə) *n., pl.* **curiae** (kyōōr'ē-ē'). Often **Curia.** The central administration of the Roman Catholic Church. [L *cūria,* curia, council.]

cu•rie (kyōōr'ē, kyōō-rē') *n.* A unit of radioactivity, the amount of any nuclide that undergoes exactly 3.7 x 10¹⁰ radioactive disintegrations per second. [< M. *Curie* (1867–1934), Polish-born French chemist.]

cu•ri•o (kyōōr′ē-ō′) *n., pl.* **-os.** An unusual object of art or bric-a-brac. [Short for CURIOSITY.]

cu•ri•os•i•ty (kyōōr′ē-ŏs′ə-tē) *n., pl.* **-ties. 1.** A desire to know or learn. **2.** That which arouses interest, as by being novel.

cu•ri•ous (kyōōr′ē-əs) *adj.* **1.** Eager to know or learn. **2.** Prying; nosy. **3.** Singular; odd. [< L *cūriōsus,* careful, diligent, inquisitive.] **—cu′ri•ous•ly** *adv.* **—cu′ri•ous•ness** *n.*

cu•ri•um (kyōōr′ē-əm) *n. Symbol* **Cm** A silvery, metallic synthetic radioactive element. Atomic number 96, longest-lived isotope Cm 247. [< M. *Curie* and her husband Pierre. See **curie.**]

curl (kûrl) *v.* **1.** To form or be twisted into ringlets, as the hair. **2.** To assume or be formed into any curved or coiled shape. **—n. 1.** Something with a spiral or coiled shape. **2.** A ringlet of hair. [< MDu *crulle,* curly.] **—curl′i•ness** *n.* **—curl′y** *adj.*

cur•lew (kûrl′yōō, kûr′lōō) *n.* A long-billed brownish, long-legged shore bird. [< OF *courlieu.*]

curl•i•cue (kûr′lǐ-kyōō′) *n.* A fancy twist or flourish, as in a signature. [CURLY + CUE¹.]

cur•rant (kûr′ənt) *n.* **1. a.** The small, sour fruit of various prickly shrubs. **b.** A shrub bearing such fruit. **2.** A small, seedless raisin. [ME *(raysons of) coraunte,* (raisins of) *Corinth,* city of Greece.]

cur•ren•cy (kûr′ən-sē) *n., pl.* **-cies. 1.** Any form of money in circulation. See *Table of Currency* on following pages. **2.** Common acceptance; prevalence.

cur•rent (kûr′ənt) *adj.* **1.** Belonging to the time now passing; now in progress. **2.** Commonly accepted; prevalent. **—n. 1.** A steady and smooth onward movement, as of water. **2.** The part of any body of liquid or gas that has a continuous onward movement. **3.** A general tendency. **4. a.** A flow of electric charge. **b.** The amount of electric charge flowing past a specified circuit point per unit time. [< L *currere,* to run.] **—cur′rent•ly** *adv.*

cur•ric•u•lum (kə-rĭk′yə-ləm) *n., pl.* **-la** (-lə) *or* **-lums. 1.** All the courses of study offered by a school. **2.** A particular course of study. [< L, a running, course.] **—cur•ric′u•lar** *adj.*

cur•ry¹ (kûr′ē) *v.* **-ried, -rying.** To groom (a horse) with a comb or brush. **—curry favor.** To seek favor by fawning or flattery. [< OF *conreer,* to prepare, equip.]

cur•ry² (kûr′ē) *n., pl.* **-ries. 1.** A pungent condiment made from a powdered blend of spices. **2.** A sauce or dish seasoned with this. **—v. -ried, -rying.** To season with curry. [Tamil *kari,* relish, sauce.]

curse (kûrs) *n.* **1. a.** An appeal to a supernatural power for evil to befall someone or something. **b.** The evil thus invoked. **2.** A scourge. **3.** Any profane oath. **—v. cursed** *or* **curst, cursing. 1.** To invoke evil upon; damn. **2.** To bring evil upon; afflict. **3.** To utter curses (at someone or something). [< OE *curs.*] **—curs′er** *n.*

curs•ed (kûr′sĭd, kûrst) *adj.* Also **curst** (kûrst). Deserving to be cursed; detestable.

cur•sive (kûr′sĭv) *adj.* Designating writing or printing in which the letters are joined together. [ML *(scripta) cursīva,* "flowing (script)."]

cur•so•ry (kûr′sə-rē) *adj.* Hasty and superficial. [LL *cursōrius,* of running.]

curt (kûrt) *adj.* **1.** Rudely brief or abrupt. **2.** Terse; concise. [L *curtus,* cut short.] **—curt′ly** *adv.* **—curt′ness** *adj.*

cur•tail (kər-tāl′) *v.* To cut short; abbreviate. [< L *curtus,* shortened.] **—cur•tail′ment** *n.*

cur•tain (kûrt′n) *n.* A piece of material hanging in a window or other opening as a decoration, shade, or screen. **—v.** To provide or shut off with or as with a curtain. [< LL *cortīna,* enclosure, curtain.]

curt•sy (kûrt′sē) *n., pl.* **-sies.** A gesture of respect made by women by bending the knees with one foot forward. [Var of COURTESY.] **—curt′sy** *v.* **(-sied, -sying).**

cur•va•ceous (kûr-vā′shəs) *adj.* Having a voluptuous figure. **—cur•va′ceous•ly** *adv.*

cur•va•ture (kûr′və-chōōr) *n.* A measure, amount, act, or instance of curving.

curve (kûrv) *n.* **1. a.** A line that deviates from straightness in a smooth, continuous fashion. **b.** A surface that deviates from planarity in a smooth, continuous fashion. **2.** Any relatively smooth bend in the shape or course of something. **—v. curved, curving.** To move in, form, or cause to form a curve. [< L *curvus,* curved.] **—curv′ed•ly** (-ĭd-lē) *adv.*

cush•ion (kōōsh′ən) *n.* **1.** A pad or pillow. **2.** Anything that absorbs shock. **—v. 1.** To provide with a cushion. **2.** To protect against or absorb the shock of. [< VL **coxīnus,* "hip rest," cushion.] **—cush′ion•y** *adj.*

Cush•it•ic (kōō-shĭt′ĭk) *n.* A group of Hamitic languages, including Somali. **—Cush•it′ic** *adj.*

cusp (kŭsp) *n.* A point or pointed end. [L *cuspis,* a point, spear.]

cus•pid (kŭs′pĭd) *n.* A tooth having one point; canine tooth. [Back-formation < BICUSPID.]

cus•pi•dor (kŭs′pə-dôr′) *n.* A spittoon. [< L *conspuere,* to spit upon.]

cuss (kŭs) *v. Informal.* To curse. **—n. 1.** A curse. **2.** An odd or perverse creature. [Var of CURSE.]

cus•tard (kŭs′tərd) *n.* A dessert of milk, sugar, eggs, and flavoring, cooked until set. [< L *crusta,* CRUST.]

cus•to•di•an (kŭs-tō′dē-ən) *n.* **1.** One who has charge of something. **2.** A janitor.

cus•to•dy (kŭs′tə-dē) *n., pl.* **-dies. 1.** The act or right of guarding. **2.** Any state of being kept or guarded, esp. imprisonment. [< L *custōdia.*] **—cus•to′di•al** (-tō′dē-əl) *adj.*

cus•tom (kŭs′təm) *n.* **1.** A practice followed as a matter of course; a convention. **2.** A habit of an individual. **3. customs.** A duty or tax on imported goods. **—adj. 1.** Made to order. **2.** Specializing in made-to-order goods. [< L *consuēscere,* to accustom.]

cus•tom•ar•y (kŭs′tə-měr′ē) *adj.* Commonly practiced or used as a matter of course; usual. **—cus′tom•ar′i•ly** *adv.*

CURRENCY
TABLE OF EXCHANGE RATES

Country	Basic Unit	Standard Subdivision	†	††
Afghanistan	afghani	100 puls	Af.	0.017
Albania	lek	100 quintars	L	0.244
Algeria	dinar	100 centimes	DA	0.256
Argentina	peso	100 centavos	$a	0.018
Australia	dollar	100 cents	$A	1.330
Austria	schilling	100 groschen	S	0.062
Bangladesh	taka	100 paise	T	0.120
Barbados	dollar	100 cents	B$	0.480
Belgium	franc	100 centimes	BF	0.029
Bolivia	peso	100 centavos	Bs	0.050
Brazil	cruzeiro	100 centavos	Cr$	0.108
Bulgaria	lev	100 stotinki	LV	0.600
Burma	kyat	100 pyas	K	0.210
Burundi	franc	100 centimes	FBu	0.013
Cambodia*				
Cameroun	franc	100 centimes	CFAF	0.004
Canada	dollar	100 cents	Can$	0.975
Central African Republic	franc	100 centimes	CFAF	0.004
Ceylon	rupee	100 cents	Cey R	0.170
Chad	franc	100 centimes	CFAF	0.004
Chile	escudo	100 centesimos	E°	0.0002
China, People's Republic of	yuan	10 chiao, 100 fen	$	0.550
China, Republic of (Taiwan)	yuan	100 cents	N.T.$	0.025
Colombia	peso	100 centavos	Col$	0.035
Congo, Republic of	franc	100 centimes	CFAF	0.004
Costa Rica	colon	100 centimos	₡	0.122
Cuba	peso	100 centavos	$	1.200
Cyprus	pound	1000 mils	£C	2.800
Czechoslovakia	koruna	100 halers	Kč	0.008
Dahomey	franc	100 centimes	CFAF	0.004
Denmark	krone	100 öre	DKr	0.187
Dominican Republic	peso	100 centavos	RD$	1.000
East Germany	ostmark	100 pfennigs	OM	0.445
Ecuador	sucre	100 centavos	S/	0.040
Egypt	pound	100 piasters	LE	2.300
El Salvador	colon	100 centavos	₡	0.400
Ethiopia	dollar	100 cents	Eth$	0.480
Finland	markka	100 pennis	Fmk	0.282
France	franc	100 centimes	Fr	0.250
Gabon	franc	100 centimes	CFAF	0.004
Gambia	dalasi	100 butut	£G	0.590
Ghana	cedi	100 pesewa	N₡	0.880
Greece	drachma	100 lepta	Dr	0.033
Guatemala	quetzal	100 centavos	Q	1.000
Guinea	syli	100 cory	S	0.048
Guyana	dollar	100 cents	G$	0.460
Haiti	gourde	100 centimes	G	0.200
Honduras	lempira	100 centavos	L	0.500
Hong Kong	dollar	100 cents	HK$	0.210
Hungary	forint	100 fillér	Ft	0.047
Iceland	krona	100 aurar	IKr	0.008
India	rupee	100 paise	R	0.120
Indonesia	rupiah	100 sen	Rp	0.002
Iran	rial	100 dinars	RI	0.015
Iraq	dinar	1000 fils	ID	3.410

*See Khmer Republic   †Abbreviation or Symbol

Country	Basic Unit	Standard Subdivision	†	††
Ireland, Republic of	pound	100 pence	£Ir.	2.250
Israel	pound	100 agorot	I£	0.160
Italy	lira	100 centesimi	Lit	0.0016
Ivory Coast	franc	100 centimes	CFAF	0.004
Jamaica	dollar	100 cents	J$	1.100
Japan	yen	100 sen	¥	0.003
Jordan	dinar	1000 fils	JD	3.220
Kenya	shilling	100 cents	K Sh.	0.140
Khmer Republic	riel	100 sen	CR	0.250
Kuwait	dinar	10 dirhams	KD	3.490
Laos	kip	100 at	K	0.002
Lebanon	pound	100 piasters	L£	0.440
Liberia	dollar	100 cents	$	1.000
Libya	dinar	1000 dirhams	Din	3.380
Luxembourg	franc	100 centimes	Lux. F.	0.029
Malagasy Republic	franc	100 centimes	FMG	0.004
Malawi, Republic of	kwacha	100 tambala	KW	1.200
Malaysia	dollar	100 cents	M$	0.420
Maldive Islands	rupee	100 larees	MRp	0.250
Mali	franc	100 centimes	MF	0.002
Malta	pound	100 cents	£M	2.500
Mauritania	ouguya	100 khoums	Oug	0.023
Mauritius	rupee	100 cents	MRp	0.170
Mexico	peso	100 centavos	Mex$	0.080
Mongolian People's Republic	tughrik	100 mongo	Tu.	0.297
Morocco	dirham	100 centimes	DH	0.249
Nepal	rupee	100 pice	NR	0.090
Netherlands	guilder	100 cents	Fls.	0.413
Netherlands Antilles	guilder	100 cents	C. Fls.	0.563
New Zealand	dollar	100 cents	$NZ	1.320
Nicaragua	cordoba	100 centavos	C$	0.144
Niger	franc	100 centimes	CFAF	0.004
Nigeria	niara	100 kobes	N	1.620
North Korea	won	100 jun	W	0.330
North Vietnam	dong	100 sau	D	0.339
Norway	krone	100 öre	NKr	0.205
Oman	riyal-omani	1000 baiza	R.S.	2.870
Pakistan	rupee	100 paisas	PR	0.100
Panama	balboa	100 centesimos	B	1.000
Paraguay	guarani	100 centimos	G	0.008
Peru	sol	100 centavos	S/	0.023
Philippines, Republic of the	peso	100 centavos	₱	0.140
Poland	zloty	100 groszy	Zl	0.050
Portugal	escudo	100 centavos	Esc	0.041
Qatar	riyal	100 dirhams	R	0.250
Rhodesia	dollar	100 cents	R$	0.870
Rumania	leu	100 bani	L	0.097
Rwanda	franc	100 centimes	RF	0.011
Saudi Arabia	riyal	100 halalas	SRI	0.283
Senegal	franc	100 centimes	CFAF	0.004
Sierra Leone	leone	100 cents	Le	1.180
Singapore	dollar	100 cents	S$	0.420
Somali Republic	shilling	100 cents	So. Sh.	0.160
South Africa, Republic of	rand	100 cents	R	1.400
South Korea	won	100 chon	W	0.002
South Vietnam	piaster	100 cents	VN$	0.001

†† **Equivalence in U.S. Dollars, August 1975**

CURRENCY (continued)

Country	Basic Unit	Standard Subdivision	†	††
Spain	peseta	100 centimos	Pta or Pts (plural)	0.179
Sudan	pound	100 piasters, 1000 milliemes	SdL	2.790
Surinam	guilder	100 cents	Sur. Fls.	0.563
Sweden	krona	100 öre	SKr	0.254
Switzerland	franc	100 centimes	SwF	0.400
Syria	pound	100 piasters	S£	0.270
Tanzania	shilling	100 cents	T. Sh.	0.140
Thailand	baht	100 satangs	B	0.050
Togo	franc	100 centimes	CFAF	0.004
Trinidad and Tobago	dollar	100 cents	TT$	0.480
Tunisia	dinar	1000 milliemes	D	2.520
Turkey	lira	100 kurus	T£	0.073
Uganda	shilling	100 cents	U. Sh.	0.140
Union of Soviet Socialist Republics	rouble	100 kopecks	R	1.449
United Kingdom of Great Britain and Northern Ireland	pound	100 pence	£	2.130
United States of America	dollar	100 cents	$	1.000
Upper Volta	franc	100 centimes	CFAF	0.004
Uruguay	peso	100 centesimos	UR$	0.0004
Venezuela	bolivar	100 centimos	B	0.232
Western Samoa	tala	100 cents	Tala	1.200
West Germany	Deutsche mark	100 pfennigs	DM	0.426
Yemen	riyal	40 bugshas	R	0.220
Yemen Democratic People's Republic	dinar	1000 fils	SYD	2.950
Yugoslavia	dinar	100 paras	Din	0.059
Zaire	zaire	100 makuta	Z	2.000
Zambia	kwacha	100 ngwee	KW	1.570

†Abbreviation or Symbol   ††Equivalence in U.S. Dollars, August 1975

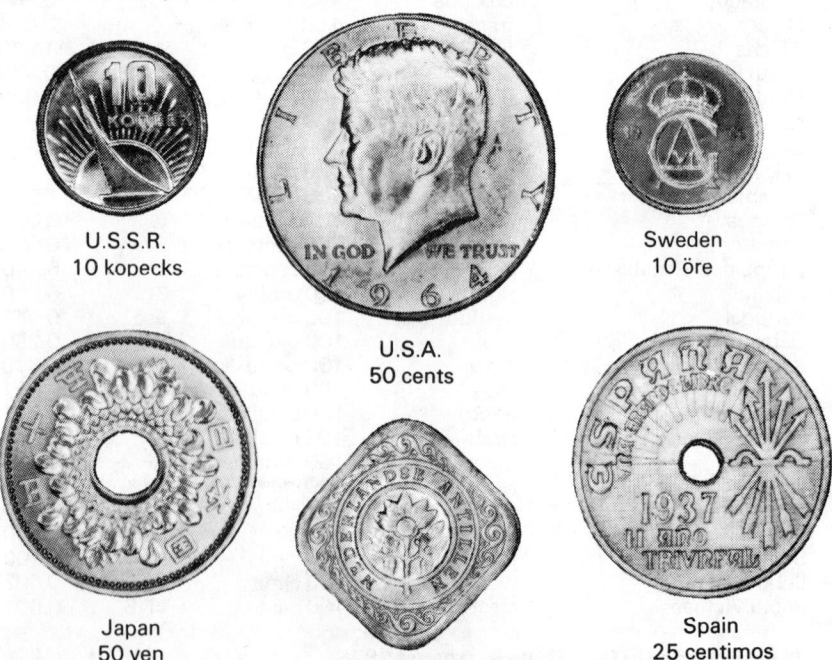

U.S.S.R.
10 kopecks

Sweden
10 öre

U.S.A.
50 cents

Japan
50 yen

Netherlands Antilles
5 cents

Spain
25 centimos

cus•tom•er (kŭs'təm-ər) *n.* 1. One who buys goods or services, esp. on a regular basis. 2. *Informal.* One with whom one must deal: *a tough customer.*

cus•tom•house (kŭs'təm-hous') *n.* A building where customs are collected.

cus•tom-made (kŭs'təm-mād') *adj.* Made to the specifications of an individual buyer.

cut (kŭt) *v.* **cut, cutting.** 1. a. To penetrate with a sharp edge. b. To penetrate injuriously. 2. To separate into parts with or as if with a sharp-edged instrument; sever. 3. To have (a new tooth) grow through the gums. 4. To fell by sawing; hew. 5. To harvest. 6. To form or shape by severing or incising. 7. To intersect; cross. 8. To reduce: *cut prices.* 9. To shorten, trim, or pare. 10. To allow incision: *Butter cuts easily.* 11. To go directly or change direction abruptly. 12. *Informal.* To fail to attend purposely: *cut a class.* 13. *Informal.* To cease; stop. —*n.* 1. The act or result of incising, severing, or separating. 2. A part that has been severed from a main body: *a cut of beef.* 3. A passage resulting from excavating or probing, as a channel. 4. A reduction: *a salary cut.* 5. The style in which a garment is cut. 6. *Informal.* A share, as of earnings. 7. *Informal.* An insult. 8. *Informal.* An unexcused absence, as from school. 9. a. An engraved block or plate. b. A print made from such a block. —**a cut above.** A little better than. [Prob < OE *cyttan.*]

cut-and-dried (kŭt'ən-drīd') *adj.* 1. Prepared in advance. 2. Ordinary; routine.

cu•ta•ne•ous (kyōō-tā'nē-əs) *adj.* Of or affecting the skin. [< L *cutis,* skin.]

cut•back (kŭt'băk') *n.* A decrease; curtailment: *a cutback in production.*

cute (kyōōt) *adj.* **cuter, cutest.** Delightfully pretty or dainty. [Short for ACUTE.] —**cute'ly** *adv.* —**cute'ness** *n.*

cu•ti•cle (kyōō'tĭ-kəl) *n.* 1. The epidermis. 2. The strip of hardened skin at the base of a fingernail or toenail. [< L *cutis,* skin.]

cut•lass (kŭt'ləs) *n.* A short, heavy sword with a curved blade. [< L *culter,* knife.]

cut•ler•y (kŭt'lĕr-ē) *n.* 1. Cutting instruments. 2. Implements used as tableware.

cut•let (kŭt'lĭt) *n.* 1. A thin slice of meat, as of veal, from the leg or ribs. 2. A flat croquette of chopped meat or fish. [< L *costa,* rib.]

cut•off (kŭt'ôf', -ŏf') *n.* 1. A designated limit or point of termination. 2. A short cut or by-pass. 3. A device for cutting off a flow of steam, water, etc.

cut-rate (kŭt'rāt') *adj.* Sold or on sale at a reduced price.

cut•ter (kŭt'ər) *n.* 1. One who cuts, esp. in tailoring. 2. A device that cuts. 3. A ship's boat for transporting stores or passengers. 4. A small, lightly armed motorboat. 5. A small sleigh.

cut•throat (kŭt'thrōt') *n.* A murderer. —*adj.* 1. Murderous. 2. Relentless; merciless.

cut•ting (kŭt'ĭng) *adj.* 1. Capable of incising or severing; sharp. 2. Piercing and cold: *a cutting wind.* 3. Sarcastic: *a cutting remark.* —*n.* A part cut off from a main body, esp. a shoot

removed from a plant for rooting or grafting.

cut•tle•bone (kŭt'l-bōn') *n.* The chalky internal shell of a cuttlefish, used for feeding cage birds or ground into powder for use as a polishing agent.

cut•tle•fish (kŭt'l-fĭsh') *n.* A ten-armed, squid-like marine mollusk that has a chalky internal shell and secretes a dark, inky fluid. [< OE *cudele,* a cuttlefish.]

cut-up (kŭt'ŭp') *n. Informal.* A mischievous person.

c.w.o. 1. cash with order. 2. chief warrant officer.

cwt. hundredweight.

–cy. *comb. form.* 1. A quality or condition: bankruptcy. 2. Office or rank: baronetcy. [< L *-cia, -tia,* and Gk *-kiā, -tiā.*]

cy•a•nide (sī'ə-nīd') *n.* Also **cy•an•id** (-nĭd). Any of various compounds containing a CN group, esp. the extremely poisonous compounds potassium cyanide and sodium cyanide.

cyano–. *comb. form.* 1. Blue or dark-blue. 2. *Chem.* Cyanide or cyanogen. [< Gk *kuanos,* dark-blue enamel, the color blue.]

cy•an•o•gen (sī-ăn'ə-jən) *n.* A colorless, flammable, highly poisonous gas, C_2N_2, used as a rocket propellant, fumigant, and military weapon.

cy•a•no•sis (sī'ə-nō'sĭs) *n. Path.* A bluish discoloration of the skin, resulting from inadequate oxygenation of the blood. —**cy'a•not'ic** (-nŏt'ĭk) *adj.*

cy•an•o•type (sī-ăn'ə-tīp') *n.* A blueprint.

cy•ber•net•ics (sī'bər-nět'ĭks) *n. (takes sing. v.).* The theoretical study of control processes in electronic, mechanical, and biological systems. [< Gk *kubernan,* to steer, guide, govern.] —**cy'ber•net'ic** *adj.*

cyc•la•men (sī'klə-mən, sĭk'lə-, -měn) *n.* A plant with showy white, pink, or red flowers. [< Gk *kuklaminos.*]

cy•cle (sī'kəl) *n.* 1. A time interval in which a characteristic, esp. a regularly repeated, event or sequence of events occurs. 2. a. A single complete execution of a periodically repeated phenomenon. b. A periodically repeated sequence of events. 3. A group of literary or musical works on a single theme. 4. A bicycle or motorcycle. —*v.* **-cled, -cling.** 1. To occur in or pass through a cycle. 2. To ride a bicycle or motorcycle. [< Gk *kuklos,* circle.]

cy•clic (sī'klĭk, sĭk'lĭk) *adj.* Also **cy•cli•cal** (-kəl). 1. Of, relating to, or moving in cycles. 2. Pertaining to compounds having atoms arranged in a ring or closed-chain structure. —**cy'cli•cal•ly** *adv.*

cy•clist (sī'klĭst) *n.* Also **cy•cler** (-klər). One who rides a bicycle, motorcycle, or similar vehicle.

cyclo–. *comb. form.* 1. Circle. 2. A cyclic compound.

cy•clo•hex•ane (sī'klō-hěk'sān') *n.* An extremely flammable, colorless, mobile liquid, C_6H_{12}, used as a solvent, paint remover, and in making nylon.

cy•cloid (sī'kloid') *adj.* Resembling a circle. —**cy•cloi'dal** *adj.*

ô paw, for/oi boy/ou out/ōō took/ōō coo/p pop/r run/s sauce/sh shy/t to/th thin/*th* the/
ŭ cut/ûr fur/v van/w wag/y yes/z size/zh vision/ə ago, item, edible, gallop, circus/

cy•clone (sī'klŏn') *n.* **1.** A type of atmospheric disturbance characterized by masses of air rapidly circulating about a low-pressure center, usually accompanied by stormy, often destructive, weather. **2.** Loosely, any violent, rotating windstorm, such as a tornado. [Prob < Gk *kuklos,* circle, CYCLE.] **—cy•clon'ic** (-klŏn'ĭk) *adj.*

cy•clo•pe•di•a (sī'klə-pē'dē-ə) *n.* Also **cy•clo•pae•di•a.** An encyclopedia. [Short for EN-CYCLOPEDIA.]

cy•clo•tron (sī'klə-trŏn') *n.* A circular accelerator in which charged particles generated at a central source are accelerated spirally outward in a plane at right angles to a fixed magnetic field by an alternating electric field.

cyg•net (sĭg'nĭt) *n.* A young swan. [< Gk *kuknos,* swan.]

Cyg•nus (sĭg'nəs) *n.* A constellation in the N Hemisphere.

cyl•in•der (sĭl'ən-dər) *n.* **1. a.** A surface generated by a straight line moving parallel to a fixed straight line and intersecting a plane curve. **b.** A solid bounded by two parallel planes and such a surface having a closed curve, esp. a circle. **2.** A chamber in which a piston moves. **3.** The rotating chamber of a revolver that holds the cartridges. [< Gk *kulindros,* roller, cylinder.] **—cy•lin'dri•cal** (sə-lĭn'drĭ-kəl) *adj.*

cym•bal (sĭm'bəl) *n.* **1.** One of a pair of brass plates struck together as percussion instruments. **2.** A single brass plate, sounded by hitting with a drumstick. [< Gk *kumbē,* hollow of a vessel, a cup.]

cyn•ic (sĭn'ĭk) *n.* One who believes all men are motivated by selfishness. [< Gk *kunikos,* "doglike," currish.] **—cyn'i•cal** *adj.* **—cyn'i•cal•ly** *adv.* **—cyn'i•cism'** (sĭn'ə-sĭz'əm) *n.*

cy•no•sure (sī'nə-shŏŏr', sĭn'ə-) *n.* A center of interest, attraction, or admiration. [< Gk *kunosoura,* "the dog's tail," Ursa Minor.]

cy•press (sī'prəs) *n.* Any of various chiefly evergreen trees with small, scalelike needles. [< Gk *kuparissos.*]

Cy•prus (sī'prəs). An island republic in the E Mediterranean. Pop. 588,000. Cap. Nicosia. **—Cyp'ri•ot** (sĭp'rē-ŏt), **Cyp'ri•ote** *n. & adj.*

Cy•ril•lic alphabet (sə-rĭl'ĭk). An old Slavic alphabet presently used in modified form for Russian and other languages.

cyst (sĭst) *n.* A pathological fluid-containing membranous sac. [< Gk *kustis,* bladder, pouch.] **—cys'tic** *adj.*

cystic fibrosis. A congenital disease of mucous glands throughout the body, usually developing during childhood and causing pancreatic insufficiency and pulmonary disorders.

–cyte. *comb. form.* A cell: **leukocyte.** [< Gk *kutos,* hollow vessel.]

cyto–. *comb. form.* Cell.

cy•tol•o•gy (sī-tŏl'ə-jē) *n.* The biology of the formation, structure, and function of cells. **—cy'to•log'i•cal** *adj.* **—cy•tol'o•gist** *n.*

cy•to•plasm (sī'tə-plăz'əm) *n.* The protoplasm outside a cell nucleus. **—cy'to•plas'mic** *adj.*

cy•to•sine (sī'tō-sēn') *n.* A pyrimidine base, $C_4H_5N_3O$, that is an essential constituent of both ribonucleic and deoxyribonucleic acids.

C.Z. Canal Zone.

czar (zär) *n.* Also **tsar, tzar.** **1.** A king or emperor, esp. one of the former emperors of Russia. **2.** A tyrant. **3.** *Informal.* One in authority; leader. [< Russ *tsar'.*]

cza•ri•na (zä-rē'nə) *n.* The wife of a czar; an empress of Russia.

Czech (chĕk) *n.* **1.** A native or inhabitant of Czechoslovakia. **2.** The Slavic language of these people. **—Czech** *adj.*

Czech•o•slo•va•ki•a (chĕk'ə-slō-vä'kē-ə, -văk'ē-ə). A republic of C Europe. Pop. 14,107,000. Cap. Prague. **—Czech'o•slo'vak, Czech'o•slo•vak'i•an** *adj. & n.*

Cyprus   Czechoslovakia

Dd

d, D (dē) *n.* **1.** The 4th letter of the English alphabet. **2.** The 4th in a series. **3. D** The lowest passing grade given to a student.
d deci-.
D 1. democrat; democratic. **2.** deuterium. **3.** The Roman numeral for 500. **4.** *Mus.* The 2nd tone in the scale of C major.
d. 1. date. **2.** daughter. **3.** deputy. **4.** died. **5.** dose. **6.** *Brit.* penny (L *denarius*).
D. 1. December. **2.** democrat; democratic. **3.** deputy. **4.** doctor (in academic degrees). **5.** dose. **6.** drachma. **7.** Dutch.
da deca-; deka-.
Da. Danish.
D.A. district attorney.
dab (dăb) *v.* **dabbed, dabbing. 1.** To apply with short, light strokes. **2.** To strike or hit lightly; pat. —*n.* **1.** A small amount. **2.** A quick, light pat. [ME *dabben.*]
D.A.B. Dictionary of American Biography.
dab·ble (dăb'əl) *v.* **-bled, -bling. 1.** To splash or spatter, as with liquid. **2.** To splash in liquid gently and playfully. **3.** To undertake something superficially or without serious intent. [< DAB[1].] —**dab'bler** *n.*
da ca·po (dä kä'pō, də). *Mus.* From the beginning Used as a direction to repeat a passage. [It.]
dace (dās) *n., pl.* **dace** or **daces.** A small freshwater fish related to the minnows. [< DART (< its swift motion).]
da·cha (dä'chə) *n.* A Russian country house.
dachs·hund (däks'hŏont, dăks'hŏond') *n.* A small dog with a long body, drooping ears, and very short legs. [G.]
Da·cron (dā'krŏn', dăk'rŏn') *n.* A trademark for a synthetic polyester textile fiber.
dac·tyl (dăk'təl) *n.* A metrical foot of one accented syllable followed by two unaccented ones. [< Gk *daktulos*, finger.] —**dac·tyl'ic** *adj.*
dad (dăd) *n. Informal.* Father. [Of baby-talk origin.]
dad·dy (dăd'ē) *n., pl.* **-dies.** Diminutive of dad.
daddy long·legs (lông'lĕgz', lŏng'-) *pl.* **daddy longlegs.** A spiderlike arachnid with a small, rounded body and long, slender legs.
da·do (dā'dō) *n., pl.* **-does. 1.** The section of a pedestal between the base and crown. **2.** The lower portion of a wall, decorated differently from the upper section. [It, a die, cube.]
daf·fo·dil (dăf'ə-dĭl) *n.* A plant cultivated for its showy, usually yellow flowers with a trumpet-shaped central part. [Prob < Du *de affodil*, the asphodel.]
daf·fy (dăf'ē) *adj.* **-fier, -fiest.** *Informal.* Silly; zany. [< obs Eng *daff*, fool.]
daft (dăft, däft) *adj.* **1.** Mad; crazy. **2.** Foolish.

[< OE *gedæfte*, mild, meek.]
dag decagram.
dag·ger (dăg'ər) *n.* **1.** A short, pointed weapon with sharp edges. **2.** *Ptg.* A reference mark (†). [< OF *dague.*]
dagger fern. An evergreen N American fern having dense clusters of lance-shaped fronds.
da·guerre·o·type (də-gâr'ə-tīp') *n.* A photograpn made by an early process on a light-sensitive silver-coated metallic plate and developed by mercury vapor. [< L. *Daguerre* (1787–1851), French artist.]
dahl·ia (dăl'yə, däl'-, dāl'-) *n.* A plant cultivated for its showy, variously colored flowers. [< A. *Dahl*, 18th-century Swedish botanist.]
Da·ho·mey (də-hō'mē). The former name for Benin.
da·hoon (də-hōōn') *n.* An evergreen tree or shrub of the SE U.S., having red fruit. [?]
dai·ly (dā'lē) *adj.* Of, pertaining to, occurring, or published every day. —*n., pl.* **-lies.** A daily publication, esp. a newspaper. —*adv.* Each day. [< OE *dæg*, DAY.]
dain·ty (dān'tē) *adj.* **-tier, -tiest. 1.** Delicately beautiful. **2.** Delicious; choice. **3.** Of refined taste. **4.** Too fastidious; squeamish. —*n., pl.* **-ties.** Something delicious; a delicacy. [< L *dignitās*, dignity, worth.] —**dain'ti·ly** *adv.*
dair·y (dâr'ē) *n., pl.* **-ies. 1.** An establishment that processes or sells milk and milk products. **2.** A farm where milk and milk products are produced. [< OE *dæge*, female breadmaker. See dheigh-.] —**dair'y** *adj.*
dairy cattle. Cows bred and raised for milk rather than for meat.
dairy farm. A farm for producing milk and milk products.
dair·y·ing (dâr'ē-ĭng) *n.* The business of running or operating a dairy.
dairy lunch. Also **dairy bar.** A restaurant that serves simple dishes that are made from dairy products.
dair·y·maid (dâr'ē-mād') *n.* A female dairy worker.
da·is (dā'ĭs, dās) *n., pl.* **-ises** (-ĭ-sĭz). A raised platform, as in a lecture hall, for honored guests. [< L *discus*, dish, quoit, DISK.]
dai·sy (dā'zē) *n., pl.* **-sies.** Any of several related plants having flowers with petallike rays surrounding a central disk, esp. a common species with white rays and a yellow center. [< OE *dægesêage*, "day's eye."]
Da·kar (dä-kär', də-). The capital of Senegal. Pop. 298,000.
Da·ko·ta (də-kō'tə) *n., pl.* **-ta** or **-tas. 1.** A member of a large group of tribes of North

---

ô paw, for/oi boy/ou out/ŏŏ took/ōō coo/p pop/r run/s sauce/sh shy/t to/th thin/*th* the/
ŭ cut/ûr fur/v van/w wag/y yes/z size/zh vision/ə ago, item, edible, gallop, circus/

American Plains Indians, commonly called Sioux. 2. Their language.

Da•lai La•ma (dä-lī′ lä′mə). Title of the former theocratic rulers of Tibet.

dale (dāl) *n.* A valley. [< OE *dæl.* See **dhel-**.]

da•leth (dä′ləth) *n.* The 4th letter of the Hebrew alphabet, representing *d(dh).*

Dal•las (dăl′əs). A city of NE Texas. Pop. 844,000.

dal•ly (dăl′ē) *v.* **-lied, -lying.** 1. To play amorously; flirt. 2. To trifle; toy. 3. To waste time. [< NF *dalier.*] —**dal′li•ance** *n.* —**dal′li•er** *n.*

Dal•ma•tian (dăl-mā′shən) *n.* A dog having a short, smooth white coat with black spots. [< *Dalmatia,* region of Yugoslavia.]

dam¹ (dăm) *n.* A barrier, esp. one constructed across a waterway to control the flow of water. —*v.* **dammed, damming.** 1. To construct a dam across. 2. To obstruct or restrain. [ME.]

dam² (dăm) *n.* A female parent, esp. of a quadruped. [< DAME.]

dam•age (dăm′ĭj) *n.* 1. Impairment of the usefulness or value of person or property; loss; harm. 2. **damages.** *Law.* Money to be paid as compensation for injury or loss. —*v.* **-aged, -aging.** To cause injury to. [< L *damnum,* loss, harm, fine.] —**dam′ag•ing•ly** *adv.*

Da•mas•cus (də-măs′kəs). The capital of Syria. Pop. 545,000.

Damascus steel. An early form of steel having wavy markings and used chiefly in sword blades; damask steel.

dam•ask (dăm′əsk) *n.* 1. A rich patterned fabric of cotton, silk, etc. 2. A fine twilled table linen. 3. **Damascus steel.** —*adj.* Made from damask or Damascus steel. [< ML *(pannus de) damasco,* "(cloth of) Damascus."]

dame (dām) *n.* 1. *Brit.* A woman's title, equivalent to that of a knight. 2. *Slang.* A woman. [< L *dominus,* master, lord.]

damn (dăm) *v.* 1. To criticize adversely; condemn. 2. *Theol.* To condemn to everlasting punishment or a similar fate. 3. To swear at by saying "damn." —*interj.* Expressive of anger or disappointment. —*n.* The saying of "damn" as a curse. —*adj.* Damned. —*adv.* Damned. [< L *damnum,* loss, damage.]

dam•na•tion (dăm-nā′shən) *n.* The act of damning or condition of being damned. —*interj.* Expressive of anger.

damned (dămd) *adj. Superl.* **damndest** or **damnedest.** 1. Condemned; doomed. 2. *Informal.* **a.** Detestable: *this damned weather.* **b.** Absolute; utter: *a damned fool.* —*adv. Informal.* Very: *a damned poor excuse.*

Dam•o•cles (dăm′ə-klēz′). A courtier forced by Dionysius the Elder, tyrant of Syracuse, to sit under a sword suspended by a single hair, to demonstrate the precariousness of a king's fortunes.

damp (dămp) *adj.* Slightly wet; moist. —*n.* 1. Moisture; humidity. 2. Foul or poisonous gas. —*v.* 1. To dampen. 2. To restrain or check. 3. To decrease the amplitude of. [< MDu. smoke, vapor.] —**damp′ness** *n.*

damp•en (dăm′pən) *v.* 1. To moisten or become moist. 2. To depress.

damp•er (dăm′pər) *n.* 1. One that restrains or

depresses. 2. An adjustable plate in a flue for controlling the draft.

dam•sel (dăm′zəl) *n.* A girl; maiden. [< L *domina,* lady, dame.]

dam•sel•fly (dăm′zəl-flī′) *n.* A slender-bodied insect related to the dragonflies.

dam•son (dăm′zən, -sən) *n.* A small, oval, bluish-black plum. [< L *(prūnum) Damascēnum,* "(plum) of Damascus."]

Dan. Daniel (Old Testament).

dance (dăns, däns) *v.* **danced, dancing.** 1. To move rhythmically to music. 2. To leap or skip about. 3. To bob up and down. —*n.* 1. A series of rhythmical motions and steps, usually to music. 2. The art of dancing. 3. A gathering of people for dancing. 4. Music composed for dancing. [< OF *danser, dancier.*] —**danc′er** *n.* —**danc′ing•ly** *adv.*

dan•de•li•on (dăn′də-lī′ən) *n.* A common weedy plant with many-rayed yellow flowers. [< OF *dent-de-lion,* "lion's tooth."]

dan•der (dăn′dər) *n. Informal.* Temper. [?]

dan•di•fy (dăn′də-fī′) *v.* **-fied, -fying.** To make resemble a dandy. —**dan′di•fi•ca′tion** *n.*

dan•dle (dănd′l) *v.* **-dled, -dling.** To move (a small child) up and down on one's knees.

dan•druff (dăn′drəf) *n.* A scaly scurf formed on and shed from the scalp. [?]

dan•dy (dăn′dē) *n., pl.* **-dies.** 1. A man who affects extreme elegance. 2. *Informal.* Something very good or agreeable. —*adj.* **-dier, -diest.** 1. Like or dressed like a dandy. 2. *Informal.* Fine; good. [Perh short for *jack-a-dandy,* pert person, fop.]

Dane (dān) *n.* A native or inhabitant of Denmark or a person of Danish ancestry.

dan•ger (dān′jər) *n.* 1. Exposure or vulnerability to harm or evil. 2. A source or instance of peril. [ME *daunger,* power, dominion, peril, damage.]

dan•ger•ous (dān′jər-əs) *adj.* 1. Involving danger. 2. Able or apt to do harm. —**dan′ger•ous•ly** *adv.* —**dan′ger•ous•ness** *n.*

dan•gle (dăng′gəl) *v.* **-gled, -gling.** To hang or cause to hang loosely and swing or sway. [Perh < Dan *dangle* or Swed *dangla.*]

dangling participle. *Gram.* A participle that lacks clear connection with the word it modifies. In the sentence *Working at my desk, the sudden noise startled me, Working at my desk* is a dangling participle.

Dan•iel (dăn′yəl). Hebrew prophet during the Babylonian captivity.

Dan•ish (dā′nĭsh) *adj.* Of or pertaining to Denmark, the Danes, or their language. —*n.* The North Germanic language of the Danes.

dank (dăngk) *adj.* Uncomfortably damp; chilly and wet. [ME.] —**dank′ness** *n.*

Dan•te A•li•ghie•ri (dän′tä ä′lē-gyä′rē). 1265–1321. Italian poet.

Dan•ube (dăn′yōōb). The major river of SE Europe. —**Dan•u′bi•an** (dăn-yōō′bē-ən) *adj.*

dap•per (dăp′ər) *adj.* 1. Neatly dressed; trim. 2. Small and active. [ME *dapyr,* elegant.]

dap•ple (dăp′əl) *v.* **-pled, -pling.** To mark or mottle with spots.

dare (dâr) *v.* **dared, daring.** 1. To have the courage required for. 2. To challenge (some-

one) to do something requiring boldness.
—**dare say.** Also **dare•say.** To consider (it) very
likely. —*n.* A challenge. [< OE *durran,* to
venture, dare. See **dhers-.**]
Usage: *Dare (v.)* is uninflected in the third
person singular in interrogative and negative
sentences: *Dare he speak up? He dare not.*
dare•dev•il (dâr′dĕv′əl) *n.* One who is recklessly bold. —**dare′dev′il** *adj.*
Dar es Sa•laam (där′ ĕs sə-läm′). The capital
of Tanzania. Pop. 129,000.
dar•ing (dâr′ĭng) *adj.* Fearless; bold.
dark (därk) *adj.* **1.** Lacking light or brightness.
2. Somber in color. **3.** Gloomy; threatening.
4. Obscure; cryptic. **5.** Ignorant; uncivilized: *a
dark era.* **6.** Evil; sinister. —*n.* **1.** Absence of
light. **2.** Night; nightfall. —**in the dark. 1.**
Secretly. **2.** Uninformed. [< OE *deorc.* See
dher-¹.] —**dark′ly** *adv.* —**dark′ness** *n.*
dark•en (där′kən) *v.* **1.** To make or become
dark or darker. **2.** To make or become sad.
—**dark′en•er** *n.*
dark horse. A little-known entrant or unexpected winner in a race or contest.
dark•room (därk′rōōm′, -rŏŏm′) *n.* A darkened or specially illuminated room in which
photographic materials are processed.
dar•ling (där′lĭng) *n.* **1.** One who is beloved.
2. A favorite. —*adj.* **1.** Beloved. **2.** Favorite.
3. Charming; pleasing. [< OE *dēorling* : DEAR
+ -LING.]
darn¹ (därn) *v.* To mend by weaving thread
across a hole. —*n.* A place repaired by darning. [F *darner.*] —**darn′er** *n.*
darn² (därn). Euphemism for **damn.**
dar•nel (där′nəl) *n.* Any of several weedy
grasses.
darning needle. 1. A long needle for darning.
2. A dragonfly.
dart (därt) *n.* **1.** A slender, pointed missile to be
thrown or shot. **2. darts** *(takes sing. v.).* A game
in which darts are thrown at a target. **3.**
Something dartlike in sharpness. **4.** A sudden
movement. **5.** A tapered tuck, as in a garment.
—*v.* To move or shoot suddenly. [< Gmc
*darôdhaz, spear.] —**dart′er** *n.*
Dar•win (där′wĭn), **Charles Robert.** 1809–
1882. British naturalist; expounded theory of

Charles Darwin

evolution by natural selection. —**Dar•win′i•an**
adj. —**Dar′win•ism′** *n.*
dash (dăsh) *v.* **1.** To break; smash; destroy.
2. To hurl, knock, or thrust violently. **3.** To
splash. **4.** To perform or complete hastily
(with *off*). **5.** To move with haste; rush. —*n.*
1. A swift blow or stroke. **2.** A splash. **3.** A
small amount of an ingredient. **4.** A sudden
movement; rush. **5.** A short foot race. **6.**
Vigor; verve. **7.** A punctuation mark (—) used
to indicate a break or omission. **8.** A long
sound or signal used in combination with the
dot, a shorter sound, and silent intervals to
represent letters or numbers. [< Scand.]
dash•board (dăsh′bôrd′, -bōrd′) *n.* A panel
under the windshield of a car, containing indicator dials and control instruments.
dash•er (dăsh′ər) *n.* The plunger of a churn or
ice-cream freezer.
dash•ing (dăsh′ĭng) *adj.* **1.** Audacious; spirited. **2.** Marked by showy elegance.
das•tard (dăs′tərd) *n.* A base, sneaking coward. [Perh < ON *dœsa,* to languish, decay.]
—**das′tard•li•ness** *n.* —**das′tard•ly** *adj.*
dat. dative.
da•ta (dā′tə, dăt′ə, dä′tə) *pl.n.* Sing. **datum**
(dā′təm, dăt′əm, dä′təm). Information, esp.
information organized for analysis or computation. [< L *datum,* "something given."]
Usage: *Data* is now used both as a plural
and as a singular collective: *These data are
inconclusive. This data is inconclusive.* The plural is more appropriate in formal usage.
data processing. The processing of data by a
computer.
date¹ (dāt) *n.* **1.** The particular time at which
something happens. **2.** The period to which
something belongs. **3.** The day of the month.
4. An inscription or statement indicating when
a thing was made or written. **5.** *Informal.*
a. An appointment to meet socially. **b.** A person so met, esp. one of the opposite sex. —**to
date.** Up to the present time. —*v.* **dated, dating.**
1. To mark with a date, as a letter. **2.** To
determine the date of. **3.** To betray the age of.
4. To originate in a particular time in the past
(with *from*). **5.** *Informal.* To make or have
social engagements with (persons of the
opposite sex). [< L *datus,* pp of *dare,* to give.]
date² (dāt) *n.* The sweet, oblong, edible fruit of
a tropical palm tree. [< Gk *daktulos,* "finger."]
dat•ed (dā′tĭd) *adj.* **1.** Marked with a date. **2.**
Old-fashioned. —**dat′ed•ness** *n.*
date•line (dāt′līn′) *n.* A phrase in a newspaper
or magazine article that gives the date and
place of its origin.
da•tive (dā′tĭv) *adj.* Designating or belonging
to a grammatical case that principally marks
the indirect object of a verb. —*n.* The dative
case. [< L *(cāsus) datīvus,* "(case) of giving."]
da•tum *sing.* of **data.**
daub (dôb) *v.* **1.** To cover or smear with an
adhesive substance. **2.** To paint crudely. —*n.*
1. The act or a stroke of daubing. **2.** A soft
adhesive coating. **3.** A crude painting. [< L
dēalbāre, to whitewash.] —**daub′er** *n.*
daugh•ter (dô′tər) *n.* **1.** One's female child.

2. A female descendant. [< OE *dohtor.* See dhughəter-.] —**daugh'ter•ly** *adj.*

daugh•ter-in-law (dô'tər-ĭn-lô') *n., pl.* **daughters-in-law.** The wife of one's son.

daunt (dônt, dänt) *v.* **1.** To intimidate. **2.** To discourage. [< L *domāre,* to tame, subdue.]

daunt•less (dônt'lĭs, dänt'-) *adj.* Not easily intimidated or discouraged.

dau•phin (dô'fĭn) *n.* The eldest son of a king of France.

dav•en•port (dăv'ən-pôrt', -pōrt') *n.* A large sofa.

Da•vid (dā'vĭd). Second king of Judah and Israel.

Da•vis (dā'vĭs), **Jefferson.** 1808–1889. President of the Confederate States of America (1861–65).

Jefferson Davis

dav•it (dăv'ĭt, dā'vĭt) *n.* Any of various small cranes used on ships to hoist boats, anchors, and cargo. [< OF *daviot.*]

daw (dô) *n.* A jackdaw. [ME *dawe.*]

daw•dle (dôd'l) *v.* **-dled, -dling.** To waste time by trifling or loitering. —**daw'dler** *n.*

dawn (dôn) *n.* **1.** The first appearance of daylight in the morning. **2.** A first appearance; beginning. —*v.* **1.** To begin to become light in the morning. **2.** To begin to appear or

develop. **3.** To begin to be perceived or understood (with *on* or *upon*). [< OE *dagian,* to dawn. See agh-².]

day (dā) *n.* **1.** The period of light between dawn and nightfall. **2.** The 24-hour period during which the earth completes one rotation on its axis. **3.** The portion of a day devoted to work. **4.** A period of activity or prominence: *a writer who has had his day.* **5.** Often **days.** A period of time; age; era. **6.** The contest or issue at hand: *carry the day.* —**call it a day.** *Informal.* To stop one's work for the day. —**day in, day out.** Continuously. [< OE *dæg.* See agh-².]

day•break (dā'brāk') *n.* The time each morning when light first appears; dawn.

day care. The providing of daytime supervision, training, medical services, and the like for children of preschool age or for the elderly. —**day'-care'** *adj.*

day•dream (dā'drēm') *n.* A dreamlike musing or fantasy. —*v.* To have daydreams.

day•light (dā'lĭt') *n.* **1. a.** The light of day. **b.** The direct light of the sun. **2.** Understanding of what was formerly obscure.

day•lights (dā'lĭts') *pl.n. Slang.* Life; wits: *scare the daylights out of him.*

day•light-sav•ing time (dā'lĭt'sā'vĭng). Time during which clocks are set one hour or more ahead of standard time.

Day of Atonement. Yom Kippur.

day•time (dā'tīm') *n.* The time between dawn and dark. —**day'time'** *adj.*

Day•ton (dāt'n). A city of SW Ohio. Pop. 262,000.

daze (dāz) *v.* **dazed, dazing. 1.** To stun, as with a blow or shock; stupefy. **2.** To dazzle, as with strong light. —*n.* A stunned or bewildered condition. [< ON *dasa.*]

daz•zle (dăz'əl) *v.* **-zled, -zling. 1.** To overpower or be overpowered with intense light. **2.** To bewilder or amaze with a spectacular display. [Freq of DAZE.] —**daz'zle** *n.*

dB decibel.

dbl. double.

dc direct current.

Note: Many compounds are formed with *de-.* Normally, *de-* combines with a second element without an intervening hyphen. Exceptions include: **a.** a second element beginning with *e,* as *de-escalate;* **b.** a second element beginning with two vowels, as *de-aerate;* **c.** a second element beginning with a capital letter, as *de-Americanize.* The following is a list of common *de-* compounds.

de•a•cid'i•fy' *v.*
de-aer'ate' *v.*
de-'aer•a'tion *n.*
de'-A•mer'i•can•i•za'tion *n.*
de'-A•mer'i•can•ize' *v.*
de•ash' *v.*
de'as•sim'i•la'tion *n.*

de•car'bon•ate' *v.*
de•cer'ti•fi•ca'tion *n.*
de•cer'ti•fy' *v.*
de•chlor'i•nate' *v.*
de•col'or *v.*
de'col•or•a'tion *n.*
de'com•mis'sion *n.*
de•com'pen•sate' *v.*
de'com•pound' *v.*

de•con•di'tion *n.*
de'con•ges'tion *n.*
de'con•ges'tive *adj.*
de•con'se•crate' *v.*
de•em'pha•size' *v.*
de•en'er•gize' *v.*
de-es'ca•late' *v.*
de-es'ca•la'tion *n.*
de•for'est *v.*
de•horn' *v.*

D.C. District of Columbia.
D.C.M. Distinguished Conduct Medal.
D.D. 1. demand draft. 2. dishonorable discharge. 3. Doctor of Divinity (Latin *Divinitatis Doctor*).
D.D.S. Doctor of Dental Science; Doctor of Dental Surgery.
DDT A colorless contact insecticide, $C_{14}H_9Cl_5$, toxic to man and animals when swallowed or absorbed through the skin. [Abbr of *d(ichloro)d(iphenyl)t(richloroethane).*]
de–. *comb. form.* 1. Reversal or undoing. 2. Removal. 3. Degradation; reduction. 4. Disparagement. [< L *dē,* from.]
dea•con (dē′kən) *n.* 1. A clergyman ranking just below a priest. 2. A lay assistant to a minister. [< Gk *diakonos,* "servant."] —**dea′con•ess** *fem.n.*
de•ac•ti•vate (dē-ăk′tə-vāt′) *v.* -vated, -vating. To render inactive. —**de•ac′ti•va′tion** *n.*
dead (dĕd) *adj.* 1. No longer alive; lifeless. 2. Inanimate. 3. Lacking feeling; unresponsive. 4. No longer in existence or use. 5. Devoid of animation or interest. 6. Not productive. 7. Weary and worn-out. 8. Lacking some important or previously evident quality. 9. Suggestive of the finality of death. 10. Exact; unerring: *dead center.* 11. a. Lacking connection to a source of electric current. b. Discharged, as a battery. —*n.* A period of greatest intensity: *the dead of winter.* —*adv.* 1. Absolutely; altogether. 2. Directly; exactly. [< OE *dēad.* See dheu-³.]
dead•beat (dĕd′bēt′) *n. Slang.* 1. One who does not pay his debts. 2. A lazy or lethargic person.
dead•en (dĕd′n) *v.* 1. To render less sensitive, intense, or vigorous. 2. To make soundproof.
dead heat. A race in which two or more contestants finish at the same time; a tie.
dead letter. An unclaimed or undelivered letter.
dead•line (dĕd′lῑn′) *n.* A time limit, as for completion of an assignment.
dead•lock (dĕd′lŏk′) *n.* A standstill resulting from the opposition of two unrelenting forces. —*v.* To bring or come to a deadlock.
dead•ly (dĕd′lē) *adj.* -lier, -liest. 1. Causing or

tending to cause death. 2. Suggestive of death. 3. Implacable; mortal. 4. Destructive in effect. 5. Absolute; unqualified. —*adv.* 1. So as to suggest death. 2. To an extreme: *deadly earnest.* —**dead′li•ness** *n.*
dead reckoning. Essentially nonobservational navigation by computations of position based on course and distance traveled from a known position.
Dead Sea. A salt lake between Israel and Jordan, 1,302 ft. below sea level.
dead weight. 1. The unrelieved weight of a heavy, motionless mass. 2. An oppressive burden or difficulty.
dead•wood (dĕd′wŏŏd′) *n.* Anything burdensome or superfluous.
deaf (dĕf) *adj.* 1. Partially or completely unable to hear. 2. Unwilling or refusing to listen; heedless. [< OE *dēaf.* See dheu-¹.] —**deaf′ly** *adv.* —**deaf′ness** *n.*
deaf•en (dĕf′ən) *v.* To make deaf.
deaf-mute (dĕf′myōōt′) *n.* Also deaf mute. One who can neither speak nor hear. —**deaf′-mute′** *adj.*
deal¹ (dēl) *v.* dealt (dĕlt), dealing. 1. To apportion or distribute. 2. To administer; deliver. 3. To distribute (playing cards) among players. 4. To be occupied or concerned; treat. 5. To behave in a specified way toward another or others. 6. To take action. 7. To do business; trade. —*n.* 1. The act of dealing. 2. a. Cards dealt in a card game; a hand. b. The right or turn of a player to distribute cards. 3. An indefinite quantity, extent, or degree. 4. *Informal.* A secret agreement, as in politics. 5. Any agreement or business transaction. 6. A bargain or favorable sale. 7. *Informal.* Treatment received, esp. as the result of an agreement. 8. *Slang.* An important issue: *big deal.* [< OE *dǣlan,* to divide, distribute. See dail-.]
deal² (dēl) *n.* Fir or pine wood. [< MDu *dele.*]
deal•er (dē′lər) *n.* 1. One engaged in buying and selling. 2. One who deals the cards in a card game.
deal•ing (dē′lῑng) *n.* 1. Often dealings. Transactions or relations with others. 2. Method or manner of conduct in relation to others.

---

de•hull′ *v.*
de•hy′dro•gen•ate′ *v.*
de•hy′dro•ge•na′tion *n.*
de•lam′i•na′tion *n.*
de•lam′i•nate′ *v.*
de•lead′ *v.*
de•lime′ *v.*
de•lint′ *v.*
de•lo′cal•ize′ *v.*
de•louse′ *v.*
de•lus′ter *v.*
de•mast′ *v.*
de•ma•te′ri•al•i•za′tion *n.*
de′ma•te′ri•al•ize′ *v.*

de•mes′mer•ize′ *v.*
de•mount′ *v.*
de•na′tion•al•i•za′tion *n.*
de•na′tion•al•ize′ *v.*
de•nat′u•ral•i•za′tion *n.*
de•nat′u•ral•ize′ *v.*
de•ni′trate′ *v.*
de•pas′ture *v.*
de•pig′ment *v.*
de•plume′ *v.*
de•po′lar•i•za′tion *n.*
de•po′lar•ize′ *v.*
de•pol′ish *v.*
de•ra′tion *v.*

de•req′ui•si′tion *v.*
de′re•strict′ *v.*
de•salt′ *v.*
de•sanc′ti•fy′ *v.*
de•sat′u•rate′ *v.*
de•scale′ *v.*
de•sil′ver *v.*
de•size′ *v.*
de•so′cial•ize′ *v.*
de•soil′ *v.*
de•sug′ar *v.*
de•sul′fur•i•za′tion *n.*
de•sul′fur•ize′ *v.*
de•vow′ *v.*
de•wool′ *v.*
de•worm′ *v.*

---

dean (dēn) *n.* **1.** An administrative officer in a university, college, or high school. **2.** The head of the chapter of canons governing a cathedral. **3.** The senior member of any body. [< LL *decānus,* "(one) set over ten."]

dean·er·y (dē′nə-rē) *n., pl.* **-ies.** The office, official residence, jurisdiction, or authority of a dean.

dear (dîr) *adj.* **1.** Beloved; precious. **2.** Highly esteemed or regarded. **3.** High-priced. —*n.* A greatly loved person; a darling. —*interj.* Expressive of surprise or distress. [< OE *dēore* < Gmc *deuriaz.*] —**dear′ly** *adv.*

Dear·born (dîr′bôrn′). A city of SE Michigan. Pop. 112,000.

dearth (dûrth) *n.* Scarcity; paucity; famine. [< DEAR.]

death (dĕth) *n.* **1.** The act of dying or state of being dead. **2.** Termination; extinction. **3.** A cause or manner of dying. [< OE *dēath.*]

death·bed (dĕth′bĕd′) *n.* **1.** The bed on which a person dies. **2.** The last hours before death.

death·blow (dĕth′blō′) *n.* A fatal blow or occurrence.

death·less (dĕth′lĭs) *adj.* Not subject to death; immortal. —**death′less·ness** *n.*

death·ly (dĕth′lē) *adj.* Resembling or characteristic of death; fatal. —*adv.* **1.** In the manner of death. **2.** Extremely; very.

Death Valley. A desert basin in E California and W Nevada.

death·watch (dĕth′wŏch′) *n.* A vigil kept beside a dying or dead person.

de·ba·cle (dĭ-bä′kəl, -băk′əl) *n.* A sudden, disastrous overthrow or collapse; ruin. [< F *débâcler,* to unbar.]

de·bar (dē-bär′) *v.* **-barred, -barring.** To exclude, forbid, or prevent. [< OF *desbarrer,* to unbar.] —**de·bar′ment** *n.*

de·bark (dĭ-bärk′) *v.* To unload; disembark. [F *débarquer.*] —**de·bar·ka′tion** *n.*

de·base (dĭ-bās′) *v.* **-based, -basing.** To lower in character, quality, or value; degrade.

de·bate (dĭ-bāt′) *v.* **-bated, -bating. 1.** To deliberate; consider. **2.** To discuss opposing points. **3.** To discuss or argue formally. —*n.* **1.** The act of debating. **2.** A formal contest in which two opposing teams defend and attack a given proposition. [< OF *debattre.*] —**de·bat′a·ble** *adj.* —**de·bat′er** *n.*

de·bauch (dĭ-bôch′) *v.* To corrupt morally. [< OF *desbaucher,* "to roughhew (timber) into a beam," separate.] —**de·bauch′er·y** *n.*

de·ben·ture (dĭ-bĕn′chər) *n.* A certificate acknowledging a debt, esp. a bond issued by a civil or governmental agency. [< L *dēbentur,* "they are due."]

de·bil·i·tate (dĭ-bĭl′ə-tāt′) *v,* **-tated, -tating.** To make feeble; weaken. [< L *dēbilis,* weak.] —**de·bil′i·ta′tion** *n.* —**de·bil′i·ta′tive** *adj.*

de·bil·i·ty (dĭ-bĭl′ə-tē) *n., pl.* **-ties.** Feebleness.

deb·it (dĕb′ĭt) *n.* An item of debt, esp. one recorded in an account. —*v.* **1.** To enter a debit in an account. **2.** To charge with a debt. [< L *dēbitum,* DEBT.]

deb·o·nair (dĕb′ə-nâr′) *adj.* **1.** Suave; urbane; gracious. **2.** Carefree; gay. [< F *de bon aire,* "of good disposition."] —**deb′o·nair′ly** *adv.*

de·brief (dē′brēf′) *v.* To question to obtain knowledge gathered on a military mission. —**de′brief′ing** *n.*

de·bris (də-brē′, dā′brē′) *n.* Also **dé·bris** (dā′-brē′). The scattered remains of something broken or destroyed. [< OF *debrisier,* to break to pieces.]

debt (dĕt) *n.* **1.** Something owed, as money, goods, or services. **2.** *Theol.* A sin; trespass. [< L *dēbitum.*] —**debt′or** *n.*

de·bunk (dĭ-bŭngk′) *v.* To expose the falseness or exaggerated claims of.

De·bus·sy (də-byōō′sē), **Claude.** 1862–1918. French composer.

de·but (dĭ-byōō′, dā-, dā′byōō′) *n.* Also **dé·but.** **1.** A first public appearance. **2.** The formal presentation of a girl to society. **3.** The beginning of a career. [F *début.*]

deb·u·tante (dĕb′yōō-tänt′, dĕb′yōō-tänt′, dā′-byōō-) *n.* Also **dé·bu·tante.** A young woman making a debut into society.

dec. deceased.

Dec. December.

deca–, deka–. *comb. form.* Ten. [< Gk *deka,* ten.]

de·cade (dĕk′ād′, dĕ-kād′) *n.* A period of 10 years.

dec·a·dence (dĕk′ə-dəns, dĭ-kā′dəns) *n.* A process, condition, or period of deterioration; decay. [< VL *dēcadere,* to decay.] —**dec′a·dent** *adj.* —**dec′a·dent·ly** *adv.*

dec·a·gon (dĕk′ə-gŏn′) *n.* A polygon with 10 sides. [< Gk *dekagōnon,* "(one) having 10 angles."]

dec·a·he·dron (dĕk′ə-hē′drən) *n., pl.* **-drons** or **-dra** (-drə). A polyhedron with 10 faces.

de·cal (dē′kăl′) *n.* A picture or design transferred by decalcomania.

de·cal·ci·fy (dē-kăl′sə-fī′) *v.* **-fied, -fying.** To remove calcium or calcareous matter, as from bones or teeth.

de·cal·co·ma·ni·a (dē′kăl-kə-mā′nē-ə) *n.* **1.** The process of transferring designs printed on specially prepared paper to glass, metal, etc. **2.** A decal. [F *décalcomanie.*]

Dec·a·logue (dĕk′ə-lôg′, -lŏg′) *n.* The **Ten Commandments.**

de·camp (dĭ-kămp′) *v.* **1.** To break camp. **2.** To depart secretly or suddenly.

de·cant (dĭ-kănt′) *v.* To pour off without disturbing the sediment, as wine. [ML *dēcanthāre.*] —**de′can·ta′tion** *n.*

de·cant·er (dĭ-kăn′tər) *n.* A decorative bottle used for serving liquids, as wine.

de·cap·i·tate (dĭ-kăp′ə-tāt′) *v.* **-tated, -tating.** To behead. [< LL *dēcapitāre.*]

de·cath·lon (dĭ-kăth′lən, -lŏn′) *n.* An athletic contest in which each contestant participates in 10 events. [< DECA- + Gk *athlon,* contest.]

de·cay (dĭ-kā′) *v.* **1.** To decompose; rot. **2.** To decrease or decline in quality or quantity. —*n.* **1.** Decomposition. **2.** Deterioration. [< VL *dēcadere,* to fall down, decay.]

de·cease (dĭ-sēs′) *v.* **-ceased, -ceasing.** To die. —*n.* Death. [< L *dēcēdere,* to depart.]

de·ceit (dĭ-sēt′) *n.* **1.** Misrepresentation; deception. **2.** A stratagem; trick. [< L *dēcipere,* DECEIVE.] —**de·ceit′ful** *adj.*

---

de•ceive (dĭ-sēv′) v. -ceived, -ceiving. To delude; mislead. [< L *dēcipere*, to take in, deceive.] —**de•ceiv′er** n.

de•cel•er•ate (dē-sĕl′ə-rāt′) v. -ated, -ating. To decrease in velocity. [DE- + (AC)CELERATE.] —**de•cel′er•a′tion** n.

De•cem•ber (dĭ-sĕm′bər) n. The 12th month of the year. December has 31 days. [< L, "the tenth month."]

de•cent (dē′sənt) adj. 1. Characterized by conformity to recognized standards of propriety. 2. Free from indelicacy; modest. 3. Adequate; passable. 4. Kind; generous. 5. Properly dressed. [< L *decēre*, to be fitting, suit.] —**de′cen•cy** (-sən-sē) n.

de•cen•tral•ize (dē-sĕn′trə-līz′) v. -ized, -izing. 1. To distribute the administrative functions of (a central authority) among local authorities. 2. To cause to withdraw from an area of concentration. —**de•cen′tral•i•za′tion** n.

de•cep•tion (dĭ-sĕp′shən) n. 1. The use of deceit. 2. The fact or state of being deceived.

de•cep•tive (dĭ-sĕp′tĭv) adj. Intended or tending to deceive. —**de•cep′tive•ly** adv.

deci-. comb. form. One-tenth. [< L *decimus*, tenth.]

de•ci•bel (dĕs′ĭ-bəl, -bĕl′) n. A unit used to express relative difference in power, usually between acoustic or electric signals, equal to one-tenth the common logarithm of the ratio of the two levels.

de•cide (dĭ-sīd′) v. -cided, -ciding. 1. To conclude, settle, or announce a verdict. 2. To influence or determine the conclusion of. 3. To make up one's mind. [< L *dēcīdere*, to cut off, determine.] —**de•cid′er** n.

de•cid•ed (dĭ-sī′dĭd) adj. 1. Unquestionable. 2. Resolute. —**de•cid′ed•ly** adv.

de•cid•u•ate (dĭ-sĭj′ōō-ĭt, -sĭd′yōō-) adj. Characterized by shedding.

de•cid•u•ous (dĭ-sĭj′ōō-əs, -sĭd′yōō-) adj. 1. Falling off at a specific season or stage of growth: *deciduous leaves.* 2. Shedding foliage at the end of the growing season: *deciduous trees.* [< L *dēcidere*, to fall off.]

dec•i•gram (dĕs′ĭ-grăm′) n. One-tenth of a gram.

dec•i•li•ter (dĕs′ə-lē′tər) n. One-tenth of a liter.

de•cil•lion (dĭ-sĭl′yən) n. 1. The cardinal number represented by 1 followed by 33 zeros. 2. Brit. The cardinal number represented by 1 followed by 60 zeros. [L *decem*, ten + (M)ILLION.] —**de•cil′lion** adj.

de•cil•lionth (dĭ-sĭl′yənth) n. 1. The ordinal number decillion in a series. 2. One of a decillion equal parts. —**de•cil′lionth** adj. & adv.

dec•i•mal (dĕs′ə-məl) n. 1. A linear array of integers that represents a fraction, every decimal place indicating a multiple of a positive or negative power of 10. For example, the decimal $.1 = \frac{1}{10}$, $.12 = \frac{12}{100}$, $.003 = \frac{3}{1000}$. 2. Any number written using base 10; a number containing a decimal point. —adj. 1. Expressed or expressible as a decimal. 2. a. Based on 10. b. Numbered or ordered by 10's. 3. Loosely, not integral; fractional. [< L *decimus*, tenth.] —**dec′i•mal•ly** adv.

decimal place. The position of a digit to the right of a decimal point, usually identified by successive ascending ordinal numbers with the digit immediately to the right of the decimal point being first.

decimal point. A period placed to the left of a decimal.

dec•i•mate (dĕs′ĭ-māt′) v. -mated, -mating. To destroy or kill a large part of. [L *decimāre*.] —**dec′i•ma′tion** n.

dec•i•me•ter (dĕs′ə-mē′tər) n. One-tenth of a meter.

de•ci•pher (dĭ-sī′fər) v. 1. To read or interpret (something ambiguous or obscure). 2. To decode. [DE- + CIPHER.] —**de•ci′pher•a•ble** adj.

de•ci•sion (dĭ-sĭzh′ən) n. 1. The passing of judgment on an issue under consideration. 2. The act of making up one's mind. 3. A conclusion or judgment reached; verdict. 4. Firmness of character or action. [< L *dēcīdere*, DECIDE.]

de•ci•sive (dĭ-sī′sĭv) adj. 1. Conclusive. 2. Resolute; determined. 3. Beyond doubt; unquestionable. —**de•ci′sive•ly** adv. —**de•ci′sive•ness** n.

deck[1] (dĕk) n. 1. a. A platform extending horizontally from one side of a ship to the other. b. Any similar platform or surface. 2. A pack of playing cards. [< MDu *decke*, roof, covering.]

deck[2] (dĕk) v. To clothe with finery; adorn. [MDu *dekken*, to cover.]

deck hand. A member of a ship's crew who works on deck.

decl. declension.

de•claim (dĭ-klām′) v. To speak loudly and with rhetorical effect. —**de•claim′er** n. —**dec′la•ma′tion** (dĕk′lə-mā′shən) n.

Declaration of Independence. A proclamation issued in 1776, declaring the independence of the 13 American colonies from Great Britain.

de•clar•a•tive (dĭ-klâr′ə-tĭv) adj. Serving to declare or state.

de•clare (dĭ-klâr′) v. -clared, -claring. 1. To state officially, formally, or authoritatively. 2. *Bridge.* To make the final bid that establishes trump or no-trump. [< L *dēclārāre*, to make clear.] —**dec′la•ra′tion** (dĕk′lə-rā′shən) n. —**de•clar′er** n.

de•clas•si•fy (dē-klăs′ə-fī′) v. To remove official security classification from (a document). —**de•clas′si•fi•ca′tion** n.

de•clen•sion (dĭ-klĕn′shən) n. 1. *Ling.* a. The systematic inflection of nouns, pronouns, and adjectives. b. A class of such words with similar inflections. 2. A descent. 3. A decline or deterioration. [< L *dēclīnāre*, DECLINE.]

de•cline (dĭ-klīn′) v. -clined, -clining. 1. To refuse to do or accept (something). 2. To slope downward. 3. To deteriorate gradually; wane. 4. *Ling.* To give the declension of. —n. 1. The process or result of declining. 2. A downward slope. 3. A disease that gradually weakens the body. [< L *dēclīnāre*, to turn aside, go down.]

de•cliv•i•ty (dĭ-klĭv′ə-tē) n., pl. -ties. A steeply descending slope. [< L *dēclīvis*, sloping down.]

ô paw, for/oi boy/ou out/ōō took/ōō coo/p pop/r run/s sauce/sh shy/t to/th thin/*th* the/
ŭ cut/ûr fur/v van/w wag/y yes/z size/zh vision/ə ago, item, edible, gallop, circus/

de•code (dē-kōd′) *v.* To convert from code into plain text. —**de•cod′er** *n.*

dé•colle•té (dā′kôl-tā′) *adj.* Having a low neckline. [< F *décolleter*, to uncover the neck.]

de•com•pose (dē′kəm-pōz′) *v.* **1.** To separate or break down into component parts or basic elements. **2.** To rot. —**de′com•po•si′tion** (-kŏm-pə-zĭsh′ən) *n.*

de•com•press (dē′kəm-prĕs′) *v.* To relieve of pressure. —**de′com•pres′sion** *n.*

de•con•ges•tant (dē′kən-jĕs′tənt) *n.* Something, as a drug, that relieves congestion.

de•con•tam•i•nate (dē′kən-tăm′ə-nāt′) *v.* To remove the contaminants or dangerous elements from.

de•con•trol (dē′kən-trōl′) *v.* To free from control.

dé•cor (dā′kôr′, dā′kôr′) *n.* Also **de•cor.** A decorative style, as of a room, home, stage setting, etc. [< F *décorer*, to decorate.]

dec•o•rate (dĕk′ə-rāt′) *v.* **-rated, -rating. 1.** To furnish or adorn with fashionable or beautiful things. **2.** To confer a medal or other honor upon. [L *decorāre.*] —**dec′o•ra′tion** *n.*

dec•o•ra•tive (dĕk′ər-ə-tĭv) *adj.* Ornamental. —**dec′o•ra•tive•ly** *adv.* —**dec′o•ra•tive•ness** *n.*

dec•o•ra•tor (dĕk′ə-rā′tər) *n.* One who decorates architectural interiors; interior decorator.

dec•o•rous (dĕk′ər-əs, dĭ-kôr′əs) *adj.* Characterized by decorum. [< L *decor,* seemliness.]

de•co•rum (dĭ-kôr′əm, dĭ-kōr′əm) *n.* Conformity to social conventions; propriety. [L *decōrum.*]

de•coy (dē′koi′, dĭ-koi′) *n.* **1.** A living or artificial animal used to entice game. **2.** One who leads another into danger, deception, or a trap. —*v.* (dĭ-koi′). To lure or entrap by or as by a decoy. [Poss < Du *de kooi,* "the cage."]

de•crease (dĭ-krēs′) *v.* **-creased, -creasing.** To diminish gradually; reduce. —*n.* (dē′krēs′). The act or process of decreasing or the resulting condition. [< L *dēcrēscere.*]

de•cree (dĭ-krē′) *n.* **1.** An authoritative order; edict. **2.** The judgment of a court. —*v.* **-creed, -creeing.** To ordain, establish, or decide by decree. [< L *dēcrētus,* pp of *dēcernere,* to decide.] —**de•cre′er** *n.*

dec•re•ment (dĕk′rə-mənt) *n.* **1.** A decrease. **2.** The amount by which something decreases.

de•crep•it (dĭ-krĕp′ĭt) *adj.* Weakened by old age, illness, or hard use; broken-down. [< L *dēcrepitus.*] —**de•crep′i•tude′** (-ĭ-t/y/ōōd′) *n.*

de•cre•scen•do (dē′krə-shĕn′dō) *n., pl.* **-dos. 1.** A gradual decrease in force or loudness. **2.** A musical passage played in a decrescendo. —*adj.* Gradually decreasing in volume or intensity. [It, "decreasing."] —**de′cre•scen′do** *adv.*

de•cry (dĭ-krī′) *v.* **-cried, -crying.** To belittle openly; censure. [< OF *descrier,* "to cry down."] —**de•cri′er** *n.*

ded•i•cate (dĕd′ə-kāt′) *v.* **-cated, -cating. 1.** To set apart for a deity or for religious purposes. **2.** To set apart for some special use. **3.** To inscribe (a literary work or artistic performance) to someone. **4.** To commit (oneself) to a particular course of thought or action. [< L

dēdicāre, to give out tidings, proclaim.] —**ded′i•ca′tion** *n.* —**ded′i•ca′tor** *n.*

de•duce (dĭ-d/y/ōōs′) *v.* **-duced, -ducing. 1.** To reach (a conclusion) by reasoning. **2.** To trace the origin of. [< L *dēdūcere,* to lead away, infer logically.] —**de•duc′i•ble** *adj.*

de•duct (dĭ-dŭkt′) *v.* To subtract. [L *dēdūcere* (pp *dēductus*), to DEDUCE.] —**de•duct′i•ble** *adj.*

de•duc•tion (dĭ-dŭk′shən) *n.* **1.** The act, process, or result of deducing. **2.** That which is or can be deducted.

deed (dēd) *n.* **1.** An act; feat; exploit. **2.** Action or performance in general: *in word and deed.* **3.** A document sealed as an instrument of bond, contract, or conveyance, esp. pertaining to property. —*v.* To transfer by means of a deed. [< OE *dæd.* See **dhē-.**]

deem (dēm) *v.* To judge; consider; think. [< OE *dēman.* See **dhē-.**]

deep (dēp) *adj.* **1.** Extending to or located at a distance below a surface. **2.** Extending from front to rear or inward from the outside. **3.** Arising from or penetrating to a depth. **4.** Far distant; obscure. **5.** Learned; profound. **6.** Intense; extreme. **7.** Dark rather than pale in shade. **8.** Low in pitch; resonant. —*n.* **1.** Any deep place on land or in a body of water, esp. in the ocean and over 3,000 fathoms in depth. **2.** The most intense or extreme part. **3. the deep.** The ocean. —*adv.* **1.** Profoundly. **2.** Well on in time; late. [< OE *dēop.* See **dheub-.**] —**deep′ly** *adv.* —**deep′ness** *n.*

deep•en (dē′pən) *v.* To make or become deep or deeper. —**deep′en•er** *n.*

deep-root•ed (dēp′rōō′tĭd, -rōōt′ĭd) *adj.* Firmly implanted.

deep-seat•ed (dēp′sē′tĭd) *adj.* Deeply rooted; ingrained.

Deep South. The southeasternmost part of the U.S.

deer (dîr) *n., pl.* **deer.** Any of various hoofed mammals of which the males characteristically have seasonally shed antlers. [< OE *dēor.* See **dheu-1.**]

deer•skin (dîr′skĭn′) *n.* **1.** Leather made from the hide of a deer. **2.** A garment made from such leather.

de•es•ca•late (dē′ĕs′kə-lāt′) *v.* To decrease or reduce the scope or intensity of (a war). —**de′-es′ca•la′tion** *n.*

def. 1. defense. **2.** definition.

de•face (dĭ-fās′) *v.* **-faced, -facing.** To spoil or mar the surface or appearance of; disfigure.

de fac•to (dē făk′tō). In reality or fact; actually. [L, "from the fact."]

de•fal•cate (dĭ-făl′kāt′, dĭ-fôl′kāt′, dĕf′əl-kāt′) *v.* **-cated, -cating.** To misuse funds; embezzle. [ML *dēfalcāre,* to cut off.] —**de′fal•ca′tion** *n.*

de•fame (dĭ-fām′) *v.* **-famed, -faming.** To attack the good name of by slander or libel. [< L *diffāmāre.*] —**def′a•ma′tion** (dĕf′ə-mā′shən) *n.* —**de•fam′er** *n.*

de•fault (dĭ-fôlt′) *n.* **1.** A failure to perform a task or fulfill an obligation. **2.** Loss by failure to appear. —*v.* **1.** To fail to do what is required. **2.** To lose by not appearing. [< VL *dēfallīre,* to fail.] —**de•fault′er** *n.*

de•feat (dĭ-fēt′) *v.* **1.** To win victory over;

vanquish. **2.** To prevent the success of; thwart. —*n.* The act of defeating or state of being defeated. [< ML *disfacere*, to undo, destroy.] —**de·feat′er** *n.*

de·feat·ism (dĭ-fē′tĭz′əm) *n.* Acceptance of the prospect of defeat. —**de·feat′ist** *n.*

def·e·cate (dĕf′ə-kāt′) *v.* -**cated, -cating.** To void feces from the bowels. [L *dēfaecāre.*] —**def′e·ca′tion** *n.* —**def′e·ca′tor** *n.*

de·fect (dē′fĕkt′, dĭ-fĕkt′) *n.* **1.** The lack of something necessary or desirable. **2.** An imperfection; fault. —*v.* (dĭ-fĕkt′). To abandon an allegiance that one had previously espoused. [< L *dēficere*, to remove from, desert, fail.] —**de·fec′tion** *n.* —**de·fec′tor** *n.*

de·fec·tive (dĭ-fĕk′tĭv) *adj.* Having a defect; lacking perfection; faulty. —**de·fec′tive·ly** *adv.* —**de·fec′tive·ness** *n.*

de·fend (dĭ-fĕnd′) *v.* **1.** To protect from danger; shield; guard. **2.** To support or maintain; justify. **3. a.** To represent (the defendant) in a civil or criminal case. **b.** To contest (a legal action or claim). [< L *dēfendere*, to ward off.] —**de·fend′a·ble** *adj.* —**de·fend′er** *n.*

de·fen·dant (dĭ-fĕn′dənt) *n. Law.* A person against whom an action is brought.

de·fense (dĭ-fĕns′) *n.* Also *chiefly Brit.* **de·fence. 1.** The act of defending. **2.** One that defends or protects. **3.** An argument in support or justification of something. **4.** A defendant and his legal counsel. —**de·fense′less** *adj.* —**de·fense′less·ly** *adv.* —**de·fen′si·ble** *adj.* —**de·fen′sive** *adj.*

de·fer¹ (dĭ-fûr′) *v.* -**ferred, -ferring.** To put off until a future time; postpone; delay. [< L *differre.*] —**de·fer′rer** *n.*

de·fer² (dĭ-fûr′) *v.* -**ferred, -ferring.** To comply with or submit to the opinion or decision of another. [< L *dēferre*, to carry away, bring to, submit.] —**de·fer′rer** *n.*

def·er·ence (dĕf′ər-əns) *n.* **1.** Courteous yielding to the opinion or wishes of another. **2.** Courteous respect. —**def′er·en′tial** *adj.* —**def′er·en′tial·ly** *adv.*

de·fer·ment (dĭ-fûr′mənt) *n.* Also **de·fer·ral** (-fûr′əl). Postponement.

de·fi·ant (dĭ-fī′ənt) *adj.* **1.** Marked by resistance to authority. **2.** Intentionally provocative. —**de·fi′ance** *n.* —**de·fi′ant·ly** *adv.*

de·fi·cient (dĭ-fĭsh′ənt) *adj.* **1.** Lacking an essential element; incomplete. **2.** Inadequate in amount or degree; insufficient. [< L *dēficere*, to remove from, desert.] —**de·fi′cien·cy** *n.* —**de·fi′cient·ly** *adv.*

def·i·cit (dĕf′ə-sĭt) *n.* The amount by which a sum of money falls short of a required or expected amount; a shortage. [< L *dēficit*, it is lacking.]

deficit spending. The spending of money obtained by borrowing.

de·file¹ (dĭ-fīl′) *v.* -**filed, -filing. 1.** To make filthy or dirty. **2.** To corrupt. **3.** To profane, as a good name. **4.** To violate the chastity of. [Prob < OF *defouler.*] —**de·file′ment** *n.* —**de·fil′er** *n.* —**de·fil′ing·ly** *adv.*

de·file² (dĭ-fīl′) *v.* -**filed, -filing.** To march in single file or in columns. —*n.* A narrow gorge, valley, etc. [F *défiler.*]

de·fine (dĭ-fīn′) *v.* -**fined, -fining. 1.** To state the precise meaning of (a word). **2.** To describe the basic qualities of. **3.** To delineate. **4.** To specify distinctly; fix definitely. [< L *dēfinire*, to set bounds to.] —**de·fin′a·ble** *adj.* —**de·fin′er** *n.*

def·i·nite (dĕf′ə-nĭt) *adj.* **1.** Having distinct limits. **2.** Known positively. **3.** Clearly defined; precise. [< L *dēfinire*, to determine, DEFINE.] —**def′i·nite·ly** *adv.*

definite article. *Gram.* The article *the*, which restricts or particularizes the noun or noun phrase following it.

def·i·ni·tion (dĕf′ə-nĭsh′ən) *n.* **1. a.** The act of defining a word, phrase, or term. **b.** The statement of the meaning of a word, phrase, or term. **2.** The act of making clear and distinct. **3.** A determining of outline, extent, or limits. [< L *dēfinire*, DEFINE.]

de·fin·i·tive (dĭ-fĭn′ə-tĭv) *adj.* **1.** Precisely defining or outlining. **2.** Determining finally; decisive. **3.** Designating a work that can stand as the most authoritative on its subject. —**de·fin′i·tive·ly** *adv.* —**de·fin′i·tive·ness** *n.*

de·flate (dĭ-flāt′) *v.* -**flated, -flating. 1. a.** To release contained air or gas from. **b.** To collapse by such a release. **2.** To lessen the confidence, pride, or certainty of. **3.** *Econ.* To reduce the value or amount of (currency), effecting a decline in prices. [DE- + (IN)FLATE.] —**de·fla′tion** *n.* —**de·fla′tor** *n.*

de·flect (dĭ-flĕkt′) *v.* To cause to swerve; turn aside. [L *dēflectere.*] —**de·flec′ta·ble** *adj.* —**de·flec′tion** *n.* —**de·flec′tive** *adj.*

de·fo·li·ate (dĭ-fō′lē-āt′) *v.* -**ated, -ating. 1.** To strip (a tree or other plant) of leaves. **2.** To cause the leaves of (a tree or other plant) to fall off, esp. by the use of a chemical spray. [< LL *dēfoliāre.*] —**de·fo′li·a′tion** *n.*

de·form (dĭ-fôrm′) *v.* **1.** To spoil the natural form of; misshape. **2.** To deface; disfigure. —**de·form′a·ble** *adj.* —**de·for′ma·tion** (dĭ-fôr′mā·shən, dĕf′ər-) *n.*

de·formed (dĭ-fôrmd′) *adj.* Misshapen.

de·form·i·ty (dĭ-fôr′mĭ-tē) *n., pl.* -**ties.** The state or condition of being deformed.

de·fraud (dĭ-frôd′) *v.* To swindle. —**de′fraud·a′tion** *n.* —**de·fraud′er** *n.*

de·fray (dĭ-frā′) *v.* To meet or satisfy by payment; pay. [< OF *desfrayer.*] —**de·fray′a·ble** *adj.* —**de·fray′al** *n.*

de·frock (dē-frŏk′) *v.* To unfrock.

de·frost (dē-frôst′, -frŏst′) *v.* **1.** To remove ice or frost from. **2.** To become free of ice or frost. —**de·frost′er** *n.*

deft (dĕft) *adj.* Skillful; adroit. [ME *defte*, orig "gentle," "meek."] —**deft′ly** *adv.*

de·funct (dĭ-fŭngkt′) *adj.* Having ceased to live or exist. [L *dēfungī*, to discharge.]

de·fuse (dē-fyōōz′) *v.* -**fused, -fusing. 1.** To remove the fuse from (an explosive device). **2.** To make less dangerous or tense.

de·fy (dĭ-fī′) *v.* -**fied, -fying. 1.** To confront or stand up to; challenge. **2.** To resist successfully; withstand. **3.** To dare (someone) to perform something deemed impossible. [< VL *disfīdāre*, to renounce one's faith.]

deg, deg. degree (thermometric).

ô paw, for/oi boy/ou out/ŏŏ took/ōō coo/p pop/r run/s sauce/sh shy/t to/th thin/*th* the/
ŭ cut/ûr fur/v van/w wag/y yes/z size/zh vision/ə ago, item, edible, gallop, circus/

De Gaulle (də gōl′), **Charles.** 1890–1970. French general and statesman; president (1945–46; 1959–69).

Charles De Gaulle

de•gauss (dē′gous′) *v.* To neutralize the magnetic field of.

de•gen•er•a•cy (dĭ-jĕn′ər-ə-sē) *n.* **1.** The state or condition of being degenerate. **2.** The process of degenerating.

de•gen•er•ate (dĭ-jĕn′ə-rāt′) *v.* -ated, -ating. To deteriorate or decay. —*adj.* (dĭ-jĕn′ər-ĭt). Morally degraded or sexually deviant. —*n.* (dĭ-jĕn′ər-ĭt). A morally degraded or sexually deviant person. [L *dēgenerāre,* to fall from one's ancestral quality.] —**de•gen′er•ate•ly** *adv.* —**de•gen′er•ate•ness** *n.* —**de•gen′er•a′tion** *n.* —**de•gen′er•a•tive** (-ə-tĭv) *adj.*

de•glu•ti•nate (dĭ-glōōt′n-āt′) *v.* -nated, -nating. To extract the gluten from: *deglutinate wheat flour.* [L *dēglūtināre.*] —**de•glu′ti•na′tion** *n.*

de•glu•ti•tion (dē′glōō-tĭsh′ən) *n.* The process or act of swallowing. [L *dēglūtīre,* to swallow down.] —**de′glu•ti′tious** *adj.*

de•grade (dĭ-grād′) *v.* -graded, -grading. **1.** To reduce in grade, rank, or status. **2.** To debase; corrupt. [< LL *dēgradāre.*] —**deg′ra•da′tion** (dĕg′rə-dā′shən) *n.* —**de•grad′ed•ly** *adv.* —**de•grad′ed•ness** *n.* —**de•grad′er** *n.*

de•gree (dĭ-grē′) *n.* **1.** One of a series of steps or stages. **2.** Relative social or official rank or position. **3.** Relative intensity. **4.** Relative condition or extent; capacity; manner. **5.** The extent or measure of a state of being, action, etc. **6.** A unit division of a temperature scale. **7.** A unit of angular measure equal in magnitude to the central angle subtended by 1/360 of the circumference of a circle. **8.** A unit of latitude or longitude, 1/360 of a great circle. **9.** The greatest sum of the exponents of the variables in a term of a polynomial or polynomial equation. **10.** An academic title given to one who has completed a course of study or as an honorary distinction. **11.** *Law.* A classification of a crime according to its seriousness. **12.** *Gram.* One of the forms used in the comparison of adjectives and adverbs. **13.** *Mus.*

One of the seven notes of a diatonic scale. [< VL *dēgradus,* "a step down."]

de•hu•man•ize (dē-hyōō′mə-nīz′) *v.* -ized, -izing. **1.** To deprive of human qualities or attributes. **2.** To render mechanical and routine. —**de•hu′man•i•za′tion** *n.*

de•hu•mid•i•fy (dē′hyōō-mĭd′ə-fī′) *v.* -fied, -fying. To decrease the humidity of. —**de′hu•mid′i•fi•ca′tion** *n.* —**de•hu•mid′i•fi′er** *n.*

de•hy•drate (dē-hī′drāt′) *v.* -drated, -drating. To remove or lose water. —**de′hy•dra′tion** *n.*

de•ice (dē-īs′) *v.* -iced, -icing. **1.** To remove the ice from, esp. by melting. **2.** To prevent the formation of ice on. —**de•ic′er** *n.*

de•i•fy (dē′ə-fī′) *v.* -fied, -fying. **1.** To raise to divine rank. **2.** To worship; idealize. [< LL *deificāre.*] —**de′i•fi•ca′tion** *n.*

deign (dān) *v.* **1.** To think it suitable to one's dignity to do something. **2.** To condescend to give or grant. [< L *dignus,* worthy.]

de•ism (dē′ĭz′əm) *n.* An 18th-century system of natural religion affirming the existence of God while denying the validity of revelation. [< L *deus,* god.] —**de′ist** *n.* —**de•is′tic** *adj.*

de•i•ty (dē′ə-tē) *n., pl.* -ties. **1.** A god or goddess. **2.** Divinity. [< L *deus,* god.]

de•ject•ed (dĭ-jĕk′tĭd) *adj.* Depressed; disheartened. [< L *dējectus,* pp of *dējicere,* to cast down.] —**de•ject′ed•ly** *adv.*

de•jec•tion (dĭ-jĕk′shən) *n.* A state of depression; melancholy.

de ju•re (dē jōōr′ē, dā yōō′rā). According to law; by right. [L.]

deka–. Variant of **deca–.**

del. delegate; delegation.

Del. Delaware.

Del•a•ware¹ (dĕl′ə-wâr′) *n., pl.* -ware or -wares. **1.** A member of a group of Algonquian-speaking North American Indian tribes, formerly inhabiting the Delaware River valley. **2.** Their language.

Del•a•ware² (dĕl′ə-wâr′). A state of the E U.S. Pop. 548,000. Cap. Dover.

de•lay (dĭ-lā′) *v.* **1.** To cause to be late. **2.** To procrastinate; linger. —*n.* **1.** The act of delaying or condition of being delayed. **2.** The period of time during which one is delayed. [< OF *deslaier.*] —**de•lay′er** *n.*

de•lec•ta•ble (dĭ-lĕk′tə-bəl) *adj.* **1.** Delightful. **2.** Delicious. [< L *dēlectāre,* to please.] —**de•lec′ta•bil′i•ty** *n.* —**de•lec′ta•bly** *adv.*

de•lec•ta•tion (dē′lĕk-tā′shən) *n.* Pleasure; delight.

del•e•gate (dĕl′ə-gāt′, -gĭt) *n.* One authorized to act as a representative for another or others. —*v.* (dĕl′ə-gāt′) -gated, -gating. **1.** To authorize and send (a person) as one's representative. **2.** To commit to one's representative. [< L *dēlēgāre,* to send away, dispatch.]

del•e•ga•tion (dĕl′ə-gā′shən) *n.* **1.** The act of delegating or condition of being delegated. **2.** A group of persons authorized to represent another or others.

de•lete (dĭ-lēt′) *v.* -leted, -leting. To strike out; omit. [L *dēlēre,* to wipe out, efface.] —**de•le′tion** *n.*

del•e•te•ri•ous (dĕl′ə-tîr′ē-əs) *adj.* Injurious; harmful. [< Gk *dēleisthai,* to harm, injure.]

—del′e·te′ri·ous·ly *adv.* —dei′e·te′ri·ous·ness *n.*

Del·hi (dĕl′ē). A city of NE India. Pop. 2,299,000.

de·lib·er·ate (dĭ-lĭb′ə-rāt′) *v.* -ated, -ating. **1.** To consider or discuss (a matter) carefully. **2.** To take careful thought; reflect. —*adj.* (dĭ-lĭb′ər-ĭt). **1.** Intentional. **2. a.** Careful in deciding. **b.** Not hastily determined: *a deliberate choice.* **3.** Slow; not hurried. [L *dēlīberāre*, to weigh well, ponder.] —**de·lib′er·ate·ly** *adv.* —**de·lib′er·ate·ness** *n.*

de·lib·er·a·tion (dĭ-lĭb′ə-rā′shən) *n.* **1.** Careful consideration. **2.** Often **deliberations.** Careful discussion of an issue. —**de·lib′er·a′tive** (-lĭb′-ə-rā′tĭv, -ər-ə-tĭv) *adj.*

del·i·ca·cy (dĕl′ĭ-kə-sē) *n., pl.* -cies. **1.** The quality of being delicate. **2.** A choice food.

del·i·cate (dĕl′ĭ-kĭt) *adj.* **1.** Pleasingly small, subtle, etc. **2.** Frail in constitution. **3.** Easily damaged. **4.** Requiring or marked by tact. **5.** Keenly sensitive or accurate. **6.** Requiring or showing careful skill. [< L *dēlicātus*, alluring, charming, dainty.] —**del′i·cate·ly** *adv.*

del·i·ca·tes·sen (dĕl′ĭ-kə-tĕs′ən) *n.* A shop that sells freshly prepared foods ready for serving. [< G *Delikatesse*, delicacy.]

de·li·cious (dĭ-lĭsh′əs) *adj.* Highly pleasing to the sense of taste. [< L *dēlicere*, to entice away, DELIGHT.] —**de·li′cious·ly** *adv.* —**de·li′cious·ness** *n.*

de·light (dĭ-līt′) *n.* **1.** Great pleasure; joy. **2.** Something that gives great pleasure or enjoyment. —*v.* **1.** To take great pleasure or joy. **2.** To give (someone) great pleasure or joy. [< L *dēlectāre*, freq of *dēlicere*, to allure.]

de·light·ful (dĭ-līt′fəl) *adj.* Greatly pleasing. —**de·light′ful·ly** *adv.* —**de·light′ful·ness** *n.*

de·lin·e·ate (dĭ-lĭn′ē-āt′) *v.* -ated, -ating. **1.** To draw or outline accurately. **2.** To describe broadly but accurately. [L *dēlīneāre*.] —**de·lin′e·a′tion** *n.* —**de·lin′e·a′tive** *adj.*

de·lin·quent (dĭ-lĭng′kwənt) *adj.* **1.** Failing to do what is required. **2.** Overdue in payment: *a delinquent account.* —*n.* One who fails to do what is required. [< L *dēlinquere*, to fail in duty, "leave undone."] —**de·lin′quen·cy** *n.*

del·i·quesce (dĕl′ə-kwĕs′) *v.* -quesced, -quescing. To dissolve and become liquid by absorbing moisture from the air. [L *dēliquēscere.*] —**del′i·ques′cent** *adj.*

de·lir·i·um (dĭ-lîr′ē-əm) *n., pl.* -ums or -ia (-ē-ə). A state of temporary mental confusion and clouded consciousness resulting from high fever, intoxication, or shock, and characterized by anxiety, tremors, hallucinations, delusions, and incoherence. [< L *dēlīrāre*, to deviate from a straight line.] —**de·lir′i·ous** *adj.* —**de·lir′i·ous·ly** *adv.* —**de·lir′i·ous·ness** *n.*

delirium tre·mens (trē′mənz). An acute delirium caused by alcohol poisoning.

de·liv·er (dĭ-lĭv′ər) *v.* **1.** To set free. **2. a.** To assist (a female) in giving birth. **b.** To assist in the birth of. **3.** To take to an intended recipient. **4.** To send forth by discharging or throwing, as a blow. **5.** To utter (a lecture). [< LL *dēlīberāre.*] —**de·liv′er·er** *n.*

de·liv·er·ance (dĭ-lĭv′ər-əns) *n.* Rescue from bondage or danger.

de·liv·er·y (dĭ-lĭv′ə-rē) *n., pl.* -ies. **1.** The act of delivering. **2.** That which is delivered. **3.** Childbirth. **4.** Manner of speaking or singing. **5.** Manner of throwing or discharging.

dell (dĕl) *n.* A small, secluded valley. [< OE. See **dhel-.**]

del·phin·i·um (dĕl-fĭn′ē-əm) *n.* A tall cultivated plant with spikes of showy, variously colored spurred flowers. [< Gk *delphinion*, larkspur.]

del·ta (dĕl′tə) *n.* **1.** The 4th letter of the Greek alphabet, representing *d.* **2.** A usually triangular alluvial deposit, as at the mouth of a river. —**del·ta′ic** (-tā′ĭk) *adj.*

del·toid (dĕl′toid′) *n.* A thick, triangular muscle covering the shoulder joint, used to raise the arm from the side. [< Gk *deltoeidēs*, triangular : DELTA + -OID.]

de·lude (dĭ-lōōd′) *v.* -luded, -luding. To mislead the mind or judgment of; deceive. [< L *dēlūdere*, to play false, deceive.]

del·uge (dĕl′yōōj) *v.* -uged, -uging. To overrun with or as with water; flood. —*n.* **1.** A flood; downpour. **2.** Anything that overwhelms as if by a flood. [< L *dīluvium*, flood.]

de·lu·sion (dĭ-l/yōō′zhən) *n.* **1.** The state of being deluded. **2.** A false belief held in spite of invalidating evidence. [< L *dēlūdere*, DELUDE.] —**de·lu′sive, de·lu′sion·al** *adj.*

de luxe (dĭ lŏŏks′, dĭ lŭks′). Luxurious; elaborate; sumptuous: *a de luxe model.* [F, "of luxury."]

delve (dĕlv) *v.* delved, delving. To search deeply and laboriously. [< OE *delfan.* See **dhelbh-.**] —**delv′er** *n.*

Dem. Democrat; Democratic.

de·mag·net·ize (dē-măg′nə-tīz′) *v.* -ized, -izing. To remove magnetic properties from. —**de·mag′net·i·za′tion** *n.*

dem·a·gogue (dĕm′ə-gôg′, -gŏg′) *n.* A leader who obtains power by means of appeals to emotions and prejudices. [Gk *dēmagōgos*, popular leader.] —**dem′a·gog′ic** (dĕm′ə-gŏj′ĭk) *adj.* —**dem′a·gogu′er·y** *n.*

de·mand (dĭ-mănd′, -mänd′) *v.* **1.** To ask for, leaving no chance for refusal. **2.** To claim as just or due. **3.** To need or require. —*n.* **1.** The act of demanding. **2.** Something demanded. **3. a.** The state of being sought after. **b.** An urgent need. [< L *dēmandāre*, to give in charge, entrust.] —**de·mand′er** *n.*

de·mand·ing (dĭ-măn′dĭng, dĭ-män′-) *adj.* **1.** Making rigorous demands. **2.** Requiring careful attention or constant effort. —**de·mand′ing·ly** *adv.*

de·mar·cate (dĭ-mär′kāt′, dē′mär-kāt′) *v.* -cated, -cating. To mark with or as with boundaries. —**de·mar′ca′tor** *n.*

de·mar·ca·tion (dē′mär-kā′shən) *n.* **1.** The setting or marking of boundaries or limits. **2.** A separation.

de·mean (dĭ-mēn′) *v.* **1.** To debase in dignity or stature. **2.** To humble (oneself).

de·mean·or (dĭ-mē′nər) *n.* A person's manner toward others.

de·ment·ed (dĭ-mĕn′tĭd) *adj.* **1.** Insane. **2.** Afflicted with dementia.

de·men·tia (dĭ-mĕn′shə, -shē-ə) *n.* Irreversible

ô paw, for/oi boy/ou out/ōō took/ōō coo/p **pop**/r run/s sauce/sh shy/t to/th thin/*th* the/ ŭ cut/ûr **fur**/v van/w wag/y yes/z size/zh vision/ə ago, item, edible, gallop, circus/

deterioration of intellectual faculties with con-comitant emotional disturbance resulting from organic brain disorder. [< L *dēmēns*, mad.]

dementia prae·cox (prē'kŏks'). Schizophrenia.

de·mer·it (dĭ-mĕr'ĭt) *n.* A mark against one's record for bad conduct or failure. [Prob < L *dēmerēre*, to deserve.]

Dem·e·rol (dĕm'ə-rôl', -rŏl') *n.* A trademark for a synthetic morphine.

de·mesne (dĭ-mān', -mēn') *n.* 1. The grounds belonging to a mansion. 2. An extensive piece of landed property. 3. Any territory; realm. [< OF *demaine*, domain.]

De·me·ter (dĭ-mē'tər). Greek goddess of agriculture.

demi-. *comb. form.* 1. Half. 2. Less than full status. [< L *dīmidius*, half.]

dem·i·god (dĕm'ē-gŏd') *n.* A mythological semidivine being, as the offspring of a god and a mortal.

dem·i·john (dĕm'ē-jŏn') *n.* A large bottle encased in wickerwork.

de·mil·i·ta·rize (dē-mĭl'ə-tə-rīz') *v.* -rized, -rizing. To eliminate or prohibit military forces in. —**de·mil'i·ta·ri·za'tion** *n.*

dem·i·monde (dĕm'ē-mŏnd, dĕm'ē-mŏnd') *n.* Any group of doubtful respectability. [F *demi-monde*, "half-world."]

de·mise (dĭ-mīz') *n.* Death. [< L *dīmittere*, to dismiss.]

dem·i·tasse (dĕm'ē-tăs', -täs') *n.* A small cup of strong black coffee. [F.]

de·mo·bil·ize (dē-mō'bə-līz') *v.* -ized, -izing. To discharge from military service or use. —**de·mo'bi·li·za'tion** *n.*

de·moc·ra·cy (dĭ-mŏk'rə-sē) *n., pl.* -cies. 1. Government by the people, exercised either directly or through elected representatives. 2. A political unit based on this form of rule. [< Gk *dēmos*, common people + -CRACY.]

dem·o·crat (dĕm'ə-krăt') *n.* An advocate of democracy.

dem·o·crat·ic (dĕm'ə-krăt'ĭk) *adj.* 1. Of, characterized by, or advocating democracy. 2. Pertaining to or promoting the interests of the people. 3. Believing in social equality; not snobbish. —**dem'o·crat'i·cal·ly** *adv.*

Democratic Party. One of the two major political parties in the U.S.

de·mog·ra·phy (dĭ-mŏg'rə-fē) *n.* The statistical study of human populations. [< Gk *dēmos*, people + -GRAPHY.] —**dem'o·graph'ic** (dĕm'ə-grăf'ĭk) *adj.* —**dem'o·graph'i·cal·ly** *adv.*

de·mol·ish (dĭ-mŏl'ĭsh) *v.* To tear down completely; destroy. [< L *dēmolīrī*, to throw down, demolish.]

dem·o·li·tion (dĕm'ə-lĭsh'ən) *n.* The act or process of demolishing, esp. destruction by explosives in warfare.

de·mon (dē'mən) *n.* 1. A devil or evil spirit. 2. One who is extremely zealous or skillful in a given activity. [< Gk *daimōn*, divine power, fate, god.]

de·mo·ni·ac (dĭ-mō'nē-ăk') *adj.* Also **de·mo·ni·a·cal** (dē'mə-nī'ə-kəl). 1. Possessed by or as by a demon. 2. Devilish; fiendish.

de·mon·stra·ble (dĭ-mŏn'strə-bəl) *adj.* Capable of being shown or proved. —**de·mon'stra·bly** *adv.*

dem·on·strate (dĕm'ən-strāt') *v.* -strated, -strating. 1. To prove or make manifest by reasoning or evidence. 2. To manifest or reveal. 3. To display, operate, and explain (a product). 4. To make a public display of opinion. [L *dēmonstrāre*, to point out.] —**dem'on·stra'tion** *n.* —**dem'on·stra'tor** *n.*

de·mon·stra·tive (dĭ-mŏn'strə-tĭv) *adj.* 1. Serving to manifest or prove. 2. Expressive of emotion, esp. affection. 3. *Gram.* Specifying the person or thing referred to, as the pronoun *these.* —*n. Gram.* A demonstrative pronoun or adjective. —**de·mon'stra·tive·ly** *adv.* —**de·mon'stra·tive·ness** *n.*

de·mor·al·ize (dĭ-môr'əl-īz', dĭ-mŏr'-) *v.* -ized, -izing. 1. To corrupt the morals of. 2. To undermine the morale of; dishearten. —**de·mor'al·i·za'tion** *n.* —**de·mor'al·iz'er** *n.*

De·mos·the·nes (dĭ-mŏs'thə-nēz'). 384?–322 B.C. Athenian orator and statesman.

de·mote (dĭ-mōt') *v.* -moted, -moting. To lower in rank or grade. [DE- + (PRO)MOTE.] —**de·mo'tion** *n.*

de·mul·cent (dĭ-mŭl'sənt) *n.* A soothing, usually mucilaginous or oily medication. [< L *dēmulcēre*, to stroke down, caress.]

de·mur (dĭ-mûr') *v.* -murred, -murring. To take exception; raise objections. [< L *dēmorārī*, to delay.] —**de·mur'ra·ble** *adj.*

de·mure (dĭ-myŏor') *adj.* -murer, -murest. 1. Modest in manner; reserved. 2. Affectedly modest. [< OF *demorer*, to stay, delay, demur.] —**de·mure'ly** *adv.* —**de·mure'ness** *n.*

den (dĕn) *n.* 1. The shelter of a wild animal; lair. 2. A residence or refuge, esp. if hidden or squalid. 3. A small room for study or relaxation. [< OE *denn* < Gmc **dan-*, low ground.]

Den. Denmark.

de·na·ture (dē-nā'chər) *v.* -tured, -turing. Also **de·na·tur·ize** (-chə-rīz') -ized, -izing. To render unfit to eat or drink, esp. to add methanol to for this purpose. —**de·na'tur·ant** *n.*

den·drite (dĕn'drīt') *n.* A branched part of a nerve cell that transmits impulses toward the cell body. [< Gk *dendron*, tree.] —**den·drit'ic** (-drĭt'ĭk) *adj.*

den·gue (dĕng'gē, dĕng'gā) *n.* An infectious tropical epidemic disease transmitted by mosquitoes and marked by fever and severe pains in the joints. [Of African origin.]

de·ni·al (dĭ-nī'əl) *n.* 1. A negative reply, as to a request. 2. Refusal to grant the truth of a statement. 3. A disavowal; repudiation. 4. Self-denial. [< DENY.]

de·nic·o·tin·ize (dē-nĭk'ə-tĭ-nīz') *v.* -ized, -izing. To remove nicotine from.

den·ier (də-nyā', dĕn'yər) *n.* A unit of fineness for rayon, nylon, and silk yarns. [ME *denere*, a small coin.]

den·i·grate (dĕn'ĭ-grāt') *v.* -grated, -grating. To belittle maliciously; defame. [L *dēnigrāre*, to blacken.] —**den'i·gra'tion** *n.*

den·im (dĕn'əm) *n.* 1. A coarse twilled cloth used for work clothes. 2. denims. Garments made of denim. [F (serge) de Nîmes, serge of Nîmes, city in France.]

ă pat/ā ate/âr care/ä bar/b bib/ch chew/d deed/ĕ pet/ē be/f fit/g gag/h hat/hw what/
ĭ pit/ī pie/îr pier/j judge/k kick/l lid, fatal/m mum/n no, sudden/ng sing/ŏ pot/ō go/

den·i·zen (dĕn′ə-zən) *n.* An inhabitant; resident. [< LL *dēintus,* from within.]

Den·mark (dĕn′märk′). A kingdom of NW Europe. Pop. 4,684,000. Cap. Copenhagen.

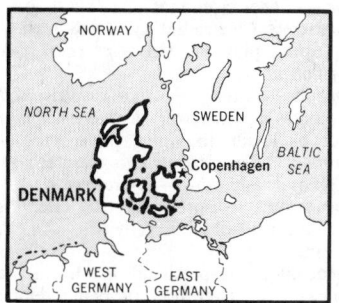

Denmark

de·nom·i·na·tion (dĭ-nŏm′ə-nā′shən) *n.* **1.** A name, esp. the name of a class or group. **2.** A unit having a specified value in a system of currency or weights. **3.** An organized group of religious congregations. —**de·nom′i·na′tion·al** *adj.* —**de·nom′i·na′tion·al·ly** *adv.*

de·nom·i·na·tor (dĭ-nŏm′ə-nā′tər) *n.* The quantity below the line indicating division in a fraction; the quantity that divides the numerator.

de·no·ta·tion (dē′nō-tā′shən) *n.* **1.** The act of denoting. **2.** The explicit meaning of a word as opposed to its connotation.

de·note (dĭ-nōt′) *v.* -noted, -noting. **1.** To reveal or indicate plainly. **2.** To refer to specifically; mean explicitly.

dé·noue·ment (dā-nōō-mäN′) *n.* The outcome or solution of the plot of a play or novel. [F, "an untying."]

de·nounce (dĭ-nouns′) *v.* -nounced, -nouncing. **1.** To express vehement disapproval of openly. **2.** To accuse formally; inform against. [< L *dēnūntiāre,* make an official announcement of.] —**de·nounce′ment** *n.* —**de·nounc′er** *n.*

Den·pa·sar (dən-pä′sär′). Also **Den Pasar.** The capital of Bali. Pop. 56,000.

dense (dĕns) *adj.* **denser, densest. 1. a.** Having relatively high density. **b.** Crowded together; compact. **2.** Thick; impenetrable. **3.** Dull; stupid. [L *dēnsus.*] —**dense′ly** *adv.*

den·si·ty (dĕn′sə-tē) *n., pl.* -ties. **1. a.** The amount of something per unit measure, esp. per unit length, area, or volume. **b.** The mass per unit volume of a substance under specified conditions of pressure and temperature. **2.** Thickness of consistency; impenetrability. **3.** Stupidity; dullness.

dent (dĕnt) *n.* A depression in a surface made by pressure or a blow. [< OE *dynt,* strike < Gmc **dunti-.*] —**dent** *v.*

dent. dental; dentist; dentistry.

den·tal (dĕnt′l) *adj.* **1.** Of or pertaining to the teeth. **2.** Of or pertaining to dentistry. [< L *dēns (dent-),* tooth.]

denti–. *comb. form.* Tooth.

den·ti·frice (dĕn′tə-frĭs) *n.* A substance for cleaning the teeth.

den·tine (dĕn′tēn′) *n.* Also **den·tin** (-tĭn). The part of a tooth between the enamel and pulp. —**den′ti·nal** *adj.*

den·tist (dĕn′tĭst) *n.* One whose profession is dentistry.

den·tist·ry (dĕn′tĭ-strē) *n.* The diagnosis, prevention, and treatment of diseases of the teeth.

den·ti·tion (dĕn-tĭsh′ən) *n.* **1.** The type, number, and arrangement of teeth. **2.** The cutting of teeth. [< L *dēns (dent-),* tooth.]

den·ture (dĕn′chər) *n.* A set of artificial teeth.

de·nude (dĭ-n/y/ōōd′) *v.* -nuded, -nuding. To divest of covering; make bare. —**den′u·da′tion** (dĕn′yōō-dā′shən) *n.*

de·nu·mer·a·ble (dĭ-n/y/ōō′mər-ə-bəl) *adj.* Capable of being put into one-to-one correspondence with the positive integers; countable. —**de·nu′mer·a·bly** *adv.*

de·nun·ci·a·tion (dĭ-nŭn′sē-ā′shən, -shē-ā′shən) *n.* The act of denouncing.

Den·ver (dĕn′vər). The capital of Colorado. Pop. 515,000.

de·ny (dĭ-nī′) *v.* -nied, -nying. **1.** To declare untrue; contradict. **2.** To refuse to recognize or acknowledge. **3.** To refuse to grant. [< L *dēnēgāre.*] —**de·ni′er** *n.*

de·o·dor·ant (dē-ō′dər-ənt) *n.* A substance used to counteract undesirable odors. [DE- + ODOR + -ANT.]

de·ox·y·ri·bo·nu·cle·ic acid (dē-ŏk′sē-rĭ-bō-n/y/ōō-klē′ĭk). A complex chromosomal constituent of living cell nuclei, the structural components of which are bonded in a sequence that determines individual hereditary characteristics.

dep. 1. depart; departure. **2.** department. **3.** deposit. **4.** deputy.

Dep. dependency (territorial).

de·part (dĭ-pärt′) *v.* **1.** To go away; leave. **2.** To vary, as from a regular course; deviate: *depart from custom.* [< OF *departir.*] —**de·par′ture** *n.*

de·part·ment (dĭ-pärt′mənt) *n.* **1.** A distinct division of a large organization, as a government, company, or college, having a specialized function. **2.** An area of special knowledge or activity; sphere. [< OF *departir,* divide, DEPART.] —**de′part·men′tal** *adj.*

de·pend (dĭ-pĕnd′) *v.* **1.** To rely, as for support or aid (with *on* or *upon*). **2.** To place trust. **3.** To be determined by (with *on* or *upon*): *depends on your taste.* [< OF *dependre,* hang down.]

de·pend·a·ble (dĭ-pĕn′də-bəl) *adj.* Reliable; trustworthy. —**de·pend′a·bil′i·ty, de·pend′a·ble·ness** *n.* —**de·pend′a·bly** *adv.*

de·pend·ence (dĭ-pĕn′dəns) *n.* Also **de·pen·dance. 1.** The state of being dependent, as for support. **2.** The state of being influenced or controlled by something else. **3.** Trust; reliance.

de·pen·den·cy (dĭ-pĕn′dən-sē) *n., pl.* -cies. Also **de·pen·dan·cy. 1.** Dependence. **2.** A territory or state under the jurisdiction of another country from which it is separated geographically.

ô paw, for/oi boy/ou out/ōō took/ōō coo/p pop/r run/s sauce/sh shy/t to/th thin/*th* the/
ŭ cut/ûr fur/v van/w wag/y yes/z size/zh vision/ə ago, item, edible, gallop, circus/

dependent / dereliction

de·pen·dent (dĭ-pĕn'dənt). Also **de·pen·dant.** *adj.* **1.** Determined by something or someone else. **2.** Subordinate. **3.** Unable to exist or function satisfactorily without the aid of another. —*n.* One who relies on another, as for support. —**de·pen'dent·ly** *adv.*

de·pict (dĭ-pĭkt') *v.* **1.** To represent in a picture or sculpture. **2.** To describe. [L *dēpingere* (pp *dēpictus*).] —**de·pic'tion** *n.*

de·pil·a·to·ry (dĭ-pĭl'ə-tôr'ē, -tōr'ē) *n., pl.* -ries. A substance used to remove hair from the body.

de·plete (dĭ-plēt') *v.* -pleted, -pleting. To use up or exhaust. [L *dēplēre* (pp *dēplētus*), to empty.] —**de·plet'a·ble** *adj.* —**de·ple'tion** *n.*

de·plore (dĭ-plôr', -plōr') *v.* -plored, -ploring. **1.** To feel or express sorrow over. **2.** To regard as very unfortunate or wrong. [<L *dēplōrāre.*] —**de·plor'a·ble** *adj.* —**de·plor'a·bly** *adv.* —**de·plor'a·ble·ness** *n.*

de·ploy (dĭ-ploi') *v.* To spread out (persons or forces) systematically over an area. [< L *displicāre*, to scatter.] —**de·ploy'ment** *n.*

de·po·nent (dĭ-pō'nənt) *n.* One who testifies under oath, esp. in writing.

de·pop·u·late (dē-pŏp'yə-lāt') *v.* -lated, -lating. To reduce sharply the population of. —**de·pop'u·la'tion** *n.* —**de·pop'u·la'tor** *n.*

de·port (dĭ-pôrt', -pōrt') *v.* **1.** To expel from a country. **2.** To behave or conduct (oneself). [< L *dēportāre*, carry off, carry away.]

de·por·ta·tion (dē'pôr-tā'shən, dē'pōr-) *n.* Expulsion from a country.

de·port·ment (dĭ-pôrt'mənt, dĭ-pōrt'-) *n.* Conduct, esp. correct conduct.

de·pose (dĭ-pōz') *v.* -posed, -posing. **1.** To remove from office or a position of power. **2.** *Law.* To testify, esp. in writing. [< OF *deposer.*] —**de·pos'a·ble** *adj.*

de·pos·it (dĭ-pŏz'ĭt) *v.* **1.** To place for safekeeping, as money in a bank. **2.** To put down in layers by a natural process. **3.** To give (money) as partial payment or security. —*n.* **1.** Something placed for safekeeping, as money in a bank. **2.** Money given as partial payment or security. **3.** Something, esp. a mineral or sediment, deposited by a natural process. [L *dēpōnere* (pp *dēpositus*), to put aside.] —**de·pos'i·tor** *n.*

dep·o·si·tion (dĕp'ə-zĭsh'ən) *n.* **1.** The act of deposing, as from office. **2.** The act of depositing. **3.** Something deposited. **4.** Testimony under oath.

de·pos·i·to·ry (dĭ-pŏz'ə-tôr'ē, -tōr'ē) *n., pl.* -ries. A place where something is deposited for safekeeping.

de·pot (dē'pō) *n.* **1.** A railroad or bus station. **2.** A warehouse. **3.** A place for the storage of military supplies. [< L *dēpositum*, deposit.]

de·prave (dĭ-prāv') *v.* -praved, -praving. To debase morally; corrupt. [< L *dēprāvāre*, to pervert.] —**de·praved'** *adj.* —**de·prav'i·ty** (-prăv'ə-tē) *n.*

dep·re·cate (dĕp'rĭ-kāt') *v.* -cated, -cating. **1.** To express disapproval of. **2.** To depreciate; belittle. [L *dēprecārī*, to ward off by prayer.] —**dep're·ca'tion** *n.* —**dep're·ca'tor** *n.*

dep·re·ca·to·ry (dĕp'rə-kə-tôr'ē, -tōr'ē) *adj.*

Also **dep·re·ca·tive** (-kā'tĭv). Expressing deprecation.

de·pre·ci·ate (dĭ-prē'shē-āt') *v.* -ated, -ating. **1.** To make or become less in price or value. **2.** To belittle. [< LL *dēpretiāre.*] —**de·pre'ci·a'tion** *n.* —**de·pre'ci·a'tor** *n.*

dep·re·date (dĕp'rə-dāt') *v.* -dated, -dating. To prey upon; plunder. [LL *dēpraedārī.*] —**dep're·da'tion** *n.*

de·press (dĭ-prĕs') *v.* **1.** To dispirit; sadden. **2.** To press down; lower: *depress a pedal.* **3.** To lower or lessen in value, price, etc. [< L *deprimere*, to press down.] —**de·pres'sive** *adj.* —**de·pres'sive·ly** *adv.* —**de·pres'sor** *n.*

de·pres·sant (dĭ-prĕs'ənt) *adj.* Serving to lower the rate of vital activities. —*n.* A depressant drug.

de·pres·sion (dĭ-prĕsh'ən) *n.* **1.** The act of depressing or condition of being depressed. **2.** An area sunk below its surroundings; hollow. **3.** A period of drastic decline in the national economy. **4.** Melancholy; dejection.

de·prive (dĭ-prīv') *v.* -prived, -priving. **1.** To take something away from; divest. **2.** To keep from the possession or enjoyment of something to which one has a right. [< ML *dēprīvāre.*] —**dep'ri·va'tion** (dĕp'rə-vā'shən) *n.*

de·pro·gram (dē-prō'grăm', -grəm) *v.* -grammed or -gramed, -gramming or -graming. To counteract the effect of a previous indoctrination based on sectarian, unusual, or esoteric notions. —**de·pro'gram'mer, de·pro'gram'er** *n.*

dept. department.

depth (dĕpth) *n.* **1.** The condition of being deep. **2.** The distance downward. **3.** Often **depths.** The deepest or most remote part of something. **4.** The most intense or worst part: *the depth of winter.* **5.** Intellectual penetration. **6.** The range of one's understanding: *beyond one's depth.* **7.** Intensity: *depth of color.*

depth charge. An explosive designed for use under water, esp. one used against submarines.

dep·u·ta·tion (dĕp'yə-tā'shən) *n.* A group appointed to represent others; delegation.

dep·u·tize (dĕp'yə-tīz') *v.* -tized, -tizing. To appoint as a deputy.

dep·u·ty (dĕp'yə-tē) *n., pl.* -ties. A person empowered to act for another. [< LL *dēputāre*, to allot.] —**dep'u·ty** *adj.*

der. derivation; derivative.

de·rail (dē-rāl') *v.* To run off or cause to run off the rails. —**de·rail'ment** *n.*

de·range (dĭ-rānj') *v.* -ranged, -ranging. **1.** To disturb the arrangement or functioning of. **2.** To make insane. [F *déranger.*] —**de·range'ment** *n.*

der·by (dûr'bē) *n., pl.* -bies. **1.** A stiff felt hat with a round crown. **2. Derby.** Any of various annual horse races. **3.** Any race with an open field of contestants. [< the 12th Earl of *Derby* (died 1834).]

der·e·lict (dĕr'ə-lĭkt) *adj.* **1.** Neglectful of duty; delinquent. **2.** Abandoned by an owner. —*n.* **1.** Abandoned property, esp. an abandoned ship. **2.** A social outcast; vagrant. [L *dērelictus*, pp of *dērelinquere*, abandon.]

der·e·lic·tion (dĕr'ə-lĭk'shən) *n.* **1.** Willful neglect, as of duty. **2.** Abandonment.

ă pat/ā ate/âr care/ä bar/b bib/ch chew/d deed/ĕ pet/ē be/f fit/g gag/h hat/hw what/ ĭ pit/ī pie/îr pier/j judge/k kick/l lid, fatal/m mum/n no, sudden/ng sing/ŏ pot/ō go/

de•ride (dĭ-rīd′) v. -rided, -riding. To speak of or treat with contemptuous mirth; scoff at. [L *dērīdēre*.] —**de•ri′sion** (dĭ-rĭzh′ən) n. —**de•ri′sive** (dĭ-rī′sĭv) adj. —**de•ri′sive•ly** adv.

der•i•va•tion (dĕr′ə-vā′shən) n. 1. The act or process of deriving or condition of being derived. 2. The source or origin of something. 3. The origin and development of a word. 4. A logical or mathematical sequence of statements indicating that a result necessarily follows from the initial assumptions.

de•riv•a•tive (dĭ-rĭv′ə-tĭv) adj. Resulting from derivation; derived. —n. Something, such as a word, derived from another.

de•rive (dĭ-rīv′) v. -rived, -riving. 1. To obtain or issue from a source. 2. To deduce; infer. 3. To trace the origin and development of something, as a word. [< L *dērīvāre*, draw off, derive.] —**de•riv′er** n.

–derm. comb. form. Skin: endoderm. [< Gk *derma*, skin.]

der•ma (dûr′mə) n. Also derm (dûrm), der•mis (dûr′mĭs). A layer of skin, the corium. [< Gk *derma*, skin.] —**der′mal** adj.

der•ma•ti•tis (dûr′mə-tī′tĭs) n. Inflammation of the skin.

dermato–. comb. form. Skin. [< Gk *derma*, skin.]

der•ma•tol•o•gy (dûr′mə-tŏl′ə-jē) n. The medical study of the physiology and pathology of the skin. —**der′ma•tol′o•gist** n.

der•o•gate (dĕr′ə-gāt′) v. -gated, -gating. To detract or disparage. [L *dērogāre*, repeal, restrict, disparage.] —**der′o•ga′tion** n.

de•rog•a•to•ry (dĭ-rŏg′ə-tôr′ē, -tōr′ē) adj. Detracting; disparaging.

der•rick (dĕr′ĭk) n. 1. A large crane for hoisting and moving heavy objects. 2. A framework over the opening of an oil well, used to support equipment.

der•ri•ère (dĕr′ē-âr′) n. The buttocks. [F, "the rear."]

der•ring-do (dĕr′ĭng-dōō′) n. Daring spirit and action. [ME *durring don,* daring to do.]

der•rin•ger (dĕr′ĭn-jər) n. A small pistol. [< H. *Deringer,* 19th-century American gunsmith.]

der•vish (dûr′vĭsh) n. A member of any of various Moslem ascetic orders. [Turk *derviş,* mendicant.]

de•sal•i•nate (dē-săl′ə-nāt′) v. -nated, -nating. To desalinize. —**de•sal′i•na′tion** n.

de•sal•in•ize (dē-săl′ə-nīz′) v. -ized, -izing. To remove salts and other chemicals from (sea water). —**de•sal′i•ni•za′tion** n.

Des•cartes (dā-kärt′), **René.** 1596–1650. French philosopher and mathematician.

de•scend (dĭ-sĕnd′) v. 1. To move to a lower level; come or go down. 2. To slope or incline downward. 3. To be derived from ancestors. [< L *dēscendere.*]

de•scen•dant (dĭ-sĕn′dənt) n. An immediate or remote offspring. —adj. Descendent.

de•scen•dent (dĭ-sĕn′dənt) adj. Also **de•scen•dant.** 1. Moving downward; descending. 2. Proceeding from an ancestor.

de•scent (dĭ-sĕnt′) n. 1. The act or an instance of descending. 2. A downward incline. 3.

Ancestral extraction; lineage. 4. A lowering or decline.

de•scribe (dĭ-skrīb′) v. -scribed, -scribing. 1. To tell about in detail; picture verbally. 2. To trace or draw the figure of. [L *dēscrībere*, to copy off, write down.] —**de•scrib′er** n.

de•scrip•tion (dĭ-skrĭp′shən) n. 1. The act, process, or technique of describing. 2. An account describing something. 3. A kind; sort: *costumes of every description.* [< L *dēscrībere*, DESCRIBE.] —**de•scrip′tive** adj.

de•scry (dĭ-skrī′) v. -scried, -scrying. To discern (something difficult to catch sight of). [ME *descrien*, cry out, proclaim, catch sight of.]

des•e•crate (dĕs′ə-krāt′) v. -crated, -crating. To subject to sacrilege; profane. [DE- + (CON)- SECRATE.] —**des′e•cra′tion** n.

de•seg•re•gate (dē-sĕg′rə-gāt′) v. -grated, -grating. To abolish racial segregation in. —**de′seg•re•ga′tion** n.

de•sen•si•tize (dē-sĕn′sə-tīz′) v. -tized, -tizing. To render insensitive. —**de•sen′si•ti•za′tion** n.

des•ert¹ (dĕz′ərt) n. A region rendered barren or partially barren by environmental extremes, esp. by low rainfall. [< L *dēserere*, to DESERT.] —**des′ert** adj.

de•sert² (dĭ-zûrt′) n. Often **deserts.** That which is deserved, esp. a punishment: *received his just deserts.*

de•sert³ (dĭ-zûrt′) v. 1. To forsake or leave; abandon. 2. To abandon one's duty or post. [< L *dēserere,* to abandon.] —**de•sert′er** n. —**de•ser′tion** n.

de•serve (dĭ-zûrv′) v. -served, -serving. To be worthy of; merit. [< L *dēservīre,* serve well.]

de•served (dĭ-zûrvd′) adj. Merited or earned. —**de•serv′ed•ly** (-vĭd-lē) adv.

de•serv•ing (dĭ-zûr′vĭng) adj. Worthy; meritorious. —**de•serv′ing•ly** adv.

des•ic•cant (dĕs′ĭ-kənt) n. A substance used to absorb moisture. [< L *dēsiccāre,* DESICCATE.]

des•ic•cate (dĕs′ĭ-kāt′) v. -cated, -cating. To make or become thoroughly dry. [L *dēsiccāre.*] —**des′ic•ca′tion** n. —**des′ic•ca′tive** adj.

de•sid•er•a•tum (dĭ-sĭd′ə-rā′təm) n., pl. -ta (-tə). Something needed and desired. [< L *dēsīderāre,* DESIRE.]

de•sign (dĭ-zīn′) v. 1. To conceive; invent. 2. To form a plan for. 3. To draw a sketch of. 4. To have as or make for a purpose; intend. —n. 1. The arrangement of the parts or details of something according to a plan. 2. A visual composition; pattern. 3. A purpose; intention; plan. 4. Often **designs.** A sinister scheme. [< L *dēsignāre,* DESIGNATE.] —**de•sign′er** n.

des•ig•nate (dĕz′ĭg-nāt′) v. -nated, -nating. 1. To indicate or specify. 2. To give a name to. 3. To appoint. —adj. (dĕz′ĭg-nĭt). Appointed but not yet installed in office. [L *dēsignāre,* designate, mark out.] —**des′ig•na′tion** n.

de•sign•ing (dĭ-zī′nĭng) adj. Conniving.

de•sir•a•ble (dĭ-zīr′ə-bəl) adj. 1. Worth seeking or having. 2. Arousing desire. 3. Advantageous; advisable. —**de•sir′a•bil′i•ty** n.

de•sire (dĭ-zīr′) v. -sired, -siring. 1. To wish or long for; crave. 2. To express a wish for. —n. 1. A wish, longing, or craving. 2. A request.

3. Something longed for. 4. Sexual appetite.
[< L *dēsiderāre*.] —de•sir'er *n.*

de•sir•ous (dĭ-zīr'əs) *adj.* Desiring.

de•sist (dĭ-zĭst') *v.* To cease doing something;
stop. [< L *dēsistere*, cease, stand off.]

desk (dĕsk) *n.* A piece of furniture with a flat
top for writing. [< L *discus*, quoit, DISK.]

Des Moines (də moin', moinz'). The capital
of Iowa. Pop. 200,000.

des•o•late (dĕs'ə-lĭt) *adj.* 1. Devoid of inhabitants; deserted. 2. Unfit for habitation; laid
waste. 3. Cheerless; dismal; gloomy. 4. Forlorn; lonely. —*v.* (dĕs'ə-lāt') -lated, -lating. To
make desolate. [< L *dēsōlāre*, abandon.]
—des'o•late•ly *adv.*

des•o•la•tion (dĕs'ə-lā'shən) *n.* 1. The act of
rendering desolate. 2. A wasteland. 3. Loneliness; wretchedness.

de•spair (dĭ-spâr') *v.* To lose all hope. —*n.*
1. Utter lack of hope. 2. That which destroys
all hope. [< L *dēspērāre*.] —de•spair'ing•ly *adv.*

des•patch. Variant of dispatch.

des•per•a•do (dĕs'pə-rä'dō, -rä'dō) *n., pl.* -does
or -dos. A desperate, dangerous criminal.
[Pseudo-Span var of DESPERATE.]

des•per•ate (dĕs'pər-ĭt) *adj.* 1. Reckless or violent because of despair. 2. Nearly hopeless;
causing despair. 3. Extreme; very great: *desperate need.* [< L *dēspērāre*, to DESPAIR.]
—des'per•ate•ly *adv.* —des'per•ate•ness *n.*

des•per•a•tion (dĕs'pə-rä'shən) *n.* 1. The condition of being desperate. 2. Recklessness
arising from despair.

des•pi•ca•ble (dĕs'pĭ-kə-bəl, dĭ-spĭk'-) *adj.*
Deserving of contempt or disdain. [< L *dē-
spicārī*, despise.] —des'pi•ca•bly *adv.*

de•spise (dĭ-spīz') *v.* -spised, -spising. To regard with contempt or disdain. [< L *dē-
spicere*, to look down on.] —de•spis'er *n.*

de•spite (dĭ-spīt') *prep.* In spite of. [< OF
despit, spite.]

de•spoil (dĭ-spoil') *v.* To deprive of possessions by force; plunder. [< L *dēspoliāre*.]
—de•spoil'er *n.* —de•spoil'ment *n.*

de•spo•li•a•tion (dĭ-spō'lē-ā'shən) *n.* The act
of despoiling or condition of being despoiled;
plunder.

de•spond (dĭ-spŏnd') *v.* To become disheartened. [L *dēspondēre*, despond, promise to give,
give up.] —de•spond'ing•ly *adv.*

de•spon•den•cy (dĭ-spŏn'dən-sē) *n., pl.* -cies.
Also de•spon•dence (-dəns). Depression of
spirits from loss of hope or courage; dejection.
—de•spon'dent *adj.* —de•spon'dent•ly *adv.*

des•pot (dĕs'pət) *n.* An autocratic ruler; tyrant. [< Gk *despotēs*.] —des•pot'ic (dĕ-spŏt'ĭk)
adj. —des•pot'i•cal•ly *adv.* —des'pot•ism' *n.*

des•sert (dĭ-zûrt') *n.* A usually sweet food
served as the last course of a meal. [< OF
desservir, clear the table.]

des•ti•na•tion (dĕs'tə-nā'shən) *n.* 1. The place
or point to which someone or something is
going. 2. An ultimate goal or purpose.

des•tine (dĕs'tĭn) *v.* -tined, -tining. 1. To determine beforehand; preordain. 2. To intend for
or direct toward a specific end or place. [< L
dēstināre, determine, destine, make firm.]

des•ti•ny (dĕs'tə-nē) *n., pl.* -nies. 1. The pre-

ordained or inevitable course of events. 2.
One's fate; lot.

des•ti•tute (dĕs'tə-t/y/ōōt') *adj.* 1. Altogether
lacking; devoid: *destitute of courage.* 2. Very
poor; penniless. [< L *dēstituere*, to set down,
desert.] —des'ti•tu'tion *n.*

de•stroy (dĭ-stroi') *v.* 1. To put an end to; ruin
completely. 2. To tear down; demolish. 3. To
kill. [< L *dēstruere* (pp *dēstructus*).]

de•stroy•er (dĭ-stroi'ər) *n.* 1. One that destroys. 2. A small, fast warship.

de•struct (dĭ-strŭkt') *n.* The intentional destruction of a space vehicle, rocket, or missile
after launching.

de•struc•ti•ble (dĭ-strŭk'tə-bəl) *adj.* Capable
of being destroyed. —de•struc'ti•bil'i•ty *n.*

de•struc•tion (dĭ-strŭk'shən) *n.* 1. The act of
destroying or state of being destroyed. 2. A
means of destroying. —de•struc'tive *adj.* —de•
struc'tive•ly *adv.* —de•struc'tive•ness *n.*

destructive distillation. The simultaneous
decomposition by heat and distillation of substances such as wood and coal to produce
useful by-products.

des•ue•tude (dĕs'wə-t/y/ōōd') *n.* A state of
disuse. [< L *dēsuēcere*, to put out of use,
become unaccustomed.]

des•ul•to•ry (dĕs'əl-tôr'ē, -tôr'ē) *adj.* Progressing aimlessly; disconnected; haphazard. [L
dēsultōrius, of a leaper.]

det. 1. *Mil.* detachment. 2. detail.

de•tach (dĭ-tăch') *v.* To separate; remove;
disconnect. [< OF *destachier*.] —de•tach'a•ble
adj. —de•tach'a•bly *adv.*

de•tached (dĭ-tăcht') *adj.* 1. Apart from
others; separate: *a detached house.* 2. Free
from emotional involvement; disinterested.

de•tach•ment (dĭ-tăch'mənt) *n.* 1. The act of
detaching or condition of being detached;
separation. 2. Disinterest; aloofness. 3. A military unit dispatched or organized for special
duty.

de•tail (dĭ-tāl', dē'tāl) *n.* 1. An individual part
or item. 2. Itemized or minute treatment of
particulars. 3. a. A group of military personnel
selected to do a specified task. b. The task
assigned. —*v.* 1. To relate item by item. 2. To
assign (military personnel) to a specified task.
[< OF, piece cut off.]

de•tain (dĭ-tān') *v.* 1. To keep from proceeding; delay or retard. 2. To keep in custody;
confine. [< L *dētinēre*, to keep back.] —de•
tain'ment *n.*

de•tect (dĭ-tĕkt') *v.* To discover or discern the
existence, presence, or fact of. [< L *dētegere*
(pp *dētectus*), uncover.] —de•tect'a•ble, de•tect'-
i•ble *adj.* —de•tec'tion *n.* —de•tec'tor *n.*

de•tec•tive (dĭ-tĕk'tĭv) *n.* One whose work is
obtaining evidence or concealed information,
as in investigating crimes.

dé•tente (dā-tänt') *n.* A relaxing of tension, as
between nations. [F, a loosening.]

de•ten•tion (dĭ-tĕn'shən) *n.* 1. The act of de-
taining or state of being detained. 2. A period
of being kept in confinement or temporary
custody. [< L *dētinēre*, DETAIN.]

de•ter (dĭ-tûr') *v.* -terred, -terring. To prevent or
discourage (someone) from acting, as through

ă pat/ā ate/âr care/ä bar/b bib/ch chew/d deed/ĕ pet/ē be/f fit/g gag/h hat/hw what/
ĭ pit/ī pie/îr pier/j judge/k kick/l lid, fatal/m mum/n no, sudden/ng sing/ŏ pot/ō go/

doubt or fear. [L *dēterrēre*, frighten from.]
—**de•ter'ment** *n.*

de•ter•gent (dĭ-tûr'jənt) *n.* A cleansing substance, esp. one made from chemical compounds other than fats and lye. [< L *dētergēre*, to wipe off.]

de•te•ri•o•rate (dĭ-tîr'ē-ə-rāt') *v.* -rated, -rating. To become or make worse. [< L *dēterior*, worse.] —**de•te'ri•o•ra'tion** *n.*

de•ter•mi•nant (dĭ-tûr'mə-nənt) *adj.* Serving to determine. —*n.* An influencing or determining factor.

de•ter•mi•nate (dĭ-tûr'mə-nĭt) *adj.* Precisely limited or defined.

de•ter•mi•na•tion (dĭ-tûr'mə-nā'shən) *n.* 1. a. The act or process of determining or being determined. b. A decision or result thus arrived at. 2. Firmness of purpose; resoluteness.

de•ter•mine (dĭ-tûr'mĭn) *v.* -mined, -mining. 1. To decide, establish, or ascertain authoritatively or conclusively. 2. To limit or regulate. 3. To affect as a causative factor; influence. 4. To resolve firmly. [< L *dētermināre*, to limit.] —**de•ter'mi•na•ble** *adj.* —**de•ter'mi•na•bly** *adv.*

de•ter•mined (dĭ-tûr'mĭnd) *adj.* Fixed in purpose; resolute; firm. —**de•ter'mined•ly** *adv.*

de•ter•min•ism (dĭ-tûr'mə-nĭz'əm) *n.* Any philosophical doctrine asserting a mechanical correspondence between determining causes and effects.

de•ter•rent (dĭ-tûr'ənt) *adj.* Serving to deter. —*n.* That which deters. —**de•ter'rence** *n.*

de•test (dĭ-tĕst') *v.* To dislike intensely; loathe; hate. [L *dētestārī*, curse, execrate.] —**de•test'a•ble** *adj.* —**de•tes•ta'tion** *n.*

de•throne (dē-thrōn') *v.* -throned, -throning. To depose from a throne. —**de•throne'ment** *n.*

det•o•nate (dĕt'n-āt') *v.* -nated, -nating. To explode or cause to explode. [L *dētonāre*, to thunder down.] —**det'o•na•ble** *adj.* —**det'o•na'tion** *n.* —**det'o•na'tor** *n.*

de•tour (dē'tŏŏr', dĭ-tŏŏr') *n.* A roundabout way, esp. one used temporarily instead of a main route. —*v.* To go or cause to go by a detour. [< OF *destorner*, to turn away.]

de•tract (dĭ-trăkt') *v.* To reduce by taking away (from); diminish. [< L *dētrahere*, to pull down, draw away.] —**de•trac'tion** *n.* —**de•trac'tive** *adj.* —**de•trac'tor** *n.*

de•train (dē-trān') *v.* To leave or cause to leave a railroad train.

det•ri•ment (dĕt'rə-mənt) *n.* 1. Harm; disadvantage. 2. A cause of this. [< L *dēterere*, to wear away.] —**det'ri•men'tal** *adj.* —**det'ri•men'tal•ly** *adv.*

de•tri•tus (dĭ-trī'təs) *n.* Fragments formed by disintegration, as of rocks. [< L *dēterere*, to wear away.]

De•troit (dĭ-troit') A city in SE Michigan. Pop. 1,511,000.

deuce (d/y/ŏŏs) *n.* 1. A two in playing cards or dice. 2. A tied tennis score necessitating the scoring of two successive points by one side to win. 3. Euphemism for the devil. [< L *duo*, two.]

Deut. Deuteronomy (Old Testament).

deu•te•ri•um (dŏŏ-tîr'ē-əm) *n.* An isotope of

hydrogen having an atomic weight of 2.0141. [< Gk *deuteros*, second.]

deuterium oxide. An isotopic form of water with composition D_2O, present in natural water as approximately one part in 6,500.

deu•ter•on (d/y/ŏŏ'tə-rŏn) *n.* The nucleus of a deuterium atom, a composite of a proton and a neutron, regarded as a single subatomic particle. [DEUTER(IUM) + -ON.]

Deut•sche mark (doi'chə märk') Also **deut•sche•mark.** The basic monetary unit of West Germany.

de•val•u•ate (dē-văl'yŏŏ-āt') *v.* -ated, -ating. Also **de•val•ue** (-văl'yŏŏ) -ued, -uing. 1. To lower the exchange value of (currency). 2. To lessen the value of. —**de•val'u•a'tion** *n.*

dev•as•tate (dĕv'ə-stāt') *v.* -tated, -tating. 1. To lay waste. 2. To overwhelm; confound. [L *dēvāstāre.*] —**dev'as•ta'tion** *n.*

de•vel•op (dĭ-vĕl'əp) *v.* 1. To bring, grow, or evolve to a more complete, complex, or desirable state. 2. To appear, disclose, or acquire gradually. 3. To elaborate; expand. 4. To make available or usable. 5. To process (a photosensitive material) chemically in order to render a recorded image visible. [< OF *desveloper.*] —**de•vel'op•er** *n.*

de•vel•op•ment (dĭ-vĕl'əp-mənt) *n.* 1. The process or result of developing. 2. An event; occurrence: *await new developments.* 3. A group of dwellings built by the same contractor.

de•vi•ant (dē'vē-ənt) *adj.* Differing from a norm or accepted standard. —*n.* A deviant individual. —**de'vi•ance** *n.*

de•vi•ate (dē'vē-āt') *v.* -ated, -ating. To move or turn away from a normal or accepted course or standard. —*n.* (dē'vē-ĭt). A deviant, esp. a sexual pervert. [LL *dēviāre.*] —**de'vi•a'tion** *n.* —**de'vi•a'tor** *n.*

de•vice (dĭ-vīs') *n.* 1. Something, as a mechanical contrivance, made for a particular purpose. 2. A scheme; trick; artifice. 3. A decorative figure or symbol. —**leave to one's own devices.** To allow to do as one pleases. [< OF *deviser*, to divide, devise.]

dev•il (dĕv'əl) *n.* 1. a. Often **Devil.** The major spirit of evil, esp. in Christian theology. b. A demon or similar evil spirit. 2. A wicked or destructively mischievous person. 3. A dashing or daring person. 4. An unfortunate person; wretch. 5. A printer's apprentice. —*v.* -iled or -illed, -iling or -illing. 1. To annoy; torment. 2. To prepare (food) with pungent seasonings. [< Gk *diabolos*, slanderer.]

dev•il•ish (dĕv'ə-lĭsh) *adj.* 1. Of or like a devil; fiendish. 2. Excessive; extreme. —*adv. Informal.* Extremely; very.

dev•il-may-care (dĕv'əl-mā-kâr') *adj.* Reckless; careless.

dev•il•ment (dĕv'əl-mənt) *n.* Mischief.

dev•il•try (dĕv'əl-trē) *n.* Also **dev•il•ry** (-əl-rē). Reckless mischief.

de•vi•ous (dē'vē-əs) *adj.* 1. Deviating from a straight or direct course; roundabout. 2. Not straightforward; deceitful: *a devious person.* [L *dēvius*, off the main road.] —**de'vi•ous•ly** *adv.* —**de'vi•ous•ness** *n.*

ô paw, for/oi boy/ou out/ŏŏ took/ōō coo/p pop/r run/s sauce/sh shy/t to/th thin/*th* the/
ŭ cut/ûr fur/v van/w wag/y yes/z size/zh vision/ə ago, item, edible, gallop, circus/

de•vise (dĭ-vīz') *v.* **-vised, -vising. 1.** To plan; invent; contrive. **2.** To transmit (real property) by will. [< L *dīvidere* (pp *dīvīsus*), to divide.] —**de•vis'er** *n.*

de•vi•tal•ize (dē-vīt'l-īz') *v.* **-ized, -izing.** To lower or destroy the vitality of.

de•void (dĭ-void') *adj.* —**devoid of.** Completely lacking; empty. [< OF *desvuidier.*]

de•volve (dĭ-vŏlv') *v.* **-volved, -volving.** To pass or be transmitted (on) to another person, as duty or authority. [< L *dēvolvere,* to roll down.] —**de•volve'ment** *n.*

De•vo•ni•an (dĭ-vō'nē-ən) *adj.* Of or belonging to the geologic time, system of rocks, or sedimentary deposits of the 4th period of the Paleozoic era, characterized by the appearance of forests and amphibians. —*n.* The Devonian period.

de•vote (dĭ-vōt') *v.* **-voted, -voting. 1.** To give or apply (oneself, one's time, etc.) entirely. **2.** To dedicate; consecrate. [L *dēvovēre,* to vow, devote.]

de•vot•ed (dĭ-vō'tĭd) *adj.* **1.** Loving; faithful. **2.** Dedicated; zealous. —**de•vot'ed•ly** *adv.*

dev•o•tee (dĕv'ə-tē', -tā') *n.* An ardent enthusiast.

de•vo•tion (dĭ-vō'shən) *n.* **1.** Ardent attachment or affection; loyalty. **2.** Religious zeal. **3. Devotions.** Prayers, esp. personal prayers. —**de•vo'tion•al** *adj.* —**de•vo'tion•al•ly** *adv.*

de•vour (dĭ-vour') *v.* **1.** To eat up greedily. **2.** To consume or destroy; swallow up. **3.** To take in greedily with the senses or mind. [< L *dēvorāre.*] —**de•vour'er** *n.*

de•vout (dĭ-vout') *adj.* **1.** Deeply religious; reverent; pious. **2.** Sincere; earnest. [< L *dēvovēre,* to vow, DEVOTE.] —**de•vout'ly** *adv.* —**de•vout'ness** *n.*

dew (d/y/ōō) *n.* **1.** Water droplets condensed from the air, usually at night, onto cool surfaces. **2.** Something resembling or suggestive of dew. [< OE *dēaw.* See dheu-².] —**dew'i•ly** *adv.* —**dew'i•ness** *n.* —**dew'y** *adj.*

dew•lap (d/y/ōō'lăp') *n.* A fold of skin hanging from the neck of certain animals.

dew point. The temperature at which air becomes saturated and produces dew.

dex•ter•i•ty (dĕk-stĕr'ə-tē) *n.* Manual or mental skill; adroitness. [< L *dexter,* skillful, on the right side.]

dex•ter•ous (dĕk'strəs) *adj.* Also **dex•trous.** Skillful, as in manipulation; adroit. —**dex'ter•ous•ly** *adv.* —**dex'ter•ous•ness** *n.*

dex•trose (dĕk'strōs') *n.* A sugar, $C_6H_{12}O_6 \cdot H_2O$, found in animal and plant tissue and derived synthetically from starch. [< L *dexter,* on the right side.]

dg decigram.

di–. *comb. form.* Twice, double, or two. [< Gk *di-,* two, twice.]

DI didymium.

dia–, di–. *comb. form.* **1.** Through or throughout. **2.** Across or by transmission. **3.** In opposite or different directions. [< Gk *dia,* through.]

dia. diameter.

di•a•be•tes (dī'ə-bē'tĭs, -tēz) *n.* Any of several metabolic disorders marked by excessive dis-

charge of urine and persistent thirst, esp. diabetes mellitus. [< Gk *diabētēs,* "a crossing over or passing through."] —**di'a•bet'ic** (-bĕt'-ĭk) *adj. & n.*

diabetes mel•li•tus (mə-lī'təs). A chronic disease of pancreatic origin, characterized by insulin deficiency, subsequent inability to utilize carbohydrates, excess sugar in the blood and urine, weakness, emaciation, and, without injection of insulin, eventual coma and death. [NL, "honey-sweet diabetes."]

di•a•bol•ic (dī'ə-bŏl'ĭk) *adj.* Also **di•a•bol•i•cal** (-ĭ-kəl). Devilish; wicked; fiendish. [< LL *diabolus,* devil.] —**di'a•bol'i•cal•ly** *adv.*

di•a•crit•i•cal (dī'ə-krĭt'ĭ-kəl). Also **di•a•crit•ic** (-ĭk). *adj.* Marking a distinction; distinguishing. —*n.* Also **diacritical mark.** A mark added to a letter to indicate a special phonetic value. [G *diakritikos,* distinguishing.]

di•a•dem (dī'ə-dĕm') *n.* A crown or headband indicative of royalty. [< Gk *diadein,* to bind on either side.]

di•aer•e•sis. Variant of **dieresis.**

diag. 1. diagonal. **2.** diagram.

di•ag•no•sis (dī'əg-nō'sĭs) *n., pl.* **-ses** (-sēz). Identification, esp. of a disease, by examination or analysis. [< Gk *diagnōsis,* discernment.] —**di'ag•nose'** *v.* **(-nosed, -nosing).** —**di'ag•nos'tic** (-nŏs'tĭk) *adj.* —**di'ag•nos'ti•cal•ly** *adv.* —**di'ag•nos•ti'cian** *n.*

di•ag•o•nal (dī-ăg'ə-nəl) *adj.* **1.** Joining two nonadjacent vertices. **2.** Slanted or oblique in direction. —*n.* A diagonal line or plane. [< Gk *diagōnios,* from angle to angle.] —**di•ag'o•nal•ly** *adv.*

di•a•gram (dī'ə-grăm') *n.* **1.** A schematic drawing or plan devised as a graphic representation of relationships between parts of a whole. **2.** *Math.* A graphic representation of an algebraic or geometric relationship. —*v.* **-grammed** or **-gramed, -gramming** or **-graming.** To represent by a diagram. [< Gk *diagramma.*] —**di'a•gram•mat'ic, di'a•gram•mat'i•cal** *adj.* —**di'a•gram•mat'i•cal•ly** *adv.*

di•al (dī'əl) *n.* **1.** A marked disk or plate on which a measurement, as of time, speed, or temperature, is indicated by a moving pointer. **2.** A rotatable disk, as of a telephone or radio, for making connections, changing frequency, etc. —*v.* **-aled** or **-alled, -aling** or **-alling. 1.** To indicate or select by means of a dial. **2.** To call on a telephone with a dial. [< ML *diālis,* daily.] —**di'al•er, di'al•ler** *n.*

dial. dialect; dialectal.

di•a•lect (dī'ə-lĕkt') *n.* **1.** A regional variety of a spoken language. **2.** A jargon. **3.** A language considered as part of a larger group of languages: *Spanish and French are Romance dialects.* [< Gk *dialektos,* speech, language, dialect.] —**di'a•lec'tal** *adj.*

di•a•lec•tic (dī'ə-lĕk'tĭk) *n.* Also **di•a•lec•tics** (-tĭks) *(takes sing. or pl. v.).* The art or process whereby contradictions are disclosed and synthetically resolved. —**di'a•lec'ti•cal, di'a•lec'tic** *adj.*

di•a•logue (dī'ə-lôg', -lŏg') *n.* Also **di•a•log. 1.** A conversation between two or more people. **2.** Conversation material in a play or

---

ă pat/ā ate/âr care/ä bar/b bib/ch chew/d deed/ĕ pet/ē be/f fit/g gag/h hat/hw what/ ĭ pit/ī pie/îr pier/j judge/k kick/l lid, fatal/m mum/n no, sudden/ng sing/ŏ pot/ō go/

narrative. **3.** An exchange of ideas or opinions. [< Gk *dialegesthai*, to converse.]

di·al·y·sis (dī-ăl′ə-sĭs) *n., pl.* **-ses** (-sēz′). The separation of molecular or particulate constituents in a solution by selective diffusion through a semipermeable membrane. [< Gk *dialuein*, to tear apart.]

di·am·e·ter (dī-ăm′ə-tər) *n.* **1. a.** A straight line segment passing through the center of a figure, esp. of a circle or sphere, and terminating at the periphery. **b.** The length of such a segment. **2.** Thickness or width as a dimension. [< Gk *diametros (grammē)*, "(line) that measures through."] —**di′a·met′ri·cal** (-ə-mĕt′rĭ-kəl), **di′a·met′ric** *adj.* —**di′a·met′ri·cal·ly** *adv.*

dia·mond (dī′mənd, dī′ə-) *n.* **1.** An extremely hard, highly refractive colorless or white crystalline allotrope of carbon, used as a gemstone when pure and chiefly in abrasives otherwise. **2.** A rhombus or lozenge. **3.** Any of a suit of playing cards marked with a red, diamond-shaped symbol. **4.** A baseball infield or playing field. [< LL *diamas (diamant-)*.]

Di·an·a (dī-ăn′ə). Roman goddess; patroness of women and wild animals.

di·a·pa·son (dī′ə-pā′sən, -zən) *n.* **1.** A full tonal range, as of an instrument or voices. **2.** One of two organ stops that establish tonal range. [< Gk *(hē) dia pasōn (khordōn sumphonia)*, (concord) through all (the notes).]

di·a·per (dī′ə-pər, dī′pər) *n.* A folded cloth or similar piece of absorbent material, used to cover the genital and anal areas of a baby. —*v.* To put a diaper on (a baby). [ME *diapre*, linen cloth with diamond pattern.]

di·aph·a·nous (dī-ăf′ə-nəs) *adj.* Delicately transparent or translucent; gauzy. [< Gk *diaphanein*, to show through.]

di·a·pho·ret·ic (dī′ə-fə-rĕt′ĭk) *adj.* Producing perspiration. —*n.* A diaphoretic medicine or agent.

di·a·phragm (dī′ə-frăm′) *n.* **1.** A muscular membranous partition separating the abdominal and thoracic cavities and functioning in respiration. **2.** Any similar membranous part that divides or separates. **3.** A thin disk, esp. in a microphone or telephone receiver, the vibrations of which convert electric to acoustic signals or acoustic to electric signals. **4.** A contraceptive consisting of a flexible disk that covers the uterine cervix. **5.** A disk having a fixed or variable opening used to restrict the amount of light traversing a lens or optical system. [< Gk *diaphrassein*, to barricade.]

di·ar·rhe·a (dī′ə-rē′ə) *n.* Also **di·ar·rhoe·a**. Pathologically excessive evacuation of watery feces. [< Gk *diarrhoia*, "a flowing through."]

di·a·ry (dī′ə-rē) *n., pl.* **-ries.** **1.** A daily record, esp. of personal experiences and observations. **2.** A book for keeping such a record. [L *diarium*, daily allowance, journal.] —**di′a·rist** *n.*

di·as·to·le (dī-ăs′tə-lē) *n.* The normal rhythmically occurring relaxation and dilatation of the heart cavities during which the cavities are filled with blood. [Gk *diastolē*, dilatation, separation.] —**di′a·stol′ic** (dī′ə-stŏl′ĭk) *adj.*

di·a·ther·my (dī′ə-thûr′mē) *n.* The therapeutic

generation of local heat in body tissues by high-frequency electromagnetic waves. —**di′a·ther′mic** *adj.*

di·a·tom (dī′ə-tŏm′, -təm) *n.* Any of various minute, unicellular algae with hard, glasslike cell walls. [< Gk *diatomos*, cut in half.]

di·a·tom·ic (dī′ə-tŏm′ĭk) *adj.* **1.** Made up of two atoms. **2.** Having two replaceable atoms or radicals.

di·a·ton·ic (dī′ə-tŏn′ĭk) *adj.* Of or pertaining to the eight tones of a standard major or minor scale. —**di′a·ton′i·cal·ly** *adv.*

di·a·tribe (dī′ə-trīb′) *n.* A bitter and abusive verbal attack. [< Gk *diatribē*, "a wearing away," "pastime."]

dib·ble (dĭb′əl) *n.* A pointed implement used to make holes in soil, as for planting bulbs. [ME *debylle*.]

dice (dīs) *pl.n. Sing.* **die** (dī). Small cubes marked on each side with from one to six dots, used in gambling games. —*v.* **diced, dicing.** **1.** To cut into small cubes. **2.** To gamble with dice. [Pl of DIE².] —**dic′er** *n.*

di·chot·o·my (dī-kŏt′ə-mē) *n., pl.* **-mies.** Division into two usually contradictory parts or categories. [< Gk *dikhotomos*, divided.] —**di·chot′o·mous** *adj.* —**di·chot′o·mous·ly** *adv.*

dick (dĭk) *n. Slang.* A detective.

dick·ens (dĭk′ənz). Euphemism for the devil.

Dick·ens (dĭk′ənz), **Charles.** 1812–1870. English novelist.

dick·er (dĭk′ər) *v.* To bargain; haggle. [Prob < earlier *dicker*, ten, ten hides.]

dick·ey (dĭk′ē) *n., pl.* **-eys.** Also **dick·y** *pl.* **-ies.** **1.** A detachable blouse or shirt front. **2.** Often **dickeybird.** Any small bird. [< *Dick*, nickname for Richard.]

Dick test (dĭk). A test of susceptibility to scarlet fever. [< G. *Dick* (born 1881), American physician.]

di·cot·y·le·don (dī′kŏt′l-ēd′n) *n.* Also **di·cot** (dī′kŏt). A plant with a pair of embryonic seed leaves that appear at germination. [DI- + COTYLEDON.] —**di′cot·y·le′don·ous** *adj.*

dict. dictionary.

dic·tate (dĭk′tāt′, dĭk-tāt′) *v.* **-tated, -tating.** **1.** To say or read aloud for recording or transcription. **2.** To issue (a command, order, etc.) authoritatively. —*n.* (dĭk′tāt′). A directive or command. [L *dictāre*, freq of *dīcere*, to say, tell.] —**dic·ta′tion** *n.*

dic·ta·tor (dĭk′tā-tər) *n.* **1.** A ruler having absolute governmental authority, esp. one considered tyrannical or oppressive. **2.** One who dictates. —**dic·ta′tor·ship′** *n.*

dic·ta·to·ri·al (dĭk′tə-tôr′ē-əl, -tōr′ē-əl) *adj.* Characteristic of or pertaining to a dictator; autocratic; highhanded. —**dic′ta·to′ri·al·ly** *adv.* —**dic′ta·to′ri·al·ness** *n.*

dic·tion (dĭk′shən) *n.* **1.** Choice and use of words in speech or writing. **2.** Distinctness of speech; enunciation. [< L *dīcere*, to say.]

dic·tion·ar·y (dĭk′shə-nĕr′ē) *n., pl.* **-ies.** A reference book containing an alphabetical list of words with definitions or equivalent translations into another language. [< L *dictiō*, diction.]

dic·tum (dĭk′təm) *n., pl.* **-ta** (-tə) or **-tums.** An authoritatively stated pronouncement or opinion. [< L *dicere,* say.]

did (dĭd). *p.t.* of do.

di·dac·tic (dī-dăk′tĭk) *adj.* **1.** Intended to provide instruction, esp. moral instruction. **2.** Inclined to moralize. [Gk *didaktikos,* skillful in teaching.] —**di·dac′ti·cal·ly** *adv.*

did·dle (dĭd′l) *v.* **-dled, -dling. 1.** To cheat; swindle. **2.** To waste time; dawdle. [Prob < Jeremy *Diddler,* a dawdling character in *Raising the Wind* (1803), a farce by J. Kenney.]

did·n't (dĭd′ənt). Contraction of *did not.*

di·do (dī′dō) *n., pl.* **-dos** or **-does.** A mischievous prank; caper. [?]

Di·do (dī′dō). Princess of Tyre; reputed founder of Carthage.

didst (dĭdst). *Archaic.* 2nd person sing. *p.t.* of do.

di·dym·i·um (dī-dĭm′ē-əm) *n. Symbol* **Di** **1.** A metallic mixture, once considered an element, composed of neodymium and praseodymium. **2.** A mixture of rare-earth elements and oxides used chiefly in manufacturing and coloring various forms of glass. [< Gk *didumos,* twin.]

die¹ (dī) *v.* **died, dying. 1.** To cease living; expire. **2.** To pass out of existence. **3.** To become faint, weak, or inoperative; subside. **4.** To desire greatly; long: *dying to go.* [< ON *deyja.*]

die² (dī) *n.* **1.** A device used for cutting out, forming, or stamping material. **2.** *Sing.* of **dice.** [< VL *datum,* "playing piece."]

die-hard (dī′härd′) *n.* Also **die·hard.** One who stubbornly resists change.

di·e·lec·tric (dī′ə-lĕk′trĭk) *n.* A nonconductor of electricity. [DI(A)- + ELECTRIC.] —**di′e·lec′tric** *adj.* —**di′e·lec′tri·cal·ly** *adv.*

di·er·e·sis (dī-ĕr′ə-sĭs, dī-îr′-) *n., pl.* **-ses** (-sēz′). Also **di·aer·e·sis. 1.** The pronunciation of adjacent vowels as separate syllables. **2.** A mark (¨) placed over a vowel to indicate this. [< Gk *diairesis,* separation.]

die·sel engine (dē′zəl, -səl). An internal-combustion engine that uses the heat of highly compressed air to ignite a spray of fuel introduced after the start of the compression stroke. [< R. *Diesel* (1858–1913), German inventor.]

di·et¹ (dī′ət) *n.* **1.** One's usual food and drink; sustenance. **2.** A restricted, often medically prescribed selection of food, as for controlling weight. —*v.* To eat according to a prescribed regimen. [< Gk *diaita,* mode of life, regimen, diet.] —**di′e·tar′y** (dī′ə-tĕr′ē) *adj.* —**di′et·er** *n.*

di·et² (dī′ət) *n.* A legislative assembly. [ME *diete,* day's journey, day for meeting.]

di·e·tet·ic (dī′ə-tĕt′ĭk) *adj.* Of or for a restricted nutritional diet. —*n.* **dietetics** *(takes sing. v.).* The study of diet and nutrition.

di·e·ti·tian (dī′ə-tĭsh′ən) *n.* Also **di·e·ti·cian.** A specialist in dietetics.

diff. difference; different.

dif·fer (dĭf′ər) *v.* **1.** To be unlike; show dissimilarity. **2.** To disagree; dissent. [< L *differre,* to be different.]

dif·fer·ence (dĭf′ər-əns, dĭf′rəns) *n.* **1.** The fact, condition, or degree of being different; dissimilarity. **2.** Distinction in choosing. **3.** A

disagreement; quarrel. **4. a.** The amount by which one quantity is greater or less than another. **b.** The amount that remains after one quantity is subtracted from another; remainder.

dif·fer·ent (dĭf′ə-rənt, dĭf′rənt) *adj.* **1.** Unlike; dissimilar. **2.** Not the same; another. **3.** Unusual; distinctive. —**dif′fer·ent·ly** *adv.*

Usage: Different from is considered preferable to *different than,* especially when what follows it is a single word or a short phrase or clause: *This exhibit is different from that* (or *different from what we expected*). *Different than* is appropriate, as an aid to conciseness, where *different from* would be clumsy: *How different things seem now than yesterday.*

dif·fer·en·tial (dĭf′ə-rĕn′shəl) *adj.* **1.** Pertaining to, showing, or constituting a difference; distinctive. **2.** Dependent on or making use of a difference. —*n. Math.* **1.** An infinitesimal increment in a variable. **2.** The product of the derivative of a function of one variable multiplied by the independent variable increment. —**dif′fer·en′tial·ly** *adv.*

differential gear. An arrangement of gears permitting the rotation of two shafts at different speeds, used on the rear axle of automotive vehicles to allow different rates of wheel rotation on curves.

dif·fer·en·ti·ate (dĭf′ə-rĕn′shē-āt′) *v.* **-ated, -ating. 1.** To constitute or perceive a difference; distinguish. **2.** To make or become different or distinct, as by modification. —**dif′fer·en′ti·a′tion** *n.*

dif·fi·cult (dĭf′ĭ-kŭlt′, -kəlt) *adj.* **1.** Hard to do, achieve, or comprehend; not easy. **2.** Hard to manage or satisfy. —**dif′fi·cult·ly** *adv.*

dif·fi·cul·ty (dĭf′ĭ-kŭl′tē, -kəl-tē) *n., pl.* **-ties. 1.** The fact or condition of being difficult. **2.** Arduous effort or trouble. **3.** A cause or state of trouble. [< L *difficultās.*]

dif·fi·dent (dĭf′ə-dənt, -dĕnt′) *adj.* Lacking self-confidence; timid. [< L *diffidere,* to mistrust.] —**dif′fi·dence** *n.* —**dif′fi·dent·ly** *adv.*

dif·fract (dĭ-frăkt′) *v.* To cause or undergo diffraction. —**dif·frac′tive** *adj.*

dif·frac·tion (dĭ-frăk′shən) *n.* Modification of the behavior of light or of other waves resulting from limitation of their lateral extent, as by an obstacle or aperture. [< L *diffringere,* to break to pieces.]

dif·fuse (dĭ-fyōōz′) *v.* **-fused, -fusing. 1.** To pour out, spread, and disperse. **2.** To be or cause to be widely dispersed. [< L *diffusus,* pp of *diffundere,* to pour out, spread.] —**dif·fuse′** (-fyōōs′) *adj.* —**dif·fu′sion** *n.*

dig (dĭg) *v.* **dug, digging. 1.** To break up, turn over, or remove (soil or something similar) with a tool. **2.** *Slang.* To understand or enjoy. —**dig in. 1.** To entrench. **2.** To begin to work. —**dig up.** To extract or reveal by digging or searching. —*n.* **1.** A poke: *a dig in the ribs.* **2.** A gibe. **3.** An archaeological excavation. **4.** **digs.** *Chiefly Brit.* Lodgings. [< OF *diguer,* "to make a dike or ditch."]

dig. digest (compilation).

di·gam·ma (dī-găm′ə) *n.* A rare Greek letter, representing *w.*

---

di·gest (dǐ-jěst′, dī-) v. **1.** To transform food into an assimilable condition, as by chemical and muscular action in the alimentary canal. **2.** To absorb mentally. **3.** To organize summarily. —n. (dī′jěst′). A synopsis of textual materials or data. [< L *dīgerere* (pp *dīgestus*), to divide, distribute, digest.] —**di·gest′i·ble** adj. —**di·ges′tion** n. —**di·ges′tive** adj.

digestive system. The alimentary canal together with accessory glands including the salivary glands, liver, and pancreas, regarded as an integrated system responsible for digestion.

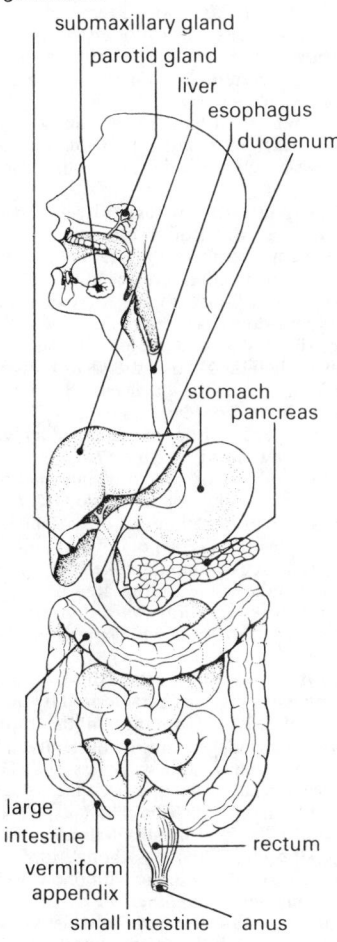

gallbladder
submaxillary gland
parotid gland
liver
esophagus
duodenum

stomach
pancreas

large
intestine
vermiform
appendix
rectum
small intestine
anus

digestive system

dig·ger (dǐg′ər) n. **1.** One that digs. **2.** *Informal.* An Australian or New Zealander.

dig·gings (dǐg′ǐngz) pl.n. **1.** An excavation site. **2.** *Chiefly Brit.* Lodgings.

dig·it (dǐj′ǐt) n. **1.** A finger or toe. **2.** The breadth of a finger, used as a unit of length, equal to about ¾ inch. **3.** Any one of the ten

Arabic number symbols, 0 through 9. [< L *digitus,* finger.] —**dig′i·tal** (dǐj′ə-təl) adj.

digital computer. A computer that performs operations with quantities represented electronically as digits.

dig·i·tal·is (dǐj′ə-tǎl′ǐs) n. A drug prepared from the seeds and leaves of the foxglove, used as a cardiac stimulant. [< L *digitus,* DIGIT.]

dig·ni·fied (dǐg′nə-fīd′) adj. Having or expressing dignity. —**dig′ni·fied′ly** adv.

dig·ni·fy (dǐg′nə-fī′) v. **-fied, -fying.** To give dignity to. [< LL *dignificāre.*]

dig·ni·tar·y (dǐg′nə-těr′ē) n., pl. **-ies.** A person of high rank.

dig·ni·ty (dǐg′nə-tē) n., pl. **-ties. 1. a.** Impressively honorable or appropriate behavior, manner, or quality. **b.** Inherent nobility and worth: *the dignity of labor.* **2.** A high rank. [< L *dignus,* worthy.]

di·graph (dī′grăf) n. A pair of letters, sometimes run together, representing a single speech sound, as *ph* in *pheasant* or *œ* in Old English *œfre,* "ever." [DI- + -GRAPH.]

di·gress (dǐ-grěs′, dī-) v. To stray from the main subject. [L *dīgredī* (pp *dīgressus*), to go aside.] —**di·gres′sion** n. —**di·gres′sive** adj.

dike (dīk) n. Also **dyke. 1.** An embankment, such as a levee. **2.** A ditch or channel. [< OE *dīc,* moat, ditch. See **dhīgw-.**] —**dik′er** n.

dil. dilute (weak).

Di·lan·tin (dī-lăn′tĭn) n. A trademark for a drug used to treat epilepsy.

di·lap·i·dat·ed (dī-lăp′ə-dā′tĭd) adj. Fallen into a state of disrepair; broken-down. [< L *dīlapidāre,* to throw away.] —**di·lap′i·da′tion** n.

di·late (dī-lāt′, dī′lāt′, dĭ-lāt′) v. **-lated, -lating.** To make or become wider or larger; expand. [< L *dīlātāre,* to enlarge, extend.] —**di·la′tion, dil′a·ta′tion** n. —**di·la′tive** adj.

dil·a·to·ry (dĭl′ə-tôr′ē, -tōr′ē) adj. Tending to delay. [< L *dīlātor,* delayer.]

di·lem·ma (dĭ-lĕm′ə) n. A choice between two equal alternatives. [< Gk *dilēmma,* ambiguous proposition.]

dil·et·tante (dĭl′ə-tänt′, -tän′tē, -tănt′, -tăn′tē, dĭl′ə-tänt′) n., pl. **-tantes** or **-tanti** (-tän′tē, -tăn′-tē). A dabbler in the arts. [It *dilettante,* "amateur."] —**dil′et·tan′tish** adj.

dil·i·gence (dĭl′ə-jəns) n. Persistent, attentive, and energetic application to a task. [< L *dīligere,* "to single out," esteem highly.] —**dil′i·gent** adj. —**dil′i·gent·ly** adv.

dill (dĭl) n. An herb with aromatic leaves and seeds used as seasoning. [< OE *dile* < Gmc **dilja.*]

dil·ly (dĭl′ē) n., pl. **-lies.** *Slang.* Something remarkable. [Poss < DELIGHTFUL.]

dil·ly-dal·ly (dĭl′ē-dăl′ē) v. **-lied, -lying. 1.** To waste time; dawdle. **2.** To vacillate. [Redupl of DALLY.]

di·lute (dī-lōōt′, dǐ-) v. **-luted, -luting.** To reduce the concentration of. —adj. Weakened; diluted. [L *dīluere,* to wash away, dilute.] —**di·lut′er** n. —**di·lu′tion** n.

dim (dǐm) adj. **dimmer, dimmest. 1. a.** Faintly lighted. **b.** Shedding a small amount of light. **2. a.** Gloomy. **b.** Lacking luster; dull. **3.** Indistinct; obscure. **4.** Lacking keenness or

---

ô paw, for/oi boy/ou out/ōō took/ōō coo/p pop/r run/s sauce/sh shy/t to/th thin/*th* the/
ŭ cut/ûr fur/v van/w wag/y yes/z size/zh vision/ə ago, item, edible, gallop, circus/

dim. / diploma

vigor. —*v.* **dimmed, dimming.** To make or become dim. [< OE *dimm* < Gmc **dim-*.] —**dim′ly** *adv.* —**dim′ness** *n.*

dim. **1.** dimension. **2.** diminished. **3.** diminutive.

dime (dīm) *n.* A U.S. or Canadian coin worth ten cents. [< L *decima (pars),* tenth (part), tithe.]

di·men·sion (dĭ-mĕn′shən) *n.* **1.** A measure of spatial extent, esp. width, height, or length. **2.** Often **dimensions.** Extent; magnitude; size; scope. **3. a.** Any of the least number of independent coordinates required to specify a point in space uniquely. **b.** A physical property, often mass, length, time, or some combination thereof, regarded as a fundamental measure. [< L *dīmēnsiō,* "a measuring."] —**di·men′sion·al** *adj.*

di·min·ish (dĭ-mĭn′ĭsh) *v.* **1.** To make or become smaller or less important. **2.** To taper. [< L *dē-,* from + *minuere,* to lessen.] —**di·min′ish·ment** *n.*

di·min·u·en·do (dĭ-mĭn′yōō-ĕn′dō) *n., pl.* **-dos** or **-does.** *Mus.* Decrescendo. [It, "diminishing."] —**di·min′u·en′do** *adj. & adv.*

dim·i·nu·tion (dĭm′ə-n/yōō′shən) *n.* The act, process, or result of diminishing.

di·min·u·tive (dĭ-mĭn′yə-tĭv) *adj.* **1.** Small. **2.** Denoting smallness or endearment, as the diminutive suffix *-let* in the word *booklet.* [< L *dēminuere,* diminish.]

dim·i·ty (dĭm′ə-tē) *n., pl.* **-ties.** A sheer, crisp cotton fabric, usually corded or checked. [< MGk *dimitos,* double-threaded.]

dim·mer (dĭm′ər) *n.* A rheostat or other device used to reduce the intensity of illumination continuously.

dim·ple (dĭm′pəl) *n.* **1.** A small natural indentation in the flesh, esp. on a chin or cheek. **2.** Any slight depression in a surface. —*v.* **-pled, -pling.** To form dimples, as by smiling. [< OE **dympel,* pool, dimple.]

dim·wit (dĭm′wĭt′) *n. Slang.* A fool. —**dim′wit′ted** *adj.* —**dim′wit′ted·ness** *n.*

din (dĭn) *n.* A medley of resounding and discordant noises. —*v.* **dinned, dinning.** —**din into.** To impress by wearying repetition: *din an idea into one's head.* [< OE *dyne.* See **dhwen-.**]

di·nar (dĭ-när′, dē′när′) *n.* The basic monetary unit of Iraq, Jordan, Kuwait, Southern Yemen, Algeria, Tunisia, and Yugoslavia. [Ar *dīnār.*]

dine (dīn) *v.* **dined, dining. 1.** To eat dinner. **2.** To give dinner to. [< VL **disjējūnāre,* to break one's fast.]

din·er (dī′nər) *n.* **1.** A person eating dinner. **2.** A railroad dining car. **3.** A restaurant like a railroad dining car.

di·nette (dī-nĕt′) *n.* A nook or alcove for meals.

din·ghy (dĭng′ē) *n., pl.* **-ghies.** Any small rowboat. [Hindi *dĭngī.*]

din·gy (dĭn′jē) *adj.* **-gier, -giest. 1.** Darkened with smoke and grime; dirty. **2.** Drab in color or appearance. **3.** Shabby; worn. —**din′gi·ly** *adv.* —**din′gi·ness** *n.*

dink·y (dĭng′kē) *adj.* **-ier, -iest. 1.** *Informal.* Of small size or consequence; insignificant. **2.**

Brit. Informal. Dainty; cute. [Prob < Scot *dink,* trim, neat.]

din·ner (dĭn′ər) *n.* **1.** The chief meal of the day, eaten at the noon hour or in the evening. **2.** banquet. [< OF *disner,* dine.]

dinner jacket. A tuxedo.

di·no·saur (dī′nə-sôr′) *n.* Any of various extinct, often gigantic reptiles of the Mesozoic era. [< Gk *deinos,* fearful, monstrous + -SAUR.]

dint (dĭnt) *n.* **1.** Force or effort; power; exertion: *by dint of hard work.* **2.** A dent. —*v.* To dent. [< OE *dynt.*]

di·o·cese (dī′ə-sĭs, -sēs′, -sēz′) *n.* The district or churches under the jurisdiction of a bishop. [< Gk *dioikēsis,* "housekeeping," administration.] —**di·oc′e·san** (dī-ŏs′ə-sən) *adj.*

di·ode (dī′ōd′) *n.* Any electronic device that restricts current flow chiefly to one direction. [DI- + -ODE.]

Di·o·nys·i·an (dī′ə-nĭsh′ən, -nĭzh′ən, -nĭs′ē-ən) *adj.* **1.** Of or relating to Dionysus. **2.** Often **dionysian.** Of an ecstatic, orgiastic, or irrational character.

Di·o·ny·sus (dī′ə-nī′səs). Greek god of wine and of an orgiastic nature cult.

di·o·ram·a (dī′ə-răm′ə, -rä′mə) *n.* A three-dimensional miniature scene.

di·ox·ide (dī-ŏk′sīd′) *n.* An oxide with two oxygen atoms per molecule.

dip (dĭp) *v.* **dipped, dipping. 1.** To plunge briefly into a liquid. **2.** To immerse in a disinfectant solution, as cattle or sheep. **3.** To scoop up (liquid). **4.** To lower and raise (a flag) in salute. **5.** To drop or sink suddenly. **6.** To slope downward; decline. **7.** To look casually into a subject or source of information. —*n.* **1.** A brief plunge or immersion. **2.** A smooth creamed preparation, as of softened cheese, into which crackers, potato chips, etc., can be dipped. **3.** An amount taken up by dipping. **4.** A candle made by repeated dipping in tallow or wax. **5.** A downward slope or sloping; a decline. **6.** A hollow; depression. [< OE *dyppan.* See **dheub-.**]

diph·the·ri·a (dĭf-thîr′ē-ə, dĭp-) *n.* An acute contagious disease characterized by the formation of false membranes in the throat and other air passages, causing difficulty in breathing, high fever, and weakness. [< Gk *diphthera,* piece of leather (< the rough false membrane).] —**diph′the·rit′ic** (-thə-rĭt′ĭk), **diph·ther′ic** (-thĕr′ĭk), **diph·the·ri·al** *adj.*

diph·thong (dĭf′thông′, -thŏng′, dĭp′-) *n.* **1.** A speech sound beginning with one vowel sound and moving to another vowel or semivowel position within the same syllable, as *oy* in the word *boy.* **2.** Either of the two Latin ligatures *æ* or *œ.* [< Gk *diphthongos.*]

dipl. diplomat; diplomatic.

dip·loid (dĭp′loid′) *adj.* **1.** Double or twofold. **2.** Having a homologous pair of chromosomes for each characteristic except sex, the total number of chromosomes being twice that of a gamete. [< Gk *diploos,* double.]

di·plo·ma (dĭ-plō′mə) *n.* **1.** A document issued by a university or other school testifying that a student has earned a degree or completed a

ă pat/ā ate/âr care/ä bar/b bib/ch chew/d deed/ĕ pet/ē be/f fit/g gag/h hat/hw what/ ĭ pit/ī pie/îr pier/j judge/k kick/l lid, fatal/m mum/n no, sudden/ng sing/ŏ pot/ō go/

course of study. **2.** A certificate conferring an honor. [< Gk *diplōma,* something doubled, folded paper.]

di•plo•ma•cy (dĭ-plō'mə-sē) *n., pl.* **-cies. 1.** The art, practice, or profession of conducting international relations. **2.** Tact or skill in dealing with people.

dip•lo•mat (dĭp'lə-măt') *n.* **1.** One appointed to represent his government in its relations with other governments. **2.** One who possesses skill in dealing with others.

dip•lo•mat•ic (dĭp'lə-măt'ĭk) *adj.* **1.** Of or relating to diplomacy. **2.** Characterized by tact in dealing with people. [< L *diplōma,* document.] **—dip'lo•mat'i•cal•ly** *adv.*

di•plo•ma•tist (dĭ-plō'mə-tĭst) *n.* A diplomat.

di•pole (dī'pōl') *n.* **1.** A pair of electric charges or magnetic poles, of equal magnitude but of opposite sign or polarity, separated by a small distance. **2.** An antenna, usually fed from the center, consisting of two equal rods extending outward in a straight line.

dip•per (dĭp'ər) *n.* **1.** One that dips. **2.** A container used for dipping, such as a long-handled cup for taking up water.

dip•py (dĭp'ē) *adj.* **-pier, -piest.** *Slang.* Foolish. [?]

dip•so•ma•ni•a (dĭp'sə-mā'nē-ə, -măn'yə) *n.* An insatiable craving for alcoholic liquors. [< Gk *dipsa,* thirst + -MANIA.] **—dip'so•ma'ni•ac** *adj. & n.*

dip•tych (dĭp'tĭk) *n.* A pair of painted or carved panels hinged together. [< Gk *diptukhos,* double-folded.]

dir. director.

dire (dīr) *adj.* **direr, direst. 1.** Dreadful and threatening. **2.** Disastrous. **3.** Ominous. [L *dīrus,* fearful, ill-omened.] **—dire'ly** *adv.*

di•rect (dĭ-rĕkt', dī-) *v.* **1.** To conduct the affairs of; manage. **2.** To take charge of with authority; control. **3.** To conduct (musicians) in a rehearsal or performance. **4.** To aim, guide, or address (something or someone) toward a goal. **5.** To give interpretative dramatic supervision to the actors in a play or film. *—adj.* **1.** Proceeding or lying in a straight course or line. **2.** Straightforward. **3.** Without intervening persons, conditions, or agencies; immediate. **4.** By action of voters, rather than through elected delegates. **5.** Absolute; total: *direct opposites.* **6.** Receiving the action of a transitive verb: *direct object.* **7.** Varying in the same manner as another quantity, esp. increasing if another quantity increases or decreasing if it decreases. *—adv.* In a direct manner; straight; directly. [< L *dīrigere* (pp *dīrectus*), to arrange in distinct lines, direct.]

direct current. An electric current flowing in one direction.

di•rec•tion (dĭ-rĕk'shən, dī-) *n.* **1.** The act or function of directing. **2.** Often **directions.** An instruction or series of instructions for doing something. **3.** A command. **4. a.** The distance-independent relationship between two points that specifies the angular position of either with respect to the other. **b.** A position to which motion or another position is referred. **c.** The line or course along which a person or thing moves. **5.** Tendency toward a particular end or goal.

di•rec•tion•al (dĭ-rĕk'shən-əl, dī-) *adj.* Of or pertaining to spatial direction. **—di•rec'tion•al'i•ty** *n.*

di•rec•tive (dĭ-rĕk'tĭv, dī-) *n.* An order or instruction.

di•rect•ly (dĭ-rĕkt'lē, dī-) *adv.* **1.** In a direct line or manner. **2.** Without anyone or anything intervening. **3.** Exactly; totally. **4.** Instantly.

di•rec•tor (dĭ-rĕk'tər, dī-) *n.* **1.** A manager. **2.** The interpretative supervisor of actors in a play or film or musicians in an orchestra or chorus. **—di•rec'tor•ship'** *n.*

di•rec•to•ry (dĭ-rĕk'tə-rē, dī-) *n., pl.* **-ries.** A book listing names and addresses.

dirge (dûrj) *n.* A funeral hymn or lament. [ME *dirige.*]

dir•ham (də-răm') *n.* The basic monetary unit of Morocco. [Ar.]

dir•i•gi•ble (dĭr'ə-jə-bəl, dĭ-rĭj'ə-bəl) *n.* A steerable lighter-than-air craft. [< L *dīrigere,* to guide, DIRECT.]

ô paw, for/oi boy/ou out/ŏŏ took/ōō coo/p pop/r run/s sauce/sh shy/t to/th thin/*th* the/ ŭ cut/ûr fur/v van/w wag/y yes/z size/zh vision/ə ago, item, edible, gallop, circus/

dirk (dûrk) *n.* A kind of dagger. [Earlier *durk, dork.*]

dirn·dl (dûrnd′l) *n.* A full-skirted dress with a tight bodice. [G.]

dirt (dûrt) *n.* **1.** Earth or soil. **2.** A soiling substance, such as mud, dust, or excrement. **3.** Something contemptible or vile. **4.** *Informal.* Malicious or scandalous gossip. **5.** Gravel, slag, or other material from which metal is extracted in mining. —*adj.* Made of dirt. [< ON *drit* < Gmc *drit-.*]

dirt·y (dûr′tē) *adj.* **-ier, -iest. 1.** Soiled, as with dirt. **2.** Obscene. **3.** Contemptibly contrary to honor or rules. **4.** Of a clouded or muddy appearance. **5.** Producing an excessive amount of radioactive fallout. **6.** Stormy: *dirty weather.* —*v.* **-ied, -ying.** To make or become soiled. —**dirt′i·ly** *adv.* —**dirt′i·ness** *n.*

dis-. *comb. form.* **1.** Negation, lack, invalidation, or deprivation. **2.** Reversal. **3.** Removal or rejection. [< L *dis,* apart, asunder.]

dis·a·bil·i·ty (dĭs′ə-bĭl′ə-tē) *n., pl.* **-ties. 1.** A disabled condition; incapacity. **2.** Something that disables or disqualifies.

dis·a·ble (dĭs-ā′bəl) *v.* **-bled, -bling. 1.** To weaken or cripple. **2.** To disqualify legally.

dis·a·buse (dĭs′ə-byōōz′) *v.* **-bused, -busing.** To free from a misconception; undeceive.

dis·ad·van·tage (dĭs′əd-văn′tĭj, -vän′tĭj) *n.* **1.** An unfavorable condition or circumstance; handicap. **2.** Detriment. —**dis·ad′van·ta′geous** *adj.* —**dis·ad′van·ta′geous·ly** *adv.*

dis·ad·van·taged (dĭs′əd-văn′tĭjd, -vän′tĭjd) *adj.* Poor.

dis·af·fect (dĭs′ə-fĕkt′) *v.* To cause to lose affection or loyalty; alienate. —**dis·af′fect′ed** *adj.* —**dis·af′fect′ed·ly** *adv.* —**dis·af·fec′tion** *n.*

dis·a·gree (dĭs′ə-grē′) *v.* **-greed, -greeing. 1.** To be different or inconsistent; fail to correspond. **2.** To have a different opinion; dissent. **3.** To dispute. **4.** To cause adverse effects. —**dis′a·gree′ment** *n.*

dis·a·gree·a·ble (dĭs′ə-grē′ə-bəl) *adj.* **1.** Unpleasant; offensive. **2.** Bad-tempered. —**dis′·a·gree′a·bly** *adv.*

dis·al·low (dĭs′ə-lou′) *v.* **1.** To refuse to allow. **2.** To reject as invalid, untrue, or improper.

dis·ap·pear (dĭs′ə-pîr′) *v.* **1.** To pass out of sight either suddenly or gradually; vanish. **2.** To become extinct. —**dis′ap·pear′ance** *n.*

dis·ap·point (dĭs′ə-point′) *v.* **1.** To fail to satisfy the hope, desire, or expectation of. **2.** To thwart. [ME *disappointen,* to remove from office, dispossess.] —**dis′ap·point′ing·ly** *adv.*

dis·ap·point·ment (dĭs′ə-point′mənt) *n.* **1. a.** The act of disappointing. **b.** The condition or feeling of being disappointed. **2.** One that disappoints.

dis·ap·pro·ba·tion (dĭs-ăp′rə-bā′shən) *n.* Disapproval.

dis·ap·prov·al (dĭs′ə-prōō′vəl) *n.* The act of disapproving; censure.

dis·ap·prove (dĭs′ə-prōōv′) *v.* **-proved, -proving. 1.** To have an unfavorable opinion (of). **2.** To refuse to approve.

dis·arm (dĭs-ärm′) *v.* **1.** To deprive of weapons. **2.** To render helpless or harmless. **3.** To overcome the hostility of. **4.** To reduce one's armaments or armed forces.

dis·ar·ma·ment (dĭs-är′mə-mənt) *n.* The reduction of armaments and armed forces by a government.

dis·arm·ing (dĭs-är′mĭng) *adj.* Tending to remove hostility; winning. —**dis·arm′ing·ly** *adv.*

dis·ar·range (dĭs′ə-rānj′) *v.* **-ranged, -ranging.** To upset the arrangement of. —**dis′ar·range′ment** *n.*

dis·ar·ray (dĭs′ə-rā′) *n.* **1.** A state of disorder; confusion. **2.** Disordered or insufficient dress. —*v.* To throw into confusion.

dis·as·so·ci·ate (dĭs′ə-sō′shē-āt′, -sē-āt′) *v.* **-ated, -ating.** To dissociate.

dis·as·ter (dĭ-zăs′tər, -zăs′tər) *n.* **1. a.** An occurrence inflicting widespread destruction and distress. **b.** A grave misfortune. **2.** A total failure. [< It *disastro,* "ill-starred."]

dis·as·trous (dĭ-zăs′trəs, -zăs′trəs) *adj.* Calamitous; ruinous. —**dis·as′trous·ly** *adv.*

dis·a·vow (dĭs′ə-vou′) *v.* To disclaim knowledge of, responsibility for, or association with; disown. —**dis′a·vow′al** *n.*

dis·band (dĭs-bănd′) *v.* To disperse or be dispersed. —**dis·band′ment** *n.*

dis·bar (dĭs-bär′) *v.* **-barred, -barring.** To expel (a lawyer) from the legal profession. —**dis·bar′ment** *n.*

---

dis′em·broil′ment *n.*

dis′em·ploy′ *v.*

dis′em·ploy′ment *n.*

dis·en·a′ble *n.*

dis′en·cour′age *v.*

dis′en·cour′age·ment *n.*

dis′en·dow′ *v.*

dis′en·dow′ment *n.*

dis′en·joy′ *v.*

dis′en·joy′ment *n.*

dis′en·roll′ *v.*

dis′en·roll′ment *n.*

dis′en·tail′ *v.*

dis′en·thrall′ *v.*

dis′en·thrall′ment *n.*

dis′en·ti′tle *v.*

dis′en·tomb′ *v.*

dis′en·tomb′ment *n.*

dis′en·trance′ *v.*

dis′en·twine′ *v.*

dis·e′qui·lib′ri·um *n.*

dis·fea′ture *v.*

dis·fel′low·ship′ *n.*

dis·for′est *v.*

dis·gar′ri·son *n. & v.*

dis·hal′low *v.*

dis·horn′ *v.*

dis′im·ag′ine *v.*

dis′im·pas′sioned *adj.*

dis′im·pris′on *v.*

dis′im·pris′on·ment *n.*

dis′im·prove′ *v.*

dis′im·prove′ment *n.*

dis′in·car′nate *adj.*

dis·in′car·na′tion *n.*

dis′in·cen′tive *n.*

dis′in·cor′po·rate′ *v.*

dis′in·cor′po·ra′tion *n.*

dis′in·fest′ *v.*

dis′in·fes·ta′tion *n.*

dis′in·flate′ *v.*

---

dis•be•lief (dĭs′bĭ-lēf′) *n.* Refusal or reluctance to believe.

dis•be•lieve (dĭs′bĭ-lēv′) *v.* **-lieved, -lieving.** To refuse to believe (in). **—dis′be•liev′er** *n.*

dis•burse (dĭs-bûrs′) *v.* **-bursed, -bursing.** To pay out, as from a fund. [OF *desbourser*.] **—dis•burse′ment, dis•bur′sal** *n.*

disc (dĭsk) *n.* **1.** Also **disk.** A phonograph record. **2.** Variant of **disk.**

disc. discount.

dis•card (dĭs-kärd′) *v.* To throw away; reject; dismiss. **—n.** (dĭs′kärd′). **1.** The act of discarding. **2.** A person or thing discarded.

dis•cern (dĭ-sûrn′, -zûrn′) *v.* **1.** To perceive (something obscure or concealed); detect. **2.** To perceive the distinctions of; discriminate. [< L *discernere,* "to separate by sifting," distinguish between.] **—dis•cern′i•ble** *adj.* **—dis•cern′ing** *adj.* **—dis•cern′ment** *n.*

dis•charge (dĭs-chärj′) *v.* **-charged, -charging.** **1.** To relieve or be relieved of a burden or contents. **2.** To unload or empty (contents). **3.** To release or dismiss, as from employment. **4.** To send or pour forth; emit. **5.** To shoot (a projectile or weapon). **6.** To perform the obligations or demands of (a duty). **7.** To acquit oneself of (an obligation). **8.** To cause or undergo electrical discharge. **—n.** (dĭs′chärj′, dĭs-chärj′). **1.** The act of removing a load or burden. **2.** The act of shooting a projectile or weapon. **3.** A pouring forth; emission. **4.** The amount or rate of emission or ejection. **5.** Something that is discharged. **6.** A relieving from an obligation. **7. a.** Dismissal or release from employment, service, etc. **b.** A document certifying such release, esp. from military service. **8. a.** The release of stored energy in a capacitor by the flow of electric current between its terminals. **b.** The conversion of chemical energy to electric energy in a storage battery. **c.** A flow of electricity in a dielectric, esp. in a rarefied gas.

dis•ci. (dĭs′ī). Alternate *pl.* of **discus.**

dis•ci•ple (dĭ-sī′pəl) *n.* **1. a.** One who subscribes to the teachings of a master and assists in spreading them. **b.** Any active adherent, as of a movement. **2.** One of the companions of Christ. [< L *discere,* to learn, to know.]

dis•ci•pli•nar•i•an (dĭs′ə-plə-nâr′ē-ən) *n.* One who enforces or believes in strict discipline. **—adj.** Disciplinary.

dis•ci•pli•nar•y (dĭs′ə-plə-něr′ē) *adj.* Pertaining to or used for discipline.

dis•ci•pline (dĭs′ə-plĭn) *n.* **1.** Training intended to produce a specified character or pattern of behavior. **2.** Controlled behavior resulting from such training. **3.** A state of order based upon submission to rules and authority. **4.** Punishment intended to correct or train. **5.** A set of rules or methods. **6.** A branch of knowledge or of teaching. **—v. -plined, -plining. 1.** To train by instruction and control. **2.** To punish. [< L *disciplīna,* instruction, knowledge.] **—dis′ci•plin′er** *n.*

disc jockey. Also **disk jockey.** A radio announcer who presents and comments on phonograph records.

dis•claim (dĭs-klām′) *v.* **1.** To deny or renounce claim to or connection with; disown. **2.** To deny the validity of; repudiate. **3.** To renounce a legal right or claim (to).

dis•claim•er (dĭs-klā′mər) *n.* A repudiation of a claim.

dis•close (dĭs-klōz′) *v.* **-closed, -closing. 1.** To expose to view, as by removing a cover; uncover. **2.** To divulge. **—dis•clos′er** *n.* **—dis•clo′sure** (-zhər) *n.*

dis•co (dĭs′kō) *n., pl.* **-cos.** *Informal.* A discotheque.

disco-. *comb. form.* A phonograph record. [< DISK.]

dis•cob•o•lus (dĭs-kŏb′ə-ləs) *n., pl.* **-li** (-lī′). A discus thrower. [< Gk *diskobolos.*]

dis•coid (dĭs′koid′) *adj.* Also **dis•coi•dal** (dĭs-koid′l). Having the shape of a disk. **—n.** A disk or an object shaped like a disk.

dis•col•or (dĭs-kŭl′ər) *v.* **1.** To alter or spoil the color of. **2.** To become changed or spoiled in color. **—dis•col′or•a′tion** *n.*

dis•com•bob•u•late (dĭs′kəm-bŏb′yə-lāt′) *v.* **-lated, -lating.** *Slang.* To throw into a state of confusion.

dis•com•fit (dĭs-kŭm′fĭt) *v.* **1.** To thwart the plans or purposes of; frustrate. **2.** To defeat in battle. **3.** To disconcert. [< VL **disconficere,* to defeat.] **—dis•com′fi•ture′** *n.*

dis•com•fort (dĭs-kŭm′fərt) *n.* **1.** The condition of being uncomfortable in body or mind.

---

dis•in•fla′tion *n.*	**dis•pau′per•ize′** *v.*	**dis•serve′** *v.*
dis′in•fla′tion•ar′ **y** *adj.*	**dis•peace′** *n.*	**dis•so′cia•bil′i•ty** *n.*
dis′in•hib′i•to′ry *adj.*	**dis•peo′ple** *v.*	**dis•so′cia•ble** *adj.*
dis′in•tox′i•ca′ **tion** *n.*	**dis′per•son′i•fy′** *v.*	**dis•so′cia•bly** *adv.*
dis′in•vest′ *v.*	**dis•pet′al** *v.*	**dis′sym•met′ri•cal** *adj.*
dis′in•vest′ment *n.*	**dis•pope′** *v.*	**dis•sym′me•try** *n.*
dis′in•vite′ *v.*	**dis•priv′i•lege** *v.*	**dis•throne′** *v.*
dis′in•volve′ *v.*	**dis•rate′** *v.*	**dis•un′i•fi•ca′tion** *n.*
dis•lus′ter *v.*	**dis′re•late′** *v.*	**dis•u′ni•form′** *adj.*
dis•mast′ *v.*	**dis′re•la′tion** *n.*	**dis•u′ni•fy′** *v.*
dis′o•blige′ *v.*	**dis•rel′ish** *v. & n.*	**dis•un′ion** *n.*
dis′o•blig′ing•ly *adv.*	**dis′re•mem′ber** *v.*	**dis•u•til′i•ty** *n.*
dis•oc′cu•pa′tion *n.*	**dis′re•spect′a•ble** *adj.*	**dis•weap′on** *v.*
	dis•roof′ *v.*	**dis•yoke′** *v.*
	dis•root′ *v.*	
	dis•seat′ *v.*	

ô paw, for/oi boy/ou out/oo took/oo coo/p pop/r run/s sauce/sh shy/t to/th thin/*th* the/
ŭ cut/ûr fur/v van/w wag/y yes/z size/zh vision/ə ago, item, edible, gallop, circus/

2. Something that disturbs one's comfort. —*v.* To make uncomfortable.

dis·com·mode (dĭs′kə-mōd′) *v.* -moded, -moding. To put to inconvenience; disturb. [F *discommoder.*]

dis·com·pose (dĭs′kəm-pōz′) *v.* -posed, -posing. 1. To disturb the composure of. 2. To put into a state of disorder. —dis′com·po′sure (-zhər) *n.*

dis·con·nect (dĭs′kə-nĕkt′) *v.* To sever the connection of or between. —dis′con·nect′ed *adj.* —dis′con·nec′tion *n.*

dis·con·cert (dĭs′kən-sûrt′) *v.* To upset the self-possession of. [< OF *desconcerter.*]

dis·con·so·late (dĭs-kŏn′sə-lĭt) *adj.* 1. Hopelessly sad. 2. Gloomy; dismal. —dis·con′so·late·ly *adv.* —dis·con′so·late·ness *n.*

dis·con·tent (dĭs′kən-tĕnt′) *n.* Absence of contentment; dissatisfaction. —*adj.* Discontented. —*v.* To make discontented.

dis·con·tent·ed (dĭs′kən-tĕn′tĭd) *adj.* Restlessly unhappy; dissatisfied. —dis′con·tent′ed·ly *adv.* —dis′con·tent′ed·ness *n.*

dis·con·tin·ue (dĭs′kən-tĭn′yōō) *v.* -ued, -uing. 1. To cause to cease. 2. To give up; abandon. 3. To come to an end. —dis′con·tin′u·ance, dis′con·tin′u·a′tion *n.*

dis·con·ti·nu·i·ty (dĭs′kŏn-tĭ-n/y/ōō′ə-tē) *n.*, *pl.* -ties. 1. A lack of continuity, logical sequence, or cohesion. 2. A break or gap.

dis·con·tin·u·ous (dĭs′kən-tĭn′yōō-əs) *adj.* Marked by breaks or interruptions; intermittent. —dis′con·tin′u·ous·ly *adv.*

dis·cord (dĭs′kôrd) *n.* 1. Lack of agreement; dissension. 2. A harsh mingling of sounds; din. 3. *Mus.* A harsh or disagreeable combination of sounds; dissonance. —*v.* (dĭs-kôrd′). To fail to agree or harmonize; clash. [< L *discors,* disagreeing.] —dis·cor′dant *adj.* —dis·cor′dant·ly *adv.*

dis·co·theque (dĭs′kə-tĕk′) *n.* Also dis·co·thèque. A nightclub featuring dancing to amplified recorded music.

dis·count (dĭs′kount′, dĭs-kount′) *v.* 1. To deduct, as from a cost or price. 2. a. To purchase or sell (a commercial paper) after deducting the interest. b. To lend money after deducting the interest. 3. To disregard as being untrustworthy or exaggerated. 4. To anticipate and make allowance for. —*n.* (dĭs′kount). 1. A reduction from the full amount of a price or debt. 2. The interest deducted in advance in purchasing or selling a commercial paper. 3. The rate of interest so deducted. 4. The act or an instance of discounting. —*adj.* Selling at prices below those set by manufacturers: *discount store.* [< ML *discomputāre.*]

dis·coun·te·nance (dĭs-koun′tə-nəns) *v.* -nanced, -nancing. 1. To view with disfavor. 2. To disconcert.

dis·cour·age (dĭs-kûr′ĭj) *v.* -aged, -aging. 1. To deprive of confidence, hope, or spirit; dishearten. 2. To dissuade or deter. 3. To hamper; hinder. —dis·cour′age·ment *n.*

dis·course (dĭs′kôrs′, -kōrs′) *n.* 1. Verbal expression in speech or writing. 2. Conversation. 3. A formal and lengthy discussion of a subject, either written or spoken. —*v.* (dĭs-kôrs′, -kōrs′) -coursed, -coursing. To speak or write

formally and at length. [< LL *discursus,* conversation.] —dis·cours′er *n.*

dis·cour·te·ous (dĭs-kûr′tē-əs) *adj.* Lacking courtesy; impolite. —dis·cour′te·ous·ly *adv.* —dis·cour′te·sy *n.*

dis·cov·er (dĭs-kŭv′ər) *v.* 1. To arrive at through search or study. 2. To be the first to find, learn of, or observe. —dis·cov′er·a·ble *adj.* —dis·cov′er·er *n.*

dis·cov·er·y (dĭs-kŭv′ə-rē) *n.*, *pl.* -ies. 1. The act or an instance of discovering. 2. Something that has been discovered.

dis·cred·it (dĭs-krĕd′ĭt) *v.* 1. To disgrace; dishonor. 2. To cast doubt on. 3. To disbelieve. —*n.* 1. Damage to one's reputation. 2. Loss of trust or belief. —dis·cred′it·a·ble *adj.*

dis·creet (dĭs-krēt′) *adj.* 1. Having a judicious reserve in speech or behavior. 2. Unpretentious. [< ML *discrētus,* "showing good judgment."] —dis·creet′ly *adv.*

dis·crep·an·cy (dĭs-krĕp′ən-sē) *n.*, *pl.* -cies. Divergence or disagreement, as between facts or claims. [< L *discrepāre,* to sound different.] —dis·crep′ant *adj.* —dis·crep′ant·ly *adv.*

dis·crete (dĭs-krēt′) *adj.* 1. Constituting a separate thing; individual. 2. Consisting of unconnected distinct parts. [< L *discrētus,* separate.] —dis·crete′ly *adv.*

dis·cre·tion (dĭs-krĕsh′ən) *n.* 1. The quality of being discreet. 2. Permission given to an individual to make decisions by his own judgment. —dis·cre′tion·ar′y, dis·cre′tion·al *adj.*

dis·crim·i·nate (dĭs-krĭm′ə-nāt′) *v.* -nated, -nating. 1. To make a clear distinction; differentiate. 2. To act on the basis of prejudice. [L *discrīmināre,* to divide, distinguish.] —dis·crim′i·nate·ly *adv.* —dis·crim′i·na′tion *n.* —dis·crim′i·na·tive, dis·crim′i·na·to′ry (dĭs-krĭm′ə-nə-tôr′ē, -tōr′ē) *adj.*

dis·crim·i·nat·ing (dĭs-krĭm′ə-nā′tĭng) *adj.* 1. Able or tending to discriminate. 2. Fastidiously selective.

dis·cur·sive (dĭs-kûr′sĭv) *adj.* 1. Moving from subject to subject in a rambling way. 2. Proceeding to a conclusion through reason rather than intuition. [< L *discursus,* "a running back and forth."] —dis·cur′sive·ly *adv.*

dis·cus (dĭs′kəs) *n.*, *pl.* -cuses or disci (dĭs′ī). A disk, typically wooden with a metal rim, thrown for distance in athletic competitions. [L, DISK.]

dis·cuss (dĭs-kŭs′) *v.* 1. To speak or write about; treat of. 2. To speak together about; talk over. [< LL *discutere* (pp *discussus*), to investigate, discuss.] —dis·cus′sion *n.*

dis·dain (dĭs-dān′) *v.* 1. To regard or treat with contempt. 2. To consider unworthy of oneself. —*n.* Scornful superiority. [< L *dēdignārī,* to scorn.] —dis·dain′ful *adj.*

dis·ease (dĭ-zēz′) *n.* 1. An abnormal condition of an organism or part, esp. as a consequence of infection, inherent weakness, or environmental stress, that impairs normal physiological functioning. 2. A condition or tendency, as of society, regarded as abnormal and pernicious. [< OF *desaise,* discomfort.] —dis·eased′ *adj.*

dis·em·bark (dĭs′ĭm-bärk′) *v.* To put, go, or

cause to go ashore from a ship. —**dis·em'·bar'ka'tion** n.

dis·em·bod·y (dĭs'ĭm-bŏd'ē) v. -ied, -ying. To free (a spirit) from the body.

dis·em·bow·el (dĭs'ĭm-bou'əl) v. To remove the entrails from.

dis·en·chant (dĭs'ĭn-chănt', -chänt') v. To free from enchantment or illusion.

dis·en·cum·ber (dĭs'ĭn-kŭm'bər) v. To relieve of encumbrances.

dis·en·gage (dĭs'ĭn-gāj') v. -gaged, -gaging. 1. To release from something that holds, connects, or obliges. 2. To free oneself. —**dis·en·gage'ment** n.

dis·en·tan·gle (dĭs'ĭn-tăng'gəl) v. -gled, -gling. To extricate or be extricated from entanglement. —**dis·en·tan'gle·ment** n.

dis·es·tab·lish (dĭs'ĭ-stăb'lĭsh) v. To remove the established status of, esp. of a nationally established church. —**dis·es·tab'lish·ment** n.

dis·es·teem (dĭs'ĭ-stēm') n. Lack of esteem.

dis·fa·vor (dĭs-fā'vər) n. 1. Disapproval. 2. The condition of being out of favor.

dis·fig·ure (dĭs-fĭg'yər) v. -ured, -uring. To spoil the appearance or shape of; deform. —**dis·fig'ur·er** n. —**dis·fig'ure·ment** n.

dis·fran·chise (dĭs-frăn'chīz') v. -chised, -chising. Also **dis·en·fran·chise** (dĭs'ĕn-frăn'-chīz'). 1. To deprive (an individual) of a right of citizenship, esp. of the right to vote. 2. To deprive (an institution) of a privilege or franchise. —**dis·fran'chise'ment** (-chīz'mənt, -chĭz-mənt) n. —**dis·fran'chis'er** n.

dis·gorge (dĭs-gôrj') v. -gorged, -gorging. 1. To bring up and expel from the throat or stomach. 2. To discharge violently; spew.

dis·grace (dĭs-grās') n. 1. Loss of honor, respect, or reputation; shame. 2. The condition of being out of favor. 3. Something that brings shame, dishonor, or disfavor. —v. -graced, -gracing. 1. To bring shame or dishonor upon. 2. To put (someone) out of favor. [< It *disgrazia*.] —**dis·grac'er** n.

dis·grace·ful (dĭs-grās'fəl) adj. Bringing or warranting disgrace; shameful.

dis·grun·tle (dĭs-grŭnt'l) v. -tled, -tling. To make discontented, resentful, or disappointed.

dis·guise (dĭs-gīz') v. -guised, -guising. 1. To modify the manner or appearance of in order to prevent recognition. 2. To dissemble: *disguise one's interest.* —n. 1. The condition of being disguised. 2. Something that serves to disguise, as a pretense. [< OF *desguisier*.]

dis·gust (dĭs-gŭst') v. 1. To excite nausea or loathing in; sicken. 2. To offend the taste or moral sense of; repel. —n. Profound aversion or repugnance. [OF *desgouster*.] —**dis·gust'ed** adj. —**dis·gust'ed·ly** adv.

dis·gust·ing (dĭs-gŭs'tĭng) adj. Acutely repugnant; loathsome. —**dis·gust'ing·ly** adv.

dish (dĭsh) n. 1. An open container, generally shallow and concave, for holding or serving food. 2. a. The food contained in a dish. b. A particular preparation of food. 3. A dishlike depression. 4. *Slang.* An attractive girl or woman. —v. —**dish out.** 1. To serve (food). 2. *Informal.* To give out; distribute. —**dish up.** To serve (food). [< L *discus*, DISK.]

dis·ha·bille (dĭs'ə-bēl', -bē') n. Also **des·ha·bille** (dĕs'-). 1. The state of being partially or very casually dressed. 2. Casual or lounging attire. [< F *déshabiller*, to undress.]

dis·har·mo·ny (dĭs-här'mə-nē) n. Lack of harmony. —**dis'har·mo'ni·ous** adj.

dis·heart·en (dĭs-härt'n) v. To diminish or destroy the courage or resolution of. —**dis·heart'en·ing·ly** adv.

di·shev·el (dĭ-shĕv'əl) v. -eled or -elled, -eling or -elling. 1. To loosen and let fall (hair or clothing) in disarray. 2. To disarrange the hair or clothing of (a person). [< OF *descheveler*, to disarrange the hair.] —**di·shev'el·ment** n.

dis·hon·est (dĭs-ŏn'ĭst) adj. 1. Lacking honesty; untrustworthy. 2. Proceeding from or gained by falseness or lack of probity. —**dis·hon'est·ly** adv. —**dis·hon'es·ty** n.

dis·hon·or (dĭs-ŏn'ər) n. 1. Loss of honor, respect, or reputation; disgrace. 2. A cause of this. —v. 1. To deprive of honor; disgrace. 2. To fail to pay, as a note. —**dis·hon'or·a·ble** adj. —**dis·hon'or·a·bly** adv.

dish·wash·er (dĭsh'wŏsh'ər, -wô'shər) n. One who or a machine that washes dishes.

dis·il·lu·sion (dĭs'ĭ-lōō'zhən) v. To free or deprive of illusion; disenchant. —n. 1. The act of disenchanting. 2. The condition of being disenchanted. —**dis'il·lu'sion·ment** n.

dis·in·cli·na·tion (dĭs-ĭn'klə-nā'shən) n. Lack of willingness or disposition.

dis·in·cline (dĭs'ĭn-klīn') v. -clined, -clining. To make or be reluctant or averse.

dis·in·fect (dĭs'ĭn-fĕkt') v. To cleanse of pathogenic microorganisms. —**dis'in·fec'tant** n.

dis·in·gen·u·ous (dĭs'ĭn-jĕn'yōō-əs) adj. Not straightforward; crafty.

dis·in·her·it (dĭs'ĭn-hĕr'ĭt) v. To prevent from inheriting.

dis·in·te·grate (dĭs-ĭn'tə-grāt') v. -grated, -grating. To separate into fragments. —**dis·in'te·gra'tor** n. —**dis·in'te·gra'tion** n.

dis·in·ter (dĭs'ĭn-tûr') v. -terred, -terring. To remove from a grave or tomb.

dis·in·ter·est·ed (dĭs-ĭn'trĭ-stĭd, -ĭn'tə-rĕs'tĭd) adj. 1. Impartial. 2. *Nonstandard.* Uninterested; indifferent. —**dis·in'ter·est·ed·ly** adv.

Usage: Disinterested differs from uninterested to the degree that lack of self-interest differs from lack of any interest. *Disinterested* is synonymous with *impartial, unbiased. Uninterested* has the sense of *indifferent, not interested.*

dis·join (dĭs-join') v. To undo; separate.

dis·joint (dĭs-joint') v. 1. To disconnect; separate. 2. To take apart at the joints. —adj. *Math.* Having no elements in common.

dis·joint·ed (dĭs-join'tĭd) adj. 1. Separated. 2. Lacking order or coherence. —**dis·joint'ed·ly** adv. —**dis·joint'ed·ness** n.

disk (dĭsk) n. 1. Also **disc.** Any thin, flat, circular plate. 2. The central part of a flower head, as of the daisy, consisting of small, densely clustered flowers. 3. Variant of **disc.** [L *discus*, quoit < Gk *diskos*.]

disk brake. A brake in which the retarding friction is generated by contact between fixed and rotating disks.

dis·like (dĭs-līk') n. An attitude or feeling of

distaste or aversion. —**dis•like′** v. (-liked, -liking).

dis•lo•cate (dĭs′lō-kāt′, dĭs-lō′kāt′) v. -cated, -cating. 1. To remove from the usual or proper relationship. 2. To displace from the normal position. 3. To throw into confusion; upset; disturb. —**dis′lo•ca′tion** n.

dis•lodge (dĭs-lŏj′) v. -lodged, -lodging. To remove forcibly from a dwelling or position.

dis•loy•al (dĭs-loi′əl) adj. Lacking in loyalty. —**dis•loy′al•ly** adv. —**dis•loy′al•ty** n.

dis•mal (dĭz′məl) adj. Causing gloom or depression. [< ML diēs malī, "bad days."] —**dis′mal•ly** adv. —**dis′mal•ness** n.

dis•man•tle (dĭs-mănt′l) v. -tled, -tling. 1. To strip of furnishings or equipment, as a house. 2. To take apart. —**dis•man′tle•ment** n.

dis•may (dĭs-mā′) v. 1. To make anxious or afraid. 2. To discourage or dishearten. —n. Apprehension; consternation. [< OF desmayer.]

dis•mem•ber (dĭs-mĕm′bər) v. 1. To cut, tear, or pull off the limbs of. 2. To separate into pieces. —**dis•mem′ber•ment** n.

dis•miss (dĭs-mĭs′) v. 1. To discharge, as from employment. 2. To direct or allow to leave. 3. To reject; repudiate. 4. To put (a claim or action) out of court without further hearing. [< L dīmittere, to send away.] —**dis•miss′al** n. —**dis•miss′i•ble** adj.

dis•mount (dĭs-mount′) v. 1. To get off or down, as from a horse or bicycle. 2. To remove (a rider) from a horse. 3. To remove (an apparatus) from its mounting. 4. To disassemble. —**dis•mount′a•ble** adj.

dis•o•be•di•ence (dĭs′ə-bē′dē-əns) n. Failure or refusal to obey. —**dis′o•be′di•ent** adj. —**dis′o•be′di•ent•ly** adv.

dis•o•bey (dĭs′ə-bā′) v. To fail or refuse to obey. —**dis′o•bey′er** n.

dis•or•der (dĭs-ôr′dər) n. 1. Lack of order. 2. A public disturbance. 3. An illness. —v. To cause disorder.

dis•or•der•ly (dĭs-ôr′dər-lē) adj. 1. Lacking order. 2. Disturbing the public peace. —**dis•or′der•li•ness** n.

dis•or•gan•ize (dĭs-ôr′gə-nīz′) v. -ized, -izing. To disrupt the organization of. —**dis•or′gan•i•za′tion** n. —**dis•or′gan•iz′er** n.

dis•o•ri•ent (dĭs-ôr′ē-ĕnt′, dĭs-ōr′-) v. To cause to lose orientation. —**dis•o′ri•en•ta′tion** n.

dis•own (dĭs-ōn′) v. To refuse responsibility or relationship to; repudiate.

dis•par•age (dĭs-păr′ĭj) v. -aged, -aging. 1. To belittle. 2. To reduce in esteem or rank. [< OF desparager, "to deprive one of his rank."] —**dis•par′age•ment** n. —**dis•par′ag•ing•ly** adv.

dis•pa•rate (dĭs′pər-ĭt, dĭs-păr′ĭt) adj. Different and distinct; dissimilar. [< L disparāre, to separate.] —**dis′pa•rate•ly** adv. —**dis•par′i•ty** (dĭs-păr′ə-tē) n.

dis•pas•sion•ate (dĭs-păsh′ən-ĭt) adj. Devoid of or unaffected by emotion. —**dis•pas′sion•ate•ly** adv.

dis•patch (dĭs-păch′). Also des•patch. v. 1. To send. 2. To perform promptly. 3. To kill. —n. 1. The act of dispatching. 2. Efficient, expeditious performance. 3. A message. 4. A shipment. 5. A news item sent to a newspaper

by a correspondent. [< OF despeechier, to set free, unshackle.] —**dis•patch′er** n.

dis•pel (dĭs-pĕl′) v. -pelled, -pelling. To drive away or scatter. [< L dispellere.]

dis•pen•sa•ble (dĭs-pĕn′sə-bəl) adj. 1. Capable of being dispensed with; unimportant. 2. Capable of being administered or distributed.

dis•pen•sa•ry (dĭs-pĕn′sə-rē) n., pl. -ries. A place at which medical supplies are dispensed.

dis•pen•sa•tion (dĭs′pən-sā′shən, dĭs′pĕn-) n. 1. The act of dispensing. 2. Something dispensed. 3. A system by which something is dispensed. 4. Exemption or release from obligation or rule. 5. Divine ordering of worldly affairs. 6. A religious system or code of commands: the Moslem dispensation.

dis•pense (dĭs-pĕns′) v. -pensed, -pensing. 1. To distribute in portions. 2. To prepare and give out (medicines). 3. To administer, as laws. 4. To exempt. [< L dispensāre, to pay out, distribute.] —**dis•pens′er** n.

dis•perse (dĭs-pûrs′) v. -persed, -persing. 1. To scatter. 2. To disseminate or distribute. [< L dispergere, to scatter on all sides.] —**dis•per′sion, dis•per′sal** n.

dis•pir•it (dĭs-pĭr′ĭt) v. To discourage.

dis•place (dĭs-plās′) v. -placed, -placing. 1. To remove from a place or position. 2. To take the place of. 3. To cause displacement of.

dis•place•ment (dĭs-plās′mənt) n. 1. The act of displacing. 2. The weight or volume of a fluid displaced by a floating body. 3. The distance from an initial position to a subsequent position assumed by a body.

dis•play (dĭs-plā′) v. To place in view; show. —n. 1. An act of displaying. 2. Something displayed. [< L displicāre, to scatter.]

dis•please (dĭs-plēz′) v. -pleased, -pleasing. To annoy or irritate. —**dis•pleas′ure** (-plĕzh′ər) n.

dis•port (dĭs-pôrt′, -pōrt′) v. To engage in an activity for diversion or amusement. [< OF desporter, "to carry away," divert.]

dis•pos•a•ble (dĭs-pō′zə-bəl) adj. 1. Designed to be discarded after use. 2. Subject to use; available. —**dis•pos′a•bil′i•ty** n.

dis•pos•al (dĭs-pō′zəl) n. 1. Order; arrangement. 2. A manner or method of disposing. 3. A throwing out or away. 4. An apparatus for disposing of something. 5. Ability or authority to dispose of something.

dis•pose (dĭs-pōz′) v. -posed, -posing. 1. To place in order; arrange. 2. To settle; conclude. 3. To incline: disposed to laughter. —**dispose of.** 1. To attend to. 2. To transfer or part with, as by selling. 3. To get rid of. [< L dispōnere, to place here and there, arrange.]

dis•po•si•tion (dĭs′pə-zĭsh′ən) n. 1. Temperament. 2. A tendency or inclination. 3. The act or manner of disposing. 4. The authority to dispose.

dis•pos•sess (dĭs′pə-zĕs′) v. To deprive of the possession of, as a house. —**dis′pos•ses′sion** n.

dis•pro•por•tion•ate (dĭs′prə-pôr′shən-ĭt, -pōr′shən-ĭt) adj. Out of proportion. —**dis′pro•por′tion** n. —**dis′pro•por′tion•ate•ly** adv.

dis•prove (dĭs-prōōv′) v. -proved, -proving. To prove to be false, invalid, or in error; refute. —**dis•proof′** (-prōōf′) n.

dis·pu·ta·tious (dĭs'pyo͞o-tā'shəs) *adj.* Inclined to dispute; contentious.

dis·pute (dĭs-pyo͞ot') *v.* **-puted, -puting. 1.** To argue; debate. **2.** To question the truth or validity of. **3.** To strive against; oppose. —*n.* **1.** An argument; debate. **2.** A quarrel. [< L *disputāre,* to reckon, discuss.] —**dis·put'a·ble** *adj.* —**dis·pu'tant** *adj. & n.* —**dis'pu·ta'tion** *n.*

dis·qual·i·fy (dĭs-kwŏl'ə-fī') *v.* **-fied, -fying.** To declare or render unqualified. —**dis·qual'i·fi·ca'tion** *n.*

dis·qui·et (dĭs-kwī'ĭt) *v.* To disturb or trouble. —*n.* Lack of peace or quiet. —**dis·qui'et·ing·ly** *adv.*

dis·qui·e·tude (dĭs-kwī'ə-t/y/o͞od') *n.* A state of worry or uneasiness.

dis·qui·si·tion (dĭs'kwə-zĭsh'ən) *n.* A formal discourse. [< L *disquīrere,* to inquire diligently.]

Dis·rae·li (dĭz-rā'lē), **Benjamin.** 1804-1881. British statesman; prime minister (1868 and 1874–80).

dis·re·gard (dĭs'rĭ-gärd') *v.* To ignore. —*n.* Willful lack of regard.

dis·re·pair (dĭs'rĭ-pâr') *n.* A condition of needing repairs; dilapidation.

dis·rep·u·ta·ble (dĭs-rĕp'yə-tə-bəl) *adj.* **1.** Not respectable. **2.** Disgraceful; discreditable.

dis·re·pute (dĭs'rĭ-pyo͞ot') *n.* Discredit; disgrace.

dis·re·spect (dĭs'rĭ-spĕkt') *n.* Lack of respect; rudeness. —**dis're·spect'ful** *adj.*

dis·robe (dĭs-rōb') *v.* **-robed, -robing.** To undress. —**dis·rob'er** *n.*

dis·rupt (dĭs-rŭpt') *v.* To throw into confusion. [L *disrumpere* (pp *disruptus*), to break asunder.] —**dis·rup'tion** *n.* —**dis·rup'tive** *adj.*

dis·sat·is·fac·tion (dĭs-săt'ĭs-făk'shən) *n.* The feeling of being displeased; discontent.

dis·sat·is·fy (dĭs-săt'ĭs-fī') *v.* **-fied, -fying.** To make discontented; displease.

dis·sect (dĭ-sĕkt', dī-, dī'sĕkt') *v.* **1.** To cut apart or separate (tissue) for anatomical study. **2.** To analyze in minute detail. [L *dissecāre,* to cut apart.] —**dis·sec'tion** *n.*

dis·sem·ble (dĭ-sĕm'bəl) *v.* **-bled, -bling. 1.** To disguise the real nature of. **2.** To simulate; feign. [< OF *dessembler,* to be different.] —**dis·sem'bler** *n.*

dis·sem·i·nate (dĭ-sĕm'ə-nāt') *v.* **-nated, -nating.** To scatter or spread widely. [L *dissēmināre.*] —**dis·sem'i·na'tion** *n.*

dis·sen·sion (dĭ-sĕn'shən) *n.* Discord; contention. [< L *dissentīre,* to DISSENT.]

dis·sent (dĭ-sĕnt') *v.* **1.** To disagree; differ. **2.** To withhold assent. —*n.* **1.** Disagreement. **2.** Political or religious nonconformity. [< L *dissentīre,* to feel apart.] —**dis·sent'er** *n.*

dis·ser·ta·tion (dĭs'ər-tā'shən) *n.* A treatise, esp. one written as a doctoral thesis. [< L *disserere,* to discuss.]

dis·ser·vice (dĭs-sûr'vĭs) *n.* A harmful action.

dis·sev·er (dĭ-sĕv'ər) *v.* To separate; break up. [< LL *dissēparāre.*]

dis·si·dent (dĭs'ə-dənt) *adj.* Publicly or violently dissenting. —*n.* A dissenter. [< L *dissidēre,* "to sit apart," dissent.] —**dis'si·dence** *n.* —**dis'si·dent·ly** *adv.*

dis·sim·i·lar (dĭ-sĭm'ə-lər) *adj.* Unlike. —**dis·sim'i·lar'i·ty** (-sĭm'ə-lăr'ə-tē) *n.*

dis·si·mil·i·tude (dĭs'ĭ-mĭl'ə-t/y/o͞od') *n.* **1.** Lack of resemblance. **2.** A point of difference. [< L *dissimilis,* different.]

dis·sim·u·late (dĭ-sĭm'yə-lāt') *v.* **-lated, -lating.** To disguise under a feigned appearance; dissemble. —**dis·sim'u·la'tion** *n.*

dis·si·pate (dĭs'ə-pāt') *v.* **-pated, -pating. 1.** To dispel or scatter. **2.** To waste; squander. **3.** To vanish; disappear. **4.** To indulge in intemperate drinking. [< L *dissipāre,* to disperse, squander.] —**dis'si·pa'tion** *n.*

dis·so·ci·ate (dĭ-sō'shē-āt', -sē-āt') *v.* **-ated, -ating.** To separate. [L *dissociāre.*] —**dis·so'ci·a'tion** *n.* —**dis·so'ci·a'tive** *adj.*

dis·so·lute (dĭs'ə-lo͞ot') *adj.* Lacking in moral restraint; debauched; abandoned. [< L *dissolūtus,* pp of *dissolvere,* DISSOLVE.] —**dis'so·lute'ly** *adv.* —**dis'so·lute'ness** *n.*

dis·so·lu·tion (dĭs'ə-lo͞o'shən) *n.* **1.** Decomposition; disintegration. **2.** Termination or extinction by deconcentration or dispersion. **3.** Death. **4.** Termination of a legal bond. **5.** Formal dismissal of an assembly. **6.** Reduction to a liquid form; liquefaction.

dis·solve (dĭ-zŏlv') *v.* **-solved, -solving. 1.** To enter or cause to enter into solution. **2.** To melt. **3.** To dispel. **4.** To break into component parts. **5.** To terminate or dismiss. **6.** To collapse emotionally. [< L *dissolvere.*]

dis·so·nance (dĭs'ə-nəns) *n.* **1.** Discord. **2.** *Mus.* A combination of tones conventionally considered to suggest unrelieved tension and to require resolution. —**dis'so·nant** *adj.* —**dis'so·nant·ly** *adv.*

dis·suade (dĭ-swād') *v.* **-suaded, -suading.** To discourage from a purpose or course of action by persuasion. [L *dissuādēre.*] —**dis·sua'sion** (-swā'zhən) *n.* —**dis·sua'sive** *adj.*

dist. 1. distance; distant. **2.** district.

dis·taff (dĭs'tăf', -täf') *n.* **1.** A staff that holds on its cleft end the unspun flax, wool, etc., in spinning. **2.** Also **distaff side.** The maternal branch of a family. [< OE *distæf* : *dis-,* bunch of flax + STAFF.]

dis·tal (dĭs'təl) *adj.* Anatomically located far from the origin or line of attachment. [DIS-T(ANT) + -AL.] —**dis'tal·ly** *adv.*

dis·tance (dĭs'təns) *n.* **1.** Separation in space or time. **2.** The length of a line segment joining two points. **3.** The interval separating any two specified instants in time. **4. a.** The degree of deviation or difference that separates two things in relationship. **b.** The degree of progress between two points in a trend or course. **5.** Coldness; aloofness. **6.** The whole way: *go the distance.* —*v.* **-tanced, -tancing.** To outrun; outstrip.

dis·tant (dĭs'tənt) *adj.* **1.** Separate in space or time. **2.** Far removed. **3.** Located at, coming from, or going to a distance. **4.** Remote in relationship: *a distant cousin.* **5.** Aloof; cold. [< L *distāre,* to be remote.] —**dis'tant·ly** *adv.*

dis·taste (dĭs-tāst') *n.* Dislike or aversion.

dis·taste·ful (dĭs-tāst'fəl) *adj.* Unpleasant; disagreeable. —**dis·taste'ful·ly** *adv.*

dis·tem·per (dĭs-tĕm'pər) *n.* An infectious,

often fatal virus disease of certain mammals, esp. dogs.

dis•tend (dĭs-tĕnd′) *v.* To expand or swell. [< L *distendere.*] —**dis•ten′si•ble** *adj.* —**dis•ten′tion, dis•ten′sion** *n.*

dis•till (dĭs-tĭl′) *v.* **1.** To subject to, or derive by means of, distillation. **2.** To separate from. **3.** To exude in drops. [< L *dēstillāre.*] —**dis•till′er** *n.* —**dis•till′er•y** *n.*

dis•til•late (dĭs′tə-lāt′, dĭs-tĭl′ĭt) *n.* The liquid condensed from vapor in distillation.

dis•til•la•tion (dĭs′tə-lā′shən) *n.* Any of various heat-dependent processes used to purify or separate a fraction of a relatively complex substance, esp. the vaporization of a liquid mixture with subsequent collection of components by differential cooling to condensation.

dis•tinct (dĭs-tĭngkt′) *adj.* **1.** Individual; discrete. **2.** Different; unlike. **3.** Readily perceived. **4.** Explicit; unquestionable. [< L *distinguere,* DISTINGUISH.] —**dis•tinct′ly** *adv.*

dis•tinc•tion (dĭs-tĭngk′shən) *n.* **1.** The act of distinguishing; differentiation. **2.** A difference. **3.** A distinguishing factor or characteristic. **4.** Personal excellence. **5.** Honor.

dis•tinc•tive (dĭs-tĭngk′tĭv) *adj.* **1.** Serving to identify; distinguishing. **2.** Characteristic. —**dis•tinc′tive•ly** *adv.* —**dis•tinc′tive•ness** *n.*

dis•tin•guish (dĭs-tĭng′gwĭsh) *v.* **1.** To recognize as being distinct. **2.** To perceive distinctly; discern. **3.** To discriminate. **4.** To set apart. **5.** To make eminent. [< L *distinguere,* to separate, distinguish.] —**dis•tin′guish•a•ble** *adj.* —**dis•tin′guish•a•bly** *adv.*

dis•tin•guished (dĭs-tĭng′gwĭsht) *adj.* **1.** Characterized by excellence or distinction; eminent. **2.** Dignified in conduct or appearance.

dis•tort (dĭs-tôrt′) *v.* **1.** To twist out of a proper or natural shape. **2.** To alter misleadingly; misrepresent. **3.** To reproduce (sound) improperly. [L *distorquēre* (pp *distortus*).] —**dis•tort′er** *n.* —**dis•tor′tion** *n.*

distr. distributor.

dis•tract (dĭs-trăkt′) *v.* **1.** To sidetrack; divert. **2.** To stir up; unsettle emotionally. [< L *distrahere* (pp *distractus*), to pull apart, draw away.] —**dis•trac′tion** *n.* —**dis•trac′tive** *adj.*

dis•traught (dĭs-trôt′) *adj.* **1.** Confused and agitated; harried. **2.** Crazed; mad. [< L *distrahere,* to DISTRACT.]

dis•tress (dĭs-trĕs′) *v.* To cause anxiety or suffering to. —*n.* **1.** Anxiety or suffering. **2.** Misfortune. **3.** Need of immediate assistance: *a ship in distress.* [< L *districtus,* pp of *distringere,* "to draw tight," hinder.]

dis•trib•ute (dĭs-trĭb′yōōt) *v.* -uted, -uting. **1.** To divide and dispense in portions. **2.** To deliver or parcel out. **3.** To spread through an area or range. **4.** To classify. [< L *distribuere.*] —**dis′-tri•bu′tion** *n.* —**dis•trib′u•tive** *adj.*

dis•trib•u•tor (dĭs-trĭb′yə-tər) *n.* Also **dis•trib•ut•er.** **1.** One that distributes. **2.** One that markets or sells merchandise, esp. a wholesaler. **3.** A device for applying electric current in proper sequence to spark plugs.

dis•trict (dĭs′trĭkt) *n.* A territorial division created for governmental or other purposes or existing by virtue of a characteristic. [< L *districtus,* pp of *distringere,* to detain, hinder.]

district attorney. The prosecuting officer of a given judicial district.

District of Columbia. The Federal District of the U.S., coextensive with the capital city of Washington. Pop. 764,000.

dis•trust (dĭs-trŭst′) *n.* Lack of trust; suspicion. —*v.* To lack confidence in; suspect. —**dis•trust′ful** *adj.* —**dis•trust′ful•ly** *adv.*

dis•turb (dĭs-tûrb′) *v.* **1.** To upset the tranquillity or settled state of. **2.** To intrude upon; interrupt. **3.** To disarrange. [< L *disturbāre.*] —**dis•tur′bance** *n.* —**dis•turb′ing•ly** *adv.*

dis•u•nite (dĭs′yōō-nīt′) *v.* To separate; divide.

dis•u•ni•ty (dĭs-yōō′nə-tē) *n.* Lack of unity; dissension.

dis•use (dĭs-yōōs′) *n.* The state of being no longer in use; desuetude.

ditch (dĭch) *n.* A trench dug in the ground. —*v. Slang.* To discard; desert. [< OE *dīc,* moat, ditch. See **dhīgw-.**]

dith•er (dĭth′ər) *n.* A state of agitation or indecision. [ME *didderen.*]

dit•to (dĭt′ō) *n., pl.* -tos. **1.** The same as before or another of the same. **2.** The pair of small marks (″) used as a symbol for the word *ditto.* [< L *dīcere,* to say.]

dit•ty (dĭt′ē) *n., pl.* -ties. A simple short song. [< L *dictātum,* "thing dictated."]

di•u•ret•ic (dī′yōō-rĕt′ĭk) *adj.* Tending to increase the discharge of urine. —*n.* A diuretic drug. [< Gk *diourein,* to pass urine.]

di•ur•nal (dī-ûr′nəl) *adj.* **1.** Pertaining to or occurring in daytime. **2.** Daily. [< L *diurnus,* of a day, daily.] —**di•ur′nal•ly** *adv.*

div. **1.** divided; division; divisor. **2.** dividend. **3.** divorced.

di•va (dē′və) *n.* An operatic prima donna. [It, "goddess."]

di•va•lent (dī-vā′lənt) *adj.* Having a valence of 2; bivalent.

di•van (dĭ-văn′, dī′văn′) *n.* A couch; sofa. [< Turk *dīvān.*]

dive (dīv) *v.* **dived** or **dove, dived, diving.** **1. a.** To plunge headfirst into water. **b.** To go toward the bottom of a body of water: *dive for pearls.* **2.** To submerge under power, as a submarine. **3.** To drop precipitously; plummet. **4.** To descend in an airplane at an acceleration exceeding that of free fall. **5.** To rush headlong. **6.** To plunge, as into an activity. —*n.* **1.** An act or instance of diving. **2.** *Slang.* A disreputable or run-down bar or nightclub. [< OE *dÿfan,* to dip, immerse, and *dūfan* to sink, dive. See **dheub-.**] —**div′er** *n.*

di•verge (dĭ-vûrj′, dī-) *v.* **-verged, -verging.** **1.** To tend in different directions from a common point. **2.** To differ, as in opinion. **3.** To deviate, as from a set course or norm. **4.** *Math.* To fail to approach a limit. [LL *dīvergere,* to turn aside.] —**di•ver′gence** *n.* —**di•ver′gent** *adj.* —**di•ver′gent•ly** *adv.*

di•vers (dī′vərz) *adj.* Various.

di•verse (dĭ-vûrs′, dī-, dī′vûrs′) *adj.* **1.** Unlike. **2.** Having variety in form; diversified. [< L *dīvertere,* to turn aside, DIVERT.] —**di•verse′ly** *adv.* —**di•verse′ness** *n.*

ă pat/ā ate/âr care/ä bar/b bib/ch chew/d deed/ĕ pet/ē be/f fit/g gag/h hat/hw what/ ĭ pit/ī pie/îr pier/j judge/k kick/l lid, fatal/m mum/n no, sudden/ng sing/ŏ pot/ō go/

di•ver•si•fy (dĭ-vûr′sə-fī′, dī-) v. -fied, -fying. 1. To make diverse; vary. 2. To spread out business activities or investments. —di•ver′si•fi•ca′tion (-fĭ-kā′shən) n.

di•ver•sion (dĭ-vûr′zhən, -shən, dī-) n. 1. A turning aside. 2. A pastime or distraction. 3. A military maneuver that draws the enemy away from a planned point of attack. —di•ver′sion•ar′y adj.

di•ver•si•ty (dĭ-vûr′sə-tē, dī-) n., pl. -ties. 1. The quality of being diverse or different; variety. 2. A point in which things differ.

di•vert (dĭ-vûrt′, dī-) v. 1. To turn aside from a course or direction; deflect. 2. To distract. 3. To amuse or entertain. [< L dīvertere, to turn aside.] —di•vert′er n.

di•vest (dĭ-vĕst′, dī-) v. 1. To strip, as of clothes. 2. To deprive, as of rights; dispossess. [< OF desvestir, to undress.]

di•vide (dĭ-vīd′) v. -vided, -viding. 1. a. To separate or become separated into parts, sections, or groups. b. To classify. 2. To set at odds; disunite. 3. To cut off; part. 4. To apportion or share. 5. a. To subject to mathematical division. b. To be an exact divisor of. 6. To branch out. —n. A watershed. [< L dīvidere.] —di•vid′a•ble adj.

div•i•dend (dĭv′ə-dĕnd′) n. 1. A quantity to be divided. 2. A share of profits received by a stockholder. 3. Informal. A bonus.

di•vid•er (dĭ-vī′dər) n. 1. a. One that divides. b. A partition. 2. dividers. A device resembling a compass, used for dividing lines and transferring measurements.

div•i•na•tion (dĭv′ə-nā′shən) n. 1. The art or practice of foretelling future events or revealing occult knowledge by means of augury or alleged supernatural agency. 2. Inspired insight or intuition.

di•vine[1] (dĭ-vīn′) adj. -viner, -vinest. 1. a. Being or having the nature of a deity. b. Of or relating to a deity. 2. Supremely good; magnificent. 3. Informal. Heavenly; perfect. —n. 1. A clergyman. 2. A theologian. [< L dīvus, divine, god.] —di•vine′ly adv.

di•vine[2] (dĭ-vīn′) v. -vined, -vining. 1. To foretell or prophesy. 2. To guess, infer, or conjecture. —di•vin′er n.

di•vin•i•ty (dĭ-vĭn′ə-tē) n. 1. The state or quality of being divine. 2. Divinity. God; the godhead. 3. Theology.

di•vis•i•ble (dĭ-vĭz′ə-bəl) adj. Capable of being divided, esp. of being divided evenly with no remainder. —di•vis′i•bil′i•ty n.

di•vi•sion (dĭ-vĭzh′ən) n. 1. The act or process of dividing or state of being divided. 2. The proportional distribution of a quantity or entity. 3. A boundary or partition. 4. One of the parts into which something is divided. 5. a. An area of activity organized as a functional unit. b. A territorial section marked off for administrative purposes. 6. A large self-contained tactical unit, as of an army. 7. a. Disagreement. b. Disunion. 8. The operation of determining how many times one quantity is contained in another. —di•vi′sion•al adj.

di•vi•sive (dĭ-vī′sĭv) adj. Creating dissension. —di•vi′sive•ly adv. —di•vi′sive•ness n.

di•vi•sor (dĭ-vī′zər) n. The quantity by which another, the dividend, is to be divided.

di•vorce (dĭ-vôrs′, -vōrs′) n. 1. The dissolution of a marriage by law. 2. A radical separation. [< L dīvortere, dīvertere, to turn aside, separate, DIVERT.] —di•vorce′ v. (-vorced, -vorcing).

di•vor•cée (dĭ-vôr′sā′, -vōr′sā′, -vôr′sā′, -vôr′sā′) n. A divorced woman.

div•ot (dĭv′ət) n. A piece of turf torn up by a golf club in striking a ball. [Scot devait.]

di•vulge (dĭ-vŭlj′) v. -vulged, -vulging. To disclose; reveal. [< L dīvulgāre, to spread abroad among the people.] —di•vulg′er n.

div•vy (dĭv′ē) v. -vied, -vying. —divvy up. Slang. To divide.

Dix•ie (dĭk′sē). The Southern states. [Orig, a ten-dollar bill issued in New Orleans.]

diz•zy (dĭz′ē) adj. -zier, -ziest. 1. Having a sensation of whirling or feeling a tendency to fall; giddy. 2. Producing or produced by giddiness. 3. Precipitate. [< OE dysig, foolish, stupid. See dheu-[1].] —diz′zi•ly adv. —diz′zi•ness n. —diz′zy v. (-zied, -zying).

DJ disc jockey.

Dja•kar•ta (jə-kär′tə). The capital of Indonesia, on the NW coast of Java. Pop. 2,907,000.

Dji•bou•ti (jĭ-boo′tē). 1. Officially, Djibouti Republic. A country of E Africa. Pop. 250,000. 2. The capital of this country. Pop. 62,000.

djin•ni, djin•ny. Variants of jinni.

dk. 1. dark. 2. deck. 3. dock.

dlr. dealer.

dlvy. delivery.

DM Deutsche mark.

DMZ demilitarized zone.

DNA deoxyribonucleic acid.

Dnie•per (nē′pər). A river of the W Soviet Union.

do (dōō) v. did, done, doing, does. 1. To perform or execute. 2. To fulfill; complete. 3. To create, compose, or make. 4. To bring about; effect. 5. To put into action; exert. 6. To deal with as is necessary. 7. To render: do equal justice. 8. To work at. 9. To solve (a problem). 10. To present (a play). 11. To have the role of; play. 12. To cover (a specified distance): do a mile in a minute. 13. To tour: do Europe. 14. To be adequate; suffice. 15. To set or style (the hair). 16. To cheat: do someone out of his inheritance. 17. To get along; fare: do well at school. 18. —Used as an auxiliary: a. In questions, negative statements, and inverted phrases: Do you understand? I did not sleep well. Little did he suspect. b. For emphasis: I do want to be sure. c. As a substitute for an antecedent verb: She tries as hard as they do. —do away with. 1. To eliminate. 2. To kill. —do for. To take care of. —do in. Slang. 1. To exhaust. 2. To kill. —do over. Informal. To redecorate. —n., pl. do's or dos. 1. Informal. A party. 2. A statement of what should be done: do's and don'ts. [< OE dōn. See dhē-.]

do. ditto.

D.O. 1. Doctor of Optometry. 2. Doctor of Osteopathy.

D.O.A. dead on arrival.

doc. document.

ô paw, for/oi boy/ou out/ōō took/ōō coo/p pop/r run/s sauce/sh shy/t to/th thin/th the/
ŭ cut/ûr fur/v van/w wag/y yes/z size/zh vision/ə ago, item, edible, gallop, circus/

doc•ile (dŏs′əl; *Brit.* dō′sīl′) *adj.* Tractable; submissive. [L *docilis.*] —**doc′ile•ly** *adv.* —**do•cil′i•ty** (dŏ-sīl′ə-tē) *n.*

dock¹ (dŏk) *n.* **1.** A slip between two piers that receives a ship. **2.** A pier or wharf. **3.** A wharflike loading platform. —*v.* **1.** To maneuver into or next to a dock. **2.** To couple (two or more spacecraft) in space. [< VL *ductia,* conduit, aqueduct.]

dock² (dŏk) *v.* **1.** To clip or cut off, as an animal's tail. **2. a.** To withhold a part of (a salary). **b.** To penalize (a worker) by such deduction. [Perh < OE *docca* < Gmc *dukk-,* bundle.]

dock³ (dŏk) *n.* The place where the defendant stands or sits in a criminal court. [Flem *docke,* cage, pen.]

dock⁴ (dŏk) *n.* A weedy plant with clusters of small, usually greenish flowers. [< OE *docce.*]

dock•age (dŏk′ĭj) *n.* **1.** Facilities for docking vessels. **2.** The charge for docking privileges.

dock•et (dŏk′ĭt) *n.* **1. a.** A brief entry of the proceedings in a court of justice. **b.** The book containing such entries. **c.** A calendar of cases awaiting court action. **2.** An agenda. **3.** A label on a package listing the contents or directions for use. [ME *doggette.*] —**dock′et** *v.*

dock•hand (dŏk′hănd′) *n.* A dock worker; longshoreman.

dock•yard (dŏk′yärd′) *n.* A place with facilities for building, repairing, or dry-docking ships.

doc•tor (dŏk′tər) *n.* **1.** One who holds the highest academic degree awarded by a university in any specified discipline. **2.** One trained in the healing arts, esp. a physician, surgeon, dentist, or veterinarian. —*v.* **1. a.** To give medical treatment to. **b.** To practice medicine. **2.** To repair, esp. in a makeshift manner. **3.** To alter or falsify. **4.** To add ingredients to. [< L, teacher.] —**doc′tor•al** *adj.*

doc•tor•ate (dŏk′tər-ĭt) *n.* The degree or status of a doctor as conferred by a university.

doc•tri•naire (dŏk′trə-nâr′) *n.* One inflexibly committed to the application of a given theory regardless of its practicality. —**doc′tri•naire′** *adj.*

doc•trine (dŏk′trĭn) *n.* **1.** Something that is taught as a body of principles. **2.** A tenet; dogma. [< L *doctrina,* teaching, learning.] —**doc′tri•nal** *adj.* —**doc′tri•nal•ly** *adv.*

doc•u•ment (dŏk′yə-mənt) *n.* A paper bearing evidence, proof, or information. —*v.* To furnish with or support by a document or documents. [< L *docēre,* to teach.] —**doc′u•men•ta′tion** *n.*

doc•u•men•ta•ry (dŏk′yə-měn′tə-rē) *adj.* **1.** Of or concerning documents. **2.** Presenting facts objectively in artistic form. —*n., pl.* -**ries.** A documentary film or television presentation.

dod•der (dŏd′ər) *v.* To shake or move shakily, as from old age. [Perh < Scand.]

dodge (dŏj) *v.* **dodged, dodging.** **1.** To avoid by moving aside. **2.** To evade by cunning or deceit. **3.** To shift suddenly. —*n.* **1.** A quick move or shift. **2.** A clever or evasive trick; stratagem. **3.** A method or technique. [?] —**dodg′er** *n.*

do•do (dō′dō) *n., pl.* -**does** or -**dos.** A large flightless bird extinct since the 17th century. [Port *doudo.*]

doe (dō) *n.* The female of a deer or of certain other animals, such as the hare. [< OE *dā.*]

do•er (dōō′ər) *n.* **1.** The agent of something. **2.** An active, energetic person.

does (dŭz). 3rd person sing. present tense of **do.**

doe•skin (dō′skĭn′) *n.* **1.** Soft leather made originally from the skin of a doe. **2.** A soft, napped woolen fabric.

does•n't (dŭz′ənt). Contraction of *does not.*

doest (dōō′əst). *Archaic.* 2nd person sing. present tense of **do.**

doeth (dōō′əth). *Archaic.* 3rd person sing. present tense of **do.**

doff (dôf, dŏf) *v.* **1.** To take off: *doff one's clothes.* **2.** To tip (one's hat). **3.** To discard. [< ME *don off* : *don,* to do + OFF.]

dog (dôg, dŏg) *n.* **1.** A domesticated carnivorous mammal related to wolves and foxes. **2.** The male of such an animal. —*v.* **dogged, dogging.** **1.** To track or trail persistently. **2.** To hound; harry. [< OE *docga.*]

dog•catch•er (dôg′kăch′ər, dŏg′-) *n.* One appointed to impound stray dogs.

doge (dōj) *n.* The chief magistrate of the former republics of Venice and Genoa. [< L *dūcere,* to lead.]

dog-ear (dôg′îr′, dŏg′-) *n.* A turned-down corner of a page of a book. —**dog′-eared′** *adj.*

dog•fight (dôg′fīt′, dŏg′-) *n.* A battle involving two or more fighter planes at close quarters.

dog•fish (dôg′fĭsh′, dŏg′-) *n.* Any of various small sharks.

dog•ged (dô′gĭd, dŏg′ĭd) *adj.* Stubborn; tenacious. —**dog′ged•ly** *adv.* —**dog′ged•ness** *n.*

dog•ger•el (dô′gər-əl, dŏg′ər-) *n.* Light verse of a loose, irregular measure. [Perh < DOG.]

dog•house (dôg′hous′, dŏg′-) *n.* A house for a dog. —**in the doghouse.** *Slang.* In disgrace; in trouble.

dog•ma (dôg′mə, dŏg′-) *n.* **1.** A system of doctrines proclaimed by a church. **2.** A tenet or body of tenets. [< Gk, decree.]

dog•mat•ic (dôg-măt′ĭk, dŏg-) *adj.* Marked by an authoritarian assertion of principles. —**dog•mat′i•cal•ly** *adv.*

dog•ma•tism (dôg′mə-tĭz′əm, dŏg′-) *n.* Dogmatic assertion of opinion or belief.

Dog Star. **1.** The star Sirius. **2.** The star Procyon.

dog•trot (dôg′trŏt′, dŏg′-) *n.* A steady trot.

dog•wood (dôg′wŏŏd′, dŏg′-) *n.* A tree with small greenish flowers surrounded by showy white or pink petallike bracts.

doi•ly (doi′lē) *n., pl.* -**lies.** A small ornamental mat. [< *Doily,* a London draper, circa 1712.]

dol. dollar.

dol•drums (dōl′drəmz′, dôl′-, dŏl′-) *n. (takes sing. v.).* **1.** Ocean regions near the equator, characterized by calms. **2.** A period of inactivity, listlessness, or depression. [Perh < OE *dol,* dull.]

dole (dōl) *n.* **1. a.** The distribution of necessities to the needy. **b.** Something so distributed. **2.** *Chiefly Brit.* Government distribution

---

ă pat/ā ate/âr care/ä bar/b bib/ch chew/d deed/ĕ pet/ē be/f fit/g gag/h hat/hw what/
ĭ pit/ī pie/îr pier/j judge/k kick/l lid, fatal/m mum/n no, sudden/ng sing/ŏ pot/ō go/

of relief payments to the unemployed. —*v.*
doled, doling. —**dole out.** To distribute in small
portions. [< OE *dāl*, share, portion. See dail-.]
dole·ful (dōl′fəl) *adj.* Mournful; sad. —**dole′-
ful·ly** *adv.* —**dole′ful·ness** *n.*
doll (dŏl) *n.* **1.** A figure representing a baby or
other human being, used as a child's toy.
2. *Slang.* An attractive young woman. —*v.*
—**doll up.** To dress up smartly. [< *Doll*, pet
name for Dorothea.]
dol·lar (dŏl′ər) *n.* The basic monetary unit of
the United States, Australia, Canada, Ethiopia, Guyana, Jamaica, Liberia, Malaysia, New
Zealand, Trinidad and Tobago, Western Samoa, and Hong Kong and Singapore, equal to
100 cents. [< G *Taler.*]
dol·lop (dŏl′əp) *n.* A lump, helping, or portion,
as of ice cream. [?]
dol·ly (dŏl′ē) *n., pl.* **-lies. 1.** A doll. **2.** A low
mobile platform that rolls on casters. **3.** A
wheeled apparatus used to move a motion-
picture or television camera. **4.** A small locomotive for use in a railroad yard, construction
site, etc.
dol·men (dŏl′mən) *n.* A prehistoric structure
consisting of two or more upright stones with a
topstone, forming a chamber. [F.]
do·lor (dō′lər) *n.* Anguish; sorrow. [< L *do-
lēre*, to feel pain, grieve.] —**do′lor·ous** *adj.*
—**do′lor·ous·ness** *n.*
dol·phin (dŏl′fĭn, dôl′-) *n.* **1.** A marine mammal related to the whales but generally smaller
and with a beaklike snout. **2.** A marine fish
with iridescent coloring. [< Gk *delphis
(delphin-).*]
dolt (dōlt) *n.* A blockhead. [Perh a var of
DULL.] —**dolt′ish** *adj.* —**dolt′ish·ly** *adv.*
–dom. *comb. form.* **1.** The condition of being:
boredom. 2. The domain, position, or rank of:
saintdom. [< OE *-dōm.*]
dom. 1. domestic. **2.** dominant. **3.** dominion.
Dom. Dominican.
do·main (dō-mān′) *n.* **1.** A territory or range of
rule or control. **2.** A sphere of action or
interest; field. [< L *dominium*, property, ownership rights.]
dome (dōm) *n.* A hemispheric roof or vault.
[< It *duomo*, (domed) cathedral.]
do·mes·tic (də-mĕs′tĭk) *adj.* **1.** Of or pertaining to the family or household. **2.** Fond of
home. **3.** Tame; domesticated. **4.** Of or pertaining to a country's internal affairs. **5.** Indigenous: *domestic wine.* —*n.* A household
servant. [< L *domus*, house.] —**do·mes′ti·cal·ly**
adv.
do·mes·ti·cate (də-mĕs′tĭ-kāt′) *v.* **-cated, -cat-
ing.** To adapt to human living conditions and
practical uses; tame: *domesticate animals.*
—**do·mes′ti·ca′tion** *n.*
do·mes·tic·i·ty (dō′mĕ-stĭs′ə-tē) *n.* Home life
or devotion to it.
dom·i·cile (dŏm′ə-sīl′) *n.* A home, dwelling
place, or legal residence. [< L *domicilium*,
habitation, abode.] —**dom′i·cile′** *v.* **(-ciled,
-ciling).**
dom·i·nance (dŏm′ə-nəns) *n.* Authority; ascendancy.
dom·i·nant (dŏm′ə-nənt) *adj.* **1.** Exercising the

most influence. **2.** Pre-eminent in position. **3.**
Producing the same phenotypic effect whether
paired with an identical or a dissimilar gene.
—**dom′i·nant·ly** *adv.*
dom·i·nate (dŏm′ə-nāt′) *v.* **-nated, -nating. 1.** To
control, govern, or rule. **2.** To occupy the
pre-eminent position in or over. **3.** To overlook from a height. [L *dominārī*, to be lord and
master.] —**dom′i·na′tion** *n.* —**dom′i·na′tor** *n.*
dom·i·neer (dŏm′ə-nîr′) *v.* **1.** To rule arrogantly; tyrannize. **2.** To be overbearing.
Do·min·i·can Republic (də-mĭn′ĭ-kən). A
country occupying E Hispaniola in the Caribbean. Pop. 3,573,000. Cap. Santo Domingo.
—**Do·min′i·can** *adj. & n.*

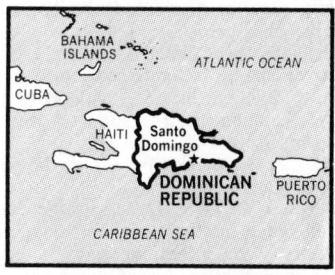

Dominican Republic

do·min·ion (də-mĭn′yən) *n.* **1.** Control or the
exercise of control; sovereignty. **2.** A sphere of
influence or control; realm; domain. **3.** Often
Dominion. Formerly, one of the self-governing
nations within the British Commonwealth of
Nations. [< L *dominium*, property, rights,
lordship.]
dom·i·no¹ (dŏm′ə-nō′) *n., pl.* **-noes** or **-nos.
1. a.** A hooded robe worn with an eye mask at
a masquerade. **b.** The mask itself. **2.** A person
wearing this costume. [< L *(benedicamos)
domino*, "(let us bless) the Lord."]
dom·i·no² (dŏm′ə-nō′) *n., pl.* **-noes** or **-nos. 1.** A
small, rectangular block marked with dots. **2.**
dominoes. The game played with a set of these
pieces. [F.]
don¹ (dŏn) *n.* A head, tutor, or fellow at a
college of Oxford or Cambridge. [< L *dominus*, lord, master.]
don² (dŏn) *v.* **donned, donning.** To put on (an
article of clothing). [Contraction of *do on.*]
Don (dŏn). A river of the SW Soviet Union.
do·nate (dō′nāt′, dō-nāt′) *v.* **-nated, -nating.** To
give to a fund or cause; contribute. [< L
dōnum, gift.] —**do·na′tion** *n.*
done (dŭn). *p.p.* of **do.** —*adj.* **1.** Finished. **2.**
Cooked adequately. **3.** Socially acceptable:
not done in polite society.
Do·netsk (də-nĕtsk′). A city of the Ukrainian
S.S.R. Pop. 774,000.
dong (dŏng) *n.* The basic monetary unit of
North Vietnam.
don·jon (dŏn′jən, dŭn′-) *n.* The main tower of
a castle. [Var of DUNGEON.]
Don Juan (dŏn′ wän′). A legendary Spanish
nobleman and libertine.

ô paw, for/oi boy/ou out/ŏŏ took/ōō coo/p pop/r run/s sauce/sh shy/t to/th thin/*th* the/
ŭ cut/ûr fur/v van/w wag/y yes/z size/zh vision/ə ago, item, edible, gallop, circus/

don•key (dŏng′kē, dŭng′-, dông′-) *n., pl.* **-keys.** 1. The domesticated ass. 2. An obstinate or stupid person.

don•ny•brook (dŏn′ē-brŏok′) *n.* A free-for-all. [< *Donnybrook,* near Dublin, Ireland.]

do•nor (dō′nər) *n.* 1. One who contributes something. 2. One who donates blood, tissue, or an organ for use in a transfusion or transplant.

Don Qui•xo•te (dŏn′ kē-hō′tē, kwĭk′sət). An idealist bent on righting incorrigible wrongs. [< Cervantes' *Don Quixote* (1605–15).]

don't (dōnt). Contraction of *do not.*

do•nut. Variant of **doughnut.**

doo•dad (dōō′dăd′) *n.* An unnamed or nondescript gadget or trinket.

doo•dle (dōōd′l) *v.* **-dled, -dling.** To draw or scribble while preoccupied. [< dial *doodle,* to trifle, fritter away time.] —**doo′dle** *n.*

doom (dōōm) *n.* 1. Condemnation to a severe penalty. 2. A terrible fate. 3. Disaster; ruin. —*v.* To condemn to ruination or death. [< OE *dōm.* See **dhē-.**]

dooms•day (dōōmz′dā′) *n.* The day of the Last Judgment.

door (dôr, dōr) *n.* 1. A movable, usually hinged, panel used to open or close an entranceway. 2. An entranceway or passage. 3. A means of access. [< OE *dor, duru,* gate, door. See **dhwer-.**]

door•jamb (dôr′jăm′, dōr′-) *n.* Either of the two vertical pieces framing a doorway.

door•knob (dôr′nŏb′, dōr′-) *n.* A handle for opening and closing a door.

door•man (dôr′măn′, -mən, dōr′-) *n.* One employed to tend the entrance of a hotel or apartment house.

door•mat (dôr′măt′, dōr′-) *n.* A mat placed before a doorway for wiping the shoes.

door•way (dôr′wā′, dōr′-) *n.* An entranceway.

dope (dōp) *n.* 1. Any of various viscous liquids. 2. *Informal.* A narcotic. 3. *Slang.* A very stupid person. 4. *Slang.* Factual information. —*v.* **doped, doping.** 1. To add or apply dope to. 2. To drug, as a horse. [Du *doop,* sauce.] —**dop′er** *n.*

Dopp•ler effect (dŏp′lər). An apparent change in the frequency of waves, as of sound or light, occurring when the source and observer are in motion relative to one another. [< C. *Doppler* (1803–1853), Austrian physicist.]

Do•ri•an (dôr′ē-ən, dōr′-) *n.* One of a Hellenic people that invaded Greece around 1100 B.C. and settled in the region of Sparta and Corinth. —**Do′ri•an** *adj.*

Dor•ic (dôr′ĭk, dōr′-) *n.* The Greek dialect of the Dorians. —*adj.* 1. Belonging to, characteristic of, or designating this dialect. 2. In the style of the Doric order.

Doric order. One of the three classical orders of architecture, characterized by heavy, fluted columns with a bold, simple cornice.

dorm (dôrm) *n. Informal.* A dormitory.

dor•mant (dôr′mənt) *adj.* 1. In a state resembling sleep. 2. In a state of suspended activity or development; inactive. [< L *dormīre,* to sleep.] —**dor′man•cy** *n.*

dor•mer (dôr′mər) *n.* A window set vertically in a gable projecting from a sloping roof. [OF *dormeor,* "bedroom window."]

dor•mi•to•ry (dôr′mə-tôr′ē, -tōr′ē) *n., pl.* **-ries.** 1. A large bedroom for a number of people. 2. A school residence hall. [< L *dormīre,* to sleep.]

dor•mouse (dôr′mous′) *n., pl.* **-mice** (-mīs′). A small, squirrellike Old World rodent. [ME *dormowse,* "sleeping mouse."]

dor•sal (dôr′səl) *adj. Anat.* In, on, or toward the back. [< L *dorsum,* back.]

Dort•mund (dôrt′mənd). A city in NW West Germany. Pop. 650,000.

dose (dōs) *n.* A specified quantity of a therapeutic agent prescribed to be taken at one time or at stated intervals. [< Gk *dosis,* a giving, dose.] —**dos′age** (dō′sĭj) *n.* —**dose** *v.* (**dosed, dosing**). —**dos′er** *n.*

dos•si•er (dŏs′ē-ā′, dôs′yā′) *n.* A file of documents pertaining to a particular person or subject. [< OF, bundle of papers having a label on the back.]

dost (dŭst). *Archaic.* 2nd person sing. present tense of **do.**

Dos•to•yev•sky (dŏs′tô-yĕf′skē), **Fyodor.** 1821–1881. Russian novelist.

dot (dŏt) *n.* 1. A spot; point. 2. Such a mark used in orthography, as the one over an *i.* 3. A short sound or signal used in combination with the dash and written as a dot to represent letters, numbers, or punctuation. 4. a. A decimal point. b. A symbol of multiplication. —**on the dot.** Absolutely punctual. —*v.* **dotted, dotting.** 1. To mark with a dot. 2. To cover with or as with dots: "*Campfires, like red, peculiar blossoms, dotted the night.*" (Stephen Crane). [< OE *dott,* head of a boil.] —**dot′ter** *n.*

do•tage (dō′tĭj) *n.* Senility. [< DOTE.]

dote (dōt) *v.* **doted, doting.** 1. To lavish excessive love or fondness. 2. To be senile. [< MDu *doten,* to be silly.] —**dot′er** *n.*

doth (dŭth). *Archaic.* 3rd person sing. present tense of **do.**

dot•tle (dŏt′l) *n.* The plug of ash left in the bowl of a pipe after it has been smoked. [< DOT.]

dot•ty (dŏt′ē) *adj.* **-tier, -tiest.** Crazy: *a dotty old lady.* [< DOTE.]

Dou•ay Version (dōō′ā). A translation of the Bible for use by Roman Catholics.

dou•ble (dŭb′əl) *adj.* 1. Twice as much in size, strength, number, or amount. 2. Composed of two parts or members. 3. Twofold; dual. 4. Designed for two: *a double bed.* 5. a. Acting two parts: *a double agent.* b. Deceitful: *double talk.* 6. Having numerous overlapping petals. —*n.* 1. Something increased twofold. 2. A duplicate; counterpart. 3. An actor's understudy. 4. A sharp turn; reversal. 5. **doubles.** A game, such as tennis, having two players on each side. 6. *Baseball.* A two-base hit. 7. *Bridge.* A bid doubling one's opponent's bid. —**on** (or **at**) **the double.** *Informal.* Immediately. —*v.* **-bled, -bling.** 1. To make twice as great. 2. To be twice as much as. 3. To fold in two. 4. To duplicate; repeat. 5. *Bridge.* To challenge with a double. 6. To turn sharply backward; reverse: *double back.* 7. To serve in an additional capacity. **8.** *Baseball.* To make a two-base hit. —*adv.* **1. a.** To twice the extent; doubly. **b.** To twice the amount: *double your money back.* **2.** Two together: *sleeping double.* **3.** In two: *bent double in pain.* [< L *duplus,* twofold, double.] —**doub'ly** *adv.* —**dou'ble·ness** *n.* —**dou'bler** *n.*

double bass. The largest member of the violin family, having a low range.

dou·ble-cross (dŭb'əl-krôs', -krŏs') *v. Slang.* To betray; deceive. —**dou'ble-cross'** *n.* —**dou'-ble-cross'er** *n.*

dou·ble-deal·ing (dŭb'əl-dē'lĭng) *adj.* Characterized by duplicity; deceitful. —*n.* Duplicity. —**doub'le-deal'er** *n.*

dou·ble-deck·er (dŭb'əl-dĕk'ər) *n.* **1.** A vehicle having two tiers for passengers. **2.** Two beds, one built above the other. **3.** A sandwich having two layers.

double knit. A jerseylike fabric knitted on a machine equipped with two sets of needles so that a double thickness of fabric is produced in which the two sides of the fabric are interlocked.

dou·ble-knit (dŭb'əl-nĭt) *adj.* Of or made of double knit.

double play. *Baseball.* A play in which two players are put out.

doub·let (dŭb'lĭt) *n.* **1.** A close-fitting jacket formerly worn by men. **2. a.** A pair of similar things. **b.** One of a pair. **3.** *Ling.* One of two words derived from the same source by different routes of transmission.

double take. A delayed reaction to the unexpected.

dou·bloon (dŭ-blōōn') *n.* An obsolete Spanish gold coin.

doubt (dout) *v.* **1.** To be uncertain or skeptical (about). **2.** To distrust. —*n.* **1.** A lack of conviction or certainty. **2.** An uncertain condition; uncertainty. **3. doubts.** Lack of trust; suspicion. —**no doubt. 1.** Certainly. **2.** Probably. [< L *dubitāre,* to waver, vibrate.] —**doubt'er** *n.*

doubt·ful (dout'fəl) *adj.* **1.** Causing doubt; uncertain. **2.** Having doubt; undecided. **3.** Questionable; suspicious. —**doubt'ful·ly** *adv.*

doubt·less (dout'lĭs) *adj.* Certain; assured. —*adv.* **1.** Certainly. **2.** Presumably. —**doubt'-less·ly** *adv.*

douche (dōōsh) *n.* **1.** A stream of water or air applied to a bodily part or cavity for cleansing or medicinal purposes. **2.** The application of a douche. **3.** A syringe or other instrument for applying a douche. —*v.* **douched, douching.** To cleanse or treat by a douche. [< It *doccia,* conduit pipe, shower, douche.]

dough (dō) *n.* **1.** A thick, pliable mixture of flour and other ingredients baked as bread, pastry, etc. **2.** *Slang.* Money. [< OE *dāg.* See **dheigh-.**] —**dough'y** *adj.*

dough·boy (dō'boi') *n.* An infantryman in World War I.

dough·nut (dō'nŭt', -nət) *n.* Also **do·nut.** A small, ring-shaped cake made of light dough that is fried in deep fat.

dough·ty (dou'tē) *adj.* **-tier, -tiest.** Courageous. [< OE *dohtig, dyhtig.*]

Doug·lass (dŭg'ləs), **Frederick,** 1817?–1895. American Negro abolitionist.

Frederick Douglass

dour (dōōr, dour) *adj.* **1.** Stern; forbidding. **2.** Glum; gloomy. [Perh < L *dūrus,* hard.] —**dour'ly** *adv.* —**dour'ness** *n.*

douse[1] (dous) *v.* **doused, dousing.** Also **dowse. 1.** To plunge into liquid; immerse. **2.** To wet thoroughly; drench; soak. [Perh < earlier *douse,* to strike, smite.]

douse[2] (dous) *v.* **doused, dousing.** To put out (a light or fire); extinguish. [Perh < DOUSE[1].]

dove[1] (dŭv) *n.* **1.** A pigeon or related bird, esp. an undomesticated species. **2.** A member of a group advocating peace. [< OE **dūfe.* See **dheu-[1].**]

dove[2] (dōv). Alternate *p.t.* of **dive.**

Do·ver (dō'vər). **1.** The capital of Delaware. Pop. 17,000. **2.** A port city of England. Pop. 36,000.

dove·tail (dŭv'tāl') *n.* **1.** A fan-shaped tenon that forms a tight interlocking joint when fitted into a corresponding mortise. **2.** A joint so formed. —*v.* **1.** To join by means of dovetails. **2.** To combine or interlock into a unified whole.

dow·a·ger (dou'ə-jər) *n.* **1.** A widow with a title derived from her husband. **2.** An elderly woman of high social station. [< L *dōs (dōt-),* dowry.]

dow·dy (dou'dē) *adj.* **-dier, -diest.** Lacking style; shabby. [< ME *doude,* slut.]

dow·el (dou'əl) *n.* A usually round pin that fits into a corresponding hole to fasten or align two adjacent pieces. —*v.* **-eled** or **-elled, -eling** or **-elling.** To fasten or align with dowels. [< MLG *dōvel,* peg, block, nail.]

dow·er (dou'ər) *n.* **1.** The part of a man's real estate allotted by law to his widow for her lifetime. **2.** A dowry. —*v.* To assign a dower to; endow.

down[1] (doun) *adv.* **1.** From a higher to a lower place. **2.** In or to a lower position, point, or condition. **3.** From an earlier to a later time. **4.** Seriously; intensely: *get down to work.* **5.** In partial payment at the time of purchase: *five dollars down.* **6.** In writing: *take down a statement.* **7.** To the source: *track down a rumor.* —*adj.* **1. a.** Moving or directed downward. **b.**

In a low position; not up. **2. a.** Sick. **b.** Low in spirit; depressed. **3.** In a competition, trailing an opponent by a specified number: *down one.* **4.** Being the first installment. **—down and out.** Lacking resources; destitute. **—down on.** *Informal.* Hostile toward. **—prep.** In a descending direction along, upon, into, or through. **—n.** **1.** A downward movement; descent. **2.** *Football.* One of four plays during which a team must advance at least ten yards to retain the ball. **—v.** **1.** To bring, put, strike, or throw down. **2.** To descend. [< OE *ofdūne,* "from the hill" < Gmc *dunaz.*]

down² (doun) *n.* **1.** Fine, soft, fluffy feathers. **2.** A similar soft covering or substance. [< ON *dūnn.*] **—down'y** *adj.*

down³ (doun) *n.* Often **downs.** A rolling, grassy upland area. [< OE *dūn,* hill.]

down•cast (doun'kăst', -kȧst') *adj.* **1.** Directed downward. **2.** Dejected; sad.

down•er (dou'nər) *n. Slang.* **1. A depressant or sedative drug, as a barbiturate. 2. A depressing experience.**

down•fall (doun'fôl') *n.* **1.** A sudden loss of wealth, reputation, etc.; ruin. **2.** A heavy or unexpected fall of rain or snow.

down•grade (doun'grād') *n.* A descending slope. **—on the downgrade.** Declining, as in influence or wealth. **—v.** To lower or minimize the importance of.

down•heart•ed (doun'här'tĭd) *adj.* Depressed; discouraged. **—down'heart'ed•ly** *adv.*

down•hill (doun'hĭl') *adv.* Down the slope of a hill; in a downward direction.

down•pour (doun'pôr', -pōr') *n.* A drenching rain.

down•right (doun'rīt') *adj.* **1.** Thorough; unequivocal. **2.** Plain; candid. **—adv.** Thoroughly; absolutely.

down•stairs (doun'stârz') *adv.* **1.** Down the stairs. **2.** To or on a lower floor. **—adj.** (doun'stârz'). Also **down•stair** (-stâr'). Located on a lower floor.

down•stream (doun'strēm') *adj.* In the direction of a stream's current. **—adv.** (doun'strēm'). Down a stream.

down-to-earth (doun'tə-ûrth') *adj.* Realistic; sensible.

down•town (doun'toun') *adv.* To, toward, or in the business center of a city or town. **—adj.** (doun'toun'). Of, relating to, or located downtown.

down•trod•den (doun'trŏd'n) *adj.* Oppressed; tyrannized.

down•ward (doun'wərd) *adv.* Also **down•wards** (-wərdz). From a higher to a lower place, level, condition, etc. **—down'ward** *adj.*

down•wind (doun'wĭnd') *adv.* In the direction in which the wind blows. **—down'wind'** *adj.*

dow•ry (dour'ē) *n., pl.* **-ries.** **1.** Money or property brought by a bride to her husband. **2.** A natural endowment or gift. [Var of DOWER.]

dowse¹ (douz) *v.* **dowsed, dowsing.** To use a divining rod, esp. to search for underground water. [?] **—dows'er** *n.*

dowse². Variant of **douse¹.**

doz. dozen.

doze (dōz) *v.* **dozed, dozing.** To sleep lightly; nap. [Prob < Scand.] **—doze** *n.* **—doz'er** *n.*

doz•en (dŭz'ən) *n.* **1.** *pl.* **-en.** A set of 12. **2.** *pl.* **-ens.** An indefinite number; a great many. **—adj.** Twelve. [< L *duodecim,* twelve.] **—doz'enth** *adj.*

dpt. department.

dr dram.

dr. **1.** debit. **2.** debtor.

Dr. **1.** doctor. **2.** drive (in street names).

drab (drăb) *adj.* **drabber, drabbest.** **1.** Of a light grayish or olive brown color. **2.** Dull; dreary. **—n.** Light grayish or olive brown. [Var of obs *drap,* cloth.] **—drab'ly** *adv.*

drach•ma (drăk'mə) *n., pl.* **-mas** or **-mae** (-mē). The basic monetary unit of Greece. [< Gk *drakhmē.*]

Dra•co (drā'kō) *n.* A constellation in the polar region of the N Hemisphere.

draft (drăft, drȧft). Also *chiefly Brit.* **draught** (drȧft). *n.* **1. a.** A current of air. **b.** A device in a flue controlling air circulation. **2. a.** A pull or traction of a load. **b.** That which is pulled or drawn. **3.** The depth of a vessel's keel below the water line. **4.** A heavy demand upon resources. **5.** A document for transferring money. **6. a.** A gulp, swallow, or inhalation. **b.** The amount taken in by such an act. **7.** The drawing of a liquid, as from a keg. **8. a.** A selection of personnel from a group, esp. conscription for military service. **b.** The body of people so selected. **9. a.** The drawing in of a fishnet. **b.** The catch. **10.** A preliminary outline, version, design, etc. **—on draft.** Tapped from a keg; not bottled. **—v.** **1.** To select from a group for an assignment, as military service. **2.** To draw up a preliminary version of or plan for. **—adj.** **1.** Used for drawing heavy loads. **2.** Drawn from a cask. [ME *draught,* a pulling, a drawing.]

draft•ee (drăf-tē', drȧf-) *n.* One drafted for military service.

draft•ing (drăf'tĭng, drȧf'-) *n.* The systematic representation and dimensional specification of mechanical and architectural structures.

drafts•man (drăfts'mən, drȧfts'-) *n.* One who draws plans or designs.

draft•y (drăf'tē, drȧf'-) *adj.* **-ier, -iest.** Having or exposed to drafts of air. **—draft'i•ly** *adv.* **—draft'i•ness** *n.*

drag (drăg) *v.* **dragged, dragging.** **1.** To pull or draw along the ground, esp. by force. **2.** To search the bottom of (a body of water), as with a grappling hook. **3.** To bring forcibly to or into. **4.** To move with reluctance, difficulty, etc. **5.** To prolong tediously (with *out*). **—n.** **1.** The act of dragging. **2.** Something dragged along the ground, as a harrow, or under water, as a grappling hook. **3.** Something that retards motion or progress. **4.** The degree of resistance involved in dragging or hauling. **5.** *Slang.* Something obnoxiously tiresome. **6.** *Slang.* A puff, as on a cigarette. [< OE *dragan* or ON *draga.* See **dhragh-.**]

drag•net (drăg'nět') *n.* **1.** A net, esp. one for trawling. **2.** A network of procedures used to apprehend criminal suspects.

drag•on (drăg'ən) *n.* **1.** A fabulous monster represented as a gigantic winged reptile with a lion's claws. **2.** A representation of this creature. [< Gk *drakôn*, serpent.]

drag·on·fly (drăg′ən-flī′) *n.* A large, narrow-bodied, four-winged insect.

dra·goon (drə-gōōn′, dră-) *n.* A heavily armed mounted trooper. —*v.* To force by the use of troops or other harsh means. [F *dragon*, carbine, "fire-breather."]

drain (drān) *v.* **1.** To draw or flow off by a gradual process. **2.** To cause liquid substance to go out from; empty. **3.** To consume totally; exhaust. —*n.* **1.** A pipe or channel by which liquid is drawn off. **2.** An act or instance of draining. [< OE *drēahnian*.]

drain·age (drā′nĭj) *n.* **1.** The action or a method of draining. **2.** A system of drains. **3.** That which is drained off.

drain·pipe (drān′pīp′) *n.* A pipe for carrying off rainwater or sewage.

drake (drāk) *n.* A male duck. [Perh < Gmc *drako*, male.]

dram (drăm) *n.* **1. a.** A unit of weight in the U.S. Customary System, an avoirdupois unit equal to 27.344 grains or 0.0625 ounce. **b.** A unit of apothecary weight, equal to 60 grains. **2.** A small draft: *a dram of cordial.* [ME *dragme*, dram, drachma.]

dra·ma (drä′mə, drăm′ə) *n.* **1. a.** A literary composition to be presented before an audience; a play. **b.** Such literature as an art. **2.** A situation of interesting, often exaggerated, conflict or emotion. [< Gk, deed, action on the stage.] —**dra·mat'ic** (drə-măt′ĭk) *adj.*

Dram·a·mine (drăm′ə-mēn′) *n.* A trademark for a drug used to treat motion sickness.

dram·a·tist (drăm′ə-tĭst, drä′mə-) *n.* A playwright.

dram·a·tize (drăm′ə-tīz′, drä′mə-) *v.* **-tized, -tizing. 1.** To adapt for presentation as a drama. **2.** To present or view in a dramatic way. —**dram'a·ti·za'tion** *n.*

drank (drăngk). *p.t.* of **drink.**

drape (drāp) *v.* **draped, draping. 1.** To dress or hang with or as with cloth in loose folds. **2.** To arrange in loose folds. **3.** To hang or rest loosely. —*n.* **1.** Often **drapes.** A drapery. **2.** The way in which cloth falls or hangs. [< LL *drappus*, cloth.]

drap·er (drā′pər) *n. Brit.* A dealer in cloth or dry goods.

drap·er·y (drā′pə-rē) *n., pl.* **-ies. 1.** Cloth arranged in loose folds. **2.** Often **draperies.** Curtains that hang straight in loose folds. **3.** *Brit.* The business of a draper.

dras·tic (drăs′tĭk) *adj.* **1.** Violently effective. **2.** Severe; extreme. [Gk *drastikos*, active, efficient.] —**dras'ti·cal·ly** *adv.*

draught. *Chiefly Brit.* Variant of **draft.**

draughts (drăfts, dräfts) *n. (takes sing. v.). Chiefly Brit.* The game of checkers.

Dra·vid·i·an (drə-vĭd′ē-ən) *n.* **1.** A large non-Indo-European family of languages, including Tamil and Malayalam. **2.** One who speaks a Dravidian language. —**Dra·vid'i·an** *adj.*

draw (drô) *v.* **drew, drawn, drawing. 1.** To pull (something) toward or after one. **2.** To pull or move (something) in a given direction or to a given position. **3.** To take or pull out, as from

a holster. **4.** To suck or take in (air). **5.** To displace (a specified depth of water) in floating. **6.** To induce to act. **7.** To attract. **8.** To extract from evidence; formulate: *draw conclusions.* **9. a.** To earn; bring in: *draw interest.* **b.** To withdraw (money). **10.** To evoke; elicit. **11.** To take or accept as a chance: *draw lots.* **12.** To distort; contract. **13.** To stretch taut. **14.** To eviscerate. **15.** To draft or sketch. —**draw out. 1.** To cause to converse easily. **2.** To prolong. —**draw up. 1.** To draft; compose (a document). **2.** To pull up to a halt. —*n.* **1.** The act or result of drawing. **2.** A special advantage. **3.** A contest ending in a tie. [< OE *dragan.* See dhragh-.]

draw·back (drô′băk′) *n.* A disadvantage; hindrance.

draw·bridge (drô′brĭj′) *n.* A bridge that can be raised or drawn aside.

draw·er *n.* **1.** (drô′ər). One who draws. **2.** (drôr). A boxlike compartment in furniture that can be drawn on slides. **3. drawers** (drôrz). Underpants.

draw·ing (drô′ĭng) *n.* **1.** The act or an instance of drawing. **2.** The art of depicting forms or figures on a surface by lines. **3.** A portrayal in lines on a surface of a form or figure.

drawing card. An attraction drawing large audiences.

drawing room. 1. A formal reception room. **2.** A private room on a railroad sleeping car. [< *withdrawing room.*]

drawl (drôl) *v.* To speak with lengthened or drawn-out vowels. [Poss a freq of DRAW.] —**drawl** *n.*

drawn (drôn). *p.p.* of **draw.** —*adj.* **1.** Pulled out of a sheath. **2.** Haggard, as from ill health. **3.** Eviscerated.

draw·string (drô′strĭng′) *n.* A cord, ribbon, etc., run through a hem or casing and pulled to tighten.

dray (drā) *n.* A low cart used for heavy loads. [< OE *dræge*, dragnet. See dhragh-.]

dread (drĕd) *v.* **1.** To be in terror of; fear greatly. **2.** To hold in awe or reverence. **3.** To anticipate with anxiety or reluctance. —*n.* **1.** Profound fear; terror. **2.** Awe; reverence. **3.** Anxious or fearful anticipation. —*adj.* **1.** Terrifying; fearsome. **2.** Awesome; revered. [< OE *drædan.*]

dread·ful (drĕd′fəl) *adj.* **1.** Inspiring dread; terrible. **2.** Extremely unpleasant. —**dread'ful·ly** *adv.* —**dread'ful·ness** *n.*

dread·nought (drĕd′nôt′) *n.* A heavily armed battleship.

dream (drēm) *n.* **1.** A series of images, ideas, etc., occurring in certain stages of sleep. **2.** A daydream; reverie. **3.** A wild fancy or hope. **4.** Anything extremely beautiful, fine, or pleasant. —*v.* **dreamed** or **dreamt** (drĕmt), **dreaming. 1.** To experience a dream or dreams. **2.** To aspire or hope (with *of*). **3.** To conceive of; imagine. **4.** To pass idly or in reverie, as time. —**dream up.** To invent; concoct. [< OE *drēam*, joy, gladness, music. See dhreugh-.] —**dream'er** *n.*

dream·y (drē′mē) *adj.* **-ier, -iest. 1.** Resembling a dream; vague. **2.** Given to daydreams or

reverie. **3.** Soothing; quiet. —**dream′i•ly** *adv.*
—**dream′i•ness** *n.*

drear•y (drîr′ē) *adj.* -ier, -iest. Also *poetic* **drear**
(drîr). **1.** Gloomy; dismal. **2.** Boring; dull. [<
OE *drēor,* blood. See **dhreu-**.] —**drear′i•ly** *adv.*
—**drear′i•ness** *n.*

dredge[1] (drĕj) *n.* **1.** A machine or implement
used to scoop or remove dirt, sand, etc., from
under water, as in deepening harbors. **2.** A
boat equipped with such a device. —*v.*
dredged, dredging. To deepen, scoop, etc., with
a dredge. [?]

dredge[2] (drĕj) *v.* **dredged, dredging.** To coat
(food) with flour, sugar, etc. [?]

dregs (drĕgz) *pl.n.* **1.** The sediment of a liquid;
lees. **2.** The basest or least desirable portion.
[< ON *dregg* (sing.).]

drench (drĕnch) *v.* To wet thoroughly; saturate. [< OE *drencan,* to give to drink, to soak.
See **dhreg-**.] —**drench′er** *n.*

dress (drĕs) *v.* **1.** To put on clothing; clothe.
2. To adorn or arrange. **3.** To wear formal
clothes. **4.** To put (troops) in ranks; align.
5. To apply therapeutic materials to (a
wound). **6.** To groom (an animal); curry. **7.**
To clean (fish or fowl), as for cooking. **8.** To
put a finish on. —**dress up.** To wear formal
clothes or finery. —*n.* **1.** Clothing; apparel.
2. A one-piece skirted outer garment for wom-
en. —*adj.* **1.** Suitable for a formal occasion: *a
dress uniform.* **2.** Requiring formal clothing: *a
dress dinner.* [< VL **dīrectiāre.*]

dress•er[1] (drĕs′ər) *n.* One that dresses or assists in dressing.

dress•er[2] (drĕs′ər) *n.* A chest of drawers. [ME
dressour, kitchen sideboard on which food was
prepared.]

dress•ing (drĕs′ĭng) *n.* **1.** Therapeutic material
applied to a wound. **2.** A sauce, as for a salad.
3. A stuffing, as for poultry.

dress•ing-down (drĕs′ĭng-doun′) *n.* A severe
scolding.

dressing gown. A robe worn informally at
home.

dress•mak•er (drĕs′mā′kər) *n.* One who
makes women's clothes. —**dress′mak′ing** *n.*

dress rehearsal. A final, uninterrupted run-
through, as of a play with costumes and stage
properties.

dress•y (drĕs′ē) *adj.* -ier, -iest. **1.** Wearing fancy
or elegant clothing. **2.** Smart; stylish.

drew (drōō). *p.t.* of **draw.**

drib•ble (drĭb′əl) *v.* -bled, -bling. **1.** To flow or
fall unsteadily; trickle. **2.** To drool. **3.** To
move (a ball) by repeated light bounces or
kicks, as in basketball or soccer. —*n.* **1.** A
trickle. **2.** A small quantity; a bit. [< DRIP.]

drib•let (drĭb′lĭt) *n.* **1.** A falling drop of liquid.
2. A small amount or portion.

dri•er[1] (drī′ər) *n.* Also **dry•er. 1.** One that dries.
2. A substance added to paint, ink, etc., to
speed drying. **3.** Variant of **dryer.**

dri•er[2]. *compar.* of **dry.**

drift (drĭft) *v.* **1.** To carry or be carried along by
or as by a current. **2.** To move about without a
goal; wander. **3.** To pile up in banks or heaps,
as by the force of the wind. —*n.* **1.** The act or
condition of drifting. **2.** Drifting material.

3. A bank or pile, as of snow, heaped up by the
wind. **4.** A trend or general meaning. **5. a.**
Lateral displacement or deviation of an object
or vehicle from a planned course. **b.** Variation
or random oscillation about a fixed setting.
6. The rate of flow of a water current. [< ON,
snowdrift, and MDu, herd, course.] —**drift′y**
adj.

drift•er (drĭf′tər) *n.* One that drifts, esp. one
who moves from place to place or job to job.

drift•wood (drĭft′wŏŏd′) *n.* Wood floating in
or washed up by water.

drill[1] (drĭl) *n.* **1. a.** An implement with cutting
edges or a pointed end for boring holes in hard
materials, usually by a rotating abrasion or
repeated blows. **b.** The hand-operated or
hand-powered holder for this tool. **2.** Disci-
plined, repetitious exercise as a means of training. **3.** A specific task or exercise designed to
develop a skill. —*v.* **1.** To make a hole in with
a drill. **2.** To train by repetition. [< MDu
drillen, to drill.]

drill[2] (drĭl) *n.* **1.** A trench or furrow in which
seeds are planted. **2.** A device for planting
seeds in holes or furrows. [?]

drill[3] (drĭl) *n.* Strong cotton or linen twill. [<
L *trilīx,* triple-twilled.]

drill press. A powered vertical drilling machine, used mainly on metals.

drink (drĭngk) *v.* **drank, drunk, drinking. 1.** To
swallow (a liquid). **2.** To soak up (liquid or
moisture); absorb. **3.** To take in eagerly
through the senses or intellect (with *in*). **4.** To
give or make (a toast). **5.** To imbibe alcoholic
liquors, esp. to excess. —*n.* **1.** Any liquid for
drinking; a beverage. **2.** An amount of liquid
swallowed. **3.** Alcoholic liquor. **4.** Excessive
indulgence in alcoholic liquor. [< OE *drincan.*
See **dhreg-**.] —**drink′a•ble** *adj.* —**drink′er** *n.*

drip (drĭp) *v.* **dripped, dripping.** To fall or allow
to fall in drops. —*n.* **1.** The process of falling
in drops. **2.** Liquid that falls in drops. **3.** The
sound made by dripping liquid. **4.** *Slang.* An
unpleasant or tiresomely boring person. [ME
drippen.]

drip•pings (drĭp′ĭngz) *pl.n.* The fat and juice
exuded from roasting meat.

drive (drīv) *v.* **drove, driven** (drĭv′ən), **driving.
1.** To push, propel, or press forcibly. **2.** To
force to work or overwork. **3.** To force or
thrust into or from a particular act or state.
4. To propel (a ball) quickly and forcefully.
5. To force to go through or penetrate. **6.** To
operate (a vehicle). **7.** To cause to function;
motivate. **8.** To carry through vigorously to a
conclusion. —**drive at.** To mean; intend. —*n.*
1. The act of driving. **2.** A road, esp. a
driveway or highway. **3.** A trip in a vehicle.
4. The means or apparatus for transmitting
motion to a machine or machine part. **5.** An
organized effort to accomplish a purpose; a
campaign. **6.** Energy; initiative. **7.** A strong
motivating tendency or instinct, esp. of sexual
or aggressive origin, that prompts activity toward a particular end. **8.** A massive and sustained military offensive. **9. a.** A quick, forceful propelling of a ball. **b.** The propelling
stroke or thrust. **10. a.** A rounding up of cattle,

ă pat/ā ate/âr care/ä bar/b **bib**/ch **chew**/d **deed**/ĕ pet/ē be/f fit/g **gag**/h hat/hw **what**/
ĭ pit/ī pie/îr pier/j **judge**/k **kick**/l lid, fatal/m **mum**/n no, sudden/ng sing/ŏ pot/ō go/

as for slaughter. **b.** A driving of logs down a river. [< OE *drīfan*. See **dhreibh-**.]

drive-in (drīv'ĭn') *n.* An establishment, as a restaurant or motion-picture theater, accommodating customers who remain in their automobiles. —**drive'-in** *adj.*

driv•el (drĭv'əl) *v.* **-eled** or **-elled, -eling** or **-elling. 1.** To slobber; drool. **2.** To flow like spittle or saliva. **3.** To talk stupidly or childishly. —*n.* **1.** Saliva flowing from the mouth. **2.** Stupid or senseless talk. [< OE *dreflian*. See **dher-¹**.] —**driv'el•er** *n.*

driv•er (drī'vər) *n.* **1.** One who drives, as a chauffeur. **2.** *Golf.* A wooden-headed club with a long shaft, used for making long shots from the tee.

drive•way (drīv'wā') *n.* An often short private road.

driz•zle (drĭz'əl) *v.* **-zled, -zling.** To rain gently in fine drops. [Perh < OE *drēosan*, to fall. See **dhreu-**.] —**driz'zle** *n.* —**driz'zly** *adj.*

drogue (drōg) *n.* A small parachute used to slow down a re-entering spacecraft or satellite prior to deployment of the main parachute. [Perh < OE *dragan*, to DRAW.]

droll (drōl) *adj.* Amusingly odd; whimsically comical. [< MDu *drol*, "little man."] —**droll'er•y** (drō'lə-rē) *n.*

–drome. *comb. form.* A place or arena, esp. a racecourse: **airdrome.** [< Gk *dromos*, race, course.]

drom•e•dar•y (drŏm'ə-dĕr'ē, drŭm'-) *n., pl.* **-ies.** The one-humped domesticated camel of N Africa and E Asia. [< Gk *dromas (dromad-)*, dromedary, runner.]

drone¹ (drōn) *n.* **1.** A male bee, esp. a honeybee. **2.** A loafer; sluggard. **3.** A pilotless, remote-control aircraft. [< OE *drān, drǣn.* See **dher-².**]

drone² (drōn) *v.* **droned, droning. 1.** To make a continuous low, dull humming sound. **2.** To speak in a monotonous tone. —*n.* A low humming or buzzing sound.

drool (drōōl) *v.* **1.** To let saliva run from the mouth; drivel. **2.** *Informal.* To make an extravagant show of appreciation. **3.** *Informal.* To talk nonsense. —*n.* **1.** Saliva; drivel. **2.** *Informal.* Silly talk. [Perh var of DRIVEL.]

droop (drōōp) *v.* **1.** To bend or hang downward. **2.** To appear dejected or listless: *The roses drooped in the heat.* —*n.* The act or condition of drooping. [< ON *drūpa.*]

drop (drŏp) *n.* **1.** The smallest quantity of liquid heavy enough to fall in a spherical or pear-shaped mass. **2.** A minute quantity. **3. drops.** Liquid medicine administered in such quantity. **4.** Something that resembles a drop. **5.** The act of falling. **6.** A swift decline or decrease, as in quality, quantity, etc. **7.** The vertical distance from a higher to a lower level. **8.** Men and equipment landed by parachute. **9.** Something arranged to be lowered, as a stage curtain. —*v.* **dropped, dropping. 1.** To fall or let fall in drops. **2.** To fall or let fall from a higher to a lower place. **3.** To become less in number, intensity, etc.; decrease. **4.** To descend. **5.** To sink into a state of exhaustion. **6.** To pass into some specified state or condi-

tion. **7.** To cease; come to an end. **8.** To say or offer casually. **9.** To lower the level of (the voice). —**drop by** (or **in**). To stop in for a short visit. —**drop off. 1.** To fall asleep. **2.** To decrease. [< OE *dropa.* See **dhreu-**.]

drop kick. A kick made by dropping a football and kicking it just as it starts to rebound. —**drop'-kick'** (drŏp'kĭk') *v.*

drop•let (drŏp'lĭt) *n.* A tiny drop.

drop out. To withdraw from school, organized society, etc.

drop•out (drŏp'out') *n.* One who has withdrawn, esp. one who leaves school before graduating.

drop•per (drŏp'ər) *n.* A small tube with a suction bulb at one end for drawing in a liquid and releasing it in drops.

drop•sy (drŏp'sē) *n.* Pathological accumulation of diluted lymph in body tissues and cavities. [< Gk *hudrōpisis.*]

dross (drôs, drŏs) *n.* **1.** Waste products or impurities formed on the surface of molten metal during smelting. **2.** Worthless material; rubbish. [< OE *drôs*, dregs. See **dher-¹.**] —**dross'i•ness** *n.* —**dross'y** *adj.*

drought (drout) *n.* Also **drouth** (drouth). A long period with no rain. [< OE *drūgath.*]

drove¹ (drōv) *p.t.* of **drive.**

drove² (drōv) *n.* A flock, herd, or large group driven or moving in a body. [< OE *drāf* < *drīfan*, to DRIVE.]

drov•er (drō'vər) *n.* A driver of cattle or sheep.

drown (droun) *v.* **1.** To kill or die by suffocating in water or other liquid. **2.** To drench or cover with a liquid. **3.** To overwhelm or muffle (a sound, noise, etc). [< Scand.]

drowse (drouz) *v.* **drowsed, drowsing.** To be half-asleep; doze. —*n.* The condition of being sleepy. [Perh < OE *drūsian*, to be sluggish. See **dhreu-**.]

drow•sy (drou'zē) *adj.* **-sier, -siest.** Having or causing a sleepy feeling. —**drow'si•ly** *adv.* —**drow'si•ness** *n.*

drub (drŭb) *v.* **drubbed, drubbing. 1.** To thrash or beat with a stick. **2.** To defeat emphatically. [Ar *dáraba*, to beat.]

drudge (drŭj) *n.* One who does tedious, menial, or unpleasant work. —*v.* **drudged, drudging.** To do the work of a drudge. [?] —**drudg'er•y** *n.*

drug (drŭg) *n.* **1.** A substance used as medicine in the treatment of disease. **2.** A narcotic, esp. one that is addictive. —**drug on the market.** A commodity for which there is little demand. —*v.* **drugged, drugging. 1.** To administer a drug to. **2.** To poison or mix (food or drink) with drugs. **3.** To stupefy or dull with or as if with a drug. [< OF *drogue*, chemical material.]

drug•gist (drŭg'ĭst) *n.* **1.** A pharmacist. **2.** One who sells drugs.

drug•store (drŭg'stôr', -stōr') *n.* A store where drugs, medical supplies, and other articles are sold.

dru•id (drōō'ĭd) *n.* Also **Dru•id.** A member of an order of priests in ancient Gaul and Britain.

drum (drŭm) *n.* **1.** A percussion instrument consisting of a hollow cylinder or hemisphere with a membrane stretched tightly over one or both ends. **2.** A sound produced by beating such an instrument. **3. a.** A metal cylinder or spool, wound with cable, wire, or heavy rope. **b.** A cylindrical or barrellike metal container. —*v.* **drummed, drumming. 1.** To beat a drum. **2.** To thump or tap rhythmically or continually. —**drum into.** To instruct by constant repetition. —**drum up.** To summon or obtain by soliciting, advertising, etc.: *drum up business.* [< MDu *tromme.*]

drum major. A person who leads a marching band.

drum•mer (drŭm'ər) *n.* **1.** One who plays a drum. **2.** A traveling salesman.

drum•stick (drŭm'stĭk') *n.* **1.** A stick for beating a drum. **2.** The lower part of the leg of a cooked fowl.

drunk (drŭngk). *p.p.* & *p.t.* of **drink.** —*adj.* **1.** Intoxicated with alcoholic liquor; inebriated. **2.** Overcome by strong feeling. —*n.* **1.** A drunken person. **2.** A bout of drinking.

Usage: Drunk (adj.) is chiefly used predicatively after a verb: *He was drunk. Drunken* is preferable to *drunk* as an attributive (before a noun): *a drunken driver; drunken driving.*

drunk•ard (drŭng'kərd) *n.* One who is habitually drunk.

drunk•en (drŭng'kən). Alternate *p.p.* of **drink.** —*adj.* **1.** Intoxicated. **2.** Pertaining to or occurring during intoxication: *drunken driving.* —See Usage note at **drunk.** —**drunk'en•ly** *adv.* —**drunk'en•ness** *n.*

dry (drī) *adj.* **drier** or **dryer, driest** or **dryest. 1.** Free from liquid or moisture. **2.** Having or characterized by little or no rain. **3.** Not under water: *dry land.* **4.** No longer yielding milk: *a dry cow.* **5.** Needing drink; thirsty. **6.** Pertaining to solid rather than liquid substances or commodities. **7.** Not sweet: *a dry wine.* **8.** Dull; boring. **9.** Matter-of-fact; impersonal. **10.** Prohibiting the sale or consumption of alcoholic beverages. —*v.* **dried, drying.** To make or become dry. —**dry up. 1.** To become dry. **2.** *Slang.* To stop talking; shut up. [< OE *drȳge* < Gmc **driug-.*] —**dry'ly, dri'ly** *adv.* —**dry'ness** *n.*

dry•ad (drī'əd, -ăd') *n.* A wood nymph.

dry cell. A primary battery cell having an electrolyte in the form of moist paste.

dry-clean (drī'klēn') *v.* To clean (clothing or fabrics) with chemical solvents having little or no water. —**dry cleaning.**

dry dock. A large floating or stationary dock used for maintaining, repairing, and altering ships.

dry•er (drī'ər). **1.** Alternate *compar.* of **dry. 2.** Variant of **drier.** —*n.* Also **drier.** An appliance for removing moisture, esp. by heating.

dry•est. Alternate *superl.* of **dry.**

dry farming. A type of farming practiced in arid areas without irrigation by maintaining a fine surface tillage or mulch that protects the natural moisture of the soil from evaporation. —**dry farm.** —**dry farmer.**

dry goods. Textiles, clothing, and related articles of trade.

Dry Ice. A trademark for solid carbon dioxide, used primarily as a refrigerant.

dry run. A trial run or rehearsal, as a military exercise without the use of live ammunition.

d.s. **1.** *Commerce.* days after sight. **2.** document signed.

DSC, D.S.C. Distinguished Service Cross.

DSM Distinguished Service Medal.

D.S.O. Distinguished Service Order.

d.s.p. died without issue (L *decessit sine prole*).

DST, D.S.T. daylight-saving time.

D.T.'s (dē'tēz') *pl.n.* Delirium tremens.

Du. Dutch.

du•al (d/y/ōō'əl) *adj.* Composed of two parts; double: *dual controls.* [< L *duo,* two.] —**du•al'i•ty** (-ăl'ə-tē) *n.* —**du'al•ly** *adv.*

du•al•ism (d/y/ōō'ə-lĭz'əm) *n.* Any doctrine viewing reality as the product of two conflicting cosmic forces. —**du'al•ist** *n.* & *adj.* —**du'al•is'tic** (-ə-lĭs'tĭk) *adj.*

dub¹ (dŭb) *v.* **dubbed, dubbing. 1.** To tap lightly on the shoulder in conferring knighthood. **2.** To name playfully; nickname. **3.** To cut, rub, etc., so as to make even or smooth. **4.** *Slang.* To execute (a golf stroke) poorly; bungle. [< OE *dubbian.* See **dheubh-.**]

dub² (dŭb) *v.* **dubbed, dubbing. 1.** To insert a new sound track, such as a translation of the original dialogue, into (a film). **2.** To insert (sound) into a film or tape (often with *in*). [Short for DOUBLE.]

dub•bin (dŭb'ĭn) *n.* Also **dub•bing** (-ĭng). An application of tallow and oil for dressing leather. [< DUB.]

du•bi•e•ty (d/y/ōō-bī'ə-tē) *n., pl.* **-ties.** A matter of doubt; an uncertainty.

du•bi•ous (d/y/ōō'bē-əs) *adj.* **1.** Fraught with uncertainty or doubt; undecided. **2.** Arousing doubt; questionable. **3.** Skeptical; doubtful. [L *dubius,* dubious, fluctuating.] —**du'bi•ous•ly** *adv.* —**du'bi•ous•ness** *n.*

Dub•lin (dŭb'lĭn). The capital of the Republic of Ireland. Pop. 537,000.

du•cal (d/y/ōō'kəl) *adj.* Pertaining to a duke or dukedom. —**du'cal•ly** *adv.*

duc•at (dŭk'ət) *n.* Any of various gold coins formerly used in Europe. [< ML *ducātūs,* duchy.]

duch•ess (dŭch'ĭs) *n.* **1.** The wife or widow of a duke. **2.** A woman holding title to a duchy.

duch•y (dŭch'ē) *n., pl.* **-ies.** The territory ruled by a duke or duchess; a dukedom.

duck¹ (dŭk) *n.* Any of various water birds with a broad, flat bill, short legs, and webbed feet. [< OE **dūcan,* to dive, DUCK.]

duck² (dŭk) *v.* **1.** To lower quickly, esp. so as to avoid something. **2.** To evade; dodge. **3.** To submerge briefly in water. [< OE **dūcan,* to dive < Gmc **dukjan.*]

duck³ (dŭk) *n.* **1.** A durable, closely woven heavy cotton or linen fabric. **2. ducks.** Clothing made of this fabric. [< MDu *doek.*]

duck•bill (dŭk'bĭl') *n.* A platypus.

duck•board (dŭk'bôrd', -bōrd') *n.* A board or boardwalk laid across a wet or muddy surface.

duck•ling (dŭk'lĭng) *n.* A young duck.

duck•pin (dŭk'pĭn') *n.* **1.** A bowling pin, shorter and squatter than a tenpin. **2. duckpins** *(takes sing. v.).* A bowling game played with these pins.

ă pat/ā ate/âr care/ä bar/b bib/ch chew/d deed/ĕ pet/ē be/f fit/g gag/h hat/hw what/ ĭ pit/ī pie/îr pier/j judge/k kick/l lid, fatal/m mum/n no, sudden/ng sing/ŏ pot/ō go/

duck•y (dŭk′ē) *adj.* -ier, -iest. *Slang.* Excellent; fine. —*n., pl.* **duckies.** Dear. Used as a term of familiarity.

duct (dŭkt) *n.* **1.** Any tubular passage through which a substance, esp. a fluid, is conveyed. **2.** A tube or pipe for electrical cables or wires. [L *ductus,* pp *dūcere,* to lead.]

duc•tile (dŭk′tĭl) *adj.* **1.** Capable of being drawn into wire or hammered thin, as metal. **2.** Readily influenced; tractable. [< L *ductus,* DUCT.] —**duc•til′i•ty** *n.*

duct•less gland (dŭkt′lĭs). An endocrine gland.

dud (dŭd) *n. Informal.* **1.** A bomb, shell, etc., that fails to explode. **2.** One that is disappointingly unsuccessful. [ME *dudde,* article of clothing, thing.]

dude (d/y/o͞od) *n.* **1.** *Informal.* An Easterner or city person staying in the West. **2.** *Informal.* A dandy. [?]

dudg•eon (dŭj′ən) *n.* A sullen or indignant anger. [?]

due (d/y/o͞o) *adj.* **1.** Payable immediately or on demand. **2.** Owed as a debt; owing. **3.** Owed by right; fitting or appropriate. **4.** Sufficient; adequate. **5.** Expected or scheduled. —**due to. 1.** Attributable to; caused by. **2.** Because of. —*n.* **1.** Something that is owed or deserved. **2. dues.** A charge or fee for membership. —*adv.* Straight; directly: *due west.* [< VL *dēbūtus,* "owed."]
Usage: *Due to* is preferably restricted to sentences in which *due* functions as an adjective following a linking verb: *His hesitancy was due to fear.* In formal usage, *due to* is not appropriate when it introduces an adverbial phrase that directly modifies a nonlinking verb: *He hesitated due to fear* (preferably *because of* or *owing to fear*).

du•el (d/y/o͞ol) *n.* **1.** A prearranged combat between two persons, fought to settle a point of honor. **2.** Any struggle between two persons, groups, etc. —*v.* -eled or -elled, -eling or -elling. To fight in a duel. [< L *duellum,* war.] —**du′el•er, du′el•ist** *n.*

du•et (d/y/o͞o-ĕt′) *n.* **1.** A musical composition written for two voices or two instruments. **2.** The two performers of such a composition. [< L *duo,* two.]

duf•fel bag (dŭf′əl). A large cloth bag for carrying personal belongings.

duf•fer (dŭf′ər) *n. Informal.* An incompetent or dull-witted person. [?]

dug[1] (dŭg) *n.* An udder, breast, or teat of a female animal. [?]

dug[2]. *p.t. & p.p.* of **dig.**

dug•out (dŭg′out′) *n.* **1.** A boat or canoe made by hollowing out a log. **2.** A shelter dug into the ground or hillside. **3.** A long sunken shelter for the players at the side of a baseball field.

Duis•burg (dü̱s′bo͝orKH′). A city of West Germany. Pop. 501,000.

duke (d/y/o͞ok) *n.* **1.** A nobleman with the highest rank, esp. a man of the highest grade of the British peerage. **2.** A prince who rules an independent duchy. [< L *dux (duc-),* leader.] —**duke′dom** *n.*

dul•cet (dŭl′sĭt) *adj.* Pleasing to the ear; gently melodious. [< L *dulcis,* sweet.]

dul•ci•mer (dŭl′sə-mər) *n.* A musical instrument with wire strings of graduated lengths, played with two padded hammers. [< OF *doulcemer,* perh "sweet song."]

dull (dŭl) *adj.* **1.** Lacking mental agility; slow to learn. **2.** Not brisk; sluggish. **3.** Not sharp; blunt. **4.** Not intensely or keenly felt. **5.** Unexciting; boring. **6.** Not bright or vivid. **7.** Cloudy; gloomy. **8.** Muffled; indistinct. —*v.* To make or become dull. [< MLG *dul.*] —**dul′ly** *adv.* —**dull′ness, dul′ness** *n.*

dull•ard (dŭl′ərd) *n.* A mentally dull person; dolt.

Du•luth (də-lo͞oth′, do͞o-). A city of NE Minnesota. Pop. 107,000.

du•ly (d/y/o͞o′lē) *adv.* **1.** In a proper manner; fittingly; properly. **2.** At the expected time; punctually. [< DUE.]

dumb (dŭm) *adj.* **1.** Lacking the power or faculty of speech; mute. **2.** Temporarily speechless from shock. **3.** *Informal.* Ignorant or stupid. [< OE. See dheu-[1].] —**dumb′ly** *adv.* —**dumb′ness** *n.*

dumb•bell (dŭm′bĕl′) *n.* **1.** A weight lifted for muscular exercise, consisting of a short bar with a metal ball at each end. **2.** *Slang.* A stupid person; dolt.

dumb•wait•er (dŭm′wā′tər) *n.* A small elevator for conveying food or other goods from one floor to another.

dum•found (dŭm′found′) *v.* Also **dumb•found.** To strike dumb with astonishment; stun; nonplus. [DUM(B) + (CON)FOUND.]

dum•my (dŭm′ē) *n., pl.* -mies. **1.** An imitation of a real object, used as a substitute. **2.** A figure imitating the human form, used for displaying clothes, as a target, etc. **3.** A blockhead; dolt. **4.** A model page to be reproduced by printing. **5.** In bridge: **a.** The partner whose exposed hand is played by the declarer. **b.** The hand thus exposed. —*adj.* Artificial; imitation. [< DUMB.]

dump (dŭmp) *v.* **1.** To drop in a large mass. **2.** To empty (material) out of a container or vehicle. **3.** To discard or foist (a problem) unceremoniously. **4.** To place (large quantities of goods) on the market at a low price. —*n.* **1.** A place where refuse is dumped. **2.** A storage place; depot. **3.** *Slang.* A dilapidated or disreputable place. [< Scand.]

dump•ling (dŭmp′lĭng) *n.* **1.** A small ball of dough cooked with stew or soup. **2.** Sweetened dough wrapped around fruit, baked, and served as a dessert. [?]

dumps (dŭmps) *pl.n. Informal.* A gloomy, melancholy state of mind: *in the dumps.* [< Du *domp,* haze, exhalation.]

dump•y (dŭm′pē) *adj.* -ier, -iest. Short and stout; squat. —**dump′i•ness** *n.*

dun[1] (dŭn) *v.* **dunned, dunning.** To ask (a debtor) persistently for payment. [?]

dun[2] (dŭn) *n.* A dull grayish brown color. [< OE *dunn.*] —**dun** *adj.*

dunce (dŭns) *n.* A dull-witted or stupid person; numskull.

dun•der•head (dŭn′dər-hĕd′) *n.* A numskull;

---

dunce. [Perh "one stunned by a thunder-stroke."]

dune (d/y/ōōn) *n.* A hill or ridge of wind-blown sand. [< MDu *dūne.*]

dung (dŭng) *n.* Animal excrement; manure. [< OE < Gmc **dung-.*]

dun·ga·ree (dŭng'gə-rē') *n.* 1. A sturdy, usually blue denim fabric. 2. dungarees. Overalls or trousers of this fabric. [Hindi *dungrī.*]

dun·geon (dŭn'jən) *n.* A dark cell used to confine prisoners. [< OF *donjon,* "keep of the lord's castle."]

dunk (dŭngk) *v.* 1. To plunge into liquid. 2. To dip (as a doughnut) into coffee or other liquid before eating it. 3. To submerge oneself briefly in water. [< OHG *dunkōn.*]

du·o (d/y/ōō'ō) *n., pl.* -os. 1. A duet. 2. A pair. [It, "two."]

du·o·dec·i·mal (d/y/ōō'ō-dĕs'ə-məl) *adj.* 1. Pertaining to or based on the number 12. 2. Of or pertaining to twelfths. —*n.* A twelfth. [< L *duodecimus,* twelfth.]

du·o·de·num (d/y/ōō'ə-dē'nəm, d/y/ōō-ŏd'-n-əm) *n., pl.* -odena (-ŏd'n-ə). The beginning portion of the small intestine, starting at the lower end of the stomach and extending to the jejunum. [< ML *intestinum duodenum digitōrum,* "intestine of twelve digits."] —**du'o·de'nal** (d/y/ōō'ə-dē'nəl, d/y/ōō-ŏd'n-əl) *adj.*

dup. duplicate.

dupe (d/y/ōōp) *n.* One who is easily deceived or used. —*v.* To make a dupe of. [F.] —**dup'er·y** *n.*

du·plex (d/y/ōō'plĕks') *n.* A house divided into two living units. [L, double.]

du·pli·cate (d/y/ōō'plĭ-kĭt) *adj.* 1. Identically copied from an original. 2. Existing in two corresponding parts; double. —*n.* An identical copy; facsimile. —*v.* (d/y/ōō'plĭ-kāt') -cated, -cating. 1. To make an exact copy of. 2. To make or perform again. [< L *duplicāre,* to make twofold.] —**du'pli·ca'tion** *n.*

du·pli·ca·tor (d/y/ōō'plĭ-kā'tər) *n.* A machine that reproduces printed or written material.

du·plic·i·ty (d/y/ōō-plĭs'ə-tē) *n., pl.* -ties. Deliberate deceptiveness; double-dealing. [< L *duplex,* twofold, DUPLEX.]

du·ra·ble (d/y/ōōr'ə-bəl) *adj.* Able to withstand wear and tear; lasting. [< L *dūrāre,* to last, endure.] —**du'ra·bil'i·ty** *n.*

du·ra ma·ter (d/y/ōōr'ə mā'tər). A tough fibrous membrane that covers the brain and spinal cord. [< ML *dūra mater (cerebrī),* "hard mother (of the brain)."]

dur·ance (d/y/ōōr'əns) *n.* Forced confinement. [< L *dūrāre,* to last.]

du·ra·tion (d/y/ōō-rā'shən) *n.* 1. Continuance in time. 2. The time during which something exists. [< L *dūrāre,* to last.]

du·ress (d/y/ōō-rĕs', d/y/ōōr'ĭs) *n.* 1. Compulsion by threat; coercion: *confessed under duress.* 2. Forcible confinement; durance. [< L *dūrus,* hard.]

dur·ing (d/y/ōōr'ĭng) *prep.* 1. Throughout the course of. 2. Within the time of; at some time in. [< L *dūrāre,* to last.]

durst (dûrst). *Archaic. p.t.* of dare.

dusk (dŭsk) *n.* The darker stage of twilight.

[< OE *dox,* dark, dusky. See dheu-¹.] —**dusk'y** *adj.*

Düs·sel·dorf (dü'səl-dôrf'). A city of W West Germany. Pop. 704,000.

dust (dŭst) *n.* 1. Fine particulate matter. 2. The earthy remains of a human body. 3. The surface of the ground. 4. Something of no worth. —*v.* 1. To remove dust (from). 2. To sprinkle with a powdery substance. [< OE *dūst.* See dheu-¹.]

dust bowl. A region reduced to aridity by drought and dust storms.

dust·er (dŭs'tər) *n.* 1. One that dusts. 2. A cloth or brush used to remove dust. 3. A smock worn to protect one's clothing from dust. 4. A woman's dress-length housecoat.

dust·pan (dŭst'păn') *n.* A short-handled, shovellike pan into which dust is swept.

dust·y (dŭs'tē) *adj.* -ier, -iest. 1. Covered with dust. 2. Like dust; powdery. 3. Tinged with gray. —**dust'i·ly** *adv.* —**dust'i·ness** *n.*

Dutch (dŭch) *adj.* Of or pertaining to the Netherlands. —*n.* 1. the Dutch (*takes pl. v.*). The people of the Netherlands. 2. The Germanic language of the Netherlands. —*adv.* So that each person pays his own way: *go Dutch.* —in Dutch. *Informal.* In trouble.

Dutch door. A door divided in half horizontally so that either part may be left open or closed.

Dutch·man (dŭch'mən) *n.* A native or inhabitant of the Netherlands, or a person of Dutch descent.

Dutch oven. An iron kettle with a tight lid, used for slow cooking.

Dutch treat. *Informal.* An outing in which each person pays his own expenses.

du·te·ous (d/y/ōō'tē-əs) *adj.* Obedient; dutiful. —**du'te·ous·ly** *adv.*

du·ti·a·ble (d/y/ōō'tē-ə-bəl) *adj.* Subject to import tax.

du·ti·ful (d/y/ōō'tĭ-fəl) *adj.* 1. Careful to perform duties. 2. Expressing a sense of duty. —**du'ti·ful·ly** *adv.* —**du'ti·ful·ness** *n.*

du·ty (d/y/ōō'tē) *n., pl.* -ties. 1. A course of action required by one's position. 2. a. Moral obligation. b. The compulsion felt to meet such obligation. 3. A service assigned or demanded of one; function; work. 4. A tax charged by a government, esp. on imports. 5. The work capability of a machine under specified conditions. —off duty. Not engaged in one's assigned work. —on duty. At one's post or work. [< DUE.]

D.V. Douay Version (of the Bible).

D.V.M. Doctor of Veterinary Medicine.

Dvoř·ák (dvôr'zhäk), **Anton.** 1841–1904. Czech composer.

dwarf (dwôrf) *n., pl.* dwarfs or dwarves (dwôrvz). An atypically small person, animal, or plant. —*v.* 1. To check the growth of; stunt. 2. To cause to appear small by comparison. —*adj.* Diminutive; undersized. [< OE *dweorh* < Gmc **dwerg-.*] —**dwarf'ism'** *n.*

dwarf star. A star such as the sun having relatively low mass and average or below average luminosity.

dwell (dwĕl) *v.* dwelt (dwĕlt) or dwelled, dwell-

ing. 1. To live; reside. **2.** To linger over; emphasize (with *on* or *upon*). [< OE *dwellan*, deceive, hinder. See **dheu-¹**.] —**dwell'er** *n.*

dwell·ing (dwĕl'ĭng) *n.* A place to live in; residence; abode.

dwin·dle (dwĭnd'l) *v.* -**dled, -dling.** To make or become gradually less until little remains. [< OE *dwīnan*, to diminish. See **dheu-³**.]

dwt. pennyweight.

Dy dysprosium.

dy·ad (dī'ăd') *n.* Two units regarded as a pair. [< Gk *duas*, pair.] —**dy·ad'ic** *adj.*

dye (dī) *n.* **1.** Any substance used to color materials. **2.** A color imparted by dyeing. —*v.* **dyed, dyeing. 1.** To color (a material) with a dye. **2.** To take on or impart color. [< OE *dēah, dēag*, hue, tinge.] —**dy'er** *n.*

dyed-in-the-wool (dīd'ĭn-*th*ə-wŏŏl') *adj.* Thoroughgoing; out-and-out.

dy·ing (dī'ĭng) *adj.* **1.** About to die. **2.** Drawing to an end. **3.** Done or uttered just before death.

dyke. Variant of **dike.**

dyn *Phys.* dyne.

dy·nam·ic (dī-năm'ĭk) *adj.* Also **dy·nam·i·cal** (-ĭ-kəl). **1.** Pertaining to energy, force, or motion in relation to force. **2.** Energetic; vigorous; forceful. —*n.* **dynamics** *(takes sing. v.).* **1. a.** The study of the relationship between motion and the forces affecting motion. **b.** The combined study of kinetics and kinematics. **2.** The physical or moral forces that produce motion and change in any field or system. **3.** Variation in force or intensity, esp. in musical sound. [< Gk *dunamis*, power.]

dy·na·mism (dī'nə-mĭz'əm) *n.* **1.** Any of various theories or philosophical systems that explain the universe in terms of force or energy. **2.** A process or mechanism responsible for the development or motion of a system. **3.** The quality of being dynamic. —**dy'na·mist** *n.* —**dy'na·mis'tic** *adj.*

dy·na·mite (dī'nə-mīt') *n.* A powerful explosive composed of nitroglycerin or another ex-

plosive compound dispersed in an absorbent medium with a combustible dope such as wood pulp and an antacid such as calcium carbonate. —*v.* -**mited, -miting.** To blow up or destroy with dynamite.

dy·na·mo (dī'nə-mō') *n., pl.* -**mos. 1.** A generator, esp. one for producing direct current. **2.** *Informal.* An extremely energetic and forceful person.

dy·na·mom·e·ter (dī'nə-mŏm'ə-tər) *n.* Any of several instruments used to measure force or power.

dy·nas·ty (dī'nə-stē) *n., pl.* -**ties. 1.** A succession of rulers from the same family or line. **2.** A family or group that maintains power for several generations. [< Gk *dunastēs*, ruler.] —**dy·nas'tic** (dī-năs'tĭk) *adj.*

dyne (dīn) *n.* A unit of force equal to the force required to impart an acceleration of one centimeter per second per second to a mass of one gram. [< Gk *dunamis*, power.]

Dy·nel (dī-nĕl') *n.* A trademark for a polymeric compound used to make a fire-resistant, insect-resistant, and easily dyed textile fiber.

dys–. *comb. form.* Diseased, difficult, faulty, or bad. [< Gk *dus-.*]

dys·en·ter·y (dĭs'ən-tĕr'ē) *n.* An infection of the lower intestinal tract producing pain, fever, and severe diarrhea, often with blood and mucus. [< Gk *dusenteria*.] —**dys'en·ter'ic** *adj.*

dys·lex·i·a (dĭs-lĕk'sē-ə) *n.* Impairment of the ability to read. [< DYS- + Gk *lexis*, speech.] —**dys·lec'tic** (-lĕk'tĭk) *adj. & n.*

dys·pep·sia (dĭs-pĕp'shə, -sē-ə) *n.* Indigestion. —**dys·pep'tic** *adj.*

dys·pro·si·um (dĭs-prō'zē-əm) *n. Symbol* **Dy** A soft, silvery metal used in nuclear research. Atomic number 66, atomic weight 162.50. [< Gk *dusprositos*, difficult to approach.]

dys·tro·phy (dĭs'trə-fē) *n.* Also **dys·tro·phi·a** (dĭs-trō'fē-ə). **1.** Defective nutrition. **2.** Any disorder caused by defective nutrition. —**dys·troph'ic** (-trŏf'ĭk, -trō'fĭk) *adj.*

dz. dozen.

Ee

e, E (ē) *n.* **1.** The 5th letter of the English alphabet. **2.** The 5th in a series.

e 1. east; eastern. **2.** electron. **3.** The base of the natural system of logarithms, approx. 2.718.

E 1. Earth. **2.** east; eastern. **3.** English. **4.** *Mus.* The 3rd tone in the scale of C major.

e. 1. east; eastern. **2.** engineer; engineering.

E. 1. east; eastern. **2.** engineer; engineering. **3.** English.

each (ēch) *adj.* One of two or more considered individually; every. —*pron.* Every one of a

group considered individually; each one. —*adv.* For or to each one; apiece. [< OE *ǣlc* < Gmc **aiwo galīkaz*, "ever alike."]

ea·ger (ē'gər) *adj.* Impatiently desirous; anxious. [< L *ācer*, sharp.] —**ea'ger·ly** *adv.* —**ea'ger·ness** *n.*

ea·gle (ē'gəl) *n.* **1.** A large bird of prey with a hooked bill and strong, soaring flight. **2.** A former gold coin of the U.S. worth ten dollars. **3.** *Golf.* A score of two below par on any hole. [< L *aquila*.]

ea·glet (ē'glĭt) *n.* A young eagle.

ô paw, for/oi boy/ou out/ŏŏ took/ōō coo/p pop/r run/s sauce/sh shy/t to/th thin/*th* the/
ŭ cut/ûr fur/v van/w wag/y yes/z size/zh vision/ə ago, item, edible, gallop, circus/

–ean. *comb. form.* Of or pertaining to or derived from: **Caesarean.** [Var of -IAN.]

ear¹ (îr) *n.* **1.** The organ of hearing in vertebrates responsible, in general, for maintaining equilibrium as well as sensing sound. **2.** The sense of hearing. **3.** Aural sensitivity, as to differences in musical pitch. **4.** Attention; heed. **5.** Anything resembling an ear. [< OE *ēare.* See **ous-.**] —**ear'less** *adj.*

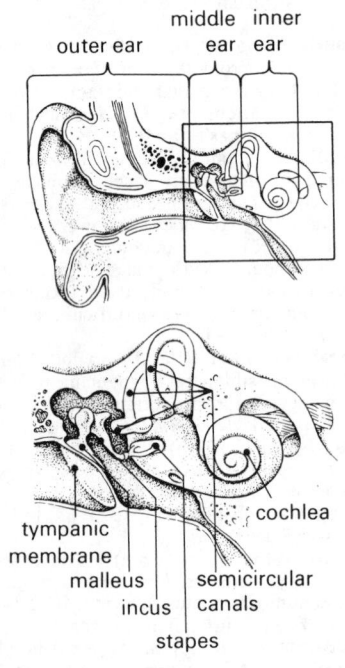

ear¹
The human ear

middle inner
outer ear   ear   ear

cochlea
tympanic membrane
malleus   semicircular
incus   canals
stapes

ear² (îr) *n.* The seed-bearing spike of a cereal plant, as corn. [< OE *ēar.* See **ak-.**]

ear·ache (îr'āk') *n.* A pain in the ear.

ear·drum (îr'drŭm') *n.* The **tympanic membrane.**

ear·flap (îr'flăp') *n.* Also **ear·lap** (-lăp'). Either of two appendages to a cap that may be turned down over the ears.

earl (ûrl) *n.* A British peer ranking above a viscount and below a marquis. [< OE *eorl,* warrior, chief, nobleman < Gmc **erilaz.*] —**earl'dom** *n.*

ear lobe. The soft, fleshy tissue at the lowest portion of the external ear.

ear·ly (ûr'lē) *adj.* **-lier, -liest. 1.** Near the beginning of a given period of time. **2.** In a period far back in time; primitive. **3.** Occurring before the usual time. **4.** Occurring in the near future. —*adv.* **1.** Near the beginning of a given period of time. **2.** Far back in time. **3.** Before the expected or arranged time: *They left early.* [< OE *ǣr,* before. See **ayer-.**] —**ear'li·ness** *n.*

ear·mark (îr'märk') *n.* An identifying mark or characteristic. —*v.* **1.** To mark distinctively for identification. **2.** To set aside for some purpose.

ear·muff (îr'mŭf') *n.* Either of a pair of ear coverings worn to protect against the cold.

earn (ûrn) *v.* **1.** To gain or deserve (salary, wages, etc.) for one's labor. **2.** To gain or acquire as a result of one's behavior. **3.** To produce (interest or return) as profit. [< OE *earnian.* See **esen-.**] —**earn'er** *n.*

ear·nest¹ (ûr'nĭst) *adj.* **1.** Determined; serious. **2.** Showing deep sincerity or feeling. **3.** Of an important or vital nature. —**in earnest.** With a purposeful or serious intent. [< OE *eornost,* zeal, seriousness. See **er-¹.**] —**ear'nest·ly** *adv.* —**ear'nest·ness** *n.*

ear·nest² (ûr'nĭst) *n.* **1.** Money paid in advance to bind a contract. **2.** A token or assurance of something to come. [< Heb *'ērābhôn,* security, pledge.]

earn·ings (ûr'nĭngz) *pl.n.* Something earned, esp. salary, wages, or profits.

ear·phone (îr'fōn') *n.* A device that converts electric signals, as from a radio receiver, to audible sound and is worn in contact with the ear.

ear·ring (îr'rĭng, -ĭng) *n.* An ornament worn on the ear lobe.

ear·shot (îr'shŏt') *n.* The range within which sound can be heard.

earth (ûrth) *n.* **1.** The land surface of the world, as distinguished from the oceans and air. **2.** The softer part of land; soil. **3. Earth.** The 3rd planet from the sun, having a sidereal period of revolution about the sun of 365.26 days at a mean distance of 92.96 million miles, an axial rotation period of 23 hours 56.07 minutes, and an average radius of 3,959 miles, and a mass of 13.17×10^{24} pounds. —**down to earth.** Realistic. [< OE *eorthe.* See **er-².**]

earth·en (ûr'thən) *adj.* Made of earth or baked clay.

earth·en·ware (ûr'thən-wâr') *n.* Pottery made from baked clay.

earth·ly (ûrth'lē) *adj.* **1.** Of the earth; terrestrial. **2.** Conceivable; possible: *no earthly meaning whatever.* —**earth'li·ness** *n.*

earth·quake (ûrth'kwāk') *n.* A trembling movement of the earth's surface.

earth science. Any of several essentially geologic sciences concerned with the origin, structure, and physical phenomena of the earth.

earth·work (ûrth'wûrk') *n.* An earthen embankment, esp. when used as a military fortification.

earth·worm (ûrth'wûrm') *n.* A round-bodied segmented worm that burrows into soil.

earth·y (ûr'thē) *adj.* **-ier, -iest. 1.** Of or like earth or soil. **2.** Crude or coarse; unrefined. —**earth'i·ness** *n.*

ear·wax (îr'wăks') *n.* The waxlike secretion of certain glands lining the canal of the outer ear.

ear·wig (îr'wĭg') *n.* An insect with pincerlike appendages protruding from the rear.

ease (ēz) *n.* **1.** Freedom from pain, worry, or agitation. **2.** Freedom from constraint or awkwardness; naturalness. **3.** Freedom from difficulty; facility. —*v.* **eased, easing. 1.** To free

---

ă pat/ā ate/âr care/ä bar/b **bib**/ch **chew**/d **deed**/ĕ pet/ē be/f fit/g **gag**/h hat/hw **what**/ ĭ pit/ī pie/îr pier/j **judge**/k **kick**/l lid, fatal/m **mum**/n no, sudden/ng sing/ŏ pot/ō go/

from pain or trouble; comfort. **2.** To alleviate or lighten (discomfort); mitigate; lessen. **3.** To slacken; loosen. **4.** To move into place slowly and carefully. **5.** To diminish in discomfort, stress, pressure, etc. [< OF *aise,* comfort, convenience.] —**ease′ment** *n.*

ea•sel (ē′zəl) *n.* An upright frame used to support an artist's canvas. [Du *ezel,* "ass."]

east (ēst) *n.* **1. a.** The direction of the earth's rotation. **b.** The point on the mariner's compass 90° clockwise from north, directly opposite west. **2.** Often **East.** The E part of any country or region. **b.** The E part of the earth, esp. Asia; the Orient. —**the East.** In the U.S.: **1.** The region E of the Mississippi and N of the Mason-Dixon line. **2.** The region E of the Alleghenies and N of the Mason-Dixon line. —*adj.* **1.** To or from the east. **2. East.** Officially designating the E part of a country, continent, or other geographic area: *East Germany.* —*adv.* In, from, or toward the east. [< OE *ēast.* See awes-.]

East Ber•lin (bûr-lĭn′). The capital of the German Democratic Republic. Pop. 1,071,000.

East Chi•na Sea (chī′nə). An arm of the Pacific Ocean off the China coast.

East•er (ē′stər) *n.* A festival in the Christian church commemorating the Resurrection of Christ. [< OE *ēastre.* See awes-.]

east•er•ly (ē′stər-lē) *adj.* **1.** Toward the east. **2.** From the east. —**east′er•ly** *adv.*

east•ern (ē′stərn) *adj.* **1.** Toward, in, or facing the east. **2.** Coming from the east. **3.** Often **Eastern.** Of or characteristic of eastern regions or the East, esp. Asia; Oriental.

east•ern•er (ē′stər-nər) *n.* **1.** A native or inhabitant of the East. **2.** Often **Easterner.** A native or inhabitant of the E U.S.

Eastern Hemisphere. The part of the earth including Europe, Africa, Asia, and Australia.

Eastern Orthodox Church. The body of modern Christian churches, including the Greek and Russian Orthodox, derived from the church of the Byzantine Empire.

East Germany. The unofficial name for the German Democratic Republic.

East In•dies (ĭn′dēz). Historically, India, SE Asia, and the Malay Archipelago. —**East Indian.**

east•ward (ēst′wərd) *adv.* Also **east•wards** (-wərdz), **east•ward•ly** (-wərd-lē). Toward the east. —*adj.* Toward, facing, or in the east. —*n.* An eastward direction or point.

eas•y (ē′zē) *adj.* **-ier, -iest. 1.** Capable of being accomplished without difficulty. **2.** Free from worry, anxiety, or pain. **3.** Pleasant and relaxing. **4.** Relaxed; easygoing; informal. **5.** Not strict; lenient. **6.** Not hurried; moderate. —*adv.* In a cautious, restrained manner. —**take it easy.** *Informal.* **1.** To relax. **2.** To remain calm. [< OF *aise,* EASE.] —**eas′i•ly** *adv.* —**eas′i•ness** *n.*

eas•y•go•ing (ē′zē-gō′ĭng) *adj.* Also **eas•y-go•ing.** Living in a carefree way.

eat (ēt) *v.* **ate, eaten, eating. 1.** To consume (food). **2.** To consume or ravage as if by eating. **3.** To erode or corrode. [< OE *etan.* See ed-.] —**eat′er** *n.*

eaves (ēvz) *pl.n.* The projecting overhang at the edge of a roof. [< OE *yfes,* eaves, edge, border. See upo.]

eaves•drop (ēvz′drŏp′) *v.* **-dropped, -dropping.** To listen secretly to a private conversation. [< ME *evesdrop,* water from the eaves.] —**eaves′drop′per** *n.*

ebb (ĕb) *n.* **1.** Ebb tide. **2.** A period of declining or diminishing. —*v.* **1.** To fall back or recede. **2.** To waste or fall away. [< OE *ebba,* low tide. See apo-.]

ebb tide. The period of a tide between high tide and a succeeding low tide.

eb•on•ite (ĕb′ə-nīt′) *n.* A hard rubber, esp. when black. [< Gk *ebenos,* EBONY.]

eb•on•y (ĕb′ə-nē) *n.* The hard, dark wood of a tropical Asian tree. —*adj.* **1.** Made of ebony. **2.** Black. [< Gk *ebenos,* ebony tree < Egypt *hebni.*]

e•bul•lient (ĭ-bŭl′yənt) *adj.* **1.** Boiling, as a liquid. **2.** Filled with excitement; exuberant. [< L *ēbullīre,* to boil over.] —**e•bul′lience** *n.* —**e•bul′lient•ly** *adv.*

eb•ul•li•tion (ĕb′ə-lĭsh′ən) *n.* **1.** The bubbling or effervescence of a liquid; a boiling. **2.** A sudden, violent outpouring, as of emotion or violence.

ec•cen•tric (ĕk-sĕn′trĭk, ĭk-) *adj.* **1.** Deviating from a conventional or established pattern. **2.** Deviating from a circular form, as in an elliptical orbit. **3.** Not situated at or in the center. **4.** Not having the same center, as a circle, cylinder, or sphere. —*n.* **1.** An odd or erratic person. **2.** A disk or wheel having its axis of revolution displaced from its center so that it is capable of imparting reciprocating motion. [< Gk *ekkentros,* not having the earth as its center.] —**ec•cen′tri•cal•ly** *adv.* —**ec′cen•tric′i•ty** (-trĭs′ə-tē) *n.*

eccles. ecclesiastic; ecclesiastical.

Eccles. Ecclesiastes (Old Testament).

ec•cle•si•as•tic (ĭ-klē′zē-ăs′tĭk) *adj.* Ecclesiastical. —*n.* A clergyman; priest. [< Gk *ekklēsia,* duly summoned assembly.]

ec•cle•si•as•ti•cal (ĭ-klē′zē-ăs′tĭ-kəl) *adj.* Of or pertaining to a church, esp. as an organized institution.

ech•e•lon (ĕsh′ə-lŏn′) *n.* **1.** A steplike formation of troops, vessels, etc. **2.** A subdivision of a military force. **3.** A level of authority in a hierarchy. [F *échelon,* "rung of a ladder."]

ech•o (ĕk′ō) *n., pl.* **-oes. 1.** Repetition of a sound by reflection of sound waves from a surface. **2.** A sound so produced. **3.** Any repetition or imitation. **4.** A reflected wave received by a radio or radar. —*v.* **1.** To repeat by or as by an echo. **2.** To resound with or emit an echo; reverberate. **3.** To imitate: *echo the teacher's ideas.* [< Gk *ēkhō.*]

é•clair (ā′klâr′, ĭ-klâr′) *n.* A light, tubular, usually iced pastry filled with cream or custard. [< OF *esclairier,* to light, flash.]

é•clat (ā-klä′) *n.* **1.** Great brilliance, as of achievement; conspicuous success. **2.** Acclaim. [< F *éclater,* to burst, explode.]

ec•lec•tic (ĭ-klĕk′tĭk) *adj.* Choosing or consisting of what appears to be the best from diverse sources. [< Gk *eklegein,* to single out.] —**ec•lec′ti•cal•ly** *adv.*

ŏ paw, for/oi boy/ou out/ŏŏ took/ōō coo/p pop/r run/s sauce/sh shy/t to/th thin/*th* the/
ŭ cut/ûr fur/v van/w wag/y yes/z size/zh vision/ə ago, item, edible, gallop, circus/

e·clipse (ĭ-klĭps′) *n.* **1. a.** The partial or complete obscuring, relative to a designated observer, of one celestial body by another. **b.** The period of time during which such an obscuring occurs. **2.** A falling into obscurity or disuse; decline. —*v.* **eclipsed, eclipsing.** To cause an eclipse or obscuring of. [< Gk *ekleipsis,* cessation, abandonment.]

eclipse
Total solar eclipse

e·clip·tic (ĭ-klĭp′tĭk) *n.* The apparent path of the sun among the stars; the intersection plane of the earth's solar orbit with the celestial sphere. [< Gk *ekleipein,* to abandon.]
ec·logue (ĕk′lôg′, -lŏg′) *n.* A pastoral poem. [< L *ecloga,* "selection."]
ecol. ecological; ecology.
e·col·o·gy (ĭ-kŏl′ə-jē) *n.* The science of the relationships between organisms and their environments. [< Gk *oikos,* house + -LOGY.] —**ec′o·log′i·cal** (ĕk′ə-lŏj′ĭ-kəl) *adj.* —**ec′o·log′i·cal·ly** *adv.* —**e·col′o·gist** *n.*
econ. economics; economist; economy.
ec·o·nom·ic (ĕk′ə-nŏm′ĭk, ē′kə-) *adj.* **1.** Of or pertaining to the production, development, and management of material wealth, as of a country or business enterprise. **2.** Of or pertaining to the necessities of life. —*n.* **economics** *(takes sing. v.).* The science of the production, distribution, and consumption of commodities. —**e·con′o·mist** (ĭ-kŏn′ə-mĭst) *n.*
ec·o·nom·i·cal (ĕk′ə-nŏm′ĭ-kəl, ē′kə-) *adj.* Not wasteful; prudent; sparing. —**ec′o·nom′i·cal·ly** *adv.*
e·con·o·mize (ĭ-kŏn′ə-mīz′) *v.* **-mized, -mizing.** To be frugal; reduce expenses; practice economy. —**e·con′o·miz′er** *n.*
e·con·o·my (ĭ-kŏn′ə-mē) *n., pl.* **-mies. 1. a.** The careful or thrifty management of resources. **b.** An instance of this. **2.** A system for the management and development of resources: *an agricultural economy.* [< Gk *oikonomos,* manager of a household.]
ec·sta·sy (ĕk′stə-sē) *n., pl.* **-sies. 1.** A state of overwhelming delight; rapture. **2.** An extreme or intense state of any emotion: *an ecstasy of anger.* [< Gk *existanai,* to displace, drive out

of one's senses.] —**ec·stat′ic** (ĕk-stăt′ĭk) *adj.* —**ec·stat′i·cal·ly** *adv.*
ecto-. *comb. form.* Outside or external part. [< Gk *ektos,* outside.]
–ectomy. *comb. form.* Removal of a part by surgery: **tonsillectomy.**
ec·to·plasm (ĕk′tə-plăz′əm) *n.* A portion of the continuous phase of cytoplasm distinguishable in some cells as a relatively rigidly jelled cortex limited on the outside by the cell membrane.
Ec·ua·dor (ĕk′wə-dôr′). A republic of NW South America. Pop. 4,485,000. Cap. Quito.

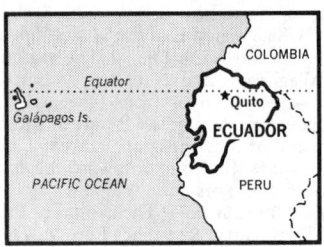

Ecuador

ec·u·men·i·cal (ĕk′yōō-mĕn′ĭ-kəl) *adj.* Pertaining to the general unity of Christians above sectarian differences. [< Gk *oikoumenikos,* of the whole world.]
ec·u·men·ism (ĕk′yōō-mĕn′ĭz′əm) *n.* A movement seeking to achieve worldwide unity among religions through greater cooperation and improved understanding.
ec·ze·ma (ĕk′sə-mə, ĕg′zə-, ĕg-zē′-, ĭg-zē′-) *n.* A noncontagious skin inflammation, marked by redness, itching, and the outbreak of lesions that become encrusted and scaly. [< Gk *ekzema,* eruption.] —**ec·zem′a·tous** (ĕg-zĕm′ə-təs, -zē′mə-təs, ĭg-) *adj.*
–ed¹. *comb. form.* Used to form the past tense of most verbs: **removed.** [< OE *-ode, -ede, -ade.*]
–ed². *comb. form.* Used to form past participles of most verbs: **hoped.** [< OE *-od, -ed, -ad.*]
–ed³. *comb. form.* Used to form adjectives from nouns and phrases: *gray-haired; thick-skinned.* [< OE *-ede.*]
ed. **1.** edition; editor. **2.** education.
ed·dy (ĕd′ē) *n., pl.* **-dies.** A current, as of water or air, moving contrary to the direction of a main current, esp. in a circular motion. [< ON *idha,* "that which flows back," whirlpool.] —**ed′dy** *v.* **(-died, -dying).**
Ed·dy (ĕd′ē), **Mary Baker.** 1821–1910. American religious leader; founder of the Church of Christ, Scientist.
e·del·weiss (ā′dəl-vīs′) *n.* An Alpine plant with whitish flowers and downy leaves. [G *Edelweiss,* "noble white."]
e·de·ma (ĭ-dē′mə) *n., pl.* **-mas** or **-mata** (-mə-tə). An excessive accumulation of serous fluid in the tissues. [< Gk *oidēma,* tumor, swelling.]
E·den (ēd′n) *n.* The first home of Adam and Eve; Paradise.
edge (ĕj) *n.* **1.** The sharp side of a cutting

blade. **2.** Keenness; zest. **3.** A rim, brink, etc., as of a cliff. **4.** A margin; border. **5.** An advantage. **—on edge. 1.** Highly tense; irritable. **2.** Impatient. *—v.* **edged, edging. 1.** To give an edge to. **2.** To move gradually. [< OE *ecg*, edge, point, sword. See **ak-**.]

edge·wise (ĕj′wīz′) *adv.* Also **edge·ways** (-wāz′). With the edge foremost.

edg·ing (ĕj′ĭng) *n.* Something that forms an edge or border.

edg·y (ĕj′ē) *adj.* **-ier, -iest.** Tense; nervous. **—edg′i·ness** *n.*

edh (ĕth) *n.* Also **eth.** An old Germanic letter representing *dh* in Scandinavian languages and *th* in Old English.

ed·i·ble (ĕd′ə-bəl) *adj.* Fit to be eaten. *—n.* Often **edibles.** Food. [< L *edere*, to eat.] **—ed′i·bil′i·ty, ed′i·ble·ness** *n.*

e·dict (ē′dĭkt′) *n.* A proclamation; decree. [< L *ēdīcere*, to speak out, proclaim.]

ed·i·fi·ca·tion (ĕd′ī-fə-kā′shən) *n.* Intellectual, moral, or spiritual improvement.

ed·i·fice (ĕd′ə-fĭs) *n.* A building, esp. one of imposing size. [< L *aedificāre*, to build.]

ed·i·fy (ĕd′ə-fī′) *v.* **-fied, -fying.** To instruct, esp. so as to encourage moral improvement. [< L *aedificāre*, to build, instruct.]

Ed·in·burgh (ĕd′n-bûr′ə). The capital of Scotland. Pop. 472,000.

Ed·i·son (ĕd′ə-sən), **Thomas Alva.** 1847–1931. American inventor.

ed·it (ĕd′ĭt) *v.* To prepare something for publication or presentation by revising, selecting, etc. [Back-formation < EDITOR.]

edit. edition; editor.

e·di·tion (ĭ-dĭsh′ən) *n.* **1.** The form in which a book is published. **2.** The entire number of copies of a publication printed at one time. **3.** One similar to an original; version.

ed·i·tor (ĕd′ə-tər) *n.* **1.** One who edits. **2.** One who supervises the policies of a publication. [< L *ēdere*, to bring forth, publish.]

ed·i·to·ri·al (ĕd′ə-tôr′ē-əl, -tōr′ē-əl) *n.* An article in a publication expressing the opinion of its editors or publishers. *—adj.* **1.** Of or pertaining to an editor. **2.** Characteristic of an editorial. **—ed′i·to′ri·al·ly** *adv.*

ed·i·to·ri·al·ize (ĕd′ə-tôr′ē-ə-līz′, -tōr′ē-ə-līz′) *v.* **-ized, -izing.** To express an opinion in or as if in an editorial.

Ed·mon·ton (ĕd′mən-tən). The capital of Alberta, Canada. Pop. 372,000.

EDP electronic data processing.

E.D.T. Eastern Daylight Time.

educ. education; educational.

ed·u·ca·ble (ĕj′ōō-kə-bəl) *adj.* Capable of being educated.

ed·u·cate (ĕj′ōō-kāt′) *v.* **-cated, -cating.** To provide with and develop knowledge, training, or skill, esp. through formal schooling; teach. [< L *ēducāre*, to bring up, educate.] **—ed′u·ca′tor** *n.*

ed·u·ca·tion (ĕj′ōō-kā′shən) *n.* **1. a.** The process of educating. **b.** The skills or knowledge so developed. **2.** The study of the teaching and learning processes; pedagogy. **—ed′u·ca′tion·al** *adj.* **—ed′u·ca′tion·al·ly** *adv.*

e·duce (ĭ-d/y/ōōs′) *v.* **educed, educing. 1.** To

draw out; elicit; evoke. **2.** To work out from given facts; deduce. [L *ēdūcere*.]

-ee¹. *comb. form.* **1.** The recipient of an action: **addressee. 2.** One who is in a specified condition: **standee.** [< L *-ātus*, **-ATE¹**.]

-ee². *comb. form.* **1.** A particular type of: **bootee. 2.** Something resembling or suggestive of: **goatee.**

EEG electroencephalogram.

eel (ēl) *n.* Any of various long, snakelike marine or freshwater fishes. [< OE *ǣl* < Gmc **ǣlaz*.]

-eer. *comb. form.* **1.** One who works with or is concerned with: **auctioneer, racketeer. 2.** One who makes or composes: **profiteer.** [< L *-ārius*, **-ARY**.]

ee·rie (îr′ē) *adj.* **-rier, -riest.** Also **ee·ry. 1.** Inspiring fear or dread. **2.** Weird; uncanny. [< OE *earg*, cowardly, timid < Gmc **arg-*.]

eff. efficiency.

ef·face (ĭ-fās′) *v.* **-faced, -facing. 1.** To obliterate or make indistinct by or as by rubbing out. **2.** To make (oneself) inconspicuous. [OF *effacer*, "to remove the face."] **—ef·face′ment** *n.* **—ef·fac′er** *n.*

ef·fect (ĭ-fĕkt′) *n.* **1.** Something brought about by a cause or agent; result. **2.** The capacity to achieve a desired result; influence. **3.** The condition of being operative or in full force. **4.** Basic meaning; purport: *He said something to that effect.* **5. effects.** Possessions; belongings. **—in effect. 1.** Actually. **2.** Virtually. **3.** In operation. **—take effect.** To become operative. *—v.* **1.** To produce as a result; bring about. **2.** To execute; make. **—See** Usage note at **affect.** [< L *effectus*, pp of *efficere*, to accomplish, perform.] **—ef·fect′er** *n.*

ef·fec·tive (ĭ-fĕk′tĭv) *adj.* **1.** Having an intended effect. **2.** Producing a desired impression; striking. **3.** Operative; in effect. **—ef·fec′tive·ly** *adv.* **—ef·fec′tive·ness** *n.*

ef·fec·tor (ĭ-fĕk′tər) *n.* An organ at the end of a nerve that activates either gland secretion or muscular contraction.

ef·fec·tu·al (ĭ-fĕk′chōō-əl) *adj.* **1.** Producing a desired effect; fully adequate. **2.** Valid; legally binding. **—ef·fec′tu·al·ly** *adv.*

ef·fem·i·nate (ĭ-fĕm′ə-nĭt) *adj.* Having qualities associated with women rather than men; unmanly. [< L *effēmināre*, "to make a woman out of."] **—ef·fem′i·na·cy** (-nə-sē) *n.*

ef·fer·ent (ĕf′ər-ənt) *adj.* Directed away from a central organ or section, esp. carrying impulses from the central nervous system to an effector. [< L *efferre*, to carry away.]

ef·fer·vesce (ĕf′ər-vĕs′) *v.* **-vesced, -vescing. 1.** To emit small bubbles of gas, as a carbonated liquid. **2.** To be lively or vivacious. [L *effervēscere*, to boil over.] **—ef′fer·ves′cence** *n.* **—ef′fer·ves′cent** *adj.*

ef·fete (ĭ-fēt′) *adj.* **1.** Exhausted of vitality or effectiveness; worn-out; spent. **2.** Decadent. [L *effētus*, worn out by childbearing.]

ef·fi·ca·cious (ĕf′ə-kā′shəs) *adj.* Capable of producing a desired effect. **—ef′fi·ca′cious·ly** *adv.* **—ef′fi·ca·cy** (-kə-sē) *n.*

ef·fi·cien·cy (ĭ-fĭsh′ən-sē) *n., pl.* **-cies. 1.** The quality of being efficient. **2.** The ratio of the effective or useful output to the total input in any system. **3.** A small apartment.

ef•fi•cient (ĭ-fish′ənt) *adj.* **1.** Acting or producing effectively with a minimum of waste or effort. **2.** Exhibiting a high ratio of output to input. —**ef•fi′cient•ly** *adv.*

ef•fi•gy (ĕf′ə-jē) *n., pl.* **-gies.** An image of a person, esp. a crude image of a despised person. [< L *effigiēs*, likeness, image.]

ef•flu•vi•um (ĭ-flōō′vē-əm) *n., pl.* **-via** (-vē-ə) or **-ums.** An often foul-smelling emanation or vapor. [< L *effluere*, to flow out.]

ef•fort (ĕf′ərt) *n.* **1.** The applied use of physical or mental energy. **2.** Exertion. **3.** An attempt. **4.** An achievement; work: *early literary efforts.* [< VL *exfortiāre*, to show strength.]

ef•front•er•y (ĭ-frŭn′tə-rē) *n., pl.* **-ies.** Impudent boldness; audacity. [< LL *effrōns*, shameless, "barefaced."]

ef•ful•gent (ĭ-fŭl′jənt) *adj.* Radiant; resplendent. [< L *effulgēre*, to shine out.] —**ef•ful′gence** *n.* —**ef•ful′gent•ly** *adv.*

ef•fu•sion (ĭ-fyōō′zhən) *n.* **1.** A pouring forth. **2.** An unrestrained outpouring. [< L *effundere*, to pour out.]

ef•fu•sive (ĭ-fyōō′sĭv) *adj.* Unrestrained in emotional expression; gushy. —**ef•fu′sive•ly** *adv.* —**ef•fu′sive•ness** *n.*

eft (ĕft) *n.* A newt, esp. a small reddish form. [< OE *efeta*, lizard.]

e.g. for example (L *exempli gratia*).

e•gad (ĭ-găd′, ē-găd′) *interj.* By God! [Euphemism for *oh God.*]

e•gal•i•tar•i•an (ĭ-găl′ə-târ′ē-ən) *adj.* Favoring absolute political and social equality. [< L *aequālis*, equal.] —**e•gal′i•tar′i•an** *n.* —**e•gal′i•tar′i•an•ism′** *n.*

egg¹ (ĕg) *n.* **1.** A female reproductive cell; ovum. **2.** The thin-shelled ovum of a bird, esp. that of a domestic fowl, used as food. **3.** *Slang.* A fellow; person: *a bad egg.* [< ON.]

egg² (ĕg) *v.* —**egg on.** To urge or incite. [< ON *eggja.*]

egg•head (ĕg′hĕd′) *n. Slang.* An intellectual; highbrow.

egg•nog (ĕg′nŏg′) *n.* A drink made with milk, beaten eggs, and often liquor.

egg•plant (ĕg′plănt′, -plänt′) *n.* **1.** A plant cultivated for its large, ovoid, purple-skinned fruit. **2.** The fruit, eaten as a vegetable.

eg•lan•tine (ĕg′lən-tīn′, -tēn′) *n.* The sweetbrier. [< VL *aquilentum*, "prickly."]

e•go (ē′gō, ĕg′ō) *n.* **1.** The self as distinguished from all others. **2.** The personality component that is conscious, most immediately controls behavior, and is most in touch with external reality. **3.** Conceit; egotism. [< L, I.]

e•go•cen•tric (ē′gō-sĕn′trĭk, ĕg′ō-) *adj.* Thinking or acting with one's self as the major concern; self-centered.

e•go•ism (ē′gō-ĭz′əm, ĕg′ō-) *n.* **1.** The belief that self-interest is the just and proper motive force. **2.** Preoccupation with one's own interests; egotism. —**e′go•ist** *n.* —**e′go•is′tic, e′go•is′ti•cal** *adj.* —**e′go•is′ti•cal•ly** *adv.*

e•go•tism (ē′gə-tĭz′əm, ĕg′ə-) *n.* **1.** The tendency to speak or write excessively about oneself. **2.** An exaggerated sense of self-im-portance; conceit. —**e′go•tist** *n.* —**e′go•tis′tic, e′go•tis′ti•cal** *adj.* —**e′go•tis′ti•cal•ly** *adv.*

e•gre•gious (ĭ-grē′jəs, -jē-əs) *adj.* Outstandingly bad; blatant; outrageous. [L *ēgregius*, "standing out from the herd."] —**e•gre′gious•ly** *adv.* —**e•gre′gious•ness** *n.*

e•gress (ē′grĕs) *n.* The way by which one goes out; exit. [< L *ēgredī*, to go out.]

e•gret (ē′grĭt, ĕg′rĭt) *n.* A heronlike, usually white wading bird with long, showy, drooping plumes. [< OProv *aigron*, heron.]

E•gypt (ē′jĭpt). Officially, United Arab Republic. A country of NE Africa. Pop. 29,059,000. Cap. Cairo.

Egypt

E•gyp•tian (ĭ-jĭp′shən) *n.* **1.** A native or inhabitant of Egypt. **2.** The extinct Hamitic language spoken by the ancient Egyptians. —**E•gyp′tian** *adj.*

E•gyp•tol•o•gy (ē′jĭp-tŏl′ə-jē) *n.* The study of the culture and artifacts of the ancient Egyptian civilization. —**E•gyp′to•log′i•cal** (ĭ-jĭp′tə-lŏj′ĭ-kəl) *adj.*

eh (ā, ĕ) *interj.* **1.** Used interrogatively. **2.** Used in asking for confirmation: *She's a flirt, eh?*

EHF extremely high frequency.

ei•der (ī′dər) *n.* A sea duck of northern regions, having soft down, **ei•der•down** (ī′dər-doun′), used to stuff quilts and pillows. [< ON *ǣdhr.*]

eight (āt) *n.* The cardinal number written 8 or in Roman numerals VIII. [< OE *eahta*. See **oktō.**] —**eight** *adj. & pron.*

eight•een (ā-tēn′) *n.* The cardinal number written 18 or in Roman numerals XVIII. —**eight•een′** *adj. & pron.*

eight•eenth (ā-tēnth′) *n.* **1.** The ordinal number 18 in a series. **2.** One of 18 equal parts. —**eight•eenth′** *adj. & adv.*

eighth (ātth, āth) *n.* **1.** The ordinal number 8 in a series. **2.** One of 8 equal parts. —**eighth** *adj. & adv.*

eight•i•eth (ā′tē-ĭth) *n.* **1.** The ordinal number 80 in a series. **2.** One of 80 equal parts. —**eight′i•eth** *adj. & adv.*

eight•y (ā′tē) *n.* The cardinal number written 80 or in Roman numerals LXXX. —**eight′y** *adj. & pron.*

ă pat/ā ate/âr care/ä bar/b bib/ch chew/d deed/ĕ pet/ē be/f fit/g gag/h hat/hw what/ ĭ pit/ī pie/îr pier/j judge/k kick/l lid, fatal/m mum/n no, sudden/ng sing/ŏ pot/ō go/

Ein·stein (īn'stīn'), **Albert**. 1879–1955. German-born American theoretical physicist.

Albert Einstein

ein·stein·i·um (īn-stī'nē-əm) *n. Symbol* **Es** A synthetic element first produced by neutron irradiation of uranium in a thermonuclear explosion. Atomic number 99, longest-lived isotope Es 254.
Eir·e (âr'ə). The Gaelic name for the Republic of Ireland.
Ei·sen·how·er (ī'zən-hou'ər), **Dwight David**. 1890–1969. American general; 34th President of the U.S. (1953–61).

Dwight David Eisenhower

ei·ther (ē'thər, ī'thər) *pron.* One or the other: *Choose either.* —*conj.* —Used before the first of two or more stated alternatives, the following alternatives being signaled by *or: Either we go now or remain here forever.* —*adj.* **1.** Any one (of two): *Wear either coat.* **2.** One and the other; each: *She wore rings on either hand.* —*adv.* Likewise; also. Used as an intensifier following negative statements: *If you don't order a dessert, I won't either.* —See Usage note at **neither**. [< OE *ǣgther, ǣghwæther.* See **kwo-**.]
e·jac·u·late (ī-jăk'yə-lāt') *v.* **-lated, -lating. 1.** To eject abruptly, esp. to discharge (semen). **2.** To utter suddenly and passionately; ex-

claim. [L *ējaculāri.*] —**e·jac'u·la'tion** *n.* —**e·jac'u·la'tor** *n.*
e·ject (ī-jĕkt') *v.* To throw out forcefully; expel; evict. [< L *ēicere* (pp *ējectus*).] —**e·jec'tion** *n.*
eke (ēk) *v.* **eked, eking.** To make or supplement with great effort or strain (with *out*): *eke out a living.* [< OE *ēacan,* to increase. See **aug-**.]
EKG electrocardiogram; electrocardiograph.
el. elevation.
e·lab·o·rate (ī-lăb'ər-īt) *adj.* Planned or executed with attention to detail; complicated. —*v.* (-ə-rāt') **-rated, -rating. 1.** To work out with care and in detail; develop thoroughly. **2.** To express oneself in greater detail. [< L *ēlabōrāre,* "to work out."] —**e·lab'o·rate·ly** *adv.* —**e·lab'o·rate·ness** *n.* —**e·lab'o·ra'tion** *n.*
é·lan (ā-läN') *n.* Enthusiasm; ardor. [< OF *eslancer,* to throw out.]
e·land (ē'lənd) *n.* A large African antelope with spirally twisted horns. [Afrik.]
e·lapse (ī-lăps') *v.* **elapsed, elapsing.** To pass; slip by, as time. [L *ēlābī* (pp *ēlapsus*).]
e·las·tic (ī-lăs'tĭk) *adj.* **1.** Returning or capable of returning to an initial form or state after deformation. **2.** Adaptable to change; flexible. **3.** Quick to recover or revive. —*n.* **1.** An elastic fabric. **2.** A rubber band. [< Gk *elastos, elatos,* beaten.] —**e·las'ti·cal·ly** *adv.* —**e·las'·tic'i·ty** (-tĭs'ə-tē) *n.*
e·late (ī-lāt') *v.* **elated, elating.** To raise the spirits of; make happy or proud. [L *ēlātus,* "carried away."] —**e·la'tion** *n.*
El·be (ĕl'bə). A river of C Europe.
el·bow (ĕl'bō) *n.* **1. a.** The joint or bend of the arm between the forearm and upper arm. **b.** The bony outer projection of this joint. **2.** Something having a bend similar to an elbow. —*v.* **1.** To push or shove, as with the elbows. **2.** To make one's way by such pushing or shoving. [< OE *elnboga,* "bow of the forearm." See **el-1**.]
elbow grease. *Informal.* Strenuous physical effort.
el·bow·room (ĕl'bō-rōōm', -rōōm') *n.* Room enough to move around or function in; ample space.
El·brus, Mount (ĕl'brōōs). The highest (18,480 ft.) mountain of Europe, in the Caucasus Mountains of the Soviet Union.
eld·er1 (ĕl'dər). Alternate *compar.* of **old.** —*n.* **1.** An older person. **2.** An older, influential man of a family, tribe, etc. **3.** One of the governing officers of a church. [< OE *ieldra, eldra.*]
eld·er2 (ĕl'dər) *n.* A shrub with clusters of small white flowers and red or blackish berries. [< OE *ellærn, ellen.*]
el·der·ber·ry (ĕl'dər-bĕr'ē) *n.* **1.** The small, edible fruit of an elder. **2.** A shrub, the elder.
el·der·ly (ĕl'dər-lē) *adj.* Approaching old age.
eld·est (ĕl'dĭst). Alternate *superl.* of **old.**
El Do·ra·do (ĕl də-rä'dō). A place of fabulous wealth.
elec. electric; electrical; electrician; electricity.
e·lect (ī-lĕkt') *v.* **1.** To select by vote for an office. **2.** To choose, esp. after deliberation. —*adj.* **1.** Chosen. **2.** Elected but not yet in-

stalled in office: *the governor-elect.* [< L *ēligere* (pp *ēlectus*), to pick out, select.]

e·lec·tion (ĭ-lĕk′shən) *n.* **1.** The act or process of electing. **2.** The fact of being elected.

e·lec·tion·eer (ĭ-lĕk′shə-nîr′) *v.* To work actively for a candidate or political party.

e·lec·tive (ĭ-lĕk′tĭv) *adj.* **1.** Filled or chosen by election. **2.** Having the power to elect. **3.** Optional. —*n.* An optional course in an academic curriculum. —**e·lec′tive·ly** *adv.*

e·lec·tor (ĭ-lĕk′tər) *n.* **1.** One who elects; a qualified voter. **2.** A member of a special group chosen to elect a person to high office. —**e·lec′tor·al** *adj.*

e·lec·tor·ate (ĭ-lĕk′tər-ĭt) *n.* The body of qualified voters.

e·lec·tric (ĭ-lĕk′trĭk) *adj.* Also **e·lec·tri·cal** (-trĭ-kəl). **1.** Of, pertaining to, producing, derived from, produced, powered, or operated by electricity. **2.** Exciting; thrilling. [< NL *electricus,* "like amber" (amber produces sparks when rubbed).] —**e·lec′tri·cal·ly** *adv.*

electrical engineering. The scientific technology of electricity, esp. the design and application of circuitry and equipment for power generation and distribution, machine control, and communications. —**electrical engineer.**

electric chair. A chair used to electrocute those sentenced to death.

electric eye. A photoelectric cell, esp. when used as a sensor for an automatic switch.

e·lec·tri·cian (ĭ-lĕk′trĭsh′ən) *n.* One whose occupation is the installation, repair, or operation of electric equipment and circuitry.

e·lec·tric·i·ty (ĭ-lĕk′trĭs′ə-tē, ē′lĕk-) *n.* **1.** The class of physical phenomena arising from the existence and interactions of electric charge. **2.** The physical science of such phenomena. **3.** Electric current used or regarded as a source of power.

e·lec·tri·fy (ĭ-lĕk′trə-fī′) *v.* **-fied, -fying. 1.** To produce electric charge on or in. **2. a.** To wire or otherwise equip for the use of electric power. **b.** To provide with electric power. **3.** To thrill, startle, or shock. —**e·lec′tri·fi·ca′tion** *n.*

electro-. *comb. form.* **1.** Electric. **2.** Electrically. **3.** Electrolysis.

e·lec·tro·car·di·o·gram (ĭ-lĕk′trō-kär′dē-ə-grăm′) *n.* The curve traced by an electrocardiograph, used to diagnose heart disease.

e·lec·tro·car·di·o·graph (ĭ-lĕk′trō-kär′dē-ə-grăf′, -gräf′) *n.* An instrument used to record electric potentials associated with the electric currents that traverse the heart.

e·lec·tro·chem·is·try (ĭ-lĕk′trō-kĕm′ĭs-trē) *n.* The science of the interaction or interconversion of electric and chemical phenomena. —**e·lec′tro·chem′i·cal** *adj.*

e·lec·tro·cute (ĭ-lĕk′trə-kyōōt′) *v.* **-cuted, -cuting.** To kill or execute with electricity. —**e·lec′tro·cu′tion** *n.*

e·lec·trode (ĭ-lĕk′trōd′) *n.* A solid electric conductor through which an electric current enters or leaves a medium such as an electrolyte, a nonmetallic solid, a molten metal, a gas, or a vacuum.

e·lec·tro·en·ceph·a·lo·gram (ĭ-lĕk′trō-ĕn-sĕf′ə-lə-grăm) *n.* A graphic record of the electrical activity of the brain as recorded by the electroencephalograph.

e·lec·tro·en·ceph·a·lo·graph (ĭ-lĕk′trō-ĕn-sĕf′ə-lə-grăf′, -grăf′) *n.* An instrument that records the electrical activity of the brain. —**e·lec′tro·en·ceph′a·lo·graph′ic** *adj.*

e·lec·trol·y·sis (ĭ-lĕk′trŏl′ə-sĭs, ē′lĕk-) *n.* **1.** Chemical change, esp. decomposition, produced in an electrolyte by an electric current. **2.** Destruction of living tissue, as hair roots, by an electric current.

e·lec·tro·lyte (ĭ-lĕk′trə-līt′) *n.* A substance that dissociates into ions in solution or when fused, thereby becoming electrically conducting.

e·lec·tro·lyt·ic (ĭ-lĕk′trə-lĭt′ĭk) *adj.* **1. a.** Pertaining to electrolysis. **b.** Produced by electrolysis. **2.** Pertaining to an electrolyte. —**e·lec′tro·lyt′i·cal·ly** *adv.*

e·lec·tro·mag·net (ĭ-lĕk′trō-măg′nĭt) *n.* A magnet consisting essentially of a soft-iron core wound with a current-carrying coil of insulated wire.

e·lec·tro·mag·net·ism (ĭ-lĕk′trō-măg′nə-tĭz′əm) *n.* Magnetism arising from electric charge in motion. —**e·lec′tro·mag′net′ic** *adj.*

e·lec·tro·mo·tive (ĭ-lĕk′trō-mō′tĭv) *adj.* Pertaining to or producing electric current.

electromotive force. The energy per unit charge that is converted reversibly from chemical, mechanical, or other forms of energy into electrical energy in a conversion device such as a battery or dynamo.

e·lec·tron (ĭ-lĕk′trŏn′) *n.* A subatomic particle having a rest mass of 9.1066×10^{-28} gram and a unit negative electric charge of approx. 1.602×10^{-19} coulomb.

e·lec·tro·neg·a·tive (ĭ-lĕk′trō-nĕg′ə-tĭv) *adj.* **1.** Having a negative electric charge. **2.** Tending to attract electrons to form a chemical bond.

e·lec·tron·ic (ĭ-lĕk′trŏn′ĭk, ē′lĕk-) *adj.* **1.** Pertaining to electrons or electronics. **2.** Based on, operated by, or otherwise involving the controlled conduction of electrons or other charge carriers, esp. in a vacuum, gas, or semiconducting material. —*n.* **electronics** *(takes sing. v.).* **1.** The science and technology of electronic phenomena. **2.** The commercial industry of electronic devices and systems. —**e·lec′tron′i·cal·ly** *adv.*

electron microscope. Any of a class of microscopes that use electrons rather than visible light to produce magnified images.

electron tube. A sealed enclosure, either highly evacuated or containing a controlled quantity of gas, in which electrons can be made sufficiently mobile to act as the principal carriers of current between at least one pair of electrodes.

electron volt. A unit of energy equal to the energy acquired by an electron falling through a potential difference of one volt, approx. 1.602×10^{-19} joule.

e·lec·tro·plate (ĭ-lĕk′trə-plāt′) *v.* To coat or cover electrolytically with a thin layer of metal.

e·lec·tro·pos·i·tive (ĭ-lĕk′trō-pŏz′ə-tĭv) *adj.*

ă pat/ā ate/âr care/ä bar/b bib/ch chew/d deed/ĕ pet/ē be/f fit/g gag/h hat/hw what/
ĭ pit/ī pie/îr pier/j judge/k kick/l lid, fatal/m mum/n no, sudden/ng sing/ŏ pot/ō go/

1. Having a positive electric charge. 2. Tending to release electrons to form a chemical bond.

e·lec·tro·scope (ĭ-lĕk′trə-skōp′) n. An instrument used to detect the presence, sign, and in some configurations the magnitude of an electric charge by the mutual attraction or repulsion of metal foils or pith balls.

e·lec·tro·stat·ic (ĭ-lĕk′trō-stăt′ĭk) adj. 1. Pertaining to stationary electric charges. 2. Produced or caused by such charges.

electrostatic generator. Any of various devices, esp. the Van de Graaff generator, that generate high voltages by accumulating large quantities of electric charge.

e·lec·tro·ther·a·py (ĭ-lĕk′trō-thĕr′ə-pē) n. Medical therapy using electric currents.

e·lec·tro·type (ĭ-lĕk′trə-tīp′) n. A duplicate metal plate used in letterpress printing, made by electroplating a lead or plastic mold of the original.

e·lec·tro·va·lence (ĭ-lĕk′trō-vā′ləns) n. Also **e·lec·tro·va·len·cy** (-lən-sē). 1. Valence characterized by the transfer of electrons from atoms of one element to atoms of another. 2. The number of electric charges lost or gained by an atom in such a transfer. —e·lec′tro·va′lent adj.

el·e·gance (ĕl′ə-gəns) n. 1. Refinement and grace. 2. Tasteful opulence, as in design. [< L ēligere, to choose out.] —el′e·gant adj. —el′e·gant·ly adv.

el·e·gi·ac (ĕl′ə-jī′ək, ĭ-lē′jē-ăk′) adj. 1. Of or pertaining to an elegy or elegies. 2. Expressing sorrow; mournful.

el·e·gy (ĕl′ə-jē) n., pl. -gies. A mournful poem, esp. one that laments the dead. [< Gk elegos, lament.]

el·e·ment (ĕl′ə-mənt) n. 1. A fundamental constituent or principle of something. 2. Math. a. A member of a set. b. A point, line, or plane. c. A part of a geometric configuration, as an angle in a triangle. 3. Chem. & Phys. A substance composed of atoms having an identical number of protons in each nucleus. See Table of Elements on following pages. 4. elements. The forces that collectively constitute the weather. 5. An environment natural to or preferred by an individual. [< L elementum, rudiment, first principle.]

el·e·men·tal (ĕl′ə-mĕnt′l) adj. 1. Of an element. 2. Fundamental or essential. 3. Resembling a force of nature in power or effect.

el·e·men·ta·ry (ĕl′ə-mĕn′tə-rē, -trē) adj. 1. Fundamental, essential, or irreducible. 2. Involving or introducing the fundamental aspects of a subject.

elementary particle. A subatomic particle hypothesized or regarded as an irreducible constituent of matter.

elementary school. A school for the first six to eight years of a child's formal education.

el·e·phant (ĕl′ə-fənt) n. A very large Asian or African mammal with a long, flexible trunk and long tusks. [< Gk elephas (elephant-).]

el·e·phan·ti·a·sis (ĕl′ə-fən-tī′ə-sĭs) n. A chronic, often extreme enlargement and hardening of the cutaneous and subcutaneous tissue, esp. of the legs and scrotum.

el·e·phan·tine (ĕl′ə-făn′tĭn, -tēn′, -tīn′) adj. 1. Of or pertaining to an elephant. 2. Ponderous; clumsy; heavy-footed.

elev. elevation.

el·e·vate (ĕl′ə-vāt′) v. -vated, -vating. 1. To raise to a higher place; lift up. 2. To promote to a higher rank. 3. To raise to a higher moral or cultural level. 4. To lift the spirits of; elate. [< L ēlevāre.]

el·e·vat·ed (ĕl′ə-vā′tĭd) adj. 1. Raised above a given level: an elevated scaffold. 2. Exalted; lofty: elevated praise. —n. Informal. An elevated railway.

elevated railway. A railway that operates on a raised structure in order to permit passage of traffic beneath it.

el·e·va·tion (ĕl′ə-vā′shən) n. 1. The act of elevating or condition of being elevated. 2. An elevated place or position. 3. The height to which something is elevated, as above sea level.

el·e·va·tor (ĕl′ə-vā′tər) n. 1. A platform or enclosure raised and lowered to transport freight or people. 2. A granary with devices for hoisting and discharging grain. 3. A movable control surface used to make an aircraft go up or down.

e·lev·en (ĭ-lĕv′ən) n. The cardinal number written 11 or in Roman numerals XI. [< OE endleofan. See oino-.] —e·lev′en adj. & pron.

e·lev·enth (ĭ-lĕv′ənth) n. 1. The ordinal number 11 in a series. 2. One of 11 equal parts. —e·lev′enth adj. & adv.

elf (ĕlf) n., pl. **elves** (ĕlvz). A small mischievous fairy. [< OE ælf.] —elf′in adj. —elf′ish adj. —elf′ish·ly adv. —elf′ish·ness n.

El Gre·co (ĕl grĕk′ō, grā′kō). 1548?–1614? Spanish painter born in Crete.

el·hi (ĕl′hī′) adj. Elementary and high school.

e·lic·it (ĭ-lĭs′ĭt) v. 1. To bring out; draw forth; evoke. 2. To bring to light. [L ēlicere.] —e·lic′i·ta′tion n. —e·lic′i·tor n.

e·lide (ĭ-līd′) v. elided, eliding. 1. To omit or slur over, as a vowel or syllable in pronunciation. 2. To leave out or suppress. [L ēlīdere, to strike out.] —e·li′sion (-lĭzh′ən) n.

el·i·gi·ble (ĕl′ə-jə-bəl) adj. Qualified; worthy of choice. [< L ēligere, to choose, ELECT.] —el′i·gi·ble n. —el′i·gi·bil′i·ty n.

E·li·jah (ĭ-lī′jə). Hebrew prophet of the 9th century B.C.

e·lim·i·nate (ĭ-lĭm′ə-nāt′) v. -nated, -nating. 1. To get rid of; remove. 2. To leave out or omit from consideration. 3. To excrete (waste products). [L ēlīmināre, "to drive outside of the threshold."] —e·lim′i·na′tion n. —e·lim′i·na·to′ry (-nə-tôr′ē, -tōr′ē) adj.

e·lite (ĭ-lēt′) n. Also **é·lite** (ā-lēt′). 1. (takes pl. v.). The superior members of a given social group. 2. A narrow and powerful clique. [< OF eslire, to choose.]

e·lit·ism (ĭ-lē′tĭz′əm) n. Also **é·lit·ism** (ā-lē′-tĭz′əm). 1. Rule or domination by an elite. 2. Belief in such rule or domination. —e·lit′ist adj. & n.

e·lix·ir (ĭ-lĭk′sər) n. A sweetened solution of alcohol and water, containing medicine. [< Ar al-iksīr.]

ô paw, for/oi boy/ou out/ŏŏ took/ōō coo/p pop/r run/s sauce/sh shy/t to/th thin/*th* the/
ŭ cut/ûr fur/v van/w wag/y yes/z size/zh vision/ə ago, item, edible, gallop, circus/

PERIODIC TABLE OF THE ELEMENTS

KEY

| Atomic Number — 1 |
| **H** — Symbol |
| Hydrogen |
| 1.00797 |

Atomic Weight (or Mass Number of most stable isotope if in parentheses)

1a

1 H Hydrogen 1.00797

2a

3 Li Lithium 6.939	4 Be Beryllium 9.0122

11 Na Sodium 22.9898	12 Mg Magnesium 24.312

		3b	4b	5b	6b	7b		8
19 K Potassium 39.102	20 Ca Calcium 40.08	21 Sc Scandium 44.956	22 Ti Titanium 47.90	23 V Vanadium 50.942	24 Cr Chromium 51.996	25 Mn Manganese 54.9380	26 Fe Iron 55.847	27 Co Cobalt 58.9332
37 Rb Rubidium 85.47	38 Sr Strontium 87.62	39 Y Yttrium 88.905	40 Zr Zirconium 91.22	41 Nb Niobium 92.906	42 Mo Molybdenum 95.94	43 Tc Technetium (97)	44 Ru Ruthenium 101.07	45 Rh Rhodium 102.905
55 Cs Cesium 132.905	56 Ba Barium 137.34	57–71* Lanthanides	72 Hf Hafnium 178.49	73 Ta Tantalum 180.948	74 W Tungsten 183.85	75 Re Rhenium 186.2	76 Os Osmium 190.2	77 Ir Iridium 192.2
87 Fr Francium (223)	88 Ra Radium (226)	89–103** **Actinides						

*Lanthanides

57 La Lanthanum 138.91	58 Ce Cerium 140.12	59 Pr Praseodymium 140.907	60 Nd Neodymium 144.24	61 Pm Promethium (145)	62 Sm Samarium 150.35	63 Eu Europium 151.96

**Actinides

89 Ac Actinium (227)	90 Th Thorium 232.038	91 Pa Protactinium (231)	92 U Uranium 238.03	93 Np Neptunium (237)	94 Pu Plutonium (244)	95 Am Americium (243)

			3a	4a	5a	6a	7a	0
								2 **He** Helium 4.0026
			5 **B** Boron 10.811	6 **C** Carbon 12.01115	7 **N** Nitrogen 14.0067	8 **O** Oxygen 15.9994	9 **F** Fluorine 18.9984	10 **Ne** Neon 20.183
	1b	2b	13 **Al** Aluminum 26.9815	14 **Si** Silicon 28.086	15 **P** Phosphorus 30.9738	16 **S** Sulfur 32.064	17 **Cl** Chlorine 35.453	18 **Ar** Argon 39.948
28 **Ni** Nickel 58.71	29 **Cu** Copper 63.546	30 **Zn** Zinc 65.37	31 **Ga** Gallium 69.72	32 **Ge** Germanium 72.59	33 **As** Arsenic 74.9216	34 **Se** Selenium 78.96	35 **Br** Bromine 79.904	36 **Kr** Krypton 83.80
46 **Pd** Palladium 106.4	47 **Ag** Silver 107.868	48 **Cd** Cadmium 112.40	49 **In** Indium 114.82	50 **Sn** Tin 118.69	51 **Sb** Antimony 121.75	52 **Te** Tellurium 127.60	53 **I** Iodine 126.9044	54 **Xe** Xenon 131.30
78 **Pt** Platinum 195.09	79 **Au** Gold 196.967	80 **Hg** Mercury 200.59	81 **Tl** Thallium 204.37	·82 **Pb** Lead 207.19	83 **Bi** Bismuth 208.980	84 **Po** Polonium (210)	85 **At** Astatine (210)	86 **Rn** Radon (222)

64 **Gd** Gadolinium 157.25	65 **Tb** Terbium 158.924	66 **Dy** Dysprosium 162.50	67 **Ho** Holmium 164.930	68 **Er** Erbium 167.26	69 **Tm** Thulium 168.934	70 **Yb** Ytterbium 173.04	71 **Lu** Lutetium 174.97
96 **Cm** Curium (247)	97 **Bk** Berkelium (247)	98 **Cf** Californium (251)	99 **Es** Einsteinium (254)	100 **Fm** Fermium (257)	101 **Md** Mendelevium (256)	102 **No** Nobelium (254)	103 **Lw** Lawrencium (257)

E·liz·a·beth I (ĭ-lĭz′ə-bəth). 1533–1603. Queen of England and Ireland (1558–1603). —**E·liz′a·be′than** (-bē′thən, -bĕth′ən) *adj.*

Elizabeth I

E·liz·a·beth II (ĭ-lĭz′ə-bəth). Born 1926. Queen of Great Britain and Northern Ireland (since 1952).

elk (ĕlk) *n., pl.* **elks** or **elk.** Either of two large deer, the wapiti or the European moose. [< ON *elgr.*]

ell (ĕl) *n.* A wing of a building at right angles to the main structure.

el·lipse (ĭ-lĭps′) *n.* A plane curve formed by the locus of points the sum of the distances of each of which from two fixed points is the same constant. [Back-formation < ELLIPSIS.]

el·lip·sis (ĭ-lĭp′sĭs) *n., pl.* **-ses** (-sēz′). **1.** The omission of a word or words not necessary for the comprehension of a sentence, as *Stop laughing* for *You stop laughing.* **2.** Marks (... or ***) used to indicate an omission. [< Gk *elleipsis,* a falling short.]

el·lip·soid (ĭ-lĭp′soid′) *n.* A geometric surface whose plane sections are all either ellipses or circles. —**el′lip·soi′dal** *adj.*

el·lip·tic (ĭ-lĭp′tĭk) *adj.* Also **el·lip·ti·cal** (-tĭ-kəl). **1. a.** Pertaining to or having the shape of an ellipse. **b.** Resembling an ellipse. **2.** *Gram.* Containing or characterized by ellipsis. —**el·lip′ti·cal·ly** *adv.*

elm (ĕlm) *n.* A shade tree with arching or curving branches. [< OE. See el-2.]

el·o·cu·tion (ĕl′ə-kyoō′shən) *n.* The art of public speaking. [< L *ēloquī,* to speak out.] —**el′o·cu′tion·ist** *n.*

e·lon·gate (ĭ-lông′gāt′, ĭ-lŏng′-) *v.* **-gated, -gating.** To lengthen; grow in length. —**e·lon′ga′tion** *n.*

e·lope (ĭ-lōp′) *v.* **eloped, eloping.** To run away with a lover, esp. to get married. [< ME *alepen,* to run away.] —**e·lope′ment** *n.*

el·o·quent (ĕl′ə-kwənt) *adj.* Persuasive and fluent in discourse. [< L *ēloquī,* to speak out.] —**el′o·quence** *n.* —**el′o·quent·ly** *adv.*

El Pas·o (ĕl păs′ō). A city of SW Texas. Pop. 277,000.

El Sal·va·dor (ĕl săl′və-dôr′). A republic of Central America. Pop. 2,859,000. Cap. San Salvador.

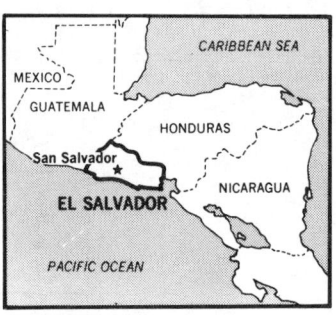

El Salvador

else (ĕls) *adj.* **1.** Other; different: *somebody else.* **2.** In addition; additional; more: *Would you like anything else?* —*adv.* **1.** In a different time, place, or manner; differently: *How else could it be done?* **2.** If not; otherwise: *Be careful, else you will make a mistake.* [< OE *elles,* otherwise, else. See al-1.]

Usage: The possessive forms of combinations employing *else* are now usually written *anyone* (or *anybody*) *else's, everyone* (or *everybody*) *else's, no one* (or *nobody*) *else's, someone* (or *somebody*) *else's.* Both *who else's* (followed by a noun) and *whose else* are used but not *whose else's.*

else·where (ĕls′hwâr′) *adv.* Somewhere or anywhere else.

e·lu·ci·date (ĭ-loō′sə-dāt′) *v.* **-dated, -dating.** To make clear or plain; clarify. [LL *ēlūcidāre.*] —**e·lu′ci·da′tion** *n.* —**e·lu′ci·da′tor** *n.*

e·lude (ĭ-loōd′) *v.* **eluded, eluding. 1.** To avoid or escape from; evade. **2.** To escape understanding or detection by; baffle. [L *ēlūdere,* "to take away from at play."]

e·lu·sive (ĭ-loō′sĭv) *adj.* Tending to elude grasp, perception, or mental retention. —**e·lu′sive·ly** *adv.* —**e·lu′sive·ness** *n.*

el·ver (ĕl′vər) *n.* A young or immature eel.

elves *pl.* of **elf.**

E·ly·si·um (ĭ-lĭzh′ē-əm, ĭ-lĭz′-) *n.* **1.** *Gk. Myth.* The abode of the blessed after death. **2.** A place or condition of ideal happiness. —**E·ly′sian** (-lĭzh′ən, -ē-ən) *adj.*

'em (əm) *pron. Informal.* Them.

em-1. Variant of **en-1** (put into).

em-2. Variant of **en-2** (into).

EM enlisted man.

e·ma·ci·ate (ĭ-mā′shē-āt′) *v.* **-ated, -ating.** To make thin, as by starvation or illness. [L *ēmaciāre.*] —**e·ma′ci·a′tion** *n.*

em·a·nate (ĕm′ə-nāt′) *v.* **-nated, -nating.** To come forth, as from a source; issue; originate. [L *ēmānāre,* flow out.] —**em′a·na′tion** *n.* —**em′a·na′tive** *adj.*

e·man·ci·pate (ĭ-măn′sə-pāt′) *v.* **-pated, -pating. 1.** To free from oppression or bondage. **2.** To

---

ă pat/ā ate/âr care/ä bar/b **bib**/ch **chew**/d **deed**/ĕ pet/ē be/f **fit**/g **gag**/h **hat**/hw **what**/ ĭ pit/ī pie/îr pier/j **judge**/k **kick**/l lid, fatal/m **mum**/n no, sudden/ng **sing**/ŏ pot/ō go/

free from any restraint. [L *ēmancipāre*, "to release from slavery or tutelage."] —e•man'ci•pa'tion *n.* —e•man'ci•pa'tor *n.*

e•mas•cu•late (ĭ-măs'kyə-lāt') *v.* -lated, -lating. **1.** To castrate. **2.** To make weak. —e•mas'cu•la'tion *n.* —e•mas'cu•la'tor *n.*

em•balm (ĕm-bäm', ĭm-) *v.* To prevent the decay of (a corpse) by treatment with preservatives. —em•balm'er *n.*

em•bank (ĕm-băngk', ĭm-) *v.* To confine, support, or protect with a bank or banks. —em•bank'ment *n.*

em•bar•go (ĕm-bär'gō, ĭm-) *n., pl.* -goes. **1.** A government order prohibiting the movement of merchant ships into or out of its ports. **2.** Any prohibition. —*v.* To impose an embargo upon. [< VL *imbarricāre*, "to place behind bars."]

em•bark (ĕm-bärk', ĭm-) *v.* **1.** To board or cause to board a vessel, esp. at the start of a journey. **2.** To set out on a venture; commence. [< LL *imbarcāre*.] —em'bar•ka'tion, em•bark'ment *n.*

em•bar•rass (ĕm-băr'əs, ĭm-) *v.* **1.** To cause to feel ill at ease. **2.** To hamper with financial difficulties. **3.** To impede. [< It *imbarrare*, "to put in bars," impede.] —em•bar'rass•ing•ly *adv.* —em•bar'rass•ment *n.*

em•bas•sy (ĕm'bə-sē) *n., pl.* -sies. **1.** The position of an ambassador. **2.** A mission to a foreign government. **3.** An ambassador and his staff. **4.** The headquarters of an ambassador. [< OProv *ambaissada*.]

em•bat•tle (ĕm-băt'l, ĭm-) *v.* -tled, -tling. To prepare or array for battle.

em•bed (ĕm-bĕd', ĭm-) *v.* -bedded, -bedding. Also im•bed (ĭm-). To fix or become fixed firmly in a surrounding mass.

em•bel•lish (ĕm-bĕl'ĭsh, ĭm-) *v.* **1.** To make more beautiful; adorn. **2.** To add fictitious details to (a statement). [< OF *embellir*.] —em•bel'lish•ment *n.*

em•ber (ĕm'bər) *n.* **1.** A piece of live coal or wood, as in a fire. **2. embers.** The smoldering remains of a fire. [< OE *æmerge*, embers, ashes.]

em•bez•zle (ĕm-bĕz'əl, ĭm-) *v.* -zled, -zling. To take (money or property) for one's own use in breach of trust. [< NF *enbesiler*.] —em•bez'zle•ment *n.* —em•bez'zler *n.*

em•bit•ter (ĕm-bĭt'ər, ĭm-) *v.* **1.** To make bitter. **2.** To arouse bitter feelings in. —em•bit'ter•ment *n.*

em•blaze (ĕm-blāz', ĭm-) *v.* -blazed, -blazing. **1.** To set on fire. **2.** To cause to glow or glitter.

em•bla•zon (ĕm-blā'zən, ĭm-) *v.* **1.** To ornament richly, esp. with heraldic devices. **2.** To make resplendent with colors. **3.** To exalt. —em•bla'zon•ment *n.*

em•blem (ĕm'bləm) *n.* **1.** An object or picture that comes to represent something else; a symbol. **2.** A distinctive badge, design, etc. [< Gk *emballein*, to throw in, insert.] —em'blem•at'ic (-blə-măt'ĭk) *adj.*

em•bod•y (ĕm-bŏd'ē, ĭm-) *v.* -ied, -ying. **1.** To invest with or as with bodily form; make corporeal. **2.** To personify. **3.** To make part of a united whole. —em•bod'i•ment *n.*

em•bold•en (ĕm-bōl'dən, ĭm-) *v.* To foster boldness in; encourage.

em•bo•lism (ĕm'bə-lĭz'əm) *n.* Obstruction or occlusion of a blood vessel by an air bubble, detached clot, bacterial mass, or other foreign body. [< Gk *emballein*, "to throw in," insert.] —em•bol'ic (ĕm-bŏl'ĭk, ĭm-) *adj.*

em•boss (ĕm-bôs', -bŏs', ĭm-) *v.* **1.** To represent (a design) in relief. **2.** To cover with or as with a raised design. [< OF *embocer*, "to put a knob in."] —em•boss'er *n.*

em•bow•er (ĕm-bou'ər, ĭm-) *v.* To enclose in a bower.

em•brace (ĕm-brās', ĭm-) *v.* -braced, -bracing. **1.** To clasp in or hold with the arms, usually in affection; hug. **2.** To encircle. **3.** To include. **4.** To take up; adopt, as a cause. **5.** To accept eagerly. —*n.* An act of embracing; an affectionate hug. [< VL *imbracchiāre*.]

em•bra•sure (ĕm-brā'zhər, ĭm-) *n.* **1.** A window or door recess. **2.** An opening for a gun in a wall or parapet.

em•broi•der (ĕm-broi'dər, ĭm-) *v.* **1.** To ornament (fabric) with needlework; make embroidery. **2.** To embellish (a narrative). [< NF *enbrouder*.]

em•broi•der•y (ĕm-broi'də-rē, ĭm-) *n., pl.* -ies. **1.** The art or act of embroidering. **2.** A piece of embroidered fabric. **3.** An embellishment.

em•broil (ĕm-broil', ĭm-) *v.* **1.** To involve in argument or hostile actions. **2.** To throw into disorder; entangle. —em•broil'ment *n.*

em•bry•o (ĕm'brē-ō') *n., pl.* -os. **1.** An organism in its earliest stages of development, as before birth or hatching. **2.** A rudimentary or beginning stage. —*adj.* Incipient; rudimentary. [< Gk *embruon*, "something that grows in the body."] —em'bry•on'ic (-ŏn'ĭk) *adj.*

em•bry•ol•o•gy (ĕm'brē-ŏl'ə-jē) *n.* The science of the formation, early growth, and development of living organisms. —em'bry•o•log'ic (-ə-lŏj'ĭk), em'bry•o•log'i•cal *adj.* —em'bry•o•log'i•cal•ly *adv.* —em'bry•ol'o•gist *n.*

em•cee (ĕm'sē') *n. Informal.* A master of ceremonies. [Short for M(ASTER OF) C(EREMONIES).] —em'cee' *v.* (-ceed, -ceeing).

e•meer. Variant of emir.

e•mend (ĭ-mĕnd') *v.* To improve (a text) by critical editing. [< L *ēmendāre*.] —e•men'da'tion *n.*

em•er•ald (ĕm'ər-əld, ĕm'rəld) *n.* **1.** A brilliant, transparent green beryl used as a gemstone. **2.** Strong yellowish green. [< OF *esmeraude*.] —em'er•ald *adj.*

e•merge (ĭ-mûrj') *v.* emerged, emerging. **1.** To rise up or come forth from or as from immersion; come into sight. **2.** To become obvious. **3.** To come into existence. [L *ēmergere*.] —e•mer'gence *n.* —e•mer'gent *adj.*

e•mer•gen•cy (ĭ-mûr'jən-sē) *n., pl.* -cies. A sudden, unexpected occurrence demanding immediate action.

e•mer•i•tus (ĭ-mĕr'ə-təs) *adj.* Retired but retaining an honorary title: *a professor emeritus.* [< L *ēmerēri*, to earn by service.]

Em•er•son (ĕm'ər-sən), **Ralph Waldo.** 1803–1882. American essayist and poet.

em•er•y (ĕm'ə-rē, ĕm'rē) *n.* A fine-grained

impure corundum used for grinding and polishing. [< Gk *smuris*, emery powder.]

e·met·ic (ĭ-mĕt'ĭk) *adj.* Causing vomiting. —*n.* An emetic agent or medicine. [< Gk *emein*, to vomit.] —**e·met'i·cal·ly** *adv.*

e·meu. Variant of **emu.**

emf, EMF electromotive force.

–emia, –hemia. *comb. form.* Blood: leukemia. [< Gk *haima*, blood.]

em·i·grate (ĕm'ĭ-grāt') *v.* **-grated, -grating.** To leave one country or region to settle in another. [L *ēmigrāre*, to move away from.] —**em'i·grant** (-grənt) *n.* —**em'i·gra'tion** *n.*

é·mi·gré (ĕm'ĭ-grā') *n.* An emigrant, esp. a refugee from a revolution.

em·i·nence (ĕm'ə-nəns) *n.* **1.** A position of superiority in achievement, position, etc. **2.** A rise of ground; hill.

em·i·nent (ĕm'ə-nənt) *adj.* **1.** Towering above others; projecting. **2.** Distinguished, as in reputation. [< L *ēminēre*, to stand out.] —**em'i·nent·ly** *adv.*

e·mir (ĕ-mîr') *n.* Also **e·meer.** A prince, chieftain, or governor, esp. in Arabia. [< Ar *'amīr*, commander.]

em·is·sar·y (ĕm'ə-sĕr'ē) *n., pl.* **-ies.** A messenger or agent. [< L *ēmittere*, to send out, EMIT.]

e·mit (ĭ-mĭt') *v.* **emitted, emitting. 1.** To release or send forth, as radiation. **2.** To utter or express. **3.** To issue with authority, esp. currency or shares of stock. [L *ēmittere*, to send out.] —**e·mis'sion** *n.* —**e·mit'ter** *n.*

e·mol·lient (ĭ-mŏl'yənt, -ē-ənt) *adj.* Having softening and soothing qualities, esp. for the skin. [< L *ēmollīre*, to soften, soothe.] —**e·mol'lient** *n.*

e·mol·u·ment (ĭ-mŏl'yə-mənt) *n.* Profit derived from one's office or employment. [< L *ēmolumentum*, orig "miller's fee for grinding grain."]

e·mote (ĭ-mōt') *v.* **emoted, emoting.** *Informal.* To express emotion or sentiment in an effusive and theatrical manner. [Back-formation < EMOTION.]

e·mo·tion (ĭ-mō'shən) *n.* **1.** Agitation of the passions or sensibilities. **2.** Any strong subjective feeling, as of joy, sorrow, reverence, hate, or love. [< L *ēmovēre*, to move out, stir up, excite.] —**e·mo'tion·al** *adj.* —**e·mo'tion·al·ism'** *n.* —**e·mo'tion·al·ly** *adv.*

em·pa·thy (ĕm'pə-thē) *n.* Understanding so intimate that the feelings, thoughts, and motives of one are readily comprehended by another. —**em'pa·thize'** *v.* **(-thized, -thizing).**

em·per·or (ĕm'pər-ər) *n.* The ruler of an empire. [< L *imperātor*, emperor, commander.]

em·pha·sis (ĕm'fə-sĭs) *n., pl.* **-ses** (sēz'). **1.** Special importance placed upon or imparted to something. **2.** Stress given to a syllable, word, or phrase. [< Gk *emphainein*, to exhibit, indicate.]

em·pha·size (ĕm'fə-sīz') *v.* **-sized, -sizing.** To give emphasis to; stress.

em·phat·ic (ĕm-făt'ĭk) *adj.* **1.** Expressed or performed with emphasis. **2.** Bold and definite. —**em·phat'i·cal·ly** *adv.*

em·phy·se·ma (ĕm'fə-sē'mə) *n.* A pathological condition of the lungs marked by labored breathing and increased susceptibility to infection. [< Gk *emphusan*, to blow in.]

em·pire (ĕm'pīr') *n.* **1.** A political unit, usually larger than a kingdom and often comprising a number of territories or nations, ruled by a single authority. **2.** Imperial rule. **3.** An extensive enterprise. [< L *imperium*, dominion, empire.]

em·pir·i·cal (ĕm-pîr'ĭ-kəl, ĭm-) *adj.* **1.** Relying on observation or experiment. **2.** Guided by experience rather than theory. [< Gk *empeira*, experience.] —**em·pir'i·cal·ly** *adv.*

em·pir·i·cism (ĕm-pîr'ə-sĭz'əm, ĭm-) *n.* **1.** The view that experience, esp. of the senses, is the only source of knowledge. **2.** The employment of empirical methods, as in science. —**em·pir'i·cist** *n.*

em·place·ment (ĕm-plās'mənt, ĭm-) *n.* A prepared position for guns within a fortification.

em·ploy (ĕm-ploi', ĭm-) *v.* **1.** To use; put to service. **2.** To devote or apply (one's time or energies) to some activity. **3.** To engage the services of; provide with a job. —*n.* Employment. [< L *implicāre*, to infold, involve.]

em·ploy·ee (ĕm-ploi'ē, ĭm-, ĕm'ploi-ē') *n.* A person who works for another in return for financial compensation.

em·ploy·er (ĕm-ploi'ər, ĭm-) *n.* A person or concern that employs persons for wages or salary.

em·ploy·ment (ĕm-ploi'mənt, ĭm-) *n.* **1.** The act of employing or state of being employed. **2.** An occupation or activity.

em·po·ri·um (ĕm-pôr'ē-əm, ĕm-pōr'-, ĭm-) *n., pl.* **-ums** or **-poria** (-pôr'ē-ə, -pōr'ē-ə). A store carrying a wide variety of merchandise. [< Gk *emporos*, merchant, traveler.]

em·pow·er (ĕm-pou'ər, ĭm-) *v.* **1.** To invest with legal power; authorize. **2.** To enable or permit.

em·press (ĕm'prĭs) *n.* **1.** A female sovereign of an empire. **2.** The wife or widow of an emperor.

emp·ty (ĕmp'tē) *adj.* **-tier, -tiest. 1.** Void of content; containing nothing. **2.** Having no occupants or inhabitants; vacant. **3.** Lacking purpose or substance; meaningless. —*v.* **-tied, -tying. 1.** To remove the contents of; make or become empty. **2.** To discharge or flow into: *The river empties into a bay.* [< OE *ǣmtig* < *ǣmetta*, rest, leisure.] —**emp'ti·ness** *n.*

emp·ty-hand·ed (ĕmp'tē-hăn'dĭd) *adj.* **1.** Bearing no gifts or possessions. **2.** Having gained nothing.

em·py·re·an (ĕm'pī-rē'ən) *n.* **1.** The highest reaches of heaven. **2.** The sky; firmament. [< Gk *empuros*, fiery.]

e·mu (ē'myōō) *n.* Also **e·meu.** A large, ostrich-like Australian bird. [Port *ema*.]

em·u·late (ĕm'yə-lāt') *v.* **-lated, -lating.** To strive to equal or excel, esp. through imitation. [< L *aemulus*, imitating.] —**em'u·la'tion** *n.*

e·mul·si·fy (ĭ-mŭl'sə-fī') *v.* **-fied, -fying.** To make into an emulsion. —**e·mul'si·fi·ca'tion** *n.* —**e·mul'si·fi'er** *n.*

e·mul·sion (ĭ-mŭl'shən) *n.* **1.** A suspension of small globules of one liquid in a second liquid with which the first will not mix, such as milk

---

fats in milk. **2.** A light-sensitive coating, usually of silver halide grains in a thin gelatin layer, on photographic film, paper, or glass. [< L *ēmulgēre,* to drain out, milk out.]

en–¹. Also **em-.** *comb. form.* **1.** Used to form verbs from nouns: **a.** To put or go into or on. **b.** To cover or imbue with. **c.** To provide with. **2.** Used to form verbs from nouns and adjectives to indicate causing to become or resemble. [< L *in-, im-.*]

en–². Also **em-.** *comb. form.* Used to form nouns and adjectives to indicate in, into, or within. [< Gk.]

–en¹. *comb. form.* **1.** Used to form verbs from adjectives to indicate being, becoming, or causing to be: **redden. 2.** Used to form verbs from nouns to indicate causing to have or gain: **lengthen.** [< OE *-nian.*]

–en². *comb. form.* Used to form adjectives from nouns to indicate made of, composed of, or resembling: **earthen.** [< OE.]

en·a·ble (ĕn-ā′bəl) *v.* **-bled, -bling.** To supply with the means, knowledge, or opportunity to do something; make possible.

en·act (ĕn-ăkt′) *v.* **1.** To pass (a bill); decree by legislative process. **2.** To act out as on a stage. —**en·act′ment** *n.* —**en·ac′tor** *n.*

en·am·el (ĭ-năm′əl) *n.* **1.** A vitreous, usually opaque coating baked on metal, ceramic ware, etc. **2.** A paint that dries to a hard, glossy surface. **3.** The hard substance covering the exposed portion of a tooth. —*v.* **-eled** or **-elled, -eling** or **-elling.** To coat or decorate with enamel. [< NF *enameler.*]

en·am·el·ware (ĭ-năm′əl-wâr′) *n.* Metal utensils coated with enamel.

en·am·or (ĭ-năm′ər) *v.* Also *chiefly Brit.* **en·am·our.** To inspire with love; captivate. [< L *amāre,* to love.]

enc. enclosed; enclosure.

en·camp (ĕn-kămp′, ĭn-) *v.* To set up or live in a camp. —**en·camp′ment** *n.*

en·cap·su·late (ĕn-kăp′sə-lāt′, ĭn-) *v.* **-lated, -lating.** Also **in·cap·su·late** (ĭn-). To encase in or as in a capsule. —**en·cap′su·la′tion** *n.*

en·case (ĕn-kās′, ĭn-) *v.* **-cased, -casing.** Also **in·case** (ĭn-). To enclose in or as in a case.

–ence, –ency. *comb. form.* Used to form nouns from adjectives ending in *-ent* to indicate action, state, quality, or condition: **reference.** [< L *-entia.*]

en·ce·phal·ic (ĕn′sə-făl′ĭk) *adj.* Pertaining to the brain.

en·ceph·a·li·tis (ĕn-sĕf′ə-lī′tĭs, ĕn′sĕf-) *n.* Inflammation of the brain. —**en·ceph′a·lit′ic** (-lĭt′ĭk) *adj.*

encephalo–. *comb. form.* The brain. [< Gk *(muelos) enkephalos,* "(marrow) in the head," the brain.]

en·ceph·a·lo·gram (ĕn-sĕf′ə-lō-grăm′) *n.* **1.** An x-ray picture of the brain. **2.** An electroencephalogram.

en·ceph·a·lon (ĕn-sĕf′ə-lŏn′) *n., pl.* **-la** (-lə). The brain of a vertebrate.

en·chain (ĕn-chān′, ĭn-) *v.* To bind with or as with chains; fetter. —**en·chain′ment** *n.*

en·chant (ĕn-chănt′, -chänt′, ĭn-) *v.* **1.** To cast under a spell; bewitch. **2.** To delight com-

pletely; enrapture. [< L *incantāre.*] —**en·chant′er** *n.* —**en·chant′ment** *n.*

en·ci·pher (ĕn-sī′fər, ĭn-) *v.* To put (a message) into cipher.

en·cir·cle (ĕn-sûr′kəl, ĭn-) *v.* **-cled, -cling. 1.** To surround. **2.** To move or go around. —**en·cir′cle·ment** *n.*

encl. enclosed; enclosure.

en·clave (ĕn′klāv′, än′-) *n.* A country or part of a country lying wholly within the boundaries of another. [< VL **inclāvāre,* to lock in with a key.]

en·close (ĕn-klōz′, ĭn-) *v.* **-closed, -closing.** Also **in·close** (ĭn-). **1.** To surround on all sides; fence in. **2.** To insert in the same container with a letter or package. —**en·clo′sure** *n.*

en·code (ĕn-kōd′, ĭn-) *v.* **-coded, -coding.** To put (a message) into code. —**en·cod′er** *n.*

en·co·mi·um (ĕn-kō′mē-əm) *n., pl.* **-ums** or **-mia** (-mē-ə). Lofty praise; a eulogy. [< Gk *enkōmion (epos),* "(speech) in praise of a conqueror."]

en·com·pass (ĕn-kŭm′pəs, ĭn-) *v.* **1.** To surround. **2.** To envelop. **3.** To include; contain.

en·core (äng′kôr′, -kôr′, än′-) *n.* **1.** A demand by an audience for an additional performance. **2.** A performance in response to such a demand. [F, still, yet, again.]

en·coun·ter (ĕn-koun′tər, ĭn-) *n.* **1.** A meeting, esp. when unplanned. **2.** A hostile confrontation. —*v.* **1.** To meet, esp. unexpectedly. **2.** To confront in battle. [< OF *encontrer,* to meet.]

en·cour·age (ĕn-kûr′ĭj, ĭn-) *v.* **-aged, -aging. 1.** To impart courage or confidence to. **2.** To give support to; foster. —**en·cour′age·ment** *n.* —**en·cour′ag·er** *n.*

en·croach (ĕn-krōch′, ĭn-) *v.* To intrude gradually on the possessions or rights of another; trespass. [< OF *encrochier,* "to catch in a hook."] —**en·croach′ment** *n.*

en·crust (ĕn-krŭst′, ĭn-) *v.* Also **in·crust** (ĭn-). To cover or surmount with a crust. —**en′crust·a′tion** *n.*

en·cum·ber (ĕn-kŭm′bər, ĭn-) *v.* **1.** To weigh down unduly; handicap. **2.** To hinder; impede. [< OF *encombrer,* to block up.] —**en·cum′brance** (-brəns) *n.*

ency., encyc. encyclopedia.

en·cyc·li·cal (ĕn-sīk′lĭ-kəl, ĭn-) *n. R.C.Ch.* A papal letter on a grave or timely subject. [< Gk *enkuklios,* circular.]

en·cy·clo·pe·di·a (ĕn-sī′klə-pē′dē-ə, ĭn-) *n.* Also **en·cy·clo·pae·di·a.** A reference work with articles on many subjects or numerous aspects of a particular field. [< Gk *enkuklios paideia,* general education.] —**en·cy′clo·pe′dic, en·cy′clo·pae′dic** *adj.* —**en·cy′clo·pe′di·cal·ly** *adv.*

end (ĕnd) *n.* **1.** An extremity; tip. **2.** A boundary; limit. **3.** The point at which something ceases or is completed; conclusion. **4.** A result; outcome. **5.** Death. **6.** A purpose; goal. **7.** A share of a responsibility: *your end of the bargain.* **8.** *Football.* Either of the players in the outermost position at the line of scrimmage. —**make (both) ends meet.** To manage to live within one's means. —**no end.** *Informal.* A great deal: *no end of trouble.* —*v.* **1.** To bring

---

ô paw, for/oi boy/ou out/ŏŏ took/ōō coo/p pop/r run/s sauce/sh shy/t to/th thin/*th* the/
ŭ cut/ûr fur/v van/w wag/y yes/z size/zh vision/ə ago, item, edible, gallop, circus/

or come to an end. **2.** To be at or form the end of. [< OE *ende.* See **anti.**]

en·dan·ger (ĕn-dān'jər, ĭn-) *v.* To expose to danger; imperil. —**en·dan'ger·ment** *n.*

endangered species. A species in danger of extinction.

en·dear (ĕn-dîr', ĭn-) *v.* To cause to be held dear; make beloved.

en·dear·ment (ĕn-dîr'mənt, ĭn-) *n.* An expression of affection.

en·deav·or (ĕn-dĕv'ər, ĭn-). Also *chiefly Brit.* **en·deav·our.** *v.* To make an earnest attempt; strive. [< ME *putten in dever,* to put in duty.] —**en·deav'or** *n.*

en·dem·ic (ĕn-dĕm'ĭk) *adj.* Prevalent in or peculiar to a particular locality or people. [< Gk *endēmios,* dwelling in a place.]

en·dive (ĕn'dīv', än'dēv') *n.* **1.** A plant with crisp, succulent leaves used in salads. **2.** A related plant with a narrow, pointed cluster of whitish leaves. [< Gk *entubioi,* chicory.]

end·less (ĕnd'lĭs) *adj.* **1.** Having no end; infinite. **2.** Formed with the ends joined; continuous. —**end'less·ly** *adv.* —**end'less·ness** *n.*

end·most (ĕnd'mōst') *adj.* Being at or closest to the end.

endo-. *comb. form.* Inside or within. [< Gk *endon,* within.]

en·do·crine (ĕn'də-krĭn, -krēn', -krīn') *adj.* **1.** Secreting internally. **2.** Pertaining to any of the endocrine glands.

endocrine gland. Any of the ductless glands, such as the thyroid or adrenal, the secretions of which pass directly into the blood stream from the cells of the gland.

en·do·me·tri·um (ĕn'dō-mē'trē-əm) *n., pl.* **-tria** (-trē-ə). The mucous membrane lining the uterus.

en·do·plasm (ĕn'dō-plăz'əm) *n.* A low-viscosity portion of the continuous phase of cytoplasm distinguishable within some cells. —**en'do·plas'mic** *adj.*

end organ. The expanded functional termination of a sensory nerve or a motor nerve in tissue.

en·dorse (ĕn-dôrs', ĭn-) *v.* **-dorsed, -dorsing.** Also **in·dorse** (ĭn-). **1.** To write one's signature on the back of (a check, stock certificate, etc.) in return for the cash or credit indicated on its face. **2.** To give approval of; sanction. [< OF *endosser,* "to put on the back of."] —**en·dorse'ment** *n.* —**en·dors'er, en·dors'or** *n.*

en·do·the·li·um (ĕn'dō-thē'lē-əm) *n., pl.* **-lia** (-lē-ə). A thin layer of flat cells that lines serous cavities, lymph vessels, and blood vessels. —**en'do·the'li·al** *adj.*

en·do·ther·mic (ĕn'dō-thûr'mĭk) *adj.* Absorbing heat.

en·dow (ĕn-dou', ĭn-) *v.* **1.** To provide with property or income. **2.** To equip with a talent or quality. [< NF *endouer.*] —**en·dow'ment** *n.*

end·plate (ĕnd'plāt') *n.* A terminal that transmits nerve impulses to a muscle.

en·due (ĕn-d/y/ōō', ĭn-) *v.* **-dued, -duing.** Also **in·due** (ĭn-). To provide with some quality or trait. [< L *indūcere,* **INDUCE,** and *induere,* to don.]

en·dur·a·ble (ĕn-d/y/ōōr'ə-bəl, ĭn-) *adj.* Ca-

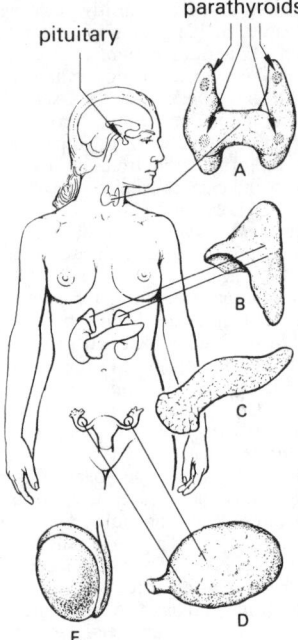

endocrine gland
A. Thyroid
B. Adrenal gland
C. Islands of Langerhans
   in pancreas
D. Ovary (in female)
E. Testis (in male)

pable of being endured; bearable; tolerable.

en·dur·ance (ĕn-d/y/ōōr'əns, ĭn-) *n.* **1.** The power to withstand hardship or stress. **2.** The state or fact of persevering.

en·dure (ĕn-d/y/ōōr', ĭn-) *v.* **-dured, -during.** **1.** To bear with tolerance; put up with. **2.** To continue in existence; last. [< LL *indūrāre,* "to harden one's heart against."]

en·dur·ing (ĕn-d/y/ōōr'ĭng, ĭn-) *adj.* Lasting; durable.

end·wise (ĕnd'wīz') *adv.* Also **end·ways** (-wāz'). **1.** On end. **2.** With the end foremost. **3.** Lengthwise.

-ene. *comb. form. Chem.* Unsaturation of an organic compound, esp. one having a double bond: ethylene. [< Gk *-ēnē.*]

en·e·ma (ĕn'ə-mə) *n.* The injection of liquid into the rectum for laxative or other therapeutic purposes. [< Gk *enienai,* to throw in, inject.]

en·e·my (ĕn'ə-mē) *n., pl.* **-mies.** **1.** One who manifests hostility toward another; a foe; an opponent. **2.** A hostile power, as a nation. [< L *inimicus.*]

en·er·get·ic (ĕn'ər-jĕt'ĭk) *adj.* Possessing, exerting, or displaying energy; vigorous. —**en'er·get'i·cal·ly** *adv.*

en·er·get·ics (ĕn'ər-jĕt'ĭks) *n. (takes sing. v.).*

ă pat/ā ate/âr care/ä bar/b bib/ch chew/d deed/ĕ pet/ē be/f fit/g gag/h hat/hw what/
ĭ pit/ī pie/îr pier/j judge/k kick/l lid, fatal/m mum/n no, sudden/ng sing/ŏ pot/ō go/

The physics of energy and its transformations.

en•er•gize (ĕn'ər-jīz') v. -gized, -gizing. To give energy to. —**en'er•giz'er** n.

en•er•gy (ĕn'ər-jē) n., pl. -gies. 1. Vigor or power in action. 2. Capacity for action or accomplishment. 3. Phys. The work that a physical system is capable of doing in changing from its actual state to a specified reference state, the total including, in general, contributions of potential energy, kinetic energy, and rest energy. [< Gk energos, active, at work.]

en•er•vate (ĕn'ər-vāt') v. -vated, -vating. To deprive of strength or vitality; weaken. [L ēnervāre, "to remove the sinews from."] —**en'er•va'tor** n.

en•fee•ble (ĕn-fē'bəl, ĭn-) v. -bled, -bling. To make feeble. —**en•fee'ble•ment** n.

en•fi•lade (ĕn'fə-lād') n. Gunfire that sweeps the length of a target, such as a column of troops. [< F enfiler, to thread.]

en•fold (ĕn-fōld', ĭn-) v. Also in•fold (ĭn-). 1. To cover with or as if with folds; envelop. 2. To embrace. —**en•fold'er** n.

en•force (ĕn-fôrs', -fōrs', ĭn-) v. -forced, -forcing. 1. To compel obedience to. 2. To impose (specified action or behavior); compel. —**en•force'a•ble** adj. —**en•force'ment** n.

en•fran•chise (ĕn-frăn'chīz', ĭn-) v. -chised, -chising. 1. To endow with the rights of citizenship, esp. the right to vote. 2. To free, as from bondage.

eng. 1. engine. 2. engineer; engineering.

Eng. England; English.

en•gage (ĕn-gāj', ĭn-) v. -gaged, -gaging. 1. To employ; hire. 2. To attract and hold the attention of. 3. To pledge (oneself), esp. by a promise to marry. 4. To enter or bring into conflict with. 5. To interlock or cause to interlock. 6. To involve oneself or become occupied. [< OF engager.] —**en•gag'er** n.

en•gage•ment (ĕn-gāj'mənt, ĭn-) n. 1. An act of engaging or the state of being engaged. 2. Betrothal. 3. A commitment to appear at a certain time; appointment. 4. Employment. 5. A battle or encounter.

en•gag•ing (ĕn-gā'jĭng, ĭn-) adj. Attractive; charming. —**en•gag'ing•ly** adv.

Eng•els (ĕng'əls), **Friedrich.** 1820–1895. German socialist; collaborated with Marx.

en•gen•der (ĕn-jĕn'dər, ĭn-) v. To bring into existence; give rise to; beget. [< L ingenerāre.]

en•gine (ĕn'jən) n. 1. a. A machine, esp. one powered by a fuel, that converts energy into mechanical motion. b. Any mechanical appliance, instrument, or tool. 2. A locomotive. [< L ingenium, inborn talent, skill.]

engine block. The cast metal block containing the cylinders of an internal-combustion engine.

en•gi•neer (ĕn'jə-nîr') n. 1. One skilled at or engaged in a branch of engineering. 2. One who operates an engine. —v. 1. To act as engineer. 2. To plan or accomplish by skillful acts or contrivance.

en•gi•neer•ing (ĕn'jə-nîr'ĭng) n. 1. The application of scientific principles to practical ends

as the design, construction, and operation of efficient and economical structures, equipment, and systems. 2. The profession of or work performed by an engineer.

Eng•land (ĭng'glənd). The largest division of the United Kingdom of Great Britain and Northern Ireland, in S Great Britain. 2. Popularly, Great Britain.

Eng•lish (ĭng'glĭsh) adj. 1. Of, pertaining to, or characteristic of England and its inhabitants. 2. Of, belonging to, or spoken or written in the English language. —n. 1. **the English** (takes pl. v.). The people of England. 2. The West Germanic language of the English divided historically into Old English, Middle English, and Modern English and now spoken in the British Isles, the United States, and numerous other countries.

English Channel. An arm of the Atlantic between England and France.

English horn. A double-reed woodwind instrument.

Eng•lish•man (ĭng'glĭsh-mən) n. A native or inhabitant of England.

engr. 1. engineer. 2. engraved; engraving.

en•graft (ĕn-grăft', -gräft', ĭn-) v. To graft (a shoot) onto a plant. —**en•graft'ment** n.

en•gram (ĕn'grăm') n. A persistent protoplasmic alteration hypothesized to occur on stimulation of living neural tissue and to account for memory.

en•grave (ĕn-grāv', ĭn-) v. -graved, -graving. 1. To carve, cut, or etch (a design or letters) into a material. 2. a. To carve, cut, or etch (a design or letters) into a block or surface used for printing. b. To print from a block or plate thus made. [EN- + GRAVE³.] —**en•grav'er** n.

en•grav•ing (ĕn-grā'vĭng, ĭn-) n. 1. The technique of one that engraves. 2. An engraved surface for printing. 3. A print made from an engraved plate or block.

en•gross (ĕn-grōs', ĭn-) v. 1. To occupy the complete attentions of. 2. a. To write or transcribe in a large, clear hand. b. To prepare the text of (an official document). [< OF en gros, in large quantity.] —**en•gross'er** n.

en•gross•ing (ĕn-grō'sĭng, ĭn-) adj. Occupying one's complete attention.

en•gulf (ĕn-gŭlf', ĭn-) v. 1. To surround completely. 2. To swallow up.

en•hance (ĕn-hăns', -häns', ĭn-) v. -hanced, -hancing. To increase, as in value or beauty. [< VL *inaltiāre, to raise.] —**en•hance'ment** n.

e•nig•ma (ĭ-nĭg'mə) n. 1. An obscure riddle. 2. A person or thing that is puzzling or inexplicable. [< Gk ainissesthai, to speak in riddles, hint.]

en•ig•mat•ic (ĕn'ĭg-măt'ĭk) adj. Also **en•ig•mat•i•cal** (-ĭ-kəl). Like an enigma; puzzling. —**en'ig•mat'i•cal•ly** adv.

en•join (ĕn-join', ĭn-) v. 1. To direct; command. 2. To forbid, esp. by legal action. [< L injungere, to join to, impose.] —**en•join'der** n.

en•joy (ĕn-joi', ĭn-) v. 1. To experience joy in. 2. To have as one's lot. [< OF enjoïr.] —**en•joy'a•ble** adj. —**en•joy'ment** n.

enl. 1. enlarged. 2. enlisted.

en•large (ĕn-lärj', ĭn-) v. -larged, -larging. To

---

make or become larger in size, scope, or detail. —en•large'ment *n.* —en•larg'er *n.*

en•light•en (ĕn-līt'n, ĭn-) *v.* **1.** To give knowledge, truth, or understanding to. **2.** To inform. —en•light'en•er *n.* —en•light'en•ment *n.*

en•list (ĕn-lĭst', ĭn-) *v.* **1.** To engage the assistance or cooperation of. **2.** To enter the armed forces voluntarily. **3.** To participate in a cause or enterprise. —en•list'ment *n.*

enlisted man. A man who has enlisted in the armed forces without an officer's commission or warrant.

en•li•ven (ĕn-lī'vən, ĭn-) *v.* To make lively; animate. —en•liv'en•ment *n.*

en masse (ĕn măs'). In one group; all together.

en•mesh (ĕn-mĕsh', ĭn-) *v.* To entangle or involve in or as if in a mesh.

en•mi•ty (ĕn'mə-tē) *n., pl.* **-ties.** Deep-seated hatred, as between rivals or opponents. [< L *inimīcus,* ENEMY.]

en•no•ble (ĕn-nō'bəl, ĭn-) *v.* **-bled, -bling.** To invest with nobility; add to the honor of. —en•no'ble•ment *n.* —en•no'bler *n.*

en•nui (än'wē') *n.* Boredom. [< L *in odiō,* "in hate," odious.]

e•nor•mi•ty (ē-nôr'mə-tē) *n., pl.* **-ties. 1.** Extreme wickedness. **2.** A monstrous offense or evil.

e•nor•mous (ē-nôr'məs) *adj.* Very great in size, number, or degree; immense. [< L *ēnormis,* unusual, immense.] —e•nor'mous•ly *adv.*

e•nough (ĭ-nŭf') *adj.* Sufficient to meet a need or satisfy a desire. —*n.* An adequate quantity. —*adv.* **1.** To a satisfactory amount or degree. **2.** Very; quite: *glad enough to leave.* [< OE *genōg.* See nek-.]

en•plane (ĕn-plān') *v.* **-planed, -planing.** To board an airplane.

en•rage (ĕn-rāj', ĭn-) *v.* **-raged, -raging.** To put in a rage; infuriate.

en•rap•ture (ĕn-răp'chər, ĭn-) *v.* **-tured, -turing.** To move to delight.

en•rich (ĕn-rĭch', ĭn-) *v.* To make rich or richer; add to the quality, value, beauty, or enjoyment of. —en•rich'ment *n.* —en•rich'er *n.*

en•roll (ĕn-rōl', ĭn-) *v.* Also **en•rol, -rolled, -rolling. 1.** To enter the name of in a register, record, or roll. **2.** To place one's name on a roll or register. —en•roll'ment *n.*

en route (än rōōt'). On the way.

en•sconce (ĕn-skŏns', ĭn-) *v.* **-sconced, -sconcing. 1.** To settle (oneself) securely or comfortably. **2.** To place or conceal in a secure place.

en•sem•ble (än-säm'bəl) *n.* **1.** A group of parts that contribute to a single effect, as: **a.** A coordinated outfit or costume. **b.** A group of musicians or other players who perform together. **2. a.** Music for two or more performers. **b.** The quality of performance by a group of actors or musicians, with respect to unity and balance of style. [< L *insimul,* at the same time.]

en•shrine (ĕn-shrīn', ĭn-) *v.* **-shrined, -shrining. 1.** To enclose in or as if in a shrine. **2.** To cherish as sacred. —en•shrine'ment *n.*

en•shroud (ĕn-shroud', ĭn-) *v.* To shroud; veil or conceal.

en•sign (ĕn'sən) *n.* **1.** (also ĕn'sīn'). A flag or banner. **2.** A commissioned officer of the lowest rank in the U.S. Navy or Coast Guard. [< L *insignia,* insignia.]

en•si•lage (ĕn'sə-lĭj) *n.* Green fodder in a silo.

en•sile (ĕn-sīl', ĭn-) *v.* **-siled, -siling. 1.** To store (fodder) in a silo. **2.** To convert (green fodder) into silage.

en•slave (ĕn-slāv', ĭn-) *v.* **-slaved, -slaving.** To make a slave of. —en•slave'ment *n.*

en•snare (ĕn-snâr', ĭn-) *v.* **-snared, -snaring.** To catch in or as if in a snare. —en•snare'ment *n.*

en•sue (ĕn-sōō', ĭn-) *v.* **-sued, -suing. 1.** To follow immediately afterward. **2.** To follow as a consequence; result. [< L *insequī,* to follow after or on.]

en•sure. Variant of **insure.**

—ent. *comb. form.* **1.** Used to form adjectives: **effervescent. 2.** Used to form nouns of agency: **referent.** [< L *-ens.*]

en•tail (ĕn-tāl', ĭn-) *v.* **1.** To have as a necessary accompaniment or consequence. **2.** To limit the inheritance of (property) to a specified, unalterable succession of heirs. —en•tail'er *n.* —en•tail'ment *n.*

en•tan•gle (ĕn-tăng'gəl, ĭn-) *v.* **-gled, -gling. 1.** To twist together so that disengagement is difficult; snarl. **2.** To complicate; confuse. **3.** To involve inextricably, as in difficulties. —en•tan'gle•ment *n.* —en•tan'gler *n.*

en•tente (än-tänt') *n.* **1.** An agreement between two or more governments for cooperative action. **2.** The parties to such an agreement. [F, "understanding."]

en•ter (ĕn'tər) *v.* **1.** To come or go into. **2.** To penetrate; pierce. **3.** To introduce; insert. **4.** To become a part or member of. **5.** To begin; embark upon. **6.** To enroll. **7.** To become a participant in. **8.** *Law.* **a.** To place formally on record. **b.** To go upon or into (real property) as a trespasser or with felonious intent. **c.** To go upon (land) to take possession of it. [< L *intrā,* within.] —en'ter•er *n.*

en•ter•i•tis (ĕn'tə-rī'tĭs) *n.* Inflammation of the intestinal tract. [< Gk *enteron,* intestines.]

en•ter•prise (ĕn'tər-prīz') *n.* **1.** An undertaking, esp. one of some scope and risk. **2.** A business. **3.** Readiness to venture; initiative. [< OF *entreprendre,* to undertake.]

en•ter•pris•ing (ĕn'tər-prī'zĭng) *adj.* Showing imagination, initiative, and boldness in action. —en'ter•pris'ing•ly *adv.*

en•ter•tain (ĕn'tər-tān') *v.* **1.** To hold the attention of; amuse. **2.** To extend hospitality toward. **3.** To hold in mind. [< VL **intertenēre,* "to hold between."] —en'ter•tain'er *n.*

en•ter•tain•ing (ĕn'tər-tā'nĭng) *adj.* Diverting; amusing. —en'ter•tain'ing•ly *adv.*

en•ter•tain•ment (ĕn'tər-tān'mənt) *n.* **1.** The act of entertaining. **2.** Something that entertains, esp. a show designed to amuse. **3.** The pleasure afforded by being entertained; amusement.

en•thrall (ĕn-thrôl', ĭn-) *v.* Also **en•thral. 1.** To hold spellbound; charm. **2.** To enslave. —en•thrall'ly *adv.* —en•thrall'ment *n.*

en•throne (ĕn-thrōn', ĭn-) *v.* **-throned, -throning. 1. a.** To seat on a throne. **b.** To invest with sovereign power. **2.** To exalt; revere. —**en•throne′ment** *n.*

en•thuse (ĕn-thōōz′, ĭn-) *v.* **-thused, -thusing.** *Informal.* **1.** To stimulate enthusiasm in. **2.** To show enthusiasm.

en•thu•si•asm (ĕn-thōō′zē-ăz′əm, ĭn-) *n.* **1. a.** Rapturous interest or excitement. **b.** Ardent fondness. **2.** Something that inspires a lively interest. [< Gk *enthousiazein,* to be inspired by a god.]

en•thu•si•ast (ĕn-thōō′zē-ăst′, ĭn-) *n.* A person filled with enthusiasm. —**en•thu′si•as′tic** *adj.* —**en•thu′si•as′ti•cal•ly** *adv.*

en•tice (ĕn-tīs′) *v.* **-ticed, -ticing.** To attract by arousing hope or desire; lure. [< VL *intitiāre,* to set on fire.] —**en•tice′ment** *n.*

en•tire (ĕn-tīr′, ĭn-) *adj.* Having no part missing or excepted; whole; complete. [< L *integer,* intact.] —**en•tire′ly** *adv.*

en•tire•ty (ĕn-tī′rə-tē, ĭn-) *n., pl.* **-ties. 1.** The state or condition of being entire; completeness. **2.** Something that is entire; a whole.

en•ti•tle (ĕn-tīt′l, ĭn-) *v.* **-tled, -tling. 1.** To give a name to. **2.** To give (one) a right.

en•ti•ty (ĕn′tə-tē) *n., pl.* **-ties. 1.** The fact of existence. **2.** Something that exists independently. [< L *ēns,* prp of *esse,* to be.]

entom. entomological; entomology.

en•tomb (ĕn-tōōm′, ĭn-) *v.* To place in or as if in a tomb; bury. —**en•tomb′ment** *n.*

en•to•mol•o•gy (ĕn′tə-mŏl′ə-jē) *n.* The scientific study of insects. [< Gk *entomon,* insect + -LOGY.] —**en′to•mo•log′i•cal** *adj.* —**en′to•mo•log′i•cal•ly** *adv.* —**en′to•mol′o•gist** *n.*

en•tou•rage (än′tōō-räzh′) *n.* A train of attendants, followers, or associates. [< OF *entour,* surroundings.]

en•tr′acte (än-träkt′) *n.* **1.** The interval between the acts of a theatrical performance. **2.** An entertainment during this interval.

en•trails (ĕn′trālz′, -trəlz) *pl.n.* The internal organs, esp. the intestines. [< L *interāneus,* internal.]

en•train (ĕn-trān′, ĭn-) *v.* To board a train.

en•trance¹ (ĕn′trəns) *n.* **1.** The act or an instance of entering. **2.** Any passage or opening that affords entry. **3.** Permission or liberty to enter; admission. [< OF *entrer,* enter.]

en•trance² (ĕn-trăns′, -träns′, ĭn-) *v.* **-tranced, -trancing.** To fill with wonder or enchantment; fascinate. —**en•trance′ment** *n.*

en•trant (ĕn′trənt) *n.* One who enters, esp. one who enters a competition.

en•trap (ĕn-trăp′, ĭn-) *v.* **-trapped, -trapping.** To catch in or as if in a trap. —**en•trap′ment** *n.*

en•treat (ĕn-trēt′, ĭn-) *v.* To ask earnestly; beseech; beg. [< OF *entraitier.*]

en•treat•y (ĕn-trē′tē, ĭn-) *n., pl.* **-ies.** An earnest request; plea.

en•trée (än′trā) *n.* Also **en•tree. 1.** Power or permission to enter; admittance; access. **2. a.** The main course of an ordinary meal. **b.** A dish served immediately before the main course or between principal courses.

en•trench (ĕn-trĕnch′, ĭn-) *v.* **1.** To provide with a trench or trenches. **2.** To establish securely. —**en•trench′ment** *n.*

en•tre•pre•neur (än′trə-prə-nûr′) *n.* A person

who organizes, operates, and assumes the risk for business ventures. [< OF *entreprendre,* to undertake.]

en•tro•py (ĕn′trə-pē) *n.* **1.** A measure of the capacity of a system to undergo spontaneous change. **2.** A measure of the randomness, disorder, or chaos in a system. [G *Entropie.*]

en•trust (ĕn-trŭst′, ĭn-) *v.* Also **in•trust** (ĭn-). **1.** To give over to another for care or performance. **2.** To commit something trustfully to. —**en•trust′ment** *n.*

en•try (ĕn′trē) *n., pl.* **-tries. 1.** The act or right of entering. **2.** A passage affording entrance. **3. a.** The inclusion of an item in a list or record. **b.** An item thus entered. **4.** A word, term, or phrase defined or treated in a dictionary or other reference book. **5.** A participant in a competition.

en•twine (ĕn-twīn′, ĭn-) *v.* **-twined, -twining.** To twine or twist around or together.

e•nu•mer•ate (ĭ-n/y/ōō′mə-rāt′) *v.* **-ated, -ating. 1.** To name one by one; to list. **2.** To count. [L *ēnumerāre,* to count out.] —**e•nu′mer•a′tion** *n.* —**e•nu′mer•a′tor** *n.*

e•nun•ci•ate (ĭ-nŭn′sē-āt′, -shē-āt′) *v.* **-ated, -ating. 1.** To pronounce or articulate (speech sounds). **2.** To state precisely or systematically. **3.** To announce; proclaim. [L *ēnunciāre.*] —**e•nun′ci•a′tion** *n.*

en•u•re•sis (ĕn′yə-rē′sĭs) *n.* Involuntary urination. [< Gk *enourein,* to urinate in.]

env. envelope.

en•vel•op (ĕn-vĕl′əp, ĭn-) *v.* **-oped, -oping. 1.** To enclose with or as if with a covering. **2.** To surround. [< OF *enveloper.*] —**en•vel′op•er** *n.* —**en•vel′op•ment** *n.*

en•ve•lope (ĕn′və-lōp′, än′-) *n.* **1.** Something that envelopes; cover. **2.** A flat paper container for a letter or similar object. [< OF *enveloper,* ENVELOP.]

en•vi•a•ble (ĕn′vē-ə-bəl) *adj.* Highly desirable. —**en′vi•a•ble•ness** *n.* —**en′vi•a•bly** *adv.*

en•vi•ous (ĕn′vē-əs) *adj.* Feeling or expressing envy. —**en′vi•ous•ly** *adv.* —**en′vi•ous•ness** *n.*

en•vi•ron•ment (ĕn-vī′rən-mənt, ĭn-) *n.* **1.** Something that surrounds; surroundings. **2.** The combination of external or extrinsic conditions that affect the growth and development of organisms. [< OF *environ,* around.] —**en•vi′ron•men′tal** (-mĕnt′l) *adj.*

en•vi•rons (ĕn-vī′rənz, ĭn-) *pl.n.* A surrounding area, esp. of a city; suburbs.

en•vis•age (ĕn-vĭz′ĭj, ĭn-) *v.* **-aged, -aging.** To have an image of; conceive of.

en•vi•sion (ĕn-vĭzh′ən) *v.* To picture in the mind.

en•voy (ĕn′voi, än′-) *n.* **1.** A messenger or other agent. **2.** A diplomatic representative of a government. [< F *envoyer,* to send.]

en•vy (ĕn′vē) *n., pl.* **-vies. 1.** A feeling of discontent and resentment aroused by another's desirable possessions or qualities, with a strong desire to have them for oneself. **2. a.** A possession of another that is strongly desired. **b.** One who possesses what another strongly desires. —*v.* **-vied, -vying.** To feel envy for. [< L *invidēre,* to look at with malice.]

en•zyme (ĕn′zīm′) *n.* Any of numerous proteins produced by living organisms and functioning as biochemical catalysts in living organisms. [< MGk *enzumos*, leavened.] —**en′zy•mat′ic** (-zə-măt′ĭk) *adj.*

eo-. *comb. form.* Early. [< Gk *ēōs*, dawn, light of day.]

E•o•cene (ē′ə-sēn′) *adj.* Of or belonging to the geologic time, rock series, or sedimentary deposits of the second epoch of the Cenozoic era, characterized by the rise of mammals. —*n.* The Eocene epoch. [EO- + -CENE.]

E•o•lith•ic (ē′ə-lĭth′ĭk) *adj.* Relating to the postulated earliest period of human culture preceding the Lower Paleolithic. —*n.* The Eolithic period.

e•on (ē′ŏn′, ē′ən) *n.* Also **ae•on.** **1.** An indefinitely long period of time; an age. **2.** The longest division of geologic time, containing two or more eras. [< Gk *aiōn.*]

-eous. *comb. form.* Having the nature of or akin to: **beauteous.** [L *-eus.*]

ep•au•let (ĕp′ə-lĕt′, ĕp′ə-lĕt′) *n.* Also **ep•au•lette.** A shoulder ornament, esp. on a uniform. [< F *épaule*, shoulder.]

é•pée (ā-pā′) *n.* Also **e•pee.** A fencing sword with a blade that has no cutting edge and tapers to a blunted point. [< L *spatha*, sword, blade.] —**é•pée′ist** *n.*

Eph. Ephesians (New Testament).

e•phem•er•al (ĭ-fĕm′ər-əl) *adj.* Lasting for a brief time; transitory. [Gk *ephēmeros.*]

epi-. *comb. form.* **1.** On, upon. **2.** Over, above. **3.** Around, covering. **4.** To, toward, close to, next to. **5.** Besides, in addition. **6.** After. **7.** Among. [Gk *epi*, upon, over, at, after.]

ep•ic (ĕp′ĭk) *n.* **1.** A long narrative poem celebrating episodes of a people's heroic tradition. **2.** A literary or dramatic composition likened to epic poetry. —*adj.* Designating or resembling an epic; grand; heroic. [< Gk *epos*, song, word.]

ep•i•cene (ĕp′ə-sēn′) *adj.* **1.** Having the characteristics of both the male and the female. **2.** Effeminate. **3.** Sexless. —*n.* An epicene person or object. [< Gk *epikoinos*, common to many, promiscuous.]

ep•i•cen•ter (ĕp′ə-sĕn′tər) *n.* **1.** The part of the earth's surface directly above the origin of an earthquake. **2.** A focal point.

ep•i•cure (ĕp′ĭ-kyŏŏr′) *n.* A person with refined taste in food and wine. [< *Epicurus* (died 270 B.C.), Greek philosopher.]

Ep•i•cu•re•an (ĕp′ĭ-kyŏŏ-rē′ən) *adj.* **1.** Devoted to the pursuit of pleasure. **2.** Suited to the tastes of an epicure.

ep•i•dem•ic (ĕp′ə-dĕm′ĭk) *adj.* Spreading rapidly among many individuals in an area. —*n.* **1.** A contagious disease that spreads rapidly. **2.** A rapid spread or development. [< Gk *epidēmos*, prevalent, common.] —**ep′i•dem′i•cal•ly** *adv.*

ep•i•der•mis (ĕp′ə-dûr′mĭs) *n.* The outer, protective layer of the skin. —**ep′i•der′mal** *adj.*

ep•i•glot•tis (ĕp′ĭ-glŏt′ĭs) *n., pl.* **-tises.** An elastic cartilage at the root of the tongue that prevents food from entering the windpipe in swallowing.

ep•i•gram (ĕp′ĭ-grăm′) *n.* A statement or short poem expressing a single thought with terseness and wit. [< Gk *epigramma*, inscription.] —**ep′i•gram•mat′ic** (-grə-măt′ĭk) *adj.* —**ep′i•gram•mat′i•cal•ly** *adv.*

ep•i•lep•sy (ĕp′ə-lĕp′sē) *n.* A nervous disorder characterized by recurring attacks of motor, sensory, or psychic malfunction with or without unconsciousness or convulsive movements. [< Gk *epilēpsia.*] —**ep′i•lep′tic** *adj. & n.* —**ep′i•lep′toid′** (-lĕp′toid′) *adj.*

ep•i•logue (ĕp′ə-lôg′, -lŏg′) *n.* Also **ep•i•log.** **1.** A short poem or speech spoken directly to the audience following the conclusion of a play. **2.** A short section at the end of any literary work. [< Gk *epilegein*, to say more.]

ep•i•neph•rine (ĕp′ə-nĕf′rēn′, -rĭn) *n.* Also **ep•i•neph•rin** (-rĭn). **1.** An adrenal hormone that stimulates autonomic nerve action. **2.** A crystalline compound, $C_9H_{13}NO_3$, isolated from adrenal glands of certain mammals or synthesized, and used as a heart stimulant and in the treatment of asthma.

e•pis•co•pa•cy (ĭ-pĭs′kə-pə-sē) *n., pl.* **-cies.** **1.** An episcopate. **2.** Church government in which bishops are the chief ministers.

e•pis•co•pal (ĭ-pĭs′kə-pəl) *adj.* **1.** Of or pertaining to a bishop or bishops. **2.** Of or advocating church government by bishops. **3.** Episcopal. Designating or pertaining to the Anglican Church or a branch of it. [< Gk *episkopos*, overseer.] —**e•pis′co•pal•ly** *adv.*

Episcopal Church. The Protestant Episcopal Church.

E•pis•co•pa•li•an (ĭ-pĭs′kə-pā′lē-ən, -pāl′yən) *adj.* Pertaining to or belonging to the Protestant Episcopal Church. —*n.* A member or adherent of the Protestant Episcopal Church. —**E•pis′co•pa′li•an•ism′** *n.*

e•pis•co•pate (ĭ-pĭs′kə-pĭt, -pāt′) *n.* **1.** The position or term of a bishop. **2.** The area of jurisdiction of a bishop; a bishopric. **3.** Bishops collectively.

ep•i•sode (ĕp′ə-sōd′) *n.* **1.** An incident or series of related events in the course of a continuous experience. **2.** A portion of a narrative that relates an event or connected events and forms a coherent story in itself. [Gk *epeisodion*, "addition."] —**ep′i•sod′ic** (-sŏd′ĭk) *adj.*

Epist. Epistle.

e•pis•tle (ĭ-pĭs′əl) *n.* **1.** A letter, esp. a formal one. **2.** Often **Epistle.** One of the letters written by an Apostle and included in the New Testament. [< Gk *epistellein*, to send to.] —**e•pis′to•lar•y** (ĭ-pĭs′tə-lăr′ē) *adj.*

ep•i•taph (ĕp′ə-tăf′, -täf′) *n.* An inscription, esp. on a tombstone, in memory of a deceased person. [< Gk *epitaphios*, "over a tomb."]

ep•i•the•li•um (ĕp′ə-thē′lē-əm) *n., pl.* **-ums** or **-lia** (-lē-ə). Membranous tissue composed of closely arranged cells and forming the covering of most internal surfaces and organs and the outer surface of an animal body. —**ep′i•the′li•al** *adj.*

ep•i•thet (ĕp′ə-thĕt′) *n.* A term used to characterize the nature of a person or thing. [< Gk *epitheton*, "an addition."]

e•pit•o•me (ĭ-pĭt′ə-mē) *n.* **1.** A summary; abridgment. **2.** One that is consummately rep-

---

ă pat/ā ate/âr care/ä bar/b **bib**/ch **chew**/d **deed**/ĕ pet/ē be/f fit/g gag/h hat/hw **what**/
ĭ pit/ī pie/îr pier/j **judge**/k **kick**/l lid, fatal/m **mum**/n no, sudden/ng sing/ŏ pot/ō go/

resentative of an entire class. [< Gk *epitemnein*, to cut short.]

e·pit·o·mize (ĭ-pĭt′ə-mīz′) *v.* **-mized, -mizing. 1.** To summarize. **2.** To typify eminently a class, type, or quality.

e plu·ri·bus u·num (ē plŏŏr′ə-bəs yŏŏ′nəm). *Latin.* One out of many. The motto of the U.S.

ep·och (ĕp′ək) *n.* **1.** A particular period of history, esp. one that is characteristic or memorable; an era. **2.** A point in time or progress that marks the beginning of such a period. **3.** A unit of geologic time that is a division of a period. **4.** An instant in time arbitrarily selected as a reference datum. [< Gk *epokhē*, pause.] **—ep′och·al** *adj.* **—ep′och·al·ly** *adv.*

ep·ox·y (ĭ-pŏk′sē) *n., pl.* **-ies.** Any of various resins capable of forming tight cross-linked polymer structures characterized by toughness, strong adhesion, and high corrosion resistance. [EP(I)- + OXY-.]

ep·si·lon (ĕp′sə-lŏn′) *n.* The 5th letter of the Greek alphabet, representing *e*.

Ep·som salts (ĕp′səm). Hydrated magnesium sulfate used as a cathartic. [< the mineral springs in *Epsom*, England.]

eq. 1. equal. **2.** equation.

eq·ua·ble (ĕk′wə-bəl, ē′kwə-) *adj.* **1.** Unvarying; even. **2.** Even-tempered. [< L *aequus*, EQUAL.] **—eq′ua·bil′i·ty** *n.* **—eq′ua·bly** *adv.*

e·qual (ē′kwəl) *adj.* **1.** Having the same capability, quantity, or effect as another. **2.** Mathematically related by a reflexive, symmetric, and transitive relationship; broadly, alike or in agreement in a specified sense with respect to specified properties. **3.** Having the same privileges, status, or rights. **4. a.** Having the requisite strength, ability, determination, etc.; qualified or disposed. **b.** Adequate in extent, amount, or degree. **—n.** One that is equal to another. **—v. equaled** or **equalled, equaling** or **equalling. 1.** To be equal to, esp. in value. **2.** To do, make, or produce something equal to. [< L *aequus*, even, level.] **—e′qual·ly** *adv.*

e·qual·i·ty (ĭ-kwŏl′ə-tē) *n., pl.* **-ties. 1.** The state or instance of being equal. **2.** A mathematical statement, usually an equation, that one thing equals another.

e·qual·ize (ē′kwə-līz′) *v.* **-ized, -izing.** To make equal or uniform. **—e′qual·iz′er** *n.*

e·qua·nim·i·ty (ē′kwə-nĭm′ə-tē, ĕk′wə-) *n.* The quality or characteristic of being even-tempered. [< L *aequanimis*, even-tempered.]

e·quate (ĭ-kwāt′) *v.* **equated, equating. 1.** To make, treat, or regard as equal or equivalent. **2.** To reduce to a standard or average; stabilize; balance. **3.** To show or state the equality of. **—e·quat′a·ble** *adj.*

e·qua·tion (ĭ-kwā′zhən, -shən) *n.* **1.** The process or act of equating or of being equated. **2.** The state of being equal; equilibrium. **3.** A linear array of mathematical symbols separated into left and right sides that are designated at least conditionally equal. **—e·qua′tion·al** *adj.* **—e·qua′tion·al·ly** *adv.*

e·qua·tor (ĭ-kwā′tər) *n.* The great circle circumscribing the earth's surface, the reckoning datum of latitudes and dividing boundary of N and S Hemispheres, formed by the inter-

section of a plane passing through the earth's center perpendicular to its axis of rotation. [ML *(circulus) aequator (diei et nocis)*, (circle) equalizing (day and night).] **—e′qua·to′ri·al** (-tôr′ē-əl, -tōr′-) *adj.*

Equatorial Guinea. A country of W Africa. Pop. 300,000. Cap. Malabo.

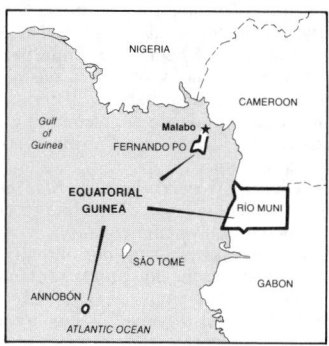

Equatorial Guinea

eq·uer·ry (ĕk′wə-rē) *n., pl.* **-ries. 1.** An officer who supervises the horses of a noble household. **2.** An attendant to the English royal household. [< OF *escuier*, riding master, squire.]

e·ques·tri·an (ĭ-kwĕs′trē-ən) *adj.* **1.** Of or pertaining to horsemanship. **2.** Depicted or represented on horseback. **—n.** One who rides a horse or performs on horseback. [< L *equus*, horse.] **—e·ques′tri·an·ism′** *n.*

e·ques·tri·enne (ĭ-kwĕs′trē-ĕn′) *n.* A female equestrian.

equi–. *comb. form.* Equality.

e·qui·an·gu·lar (ē′kwē-ăng′gyə-lər) *adj.* Having all angles equal.

e·qui·dis·tant (ē′kwə-dĭs′tənt) *adj.* Equally distant. **—e′qui·dis′tant·ly** *adv.*

e·qui·lat·er·al (ē′kwə-lăt′ər-əl) *adj.* Having all sides or faces equal.

e·qui·lib·ri·um (ē′kwə-lĭb′rē-əm) *n.* Any condition in which all acting influences are cancelled by others resulting in a stable, balanced, or unchanging system. [L *aequilibrium*, even balance.]

e·quine (ē′kwīn′) *adj.* Of, pertaining to, or characteristic of a horse. [< L *equus*, horse.]

e·qui·noc·tial (ē′kwə-nŏk′shəl, ĕk′wə-) *adj.* Pertaining to an equinox.

e·qui·nox (ē′kwə-nŏks′, ĕk′wə-) *n.* Either of the two times during a year when the sun crosses the celestial equator and when the length of day and night are approx. equal. [< L *aequinoctium*, "equal night."]

e·quip (ĭ-kwĭp′) *v.* **equipped, equipping. 1.** To supply with material necessities. **2.** To supply with intellectual, emotional, or spiritual essentials. [< OF *esquipper*, to put to sea, embark.]

equip. equipment.

eq·ui·page (ĕk′wə-pĭj) *n.* An elegantly equipped carriage.

---

e·quip·ment (ĭ-kwĭp′mənt) *n.* **1.** The act of equipping or the state of being equipped. **2.** That with which a person, organization, or thing is equipped; furnishings.

e·qui·poise (ē′kwə-poiz′, ĕk′wə-) *n.* **1.** Balance; equilibrium. **2.** A counterbalance.

eq·ui·ta·ble (ĕk′wə-tə-bəl) *adj.* Exhibiting equity; impartial; just. —**eq′ui·ta·bly** *adv.*

eq·ui·ta·tion (ĕk′wə-tā′shən) *n.* The learning and practice of riding a horse; horsemanship.

eq·ui·ty (ĕk′wə-tē) *n., pl.* **-ties. 1.** The state, ideal, or quality of being just, impartial, and fair. **2.** The residual value of a business or property beyond any liability therein. **3.** A system of jurisprudence supplementing common law. [< L *aequitās* < *aequus,* EQUAL.]

equiv. equivalent.

e·quiv·a·lence (ĭ-kwĭv′ə-ləns) *n.* Also **e·quiv·a·len·cy** (-lən-sē) *pl.* **-cies.** The state or condition of being equivalent; equality.

e·quiv·a·lent (ĭ-kwĭv′ə-lənt) *adj.* Equal; similar in effects; practically equal; tantamount. —*n.* That which is equivalent. [< LL *aequivalēre,* to be equal in value.] —**e·quiv·a·lent·ly** *adv.*

equivalent weight. The number of parts by weight of any element combining with or replacing the equivalent of half the atomic weight of oxygen or with one atomic weight of hydrogen.

e·quiv·o·cal (ĭ-kwĭv′ə-kəl) *adj.* **1.** Capable of two interpretations; ambiguous. **2.** Of uncertain outcome; indeterminate. **3.** Questionable; not genuine. [< LL *aequivocus.*] —**e·quiv′o·cal·ly** *adv.* —**e·quiv′o·cal·ness** *n.*

e·quiv·o·cate (ĭ-kwĭv′ə-kāt′) *v.* **-cated, -cating.** To speak in ambiguities; hedge. —**e·quiv′o·ca′tion** *n.* —**e·quiv′o·ca′tor** *n.*

–er[1]. *comb. form.* **1.** One that performs the action indicated by the root verb: **blender. 2.** Geographic origin or residence: **westerner.** [< L *-ārius.*]

–er[2], **–r.** *comb. form.* Used to form the comparative degree of adjectives and adverbs: **slower.** [< OE *-re, -ra.*]

Er erbium.

e·ra (îr′ə, ĕr′ə) *n.* **1.** A period of time that utilizes a specific point in history as the basis of its chronology. **2.** A distinctive or notable period of time. **3.** The longest division of geologic time comprising one or more periods. [< L *aera,* "counters for calculating."]

ERA Equal Rights Amendment.

e·rad·i·cate (ĭ-răd′ĭ-kāt′) *v.* **-cated, -cating. 1.** To uproot; destroy. **2.** To remove all traces of; erase. **3.** To pull or tear up by the roots. [L *ērādicāre,* to pluck up by the roots.] —**e·rad′i·ca′tion** *n.* —**e·rad′i·ca′tor** *n.*

e·rase (ĭ-rās′) *v.* **erased, erasing. 1.** To remove; rub, wipe, scrape, or blot out; efface. **2.** To remove all traces of. [L *ērādere* (pp *ērāsus*), to scrape out.] —**e·ras′er** *n.* —**e·ra′sure** *n.*

E·ras·mus (ĭ-răz′məs), **Desiderius.** 1466?–1536. Dutch humanist.

er·bi·um (ûr′bē-əm) *n. Symbol* **Er** A soft, malleable, silvery element, used in metallurgy, nuclear research, and to color glass and porcelain. Atomic number 68, atomic weight

167.26. [< *Ytterby,* Sweden.]

ere (âr). *Archaic. prep.* Previous to; before. —*conj.* **1.** Before. **2.** Rather than. [< OE *ær,* before. See **ayer-.**]

e·rect (ĭ-rĕkt′) *adj.* Directed or pointing upward; standing upright; vertical. —*v.* **1.** To raise, as a building; construct. **2.** To raise upright; set on end. **3.** To put together; assemble. **4.** To set up; establish. **5.** *Physiol.* To become rigid and upright. [< L *ērectus,* pp of *ērigere,* to raise up, set up.] —**e·rec′tion** *n.*

er·e·mite (ĕr′ə-mīt′) *n.* A hermit, esp. a religious recluse. [ME *(h)ermite,* hermit.]

erg (ûrg) *n.* A unit of energy or work equal to the work done by a force of one dyne acting over a distance of one centimeter. [Gk *ergon,* work.]

er·go (ûr′gō, âr′-) *conj. & adv.* Consequently. [L *ergō,* therefore.]

er·gos·ter·ol (ûr′gŏs′tə-rôl′, -rōl′, -rŏl′) *n.* A crystalline compound, $C_{28}H_{14}O$, synthesized by yeast from sugars or derived from ergot.

er·got (ûr′gət, -gŏt′) *n.* **1.** A fungus that infects cereal plants. **2.** The dried black filaments of such a fungus, used medicinally. [F, "cock's spur."]

E·rie, Lake (îr′ē). The fourth largest of the Great Lakes.

er·mine (ûr′mĭn) *n.* **1.** A weasel with fur that turns white in winter. **2.** The white fur of this animal. [< ML *(mūs) Armenius,* "Armenian (mouse)."]

e·rode (ĭ-rōd′) *v.* **eroded, eroding.** To wear away by or as if by erosion. [L *ērōdere,* to gnaw off, eat away.] —**e·ro′dent** *adj.*

Er·os (îr′ŏs′, ĕr′-). Greek god of love, son of Aphrodite.

e·ro·sion (ĭ-rō′zhən) *n.* The group of natural processes including weathering, dissolution, abrasion, corrosion, and transportation by which earthy or rock material is removed from any part of the earth's surface.

e·rot·ic (ĭ-rŏt′ĭk) *adj.* Of or concerning sexual love and desire; amatory. [Gk *erōtikos,* of or caused by love.] —**e·rot′i·cal·ly** *adv.*

err (ûr, ĕr) *v.* **1.** To deviate from proper course or aim. **2.** To make an error. **3.** To sin. [< L *errāre,* to wander.]

er·rand (ĕr′ənd) *n.* **1.** A short trip taken for a specific purpose. **2.** The purpose of such a trip. [< OE *ǣrende,* message < Gmc **arund-jam.*]

er·rant (ĕr′ənt) *adj.* **1.** Roving, esp. in search of adventure. **2.** Straying from a proper course or standard; erring. [< OF *errer,* to travel, err; *errer,* to err.] —**er′rant·ly** *adv.*

er·ra·ta (ĭ-rä′tə, ĭ-rā′-) *pl.n. Sing.* **-tum** (-təm). A list of corrections appended to a book. [< L *errāre,* to wander, ERR.]

er·rat·ic (ĭ-răt′ĭk) *adj.* **1.** Without a fixed or regular course; inconsistent. **2.** Unconventional; eccentric. [< L *errāticus,* wandering, straying.] —**er·rat′i·cal·ly** *adv.*

er·ro·ne·ous (ĭ-rō′nē-əs) *adj.* Mistaken; false. —**er·ro′ne·ous·ly** *adv.* —**er·ro′ne·ous·ness** *n.*

er·ror (ĕr′ər) *n.* **1.** An unintentional deviation from what is correct, right, or true; mistake. **2.** The condition of having incorrect or false

---

ă pat/ā ate/âr care/ä bar/b bib/ch chew/d deed/ĕ pet/ē be/f fit/g gag/h hat/hw what/ ĭ pit/ī pie/îr pier/j judge/k kick/l lid, fatal/m mum/n no, sudden/ng sing/ŏ pot/ō go/

knowledge. **3.** A transgression; wrongdoing. **4.** *Baseball.* A defensive or fielding misplay. [< L *errāre*, to ERR.]

er·satz (ĕr-zäts′, ĕr′zäts′) *adj.* Substitute; artificial. —*n.* A substitute, esp. an inferior imitation. [< G, compensation, replacement.]

erst (ûrst) *adv. Archaic.* **1.** At first. **2.** Formerly. [< OE *ǣrest*. See ayer-.]

erst·while (ûrst′hwīl′) *adj.* Former. —*adv. Archaic.* Formerly.

e·ruct (ĭ-rŭkt′) *v.* **1.** To belch. **2.** To emit violently, as a volcano. [L *ēructāre.*] —**e·ruc′ta′tion** *n.*

er·u·dite (ĕr′/y/ōō-dīt′) *adj.* Deeply learned. [< L *ērudīre*, "to take the roughness out of," teach.] —**er′u·dite′ly** *adv.* —**er′u·di′tion** *n.*

e·rupt (ĭ-rŭpt′) *v.* **1.** To emerge or eject violently. **2.** To become violently active. **3. a.** To pierce the gum, as a tooth. **b.** To appear on the skin, as a blemish. [L *ērumpere* (pp *ēruptus*), to break out.] —**e·rup′tion** *n.* —**e·rup′tive** *adj.* —**e·rup′tive·ly** *adv.*

–ery, –ry. *comb. form.* Used to form nouns from verbs or other nouns to indicate: **1.** A certain activity: **hatchery. 2.** Certain things or persons: **nunnery. 3.** A collection or class of objects: **finery. 4.** A craft, study, or practice: **husbandry. 5. a.** Certain characteristics: **snobbery. b.** A kind of behavior: **knavery. 6.** Condition or status: **slavery.** [< L *-ārius.*]

er·y·the·ma (ĕr′ə-thē′mə) *n.* A redness of the skin, as caused by chemical poisoning or sunburn. [< Gk *eruthros*, red.]

erythro–. *comb. form.* Red. [< Gk *eruthros*, red.]

e·ryth·ro·cyte (ĭ-rĭth′rə-sīt′) *n.* The yellowish, nonnucleated, disk-shaped blood cell that contains hemoglobin and is responsible for the color of blood.

Es einsteinium.

–es[1]. *comb. form.* The plural form: **trusses, Negroes, ladies.**

–es[2]. *comb. form.* The 3rd person sing. form of the present indicative: **guesses, does.**

es·ca·late (ĕs′kə-lāt′) *v.* **-lated, -lating.** To increase, enlarge, or intensify. —**es′ca·la′tion** *n.*

es·ca·la·tor (ĕs′kə-lā′tər) *n.* A moving stairway consisting of steps attached to a continuously circulating belt. [Poss F *escalade*, a scaling + (ELEV)ATOR.]

es·cal·lop. Variant of **scallop.**

es·ca·pade (ĕs′kə-pād′) *n.* A carefree or reckless adventure. [< OIt *scappare*, to escape.]

es·cape (ĕ-skāp′, ĭ-skāp′) *v.* **-caped, -caping. 1.** To break from confinement; get free. **2.** To succeed in avoiding (capture, danger, or harm). **3.** To elude: *The meaning escaped him.* —*n.* **1.** The act, an instance, or a means of escaping. **2.** Temporary freedom from trouble. —*adj.* Affording a means of escape: *an escape clause.* [< ONF *escaper*, "to take off one's cloak."] —**es·cap′a·ble** *adj.*

es·cap·ee (ĕs-kā′pē′, ĕ-skā′pē, ĭ-skā′pē) *n.* One that has escaped, esp. a prisoner.

es·cape·ment (ĕ-skāp′mənt, ĭ-skāp′-) *n.* A mechanism used esp. in timepieces to control the wheel movement and provide periodic energy impulses to a pendulum or balance.

escape velocity. The minimum velocity that a body must attain to overcome the gravitational attraction of another body, such as the earth.

es·cap·ism (ĕ-skā′pĭz′əm, ĭ-skā′-) *n.* The habit or tendency of escaping from unpleasant realities through fantasy or entertainment. —**es·cap′ist** *n.*

es·ca·role (ĕs′kə-rōl′) *n.* A salad plant having leaves with irregular, frilled edges. [< L *esca*, food.]

es·carp·ment (ĕ-skärp′mənt, ĭ-skärp′-) *n.* A steep slope or long cliff.

–escence. *comb. form.* A beginning or continuing state: **luminescence.** [< -ESCENT.]

–escent. *comb. form.* Beginning to be or exhibit: **phosphorescent.** [< L *-ēscēns.*]

es·chew (ĕs-chōō′) *v.* To take care to avoid; shun. [< OF *eschiuver*, to shun, avoid.]

es·cort (ĕs′kôrt′) *n.* **1.** One or more persons or vehicles accompanying another to give guidance or protection or to pay honor. **2.** A male companion of a woman in public. —*v.* (ĕs-kôrt′). To accompany as an escort. [< VL **excorrigere*, to conduct, escort.]

es·crow (ĕs′krō, ĕ-skrō′, ĭ-skrō′) *n.* The state of a written agreement, such as a deed, put into the custody of a third party until certain conditions are fulfilled. [< OF *escroe*, strip of parchment, scroll.]

es·cu·do (ĕ-skōō′dō, ĭ-skōō′-) *n., pl.* **-dos. 1.** The basic monetary unit of Portugal. **2.** The basic monetary unit of Chile.

es·cutch·eon (ĕ-skŭch′ən, ĭ-) *n.* A shield or shield-shaped emblem bearing a coat of arms. [< L *scūtum*, shield.]

–ese. *comb. form.* **1.** A native or inhabitant: **Sudanese. 2.** A language or dialect: **Japanese. 3.** A literary style or diction: **journalese.** [< L *-ēnsis*, "originating in."]

Es·ki·mo (ĕs′kə-mō′) *n., pl.* **-mo** or **-mos. 1.** One of a people native to the Arctic coastal regions of North America and parts of Greenland and NE Siberia. **2.** The language spoken by these people. —**Es′ki·mo′** *adj.*

Es·ki·mo-Al·e·ut (ĕs′kə-mō′ăl′ē-ōōt′) *n.* A family of languages spoken chiefly among the Eskimos and the people of the Aleutian Islands.

e·soph·a·gus (ĭ-sŏf′ə-gəs) *n., pl.* **-gi** (-jī′). A muscular, membranous tube for the passage of food from the pharynx to the stomach. [< Gk *oisophagos*, gullet.] —**e·so·phag′e·al** (ē′sŏ-făj′ē-əl, ĭ-sŏf′ə-jē′əl) *adj.*

es·o·ter·ic (ĕs′ə-tĕr′ĭk) *adj.* **1.** Intended for or understood by only a small group. **2.** Confidential; private. [< Gk *esōterikos*.]

ESP extrasensory perception.

esp. especially.

es·pa·drille (ĕs′pə-drĭl′) *n.* A sandal with a rope sole and a canvas upper. [< Prov *espardilho.*]

es·pal·ier (ĕ-spăl′yər, -yā′, ĭ-spăl′-) *n.* A fruit tree or shrub trained to grow flat against a wall, often in a symmetrical pattern. [< It *spalliera*, applied to shoulder supports.] —**es·pal′ier** *v.*

es·pe·cial (ĕ-spĕsh′əl, ĭ-spĕsh′-) *adj.* Special;

exceptional; particular. —**es•pe′cial•ly** *adv.*

Es•pe•ran•to (ĕs′pə-răn′tō, -rän′tō) *n.* An artificial international language based on word roots common to many European languages. [< Dr. L.L. Zamenhof (died 1917), Polish philologist who wrote under the name of Dr. *Esperanto*, "one who hopes."]

es•pi•o•nage (ĕs′pē-ə-näzh′, -nĭj) *n.* The act or practice of spying. [< OIt *spia*, spy.]

es•pla•nade (ĕs′plə-näd′, -nād′) *n.* A flat, open stretch of pavement or grass used as a promenade. [< It *spianare*, to level.]

es•pouse (ĕ-spouz′, ĭ-spouz′) *v.* **-poused, -pous-ing. 1.** To marry. **2.** To give one's loyalty or support to; adopt. [< L *spondēre*, to promise solemnly.] —**es•pou′sal** *n.* —**es•pous′er** *n.*

es•prit (ĕ-sprē′) *n.* **1.** Spirit. **2.** Liveliness of mind and expression. [< L *spīritus*, SPIRIT.]

esprit de corps (də kôr′). A common spirit of devotion and enthusiasm among members of a group.

es•py (ĕ-spī′, ĭ-spī′) *v.* **-pied, -pying.** To catch sight of; glimpse. [< OF *espier*, to spy.]

—esque. *comb. form.* Possession of a specified manner or quality: **statuesque.** [< Gmc *-iskaz.*]

es•quire (ĕs′kwîr′) *n.* **1.** A candidate for knighthood serving as attendant to a knight. **2.** A member of the English gentry ranking just below a knight. **3. Esquire.** A title of courtesy placed after a man's full name. [< OF *esquier, escuier*, squire, "shield-carrier."]

—ess. *comb. form.* A female: **lioness.** [< Gk *-issa.*]

es•say (ĕs′ā, ĕ-sā′) *v.* To make an attempt at; try; try out. —*n.* (ĕs′ā, ĕ-sā′). **1.** An attempt; endeavor. **2.** A short literary composition on a single subject, usually presenting the author's personal views. [< OF *essai*, a trial.]

es•say•ist (ĕs′ā′ĭst) *n.* A writer of essays.

Es•sen (ĕs′ən). A city of NW West Germany. Pop. 728,000.

es•sence (ĕs′əns) *n.* **1.** The intrinsic or indispensable properties of a thing. **2.** A concentrated extract of a substance that retains its fundamental properties. **3.** A perfume. [< L *esse*, to be.]

es•sen•tial (ĭ-sĕn′shəl) *adj.* **1.** Constituting or part of the essence of something; basic. **2.** Of the greatest importance; indispensable. —*n.* An essential thing. —**es•sen′tial•ly** *adv.*

—est¹. *comb. form.* The superlative degree of adjectives and adverbs: **earliest.** [< Gmc *-istaz.*]

—est², -st. *comb. form.* The archaic 2nd person sing. form of the present and past indicative tenses: **comest.** [< OE.]

EST Eastern Standard Time.

est. **1.** established. **2.** estimate.

es•tab•lish (ĕ-stăb′lĭsh, ĭ-stăb′-) *v.* **1.** To make firm or secure. **2.** To settle securely in a position. **3.** To cause to be recognized and accepted. **4.** To found or create. **5.** To prove the truth of. [< L *stabilīre*, to establish.]

es•tab•lish•ment (ĕ-stăb′lĭsh-mənt, ĭ-stăb′-) *n.* **1.** The act of establishing or condition of being established. **2.** A business firm or residence, including its members, staff, and possessions.

3. the Establishment. An exclusive or powerful group in control of society or a field of activity.

es•tate (ĕ-stāt′, ĭ-stāt′) *n.* **1.** A sizable piece of land with a large house. **2.** All of one's possessions, esp. those left by a deceased person. **3.** A stage, condition, or status of life. [< OF *estat*, state.]

es•teem (ĕ-stēm′, ĭ-stēm′) *v.* **1.** To regard favorably; respect; prize. **2.** To judge to be; consider. —*n.* Favorable regard; respect. [< L *aestimāre*, to ESTIMATE.]

es•ter (ĕs′tər) *n.* Any of a class of organic compounds chemically corresponding to inorganic salts. [< G *Essigäther*, "vinegar ether."]

es•thet•ics (ĕs-thĕt′ĭks) *n.* Aesthetics. —**es′thete′** (-thēt′) *n.* —**es•thet′ic** *adj.*

es•ti•mate (ĕs′tə-māt′) *v.* **-mated, -mating. 1.** To make a judgment as to the likely cost, quantity, or extent of; calculate approximately. **2.** To evaluate. —*n.* (ĕs′tə-mĭt). **1.** A tentative evaluation or rough calculation. **2. a.** A preliminary calculation of the cost of work to be undertaken. **b.** The written statement of such a calculation. **3.** An opinion. [L *aestimāre.*] —**es′ti•ma•ble** (-tə-mə-bəl) *adj.* —**es′ti•ma′tion** *n.* —**es′ti•ma′tor** *n.*

Es•to•ni•a (ĕs-tō′nē-ə). A constituent republic of the Soviet Union, on the Baltic. Pop. 1,357,000. Cap. Tallinn.

Es•to•ni•an (ĕs-tō′nē-ən) *n.* **1.** A native or inhabitant of Estonia. **2.** The Finno-Ugric language of Estonia. —**Es•to′ni•an** *adj.*

es•trange (ĕs-trānj′) *v.* **-tranged, -tranging. 1.** To remove from an accustomed place or relation. **2.** To alienate the affections of. [< L *extrāneus*, STRANGE.] —**es•trange′ment** *n.*

es•tro•gen (ĕs′trə-jən) *n.* Any of several steroid hormones produced chiefly by the ovary and responsible for the development and maintenance of female secondary sex characteristics. —**es′tro•gen′ic** (-jĕn′ĭk) *adj.*

es•tu•ar•y (ĕs′chŏō-ĕr′ē) *n., pl.* **-ies. 1.** The wide lower course of a river where its current is met by the tides. **2.** An inland arm of the sea that meets the mouth of a river. [L *aestuārium*, estuary, tidal channel.]

ET Eastern Time.

e•ta (ā′tə, ē′tə) *n.* The 7th letter of the Greek alphabet, representing *ē.*

e.t.a. estimated time of arrival.

et al. and others (L *et alii*).

etc. et cetera.

et cet•er•a (ĕt sĕt′ər-ə, -sĕt′rə). Also **et•cet•er•a, et caet•er•a.** And other unspecified things of the same class; and so forth. [L, "and other (things)."]

etch (ĕch) *v.* **1.** To wear away with or as if with acid. **2.** To make (a pattern) on a surface with acid. **3.** To impress or imprint clearly. [< G *ätzen*, to etch, bite.] —**etch′er** *n.*

etch•ing (ĕch′ĭng) *n.* **1.** The art of preparing etched metal plates. **2.** A design etched on a plate. **3.** An impression made from an etched plate.

e•ter•nal (ĭ-tûr′nəl) *adj.* **1.** Without beginning or end. **2.** Lasting; timeless. **3.** Seemingly endless; interminable. **4.** Of or relating to ex-

---

ă pat/ā ate/âr care/ä bar/b bib/ch chew/d deed/ĕ pet/ē be/f fit/g gag/h hat/hw what/ ĭ pit/ī pie/îr pier/j judge/k kick/l lid, fatal/m mum/n no, sudden/ng sing/ŏ pot/ō go/

istence after death. [< L *aeternus*, eternal.]
—e•ter′nal•ly *adv.*

e•ter•ni•ty (ĭ-tûr′nə-tē) *n.* **1.** The totality of time without beginning or end. **2.** The state or quality of being eternal. **3.** Afterlife; immortality.

eth. Variant of **edh.**

—eth¹, –th. *comb. form.* The archaic 3rd person sing. form of the present indicative tense: *praiseth.* [< OE.]

—eth². Variant of **-th².**

eth•ane (ĕth′ān′) *n.* A colorless, odorless gas, C_2H_6, occurring as a constituent of natural gas and used as a fuel and refrigerant. [ETH(YL) + -ANE.]

eth•a•nol (ĕth′ə-nôl′, -nŏl′, -nōl′) *n.* A colorless flammable liquid, C_2H_5OH, obtained from fermentation of sugars and starches, and used as a solvent, in drugs, and in intoxicating beverages.

e•ther (ē′thər) *n.* Also **ae•ther. 1.** Any of a class of organic compounds in which two hydrocarbon groups are linked by an oxygen atom. **2.** A highly flammable liquid, $C_4H_{10}O$, widely used in industry and as an anesthetic. **3.** The regions of space beyond the earth's atmosphere; the clear sky; the heavens. **4.** An all-pervading, infinitely elastic, massless medium formerly postulated as the medium of propagation of electromagnetic waves. [< L *aether,* the upper or bright air, ether.]

e•the•re•al (ĭ-thîr′ē-əl) *adj.* **1.** Highly refined; delicate. **2.** Heavenly; spiritual.

eth•ic (ĕth′ĭk) *n.* A principle of right or good conduct, or a body of such principles. —*n.*

ethics. 1. *(takes sing. v.).* The study of the general nature of morals and of specific moral choices. **2.** *(takes pl. v.).* **a.** The rules or standards governing the conduct of the members of a profession. **b.** Any set of moral principles or values. **c.** The moral quality of a course of action; propriety. [< Gk *ēthikos,* ethical.]

eth•i•cal (ĕth′ĭ-kəl) *adj.* **1.** Of or dealing with ethics. **2.** In accordance with the accepted principles governing the conduct of a group. —eth′i•cal•ly *adv.*

E•thi•o•pi•a (ē′thē-ō′pē-ə). **An independent country in E Africa. Pop. 27,000,000. Cap. Addis Ababa.** —E′thi•o′pi•an *adj. & n.*

eth•nic (ĕth′nĭk) *adj.* Of or pertaining to a

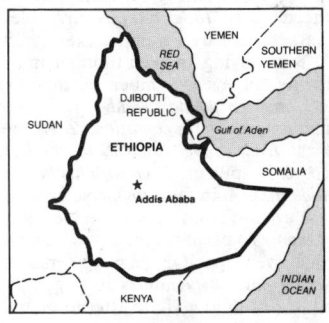

Ethiopia

social group that claims or is accorded special status on the basis of complex, often variable traits including religious, linguistic, ancestral, or physical characteristics. [< Gk *ethnikos,* of a national group, foreign.]

eth•nic•i•ty (ĕth-nĭs′ĭ-tē) *n.* **1.** The condition of belonging to a particular ethnic group. **2.** Ethnic pride.

eth•nol•o•gy (ĕth-nŏl′ə-jē) *n.* The anthropological study of socio-economic systems and cultural heritage, esp. of cultural origins and factors influencing cultural growth and change, in technologically primitive societies. —eth′no•log′ic (ĕth′nə-lŏj′ĭk), eth′no•log′i•cal *adj.* —eth•nol′o•gist *n.*

eth•yl (ĕth′əl) *n.* **1.** An organic radical, C_2H_5. **2. Ethyl. a.** A trademark for a gasoline containing an antiknock substance, tetraethyl lead. **b.** A trademark for any of various additives for hydrocarbon fuels and lubricants. [ETH(ER) + -YL.]

ethyl alcohol. Ethanol.

eth•yl•ene (ĕth′ə-lēn′) *n.* **1.** A colorless, flammable gas, C_2H_4, derived from natural gas and petroleum. **2.** An organic radical, C_2H_4.

ethylene glycol. A colorless, syrupy alcohol, $C_2H_6O_2$, used as an antifreeze in cooling and heating systems.

e•ti•ol•o•gy (ē′tē-ŏl′ə-jē) *n., pl.* **-gies. 1.** The study of causes, origins, or reasons. **2.** The cause of a disease or disorder as determined by medical diagnosis. [< Gk *aitiologia,* a giving the cause of.] —e′ti•o•log′i•cal (-ə-lŏj′ĭ-kəl) *adj.* —e′ti•o•log′i•cal•ly *adv.*

et•i•quette (ĕt′ə-kĕt′, -kĭt) *n.* **1.** The body of prescribed social usages. **2.** Any special code of behavior or courtesy. [F *étiquette,* prescribed routine.]

E•tru•ri•a (ĭ-trŏŏr′ē-ə). An ancient country of west-central Italy.

E•trus•can (ĭ-trŭs′kən) *n.* **1.** One of a people of ancient Etruria. **2.** The extinct ancient language of the Etruscans, of undetermined linguistic affiliation. —E•trus′can *adj.*

—ette. *comb. form.* **1.** Small or diminutive: **kitchenette. 2.** An imitation of: *leatherette.* **3.** Female or feminine: **usherette.** [< OF.]

e•tude (ā′t/y/ŏŏd′) *n.* A musical piece for the development of a given point of technique. [< OF *estudie,* study.]

etym. etymology.

et•y•mol•o•gy (ĕt′ə-mŏl′ə-jē) *n., pl.* **-gies. 1.** The origin and historical development of a word. **2.** An account of the history of a specific word. **3.** The branch of linguistics that studies the derivation of words. [< Gk *etumologia.*] —et′y•mo•log′i•cal (-mə-lŏj′ĭ-kəl) *adj.* —et′y•mol′o•gist *n.*

eu-. *comb. form.* **1.** Well or beneficial. **2.** Derivative of a specified substance. [< Gk *eus,* good.]

Eu europium.

eu•ca•lyp•tus (yŏŏ′kə-lĭp′təs) *n., pl.* **-tuses.** Any of various Australian trees yielding valuable timber and an aromatic medicinal oil. [< EU- + Gk *kaluptos,* covered.]

Eu•cha•rist (yŏŏ′kər-ĭst) *n.* **1.** The Christian sacrament commemorating Christ's Last Sup-

---

ō paw, for/oi boy/ou out/ŏŏ took/ŏŏ coo/p pop/r run/s sauce/sh shy/t to/th thin/*th* the/
ŭ cut/ûr fur/v van/w wag/y yes/z size/zh vision/ə ago, item, edible, gallop, circus/

per; Communion; Holy Communion. **2.** The consecrated elements of bread and wine used in this sacrament. [< Gk *eukharistos,* grateful.] **—Eu′cha·ris′tic, Eu′cha·ris′ti·cal** *adj.*

eu·chre (yōō′kər) *n.* A card game played with the 32 highest cards of the deck. [?]

Eu·clid (yōō′klĭd). Greek mathematician of the 3rd century B.C. **—Eu·clid′e·an** *adj.*

eu·gen·ics (yōō-jĕn′ĭks) *n. (takes sing. v.).* The study of hereditary improvement, esp. of human improvement by genetic control. [< Gk *eugenēs,* well-born.] **—eu·gen′ic** *adj.*

eu·lo·gy (yōō′lə-jē) *n., pl.* **-gies. 1.** A public tribute to a person or thing, esp. an oration honoring one recently deceased. **2.** Great praise or commendation. [Prob < Gk *eulogia,* praise.] **—eu′lo·gis′tic** *adj.*

eu·nuch (yōō′nək) *n.* A castrated man. [< Gk *eunoukhos,* "bed-watcher," eunuch.]

eu·phe·mism (yōō′fə-mĭz′əm) *n.* An inoffensive term substituted for one considered offensively explicit. [< Gk *euphēmia,* use of good words.] **—eu′phe·mis′tic** (-mĭs′tĭk) *adj.*

eu·pho·ny (yōō′fə-nē) *n., pl.* **-nies.** Agreeable sound, esp. in the phonetic quality of words. **—eu·pho′ni·ous** (-fō′nē-əs) *adj.*

eu·pho·ri·a (yōō-fôr′ē-ə, -fōr′ē-ə) *n.* A feeling of great happiness or well-being. [< Gk *euphoros,* easy to bear, well-borne.] **—eu·phor′ic** *adj.* **—eu·phor′i·cal·ly** *adv.*

Eu·phra·tes (yōō-frā′tēz). A river of SW Asia.

Eur. Europe; European.

Eur·a·sia (yōō-rā′zhə). The continents of Europe and Asia.

Eur·a·sian (yōō-rā′zhən) *adj.* **1.** Of or pertaining to Eurasia. **2.** Of mixed European and Asian ancestry. **—***n.* A person of Eurasian ancestry.

eu·re·ka (yōō-rē′kə) *interj.* Expressive of triumphant discovery. [Gk *heurēka,* "I have found (it)."]

Eu·rip·i·des (yōō-rĭp′ə-dēz′). 480?–406 B.C. Greek tragic poet.

Eu·rope (yōōr′əp). A continent consisting of the section of Eurasia that extends westward from the Urals. **—Eu′ro·pe′an** *adj. & n.*

European Economic Community. The official name for the **Common Market.**

eu·ro·pi·um (yōō-rō′pē-əm) *n. Symbol* **Eu** A soft, silvery-white element used to absorb neutrons in research. Atomic number 63, atomic weight 151.96.

Eu·sta·chian tube (yōō-stā′shən, -stā′kē-ən, -stā′shē-ən). A bony and cartilaginous tube through which the tympanic cavity communicates with the nasal part of the pharynx. [< B. *Eustachio* (died 1517), Italian anatomist.]

eu·tha·na·sia (yōō′thə-nā′zhə, -shə) *n.* **1.** The act of killing a person painlessly for reasons of mercy. **2.** A painless death. [Gk.]

eu·then·ics (yōō-thĕn′ĭks) *n. (often takes sing. v.).* The study of the improvement of human functioning and well-being by adjustment of environment. [< Gk *euthenein,* to flourish, thrive.] **—eu·then′ist** *n.*

eV electron volt.

EVA extravehicular activity.

e·vac·u·ate (ĭ-văk′yōō-āt′) *v.* **-ated, -ating. 1. a.** To remove the contents of. **b.** To create a vacuum in. **2.** To excrete or discharge waste matter from (the bowels). **3.** To withdraw, esp. from a threatened area. [L *ēvacuāre,* to empty out.]´ **—e·vac′u·a′tion** *n.* **—e·vac′u·a′tor** *n.*

e·vac·u·ee (ĭ-văk′yōō-ē′) *n.* One evacuated from a threatened area.

e·vade (ĭ-vād′) *v.* **evaded, evading.** To escape or avoid by cleverness or deceit. [< L *ēvādere,* to evade, go out.] **—e·vad′er** *n.*

e·val·u·ate (ĭ-văl′yōō-āt′) *v.* **-ated, -ating.** To ascertain, judge, or fix the value or worth of. **—e·val′u·a′tion** *n.* **—e·val′u·a′tor** *n.*

ev·a·nes·cent (ĕv′ə-nĕs′ənt) *adj.* Vanishing or likely to vanish; transitory; fleeting. **—ev′-a·nes′cence** *n.* **—ev′a·nes′cent·ly** *adv.*

e·van·gel·i·cal (ē′văn-jĕl′ĭ-kəl) *adj.* Also **e·van·gel·ic** (-jĕl′ĭk). **1.** Pertaining to the Christian Gospel, esp. the Gospels of the New Testament. **2.** Of or pertaining to a Protestant group emphasizing the authority of the Gospel. [< Gk *evangelos,* bringing good news.]

e·van·gel·ism (ĭ-văn′jə-lĭz′əm) *n.* The zealous preaching and dissemination of the Gospel, as through missionary work.

e·van·gel·ist (ĭ-văn′jə-lĭst) *n.* **1.** Often **Evangelist.** Any of the authors of the New Testament Gospels, Matthew, Mark, Luke, or John. **2.** A Protestant who practices evangelism. **—e·van′gel·is′tic** *adj.*

Ev·ans·ville (ĕv′ənz-vĭl, -vəl). A city of SW Indiana. Pop. 102,000.

e·vap·o·rate (ĭ-văp′ə-rāt′) *v.* **-rated, -rating. 1. a.** To change into a vapor. **b.** To remove or be removed in, or as, a vapor. **2.** To vanish. **—e·vap′o·ra′tion** *n.* **—e·vap′o·ra′tor** *n.*

e·va·sion (ĭ-vā′zhən) *n.* **1.** The act of evading. **2.** A means of evading.

e·va·sive (ĭ-vā′sĭv) *adj.* **1.** Characterized by evasion. **2.** Intentionally vague: *an evasive statement.* **—e·va′sive·ness** *n.*

eve (ēv) *n.* **1.** The evening or day preceding a holiday. **2.** The period immediately preceding a certain event: *the eve of war.* **3.** *Poetic.* Evening.

Eve (ēv). The first woman; wife of Adam. Genesis 3:20.

e·ven (ē′vən) *adj.* **1. a.** Flat: *an even floor.* **b.** Smooth. **c.** Level: *The picture is even with the window.* **2.** Uniform; steady; regular: *an even rate of speed.* **3.** Tranquil; calm: *an even temper.* **4.** Equal in degree, extent, or amount; balanced. **5. a.** *Math.* Exactly divisible by 2. **b.** Characterized by a number exactly divisible by 2. **6. a.** Having an even number in a series. **b.** Having an even number of members. **7.** Exact: *an even pound.* **—***adv.* **1.** To a higher degree: *an even worse condition.* **2.** At the same time as: *Even as we watched, the building collapsed.* **3.** In spite of: *Even with his head start, I overtook him.* **4.** In fact: *unhappy, even weeping.* **—break even.** To have neither losses nor gains. **—get even.** To exact revenge. **—***v.* To make or become even. [< OE *efen* < Gmc **ibnaz.*] **—e′ven·ly** *adv.* **—e′ven·ness** *n.*

eve·ning (ēv′nĭng) *n.* Late afternoon and early night. [< OE *æfen,* evening. See **apo-.**]

evening star. Any planet that crosses the local

meridian before midnight, esp. Mercury or Venus when either is prominent in the west shortly after sunset.

e·vent (ĭ-vĕnt′) *n.* **1.** An occurrence or incident, esp. a significant one. **2.** One of the items in a sports program. [< L *ēvenīre,* to come out, happen.]

e·vent·ful (ĭ-vĕnt′fəl) *adj.* **1.** Full of or abounding in events. **2.** Important; momentous. —**e·vent′ful·ly** *adv.* —**e·vent′ful·ness** *n.*

e·ven·tu·al (ĭ-vĕn′chōō-əl) *adj.* Occurring at an unspecified time in the future: *his eventual death.* [< EVENT.] —**e·ven′tu·al·ly** *adv.*

e·ven·tu·al·i·ty (ĭ-vĕn′chōō-ăl′ə-tē) *n., pl.* **-ties.** Something that may occur.

ev·er (ĕv′ər) *adv.* **1.** At all times: *He is ever courteous.* **2.** At any time: *Have you ever seen him?* **3.** In any way: *How could you ever treat him so?* [< OE *æfre.* See **aiw-.**]

Ev·er·est, Mount (ĕv′ər-ĭst, ĕv′rĭst). The highest mountain (29,028 ft.) in the world, in the Himalayas.

ev·er·glade (ĕv′ər-glād′) *n.* A tract of usually submerged swampland.

ev·er·green (ĕv′ər-grēn′) *adj.* Having or characterizing foliage that remains green throughout the year. —*n.* An evergreen tree or plant.

ev·er·last·ing (ĕv′ər-lăs′tĭng, -läs′tĭng) *adj.* Lasting forever; eternal.

ev·er·more (ĕv′ər-môr′, -mōr′) *adv.* Forever; always.

eve·ry (ĕv′rē, -ə-rē) *adj.* **1.** Each without exception: *every student in the class.* **2.** Not lacking anything necessary; complete. —*adv.* —Used as an intensifier: *every once in a while.* —**every other.** Each second: *Every other door is unmarked.* [< OE *æfre ælc,* "ever each," every.]

eve·ry·bod·y (ĕv′rē-bŏd′ē) *pron.* Every person; everyone.

eve·ry·day (ĕv′rē-dā′) *adj.* **1.** Suitable for ordinary days. **2.** Commonplace; usual.

eve·ry·one (ĕv′rē-wŭn′) *pron.* Every person; everybody.

eve·ry·place (ĕv′rē-plās′) *adv.* Everywhere.

eve·ry·thing (ĕv′rē-thĭng′) *pron.* All things that exist or are relevant.

eve·ry·where (ĕv′rē-hwâr′) *adv.* In every place.

e·vict (ĭ-vĭkt′) *v.* To expel (a tenant) by legal process; force out. [< L *ēvincere,* to conquer, overcome.] —**e·vic′tion** *n.* —**e·vic′tor** *n.*

ev·i·dence (ĕv′ə-dəns) *n.* **1.** The data on which a judgment can be based or proof established. **2.** That which serves to indicate: *His reaction was evidence of guilt.* —*v.* **-denced, -dencing.** To indicate clearly.

ev·i·dent (ĕv′ə-dənt) *adj.* Easily recognized or perceived; obvious. [< L *ēvidēns,* evident, clear.] —**ev′i·dent·ly** *adv.* —**ev′i·dent·ness** *n.*

e·vil (ē′vəl) *adj.* **1.** Morally bad or wrong; wicked. **2.** Injurious; harmful. —*n.* **1.** That which is morally bad or wrong; wickedness. **2.** That which causes misfortune, suffering, etc. [< OE *yfel.* See **upo.**] —**e′vil·ly** *adv.*

e·vince (ĭ-vĭns′) *v.* **evinced, evincing.** To show or demonstrate; manifest. [L *ēvincere,* to conquer, prove.] —**e·vin′ci·ble** *adj.*

e·vis·cer·ate (ĭ-vĭs′ə-rāt′) *v.* **-ated, -ating. 1.** To remove the entrails of. **2.** To take away a vital part of. [L *ēviscerāre.*] —**e·vis′cer·a′tion** *n.*

e·voke (ĭ-vōk′) *v.* **evoked, evoking.** To summon or call forth, as memories; elicit. [L *ēvocāre,* to call forth, summon.] —**ev′o·ca′tion** (ĕv′ə-kā′shən) *n.* —**e·vok′er** *n.*

ev·o·lu·tion (ĕv′ə-lōō′shən) *n.* **1.** A gradual process in which something changes, esp. into a more complex form. **2.** The biological theory or process whereby organisms change with passage of time so that descendants differ from their ancestors. **3.** The extraction of a root of a mathematical quantity. [< L *ēvolvere,* EVOLVE.] —**ev′o·lu′tion·ar·y** *adj.* —**ev′o·lu′tion·ism** *n.* —**ev′o·lu′tion·ist** *n.*

e·volve (ĭ-vŏlv′) *v.* **evolved, evolving. 1.** To develop or achieve gradually. **2.** To develop biologically by evolutionary processes. [L *ēvolvere,* to roll out, unfold.]

ewe (yōō) *n.* A female sheep. [< OE *ēowu.* See **owi-.**]

E·we (ā′vā, ā′wā) *n.* The Niger-Congo language of Togo, Ghana, and parts of Dahomey.

ew·er (yōō′ər) *n.* A wide-mouthed pitcher. [< VL **aquāria.*]

ex-¹. *comb. form.* **1.** Removal out of or from. **2.** Former. [< L *ex,* out, out of.]

ex-². *comb. form.* Out of. [< Gk *ex.*]

ex. 1. example. **2.** express. **3.** extra.

Ex. Exodus (Old Testament).

ex·ac·er·bate (ĕg-zăs′ər-bāt′, ĭg-, ĕk-săs′-, ĭk-) *v.* **-bated, -bating.** To increase the severity of; aggravate, as a pain, emotion, etc. [L *exacerbāre,* aggravate, make harsh.] —**ex·ac′er·bat′ing·ly** *adv.* —**ex·ac′er·ba′tion** *n.*

ex·act (ĕg-zăkt′, ĭg-) *adj.* Strictly accurate; precise. —*v.* **1.** To force the payment of; extort. **2.** To call for; require. [L *exactus,* pp of *exigere,* "to drive out," require.] —**ex·act′ly** *adv.* —**ex·act′ness** *n.*

ex·act·ing (ĕg-zăk′tĭng, ĭg-) *adj.* **1.** Making great demands. **2.** Requiring great effort or attention. —**ex·act′ing·ly** *adv.*

ex·ac·ti·tude (ĕg-zăk′tə-t/yōōd′, ĭg-) *n.* The state or quality of being exact.

ex·ag·ger·ate (ĕg-zăj′ə-rāt′, ĭg-) *v.* **-ated, -ating.** To enlarge (something) disproportionately; overstate. [L *exaggerāre,* to pile up, exaggerate.] —**ex·ag′ger·a′tion** *n.*

ex·alt (ĕg-zôlt′, ĭg-) *v.* **1.** To raise in position, status, etc.; elevate. **2.** To glorify; praise. **3.** To fill with pride, delight, etc.; elate. [< L *exaltāre,* to lift up, exalt.] —**ex′al·ta′tion** *n.*

ex·am (ĕg-zăm′, ĭg-) *n. Informal.* An examination.

exam. examination.

ex·am·i·na·tion (ĕg-zăm′ə-nā′shən, ĭg-) *n.* **1.** The act of examining. **2.** A set of questions testing knowledge.

ex·am·ine (ĕg-zăm′ĭn, ĭg-) *v.* **-ined, -ining. 1.** To inspect or analyze (a person, thing, or situation) in detail. **2.** To test knowledge or skills by questioning. **3.** To interrogate formally to elicit facts. [< L *exāmen,* a weighing, consideration.] —**ex·am′in·er** *n.*

ex·am·ple (ĕg-zăm′pəl, -zäm′pəl, ĭg-) *n.* **1.** One representative of a group; a sample. **2.**

Something worthy of imitation; a model. **3.** Something that serves as a warning. **4.** Something that illustrates a principle. [< L *exemplum*, "(something) taken out," example.]

ex·as·per·ate (ĕg-zăs′pə-rāt′, ĭg-) *v.* **-ated, -ating.** To make angry or irritated; tax the patience of. [L *exasperāre*, to exasperate, make rough.] —**ex·as′per·a′tion** *n.*

exc. 1. excellent. **2.** except.

ex·ca·vate (ĕk′skə-vāt′) *v.* **-vated, -vating. 1.** To dig out; hollow out. **2.** To remove (soil) by digging or scooping out. **3.** To uncover by digging. [L *excavāre*, to hollow out.] —**ex′ca·va′tion** *n.* —**ex′ca·va′tor** *n.*

ex·ceed (ĕk-sēd′, ĭk-) *v.* **1.** To be greater than; surpass. **2.** To go or be beyond the limits of. [< L *excēdere*, to depart, go out.]

ex·ceed·ing (ĕk-sē′dĭng, ĭk-) *adj.* Extreme; extraordinary. —**ex·ceed′ing·ly** *adv.*

ex·cel (ĕk-sĕl′, ĭk-) *v.* **-celled, -celling.** To be better than (others); surpass; outdo. [< L *excellere*.]

ex·cel·lence (ĕk′sə-ləns) *n.* **1.** The state or quality of excelling. **2.** Something in which a person or thing excels.

Ex·cel·len·cy (ĕk′sə-lən-sē) *n., pl.* **-cies.** A title of honor for certain high officials.

ex·cel·lent (ĕk′sə-lənt) *adj.* Of the highest quality; exceptionally good; superb. —**ex′cel·lent·ly** *adv.*

ex·cel·si·or (ĕk-sĕl′sē-ər, ĭk-) *n.* Wood shavings used for packing, stuffing, etc.

ex·cept (ĕk-sĕpt′, ĭk-) *prep.* With the exclusion of; but. —*conj.* Were it not for the fact that; only. —*v.* To leave out; exclude. [< L *excipere*, to take out.]

ex·cept·ing (ĕk-sĕp′tĭng, ĭk-) *prep.* Excluding; except.

ex·cep·tion (ĕk-sĕp′shən, ĭk-) *n.* **1.** The act of excepting. **2.** A case that does not conform to normal rules. **3.** An objection.

ex·cep·tion·a·ble (ĕk-sĕp′shən-ə-bəl, ĭk-) *adj.* Open to exception; objectionable.

ex·cep·tion·al (ĕk-sĕp′shən-əl, ĭk-) *adj.* Uncommon; extraordinary. —**ex·cep′tion·al′i·ty** *n.* —**ex·cep′tion·al·ly** *adv.*

ex·cerpt (ĕk′sûrpt′) *n.* A passage selected or quoted from a speech, book, etc. [L *excerptum*, "something picked out," excerpt.]

ex·cess (ĕk-sĕs′, ĭk-, ĕk′sĕs′) *n.* **1.** An amount beyond what is required; superfluity. **2.** Intemperance; overindulgence. —*adj.* Being more than is required. [< L *excessus*, pp of *excēdere*, to EXCEED.]

ex·ces·sive (ĕk-sĕs′ĭv, ĭk-) *adj.* Exceeding a reasonable degree or amount. —**ex·ces′sive·ly** *adv.* —**ex·ces′sive·ness** *n.*

exch. exchange.

ex·change (ĕks-chānj′, ĭks-) *v.* **-changed, -changing. 1.** To give and receive reciprocally; trade. **2.** To replace (one thing by another). —*n.* **1.** An act or instance of exchanging. **2.** A place where things are exchanged, esp. a center where securities are traded. **3.** A central system that establishes connections between individual telephones. [< VL *excambiāre*.]

ex·cheq·uer (ĕks-chĕk′ər, ĭks-, ĕks′chĕk′ər) *n.* A treasury, as of a nation or organization. [<

OF *eschequier*, chessboard, counting table.]

ex·cise¹ (ĕk′sīz′, ĕk-sīz′, ĭk-) *n.* A tax on the production, sale, or consumption of certain commodities within a country. [Obs Du *excijs*.] —**ex′cise′** *v.* **(-cised, -cising).**

ex·cise² (ĕk-sīz′, ĭk-) *v.* **-cised, -cising.** To remove by cutting. [L *excīdere* (pp *excīsus*), to cut out.] —**ex·ci′sion** (ĕk-sĭzh′ən, ĭk-) *n.*

ex·cite (ĕk-sīt′, ĭk-) *v.* **-cited, -citing. 1.** To stimulate; stir to activity. **2.** To arouse strong feeling in (a person); provoke. **3.** *Phys.* To increase the energy of. [< L *excitāre*.] —**ex·cit′ed·ly** *adv.* —**ex·cite′ment** *n.*

ex·claim (ĕks-klām′, ĭks-) *v.* To cry out or speak suddenly or vehemently. [< L *exclāmāre*, to call out.] —**ex·claim′er** *n.* —**ex′cla·ma′tion** (-klə-mā′shən) *n.* —**ex·clam′a·tor′y** (-klăm′ə-tôr′ē, -tōr′ē) *adj.*

exclamation point. A punctuation mark (!) used after an exclamation.

ex·clude (ĕks-klōōd′, ĭks-) *v.* **-cluded, -cluding. 1.** To prevent from entering a place, group, etc.; bar. **2.** To force out; expel. [< L *exclūdere*.] —**ex·clud′er** *n.* —**ex·clu′sion** *n.*

ex·clu·sive (ĕks-klōō′sĭv, ĭks-) *adj.* **1.** Not divided or shared with others. **2.** Admitting only certain people; select. **3.** Expensive; chic: *exclusive shops.* —**ex·clu′sive·ly** *adv.* —**ex·clu′sive·ness, ex′clu·siv′i·ty** (-sĭv′ĭ-tē) *n.*

ex·com·mu·ni·cate (ĕks′kə-myōō′nĭ-kāt′) *v.* **-cated, -cating.** To cut off from the church by ecclesiastical authority. —**ex′com·mu·ni·ca′tion** *n.* —**ex′com·mu′ni·ca′tor** *n.*

ex·co·ri·ate (ĕk-skôr′ē-āt′, ĕk-skōr′-, ĭk-) *v.* **-ated, -ating. 1.** To tear or wear off the skin of. **2.** To censure strongly; denounce. [< L *excoriāre*, to strip of skin.] —**ex·co′ri·a′tion** *n.*

ex·cre·ment (ĕk′skrə-mənt) *n.* Bodily waste, esp. fecal matter. [< L *excernere*, to sift out.] —**ex′cre·ment′al** (-mĕn′təl) *adj.*

ex·cres·cence (ĕk-skrĕs′əns, ĭk-) *n.* An abnormal outgrowth or enlargement. [< L *crēscere*, to grow out.]

ex·cre·ta (ĕk-skrē′tə, ĭk-) *pl.n.* Wastes excreted from the body. —**ex·cre′tal** *adj.*

ex·crete (ĕk-skrēt′, ĭk-) *v.* **-creted, -creting.** To eliminate (waste matter) from the blood, tissues, or organs. [L *excernere* (pp *excrētus*), to sift out.] —**ex·cre′tion** *n.* —**ex′cre·tor′y** (ĕk′skrə-tôr′ē, -tōr′ē) *adj.*

ex·cru·ci·at·ing (ĕk-skrōō′shē-ā′tĭng, ĭk-) *adj.* Intensely painful. [< L *excruciāre*, to torment.] —**ex·cru′ci·at′ing·ly** *adv.*

ex·cul·pate (ĕk′skŭl-pāt′, ĕk-skŭl′-, ĭk-) *v.* **-pated, -pating.** To clear of a charge; exonerate. [ML *exculpāre*.] —**ex′cul·pa′tion** *n.*

ex·cur·sion (ĕk-skûr′zhən, ĭk-) *n.* **1.** A short journey; outing. **2.** A short, inexpensive pleasure tour. **3.** Movement from an average position or axis. [< L *excurrere*, to run out.]

ex·cuse (ĕk-skyōōz′, ĭk-) *v.* **-cused, -cusing. 1.** To grant pardon to; forgive. **2.** To overlook; condone. **3.** To justify. **4.** To free, as from an obligation. —*n.* (ĕk-skyōōs′, ĭk-). **1.** An explanation to elicit pardon. **2.** A ground for being excused. [< L *excūsāre*.] —**ex·cus′a·ble** *adj.* —**ex·cus′a·ble·ness** *n.*

exec. 1. executive. **2.** executor.

ă pat/ā ate/âr care/ä bar/b **bib**/ch **chew**/d **deed**/ĕ pet/ē be/f fit/g **gag**/h **hat**/hw **what**/ ĭ pit/ī pie/îr pier/j **judge**/k **kick**/l lid, fatal/m **mum**/n no, sudden/ng sing/ŏ pot/ō go/

ex·e·cra·ble (ĕk'sĭ-krə-bəl) *adj.* **1.** Abominable; detestable. **2.** Extremely inferior. [< L *exsecrārī,* to EXECRATE.] —**ex'e·cra·bly** *adv.*

ex·e·crate (ĕk'sĭ-krāt') *v.* -**crated, -crating. 1.** To inveigh against; denounce. **2.** To abominate; abhor. [L *exsecrārī,* to curse, execrate.] —**ex'e·cra'tion** *n.* —**ex'e·cra'tor** *n.*

ex·e·cute (ĕk'sĭ-kyōōt') *v.* -**cuted, -cuting. 1.** To carry out; perform. **2.** To legalize, as by signing and sealing: *execute a deed.* **3.** To carry out what is required by: *execute a will.* **4.** To subject to capital punishment. [< L *exsequī,* execute, follow to the end.] —**ex'e·cu'tion** *n.*

ex·e·cu·tion·er (ĕk'sĭ-kyōō'shən-ər) *n.* One who administers capital punishment.

ex·ec·u·tive (ĕg-zĕk'yə-tĭv, ĭg-) *n.* **1.** One having administrative authority in an organization. **2.** The branch of government charged with putting into effect a country's laws. —*adj.* **1.** Pertaining to or suited for carrying out plans, duties, etc. **2.** Of or pertaining to the executive branch of a government.

ex·ec·u·tor (ĕg-zĕk'yə-tər, ĭg-) *n.* One appointed by a testator to execute his will. —**ex·ec'u·trix'** (-trĭks') *fem.n.*

ex·e·ge·sis (ĕk'sə-jē'sĭs) *n., pl.* -**ses** (-sēz). Critical explanation or analysis of a text. [< Gk *exēgeisthai,* to show the way.]

ex·em·plar (ĕg-zĕm'plär, -plər, ĭg-) *n.* One that is worthy of being copied; a model. [< L *exemplum,* example.] —**ex·em'pla·ry** (-plə-rē) *adj.*

ex·em·pli·fy (ĕg-zĕm'plə-fī', ĭg-) *v.* -**fied, -fying. 1.** To illustrate by example. **2.** To serve as an example of. —**ex·em'pli·fi·ca'tion** *n.*

ex·empt (ĕg-zĕmpt', ĭg-) *v.* To free from an obligation or duty required of others. [< L *eximere,* to take out.] —**ex·empt'** *adj.* —**ex·empt'i·ble** *adj.* —**ex·emp'tion** *n.*

ex·er·cise (ĕk'sər-sīz') *n.* **1.** An act of employing or putting into use. **2.** Physical activity to develop fitness. **3.** A lesson, problem, etc., designed to increase some skill. **4.** Often **exercises.** A public ceremony with speeches and other formalities: *graduation exercises.* —*v.* -**cised, -cising. 1.** To put into operation; employ. **2.** To subject to or engage in exercises for physical fitness. **3.** To worry or upset: *exercised by his wife's illness.* [< L *exercēre,* to drive on; practice.]

ex·ert (ĕg-zûrt', ĭg-) *v.* **1.** To put into vigorous action. **2.** To bring to bear: *exert influence.* [L *exserere,* to stretch out.] —**ex·er'tion** *n.*

ex·hale (ĕks-hāl', ĕk-sāl', ĭk-sāl') *v.* -**haled, -haling. 1.** To breathe out. **2.** To emit (vapor, smoke, etc.). [< L *exhālāre,* to breathe out.] —**ex'ha·la'tion** (ĕks'hə-lā'shən) *n.*

ex·haust (ĕg-zôst', ĭg-) *v.* **1.** To let out or draw off (air or fumes). **2.** To use up; expend. **3.** To wear out completely; tire. **4.** To deal with comprehensively: *exhaust a topic.* —*n.* **1.** Vapor or fumes exhausted. **2.** An apparatus or channel for exhausting gases. [< L *exhaurīre,* to draw out.] —**ex·haust'i·ble** *adj.* —**ex·haus'tion** (ĕg-zôs'chən, ĭg-) *n.*

ex·haus·tive (ĕg-zôs'tĭv, ĭg-) *adj.* Comprehensive; thorough: *an exhaustive survey.*

ex·hib·it (ĕg-zĭb'ĭt, ĭg-) *v.* To show; display,

esp. to public view. —*n.* **1.** An act of exhibiting. **2.** That which is exhibited. **3.** Something formally introduced as evidence in court. [< L *exhibēre,* to hold forth.] —**ex'hi·bi'tion** (ĕk'sə-bĭsh'ən) *n.*

ex·hi·bi·tion·ism (ĕk'sə-bĭsh'ə-nĭz'əm) *n.* The practice of behaving so as to attract attention. —**ex'hi·bi'tion·ist** *n.* —**ex'hi·bi'tion·is'tic** *adj.*

ex·hil·a·rate (ĕg-zĭl'ə-rāt', ĭg-) *v.* -**rated, -rating. 1.** To make cheerful; elate. **2.** To invigorate. [L *exhilarāre.*] —**ex·hil'a·ra'tion** *n.*

ex·hort (ĕg-zôrt', ĭg-) *v.* To urge by strong argument or appeal; admonish earnestly. [< L *exhortārī.*] —**ex'hor·ta'tion** *n.*

ex·hume (ĕg-zyōōm', ĭg-, ĕks-hyōōm') *v.* -**humed, -huming.** To remove from a grave. [< ML *exhumāre.*] —**ex'hu·ma'tion** *n.*

ex·i·gen·cy (ĕk'sə-jən-sē) *n., pl.* -**cies.** Also **ex·i·gence** (-jəns). **1.** A situation demanding immediate attention. **2.** Often **exigencies.** Urgent requirements; pressing needs. [< L *exigere,* to demand.] —**ex'i·gent** *adj.*

ex·ile (ĕg'zīl', ĕk'sīl') *n.* **1.** Enforced removal from one's native country by decree; banishment. **2.** One who has been separated from his country. —*v.* -**iled, -iling.** To send (someone) into exile. [< L *exilium.*]

ex·ist (ĕg-zĭst', ĭg-) *v.* **1.** To have being or life; be or live. **2.** To occur. [L *exsistere,* to exist, emerge.] —**ex·is'tence** *n.* —**ex·is'tent** *adj.*

ex·is·ten·tial·ism (ĕg'zĭ-stĕn'shə-lĭz'əm, ĕk'sĭ-) *n.* A body of ethical thought based on the philosophical analysis of existence and an affirmation of the freedom and responsibility of the individual. —**ex'is·ten'tial·ist** *adj. & n.*

ex·it (ĕg'zĭt, ĕk'sĭt) *n.* **1.** The departure of a performer from the stage. **2.** The act of going out. **3.** A way out. [< L *exīre,* to go out.]

exo-. *comb. form.* Outside of, external, or beyond. [Gk *exō,* outside of.]

ex·o·bi·ol·o·gy (ĕk'sō-bī-ŏl'ə-jē) *n.* Extraterrestrial biology.

ex·o·crine (ĕk'sə-krĭn', -krēn', -krīn') *adj.* Involving a glandular secretion through a duct. [EXO- + Gk *krinein,* to separate.]

Exod. Exodus (Old Testament).

ex·o·dus (ĕk'sə-dəs) *n.* **1.** A departure, usually of a large number of people. **2. the Exodus.** The departure of the Israelites from Egypt. [< Gk *exodos,* a going out.]

ex of·fi·ci·o (ĕks' ə-fĭsh'ē-ō'). By virtue of office or position.

ex·on·er·ate (ĕg-zŏn'ə-rāt', ĭg-) *v.* -**ated, -ating.** To free from a charge; declare blameless. [< L *exonerāre,* to free from a burden.] —**ex·on'er·a'tion** *n.* —**ex·on'er·a'tor** *n.*

ex·or·bi·tant (ĕg-zôr'bə-tənt, ĭg-) *adj.* Out of all bounds; excessive; immoderate. [< LL *exorbitāre,* to deviate.] —**ex·or'bi·tance** *n.* —**ex·or'bi·tant·ly** *adv.*

ex·or·cise (ĕk'sôr-sīz', ĕk'sər-) *v.* -**cised, -cising.** Also **ex·or·cize. 1.** To expel (an evil spirit) by or as by incantation. **2.** To free from evil spirits. [< Gk *exorkizein.*] —**ex'or·cis'er** *n.* —**ex'or·cism'** (-sĭz'əm) *n.*

ex·o·ther·mic (ĕk'sō-thûr'mĭk) *adj.* Releasing heat.

ex·ot·ic (ĕg-zŏt'ĭk, ĭg-) *adj.* **1.** Not indigenous;

ŏ paw, for/oi boy/ou out/ŏŏ took/ōō coo/p pop/r run/s sauce/sh shy/t to/th thin/*th* the/
ŭ cut/ûr fur/v van/w wag/y yes/z size/zh vision/ə ago, item, edible, gallop, circus/

foreign. 2. Having the charm of the unfamiliar. [< Gk *exōtikos*.] —ex•ot′ic *n.*
exp. 1. expenses. **2.** export; exported; exporter. **3.** express.
ex•pand (ĕk-spănd′, ĭk-) *v.* **1.** To unfold; spread out. **2.** To increase in size, extent, etc. **3.** To express more fully; expatiate. [< L *expandere.*] —ex•pand′er *n.*
ex•panse (ĕk-spăns′, ĭk-) *n.* A wide and open extent, as of land or sky.
ex•pan•sion (ĕk-spăn′shən, ĭk-) *n.* **1.** The act or process of expanding or state of being expanded. **2.** A part produced by expanding. **3.** The extent to which something has expanded.
ex•pan•sive (ĕk-spăn′sĭv, ĭk-) *adj.* **1.** Capable of expanding. **2.** Wide; sweeping. **3.** Open and generous; outgoing. —ex•pan′sive•ly *adv.*
ex•pa•ti•ate (ĕk-spā′shē-āt′, ĭk-) *v.* -ated, -ating. To speak or write at length on a subject. [L *exspatiāri,* to spread out, expatiate.] —ex•pa′ti•a′tor *n.*
ex•pa•tri•ate (ĕks-pā′trē-āt′) *v.* -ated, -ating. **1.** To banish; exile. **2.** To leave one's own country to reside in another. —*n.* (ĕks-pā′trē-ĭt, -āt′). An expatriated person. [ML *expatriāre.*] —ex•pa′tri•a′tion *n.*
ex•pect (ĕk-spĕkt′, ĭk-) *v.* **1.** To look forward to the probable occurrence of. **2.** To consider reasonable or due. [L *exspectāre,* to look out (for), expect.] —ex•pect′er *n.*
ex•pec•tan•cy (ĕk-spĕk′tən-sē, ĭk-) *n., pl.* -cies. **1.** Expectation. **2.** Something expected: *a life expectancy of seventy years.*
ex•pec•tant (ĕk-spĕk′tənt, ĭk-) *adj.* Expecting. —ex•pec′tant•ly *adv.*
ex•pec•ta•tion (ĕk′spĕk-tā′shən) *n.* **1.** The act or state of expecting. **2.** Eager anticipation. **3.** expectations. Prospects of success, profit, etc. **4.** Something expected.
ex•pec•to•rate (ĕk-spĕk′tə-rāt′, ĭk-) *v.* -rated, -rating. To eject from the mouth; spit. [L *expectorāre,* to drive from the breast.] —ex•pec′to•ra′tion *n.* —ex•pec′to•ra′tor *n.*
ex•pe•di•en•cy (ĕk-spē′dē-ən-sē) *n., pl.* -cies. Also **ex•pe•di•ence** (-dē-əns). **1.** Appropriateness to a purpose. **2.** Adherence to self-serving means. **3.** An expedient.
ex•pe•di•ent (ĕk-spē′dē-ənt) *adj.* **1.** Appropriate to a particular purpose. **2.** Serving to promote one's interest without regard for principle. —*n.* Something expedient. [< L *expedīre,* to free, make ready.] —ex•pe′di•en′tial (-ĕn′shəl) *adj.* —ex•pe′di•ent•ly *adv.*
ex•pe•dite (ĕk′spə-dīt′) *v.* -dited, -diting. **1.** To speed the progress of; facilitate. **2.** To perform quickly. [< L *expedīre,* to free the feet.] —ex′pe•dit′er, ex′pe•di′tor *n.*
ex•pe•di•tion (ĕk′spə-dĭsh′ən) *n.* **1. a.** A trip, march, etc., made by an organized group, as for investigation or military action. **b.** The group thus engaged. **2.** Speed in performance; promptness. [< L *expedīre,* to extricate.]
ex•pe•di•tion•ar•y (ĕk′spə-dĭsh′ə-nĕr′ē) *adj.* Constituting a military expedition.
ex•pe•di•tious (ĕk′spə-dĭsh′əs) *adj.* Acting or done with speed and efficiency. —ex′pe•di′tious•ly *adv.* —ex′pe•di′tious•ness *n.*

ex•pel (ĕk-spĕl′, ĭk-) *v.* -pelled, -pelling. **1.** To force or drive out; eject forcefully. **2.** To dismiss by official decision. [< L *expellere.*]
ex•pend (ĕk-spĕnd′, ĭk-) *v.* To pay out; spend; use up; consume. [< L *expendere,* to pay out.]
ex•pend•a•ble (ĕk-spĕn′də-bəl, ĭk-) *adj.* **1.** Capable of being expended. **2.** Subject to discard or sacrifice; not essential.
ex•pen•di•ture (ĕk-spĕn′də-chər, ĭk-) *n.* **1.** The act or process of expending. **2.** An amount expended, esp. of money.
ex•pense (ĕk-spĕns′, ĭk-) *n.* **1.** An expending; expenditure. **2.** Often **expenses.** Money paid, needed, or provided for a purpose. **3.** Cost; sacrifice.
ex•pen•sive (ĕk-spĕn′sĭv, ĭk-) *adj.* High-priced; costly. —ex•pen′sive•ly *adv.*
ex•pe•ri•ence (ĕk-spîr′ē-əns, ĭk-) *n.* **1.** Apprehension through the mind, senses, or emotions. **2. a.** Activity or practice through which knowledge or skill is gained. **b.** Knowledge or skill thus gained. **3. a.** An event, circumstance, etc., undergone or lived through. **b.** The sum or cumulative effect of such events. —*v.* -enced, -encing. To have as an experience; undergo. [< L *experīrī,* to try, test.]
ex•pe•ri•enced (ĕk-spîr′ē-ənst, ĭk-) *adj.* Skilled through frequent experience.
ex•per•i•ment (ĕk-spĕr′ə-mənt, -mĕnt′, ĭk-) *n.* A test made to demonstrate a known truth, examine the validity of a hypothesis, or determine the efficacy of something previously untried. —*v.* To conduct an experiment; try or test. [< L *experīrī,* to try, test.] —ex•per′i•men′tal *adj.* —ex•per′i•men′tal•ly *adv.* —ex•per′i•men•ta′tion *n.*
ex•pert (ĕk′spûrt′) *n.* A person with a high degree of skill or specialized knowledge. —*adj.* (ĭk-spûrt′, ĕk′spûrt). Highly skilled or knowledgeable. [< L *expertus,* pp of *experīrī,* to try.] —ex•pert′ly *adv.* —ex•pert′ness *n.*
ex•per•tise (ĕk′spûr-tēz′) *n.* Specialized knowledge or skill.
ex•pi•ate (ĕk′spē-āt′) *v.* -ated, -ating. To make atonement for. [L *expiāre.*] —ex′pi•a′tion *n.*
ex•pire (ĕk-spīr′, ĭk-) *v.* -pired, -piring. **1.** To die. **2.** To come to an end; terminate. **3.** To exhale; breathe out. [< L *exspīrāre,* to breathe out, expire.] —ex′pi•ra′tion *n.*
ex•plain (ĕk-splān′, ĭk-) *v.* **1.** To make plain or comprehensible. **2.** To offer reasons for; account for. [< L *explānāre,* to explain, to spread out.] —ex•plain′a•ble *adj.* —ex′pla•na′tion (-splə-nā′shən) *n.* —ex•plan′a•to′ry (-splăn′ə-tôr′ē, -tōr′ē) *adj.*
ex•ple•tive (ĕks′plĭ-tĭv) *n.* An exclamation or oath. [< L *explētus,* pp of *explēre,* to fill out.]
ex•pli•ca•ble (ĕks′plĭ-kə-bəl) *adj.* Capable of being explained.
ex•pli•cate (ĕks′plĭ-kāt′) *v.* -cated, -cating. To explain, esp. in detail. [L *explicāre,* to unfold, explicate.] —ex′pli•ca′tion *n.*
ex•plic•it (ĕk-splĭs′ĭt, ĭk-) *adj.* Precisely expressed; clear and specific. [< L *explicāre,* to EXPLICATE.] —ex•plic′it•ly *adv.*
ex•plode (ĕk-splōd′, ĭk-) *v.* -ploded, -ploding. **1.** To cause or undergo an explosion. **2.** To burst or cause to burst by explosion. **3.** To

burst forth or break out suddenly. **4.** To expose as false or unreliable: *explode a hypothesis.* [L *explōdere*, drive out by clapping.]

ex·ploit (ĕks'ploit') *n.* A noteworthy act or deed; feat. —*v.* (ĕk-sploit', ĭk-). **1.** To utilize fully or advantageously. **2.** To make selfish or unethical use of. [< OF, achievement.] —**ex·ploit'a·ble, ex·ploit'a·tive** *adj.* —**ex'ploi·ta'tion** *n.* —**ex·ploit'er** *n.*

ex·plore (ĕk-splôr', -splōr', ĭk-) *v.* **-plored, -ploring. 1.** To investigate systematically. **2.** To travel into or range over (an area) for the purpose of discovery. [L *explōrāre*, to search out.] —**ex'plo·ra'tion** *n.* —**ex·plor'a·to'ry** (-ə-tôr'ē, -tōr'ē) *adj.* —**ex·plor'er** *n.*

ex·plo·sion (ĕk-splō'zhən, ĭk-) *n.* **1. a.** A sudden rapid, violent release of mechanical, chemical, or nuclear energy. **b.** The loud sound accompanying such a release. **2.** A sudden outburst, increase, etc. [< L *explōdere*, to EXPLODE.]

ex·plo·sive (ĕk-splō'sĭv, ĭk-) *adj.* **1.** Of, pertaining to, or causing an explosion. **2.** Tending to explode. —*n.* A substance that explodes or causes 'explosion. —**ex·plo'sive·ly** *adv.* —**ex·plo'sive·ness** *n.*

ex·po·nent (ĕk-spō'nənt, ĭk-) *n.* **1.** One that expounds, interprets, or advocates. **2.** A number or symbol, as *3* in $(x+y)^3$, placed to the right of and above another number, symbol, or expression, denoting the power to which the latter is to be raised. —**ex'po·nen'tial** (-nĕn'shəl) *adj.* —**ex'po·nen'tial·ly** *adv.*

ex·port (ĕk-spôrt', -spōrt', ĭk-, ĕks'pôrt', -pōrt') *v.* To send abroad, esp. for trade or sale. —*n.* (ĕks'pôrt, -pōrt). **1.** The act of exporting. **2.** Something exported. [L *exportāre*, to carry out.] —**ex'por·ta'tion** *n.* —**ex·port'er** *n.*

ex·pose (ĕk-spōz', ĭk-) *v.* **-posed, -posing. 1.** To make visible or known; reveal. **2.** To subject; lay open, as to an influence or danger. **3.** To subject (a photographic film) to the action of light. [< L *expōnere*, to expose, EXPOUND.] —**ex·pos'er** *n.*

ex·po·sé (ĕk'spō-zā') *n.* A public revelation of something discreditable.

ex·po·si·tion (ĕk'spə-zĭsh'ən) *n.* **1.** A setting forth of meaning or intent. **2.** The presentation of information in clear, precise form. **3.** A public exhibition of broad scope. [< L *expōnere*, to EXPOUND.] —**ex·pos'i·tor** *n.* —**ex·pos'i·to'ry** (-tôr'ē, -tōr'ē) *adj.*

ex post fac·to (ĕks' pōst' făk'tō) Formulated or operating retroactively. [L.]

ex·pos·tu·late (ĕk-spŏs'chōō-lāt', ĭk-) *v.* **-lated, -lating.** To reason earnestly with someone, esp. to dissuade. [L *expostulāre*, to demand strongly.] —**ex·pos'tu·la'tion** *n.*

ex·po·sure (ĕk-spō'zhər, ĭk-) *n.* **1.** An act or instance of exposing or being exposed. **2.** A position in relation to direction or weather conditions: *a southern exposure.* **3.** The act or time of exposing a photographic film or plate.

ex·pound (ĕk-spound', ĭk-) *v.* To give a detailed statement (of); explain; elucidate; hold forth. [< L *expōnere*, to put forth, expose.] —**ex·pound'er** *n.*

ex·press (ĕk-sprĕs', ĭk-) *v.* **1.** To make known

or indicate, as by words, facial aspect, or symbols. **2.** To press out, as juice. **3.** To send by rapid transport. —*adj.* **1.** Clearly stated or intended; explicit. **2.** Used or adapted for speedy, direct transportation. —*adv.* By express transportation. —*n.* **1.** Transportation by express. **2.** An express train, bus, etc. [< VL *expressāre*, to press out, express.] —**ex·press'i·ble** *adj.* —**ex·press'ly** *adv.*

ex·pres·sion (ĕk-sprĕsh'ən, ĭk-) *n.* **1.** Communication of an idea, emotion, etc., esp. by words. **2.** A symbol; sign; indication. **3.** A manner of expressing, esp. in speaking or performing. **4.** A facial aspect or tone of voice conveying feeling. **5.** A word or phrase. **6.** A symbolic mathematical form, such as an equation. —**ex·pres'sion·ist** *n.* & *adj.* —**ex·pres'sion·is'tic** *adj.* —**ex·pres·sion·is'ti·cal·ly** *adv.*

ex·pres·sive (ĕk-sprĕs'ĭv, ĭk-) *adj.* **1.** Expressing or tending to express. **2.** Eloquent or forceful in expression. —**ex·pres'sive·ly** *adv.* —**ex·pres'sive·ness** *n.*

ex·press·way (ĕk-sprĕs'wā', ĭk-) *n.* A major divided highway designed for fast travel.

ex·pro·pri·ate (ĕks-prō'prē-āt') *v.* **-ated, -ating.** To acquire or take (property) from another, as for public use. [ML *expropriāre*.] —**ex·pro'pri·a'tion** *n.* —**ex·pro'pri·a'tor** *n.*

ex·pul·sion (ĕk-spŭl'shən, ĭk-) *n.* The act of expelling or state of being expelled.

ex·punge (ĕk-spŭnj', ĭk-) *v.* **-punged, -punging.** To erase; strike out. [L *expungere*, to prick out, erase.] —**ex·pung'er** *n.*

ex·pur·gate (ĕks'pər-gāt', -pûr'-) *v.* **-gated, -gating.** To amend by removing obscene or objectionable parts, esp. from a text. [L *expurgāre*, to purge out, purify.] —**ex'pur·ga'tion** *n.* —**ex'pur·ga'tor** *n.*

ex·qui·site (ĕks'kwĭ-zĭt) *adj.* **1.** Showing a high degree of craft or excellence. **2.** Delicately or poignantly beautiful. **3.** Acutely discriminating, as in taste. **4.** Keen; intense. [< L *exquirere*, to search out.] —**ex'qui·site·ly** *adv.*

ext. 1. extension. **2.** external. **3.** extinct. **4.** extra. **5.** extract.

ex·tant (ĕk'stənt, ĕk-stănt', ĭk-) *adj.* Still in existence; not destroyed or extinct. [< L *exstāre*, to stand out, exist.]

ex·tem·po·ra·ne·ous (ĕk-stĕm'pə-rā'nē-əs, ĭk-) *adj.* Not rehearsed or prepared in advance; impromptu. [< L *ex tempore*, EXTEMPORE.] —**ex·tem'po·ra'ne·ous·ly** *adv.*

ex·tem·po·re (ĕk-stĕm'pə-rē, ĭk-) *adj.* Extemporaneous. —*adv.* Extemporaneously. [L *ex tempore.*]

ex·tem·po·rize (ĕk-stĕm'pə-rīz', ĭk-) *v.* **-rized, -rizing.** To do or perform (something) extemporaneously; improvise.

ex·tend (ĕk-stĕnd', ĭk-) *v.* **1.** To spread, stretch, or enlarge to greater length, area, or scope. **2.** To exert to full capacity. **3.** To offer; tender. [< L *extendere*.] —**ex·tend'i·bil'i·ty** *n.* —**ex·tend'i·ble, ex·ten'si·ble** *adj.*

ex·ten·sion (ĕk-stĕn'shən, ĭk-) *n.* **1.** The act of extending or condition of being extended. **2.** The degree or range to which something can be extended. **3.** An extended or added part.

ex·ten·sive (ĕk-stĕn'sĭv, ĭk-) *adj.* Great in extent, range, or amount. —**ex·ten'sive·ly** *adv.*

ex·tent (ĕk-stĕnt', ĭk-) *n.* **1.** The distance or area over which something extends; size or space. **2.** Range or degree to which something extends; scope.

ex·ten·u·ate (ĕk-stĕn'yōō-āt', ĭk-) *v.* **-ated, -ating.** To excuse by minimizing the seriousness of: *extenuate his guilt.* [L *extenuāre,* to thin out, lessen.] —**ex·ten'u·a'tion** *n.*

ex·te·ri·or (ĕk-stîr'ē-ər, ĭk-) *adj.* Outer; external. —*n.* An outer part, surface, or aspect. [< L *exterus,* outward, outside.]

ex·ter·mi·nate (ĕk-stûr'mə-nāt', ĭk-) *v.* **-nated, -nating.** To destroy completely; wipe out. [L *extermināre,* to drive out.] —**ex·ter'mi·na'tion** *n.* —**ex·ter'mi·na'tor** *n.*

ex·ter·nal (ĕk-stûr'nəl, ĭk-) *adj.* **1.** Of or on the outside or an outer part. **2.** Acting or coming from the outside. **3.** Having material existence; not imaginary. **4.** Outward; superficial. **5.** Not internal or domestic; foreign. —*n.* **externals.** External parts or aspects. [< L *exterus,* outward.] —**ex·ter'nal·ly** *adv.*

ex·tinct (ĕk-stĭngkt', ĭk-) *adj.* **1.** No longer existing in living or active form; having died out. **2.** Completely gone or destroyed; extinguished. [< L *exstinguere,* to EXTINGUISH.] —**ex·tinc'tion** *n.*

ex·tin·guish (ĕk-stĭng'gwĭsh, ĭk-) *v.* **1.** To put out (a fire, light, etc.). **2.** To put an end to, as hope; destroy. [L *exstinguere.*]

ex·tin·guish·er (ĕk-stĭng'gwĭ-shər, ĭk-) *n.* One that extinguishes, esp. a device for spraying fire-extinguishing chemicals.

ex·tir·pate (ĕk'stər-pāt', ĕk-stûr'-, ĭk-) *v.* **-pated, -pating. 1.** To root up or out. **2.** To destroy wholly; exterminate. [L *exstirpāre,* to pluck up by the roots.] —**ex'tir·pa'tion** *n.*

ex·tol (ĕk-stōl', ĭk-) *v.* **-tolled, -tolling.** Also **ex·toll.** To praise highly; eulogize. [< L *extollere,* to lift up.] —**ex·tol'ler** *n.*

ex·tort (ĕk-stôrt', ĭk-) *v.* To obtain (money, information, etc.) by coercion or intimidation. [< L *extorquēre,* to twist out.] —**ex·tor'tion** *n.* —**ex·tor'tion·ist, ex·tor'tion·er** *n.*

ex·tra (ĕk'strə) *adj.* More than what is usual, expected, etc.; additional. —*n.* **1.** Something additional, as an accessory for which an added charge is made. **2.** A special edition of a newspaper. **3.** An additional worker, esp. an actor hired to play a minor part. —*adv.* Very; unusually. [Prob short for EXTRAORDINARY.]

extra-. *comb. form.* Outside a boundary or scope. [< L *extrā,* outside, beyond.]

ex·tract (ĕk-străkt', ĭk-) *v.* **1.** To draw forth or pull out by or as by force. **2.** To obtain by chemical or mechanical action, as by pressure, distillation, etc. **3.** To pick out, as a literary passage, for separate mention or publication. **4.** *Math.* To determine or calculate (a root). —*n.* (ĕk'străkt). **1.** A literary excerpt. **2.** An extracted substance or concentrated preparation, as of a food. [< L *extrahere* (pp *extractus*), to draw out.] —**ex·trac'tor** *n.*

ex·trac·tion (ĕk-străk'shən, ĭk-) *n.* **1.** The act of extracting or condition of being extracted. **2.** Something obtained by extracting. **3.** Descent; lineage.

ex·tra·cur·ric·u·lar (ĕk'strə-kə-rĭk'yə-lər) *adj.* Not part of the regular curriculum, esp. of a school.

ex·tra·dite (ĕk'strə-dīt') *v.* **-dited, -diting.** To surrender or obtain the surrender of (an alleged criminal) for trial by another authority. [< L *ex-,* out + *trāditiō,* a surrendering.] —**ex'tra·di'tion** (-dĭsh'ən) *n.*

ex·tra·ga·lac·tic (ĕk'strə-gə-lăk'tĭk) *adj.* Located or originating beyond the Galaxy.

ex·tra·mar·i·tal (ĕk'strə-măr'ə-təl) *adj.* Adulterous.

ex·tra·ne·ous (ĕk-strā'nē-əs, ĭk-) *adj.* **1.** Coming from without; foreign. **2.** Not essential or relevant. [L *extrāneus,* strange.] —**ex·tra'ne·ous·ly** *adv.* —**ex·tra'ne·ous·ness** *n.*

ex·traor·di·nar·y (ĕk-strôr'də-nĕr'ē, ĭk-, ĕk'strə-ôr'-) *adj.* Beyond what is ordinary or usual; exceptional; remarkable. —**ex·traor'di·nar'i·ly** *adv.*

ex·trap·o·late (ĕk-străp'ə-lāt', ĭk-) *v.* **-lated, -lating.** To infer (unknown information) from known information. —**ex·trap'o·la'tion** *n.*

ex·tra·sen·so·ry (ĕk'strə-sĕn'sə-rē) *adj.* Not perceptible by or beyond the range of the normal senses.

ex·tra·ter·res·tri·al (ĕk'strə-tə-rĕs'trē-əl) *adj.* Outside the earth or its atmosphere.

ex·trav·a·gant (ĕk-străv'ə-gənt, ĭk-) *adj.* **1.** Spending too much; wasteful; prodigal. **2.** Immoderate; excessive. [< ML *extrāvagārī,* to wander beyond.] —**ex·trav'a·gance, ex·trav'a·gant·ness** *n.* —**ex·trav'a·gant·ly** *adv.*

ex·trav·a·gan·za (ĕk-străv'ə-găn'zə, ĭk-) *n.* An elaborate, spectacular entertainment.

ex·tra·ve·hic·u·lar activity (ĕk'strə-vē-hĭk'yə-lər). Activity or maneuvers performed by an astronaut outside a spacecraft in space.

ex·treme (ĕk-strēm', ĭk-) *adj.* **1.** Outermost or farthest; most remote. **2.** Final; last. **3.** Very great; intense. **4.** To the utmost degree; radical. **5.** Drastic; severe. —*n.* **1.** The greatest or utmost degree. **2.** Either of the two ends of a scale, series, or range. **3.** An extreme condition. **4.** A drastic expedient. [< L *extrēmus.*] —**ex·treme'ly** *adv.* —**ex·treme'ness** *n.*

ex·trem·ist (ĕk-strē'mĭst, ĭk-) *n.* One who advocates or resorts to extreme measures.

ex·trem·i·ty (ĕk-strĕm'ə-tē, ĭk-) *n., pl.* **-ties. 1.** The outermost or farthest point or part. **2.** The utmost degree. **3.** Grave danger, necessity, or distress. **4.** An extreme or severe measure. **5.** A bodily limb or appendage, esp. a hand or foot.

ex·tri·cate (ĕk'strĭ-kāt') *v.* **-cated, -cating.** To release from entanglement or difficulty; disengage. [L *extrīcāre.*] —**ex'tri·ca'tion** *n.*

ex·trin·sic (ĕk-strĭn'sĭk, -zĭk, ĭk-) *adj.* **1.** Not inherent or essential. **2.** Originating from without; external. [LL *extrinsecus,* outer.] —**ex·trin'si·cal·ly** *adv.*

ex·tro·vert (ĕk'strə-vûrt') *n.* One interested in others or in the environment as opposed to, or to the exclusion of, self. [< EXTRA- + L *vertere,* to turn.] —**ex'tro·ver'sion** *n.* —**ex'tro·ver'sive** *adj.* —**ex'tro·vert'ed** *adj.*

ex·trude (ĕk-strōōd', ĭk-) *v.* **-truded, -truding. 1.** To push or thrust out. **2.** To shape (metal, plastic, etc.) by forcing through a die. [L *extrūdere*, to thrust out.] —**ex•tru′sion** *n.*

ex•u•ber•ant (ĕg-zōō′bər-ənt, ĭg-) *adj.* **1.** Full of unrestrained high spirits. **2.** Lavish; profuse. **3.** Growing abundantly; luxuriant. [< L *exūberāre*, to overflow.] —**ex•u′ber•ance** *n.* —**ex•u′ber•ant•ly** *adv.*

ex•u•date (ĕks′yōō-dāt′) *n.* An exuded substance; exudation.

ex•ude (ĕg-zōōd′, ĭg-, ĕk-sōōd′, ĭk-) *v.* **-uded, -uding. 1.** To ooze or pour forth gradually.

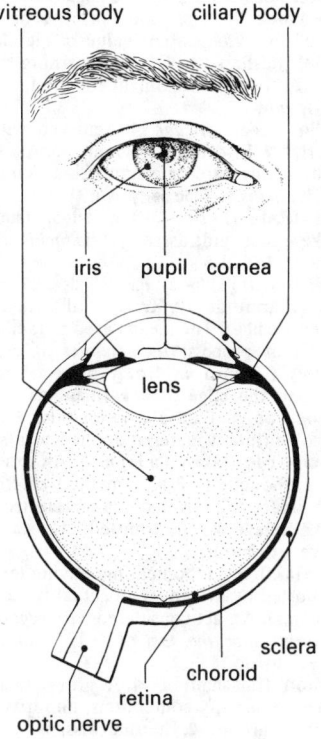

vitreous body   ciliary body

iris   pupil   cornea

lens

sclera

choroid

retina

optic nerve

eye
Anterior view and
cross section of the
human eye

2. To emit; give off. [L *exsūdāre*, to sweat out, exude.] —**ex′u•da′tion** *n.*

ex•ult (ĕg-zŭlt′, ĭg-) *v.* To rejoice greatly, as in triumph. [L *exsultāre*, freq of *exsilīre*, to leap up, rejoice.] —**ex•ul′tant** *adj.* —**ex′ul•ta′tion** *n.*

ex•ur•bi•a (ĕk-sûr′bē-ə, ĕg-zûr′-) *n.* A usually prosperous residential area beyond the suburbs of a city. —**ex•ur′ban•ite** (-bə-nīt) *n.*

—ey¹. Variant of -y¹.

—ey². Variant of -y³.

eye (ī) *n.* **1.** An organ of vision or of light sensitivity. **2.** Sight; vision. **3.** A look; gaze. **4.** Ability to perceive or discern. **5.** Viewpoint; opinion. **6.** Something suggestive of an eye. —**make eyes at.** To gaze at flirtatiously. —**see eye to eye.** To be in agreement. —*v.* **eyed, eyeing** or **eying.** To look at; regard. [< OE *ēage.* See **okw-**.] —**ey′er** *n.*

eye•ball (ī′bôl′) *n.* The ball-shaped portion of the eye enclosed by the socket and eyelids.

eye•brow (ī′brou′) *n.* The hairs covering the bony ridge over the eye.

eye•ful (ī′fōōl′) *n.* **1.** An amount that fills an eye. **2.** A close or revealing look. **3.** A pleasing or striking sight.

eye•glass (ī′glăs′, -gläs′) *n.* **1.** A lens used to aid vision. **2. eyeglasses.** A pair of mounted lenses worn to correct faulty vision.

eye•lash (ī′lăsh′) *n.* One of the hairs fringing the edge of an eyelid.

eye•let (ī′lĭt) *n.* **1.** A small, often edged or rimmed hole used for fastening with a cord or hook or to decorate fabric. **2.** A metal ring designed to reinforce such a hole. [< OF *oillet*, dim of *oil*, eye.]

eye•lid (ī′lĭd′) *n.* Either of two folds of skin and muscle that can be closed over an eye.

eye•piece (ī′pēs′) *n.* The lens or lens group closest to the eye, as in a microscope.

eye shadow. A tinted cosmetic applied to the eyelids.

eye•sight (ī′sīt′) *n.* The faculty or range of sight; vision.

eye•sore (ī′sôr′, -sōr′) *n.* Something offensive to look at.

eye•strain (ī′strān′) *n.* Fatigue of the ciliary muscle or of the extrinsic muscles of the eyeball.

eye•tooth (ī′tōōth′) *n.* A canine tooth of the upper jaw. [Perh because it lies immediately under the eye.]

eye•wit•ness (ī′wĭt′nəs) *n.* One who has personally seen something and can bear witness to the fact.

ô paw, for/oi boy/ou out/ōō took/ōō coo/p pop/r run/s sauce/sh shy/t to/th thin/*th* the/ ŭ cut/ûr fur/v van/w wag/y yes/z size/zh vision/ə ago, item, edible, gallop, circus/

Ff

f, F (ĕf) *n.* **1.** The 6th letter of the English alphabet. **2.** The 6th in a series. **3. F** A failing grade.
f *Mus.* forte.
F **1.** Fahrenheit. **2.** farad. **3.** fluorine. **4.** *Mus.* forte. **5.** *Mus.* The 4th tone in the scale of C major.
F. French.
fa•ble (fā′bəl) *n.* **1.** A fictitious story, often with animal characters, designed to teach a lesson. **2.** A story about legendary persons and exploits. **3.** A falsehood. [< L *fābula*, narration, account.] —**fab′u•list** (făb′yə-lĭst) *n.*
fa•bled (fā′bəld) *adj.* **1.** Made known by fable; legendary. **2.** Existing only in fable; fictitious.
fab•ric (făb′rĭk) *n.* **1.** A structure; framework. **2.** Cloth made by joining fibers, as by weaving, knitting, etc. [< L *fabrica*, workshop, a trade.]
fab•ri•cate (făb′rĭ-kāt′) *v.* **-cated, -cating. 1.** To make or fashion. **2.** To construct; assemble; manufacture. **3.** To make up (a deception). [< L *fabrica*, workshop.] —**fab′ri•ca′tion** *n.*
fab•u•lous (făb′yə-ləs) *adj.* **1.** Of the nature of a fable; legendary. **2.** Told of or celebrated in fables. **3.** Barely credible; astonishing.
fac. 1. facsimile. **2.** *Ed.* faculty.
fa•çade (fə-säd′) *n.* Also **fa•cade. 1.** The main face or front of a building. **2.** A superficial or false outward appearance. [< VL **facia*, face.]
face (fās) *n.* **1.** The surface of the front of the head. **2.** A facial expression; countenance. **3.** A grimace. **4.** An outward appearance; aspect. **5.** Dignity; prestige. **6.** Effrontery; impudence. **7.** A planar surface bounding a solid. **8.** The appearance and geological surface features of an area of land; topography. —**face to face. 1.** In each other's presence. **2.** Directly confronting: *face to face with death.* —*v.* **faced, facing. 1.** To turn or be turned in the direction of. **2.** To front upon: *a window facing the south.* **3. a.** To meet; encounter. **b.** To confront; meet boldly. **4.** To furnish with a surface or cover of a different material. **5.** To provide the edges of (a cloth or garment) with finishing or trimming. —**face up to. 1.** To recognize the existence or importance of. **2.** To confront bravely. [< L *faciēs*, form, shape, face.] —**face′less** *adj.*
face lifting. Also **face-lift** (fās′lĭft′). Plastic surgery for tightening facial tissues.
fac•et (făs′ĭt) *n.* **1.** One of the flat surfaces cut on a gemstone. **2.** A small planar or rounded smooth surface on a bone or tooth. **3.** An aspect; phase. [< F *face*, face.]
fa•ce•tious (fə-sē′shəs) *adj.* Playfully jocular; flippant. [< L *facētus*, elegant, facetious.] —**fa•ce′tious•ly** *adv.* —**fa•ce′tious•ness** *n.*
face value. 1. The value printed on a bill, bond, etc. **2.** Apparent value or significance.
fa•cial (fā′shəl) *adj.* Of or concerning the face. —*n.* A cosmetic treatment for the face. —**fa′cial•ly** *adv.*
fac•ile (făs′əl, -ĭl) *adj.* **1.** Achieved with little effort. **2.** Effortlessly fluent. **3.** Arrived at without due care or examination; superficial. [< L *facilis.*] —**fac′ile•ly** *adv.*
fa•cil•i•tate (fə-sĭl′ə-tāt′) *v.* **-tated, -tating.** To make easier; aid; assist. [< L *facilis,* FACILE.] —**fa•cil′i•ta′tion** *n.*
fa•cil•i•ty (fə-sĭl′ə-tē) *n., pl.* **-ties. 1.** Ease in doing; aptitude. **2.** Ready skill; fluency. **3.** Often **facilities.** The means used to facilitate an action or process: *the facilities of a library.*
fac•ing (fā′sĭng) *n.* **1. a.** A piece of material sewn to the edge of a garment as lining or decoration. **b.** Fabric used for this. **2.** A coating of different material applied to a surface.
fac•sim•i•le (făk-sĭm′ə-lē) *n.* **1.** An exact copy or reproduction. **2. a.** A method of transmitting images or printed matter electronically. **b.** An image so transmitted. [L *fac simile,* make (it) similar.]
fact (făkt) *n.* **1.** Something having existence supported by evidence; an actuality. **2.** Truth; reality. **3.** An act considered with regard to its legality: *after the fact.* [< L *factus,* pp of *facere,* to do.]
fac•tion (făk′shən) *n.* **1.** A group forming a cohesive, usually contentious, minority within a larger group. **2.** Internal dissension. [< L *factiō,* an acting (together).] —**fac′tion•al** *adj.* —**fac′tion•al•ism′** *n.*
fac•tious (făk′shəs) *adj.* **1.** Produced or characterized by faction. **2.** Creating or promoting faction. —**fac′tious•ness** *n.*
fac•ti•tious (făk-tĭsh′əs) *adj.* Artificial; false. [L *factīcius,* made by art.] —**fac•ti′tious•ly** *adv.* —**fac•ti′tious•ness** *n.*
fac•tor (făk′tər) *n.* **1.** One who acts for another; an agent. **2.** One that actively contributes to a result or process. **3.** One of two or more quantities having a designated product: *2 and 3 are factors of 6.* —*v. Math.* To determine the factors of. [< L *factus,* FACT.] —**fac′tor•ship′** *n.*
fac•to•ry (făk′tə-rē) *n., pl.* **-ries.** A building or buildings in which goods are manufactured. [< FACTOR.]
fac•to•tum (făk-tō′təm) *n.* An employee with a wide range of duties. [< L *fac tōtum,* do everything.]

ă pat/ā ate/âr care/ä bar/b bib/ch chew/d deed/ĕ pet/ē be/f fit/g gag/h hat/hw what/
ĭ pit/ī pie/îr pier/j judge/k kick/l lid, fatal/m mum/n no, sudden/ng sing/ŏ pot/ō go/

fac·tu·al (făk′chōō-əl) *adj.* **1.** Of the nature of fact; actual. **2.** Of or containing facts. —**fac′-tu·al·ly** *adv.*

fac·ul·ty (făk′əl-tē) *n., pl.* -**ties. 1.** An inherent power or ability. **2.** A special aptitude. **3.** A division of learning at a college or university. **4.** The teachers in a college or school. [< L *facultās,* power, capability.]

fad (făd) *n.* A briefly popular fashion. [?] —**fad′dish** *adj.*

fade (fād) *v.* **faded, fading. 1.** To lose or cause to lose brightness or brilliance; dim. **2.** To lose strength or freshness; wither. **3.** To disappear gradually; vanish. [< VL **fatidus,* faded.] —**fad′ed·ly** *adv.*

fad·ing (fā′dĭng) *n.* Fluctuation in the strength of received radio signals because of variations in the transmission medium.

fae·ces. Variant of **feces.**

fa·er·ie (fā′ə-rē, fâr′ē) *n.* Also **fa·er·y** *pl.* -**ies.** *Archaic.* **1.** A fairy. **2.** Fairyland.

fag[1] (făg) *v.* **fagged, fagging.** To work to exhaustion; weary or become weary from toil or long work. [?]

fag[2] (făg) *n. Slang.* A cigarette. [< ME *fagge.*]

fag·ot (făg′ət) *n.* Also **fag·got.** A bundle of twigs or sticks. [< Gk *phakelos.*]

fag·ot·ing (făg′ə-tĭng) *n.* Also **fag·got·ing.** Openwork stitching in which threads are tied in clusters or crisscrossed between two edges.

Fahr·en·heit (făr′ən-hīt′) *adj.* Pertaining to a temperature scale that registers the freezing point of water as 32°F and the boiling point as 212°F under standard atmospheric pressure. [< G. *Fahrenheit* (1686–1736), German physicist.]

fa·ience (fī-äns′, fā-) *n.* Also **fa·ïence.** Earthenware decorated with opaque, colorful glazes.

fail (fāl) *v.* **1.** To be deficient or unsuccessful. **2.** To decline, weaken, or cease to function. **3.** To disappoint or forsake. **4.** To omit or neglect: *failed to appear.* **5.** To give or receive an unacceptable grade (in a test, course, etc.). [< L *fallere,* to deceive, disappoint, fail.]

fail·ing (fā′lĭng) *n.* A fault or weakness; shortcoming. —*prep.* In the absence of.

faille (fāl, fīl) *n.* A ribbed fabric of silk, rayon, etc. [< OF.]

fail-safe (fāl′sāf′) *adj.* **1.** Capable of compensating automatically for a failure. **2.** Acting to stop a military attack on the occurrence of a predetermined condition.

fail·ure (fāl′yər) *n.* **1.** The act, condition, or fact of failing: *the failure of an experiment.* **2.** One that has failed.

fain (fān) *adv. Archaic.* Preferably; gladly. [< OE *fægen,* joyful.]

faint (fānt) *adj.* **1.** Lacking strength or vigor; feeble. **2.** Indistinct; dim. **3.** Suddenly dizzy and weak. —*n.* An abrupt, usually brief loss of consciousness. —*v.* To fall into a faint. [< OF *feindre, faindre,* feign.] —**faint′er** *n.* —**faint′ly** *adv.* —**faint′ness** *n.*

faint-heart·ed (fānt′här′tĭd) *adj.* Lacking conviction or courage; timid. —**faint′heart′ed·ly** *adv.* —**faint′heart′ed·ness** *n.*

fair[1] (fâr) *adj.* **1.** Beautiful; lovely. **2.** Clear and sunny. **3.** Light in color, as hair. **4.** Just;

equitable. **5.** Consistent with rules; permissible. **6.** Moderately good. **7.** Unblemished; clean. **8.** Favorable; propitious. —*adv.* **1.** In a fair manner; properly. **2.** Directly; squarely. [< OE *fæger.*] —**fair′ness** *n.*

fair[2] (fâr) *n.* **1.** A regularly held gathering for buying and selling goods. **2.** A public exhibition at which various products, handicrafts, etc., are displayed or judged competitively. **3.** A fund-raising sale or bazaar, as for charity. [< L *fēriæ,* holidays.]

fair-haired (fâr′hârd′) *adj.* **1.** Having blond hair. **2.** Favorite: *mother's fair-haired boy.*

fair·ly (fâr′lē) *adv.* **1.** In a fair or just manner. **2.** Moderately; rather. **3.** Completely; altogether.

fair-trade (fâr′trād′) *adj.* Of or designating an agreement under which distributors sell products at no less than a minimum price set by the manufacturer.

fair·way (fâr′wā′) *n.* The mowed part of a golf course between each tee and putting green.

fair·y (fâr′ē) *n., pl.* -**ies.** A supernatural being of folklore often represented as a tiny person with magical powers. [< L *fāta,* the Fates, pl of *fātum,* FATE.]

fair·y·land (fâr′ē-lănd′) *n.* **1.** The imaginary land of the fairies. **2.** Any charming, enchanting place.

fairy tale. 1. A story about fairies. **2.** A fictitious, fanciful story or explanation.

fait ac·com·pli (fĕ′tà-kôN-plē′) *pl.* **faits accomplis** (fĕ′tà-kôN-plē′). An accomplished fact. [F.]

faith (fāth) *n.* **1. a.** Confident belief; trust. **b.** Belief in God; religious conviction. **2.** Loyalty; allegiance. **3.** A system of religious beliefs. —**bad faith.** Deceit; insincerity. —**good faith.** Sincerity; honesty. —**in faith.** *Archaic.* Indeed; truly. [< L *fidēs.*]

faith·ful (fāth′fəl) *adj.* **1.** Loyal. **2.** Truthful; accurate. —**faith′ful·ly** *adv.* —**faith′ful·ness** *n.*

faith·less (fāth′lĭs) *adj.* Failing in faith or loyalty; untrue. —**faith′less·ly** *adv.* —**faith′less·ness** *n.*

fake (fāk) *adj.* Not genuine; false; fraudulent. —*n.* **1.** Something not genuine or authentic; a counterfeit. **2.** An impostor; fraud. —*v.* **faked, faking. 1.** To contrive and present as genuine; counterfeit. **2.** To pretend; feign. [?] —**fak′er** *n.* —**fak′er·y** *n.*

fa·kir (fə-kîr′, fā′kər) *n.* A Moslem or Hindu religious mendicant, esp. one who performs feats of magic or endurance. [Ar *faqīr.*]

fal·con (făl′kən, fôl′-, fô′-) *n.* A long-winged, swift-flying hawk, esp. one trained to hunt small game. [< LL *falcō.*]

fal·con·er (făl′kə-nər, fôl′-, fô′-) *n.* One who trains or hunts with falcons. —**fal′con·ry** *n.*

fall (fôl) *v.* **fell, fallen, falling. 1.** To move under the influence of gravity, esp. to drop without restraint. **2.** To come down from an erect position; collapse. **3.** To be killed or severely wounded in battle. **4.** To hang down: *Her hair fell in ringlets.* **5.** To assume an expression of disappointment: *Her face fell.* **6.** To be conquered or overthrown. **7.** To slope. **8.** To diminish. **9.** To decline in rank, status, or importance. **10.** To err or sin. **11.** To pass into a less active condition: *The crowd fell silent.* **12.** To arrive and pervade: *A hush fell on the crowd.* **13.** To occur at a specified time or place. **14.** To be allotted: *The task fell to him.* **15.** To divide naturally: *They fall into three categories.* **16.** To be directed by chance: *His gaze fell on a book.* **17.** To be uttered as if involuntarily. —**fall back on.** To resort to. —**fall for. 1.** To become infatuated with. **2.** To be deceived by. —**fall off.** To decline. —**fall short.** To fail to attain a specified level. —**fall through.** To fail; miscarry. —*n.* **1.** The act or an instance of falling. **2.** That which has fallen: *a fall of hail.* **3. a.** The amount of what has fallen: *a light fall of rain.* **b.** The distance that something falls. **4.** Often **Fall.** Autumn. **5.** Often **falls.** A waterfall. **6.** A woman's hair piece with long, free-hanging hair. **7.** An overthrow or collapse: *the fall of a government.* **8.** A decline or reduction. **9.** A loss of moral innocence. [< OE *feallan.* See **phol-**.]

fal·la·cious (fə-lā′shəs) *adj.* **1.** Containing or based on a fallacy. **2.** Deceptive in appearance or meaning. —**fal·la′cious·ly** *adv.*

fal·la·cy (făl′ə-sē) *n., pl.* **-cies. 1.** An erroneous idea or opinion. **2.** Incorrectness of reasoning or belief. [< L *fallere,* to deceive.]

fal·li·ble (făl′ə-bəl) *adj.* Capable of erring. [< L *fallere,* to deceive.] —**fal′li·bly** *adv.*

fall·ing-out (fôl′ĭng-out′) *n., pl.* **fallings-out** or **falling-outs.** A disagreement or quarrel.

falling sickness. Epilepsy.

falling star. A meteor.

Fal·lo·pi·an tube (fə-lō′pē-ən). Either of a pair of slender ducts that connect the uterus to the region of each of the ovaries in the female reproductive system of humans and higher vertebrates. [< G. *Fallopio* (1523–1562), Italian anatomist.]

fall out. 1. To quarrel; become estranged. **2.** To happen; occur.

fall·out (fôl′out′) *n.* **1. a.** The slow descent of minute particles of radioactive debris in the atmosphere following a nuclear explosion. **b.** The particles so descending. **c.** Such particles collectively. **2.** Any incidental results or side effects: *the technological fallout of the space program; political fallout.*

fal·low (făl′ō) *adj.* Plowed and tilled but left unseeded during a growing season. —**lie fallow.** To remain unused or inactive. [< OE *fealh,* arable land.] —**fal′low·ness** *n.*

fallow deer. An Old World deer with a white-spotted summer coat and broad, flat antlers. [< OE *fealo,* sallow. See **pel-²**.]

false (fôls) *adj.* **falser, falsest. 1.** Contrary to fact or truth. **2.** Insincere: *false promises.* **3.** Not faithful: *a false lover.* **4.** Not real or natural; artificial. **5.** *Mus.* Of incorrect pitch. —**play** (a person) **false.** To betray. [< L *falsus,* pp of *fallere,* to deceive.] —**false′ly** *adv.* —**false′ness** *n.*

false·hood (fôls′hŏŏd′) *n.* **1.** Contradiction to or disparity with truth or fact. **2.** An untrue statement; lie.

fal·set·to (fôl-sĕt′ō) *n., pl.* **-tos.** A typically male singing voice when artificially producing tones in an upper register beyond its normal range. —**fal·set′to** *adj & adv.*

fal·si·fy (fôl′sə-fī′) *v.* **-fied, -fying. 1.** To state untruthfully. **2.** To alter (a document) in order to deceive. —**fal′si·fi·ca′tion** *n.*

fal·si·ty (fôl′sə-tē) *n., pl.* **-ties. 1.** The condition of being false. **2.** A lie.

fal·ter (fôl′tər) *v.* **1.** To waver or weaken in purpose, force, etc. **2.** To stammer. **3.** To stumble. [ME *falteren.*] —**fal′ter·ing·ly** *adv.*

fame (fām) *n.* Great reputation and recognition; public esteem; renown. [< L *fāma,* talk, reputation.] —**famed** *adj.*

fa·mil·ial (fə-mĭl′yəl) *adj.* Of, pertaining to, or passed on in a family: *a familial trait.*

fa·mil·iar (fə-mĭl′yər) *adj.* **1.** Of frequent instance or occurrence; common. **2.** Having knowledge of something: *familiar with those roads.* **3.** Friendly; intimate: *on familiar terms.* **4.** Taking undue liberties. [< L *familia,* FAMILY.] —**fa·mil′iar·ly** *adv.*

fa·mil·i·ar·i·ty (fə-mĭl′yăr′ə-tē, -ē-ăr′ə-tē) *n., pl.* **-ties. 1.** Substantial acquaintance with something. **2.** Close friendship. **3.** Undue liberty; boldness.

fa·mil·iar·ize (fə-mĭl′yə-rīz′) *v.* **-ized, -izing.** To make (oneself or another) acquainted with.

fam·i·ly (făm′ə-lē, făm′lē) *n., pl.* **-lies. 1.** Parents and their children. **2.** A group of persons related by blood or marriage. **3.** Lineage; ancestry. **4.** A group or category of like things, as related organisms. —*adj.* Pertaining to family: *a family reunion.* [< L *familia,* family, household.]

family tree. A genealogical diagram of a family.

fam·ine (făm′ĭn) *n.* **1.** A drastic and wide-reaching shortage of food. **2.** A drastic shortage of anything. [< L *fames,* hunger.]

fam·ished (făm′ĭsht) *adj.* Extremely hungry; starving.

fa·mous (fā′məs) *adj.* **1.** Widely known; publicly acclaimed. **2.** *Informal.* Excellent. [< L *fāma,* FAME.] —**fa′mous·ly** *adv.*

fan¹ (făn) *n.* **1.** A hand-waved implement for creating a cooling breeze. **2. a.** An array of thin, rigid blades attached to a central hub. **b.** A machine that rotates one or more such arrays on electrically powered shafts in order to move air. —*v.* **fanned, fanning. 1.** To direct a current of air upon. **2.** To stir up: *fan resentment.* **3.** *Baseball.* To strike out. **4.** To spread like a fan (with *out*). [< L *vannus.*]

fan² (făn) *n. Informal.* An ardent admirer. [Short for FANATIC.]

fa·nat·ic (fə-năt′ĭk) *n.* A person possessed by an excessive or irrational zeal. —*adj.* Variant of **fanatical.** [< L *fānāticus,* of a temple, inspired by a god, mad.]

fa·nat·i·cal (fə-năt′ĭ-kəl) *adj.* Also **fa·nat·ic. 1.** Driven by fanaticism. **2.** Characteristic of a fanatic. —**fa·nat′i cal·ly** *adv.*

fa·nat·i·cism (fə-năt′ə-sĭz′əm) *n.* Excessive or irrational zeal.

fan·ci·er (făn′sē-ər) *n.* One who has a special enthusiasm, as raising a specific kind of plant or animal.

fan·ci·ful (făn′sĭ-fəl) *adj.* **1.** Created in the fan-

ă pat/ā ate/âr care/ä bar/b bib/ch chew/d deed/ĕ pet/ē be/f fit/g gag/h hat/hw what/
ĭ pit/ī pie/îr pier/j judge/k kick/l lid, fatal/m mum/n no, sudden/ng sing/ŏ pot/ō go/

cy; unreal. **2.** Showing invention or whimsy in design. —**fan′ci•ful•ly** *adv.*

fan•cy (făn′sē) *n., pl.* **-cies. 1.** The light invention or play of the mind through which whims, images, etc., are summoned up. **2.** An associative image. **3.** An unfounded opinion. **4.** A capricious idea. **5.** Capricious or sudden liking. **6.** Taste or preference. —*adj.* **-cier, -ciest. 1.** Decorative; elegant: *a fancy hat.* **2.** Illusory: *fancy notions.* **3.** Executed with great skill. **4.** Of superior grade: *fancy preserves.* **5.** Excessive or exorbitant: *a fancy bid.* —*v.* **-cied, -cying. 1.** To visualize; imagine. **2.** To take to or like. **3.** To suppose; guess. [< FANTASY.] —**fan′ci•ly** *adv.* —**fan′ci•ness** *n.*

fan•cy-free (făn′sē-frē′) *adj.* Without commitment; unattached.

fan•cy•work (făn′sē-wûrk′) *n.* Decorative needlework.

fan•dan•go (făn-dăng′gō) *n., pl.* **-gos.** An animated Spanish dance. [Span.]

fan•fare (făn′fâr′) *n.* **1.** A flourish of trumpets. **2.** Spectacular display. [F.]

fang (făng) *n.* A long, pointed tooth, as one with which a venomous snake injects its venom. [< OE, plunder. See **pag-**.] —**fanged** *adj.*

fan•light (făn′līt′) *n.* A half-circle window with sash bars arranged like the ribs of a fan.

fan•ta•sia (făn-tā′zhə, -zhē-ə, făn′tə-zē′ə) *n.* A free-form musical composition. [< FANTASY.]

fan•tas•tic (făn-tăs′tĭk) *adj.* **1.** Bizarre; grotesque. **2.** Unreal; illusory. **3.** Capricious or eccentric: *a fantastic old person.* **4.** *Informal.* Wonderful or superb. [< LL *phantasticus,* imaginary.] —**fan•tas′ti•cal•ly** *adv.*

fan•ta•sy (făn′tə-sē, -zē) *n., pl.* **-sies. 1.** Imagination. **2.** A product of the imagination; illusion. **3.** A delusion. **4.** A capricious or whimsical notion or idea; conceit. **5.** A daydream. **6.** A fantasia. [< Gk *phantasia,* appearance, faculty of imagination.]

far (fär) *adv.* **farther** or **further, farthest** or **furthest. 1.** To, from, or at considerable distance. **2.** To or at a specific distance or degree. **3.** To a considerable degree; much: *far better.* **4.** Not at all: *far from happy.* —**as far as.** To the extent that: *as far as I know.* —**by far.** To a considerable or evident degree. —**far and away.** Definitely. —**far and wide.** Everywhere. —**far be it from me.** I neither hope nor dare. —**go far. 1.** To be successful. **2.** To last a long time. **3.** To tend strongly. —**in so far** (or **insofar**) **as.** To the degree or extent that. —**so far. 1.** Up to now. **2.** To a limited extent. —**so far as.** To the extent that: *so far as I can tell.* —*adj.* **farther** or **further, farthest** or **furthest. 1.** Distant: *a far country.* **2.** More distant; opposite: *the far corner.* **3.** Long: *a far trek.* [< OE *feor.* See **per¹.**]

fa•rad (făr′əd, -ăd′) *n.* A unit of capacitance, equal to the capacitance of a capacitor having a charge of 1 coulomb on each plate and a potential difference of 1 volt between the plates. [< M. *Faraday* (1791–1867), British scientist.]

far•a•way (fär′ə-wā′) *adj.* **1.** Distant; remote. **2.** Abstracted.

farce (färs) *n.* **1.** A play marked by slapstick

humor and wild improbabilities of plot. **2.** An empty show; mockery. [< L *farcire,* to stuff.] —**far′ci•cal** *adj.*

fare (fâr) *v.* **fared, faring. 1.** To get along. **2.** To turn out; go: *How does it fare with you?* —*n.* **1.** A transportation charge. **2.** A passenger transported for a fee. **3.** Food and drink; diet. [< OE *faran,* to go. See **per-².**]

Far East. An area including China, Japan, and Korea.

fare•well (fâr′wĕl′) *interj.* Good-by. —*n.* (fâr′wĕl′). **1.** A good-by. **2.** A leave-taking. —*adj.* (fâr′wĕl′). Parting: *a farewell party.* [< FARE + WELL.]

far-fetched (fär′fĕcht′) *adj.* Improbable.

far-flung (fär′flŭng′) *adj.* **1.** Wide-ranging. **2.** Remote; distant.

fa•ri•na (fə-rē′nə) *n.* Fine meal, as of cereal grain, often used as a cooked cereal or in puddings. [L *farina,* ground corn, meal.]

far•i•na•ceous (făr′ə-nā′shəs) *adj.* **1.** Made from, rich in, or consisting of starch. **2.** Having a mealy or powdery texture.

farm (färm) *n.* A tract of land for producing crops or raising livestock. —*v.* **1.** To raise crops or livestock as a business. **2.** To use (land) for this purpose. —**farm out.** To send out (work) to be done elsewhere. [ME *ferme,* lease, rent.]

farm•er (fär′mər) *n.* One who operates a farm.

farm hand. A hired farm laborer.

farm•house (färm′hous′) *n.* The farmer's dwelling on a farm.

farm•stead (färm′stĕd′) *n.* A farm, including its land and buildings.

far-off (fär′ôf′, -ŏf′) *adj.* Remote in space or time; distant.

far-out (fär′out′) *adj. Slang.* Extremely unconventional.

far•ra•go (fə-rä′gō, -rä′gō) *n., pl.* **-goes.** A medley; conglomeration. [L *farrago,* mixed fodder for cattle.]

far-reach•ing (fär′rē′chĭng) *adj.* Having a wide range or effect.

far•row (făr′ō) *n.* A litter of pigs. —*v.* To give birth to (a farrow). [Perh < OE *fearh,* little pig.]

far•see•ing (fär′sē′ĭng) *adj.* Foresighted; prudent.

far•sight•ed (fär′sī′tĭd) *adj.* **1.** Able to see objects better from a distance than from short range. **2.** Planning prudently for the future; foresighted. —**far′sight′ed•ness** *n.*

far•ther (fär′thər) *adv.* **1.** To a greater distance. **2.** Further. —*adj.* **1.** More distant. **2.** Additional. [< FURTHER.]

far•thest (fär′thĭst) *adj.* Most remote or distant. —*adv.* To or at the most distant or remote point in space or time.

f.a.s., F.A.S. free alongside ship.

fas•ci•cle (făs′ĭ-kəl) *n.* Also **fas•ci•cule** (-kyōōl′). One of the separately published installments of a book. [< L *fascis,* a bundle.]

fas•ci•nate (făs′ə-nāt′) *v.* **-nated, -nating. 1.** To attract irresistibly. **2.** To spellbind or mesmerize. [L *fascinare,* to enchant, bewitch.] —**fas′ci•nat′ing•ly** *adv.* —**fas′ci•na′tion** *n.*

fas•cism (făsh′ĭz′əm) *n.* A system of government that exercises a dictatorship of the extreme right, typically through the merging of state and business leadership, together with a belligerent nationalism. [< It *fascio,* bundle, group.] **—fas′cist** *n.* & *adj.*

fash·ion (făsh′ən) *n.* **1.** The configuration or aspect of something. **2.** Kind; sort. **3.** Manner; way. **4.** The current style. **—after** (or **in**) **a fashion.** In some way or other. *—v.* **1.** To make into a particular shape or form. **2.** To make suitable; adapt. [< L *factiō,* "a making."] **—fash′ion·er** *n.*

fash·ion·a·ble (făsh′ən-ə-bəl) *adj.* **1.** Currently stylish. **2.** Associated with the world of fashion. **—fash′ion·a·bly** *adv.*

fast[1] (făst, fäst) *adj.* **1.** Swift; rapid. **2.** Accomplished in little time: *a fast visit.* **3.** Indicating a time ahead of the correct time: *a fast clock.* **4.** Adapted to rapid travel: *a fast turnpike.* **5.** Flouting conventional mores, esp. in sexual matters. **6.** Resistant: *acid-fast.* **7.** Firmly fixed or fastened. **8.** Secure. **9.** Loyal; constant: *fast friends.* **10.** Proof against fading. **11.** Deep; sound: *a fast sleep.* **12.** *Photog.* **a.** Compatible with a high shutter speed: *a fast lens.* **b.** Designed for short exposure; highly sensitive: *fast film.* *—adv.* **1.** Firmly; securely; tightly. **2.** Deeply; soundly: *fast asleep.* **3.** Quickly; rapidly. **4.** In a dissipated way: *living fast.* [< OE *fæst.* See **past-**.]

fast[2] (făst, fäst) *v.* To abstain from eating all or certain foods. *—n.* The act or a period of fasting. [< OE *fæstan,* to hold fast, abstain from food. See **past-**.]

fas·ten (făs′ən, fäs′-) *v.* **1.** To attach or become attached to something else; join; connect. **2. a.** To make fast or secure. **b.** To close, as by shutting. **3.** To fix or direct steadily, as the gaze. [< OE *fastnian,* to settle, establish, make fast. See **past-**.] **—fas′ten·er** *n.*

fast-food (făst′fōod′, fäst′-) *adj.* Specializing in foods prepared and served quickly: *a fast-food restaurant.*

fas·tid·i·ous (fă-stĭd′ē-əs, fə-) *adj.* **1.** Careful in all details; exacting; meticulous. **2.** Difficult to please. **3.** Easily disgusted. [< L *fastīdium,* a loathing.] **—fas·tid′i·ous·ness** *n.*

fast·ness (făst′nĭs, fäst′-) *n.* **1. a.** A fortified place. **b.** A secret place. **2.** The condition or quality of being fast.

fat (făt) *n.* **1. a.** Any of various energy-rich semisolid organic compounds occurring widely in animal and plant tissue. **b.** Organic tissue containing such substances. **c.** A solidified animal or vegetable oil. **2.** Plumpness; obesity. **3.** The best part of something: *the fat of the land.* *—adj.* **1.** Plump; obese. **2.** Oily; greasy. **3.** Abounding in desirable elements. **4.** Fertile or productive; rich. **5.** Ample; well-stocked: *a fat larder.* **6.** Thick; broad; large: *a fat plank.* [< OE *fætt.* See **peyə-**.] **—fat′ly** *adv.* **—fat′ness** *n.* **—fat′ty** *adj.*

fa·tal (fāt′l) *adj.* **1.** Deadly; mortal. **2.** Ruinous; disastrous. **3.** Most decisive; fateful. **4.** Controlling destiny. [< L *fātum,* FATE.] **—fa′tal·ly** *adv.* **—fa′tal·ness** *n.*

fa·tal·ism (fāt′l-ĭz′əm) *n.* The belief that all events are predetermined by fate. **—fa′tal·ist** *n.*

—fa′tal·is′tic *adj.* **—fa′tal·is′ti·cal·ly** *adv.*

fa·tal·i·ty (fā-tăl′ə-tē, fə-) *n., pl.* **-ties. 1.** An accidental death. **2.** Liability to disaster.

fat·back (făt′băk′) *n.* A dried and salt-cured strip of fat taken from the upper part of a side of pork.

fate (fāt) *n.* **1.** The supposed force, principle, or power that predetermines events. **2.** Lot; fortune. **3.** A final result; outcome. **4.** Doom or ruin. **5. the Fates.** *Gk.&Rom.Myth.* The three goddesses who govern human destiny. [< L *fātum,* neut pp of *fārī,* to speak.]

fat·ed (fā′tĭd) *adj.* Governed or condemned by fate.

fate·ful (fāt′fəl) *adj.* **1.** Affecting one's future. **2.** Controlled by fate. **3.** Ruinous; fatal. **4.** Portentous; ominous. **—fate′ful·ly** *adv.*

fath. fathom.

fa·ther (fä′thər) *n.* **1.** A male parent. **2.** A male ancestor; forefather. **3.** An originator. **4. Father.** God, esp. as the first member of the Trinity. **5.** Any elderly or venerable man. **6.** Often **Father.** One of the authoritative early codifiers of Christian doctrines and observances. **7.** A title for a Roman Catholic or Anglican priest. **8.** A leading citizen: *town fathers. —v.* **1.** To beget. **2.** To act or serve as a father to. [< OE *fæder.* See **pəter-**.] **—fa′ther·less** *adj.* **—fa′ther·ly** *adj.* & *adv.*

fa·ther·hood (fä′thər-hōod′) *n.* The condition of being a father; paternity.

fa·ther-in-law (fä′thər-ĭn-lô′) *n., pl.* **fathers-in-law.** The father of one's husband or wife.

fath·om (făth′əm) *n., pl.* **-oms** or **-om.** A unit of length equal to 6 feet, used principally in the measurement of marine depths. *—v.* **1.** To determine the depth of; sound. **2.** To understand. [< OE *fæthm,* a measure of length. See **pet-**[2].] **—fath′om·a·ble** *adj.*

fath·om·less (făth′əm-lĭs) *adj.* Too deep to be fathomed.

fa·tigue (fə-tēg′) *n.* **1.** Weakness or weariness resulting from exertion or prolonged stress. **2.** Manual or menial labor assigned to soldiers. **3. fatigues.** Military dress for work and field duty. *—v.* **-tigued, -tiguing.** To tire out; weary. [< L *fatīgāre,* to fatigue.]

fat·ten (făt′n) *v.* To make or become fat.

fatty acid. Any of a large group of organic acids having the general formula $C_nH_{2n+1}CO-OH$, esp. any of a commercially important subgroup obtained from animals and plants.

fa·tu·i·ty (fə-t/y/ōo′ə-tē) *n.* Stupidity or foolishness. [< L *fatuus,* FATUOUS.]

fat·u·ous (făch′ōo-əs) *adj.* Stupid; asinine; inane. [L *fatuus.*] **—fat′u·ous·ly** *adv.*

fau·cet (fô′sĭt) *n.* A device for drawing a flow of a liquid, as from a pipe. [< OF *fausser,* damage, break into, make false.]

Faulkner (fôk′nər), **William Cuthbert.** 1897-1962. American author.

fault (fôlt) *n.* **1.** A failing, defect, or impairment. **2.** A mistake or minor transgression. **3.** Responsibility for something wrong. **4.** A break in the continuity of a rock formation, caused by a shifting or dislodging of the earth's crust, in which adjacent surfaces are differentially displaced parallel to the plane of

---

ă pat/ā ate/âr care/ä bar/b bib/ch chew/d deed/ĕ pet/ē be/f fit/g gag/h hat/hw what/ ĭ pit/ī pie/îr pier/j judge/k kick/l lid, fatal/m mum/n no, sudden/ng sing/ŏ pot/ō go/

fracture. **5.** A bad service, as in tennis. **—at fault.** Guilty. **—find fault.** To carp. **—to a fault.** Excessively. **—v. 1.** To find a fault in. **2.** To produce a geological fault in. **3.** To commit a fault; err. [< L *fallere,* to fail, deceive.] **—fault′i•ly** *adv.* **—fault′less** *adj.* **—fault′less•ly** *adv.* **—fault′y** *adj.*

faun (fôn) *n.* One of a group of ancient Italian rural deities represented as part man and part goat.

fau•na (fô′nə) *n., pl.* **-nas** or **-nae** (-nē′). Animals, esp. of a region or time. [< L *Faunus,* Roman god of nature.]

Faust (foust). A legendary magician who sold his soul to the devil in exchange for power and knowledge. **—Faust′i•an** *adj.*

faux pas (fō pä′) *pl.* **faux pas** (fō päz′). A social blunder. [F, "false step."]

fa•vor (fā′vər) *n.* **1.** A friendly attitude. **2.** An act of kindness. **3.** An indulgence. **4. a.** Friendly regard shown by a superior. **b.** A state of being held in such regard. **5.** Approval or support. **6. favors.** Sexual privileges. **7.** A token of love. **8.** A small, decorative gift handed out at a party. **9.** Advantage; benefit. **—v. 1.** To oblige. **2.** To like. **3.** To support. **4.** To aid or facilitate. **5.** To resemble: *She favors her father.* **6.** To be gentle with; spare: *favor a sore foot.* [< L *favēre,* to favor.]

fa•vor•a•ble (fā′vər-ə-bəl, fāv′rə-) *adj.* **1.** Advantageous; helpful. **2.** Propitious; encouraging. **3.** Manifesting approval. **—fa′vor•a•ble•ness** *n.* **—fa′vor•a•bly** *adv.*

fa•vor•ite (fā′vər-ĭt, fāv′rĭt) *n.* **1. a.** A person or thing liked above all others. **b.** A person esp. indulged by a superior: *a favorite of the king.* **2.** A contestant regarded as most likely to win. **—fa′vor•ite** *adj.*

fa•vor•it•ism (fā′vər-ə-tĭz′əm, fāv′rə-) *n.* Partiality.

fawn¹ (fôn) *v.* **1.** To exhibit affection, as a dog. **2.** To seek favor by obsequious behavior. [< OE *fægen,* FAIN.]

fawn² (fôn) *n.* **1.** A young deer. **2.** Grayish or yellowish brown. [< L *fētus,* offspring, a giving birth.]

fay (fā) *n.* A fairy or sprite. [< L *fāta,* the Fates, pl of *fātum,* FATE.]

faze (fāz) *v.* **fazed, fazing.** To daunt or disconcert. [< OE *fēsian,* to drive off.]

FBI, F.B.I. Federal Bureau of Investigation.

fcap., fcp. foolscap.

FCC Federal Communications Commission.

FDA Food and Drug Administration.

Fe iron (L *ferrum*)

fe•al•ty (fē′əl-tē) *n., pl.* **-ties. 1.** Loyalty. **2.** The obligation of feudal allegiance. [< L *fidēlitās,* faithfulness.]

fear (fîr) *n.* **1.** A feeling of alarm or disquiet caused by awareness or expectation of danger. **2.** An instance or manifestation of such a feeling. **3.** A state of dread. **4.** Concern; solicitude. **—v. 1.** To be afraid of. **2.** To be apprehensive. **3.** To be in awe of. **4.** To suspect: *I fear you are wrong.* [< OE *fǣr,* danger, sudden calamity. See per-³.] **—fear′ful** *adj.* **—fear′ful•ly** *adv.* **—fear′ful•ness** *n.* **—fear′less** *adj.* **—fear′less•ly** *adv.* **—fear′less•ness** *n.*

fear•some (fîr′səm) *adj.* **1.** Frightening; awesome. **2.** Frightened; timid.

fea•si•ble (fē′zə-bəl) *adj.* **1.** Capable of being accomplished or brought about; practicable. **2.** Suitable. **3.** Likely or reasonable: *a feasible excuse.* [< L *facere,* to do.] **—fea′si•bil′i•ty, fea′si•ble•ness** *n.* **—fea′si•bly** *adv.*

feast (fēst) *n.* **1.** A large and elaborate meal; banquet. **2.** A religious festival. **—v. 1.** To entertain or feed sumptuously. **2.** To delight; gratify. **3.** To partake of a feast. [< L *fēstus,* joyous, festal.] **—feast′er** *n.*

feat (fēt) *n.* A particularly remarkable exploit or achievement. [< L *factum,* something done.]

feath•er (fĕth′ər) *n.* **1.** One of the light, hollow-shafted structures forming the external covering of birds. **2. feathers.** Clothing; attire. **3.** Character; kind: *birds of a feather.* **—in fine** (or **good**) **feather.** In fine fettle. **—v. 1.** To cover, dress, or line with feathers. **2.** To fit (an arrow) with a feather. [< OE *fether.* See pet-¹.] **—feath′er•i•ness** *n.* **—feath′er•y** *adj.*

feather bed. A mattress stuffed with feathers or down.

feath•er•bed (fĕth′ər-bĕd′) *v.* **-bedded, -bedding. 1.** To employ more workers than are actually needed for a given purpose or to limit their production. **2.** To be so employed.

feath•er•weight (fĕth′ər-wāt′) *n.* **1.** A boxer weighing between 118 and 127 pounds. **2.** One that weighs very little.

fea•ture (fē′chər) *n.* **1. a.** The shape or aspect of the face: *hard of feature.* **b. features.** The face or its lineaments: *regular features.* **2.** Any prominent or distinctive characteristic. **3.** The main presentation at a motion-picture theater. **4.** A prominent article in a newspaper or periodical. **5.** Anything advertised as a sales inducement. **—v. -tured, -turing. 1.** To make prominent; publicize. **2.** To be a prominent part of. **3.** To draw the features of. [< L *factūra,* a making, formation < *facere,* to do.]

Feb. February.

feb•rile (fĕb′rəl, fē′brəl) *adj.* Of or having fever. [< L *febris,* FEVER.]

Feb•ru•ar•y (fĕb′rōō-ĕr′ē, fĕb′yōō-) *n., pl.* **-ies** or **-ys.** The 2nd month of the year. February has 28 days, 29 in leap years. [< L *februa,* festival of purification held on February 15.]

fe•ces (fē′sēz) *pl.n.* Also **fae•ces.** Waste excreted from the bowels; excrement. [< L *faex* (*faec-*), dregs.] **—fe′cal** *adj.*

feck•less (fĕk′lĭs) *adj.* **1.** Feeble; ineffectual. **2.** Careless; irresponsible. [< EFFECT + -LESS.]

fe•cund (fē′kənd, fĕk′ənd) *adj.* Fertile; productive; prolific. [< L *fēcundus.*] **—fe•cun′di•ty** (fĭ-kŭn′də-tē) *n.*

fe•cun•date (fē′kən-dāt′, fĕk′ən-) *v.* **-dated, -dating.** To impregnate; fertilize.

fed (fĕd). *p.t.* & *p.p.* of **feed.**

fed. federal; federated; federation.

fed•er•al (fĕd′ər-əl) *adj.* **1.** Of or constituting a union of states recognizing the sovereignty of a central authority while retaining certain residual powers. **2.** Of or pertaining to the central government of a federation. **3. Federal. a.** Of or pertaining to the central government

---

ô paw, for/oi boy/ou out/ŏŏ took/ōō coo/p pop/r run/s sauce/sh shy/t to/th thin/*th* the/
ŭ cut/ûr fur/v van/w wag/y yes/z size/zh vision/ə ago, item, edible, gallop, circus/

of the U.S. **b.** Of or supporting the Federal government during the Civil War; pro-Union. —*n.* A supporter of federation or federal government. [< L *foedus (foeder-),* league, treaty.]

fed·er·al·ism (fĕd′ər-ə-lĭz′əm) *n.* **1.** The doctrine or system of federal government. **2.** The advocacy of such a government.

fed·er·al·ist (fĕd′ər-ə-lĭst) *n.* **1.** An advocate of federalism. **2. Federalist.** A member of a U.S. political party of the 1790's, advocating a strong federal government.

fed·er·al·ize (fĕd′ər-ə-līz′) *v.* **-ized, -izing. 1.** To unite in a federal union. **2.** To put under federal control. —**fed′er·al·i·za′tion** *n.*

fed·er·ate (fĕd′ə-rāt′) *v.* **-ated, -ating.** To join or unite in a league, federal union, or similar association. —**fed′e·ra′tion** *n.*

fe·do·ra (fĭ-dôr′ə, -dōr′ə) *n.* A soft felt hat with a crown creased lengthwise and a brim. [< *Fédora,* play by Victorien Sardou (1831–1908), French playwright.]

fee (fē) *n.* **1.** A fixed charge. **2.** A payment for professional services. **3.** *Law.* An inherited or heritable estate in land. **4.** An estate in land held from a feudal lord. [< Frank **fehu-ōd,* payment.]

fee·ble (fē′bəl) *adj.* **-bler, -blest. 1.** Frail or infirm. **2.** Lacking vigor or force; ineffective. **3.** Faint; slight: *a feeble cry.* [< L *flēbilis,* to be wept over, lamentable.] —**fee′ble·ness** *n.* —**fee′bly** *adv.*

fee·ble-mind·ed (fē′bəl-mīn′dĭd) *adj.* Mentally deficient. —**fee′ble·mind′ed·ness** *n.*

feed (fēd) *v.* **fed, feeding. 1.** To give food to or provide as food or nourishment. **2.** To eat. **3.** To supply a flow of (a material to be consumed or utilized). —**be fed up.** To be out of patience and disgusted. —*n.* **1.** Food for animals. **2.** *Informal.* A meal. **3. a.** Material supplied, as to a machine. **b.** An apparatus that supplies such material. [< OE *fēdan.* See **pā-.**] —**feed′a·ble** *adj.* —**feed′er** *n.*

feed·back (fēd′băk′) *n.* The return of a portion of the output of any process or system to the input.

feel (fēl) *v.* **felt, feeling. 1.** To perceive, give, or produce through the sense of touch. **2. a.** To touch. **b.** To examine by touching. **3. a.** To experience (an emotion). **b.** To be aware of; sense. **c.** To suffer from. **4.** To believe or consider. **5.** To have compassion or sympathy. —*n.* **1.** Perception by touching or feeling. **2.** The sense of touch. **3.** The nature or quality of something perceived. [< OE *fēlan.* See **pōl-.**]

feel·er (fē′lər) *n.* **1.** An exploratory suggestion or remark. **2.** A sensory organ such as an antenna or tentacle.

feel·ing (fē′lĭng) *n.* **1. a.** The sensation involving perception by touch. **b.** A sensation perceived by touch. **c.** Any physical sensation. **2. a.** Any affective state or disposition. **b.** Emotion: *a deep feeling.* **3.** An awareness; impression. **4. feelings.** Sensibilities. **5.** Opinion. **6.** Sympathy. **7.** A bent; aptitude. —*adj.* **1. a.** Sensitive. **b.** Easily moved emotionally. **2.** Sympathetic. —**feel′ing·ly** *adv.*

feet. *pl.* of **foot.**

feign (fān) *v.* To give a false appearance (of);

pretend; sham. [< OF *feindre* < L *fingere,* to form, shape.] —**feign′er** *n.*

feint (fānt) *n.* A feigned attack designed to draw defensive action away from an intended target. —**feint** *v.*

feld·spar (fĕld′spär′, fĕl′-) *n.* Any of a group of abundant rock-forming minerals consisting of silicates of aluminum with potassium, sodium, calcium, and rarely barium. [Part trans of obs G *Feldspath,* "field spar."]

fe·lic·i·tate (fĭ-lĭs′ə-tāt′) *v.* **-tated, -tating.** To congratulate. [< L *fēlīx,* happy.] —**fe·lic′i·ta′tion** *n.* —**fe·lic′i·ta′tor** *n.*

fe·lic·i·tous (fĭ-lĭs′ə-təs) *adj.* **1.** Well-chosen; apt. **2.** Having an appropriate and agreeable manner or style. —**fe·lic′i·tous·ly** *adv.*

fe·lic·i·ty (fĭ-lĭs′ə-tē) *n., pl.* **-ties. 1.** Great happiness. **2.** Something that causes or produces happiness. **3. a.** Aptness of expression. **b.** An instance of this.

fe·line (fē′līn′) *adj.* **1.** Of or pertaining to cats or related animals, such as lions and tigers. **2.** Catlike, as in slyness or suppleness. —*n.* A feline animal. [< L *fēlēs,* cat.]

fell¹ (fĕl) *v.* **1.** To cut or knock down. **2.** To sew or finish (a seam) with the raw edges flattened and turned under. [< OE *fellan, fyllan,* strike down, fell. See **phol-.**]

fell² (fĕl) *adj.* **1.** Cruel; fierce; unsparing. **2.** Deadly; lethal. [< ML *fellō,* wicked person, felon.] —**fell′ness** *n.*

fell³ (fĕl). *p.t.* of **fall.**

fel·lah (fĕl′ə, fə-lä′) *n.* A peasant or agricultural laborer in Arab countries. [Ar *fellāh.*]

fel·low (fĕl′ō) *n.* **1.** A man or boy. **2.** Any human being. **3.** A comrade; associate. **4. a.** An equal; peer. **b.** One of a pair; mate. **5.** A member of a learned society. **6.** A recipient of a grant for advanced study. [< ON *fēlagi,* fellow, one who lays down money.]

fel·low·ship (fĕl′ō-shĭp′) *n.* **1.** Companionship, comradeship, or friendship. **2.** A union of friends or equals. **3. a.** A graduate stipend. **b.** A foundation awarding such grants.

fellow traveler. One who sympathizes with an organized group, as the Communist Party, without actually joining it.

fel·ly (fĕl′ē) *n., pl.* **-lies.** Also **fel·loe** (fĕl′ō). The rim of a wheel supported by spokes. [< OE *felg* < Gmc **felgam.*]

fel·on¹ (fĕl′ən) *n.* One who has committed a felony. [< VL **fellō.*]

fel·on² (fĕl′ən) *n.* An infection at the end of a finger near the nail. [Poss < L *fel,* bile, venom.]

fel·o·ny (fĕl′ə-nē) *n., pl.* **-nies.** Any of several crimes, such as murder, rape, or burglary. —**fe·lo′ni·ous** (fə-lō′nē-əs) *adj.*

felt¹ (fĕlt) *n.* **1.** A fabric of matted, compressed fibers, as wool or fur. **2.** Any material resembling this. [< OE. See **pel-¹.**]

felt² (fĕlt). *p.t. & p.p.* of **feel.**

fem. feminine.

fe·male (fē′māl′) *adj.* **1.** Of, pertaining to, or designating the sex that produces ova or bears young. **2.** Characteristic of or appropriate to this sex; feminine. **3.** Consisting of members of this sex. —*n.* A female person, plant, or animal. [< L *fēmina,* woman, female.] —**fe′-male·ness** *n.*

fem·i·nine (fĕm′ə-nĭn) *adj.* **1.** Of or belonging to the female sex. **2.** Characterized by qualities attributed to women. **3.** Indicating or belonging to the gender of words or grammatical forms that are classified as female. —*n.* **1.** The feminine gender. **2.** A word or form belonging to that gender. [< L *fēmina,* FEMALE.] —**fem′i·nin′i·ty** *n.*

fem·i·nism (fĕm′ə-nĭz′əm) *n.* Militant advocacy of equal rights and status for women.

fe·mur (fē′mər) *n., pl.* -**murs** or **femora** (fĕm′ər-ə). **1.** The proximal bone of the lower or hind limb in vertebrates, situated between the pelvis and knee in humans. **2.** The thigh. [L, thigh.] —**fem′o·ral** (fĕm′ər-əl) *adj.*

fen (fĕn) *n.* Low, flat, swampy land; bog; marsh. [< OE *fenn.*]

fe·na·gle. Variant of **finagle.**

fence (fĕns) *n.* **1.** An enclosure, barrier, or boundary made of posts, boards, wire, stakes, or rails. **2. a.** A receiver of stolen goods. **b.** A place where such goods are received and sold. —**on the fence.** *Informal.* Undecided as to which of two sides to support; neutral. —*v.* **fenced, fencing. 1.** To surround, close in, or close off by means of a fence. **2.** To practice the art of fencing. **3.** To avoid giving direct answers; be evasive. **4.** To act as a fence for stolen goods. [< DEFENSE.]

fenc·er (fĕn′sər) *n.* One who fences, as with a foil.

fenc·ing (fĕn′sĭng) *n.* **1.** The art or practice of using a foil or saber. **2.** Material used in the construction of fences.

fend (fĕnd) *v.* To ward off, deflect, or repel. —**fend for oneself.** To provide for oneself. [< DEFEND.]

fend·er (fĕn′dər) *n.* **1.** A guard device over the wheel of an automobile. **2.** A screen in front of a fireplace.

fen·nel (fĕn′əl) *n.* **1.** A plant with aromatic seeds used as flavoring. **2.** The seeds or edible stalks of this plant. [< L *fēnum,* hay.]

—**fer.** *comb. form.* Agency, bearing, or production: *aquifer.* [< L *ferre,* to carry, bear.]

fer·ment (fûr′mĕnt′) *n.* **1.** Something that causes fermentation, as a yeast or enzyme. **2.** A state of agitation or unrest. —*v.* (fər-mĕnt′). **1.** To produce by or as if by fermentation. **2.** To undergo or cause to undergo fermentation. **3.** To be turbulent; seethe. [< L *fermentum.*] —**fer·ment′a·ble** *adj.*

fer·men·ta·tion (fûr′mĕn-tā′shən) *n.* **1.** Chemical splitting of complex organic compounds into relatively simple substances, esp. the conversion of sugar to carbon dioxide and alcohol by yeast. **2.** Unrest; commotion.

fer·mi·um (fûr′mē-əm) *n. Symbol* **Fm** A synthetic metallic element. Atomic number 100, longest-lived isotope Fm 257. [< E. *Fermi* (1901–1954), Italian-born American physicist.]

fern (fûrn) *n.* Any of numerous flowerless plants characteristically having fronds with divided leaflets and reproducing by means of spores. [< OE *fearn.*]

fe·ro·cious (fə-rō′shəs) *adj.* **1.** Extremely savage; fierce. **2.** Extreme; relentless. [< L *ferōx,* wild, fierce.] —**fe·ro′cious·ly** *adv.*

fe·roc·i·ty (fə-rŏs′ə-tē) *n., pl.* -**ties.** The condition or quality of being ferocious.

—**ferous.** *comb. form.* Bearing, producing, or containing: *crystalliferous.* [< -FER + -OUS.]

fer·ret[1] (fĕr′ĭt) *n.* **1.** A domesticated, usually white form of the Old World polecat, often trained to hunt rats or rabbits. **2.** A related weasellike North American mammal. —*v.* **1.** To hunt with a ferret. **2.** To drive out; expel. **3.** To uncover and bring to light by searching (with *out*). [< VL **fūrittus,* little thief.] —**fer′ret·er** *n.* —**fer′ret·y** *adj.*

fer·ret[2] (fĕr′ĭt) *n.* Also **fer·ret·ing** (-ĭng). A narrow piece of tape used to bind or edge fabric. [Prob < It *fioretti,* floss silk.]

fer·ric (fĕr′ĭk) *adj.* Of or containing iron, esp. with valence 3. [FERR(O)- + -IC.]

ferric oxide. A dark compound, Fe_2O_3, occurring naturally as hematite ore and rust.

Fer·ris wheel. Also **fer·ris wheel.** A large upright, rotating wheel having suspended cars in which passengers ride for amusement. [< G. *Ferris* (1859–1896), American engineer.]

fer·rite (fĕr′īt) *n.* Any of a group of nonmetallic, ceramiclike, usually ferromagnetic compounds of ferric oxide with other oxides.

ferro-. *comb. form.* Iron. [< L *ferrum,* iron.]

fer·ro·mag·net·ic (fĕr′ō-măg′nĕt′ĭk) *adj.* Pertaining to or characteristic of substances, such as iron, nickel, cobalt, and various alloys, that acquire high magnetization in relatively weak magnetic fields. —**fer′ro·mag′net** *n.* —**fer′ro·mag′ne·tism′** *n.*

fer·ro·type (fĕr′ə-tīp′) *n.* **1.** A positive photograph made directly on an iron plate varnished with a thin sensitized film. **2.** The process by which such photographs are made.

fer·rous (fĕr′əs) *adj.* Of or containing iron, esp. with valence 2.

ferrous oxide. A black powdery compound, FeO, used in the manufacture of steel.

fer·rule (fĕr′əl, -ōōl′) *n.* A metal ring or cap attached to or near the end of a cane or wooden handle to prevent splitting. [< L *viriola,* little bracelet.]

fer·ry (fĕr′ē) *n., pl.* -**ries. 1.** A service for transport across a body of water. **2.** A ferryboat. **3.** The place of embarkation of a ferryboat. **4.** A service for transporting people or goods by aircraft, usually over short distances. —*v.* -**ried, -rying. 1.** To transport across a body of water. **2.** To cross on a ferry. **3.** To transport from one place to another. [Prob < ON *ferja.*]

fer·ry·boat (fĕr′ē-bōt′) *n.* A boat used to ferry passengers or goods.

fer·ry·man (fĕr′ē-mən) *n.* One who operates a ferry.

fer·tile (fûrt′l) *adj.* **1.** Capable of initiating, sustaining, or supporting reproduction. **2.** Rich in material needed to sustain plant growth: *fertile soil.* **3.** Highly or continuously productive; prolific: *a fertile imagination.* [< L *ferre,* to bear, carry, produce.] *adv.* —**fer·til′i·ty, fer′tile·ness** *n.*

fer·til·ize (fûrt′l-īz′) *v.* -**ized, -izing. 1.** To initiate biological reproduction, esp. to provide with sperm or pollen. **2.** To make fertile, as by spreading fertilizer. —**fer′til•i•za′tion** *n.*

fer•til•iz•er (fûrt′l-ī′zər) *n.* **1.** One that fertilizes. **2.** Any of a large number of natural and synthetic materials, including manure and nitrogen, phosphorus, and potassium compounds, spread on or worked into soil to increase its fertility.

fer•ule (fĕr′əl, -ōōl′) *n.* A baton, cane, or stick used in punishing children. [L *ferula,* giant fennel.]

fer•ven•cy (fûr′vən-sē) *n.* Fervor.

fer•vent (fûr′vənt) *adj.* **1.** Passionate; ardent. **2.** Extremely hot; glowing. [< L *fervēre,* to boil, glow.] —**fer′vent•ly** *adv.*

fer•vid (fûr′vĭd) *adj.* **1.** Zealous; impassioned. **2.** Extremely hot; burning. [< L *fervēre,* to glow, boil.] —**fer′vid•ly** *adv.*

fer•vor (fûr′vər) *n.* **1.** Ardor; enthusiasm. **2.** Intense heat. [< L *fervēre,* to boil.]

fes•tal (fĕs′təl) *adj.* Festive. [< L *fēsta,* FEAST.]

fes•ter (fĕs′tər) *v.* **1.** To generate pus; suppurate. **2.** To form an ulcer. **3.** To be or become a source of irritation; rankle. [< L *fistula,* FISTULA.]

fes•ti•val (fĕs′tə-vəl) *n.* **1.** A day of religious feasting or special observances. **2.** A programmed series of related cultural events: *a film festival.* **3.** Conviviality; revelry. [< L *fēstivus,* FESTIVE.]

fes•tive (fĕs′tĭv) *adj.* **1.** Of or appropriate to a feast or festival. **2.** Merry; joyous. [L *fēstivus* < *fēstus,* joyous.] —**fes′tive•ly** *adv.*

fes•tiv•i•ty (fĕs-tĭv′ə-tē) *n., pl.* -**ties.** **1.** A joyous feast, holiday, or celebration; festival. **2.** The joy or gaiety of a festival. **3. festivities.** Festive activities.

fes•toon (fĕs-tōōn′) *n.* **1.** A decorative garland suspended in a curve between two points. **2.** A sculptured representation of this. —*v.* **1.** To decorate with or as with festoons. **2.** To form festoons. [< It *festone,* festal ornament.]

fe•tal (fēt′l) *adj.* Also **foe•tal** (fēt′l). Pertaining to the nature of a fetus.

fetch (fĕch) *v.* **1.** To go after and return with. **2.** To cause to come forth. **3. a.** To draw in (breath); inhale. **b.** To heave (a sigh). **4.** To strike or deal (a blow). [< OE *feccan.*] —**fetch′er** *n.*

fetch•ing (fĕch′ĭng) *adj.* Attractive; captivating. —**fetch′ing•ly** *adv.*

fete (fāt) *n.* Also **fête.** **1.** A festival. **2.** An elaborate outdoor party. **3.** Any elaborate party. —*v.* **feted, feting. 1.** To honor or celebrate with a fete. **2.** To pay honor to. [< OF *feste,* feast.]

fet•id (fĕt′ĭd, fē′tĭd) *adj.* Foul-smelling; stinking. [< L *fētēre,* to stink.]

fet•ish (fĕt′ĭsh) *n.* **1.** An object believed to have magical power. **2.** An object of obsessive attention or reverence. [< L *factītius,* made by art.] —**fet′ish•ism′** *n.* —**fet′ish•ist** *n. & adj.*

fet•lock (fĕt′lŏk′) *n.* A projection above and behind the hoof of a horse or related animal. [ME *fitlok.*]

fet•ter (fĕt′ər) *n.* **1.** A chain or shackle attached to the ankles. **2. fetters.** Anything that serves to restrict; restraint. —*v.* **1.** To shackle. **2.** To

restrict or confine. [< OE *feter.* See **ped-**[1].]

fet•tle (fĕt′l) *n.* Condition: *in fine fettle.* [< ME *fetlen,* to shape, make ready.]

fe•tus (fē′təs) *n., pl.* -**tuses.** Also **foe•tus** (fē′təs). The unborn young of a viviparous vertebrate; in humans, the unborn young from the end of the eighth week to the moment of birth as distinguished from the earlier embryo. [L *fētus,* pregnancy, fetus.]

feud (fyōōd) *n.* A protracted quarrel; vendetta. [< OHG *fēhida.*] —**feud** *v.*

feu•dal (fyōōd′l) *adj.* **1.** Pertaining to or characteristic of feudalism. **2.** Of or pertaining to a medieval fee. [< ML *feudum,* a feudal estate.] —**feu′dal•ly** *adv.*

feu•dal•ism (fyōōd′l-ĭz′əm) *n.* The political system of Europe from the 9th to about the 15th century A.D., based on the relation of lord to vassal as a result of land being held on condition of homage and service. —**feu′dal•ist** *n.* —**feu′dal•is′tic** *adj.*

feu•da•to•ry (fyōō′də-tôr′ē, -tōr′ē) *n., pl.* -**ries.** **1.** A vassal. **2.** A feudal fee. —*adj.* **1.** Of or characteristic of a feudal relationship. **2.** Owing feudal allegiance.

fe•ver (fē′vər) *n.* **1.** Abnormally high body temperature. **2.** A disease characterized by abnormally high body temperatures. **3.** Heightened activity or excitement; agitation. **4.** A contagious, short-lived enthusiasm; craze. [< L *febris.*] —**fe′ver•ish** *adj.* —**fe′ver•ish•ly** *adv.* —**fe′ver•ish•ness** *n.*

few (fyōō) *adj.* **fewer, fewest.** Amounting to or consisting of a small number. —*n. (takes pl. v.).* **1.** A small number of persons or things. **2.** A select group or elite: *the happy few.* —*pron. (takes pl. v.).* A small number. [< OE *fēa, fēawe.* See **pōu-**.] —**few′ness** *n.*

Usage: Fewer, in contrast to *less,* is the preferred term in most examples involving reference to numbers or units considered individually and therefore capable of being counted or enumerated. *Less* refers to collective quantity or to something abstract: *fewer people, less noise; fewer chances, less opportunity.*

fey (fā) *adj.* **1.** *Scot.* **a.** Fated to die soon. **b.** Marked by a sense of approaching death. **2.** Clairvoyant. **3.** Enchanted; elfin. [< OE *fǣge.* See **peig-**[2].]

fez (fĕz) *n., pl.* **fezzes.** A man's felt cap in the shape of a truncated cone, usually red with a black tassel, worn chiefly in the E Mediterranean region. [< *Fez,* Morocco.]

ff. **1.** folios. **2.** following.

FHA Federal Housing Administration.

fi•an•cé (fē′än-sā′, fē-än′sā′) *n.* A man engaged to be married. [< OF *fier,* to trust.]

fi•an•cée (fē′än-sā′, fē-än′sā′) *n.* A woman engaged to be married.

fi•as•co (fē-ăs′kō) *n., pl.* -**coes** or -**cos.** A complete failure. [< It *(far) fiasco,* "(to make) a bottle."]

fi•at (fī′ăt′, -ət, fē′ăt′) *n.* An arbitrary order or decree. [L *fiat,* "let it be done."]

fib (fĭb) *n.* An inconsequential lie. —*v.* **fibbed, fibbing.** To tell a fib. [?] —**fib′ber** *n.*

fi•ber (fī′bər) *n.* Also *chiefly Brit.* **fi•bre.** **1.** Any

---

ă pat/ā ate/âr care/ä bar/b bib/ch chew/d deed/ĕ pet/ē be/f fit/g gag/h hat/hw what/
ĭ pit/ī pie/îr pier/j judge/k kick/l lid, fatal/m mum/n no, sudden/ng sing/ŏ pot/ō go/

slender, elongated structure; a filament or strand, as of plant, muscle, or nerve tissue, or a synthetic substance. **2.** Internal strength; toughness: *moral fiber.* [< L *fibra.*]

fi·ber·board (fī′bər-bôrd′, -bōrd′) *n.* A building material composed of wood or other plant fibers compressed into rigid sheets.

fiber glass. A composite material consisting of glass fibers in resin.

fi·broid (fī′broid′) *adj.* Resembling or composed of fibrous tissue.

fi·bro·sis (fī-brō′sĭs) *n.* The formation of fibrous tissue, as in a reparative or reactive process, in excess of amounts normally present.

fi·brous (fī′brəs) *adj.* Consisting of or resembling fibers.

fib·u·la (fĭb′yə-lə) *n., pl.* **-lae** (-lē′) or **-las.** The outer and smaller of two bones of the leg. [L *fibula.*]

–fic, *comb. form.* The making, causing, or creating of: **terrific.** [< L *-ficus* < *facere,* to do, make.]

fi·chu (fĭsh′ōō) *n.* A woman's triangular scarf worn over the shoulders and crossed or tied in front. [F.]

fick·le (fĭk′əl) *adj.* Changeable; inconstant; capricious. [< OE *ficol,* false. See **peig-**[2].] —**fick′le·ness** *n.*

fic·tion (fĭk′shən) *n.* **1.** Something invented or imagined. **2. a.** The category of literature with imaginary characters and events, including novels, short stories, etc. **b.** A work of this category. [< L *fictiō,* a making, fashioning.] —**fic′tion·al** *adj.* —**fic′tion·al·ly** *adv.*

fic·ti·tious (fĭk-tĭsh′əs) *adj.* **1.** Nonexistent; imaginary; unreal. **2.** Purposefully deceptive; false: *a fictitious name.*

fid·dle (fĭd′l) *n.* A violin. —*v.* **1.** *Informal.* To play a violin. **2.** To fidget. [< L *vītulārī,* to celebrate a victory.] —**fid′dler** *n.*

fid·dle·sticks (fĭd′l-stĭks′) *interj.* Expressive of mild annoyance or impatience.

fi·del·i·ty (fĭ-dĕl′ə-tē, fī-) *n., pl.* **-ties. 1.** Faithfulness; loyalty. **2.** Truthfulness; accuracy. **3.** The degree to which an electronic system accurately reproduces at its output the essential characteristics of its input signal. [< L *fidēs,* faith.]

fidg·et (fĭj′ĭt) *v.* **1.** To move nervously or restlessly. **2.** To play or fuss; fiddle (with *with*). —*n.* **1.** Often **fidgets.** A condition of restlessness. **2.** One who fidgets. [Prob < ON *fikjast.*] —**fidg′et·i·ness** *n.* —**fidg′et·y** *adj.*

fi·du·ci·ar·y (fĭ-d/yōō′shē-ĕr′ē, fī-) *adj.* **1.** Pertaining to the holding of something in trust. **2.** Held in trust. —*n., pl.* **-ies.** A trustee. [< L *fidūcia,* trust.]

fie (fī) *interj.* Expressive of distaste or shock. [< L *fī.*]

fief (fēf) *n.* A feudal estate. [< OF *fief,* fee.]

field (fēld) *n.* **1.** A broad, level expanse of open land. **2.** A piece of land devoted to a particular crop. **3.** A portion of land containing a specified natural resource: *an oil field.* **4.** An airfield or airport. **5.** A background area, as on a flag. **6.** *Sports.* **a.** An area in which a sports event takes place; ground; stadium. **b.** All the contestants in an event. **7.** An area of activity or knowledge. **8.** A battlefield. **9.** A region of space characterized by a physical property, such as gravitational force, having a determinable value at every point in the region. —*v. Sports.* **1.** To retrieve (a ball) and perform the required maneuver. **2.** To put (a team) into a contest. [< OE *feld.* See **pelə-**.] —**field′er** *n.*

field glass. Often **field glasses.** A portable binocular instrument used esp. for viewing distant objects.

field goal. 1. *Football.* A score worth three points made by kicking the ball over the crossbar and between the goal posts. **2.** *Basketball.* A score worth two points made by throwing the ball through the basket in regulation play.

field magnet. A magnet used to provide a magnetic field in an electrical device such as a generator or motor.

field marshal. An officer ranking just below the commander in chief in some European armies.

field of force. A region of space throughout which the force produced by a single agent, such as an electric current, is operative.

fiend (fēnd) *n.* **1.** An evil spirit; demon. **2.** A diabolically evil or wicked person. **3.** *Informal.* An addict: *a dope fiend; a crossword-puzzle fiend.* [< OE *fēond.*] —**fiend′ish** *adj.* —**fiend′ish·ly** *adv.* —**fiend′ish·ness** *n.*

fierce (fîrs) *adj.* **1.** Having a savage and violent nature; ferocious. **2.** Extremely severe or violent; terrible. [< L *ferus,* wild.] —**fierce′ly** *adv.* —**fierce′ness** *n.*

fier·y (fîr′ē, fī′ə-rē) *adj.* **-ier, -iest. 1.** Consisting of or containing fire. **2.** Of or like fire. **3.** Charged with emotion; fervent. **4.** Emotionally volatile; tempestuous. —**fier′i·ly** *adv.* —**fier′i·ness** *n.*

fi·es·ta (fē-ĕs′tə) *n.* **1.** A religious feast or holiday. **2.** Any celebration or festival. [< L *fēstus,* joyous, festive.]

fife (fīf) *n.* A musical instrument similar to a flute but higher in range, used primarily to accompany drums. [< OHG *pfiffa.*]

fif·teen (fĭf-tēn′) *n.* The cardinal number written ten 15 or in Roman numerals XV. [< OE *fiftēne.* See **penkwe.**] —**fif·teen′** *adj. & pron.*

fif·teenth (fĭf-tēnth′) *n.* **1.** The ordinal number 15 in a series. **2.** One of 15 equal parts. —**fif·teenth′** *adj. & adv.*

fifth (fĭfth) *n.* **1.** The ordinal number 5 in a series. **2.** One of 5 equal parts. **3.** One-fifth of a gallon of liquor; four-fifths of a quart. [< OE *fifta.* See **penkwe.**] —**fifth** *adj. & adv.*

fif·ti·eth (fĭf′tē-ĭth) *n.* **1.** The ordinal number 50 in a series. **2.** One of 50 equal parts. —**fif′ti·eth** *adj. & adv.*

fif·ty (fĭf′tē) *n.* The cardinal number written 50 or in Roman numerals L. [< OE *fiftig.* See **penkwe.**] —**fif′ty** *adj. & pron.*

fif·ty-fif·ty (fĭf′tē-fĭf′tē) *adj. Informal.* Divided or shared in two equal portions. —**fif′ty-fif′ty** *adv.*

fig (fĭg) *n.* **1.** The pear-shaped, many-seeded, edible fruit of a widely cultivated tree. **2.** A

ô paw, for/oi boy/ou out/ōō took/ōō coo/p pop/r run/s sauce/sh shy/t to/th thin/*th* the/
ŭ cut/ûr fur/v van/w wag/y yes/z size/zh vision/ə ago, item, edible, gallop, circus/

tree bearing such fruit. **3.** A trivial amount; whit: *not care a fig.* [< L *ficus.*]

fig. figurative; figuratively; figure.

fight (fīt) *v.* **fought, fighting. 1.** To participate in combat or battle. **2.** To struggle; contend (with). **3.** To quarrel; argue. **4.** To box or wrestle (against) in a ring. **5.** To try to prevent; oppose. **6.** To wage (a battle). **7.** To make (one's way), as by combat. **—fight off. 1.** To defend against or drive back (a hostile force). **2.** To struggle to avoid: *fight off temptation.* **—n. 1.** A battle; combat. **2.** A struggle, quarrel, or conflict. **3.** A boxing match; a bout. **4.** Inclination to fight; pugnacity. [< OE *feohtan.*]

fight·er (fī'tər) *n.* **1.** One engaged in fighting; a combatant. **2.** A pugilist. **3.** A pugnacious or determined person. **4.** A fast, maneuverable combat aircraft.

fig·ment (fĭg'mənt) *n.* **1.** Something imagined. **2.** An arbitrary notion. [< L *fingere,* to mold, fashion.]

fig·ur·a·tive (fĭg'yər-ə-tĭv) *adj.* **1.** Based on figures of speech; not literal; metaphorical. **2.** Represented by a figure; emblematic. **—fig'ur·a·tive·ly** *adv.* **—fig'ur·a·tive·ness** *n.*

fig·ure (fĭg'yər) *n.* **1.** A written symbol representing anything other than a letter, esp. a number. **2. figures.** Mathematical calculation involving the use of such symbols. **3.** An amount represented in numbers. **4.** The outline, form, or silhouette of a thing, esp. of a human body. **5.** An individual, esp. a well-known personage. **6.** The impression an individual makes: *He cuts a dashing figure.* **7.** A diagram, design, or pattern. **8.** A group of steps in a dance. **9.** An expression, as a simile. **—v. 1.** To calculate with numbers; compute. **2.** To make a likeness of; represent. **3.** To adorn with a design. **4.** *Informal.* To conclude, believe, or predict. **5.** To be an element; have mention, pertinence, or importance. **—figure on** (or **upon**). *Informal.* **1.** To depend on. **2.** To plan on; expect. **—figure out.** *Informal.* To solve, decipher, or comprehend. [< L *figūra,* form, shape, figure.]

fig·ure·head (fĭg'yər-hĕd') *n.* **1.** A person holding nominal leadership but having no actual authority. **2.** A carved figure on the prow of a ship.

fig·u·rine (fĭg'yə-rēn') *n.* A small sculptured figure; statuette.

Fi·ji (fē'jē). A British colony in the SW Pacific Ocean. Pop. 456,000.

fil·a·gree. Variant of filigree.

fil·a·ment (fĭl'ə-mənt) *n.* **1.** A fine, thin thread or threadlike structure. **2.** A fine wire heated electrically to incandescence in an electric lamp. [< L *filum,* thread.] **—fil'a·men'ta·ry** *adj.* **—fil'a·men'tous** *adj.*

fil·bert (fĭl'bərt) *n.* The rounded, smooth-shelled edible nut of an Old World hazel. [< NF (*noix de*) *filbert,* "nut of Saint *Philibert*" (died A.D. 684), Frankish abbot.]

filch (fĭlch) *v.* To steal; pilfer. [ME *filchen.*] **—filch'er** *n.*

file[1] (fīl) *n.* **1.** A receptacle for keeping papers, cards, etc., in useful order. **2.** A collection of objects kept thus: *the accounts-due file.* **3.** A line of persons, animals, or things positioned one behind another. **—on file.** Catalogued in a file; on hand. **—v. 1.** To put in useful order; catalogue. **2.** To enter (as a legal document) on public record. **3.** To transmit (copy) to a newspaper. **4.** To march or walk in a line. [< L *fīlum,* thread.] **—fil'er** *n.*

file[2] (fīl) *n.* **1.** A tool with hardened ridged surfaces, used in smoothing, polishing, grinding, or boring. **2.** *Brit. Slang.* A deceitful, cunning person. **—v.** **filed, filing.** To work with or as if with a file. [< OE *fēol, fil.* See peig-[1].] **—fil'er** *n.*

file clerk. One who is employed to maintain the files of an office.

fi·let mi·gnon (fĭ-lā' mĭn-yŏn'). A small, round, very choice cut of beef from the loin. [F, "small or dainty fillet."]

fil·i·al (fĭl'ē-əl) *adj.* Of, pertaining to, or befitting a son or daughter: *filial obedience.* [< L *filius,* son.]

fil·i·bus·ter (fĭl'ə-bŭs'tər) *n.* **1.** Obstructionist tactics, such as the making of prolonged speeches, for the purpose of delaying legislative action. **2.** An adventurer who engages in a private military action in a foreign country. [Orig "freebooter."] **—fil'i·bus'ter** *v.* **—fil'i·bus'-ter·er** *n.*

fil·i·gree (fĭl'ə-grē') *n.* Also **fil·a·gree, fil·la·gree.** Delicate ornamental work made from gold, silver, or other fine twisted wire. **—adj.** Made of or resembling filigree. [< F *filigrane.*]

fil·ing (fī'lĭng) *n.* Often **filings.** A particle or shaving removed by a file.

Fil·i·pi·no (fĭl'ə-pē'nō) *n., pl.* **-nos.** A native, citizen, or inhabitant of the Philippines. **—adj.** Of, relating to, or pertaining to the Philippines or Filipinos.

fill (fĭl) *v.* **1.** To make or become full. **2.** To stop or plug up. **3.** To satisfy; fulfill: *fill the requirements.* **4.** To supply the necessary materials for: *fill a prescription.* **5.** To supply (an empty space) with material. **6.** To put someone into (a specific office or position). **7.** To occupy (a specific office or position). **—fill in. 1.** To write in. **2.** To act as a substitute. **—fill out. 1.** To complete (a document). **2.** To become fuller or rounder. **—fill up.** To make or become full. **—n. 1.** A full supply: *eat one's fill.* **2.** A built-up piece of land; embankment. **—have one's fill.** To have enough or too much; be thoroughly sated or weary. [< OE *fyllan.* See pel-[5].] **—fill'er** *n.*

fil·let (fĭl'ĭt) *n.* **1.** A narrow strip of ribbon or similar material. **2.** (*often* fĭ-lā', fĭl'ā). Also **fi·let.** A strip or slice of boneless meat or fish. **—v. 1.** (fĭl'ĭt), **filleted** (fĭl'ĭt-ĭd), **filleting** (fĭl'ĭt-ĭng). To bind or decorate with or as with a fillet. **2.** (fĭ-lā', fĭl'ā), **filleted** (fĭ-lād', fĭl'ād'), **filleting** (fĭ-lā'ĭng, fĭl'ā'ĭng). Also **fi·let.** To slice, bone, or make into a fillet or fillets. [< L *fīlum,* thread.]

fill·ing (fĭl'ĭng) *n.* **1.** Something used to fill a space, cavity, or container. **2.** The threads that cross the warp in weaving; weft.

fil·lip (fĭl'əp) *n.* **1.** A snap of the fingers. **2.** An incentive; stimulus. [Imit.] **—fil'lip** *v.*

Fill·more (fĭl′môr′, -mōr′), **Millard.** 1800–1874. 13th President of the U.S. (1850–53).

Millard Fillmore

fil·ly (fĭl′ē) *n., pl.* **-lies.** A young female horse. [< ON *fylja.*]

film (fĭlm) *n.* **1.** A thin skin or membrane. **2.** Any thin covering or coating. **3.** A thin sheet or strip of flexible cellulose material coated with a photosensitive emulsion, used to make photographic negatives or transparencies. **4. a.** A motion picture. **b.** Motion pictures collectively regarded as an art. —*v.* **1.** To cover with a film. **2.** To make a motion picture of. [< OE *filmen.* See **pel-⁴.**] —**film′i·ly** *adv.* —**film′i·ness** *n.* —**film′y** *adj.*

film·dom (fĭlm′dəm) *n.* The motion picture industry or those in it.

film·go·er (fĭlm′gō′ər) *n.* One who goes to see motion pictures.

fil·ter (fĭl′tər) *n.* **1.** Any porous substance through which a liquid or gas is passed in order to remove certain constituents. **2.** A device containing or consisting of such a substance so used. **3.** Any of various electric, electronic, acoustic, or optical devices used to reject signals, vibrations, or radiations of certain frequencies while passing others. —*v.* **1.** To pass through a filter. **2.** To remove by passing through a filter. [< Frank **filtir.*] —**fil·tra′tion** *n.*

fil·ter·a·ble (fĭl′tər-ə-bəl, fĭl′trə-) *adj.* Also **fil·tra·ble. 1.** Capable of being filtered, esp. capable of being removed by filtering. **2.** Sufficiently minute to pass through a fine filter, thereby maintaining the infectivity of the filtrate, as certain viruses and some bacteria. —**fil′ter·a·bil′i·ty** *n.*

filth (fĭlth) *n.* **1.** Foul or dirty matter. **2.** A dirty or foul condition. **3.** Obscene material or language. [< OE *fÿlth,* putrid matter. See **pu-.**] —**filth′i·ness** *n.* —**filth′y** *adj.*

fil·trate (fĭl′trāt′) *n.* The portion of the material subjected to filtration that passes through the filter.

fin (fĭn) *n.* **1.** One of the membranous swimming and balancing appendages extending from the body of a fish, whale, etc. **2.** Some-

thing resembling a fin in shape or function. [< OE *finn.*]

fin. 1. finance; financial. **2.** finish.

Fin. Finland; Finnish.

fi·na·gle (fĭ-nā′gəl) *v.* **-gled, -gling.** Also **fe·na·gle.** *Informal.* To use or achieve by dubious or crafty methods. [?] —**fi·na′gler** *n.*

fi·nal (fī′nəl) *adj.* **1.** Concluding; last; ultimate. **2.** Decisive; conclusive; unalterable. —*n.* **1.** The last of a series of athletic contests. **2.** The last examination of an academic course. [< L *finis,* end.] —**fi·nal′i·ty** (fī-năl′ə-tē, fĭ-) *n.* —**fi′nal·ly** *adv.*

fi·na·le (fĭ-năl′ē, -nä′lē) *n.* The concluding part, esp. of a musical composition. [It, "final."]

fi·nal·ist (fī′nəl-ĭst) *n.* A contestant in the final session of a competition.

fi·nal·ize (fī′nə-līz′) *v.* **-ized, -izing.** To put into final form; complete.

fi·nance (fĭ-năns′, fī′năns′, fī′năns′) *n.* **1.** The science of the management of money. **2.** **fi·nances.** Monetary resources. —*v.* To supply the funds or capital for. [< OF *finer,* to end, settle.] —**fi·nan′cial** *adj.* —**fi·nan′cial·ly** *adv.*

fin·an·cier (fĭn′ən-sîr′, fī-năn′-, fī′năn-) *n.* One who is occupied with or expert in large-scale financial affairs.

finch (fĭnch) *n.* Any of various small related birds with a short, stout bill, such as a goldfinch, cardinal, or canary. [< OE *finc.* See **sping-.**]

find (fīnd) *v.* **found, finding. 1.** To come upon by accident or after a search. **2.** To attain: *found contentment at last.* **3.** To determine; ascertain. **4.** To consider; regard. **5.** To recover; regain. **6.** To declare as a verdict or conclusion. —*n.* **1.** An act of finding. **2.** That which is found, esp. a rare or valuable discovery. [< OE *findan.* See **pent-.**]

find·er (fīn′dər) *n.* **1.** One that finds. **2.** A device on a camera that indicates what will appear in the field of view of the lens.

find·ing (fīn′dĭng) *n.* **1.** The discovery of something. **2.** Often **findings.** A conclusion reached after investigation.

fine¹ (fīn) *adj.* **finer, finest. 1.** Of superior quality, skill, or appearance. **2.** Most enjoyable; pleasant. **3.** Sharp: *a blade with a fine edge.* **4.** Consisting of extremely small particles: *fine dust.* **5.** Subtle or precise: *a fine shade of meaning.* **6.** Of refined manners; elegant. **7.** Having no clouds; clear: *a fine day.* **8.** *Informal.* Quite well; in satisfactory health. —*adv.* *Informal.* Very well: *doing fine.* [< L *finis,* the end.] —**fine′ly** *adv.* —**fine′ness** *n.*

fine² (fīn) *n.* A sum of money imposed as a penalty for an offense. —*v.* **fined, fining.** To impose a fine on. [< L *finis,* limit, end.]

fine art. Often **fine arts.** Art produced primarily for beauty rather than utility.

fin·er·y (fī′nə-rē) *n.* Elaborate adornment; fine clothing and accessories.

fi·nesse (fĭ-nĕs′) *n.* **1.** Artful delicacy of performance or behavior. **2.** Subtlety; tact. [< OF *fin,* fine.]

fin·ger (fĭng′gər) *n.* **1.** One of the five digits of the hand. **2.** Something resembling a finger.

—*v.* To touch with the fingers; handle. [< OE. See **penkwe**.]

fin•ger•board (fĭng'gər-bôrd', -bōrd') *n.* The part of a stringed instrument against which the strings are pressed in playing.

finger bowl. A small basin to hold water for rinsing the fingers at table.

fin•ger•ing (fĭng'gər-ĭng) *n.* The indication on a musical score of which fingers are to be used in playing.

fin•ger•ling (fĭng'gər-lĭng) *n.* A young or small fish.

fin•ger•nail (fĭng'gər-nāl') *n.* A thin, horny, transparent plate on the tip of each finger.

fin•ger•print (fĭng'gər-prĭnt') *n.* An ink impression of the pattern of ridges on the surface of a finger. —*v.* To take the fingerprints of.

fin•ick•y (fĭn'ĭ-kē) *adj.* Highly fastidious; difficult to please; very fussy.

fi•nis (fĭn'ĭs, fī'nĭs) *n.* The end. [< L *finis.*]

fin•ish (fĭn'ĭsh) *v.* **1.** To attain the end of; terminate; complete. **2.** To reach the end of a task or undertaking. **3.** To consume all of; use up: *finish a pie.* **4.** To give (as wood or cloth) a desired surface texture. —*n.* **1.** The conclusion of something; end. **2.** Surface texture. **3.** The material used in surfacing or finishing something. **4.** Smoothness of execution; perfection. **5.** Polish or refinement in speech, manners, etc. [< L *finis,* end.] —**fin'ish•er** *n.*

fi•nite (fī'nīt') *adj.* **1.** Having boundaries; limited. **2.** Neither infinite nor infinitesimal. [< L *finīre,* to limit, finish.] —**fi'nite•ly** *adv.* —**fi'nite•ness** *n.*

Fin•land (fĭn'lənd). A republic of north-central Europe. Pop. 4,598,000. Cap. Helsinki.

Finland

Finn (fĭn) *n.* A native or inhabitant of Finland.

Finn•ish (fĭn'ĭsh) *adj.* Of or pertaining to Finland, its language, or its people. —*n.* The Uralic language spoken by the Finns.

Fin•no-U•gric (fĭn'ō-/y/ōō'grĭk) *n.* Also **Fin•no-U•gri•an** (-/y/ōō'grē-ən). A subfamily of Uralic, including Hungarian and Finnish. —**Fin'no-U'gric** *adj.*

fin•ny (fĭn'ē) *adj.* **1.** Having fins, as a fish. **2.** Finlike.

fiord. Variant of **fjord.**

fir (fûr) *n.* **1.** An evergreen tree with somewhat flattened needles. **2.** The wood of such a tree. [< OE *fyrh, furh.* See **perkwu-**.]

fire (fīr) *n.* **1.** A rapid, persistent chemical reaction that releases heat and light, esp. the exothermic combination of a combustible substance with oxygen. **2.** A destructive burning: *a forest fire.* **3.** Ardor; enthusiasm. **4.** The discharge of firearms; firing. —**catch fire.** To become ignited. —**hang fire. 1.** To fail to fire, as a gun. **2.** To be delayed, as an event or decision. —**on fire.** Burning; ablaze. —**open fire.** To commence shooting. —**under fire.** Under attack. —*v.* **fired, firing. 1.** To ignite. **2.** To maintain a fire in. **3.** To bake in a kiln. **4.** To arouse; stimulate. **5.** To detonate or shoot (a weapon). **6.** *Informal.* To hurl suddenly and forcefully: *fire a ball.* **7.** *Informal.* To discharge from a position; dismiss. [< OE *fȳr.* See **pūr-**.]

fire•arm (fīr'ärm') *n.* Any weapon capable of firing a missile, esp. a pistol or rifle.

fire•ball (fīr'bôl') *n.* **1.** A ball of fire. **2.** A highly luminous, intensely hot cloud generated by a nuclear explosion.

fire•brand (fīr'brănd') *n.* **1.** A piece of burning wood. **2.** A person who stirs up trouble.

fire•bug (fīr'bŭg') *n. Informal.* One who deliberately sets fires; pyromaniac.

fire•crack•er (fīr'krăk'ər) *n.* A small explosive charge in a cylinder of heavy paper, used to make noise, as at celebrations.

fire•damp (fīr'dămp') *n.* **1.** A combustible gas, chiefly methane, occurring naturally in coal mines and forming explosive mixtures with air. **2.** The explosive mixture itself.

fire drill. A practice exercise in the exit procedure to be followed in case of fire.

fire engine. A motor truck that carries firemen and equipment to fight a fire.

fire escape. An outside stairway attached to a building, used for emergency exit in the event of fire.

fire extinguisher. A portable apparatus containing chemicals used to extinguish a small fire.

fire•fly (fīr'flī') *n.* A night-flying beetle with luminous abdominal organs that produce a flashing light.

fire irons. The equipment used to tend a fireplace, including tongs, a shovel, etc.

fire•man (fīr'mən) *n.* **1.** A man employed to fight fires. **2.** A man who tends fires; stoker.

fire•place (fīr'plās') *n.* **1.** An open recess for holding a fire at the base of a chimney; hearth. **2.** A structure, usually of stone or brick, for holding an outdoor fire.

fire•plug (fīr'plŭg') *n.* A pipe from which water can be drawn for extinguishing a fire; a hydrant.

fire•pow•er (fīr'pou'ər) *n.* The capacity, as of a military unit, for discharging fire.

fire•proof (fīr'prōof') *adj.* Capable of withstanding damage by fire. —*v.* To make fire-proof.

fire·side (fīr'sīd') *n.* **1.** The area around a fireplace. **2.** Home.

fire·trap (fīr'trăp') *n.* A building susceptible to catching fire or difficult to escape from in the event of fire.

fire·wood (fīr'wŏŏd') *n.* Wood used as fuel.

fire·work (fīr'wûrk') *n.* Often **fireworks.** An explosive used to generate colored lights, smoke, and noise for amusement.

firing line. The line of positions from which fire is directed against a target.

firing pin. The part of the bolt of a firearm that strikes the primer and explodes the charge of the projectile.

firing squad. A detachment assigned to execute condemned persons.

firm[1] (fûrm) *adj.* **1.** Unyielding to pressure; solid. **2.** Securely fixed in place. **3.** Indicating determination or resolution. **4.** Constant; steadfast: *a firm ally.* **5.** Definite; final: *a firm bargain.* **6.** Unfluctuating; steady, as prices. —*v.* To make or become firm. —*adv.* Resolutely; unwaveringly: *stand firm.* [< L *firmus.*] —**firm'ly** *adv.* —**firm'ness** *n.*

firm[2] (fûrm) *n.* A commercial partnership of two or more persons. [< It, *firmare,* "to confirm by signature."]

fir·ma·ment (fûr'mə-mənt) *n.* The vault or expanse of the heavens; sky. [< L *firmāmentum,* a strengthening, support.]

first (fûrst) *adj.* **1.** Coming or located before all others. **2.** Prior to all others; earliest. **3.** Foremost in importance or quality. —**in the first place.** To begin with. —*adv.* **1.** Before or above all others in time or rank. **2.** For the first time. **3.** Preferably; rather. —*n.* **1.** The ordinal number one in a series. **2.** The one coming, occurring, or ranking first. **3.** The beginning; outset: *from the first.* **4.** The lowest forward gear in an automotive vehicle. **5.** The winning position in a contest. [< OE *fyrst.* See per[1].]

first aid. Emergency treatment administered before professional medical care is available.

first-born (fûrst'bôrn') *adj.* First in order of birth. —*n.* The first-born child.

first class. 1. The most expensive class of accommodations on a train, passenger ship, or airplane. **2.** A class of mail sealed against inspection.

first-class (fûrst'klăs') *adj.* **1.** The most expensive; preferential, as accommodations. **2.** Of the highest quality; first-rate. —**first'-class'** *adv.*

first·hand (fûrst'hănd') *adj.* Received from the original source: *firsthand information.* —**first'hand'** *adv.*

first·ly (fûrst'lē) *adv.* In the first place; to begin with.

first mate. A ship's officer ranking immediately below the captain.

first person. A set of grammatical forms designating the speaker or writer of the sentence in which they appear.

first-rate (fûrst'rāt') *adj.* Foremost in quality or rank. —*adv. Informal.* Excellently.

first sergeant. In the U.S. Army, the highest ranking noncommissioned officer of a company or other military unit.

firth (fûrth) *n. Chiefly Scot.* A narrow inlet of the sea. [< ON *fjördhr.*]

fis·cal (fĭs'kəl) *adj.* **1.** Of or pertaining to the public treasury or finances. **2.** Of or pertaining to finances in general. [< L *fiscus,* treasury, basket.] —**fis'cal·ly** *adv.*

fish (fĭsh) *n., pl.* **fish** or **fishes. 1.** Any of numerous cold-blooded aquatic vertebrates characteristically having fins, gills, and a streamlined body. **2.** The edible flesh of a fish. **3.** Often **the Fish** or **the Fishes.** Pisces. —*v.* **1.** To catch or try to catch fish. **2.** To draw or pull up, as by fishing (with *out*). **3.** To seek something indirectly: *fish for compliments.* [< OE *fisc.* See **peisk-.**]

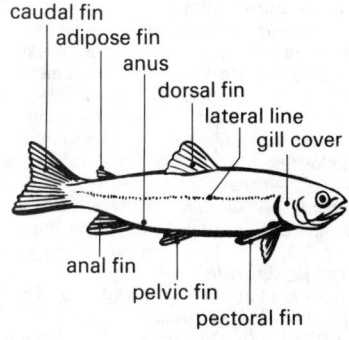

caudal fin
adipose fin
anus
dorsal fin
lateral line
gill cover
anal fin
pelvic fin
pectoral fin

fish

fish·bowl (fĭsh'bōl') *n.* **1.** A bowl in which live fish are kept. **2.** Something that can be seen through on all sides or at all points.

fish·er·man (fĭsh'ər-mən) *n.* One who fishes as an occupation or sport.

fish·er·y (fĭsh'ə-rē) *n., pl.* **-ies. 1.** The industry of catching fish. **2.** A fishing ground. **3.** A hatchery for fish.

fish·hook (fĭsh'hŏŏk') *n.* A barbed hook for catching fish.

fish·ing (fĭsh'ĭng) *n.* The business or sport of catching fish.

fishing rod. A rod used with a line for catching fish.

fish story. *Informal.* An implausible and boastful story.

fish·wife (fĭsh'wīf') *n.* **1.** A woman who sells fish. **2.** A coarse, abusive woman.

fish·y (fĭsh'ē) *adj.* **-ier, -iest. 1.** Resembling or suggestive of fish. **2.** Cold or expressionless: *a fishy stare.* **3.** *Informal.* Questionable; inspiring suspicion. —**fish'i·ness** *n.*

fis·sile (fĭs'əl, fĭs'īl') *adj.* **1.** Capable of being split. **2.** *Phys.* Fissionable, esp. by neutrons of all energies. —**fis·sil'i·ty** (fĭ-sĭl'ə-tē) *n.*

fis·sion (fĭsh'ən) *n.* **1.** The act or process of splitting into parts. **2.** A nuclear reaction in which an atomic nucleus splits into fragments, usually two fragments of comparable mass, with the evolution of approx. 100 million to several hundred million electron volts of energy. **3.** An asexual reproductive process in which a unicellular organism splits into two or more independently maturing daughter cells. [< L *fissus,* pp of *findere,* to split.] —**fis′sion‑a‑ble** *adj.*

fis‑sure (fish′ər) *n.* A narrow groove, crack, or cleft. [< L *fissus,* split.]

fist (fĭst) *n.* The hand closed tightly, with the fingers bent against the palm. [< OE *fӯst.* See penkwe.]

fist‑i‑cuffs (fĭs′tĭ‑kŭfs′) *pl.n.* **1.** A fist fight. **2.** Boxing. [< FIST + CUFF[2].]

fis‑tu‑la (fĭs′chōō‑lə) *n., pl.* **-las** or **-lae** (-lē′). An abnormal bodily duct or passage from an abscess, cavity, or hollow organ. [< L.] —**fis′tu‑lous** *adj.*

fit[1] (fĭt) *v.* **fitted** or **fit, fitted, fitting. 1.** To be the proper size and shape (for). **2.** To be suitable (to). **3.** To adjust; adapt. **4.** To equip; outfit (with *up* or *out*). **5.** To provide a place or time for (with *in* or *into*). —*adj.* **fitter, fittest. 1.** Suited or adequate to a given circumstance. **2.** Appropriate; proper. **3.** Physically sound; healthy. —*n.* **1.** Adjustment or alteration to a given pattern or standard. **2.** The manner in which clothing fits. [< ME *fitten,* to arrange.] —**fit′ly** *adv.* —**fit′ness** *n.*

fit[2] (fĭt) *n.* **1.** A sudden violent attack, as of coughing. **2.** A sudden, violent outburst of emotion. **3.** A sudden period of vigorous activity. [< OE *fitt,* conflict.]

fitch (fĭch) *n.* The fur of the Old World polecat. [Prob < MDu *vitsau.*]

fit‑ful (fĭt′fəl) *adj.* Occurring in or characterized by fits; intermittent; irregular. —**fit′ful‑ly** *adv.* —**fit′ful‑ness** *n.*

fit‑ting (fĭt′ĭng) *adj.* Suitable; appropriate. —*n.* **1.** A trying on for fit, as of clothes. **2.** Often **fittings.** Furnishings or accessories. —**fit′ting‑ly** *adv.* —**fit′ting‑ness** *n.*

five (fīv) *n.* The cardinal number written 5 or in Roman numerals V. [< OE *fīf.* See penkwe.] —**five** *adj. & pron.*

fix (fĭks) *v.* **1.** To place or fasten securely. **2.** To put into a stable or unalterable form, as: **a.** To make a substance nonvolatile or solid. **b.** To convert (nitrogen) into stable, biologically assimilable compounds. **c.** To prevent discoloration of (a photographic image) by washing or coating with a chemical preservative. **3.** To direct (as the gaze) steadily. **4.** To establish definitely; specify: *fix a time.* **5.** To ascribe; place: *fix blame.* **6.** To rectify; adjust. **7.** To set right; repair. **8.** To make ready; put together; prepare. **9.** *Informal.* To take revenge upon; get even with. **10.** To prearrange the outcome of (a contest) by unlawful means. —**fix up.** *Informal.* **1.** To set in order. **2.** To provide with; furnish. —*n.* **1.** A predicament; dilemma. **2.** A position, as of a ship or aircraft, as determined by observations or radio. **3.** An instance of collusion to predetermine a result. **4.** *Slang.* An intravenous injection of heroin. [< L *fixus,* pp of *figere,* to fasten.] —**fix′a‑ble** *adj.* —**fix′er** *n.*

fix‑a‑tion (fĭk‑sā′shən) *n.* A strong attachment to a person or thing, esp. such an attachment

formed in childhood or infancy and persisting in immature or neurotic behavior.

fix‑a‑tive (fĭk′sə‑tĭv) *adj.* Tending to render permanent, firm, or stable. —*n.* Something that fixes or preserves, esp. a liquid preservative applied to art work, such as charcoal drawings.

fixed (fĭkst) *adj.* **1.** Firmly in position; stationary. **2. a.** Nonvolatile: *fixed oils.* **b.** In a stable combined form. **3.** Not subject to variation; constant. **4.** Stubbornly held to: *a fixed notion.* —**fix′ed‑ly** (fĭk′sĭd‑lē) *adv.*

fix‑ings (fĭk′sĭngz) *pl.n. Informal.* Accessories; trimmings.

fix‑ture (fĭks′chər) *n.* **1.** Something attached as a permanent appendage, apparatus, or appliance. **2.** One long established in a place, position, or function.

fizz (fĭz) *v.* To make a hissing or bubbling sound. —*n.* **1.** A hissing or bubbling sound. **2.** An effervescent beverage. [Imit.]

fiz‑zle (fĭz′əl) *v.* **-zled, -zling. 1.** To fizz. **2.** To fail or die out, esp. after a hopeful beginning. —*n.* A failure; fiasco. [Prob freq of obs *fist,* to break wind.]

fjord, fiord (fyôrd, fyōrd) *n.* A long, narrow inlet from the sea between steep cliffs or slopes. [< ON *fjördhr.*]

fl fluid.

fl. 1. floor. **2.** fluid.

Fla. Florida.

flab‑ber‑gast (flăb′ər‑găst′) *v.* To overwhelm with astonishment; astound. [?]

flab‑by (flăb′ē) *adj.* **-bier, -biest. 1.** Lacking firmness; flaccid: *flabby skin.* **2.** Lacking force; feeble. [< FLAP.] —**flab′bi‑ly** *adv.* —**flab′bi‑ness** *n.*

flac‑cid (flăk′sĭd) *adj.* Lacking firmness; flabby. [< L *flaccus,* hanging, flabby.]

fla‑con (flăk′ən, -ŏn′) *n.* A small stoppered bottle. [< L *flascō,* FLASK.]

flag[1] (flăg) *n.* **1.** An often rectangular piece of fabric used as a symbol, signal, etc. **2.** Something resembling a flag in appearance or function. —*v.* **flagged, flagging. 1.** To mark with a flag. **2.** To signal with or as with a flag. [?]

flag[2] (flăg) *n.* A wild iris or similar plant. [ME *flagge,* rush, reed.]

flag[3] (flăg) *v.* **flagged, flagging. 1.** To hang limply; droop. **2.** To become languid; tire. **3.** To decline in interest; grow dull. [?]

flag[4] (flăg) *n.* Flagstone. [Prob < ON *flaga,* slab of stone.]

flag‑el‑late (flăj′ə‑lāt′) *v.* **-lated, -lating.** To whip or flog; scourge. [L *flagellāre.*] —**flag′el‑la′tion** *n.* —**flag′el‑la′tor** *n.*

flag‑on (flăg′ən) *n.* A vessel for liquids, usually having a handle and spout. [< LL *flascō,* bottle, FLASK.]

flag‑pole (flăg′pōl′) *n.* A pole on which a flag is hoisted; flagstaff.

fla‑grant (flā′grənt) *adj.* Extremely or deliberately conspicuous; shocking. [< L *flagrāre,* to burn, blaze.] —**fla′gran‑cy, fla′grance** *n.* —**fla′grant‑ly** *adv.*

flag‑ship (flăg′shĭp′) *n.* A ship bearing the flag of a fleet or squadron commander.

flag‑staff (flăg′stăf′, -stäf′) *n.* A flagpole.

ă pat/ā ate/âr care/ä bar/b bib/ch chew/d deed/ĕ pet/ē be/f fit/g gag/h hat/hw what/
ĭ pit/ī pie/îr pier/j judge/k kick/l lid, fatal/m mum/n no, sudden/ng sing/ŏ pot/ō go/

A	N
B	O
C	P
D	Q
E	R
F	S
G	T
H	U
I	V
J	W
K	X
L	Y
M	Z

black blue white yellow red
International Code flags

flag·stone (flăg′stōn′) *n.* A flat, evenly layered paving stone.

flail (flāl) *n.* A manual threshing device. —*v.* To beat, thrash, or strike with or as with a flail. [< L *flagrum,* whip.]

flair (flâr) *n.* **1.** A natural talent or aptitude; bent; knack. **2.** Instinctive discernment; keenness. [< L *frāgrāre,* to emit a smell.]

flak (flăk) *n.* **1.** Antiaircraft artillery. **2.** The bursting shells fired from such artillery. [G.]

flake (flāk) *n.* **1.** A flat, thin piece or layer; chip. **2.** A small loose fragment; bit. —*v.* **flaked, flaking.** To form into or come off in flakes. [< Scand.] —**flak′y** *adj.*

flam·boy·ant (flăm-boi′ənt) *adj.* **1.** Highly elaborate; showy. **2.** Richly colored; vivid; resplendent. [< OF *flamboyer,* to blaze.] —**flam·boy′ance** *n.* —**flam·boy′ant·ly** *adv.*

flame (flām) *n.* **1.** The zone of burning gases and fine suspended matter associated with the combustion of a substance. **2.** The condition of active, blazing combustion. **3.** Something flamelike in appearance. **4.** A violent or intense passion; a burning emotion. **5.** *Informal.* A sweetheart. —*v.* **flamed, flaming. 1.** To burn brightly; blaze. **2.** To burst into or as into flame. [< L *flamma.*]

fla·men·co (flə-měng′kō) *n.* A dance style of Spanish Gypsies, characterized by forceful, often improvised rhythms. [Span, resembling a Gypsy, Flemish.]

flame·out (flām′out′) *n.* Failure of a jet aircraft engine in flight.

flame thrower. A weapon that projects a stream of ignited incendiary fuel.

fla·min·go (flə-mǐng′gō) *n., pl.* **-gos** or **-goes.** A long-legged, long-necked tropical wading bird with reddish or pinkish plumage. [Prob < Prov *flamenc,* prob "fire bird."]

flam·ma·ble (flăm′ə-bəl) *adj.* Easily ignitable and capable of burning with great rapidity. [< L *flamma,* FLAME.]

Flan·ders (flăn′dərz). A region of NW Europe, including part of N France and W Belgium.

flange (flănj) *n.* A protruding rim, edge, etc., as on a wheel, used to strengthen an object or hold it in place. [?]

flank (flăngk) *n.* **1.** The section of flesh between the last rib and the hip; side. **2.** A cut of meat from this section of an animal. **3.** A side or lateral part. **4.** The right or left side of a military formation. —*v.* **1.** To be at the flank or side of. **2.** To attack or maneuver around the flank of. [< Frank **hlanca,* side.]

flan·nel (flăn′əl) *n.* A soft woven cloth of wool or a wool blend. [Prob < W *gwlanen,* "woolen cloth."] —**flan′nel·ly** *adj.*

flan·nel·ette (flăn′ə-lět′) *n.* A soft, napped cotton cloth.

flap (flăp) *v.* **flapped, flapping. 1.** To wave up and down, as wings; flutter; beat. **2.** To swing or sway loosely. **3.** To hit with something broad and flat; slap. —*n.* **1.** A flat, loose appendage attached on one side, as of an envelope or pocket. **2.** The action or sound of flapping. **3.** A blow given with something flat; a slap. **4.** A variable control surface on the trailing edge of an aircraft wing, used primarily to increase lift or drag. [ME *flappen.*]

flap·jack (flăp′jăk′) *n.* A pancake.

flap·per (flăp′ər) *n. Informal.* An ostentatiously unconventional young woman of the 1920's.

flare (flâr) *v.* **flared, flaring. 1.** To flame up with a bright, wavering light; blaze unsteadily. **2.** To erupt into emphatic emotion or activity (with *out* or *up*). **3.** To expand outward, as a bell. —*n.* **1.** A brief, wavering blaze. **2.** A pyrotechnic device that produces a bright light, as for signaling. **3.** An outbreak, as of emotion or activity. **4.** An expanding contour. [?]

flare-up (flâr′ŭp′) *n.* A sudden outbreak, as of flame, emotion, etc.

flash (flăsh) *v.* **1.** To occur or emerge suddenly in or as in flame. **2.** To appear or cause to appear briefly. **3.** To be lighted intermittently; sparkle. **4.** To cause (light) to appear in intermittent bursts. **5.** To move rapidly. **6.** To signal with light. **7.** To communicate (information) at great speed. **8.** To display ostentatiously; flaunt. —*n.* **1.** A sudden brief, intense display of light. **2.** A sudden, brief display, as of a mental faculty. **3.** An instant: *in a flash.* **4.** A brief news dispatch or transmission. **5. a.** Instantaneous illumination for photography. **b.** Any equipment or device used to produce such illumination. [ME *flashen,* to splash, burst into flame.]

flash·back (flăsh′băk′) *n.* A reversion to an event occurring earlier in a narrative.

flash bulb. A glass bulb filled with finely shredded aluminum or magnesium foil that is ignited by electricity to produce a short-duration high-intensity light flash for taking photographs.

flash flood. A sudden flood.

flash gun. A dry-cell-powered photographic apparatus that holds and electrically triggers a flash bulb.

flash·ing (flăsh′ĭng) *n.* Sheet metal used to weatherproof the joints and angles of a roof.

flash lamp. An electric lamp for producing a high-intensity light of very short duration for use in photography.

flash·light (flăsh′līt′) *n.* **1.** A small, portable lamp having a bulb and dry batteries. **2.** A brief, brilliant flood of light, as from a photographic lamp.

flash point. The lowest temperature at which the vapor of a combustible liquid can be made to ignite momentarily in air.

flash tube. A gas discharge tube used in an electronic flash to produce a brief, intense pulse of light.

flash unit. 1. An electronic flash system containing both power supply and flash tube in a single compact unit. **2. a.** A flash gun. **b.** A flash gun and reflector.

flash·y (flăsh′ē) *adj.* **-ier, -iest. 1.** Momentarily brilliant. **2.** Showy; gaudy.

flask (flăsk, fläsk) *n.* A small bottle-shaped container. [< LL *flascō.*]

flat¹ (flăt) *adj.* **flatter, flattest. 1. a.** Having no curves. **b.** Having a smooth, even, level surface. **2.** Shallow; low: *a flat box.* **3.** Lying

prone; prostrate. **4.** Unequivocal; absolute: *a flat refusal.* **5.** Fixed: *a flat rate.* **6.** Uninteresting; dull; vapid. **7.** Lacking zest; flavorless. **8.** Deflated, as a tire. **9.** *Mus.* **a.** Being one half step lower than the corresponding natural key. **b.** Being below the intended pitch. —*adv.* **1. a.** Horizontally; level with the ground. **b.** Prostrate. **2.** So as to be flat. **3.** Directly; completely. **4.** *Mus.* Below the intended pitch. —*n.* **1.** A flat object, surface, or part. **2.** Often **flats.** A stretch of level ground. **3.** A shallow frame or box for seeds or seedlings. **4.** A deflated tire. **5. flats.** Women's shoes with flat heels. **6.** *Mus.* **a.** A sign (♭) affixed to a note to indicate that it is to be lowered by a half step. **b.** A note that is lowered a half step. —*v.* **flatted, flatting. 1.** To make flat; flatten. **2.** *Mus.* **a.** To lower (a note) a half step. **b.** To sing or play below the proper pitch. [< ON *flatr.*] —**flat′ly** *adv.* —**flat′ness** *n.*

flat² (flăt) *n.* An apartment on one floor of a building. [< OE *flett,* floor, ground, hall. See **plat-.**]

flat·boat (flăt′bōt′) *n.* A flat-bottomed boat used for transporting freight.

flat·car (flăt′kär′) *n.* A railroad car without sides or roof.

flat·fish (flăt′fĭsh′) *n.* A fish, as a flounder or sole, having a flattened body with the eyes on the upper side.

flat·foot (flăt′fŏŏt′) *n.* **1.** *pl.* **-feet.** A condition in which the arch of the foot is broken down so that the entire sole makes contact with the ground. **2.** *pl.* **-foots.** *Slang.* A policeman. —**flat′-foot′ed** *adj.*

flat·i·ron (flăt′ī′ərn) *n.* An externally heated iron for pressing clothes.

flat·ten (flăt′n) *v.* To make or become flat or flatter. —**flat′ten·er** *n.*

flat·ter (flăt′ər) *v.* **1.** To compliment excessively and often insincerely. **2.** To please or gratify the vanity of. **3.** To portray favorably. [< Frank **flat,* flat part of a person's hand.] —**flat′ter·er** *n.* —**flat′ter·ing** *adj.*

flat·ter·y (flăt′ə-rē) *n., pl.* **-ies. 1.** The act or practice of flattering. **2.** Insincere praise.

flat·u·lent (flăch′ōō-lənt) *adj.* **1.** Having or causing excessive gas in the digestive tract. **2.** Inflated with self-importance; pompous. [< L *flātus,* a breaking wind.] —**flat′u·lence** *n.* —**flat′u·lent·ly** *adv.*

flat·ware (flăt′wâr′) *n.* Tableware that is fairly flat and fashioned usually of a single piece.

Flau·bert (flō-bâr′), **Gustave.** 1821–1880. French novelist.

flaunt (flônt) *v.* To exhibit ostentatiously; show off. [?] —**flaunt′er** *n.*

fla·vor (flā′vər). Also *chiefly Brit.* **fla·vour.** *n.* **1.** Distinctive taste; savor. **2.** A characteristic quality. **3.** A seasoning. —*v.* To give flavor to. [< L *flātus,* a blowing, breeze.]

fla·vor·ing (flā′vər-ĭng) *n.* A substance that imparts flavor, as an extract.

flaw (flô) *n.* **1.** An imperfection; defect. **2.** A small fissure; crack. [< ON *flaga,* slab or layer of stone.] —**flaw′less** *adj.*

flax (flăks) *n.* **1.** A widely cultivated plant with blue flowers, seeds that yield linseed oil, and slender stems that yield a fine, light-colored textile fiber. **2.** The fiber obtained from this plant. [< OE *fleax, flæx.* See **plek-**.]

flax•en (flăk'sən) *adj.* **1.** Made of flax. **2.** Having the pale-yellow color of flax fiber.

flay (flā) *v.* **1.** To strip off the skin of. **2.** To assail with stinging criticism. [< OE *flēan.* See **plēk-**.] —**flay′er** *n.*

flea (flē) *n.* Any of various small, wingless, leaping, bloodsucking insects that are parasitic on warm-blooded animals. [< OE *flēah.* See **plou-**.]

fleck (flĕk) *n.* **1.** A tiny mark or spot. **2.** A small bit or flake. **3.** A small patch of color or light. —*v.* To spot or streak. [Prob < ON *flekkr,* spot, stain.] —**fleck′y** *adj.*

fledg•ling (flĕj'lĭng) *n.* Also **fledge•ling.** **1.** A young bird with newly developed flight feathers. **2.** One that is young and inexperienced.

flee (flē) *v.* **fled, fleeing.** **1.** To run away, as from trouble or danger. **2.** To pass swiftly away; vanish. [< OE *flēon.*] —**fle′er** *n.*

fleece (flēs) *n.* **1.** The coat of wool of a sheep or similar animal. **2.** Any soft, woolly covering or mass. —*v.* **fleeced, fleecing.** **1.** To shear the fleece from. **2.** To swindle. [< OE *flēos.* See **pleus-**.] —**fleec′i•ness** *n.* —**fleec′y** *adj.*

fleet¹ (flēt) *n.* **1.** A number of warships operating together under one command. **2.** Any group of vehicles owned or operated as a unit. [< OE *flēotan,* to float. See **pleu-**.]

fleet² (flēt) *adj.* Moving swiftly; rapid or nimble. [Prob < OE *flēotan,* to float.] —**fleet′ing** *adj.* —**fleet′ly** *adv.* —**fleet′ness** *n.*

Flem. Flemish.

Flem•ish (flĕm′ĭsh) *n.* **1.** The people of Flanders. **2.** Their Germanic language, related to Dutch. —**Flem′ish** *adj.*

flesh (flĕsh) *n.* **1.** The soft tissue of the body, esp. skeletal muscle distinguished from bone and viscera. **2.** Meat. **3.** The pulpy part of a fruit or vegetable. **4.** Excess tissue; fat. **5.** The physical being as distinguished from the mind or soul. **6.** One's family; kin. [< OE *flæsc.* See **plēk-**.]

flesh•ly (flĕsh′lē) *adj.* **-lier, -liest.** **1.** Of or pertaining to the body; corporeal. **2.** Carnal; sensual. **3.** Not spiritual; worldly.

flesh•y (flĕsh′ē) *adj.* **-ier, -iest.** **1.** Consisting of or like flesh. **2.** Corpulent; plump. **3.** Firm and pulpy, as fruit. —**flesh′i•ness** *n.*

fleur-de-lis, fleur-de-lys (flûr′də-lē′, floor′-) *n., pl.* **fleurs-de-lis, fleurs-de-lys** (flûr′də-lēz′, floor′-). A stylized three-petaled representation of an iris flower. [< OF *flor de lis,* lily flower.]

flew (floo). *p.t.* of **fly¹.**

flex (flĕks) *v.* **1.** To bend (something pliant). **2.** To contract (a muscle). [L *flectere* (pp *flexus*), to bend.]

flex•i•ble (flĕk′sə-bəl) *adj.* **1.** Capable of being flexed. **2.** Capable of or responsive to change; adaptable. —**flex′i•bil′i•ty** *n.* —**flex′i•bly** *adv.*

flex•time (flĕks′tīm′) *n.* Also **flex•i•time** (flĕk′sə-tīm′). An arrangement by which employees set their own work schedule whenever possible.

flib•ber•ti•gib•bet (flĭb′ər-tē-jĭb′ĭt) *n.* A scatterbrained person. [?]

flick (flĭk) *n.* **1.** A light, quick motion or touch. **2.** A light splash or daub. —*v.* **1.** To touch or move with a light, quick motion. **2.** To flutter or dart. [Perh imit.]

flick•er (flĭk′ər) *v.* **1.** To move waveringly; flutter. **2.** To yield irregular, intermittent light. —*n.* **1.** A tremor or flutter. **2.** A brief or wavering light. **3.** A brief sensation. [< OE *flicorian,* to flutter, hover.]

flied. *Baseball. p.t. & p.p.* of **fly¹.**

fli•er (flī′ər) *n.* Also **fly•er.** **1.** One that flies. **2.** A daring financial venture. **3.** A circular for mass distribution.

flight¹ (flīt) *n.* **1.** Motion through the earth's atmosphere or through space. **2.** Locomotion through the air by means of wings. **3.** A group flying together, as of birds or aircraft. **4.** A scheduled airline run. **5.** A soaring, as of the imagination. **6. a.** A series of stairs. **b.** Stairs between landings. [< OE *flyht.* See **pleu-**.]

flight² (flīt) *n.* A running away. [< OE **flyht.* See **pleu-**.]

flight•y (flī′tē) *adj.* **-ier, -iest.** Capriciously unstable; skittish. —**flight′i•ness** *n.*

flim•flam (flĭm′flăm′) *n. Informal.* Humbug; deception. [< Scand.] —**flim′flam′** *v.* **(-flammed, -flamming).**

flim•sy (flĭm′zē) *adj.* **-sier, -siest.** **1.** Not strong or substantial. **2.** Implausible; unconvincing. [?] —**flim′si•ly** *adv.* —**flim′si•ness** *n.*

flinch (flĭnch) *v.* To shrink or wince, as from pain or fear. [OF *flenchir* < Gmc.]

fling (flĭng) *v.* **flung, flinging.** **1.** To throw or move suddenly and forcefully. **2.** To put or abandon energetically. —*n.* **1.** A toss; a throw. **2.** A short period of indulging one's impulses; a spree. **3.** *Informal.* A brief attempt. [< Scand.] —**fling′er** *n.*

flint (flĭnt) *n.* **1.** A very hard quartz that sparks when struck with steel. **2.** A small solid cylinder of a spark-producing alloy. [< OE. See **splei-**.]

Flint (flĭnt). A city of SE Michigan. Pop. 197,000.

flint•lock (flĭnt′lŏk′) *n.* **1.** An obsolete gunlock in which a flint sparks the charge. **2.** A gun with such a gunlock.

flip (flĭp) *v.* **flipped, flipping.** **1.** To toss or turn with a light quick motion. **2.** *Slang.* To be delighted or crazed. —*n.* A quick turn or motion. —*adj.* Flippant; pert. [?]

flip•pant (flĭp′ənt) *adj.* Marked by disrespectful levity; pert; saucy. —**flip′pan•cy** *n.* —**flip′pant•ly** *adv.*

flip•per (flĭp′ər) *n.* **1.** A wide, flat limb, as of a seal, adapted for swimming. **2.** A flattened rubber foot covering used in swimming.

flirt (flûrt) *v.* **1.** To amuse oneself in light, playful courtship. **2.** To deal triflingly; toy: *flirt with danger.* **3.** To move jerkily; dart. —*n.* **1.** One given to flirting. **2.** An abrupt jerking movement. [?] —**flir•ta′tion** (-tā′shən) *n.* —**flir•ta′tious** *adj.* —**flir•ta′tious•ly** *adv.*

flit (flĭt) *v.* **flitted, flitting.** To move about rapidly and nimbly; dart. [< ON *flytja,* to convey.]

float (flōt) *v.* **1. a.** To remain or cause to remain suspended within or on the surface of a fluid without sinking. **b.** To be or cause to be suspended unsupported in space. **2.** To move from position to position at random; drift. **3.** To move easily and lightly as if· suspended. **4.** To release (a security) for sale. —*n.* **1.** Something that floats. **2.** A small floating object on a fishing line. **3.** A large, flat vehicle bearing an exhibit in a parade. [< OE *flotian.* See **pleu-**.] —**float′er** *n.*

float·ing rib (flō′tĭng). One of the four lower ribs that, unlike the other ribs, are not attached at the front.

flock (flŏk) *n.* **1.** A group of animals, as birds or sheep, that live, travel, or feed together. **2.** A group of people under the leadership of one person. **3.** A large crowd or number. —*v.* To congregate or travel in a flock or crowd. [< OE *flocc* < Gmc **flugnaz.*]

floe (flō) *n.* **1.** A large, flat mass of ice formed on the surface of a body of water. **2.** A segment separated from such an ice mass. [Prob < ON *flō,* stratum, coating.]

flog (flŏg, flôg) *v.* **flogged, flogging.** To beat harshly with a whip or rod. [Perh short for L *flagellāre,* to whip.] —**flog′ger** *n.*

flood (flŭd) *n.* **1.** An overflowing of water onto land that is normally dry. **2.** Also **flood tide.** The rising tide. **3.** Any abundant flow or outpouring. **4. the Flood.** The universal deluge recorded in the Bible. Genesis 7. —*v.* **1.** To cover or submerge with a flood; inundate. **2.** To fill with an abundance or excess. [< OE *flōd.* See **pleu-**.]

flood·gate (flŭd′gāt′) *n.* A gate used to control the flow of a body of water.

flood·light (flŭd′līt′) *n.* **1.** Artificial light in an intensely bright and broad beam. **2.** A unit that produces such a beam. —*v.* To illuminate with a floodlight.

flood plain. A plain bordering a river, subject to flooding.

floor (flôr, flōr) *n.* **1.** The surface of a room on which one stands. **2.** The ground or lowermost surface, as of a forest or ocean. **3.** The lower part of a room, as a legislative chamber, where business is conducted. **4.** The right to address an assembly. **5.** A story of a building. —*v.* **1.** To provide with a floor. **2.** To knock down. **3.** To stun; overwhelm. [< OE *flōr.* See **pelə-**.] —**floor′er** *n.*

floor·ing (flôr′ĭng, flōr′-) *n.* **1. a.** Floors collectively. **b.** A floor. **2.** Material used in making floors.

floor show. The entertainment presented in a nightclub.

floor·walk·er (flôr′wô′kər, flōr′-) *n.* An employee of a department store who supervises sales personnel.

floo·zy (floō′zē) *n., pl.* **-zies.** Also **floo·zie.** *Slang.* A cheap prostitute. [?]

flop (flŏp) *v.* **flopped, flopping. 1.** To fall down heavily and noisily; plop. **2.** To move about in a clumsy, noisy way. **3.** *Informal.* To fail utterly. —*n.* **1.** The action or sound of flopping. **2.** *Informal.* An utter failure. [Var of FLAP.]

flop·house (flŏp′hous′) *n.* A cheap hotel.

flo·ra (flôr′ə, flōr′ə) *n., pl.* **-ras** or **-rae** (flôr′ē′,

flōr′ē′). Plants, esp. of a region or time. [< L *flōs (flōr-),* flower.]

flo·ral (flôr′əl, flōr′-) *adj.* Of or pertaining to flowers. —**flo′ral·ly** *adv.*

Flor·ence (flôr′əns, flŏr′-). A city of N Italy. Pop. 456,000. —**Flor′en·tine′** (-ən-tēn′, -tīn′) *adj. & n.*

flo·ret (flôr′ĭt, flōr′-) *n.* A small flower, usually part of a dense cluster.

flor·id (flôr′ĭd, flŏr′-) *adj.* **1.** Flushed with rosy color; ruddy. **2.** Heavily embellished; flowery. [< L *flōs (flōr-),* FLOWER.]

Flor·i·da (flôr′ə-də, flŏr′-). A state of the SE U.S. Pop. 6,789,000. Cap. Tallahassee.

flor·in (flôr′ĭn, flŏr′-) *n.* **1.** A guilder. **2.** A British coin worth two shillings. [< It *fiore,* flower.]

flo·rist (flôr′ĭst, flōr′-, flŏr′-) *n.* One whose business is the raising or selling of flowers.

floss (flôs, flŏs) *n.* **1.** Short fibers or waste silk from the cocoon of a silkworm. **2.** A soft, loosely twisted thread. **3.** Any soft, silky, fibrous substance. [Poss < OF *flosche,* down.]

floss·y (flô′sē, flŏs′ē) *adj.* **-ier, -iest. 1.** Made of or resembling floss; silky. **2.** *Slang.* Ostentatiously stylish; flashy.

flo·ta·tion (flō-tā′shən) *n.* Any of several processes in which different pulverized materials, notably minerals, are separated from a fluid mixture by agitation.

flo·til·la (flō-tĭl′ə) *n.* **1.** A fleet of small ships. **2.** A small fleet. [< ON *floti,* raft, fleet.]

flot·sam (flŏt′səm) *n.* Floating wreckage or cargo from a ship. [< VL **flottāre,* to float.]

flounce[1] (flouns) *n.* A strip of gathered or pleated material secured on its upper edge to another surface, such as a garment. [< OF *froncir,* to wrinkle.]

flounce[2] (flouns) *v.* **flounced, flouncing. 1.** To move with exaggerated motions expressive of displeasure or impatience. **2.** To flounder. —*n.* The act or motion of flouncing. [?]

floun·der[1] (floun′dər) *v.* **1.** To move clumsily or awkwardly. **2.** To proceed clumsily and in confusion. [Prob blend of FOUNDER and BLUNDER.] —**floun′der** *n.*

floun·der[2] (floun′dər) *n.* Any of various marine flatfishes used as food. [Prob < Scand.]

flour (flour) *n.* **1.** A fine, powdery substance obtained by grinding grain, esp. wheat. **2.** Any similar soft, fine powder. —*v.* To cover or coat with flour. [ME, finer meal, farina, flower.] —**flour′y** *adj.*

flour·ish (flûr′ĭsh) *v.* **1.** To grow well or abundantly; thrive. **2.** To fare well; succeed. **3.** To be in one's prime. **4.** To make bold, sweeping movements. —*n.* **1.** An embellishment or ornamentation. **2.** A dramatic action or gesture. [< L *flōrēre,* to bloom.]

flout (flout) *v.* To show contempt for; scoff at. —*n.* A contemptuous action or remark. [Prob < ME *flouten,* to play the flute.]

flow (flō) *v.* **1.** To move or run freely in or as in a stream. **2.** To circulate, as the blood in the body. **3.** To proceed steadily and continuously. **4.** To appear smooth, harmonious, or graceful. **5.** To rise, as the tide. **6.** To arise;

ă pat/ā ate/âr care/ä bar/b bib/ch chew/d deed/ĕ pet/ē be/f fit/g gag/h hat/hw what/ ĭ pit/ī pie/îr pier/j judge/k kick/l lid, fatal/m mum/n no, sudden/ng sing/ŏ pot/ō go/

derive. **7.** To abound or be plentiful. **8.** To hang loosely and gracefully. —*n.* **1. a.** The smooth motion characteristic of fluids. **b.** The act of flowing. **2.** A stream. **3. a.** A continuous outpouring: *a flow of ideas.* **b.** A continuous movement or circulation: *the flow of traffic.* **4.** The amount that flows in a given period of time. **5.** The rising of the tide. [< OE *flōwan.* See **pleu-.**]

flow•er (flou′ər) *n.* **1.** The reproductive structure of a seed-bearing plant, characteristically having specialized male and female organs and often colorful petals. **2.** A plant conspicuous for its blossoms. **3.** The period or an example of highest development; peak. **4.** Often **flowers.** *Chem.* A fine powder produced by condensation or sublimation. —*v.* **1.** To produce flowers; bloom. **2.** To develop fully; reach a peak. [< L *flōs (flōr-).*]

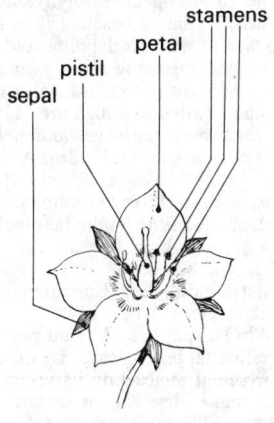

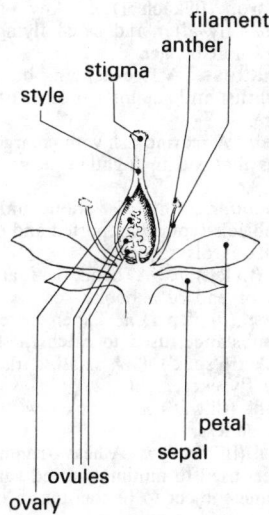

flower
Flower *(above)* and cross section showing details

flow•er•y (flou′ə-rē) *adj.* **-ier, -iest. 1.** Abounding in or suggestive of flowers. **2.** Full of ornate expressions: *a flowery speech.*

flown (flōn). *p.p.* of **fly¹.**

flu (flōō) *n. Informal.* Influenza.

fluc•tu•ate (flŭk′chōō-āt′) *v.* **-ated, -ating. 1.** To vary irregularly. **2.** To rise and fall like waves. [L *fluctuāre.*] —**fluc′tu•a′tion** *n.*

flue (flōō) *n.* A pipe, tube, or channel through which air, gas, steam, or smoke can pass, as in a chimney. [?]

flu•ent (flōō′ənt) *adj.* **1.** Having facility in the use of a language. **2.** Effortless; polished. **3.** Flowing or capable of flowing; fluid. [< L *fluere,* to flow.] —**flu′en•cy** *n.* —**flu′ent•ly** *adv.*

fluff (flŭf) *n.* **1.** Light down or nap. **2.** Something having a light, soft, or frothy consistency or appearance. **3.** Something of little consequence. **4.** *Informal.* An error or blunder, as by an actor. —*v.* **1.** To make light and puffy by shaking or patting into a soft, loose mass: *fluff a pillow.* **2.** *Informal.* To misread or blunder. [< F *velu,* velvety.] —**fluff′y** *adj.*

flu•id (flōō′ĭd) *n.* A substance that exists, or is regarded as existing, as a continuum characterized by low resistance to flow and the tendency to assume the shape of its container. —*adj.* **1.** Characteristic of a fluid, esp. flowing easily. **2.** Used in the measurement of fluids. **3.** Smooth and effortless. **4.** Easily changed or tending to change. **5.** Convertible into cash: *fluid assets.* [< L *fluere,* to flow.] —**flu•id′i•ty, flu′id•ness** *n.* —**flu′id•ly** *adv.*

fluid dram. One-eighth of a fluid ounce.

flu•id•ics (flōō-ĭd′ĭks) *n.* *(takes sing. v.).* The technology of fluids used as nonmoving, nonelectrical components of control and sensing systems.

fluid ounce. 1. A U.S. Customary System unit of volume or capacity, used in liquid measure, equal to 1.804 cubic inches. **2.** A corresponding British Imperial System unit, used in liquid and dry measure, equal to 1.734 cubic inches.

fluke¹ (flōōk) *n., pl.* **fluke** or **flukes.** Any of various flatfishes. [< OE *flōc.*]

fluke² (flōōk) *n.* **1.** The triangular blade at the end of either arm of an anchor. **2.** A barb or barbed head, as on a harpoon. **3.** One of the two flattened divisions of a whale's tail. [Prob < FLUKE¹.]

fluke³ (flōōk) *n.* An accidental stroke of good luck. [?] —**fluk′i•ness** *n.* —**fluk′y** *adj.*

flume (flōōm) *n.* **1.** A narrow gorge, usually with a stream flowing through it. **2.** An artificial channel for a stream of water, as for conveying logs. [< L *fluere,* to flow.]

flung (flŭng). *p.t.* & *p.p.* of **fling.**

flunk (flŭngk) *v. Informal.* To fail an examination, course, etc. [?]

flun•ky (flŭng′kē) *n., pl.* **-kies.** Also **flun•key** *pl.* **-keys. 1.** A lackey. **2.** An obsequious or fawning person; a toady. [?]

flu•o•resce (flōō-ə-rĕs′, flôr-ĕs′) *v.* **-resced, -rescing.** To undergo, produce, or show fluorescence.

flu•o•res•cence (flōō-ə-rĕs′əns, flôr-ĕs′-) *n.* **1.** The emission of electromagnetic radiation, esp. of visible light, resulting from the absorption of incident radiation and persisting only as long as the stimulating radiation is continued. **2.** The radiation emitted during fluorescence. [< L *fluere*, to flow + -ESCENCE.] —**flu·o·res′cent** *adj.*

fluorescent lamp. A lamp consisting of a glass tube, the inner wall of which is coated with a material that fluoresces when bombarded with secondary radiation generated within the tube.

flu·o·ri·date (flŏŏr′ə-dāt′, flŏŏ′ər-ə-) *v.* **-dated, -dating.** To add a fluorine compound to (a water supply) for the purpose of preventing tooth decay. —**flu′o·ri·da′tion** *n.*

flu·o·ride (flŏŏ′ə-rīd′, flŏŏr′īd′) *n.* Any binary compound of fluorine with another element.

flu·o·rine (flŏŏ′ə-rēn′, flŏŏr′ēn′, -ĭn) *n. Symbol* **F** A pale-yellow, highly corrosive, highly poisonous gaseous element, the most electronegative and most reactive of all the elements. Atomic number 9, atomic weight 18.9984. [< L *fluor*, fluid, flowing.]

flu·o·ro·scope (flŏŏr′ə-skōp′, flŏŏ′ər-ə-) *n.* A mounted fluorescent screen on which the contents or internal structure of an optically opaque object may be continuously viewed as shadows formed by differential transmission of x rays through the object.

flur·ry (flûr′ē) *n., pl.* **-ries.** **1.** A sudden gust of wind. **2.** A light snowfall. **3.** A sudden burst of bustling activity; a stir. —*v.* **-ried, -rying.** **1.** To agitate or confuse; fluster. **2.** To move or come down in a flurry. [< obs *flurr*, to whirl up, scatter.] —**flur′ried·ly** *adv.*

flush¹ (flŭsh) *v.* **1.** To flow suddenly and abundantly. **2.** To redden; blush. **3.** To glow, esp. with a reddish color. **4.** To wash out or clean by a rapid, brief gush of water. **5.** To excite or elate. —*n.* **1.** A brief but copious flow or gushing, as of water. **2.** A reddish tinge; a blush. **3.** A feeling of animation or exhilaration. **4.** A sudden freshness, development, or growth. —*adj.* **1.** Having a reddish color; blushing. **2.** Abundant; plentiful. **3.** Prosperous; affluent. **4. a.** Having surfaces in the same plane; even. **b.** Arranged with adjacent sides, surfaces, or edges close together. **5.** Direct; straightforward. —*adv.* **1.** So as to be even, in one plane, or aligned with a margin. **2.** Squarely; solidly: *a hit flush on the face.* [Prob < FLUSH³.]

flush² (flŭsh) *n.* A hand in certain card games in which all the cards are of the same suit. [< L *fluxus*, a flow, FLUX.]

flush³ (flŭsh) *v.* To cause to fly from cover, as a game bird. [Poss < OE **flyscan*.]

flus·ter (flŭs′tər) *v.* To make confused or agitated; upset. —*n.* A state of agitation or confusion. [Poss < Scand.]

flute (flŏŏt) *n.* **1.** A high-pitched tubular woodwind instrument. **2.** One of the long parallel grooves incised on the shaft of a column. **3.** A groove in cloth, as a pleat. [< OF *flaute*.]

flut·ist (flŏŏ′tĭst) *n.* One who plays the flute.

flut·ter (flŭt′ər) *v.* **1.** To wave or flap lightly, rapidly, and irregularly. **2.** To fly with a quick, light flapping of the wings. **3.** To vibrate or beat rapidly or erratically. **4.** To move quickly or behave in a restless or excited manner. —*n.*

1. An act of fluttering; a quick flapping. **2.** A condition of nervous excitement or agitation. **3.** A commotion; flurry. [< OE *floterian*. See **pleu-**.] —**flut′ter·er** *n.* —**flut′ter·y** *adj.*

flux (flŭks) *n.* **1. a.** A flow or flowing. **b.** A continued flow or flood. **2.** Change regarded as an abstract influence or condition persisting in time. **3.** A substance applied to prevent oxide formation and facilitate flowing, as of solder. —*v.* **1.** To melt; fuse. **2.** To apply a flux to. **3.** To flow; stream. [< L *fluxus*, pp of *fluere*, to flow.]

fly¹ (flī) *v.* **flew, flown, flying.** **1.** To engage in flight, esp.: **a.** To move through the air with the aid of wings or winglike parts. **b.** To travel by air. **c.** To pilot an aircraft. **2.** To rise, float, or cause to float in the air. **3.** To flee; try to escape. **4.** To hasten; rush. **5.** To pass by swiftly. **6.** To disappear rapidly; vanish. **7.** *p.t. & p.p.* **flied.** To bat a baseball in a high arc. —*n., pl.* **flies.** **1.** An overlapping fold of cloth that hides the fastening on a garment. **2.** A cloth flap that covers an entrance, as of a tent. **3.** A baseball batted in a high arc. **4.** **flies.** The area directly over the stage and behind the proscenium of a theater. **5.** *Brit.* A one-horse carriage. [< OE *flēogan*. See **pleu-**.]

fly² (flī) *n., pl.* **flies.** **1.** Any of numerous winged insects, esp. one of the family that includes the housefly. **2.** A fishing lure simulating a fly. [< OE *flēoge*. See **pleu-**.]

fly·blown (flī′blōn′) *adj.* Contaminated by or as by flies.

fly·by (flī′bī′) *n., pl.* **-bys.** A flight passing close to a specified target or position, esp. a maneuver in which a spacecraft passes close to a planet to make observations without landing.

fly-by-night (flī′bī-nīt′) *adj.* **1.** Of unreliable business character. **2.** Dubious and temporary.

fly·catch·er (flī′kăch′ər) *n.* Any of various birds that fly after and catch flying insects.

fly·er. Variant of **flier.**

flying buttress. A free-standing buttress that resists thrust and supports another part of the structure.

flying fish. A marine fish with enlarged, winglike fins that aid in flightlike leaps from the water.

flying saucer. Any of various unidentified flying objects typically reported and described as luminous disks.

fly·leaf (flī′lēf′) *n.* A blank leaf at the beginning or end of a book.

fly·pa·per (flī′pā′pər) *n.* Paper coated with a sticky substance, used to catch flies.

fly·speck (flī′spĕk′) *n.* A small, dark speck or stain of fly excrement.

fly·weight (flī′wāt′) *n.* A boxer weighing 112 pounds or less.

fly·wheel (flī′hwēl′) *n.* A heavy-rimmed rotating wheel used to minimize speed variation in a machine subject to fluctuation in drive and load.

Fm fermium.

FM frequency modulation.

fm. fathom.

fn. footnote.

ă pat/ā ate/âr care/ä bar/b bib/ch chew/d deed/ĕ pet/ē be/f fit/g gag/h hat/hw what/ ĭ pit/ī pie/îr pier/j judge/k kick/l lid, fatal/m mum/n no, sudden/ng sing/ŏ pot/ō go/

f-num·ber (ĕf'nŭm'bər) *n.* The ratio of focal length to the effective aperture diameter in a lens or lens system.

foal (fōl) *n.* The young offspring of a horse or other equine animal, esp. when under a year old. —*v.* To give birth to (a foal). [< OE *fola.* See **pou-**.]

foam (fōm) *n.* 1. A mass of gas bubbles in a liquid-film matrix. 2. Any of various light, bulky, more or less rigid materials used as thermal or mechanical insulators, esp. in packaging and containers. —*v.* To form or come forth in foam. [< OE *fām.* See **spoimo-**.] —**foam'i·ness** *n.* —**foam'y** *adj.*

foam rubber. A light, firm, spongy rubber containing several times the volume of air ordinarily found in rubber.

fob¹ (fŏb) *n.* 1. A short chain or ribbon attached to a pocket watch. 2. An ornament attached to such a chain or ribbon. [Prob < Gmc.]

fob² (fŏb) *v.* **fobbed, fobbing.** —**fob off. 1.** To dispose of (goods) by fraud. 2. To put off or appease by deceitful or evasive means. [ME *fobben.*]

f.o.b., F.O.B. free on board.

focal length. The distance of the focal point from the surface of a lens or mirror.

focal point. A point on the axis of symmetry of an optical system to which parallel incident rays converge or from which they appear to diverge after passing through the system.

fo·cus (fō'kəs) *n., pl.* **-cuses** or **-ci** (-sī'). 1. A point to which something converges or from which it diverges. 2. *Opt.* **a. Focal point. b. Focal length. c.** The distinctness or clarity with which an optical system renders an image. **d.** Adjustment for distinctness or clarity. 3. A center of interest or activity. —*v.* **-cused** or **-cussed, -cusing** or **-cussing. 1. a.** To produce a clear image of. **b.** To adjust the setting of (a lens) to produce a clear image. 2. To concentrate on. 3. To converge at a focus. [L, fireplace, hearth (the center of the home).] —**fo'cal** *adj.* —**fo'cal·ly** *adv.*

fod·der (fŏd'ər) *n.* Feed for livestock, as coarsely chopped stalks and leaves of corn. [< OE *fōdor.* See **pā-**.]

foe (fō) *n.* **1. a.** A personal enemy. **b.** An enemy in war. 2. An adversary; opponent. [< OE *gefāh,* hostile. See **peig-²**.]

foe·tal. Variant of **fetal.**

foe·tus. Variant of **fetus.**

fog (fôg, fŏg) *n.* 1. Condensed water vapor in cloudlike masses close to the ground, limiting visibility. 2. Confusion or bewilderment. 3. A dark blur on a developed photographic negative. —*v.* **fogged, fogging.** To cover or be obscured by or as by fog. —**fog'gi·ly** *adv.* —**fog'gi·ness** *n.* —**fog'gy** *adj.*

fog·horn (fôg'hôrn', fŏg'-) *n.* A horn used by ships and coastal installations to sound warning signals in fog or darkness.

fo·gy (fō'gē) *n., pl.* **-gies.** Also **fo·gey** *pl.* **-geys.** A person of old-fashioned habits and attitudes. [?] —**fo'gy·ish** *adj.*

foi·ble (foi'bəl) *n.* A minor weakness of character. [< OF *feble,* feeble.]

foil¹ (foil) *v.* To prevent from being successful; thwart. [< ME *foilen,* to trample.]

foil² (foil) *n.* 1. A thin, flexible leaf or sheet of metal. 2. Any person or thing that, by contrast, enhances the characteristics of another. [< L *folium,* leaf.]

foil³ (foil) *n.* A fencing sword with a thin, flexible blade tipped with a blunt point. [?]

foist (foist) *v.* 1. To pass off (something inferior) as genuine, valuable, or worthy. 2. To impose (something or someone unwanted) upon another, as by coercion. 3. To insert fraudulently or deceitfully. [< Du *vuist,* fist.]

fol. 1. folio. 2. following.

fold¹ (fōld) *v.* 1. To bend over or double up so that one part lies on another. 2. To bring from an extended to a closed position. 3. To place together and intertwine: *fold one's arms.* 4. To wrap; envelop. 5. To mix in (an ingredient) by slowly and gently turning one part over another, as in cooking. 6. *Informal.* To fail or collapse. —*n.* 1. The act or an instance of folding. 2. The junction of two folded parts. [< OE *fealdan.* See **pel-³**.]

fold² (fōld) *n.* 1. A fenced enclosure for domestic animals, esp. sheep. 2. A flock of sheep. 3. Any group of people with common beliefs, aims, or loyalties. —*v.* To place or keep (sheep) in a fold. [< OE *fald.*]

–fold. *comb. form.* A specified number of parts: *fivefold.* [< OE *-feald.* See **pel-³**.]

fold·er (fōl'dər) *n.* 1. A group of folded, printed sheets gathered together but not fastened. 2. A folded piece of cardboard or thick paper used as a container.

fol·de·rol (fŏl'də-rŏl') *n.* 1. Foolish talk or procedure; nonsense. 2. A trifle; gewgaw.

fo·li·age (fō'lē-ĭj) *n.* Plant leaves collectively. [< L *folium,* leaf.]

fo·li·ar (fō'lē-ər) *adj.* Of or pertaining to a leaf or leaves.

fo·li·o (fō'lē-ō') *n., pl.* **-os.** 1. A large sheet of paper folded once in the middle. 2. A book of the largest common size having such folded sheets. 3. A page number in a book. [< L *folium,* leaf.]

folk (fōk) *n., pl.* **folk** or *informal* **folks. 1.** A people; a nation. 2. People of a specified group or kind: *city folk.* 3. **folks.** *Informal.* The members of one's family. 4. **folks.** *Informal.* People in general. —*adj.* Of, occurring in, or originating among the common people: *folk music.* [< OE *folc,* the people, nation < Gmc **folkam.*]

folk·lore (fōk'lôr', -lōr') *n.* The body of orally preserved traditions, beliefs, tales, etc., of a people. —**folk'lor·ist** *n.*

folk·sy (fōk'sē) *adj.* **-sier, -siest.** *Informal.* 1. Casual; unpretentious. 2. Sociable; congenial.

fol·li·cle (fŏl'ĭ-kəl) *n.* 1. An approximately spherical group of cells containing a cavity. 2. A vascular body in the ovary containing ova. [< L *follis,* bellows.]

fol·low (fŏl'ō) *v.* 1. To come or go after. 2. To pursue. 3. To accompany; attend. 4. To move along the course of. 5. To obey; comply with. 6. To succeed to the place or position of. 7. To engage in. 8. To result; ensue. 9. To be attentive to. **10.** To grasp the meaning or logic of; understand. [< OE *folgian* and *fylgan* < Gmc **fulg-*.]

fol·low·er (fŏl'ō-ər) *n.* **1.** One that follows another. **2.** An attendant or subordinate. **3.** One who subscribes to the teachings of another; an adherent.

fol·low·ing (fŏl'ō-ĭng) *adj.* **1.** Coming next in time or order. **2.** Now to be enumerated. —*n.* A group or gathering of followers.

fol·ly (fŏl'ē) *n., pl.* **-lies. 1.** Lack of good judgment. **2. a.** An act or instance of foolishness. **b.** A costly undertaking having an absurd or ruinous outcome. [< OF *fol*, foolish.]

fo·ment (fō-měnt') *v.* **1.** To arouse; stir up; instigate. **2.** To treat with heat and moisture. [< L *fōmentum*, warm application.]

fond (fŏnd) *adj.* **1.** Affectionate; tender. **2.** Having a tender interest or affection (with *of*). **3.** Foolishly affectionate; doting. **4.** Cherished; dear. [Prob < ME *fon*, a fool.] —**fond'ly** *adv.* —**fond'ness** *n.*

fon·dle (fŏnd'l) *v.* **-dled, -dling.** To handle or stroke affectionately; caress.

font¹ (fŏnt) *n.* **1.** A receptacle for holy or baptismal water. **2.** *Archaic.* A fountain or spring. **3.** Any source of abundance. [< L *fons (font-)*, spring, fountain.]

font² (fŏnt) *n.* A complete set of printing type of one size and face. [< OF *fondre*, to melt, cast.]

food (fōōd) *n.* **1.** Any material, usually of plant or animal origin, that is taken in and assimilated by an organism to maintain life and growth. **2.** A specified kind of nourishment. **3.** Solid nourishment as distinguished from liquid nourishment. **4.** Anything that nourishes or sustains. [< OE *fōda*. See **pā-.**]

food stamp. A stamp issued by the government and sold or given to low-income persons to be redeemed for food.

food·stuff (fōōd'stŭf') *n.* Any substance suitable for food, esp. after processing.

fool (fōōl) *n.* **1.** One deficient in judgment, sense, or understanding. **2.** A jester; buffoon. **3.** One who can be easily deceived; a dupe. —*v.* **1.** To deceive or misinform; trick; dupe. **2.** To act or speak in jest; play; joke. —**fool around.** To engage in useless or trifling activity. —**fool with.** To toy or tamper with. [< L *follis*, "bellows," windbag.]

fool·er·y (fōō'lə-rē) *n., pl.* **-ies. 1.** Foolish behavior or speech. **2.** A prank or trick.

fool·har·dy (fōōl'här'dē) *adj.* **-dier, -diest.** Unwisely bold; rash. —**fool'har'di·ness** *n.*

fool·ish (fōō'lĭsh) *adj.* **1.** Having or resulting from poor judgment; unwise. **2.** Silly; ridiculous; inane. **3.** Abashed; embarrassed. —**fool'ish·ly** *adv.* —**fool'ish·ness** *n.*

fool·proof (fōōl'prōōf') *adj.* Designed to be proof against human error or misuse.

fools·cap (fōōlz'kăp') *n.* A sheet of paper approx. 13 × 16 inches.

fool's gold. Pyrite or any similar mineral found in gold-colored veins or nuggets, sometimes mistaken for gold.

foot (fōōt) *n., pl.* **feet** (fēt). **1.** The lower extremity of the leg that is in direct contact with the ground in standing or walking. **2.** Something resembling or suggestive of a foot in position or function, as the bottom or lowest part or the end opposite the head. **3.** *Pros.* A metric unit consisting of a stressed or unstressed syllable or syllables. **4.** A unit of length equal to ⅓ yard or 12 inches. —**on foot.** Walking or standing; not riding. —**under foot.** Obstructing free movement; in the way. —*v.* **1.** To go on foot; walk. **2.** To dance. **3.** To move steadily; proceed. **4.** To add up; total: *Foot up the bill.* **5.** *Informal.* To pay. [< OE *fōt.* See **ped-¹.**]

Usage: Foot and *feet*, as units of measure, are employed typically in the following: *a four-foot plank; a plank four feet long* (or *four feet in length*); *a man six feet tall; a ledge two feet below.*

foot·age (fōōt'ĭj) *n.* **1.** The length of something expressed in feet. **2.** A portion of motion-picture film.

foot·ball (fōōt'bôl') *n.* **1. a.** A game played with a ball on a rectangular field by opposing teams of 11 players each. **b.** The ball used in this game, an inflated ellipsoid. **2.** *Chiefly Brit.* **a.** **Rugby football. b.** Soccer.

foot·board (fōōt'bôrd', -bôrd') *n.* **1.** A board or small raised platform on which to support the feet. **2.** An upright board across the foot of a bedstead.

foot·bridge (fōōt'brĭj') *n.* A narrow bridge for pedestrians.

foot·ed (fōōt'ĭd) *adj.* **1.** Having a foot or feet. **2.** Having a specified kind or number of feet: *web-footed.*

foot·fall (fōōt'fôl') *n.* **1.** A footstep. **2.** The sound made by a footstep or footsteps.

foot·hill (fōōt'hĭl') *n.* A low hill near the base of a mountain.

foot·hold (fōōt'hōld') *n.* **1.** A place affording support for the foot in climbing or standing. **2.** A firm or secure position enabling one to advance.

foot·ing (fōōt'ĭng) *n.* **1.** A secure placement of the feet. **2.** A place on which one can stand or move securely. **3.** A basis; foundation. **4. a.** The totaling up of a column of figures. **b.** The sum of such a column.

foot·less (fōōt'lĭs) *adj.* **1.** Without feet. **2.** Without a firm support or basis. **3.** Clumsy; inept. —**foot'less·ness** *n.*

foot·lights (fōōt'līts') *pl.n.* **1.** A row of lights along the front of a stage floor. **2.** The theater as a profession.

foot·lock·er (fōōt'lŏk'ər) *n.* A small trunk for storing personal belongings.

foot·loose (fōōt'lōōs') *adj.* Having no attachments or ties; free.

foot·man (fōōt'mən) *n.* A male servant employed to wait on table, attend the door, and run errands.

foot·note (fōōt'nōt') *n.* A note of comment or reference, often placed at the bottom of a page.

foot·path (fōōt'păth', -päth') *n., pl.* **-paths** (-păthz', -päthz', -păths', -päths'). A narrow path for people on foot.

foot·pound (fōōt'pound') *n.* A unit of work

equal to the work done by a force of one pound acting through a distance of one foot in the direction of the force.

foot·print (fŏŏt′prĭnt′) n. An outline or indentation of a foot.

foot·rest (fŏŏt′rĕst′) n. A support on which to rest the feet.

foot soldier. A soldier who fights on foot; infantryman.

foot·step (fŏŏt′stĕp′) n. 1. A step with the foot. 2. The distance covered by one step. 3. The sound of a foot stepping. 4. A footprint. 5. A step up or down.

foot·stool (fŏŏt′stōōl′) n. A low stool for supporting the feet.

foot·wear (fŏŏt′wâr′) n. Anything worn on the feet, as shoes.

foot·work (fŏŏt′wûrk′) n. The manner in which the feet are employed, as in boxing.

fop (fŏp) n. A man who is preoccupied with clothes and manners; a dandy. [ME, a fool.] —**fop′per·y** n. —**fop′pish** adj.

for (fôr, unstressed fər) prep. 1. —Used to indicate a recipient: a letter for me. 2. As a result of: weep for joy. 3. To the extent or through the duration of. 4. In order to go to or reach: start for home. 5. a. With an aim or view to: swim for fun. b. So as to find, get, have, keep, or save. 6. In preparation toward: study for the ministry. 7. In the amount or at the price of. 8. In response to or requital of. 9. In view of the normal character of: short for a novel. 10. At a stated time: a date for 6 o'clock. 11. In the service or hire of. 12. In honor or behalf of. 13. In favor, defense, or support of. 14. In place of. 15. With effect on or by way of affecting. 16. In coincidence or conjunction with: one bad egg for every good one. 17. As against: pound for pound. 18. As being: took him for a fool. 19. As the duty or task of; up to: It's for him to decide. 20. —Used with an infinitive preceded by its subject as an equivalent for a corresponding noun clause: a job for us to do. 21. Despite (with all): For all his learning he's a bore. —conj. For this reason; namely. [< OE. See per¹.]

for. 1. foreign. 2. forestry.

fo·ra. Alternate pl. of **forum.**

for·age (fôr′ĭj, fŏr′-) n. 1. Food for animals, as that obtained by grazing. 2. A search for food or supplies. —v. **-aged, -aging.** 1. To search for food or supplies. 2. To raid; plunder. 3. To rummage through, esp. in search of provisions. [< OF feurre, fodder.]

fo·ra·men (fə-rā′mən) n., pl. **-ramina** (-răm′ə-nə) or **-mens.** An anatomical aperture or perforation. [< L forāmen, an opening.]

for·ay (fôr′ā′) n. 1. A raid, as for plunder. 2. A venture in some field. [< OF forrier, plunderer.] —**for′ay′** v.

for·bear¹ (fôr-bâr′) v. **-bore, -borne, -bearing.** 1. To refrain or desist from. 2. To be tolerant or patient. [< OE forberan, to bear, endure.] —**for·bear′ance** n. —**for·bear′er** n.

for·bear². Variant of **forebear.**

for·bid (fər-bĭd′, fôr-) v. **-bade** (-băd′, -bād′) or **-bad** (-băd′), **-bidden** (-bĭd′n) or **-bid, -bidding.** 1. To command (someone) not to do some-

thing. 2. To prohibit; interdict. 3. To preclude. [< OE forbēodan.]

for·bid·ding (fər-bĭd′ĭng, fôr-) adj. 1. Unfriendly; disagreeable: a desolate and forbidding landscape. 2. Grim; ominous.

force (fôrs, fōrs) n. 1. Strength; power. 2. The exertion of such power. 3. Intellectual vigor or persuasiveness, as of a statement. 4. A body of persons organized for a certain purpose, esp. for the use of military power. 5. A vector quantity that tends to produce an acceleration of a body in the direction of its application. —**in force.** 1. In full strength. 2. In effect; operative. —v. **forced, forcing.** 1. To compel to perform an action. 2. To obtain by force; extort. 3. To produce by effort: force a tear from one's eye. 4. To move (something) against resistance. 5. To break down or open by force: force a lock. 6. To inflict or impose. 7. To cause to grow rapidly by artificial means. [< L fortis, strong.]

force field. Field of force.

force·ful (fôrs′fəl, fōrs′-) adj. Effective; persuasive. —**force′ful·ly** adv.

for·ceps (fôr′səps) n., pl. **-ceps.** An instrument used for grasping, manipulating, or extracting. [L forceps, fire tongs, pincers.]

for·ci·ble (fôr′sə-bəl, fōr′-) adj. Effected through or characterized by force. —**for′ci·ble·ness** n. —**for′ci·bly** adv.

ford (fôrd, fōrd) n. A shallow place in a body of water where a crossing can be made on foot or on horseback. —v. To cross at such a shallow place. [< OE. See per-².]

Ford (fôrd, fōrd), **Gerald Rudolph.** Original name, Leslie Lynch King, Jr. Born 1913. 38th President of the U.S. (1974–77).

Ford (fôrd, fōrd), **Henry.** 1863–1947. American automobile designer and manufacturer.

fore (fôr, fōr) adj. Located at or toward the front; anterior. —n. The front part. —adv. Toward or at the bow of a ship; forward. —interj. Expressive of a warning to those ahead that a golf ball is about to be driven in their direction. [< OE, beforehand. See per¹.]

fore-. comb. form. 1. Before in time. 2. The front or first part.

fore-and-aft (fôr′ən-ăft′, -äft′, fōr′-) adj. Parallel with the keel of a ship.

fore·arm¹ (fôr-ärm′, fōr-) v. To prepare in advance for some conflict.

fore·arm² (fôr′ärm′, fōr′-) n. The part of the arm between the wrist and elbow.

fore·bear (fôr′bâr′, fōr′-) n. Also **fore·bear.** An ancestor; forefather. [< FORE- + ME bear, "be-er."]

fore·bode (fôr-bōd′, fōr-) v. **-boded, -boding.** 1. To indicate the threatening likelihood of; portend. 2. To have a premonition of (a future misfortune). —**fore·bod′ing** n. & adj.

fore·cast (fôr′kăst′, -käst′, fōr′-) v. **-cast** or **-casted, -casting.** 1. To estimate or calculate in advance, esp. to predict the weather. 2. To serve as an advance indication of; foreshadow. —n. A prediction. —**fore′cast′er** n.

fore·cas·tle (fōk′səl, fôr′kăs′əl, -käs′əl, fōr′-) n. 1. The section of the upper deck of a ship located at the bow. 2. A superstructure at the

---

ô paw, for/oi boy/ou out/ŏŏ took/ōō coo/p pop/r run/s sauce/sh shy/t to/th thin/th the/
ŭ cut/ûr fur/v van/w wag/y yes/z size/zh vision/ə ago, item, edible, gallop, circus/

bow of a merchant ship, where the crew is housed.

fore·close (fôr-klōz′, fōr-) v. **-closed, -closing.**
1. To deprive (a mortgagor) of possession of mortgaged property, as when he has failed in his payments. **2.** To shut out; bar.

fore·clo·sure (fôr-klō′zhər, fōr-) n. The act of foreclosing, esp. a legal proceeding by which a mortgage is foreclosed.

fore·fa·ther (fôr′fä′thər, fōr′-) n. An ancestor.

fore·fin·ger (fôr′fĭng′gər, fōr′-) n. The index finger.

fore·foot (fôr′fŏŏt′, fōr′-) n. One of the front feet of an animal.

fore·front (fôr′frŭnt′, fōr′-) n. **1.** The foremost part or area of something. **2.** The position of most importance.

fore·go¹ (fôr-gō′, fōr-) v. To precede.

fore·go². Variant of **forgo.**

fore·go·ing (fôr-gō′ĭng, fōr-, fôr′gō′ĭng, fōr′-) adj. Just past; preceding.

fore·gone (fôr′gôn′, -gŏn′, fōr′-) adj. Having gone or been completed previously. [pp of FOREGO¹.]

fore·ground (fôr′ground′, fōr′-) n. **1.** The part of a view or picture that is nearest to the viewer. **2.** The most important position.

fore·hand (fôr′hănd′, fōr′-) adj. Made with the hand moving palm forward: *a forehand tennis stroke.* —**fore′hand** n.

fore·head (fôr′ĭd, fōr′-, fôr′hĕd′, fōr′-) n. The part of the face between the eyebrows and the normal hairline.

for·eign (fôr′ĭn, fŏr′-) adj. **1.** Located away from one's native country: *foreign parts.* **2.** Of a country other than one's own: *a foreign custom.* **3.** Conducted or involved with other nations: *foreign trade.* **4.** Situated in an abnormal or improper place. **5.** Not germane; extraneous. [< L *forās,* out of doors, abroad.] —**for′eign·ness** n.

for·eign·er (fôr′ə-nər, fŏr′-) n. A person from a foreign country.

Foreign Office. The official name, in several countries, of the department in charge of foreign affairs.

fore·knowl·edge (fôr-nŏl′ĭj, fōr′-) n. Knowledge of something prior to its occurrence.

fore·leg (fôr′lĕg′, fōr′-) n. One of the front legs of an animal.

fore·limb (fôr′lĭm′, fōr′-) n. An anterior appendage such as a leg, wing, or flipper.

fore·lock (fôr′lŏk′, fōr′-) n. A lock of hair that falls on the forehead.

fore·man (fôr′mən, fōr′-) n. **1.** A man who has charge of a group of workers. **2.** The spokesman for a jury.

fore·mast (fôr′məst, -măst′, -mäst′, fōr′-) n. The forward mast on a sailing vessel.

fore·most (fôr′mōst′, fōr′-) adj. Ahead of all others, esp. in position or rank. [< OE *formest,* superl of *forma,* first. See per¹.] —**fore′most** adv.

fore·noon (fôr′nōōn′, fōr′-, fôr-nōōn′, fōr′-) n. The period of time between sunrise and noon.

fo·ren·sic (fə-rĕn′sĭk) adj. **1.** Of or employed in legal proceedings: *forensic medicine.* **2.** Of debate or argument; rhetorical. —n. **forensics.**

(takes sing. v.). The art of formal debate. [< L *forēnsis,* of a market or forum.]

fore·or·dain (fôr-ôr-dān′, fōr′-) v. To appoint or ordain beforehand; predestine.

fore·quar·ter (fôr′kwôr′tər, fōr′-) n. The region including the front leg and shoulder of an animal or side of meat.

fore·run·ner (fôr′rŭn′ər, fōr′-) n. **1.** A predecessor. **2.** One that provides advance notice of the coming of others; harbinger.

fore·sail (fôr′səl, -sāl′, fōr′-) n. *Naut.* The principal sail hung to the foremast.

fore·see (fôr-sē′, fōr-) v. To see or know beforehand. —**fore·see′a·ble** adj.

fore·shad·ow (fôr-shăd′ō, fōr-) v. To present an indication or suggestion of beforehand.

fore·shore (fôr′shôr′, fôr′shōr′) n. The part of a shore covered at high tide.

fore·short·en (fôr-shôrt′n, fōr-) v. To represent the long axis of (an object) by contracting its lines so as to produce an illusion of projection or extension in space.

fore·sight (fôr′sīt′, fōr′-) n. **1.** The act or ability of foreseeing. **2.** The act of looking forward. **3.** Concern or prudence with respect to the future. —**fore′sight′ed** adj.

fore·skin (fôr′skĭn′, fōr′-) n. The prepuce.

for·est (fôr′ĭst, fŏr′-) n. A dense growth of trees covering a large area. [< LL *forestis (silva),* outside (forest).]

fore·stall (fôr-stôl′, fōr-) v. **1.** To prevent or take precautionary measures against beforehand. **2.** To deal with beforehand; anticipate. [< OE *foresteall,* waylaying, interception.]

for·est·ry (fôr′ĭ-strē, fŏr′-) n. The science of maintaining and developing forests. —**for′est·er** n.

fore·taste (fôr′tāst′, fōr′-) n. An advance realization. —**fore′taste′** v.

fore·tell (fôr-tĕl′, fōr-) v. To tell of or indicate beforehand; predict.

fore·thought (fôr′thôt′, fōr′-) n. **1.** Deliberation or planning beforehand. **2.** Preparation for the future.

for·ev·er (fôr-ĕv′ər, fər-) adv. **1.** Eternally. **2.** Incessantly.

for·ev·er·more (fôr-ĕv′ər-môr′, -mōr′, fər-) adv. Forever.

fore·warn (fôr-wôrn′, fōr-) v. To warn in advance.

fore·word (fôr′wûrd′, -wərd, fōr′-) n. A preface or introductory note.

for·feit (fôr′fĭt) n. **1.** Something surrendered as punishment; a penalty or fine. **2.** Something placed in escrow and then redeemed after payment of a fine. **3.** A forfeiture. —v. To surrender or be forced to surrender as a forfeit. [< OF *forsfaire,* to commit a crime.]

for·fei·ture (fôr′fĭ-chŏŏr′) n. **1.** The act of forfeiting. **2.** Something forfeited.

for·gath·er (fôr-găth′ər, fōr-) v. To gather together; assemble.

for·gave (fər-gāv′, fôr-) p.t. of **forgive.**

forge¹ (fôrj, fōrj) n. A furnace or hearth where metals are heated or wrought; smithy. —v. **forged, forging. 1.** To form (metal) by heating and hammering. **2.** To give form or shape to: *forge a treaty.* **3.** To fashion or reproduce for

---

ă pat/ā ate/âr care/ä bar/b bib/ch chew/d deed/ĕ pet/ē be/f fit/g gag/h hat/hw what/
ĭ pit/ī pie/îr pier/j judge/k kick/l lid, fatal/m mum/n no, sudden/ng sing/ŏ pot/ō go/

fraudulent purposes: *forge a signature.* [< L *fabrica*, smithy, artisan's workshop.] —**forge'-a·ble** *adj.* —**forg'er** *n.*

forge² (fôrj, fōrj) *v.* **forged, forging. 1.** To advance gradually but firmly. **2.** To advance with an abrupt increase of speed. [Perh a var of FORCE.]

for·ger·y (fôr'jə-rē, fōr'-) *n., pl.* **-ies. 1.** The production of something counterfeit or forged. **2.** Something forged.

for·get (fər-gĕt', fôr-) *v.* **-got** (-gŏt'), **-gotten** (-gŏt'n) or **-got, -getting. 1.** To be unable to remember or call to mind. **2.** To treat with inattention; neglect. **3.** To fail or neglect to become aware at the proper moment. —**forget oneself.** To lose one's reserve or self-restraint. [< OE *forgietan.* See **ghend-**.] —**for·get'ful** *adj.* —**for·get'ful·ness** *n.*

for·get-me-not (fər-gĕt'mē-nŏt', fôr-) *n.* A low-growing plant with small blue flowers.

for·give (fər-gĭv', fôr-) *v.* **-gave, -given, -giving. 1.** To excuse for a fault or offense. **2.** To renounce resentment against. **3.** To absolve from payment of. [< OE *forgiefan.*] —**for·giv'a·ble** *adj.* —**for·give'ness** *n.*

for·go (fôr-gō') *v.* **-went, -gone** (-gôn', -gŏn'), **-going.** Also **forego.** To relinquish; abstain from; forsake. —**for·go'er** *n.*

fo·rint (fôr'ĭnt) *n.* The basic monetary unit of Hungary.

fork (fôrk) *n.* **1.** An implement with two or more prongs used for raising, carrying, piercing, etc. **2.** A pronged utensil for serving or eating food. **3. a.** A bifurcation into branches. **b.** The point at which this occurs. **c.** One of the branches. —*v.* **1.** To raise, carry, etc., with a fork. **2.** To give the shape of a fork to. **3.** To divide into branches. [< L *furca*, two-pronged fork.]

forked (fôrkt, fôr'kĭd) *adj.* Containing or shaped like a fork.

fork lift. A vehicle with a power-operated pronged platform for lifting and carrying loads.

for·lorn (fôr-lôrn', fər-) *adj.* **1.** Deserted; abandoned. **2.** Wretched or pitiful. **3.** Nearly hopeless. [< OE *forlēosan*, to abandon. See **leu-**.] —**for·lorn'ly** *adv.*

form (fôrm) *n.* **1.** The contour and structure of something. **2.** The body, esp. of a person. **3.** The essence of something. **4.** The mode in which a thing exists; kind; variety: *a form of animal life.* **5.** Procedure as determined by regulation or custom. **6.** Manners as governed by etiquette. **7.** Performance according to recognized criteria. **8.** Fitness with regard to health or training. **9.** A fixed order of words or procedures, as in a ceremony. **10.** A document with blanks for the insertion of requested information. **11.** Style or manner in literary or musical composition. **12.** The structure of a work of art. **13.** A model for making a mold. **14.** A grade in a British school or in some American private schools. —*v.* **1.** To shape or become shaped. **2.** To shape into or assume a particular form. **3.** To develop by instruction or precept: *form the mind.* **4.** To develop; acquire: *form a habit.* **5.** To constitute a part

of. **6.** To develop in the mind: *form an opinion.* **7.** To draw up; arrange. [< L *fōrma*, form, contour, shape.]

–form. *comb. form.* Having the form of: **cuneiform.**

for·mal (fôr'məl) *adj.* **1.** Pertaining to the extrinsic aspect of something. **2.** Pertaining to the essential form of something: *a formal principle.* **3.** Following accepted conventions or proper form. **4.** Characterized by strict observation of forms. **5.** Stiff or cold: *a formal manner.* **6.** Done for the sake of form only: *a purely formal greeting.* —*n.* An occasion requiring formal attire. [< L *fōrmālis*, of or for form.] —**for'mal·ly** *adv.*

for·mal·de·hyde (fôr-măl'də-hīd') *n.* A colorless, gaseous compound, HCHO, used in aqueous solution as a preservative and disinfectant. [< FORM(IC ACID) + ALDEHYDE.]

for·mal·ism (fôr'mə-lĭz'əm) *n.* Rigorous or excessive adherence to recognized forms.

for·mal·i·ty (fôr-măl'ə-tē) *n., pl.* **-ties. 1.** The quality or condition of being formal. **2.** Rigorous or ceremonious adherence to established rules. **3.** An established form.

for·mal·ize (fôr'mə-līz') *v.* **-ized, -izing. 1.** To give a definite form or shape to. **2.** To render formal. **3.** To give formal endorsement to.

for·mat (fôr'măt') *n.* **1.** A plan for the organization and arrangement of something. **2.** The layout of a publication. [< L *fōrma*, FORM.]

for·ma·tion (fôr-mā'shən) *n.* **1.** The process of forming. **2.** Something that is formed. **3.** The manner in which something is formed. **4.** A specified arrangement, as of troops.

for·ma·tive (fôr'mə-tĭv) *adj.* **1.** Forming or capable of forming. **2.** Pertaining to growth or development: *a formative stage.*

for·mer (fôr'mər) *adj.* **1.** Occurring earlier in time. **2.** Coming before in place or order. **3.** Of the first or first mentioned of two. —See Usage note at **latter.** [< OE *forma*, first. See **per¹**.]

for·mer·ly (fôr'mər-lē) *adv.* At a former time; once.

form-fit·ting (fôrm'fĭt'ĭng) *adj.* Closely fitted to the body.

For·mi·ca (fôr-mī'kə) *n.* A trademark for any of various high-pressure laminated plastic sheets, used esp. for chemical and heat-resistant surfaces.

for·mic acid (fôr'mĭk). A colorless caustic fuming liquid, HCOOH, used in fumigants, insecticides, and refrigerants. [< L *formica*, ant.]

for·mi·da·ble (fôr'mə-də-bəl) *adj.* **1.** Arousing dread or awe. **2.** Difficult to surmount. [< L *formīdō*, fright, fear.] —**for'mi·da·bly** *adv.*

For·mo·sa (fôr-mō'sə). The former name for **Taiwan.**

for·mu·la (fôr'myə-lə) *n., pl.* **-las** or **-lae** (-lē'). **1.** A set form of words or symbols for use in a ceremony. **2.** A hackneyed expression; a cliché. **3.** A symbolic representation of the composition, or of the composition and structure, of a chemical compound. **4.** A recipe. **5.** A liquid food prescribed for an infant. **6.** A mathematical statement, as an equation, of

some logical relation. [< L *fōrma*, FORM.]
—for'mu·la'ic (fôr'myə-lā'ĭk) *adj.*

for·mu·late (fôr'myə-lāt') *v.* -lated, -lating. 1. To state as a formula. 2. To express in systematic terms. 3. To prepare according to a formula. —for'mu·la'tion *n.*

for·ni·ca·tion (fôr'nĭ-kā'shən) *n.* Sexual intercourse between a man and woman not married to each other. —for'ni·cate *v.* (-cated, -cating).

for·sake (fôr-sāk', fər-) *v.* -sook (-sŏŏk'), -saken (-sā'kən), -saking. 1. To give up; renounce. 2. To leave altogether; abandon. [< OE *forsacan*. See **sāg-.**] —for·sak'er *n.*

for·sooth (fôr-sŏŏth', fər-) *adv. Archaic.* In truth; indeed.

for·swear (fôr-swâr') *v.* -swore (-swôr', -swōr'), -sworn (-swôrn', -swōrn'), -swearing. 1. To renounce or forsake unalterably. 2. To repudiate unalterably. 3. To commit perjury.

for·syth·i·a (fôr-sĭth'ē-ə, fər-) *n.* A widely cultivated shrub with early-blooming yellow flowers. [< W. *Forsyth* (1737–1804), English botanist.]

fort (fôrt, fōrt) *n.* A fortified place, esp. a permanent post. [< L *fortis*, strong.]

forte¹ (fôrt, fōrt, fôr'tā) *n.* Something in which a person excels. [< OF *fort*, "strong."]

for·te² (fôr'tā) *adv. Mus.* Loudly; forcefully. [It, "strongly."] —for'te *adj.*

forth (fôrth, fōrth) *adv.* 1. Forward; onward. 2. Out into view. [< OE. See **per¹.**]

forth·com·ing (fôrth-kŭm'ĭng, fōrth-) *adj.* 1. About to appear: *the forthcoming elections.* 2. Available when required.

forth·right (fôrth'rīt', fōrth'-) *adj.* Straightforward; frank; candid.

forth·with (fôrth'wĭth', -wĭth', fōrth'-) *adv.* At once; immediately.

for·ti·eth (fôr'tē-ĭth) *n.* 1. The ordinal number 40 in a series. 2. One of 40 equal parts. —for'ti·eth *adj. & adv.*

for·ti·fy (fôr'tə-fī') *v.* -fied, -fying. 1. To strengthen and secure (a position) with military defenses. 2. To impart physical strength to. 3. To give moral or mental strength to; encourage. 4. To strengthen or increase the content of (a substance), as by adding vitamins to food or alcohol to wine. [< L *fortis*, strong.] —for'ti·fi·ca'tion *n.* —for'ti·fi'er *n.*

for·tis·si·mo (fôr-tĭs'ə-mō') *adv. Mus.* Very loudly. [It.] —for·tis'si·mo' *adj.*

for·ti·tude (fôr'tə-t/y/ōod') *n.* Strength of mind that allows one to endure adversity with courage. [< L *fortis*, strong.]

Fort-La·my (fôr'lə-mē') The former name for N'Djamena.

fort·night (fôrt'nīt', -nĭt) *n.* A period of 14 days; two weeks. [< OE *fēowertiene niht* : FOURTEEN + NIGHT.]

fort·night·ly (fôrt'nīt'lē) *adj.* Happening or appearing once in every two weeks. —fort'night'ly *adv.*

for·tress (fôr'trĭs) *n.* A fort. [< L *fortis*, strong.]

for·tu·i·tous (fôr-t/y/ōo'ə-təs) *adj.* Happening by accident or chance. [< L *forte*, by chance.]

for·tu·i·ty (fôr-t/y/ōo'ə-tē) *n., pl.* -ties. 1. An accidental occurrence; chance. 2. The quality or condition of being fortuitous.

for·tu·nate (fôr'chə-nĭt) *adj.* 1. Occurring by good fortune. 2. Lucky.

for·tune (fôr'chən) *n.* 1. A hypothetical force that governs the events of one's life. 2. Good or bad luck. 3. Luck, esp. when good; success. 4. Wealth or riches. [< L *fors*, chance, luck.]

for·tune-tell·er (fôr'chən-tĕl'ər) *n.* A person who, usually for a fee, will undertake to predict one's future. —for'tune-tell'ing *n. & adj.*

Fort Wayne (wān). A city in NE Indiana. Pop. 162,000.

Fort Worth (wûrth). A city in NE Texas. Pop. 356,000.

for·ty (fôr'tē) *n.* The cardinal number written 40 or in Roman numerals XL. [< OE *fēowertig*. See **kwetwer-.**] —for'ty *adj. & pron.*

fo·rum (fôr'əm, fōr'-) *n., pl.* -rums or fora (fôr'ə, fōr'ə). 1. The public square or marketplace of an ancient Roman city. 2. Any public place or medium for open discussion. 3. A court of law. [< L, forum, place out-of-doors.]

for·ward (fôr'wərd) *adj.* 1. a. At, near, or belonging to the front. b. Going, tending, or moving toward the front. 2. Ardently inclined; eager. 3. Bold; fresh: *a forward woman.* 4. Progressive: *a forward new nation.* 5. Advanced in development. 6. For the future; completed or made in advance. —*adv.* 1. Also for·wards (-wərdz). Toward or tending to the front; frontward: *step forward.* 2. In or toward the future: *I look forward to seeing you.* 3. Into view or prominence; forth: *Come forward out of the shadows so I can see you.* —*n.* A player in the front lines, as in basketball. —*v.* 1. To send on to a subsequent destination: *forward mail.* 2. To advance; promote. [< FORE- + -WARD.] —for'ward·er *n.*

for·went (fôr-wĕnt', fōr-). *p.t.* of forgo.

fos·sil (fŏs'əl) *n.* 1. A remnant or trace of an organism of a past geological age embedded in the earth's crust. 2. One that is outdated. —*adj.* 1. Of or pertaining to fossils. 2. Derived from fossils: *Coal is a fossil fuel.* [< L *fossilis*, dug up.]

fos·sil·ize (fŏs'ə-līz') *v.* -ized, -izing. To convert into or become a fossil.

fos·ter (fôs'tər, fŏs'-) *v.* 1. To bring up; rear. 2. To encourage; cultivate. —*adj.* Receiving, sharing, or affording parental care although not related through legal or blood ties: *a foster child.* [< OE *fōstor*, food. See **pā-.**]

fought (fôt). *p.t. & p.p.* of fight.

foul (foul) *adj.* 1. Offensive to the senses; disgusting. 2. Having an offensive odor. 3. Spoiled; rotten. 4. Dirty; filthy. 5. Immoral; wicked. 6. Vulgar; obscene. 7. Unpleasant: *a foul day.* 8. Unfair; dishonorable: *win by foul means.* 9. *Sports.* a. Designating lines that limit the playing area: *foul lines.* b. Contrary to the rules or outside the limits set. 10. Entangled, as a rope. —*n.* 1. *Sports.* a. A foul ball, hit, move, etc. b. An infraction of the rules. 2. An entanglement or collision. —*adv.* In a foul manner. —*v.* 1. To make or become foul; soil. 2. To bring into dishonor. 3. To

---

ă pat/ā ate/âr care/ä bar/b bib/ch chew/d deed/ĕ pet/ē be/f fit/g gag/h hat/hw what/
ĭ pit/ī pie/îr pier/j judge/k kick/l lid, fatal/m mum/n no, sudden/ng sing/ŏ pot/ō go/

clog or obstruct. **4.** To entangle or become entangled, as a rope. **5.** *Sports.* To commit a foul. [< OE *fūl.* See **pu-.**] —**foul′ly** *adv.* —**foul′ness** *n.*

fou·lard (fōō-lärd′) *n.* A lightweight twill or plain-woven fabric of silk usually having a printed design. [F.]

foul-mouthed (foul′mou*th*d′, -moutht′) *adj.* Using obscene language.

foul play. Unfair action, esp. when involving violence.

found[1] (found) *v.* **1.** To originate or establish; set up, as a college. **2.** To establish the foundation of. **3.** To have a foundation or base (with *on* or *upon*). [< L *fundāre,* to lay the foundation for.] —**found′er** *n.*

found[2] (found) *v.* **1.** To melt (a metal) and pour into a mold. **2.** To make (objects) in this fashion; cast. [< L *fundere,* to pour, melt.] —**found′er** *n.*

found[3] (found). *p.t.* & *p.p.* of **find.**

foun·da·tion (foun-dā′shən) *n.* **1.** The act of founding or state of being founded. **2.** The basis on which a thing stands; an underlying support. **3.** An endowment. **4.** An endowed institution. —**foun·da′tion·al** *adj.*

foun·der (foun′dər) *v.* **1.** To go lame, as a horse. **2.** To fail utterly; collapse or break down. **3.** To sink below the water. [< VL **fundorāre,* to submerge.]

found·ling (found′lĭng) *n.* A child abandoned by unknown parents. [Prob < ME *finden,* to find.]

foun·dry (foun′drē) *n., pl.* **-dries.** An establishment in which the founding of metals is done.

fount (fount) *n.* **1.** A fountain. **2.** Any source. [Prob < FOUNTAIN.]

foun·tain (foun′tən) *n.* **1.** A spring, esp. the source of a stream. **2.** Any source. **3. a.** An artificially created jet of water. **b.** A device that produces such a jet: *a drinking fountain.* **4.** A container for liquid that can be siphoned off as needed. [< L *fons (font-),* spring.]

foun·tain·head (foun′tən-hĕd′) *n.* A principal source or origin.

fountain pen. A pen containing an ink reservoir that feeds the writing point.

four (fôr, fōr) *n.* The cardinal number written 4 or in Roman numerals IV. [< OE *fēower.* See **four** *adj* & *pron.*

four-flush·er (fôr′flŭsh′ər, fōr′-) *n. Slang.* A bluffer; faker.

four-in-hand (fôr′ĭn-hănd′, fōr′-) *n.* **1.** A team of four horses driven by one person. **2.** A necktie tied in a slipknot with the ends left hanging and overlapping.

four-post·er (fôr′pō′stər, fōr′-) *n.* A bed having tall corner posts originally intended to support curtains or a canopy.

four·score (fôr′skôr′, fōr′skōr′) *adj.* Four times 20; 80.

four·some (fôr′səm, fōr′-) *n.* **1.** Any group of four persons. **2.** Any game played by four persons, two on each side.

four·square (fôr′skwâr′, fōr′-) *adj.* **1.** Square. **2.** Unyielding; firm. **3.** Forthright; frank. —**four′square′** *adv.*

four·teen (fôr-tēn′, fōr-) *n.* The cardinal number written 14 or in Roman numerals XIV. [< OE *fēowertiene.*] —**four·teen′** *adj.* & *pron.*

four·teenth (fôr-tēnth′, fōr-) *n.* **1.** The ordinal number 14 in a series. **2.** One of 14 equal parts. —**four·teenth′** *adj.* & *adv.*

fourth (fôrth, fōrth) *n.* **1.** The ordinal number 4 in a series. **2.** One of 4 equal parts. [< OE *fēowertha.*] —**fourth** *adj.* & *adv.*

fourth dimension. Time regarded as a coordinate dimension and required by geometry, along with three spatial dimensions, to specify completely the location of any event.

Fourth of July. Independence Day.

fowl (foul) *n., pl.* **fowl** or **fowls.** **1.** A bird used as food or hunted as game, esp. the common domesticated chicken. **2.** The edible flesh of such a bird. —*v.* To hunt wild fowl. [< OE *fugol.* See **pleu-.**] —**fowl′er** *n.*

fox (fŏks) *n.* **1.** A mammal related to the dogs and wolves, having a pointed snout and a long, bushy tail. **2.** The fur of a fox. **3.** A crafty or sly person. —*v.* To trick by ingenuity or cunning. [< OE. See **puk-.**]

foxed (fŏkst) *adj.* Discolored with yellowish-brown stains, as an old book.

fox·glove (fŏks′glŭv′) *n.* A plant with a long cluster of large, tubular, pinkish-purple flowers, and leaves that are the source of the medicinal drug digitalis.

fox·hole (fŏks′hōl′) *n.* A pit dug for refuge against enemy fire.

fox terrier. A small dog with a smooth or wire-haired white coat with dark markings.

fox trot. A ballroom dance in $^2/_4$ or $^4/_4$ time. —**fox′-trot′** *v.*

fox·y (fŏk′sē) *adj.* **-ier, -iest.** Suggestive of a fox; sly; clever. —**fox′i·ness** *n.*

foy·er (foi′ər, foi′ā′) *n.* **1.** The lobby of a public building. **2.** The entrance hall of a private dwelling. [< L *focus,* hearth, fireplace.]

fp freezing point.

fp. foolscap.

Fr francium.

fr. from.

Fr. 1. father (clergyman). **2.** France; French. **3.** friar. **4.** Friday (unofficial).

fra·cas (frā′kəs) *n.* A brawl. [< It *fracasso.*]

frac·tion (frăk′shən) *n.* **1.** A small part of something. **2.** A disconnected piece of something. **3.** *Math.* An indicated quotient of two quantities. **4.** *Chem.* A component separated by distillation, crystallization, etc. [< L *fractus,* pp of *frangere,* to break.] —**frac′tion·al** *adj.*

frac·tious (frăk′shəs) *adj.* **1.** Inclined to make trouble; unruly. **2.** Cranky; irritable.

frac·ture (frăk′chər) *n.* **1. a.** An act, process, or manner of breaking. **b.** The condition of being broken. **2.** A break, rupture, or crack, as in bone or cartilage. —*v.* **-tured, -turing.** To break; crack. [< L *fractus,* broken.]

frag·ile (frăj′əl, -īl′) *adj.* **1.** Easily broken or damaged; brittle. **2.** Physically weak; frail. **3.** Suggesting fragility; light. **4.** Tenuous; flimsy. [< L *fragilis* < *frangere,* to break.] —**frag′ile·ly** *adv.* —**fra·gil′i·ty** (frə-jĭl′ə-tē), **frag′ile·ness** *n.*

frag·ment (frăg′mənt) *n.* **1.** A part broken off. **2.** Something incomplete, as a manuscript. [< L *frangere,* to break.] —**frag′men·ta′tion** *n.*

ô paw, for/oi boy/ou out/ōō took/ōō coo/p pop/r run/s sauce/sh shy/t to/th thin/*th* the/
ŭ cut/ûr fur/v van/w wag/y yes/z size/zh vision/ə ago, item, edible, gallop, circus/

frag·men·tar·y (frăg′mən-tĕr′ē) *adj.* Consisting of fragments. —**frag′men·tar′i·ly** *adv.*

fra·grant (frā′grənt) *adj.* Having a pleasing odor. [< L *fragrāre*, to emit an odor.] —**fra′grance** *n.* —**fra′grant·ly** *adv.*

frail (frāl) *adj.* 1. Having a delicate constitution. 2. Slight; weak. 3. Easily broken. 4. Morally weak. [< L *fragilis*, FRAGILE.]

frail·ty (frāl′tē) *n., pl.* -ties. 1. The condition or quality of being frail. 2. Often **frailties.** A fault arising from human weakness.

frame (frām) *v.* **framed, framing.** 1. To construct; build. 2. To design; draw up. 3. To arrange or adjust for a purpose: *The question was framed to draw only one answer.* 4. To put into words; compose. 5. To provide with a frame; enclose. 6. *Slang.* To rig evidence or events so as to incriminate (a person) falsely. —*n.* 1. Something composed of parts fitted and joined together; a structure, such as: **a.** A skeletal structure: *the frame of a house.* **b.** An open structure or rim: *a window frame.* **c.** The human body. 2. A machine built upon or utilizing a frame. 3. The general structure of something: *the frame of government.* 4. A single exposure on a roll of motion-picture film. [< OE *framian*, to benefit, avail. See **per¹.**] —**fram′er** *n.*

frame-up (frām′ŭp′) *n.* A fraudulent scheme, esp. one involving falsified charges or evidence.

frame·work (frām′wûrk′) *n.* 1. A structure for supporting or enclosing something. 2. A basic system or design.

franc (frăngk) *n.* The basic monetary unit of France, Belgium, Burundi, Cameroun, Central African Empire, Chad, Congo, Benin, Gabon, Guinea, Ivory Coast, Luxembourg, Malagasy Republic, Mali, Mauritania, Niger, Rwanda, Senegal, Switzerland, Togo, Upper Volta, and of various overseas departments and territories of France. [OF.]

France (frăns, fräns). A republic of W Europe. Pop. 48,700,000. Cap. Paris.

France

fran·chise (frăn′chīz) *n.* 1. A privilege granted a person or group; a charter. 2. A consti-

tutional or statutory right, as the suffrage. 3. Authorization granted by a manufacturer to a distributor or dealer. [< OF *franc,* free, FRANK.]

Fran·cis of As·si·si (frăn′sĭs, frän′-; ə-sē′zē), **Saint.** 1182?–1226. Italian monk; founder of a religious order.

fran·ci·um (frăn′sē-əm) *n. Symbol* **Fr** An extremely unstable radioactive metallic element. Atomic number 87, longest-lived isotope Fr 223. [< FRANCE.]

Fran·co (fräng′kō, fräng′-), **Francisco.** 1892–1975. Spanish statesman (1939–75).

Franco–. *comb. form.* French.

frank (frăngk) *adj.* Open and sincere in expression; straightforward. —*v.* 1. To put an official mark (on a piece of mail) so that it can be sent and delivered free. 2. To send (mail) free of charge. —*n.* 1. A mark or signature on a piece of mail indicating the right to send it free. 2. The right to send mail free. [< OF *franc,* free.]

Frank·en·stein monster (frăng′kən-stīn′). Also **Frank·en·stein's monster** (-stīnz′). A creation that slips from the control of and destroys its creator. [< Mary Shelley's novel *Frankenstein* (1818).]

Frank·fort (frăngk′fərt). The capital of Kentucky. Pop. 21,000.

Frank·furt am Main (frängk′fŏŏrt′ äm mīn′). A city of West Germany. Pop. 692,000.

frank·furt·er (frăngk′fər-tər) *n.* A smoked sausage of beef or beef and pork made in long, reddish links. [< FRANKFURT.]

frank·in·cense (frăngk′ĭn-sĕns′) *n.* An aromatic gum resin used chiefly as incense. [< OF *franc encens.*]

Frank·lin (frăngk′lĭn), **Benjamin.** 1706–1790. American statesman, author, and scientist.

Benjamin Franklin

frank·ly (frăngk′lē) *adv.* 1. In a frank manner. 2. In truth: *Frankly, I don't care.*

frank·ness (frăngk′nĭs) *n.* Openness and directness of speech; candor.

fran·tic (frăn′tĭk) *adj.* Emotionally distraught;

ă pat/ā ate/âr care/ä bar/b bib/ch chew/d deed/ĕ pet/ē be/f fit/g gag/h hat/hw what/
ĭ pit/ī pie/îr pier/j judge/k kick/l lid, fatal/m mum/n no, sudden/ng sing/ŏ pot/ō go/

frenzied. [< FRENETIC.] —fran′ti•cal•ly *adv.*

frap•pé (fră-pā′, frăp) *n.* **1.** A frozen mixture similar to sherbet. **2.** A beverage poured over shaved ice. **3.** A milk shake with ice cream. [< OF *fraper*, to strike.]

fra•ter•nal (frə-tûr′nəl) *adj.* **1.** Pertaining to brothers; brotherly. **2.** Pertaining to or constituting a fraternity. **3.** Pertaining to a twin or twins developed from separately fertilized ova. [< L *frāter*, brother. See **bhrāter-**.] —fra•ter′-nal•ism′ *n.* —fra•ter′nal•ly *adv.*

fra•ter•ni•ty (frə-tûr′nə-tē) *n., pl.* **-ties. 1.** A body of men linked together by similar interests or professions. **2.** A chiefly social organization of male college students. **3.** Brotherhood; brotherliness.

frat•er•nize (frăt′ər-nīz′) *v.* **-nized, -nizing. 1.** To associate with others in a congenial way. **2.** To associate with the people of an enemy or conquered country. —frat′er•ni•za′tion *n.*

frat•ri•cide (frăt′rə-sīd′) *n.* **1.** The killing of one's brother or sister. **2.** One who has killed his brother or sister. [< L *frāter*, brother + -CIDE.] —frat′ri•ci′dal *adj.*

fraud (frôd) *n.* **1.** A deliberate deception for unfair or unlawful gain. **2.** A swindle; trick. **3.** One who practices deception; an impostor. [< L *fraus.*]

fraud•u•lent (frô′jə-lənt) *adj.* **1.** Engaging in fraud; deceitful. **2.** Constituting or gained by fraud. —fraud′u•lence *n.* —fraud′u•lent•ly *adv.*

fraught (frôt) *adj.* Attended; accompanied: *an occasion fraught with peril.* [< MDu *vracht*, freight.]

fray¹ (frā) *n.* **1.** A fight; brawl. **2.** A heated dispute. [< ME *fraien*, to frighten.]

fray² (frā) *v.* **1.** To unravel, wear away, or tatter by or through rubbing. **2.** To strain; chafe. [< L *fricāre*, to rub.]

fraz•zle (frăz′əl) *v.* **-zled, -zling.** *Informal.* **1.** To fray; wear ragged. **2.** To wear out the nerves of.

freak (frēk) *n.* **1.** A person, thing, or occurrence that is abnormal or very unusual. **2.** A whim; vagary. [?] —freak′ish *adj.*

freck•le (frĕk′əl) *n.* A small precipitation of pigment in the skin. —*v.* **-led, -ling.** To make or become dotted with freckles. [< ON *frekrnur* (pl).] —freck′ly *adv.*

Fred•er•ic•ton (frĕd′rĭk-tən). The capital of New Brunswick, Canada. Pop. 20,000.

free (frē) *adj.* **freer, freest. 1.** At liberty; not bound or constrained. **2.** Not under obligation or necessity. **3. a.** Politically independent. **b.** Governed by consent and possessing civil liberties. **4. a.** Not affected by a given condition or circumstance. **b.** Exempt: *duty-free.* **5.** Not literal: *a free translation.* **6.** Costing nothing; gratuitous. **7. a.** Unoccupied. **b.** Unobstructed. **8.** Guileless; frank. **9.** Taking undue liberties. **10.** Liberal or lavish. —*adv.* **1.** In a free manner. **2.** Without charge. —*v.* **freed, freeing. 1.** To set at liberty. **2.** To rid or release. **3.** To disengage; untangle. [< OE *frēo*. See **prī-**.] —free′ly *adv.* —free′ness *n.*

free•boot•er (frē′boō′tər) *n.* One who plunders; pirate.

freed•man (frēd′mən) *n.* A man freed from bondage.

free•dom (frē′dəm) *n.* **1.** The condition of being free. **2.** Political independence. **3.** Facility, as of motion. **4.** Frankness. **5.** Unrestricted use or access.

free enterprise. The freedom to operate businesses competitively with minimal government regulation.

free fall. The fall of a body within the atmosphere without a drag-producing device such as a parachute.

free-for-all (frē′fər-ôl′) *n.* A brawl in which many take part.

free•hand (frē′hănd′) *adj.* Drawn without the aid of mechanical devices.

free•hold (frē′hōld′) *n.* **1.** An estate held in fee or for life. **2.** The tenure by which such an estate is held. —free′hold′er *n.*

free lance. One who sells his services without a long-term commitment to any employer. —free′-lance′ *v.* (-lanced, -lancing). —free′-lance′ *adj.*

free•man (frē′mən) *n.* **1.** One not in slavery or serfdom. **2.** One having the rights or privileges of a citizen.

Free•ma•son (frē′mā′sən) *n.* A member of the Free and Accepted Masons, an international secret fraternity. —Free′ma′son•ry *n.*

fre•er (frē′ər). *comp.* of **free.**

fre•est (frē′ĭst). *superl.* of **free.**

free•stand•ing (frē′stăn′dĭng) *adj.* Standing without support or attachment.

free•stone (frē′stōn′) *n.* **1.** A stone soft enough to be cut easily without shattering. **2.** A fruit, esp. a peach, with a stone that does not adhere to the pulp.

free•think•er (frē′thĭng′kər) *n.* One who has rejected authority and dogma, esp. in his religious thinking. —free′think′ing *adj. & n.*

Free•town (frē′toun′). The capital of Sierra Leone. Pop. 128,000.

free trade. Trade without protective customs tariffs between nations.

free verse. Verse without a conventional metrical pattern and with an irregular rhyme or none.

free•way (frē′wā′) *n.* A highway with several lanes; expressway.

free•wheel•ing (frē′hwē′lĭng) *adj.* **1.** Free of restraints or rules in organization, methods, or procedure. **2.** Heedless; carefree.

free will. 1. Free choice. **2.** The belief that man's choices are or can be voluntary.

freeze (frēz) *v.* **froze, frozen, freezing. 1. a.** To pass or cause to pass from liquid to solid by loss of heat. **b.** To acquire a surface of ice from cold. **2.** To preserve by subjecting to cold. **3.** To make or become inoperative through the formation of frost or ice. **4.** To damage or be damaged by cold. **5. a.** To be at that degree of temperature at which ice forms. **b.** To be uncomfortably cold. **6.** To make or become rigid or inflexible. **7.** To become paralyzed through fear or shyness. **8.** To become icily silent. **9.** To fix (prices or wages) at a current level. **10.** To prohibit further manufacture or use of. **11.** To prevent or restrict the exchange, liquidation, or granting of by law. **12.** To anesthetize by freezing. —*n.* **1.** An act of freezing. **2.** A spell of cold weather; frost. [< OE *frēosan.* See **preus-**.]

freeze-dry (frēz′drī′) *v.* To preserve by rapid freezing and drying in a high vacuum.

freez·er (frē′zər) *n.* One that freezes, esp. an insulated cabinet or room for the rapid freezing and storing of perishable food.

freezing point. 1. The temperature at which a liquid of specified composition solidifies under a specified pressure. **2.** The temperature at which the liquid and solid phases of a substance of specified composition are in equilibrium at atmospheric pressure.

freight (frāt) *n.* **1.** Goods carried by a vessel or vehicle; cargo. **2.** The commercial transportation of goods. **3.** The charge for transporting goods by cargo carrier. **4.** A railway train carrying goods only. —*v.* **1.** To convey commercially as cargo. **2.** To load with cargo. [< MDu *vrecht,* cargo.]

freight·er (frā′tər) *n.* A ship for carrying freight.

French (frĕnch) *n.* **1.** The Romance language spoken by the people of France, W Switzerland, and S Belgium. **2. the French** *(takes pl. v.).* The people of France. —**French** *adj.* —**French′man** *n.*

French dressing. A seasoned oil and vinegar salad dressing.

French fry. To fry in deep fat.

French Gui·an·a (gē-ăn′ə, -ä′nə). An overseas department of France in N South America between Surinam and Brazil. Pop. 34,000. Cap. Cayenne.

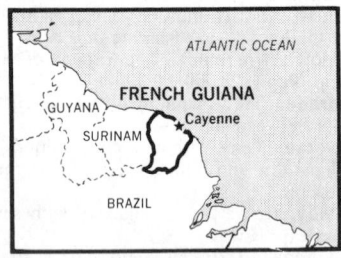

French Guiana

French horn. A brass wind instrument that tapers from a narrow mouthpiece to a flaring bell.

French leave. An unauthorized departure.

French toast. Sliced bread soaked in a milk and egg batter and lightly fried.

fre·net·ic (frə-nĕt′ĭk) *adj.* Also **fre·net·i·cal** (-ĭ-kəl), **phre·net·ic, phre·net·i·cal.** Frantic; frenzied. [< Gk *phrenitis,* brain disease, insanity.] —**fre·net′i·cal·ly** *adv.*

fren·zy (frĕn′zē) *n., pl.* -**zies. 1.** A seizure of violent agitation. **2.** Temporary madness. [< L *phrenēsis.*] —**fren′zied** *adj.*

Fre·on (frē′ŏn′) *n.* A trademark for a gas or liquid used as a working fluid in refrigeration and air conditioning and as an aerosol propellant.

freq. 1. frequentative. **2.** frequently.

fre·quen·cy (frē′kwən-sē) *n., pl.* -**cies. 1.** The number of times a phenomenon occurs within a specified interval, esp. the number of repetitions per unit time of a complete waveform, as of an electric current. **2.** The property or condition of occurring repeatedly in short intervals.

frequency modulation. The encoding of a carrier wave by variation of its frequency in accordance with an input signal.

fre·quent (frē′kwənt) *adj.* Occurring or appearing often or at close intervals. —*v.* (frē-kwĕnt′, frē′kwənt). To pay frequent visits to. [< L *frēquens,* full, frequent.] —**fre·quent′er** *n.* —**fre′quent·ly** *adv.* —**fre′quent·ness** *n.*

fre·quen·ta·tive (frē-kwĕn′tə-tĭv) *n.* A verb that denotes repeated action, such as *flicker.* —**fre·quen′ta·tive** *adj.*

fres·co (frĕs′kō) *n., pl.* -**coes** or -**cos. 1.** The art of painting with earth colors on wet plaster. **2.** A painting thus executed. [< It *fresco,* fresh.] —**fres′co·er, fres′co·ist** *n.*

fresh (frĕsh) *adj.* **1.** New to one's experience; novel; original. **2.** Recently made, produced, or harvested; not stale: *fresh bread.* **3.** Not preserved, as by canning or freezing. **4.** Not saline: *fresh water.* **5.** Not yet used; clean. **6.** Additional: *a fresh start.* **7.** Bright and clear; not dull or faded. **8.** Inexperienced: *fresh recruits.* **9.** Having just arrived: *fresh from Paris.* **10.** Refreshed. **11.** Cool and invigorating: *fresh morning air.* **12.** Fairly strong; brisk: *a fresh wind.* **13.** *Informal.* Bold and saucy; impudent. —*adv.* Recently; newly: *fresh-baked bread.* [< Gmc **friskaz.*] —**fresh′ly** *adv.* —**fresh′ness** *n.*

fresh·en (frĕsh′ən) *v.* To make or become fresh. —**fresh′en·er** *n.*

fresh·et (frĕsh′ĭt) *n.* **1.** A sudden overflow of a stream from heavy rain or a thaw. **2.** A stream of fresh water that empties into a body of salt water.

fresh·man (frĕsh′mən) *n.* **1.** A student in the first year of high school or college. **2.** Any beginner.

fresh·wa·ter (frĕsh′wô′tər, -wŏt′ər) *adj.* Of, pertaining to, living in, or consisting of water that is not salty.

Fres·no (frĕz′nō). A city of C California. Pop. 134,000.

fret¹ (frĕt) *v.* **fretted, fretting. 1.** To be or cause to be uneasy or vexed; worry. **2. a.** To gnaw at or wear away. **b.** To become worn or corroded. **3.** To disturb the surface of (water); agitate. —*n.* **1.** A hole, worn spot, or path made by abrasion or erosion. **2.** Irritation; annoyance. [< OE *fretan,* to irritate < Gmc **fraitan,* to eat up.]

fret² (frĕt) *n.* A ridge set across the fingerboard of a stringed instrument. [?]

fret³ (frĕt) *n.* A design within a band or border, consisting esp. of a geometrical pattern. [< OF *frete,* embossed work.]

fret·ful (frĕt′fəl) *adj.* Inclined to fret; peevish; troubled. —**fret′ful·ly** *adv.* —**fret′ful·ness** *n.*

fret·work (frĕt′wûrk′) *n.* Ornamental work consisting of three-dimensional frets; geometric openwork.

Freud (froid), **Sigmund.** 1856–1939. Austrian physician; founder of psychoanalysis. —**Freu′di·an** (froi′dē-ən) *adj. & n.*

Sigmund Freud

Fri. Friday.

fri·a·ble (frī′ə-bəl) *adj.* Readily crumbled; brittle. [< L *friāre,* to crumble.] —**fri′a·bil′i·ty, fri′a·ble·ness** *n.*

fri·ar (frī′ər) *n.* A member of a Roman Catholic order, usually mendicant. [< L *frāter,* brother.]

fric·as·see (frĭk′ə-sē′) *n.* Poultry cut into pieces, stewed, and served with a gravy. —*v.* **-seed, -seeing.** To prepare as a fricassee. [< F *fricasser,* to fry.]

fric·tion (frĭk′shən) *n.* **1.** The rubbing of one object or surface against another. **2.** A conflict; a clashing. **3.** *Phys.* A force tangential to the common boundary of two bodies in contact that resists the motion or tendency to motion of one relative to the other. [< L *fricāre,* to rub.] —**fric′tion·al** *adj.*

friction tape. A moisture-resistant adhesive tape, used chiefly to insulate electrical conductors.

Fri·day (frī′dē, -dā′) *n.* The 6th day of the week. [< OE *frīgedæg.* See **prī-.**]

fried (frīd). *p.t. & p.p.* of **fry**[1].

friend (frĕnd) *n.* **1.** A person one knows, likes, and trusts. **2.** A favored companion; comrade. **3.** One who supports a group or cause. **4. Friend.** A member of the Society of Friends; Quaker. [< OE *frēond.* See **prī-.**] —**friend′less** *adj.* —**friend′ship′** *n.*

friend·ly (frĕnd′lē) *adj.* **-lier, -liest. 1.** Of or befitting a friend. **2.** Favorably disposed; not antagonistic. **3.** Warm; comforting. —**friend′li·ness** *n.*

fri·er. Variant of **fryer.**

frieze (frēz) *n.* A decorative horizontal band, as along the upper part of a wall in a room. [< ML *frisium, frigium,* fringe.]

frig·ate (frĭg′ĭt) *n.* **1.** A sailing war vessel of the 17th, 18th, and 19th centuries. **2.** A U.S. warship of approx. 5,000 to 7,000 tons. [< It *fregata.*]

fright (frīt) *n.* **1.** Sudden, intense fear. **2.**

Informal. Something extremely unsightly or distressing. [< OE *fryhto* < Gmc **furht-.*]

fright·en (frīt′n) *v.* **1.** To make suddenly afraid. **2.** To drive or force by arousing fear: *frightened into confessing.*

fright·ful (frīt′fəl) *adj.* **1.** Causing disgust or shock. **2.** Causing fright. **3.** *Informal.* Excessive; extreme. —**fright′ful·ly** *adv.*

frig·id (frĭj′ĭd) *adj.* **1.** Extremely cold. **2.** Lacking warmth of feeling; cold in manner. [< L *frigus,* cold.] —**fri·gid′i·ty** (frĭ-jĭd′ə-tē) *n.*

Frigid Zone. The area within the Arctic Circle or that within the Antarctic Circle.

frill (frĭl) *n.* **1.** A ruffled, gathered, or pleated border or edging. **2.** *Informal.* Anything superfluous. [?] —**fril′li·ness** *n.* —**fril′ly** *adj.*

fringe (frĭnj) *n.* **1.** A decorative border or edging of hanging threads, cords, or strips. **2.** A marginal or peripheral part; edge. —*v.* **fringed, fringing. 1.** To decorate with a fringe. **2.** To grow or occur along the edge of. [< LL *fimbria.*] —**fringe′less** *adj.*

fringe benefit. An employment benefit given in addition to one's wages.

frip·per·y (frĭp′ə-rē) *n., pl.* **-ies. 1.** Excessively ornamented dress. **2.** Pretentious elegance. [< OF *frepe, felpe,* frill.]

Fris. Frisian.

Fri·sian (frĭzh′ən, frē′zhən) *n.* **1.** A native or inhabitant of the Frisian Islands. **2.** The Germanic language spoken by the Frisian people. —**Fri′sian** *adj.*

Frisian Islands. A chain of islands in the North Sea, belonging to the Netherlands, West Germany, and Denmark.

frisk (frĭsk) *v.* **1.** To move about briskly and playfully. **2.** To search (a person) for concealed weapons by passing the hands over clothes or through pockets. [< Gmc **friskaz,* FRESH.] —**frisk′er** *n.*

frisk·y (frĭs′kē) *adj.* **-ier, -iest.** Lively and playful. —**frisk′i·ly** *adv.* —**frisk′i·ness** *n.*

frit·ter[1] (frĭt′ər) *v.* —**fritter away.** To reduce or squander little by little. [Prob < obs *fritter,* to break in pieces.]

frit·ter[2] (frĭt′ər) *n.* A small cake made of batter, often containing fruit, vegetables, or fish, fried in deep fat. [< L *frīgere,* to FRY.]

friv·o·lous (frĭv′ə-ləs) *adj.* **1.** Unworthy of serious attention. **2.** Marked by flippancy. [< L *frivolus.*] —**fri·vol′i·ty** (-vŏl′ə-tē) *n.*

frizz (frĭz) *v.* Also **friz.** To form or be formed into small, tight curls or tufts. —*n.* Hair or fabric in tight curls. [F *friser,* to curl.] —**frizz′zi·ly** *adv.* —**friz′zi·ness** *n.* —**friz′zy** *adj.*

friz·zle[1] (frĭz′əl) *v.* **-zled, -zling. 1.** To fry until crisp and curled. **2.** To fry or sear with a sizzling noise. [Perh blend of FRY and SIZZLE.]

friz·zle[2] (frĭz′əl) *v.* **-zled, -zling.** To frizz. —*n.* A small, tight curl. —**friz′zly** *adj.*

fro (frō) *adv.* Away; back: *to and fro.* [< ON *frā.*]

frock (frŏk) *n.* **1.** A long, loose outer garment; smock. **2.** A robe worn by monks and other clerics. **3.** A woman's dress. [< Gmc **hrok-.*]

frog (frôg, frŏg) *n.* **1.** Any of various tailless, chiefly aquatic amphibians with a smooth, moist skin and long hind legs adapted for

ô paw, for/oi boy/ou out/ōō took/ōō coo/p pop/r run/s sauce/sh shy/t to/th thin/*th* the/
ŭ cut/ûr fur/v van/w wag/y yes/z size/zh vision/ə ago, item, edible, gallop, circus/

leaping. **2.** An ornamental looped braid or cord with a button or knot for fastening a garment. **3.** *Informal.* Hoarseness in the throat. [< OE *frogga.* See preu-.]

frog·man (frôg′măn′, -mən, frŏg′-) *n.* A swimmer equipped to execute extended underwater, esp. military, maneuvers.

frol·ic (frŏl′ĭk) *n.* **1.** Gaiety; merriment. **2.** A prank or trick. —*v.* **-icked, -icking.** To engage in merrymaking, joking, or teasing. [< MDu *vrolijc.*] —**frol′ick·er** *n.*

frol·ic·some (frŏl′ĭk-səm) *adj.* Full of high-spirited fun; playful.

from (frŭm, frŏm) *prep.* **1.** Beginning at a specified place or time. **2.** With a specified point as the first of two limits. **3.** With a person, place, or thing as the source or instrument. **4.** Out of. **5.** Out of the control or possession of. **6.** So as not to be engaged in: *keep him from making a mistake.* **7.** Measured by reference to: *far from home.* **8.** As opposed to: *know right from wrong.* —See Usage note at **different.** [< OE *from, fram.* See per¹.]

frond (frŏnd) *n.* The usually divided leaf of a fern, palm, etc. [L *frôns.*]

front (frŭnt) *n.* **1.** The forward part or surface. **2.** The location or position directly ahead: *in front of the fountain.* **3.** The position of leadership or superiority. **4.** The first part. **5.** Demeanor or bearing: *a brave front.* **6.** A false appearance or manner. **7.** Land bordering a lake, river, or street: *on the lake front.* **8.** *Mil.* **a.** The most forward line of combat force. **b.** The area of contact between opposing combat forces. **9.** *Meteorol.* The interface between air masses at different temperatures. **10.** An apparently respectable person under whose cover secret or illegal business is carried on. —*adj.* Of, pertaining to, aimed at, or located in the front. —*v.* **1.** To face; have a front (on). **2.** To serve as a front for. [< L *frôns.*] —**fron′tal** *adj.*

front·age (frŭn′tĭj) *n.* **1.** The front part of a piece of property. **2.** The dimensions of such a part. **3.** The direction in which something faces. **4.** Land adjacent to something.

frontal bone. A cranial bone with a vertical portion corresponding to the forehead and a horizontal portion that partially forms the roofs of the orbital and nasal cavities.

fron·tier (frŭn-tîr′) *n.* **1.** An international border or the area along it. **2.** A region just beyond or at the edge of a settled area. **3.** Any underdeveloped area or field, as of scientific research. [< OF *front,* front.] —**fron·tier′** *adj.* —**fron·tiers′man** *n.*

fron·tis·piece (frŭn′tĭs-pēs′) *n.* An illustration that faces or immediately precedes the title page of a book. [< LL *frontispicium,* "examination of the front."]

frost (frôst, frŏst) *n.* **1.** A covering of minute ice crystals formed from frozen water vapor. **2.** The atmospheric conditions when the temperature is below the freezing point of water. —*v.* **1.** To cover or become covered with frost. **2.** To damage or kill by frost. **3.** To cover or decorate with icing. [< OE *frost, forst.* See preus-.] —**frost′i·ness** *n.* —**frost′y** *adj.*

Frost (frôst, frŏst), **Robert.** 1875–1963. American poet.

frost·bite (frôst′bīt′, frŏst′-) *n.* Local tissue destruction resulting from freezing. —*v.* To injure or damage by freezing.

frost·ing (frôs′tĭng, frŏs′-) *n.* **1.** Icing. **2.** A roughened or speckled surface on glass or metal.

froth (frôth, frŏth) *n.* **1.** A mass of bubbles in or on a liquid; foam. **2.** A salivary foam released as a result of disease or exhaustion. **3.** Anything unsubstantial; triviality. —*v.* To exude or expel froth; to foam. [< ON *frodha.*] —**froth′i·ly** *adv.* —**froth′i·ness** *n.* —**froth′y** *adj.*

frou-frou (frōō′frōō) *n.* **1.** A rustling sound, as of silk. **2.** Fussy or showy dress or ornamentation. [F.]

fro·ward (frō′wərd, frō′ərd) *adj.* Stubbornly contrary and disobedient. [< FRO + -WARD.]

frown (froun) *v.* **1.** To wrinkle the brow, as in thought or displeasure. **2.** To regard with disapproval or distaste (with *on* or *upon*). —*n.* A wrinkling of the brow in thought or displeasure. [< OF *froigner.*] —**frown′er** *n.*

frow·zy (frou′zē) *adj.* **-zier, -ziest.** Also **frou·zy, frow·sy.** Unkempt in appearance; slovenly. [?] —**frow′zi·ness** *n.*

froze (frōz) *p.t.* of **freeze.**

fro·zen (frō′zən). *p.p.* of **freeze.** —*adj.* **1.** Made into, covered with, or surrounded by ice. **2.** Very cold. **3.** Preserved by freezing. **4.** Rendered immobile. **5.** Expressive of cold unfriendliness or disdain. **6. a.** Kept at an arbitrary level. **b.** Incapable of being withdrawn, sold, or liquidated: *frozen assets.*

FRS Federal Reserve System.

frt. freight.

fruc·tose (frŭk′tōs′, frōōk′-) *n.* A very sweet sugar, $C_6H_{12}O_6$, occurring in many fruits and honey. [L *frūctus,* FRUIT + -OSE.]

fru·gal (frōō′gəl) *adj.* Avoiding unnecessary expenditure of money; thrifty. [< L *frūgi,* useful, worthy.] —**fru·gal′i·ty** (-găl′ə-tē) *n.* —**fru′gal·ly** *adv.*

fruit (frōōt) *n., pl.* **fruit** or **fruits.** **1.** The ripened seed-bearing structure of a plant, esp. when fleshy and edible. **2.** A plant crop or product. **3.** Result; issue; outcome: *the fruit of labor.* —*v.* To produce fruit. [< L *frūctus,* enjoyment, use, fruit < pp of *fruī,* to enjoy, to eat fruit.]

fruit·ful (frōōt′fəl) *adj.* **1.** Producing fruit. **2.** Producing results; profitable.

fru·i·tion (frōō-ĭsh′ən) *n.* **1.** Enjoyment from use or possession. **2. a.** The condition of bearing fruit. **b.** The achievement of something desired or worked for. [< L *fruī,* to enjoy, eat fruit.]

fruit·less (frōōt′lĭs) *adj.* **1.** Producing no fruit. **2.** Having negligible or no results.

fruit·y (frōō′tē) *adj.* **-ier, -iest.** Tasting or smelling of fruit. —**fruit′i·ness** *n.*

frus·trate (frŭs′trāt′) *v.* **-trated, -trating.** **1. a.** To prevent from accomplishing a purpose or fulfilling a desire. **b.** To cause feelings of discouragement or bafflement in. **2.** To nullify. [< L *frūstrāre,* to disappoint.] —**frus·tra′tion** *n.*

fry¹ (frī) *v.* **fried, frying.** To cook over direct heat in hot oil or fat. —*n., pl.* **fries. 1.** A dish of any fried food. **2.** A social gathering featuring fried food: *a fish fry.* [< L *frigere.*]

fry² (frī) *pl.n.* **1.** Young, recently hatched fish. **2.** Young individuals. [Perh < OF *freier,* to spawn, to rub.]

fry·er (frī'ər) *n.* Also **fri·er.** One that fries.

f-stop (ĕf'stŏp') *n.* **1.** A camera lens aperture setting calibrated to a corresponding f-number. **2.** An f-number.

ft foot.

ft. fort.

FTC Federal Trade Commission.

ft-lb foot-pound.

fuch·sia (fyōō'shə) *n.* A widely cultivated plant with showy, drooping, usually red and purple flowers. [< L. *Fuchs* (1501–1566), German botanist.]

fud·dle (fŭd'l) *v.* **-dled, -dling.** To muddle with or as if with liquor. [?]

fudge (fŭj) *n.* **1.** A soft rich candy made of sugar, butter, and flavoring. **2.** Nonsense; humbug. —*v.* **fudged, fudging.** To fake or falsify. [Prob var of archaic *fadge.*]

fueh·rer. Variant of **führer.**

fu·el (fyōō'əl) *n.* **1.** Anything consumed to produce energy, as: **a.** A material such as wood, coal, gas, or oil burned to produce heat. **b.** Fissionable material used in a nuclear reactor. **2.** Anything that maintains or heightens an activity or an emotion. —*v.* **-eled** or **-elled, -eling** or **-elling.** To provide with or take in fuel. [< L *focus,* fire, hearth.]

fuel cell. An electrochemical cell in which the energy of a reaction between a fuel such as liquid hydrogen and an oxidant such as liquid oxygen is converted directly and continuously into the energy of direct electric current.

fuel injection. Any of several methods or mechanical systems by which a fuel is vaporized and sprayed into the cylinders of a diesel or other internal-combustion engine.

fu·gi·tive (fyōō'jə-tĭv) *adj.* **1.** Running or having run away; fleeing, as from justice. **2.** Passing quickly; fleeting: *fugitive hours.* —*n.* One who flees; a runaway. [< L *fugere,* to flee.] —**fu'gi·tive·ly** *adv.*

fugue (fyōōg) *n.* A polyphonic musical form in which a theme stated sequentially and in imitation is developed in contrapuntal form. [< L *fuga,* flight.] —**fu'gal** *adj.*

füh·rer (fyōōr'ər) *n.* Also **fueh·rer.** A leader, esp. one exercising the powers of a tyrant, as Adolf Hitler. [G.]

-ful *comb. form.* **1.** Fullness or abundance: *playful.* **2.** Having the characteristics of: *masterful.* **3.** Tendency or ability: *useful.* **4.** The amount or number that will fill: *armful.* [< OE *full,* FULL.]

Usage: The plurals of nouns that end in *-ful* are most often indicated, esp. in writing, by the addition of the letter *s: glassfuls; spoonfuls; tablespoonfuls; teaspoonfuls.*

ful·crum (fōōl'krəm, fŭl'-) *n., pl.* **-crums** or **-cra** (-krə). **1.** The point or support on which a lever turns. **2.** Something through or by means of which vital powers are exercised. [L, bedpost, support.]

ful·fill (fōōl-fĭl') *v.* Also **ful·fil. -filled, -filling. 1.** To bring into actuality; effect. **2.** To satisfy. **3.** To go to the end of (a period of time); complete. [< OE *fullfyllan,* to fill full.] —**ful·fill'er** *n.* —**ful·fill'ment** *n.*

full¹ (fōōl) *adj.* **1.** Containing all that is normal or possible; complete. **2.** Of maximum or highest degree. **3.** Having a great deal or many: *full of errors.* **4.** Totally qualified or unanimously accepted: *a full member.* **5. a.** Rounded in shape. **b.** Of generous proportions; wide. **6.** Satiated, esp. with food or drink. **7.** Having depth and body. —*adv.* **1.** To a complete extent; entirely: *full well.* **2.** Directly: *full in the path of the moon.* —*n.* The maximum or complete size, amount, or development. [< OE. See pel-⁵.]

full² (fōōl) *v.* To increase or cause to increase the weight and bulk of (cloth) by shrinking and beating or pressing. [< VL *fullāre.*]

full·back (fōōl'băk') *n. Football.* A backfield player whose position is usually behind the quarterback and halfbacks.

full-blood·ed (fōōl'blŭd'ĭd) *adj.* **1.** Of unmixed breed or ancestry. **2.** Not pale or anemic. **3.** Vigorous and virile.

full-blown (fōōl'blōn') *adj.* **1.** In full blossom. **2.** Fully developed or matured.

full-bod·ied (fōōl'bŏd'ēd) *adj.* Having richness of flavor.

full dress. The attire appropriate for formal events.

full-fledged (fōōl'flĕjd') *adj.* **1.** Having fully developed adult plumage. **2.** Having full status or rank.

full moon. 1. The phase of the moon when it is visible as a fully illuminated disk. **2.** The period of the month when this occurs.

full-scale (fōōl'skāl') *adj.* **1.** Of the actual or full size. **2.** Employing all resources.

ful·ly (fōōl'ē) *adv.* **1.** Totally. **2.** Adequately; sufficiently. **3.** At least.

ful·mi·nate (fŭl'mə-nāt', fōōl'-) *v.* **-nated, -nating. 1.** To denounce severely. **2.** To explode. [< L *fulmināre,* to strike with lightning.] —**ful'mi·na'tion** *n.*

ful·some (fōōl'səm) *adj.* **1.** Offensively excessive or insincere. **2.** Loathsome; disgusting. [< FULL + -SOME.] —**ful'some·ly** *adv.* —**ful'some·ness** *n.*

fum·ble (fŭm'bəl) *v.* **-bled, -bling. 1.** To touch or handle nervously or idly. **2.** To grope awkwardly and uncertainly; blunder. **3.** *Sports.* To mishandle or drop a ball. —*n.* **1.** The act or instance of fumbling. **2.** *Sports.* A ball that has been fumbled. [Perh < Scand.]

fume (fyōōm) *n.* **1.** An exhalation of smoke, vapor, or gas, esp. an irritating or disagreeable exhalation. **2.** A strong or acrid odor. —*v.* **fumed, fuming. 1.** To subject to or treat with fumes. **2.** To give off in or as in fumes. **3.** To feel or show agitation or anger. [< L *fūmus,* smoke, steam.]

fu·mi·gate (fyōō'mĭ-gāt') *v.* **-gated, -gating.** To subject to smoke or fumes, usually in order to exterminate vermin or insects. —**fu'mi·ga'tion** *n.* —**fu'mi·ga'tor** *n.*

fun (fŭn) *n.* **1.** A source of enjoyment or pleasure. **2.** Enjoyment; amusement. **—make fun of.** To ridicule. [Perh < ME *fonnen*, to make fun of.]

func·tion (fŭngk'shən) *n.* **1.** The natural or proper action for which a person, office, mechanism, or organ is fitted or employed. **2. a.** Assigned duty or activity. **b.** Specific occupation or role. **3.** An official ceremony or elaborate social occasion. **4.** *Math.* **a.** A variable so related to another that for each value assumed by one there is a value determined for the other. **b.** A rule of correspondence between two sets such that there is a unique element in one set assigned to each element in the other. *—v.* To have or perform a function; serve. [< L *functus,* pp of *fungī,* to perform.]

func·tion·al (fŭngk'shən-əl) *adj.* **1.** Of or pertaining to a function or functions. **2.** Designed for or adapted to a particular function. **3.** Capable of performing; operative. **4.** Pertaining to a disease having no apparent physiological or structural cause.

func·tion·ar·y (fŭngk'shə-něr'ē) *n., pl.* **-ies.** One who holds an office or trust; an official.

fund (fŭnd) *n.* **1.** A source of supply; a stock. **2.** A sum of money set aside for a specific purpose. **3. funds.** Available money; ready cash. **4.** An organization established to administer a fund. *—v.* **1.** To provide funds for. **2.** To convert (a debt), as into a long-term debt, with fixed interest payments. [< L *fundus,* bottom, landed property.]

fun·da·men·tal (fŭn'də-měnt'l) *adj.* **1. a.** Elemental; basic. **b.** Central; key. **2.** Generative; primary. **3.** *Phys.* **a.** Of or pertaining to the component of lowest frequency of a periodic wave or quantity. **b.** Of or pertaining to the lowest possible frequency of a vibrating element or system. [< L *fundus,* bottom.] **—fun'da·men'tal** *n.* **—fun'da·men'tal·ly** *adv.*

fun·da·men·tal·ism (fŭn'də-měnt'l-ĭz'əm) *n.* A Protestant movement holding the Bible to be the sole historical and prophetic authority. **—fun'da·men'tal·ist** *n. & adj.*

fu·ner·al (fyōō'nər-əl) *n.* **1.** The ceremonies held in connection with the burial or cremation of the dead. **2.** A group accompanying a body to the grave. [< L *fūnus (fūner-),* funeral, death.] **—fu'ner·al** *adj.*

fu·ner·ar·y (fyōō'nə-rěr'ē) *adj.* Of or suitable for a funeral.

fu·ne·re·al (fyōō-nîr'ē-əl) *adj.* **1.** Of or suitable for a funeral. **2.** Mournful.

fun·gal (fŭng'gəl) *adj.* Of or pertaining to a fungus; fungous.

fun·gus (fŭng'gəs) *n., pl.* **fungi** (fŭn'jī') or **-guses.** Any of a large group of plants without chlorophyll, including the yeasts, molds, smuts, and mushrooms. [L.] **—fun'goid'** (-goid') *adj.* **—fun'gous** *adj.*

fu·nic·u·lar (fyōō-nĭk'yə-lər, fə-) *n.* A cable railway on a steep incline, esp. one with simultaneously ascending and descending cars. [< L *fūnis,* rope.]

fun·nel (fŭn'əl) *n.* **1.** A conical utensil with a small hole or narrow tube at the apex used to channel a substance into a small-mouthed container. **2.** A shaft or flue; smokestack. *—v.*

To move or cause to move through or as through a funnel. [< L *infundere,* to pour in.]

fun·ny (fŭn'ē) *adj.* **-nier, -niest. 1.** Causing laughter or amusement; mirthful. **2.** Strange; odd; curious. *—n.* **funnies.** Comic strips.

fur (fûr) *n.* **1.** The thick, soft hair covering the body of various animals, as a fox, beaver, or cat. **2.** The pelt or pelts of such an animal, used for garments or trimming. **3.** A furlike coating. *—adj.* Made of fur. [< OF *forre,* lining.] **—furred** *adj.*

fur·be·low (fûr'bə-lō') *n.* **1.** A ruffle on a garment. **2.** Any small piece of showy ornamentation. [< F *falbala.*]

fur·bish (fûr'bĭsh) *v.* **1.** To brighten by cleaning or rubbing. **2.** To renovate. [< OF *fourbir.*]

fur·cu·la (fûr'kyə-lə) *n., pl.* **-lae** (-lē'). Also **fur·cu·lum** (fûr'kyə-ləm) *pl.* **-la** (-lə). A forked process or bone, esp. the wishbone of a bird. [< L *furca,* FORK.]

fu·ri·ous (fyŏōr'ē-əs) *adj.* Extremely angry; raging; fierce. [< L *furia,* FURY.]

furl (fûrl) *v.* **1.** To roll up and secure (a flag or sail) to a pole, yard, or mast. **2.** To fold. [< OF *ferlier.*] **—furl'er** *n.*

fur·long (fûr'lông', -lŏng') *n.* A unit of length, equal to ⅛ mile or 220 yards. [< OE *furlang,* "a furrow long."]

fur·lough (fûr'lō) *n.* A leave of absence; a vacation, esp. one granted to enlisted personnel of the armed forces. [Du *verlof,* leave, permission.] **—fur'lough** *v.*

fur·nace (fûr'nĭs) *n.* An enclosure in which heat is generated by the combustion of a suitable fuel. [< L *fornāx.*]

fur·nish (fûr'nĭsh) *v.* **1.** To provide furniture for. **2.** To supply; give. [< OF *furnir.*]

fur·nish·ings (fûr'nĭsh-ĭngz) *pl.n.* **1.** The furniture in a home or office. **2.** Wearing apparel and accessories.

fur·ni·ture (fûr'nə-chər) *n.* Movable articles in a room or establishment. [< OF *furnir,* to FURNISH.]

fu·ror (fyŏōr'ôr', -ôr') *n.* **1.** Violent anger; frenzy. **2.** A state of intense excitement. **3.** A public disorder or uproar. [< L *furere,* rage.]

fur·ri·er (fûr'ē-ər) *n.* One who dresses, designs, sells, or repairs furs.

fur·ring (fûr'ĭng) *n.* Strips of wood or metal applied to a wall to provide a level surface.

fur·row (fûr'ō) *n.* **1.** A trench or similar depression made in the ground by a plow or other implement. **2.** A deep wrinkle in the skin, as on the forehead. [< OE *furh.* See **perk-.**] **—fur'row** *v.* **—fur'row·y** *adj.*

fur·ry (fûr'ē) *adj.* **-rier, -riest. 1.** Consisting of or covered with fur. **2.** Resembling fur.

fur·ther (fûr'*th*ər) *adj.* **1.** More distant in time, degree, or space. **2.** Additional. *—adv.* **1.** To a great extent; more. **2.** In addition; furthermore. **3.** At or to a more distant point in space or time. *—v.* To help the progress of; advance. [< OE *furthor.* See **per¹.**] **—fur'ther·ance** *n.*

fur·ther·more (fûr'*th*ər-môr', -mōr') *adv.* Moreover; in addition.

ă pat/ā ate/âr care/ä bar/b bib/ch chew/d deed/ĕ pet/ē be/f fit/g gag/h hat/hw what/ ĭ pit/ī pie/îr pier/j judge/k kick/l lid, fatal/m mum/n no, sudden/ng sing/ŏ pot/ō go/

fur·ther·most (fûr′thər-mōst′) *adj.* Most distant or remote.

fur·thest (fûr′thĭst) *adj.* Most distant in time, degree, or space. —*adv.* 1. To the greatest extent or degree. 2. At or to the most distant point in space or time.

fur·tive (fûr′tĭv) *adj.* Characterized by stealth; surreptitious; sly. [< L *fūr*, thief.] —**fur′tive·ly** *adv.* —**fur′tive·ness** *n.*

fu·ry (fyŏŏr′ē) *n., pl.·* -ies. 1. Violent anger; rage. 2. Uncontrolled action; turbulence. [< L *furere*, to rage.]

furze (fûrz) *n.* Gorse. [< OE *fyrs*. See **pŭro-**.]

fuse[1] (fyŏŏz) *n.* 1. A length of readily combustible material that is lighted at one end to detonate an explosive at the other. 2. Variant of **fuze**. [< L *fūsus*, spindle.]

fuse[2] (fyŏŏz) *v.* **fused, fusing.** 1. To liquefy by heating; melt. 2. To mix together by or as by melting; blend. —*n.* A device containing an element · that protects an electric circuit by melting when overloaded, thereby opening the circuit. [L *fundere* (pp *fūsus*), to pour, melt.] —**fu′si·ble** *adj.* —**fu′si·ble·ness** *n.*

fu·see (fyŏŏ-zē′) *n.* Also **fu·zee.** 1. A friction match with a large head capable of burning in a wind. 2. A colored flare used as a railway warning signal. 3. A fuse for detonating explosives. [< L *fūsus*, FUSE.]

fu·se·lage (fyŏŏ′sə-läzh′, fyŏŏ′zə-) *n.* The central body of an airplane to which the wings and tail assembly are attached. [< F *fuseau*, spindle.]

fu·sil·lade (fyŏŏ′sə-lād′, -läd′, fyŏŏ′zə-) *n.* 1. A simultaneous or rapid discharge of many firearms. 2. Any rapid outburst. [< F *fusiller*, to shoot.]

fu·sion (fyŏŏ′zhən) *n.* 1. Liquefying or melting together by heat. 2. A union resulting from fusing. 3. The merging of different elements into a union. 4. A nuclear reaction in which nuclei combine to form more massive nuclei with the simultaneous release of energy. [< L *fūsus*, pp of *fundere*, to pour, melt.]

fuss (fŭs) *n.* 1. Needlessly nervous or useless activity; commotion. 2. Needless worry. 3. Objection; protest. 4. A quarrel. —*v.* 1. To trouble or worry over trifles. 2. To be excessively careful or solicitous. [?]

fuss-budg·et (fŭs′bŭj′ĭt) *n.* One who fusses over trifles.

fuss·y (fŭs′ē) *adj.* -ier, -iest. 1. Given to fussing; easily upset. 2. Fastidious; meticulous. 3. Full of superfluous details or trimmings.

fus·tian (fŭs′chən) *n.* 1. A coarse, sturdy cloth. 2. Pretentious or pompous language. [< ML *fustāneus*, cloth.]

fus·ty (fŭs′tē) *adj.* -tier, -tiest. 1. Smelling of mildew or decay. 2. Old-fashioned; antique. [< OF *fuste*, barrel, stale odor of a barrel.]

fut. *Gram.* future.

fu·tile (fyŏŏt′l, fyŏŏ′tīl′) *adj.* 1. Having no useful result; ineffectual. 2. Unproductive; frivolous. [< L *fūtilis*, untrustworthy, useless.] —**fu′tile·ly** *adv.* —**fu·til′i·ty** (-tĭl′ə-tē) *n.*

fu·ture (fyŏŏ′chər) *n.* 1. The indefinite period of time yet to be. 2. That which will happen in time to come. 3. The prospective condition of a person or thing. 4. Prospects of advancement; chances of success. 5. *Gram.* a. A verb tense used to express action in the future. b. A verb in this tense. [< L *fūtūrus*.] —**fu′ture** *adj.*

future shock. The dizzying disorientation suffered by people and brought on by the overwhelmingly rapid changes of modern society.

fu·tu·ri·ty (fyŏŏ-t/y/ŏŏr′ə-tē, fyŏŏ-chŏŏr′-) *n., pl.* -ties. 1. The future. 2. A future event or possibility.

fuze (fyŏŏz) *n.* Also **fuse.** A mechanical or electrical mechanism used to detonate an explosive. [Var of FUSE[1].]

fu·zee. Variant of fusee.

fuzz[1] (fŭz) *n.* A mass of fine, light particles, fibers, or hairs. [Perh < FUZZY.]

fuzz[2] (fŭz) *n. Slang.* The police. [?]

fuzz·y (fŭz′ē) *adj.* -ier, -iest. 1. Covered with or resembling fuzz. 2. Indistinct; blurred; confused. [Perh < LG *fussig*, spongy.]

–fy. *comb. form.* A making or forming into: **nitrify.** [< L *-ficus*, -FIC.]

Gg

g, G (jē) *n.* 1. The 7th letter of the English alphabet. 2. The 7th in a series.

g 1. acceleration of gravity. 2. gram.

G 1. giga-. 2. gravitation constant. 3. *Mus.* The 5th tone in the scale of C major. 4. *Slang.* grand.

G. gulf.

Ga gallium.

Ga. Georgia.

G.A. general assembly.

gab (găb) *v.* **gabbed, gabbing.** To talk easily or excessively about trivial matters; chatter. —*n.* Chatter; prattle. —**gift of gab.** A talent for speaking easily or well. [Perh < Scot *gab*, mouthful, lump.] —**gab′ber** *n.*

gab·ar·dine (găb′ər-dēn′, găb′ər-dēn′) *n.* A worsted cotton, wool, or rayon twill, used in making dresses, suits, and coats. [Var of earlier *gaberdine* < OF *gallevardine*, "pilgrim's frock."]

gab·ble (găb′əl) *v.* -bled, -bling. 1. To speak rapidly or incoherently. 2. To make rapid, repeated cackling noises, as a goose or duck. [MDu *gabbelen*.] —**gab′ble** *n.*

gab•by (găb′ē) *adj.* **-bier, -biest.** Tending to talk excessively.

ga•ble (gā′bəl) *n.* A triangular wall section at the ends of a pitched roof. [< OF.] —**ga′bled** *adj.*

Ga•bon (gȧ-bôN′). A republic of west-central Africa. Pop. 462,000. Cap. Libreville.

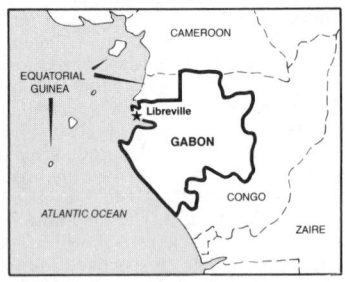

Gabon

Gab•o•ro•ne (găb′ə-rō′nə). The capital of Botswana. Pop. 18,000.

Ga•bri•el (gā′brē-əl). Biblical archangel who acted as the messenger of God.

gad (găd) *v.* **gadded, gadding.** To roam about restlessly or excitedly; rove. [ME *gadden*.] —**gad′der** *n.*

gad•a•bout (găd′ə-bout′) *n.* One who gads, esp. one who goes about seeking gossip or excitement.

gad•fly (găd′flī′) *n.* **1.** A fly that bites or annoys livestock and other animals. **2.** One that acts as a provocative stimulus. [GAD + FLY.]

gadg•et (găj′ĭt) *n. Informal.* A small specialized mechanical device. [Poss < F *gâchette*, catch (of a lock).] —**gadg′et•ry** *n.*

gad•o•lin•i•um (găd′l-ĭn′ē-əm) *n. Symbol* **Gd** A silvery-white malleable, ductile metallic element, used to improve the high-temperature characteristics of iron, chromium, and related metallic alloys. Atomic number 64, atomic weight 157.25. [< J. *Gadolin* (1760–1852), Finnish chemist.]

Gael (gāl) *n.* A Gaelic-speaking Celt of Scotland, Ireland, or the Isle of Man.

Gael. Gaelic.

Gael•ic (gā′lĭk) *n.* **1.** The Goidelic family of the Celtic languages. **2.** One of the languages of the Gaels. —*adj.* Of or pertaining to the Gaels or their languages.

gaff (găf) *n.* **1.** An iron hook attached to a pole and used to land and maneuver large fish. **2.** A spar used to extend the top edge of a fore-and-aft sail. **3.** Harshness of treatment; abuse. [< OProv *gaf.*]

gaffe (găf) *n.* A clumsy social error; a faux pas. [< F *gaffer*, to hook, hence to blunder.]

gaf•fer (găf′ər) *n.* An old man or rustic. [< GODFATHER.]

gag (găg) *n.* **1.** Something forced into or put over the mouth to prevent the utterance of

sound. **2.** Any obstacle to free speech. **3.** A device placed in the mouth to keep it open, as in dentistry. **4. a.** A practical joke. **b.** A comic remark. —*v.* **gagged, gagging.** **1.** To prevent from uttering sounds by using a gag. **2.** To repress (free speech). **3.** To keep (the mouth) open by using a gag. **4.** To block off or stop up, as a pipe or valve. **5.** To choke or retch. [ME *gaggen*, to suffocate.]

gage (gāj) *n.* **1.** Something deposited or given as security; a pledge. **2.** Something, as a glove, thrown down as a challenge to fight. **3.** Any test or challenge. [< Frank **wadi.*]

gag•gle (găg′əl) *n.* **1.** A flock of geese. **2.** A gabbling or cackling sound. [ME *gagelen.*]

gai•e•ty (gā′ə-tē) *n.* **1.** A state of being gay or merry. **2.** Festivity; merriment.

gai•ly (gā′lē) *adv.* **1.** In a joyful or cheerful manner. **2.** Colorfully; showily.

gain (gān) *v.* **1.** To become the owner of; acquire; get. **2.** To win. **3.** To earn. **4.** To build up an increase of, as weight. **5.** To arrive at. **6.** To advance or progress. —*n.* Something gained; a profit; advantage; increase. [< OF *gaaignier.*]

gain•ful (gān′fəl) *adj.* Profitable; lucrative. —**gain′ful•ly** *adv.* —**gain′ful•ness** *n.*

gain•say (gān-sā′) *v.* **-said** (-sĕd′), **-saying.** **1.** To deny. **2.** To contradict. [ME *gaynsayen,* "to say against."] —**gain•say′er** *n.*

gait (gāt) *n.* A way of moving on foot; a manner of walking or running; specifically, such a motion of a horse, as a canter, trot, or walk. [< ON *gata,* path, street.] —**gait′ed** *adj.*

gai•ter (gā′tər) *n.* **1.** A leather or heavy cloth covering for the ankle or legs; a legging; spat. **2.** An ankle-high shoe with elastic sides. **3.** An overshoe with a cloth top. [< OF *guestre.*]

gal (găl) *n. Informal.* A girl.

gal. gallon.

Gal. Galatians (New Testament).

ga•la (gā′lə, găl′ə, gä′lə) *n.* A festive occasion or celebration. —*adj.* Festive. [It.]

Gal•a•had (găl′ə-hăd′) *n.* A model of chivalrous virtue. [< Sir *Galahad,* knight of Arthurian legend who achieved the quest of the Holy Grail.]

gal•ax•y (găl′ək-sē) *n., pl.* **-ies.** **1. a.** Any of numerous large-scale aggregates of stars, gas, and dust, containing an average of 100 billion solar masses and ranging in diameter from 1,500 to 300,000 light-years. **b. The Galaxy.** The galaxy of which the earth's sun is a part, the **Milky Way.** **2.** An assembly of brilliant, beautiful, or distinguished persons or things. [< Gk *galaxias (kuklos),* "milky (circle).")] —**ga•lac′tic** *adj.*

gale (gāl) *n.* **1. a.** A very strong wind. **b.** A wind having a speed between 32 and 63 miles per hour. **2.** A forceful outburst, as of laughter. [Prob short for *gale wind,* "bad wind."]

ga•le•na (gə-lē′nə) *n.* A gray mineral, essentially PbS, the principal ore of lead. [L *galēna,* lead ore.]

Gal•i•le•o (găl′ə-lā′ō). 1564–1642. Italian scientist and astronomer.

gall¹ (gôl) *n.* **1. a.** Liver bile. **b.** The gallbladder. **2.** Rancor; bitterness; resentment. **3.**

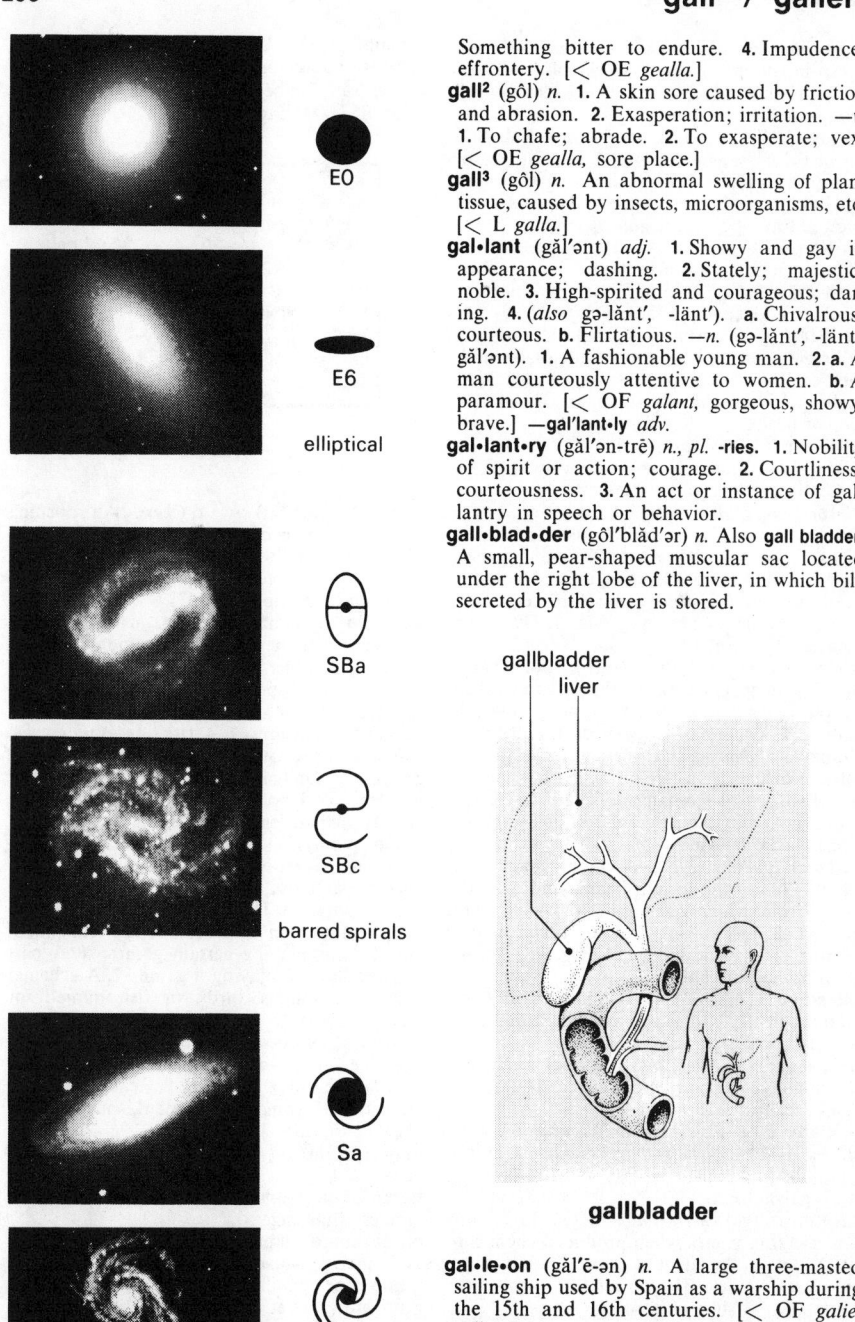

galaxy
Diagrams and letter codes
beneath each group
identify galactic types

EO

E6

elliptical

SBa

SBc

barred spirals

Sa

Sc

spirals

Something bitter to endure. **4.** Impudence; effrontery. [< OE *gealla*.]

gall² (gôl) *n.* **1.** A skin sore caused by friction and abrasion. **2.** Exasperation; irritation. —*v.* **1.** To chafe; abrade. **2.** To exasperate; vex. [< OE *gealla*, sore place.]

gall³ (gôl) *n.* An abnormal swelling of plant tissue, caused by insects, microorganisms, etc. [< L *galla.*]

gal·lant (găl′ənt) *adj.* **1.** Showy and gay in appearance; dashing. **2.** Stately; majestic; noble. **3.** High-spirited and courageous; daring. **4.** (*also* gə-lănt′, -länt′). **a.** Chivalrous; courteous. **b.** Flirtatious. —*n.* (gə-lănt′, -länt′, găl′ənt). **1.** A fashionable young man. **2. a.** A man courteously attentive to women. **b.** A paramour. [< OF *galant*, gorgeous, showy, brave.] —**gal′lant·ly** *adv.*

gal·lant·ry (găl′ən-trē) *n., pl.* **-ries. 1.** Nobility of spirit or action; courage. **2.** Courtliness; courteousness. **3.** An act or instance of gallantry in speech or behavior.

gall·blad·der (gôl′blăd′ər) *n.* Also **gall bladder.** A small, pear-shaped muscular sac located under the right lobe of the liver, in which bile secreted by the liver is stored.

gallbladder
liver

gallbladder

gal·le·on (găl′ē-ən) *n.* A large three-masted sailing ship used by Spain as a warship during the 15th and 16th centuries. [< OF *galie*, galley.]

gal·ler·y (găl′ə-rē) *n., pl.* **-ies. 1.** A long balcony, often with a roof. **2.** Any enclosed narrow passageway, esp. one used for a specified purpose: *a shooting gallery.* **3.** A porch; verandah. **4. a.** The balcony of a theater. **b.** The seats in such a section. **c.** The audience occupying these seats. **d.** Any similar balcony, as in a church. **5.** Any large audience, as in a stadium or legislative assembly. **6. a.** A building or hall in which artistic work is displayed. **b.** An institution that sells works of art. **7.** An underground tunnel or other passageway. [< ML *galeria.*]

gal·ley (găl′ē) *n.* **1.** A large medieval ship propelled by sails and oars. **2.** The kitchen of a ship or airliner. **3.** *Ptg.* **a.** A long tray used for holding composed type. **b.** A proof from such a tray. [< MGk *galea.*]

Gal·lic (găl′ĭk) *adj.* Of or pertaining to ancient Gaul or modern France; French.

gal·li·mau·fry (găl′ə-mô′frē) *n., pl.* -**fries.** A jumble; hodgepodge. [F *galimafrée.*]

gal·li·um (găl′ē-əm) *n. Symbol Ga* A rare metallic element used in semiconductor technology and as a component of various low-melting alloys. Atomic number 31, atomic weight 69.72. [< L *gallus,* cock.]

gal·li·vant (găl′ə-vănt′, găl′ə-vănt′) *v.* **1.** To roam about aimlessly or frivolously; traipse. **2.** To flirt. [Perh var of GALLANT.]

gal·lon (găl′ən) *n.* **1.** A U.S. Customary System unit of volume or capacity, used in liquid measure, equal to 4 quarts or 231 cubic inches. **2.** A British Imperial System unit of volume, used in liquid and dry measure, equal to 277.420 cubic inches. [< ML *gallēta,* jug, measure for wine.]

gal·lop (găl′əp) *n.* A three-beat gait of a horse or other quadruped, faster than a canter and slower than a run. —*v.* **1.** To move or ride at a gallop. **2.** To move or progress rapidly. [< Frank **walahlaupan,* "to run well."]

Gal·lo-Ro·man (găl′ō-rō′mən) *n.* **1.** A native or inhabitant of Roman Gaul. **2.** The Vulgar Latin spoken by the Romanized inhabitants of Gaul. —**Gal′lo-Ro′man** *adj.*

gal·lows (găl′ōz) *n., pl.* -**lowses** or -**lows.** **1.** A frame having two upright beams and a crossbeam from which condemned prisoners are hanged. **2.** Any similar structure used for supporting or suspending. [< OE *gealga,* cross, gallows. See **ghalgh-.**]

gall·stone (gôl′stōn′) *n.* A small, hard concretion, chiefly cholesterol crystals, formed in the gallbladder or in a bile duct.

ga·lore (gə-lôr′, -lōr′) *adj.* In great numbers; in abundance: *opportunites galore.* [Ir Gael *go leór.*]

ga·losh·es (gə-lŏsh′ĭz) *pl.n.* Waterproof overshoes. [Prob < L *gallica (solea),* "Gaulish (sandal)."]

galv. galvanized.

gal·van·ic (găl-văn′ĭk) *adj.* **1.** Of direct-current electricity, esp. when produced chemically. **2.** Having the effect of or produced as if by an electric shock. [F *galvanique.*] —**gal·van′i·cal·ly** *adv.* —**gal′va·nism′** *n.*

gal·va·nize (găl′və-nīz′) *v.* -**nized, -nizing. 1.** To stimulate or shock with an electric current. **2.** To arouse to awareness or action; spur; startle. **3.** To coat (iron or steel) with rust-resistant zinc. —**gal′va·ni·za′tion** *n.* —**gal′va·niz′er** *n.*

gal·va·nom·e·ter (găl′və-nŏm′ə-tər) *n.* A device for detecting or measuring small electric currents by means of mechanical effects produced by the current to be measured.

Ga·ma (găm′ə), **Vasco da.** 1469?-1524. Portuguese navigator.

Gam·bi·a (găm′bē-ə). A republic of W Africa. Pop. 357,000. Cap. Banjul.

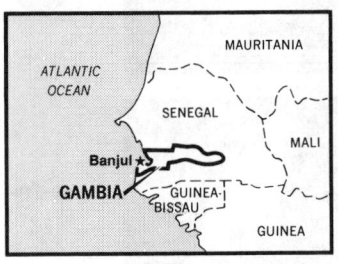

Gambia

gam·bit (găm′bĭt) *n.* **1.** *Chess.* An opening move in which one or more pieces are sacrificed in order to gain a favorable position. **2.** An opening remark or stratagem. [< It *gambetto,* "a tripping up."]

gam·ble (găm′bəl) *v.* -**bled, -bling. 1. a.** To wager; bet money on the outcome of a game, contest, or other event. **b.** To play a game of chance. **2.** To speculate. **3.** To expose to hazard; risk. —*n.* **1.** A bet, wager, or other gambling venture. **2.** A risk. [< OE *gamen,* amusement, GAME.] —**gam′bler** *n.*

gam·bol (găm′bəl) *v.* -**boled** or -**bolled, -boling** or -**bolling.** To leap about playfully; frolic; skip. [< It *gamba,* leg.] —**gam′bol** *n.*

game¹ (gām) *n.* **1.** A way of amusing oneself; a pastime; diversion. **2.** A sport or other competitive activity. **3.** A single instance of such an activity. **4.** The total number of points required to win a game. **5.** The equipment needed for playing certain games. **6.** A particular style of playing a game. **7.** A scheme; plan. **8.** Animals, birds, or fish hunted for food or sport. **9.** An object of ridicule or scorn. **10.** A vocation or business, esp. a competitive one. —*adj.* **gamer, gamest. 1.** Plucky and unyielding; resolute. **2.** Ready and willing. [< OE *gamen,* amusement, sport < Gmc **gam-,* to enjoy.]

game² (gām) *adj.* Lame. [Perh < F *gambi,* crooked.]

game·cock (gām′kŏk′) *n.* A rooster trained for cockfighting.

game·some (gām′səm) *adj.* Frolicsome; playful; merry. —**game′some·ly** *adv.*

game·ster (gām′stər) *n.* A habitual gambler.

gam·ete (găm′ēt, gə-mēt′) *n.* A germ cell, esp. a mature sperm or egg, capable of participating in fertilization. [< Gk *gametē,* wife, and *gametēs,* husband.]

game theory. The mathematical analysis of abstract models of strategic competition.

gam·in (găm′ĭn) *n.* A boy who roams the streets; street urchin; waif. [F.]

ga·mine (gă-mēn′) *n.* A girl or woman having elfin appeal. [< GAMIN.]

gam·ma (găm′ə) *n.* **1.** The 3rd letter of the

ă pat/ā ate/âr care/ä bar/b **bib**/ch **chew**/d **deed**/ĕ pet/ē be/f fit/g **gag**/h **hat**/hw **what**/
ĭ pit/ī pie/îr pier/j **judge**/k **kick**/l lid, fatal/m **mum**/n no, sudden/ng **sing**/ŏ pot/ō go/

Greek alphabet, representing *g(n).* **2. A gamma ray.**

gamma globulin. Any of several globulin fractions of blood serum associated with immune bodies and used to treat measles, poliomyelitis, infectious hepatitis, and other infectious diseases.

gamma ray. Any electromagnetic radiation with energy greater than several hundred thousand electron volts.

gam·mon (găm′ən) *n.* **1.** A cured or smoked ham. **2.** The lower part of a side of bacon. [ONF *gambon.*]

gam·ut (găm′ət) *n.* The complete range of anything; extent. [< ML *gamma ut,* notes named after syllables in a Latin hymn.]

gam·y (gā′mē) *adj.* **-ier, -iest. 1.** Having the flavor or odor of game, esp. game that has been hung too long. **2.** Plucky; hardy.

–gamy. *comb. form.* Marriage or sexual union: *allogamy.* [< Gk *gamos,* marriage.]

gan·der (găn′dər) *n.* **1.** A male goose. **2.** *Slang.* A quick look; glance. [< OE *gandra, ganra.* See **ghans-.**]

Gan·dhi (gän′dē, găn′-), **Mohandas Karamchand.** Called "Mahatma." 1869–1948. Hindu nationalist and spiritual leader.

Mahatma Gandhi

gang (găng) *n.* **1.** A group of people who associate or work together. **2.** A set, esp. of matched tools. —*v.* To band together as a group or gang. —**gang up (on).** To harass or attack as a group. [< OE *gang,* a going. See **ghengh-.**]

Gan·ges (găn′jēz′). A river in N India and Bangladesh.

gan·gling (găng′glĭng) *adj.* Also **gang·ly** (-glē), **-lier, -liest.** Tall, thin, and ungraceful; lanky. [< dial *gang,* to go, straggle.]

gan·gli·on (găng′glē-ən) *n., pl.* **-glia** (-glē-ə) or **-ons.** A group of nerve cells, such as one located outside the brain or spinal cord, in vertebrates. [Gk, cystlike tumor, nerve bundle, ganglion.] —**gan′gli·on′ic** (-ŏn′ĭk) *adj.*

gang·plank (găng′plăngk′) *n.* A removable

bridgelike structure between a ship and a pier.

gan·grene (găng′grēn′, găng-grēn′) *n.* Death and decay of bodily tissue caused by failure of blood supply, injury, or disease. [< Gk *gangraina.*] —**gan′gre·nous** (-grə-nəs) *adj.*

gang·ster (găng′stər) *n.* A member of an organized group of criminals; racketeer.

Gang·tok (gŭng′tŏk). The capital of Sikkim. Pop. 7,000.

gang·way (găng′wā′) *n.* **1.** A passageway, as through a crowd or an obstructed area. **2.** A gangplank.

gan·net (găn′ĭt) *n.* A large sea bird of northern coastal regions with white plumage and black wing tips. [< OE *ganot.* See **ghans-.**]

gan·try (găn′trē) *n., pl.* **-tries.** A frame or support, esp. a large vertical structure used in assembling or servicing rockets. [< L *canthērius,* rafter.]

GAO General Accounting Office.

gaol. *Chiefly Brit.* Variant of **jail.**

gap (găp) *n.* **1.** An opening, as in a partition or wall; fissure; cleft. **2.** A break or pass through mountains. **3.** An interval; hiatus: *a gap in his report.* **4.** A conspicuous difference; disparity. [< ON, chasm.]

gape (gāp, găp) *v.* **gaped, gaping. 1.** To open the mouth wide; yawn. **2.** To stare wonderingly, as with the mouth open. **3.** To open widely. —*n.* **1.** An act or instance of gaping. **2.** A large opening. [< ON *gapa,* to open the mouth.] —**gap′er** *n.*

gap·ing (gā′pĭng) *adj.* Deep and wide open: *a gaping wound.* —**gap′ing·ly** *adv.*

gar (gär) *n.* Also **gar·fish** (gär′fĭsh′). A fish having an elongated body covered with bony plates and a long snout. [< OE *gār,* spear.]

GAR, G.A.R. Grand Army of the Republic.

ga·rage (gə-räzh′, -räj′) *n.* **1.** A structure for housing cars. **2.** A commercial establishment where cars are repaired and serviced. [< OF *garer,* to protect, guard.] —**ga·rage′** *v.* (**-raged, -raging**).

garb (gärb) *n.* Clothing, esp. the distinctive attire of one's occupation or station. —*v.* To clothe; dress; array. [< It *garbo,* grace, elegance of dress.]

gar·bage (gär′bĭj) *n.* **1.** Food wastes, as from a kitchen. **2.** Refuse; rubbish. [ME, offal of an animal.]

gar·ble (gär′bəl) *v.* **-bled, -bling.** To distort or scramble (an account or message) so as to be unintelligible; jumble. [< Ar *gharbala,* to sift.] —**gar′bler** *n.*

gar·den (gärd′n) *n.* **1.** A plot of land used for growing flowers, vegetables, or fruit. **2.** A planted tract used for public enjoyment. **3.** A yard; lawn. **4.** A fertile, well-cultivated region. —*adj.* Of, pertaining to, or found in a garden. —*v.* To work in a garden. [< VL **(hortus) gardīnus,* "enclosed (garden)."]

gar·den·er (gärd′nər, gärd′n-ər) *n.* A person who works in or tends a garden.

gar·de·ni·a (gär-dēn′yə, -dē′nē-ə) *n.* **1.** A shrub with glossy, evergreen leaves and large, fragrant white flowers. **2.** The flower of this shrub. [< Dr. A. *Garden* (1731–1790), Scottish naturalist.]

ô **paw,** for/oi **boy**/ou **out**/ŏŏ **took**/ōō **coo**/p **pop**/r **run**/s **sauce**/sh **shy**/t **to**/th **thin**/*th* **the**/ ŭ **cut**/ûr **fur**/v **van**/w **wag**/y **yes**/z **size**/zh **vision**/ə **ago, item, edible, gallop, circus/**

Gar·field (gär′fēld′), **James Abram.** 1831–1881. 20th President of the U.S. (1881).

James A. Garfield

gar·gan·tu·an (gär-găn′chōō-ən) *adj.* Of immense size or volume. [< the hero of Rabelais' *Gargantua and Pantagruel.*]

gar·gle (gär′gəl) *v.* **-gled, -gling. 1.** To exhale through a soothing or medicated liquid held in the back of the mouth, with the head tilted back. **2.** To produce the sound of gargling when speaking or singing. —*n.* A medicated solution for gargling. [< OF *gargouille*, throat, gargoyle.]

gar·goyle (gär′goil′) *n.* A roof spout carved to represent a grotesque human or animal figure. [< L *gurguliō*, windpipe.]

Gar·i·bal·di (găr′ə-bôl′dē), **Giuseppe.** 1807–1882. Italian general and nationalist leader.

gar·ish (gâr′ĭsh) *adj.* Marked by strident color or excessive ornamentation; gaudy. [?] —**gar′ish·ly** *adv.* —**gar′ish·ness** *n.*

gar·land (gär′lənd) *n.* **1.** A crown or wreath of flowers, leaves, etc. **2.** Something resembling a garland. —*v.* To embellish with a garland. [< OF *garlande.*]

gar·lic (gär′lĭk) *n.* **1.** A plant related to the onion, having a bulb with a strong, distinctive odor and flavor. **2.** The bulb of this plant used as a seasoning. [< OE *gārlēac*, "spear leek."]

gar·lick·y (gär′lĭk-ē) *adj.* Containing, tasting of, or redolent of garlic, esp. too much garlic: *a garlicky dish.*

gar·ment (gär′mənt) *n.* An article of clothing, esp. of outer clothing. [< OF *garnement*, "equipment."]

gar·ner (gär′nər) *v.* To amass; acquire. [< L *grānārium*, granary.]

gar·net (gär′nĭt) *n.* **1.** Any of several common, widespread silicate minerals, colored red, brown, black, green, yellow, or white, and used as gemstones and abrasives. **2.** Dark to very dark red. [< OF *grenat*, garnet, pomegranate-colored.]

gar·nish (gär′nĭsh) *v.* To embellish; adorn. —*n.* An embellishment, usually savory, for a dish of food or a drink. [< OF *guarnir*, to adorn.]

gar·nish·ee (gär′nĭ-shē′) *v.* **-eed, -eeing.** *Law.* To attach (a debtor's pay) by garnishment.

gar·nish·ment (gär′nĭsh-mənt) *n.* *Law.* A proceeding whereby money or property due or belonging to a debtor but in the possession of another is applied to the payment of the debt to the plaintiff.

gar·ret (găr′ĭt) *n.* An attic; loft. [< OF *guarir*, to defend, protect.]

gar·ri·son (găr′ĭ-sən) *n.* **1.** A permanent military post. **2.** The troops stationed at such a post. —*v.* To assign (troops) to a military post. [< OF *guarir*, to protect.]

gar·ru·lous (găr′/y/ə-ləs) *adj.* Talkative; loquacious; wordy. [< L *garrīre*, to chatter.] —**gar·ru′li·ty** (gə-rōō′lə-tē), **gar′ru·lous·ness** *n.*

gar·ter (gär′tər) *n.* An elasticized band or suspender to hold up hose. [< Gaul *garr-, leg.]

garter snake. A nonvenomous North American snake with longitudinal stripes.

Gar·y (gâr′ē). A city of NW Indiana. Pop. 178,000.

gas (găs) *n., pl.* **gases** or **gasses. 1. a.** The state of matter distinguished from the solid and liquid states by very low density and viscosity, the ability to diffuse readily, and the spontaneous tendency to become distributed uniformly throughout any container. **b.** A substance in this state. **2.** Gasoline. **3.** *Slang.* Something providing great excitement. —*v.* **gassed, gassing. 1.** To supply with gas or gasoline. **2.** To treat with gas. **3.** To poison with gas. [Du.]

gas chamber. A sealed enclosure in which prisoners are executed by a poisonous gas.

gas·e·ous (găs′ē-əs, -yəs, găsh′əs) *adj.* Of, pertaining to, or existing as a gas.

gash (găsh) *n.* A long, deep cut or wound; a slash. [Prob < Gk *kharassein*, to carve, cut.] —**gash** *v.*

gas·ket (găs′kĭt) *n.* Any of a wide variety of seals or packings used between matched machine parts or around pipe joints to prevent the escape of a gas or fluid. [F *garcette*, "little girl," rope.]

gas·light (găs′līt′) *n.* **1.** Light produced by burning illuminating gas. **2.** A gas-burning lamp.

gas mask. A respirator covering the face and having a chemical air filter to protect against poisonous gases.

gas·o·line (găs′ə-lēn′, găs′ə-lēn′) *n.* A volatile mixture of flammable liquid hydrocarbons derived chiefly from crude petroleum and used principally as a fuel for internal-combustion engines, and as a solvent, illuminant, and thinner.

gasp (găsp, gäsp) *v.* **1.** To draw in the breath sharply, as from shock. **2.** To breathe convulsively or laboriously. [< ON *geispa*.] —**gasp** *n.*

gas·sy (găs′ē) *adj.* **-sier, -siest.** Containing, full of, or resembling gas.

gas·tric (găs′trĭk) *adj.* Pertaining to the stomach. [< Gk *gastēr*, belly, womb.]

gastric juice. The colorless, watery, acidic digestive fluid secreted by the stomach glands.

ă pat/ā ate/âr care/ä bar/b bib/ch chew/d deed/ĕ pet/ē be/f fit/g gag/h hat/hw what/
ĭ pit/ī pie/îr pier/j judge/k kick/l lid, fatal/m mum/n no, sudden/ng sing/ŏ pot/ō go/

gas•tri•tis (găs-trī'tĭs) *n.* Chronic or acute inflammation of the stomach.

gastro–. *comb. form.* The stomach.

gas•tro•en•ter•i•tis (găs'trō-ĕn'tə-rī'tĭs) *n.* Inflammation of the mucous membrane of the stomach and intestine.

gas•tro•in•tes•ti•nal (găs'trō-ĭn-tĕs'tə-nəl) *adj.* Of or pertaining to the stomach and intestines.

gas•tron•o•my (găs-trŏn'ə-mē) *n.* 1. The art of good eating. 2. Cooking, as of a particular region. —**gas'tro•nom'ic** (găs'trə-nŏm'ĭk) *adj.* —**gas'tro•nom'i•cal•ly** *adv.*

gas•tro•pod (găs'trə-pŏd') *n.* Also *rare* **gas•ter•o•pod** (-tər-ə-pŏd'). A snail or related mollusk having a single, usually coiled shell and a broad, muscular organ of locomotion. [< NL *Gastropoda,* "belly-footed creatures."]

gas•works (găs'wûrks') *n. (takes sing. v.).* A factory where gas for heating and lighting is produced.

gat (găt). *Archaic. p.t.* of **get.**

gate (gāt) *n.* 1. A structure, usually hinged, that serves as a door in a wall or fence. 2. The total admission receipts or attendance at a public spectacle. 3. A circuit extensively used in computers that has an output dependent on some function of its input. [< OE *geat* < Gmc **gatam.*]

gate•crash•er (gāt'krăsh'ər) *n. Slang.* One who gains admittance without being invited or enters without paying admission.

gate•keep•er (gāt'kē'pər) *n.* A person in charge of a gate.

gate•way (gāt'wā') *n.* 1. A structure, as an arch, framing an entrance that may be closed by a gate. 2. Something that serves as an entrance or means of access.

gath•er (găth'ər) *v.* 1. To bring or come together. 2. To accumulate gradually; collect. 3. To harvest or pick. 4. To increase by degrees: *gather velocity.* 5. To pull (cloth) along a thread to create small folds. 6. To draw (a garment) about or closer to something. 7. To infer: *I gather he's ready.* —*n.* 1. An act or instance of gathering. 2. Often **gathers.** A small tuck or pucker in cloth. [< OE *gaderian,* to come together. See **ghedh–.**] —**gath'er•er** *n.* —**gath'er•ing** *n.*

gauche (gōsh) *adj.* Lacking social grace; awkward. [F, "left," "askew."]

gau•che•rie (gō'shə-rē') *n.* An awkward or graceless action.

Gau•cho (gou'chō) *n., pl.* **-chos.** A cowboy of the South American pampas.

gaud•y (gô'dē) *adj.* **-ier, -iest.** Characterized by tasteless or showy colors. [< L *gaudēre,* to delight in.] —**gaud'i•ly** *adv.*

gauge (gāj) *n.* 1. a. A standard or scale of measurement. b. A standard dimension, quantity, or capacity. 2. An instrument for measuring or testing. 3. A means of evaluating: *a gauge of character.* —*v.* **gauged, gauging.** 1. To measure precisely. 2. To determine the capacity or contents of. 3. To evaluate: *gauge ability.* [< Frank **galga,* cross, perch, windlass.] —**gaug'er** *n.*

Gau•guin (gō-găN'), **Paul.** 1848–1903. French painter.

Gaul¹ (gôl). A region of the Roman Empire in W Europe.

Gaul² (gôl) *n.* 1. A Celt of ancient Gaul. 2. A Frenchman.

Gaul•ish (gô'lĭsh) *n.* The Celtic language of ancient Gaul.

gaunt (gônt) *adj.* 1. Very thin and bony; emaciated. 2. Bleak; desolate. [Prob < Scand.] —**gaunt'ly** *adv.* —**gaunt'ness** *n.*

gaunt•let¹ (gônt'lĭt, gänt'-) *n.* 1. A protective glove. 2. A challenge: *fling down the gauntlet.* [< Frank **want,* mitten.]

gaunt•let² (gônt'lĭt, gänt'-) *n.* 1. A double line of men armed with clubs with which to beat a person forced to run between them. 2. An ordeal in which one comes under fire from several quarters: *run the gauntlet.* [< OSwed *gatulop,* "passageway."]

gauze (gôz) *n.* A thin, transparent fabric with a loose open weave. [< OF *gaze.*] —**gauz'i•ly** *adv.* —**gauz'i•ness** *n.* —**gauz'y** *adj.*

gave (gāv). *p.t.* of **give.**

gav•el (găv'əl) *n.* The mallet used by a presiding officer or auctioneer to signal for attention or order. [?]

gawk (gôk) *n.* An awkward, stupid person. —*v.* To stare stupidly. —**gawk'y** *adj.*

gay (gā) *adj.* 1. Light-hearted; lively. 2. Given to social pleasures. 3. *Slang.* Homosexual. —*n.* A homosexual. [< OF *gai.*]

gaze (gāz) *v.* **gazed, gazing.** To look with fixed attention; stare. [Prob < Scand.] —**gaze** *n.*

ga•zelle (gə-zĕl') *n.* Any of various slender, swift-running horned mammals of Africa and Asia. [Prob < Ar *ghazāl.*]

ga•zette (gə-zĕt') *n.* 1. A newspaper. 2. An official journal. [< It *gazetta.*]

gaz•et•teer (găz'ə-tîr') *n.* A geographic dictionary or index.

G.B. Great Britain.

G clef. The treble clef.

Gd gadolinium.

gds. goods.

Ge germanium.

gear (gîr) *n.* 1. a. A toothed wheel or other machine element that meshes with another toothed element to transmit motion or change speed or direction. b. A transmission configuration for a specific ratio of engine to axle torque in a motor vehicle. 2. Equipment, as tools or clothing, required for a particular activity. —*v.* 1. a. To provide with or connect by gears. b. To put into gear. 2. To adjust or adapt. [< ON *gervi.*]

gear•box (gîr'bŏks') *n.* An automotive transmission.

gear•ing (gîr'ĭng) *n.* A system of gears and associated machine elements.

gear•shift (gîr'shĭft') *n.* A mechanism for changing from one gear to another in a transmission.

gee (jē) *interj.* Expressive of mild surprise. [Euphemistic shortening of JESUS.]

geese. *pl.* of **goose.**

gee•zer (gē'zər) *n. Slang.* An eccentric old man.

Gei•ger counter (gī'gər). An electronic instrument used to detect, measure, and record

---

ô paw, for/oi boy/ou out/ōō took/ōō coo/p pop/r run/s sauce/sh shy/t to/th thin/*th* the/
ŭ cut/ûr fur/v van/w wag/y yes/z size/zh vision/ə ago, item, edible, gallop, circus/

nuclear emanations, cosmic rays, and artificially produced subatomic particles. [< H. *Geiger* (1882–1945), German physicist.]

gei•sha (gā′shə, gē′-) *n., pl.* **-sha** or **-shas.** A Japanese girl trained to provide entertainment, as singing or dancing, for men. [Jap, "artist."]

gel (jĕl) *n.* A colloid in which the disperse phase has combined with the continuous phase to produce a semisolid such as a jelly. [Short for GELATIN.]

gel•a•tin (jĕl′ə-tən) *n.* Also **gel•a•tine.** A transparent, brittle protein formed by boiling the specially prepared skin, bones, and connective tissue of animals, and used in foods, drugs, and photographic film. [< L *gelāre,* to freeze, congeal.] **—ge•lat′i•nous** (jə-lăt′n-əs) *adj.*

geld (gĕld) *v.* To castrate (a horse or other animal). [< ON *gelda.*]

geld•ing (gĕl′dĭng) *n.* A castrated animal, esp. a horse.

gel•id (jĕl′ĭd) *adj.* Very cold; icy. [< L *gelū,* cold, frost.] **—gel′id•ly** *adv.*

gem (jĕm) *n.* **1.** A precious or semiprecious stone, esp. one that has been cut and polished. **2.** Something that is valued highly. [< L *gemma,* bud, precious stone.]

Gem•i•ni (jĕm′ə-nī′, -nē′) *n.* **1.** A constellation in the N Hemisphere. **2.** The 3rd sign of the zodiac. [< L *geminus,* twin.]

gem•stone (jĕm′stōn′) *n.* A precious or semiprecious stone that can be used as a jewel when cut and polished.

–gen, –gene. *comb. form.* **1.** That which produces: **oxygen. 2.** Something produced: **antigen.** [< Gk *-genēs,* born.]

gen. **1.** gender. **2.** genitive. **3.** genus.

Gen. **1.** general (military rank). **2.** Genesis (Old Testament).

gen•darme (zhän′därm′) *n.* A member of the French national police. [< F *gens d'armes,* "men of arms."]

gen•der (jĕn′dər) *n. Gram.* Any of two or more categories, as masculine, feminine, and neuter, into which words are divided and that determine agreement with or selection of modifiers or grammatical forms. [< L *genus (gener-),* race, kind.]

gene (jēn) *n.* A functional hereditary unit that occupies a fixed location on a chromosome, has a specific influence on phenotype, and is capable of mutation to various allelic forms. [< -GEN.]

–gene. Variant of -gen.

ge•ne•al•o•gy (jē′nē-ăl′ə-jē, -ŏl′ə-jē, jĕn′ē-) *n., pl.* **-gies. 1.** A record or table of ancestry. **2.** The study of ancestry. [< Gk *genea,* race, generation + -LOGY.] **—ge′ne•a•log′i•cal** (-ə-lŏj′ĭ-kəl) *adj.* **—ge′ne•al′o•gist** *n.*

gen•e•ra. *pl.* of **genus.**

gen•er•al (jĕn′ər-əl) *adj.* **1.** Of, pertaining to, or applicable to the whole or every member of a group. **2.** Widespread; prevalent. **3.** Being usually the case; true in most instances. **4.** Diversified: *general studies.* **5.** Lacking detail or precision: *a general grasp of a subject.* **6.** Chief within a particular sphere: *the general manager.* **—n. 1.** An officer of the second-highest rank in the U.S. Army or Air Force

and the highest rank in the Marine Corps. **2.** A military officer, as in England or Canada, holding a rank just below field marshal. **—in general.** For the most part. [< L *generālis,* relating to all.] **—gen′er•al•ly** *adv.*

gen•er•al•is•si•mo (jĕn′ər-ə-lĭs′ə-mō′) *n., pl.* **-mos.** The commander in chief of all the armed forces in certain countries.

gen•er•al•i•ty (jĕn′ə-răl′ə-tē) *n., pl.* **-ties. 1.** The condition or quality of being general. **2.** An observation or principle having general application. **3.** An imprecise or vague statement or idea.

gen•er•al•ize (jĕn′ər-ə-līz′) *v.* **-ized, -izing. 1.** To render general rather than specific. **2.** To draw inferences or a general conclusion from. **3.** To speak or think in generalities. **—gen′er•al•i•za′tion** *n.*

General of the Air Force. An officer having the highest rank in the U.S. Air Force.

General of the Army. An officer having the highest rank in the U.S. Army.

general relativity. The geometric theory of gravitation developed by Albert Einstein, incorporating and extending the special theory of relativity to accelerated frames of reference and introducing the principle that gravitational and inertial forces are equivalent.

gen•er•ate (jĕn′ə-rāt′) *v.* **-ated, -ating.** To bring into existence; produce. [L *generāre.*] **—gen′er•a′tive** (-ə-rā′tĭv, -ə-rə-tĭv) *adj.*

gen•er•a•tion (jĕn′ə-rā′shən) *n.* **1.** The act or process of generating. **2.** Offspring having common parentage and constituting a stage of descent. **3.** A group of contemporaneous individuals. **4.** The average time interval between the birth of parents and the birth of their offspring.

gen•er•a•tor (jĕn′ə-rā′tər) *n.* One that generates, esp. a machine that converts mechanical energy into electrical energy.

ge•ner•ic (jĭ-nĕr′ĭk) *adj.* **1.** Of or descriptive of an entire group or class. **2.** *Biol.* Of or relating to a genus. [< L *genus (gener-),* race, kind.] **—ge•ner′i•cal•ly** *adv.*

gen•er•ous (jĕn′ər-əs) *adj.* **1.** Liberal in giving; munificent. **2.** Abundant; ample. **3.** Lacking pettiness; magnanimous. [< L *generōsus,* of noble birth, magnanimous.] **—gen′er•os′i•ty** (-ə-rŏs′ə-tē) *n.* **—gen′er•ous•ly** *adv.*

gen•e•sis (jĕn′ə-sĭs) *n., pl.* **-ses** (-sēz′). The coming into being of anything; origin. [< Gk, generation, origin.]

–genesis. *comb. form.* Generation: **parthenogenesis.**

ge•net•i•cist (jə-nĕt′ə-sĭst) *n.* One who specializes in genetics.

ge•net•ics (jə-nĕt′ĭks) *n. (takes sing. v.).* The biology of heredity, esp. the study of hereditary transmission and variation. **—ge•net′ic** *adj.* **—ge•net′i•cal•ly** *adv.*

Ge•ne•va (jə-nē′və). A city of SW Switzerland. Pop. 174,000.

Gen•ghis Khan (jĕn′gĭz kän′, jĕng′gĭs, gĕng′-gĭs). 1162?–1227. Founder of the Mongol empire.

gen•ial (jĕn′yəl, jē′nē-əl) *adj.* **1.** Cheerful and friendly; kindly. **2.** Giving warmth; mild: *a* *genial climate.* [L *geniālis,* of generation or birth, nuptial, festive.] —**ge′ni•al′i•ty** (jē′nē-ăl′ə-tē) *n.* —**gen′ial•ly** *adv.*

ge•nie (jē′nē) *n.* A supernatural creature who does one's bidding. [< L *genius,* GENIUS.]

gen•i•tal (jĕn′ə-təl) *adj.* 1. Of or relating to biological reproduction. 2. Of or pertaining to the genitals.

gen•i•ta•li•a (jĕn′ə-tā′lē-ə, -tāl′yə) *pl.n.* The reproductive organs, esp. the external sex organs. [L *genitālia (membra),* genital (members).]

gen•i•tals (jĕn′ə-təlz) *pl.n.* Genitalia.

gen•i•tive (jĕn′ə-tĭv) *Gram. adj.* Of or pertaining to a case that expresses possession or source. —*n.* The genitive case. [< L *(casus) genitīvus,* "case of origin."]

gen•i•to•u•ri•nar•y (jĕn′ə-tō-yŏŏr′ə-nĕr′ē) *adj.* Of or pertaining to the genital and urinary organs or their functions.

gen•ius (jĕn′yəs) *n., pl.* **-iuses.** 1. a. Exceptional intellectual and creative power. b. One who possesses such power. 2. The prevailing spirit or character, as of a place, time, or group. [L, deity of generation and birth.]

genl. general.

Gen•o•a (jĕn′ō-ə). A city of NW Italy. Pop. 784,000.

gen•o•cide (jĕn′ə-sīd′) *n.* The systematic annihilation of a racial, political, or cultural group. [Gk *genos,* race + -CIDE.] —**gen′o•ci′dal** (-sīd′l) *adj.*

gen•o•type (jĕn′ə-tīp′) *n.* 1. The genetic constitution of an organism, esp. as distinguished from its physical appearance. 2. A group or class of organisms having the same genetic constitution. —**gen′o•typ′ic** (-tĭp′ĭk) *adj.*

–genous. *comb. form.* Generating or generated by: **androgenous.** [< -GEN.]

gen•re (zhän′rə) *n.* 1. Type; class. 2. A style of painting in which scenes and subjects of everyday life are depicted. 3. A distinctive class or category of literary composition. [< L *genus (gener-),* race, kind.]

gent (jĕnt) *n. Informal.* A man; fellow. [< GENTLEMAN.]

gen•teel (jĕn-tēl′) *adj.* 1. Refined in manner; polite. 2. Fashionable; elegant. 3. Striving to convey an appearance of respectability. 4. Marked by affected and somewhat prudish refinement. [OF *gentil,* gentle.]

gen•tian (jĕn′shən) *n.* Any of various plants characteristically having showy blue flowers. [< L *gentiāna.*]

gentian violet. A purple dye used chiefly as a biological stain and bactericide.

Gen•tile (jĕn′tīl) *n.* A Christian as distinguished from a Jew. [< LL *gentīlis,* pagan.]

gen•til•i•ty (jĕn-tĭl′ə-tē) *n.* 1. The condition of being genteel. 2. Gentle birth.

gen•tle (jĕnt′l) *adj.* **-tler, -tlest.** 1. Considerate or kindly. 2. Not harsh, severe, or violent; soft. 3. Easily managed or handled: *a gentle horse.* 4. Not steep: *a gentle incline.* 5. Of good family; well-born. —*v.* **-tled, -tling.** To make gentle. [< L *gentīlis,* of the same clan, of noble birth.] —**gen′tle•ness** *n.*

gen•tle•man (jĕnt′l-mən) *n.* 1. A polite or con-

siderate man. 2. **gentlemen.** A form of address for a group of men. [GENTLE + MAN.] —**gen′-tle•man•ly** *adj.*

gen•try (jĕn′trē) *n.* 1. People of good birth and superior social position. 2. The upper middle classes in England. [< OF *gentil,* gentle.]

gen•u•flect (jĕn′yə-flĕkt′) *v.* To bend the knee in a kneeling or half-kneeling position, as in worship. [LL *genuflectere.*] —**gen′u•flec′tion** *n.*

gen•u•ine (jĕn′yōō-ĭn) *adj.* 1. Not artificial; real. 2. Sincere; frank. [L *genuīnus.*]

ge•nus (jē′nəs) *n., pl.* **genera** (jĕn′ə-rə). 1. A category of related organisms usually including several species. 2. Any class or kind with common attributes. [L, birth, race, kind.]

geo–. *comb. form.* The earth. [< Gk *gē,* earth.]

ge•o•cen•tric (jē′ō-sĕn′trĭk) *adj.* 1. Of or from the center of the earth. 2. Having the earth as a center. —**ge′o•cen′tri•cal•ly** *adv.*

ge•o•des•ic dome (jē′ə-dĕs′ĭk). A domed or vaulted structure of lightweight straight elements that form interlocking polygons.

geog. geographer; geographic; geography.

ge•og•ra•phy (jē-ŏg′rə-fē) *n., pl.* **-phies.** 1. The study of the earth and its features and of the distribution on the earth of life, including human life and the effects of human activity. 2. The geographic characteristics of any area. —**ge•og′ra•pher** *n.* —**ge′o•graph′ic** (-ə-grăf′ĭk), **ge′o•graph′i•cal** *adj.* —**ge′o•graph′i•cal•ly** *adv.*

geol. geologic; geologist; geology.

ge•ol•o•gy (jē-ŏl′ə-jē) *n., pl.* **-gies.** 1. The scientific study of the origin, history, and structure of the earth. 2. The structure of a specific region of the earth's surface. —**ge′o•log′ic** (jē′ə-lŏj′ĭk), **ge′o•log′i•cal** *adj.* —**ge′o•log′i•cal•ly** *adv.* —**ge•ol′o•gist** *n.*

geom. geometric; geometry.

geometric progression. A sequence of terms, such as 1, 3, 9, 27, 81, each of which is a constant multiple of the immediately preceding term.

ge•om•e•try (jē-ŏm′ə-trē) *n., pl.* **-tries.** 1. The mathematics of the properties, measurement, and relationships of points, lines, angles, surfaces, and solids. 2. Configuration; arrangement. 3. A surface shape. [< Gk *geōmetrein,* to measure land.] —**ge′o•met′ric** (jē′ə-mĕt′rĭk) *adj.* —**ge′o•met′ri•cal•ly** *adv.* —**ge•om′e•tri′cian** (jē-ŏm′ə-trĭsh′ən, jē′ə-mə-), **ge•om′e•ter** *n.*

George III (jôrj). King of Great Britain and Ireland (1760–1820).

George•town (jôrj′toun). The capital of Guyana. Pop. 78,000.

Geor•gia (jôr′jə). 1. A S state of the U.S. Pop. 4,560,000. Cap. Atlanta. 2. The Georgian S.S.R. —**Geor′gian** *adj. & n.*

Georgian Soviet Socialist Republic. A constituent republic of the U.S.S.R., S of the Caucasus Mountains. Pop. 4,638,000. Cap. Tbilisi.

ge•o•stroph•ic (jē′ō-strŏf′ĭk) *adj.* Of or pertaining to force caused by the earth's rotation.

ge•o•ther•mal (jē′ō-thûr′məl) *adj.* Also **ge•o•ther•mic** (-mĭk). Pertaining to the internal heat of the earth.

ger. gerund.

Ger. German; Germany.

ô paw, for/oi boy/ou out/ōō took/ōō coo/p pop/r run/s sauce/sh shy/t to/th thin/*th* the/
ŭ cut/ûr fur/v van/w wag/y yes/z size/zh vision/ə ago, item, edible, gallop, circus/

GEOLOGIC TIME SCALE

ERA	PERIOD	EPOCH	YEARS BEFORE THE PRESENT
	Quarternary	Holocene (Recent)	
		———————	11,000
		Pleistocene (Glacial)	
			500,000 to 2,000,000
Cenozoic		Pliocene	
			13,000,000
		Miocene	
			25,000,000
	Tertiary	Oligocene	
			36,000,000
		Eocene	
			58,000,000
		Paleocene	
			63,000,000
Mesozoic	Cretaceous		
			135,000,000
	Jurassic		
			180,000,000
	Triassic		
			230,000,000
	Permian		
			280,000,000
	Carboniferous — Pennsylvanian (Upper Carboniferous)		
			310,000,000
	Carboniferous — Mississippian (Lower Carboniferous)		
Paleozoic			345,000,000
	Devonian		
			405,000,000
	Silurian		
			425,000,000
	Ordovician		
			500,000,000
	Cambrian		
			600,000,000
Precambrian			

ă pat/ā ate/âr care/ä bar/b bib/ch chew/d deed/ĕ pet/ē be/f fit/g gag/h hat/hw what/
ĭ pit/ī pie/îr pier/j judge/k kick/l lid, fatal/m mum/n no, sudden/ng sing/ŏ pot/ō go/

ge•ra•ni•um (jĭ-rā′nē-əm) *n.* **1.** A widely cultivated plant with rounded leaves and showy clusters of red, pink, or white flowers. **2.** A related plant with divided leaves and pink or purplish flowers. [< Gk *geranion,* "small crane."]

ger•bil (jûr′bĭl) *n.* A mouselike rodent of desert regions of Africa and Asia Minor. [< Ar *yerbŏ′,* flesh of the loins.]

ger•i•at•rics (jĕr′ē-ăt′rĭks) *n. (takes sing. v.).* The medical study of the physiology and pathology of old age. —**ger′i•at′ric** *adj. & n.*

germ (jûrm) *n.* **1.** A small organic structure or cell from which a new organism may develop. **2.** Something that may serve as the basis of further development. **3.** A microorganism, esp. a pathogen. [< L *germen,* offshoot, sprout, fetus.]

Ger•man (jûr′mən) *n.* **1.** A native or citizen of Germany. **2.** The West Germanic language spoken in Germany, Austria, and part of Switzerland. —**Ger′man** *adj.*

German Democratic Republic. See **Germany.**

ger•mane (jər-mān′) *adj.* Significantly related; pertinent. [< L *germānus,* "of the same race."] —**ger•mane′ly** *adj.* —**ger•mane′ness** *n.*

German Federal Republic. See **Germany.**

Ger•man•ic (jûr-măn′ĭk) *adj.* **1.** Of, pertaining to, or characteristic of Germany, the German people, or their culture. **2.** Of or pertaining to Germanic or to people who speak a Germanic language. —*n.* A branch of the Indo-European language family, divided into North Germanic (including Scandinavian), West Germanic (including German, Dutch, Flemish, Frisian, English, and Yiddish), and East Germanic (including Gothic).

ger•ma•ni•um (jər-mā′nē-əm) *n. Symbol* **Ge** A brittle, crystalline, gray-white semi-conducting element, widely used as a semiconductor and as an alloying agent and catalyst. Atomic number 32, atomic weight 72.59. [< L *germānus,* germane.]

German measles. A mild, contagious, eruptive disease caused by a virus spread in droplet sprays from the nose and throat.

German silver. Formerly, an alloy, **nickel silver.**

Ger•ma•ny (jûr′mə-nē). A nation of C Europe

Germany

divided since 1949 into two states: **a. German Democratic Republic** (East Germany). Pop. 17,136,000. Cap. East Berlin. **b. German Federal Republic** (West Germany). Pop. 57,974,000. Cap. Bonn.

germ cell. A cell having reproduction as its principal function, esp. an egg or sperm cell.

ger•mi•cide (jûr′mə-sīd′) *n.* Any agent that kills germs. —**ger′mi•ci′dal** (-sīd′l) *adj.*

ger•mi•nal (jûr′mə-nəl) *adj.* **1.** Pertaining to a germ cell. **2.** Pertaining to the earliest stage of development.

ger•mi•nate (jûr′mə-nāt′) *v.* **-nated, -nating.** To begin to grow; sprout. [< L *germen,* sprout, GERM.] —**ger′mi•na′tion** *n.*

Ge•ron•i•mo (jə-rŏn′ə-mō′). 1829–1909. American Indian leader; chief of the Apaches.

Geronimo

ger•ry•man•der (jĕr′ē-măn′dər, gĕr′-) *v.* To divide into voting districts that give unfair advantage to one political party.

Gersh•win (gûrsh′wĭn), **George.** 1898–1937. American composer.

ger•und (jĕr′ənd) *n.* A verbal form that can be used as a noun, in English ending in *-ing,* as *cooking* in *I don't like cooking.* [< L *gerundum,* acting, carrying.]

ge•stalt, Ge•stalt (gə-shtält′, -shtôlt′) *n., pl.* **-stalts** or **-stalten** (-shtält′n, -shtôlt′n). A unified physical, psychological, or symbolic configuration having properties that cannot be derived from its parts. [G, form, shape.]

Ge•sta•po (gə-stä′pō) *n.* The German internal security police under the Nazi regime.

ges•ta•tion (jĕ-stā′shən) *n.* The development and carrying of offspring in the uterus. [< L *gerere,* to carry, bear.]

ges•tic•u•late (jĕ-stĭk′yə-lāt′) *v.* **-lated, -lating.** To make gestures, esp. while speaking. [L *gesticulāri.*] —**ges•tic′u•la′tion** *n.*

ges•ture (jĕs′chər) *n.* **1.** A motion of the limbs or body made as an expression of thought or emphasis. **2.** An action or statement made as an indication of intention or attitude. —*v.* **-tured, -turing.** To make or signal by gestures. [ML *gestūra,* bearing, carriage.]

ô paw, for/oi boy/ou out/ŏŏ took/ōō coo/p pop/r run/s sauce/sh shy/t to/th thin/*th* the/ ŭ cut/ûr fur/v van/w wag/y yes/z size/zh vision/ə ago, item, edible, gallop, circus/

get (gĕt) *v.* **got, got** or **gotten, getting. 1.** To obtain or acquire. **2.** To procure; secure. **3.** To go after; fetch. **4.** To make contact with by or as if by radio or telephone. **5.** To earn: *get a reward.* **6.** To receive: *get a present.* **7.** To buy. **8.** To catch; contract: *get chicken pox.* **9.** To reach by calculation: *If you add them, you'll get 1,000.* **10.** To have obtained or received and now have: *I've got a large collection of books.* **11.** To understand: *Do you get his point?* **12.** *Informal.* To register, as by eye or ear: *I didn't get your name.* **13.** To cause to become or to be in a specific condition: *He can't get the hook loose.* **14.** To cause to move, come, or go: *Get that dog out of here!* **15.** To bring or take: *I'll get him in here.* **16.** To prevail upon: *I'll get my friend to agree.* **17.** To capture: *The police got him.* **18.** *Slang.* To reciprocate by causing harm: *I'll get you for that remark.* **19.** *Informal.* To strike or hit: *That blow got him on the chin.* **20.** *Slang.* To puzzle: *Her attitude gets me.* **21.** To have the obligation: *I have got to go.* **22.** To become or grow. —Used as a linking verb: *I got well again.* **23.** To arrive: *When will we get to New York?* **24.** To betake oneself: *Get out!* **25.** *Informal.* To start: *Get going!* **—get across.** To make or be understandable or clear: *Am I getting this across to you?* **—get ahead.** To be successful. **—get along. 1.** To be mutually congenial. **2.** To manage with reasonable success. **3.** To advance in years. **—get around. 1.** To avoid doing or encountering; circumvent. **2.** *Informal.* To convince or gain the favor of by flattering or cajoling. **—get at. 1.** To determine; ascertain: *I'm trying to get at his point.* **2.** To reach: *It's under the desk and I can't get at it.* **3.** To lead up to or arrive at, as a conclusion or meaning: *Do you understand what I'm getting at?* **—get away with.** *Informal.* To be successful in avoiding retribution or the discovery of something done. **—get back at.** *Informal.* To retaliate or have revenge against. **—get by.** To manage; survive: *We'll get by.* **—get down to.** To concentrate on. **—get in. 1.** To enter or be allowed to enter. **2.** To arrive. **—get it. 1.** To comprehend; understand. **2.** *Informal.* To be punished or scolded. **—get nowhere.** To make no progress; have no success. **—get off. 1.** To get down from or out of. **2.** To leave; depart. **3.** To write and send, as a letter. **—get on. 1.** To climb up onto or into; enter. **2.** To get along. **3.** To advance: *He's getting on in years.* **—get out of. 1.** To derive or draw: *He gets out of it what he can.* **2.** To avoid or get around. **—get over.** To recover from (a sorrow, illness, etc.). **—get there.** *Informal.* To attain one's goal. **—get through to. 1.** To make contact with. **2.** To make understandable to. **—get to. 1.** To be able to: *I hope I get to go.* **2.** To reach: *We never got to that point.* **3.** *Informal.* To happen to start: *Then we got to remembering good times.* [< ON *geta.*] **—get'-a·ble, get'ta·ble** *adj.*

get·a·way (gĕt'ə-wā') *n.* **1.** An act or instance of escaping. **2.** A start, as of a race. *—adj.* Used for escape: *a getaway car.*

get-to·geth·er (gĕt'tə-gĕth'ər) *n.* An informal social gathering.

Get·tys·burg (gĕt'ĭz-bûrg). A town in S Pennsylvania, the site of a major Civil War battle. Pop. 8,000.

get-up (gĕt'ŭp') *n.* An outfit or costume, esp. one remarkable in some way.

GeV *Phys.* Giga (10⁹) electron volts.

gew·gaw (gyoo'gô') *n.* A trinket; bauble. [?]

gey·ser (gī'zər) *n.* A natural hot spring that intermittently ejects a column of water and steam. [< ON *geysa,* to gush.]

Gha·na (gä'nə). A republic in W Africa. Pop. 7,600,000. Cap. Accra. **—Gha·na'ian, Gha'ni·an** (gə-nā'ən) *adj. & n.*

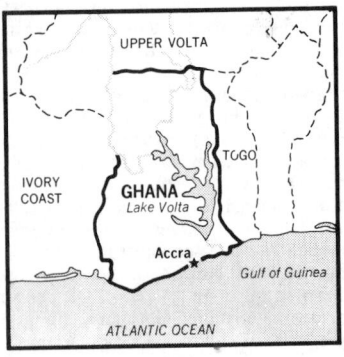

Ghana

ghast·ly (găst'lē, gäst'-) *adj.* **-lier, -liest. 1.** Terrifying; dreadful. **2.** Deathly pale. **3.** Extremely unpleasant. [< OE *gāst,* soul, ghost.]

gher·kin (gûr'kĭn) *n.* A small cucumber, esp. one used for pickling. [Du *agurkje.*]

ghet·to (gĕt'ō) *n., pl.* **-tos** or **-toes.** A section of a city to which an ethnic or economically depressed minority group is restricted, as by poverty or social pressure. [It.]

ghost (gōst) *n.* **1.** The disembodied spirit of a dead person, supposed to haunt living persons or former habitats. **2.** A slight trace or vestige. **3.** A faint secondary photographic or television image. **—give up the ghost.** To die. [< OE *gāst.* See **gheis-**.] **—ghost'ly** *adj.*

ghost·writ·er (gōst'rī'tər) *n.* A person who writes for another who is credited with authorship. **—ghost'write'** *v.*

ghoul (gool) *n.* **1.** An evil spirit supposed to plunder graves and feed on corpses. **2.** A grave robber. [Ar *ghūl.*] **—ghoul'ish** *adj.*

GHQ general headquarters.

gi gill[2].

GI (jē'ī') *n., pl.* **GIs** or **GI's.** An enlisted man in the U.S. armed forces. *—adj.* **1.** Pertaining to or characteristic of a GI or U.S. military procedures. **2.** Issued by an official U.S. military supply department.

GI Government Issue.

gi·ant (jī'ənt) *n.* **1.** A legendary manlike being of enormous size and strength. **2.** One of unusually great size or importance. *—adj.* Gigantic; huge. [< L *gigās (gigant-).*] **—gi'ant·ess** *fem.n.*

ă pat/ā ate/âr care/ä bar/b bib/ch chew/d deed/ĕ pet/ē be/f fit/g gag/h hat/hw what/
ĭ pit/ī pie/îr pier/j judge/k kick/l lid, fatal/m mum/n no, sudden/ng sing/ŏ pot/ō go/

gib·ber (jĭb′ər, gĭb′-) *v.* To chatter unintelligibly. [Imit.]

gib·ber·ish (jĭb′ər-ĭsh, gĭb′-) *n.* Rapid, meaningless talk.

gib·bet (jĭb′ĭt) *n.* A gallows. —*v.* **1.** To hang on a gibbet. **2.** To expose to public ridicule. [< OF *gibe*, staff, club.]

gib·bon (gĭb′ən) *n.* An ape of tropical Asia with a slender body and long arms.

gib·bous (gĭb′əs) *adj.* More than half but less than fully illuminated: *the gibbous moon.* [< LL *gibbus,* hump.]

gibe (jīb) *v.* **gibed, gibing.** Also **jibe.** To make mocking remarks; taunt. —*n.* Also **jibe.** A taunt. —**gib′er** *n.* —**gib′ing·ly** *adv.*

gib·let (jĭb′lĭt) *n.* Often **giblets.** The edible heart, liver, or gizzard of a fowl. [< OF *gibelet.*]

Gib·ral·tar, Strait of (jĭ-brôl′tər). A waterway connecting the Mediterranean with the Atlantic Ocean.

gid·dy (gĭd′ē) *adj.* **-dier, -diest. 1. a.** Lightheaded; dizzy. **b.** Causing dizziness: *giddy heights.* **2.** Frivolous; flighty. [< OE *gydig,* possessed by a god, insane. See **gheu(ə)-.**] —**gid′di·ly** *adv.* —**gid′di·ness** *n.*

gift (gĭft) *n.* **1.** Something given; a present. **2.** The act or power of giving. **3.** A natural ability; talent. [< ON.]

gift·ed (gĭf′tĭd) *adj.* Having or showing great natural ability; talented.

gig¹ (gĭg) *n.* **1.** A light, two-wheeled horse-drawn carriage. **2.** A long, light ship's boat. [ME *gigg,* giddy girl, something that whirls.]

gig² (gĭg) *n.* A pronged spear for fishing. —*v.* **gigged, gigging.** To fish or catch with a gig.

gig³ (gĭg) *n. Slang.* A job, esp. a booking for a jazz musician.

giga–. *comb. form.* Indicates one billion (10⁹); for example, *gigavolt,* or one billion volts. [< Gk *gigas,* giant.]

gi·gan·tic (jī-găn′tĭk) *adj.* Unusually large; enormous; huge. [< L *gigās (gigant-),* GIANT.] —**gi·gan′ti·cal·ly** *adv.*

gi·gan·tism (jī-găn′tĭz′əm) *n.* Excessive growth of the body or any of its parts as a result of oversecretion of the pituitary growth hormone.

gig·gle (gĭg′əl) *v.* **-gled, -gling.** To laugh with high-pitched, convulsive sounds. —*n.* A high-pitched, spasmodic laugh. [Imit.] —**gig′-gler** *n.* —**gig′gling·ly** *adv.* —**gig′gly** *adj.*

gig·o·lo (jĭg′ə-lō′, zhĭg′-) *n., pl.* **-los.** A man paid to be a woman's escort or lover. [< F *gigolette,* dance-hall pickup.]

Gi·la monster (hē′lə). A venomous lizard of the SW U.S.

gild (gĭld) *v.* **gilded** or **gilt, gilding. 1.** To cover with or as with a thin layer of gold. **2.** To give a deceptively attractive appearance to. [< OE *gyldan.*] —**gild′er** *n.*

gill¹ (gĭl) *n.* The respiratory organ of fishes and various aquatic invertebrates. [ME *gille.*]

gill² (jĭl) *n.* **1.** A U.S. Customary System unit of volume or capacity used in liquid measure, equal to 4 fluid ounces (¼ pint) or 7.216 cubic inches. **2.** A corresponding British Imperial System unit used in dry and liquid measure,

equal to 5 fluid ounces (¼ pint) or 8.670 cubic inches. [< LL *gillo,* water pot.]

gil·ly·flow·er (gĭl′ē-flou′ər) *n.* Also **gil·li·flow·er.** A carnation or other plant with fragrant flowers. [< Gk *karuophullon,* "leaf nut."]

gilt (gĭlt). Alternate *p.t.* & *p.p.* of **gild.** —*adj.* Gilded. —*n.* A thin layer of gold or similar material applied in gilding.

gim·crack (jĭm′krăk′) *n.* A cheap, showy, useless object. —**gim′crack′** *adj.*

gim·el (gĭm′əl) *n.* The 3rd letter of the Hebrew alphabet, representing *g(gh).*

gim·let (gĭm′lĭt) *n.* A small screw-tipped hand tool for boring holes. [< OF *guimbelet.*] —**gim′let** *v.*

gim·mick (gĭm′ĭk) *n.* **1.** A tricky, deceptive, often dishonest device. **2.** A concealed disadvantage; catch. **3.** An attention-getting stratagem or inducement. **4.** A gadget. [?] —**gim′mick·ry** *n.* —**gim′mick·y** *adj.*

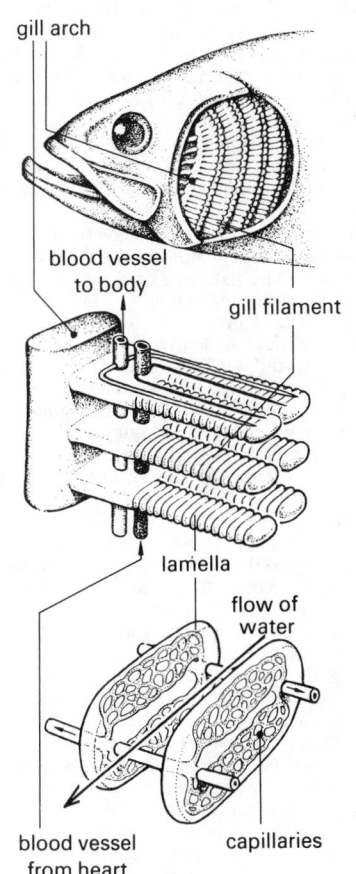

gill arch

blood vessel to body

gill filament

lamella

flow of water

blood vessel from heart

capillaries

gill¹
Gill of a fish
with gill cover removed
and enlarged portions
showing structural details

gin¹ (jĭn) *n.* An alcoholic liquor distilled from grain and flavored with juniper berries. [< L *jūniperus,* JUNIPER.]

gin² (jĭn) *n.* A mechanical device, esp. one used to remove the seeds from cotton fibers. —*v.* **ginned, ginning.** To remove seeds from (cotton) with such a gin. [< ENGINE.]

gin·ger (jĭn′jər) *n.* **1.** The pungent, aromatic root of a tropical Asian plant, used as flavoring. **2.** The plant itself. **3.** *Informal.* Liveliness; pep. —*v.* **ginger up.** *Informal.* To make more lively. [< Sk *śṛṅgaveram.*]

ginger ale. An effervescent soft drink flavored with ginger.

gin·ger·bread (jĭn′jər-brĕd′) *n.* **1.** A dark molasses cake flavored with ginger. **2.** Elaborate, often tasteless ornamentation. [< ML *gingiber,* ginger.]

gin·ger·ly (jĭn′jər-lē) *adj.* Cautiously or timidly careful. —*adv.* Cautiously; carefully; timidly. [Orig "daintily."]

gin·ger·y (jĭn′jə-rē) *adj.* **1.** Having the spicy flavor of ginger. **2.** Sharp; biting.

ging·ham (gĭng′əm) *n.* A cotton fabric with a woven, often checked pattern. [Du *gingang.*]

gin·gi·va (jĭn-jī′və, jĭn′jə-) *n. Anat.* The gum. [< L *gingīva,* gum.]

gin·gi·val (jĭn-jī′vəl, jĭn′jə-) *adj.* Pertaining to the gums.

gin·gi·vi·tis (jĭn′jə-vī′tĭs) *n.* Inflammation of the gums.

gink·go (gĭng′kō) *n., pl.* **-goes.** A widely planted Chinese tree with fan-shaped leaves. [Jap *ginkyō.*]

gin mill. *Slang.* A saloon.

gip. Variant of **gyp.**

Gip·sy. Variant of **Gypsy.**

gi·raffe (jĭ-răf′, -räf′) *n.* An African mammal with a very long neck and legs and a distinctively marked coat. [< Ar *zirāfah.*]

gird (gûrd) *v.* **girded** or **girt** (gûrt), **girding.** **1.** To encircle with or as with a belt or band. **2.** To equip or prepare for action. [< OE *gyrdan.* See **gher-².**]

gird·er (gûr′dər) *n.* A strong horizontal beam used as a main support in building.

gir·dle (gûrd′l) *n.* **1.** A belt, sash, or similar encircling band. **2.** A supporting undergarment worn over the waist and hips. —*v.* **-dled, -dling.** To encircle with or as with a belt. [< OE *gyrdel.* See **gher-².**]

girl (gûrl) *n.* **1.** A female child or young unmarried woman. **2.** *Informal.* Any woman. **3.** A sweetheart. **4.** A female servant. [ME *girle.*] —**girl′hood** *n.* —**girl′ish** *adj.*

girth (gûrth) *n.* **1.** Size measured by encircling something; circumference. **2.** A strap encircling an animal's body to secure a load or saddle. [< ON *györdh,* girdle.]

gist (jĭst) *n.* The central idea, as of an argument or speech. [< OF *(cest action) gist,* (this action) lies.]

give (gĭv) *v.* **gave, given, giving.** **1. a.** To make a present of: *give flowers.* **b.** To make gifts: *give generously to charity.* **c.** To deliver in exchange or in recompense: *give five dollars for the book.* **2.** To entrust or to place in the hands of: *Give me the scissors.* **3.** To convey: *Give him*

my best wishes. **4.** To grant: *give permission.* **5.** To expose or subject one to: *She gave him the measles.* **6.** To produce: *This cow gives three gallons of milk per day.* **7.** To provide (something required or expected): *give one's name and address.* **8.** To administer: *give a spanking.* **9.** To accord; concede: *give the benefit of the doubt to.* **10.** To relinquish; yield: *give ground.* **11.** To emit or issue: *give a sigh.* **12.** To allot; assign: *give her five minutes to finish.* **13.** To award: *give first prize to.* **14.** To submit for consideration or acceptance; tender: *give an opinion.* **15.** To stage: *give a dinner party.* **16.** To afford a view of or access to; open: *The French doors give onto a terrace.* —**give back.** To return. —**give in.** **1.** To cease opposition; concede. **2.** To hand in; submit: *give in a report.* —**give it to.** *Informal.* To scold or thrash soundly. —**give out.** **1.** To distribute. **2.** To break down; fail. —**give rise to.** To cause; occasion. —**give up.** **1.** To surrender: *give yourself up.* **2.** To stop: *give up smoking.* **3.** To relinquish: *give up hope.* **4.** To abandon hope for: *give her up as lost.* —**give way.** **1.** To make room for: *give way to an oncoming car.* **2.** To collapse: *The ladder gave way.* **3.** To abandon oneself: *give way to hysteria.* —*n. Informal.* Resilient springiness: *The mattress has lots of give.* [< OE *giefan.* See **ghabh-.**] —**give′a·ble** *adj.* —**giv′er** *n.*

give-and-take (gĭv′ən-tāk′) *n.* Lively exchange of ideas or conversation.

give·a·way (gĭv′ə-wā′) *n. Informal.* **1.** Something given away at no charge. **2.** Something that betrays or exposes, often accidentally or unintentionally.

giv·en (gĭv′ən) *adj.* **1.** Specified: *a given date.* **2.** Accepted as a fact; acknowledged. **3.** Habitually inclined: *given to shyness.* **4.** Bestowed; presented.

giz·zard (gĭz′ərd) *n.* A muscular enlargement of the digestive tract in birds. [< L *gigeria,* cooked entrails of poultry.]

Gk. Greek.

gl. gloss.

gla·cial (glā′shəl) *adj.* **1.** Of or pertaining to a glacier. **2.** Often **Glacial.** Characterized or dominated by the existence of glaciers, as the Pleistocene epoch. **3.** Extremely cold. —**gla′cial·ly** *adv.*

gla·cier (glā′shər) *n.* A huge mass of laterally limited, moving ice originating from compacted snow. [< L *glaciēs,* ice.]

glad (glăd) *adj.* **gladder, gladdest.** **1.** Feeling, showing, or giving joy and pleasure; happy. **2.** Pleased; willing: *glad to help.* [< OE *glæd.*] —**glad′ly** *adv.* —**glad′ness** *n.*

glad·den (glăd′n) *v.* To make or become glad.

glade (glād) *n.* An open space in a forest. [Perh < GLAD.]

glad·i·a·tor (glăd′ē-ā′tər) *n.* **1.** A professional combatant, slave, etc., who engaged in mortal combat for public entertainment in ancient Rome. **2.** One engaged in fighting or controversy. [< L *gladius,* sword.] —**glad′i·a·to′ri·al** (-ə-tôr′ē-əl, -tōr′ē-əl) *adj.*

glad·i·o·lus (glăd′ē-ō′ləs) *n., pl.* **-li** (-lī′, -lē′) or **-luses.** A widely cultivated plant with sword-

---

shaped leaves and a spike of showy, variously colored flowers. [< L *gladius,* sword.]

glad•some (glăd′səm) *adj.* Glad; joyful.

glam•or•ize (glăm′ə-rīz′) *v.* -ized, -izing. Also **glam•our•ize.** To make or portray as glamorous. —**glam′or•i•za′tion** *n.*

glam•our (glăm′ər) *n.* Also **glam•or.** Alluring charm and excitement. [Scot var of GRAMMAR.] —**glam′or•ous, glam′our•ous** *adj.*

glance (glăns, gläns) *v.* **glanced, glancing.** 1. To strike and be deflected. 2. To look briefly. 3. To shine briefly; glint. —*n.* 1. A quick look. 2. A flash; gleam. 3. A glancing impact or motion. [< OF *glacier,* to slide.]

gland (glănd) *n.* An organ or structure that secretes a substance, esp. one that extracts specific substances from the blood for subsequent secretion. [< L *glāns (gland-),* acorn.] —**glan′du•lar** (glăn′jə-lər) *adj.*

glans cli•tor•i•dis (glănz klī-tôr′ə-dĭs, klī-). The small mass of erectile tissue at the tip of the clitoris.

glans penis. The head or tip of the penis.

glare (glâr) *v.* **glared, glaring.** 1. To stare fixedly and angrily. 2. To shine intensely and blindingly. —*n.* 1. A fixed, angry stare. 2. An intense and blinding light. [ME *glaren.*]

glar•ing (glâr′ĭng) *adj.* 1. Staring fixedly and angrily. 2. Blindingly bright; dazzling. 3. Obtrusively conspicuous. —**glar′ing•ly** *adv.*

Glas•gow (glăs′gō, -kō, gläs′-). A city of SW Scotland. Pop. 1,796,000.

glass (glăs, gläs) *n.* 1. Any of a large class of materials that solidify from the molten state without crystallization, are generally transparent or translucent, and are regarded physically as supercooled liquids rather than true solids. 2. Also **glass•ware** (glăs′wâr′, gläs′-). Objects made of glass. 3. Something made of glass, as a drinking vessel or mirror. 4. Often **glasses.** A device containing a lens or lenses and used as an aid to vision. 5. Also **glass•ful** (glăs′fŏŏl′, gläs′-). The quantity contained by a drinking glass. [< OE *glæs.*]

glass•y (glăs′ē, gläs′ē) *adj.* -ier, -iest. 1. Of or like glass. 2. Lifeless; expressionless: *a glassy grin.* —**glass′i•ly** *adv.* —**glass′i•ness** *n.*

glau•co•ma (glô-kō′mə, glou-) *n.* A disease of the eye characterized by high intraocular pressure, damaged optic disk, hardening of the eyeball, and partial or complete loss of vision. [L *glaucōma,* cataract.] —**glau•co′ma•tous** *adj.*

glaze (glāz) *n.* A thin, smooth, glassy coating, as on ceramics or ice. —*v.* **glazed, glazing.** 1. To furnish with glass, as a window. 2. To apply a glaze to. 3. To become glassy. [< ME *glas,* glass.] —**glaz′er** *n.*

gla•zier (glā′zhər) *n.* One who cuts and fits window glass.

gleam (glēm) *n.* 1. A brief flash or subdued glow of light. 2. A brief or dim indication: *a gleam of intelligence.* —*v.* 1. To flash or glow. 2. To show briefly or faintly. [< OE *glæm.*]

glean (glēn) *v.* 1. To gather (grain) left behind by reapers. 2. To collect bit by bit, as knowledge. [< LL *glennāre.*] —**glean′er** *n.*

glee (glē) *n.* 1. Merriment; joy. 2. An unaccompanied part song for three or more voices.

[< OE *glēo.*] —**glee′ful** *adj.* —**glee′ful•ly** *adv.*

glee club. A group of singers who perform part songs or choral music.

glen (glĕn) *n.* A narrow, high-walled valley. [< Scot Gael *gleann.*]

Glen•dale (glĕn′dāl′). A city in SW California. Pop. 119,000.

glib (glĭb) *adj.* **glibber, glibbest.** Easy, fluent, and often superficial, as in speech. [Prob < MLG *glibberich,* slippery.] —**glib′ly** *adv.* —**glib′ness** *n.*

glide (glīd) *v.* **glided, gliding.** 1. To move or pass smoothly and easily. 2. To fly without propulsion. —*n.* 1. A smooth, effortless movement. 2. An act of flying without propulsion. [< OE *glīdan.*]

glid•er (glī′dər) *n.* 1. One that glides. 2. A light, engineless aircraft designed for long periods of gliding. 3. A swinging couch suspended from a vertical frame.

glim•mer (glĭm′ər) *v.* To emit a dim, flickering light. —*n.* 1. A dim, flickering light. 2. A faint indication. [Prob < Scand.]

glimpse (glĭmps) *n.* A brief, hasty look. —*v.* **glimpsed, glimpsing.** To catch a brief, hasty view of. [< Gmc.]

glint (glĭnt) *n.* A brief flash of light; a sparkle. —*v.* To gleam; sparkle. [< Scand.]

glis•ten (glĭs′ən) *v.* To shine or reflect lustrously; gleam. [< OE *glisnian.*] —**glis′ten** *n.*

glit•ter (glĭt′ər) *v.* To sparkle brilliantly. —*n.* 1. A sparkling light or brightness. 2. Brilliant or showy splendor. 3. Small pieces of decorative material. [< ON *glitra.*]

gloam•ing (glō′mĭng) *n.* Twilight. [< OE *glōm,* dusk.]

gloat (glōt) *v.* To show smug, triumphant, or malicious pleasure or satisfaction. [Perh < Scand.]

glob (glŏb) *n.* A small drop or rounded mass. [< L *globus,* GLOBE.]

glob•al (glō′bəl) *adj.* Of or pertaining to the entire earth; worldwide. —**glob′al•ly** *adv.*

globe (glōb) *n.* 1. A spherical object, as a representation of the earth. 2. The earth. 3. A globelike article, as a fishbowl. [< L *globus.*]

globe•trot•ter (glōb′trŏt′ər) *n.* One who travels widely.

glob•ule (glŏb′yōōl) *n.* A very small spherical mass, esp. of liquid. [< L *globus,* GLOBE.] —**glob′u•lar** (-yə-lər) *adj.*

glob•u•lin (glŏb′yə-lən) *n.* Any of a class of simple proteins that are found extensively in blood, milk, muscle, and plant seeds.

glock•en•spiel (glŏk′ən-spēl′, -shpēl′) *n.* A musical instrument having a series of metal bars played with two light hammers. [G, "play of bells."]

gloom (glōōm) *n.* 1. Partial or total darkness. 2. A melancholy or dejected state or atmosphere. [ME *gloumben,* to look glum, become dark.] —**gloom′i•ly** *adv.* —**gloom′y** *adj.*

glo•ri•fy (glôr′ə-fī′, glōr′-) *v.* -fied, -fying. 1. To invest with glory; make glorious. 2. To offer glory to; worship; extol. 3. To exaggerate or overestimate the glory or excellence of. —**glo′ri•fi•ca′tion** *n.* —**glo′ri•fi′er** *n.*

glo•ri•ous (glôr′ē-əs, glōr′-) *adj.* 1. Having, de-

ŏ paw, for/oi boy/ou out/ŏŏ took/ōō coo/p pop/r run/s sauce/sh shy/t to/th thin/*th* the/
ŭ cut/ûr fur/v van/w wag/y yes/z size/zh vision/ə ago, item, edible, gallop, circus/

serving, or imparting glory; illustrious. **2.** Magnificent; resplendent. **3.** Delightful. —**glo'ri·ous·ly** *adv.* —**glo'ri·ous·ness** *n.*

glo·ry (glôr'ē, glōr'ē) *n., pl.* **-ries. 1.** Great honor or distinction; renown. **2.** Adoration and praise offered in worship. **3.** Magnificent splendor. **4.** A praiseworthy attribute. **5.** The height of achievement, triumph, etc. —*v.* **-ried, -rying.** To rejoice triumphantly; exult. [< L *glōria.*]

gloss¹ (glôs, glŏs) *n.* **1.** Surface shine; luster. **2.** A superficially attractive appearance. —*v.* —**gloss over.** To attempt to excuse or ignore, as a fault or error. [Prob < Scand.] —**gloss'i·ness** *n.* —**gloss'y** *adj.*

gloss² (glôs, glŏs) *n.* **1.** A brief explanatory note or translation of a difficult or technical expression. **2.** A translation or commentary accompanying a text. —*v.* To annotate or translate briefly. [< Gk *glōssa,* tongue, language.] —**gloss'er** *n.*

glos·sa·ry (glôs'ə-rē, glŏs'-) *n., pl.* **-ries.** A collection of specialized terms with accompanying definitions. [< L *glōssa,* GLOSS².]

glottal stop. A speech sound produced by a momentary closure of the glottis, followed by an explosive release.

glot·tis (glŏt'ĭs) *n., pl.* **-tises** or **glottides** (glŏt'ə-dēz'). The space between the vocal cords at the upper part of the larynx. [< Gk *glōtta, glōssa,* tongue, language.] —**glot'tal** *adj.*

glove (glŭv) *n.* **1.** A fitted covering for the hand, having a separate sheath for each finger. **2.** An oversized padded leather covering for the hand, as one used by a baseball player or boxer. [< OE *glōf.* See **lep-.**] —**gloved** *adj.*

glow (glō) *v.* **1.** To shine brightly and steadily, esp. without a flame. **2.** To have a bright or ruddy color. **3.** To be exuberant or radiant, as with pride. —*n.* **1.** A light produced by or as by a body heated to luminosity. **2.** Brilliance or warmth of color, esp. redness. **3.** A sensation of physical warmth. **4.** A warm feeling of emotion. [< OE *glōwan.*]

glow·er (glou'ər) *v.* To look or stare angrily or sullenly. —*n.* An angry, sullen, or threatening stare. [Prob < Scand.]

glow·ing (glō'ĭng) *adj.* **1.** Incandescent; luminous. **2.** Having a warm or ruddy color. **3.** Ardently enthusiastic or favorable.

glow·worm (glō'wûrm') *n.* The luminous larva or grublike female of a firefly.

glu·cose (glōō'kōs') *n.* **1.** A sugar, dextrose. **2.** A colorless to yellowish syrupy mixture of dextrose and maltose with about 20% water, used in confectionery, alcoholic fermentation, tanning, and treating tobacco. [< Gk *gleukos,* sweet new wine, must.]

glue (glōō) *n.* An adhesive substance or solution used to join or bond. —*v.* **glued, gluing.** To stick or fasten with or as with glue. [< L *glūten.*]

glum (glŭm) *adj.* **glummer, glummest.** Dejected; gloomy. [< GLOOM.] —**glum'ly** *adv.* —**glum'ness** *n.*

glut (glŭt) *v.* **glutted, glutting. 1.** To eat or fill to excess; satiate. **2.** To flood (a market) with a supply that exceeds demand. —*n.* An ex-

cessive amount or supply; an oversupply. [Prob < L *gluttīre,* to swallow.]

glu·ten (glōōt'n) *n.* A glutinous, nutritious mixture of plant proteins occurring in cereal grains. [L *glūten,* glue.]

glu·te·us (glōō'tē-əs, glōō-tē'-) *n., pl.* **-tei** (-tē-ī', tē'ī'). Any of three large muscles of the buttocks. [< Gk *gloutos,* buttock.]

glu·ti·nous (glōōt'n-əs) *adj.* Sticky; adhesive. [< L *glūten,* glue.] —**glu'ti·nous·ly** *adv.*

glut·ton (glŭt'n) *n.* One that eats or consumes to excess. [< L *gluttō.*] —**glut'ton·ous** *adj.* —**glut'ton·ous·ly** *adv.* —**glut'ton·y** *n.*

glyc·er·ol (glĭs'ə-rôl', -rōl', -rŏl') *n.* A syrupy liquid, $C_3H_8O_3$, obtained from fats and oils and used as a solvent, antifreeze, and sweetener, and in making dynamite, liquid soaps, and lubricants. [< Gk *glukeros,* sweet.]

gly·co·gen (glī'kə-jən) *n.* A white powder, $(C_6H_{10}O_5)_n$, occurring as the chief animal storage carbohydrate, primarily in the liver. [< Gk *glukus,* sweet + -GEN.] —**gly'co·gen'ic** *adj.*

gm gram.

gnarl (närl) *n.* A protruding knot on a tree. —**gnarled** *adj.*

gnash (năsh) *v.* To grind (the teeth) together. [Prob < Scand.]

gnat (năt) *n.* Any of various small, winged, biting insects. [< OE *gnæt.*]

gnaw (nô) *v.* **gnawed, gnawed** or **gnawn, gnawing. 1.** To consume, wear away, or produce by nibbling: *gnaw a hole.* **2.** To afflict or irritate. [< OE *gnagan.*] —**gnaw'er** *n.* —**gnaw'ing·ly** *adv.*

gneiss (nīs) *n.* A banded metamorphic rock, usually of the same composition as granite. [G *Gneis.*]

gnome (nōm) *n.* One of a race of dwarfs said to live underground and guard treasure hoards. [F.]

GNP gross national product.

gnu (n/y/ōō) *n.* A large bearded African antelope, with curved horns.

go (gō) *v.* **went, gone, going. 1.** To proceed. **2.** To move or start to move. **3.** To move to or from a given place, or out of someone's presence. **4.** —Used in the form *be going* followed by an infinitive to indicate the indefinite future: *He's going to go home.* **5.** To engage in a specified activity: *go riding.* **6.** To function. **7.** To make a specified sound: *The glass went crack.* **8.** To belong (somewhere). **9.** To extend or spread. **10.** To be allotted. **11.** To serve: *It all goes to show.* **12.** To harmonize: *The rug goes well with this room.* **13.** To die. **14.** To come apart or cave in. **15.** To fail: *Her eyes are going.* **16.** To be used up. **17.** To disappear. **18.** To be abolished: *War must go.* **19.** To pass, as time. **20.** To become: *go crazy.* **21.** To be or continue to be: *go unchallenged.* **22.** To fare. **23.** To hold out or endure: *go without water.* **24.** To wager; bid. **25.** To furnish: *go bail for a client.* **26.** To participate to the extent of: *go halves on a deal.* —*n., pl.* **goes.** *Informal.* **1.** A try. **2.** Bargain; deal: *no go.* —**on the go.** Constantly busy. [< OE *gān.* See **ghē-.**]

GO general order.

goad (gōd) *n.* **1.** A pointed stick used for

prodding animals. **2.** A stimulus; spur. [< OE *gād.*] —**goad** *v.*

goal (gōl) *n.* **1.** An end; objective. **2.** The finish line of a race. **3.** *Sports.* **a.** A specified place into which players endeavor to advance a ball or puck. **b.** The score awarded for such an act. [Prob < OE *gāl*, obstacle.]

goal·keep·er (gōl'kē'pər) *n.* Also **goal·ie** (gōl'ē). A player assigned to protect the goal in various sports.

goal post. One of a pair of posts joined with a crossbar forming the goal at each end of a football field.

goat (gōt) *n.* **1.** A horned, bearded mammal originally of mountainous regions and now widely domesticated. **2. Goat.** Capricornus. [< OE *gāt.* See **ghaido-.**]

goat·ee (gō-tē') *n.* A small pointed chin beard. [< GOAT + -EE.]

goat·skin (gōt'skin') *n.* The skin of a goat, used for leather.

gob[1] (gŏb) *n.* A lump or mass. [< OF *gobe*, mouthful, lump.]

gob[2] (gŏb) *n.* *Slang.* A sailor. [?]

gob·bet (gŏb'ĭt) *n.* A chunk, morsel, or lump. [< OF *gobe*, GOB[1].]

gob·ble[1] (gŏb'əl) *v.* **-bled, -bling. 1.** To devour greedily. **2.** To snatch; grab. [Freq of ME *gobben*, to drink greedily.]

gob·ble[2] (gŏb'əl) *v.* **-bled, -bling.** To make the guttural sound of a male turkey.

gob·ble·dy·gook (gŏb'əl-dē-gŏŏk') *n.* Also **gob·ble·de·gook.** Unintelligible jargon. [< GOBBLE.]

gob·bler (gŏb'lər) *n.* A male turkey.

go-be·tween (gō'bĭ-twēn') *n.* An intermediary.

Go·bi Desert (gō'bē). A desert in east-central Asia.

gob·let (gŏb'lĭt) *n.* A drinking glass with a stem and base. [< OF *gobel*, cup.]

gob·lin (gŏb'lən) *n.* A grotesque elf or sprite said to work mischief or evil. [< MHG *kobolt*, goblin.]

go-cart (gō'kärt') *n.* A small toy wagon.

god (gŏd) *n.* **1.** A being of supernatural powers or attributes, believed in and worshiped by a people. **2.** One that is worshiped or idealized as a god. **3. God.** A being conceived as the perfect, omnipotent, omniscient originator and ruler of the universe, the principal object of faith and worship in monotheistic religions. [< OE. See **gheu(ə)-.**]

god·child (gŏd'chīld') *n.* One for whom another serves as sponsor at baptism.

god·daugh·ter (gŏd'dô'tər) *n.* A female godchild.

god·dess (gŏd'ĭs) *n.* **1.** A female deity. **2.** A woman of great beauty.

god·fa·ther (gŏd'fä'thər) *n.* A man who sponsors a child at its baptism.

god·head (gŏd'hĕd') *n.* **1.** Divinity. **2. Godhead.** The essential and divine nature of God.

god·less (gŏd'lĭs) *adj.* **1.** Recognizing or worshiping no god. **2.** Irreverent; wicked. —**god'less·ly** *adv.* —**god'less·ness** *n.*

god·like (gŏd'līk') *adj.* Resembling a god or God.

god·ly (gŏd'lē) *adj.* **-lier, -liest. 1.** Having reverence for God; pious; devout. **2.** Divine. —**god'li·ness** *n.*

god·moth·er (gŏd'mŭth'ər) *n.* A woman who sponsors a child at its baptism.

god·par·ent (gŏd'pâr'ənt) *n.* A godfather or godmother.

god·send (gŏd'sĕnd') *n.* An unexpected boon or stroke of luck. [ME *goddes sand*, God's message.]

god·son (gŏd'sŭn') *n.* A male godchild.

God·speed (gŏd'spēd') *n.* Success or good fortune.

Godt·haab (gôt'hôp'). The capital of Greenland. Pop. 1,400.

Goe·the (gœ'tə), **Johann Wolfgang von.** 1749–1832. German poet.

go-get·ter (gō'gĕt'ər) *n.* *Informal.* An enterprising, hustling person.

gog·gle (gŏg'əl) *v.* **-gled, -gling.** To stare with wide and bulging eyes. —*n.* **goggles.** A pair of large eyeglasses worn as a protection against wind, dust, or glare. [ME *gogelen*, to roll the eyes.] —**gog'gly** *adj.*

Goi·del·ic (goi-dĕl'ĭk) *n.* A group of Celtic languages, including Irish Gaelic and Scottish Gaelic. —**Goi·del'ic** *adj.*

goi·ter (goi'tər) *n.* Also **goi·tre.** A chronic, noncancerous enlargement of the thyroid gland, visible as a swelling at the front of the neck. [< L *guttur*, throat.] —**goi'trous** (-trəs) *adj.*

gold (gōld) *n.* **1.** *Symbol* **Au** A soft, yellow, corrosion-resistant, highly malleable and ductile metallic element that is used as an international monetary standard, in jewelry, for decoration, and as a plated coating on a wide variety of electrical and mechanical components. Atomic number 79, atomic weight 196.967. **2. a.** Coinage made of gold. **b.** A gold standard. **3.** Money; riches. **4.** Moderate to vivid yellow. [< OE. See **ghel-**[2].]

gold·brick (gōld'brĭk') *n.* Also **gold·brick·er** (-ər). *Slang.* One who avoids assigned duties or work; a shirker. —**gold'brick'** *v.*

gold·en (gōl'dən) *adj.* **1.** Made of or containing gold. **2. a.** Having the color of gold. **b.** Lustrous; radiant. **c.** Suggestive of gold: *a golden voice.* **3.** Of the greatest value or importance; precious. **4.** Marked by prosperity. **5.** Very favorable or advantageous; excellent: *a golden opportunity.* —**gold'en·ly** *adv.*

gold·en·rod (gōl'dən-rŏd') *n.* A North American plant with branching clusters of small yellow flowers.

gold·finch (gōld'fĭnch') *n.* A small New World bird having yellow plumage with a black forehead, wings, and tail.

gold·fish (gōld'fĭsh') *n.* A reddish or brass-colored freshwater fish often kept in home aquariums.

gold·smith (gōld'smĭth') *n.* One who fashions or deals in gold articles.

golf (gŏlf, gôf) *n.* A game played on a course having nine or eighteen holes, the object being to propel a small ball with the use of a club into each hole with as few strokes as possible. [ME.] —**golf** *v.* —**golf'er** *n.*

ô paw, for/oi boy/ou out/ŏŏ took/ōō coo/p pop/r run/s sauce/sh shy/t to/th thin/*th* the/
ŭ cut/ûr fur/v van/w wag/y yes/z size/zh vision/ə ago, item, edible, gallop, circus/

Go•li•ath (gə-lī'əth). The Philistine giant slain by David. I Samuel 17:4–51.

–gon. *comb. form.* Having a designated number of angles: **pentagon.** [< Gk *gōnia*, angle.]

go•nad (gō'năd', gŏn'ăd') *n.* The organ that produces gametes; a testis or ovary. [< Gk *gonos*, offspring, genitals.]

gon•do•la (gŏn'd'l-ə, gŏn-dō'lə) *n.* **1.** A narrow barge used on the canals of Venice. **2.** Also **gondola car.** An open, shallow freight car. **3.** A structure suspended from and carried aloft by a balloon. [It, roll, rock.]

gon•do•lier (gŏnd'l-îr') *n.* The boatman of a gondola.

gone (gôn, gŏn) *adj.* **1.** Past; bygone. **2. a.** Advanced. **b.** Pregnant. **3.** Dying or dead. **4.** Ruined; lost. **5.** Carried away; absorbed. **6.** Used up; exhausted. **7.** *Slang.* Infatuated: *gone on the girl.*

gon•er (gôn'ər, gŏn'-) *n.* *Slang.* One who is ruined or doomed.

gon•fa•lon (gŏn'fə-lən) *n.* A banner suspended from a crosspiece. [It *gonfalone*, standard.]

gong (gông, gŏng) *n.* A rimmed metal disk that produces a loud, sonorous tone when struck. [Malay *gōng* (imit.).]

gon•or•rhe•a (gŏn'ə-rē'ə) *n.* An infectious disease of the genitourinary tract, rectum, and cervix, caused by a bacterium and transmitted chiefly by sexual intercourse. [< Gk *gonorrhoia*.]

goo (gōō) *n.* *Informal.* **1.** A sticky wet substance. **2.** Sentimental drivel. **—goo'ey** *adj.*

goo•ber (gōō'bər) *n.* A peanut.

good (gōŏd) *adj.* **better, best. 1.** Having positive or desirable qualities. **2.** Suitable; serviceable. **3. a.** Not spoiled. **b.** Whole; sound. **4.** Superior to the average: *a good student.* **5. a.** Of high quality. **b.** Discriminating: *good taste.* **6.** Suitable for formal occasions: *good clothes.* **7.** Beneficial; salutary: *a good night's rest.* **8.** Competent; skilled. **9.** Complete; thorough. **10. a.** Safe; sure. **b.** Valid or sound. **c.** Genuine; real. **11. a.** Ample; substantial. **b.** Bountiful. **12.** Full: *a good mile from here.* **13. a.** Pleasant; enjoyable. **b.** Propitious; favorable. **14. a.** Virtuous; upright. **b.** Benevolent; cheerful. **c.** Loyal; staunch. **15. a.** Well-behaved; obedient. **b.** Socially correct; proper. **—as good as.** Practically; virtually; nearly. **—make good. 1.** To fulfill a commitment. **2.** To compensate for or replace. **3.** To prove; verify. **4.** *Informal.* To succeed; do well. **—***n.* **1. a.** That which is good. **b.** The valuable or useful part. **2.** Welfare; benefit: *the common good.* **3.** Goodness; virtue; merit. **—for good.** Forever; permanently. **—***adv.* *Informal.* Well. [< OE *gōd.* See **ghedh-**.]

Usage: Good occurs frequently after linking verbs such as *be, feel, seem, smell, sound,* and *taste: The news sounds good.* In such usage, acceptable on all levels, *good* is an adjective that qualifies the subject of the verb. Except in distinctly informal usage, *good* does not function as an adverb by qualifying verbs directly; instead, *well* is used: *He dances well* (not *good*). *Things are not going well.*

good-by, good-bye (gōŏd'bī') *interj.* Farewell.

[Contraction of *God be with you.*] **—good'-by', good'-bye'** *n.*

Good Friday. The Friday before Easter, observed in commemoration of the Crucifixion.

Good Hope, Cape of. A promontory on the SW coast of South Africa.

good•ly (gōŏd'lē) *adj.* **-lier, -liest. 1.** Of pleasing appearance. **2.** Somewhat large; considerable. **—good'li•ness** *n.*

good•man (gōŏd'mən) *n.* *Archaic.* **1.** The male head of a household; husband. **2. Goodman.** Mister: *Goodman Jones.*

good•ness (gōŏd'nĭs) *n.* **1.** The state or quality of being good. **2.** Virtuousness; rectitude. **3.** Kindness; benevolence. **4.** A euphemism for God: *Thank goodness!*

goods (gōŏdz) *pl.n.* **1.** Merchandise; wares. **2.** Portable personal property. **3.** Cloth. [Pl of GOOD.]

Good Sa•mar•i•tan (sə-măr'ĭ-tən). A compassionate person. [< the parable of the *good Samaritan.* Luke 10:30–37.]

Good•wife (gōŏd'wīf') *n.* *Archaic.* Mrs.: *Goodwife Jones.*

good will. Also **good•will** (gōŏd'wĭl'). **1.** Benevolence. **2.** Cheerful willingness. **3.** The favorable disposition of clients or customers, reckoned as an intangible asset.

good•y¹ (gōŏd'ē) *n.*, *pl.* **-ies.** Something delectable or attractive.

good•y² (gōŏd'ē) *n.* Also **Good•y.** *Obs.* Goodwife; Mrs.: *Goody Garlick.*

good•y-good•y (gōŏd'ē-gōŏd'ē) *adj.* Affectedly sweet or good. **—good'y-good'y** *n.*

goof (gōōf) *Slang. v.* To blunder. **—goof off.** To waste or kill time. **—goof up.** To bungle. **—***n.* **1.** A blunder. **2.** A ludicrously incompetent or stupid person. [< OF *goffe*, awkward.] **—goof'i•ness** *n.* **—goof'y** *adj.*

gook (gōŏk, gōōk) *n.* *Slang.* A sludgy or slimy substance. [Perh < ME *gowke*, cuckoo.]

goon (gōōn) *n.* **1.** A thug hired for purposes of intimidation. **2.** *Slang.* **a.** An oaf. **b.** A dullard; bore. [?]

goose (gōōs) *n.*, *pl.* **geese** (gēs). **1.** A water bird related to the ducks and swans. **2.** The female of such a bird. **3.** The edible flesh of such a bird. **4.** *Informal.* A silly person. [< OE *gōs.* See **ghans-**.]

goose•ber•ry (gōōs'bĕr'ē, -bə-rē, gōōz'-) *n.* **1.** The edible greenish berry of a spiny shrub. **2.** A shrub bearing such berries.

goose flesh. Momentary roughness of skin in response to cold or fear.

G.O.P. Grand Old Party (Republican Party of the U.S.).

go•pher (gō'fər) *n.* Any of various burrowing North American rodents with pocketlike cheek pouches. [< earlier *magopher.*]

gore¹ (gôr) *v.* **gored, goring.** To stab with a horn or tusk. [< OE *gār*, spear.]

gore² (gôr) *n.* A triangular or tapering piece of cloth, as in a skirt, umbrella, or sail. [< OE *gāra*, triangular piece of land.]

gore³ (gôr) *n.* Blood, esp. from a wound. [< OE *gor*, dung, dirt.]

gorge (gôrj) *n.* **1.** A deep, narrow ravine. **2.** The throat; gullet. **3.** A mass obstructing a

narrow passage: *an ice gorge.* —*v.* **gorged,
gorging. 1.** To stuff; satiate; glut. **2.** To eat
greedily. [< L *gurges*, whirlpool, throat.]
gor•geous (gôr′jəs) *adj.* **1.** Resplendent; magnificent. **2.** Strikingly beautiful. [< OF *gor-
gias*, stylish, fine.] —**gor′geous•ly** *adv.* —**gor′-
geous•ness** *n.*
go•ril•la (gə-rĭl′ə) *n.* A large African ape with
a stocky body and dark hair. [< Gk *Gorillai*,
African tribe of hairy men.]
Gor•ki (gôr′kē), **Maxim.** 1868–1936. Russian
novelist and playwright.
Gor•kiy (gôr′kē). Also **Gor•ki, Gor•ky.** A city of
the U.S.S.R., on the Volga. Pop. 1,170,000.
gorse (gôrs) *n.* A spiny European shrub with
fragrant yellow flowers. [< OE *gorst, gors.*]
go•ry (gôr′ē, gōr′ē) *adj.* **-rier, -riest. 1.** Bloody;
bloodstained. **2.** Bloodcurdling; sensational:
the gory details. —**gor′i•ly** *adv.*
gos•hawk (gŏs′hôk′) *n.* A large hawk with
broad, rounded wings and gray or brownish
plumage. [< OE *gôs*, GOOSE + *heafoc*, HAWK.]
gos•ling (gŏz′lĭng) *n.* A young goose.
gos•pel (gŏs′pəl) *n.* **1.** Often **Gospel.** The
teachings of Christ and the Apostles. **2. Gospel.** Any of the first four books of the New
Testament. **3.** Something accepted as unquestionably true. [< OE *godspell*, "good news."]
gos•sa•mer (gŏs′ə-mər) *n.* **1.** A fine film of
floating cobwebs. **2.** A sheer gauzy fabric.
3. Anything delicate, light, or insubstantial.
[ME *gossomer.*] —**gos′sa•mer** *adj.*
gos•sip (gŏs′əp) *n.* **1.** Trivial rumor of a personal nature. **2.** One who habitually engages
in such talk. **3.** Casual, chatty talk. —*v.* To
engage in or spread gossip. [< OE *god*, GOD
+ *sibb*, kinsman.] —**gos′sip•y** *adj.*
got (gŏt). *p.t.* & *p.p.* of **get.**
Goth (gŏth) *n.* **1.** One of a Germanic people
that settled near the Elbe River and invaded
the Roman Empire in the early centuries of
the Christian era. **2.** An uncultured or uncivilized person; barbarian.
Goth. Gothic.
Goth•ic (gŏth′ĭk) *adj.* **1. a.** Of or pertaining to
the Goths or their language. **b.** Germanic.
2. Of or pertaining to an architectural style of
W Europe from the 12th through the 15th
century. —*n.* **1.** The extinct East Germanic
language of the Goths. **2.** Gothic art or architecture.
got•ten (gŏt′n). Alternate *p.p.* of **get.**
gouge (gouj) *n.* **1.** A chisel with a rounded,
troughlike blade. **2.** A groove or hole scooped
with or as if with a gouge. —*v.* **gouged, gouging.
1.** To cut or scoop out with or as if with a
gouge. **2.** *Slang.* To extort or cheat. [< LL
gubia.] —**goug′er** *n.*
gou•lash (gōō′läsh, -lăsh) *n.* A meat and vegetable stew seasoned mainly with paprika.
[Hung *gulyás (hus)*, "herdsman's meat."]
gourd (gôrd, gōrd, gōōrd) *n.* **1.** A vine related
to the pumpkin, squash, and cucumber, bearing fruits with a hard rind. **2.** The fruit of such
a vine. **3.** The dried, hollowed-out shell of
such a fruit, used as a utensil. [< L *cucurbita.*]
gourde (gōōrd) *n.* The basic monetary unit of
Haiti. [< L *gurdus*, heavy, dull.]

gour•mand (gōōr′mənd) *n.* **1.** A glutton. **2.** A
gourmet. [< OF, glutton.]
gour•met (gōōr-mā′) *n.* A connoisseur of fine
food and drink; epicure. [F.]
gout (gout) *n.* **1.** A disturbance of the uric-acid
metabolism occurring predominantly in males
and marked by arthritic attacks. **2.** A blob,
clot, or splash: *bleeding great gouts of blood.*
[< L *gutta*, drop.] —**gout′y** *adj.*
gov. 1. government. **2.** governor.
gov•ern (gŭv′ərn) *v.* **1.** To control; guide; direct. **2.** To rule by exercise of sovereign authority. **3.** To regulate or determine. **4.** To
restrain. [< L *gubernāre*, to direct, steer < Gk
kubernan.] —**gov′ern•a•bil′i•ty, gov′ern•a•ble•
ness** *n.* —**gov′ern•a•ble** *adj.* —**gov′ern•ance** *n.*
gov•ern•ess (gŭv′ər-nĭs) *n.* A woman who
supervises and trains the children of a private
household.
gov•ern•ment (gŭv′ərn-mənt) *n.* **1.** The administration of public policy in a political unit.
2. The office, function, or authority whereby
political power is exercised. **3.** A prevailing
political system or policy. **4.** A governing
body. —**gov′ern•ment′al** (-mĕnt′l) *adj.*
gov•er•nor (gŭv′ər-nər) *n.* **1.** The chief executive of a state in the U.S. or of some analogous
political unit. **2.** A manager or administrative
head in certain institutions or organizations.
3. A military commandant. **4.** A feedback device providing automatic control on a machine. —**gov′er•nor•ship′** *n.*
govt. government.
gown (goun) *n.* **1.** A loose, flowing garment, as
a robe or nightgown. **2.** A woman's formal
dress. **3.** A distinctive outer robe worn on
official or ceremonial occasions, as by a judge
or clergyman. **4.** Students and professors as
distinguished from townspeople: *town and
gown.* [< LL *gunna*, robe, fur.]
G.P. general practitioner.
GPO general post office.
GQ general quarters.
gr. 1. grade. **2.** gross.
Gr. Greece; Greek.
Graaf•i•an follicle (grä′fē-ən). Any of the follicles in the mammalian ovary, containing a
maturing ovum. [< R. de *Graaf* (1641–1673),
Dutch anatomist.]
grab (grăb) *v.* **grabbed, grabbing. 1.** To grasp
suddenly; snatch; seize. **2.** To obtain or appropriate unscrupulously. [MDu and MLG
grabben.] —**grab** *n.* —**grab′ber** *n.*
grace (grās) *n.* **1.** Beauty or charm of movement, form, or proportion. **2.** Fitness or propriety. **3. a.** Good will. **b.** Mercy; clemency.
4. Temporary immunity or respite: *a period of
grace.* **5. a.** Divine love and protection bestowed freely upon mankind. **b.** The state of
being thus protected or sanctified. **c.** A virtue
or gift granted by God. **6.** A short prayer at
mealtime. **7.** Often **Grace.** A title of courtesy
for a duke, duchess, or archbishop: *His Grace
the Duke of Leeds.* —**in the good** (or **bad**) **graces
of.** In (or out) of favor with. —**with good** (or
bad) **grace.** In a willing (or grudging) manner.
—*v.* **graced, gracing. 1.** To honor or favor. **2.**
To embellish. [< L *grātia*, pleasure, favor.]

—grace'ful *adj.* —grace'ful•ly *adv.* —grace'ful•ness *n.* —grace'less *adj.*

gra•cious (grā'shəs) *adj.* 1. Generous, tactful, and courteous. 2. Merciful; compassionate. 3. Marked by qualities associated with taste and breeding. 4. Graceful. —*interj.* Expressive of surprise or mild emotion. —gra'cious•ly *adv.* —gra'cious•ness *n.*

grack•le (grăk'əl) *n.* Any of several New World blackbirds with iridescent blackish plumage. [< L *grāculus,* jackdaw.]

grad (grăd) *n. Informal.* A graduate of a school or college.

gra•da•tion (grā-dā'shən) *n.* 1. a. A progression of successive stages. b. A degree or stage in such a progression. 2. Advancement by regular stages. 3. The act of arranging in grades. —gra•da'tion•al *adj.*

grade (grād) *n.* 1. A stage or degree in a process. 2. A position in a scale. 3. A homogeneously ranked group or class. 4. a. An elementary school class. b. the grades. Elementary school. 5. A mark indicating a student's level of accomplishment. 6. A military, naval, or civil-service rank. 7. A degree of slope. 8. A slope or gradual inclination, esp. of a road or railroad track. —*v.* graded, grading. 1. To arrange in degrees; rank; sort. 2. To assign an academic grade to. 3. To level or smooth to a desired gradient: *grade a road.* [< L *gradus,* step.]

—grade. *comb. form.* Progression or movement: retrograde. [< L *gradī,* to step, go.]

gra•di•ent (grā'dē-ənt) *n.* 1. A rate of inclination. 2. An incline. 3. The maximum rate at which a variable physical quantity changes in value per unit change in position.

grad•u•al (grăj'ōō-əl) *adj.* Occurring or proceeding by stages or degrees. [< L *gradus,* GRADE.] —grad'u•al•ly *adv.*

grad•u•al•ism (grăj'ōō-ə-lĭz'əm) *n.* The policy of advancing toward a goal by gradual stages.

grad•u•ate (grăj'ōō-āt') *v.* -ated, -ating. 1. To grant or be granted an academic degree or diploma. 2. To divide into categories, steps, or grades. 3. To divide into marked intervals, esp. for use in measurement. —*n.* (grăj'ōō-ĭt). 1. A recipient of an academic degree or diploma. 2. A graduated container. —*adj.* (grăj'ōō-ĭt). 1. Possessing an academic degree or diploma. 2. Of or relating to studies beyond a bachelor's degree. [< L *gradus,* GRADE.]

Usage: Either *graduated* or *was graduated* is possible in sentences such as *She graduated* (or *was graduated*) *from college. From* is necessary in either case. *She graduated college* is not acceptable usage.

grad•u•a•tion (grăj'ōō-ā'shən) *n.* 1. The conferring or receipt of an academic degree or diploma. 2. A commencement ceremony. 3. A division mark or interval on a graduated scale. 4. Division into stages or degrees.

graf•fi•to (grə-fē'tō) *n., pl.* -ti (-tē). A crude drawing or inscription, as on a wall. [< It *graffiare,* to scratch.]

graft¹ (grăft, gräft) *v.* 1. To unite (a shoot, bud, or plant) with a growing plant by insertion or placing in close contact. 2. To transplant or implant (tissue) into a bodily part. —*n.* 1. a. A detached shoot or bud grafted onto a growing plant. b. The point of union of such graft parts. 2. Material, esp. tissue or an organ, grafted onto a bodily part. [< OF *grafe,* pencil, shoot for grafting.]

graft² (grăft, gräft) *n.* 1. The unscrupulous use of one's position to derive profit or advantages. 2. Money or advantage thus gained. —graft *v.* —graft'er *n.*

gra•ham (grā'əm) *adj.* Made from or consisting of whole-wheat flour. [< S. *Graham* (1794–1851), American vegetarian.]

Grail (grāl) *n.* The cup or dish assertedly used by Christ at the Last Supper, thereafter constituting an object of chivalrous quests. [< ML *gradālis,* dish.]

grain (grān) *n.* 1. A small, hard seed, esp. of a cereal grass, as wheat, rice, etc. 2. The seeds of such plants. 3. Cereal grasses collectively. 4. A relatively small discrete mass of particles or crystals: *a grain of sand.* 5. A tiny quantity: *a grain of truth.* 6. A U.S. Customary System avoirdupois unit of weight equal to 0.002285 ounce or 0.036 dram. 7. The arrangement of the fibrous tissue in wood. 8. Texture. 9. Temperament; nature. [< L *grānum,* seed.] —grain'i•ness *n.* —grain'y *adj.*

grain alcohol. Ethanol.

gram (grăm) *n.* Also *chiefly Brit.* gramme. A metric unit of mass and weight equal to one-thousandth of a kilogram. [< LL *gramma,* small unit.]

—gram¹. *comb. form.* Something written or drawn: telegram. [< Gk *gramma,* letter, and *grammē,* line.]

—gram². *comb. form.* A gram: kilogram.

gram. grammar.

gram-at•om (grăm'ăt'əm) *n.* The mass in grams of an element numerically equal to the atomic weight.

gram•mar (grăm'ər) *n.* 1. The study of syntax and word inflection. 2. A book containing the syntactic and inflectional rules for a given language. 3. a. A normative system of usage rules for pedagogical or reference purposes. b. Writing or speech judged with regard to such rules: *bad grammar.* [< Gk *gramma,* letter.] —gram•mar'i•an (grə-mâr'ē-ən) *n.* —gram•mat'i•cal (grə-măt'ĭ-kəl) *adj.* —gram•mat'i•cal•ly *adv.*

grammar school. 1. An elementary school. 2. A British secondary or preparatory school.

gramme. *Chiefly Brit.* Variant of gram.

gram-mo•lec•u•lar weight (grăm'mə-lĕk'yə-lər). *Chem.* A mole.

gram molecule. *Chem.* A mole.

Gram-neg•a•tive (grăm'nĕg'ə-tĭv) *adj.* Of or being a microorganism that does not retain the purple dye used in Gram's method.

gram•o•phone (grăm'ə-fōn') *n.* A phonograph.

Gram-pos•i•tive (grăm'pŏz'ə-tĭv) *adj.* Of or being a microorganism that retains the purple dye used in Gram's method.

gram•pus (grăm'pəs) *n., pl.* -puses. A whalelike marine mammal. [< OF *graspois, craspois,* fat fish.]

Gram's method (grămz). A differential staining technique using the retention or lack of retention of a purple dye to classify bacteria. [< H. *Gram* (1855–1938), Danish physician.]
gran·a·ry (grăn'ə-rē, grā'nə-) *n., pl.* **-ries.** A building for storing threshed grain.
grand (grănd) *adj.* **1.** Large and impressive in size, scope, or extent. **2.** Magnificent; sumptuous. **3.** Having higher rank than others of the same category. **4.** Principal; main: *grand ballroom.* **5.** Illustrious. **6. a.** Pretentious. **b.** Calculated to impress: *a grand manner.* **7.** Dignified and admirable. **8.** Stately; regal. **9.** Lofty; noble. **10.** Inclusive; complete: *grand total.* —*n.* **1.** A grand piano. **2.** *Slang.* A thousand dollars. [< L *grandis,* grand, full-grown.] —**grand'ly** *adv.* —**grand'ness** *n.*
gran·dam (grăn'dăm', -dəm) *n.* **1.** A grandmother. **2.** An old woman.
Grand Canyon. A gorge formed by the Colorado River in NW Arizona.
grand·child (grănd'chīld') *n.* A child of one's son or daughter.
grand·daugh·ter (grăn'dô'tər) *n.* The daughter of one's son or daughter.
gran·dee (grăn-dē') *n.* A nobleman of the highest rank in Spain or Portugal. [< Port *grande,* "great (one)."]
gran·deur (grăn'jər, -jŏŏr) *n.* Greatness; splendor; majesty.
grand·fa·ther (grănd'fä'*th*ər) *n.* **1.** The father of one's mother or father. **2.** An ancestor.
gran·dil·o·quence (grăn-dĭl'ə-kwəns) *n.* Pompous or bombastic eloquence. —**gran·dil'o·quent** *adj.* —**gran·dil'o·quent·ly** *adv.*
gran·di·ose (grăn'dē-ōs', grăn'dē-ōs') *adj.* **1.** Grand and imposing. **2.** Affectedly grand. —**gran'di·ose'ly** *adv.* —**gran'di·os'i·ty** (-ŏs'ə-tē), **gran'di·ose'ness** *n.*
grand·ma (grănd'mä', grăn'mä', grăm'mä', grăm'ə) *n. Informal.* Grandmother.
grand mal (grän mäl') A form of epilepsy characterized by severe seizures involving spasms and loss of consciousness.
grand·moth·er (grănd'mŭ*th*'ər) *n.* **1.** The mother of one's father or mother. **2.** A female ancestor.
grand·pa (grănd'pä', grăm'pä', grăm'pə) *n. Informal.* Grandfather.
grand·par·ent (grănd'pâr'ənt, grăn'-) *n.* A parent of one's mother or father.
grand piano. A piano having the strings strung in a horizontal harp-shaped frame.
Grand Rapids (răp'ĭdz). A city of S Michigan. Pop. 177,000.
grand·son (grănd'sŭn', grăn'-) *n.* The son of one's son or daughter.
grand·stand (grănd'stănd', grăn'-) *n.* A roofed stand for spectators at a stadium or racetrack.
grange (grānj) *n.* **1.** Grange. **a.** The Patrons of Husbandry, a U.S. farmers' association. **b.** One of its branch lodges. **2.** *Archaic.* A manor house. [< L *grānum,* GRAIN.]
gran·ite (grăn'ĭt) *n.* A common, coarse-grained, light-colored, hard igneous rock consisting chiefly of quartz, orthoclase, and mica, used in monuments and for building. [It *granito,* "grained."] —**gra·nit'ic** (grə-nĭt'ĭk) *adj.*

gran·ny (grăn'ē) *n., pl.* **-nies. 1.** A grandmother. **2.** A fuss-budget. **3.** *Southern U.S.* A midwife.
grant (grănt, gränt) *v.* **1.** To allow; consent to. **2.** To accord, as a favor. **3. a.** To bestow; confer. **b.** To transfer (property) by a deed. **4.** To concede; acknowledge. —*n.* **1.** The act of granting. **2.** Something granted. **3. a.** A transfer of property by deed. **b.** The instrument of such transfer. **c.** Land thus bestowed. [< OF *greanter, creanter,* to insure, guarantee.]
Grant (grănt), **Ulysses S(impson).** 1822–1885. American general; 18th President of the U.S. (1869–77).

Ulysses S. Grant

gran·u·lar (grăn'yə-lər) *adj.* **1.** Composed of granules or grains. **2.** Grainy. —**gran'u·lar'i·ty** *n.* —**gran'u·lar·ly** *adv.*
gran·u·late (grăn'yə-lāt') *v.* **-lated, -lating. 1.** To form into grains or granules. **2.** To make rough and grainy. —**gran'u·la'tion** *n.*
gran·ule (grăn'yōōl) *n.* A small grain or pellet; particle.
grape (grāp) *n.* **1.** A juicy, smooth-skinned, edible fruit borne in clusters on a woody vine. **2.** A vine bearing such fruit. **3.** Grapeshot. [< OF, bunch of grapes, hook.]
grape·fruit (grāp'frōōt') *n.* **1.** A large, round, yellow-skinned, acid-flavored citrus fruit. **2.** A tree bearing such fruit.
grape·shot (grāp'shŏt') *n.* A cluster of iron balls formerly used as a cannon charge.
grape sugar. Dextrose.
grape·vine (grāp'vīn') *n.* **1.** A vine on which grapes grow. **2.** An informal means of transmitting information or rumor. **3.** Gossip; rumor.
graph (grăf, gräf) *n.* **1.** A drawing that exhibits a relationship between two sets of numbers. **2.** Any pictorial device, as a bar graph, used to display numerical relationships. —*v.* **1.** To represent by a graph. **2.** To plot (a function) on a graph.
–graph. *comb. form.* **1.** An apparatus that

writes or records: **seismograph.** 2. Something drawn or written: **monograph.** [< Gk *graphein*, to write.]

graph·ic (grăf′ĭk) *adj.* Also **graph·i·cal** (-ĭ-kəl). 1. Written, printed, drawn, or engraved. 2. Vividly outlined or set forth: *a graphic account.* 3. Of or pertaining to the graphic arts. [< Gk *graphein*, to write.] —**graph′i·cal·ly** *adv.*

graphic arts. Any of the fine or applied visual arts, as painting, drawing, etc.

graph·ite (grăf′īt′) *n.* The soft, steel-gray to black, hexagonally crystallized allotrope of carbon, used in lead pencils, lubricants, paints, and coatings. [< Gk *graphein*, to write.] —**gra·phit′ic** (-fĭt′ĭk) *adj.*

—**graphy.** *comb. form.* 1. A method of graphic representation: **stenography.** 2. A descriptive science of a specific subject or field: **oceanography.**

grap·nel (grăp′nəl) *n.* A small anchor with three or more flukes. [< OF *grapon*, anchor, hook.]

grap·ple (grăp′əl) *n.* 1. a. A clawed implement formerly used to hold an enemy ship alongside for boarding. b. A grapnel. 2. Hand-to-hand combat. —*v.* **-pled, -pling.** 1. To lay hold on, make fast, or drag with or as if with a grapple. 2. To seize firmly with the hands. 3. a. To come to grips; wrestle. b. To attempt to cope: *grapple with a problem.* [< OProv *grapa*, hook.] —**grap′pler** *n.*

grasp (grăsp) *v.* 1. To take hold of or seize. 2. To hold with the hand; clasp. 3. To comprehend. —*n.* 1. Hold; control; grip. 2. The ability to seize or reach. 3. Comprehension. [< OE **grapsan.*]

grasp·ing (grăs′pĭng) *adj.* Greedy; avaricious. —**grasp′ing·ly** *adv.* —**grasp′ing·ness** *n.*

grass (grăs, gräs) *n.* 1. Any of numerous plants with narrow leaves, jointed stems, and spikes or clusters of inconspicuous flowers. 2. Such plants collectively. 3. Ground, as a lawn or pasture, covered with such plants. 4. *Slang.* Marijuana. [< OE *græs.* See **ghrē-.**] —**grass′y** *adj.*

grass·hop·per (grăs′hŏp′ər, gräs′-) *n.* Any of various related insects with long hind legs adapted for jumping.

grass·land (grăs′lănd′, gräs′-) *n.* An area, such as a prairie, of grass or grasslike vegetation.

grass·roots (grăs′rōōts′, -rŏŏts′, gräs′-) *pl.n.* 1. The rural electorate. 2. The groundwork or source of something. —**grass′roots′** *adj.*

grate¹ (grāt) *v.* **grated, grating.** 1. To shred or pulverize by rubbing. 2. To make or cause to make a rasping sound. 3. To irritate. —*n.* A rasping noise. [< OF *grater*, to scrape.] —**grat′er** *n.* —**grat′ing·ly** *adv.*

grate² (grāt) *n.* 1. A framework of parallel bars over an opening. 2. Such a framework of metal, used to hold burning fuel. [< L *crātis*, frame, wicker basket.]

grate·ful (grāt′fəl) *adj.* 1. Appreciative; thankful. 2. Expressing gratitude. 3. Agreeable; pleasing. [< L *grātus*, pleasing, favorable.] —**grate′ful·ly** *adv.* —**grate′ful·ness** *n.*

grat·i·fy (grăt′ə-fī′) *v.* **-fied, -fying.** To please, favor, or indulge. —**grat′i·fi·ca′tion** *n.*

grat·ing¹ (grā′tĭng) *adj.* 1. Rasping. 2. Irritating. —**grat′ing·ly** *adv.*

grat·ing² (grā′tĭng) *n.* A grill; grate.

gra·tis (grā′tĭs, grăt′ĭs) *adv.* Without charge; free. [< L *grātus*, favorable.] —**gra′tis** *adj.*

grat·i·tude (grăt′ə-t/y/ōōd′) *n.* Thankfulness. [< L *grātus*, favorable.]

gra·tu·i·tous (grə-t/y/ōō′ə-təs) *adj.* 1. Free; gratis. 2. Unnecessary or unwarranted: *gratuitous criticism.* [L *grātuītus*, given as a favor.] —**gra·tu′i·tous·ly** *adv.*

gra·tu·i·ty (grə-t/y/ōō′ə-tē) *n., pl.* **-ties.** A tip for service.

grau·pel (grou′pəl) *n.* Precipitation consisting of pellets of snow. [< G *Graupe*, hulled grain.]

grave¹ (grāv) *n.* An excavation for the interment of a corpse; burial place. [< OE *græf.* See **ghrebh-.**]

grave² (grāv) *adj.* **graver, gravest.** 1. Extremely serious; important; weighty. 2. Fraught with danger; critical. [< L *gravis*, heavy, weighty.] —**grave′ly** *adv.* —**grave′ness** *n.*

grave³ (grāv) *v.* **graved, graven** (grā′vən), **graving.** To sculpt or carve; engrave. [< OE *grafan.* See **ghrebh-.**] —**grav′er** *n.*

grav·el (grăv′əl) *n.* Any unconsolidated mixture of rock or rocklike fragments. [< OF *grave.*]

grave·stone (grāv′stōn′) *n.* A tombstone.

grave·yard (grāv′yärd′) *n.* A cemetery.

grav·id (grăv′ĭd) *adj.* Pregnant. [< L *gravidus.*]

grav·i·met·ric (grăv′ə-mĕt′rĭk) *adj.* Pertaining to measurement by weight.

grav·i·tate (grăv′ə-tāt′) *v.* **-tated, -tating.** 1. To move in response to the force of gravity. 2. To be attracted by or toward.

grav·i·ta·tion (grăv′ə-tā′shən) *n.* 1. a. The natural phenomenon of attraction between massive bodies. b. The degree of such attraction; broadly, gravity. 2. A movement toward a source of attraction: *the gravitation of the middle class to the suburbs.* —**grav′i·ta′tion·al** *adj.*

grav·i·ton (grăv′ə-tŏn′) *n.* A particle postulated to be the quantum of gravitational interaction, and presumed to have zero electric charge and zero rest mass.

grav·i·ty (grăv′ə-tē) *n.* 1. a. The force of gravitation, being, for any two sufficiently massive bodies, directly proportional to the product of their masses and inversely proportional to the square of the distance between them; esp. the attractive central gravitational force exerted by a celestial body such as the earth. b. Loosely, gravitation. c. *Rare.* Weight. 2. Graveness; seriousness. [< L *gravis*, heavy, GRAVE.]

gra·vure (grə-vyŏŏr′) *n.* A method of printing using photomechanically prepared plates or cylinders; photogravure. [< F *graver*, to engrave, dig into.]

gra·vy (grā′vē) *n., pl.* **-vies.** 1. The juices that drip from cooking meat. 2. A sauce made from these juices. [< OF *grain*, spice, grain.]

gravy boat. An elongated dish or pitcher for serving gravy.

gray (grā). Also **grey.** *adj.* 1. Of a neutral color ranging between black and white. 2. Dull or

---

ă pat/ā ate/âr care/ä bar/b **bib**/ch **chew**/d **deed**/ĕ pet/ē be/f **fit**/g **gag**/h **hat**/hw **what**/ ĭ pit/ī pie/îr pier/j **judge**/k **kick**/l lid, fatal/m **mum**/n **no**, sudden/ng **sing**/ŏ pot/ō **go**/

dark; gloomy. **3.** Having gray hair. —*n.* **1.** A neutral color ranging between black and white. **2.** An object or animal of this color. [< OE *græg.* See gher-⁴.] —**gray′ish** *adj.*

gray matter. The brownish-gray nerve tissue of the brain and spinal cord.

graze¹ (grāz) *v.* **grazed, grazing. 1.** To feed on growing grass and herbage. **2.** To put (livestock) out to graze. [< OE *græs*, GRASS.]

graze² (grāz) *v.* **grazed, grazing.** To touch or scrape lightly in passing. —**graz′ing·ly** *adv.*

grease (grēs) *n.* **1.** Melted animal fat. **2.** Any thick oil or viscous lubricant. —*v.* **greased, greasing.** To coat, smear, lubricate, or soil with grease. [< L *crassus*, fat.]

grease paint. Theatrical make-up.

greas·y (grē′sē, -zē) *adj.* **-ier, -iest. 1.** Coated or soiled with grease. **2.** Containing grease; oily.

great (grāt) *adj.* **1.** Extremely large; bulky; big. **2.** Remarkable; outstanding: *a great work of art.* **3.** Eminent; distinguished: *a great leader.* **4.** *Informal.* First-rate; very good: *a great book.* **5.** Being one generation removed from the relative specified: *a great-grandfather.* —*adv. Informal.* Very well. [< OE *grēat*, thick, coarse. See ghreu-.] —**great′ness.** *n.*

Great Bear. Ursa Major.

Great Brit·ain (brĭt′n). An island off the W coast of Europe, comprising England, Scotland, and Wales.

great circle. A circle that is the intersection of the surface of a sphere with a plane passing through the center of the sphere.

Great Dane. A large, powerful dog with a smooth, short coat.

Greater An·til·les (ăn-tĭl′ēz). An island group of the West Indies, including Cuba, Jamaica, Hispaniola, and Puerto Rico.

great-grand·child (grāt′grănd′chīld′) *n.* Any of the children of a grandchild.

great-grand·par·ent (grāt′grănd′pâr′ənt) *n.* Either of the parents of any grandparent.

great-heart·ed (grāt′här′tĭd) *adj.* **1.** Courageous in spirit; stouthearted. **2.** Unselfish; magnanimous.

Great Lakes. The largest group of freshwater lakes in the world, in C North America.

great·ly (grāt′lē) *adv.* To a great degree.

Great Salt Lake. A highly saline lake in N Utah.

Great Smoky Mountains. A range of the S Appalachians.

grebe (grēb) *n.* A diving bird with lobed, fleshy membranes along each toe. [F *grèbe.*]

Gre·cian (grē′shən) *adj.* Greek. —*n.* A native of Greece.

Gre·co-Ro·man (grē′kō-rō′mən, grĕk′ō-) *adj.* Of or pertaining to both Greece and Rome.

Greece (grēs). A nation of SE Europe. Pop. 8,550,000. Cap. Athens.

greed (grēd) *n.* A rapacious desire for more than one needs or deserves; avarice.

greed·y (grē′dē) *adj.* **-ier, -iest.** Excessively eager to acquire; covetous; avaricious. [< OE *grædig.*] —**greed′i·ly** *adv.* —**greed′i·ness** *n.*

Greek (grēk) *n.* **1.** The language of the Hellenes, constituting the Hellenic group of Indo-European. (In the etymologies of this Dictionary, *Greek* is used to mean **Ancient Greek.**) **2.** An indigenous inhabitant of Greece. —*adj.* Of or pertaining to Greece, the Hellenes, their language, or their culture.

Greek Church. A branch of the Eastern Orthodox Church that is the national church of Greece.

green (grēn) *n.* **1.** Any of a group of colors whose hue is that of the emerald or somewhat less yellow than that of growing grass. **2.** Leafy plants or plant parts used as food or for decoration. **3.** A grassy lawn or plot: *a putting green.* —*adj.* **1.** Of the color green. **2.** Abounding in green growth or foliage. **3.** Not ripe; immature. **4.** Lacking experience. —*v.* To make or become green. [< OE *grēne.* See ghrē-.] —**green′ish** *adj.* —**green′ness** *n.*

green·back (grēn′băk′) *n.* Any official note of U.S. currency.

green·er·y (grē′nə-rē) *n.* Green plants or foliage.

green-eyed (grēn′īd′) *adj.* **1.** Having green eyes. **2.** Jealous; envious.

green·horn (grēn′hôrn′) *n.* An inexperienced or immature person. [Orig, a young animal with immature horns.]

green·house (grēn′hous′) *n.* A usually glass-enclosed structure in which plants requiring controlled temperature are grown.

Green·land (grēn′lənd, -lănd′). An island in the N Atlantic and Arctic, constituting an

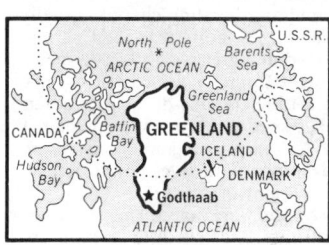

Greenland

Greece

integral part of Denmark. Pop. 36,000. Cap. Godthaab.

Greens·bo·ro (grĕnz'bûr'ō). A city of north-central North Carolina. Pop. 120,000.

green·sward (grēn'swôrd') *n.* Turf on which the grass is green.

green thumb. A knack for making plants thrive.

green turtle. A large marine turtle having edible flesh.

Green·wich time (grĭn'ĭj, -ĭch, grĕn'-). Mean solar time for the meridian at Greenwich, England, used as a basis for calculating time throughout most of the world; Greenwich mean time.

green·wood (grēn'wŏŏd') *n.* A leafy wood or forest.

greet (grēt) *v.* 1. To address in a friendly way; welcome. 2. To receive: *greet a joke with laughter.* 3. To present itself to: *A din greeted our ears.* [< OE *grētan.* See gher-³.]

greet·ing (grē'tĭng) *n.* A gesture or word of welcome or salutation.

gre·gar·i·ous (grĭ-gâr'ē-əs) *adj.* 1. Tending to live or move in herds. 2. Seeking and enjoying the company of others; sociable. [< L *grex,* herd, flock.] —**gre·gar'i·ous·ly** *adv.*

Gre·go·ri·an calendar (grĭ-gôr'ē-ən, grĭ-gōr'-). The calendar now in use throughout most of the world, introduced by Pope Gregory XIII in 1582.

gre·nade (grə-nād') *n.* A missile containing priming and bursting charges, usually thrown by hand. [< POMEGRANATE.]

gren·a·dier (grĕn'ə-dîr') *n.* A member of a regiment formerly armed with grenades.

gren·a·dine (grĕn'ə-dēn', grĕn'ə-dēn') *n.* A thick, sweet syrup made from pomegranates.

grew (grōō). *p.t.* of **grow.**

grew·some. Variant of **gruesome.**

grey. Variant of **gray.**

grey·hound (grā'hound') *n.* A large, slender, swift-running dog with a smooth coat and a narrow head. [< OE *grīghund.*]

grid (grĭd) *n.* 1. A grating or gridiron. 2. A pattern of lines forming squares on a map, used as a reference for locating points. 3. a. A system of electric cables and power stations over a large area. b. A corrugated or per-forated conducting plate in a storage battery. c. A structure of fine wires located between the plate and filament in an electron tube. [Short for GRIDIRON.]

grid·dle (grĭd'l) *n.* A flat pan used for cooking by dry heat. [< L *crātis,* wickerwork.]

grid·dle·cake (grĭd'l-kāk') *n.* A pancake.

grid·i·ron (grĭd'ī'ərn) *n.* 1. A framework of parallel metal bars used for broiling. 2. Any framework or network suggestive of a gridiron. 3. A football field. [Perh < GRIDDLE.]

grief (grēf) *n.* 1. Intense mental anguish; acute sorrow. 2. A source of grief.

griev·ance (grē'vəns) *n.* 1. A circumstance re-garded as just cause for protest. 2. A com-plaint based on such a circumstance.

grieve (grēv) *v.* grieved, grieving. 1. To cause grief to; distress. 2. To be sorrowful; lament; mourn. [< L *gravāre,* to oppress, weigh upon.]

griev·ous (grē'vəs) *adj.* 1. Causing or express-ing grief, pain, or anguish. 2. Serious or dire; grave. —**griev'ous·ly** *adv.*

grif·fin (grĭf'ən) *n.* Also **grif·fon, gry·phon.** A mythical beast with the head and wings of an eagle and the body of a lion. [< Gk *grups.*]

grill (grĭl) *n.* 1. A cooking utensil containing metal bars; gridiron. 2. Food cooked on a grill. 3. A grillroom. 4. Variant of **grille.** —*v.* 1. To broil on a grill. 2. *Informal.* To question relentlessly; cross-examine. [< L *crātis,* wick-erwork.]

grille (grĭl) *n.* Also **grill.** A metal grating used as a screen, as in a window or gate.

grill·room (grĭl'rōōm', -rŏŏm') *n.* A restaurant or room in a restaurant where grilled foods are served.

grim (grĭm) *adj.* grimmer, grimmest. 1. Unre-lenting; rigid; stern. 2. Uninviting in aspect; forbidding; 'terrible. 3. Ghastly; sinister. 4. Ferocious; savage. [< OE, fierce, severe. See ghrem-.] —**grim'ly** *adv.* —**grim'ness** *n.*

gri·mace (grĭ-mās', grĭm'ĭs) *n.* A contortion of the face expressing pain, contempt, or disgust. [< Frank **grima,* mask.] —**gri·mace'** *v.* (-maced, -macing).

grime (grīm) *n.* Black dirt or soot clinging to or ingrained in a surface. [< MDu *grime.*] —**grim'y** *adj.*

grin (grĭn) *v.* grinned, grinning. To smile broad-ly, showing the teeth. —*n.* The expression produced by grinning. [< OE *grennian,* to grimace.] —**grin'ner** *n.*

grind (grīnd) *v.* ground, grinding. 1. To crush into fine particles. 2. To shape, sharpen, or refine with friction: *grind a lens.* 3. To rub together; gnash: *grind the teeth.* 4. To move with noisy friction: *grind to a halt.* 5. To bear down on harshly; crush. 6. To operate or produce by turning a crank. 7. To produce mechanically or without inspiration (with *out*). 8. *Informal.* To devote oneself to study or work. —*n.* 1. The act of grinding. 2. A specif-ic degree of pulverization, as of coffee beans. 3. *Informal.* a. A laborious task, routine, or study. b. One who works or studies exces-sively. [< OE *grindan.* See ghren-.] —**grind'er** *n.* —**grind'ing·ly** *adv.*

grind·stone (grīnd'stōn') *n.* A revolving stone disk used for grinding, polishing, or sharpen-ing tools.

grip¹ (grĭp) *n.* 1. A tight hold; a firm grasp. 2. A manner of grasping and holding. 3. A part to be grasped and held; handle. 4. A suitcase or valise. —**come to grips.** 1. To fight in hand-to-hand combat. 2. To deal actively and conclusively, as with a problem. —*v.* gripped, gripping. 1. To grasp and maintain a tight hold on. 2. To hold the attention of. [< OE *gripa,* grasp, and *gripa,* handful. See ghreib-.] —**grip'ping·ly** *adv.*

grip². Variant of **grippe.**

gripe (grīp) *v.* griped, griping. 1. To cause or suffer sharp pain in the bowels. 2. *Informal.* To irritate; annoy. 3. *Informal.* To complain naggingly; grumble. —*n.* 1. *Informal.* A com-plaint. 2. **gripes.** Sharp, repeated pains in the bowels. [< OE *grīpan.* See ghreib-.]

grippe (grĭp) *n.* Also **grip.** Influenza. [< Frank *gripan.*] —**grip′py** *adj.*
gris•ly (grĭz′lē) *adj.* -lier, -liest. Horrifying; repugnant; gruesome. [< OE *grislīc.*]
grist (grĭst) *n.* Grain to be ground or already ground. [< OE *grist.* See **ghren-.**]
gris•tle (grĭs′əl) *n.* Cartilage, esp. in meat. [< OE < Gmc *gristil-.*] —**gris′tly** *adj.*
grit (grĭt) *n.* **1. a.** Minute rough granules, as of sand or stone. **b.** A material composed of such granules. **c.** The texture of such a material. **2.** *Informal.* Indomitable spirit; pluck. —*v.* **gritted, gritting.** To clamp (the teeth) together. [< OE *grēot.* See **ghreu-.**] —**grit′ty** *adj.*
grits (grĭts) *pl.n.* Coarsely ground grain, esp. corn. [< OE *grytt,* bran.]
griz•zle (grĭz′əl) *v.* -zled, -zling. To make or become gray. [< Frank *gris,* gray.]
griz•zly (grĭz′lē) *adj.* -zlier, -zliest. Grayish or flecked with gray. —*n., pl.* -zlies. Also **grizzly bear.** A large grayish bear of NW North America.
groan (grōn) *v.* To voice a deep, wordless, prolonged sound expressive of pain, grief, annoyance, or disapproval. —*n.* The sound made in groaning; a moan. [< OE *grānian.*]
groats (grōts) *pl.n.* Hulled, usually crushed grain, esp. oats. [< OE *grotan.*]
gro•cer (grō′sər) *n.* A storekeeper who sells foodstuffs and sundry household supplies. [< OF *grossier,* wholesale dealer.]
gro•cer•y (grō′sə-rē) *n., pl.* -ies. **1.** A store selling foodstuffs and household supplies. **2. groceries.** Commodities sold by a grocer.
grog (grŏg) *n.* Alcoholic liquor, esp. rum diluted with water.
grog•gy (grŏg′ē) *adj.* -gier, -giest. Unsteady and dazed; shaky. —**grog′gi•ly** *adv.*
groin (groin) *n.* **1.** The crease at the junction of the thigh with the trunk, together with the adjacent region. **2.** *Archit.* The curved edge at the junction of two intersecting vaults. [Perh < OE *grynde,* abyss, depression.]
grom•met (grŏm′ĭt) *n.* A reinforced eyelet in cloth, leather, etc., through which a fastener can be passed. [Obs F *grommette,* bridle ring.]
groom (grōōm) *n.* **1.** A man or boy employed to take care of horses. **2.** A bridegroom. —*v.* **1.** To make neat and trim. **2.** To clean and brush (an animal). **3.** To train, as for a specific position.
groove (grōōv) *n.* **1.** A long, narrow furrow or channel. **2.** A settled, humdrum routine; rut. —*v.* **grooved, grooving.** To cut a groove in. [< MDu *groeve,* ditch.]
grope (grōp) *v.* **groped, groping. 1.** To reach about uncertainly; feel one's way. **2.** To search blindly or uncertainly. [< OE *grāpian.* See **ghreib-.**] —**grop′ing•ly** *adv.*
gros•beak (grōs′bēk′) *n.* Any of several often colorful birds with a thick, rounded bill.
gross (grōs) *adj.* **1.** Exclusive of deductions: *gross profits.* **2.** Glaringly obvious; flagrant. **3.** Coarse; vulgar. **4.** Overweight; corpulent. —*n., pl.* **gross. 1.** Twelve dozen. **2.** A group of 12 dozen items. —*v.* To earn a total of before deductions. [< L *grossus,* thick.] —**gross′ly** *adv.* —**gross′ness** *n.*

gro•tesque (grō-tĕsk′) *adj.* **1.** Characterized by ludicrous or incongruous distortion. **2.** Extravagant; outlandish; bizarre. [< OIt *(pittura) grottesca,* "grottolike (painting)."] —**gro•tesque′ly** *adv.* —**gro•tesque′ness** *n.*
grot•to (grŏt′ō) *n., pl.* -toes or -tos. **1.** A small cave or cavern. **2.** An artificial cavelike structure or excavation. [< L *crypta,* vault, CRYPT.]
grouch (grouch) *v.* To grumble or sulk. —*n.* **1.** A grumbling or sulky mood. **2.** A habitually complaining or irritable person. [ME *grutchen,* to grudge.] —**grouch′y** *adj.*
ground¹ (ground) *n.* **1.** The solid surface of the earth. **2.** Soil; earth. **3.** Often **grounds.** An area of land designated for a particular purpose. **4. grounds.** The land surrounding a building. **5.** Often **grounds.** The foundation or basis for an argument, belief, or action. **6.** A background. **7. grounds.** The sediment at the bottom of a liquid, esp. coffee. **8. a.** The position or portion of an electric circuit that is at zero potential with respect to the earth. **b.** A conducting connection to such a position or to the earth. **c.** A large conducting body, such as the earth, used as a return for electric currents and as an arbitrary zero of potential. —*v.* **1.** To place or set on the ground. **2.** To provide a basis for; substantiate; justify. **3.** To instruct in fundamentals; school. **4.** To prevent (an aircraft, pilot, or crew) from flying. **5.** To connect (an electric circuit) to a ground. **6.** To run (a vessel) aground. [< OE *grund* < Gmc *grunduz.*]
ground² (ground). *p.t.* & *p.p.* of **grind.**
ground hog. A woodchuck.
ground•less (ground′lĭs) *adj.* Having no ground or foundation; unsubstantiated. —**ground′less•ly** *adv.* —**ground′less•ness** *n.*
ground water. Water beneath the earth's surface between saturated soil and rock that supplies wells and springs.
ground•work (ground′wûrk′) *n.* A foundation; basis; preliminary work.
group (grōōp) *n.* A number of individuals or things considered together because of certain similarities. —*v.* To place in or form a group or groups. [< It *gruppo,* "knot."]
group•er (grōō′pər) *n.* Any of various large, chiefly tropical marine fishes. [Port *garoupa.*]
grouse¹ (grous) *n., pl.* **grouse.** A plump, chicken-like bird with mottled brown or grayish plumage. [?]
grouse² (grous) *v.* **groused, grousing.** *Informal.* To complain; grumble. [?]
grove (grōv) *n.* A small group of trees lacking dense undergrowth. [< OE *grāf.*]
grov•el (grŭv′əl, grŏv′-) *v.* To humble oneself in a servile manner; cringe. [< ON *ā grūfu,* prone.] —**grov′el•er** *n.*
grow (grō) *v.* **grew, grown** (grōn), **growing. 1.** To increase in size by natural processes. **2.** To cultivate; raise: *grow tulips.* **3.** To develop and reach maturity. **4.** To be capable of growth; thrive; flourish. **5.** To become: *grow angry; grow cold.* —**grow up. 1.** To reach maturity; become an adult. **2.** To come into being; develop. [< OE *grōwan.* See **ghrē-.**]
growl (groul) *n.* A low, guttural, menacing

sound, as of an angry dog. —v. To utter or express by such a sound. [Perh imit.]

grown (grōn) *adj.* Mature; adult.

grown-up (grōn'ŭp') *adj.* Characteristic of or suitable for an adult. —**grown'up'** *n.*

growth (grōth) *n.* **1. a.** The process of growing or developing. **b.** A stage in the process of growing. **2.** An increase, as in size or number. **3.** Something that has grown: *a new growth of grass.* **4.** An abnormal tissue formation.

grub (grŭb) *v.* **grubbed, grubbing. 1.** To clear of roots. **2.** To dig up by the roots. **3. a.** To search laboriously; rummage. **b.** To toil arduously; drudge: *grub for a living.* **4.** *Slang.* To obtain by importunity: *grub a cigarette.* —*n.* **1.** The thick, wormlike larva of certain insects. **2.** *Slang.* Food. [< OE *grybban. See ghrebh-.] —**grub'ber** *n.*

grub•by (grŭb'ē) *adj.* **-bier, -biest.** Dirty; unkempt. —**grub'bi•ness** *n.*

grub•stake (grŭb'stāk') *n.* Supplies or funds advanced to a mining prospector in return for a promised share of the profits.

grudge (grŭj) *v.* **grudged, grudging.** To be reluctant to give or admit. —*n.* A deep-seated feeling of resentment or rancor. [Prob < MHG *grunzen,* to grunt.] —**grudg'ing•ly** *adv.*

gru•el (grōō'əl) *n.* A thin, watery porridge. —*v.* To exhaust. [< OF *gru,* groats, oatmeal.] —**gru'el•ing** *adj.* —**gru'el•ing•ly** *adv.*

grue•some (grōō'səm) *adj.* Also **grew•some.** Causing horror and repugnance; frightful and shocking. [< obs *grue,* to shiver.] —**grue'-some•ly** *adv.* —**grue'some•ness** *n.*

gruff (grŭf) *adj.* **1.** Brusque and stern in speech or manner. **2.** Harsh; hoarse. [Du *grof.*] —**gruff'ly** *adv.* —**gruff'ness** *n.*

grum•ble (grŭm'bəl) *v.* **-bled, -bling.** To mumble in discontent. —*n.* A grumbling utterance. [< ME *grummen.*] —**grum'bler** *n.*

grump•y (grŭm'pē) *adj.* **-ier, -iest.** Fretful and peevish; irritable; cranky. [< dial *grump,* ill-tempered.] —**grump'i•ness** *n.*

grun•ion (grŭn'yən) *n.* A small fish of California coastal waters that spawns along beaches during high tides at the time of the full moon. [Perh < L *grunnire,* to grunt.]

grunt (grŭnt) *v.* To utter (with) a low, guttural sound, as does a hog. —*n.* A low, guttural sound. [< OE *grunnettan.*]

gry•phon. Variant of **griffin.**

gtd. guaranteed.

GU genitourinary.

Gua•da•la•ja•ra (gwŏd'l-ə-här'ə). A city of west-central Mexico. Pop. 978,000.

Guam (gwŏm). An island of the U.S. in the W Pacific. Pop. 72,000.

gua•nine (gwä'nēn') *n.* A purine, $C_5H_5N_5O$, that is a constituent of both ribonucleic and deoxyribonucleic acids. [< GUANO.]

gua•no (gwä'nō) *n.* A substance composed chiefly of the dung of sea birds or bats, used as fertilizer. [< Quechua *huanu,* dung.]

guar. guaranteed.

gua•ra•ni (gwär'ə-nē') *n., pl.* **-ni** or **-nis.** The basic monetary unit of Paraguay.

Gua•ra•ni (gwär'ə-nē') *n.* **1.** A group of South American Indians of Paraguay, Bolivia, and S

Brazil. **2.** The Tupi-Guarani language of these people.

guar•an•tee (găr'ən-tē') *n.* **1.** A formal assurance that something is as represented or that a specified act will be performed. **2.** A guaranty. **3.** A guarantor. —*v.* **-teed, -teeing.** **1.** To assume responsibility for the debt or default of. **2.** To undertake to accomplish something. **3.** To furnish security for. [Perh < Frank *wār-jan,* to vouch for the truth of.]

guar•an•tor (găr'ən-tər, -tôr') *n.* One that gives a guarantee or guaranty.

guar•an•ty (găr'ən-tē) *n., pl.* **-ties. 1.** An undertaking to answer for another's debts or obligations in the event of default. **2. a.** Anything held as security for something. **b.** The act of providing such security. **3.** A guarantor.

guard (gärd) *v.* **1.** To protect from harm; watch over. **2.** To watch over to prevent escape. **3.** To keep watch at (a door or gate). **4.** To take precautions: *guard against infection.* —*n.* **1.** One that guards. **2.** A body of persons who serve on ceremonial occasions: *an honor guard.* **3.** Watchful care: *under close guard.* **4.** A defensive posture or stance. **5.** *Football.* One of the two players on either side of the center. **6.** *Basketball.* Either of the two defensive players. **7.** Any device that prevents injury, damage, or loss. [< OF *garder, guarder.*] —**guard'er** *n.*

guard•ed (gär'dĭd) *adj.* **1.** Kept safe; protected. **2.** Cautious; restrained: *guarded words.* —**guard'ed•ly** *adv.*

guard•house (gärd'hous') *n.* **1.** A building occupied by a guard. **2.** A military detention house.

guard•i•an (gär'dē-ən) *n.* **1.** One who guards; a custodian. **2.** A person legally responsible for the care of one incompetent to manage his own affairs, as a child during its minority. —**guard'i•an•ship'** *n.*

guards•man (gärdz'mən) *n.* A member of a regiment of guards.

Gua•te•ma•la (gwä'tə-mä'lə). **1.** A republic in Central America. Pop. 4,343,000. **2.** Also **Guatemala City.** The capital of this republic. Pop. 573,000. —**Gua'te•ma'lan** *adj. & n.*

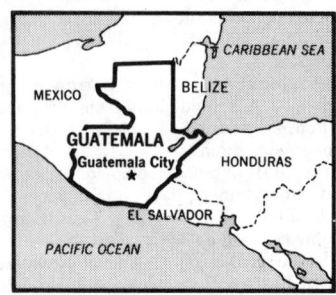

Guatemala

gua•va (gwä'və) *n.* The yellow-skinned fruit of a tropical American tree, used for jellies and preserves. [Span.]

ă pat/ā ate/âr care/ä bar/b **bib**/ch **chew**/d **deed**/ĕ pet/ē be/f fit/g gag/h hat/hw what/
ĭ pit/ī pie/îr pier/j **judge**/k **kick**/l lid, fatal/m **mum**/n no, sudden/ng sing/ŏ pot/ō go/

gu·ber·na·to·ri·al (g/y/ōō′bər-nə-tôr′ē-əl, -tôr′ē-əl) *adj.* Of or relating to a governor.

guer·don (gûrd′n) *n. Poetic.* A reward; requital. [< OF.]

guer·ril·la, gue·ril·la (gə-rĭl′ə) *n.* A member of an irregular military force that seeks to immobilize and isolate the superior forces of an occupying enemy. —*adj.* Of or by guerrillas: *guerrilla warfare.* [< Span *guerra,* war.]

guess (gĕs) *v.* **1.** To predict (a result or event) or assume (a fact) without sufficient information. **2.** To estimate or judge correctly. **3.** To suppose. —*n.* **1.** An instance of guessing. **2.** A conjecture arrived at by guessing. [Prob < Scand.] —**guess′er** *n.*

guess·work (gĕs′wûrk′) *n.* **1.** The process of making guesses. **2.** An instance of inference by guessing.

guest (gĕst) *n.* **1.** A recipient of hospitality at the home or table of another. **2.** A patron of a restaurant, hotel, etc. [< ON *gestr.*]

guf·faw (gə-fô′) *n.* A hearty or coarse burst of laughter. [Imit.] —**guf·faw′** *v.*

Gui·an·a (gē-ăn′ə, -ä′nə). A region of NE South America, including SE Venezuela, part of N Brazil, and French Guiana, Surinam, and Guyana.

gui·dance (gīd′əns) *n.* **1.** An act or instance of guiding. **2.** Counseling, as on vocational, educational, or marital problems.

guide (gīd) *n.* **1.** One who shows the way by leading or directing, esp. a person employed to guide a tour, group, etc. **2.** Any sign or mark that serves to direct. **3.** An example or model to be followed. **4.** A book or manual that serves to instruct or direct. **5.** Any device that acts as an indicator or regulates the motion of something. —*v.* **guided, guiding. 1.** To show the way to; conduct; lead; direct. **2.** To direct the course of; steer. **3.** To manage the affairs of; govern. [< OProv *guidar,* to show the way.] —**guid′er** *n.*

guide·book (gīd′bŏŏk′) *n.* A handbook of information for travelers.

guide·line (gīd′līn′) *n.* **1.** A mark used as a guide in lettering or drawing. **2.** A statement of general policy.

guided missile. Any missile capable of being guided while in flight.

guide·post (gīd′pōst′) *n.* A post with a directional sign.

gui·don (gī′dŏn′, gīd′n) *n.* A small flag carried as a standard by a military unit. [< It *guida,* guide.]

guild (gĭld) *n.* An association of persons of the same trade for the furtherance of some purpose, esp. in medieval times, a society of merchants or artisans. [< ON *gildi,* payment, fraternity.]

guil·der (gĭl′dər) *n.* The basic monetary unit of the Netherlands, Surinam, and the Netherlands Antilles.

guile (gīl) *n.* Insidious, treacherous cunning; craftiness. [< OF.] —**guile′ful** *adj.*

guile·less (gīl′lĭs) *adj.* Free of guile; simple; artless. —**guile′less·ness** *n.*

guil·lo·tine (gĭl′ə-tēn′, gē′ə-) *n.* A machine with a heavy blade that falls between upright

guides to behead a condemned prisoner. —*v.* (gĭl′ə-tēn′) **-tined, -tining.** To behead with a guillotine. [< J. *Guillotin* (1738–1814), French doctor.]

guilt (gĭlt) *n.* **1.** The fact of being responsible for an offense or wrongdoing. **2.** Remorseful awareness of having done something wrong. [< OE *gylt.*] —**guilt′less** *adj.*

guilt·y (gĭl′tē) *adj.* **-ier, -iest. 1.** Responsible for some reprehensible act. **2.** At fault; delinquent; culpable. **3.** Prompted by or showing a sense of guilt: *a guilty conscience.* —**guilt′i·ly** *adv.* —**guilt′i·ness** *n.*

guin·ea (gĭn′ē) *n. Brit.* The sum of one pound and one shilling.

Guin·ea, Republic of (gĭn′ē). A country of W Africa. Pop. 3,420,000. Cap. Conakry.

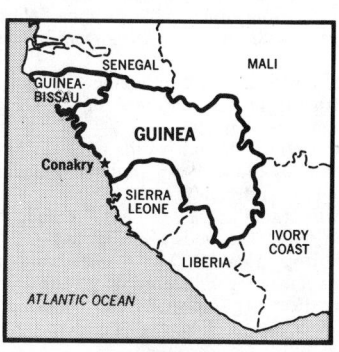

Guinea
Guinea-Bissau

Guin·ea-Bis·sau (gĭn′ē-bĭ-sou′). A country of W Africa. Pop. 535,000. Cap. Bissau.

guinea fowl. Also **guinea hen.** A domesticated pheasantlike bird having blackish plumage marked with many small white spots.

guinea pig. 1. A variously colored, seemingly tailless rodent often kept as a pet or used for biological experiments. **2.** A subject for experimentation.

guise (gīz) *n.* **1.** Outward appearance; aspect. **2.** False appearance; pretense. **3.** Mode of dress; garb. [< OF, manner.]

gui·tar (gĭ-tär′) *n.* A stringed musical instrument, generally shaped like a violin, played by strumming or plucking. [< Ar *qitār.*] —**gui·tar′ist** *n.*

gulch (gŭlch) *n.* A small, shallow canyon with smoothly inclined slopes and steep sides; a small ravine. [?]

gul·den (gŏŏl′dən) *n.* A guilder.

gulf (gŭlf) *n.* **1.** A large area of a sea or ocean partially enclosed by land. **2.** A deep, wide chasm; abyss. **3.** A separating distance; wide gap. —*v.* To swallow; engulf. [< Gk *kolphos,* bosom, fold, bay.]

gull¹ (gŭl) *n.* Any of various chiefly coastal water birds with long wings, webbed feet, and usually gray and white plumage. [ME.]

gull² (gŭl) *n.* A gullible person; dupe. —*v.* To deceive; dupe.

ô paw, for/oi boy/ou out/ŏŏ took/ōō coo/p pop/r run/s sauce/sh shy/t to/th thin/*th* the/
ŭ cut/ûr fur/v van/w wag/y yes/z size/zh vision/ə ago, item, edible, gallop, circus/

gul·let (gŭl′ĭt) *n.* 1. The esophagus. 2. The throat. [< L *gula*, throat.]

gul·li·ble (gŭl′ə-bəl) *adj.* Easily deceived or duped; credulous. —**gul′li·bil′i·ty** *n.*

Gul·li·ver (gŭl′ə-vər), **Lemuel.** Hero of Swift's *Gulliver's Travels* (1726).

gul·ly (gŭl′ē) *n., pl.* **-lies.** A deep channel cut in the earth by running water. [< GULLET.]

gulp (gŭlp) *v.* 1. To choke or gasp, as in nervousness. 2. To swallow in large amounts. —*n.* 1. The act of gulping. 2. A large mouthful. 3. A convulsive attempt to swallow. [< MDu *gulpen*.] —**gulp′er** *n.*

gum¹ (gŭm) *n.* 1. Any of various viscous plant substances that dry into water-soluble, noncrystalline, brittle solids. 2. Also **gum tree.** Any of various trees yielding gum. 3. Chewing gum. —*v.* **gummed, gumming.** 1. To cover, seal, or fill with gum. 2. To become sticky or clogged with gum. [< Gk *kommi.*] —**gum′my** *adj.*

gum² (gŭm) *n.* The firm connective tissue that surrounds the bases of the teeth. [< OE *gōma*, palate, jaw. See **ghēu-**.]

gum arabic. A gum exuded by various African trees and used esp. in the manufacture of mucilage and candies.

gum·bo (gŭm′bō) *n., pl.* **-bos.** A soup thickened with okra pods. [< Bantu.]

gum·drop (gŭm′drŏp′) *n.* A small candy made of sweetened gum arabic or gelatin.

gump·tion (gŭmp′shən) *n. Informal.* 1. Shrewdness. 2. Boldness of enterprise; initiative. [?]

gum·shoe (gŭm′shoō′) *n.* 1. A rubber overshoe. 2. *Slang.* A detective.

gun (gŭn) *n.* 1. A weapon consisting essentially of a metal tube from which a projectile is fired. 2. A portable firearm. 3. A device that shoots a projectile. —*v.* **gunned, gunning.** 1. To shoot (with *down*). 2. To open the throttle of: *gun an engine.* —**gun for.** To seek to catch or obtain. [ME *gunne.*] —**gun′ner** *n.*

gun·boat (gŭn′bōt′) *n.* A small armed vessel.

gun·cot·ton (gŭn′kŏt′n) *n.* Nitrocellulose.

gun·fire (gŭn′fīr′) *n.* The firing of guns.

gun·lock (gŭn′lŏk′) *n.* A device for igniting the charge of a firearm.

gun·man (gŭn′mən) *n.* A professional killer.

gun·nel. Variant of **gunwale.**

gun·ner·y (gŭn′ə-rē) *n.* The science of constructing and operating guns.

gun·ny (gŭn′ē) *n.* 1. A coarse fabric made of jute or hemp. 2. Burlap. [< Sk *goṇi*, sack.]

gunny sack. A sack made of burlap or gunny.

gun·pow·der (gŭn′pou′dər) *n.* An explosive powder used to propel projectiles from guns.

gun·shot (gŭn′shŏt′) *n.* 1. Shot fired from a gun. 2. The range of a gun: *within gunshot.*

gun-shy (gŭn′shī′) *adj.* Afraid of gunfire.

gun·smith (gŭn′smĭth′) *n.* One who makes or repairs firearms.

gun·wale (gŭn′əl) *n.* Also **gun·nel.** The upper edge of a ship's side.

gup·py (gŭp′ē) *n., pl.* **-pies.** A small, brightly colored tropical freshwater fish. [< R.J.L. *Guppy* of Trinidad.]

gur·gle (gûr′gəl) *v.* **-gled, -gling.** 1. To flow in a broken, uneven current making intermittent low sounds. 2. To make such sounds. [< L *gurguliō*, gullet.] —**gur′gle** *n.*

gu·ru (goō-roō′, goō′roō′) *n.* Also **Gu·ru.** *Hinduism.* A spiritual teacher.

gush (gŭsh) *v.* 1. To emit or flow forth suddenly and violently. 2. To make an effusive display of sentiment or enthusiasm. —*n.* A sudden, violent, or copious outflow. [Perh < Scand.]

gush·er (gŭsh′ər) *n.* 1. One that gushes. 2. A gas or oil well with an abundant flow.

gush·y (gŭsh′ē) *adj.* **-ier, -iest.** Characterized by excessive sentiment. —**gush′i·ly** *adv.*

gus·set (gŭs′ĭt) *n.* A triangular insert for strengthening or enlarging a garment. [< OF *gousset*, armpit, piece of armor.]

gust (gŭst) *n.* 1. A violent, abrupt rush of wind. 2. An abrupt outburst of emotion. [< ON *gustr.*] —**gust′i·ly** *adv.* —**gust′y** *adj.*

gus·ta·to·ry (gŭs′tə-tôr′ē, -tōr′ē) *adj.* Pertaining to the sense of taste.

gus·to (gŭs′tō) *n.* Vigorous enjoyment; relish; zest. [< L *gustus*, taste.]

gut (gŭt) *n.* 1. The alimentary canal or a portion thereof, esp. the intestine or stomach. 2. **guts.** The bowels; entrails; viscera. 3. **guts.** The essential contents of something. 4. **guts.** *Slang.* Courage; fortitude. —*v.* **gutted, gutting.** 1. To eviscerate; disembowel. 2. To destroy the interior of: *gut a house.* [< OE *guttas.*]

Gu·ten·berg (goōt′n-bûrg′), **Johann.** 1400?–1468? German inventor of movable type.

Johann Gutenberg

gut·ta-per·cha (gŭt′ə-pûr′chə) *n.* A rubbery substance derived from the latex of certain tropical trees, used as electrical insulation and for waterproofing. [Malay *gĕtah percha.*]

gut·ter (gŭt′ər) *n.* A channel for draining off

ă pat/ā ate/âr care/ä bar/b bib/ch chew/d deed/ĕ pet/ē be/f fit/g gag/h hat/hw what/
ĭ pit/ī pie/îr pier/j judge/k kick/l lid, fatal/m mum/n no, sudden/ng sing/ŏ pot/ō go/

water, as at the edge of a street or under the border of a roof. [< L *gutta*, drop.]

gut·ter·snipe (gŭt'ər-snīp') *n.* A street urchin.

gut·tur·al (gŭt'ər-əl) *adj.* **1.** Of or pertaining to the throat. **2.** Produced in the throat. [< L *guttur*, throat.] —**gut'tur·al·ly** *adv.*

guy¹ (gī) *n.* A rope, cord, or cable used to steady or guide something. —*v.* To steady or guide with a guy. [Prob < LG.]

guy² (gī) *n. Informal.* A man; fellow.

Guy·a·na (gī-än'ə). A republic of N South America. Pop. 628,000. Cap. Georgetown.

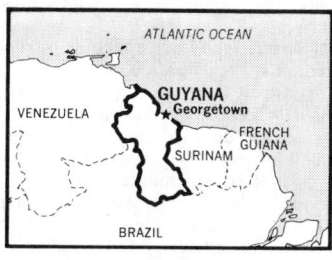

Guyana

guz·zle (gŭz'əl) *v.* **-zled, -zling.** To drink greedily or inordinately. [Poss < OF *gosier*, throat.]

gym (jĭm) *n. Informal.* A gymnasium.

gym·na·si·um. *n.* **1.** (jĭm-nā'zē-əm). *pl.* **-ums** or **-sia** (-zē-ə). A room or building equipped for gymnastics and sports. **2.** (gĭm-nä'zē-ōōm'). *pl.* **-ums** or **-sia.** An academic high school in various C European countries. [< Gk *gumnazein*, "to train naked," practice gymnastics.]

gym·nas·tics (jĭm-năs'tĭks) *pl.n.* Body-building exercises, esp. those performed with special apparatus in a gymnasium. —**gym'nast'** *n.* —**gym·nas'tic** *adj.* —**gym·nas'ti·cal·ly** *adv.*

gyn. gynecology.

gy·ne·col·o·gy (gī'nə-kŏl'ə-jē, jī'-, jĭn'ə-) *n.* The medical science of disease, reproductive physiology, and endocrinology in females. [Gk *gunē*, woman + -LOGY.] —**gy'ne·co·log'i·cal** (-kə-lŏj'ĭ-kəl) *adj.* —**gy'ne·col'o·gist** *n.*

gyp (jĭp) *v.* **gypped, gypping.** Also **gip.** *Informal.* To swindle, cheat, or defraud. —*n.* **1.** A swindle. **2.** A swindler. [Prob short for GYP-SY.] —**gyp'per** *n.*

gyp·sum (jĭp'səm) *n.* A white mineral, $CaSO_4 \cdot 2H_2O$, used in the manufacture of plaster of Paris, plaster, and some cements. [< Gk *gupsos*.]

Gyp·sy (jĭp'sē) *n., pl.* **-sies.** Also **Gip·sy. 1.** One of a nomadic people originally migrating to Europe from the border region between Iran and India in the 14th or 15th century. **2.** The Indic language spoken by this people; Romany. **3. gypsy.** One that resembles a Gypsy in appearance or behavior.

gy·rate (jī'rāt') *v.* **-rated, -rating. 1.** To revolve on or around a center or axis. **2.** To circle or spiral. [< L *gȳrus*, circle.] —**gy·ra'tion** *n.* —**gy'ra·tor** *n.*

gyr·fal·con (jûr'făl'kən, -fôl'kən, -fô'kən) *n.* A large falcon of northern regions, with white or grayish plumage. [< ON *geirfalki*.]

gy·ro (jī'rō) *n., pl.* **-ros.** A gyroscope.

gyro-. *comb. form.* **1.** Gyrating. **2.** Spiral. [< Gk *guros*, circle.]

gy·ro·com·pass (jī'rō-kŭm'pəs, -kŏm'pəs) *n.* A navigational device in which a north-south orientation of a gyroscope's spin axis is maintained.

gy·ro·scope (jī'rə-skōp') *n.* A spinning mass, typically a disk or wheel, suspended so that its spin axis maintains a fixed angular orientation when not subjected to external torques. —**gy'ro·scop'ic** (-skŏp'ĭk) *adj.* —**gy'ro·scop'i·cal·ly** *adv.*

gyve (jīv) *n.* Often **gyves.** A shackle or fetter, esp. for the leg. —*v.* **gyved, gyving.** To shackle or fetter. [ME.]

Hh

h, H (āch) *n.* **1.** The 8th letter of the English alphabet. **2.** The 8th in a series. **3. H** Anything shaped like the letter **H.**

h 1. hecto-. **2.** hour.

H 1. henry. **2.** hydrogen.

h. height.

H. height.

ha (hä) *interj.* Also **hah.** Expressive of surprise, wonder, triumph, etc.

ha hectare.

Hab. Habakkuk (Old Testament).

ha·be·as cor·pus (hā'bē-əs kôr'pəs). A writ issued to bring a party before a court to prevent unlawful restraint. [< ML *habeas corpus*, "you shall have the body."]

hab·er·dash·er (hăb'ər-dăsh'ər) *n.* A dealer in men's furnishings, as hats, shirts, etc. [< NF *hapertas*, fabric, cloth.]

hab·er·dash·er·y (hăb'ər-dăsh'ə-rē) *n., pl.* **-ies.** A haberdasher's shop.

hab·it (hăb'ĭt) *n.* **1.** A pattern of behavior acquired by frequent repetition. **2.** Customary manner or practice. **3.** An addiction. **4.** A distinctive dress or costume. [< L *habitus*, pp of *habēre*, to hold, have.]

hab·it·a·ble (hăb'ə-tə-bəl) *adj.* Suitable to live

ô paw, for/oi boy/ou out/ōō took/ōō coo/p pop/r run/s sauce/sh shy/t to/th thin/*th* the/
ŭ cut/ûr fur/v van/w wag/y yes/z size/zh vision/ə ago, item, edible, gallop, circus/

in. [< L habitāre, to inhabit.] —hab'i·ta·bil'i·ty, hab'i·ta·ble·ness n.

hab·i·tat (hăb'ə-tăt') n. 1. The area or type of environment in which a plant or animal normally lives or occurs. 2. The place where a person or thing is most likely to be found. [< L habitāre, to inhabit.]

hab·i·ta·tion (hăb'ə-tā'shən) n. 1. The act of inhabiting. 2. a. Natural environment or locality. b. Place of abode.

hab·it-form·ing (hăb'ĭt-fôr'mĭng) adj. Leading to physiological addiction.

ha·bit·u·al (hə-bĭch'ōō-əl) adj. 1. Established by or acting according to habit. 2. Inveterate. 3. Customary; usual. —ha·bit'u·al·ly adv.

ha·bit·u·ate (hə-bĭch'ōō-āt') v. -ated, -ating. To accustom by repetition or exposure. —ha·bit'u·a'tion n.

hab·i·tude (hăb'ə-t/y/ōōd') n. A customary behavior or manner.

ha·bit·u·é (hə-bĭch'ōō-ā', hə-bĭch'ōō-ā') n. One who frequents a certain place.

ha·ci·en·da (hä'sē-ĕn'də) n. 1. In Spanish-speaking countries, a large estate. 2. The main house of such an estate. [Span, domestic work, landed property.]

hack¹ (hăk) v. 1. To cut with irregular and heavy blows; chop roughly. 2. To cough in short, dry-throated spasms. —n. 1. A notch made by hacking. 2. A tool used for hacking. 3. A rough, dry cough. [< OE (tō)haccian, to cut to pieces.]

hack² (hăk) n. 1. A horse for hire. 2. A worn-out horse. 3. A vehicle for hire. 4. One hired to do routine writing. 5. A taxicab. —v. To employ or work as a hack. —adj. 1. For or by a hack. 2. Banal; trite. [Short for HACKNEY.]

hack·le (hăk'əl) n. 1. One of the long, slender feathers on the neck of a bird, esp. a rooster. 2. hackles. Hairs at the back of the neck, as on a dog, that can rise with anger, fear, etc. [ME hakell.]

hack·ney (hăk'nē) n., pl. -neys. 1. A horse for riding or driving. 2. A coach or carriage for hire. —v. To cause to become banal and trite. [< Hackney, England.]

hack·neyed (hăk'nēd) adj. Overused; trite; banal.

hack·saw (hăk'sô') n. A saw with a tough, fine-toothed blade stretched taut in a frame, used for cutting metal.

had (hăd). p.t. & p.p. of have.

had·dock (hăd'ək) n., pl. -dock or -docks. A food fish of Atlantic waters, related to and resembling the cod. [< OF hadot.]

Ha·des (hā'dēz) n. 1. The nether world of Greek mythology. 2. Often hades. Hell.

had·n't (hăd'ənt). Contraction of had not.

hadst (hădst). Archaic. p.t. & p.p. of have.

haf·ni·um (hăf'nē-əm) n. Symbol Hf A brilliant, silvery metallic element used in nuclear reactor control rods and in the manufacture of tungsten filaments. Atomic number 72, atomic weight 178.49. [< Hafnia, L name for Copenhagen.]

haft (hăft, häft) n. A handle or hilt, as of a sword or knife. [< OE hæft.]

hag (hăg) n. 1. An ugly old woman. 2. A witch; sorceress. [Prob < OE hægtesse, witch.]

hag·gard (hăg'ərd) adj. Appearing worn and exhausted; emaciated; gaunt. [OF hagard, untamed hawk.]

hag·gle (hăg'əl) v. -gled, -gling. To argue or dispute in an attempt to bargain. [< ON höggva, to cut.] —hag'gler n.

Hag·i·og·ra·pha (hăg'ē-ŏg'rə-fə, hā'jē-) n. The third of the three ancient Jewish divisions of the Old Testament, including those books not in the Torah or the Prophets.

hag·i·og·ra·phy (hăg'ē-ŏg'rə-fē, hā'jē-) n. Biography of saints. [Gk hagios, holy + -GRAPHY.]

Hague, The (hāg). The de facto capital of the Netherlands. Pop. 602,000.

hah. Variant of ha.

hail¹ (hāl) n. 1. a. Precipitation in the form of pellets of ice and hard snow. b. A hailstone. 2. Something with the effect of a shower of hail. —v. 1. To precipitate hail. 2. To pour down or forth. [< OE hagol. See kaghlo-.]

hail² (hāl) v. 1. a. To salute or greet. b. To acclaim enthusiastically. 2. To signal or call out to. —n. 1. A greeting or expression of acclaim. 2. Hailing distance. —interj. Expressive of greeting or tribute. [< ON heill, whole, healthy.]

Hai·le Se·las·sie (hī'lē sə-lăs'ē, sə-lä'sē). 1891-1975. Emperor of Ethiopia (1930-74); deposed.

hail·stone (hāl'stōn') n. A hard pellet of snow and ice.

hair (hâr) n. 1. A fine, threadlike outgrowth, esp. from the skin of a mammal. 2. A covering of such outgrowth, as on the human head. 3. A minute distance or narrow margin. —adj. 1. Made of or with hair. 2. For the hair: a hair dryer. [< OE hēr < Gmc *hēram.] —haired (hârd) adj.

hair·breadth (hâr'brĕdth') adj. Extremely close. —n. Variant of hairsbreadth.

hair·brush (hâr'brŭsh') n. A brush for grooming the hair.

hair·cloth (hâr'klôth', -klŏth') n. A stiff, wiry fabric usually having a cotton or linen warp with a horsehair filler.

hair·cut (hâr'kŭt') n. 1. A cutting of the hair. 2. The style in which hair is cut.

hair·do (hâr'dōō') n., pl. -dos. A hair style; coiffure.

hair·dress·er (hâr'drĕs'ər) n. A person who cuts or arranges women's hair.

hair·line (hâr'līn') n. 1. The outline of the growth of hair on the head. 2. A very slender line.

hair·pin (hâr'pĭn') n. A thin U-shaped pin used to keep the hair in place. —adj. Doubled back in a deep U: a hairpin curve.

hair-rais·ing (hâr'rā'zĭng) adj. Horrifying.

hairs·breadth, hair's-breadth (hârz'brĕdth') n. Also hair·breadth (hâr'brĕdth'). A small space or distance; narrow margin.

hair·split·ting (hâr'splĭt'ĭng) n. The making of unreasonably fine distinctions; quibbling. —adj. Concerned with petty distinctions. —hair'split'ter n.

ă pat/ā ate/âr care/ä bar/b bib/ch chew/d deed/ĕ pet/ē be/f fit/g gag/h hat/hw what/ ĭ pit/ī pie/îr pier/j judge/k kick/l lid, fatal/m mum/n no, sudden/ng sing/ŏ pot/ō go/

hair•spring (hâr'sprĭng') *n.* A fine coiled spring that regulates the movement of the balance wheel in a watch or clock.
hair•y (hâr'ē) *adj.* -ier, -iest. 1. Covered with hair. 2. Of or like hair. —**hair'i•ness** *n.*
Hai•ti (hā'tē). A republic of the West Indies. Pop. 4,660,000. Cap. Port-au-Prince. —**Hai'ti•an** *adj. & n.*

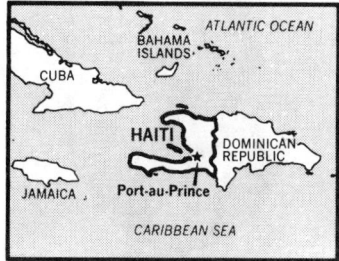

Haiti

hake (hāk) *n., pl.* **hake** or **hakes.** A marine food fish related to and resembling the cod. [ME.]
hal•berd (hăl'bərd) *n.* A weapon of the 15th and 16th centuries having an axlike blade and a steel spike mounted on the end of a long shaft. [< MHG *helmbarde,* "handle ax."]
hal•cy•on (hăl'sē-ən) *adj.* Calm and peaceful; tranquil. [< Gk *halkuōn,* a mythical bird.]
hale¹ (hāl) *adj.* **haler, halest.** Sound in health; robust. [< OE *hāl.* See **kailo-.**]
hale² (hāl) *v.* **haled, haling.** To compel to go; force. [< MLG *halen,* to pull.]
Hale (hāl), **Nathan.** 1755–1776. American army officer; hanged by the British for spying.
half (hăf, häf) *n., pl.* **halves** (hăvz, hävz). 1. One of two equal parts. 2. A part of something approximately equal to the remainder. —*adj.* 1. Being a half. 2. Being approximately a half. 3. Partial; incomplete. —*adv.* 1. To the extent of exactly or nearly 50%. 2. Not completely; partly. —**go halves.** To share equally. [< OE *healf.*]
half•back (hăf'băk', häf'-) *n. Football.* One of the two players positioned near the flanks behind the line of scrimmage.
half-breed (hăf'brēd', häf'-) *n.* A person having parents of different ethnic types.
half brother. A brother related through one parent only.
half-caste (hăf'kăst', häf'käst') *n.* A person of mixed racial descent.
half•heart•ed (hăf'här'tĭd, häf'-) *adj.* Lacking interest or enthusiasm; uninspired. —**half'-heart'ed•ly** *adv.*
half-life (hăf'līf', häf'-) *n.* The time required for half the nuclei in a sample of a specific isotopic species to undergo **radioactive decay.**
half-line (hăf'līn', häf'-) *n.* A straight line extending in just one direction from a given point.
half-mast (hăf'măst', häf'mäst') *n.* The position about halfway up a mast or pole at which

a flag is flown as a sign of mourning or distress.
half-moon (hăf'mo͞on', häf'-) *n.* 1. The moon when only half its disk is illuminated. 2. Something shaped like a crescent. —**half'moon'** *adj.*
half-plane (hăf'plān', häf'-) *n.* The part of a plane lying to one side of a line in the plane.
half sister. A sister related through one parent only.
half step. *Mus.* An interval equal to half a tone in the diatonic scale.
half tide. The tide at a time halfway between high tide and low tide.
half-track (hăf'trăk', häf'-) *n.* A military motor vehicle with caterpillar treads.
half-truth (hăf'tro͞oth', häf'-) *n.* A statement that is only partially true, usually intended to deceive.
half•way (hăf'wā', häf'-) *adj.* 1. Midway between two points or conditions; in the middle. 2. Partial; *halfway measures for solving the problem.* —**half'way'** *adv.*
half-wit (hăf'wĭt', häf'-) *n.* 1. A mentally retarded person. 2. A stupid, foolish, or frivolous person. —**half'wit'ted** *adj.*
hal•i•but (hăl'ə-bət, hŏl'-) *n., pl.* **-but** or **-buts.** A large, edible flatfish of northern marine waters. [ME *halybutte.*]
hal•ide (hăl'īd', -ĭd, hā'līd', -lĭd) *n.* A binary chemical compound of a halogen with a more electropositive element or group.
Hal•i•fax (hăl'ə-făks'). The capital of Nova Scotia. Pop. 93,000.
hal•i•to•sis (hăl'ə-tō'sĭs) *n.* Foul-smelling breath. [< L *halitus,* breath + -OSIS.]
hall (hôl) *n.* 1. a. A corridor; hallway. b. A large entrance room; lobby. 2. A large public building. 3. A large room for meetings, meals, etc. 4. A college or university building. 5. a. The main house on a landed estate. b. The main residence of a medieval nobleman. [< OE *heall.* See **kel-⁴.**]
hal•lah. Variant of **challah.**
hal•le•lu•jah (hăl'ə-lo͞o'yə) *interj.* Expressive of praise or joy. —*n.* An expression or exclamation of "hallelujah." [Heb *hallelūyāh,* praise the Lord.]
hall•mark (hôl'märk') *n.* 1. A mark placed on an article to indicate purity, quality, etc. 2. Any indication of quality or excellence.
hal•loo (hə-lo͞o') *interj.* Used to attract attention. —*n.* A shout or call of "halloo." [Perh < OF *halloer.*]
hal•low (hăl'ō) *v.* 1. To make or set apart as holy; consecrate. 2. To honor as being holy; revere. [< OE *hālgian.* See **kailo-.**] —**hal'lowed** *adj.*
Hal•low•een (hăl'ō-ēn') *n.* The eve of All Saints' Day, falling on October 31. [Short for *All Hallow E'en.*]
hal•lu•ci•na•tion (hə-lo͞o'sə-nā'shən) *n.* 1. False perception with a characteristically compelling sense of the reality of objects or events perceived in the absence of relevant and adequate stimuli. 2. The complex of material so perceived. 3. Any false or mistaken idea; delusion. [< L *hallūcinārī,* to wander in

---

ô paw, for/oi boy/ou out/o͞o took/o͞o coo/p pop/r run/s sauce/sh shy/t to/th thin/*th* the/
ŭ cut/ûr fur/v van/w wag/y yes/z size/zh vision/ə ago, item, edible, gallop, circus/

mind.] —hal·lu'ci·nate' v. (-nated, -nating). —hal·lu'ci·na·to'ry (-tôr'ē, -tōr'ē) adj.

hal·lu·cin·o·gen (hə-lōō'sə-nə-jən) n. A drug that induces hallucination. —hal·lu'cin·o·gen'ic adj.

hall·way (hôl'wā') n. 1. A corridor or passageway. 2. An entrance hall.

ha·lo (hā'lō) n., pl. -los or -loes. 1. A disk or ring of light surrounding the head, as in a representation of a holy person. 2. A circular band of colored light around a light source, as around the sun or moon. [< Gk halōs.]

hal·o·gen (hăl'ə-jən) n. Any of a group of five chemically related nonmetallic elements that includes fluorine, chlorine, bromine, iodine, and astatine. [< Gk hals, salt + -GEN.]

halt¹ (hôlt) n. A suspension of movement or progress; a stop. [< OHG haltan, to stop.]

halt² (hôlt) v. To limp or hobble. —adj. Archaic. Lame; crippled. [< OE healtian. See kel-².]

hal·ter (hôl'tər) n. 1. A rope or leather strap that fits around the head or neck of an animal, such as a horse, used to lead or secure it. 2. A noose used for execution by hanging. 3. A bodice for women held in place by ties behind the neck and across the back. —v. To put a halter on; control with a halter. [< OE hælftre. See kelp-.]

halt·ing (hôl'tĭng) adj. 1. Limping; lame. 2. Uncertain or faltering. —halt'ing·ly adv.

halve (hăv, häv) v. halved, halving. 1. To separate or divide into two equal parts. 2. To lessen or reduce by half. 3. Informal. To share equally.

halves. pl. of half.

hal·yard (hăl'yərd) n. A rope used to raise or lower a sail, flag, or yard. [< ME halen, to pull.]

ham (hăm) n. 1. A cut of meat consisting of the thigh of the hind leg of a hog. 2. The back of the knee. 3. The back of the thigh. 4. hams. The buttocks. 5. Slang. An actor who overacts or exaggerates excessively. 6. Informal. A licensed amateur radio operator. —v. hammed, hamming. To exaggerate or overdo. [< OE hamm.]

Ham·burg (hăm'bûrg). A port of N West Germany. Pop. 1,851,000.

ham·burg·er (hăm'bûr'gər) n. 1. Ground or chopped meat, usually beef. 2. A cooked patty of such meat. 3. A sandwich made with such a patty. [< HAMBURG.]

Ham·il·ton (hăm'əl-tən), **Alexander.** 1755–1804. American statesman.

Ham·ite (hăm'īt') n. A member of a group of related peoples of N and NE Africa, including the Berbers and the descendants of the ancient Egyptians.

Ha·mit·ic (hă-mĭt'ĭk) adj. Of or relating to the Hamites or the language of the Hamites. —n. A group of North African languages related to Semitic, including the Berber dialects and ancient Egyptian.

Ham·i·to-Se·mit·ic (hăm'ə-tō-sə-mĭt'ĭk) n. Afro-Asiatic.

ham·let (hăm'lĭt) n. A small village. [< OF hamelet.]

Ham·mar·skjöld (häm'är-shœld'), **Dag.** 1905–1961. Swedish diplomat; secretary-general of the UN (1953–61).

Dag Hammarskjöld

ham·mer (hăm'ər) n. 1. A hand tool used to exert an impulsive force by striking. 2. Any tool or device of analogous function or action, as: a. The part of a gunlock that hits the primer or firing pin or explodes the percussion cap. b. One of the padded wooden pieces of a piano that strike the strings. c. Any part of an apparatus that strikes a gong or bell, as in a clock. —v. 1. To strike; pound. 2. To shape or flatten with a hammer. [< OE hamor.]

ham·mer·head (hăm'ər-hĕd') n. 1. A large shark having the sides of the head elongated into large extensions with the eyes at the ends. 2. The head of a hammer.

ham·mer·toe (hăm'ər-tō') n. A toe, usually the second, that is congenitally bent downward.

ham·mock (hăm'ək) n. A hanging, easily swung cot or bed, suspended by cords between two supports. [Span hamaca.]

ham·per¹ (hăm'pər) v. To restrain movement, action, etc.; impede. [ME hamperen.]

ham·per² (hăm'pər) n. A large, usually covered basket. [< ME hanaper.]

ham·ster (hăm'stər) n. A rodent with large cheek pouches and a short tail, often kept as a pet or used in laboratory research. [< OHG hamustro < Slav.]

ham·string (hăm'strĭng') n. 1. Either of two tendons at the rear hollow of the human knee. 2. The large sinew in the back of the hock of a quadruped. —v. -strung (-strŭng'), -stringing. 1. To cut the hamstring of (an animal or person) and thereby cripple. 2. To hinder the efficiency of.

ham·u·lus (hăm'yə-ləs) n., pl. -li (-lī'). A small hooklike projection or process, as at the end of a bone. [< L hāmus, hook.]

hand (hănd) n. 1. The terminal part of the arm below the wrist. 2. A unit of length equal to 4 in., used esp. to specify the height of a horse. 3. Something suggesting the shape or function of the human hand. 4. A pointer on a clock or instrument. **5.** A lateral direction: *at my right hand.* **6.** Handwriting; penmanship. **7.** A round of applause. **8.** Physical assistance; help. **9.** *Card Games.* **a.** The cards held by or dealt to a player. **b.** A round of play. **10.** A laborer. **11.** A person who is part of a group or crew. **12.** A participant; contributor. **13.** Skill; ability. **14.** Often **hands.** **a.** Possession or keeping. **b.** Control. **15.** A source of information: *at first hand.* **16.** A pledge to marry. —**at hand. 1.** Close by; near; easily accessible. **2.** Soon in time. —**by hand.** Performed by using the hands as opposed to mechanical means. —**hands down.** With no trouble; easily. —**in hand. 1.** Under control. **2.** Presently accessible. **3.** In preparation. —**on hand.** Available. —**on the other hand.** As another point of view. —**out of hand.** Out of control. —*adj.* **1.** Of or pertaining to the hand. **2.** Made to be transported in one's hand. **3.** Performed, operated, or made by hand; manual. —*v.* **1.** To give or pass with or as with the hands. **2.** To aid, direct, or conduct with the hands. **3.** *Naut.* To roll up and secure (a sail); furl. —**hand down. 1.** To give as an inheritance. **2.** To pronounce a court decision. —**hand it to.** *Slang.* To give credit to. [< OE < Gmc *handuz.]

hand•bag (hănd′băg′) *n.* A woman's bag for carrying articles such as money, keys, etc.
hand•ball (hănd′bôl′) *n.* **1.** A game played by batting a ball against the wall with the hands. **2.** The small rubber ball used in this game.
hand•bill (hănd′bĭl′) *n.* A printed sheet or pamphlet distributed by hand.
hand•book (hănd′bŏŏk′) *n.* A manual or small reference book providing specific information or instruction.
hand•car (hănd′kär′) *n.* A small open hand-propelled railroad car.
hand•cart (hănd′kärt′) *n.* A small, usually two-wheeled, cart pulled or pushed by hand.
hand•clasp (hănd′klăsp′, -kläsp′) *n.* The act of clasping the hand of another person.
hand•cuff (hănd′kŭf′) *n.* Often **handcuffs.** A restraining device consisting of a pair of strong, connected hoops that can be locked about the wrist. —*v.* To restrain with handcuffs.
hand•ed (hăn′dĭd) *adj.* **1.** Of or pertaining to dexterity or preference as regards a hand or hands: *one-handed; left-handed.* **2.** Pertaining to a specified number of people: *a four-handed card game.*
Han•del (hănd′l), **George Frederick.** 1685–1759. German-born British composer.
hand•ful (hănd′fŏŏl′) *n., pl.* **-fuls. 1.** The quantity or number that can be held in the hand. **2.** A small but undefined quantity or number. **3.** *Informal.* A person or thing difficult to control.
hand grenade. A small grenade to be thrown by the hand.
hand•i•cap (hăn′dē-kăp′) *n.* **1.** A race or contest in which advantages or compensations are given different contestants to equalize the chances of winning. **2.** Such an advantage or penalty. **3.** An anatomical, physiological, or

mental deficiency that prevents or restricts normal achievement. —*v.* **-capped, -capping. 1.** To assign a handicap or handicaps to (a contestant). **2.** To hinder. [< earlier *hand in cap.*] —**hand′i•cap′per** *n.*
hand•i•craft (hăn′dē-krăft′, -krăft′) *n.* **1.** Skill with the hands. **2.** A trade, craft, or occupation requiring such skill. **3.** The work so produced.
hand•i•work (hăn′dē-wûrk′) *n.* **1.** Work performed by hand. **2.** Work accomplished by a single person. **3.** The results of one's efforts.
hand•ker•chief (hăng′kər-chĭf′) *n.* A small square of cloth used in wiping the nose, mouth, etc.
han•dle (hănd′l) *v.* **-dled, -dling. 1.** To touch, lift, or turn with the hands. **2.** To operate with the hands; manipulate. **3.** To manage; deal with or in: *handle corporation law.* —*n.* A part that is held or manipulated with the hand. [< OE *handlian.*]
han•dle•bar (hănd′l-bär′) *n.* Often **handlebars.** A curved metal steering bar, as on a bicycle.
hand•made (hănd′mād′) *adj.* Made or prepared by hand rather than by machine.
hand•maid (hănd′mād′) *n.* A female attendant.
hand•out (hănd′out′) *n.* Food, clothing, or money donated to a beggar or destitute person.
hand-pick (hănd′pĭk′) *v.* To select carefully or personally.
hand•rail (hănd′rāl′) *n.* A narrow rail to be grasped for support.
hand•shake (hănd′shāk′) *n.* The grasping of right hands by two people as a gesture of greeting, leave-taking, etc.
hand•some (hăn′səm) *adj.* **1.** Pleasing and dignified in appearance. **2.** Generous; liberal: *a handsome reward.* **3.** Marked by great skill: *a handsome piece of work.* [ME *handsom,* easy to handle.] —**hand′some•ly** *adv.*
hand•spring (hănd′sprĭng′) *n.* A gymnastic feat in which the body is flipped forward or backward, landing first on the hands, then on the feet.
hand-to-hand (hănd′tə-hănd′) *adj.* At close quarters.
hand•writ•ing (hănd′rī′tĭng) *n.* **1.** Writing done with the hand. **2.** The writing characteristic of a particular person.
hand•y (hăn′dē) *adj.* **-ier, -iest. 1.** Manually adroit. **2.** Readily accessible. **3.** Easy to use. [< HAND.] —**hand′i•ly** *adv.* —**hand′i•ness** *n.*
hand•y•man (hăn′dē-măn′) *n.,* One who does odd jobs.
hang (hăng) *v.* **hung** or **hanged, hanging. 1.** To fasten or be fastened from above with no support from below. **2.** To suspend or be suspended so as to allow free movement at or about the point of suspension. **3.** To execute or be executed by suspending by the neck. **4.** To attach at an appropriate angle. **5. a.** To furnish by suspending objects about: *hang the room with curtains.* **b.** To attach to a wall: *hang wallpaper.* **6.** To hold downward. **7.** To deadlock (a jury). —**hang around.** To loiter. —**hang back.** To lag or hold back. —**hang on.**

1. To cling to something. 2. To persevere. —*n.* 1. The way in which something hangs. 2. *Informal.* The proper method for doing something. [< OE *hōn,* to hang, suspend, and *hangian,* to hang, be hung, and < ON *hanga,* to cause to hang. See **konk-**.]

Usage: Hanged is preferable to *hung* as the past tense and past participle when the verb is used in the sense of capital punishment. In other senses of the verb, *hung* is the customary form as past tense and past participle.

han·gar (hăng'ər) *n.* A shed or shelter, esp. for aircraft. [< OF.]

hang·dog (hăng'dôg', -dŏg') *adj.* 1. Shamefaced or guilty. 2. Downcast; intimidated.

hang·er (hăng'ər) *n.* 1. One that hangs. 2. A contrivance to which something hangs or by which something is hung.

hang·er-on (hăng'ər-ŏn', -ôn') *n., pl.* **hangers-on** (hăng'ərz-). A sycophant.

hang·ing (hăng'ĭng) *n.* 1. An execution on a gallows. 2. Something hung, as drapery. —**hang'ing** *adj.*

hang·man (hăng'mən) *n.* One employed to execute prisoners by hanging.

hang·nail (hăng'nāl') *n.* A small, partly detached piece of dead skin at the side or base of a fingernail.

hang·out (hăng'out') *n.* A frequently visited place.

hang·o·ver (hăng'ō'vər) *n.* 1. Unpleasant physical effects following the heavy use of alcohol. 2. A vestige; holdover.

hang up. 1. To suspend on a hook or hanger. 2. To replace (a telephone receiver) on its cradle. 3. To end a telephone conversation.

hang-up (hăng'ŭp') *n. Informal.* An inhibition.

hank (hăngk) *n.* A coil or loop. [< Scand.]

han·ker (hăng'kər) *v.* To have a longing; crave. [< dial *hank.*]

han·ky-pan·ky (hăng'kē-păng'kē) *n. Slang.* Devious or mischievous activity.

Ha·noi (hä-noi', hă-). The capital of Vietnam. Pop. 415,000.

Han·o·ver (hăn'ō'vər). A city of N West Germany. Pop. 571,000.

han·som (hăn'səm) *n.* A two-wheeled covered carriage with the driver's seat above and behind. [< English architect J.A. *Hansom* (1803–1882).]

Ha·nuk·kah, Ha·nu·kah. Variants of **Chanukah.**

hap·haz·ard (hăp-hăz'ərd) *adj.* Dependent upon or characterized by mere chance. —*n.* Mere chance; fortuity. [HAP + HAZARD.] —**hap·haz'ard·ly** *adv.* —**hap·haz'ard·ness** *n.*

hap·less (hăp'lĭs) *adj.* Luckless; unfortunate.

hap·loid (hăp'loid') *adj.* Having the number of chromosomes present in the normal germ cell, equal to half the number in the normal somatic cell. [Gk *haploeidēs,* single.]

hap·ly (hăp'lē) *adv. Archaic.* By chance; perhaps.

hap·pen (hăp'ən) *v.* 1. To take place. 2. To take place by chance. 3. To come upon something by chance. 4. To appear by chance; turn up. [< HAP.]

hap·pen·ing (hăp'ə-nĭng) *n.* 1. An event. 2.

An improvised spectacle.

hap·py (hăp'ē) *adj.* **-pi·er, -pi·est.** 1. Characterized by good fortune; prosperous. 2. Having or demonstrating pleasure; gratified. 3. Appropriate: *a happy turn of phrase.* [< HAP.] —**hap'pi·ly** *adv.* —**hap'pi·ness** *n.*

hap·py-go-luck·y (hăp'ē-gō-lŭk'ē) *adj.* Carefree.

ha·ra-ki·ri (hăr'ə-kîr'ē) *n.* Ritual suicide by disembowelment. [Jap.]

ha·rangue (hə-răng') *n.* 1. A long, pompous speech. 2. A speech characterized by strong feeling or vehement expression. [< ML *harenga.*] —**ha·rangue'** *v.* (**-rangued, -ranguing**). —**ha·rangu'er** *n.*

har·ass (hăr'əs, hə-răs') *v.* 1. To disturb or irritate persistently. 2. To wear out; exhaust. 3. To enervate (an enemy) by repeated raids. [< OF *harer,* to set a dog on.] —**har'ass·er** *n.* —**har'ass·ment** *n.*

Har·bin (här'bən). A city of NE China, in Manchuria. Pop. 1,595,000.

har·bin·ger (här'bən-jər) *n.* A forerunner. [< OS *heriberga,* lodging.]

har·bor (här'bər). Also *chiefly Brit.* **har·bour.** *n.* 1. A sheltered part of a body of water deep enough to provide anchorage for ships; a port. 2. Any protected place; a refuge. —*v.* 1. To give shelter to; protect; keep. 2. To hold a thought or feeling about. [< OE *hereborg.*]

hard (härd) *adj.* 1. Resistant to pressure; not easily penetrated; rigid. 2. Physically or mentally toughened. 3. Difficult to do, understand, or endure. 4. Powerful; intense: *a hard blow.* 5. Energetic. 6. Bitter; severe; harsh. 7. Callous; unfeeling. 8. Cruel; unjust. 9. Real: *hard facts.* 10. Having a high alcoholic content. 11. Containing salts that interfere with the lathering of soap. 12. Backed by bullion rather than by credit: *hard currency.* —**hard and fast.** Defined and invariable: *hard and fast rules.* —**hard of hearing.** Deaf to some degree. —**hard up.** In need; poor. [< OE. See **kar-**.] —**hard** *adv.*

hard-bit·ten (härd'bĭt'n) *adj.* Obdurate; toughened.

hard-boiled (härd'boild') *adj.* 1. Cooked by boiling to a solid consistency, as eggs. 2. Callous; unfeeling.

hard cash. Available money; cash.

hard cider. Fermented cider.

hard-core (härd'kôr') *adj.* Also **hard-core.** 1. Stubbornly resistant or inveterate: *a hard-core criminal.* 2. Held to constitute an intractable social problem: *hard-core poverty.*

hard drug. Any dangerously addictive drug, such as heroin.

hard·en (härd'n) *v.* 1. To make or become firm or firmer. 2. To toughen mentally or physically. 3. To make unfeeling or cold in spirit. —**hard'en·er** *n.*

hard·head·ed (härd'hĕd'ĭd) *adj.* 1. Stubborn; willful. 2. Realistic; practical —**hard'head'ed·ly** *adv.* —**hard'head'ed·ness** *n.*

hard-heart·ed (härd'härt'ĭd) *adj.* Unfeeling; cold; pitiless. —**hard'heart'ed·ly** *adv.*

har·di·hood (här'dē-hŏŏd') *n.* Boldness and daring; audacity.

Har·ding (här'dĭng), **Warren Gamaliel.** 1865–1923. 29th President of the U.S. (1921–23).

Warren G. Harding

hard·ly (härd'lē) *adv.* **1.** Barely; just. **2.** To almost no degree. **3.** Probably or almost surely not.
Usage: Hardly has the force of a negative; therefore it is not used with another negative: *I could hardly see* (not *couldn't hardly*). *Hardly* is idiomatically followed by clauses introduced by *when* or, less often, *before*, but not by *than* or *until*: *We were hardly seated when* (or *before*) *the fire broke out.*
hard·ness (härd'nĭs) *n.* **1.** The quality or condition of being hard. **2.** The relative resistance of a substance to denting, scratching, or bending.
hard palate. The relatively hard, bony anterior portion of the palate.
hard·pan (härd'păn') *n.* A layer of hard subsoil or clay.
hard rubber. A relatively inelastic rubber made with 30 to 50% sulfur.
hard-shell (härd'shĕl') *adj.* Unyieldingly orthodox; uncompromising; confirmed.
hard·ship (härd'shĭp') *n.* **1.** Extreme privation; suffering. **2.** A cause of privation or difficulty.
hard·tack (härd'tăk') *n.* A hard biscuit made only with flour and water.
hard·top (härd'tŏp') *n.* An automobile with a fixed hard top, designed to look like a convertible.
hard·ware (härd'wâr') *n.* **1.** Metal goods and utensils. **2. a.** A computer and the associated physical equipment directly involved in communications or data processing. **b.** Broadly, machines and other physical equipment directly involved in performing an industrial, technological, or military function.
hard·wood (härd'wood') *n.* The wood of a broad-leaved flowering tree as distinguished from that of a conifer.
har·dy (här'dē) *adj.* **-dier, -diest. 1.** Stalwart and rugged; strong. **2.** Capable of surviving severe cold, drought, etc., as a plant. **3.** Courageous;

stouthearted. **4.** Audacious; hotheaded. [< OF *hardir,* to become bold, make hard.] **—har'di·ly** *adv.* **—har'di·ness** *n.*
hare (hâr) *n.* A mammal related to and resembling the rabbits but usually larger and with longer ears and legs. [< OE *hara.* See kas-.]
hare·brained (hâr'brānd') *adj.* Giddy; flighty.
hare·lip (hâr'lĭp') *n.* A congenital fissure or pair of fissures in the upper lip.
har·em (hâr'əm, här'-) *n.* **1.** A house or section of a house reserved for women in a Moslem household. **2.** The women occupying a harem. [Ar *ḥarīm,* sacred, forbidden place.]
hark (härk) *v.* To listen attentively. [< OE **heorcian.* See keu-.]
har·le·quin (här'lə-kwən, -kən) *n.* **1.** Harlequin. A character in comedy, traditionally presented in a mask and parti-colored tights. **2.** A clown; buffoon. [Prob < OE *Herla cyning,* King *Herla,* a mythical figure.]
har·lot (här'lət) *n.* A prostitute. [< OF, young fellow, vagabond.]
harm (härm) *n.* **1.** Injury or damage. **2.** Wrong; evil. **—v.** To damage; injure; impair. [< OE *hearm.* See kormo-.] **—harm'ful** *adj.* **—harm'less** *adj.*
har·mon·ic (här-mŏn'ĭk) *adj.* Of or pertaining to musical harmony or harmonics. **—n. 1.** A musical overtone. **2. harmonics** (*takes sing. v.*). The study of the physical properties of musical sound. **—har·mon'i·cal·ly** *adv.*
har·mon·i·ca (här-mŏn'ĭ-kə) *n.* A small musical instrument played by exhaling or inhaling through a row of reeds.
har·mo·ni·ous (här-mō'nē-əs) *adj.* **1.** Characterized by agreement or accord. **2.** Consisting of pleasingly combined elements. **3.** Marked by harmony of sound.
har·mo·ni·um (här-mō'nē-əm) *n.* An organlike keyboard instrument with metal reeds.
har·mo·nize (här'mə-nīz') *v.* **-nized, -nizing. 1.** To be in or bring into agreement or harmony. **2.** To sing or play in harmony.
har·mo·ny (här'mə-nē) *n., pl.* **-nies. 1.** Agreement or accord, as of feeling. **2.** A pleasing combination of parts or elements. **3.** Combination and progression of chords in musical structure. [< Gk *harmonia.*]
har·ness (här'nĭs) *n.* Gear by which a draft animal pulls a vehicle or implement. **—in harness.** Engaged in one's usual work. **—v. 1.** To put a harness on. **2.** To control and direct the force of. [< OF *harneis,* military gear.] **—har'ness·er** *n.*
harp (härp) *n.* A musical instrument having an upright frame with strings played by plucking. **—v.** To play a harp. **—harp on.** To discourse tediously on. [< OE *hearpe* < Gmc **harpōn-.*] **—harp'er** *n.* **—harp'ist** *n.*
har·poon (här-pōōn') *n.* A spearlike weapon with a barbed head, used esp. in whaling. **—v.** To strike with or as if with a harpoon. [< L *harpē,* sickle.]
harp·si·chord (härp'sĭ-kôrd', -kôrd') *n.* A keyboard instrument in which the strings are sounded by means of a plucking mechanism. [< It *arpicordo,* "harp string."]

ŏ paw, for/oi boy/ou out/oo took/oo coo/p pop/r run/s sauce/sh shy/t to/th thin/*th* the/
ŭ cut/ûr fur/v van/w wag/y yes/z size/zh vision/ə ago, item, edible, gallop, circus/

har•py (här′pē) *n., pl.* **-pies. 1.** A shrewish woman. **2.** A predatory person. **3. Harpy.** A voracious monster having a woman's head and a bird's body. [< Gk *harpuiai,* "snatchers."]

har•que•bus (här′kə-bəs, -kwĭ-bŭs′) *n.* A heavy 16th-century gun.

har•ri•dan (hăr′ə-dən) *n.* A disagreeable old woman.

har•ri•er¹ (hăr′ē-ər) *n.* **1.** One that harries. **2.** A slender, narrow-winged hawk.

har•ri•er² (hăr′ē-ər) *n.* A small hound formerly used to hunt hares. [< HARE.]

Har•ris•burg (hăr′ĭs-bûrg, hâr′-). The capital of Pennsylvania. Pop. 66,000.

Har•ri•son (hăr′ĭ-sən). **1. Benjamin.** 1833–1901. 23rd President of the U.S. (1889–93). **2. William Henry.** 1773–1841. 9th President of the U.S. (1841).

Benjamin Harrison

William Henry Harrison

har•row (hăr′ō) *n.* An implement having a heavy frame with teeth or upright disks, used to break up plowed ground. —*v.* **1.** To break up (soil) with a harrow. **2.** To distress greatly; torment. [ME *harwe.*]

har•ry (hăr′ē) *v.* **-ried, -rying. 1.** To raid; sack; pillage. **2.** To distress by constant attacks; harass. [< OE *hergian.*]

harsh (härsh) *adj.* **1.** Severe; stern. **2.** Unpleasant; irritating. [ME *harsk.*] —**harsh′ly** *adv.* —**harsh′ness** *n.*

hart (härt) *n.* An adult male deer. [< OE *heorot.* See ker-¹.]

Hart•ford (härt′fərd). The capital of Connecticut. Pop. 156,000.

har•um-scar•um (hâr′əm-skâr′əm) *adv.* Recklessly. —*adj.* Rash; irresponsible. —*n.* A scatterbrain.

har•vest (här′vĭst) *n.* **1.** The gathering in of a crop. **2.** A gathered crop. —*v.* **1.** To gather (a crop). **2.** To gain, win, or acquire as by gathering; reap. [< OE *hærfest,* autumn. See kerp-.] —**har′vest•er** *n.*

harvest moon. The full moon that occurs nearest the autumnal equinox.

has (hăz). 3rd person sing. present indicative of **have.**

has-been (hăz′bĭn′) *n.* One no longer popular or successful.

ha•sen•pfef•fer (hä′sən-fĕf′ər) *n.* A highly seasoned rabbit stew. [G, "rabbit pepper."]

hash¹ (hăsh) *n.* **1.** Chopped meat and potatoes mixed together and browned. **2.** A jumble; hodgepodge. —*v.* **1.** To chop up; mince. **2.** To discuss; go over: *hash over future plans.* [< F *hacher,* to mince.]

hash² (hăsh) *n. Informal.* Hashish.

hash•ish (hăsh′ēsh′, -ĭsh) *n.* A narcotic extract prepared from the flowers of the hemp plant; hash. [Ar *ḥashīsh,* hemp.]

hash mark. *Mil. Slang.* A service stripe on the sleeve of an enlisted man's uniform.

Has•i•dim. Variant of **Chassidim.**

has•n't (hăz′ənt). Contraction of *has not.*

hasp (hăsp, häsp) *n.* A hinged metal fastener that fits over a staple and is secured by a pin, bolt, or padlock. [< OE *hæspe,* fastening, hinge.]

Has•si•dim. Variant of **Chassidim.**

has•sle (hăs′əl) *n.* **1.** An argument or fight. **2.** Trouble; bother. [Perh blend of HAGGLE + TUSSLE.]

has•sock (hăs′ək) *n.* A cushion used as a footstool or for kneeling. [< OE *hassuc,* clump of matted vegetation.]

hast (hăst). *Archaic.* 2nd person sing. present indicative of **have.**

haste (hāst) *n.* **1.** Swiftness; rapidity. **2.** Eagerness or necessity to move swiftly; urgency. **3.** Careless or headlong hurrying. [< OF < Gmc **haifsti-.*]

has•ten (hā′sən) *v.* To move or cause to move swiftly; hurry.

hast•y (hā′stē) *adj.* **-ier, -iest. 1.** Characterized by speed; swift. **2.** Done too quickly to be accurate or wise; rash. —**hast′i•ly** *adv.* —**hast′i•ness** *n.*

hat (hăt) *n.* A covering for the head, esp. one with a shaped crown and brim. [< OE *hæt.* See kadh-.]

hatch¹ (hăch) *n.* **1. a.** An opening in the deck of a ship leading to the hold. **b.** A hatchway. **2.** Any small door or opening. [< OE *hæcc,* hatch, wicket < Gmc **khak-.*]

ă pat/ā ate/âr care/ä bar/b bib/ch chew/d deed/ĕ pet/ē be/f fit/g gag/h hat/hw what/
ĭ pit/ī pie/îr pier/j judge/k kick/l lid, fatal/m mum/n no, sudden/ng sing/ŏ pot/ō go/

hatch² (hăch) *v.* **1.** To emerge from or cause to emerge from an egg. **2.** To cause (an egg or eggs) to produce young. **3.** To originate or formulate. [< OE *hæccan.*]

hatch·er·y (hăch'ə-rē) *n., pl.* **-ies.** A place where eggs, as of fish or domestic fowl, are hatched.

hatch·et (hăch'ĭt) *n.* **1.** A short-handled ax. **2.** A tomahawk. [< OF *hache*, ax.]

hatch·way (hăch'wā') *n.* **1.** An opening in the deck of a ship leading to a hold or lower deck. **2.** A ladder within such an opening.

hate (hāt) *v.* **hated, hating. 1.** To loathe; detest. **2.** To dislike; wish to shun. —*n.* **1.** Strong dislike; animosity. **2.** An object of hatred. [< OE *hatian.* See **kād-.**] —**hate'ful** *adj.*

hath (hăth). *Archaic.* 3rd person sing. present indicative of **have.**

ha·tred (hā'trĭd) *n.* Violent dislike or animosity; abhorrence. [< OE *hete*, hate.]

hat·ter (hăt'ər) *n.* One who makes, repairs, or sells hats.

hau·berk (hô'bûrk) *n.* A tunic of chain mail. [< OF *hauberc.*]

haugh·ty (hô'tē) *adj.* **-tier, -tiest.** Proud and vain to the point of arrogance. [< OF *haut*, "high."] —**haugh'ti·ly** *adv.* —**haugh'ti·ness** *n.*

haul (hôl) *v.* **1.** To pull or drag; tug. **2.** To provide transportation; cart. —*n.* **1.** The act of hauling. **2. a.** The distance over which something is carted. **b.** The load carted. **3.** An amount collected or acquired; take: *a haul of fish.* [< OF *haler*, to pull.]

haul·age (hô'lĭj) *n.* **1.** The act or process of hauling. **2.** The charge made for hauling.

haunch (hônch, hänch) *n.* The hip, buttock, and upper thigh. [< OF *hanche* < Gmc *hanka.*]

haunt (hônt, hänt) *v.* **1.** To visit or appear to in the form of a ghost. **2.** To frequent. **3.** To recur to continually. **4.** To linger or remain in profusion; pervade. —*n.* A place much frequented. [< OF *hanter.*]

Hau·sa (hou'sə, -zə) *n., pl.* **-sa.** Also **Haus·sa.** **1.** One of a Negroid people of the Sudan and Nigeria. **2.** Their language.

hau·teur (hō-tûr') *n.* Haughtiness; arrogance. [< F *haut*, high, pious.]

Ha·van·a (hə-văn'ə). The capital of Cuba. Pop. 800,000.

have (hăv) *v.* **had, having, has.** —Used as an auxiliary before a past participle to form the past, present, and future perfect tenses. **1.** To possess; own. **2.** To stand in relationship to. **3.** To be obliged to. **4.** To hold in one's mind; entertain. **5. a.** To win a victory over. **b.** To cheat or trick. **6.** To possess sexually. **7.** To keep in a specified place. **8.** To accept or take. **9.** To partake of; consume. **10.** To be made of, consist of, or contain. **11.** To exercise or exhibit: *have mercy.* **12.** To allow; permit. **13.** To cause to. **14.** To carry out or stage. **15.** To experience: *have a good summer.* **16.** To beget or give birth to. **17.** To be in command of: *have the necessary technique.* **18.** To receive as a guest. —*n.* One of a class enjoying material comforts: *the haves and the have-nots.* [< OE *habban.* See **kap-.**]

ha·ven (hā'vən) *n.* **1.** A harbor or port. **2.** A place of sanctuary. [< OE *hæfen.*]

have-not (hăv'nŏt') *n.* One having little or no property.

have·n't (hăv'ənt). Contraction of *have not.*

hav·er·sack (hăv'ər-săk') *n.* A canvas bag worn over one shoulder to transport supplies on a hike. [< G *Habersack*, "bag for oats."]

hav·oc (hăv'ək) *n.* Widespread destruction or confusion. [< OF *havot*, plunder.]

haw (hô) *n.* **1.** The fruit of a hawthorn. **2.** A hawthorn. [< OE *haga*, hawthorn, hedge.]

Ha·wai·i (hə-wä'ē, -wä'yə). A state of the U.S.; an island group in the C Pacific. Pop. 770,000. Cap. Honolulu.

Ha·wai·ian (hə-wä'yən) *n.* **1.** A native or inhabitant of Hawaii. **2.** The Polynesian language of Hawaii. —**Ha·wai'ian** *adj.*

hawk¹ (hôk) *n.* **1.** Any of various day-flying birds of prey characteristically having a short, hooked bill and strong claws adapted for seizing. **2.** A member of a group advocating a militaristic foreign policy. [< OE *heafoc.* See **kap-.**]

hawk² (hôk) *v.* To peddle (wares), esp. in the streets. [Prob < MLG *höken*, to peddle.] —**hawk'er** *n.*

haw·ser (hô'zər) *n. Naut.* A rope or cable used in mooring or towing a ship. [< OF *haucier*, to lift.]

haw·thorn (hô'thôrn') *n.* A thorny tree or shrub with white or pinkish flowers and reddish fruit. [< HAW + THORN.]

Haw·thorne (hô'thôrn'), **Nathaniel.** 1804–1864. American novelist.

hay (hā) *n.* Grass or other forage plants cut and dried for fodder. —*v.* To cut and process grass and herbage to make hay. [< OE *hieg.* See **kau-.**]

hay·cock (hā'kŏk') *n.* A conical mound of hay.

Hay·dn (hīd'n), **Franz Joseph.** 1732–1809. Austrian composer.

Hayes (hāz), **Rutherford B(irchard).** 1822–1893. 19th President of the U.S. (1877–81).

Rutherford B. Hayes

hay fever. An acute allergic condition of the mucous membranes of the upper respiratory tract and the eyes, caused by abnormal sensitivity to certain airborne pollens, esp. of the ragweed and related plants.

hay·fork (hā′fôrk′) *n.* **1.** A hand tool for pitching hay. **2.** A machine-operated fork for moving hay.

hay·loft (hā′lôft′, -lŏft′) *n.* A loft for storing hay.

hay·mow (hā′mou′) *n.* A hayloft.

hay·seed (hā′sēd′) *n. Slang.* A country bumpkin.

hay·stack (hā′stăk′) *n.* Hay piled into a stack for outdoor storage.

hay·wire (hā′wīr′) *adj. Informal.* **1.** Not functioning properly; broken. **2.** Crazy.

haz·ard (hăz′ərd) *n.* **1.** A chance or accident. **2.** A danger; risk. **3.** An obstacle on a golf course. —*v.* To run the risk of; venture. [< Span *azar*, unlucky throw of the dice.] —**haz′ard·ous** *adj.* —**haz′ard·ous·ly** *adv.*

haze¹ (hāz) *n.* **1.** Atmospheric moisture, dust, smoke, and vapor suspended to form a partially opaque condition. **2.** A vague state of mind. [< HAZY.]

haze² (hāz) *v.* **hazed, hazing.** To persecute or harass with humiliating tasks or practical jokes. [?]

ha·zel (hā′zəl) *n.* **1.** A shrub or small tree bearing smooth-shelled edible nuts enclosed in a leafy husk. **2.** Light or yellowish brown. [< OE *hæsel.* See **koselo-**.] —**ha′zel** *adj.*

ha·zel·nut (hā′zəl-nŭt′) *n.* The nut of a hazel.

haz·y (hā′zē) *adj.* **-ier, -iest. 1.** Marked by the presence of haze. **2.** Vague; confused. [?] —**haz′i·ly** *adv.* —**haz′i·ness** *n.*

H-bomb (āch′bŏm′) *n.* A hydrogen bomb.

hdqrs. headquarters.

he¹ (hē) *pron.* The 3rd person sing. pronoun in the nominative case, masculine gender. **1.** —Used to represent the male person last mentioned. **2.** —Used to represent any person whose sex is not specified: *He who hesitates is lost.* —*n.* A male animal or person: *Is the cat a he?* [< OE *hē, he.* See **ko-**.]

he² (hā) *n.* The 5th letter of the Hebrew alphabet, representing *h.*

He helium.

head (hĕd) *n.* **1.** The upper or anterior bodily extremity, containing the brain or the principal ganglia and in vertebrates the eyes, ears, nose, mouth, and jaws. **2. a.** Intellect; mind. **b.** Aptitude. **3.** Self-control. **4.** Freedom of choice or action: *Give him his head.* **5.** The obverse side of a coin. **6. a.** Each individual within a group. **b.** *pl.* **head.** A single animal within a herd. **7.** A leader; chief. **8.** The foremost position: *the head of the line.* **9.** A turning point; crisis. **10.** A projecting or striking part of something. **11.** The upper or higher end of something. **12.** Either end, as of a drum. **13.** Pressure: *a head of steam.* **14.** A rounded, compact mass of leaves, as of cabbage, or flowers, as of clover. —**go to one's head. 1.** To make one lightheaded. **2.** To increase one's conceit. —*adj.* **1.** Foremost in importance. **2.** Placed at the top or front. **3.** Coming from the front: *head winds.* —*v.* **1.** To be chief of; command. **2.** To assume or be placed in the first or foremost position of. **3.** To aim: *head the horse for home.* **4.** To proceed or set out: *head for town.* [< OE *hēafod.* See **kaput**.]

head·ache (hĕd′āk′) *n.* **1.** A pain in the head. **2.** *Informal.* Something that bothers.

head·band (hĕd′bănd′) *n.* A band worn around the head.

head·dress (hĕd′drĕs′) *n.* Something worn on the head, as a covering or ornament.

head·first (hĕd′fûrst′) *adv.* **1.** With the head leading; headlong. **2.** Impetuously.

head·gear (hĕd′gîr′) *n.* A covering for the head, such as a hat or helmet.

head·ing (hĕd′ĭng) *n.* **1.** A word or words at the beginning of a chapter, paragraph, etc. **2.** The course or direction of movement of a ship or aircraft.

head·land (hĕd′lənd, -lănd′) *n.* A point of land extending out into a body of water; promontory.

head·light (hĕd′līt′) *n.* A lamp mounted on the front of a vehicle.

head·line (hĕd′līn′) *n.* The title or caption of a newspaper article, set in large type.

head·lock (hĕd′lŏk′) *n.* A wrestling hold in which the head of one wrestler is locked under the arm of the other.

head·long (hĕd′lông′, -lŏng′) *adv.* **1.** With the head leading; headfirst. **2.** Impetuously. **3.** At breakneck speed. —**head′long′** *adj.*

head·mas·ter (hĕd′măs′tər, -mäs′tər) *n.* A male principal of a private school.

head·mis·tress (hĕd′mĭs′trĭs) *n.* A woman principal of a private school.

head·phone (hĕd′fōn′) *n.* A receiver, as for a radio, held to the ear by a headband.

head·quar·ters (hĕd′kwôr′tərz) *pl.n. (often takes sing. v.).* The command center, as of a military unit.

head·rest (hĕd′rĕst′) *n.* A support for the head.

head·set (hĕd′sĕt′) *n.* A pair of headphones.

head·stall (hĕd′stôl′) *n.* The section of a bridle that fits over the horse's head.

head·stone (hĕd′stōn′) *n.* A stone set at the head of a grave.

head·strong (hĕd′strông′, -strŏng′) *adj.* Willful; obstinate.

head·wait·er (hĕd′wā′tər) *n.* A waiter in charge of other waiters in a restaurant.

head·wa·ters (hĕd′wô′tərz, -wŏt′ərz) *pl.n.* The waters from which a river rises.

head·way (hĕd′wā′) *n.* **1.** Movement forward. **2.** Progress. **3.** Clearance overhead.

head·y (hĕd′ē) *adj.* **-ier, -iest. 1.** Intoxicating. **2.** Headstrong; obstinate. —**head′i·ly** *adv.*

heal (hēl) *v.* **1.** To restore or return to health; cure. **2.** To set right; amend. [< OE *hælen.* See **kailo-**.] —**heal′er** *n.*

health (hĕlth) *n.* **1.** The state of an organism with respect to functioning, disease, and abnormality at any given time. **2.** Optimal functioning with freedom from disease and abnormality. **3.** A wish for someone's good health, expressed as a toast. **4.** Flourishing condition; vitality. [< OE *hælth.* See **kailo-**.]

ă pat/ā ate/âr care/ä bar/b bib/ch chew/d deed/ĕ pet/ē be/f fit/g gag/h hat/hw what/
ĭ pit/ī pie/îr pier/j judge/k kick/l lid, fatal/m mum/n no, sudden/ng sing/ŏ pot/ō go/

health•ful (hĕlth'fəl) *adj.* **1.** Conducive to good health. **2.** Healthy. —**health'ful•ly** *adv.*

health•y (hĕl'thē) *adj.* **-ier, -iest. 1.** Possessing good health. **2.** Conducive to good health; healthful. **3.** Indicative of a constructive frame of mind: *a healthy attitude.* **4.** Sizable; considerable: *a healthy portion.* —**health'i•ly** *adv.* —**health'i•ness** *n.*

heap (hēp) *n.* **1.** A group of things haphazardly gathered; a pile. **2.** Often **heaps.** A great deal; lots. —*v.* **1.** To put or throw in a heap. **2.** To fill to overflowing. [< OE *hēap.*]

hear (hîr) *v.* **heard** (hûrd), **hearing. 1.** To perceive by the ear. **2.** To listen attentively. **3.** To learn. **4.** To listen to in an official capacity, as in a court. [< OE *hīeran.* See **keu-.**]

hear•ing (hîr'ĭng) *n.* **1.** The capacity to hear. **2.** The range of audibility. **3.** An opportunity to be heard. **4.** A preliminary examination of an accused person. **5.** A session, as of an investigative committee, at which testimony is taken.

heark•en (här'kən) *v. Poetic.* To listen attentively; give heed. [< OE **heorcian,* to hark, hear. See **keu-.**]

hear•say (hîr'sā') *n.* Information or a rumor heard from another.

hearse (hûrs) *n.* A vehicle for conveying a dead body to a cemetery. [ME *herse,* frame for holding candles.]

heart (härt) *n.* **1.** *Anat.* The hollow muscular organ that pumps blood received from the veins into the arteries, thereby supplying the entire circulatory system. **2.** The heart regarded as the seat of emotions, as: **a.** Mood. **b.** Compassion. **c.** Affection. **d.** Character or fortitude. **3. a.** The innermost area or part. **b.** The essence: *the heart of the problem.* **4.** Any of a suit of playing cards marked with a red, heart-shaped symbol. —**at heart.** Essentially; fundamentally. —**by heart.** By rote. [< OE *heorte.* See **kerd-.**]

heart•ache (härt'āk') *n.* Emotional anguish; deep sorrow.

heart attack. 1. Partial failure of the pumping action of the heart. **2.** Any seizure of abnormal heart functioning, as a coronary thrombosis.

heart•beat (härt'bēt') *n.* A single complete pulsation of the heart.

heart•break (härt'brāk') *n.* Intense grief or disappointment. —**heart'break'ing** *adj.*

heart•burn (härt'bûrn') *n.* A burning sensation in the stomach and esophagus, caused by excess acidity of stomach fluids.

heart•en (härt'n) *v.* To give strength or hope to; encourage.

heart•felt (härt'fĕlt') *adj.* Deeply or sincerely felt.

hearth (härth) *n.* **1.** The floor of a fireplace, usually extending into a room. **2.** The fireside; family life. **3.** The lowest part of a blast furnace or cupola, from which the molten metal flows. [< OE *heorth.* See **ker-³.**]

hearth•stone (härth'stōn') *n.* **1.** Stone used in constructing a hearth. **2.** The fireside; home.

heart•less (härt'lĭs) *adj.* Without compassion; pitiless; cruel. —**heart'less•ly** *adv.*

heart-rend•ing (härt'rĕn'dĭng) *adj.* Causing anguish or deep sympathy.

heart•sick (härt'sĭk') *adj.* Profoundly disappointed; despondent; unhappy.

heart•strings (härt'strĭngz') *pl.n.* The deepest feelings or affections.

heart-to-heart (härt'tə-härt') *adj.* Personal and candid.

heart•y (här'tē) *adj.* **-ier, -iest. 1.** Expressed with warmth of feeling; exuberant. **2.** Complete or thorough. **3.** Vigorous; robust. **4.** Nourishing. —**heart'i•ly** *adv.*

heat (hēt) *n.* **1.** Energy associated with the motion of atoms or molecules in solids and capable of being transmitted through solid and fluid media by conduction, through fluid media by convection, and through empty space by radiation. **2.** The perceptible, sensible, or measurable effect of such energy so transmitted, esp. a physiological sensation of being hot. **3.** A recurrent condition of sexual activity in female mammals. **4.** One of a series of efforts. **5.** *Slang.* Pressure, as from police pursuing criminals. —*v.* **1.** To make or become warm or hot. **2.** To excite the feelings of. [< OE *hǣtu.* See **kai-.**]

heat•er (hē'tər) *n.* An apparatus that provides heat.

heath (hēth) *n.* **1.** An open, uncultivated tract of land covered with heather or similar plants. **2.** A plant, as heather, that grows on such land. [< OE *hǣth.* See **kaito-.**]

hea•then (hē'thən) *n., pl.* **-thens** or **-then. 1.** One who adheres to a religion that does not acknowledge the God of Judaism, Christianity, or Islam. **2.** One who is regarded as irreligious, uncivilized, or unenlightened. [< OE *hǣthen.* See **kaito-.**] —**hea'then, hea'then•ish** *adj.* —**hea'then•dom** (-dəm) *n.*

heath•er (hĕth'ər) *n.* A low-growing evergreen shrub having small purplish flowers and forming dense masses. [Prob < HEATH.]

heave (hēv) *v.* **heaved** or *chiefly naut.* **hove, heaving. 1.** To raise or lift. **2.** To throw, esp. with great effort. **3.** *Naut.* **a.** To pull on or haul. **b.** To push. **4.** *Naut.* To come to be in a specified position: *The ship hove alongside.* **5.** To breathe or emit: *heaved a sigh.* **6.** To rise up or swell. **7.** *Informal.* To vomit. —*n.* **1.** The act or strain of heaving. **2.** *Informal.* A throw. **3. heaves** *(takes sing. or pl. v.).* A respiratory disease of horses characterized by coughing and irregular breathing. [< OE *hebban.* See **kap-.**]

heav•en (hĕv'ən) *n.* **1.** *Often* **heavens.** The sky or universe as seen from the earth. **2.** The abode of God, the angels, and the souls granted salvation. **3. a. Heaven.** The divine providence. **b.** *Often* **heavens.** A euphemism for God: *Good heavens!* **4.** The celestial powers; the gods: *The heavens favored our plan.* **5.** A place or thing that affords supreme happiness. [< OE *heofon.*] —**heav'en•ly** *adj.* —**heav'en•ward** *adv. & adj.*

heav•y (hĕv'ē) *adj.* **-ier, -iest. 1.** Having relatively great weight. **2.** Having relatively high density. **3. a.** Large in number or volume: *heavy rainfall; a heavy turnout.* **b.** Intense or sustained: *heavy activity.* **4.** Dense or thick: *heavy fog; a heavy coat.* **5. a.** Concerted or powerful; severe: *a heavy blow.* **b.** Rough; violent: *heavy seas.* **6. a.** To a great or habitual degree. **b.** On a large scale. **7.** Of great import or seriousness. **8. a.** Hard to do. **b.** Oppressive: *heavy taxes.* **9. a.** Copious: *a heavy breakfast.* **b.** Not easily or quickly digested. **10.** Having large or marked physical features. **11.** Weighed with concern or sadness: *a heavy heart.* **12.** Ponderous. **13. a.** Weighed down; laden. **b.** Showing weariness. **14.** Involving large-scale manufacturing: *heavy industry.* **15.** Bearing heavy arms or armor. —*adv.* Heavily. —*n., pl.* **-ies. 1.** A villain in a story or play. **2.** An actor who portrays villains or scoundrels in plays. [< OE *hefig.* See kap-.] —**heav′i·ly** *adv.* —**heav′i·ness** *n.*

heav·y-dut·y (hĕv′ē-d/y/ōō′tē) *adj.* Made for hard use: *heavy-duty equipment.*

heav·y-hand·ed (hĕv′ē-hăn′dĭd) *adj.* **1.** Clumsy. **2.** Tactless. **3.** Oppressive.

heav·y·set (hĕv′ē-sĕt′) *adj.* Having a heavy, compact build.

heavy water. Any of several isotopic varieties of water, esp. **deuterium oxide.**

heav·y·weight (hĕv′ē-wāt′) *n.* **1.** One of above average weight. **2.** One that competes in the heaviest class, esp. a boxer weighing more than 175 pounds.

Heb. 1. Hebrew. **2.** Hebrews (New Testament).

Hebr. Hebrew.

He·bra·ic (hĭ-brā′ĭk) *adj.* Also **He·bra·i·cal** (-ĭ-kəl). Of or characteristic of the Hebrews or their language or culture. —**He′bra·ism′** (hē′brā-ĭz′əm, hē′brə-) *n.*

He·brew (hē′brōō) *n.* **1.** One of the Semitic people claiming descent from Abraham, Isaac, and Jacob; an Israelite. **2. a.** The Semitic language of the ancient Hebrews, used in most of the Old Testament. **b.** Any of various later forms of this language, esp. the form now spoken in Israel. —*adj.* Relating or pertaining to Hebrews.

Hebrew Scriptures. The Pentateuch, the Prophets, and the Hagiographa, forming the covenant between God and the Jewish people that is the foundation and Bible of Judaism.

heck (hĕk). Euphemism for hell.

heck·le (hĕk′əl) *v.* **-led, -ling.** To harass persistently, as with questions or objections. [< OE *hæcel,* "comb for flax."] —**heck′ler** *n.*

hec·tare (hĕk′târ′) *n.* A metric unit of area equal to 100 ares or 2.471 acres. [< Gk *hekaton,* hundred.]

hec·tic (hĕk′tĭk) *adj.* **1.** Characterized by feverish activity, confusion, or haste. **2.** Of or having an undulating fever, as in diseases such as tuberculosis or septicemia. **3.** Flushed. [< Gk *hektikos,* formed by habit, consumptive, hectic.] —**hec′ti·cal·ly, hec′tic·ly** *adv.*

hec·tor (hĕk′tər) *v.* To intimidate or dominate in a blustering way.

Hec·tor (hĕk′tər) *n.* Trojan prince and champion slain by Achilles in Homer's *Iliad.*

he'd (hĕd). **1.** Contraction of *he had.* **2.** Contraction of *he would.*

hedge (hĕj) *n.* A row of closely planted shrubs forming a boundary. —*v.* **hedged, hedging. 1.** To enclose or bound with or as if with hedges. **2.** To counterbalance (a bet) with other transactions, so as to limit risk. **3.** To avoid committing oneself, as by making evasive statements. [< OE *hecg.* See kagh-.]

hedge·hog (hĕj′hŏg′, -hŏg′) *n.* A small Old World mammal having the back covered with dense spines.

hedge·hop (hĕj′hŏp′) *v.* To fly an airplane close to the ground.

he·don·ism (hēd′n-ĭz′əm) *n.* **1.** Pursuit of or devotion to pleasure. **2.** The ethical doctrine that only that which is pleasant is intrinsically good. [< Gk *hēdonē,* pleasure.] —**he′don·ist** *n.* —**he′don·is′tic** *adj.*

heed (hēd) *v.* To pay attention (to). —*n.* Close attention or consideration. [< OE *hēdan.* See kadh-.] —**heed′ful** *adj.* —**heed′ful·ly** *adv.* —**heed′less** *adj.* —**heed′less·ly** *adv.*

heel¹ (hēl) *n.* **1.** The rounded posterior portion of the human foot under and behind the ankle. **2.** A similar or corresponding part, as in animals. **3.** That part of footwear which covers the heel. **4.** A lower, rearward surface of a thing. **5.** *Slang.* A dishonorable man. —*v.* **1.** To furnish with a heel or heels. **2.** *Slang.* To furnish (a person) with something, esp. money. **3.** To follow at the heels of. [< OE *hēla.* See kenk-¹.] —**heel′less** *adj.*

heel² (hēl) *v.* To tip or cause to tip to one side, esp. a ship. —*n.* A tilting to one side; list. [Prob < OE *hieldan.*]

heft (hĕft) *n. Informal.* Weight; heaviness. —*v.* **1.** To determine the weight of by lifting. **2.** To hoist; heave. [< HEAVE.]

heft·y (hĕf′tē) *adj.* **-ier, -iest. 1.** Heavy. **2.** Large and powerful.

He·gel (hā′gəl), **Georg Wilhelm Friedrich.** 1770–1831. German philosopher.

he·gem·o·ny (hĭ-jĕm′ə-nē, hĕj′ə-mō′nē) *n., pl.* **-nies.** Predominance, esp. that of one state over others. [Gk *hēgemonia,* authority, rule.]

he·gi·ra (hĭ-jī′rə, hĕj′ər-ə) *n.* A flight, as from danger. [Ar *(al)hijrah,* abandonment of Mecca, flight.]

heif·er (hĕf′ər) *n.* A young cow, esp. one that has not borne a calf. [< OE *hēahfore,* young ox.]

height (hīt) *n.* **1.** The highest or uppermost point. **2.** The most advanced degree; point of highest intensity. **3. a.** The distance from the base to the top of something. **b.** The elevation of something above a given level; altitude. **4.** Stature, esp. of the human body. **5.** An eminence. [< OE *hēhthu, hīehthu.*]

height·en (hīt′n) *v.* **1.** To make or become greater in quantity or degree; intensify. **2.** To make or become high or higher.

Hei·ne (hī′nə), **Heinrich.** 1797–1856. German poet and critic.

hei·nous (hā′nəs) *adj.* Grossly wicked or reprehensible. [< OF *haïr,* to hate.]

heir (âr) *n.* A person who inherits or is entitled by law to inherit the property, title, or office of another. [< L *hērēs.*]

heir apparent. An heir whose right to in-

ă pat/ā ate/âr care/ä bar/b **bib**/ch **chew**/d **deed**/ĕ pet/ē be/f **fit**/g **gag**/h **hat/hw what**/
ĭ pit/ī **pie**/îr **pier**/j **judge**/k **kick**/l lid, fatal/m **mum**/n no, sudden/ng **sing**/ŏ pot/ō go/

heritance is indefeasible by law provided he survives his ancestor.

heir·ess (âr′ĭs) *n.* A female heir.

heir·loom (âr′lōōm′) *n.* 1. A possession passed down in a family through succeeding generations. 2. *Law.* An article of personal property included in an inherited estate.

heist (hīst) *v. Slang.* To rob; steal. —*n. Slang.* A robbery. [Dial var of HOIST.]

held (hĕld). *p.t.* & *p.p.* of **hold.**

Hel·e·na (hĕl′ə-nə). The capital of Montana. Pop. 20,000.

Helen of Troy. *Gk.Myth.* A daughter of Zeus and queen of Sparta whose abduction by Paris caused the Trojan War.

hel·i·cal (hĕl′ĭ-kəl) *adj.* Shaped like a helix.

hel·i·cop·ter (hĕl′ĭ-kŏp′tər) *n.* An aircraft that derives its lift from blades that rotate about an approximately vertical central axis. [F *hélicoptère,* "spiral wing."]

helio–. *comb. form.* The sun. [< Gk *hēlios,* the sun.]

he·li·o·cen·tric (hē′lē-ō-sĕn′trĭk) *adj.* Having the sun as a center. —**he′li·o·cen·tric′i·ty** (-sĕn-trĭs′ə-tē) *n.*

he·li·o·graph (hē′lē-ə-grăf′, -gräf′) *n.* A signaling apparatus that reflects sunlight with a movable mirror.

he·li·o·trope (hē′lē-ə-trōp′) *n.* A cultivated plant with small, fragrant, purplish flowers.

hel·i·port (hĕl′ə-pôrt′, -pōrt′) *n.* An airport for helicopters.

he·li·um (hē′lē-əm) *n. Symbol* **He** A colorless, odorless, tasteless, inert gaseous element used to provide lift for balloons and as an inert component of various artificial atmospheres. Atomic number 2, atomic weight 4.0026. [< Gk *hēlios,* the sun.]

he·lix (hē′lĭks) *n., pl.* **-lixes** or **helices** (hĕl′ə-sēz′, hē′lə-). 1. A three-dimensional curve that lies on a cylinder or cone and cuts the elements at a constant angle. 2. Any spiral or helical object. [< Gk, spiral.]

hell (hĕl) *n.* 1. The abode of the dead; the underworld where departed souls were believed to dwell. 2. The place or state of torture and punishment for the wicked after death. 3. The infernal powers of evil and darkness. 4. a. Torment; anguish. b. Something that causes agony. —**a** (or **one**) **hell of a.** *Informal.* Unusually (bad, good, hard, etc.). —**raise hell.** *Slang.* To cause a disturbance or trouble. —*interj. Slang.* Expressive of acute anger, disgust, or impatience. [< OE. See kel-⁴.]

he'll (hĕl). 1. Contraction of *he will.* 2. Contraction of *he shall.*

hell-bent (hĕl′bĕnt′) *adj.* Impetuously bent on doing something.

hell·cat (hĕl′kăt′) *n.* A furious and evil woman.

hel·le·bore (hĕl′ə-bôr′, -bōr′) *n.* Any of several chiefly poisonous plants with white or greenish flowers. [< Gk *helleboros,* perh "eaten by fawns."]

Hel·lene (hĕl′ēn′) *n.* Also **Hel·le·ni·an** (hĕ-lē′nē-ən). A Greek. [< Gk *Hellēn.*]

Hel·len·ic (hĕ-lĕn′ĭk) *adj.* Of or relating to the ancient Greeks or their language.

hell·gram·mite (hĕl′grə-mīt′) *n.* A large, brownish aquatic insect larva, often used as fishing bait. [?]

hell·hole (hĕl′hōl′) *n.* A place of extreme wretchedness and squalor.

hel·lion (hĕl′yən) *n. Informal.* A mischievous, unrestrainable person. [?]

hell·ish (hĕl′ĭsh) *adj.* 1. Of or relating to hell. 2. *Informal.* Like hell; devilish. —**hell′ish·ly** *adv.* —**hell′ish·ness** *n.*

hel·lo (hĕ-lō′, hə-) *interj.* 1. Used to greet another or summon their attention. 2. Expressive of surprise. —*n., pl.* **-loes.** A calling or greeting of "hello." [Var of earlier *holla,* stop!]

helm (hĕlm) *n.* 1. The tiller, wheel, or whole steering gear of a ship. 2. A position of leadership or control. [< OE *helma.* See **kelp-.**]

hel·met (hĕl′mĭt) *n.* 1. A protective head covering of metal, used in combat or warfare. 2. A protective head covering of hard material, as leather or plastic, worn by policemen, firemen, etc. [< Frank **helm.*]

helms·man (hĕlmz′mən) *n.* One who steers a ship.

hel·ot (hĕl′ət, hē′lət) *n.* A serf; bondsman. [< Gk *Heilōtes,* a class of Spartan serfs.]

help (hĕlp) *v.* 1. To give assistance (to); aid. 2. To contribute to; further. 3. To give relief to. 4. To improve; benefit. 5. To be able to prevent, change, or rectify: *I cannot help her laziness.* 6. To refrain from; avoid: *He cannot help laughing.* 7. To wait on; serve. —**cannot help but.** To be compelled to. —*n.* 1. Aid; assistance. 2. Relief; remedy. 3. One that helps. 4. a. A person employed to assist. b. Such employees collectively. [< OE *helpan.* See **kelb-.**] —**help′er** *n.*

Usage: The construction *cannot help but* is a less formal variant of *cannot help* plus gerund and of *cannot but* plus infinitive without *to.* All three express substantially the same idea: *One cannot help but admire his courage. One cannot help admiring his courage. One cannot but admire his courage.*

help·ful (hĕlp′fəl) *adj.* Providing help; useful; beneficial. —**help′ful·ly** *adv.* —**help′ful·ness** *n.*

help·ing (hĕl′pĭng) *n.* A portion of food for one person.

help·less (hĕlp′lĭs) *adj.* 1. Unable to manage by oneself; defenseless; dependent. 2. Lacking power to help; impotent. —**help′less·ly** *adv.* —**help′less·ness** *n.*

help·mate (hĕlp′māt′) *n.* A helper, esp. a spouse.

help·meet (hĕlp′mēt′) *n.* A helpmate.

Hel·sin·ki (hĕl′sĭng′kē). The capital of Finland. Pop. 470,000.

hel·ter-skel·ter (hĕl′tər-skĕl′tər) *adv.* 1. In disorderly haste. 2. Haphazardly. 3. In confusion. —*adj.* 1. Carelessly hurried and confused. 2. Haphazard. [?]

helve (hĕlv) *n.* A handle of a wagon or tool. [< OE *hielfe.*]

hem¹ (hĕm) *n.* An edge or border of a piece of cloth, esp. a finished edge made by folding under and stitching down the selvage or raw edge. —*v.* **hemmed, hemming.** 1. To fold back and stitch down the edge of. 2. To encircle

---

ô paw, for/oi boy/ou out/ŏŏ took/ōō coo/p pop/r run/s sauce/sh shy/t to/th thin/*th* the/ ŭ cut/ûr fur/v van/w wag/y yes/z size/zh vision/ə ago, item, edible, gallop, circus/

and confine; shut in; enclose. [<OE *hemm.* See **kem-².**] —**hem′mer** *n.*

hem² (hĕm) *n.* A short cough or clearing of the throat made to gain attention, fill a pause, etc. —*v.* **hemmed, hemming.** To utter this sound. —**hem and haw.** To be hesitant and indecisive in speech. [Imit.]

he-man (hē′măn′) *n. Informal.* A strong, virile man.

hem·a·tite (hĕm′ə-tīt′, hē′mə-) *n.* A blackish-red to brick-red mineral, essentially Fe_2O_3, the chief ore of iron. [< Gk *(lithos) haimatitēs,* "bloodlike (stone)."]

hemato–. *comb. form.* Blood. [< Gk *haima,* blood.]

he·ma·tol·o·gy (hē′mə-tŏl′ə-jē, hĕm′ə-) *n.* The science encompassing the generation, anatomy, physiology, pathology, and therapeutics of blood. —**he′ma·tol′o·gist** *n.*

heme (hēm) *n.* The nonprotein, ferrous-iron-containing component of hemoglobin, having composition $C_{34}H_{32}FeN_4O_4$.

hemi–. *comb. form.* Half. [< Gk *hēmi-.*]

–hemia. Variant of -emia.

Hem·ing·way (hĕm′ĭng-wā′), **Ernest.** 1899–1961. American novelist.

hem·i·sphere (hĕm′ə-sfîr′) *n.* **1. a.** A half of a sphere bounded by a great circle. **b.** A symmetric half of an approximately symmetrical object. **2.** Either the N or S half of the earth as divided by the equator or the E or W half as divided by a meridian. —**hem′i·spher′ic** (-sfîr′ĭk, -sfĕr′ĭk), **hem′i·spher′i·cal** *adj.*

hem·lock (hĕm′lŏk′) *n.* **1. a.** An evergreen tree with short, flat needles and small cones. **b.** The wood of such a tree. **2. a.** A poisonous plant with compound leaves and small whitish flowers. **b.** A poison obtained from this plant. [< OE *hemlic.*]

hemo–. *comb. form.* Blood. [< Gk *haima,* blood.]

he·mo·glo·bin (hē′mə-glō′bən, hĕm′ə-) *n.* The oxygen-bearing, iron-containing protein in vertebrate red blood cells, consisting of about 6% heme and 94% globin. [< HEMATO- + GLOBULIN.]

he·mo·phil·i·a (hē′mə-fĭl′ē-ə, hĕm′ə-) *n.* A hereditary plasma-coagulation disorder, principally affecting males but transmitted by females and characterized by excessive, sometimes spontaneous, bleeding. —**he′mo·phil′i·ac′** (-ăk′) *adj. & n.*

hem·or·rhage (hĕm′ə-rĭj) *n.* Bleeding, esp. copious discharge of blood from the vessels. —*v.* **-rhaged, -rhaging.** To bleed copiously. —**hem′or·rhag′ic** (-răj′ĭk) *adj.*

hem·or·rhoid (hĕm′ə-roid′) *n.* **1.** An itching or painful mass of dilated veins in swollen anal tissue. **2. hemorrhoids.** The pathological condition in which such swollen masses occur. [< Gk *haimorrhoos,* flowing with blood.]

he·mo·stat (hē′mə-stăt′) *n.* Any agent that stops bleeding, esp. a clamplike instrument used in surgery.

hemp (hĕmp) *n.* **1.** A tall Asian plant with stems that yield a coarse fiber used in cordage. **2.** The fiber of this plant. [< OE *hænep.*] —**hemp′en** *adj.*

hem·stitch (hĕm′stĭch′) *n.* A decorative stitch made by drawing out several parallel threads and catching together the cross threads in uniform groups, thus creating an open design. —*v.* To ornament with this stitch.

hen (hĕn) *n.* A female bird, esp. the adult female of the domestic fowl. [< OE. See **kan-.**]

hence (hĕns) *adv.* **1. a.** For this reason; therefore. **b.** From this source. **2.** From now. **3.** Forth from this place. [< OE *heonane,* from here, away. See **ko-.**]

hence·forth (hĕns′fôrth′) *adv.* Also **hence·for·ward** (hĕns′fôr′wərd). From now on; from this time forth.

hench·man (hĕnch′mən) *n.* **1.** A loyal and trusted follower or subordinate. **2.** One who supports a political figure chiefly out of self-seeking interests. [ME *hengestman,* prob groom.]

hen·na (hĕn′ə) *n.* **1. a.** A cosmetic dyestuff obtained from the leaves of a Middle Eastern shrub. **b.** The shrub itself. **2.** Strong reddish brown. —*v.* To dye or rinse (hair) with henna. [Ar *ḥinnā′.*]

hen·peck (hĕn′pĕk′) *v. Informal.* To afflict (one's husband) with persistent nagging.

hen·ry (hĕn′rē) *n., pl.* **-ries** or **-rys.** The unit of inductance in which an induced electromotive force of one volt is produced when the current is varied at the rate of one ampere per second. [< J. *Henry* (1797–1878), American physicist.]

Hen·ry VIII (hĕn′rē). 1491–1547. King of England (1509–47); broke with Rome (1533).

Hen·ry (hĕn′rē), **Patrick.** 1736–1799. American Revolutionary leader and orator.

hep. Variant of **hip².**

he·pat·i·ca (hĭ-păt′ĭ-kə) *n.* A North American woodland plant with three-lobed leaves and lavender or white flowers. [< ML *hēpatica,* liverwort.]

hep·a·ti·tis (hĕp′ə-tī′tĭs) *n.* Inflammation of the liver characterized by jaundice and usually accompanied by fever and other systemic manifestations. [< Gk *hēpar (hēpat-),* liver + -ITIS.]

her (hûr; *unstressed* hər, ər). **I.** —*pron.* The objective case of the 3rd person pronoun *she,* used as the direct or indirect object of a verb or as the object of a preposition. **II.** The possessive form of the pronoun *she,* used attributively: *her* umbrella. [< OE *hire.* See **ko-.**]

He·ra (hîr′ə). *Gk. Myth.* The sister and wife of Zeus.

her·ald (hĕr′əld) *n.* **1.** One who proclaims important news. **2.** One that announces or gives indication of something to come. **3.** An official formerly charged with making royal proclamations. —*v.* To proclaim; usher in. [< OF *herault* < Gmc.]

he·ral·dic (hə-răl′dĭk) *adj.* Of or pertaining to heralds or heraldry.

her·ald·ry (hĕr′əl-drē) *n., pl.* **-ries. 1. a.** The profession of devising, granting, and blazoning arms and tracing pedigrees. **b.** The history and description of armorial bearings. **2.** Armorial ensigns. **3.** Pomp and ceremony.

herb (ûrb, hûrb) *n.* **1.** A plant that has a fleshy rather than woody stem and that generally dies back at the end of each growing season. **2.** An often aromatic plant used in medicine or as seasoning. [< L *herba*.]

her•ba•ceous (hûr-bā′shəs) *adj.* Of herbs as distinguished from woody plants.

herb•age (ûr′bĭj, hûr′-) *n.* **1.** Grass or leafy plants used esp. for pasturage. **2.** The fleshy, often edible parts of plants.

herb•al (hûr′bəl, ûr′-) *adj.* Of or relating to medicinal or culinary herbs.

her•bi•vore (hûr′bə-vôr′, -vōr′) *n.* A herbivorous animal.

her•biv•o•rous (hûr-bĭv′ər-əs) *adj.* Feeding on plants.

Her•cu•les (hûr′kyə-lēz′) *n.* **1.** Often **hercules.** A man of prodigious strength. **2.** A constellation in the N Hemisphere. [< *Hercules,* Greco-Roman mythological hero noted for his strength.] **—Her′cu•le′an** *adj.*

herd (hûrd) *n.* **1.** A group of animals, as domestic cattle or elephants, that remain or are kept together. **2.** A number of people banded together. *—v.* **1.** To congregate in a herd. **2.** To gather, keep, or drive (animals) in a herd. [< OE *heord.* See **kerdh-**.]

herd•er (hûr′dər) *n.* **1.** One who tends or drives a herd. **2.** Also **herds•man** (hûrdz′mən). One who owns or breeds livestock.

here (hîr) *adv.* **1.** At or in this place. **2.** At this time. **3.** At or on this point or detail. **4.** In the present life or condition. **5.** To this place; hither. *—interj.* Used as a response to a roll call or summons. [< OE *hēr.* See **ko-**.]

here•a•bout (hîr′ə-bout′) *adv.* Also **here•a•bouts** (-bouts′). In this general vicinity; around here.

here•af•ter (hîr-ăf′tər, -äf′tər) *adv.* **1.** After this; henceforth. **2.** In the afterlife. *—n.* Life after death.

here•by (hîr-bī′) *adv.* By this means.

he•red•i•tar•y (hə-rĕd′ə-tĕr′ē) *adj.* **1.** *Law.* **a.** Passing down by inheritance. **b.** Having title or possession through inheritance. **2.** Genetically transmitted or transmissible. **3.** Derived from or fostered by one's ancestors; traditional. **—he•red′i•tar′i•ly** *adv.*

he•red•i•ty (hə-rĕd′ə-tē) *n., pl.* **-ties. 1.** The genetic transmission of characteristics from parents to offspring. **2.** The totality of characteristics and associated potentialities so transmitted to an individual organism. [< L *hērēs (hērēd-),* heir.]

here•in (hîr-ĭn′) *adv.* In or into this.

here•of (hîr-ŭv′, -ŏv′) *adv.* Pertaining to this.

here•on (hîr-ŏn′, -ôn′) *adv.* Hereupon.

her•e•sy (hĕr′ə-sē) *n., pl.* **-sies. 1.** An opinion or doctrine at variance with established beliefs, esp. dissension from or denial of Roman Catholic dogma by a professed believer or baptized church member. **2.** Adherence to such dissenting opinion. [< Gk *hairesis,* "a taking," faction.]

her•e•tic (hĕr′ə-tĭk) *n.* One who holds controversial opinions, esp. one who publicly dissents from the officially accepted dogma of the Roman Catholic Church. [< Gk *hairetikos,* able to choose, factious.] **—he•ret′i•cal** (hə-rĕt′ĭ-kəl) *adj.* **—he•ret′i•cal•ly** *adv.*

here•to (hîr-tōō′) *adv.* To this place or matter.

here•to•fore (hîr′tə-fôr′, -fōr′) *adv.* Up to the present time; before this.

here•un•to (hîr-ŭn′tōō) *adv.* Hereto.

here•up•on (hîr′ə-pŏn′, -pôn′) *adv.* **1.** Following instantly upon this. **2.** On this point or matter.

here•with (hîr-wĭth′, -wĭ*th*′) *adv.* **1.** Along with this. **2.** By this means; hereby.

her•i•ta•ble (hĕr′ə-tə-bəl) *adj.* Capable of being inherited.

her•i•tage (hĕr′ə-tĭj) *n.* **1.** Property that is or can be inherited. **2.** Something other than property passed down from preceding generations; legacy; tradition. **3.** Birthright. [< L *hērēs (hērēd-),* heir.]

her•maph•ro•dite (hər-măf′rə-dīt′) *n.* One having the sex organs and often the secondary sex characteristics of both male and female. [< Gk *Hermaphroditos,* the son of Hermes and Aphrodite, who became united in one body with a nymph.] **—her•maph′ro•dit′ic** (-dĭt′ĭk) *adj.* **—her•maph′ro•dit′i•cal•ly** *adv.*

Her•mes (hûr′mēz′). Greek god of commerce, invention, cunning, and theft.

her•met•ic (hər-mĕt′ĭk) *adj.* Also **her•met•i•cal** (-ĭ-kəl). **1.** Completely sealed, esp. against the escape or entry of air. **2.** Impervious to outside interference or influence. **—her•met′i•cal•ly** *adv.*

her•mit (hûr′mĭt) *n.* One who has withdrawn from society and lives a solitary existence. [< Gk *erēmitēs,* "(one) of the desert."]

her•mit•age (hûr′mə-tĭj) *n.* **1.** The habitation of a hermit. **2.** A retreat; hideaway.

her•ni•a (hûr′nē-ə) *n., pl.* **-as** or **-niae** (-nē-ē′). Protrusion of an organ, organic part, or any bodily structure through the wall that normally contains it. [< L.]

her•ni•ate (hûr′nē-āt′) *v.* **-ated, -ating.** To protrude through an abnormal bodily opening. [HERNI(A) + -ATE[1].]

he•ro (hîr′ō) *n., pl.* **-roes. 1.** In mythology and legend, a man celebrated for his strength and bold exploits. **2.** Any man noted for his special achievements. **3.** The principal male character in a novel, poem, or dramatic work. [< Gk *hērōs.*]

He•rod•o•tus (hĭ-rŏd′ə-təs). Greek historian of the 5th century B.C.

he•ro•ic (hĭ-rō′ĭk) *adj.* Also **he•ro•i•cal** (-ĭ-kəl). **1.** Of or appropriate to a hero or heroes; courageous; noble. **2.** Calling for heroism; involving risk. **3.** Impressive in size or scope; on a grand or grandiose scale. *—n.* **heroics.** Melodramatic behavior or language. **—he•ro′i•cal•ly** *adv.* **—he•ro′i•cal•ness** *n.*

her•o•in (hĕr′ō-ən) *n.* A highly addictive narcotic, $C_{17}H_{17}NO(C_2H_3O_2)_2$, derived from morphine.

her•o•ine (hĕr′ō-ĭn) *n.* **1.** The female counterpart of a hero. **2.** The principal female character in a literary or dramatic work.

her•o•ism (hĕr′ō-ĭz′əm) *n.* **1.** The condition or quality of being a hero. **2.** Courage; gallantry.

he•ron (hĕr′ən) *n.* A wading bird with a long neck, long legs, and a long, pointed bill. [< OF *hairon.*]

ô paw, for/oi boy/ou out/ōō took/ōō coo/p pop/r run/s sauce/sh shy/t to/th thin/*th* the/ ŭ cut/ûr fur/v van/w wag/y yes/z size/zh vision/ə ago, item, edible, gallop, circus/

her·pes zos·ter (hûr′pēz′ zŏs′tər, zōs′-). A viral infection with eruption of vesicles along a nerve path on one side of the body, often involving severe neuralgia. [NL, "girdle herpes."]

her·ring (hĕr′ĭng) n., pl. -ring or -rings. A commercially important food fish of Atlantic and Pacific waters. [< OE *hæring* < Gmc *hēringaz.*]

her·ring·bone (hĕr′ĭng-bōn′) n. 1. A pattern consisting of rows of slanted parallel lines, with the direction of the slant alternating row by row. 2. A fabric woven in this pattern.

hers (hûrz). The possessive form of the pronoun *she*, used as a predicate adjective or as a substantive: *The gloves are hers. My husband is a doctor and hers is a lawyer.* —**of hers.** Belonging to her: *a friend of hers.*

her·self (hûr-sĕlf′) pron. A form of the 3rd person sing. feminine pronoun: 1. —Used reflexively: *She hurt herself.* 2. —Used for emphasis: *She did it herself.* 3. —Used to indicate one's normal or proper state: *She hasn't been herself lately.* —**by herself.** 1. Alone. 2. Without help.

hertz (hûrts) n. A unit of frequency equal to one cycle per second. [< H. *Hertz* (1857–1894), German physicist.]

he's (hēz). 1. Contraction of *he is.* 2. Contraction of *he has.*

hes·i·tant (hĕz′ə-tənt) adj. Inclined or tending to hesitate. —**hes′i·tan·cy** n.

hes·i·tate (hĕz′ə-tāt′) v. -tated, -tating. 1. To be slow or reluctant to act or decide; waver; demur. 2. To pause briefly, as in uncertainty. 3. To falter. [L *haesitāre*, to stick fast, hesitate.] —**hes′i·tat′er** n. —**hes′i·tat′ing·ly** adv. —**hes′i·ta′tion** n.

hetero–. comb. form. Other, another, or different. [< Gk *heteros*, other.]

het·er·o·cy·clic (hĕt′ər-ō-sī′klĭk, -sĭk′lĭk) adj. Chem. Containing more than one kind of atom joined in a ring.

het·er·o·dox (hĕt′ər-ə-dŏks′) adj. 1. Not in agreement with accepted beliefs, esp. departing from church doctrine or dogma. 2. Holding unorthodox opinions. [< Gk *heterodoxos*, differing in opinion.] —**het′er·o·dox′y** n.

het·er·o·ge·ne·ous (hĕt′ər-ə-jē′nē-əs, -jēn′yəs) adj. Also **het·er·og·e·nous** (hĕt′ə-rŏj′ə-nəs). Consisting of or involving parts that are unlike or without interrelation; having dissimilar elements; not homogeneous. [< HETERO- + Gk *genos*, kind, sex.] —**het′er·o·ge·ne′i·ty** (-ə-rō-jə-nē′ə-tē) n.

het·er·o·sex·u·al (hĕt′ə-rō-sĕk′shōō-əl) adj. 1. Characterized by attraction to the opposite sex. 2. Pertaining to different sexes. —n. A heterosexual person.

heth (KHĕt, KHĕth, KHĕs) n. Also **cheth.** The 8th letter in the Hebrew alphabet, representing *ẖ.*

hew (hyōō) v. **hewed, hewn** (hyōōn) or **hewed, hewing.** 1. To make or shape with or as with an ax, knife, etc. 2. To cut down with an ax. 3. To adhere or conform; hold. [< OE *hēawan.* See kau-.] —**hew′er** n.

HEW Department of Health, Education, and Welfare.

hex (hĕks) n. 1. An evil spell; curse. 2. A bad influence on or dominating control over someone or something. —v. 1. To bewitch. 2. To wish or bring bad luck to. [< G *Hexe*, witch.]

hex. hexagon; hexagonal.

hexa–. comb. form. Six. [< Gk *hex*, six.]

hex·a·chlo·ro·phene (hĕk′sə-klôr′ə-fēn′, -klôr′ə-fēn′) n. A white powder, $(C_6HCl_3OH)_2$-CH_2, used as a bactericidal agent in soaps, cosmetics, and skin medications.

hex·a·gon (hĕk′sə-gŏn′) n. A polygon having six sides. —**hex·ag′o·nal** (-săg′ə-nəl) adj.

hex·a·he·dron (hĕk′sə-hē′drən) n., pl. -drons or -dra (-drə). A polyhedron with six faces. —**hex′a·he′dral** adj.

hex·am·e·ter (hĕk-săm′ə-tər) n. A verse line consisting of six feet.

hey (hā) interj. 1. Expressive of surprise, appreciation, etc. 2. Used to attract attention: *Hey, you!* [ME *hei, hay.*]

hey·day (hā′dā′) n. The period of greatest popularity, success, fashion, power, etc.; prime. [Prob < HEY.]

hf high frequency.

Hf hafnium.

Hg mercury (L *hydrargyrum*).

HG High German.

hgt. height.

hi (hī) interj. Expressive of greeting. [ME *hy.*]

H.I. Hawaiian Islands.

hi·a·tus (hī-ā′təs) n., pl. -tuses or -tus. 1. A gap or missing section. 2. An interruption in time; break. 3. *Anat.* A separation, aperture, or fissure. [L *hiātus*, a gaping, gap.]

hi·ba·chi (hĭ-bä′chē) n., pl. -chis. A portable charcoal-burning brazier. [Jap.]

hi·ber·nate (hī′bər-nāt′) v. -nated, -nating. To pass the winter in a dormant or torpid state. [L *hibernāre.*] —**hi′ber·na′tion** n.

hi·bis·cus (hi-bĭs′kəs) n. Any of various chiefly tropical plants or shrubs with large, showy, variously colored flowers. [< Gk *hibiskos*, marshmallow.]

hic·cup (hĭk′ŭp). Also **hic·cough.** n. 1. A spasm of the diaphragm resulting in a sudden, abortive inhalation that is stopped by a spasmodic glottal closure. 2. **the hiccups.** An attack of such spasms. —v. -cupped, -cupping. To have the hiccups. [Earlier *hicket, hickop.*]

hick (hĭk) n. *Informal.* A gullible, provincial person; yokel. —adj. Rural. [< *Hick*, pet form of *Richard.*]

hick·o·ry (hĭk′ə-rē) n., pl. -ries. 1. Any of several North American trees having smooth or shaggy bark, compound leaves, hard-shelled, edible nuts, and hard wood. 2. The wood of such a tree. [< Virginian native name.]

hi·dal·go (hĭ-dăl′gō) n., pl. -gos. A member of the minor nobility in Spain. [Span.]

hide¹ (hīd) v. **hid** (hĭd), **hidden** (hĭd′n) or **hid, hiding.** 1. To put or keep out of sight; secrete; conceal. 2. To avert (one's gaze) in shame or grief. 3. To seek refuge. [< OE *hȳdan.* See skeu-.] —**hid′er** n.

hide² (hīd) n. The skin of an animal, esp. the thick, tough skin of a large animal. [< OE *hȳd.* See skeu-.]

hide-and-seek (hīd′n-sēk′) n. A 'children's

ă pat/ā ate/âr care/ä bar/b bib/ch chew/d deed/ĕ pet/ē be/f fit/g gag/h hat/hw what/ ĭ pit/ī pie/îr pier/j judge/k kick/l lid, fatal/m mum/n no, sudden/ng sing/ŏ pot/ō go/

game in which one player tries to find and catch others who are hiding.

hide·a·way (hĭd'ə-wā') *n.* **1.** A place of concealment; hide-out. **2.** A secluded place.

hide·bound (hĭd'bound') *adj.* Bigoted.

hid·e·ous (hĭd'ē-əs) *adj.* **1.** Physically repulsive; ugly. **2.** Repugnant to the moral sense; despicable. [< OF *hisde*, fear, horror.]

hide-out (hĭd'out') *n.* A place of shelter or concealment.

hie (hī) *v.* **hied, hieing** or **hying.** To go quickly; hasten. [< OE *hīgian*, to strive, hurry.]

hi·er·ar·chy (hī'ə-rär'kē, hī'rär'-) *n., pl.* **-chies. 1.** A body of persons, esp. clergy, classified according to rank or authority. **2.** A body of entities arranged in a graded series. [< Gk *hierarkhēs*, high priest.] —**hi'er·ar'chi·cal, hi'er·ar'chic** *adj.* —**hi'er·ar'chi·cal·ly** *adv.*

hi·er·o·glyph·ic (hī'ər-ə-glĭf'ĭk, hī'rə-) *n.* **1.** A picture or symbol used in writing, esp. in the writing system of ancient Egypt. **2.** **hieroglyphics.** Illegible or undecipherable symbols. [< Gk *hierogluphikos*, written in hieroglyphics.]

hi-fi (hī'fī') *n.* **1.** High fidelity. **2.** An electronic system for reproducing high-fidelity sound. [HI(GH) FI(DELITY).]

hig·gle·dy-pig·gle·dy (hĭg'əl-dē-pĭg'əl-dē) *adv.* In utter disorder or confusion. [Rhyming and jingling formation prob based on PIG.]

high (hī) *adj.* **1.** Tall; elevated. **2.** Being at or near a peak or culmination. **3.** Far removed in time; remote. **4.** Piercing in tone or sound. **5.** Situated far from the equator. **6.** Of great moment or importance; serious; weighty: *high treason.* **7.** Lofty or exalted in quality. **8.** Of great quantity, magnitude, or degree. **9.** Costly; expensive. **10.** In a state of excitement or euphoria. **11.** *Slang.* Intoxicated. —*n.* **1.** A high place or region. **2.** The transmission gear of an automotive vehicle producing maximum speed. **3.** A center of high atmospheric pressure. **4.** *Slang.* Intoxication or euphoria. [< OE *hēah.*] —**high'ly** *adv.*

high·ball (hī'bôl') *n.* A mixed alcoholic beverage served in a tall glass.

high·born (hī'bôrn') *adj.* Of noble birth.

high·boy (hī'boi') *n.* A tall chest of drawers supported on four legs.

high·bred (hī'brĕd') *adj.* Of superior breed or stock.

high·brow (hī'brou') *n.* One who has or affects superior learning or culture. —**high'brow'** *adj.*

high-class (hī'klăs', -kläs') *adj.* First-class.

high·er-up (hī'ər-ŭp') *n. Informal.* One who has a higher rank, position, or status.

high·fa·lu·tin, hi·fa·lu·tin (hī'fə-lōōt'n) *adj. Informal.* Pompous or pretentious.

high fidelity. The electronic reproduction of sound, esp. from broadcast, recorded, or tapeo sources, with minimal distortion. —**high'-fi·del'i·ty** *adj.*

high-flown (hī'flōn') *adj.* **1.** Lofty; exalted. **2.** Pretentious; inflated.

high frequency. A radio frequency in the range between 3 and 30 megacycles per second.

High German. 1. German as spoken and writ-

ten in S Germany. **2.** German.

high·hand·ed (hī'hăn'dĭd) *adj.* In an arrogant or arbitrary manner. —**high'hand'ed·ly** *adv.* —**high'hand'ed·ness** *n.*

high·land (hī'lənd) *n.* **1.** Elevated land. **2. highlands.** A mountainous or hilly region or part of a country.

high·land·er (hī'lən-dər) *n.* **1.** One who lives in a highland area. **2. Highlander.** An inhabitant of The Highlands.

High·lands, The (hī'ləndz). A mountainous region of N and W Scotland.

high·light (hī'līt') *n.* An outstanding event or prominent detail. —*v.* **1.** To give prominence to. **2.** To be the highlight of.

high-mind·ed (hī'mīn'dĭd) *adj.* Characterized by morally lofty ideals or conduct; magnanimous. —**high'-mind'ed·ly** *adv.*

high·ness (hī'nĭs) *n.* **1.** Tallness; height. **2. Highness.** A title of honor for royalty.

high profile. *Informal.* A conspicuous, well-publicized presence or stance.

high-rise (hī'rīz') *adj.* Designating a building with many stories.

high·road (hī'rōd') *n.* **1.** *Chiefly Brit.* A main road; highway. **2.** A direct or sure path.

high school. A school that usually includes grades 9 through 12. —**high'-school'** *adj.*

high seas. The open waters of an ocean or sea beyond the limits of national territorial jurisdiction.

high-sound·ing (hī'soun'dĭng) *adj.* Pompous.

high-spir·it·ed (hī'spĭr'ə-tĭd) *adj.* **1.** Brave. **2.** Vivacious. —**high'-spir'it·ed·ness** *n.*

high-strung (hī'strŭng') *adj.* Acutely nervous and sensitive.

high-ten·sion (hī'tĕn'shən) *adj.* Having a high voltage.

high tide. 1. The tide when the water reaches its highest level. **2.** The time at which this occurs.

high-toned (hī'tōnd') *adj.* **1.** Intellectually or socially superior. **2.** Elegant or slick.

high·way (hī'wā') *n.* A main public road.

high·way·man (hī'wā'mən) *n.* A robber who holds up travelers on a highway.

hi·jack (hī'jăk') *v.* **1.** To rob (a vehicle) by stopping it in transit. **2.** To seize forcibly or commandeer (a moving vehicle). —**hi'jack'er** *n.*

hike (hīk) *v.* **hiked, hiking. 1.** To go on an extended walk, esp. for pleasure. **2.** To raise or go up, as prices. **3.** To be raised, caught up, or uneven. **4.** To raise with a sudden motion; hitch. —*n.* **1.** A walk or march. **2.** A rise as in prices. [?] —**hik'er** *n.*

hi·lar·i·ous (hĭ-lâr'ē-əs, hī-) *adj.* Boisterously funny or merry. [< L *hilaris.*]

hi·lar·i·ty (hĭ-lăr'ə-tē, hī-) *n.* Boisterous merriment. [< Gk *hilaros*, cheerful.]

hill (hĭl) *n.* **1.** A well-defined, naturally elevated area of land smaller than a mountain. **2.** A heap, pile, or mound. [< OE *hyll.* See **kel-⁶.**] —**hill'i·ness** *n.* —**hill'y** *adj.*

hill·bil·ly (hĭl'bĭl'ē) *n., pl.* **-lies.** *Informal.* A person from a rural mountainous area. —**hill'bil'ly** *adj.*

hill·ock (hĭl'ək) *n.* A small hill.

hill·side (hĭl'sīd') *n.* The side or slope of a hill.

ô paw, for/oi boy/ou out/ŏŏ took/ōō coo/p pop/r run/s sauce/sh shy/t to/th thin/*th* the/
ŭ cut/ûr fur/v van/w wag/y yes/z size/zh vision/ə ago, item, edible, gallop, circus/

hill·top (hĭl'tŏp') *n.* The crest or top of a hill.

hilt (hĭlt) *n.* The handle of a weapon or tool, esp. of a sword or dagger. —**to the hilt.** Completely. [< OE < Gmc *hilt-.]

him (hĭm) *pron.* The objective case of the 3rd person pronoun *he,* used as the direct or indirect object of a verb or as the object of a preposition. [< OE. See ko-.]

Hi·ma·la·yas (hĭm'ə-lā'əz, hĭ-mäl'yəz). A mountain range of south-central Asia. Highest elevation, Mount Everest (29,028 ft.).

him·self (hĭm-sĕlf') *pron.* A form of the 3rd person sing. masculine pronoun: **1.** —Used reflexively: *He hurt himself.* **2.** —Used for emphasis: *He did it himself.* **3.** —Used to indicate one's normal or proper state: *He hasn't been himself lately.* —**by himself. 1.** Alone. **2.** Without help.

hind¹ (hīnd) *adj.* Located at the rear; posterior: *hind legs.* [Perh < OE *hinder,* behind, or *hindan,* from behind.]

hind² (hīnd) *n.* The female of the Old World deer. [< OE. See kem-¹.]

hin·der (hĭn'dər) *v.* **1.** To hold back; hamper. **2.** To obstruct or delay the progress of; prevent. [< OE *hindrian.*] —**hin'der·er** *n.*

Hin·di (hĭn'dē) *n.* **1. a.** A group of Indic dialects spoken in N India. **b.** A literary language based upon these dialects. **2.** One who speaks a Hindi dialect. —**Hin'di** *adj.*

hind·most (hīnd'mōst') *adj.* Also **hin·der·most** (hīn'dər-). Farthest to the rear; most remote; last.

hind·quar·ter (hīnd'kwôr'tər) *n.* **1.** The hind leg and posterior part of a side of meat. **2.** The rump of a four-footed animal.

hin·drance (hĭn'drəns) *n.* **1.** The act of hindering. **2.** One that hinders.

hind·sight (hīnd'sīt') *n.* Perception of events after they have occurred.

Hin·du (hĭn'dōo) *n.* **1.** A native of India, esp. N India. **2.** A believer in Hinduism. —**Hin'du** *adj.*

Hin·du·ism (hĭn'dōo-ĭz'əm) *n.* A syncretistic body of religious, philosophical, and social doctrines native to India.

Hindu Kush (kōosh). A mountain range of C Asia.

Hin·du·sta·ni (hĭn'dōo-stä'nē, -stăn'ē) *n.* **1.** A subdivision of Indic, including Urdu and Hindi. **2.** One who speaks a Hindustani language. —**Hin'du·sta'ni** *adj.*

hinge (hĭnj) *n.* **1.** A flexible device permitting pivoting of a part, as a door, on a stationary frame. **2.** A similar structure or part. —*v.* **hinged, hinging. 1.** To attach to or equip with a hinge or hinges. **2.** To depend; be contingent. [ME *heng.*] —**hinge'less** *adj.*

hint (hĭnt) *n.* **1.** A subtle suggestion or slight indication; clue. **2.** A barely perceptible amount. —*v.* **1.** To make known by a hint. **2.** To give a hint or hints. [?] —**hint'er** *n.*

hin·ter·land (hĭn'tər-lănd') *n.* **1.** The land directly adjacent to a coast. **2.** A region remote from urban areas. [G.]

hip¹ (hĭp) *n.* **1.** The laterally projecting prominence of the pelvis or pelvic region from the waist to the thigh. **2.** The hip joint. [< OE *hype.*] —**hip'py** *adj.*

hip² (hĭp) *adj.* **hipper, hippest.** Also **hep** (hĕp). *Slang.* **1.** Aware of advanced tastes and attitudes. **2.** Cognizant; wise. [?]

hip³ (hĭp) *n.* The berrylike fruit of a rose. [< OE *hēope.*]

hip·bone (hĭp'bōn') *n.* The innominate bone.

hip joint. The joint between the innominate bone and the femur.

hip·pie (hĭp'ē) *n.* Also **hippy** *pl.* **-pies.** A member of a loosely knit nonconformist group, esp. one that rejects conventional social mores. [< HIP².] —**hip'pie** *adj.*

Hip·poc·ra·tes (hĭ-pŏk'rə-tēz'). 460?–377? B.C. Greek physician.

hip·po·drome (hĭp'ə-drōm') *n.* An arena, esp. for horse shows. [< Gk *hippodromos.*]

hip·po·pot·a·mus (hĭp'ə-pŏt'ə-məs) *n., pl.* **-muses** or **-mi** (-mī'). A large African river mammal with dark, almost hairless skin and a broad, wide-mouthed muzzle. [< Gk *hippos ho potamios,* "horse of the river."]

hip·py. Variant of **hippie.**

hire (hīr) *v.* **hired, hiring. 1.** To engage the services of (a person) for a fee; employ. **2.** To rent. **3.** To rent out. —*n.* **1.** The payment for services or use of something. **2.** The act of hiring. **3.** The condition or fact of being hired. [< OE *hȳrian* < Gmc *khūrjan.*]

hire·ling (hīr'lĭng) *n.* A mercenary.

Hi·ro·shi·ma (hīr'ə-shē'mə, hĭ-rō'shĭ-mə). A city of SW Honshu, Japan. Pop. 485,000.

hir·sute (hûr'sōot', hûr'sōot') *adj.* Hairy. [L *hirsūtus.*] —**hir'sute'ness** *n.*

his (hĭz). The possessive form of the pronoun *he:* **1.** —Used attributively: *his wallet.* **2.** —Used as a predicate adjective or as a substantive: *The boots are his. If you can't find your hat, take his.* —**of his.** Belonging to him: *a friend of his.* [< OE. See ko-.]

His·pa·nio·la (hĭs'pən-yō'lə). An island of the West Indies, occupied in the W by Haiti and in the E by the Dominican Republic.

hiss (hĭs) *n.* **1.** A sharp, sibilant sound similar to a sustained *s.* **2.** This sound as an expression of disapproval or contempt. —*v.* **1.** To make a hiss. **2.** To direct hisses at in disapproval. [ME *hissen* (imit.).] —**hiss'er** *n.*

hist. historian; historical; history.

his·ta·mine (hĭs'tə-mēn', -mĭn) *n.* A white crystalline compound, $C_5H_9N_3$, found in plant and animal tissue, a stimulant of gastric secretion. —**his'ta·min'ic** (-mĭn'ĭk) *adj.*

histo–. *comb. form.* Bodily tissue. [< Gk *histos,* web, beam, mast.]

his·to·gram (hĭs'tə-grăm') *n.* A graphic representation of a frequency distribution in which the widths of contiguous vertical bars are proportional to the class widths of the variable and the heights of the bars are proportional to the class frequencies. [HISTO(RY) + -GRAM.]

his·tol·o·gy (hĭ-stŏl'ə-jē) *n.* **1.** The study of the microscopic structure of animal and plant tissues. **2.** The microscopic structure of tissue.

his·tol·y·sis (hĭ-stŏl'ə-sĭs) *n.* The breakdown and disintegration of organic tissue. —**his'to·lyt'ic** (hĭs'tə-lĭt'ĭk) *adj.* —**his'to·lyt'i·cal·ly** *adv.*

his·to·ri·an (hĭ-stôr'ē-ən, hĭ-stŏr'-) *n.* A writer or student of history.

ă pat/ā ate/âr care/ä bar/b bib/ch chew/d deed/ĕ pet/ē be/f fit/g gag/h hat/hw what/
ĭ pit/ī pie/îr pier/j judge/k kick/l lid, fatal/m mum/n no, sudden/ng sing/ŏ pot/ō go/

his·tor·ic (hĭ-stôr'ĭk, hĭ-stŏr'-) *adj.* Having importance in or influence on history; famous.
his·tor·i·cal (hĭ-stôr'ĭ-kəl, hĭ-stŏr'-) *adj.* **1.** Of or relating to history. **2.** Based on or concerned with events in history. **3.** Historic. —**his·tor'i·cal·ly** *adv.*
his·to·ry (hĭs'tə-rē) *n., pl.* -ries. **1.** A narrative of events; a story; chronicle. **2.** A chronological record of events. **3.** The branch of knowledge that records and analyzes past events. **4.** The events of the past. **5.** An interesting past. **6.** That which is not of current concern. **7.** A record of a patient's medical background. [< Gk *histōr*, learned man.]
his·tri·on·ic (hĭs'trē-ŏn'ĭk) *adj.* **1.** Of or pertaining to actors or acting. **2.** Overemotional or dramatic; theatrical; affected. —*n.* **histrionics** *(takes pl. v.).* Exaggerated emotional behavior calculated for effect. [< LL *histriō*, actor.] —**his'tri·on'i·cal·ly** *adv.*
hit (hĭt) *v.* **hit, hitting. 1.** To come or cause to come in contact with forcefully; strike. **2.** To affect adversely. **3.** To arrive at. **4.** To appeal. **5.** To propel with a blow. **6.** *Baseball.* To bat; succeed in getting (a base hit). —*n.* **1.** A collision or impact. **2.** A successfully executed shot, blow, or throw. **3.** A successful or popular venture. **4.** *Baseball.* A base hit. [< ON *hitta*, to hit.] —**hit'ter** *n.*
hit-and-run (hĭt'n-rŭn') *adj.* Designating or involving the driver of a motor vehicle who drives on after striking a pedestrian or another vehicle.
hitch (hĭch) *v.* **1.** To fasten with a loop, hook, or noose; tie. **2.** To connect or attach. **3.** *Informal.* To join or be united in marriage. **4.** To raise by pulling or jerking. **5.** To hitchhike (a ride). —*n.* **1.** A kind of knot. **2.** A short jerking motion. **3.** An impediment or delay. **4.** A term of military service. [ME *hytchen*, to lift with a jerk.] —**hitch'er** *n.*
hitch·hike (hĭch'hīk') *v.* To solicit or get (a free ride) along a road. —**hitch'hik'er** *n.*
hith·er (hĭth'ər) *adv.* To or toward this place. —*adj.* Located toward this side; nearer. [< OE *hider.* See **ko-**.]
hith·er·to (hĭth'ər-tōo') *adv.* Until this time.
Hit·ler (hĭt'lər), **Adolf.** 1889–1945. Austrian-

Adolf Hitler

born Nazi leader; dictator of German Reich (1933–45).
Hit·tite (hĭt'īt') *n.* **1.** One of an ancient people living in Asia Minor and N Syria about 2000–1200 B.C. **2.** An extinct Indo-European language spoken by these people. —*adj.* Of or pertaining to the Hittites, their culture, or their language.
hive (hīv) *n.* **1.** A structure for housing bees, esp. honeybees. **2.** A colony of bees. **3.** A place swarming with active people. —*v.* **hived, hiving.** To collect or go into a hive. [< OE *hȳf.*]
hives (hīvz) *n.* Urticaria. [?]
H.M. His (or Her) Majesty.
H.M.S. His (or Her) Majesty's Ship.
Ho holmium.
ho. house.
hoard (hôrd, hōrd) *n.* A hidden or stored fund or supply guarded for future use; a cache. —*v.* To accumulate a hoard. [< OE *hord.* See **skeu-**.] —**hoard'er** *n.*
hoar·frost (hôr'frôst', -frŏst', hōr'-) *n.* Frozen dew that forms a white coating on a surface. [< OE *hār.* See **kei-²**.]
hoarse (hôrs, hōrs) *adj.* **hoarser, hoarsest.** Low and grating in sound; husky; croaking. [< ON *hās* < Gmc **hairsa-.*] —**hoarse'ly** *adv.*
hoars·en (hôr'sən, hōr'-) *v.* To cause to be or become hoarse.
hoar·y (hôr'ē, hōr'ē) *adj.* -ier, -iest. **1.** Gray or white with or as with age. **2.** Very old; ancient. —**hoar'i·ness** *n.*
hoax (hōks) *n.* An act intended to deceive or trick. —*v.* To deceive, cheat, or trick by using a hoax. [Perh short for HOCUS-POCUS.] —**hoax'er** *n.*
hob (hŏb) *n.* A hobgoblin. —**play** (or **raise**) **hob.** To make mischief or trouble.
hob·ble (hŏb'əl) *v.* -bled, -bling. **1.** To walk or move awkwardly or with difficulty; limp. **2.** To fetter; restrain; impede. —*n.* **1.** An awkward, clumsy, or irregular walk or gait. **2.** A device used to hobble an animal. [ME *hoblen.*] —**hob'bler** *n.*
hob·ble·de·hoy (hŏb'əl-dē-hoi') *n.* A gawky adolescent. [?]
hobble skirt. A type of long skirt, popular between 1910 and 1914, that was so narrow below the knees that it restricted the wearer's normal stride.
hob·by (hŏb'ē) *n., pl.* -bies. An activity or interest engaged in primarily for pleasure; a pastime. [ME *hoby*, a hobbyhorse, something one pursues.] —**hob'by·ist** *n.*
hob·by·horse (hŏb'ē-hôrs') *n.* **1.** A child's toy consisting of a long stick with an imitation horse's head on one end. **2.** A rocking horse. **3.** A favorite topic or hobby.
hob·gob·lin (hŏb'gŏb'lən) *n.* **1.** A mischievous or evil goblin. **2.** A bugbear.
hob·nail (hŏb'nāl') *n.* A short nail used to protect the soles of shoes or boots.
hob·nob (hŏb'nŏb') *v.* -nobbed, -nobbing. To associate familiarly (with *with*). [< earlier *hab or nab*, hit or miss.]
ho·bo (hō'bō) *n., pl.* -boes or -bos. A tramp; vagrant. [?]

ô paw, for/oi boy/ou out/ōo took/ōo coo/p pop/r run/s sauce/sh shy/t to/th thin/*th* the/
ŭ cut/ûr fur/v van/w wag/y yes/z size/zh vision/ə ago, item, edible, gallop, circus/

Ho Chi Minh (hō′ chē′ mǐn′). 1890?–1969. President of Vietnam (1945–54) and of North Vietnam (1954–69).

Ho Chi Minh

Ho Chi Minh City. The official name for Saigon.

hock¹ (hŏk) n. The joint of the hind leg of a horse or other four-footed animal that corresponds to the human ankle. [< OE *hōh,* heel. See **kenk-¹.**]

hock² (hŏk) v. To pawn. —n. The state of being pawned. [< Du *hok,* prison.]

hock•ey (hŏk′ē) n. A game played on ice in which two opposing teams of skaters, using curved sticks, try to drive a puck into the opponents' goal. [?]

ho•cus-po•cus (hō′kəs-pō′kəs) n. 1. Nonsense words or phrases used as a formula by conjurers. 2. Deception or chicanery.

hod (hŏd) n. 1. A trough carried over the shoulder for transporting loads, as of bricks. 2. A coal scuttle. [Perh < OF *hotte.*]

hodge•podge (hŏj′pŏj′) n. A mixture of dissimilar ingredients. [< OF *hochepot,* "a gathering."]

Hodg•kin's disease (hŏj′kĭnz). A usually chronic, progressive, ultimately fatal disease of unknown etiology, marked by inflammatory enlargement of the lymph nodes, spleen, liver, and kidneys, and occurring approximately twice as often in adult males as females. [< T. *Hodgkin* (1798–1866), English physician.]

hoe (hō) n. A tool with a flat blade and a long handle, used for weeding, cultivating, and gardening. [< Frank **hauwa.*] —**hoe** v. (**hoed,** **hoeing**). —**ho′er** n.

hog (hŏg, hŏg) n. 1. A pig, esp. a full-grown domesticated pig. 2. A self-indulgent, gluttonous, or vulgar person. —v. **hogged, hogging.** To take more than one's share of. [< OE *hogg* < Celt. See **su-.**] —**hog′gish** adj.

hogs•head (hŏgz′hĕd′, hŏgz′-) n. 1. Any of various units of volume or capacity ranging from 62.5 to 140 gallons, esp. a unit used in the U.S., equal to 63 gallons. 2. A barrel or cask with such capacity.

hog-tie (hŏg′tī′, hŏg′-) v. Also **hog•tie.** 1. To tie together the legs of. 2. To impede in movement or action.

hog•wash (hŏg′wŏsh′, -wôsh′, hŏg′-) n. 1. Garbage fed to hogs; swill. 2. Worthless, false, or ridiculous speech or writing.

hoi pol•loi (hoi′ pə-loi′). The common people. [Gk *hoi polloi,* the many, the masses.]

hoist (hoist) v. To raise or haul up. —n. 1. An apparatus for lifting heavy or cumbersome objects. 2. A pull; lift. 3. The height or vertical dimension of a raised flag. [Var of dial *hoise.*] —**hoist′er** n.

Hok•kai•do (hŏ-kī′dō). The second-largest island of Japan, situated N of Honshu.

ho•kum (hō′kəm) n. Nonsense; fakery. [Perh < HOCUS-POCUS.]

hold¹ (hōld) v. **held, holding.** 1. To have and keep in possession; grasp; clasp. 2. To support; keep up; maintain in a certain position or relationship. 3. To contain; be filled by. 4. To own. 5. To maintain for use; wield. 6. To restrain. 7. To retain the attention or interest of. 8. To detain; delay. 9. To have the position of; occupy. 10. To cause to keep; obligate. 11. To keep in one's mind or heart. 12. a. To believe; regard. b. To assert; affirm. 13. To cause to take place; put on. 14. To assemble; convene. 15. To stand up under stress; last. 16. To be valid, applicable, or true. —n. 1. The act or a means of grasping; a grip; clasp. 2. A means of obtaining or controlling something. 3. Something held onto, as for support. 4. A container. 5. A strong influence or power. 6. A prison cell. 7. A temporary halt, as in a countdown; pause. [< OE *healdan.*] —**hold′er** n.

hold² (hōld) n. The interior of a ship below decks where cargo is stored. [Var of ME *hole,* hole.]

hold•ing (hōl′dĭng) n. 1. Land rented or leased from another. 2. Often **holdings.** Legally possessed property.

hold•up (hōld′ŭp′) n. 1. A suspension of activity; delay. 2. A robbery, esp. an armed robbery.

hole (hōl) n. 1. A cavity in a solid. 2. An opening or perforation through something; a gap; aperture. 3. A hollow place. 4. An animal's burrow or similar dwelling place. 5. An ugly, squalid, or depressing dwelling. 6. A fault or flaw. 7. A bad situation; predicament. 8. *Golf.* The small pit lined with a cup into which the ball must be hit. 9. A vacant electron energy state manifested as a positive charge carrier with magnitude equal to that of the electron. [< OE *hol,* hollow place. See **kel-⁴.**] —**hole** v. (**holed, holing**).

hol•i•day (hŏl′ə-dā′) n. 1. A day on which a particular event is celebrated. 2. A religious feast day. 3. A day off. 4. *Chiefly Brit.* A vacation. [< OE *hālig,* HOLY + *dæg,* DAY.] —**hol′i•day** adj.

ho•li•er-than-thou (hō′lē-ər-*th*ən-thou′) adj. Showing an attitude of superior virtue.

ho•li•ness (hō′lē-nĭs) n. 1. The quality of

being holy. **2. Holiness.** A title of address used for the pope.

Hol·land (hŏl′ənd). The Netherlands.

hol·lan·daise sauce (hŏl′ən-dāz′, hŏl′ən-dāz′). A creamy sauce of butter, egg yolks, and lemon or vinegar. [< F *Hollandais,* Dutch.]

hol·ler (hŏl′ər) *v.* To yell or shout.

hol·low (hŏl′ō) *adj.* **1.** Having a cavity or space within: *a hollow wall.* **2.** Concave; sunken. **3.** Without substance or validity. **4.** Reverberating: *a hollow sound.* —*n.* **1.** A cavity or space within something. **2.** A concave surface or area. **3.** A valley. —*v.* To make or become hollow. [< OE *holh,* hole, hollow place. See **kel-⁴.**] —**hol′low·ness** *n.*

hol·ly (hŏl′ē) *n., pl.* **-lies.** A tree or shrub characteristically having prickly-edged evergreen leaves and bright-red berries. [< OE *holen.* See **kel-⁵.**]

hol·ly·hock (hŏl′ē-hŏk′) *n.* A tall plant widely cultivated for its showy spike of large, variously colored flowers. [< HOLY + OE *hoc,* a mallow.]

Hol·ly·wood (hŏl′ē-wŏŏd′). A district of Los Angeles, California; center of the U.S. motion-picture industry.

hol·mi·um (hōl′mē-əm) *n.* *Symbol* **Ho** A relatively soft, malleable metallic element. Atomic number 67, atomic weight 164.930. [< *Stockholm,* Sweden.]

holo-. *comb. form.* Whole or entirely. [< Gk *holos,* whole, entire.]

hol·o·caust (hŏl′ə-kôst′, hō′lə-) *n.* Great or total destruction by fire. [< Gk *holokaustos,* burnt whole.]

Hol·o·cene (hŏl′ə-sēn′, hō′lə-) *adj.* Of or belonging to the geologic time or sedimentary deposits of the more recent of the two epochs of the Quaternary period, extending from the end of the Pleistocene to the present. —*n.* The Holocene epoch.

hol·o·crine (hŏl′ə-krĭn, -krēn′, -krīn′, hō′lə-) *adj.* Pertaining to a gland whose secretion is formed by the degeneration of the gland's cells. [HOLO- + Gk *krinein,* to separate.]

hol·o·gram (hŏl′ə-grăm′, hō′lə-) *n.* **1.** The pattern produced on a photosensitive medium by holography. **2.** The photosensitive medium so exposed and developed.

hol·o·graph¹ (hŏl′ə-grăf′, -gräf′, hō′lə-) *n.* **1.** A document written wholly in the handwriting of the person whose signature it bears. **2.** A hologram.

ho·lo·graph² (hŏl′ə-grăf′, -gräf′, hō′lə-) *v.* **1.** To produce an image of (a physical object) by holography. **2.** To form a hologram of (a physical object).

ho·log·ra·phy (hō-lŏg′rə-fē, hə-) *n.* The technique of producing images by wave front reconstruction, esp. by using lasers to record on a photographic plate the diffraction pattern from which a three-dimensional image can be projected.

hol·ster (hōl′stər) *n.* A leather case shaped to hold a pistol. [Du.]

ho·ly (hō′lē) *adj.* **-lier, -liest. 1.** Belonging to, derived from, or associated with a divine

power. **2.** Living according to a religious system. **3.** Specified or set apart for a religious purpose: *a holy hour.* [< OE *hālig.* See **kailo-.**]

Holy Communion. The Eucharist.

Holy Ghost. The third person of the Christian Trinity; Holy Spirit.

Holy Grail. The Grail.

Holy Land. See Palestine.

Holy Spirit. The Holy Ghost.

holy water. Water blessed by a priest.

hom·age (hŏm′ĭj, ŏm′-) *n.* Honor or respect publicly expressed to a person or idea. [< L *homō,* man.]

Hom·burg (hŏm′bûrg′) *n.* A man's felt hat having a dented crown and a shallow brim. [< *Homburg,* West Germany.]

home (hōm) *n.* **1.** The place where one resides. **2.** A house. **3.** A family living in a dwelling. **4.** A customary environment; habitat. **5.** A place of origin. **6.** A headquarters. **7.** An objective or place of safety in some games. **8.** An institution where people are cared for: *a nursing home.* —*adj.* **1.** Of or pertaining to a household or house. **2.** Of or pertaining to a headquarters: *a home office.* **3.** Taking place in the city where a team is franchised: *a home game.* —*adv.* **1.** At or to one's home. **2.** On target: *The arrow struck home.* **3.** To the center or heart of something; deeply. —**at home. 1.** In one's own house, locale, etc. **2.** At ease; comfortable: *feel at home.* **3.** Having an easy competence and familiarity: *at home in French.* [< OE *hām.* See **kei-¹.**]

home base. 1. *Baseball.* The plate. **2.** A base of operations.

home·bod·y (hōm′bŏd′ē) *n.* One who likes to stay or work at home.

home·com·ing (hōm′kŭm′ĭng) *n.* **1.** A coming to or returning home. **2.** An annual event for visiting alumni, as in a college.

home economics. The art of home management, including household budgets, clothing, child care, cooking, etc.

home·land (hōm′lănd′) *n.* **1.** The land of one's allegiance. **2.** The place of origin of a people.

home·ly (hōm′lē) *adj.* **-lier, -liest. 1.** Of a nature associated with the home; familiar. **2.** Not attractive or good-looking: *a homely girl.* —**home′li·ness** *n.*

home·made (hōm′mād′) *adj.* **1.** Made or prepared in the home. **2.** Crudely or simply made.

home·mak·er (hōm′mā′kər) *n.* One who manages a household, esp. a housewife.

ho·me·o·sta·sis (hō′mē-ō-stā′sĭs, hŏm′ē-) *n.* A state of physiological equilibrium produced by a balance of functions and of chemical composition within an organism.

home plate. *Baseball.* The plate.

hom·er (hō′mər) *n.* *Baseball.* A home run.

Ho·mer (hō′mər). Greek epic poet traditionally believed to have been author of the *Iliad* and the *Odyssey.* —**Ho·mer′ic** (-mĕr′ĭk) *adj.*

home·room (hōm′rōōm′, -rŏŏm′) *n.* A classroom to which pupils of the same grade are required to report each day.

home run. *Baseball.* A hit that allows the batter to make a complete circuit of the diamond and score a run.

ô paw, for/oi boy/ou out/ŏŏ took/ōō coo/p pop/r run/s sauce/sh shy/t to/th thin/*th* the/
ŭ cut/ûr fur/v van/w wag/y yes/z size/zh vision/ə ago, item, edible, gallop, circus/

home·sick (hōm'sĭk') *adj.* Longing for home.
—**home'sick'ness** *n.*
home·spun (hōm'spŭn') *adj.* 1. Spun or made
at home. 2. Made of a homespun fabric. 3.
Simple and homely; unpretentious. —*n.* A
plain coarse woolen cloth.
home·stead (hōm'stĕd') *n.* A house, esp. a
farmhouse, with adjoining buildings and land.
home·stretch (hōm'strĕch') *n.* 1. The portion
of a racetrack from the last turn to the finish
line. 2. The final stages of an undertaking.
home·ward (hōm'wərd) *adv.* Also **home·wards**
(-wərdz). Toward home. —**home'ward** *adj.*
home·work (hōm'wûrk') *n.* 1. Work, esp.
schoolwork, done at home. 2. Any work of a
preparatory or preliminary nature.
home·y (hō'mē) *adj.* **-ier, -iest.** Also **hom·y.**
Informal. Having a feeling of home; homelike.
—**hom'ey·ness** *n.*
hom·i·cide (hŏm'ə-sīd', hō'mə-) *n.* 1. The killing of one person by another. 2. A person who
kills another person. [< L *homō,* man +
-CIDE.] —**hom'i·ci'dal** *adj.*
hom·i·ly (hŏm'ə-lē) *n., pl.* **-lies.** 1. A sermon.
2. A moralizing lecture or admonition. [< Gk
homilia, discourse.]
hom·ing (hō'mĭng) *adj.* 1. Having the faculty
of returning home, esp. from a distance.
2. Assisting in guiding a craft home: *a homing
guidance system.*
hom·i·ny grits (hŏm'ə-nē). A coarse white
meal of corn kernels. [Perh < Algon.]
homo-. *comb. form.* Same or like. [< Gk
homos, same.]
ho·mo·ge·ne·ous (hō'mə-jē'nē-əs, -jēn'yəs,
hŏm'ə-) *adj.* 1. Like in nature or kind. 2.
Uniform in composition throughout. [<
HOMO- + Gk *-genēs,* born +-OUS.] —**ho'mo·
ge·ne'i·ty** (hō'mō-ji-nē'ə-tē) *n.* —**ho'mo·ge'ne·
ous·ly** *adv.* —**ho'mo·ge'ne·ous·ness** *n.*
ho·mog·en·ize (hō-mŏj'ə-nīz', hə-) *v.* **-ized,
-izing.** 1. To make homogeneous. 2. a. To reduce to particles and disperse throughout a
fluid. b. To make uniform in consistency, esp.
to render (milk) uniform in consistency by
emulsifying the fat content. —**ho·mog'en·i·
za'tion** *n.* —**ho·mog'en·iz'er** *n.*
hom·o·graph (hŏm'ə-grăf', -gräf', hō'mə-) *n.*
A word spelled the same as another but differing in meaning and origin.
ho·mol·o·gous (hō-mŏl'ə-gəs, hə-) *adj.* Corresponding or similar in position, structure,
etc. [Gk *homologos,* agreeing.]
hom·o·nym (hŏm'ə-nĭm', hō'mə-) *n.* One of
two or more words that have the same sound
and often the same spelling but differ in meaning. —**hom'o·nym'ic** *adj.*
hom·o·phone (hŏm'ə-fōn', hō'mə-) *n.* A word
having the same sound as another but differing from it in spelling, origin, and meaning.
ho·mo·sex·u·al·i·ty (hō'mə-sĕk'shōō-ăl'ə-tē,
hŏm'ə-) *n.* 1. Sexual desire for others of one's
own sex. 2. Sexual activity with another of the
same sex. —**ho'mo·sex'u·al** *adj. & n.*
ho·mun·cu·lus (hō-mŭng'kyə-ləs) *n., pl.* **-li**
(-lī'). A small man. [< L *homō,* man.]
hon. honorary.
Hon. Honorable (title).

Hon·du·ras (hŏn-d/y/ōōr'əs). A republic of
Central America. Pop. 2,315,000. Cap. Teguci-
galpa. —**Hon·du'ran** *adj. & n.*

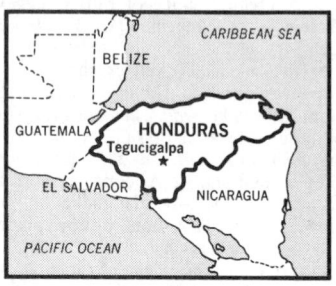

Honduras

hone (hōn) *n.* A fine-grained whetstone. —*v.*
honed, honing. To sharpen on or as on a hone.
[< OE *hān,* stone. See kē-.]
hon·est (ŏn'ĭst) *adj.* 1. Not lying, cheating,
stealing, or taking unfair advantage; honorable. 2. Not characterized by deception or
fraud; genuine. 3. Having or manifesting integrity and truth. 4. Unpretentious; simple.
—**honest to goodness.** 1. Absolutely genuine.
2. Expressive of surprise, affirmation, etc. [<
L *honōs,* HONOR.] —**hon'est·ly** *adv.* —**hon'es·ty,**
hon'est·ness *n.*
hon·ey (hŭn'ē) *n., pl.* **-eys.** 1. A sweet, thick
yellowish fluid produced by bees from the
nectar of flowers. 2. A sweet substance or
quality. 3. *Informal.* Sweet one; dear. [< OE
hunig. See kenəko-.] —**hon'ey** *adj.*
hon·ey·bee (hŭn'ē-bē') *n.* A bee that produces
honey.
hon·ey·comb (hŭn'ē-kōm') *n.* 1. A structure
of six-sided cells constructed from beeswax by
honeybees to hold honey and eggs. 2. Something resembling this. —*v.* To fill with holes;
riddle: *His story was honeycombed with lies.*
hon·ey·dew (hŭn'ē-d/y/ōō') *n.* A sweet,
sticky substance, as that excreted by aphids.
honeydew melon. A melon with a smooth,
whitish rind and green flesh.
hon·eyed (hŭn'ēd) *adj.* Sweet; sugary: *honeyed
words.*
hon·ey·moon (hŭn'ē-mōōn') *n.* A holiday or
trip taken by a newly married couple. —*v.* To
spend a honeymoon.
hon·ey·suck·le (hŭn'ē-sŭk'əl) *n.* A shrub or
vine with tubular, often fragrant yellowish,
white, or pink flowers.
Hong Kong (hŏng' kŏng', hông' kông'). A
British Crown Colony on the S coast of China.
Pop. 3,982,000. Cap. Victoria.
honk (hŏngk, hôngk) *n.* A raucous, resonant
sound, as that made by a wild goose or an
automobile horn. [Imit.] —**honk** *v.*
honk·y-tonk (hŏng'kē-tôngk', hông'kē-tŏngk')
n. Slang. A cheap, noisy bar. [?]
Hon·o·lu·lu (hŏn'ə-lōō'lōō). The capital of
Hawaii. Pop. 320,000.
hon·or (ŏn'ər). Also *chiefly Brit.* **hon·our.** *n.*

ă pat/ā ate/âr care/ä bar/b bib/ch chew/d deed/ĕ pet/ē be/f fit/g gag/h hat/hw what/
ĭ pit/ī pie/îr pier/j judge/k kick/l lid, fatal/m mum/n no, sudden/ng sing/ŏ pot/ō go/

1. Esteem; respect. **2. a.** Glory; distinction. **b.** A token or gesture of respect or distinction: *the place of honor.* **3.** Great privilege. **4.** Honor. A title of address often accorded to mayors and judges. **5.** Personal integrity maintained without legal or other obligation. **6. honors. a.** Special recognition for unusual academic achievement. **b.** A program of individual advanced study for exceptional students. —*v.* **1. a.** To esteem. **b.** To show respect for. **2.** To confer distinction upon. **3.** To accept or pay as valid (as a check). [< L *honor, honōs.*]

hon·or·a·ble (ŏn′ər-ə-bəl) *adj.* **1.** Deserving respect. **2.** Bestowing honor or recognition: *honorable mention.* **3.** Possessing integrity. **4.** Honorable. A title of respect for certain high officials: *the Honorable Mayor.* —**hon′or·a·ble·ness** *n.* —**hon′or·a·bly** *adv.*

hon·o·rar·i·um (ŏn′ə-râr′ē-əm) *n., pl.* **-ums** or **-ia** (-ē-ə). A payment given a professional person for services for which fees are not legally or traditionally required.

hon·or·ar·y (ŏn′ə-rěr′ē) *adj.* Conferred as an honor without the usual duties, privileges, etc.: *an honorary degree.*

hon·or·if·ic (ŏn′ə-rĭf′ĭk) *adj.* Conferring or showing respect or honor. —*n.* A term conveying respect, used esp. when addressing a social superior. —**hon′or·if′i·cal·ly** *adv.*

Hon·shu (hŏn′shōō). The largest island of Japan.

hood[1] (hŏod) *n.* **1.** A loose, pliable covering for the head and neck. **2.** Something resembling a hood in shape or function. **3.** The hinged metal lid over an automobile engine. [< OE *hōd.* See **kadh-.**] —**hood′ed** *adj.*

hood[2] (hŏod) *n. Slang.* A hoodlum; thug.

-hood. *comb. form.* **1.** The state, condition, or quality of being: **manhood. 2.** All the members of a grouping of a specified nature: **neighborhood.** [< OE *-hād.*]

hood·lum (hŏod′ləm, hōod′-) *n.* A gangster; thug. [?] —**hood′lum·ism′** *n.*

hood·wink (hŏod′wĭngk′) *v.* To deceive; trick; take in.

hoo·ey (hōō′ē) *n. Slang.* Nonsense. [?]

hoof (hŏof, hōof) *n., pl.* **hoofs** or **hooves** (hōovz, hŏovz). **1.** The horny covering of the foot of horses, cattle, deer, etc. **2.** The foot of such an animal. —*v.* —**hoof it.** *Slang.* To go on foot; walk. [< OE *hōf.* See **kapho-.**] —**hoofed** *adj.*

hook (hŏok) *n.* **1.** A curved or sharply bent device, usually of metal, used to catch, drag, suspend, or fasten something. **2.** Something shaped like a hook. **3.** *Boxing.* A short swinging blow delivered with a crooked arm. —**by hook or (by) crook.** By whatever means possible, fair or unfair. —**hook, line, and sinker.** Without reservation; entirely. —**off the hook. 1.** *Slang.* Freed, as from blame or a vexatious obligation. **2.** Off the cradle, as a telephone receiver. —*v.* **1.** To get hold of or catch with or as with a hook. **2.** *Slang.* To become addicted. **3.** *Slang.* To steal; snatch. **4.** To fasten by means of a hook and eye. [< OE *hōc.* See **keg-.**]

hook·ah (hŏok′ə) *n.* A smoking pipe with a long tube passing through an urn of water that cools the smoke as it is drawn through. [< Ar *ḥuqqah.*]

hook and eye. A clothes fastener consisting of a small hook with a corresponding loop.

hook up. 1. To connect a mechanism and a source of power. **2.** *Slang.* To form a tie or connection. **3.** To fasten together with a hook or hooks.

hook·up (hŏok′ŭp′) *n.* **1.** A system of electrical interconnections. **2.** Any configuration of parts or devices acting together.

hook·worm (hŏok′wûrm′) *n.* A parasitic worm with hooked mouth parts that fasten to the intestinal tract.

hook·y (hŏok′ē) *n. Informal.* Truancy: *play hooky.*

hoop (hōop, hŏop) *n.* **1.** A circular band of metal put around a cask or barrel to bind the staves together. **2.** Anything resembling such a band, as: **a.** A large ring used as a plaything. **b.** A ringlike earring. [< OE *hōp* < Gmc **hōpaz.*] —**hoop′less** *adj.*

hoop·la (hōop′lä′, hŏop′-) *n. Slang.* **1.** Boisterous commotion or excitement. **2.** Talk intended to mislead or confuse. [F *houp-là.*]

hoo·poe (hōo′pōo, -pō) *n.* An Old World bird with a fanlike crest and a long, slender bill. [< L *upupa* (imit.).]

hoo·ray. Variant of **hurrah.**

hoose·gow (hōos′gou′) *n. Slang.* A jail. [< Span *juzgar,* to judge.]

hoot (hōot) *v.* **1.** To utter the hollow, raucous cry of an owl. **2.** To make a loud derisive or contemptuous cry. **3.** To shout down or drive off with jeering cries. —*n.* **1.** The characteristic cry of an owl. **2.** A cry of contempt or derision. —**not give a hoot.** Not to care at all. [Imit.] —**hoot′er** *n.*

hoot·en·an·ny (hōot′n-ăn′ē) *n., pl.* **-nies.** A gathering of folk singers, typically with audience participation. [?]

hoot owl. Any of various owls having a hooting cry.

Hoo·ver (hōo′vər), **Herbert Clark.** 1874–1964. 31st President of the U.S. (1929–33).

Herbert Hoover

hooves. Alternate *pl.* of **hoof.**

ô paw, for/oi boy/ou out/ŏŏ took/ōō coo/p pop/r run/s sauce/sh shy/t to/th thin/*th* the/
ŭ cut/ûr fur/v van/w wag/y yes/z size/zh vision/ə ago, item, edible, gallop, circus/

hop¹ (hŏp) *v.* **hopped, hopping. 1.** To move with light bounding skips or leaps. **2.** To jump on one foot. **3.** To jump aboard: *hop a freight.* —*n.* **1.** A light springy jump, esp. on one foot. **2.** *Informal.* A dance. **3.** A short airplane trip. [< OE *hoppian.*] —**hop′ping·ly** *adv.*

hop² (hŏp) *n.* **1.** A twining vine with lobed leaves and green, conelike flowers. **2. hops.** The dried flowers of this plant, used as flavoring in brewing beer. —*v.* **hopped, hopping.** —**hop up.** *Slang.* **1.** To increase the power or energy of. **2.** To stimulate or excite. [< MDu *hoppe.*]

hope (hŏp) *v.* **hoped, hoping.** To desire (something) with some confidence of fulfillment. —**hope against hope.** To persist in hoping for something against the odds. —*n.* **1.** A desire supported by some confidence of its fulfillment. **2.** A ground for expectation. **3.** That which is desired. **4.** That in which one places one's confidence. **5.** Expectation; confidence. [< OE *hopian.*] —**hop′er** *n.*

hope·ful (hŏp′fəl) *adj.* **1.** Having or manifesting hope. **2.** Inspiring hope. —*n.* A person who aspires to success or shows promise of succeeding. —**hope′ful·ness** *n.*

hope·ful·ly (hŏp′fə-lē) *adv.* **1.** In a hopeful manner. **2.** In such a manner as to be hoped; let us hope.
Usage: Hopefully, as used to mean *in such a manner as to be hoped* or *let us hope,* is still unacceptable to a substantial number of authorities on grammar and usage.

hope·less (hŏp′lĭs) *adj.* **1.** Having no hope; despairing. **2.** Offering no hope. **3.** Incurable. **4.** Insoluble; discouraging; impossible. —**hope′less·ly** *adv.* —**hope′less·ness** *n.*

Ho·pi (hŏ′pē) *n., pl.* **-pi** or **-pis. 1.** A member of a tribe of Uto-Aztecan-speaking North American Indians now inhabiting a reservation in NE Arizona. **2.** The language of these people.

hop·per (hŏp′ər) *n.* **1.** One that hops, esp. a hopping insect. **2.** A receptacle in which materials are stored in readiness for dispensation and use.

hop·scotch (hŏp′skŏch′) *n.* A children's game in which players toss an object into succeeding sections of a figure on the ground, then hop through the figure and back on one foot as they retrieve the object.

hor. horizontal.

Hor·ace (hôr′ĭs, hŏr′-). 65–8 B.C. Latin poet. —**Ho·ra′tian** (hə-rā′shən) *adj.*

horde (hôrd, hŏrd) *n.* A throng or swarm. [< Turk *ordŭ,* camp.]

hore·hound (hôr′hound′, hŏr′-) *n.* A downy, aromatic plant yielding a bitter extract used as candy flavoring and as a cough remedy. [< OE *hār,* hoarfrost + *hūne,* horehound.]

ho·ri·zon (hə-rī′zən) *n.* **1.** The apparent intersection of the earth and sky as seen by an observer. **2.** The range of an individual's knowledge, experience, etc. [< Gk *horizein,* to divide, separate.]

hor·i·zon·tal (hôr′ə-zŏnt′l, hŏr′-) *adj.* **1.** Of, relating to, or near the horizon. **2.** Parallel to or in the plane of the horizon. **3.** Occupying or restricted to the same level in a hierarchy.

4. Flat. —*n.* Anything horizontal. —**hor′i·zon′tal·ly** *adv.*

hor·mone (hôr′mōn′) *n.* A substance formed by one organ and conveyed, as by the blood stream, to another, which it stimulates to function by means of its chemical activity. [< Gk *horman,* to urge on.] —**hor′mo′nal** *adj.*

horn (hôrn) *n.* **1.** One of the hard, usually permanent structures projecting from the head of cattle, sheep, goats, etc. **2.** A structure, object, or part suggestive of a horn. **3.** The hard, smooth material forming the outer covering of the horns of cattle or related animals. **4.** A container made from a horn: *a powder horn.* **5.** *Mus.* **a.** A wind instrument made of brass. **b.** A French horn. **6.** A device that produces a sound similar to that of a sounded animal horn. —*v.* —**horn in.** *Slang.* To join without being invited; intrude. [< OE. See **ker-¹.**] —**horned** *adj.* —**horn′y** *adj.*

Horn, Cape. The southernmost point of South America.

horn·blende (hôrn′blĕnd′) *n.* A common green or bluish-green to black mineral formed in the late stages of cooling in igneous rock. [G.]

hor·net (hôr′nĭt) *n.* A large, stinging wasp. [< OE *hyrnet.* See **ker-¹.**]

horn of plenty. A cornucopia.

ho·rol·o·gy (hô-rŏl′ə-jē, hō-) *n.* **1.** The science of measuring time. **2.** The art of making timepieces. [< Gk *hōrologos,* "hour-teller."] —**hor′o·log′i·cal** *adj.* —**ho·rol′o·gist** *n.*

hor·o·scope (hôr′ə-skōp′, hŏr′-) *n. Astrol.* A forecast of a person's future. [< Gk *hōroskopos,* astrologer, "hour-observer."]

hor·ren·dous (hô-rĕn′dəs, hō-) *adj.* Hideous; dreadful. [< L *horrēre,* to tremble.] —**hor·ren′dous·ly** *adv.*

hor·ri·ble (hôr′ə-bəl, hŏr′-) *adj.* **1.** Causing horror. **2.** Unpleasant; offensive. —**hor′ri·ble·ness** *n.* —**hor′ri·bly** *adv.*

hor·rid (hôr′ĭd, hŏr′-) *adj.* **1.** Causing horror. **2.** Unpleasant; offensive. —**hor′rid·ly** *adv.* —**hor′rid·ness** *n.*

hor·ri·fy (hôr′ə-fī′, hŏr′-) *v.* **-fied, -fying. 1.** To cause to feel horror. **2.** To cause unpleasant surprise; shock.

hor·ror (hôr′ər, hŏr′-) *n.* **1.** An intense feeling of repugnance and fear; terror. **2.** Intense dislike; abhorrence. **3.** That which causes horror. [< L *horrēre,* to tremble, be in horror.]

hors d'oeuvre (ôr dûrv′) *pl.* **hors d'oeuvres** (ôr dûrvz′) or **hors d'oeuvre.** An appetizer or canapé served with cocktails or before a meal. [F, side dish, "outside of work."]

horse (hôrs) *n.* **1.** A large hoofed mammal with a long mane and tail, domesticated for riding and to pull vehicles or carry loads. **2.** A supportive frame or device, usually having four legs. **3.** Often **horses.** Horsepower. —*v.* **horsed, horsing.** —**horse around.** To engage in horseplay. [< OE *hors* < Gmc **hors-.*]

horse·back (hôrs′băk′) *adv.* On the back of a horse.

horse chestnut. 1. A tree with erect clusters of white flowers and brown, shiny, inedible nuts. **2.** The nut of such a tree.

ă pat/ā ate/âr care/ä bar/b bib/ch chew/d deed/ĕ pet/ē be/f fit/g gag/h hat/hw what/
ĭ pit/ī pie/îr pier/j judge/k kick/l lid, fatal/m mum/n no, sudden/ng sing/ŏ pot/ō go/

horse•flesh (hôrs'flĕsh') *n.* **1.** Edible horse meat. **2.** Riding or racing horses.

horse•fly (hôrs'flī') *n.* Also **horse fly.** A large bloodsucking fly.

horse•hair (hôrs'hâr') *n.* **1.** The hair from a horse's mane or tail. **2.** Cloth made of horsehair.

horse•man (hôrs'mən) *n.* A man who rides a horse or is skilled at horsemanship. **—horse'-wom'an** *fem.n.*

horse•man•ship (hôrs'mən-shĭp') *n.* The art of horseback riding.

horse•play (hôrs'plā') *n.* Rowdy, prankish play.

horse•pow•er (hôrs'pou'ər) *n.* A U.S. Customary System unit of power, equal to 745.7 watts.

horse•rad•ish (hôrs'răd'ĭsh) *n.* **1.** A coarse plant with a thick, whitish, pungent root. **2.** The grated root of this plant, used as a condiment.

horse•shoe (hôrs'shōō', hôrsh'-) *n.* **1.** A narrow U-shaped iron plate fitted and nailed to a horse's hoof. **2. horseshoes.** A game in which players try to toss horseshoes around a stake.

hors•y (hôr'sē) *adj.* **-ier, -iest. 1.** Of, pertaining to, or characteristic of a horse. **2.** Devoted to horses and horsemanship: *the horsy crowd.*

hort. horticultural; horticulture.

hor•ta•to•ry (hôr'tə-tôr'ē, -tōr'ē) *adj.* Characterized by or expressing exhortation.

hor•ti•cul•ture (hôr'tə-kŭl'chər) *n.* The science or art of cultivating plants, esp. garden plants. [L *hortus,* garden + (AGRI)CULTURE.] **—hor'ti•cul'tur•al** *adj.* **—hor'ti•cul'tur•ist** *n.*

Hos. Hosea (Old Testament).

ho•san•na (hō-zăn'ə) *interj.* Expressive of praise or adoration to God or the Messiah. [< Heb *hosha'nā,* "save us!"]

hose (hōz) *n.* **1.** *pl.* **hose. a.** Stockings. **b.** Socks. **2.** *pl.* **hoses.** A flexible tube for conveying liquids or gases under pressure. **—v. hosed, hosing.** To water, drench, or wash with a hose. [< OE *hosa,* leg covering. See **skeu-**.]

ho•sier•y (hō'zhə-rē) *n.* Stockings and socks; hose.

hosp. hospital.

hos•pice (hŏs'pĭs) *n.* A shelter or lodging for travelers, children, or the destitute, often maintained by a monastic order. [<L *hospitium,* hospitality.]

hos•pi•ta•ble (hŏs'pə-tə-bəl, hŏs-pĭt'ə-bəl) *adj.* Welcoming guests or strangers with warmth and generosity. [< L *hospes (hospit-),* HOST.] **—hos'pi•ta•ble•ness** *n.* **—hos'pi•ta•bly** *adv.*

hos•pi•tal (hŏs'pə-təl) *n.* An institution providing medical or surgical care and treatment for the sick and injured. [< L *hospitālis,* of a guest.]

hos•pi•tal•i•ty (hŏs'pə-tăl'ə-tē) *n., pl.* **-ties. 1.** The act or practice of being hospitable. **2.** An instance of being hospitable.

hos•pi•tal•i•za•tion (hŏs'pə-tə-lə-zā'shən, -lĭ-zā'shən) *n.* **1.** The state of being hospitalized. **2.** A form of insurance that helps pay a patient's hospital expenses.

hos•pi•tal•ize (hŏs'pə-tə-līz') *v.* **-ized, -izing.** To put (a person) into a hospital.

host¹ (hōst) *n.* **1.** One who entertains guests. **2.** An organism on or in which a parasite lives. **—v.** *Informal.* To serve as host for (a party, reception, etc.). [< L *hospes (hospit-),* guest, host, stranger.]

host² (hōst) *n.* **1.** An army. **2.** A great number. [< L *hostis,* stranger, enemy.]

host³ (hōst) *n.* Also **Host.** *Eccles.* The consecrated bread or wafer of the Eucharist. [< L *hostia,* sacrifice, victim.]

hos•tage (hŏs'tĭj) *n.* A person held as a security for the fulfillment of certain terms. [< OF *hoste,* guest, host, and < L *obses (obsid-),* a hostage.] **—hos'tage•ship'** *n.*

hos•tel (hŏs'təl) *n.* A supervised, inexpensive lodging house for youthful travelers. [< ML *hospitāle,* inn.]

host•ess (hōs'tĭs) *n.* A woman who acts as a host.

hos•tile (hŏs'təl; *chiefly Brit.* hŏs'tīl') *adj.* **1.** Of or pertaining to an enemy. **2.** Feeling or showing enmity. [< L *hostis,* HOST.]

hos•til•i•ty (hŏ-stĭl'ə-tē) *n., pl.* **-ties. 1.** The state of being hostile. **2. hostilities.** Overt warfare.

hot (hŏt) *adj.* **hotter, hottest. 1. a.** Possessing great heat. **b.** Yielding much heat. **c.** At a high temperature. **2.** Warmer than is normal or desirable. **3.** Pungent; spicy. **4. a.** Charged or as if charged with electricity. **b.** Radioactive. **5.** Angry: *a hot dispute.* **6.** *Slang.* Recently stolen: *hot goods.* **7.** *Informal.* **a.** New; fresh: *hot off the press.* **b.** Currently popular: *a hot sales item.* **8.** *Slang.* **a.** Performing with unusual skill. **b.** Lucky. **—hot under the collar.** Angry. **—in hot water.** In trouble. [< OE *hāt.* See **kai-**.] **—hot'ly** *adv.* **—hot'ness** *n.*

hot air. *Slang.* Boastful nonsense.

hot•bed (hŏt'bĕd') *n.* **1.** A glass-covered, heated bed of soil used for raising tender plants. **2.** An environment conducive to rapid, vigorous growth, esp. of something bad: *a hotbed of intrigue.*

hot cake. A pancake. **—sell (or go) like hot cakes.** To be in great demand.

hot dog. A frankfurter, usually served in a long soft roll.

ho•tel (hō-tĕl') *n.* A public house that provides lodging and usually board. [< OF *hostel,* hostel.]

hot•head•ed (hŏt'hĕd'ĭd) *adj.* **1.** Having a fiery temper. **2.** Impetuous; rash. **—hot'head'ed•ly** *adv.* **—hot'head'ed•ness** *n.*

hot•house (hŏt'hous') *n.* A heated greenhouse for plants.

hot line. A direct communications link, as a telephone line, especially one between heads of government for use in time of crisis, as to prevent unintentional war.

hot plate. A table-top cooking device having one or two burners.

hot rod. *Slang.* An automobile rebuilt or remodeled for increased speed and acceleration. **—hot rodder.**

hot•shot (hŏt'shŏt') *n.* *Slang.* An ostentatiously skillful person.

hound (hound) *n.* **1.** Any of various dogs originally bred and used for hunting. **2.** An en-

ô paw, for/oi boy/ou out/ŏŏ took/ōō coo/p pop/r run/s sauce/sh shy/t to/th thin/*th* the/
ŭ cut/ûr fur/v van/w wag/y yes/z size/zh vision/ə ago, item, edible, gallop, circus/

hour / hue¹

thusiast or addict: *a coffee hound.* —*v.* To pursue relentlessly and tenaciously. [< OE *hund.* See kwon-.] —**hound′er** *n.*

hour (our) *n.* **1.** The 24th part of a day. **2.** The time of day. **3. a.** A customary time: *dinner hour.* **b. hours.** A specified period: *banking hours.* [< Gk *hōra,* time, season.]

hour•glass (our′glăs′, -gläs′) *n.* An instrument that measures time by the trickling of sand from an upper to a lower glass compartment.

hour•ly (our′lē) *adj.* Every hour. —**hour′ly** *adv.*

house (hous) *n., pl.* **houses** (hou′zĭz). **1.** A structure serving as a dwelling for one or several families. **2.** A building having a specified function. **3.** A household. **4. House.** A noble family: *House of Orange.* **5.** A commercial firm: *banking house.* **6. a.** A theater. **b.** A theater audience. **7.** A legislative assembly. —*v.* (houz) **housed, housing. 1.** To provide living or working quarters for. **2.** To contain. [< OE *hūs* < Gmc **hūsam.*]

house•boat (hous′bōt′) *n.* A wide, flat-bottomed boat equipped for use as a domicile.

house•break•ing (hous′brā′kĭng) *n.* The unlawful breaking into of another's domicile for the purpose of committing a felony. —**house′break′er** *n.*

house•bro•ken (hous′brō′kən) *adj.* Trained to control excretory functions, as a pet.

house•coat (hous′kōt′) *n.* A woman's garment with a long skirt, worn at home.

house•fly (hous′flī′) *n.* A common fly that frequents human dwellings and is a transmitter of a wide variety of diseases.

house•hold (hous′hōld′) *n.* A domestic establishment including the members of a family and others living under the same roof. —**house′hold′** *adj.*

household word. A commonly used word, phrase, or name.

house•keep•er (hous′kē′pər) *n.* One who has charge of domestic tasks in a household. —**house′keep′ing** *n.*

house•warm•ing (hous′wôr′mĭng) *n.* A party to celebrate the occupancy of a new home.

house•wife (hous′wīf′) *n.* **1.** A woman who manages her own household. **2.** (hŭz′ĭf). *Chiefly Brit.* A pocket container for sewing equipment. —**house′wife′li•ness** *n.* —**house′-wife′ly** *adj.* —**house′wif′er•y** *n.*

house•work (hous′wûrk′) *n.* The tasks performed in housekeeping.

hous•ing (hou′zĭng) *n.* **1. a.** Protective shelter; a dwelling. **b.** Dwellings collectively. **2.** A protective covering for something, as a mechanical part.

Hous•ton (hyōō′stən). A city of SE Texas. Pop. 1,213,000.

hove (hōv). *Chiefly naut.* Alternate *p.t.* & *p.p.* of **heave.**

hov•el (hŭv′əl, hŏv′-) *n.* A small, miserable dwelling. [ME.]

hov•er (hŭv′ər, hŏv′-) *v.* **1.** To fly or float as if suspended. **2.** To linger close to a place. **3.** To pause or waver uncertainly. [ME *hoveren.*]

hov•er•craft (hŭv′ər-krăft′, -kräft′, hŏv′-) *n.* A motorized vehicle capable of low-level flight on a cushion of air.

how (hou) *adv.* **1.** In what manner or way; by what means. **2.** In what state or condition. **3.** To what extent, amount, or degree: *How do you like that?* **4.** For what effect or purpose; why. **5.** For what price: *How are these shirts sold on sale?* **6.** With what meaning: *How should I interpret this?* —**how come?** Why? [< OE *hū.* See kwo-.]

how•be•it (hou-bē′ĭt) *adv. Archaic.* Be that as it may. —*conj. Obs.* Although.

how•dah (hou′də) *n.* A covered seat, usually enclosed, on the back of an elephant or camel. [< Ar *haudaj,* camel's burden.]

how-do-you-do (hou′də-yə-dōō′) *n.* Also **how-d′ye-do** (hou′dyə-dōō′, hou′dē-). *Informal.* A predicament.

how•ev•er (hou-ev′ər) *adv.* **1.** By whatever manner or means. **2.** To whatever degree or extent. —*conj.* Nevertheless; yet.

how•it•zer (hou′ĭt-sər) *n.* A cannon that delivers shells in a high trajectory. [< Czech *houfnice,* catapult.]

howl (houl) *v.* **1.** To utter a long-drawn, mournful cry, as of a wolf. **2.** To utter or produce a similar sound or outcry. —*n.* **1.** A long-drawn wailing sound. **2.** *Slang.* Something uproariously funny. [Perh < MDu *hūlen.*]

howl•er (hou′lər) *n.* **1.** One that howls. **2.** A ridiculous blunder.

howl•ing (hou′lĭng) *adj.* **1.** Characterized by howls. **2.** Very great; vast.

how•so•ev•er (hou′sō-ev′ər) *adv.* **1.** To whatever degree or extent. **2.** By whatever means.

hoy•den (hoid′n) *n.* A boisterous girl. [Prob < MDu *heiden,* "heathen."]

hp horsepower.

HQ, h.q., H.Q. headquarters.

hr. hour.

H.R. House of Representatives.

ht height.

hub (hŭb) *n.* **1.** The center portion of a wheel or wheellike part. **2.** A center of activity or interest.

hub•bub (hŭb′ŭb′) *n.* A confused din or uproar. [Ir *hooboobbes.*]

hub•cap (hŭb′kăp′) *n.* A round metal covering clamped over the hub of an automobile wheel.

hu•bris (hyōō′brĭs) *n.* Overbearing pride or presumption. [Gk, insolence, outrage.]

huck•le•ber•ry (hŭk′əl-bĕr′ē) *n.* **1.** A glossy, blackish, edible berry related to the blueberry. **2.** A shrub bearing such berries.

huck•ster (hŭk′stər) *n.* **1.** A peddler. **2.** One who publicizes a commercial product.

hud•dle (hŭd′əl) *v.* **-dled, -dling. 1.** To crowd in a close group. **2.** To hunch up; crouch. **3.** To gather together, as for a conference. —*n.* **1.** A closely crowded group. **2.** A brief gathering together for consultation, as of football players between plays. [?] —**hud′dler** *n.*

Hud•son Bay (hŭd′sən). A part of the Atlantic extending into east-central Canada.

Hudson River. A river of New York State.

hue¹ (hyōō) *n.* **1.** The dimension of color that is referred to a scale of perceptions ranging from red through yellow, green, and blue, and (circularly) back to red. **2.** A particular grada-

---

ă pat/ā ate/âr care/ä bar/b bib/ch chew/d deed/ĕ pet/ē be/f fit/g gag/h hat/hw what/
ĭ pit/ī pie/îr pier/j judge/k kick/l lid, fatal/m mum/n no, sudden/ng sing/ŏ pot/ō go/

tion of color; tint; shade. **3.** Color. [< OE *hēo*, appearance, color, beauty. See **kei-²**.]

hue² (hyōō) *n.* —**hue and cry.** A loud outcry, as of pursuit or protest. [< OF *huer*, to cry out (imit).]

huff (hŭf) *n.* A fit of anger or offended annoyance. —*v.* To puff; blow; breathe heavily. [Imit.] —**huf′fi·ness** *n.* —**huf′fy** *adj.*

hug (hŭg) *v.* **hugged, hugging. 1.** To clasp or hold closely; embrace. **2.** To keep or hold close to. **3.** To cling to; cherish. —*n.* A close embrace. [< Scand.] —**hug′ger** *n.*

huge (hyōōj) *adj.* **huger, hugest.** Very large; enormous. [< OF *ahuge*.] —**huge′ly** *adv.* —**huge′ness** *n.*

hug·ger·mug·ger, hug·ger-mug·ger (hŭg′ər-mŭg′ər) *n.* **1.** Confused disorder. —*adj.* **1.** Disordered; jumbled. **2.** Secret; clandestine. [?]

Hu·go (hyōō′gō), **Victor.** 1802–1885. French poet.

Hu·gue·not (hyōō′gə-nŏt′) *n.* A French Protestant of the 16th and 17th centuries.

huh (hŭ) *interj.* Expressive of surprise, interrogation, or contempt.

hu·la (hōō′lə) *n.* A Polynesian dance characterized by undulating movements of the hips, arms, and hands.

hulk (hŭlk) *n.* **1.** The hull of a ship, esp. an old or wrecked ship. **2.** A large, clumsy person or object. [< Gk *holkas*, "ship that is towed."]

hulk·ing (hŭl′kĭng) *adj.* Massive and clumsy.

hull (hŭl) *n.* **1.** The dry or leafy outer covering of a fruit, seed, or nut. **2. a.** The main body of a ship. **b.** The outer casing of a rocket, missile, or spacecraft. —*v.* To remove the hulls of (fruit or seeds). [< OE *hulu*. See **kel-⁴**.]

hul·la·ba·loo (hŭl′ə-bə-lōō′) *n.* A loud, confused noise; uproar.

hum (hŭm) *v.* **hummed, humming 1.** To produce a continuous droning sound. **2.** To sing with closed lips. **3.** To be full of activity. —*n.* A continuous droning sound. —**hum′mer** *n.*

hu·man (hyōō′mən) *adj.* **1.** Of, relating to, or characteristic of mankind or of persons. **2.** Having the form or qualities characteristic of man. —*n.* Also **human being.** A person. [< L *hūmānus*.] —**hu′man·ness** *n.*

hu·mane (hyōō-mān′) *adj.* **1.** Having or showing sympathetic concern for others; compassionate; kind. **2.** Of or pertaining to the humanities. [ME *humaine*, human.] —**hu·mane′ly** *adv.* —**hu·mane′ness** *n.*

hu·man·ism (hyōō′mə-nĭz′əm) *n.* **1.** An attitude or system of thought asserting the primacy of man over metaphysical or abstract principles. **2. Humanism.** Study of classical texts as pursued during the Renaissance. —**hu′man·ist** *n.* & *adj.* —**hu′man·is′tic** *adj.*

hu·man·i·tar·i·an (hyōō-măn′ə-târ′ē-ən) *n.* One devoted to the promotion of human welfare. —*adj.* Concerned with human welfare. —**hu·man′i·tar′i·an·ism′** *n.*

hu·man·i·ty (hyōō-măn′ə-tē) *n.* **1.** Human beings collectively; mankind. **2.** The condition or quality of being human. **3.** Humane quality; kindness; mercy. **4. the humanities.** Philosophy, literature, and the fine arts as distinguished from the sciences.

hu·man·ize (hyōō′mə-nīz′) *v.* **-ized, -izing.** To make human or humane. —**hu′man·i·za′tion** *n.*

hu·man·kind (hyōō′mən-kīnd′) *n.* The human race; mankind.

hu·man·ly (hyōō′mən-lē) *adv.* **1.** In a human way. **2.** By human means or powers.

hu·man·oid (hyōō′mə-noid′) *adj.* Resembling a human being in appearance. —*n.* An android.

hum·ble (hŭm′bəl) *adj.* **-bler, -blest. 1.** Showing awareness of one's shortcomings; not proud; meek. **2.** Deeply respectful. **3.** Not high in station; lowly. —*v.* **-bled, -bling. 1.** To make humble in spirit. **2.** To bring low; abase. [< L *humilis*, low, lowly, base.] —**hum′ble·ness** *n.* —**hum′bly** *adv.*

hum·bug (hŭm′bŭg′) *n.* **1.** A hoax; fake. **2.** An impostor; charlatan. **3.** Nonsense; rubbish. —*v.* **-bugged, -bugging.** To trick; cheat. [?] —**hum′bug′ger** *n.*

hum·ding·er (hŭm′dĭng′ər) *n. Informal.* Something extraordinary.

hum·drum (hŭm′drŭm′) *adj.* Monotonous; uneventful. —**hum′drum′ness** *n.*

hu·mer·us (hyōō′mər-əs) *n., pl.* **-meri** (-mə-rī′). The long bone of the upper arm, extending from the shoulder to the elbow. [< L, upper arm, shoulder.] —**hu′mer·al** *adj.*

hu·mid (hyōō′mĭd) *adj.* Having a high concentration of water vapor or moisture. [< L *hūmēre*, to be moist.] —**hu·mid′i·ty** *n.*

hu·mid·i·fy (hyōō-mĭd′ə-fī′) *v.* **-fied, -fying.** To make humid. —**hu·mid′i·fi′er** *n.*

hu·mi·dor (hyōō′mə-dôr′) *n.* A storage case for tobacco products, esp. cigars, equipped with a humidifying device.

hu·mil·i·ate (hyōō-mĭl′ē-āt′) *v.* **-ated, -ating.** To destroy the dignity or pride of; shame; disgrace. [< L *humilis*, HUMBLE.] —**hu·mil′i·at′ing·ly** *adv.* —**hu·mil′i·a′tion** *n.*

hu·mil·i·ty (hyōō-mĭl′ə-tē) *n.* The quality or condition of being humble.

hum·ming·bird (hŭm′ĭng-bûrd′) *n.* A very small, long-billed, often brilliantly colored bird.

hum·mock (hŭm′ək) *n.* A low mound or ridge; knoll. [?]

hu·mor (hyōō′mər). Also *Brit.* **hu·mour.** *n.* **1.** The quality of being laughable or comical. **2.** Ability to perceive or express what is comical, witty, etc. **3.** State of mind; mood; disposition. **4.** Capricious impulse; whim. **5.** Any of various bodily fluids. —*v.* To comply with the whims of; indulge. [ME *humour*, one of the four principal bodily fluids that affected mental disposition.]

hu·mor·ist (hyōō′mər-ĭst) *n.* **1.** One with a sharp sense of humor. **2.** A performer or writer of comedy.

hu·mor·ous (hyōō′mər-əs) *adj.* Comical; funny. —**hu′mor·ous·ly** *adv.* —**hu′mor·ous·ness** *n.*

hump (hŭmp) *n.* **1.** A rounded protuberance, as on the back of a camel. **2.** A hill or hummock. —**over the hump.** Past the worst or most difficult part. —*v.* To make into a hump; to round. [Short for earlier *humpback(ed)*, poss < HUNCHBACK(ED).]

hump·back (hŭmp′băk′) *n.* **1.** An abnormally

---

curved or humped back. **2.** One having such a back; a hunchback. —**hump'backed'** *adj.*

humph (hŭmf) *interj.* Expressive of doubt, displeasure, or contempt.

hu·mus (hyōō'məs) *n.* Dark-colored partially or wholly decayed vegetable matter forming a nutrient constituent of soil. [L, earth, ground, soil.]

Hun (hŭn) *n.* One of a nomadic Asiatic people who invaded Europe in the 4th and 5th centuries A.D.

Hun. Hungarian; Hungary.

hunch (hŭnch) *v.* **1.** To arch or draw up into a hump. **2.** To push or thrust forward. —*n.* An intuitive premonitory feeling. [?]

hunch·back (hŭnch'băk') *n.* **1.** One having an abnormally curved or humped back; a hump-back. **2.** An abnormally curved or humped back. —**hunch'backed'** *adj.*

hun·dred (hŭn'drĭd) *n. pl.* **-dreds** or **-dred. 1.** The cardinal number written 100 or in Roman numerals C. **2.** The number in the third position left of the decimal point in an Arabic numeral. **3. hundreds.** The numbers between 100 and 999: *in the hundreds.* [< OE *hundred, hund.*] —**hun'dred** *adj. & pron.*

hun·dredth (hŭn'drĭdth) *n.* **1.** The ordinal number 100 in a series. **2.** One of 100 equal parts. —**hun'dredth** *adj. & adv.*

hun·dred·weight (hŭn'drĭd-wāt') *n., pl.* **-weight** or **-weights. 1.** A U.S. Customary System unit of weight equal to 100 pounds. **2.** A British Imperial System unit of weight equal to 112 pounds.

hung (hŭng). Alternate *p.t. & p.p.* of **hang.** See Usage note at **hang.**

Hung. Hungarian; Hungary.

Hun·gar·i·an (hŭng·gâr'ē-ən) *n.* **1.** A citizen or native of Hungary. **2.** The Finno-Ugric language spoken in Hungary. —**Hun'gar'i·an** *adj.*

Hun·ga·ry (hŭng'gə-rē). A republic of C Europe. Pop. 10,123,000. Cap. Budapest.

Hungary

hun·ger (hŭng'gər) *n.* **1.** A strong desire or need for food. **2.** Weakness or discomfort caused by lack of food. **3.** A strong desire; craving. —*v.* **1.** To be hungry. **2.** To have a strong desire; yearn. [< OE *hungor.* See kenk-2.] —**hun'ger·less** *adj.*

hun·gry (hŭng'grē) *adj.* **-grier, -griest. 1. a.** Desiring food. **b.** Weak or uncomfortable from lack of food. **2.** Feeling or showing a strong desire for something. —**hun'gri·ly** *adv.*

hunk (hŭngk) *n.* A large piece; chunk.

hun·ker (hŭng'kər) *v.* To squat with one's weight resting on the calves. [Prob < Scand.]

hun·ky-do·ry (hŭng'kē-dôr'ē, -dōr'ē) *adj. Informal.* Quite satisfactory; fine. [< MDu *honc,* hiding place.]

Hun·nish (hŭn'ĭsh) *adj.* **1.** Of or pertaining to the Huns. **2.** Often **hunnish.** Barbarous. —**Hun'nish·ness** *n.*

hunt (hŭnt) *v.* **1.** To pursue (animals) for food, sport, etc. **2.** To make a search (for); seek. **3.** To chase and harass. **4.** To swing back and forth or oscillate, as an indicator on an instrument panel. —*n.* **1.** The act or sport of hunting. **2.** A group or expedition organized for hunting. **3.** A search or pursuit. [< OE *huntian* < Gmc **huntjan.*] —**hunt'er** *n.* —**hunt'ress** *fem.n.*

hunts·man (hŭnts'mən) *n.* One who hunts, esp. one who manages a pack of hunting hounds.

hur·dle (hûrd'l) *n.* **1.** A framelike barrier to be jumped over in obstacle races. **2.** Any obstacle or problem that must be overcome. —*v.* **-dled, -dling. 1.** To jump over (a barrier). **2.** To overcome (an obstacle). [< OE *hyrdel.* See kert-.] —**hur'dler** *n.*

hur·dy-gur·dy (hûr'dē-gûr'dē) *n., pl.* **-dies.** A musical instrument, as a barrel organ, played by turning a crank. [Prob imit.]

hurl (hûrl) *v.* **1.** To throw forcefully; fling. **2.** To utter vehemently: *hurl insults.* [ME *hourlen,* to throw, rush on.] —**hurl** *n.* —**hurl'er** *n.*

hur·ly-bur·ly (hûr'lē-bûr'lē) *n., pl.* **-lies.** Commotion; tumult. [< HURL.]

Hu·ron (hyŏŏr'ən, -ŏn') *n., pl.* **-ron** or **-rons. 1.** A member of a confederation of four tribes of Iroquoian-speaking North American Indians formerly inhabiting the St. Lawrence Valley region. **2.** The Iroquoian language spoken among these tribes. —**Hu'ron** *adj.*

Huron, Lake. The second largest of the Great Lakes.

hur·rah (hŏŏ-rä', -rô') *interj.* Also **hoo·ray** (-rā'), **hur·ray** (-rā'). Expressive of approval, elation, or victory. —**hur·rah'** *n.*

hur·ri·cane (hûr'ə-kān') *n.* A severe tropical cyclone with winds exceeding 75 miles per hour and usually involving heavy rains. [< Carib *huracan, furacan.*]

hur·ry (hûr'ē) *v.* **-ried, -rying. 1.** To move or cause to move with speed or haste. **2.** To proceed or press to proceed with great or undue rapidity; rush. —*n., pl.* **-ries. 1.** The act of hurrying. **2.** Haste; a rush. [Prob imit.] —**hur'ried·ly** *adv.* —**hur'ried·ness** *n.*

hurt (hûrt) *v.* **hurt, hurting. 1.** To feel or cause to feel physical pain. **2.** To offend; distress. **3.** To damage; harm. —*n.* **1.** Physical pain or injury. **2.** Anguish; distress. **3.** Damage; harm. [< OF *hurter.*] —**hurt'ful** *adj.*

hur·tle (hûrt'l) *v.* **-tled, -tling. 1.** To move with forceful, often noisy speed. **2.** To collide violently; crash. [< ME *hurten,* to strike, hurt.]

Hus (hōōs), **Jan.** 1369?–1415. Bohemian religious reformer.

hus•band (hŭz'bənd) *n.* A married man; male spouse. —*v.* To expend wisely or economically. [< OE *húsbonda,* master of a household, husband.]

hus•band•man (hŭz'bənd-mən) *n.* A farmer.

hus•band•ry (hŭz'bən-drē) *n.* 1. Farming; agriculture. 2. Careful management of resources.

hush (hŭsh) *v.* 1. To make or become silent. 2. To quell; calm. 3. To suppress; conceal. —*n.* A silence; stillness.

hush•pup•py (hŭsh'pŭp'ē) *n. Southern U.S.* A fried cornmeal fritter.

husk (hŭsk) *n.* 1. A thin or leaflike outer envelope, as of an ear of corn or a nut. 2. An often worthless or discarded outer shell. —*v.* To remove the husk from. [Prob < MDu *hûs,* house.] —**husk'er** *n.*

husk•y¹ (hŭs'kē) *adj.* -ier, -iest. Hoarse; throaty. [Orig "dry as a husk."] —**husk'i•ly** *adv.* —**husk'i•ness** *n.*

husk•y² (hŭs'kē) *adj.* -ier, -iest. Large and strong; burly. [< HUSKY¹.] —**husk'i•ness** *n.*

hus•ky³ (hŭs'kē) *n., pl.* -kies. An Arctic sled dog with a dense, furry coat. [Prob a shortened var of ESKIMO.]

hus•sar (hŏŏ-zär') *n.* A member of a cavalry regiment with a usually much ornamented dress uniform. [Hung *huszár,* "freebooter," hussar.]

hus•sy (hŭz'ē, hŭs'ē) *n., pl.* -sies. 1. A saucy girl. 2. A strumpet; trollop. [Var of HOUSEWIFE.]

hus•tle (hŭs'əl) *v.* -tled, -tling. 1. To jostle; shove. 2. To hurry along. 3. To work busily. 4. *Slang.* To make money by questionable means. —*n.* Busy activity. [< MDu *hutsen,* to shake.] —**hus'tler** *n.*

hut (hŭt) *n.* A makeshift or crude dwelling; shack. [OF *hutte.*]

hutch (hŭch) *n.* 1. A coop for small animals, esp. rabbits. 2. A cupboard surmounted by usually open shelves. [< OF *huche,* chest.]

huz•za (hə-zä'). Also **huz•zah.** *n.* A shout of encouragement or triumph; a cheer. —**huz•za'** *interj.*

hy•a•cinth (hī'ə-sĭnth) *n.* A bulbous plant with a cluster of variously colored, fragrant flowers. [< Gk *huakinthos,* wild hyacinth.]

hy•ae•na. Variant of hyena.

hy•brid (hī'brĭd) *n.* 1. The offspring of genetically dissimilar parents or stock, as that of plants or animals of different varieties, species, etc. 2. Something of mixed origin or composition. [L *hybrida,* hybrid, mongrel.] —**hy'brid** *adj.* —**hy'brid•ism'** *n.*

hy•brid•ize (hī'brĭ-dīz') *v.* -ized, -izing. To produce or cause to produce a hybrid. —**hy'brid•i•za'tion** *n.*

hy•dran•ge•a (hī-drān'jē-ə, -jə) *n.* A shrub with large, flat-topped or rounded clusters of white, pink, or blue flowers. [< HYDR(O)- + Gk *angos,* vessel.]

hy•drant (hī'drənt) *n.* An upright pipe serving as an outlet from a water main. [HYDR(O)- + -ANT.]

hy•drate (hī'drāt') *n.* A compound containing water combined in a definite ratio, regarded as

being retained in its molecular state. —*v.* -drated, -drating. To form a hydrate. —**hy•dra'tion** *n.* —**hy'dra'tor** (-drā'tər) *n.*

hy•drau•lic (hī-drô'lĭk) *adj.* 1. Of, involving, or operated by a fluid, esp. water, under pressure. 2. Setting and hardening under water: *hydraulic cement.* 3. Of or pertaining to hydraulics. —*n.* **hydraulics** *(takes sing. v.).* The physical science and technology of the static and dynamic behavior of fluids. [< Gk *hudraulis,* a water organ.] —**hy•drau'li•cal•ly** *adv.*

hydraulic brake. A brake in which the braking force is transmitted to the braking surface by a compressed fluid.

hydro–. *comb. form.* 1. Water. 2. Liquid. 3. Composed of or combined with hydrogen. [< Gk *hudōr,* water.]

hy•dro•car•bon (hī'drə-kär'bən) *n.* An organic compound, such as benzene or methane, that contains only carbon and hydrogen.

hy•dro•ceph•a•ly (hī'drō-sĕf'ə-lē) *n.* A usually congenital condition in which an abnormal accumulation of fluid in the cerebral ventricles causes enlargement of the skull and compression of the brain. —**hy'dro•ce•phal'ic** (-sə-făl'ĭk) *adj.*

hy•dro•chlo•ric acid (hī'drə-klôr'ĭk, -klōr'ĭk). A clear, colorless, highly acidic aqueous solution of hydrogen chloride, HCl, used in petroleum production, ore reduction, food processing, pickling, and metal cleaning.

hy•dro•dy•nam•ics (hī'drō-dī-năm'ĭks) *n.* *(takes sing. v.).* The dynamics of fluids, esp. incompressible fluids, in motion. —**hy'dro•dy•nam'ic** *adj.*

hy•dro•e•lec•tric (hī'drō-ĭ-lĕk'trĭk) *adj.* Generating electricity by conversion of the energy of running water. —**hy'dro•e•lec'tric'i•ty** (-ĭ-lĕk'trĭs'ə-tē) *n.*

hy•dro•foil (hī'drə-foil') *n.* 1. One of a set of blades attached to the hull of a boat to lift it out of the water for efficient high-speed operation. 2. A boat equipped with hydrofoils; hydroplane.

hy•dro•gen (hī'drə-jən) *n.* *Symbol* **H** A colorless, highly flammable gaseous element used in the production of synthetic ammonia and methanol, in petroleum refining, as a reducing atmosphere, in oxyhydrogen torches, and in rocket fuels. Atomic number 1, atomic weight 1.00797. [F *hydrogène,* "water generating."] —**hy•drog'e•nous** (-drŏj'ə-nəs) *adj.*

hy•dro•gen•ate (hī'drə-jə-nāt', hī-drŏj'ə-) *v.* -ated, -ating. To combine with or subject to the action of hydrogen. —**hy'dro•gen•a'tion** *n.*

hydrogen bomb. An explosive weapon of great destructive power derived from the fusion of nuclei of various hydrogen isotopes in the formation of helium nuclei.

hydrogen bond. An essentially ionic chemical bond between a strongly electronegative atom and a hydrogen atom already bonded to another strongly electronegative atom.

hydrogen peroxide. A colorless, heavy, strongly oxidizing liquid, H_2O_2, an essentially unstable compound, used principally in aqueous solution as an antiseptic, bleaching agent, oxidizing agent, and laboratory reagent.

ô paw, for/oi boy/ou out/ŏŏ took/ōō coo/p pop/r run/s sauce/sh shy/t to/th thin/*th* the/
ŭ cut/ûr fur/v van/w wag/y yes/z size/zh vision/ə ago, item, edible, gallop, circus/

hy·drol·y·sis (hĭ-drŏl′ə-sĭs) *n.* Decomposition of a chemical compound by reaction with water. —**hy′dro·ly′tic** (hī′drə-lĭt′ĭk) *adj.* —**hy′dro·lyze′** *v.* (-lyzed, -lyzing.)

hy·drom·e·ter (hĭ-drŏm′ə-tər) *n.* A sealed graduated tube, weighted at one end, that sinks in a fluid to a depth used as a measure of the fluid's specific gravity.

hy·dro·pho·bi·a (hī′drə-fō′bē-ə) *n.* Rabies.

hy·dro·plane (hī′drə-plān′) *n.* 1. A seaplane. 2. A motorboat designed to skim the water at high speeds. 3. A hydrofoil.

hy·dro·stat·ic (hī′drə-stăt′ĭk) *adj.* Also **hy·dro·stat·i·cal** (-ĭ-kəl). Pertaining to hydrostatics. —*n.* **hydrostatics** (*takes sing. v.*). The statics of fluids, esp. incompressible fluids.

hy·dro·ther·a·py (hī′drō-thĕr′ə-pē) *n.* The medical use of water in the treatment of certain diseases.

hy·drous (hī′drəs) *adj.* Containing water.

hy·drox·ide (hĭ-drŏk′sīd′) *n.* A chemical compound containing the univalent group OH. [HYDR(O)- + OXIDE.]

hy·e·na (hī-ē′nə) *n.* Also **hy·ae·na.** A carnivorous African and Asian mammal with powerful jaws. [< Gk *huaina* < *hus,* swine.]

hy·giene (hī′jēn′) *n.* The science or principles of health and the prevention of disease. [< Gk *hugiēs,* healthy.] —**hy′gi·en′ic** *adj.*

hygro–. *comb. form.* Wet. [< Gk *hugros,* wet, moist.]

hy·grom·e·ter (hī-grŏm′ə-tər) *n.* Any of several instruments that measure atmospheric humidity. —**hy·grom′e·try** *n.*

hy·gro·scop·ic (hī′grə-skŏp′ĭk) *adj.* Readily absorbing moisture, as from the atmosphere.

hy·men (hī′mən) *n.* A membranous fold of tissue partly or completely occluding the vaginal external orifice. [< Gk *humēn,* membrane.]

hy·me·ne·al (hī′mə-nē′əl) *adj.* Of or pertaining to a wedding or marriage. [< Gk *Humēn,* god of marriage.]

hymn (hĭm) *n.* A song of praise or thanksgiving, esp. to God. [< Gk *humnos.*]

hym·nal (hĭm′nəl) *n.* A book or collection of hymns.

hy·oid bone (hī′oid′). A U-shaped bone between the mandible and larynx.

hyp. 1. hypotenuse. 2. hypothesis.

hyper–. *comb. form.* 1. Over, above, or in great amount. 2. In abnormal excess. [< Gk *huper,* over, above, beyond.]

hy·per·bar·ic (hī′pər-băr′ĭk) *adj.* Employing pressures higher than normal atmospheric pressure.

hy·per·bo·la (hī-pûr′bə-lə) *n.* A plane curve having two branches, formed by the locus of points related to two given points such that the difference in the distances of each point from the two given points is a constant. [< Gk *huperbolē,* "a throwing beyond," excess.]

hy·per·bo·le (hī-pûr′bə-lē) *n.* Exaggeration used as a figure of speech. [< Gk *huperbolē,* excess.]

hy·per·bol·ic (hī′pər-bŏl′ĭk) *adj.* 1. Of or employing hyperbole. 2. Of or having the form of a hyperbola. —**hy′per·bol′i·cal·ly** *adv.*

hy·per·bo·re·an (hī′pər-bôr′ē-ən, -bōr′ē-ən, -bə-rē′ən) *adj.* Of the far north.

hy·per·crit·i·cal (hī′pər-krĭt′ĭ-kəl) *adj.* Overcritical. —**hy′per·crit′i·cal·ly** *adv.*

hy·per·o·pi·a (hī′pər-ō′pē-ə) *n.* A refractive defect of the eye in which vision is better for distant than for near objects.

hy·per·sen·si·tive (hī′pər-sĕn′sə-tĭv) *adj.* Abnormally sensitive. —**hy′per·sen′si·tiv′i·ty,** **hy′per·sen′si·tive·ness** *n.*

hy·per·son·ic (hī′pər-sŏn′ĭk) *adj.* Pertaining to speed equal to or exceeding five times the speed of sound.

hy·per·ten·sion (hī′pər-tĕn′shən) *n.* 1. Abnormally high arterial blood pressure. 2. A state of high emotional tension.

hy·per·thy·roid·ism (hī′pər-thī′roi-dĭz′əm) *n.* Pathologically excessive production of thyroid hormones. —**hy′per·thy′roid′** *adj. & n.*

hy·phen (hī′fən) *n.* A punctuation mark (-) used to connect the parts of a compound word or between syllables of a divided word. [< Gk *huphen,* in the same word.]

hy·phen·ate (hī′fə-nāt′) *v.* -ated, -ating. To divide or connect with a hyphen. —**hy′phen·a′tion** *n.*

hyp·no·sis (hĭp-nō′sĭs) *n.* An artificially induced sleeplike condition in which an individual is extremely responsive to suggestion. [< Gk *hupnos,* sleep + -OSIS.] —**hyp′no·tize′** (hĭp′nə-tīz′) *v.* (-tized, -tizing).

hyp·not·ic (hĭp-nŏt′ĭk) *adj.* 1. Of or inducing hypnosis. 2. Inducing sleep. —*n.* 1. A hypnotic agent. 2. A hypnotized person. —**hyp·not′i·cal·ly** *adv.*

hyp·no·tism (hĭp′nə-tĭz′əm) *n.* The theory or practice of inducing hypnosis. —**hyp′no·tist** *n.*

hy·po (hī′pō) *n., pl.* -pos. *Informal.* A hypodermic syringe or injection.

hypo–. *comb. form.* 1. Below or beneath. 2. At a lower point. 3. Abnormally low. 4. Deficient. [< Gk *hupo,* under, beneath.]

hy·po·chon·dri·a (hī′pə-kŏn′drē-ə) *n.* The persistent neurotic conviction that one is or is likely to become ill. [< Gk *hupokhondrion,* belly, abdomen.] —**hy′po·chon′dri·ac′** *n. & adj.*

hy·poc·ri·sy (hĭ-pŏk′rə-sē) *n.* The feigning of beliefs, feelings, or virtues that one does not hold or possess. [< Gk *hupokrisis,* playing of a part on the stage.]

hyp·o·crite (hĭp′ə-krĭt′) *n.* A person given to hypocrisy. —**hyp′o·crit′i·cal** *adj.* —**hyp′o·crit′i·cal·ly** *adv.*

hy·po·der·mic (hī′pə-dûr′mĭk) *adj.* 1. Just beneath the epidermis. 2. Injected beneath the skin. —*n.* A hypodermic injection.

hy·pot·e·nuse (hī-pŏt′n/y/ōōs′) *n.* The side of a right triangle opposite the right angle. [< Gk *hupoteinousa,* line subtending the right angle.]

hypoth. hypothesis.

hy·po·thal·a·mus (hī′pō-thăl′ə-məs) *n.* The part of the brain that lies below the thalamus and functions to regulate bodily temperature, certain metabolic processes, and other autonomic activities.

hy·poth·e·sis (hī-pŏth′ə-sĭs) *n., pl.* -ses (-sēz′). An assumption subject to verification or proof, as a conjecture that accounts for a set of facts and can be used as a basis for further investigation. [< Gk *hupothesis,* proposal.]

hy·poth·e·size (hī-pŏth′ə-sīz′) *v.* **-sized, -sizing.** To assert as or form a hypothesis.

hy·po·thet·i·cal (hī′pə-thĕt′ĭ-kəl) *adj.* Of or based on a hypothesis; conjectural. —**hy′po·thet′i·cal·ly** *adv.*

hy·po·thy·roid·ism (hī′pō-thī′roi-dĭz′əm) *n.* Insufficient production of thyroid hormones.

hys·sop (hĭs′əp) *n.* A bushy, aromatic plant with spikes of small blue flowers. [< Gk *hussōpos.*]

hys·ter·ec·to·my (hĭs′tə-rĕk′tə-mē) *n., pl.* **-mies.** Total or partial surgical removal of the uterus.

hys·ter·e·sis (hĭs′tə-rē′sĭs) *n., pl.* **-ses** (-sēz′). *Phys.* Failure of a property changed by an external agent to return to its original value when the cause of the change is removed. [< Gk *husterēsis,* a shortcoming.]

hys·ter·i·a (hĭ-stĕr′ē-ə) *n.* **1.** A neurosis characterized by symbolic physiological symptoms, hallucination, somnambulism, amnesia, and other mental aberrations. **2.** Uncontrollable fear or other strong emotion. [< Gk *husterikos,* suffering in the womb.] —**hys·ter′ic** *n. & adj.* —**hys·ter′i·cal** *adj.* —**hys·ter′i·cal·ly** *adv.*

hys·ter·ics (hĭ-stĕr′ĭks) *n. (takes sing. v.).* A fit of uncontrollable laughing and crying.

Hz hertz.

Ii

I, I (ī) *n.* **1.** The 9th letter of the English alphabet. **2.** The 9th in a series.

I **1.** *Math.* imaginary unit. **2.** The Roman numeral for one.

I **1.** iodine. **2.** The Roman numeral for one.

i. **1.** interest. **2.** intransitive.

i. island.

I (ī) *pron.* The 1st person sing. pronoun in the nominative case, used to represent the speaker or writer. [< OE *ic.* See **eg.**]

Ia. Iowa (unofficial).

–ial. *comb. form.* Of, pertaining to, or characterized by: managerial. [< L *-iālis.*]

i·amb (ī′ămb′) *n.* A metrical foot consisting of an unstressed syllable followed by a stressed syllable. —**i·am′bic** *adj. & n.*

–ian. *comb. form.* Of, belonging to, or resembling: Bostonian. [< L *-iānus.*]

–iatrics. *comb. form.* Medical treatment: pediatrics. [< Gk *iatros,* healer.]

–iatry. *comb. form.* Medical treatment: psychiatry.

I·be·ri·a (ī-bîr′ē-ə). The ancient name for the Spanish-Portuguese peninsula. —**I·be′ri·an** *adj. & n.*

i·bex (ī′bĕks′) *n.* An Old World mountain goat with long, curving horns. [L.]

ibid. ibidem.

i·bi·dem (ĭb′ə-dĕm′, ĭ-bī′dəm) *adv.* In the same place, as in a book cited before. [L.]

i·bis (ī′bĭs) *n.* A large wading bird with a long, downward-curving bill. [< Gk < Egypt *hĭb.*]

–ible. Variant of **-able.**

Ib·sen (ĭb′sən), **Henrik.** 1828–1906. Norwegian dramatist.

–ic. *comb. form.* **1.** Used to form adjectives meaning of, pertaining to, or characteristic of: Gaelic. **2.** *Chem.* Having or taking a valence higher than in corresponding *-ous* compounds: ferric. [< L *-icus.*]

ICBM intercontinental ballistic missile.

ICC Interstate Commerce Commission.

ice (īs) *n.* **1.** Water frozen solid. **2.** A dessert of sweetened and flavored crushed ice. —**break the ice.** To relax a tense or formal atmosphere. —*v.* **iced, icing.** **1.** To form ice. **2.** To coat with ice. **3.** To chill or freeze. **4.** To cover with icing. [< OE *is.* See **eis-².**] —**i′ci·ly** *adv.* —**i′cy** *adj.*

ice·berg (īs′bûrg′) *n.* A massive floating body of ice broken away from a glacier.

ice·bound (īs′bound′) *adj.* **1.** Locked in by ice, as a ship. **2.** Obstructed by ice, as a waterway.

ice·box (īs′bŏks′) *n.* A refrigerator.

ice·break·er (īs′brā′kər) *n.* A ship built for breaking a passage through icebound waters.

ice cap. An extensive perennial cover of ice and snow.

ice cream. A food prepared from a frozen mixture of milk products with sweetening.

Icel. Iceland; Icelandic.

Ice·land (īs′lənd). An island republic in the

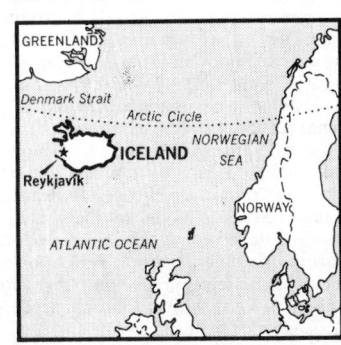

Iceland

ô paw, for/oi bôy/ou out/ŏŏ took/ōō coo/p pop/r run/s sauce/sh shy/t to/th thin/*th* the/
ŭ cut/ûr fur/v van/w wag/y yes/z size/zh vision/ə ago, item, edible, gallop, circus/

North Atlantic. Pop. 200,000. Cap. Reykjavik. —Ice′land•er n.

Ice•land•ic (īs-lăn′dĭk) adj. Of or pertaining to Iceland, its inhabitants, or their language. —n. The Germanic language of Iceland as spoken since the 16th century.

ice pick. An awl for chipping ice.

ice point. The temperature at which pure water and ice are in equilibrium in a mixture at one atmosphere of pressure.

ice-skate (īs′skāt′) v. -skated, -skating. To skate on ice. —ice skater.

ice water. Very cold or iced drinking water.

ichthyo-. comb. form. Fish. [< Gk ikhthus, fish.]

ich•thy•ol•o•gy (ĭk′thē-ŏl′ə-jē) n. Zoology specializing in the study of fishes. —ich′thy•ol′o•gist n.

–ician. comb. form. One who practices or is a specialist in a given field: mortician.

i•ci•cle (ī′sĭ-kəl) n. A tapering spike of ice formed by the freezing of dripping water. [< ICE + OE gicel, icicle (see yeg-).]

ic•ing (ī′sĭng) n. A sweet glaze for cakes and cookies.

ICJ International Court of Justice.

i•con (ī′kŏn′) n. Also i•kon. A religious image painted on a panel. [< Gk eikōn, likeness, image.]

i•con•o•clast (ī-kŏn′ə-klăst′) n. Any attacker of established ideas and usages. [< MGk eikonoklastēs, "image breaker."] —i•con′o•clas′tic (-klăs′tĭk) adj.

–ics. comb. form. 1. The science or art of: acoustics. 2. The act or practices of: hysterics. [< -IC.]

id (ĭd) n. The division of the psyche associated with instinctual impulses and primitive needs. [< L, it.]

I'd (īd). 1. Contraction of I had. 2. Contraction of I would. 3. Contraction of I should.

id. idem.

Id. Idaho (unofficial).

i.d. inside diameter.

I.D. identification.

I•da•ho (ī′də-hō). A state of the NW U.S. Pop. 713,000. Cap. Boise.

–ide, –id. comb. form. Used to form the names of chemical compounds: chloride. [< F acide, acid.]

i•de•a (ī-dē′ə) n. 1. A mental representation forming an object of thought. 2. A product of thought, as: a. An opinion. b. A plan or method. c. A notion; fancy. 3. The gist or purpose of something. 4. The Platonic archetype of which a corresponding being in phenomenal reality is assertedly an imperfect replica. [< Gk, form, model, class, notion.]

i•de•al (ī-dē′əl, ī-dēl′) n. 1. a. A standard of absolute perfection, excellence, or beauty. b. One regarded as a model of these qualities. 2. An ultimate object; goal. 3. An honorable or worthy principle. —adj. 1. Perfect or near-perfect. 2. Existing only in the mind; visionary. 3. Existing as a Platonic archetype. [< L idea, model, idea.] —i•de•al′ly adv.

i•de•al•ism (ī-dē′ə-lĭz′əm) n. 1. Pursuit of one's ideals. 2. Any theory identifying reality with perception or ideation. —i•de′al•ist n. —i•de′al•is′tic adj. —i•de′al•is′ti•cal•ly adv.

i•de•al•ize (ī-dē′ə-līz′) v. -ized, -izing. To regard or represent as ideal. —i•de′al•i•za′tion n.

i•de•a•tion (ī′dē-ā′shən) n. The process of forming and relating ideas. —i′de•a′tion•al adj.

i•dem (ī′dĕm′). Used to indicate a reference previously given or mentioned. [L idem, idem, the same.]

i•den•ti•cal (ī-dĕn′tĭ-kəl) adj. 1. Being the same. 2. Being exactly equal. 3. Developed from the same ovum. [< LL identitās, identity.] —i•den′ti•cal•ly adv.

i•den•ti•fi•ca•tion (ī-dĕn′tə-fĭ-kā′shən) n. 1. The act of identifying or state of being identified. 2. Documentary proof of one's identity.

i•den•ti•fy (ī-dĕn′tə-fī′) v. -fied, -fying. 1. To ascertain or establish the identity of. 2. To be or cause to be identical; regard as the same. 3. To associate with, as a political party, business, etc. —i•den′ti•fi′a•ble adj.

i•den•ti•ty (ī-dĕn′tə-tē) n., pl. -ties. 1. The collective aspect of the set of characteristics by which a person or thing is recognized or known. 2. Sameness of character, quality, or condition. 3. Personal individuality. 4. An equality satisfied by all values of the variables for which the expressions involved are defined. [LL identitās < L idem, the same, IDEM.]

ideo-. comb. form. Idea.

i•de•ol•o•gy (ī′dē-ŏl′ə-jē, ĭd′ē-) n., pl. -gies. The body of ideas reflecting the social needs and aspirations of an individual, group, or culture. —i′de•o•log′i•cal adj.

ides (īds) n. (takes sing. v.). The 15th day of March, May, July, or October or the 13th day of the other months in the ancient Roman calendar. [< L īdūs.]

id est (ĭd ĕst′). Latin. That is.

id•i•o•cy (ĭd′ē-ə-sē) n., pl. -cies. 1. Subnormal intellectual development or ability characterized by intelligence in the lowest measurable range. 2. Extreme folly or stupidity.

id•i•om (ĭd′ē-əm) n. 1. A speech form that is peculiar to itself within the usage of a given language. 2. A specialized vocabulary; jargon: legal idiom. [< Gk idiōma, peculiarity, idiom.] —id′i•o•mat′ic adj.

id•i•o•syn•cra•sy (ĭd′ē-ō-sĭng′krə-sē) n., pl. -sies. A structural or behavioral peculiarity. [< Gk idios, peculiar + sunkrasis, mixture.] —id′i•o•syn•crat′ic (-sĭn-krăt′ĭk) adj.

id•i•ot (ĭd′ē-ət) n. 1. A mentally deficient person having intelligence in the lowest measurable range, being unable to guard against common dangers, and incapable of learning connected speech. 2. An imbecile; blockhead. [< Gk idios, peculiar, private.] —id′i•ot′ic adj.

i•dle (īd′l) adj. idler, idlest. 1. Inactive. 2. Lazy; shiftless. 3. Useless or groundless: idle talk. —v. idled, idling. 1. To pass time without working. 2. To move lazily. 3. To run or cause to run at a slow speed or out of gear: The motor is idling. 4. To cause to be unemployed or inactive. [< OE īdel < Gmc *idal.] —i′dle•ness n. —i′dler n. —i′dly adv.

i•dol (īd′l) n. 1. An image used as an object of

worship. **2.** One that is adored. [< Gk *eidōlon*, image, form.]

i·dol·a·try (ī-dŏl′ə-trē) *n.* **1.** The worship of idols. **2.** Blind devotion. —**i·dol′a·ter** *n.* —**i·dol′a·trous** *adj.*

i·dol·ize (īd′l-īz′) *v.* **-ized, -izing. 1.** To regard with blind admiration or devotion. **2.** To worship as an idol.

i·dyll (īd′l) *n.* Also **i·dyl. 1.** A short poem about rustic life. **2.** A scene or event of rural simplicity. **3.** A romantic interlude. [< Gk *eidos*, form, picture.] —**i·dyl′lic** *adj.*

i.e. id est.

if (ĭf) *conj.* **1.** —Used to introduce a subjunctive clause, meaning: **a.** In the event that. **b.** Granting that. **c.** On condition that. **2.** —Used to introduce a negative conditional clause, meaning even though: *a handsome if useless trinket.* **3.** —Used to introduce an indirect question, meaning whether: *Ask if he will come.* —*n.* A condition or stipulation. [< OE *gif.*]

ig·loo (ĭg′lōō) *n., pl.* **-loos.** Also **ig·lu.** An Eskimo house, sometimes built of ice blocks. [Esk *iglu,* house.]

ig·ne·ous (ĭg′nē-əs) *adj.* **1.** Characteristic of fire. **2.** Solidified from a molten state. [< L *ignis,* fire.]

ig·nite (ĭg-nīt′) *v.* **-nited, -niting. 1. a.** To cause to burn. **b.** To begin to burn. **2.** To arouse or kindle. [< L *ignis,* fire.]

ig·ni·tion (ĭg-nĭsh′ən) *n.* **1.** An act or instance of igniting. **2.** An electrical system that ignites the fuel mixture in an internal-combustion engine.

ig·no·ble (ĭg-nō′bəl) *adj.* **1.** Dishonorable; base. **2.** Not of the nobility; common. —**ig·no′ble·ness** *n.* —**ig·no′bly** *adv.*

ig·no·min·i·ous (ĭg′nō-mĭn′ē-əs) *adj.* **1.** Characterized by dishonor. **2.** Despicable. **3.** Degrading; debasing. [< L *ignōminia,* dishonor.] —**ig′no·min′i·ous·ly** *adv.* —**ig′no·min′y** *n.*

ig·no·ra·mus (ĭg′nə-rā′məs) *n.* An ignorant person.

ig·no·rance (ĭg′nər-əns) *n.* The condition of being ignorant; lack of knowledge.

ig·no·rant (ĭg′nər-ənt) *adj.* **1.** Without education or knowledge. **2.** Exhibiting lack of education or knowledge. **3.** Unaware or uninformed. [< L *ignōrāre,* to be ignorant, IGNORE.] —**ig′no·rant·ly** *adv.*

ig·nore (ĭg-nôr′, -nōr′) *v.* **-nored, -noring.** To refuse to pay attention to; disregard. [< L *ignōrāre,* not to know, disregard.]

i·gua·na (ĭ-gwä′nə) *n.* A large tropical American lizard. [< Arawak *iwana.*]

i·kon. Variant of **icon.**

il·e·um (ĭl′ē-əm) *n., pl.* **-ea** (-ē-ə). The portion of the small intestine extending from the jejunum to the cecum. [< L *īleum,* groin, flank.] —**il′e·al** *adj.*

I.L.G.W.U. International Ladies′ Garment Workers′ Union.

il·i·um (ĭl′ē-əm) *n., pl.* **-ia** (-ē-ə). The uppermost and widest bone of each of the sides of the pelvis.

ilk (ĭlk) *n.* Type or kind: *a remark of that ilk.* [< OE *ilca,* same.]

ill (ĭl) *adj.* **worse, worst. 1.** Not healthy; sick. **2.** Resulting in suffering; distressing. **3.** Hostile. **4.** Unpropitious. **5.** Not up to recognized standards of excellence or conduct. **6.** Harmful; cruel. —*adv.* **worse, worst. 1.** In an ill manner; not well. **2.** Scarcely or with difficulty. —*n.* **1.** Evil. **2.** Disaster or harm. [< ON *illr,* bad.]

I′ll (īl). **1.** Contraction of *I will.* **2.** Contraction of *I shall.*

ill. illustrated; illustration.

Ill. Illinois.

ill-ad·vised (ĭl′əd-vīzd′) *adj.* Unwise; reckless. —**ill′-ad·vis′ed·ly** *adv.*

ill-bred (ĭl′brĕd′) *adj.* Badly brought up; impolite.

il·le·gal (ĭ-lē′gəl) *adj.* Prohibited by law. —**il′le·gal′i·ty** *n.* —**il·le′gal·ly** *adv.*

il·leg·i·ble (ĭ-lĕj′ə-bəl) *adj.* Not legible or decipherable. —**il·leg′i·bil′i·ty** *n.* —**il·leg′i·bly** *adv.*

il·le·git·i·mate (ĭl′ĭ-jĭt′ə-mĭt) *adj.* **1.** Against the law; illegal. **2.** Born out of wedlock; bastard. **3.** Illogical. —**il′le·git′i·ma·cy** *n.* —**il′le·git′i·mate·ly** *adv.*

ill-fat·ed (ĭl′fā′tĭd) *adj.* Doomed or unlucky.

ill-fa·vored (ĭl′fā′vərd) *adj.* **1.** Having an ugly face. **2.** Objectionable; offensive.

ill-got·ten (ĭl′gŏt′n) *adj.* Obtained by dishonest means.

ill-hu·mored (ĭl′hyōō′mərd) *adj.* Irritable and surly.

il·lib·er·al (ĭ-lĭb′ər-əl) *adj.* Narrow-minded; bigoted.

il·lic·it (ĭ-lĭs′ĭt) *adj.* Not sanctioned by custom or law; unlawful. [L *illicitus,* not allowed.] —**il·lic′it·ly** *adv.* —**il·lic′it·ness** *n.*

Il·li·nois¹ (ĭl′ə-noi′, -noiz′) *n., pl.* **-nois. 1.** A member of a confederacy of Algonquian-speaking Indian tribes that inhabited Illinois and parts of Iowa, Wisconsin, and Missouri. **2.** The language of these peoples.

Il·li·nois² (ĭl′ə-noi′, -noiz′). A Midwestern state of the U.S. Pop. 11,113,976. Cap. Springfield. —**Il′li·nois′an** *adj. & n.*

il·lit·er·a·cy (ĭ-lĭt′ər-ə-sē) *n., pl.* **-cies. 1.** Inability to read and write. **2.** An error characteristic of this condition.

il·lit·er·ate (ĭ-lĭt′ər-ĭt) *adj.* **1.** Unable to read and write. **2. a.** Marked by inferiority to an expected standard of familiarity with language and literature. **b.** Violating prescribed standards of speech or writing. —**il·lit′er·ate** *n.*

ill-man·nered (ĭl′măn′ərd) *adj.* Impolite; rude.

ill-na·tured (ĭl′nā′chərd) *adj.* Disagreeable; surly.

ill·ness (ĭl′nĭs) *n.* Sickness.

il·log·i·cal (ĭ-lŏj′ĭ-kəl) *adj.* Contradicting logic. —**il·log′i·cal′i·ty** *n.* —**il·log′i·cal·ly** *adv.*

ill-starred (ĭl′stärd′) *adj.* Ill-fated; unlucky.

ill-tem·pered (ĭl′tĕm′pərd) *adj.* Quarrelsome; irritable.

il·lu·mi·nate (ĭ-lōō′mə-nāt′) *v.* **-nated, -nating. 1.** To provide or brighten with light. **2.** To decorate (a manuscript) with pictures or designs in brilliant colors. **3.** To clarify. **4.** To enlighten. [L *illūmināre.*] —**il·lu′mi·na′tion** *n.* —**il·lu′mi·na′tor** *n.*

illus. illustrated; illustration.

ô paw, for/oi boy/ou out/ŏŏ took/ōō coo/p pop/r run/s sauce/sh shy/t to/th thin/*th* the/
ŭ cut/ûr fur/v van/w wag/y yes/z size/zh vision/ə ago, item, edible, gallop, circus/

ill-use (ĭl′yōōz′) *v.* To maltreat. —*n.* (ĭl′yōōs′). Also **ill-us•age** (-yōō′sĭj). Bad or unjust treatment.

il•lu•sion (ĭ-lōō′zhən) *n.* 1. An erroneous perception of reality. 2. An erroneous concept; misconception. [< L *illūdere*, to mock.]

il•lu•sive (ĭ-lōō′sĭv) *adj.* Illusory. [< ILLUSION.] —**il•lu′sive•ness** *n.*

il•lu•so•ry (ĭ-lōō′sə-rē) *adj.* Of the nature of an illusion.

il•lus•trate (ĭl′ə-strāt′, ĭ-lŭs′trāt′) *v.* -trated, -trating. 1. a. To clarify by use of example or comparison. b. To exemplify. 2. To provide (a text) with explanatory or decorative pictures, photographs, or diagrams. [L *illūstrāre*.] —**il′lus•tra′tor** *n.*

il•lus•tra•tion (ĭl′ə-strā′shən) *n.* 1. a. The act of illustrating. b. The state of being illustrated. 2. An explanatory example. 3. Visual matter used to elucidate or ornament a text.

il•lus•tra•tive (ĭ-lŭs′trə-tĭv, ĭl′ə-strā′tĭv) *adj.* Serving to elucidate or exemplify. —**il•lus′tra•tive•ly** *adv.*

il•lus•tri•ous (ĭ-lŭs′trē-əs) *adj.* Eminent; celebrated; famous. —**il•lus′tri•ous•ly** *adv.* —**il•lus′tri•ous•ness** *n.*

ill will. Hostility; enmity.

il•ly (ĭl′lē) *adv. Regional.* Badly; ill.

ILO International Labor Organization.

ILS instrument landing system.

I'm (īm). Contraction of *I am.*

im•age (ĭm′ĭj) *n.* 1. A sculptured likeness. 2. An optically formed duplicate, counterpart, or other representative reproduction of an object. 3. One that closely resembles another: *the image of his uncle.* 4. The concept of someone or something that is held by or projected to the public. 5. A personification of something specified: *He is the image of health.* 6. A mental picture. 7. A representation to the mind by speech or writing. —*v.* -aged, -aging. 1. To make a likeness of. 2. a. To mirror; reflect. b. To project. 3. To symbolize. 4. To conjure up; imagine. [< L *imāgō.*]

im•age•ry (ĭm′ĭj-rē) *n., pl.* -ries. 1. Mental images. 2. Diction conveying poetic images.

im•ag•i•na•ble (ĭ-măj′ə-nə-bəl) *adj.* Capable of being conceived of by the imagination. —**im•ag′i•na•bly** *adv.*

im•ag•i•nar•y (ĭ-măj′ə-nĕr′ē) *adj.* 1. Existing only in the imagination. 2. Of, involving, or being an imaginary number.

imaginary number. A complex number in which the real part is zero and the coefficient of the imaginary unit is not zero.

imaginary unit. The positive square root of –1.

im•ag•i•na•tion (ĭ-măj′ə-nā′shən) *n.* 1. The process or power of forming a mental image of something that is not or has not been seen or experienced. 2. Creativity or resourcefulness. 3. Popular acceptation or belief. —**im•ag′i•na•tive** *adj.* —**im•ag′i•na•tive•ly** *adv.*

im•ag•ine (ĭ-măj′ən) *v.* -ined, -ining. 1. To form a mental picture of; fancy. 2. To think; suppose. [< L *imāginārī*, to picture to oneself < *imāgō*, IMAGE.]

im•be•cile (ĭm′bə-sĭl, -səl) *n.* 1. A feebleminded person. 2. A dolt. [< L *imbēcillus,*

"without support," feeble.] —**im′be•cile, im′be•cil′ic** (-sĭl′ĭk) *adj.* —**im′be•cil′i•ty** *n.*

im•bed. Variant of embed.

im•bibe (ĭm-bīb′) *v.* -bibed, -bibing. 1. To consume by drinking. 2. To take in; absorb. 3. To assimilate in the mind. [< L *imbibere*, to drink in.] —**im•bib′er** *n.*

im•bro•glio (ĭm-brōl′yō) *n., pl.* -glios. 1. a. A confused or difficult situation; predicament; mess. b. A deeply embarrassing misunderstanding. 2. A confused heap; a tangle. [It.]

im•brue (ĭm-brōō′) *v.* -brued, -bruing. To stain or drench. [< OF *embruer*, to soak.]

im•bue (ĭm-byōō′) *v.* -bued, -buing. 1. To dye or stain deeply. 2. To permeate or pervade. [L *imbuere*, to moisten, stain.]

im•i•tate (ĭm′ə-tāt′) *v.* -tated, -tating. 1. To copy or emulate. 2. To mimic, ape, or counterfeit. 3. To reproduce. 4. To resemble. [L *imitārī.*] —**im′i•ta′tor** (-tā′tər) *n.*

im•i•ta•tion (ĭm′ə-tā′shən) *n.* 1. An act of imitating. 2. Something derived or copied from an original. 3. A counterfeit.

im•i•ta•tive (ĭm′ə-tā′tĭv) *adj.* 1. Of or involving imitation. 2. Derivative; copied. 3. Tending to imitate. 4. Onomatopoeic. —**im′i•ta′tive•ly** *adv.* —**im′i•ta′tive•ness** *n.*

im•mac•u•late (ĭ-măk′yə-lĭt) *adj.* 1. Spotless; pure. 2. Free from sin or error. 3. Impeccably clean. [< L *immaculātus*, not stained.] —**im•mac′u•late•ly** *adv.* —**im•mac′u•late•ness** *n.*

im•ma•nent (ĭm′ə-nənt) *adj.* 1. Intrinsic to subjective reality. 2. Dwelling at the inmost heart of nature and of the human soul. [< L *immanēre*, to remain in.] —**im′ma•nence** *n.*

im•ma•te•ri•al (ĭm′ə-tîr′ē-əl) *adj.* 1. Having no material body. 2. Inconsequential; trifling.

im•ma•ture (ĭm′ə-tyōōr′, -chōōr′) *adj.* 1. Not fully grown or developed. 2. Exhibiting less than normal maturity. —**im′ma•tur′i•ty** *n.*

im•meas•ur•a•ble (ĭ-mĕzh′ər-ə-bəl) *adj.* Vast; limitless. —**im•meas′ur•a•bly** *adv.*

im•me•di•a•cy (ĭ-mē′dē-ə-sē) *n.* 1. Directness. 2. Urgency.

im•me•di•ate (ĭ-mē′dē-ĭt) *adj.* 1. Being without mediation or interposition; direct. 2. Intuitive. 3. Next in line or relation. 4. Occurring or accomplished without delay; instant. 5. Near to the present. 6. Near at hand. [LL *immediātus.*] —**im•me′di•ate•ly** *adv. & conj.* —**im•me′di•ate•ness** *n.*

im•me•mo•ri•al (ĭm′ə-môr′ē-əl, -mōr′ē-əl) *adj.* Reaching beyond memory, tradition, or recorded history. —**im′me•mo′ri•al•ly** *adv.*

im•mense (ĭ-mĕns′) *adj.* Vast; huge. [< L *immēnsus*, immeasurable.] —**im•mense′ly** *adv.* —**im•men′si•ty** *n.*

im•merse (ĭ-mûrs′) *v.* -mersed, -mersing. 1. To plunge into a fluid. 2. To baptize by submerging in water. 3. To absorb; engross. [L *immergere*, to dip in.] —**im•mer′sion** *n.*

im•mi•grant (ĭm′ĭ-grənt) *n.* 1. One who immigrates. 2. An organism that appears where it was formerly unknown. —**im′mi•grant** *adj.*

im•mi•grate (ĭm′ĭ-grāt′) *v.* -grated, -grating. To settle permanently in a foreign country. [L *immigrāre*, to remove into, go in.] —**im′mi•gra′tion** *n.*

ă pat/ā ate/âr care/ä bar/b bib/ch chew/d deed/ĕ pet/ē be/f fit/g gag/h hat/hw what/ ĭ pit/ī pie/îr pier/j judge/k kick/l lid, fatal/m mum/n no, sudden/ng sing/ŏ pot/ō go/

im·mi·nent (ĭm′ə-nənt) *adj.* About to occur; impending. [< L *imminēre,* to project over or toward, threaten.] —**im′mi·nence** *n.* —**im′mi·nent·ly** *adv.*

im·mo·bile (ĭ-mō′bəl, -bēl′) *adj.* **1. a.** Unable to move. **b.** Incapable of being moved. **2.** Not moving. —**im′mo·bil′i·ty** *n.* —**im·mo′bi·lize** *v.* (**-lized, -lizing**). —**im·mo′bi·li·za′tion** *n.*

im·mod·er·ate (ĭ-mŏd′ər-ĭt) *adj.* Extreme or excessive. —**im·mod′er·ate·ly** *adv.* —**im·mod′er·ate·ness, im·mod′er·a′tion** *n.*

im·mod·est (ĭ-mŏd′ĭst) *adj.* **1.** Lacking modesty: *immodest boasting.* **2.** Indecent; brazen. —**im·mod′est·ly** *adv.* —**im·mod′es·ty** *n.*

im·mo·late (ĭm′ə-lāt′) *v.* **-lated, -lating.** To kill as a sacrifice. [L *immolāre.*] —**im′mo·la′tion** *n.*

im·mor·al (ĭ-môr′əl, ĭ-mŏr′-) *adj.* **1.** Contrary to established morality. **2.** Licentious or dissolute. —**im′mor·al′i·ty** (ĭm′ô-răl′ə-tē) *n.* —**im·mor′al·ly** *adv.*

im·mor·tal (ĭ-môrt′l) *adj.* **1.** Not subject to death. **2.** Having eternal fame; imperishable. **3.** Of or pertaining to immortality. —*n.* **1.** One exempt from death. **2.** One whose fame is enduring. **3. Immortals.** The gods of the Greek and Roman pantheon. —**im·mor′tal·ly** *adv.*

im·mor·tal·i·ty (ĭm′ôr-tăl′ə-tē) *n.* The quality or condition of being immortal, esp. eternal life.

im·mor·tal·ize (ĭ-môrt′l-īz′) *v.* **-ized, -izing.** To make immortal.

im·mov·a·ble (ĭ-mōō′və-bəl) *adj.* **1.** Incapable of being moved. **2.** Unyielding; steadfast. **3.** Unimpressionable or impassive. —**im·mov′a·bil′i·ty** *n.* —**im·mov′a·bly** *adv.*

im·mune (ĭ-myōōn′) *adj.* **1. a.** Exempt. **b.** Not affected or responsive. **2.** Resistant to a disease. [L *immūnis.*] —**im·mu′ni·ty** *n.*

im·mu·nize (ĭm′yə-nīz′) *v.* **-nized, -nizing.** To render immune. —**im′mu·ni·za′tion** *n.*

im·mure (ĭ-myōōr′) *v.* **-mured, -muring. 1.** To imprison. **2.** To entomb in a wall. [ML *immūrāre.*] —**im·mure′ment** *n.*

im·mu·ta·ble (ĭ-myōō′tə-bəl) *adj.* Not susceptible to change. [< L *immūtābilis.*] —**im·mu′ta·bil′i·ty** *n.* —**im·mu′ta·bly** *adv.*

imp (ĭmp) *n.* **1.** A mischievous child. **2.** A small demon. [< OE *impa,* young shoot, sapling < ML *impotus,* graft.]

imp. 1. imperative. **2.** imperfect. **3.** imperial. **4.** import; imported. **5.** important.

im·pact (ĭm′păkt′) *n.* **1.** A collision. **2.** The effect of one thing upon another. —*v.* (ĭm-păkt′). **1.** To pack firmly together. **2.** To collide. [< L *impingere,* to strike against, IM-PINGE.] —**im·pac′tion** *n.*

im·pact·ed (ĭm-păk′tĭd) *adj.* **1.** Wedged together at the broken ends. **2.** Placed in the alveolus in a manner prohibiting eruption into a normal position: *an impacted tooth.*

im·pair (ĭm-pâr′) *v.* To diminish in strength, value, quantity, or quality. [< VL *impējōrāre,* to make worse.] —**im·pair′ment** *n.*

im·pa·la (ĭm-pä′lə) *n.* An African antelope with ridged, curved horns. [Zulu.]

im·pale (ĭm-pāl′) *v.* **-paled, -paling. 1.** To pierce or fix by piercing with a sharp point. **2.** To execute by means of a stake driven upward through the body. [ML *impālāre.*] —**im·pale′ment** *n.* —**im·pal′er** *n.*

im·pal·pa·ble (ĭm-păl′pə-bəl) *adj.* **1.** Intangible. **2.** Imperceptible. —**im·pal′pa·bly** *adv.*

im·pan·el (ĭm-păn′əl) *v.* To enroll (a jury).

im·part (ĭm-pärt′) *v.* **1.** To transmit. **2.** To disclose.

im·par·tial (ĭm-pär′shəl) *adj.* Unbiased; unprejudiced. —**im′par·ti·al′i·ty** (-shē-ăl′ə-tē) *n.* —**im·par′tial·ly** *adv.*

im·passe (ĭm′păs′) *n.* **1.** A dead-end road; cul-de-sac. **2.** A deadlock or dilemma.

im·pas·si·ble (ĭm-păs′ə-bəl) *adj.* **1.** Not subject to pain. **2.** Impassive. [< LL *impassibilis.*] —**im·pas′si·bil′i·ty** *n.* —**im·pas′si·bly** *adv.*

im·pas·sioned (ĭm-păsh′ənd) *adj.* Filled with passion; ardent.

im·pas·sive (ĭm-păs′ĭv) *adj.* Revealing no emotion; expressionless. —**im·pas′sive·ly** *adv.* —**im′pas·siv′i·ty** *n.*

im·pa·tience (ĭm-pā′shəns) *n.* **1.** The inability to wait patiently. **2.** Restive eagerness, desire, or anticipation. —**im·pa′tient** *adj.* —**im·pa′tient·ly** *adv.*

im·peach (ĭm-pēch′) *v.* **1.** To charge with malfeasance in office before a proper tribunal. **2.** To challenge or discredit. [< LL *impedicāre,* to entangle, put in fetters.] —**im·peach′a·ble** *adj.* —**im·peach′er** *n.* —**im·peach′ment** *n.*

im·pec·ca·ble (ĭm-pĕk′ə-bəl) *adj.* **1.** Irreproachable; flawless. **2.** Not capable of sin or wrongdoing. [L *impeccābilis,* not liable to sin.] —**im·pec′ca·bly** *adv.* —**im·pec′ca·bil′i·ty** *n.*

im·pe·cu·ni·ous (ĭm′pĭ-kyōō′nē-əs) *adj.* Lacking money; penniless. [IN- + L *pecūnia,* money.] —**im′pe·cu′ni·ous·ly** *adv.*

im·pe·dance (ĭm-pē′dəns) *n.* A measure of the total opposition to current flow in an alternating-current circuit. [< IMPEDE.]

im·pede (ĭm-pēd′) *v.* **-peded, -peding.** To obstruct the way of; block. [L *impedīre,* to entangle, fetter.] —**im·ped′er** *n.*

im·ped·i·ment (ĭm-pĕd′ə-mənt) *n.* A hindrance; obstruction; block.

im·ped·i·men·ta (ĭm-pĕd′ə-mĕn′tə) *pl.n.* Objects, as provisions or baggage, that impede or encumber.

im·pel (ĭm-pĕl′) *v.* **-pelled, -pelling.** To urge; compel. [L *impellere,* to drive on or against.]

im·pend (ĭm-pĕnd′) *v.* **1.** To hang or hover menacingly. **2.** To be about to take place. [L *impendēre.*]

im·pend·ing (ĭm-pĕn′dĭng) *adj.* Approaching; imminent.

im·pen·e·tra·ble (ĭm-pĕn′ə-trə-bəl) *adj.* **1.** Not capable of being entered. **2.** Incomprehensible; inscrutable. —**im·pen′e·tra·ble·ness, im·pen′e·tra·bil′i·ty** *n.* —**im·pen′e·tra·bly** *adv.*

im·pen·i·tent (ĭm-pĕn′ə-tənt) *adj.* Not penitent; unrepentant. —**im·pen′i·tence** *n.*

im·per·a·tive (ĭm-pĕr′ə-tĭv) *adj.* **1.** Expressing a command or plea. **2.** Urgent or obligatory. [< L *imperāre,* "to prepare against (an occasion)," to command.] —**im·per′a·tive** *n.* —**im·per′a·tive·ly** *adv.*

im·per·cep·ti·ble (ĭm′pər-sĕp′tə-bəl) *adj.* Not perceptible or barely perceptible. —**im′per·cep′ti·ble·ness** *n.* —**im′per·cep′ti·bly** *adv.*

im·per·fect (ĭm-pûr′fĭkt) *adj.* **1.** Not perfect. **2.** Of or being a verb tense expressing continuous or incomplete action. —*n.* **1.** The imperfect tense. **2.** A verb in this tense. —**im·per′fect·ly** *adv.* —**im·per′fect·ness** *n.*

im·per·fec·tion (ĭm′pər-fĕk′shən) *n.* **1.** The quality or condition of being imperfect. **2.** A defect; flaw.

im·per·fo·rate (ĭm-pûr′fər-ĭt) *adj.* **1.** Not perforated; having no opening. **2.** Not perforated into perforated rows. —*n.* An imperforate stamp.

im·pe·ri·al[1] (ĭm-pîr′ē-əl) *adj.* **1.** Of or pertaining to an empire or emperor. **2.** Designating a nation or government having sovereign rights over colonies or dependencies. [< L *imperium*, command, EMPIRE.]

im·pe·ri·al[2] (ĭm-pîr′ē-əl) *n.* A pointed beard grown from the lower lip.

im·pe·ri·al·ism (ĭm-pîr′ē-ə-lĭz′əm) *n.* The policy of extending economic and political hegemony over other nations. —**im·pe′ri·al·ist** *n. & adj.* —**im·pe′ri·al·is′tic** *adj.*

im·per·il (ĭm-pĕr′əl) *v.* **-iled** or **-illed, -iling** or **-illing.** To endanger. —**im·per′il·ment** *n.*

im·pe·ri·ous (ĭm-pîr′ē-əs) *adj.* **1.** Domineering; overbearing. **2.** Urgent; pressing. [< L *imperium*, EMPIRE.] —**im·pe′ri·ous·ly** *adv.* —**im·pe′ri·ous·ness** *n.*

im·per·ish·a·ble (ĭm-pĕr′ĭ-shə-bəl) *adj.* Not perishable. —**im·per′ish·a·bly** *adv.*

im·per·ma·nent (ĭm-pûr′mə-nənt) *adj.* Not permanent; transient. —**im·per′ma·nence** *n.*

im·per·me·a·ble (ĭm-pûr′mē-ə-bəl) *adj.* Not permeable. —**im·per′me·a·bly** *adv.*

im·per·son·al (ĭm-pûr′sə-nəl) *adj.* **1.** Not personal. **2.** Exhibiting no emotion. —**im·per′son·al′i·ty** *n.* —**im·per′son·al·ly** *adv.*

im·per·son·ate (ĭm-pûr′sə-nāt′) *v.* **-ated, -ating.** To act the character or part of. —**im·per′son·a′tion** *n.* —**im·per′son·a′tor** *n.*

im·per·ti·nence (ĭm-pûrt′n-əns) *n.* Insolence.

im·per·ti·nent (ĭm-pûrt′n-ənt) *adj.* **1.** Impudent; insolent. **2.** Not pertinent; irrelevant. —**im·per′ti·nent·ly** *adv.*

im·per·turb·a·ble (ĭm′pər-tûr′bə-bəl) *adj.* Not capable of being perturbed. —**im′per·turb′a·bil′i·ty** *n.* —**im′per·turb′a·bly** *adv.*

im·per·vi·ous (ĭm-pûr′vē-əs) *adj.* **1.** Incapable of being penetrated. **2.** Incapable of being affected. —**im·per′vi·ous·ly** *adv.*

im·pe·ti·go (ĭm′pə-tī′gō, -tē′gō) *n.* A contagious skin disease characterized by superficial pustules that burst and form characteristic thick yellow crusts. [L *impetīgō*, "an attack" < *impetere*, to attack.]

im·pet·u·os·i·ty (ĭm-pĕch′ōō-ŏs′ə-tē) *n.* Also **im·pet·u·ous·ness** (-əs-nĭs). The quality or condition of being impetuous.

im·pet·u·ous (ĭm-pĕch′ōō-əs) *adj.* **1.** Impulsive; brash. **2.** Having great impetus; rushing with violence. [< L *impetus*, IMPETUS.] —**im·pet′u·ous·ly** *adv.*

im·pe·tus (ĭm′pə-təs) *n., pl.* **-tuses. 1. a.** An impelling force; impulse. **b.** Something that incites; a stimulus. **2.** Force or energy associated with a moving body. [L, attack.]

im·pi·e·ty (ĭm-pī′ə-tē) *n., pl.* **-ties. 1.** The quality or state of being impious. **2.** An impious act. **3.** Undutifulness.

im·pinge (ĭm-pĭnj′) *v.* **-pinged, -pinging. 1.** To collide; dash. **2.** To encroach; trespass. [L *impingere*, to push against.]

im·pi·ous (ĭm′pē-əs, ĭm-pī′-) *adj.* Not pious; irreverent. —**im′pi·ous·ly** *adv.*

imp·ish (ĭm′pĭsh) *adj.* Mischievous. —**imp′ish·ly** *adv.* —**imp′ish·ness** *n.*

im·pla·ca·ble (ĭm-plă′kə-bəl, -plăk′ə-bəl) *adj.* Inexorable. —**im·pla′ca·bly** *adv.*

im·plant (ĭm-plănt′, -plänt′) *v.* **1.** To fix or set firmly. **2.** To inculcate; instill. **3.** To insert or embed in living tissue.

im·plau·si·ble (ĭm-plô′zə-bəl) *adj.* Not plausible. —**im·plau′si·bil′i·ty, im·plau′si·ble·ness** *n.* —**im·plau′si·bly** *adv.*

im·ple·ment (ĭm′plə-mənt) *n.* A tool or utensil. —*v.* To carry into effect. [< L *implēre*, to fill up, fulfill.] —**im′ple·men·ta′tion** *n.*

im·pli·cate (ĭm′plĭ-kāt′) *v.* **-cated, -cating. 1.** To involve intimately or incriminatingly. **2.** To imply. [L *implicāre*.] —**im′pli·ca′tion** *n.*

im·plic·it (ĭm-plĭs′ĭt) *adj.* **1.** Implied or understood. **2.** Inherent or contained in the nature of something. **3.** Having no doubts or reservations; unquestioning. [< L *implicāre*, to involve, IMPLICATE.] —**im·plic′it·ly** *adv.* —**im·plic′it·ness** *n.*

im·plode (ĭm-plōd′) *v.* **-ploded, -ploding.** To undergo implosion.

im·plore (ĭm-plôr′, -plōr′) *v.* **-plored, -ploring.** To entreat; beseech. [L *implōrāre*, to invoke with tears.] —**im·plo′ra·tion** *n.*

im·plo·sion (ĭm-plō′zhən) *n.* A more or less violent collapse inward. [IN- (in) + (EX)PLO-SION.]

im·ply (ĭm-plī′) *v.* **-plied, -plying. 1.** To involve or suggest by logical necessity; entail. **2.** To express indirectly. —See Usage note at **infer.** [< L *implicāre*, infold, involve, IMPLICATE.]

im·po·lite (ĭm′pə-lit′) *adj.* Discourteous; rude.

im·pol·i·tic (ĭm-pŏl′ə-tĭk) *adj.* Not wise or expedient. —**im·pol′i·tic·ly** *adv.*

im·pon·der·a·ble (ĭm-pŏn′dər-ə-bəl) *adj.* Incapable of being weighed or measured with preciseness.

im·port (ĭm-pôrt′, -pōrt′, ĭm′pôrt′, -pōrt′) *v.* **1.** To bring in from a foreign country for trade or sale. **2.** To mean; signify. —*n.* (ĭm′pôrt′, -pōrt′). **1.** Meaning; signification. **2.** Importance; significance. [< L *importāre*, to carry in.] —**im·port′a·ble** *adj.* —**im·port′er** *n.*

im·por·tance (ĭm-pôr′təns) *n.* The condition or quality of being important; significance; consequence.

im·por·tant (ĭm-pôr′tənt) *adj.* **1.** Significant; noteworthy. **2.** Having an air of importance. [< L *importāre*, to IMPORT.] —**im·por′tant·ly** *adv.*

im·por·ta·tion (ĭm′pôr-tā′shən, ĭm′pōr-) *n.* **1.** The act or occupation of importing. **2.** Something imported; import.

im·por·tu·nate (ĭm-pôr′chōō-nĭt) *adj.* Stubbornly or unreasonably persistent. —**im·por′tu·nate·ly** *adv.* —**im·por′tu·nate·ness** *n.*

im·por·tune (ĭm′pôr-t/y/ōōn′, ĭm-pôr′chən) *v.* **-tuned, -tuning.** To beset with repeated and

---

ă pat/ā ate/âr care/ä bar/b bib/ch chew/d deed/ĕ pet/ē be/f fit/g gag/h hat/hw what/
ĭ pit/ī pie/îr pier/j judge/k kick/l lid, fatal/m mum/n no, sudden/ng sing/ŏ pot/ō go/

insistent requests. [< L *importūnus*, "without a port," unsuitable.] —im′por·tu′ni·ty *n.*

im·pose (ĭm-pōz′) *v.* -posed, -posing. 1. To establish or apply as compulsory; levy. 2. To apply or make prevail by or as if by authority. 3. To obtrude. 4. To pass off on others. 5. To take unfair advantage of. [< L *impōnere*, to put on.] —im·pos′er *n.*

im·pos·ing (ĭm-pō′zĭng) *adj.* Impressive.

im·po·si·tion (ĭm′pə-zĭsh′ən) *n.* 1. The act of imposing. 2. Something imposed, as a tax, undue burden, etc.

im·pos·si·ble (ĭm-pŏs′ə-bəl) *adj.* 1. Not capable of existing or happening. 2. Unacceptable. 3. Having little likelihood of happening or being accomplished. 4. Not capable of being dealt with or tolerated; objectionable. —im·pos′si·bil′i·ty *n.* —im·pos′si·bly *adv.*

im·post (ĭm′pōst′) *n.* A tax. [< L *impōnere*, IMPOSE.]

im·pos·tor (ĭm-pŏs′tər) *n.* A person who deceives under an assumed identity. [< L *impōnere*, IMPOSE.]

im·pos·ture (ĭm-pŏs′chər) *n.* Deception or fraud, esp. assumption of a false identity.

im·po·tent (ĭm′pə-tənt) *adj.* 1. Lacking physical strength or vigor. 2. Powerless; ineffectual. 3. Incapable of sexual intercourse. —im′po·tence *n.* —im′po·tent·ly *adv.*

im·pound (ĭm-pound′) *v.* 1. To confine in a pound. 2. To seize and retain in legal custody.

im·pov·er·ish (ĭm-pŏv′ər-ĭsh) *v.* 1. To reduce to poverty. 2. To deprive of natural richness or strength. —im·pov′er·ish·ment *n.*

im·prac·ti·ca·ble (ĭm-prăk′tĭ-kə-bəl) *adj.* Not capable of being done or carried out.

im·prac·ti·cal (ĭm-prăk′tĭ-kəl) *adj.* 1. Unwise to implement or maintain in practice. 2. Incapable of dealing efficiently with practical matters. 3. Impracticable.

im·pre·cate (ĭm′prə-kāt′) *v.* -cated, -cating. To invoke (evil or a curse) upon. [L *imprecārī*.] —im′pre·ca′tion *n.* —im′pre·ca′tor *n.*

im·pre·cise (ĭm′prĭ-sīs′) *adj.* Not precise. —im′pre·cise′ly *adv.*

im·preg·na·ble (ĭm-prĕg′nə-bəl) *adj.* Able to resist capture or entry by force.

im·preg·nate (ĭm-prĕg′nāt′) *v.* -nated, -nating. 1. To make pregnant; inseminate. 2. To fertilize (an ovum). 3. To fill throughout or saturate. —im′preg′na′tion *n.*

im·pre·sa·ri·o (ĭm′prə-sär′ē-ō′, -sâr′ē-ō′) *n., pl.* -rios. One who sponsors or produces entertainment, esp. the director of an opera company. [< It *imprendere*, to undertake.]

im·press¹ (ĭm-prĕs′) *v.* 1. To produce or apply with pressure. 2. To mark or stamp with pressure. 3. To establish firmly in the mind. 4. To affect or influence deeply or forcibly. —n. (ĭm′prĕs′). 1. The act of impressing. 2. A mark or pattern produced by impressing. 3. A stamp or seal meant to be impressed.

im·press² (ĭm-prĕs′) *v.* 1. To force into military service. 2. To confiscate.

im·pres·sion (ĭm-prĕsh′ən) *n.* 1. An imprint made on a surface by pressure. 2. An effect produced upon the mind. 3. A vague notion, remembrance, or belief.

im·pres·sion·a·ble (ĭm-prĕsh′ən-ə-bəl) *adj.* Readily influenced.

im·pres·sion·ism (ĭm-prĕsh′ə-nĭz′əm) *n.* A theory or style of painting, literature, or music which aims to reflect subjective impressions rather than objective reality. —im·pres′sion·ist *n. & adj.* —im·pres′sion·ist′ic *adj.*

im·pres·sive (ĭm-prĕs′ĭv) *adj.* Commanding attention; making strong impressions. —im·pres′sive·ly *adv.* —im·pres′sive·ness *n.*

im·pri·ma·tur (ĭm′prə-mä′tər, -mä′tər) *n.* 1. Official approval or license to print or publish. 2. Official sanction; authorization. [< L *imprimere*, to print, impress.]

im·print (ĭm-prĭnt′) *v.* To produce or impress (a mark or pattern) on a surface. —n. (ĭm′-prĭnt′). 1. A mark or pattern produced by imprinting. 2. A distinguishing manifestation: *the imprint of defeat.* 3. The publisher's name, often with other information, printed on a title page. [< L *imprimere*, to print.]

im·pris·on (ĭm-prĭz′ən) *v.* To put in or as if in prison. —im·pris′on·ment *n.*

im·prob·a·ble (ĭm-prŏb′ə-bəl) *adj.* Not probable; doubtful or unlikely. —im·prob′a·bil′i·ty *n.* —im·prob′a·bly *adv.*

im·promp·tu (ĭm-prŏmp′t/y/ō̄o) *adj.* Not rehearsed; extempore. [< L *in promptū*, in readiness.] —im·promp′tu *adv.*

im·prop·er (ĭm-prŏp′ər) *adj.* 1. Not suited to the given circumstances. 2. Unseemly; indecorous. 3. Not consistent with fact; incorrect. —im·prop′er·ly *adv.* —im·prop′er·ness *n.*

im·pro·pri·e·ty (ĭm′prə-prī′ə-tē) *n., pl.* -ties. 1. The quality of being improper. 2. An improper act or usage.

im·prove (ĭm-prōōv′) *v.* -proved, -proving. 1. To make or become better. 2. To increase the productivity or value of (land). [NF *emprouer*, to turn to profit.]

im·prove·ment (ĭm-prōōv′mənt) *n.* 1. The act or procedure of improving. 2. The state of being improved. 3. A change or addition that improves.

im·prov·i·dent (ĭm-prŏv′ə-dənt) *adj.* Not providing for the future; thriftless. —im·prov′i·dence *n.* —im·prov′i·dent·ly *adv.*

im·pro·vise (ĭm′prə-vīz′) *v.* -vised, -vising. 1. To invent, compose, or recite without preparation. 2. To make or provide from available materials. [< L *imprōvīsus*, not foreseen.] —im·pro′vi·sa′tion *n.* —im′pro·vis′er *n.*

im·pru·dent (ĭm-prōō′dənt) *adj.* Not prudent; unwise or injudicious. —im·pru′dence *n.*

im·pu·dent (ĭm′pyə-dənt) *adj.* Impertinent; rude; disrespectful. [< L *impudēns.*] —im′pu·dence *n.*

im·pugn (ĭm-pyōōn′) *v.* To oppose or attack as false; criticize; refute. [< L *impugnāre*, to fight against.] —im·pugn′er *n.*

im·pulse (ĭm′pŭls′) *n.* 1. An impelling force or the motion it produces. 2. A sudden inclination or urge. 3. A motivating propensity; drive; instinct. 4. A transmission of energy from one neuron to another. [L *impulsus*, pp of *impellere*, IMPEL.]

im·pul·sive (ĭm-pŭl′sĭv) *adj.* 1. Inclined to act on impulse rather than thought. 2. Produced as a result of impulse; precipitate; uncalculated. **3.** Having force or power to impel or incite; forceful. **4.** *Phys.* Acting within brief time intervals. —**im·pul′sive·ly** *adv.* —**im·pul′sive·ness** *n.*

im·pu·ni·ty (ĭm-pyōō′nə-tē) *n.* **1.** Exemption from punishment or penalty. **2.** Immunity or preservation from recrimination, regret, etc. [< L *impūnis*, not punished.]

im·pure (ĭm-pyŏŏr′) *adj.* **1.** Not pure or clean; contaminated. **2.** Immoral or obscene. **3.** Mixed with another substance; alloyed; adulterated. —**im·pure′ly** *adv.* —**im·pu′ri·ty** *n.*

im·pute (ĭm-pyōōt′) *v.* **-puted**, **-puting**. To ascribe or attribute (a crime or fault) to another. [< L *imputāre*, to bring into the reckoning.] —**im·put′a·ble** *adj.* —**im·pu·ta′tion** *n.*

in (ĭn) *prep.* **1. a.** Within the confines of; inside. **b.** Within the area covered by. **2.** On. **3.** As a part, aspect, or property of. **4.** During. **5.** At the position or business of. **6.** After the pattern or form of. **7.** Into. **8.** Out of: *said in anger.* **9.** As part of the act or process of: *in hot pursuit.* **10.** With the attribute of: *in silence.* **11. a.** By means of: *paid in cash.* **b.** Through the medium of. **12.** Within the category of. **13.** With reference to. —*adv.* **1.** To or toward the inside or center. **2.** Into a given place or position. **3.** Indoors. **4.** Into a given activity together: *joined in and sang.* **5.** Inward: *caved in.* —*adj.* **1.** Prestigious or appealing to a clique. **2.** Available or at home: *He wasn't in.* **3.** Incoming or incumbent. —*n.* **1.** One in power or having the advantage. **2.** *Informal.* Influence. [< OE *in, inn.* See **en.**]

in-.[1] *comb. form.* Not, lacking, or without. [< L.]

in-.[2] *comb. form.* **1.** In, into, within, or inward. **2.** Intensive action. **3.** Causative function. [< L.]

-in. *comb. form.* **1.** Enzyme: **rennin. 2.** Names of drugs and other pharmaceutical products: **aspirin. 3.** Variant of **-ine**[2]. [< L *-īnus*, belonging to.]

In inch.

In indium.

in. inch.

in·a·bil·i·ty (ĭn′ə-bĭl′ə-tē) *n.* Lack of ability or means.

in ab·sen·ti·a (ĭn ăb-sĕn′shē-ə, -shə) *Latin.* In one's absence; while or although not present.

in·ac·ces·si·ble (ĭn′ăk-sĕs′ə-bəl) *adj.* Not accessible; unapproachable.

in·ac·cu·rate (ĭn-ăk′yər-ĭt) *adj.* **1.** Not accurate. **2.** Mistaken or incorrect. —**in·ac′cu·ra·cy** *n.* —**in·ac′cu·rate·ly** *adv.*

in·ac·tion (ĭn-ăk′shən) *n.* Lack or absence of action.

in·ac·tive (ĭn-ăk′tĭv) *adj.* **1.** Not active or not tending to be active. **2.** Retired from duty or service. —**in·ac′tive·ly** *adv.* —**in·ac·tiv′i·ty** *n.*

in·ad·e·quate (ĭn-ăd′ĭ-kwĭt) *adj.* Not adequate; insufficient. —**in·ad′e·qua·cy** *n.*

in·ad·mis·si·ble (ĭn′əd-mĭs′ə-bəl) *adj.* Not admissible. —**in′ad·mis′si·bil′i·ty** *n.*

in·ad·ver·tent (ĭn′əd-vûr′tənt) *adj.* **1.** Not duly attentive. **2.** Accidental; unintentional. —**in′ad·ver′tence** *n.* —**in′ad·ver′tent·ly** *adv.*

in·ad·vis·a·ble (ĭn′əd-vī′zə-bəl) *adj.* Inexpedient; unwise; not recommended. —**in′ad·vis′a·bil′i·ty** *n.* —**in′ad·vis′a·bly** *adv.*

in·al·ien·a·ble (ĭn-āl′yə-nə-bəl) *adj.* Not to be transferred to another; not alienable. —**in·al′ien·a·bly** *adv.*

in·ane (ĭn-ān′) *adj.* Lacking sense or substance; empty; silly: *an inane comment.* [L *inānis*, empty, vain.] —**in·an′i·ty** (-ăn′ə-tē) *n.*

in·an·i·mate (ĭn-ăn′ə-mĭt) *adj.* Not having the qualities associated with active, living organisms; not animate. —**in·an′i·mate·ly** *adv.*

in·ap·pli·ca·ble (ĭn-ăp′lĭ-kə-bəl) *adj.* Not applicable. —**in·ap′pli·ca·bil′i·ty** *n.*

in·ap·pre·ci·a·ble (ĭn′ə-prē′shē-ə-bəl) *adj.* Insignificant; negligible. —**in′ap·pre′ci·a·bly** *adv.*

in·ap·pre·ci·a·tive (ĭn′ə-prē′shə-tĭv, -shē-ā′-tĭv) *adj.* Showing no appreciation.

in·ap·pro·pri·ate (ĭn′ə-prō′prē-ĭt) *adj.* Not appropriate. —**in′ap·pro′pri·ate·ly** *adv.*

in·ar·tic·u·late (ĭn′är-tĭk′yə-lĭt) *adj.* **1.** Incomprehensible as speech or language. **2.** Unable to speak; speechless. **3.** Unable to speak with clarity or eloquence. **4.** Unexpressed: *inarticulate sorrow.* —**in′ar·tic′u·late·ly** *adv.* —**in′ar·tic′u·late·ness** *n.*

in·as·much as (ĭn′əz-mŭch′). Because of the fact that; since.

in·at·ten·tion (ĭn′ə-tĕn′shən) *n.* Lack of attention or notice; neglect. —**in′at·ten′tive** *adj.*

in·au·di·ble (ĭn-ô′də-bəl) *adj.* Incapable of being heard; not audible. —**in·au′di·bly** *adv.*

in·au·gu·ral (ĭn-ô′gyər-əl) *adj.* Of, relating to, or characteristic of an inauguration. —*n.* A speech made at an inauguration.

in·au·gu·rate (ĭn-ô′gyə-rāt′) *v.* **-rated**, **-rating**. **1.** To induct into office by a formal ceremony. **2.** To begin or start officially. **3.** To open with a ceremony; dedicate. [L *inaugurāre*, to take omens from the flight of birds, to consecrate, install.] —**in·au′gu·ra′tion** *n.*

in·aus·pi·cious (ĭn′ô-spĭsh′əs) *adj.* Not auspicious; ill-omened. —**in′aus·pi′cious·ly** *adv.*

in·board (ĭn′bôrd′, -bōrd′) *adj.* **1.** Within the hull of a ship. **2.** Near the fuselage of an aircraft: *inboard engines.* —**in′board′** *adv.*

in·born (ĭn′bôrn′) *adj.* Present at birth; inherited; hereditary.

in·bound (ĭn′bound′) *adj.* Homeward bound or incoming.

in·bred (ĭn′brĕd′) *adj.* **1.** Produced by inbreeding. **2.** Inborn; innate.

in·breed (ĭn′brēd′, ĭn-brēd′) *v.* To produce by the continued breeding of closely related individuals.

inc. 1. incorporated. **2.** increase.

Inc. incorporated.

In·ca (ĭng′kə) *n., pl.* **-ca** or **-cas.** A member of a powerful Indian people that ruled Peru before the Spanish conquest.

in·cal·cu·la·ble (ĭn-kăl′kyə-lə-bəl) *adj.* **1.** Not calculable; indeterminate. **2.** Incapable of being foreseen; unpredictable; uncertain. —**in·cal′cu·la·ble·ness** *n.* —**in·cal′cu·la·bly** *adv.*

in·can·des·cent (ĭn′kən-dĕs′ənt) *adj.* **1.** Emitting visible light as a result of being heated. **2.** Shining brilliantly; very bright. —**in′can·des′cence** *n.* —**in′can·des′cent·ly** *adv.*

ă pat/ā ate/âr care/ä bar/b bib/ch chew/d deed/ĕ pet/ē be/f fit/g gag/h hat/hw what/ ĭ pit/ī pie/îr pier/j judge/k kick/l lid, fatal/m mum/n no, sudden/ng sing/ŏ pot/ō go/

in·can·ta·tion (ĭn'kăn-tā'shən) *n.* **1.** A recitation of verbal charms or spells to produce a magical effect. **2.** The words, phrases, or sounds used in this manner. [< L *incantāre*, ENCHANT.]

in·ca·pa·ble (ĭn-kā'pə-bəl) *adj.* **1.** Not capable; not able. **2.** Legally unqualified; ineligible. —**in·ca'pa·bil'i·ty** *n.* —**in·ca'pa·bly** *adv.*

in·ca·pac·i·tate (ĭn'kə-păs'ĭ-tāt') *v.* **-tated, -tating. 1.** To deprive of strength or ability. **2.** To make legally ineligible; disqualify. —**in'ca·pac'i·ta'tion** *n.*

in·ca·pac·i·ty (ĭn'kə-păs'ə-tē) *n., pl.* **-ties. 1.** Lack of strength or ability. **2.** That which renders legally ineligible; disqualification.

in·cap·su·late. Variant of encapsulate.

in·car·cer·ate (ĭn-kär'sə-rāt') *v.* **-ated, -ating.** To put in jail. [L *incarcerāre.*] —**in·car'cer·a'tion** *n.* —**in·car'cer·a·tor** *n.*

in·car·nate (ĭn-kär'nĭt) *adj.* **1.** Invested with bodily nature and form. **2.** Personified: *wisdom incarnate.* —*v.* (ĭn-kär'nāt') **-nated, -nating. 1.** To give bodily form to. **2.** To embody or personify. [LL *incarnāre*, to make flesh.] —**in'car·na'tion** *n.*

in·case. Variant of encase.

in·cen·di·ar·y (ĭn-sĕn'dē-ĕr'ē) *adj.* **1.** Of or involving arson. **2.** Producing intensely hot fire, as a military weapon. **3.** Tending to inflame; inflammatory. [< L *incendium*, burning.] —**in·cen'di·ar'y** *n.*

in·cense¹ (ĭn-sĕns') *v.* **-censed, -censing.** To infuriate; enrage. [< L *incendere*, to set on fire, enrage.]

in·cense² (ĭn'sĕns') *n.* **1.** An aromatic substance burned to produce a pleasant odor. **2.** The smoke or odor thus produced. [< L *incendere*, to set on fire.]

in·cen·tive (ĭn-sĕn'tĭv) *n.* Something inciting to action or effort. [< L *incentīvus*, that sets the tune, inciting.]

in·cep·tion (ĭn-sĕp'shən) *n.* The beginning of something. [< L *incipere*, to take in hand, begin.] —**in·cep'tive** *adj.*

in·cer·ti·tude (ĭn-sûr'tə-t/y/ōōd') *n.* **1.** Uncertainty; doubt. **2.** Insecurity or instability.

in·ces·sant (ĭn-sĕs'ənt) *adj.* Continuing without interruption; unceasing. —**in·ces'sant·ly** *adv.*

in·cest (ĭn'sĕst) *n.* Sexual union between persons so closely related that their marriage is illegal. [< L *incestus*, "unchaste."] —**in·ces'tu·ous** *adj.*

inch (ĭnch) *n.* A unit of length equal to ¹/₁₂ of a foot. —*v.* To move by inches or small degrees. [< L *unica*, twelfth part, inch.]

in·cho·ate (ĭn-kō'ĭt) *adj.* **1.** In an initial or early stage; incipient. **2.** Lacking order or form. [< L *inchoāre*, to begin, orig "to harness."]

inch·worm (ĭnch'wûrm') *n.* A caterpillar that moves by alternately looping and stretching out its body.

in·ci·dence (ĭn'sə-dəns) *n.* The extent or frequency of the occurrence of something.

in·ci·dent (ĭn'sə-dənt) *n.* **1.** A definite, distinct occurrence; an event. **2.** A relatively minor occurrence that precipitates a crisis. —*adj.*

1. Tending to arise or occur in connection with: *a melancholy incident to his profession.* **2.** Falling upon; striking: *incident radiation.* [< L *incidere*, to fall upon, happen to.]

in·ci·den·tal (ĭn'sə-dĕnt'l) *adj.* Occurring as a fortuitous or minor concomitant. —*n.* Often **incidentals.** A minor concomitant circumstance, expense, etc.

in·ci·den·tal·ly (ĭn'sə-dĕnt'l-ē) *adv.* **1.** Casually; by chance. **2.** Parenthetically.

in·cin·er·ate (ĭn-sĭn'ə-rāt') *v.* **-ated, -ating.** To consume by burning. [ML *incinerāre.*] —**in·cin'er·a'tion** *n.*

in·cin·er·a·tor (ĭn-sĭn'ə-rā'tər) *n.* A furnace or other apparatus for burning waste.

in·cip·i·ent (ĭn-sĭp'ē-ənt) *adj.* In an initial or early stage; just beginning to exist or appear. [L *incipiēns*, beginning.] —**in·cip'i·ence** *n.*

in·cise (ĭn-sīz') *v.* **-cised, -cising. 1.** To cut into or mark with a sharp instrument. **2.** To cut (designs or writing) into a surface; engrave; carve. [<L *incidere.*]

in·ci·sion (ĭn-sĭzh'ən) *n.* **1.** A surgical cut into soft tissue. **2.** The scar resulting from such a cut.

in·ci·sive (ĭn-sī'sĭv) *adj.* **1.** Cutting; penetrating. **2.** Trenchant. —**in·ci'sive·ly** *adv.*

in·ci·sor (ĭn-sī'zər) *n.* A tooth adapted for cutting.

in·cite (ĭn-sīt') *v.* **-cited, -citing.** To provoke to action; stir up or urge on. [< L *incitāre*, to urge.] —**in·cite'ment** *n.* —**in·cit'er** *n.*

incl. including; inclusive.

in·clem·ent (ĭn-klĕm'ənt) *adj.* **1.** Stormy. **2.** Severe or unmerciful. [L *inclēmēns.*] —**in·clem'en·cy** *n.*

in·cli·na·tion (ĭn'klə-nā'shən) *n.* **1.** The act of inclining. **2.** A slope; slant. **3.** A tendency; propensity. **4.** A preference or leaning.

in·cline (ĭn-klīn') *v.* **-clined, -clining. 1.** To lean; slant; slope. **2.** To lower or bend (the head or body) in a nod or bow. **3.** To influence (someone or something) to have a certain preference; dispose. **4.** To tend toward a particular state or condition. —*n.* (ĭn'klīn'). An inclined surface; a slope. [L *inclināre.*]

in·close. Variant of enclose.

in·clude (ĭn-klōōd') *v.* **-cluded, -cluding. 1.** To have as part of a whole; contain. **2.** To consider with or put into a general category. [< L *inclūdere*, to shut in.] —**in·clu'sion** *n.*

in·clu·sive (ĭn-klōō'sĭv) *adj.* **1.** Taking everything into account; comprehensive. **2.** Including the limits specified: *from 11 to 20 inclusive.* —**in·clu'sive·ly** *adv.* —**in·clu'sive·ness** *n.*

in·cog·ni·to (ĭn-kŏg'nə-tō', ĭn'kŏg'nē'tō) *adv.* In a nonofficial capacity or with one's identity concealed. [< L *incognitus*, unknown.] —**in·cog'ni·to'** *adj.*

in·co·her·ent (ĭn'kō-hîr'ənt) *adj.* **1.** Not coherent; disordered; unconnected. **2.** Unable to express one's thoughts in an orderly manner. —**in'co·her'ence** *n.* —**in'co·her'ent·ly** *adv.*

in·com·bus·ti·ble (ĭn'kəm-bŭs'tə-bəl) *adj.* Incapable of burning.

in·come (ĭn'kŭm') *n.* Money received for labor or services, from the sale of property, or from investments. [ME, a coming in, entry.]

ô paw, for/oi boy/ou out/ōō took/ōō coo/p pop/r run/s sauce/sh shy/t to/th thin/*th* the/
ŭ cut/ûr fur/v van/w wag/y yes/z size/zh vision/ə ago, item, edible, gallop, circus/

income tax. A graduated tax levied on annual income.

in·com·ing (ĭn'kŭm'ĭng) *adj.* 1. Coming in; entering. 2. About to take office: *the incoming president.*

in·com·men·su·rate (ĭn'kə-mĕn'shər-ĭt, -sər-ĭt) *adj.* Not commensurate; unequal; disproportionate: *a reward incommensurate with his efforts.* —in'com·men'su·rate·ly *adv.*

in·com·mode (ĭn'kə-mōd') *v.* -moded, -moding. To inconvenience; disturb. [< L *incommodus,* inconvenient.]

in·com·mo·di·ous (ĭn'kə-mō'dē-əs) *adj.* Inconvenient; uncomfortable.

in·com·mu·ni·ca·do (ĭn'kə-myōō'nĭ-kä'dō) *adj.* Without the means or right to communicate with others, as one held in confinement. —in'com·mu'ni·ca'do *adv.*

in·com·pa·ra·ble (ĭn-kŏm'pər-ə-bəl) *adj.* 1. Incapable of being compared. 2. Beyond compare; unsurpassed; matchless.

in·com·pat·i·ble (ĭn'kəm-păt'ə-bəl) *adj.* Not compatible; inharmonious; antagonistic. —in'com·pat'i·bil'i·ty *n.* —in'com·pat'i·bly *adv.*

in·com·pe·tent (ĭn-kŏm'pə-tənt) *adj.* Not competent. —*n.* An incompetent person. —in·com'pe·tence *n.* —in·com'pe·tent·ly *adv.*

in·com·plete (ĭn'kəm-plēt') *adj.* Not complete. —in'com·plete'ly *adv.*

in·com·pre·hen·si·ble (ĭn'kŏm-prĭ-hĕn'sə-bəl, ĭn-kŏm'-) *adj.* Not understandable; unintelligible. —in'com·pre·hen'sion *n.*

in·com·press·i·ble (ĭn'kəm-prĕs'ə-bəl) *adj.* Incapable of being compressed. —in'com·press'i·bil'i·ty *n.*

in·con·ceiv·a·ble (ĭn'kən-sē'və-bəl) *adj.* Incapable of being conceived of; unimaginable.

in·con·clu·sive (ĭn'kən-klōō'sĭv) *adj.* Not conclusive. —in'con·clu'sive·ly *adv.*

in·con·gru·ous (ĭn-kŏng'grōō-əs) *adj.* 1. Inappropriate; out of place. 2. Not harmonious; incompatible. 3. Inconsistent; illogical. —in'con·gru'i·ty *n.* —in·con'gru·ous·ly *adv.*

in·con·se·quen·tial (ĭn-kŏn'sə-kwĕn'shəl) *adj.* Without consequence; lacking importance.

in·con·sid·er·a·ble (ĭn'kən-sĭd'ər-ə-bəl) *adj.* Small; unimportant.

in·con·sid·er·ate (ĭn'kən-sĭd'ər-ĭt) *adj.* Not considerate. —in'con·sid'er·ate·ly *adv.*

in·con·sis·tent (ĭn'kən-sĭs'tənt) *adj.* Not consistent; erratic; contradictory. —in'con·sis'ten·cy *n.* —in'con·sis'tent·ly *adv.*

in·con·sol·a·ble (ĭn'kən-sō'lə-bəl) *adj.* Incapable of being consoled.

in·con·spic·u·ous (ĭn'kən-spĭk'yōō-əs) *adj.* Not readily noticeable. —in'con·spic'u·ous·ly *adv.* —in'con·spic'u·ous·ness *n.*

in·con·stant (ĭn-kŏn'stənt) *adj.* 1. Not constant. 2. Fickle. —in·con'stan·cy *n.*

in·con·test·a·ble (ĭn'kən-tĕs'tə-bəl) *adj.* Indisputable; unquestionable. —in'con·test'a·bil'i·ty *n.* —in'con·test'a·bly *adv.*

in·con·ti·nent (ĭn-kŏn'tə-nənt) *adj.* Not continent; lacking self-restraint. —in·con'ti·nence *n.* —in·con'ti·nent·ly *adv.*

in·con·tro·vert·i·ble (ĭn'kŏn-trə-vûr'tə-bəl) *adj.* Indisputable; unquestionable.

in·con·ven·ience (ĭn'kən-vēn'yəns) *n.* 1. The state of being inconvenient; trouble; difficulty. 2. Something that causes difficulty, trouble, or discomfort. —*v.* -ienced, -iencing. To cause inconvenience to; trouble; bother.

in·con·ven·ient (ĭn'kən-vēn'yənt) *adj.* Not convenient; awkward; inopportune.

in·cor·po·rate (ĭn-kôr'pə-rāt') *v.* -rated, -rating. 1. To form or form into a legal corporation. 2. To combine together into a united whole. [< LL *incorporāre,* to form into a body.] —in·cor'po·ra'tion *n.* —in·cor'po·ra'tor *n.*

in·cor·po·re·al (ĭn'kôr-pôr'ē-əl, -pōr'ē-əl) *adj.* Lacking material form or substance.

in·cor·rect (ĭn'kə-rĕkt') *adj.* 1. Not correct; erroneous. 2. Improper; unbecoming. —in'cor·rect'ly *adv.* —in'cor·rect'ness *n.*

in·cor·ri·gi·ble (ĭn-kôr'ə-jə-bəl, ĭn-kŏr'-) *adj.* Incapable of being corrected or reformed. —*n.* A person that will not be tamed or corrected. —in·cor'ri·gi·bly *adv.*

in·cor·rupt·i·ble (ĭn'kə-rŭp'tə-bəl) *adj.* Incapable of being corrupted; not subject to bribery or corruption. —in'cor·rupt'i·bly *adv.*

in·crease (ĭn-krēs') *v.* -creased, -creasing. To make or become greater or larger. —*n.* (ĭn'krēs'). 1. Augmentation; enlargement; multiplication. 2. The amount of such increase; increment. [< L *incrēscere,* to grow in or on.] —in·creas'er *n.* —in·creas'ing·ly *adv.*

in·cred·i·ble (ĭn-krĕd'ə-bəl) *adj.* Unbelievable. —in·cred'i·ble·ness *n.* —in·cred'i·bly *adv.*

in·cred·u·lous (ĭn-krĕj'ə-ləs) *adj.* 1. Disbelieving; skeptical. 2. Expressing disbelief. —in'cre·du'li·ty (-krə-d/y/ōō'lə-tē) *n.*

in·cre·ment (ĭn'krə-mənt) *n.* 1. An increase in number, size, or extent. 2. Something added or gained. [< L *incrēmentum* < *incrēscere,* to INCREASE.]

in·crim·i·nate (ĭn-krĭm'ə-nāt') *v.* -nated, -nating. To charge with or involve in a crime. —in·crim'i·na'tion *n.*

in·crust. Variant of **encrust.**

in·cu·bate (ĭn'kyə-bāt', ĭng'-) *v.* -bated, -bating. 1. To warm and hatch (eggs), as by bodily heat. 2. To maintain in favorable environmental conditions for development. [L *incubāre,* to hatch, lie down upon.] —in'cu·ba'tion *n.* —in'cu·ba'tive *adj.*

in·cu·ba·tor (ĭn'kyə-bā'tər, ĭng'-) *n.* 1. A cabinet in which a uniform temperature can be maintained, used in growing bacterial cultures. 2. An apparatus for maintaining a premature infant in an environment of controlled temperature, humidity, and oxygen.

in·cu·bus (ĭn'kyə-bəs, ĭng'-) *n., pl.* -buses or -bi (-bī'). 1. An evil spirit believed to descend upon sleeping women. 2. A nightmare. [< L *incubāre,* to lie down upon, INCUBATE.]

in·cu·des. pl. of **incus.**

in·cul·cate (ĭn-kŭl'kāt') *v.* -cated, -cating. To teach or impress by forceful urging; instill. [L *inculcāre,* to impress upon.] —in·cul'ca'tion *n.*

in·cul·pa·ble (ĭn-kŭl'pə-bəl) *adj.* Free from guilt; blameless.

in·cul·pate (ĭn-kŭl'pāt') *v.* -pated, -pating. To incriminate. [LL *inculpāre.*]

in·cum·bent (ĭn-kŭm'bənt) *adj.* 1. Required; obligatory. 2. Holding a specified office. —*n.*

ă pat/ā ate/âr care/ä bar/b bib/ch chew/d deed/ĕ pet/ē be/f fit/g gag/h hat/hw what/
ĭ pit/ī pie/îr pier/j judge/k kick/l lid, fatal/m mum/n no, sudden/ng sing/ŏ pot/ō go/

A person who holds an office. [< L *incumbere*, to lean upon.] —**in•cum'ben•cy** n.

in•cu•nab•u•lum (ĭn'kyōō-năb'yə-ləm) n., pl. **-la** (-lə). A book printed in the earliest stages of movable type (before 1500). [< L *incūnābula*, swaddling clothes, cradle.]

in•cur (ĭn-kûr') v. **-curred, -curring**. To become subject to; bring upon oneself. [L *incurrere*, to run into.]

in•cur•a•ble (ĭn-kyŏŏr'ə-bəl) adj. Not curable, as a disease. —**in•cur'a•bly** adv.

in•cur•sion (ĭn-kûr'zhən, -shən) n. **1.** A sudden attack or invasion; a raid. **2.** A running or entering into. [< L *incurrere*, to run into, attack, INCUR.]

in•cus (ĭng'kəs) n., pl. **incudes** (ĭn-kyōō'dēz). An anvil-shaped bone in the middle ear.

Ind. 1. independence; independent. **2.** index. **3.** industrial; industry.

Ind. 1. India. **2.** Indian. **3.** Indiana.

in•debt•ed (ĭn-dĕt'ĭd) adj. Obligated to another; beholden. —**in•debt'ed•ness** n.

in•de•cent (ĭn-dē'sənt) adj. Offensive to good taste; unseemly. —**in•de'cen•cy** n. —**in•de'cent•ly** adv.

in•de•ci•pher•a•ble (ĭn'dĭ-sī'fər-ə-bəl) adj. Incapable of being deciphered.

in•de•ci•sion (ĭn'dĭ-sĭzh'ən) n. Irresolution.

in•de•ci•sive (ĭn'dĭ-sī'sĭv) adj. Not decisive; vacillating; hesitant. —**in•de•ci'sive•ly** adv. —**in•de•ci'sive•ness** n.

in•dec•o•rous (ĭn-dĕk'ər-əs) adj. Lacking propriety or good taste; unseemly. —**in•dec'o•rous•ly** adv. —**in•dec'o•rous•ness** n.

in•deed (ĭn-dēd') adv. **1.** Truly; certainly. **2.** In fact; in reality. **3.** Admittedly; unquestionably. —*interj.* Expressive of surprise, skepticism, or irony. [ME *in dede*, in reality.]

indef. indefinite.

in•de•fat•i•ga•ble (ĭn'dĭ-făt'ə-gə-bəl) adj. Untiring; tireless. —**in'de•fat'i•ga•bly** adv.

in•de•fen•si•ble (ĭn'dĭ-fĕn'sə-bəl) adj. **1.** Not capable of being defended. **2.** Inexcusable. **3.** Untenable. —**in'de•fen'si•bly** adv.

in•de•fin•a•ble (ĭn'dĭ-fī'nə-bəl) adj. Not capable of being defined, described, or analyzed. —n. Something that cannot be defined.

in•def•i•nite (ĭn-dĕf'ə-nĭt) adj. Not definite; unclear; uncertain. —**in•def'i•nite•ly** adv.

indefinite article. *Gram.* An article, as English *a* or *an,* that does not fix the identity of the noun it modifies.

in•del•i•ble (ĭn-dĕl'ə-bəl) adj. **1.** Making a mark not easily erased. **2.** Permanent; lasting. [L *indēlēbilis.*] —**in•del'i•bly** adv.

in•del•i•cate (ĭn-dĕl'ĭ-kĭt) adj. **1.** Offensive to propriety; coarse. **2.** Tactless. —**in•del'i•ca•cy** n. —**in•del'i•cate•ly** adv.

in•dem•ni•fy (ĭn-dĕm'nə-fī') v. **-fied, -fying. 1.** To protect against possible damage; insure. **2.** To make compensation to for incurred damage. —**in•dem'ni•fi•ca'tion** n.

in•dem•ni•ty (ĭn-dĕm'nə-tē) n., pl. **-ties. 1.** Insurance against possible damage or loss. **2.** Compensation for damage or loss incurred; indemnification. [< L *indemnis,* unhurt.]

in•dent[1] (ĭn-dĕnt') v. **1.** To notch or serrate the edge of; make jagged. **2.** To set in (the first line of a paragraph) from the margin. [ME *indenten,* to make a toothlike incision into.]

in•dent[2] (ĭn-dĕnt') v. To press down upon so as to form an impression. —n. An indentation. [< IN- + DENT.]

in•den•ta•tion (ĭn'dĕn'tā'shən) n. **1.** The act of indenting or condition of being indented. **2.** A notch or jagged cut in an edge, as in certain leaves. **3.** A deep recess in a border, coastline, or other boundary. **4.** The blank space between a margin and the beginning of an indented line.

in•den•tion (ĭn-dĕn'shən) n. **1.** The act of indenting or the condition of being indented. **2.** The blank space between a margin and the beginning of an indented line.

in•den•ture (ĭn-dĕn'chər) n. **1.** A written contract. **2.** Often **indentures.** A contract binding one party into the service of another for a specified term. —v. **-tured, -turing.** To bind by indenture.

Independence Day. July 4, a holiday celebrating the adoption of the Declaration of Independence.

in•de•pend•ent (ĭn'dĭ-pĕn'dənt) adj. **1.** Politically autonomous; self-governing. **2.** Free from the influence, guidance, or control of others; self-reliant. **3.** Not committed to one political party. **4.** Not dependent on or affiliated with. **5.** Financially self-sufficient. —n. One that is independent, esp. a voter not committed to any one political party. —**in'de•pen'dence** n. —**in'de•pend'ent•ly** adv.

in-depth (ĭn'dĕpth') adj. Detailed; thorough: *an in-depth study.*

in•de•scrib•a•ble (ĭn'dĭ-skrī'bə-bəl) adj. Beyond description. —**in'de•scrib'a•bil'i•ty** n. —**in'de•scrib'a•bly** adv.

in•de•struc•ti•ble (ĭn'dĭ-strŭk'tə-bəl) adj. Not capable of being destroyed; unbreakable. —**in'de•struc'ti•bil'i•ty, in'de•struc'ti•ble•ness** n. —**in'de•struc'ti•bly** adv.

in•de•ter•mi•na•ble (ĭn'dĭ-tûr'mə-nə-bəl) adj. Not capable of being ascertained or decided. —**in'de•ter'mi•na•bly** adv.

in•de•ter•mi•na•cy (ĭn'dĭ-tûr'mə-nə-sē) n. The state or quality of being indeterminate.

in•de•ter•mi•nate (ĭn'dĭ-tûr'mə-nĭt) adj. **1.** Not precisely or quantitatively determined. **2.** Lacking clarity or precision. —**in'de•ter'mi•nate•ly** adv. —**in'de•ter'mi•nate•ness, in'de•ter'mi•na'tion** (-nā'shən) n.

in•dex (ĭn'dĕks') n., pl. **-dexes** or **-dices** (-də-sēz'). **1.** An alphabetized listing of the names, places, and subjects in a printed work, giving the page on which each can be found. **2.** Anything that reveals or indicates; a sign; token. **3.** A number or symbol used to indicate an operation or relationship involving a particular mathematical expression. **4.** A number derived from a formula used to characterize a set of data: *cost-of-living index.* —v. **1.** To furnish with an index. **2.** To enter (an item) in an index. [L, forefinger, indicator.]

index finger. The finger next to the thumb.

index of refraction. The ratio of the speed of light in a vacuum to the speed of light in a medium under consideration.

ô paw, for/oi boy/ou out/ŏŏ took/ōō coo/p pop/r run/s sauce/sh shy/t to/th thin/*th* the/
ŭ cut/ûr fur/v van/w wag/y yes/z size/zh vision/ə ago, item, edible, gallop, circus/

In·di·a (ĭn'dē-ə). **1.** A subcontinent of S Asia. **2.** A republic occupying most of this subcontinent. Pop. 476,278,000. Cap. New Delhi.

India

India ink. A black liquid ink.

In·di·an (ĭn'dē-ən) *n.* **1.** A native or inhabitant of India or the East Indies. **2.** A member of any of the aboriginal peoples of the Americas. —**In'di·an** *adj.*

In·di·an·a (ĭn'dē-ăn'ə). A Midwestern state of the U.S. Pop. 5,194,000. Cap. Indianapolis. —**In'di·an'i·an** *n. & adj.*

In·di·an·ap·o·lis (ĭn'dē-ə-năp'ə-lĭs). The capital of Indiana. Pop. 745,000.

Indian Ocean. The ocean between Africa and Australia.

Indian pipe. A waxy white woodland plant with scalelike leaves and a single nodding flower.

Indian summer. A period of mild weather occurring in late autumn or early winter.

In·dic (ĭn'dĭk) *n.* A branch of the Indo-European languages that includes Sanskrit. —**In'dic** *adj.*

Indic. indicative.

In·di·cate (ĭn'dĭ-kāt') *v.* -cated, -cating. **1.** To demonstrate or point out. **2.** To serve as a sign, symptom, or token of; signify. **3.** To suggest the necessity or advisability of. **4.** To state, disclose, or express briefly. [< L *index*, INDEX.] —**In'di·ca'tion** *n.*

In·dic·a·tive (ĭn-dĭk'ə-tĭv) *adj.* **1.** Serving to point out or indicate. **2.** *Gram.* Pertaining to or designating a verbal mood used to indicate that the denoted act or condition is an objective fact. —*n. Gram.* The indicative mood. —**In·dic'a·tive·ly** *adv.*

In·di·ca·tor (ĭn'dĭ-kā'tər) *n.* **1.** One that indicates, esp. a device used to monitor the operation or condition of a system. **2.** A substance such as litmus that indicates the presence, absence, or concentration of a substance, or the degree of reaction between two or more substances, by means of a characteristic change, esp. in color.

In·di·ces. Alternate *pl.* of **index.**

In·dict (ĭn-dīt') *v.* **1.** To accuse of a crime; charge. **2.** To make a formal accusation against by the findings of a grand jury. [< L *indīcere*, to proclaim.] —**in·dict'ment** *n.*

in·dif·fer·ent (ĭn-dĭf'ər-ənt) *adj.* **1.** Having no partiality or bias. **2.** Of no great importance; insignificant. **3.** Having no marked feeling for one way or the other. **4.** Having no particular interest in or concern for; apathetic. **5.** Neither good nor bad; mediocre. —**in·dif'fer·ence** *n.* —**in·dif'fer·ent·ly** *adv.*

in·dig·e·nous (ĭn-dĭj'ə-nəs) *adj.* Living naturally in an area; native. [< L *indigena*, native.]

in·di·gent (ĭn'də-jənt) *adj.* Lacking the means of subsistence; impoverished; needy. —*n.* A destitute or needy person. [< L *indigēre*, to lack.] —**in'di·gence** *n.* —**in'di·gent·ly** *adv.*

in·di·gest·i·ble (ĭn'dĭ-jĕs'tə-bəl, ĭn'dī-) *adj.* Difficult or impossible to digest.

in·di·ges·tion (ĭn'dĭ-jĕs'chən, ĭn'dī-) *n.* **1.** The inability to digest food. **2.** Discomfort or illness resulting from this.

in·dig·nant (ĭn-dĭg'nənt) *adj.* Feeling or expressing indignation. [< L *indignus*, unworthy.] —**in·dig'nant·ly** *adv.*

in·dig·na·tion (ĭn'dĭg-nā'shən) *n.* Anger aroused by something unjust.

in·dig·ni·ty (ĭn-dĭg'nə-tē) *n., pl.* -ties. An offense to one's dignity; affront.

in·di·go (ĭn'dĭ-gō') *n., pl.* -gos or -goes. **1.** A plant that yields a blue dyestuff. **2.** A blue dye obtained from such a plant or produced synthetically. **3.** Dark blue. [< Gk *indikon (pharmakon)*, "Indian (dye)."]

in·di·rect (ĭn'dĭ-rĕkt', -dī-rĕkt') *adj.* **1.** Not taking a direct course; roundabout. **2.** Not straight to the point; circumlocutory. **3.** Not immediate; secondary. —**in'di·rec'tion** *n.* —**in·di·rect'ly** *adv.*

indirect object. A grammatical object indirectly affected by the action of a verb.

in·dis·creet (ĭn'dĭs-krēt') *adj.* Lacking discretion; injudicious; imprudent.

in·dis·cre·tion (ĭn'dĭs-krĕsh'ən) *n.* **1.** Lack of discretión. **2.** An indiscreet act or remark.

in·dis·crim·i·nate (ĭn'dĭs-krĭm'ə-nĭt) *adj.* **1.** Not discriminating. **2.** Random; haphazard. **3.** Confused; motley. —**in'dis·crim'i·nate·ly** *adv.* —**in'dis·crim'i·nate·ness** *n.*

in·dis·pen·sa·ble (ĭn'dĭs-pĕn'sə-bəl) *adj.* Absolutely necessary; essential. —**in'dis·pen·sa·bil'i·ty** *n.* —**in'dis·pen'sa·bly** *adv.*

in·dis·posed (ĭn'dĭs-pōzd') *adj.* **1.** Mildly ill. **2.** Disinclined; unwilling. —**in'dis·po·si'tion** *n.*

in·dis·put·a·ble (ĭn'dĭs-pyoō'tə-bəl) *adj.* Beyond doubt; undeniable. —**in'dis·put'a·ble·ness** *n.* —**in'dis·put'a·bly** *adv.*

in·dis·sol·u·ble (ĭn'dĭ-sŏl'yə-bəl) *adj.* **1.** Impossible to break or undo; binding. **2.** Incapable of being dissolved, disintegrated, or decomposed. —**in'dis·sol'u·bly** *adv.*

in·dis·tinct (ĭn'dĭs-tĭngkt') *adj.* **1.** Not clearly delineated. **2.** Faint; dim. —**in'dis·tinct'ly** *adv.*

in·dis·tin·guish·a·ble (ĭn'dĭs-tĭng'gwĭ-shə-bəl) *adj.* **1.** Not readily perceptible. **2.** Without distinctive qualities.

in·di·um (ĭn'dē-əm) *n. Symbol* **In** A soft, malleable, silvery-white metallic element used as a plating over silver in making mirrors and in transistor compounds. Atomic number 49,

---

ă pat/ā ate/âr care/ä bar/b bib/ch chew/d deed/ĕ pet/ē be/f fit/g gag/h hat/hw what/
ĭ pit/ī pie/îr pier/j judge/k kick/l lid, fatal/m mum/n no, sudden/ng sing/ŏ pot/ō go/

atomic weight 114.82. [< L *indicum*, indigo.]

in·di·vid·u·al (ĭn′də-vĭj′ōō-əl) *adj.* **1.** Of or relating to a single human being. **2.** By or for one person: *an individual portion.* **3.** Existing as a distinct entity; single; separate. **4.** Distinguished by particular attributes; distinctive. **5.** Indivisible; inseparable. —*n.* **1.** A single person or organism considered separately. **2.** A particular person. [< L *indīviduus*, indivisible.] —**in′di·vid′u·al·ly** *adv.*

in·di·vid·u·al·ism (ĭn′də-vĭj′ōō-ə-lĭz′əm) *n.* **1.** Individuality. **2.** The doctrine that the interests of the individual take precedence over those of the state.

in·di·vid·u·al·ist (ĭn′də-vĭj′ōō-ə-lĭst) *n.* **1.** A person of independent thought and action. **2.** One who advocates individualism. —**in′di·vid′u·al·is′tic** *adj.*

in·di·vid·u·al·i·ty (ĭn′də-vĭj′ōō-ăl′ə-tē) *n.* **1.** The quality of being individual. **2.** The aggregate of distinguishing attributes of a person or thing.

in·di·vid·u·al·ize (ĭn′dĭ-vĭj′ōō-ə-līz′) *v.* **-ized, -izing. 1.** To give individuality to. **2.** To consider individually; particularize. **3.** To modify to suit a particular individual.

in·di·vis·i·ble (ĭn′də-vĭz′ə-bəl) *adj.* Incapable of being divided. —**in′di·vis′i·bil′i·ty** *n.*

In·do·chi·na (ĭn′dō-chī′nə). A peninsula in SE Asia. —**In′do·chi′nese′** *adj. & n.*

in·doc·tri·nate (ĭn-dŏk′trə-nāt′) *v.* **-nated, -nating. 1.** To instruct in a body of doctrine. **2.** To teach to accept a system of thought uncritically. —**in·doc′tri·na′tion** *n.*

In·do-Eu·ro·pe·an (ĭn′dō-yōōr′ə-pē′ən) *adj.* Belonging to or constituting a family of languages that includes the Germanic, Celtic, Italic, Baltic, Slavic, Greek, Armenian, Iranian, and Indic groups. —*n.* **1.** The Indo-European family of languages. **2.** Proto-Indo-European. See *Table of Indo-European Languages* on following pages. **3.** A member of the presumed prehistoric people who spoke Proto-Indo-European.

In·do-I·ra·ni·an (ĭn′dō-ĭ-rä′nē-ən, -ĭ-rā′nē-ən) *n.* The branch of Indo-European including Indic and Iranian. —**In′do-I·ra′ni·an** *adj.*

in·do·lent (ĭn′də-lənt) *adj.* Disinclined to work; habitually lazy. [LL *indolēns*, painless.] —**in′do·lence** *n.* —**in′do·lent·ly** *adv.*

in·dom·i·ta·ble (ĭn-dŏm′ə-tə-bəl) *adj.* Incapable of being overcome or subdued; unconquerable. [LL *indomitābilis*, untamable.]

In·do·ne·sia (ĭn′də-nē′zhə, -shə). A republic in the Malay Archipelago, comprising Java, Sumatra, part of Borneo, and other islands. Pop. 102,200,000. Cap. Djakarta, on Java.

In·do·ne·sian (ĭn′də-nē′zhən, -shən) *n.* **1.** A native or inhabitant of Indonesia. **2.** The national language of Indonesia. —**In′do·ne′sian** *adj.*

in·door (ĭn′dôr′, -dōr′) *adj.* Pertaining to, situated in, or carried on within the interior of a house.

in·doors (ĭn-dôrz′, -dōrz′) *adv.* In or into a house or other building.

in·dorse. Variant of **endorse.**

in·du·bi·ta·ble (ĭn-d/y/ōō′bə-tə-bəl) *adj.* Too

apparent to be doubted; unquestionable. —**in·du′bi·ta·bly** *adv.*

in·duce (ĭn-d/y/ōōs′) *v.* **-duced, -ducing. 1.** To persuade; prevail upon. **2.** To stimulate the occurrence of; cause. **3.** To infer by inductive reasoning. [< L *indūcere.*]

in·duce·ment (ĭn-d/y/ōōs′mənt) *n.* **1.** The act or process of inducing. **2.** An incentive; motive.

in·duct (ĭn-dŭkt′) *v.* **1.** To place formally in office; install. **2.** To admit as a member of; initiate. **3.** To call into military service. [< L *indūcere,* to lead in, INDUCE.] —**in′duc·tee′** *n.*

in·duc·tance (ĭn-dŭk′təns) *n.* A circuit element, typically a conducting coil, in which electromotive force is generated by induction.

in·duc·tion (ĭn-dŭk′shən) *n.* **1.** The act of inducting or being inducted. **2. a.** The generation of electromotive force in a closed circuit by a varying magnetic flux through the circuit. **b.** The charging of an isolated conducting object by momentarily grounding it while a charged body is nearby. **3. a.** Reasoning from the particular to the general. **b.** *Math.* A deductive method of proof in which verification of a proposition consists of proving the first case and the case immediately following an arbitrary case for which the proposition is assumed to be correct.

in·duc·tive (ĭn-dŭk′tĭv) *adj.* **1.** Of or utilizing induction: *inductive method.* **2.** Of or arising from inductance. —**in·duc′tive·ly** *adv.*

in·due. Variant of **endue.**

in·dulge (ĭn-dŭlj′) *v.* **-dulged, -dulging. 1.** To yield to the desires and whims of; pamper. **2.** To gratify; satisfy: *indulge a craving for chocolate.* **3.** To allow oneself some special pleasure (with *in*). [L *indulgēre,* to grant as a favor.] —**in·dulg′er** *n.*

in·dul·gence (ĭn-dŭl′jəns) *n.* **1.** The act of indulging or state of being indulgent. **2.** Something indulged in. **3.** Something granted as a favor or privilege. **4.** Liberal or lenient treatment; tolerance. **5.** *R.C.Ch.* The remission of temporal punishment due for a sin after the guilt has been forgiven.

in·dul·gent (ĭn-dŭl′jənt) *adj.* Given to indulgence; lenient. —**in·dul′gent·ly** *adv.*

In·dus (ĭn′dəs). A river of S Asia flowing through West Pakistan.

in·dus·tri·al (ĭn-dŭs′trē-əl) *adj.* **1.** Of or per-

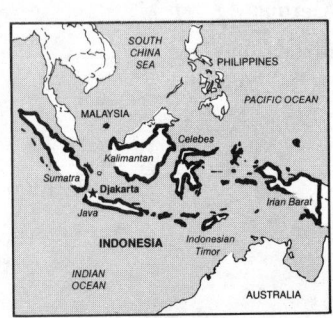

Indonesia

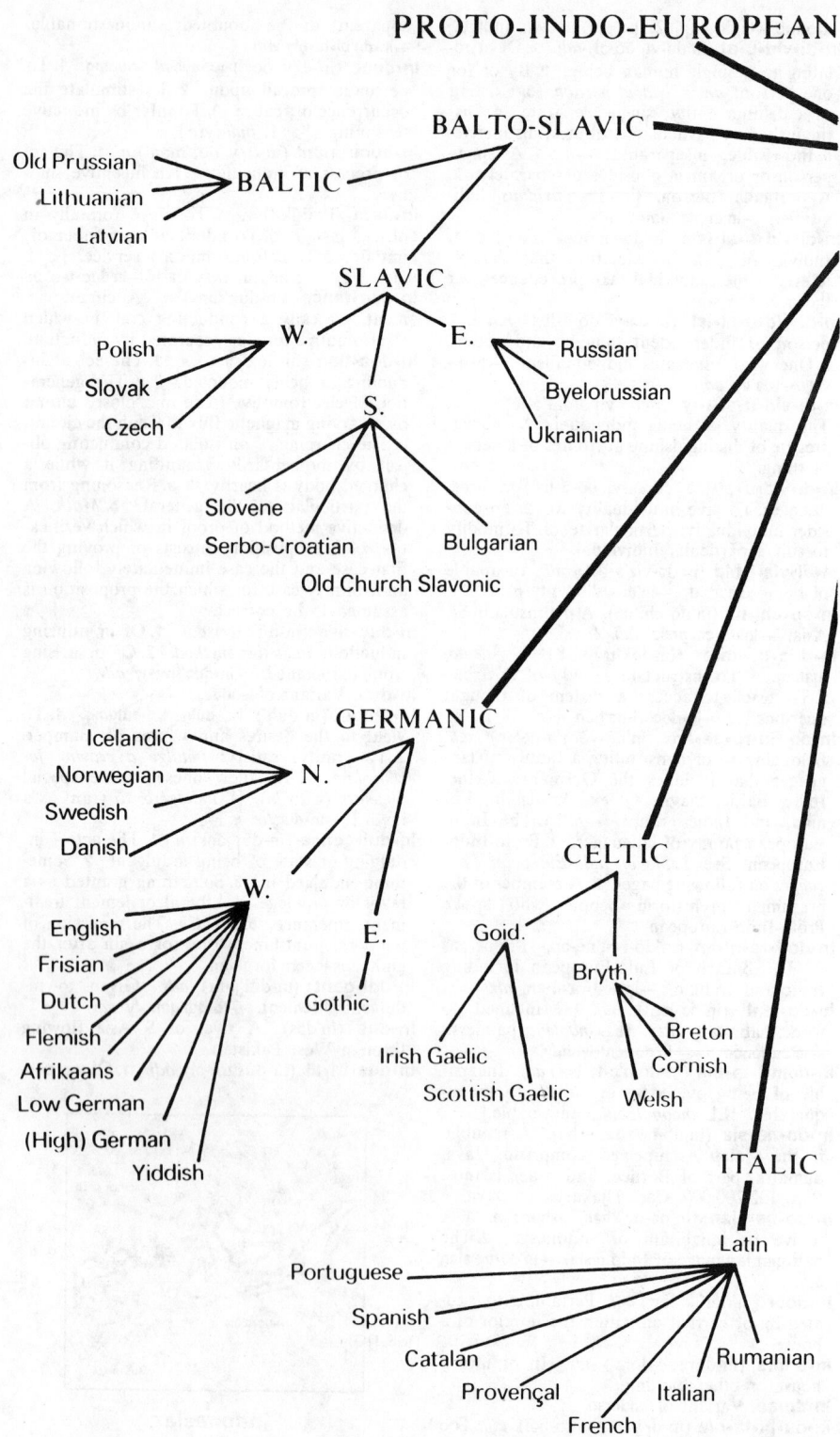

PROTO-INDO-EUROPEAN

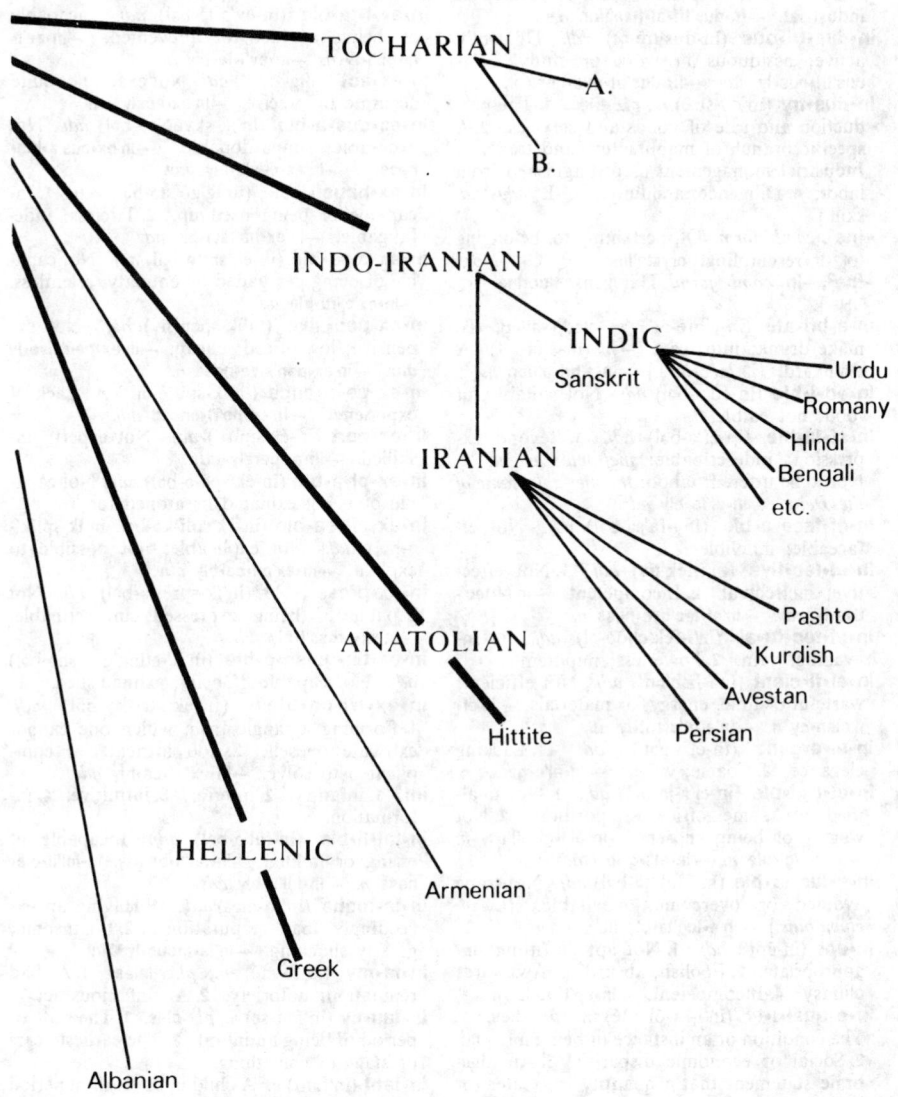

TOCHARIAN

A.

B.

INDO-IRANIAN

INDIC

Sanskrit

Urdu
Romany
Hindi
Bengali
etc.

IRANIAN

Pashto
Kurdish
Avestan
Persian

ANATOLIAN

Hittite

HELLENIC

Armenian

Greek

Albanian

THE INDO-EUROPEAN FAMILY OF LANGUAGES, of which English is a member, is descended from a prehistoric language, Proto-Indo-European, spoken in a region that has not yet been identified, possibly in the fifth millennium B.C. The chart shows the principal languages of the family, arranged in a diagrammatic form that displays their genetic relationships and loosely suggests their geographic distribution. This Dictionary contains an Appendix listing some of the Indo-European roots underlying English words.

taining to industry. **2.** Having highly developed industries: *an industrial nation.*

in·dus·tri·al·ist (ĭn-dŭs'trē-ə-lĭst) *n.* One owning or managing an industrial enterprise.

in·dus·tri·al·ize (ĭn-dŭs'trē-ə-līz') *v.* **-ized, -izing. 1.** To develop industry in. **2.** To become industrial. —**in·dus'tri·al·i·za'tion** *n.*

in·dus·tri·ous (ĭn-dŭs'trē-əs) *adj.* Diligently active; assiduous in work or study. —**in·dus'tri·ous·ly** *adv.* —**in·dus'tri·ous·ness** *n.*

in·dus·try (ĭn'də-strē) *n., pl.* **-tries. 1.** The production and sale of goods and services. **2.** A specific branch of manufacture and trade. **3.** Industrial management as distinguished from labor. **4.** Diligence; assiduity. [< L *industria,* skill.]

–ine¹. *comb. form.* Of, pertaining to, belonging to, or resembling: **crystalline.** [< Gk *-inos.*]

–ine², –in. *comb. form.* Halogens: **fluorine.** [< -INE.]

in·e·bri·ate (ĭn-ē'brē-āt') *v.* **-ated, -ating.** To make drunk; intoxicate. —*n.* (ĭn-ē'brē-ĭt). A drunkard. [L *inēbriāre.*] —**in·e'bri·a'tion** *n.*

in·ed·i·ble (ĭn-ĕd'ə-bəl) *adj.* Not suitable for food; not edible.

in·ef·fa·ble (ĭn-ĕf'ə-bəl) *adj.* **1.** Beyond expression; indescribable: *ineffable delight.* **2.** Not to be uttered; taboo: *the ineffable name of the Deity.* —**in·ef'fa·bly** *adv.*

in·ef·face·a·ble (ĭn'ĭ-fā'sə-bəl) *adj.* Not effaceable; indelible.

in·ef·fec·tive (ĭn'ĭ-fĕk'tĭv) *adj.* **1.** Not effective; ineffectual. **2.** Incompetent. —**in·ef·fec'tive·ly** *adv.* —**in·ef·fec'tive·ness** *n.*

in·ef·fec·tu·al (ĭn'ĭ-fĕk'chōō-əl) *adj.* **1.** Unavailing; vain. **2.** Powerless; impotent.

in·ef·fi·cient (ĭn'ĭ-fĭsh'ənt) *adj.* Not efficient; wasteful of time, energy, or materials. —**in·ef·fi'cien·cy** *n.* —**in·ef·fi'cient·ly** *adv.*

in·el·e·gant (ĭn-ĕl'ə-gənt) *adj.* **1.** Lacking elegance. **2.** Coarse; vulgar. —**in·el'e·gance** *n.*

in·el·i·gi·ble (ĭn-ĕl'ə-jə-bəl) *adj.* **1.** Not qualified for some office or position. **2.** Not worthy of being chosen. —**in·el'i·gi·bil'i·ty** *n.* —**in·el'i·gi·ble** *n.* —**in·el'i·gi·bly** *adv.*

in·e·luc·ta·ble (ĭn'ĭ-lŭk'tə-bəl) *adj.* Not to be avoided or overcome; inevitable. [L *inēluctābilis.*] —**in·e·luc'ta·bly** *adv.*

in·ept (ĭn-ĕpt') *adj.* **1.** Not apt or fitting; inappropriate. **2.** Foolish; absurd. **3.** Awkward; clumsy. **4.** Incompetent. —**in·ept'i·tude'** *n.*

in·e·qual·i·ty (ĭn'ĭ-kwŏl'ə-tē) *n., pl.* **-ties. 1.** The condition or an instance of being unequal. **2.** Social or economic disparity. **3.** An algebraic statement that a quantity is greater (or less) than another.

in·eq·ui·ta·ble (ĭn-ĕk'wə-tə-bəl) *adj.* Not equitable; unfair. —**in·eq'ui·ta·bly** *adv.*

in·eq·ui·ty (ĭn-ĕk'wə-tē) *n., pl.* **-ties. 1.** Lack of equity; injustice; unfairness. **2.** An instance of injustice or unfairness.

in·ert (ĭn-ûrt') *adj.* **1.** Unable to move or act. **2.** Sluggish; lethargic. **3. a.** Exhibiting no chemical activity. **b.** Exhibiting chemical activity under special conditions only. [L *iners,* inactive, unskilled.]

in·er·tia (ĭn-ûr'shə) *n.* **1.** The tendency of a body to resist acceleration. **2.** Resistance to motion, action, or change. —**in·er'tial** *adj.*

in·es·cap·a·ble (ĭn'ə-skā'pə-bəl) *adj.* That cannot be escaped; inevitable.

in·es·ti·ma·ble (ĭn-ĕs'tə-mə-bəl) *adj.* **1.** Incapable of being estimated. **2.** Of incalculable value. —**in·es'ti·ma·bly** *adv.*

in·ev·i·ta·ble (ĭn-ĕv'ə-tə-bəl) *adj.* Incapable of being avoided or prevented. —**in·ev'i·ta·bil'i·ty** *n.* —**in·ev'i·ta·bly** *adv.*

in·ex·act (ĭn'ĭg-zăkt') *adj.* Not exact; not quite accurate or precise. —**in·ex·act'ly** *adv.*

in·ex·cus·a·ble (ĭn'ĭk-skyōō'zə-bəl) *adj.* Not excusable; unpardonable. —**in·ex·cus'a·ble·ness** *n.* —**in·ex·cus'a·bly** *adv.*

in·ex·haust·i·ble (ĭn'ĭg-zô'stə-bəl) *adj.* **1.** Incapable of being used up. **2.** Tireless; indefatigable. —**in·ex·haust'i·bly** *adv.*

in·ex·o·ra·ble (ĭn-ĕk'sər-ə-bəl) *adj.* Not capable of being persuaded by entreaty; relentless. —**in·ex'o·ra·bly** *adv.*

in·ex·pen·sive (ĭn'ĭk-spĕn'sĭv) *adj.* Not expensive; low-priced; cheap. —**in·ex'pen·sive·ly** *adv.* —**in·ex·pen'sive·ness** *n.*

in·ex·pe·ri·ence (ĭn'ĭk-spîr'ē-əns) *n.* Lack of experience. —**in·ex·pe'ri·enced** *adj.*

in·ex·pert (ĭn-ĕk'spûrt') *adj.* Not expert; unskilled. —**in·ex'pert'ly** *adv.*

in·ex·pi·a·ble (ĭn-ĕk'spē-ə-bəl) *adj.* Not capable of being expiated or atoned for.

in·ex·pli·ca·ble (ĭn-ĕk'splĭ-kə-bəl, ĭn'ĭk-splĭk'-ə-bəl) *adj.* Not explicable; not possible to explain. —**in·ex'pli·ca·bly** *adv.*

in·ex·press·i·ble (ĭn'ĭk-sprĕs'ə-bəl) *adj.* Not capable of being expressed; indescribable. —**in·ex·press'i·bly** *adv.*

in·ex·tin·guish·a·ble (ĭn'ĭk-stĭng'gwĭ-shə-bəl) *adj.* Not capable of being extinguished.

in·ex·tri·ca·ble (ĭn-ĕk'strĭ-kə-bəl) *adj.* **1.** Forming a tangle from which one cannot extricate oneself. **2.** Too intricate or complicated to solve. —**in·ex'tri·ca·bly** *adv.*

inf. 1. infantry. **2.** inferior. **3.** infinitive. **4.** information.

in·fal·li·ble (ĭn-făl'ə-bəl) *adj.* Incapable of erring or failing. —**in·fal'li·bil'i·ty, in·fal'li·ble·ness** *n.* —**in·fal'li·bly** *adv.*

in·fa·mous (ĭn'fə-məs) *adj.* **1.** Having an exceedingly bad reputation. **2.** Loathsome; grossly shocking. —**in'fa·mous·ly** *adv.*

in·fa·my (ĭn'fə-mē) *n., pl.* **-mies. 1.** A bad reputation; notoriety. **2.** An infamous act.`

in·fan·cy (ĭn'fən-sē) *n., pl.* **-cies. 1.** The state or period of being an infant. **2.** The earliest years or stage of something.

in·fant (ĭn'fənt) *n.* A child in the earliest period of its life; a baby. —*adj.* **1.** Of or for infants or very young children. **2.** Young and growing: *an infant enterprise.* [< L *infāns,* "(one) unable to speak."]

in·fan·tile (ĭn'fən-tīl', -tĭl) *adj.* **1.** Of or relating to infants or infancy. **2.** Babyish; childish.

infantile paralysis. Poliomyelitis.

in·fan·try (ĭn'fən-trē) *n., pl.* **-tries.** The branch of an army made up of units trained to fight on foot. [< It *infante,* youth, foot soldier.] —**in'fan·try·man** *n.*

in·fat·u·ate (ĭn-făch'ōō-āt') *v.* **-ated, -ating.** To inspire with foolish and unreasoning passion

---

ă pat/ā ate/âr care/ä bar/b bib/ch chew/d deed/ĕ pet/ē be/f fit/g gag/h hat/hw what/
ĭ pit/ī pie/îr pier/j judge/k kick/l lid, fatal/m mum/n no, sudden/ng sing/ŏ pot/ō go/

or attraction. [L *infatuāre*.] —**in•fat'u•a'tion** *n.*

in•fect (ĭn-fĕkt') *v.* **1.** To contaminate with pathogenic microorganisms. **2.** To communicate a disease to. **3.** To affect as if by contagion: *His laughter infected us all.* [< L *inficere*, to work in, dye, taint.]

in•fec•tion (ĭn-fĕk'shən) *n.* **1.** Invasion of a bodily part by pathogenic microorganisms. **2.** The pathological state resulting from such invasion. **3.** An infectious disease.

in•fec•tious (ĭn-fĕk'shəs) *adj.* **1.** Capable of causing infection. **2.** Capable of being transmitted by infection, as a disease. **3.** Caused by a microorganism, as a disease. **4.** Tending to spread easily or catch on. —**in•fec'tious•ly** *adv.* —**in•fec'tious•ness** *n.*

in•fec•tive (ĭn-fĕk'tĭv) *adj.* Capable of producing infection. —**in•fec'tive•ness** *n.*

in•fe•lic•i•tous (ĭn'fə-lĭs'ə-təs) *adj.* **1.** Not happy; unfortunate; sad. **2.** Inappropriate; inopportune. —**in'fe•lic'i•ty** *n.*

in•fer (ĭn-fûr') *v.* **-ferred, -ferring. 1.** To conclude from evidence; deduce. **2.** To have as a logical consequence. [< L *inferre*, to bring in, introduce.] —**in•fer'a•ble** *adj.*

Usage: Infer and *imply*, in their most frequently used senses, are carefully distinguished in modern usage. To *imply* is to state indirectly, hint, or intimate. To *infer* is to draw a conclusion or make a deduction based on facts or indications. In these senses the words are not interchangeable.

in•fer•ence (ĭn'fər-əns) *n.* **1.** The act or process of inferring. **2.** Something inferred; a conclusion based on a premise. —**in'fer•en'tial** *adj.* —**in'fer•en'tial•ly** *adv.*

in•fe•ri•or (ĭn-fîr'ē-ər) *adj.* **1.** Situated under or beneath. **2.** Low or lower in order, degree, or rank. **3.** Low or lower in quality. —*n.* A person of lesser rank or status than others. [< L *inferus*, low.] —**in•fe'ri•or'i•ty** (-ôr'ə-tē, -ŏr'ə-tē) *n.*

in•fer•nal (ĭn-fûr'nəl) *adj.* **1.** Of or relating to hell. **2.** Abominable; damnable. [< LL *infernus*, hell < L, lower.]

in•fer•no (ĭn-fûr'nō) *n., pl.* **-nos. 1.** Hell. **2.** Any place likened to hell.

in•fer•tile (ĭn-fûrt'l) *adj.* Not fertile; unproductive; barren.

in•fest (ĭn-fĕst') *v.* To overrun in large numbers so as to be harmful or unpleasant. [< L *infestus*, hostile.] —**in'fes•ta'tion** *n.*

in•fi•del (ĭn'fə-dəl, -dĕl') *n.* **1.** One who has no religious beliefs. **2.** One who does not accept a certain religion, esp. Christianity or Islam. [< L *infidēlis*, unfaithful.] —**in'fi•del** *adj.*

in•fi•del•i•ty (ĭn'fə-dĕl'ə-tē) *n., pl.* **-ties. 1.** Lack of religious faith. **2.** Lack of fidelity; unfaithfulness.

in•field (ĭn'fēld') *n.* **1.** The area of a baseball field within the base lines. **2.** The defensive positions of first base, second base, third base, and shortstop. —**in'field'er** *n.*

in•fight•ing (ĭn'fī'tĭng) *n.* **1.** Fighting at close range. **2.** Conflict, as within an organization, that is generally concealed from outsiders.

in•fil•trate (ĭn-fĭl'trāt', ĭn'fĭl-) *v.* **-trated, -trating. 1.** To pass or cause (a liquid or gas) to pass into. **2.** To pass, enter, or join surreptitiously. —**in'fil•tra'tion** *n.*

infin. infinitive.

in•fi•nite (ĭn'fə-nĭt) *adj.* **1.** Having no boundaries or limits. **2.** *Math.* Existing beyond or being greater than any arbitrarily large value. **3.** Unlimited in spatial extent. **4.** Continuing endlessly in time. —*n.* Something infinite. —**in'fi•nite•ly** *adv.* —**in'fi•nite•ness** *n.*

in•fin•i•tes•i•mal (ĭn'fĭn-ə-tĕs'ə-məl) *adj.* **1.** Immeasurably or incalculably minute. **2.** *Math.* Capable of having values arbitrarily close to zero. —**in'fin•i•tes'i•mal•ly** *adv.*

in•fin•i•tive (ĭn-fĭn'ə-tĭv) *n.* An uninflected verb form used: **1.** Preceded by *to:* **a.** As a substantive with some verbal aspects, such as connection with an object: *To go willingly is to show strength.* **b.** In verb phrases: *He wished to go.* **2.** With certain verbs without *to: He may go.* [< L *infinītus*, infinite.] —**in•fin'i•tive** *adj.*

in•fin•i•ty (ĭn-fĭn'ə-tē) *n., pl.* **-ties. 1.** The quality or condition of being infinite. **2.** Unbounded space, time, or quantity. **3.** An indefinitely large number.

in•firm (ĭn-fûrm') *adj.* **1.** Weak in body, esp. from old age; feeble. **2.** Not stable; insecure.

in•fir•ma•ry (ĭn-fûr'mə-rē) *n., pl.* **-ries.** A place for the care of the sick or injured.

in•fir•mi•ty (ĭn-fûr'mə-tē) *n., pl.* **-ties. 1.** Feebleness. **2.** An unhealthy state; a malady.

in•fix (ĭn'fĭks') *n. Ling.* An inflectional or derivational element inserted into the body of a word.

in•flame (ĭn-flām') *v.* **-flamed, -flaming. 1.** To set on fire. **2.** To arouse to strong emotion. **3.** To intensify. **4.** To produce or be affected by inflammation.

in•flam•ma•ble (ĭn-flăm'ə-bəl) *adj.* **1.** Tending to ignite easily; flammable. **2.** Easily aroused to strong emotion.

in•flam•ma•tion (ĭn'flə-mā'shən) *n.* Localized heat, redness, swelling, and pain as a result of irritation, injury, or infection.

in•flam•ma•to•ry (ĭn-flăm'ə-tôr'ē, -tōr'ē) *adj.* **1.** Arousing strong emotion. **2.** Characterized or caused by inflammation.

in•flate (ĭn-flāt') *v.* **-flated, -flating. 1.** To fill and swell with a gas. **2.** To cause to increase or puff up. **3.** To raise or expand abnormally, as prices, wages, etc. [L *inflāre*, to blow into.]

in•fla•tion (ĭn-flā'shən) *n.* **1.** The act of inflating or state of being inflated. **2.** An abnormal increase in available currency and credit, resulting in a rise in price levels. —**in•fla'tion•ar'y** (-shə-nĕr'ē) *adj.*

in•flect (ĭn-flĕkt') *v.* **1.** To alter (the voice) in tone or pitch; modulate. **2.** *Gram.* To subject to or be modified by inflection. [< L *inflectere*, to bend, warp, change.]

in•flec•tion (ĭn-flĕk'shən) *n.* **1.** An alteration in pitch or tone of voice. **2.** *Gram.* **a.** An alteration of the form of a word to indicate different grammatical and syntactic relations. **b.** An element added to a word to denote a grammatical function. —**in•flec'tion•al** *adj.*

in•flexed (ĭn-flĕkst') *adj.* Bent or curved inward or downward, as petals or sepals.

in•flex•i•ble (ĭn-flĕk'sə-bəl) *adj.* **1.** Not flexible; rigid. **2.** Incapable of being changed; unalterable. **3.** Unyielding. —**in•flex′i•bil′i•ty** *n.* —**in•flex′i•bly** *adv.*

in•flict (ĭn-flĭkt′) *v.* **1.** To cause or carry out by aggressive action. **2.** To impose. **3.** To afflict. [L *inflīgere.*] —**in•flic′tion** *n.*

in•flu•ence (ĭn′flōō-əns) *n.* **1.** A power indirectly or intangibly affecting a person or course of events. **2. a.** Power to sway or affect based on prestige, wealth, etc. **b.** A person or thing exercising such power. —*v.* -**enced,** -**encing. 1.** To have power over; affect. **2.** To modify. [< L *influere,* to flow in.] —**in′flu•enc•er** *n.* —**in′flu•en′tial** (-ĕn′shəl) *adj.*

in•flu•en•za (ĭn′flōō-ĕn′zə) *n.* An acute infectious viral disease characterized by inflammation of the respiratory tract, fever, muscular pain, and intestinal irritation. [< ML *influentia,* influence.]

in•flux (ĭn′flŭks′) *n.* A flowing in. [< L *influere,* to flow in.]

in•fold (ĭn-fōld′) *v.* **1.** To fold inward. **2.** Variant of **enfold.** —**in•fold′er** *n.*

in•form (ĭn-fôrm′) *v.* **1.** To impart information to; tell. **2.** To disclose or give often incriminating information. [< L *informāre,* to give form to.] —**in•form′ant, in•form′er** *n.*

in•for•mal (ĭn-fôr′məl) *adj.* **1.** Completed or performed without ceremony or formality. **2.** Of, for, pertaining to, or appropriate to ordinary use; casual. —**in′for•mal′i•ty** (ĭn′fôr-mǎl′ə-tē) *n.* —**in•for′mal•ly** *adv.*

in•for•ma•tion (ĭn′fər-mā′shən) *n.* **1.** The act of informing or condition of being informed; communication of knowledge. **2.** Knowledge derived from study, experience, or instruction. **3.** Knowledge of a specific event or situation; news. —**in′for•ma′tion•al** *adj.*

in•form•a•tive (ĭn-fôr′mə-tĭv) *adj.* Providing information; instructive.

infra-. *comb. form.* **1.** Below; beneath. **2.** After; later. [L *infrā,* below, beneath.]

in•frac•tion (ĭn-frǎk′shən) *n.* The act of breaching; infringement; violation.

in•fra•red (ĭn′frə-rĕd′) *adj.* Pertaining to electromagnetic radiation having wavelengths greater than those of visible light and shorter than those of microwaves.

in•fra•son•ic (ĭn′frə-sŏn′ĭk) *adj.* Generating or using waves or vibrations with frequencies below the limit of audible sound.

in•fre•quent (ĭn-frē′kwənt) *adj.* **1.** Not frequent; rare. **2.** Not steady; occasional. —**in•fre′quence** *n.* —**in•fre′quent•ly** *adv.*

in•fringe (ĭn-frĭnj′) *v.* -**fringed,** -**fringing. 1.** To break or ignore the terms or obligations of an agreement, law, etc.; violate. **2.** To trespass; encroach. [L *infringere.*] —**in•fringe′ment** *n.*

in•fu•ri•ate (ĭn-fyŏŏr′ē-āt′) *v.* -**ated,** -**ating.** To make furious; enrage. [ML *infuriāre,* to enrage.]

in•fuse (ĭn-fyōōz′) *v.* -**fused,** -**fusing. 1.** To fill; imbue. **2.** To instill; inculcate. **3.** To steep or soak without boiling. [< L *infundere,* to pour in.] —**in•fus′er** *n.*

in•fus•i•ble (ĭn-fyōō′zə-bəl) *adj.* Incapable of being fused or melted; resistant to heat.

in•fu•sion (ĭn-fyōō′zhən) *n.* **1.** The act or proc-

ess of infusing. **2.** An admixture. **3.** The liquid product obtained by infusing.

–ing[1]. *comb. form.* Used to form: **1.** The present participle of verbs: **hoping. 2.** Participial adjectives: **crippling. 3.** Adjectives resembling participial adjectives but not derived from verbs: **swashbuckling.** [< OE -*ende.*]

–ing[2]. *comb. form.* Used to form nouns from verbs, nouns, and other parts of speech. **1.** The act, process, or art of performing an action designated by a root verb: **thinking. 2.** The one that accomplishes such an action: **coating. 3.** Something necessary for the performance of such an action: **mooring. 4.** The result of such an action: **drawing. 5.** Belonging to or connected with the character of the noun root: **boarding. 6.** An action upon or involving the noun root: **sounding.** [< OE.]

in•gen•ious (ĭn-jēn′yəs) *adj.* **1.** Owing to or displaying ingenuity. **2.** Resourceful; clever. [< L *ingenium,* inborn talent, skill.]

in•gé•nue (ăn′zhə-n/y/ōō′) *n.* **1.** An artless, innocent girl or young woman. **2.** An actress playing an ingénue. [< L *ingenuus,* INGENUOUS.]

in•ge•nu•i•ty (ĭn′jə-n/y/ōō′ə-tē) *n.* Inventive skill or imagination; cleverness. [< L *ingenuus,* INGENUOUS.]

in•gen•u•ous (ĭn-jĕn′yōō-əs) *adj.* **1.** Without sophistication; artless; innocent. **2.** Open or honest; frank; candid. [L *ingenuus,* native, noble, honest.] —**in•gen′u•ous•ly** *adv.*

in•gest (ĭn-jĕst′) *v.* To take in by or as if by swallowing. [L *ingerere,* to carry in.] —**in•ges′tion** *n.*

in•glo•ri•ous (ĭn-glôr′ē-əs, ĭn-glōr′-) *adj.* Ignominious; dishonorable.

in•got (ĭng′gət) *n.* A mass of metal shaped for convenient storage or transportation. [< IN + OE *geotan,* to pour, cast in metal.]

in•grained (ĭn-grānd′) *adj.* **1.** Imbued; deepseated: *ingrained faults.* **2.** Complete; utter.

in•grate (ĭn′grāt′) *n.* An ungrateful person. [< L *ingrātus,* ungrateful.]

in•gra•ti•ate (ĭn-grā′shē-āt′) *v.* -**ated,** -**ating.** To bring (oneself) purposely into the favor of another. —**in•gra′ti•a′tion** *n.*

in•grat•i•tude (ĭn-grăt′ə-t/y/ōōd′) *n.* Ungratefulness.

in•gre•di•ent (ĭn-grē′dē-ənt) *n.* **1.** Something added or required to form a mixture or compound. **2.** A component or constituent. [< L *ingredī,* to enter into.]

in•gress (ĭn′grĕs′) *n.* An entrance or entering. [< L *ingredī,* to enter into.]

in•grown (ĭn′grōn′) *adj.* Grown abnormally into the flesh.

in•gui•nal (ĭng′gwə-nəl) *adj.* Of or located in the groin. [< L *inguen,* groin.]

in•hab•it (ĭn-hăb′ĭt) *v.* To live or reside in. [< L *inhabitāre.*] —**in•hab′i•ta•ble** *adj.*

in•hab•i•tant (ĭn-hăb′ə-tənt) *n.* A permanent resident.

in•ha•la•tor (ĭn′hə-lā′tər) *n.* A device that produces a vapor to ease breathing or medicate by inspiration.

in•hale (ĭn-hāl′) *v.* -**haled,** -**haling.** To draw in by breathing; breathe in. [L *inhālāre.*] —**in•ha′lant**

ă pat/ā ate/âr care/ä bar/b bib/ch chew/d deed/ĕ pet/ē be/f fit/g gag/h hat/hw what/
ĭ pit/ī pie/îr pier/j judge/k kick/l lid, fatal/m mum/n no, sudden/ng sing/ŏ pot/ō go/

adj. & n. —in'ha•la'tion (ĭn'hə-lā'shən) n. —in•
hal'er n.

in•here (ĭn-hîr') v. -hered, -hering. To be inherent or innate. [L inhaerēre.]

in•her•ent (ĭn-hîr'ənt, -hĕr'ənt) adj. Existing
as an essential part; intrinsic. —in•her'ent•ly
adv.

in•her•it (ĭn-hĕr'ĭt) v. 1. To receive, esp. by
legal succession or will. 2. To receive (a character or characteristic) genetically from an
ancestor. [< L inhērēdĭtāre.] —in•her'it•a•ble
adj. —in•her'i•tor n.

in•her•i•tance (ĭn-hĕr'ə-təns) n. 1. The act of
inheriting. 2. That which is inherited or to be
inherited; legacy. 3. a. The process of genetic
transmission of characters or characteristics.
b. The configuration of characters or characteristics so inherited.

in•hib•it (ĭn-hĭb'ĭt) v. 1. To restrain; repress.
2. To prohibit; forbid. [< L inhibēre, to restrain, hold in.] —in'hi•bi'tion n.

in•hib•i•tor (ĭn-hĭb'ə-tər) n. A substance used
to retard or halt an undesirable reaction such
as rusting.

in•hos•pi•ta•ble (ĭn-hŏs'pĭ-tə-bəl, ĭn'hŏ-spĭt'-
ə-bəl) adj. 1. Unfriendly. 2. Not affording
shelter or sustenance; barren.

in•hu•man (ĭn-hyōō'mən) adj. 1. Not human.
2. Lacking kindness or sympathy; cruel. 3.
Not of ordinary human form.

in•hu•mane (ĭn'hyōō-mān') adj. Not humane;
lacking in pity or compassion.

in•hu•man•i•ty (ĭn'hyōō-măn'ə-tē) n., pl. -ties.
1. Lack of pity or compassion. 2. An inhuman
or cruel act.

in•im•i•cal (ĭn-ĭm'ĭ-kəl) adj. 1. Harmful; adverse. 2. Unfriendly; hostile. [< L inimícus,
enemy.] —in•im'i•cal•ly adv.

in•im•i•ta•ble (ĭn-ĭm'ĭ-tə-bəl) adj. Defying imitation; matchless. —in•im'i•ta•bly adv.

in•iq•ui•ty (ĭ-nĭk'wə-tē) n., pl. -ties. 1. Moral
turpitude or sin; wickedness. 2. A grossly immoral act; a sin. [< L iníquus, unjust.] —in•
iq'ui•tous adj. —in•iq'ui•tous•ly adv.

in•i•tial (ĭ-nĭsh'əl) adj. Occurring first. —n.
1. Often initials. The first letter or letters of a
person's name. 2. The first letter of a word.
—v. -tialed, -tialing. To mark or sign with one's
own initials. [< L initium, beginning.] —in•
i'tial•ly adv.

in•i•ti•ate (ĭ-nĭsh'ē-āt') v. -ated, -ating. 1. To
begin or originate. 2. To introduce (a person)
to a new field, interest, skill, etc. 3. To admit
into membership, as with ceremonies. —n.
(ĭ-nĭsh'ē-ĭt). 1. One who has been initiated.
2. A novice; beginner. —in•i'ti•ate (-ē-ĭt) adj.
—in•i'ti•a'tion n. —in•i'ti•a'tor n.

in•i•ti•a•tive (ĭ-nĭsh'ē-ə-tĭv, -ē'ə-tĭv, -nĭsh'ə-tĭv)
n. 1. The ability to begin or follow through
with a plan; enterprise. 2. The first step or
action; opening move. 3. The procedure by
which citizens can propose a law by petition
and ensure its submission to the electorate.

in•ject (ĭn-jĕkt') v. 1. To force or drive (a fluid)
into. 2. To introduce (a comment or new
element) into conversation or consideration.
[L injicere, to throw or put in.] —in•jec'tion n.

in•junc•tion (ĭn-jŭngk'shən) n. 1. A command,

directive, or order. 2. A court order enjoining
or prohibiting a party from a specific course of
action. [< L injungere, to enjoin.]

in•jure (ĭn'jər) v. -jured, -juring. 1. To harm;
hurt; damage. 2. To commit an offense
against; wrong. —in'jur•er n.

in•ju•ry (ĭn'jə-rē) n., pl. -ries. 1. Damage of or
to a person, property, reputation, or thing.
2. A specific damage or wound. [< L injúrius,
unjust, wrongful.] —in•ju'ri•ous (ĭn-jōōr'ē-əs)
adj. —in•ju'ri•ous•ly adv.

in•jus•tice (ĭn-jŭs'tĭs) n. 1. Lack of justice.
2. A specific unjust act; a wrong.

ink (ĭngk) n. A pigmented liquid or paste used
esp. for writing or printing. [< Gk enkauston,
purple ink.]

ink•ling (ĭngk'lĭng) n. 1. A hint or intimation.
2. A vague idea or notion. [< ME inkle, to
mutter.]

ink•well (ĭngk'wĕl') n. A small reservoir for
ink.

ink•y (ĭng'kē) adj. -ier, -iest. 1. Of or containing
ink. 2. Dark or murky. 3. Stained with ink.

in•laid (ĭn'lād', ĭn-lād') adj. Decorated with a
pattern set into a surface.

in•land (ĭn'lənd) adj. 1. Of or located in the
interior part of a land mass. 2. Operating or
applying within the borders of a country.
—adv. In, toward, or into the interior of a
country. —n. The interior of a country.

in•law (ĭn'lô') n. Any relative by marriage. [<
-IN-LAW.]

–in-law. comb. form. Parental, filial, or fraternal relation through marriage: **father-in-law.**

in•lay (ĭn-lā', ĭn'lā') v. To set into a surface to
form a design. —n. (ĭn'lā'). 1. An inlaid object
or design. 2. A solid filling, as of gold, fitted to
a cavity in a tooth and cemented in place.

in•let (ĭn'lĕt, -lĭt) n. 1. A narrow channel or
pocket of water. 2. A stream or bay leading
inland.

in•mate (ĭn'māt') n. 1. A resident in a building.
2. A person confined to an institution, as a
prison. [Perh INN + MATE.]

in•most (ĭn'mōst') adj. Innermost.

inn (ĭn) n. 1. A public lodging house; hotel.
2. A tavern or restaurant. [< OE. See en.]

in•nards (ĭn'ərdz) pl.n. Informal. 1. Internal
bodily organs; viscera. 2. Any inner parts.
[Var of INWARDS.]

in•nate (ĭ-nāt', ĭn'āt') adj. 1. Possessed at birth;
inborn. 2. Possessed as an essential characteristic; inherent. [< L innāscī, to be born
in.] —in•nate'ly adv. —in•nate'ness n.

in•ner (ĭn'ər) adj. 1. Located further inside.
2. Occurring within. 3. Pertaining to the soul
or mind. 4. More exclusive, private, or important. [< OE innera, innra.]

inner city. The older, central part of a city,
especially when characterized by crowded,
rundown low-income neighborhoods.

in•ner-cit•y (ĭn'ər-sĭt'ē) adj. Of or in an inner
city.

inner ear. The part of the ear that contains the
semicircular canals and cochlea.

in•ner•most (ĭn'ər-mōst') adj. 1. Farthest within. 2. Most intimate.

in•ner•vate (ĭ-nûr'vāt', ĭn'ər-) v. -vated, -vating.

ō paw, for/oi boy/ou out/ōō took/ōō coo/p pop/r run/s sauce/sh shy/t to/th thin/*th* the/
ŭ cut/ûr fur/v van/w wag/y yes/z size/zh vision/ə ago, item, edible, gallop, circus/

To supply (a bodily part) with nerves. —**in·ner·va'tion** *n.*

in·ning (ĭn'ĭng) *n. Baseball.* A division or period of a game in which each team has a turn at bat. [< IN.]

inn·keep·er (ĭn'kē'pər) *n.* One who manages an inn.

in·no·cent (ĭn'ə-sənt) *adj.* **1.** Uncorrupted by evil or wrongdoing; pure. **2.** Not guilty of a crime. **3.** Harmless. **4.** Not experienced or worldly; naive. **5.** Without deception or guile. [< L *innocēns.*] —**in'no·cence** *n.* —**in'no·cent** *n.* —**in'no·cent·ly** *adv.*

in·noc·u·ous (ĭ-nŏk'yŏŏ-əs) *adj.* **1.** Having no adverse effect; harmless. **2.** Lacking import; insignificant. [< L *innocuus.*]

in·nom·i·nate bone (ĭ-nŏm'ə-nĭt). A large flat bone forming the lateral half of the pelvis; hipbone.

in·no·vate (ĭn'ə-vāt') *v.* **-vated, -vating.** To begin or introduce (something new). [L *innovāre,* to renew.] —**in'no·va'tion** *n.* —**in'no·va'tive** *adj.* —**in'no·va'tor** *n.*

in·nu·en·do (ĭn'yŏŏ-ĕn'dō) *n., pl.* **-does.** An indirect, subtle, often derogatory implication. [< L *innuere,* to nod to.]

in·nu·mer·a·ble (ĭ-n/y/ŏŏ'mər-ə-bəl) *adj.* Too many to be counted.

in·oc·u·late (ĭ-nŏk'yə-lāt') *v.* **-lated, -lating.** To introduce the virus of a disease or other antigenic material into (the body) in order to immunize, cure, or experiment. [< L *inoculāre,* to engraft.] —**in·oc'u·la'tion** *n.*

in·of·fen·sive (ĭn'ə-fĕn'sĭv) *adj.* Giving no offense; unobjectionable.

in·op·er·a·ble (ĭn-ŏp'ər-ə-bəl) *adj.* **1.** Not operable. **2.** Not susceptible to surgery.

in·op·er·a·tive (ĭn-ŏp'ər-ə-tĭv) *adj.* Not working or functioning.

in·op·por·tune (ĭn-ŏp'ər-t/y/ŏŏn') *adj.* Inconvenient; ill-timed. —**in'op'por·tune'ly** *adv.*

in·or·di·nate (ĭn-ôrd'n-ĭt) *adj.* **1.** Immoderate; unrestrained. **2.** Not regulated; disorderly. [< L *inordinātus.*] —**in·or'di·nate·ly** *adv.*

in·or·gan·ic (ĭn'ôr-găn'ĭk) *adj.* **1.** Involving neither organic life nor the products of organic life. **2.** Relating to the chemistry of compounds not usually classified as organic. —**in'or·gan'i·cal·ly** *adv.*

in·pa·tient (ĭn'pā'shənt) *n.* A patient living in a hospital.

in·put (ĭn'pŏŏt') *n.* Anything put into a system or expended in its operation to achieve a result or output.

in·quest (ĭn'kwĕst') *n.* **1.** A judicial inquiry, usually before a jury. **2.** An investigation.

in·qui·e·tude (ĭn-kwī'ə-t/y/ŏŏd') *n.* **1.** Restlessness. **2.** Uneasiness.

in·quire (ĭn-kwīr') *v.* **-quired, -quiring.** **1.** To ask or ask about. **2.** To examine closely; investigate. [< L *inquīrere.*] —**in·quir'er** *n.* —**in·quir'ing·ly** *adv.*

in·quir·y (ĭn'kwĭr'ē, ĭn'kwə-rē) *n., pl.* **-ies.** **1.** The act of inquiring. **2.** A question; query. **3.** A close examination.

in·qui·si·tion (ĭn'kwə-zĭsh'ən) *n.* **1.** An official investigation, as an inquest. **2. Inquisition.** A former Roman Catholic tribunal directed at the suppression of heresy. **3.** Any severe scrutiny. —**in'qui·si'tion·al** *adj.* —**in·quis'i·tor** *n.*

in·quis·i·tive (ĭn-kwĭz'ə-tĭv) *adj.* **1.** Unduly curious. **2.** Eager to learn.

in·road (ĭn'rōd') *n.* **1.** An invasion; raid; incursion. **2.** An encroachment; intrusion.

in·rush (ĭn'rŭsh') *n.* A sudden rushing in; influx.

ins. insurance.

in·sane (ĭn-sān') *adj.* **1.** Of, exhibiting, or afflicted with mental disorder. **2.** Used by or for the mentally deranged. **3.** Very foolish; wild. —**in·sane'ly** *adv.* —**in·san'i·ty** (-săn'ə-tē) *n.*

in·sa·tia·ble (ĭn-sā'shə-bəl, -shē-ə-bəl) *adj.* Incapable of being satiated.

in·sa·ti·ate (ĭn-sā'shē-ĭt) *adj.* Not satisfied; insatiable. —**in·sa'ti·ate·ly** *adv.*

in·scribe (ĭn-skrīb') *v.* **-scribed, -scribing.** **1.** To write, print, or engrave (words or letters) on a surface. **2.** To mark or engrave with words or letters. **3.** To enter (a name) on a list. **4.** To dedicate to another, as a book. **5.** To enclose (a polygon or polyhedron) within a closed configuration of lines, curves, or surfaces so that every vertex of the enclosed figure is incident on the enclosing configuration. [L *inscrībere.*] —**in·scrib'er** *n.*

in·scrip·tion (ĭn-skrĭp'shən) *n.* **1.** The act or an instance of inscribing. **2.** That which is inscribed.

in·scru·ta·ble (ĭn-skrŏŏ'tə-bəl) *adj.* Impenetrable; enigmatic. —**in·scru'ta·bil'i·ty, in·scru'ta·ble·ness** *n.* —**in·scru'ta·bly** *adv.*

in·sect (ĭn'sĕkt') *n.* Any of numerous usually small, usually winged invertebrate animals having three pairs of legs and a three-segmented body. [< L *insecāre,* to cut into.]

in·sec·ti·cide (ĭn-sĕk'tə-sīd') *n.* A substance used to kill insects.

in·sec·tiv·o·rous (ĭn'sĕk-tĭv'ər-əs) *adj.* Feeding on insects.

in·se·cure (ĭn'sĭ-kyŏŏr') *adj.* **1.** Not secure or safe. **2.** Unstable; shaky. **3.** Apprehensive or lacking self-confidence. —**in'se·cure'ly** *adv.* —**in'se·cu'ri·ty, in'se·cure'ness** *n.*

in·sem·i·nate (ĭn-sĕm'ə-nāt') *v.* **-nated, -nating.** To introduce semen into the uterus of. —**in·sem'i·na'tion** *n.* —**in·sem'i·na'tor** *n.*

in·sen·sate (ĭn-sĕn'sāt', -sĭt) *adj.* **1.** Inanimate. **2.** Inhuman; unfeeling. **3.** Lacking sense; foolish. —**in·sen'sate'ly** *adv.*

in·sen·si·ble (ĭn-sĕn'sə-bəl) *adj.* **1.** Imperceptible; inappreciable. **2.** Unconscious. **3. a.** Unsusceptible to or unaffected by. **b.** Incognizant. **c.** Indifferent; callous. —**in·sen'si·bil'i·ty** *n.* —**in·sen'si·bly** *adv.*

in·sen·ti·ent (ĭn-sĕn'shənt) *adj.* Without sensation or consciousness. —**in·sen'ti·ence** *n.*

in·sep·a·ra·ble (ĭn-sĕp'ər-ə-bəl) *adj.* Incapable of being separated. —**in·sep'a·ra·bil'i·ty, in·sep'a·ra·ble·ness** *n.* —**in·sep'a·ra·bly** *adv.*

in·sert (ĭn-sûrt') *v.* **1.** To put, or thrust into. **2.** To introduce into; interpolate. —*n.* (ĭn'sûrt'). Something inserted or intended for insertion. [L *inserere.*] —**in·ser'tion** *n.*

in·set (ĭn-sĕt') *v.* To insert; set in. —**in'set'** *n.*

in·side (ĭn-sīd', ĭn'sīd') *n.* **1.** The inner or interior part. **2.** An inner side or surface. **3.**

insides. *Informal.* a. The inner organs; entrails. b. The inner parts or workings. 4. *Slang.* A position of confidence or influence. —*adj.* 1. Inner; interior. 2. For the interior. —*adv.* (ĭn'sīd'). Into or in the interior; within. —*prep.* (ĭn'sīd'). 1. Within: *inside an hour.* 2. Into: *go inside the house.*

in·sid·er (ĭn-sī'dər) *n.* One having a position of confidence or influence.

in·sid·i·ous (ĭn-sĭd'ē-əs) *adj.* 1. Working or spreading harmfully in a subtle or stealthy manner. 2. Intended to entrap; treacherous. 3. Sly; beguiling. [L *insidiōsus,* "lying in wait for."] —**in·sid'i·ous·ly** *adv.*

in·sight (ĭn'sīt') *n.* 1. The capacity to discern the true nature of a situation. 2. An elucidating glimpse.

in·sig·ni·a (ĭn-sĭg'nē-ə) *n., pl.* **-nia** or **-as.** Also **in·sig·ne** (-nē). 1. A badge of office, rank, etc.; emblem. 2. A distinguishing sign. [< L *insignis,* distinguished, marked.]

in·sig·nif·i·cant (ĭn'sĭg-nĭf'ĭ-kənt) *adj.* 1. Trivial. 2. Small. 3. Meaningless. —**in'sig·nif'i·cance** *n.* —**in'sig·nif'i·cant·ly** *adv.*

in·sin·cere (ĭn'sĭn-sîr') *adj.* Not sincere; hypocritical. —**in'sin·cere'ly** *adv.* —**in'sin·cer'i·ty** (-sĕr'ə-tē) *n.*

in·sin·u·ate (ĭn-sĭn'yōō-āt') *v.* **-ated, -ating.** 1. a. To introduce gradually and insidiously. b. To edge or worm (oneself) by subtle and artful means. 2. To hint covertly. [L *insinuāre,* to wind one's way into.] —**in·sin'u·a'tion** *n.*

in·sip·id (ĭn-sĭp'ĭd) *adj.* 1. Lacking flavor or zest; tasteless. 2. Uninteresting; dull; vapid. [LL *insipidus.*] —**in·sip'id·ly** *adv.*

in·sist (ĭn-sĭst') *v.* 1. To keep resolutely to or emphasize an assertion, demand, or course. 2. To assert or demand vehemently and persistently. [L *insistere,* to stand on.] —**in·sis'tence, in·sis'ten·cy** *n.* —**in·sis'tent** *adj.*

in·so·far (ĭn'sō-fär') *adv.* —**insofar as.** To such an extent.

in·sole (ĭn'sōl') *n.* 1. The inner sole of a shoe or boot. 2. An extra strip put inside a shoe for comfort.

in·so·lent (ĭn'sə-lənt) *adj.* 1. Insulting in manner or speech; arrogant. 2. Audaciously impudent. [< L *insolēns.*] —**in'so·lence** *n.*

in·sol·u·ble (ĭn-sŏl'yə-bəl) *adj.* 1. Incapable of being dissolved. 2. Incapable of being solved or explained. —**in·sol'u·bil'i·ty** *n.*

in·sol·vent (ĭn-sŏl'vənt) *adj.* Unable to meet debts or discharge liabilities; bankrupt. —**in·sol'ven·cy** *n.*

in·som·ni·a (ĭn-sŏm'nē-ə) *n.* Chronic inability to sleep. [< L *insomnis,* sleepless.] —**in·som'ni·ac'** (-ăk') *n.*

in·so·much (ĭn'sō-mŭch') *adv.* 1. To such extent or degree. 2. **insomuch as.** Since.

in·sou·ci·ant (ĭn-sōō'sē-ənt) *adj.* Blithely indifferent; carefree. [F.] —**in·sou'ci·ance** *n.*

insp. inspected; inspector.

in·spect (ĭn-spĕkt') *v.* 1. To examine carefully and critically. 2. To review or examine officially. [< L *inspicere,* to look into.] —**in·spec'tion** *n.* —**in·spec'tor** *n.*

in·spi·ra·tion (ĭn'spə-rā'shən) *n.* 1. The act of inspiring. 2. The condition of being inspired.

3. An inspiring agency or influence. 4. Something that is inspired. 5. Inhalation. —**in'spi·ra'tion·al** *adj.* —**in'spi·ra'tion·al·ly** *adv.*

in·spire (ĭn-spīr') *v.* **-spired, -spiring.** 1. To animate the mind or emotions of. 2. To stimulate and influence. 3. To elicit; create. 4. To inhale. [< L *inspīrāre,* to breathe into.]

in·spir·it (ĭn-spîr'ĭt) *v.* To instill courage or life into; animate.

inst. 1. instant. 2. institute; institution.

in·sta·bil·i·ty (ĭn'stə-bĭl'ə-tē) *n., pl.* **-ties.** Lack of stability.

in·stall (ĭn-stôl') *v.* Also **in·stal, -stalled, -stalling.** 1. To set in position and adjust for use. 2. To put in an office, rank, or position. 3. To establish (oneself or another) in a place or condition indicated. —**in'stal·la'tion** *n.*

in·stall·ment (ĭn-stôl'mənt) *n.* Also **in·stal·ment.** 1. One of several successive payments of a debt. 2. A portion of anything issued or presented at intervals.

in·stance (ĭn'stəns) *n.* 1. A case or example. 2. A step in a series of events; occasion. 3. A prompting; request. —*v.* **-stanced, -stancing.** To offer as an example; cite.

in·stant (ĭn'stənt) *n.* 1. A very brief time; a moment. 2. A particular point in time. —*adj.* 1. Immediate. 2. Imperative; urgent. 3. Prepared for rapid completion with minimal effort. [< L *instāre,* to stand upon, be present.]

in·stan·ta·ne·ous (ĭn'stən-tā'nē-əs) *adj.* Occurring without perceptible delay or at a specific instant. —**in'stan·ta'ne·ous·ly** *adv.*

in·stant·ly (ĭn'stənt-lē) *adv.* At once.

in·stead (ĭn-stĕd') *adv.* As an alternative or substitute. —**instead of.** In lieu of; rather than. [< IN + STEAD.]

in·step (ĭn'stĕp') *n.* The arched medial portion of the human foot. [Prob IN + STEP.]

in·sti·gate (ĭn'stĭ-gāt') *v.* **-gated, -gating.** 1. To urge on; goad. 2. To incite. [L *instīgāre.*] —**in'sti·ga'tion** *n.* —**in'sti·ga'tor** *n.*

in·still (ĭn-stĭl') *v.* Also **in·stil, -stilled, -stilling.** 1. To introduce gradually; implant. 2. To pour in drop by drop. [L *instillāre,* to drip in.] —**in·still'er** *n.* —**in·still'ment** *n.*

in·stinct (ĭn'stĭngkt') *n.* 1. a. The innate aspect of behavior that is unlearned, complex, and normally adaptive. b. A powerful motivation or impulse. 2. An innate aptitude. [< L *instinguere,* to instigate, urge on.] —**in·stinc'tive** *adj.* —**in·stinc'tive·ly** *adv.* —**in·stinc'tu·al** (-chōō-əl) *adj.*

in·sti·tute (ĭn'stə-t/y/ōōt') *v.* **-tuted, -tuting.** 1. a. To establish; organize. b. To initiate; begin. 2. To invest in a position. —*n.* 1. An authoritative principle. 2. An organization founded to promote some cause. 3. An educational institution. 4. A seminar or workshop. [< L *instituere,* to establish, ordain.]

in·sti·tu·tion (ĭn'stə-t/y/ōō'shən) *n.* 1. The act of instituting. 2. An established custom or practice. 3. a. An organization, esp. one dedicated to public service. b. The building or buildings housing such an organization. 4. A place of confinement, as a mental asylum. —**in'sti·tu'tion·al** *adj.*

in·sti·tu·tion·al·ize (ĭn'stə-t/y/ōō'shən-ə-līz')

v. **-ized, -izing. 1.** To make into an institution. **2.** To confine in an institution.

instr. 1. instructor. **2.** instrument.

in•struct (ĭn-strŭkt′) *v.* **1.** To teach; educate. **2.** To direct; give orders to. [< L *instruere*, to build, prepare, instruct.] —**in•struc′tive** *adj.*

in•struc•tion (ĭn-strŭk′shən) *n.* **1.** The act or practice of instructing; education. **2. a.** Imparted knowledge. **b.** A lesson. **3. instructions.** Directions; orders. —**in•struc′tion•al** *adj.*

in•struc•tor (ĭn-strŭk′tər) *n.* One who instructs, esp. a college teacher below the rank of assistant professor. —**in•struc′tor•ship′** *n.*

in•stru•ment (ĭn′strə-mənt) *n.* **1.** A means by which something is done. **2.** A usually small precision tool. **3.** A recording or measuring device functioning as part of a control system. **4.** A device for producing music. **5.** A legal document. —*v.* **1.** To equip with instruments. **2.** To address a legal document to. [< L *instruere*, to prepare, INSTRUCT.]

in•stru•men•tal (ĭn′strə-mĕnt′l) *adj.* **1.** Serving as an instrument. **2.** Pertaining to or accomplished with an instrument. **3.** Performed on or written for a musical instrument. —**in′stru•men′tal•ly** *adv.*

in•stru•men•tal•ist (ĭn-strə-mĕnt′l-ĭst) *n.* One who plays a musical instrument.

in•stru•men•tal•i•ty (ĭn′strə-mĕn-tăl′ə-tē) *n., pl.* **-ties.** Agency; means.

in•stru•men•ta•tion (ĭn′strə-mĕn-tā′shən) *n.* **1.** The application or use of instruments. **2.** The arrangement or composition of music for instruments.

in•sub•or•di•nate (ĭn′sə-bôrd′n-ĭt) *adj.* Not submissive to authority. —**in′sub•or′di•nate•ly** *adv.* —**in′sub•or′di•na′tion** *n.*

in•sub•stan•tial (ĭn′səb-stăn′shəl) *adj.* **1.** Imaginary. **2.** Not firm or solid.

in•suf•fer•a•ble (ĭn-sŭf′ər-ə-bəl) *adj.* Not endurable; intolerable. —**in•suf′fer•a•bly** *adv.*

in•suf•fi•cient (ĭn′sə-fĭsh′ənt) *adj.* Not sufficient; inadequate. —**in′suf•fi′cien•cy** *n.*

in•su•lar (ĭn′sə-lər, ĭns′yə-) *adj.* **1.** Of, constituting, or characteristic of an island or island life. **2.** Circumscribed and detached in outlook and experience. [< L *insula*, island.] —**in′su•lar′i•ty** (-lăr′ə-tē) *n.*

in•su•late (ĭn′sə-lāt′, ĭns′yə-) *v.* **-lated, -lating. 1.** To detach; isolate. **2.** To prevent the passage of heat, electricity, or sound into or out of (a body or region), esp. by interposition of an appropriate insulator. [< L *insula*, island.] —**in′su•la′tion** *n.*

in•su•la•tor (ĭn′sə-lā′tər, ĭns′yə-) *n.* A material or device that insulates.

in•su•lin (ĭn′sə-lən, ĭns′yə-) *n.* A pancreatic hormone that regulates carbohydrate metabolism by controlling blood glucose levels. [< L *insula*, island.]

in•sult (ĭn-sŭlt′) *v.* To speak to or treat in a callous or contemptuous way. —*n.* (ĭn′sŭlt′). An offensive remark or act. [< L *insultāre*, to leap on, jump over.]

in•su•per•a•ble (ĭn-sōō′pər-ə-bəl) *adj.* Incapable of being overcome; insurmountable. —**in•su′per•a•bly** *adv.*

in•sup•port•a•ble (ĭn′sə-pôr′tə-bəl, -pôr′-

tə-bəl) *adj.* **1.** Unbearable; intolerable. **2.** Unjustifiable.

in•sur•ance (ĭn-shōōr′əns) *n.* **1. a.** The act, business, or means of insuring persons or property. **b.** The state of being insured. **2.** A contract binding a company to indemnify an insured party against specified loss. **3.** The sum for which something is insured.

in•sure (ĭn-shōōr′) *v.* **-sured, -suring. 1.** To protect against loss, damage, etc., with insurance. **2.** Also **en•sure** (ĕn-). To guarantee. [< NF *enseurer*, to guarantee.] —**in•sur′er** *n.*

in•sur•gent (ĭn-sûr′jənt) *adj.* Rising in revolt against civil authority or a government in power. —*n.* One who revolts against authority. [< L *insurgere*, to rise up.] —**in•sur′gence, in•sur′gen•cy** *n.*

in•sur•mount•a•ble (ĭn′sər-moun′tə-bəl) *adj.* Incapable of being surmounted; insuperable.

in•sur•rec•tion (ĭn′sə-rĕk′shən) *n.* An act of open revolt against civil authority or a constituted government. [< L *insurgere*, to rise up.] —**in′sur•rec′tion•ist** *n.*

int. 1. interest. **2.** interior. **3.** international.

in•tact (ĭn-tăkt′) *adj.* **1.** Not impaired in any way. **2.** Having all parts; whole. [< L *intactus*, untouched.] —**in•tact′ness** *n.*

in•ta•glio (ĭn-tăl′yō) *n., pl.* **-glios.** A figure or design incised beneath the surface of a hard material, as stone. [It.]

in•take (ĭn′tāk′) *n.* **1.** An opening through which a fluid is admitted to a container or conduit. **2. a.** The act of taking in. **b.** That which is taken in.

in•tan•gi•ble (ĭn-tăn′jə-bəl) *adj.* Not tangible; elusive. —*n.* Something intangible. —**in•tan′-gi•bil′i•ty** *n.* —**in•tan′gi•bly** *adv.*

in•te•ger (ĭn′tə-jər) *n.* **1.** Any member of the set of positive whole numbers (1, 2, 3, ...), negative whole numbers (–1, –2, –3, ...), and zero (0). **2.** Any intact unit. [L, whole.]

in•te•gral (ĭn′tə-grəl) *adj.* **1.** Essential for completion; constituent. **2.** Whole; entire; intact. **3.** Expressed or expressible as or in terms of integers. —*n.* A complete unit; a whole. [< L *integer*, whole.] —**in′te•gral•ly** *adv.*

in•te•grate (ĭn′tə-grāt′) *v.* **-grated, -grating. 1.** To make into a whole; unify. **2.** To join together; unite. **3.** To open to all ethnic groups; desegregate. [L *integrāre*, to make complete.] —**in′te•gra′tion** *n.* —**in′te•gra′tive** *adj.*

in•teg•ri•ty (ĭn-tĕg′rə-tē) *n.* **1.** Rigid adherence to a code of values; probity. **2.** Soundness; completeness; unity. [< L *integritās*, completeness, purity.]

in•teg•u•ment (ĭn-tĕg′yōō-mənt) *n.* An outer covering, as skin or a seed coat. [< L *integere*, to cover.]

in•tel•lect (ĭn′tə-lĕkt′) *n.* **1. a.** The ability to learn, reason, and think abstractly. **b.** The capacity for knowledge and understanding. **2.** A person of great intellectual ability. [< L *intellegere*, to perceive, choose between.]

in•tel•lec•tu•al (ĭn′tə-lĕk′chōō-əl) *adj.* **1. a.** Of the intellect. **b.** Rational. **2.** Appealing to or engaging the intellect. **3.** Having superior intelligence. —**in′tel•lec′tu•al** *n.* —**in′tel•lec′tu•al•ly** *adv.*

ă pat/ā ate/âr care/ä bar/b bib/ch chew/d deed/ĕ pet/ē be/f fit/g gag/h hat/hw what/
ĭ pit/ī pie/îr pier/j judge/k kick/l lid, fatal/m mum/n no, sudden/ng sing/ŏ pot/ō go/

in·tel·lec·tu·al·ize (ĭn′tə-lĕk′chōō-ə-līz′) v. -ized, -izing. 1. To make rational. 2. To avoid emotional insight into (an emotional problem) by performing an intellectual analysis. —in′tel·lec′tu·al·i·za′tion n.

in·tel·li·gence (ĭn-tĕl′ə-jəns) n. 1. a. The capacity to acquire and apply knowledge. b. The faculty of thought and reason. 2. Information; news. 3. a. Secret information, esp. about an enemy. b. An agency engaged in seeking such information.

intelligence quotient. The ratio of tested mental age to chronological age, usually expressed as a quotient multiplied by 100.

in·tel·li·gent (ĭn-tĕl′ə-jənt) adj. 1. Having intelligence. 2. Having a high degree of intelligence. 3. Showing intelligence. —in·tel′li·gent·ly adv.

in·tel·li·gent·si·a (ĭn-tĕl′ə-jĕnt′sē-ə, -gĕnt′sē-ə) n. The intellectual class of a society.

in·tel·li·gi·ble (ĭn-tĕl′ə-jə-bəl) adj. Comprehensible. —in·tel′li·gi·bil′i·ty n. —in·tel′li·gi·bly adv.

in·tem·per·ance (ĭn-tĕm′pər-əns) n. Lack of temperance, as in the indulgence of an appetite. —in·tem′per·ate adj.

in·tend (ĭn-tĕnd′) v. 1. To have in mind; plan. 2. To design for a specific purpose. 3. To mean. [< L intendere, to stretch toward, direct one's mind to.]

in·tense (ĭn-tĕns′) adj. 1. Of great intensity. 2. Extreme in degree, strength, or size. 3. Involving or showing strain. 4. Deeply felt; profound. [< L intensus, stretched tight.] —in·tense′ly adv. —in·tense′ness n.

in·ten·si·fy (ĭn-tĕn′sə-fī′) v. -fied, -fying. To make or become intense or more intense. —in·ten′si·fi·ca′tion n.

in·ten·si·ty (ĭn-tĕn′sə-tē) n., pl. -ties. 1. Exceptionally great concentration, power, or force. 2. a. The measure of effectiveness of a force field given by the force per unit test element. b. The energy transferred by a wave per unit time across a unit area perpendicular to the direction of propagation.

in·ten·sive (ĭn-tĕn′sĭv) adj. 1. Of, pertaining to, or characterized by intensity. 2. Concentrated and exhaustive. —n. Gram. A word that serves to emphasize another word or expression. —in·ten′sive·ly adv.

in·tent (ĭn-tĕnt′) n. 1. That which is intended; aim; purpose. 2. The state of mind operative at the time of an action; volition. 3. a. Meaning; purport. b. Connotation. —adj. 1. Firmly fixed; concentrated. 2. Engrossed. 3. Determined. [< L intendere, to INTEND.]

in·ten·tion (ĭn-tĕn′shən) n. 1. A plan of action; design. 2. An aim that guides action; object.

in·ten·tion·al (ĭn-tĕn′shə-nəl) adj. Deliberate; intended. —in·ten′tion·al·ly adv.

in·ter (ĭn-tûr′) v. -terred, -terring. To place in a grave; bury. [< L in, in + terra, earth, ground.]

inter-. comb. form. 1. Between or among. 2. Mutually or together. [< L inter, among.]

in·ter·act (ĭn′tər-ăkt′) v. To act on each other. —in′ter·ac′tion n. —in′ter·ac′tive adj.

in·ter·breed (ĭn′tər-brēd′) v. 1. To crossbreed;

hybridize. 2. To breed within a narrow range; inbreed.

in·ter·ca·lar·y (ĭn-tûr′kə-lĕr′ē) adj. 1. Intercalated. 2. Interpolated.

in·ter·ca·late (ĭn-tûr′kə-lāt′) v. -lated, -lating. 1. To add (a day or month) to a calendar. 2. To insert, interpose, or interpolate. [L intercalāre, to proclaim the insertion of a day.] —in·ter′ca·la′tion n.

in·ter·cede (ĭn′tər-sēd′) v. -ceded, -ceding. 1. To plead on another's behalf. 2. To mediate. [L intercēdere, to come between.]

in·ter·cel·lu·lar (ĭn′tər-sĕl′yə-lər) adj. Among or between cells.

in·ter·cept (ĭn′tər-sĕpt′) v. 1. To stop or interrupt the progress of. 2. To intersect. 3. Math. To cut off or bound a part of (a line, plane, surface, or solid). —n. (ĭn′tər-sĕpt′). Math. The distance from the origin of co-ordinates along a coordinate axis to the point at which a line, curve, or surface intersects the axis. [L intercipere, to intercept, seize in transit.] —in′ter·cep′tive adj.

in·ter·cep·tor (ĭn′tər-sĕp′tər) n. A fast-climbing, highly maneuverable fighter plane designed to intercept enemy aircraft.

in·ter·ces·sion (ĭn′tər-sĕsh′ən) n. 1. Entreaty in favor of another. 2. Mediation. [< L intercēdere, INTERCEDE.] —in′ter·ces′sion·al adj. —in′ter·ces′sor n. —in′ter·ces′so·ry adj.

in·ter·change (ĭn′tər-chānj′) v. 1. To switch each into the place of the other; change places. 2. To exchange. 3. To alternate. —n. (ĭn′tər-chānj′). 1. An exchange. 2. Alternation. 3. A highway intersection designed to permit traffic to move freely from one road to another. —in′ter·change′a·ble adj.

in·ter·col·le·giate (ĭn′tər-kə-lē′jĭt, -jē-ĭt) adj. Involving two or more colleges.

in·ter·com (ĭn′tər-kŏm′) n. An intercommunication system, as between two rooms.

in·ter·com·mu·ni·cate (ĭn′tər-kə-myōō′nə-kāt′) v. -cated, -cating. 1. To communicate with each other. 2. To be adjoined, as rooms.

in·ter·con·ti·nen·tal (ĭn′tər-kŏn′tə-nĕnt′l) adj. 1. Extending or carried on from one continent to another. 2. Capable of flight from one continent to another.

in·ter·cos·tal (ĭn′tər-kŏst′l) adj. Located or occurring between the ribs. [< INTER- + L costa, rib.]

in·ter·course (ĭn′tər-kôrs′, -kōrs′) n. 1. Social interchange; communication. 2. Coitus.

in·ter·dict (ĭn′tər-dĭkt′) v. To prohibit or place under an ecclesiastical or legal sanction. —n. An ecclesiastical or legal prohibition. [< L interdīcere, to forbid.] —in′ter·dic′tion n.

in·ter·est (ĭn′trĭst, -tər-ĭst) n. 1. a. A feeling of curiosity, fascination, or absorption. b. The cause of such a feeling. 2. Often interests. Advantage; self-interest. 3. A right, claim, or legal share in something. 4. A charge for a financial loan, usually a percentage of the amount loaned. 5. Often interests. A group sharing in a financial enterprise. —v. 1. To arouse the curiosity or hold the attention of. 2. To cause to become concerned with. [< L interesse, "to be in between," be of concern.]

ô paw, for/oi boy/ou out/ōō took/ōō coo/p pop/r run/s sauce/sh shy/t to/th thin/th the/ ŭ cut/ûr fur/v van/w wag/y yes/z size/zh vision/ə ago, item, edible, gallop, circus/

in·ter·face (ĭn′tər-fās′) *n.* A surface forming a common boundary between adjacent regions.
in·ter·fere (ĭn′tər-fîr′) *v.* **-fered, -fering. 1.** To hinder; impede. **2.** *Football.* To impede illegally the catching of a pass. **3.** To intrude in the affairs of others; meddle. **4.** To inhibit clear reception of broadcast signals. [OF *(s′)entreferir,* to strike each other.] **—in′ter·fer′ence** *n.* **—in′ter·fer′er** *n.*
in·ter·fer·on (ĭn′tər-fîr′ŏn) *n.* A cellular protein produced in response to, and acting to prevent reproduction of, an infectious viral form within an infected cell. [INTERFER(E) + -ON.]
in·ter·ga·lac·tic (ĭn′tər-gə-lăk′tĭk) *adj.* Between galaxies.
in·ter·im (ĭn′tər-ĭm) *n.* An intervening period of time. **—adj.** Temporary. [L, in the meantime.]
in·te·ri·or (ĭn-tîr′ē-ər) *adj.* **1.** Situated inside; inner. **2.** Inland. **—n.** **1.** The inner area of something; inside. **2.** A representation of the inside of a building. **3.** The inland part, as of a country. [L.] **—in·te′ri·or·ly** *adv.*
interior decorator. One who plans and executes the layout and decoration of an architectural interior.
interj. interjection.
in·ter·ject (ĭn′tər-jĕkt′) *v.* To interpose parenthetically; insert. [L *interjicere,* to throw between.] **—in′ter·jec′tor** *n.*
in·ter·jec·tion (ĭn′tər-jĕk′shən) *n.* **1.** An exclamation. **2.** A part of speech consisting of exclamatory words capable of standing alone, as *oh!* **—in′ter·jec′tion·al** *adj.*
in·ter·lace (ĭn′tər-lās′) *v.* **1.** To interweave; intertwine. **2.** To intersperse.
in·ter·lard (ĭn′tər-lärd′) *v.* To insert at intervals; intersperse. [OF *entrelarder,* to alternate layers of fat and lean.]
in·ter·leaf (ĭn′tər-lēf′) *n.* A blank leaf inserted between the regular pages of a book.
in·ter·leave (ĭn′tər-lēv′) *v.* **-leaved, -leaving.** To provide with an interleaf.
in·ter·lin·e·ar (ĭn′tər-lĭn′ē-ər) *adj.* Inserted between the lines of a text.
in·ter·lock (ĭn′tər-lŏk′) *v.* To unite firmly or join closely, as by dovetailing.
in·ter·loc·u·tor (ĭn′tər-lŏk′yə-tər) *n.* One taking part in a conversation. [< L *interloqui,* to speak between.]
in·ter·loc·u·to·ry (ĭn′tər-lŏk′yə-tôr′ē, -tōr′ē) *adj.* A temporary decree made during the course of a legal action. **—adj.** Relating to such a decree.
in·ter·lope (ĭn′tər-lōp′) *v.* **-loped, -loping.** To interfere; intrude; meddle. [< INTER- + MDu *loopen,* to run.] **—in′ter·lop′er** *n.*
in·ter·lude (ĭn′tər-lōōd′) *n.* **1.** An intervening period of time; interval. **2.** An entertainment between the acts of a play. **3.** A short musical piece inserted between parts of a longer composition. [< ML *interlūdium,* performance between acts.]
in·ter·lu·nar (ĭn′tər-lōō′nər) *adj.* Of or relating to the period between the old and new moon when the moon is not visible.
in·ter·mar·ry (ĭn′tər-măr′ē) *v.* **1.** To marry one

of another group. **2.** To be bound together by the marriages of members. **3.** To marry within one's own group. **—in′ter·mar′riage** *n.*
in·ter·me·di·ar·y (ĭn′tər-mē′dē-ĕr′ē) *n., pl.* **-ies.** A mediator or agent. **—adj.** **1.** Acting as a mediator. **2.** In between; intermediate.
in·ter·me·di·ate (ĭn′tər-mē′dē-ĭt) *adj.* In between; in the middle. **—n.** **1.** One that is intermediate. **2.** An intermediary.
in·ter·ment (ĭn-tûr′mənt) *n.* The act or ritual of interring.
in·ter·mez·zo (ĭn′tər-mĕt′sō, -mĕd′zō) *n., pl.* **-zos. 1.** A short movement separating the major sections of a symphonic work. **2.** A short independent instrumental composition.
in·ter·mi·na·ble (ĭn-tûr′mə-nə-bəl) *adj.* Tiresomely protracted; endless. **—in·ter′mi·na·bly** *adv.*
in·ter·min·gle (ĭn′tər-mĭng′gəl) *v.* To mix or mingle.
in·ter·mis·sion (ĭn′tər-mĭsh′ən) *n.* A temporary suspension of activity, as the period between the acts of a theatrical performance.
in·ter·mit (ĭn′tər-mĭt′) *v.* **-mitted, -mitting.** To suspend activity temporarily or repeatedly. [L *intermittere,* to interrupt at intervals.]
in·ter·mit·tent (ĭn′tər-mĭt′ənt) *adj.* Stopping and starting at intervals. **—in′ter·mit′tent·ly** *adv.*
in·ter·mix (ĭn′tər-mĭks′) *v.* To mix together. **—in′ter·mix′ture** *n.*
in·tern (ĭn′tûrn′) *n.* Also **in·terne.** An advanced student or recent graduate, as of a medical school, undergoing supervised practical training. **—v.** **1.** To train or serve as an intern. **2.** (ĭn-tûrn′). To detain or confine, esp. in wartime. [< L *internus,* INTERNAL.] **—in′tern·ship′** *n.*
in·ter·nal (ĭn-tûr′nəl) *adj.* **1.** Inner; interior. **2.** Intrinsic; inherent. **3.** Within the body. **4.** Of or relating to the domestic affairs of a country. [< L *internus < inter,* in.] **—in′ter·nal′i·ty** *n.* **—in·ter′nal·ly** *adv.*
in·ter·nal-com·bus·tion engine (ĭn-tûr′nəl-kəm-bŭs′chən). An engine in which fuel is burned within the engine proper rather than in an external furnace as in a steam engine.
internal medicine. The medical study and treatment of nonsurgical constitutional diseases in adults.
in·ter·na·tion·al (ĭn′tər-năsh′ən-əl) *adj.* Of, relating to, or involving two or more nations or nationalities. **—n.** **International.** Any of three successive international associations of Marxist parties. **—in′ter·na′tion·al·ly** *adv.*
in·ter·na·tion·al·ism (ĭn′tər-năsh′ən-ə-lĭz′əm) *n.* A theory or policy of promoting cooperation among nations, esp. in politics and economy. **—in′ter·na′tion·al·ist** *n.*
in·ter·na·tion·al·ize (ĭn′tər-năsh′ən-ə-līz′) *v.* **-ized, -izing.** To put under international control. **—in′ter·na′tion·al·i·za′tion** *n.*
International System. A system of units used for scientific work, based on the metric system with the addition of units of time, electric current, temperature, and luminous intensity.
in·terne. Variant of **intern.**
in·ter·ne·cine (ĭn′tər-nĕs′ēn′, -ən, -nē′sĭn′) *adj.* **1.** Mutually destructive. **2.** Relating to struggle

within a group. [< L *internecāre*, to slaughter.]

in·tern·ee (ĭn'tûr-nē') *n.* One who is interned, esp. during a war.

in·ter·nist (ĭn-tûr'nĭst) *n.* A physician who specializes in internal medicine.

in·tern·ment (ĭn-tûrn'mənt) *n.* The act of interning or state of being interned.

in·ter·phase (ĭn'tər-fāz') *n.* A period or stage between two successive mitotic divisions of a cell nucleus.

in·ter·plan·e·tar·y (ĭn'tər-plăn'ə-tĕr'ē) *adj.* Between planets.

in·ter·play (ĭn'tər-plā') *n.* Reciprocal action and reaction; interaction. —*v.* To act or react on each other.

in·ter·po·late (ĭn-tûr'pə-lāt') *v.* -lated, -lating. 1. To insert or introduce between other things or parts. 2. To change (a text) by introducing new or false material. 3. *Math.* To determine a value of (a function) between known values by a procedure or algorithm different from that specified by the function itself. [< L *interpolāre.*] —**in·ter'po·la'tion** *n.* —**in·ter'po·lat'or** *n.*

in·ter·pose (ĭn'tər-pōz') *v.* -posed, -posing. 1. To insert or introduce between parts. 2. To introduce or interject (a remark, question, etc.) during a conversation or speech. 3. To intrude. 4. To intervene. [< L *interpōnere*, to place between.] —**in'ter·pos'er** *n.* —**in'ter·po·si'tion** (-pə-zĭsh'ən) *n.*

in·ter·pret (ĭn-tûr'prĭt) *v.* 1. To clarify; elucidate. 2. To expound the significance of. 3. To represent through art. 4. To translate. 5. To offer an explanation. [< L *interpretāri.*] —**in·ter'pret·a·ble** *adj.* —**in·ter'pret·er** *n.*

in·ter·pre·ta·tion (ĭn-tûr'prə-tā'shən) *n.* 1. An explanation. 2. A concept of a work of art as expressed by its representation or performance. —**in·ter'pre·ta'tion·al** *adj.*

in·ter·pre·ta·tive (ĭn-tûr'prə-tā'tĭv) *adj.* Also **in·ter·pre·tive** (-prə-tĭv). Expository; explanatory. —**in·ter'pre·ta'tive·ly** *adv.*

in·ter·reg·num (ĭn'tər-rĕg'nəm) *n., pl.* -nums or -na (-nə). 1. The interval of time between two successive reigns or governments. 2. A pause in continuity. —**in'ter·reg'nal** *adj.*

in·ter·re·late (ĭn'tər-rĭ-lāt') *v.* To place in or come into a mutual relationship. —**in'ter·re·la'tion** *n.* —**in'ter·re·la'tion·ship'** *n.*

interrog. interrogative.

in·ter·ro·gate (ĭn-tĕr'ə-gāt') *v.* -gated, -gating. To examine by formal questioning. [L *interrogāre*, to consult, question.] —**in·ter'ro·ga'tion** *n.* —**in·ter'ro·ga'tor** *n.*

in·ter·rog·a·tive (ĭn'tə-rŏg'ə-tĭv) *adj.* 1. Of the nature of a question. 2. Designating a word or form used in asking a question. —**in'ter·rog'·a·tive** *n.* —**in'ter·rog'a·tive·ly** *adv.*

in·ter·rog·a·to·ry (ĭn'tə-rŏg'ə-tôr'ē, -tōr'ē) *adj.* Interrogative. —**in'ter·rog'a·tor'i·ly** *adv.*

in·ter·rupt (ĭn'tə-rŭpt') *v.* 1. To break the continuity or uniformity of. 2. To hinder or stop by breaking in upon. 3. To break in upon an action or discourse. [< L *interrumpere*, to break in.] —**in'ter·rup'tion** *n.*

in·ter·scho·las·tic (ĭn'tər-skə-lăs'tĭk) *adj.* Between or among schools.

in·ter·sect (ĭn'tər-sĕkt') *v.* 1. To cut across or through. 2. To form an intersection with.

in·ter·sec·tion (ĭn'tər-sĕk'shən) *n.* 1. The point or points common to two or more geometric figures. 2. a. The act or process of intersecting. b. A place where things intersect.

in·ter·sperse (ĭn'tər-spûrs') *v.* -spersed, -spersing. To scatter or distribute among other things at irregular intervals. [L *interspergere*, to scatter among.] —**in'ter·sper'sion** (-spûr'zhən, -shən) *n.*

in·ter·state (ĭn'tər-stāt') *adj.* Pertaining to, existing between, or connecting two or more states.

in·ter·stel·lar (ĭn'tər-stĕl'ər) *adj.* Between the stars.

in·ter·stice (ĭn-tûr'stĭs) *n., pl.* -stices (-stĭ-sēz', -sĭz). A small space between things or parts; crevice. [< L *intersistere*, to stand in the middle of.] —**in'ter·sti'tial** (ĭn'tər-stĭsh'əl) *adj.* —**in'ter·sti'tial·ly** *adv.*

in·ter·tid·al (ĭn'tər-tīd'l) *adj.* Of or being the region between the extremes of high and low tide.

in·ter·twine (ĭn'tər-twīn') *v.* 1. To twist or braid together. 2. To interweave with one another. —**in'ter·twine'ment** *n.*

in·ter·ur·ban (ĭn'tər-ûr'bən) *adj.* Pertaining to or connecting cities.

in·ter·val (ĭn'tər-vəl) *n.* 1. A space between two objects, points, or units. 2. The temporal duration between two specified instants, events, or states. 3. a. A set consisting of all the numbers between, and sometimes including, a pair of given numbers. b. A set of numbers greater than or less than, and sometimes including, a given number. 4. The difference in pitch between two tones. [< L *intervallum*, space between ramparts.]

in·ter·vene (ĭn'tər-vēn') *v.* -vened, -vening. 1. To enter or occur extraneously. 2. To occur between two things or two periods of time. 3. To come between so as to modify. 4. To interfere in the affairs of another nation. [L *intervenīre*, to come between.] —**in'ter·ven'er** *n.* —**in'ter·ven'tion** (-vĕn'shən) *n.*

in·ter·view (ĭn'tər-vyōō') *n.* 1. a. A face-to-face meeting. b. Such a meeting arranged for formal discussion. 2. A conversation between a reporter and one from whom he seeks information. —**in'ter·view'** *v.*

in·ter·weave (ĭn'tər-wēv') *v.* 1. To weave together. 2. To intertwine.

in·tes·tate (ĭn-tĕs'tāt', -tĭt) *adj.* 1. Having made no legal will. 2. Not disposed of by a legal will. —**in·tes'ta·cy** (-tə-sē) *n.*

in·tes·tine (ĭn-tĕs'tən) *n.* The portion of the alimentary canal extending from the stomach to the anus. [< L *intestīnus*, internal.] —**in·tes'ti·nal** *adj.* —**in·tes'ti·nal·ly** *adv.*

in·ti·mate¹ (ĭn'tə-mĭt) *adj.* 1. Marked by close acquaintance or familiarity. 2. Essential; innermost. 3. Characterized by informality and privacy. 4. Very personal; private. —*n.* A close friend or confidant. [< LL *intimāre*, to put in, INTIMATE².] —**in'ti·ma·cy, in'ti·mate·ness** *n.* —**in'ti·mate·ly** *adv.*

in·ti·mate² (ĭn'tə-māt') *v.* -mated, -mating. To

imply subtly. [LL *intimāre,* to put or bring in.] —**in′ti•mat′er** *n.* —**in′ti•ma′tion** *n.*

in•tim•i•date (ĭn-tĭm′ə-dāt′) *v.* -**dated,** -**dating.** 1. To make timid; frighten. 2. To discourage or inhibit by or as by threats.

Intl. international.

in•to (ĭn′tōō) *prep.* 1. To the inside of. 2. To the occupation of: *go into banking.* 3. To the condition or form of. 4. So as to be in or within. 5. To a time or place in the course of: *well into the week.* 6. Against: *ram into a tree.* 7. Toward.

in•tol•er•a•ble (ĭn-tŏl′ər-ə-bəl) *adj.* Insupportable; unbearable. —**in•tol′er•a•bly** *adv.*

in•tol•er•ant (ĭn-tŏl′ər-ənt) *adj.* Not tolerant, esp.: **a.** Bigoted. **b.** Irritable. **c.** Unable to endure. —**in•tol′er•ance** *n.*

in•to•na•tion (ĭn′tō-nā′shən) *n.* 1. **a.** The act of intoning. **b.** An intoned utterance. 2. A manner of producing or uttering tones, esp. with regard to accuracy of pitch.

in•tone (ĭn-tōn′) *v.* -**toned,** -**toning.** 1. To recite in a singing voice. 2. To utter in a monotone. —**in•ton′er** *n.*

in to•to (ĭn tō′tō). Totally; altogether. [L.]

in•tox•i•cant (ĭn-tŏk′sĭ-kənt) *n.* An agent that intoxicates, esp. an alcoholic beverage.

in•tox•i•cate (ĭn-tŏk′sĭ-kāt′) *v.* -**cated,** -**cating.** 1. To induce, esp. with ingested alcohol, effects ranging from exhilaration to stupefaction. 2. To stimulate or excite. [ML *intoxicāre,* to put poison in.] —**in•tox′i•ca′tion** *n.*

intra–. *comb. form.* In, within, or inside of. [< L *intrā,* on the inside, within.]

in•trac•ta•ble (ĭn-trăk′tə-bəl) *adj.* Difficult to manage or govern; stubborn.

in•tra•cu•ta•ne•ous (ĭn′trə-kyōō-tā′nē-əs) *adj.* Within the skin.

in•tra•mu•ral (ĭn′trə-myōōr′əl) *adj.* Existing within the bounds of an institution, esp. a school. —**in′tra•mu′ral•ly** *adv.*

in•tran•si•gent (ĭn-trăn′sə-jənt) *adj.* Refusing to moderate an extreme position; uncompromising. [< Span *los intransigentes,* "the uncompromising."] —**in•tran′si•gence** *n.* —**in•tran′si•gent•ly** *adv.*

in•tran•si•tive (ĭn-trăn′sə-tĭv) *adj.* Designating a verb or verb construction that does not require a direct object to complete its meaning. —**in•tran′si•tive•ness** *n.*

in•tra•state (ĭn′trə-stāt′) *adj.* Within the boundaries of a state.

in•tra•u•ter•ine (ĭn′trə-yōō′tər-ĭn, -tə-rīn′) *adj.* Within the uterus.

in•tra•ve•nous (ĭn′trə-vē′nəs) *adj.* Within a vein or veins. —**in′tra•ve′nous•ly** *adv.*

in•trep•id (ĭn-trĕp′ĭd) *adj.* Resolutely courageous; fearless; bold. [< L *intrepidus.*] —**in′-tre•pid′i•ty** (-trə-pĭd′ə-tē) *n.* —**in•trep′id•ly** *adv.*

in•tri•cate (ĭn′trĭ-kĭt) *adj.* 1. Having many complexly arranged elements. 2. Difficult to solve or comprehend. [< L *intrīcāre,* to entangle.] —**in′tri•ca•cy** *n.* —**in′tri•cate•ly** *adv.*

in•trigue (ĭn′trēg′, ĭn-trēg′) *n.* 1. **a.** A covert or underhand scheme. **b.** The use of such schemes. 2. A clandestine love affair. 3. Mystery; suspense. —*v.* (ĭn-trēg′) -**trigued,** -**triguing.** 1. To engage in covert schemes. 2. To arouse

the interest or curiosity of. [< L *intrīcāre,* to entangle.] —**in•tri′guer** *n.*

in•trin•sic (ĭn-trĭn′sĭk) *adj.* Pertaining to the essential nature of a thing. [< L *intrinsecus,* inwardly, on the inside.] —**in•trin′si•cal•ly** *adv.*

intro–. *comb. form.* 1. In or into. 2. Inward. [< L *intrō,* to the inside, inwardly.]

intro. introduction; introductory.

in•tro•duce (ĭn′trə-d/y/ōōs′) *v.* -**duced,** -**ducing.** 1. To identify and present, esp. to make (strangers) acquainted. 2. To present and recommend, as a plan. 3. To originate. 4. To insert or inject. 5. To inform of something for the first time. 6. To preface. [L *intrōdūcere,* to lead in.] —**in′tro•duc′er** *n.* —**in′tro•duc′tion** (-dŭk′shən) *n.* —**in′tro•duc′to•ry** *adj.*

in•tro•spec•tion (ĭn′trə-spĕk′shən) *n.* Contemplation of one's own thoughts and sensations; self-examination. —**in′tro•spec′tive** *adj.* —**in′-tro•spec′tive•ness** *n.*

in•tro•vert (ĭn′trə-vûrt′) *n.* One whose thoughts and interests are directed inward. [< INTRO- + L *vertere,* to turn.] —**in′tro•ver′sion** *n.*

in•trude (ĭn-trōōd′) *v.* -**truded,** -**truding.** To come in rudely or inappropriately; enter as an improper or unwanted element. [L *intrūdere,* to thrust in.] —**in•trud′er** *n.* —**in•tru′sion** *n.* —**in•tru′sive** *adj.* —**in•tru′sive•ly** *adv.*

in•trust. Variant of **entrust.**

in•tu•it (ĭn-t/y/ōō′ĭt) *v.* To know or sense by intuition.

in•tu•i•tion (ĭn′t/y/ōō-ĭsh′ən) *n.* 1. **a.** The act or faculty of knowing without the use of rational processes. **b.** Knowledge so gained. 2. Sharp insight. [< L *intuērī,* to look at, contemplate.] —**in•tu′i•tive** *adj.*

in•un•date (ĭn′ŭn-dāt′) *v.* -**dated,** -**dating.** To overwhelm or cover with or as with a flood. [L *inundāre,* "to flow in."] —**in′un•da′tion** *n.*

in•ure (ĭn-yōōr′) *v.* -**ured,** -**uring.** To make used to something undesirable by prolonged subjection. —**in•ure′ment** *n.*

inv. invoice.

in•vade (ĭn-vād′) *v.* -**vaded,** -**vading.** 1. To enter by force in order to conquer or overrun. 2. To encroach or intrude upon. 3. To infest. 4. To enter and spread harm through. [< L *invādere,* "to go in."] —**in•vad′er** *n.*

in•va•lid¹ (ĭn′və-lĭd) *n.* A chronically ill or disabled person. —*adj.* Disabled by illness or injury.

in•val•id² (ĭn-văl′ĭd) *adj.* 1. Null; legally ineffective. 2. Falsely based or reasoned; unjustified. —**in•val′id•ly** *adv.*

in•val•i•date (ĭn-văl′ə-dāt′) *v.* To make void; render invalid. —**in•val′i•da′tion** *n.*

in•val•u•a•ble (ĭn-văl′yōō-ə-bəl) *adj.* 1. Having great value; priceless. 2. Of inestimable use or help. —**in•val′u•a•bly** *adv.*

in•var•i•a•ble (ĭn-vâr′ē-ə-bəl) *adj.* Not changing or subject to change; constant. —**in•var′i•a•bil′i•ty** *n.* —**in•var′i•a•bly** *adv.*

in•var•i•ant (ĭn-vâr′ē-ənt) *adj.* Unaffected by a designated mathematical operation. —**in•var′i•ance** *n.* —**in•var′i•ant** *n.*

in•va•sion (ĭn-vā′zhən) *n.* 1. The act of invading, esp. entrance by force. 2. The onset of something harmful, as a disease.

ă pat/ā ate/âr care/ä bar/b **bib**/ch **chew**/d **deed**/ĕ pet/ē be/f fit/g gag/h hat/hw **what**/ ĭ pit/ī pie/îr pier/j **judge**/k **kick**/l lid, fatal/m **mum**/n no, sudden/ng sing/ŏ pot/ō go/

in·va·sive (ĭn-vā'sĭv) *adj.* Tending to spread, esp. tending to invade healthy tissue.

in·vec·tive (ĭn-věk'tĭv) *n.* **1.** An abusive expression. **2.** Vehement denunciation; vituperation. [< L *invehere*, to attack, INVEIGH.]

in·veigh (ĭn-vā') *v.* To protest vehemently; rail. [< L *invehere*, to carry in, assail.]

in·vei·gle (ĭn-vē'gəl, ĭn-vā'-) *v.* **-gled, -gling.** **1.** To lead astray or win over by deceitful flattery. **2.** To obtain by cajolery. [< OF *aveugler*, to blind.] —**in·vei'gler** *n.*

in·vent (ĭn-věnt') *v.* **1.** To conceive of or devise first; originate. **2.** To fabricate; make up. [< L *invenire*, to come upon.] —**in·ven'tor** *n.*

in·ven·tion (ĭn-věn'shən) *n.* **1.** The act or process of inventing. **2.** A new device or process developed from study and experimentation. **3.** A mental fabrication; falsehood. **4.** Skill at inventing; inventiveness.

in·ven·tive (ĭn-věn'tĭv) *adj.* **1.** Of or characterized by invention. **2.** Adept or skillful at inventing. —**in·ven'tive·ness** *n.*

in·ven·to·ry (ĭn'vən-tôr'ē, -tōr'ē) *n., pl.* **-ries.** **1.** A detailed list of things, esp. a periodic survey of goods and materials in stock. **2.** The process of making such a survey. **3.** The items so listed. **4.** The quantity of goods so determined. [< L *invenire*, to come upon, INVENT.] —**in'ven·to'ry** *v.* **(-ried, -rying).**

in·ver·ness (ĭn'vər-nĕs') *n.* A loose overcoat with a detachable cape. [< *Inverness*, Scotland.]

in·verse (ĭn-vûrs', ĭn'vûrs') *adj.* Reversed in order, nature, or effect. —*n.* That which is opposite, as in sequence or character; the reverse. [< L *invertere*, INVERT.] —**in·verse'ly** *adv.*

in·ver·sion (ĭn-vûr'zhən, -shən) *n.* **1.** The act of inverting or state of being inverted. **2.** An interchange of position, order, etc. **3.** Homosexuality. **4.** *Meteorol.* A state in which the air temperature increases with increasing altitude, holding surface air down along with its pollutants.

in·vert (ĭn-vûrt') *v.* **1.** To turn inside out or upside down. **2.** To reverse the position, order, or condition of. [L *invertere*, to turn inside out or upside down.] —**in·vert'i·ble** *adj.*

in·ver·te·brate (ĭn-vûr'tə-brĭt, -brāt') *adj.* Having no backbone or spinal column; not vertebrate. —**in·ver'te·brate** *n.*

in·vest (ĭn-věst') *v.* **1.** To commit (money or capital) in order to gain profit or interest. **2.** To spend or utilize (time or effort) for future benefit. **3.** To endow with rank, authority, or power. **4.** To inaugurate; install in office. **5.** *Rare.* To clothe. **6.** To cover completely; envelop. [< L *investire*, to clothe in, surround.] —**in·ves'tor** *n.*

in·ves·ti·gate (ĭn-věs'tĭ-gāt') *v.* **-gated, -gating.** To observe or inquire into in detail; examine systematically. [L *investigāre*, to trace out.] —**in·ves'ti·ga'tion** *n.* —**in·ves'ti·ga'tor** *n.*

in·ves·ti·ture (ĭn-věs'tə-choor') *n.* The act or ceremony of conferring the authority and symbols of a high office.

in·vest·ment (ĭn-věst'mənt) *n.* **1.** The act of investing or state of being invested. **2.** An amount invested. **3.** Property acquired for future income. **4.** Investiture. **5.** An outer covering or layer.

in·vet·er·ate (ĭn-vět'ər-ĭt) *adj.* **1.** Firmly established by long standing. **2.** Persisting in an ingrained habit: *an inveterate liar.* [< L *inveterāre*, to render old.] —**in·vet'er·a·cy** (-ər-ə-sē) *n.* —**in·vet'er·ate·ly** *adv.*

in·vid·i·ous (ĭn-vĭd'ē-əs) *adj.* **1.** Tending to rouse ill will or animosity. **2.** Containing or implying a slight. [< L *invidia*, envy.] —**in·vid'i·ous·ly** *adv.*

in·vig·or·ate (ĭn-vĭg'ə-rāt') *v.* **-ated, -ating.** To impart vigor or vitality to. —**in·vig'or·a'tion** *n.*

in·vin·ci·ble (ĭn-vĭn'sə-bəl) *adj.* Unconquerable. —**in·vin'ci·bil'i·ty** *n.* —**in·vin'ci·bly** *adv.*

in·vi·o·la·ble (ĭn-vī'ə-lə-bəl) *adj.* **1.** Safe from violation or profanation. **2.** Impregnable. —**in·vi'o·la·bil'i·ty** *n.* —**in·vi'o·la·bly** *adv.*

in·vi·o·late (ĭn-vī'ə-lĭt) *adj.* Not violated; intact. —**in·vi'o·late·ly** *adv.*

in·vis·i·ble (ĭn-vĭz'ə-bəl) *adj.* **1.** Incapable of being seen; not visible. **2.** Not accessible to view; hidden. **3.** Inconspicuous. —**in·vis'i·bil'i·ty, in·vis'i·ble·ness** *n.* —**in·vis'i·bly** *adv.*

in·vite (ĭn-vīt') *v.* **-vited, -viting.** **1.** To request the presence or participation of. **2.** To request formally. **3.** To welcome. **4.** To tend to bring on; provoke. **5.** To lure; entice. [< L *invītāre*.] —**in·vi·ta'tion** *n.*

in·vit·ing (ĭn-vī'tĭng) *adj.* Attractive; tempting.

in·vo·ca·tion (ĭn'və-kā'shən) *n.* **1.** The act of invoking, esp. an appeal to a higher power. **2.** A prayer or other formula used in invoking.

in·voice (ĭn'vois') *n.* A detailed list of goods shipped or services rendered, with an account of all costs; a bill. [< OF *envoy*, a sending.]

in·voke (ĭn-vōk') *v.* **-voked, -voking.** **1.** To call upon (a higher power) for assistance. **2.** To appeal to; petition. **3.** To call for earnestly; solicit. **4.** To conjure. **5.** To cite in support of one's cause. [< L *invocāre*, "to call upon."]

in·vol·un·tar·y (ĭn-vŏl'ən-tĕr'ē) *adj.* **1.** Not performed willingly. **2.** Not subject to control. —**in·vol'un·tar'i·ly** *adv.* —**in·vol'un·tar'i·ness** *n.*

in·vo·lu·tion (ĭn'və-loo'shən) *n.* **1.** The act of involving or state of being involved. **2.** Anything internally complex or involved. **3.** The multiplying of a quantity by itself a specified number of times; raising to a power.

in·volve (ĭn-vŏlv') *v.* **-volved, -volving.** **1.** To contain or include. **2.** To have as a necessary feature or consequence. **3.** To draw in; embroil. **4.** To engross completely. **5.** To make complex; complicate. [< L *involvere*, to enwrap, "roll in."] —**in·volve'ment** *n.*

in·vul·ner·a·ble (ĭn-vŭl'nər-ə-bəl) *adj.* **1.** Immune to attack; impregnable. **2.** Incapable of being damaged, injured, or wounded. —**in·vul'ner·a·bil'i·ty** *n.* —**in·vul'ner·a·bly** *adv.*

in·ward (ĭn'wərd) *adj.* **1.** Located inside; inner. **2.** Directed or moving toward the interior. **3.** Existing in the mind. —*adv.* Also **in·wards** (-wərdz). **1.** Toward the inside or center. **2.** Toward the mind or the self.

in·ward·ly (ĭn'wərd-lē) *adv.* **1.** On or in the inside; within. **2.** Privately; to oneself.

i·o·dide (ī'ə-dīd') *n.* A binary compound of

iodine with a more electropositive atom or group.

i•o•dine (ī'ə-dīn', -dĭn, -dēn') *n. Symbol* **I** **1.** A lustrous, grayish-black, corrosive, poisonous element having radioactive isotopes, esp. I 131, used as tracers and in thyroid disease diagnosis and therapy, and compounds used as germicides, antiseptics, and dyes. Atomic number 53, atomic weight 126.9044. **2.** A tincture of iodine and sodium iodide, NaI, or potassium iodide, KI, used as an antiseptic. [< Gk *iōdēs, ioeidēs,* violet-colored.]

i•o•dize (ī'ə-dīz') *v.* **-dized, -dizing.** To treat or combine with iodine or an iodide.

i•on (ī'ən, ī'ŏn') *n.* An atom, group of atoms, or molecule having a net electric charge acquired by gaining or losing electrons from an initially neutral configuration. [< Gk, "going (particle)."] **—i•on•ic** (ī-ŏn'ĭk) *adj.*

Ionic bond. A chemical bond formed by the complete transfer of one or more electrons from one kind of atom to another.

Ionic order. One of the three classical orders of architecture, characterized by two opposed volutes in the capital.

i•on•ize (ī'ə-nīz') *v.* **-ized, -izing.** To convert totally or partially into ions. **—i'on•i•za'tion** *n.*

i•on•o•sphere (ī-ŏn'ə-sfîr') *n.* An electrically conducting set of layers of the earth's atmosphere, extending from altitudes of approx. 30 miles to more than 250 miles.

i•o•ta (ī-ō'tə) *n.* **1.** The 9th letter of the Greek alphabet, representing *i.* **2.** A very small amount.

IOU (ī'ō-yōō') *n., pl.* **IOU's, IOUs.** A promise to pay a debt.

I•o•wa¹ (ī'ə-wə). A Midwestern state of the U.S. Pop. 2,825,000. Cap. Des Moines.

I•o•wa² (ī'ə-wə) *n., pl.* **-wa** or **-was. 1.** A member of a tribe of Siouan-speaking North American Indians formerly inhabiting the region of Minnesota, Iowa, and Missouri. **2.** The language of this tribe. **—I'o•wa** *adj.*

IPA International Phonetic Alphabet.

ip•so fac•to (ĭp'sō făk'tō). By the fact itself; by that very fact. [L.]

IQ intelligence quotient.

Ir 1. iridium. **2.** Irish.

I•ran (ĭ-răn', ē-rän'). Formerly **Per•sia** (pûr'zhə, -shə). A kingdom of SW Asia. Pop. 22,860,000. Cap. Teheran.

Iran

I•ra•ni•an (ĭ-rä'nē-ən) *n.* **1.** A native or inhabitant of Iran. **2.** A group of languages including Persian and Pashto and forming a subbranch of Indo-Iranian. **—I•ra'ni•an** *adj.*

I•raq (ĭ-răk', ē-räk'). Also **I•rak.** A republic of SW Asia. Pop. 8,262,000. Cap. Baghdad. **—I•ra'qi** *adj. & n.*

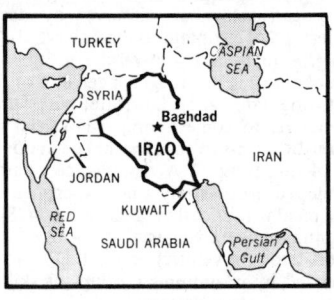

Iraq

i•ras•ci•ble (ĭ-răs'ə-bəl, i-răs'-) *adj.* Prone to outbursts of temper; easily angered. [< L *irāsci,* to get angry.] **—i•ras'ci•bil'i•ty** *n.*

i•rate (ī'rāt, ī-rāt') *adj.* Angry; enraged. **—i'rate•ly** *adv.*

IRBM Intermediate Range Ballistic Missile.

ire (īr) *n.* Wrath; anger. [< L *ira,* anger.]

Ire. Ireland.

ire•ful (īr'fəl) *adj.* Full of ire; angry; wrathful. **—ire'ful•ly** *adv.*

Ire•land (īr'lənd). **1.** One of the British Isles, divided into the Republic of Ireland and Northern Ireland. **2.** A republic occupying most of Ireland. Pop. 2,849,000. Cap. Dublin.

Republic of Ireland

ir•i•des•cent (îr'ə-dĕs'ənt) *adj.* Producing a display of lustrous, rainbowlike colors. [L *iris,* rainbow, iris + -ESCENT.] **—ir'i•des'cence** *n.*

i•rid•i•um (ĭ-rĭd'ē-əm, ī-rĭd'-) *n. Symbol* **Ir** A very hard and brittle, exceptionally corrosion-resistant, whitish-yellow metallic element used to harden platinum and in high-temperature materials, electrical contacts, and wear-resistant bearings. Atomic number 77, atomic weight 192.2. [< Gk *iris,* rainbow, IRIS.]

i•ris (ī'rĭs) *n., pl.* **irises** or **irides** (ī'rə-dēz', îr'ə-).

1. The pigmented, round, contractile membrane of the eye, situated between the cornea and lens, and perforated by the pupil. **2.** A plant with narrow, sword-shaped leaves and showy, variously colored flowers. [< Gk, rainbow, iris of the eye.]

I•rish (ī'rĭsh) *adj.* **1. the Irish** *(takes pl. v.).* **a.** The inhabitants of Ireland. **b.** People of immediate Irish descent. **2.** The Celtic language spoken in Ireland. —**I'rish** *adj.*

Irish Gaelic. The Goidelic language of Ireland.

I•rish•man (ī'rĭsh-mən) *n.* A man of Irish birth or descent.

irk (ûrk) *v.* To vex; irritate. [ME *irken.*]

irk•some (ûrk'səm) *adj.* Wearisome; tedious.

i•ron (ī'ərn) *n.* **1.** *Symbol* **Fe** A silvery-white, lustrous, malleable, ductile, magnetic or magnetizable, metallic element used alloyed in many important structural materials. Atomic number 26, atomic weight 55.847. **2.** Great hardness or strength. **3.** An implement made of iron alloy or similar metal. **4.** A golf club with a metal head. **5.** An appliance with a weighted flat bottom, used when heated to press fabric. **6. irons.** Fetters; shackles. —*adj.* Of or like iron. —*v.* To press (fabric) with a heated iron. —**iron out.** To settle through discussion or compromise. [< OE *iren, īsen.*]

Iron Age. A period of human culture succeeding the Bronze Age, characterized by the introduction of iron metallurgy, in Europe beginning around the 8th century B.C.

i•ron•bound (ī'ərn-bound') *adj.* Rigid and unyielding.

i•ron•clad (ī'ərn-klăd') *adj.* **1.** Sheathed with protective iron plates. **2.** Rigid: *an ironclad rule.*

i•ron•ic (ī-rŏn'ĭk) *adj.* Also **i•ron•ic•al** (-ĭ-kəl). **1.** Characterized by or constituting irony. **2.** Given to irony. —**i•ron'i•cal•ly** *adv.*

Iron lung. A tank in which the body is enclosed and by means of which pressure is regularly increased and decreased to provide artificial respiration.

i•ron•ware (ī'ərn-wâr') *n.* Iron utensils and other products made of iron.

i•ron•work (ī'ərn-wûrk') *n.* Work in iron, as gratings and rails.

i•ron•works (ī'ərn-wûrks') *n. (takes sing. v.).* An establishment where iron is smelted or where heavy iron products are made.

i•ro•ny (ī'rə-nē) *n., pl.* **-nies. 1.** The use of words to convey the opposite of their literal meaning. **2.** Incongruity between what might be expected and what actually occurs. [< Gk *eirōneia,* dissembling, feigned ignorance.]

Ir•o•quoi•an (ĭr'ə-kwoi'ən) *n.* **1.** A family of North American Indian languages spoken in Canada and the E U.S. **2.** A member of a tribe using a language of this family. —**Ir'o•quoi'an** *adj.*

Ir•o•quois (ĭr'ə-kwoi', -kwoiz') *n., pl.* **-quois. 1.** A member of any of several Iroquoian-speaking North American Indian tribes formerly inhabiting New York State. **2.** Any of the languages spoken among these tribes.

ir•ra•di•ate (ĭ-rā'dē-āt') *v.* **-ated, -ating. 1.** To

expose to or treat with radiation. **2.** To emit in a manner analogous to the emission of light. —**ir•ra'di•a'tion** *n.*

ir•ra•tion•al (ĭ-răsh'ən-əl) *adj.* **1. a.** Not endowed with reason. **b.** Incoherent, as from shock. **c.** Illogical. **2.** Incapable of being expressed as an integer or a quotient of integers. —**ir•ra'tion•al•ly** *adv.* —**ir•ra'tion•al•ness** *n.*

Ir•ra•wad•dy (ĭr'ə-wä'dē). A river of Burma.

ir•re•claim•a•ble (ĭr'ĭ-klā'mə-bəl) *adj.* Incapable of being reclaimed.

ir•rec•on•cil•a•ble (ĭ-rĕk'ən-sī'lə-bəl, ĭ-rĕk'-ən-sī'-) *adj.* **1.** Incapable of being reconciled; implacably hostile. **2.** Incompatible; incongruous. —**ir•rec'on•cil'a•bly** *adv.*

ir•re•cov•er•a•ble (ĭr'ĭ-kŭv'ər-ə-bəl) *adj.* Incapable of being recovered; irreparable.

ir•re•deem•a•ble (ĭr'ĭ-dē'mə-bəl) *adj.* **1.** Incapable of being bought back or paid off. **2.** Not convertible into coin. **3.** Incapable of being saved or reformed.

ir•re•den•tist (ĭr'ĭ-dĕn'tĭst) *n.* One who advocates the recovery of territory culturally or historically related to his nation but now subject to a foreign government. [It *irredentista.*]

ir•re•duc•i•ble (ĭr'ĭ-d/y/ōō'sə-bəl) *adj.* Incapable of being reduced to a desired, simpler, or smaller form or amount.

ir•ref•u•ta•ble (ĭ-rĕf'yə-tə-bəl, ĭr'ĭ-fyōō'tə-bəl) *adj.* Incapable of being refuted.

irreg. irregular.

ir•re•gard•less (ĭr'ĭ-gärd'lĭs) *adv. Nonstandard.* Regardless.

Usage: Irregardless, a double negative, is only acceptable when the intent is clearly humorous.

ir•reg•u•lar (ĭ-rĕg'yə-lər) *adj.* **1.** Not according to accepted rules, practice, or order. **2.** Not straight, uniform, or symmetrical. **3.** Of uneven rate, occurrence, or duration. **4.** Asymmetrically arranged or atypical. —*n.* A guerrilla. —**ir•reg'u•lar'i•ty** *n.* —**ir•reg'u•lar•ly** *adv.*

ir•rel•e•vant (ĭ-rĕl'ə-vənt) *adj.* Having no applications or effects in a specified circumstance. —**ir•rel'e•vance** *n.*

ir•re•li•gious (ĭr'ĭ-lĭj'əs) *adj.* Indifferent or hostile to religion. —**ir•re•lig'ious•ness** *n.*

ir•re•me•di•a•ble (ĭr'ĭ-mē'dē-ə-bəl) *adj.* Impossible to remedy; incurable.

ir•re•mov•a•ble (ĭr'ĭ-mōō'və-bəl) *adj.* Not removable. —**ir're•mov'a•bly** *adv.*

ir•rep•a•ra•ble (ĭ-rĕp'ər-ə-bəl) *adj.* Incapable of being repaired, rectified, or amended.

ir•re•place•a•ble (ĭr'ĭ-plā'sə-bəl) *adj.* Incapable of being replaced.

ir•re•pres•si•ble (ĭr'ĭ-prĕs'ə-bəl) *adj.* Impossible to control or restrain.

ir•re•proach•a•ble (ĭr'ĭ-prō'chə-bəl) *adj.* Beyond reproach. —**ir're•proach'a•bly** *adv.*

ir•re•sis•ti•ble (ĭr'ĭ-zĭs'tə-bəl) *adj.* **1.** Impossible to resist. **2.** Having an overpowering appeal.

ir•res•o•lute (ĭ-rĕz'ə-lōōt') *adj.* **1.** Unresolved as to action or procedure. **2.** Vacillating; indecisive. —**ir•res'o•lute'ly** *adv.*

ir•re•spec•tive (ĭr'ĭ-spĕk'tĭv) *adj.* Regardless of; without consideration of.

ir•re•spon•si•ble (ĭr'ĭ-spŏn'sə-bəl) *adj.* Unre-

ô paw, for/oi boy/ou out/ōō took/ōō coo/p pop/r run/s sauce/sh shy/t to/th thin/*th* the/
ŭ cut/ûr fur/v van/w wag/y yes/z size/zh vision/ə ago, item, edible, gallop, circus/

liable. —ir're·spon'si·bil'i·ty, ir're·spon'si·ble·ness *n.* —ir're·spon'si·bly *adv.*

ir·re·triev·a·ble (ĭr'ĭ-trē'və-bəl) *adj.* Incapable of being retrieved or recovered.

ir·rev·er·ence (ĭ-rĕv'ər-əns) *n.* 1. Want of reverence or due respect. 2. A disrespectful act or remark. —ir·rev'er·ent *adj.*

ir·re·vers·i·ble (ĭr'ĭ-vûr'sə-bəl) *adj.* Incapable of being reversed. —ir're·vers'i·bly *adv.*

ir·rev·o·ca·ble (ĭ-rĕv'ə-kə-bəl) *adj.* Incapable of being retracted or revoked.

ir·ri·gate (ĭr'ĭ-gāt') *v.* -gated, -gating. 1. To supply (dry land) with water by artificial means. 2. To wash out with water or a medicated fluid. [L *irrigāre*, to lead water to.] —ir'ri·ga'tion *n.* —ir'ri·ga'tor *n.*

ir·ri·ta·ble (ĭr'ə-tə-bəl) *adj.* 1. Easily annoyed; ill-tempered. 2. Responsive or abnormally sensitive, as to stimuli. [< L *irritāre*, IRRITATE.] —ir'ri·ta·bil'i·ty *n.* —ir'ri·ta·bly *adv.*

ir·ri·tate (ĭr'ə-tāt') *v.* -tated, -tating. 1. a. To exasperate; vex. b. To provoke. 2. To chafe or inflame. [L *irritāre*.] —ir'ri·tant *adj. & n.* —ir'ri·tat'ing·ly *adv.* —ir'ri·ta'tion *n.*

ir·rupt (ĭ-rŭpt') *v.* To break or burst in; make an invasion. [L *irrumpere*.] —ir·rup'tion *n.*

Ir·ving (ûr'vĭng), **Washington.** 1783–1859. American author.

is (ĭz). 3rd person sing. present indicative of the verb **be.** —**as is.** In its present state; as it stands. [< OE. See **es-**.]

Isa. Isaiah (Old Testament).

I·saac (ī'zək). Hebrew patriarch, son of Abraham and father of Jacob. Genesis 21:1–4.

I·sa·iah (ī-zā'ə, ī-zī'ə). Hebrew prophet of the 8th century B.C.

-ise. *Chiefly Brit.* Variant of **-ize.**

-ish. *comb. form.* 1. a. Of the nationality of: **Finnish.** b. Having the qualities or character of: **sheepish.** c. Tending to or preoccupied with: **selfish.** d. Somewhat near or approximately: *fortyish.* 2. Somewhat: **greenish.** [< OE *-isc.*]

i·sin·glass (ī'zĭng-glăs', -gläs', ī'zən-) *n.* A transparent, almost pure gelatin prepared from the air bladder of certain fishes. [< MDu *huusblase,* "sturgeon bladder."]

I·sis (ī'sĭs). Egyptian goddess of fertility; sister and wife of Osiris.

isl. island.

Is·lam (ĭs'ləm, ĭz'-, ĭs-läm') *n.* 1. A religion based upon the teachings of the prophet Mohammed and believing in one God (Allah); the Moslem religion. 2. Moslems or Moslem nations viewed collectively. —Is·lam'ic *adj.*

Is·lam·a·bad (ĭs-lä'mə-bäd', ĭz-). The capital of Pakistan in N West Pakistan. Pop. 50,000.

is·land (ī'lənd) *n.* 1. A land mass smaller than a continent and surrounded by water. 2. Anything completely isolated or surrounded. [< OE *iegland, iland.* See akwā-.]

is·land·er (ī'lən-dər) *n.* An inhabitant of an island.

islands of Lang·er·hans (läng'ər-häns'). Also **islets of Lang·er·hans.** Irregular masses of small cells that lie in the interstitial tissue of the pancreas and secrete insulin. [< P. *Langerhans* (1847–1888), German physician.]

isle (īl) *n.* An island, esp. a small one. [< L *insula.*]

is·let (ī'lĭt) *n.* A little island.

ism (ĭz'əm) *n. Informal.* A distinctive doctrine or cause.

-ism. *comb. form.* 1. An action, practice, or process: **favoritism.** 2. A state or condition of being: **parallelism.** 3. A characteristic behavior or quality: **individualism.** 4. A distinctive usage or feature: *Latinism.* 5. A doctrine, theory, system, or principle: **pacifism, militarism.** [< Gk *-ismos.*]

is·n't (ĭz'ənt). Contraction of *is not.*

iso-. *comb. form.* 1. Equal, identical, or similar. 2. *Chem.* Isomeric. [< Gk *isos,* equal.]

i·so·bar (ī'sə-bär') *n.* A line on a map connecting points of equal pressure. —i'so·bar'ic *adj.*

i·so·late (ī'sə-lāt', ĭs'ə-) *v.* -lated, -lating. 1. To separate from a group or whole and set apart. 2. To render free of external influence. [< LL *insulātus,* converted into an island.] —i'so·la'tion *n.* —i'so·la'tor *n.*

i·so·la·tion·ism (ī'sə-lā'shə-nĭz'əm, ĭs'ə-) *n.* A national policy of remaining aloof from political entanglements with other countries. —i'so·la'tion·ist *n. & adj.*

i·so·mer (ī'sə-mər) *n.* 1. A compound having the same percentage composition and molecular weight as another compound but differing in chemical or physical properties. 2. An atom the nucleus of which can exist in any of several bound excited states for a measurable period of time. —i'so·mer'ic *adj.* —i·som'er·ism' (ī-sŏm'ə-rĭz'əm) *n.*

i·so·met·ric (ī'sə-mĕt'rĭk) *adj.* Also **i·so·met·ri·cal** (-rĭ-kəl). 1. Exhibiting equality in dimensions or measurements. 2. Involving muscular contraction occurring when the ends of the muscle are fixed in place so that significant increases in tension occur without appreciable increases in length. [< Gk *isometros,* of equal measure.]

isometric exercise. Exercise involving isometric contraction.

i·so·oc·tane (ī'sō-ŏk'tān') *n.* A highly flammable liquid, C_8H_{18}, used to determine the octane numbers of fuels.

i·so·prene (ī'sə-prēn') *n.* A colorless volatile liquid, C_5H_8, used chiefly to make synthetic rubber.

i·so·pro·pyl alcohol (ī'sə-prō'pəl). A clear, colorless, mobile flammable liquid, C_3H_8O, used in antifreeze compounds, lotions and cosmetics, and as a solvent.

i·sos·ce·les (ī-sŏs'ə-lēz') *adj.* Having two equal sides: *isosceles triangle.* [< Gk *isoskelēs,* "having equal legs."]

i·so·ther·mal (ī'sə-thûr'məl) *adj.* With or at equal temperatures. —i'so·therm' *n.*

i·so·tope (ī'sə-tōp') *n.* One of two or more atoms, the nuclei of which have the same number of protons but different numbers of neutrons. —i'so·top'ic (-tŏp'ĭk) *adj.* —i'so·top'i·cal·ly *adv.*

i·so·trop·ic (ī'sə-trŏp'ĭk) *adj.* Invariant with respect to direction. —i·sot'ro·py (ī-sŏt'rə-pē), i·sot'ro·pism' *n.*

ă pat/ā ate/âr care/ä bar/b bib/ch chew/d deed/ĕ pet/ē be/f fit/g gag/h hat/hw what/ ĭ pit/ī pie/îr pier/j judge/k kick/l lid, fatal/m mum/n no, sudden/ng sing/ŏ pot/ō go/

Is·ra·el¹ (ĭz′rē-əl). A republic on the E coast of the Mediterranean. Pop. 2,565,000. Cap. Jerusalem. **—Is·rae′li** *adj. & n.*

Israel¹

Is·ra·el² (ĭz′rē-əl) *n.* **1.** The descendants of Jacob. **2.** The whole Hebrew people, past, present, and future, regarded as the chosen people of Jehovah by virtue of the covenant of Jacob. **3.** The Christian church, regarded as the heir to the ancient covenant.
Is·ra·el³ (ĭz′-rē-əl). A name of the patriarch Jacob.
Is·ra·el·ite (ĭz′rē-ə-līt′) *n.* A Hebrew. **—Is′ra·el·ite′** *adj.*
Is·su·ance (ĭsh′ŏŏ-əns) *n.* An act of issuing.
Is·sue (ĭsh′ŏŏ) *n.* **1.** An act or instance of flowing, passing, or giving out. **2.** Something produced, published, or offered, as stamps or coins. **3.** The result of an action. **4.** Proceeds from estates or fines. **5.** Something proceeding from a specified source. **6.** Offspring. **7.** A point of discussion. **8.** An outlet. **9.** A discharge, as of blood. **—at issue.** In dispute. **—take issue.** To disagree. **—v. -sued, -suing. 1.** To go or come out. **2.** To come forth or cause to come forth. **3.** To give or distribute, as supplies. **4.** To be descended. **5.** To result from. **6.** To result in. **7.** To publish or be published. **8.** To circulate or be circulated, as coins. [< VL *exūta,* "exit."] **—is′su·er** *n.*
-ist. *comb. form.* **1.** One who does, makes, produces, etc.: **dramatist. 2.** One who is skilled or trained in a specified field: **industrialist. 3.** An adherent or proponent of a doctrine, system, or school of thought: *Platonist.* **4.** A person characterized by a certain trait: **sadist.** [< Gk *-istēs.*]
Is·tan·bul (ĭs′tăn-bŏŏl′, ĭs′tän-). A city of European Turkey. Pop. 1,467,000.
isth·mus (ĭs′məs) *n., pl.* **-muses** or **-mi** (-mĭ′). **1.** A narrow strip of land connecting two larger masses of land. **2.** *Anat.* **a.** A narrow strip of tissue joining two larger organs or parts of an organ. **b.** A narrow passage connecting two larger cavities. [< Gk *isthmos.*]

it (ĭt) *pron.* The 3rd person sing. pronoun, neuter gender. **1.** —Used to represent the thing last mentioned: *I haven't seen it.* **2.** —Used as the subject of an impersonal verb: *It is raining.* **3.** —Used to represent a word, phrase, or clause that follows: *It is he.* **4.** *Informal.* The best or ultimate in something: *That steak was really it!* **—n.** In the game of tag, the player who must catch the others. [OE *hit.* See **ko-.**]
It., Ital. Italian; Italy.
ital. italic.
I·tal·ian (ĭ-tăl′yən) *adj.* Of Italy, its people, or their language. **—n. 1.** An inhabitant of Italy, or a person of Italian descent. **2.** The Romance language of Italy.
i·tal·ic (ĭ-tăl′ĭk, ī-tăl′-) *adj.* Being a type with the letters slanting to the right, used to emphasize a word or passage. **—i·tal′ic** *n.*
I·tal·ic (ĭ-tăl′ĭk) *n.* A branch of Indo-European, including Latin and Osco-Umbrian.
i·tal·i·cize (ĭ-tăl′ĭ-sīz′) *v.* **-cized, -cizing.** To print in italic type.
It·a·ly (ĭt′ə-lē). A republic of S Europe. Pop.

Italy

50,849,000. Cap. Rome.
itch (ĭch) *n.* **1.** A skin sensation causing a desire to scratch. **2.** A contagious skin disease marked by itching. **3.** A restless craving. [< OE *giccan* < Gmc **juk-.*] **—itch** *v.* **—itch′i·ness** *n.* **—itch′y** *adj.*
-ite. *comb. form.* **1.** A native or resident of a specified place: *New Jerseyite.* **2.** An adherent of someone specified: *Trotskyite.* **3.** A mineral or rock: **graphite. 4.** A commercial product: **Lucite.** [< Gk *-ītēs.*]
i·tem (ī′təm) *n.* **1.** A single unit in a list, account, or series. **2. a.** A bit of information. **b.** A short piece in a newspaper. [< L *ita,* so.]
i·tem·ize (ī′tə-mīz′) *v.* **-ized, -izing.** To set down item by item; list.
it·er·ate (ĭt′ə-rāt′) *v.* **-ated, -ating.** To say or perform again; repeat. [< L *iterum,* again.] **—it′er·a′tion** *n.*
i·tin·er·ant (ī-tĭn′ər-ənt, ĭ-tĭn′-) *adj.* Traveling from place to place, esp. to perform some duty or work. **—n.** One who so travels. [< L *iter,* journey.]
i·tin·er·ar·y (ī-tĭn′ə-rĕr′ē, ĭ-tĭn′-) *n., pl.* **-ies.**

1. A route or proposed route of a journey. 2. An account or record of a journey. 3. A travelers' guidebook.

–itis. *comb. form.* Inflammation of or inflammatory disease: **bronchitis.** [< Gk.]

its (ĭts). The possessive form of the pronoun *it*, used attributively.

it's (ĭts). 1. Contraction of *it is.* 2. Contraction of *it has.*

it•self (ĭt-sĕlf′) *pron.* A form of the 3rd person sing. neuter pronoun: 1. —Used reflexively: *This radio turns itself off.* 2. —Used for emphasis: *The trouble is in the machine itself.* —**by itself.** 1. Alone. 2. Without help.

–ity. *comb. form.* A state or quality: **authenticity.** [< L *-itās.*]

IUD intrauterine device.

–ium. *comb. form.* The name of an element or chemical group: **ammonium.** [< Gk *-ion*, dim suffix.]

IV intravenous.

I've (īv). Contraction of *I have.*

–ive. *comb. form.* Having a tendency toward or inclination to perform some action: **disruptive.** [< L *-īvus.*]

i•vo•ry (ī′və-rē, ī′vrē) *n., pl.* **-ries.** 1. The hard, smooth, yellowish-white substance forming the tusks of certain animals, esp. elephants. 2. A substance resembling ivory. 3. Creamy white. [< L *ebur.*] —**i′vo•ry** *adj.*

Ivory Coast. A republic of W Africa. Pop. 3,750,000. Cap. Abidjan.

ivory tower. A place or attitude of intellectual retreat.

i•vy (ī′vē) *n., pl.* **ivies.** 1. A climbing or trailing plant with lobed, evergreen leaves. 2. Any of various similar plants. [< OE *ĭfig* < Gmc *ibahs.*] —**i′vied** *adj.*

IWW Industrial Workers of the World.

–ize. Also *chiefly Brit.* **-ise.** *comb. form.* 1. a. To cause to be or to become; make into: **dramatize.** b. To make conform with: **Anglicize.** c. To treat or regard as: **idolize.** 2. To cause to acquire a specified quality: **sterilize.** 3. To become or become similar to: **materialize.** 4. a. To subject to: **anesthetize.** b. To affect with: **galvanize, magnetize.** 5. To do or follow some practice: **pasteurize.** [< LL *-izāre* < Gk *-izein.*]

Ivory Coast

Jj

j, J (jā) *n.* 1. The 10th letter of the English alphabet. 2. The 10th in a series.

J joule.

J. 1. journal. 2. judge.

J.A. judge advocate.

jab (jăb) *v.* **jabbed, jabbing.** 1. To poke abruptly, esp. with something sharp. 2. To stab or pierce. —*n.* A quick stab or blow. [< ME *jobben.*] —**jab′bing•ly** *adv.*

jab•ber (jăb′ər) *v.* To talk rapidly, unintelligibly, or idly. —**jab′ber** *n.*

jab•ot (zhă-bō′, jă-) *n.* A cascade of frills down the front of a shirt or blouse. [F.]

jac•a•ran•da (jăk′ə-răn′də) *n.* 1. A tropical American tree with feathery leaves and clusters of pale-purple flowers. 2. Rosewood. [Port *jacarandá.*]

jack (jăk) *n.* 1. Any of several mechanical devices, esp. one for raising heavy objects a short distance, as by leverage. 2. A socket that accepts a plug at one end and attaches to circuitry at the other. 3. A playing card showing the figure of a knave. [Transferred use of the name *Jack.*]

jack•al (jăk′əl, -ôl′) *n.* A doglike carnivorous mammal of Africa and Asia. [< Pers *shagāl.*]

jack•ass (jăk′ăs′) *n.* 1. A male ass or donkey. 2. A foolish or stupid person.

jack•daw (jăk′dô′) *n.* A crowlike Eurasian bird.

jack•et (jăk′ĭt) *n.* 1. A short coat, usually hip-length. 2. An outer covering or casing, as the dust jacket of a book. [< OF *jaque*, short jacket.] —**jack′et•less** *adj.*

jack-in-the-pul•pit (jăk′ĭn-thə-poŏl′pĭt, -pŭl′pĭt) *n.* A plant with a leaflike part enclosing a clublike flower stalk.

jack•knife (jăk′nīf′) *n.* 1. A large pocketknife. 2. A dive executed by bending at the waist and touching the feet with the hands before straightening out. —*v.* **-knifed, -knifing.** 1. To bend or fold like a jackknife. 2. To form a 90°angle. [Prob JACK + KNIFE.]

jack-of-all-trades (jăk′əv-ôl′trādz′) *n., pl.*

ă pat/ā ate/âr care/ä bar/b bib/ch chew/d deed/ĕ pet/ē be/f fit/g gag/h hat/hw what/
ĭ pit/ī pie/îr pier/j judge/k kick/l lid, fatal/m mum/n no, sudden/ng sing/ŏ pot/ō go/

jacks-of-all-trades. One who can do many different kinds of work.
jack-o'-lan·tern (jăk'ə-lăn'tərn) *n.* A lantern made from a hollowed pumpkin with a carved face.
jack·pot (jăk'pŏt') *n.* **1.** The cumulative stakes in various gambling games. **2.** A top prize or reward.
jack rabbit. A large hare of W North America. [JACK(ASS) + RABBIT.]
Jack·son (jăk'sən). The capital of Mississippi. Pop. 154,000.

Andrew Jackson

Jack·son (jăk'sən), **Andrew.** 1767–1845. 7th President of the U.S. (1829–37).
Jack·son·ville (jăk'sən-vĭl). A city of N Florida. Pop. 201,000.
Ja·cob (jā'kəb). Hebrew patriarch, son of Isaac. Genesis 25–50.
jade¹ (jād) *n.* Either of two distinct minerals, nephrite and jadeite, that are generally pale green or white and are used mainly as gemstones. [< Span *(piedra de) ijada,* "(stone of the) flank."]
jade² (jād) *n.* **1.** A broken-down horse; nag. **2.** A worthless woman. —*v.* **jaded, jading. 1.** To exhaust or wear out. **2.** To become weary or sated. [ME.] —**jad'ish** *adj.*
jad·ed (jā'dĭd) *adj.* **1.** Wearied; spiritless with fatigue. **2.** Dulled as by surfeit; sated. —**jad'ed·ly** *adv.* —**jad'ed·ness** *n.*
jade·ite (jā'dīt') *n.* A rare, emerald to light-green, white, red-brown, yellow-brown, or violet jade, $NaAlSi_2O_6$.
jag¹ (jăg) *n.* Also **jagg.** A sharp projection; barb. [ME *jagge.*] —**jag'less** *adj.*
jag² (jăg) *n. Slang.* A bout or spree: *a crying jag.* [?]
jag·ged (jăg'ĭd) *adj.* Toothed or serrated; having jags. —**jag'ged·ly** *adv.*
jag·uar (jăg'wär', -yōō-är') *n.* A large, leopard-like tropical American wild-cat.
Jah·weh. Variant of **Yahweh.**
jai a·lai (hī' lī', hī' ə-lī', hī' ə-lī'). A court game

in which players use a long hand-shaped basket strapped to the wrist to propel a ball against a wall. [< Basque.]
jail (jāl). Also *chiefly Brit.* **gaol.** *n.* A prison for the confinement of persons in lawful detention. —*v.* To detain in custody; imprison. [< L *cavea,* a hollow, den, coop.]
jail·bird (jāl'bûrd') *n. Informal.* A prisoner or ex-convict.
jail·er (jā'lər) *n.* Also **jail·or.** The keeper of a jail.
ja·lop·y (jə-lŏp'ē) *n., pl.* **-ies.** Also **ja·lop·py.** *Informal.* An old, dilapidated automobile. [?]
ja·lou·sie (jăl'ōō-sē) *n.* A blind or shutter having adjustable horizontal slats. [F, "jealousy."]
jam¹ (jăm) *v.* **jammed, jamming. 1.** To drive or wedge forcibly; squeeze into a tight position. **2.** To activate or apply suddenly: *jam the brakes on.* **3.** To become or cause to become locked, stuck, or unworkable. **4.** To pack to excess; cram. **5.** To block or clog. **6.** To interfere with the reception of (broadcast signals) by electronic means. —*n.* **1.** The act of jamming or condition of being jammed. **2.** A crush or congestion. **3.** *Informal.* A predicament.
jam² (jăm) *n.* A preserve made by boiling fruit with sugar.
Ja·mai·ca (jə-mā'kə). An island and nation in the Caribbean. Pop. 1,613,000. Cap. Kingston. —**Ja·mai'can** *n. & adj.*

Jamaica

jamb (jăm) *n.* The vertical posts or pieces of a door or window frame. [< Gk *kampē,* joint.]
jam·bo·ree (jăm'bə-rē') *n.* **1.** A noisy celebration. **2.** A large assembly. [?]
Jan. January.
jan·gle (jăng'gəl) *v.* **-gled, -gling. 1.** To make or cause to make a harsh, metallic sound. **2.** To grate on or jar (the nerves). —*n.* A harsh, metallic sound. [< OF *jangler.*] —**jan'gler** *n.* —**jan'gly** *adj.*
jan·i·tor (jăn'ə-tər) *n.* One who attends to the maintenance or cleaning of a building. [< L *jānus,* arched passage.]
Jan·u·ar·y (jăn'yōō-ĕr'ē) *n., pl.* **-ies.** The 1st month of the year. January has 31 days. [< L *Jānuārius (mensis),* "(month of) Janus."]
Ja·nus (jā'nəs). The Roman god of portals, depicted with two faces looking in opposite directions.

Ja·nus-faced (jā′nəs-fāst′) *adj.* Hypocritical.

Jap. Japan; Japanese.

Ja·pan (jə-păn′). A country of Asia occupying an archipelago off the NE coast of the continent. Pop. 93,419,000. Cap. Tokyo.

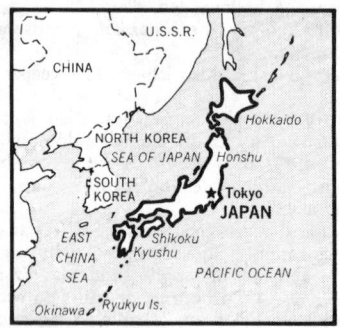

Japan

Jap·a·nese (jăp′ə-nēz′, -nēs′) *n., pl.* **-nese.** 1. A native or inhabitant of Japan. 2. The language of Japan. —**Jap′a·nese′** *adj.*

jar[1] (jär) *n.* A cylindrical glass or earthenware vessel with a wide mouth. [< Ar *jarrah*, large earthen vase.]

jar[2] (jär) *v.* **jarred, jarring.** 1. To make or utter a harsh sound. 2. To disturb. 3. To shake from impact. 4. To clash; conflict. 5. To bump or cause to move or shake. —*n.* 1. A jolt. 2. A harsh, grating sound. [Prob imit.]

jar·di·nière (järd′n-îr′) *n.* A large, decorative stand or pot for plants. [< VL *gardinus*, GARDEN.]

jar·gon (jär′gən) *n.* 1. Nonsensical or incoherent utterance. 2. The specialized or technical language of a group or profession. [< OF *jargoun*, "twittering."]

Jas. James (New Testament).

jas·mine (jăz′mən) *n.* Also **jes·sa·mine** (jĕs′ə-mĭn). Any of several vines or shrubs with fragrant, usually yellow or white flowers. [< Pers *yasmīn*.]

jas·per (jăs′pər) *n.* An opaque reddish, brown, or yellow quartz. [< Gk *iaspis*.]

jaun·dice (jôn′dĭs, jän′-) *n.* Yellowish discoloration of tissues and bodily fluids with bile pigment. [< L *galbinus*, greenish yellow.]

jaun·diced (jôn′dĭst, jän′-) *adj.* 1. Affected with jaundice. 2. Affected by envy, jealousy, malice, etc.

jaunt (jônt, jänt) *n.* A short trip or outing. [?]

jaun·ty (jôn′tē, jän′-) *adj.* **-tier, -tiest.** 1. Dapper in appearance; natty. 2. Having a buoyant or self-confident air. [Earlier *jentee*, elegant, "genteel."] —**jaun′ti·ly** *adv.* —**jaun′ti·ness** *n.*

Jav. Javanese.

Ja·va (jä′və, jăv′ə). An island of Indonesia. Pop. 63,000,000.

Jav·a·nese (jăv′ə-nēz′, -nēs′) *n., pl.* **-nese.** 1. A native of Java. 2. The Indonesian language spoken in Java. —**Jav′a·nese′** *adj.*

jave·lin (jăv′lən, jăv′ə-) *n.* 1. A light spear thrown as a weapon. 2. A spear used in con-

tests of distance throwing. [< OF *javelot*.]

jaw (jô) *n.* 1. Either of two bony or cartilaginous structures in most vertebrates forming the framework of the mouth and holding the teeth. 2. Either of two opposed hinged parts in a mechanical device. 3. **jaws.** A dangerous confrontation: *the jaws of death.* [ME *iawe*.] —**jaw′less** *adj.*

jaw·bone (jô′bōn′) *n.* Any bone of the jaw, esp. the bone of the lower jaw. —*v.* **-boned, -boning.** *Informal.* To urge voluntary compliance or to comply voluntarily, as with governmental guidelines limiting prices and wages. —*adj. Informal.* Urging voluntary compliance: *jawbone controls.*

jaw·break·er (jô′brā′kər) *n.* 1. A kind of very hard candy. 2. *Slang.* A word very difficult to pronounce.

jay (jā) *n.* Any of various birds related to the crows, often having a loud, harsh call. [< LL *gāius* and *gāia*.]

jay·walk (jā′wôk′) *v.* To cross a street without regard to traffic rules. —**jay′walk′er** *n.*

jazz (jăz) *n.* 1. A kind of native American music, in most styles having a strong rhythmic understructure with solo and ensemble improvisations. 2. *Slang.* **a.** Extreme exaggeration. **b.** Nonsense. [?]

jazz·y (jăz′ē) *adj.* **-ier, -iest.** 1. Resembling jazz. 2. *Slang.* Showy; flashy: *a jazzy red car.* —**jazz′i·ly** *adv.* —**jazz′i·ness** *n.*

J.C.S. Joint Chiefs of Staff.

jct. junction.

jeal·ous (jĕl′əs) *adj.* 1. Fearful of loss of position or affection. 2. Resentful in rivalry; envious. 3. Possessively watchful; vigilant. [< Gk *zēlos*, zèal.] —**jeal′ous·ly** *adv.* —**jeal′ous·y, jeal′ous·ness** *n.*

jeans (jēnz) *pl.n.* Pants made from strong, twilled cotton material. [< Genoa, where it was first made.]

jeep (jēp) *n.* A small, durable motor vehicle used esp. by the armed forces. [Orig *G.P.*, "general purpose."]

jeer (jîr) *v.* To speak or shout derisively; mock; taunt. [?] —**jeer** *n.* —**jeer′ing·ly** *adv.*

Jef·fer·son (jĕf′ər-sən), **Thomas.** 1743–1826.

Thomas Jefferson

ă pat/ā ate/âr care/ä bar/b bib/ch chew/d deed/ĕ pet/ē be/f fit/g gag/h hat/hw what/
ĭ pit/ī pie/îr pier/j judge/k kick/l lid, fatal/m mum/n no, sudden/ng sing/ŏ pot/ō go/

3rd President of the U.S. (1801–09). —**Jef'fer•so'ni•an** (-sō'nē-ən) *adj.*

Jef•fer•son City (jĕf'ər-sən). The capital of Missouri. Pop. 32,000.

Je•ho•vah (jĭ-hō'və). God, esp. in Christian translations of the Old Testament.

Je•june (jə-jōōn') *adj.* **1.** Not nourishing; insubstantial. **2.** Not interesting. **3.** Childish. [< L *jējūnus*, hungry, fasting.]

Je•ju•num (jə-jōō'nəm) *n., pl.* **-na** (-nə). The section of the small intestine between the duodenum and the ileum. [ML *jējūnum (intestīnum),* "the fasting (intestine)."]

jell (jĕl) *v.* **1.** To become or cause to become firm or gelatinous; congeal. **2.** *Informal.* To take shape or fall into place; crystallize.

jel•ly (jĕl'ē) *n., pl.* **-lies. 1.** A soft, resilient food usually made by the setting of a liquid containing pectin or gelatin. **2.** Any substance with the consistency of jelly. —*v.* **-lied, -lying.** To make into or become jelly. [< L *gelāre,* to freeze.]

jel•ly•fish (jĕl'ē-fĭsh') *n.* **1.** A gelatinous, freeswimming, often umbrella-shaped marine organism. **2.** *Informal.* A person who lacks force of character.

jen•ny (jĕn'ē) *n., pl.* **-nies.** A spinning jenny.

jeop•ard•ize (jĕp'ər-dīz') *v.* **-ized, -izing.** To invite loss of or injury to; imperil.

jeop•ard•y (jĕp'ər-dē) *n., pl.* **-ies. 1.** Danger or risk of loss or injury. **2.** *Law.* A defendant's risk or danger of conviction. [< OF *jeu parti,* "divided play, even chance."]

Jer. Jeremiah (Old Testament).

Jer•e•mi•ad (jĕr'ə-mī'əd) *n.* An elaborate lamentation.

Jer•e•mi•ah (jĕr'ə-mī'ə). Hebrew prophet of the 7th and 6th centuries B.C.

jerk (jûrk) *v.* To move by or with a sharp, suddenly abrupt motion. —*n.* **1.** A sudden, abrupt motion, such as a yank, twist, or lurch. **2.** A sudden spasmodic muscular movement. **3.** *Slang.* A stupid or fatuous person. [?] —**jerk'i•ly** *adv.* —**jerk'i•ness** *n.* —**jerk'y** *adj.*

jer•kin (jûr'kən) *n.* A short, close-fitting coat or jacket, usually sleeveless. [?]

jerk•wa•ter (jûrk'wô'tər, -wŏt'ər) *adj. Informal.* Remote, small, and insignificant: *a jerkwater town.*

jer•ry•build (jĕr'ē-bĭld') *v.* **-built** (-bĭlt'), **-building.** To build flimsily and cheaply. [?]

jer•sey (jûr'zē) *n., pl.* **-seys. 1.** A soft, plainknitted fabric. **2.** A knitted pullover shirt. **3.** A close-fitting knitted jacket or sweater. [< *Jersey,* one of the Channel Islands.]

Jersey City. A city of NE New Jersey. Pop. 276,000.

Je•ru•sa•lem (jə-rōō'sə-ləm, -zə-ləm). The capital of ancient and modern Israel. Pop. 248,000.

jes•sa•mine. Variant of **jasmine.**

jest (jĕst) *n.* **1.** Something said or done to provoke amusement and laughter. **2.** A frivolous attitude: *spoken in jest.* —*v.* To act or speak playfully; joke. [< L *gesta,* exploits.]

jest•er (jĕs'tər) *n.* One given to jesting, esp. a fool or buffoon at medieval courts.

Jes•u•it (jĕzh'ōō-ĭt, jĕz'yōō-) *n.* A member of the Society of Jesus, a Roman Catholic order.

Je•sus (jē'zəs). Also, in various contexts, "Jesus of Nazareth," "Christ," "Jesus Christ," or "Christ Jesus." 4? B.C.–A.D. 29? Son of Mary; founder of the Christian religion; regarded by Christians as the son of God and the Messiah.

jet[1] (jĕt) *n.* **1.** A dense black coal that takes a high polish and is used for jewelry. **2.** A deep black. [< Gk *gagatēs,* "stone of *Gagai*" (town in Asia Minor).] —**jet** *adj.*

jet[2] (jĕt) *n.* **1. a.** A high-velocity fluid stream forced under pressure out of a small-diameter opening. **b.** Something emitted in or as if in such a stream. **c.** An outlet for emitting such a stream. **2.** A jet-propelled vehicle, esp. a jet-propelled aircraft. —*v.* **jetted, jetting. 1.** To propel outward under pressure. **2.** To travel by jet plane. [< L *jacere,* to throw.]

jet engine. 1. Any engine that develops thrust by ejecting a jet, esp. of gaseous combustion products. **2.** Such an engine equipped to consume atmospheric oxygen as distinguished from rocket engines with self-contained fuel-oxidizer systems.

jet•sam (jĕt'səm) *n.* **1.** Cargo thrown overboard to lighten a ship in distress. **2.** Discarded odds and ends. [< JETTISON.]

jet•ti•son (jĕt'ĭ-sən, -zən) *v.* **1.** To cast off or overboard. **2.** To discard. [< L *jactāre,* to throw.]

jet•ty (jĕt'ē) *n., pl.* **-ties. 1.** A structure projecting into a body of water to influence the current or tide or protect a harbor or shoreline. **2.** A wharf. [< OF *jeter,* to throw, project.]

Jew (jōō) *n.* **1.** An adherent of Judaism. **2.** A descendant of the Hebrew people.

jew•el (jōō'əl) *n.* **1.** An ornament of precious metal or gems. **2.** A precious stone; a gem. **3.** A small gem or gem substitute used as a bearing in a watch. **4.** A treasured or esteemed person or thing. —*v.* **1.** To adorn with jewels. **2.** To fit with jewels, as a watch. [< NF *juel.*] —**jew'el•ry** *n.*

jew•el•er (jōō'ə-lər) *n.* Also *chiefly Brit.* **jew•el•ler.** One who makes, repairs, or deals in jewelry.

Jew•ish (jōō'ĭsh) *adj.* **1.** Of, concerning, or characteristic of the Jews, their customs, or their religion. **2.** Yiddish. —*n.* Yiddish.

Jew•ry (jōō'rē) *n.* Jews collectively.

jez•e•bel (jĕz'ə-bĕl', -bəl) *n.* Also **Jez•e•bel.** A scheming, wicked woman. [< *Jezebel,* wicked queen of Israel.]

jg junior grade.

jib (jĭb) *n.* A triangular sail attached to the forward mast of a sailing vessel. [?]

jibe[1] (jīb) *v.* **jibed, jibing.** *Informal.* To be in accord; agree. [?]

jibe[2]. Variant of **gibe.**

jif•fy (jĭf'ē) *n., pl.* **-fies.** *Informal.* A moment; no time at all. [?]

jig (jĭg) *n.* **1.** Any of various lively dances in triple time. **2.** A device for guiding a tool or holding machine work in place. —*v.* **jigged, jigging. 1.** To dance a jig. **2.** To move or bob up and down jerkily and rapidly. [?]

ô paw, for/oi boy/ou out/ŏŏ took/ōō coo/p pop/r run/s sauce/sh shy/t to/th thin/*th* the/
ŭ cut/ûr fur/v van/w wag/y yes/z size/zh vision/ə ago, item, edible, gallop, circus/

jig·ger (jĭg′ər) *n.* **1.** A small measure for liquor, usually holding 1½ ounces. **2.** A short golf club with an iron head. **3.** A short mast set in the stern of a yawl or ketch. **4.** A trivial article whose name eludes one.

jig·gle (jĭg′əl) *v.* -gled, -gling. To move lightly and jerkily up and down or to and fro. —*n.* A jiggling motion.

jig·saw (jĭg′sô′) *n.* A saw used to cut sharp curves.

jigsaw puzzle. A game consisting of the reassembly of a picture on cardboard or wood that has been cut into numerous interlocking pieces.

jilt (jĭlt) *v.* To discard (a lover) unexpectedly. —*n.* A woman who discards a lover.

Jim Crow. *Slang.* The systematic practice of segregating and suppressing Negroes. —**Jim′-Crow′** *adj.*

jim·my (jĭm′ē) *n., pl.* -mies. A short crowbar with curved ends, often regarded as a burglar's tool. —**jim′my** *v.* (-mied, -mying).

jim·son·weed (jĭm′sən-wēd′) *n.* A coarse, poisonous plant with large, trumpet-shaped white or purplish flowers. [< *Jamestown*, Virginia.]

jin·gle (jĭng′gəl) *v.* -gled, -gling. To make or cause to make a tinkling or ringing metallic sound. —*n.* **1.** Such a sound. **2.** Something resembling or suggesting such a sound. **3.** A simple, repetitious, catchy rhyme.

jin·go (jĭng′gō) *n., pl.* -goes. An extreme and belligerent nationalist; a blatant patriot. —**jin′go·ish**, **jin′go·is′tic** *adj.* —**jin′go·ism′** *n.* —**jin′go·ist** *n.*

jink (jĭngk) *v.* To make a quick, evasive turn. —*n.* **1.** A sudden evasive turn. **2.** jinks. Rambunctious play: *high jinks.* [?]

jin·ni (jĭn′ē, jĭ-nē′) *n., pl.* jinn (jĭn). Also **djin·ni** *pl.* djinn. A supernatural being in Moslem folklore.

jin·rik·sha (jĭn-rĭk′shô) *n.* A two-wheeled Oriental carriage drawn by one or two men. [Jap *jinrikisha.*]

jinx (jĭngks). *Informal. n.* Something or someone believed to bring bad luck. —*v.* To bring bad luck to. [Poss < Gk *iunx*, a bird used in magic.]

jit·ney (jĭt′nē) *n., pl.* -neys. *Informal.* A small vehicle that transports passengers for a low fare. [?]

jit·ter (jĭt′ər) *v. Informal.* To be nervous or uneasy; fidget. [?] —**jit′ter·y** *adj.*

jit·ter·bug (jĭt′ər-bŭg′) *n.* **1.** A strenuous dance performed to quick-tempo jazz or swing music. **2.** A performer of this dance. —*v.* -bugged, -bugging. To dance the jitterbug.

jit·ters (jĭt′ərz) *pl.n. Informal.* A fit of nervousness.

jiu·jit·su, jiu·jut·su. Variants of **jujitsu.**

jive (jīv) *n. Slang.* **1.** Jazz or swing music. **2.** The jargon of jazz musicians and enthusiasts. **3.** Deceptive or glib talk. [?]

jnt. joint.

Joan of Arc (jōn′; ärk′), **Saint.** 1412–1431. French national heroine.

job (jŏb) *n.* **1.** An action requiring some exertion; an undertaking. **2.** An activity performed for payment, esp. one performed regularly as one's occupation. **3. a.** A piece of work to be done for a fee. **b.** The object to be worked on. **c.** Anything resulting from work. **4.** A position in which one is employed. —*v.* jobbed, jobbing. **1.** To work by the piece. **2.** To act as a middleman or jobber. **3.** To subcontract (work). **4.** To transact (official business) dishonestly for private profit. [?] —**job′less** *adj.* —**job′less·ness** *n.*

Job (jōb). The righteous sufferer of the Old Testament book of Job.

job·ber (jŏb′ər) *n.* **1.** One who buys merchandise from manufacturers and sells it to retailers. **2.** A person who works by the piece. **3.** A public official who exploits his position for personal gain.

job·ber·y (jŏb′ə-rē) *n.* Corruption among public officials.

job·hold·er (jŏb′hōl′dər) *n.* One who has a regular or steady job.

job lot. **1.** Miscellaneous merchandise sold in one lot. **2.** Any collection of cheap or almost worthless items.

job printer. A printer who does miscellaneous work, as circulars and cards.

jock·ey (jŏk′ē) *n., pl.* -eys. One who rides horses in races, esp. professionally. —*v.* **1.** To ride (a horse) as jockey. **2.** To direct or maneuver by cleverness or skill. **3.** To maneuver for position or a certain advantage.

jo·cose (jō-kōs′) *adj.* Merry; humorous. [< L *jocus*, jest, joke.] —**jo·cose′ly** *adv.*

jo·cos·i·ty (jō-kŏs′ə-tē) *n., pl.* -ties. **1.** The state or quality of being jocose. **2.** A jocose remark or act.

joc·u·lar (jŏk′yə-lər) *adj.* Humorous; facetious; merry. [< L *jocus*, jest, joke.] —**joc′u·lar·ly** *adv.*

joc·u·lar·i·ty (jŏk′yə-lăr′ə-tē) *n., pl.* -ties. **1.** The state or quality of being jocular. **2.** Playful humor. **3.** A jocular remark.

joc·und (jŏk′ənd, jō′kənd) *adj.* Cheerful; merry; gay. [< L *jūcundus*, agreeable.] —**joc′und·ly** *adv.*

jo·cun·di·ty (jō-kŭn′də-tē) *n., pl.* -ties. **1.** The state or quality of being jocund. **2.** A jocund remark or act.

jodh·pur boots (jŏd′pər). Short ankle-height leather boots worn with jodhpurs.

jodh·purs (jŏd′pərz) *pl.n.* Riding breeches that fit tightly at the knees and ankles. [< *Jodhpur*, India.]

jog¹ (jŏg) *v.* jogged, jogging. **1.** To jolt. **2.** To nudge. **3.** To run or ride at a steady slow trot. **4.** To proceed in a carefree way. —*n.* **1.** A jolt. **2.** A nudge. **3.** A trot. [?]

jog² (jŏg) *n.* **1.** A protruding or receding part in a surface or line. **2.** An abrupt change in direction. [Perh var of JAG¹.]

jog·gle (jŏg′əl) *v.* -gled, -gling. To shake or jar slightly. —**jog′gle** *n.*

Jo·han·nes·burg (jō-hăn′ĭs-bûrg′, yō-hä′nĭs-). A city of the Republic of South Africa, in the NE. Pop. 1,153,000.

John, **Saint.** Called "the Evangelist," "the Divine." Christian apostle; reputed author of the 4th Gospel.

ă pat/ā ate/âr care/ä bar/b bib/ch chew/d deed/ĕ pet/ē be/f fit/g gag/h hat/hw what/ ĭ pit/ī pie/îr pier/j judge/k kick/l lid, fatal/m mum/n no, sudden/ng sing/ŏ pot/ō go/

John Doe (jŏn' dō'). A name used in legal proceedings to designate a fictitious or unidentified person.

john•ny•cake (jŏn'ē-kāk') n. A small breadlike cake made with white cornmeal cooked on a griddle or baked.

John•son (jŏn'sən). **1. Andrew.** 1808–1875. 17th President of the U.S. (1865–69). **2. Lyndon Baines.** 1908–1973. 36th President of the U.S. (1963–69). **3. Samuel.** 1709–1784. English author, critic, and lexicographer.

Andrew Johnson

Lyndon Baines Johnson

John the Baptist, Saint. Baptizer of Jesus.
join (join) v. **1.** To put or bring together: *join hands.* **2.** To put or bring into close association: *joined in marriage.* **3.** To connect, as with a straight line. **4.** To form a junction with; combine with. **5.** To come or act together. **6.** To take part; participate. [< L *jungere.*]

join•er (joi'nər) n. **1.** One that joins. **2.** *Chiefly Brit.* A carpenter.

joint (joint) n. **1.** A point or position at which two or more things are joined. **2.** A point of connection or articulation between more or less movable bodily parts. **3.** A cut of meat for roasting. **4.** *Slang.* Any public establishment or dwelling. **5.** *Slang.* A marijuana cigarette. —*adj.* Shared by or common to two or more.

joist (joist) n. A horizontal beam set from wall to wall to support the boards of a floor or ceiling. [< L *jacēre,* to lie down.]

joke (jōk) n. **1.** An amusing remark or story. **2.** A mischievous trick. **3.** A ludicrous incident or situation. **4.** A triviality: *His accident was no joke.* **5.** A laughingstock. —*v.* **joked, joking. 1.** To tell or play jokes. **2.** To speak in fun; be facetious. [L *jocus,* jest, joke.] —**joke'less** *adj.* —**jok'ing•ly** *adv.*

jok•er (jō'kər) n. **1.** One who tells or plays jokes. **2.** A playing card, usually printed with a picture of a jester, typically used as a wild card. **3.** An element in a situation that acts in an unexpected way.

jol•li•fi•ca•tion (jŏl'ə-fĭ-kā'shən) n. Festivity; merrymaking.

jol•li•ty (jŏl'ə-tē) n. Merriment.

jol•ly (jŏl'ē) *adj.* -**lier,** -**liest. 1.** Merry. **2.** Festive. —*adv. Brit. Informal.* Very: *a jolly good cook.* [< OF *jolif, joli,* gay, pleasant.]

jolt (jōlt) v. **1.** To bump into; jostle. **2.** To shake or knock about. **3.** To jar with or as if with a sudden, sharp blow. —*n.* **1.** A sudden jarring or jerking. **2.** A sudden shock or reversal. [?] —**jolt'er** *n.* —**jolt'y** *adj.*

Jo•nah (jō'nə) n. One thought to bring bad luck. [< *Jonah,* Old Testament prophet whose disobedience to God caused a storm to endanger the ship in which he was traveling. Jonah 1:4.]

Jones (jōnz), **John Paul.** 1747–1792. Scottish-born American naval officer in the Revolutionary War.

jon•quil (jŏng'kwĭl, jŏn'-) n. A cultivated plant related to the daffodil, having short-tubed, fragrant yellow flowers. [< Span *junco,* rush, reed.]

Jon•son (jŏn'sən), **Ben(jamin).** 1573–1637. English poet and dramatist.

Jor•dan (jôrd'n). **1.** The principal river of Israel and Jordan. **2.** A kingdom in NW Arabia. Pop. 1,935,000. Cap. Amman. —**Jor•da'ni•an** (jôr-dā'nē-ən) *adj. & n.*

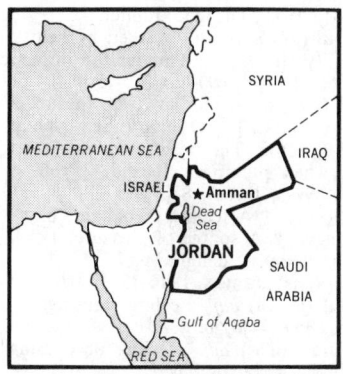

Jordan

Jo•seph (jō'zəf). **1.** Son of Jacob; sold into slavery in Egypt, he became the pharaoh's

---

ô paw, for/oi boy/ou out/ŏŏ took/ōō coo/p pop/r run/s sauce/sh shy/t to/th thin/*th* the/ ŭ cut/ûr fur/v van/w wag/y yes/z size/zh vision/ə ago, item, edible, gallop, circus/

chief official. Genesis 30–46. **2.** Husband of Mary, mother of Jesus. Matthew 1:16.

josh (jŏsh) *v.* To tease; joke. [?]

Josh. Joshua (Old Testament).

jos·tle (jŏs′əl) *v.* **-tled, -tling. 1.** To come in contact or collide. **2.** To make one's way by pushing or elbowing. *—n.* A rough push or shove. [< OF *juster,* to joust.]

jot (jŏt) *n.* The smallest bit or particle; iota. *—v.* **jotted, jotting.** To write down briefly and hastily. [< Gk *iōta,* IOTA.]

joule (joul, jool) *n.* **1.** The International System unit of energy equal to the work done when a current of 1 ampere is passed through a resistance of 1 ohm for 1 second. **2.** A unit of energy equal to the work done when the point of application of a force of 1 newton is displaced 1 meter in the direction of the force. [< J.P. *Joule* (1818–1889), British physicist.]

jounce (jouns) *v.* **jounced, jouncing.** To move with bumps and jolts. [ME *jouncen.*] **—jounce** *n.* **—jounc′y** *adj.*

jour. journal.

jour·nal (jûr′nəl) *n.* **1.** A daily record of occurrences or transactions, as a diary or ship's log. **2.** A newspaper. **3.** A specialized periodical. **4.** The part of a shaft or axle supported by a bearing. [< OF, "daily."]

jour·nal·ese (jûr′nə-lēz′, -lēs′) *n.* The slick, superficial style of writing often held to be characteristic of newspapers and magazines.

jour·nal·ism (jûr′nə-līz′əm) *n.* **1.** The collecting, writing, editing, and publishing of news in periodicals. **2.** Material written for publication in a periodical. **—jour′nal·ist** *n.* **—jour′nal·is′tic** *adj.* **—jour′nal·is′ti·cal·ly** *adv.*

jour·ney (jûr′nē) *n., pl.* **-neys.** Travel from one place to another; a trip. *—v.* To travel. [ME, period of travel, a day's traveling.]

jour·ney·man (jûr′nē-mən) *n.* A workman who has served his apprenticeship.

joust (jŭst, joust, joost) *n.* **1.** A combat with lances between two mounted knights. **2. jousts.** A series of these matches; a tournament. *—v.* To engage in such combat. [< VL **juxtāre,* to come together.]

Jove (jōv) *n.* The god Jupiter.

jo·vi·al (jō′vē-əl) *adj.* Marked by hearty conviviality." [Orig "born under the influence of Jupiter."] **—jo′vi·al′i·ty** (-ăl′ə-tē) *n.*

jowl[1] (joul) *n.* **1.** The jaw, esp. the lower jaw. **2.** The cheek. [< OE *ceafl.* See geph-.]

jowl[2] (joul) *n.* The flesh under the lower jaw, esp. when plump or flaccid. [Prob < OE *ceole, ceolu,* throat. See gwel-[1].]

joy (joi) *n.* **1.** A feeling of delight; happiness; gladness. **2.** A source of pleasure. [< L *gaudium,* gladness, delight.]

Joyce (jois), **James.** 1882–1941. Irish novelist.

joy·ful (joi′fəl) *adj.* Feeling, causing, or indicating joy. **—joy′ful·ly** *adv.*

joy·ous (joi′əs) *adj.* Feeling or causing joy; joyful. **—joy′ous·ly** *adv.*

J.P. justice of the peace.

Jr., Jr. junior.

ju·bi·lant (joo′bə-lənt) *adj.* **1.** Exultingly joyful. **2.** Expressing joy. [< L *jūbilāre,* to raise a shout of joy.] **—ju′bi·lant·ly** *adv.*

ju·bi·la·tion (joo′bə-lā′shən) *n.* The state of being jubilant; exultation.

ju·bi·lee (joo′bə-lē′) *n.* **1. a.** A special anniversary, esp. a 50th anniversary. **b.** The celebration of such an anniversary. **2.** A season or occasion of joyful celebration. **3.** Jubilation; rejoicing. [< LGk *iōbēlos,* jubilee.]

Ju·da·ic (joo-dā′ĭk) *adj.* Also **Ju·da·i·cal** (-ĭ-kəl).** Of or pertaining to Jews or Judaism.

Ju·da·ism (joo′dē-ĭz′əm) *n.* The monotheistic religion of the Jewish people.

Ju·das (joo′dəs) *n.* A betrayer in the guise of a friend. [< *Judas* Iscariot, Apostle who betrayed Jesus.]

Judg. Judges (Old Testament).

judge (jŭj) *v.* **judged, judging. 1. a.** To pass judgment upon in a court of law. **b.** To sit in judgment upon; hear. **2.** To determine authoritatively after deliberation; decide. **3.** To form an opinion about. **4.** To criticize; censure. **5.** To think; consider; suppose. *—n.* **1.** A public official who hears and decides cases brought before a court of law; justice; magistrate. **2.** An appointed arbiter in a contest or competition. **3.** One whose critical judgment or opinion is sought; a connoisseur. [< L *jūdex (jūdic-),* judge.] **—judg′er** *n.*

judg·ment (jŭj′mənt) *n.* Also **judge·ment. 1. a.** The ability to perceive and distinguish relationships or alternatives; discernment. **b.** The capacity to make reasonable decisions. **2.** A formal decision, as of an arbiter in a contest. **3.** An estimation. **4.** An idea; opinion; thought. **5.** Criticism; censure. **6.** A judicial decision. **—judg·men′tal** *adj.*

ju·di·ca·ture (joo′dĭ-kə-choor′) *n.* **1.** The administering of justice. **2.** A system of law courts and their judges.

ju·di·cial (joo-dĭsh′əl) *adj.* **1.** Of, pertaining to, or proper to courts of law or the administration of justice. **2.** Decreed by or proceeding from a court. **3.** Relative to, characterized by, or expressing judgment.

ju·di·ci·ar·y (joo-dĭsh′ē-ĕr′ē) *adj.* Of or pertaining to courts, judges, or judicial decisions. *—n., pl.* **-ies. 1.** The judicial branch of government. **2.** A system of courts of justice and their judges. **—ju·di′ci·ar′i·ly** *adv.*

ju·di·cious (joo-dĭsh′əs) *adj.* Having or exhibiting sound judgment. **—ju·di′cious·ly** *adv.* **—ju·di′cious·ness** *n.*

ju·do (joo′dō) *n.* A modern form of jujitsu applying principles of balance and leverage. [Jap *jūdō.*] **—ju′do·ist** *n.*

jug (jŭg) *n.* **1.** A small pitcher. **2.** A tall, often rounded vessel with a small mouth, a handle, and usually a stopper, for holding liquids. **3.** *Slang.* A jail. [< *Jug,* pet form of Joan or Judith.]

jug·ger·naut (jŭg′ər-nôt′) *n.* Anything that draws blind and destructive devotion, such as a belief.

jug·gle (jŭg′əl) *v.* **-gled, -gling. 1.** To keep (two or more objects) in the air at one time by alternately tossing and catching them. **2.** To manipulate in order to deceive. [< L *joculārī,* to jest.] **—jug′gler** *n.* **—jug′gling·ly** *adv.*

jug·u·lar (jŭg′yə-lər) *adj.* Of or located in the

ă pat/ā ate/âr care/ä bar/b bib/ch chew/d deed/ĕ pet/ē be/f fit/g gag/h hat/hw what/
ĭ pit/ī pie/îr pier/j judge/k kick/l lid, fatal/m mum/n no, sudden/ng sing/ŏ pot/ō go/

region of the neck or throat. —*n.* A jugular vein. [< L *jugulum,* collarbone.]

juice (jōos) *n.* **1. a.** Any fluid naturally contained in plant or animal tissue. **b.** Any bodily secretion. **2.** *Slang.* **a.** Electric current. **b.** Fuel for an engine. —*v.* **juiced, juicing.** To extract the juice from. [< L *jūs,* broth, sauce, juice.] —**juice'less** *adj.*

juic•y (jōo'sē) *adj.* **-ier, -iest. 1.** Full of juice; succulent. **2.** Richly interesting; lively; racy.

ju•jit•su (jōo-jĭt'sōo) *n.* Also **ju•jut•su, jiu•jit•su, jiu•jut•su.** A Japanese art of hand-to-hand combat that forces an opponent to use his weight and strength against himself. [Jap *jūjitsu.*]

ju•jube (jōo'jōob') *n.* **1.** The fleshy, edible fruit of a spiny tree. **2.** A chewy, fruit-flavored candy or lozenge. [< L *zizyphum.*]

juke box (jōok). A coin-operated phonograph. [< earlier *juke-house,* a brothel.]

ju•lep (jōo'lĭp) *n.* A sweetened alcoholic drink made with shaved ice and usually garnished with mint leaves. [< Pers *gulāb,* "rose water."]

Ju•ly (jōo-lī', jōo-) *n., pl.* **-lys.** The 7th month of the year. July has 31 days. [< L *Jūlius (mēnsis),* (month of) Julius Caesar.]

jum•ble (jŭm'bəl) *v.* **-bled, -bling. 1.** To move, mix, or mingle in a confused, disordered manner. **2.** To confuse. [?] —**jum'ble** *n.*

jum•bo (jŭm'bō) *n., pl.* **-bos.** An unusually large person, animal, or thing. [< *Jumbo,* a large elephant exhibited by P.T. Barnum.] —**jum'bo** *adj.*

jump (jŭmp) *v.* **1.** To spring off the ground or another base by a muscular effort of the legs and feet; leap; leap over. **2.** To throw oneself down, off, out, or into something. **3.** To spring at or upon with the intent to assail or censure. **4.** To arrive at hastily or haphazardly: *jump to conclusions.* **5.** To grab at eagerly: *jump at a bargain.* **6.** To start involuntarily. **7.** To rise suddenly and pronouncedly. **8.** To skip over, leaving a break in continuity. **9.** *Checkers.* To take (an opponent's piece) by moving over it with one's own checker. **10.** To leave (a course or track) through mishap. **11.** *Slang.* To have a lively, pulsating quality. —*n.* **1.** The act of jumping; a leap. **2.** A sudden, pronounced rise. **3.** A level: *a jump ahead of the others.* **4.** An involuntary nervous movement. [Prob imit.] —**jump'a•ble** *adj.*

jump•er¹ (jŭm'pər) *n.* **1.** One that jumps. **2.** A wire used temporarily to complete or by-pass an electric circuit.

jump•er² (jŭm'pər) *n.* A sleeveless dress worn over a blouse or sweater. [Prob < Brit dial *jump, jup,* man's loose jacket.]

jump•y (jŭm'pē) *adj.* **-ier, -iest.** Fitful, nervous, or on edge. —**jump'i•ness** *n.*

Jun., Jun. junior.

junc. junction.

jun•co (jŭng'kō) *n., pl.* **-cos.** A North American bird with predominantly gray plumage. [Span "rush," junco.]

junc•tion (jŭngk'shən) *n.* **1.** The act or process of joining or condition of being joined. **2.** A place where two things join or meet. [< L *junctus,* pp of *jungere,* to join.]

junc•ture (jŭngk'chər) *n.* **1.** The act of joining or condition of being joined. **2.** The line or point where two things are joined; junction. **3.** A point or interval in time.

June (jōon) *n.* The 6th month of the year. June has 30 days. [< L *Jūnius (mēnsis),* (month consecrated to) the goddess JUNO.]

Ju•neau (jōo'nō). The capital of Alaska. Pop. 7,000.

jun•gle (jŭng'gəl) *n.* **1.** Land densely overgrown with tropical vegetation and trees. **2.** Any dense thicket or growth. **3.** Any place requiring intense or ruthless struggle for survival. [< Sk *jāngala,* "dry," desert.]

jun•ior (jōon'yər) *adj.* **1.** Younger. Used to distinguish a son from a father of the same name: *William Jones, Jr.* **2.** Designed for youthful persons: *junior dress sizes.* **3.** Lower in rank or shorter in length of tenure. **4.** Designating the 3rd year of a U.S. high school or college. —*n.* **1.** A younger person. **2.** A subordinate. **3.** One in his junior year of high school or college. [L *jūnior.*]

junior college. A U.S. college offering a two-year course.

junior high school. A U.S. school including the 7th, 8th, and sometimes 9th grades.

ju•ni•per (jōo'nə-pər) *n.* An evergreen tree or shrub with scalelike foliage and aromatic, berrylike fruit. [< L *jūniperus.*]

junk¹ (jŭngk) *n.* **1.** Scrapped materials that can be converted into usable stock. **2.** Rubbish; trash. —*v.* To throw away or desert as useless. [< ME *jonke.*]

junk² (jŭngk) *n.* A Chinese flat-bottomed sailing ship. [< Malay *jong,* seagoing ship.]

jun•ket (jŭng'kĭt) *n.* **1.** A sweet food made from flavored milk and rennet. **2.** An outing. **3.** A trip taken by an official and underwritten with public funds. [ME *jonket,* a kind of egg custard.]

Ju•no (jōo'nō). Chief goddess of the Roman pantheon; sister and wife of Jupiter.

jun•ta (hōon'tə, hōon'-, jŭn'-) *n.* Those holding state power in a country, esp. after a coup d'état. [< VL **juncta,* "joined."]

Ju•pi•ter (jōo'pə-tər) *n.* **1.** The supreme god of the Roman pantheon; Jove. **2.** The 5th planet from the sun, having a diameter of approx. 86,000 miles, a mass approx. 318 times that of Earth, and a sidereal period of revolution about the sun of 11.86 years at a mean distance of 483 million miles.

Ju•ras•sic (jōo-răs'ĭk) *adj.* Of or belonging to the geologic time, rock systems, or sedimentary deposits of the second period of the Mesozoic era. —*n.* The Jurassic period. [< the *Jura* Mountains along the French-Swiss border.]

ju•rid•i•cal (jōo-rĭd'ĭ-kəl) *adj.* Also **ju•rid•ic** (-ĭk). Of or pertaining to the law. [< L *jūs,* law + *dīcere,* to say.]

ju•ris•dic•tion (jōor-əs-dĭk'shən) *n.* **1.** The authority to interpret and apply the law. **2.** The extent or range of such authority. [< L *jūrisdictiō.*] —**ju'ris•dic'tion•al** *adj.*

ju•ris•pru•dence (jōor'əs-prōo'dəns) *n.* **1.** The science or philosophy of law. **2.** A system of

---

ô paw, for/oi boy/ou out/ōo took/ōo coo/p pop/r run/s sauce/sh shy/t to/th thin/*th* the/
ŭ cut/ûr fur/v van/w wag/y yes/z size/zh vision/ə ago, item, edible, gallop, circus/

laws. [< LL *jūrisprūdentia,* "skill in law."]
ju•rist (jŏŏr′əst) *n.* One skilled in the law. [<
L *jūs (jūr-),* law.]
ju•ror (jŏŏr′ər, -ôr′) *n.* One who serves on a
jury.
ju•ry (jŏŏr′ē) *n., pl.* **-ries.** **1.** A group of persons
forming a body sworn to judge and give a
verdict on some matter, esp. one summoned to
a court of law. **2.** A committee formed to
judge a competition. [< L *jūrāta,* "thing
sworn."] —**ju′ry•less** *adj.*
just (jŭst) *adj.* **1.** Honorable and fair in one's
dealings and actions; equitable. **2.** Properly
due or merited. **3.** Legitimate. **4.** Suitable; fitting. **5.** Sound; well-founded; accurate. **6.**
Righteous. —*adv.* (jŭst; *unstressed* jəst, jĭst).
1. Precisely; exactly. **2.** Only a moment ago.
3. By a narrow margin; barely. **4.** But a little
distance. **5.** Merely; only. **6.** Simply; certainly: *It's just beautiful!* [< L *jŭstus.*] —**just′ly**
adv. —**just′ness** *n.*
jus•tice (jŭs′tĭs) *n.* **1.** Moral rightness; equity.
2. Honor; fairness. **3.** The administration and
procedure of law. **4.** A judge. [< L *jŭstus,*
JUST.] —**jus′tice•less** *adj.*

justice of the peace. A magistrate of a state
court system, having authority chiefly to act
on minor offenses, perform marriages, etc.
jus•ti•fy (jŭs′tə-fī′) *v.* **-fied, -fying.** **1.** To demonstrate to be just, right, or valid. **2.** To show
to be well-founded; warrant. **3.** To declare
free of blame; absolve. [< LL *jūstificāre,* to
do justice toward, forgive.] —**jus′ti•fi′a•ble** *adj.*
—**jus′ti•fi′a•bly** *adv.* —**jus′ti•fi•ca′tion** *n.*
jut (jŭt) *v.* **jutted, jutting.** To project; protrude.
[Var of JET².] —**jut′ting•ly** *adv.*
jute (jŏŏt) *n.* **1.** The fiber of an Asian plant,
used for sacking and cordage. **2.** The plant
itself. [< Sk *jūṭa.*]
Jute (jŏŏt) *n.* A member of any of several
Germanic tribes, some of whom invaded Britain in the 5th century A.D.
juv. juvenile.
ju•ve•nile (jŏŏ′və-nəl, -nīl′) *adj.* **1.** Not yet
adult; young. **2.** Immature. —*n.* A young
person; child. [< L *juvenis,* young, a youth.]
jux•ta•pose (jŭk′stə-pōz′) *v.* **-posed, -posing.** To
situate side by side; place together. —**jux′-
ta•po•si′tion** (-pə-zĭsh′ən) *n.*
J.V. junior varsity.

Kk

k, K (kā) *n.* The 11th letter of the English
alphabet.
K **1.** karat. **2.** kilo-.
K **1.** Kelvin (temperature scale). **2.** potassium.
ka•bob (kə-bŏb′) *n.* Shish kebab.
Ka•bul (kä′bŏŏl). The capital of Afghanistan.
Pop. 450,000.
Kaf•ka (käf′kä), **Franz.** 1883–1924. Austrian
novelist.
Kai•ser (kī′zər) *n.* The title of the ruler of
Germany (1871–1918). [< L *Caesar,* Caesar.]
ka•la-a•zar (kä′lä-ä-zär′) *n.* A chronic, usually
fatal disease occurring in Asia, esp. in India,
caused by a protozoan parasite and characterized by irregular fever, enlargement of the
spleen, hemorrhages, dropsy, and emaciation.
[Hindi *kālā-āzār,* "black disease."]
kale (kāl) *n.* A variety of cabbage with
crinkled leaves that do not form a tight head.
[< L *caulis,* cabbage.]
ka•lei•do•scope (kə-lī′də-skōp′) *n.* **1.** A small
tube in which mirrors reflect light transmitted
through bits of loose colored glass contained
at one end, causing them to appear as symmetrical designs when viewed at the other.
2. A constantly changing set of colors. **3.** A
series of changing phases or events. [Gk *kalos,*
beautiful + *eidos,* form + -SCOPE.] —**ka•lei′-
do•scop′ic** (-skŏp′ĭk) *adj.*
ka•mi•ka•ze (kä′mĭ-kä′zē) *n.* **1.** A Japanese
pilot trained to make a suicidal crash attack.

2. An airplane used in such an attack. [Jap,
"divine wind."]
Kam•pa•la (käm-pä′lə). The capital of Uganda. Pop. 45,000.
kan•ga•roo (kăng′gə-rŏŏ′) *n.* An Australian
marsupial with large hind limbs adapted for
leaping and a long, tapered tail. [Prob < a
native name in Australia.]
Kan•sas (kăn′zəs). A state of the C U.S. Pop.
2,249,000. Cap. Topeka.
Kansas City. **1.** A city of NE Kansas. Pop.
168,000. **2.** A city of NW Missouri. Pop.
507,000.
Kant (kănt, känt), **Immanuel.** 1724–1804.
German philosopher. —**Kant′i•an** *adj.*
ka•o•lin (kā′ə-lĭn) *n.* Also **ka•o•line.** A fine
whitish clay used in ceramics and refractories.
[< Mand Chin *kao¹ ling³,* "high mountain."]
kaph (käf) *n.* Also **caph.** The 11th letter of the
Hebrew alphabet, representing *k(kh).*
ka•pok (kā′pŏk′) *n.* A silky fiber obtained
from the fruit of a tropical tree and used as
filling for pillows, life preservers, etc. [Malay.]
kap•pa (kăp′ə) *n.* The 10th letter of the Greek
alphabet, representing *k.*
Ka•ra•chi (kə-rä′chē). A city of S West Pakistan. Pop. 1,913,000.
Kar•a•kor•am (kăr′ə-kôr′əm). A mountain
range of S Asia.
kar•a•kul (kăr′ə-kəl) *n.* Also **car•a•cul.** **1.** Fur
made from the curled, glossy pelt of the lamb

ă pat/ā ate/âr care/ä bar/b **bib**/ch **chew**/d **deed**/ĕ pet/ē be/f fit/g gag/h hat/hw **what**/
ĭ pit/ī pie/îr pier/j judge/k **kick**/l lid, fatal/m **mum**/n no, sudden/ng sing/ŏ pot/ō go/

of an Asian sheep. **2.** The sheep itself. [< *Kara Kul,* lake in Tadzhik S.S.R.]

kar·at (kăr′ət) *n.* Also **car·at.** A measure comprising 24 units used to specify the proportion of pure gold in an alloy; for example, 12 karat gold is 50% pure gold. [< CARAT.]

ka·ra·te (kə-rä′tē, kä-rä′tä) *n.* A Japanese system of unarmed self-defense that stresses efficiently struck blows. [Jap, "empty-handed."]

kar·ma (kär′mə) *n.* **1.** *Hinduism* & *Buddhism.* The sum and consequences of a person's actions during the successive phases of his existence. **2.** Fate; destiny. [Sk *karman,* act, deed.] —**kar′mic** (-mĭk) *adj.*

karyo-. *comb. form.* The nucleus of a living cell. [< Gk *karuon,* kernel, nut.]

kar·y·og·a·my (kăr′ē-ŏg′ə-mē) *n.* The coming together and fusing of gamete nuclei.

Kat·man·du (kät′män-dōō′). The capital of Nepal. Pop. 123,000.

ka·ty·did (kā′tē-dĭd′) *n.* A green insect related to the grasshoppers, having specialized organs that produce a distinctive sound when rubbed together. [Imit.]

kay·ak (kī′ăk′) *n.* An Eskimo canoe with a deck covering that closes around the waist of the paddler. [Eskimo *qajaq.*]

kay·o (kā′ō, kā′ō′). *Slang. n., pl.* **-os.** A knockout. —*v.* To knock out.

Ka·zakh Soviet Socialist Republic (kə-zäk′). A constituent republic of the Soviet Union, NE of the Caspian Sea. Pop. 12,850,000.

Ka·zan (kə-zän′). A city of the Soviet Union, on the Volga. Pop. 869,000.

ka·zoo (kə-zōō′) *n.* A toy musical instrument in which a paper membrane is vibrated by the performer's voice. [Prob imit.]

kc kilocycle.

K.C. **1.** King's Counsel. **2.** Knights of Columbus.

Keats (kēts), **John.** 1795–1821. English poet.

ke·bab (kə-bŏb′) *n.* Also **ke·bob. Shish kebab.**

keel (kēl) *n.* **1.** The principal structural member of a ship, extending from bow to stern and forming the backbone of the vessel, to which the frames are attached. **2.** Any similarly shaped structure. —*v.* —**keel over. 1.** To capsize. **2.** To faint. [< ON *kjölr.*]

keen (kēn) *adj.* **1.** Having a sharp cutting edge. **2.** Intellectually acute. **3.** Acutely sensitive: *a keen sense of smell.* **4.** Sharp; vivid. **5.** Intense; piercing. **6.** Pungent; acrid. **7.** Eager; enthusiastic. **8.** *Slang.* Great; splendid. [< OE *cēne,* wise, bold < Gmc *kônjaz.*] —**keen′ly** *adv.* —**keen′ness** *n.*

keep (kēp) *v.* **kept, keeping. 1.** To retain possession of. **2.** To store; put customarily. **3.** To take in one's charge temporarily. **4.** To provide with the necessities of life; support; raise and feed. **5.** To manage; tend; maintain. **6.** To remain, continue, or cause to continue in some condition or position. **7.** To preserve and protect; save. **8.** To detain; confine. **9.** To adhere to; fulfill. **10.** To refrain from divulging. **11.** To celebrate. **12.** To remain fresh or unspoiled. —**keep from.** To deter or prevent. —*n.* **1.** Care; charge. **2.** Means of support. **3. a.** The main tower or donjon of a

castle. **b.** A jail. [< OE *cēpan,* to seize, hold, guard.] —**keep′er** *n.*

keep·sake (kēp′sāk′) *n.* Something given or kept as a reminder; memento.

keg (kĕg) *n.* A small cask. [< ON *kaggi.*]

Kel·ler (kĕl′ər), **Helen.** 1880–1968. American author; deaf and blind from infancy.

kelp (kĕlp) *n.* Any of various brown, often very large seaweeds. [ME *culpe.*]

Kelt. Variant of **Celt.**

Kelt·ic. Variant of **Celtic.**

Kel·vin (kĕl′vĭn) *adj.* Pertaining to a scale of temperature, the zero point of which is approx. –273.16°C. [< Lord *Kelvin* (1824–1907), British physicist.]

ken (kĕn) *v.* **kenned** or **kent** (kĕnt), **kenning.** *Chiefly Scot.* To know (a person or thing). —*n.* **1.** Understanding. **2.** View; sight. [< OE *cennan,* to make known.]

Ken·ne·dy (kĕn′ə-dē), **John Fitzgerald.** 1917–1963. 35th President of the U.S. (1961–63).

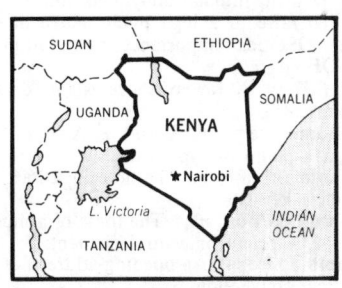

John F. Kennedy

ken·nel (kĕn′əl) *n.* **1.** A shelter for a dog. **2.** An establishment where dogs are bred or boarded. [< L *canis,* dog.]

Ken·tuck·y (kən-tŭk′ē). A state of the eastcentral U.S. Pop. 3,219,000. Cap. Frankfort.

Ken·ya (kĕn′yə, kĕn′-). A republic in eastcentral Africa. Pop. 9,365,000. Cap. Nairobi.

Kenya

Kep·ler (kĕp′lər), **Johannes.** 1571–1630. German astronomer and mathematician.

kept (kĕpt). *p.t.* & *p.p.* of **keep.**

ker·a·tin (kĕr′ə-tən) *n.* A tough, fibrous protein forming the outer layer of epidermal structures such as hair, nails, horns, and hoofs. [Gk *keras*, horn + -IN.] —**ke·rat′i·nous** (kə-răt′n-əs) *adj.*

kerb. *Brit.* Variant of **curb.**

ker·chief (kûr′chĭf) *n.* 1. A woman's square scarf, often worn as a head covering. 2. A handkerchief. [< OF *couvrechef,* "head covering."]

Ke·ren·sky (kə-rĕn′skē), **Aleksandr Fyodorovich.** 1881–1970. Russian revolutionary leader; prime minister (July–November 1917).

ker·nel (kûr′nəl) *n.* 1. A grain or seed, as of a cereal grass. 2. The inner, often edible part of a nut or fruit stone. 3. A nucleus; essence; core. [< OE *corn,* corn, berry, seed.]

ker·o·sene (kĕr′ə-sēn′, kĕr′ə-sēn′) *n.* Also **ker·o·sine.** A thin oil distilled from petroleum or shale oil, used as a fuel and alcohol denaturant. [Gk *kēros,* wax + -ENE.]

ketch (kĕch) *n.* A two-masted fore-and-aft-rigged sailing vessel with a smaller mast aft of the mainmast and in front of the tiller. [Earlier *catch.*]

ketch·up (kĕch′əp, kăch′-) *n.* Also **catch·up** (kăch′əp, kĕch′-), **cat·sup** (kăt′səp, kăch′əp, kĕch′-). A condiment consisting of a thick, smooth-textured, spicy tomato sauce. [Malay *kechap.*]

ket·tle (kĕt′l) *n.* A metal pot for boiling. [< L *catillus,* small bowl.]

ket·tle·drum (kĕt′l-drŭm′) *n.* A large copper or brass drum with a parchment head.

key¹ (kē) *n.* 1. A notched metallic implement designed to open or close a lock. 2. Any means of control, esp. of entry or possession. 3. a. A small instrument for winding a spring. b. A slotted metal strip used to open cans. 4. a. A crucial fact. b. A set of answers to a test. c. A table, gloss, or cipher for decoding or interpreting. 5. A pin inserted to lock together mechanical or structural parts. 6. a. A control button or lever on a hand-operated machine. b. A button or lever on a musical instrument, used to produce or modulate a sound. 7. *Mus.* A tonal system consisting of seven tones in fixed relationship to a tonic; tonality. 8. The pitch of a voice or other sound. 9. A general tone or level of intensity. —*v.* To bring into harmony; coordinate. —**key up.** To raise to a high pitch; make intense. —*adj.* Of crucial importance; essential; major. [< OE *cæg(e).*]

key² (kē) *n.* A low offshore island or reef. [Span *cayo.*]

key·board (kē′bôrd′, -bōrd′) *n.* A set of keys, as on a piano or typewriter.

key·hole (kē′hōl′) *n.* The hole in a lock into which a key fits.

key·note (kē′nōt′) *n.* 1. The tonic of a musical key. 2. A prime or central element.

keynote address. An opening address, as at a political convention.

key punch. A keyboard machine that is used

to punch holes in cards or tapes for data-processing systems.

key signature. The group of sharps or flats placed to the right of the clef on a musical staff to identify the key.

key·stone (kē′stōn′) *n.* The central wedge-shaped stone of an arch that locks the others together.

kg kilogram.

khak·i (kăk′ē, kä′kē) *n., pl.* -**is.** 1. Light olive brown or light yellowish brown. 2. A cloth of this color. 3. **khakis.** A uniform of this cloth. [Urdu *khākī,* dusty.] —**khak′i** *adj.*

khan (kän, kăn) *n.* 1. A title of respect in India and some central Asian countries. 2. **Khan.** The title of the rulers of Mongol, Tartar, or Turkish tribes who succeeded Genghis Khan. [< Turk *khān.*]

Khar·kov (kär′kôf, -kôv). A city of the Soviet Union in the E Ukrainian S.S.R. Pop. 1,223,000.

Khar·toum (kär-tōōm′). The capital of Sudan. Pop. 584,000.

khe·dive (kə-dēv′) *n.* The title of the Turkish viceroys of Egypt from 1867 to 1914.

Khmer Republic (kmĕr). A former name for **Cambodia,** a country of SE Asia.

kib·butz (kĭ-bōōts′) *n., pl.* -**butzim** (-bōōt′sĕm′). A collective farm or settlement in Israel. [Heb *qibbūtz,* "gathering."]

kib·itz (kĭb′ĭts) *v. Informal.* To act as a kibitzer. [Yid *kibitsen.*]

kib·itz·er (kĭb′ĭt-sər) *n. Informal.* An onlooker who offers unwanted advice, esp. at a card game.

kick (kĭk) *v.* 1. To strike or strike out with the foot or feet. 2. *Sports.* To strike a ball with the foot. 3. To recoil, as a gun when fired. 4. *Informal.* To object vigorously; complain; protest. —*n.* 1. The act of kicking. 2. *Slang.* A stimulating or intoxicating impact. 3. *Slang.* A temporary concentration of interest. [ME *kiken.*]

kick·back (kĭk′băk′) *n.* 1. A sharp response or reaction; repercussion. 2. *Slang.* A percentage payment to a person able to influence or control a source of income.

kick off. *Football.* To put the ball in play by kicking it toward the opposing team.

kick·off (kĭk′ôf′, -ŏf′) *n.* 1. A kick in football or soccer with which play is begun. 2. A beginning.

kid (kĭd) *n.* 1. A young goat. 2. Also **kid·skin** (kĭd′skĭn′). Leather made from the skin of a young goat. 3. *Slang.* A child. —*adj.* 1. Made of kid. 2. *Informal.* Younger: *my kid brother.* —*v.* **kidded, kidding.** *Informal.* 1. To mock playfully. 2. To deceive in fun. [< ON *kidh* < Gmc **kidhja-.*] —**kid′der** *n.*

kid·nap (kĭd′năp′) *v.* -**naped** or -**napped,** -**naping** or -**napping.** To abduct and detain (a person), often for ransom. [< KID + earlier *nap,* to seize.] —**kid′nap′er, kid′nap′per** *n.*

kid·ney (kĭd′nē) *n., pl.* -**neys.** 1. Either of a pair of structures in the dorsal region of the vertebrate abdominal cavity, functioning to maintain proper water balance, regulate acid-base concentration, and excrete metabolic

---

ă pat/ā ate/âr care/ä bar/b bib/ch chew/d deed/ĕ pet/ē be/f fit/g gag/h hat/hw what/
ĭ pit/ī pie/îr pier/j judge/k kick/l lid, fatal/m mum/n no, sudden/ng sing/ŏ pot/ō go/

wastes as urine. **2.** Disposition; temperament. [ME *kydney.*]

Ki·ev (kē-ĕv′, kĕ′ĕf′). The capital of the Ukrainian S.S.R. Pop. 1,632,000.

Ki·ga·li (kĭ-gä′lē). The capital of Rwanda. Pop. 4,000.

Kil·i·man·ja·ro (kĭl′ə-mən-jär′ō). The highest mountain (19,565 ft.) in Africa, in NE Tanzania.

kill (kĭl) *v.* **1. a.** To put to death; slay. **b.** To deprive of life. **2. a.** To put an end to. **b.** To thwart; veto: *kill a congressional bill.* **3.** To use up: *kill two hours.* **4.** To cause extreme discomfort to. **5.** To mark for deletion; rule out. —*n.* **1.** The act of killing. **2.** That which is killed or destroyed, as an animal in hunting. [< OE *cyllan.* See gwel-².] —**kill′er** *n.*

kill·deer (kĭl′dîr′) *n., pl.* **-deers** or **-deer.** A bird with a banded breast and a distinctive cry.

kill·ing (kĭl′ĭng) *n.* **1.** A murder; homicide. **2.** A sudden large profit. —*adj.* **1.** Fatal. **2.** Exhausting. **3.** *Informal.* Hilarious.

kill·joy (kĭl′joi′) *n.* One who spoils the fun of others.

kiln (kĭl, kĭln) *n.* An oven for hardening, burning, or drying, esp. one used to bake or fire ceramics. [< L *culīna,* kitchen.]

ki·lo (kē′lō, kĭl′ō) *n., pl.* **-los.** **1.** A kilogram. **2.** A kilometer.

kilo-. *comb. form.* 1,000 (10³). [< Gk *khilioi,* thousand.]

kil·o·cy·cle (kĭl′ə-sī′kəl) *n.* **1.** A unit equal to 1,000 cycles. **2.** Loosely, 1,000 cycles per second.

kil·o·gram (kĭl′ə-grăm′) *n.* The fundamental unit of mass in the International System, about 2.2046 pounds.

kil·o·me·ter (kĭl′ə-mē′tər, kĭ-lŏm′ə-tər) *n.* One thousand meters, approx. 0.62137 mile.

kil·o·ton (kĭl′ə-tŭn′) *n.* **1.** One thousand tons. **2.** An explosive force equivalent to that of 1,000 tons of TNT.

kil·o·watt (kĭl′ə-wŏt′) *n.* One thousand watts.

kil·o·watt-hour (kĭl′ə-wŏt′our′) *n.* The total energy developed by a power of one kilowatt acting for one hour.

kilt (kĭlt) *n.* A skirt with deep pleats, usually of a tartan wool, worn esp. as part of the dress for men in the Scottish Highlands. [< Scand.]

kil·ter (kĭl′tər) *n.* Proper condition: *out of kilter.* [?]

ki·mo·no (kə-mō′nə, -nō) *n., pl.* **-nos.** **1.** A wide-sleeved Japanese robe, worn with a broad sash. **2.** A dressing gown resembling this. [Jap, "thing for wearing."]

kin (kĭn) *n.* One's relatives collectively. [< OE *cynn.* See gen∂-.]

-kin. *comb. form.* Small or diminutive: **lambkin.** [< MDu < Gmc *-kin.*]

kin·aes·the·sia. Variant of **kinesthesia.**

kind¹ (kīnd) *adj.* Showing sympathy, concern, or understanding. [< OE *gecynde,* natural, innate. See gen∂-.]

kind² (kīnd) *n.* A class or category of similar or related individuals; sort; type. [< OE *cynd, gecynd,* birth, nature, race. See gen∂-.]

Usage: Kind, denoting a single variety, is used with singular elements in examples such

as *This kind of book has little value* (preferable to *these kind of books have*). *Kind* is used acceptably with a plural noun and verb in questions such as *What kind of books are these?* The plural *kinds* is always used, with a plural verb, in examples such as *All kinds of difficulty were involved.*

kin·der·gar·ten (kĭn′dər-gärt′n) *n.* A class for four- to six-year-old children that serves as an introduction to schooling. [G, "children's garden."]

kind·heart·ed (kīnd′här′tĭd) *adj.* Showing a kind nature. —**kind′heart′ed·ly** *adv.* —**kind′heart′ed·ness** *n.*

kin·dle (kĭnd′l) *v.* **-dled, -dling.** **1.** To start (a fire); begin to burn. **2.** To glow or cause to glow. **3.** To arouse; inspire. [< ON *kynda.*]

kind·less (kīnd′lĭs) *adj.* **1.** Heartless; cruel. **2.** *Obs.* Inhuman.

kind·li·ness (kīnd′lē-nĭs) *n.* **1.** The quality of being kindly. **2.** A kindly deed.

kin·dling (kĭnd′lĭng) *n.* Material, such as dry sticks of wood, used to start a fire.

kindling point. The minimum temperature at which a substance will continue to burn without additional application of heat.

kind·ly (kīnd′lē) *adj.* **-lier, -liest.** Showing sympathy, considerateness, or helpfulness. —*adv.* **1.** In a kind way or manner. **2.** Please; accommodatingly: *Would you kindly refrain from doing that?*

kind·ness (kīnd′nĭs) *n.* **1.** The quality or state of being kind. **2.** An instance of kind behavior.

kin·dred (kĭn′drĭd) *n.* **1.** A group of related persons. **2.** A person's relatives. —*adj.* Being similar or related. [< KIN + OE *rǣden,* condition.] —**kin′dred·ness** *n.*

kine (kīn) *pl.n.* Cows; cattle.

kin·e·mat·ics (kĭn′ə-măt′ĭks) *n.* *(takes sing. v.).* The study of motion exclusive of the influences of mass and force. [< Gk *kinein,* to move.] —**kin′e·mat′ic, kin′e·mat′i·cal** *adj.* —**kin′e·mat′i·cal·ly** *adv.*

kin·e·scope (kĭn′ə-skōp′) *n.* **1.** A cathode-ray tube that translates received TV signals into a visible picture. **2.** A film of a transmitted TV program.

kin·es·the·sia (kĭn′əs-thē′zhə) *n.* Also **kin·aes·the·sia.** The sensation of bodily position, presence, or movement.

ki·net·ic (kĭ-nĕt′ĭk) *adj.* Of or produced by motion. —*n.* **kinetics** *(takes sing. v.).* **1.** The study of all aspects of motion, comprising both kinematics and dynamics. **2.** The study of the relationship between motion and the forces affecting motion. [Gk *kinētikos* < *kinein,* to move.]

kinetic energy. Energy associated with motion.

kin·folk, kin·folks. Variants of **kinsfolk.**

king (kĭng) *n.* **1.** A male monarch. **2.** The most eminent of a group, category, etc. **3.** A playing card bearing a picture of a king. **4.** *Chess.* The principal piece. [< OE *cyning.* See gen∂-.] —**king′li·ness** *n.* —**king′ly** *adj.*

King James Bible (jāmz). A translation of the Bible for use by Protestants.

ô paw, for/oi boy/ou out/o͞o took/o͞o coo/p pop/r run/s sauce/sh shy/t to/th thin/*th* the/
ŭ cut/ûr fur/v van/w wag/y yes/z size/zh vision/ə ago, item, edible, gallop, circus/

King (kĭng), **Martin Luther, Jr.** 1929–1968. American Baptist minister and civil-rights leader; assassinated.

Martin Luther King, Jr.

king·dom (kĭng'dəm) *n.* **1.** A country nominally or actually ruled by a king or queen. **2.** An area in which one thing is dominant. **3.** A broad, general category of living or natural forms: *animal kingdom; plant kingdom.*

king·fish·er (kĭng'fĭsh'ər) *n.* A crested, large-billed bird that feeds on fish.

king·let (kĭng'lĭt) *n.* A small bird with a red or yellow head patch.

king·pin (kĭng'pĭn') *n.* **1.** *Bowling.* The foremost or central pin. **2.** A person of central importance. **3.** A vertical bolt used as a pivot.

Kings·ton (kĭngz'tən). The capital of Jamaica. Pop. 123,000.

kink (kĭngk) *n.* **1.** A small, tight curl or twist. **2.** A painful muscle spasm, as in the neck or back. **3.** A slight flaw, as in a plan. —*v.* To form kinks (in). [LG *kinke,* a twist in a rope.] —**kink'i·ness** *n.* —**kink'y** *adj.*

kink·a·jou (kĭng'kə-joō') *n.* A furry, long-tailed tropical American mammal. [< Algon.]

kins·folk (kĭnz'fōk') *pl.n.* Also *informal* **kin·folk** (kĭn'-). **kin·folks** (-fōks). Members of a family.

Kin·sha·sa (kĭn-shä'sä). The capital of Zaire. Pop. 1,323,000.

kin·ship (kĭn'shĭp') *n.* **1.** The state of being related by blood. **2.** A close connection or relationship.

kins·man (kĭnz'mən) *n.* A male blood relation. —**kins'wo·man** *fem.n.*

ki·osk (kē-ŏsk', kē'ŏsk') *n.* A small structure used as a newsstand, refreshment booth, etc. [< Turk *köshk,* pavilion.]

kip (kĭp) *n., pl.* **kip.** The basic monetary unit of Laos.

Kip·ling (kĭp'lĭng), **Rudyard.** 1865-1936. English author.

kip·per (kĭp'ər) *n.* A herring that has been split, salted, and smoked. [< OE *cypera.*]

Kir·ghiz Soviet Socialist Republic (kĭr-gēz'). A constituent republic of the Soviet Union, in

C Asia. Pop. 2,933,000.

kis·met (kĭz'mĭt, kĭs'-) *n.* Fate; fortune. [Turk *kismet.*]

kiss (kĭs) *v.* To touch with the lips as a sign of affection, greeting, etc. —*n.* **1.** A touching with the lips. **2.** A small piece of candy. [< OE *cyssan.* See kus-.]

kit (kĭt) *n.* **1. a.** A set of instruments or equipment used for a specific purpose. **b.** A container for such a set. **2.** A set of parts or materials to be assembled. [< MDu *kitte,* jug, tankard.]

kitch·en (kĭch'ən) *n.* **1.** An area in which food is cooked or prepared. **2.** A department, as of an institution, that prepares, cooks, and serves food. [< L *coquīnus,* of cooking.]

kitch·en·ette (kĭch'ə-nĕt') *n.* A small kitchen.

kitch·en·ware (kĭch'ən-wâr') *n.* Utensils for kitchen use.

kite (kīt) *n.* **1.** A light framework covered with paper or cloth and designed to hover in the wind at the end of a long string. **2.** A predatory bird with a long, often forked tail. [< OE *cȳta,* kite bird < Gmc *kūtja-.*]

kith (kĭth) *n.* Friends and neighbors: *kith and kin.* [< OE *cȳth,* "knowledge," "acquaintance," friend.]

kit·ten (kĭt'n) *n.* A young cat. [< LL *cattus,* cat.]

kit·ten·ish (kĭt'n-ĭsh) *adj.* Playful; flirtatious; coy. —**kit'ten·ish·ly** *adv.*

kit·ty[1] (kĭt'ē) *n., pl.* **-ties.** A pool or fund of money. [< KIT.]

kit·ty[2] (kĭt'ē) *n., pl.* **-ties.** *Informal.* A kitten or cat.

K.K.K. Ku Klux Klan.

klep·to·ma·ni·a (klĕp'tə-mā'nē-ə) *n.* An obsessive impulse to steal, esp. in the absence of economic necessity. [< Gk *kleptein,* to steal + -MANIA.] —**klep'to·ma'ni·ac'** *n.*

klutz (klŭts) *n.* **1.** A clumsy or dim-witted person. **2.** A bungler. [< MHG *kloz,* block, lump. See gel-[1].]

km kilometer.

kn. knot.

knack (năk) *n.* **1.** A clever way of doing something. **2.** A specific talent for something. [ME *knak.*]

knap·sack (năp'săk') *n.* A case or bag worn on the back to carry supplies and equipment. [LG.]

knave (nāv) *n.* **1.** An unprincipled, crafty man. **2.** *Card Games.* A jack. [< OE *cnafa,* boy, lad < Gmc *knabōn-.*] —**knav'er·y** *n.* —**knav'ish** *adj.* —**knav'ish·ly** *adv.*

knead (nēd) *v.* **1.** To mix and work (a substance) into a uniform mass. **2.** To massage. [< OE *cnedan.*] —**knead'er** *n.*

knee (nē) *n.* The joint or region between the upper and lower parts of the human leg. [< OE *cnēo.* See genu-[1].]

knee·cap (nē'kăp') *n.* The patella.

kneel (nēl) *v.* **knelt** (nĕlt) or **kneeled, kneeling.** To fall or rest on bent knees. [< OE *cnēowlian.* See genu-[1].]

knell (nĕl) *v.* **1.** To ring or sound a bell, esp. for a funeral; toll. **2.** To signal, summon, or proclaim by tolling. —*n.* **1.** The slow, solemn

---

ă pat/ā ate/âr care/ä bar/b bib/ch chew/d deed/ĕ pet/ē be/f fit/g gag/h hat/hw what/
ĭ pit/ī pie/îr pier/j judge/k kick/l lid, fatal/m mum/n no, sudden/ng sing/ŏ pot/ō go/

sounding of a bell. **2.** An omen of sorrow or death. [< OE *cnyllan.*]

knew (n/y/ōō). *p.t.* of **know.**

knick·ers (nĭk′ərz) *pl.n.* Also **knick·er·bock·ers** (-ər-bŏk′ərz). Full breeches gathered just below the knee.

knick·knack (nĭk′năk′) *n.* A small ornamental article. [Redupl of KNACK.]

knife (nīf) *n., pl.* **knives** (nīvz). **1.** A cutting instrument consisting of a sharp blade with a handle. **2.** Any cutting edge or blade. —*v.* **knifed, knifing. 1.** To use a knife on, esp. to cut, stab, or wound. **2.** *Informal.* To betray by underhand means. [< OE *cníf.*]

knight (nīt) *n.* **1.** A medieval gentleman-soldier. **2.** The holder of a nonhereditary dignity conferred by a sovereign. **3.** A member of any of several orders or brotherhoods. **4.** A chess piece usually representing a horse's head. —*v.* To raise (a person) to knighthood. [< OE *cniht,* orig "boy," "servant" < Gmc **knihtas.*] —**knight′hood** *n.* —**knight′ly** *adj.*

knit (nĭt) *v.* **knit** or **knitted, knitting. 1.** To make (a fabric or garment) by intertwining yarn or thread in a series of connected loops. **2.** To join closely. **3.** To draw (the brows) together in wrinkles. —*n.* A fabric or garment made by knitting. [< OE *cnyttan,* to tie in a knot.]

knob (nŏb) *n.* **1.** A rounded protuberance on a surface or extremity. **2.** A rounded handle. [< MLG *knobbe,* tree knot, knob.] —**knobbed** *adj.* —**knob′bi·ness** *n.* —**knob′by** *adj.*

knock (nŏk) *v.* **1.** To strike with a blow or series of blows. **2.** To produce by hitting: *knock a hole in the wall.* **3.** *Slang.* To criticize adversely. **4.** To collide; bump. **5.** To make the pounding noise of a laboring or defective engine. —**knock about** (or **around**). **1.** To be physically brutal with. **2.** To wander aimlessly from place to place. **3.** To discuss. —**knock off. 1.** To rest from or cease work. **2.** To accomplish or consume easily. **3.** To deduct; eliminate. **4.** *Slang.* To kill. [< OE *cnocian.*] —**knock** *n.*

knock·er (nŏk′ər) *n.* A fixture used for knocking on a door.

knock-knee (nŏk′nē′) *n.* An abnormal condition in which one or both knees are turned toward the other. —**knock′-kneed′** *adj.*

knock out. 1. To render unconscious. **2.** *Boxing.* To defeat (an opponent) by knocking him to the canvas for a count of ten. **3.** To exhaust (oneself or another).

knock·out (nŏk′out′) *n.* **1.** A blow that induces unconsciousness. **2.** *Boxing.* The knocking out of an opponent. **3.** *Slang.* Something very impressive or attractive.

knoll (nōl) *n.* A small rounded hill. [< OE *cnoll.*]

knot (nŏt) *n.* **1.** A compact intersection of interlaced string, rope, etc. **2.** Any tie or bond, esp. a marriage bond. **3.** A cluster of persons or things. **4.** A difficulty; problem. **5.** A hard, dark marking at a point from which a tree branch grows. **6.** A growth on or enlargement of a gland, muscle, etc. **7.** A unit of speed, one nautical mile per hour, about 1.15 statute miles per hour. —**tie the knot.** To get married. —*v.*

knotted, knotting. 1. To make or become snarled or entangled. **2.** To form a knot or knots (in). [< OE *cnotta.*]

knot·hole (nŏt′hōl′) *n.* A hole in a piece of lumber where a knot has dropped out or been removed.

knot·ty (nŏt′ē) *adj.* **-tier, -tiest. 1.** Having knots. **2.** Covered with knots; gnarled. **3.** Difficult to understand or solve; intricate. —**knot′ti·ly** *adv.* —**knot′ti·ness** *n.*

know (nō) *v.* **knew, known, knowing. 1.** To perceive directly with the senses or mind; be aware of as true or factual. **2.** To be capable of: *know how to swim.* **3.** To have a practical understanding of. **4.** To be subjected to. **5.** To have firmly secured in the mind or memory. **6.** To be able to distinguish. **7.** To be acquainted or familiar with. [< OE *(ge)cnāwan.* See gnō-.]

Usage: Know, esp. in negative constructions, is often followed by clauses introduced by *that, whether,* or *if,* but not by *as: I don't know that* (not *as) I can.*

know-how (nō′hou′) *n. Informal.* Skill or ingenuity.

know·ing (nō′ĭng) *adj.* **1.** Possessing or showing knowledge or understanding. **2.** Suggestive of secret or private information: *a knowing glance.* **3.** Clever; shrewd. —**know′ing·ly** *adv.* —**know′ing·ness** *n.*

know-it-all (nō′ĭt-ôl′) *n. Informal.* One who talks as if he knew everything.

knowl·edge (nŏl′ĭj) *n.* **1.** The state or fact of knowing. **2.** Familiarity, awareness, or understanding gained through experience or study. **3.** That which is known; the sum or range of what has been perceived, discovered, or inferred. **4.** Learning; erudition.

knowl·edge·a·ble (nŏl′ĭ-jə-bəl) *adj.* Well-informed.

Knox·ville (nŏks′vĭl). A city of E Tennessee. Pop. 172,000.

Knt. knight.

knuck·le (nŭk′əl) *n.* Any joint or region around a joint of a finger, esp. one of the joints connecting the fingers to the hand. —*v.* **-led, -ling.** To press or rub with the knuckles. —**knuckle down.** To apply oneself earnestly. —**knuckle under.** To yield to pressure; give. [< MLG *knökel.*]

knuck·le·bone (nŭk′əl-bōn′) *n.* A knobbed bone, as of a knuckle or joint.

ko·a·la (kō-ä′lə) *n.* Also **koala bear.** A furry, tree-dwelling Australian marsupial. [< native Australian name *kūlla.*]

Ko·be (kō′bĕ, -bā′). A city of Japan, on Honshu. Pop. 1,181,000.

kohl·ra·bi (kōl-rä′bē, kōl′rä′-) *n.* A plant with a thickened, turniplike stem base that is eaten as a vegetable. [< It *cavolo rapa,* "cabbage turnip."]

ko·la. Variant of **cola.**

ko·lin·sky (kə-lĭn′skē) *n.* The fur of a Eurasian mink. [< *Kola,* district in NW U.S.S.R.]

Ko·ran (kô-răn′, -rän′, kō-) *n.* The sacred text of Islam, believed to contain the revelations made by Allah to Mohammed. [Ar *qur'ān,* reading, recitation.]

ô **paw,** for/oi **boy**/ou **out**/ŏŏ **took**/ōō **coo**/p **pop**/r **run**/s **sauce**/sh **shy**/t **to**/th **thin**/*th* **the**/
ŭ **cut**/ûr **fur**/v **van**/w **wag**/y **yes**/z **size**/zh **vision**/ə **ago, item, edible, gallop, circus**/

Ko·re·a (kô-rē′ə, kō-). A country of E Asia, divided since 1948 into two states: **a.** the People's Democratic Republic of Korea (North Korea). Pop. 10,930,000. Cap. Pyongyang. **b.** the Republic of Korea (South Korea). Pop. 28,155,000. Cap. Seoul.

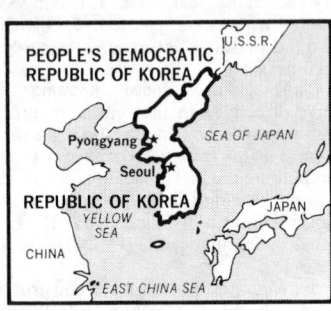

Korea

Ko·re·an (kô-rē′ən, kō-) *adj.* Of or pertaining to Korea, its inhabitants, or their language. —*n.* **1.** A native of Korea. **2.** The language of Korea.

Korean War. A military action between North Korea and United Nations forces (June 1950 –July 1953).

ko·ru·na (kôr′ōō-nä′) *n., pl.* **-ny** (-ně) or **-nas.** The basic monetary unit of Czechoslovakia.

ko·sher (kō′shər) *adj.* **1.** Conforming to or prepared in accordance with Jewish dietary laws. **2.** *Slang.* Proper; legitimate. [< Heb *kāshêr,* proper.]

Ko·sy·gin (kə-sē′gĭn), **Aleksei Nikolayevich.** Born 1904. Premier of the Soviet Union (since 1964).

kow·tow (kou′tou′, kô′-) *n.* A Chinese salutation in which one touches the forehead to the ground. —*v.* **1.** To perform a kowtow. **2.** To show servile deference. [Mand Chin *k'o¹ t'-ou².*] —**kow′tow′er** *n.*

KP kitchen police.

Kr krypton.

Kra·ków (krä′kou′, krăk′ou′, krä′kō). A city in S Poland. Pop. 509,000.

Krem·lin (krěm′lən) *n.* **1.** The citadel of Moscow, housing the offices of the Soviet government. **2.** The executive branch of the Soviet government. [< Russ *kreml′,* citadel.]

Krish·na (krĭsh′nə). *Hinduism.* The 8th and principal avatar of Vishnu.

kro·na¹ (krō′nə) *n., pl.* **-nur** (-nər). The basic monetary unit of Iceland.

kro·na² (krō′nə) *n., pl.* **-nor** (-nôr′). The basic monetary unit of Sweden.

kro·ne (krō′nə) *n., pl.* **-ner** (-nər). The basic monetary unit of Denmark and Norway.

kryp·ton (krĭp′tŏn′) *n. Symbol* **Kr** A whitish, inert gaseous element used chiefly in gas-

discharge lamps, fluorescent lamps, and electronic flash tubes. Atomic number 36, atomic weight 83.80. [< Gk *kruptos,* hidden.]

kt. karat.

Kua·la Lum·pur (kwä′lə lōōm′pŏŏr). The capital of Malaysia. Pop. 316,000.

Ku·blai Khan (kōō′blī kän′). 1216–1294. Founder of Mongol dynasty in China; grandson of Genghis Khan.

ku·dos (kyōō′dŏs′, -dōs′) *n.* Acclaim or prestige in recognition of achievement. [< Gk, glory, fame.]

Kui·by·shev (kwē′bə-shěf′, -shěv′). A city of the Soviet Union, on the Volga. Pop. 1,047,000.

kum·quat (kŭm′kwŏt′) *n.* **1.** A small, thin-skinned, edible orangelike fruit. **2.** A tree bearing such fruit. [Cant *kam kwat.*]

kung fu (kŏŏng′ fōō′, gŏŏng′-). A Chinese system of self-defense resembling the Japanese system karate. [<Mand *ch¹üan² fa³,* "boxing principles."]

Kurd·ish (kûr′dĭsh, kŏŏr′-) *n.* The Iranian language of the Kurds, a nomadic Moslem people of SW Asia. —**Kurd′ish** *adj.*

Ku·wait (kōō-wāt′, -wīt′). **1.** A republic at the head of the Persian Gulf. Pop. 468,000. **2.** The capital of this republic. Pop. 100,000.

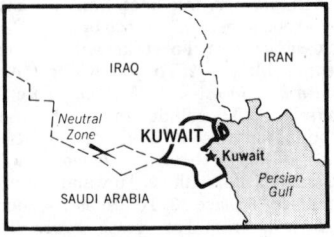

Kuwait

kW kilowatt.

Kwa (kwä) *n.* A branch of the Niger-Congo language family. —**Kwa** *adj.*

kwa·cha (kwä′chä′) *n.* The basic monetary unit of Zambia.

kwash·i·or·kor (kwäsh′ē-ôr′kôr, kwä′shē-) *n.* Severe malnutrition, occurring esp. in African children, characterized by anemia, edema, potbelly, depigmentation of the skin, and loss of hair or change in hair color. [Native word in Ghana.]

kWh kilowatt-hour.

Ky. Kentucky.

kyat (kyät, kě-ät′) *n.* The basic monetary unit of Burma.

Kyo·to (kyō′tō, kē-ō′-). A city of Japan, in S Honshu. Pop. 1,376,000.

Kyu·shu (kyōō′shōō). The southernmost island of Japan.

ă pat/ā ate/âr care/ä bar/b bib/ch chew/d deed/ĕ pet/ē be/f fit/g gag/h hat/hw what/
ĭ pit/ī pie/îr pier/j judge/k kick/l lid, fatal/m mum/n no, sudden/ng sing/ŏ pot/ō go/

L l

l, L (ĕl) *n.* **1.** The 12th letter of the English alphabet. **2. L** Anything shaped like the letter **L.**

l liter.

L 1. large. **2.** The Roman numeral for 50.

l. 1. left. **2.** length. **3.** line.

L. 1. lake. **2.** Latin.

La lanthanum.

La. Louisiana.

L.A. Los Angeles.

lab (lăb) *n. Informal.* A laboratory.

lab. laboratory.

la·bel (lā′bəl) *n.* Anything functioning as a means of identification, esp. a small piece of paper attached to an article to designate its origin, owner, contents, etc. —*v.* **-beled** or **-belled, -beling** or **-belling. 1.** To attach a label to. **2.** To classify or designate. [< OF, ribbon, strip < Gmc.] —**la′bel·er, la′bel·ler** *n.*

la·bi·al (lā′bē-əl) *adj.* Of or pertaining to the lips or labia. —**la′bi·al·ly** *adv.*

la·bi·um (lā′bē-əm) *n., pl.* **-bia** (-bē-ə). Any of four folds of tissue of the female external genitalia. [< L, lip.]

la·bor (lā′bər). Also *chiefly Brit.* **la·bour.** *n.* **1.** Physical or mental exertion of a practical nature; work. **2.** Work for wages. **3.** Workers collectively. **4.** The physical efforts of childbirth. —*v.* **1.** To work. **2.** To strive painstakingly. **3.** To proceed slowly; plod. **4.** To be hampered: *labor under a misconception.* **5.** To deal with in exhaustive detail. [< L.] —**la′bor·er** *n.* —**la′bor·ing·ly** *adv.*

lab·o·ra·to·ry (lăb′rə-tôr′ē, -tōr′ē) *n., pl.* **-ries. 1.** A place equipped for scientific experimentation, research, or testing. **2.** A place where drugs and chemicals are manufactured. [< L *labor,* LABOR.] —**lab′o·ra·to′ri·al** *adj.*

Labor Day. The first Monday in September, a legal holiday in honor of the workingman.

la·bored (lā′bərd) *adj.* Showing labor; lacking natural ease. —**la′bored·ly** *adv.*

la·bo·ri·ous (lə-bôr′ē-əs, lə-bōr′-) *adj.* Requiring long, hard work. —**la·bo′ri·ous·ly** *adv.*

Lab·ra·dor (lăb′rə-dôr′). A peninsula of NE Canada.

la·bur·num (lə-bûr′nəm) *n.* A tree or shrub cultivated for its drooping clusters of yellow flowers. [L.]

lab·y·rinth (lăb′ə-rĭnth′) *n.* An intricate structure of interconnecting passages. [< Gk *laburinthos.*] —**lab′y·rin′thine** (-rĭn′thĭn′, -thēn′) *adj.*

lac (lăk) *n.* A resinous secretion of an Asian insect used in making shellac. [< Sk *lākshā.*]

lace (lās) *n.* **1.** A cord threaded through eyelets or around hooks on two opposite edges to draw and tie them together. **2.** A delicate fabric woven in a weblike pattern. —*v.* **laced, lacing. 1.** To thread a cord through the eyelets or around the hooks of. **2.** To draw together and tie the laces of. **3.** To add liquor to (a beverage). —**lace into.** To attack; assail. [< L *laqueus,* noose, trap.] —**lac′er** *n.* —**lac′y** *adj.*

lac·er·ate (lăs′ə-rāt′) *v.* **-ated, -ating.** To tear; mangle. [< L *lacer,* torn, rent, mangled.] —**lac′er·a′tion** *n.* —**lac′er·a′tive** *adj.*

lach·ry·mal (lăk′rə-məl) *adj.* Also **lac·ri·mal.** Pertaining to tears or tear-producing glands. [< L *lacrima,* tear.]

lach·ry·mose (lăk′rə-mōs′) *adj.* Weeping or inclined to weep; tearful.

lack (lăk) *n.* A deficiency or absence. —*v.* **1.** To be entirely without or have very little of. **2.** To be wanting or deficient. [ME *lac, lacke.*]

lack·a·dai·si·cal (lăk′ə-dā′zĭ-kəl) *adj.* Lacking spirit or interest. [< the phrase *alack the day.*] —**lack′a·dai′si·cal·ly** *adv.*

lack·ey (lăk′ē) *n., pl.* **-eys. 1.** A footman. **2.** A servile follower; toady. [< OF *laquais.*]

lack·lus·ter (lăk′lŭs′tər) *adj.* Lacking luster, brightness, or vitality.

la·con·ic (lə-kŏn′ĭk) *adj.* Sparing of words; terse. [< Gk *Lakōnikos,* of the Spartans (known for their brevity of speech).] —**la·con′i·cal·ly** *adv.*

lac·quer (lăk′ər) *n.* Any of various clear or colored synthetic or resinous coatings used to give wood and metal surfaces a high gloss. [< Hindi *lākh,* lac.] —**lac′quer** *v.*

lac·ri·mal. Variant of **lachrymal.**

la·crosse (lə-krôs′, -krŏs′) *n.* A game played on a field by two teams using long-handled racquets and a hard rubber ball. [< F *la crosse,* a hooked stick.]

lac·ta·ry (lăk′tə-rē) *adj.* Of or pertaining to milk. [< L *lac (lact-),* milk.]

lac·tate (lăk′tāt′) *v.* **-tated, -tating.** To secrete or produce milk. —**lac·ta′tion** *n.*

lac·te·al (lăk′tē-əl) *adj.* Of or like milk; milky. —**lac′te·al·ly** *adv.*

lac·tic (lăk′tĭk) *adj.* Of or derived from milk.

lactic acid. A hygroscopic syrupy liquid, $C_3H_6O_3$, present in sour milk, molasses, various fruits, and wines.

lacto-. *comb. form.* Milk. [< L *lac (lact-).*]

lac·to·ba·cil·lus (lăk′tō-bə-sĭl′əs) *n., pl.* **-cilli** (-sĭl′ī′). Any of various bacilli that ferment lactic acid from carbohydrates.

lac·to·pro·te·in (lăk′tō-prō′tē-ən, -prō′tēn′) *n.* Any protein normally present in milk.

lac·tose (lăk′tōs′) *n.* A white crystalline sugar,

ô paw, for/oi boy/ou out/ŏŏ took/ōō coo/p pop/r run/s sauce/sh shy/t to/th thin/*th* the/
ŭ cut/ûr fur/v van/w wag/y yes/z size/zh vision/ə ago, item, edible, gallop, circus/

$C_{12}H_{22}O_{11}$, made from whey and used in pharmaceuticals, infant foods, and confections.

la·cu·na (lə-kyōō′nə) *n., pl.* -nae (-nē) or -nas. **1.** An empty space; gap. **2.** *Anat.* A cavity or depression. [L *lacuna*, pool.]

lad (lăd) *n.* A young man. [ME *ladde*.]

lad·der (lăd′ər) *n.* **1.** A device consisting of two long structural members crossed by parallel rungs, used to climb or descend. **2.** A series of ranked levels: *high on the executive ladder.* [< OE *hlædder.* See **klei-**.]

lad·en (lăd′n) *adj.* Weighed down; oppressed: *laden with grief.* [< OE *hladan,* to load.]

lad·ing (lā′dĭng) *n.* Cargo; freight: *a bill of lading.*

La·di·no (lə-dē′nō) *n.* A Romance language, derived from Spanish with Hebrew elements and modifications, spoken by Sephardic Jews. [< L *Latinus,* Latin.]

la·dle (lād′l) *n.* A long-handled spoon with a deep bowl for serving liquids. —*v.* -**dled,** -**dling.** To lift out with a ladle. [< OE *hladan,* to draw out, load.] —**la′dler** *n.*

la·dy (lā′dē) *n., pl.* -**dies. 1.** A woman of refinement and good manners. **2.** The female head of a household: *the lady of the house.* **3.** A polite term for any adult member of the feminine sex. **4. Lady.** *Brit.* The general feminine title of nobility and other rank. [< OE *hlæfdige,* "kneader of bread," lady. See **dheigh-**.]

la·dy·bug (lā′dē-bŭg′) *n.* Also **la·dy·bird** (lā′dē-bûrd′), **lady beetle.** A small, usually reddish, black-spotted beetle.

la·dy·fin·ger (lā′dē-fĭng′gər) *n.* A small oval sponge cake.

la·dy′s-slip·per (lā′dēz-slĭp′ər) *n.* An orchid with an inflated, pouchlike lip.

La·e·trile (lā′ə-trĭl) *n.* The name of a chemical believed by some people to be an antineoplastic agent.

La·fay·ette (lä′fē-ĕt′, lăf′ē-), **Marquis de.** 1757–1834. French political leader; commanded American troops in the Revolutionary War.

lag (lăg) *v.* **lagged, lagging. 1.** To fail to keep up a pace; fall behind. **2.** To fail or slacken; flag. —*n.* **1.** A falling behind; retardation. **2.** An interval resulting from this. [?]

la·ger (lä′gər) *n.* Also **lager beer.** Beer aged up to six months to allow sedimentation. [< G *Lager(bier)* (beer) for storing.]

lag-gard (lăg′ərd) *n.* One who lags; a dawdler.

la·gniappe (lăn-yăp′, lăn′yăp′) *n.* An extra or unexpected gift. [< Amer Span *la ñapa.*]

la·goon (lə-gōōn′) *n.* A body of brackish water, esp. one separated from the sea by sandbars or coral reefs. [< L *lacuna,* pool, cavity < *lacus,* LAKE.] —**la·goon′al** *adj.*

La·gos (lā′gŏs′, -gəs). The capital of Nigeria. Pop. 450,000.

La·hore (lə-hôr′, -hōr′). A city of NE West Pakistan. Pop. 1,296,000.

laid (lād). *p.t. & p.p.* of **lay¹.**

lain (lān). *p.p.* of **lie¹.**

lair (lâr) *n.* The den or dwelling of a wild animal. [< OE *leger.*]

lais·sez faire (lĕs′ā fâr′). Also **lais·ser faire.** Noninterference, esp. the doctrine that gov-

ernment should not interfere with commerce. [F, "allow (them) to do."] —**lais′sez-faire′** *adj.* —**lais′sez-faire′ism′** *n.*

la·i·ty (lā′ə-tē) *n.* **1.** Laymen collectively as distinguished from the clergy. **2.** Those outside a given profession, art, etc.; nonprofessionals.

lake (lāk) *n.* **1.** A relatively large inland body of water. **2.** A large pool of other liquid. [< L *lacus,* basin for water.]

lam¹ (lăm) *v.* **lammed, lamming.** *Slang.* To thrash; wallop. [< Scand.]

lam² (lăm) *v.* **lammed, lamming.** *Slang.* To depart swiftly. —*n.* —**on the lam.** In flight, esp. from the law. [?]

Lam. Lamentations (Old Testament).

la·ma (lä′mə) *n.* A Buddhist monk of Tibet or Mongolia.

lamb (lăm) *n.* **1.** A young sheep. **2.** The flesh of a young sheep used as meat. **3.** A mild-mannered or naive person. **4. the Lamb** or **Lamb of God.** Christ. —*v.* To give birth to a lamb. [< OE < Gmc *lambiz-.]

lam·baste (lăm-bāst′) *v.* -**basted,** -**basting. 1.** To thrash; whip. **2.** To scold sharply.

lamb·da (lăm′də) *n.* The 11th letter of the Greek alphabet, representing *l.*

lam·bent (lăm′bənt) *adj.* **1.** Flickering or

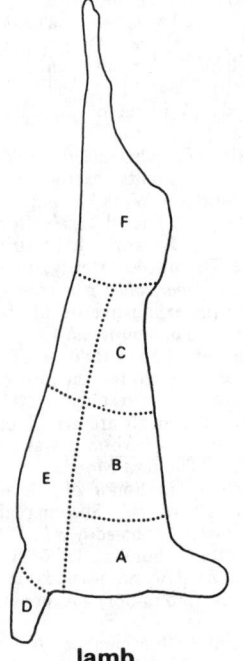

lamb
A. Shoulder
B. Ribs
C. Loin
D. Shank
E. Breast
F. Leg

glowing gently. **2.** Light, effortless, and brilliant: *lambent wit.* [< L *lambere*, to lick, lap.] —**lam'ben•cy** *n.* —**lam'bent•ly** *adv.*

lamb•kin (lăm'kĭn) *n.* **1.** A little lamb. **2.** A small, endearing child.

lame (lām) *adj.* **lamer, lamest. 1.** Crippled, esp. in a leg or foot so as to impair ability to walk. **2.** Ineffectual; unsatisfactory: *a lame excuse.* —*v.* **lamed, laming.** To cause to become lame. [< OE *lama*. See **lem-**.] —**lame'ly** *adv.* —**lame'ness** *n.*

la•mé (lă-mā') *n.* A fabric woven with metallic threads. [F.]

la•med (lä'mĕd', -mĭd) *n.* Also **la•medh.** The 12th letter of the Hebrew alphabet, representing *l.*

lame duck. 1. An elected officeholder continuing in office during the period between the election and inauguration of a successor. **2.** A helpless person; weakling.

la•mel•la (lə-mĕl'ə) *n., pl.* **-lae** (-lē) or **-las.** A thin scale, plate, or layer. [< L *lamella.*]

la•ment (lə-mĕnt') *v.* **1.** To express sorrow or deep regret (over); mourn. **2.** To wail; complain. —*n.* **1.** An expression of sorrow or mourning. **2.** A dirge or elegy. [< L *lamentum,* expression of sorrow.] —**lam'en•ta'tion** (lăm'ən-tā'shən) *n.* —**la•ment'er** *n.*

lam•en•ta•ble (lăm'ən-tə-bəl, lə-mĕn'-) *adj.* To be lamented; grievous; deplorable. —**lam'en•ta•bly** *adv.*

lam•i•na (lăm'ə-nə) *n., pl.* **-nae** (-nē') or **-nas.** A thin plate, sheet, or layer. [< L *lamina,* thin plate.] —**lam'i•nar, lam'i•nal** *adj.*

lam•i•nate (lăm'ə-nāt') *v.* **-nated, -nating. 1.** To form into or bond together in thin layers. **2.** To divide into thin layers. —**lam'i•na'tion** *n.*

lamp (lămp) *n.* **1.** A device, as one equipped with an electric bulb or wick, for providing light. **2.** A similar device, as for therapeutic radiation. [< Gk *lampein,* to shine.]

lamp•black (lămp'blăk') *n.* A gray or black pigment made from soot.

lam•poon (lăm-pōōn') *n.* Broad satire, esp. satire intended as personal ridicule. —*v.* To ridicule in a lampoon. [F.] —**lam•poon'er, lam•poon'ist** *n.* —**lam•poon'er•y** *n.*

lam•prey (lăm'prē) *n., pl.* **-preys.** An eellike primitive fish with a jawless sucking mouth. [< ML *lamprēda.*]

la•na•i (lə-nī') *n.* A porch or patio. [Hawaiian.]

lance (lăns, läns) *n.* **1.** A thrusting weapon with a long shaft and a sharp metal head. **2.** A similar implement. —*v.* **lanced, lancing. 1.** To pierce with a lance. **2.** To cut into with a lancet. [< L *lancea.*]

lance corporal. An enlisted man in the U.S. Marine Corps ranking above a private first class and below a corporal. [< OIt *lancia spezzata,* old soldier, "broken lance."]

Lan•ce•lot (lăn'sə-lət, -lŏt', län'-). Knight of Arthurian legend; lover of Guinevere.

lanc•er (lăn'sər, län'-) *n.* A cavalryman armed with a lance.

lan•cet (lăn'sĭt, län'-) *n.* A surgical knife with a short, wide, pointed double-edged blade. [< LANCE.]

land (lănd) *n.* **1. a.** The solid part of the earth's surface. **b.** A portion or region of this. **2.** Earth; soil. **3.** A nation, country, or realm. **4.** A tract owned or sold as property. —*v.* **1.** To put or arrive on land after traveling by water or air. **2.** To arrive or cause to arrive at a certain place. **3.** To come to rest; alight. **4.** To catch by or as by fishing. [< OE. See **lendh-**.]

land•ed (lăn'dĭd) *adj.* **1.** Owning land: *landed gentry.* **2.** Consisting of land: *a landed estate.*

land•fall (lănd'fôl') *n.* **1.** The sighting or reaching of land on a voyage. **2.** The land thus sighted.

land grant. A government grant of public land for a railroad, highway, or state college. —**land'-grant'** *adj.*

land•hold•er (lănd'hōl'dər) *n.* One who owns land. —**land'hold'ing** *n.*

land•ing (lăn'dĭng) *n.* **1.** The act or process of coming to land or rest, as at the end of a voyage or flight. **2.** A site for landing. **3.** A platform at the top, bottom, or between flights of a staircase.

landing field. A tract of land providing a runway for aircraft.

landing gear. The structure that supports an aircraft and its load on the ground.

landing strip. An aircraft runway without airport facilities.

land•locked (lănd'lŏkt') *adj.* **1.** Surrounded or nearly surrounded by land. **2.** Confined to inland waters: *landlocked salmon.*

land•lord (lănd'lôrd') *n.* **1.** One who owns and leases land, buildings, or dwelling units. **2.** A man who runs a rooming house or inn. —**land'la'dy** (-lā'dē) *fem.n.*

land•lub•ber (lănd'lŭb'ər) *n.* One unfamiliar with the sea or seamanship.

land•mark (lănd'märk') *n.* **1.** A fixed marker indicating a boundary line. **2.** A prominent and identifying feature of a landscape. **3.** A historically significant event, building, or site.

land-poor (lănd'pŏŏr') *adj.* Owning much unprofitable land but lacking the capital to improve or maintain it.

land•scape (lănd'skāp') *n.* **1.** A view or vista of scenery on land. **2.** A pictorial representation of such a scene. —*v.* **-scaped, -scaping.** To improve the appearance of (a piece of ground) by contouring and decorative planting. —**land'scap'er** *n.*

land•slide (lănd'slīd') *n.* **1. a.** The dislodging and fall of a mass of earth and rock. **b.** The dislodged mass. **2.** An overwhelming majority of votes.

land•ward (lănd'wərd) *adv.* Also **land•wards** (-wərdz). Toward the land. —**land'ward** *adj.*

lane (lān) *n.* **1.** A narrow way or road. **2.** A limited passageway or course designated for vehicles, ships, etc. [< OE.]

lang. language.

Lang•er•hans, islands of. See **islands of Langerhans.**

lan•guage (lăng'gwĭj) *n.* **1. a.** The aspect of human behavior that involves the use of vocal sounds in meaningful patterns and, when they exist, corresponding written symbols to form,

---

ô paw, for/oi boy/ou out/ŏŏ took/ōō coo/p pop/r run/s sauce/sh shy/t to/th thin/*th* the/
ŭ cut/ûr fur/v van/w wag/y yes/z size/zh vision/ə ago, item, edible, gallop, circus/

express, and communicate thoughts and feelings. **b.** A historically established pattern of such behavior that offers substantial communication only within the culture it defines: *the English language.* **2.** Any system of signs, symbols, etc., used for communication. **3.** The special vocabulary, usage, or style of a particular group or individual. **4.** Any particular manner of utterance: *gentle language.* **5.** The manner or means of communication between living creatures other than man. [< L *lingua,* tongue, language.]

lan·guid (lăng'gwĭd) *adj.* **1.** Lacking energy or vitality; weak. **2.** Listless; spiritless; apathetic. **3.** Slow; sluggish. [< L *languēre,* to LANGUISH.] —**lan'guid·ly** *adv.* —**lan'guid·ness** *n.*

lan·guish (lăng'gwĭsh) *v.* **1.** To lose strength or vigor; flag. **2.** To become listless or disconsolate; pine. **3.** To affect a mawkish air of longing or wistfulness. [< L *languēre,* to be faint or weak.] —**lan'guish·er** *n.*

lan·guor (lăng'gər) *n.* **1.** Languidness; lassitude; indolence. —**lan'guor·ous** *adj.* —**lan'guor·ous·ly** *adv.* —**lan'guor·ous·ness** *n.*

lank (lăngk) *adj.* **1.** Long and lean; gaunt. **2.** Long, straight, and limp: *lank hair.* [< OE *hlanc,* loose, hollow. See kleng-.]

lank·y (lăng'kē) *adj.* -ier, -iest. Tall, thin, and ungainly. —**lank'i·ly** *adv.* —**lank'i·ness** *n.*

lan·o·lin (lăn'ə-lən) *n.* A yellowish-white fatty substance obtained from wool and used in soaps, cosmetics, and ointments. [< L *lāna,* wool + -OL + -IN.]

Lan·sing (lăn'sĭng). The capital of Michigan. Pop. 132,000.

lan·tern (lăn'tərn) *n.* A case with transparent or translucent sides for holding and protecting a light. [< Gk *lamptēr,* lantern, torch.]

lan·tha·nide (lăn'thə-nīd') *n.* A rare-earth element. [< LANTHANUM.]

lan·tha·num (lăn'thə-nəm) *n. Symbol* **La** A soft, silvery-white metallic element used in glass manufacture and lighting. Atomic number 57, atomic weight 138.91. [< Gk *lanthanein,* to hide.]

lan·yard (lăn'yərd) *n.* A short rope or cord used to secure nautical rigging or worn to carry a knife, whistle, etc. [< OF *lasne,* thong, strap.]

La·os (lä'ōs, lous, lä'ŏs'). A kingdom of SE Asia. Pop. 3,000,000. Caps. Luang Prabang and Vientiane. —**Lao** (lou) *adj. & n.* —**La·o'tian** (lā-ō'shən, lou'shən) *adj. & n.*

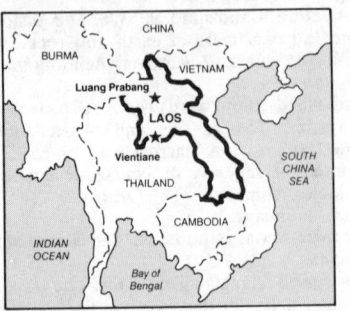

Laos

Lao-tse (lou'dzŭ'). 604?-531 B.C. Chinese philosopher.

lap[1] (lăp) *n.* **1.** The front part of a seated person extending from the lower trunk to the knees. **2.** The part of a garment covering this area. **3.** A place of nurture or control: *the lap of luxury; the lap of the gods.* [< OE *læppa,* flap of a garment.]

lap[2] (lăp) *v.* **lapped, lapping. 1.** To fold or wrap over or around something. **2.** To place or extend so as to overlap. —*n.* **1.** An overlapping part. **2.** A complete turn or circuit, as of a racecourse. [Prob < LAP[1].]

lap[3] (lăp) *v.* **lapped, lapping. 1.** To lift and take in (a liquid or food) with the tongue. **2.** To wash or splash with a light slapping sound. —**lap up.** To take in eagerly. —*n.* The act or sound of lapping. [< OE *lapian.* See lab-.] —**lap'per** *n.*

La Paz (lə păz', päz'). A capital of Bolivia. Pop. 361,000.

lap dog. A small, easily held pet dog.

la·pel (lə-pĕl') *n.* A part of a coat, jacket, etc., folded back against the chest from the opening at the neckline. [< LAP[1].]

lap·i·dar·y (lăp'ə-dĕr'ē) *n., pl.* -ies. One who cuts, polishes, or engraves gems. —*adj.* Of or relating to precious stones or the art of working with them. [L *lapidārius,* stoneworker.]

lap·in (lăp'ən) *n.* Rabbit fur, esp. when sheared. [F.]

lap·is laz·u·li (lăp'ĭs lăz'yōō-lē). An opaque, deep-blue gemstone. [< ML.]

Lap·land (lăp'lănd). A region comprising the areas of N Scandinavia and Finland and the NW Soviet Union lying above the Arctic Circle.

Lapp (lăp) *n.* **1.** Also **Lap·land·er** (lăp'lăn'dər). One of a people of nomadic tradition who inhabit Lapland. **2.** Also **Lap·pish** (lăp'ĭsh). The Finno-Ugric language of this people.

lap·pet (lăp'ĭt) *n.* A decorative flap or loose fold on a garment. [< LAP[1].]

lapse (lăps) *v.* **lapsed, lapsing. 1.** To fall away gradually; decline; subside. **2.** To become invalid, as through neglect or the passage of time. **3.** To elapse. —*n.* **1.** A slipping into a lower state; decline. **2.** A minor slip or failure. **3.** A passing or interval of time. **4.** The termination of a right or privilege through disuse or other failure. [< L *lābī* (pp *lapsus*), to slide.] —**laps'er** *n.*

lap·wing (lăp'wĭng) *n.* A crested Old World bird related to the plovers. [< OE *hlēapewince.*]

lar·board (lär'bərd) *n. Naut.* The port side. [ME *ladborde,* prob "the loading side."] —**lar'board** *adj.*

lar·ce·ny (lär'sə-nē) *n., pl.* -nies. The crime of stealing; theft. [< L *latrōcinium,* military service for pay.] —**lar'ce·nous** *adj.*

larch (lärch) *n.* A cone-bearing tree with deciduous needles and heavy, durable wood. [< L *larix.*]

lard (lärd) *n.* The white rendered fat of a hog. —*v.* **1.** To insert strips of fat in (lean, uncooked meat). **2.** To enrich or add to (speech or writing). [< L *lārdum.*] —**lard′y** *adj.*

lar·der (lär′dər) *n.* A storage place for food. [< LARD.]

la·res and pe·na·tes (lâr′ēz; pĕ-nä′tēz, -nä′tēz). **1.** Ancient Roman household gods. **2.** One's household possessions.

large (lärj) *adj.* **larger, largest. 1.** Of considerable size, capacity, etc.; big. **2.** Broad in scope; comprehensive. —**at large. 1.** At liberty; free. **2.** At length; in detail. **3.** Not representing or assigned to a specific country, district, etc. [< L *largus,* generous, bountiful.] —**large′ness** *n.*

large intestine. The lower portion of the intestine, extending to the anus.

large·ly (lärj′lē) *adv.* **1.** For the most part; mainly. **2.** In a large manner.

lar·gess (lär-jĕs′, lär′jĭs, -jĕs′) *n.* Also **lar·gesse. 1.** Liberality in giving. **2.** Something generously bestowed.

larg·ish (lär′jĭsh) *adj.* Fairly large.

lar·go (lär′gō) *adv. Mus.* Slowly and solemnly. [It, slow, "broad."] —**lar′go** *adj. & n.*

lar·i·at (lär′ē-ət) *n.* A rope with a running noose; a lasso. [Span *la reata.*]

lark¹ (lärk) *n.* **1.** An Old World bird with a sustained, melodious song. **2.** Any of several similar birds. [< OE *lǣwerce* < Gmc *larwarikōn.*]

lark² (lärk) *n.* A carefree romp or prank. —*v.* To romp; frolic. [< ON *leika,* to play.]

lark·spur (lärk′spûr′) *n.* A plant with spurred, usually blue or purplish flowers.

lar·rup (lär′əp) *v. Informal.* To flog; thrash; beat. [?]

lar·va (lär′və) *n., pl.* **-vae** (-vē). **1.** The wingless, often wormlike form of a newly hatched insect. **2.** The newly hatched stage of any of various animals that differ markedly in the adult form, as a tadpole. [L *lārva,* disembodied spirit, mask.] —**lar′val** *adj.*

lar·yn·gi·tis (lăr′ən-jī′tĭs) *n.* Inflammation of the larynx.

lar·ynx (lăr′ĭngks) *n., pl.* **larynges** (lə-rĭn′jēz) or **-ynxes.** The upper part of the respiratory tract between the pharynx and the trachea, containing the vocal cords. [< Gk *larunx.*] —**la·ryn′ge·al** (lə-rĭn′jē-əl) *adj.*

la·sa·gna (lə-zän′yə) *pl.n.* Also **la·sa·gne.** Flat wide noodles, usually baked with tomato sauce and cheese. [It.]

las·civ·i·ous (lə-sĭv′ē-əs) *adj.* Lewd; lecherous. [< L *lascivus,* wanton, lustful.] —**las·civ′i·ous·ly** *adv.* —**las·civ′i·ous·ness** *n.*

la·ser (lā′zər) *n.* Any of several devices that convert incident electromagnetic radiation of mixed frequencies to one or more discrete frequencies of highly amplified and coherent radiation. [L(ight) a(mplification by) s(timulated) e(mission of) r(adiation).] —**lase** *v.* **(lased, lasing).**

lash¹ (lăsh) *n.* **1.** A whip or thong of a whip. **2.** A stroke or blow with or as with a whip. **3.** An eyelash. —*v.* **1.** To strike with or as with a whip. **2.** To wave or thrash vigorously, as a tail. **3.** To make a violent verbal attack. [ME *lashe.*] —**lash′er** *n.*

lash² (lăsh) *v.* To secure or bind, as with a rope. [< L *laqueus,* snare.] —**lash′er** *n.*

lass (lăs) *n.* A girl or young woman. [ME *lasse.*]

las·sie (lăs′ē) *n.* A girl.

las·si·tude (lăs′ə-t/y/ōōd′) *n.* A state of listless weakness or exhaustion. [< L *lassus,* tired, weary.]

las·so (lăs′ō) *n., pl.* **-sos** or **-soes.** A long rope or thong with a running noose at one end, used esp. to catch horses and cattle. [< L *laqueus,* snare.] —**las′so** *v.*

last¹ (lăst, läst) *adj.* **1.** Being, coming, or remaining after all others. **2.** Most recent; latest. **3.** Conclusive and authoritative. **4.** Least likely or expected: *the last man we would have suspected.* —*adv.* **1.** After all others. **2.** Most recently. **3.** In conclusion. —*n.* **1.** One that is last. **2.** The end. —**at last.** Finally. [< OE *latost.* See **lēi-**.] —**last′ly** *adv.*

last² (lăst, läst) *v.* **1.** To continue in existence; endure. **2.** To continue to be adequate or sufficient. [< OE *lǣstan.* See **leis-**.]

last³ (lăst, läst) *n.* A foot-shaped block or form used in making or repairing shoes. [< OE *lāst,* sole, footprint. See **leis-**.]

Las·tex (lăs′tĕks) *n.* A trademark for a yarn of elastic rubber wound with rayon, nylon, silk, or cotton. [(E)las(tic) + tex(tile).]

Last Judgment. The final judgment by God of all mankind.

Last Supper. Christ's supper with his disciples on the night before his Crucifixion.

lat. latitude.

Lat. Latin.

lat·a·ki·a (lăt′ə-kē′ə) *n.* A type of Turkish tobacco.

latch (lăch) *n.* A fastening or lock, as for a door or gate. —*v.* To close with a latch. —**latch on to.** *Informal.* **1.** To get hold or possession of. **2.** To cling to. [< OE *lǣccan,* to grasp. See **slagw-**.]

late (lāt). **later, latest.** *adj.* **1.** Coming, occurring, or remaining after the usual or expected time. **2.** Being or occurring toward the end. **3.** Recent. **4.** Recently deceased: *the late Mr. Foster.* —*adv.* **1.** After the usual or expected time. **2.** At or into an advanced period or part. **3.** Recently. —**of late.** Recently. [< OE *lǣt.* See **lēi-**.] —**late′ly** *adv.* —**late′ness** *n.*

Late Greek. Greek from the 4th to the 9th century A.D.

Late Latin. Latin from the 3rd to the 7th century A.D.

la·tent (lā′tənt) *adj.* Present or potential but not manifest. [< L *latēre,* to lie hidden, be concealed.] —**la′ten·cy** *n.* —**la′tent·ly** *adv.*

lat·er·al (lăt′ər-əl) *adj.* Of, at, on, or toward the side. —*n.* Also **lateral pass.** A football pass thrown sideways. [< L *latus (later-),* side.] —**lat′er·al·ly** *adv.*

la·tex (lā′tĕks′) *n.* **1.** The milky, viscous sap of certain trees and plants, as the rubber tree. **2.** An emulsion of rubber or plastic globules in water, used in paints, adhesives, etc. [< L, fluid.] —**la′tex′** *adj.*

lath (lăth) *n.* **1.** A narrow, thin strip of wood, used esp. in making a supporting structure for

plaster. **2.** A similarly used building material.
[< OE *lætt*.]

lathe (lāth) *n.* A machine on which a piece is spun and shaped by a fixed cutting or abrading tool. [?] —**lathe** *v.* (**lathed, lathing**).

lath·er (lăth'ər) *n.* **1.** Foam or froth, esp. that formed by soap and water. **2.** Frothy sweat. **3.** A dither. —*v.* **1.** To produce lather. **2.** To apply lather to. [< OE *lēathor*, washing soda. See lou-.] —**lath'er·y** *adj.*

Lat·in (lăt'n) *adj.* **1.** Of or relating to ancient Rome, its culture, or its language. **2.** Of or relating to peoples using Romance languages. —*n.* **1.** The Italic dialect of ancient Rome. **2.** A member of a Latin people. [< L *Latīnus* < *Latium*, region surrounding Rome.]

Latin America. The Spanish- or Portuguese-speaking countries of the Western Hemisphere. —**Lat'in-A·mer'i·can** *adj.*

lat·i·tude (lăt'ə-t/y/ōōd') *n.* **1.** Extent; range. **2.** Freedom from limitations. **3. a.** The angular distance N or S of the equator, measured in degrees along a meridian. **b.** A region considered in relation to this distance. [< L *lātus*, wide.] —**lat'i·tu'din·al** *adj.*

lat·i·tu·di·nar·i·an (lăt'ə-t/y/ōōd'n-âr'ē-ən) *n.* One favoring freedom of thought and behavior. —**lat'i·tu'di·nar'i·an·ism'** *n.*

la·trine (lə-trēn') *n.* A communal toilet. [< L *latrīna* < *lavāre*, to wash.]

–latry. *comb. form.* Worship: *bibliolatry.* [< Gk *latreia.*]

lat·ter (lăt'ər) *adj.* **1.** Second of two persons or things mentioned. **2.** Further advanced; later. **3.** Closer to the end. [< OE *lætra*. See lēi-.] —**lat'ter·ly** *adv.*

> *Usage:* Latter, in contrast with *former*, is acceptable only in contexts limited to two. Otherwise, *last-named* is more appropriate.

lat·ter-day (lăt'ər-dā') *adj.* Of present or recent time.

Latter-day Saint. A Mormon.

lat·tice (lăt'ĭs) *n.* **1.** An open framework made of interwoven strips, as of wood or metal. **2.** Something resembling this, as a window. **3.** *Phys.* A regular periodic configuration throughout an area or space. [< OF *latte*, lath.] —**lat'ticed** *adj.* —**lat'tice·work'** *n.*

Lat·vi·a (lăt'vē-ə). A constituent republic of the Soviet Union, on the Baltic. Pop. 2,365,000. Cap. Riga.

Lat·vi·an (lăt'vē-ən) *n.* **1.** A native of Latvia. **2.** The Baltic language of these people; Lettish. —**Lat'vi·an** *adj.*

laud (lôd) *v.* To praise; extol. —*n.* **1.** Praise. **2. lauds.** A morning church service at which psalms of praise are sung. [L *laudāre*, to praise.] —**laud'er** *n.*

laud·a·ble (lô'də-bəl) *adj.* Praiseworthy; commendable. —**laud'a·bly** *adv.*

lau·da·num (lôd'n-əm) *n.* A tincture of opium. [NL.]

laud·a·to·ry (lô'də-tôr'ē, -tōr'ē) *adj.* Expressing praise. —**laud'a·to'ri·ly** *adv.*

laugh (lăf, läf) *v.* **1.** To produce inarticulate sounds expressive of mirth, joy, or derision. **2.** To drive or influence by or as by laughing: *laughed him off the stage.* —*n.* **1.** The sound or

act of laughing: *had a good laugh.* **2.** Something amusing or ridiculous. [< OE *hliehhan*. See klēg-.] —**laugh'a·ble** *adj.*

laugh·ing·stock (lăf'ĭng-stŏk', läf'-) *n.* An object of ridicule; butt.

laugh·ter (lăf'tər, läf'-) *n.* The sound or action of laughing.

launch¹ (lônch, länch) *v.* **1.** To set in motion; propel. **2.** To move (a boat) into the water. **3.** To put into action; inaugurate; initiate. —*n.* An act of launching. [< OF *lancier*, to hurl < *lance*, lance.]

launch² (lônch, länch) *n.* An open motorboat. [< Malay *lancha.*]

launch·er (lôn'chər, län'-) *n.* A device for launching a grenade or rocket shell.

launching pad. A platform from which a, rocket or space vehicle is launched.

launch vehicle. *Aerospace.* A booster.

laun·der (lôn'dər, län'-) *v.* **1.** To wash or wash and iron (clothes or linens). **2.** To conceal the source of (money), as by channeling it through an intermediary. [<L *lavanda*, things that need washing <*lavāre*, to LAVE.] —**laun'der·er** *n.* —**laun'dress** (-drĭs) *fem.n.*

laun·dry (lôn'drē, län'-) *n., pl.* **-dries. 1.** Soiled or laundered clothes. **2.** A place where laundering is done.

lau·re·ate (lôr'ē-ĭt) *n.* One receiving highest honors, as a poet or scientist. [L *laureātus*, crowned with laurel.] —**lau're·ate** *adj.*

lau·rel (lôr'əl, lŏr'-) *n.* **1.** A shrub or tree of the Mediterranean region, having aromatic evergreen leaves. **2.** Any of several similar shrubs or trees. **3.** Often **laurels.** A wreath of laurel leaves. **4. laurels.** Honor; glory. [< L *laurus.*]

la·va (lä'və, lăv'ə) *n.* **1.** Molten rock from a volcano or geologic fissure. **2.** The rock formed by the cooling and solidifying of this substance. [It, lava stream from Vesuvius.]

lav·a·liere (lăv'ə-lîr') *n.* A pendant worn on a chain around the neck. [< Louise de *La Vallière*, a mistress of Louis XIV.]

lav·a·to·ry (lăv'ə-tôr'ē) *n., pl.* **-ries.** A room equipped with washing and toilet facilities. [< L *lavāre*, LAVE.]

lave (lāv) *v.* **laved, laving.** To wash; bathe. [< L *lavāre.*]

lav·en·der (lăv'ən-dər) *n.* **1.** Any of various aromatic plants having small fragrant purplish flowers. **2.** Pale to light purple. [< ML *lavendula.*] —**lav'en·der** *adj.*

lav·ish (lăv'ĭsh) *adj.* Extravagant; profuse. —*v.* To give forth unstintingly. [< OF *lavasse*, torrent of rain.] —**lav'ish·er** *n.* —**lav'ish·ly** *adv.* —**lav'ish·ness** *n.*

La·voi·sier (lä-vwä-zyā'), **Antoine.** 1743–1794. French chemist.

law (lô) *n.* **1.** A rule established by authority, society, or custom. **2.** A body of such rules. **3.** The science or study of such rules; jurisprudence. **4.** A judicial system or its workings. **5.** A formulation or generalization based on observed phenomena. **6.** A code of ethics or behavior. **7.** Avowed or undisputed authority. [< OE *lagu*, code of rules.]

law·ful (lô'fəl) *adj.* Allowed or established by law. —**law'ful·ly** *adv.*

ă pat/ā ate/âr care/ä bar/b bib/ch chew/d deed/ĕ pet/ē be/f fit/g gag/h hat/hw what/
ĭ pit/ī pie/îr pier/j judge/k kick/l lid, fatal/m mum/n no, sudden/ng sing/ŏ pot/ō go/

law•giv•er (lô'gĭv'ər) *n.* 1. One who gives a code of laws to a people. 2. A legislator.
law•less (lô'lĭs) *adj.* 1. Not governed by law. 2. Heedless of or contrary to law. 3. Disorderly; unbridled. —**law'less•ly** *adv.* —**law'less• ness** *n.*
law•mak•er (lô'mā'kər) *n.* A legislator.
lawn[1] (lôn) *n.* A closely mown area planted with grass. [< OF *launde,* heath.]
lawn[2] (lôn) *n.* A very fine, thin cotton or linen fabric. [Prob < *Laon,* France, linen-manufacturing town.]
law•ren•ci•um (lô-rĕn'sē-əm, lō-) *n. Symbol* **Lw** A synthetic radioactive element having a single isotope, Lw 257. Atomic number 103. [< E. *Lawrence* (1901–1958), American physicist.]
law•suit (lô'soot') *n.* A case brought before a law court.
law•yer (lô'yər) *n.* One who gives legal advice and assistance to clients and represents them in court.
lax (lăks) *adj.* 1. Negligent; remiss. 2. Not strict. 3. Not tense or taut; slack. 4. Loose. [< L *laxus,* slack, loose.] —**lax'i•ty, lax'ness** *n.* —**lax'ly** *adv.*
lax•a•tive (lăk'sə-tĭv) *n.* A drug stimulating bowel evacuation. [< L *laxus,* loose, LAX.] —**lax'a•tive** *adj.*
lay[1] (lā) *v.* **laid, laying.** 1. a. To place or rest on a surface. b. *Nonstandard.* To recline; lie. 2. To knock down: *laid him out flat.* 3. To calm; allay. 4. To produce and deposit (eggs). 5. To bet: *laid his life on it.* 6. To spread: *lay paint on a canvas.* 7. To apply, assign, or locate. 8. To bring into a specified condition. 9. To set or place in a desired position. 10. To prepare; contrive: *lay plans.* 11. To sink in the ground: *lay a cable.* 12. To impose: *laid a heavy fine on him.* 13. To put forth or submit: *laid the case before us.* —*n.* The relative position or arrangement of something. [< OE *lecgan.* See **legh-.**]
lay[2] (lā) *adj.* 1. Of or belonging to the laity. 2. Nonprofessional. [< Gk *laos,* the people.]
lay[3] (lā) *n.* 1. A ballad. 2. A song. [< OF *lai.*]
lay[4] (lā). *p.t.* of **lie**[1].
lay•er (lā'ər) *n.* 1. A single thickness, coating, or stratum. 2. One that lays, esp. a hen. [< ME *leyen,* to lay.]
lay•ette (lā-ĕt') *n.* Clothing and other equipment for a newborn child. [< OF *laie,* box.]
lay•man (lā'mən) *n.* 1. A member of the laity. 2. A nonprofessional.
lay off. 1. To suspend from employment, as during a slack period. 2. To mark off; chart. 3. *Slang.* a. To give up (a habitual indulgence). b. To desist.
lay•off (lā'ôf', -ŏf') *n.* 1. Temporary dismissal of employees. 2. A period of inactivity.
lay out. 1. To put or spread out. 2. To arrange according to plan. 3. To spend; supply (money). 4. To prepare for burial. 5. To knock down; prostrate.
lay•out (lā'out') *n.* 1. An arrangement or plan. 2. A set of tools.
lay over. To stop at some place in the course of a journey because of scheduling requirements.

lay•o•ver (lā'ō'vər) *n.* A stop imposed by the scheduling of a carrier.
la•zar (lā'zər) *n.* A leper. [< ML *Lazarus,* LAZARUS.]
Laz•a•rus (lăz'ər-əs). 1. A man raised from the dead by Jesus. John 11:1–44. 2. The diseased beggar in the parable of the rich man and the beggar. Luke 16:19–31.
laze (lāz) *v.* **lazed, lazing.** To loaf; idle. [Back-formation < LAZY.]
la•zy (lā'zē) *adj.* **-zier, -ziest.** 1. Indolent; slothful. 2. Slow-moving; sluggish. [?] —**la'zi•ly** *adv.* —**la'zi•ness** *n.*
lazy Susan. A revolving tray for condiments or relishes.
lb pound (L *libra*).
l.c. *Ptg.* lower-case.
L.C. Library of Congress.
L/C letter of credit.
l.c.d. lowest common denominator.
l.c.m. least common multiple.
lea (lē, lā) *n.* Grassland; meadow. [< OE *lēah, lēa.*]
leach (lēch) *v.* To remove, or be removed from, by the action of a percolating liquid. [Prob < OE *leccan,* to moisten.] —**leach'er** *n.*
lead[1] (lēd) *v.* **led, leading.** 1. To guide, conduct, escort, or direct. 2. To influence; induce. 3. To be ahead or at the head of: *His name lea the list.* 4. To pursue; live: *lead a hectic life.* 5. To tend toward a certain goal or result: *lea to complications.* 6. To make the initial play, as in a card game. —**lead astray.** To lead into error or wrongdoing. —**lead on.** To draw along; lure; entice. —**lead up to.** 1. To result in by a series of steps. 2. To proceed toward (one's true purpose or subject) with lengthy or evasive preliminary remarks. —*n.* 1. The first place; foremost position. 2. The margin by which one is ahead. 3. A clue. 4. Command; leadership. 5. An example; precedent. 6. The principal role in a play. 7. a. The prerogative or turn to make the first play in a card game. b. The card played. 8. A leash for leading an animal. [< OE *lǣdan.* See **leith-.**] —**lead'er** *n.* —**lead'er•ship'** *n.*
lead[2] (lĕd) *n.* 1. *Symbol* **Pb** A soft, bluish-white, dense metallic element, used in solder and type metal, bullets, radiation shielding, and paints. Atomic number 82, atomic weight 207.19. 2. A weight used to make soundings. 3. A thin metal strip used to separate lines of type. 4. A thin stick of graphitic marking substance in a pencil. —*v.* 1. To cover, line, or weight with lead. 2. To secure (window glass) with lead. [< OE *lēad* < Gmc **lauda.*]
lead•en (lĕd'n) *adj.* 1. Made of lead. 2. Heavy and inert. 3. Dull; sluggish. 4. Weighted down; depressed: *a leaden heart.* 5. Dull, dark gray. —**lead'en•ly** *adv.*
lead-time (lēd'tīm') *n.* The time needed or available between the decision to start a project and the completion of the work.
leaf (lēf) *n., pl.* **leaves** (lēvz). 1. A usually green, flattened plant structure attached to a stem and functioning as a principal organ of photosynthesis. 2. A leaflike part. 3. Leaves collectively; foliage. 4. One of the sheets con-

---

ô paw, for/oi boy/ou out/oo took/oo coo/p pop/r run/s sauce/sh shy/t to/th thin/*th* the/
ŭ cut/ûr fur/v van/w wag/y yes/z size/zh vision/ə ago, item, edible, gallop, circus/

stituting the pages of a book. **5.** A very thin sheet of gold. **6.** A movable section of a table top. **7.** A movable section of a folding door, shutter, or gate. *—v.* **1.** To produce leaves. **2.** To turn pages rapidly: *leaf through a book.* [< OE *léaf.* See leup-.] —**leaf′y** *adj.*

leaf·let (lēf′lĭt) *n.* **1.** A small leaf or leaflike part. **2.** A printed handbill, circular, or flier.

leaf spring. A spring consisting of several metallic strips joined to act as a single unit.

league[1] (lēg) *n.* **1.** An association or alliance, as of states or persons, for common action. **2.** *Informal.* A class of competition: *out of his league.* [< L *ligāre,* to bind.] —**league** *v.* **(leagued, leaguing).**

league[2] (lēg) *n.* A unit of distance equal to three miles. [< LL *leuga.*]

leak (lēk) *n.* **1. a.** A flaw, crack, or hole permitting accidental admission or escape of fluid or light. **b.** Such admission or escape. **2.** A secret or accidental disclosure of confidential information. *—v.* **1.** To escape or pass through a leak. **2.** To allow something passage through a leak. **3.** To disclose or become known through a breach of secrecy. [ME *leke.*] —**leak′i·ness** *n.* —**leak′y** *adj.*

leak·age (lē′kĭj) *n.* **1.** The process of leaking. **2.** The thing or amount that escapes by leaking.

lean[1] (lēn) *v.* **leaned** or **leant** (lĕnt), **leaning.** **1.** To bend away from the vertical; incline. **2.** To incline one's weight so as to be supported. **3.** To rely on for assistance or support. **4.** To have a tendency or preference. [< OE *hleonian.* See klei-.]

lean[2] (lēn) *adj.* **1.** Not fleshy; thin. **2.** Containing little or no fat: *lean meat.* **3.** Not productive: *lean years.* *—n.* Meat with little or no fat. [< OE *hlǽne* < Gmc **hlainjaz.*] —**lean′ly** *adv.* —**lean′ness** *n.*

lean·ing (lē′nĭng) *n.* A tendency; inclination.

lean-to (lēn′tōō′) *n., pl.* **-tos.** **1.** A shed with a single-pitch roof attached to the side of a building. **2.** A simple shelter resembling this.

leap (lēp) *v.* **leaped** or **leapt** (lĕpt, lēpt), **leaping.** **1.** To jump off the ground; hurdle. **2.** To jump forward; vault; bound. *—n.* A jump or bound. [< OE *hlēapan.*] —**leap′er** *n.*

leap·frog (lēp′frôg′, -frŏg′) *n.* A game in which one player bends over while the next jumps over him straddle-legged.

leap year. A year having 366 days with February 29 as the extra day.

learn (lûrn) *v.* **learned** or **learnt** (lûrnt), **learning.** **1.** To gain knowledge, comprehension, or mastery through experience or study. **2.** To memorize. **3.** To become informed. [< OE *leornian.* See leis-.] —**learn′er** *n.*

learn·ed (lûr′nĭd) *adj.* Erudite; scholarly.

learn·ing (lûr′nĭng) *n.* Erudition.

lease (lēs) *n.* **1.** A contract granting use or occupation of land or holdings during a specified period in exchange for rent. **2.** An extension under improved circumstances: *a new lease on life.* *—v.* **leased, leasing.** **1.** To grant by lease. **2.** To hold under lease. [< L *laxāre,* to let go, loosen < *laxus,* LAX.]

lease·hold (lēs′hōld′) *n.* **1.** Possession by lease.

2. Property held by lease. —**lease′hold′er** *n.*

leash (lēsh) *n.* A restraining chain, strap, etc., attached to the collar or harness of an animal. [< OF *laissier,* to loosen, let (a dog run slack).] —**leash** *v.*

least (lēst). Alternate *superl.* of **little.** *—adj.* **1.** Lowest in importance or rank. **2.** Smallest in magnitude or degree. *—adv.* In the smallest degree. *—n.* The smallest; slightest. [< OE *lǽst* < Gmc **loisiz,* little.]

least common multiple. The least quantity that is exactly divisible by each of two or more designated quantities.

leath·er (lĕth′ər) *n.* The dressed or tanned hide of an animal, usually with the hair removed. [< OE *lether-.* See letro-.] —**leath′er** *adj.* —**leath′ern** *adj.*

leath·er·neck (lĕth′ər-nĕk′) *n. Slang.* A marine.

leath·er·y (lĕth′ə-rē) *adj.* Resembling leather; tough or weathered.

leave[1] (lēv) *v.* **left, leaving.** **1.** To go out or away from; depart. **2. a.** To let or cause to remain. **b.** To deliver. **3.** To have as a remainder. **4.** To forgo moving or interfering with. **5.** To bequeath. **6.** To abandon; forsake. [< OE *lǽfan.* See leip-.]

leave[2] (lēv) *n.* **1.** Permission. **2.** Official permission to be absent from duty. **3.** Farewell or departure: *take leave.* [< OE *léaf.*]

leaved (lēvd) *adj.* Having a specified number or kind of leaves: *three-leaved; wide-leaved.*

leav·en (lĕv′ən) *n.* **1.** A substance, such as yeast, used to produce fermentation in batters and doughs. **2.** An element that works to lighten or enliven a whole. *—v.* **1.** To raise dough, as with yeast. **2.** To pervade with a lightening or enlivening influence. [Prob < L *levāre,* to raise.]

leaves. *pl.* of **leaf.**

leave-tak·ing (lēv′tā′kĭng) *n.* Departure.

leav·ings (lē′vĭngz) *pl.n.* Leftovers; residue.

Leb·a·non (lĕb′ə-nən). A republic on the E Mediterranean. Pop. 2,152,000. Cap. Beirut. —**Leb′a·nese′** (-nēz′, -nēs′) *adj. & n.*

Lebanon

lech·er (lĕch′ər) *n.* A man given to inordinate sexual indulgence. [< OF *lechier,* to live in debauchery, lick.] —**lech′er·ous** *adj.* —**lech′er·ous·ly** *adv.* —**lech′er·y** *n.*

lec·tern (lĕk′tərn) *n.* A reading stand for a public speaker. [< L *lectus*, pp of *legere*, to read.]

lec·ture (lĕk′chər) *n.* **1.** An instructional exposition of a given subject delivered before an audience or class. **2.** A solemn scolding. [< L *lectus*, pp of *legere*, to read.] —**lec′ture** *v.* (-tured, -turing). —**lec′tur·er** *n.*

led (lĕd). *p.t.* & *p.p.* of **lead**[1].

ledge (lĕj) *n.* **1.** A shelflike projection on a wall or cliff. **2.** A reef. [ME *legge*, a raised strip or bar.] —**ledge′less** *adj.*

ledg·er (lĕj′ər) *n.* A book in which monetary transactions are posted in the form of debits and credits. [ME *legger*, book remaining in one place.]

lee (lē) *n.* **1.** The side or quarter away from the wind. **2.** Cover; shelter. [< OE *hlēo*, covering, shelter. See kel-[1].] —**lee** *adj.*

Lee (lē), **Robert E(dward).** 1807–1870. Commander in chief of the Confederate armies in the Civil War.

leech (lēch) *n.* **1.** Any of various aquatic bloodsucking worms, of which one kind was formerly used by physicians to bleed their patients. **2.** A hanger-on or parasite. [< OE *lǽce*.]

Leeds (lēdz). A city of N England. Pop. 509,000.

leek (lēk) *n.* A vegetable related to the onion, having a white, slender bulb and dark-green leaves. [< OE *lēac*.]

leer (lîr) *n.* A suggestive, cunning, or malicious look. [Prob < *leer*, cheek.] —**leer** *v.*

leer·y (lîr′ē) *adj.* -**ier**, -**iest.** Distrustful; wary. [< LEER.] —**leer′i·ness** *n.*

lees (lēz) *pl.n.* Dregs. [< ML *lia*, sediment.]

lee·ward (lē′wərd, lōō′ərd) *adj.* Located away from the wind. —**lee′ward** *n.* & *adv.*

lee·way (lē′wā′) *n.* **1.** The drift of a ship to leeward of true course. **2.** A margin of freedom or variation; latitude.

left[1] (lĕft) *adj.* **1.** Of, at, or on the side of the body that faces north when the subject is facing east. **2.** Of, at, or on the corresponding side of anything that can be said to have a front. **3.** Often **Left.** Of or belonging to the political Left. —*n.* **1.** The direction or position on the left side of something. **2.** The left side or hand. **3.** A turn in this direction: *take a left.* **4. the Left.** The persons and groups pursuing egalitarian political goals by reformist or revolutionary means. —*adv.* Toward or on the left. [< OE *left, lyft.*]

left[2] (lĕft). *p.t.* & *p.p.* of **leave.**

left-hand (lĕft′hănd′) *adj.* **1.** Of, at, or on the left. **2.** Intended for the left hand.

left-hand·ed (lĕft′hăn′dĭd) *adj.* **1.** Having more dexterity in the left hand than in the right. **2.** Done with the left hand. **3.** Awkward; maladroit. —*adv.* With the left hand. —**left′-hand′ed·ly** *adv.* —**left′-hand′ed·ness** *n.*

left·ist (lĕf′tĭst) *n.* Also **Left·ist.** One espousing the ideology of the Left. —**left′ist** *adj.*

left·o·vers (lĕft′ō′vərz) *n.* Food left over from one meal and saved for another.

left wing. The leftist faction of a group. —**left′-wing′** *adj.* —**left′-wing′er** *n.*

leg (lĕg) *n.* **1.** A limb of an animal, used for locomotion or support. **2.** Something resembling a leg in shape or function. **3.** The part of a pair of trousers that covers the leg. **4.** A stage of a journey or course. —*v.* **legged, legging.** To use one's legs, esp. to run: *legged it out of there.* [< ON *leggr.*]

leg. 1. legal. **2.** legislation; legislative; legislature.

leg·a·cy (lĕg′ə-sē) *n., pl.* -**cies.** **1.** A bequest. **2.** Something handed down from an ancestor or predecessor, or from the past. [< L *lēgāre*, to depute, bequeath.]

le·gal (lē′gəl) *adj.* **1.** Of or relating to law or lawyers. **2. a.** Authorized or permitted by law. **b.** Established by law; statutory. **3.** Enforced by law. [< L *lēx* (*lēg-*), law.] —**le·gal′i·ty** (lē-găl′ə-tē) *n.* —**le′gal·i·za′tion** *n.* —**le′gal·ize′** *v.* (-ized, -izing). —**le′gal·ly** *adv.*

le·gal·ism (lē′gə-lĭz′əm) *n.* Strict, literal adherence to law. —**le′gal·is′tic** *adj.*

leg·ate (lĕg′ĭt) *n.* An official emissary, esp. of the pope. [< L *lēgāre*, to depute, send on an embassy.] —**leg′ate·ship′** *n.*

leg·a·tee (lĕg′ə-tē′) *n.* The inheritor of a legacy.

le·ga·tion (lə-gā′shən) *n.* **1.** A diplomatic mission headed by a minister. **2.** The premises occupied by the minister and his staff.

le·ga·to (lə-gä′tō) *adv. Mus.* In a connected style. [It, "connected," "bound."] —**le·ga′to** *adj.* & *n.*

leg·end (lĕj′ənd) *n.* **1.** An unverifiable popular story handed down from the past. **2.** An inscription on an object. **3.** An explanatory caption. [< L *legere*, to collect, gather, read.] —**leg′en·dar′i·ly** *adv.* —**leg′en·dar′y** *adj.*

leg·er·de·main (lĕj′ər-də-mān′) *n.* Sleight of hand. [< OF *leger de main*, "light of hand."]

leg·ged (lĕg′ĭd, lĕgd) *adj.* Having a specified number or kind of legs: *six-legged; long-legged.*

leg·gings (lĕg′ĭngz) *pl.n.* Leg coverings, as gaiters or puttees.

leg·horn (lĕg′hôrn′, -ərn) *n.* **1. a.** Finely plaited, bleached straw. **b.** A hat made from this. **2.** Often **Leghorn.** One of a breed of domestic fowl noted for egg production. [< *Leghorn,* Italy.]

leg·i·ble (lĕj′ə-bəl) *adj.* Capable of being read. [< L *legere*, to read.] —**leg′i·bil′i·ty, leg′i·ble·ness** *n.* —**leg′i·bly** *adv.*

le·gion (lē′jən) *n.* **1.** The major unit of the Roman army, comprising 3,000 to 6,000 foot soldiers and 100 to 200 mounted soldiers. **2.** A multitude. [< L *legere*, "to gather," levy troops.] —**le′gion·ar′y** *n.*

le·gion·naire (lē′jə-nâr′) *n.* A member of the American Legion, an ex-servicemen's organization.

legis. legislation; legislative; legislature.

leg·is·late (lĕj′ĭs-lāt′) *v.* -**lated, -lating.** To pass a law or create by legislation. —**leg′is·la′tor** *n.*

leg·is·la·tion (lĕj′ĭs-lā′shən) *n.* **1.** The action of making laws. **2.** Laws made by a legislative body.

leg·is·la·tive (lĕj′ĭs-lā′tĭv) *adj.* **1.** Of or relating to a legislature. **2.** Having the power to make laws. —**leg′is·la′tive·ly** *adv.*

leg·is·la·ture (lĕj′ĭs-lā′chər) *n.* A body of persons vested with the power to legislate.

le·git·i·mate (lə-jĭt′ə-mĭt) *adj.* **1.** In compliance with the law; lawful. **2.** In accordance with accepted standards. **3.** Reasonable: *a legitimate solution.* **4.** Authentic; genuine. **5.** Born in wedlock. —*v.* (lə-jĭt′ə-māt′) -**mated**, -**mating.** To justify as legitimate. [< L *lēgitimus,* lawful, legal.] —**le·git′i·ma·cy** (-mə-sē) *n.* —**le·git′i·mate·ly** *adv.*

leg·ume (lĕg′yo͞om′, lə-gyo͞om′) *n.* **1.** A bean, pea, or related plant bearing pods that split in two when mature. **2.** The pod or seeds of such a plant, esp. when used as food. [< L *legūmen,* pulse, bean.] —**le·gu′mi·nous** *adj.*

lei[1] (lā, lā′ē) *n.* A garland of flowers. [Hawaiian.]

lei[2]. *pl.* of **leu.**

Leip·zig (līp′sĭg, -sĭk). A city of S East Germany. Pop. 595,000.

lei·sure (lē′zhər, lĕzh′ər) *n.* **1.** Freedom from time-consuming work or duties. **2.** Free time. —**at one's leisure.** At one's convenience. —*adj.* **1.** Not spent in compulsory activity: *leisure hours.* **2.** Having leisure: *the leisure class.* [< L *licere,* to be lawful, be permitted.] —**lei′sured** *adj.* —**lei′sure·ly** *adj. & adv.*

leit·mo·tif (līt′mō-tēf′) *n.* Also **leit·mo·tiv.** A dominant recurrent theme. [G *Leitmotiv,* "leading motif."]

lek (lĕk) *n.* The basic monetary unit of Albania.

lem·ming (lĕm′ĭng) *n.* A rodent of northern regions, noted for its periodic mass migrations. [Norw.]

lem·on (lĕm′ən) *n.* **1.** An egg-shaped yellow citrus fruit with acid, juicy pulp. **2.** A tree bearing such fruit. [< Pers *līmūn.*]

lem·on·ade (lĕm′ə-nād′) *n.* A drink of lemon juice, water, and sugar.

lem·pi·ra (lĕm-pîr′ə) *n.* The basic monetary unit of Honduras.

le·mur (lē′mər) *n.* A small African primate with large eyes, soft fur, and a long tail. [< L *lemurēs,* the spirits of the dead in ancient Rome.]

Le·na (lē′nə, lā′-). A river of the E Soviet Union.

lend (lĕnd) *v.* **lent, lending. 1.** To give out or allow the use of temporarily on condition that the same or its equivalent be returned. **2.** To impart. **3.** To provide: *lend a helping hand.* **4.** To accommodate. [< OE *lǣnan,* to lend, give. See **leikw-.**] —**lend′er** *n.*

length (lĕngkth, lĕngth) *n.* **1. a.** The measure of something along its greatest dimension. **b.** The measure of something from back to front as distinguished from its width or height. **2.** Measured distance or dimension. **3.** Duration or extent. [< OE *lengthu.*] —**length′y** *adj.*

length·en (lĕngk′thən, lĕng′-) *v.* To make or become longer. —**length′en·er** *n.*

length·wise (lĕngkth′wīz′, lĕngth′-) *adv.* In or along the direction of the length. —**length′wise′** *adj.*

le·ni·ent (lē′nē-ənt, lēn′yənt) *adj.* Gentle or

liberal. [< L *lēnis,* soft.] —**le′ni·en·cy, le′ni·ence** *n.* —**le′ni·ent·ly** *adv.*

Le·nin (lĕn′ĭn, -ēn′), **Vladimir Ilyich.** 1870–1924. Russian revolutionary leader; founder of the modern Soviet state. —**Len′in·ist** *n. & adj.*

Lenin

Len·in·grad (lĕn′ĭn-grăd′). A city of the W Soviet Union. Pop. 3,950,000.

len·i·tive (lĕn′ə-tĭv) *adj.* Easing pain or discomfort. [< L *lēnīre,* to soothe, soften.]

lens (lĕnz) *n.* **1.** A piece of glass or other transparent material made so that either or both of its opposite surfaces are curved, used to make light rays converge or diverge to form an image. **2.** A combination of two or more such lenses used to form an image for viewing or photographing. **3.** A transparent part of the eye that focuses light rays to form an image on the retina. [< L *lēns,* LENTIL.]

lent (lĕnt). *p.t. & p.p.* of **lend.**

Lent (lĕnt) *n.* The 40 weekdays before Easter (beginning on Ash Wednesday), observed as a season of penitence. [< OE *lengten.*]

len·til (lĕn′təl) *n.* **1.** The round, flattened, edible seed of a pealike Old World plant. **2.** The plant itself. [< L *lēns.*]

len·to (lĕn′tō) *adv. Mus.* Slowly. [< L *lentus,* pliant, tenacious, slow.] —**len′to** *adj.*

Le·o (lē′ō) *n.* **1.** A constellation in the N Hemisphere near Cancer and Virgo. **2.** The 5th sign of the zodiac. [< L *leō,* lion.]

Le·o·nar·do da Vin·ci (lē′ə-när′dō də vĭn′chē). 1452–1519. Florentine artist and engineer.

le·one (lē-ōn′) *n.* The basic monetary unit of Sierra Leone.

le·o·nine (lē′ə-nīn′) *adj.* Resembling or characteristic of a lion.

leop·ard (lĕp′ərd) *n.* **1.** A large wild cat of Africa and Asia, usually having a tawny black-spotted coat. **2.** The pelt of a leopard. [< LGk *leopardos,* "lion pard."]

le·o·tard (lē′ə-tärd′) *n.* **1.** A snugly fitting garment worn by dancers or acrobats. **2. leotards.** Tights. [< J. *Léotard,* 19th-century French aerialist.]

ă pat/ā ate/âr care/ä bar/b bib/ch chew/d deed/ĕ pet/ē be/f fit/g gag/h hat/hw what/ ĭ pit/ī pie/îr pier/j judge/k kick/l lid, fatal/m mum/n no, sudden/ng sing/ŏ pot/ō go/

lep•er (lĕp′ər) *n.* One afflicted with leprosy.

lep•re•chaun (lĕp′rə-kôn′, -kŏn′) *n.* An elf of Irish folklore. [< OIr *luchorpán,* "small body."]

lep•ro•sy (lĕp′rə-sē) *n.* A chronic infectious disease caused by a bacillus and ranging in severity from noncontagious and spontaneously remitting forms to contagious, malignant forms with progressive tissue degeneration. [< Gk *lepros,* scaly.] —**lep′rous** *adj.*

les•bi•an (lĕz′bē-ən) *n.* A female homosexual. [< *Lesbos,* island in the Aegean.] —**les′bi•an** *adj.* —**les′bi•an•ism′** *n.*

le•sion (lē′zhən) *n.* A wound, injury, or mass of diseased tissue. [< L *laedere,* to injure, damage.]

Le•so•tho (lə-sō′tō). A kingdom of S Africa. Pop. 745,000. Cap. Maseru.

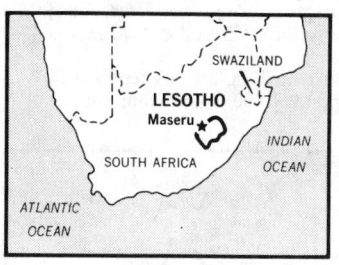

Lesotho

less (lĕs). Alternate comparative of **little.** —*adj.* **1.** Smaller. **2.** Lower in importance, esteem, or rank. —*adv.* To a smaller extent, degree, or frequency. —*n.* A smaller amount. —*prep.* Minus. See Usage note at **few.** [< OE *lǣssa* (adj) and *lǣs* (adv and noun) < Gmc *loisiz,* little.]

-less. *comb. form.* Lack of, free of, or not having: **sleepless.** [< OE *lēas,* lacking, free from.]

les•see (lĕ-sē′) *n.* A tenant holding a lease.

less•en (lĕs′ən) *v.* To make or become less.

less•er (lĕs′ər) *adj.* Smaller in size, amount, value, or importance.

Lesser An•til•les (ăn-tĭl′ēz). An island group in the West Indies.

les•son (lĕs′ən) *n.* **1.** Something learned or to be learned. **2. a.** A period of instruction; a class. **b.** An instructional exercise. **3.** An edifying example or experience. **4.** A reprimand or punishment. **5.** A reading from sacred writings as part of a religious service. [< L *lectiō,* a reading.]

les•sor (lĕs′ôr′, lĕ-sôr′) *n.* One who lets property under a lease.

lest (lĕst) *conj.* For fear that. [< OE *lǣs,* LESS.]

let[1] (lĕt) *v.* **let, letting. 1.** To allow. **2.** To cause to: *He let me know the results.* **3.** —Used in the imperative: **a.** By way of exhortation, command, or warning: *Let's go.* **b.** By way of expressing an assumption or hypothesis: *Let x equal y.* **4.** To rent or lease. [< OE *lǣtan,* to leave behind, leave undone. See **lēi-.**]

let[2] (lĕt) *n.* **1.** Obstacle: *without let or hindrance.*

2. A stroke in tennis or a similar net game that is invalid. [< OE *lettan,* to hinder. See **lēi-.**]

-let. *comb. form.* **1.** Diminutive size or minor status: **starlet. 2.** An article worn on some part of the body: **bracelet.** [< OF *-elet.*]

let down. 1. To lower. **2.** To disappoint.

let•down (lĕt′doun′) *n.* **1.** A slackening, as of effort. **2.** A disappointment.

le•thal (lē′thəl) *adj.* Fatal or deadly. [< L *lēthum,* death.] —**le•thal′i•ty** (lē-thăl′ə-tē) *n.*

leth•ar•gy (lĕth′ər-jē) *n., pl.* **-gies. 1.** Sluggishness and indifference. **2.** A state of pathological drowsiness. [< Gk *lēthargos,* forgetful.] —**le•thar′gic** (lə-thär′jĭk) *adj.*

let's (lĕts). Contraction of *let us.*

let•ter (lĕt′ər) *n.* **1.** A written symbol representing a speech sound and constituting a unit of an alphabet. **2.** A written or printed communication. **3.** The literal meaning of something. **4. letters.** Literature or learning. —*v.* To write letters on; inscribe. [< L *littera,* letter.] —**let′ter•er** *n.*

let•tered (lĕt′ərd) *adj.* **1. a.** Literate. **b.** Erudite. **2.** Inscribed with letters.

let•ter•head (lĕt′ər-hĕd′) *n.* **1.** Stationery with a printed or engraved heading. **2.** The heading itself.

let•ter-per•fect (lĕt′ər-pûr′fĭkt) *adj.* Correct to the last detail.

let•ter•press (lĕt′ər-prĕs′) *n.* **1. a.** The process of printing from a raised inked surface. **b.** Anything printed in this fashion. **2.** Text as distinct from graphic ornamentation.

Let•tish (lĕt′ĭsh) *n.* Latvian. —**Let′tish** *adj.*

let•tuce (lĕt′əs) *n.* A plant cultivated for its crisp, edible leaves, eaten as salad. [< L *lac (lact-),* milk (< its milky juice).]

let up. 1. To slacken; lessen. **2.** To stop.

let-up (lĕt′ŭp′) *n.* **1.** A slackening or slowdown. **2.** A pause.

le•u (lē′ōō) *n., pl.* **lei** (lē′ī). The basic monetary unit of Rumania.

leu•ke•mi•a (lōō-kē′mē-ə) *n.* Any of a group of usually fatal diseases involving uncontrolled proliferation of leukocytes. [< LEUK(O)- + -EMIA.]

leuko-. *comb. form.* **1.** White or colorless. **2.** Leukocyte. [< Gk *leukos,* clear, white.]

leu•ko•cyte (lōō′kə-sīt′) *n.* Also **leu•co•cyte.** Any of the white or colorless nucleated cells occurring in blood.

lev (lĕf) *n., pl.* **leva** (lĕv′ə). The basic monetary unit of Bulgaria.

Lev. Leviticus (Old Testament).

Le•vant (lə-vănt′). The countries on the E Mediterranean. —**Le•van′tine** *adj. & n.*

lev•ee (lĕv′ē) *n.* **1.** An embankment raised to prevent a river from overflowing. **2.** A landing place on a river. [< OF *levee,* "raising."]

lev•el (lĕv′əl) *n.* **1.** Relative position or rank on a scale. **2.** A natural or proper position, place, or stage. **3.** Position along a vertical axis; elevation; height. **4. a.** A horizontal line or plane at right angles to the plumb. **b.** The position or height of such a line or plane: *eye level.* **5.** A flat, horizontal surface. **6.** A tract of land of uniform elevation. **7.** An instrument for ascertaining whether a surface is horizontal. —*adj.* **1.** Having a flat, smooth surface. **2.** Horizontal. **3.** At the same height as another; even. **4.** Uniform; consistent. **5.** Steady; cool. —*v.* **-eled** or **-elled, -eling** or **-elling. 1.** To make or become horizontal, flat, or even. **2.** To knock down or raze. **3.** To equalize. **4.** To aim or direct. [< L *libella,* level, water level, plumb line.] —**lev′el·er** *n.* —**lev′el·ly** *adv.* —**lev′el·ness** *n.*

lev·el·head·ed (lĕv′əl-hĕd′ĭd) *adj.* Cool and steady of judgment. —**lev′el·head′ed·ness** *n.*

le·ver (lĕv′ər, lē′vər) *n.* A simple machine consisting of a rigid body pivoted on a fixed fulcrum. —*v.* To move or lift with a lever. [< OF *lever,* to raise.]

le·ver·age (lĕv′ər-ĭj, lē′vər-) *n.* **1.** The mechanical advantage of a lever. **2.** Positional advantage.

le·vi·a·than (lə-vī′ə-thən) *n.* **1.** A huge sea monster. **2.** Anything unusually large for its kind. [< Heb *libhyāthān.*]

lev·i·tate (lĕv′ə-tāt′) *v.* **-tated, -tating.** To rise or raise in the air in apparent defiance of gravity. [< LEVITY.] —**lev′i·ta′tion** *n.*

lev·i·ty (lĕv′ə-tē) *n., pl.* **-ties.** Lightness of speech or manner; frivolity. [< L *levis,* light.]

lev·y (lĕv′ē) *v.* **-ied, -ying. 1.** To impose or collect (a tax). **2.** To draft into military service. **3.** To wage (a war). **4.** To confiscate property. —*n.* **1.** The act or process of levying. **2.** Money, troops, or property levied. [< OE *levee,* a raising.] —**lev′i·er** *n.*

lewd (lōōd) *adj.* **1.** Licentious; lustful. **2.** Obscene. [< OE *lǣwede,* lay (nonclergy).] —**lewd′ly** *adv.* —**lewd′ness** *n.*

lex. lexicon.

lex·i·cog·ra·phy (lĕk′sĭ-kŏg′rə-fē) *n.* **1.** The writing or compilation of a dictionary. **2.** The principles underlying the making of dictionaries. [LEXICO(N) + -GRAPHY.] —**lex′i·cog′-ra·pher** *n.* —**lex′i·co·graph′ic** (-kō-grăf′ĭk), **lex′i·co·graph′i·cal** *adj.* —**lex′i·co·graph′i·cal·ly** *adv.*

lex·i·con (lĕk′sĭ-kŏn′) *n.* **1.** A dictionary. **2.** A vocabulary used in a particular profession, subject, or style. [< Gk *lexikon (biblion),* (book) pertaining to words.] —**lex′i·cal** *adj.*

lf 1. lightface. **2.** low frequency.

LG Low German.

lg., lge. large.

Lha·sa (lä′sə, lăs′ə). The capital of Tibet. Pop. 80,000.

Li lithium.

L.I. Long Island.

li·a·bil·i·ty (lī′ə-bĭl′ə-tē) *n., pl.* **-ties. 1.** The state of being liable. **2. liabilities.** Debts. **3.** A hindrance or drawback.

li·a·ble (lī′ə-bəl) *adj.* **1.** Legally obligated; responsible. **2.** Susceptible; subject. **3.** Likely; apt. [Perh < OF *lier,* to bind.]

li·ai·son (lē′ā-zŏn′, lē-ā′zŏn′, lē′ə-) *n.* **1.** Communication between groups or units. **2. a.** A close relationship. **b.** An illicit relationship. [F, "binding."]

li·an·a (lē-ăn′ə, -ä′nə) *n.* A high-climbing tropical woody vine. [French *liane.*]

li·ar (lī′ər) *n.* One who tells lies.

li·ba·tion (lī-bā′shən) *n.* **1.** A sacrificial pouring of a liquid or the liquid thus poured.

2. *Informal.* An alcoholic drink. [< L *lībāre,* to taste, pour out as an offering.]

li·bel (lī′bəl) *n.* **1.** A written, printed, or pictorial statement that unjustly damages a person's reputation. **2.** The action or crime of presenting such a statement to the public. —*v.* **-beled** or **-belled, -beling** or **-belling.** To defame or malign. [< L *libellus,* a little book.] —**li′bel·er** *n.* —**li′bel·ous** *adj.*

lib·er·al (lĭb′ər-əl, lĭb′rəl) *adj.* **1.** Favoring individual freedom and nonrevolutionary reform. **2.** Broad-minded or tolerant. **3.** Generous. **4.** Bountiful: *a liberal serving.* **5.** Not literal. **6.** Of or relating to the cultivation of general knowledge and the humanities: *liberal arts.* —*n.* One holding liberal political or cultural views. [< L *liber,* free.] —**lib′er·al·ism′** *n.* —**lib′er·al′i·ty** (lĭb′ə-răl′ə-tē). —**lib′er·al·ize′** *v.* (**-ized, -izing**). —**lib′er·al·ly** *adv.*

lib·er·ate (lĭb′ə-rāt′) *v.* **-ated, -ating.** To give liberty to; set free. [< L *liber,* free.] —**lib′er·a′tor** *n.* —**lib′er·a′tor** *n.*

Li·be·ri·a (lī-bîr′ē-ə). A republic of W Africa. Pop. 1,066,000. Cap. Monrovia.

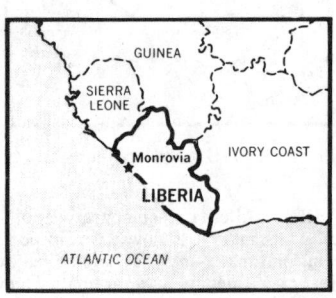

Liberia

lib·er·tine (lĭb′ər-tēn′) *n.* A dissolute person. [< L *liber,* free.]

lib·er·ty (lĭb′ər-tē) *n., pl.* **-ties. 1. a.** The condition of being free from restriction or control; freedom. **b.** The right to act as one chooses. **2.** Freedom from confinement or servitude. **3.** Permission to do something; authorization or privilege. **4.** Often **liberties.** Unwarranted familiarity. **5.** Authorized leave from naval duty. [< L *liber,* free.]

li·bi·do (lǐ-bē′dō, -bǐ′dō) *n., pl.* **-dos. 1.** The psychic and emotional energy associated with instinctual biological drives. **2.** The sexual drive. [< L *libidō,* desire, lust.] —**li·bid′i·nal** (lǐ-bǐd′n-əl) *adj.* —**li·bid′i·nous** *adj.*

Li·bra (lī′brə, lē′-) *n.* **1.** A constellation in the S Hemisphere. **2.** The 7th sign of the zodiac. [< L *libra,* balance.]

li·brar·i·an (lī-brâr′ē-ən) *n.* A custodian of a library.

li·brar·y (lī′brĕr′ē) *n., pl.* **-ies. 1.** A repository for literary and artistic materials, such as books, records, prints, etc., kept for reading or reference. **2.** A permanent collection of such materials. [< L *liber,* book.]

li·bret·to (lǐ-brĕt′ō) *n., pl.* **-tos** or **-bretti** (-brĕt′ē). The text of an opera or other dramatic musical

---

ă pat/ā ate/âr care/ä bar/b bib/ch chew/d deed/ĕ pet/ē be/f fit/g gag/h hat/hw what/ ĭ pit/ī pie/îr pier/j judge/k kick/l lid, fatal/m mum/n no, sudden/ng sing/ŏ pot/ō go/

work as distinct from the musical score. [< It *libro*, book.] —**li·bret'tist** *n.*

Li·bre·ville (lē'brə-vēl'). The capital of Gabon. Pop. 46,000.

Lib·y·a (lĭb'ē-ə). A country of N Africa, on the Mediterranean Sea. Pop. 2,580,000. Cap. Tripoli. —**Lib'yan** *adj. & n.*

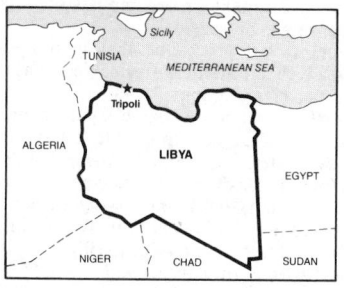

Libya

lice. *pl.* of **louse.**

li·cense (lī'səns). Also *chiefly Brit.* **li·cence.** *n.* **1. a.** Official permission to do or own a specified thing. **b.** Documentary evidence of this. **2.** Unusual freedom justified by extenuating circumstance. **3.** Studied and purposeful irregularity or deviation: *poetic license.* **4.** Excessive or undisciplined freedom. [< L *licēre*, to be lawful, be permitted.] —**li'cens·a·ble** *adj.* —**li'cense** *v.* (**-censed, -censing**).

li·cen·see (lī'sən-sē') *n.* The holder of a license.

li·cen·ti·ate (lī-sĕn'shē-ĭt, -āt') *n.* One who is granted a license, as by a university, to practice a specified profession.

li·cen·tious (lī-sĕn'shəs) *adj.* Lacking moral discipline or sexual restraint; lewd. [< L *licentia*, freedom, license.] —**li·cen'tious·ly** *adv.*

li·chee. Variant of **litchi.**

li·chen (lī'kən) *n.* A plant consisting of a fungus in close combination with certain algae and forming a scaly or branching growth on rocks or tree trunks. [< Gk *leikhēn*, "licker."]

lic·it (lĭs'ĭt) *adj.* Lawful. [< L *licēre*, to be permitted.] —**lic'it·ly** *adv.*

lick (lĭk) *v.* **1.** To pass the tongue over. **2.** To flicker over like a tongue. **3.** To thrash or defeat. —*n.* **1.** The act of licking. **2.** A small quantity. **3.** A place frequented by animals that lick an exposed salt deposit. **4.** A blow. [< OE *liccian.* See **leigh-.**] —**lick'er** *n.*

lick·e·ty-split (lĭk'ə-tē-splĭt') *adv.* With great speed. [< LICK and SPLIT.]

lic·o·rice (lĭk'ər-ĭs, -ĭsh) *n.* Also *chiefly Brit.* **li·quo·rice. 1.** A plant with a sweet, distinctively flavored root. **2.** The root of this plant, used as a flavoring. **3.** A candy made from or flavored with this root. [< Gk *glukurrhiza*, "sweetroot."]

lid (lĭd) *n.* **1.** A cover for any hollow receptacle. **2.** An eyelid. [< OE *hlid*, covering, gate, opening. See **klei-.**] —**lid'ded** *adj.*

lie¹ (lī) *v.* **lay, lain, lying. 1.** To assume or maintain a prostrate or recumbent position;

recline. **2.** To be or remain in a specific condition. **3.** To occupy a place. **4.** To extend. —*n.* The position in which something is situated. [< OE *licgan.* See **legh-.**]

lie² (lī) *n.* A deliberate falsehood. —*v.* **lied, lying.** To tell a lie or convey a false image or impression; prevaricate. [< OE *lēogan.* See **leugh-.**]

Liech·ten·stein (lĭkH'tən-shtīn). A principality of C Europe. Pop. 19,000. Cap. Vaduz.

lied (lēd) *n., pl.* **lieder** (lē'dər). A German art song.

lie detector. A polygraph used to detect lying.

lief (lēf) *adv.* Readily; willingly. [< OE *lēof*, beloved.]

liege (lēj) *n.* **1.** A feudal lord. **2.** A vassal. —*adj.* **1.** Being in the feudal relationship with another: *liege lord.* **2.** Loyal. [< ML *lētus, lītus*, serf.]

lien (lēn, lē'ən) *n.* The right to take and hold or sell the property of a debtor as security or payment for a debt. [< L *ligāre*, to bind.]

lieu (lōō) *n. Archaic.* Place; stead. —**in lieu of.** In place of; instead of. [< L *locus*, place, LOCUS.]

lieu·ten·ant (lōō-tĕn'ənt) *n.* **1.** One of two ranks held by military officers: **a.** A *second lieutenant*, the lowest-ranking commissioned officer; **b.** A *first lieutenant*, an officer ranking next below a captain. **2.** One of two ranks held by naval officers: **a.** A *lieutenant junior grade*, an officer ranking just above an ensign; **b.** A *lieutenant senior grade*, an officer ranking next below a lieutenant commander. **3.** One who acts in place of his superior; a deputy. [< OF, a rank.] —**lieu·ten'an·cy** *n.*

lieutenant colonel. A military officer ranking next below a colonel.

lieutenant commander. A naval officer ranking next below a commander.

lieutenant general. A military officer ranking next below a general.

life (līf) *n., pl.* **lives** (līvz). **1.** The quality manifested in functions such as metabolism, growth, response to stimulation, and reproduction, by which living organisms are distinguished from dead organisms or inanimate matter. **2.** Living organisms collectively: *plant life.* **3.** A living being. **4.** The interval between the birth or inception of an organism and its death. **5.** A biography. **6.** Human activities and relationships: *everyday life.* **7.** A manner of living: *country life.* **8.** Animation; liveliness. [< OE *līf.* See **leip-.**]

life·blood (līf'blŭd') *n.* The indispensable vital part of a thing.

life·boat (līf'bōt') *n.* A boat used for rescue at sea.

life buoy. A buoy.

life·guard (līf'gärd') *n.* An expert swimmer employed to safeguard bathers.

life history. The history of changes undergone by an organism.

life line. 1. A line thrown to a person in danger of drowning. **2.** Any means or route by which necessary supplies are transported.

life·long (līf'lông', -lŏng') *adj.* Continuing for a lifetime.

life preserver. A device designed to keep a person afloat in the water.

life·style (līf′stīl′) *n.* Also **life-style, life style.** A way of life or style of living that reflects the attitudes and values of an individual or culture.

life·time (līf′tīm′) *n.* 1. The time during which an individual is alive. 2. The time during which an object, property, process, or phenomenon persists.

lift (lĭft) *v.* 1. a. To raise; elevate. b. To ascend; rise. 2. a. To revoke; rescind. b. To put an end to. 3. *Informal.* To steal. 4. To pay off (a debt). —*n.* 1. The act or process of raising or rising. 2. Power or force available for raising. 3. A load. 4. The extent or height something is raised. 5. A rise in the level of the ground. 6. A rising of spirits. 7. A machine designed to raise or carry something. 8. *Chiefly Brit.* An elevator. 9. Help or a ride along one's way. 10. The component of the aerodynamic force acting on an aircraft, perpendicular to the relative wind and normally exerted in an upward direction. [< ON *lypta.*]

lift·off (lĭft′ôf′, -ŏf′) *n.* The initial part of the flight of a rocket or other craft.

lig·a·ment (lĭg′ə-mənt) *n.* A sheet or band of tough, fibrous tissue connecting bones or cartilages, or supporting an organ. [< L *ligamentum,* bond, bandage.]

lig·a·ture (lĭg′ə-chŏŏr′) *n.* 1. A cord, wire, or bandage used for binding or constricting. 2. A character combining two or more letters, such as æ. 3. *Mus.* A slur. [< L *ligāre,* to bind.]

light¹ (līt) *n.* 1. Electromagnetic radiation that may be perceived by the human eye. 2. The sensation of the perception of such radiation; brightness. 3. A source of illumination, such as the sun or an electric lamp. 4. The illumination derived from such a source. 5. Daylight. 6. Dawn; daybreak. 7. A means or agent, as a match or cigarette lighter, for igniting a fire. 8. A way of regarding something; aspect: *see the situation in a different light.* 9. A prominent or distinguished person. —**in (the) light of.** In consideration of. —**shed (or throw) light on.** To provide information about. —*v.* **lighted** or **lit, lighting.** 1. To set on fire; ignite. 2. To cause to give out light: *light a lamp.* 3. To illuminate. 4. To start to burn; be ignited. —**light up.** 1. To become or cause to become light, bright, animated, or cheerful. 2. *Informal.* To start smoking a cigarette, cigar, or pipe. —*adj.* 1. Characterized by or filled with light; radiant; bright. 2. Mixed with white; pale: *light colors.* [< OE *lēoht, līht.* See **leuk-.**]

light² (līt) *adj.* 1. Not heavy. 2. Of relatively low density. 3. Having less force, quantity, intensity, or volume than normal. 4. Moderate; mild. 5. Not serious or profound. 6. Free from worries or troubles; blithe. 7. Frivolous; silly; trivial. 8. Quick to change or be swayed; fickle. 9. Suffering from mild delirium or faintness; dizzy. 10. Moving quickly and easily; graceful. —**make light of.** To regard as insignificant or petty. —*adv.* 1. Lightly. 2. Without additional weight or burdens: *trav-*

eling light. —*v.* **lighted** or **lit, lighting.** 1. To get down, as from a mount or vehicle; dismount. 2. To land. 3. To come upon unexpectedly. [< OE *lēoht, līht.* See **legwh-.**] —**light′ly** *adv.* —**light′ness** *n.*

light·en¹ (līt′n) *v.* To make or become light or lighter; brighten. —**light′en·er** *n.*

light·en² (līt′n) *v.* 1. To make or become less heavy. 2. To make or become less oppressive, burdensome, or severe.

light·er¹ (lī′tər) *n.* 1. One that ignites something. 2. A mechanical device for lighting a cigarette, cigar, or pipe.

light·er² (lī′tər) *n.* A barge used to unload cargo from a larger ship unable to navigate in shallow water. [< MDu *lichten,* to unload.]

light·face (līt′fās′) *n. Ptg.* A typeface having relatively thin, light lines. —**light′faced′** *adj.*

light·head·ed (līt′hĕd′ĭd) *adj.* 1. Delirious, giddy, or faint. 2. Frivolous; silly.

light·heart·ed (līt′här′tĭd) *adj.* Blithe; carefree; gay. —**light′heart′ed·ly** *adv.* —**light′heart′ed·ness** *n.*

light·house (līt′hous′) *n.* A tall structure topped by a powerful light used for guiding ships.

light·ing (lī′tĭng) *n.* 1. The state of being lighted; illumination. 2. The method or equipment used to provide artificial illumination.

light·ning (līt′nĭng) *n.* A large-scale high-tension natural electric discharge in the atmosphere. —*adj.* Very fast or sudden, like a flash of lightning. [< LIGHT¹.]

lightning rod. A grounded metal rod placed high on a structure to prevent damage by conducting lightning to ground.

light·weight (līt′wāt′) *n.* A person weighing relatively little, esp. a fighter weighing between 127 and 135 pounds. —*adj.* Weighing relatively little; not heavy.

light-year (līt′yîr′) *n.* Also **light year.** The distance that light travels in one year, approx. 5.878 trillion (5.878 × 10¹²) miles.

lig·nite (lĭg′nīt′) *n.* A low-grade, brownish-black coal. [< L *lignum,* wood.]

lig·num vi·tae (lĭg′nəm vī′tē) 1. A tropical American tree with very hard, heavy wood. 2. The wood of such a tree. [< LL, "tree or wood of life."]

lig·ro·in (lĭg′rō-ən) *n.* A volatile, flammable fraction of petroleum, obtained by distillation, and used as a solvent. [?]

lik·a·ble (lī′kə-bəl) *adj.* Also **like·a·ble.** Pleasing; attractive. —**lik′a·ble·ness** *n.*

like¹ (līk) *v.* **liked, liking.** 1. To find pleasant; enjoy. 2. To want, wish, or prefer. 3. To be fond of. —*n.* —**likes and dislikes.** Preferences, predilections, and aversions. [< OE *lician,* to please, be sufficient < Gmc *līkjan.*]

like² (līk) *prep.* 1. Similar or similarly to. 2. In the typical manner of: *That's not like you.* 3. Disposed to: *feel like eating.* 4. Indicative of: *It looks like rain.* —*adj.* 1. Similar. 2. Equivalent; equal. —*adv.* As if: *He ran like crazy.* —*n.* Similar or related persons or things: *bills, coins, and the like.* —**the likes of.** *Informal.* An equivalent to a person or thing: *never seen the likes of him.* —*conj.* Non-

ă pat/ā ate/âr care/ä bar/b bib/ch chew/d deed/ĕ pet/ē be/f fit/g gag/h hat/hw what/
ĭ pit/ī pie/îr pier/j judge/k kick/l lid, fatal/m mum/n no, sudden/ng sing/ŏ pot/ō go/

standard. **1.** In the same way that; as: *Tell it like it is.* **2.** As if: *It rained like the skies were falling.* [< OE *lic* < Gmc **līk-.*]

Usage: Like, as a conjunction, is not appropriate to formal usage except when it introduces an elliptical clause in which a verb is not expressed: *He took to politics like a fish to water. The dress looked like new.* If these examples were recast to include full clauses containing verbs, *like* would preferably be replaced, in formal usage, by *as, as if,* or *as though: took to politics as a fish takes to water; dress looked as if it were new.*

like·li·hood (līk'lē-hŏŏd') *n.* **1.** The state of being likely or probable; probability. **2.** Something that is probable.

like·ly (līk'lē) *adj.* **-lier, -liest. 1.** Apparently destined; apt: *likely to be successful.* **2.** Expected to occur. **3.** Credible; plausible: *a likely excuse.* **4.** Apparently suitable: *a likely place.* **5.** Apparently capable of doing well; promising: *a likely lad.* —*adv.* Probably. [< ON *līkr,* like.]

Usage: Likely, as an adverb, is preferably preceded by a qualifying word such as *quite, very,* or *most: He will very likely arrive on Friday.*

lik·en (lī'kən) *v.* To see, mention, or show as like or similar; compare.

like·ness (līk'nĭs) *n.* **1.** A resemblance. **2.** A semblance; guise. **3.** A representation of something; an image.

like·wise (līk'wīz') *adv.* **1.** In the same way; similarly. **2.** As well; also; too.

lik·ing (lī'kĭng) *n.* **1.** A feeling of attraction, tenderness, or love; fondness; affection. **2.** Preference; inclination.

li·lac (lī'lək, -lŏk') *n.* **1.** A shrub widely cultivated for its clusters of fragrant purplish or white flowers. **2.** Pale purple. [< Ar *līlak.*] —**li'lac** *adj.*

Li·long·we (lē-lông'wä). The capital of Malawi. Pop. 20,000.

lilt (lĭlt) *n.* **1.** A light, happy tune. **2.** A cheerful or lively manner of speaking, in which the pitch of the voice varies pleasantly. **3.** A light or resilient manner of walking. [< ME *lulten,* to sound, sing.]

lil·y (lĭl'ē) *n., pl.* **-ies. 1.** Any of various related plants with showy, often trumpet-shaped flowers. **2.** Any of various similar plants. [< L *līlium.*]

lily of the valley *pl.* **lilies of the valley.** A plant with a slender cluster of fragrant, bell-shaped white flowers.

lily pad. One of the broad, floating leaves of a water lily.

lim. limit.

Li·ma (lē'mə). The capital of Peru. Pop. 1,716,000.

li·ma bean (lī'mə). **1.** A plant having flat pods containing large, light-green, edible seeds. **2.** The seed of such a plant. [< LIMA.]

limb (lĭm) *n.* **1.** One of the jointed appendages of an animal, used for locomotion or grasping, as an arm, leg, or wing. **2.** A large tree branch. [< OE *lim.*]

lim·ber (lĭm'bər) *adj.* **1.** Bending or flexing readily; pliable. **2.** Capable of moving or bending easily; agile. —*v.* —**limber up.** To make (oneself) limber. [?] —**lim'ber·ly** *adv.* —**lim'ber·ness** *n.*

lim·bo (lĭm'bō) *n., pl.* **-bos. 1.** Often **Limbo.** *Theol.* The abode of souls kept from Heaven through circumstance, such as lack of baptism. **2.** A region or condition of oblivion or neglect. [< ML *in limbō,* "(region) on the border (of hell)."]

lime¹ (lĭm) *n.* **1.** A green, egg-shaped citrus fruit with acid juice used as flavoring. **2.** A tree bearing such fruit. [< Ar *līmah.*]

lime² (lĭm) *n.* An Old World linden tree.

lime³ (lĭm) *n.* **1. Calcium oxide. 2.** Birdlime. [< OE *līm.*]

lime·light (līm'līt') *n.* **1.** A bright light produced by directing a flame at a cylinder of heated lime, formerly used in the theater. **2. the limelight.** A focus of public attention or notoriety.

lim·er·ick (lĭm'ər-ĭk) *n.* A light humorous or nonsensical verse of five lines with the rhyme scheme *aabba.*

lime·stone (līm'stōn') *n.* A shaly or sandy sedimentary rock composed chiefly of calcium carbonate.

lim·it (lĭm'ĭt) *n.* **1.** The point, edge, or line where something ends. **2. limits.** Bounds: *city limits.* **3.** The greatest amount or number allowed. —*v.* To confine or restrict within limits. [< L *līmes,* boundary.] —**lim'it·a·ble** *adj.* —**lim'i·ta'tion** *n.* —**lim'i·ta'tive** *adj.* —**lim'it· less** *adj.* —**lim'it·less·ly** *adv.*

lim·it·ed (lĭm'ĭ-tĭd) *adj.* **1.** Having a limit or limits. **2.** *Chiefly Brit.* Limiting the liability of each stockholder to his actual investment: *a limited company.* **3.** Designating trains or buses that make few stops. —**lim'it·ed·ly** *adv.* —**lim'it·ed·ness** *n.*

limn (lĭm) *v. Archaic.* **1.** To describe. **2.** To depict by painting or drawing. [< L *lūmināre,* to illuminate.] —**lim'ner** (lĭm'nər) *n.*

lim·ou·sine (lĭm'ə-zēn', lĭm'ə-zēn') *n.* A large, luxurious automobile with an enclosed passenger compartment. [Orig a kind of coat < *Limousin,* France.]

limp (lĭmp) *v.* To walk lamely, as if favoring one leg. —*n.* An irregular, jerky, or awkward gait. —*adj.* Lacking rigidity; flabby. [Prob short for obs *limphalt,* lame.] —**limp'ly** *adv.* —**limp'ness** *n.*

lim·pet (lĭm'pĭt) *n.* **1.** A marine mollusk that has a tent-shaped shell and adheres to rocks of tidal areas. **2.** One who clings persistently. [< OE *lempedu* < ML *lamprēda,* LAMPREY.]

lim·pid (lĭm'pĭd) *adj.* Crystal clear; transparent. [< L *limpidus.*] —**lim·pid'i·ty, lim'pid·ness** *n.* —**lim'pid·ly** *adv.*

lin. 1. lineal. **2.** linear.

lin·age (lī'nĭj) *n.* Also **line·age.** The number of lines of printed or written material.

linch·pin (lĭnch'pĭn') *n.* A locking pin inserted through the end of an axle to prevent a wheel from slipping off. [< OE *lynis,* linchpin + PIN.]

Lin·coln (lĭng'kən). The capital of Nebraska. Pop. 150,000.

ô paw, for/oi boy/ou out/ŏŏ took/ōō coo/p pop/r run/s sauce/sh shy/t to/th thin/*th* the/
ŭ cut/ûr fur/v van/w wag/y yes/z size/zh vision/ə ago, item, edible, gallop, circus/

Lin·coln (lĭng′kən), **Abraham.** 1809–1865. 16th President of the U.S. (1861–65).

Abraham Lincoln

lin·den (lĭn′dən) *n.* A shade tree with heart-shaped leaves and yellowish, often fragrant flowers. [Perh < OE *linde*, the linden.]

line¹ (lĭn) *n.* **1. a.** The locus of a point having one degree of freedom; a curve. **b.** A set of points *(x, y)* that satisfy the equation $ax + by + c = 0$, where a and b are not both zero. **2.** A thin, continuous mark, as that made by a pen, pencil, or brush. **3.** A crease in the skin; wrinkle. **4.** A border or limit. **5.** A contour or outline. **6.** A cable, rope, string, cord, wire, etc. **7.** An electric-power transmission cable. **8.** A telephone connection. **9.** A system of transportation, esp. a company owning such a system. **10.** A course of progress or movement: *line of flight.* **11.** A general manner or course of procedure: *different lines of thought.* **12.** An official or prescribed policy: *the party line.* **13.** Alignment: *bring the wheels into line.* **14. a.** One's trade or occupation. **b.** The range of one's competence: *out of my line.* **15.** Merchandise of a similar nature: *a line of small tools.* **16.** A group of persons or things arranged in a row: *stand in line.* **17.** A row of words printed or written across a page. **18.** A brief letter; a note. **19.** Often **lines.** The dialogue of a play or other theatrical presentation. **20.** A calculated or glib way of speaking. **21.** *Football.* **a.** A line of scrimmage. **b.** The linemen. —**hold the line.** To stand firm. —**in line for.** Next in order for. —**in line with.** In accordance with. —**out of line. 1.** Not in agreement or conformity. **2.** In an uncalled-for manner. —*v.* **lined, lining. 1.** To mark with lines. **2.** To place in a series or row. **3.** To form a bordering line along: *Small stalls lined the alleys.* [< L *linea*, thread, line < *linum*, flax.] —**line′less** *adj.*

line² (lĭn) *v.* **lined, lining.** To sew or fit a covering to the inside surface of. [< L *linum*, flax.]

lin·e·age¹ (lĭn′ē-ĭj) *n.* Direct descent from a particular ancestor; ancestry.

line·age². Variant of **linage.**

lin·e·al (lĭn′ē-əl) *adj.* **1.** Being in the direct line of descent from an ancestor. **2.** Linear.

lin·e·a·ment (lĭn′ē-ə-mənt) *n.* A distinctive shape, contour, or line, esp. of the face.

lin·e·ar (lĭn′ē-ər) *adj.* **1.** Of or resembling a line or lines. **2.** Narrow and elongated: *a linear leaf.* —**lin′e·ar·ly** *adv.*

line drive. *Baseball.* A batted ball hit in a roughly straight horizontal line.

line·man (lĭn′mən) *n.* **1.** One who installs or repairs telephone, telegraph, or other electric power lines. **2.** *Football.* A player positioned on the forward line.

lin·en (lĭn′ən) *n.* **1.** Thread or cloth made of flax. **2.** Garments or articles made from this cloth. [< OE *līnen*, "made of flax" < Gmc *līnin*.] —**lin′en** *adj.*

lin·er (lī′nər) *n.* A commercial ship or airplane, esp. one carrying passengers on a regular route.

lines·man (līnz′mən) *n.* **1.** A football official who marks the downs and the position of the ball. **2.** An official in various court games whose chief duty is to call shots that fall out of bounds.

line up. 1. To form or take a place in a line. **2.** To put into alignment.

line-up (līn′ŭp′) *n.* Also **line·up. 1.** A line of persons formed for inspection or identification. **2.** The members of a team chosen to start a game.

–ling. *comb. form.* **1.** One who belongs to or is connected with: **hireling. 2.** One who has a specified quality: **underling. 3.** A diminutive: **duckling.** [< OE < Gmc *-linga-*.]

ling. linguistics.

lin·ger (lĭng′gər) *v.* **1.** To remain as though reluctant to leave; tarry. **2.** To persist: *The memory still lingers.* **3.** To be tardy in acting; procrastinate. [< ON *lengja*.]

lin·ge·rie (län′zhə-rā′, län′zhə-rē) *n.* Women's underwear. [< L *līnum*, flax.]

lin·go (lĭng′gō) *n., pl.* **-goes.** Language that is unintelligible through being foreign or a special jargon. [Port *lingoa*, "tongue," language.]

lin·gua fran·ca (lĭng′gwə frăng′kə). A language used as a medium of communication between peoples of different languages. [It, "the Frankish tongue."]

lin·guist (lĭng′gwĭst) *n.* **1.** One who speaks several languages. **2.** A specialist in linguistics. [< L *lingua*, language.]

lin·guis·tics (lĭng-gwĭs′tĭks) *n.* *(takes sing. v.)* The science of language; the study of the nature and structure of human speech. —**lin·guis′tic** *adj.* —**lin·guis′ti·cal·ly** *adv.*

lin·i·ment (lĭn′ə-mənt) *n.* A soothing medicinal fluid applied to the skin, esp. by rubbing. [< L *linere*, to anoint.]

lin·ing (lī′nĭng) *n.* **1.** An interior covering or coating. **2.** A layer of material sewn into the inside of a garment.

link (lĭngk) *n.* **1.** One of the rings or loops forming a chain. **2.** Anything resembling a chain link in its physical arrangement. **3.** Anything that serves to connect; a bond or tie. —*v.* To connect or become connected with or as if with links. [< ON *hlekkr*, link, ring.]

ă pat/ā ate/âr care/ä bar/b bib/ch chew/d deed/ĕ pet/ē be/f fit/g gag/h hat/hw what/
ĭ pit/ī pie/îr pier/j judge/k kick/l lid, fatal/m mum/n no, sudden/ng sing/ŏ pot/ō go/

link·age (lĭng'kĭj) *n.* **1.** The act or process of linking. **2.** The state or condition of being linked. **3.** A system of interconnected machine elements used to transmit power or motion.

links (lĭngks) *pl.n.* A golf course. [< OE *hlinc,* ridge. See **kleng-**.]

lin·net (lĭn'ĭt) *n.* A small, brownish Old World songbird. [< OF *lin,* flax (the bird feeds on linseeds).]

li·no·le·um (lĭ-nō'lē-əm) *n.* A durable, washable material made in sheets, used as a floor and counter-top covering. [L *līnum,* flax + *oleum,* OIL.]

Li·no·type (lī'nə-tīp') *n.* A trademark for a keyboard-operated machine that sets an entire line of type on a single metal slug. [LINE + TYPE.]

Lin Pi·ao (lĭn' byou'). Born 1908. Vice-chairman of Chinese Communist Party.

Lin Piao

lin·seed (lĭn'sēd') *n.* The seed of flax, esp. as the source of a yellowish oil, **linseed oil,** used as a drying agent in paints, varnishes, etc. [< L *līnum,* flax + SEED.]

lint (lĭnt) *n.* Clinging bits of fiber and fluff; fuzz. [< L *līnum,* flax.] —**lint'y** *adj.*

lin·tel (lĭnt'l) *n.* The horizontal beam that forms the top of a window or door frame. [< L *līmen,* threshold.]

li·on (lī'ən) *n.* **1.** A very large carnivorous cat of Africa and India, having a short tawny coat and a thick mane in the male. **2. Lion.** Leo. —**the lion's share.** The greatest or best part of a whole. [< Gk *leōn.*] —**li'on·ness** *fem.n.*

li·on·ize (lī'ə-nīz') *v.* **-ized, -izing.** To look upon or treat (a person) as a celebrity.

lip (lĭp) *n.* **1.** Either of two fleshy, muscular folds that together surround the opening of the mouth. **2.** A part that similarly encircles or bounds an opening. **3.** A protruding part or division of a flower. **4.** The tip of a pouring spout. **5.** *Slang.* Insolent talk. [< OE *lippa.* See **leb-**.] —**lip'less** *adj.*

lip reading. The interpretation of inaudible speech by watching lip and facial movements.

lip·stick (lĭp'stĭk') *n.* A stick of waxy lip coloring enclosed in a small cylindrical case.

liq. 1. liquid. **2.** liquor.

liq·ue·fy (lĭk'wə-fī') *v.* **-fied, -fying.** Also **liq·ui·fy.** To become or cause to become liquid. —**liq'ue·fac'tion** (-făk'shən) *n.*

li·queur (lĭ-kûr', -kyŏŏr') *n.* A sweet, syrupy alcoholic beverage. [< OF *licour,* liquid, liquor.]

liq·uid (lĭk'wĭd) *n.* A substance capable of flowing or of being poured. —*adj.* **1.** Of or being a liquid. **2.** Liquefied, esp.: **a.** Melted by heating: *liquid wax.* **b.** Condensed by cooling: *liquid oxygen.* **3.** Readily converted into cash: *liquid assets.* [< L *liquēre,* to be liquid.]

liq·ui·date (lĭk'wə-dāt') *v.* **-dated, -dating. 1.** To pay off or settle (a debt). **2.** To wind up the affairs of (a business firm). **3.** To convert (assets) into cash. **4.** To do away with; kill. —**liq'ui·da'tion** *n.* —**liq'ui·da'tor** *n.*

liq·uor (lĭk'ər) *n.* **1.** An alcoholic beverage made by distillation rather than fermentation. **2.** A liquid substance or solution. [< L *liquēre,* to be liquid.] —**liq'uor·y** *adj.*

li·quo·rice. *Chiefly Brit.* Variant of **licorice.**

li·ra (lîr'ə) *n.* **1.** *pl.* **-ras** or **-re.** The basic monetary unit of Italy. **2.** *pl.* **-re** or **-ras.** The basic monetary unit of Turkey. [< L *lībra,* balance, measure.]

Lis·bon (lĭz'bən). The capital of Portugal. Pop. 802,000.

lisle (līl) *n.* A fine, smooth, tightly twisted thread spun from long-stapled cotton. [< *Lille,* France.]

lisp (lĭsp) *n.* A speech defect characterized by the substitution of the sounds (th) and (*th*) for the sibilants (s) and (z). [< OE *wlisp,* a lisping.] —**lisp** *v.* —**lisp'er** *n.*

lis·some (lĭs'əm), *adj.* **1.** Lithe; supple. **2.** Agile; nimble. [Var of LITHESOME.] —**lis'some·ly** *adv.* —**lis'some·ness** *n.*

list¹ (lĭst) *n.* A printed or written series of persons or things, often arranged in a particular order. —*v.* **1.** To make a list of; itemize. **2.** To enter in a list. [OF *liste,* band, strip of paper.]

list² (lĭst) *n.* An inclination to one side, as of a ship; a tilt. —*v.* To lean or tilt to one side. [?]

lis·ten (lĭs'ən) *v.* **1.** To apply oneself to hearing something. **2.** To pay attention. [< OE *hlysnan.* See **kleu-**.] —**lis'ten·er** *n.*

list·ing (lĭs'tĭng) *n.* **1.** An act of making or entering in a list. **2.** An entry in a list.

list·less (lĭst'lĭs) *adj.* Marked by lack of energy or enthusiasm; indifferent; languid. [< OE *lystan,* to be pleasing (see **las-**) + -LESS.] —**list'less·ly** *adv.* —**list'less·ness** *n.*

Liszt (lĭst), **Franz.** 1811–1886. Hungarian pianist and composer.

lit (lĭt). **1.** Alternate *p.t.* & *p.p.* of **light¹. 2.** Alternate *p.t.* & *p.p.* of **light².**

lit. 1. literal; literally. **2.** literary; literature.

lit·a·ny (lĭt'n-ē) *n., pl.* **-nies.** A prayer consisting of phrases recited by a leader alternating with responses by the congregation. [< Gk *litaneia,* entreaty.]

li·tchi (lē'chē) *n.* Also **li·chee. 1.** A Chinese tree bearing edible fruit. **2.** Also **litchi nut.** The thin-shelled, fleshy fruit of this tree. [Cant *lai chi.*]

li·ter (lē′tər) *n.* Also *chiefly Brit* **li·tre.** A metric unit of volume, approx. 1.056 liquid quart or 0.908 dry quart. [< Gk *litra,* a unit of weight.]

lit·er·a·cy (lĭt′ər-ə-sē) *n.* The ability to read and write.

lit·er·al (lĭt′ər-əl) *adj.* **1.** Upholding the exact meaning of a word or the words of a text. **2.** Word for word; verbatim: *a literal translation.* **3.** Concerned chiefly with facts; prosaic. [< L *littera,* letter.] —**lit′er·al·ly** *adv.*

lit·er·ar·y (lĭt′ə-rĕr′ē) *adj.* **1.** Of or relating to literature. **2. a.** Found in or appropriate to literature: *a literary style.* **b.** Employed chiefly in writing rather than speaking: *literary language.* —**lit′er·ar′i·ness** *n.*

lit·er·ate (lĭt′ər-ĭt) *adj.* **1.** Able to read and write. **2.** Knowledgeable; educated. [< L *literātus,* acquainted with writings, learned.]

lit·e·ra·ti (lĭt′ə-rä′tē, -rä′tī′) *pl.n.* The literary intelligentsia.

lit·er·a·ture (lĭt′ər-ə-chŏŏr′) *n.* **1.** Imaginative or creative writing; belles-lettres. **2.** The body of written work produced in a given field: *medical literature.* **3.** Printed material of any kind, as for a political campaign. [< L *literātus,* LITERATE.]

lith. lithograph; lithographic; lithography.

lithe (līth) *adj.* **1.** Supple; limber. **2.** Marked by effortless grace. [< OE *līthe,* flexible, mild. See **lento-**.] —**lithe′ly** *adv.*

lithe·some (līth′səm) *adj.* Lithe; lissome.

–lithic. *comb. form.* Stone: **Neolithic.**

lith·i·um (lĭth′ē-əm) *n. Symbol* **Li** A soft, silvery, highly reactive metallic element, used as a heat transfer medium, in thermonuclear weapons, and in various alloys. Atomic number 3, atomic weight 6.939.

litho-. *comb. form.* Stone. [< Gk *lithos,* stone.]

litho., lithog. lithograph; lithographic; lithography.

lith·o·graph (lĭth′ə-grăf′, -gräf′) *n.* A print produced by lithography. —**lith′o·graph′** *v.* —**li·thog′raph·er** (lĭ-thŏg′rə-fər) *n.* —**lith′o·graph′ic** *adj.* —**lith′o·graph′i·cal·ly** *adv.*

li·thog·ra·phy (lĭ-thŏg′rə-fē) *n.* A printing process in which an image is rendered on a surface and treated so that it will retain ink while the other areas will repel ink.

Lith·u·a·ni·a (lĭth′ŏŏ-ā′nē-ə). A Baltic republic of the Soviet Union. Pop. 3,129,000. Cap. Vilnius.

Lith·u·a·ni·an (lĭth′ŏŏ-ā′nē-ən) *n.* **1.** An inhabitant or native of Lithuania. **2.** The Baltic language of the Lithuanians. —**Lith′u·a′ni·an** *adj.*

lit·i·gant (lĭt′ĭ-gənt) *n.* One engaged in a lawsuit.

lit·i·gate (lĭt′ĭ-gāt′) *v.* **-gated, -gating.** To engage in or subject (something) to legal proceedings. [L *lītigāre,* to dispute, quarrel, sue.] —**lit′i·ga′tion** *n.* —**lit′i·ga′tor** *n.*

li·ti·gious (lĭ-tĭj′əs) *adj.* Given to or characterized by litigation. —**li·ti′gious·ness** *n.*

lit·mus (lĭt′məs) *n.* A blue, amorphous powder derived from certain lichens that turns red with increasing acidity and blue with increas-

ing alkalinity. [Perh < ON *litmosi,* "dye moss."]

litmus paper. An unsized white paper impregnated with litmus.

li·tre. *Chiefly Brit.* Variant of **liter.**

lit·ter (lĭt′ər) *n.* **1.** A conveyance consisting of a couch mounted between shafts, carried by men or animals. **2.** A stretcher for the sick or wounded. **3.** Straw or other material used as bedding for animals. **4.** The young produced at one birth by certain mammals. **5.** Discarded waste materials or scraps. —*v.* **1.** To make untidy by discarding rubbish carelessly. **2.** To scatter (litter) about. [< L *lectus,* bed.]

lit·ter·bug (lĭt′ər-bŭg′) *n.* Slang. One who litters public areas.

lit·tle (lĭt′l) *adj.* **-tler, -tlest. 1.** Small in size, quantity, or degree. **2.** Also *compar.* **less,** *superl.* **least. a.** Short in extent or duration; brief: *little time.* **b.** Unimportant; trivial; insignificant. **3.** Without much force; weak. **4.** Narrow; petty. **5.** Without much power or influence. **6. a.** Appealing; endearing: *a little rascal.* **b.** Contemptible. —*adv.* **less, least.** Not much: *He sleeps little.* —*n.* A small quantity: *Give me a little.* [< OE *lȳtel.* See **leud-**.] —**lit′-tle·ness** *n.*

Little Bear. Ursa Minor.

Little Dipper. Ursa Minor.

Little Rock. The capital of Arkansas. Pop. 129,000.

lit·to·ral (lĭt′ər-əl) *adj.* Of or existing on a shore. —*n.* A shore or coastal region. [< L *lītus (lītor-),* shore.]

lit·ur·gy (lĭt′ər-jē) *n., pl.* **-gies.** The system of public worship in the Christian church. [< Gk *leitourgos,* public servant, minister.] —**li·tur′gi·cal** (lĭ-tûr′jĭ-kəl) *adj.*

liv·a·ble (lĭv′ə-bəl) *adj.* Also **live·a·ble 1.** Fit to live in; habitable. **2.** Worth living; endurable.

live[1] (lĭv) *v.* **lived, living. 1.** To have life; continue to remain alive. **2.** To reside. **3.** To pass; spend: *live a full life.* **4.** To pass life in a particular manner. **5.** To remain in human memory, usage, or general acceptance. —**live down.** To overcome (an adversity) by acceptance over a period of time. —**live up to.** To satisfy (an ideal), justify (an explanation), or fulfill (a bargain). —**live with.** To put up with (a continuing adverse factor). [< OE *libban, lifian.* See **leip-**.]

live[2] (līv) *adj.* **1.** Having life. **2.** Of current interest: *a live topic.* **3.** Glowing; burning: *a live coal.* **4.** Ignitable or explosive: *live ammunition.* **5.** Energized. **6.** Broadcast at the time of occurrence. [Short for ALIVE.]

live·li·hood (līv′lē-hŏŏd′) *n.* Means of support; subsistence. [< OE *līf,* LIFE + *lād,* course (see **leith-**).]

live·ly (līv′lē) *adj.* **-lier, -liest. 1.** Full of life; vigorous. **2.** Full of activity, spirit, or excitement. **3.** Intense; keen. **4.** Cheerful. **5.** Bouncing readily upon impact, as a ball. —*adv.* In a vigorous, energetic, or spirited manner. [< OE *līf,* LIFE.] —**live′li·ness** *n.*

liv·en (lī′vən) *v.* To become or cause to become lively or livelier. —**li′ven·er** *n.*

live oak (līv). An evergreen American oak.

liv·er (lĭv′ər) *n.* A large gland that secretes bile and acts in the formation of blood and metabolism of carbohydrates, fats, proteins, minerals, and vitamins. [< OE *lifer.* See **leip-.**]

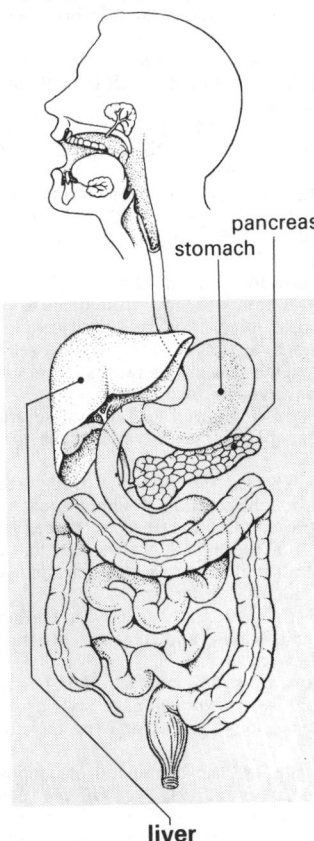

pancreas

stomach

liver

liv·er·ied (lĭv′ə-rēd) *adj.* Wearing livery, esp. as a servant.

Liv·er·pool (lĭv′ər-pōōl). A city of NW England. Pop. 722,000. —**Liv′er·pud′li·an** (-pŭd′lē-ən) *adj. & n.*

liv·er·wort (lĭv′ər-wûrt′, -wôrt′) *n.* 1. Any of various green nonflowering plants related to the mosses. 2. The hepatica.

liv·er·wurst (lĭv′ər-wûrst′) *n.* A type of sausage made with or containing chopped liver.

liv·er·y (lĭv′ə-rē) *n., pl.* **-ies.** 1. The uniform worn by male servants. 2. a. The boarding and care of horses. b. The hiring out of horses and carriages. [< OF *livree,* "something delivered or given," allowance granted to servants.]

liv·er·y·man (lĭv′ə-rē-mən) *n.* A keeper or employee of a livery stable.

lives. *pl.* of **life.**

live·stock (lĭv′stŏk′) *n.* Domestic animals, as cattle, horses, or sheep, raised for home use or profit.

liv·id (lĭv′ĭd) *adj.* 1. Discolored, as from a bruise. 2. Ashen or pallid, as with anger. [< L *līvēre,* to be bluish.] —**liv′id·ly** *adv.*

liv·ing (lĭv′ĭng) *adj.* 1. Possessing life; alive. 2. In active function or use: *living languages.* 3. Of or relating to persons who are alive. 4. Of or characteristic of daily life. —*n.* 1. The state or condition of being alive. 2. A means of maintaining life; livelihood. 3. A manner or style of life: *plain living.* 4. **the living.** Those who are alive.

living room. A room for general use and the reception and entertainment of guests in a household.

liz·ard (lĭz′ərd) *n.* 1. Any of various reptiles having a long, scaly body, four legs, and a tapering tail. 2. Leather made from the skin of a lizard. [< L *lacertus, lacerta.*]

ll. lines.

lla·ma (lä′mə) *n.* A South American mammal kept as a beast of burden and for its wool. [< Quechua.]

lla·no (län′ō, lä′nō) *n., pl.* **-nos.** A large, grassy, almost treeless plain in Latin America and the SW U.S. [< L *plānum,* a plain.]

LL.B. Bachelor of Laws (L *Legum Baccalaureus*).

LL.D. Doctor of Laws (L *Legum Doctor*).

lo (lō) *interj.* Expressive of surprise: *lo and behold.*

load (lōd) *n.* 1. a. A supported weight or mass. b. The overall force to which a structure is subjected. 2. Material transported by a vehicle or animal. 3. The share of work allocated to an individual, machine, or group. 4. A responsibility regarded as an oppressive weight. 5. Often **loads.** *Informal.* Any large amount or quantity. —*v.* 1. To place (a load) in or on (a structure, device, or conveyance). 2. To take on or receive a load. 3. To weigh down with; burden; oppress. 4. To charge (a firearm) with ammunition. 5. To insert (film, tape, etc.) into (a holder or magazine). 6. To raise the power demand in (a circuit). [< OE *lād,* way, course, conveyance. See **leith-.**]

loaf[1] (lōf) *n., pl.* **loaves** (lōvz). A shaped mass of bread or other food baked in one piece. [< OE *hlāf* < Gmc **hlaibaz.*]

loaf[2] (lōf) *v.* 1. To spend time lazily or aimlessly. 2. To waste time on a job. 3. To spend (time) idly.

loaf·er (lō′fər) *n.* 1. One who loafs. 2. A casual moccasinlike shoe.

loam (lōm) *n.* Soil consisting mainly of sand, clay, silt, and organic matter. [< OE *lām.*]

loan (lōn) *n.* 1. A sum of money lent at interest. 2. Anything lent for temporary use. —*v.* To lend. [< ON *lān.*] —**loan′er** *n.*

loan-word (lōn′wûrd′) *n.* Also **loan word, loanword.** A word adopted from another language and at least partly naturalized; for example, *encore, kindergarten.*

loath (lōth, lō*th*) *adj.* Unwilling; reluctant; disinclined. [< OE *lāth,* hateful, loathsome. See **leit-.**] —**loath′ness** *n.*

loathe (lō*th*) *v.* **loathed, loathing.** To detest greatly; abhor. [< OE *lāthian.* See **leit-.**] —**loath′er** *n.*

loath·ing (lō′*th*ĭng) *n.* Abhorrence.

ô paw, for/oi boy/ou out/ōō took/ōō coo/p pop/r run/s sauce/sh shy/t to/th thin/*th* the/
ŭ cut/ûr fur/v van/w wag/y yes/z size/zh vision/ə ago, item, edible, gallop, circus/

loath·some (lō*th*'səm, lōth'-) *adj.* Abhorrent; repulsive; disgusting. —**loath'some·ly** *adv.*
loaves. *pl.* of **loaf**[1].
lob (lŏb) *v.* **lobbed, lobbing.** To hit, toss, or propel (something) slowly in a high arc. —*n.* A ball thus hit or thrown. [Prob < LG.]
lob·by (lŏb'ē) *n., pl.* **-bies.** 1. A hall, foyer, or waiting room in a hotel, apartment house, or theater. 2. A group of private persons engaged in influencing legislation. —*v.* **-bied, -bying.** To seek to influence legislators in favor of some special interest. [ML *lobium,* a monastic cloister.] —**lob'by·ism** *n.* —**lob'by·ist** *n.*
lobe (lōb) *n.* 1. A rounded projection, esp. an anatomical part. 2. A structurally bounded subdivision of an organ or part. [< Gk *lobos.*] —**lo'bar** *adj.*
lo·bot·o·my (lō-bŏt'ə-mē, lə-) *n., pl.* **-mies.** Surgical incision into a lobe, esp. one in the brain.
lob·ster (lŏb'stər) *n.* 1. A large, edible marine crustacean with five pairs of legs, of which the first pair is large and clawlike. 2. Any of several related crustaceans. [< L *locusta,* locust, lobster.]
lo·cal (lō'kəl) *adj.* 1. Of or relating to a place. 2. Pertaining to, existing in, or serving a locality: *local government.* 3. Of or affecting a limited part of the body. 4. Making many stops: *a local train.* —*n.* 1. A public conveyance that stops at all stations. 2. A local branch of an organization, esp. of a labor union. [< L *locus,* place, LOCUS.] —**lo'cal·ly** *adv.*
lo·cale (lō-kăl', -käl') *n.* A locality, with reference to some event.
lo·cal·i·ty (lō-kăl'ə-tē) *n., pl.* **-ties.** 1. A neighborhood, place, or district. 2. A site, as of an event.
lo·cal·ize (lō'kə-līz') *v.* **-ized, -izing.** To confine or restrict to a particular area or part.
lo·cate (lō'kāt, lō-kāt') *v.* **-cated, -cating.** 1. To determine the position of: *locate Albany on the map.* 2. To find by searching: *locate the source of error.* 3. To station, situate, or place. [< L *locus,* place, LOCUS.] —**lo'ca·tor** *n.*
lo·ca·tion (lō-kā'shən) *n.* 1. A place where something is located. 2. A site away from the grounds of a motion-picture studio, where a scene is shot: *make a movie on location.*
loc. cit. In the place cited (L *locō citātō*).
loch (lŏKH, lŏk) *n. Scot.* 1. A lake. 2. An arm of the sea similar to a fjord. [< Scot Gael.]
lo·ci. *pl.* of **locus.**
lock[1] (lŏk) *n.* 1. A key- or combination-operated mechanism used to secure a door, lid, etc. 2. A section of a canal closed off with gates for the purpose of raising or lowering the water level. 3. A mechanism in a firearm for exploding its charge of ammunition. —*v.* 1. To fasten or become fastened with a lock. 2. a. To confine or safeguard by putting behind a lock. b. To put in jail (with *up*). 3. To clasp or embrace tightly. 4. To entangle in struggle or battle. 5. To become entangled; interlock. 6. To jam or force together so as to make unmovable. 7. To become rigid or unmovable. [< OE *loc.*] —**lock'less** *adj.*
lock[2] (lŏk) *n.* 1. A strand or curl of hair. 2.

locks. The hair of the head. [< OE *locc.*]
lock·er (lŏk'ər) *n.* An enclosure that can be locked, esp. one in a gymnasium or public place, for the safekeeping of clothing and valuables.
lock·et (lŏk'ĭt) *n.* A small ornamental case for a picture or keepsake, usually worn as a pendant.
lock·jaw (lŏk'jô') *n. Path.* 1. Tetanus. 2. A symptom of tetanus, in which the jaw muscles go into spasm.
lock·out (lŏk'out') *n.* The closing down of a plant by an employer to coerce the workers into meeting his terms.
lock·smith (lŏk'smĭth') *n.* One who makes or repairs locks.
lo·co (lō'kō) *adj. Slang.* Mad; insane. [< Span.]
lo·co·mo·tion (lō'kə-mō'shən) *n.* The act of moving or ability to move from place to place. [< L *locus,* place, LOCUS + MOTION.]
lo·co·mo·tive (lō'kə-mō'tĭv) *n.* A self-propelled engine that moves railroad cars. —*adj.* Of or involved in locomotion.
lo·co·weed (lō'kō-wēd') *n.* Any of several W American plants that are poisonous to livestock.
lo·cus (lō'kəs) *n., pl.* **-ci** (-sī'). 1. A place. 2. The set or configuration of all points satisfying geometric conditions. [L *locus,* place.]
lo·cust[1] (lō'kəst) *n.* 1. A grasshopper that travels in destructive swarms. 2. A cicada. [< L *lōcusta,* locust, lobster.]
lo·cust[2] (lō'kəst) *n.* A tree with featherlike compound leaves and clusters of fragrant white flowers.
lo·cu·tion (lō-kyōō'shən) *n.* 1. A particular word, phrase, or expression. 2. Style of speaking; phraseology. [< L *loqui* (pp *locūtus*), to speak.]
lode (lōd) *n.* A vein of mineral ore deposited between layers of rock. [< OE *lād,* course, way. See **leith-**.]
lode·star (lōd'stär') *n.* A star that is used as a point of reference, esp. the North Star. [ME *loode sterre,* "guiding star."]
lode·stone (lōd'stōn') *n.* A magnetized piece of magnetite.
lodge (lŏj) *n.* 1. A cottage or cabin used as a temporary abode by a caretaker, gatekeeper, etc. 2. An inn. 3. a. A local chapter of certain fraternal organizations. b. The meeting hall of such a society. —*v.* **lodged, lodging.** 1. To provide with or rent quarters temporarily, esp. for sleeping. 2. To live in a rented room or rooms. 3. To register (a charge): *lodge a complaint.* 4. To vest (authority or power). 5. To be or become embedded. [< OF *loge,* shed, small house.] —**lodge'a·ble** *adj.*
lodg·er (lŏj'ər) *n.* One who rents and lives in a furnished room or rooms; roomer.
lodg·ing (lŏj'ĭng) *n.* Often **lodgings.** Sleeping accommodations.
Łódź (lōōj). A city of C Poland. Pop. 700,000.
loft (lôft, lŏft) *n.* 1. A large, usually unpartitioned floor over a commercial building. 2. An open space under a roof; attic. 3. A gallery or balcony, as in a church: *a choir loft.*

ă pat/ā ate/âr care/ä bar/b bib/ch chew/d deed/ě pet/ē be/f fit/g gag/h hat/hw what/
ĭ pit/ī pie/îr pier/j judge/k kick/l lid, fatal/m mum/n no, sudden/ng sing/ŏ pot/ō go/

—*v.* To send (a ball) in a high arc. [< ON *lopt*, air, attic.]

loft•y (lôf′tē, lŏf′-) *adj.* **-ier, -iest. 1.** Of imposing height; towering. **2.** Elevated in character; noble. **3.** Arrogant; haughty. —**loft′i•ly** *adv.* —**loft′i•ness** *n.*

log (lôg, lŏg) *n.* **1.** A trunk or section of a trunk of a fallen or felled tree. **2.** A device used to determine the speed of a ship through water. **3.** A record of a ship's speed, progress, etc. **4.** Any record of performance, as the flight record of an aircraft. —*v.* **logged, logging. 1.** To cut (trees) into logs. **2. a.** To enter (something) in a ship's or aircraft's log. **b.** To travel (a specified distance, time, or speed). [ME *logge*.] —**log′ger** *n.*

log logarithm.

–log. Variant of **-logue.**

lo•gan•ber•ry (lō′gən-bĕr′ē) *n.* An edible, blackberrylike red fruit. [< J. *Logan* (1841–1928), American horticulturist.]

log•a•rithm (lô′gə-rĭ*th*′əm, lŏg′ə-) *n.* The exponent indicating the power to which a fixed number, the base, must be raised to produce a given number. [< Gk *logos*, reckoning, ratio + *arithmos*, number.] —**log′a•rith′mic** (-rĭ*th*′mĭk), **log′a•rith′mi•cal** *adj.*

loge (lōzh) *n.* **1.** A small compartment, esp. a box in a theater. **2.** The front rows of a theater's mezzanine. [< OF, shed, small house.]

log•ger•head (lô′gər-hĕd′, lŏg′ər-) *n.* —**at loggerheads.** In a head-on dispute. [< LOG + HEAD.]

log•ging (lô′gĭng, lŏg′ĭng) *n.* The work of felling and trimming trees and transporting the logs to a mill.

log•ic (lŏj′ĭk) *n.* **1.** The study of the principles of reasoning. **2.** Valid reasoning, esp. as distinguished from invalid or irrational argumentation. [< Gk *logos*, speech, reason.]

log•i•cal (lŏj′ĭ-kəl) *adj.* **1.** Pertaining to or in accordance with logic. **2.** Showing consistency of reasoning. **3.** Reasonable on the basis of earlier statements or events. **4.** Able to reason clearly. —**log′i•cal•ly** *adv.*

lo•gi•cian (lō-jĭsh′ən) *n.* A practitioner of a system of logic.

lo•gis•tics (lō-jĭs′tĭks) *n.* *(takes sing. v.).* The procurement, distribution, maintenance, and replacement of materiel and personnel. —**lo•gis′tic, lo•gis′ti•cal** *adj.*

log•jam (lôg′jăm′, lŏg′-) *n.* Also **log-jam, log jam. 1.** A mass of floating logs crowded immovably together. **2.** A deadlock in negotiations, debates, etc.

logo–. *comb. form.* Word or speech. [< Gk *logos*, speech, word, reason.]

log•roll•ing (lôg′rō′lĭng, lŏg′-) *n.* Also **log-roll-ing.** The trading of votes among legislators to achieve passage of projects of interest to one another.

–logue, –log. *comb. form.* Speech, discourse, or recitation: *travelogue.* [< Gk *legein*, to speak.]

lo•gy (lō′gē) *adj.* **-gier, -giest.** Sluggish; lethargic. [Perh < Du *log*.] —**lo′gi•ness** *n.*

–logy. *comb. form.* **1.** Discourse or expression:

phraseology. **2.** The science, theory, or study of: paleontology. [< Gk *logos*, word, speech.]

loin (loin) *n.* **1.** The part of the side and back between the ribs and pelvis. **2.** A cut of meat from this part of an animal. **3. loins.** The region of the thighs and groin. [< L *lumbus*.]

loin•cloth (loin′klôth′, -klŏth′) *n.* A strip of cloth worn around the loins.

Loire (lwàr). A river of France.

loi•ter (loi′tər) *v.* **1.** To stand idly about; loaf. **2.** To proceed slowly or with many stops. [ME *loyteren.*] —**loi′ter•er** *n.* —**loi′ter•ing•ly** *adv.*

loll (lŏl) *v.* **1.** To recline in an indolent manner. **2.** To hang or droop laxly. [ME *lollen.*]

lol•li•pop (lŏl′ē-pŏp′) *n.* Also **lol•ly•pop.** A piece of hard candy on the end of a stick. [Perh < LOLL, to hang out (the tongue) + POP.]

Lo•mé (lō′mā′). The capital of Togo. Pop. 80,000.

Lon•don (lŭn′dən). The capital of the United Kingdom, in SE. England. Pop. 7,990,000.

lone (lōn) *adj.* **1.** Solitary: *a lone tree.* **2.** Isolated; unfrequented. [Short for ALONE.]

lone•ly (lōn′lē) *adj.* **-lier, -liest. 1.** Without companions or companionship; solitary. **2.** Unfrequented; desolate. **3.** Dejected by the awareness of being alone. [< LONE.] —**lone′li•ly** *adv.* —**lone′li•ness** *n.*

lon•er (lō′nər) *n.* *Informal.* One who avoids other people.

lone•some (lōn′səm) *adj.* **1.** Dejected by being lonely. **2.** Offering solitude; secluded.

long¹ (lông, lŏng) *adj.* **1.** Having great length. **2.** Of relatively great duration: *a long time.* **3.** Of a specified length or duration: *a mile long; an hour long.* **4.** Concerned with distant issues; far-reaching: *a long view.* **5.** Risky; chancy: *long odds.* **6.** Having an abundance or excess of: *long on hope.* —**in the long run.** Ultimately; eventually. —*adv.* **1.** For an extended period of time. **2.** For or throughout a specified period: *all night long.* **3.** At a distant point in time: *long before we were born.* —**as (or so) long as. 1.** Since; inasmuch as. **2.** During the time that. —**no longer.** Not now as formerly; no more. Soon. —**the long and the short of.** The substance; gist. [< OE *lang.* See del-¹.]

long² (lông, lŏng) *v.* To yearn; desire greatly. [< OE *langian*, "to seem long (to some)," yearn for. See del-¹.]

long. longitude.

long distance. Telephone service between distant points. —**long′-dis′tance** *adj.*

long-drawn (lông′drôn′, lŏng′-) *adj.* Prolonged.

lon•gev•i•ty (lŏn-jĕv′ə-tē) *n.* Long duration of life. —**lon•ge′vous** (-jē′vəs) *adj.*

Long•fel•low (lông′fĕl′ō, lŏng′-), **Henry Wadsworth.** 1807–1882. American poet.

long•hair (lông′hâr′, lŏng′-) *n.* One dedicated to the arts and esp. to classical music. —**long′-hair′, long′haired′** *adj.*

long•hand (lông′hănd′, lŏng′-) *n.* Ordinary handwriting.

long•ing (lông′ĭng, lŏng′-) *n.* A persistent . yearning or desire that cannot be fulfilled.

ô paw, for/oi boy/ou out/o͞o took/o͞o coo/p pop/r run/s sauce/sh shy/t to/th thin/*th* the/
ŭ cut/ûr fur/v van/w wag/y yes/z size/zh vision/ə ago, item, edible, gallop, circus/

—*adj.* Showing such a yearning: *longing eyes.* —**long'ing•ly** *adv.*

Long Island. An island of SE New York State.

lon•gi•tude (lŏn'jə-t/y/ōōd') *n.* Angular distance E or W, generally measured with respect to the prime meridian at Greenwich, England. —**lon'gi•tu'di•nal** *adj.* —**lon'gi•tu'di•nal•ly** *adv.*

long-lived (lông'lĭvd', -lĭvd', lŏng'-) *adj.* Having a long life. —**long'-lived'ness** *n.*

long-play•ing (lông'plā'ĭng, lŏng'-) *adj.* Relating to or being a microgroove phonograph record, esp. one turning at 33⅓ revolutions per minute.

long-range (lông'rānj', lŏng'-) *adj.* **1.** Involving a span of time: *long-range planning.* **2.** Designed to shoot over long distances.

long•shore•man (lông'shôr'mən, -shōr'mən, lŏng'-) *n.* A dock worker who loads and unloads ships.

long shot. An entry, as in a horse race, with only a slight chance of winning.

long-stand•ing (lông'stăn'dĭng, lŏng'-) *adj.* Of long duration.

long-suf•fer•ing (lông'sŭf'ər-ĭng, lŏng'-) *adj.* Patiently enduring wrongs or difficulties.

long-term (lông'tûrm', lŏng'-) *adj.* Involving or maturing after a number of years: *a long-term investment.*

long ton. A unit of weight, a ton.

long-wind•ed (lông'wĭn'dĭd, lŏng'-) *adj.* Wearisomely verbose. —**long'wind'ed•ly** *adv.* —**long'wind'ed•ness** *n.*

look (lŏŏk) *v.* **1.** To employ one's eyes in seeing. **2.** To turn one's eyes on. **3.** To seem or appear to be: *look morose.* **4.** To face in a specified direction. **5.** To have an appearance in conformity with: *look one's age.* —**look after.** To take care of. —**look down on** (or **upon**). To regard with contempt or condescension. —**look for. 1.** To search for. **2.** To expect. —**look forward to.** To anticipate eagerly. —**look into.** To investigate. —**look over.** To inspect, esp. casually. —**look up. 1.** To search for and find, as in a reference book. **2.** To locate and call upon; visit. **3.** *Informal.* To improve. —**look up to.** To admire. —*n.* **1.** The action of looking; a gaze or glance. **2.** Appearance or aspect. **3. looks.** Physical appearance, esp. when pleasing. [< OE *lōcian* < Gmc *lōkōjan.*] —**look'er** *n.*

looking glass. A mirror.

look•out (lŏŏk'out') *n.* **1.** The act of observing or keeping watch. **2.** A high place or structure commanding a wide view for observation. **3.** One who keeps watch.

loom[1] (lōōm) *v.* **1.** To come into view as a massive, distorted, or indistinct image. **2.** To appear to the mind in a magnified and threatening form. **3.** To seem imminent; impend. [Prob of LG origin.]

loom[2] (lōōm) *n.* A machine from which cloth is produced by interweaving thread or yarn at right angles. [< OE *gelōma,* utensil, tool.]

loon[1] (lōōn) *n.* A diving bird with mottled plumage and an eerie, laughlike cry. [Prob < ON *lomr.*]

loon[2] (lōōn) *n.* A simple-minded or mad person. [ME *loun, lown.*]

loon•y (lōō'nē) *adj.* **-ier, -iest.** *Informal.* So odd as to appear demented. —**loon'i•ness** *n.*

loop (lōōp) *n.* **1.** A length of line, thread, etc., that is folded over and joined at the ends. **2.** Any roughly oval, closed, or nearly closed turn or figure. —*v.* **1.** To form or form into a loop or loops. **2.** To fasten, join, or encircle with a loop or loops. —**loop the loop.** To make a vertical loop or loops in the air, as an aircraft. [ME *loupe.*]

loop•hole (lōōp'hōl') *n.* **1.** A small hole or slit in a wall. **2.** An omission or ambiguity that provides a means of evasion.

loose (lōōs) *adj.* **looser, loosest. 1.** Not fastened; unbound. **2.** Not taut or drawn up tightly; slack. **3.** Not tight-fitting or tightly fitted. **4.** Not compact or dense. **5.** Lacking a sense of restraint or responsibility; idle: *loose talk.* **6.** Licentious; immoral. **7.** Not literal or exact: *a loose translation.* —**at loose ends.** Without plans or direction. —*adv.* In a loose manner. —*v.* **loosed, loosing. 1.** To let loose; set free; release. **2.** To become loose. **3.** To undo, untie, or unwrap. **4.** To release pressure on; make less tight, firm, or compact. **5.** To let fly (a missile). [< ON *lauss, louss.*] —**loose'ly** *adv.* —**loose'ness** *n.*

loos•en (lōō'sən) *v.* **1.** To make or become loose or looser. **2.** To free from restraint, pressure, or strictness. —**loos'en•er** *n.*

loot (lōōt) *n.* **1.** Valuables pillaged in time of war; spoils. **2.** *Informal.* Goods stolen or illicitly obtained. —*v.* To pillage or engage in pillage. [< Sk *lōptra,* booty.] —**loot'er** *n.*

lop[1] (lŏp) *v.* **lopped, lopping. 1.** To cut off branches or twigs from; trim. **2.** To cut off (a part), esp. with a single swift blow. [?]

lop[2] (lŏp) *v.* **lopped, lopping.** To hang loosely; droop.

lope (lōp) *v.* **loped, loping.** To run or ride with a steady, easy gait. —*n.* A steady, easy gait. [< ON *hlaupa,* to leap.] —**lop'er** *n.*

lop•sid•ed (lŏp'sī'dĭd) *adj.* Heavier, larger, or higher on one side than the other; not symmetrical. —**lop'sid•ed•ness** *n.*

lo•qua•cious (lō-kwā'shəs) *adj.* Very talkative. [< L *loquī,* to speak.] —**lo•qua'cious•ness, lo•quac'i•ty** (-kwăs'ə-tē) *n.*

lord (lôrd) *n.* **1.** A person having dominion over others; a ruler or master. **2. Lord.** *Brit.* The general masculine title of nobility and other rank. **3. Lord.** God. Also used in exclamations, as *Good Lord!* —*v.* To play the lord; domineer: *lording it over the newcomers.* [< OE *hlāfweard,* "keeper of the bread": *hlāf,* LOAF + *weard,* keeper, WARD.]

Lord Chancellor *pl.* **Lords Chancellor.** Also **Lord High Chancellor.** The presiding officer of the House of Lords.

lord•ly (lôrd'lē) *adj.* **-lier, -liest. 1.** Pertaining to a lord. **2.** Dignified; noble. **3.** Arrogant; haughty. —**lord'li•ness** *n.*

Lord's Day, Lord's day. The Sabbath; Sunday.

lord•ship (lôrd'shĭp') *n.* **1. Lordship.** A form of address or a title for a British nobleman, judge, or bishop: *His Lordship.* **2.** The position, authority, or territory of a lord.

ă pat/ā ate/âr care/ä bar/b bib/ch chew/d deed/ě pet/ē be/f fit/g gag/h hat/hw what/ ĭ pit/ī pie/îr pier/j judge/k kick/l lid, fatal/m mum/n no, sudden/ng sing/ŏ pot/ō go/

Lord's Prayer. The prayer taught by Jesus to his disciples. Matthew 6:9–13.

lore (lôr, lōr) *n.* Accumulated fact, tradition, or belief about a particular subject. [< OE *lār.* See **leis-.**]

lor•gnette (lôrn-yĕt') *n.* Eyeglasses or opera glasses with a short handle. [< OF *lorgne,* squinting.]

lor•ry (lôr'ē, lŏr'ē) *n., pl.* **-ries.** *Chiefly Brit.* A motor truck.

Los An•ge•les (lôs ăn'jə-ləs, -lēz', lŏs). A city of SW California. Pop. 2,782,000.

lose (lōōz) *v.* **lost** (lôst, lŏst), **losing.** **1.** To be unable to find; mislay. **2.** To be unable to maintain or keep. **3.** To be deprived of: *lose a friend.* **4.** To fail to win; be defeated. **5.** To fail to take advantage of: *lose a chance.* **6.** To rid oneself of. **7.** To allow (oneself) to become engrossed, as in a book. **8.** To result in the loss of: *Failure to reply lost her a job.* **9.** To suffer loss. [< OE *los,* loss, destruction. See **leu-.**]

loss (lôs, lŏs) *n.* **1.** The act or an instance of losing. **2.** Something or someone that is lost. **3. losses.** Casualties. **—at a loss.** Perplexed; puzzled. [< OE *los,* destruction, loss. See **leu-.**]

lost (lôst, lŏst) *adj.* **1.** Strayed or missing. **2.** No longer possessed. **3.** No longer visible. **4.** Not taken advantage of: *a lost opportunity.* **5.** Bewildered; helpless. [< the pp of LOSE.]

lot (lŏt) *n.* **1.** An object used in making a determination by chance. **2.** The use of lots for selection. **3.** One's fortune in life; fate. **4.** A number of people or things. **5.** Often **lots.** A large amount or number. **6.** A piece of land having fixed boundaries. **—adv.** Very much: *Thanks a lot.* [< OE *hlot.*]

Lo•thar•i•o (lō-thâr'ē-ō) *n., pl.* **-os.** A libertine; rake. [< *Lotario,* seducer in *The Fair Penitent* (1703), by Nicholas Rowe.]

lo•tion (lō'shən) *n.* A liquid for external application, esp. one containing a substance in suspension. [< L *lōtiō,* washing.]

lot•ter•y (lŏt'ə-rē) *n., pl.* **-ies.** A contest in which lots are distributed or sold and the winners determined in a chance drawing. [< MDu *lot,* lot.]

lo•tus (lō'təs) *n., pl.* **-tuses.** **1.** An Oriental water lily with pinkish flowers and large leaves. **2.** Any of several similar or related plants. **3.** A fruit said in Greek legend to produce a drugged, indolent state in those who eat it. [< Gk *lōtos,* a kind of fruit.]

loud (loud) *adj.* **1.** Characterized by high volume and intensity of sound. **2.** Producing or capable of producing a sound of high volume and intensity. **3.** Having offensively bright colors. [< OE *hlūd.* See **kleu-.**] **—loud, loud'ly** *adv.* **—loud'ness** *n.*

Usage: Loud (adverb) and *loudly* are often used interchangeably after certain common verbs, such as *laugh, play, roar, say, scream, shout, sing,* and *talk. Loudly* occurs more frequently in formal usage, esp. in writing. *Loudly* is the idiomatic form after verbs such as *boast, brag, insist,* and *proclaim.*

loud-mouth (loud'mouth') *n.* One whose speech is loud and irritating or indiscreet.

loud-speak•er (loud'spē'kər) *n.* Also **loud-speak•er.** A device that converts electric signals to audible sound.

Lou•is XIV (lōō'ē). 1638–1715. King of France (1643–1715).

Lou•is XVI (lōō'ē). 1754–1793. King of France (1774–92).

Lou•i•si•an•a (lōō-ē'zē-ăn'ə). A state of the S U.S. Pop. 3,643,000. Cap. Baton Rouge.

Louisiana French. French as spoken by descendants of the original settlers of Louisiana.

Lou•is•ville (lōō'ē-vĭl). A city of N Kentucky. Pop. 361,000.

lounge (lounj) *v.* **lounged, lounging.** To stand, sit, or lie in a lazy, relaxed way. **—n.** **1.** A comfortably furnished waiting room, as in a hotel or theater. **2.** A long couch. [?]

loupe (lōōp) *n.* A magnifying glass set in an eyepiece, used by watchmakers and jewelers. [< OF *loupe,* imperfect gem.]

lour. Variant of **lower¹.**

Lou•ren•ço Mar•ques (lō-rān'sōō mər-käsh'). The capital of Mozambique. Pop. 79,000.

louse (lous) *n.* **1.** *pl.* **lice** (līs). A small, wingless insect that lives as a parasite on various animals, including man. **2.** *pl.* **louses.** *Slang.* A mean or despicable person. **—v.** **loused, lousing.** *Slang.* To bungle (with *up*). [< OE *lūs, lỹs.* See **lus-.**]

lous•y (lou'zē) *adj.* **-ier, -iest.** **1.** Infested with lice. **2.** *Slang.* Mean; nasty. **3.** *Slang.* Inferior; worthless. **4.** *Slang.* Having a surfeit of: *lousy with money.* **—lous'i•ly** *adv.* **—lous'i•ness** *n.*

lout (lout) *n.* An awkward, stupid fellow; oaf. [Perh < ON *lūtr,* bent low.] **—lout'ish** *adj.*

lou•ver (lōō'vər) *n.* Also **lou•vre.** **1.** An opening fitted with fixed or movable slanted slats. **2.** One of the slats used in a louver. [< OF *lovier.*] **—lou'vered** *adj.*

love (lŭv) *n.* **1. a.** An intense affectionate concern for another person. **b.** A passionate attraction to another person. **2.** A beloved person. **3.** A strong liking or enthusiasm for something. **4.** A zero score in tennis. **—in love.** Enamored. **—v.** **loved, loving.** **1.** To feel love for. **2.** To like enthusiastically. [< OE *lufu.* See **leubh-.**] **—lov'a•ble, love'a•ble** *adj.*

love•bird (lŭv'bûrd') *n.* A small parrot often kept as a cage bird.

love•lorn (lŭv'lôrn') *adj.* Bereft of love or one's lover. **—love'lorn'ness** *n.*

love•ly (lŭv'lē) *adj.* **-lier, -liest.** **1.** Having pleasing or attractive qualities; beautiful. **2.** Enjoyable; delightful. **—love'li•ness** *n.*

lov•er (lŭv'ər) *n.* **1.** A person in love with another. **2. lovers.** A couple in love with each other. **3.** A paramour. **4.** One who is fond of or devoted to something.

love seat. A small sofa or double chair that seats two people.

love•sick (lŭv'sĭk') *adj.* **1.** Stricken, as if with illness, by love. **2.** Showing a lover's yearning. **—love'sick'ness** *n.*

lov•ing (lŭv'ĭng) *adj.* Feeling or exhibiting love; affectionate. **—lov'ing•ly** *adv.*

loving cup. A large, ornamental cup given as an award in sporting events and similar affairs.

low¹ (lō) *adj.* **1.** Having little height. **2.** Situ-

ō paw, for/oi boy/ou out/ōō took/ōō coo/p pop/r run/s sauce/sh shy/t to/th thin/*th* the/ ŭ cut/ûr fur/v van/w wag/y yes/z size/zh vision/ə ago, item, edible, gallop, circus/

ated below normal height. **3.** Situated below surrounding surfaces. **4.** Of less than usual or average depth. **5.** Of inferior quality or character. **6.** Of inferior or relatively simple status. **7.** Morally base. **8.** Emotionally or mentally depressed. **9.** Below average in degree or intensity. **10.** Below an average or standard figure. **11.** Being a sound produced by a relatively small frequency of vibrations. **12.** Not loud. **13.** Depreciatory; disparaging: *a low o-pinion of his qualities.* —*adv.* **1.** In a low position, level, etc. **2.** In or to a reduced or degraded condition. **3.** At or to a low volume, intensity, etc. **4.** At a small price: *bought low, sold high.* —*n.* **1.** A low level, position, or degree. **2.** A region of depressed barometric pressure. **3.** The gear arrangement that produces the lowest range of output speeds, as in an automotive transmission. [< ON *lāgr*.] —**low'ness** *n.*

low² (lō) *v.* To moo. [< OE *hlōwan.* See kel-³.] —**low** *n.*

low·boy (lō'boi') *n.* A low, tablelike chest of drawers.

low·brow (lō'brou') *n. Informal.* One having uncultivated tastes. —**low'brow'** *adj.*

Low Countries. Belgium, the Netherlands, and Luxembourg.

low-down (lō'doun') *adj.* Mean; unfair.

low·down (lō'doun') *n. Slang.* All the facts; the whole truth.

Low·ell (lō'əl), **James Russell.** 1819–1891. American poet, essayist, and diplomat.

low·er¹ (lou'ər) *v.* Also **lour. 1.** To look angry or sullen; scowl. **2.** To appear dark and threatening, as the weather. [ME *l(o)uren.*]

low·er² (lō'ər) *adj.* **1.** Below someone or something, as in rank, position, etc. **2.** Lower. *Geol. & Archaeol.* Being an earlier division of the period named. **3.** Denoting the larger house of a bicameral legislature. —*v.* **1.** To let or move something down to a lower level. **2.** To reduce in value, degree, etc.

Lower Carboniferous. *Geol.* Mississippian.

low·er-case (lō'ər-kās') *adj.* Of or pertaining to small letters as distinguished from capitals.

lower class. Often **lower classes.** The class or classes of lower than middle rank in a society. —**low'er-class'** *adj.*

lowest common denominator. The least common multiple of the denominators of a set of fractions.

low frequency. A radio frequency in the range from 30 to 300 kilocycles per second.

Low German. 1. Any of several German dialects spoken in N Germany. **2.** All of the West Germanic languages except High German.

low-keyed (lō'kēd') *adj.* Restrained, as in style or quality.

low·land (lō'lənd) *n.* An area of land that is low in relation to the surrounding country. —**low'land** *adj.*

Low·land (lō'lənd) *n.* The English dialect of the Scottish Lowlands. —*adj.* Of or from the Scottish Lowlands.

Low·lands, The (lō'ləndz). The lowlands of E and S Scotland.

low·ly (lō'lē) *adj.* -**lier**, -**liest. 1.** Having a low

rank or position. **2.** Plain; undistinguished. —**low'li·ness** *n.* —**low'ly** *adv.*

low-mind·ed (lō'mīn'dĭd) *adj.* Exhibiting a coarse, vulgar character. —**low'-mind'ed·ly** *adv.* —**low'-mind'ed·ness** *n.*

low profile. Unobtrusive, restrained behavior or stance, esp. an avoidance of militancy or intervention.

low relief. Sculptural relief that projects very little from the background.

low tide. 1. The tide at its lowest ebb. **2.** The time of this ebb.

lox¹ (lŏks) *n.* Smoked salmon. [Yid.]

lox² (lŏks) *n.* Liquid oxygen.

loy·al (loi'əl) *adj.* **1.** Steadfast in allegiance to one's homeland or government. **2.** Faithful to a person, ideal, etc. [< L *lēgālis*, legal.] —**loy'al·ly** *adv.* —**loy'al·ty, loy'al·ness** *n.*

loz·enge (lŏz'ĭnj) *n.* **1.** A four-sided planar figure with a diamondlike shape. **2.** A lozenge-shaped medicated drop for the mouth or throat. [< Gaul **lausa*, flat stone.]

LP (ĕl'pē') *adj.* Long-playing. —*n., pl.* **LP's** or **LPs.** A trademark for a long-playing record.

LSD Lysergic acid diethylamide; specifically, this chemical taken as a hallucinogen.

lt. light.

Lt. lieutenant.

Lt. Col. lieutenant colonel.

Lt. Comdr. lieutenant commander.

ltd., Ltd. limited.

Lt. Gen. lieutenant general.

Lu lutetium.

Lu·an·da (lōō-än'də). The capital of Angola. Pop. 245,000.

Luang Pra·bang (lwäng' prä-bäng'). A capital of Laos. Pop. 8,000.

lu·au (lōō-ou') *n.* An elaborate Hawaiian feast.

lub. lubricant; lubrication.

Lub·bock (lŭb'ək). A city of NW Texas. Pop. 129,000.

lu·bri·cant (lōō'brĭ-kənt) *n.* Any of various materials, such as grease, machine oil, or graphite, that reduce friction when applied as a coating to moving parts.

lu·bri·cate (lōō'brĭ-kāt') *v.* -**cated**, -**cating.** To apply a lubricant to. [< L *lūbricus*, slippery.] —**lu'bri·ca'tion** *n.*

lu·bri·cous (lōō'brĭ-kəs) *adj.* Also **lu·bri·cious** (lōō-brĭsh'əs). Characterized by lewdness. [< L *lūbricus*, slippery.]

lu·cid (lōō'sĭd) *adj.* **1.** Easily understood; clear. **2.** Rational; clear-minded. [< L *lūcidus* < *lūcēre*, to shine.] —**lu·cid'i·ty, lu'cid·ness** *n.* —**lu'cid·ly** *adv.*

Lu·ci·fer (lōō'sə-fər). The archangel cast from Heaven for leading a revolt of the angels; Satan.

Lu·cite (lōō'sīt') *n.* A trademark for a transparent, thermoplastic, acrylic resin.

luck (lŭk) *n.* **1.** The fortuitous happening of fortunate or adverse events; fortune. **2.** Good fortune. [Perh < LG *luk* or MDu *luc.*]

luck·y (lŭk'ē) *adj.* -**ier**, -**iest.** Having or resulting in good luck; fortunate. —**luck'i·ly** *adv.* —**luck'-i·ness** *n.*

lu·cra·tive (lōō'krə-tĭv) *adj.* Producing wealth; profitable. [< L *lucrum*, LUCRE.]

ă pat/ā ate/âr care/ä bar/b bib/ch chew/d deed/ĕ pet/ē be/f fit/g gag/h hat/hw what/
ĭ pit/ī pie/îr pier/j judge/k kick/l lid, fatal/m mum/n no, sudden/ng sing/ŏ pot/ō go/

lu·cre (lōō′kər) *n.* Money; profits. [< L *lucrum,* gain, profit.]

lu·di·crous (lōō′dĭ-krəs) *adj.* Laughable because of obvious absurdity or incongruity. [L *lūdicrus,* done playfully.] —**lu′di·crous·ly** *adv.* —**lu′di·crous·ness** *n.*

lug¹ (lŭg) *n.* **1.** An earlike handle or projection used as a hold or support. **2.** *Mach.* A nut, esp. one closed at one end to serve as a cap. **3.** *Slang.* A clumsy fool. [ME *lugge,* flap, ear.]

lug² (lŭg) *v.* **lugged, lugging.** To drag or carry (something) laboriously. [Perh < Scand.]

lug·gage (lŭg′ĭj) *n.* Baggage, esp. suitcases. [Prob LUG + (BAG)GAGE.]

lu·gu·bri·ous (lōō-g/y/ōō′brē-əs) *adj.* Mournful, esp. to a ludicrous degree. [L *lūgubris.*] —**lu·gu′bri·ous·ly** *adv.*

Luke (lōōk), **Saint.** Christian apostle, reputed author of the 3rd Gospel and Acts.

luke·warm (lōōk′wôrm′) *adj.* **1.** Mildly warm; tepid. **2.** Halfhearted; indifferent. [ME.]

lull (lŭl) *v.* **1.** To cause to sleep or rest; soothe. **2.** To deceive into trustfulness. —*n.* A relatively calm or inactive period. [ME *lullen.*]

lull·a·by (lŭl′ə-bī′) *n., pl.* -**bies.** A song with which to lull a child to sleep. [Perh LULL + (GOOD-)BY.]

lum·ba·go (lŭm-bā′gō) *n.* A painful inflammatory rheumatism of the tendons and muscles of the lumbar region.

lum·bar (lŭm′bər, -bär′) *adj.* Of or situated in the part of the back and sides between the lowest ribs and pelvis. [< L *lumbus,* loin.]

lum·ber¹ (lŭm′bər) *n.* **1.** Timber sawed into boards, planks, etc. **2.** Anything useless or cumbersome. —**lum′ber** *adj.*

lum·ber² (lŭm′bər) *v.* To walk or move heavily or clumsily. [Perh < Scand.]

lum·ber·jack (lŭm′bər-jăk′) *n.* One who fells trees and transports the timber to a mill.

lum·ber·yard (lŭm′bər-yärd′) *n.* An establishment that sells lumber and other building materials.

lu·mi·nar·y (lōō′mə-nĕr′ē) *n., pl.* -**ies.** **1.** An object, as a celestial body, that gives light. **2.** A person notable in a specific field. [< L *lūmen,* light.]

lu·mi·nesce (lōō′mə-nĕs′) *v.* -**nesced, -nescing.** To be or become luminescent.

lu·mi·nes·cence (lōō′mə-nĕs′əns) *n.* **1.** The emission of light, as in phosphorescence and fluorescence, by means of essentially nonthermal effects. **2.** The light so emitted. —**lu′mi·nes′cent** *adj.*

lu·mi·nos·i·ty (lōō′mə-nŏs′ə-tē) *n.* **1.** The condition or quality of being luminous. **2.** Something luminous.

lu·mi·nous (lōō′mə-nəs) *adj.* **1.** Emitting light, esp. self-generated light. **2.** Full of light. [< L *lūmen,* light.] —**lu′mi·nous·ly** *adv.*

lum·mox (lŭm′əks) *n.* An oaf. [?]

lump¹ (lŭmp) *n.* **1.** An irregularly shaped mass or piece. **2.** *Path.* A swelling or small, palpable mass. **3.** An aggregate; collection. —*v.* To put together in a single group or pile. [ME.] —**lump′i·ness** *n.* —**lump′y** *adj.*

lump² (lŭmp) *v. Informal.* To tolerate: *like it or lump it.* [?]

lu·na·cy (lōō′nə-sē) *n., pl.* -**cies.** **1.** Insanity. **2.** Foolish conduct.

lu·nar (lōō′nər) *adj.* Of or pertaining to the moon. [< L *lūna,* moon.]

lunar excursion module. Also **lunar module.** A spacecraft designed to transport astronauts orbiting the moon to the lunar surface and back.

lu·na·tic (lōō′nə-tĭk) *adj.* **1.** Of or for the insane. **2.** Wildly foolish. [< L *lūnāticus,* "moonstruck," crazy.] —**lu′na·tic** *n.*

lunch (lŭnch) *n.* A meal eaten at midday. [Orig "chunk, thick piece of food."] —**lunch** *v.*

lunch·eon (lŭn′chən) *n.* A lunch, esp. a party at which lunch is served.

lunch·eon·ette (lŭn′chə-nĕt′) *n.* A small restaurant that serves simple meals.

lung (lŭng) *n.* Either of two spongy, saclike thoracic organs in most vertebrates, functioning to remove carbon dioxide from the blood and provide it with oxygen. [< OE *lungen.*]

lunge (lŭnj) *n.* Any sudden forward movement or plunge. —*v.* **lunged, lunging.** To move with a lunge. [< OF *allonger,* to lengthen, extend.]

lu·pine (lōō′pən) *n.* Also **lu·pin.** A plant with compound leaves and long clusters of variously colored flowers.

lu·pus (lōō′pəs) *n.* Any of several diseases of the skin and mucous membranes, many causing disfiguring lesions. [< L, wolf.]

lurch¹ (lûrch) *v.* **1.** To stagger. **2.** To roll or tip abruptly. —*n.* **1.** A staggering movement. **2.** An abrupt rolling or tipping. [?]

lurch² (lûrch) *n.* A position of difficulty. [< F *lourche,* a game, "defeat."]

lure (lōōr) *n.* **1.** Anything that attracts with the prospect of pleasure or reward. **2.** An artificial bait used in catching fish. —*v.* **lured, luring.** To attract by wiles; entice. [< OF *loirre,* bait < Gmc *lōthr.*] —**lur′ing·ly** *adv.*

lu·rid (lōōr′ĭd) *adj.* Causing shock or horror; sensational. [L *lūridus,* pallid, ghastly.]

lurk (lûrk) *v.* **1.** To lie in wait, as in ambush. **2.** To move furtively. [ME *lurken.*]

Lu·sa·ka (lōō-sä′kə). The capital of Zambia. Pop. 122,000.

lus·cious (lŭsh′əs) *adj.* **1.** Pleasant to taste or smell; delicious. **2.** Sensually appealing.

lush¹ (lŭsh) *adj.* **1.** Characterized by luxuriant growth or vegetation. **2.** Luxurious; opulent. [ME *lusch,* lax, soft.] —**lush′ness** *n.*

lush² (lŭsh) *n. Slang.* A drunkard. [?]

lust (lŭst) *n.* **1.** Sexual craving, esp. when excessive. **2.** Any overwhelming craving. —*v.* To have an inordinate desire, esp. a sexual desire. [< OE. See las-.] —**lust′ful** *adj.*

lus·ter (lŭs′tər) *n.* Also *chiefly Brit.* **lus·tre.** **1.** Soft reflected light; sheen; gloss. **2.** Brilliance or radiance. **3.** Splendor; glory. [< L *lūstrāre,* to purify, make bright.] —**lus′trous** (-trəs) *adj.*

lust·y (lŭs′tē) *adj.* -**ier, -iest.** Full of vigor; robust. —**lust′i·ly** *adv.* —**lust′i·ness** *n.*

lute (lōōt) *n.* A stringed instrument with a fretted fingerboard and a body shaped like half a pear. [< Ar *al-'ud,* "the wood."]

lu·te·ti·um (lōō-tē′shē-əm) *n.* Also **lu·te·ci·um.** *Symbol* **Lu** A silvery-white rare-earth element

---

ô paw, for/oi boy/ou out/ōō took/ōō coo/p pop/r run/s sauce/sh shy/t to/th thin/*th* the/
ŭ cut/ûr fur/v van/w wag/y yes/z size/zh vision/ə ago, item, edible, gallop, circus/

used in nuclear technology. Atomic number 71, atomic weight 174.97. [< *Lūtétia*, Latin name for Paris.]

Lu·ther (lōō'thər), **Martin.** 1483–1546. German theologian and religious reformer.

Martin Luther

Lu·ther·an (lōō'thər-ən) *adj.* Of or relating to the branch of the Protestant Church adhering to the views of Martin Luther. —**Lu'ther·an** *n.*

Lux·em·bourg (lŭk'səm-bûrg). Also **Lux·em·burg.** 1. A grand duchy in W Europe. Pop. 331,000. 2. The capital of this grand duchy. Pop. 77,000.

Luxembourg

lux·u·ri·ant (lŭg-zhōōr'ē-ənt, lŭk-shōōr'-) *adj.* 1. Growing abundantly, vigorously, or lushly. 2. Elaborate; ornate; florid. —**lux·u'ri·ance** *n.*

lux·u·ri·ate (lŭg-zhōōr'ē-āt', lŭk-shōōr'-) *v.* **-ated, -ating.** To take luxurious pleasure; indulge oneself. —**lux·u'ri·a'tion** *n.*

lux·u·ri·ous (lŭg-zhōōr'ē-əs, lŭk-shōōr'-) *adj.* 1. Fond of or given to luxury. 2. Characterized by luxury. —**lux·u'ri·ous·ly** *adv.*

lux·u·ry (lŭg'zhə-rē, lŭk'shə-) *n., pl.* **-ries.** 1. Something not absolutely necessary that provides comfort or enjoyment. 2. The enjoyment of sumptuous living. [< L *luxus,* excess, extravagance.]

lv. leave.

Lw lawrencium.

–ly¹. *comb. form.* 1. A characteristic or resem-

blance: **sisterly.** 2. Occurrence at specified intervals: **monthly.** [< OE *-lic,* "having the form of."]

–ly². *comb. form.* 1. In a specified manner: **gradually.** 2. At every specified interval: **daily.** [< OE *-lic,* -LY.]

ly·ce·um (lī-sē'əm) *n.* 1. A hall in which lectures, concerts, etc., are presented. 2. An organization sponsoring such presentations.

lye (lī) *n.* 1. The liquid obtained by leaching wood ashes. 2. **Potassium hydroxide.** 3. **Sodium hydroxide.** [< OE *lēag.* See lou-.]

ly·ing (lī'ĭng). 1. *pres.p.* of **lie¹.** 2. *pres.p.* of **lie².**

lymph (lĭmf) *n.* A clear, watery, sometimes faintly yellowish liquid that contains white blood cells and some red blood cells and acts to remove bacteria and certain proteins from the tissues, transport fat from the intestines, and supply lymphocytes to the blood. [L *lympha, limpa,* water.]

lym·phat·ic (lĭm-făt'ĭk) *adj.* Of or relating to lymph or the lymphatic system. —*n.* A vessel that conveys lymph.

lymphatic system. The interconnected system of spaces and vessels between tissues and organs by which lymph is circulated throughout the body.

lymph node. Any of numerous oval or round bodies that supply lymphocytes to the circulatory system and remove bacteria and foreign particles from the lymph.

lym·phoid (lĭm'foid') *adj.* Of or pertaining to lymph, lymphatic tissue, or the lymphatic system.

lynch (lĭnch) *v.* To execute, esp. by hanging, without due process of law. [< C. *Lynch* (1736–1796), Virginia planter and justice of the peace.] —**lynch'er** *n.*

lynx (lĭngks) *n.* A wild cat with thick, soft fur, a short tail, and tufted ears. [< Gk *lunx.*]

lynx-eyed (lĭngks'īd') *adj.* Keen of vision.

Ly·on (lē'ôɴ'). A city of east-central France. Pop. 529,000.

Ly·ra (lī'rə) *n.* A constellation in the N Hemisphere. [L *lyra,* lyre.]

lyre (līr) *n.* A stringed instrument of the harp family used esp. in ancient Greece. [< Gk *lura.*]

lyr·ic (lĭr'ĭk) *adj.* 1. Of or relating to poetry that is a direct, often songlike expression of the poet's thoughts and feelings. 2. Exuberant; unrestrained. —*n.* 1. A lyric poem. 2. **lyrics.** The words of a song. [< Gk *lura,* LYRE.] —**lyr'i·cal** *adj.* —**lyr'i·cal·ly** *adv.*

lyr·i·cist (lĭr'ə-sĭst) *n.* A writer of lyrics.

ly·ser·gic acid (lĭ-sûr'jĭk, lī-). A crystalline alkaloid, $C_{16}H_{16}N_2O_2$, derived from ergot and used in medical research.

lysergic acid di·eth·yl·am·ide (dī'ĕth-əl-ăm'-ĭd'). A hallucinogenic drug, $C_{20}H_{25}N_3O$, derived from lysergic acid.

ly·sin (lī'sĭn) *n.* A specific antibody that acts to destroy blood cells, tissues, or microorganisms.

–lysis. *comb. form.* Dissolving or decomposition: **hydrolysis.** [< Gk *lusis,* a loosing.]

–lyte. *comb. form.* A substance that can be decomposed by a specific process: **electrolyte.** [< Gk *luein,* to loosen.]

ă pat/ā ate/âr care/ä bar/b bib/ch chew/d deed/ĕ pet/ē be/f fit/g gag/h hat/hw what/
ĭ pit/ī pie/îr pier/j judge/k kick/l lid, fatal/m mum/n no, sudden/ng sing/ŏ pot/ō go/

Mm

m, M (ĕm) *n.* The 13th letter of the English alphabet.

m 1. male. 2. *Phys.* mass. 3. medium. 4. meter (measure). 5. milli-.

M 1. male. 2. *Phys.* mass. 3. medium. 4. mega-. 5. The Roman numeral for 1,000 (L *mille*).

m. 1. male. 2. medium. 3. mile.

M. 1. male. 2. master (in titles). 3. medium. 4. minim (liquid measure). 5. Monday.

ma (mä, mô) *n. Informal.* Mother. [Short for MAMA.]

M.A. 1. Master of Arts (L *Magister Artium*). 2. mental age.

Ma'am (măm). A contraction of *Madam.*

ma·ca·bre (mə-kä′brə, -bər) *adj.* Suggesting or concerned unduly with the horror of death; gruesome; ghastly.

mac·ad·am (mə-kăd′əm) *n.* A pavement of layers of compacted small stones bound with tar or asphalt. [< J. *McAdam* (1756–1836), Scottish engineer.] —**mac·ad′am·ize′** *v.* (**-ized, -izing**). —**mac·ad·am·iz′er** *n.*

mac·a·ro·ni (măk′ə-rō′nē) *pl.n.* Also **mac·ca·ro·ni.** Dried, usually tube-shaped pieces of pasta, prepared for eating by boiling. [< obs It *maccaroni.*]

mac·a·roon (măk′ə-rōōn′, măk′ə-rōōn′) *n.* A cooky made with almond paste or coconut. [< It *maccarone,* macaroni.]

Mac·Ar·thur (mək-är′thər), **Douglas.** 1880–1964. American General of the Army.

ma·caw (mə-kô′) *n.* A large, often brightly colored tropical American parrot. [Port *macaú.*]

mace¹ (mās) *n.* 1. A heavy medieval war club with a spiked metal head. 2. A ceremonial staff used as a symbol of authority. [< L *mateola,* rod, club.]

mace² (mās) *n.* A spice made from the seed covering of the nutmeg. [< Gk *makir,* an Indian spice.]

Mace (mās) *n.* **Chemical mace.**

Mac·e·do·ni·a (măs′ə-dō′nē-ə). 1. An ancient kingdom, N of Greece. 2. A Balkan region consisting of parts of Greece, Bulgaria, and Yugoslavia.

mac·er·ate (măs′ə-rāt′) *v.* **-ated, -ating.** 1. To soften by soaking or steeping in a liquid. 2. To separate into constituents by soaking. 3. To emaciate, usually by starvation. [L *mācerāre,* to soften.] —**mac′er·a′tion** *n.* —**mac′er·a′tor,** **mac′er·at′er** *n.*

mach. machine; machinery; machinist.

ma·chet·e (mə-shĕt′ē, -chĕt′ē) *n.* A large, broad-bladed knife used esp. for cutting vegetation. [< Span *macho,* ax, club.]

Mach·i·a·vel·li (măk′ē-ə-vĕl′ē), **Niccolò.** 1469–1527. Florentine statesman and political theorist. —**Mach′i·a·vel′li·an** *adj.*

mach·i·na·tion (măk′ĭ-nā′shən, măsh′ĭ-) *n.* 1. The act of plotting. 2. A hostile intrigue.

ma·chine (mə-shēn′) *n.* 1. a. Any system formed and connected to alter, transmit, and direct applied forces to accomplish a specific objective. b. A simple device, as a lever, pulley, or inclined plane, that alters an applied force. 2. Any system or device, as an electronic computer, that assists in the performance of a human task. 3. A powerful political group whose members appear to be under the control of one or more leaders. —*v.* **-chined, -chining.** To cut, shape, or finish by machine. [< Doric Gk *mākhos,* contrivance, means.]

machine gun. A gun that fires rapidly and repeatedly when the trigger is pressed.

ma·chin·er·y (mə-shē′nər-ē, -shēn′rē) *n., pl.* **-ies.** 1. Machines or machine parts collectively. 2. The working parts of a particular machine. 3. Any system of related elements that operates in a definable manner.

ma·chin·ist (mə-shē′nĭst) *n.* One who makes, operates, or repairs machines.

ma·chis·mo (mä-chēz′mō) *n.* An exaggerated sense of masculinity. [< Span *macho,* masculine, virile + -ISM.]

Mach number. Also **mach number.** The ratio of the speed of an object to the speed of sound in the surrounding medium. [< E. *Mach* (1836–1916), Austrian physicist.]

ma·cho (mä′chō) *adj.* Characterized by machismo. —*n.,pl.* **-chos.** 1. A male characterized by machismo. 2. Machismo. [Span]

mac·in·tosh. Variant of **mackintosh.**

Mac·ken·zie (mə-kĕn′zē). A river of NW Canada.

mack·er·el (măk′ər-əl, măk′rəl) *n., pl.* **-el** or **-els.** Any of several widely distributed marine food fishes. [< OF *maquerel.*]

mack·i·naw (măk′ə-nô′) *n.* A short coat of heavy woolen material, usually plaid. [< *Mackinac,* island in Michigan.]

mack·in·tosh (măk′ĭn-tŏsh′) *n.* Also **mac·in·tosh.** *Chiefly Brit.* A raincoat. [< C. *Macintosh* (1766–1843), Scottish chemist.]

macro-. *comb. form.* 1. Largeness or length in extent or size. 2. Abnormal largeness or over-development. [< Gk *makros,* large, long.]

mac·ro·cosm (măk′rō-kŏz′əm) *n.* 1. The universe itself or the concept of universe. 2. A system regarded as an entity containing subsystems. —**mac′ro·cos′mic** *adj.*

mac·ro·mol·e·cule (măk′rō-mŏl′ə-kyōōl) *n.*

A polymer, esp. one composed of more than 100 repeated monomers.

ma•cron (mā'krŏn', -krən) *n.* A mark (ˉ) placed above a vowel to indicate a long sound, as the (ā) in *make.* [< Gk *makros,* long.]

mac•ro•scop•ic (măk'rə-skŏp'ĭk) *adj.* Also **mac•ro•scop•i•cal** (-ĭ-kəl). **1.** Large enough to be perceived or examined without instrumentation, esp. as by the unaided eye. **2.** Pertaining to observations made without magnifying instruments, esp. as by the unaided eye. —**mac'ro•scop'i•cal•ly** *adv.*

mac•u•late (măk'yə-lāt') *v.* **-lated, -lating.** To spot, blemish, or pollute.

mad (măd) *adj.* **madder, maddest. 1.** Suffering from a disorder of the mind; insane. **2.** Marked by extreme excitement, confusion, or agitation; frantic: *a mad scramble for the bus.* **3.** *Informal.* Showing strong liking or enthusiasm: *mad about sports.* **4.** Angry; resentful. **5.** Lacking restraint or reason; wildly foolish. **6.** Affected by rabies. [< OE *gemād.* See **mei-**.] —**mad'ly** *adv.* —**mad'ness** *n.*

Mad•a•gas•car (măd'ə-găs'kər). An island in the Indian Ocean, coextensive with the Malagasy Republic.

Mad•am (măd'əm) *n.* **1.** *pl.* **Mesdames** (mā-däm'). A title of courtesy used as a form of address to a woman. **2. madam.** A woman who manages a brothel. [< MADAME.]

Mad•ame (măd'əm, mə-däm') *n., pl.* **Mesdames** (mā-däm'). **1.** The French title of courtesy for a married woman. **2.** A title of courtesy or distinction indicating rank or office: *Madame Ambassador.* [< OF *ma dame,* my lady.]

mad•cap (măd'kăp') *n.* A rash or impulsive person, especially a girl. —*adj.* Rash; impulsive; wild. [MAD + CAP.]

mad•den (măd'n) *v.* **1.** To make frantic or insane. **2.** To make or become angry.

mad•der (măd'ər) *n.* **1.** An Old World plant with small, yellow flowers and a red, fleshy root. **2.** A red dye obtained from the root of this plant. [< OE *mædere.*]

made (mād). *p.t. & p.p.* of **make.**

made-to-or•der (măd'tōō-ôr'dər) *adj.* Made in accordance with a customer's instructions; custom-made.

made-up (măd'ŭp') *adj.* **1.** Fabricated; fictitious; invented: *a made-up story.* **2.** Marked by the use of cosmetics or make-up: *a made-up actress.*

mad•house (măd'hous') *n.* **1.** An insane asylum. **2.** *Informal.* A place of great disorder.

Mad•i•son (măd'ĭ-sən). The capital of Wisconsin. Pop. 173,000.

Mad•i•son (măd'ĭ-sən), **James.** 1751–1836. 4th President of the U.S. (1809–17).

mad•man (măd'măn', -mən) *n.* **1.** An insane person. **2.** A frantic person.

Ma•don•na (mə-dŏn'ə) *n.* **1.** The Virgin Mary. **2.** An artistic representation of the Virgin Mary.

Ma•dras (mə-drăs', -dräs'). A city of SE India. Pop. 1,729,000.

ma•dras (măd'rəs, mə-drăs', -dräs') *n.* A fine cotton cloth, usually with a plaid or striped pattern. [< MADRAS.]

Ma•drid (mə-drĭd'). The capital of Spain. Pop. 2,559,000.

mad•ri•gal (măd'rĭ-gəl) *n.* **1.** An unaccompanied vocal composition for two or three voices in simple harmony. **2.** A polyphonic part song, usually unaccompanied. [< It *madriale,* "(piece) without accompaniment."]

mad•ri•lène (măd'rĭ-lĕn) *n.* Also **mad•ri•lene.** A consommé flavored with tomato, generally chilled. [< Span *madrileño,* of Madrid.]

mael•strom (māl'strəm) *n.* **1.** A whirlpool of extraordinary size or violence. **2.** A situation that resembles such a whirlpool in violence, turbulence, etc. [< Du *maelstrom,* "whirlstream."]

maes•tro (mīs'trō) *n., pl.* **-tros.** A master in any art, esp. music. [< L *magister,* master.]

mag. **,1.** magazine. **2.** magnetism. **3.** magnitude.

mag•a•zine (măg'ə-zēn', măg'ə-zēn') *n.* **1.** A place for storage, esp. of ammunition. **2.** A periodical containing articles, stories, etc. **3. a.** A compartment in some types of firearms for holding cartridges. **b.** A compartment in a camera for holding film. [< Ar *makhzan,* storehouse.]

Ma•gel•lan (mə-jĕl'ən), **Ferdinand.** 1480?–1521. Portuguese navigator; commander of Spanish expedition that was first to circumnavigate the world.

Ma•gen Da•vid (mä'gən dä'vĭd, mü'gən dŭ'vĭd). A six-pointed star, used as a symbol of Judaism. [Heb *māgen Dāwid,* shield of (King) David.]

ma•gen•ta (mə-jĕn'tə) *n.* Moderate to vivid purplish red. [< the battle of *Magenta* (1859).]

mag•got (măg'ət) *n.* The soft-bodied, wormlike larva of a fly, as the housefly. [ME *magot,* maked.] —**mag'got•y** *adj.*

Ma•gi (mā'jī') *pl.n.* The three wise men from the East who paid homage to the infant Jesus. [< L *magus,* sorcerer.]

mag•ic (măj'ĭk) *n.* **1.** The art that purports to produce supernatural effects, as with charms, spells, etc. **2.** Any mysterious or overpowering quality that lends enchantment. **3.** The exercise of sleight of hand, as for entertainment.

James Madison

[< OPers *maguš,* sorcerer.] —**mag′ic, mag′i•cal** *adj.* —**ma•gi′cian** (mə-jĭsh′ən) *n.*

mag•is•te•ri•al (măj′ĭs-tîr′ē-əl) *adj.* 1. Authoritative; commanding. 2. Of or pertaining to a magistrate or his functions. [< L *magister,* master.] —**mag′is•te′ri•al•ly** *adv.*

mag•is•trate (măj′ĭs-trāt′, -trĭt) *n.* A civil officer with power to administer the law. [< L *magister,* master.]

mag•ma (măg′mə, mäg′-) *n., pl.* **-mata** (măg′-mä′tə, mäg′-) or **-mas.** The molten matter under the earth's crust, from which igneous rock is formed by cooling. [< Gk, unguent.]

Mag•na Char•ta, Mag•na Car•ta (măg′nə kär′tə). The charter of English political and civil liberties granted in 1215.

mag•nan•i•mous (măg-năn′ə-məs) *adj.* Generous and noble in forgiving; above revenge or resentment. [L *magnanimus,* "great-souled."] —**mag′na•nim′i•ty** (-nə-nĭm′ĭ-tē) *n.* —**mag•nan′i•mous•ly** *adv.*

mag•nate (măg′nāt′) *n.* A powerful or influential man. [< L *magnus,* great.]

mag•ne•sia (măg-nē′zhə, -shə) *n.* **Magnesium oxide.** [< Gk *Magnēsia,* name of an area of Greece.] —**mag•ne′sian** *adj.*

mag•ne•si•um (măg-nē′zē-əm, -shəm) *n. Symbol* **Mg** A light, silvery, moderately hard metallic element used in structural alloys, pyrotechnics, flash photography, and incendiary bombs. Atomic number 12, atomic weight 24.312.

magnesium oxide. A white, powdery compound, MgO, having a high melting point and used in high-temperature refractories and electric insulation.

magnesium sulfate. A colorless crystalline compound, $MgSO_4$, used in fireproofing, matches, explosives, and fertilizers.

mag•net (măg′nĭt) *n.* 1. A body that attracts iron and certain other materials by virtue of a surrounding field of force produced by the motion of its atomic electrons and the alignment of its atoms. 2. Anything that attracts. [< Gk *Magnēs lithos,* "the Magnesian stone."]

mag•net•ic (măg-nĕt′ĭk) *adj.* 1. Of or relating to magnetism or magnets. 2. Having the properties of a magnet; exhibiting magnetism. 3. Relating to the magnetic poles of the earth. 4. Capable of being magnetized or of being attracted by a magnet. 5. Exerting attraction.

magnetic compass. An instrument using a magnetic needle to show direction relative to the earth's magnetic field.

magnetic field. A condition in a region of space established by the presence of a magnet or an electric current and characterized by the existence of a detectable magnetic force at every point in the region.

magnetic needle. A needle-shaped bar magnet usually suspended on a low-friction mounting and used in various instruments, esp. in the magnetic compass, to indicate the alignment of a local magnetic field.

magnetic north. The direction of the earth's magnetic pole, to which the north-seeking pole of a magnetic needle points when free from local magnetic influence.

magnetic pickup. A type of phonograph pickup that utilizes a coil in a magnetic field to convert motions of the stylus into electric impulses.

magnetic pole. 1. Either of two limited regions in a magnet at which the magnet's field is most intense. 2. Either of two variable points on the earth, close to but not coinciding with the geographic poles, where the earth's magnetic field is most intense.

magnetic recording. The recording of a signal, such as sound or computer instructions, in the form of a magnetic pattern.

magnetic storm. A severe but transitory fluctuation in the earth's magnetic field.

magnetic tape. A plastic tape coated with magnetic material for use in magnetic recording.

mag•net•ism (măg′nə-tĭz′əm) *n.* 1. The class of phenomena exhibited by the field of force produced by a magnet or electric current. 2. The study of magnets and their effects. 3. The force exerted by a magnetic field. 4. Power to attract.

mag•net•ite (măg′nə-tīt′) *n.* A magnetic black iron oxide, Fe_3O_4, an important ore of iron.

mag•net•ize (măg′nə-tīz′) *v.* **-ized, -izing.** 1. To make magnetic. 2. To attract. —**mag′net•i•za′tion** *n.* —**mag′net•iz′er** *n.*

mag•ne•to (măg-nē′tō) *n., pl.* **-tos.** A small generator of alternating current using permanent magnets, used in the ignition systems of some internal-combustion engines.

mag•ni•fi•ca•tion (măg′nĭ-fĭ-kā′shən) *n.* 1. a. The act of magnifying or state of being magnified. b. The process of enlarging the size of something, as an optical image. c. Something magnified; an enlarged representation, image, or model. 2. *Opt.* The ratio of image size to object size.

mag•nif•i•cent (măg-nĭf′ĭ-sənt) *adj.* 1. Splendid; lavish; sumptuous. 2. Noble in thought or deed; exalted. 3. Impressive. [< L *magnificus,* "great in deeds."] —**mag•nif′i•cence** *n.* —**mag•nif′i•cent•ly** *adv.*

mag•ni•fi•er (măg′nĭ-fī′ər) *n.* A magnifying glass or other system of components that magnifies.

mag•ni•fy (măg′nĭ-fī′) *v.* **-fied, -fying.** 1. To make greater in size; enlarge. 2. To exaggerate. 3. To increase the apparent size of, esp. by means of a lens. 4. To glorify. [< L *magnificāre,* to make great.]

magnifying glass. A converging lens that enlarges the image of an object.

mag•ni•tude (măg′nĭ-t/y/ōōd′) *n.* 1. Greatness in size, extent, or significance. 2. Size; quantity. 3. The relative brightness of a celestial body designated on a numerical scale, where 6 denotes faint visibility and decreases of 1 unit represent an increase in apparent brightness by a factor of 2.512. [< L *magnus,* great.]

mag•no•lia (măg-nōl′yə) *n.* A tree or shrub with large, showy, usually white or pinkish flowers. [< P. *Magnol* (1638–1715), French botanist.]

mag•pie (măg′pī) *n.* A long-tailed, loud-

ô paw, for/oi boy/ou out/ŏŏ took/ōō coo/p pop/r run/s sauce/sh shy/t to/th thin/*th* the/
ŭ cut/ûr fur/v van/w wag/y yes/z size/zh vision/ə ago, item, edible, gallop, circus/

voiced, chiefly black and white bird related to the crows and jays.

Mag·yar (măg'yär', mäg'-) *n.* Hungarian. —**Mag'yar** *adj.*

ma·ha·ra·jah, ma·ha·ra·ja (mä'hə-rä'jä, -zhä) *n.* A king or prince in India. [< Sk *mahārājā,* "great king."]

ma·ha·ra·ni, ma·ha·ra·nee (mä'hə-rä'nē) *n.* A queen or princess in India. [< Sk *mahārājnī,* "great queen."]

ma·hat·ma (mä-hät'mä, mə-hät'mə) *n.* 1. One venerated for great knowledge and love of humanity. 2. **Mahatma.** A Hindu title of respect for a man renowned for spirituality. [Sk *mahātman,* "great soul."]

Mah·di (mä'dē). The Islamic messiah.

Ma·hi·can (mə-hē'kən) *n., pl.* **-can** or **-cans.** Also **Mo·hi·can** (mō-hē'kən, mə-). A member of a tribe or confederacy of Algonquian-speaking Indians that formerly lived in N New York State.

mah·jong (mä'zhŏng', -zhông') *n.* Also **mah·jongg.** A game of Chinese origin played with tiles resembling dominoes.

ma·hog·a·ny (mə-hŏg'ə-nē) *n., pl.* **-nies.** 1. A tropical American tree with hard, reddish-brown wood. 2. The wood of such a tree. 3. Any of several similar trees or their wood.

ma·hout (mə-hout') *n.* The keeper and driver of an elephant. [< Sk *mahāmātra,* "of great measure."]

maid (mād) *n.* 1. A girl or an unmarried woman. 2. A female servant. [< MAIDEN.]

maid·en (mād'n) *n.* An unmarried girl or woman. —*adj.* 1. Of, pertaining to, or befitting a maiden. 2. First or earliest: *a maiden voyage.* [< OE *mægden.* See maghu-.] —**maid'en·hood'** *n.* —**maid'en·ly** *adj.*

maid·en·hair (mād'n-hâr') *n.* A fern having feathery fronds with fan-shaped leaflets.

maid of honor *pl.* **maids of honor.** The chief unmarried female attendant of a bride.

Mai·du (mī'dōō) *n., pl.* **-du** or **-dus.** 1. A member of a Penutian-speaking Indian tribe, formerly living in the Sacramento Valley area of California. 2. The language of this tribe. [Maidu, "man."] —**Mai'du** *adj.*

mail[1] (māl) *n.* 1. a. Letters, packages, etc., handled by a postal system. b. Postal material for a specific person or organization. 2. A postal system. —*v.* To send by mail. [< OF *male,* pouch, bag.] —**mail'er** *n.*

mail[2] (māl) *n.* Armor made of small overlapping metal rings, loops of chain, or scales. [< L *macula,* spot, mesh.]

mail·box (māl'bŏks') *n.* 1. A public box for deposit of outgoing mail. 2. A private box for incoming mail.

mail·man (māl'măn', -mən) *n.* One who delivers mail.

maim (mām) *v.* 1. To mutilate; disable; cripple. 2. To impair. [< OF *mahaignier,* to wound.]

main (mān) *adj.* 1. Most important; principal; major. 2. Exerted to the utmost; sheer; utter. —*n.* 1. The principal part or point. 2. The principal pipe or conduit in a utility system. 3. Physical strength: *might and main.* [< OE

mægen, strength. See magh-.] —**main'ly** *adv.*

Maine (mān). A state of the NE U.S. Pop. 994,000. Cap. Augusta.

main·land (mān'lănd', -lənd) *n.* The principal land mass of a country or continent.

main·mast (mān'məst) *n.* The principal mast of a vessel.

main·sail (mān'səl) *n.* The principal sail of a vessel, as one set from the mainmast.

main·spring (mān'sprĭng') *n.* 1. The principal spring in a mechanical device, esp. in a watch or clock. 2. A chief motivating force.

main·stay (mān'stā') *n.* 1. A rope that supports a mainmast. 2. A principal support.

main·stream (mān'strēm') *n.* The prevailing direction of a movement or influence.

main·tain (mān-tān') *v.* 1. To continue; carry on. 2. To preserve or retain. 3. To keep in repair. 4. To provide for; support. 5. To defend or sustain. 6. To assert or declare. [< L *manū tenēre,* "to hold in the hand."] —**main'te·nance** (mān'tə-nəns) *n.*

main top·sail (tŏp'səl). The sail that is set above the mainsail.

maî·tre d'hô·tel (mě'tr' dō-tĕl') *pl.* **maîtres d'hôtel** (mě'tr' dō-tĕl'). 1. A head steward. 2. A headwaiter. [F, "master of hotel."]

maize (māz) *n.* Corn. [< Taino *mahiz.*]

Maj. major.

maj·es·ty (măj'ĭs-tē) *n., pl.* **-ties.** 1. Sovereign greatness, power, and authority. 2. **Majesty.** A title used in speaking of or to a monarch: *at His Majesty's request.* 3. Regal dignity, splendor, and grandeur. [< L *mājestās,* authority, grandeur.] —**ma·jes'tic** (mə-jĕs'tĭk) *adj.*

Maj. Gen. major general.

ma·jor (mā'jər) *adj.* 1. Greater in importance, rank, or extent. 2. Serious or dangerous: *a major illness.* 3. *Mus.* Of or based on a major scale. —*n.* 1. A military officer ranking next above a captain. 2. a. The principal field of specialization of a college student. b. A student specializing in such a field. —*v.* To pursue academic studies in a major field. [< L *mājor,* greater.]

ma·jor·do·mo (mā'jər-dō'mō) *n., pl.* **-mos.** A head steward or butler. [< ML *mājor domūs,* "head of the house."]

major general. A military officer who ranks next above a brigadier general.

ma·jor·i·ty (mə-jôr'ĭ-tē, mə-jŏr'-) *n., pl.* **-ties.** 1. The greater number or part of something. 2. a. A number more than half of a total. b. The number of votes cast in any election above the total of all other votes cast. 3. The status of legal age.

major scale. *Mus.* A diatonic scale having half steps between the 3rd and 4th and the 7th and 8th tones.

make (māk) *v.* **made, making.** 1. To create; construct; form; shape. 2. To cause to be, become, or seem. 3. To compel. 4. To appoint. 5. To perform. 6. To do; execute. 7. To arrive at. 8. To acquire. 9. To achieve; attain. 10. To prepare. 11. To provide. 12. To develop into. 13. To admit of being transformed into. 14. To constitute. 15. To behave or act in a specified manner. 16. To set out; proceed.

ă pat/ā ate/âr care/ä bar/b bib/ch chew/d deed/ĕ pet/ē be/f fit/g gag/h hat/hw what/
ĭ pit/ī pie/îr pier/j judge/k kick/l lid, fatal/m mum/n no, sudden/ng sing/ŏ pot/ō go/

—**make away with.** To carry off, esp. to steal.
—**make out. 1.** To discern or see, esp. with difficulty. **2.** To comprehend. **3.** To write out or draw up. **4.** To attempt to prove or imply. **5.** *Slang.* To get along; succeed. **6.** *Slang.* To neck; pet. —*n.* **1.** The style or manner in which a thing is made. **2.** A specific line of manufactured goods. **3.** The physical or moral nature of a person. **4.** The yield or output, as of a factory. [< OE *macian.* See **mag-.**] —**mak'er** *n.*

make believe. To feign; pretend.

make-be·lieve (māk'bĭ-lēv') *n.* **1.** Playful pretense. **2.** *Psychol.* A tendency to live in a world of fantasy. —**make'-be·lieve'** *adj.*

make·shift (māk'shĭft') *n.* A temporary or expedient substitute. —**make'shift'** *adj.*

make up. 1. To construct. **2.** To arrange or organize. **3.** To apply cosmetics. **4.** To decide. **5.** To constitute; amount to. **6.** To invent or improvise. **7.** To compensate for; fill a deficiency. **8.** To resolve a personal difference.

make-up (māk'ŭp') *n.* Also **make·up. 1.** The way in which something is arranged or constructed. **2.** One's constitution, temperament, or disposition. **3.** Cosmetics.

mal-. *comb. form.* Bad, badly, or wrongly. [< L *malus,* bad.]

Mal. 1. Malachi (Old Testament). **2.** Malay; Malayan.

Ma·la·bo (mə-lä'bō). The capital of Equatorial Guinea. Pop. 38,000.

mal·ad·just·ment (măl'ə-jŭst'mənt) *n.* **1.** Faulty adjustment, as in a machine. **2.** Inability to adjust personality needs to environmental demands. —**mal·ad·just'ed** *adj.*

mal·a·droit (măl'ə-droit') *adj.* **1.** Awkward; clumsy. **2.** Tactless. —**mal'a·droit'ly** *adv.*

mal·a·dy (măl'ə-dē) *n., pl.* **-dies.** A disease, disorder, or ailment. [< L *male habitus,* "ill-kept."]

Mal·a·gas·y (măl'ə-găs'ē) *n.* **1.** A native of the Malagasy Republic. **2.** The language spoken in the Malagasy Republic. —**Mal'a·gas'y** *adj.*

Malagasy Republic. A country occupying the island of Madagascar. Pop. 5,862,000. Cap. Tananarive.

mal·aise (măl-āz') *n.* A feeling of illness or depression. [F.]

mal·a·prop·ism (măl'ə-prŏp-ĭz'əm) *n.* A humorous misuse of a word. [< Mrs. *Malaprop* in Sheridan's play *The Rivals* < MALA-PROPOS.]

ma·lar·i·a (mə-lâr'ē-ə) *n.* A disease characterized by cycles of chills, fever, and sweating, transmitted by the bite of an infected mosquito. [It *mal'aria,* foul air.] —**ma·lar'i·al, ma·lar'i·an, ma·lar'i·ous** *adj.*

ma·lar·key (mə-lär'kē) *n.* Also **ma·lar·ky.** *Slang.* Nonsense. [?]

Ma·la·wi (mə-lä'wē). A republic of SE Africa. Pop. 4,530,000. Cap. Lilongwe.

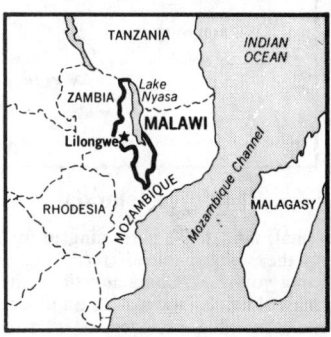

Malawi

Ma·lay (mā'lā', mə-lā') *n.* **1.** One of a people inhabiting the Malay Peninsula, other parts of Malaysia, Indonesia, and some adjacent areas. **2.** The language of the Malays. —*adj.* **1.** Of or pertaining to the Malays or their language. **2.** Of or pertaining to Malaysia. —**Ma·lay'an** *adj. & n.*

Mal·a·ya·lam (măl'ə-yä'ləm) *n.* A Dravidian language spoken in SW India.

Malay Archipelago. A group of islands in the Indian and Pacific Oceans, including Sumatra, Java, Borneo, and other islands.

Malay Peninsula. A peninsula of SE Asia.

Ma·lay·sia (mə-lā'zhə, -shə). A country of SE

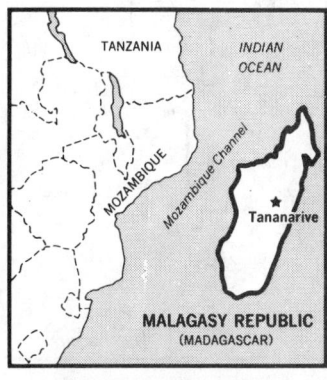

Malagasy Republic

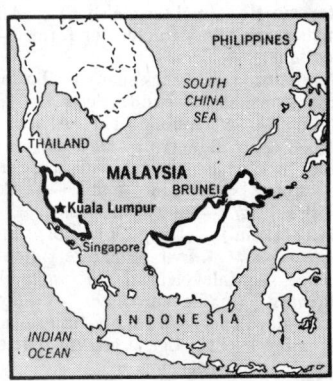

Malaysia

ô paw, for/oi boy/ou out/ŏŏ took/ōō coo/p pop/r run/s sauce/sh shy/t to/th thin/*th* the/
ŭ cut/ûr fur/v van/w wag/y yes/z size/zh vision/ə ago, item, edible, gallop, circus/

Asia. Pop. 9,137,000. Cap. Kuala Lumpur.
—Ma·lay'sian *adj. & n.*

mal·con·tent (măl'kən-tĕnt') *adj.* Discontented. —*n.* A discontented person.

Mal·dive Islands (măl'dīv'). A sultanate in the Indian Ocean. Pop. 96,000. Cap. Malé.

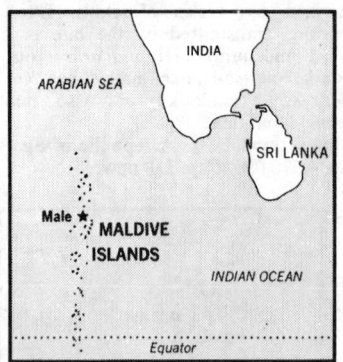

Maldive Islands

male (māl) *adj.* **1.** Of, pertaining to, or designating the sex capable of fertilizing ova or begetting young. **2.** Characteristic of the male sex; masculine. **3.** Designating an object, such as an electric plug, designed for insertion into a fitted bore or socket. —*n.* One that is male. [< L *masculus,* dim of *mas,* male.]

Ma·lé (mä'lā). The capital of the Maldive Islands. Pop. 11,000.

mal·e·dic·tion (măl'ə-dĭk'shən) *n.* **1.** A curse. **2.** Slander; calumny.

mal·e·fac·tor (măl'ə-făk'tər) *n.* **1.** A criminal. **2.** One who does evil. [< L *malefacere,* to do wrong.] —**mal'e·fac'tion** *n.*

ma·lef·ic (mə-lĕf'ĭk) *adj.* **1.** Baleful. **2.** Malicious. [L *maleficus,* wrongdoing.]

ma·lev·o·lent (mə-lĕv'ə-lənt) *adj.* **1.** Having or exhibiting ill will or malice. **2.** Having an evil influence. [L *malevolēns.*] —**ma·lev'o·lence** *n.* —**ma·lev'o·lent·ly** *adv.*

mal·fea·sance (măl-fē'zəns) *n.* Wrongdoing, esp. if contrary to official obligations. [MAL- + OF *faisance,* doing.] —**mal·fea'sant** *adj. & n.*

mal·for·ma·tion (măl'fôr-mā'shən) *n.* An abnormal or irregular structure or form. —**mal·formed'** *adj.*

mal·func·tion (măl-fŭngk'shən) *v.* To fail to function normally. —**mal·func'tion** *n.*

Ma·li (mä'lē). A republic of W Africa. Pop. 4,485,000. Cap. Bamako. —**Ma'li** *adj.*

mal·ice (măl'ĭs) *n.* Ill will with a desire to harm; spite. [< L *malus,* bad.] —**ma·li'cious** (mə-lĭsh'əs) *adj.* —**ma·li'cious·ly** *adv.*

ma·lign (mə-līn') *v.* To speak evil of; slander; defame. —*adj.* **1.** Evil in nature, intent, or influence. **2.** Malevolent. [< L *malus,* bad.]

ma·lig·nant (mə-lĭg'nənt) *adj.* **1.** Showing great malevolence. **2.** Highly injurious. **3.** Designating a pathological growth that tends to spread. —**ma·lig'nan·cy** *n.*

ma·lig·ni·ty (mə-lĭg'nə-tē) *n., pl.* **-ties. 1. a.** Intense ill will; great malice. **b.** An instance of

great malice. **2.** The quality of being highly evil or injurious.

ma·lin·ger (mə-lĭng'gər) *v.* To feign illness to avoid duty or work. [< OF *malingre.*] —**ma·lin'ger·er** *n.*

mall (môl, măl) *n.* **1.** A shady public walk or promenade. **2.** A street lined with shops and closed to vehicles. **3.** A median strip dividing a road or highway. [< The *Mall,* a tree-lined street in London.]

mal·lard (măl'ərd) *n.* A wild duck of which the male has a green head and neck. [< OF *mallart.*]

mal·le·a·ble (măl'ē-ə-bəl) *adj.* **1.** Capable of being shaped or formed, as by hammering or pressure. **2.** Tractable; pliable. [< ML *malleāre,* to hammer.] —**mal'le·a·bil'i·ty** *n.* —**mal'le·a·bly** *adv.*

mal·let (măl'ĭt) *n.* **1.** A short-handled hammer, usually with a cylindrical wooden head, used chiefly to drive a chisel or wedge. **2.** A longer-handled hammer, as for use in croquet and polo. [< L *malleus,* hammer.]

mal·le·us (măl'ē-əs) *n., pl.* **mallei** (măl'ē-ī', -ē-ē'). The largest of three small bones in the middle ear.

mal·low (măl'ō) *n.* Any of various related plants usually having pink or white, often showy flowers. [< L *malva.*]

mal·nour·ished (măl-nûr'ĭsht) *adj.* Suffering from improper nutrition or insufficient food.

mal·nu·tri·tion (măl'n/y/ōō-trĭsh'ən) *n.* Poor nutrition, esp. because of insufficient or poorly balanced diet.

mal·oc·clu·sion (măl'ə-klōō'zhən) *n.* Faulty closure of teeth.

mal·o·dor·ous (măl-ō'dər-əs) *adj.* Having a bad odor; ill-smelling. —**mal·o'dor·ous·ly** *adv.* —**mal·o'dor·ous·ness** *n.*

mal·prac·tice (măl-prăk'tĭs) *n.* Improper or negligent conduct or treatment, esp. by a physician. —**mal'prac·ti'tion·er** *n.*

malt (môlt) *n.* **1.** Soaked, sprouted, and dried grain, usually barley, used chiefly in brewing and distilling. **2.** Any alcoholic beverage brewed from malt. [< OE *mealt.* See mel-.]

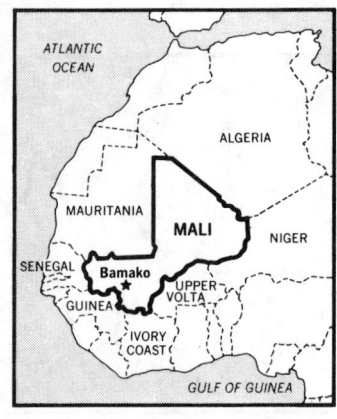

Mali

Mal•ta (môl'tə). An island nation in the Mediterranean. Pop. 324,000. Cap. Valletta.

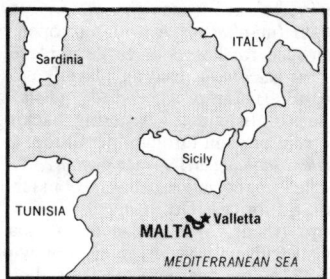

Malta

Mal•tese (môl-tēz', -tēs') *adj.* Pertaining to Malta, its inhabitants, or the language spoken in Malta. —*n., pl.* **-tese.** **1.** A native of Malta. **2.** The language of Malta, a dialect of North Arabic with elements of Italian.

mal•tose (môl'tōs', -tōz') *n.* A sugar, $C_{12}H_{22}O_{11} \cdot H_2O$. [< MALT + -OSE.]

mal•treat (măl-trēt') *v.* To treat cruelly; handle roughly. —**mal•treat′ment** *n.*

ma•ma (mä'mə, mə-mä') *n.* Also **mam•ma.** *Informal.* Mother. [Baby talk.]

mam•ba (mäm'bə) *n.* A venomous tropical African snake.

mam•mal (măm'əl) *n.* Any of a group of warm-blooded vertebrate animals, including man, characterized by the presence of hair and by milk-producing glands in the females. [< L *mamma,* breast.] —**mam•mal′i•an** (mă-mā'lē-ən) *adj. & n.*

mam•ma•ry (măm'ər-ē) *adj.* Of or pertaining to a breast or milk-producing organ.

mam•mo•gram (măm'ə-grăm') *n.* An x-ray photograph or radiograph of the breast. [L *mamma,* breast + -GRAM.]

mam•mog•ra•phy (mə-mŏg'rə-fē) *n.* Examination of the breast by x-rays in order to detect tumors before they can be felt by hand. [L *mamma,* breast +-GRAPHY.]

mam•mon (măm'ən) *n.* Also **Mam•mon.** Money personified as a false god. [< Aram *māmōnā,* riches.]

mam•moth (măm'əth) *n.* An extinct elephant that formerly existed throughout the N Hemisphere. —*adj.* Huge; gigantic. [Obs Russ *mammot'.*]

man (măn) *n., pl.* **men** (mĕn). **1.** An adult male human being. **2.** A human being; a person. **3.** Mankind. **4.** A male human being having qualities considered characteristic of manhood. **5.** A husband, lover, or sweetheart. **6.** Any workman, servant, or subordinate. **7.** Any of the pieces used in board games, as chess. —*v.* **manned, manning.** **1.** To supply or furnish with men for defense, service, etc. **2.** To strengthen; fortify. [< OE *mann.* See man-.]

Man, Isle of (măn). A British island between Britain and Ireland. —**Manx** *adj. & n.*

Man. Manitoba.

man•a•cle (măn'ə-kəl) *n.* **1.** Often **manacles.** A restraining device, as handcuffs, for the hands. **2.** Anything that confines or restrains. —*v.* **-cled, -cling.** To restrain with manacles. [< L *manicula,* little hand, handle.]

man•age (măn'ĭj) *v.* **-aged, -aging.** **1.** To direct, control, or handle. **2.** To administer or regulate. **3.** To make submissive. **4.** To contrive or arrange. **5.** To get along. [Prob < VL *manidiāre,* to handle.] —**man′age•a•ble** *adj.* —**man′age•a•bil′i•ty** *n.* —**man′age•a•bly** *adv.*

man•age•ment (măn'ĭj-mənt) *n.* **1.** The act or practice of managing. **2.** The person or persons who manage a business. **3.** Skill in managing.

man•ag•er (măn'ĭj-ər) *n.* **1.** One who manages. **2.** One in charge of the business affairs or training of a person or group. —**man′a•ger′i•al** (măn'ə-jîr'ē-əl) *adj.*

Ma•na•gua (mä-nä'gwä). The capital of Nicaragua. Pop. 275,000.

ma•ña•na (mä-nyä'nä) *n.* Some indefinite time in the future. [Span, tomorrow.]

man•a•tee (măn'ə-tē') *n.* A large aquatic mammal of warm Atlantic coastal waters. [Span *manati.*]

Man•ches•ter (măn'chĕs'tər, -chĭs-tər). A city of NW England. Pop. 638,000.

Man•chu (măn'chōō, măn-chōō') *n., pl.* **-chu** or **-chus.** **1.** One of a nomadic Mongoloid people, native to Manchuria, who ruled China from 1644 to 1911. **2.** The Tungusic language of the Manchu. —**Man′chu** *adj.*

Man•chu•ri•a (măn-chōōr'ē-ə). The northernmost region and administrative division of China. —**Man•chu′ri•an** *adj. & n.*

Manchuria

man•da•rin (măn'də-rĭn) *n.* **1.** In imperial China, a high-ranking public official. **2. Mandarin. a. Mandarin Chinese. b.** In imperial China, the dialect used by mandarins and other officials of the empire. [< Sk *mantrin,* counselor.]

Mandarin Chinese. The national language of China, based on the principal dialect spoken in the area around Peking.

man•date (măn'dāt') *n.* **1.** An authoritative command or instruction. **2.** The wishes of a political electorate, expressed to its representatives. **3. a.** A commission from the League of Nations authorizing a nation to administer a territory. **b.** Any region under such administration. [< L *mandāre*, to command.]

man·da·to·ry (măn′də-tôr′ē, -tōr′ē) *adj.* **1.** Of or pertaining to a mandate. **2.** Required; obligatory.

Man·de (măn′dā) *n., pl.* **-de** or **-des.** **1.** A people of W Africa in the upper Niger valley. **2.** A branch of the Niger-Congo language family.

man·di·ble (măn′də-bəl) *n.* A jaw or jawlike part, esp. the lower jaw in vertebrates. [< L *mandere*, to chew.] —**man·dib′u·lar** (măn-dĭb′-yə-lər) *adj.*

Man·din·go (măn-dĭng′gō) *n., pl.* **-gos** or **-goes.** **1.** A member of any of various Negroid peoples inhabiting the region of the upper Niger River valley of W Africa. **2.** Any language or dialect of the Mandingos.

man·do·lin (măn′də-lĭn, măn′də-lĭn′) *n.* A stringed musical instrument with a usually pear-shaped wooden body and a fretted neck. [< It *mandola, mandora*, lute.]

man·drag·o·ra (măn-drăg′ə-rə) *n. Chiefly Poetic.* The mandrake or a narcotic prepared from it.

man·drake (măn′drāk′) *n.* **1.** A Eurasian plant with a branched root thought to resemble the human body and believed to have magical powers. **2.** The **May apple.** [< Gk *mandragoras.*]

man·drel, man·dril (măn′drəl) *n.* **1.** A spindle or axle used to secure or support material being machined or milled. **2.** A shaft on which a working tool is mounted. [Prob < F *mandrin*, a lathe.]

man·drill (măn′drĭl) *n.* A large African monkey with brilliantly colored markings on the face and buttocks. [MAN + DRILL.]

mane (mān) *n.* The long hair growing from the neck of a horse, male lion, etc. [< OE *manu.* See **mon-**.]

ma·nège (mă-nĕzh′) *n.* Also **ma·nege.** The art of training or managing horses. [< It *maneggiare*, to manage.]

ma·nes, Ma·nes (mā′nēz, mä′nās) *pl.n.* **1.** The deified spirits of the dead. **2.** *(takes sing. v.).* Any revered spirit of one who has died. [L *mānēs*, prob "the good ones."]

Ma·net (mȧ-nā′), **Edouard.** 1832–1883. French painter.

ma·neu·ver (mə-n/y/o͞o′vər). Also *chiefly Brit.* **ma·noeu·vre.** *n.* **1. a.** A strategic or tactical military movement. **b.** Often **maneuvers.** A large-scale military training exercise simulating combat. **2. a.** A procedure requiring skill. **b.** A controlled change in the path of a vehicle. **3.** A stratagem. —*v.* **1.** To perform a military maneuver. **2.** To change tactics. **3.** To scheme. **4.** To manipulate into a desired position. [< L *manū operārī*, to work by hand.] —**ma·neu′ver·a·bil′i·ty** *n.*

man·ful (măn′fəl) *adj.* Displaying manly qualities; brave and resolute. —**man′ful·ly** *adv.* —**man′ful·ness** *n.*

man·ga·nese (măng′gə-nēz′, -nēs′) *n. Symbol* **Mn** A gray-white, brittle metallic element, alloyed with steel to increase strength, hardness, wear resistance, and other properties. Atomic number 25, atomic weight 54.9380. [< It.]

mange (mānj) *n.* A skin disease, esp. of animals, caused by parasitic mites and characterized by itching and loss of hair. [< OF *mangier*, to eat.] —**man′gy** *adj.*

man·ger (mān′jər) *n.* A trough or open box in which feed for horses or cattle is placed. [< VL **mandūcātōria*, feeding place.]

man·gle¹ (măng′gəl) *v.* **-gled, -gling. 1.** To mutilate or disfigure by battering, hacking, etc. **2.** To ruin or spoil through ineptitude. [< NF *mangler, mahangler.*] —**man′gler** *n.*

man·gle² (măng′gəl) *n.* A laundry machine for pressing fabrics. [Du *mangel.*]

man·go (măng′gō) *n., pl.* **-goes** or **-gos. 1.** A tropical fruit with sweet, juicy, yellow-orange flesh. **2.** A tree bearing such fruit. [< Tamil *mānkāy.*]

man·grove (măn′grōv′, măng′grōv′) *n.* A tropical evergreen tree that has stiltlike roots and forms dense thickets along tidal shores. [< Port *mangue.*]

man·han·dle (măn′hăn′dəl) *v.* To handle roughly. —**man′han′dler** *n.*

Man·hat·tan¹ (măn-hăt′n, mən-) *n., pl.* **-tan** or **-tans.** A member of a tribe of Algonquian-speaking Indians, formerly inhabiting the area that is now roughly New York City.

Man·hat·tan² (măn-hăt′n, mən-). A borough of New York City. Pop. 1,698,000.

man·hole (măn′hōl′) *n.* A hole through which one enters a sewer, boiler, etc.

man·hood (măn′ho͝od) *n.* **1.** The state or condition of being an adult male. **2.** The composite of manly qualities, as courage and determination. **3.** Men collectively.

man-hour (măn′our′) *n., pl.* **man-hours.** A unit equal to the work a man can produce in one hour.

man·hunt (măn′hŭnt′) *n., pl.* **manhunts.** An organized search for someone, esp. a fugitive criminal.

ma·ni·a (mā′nē-ə, mān′yə) *n.* **1.** An inordinately intense enthusiasm; craze. **2.** A manifestation of manic-depressive psychosis. [< Gk.] —**man′ic** (măn′ĭk) *adj.*

–mania. *comb. form.* An exaggerated desire for, pleasure in, or excitement induced by (something): **monomania.**

In the following list, the English meaning is indicated for the form with which **-mania** is combined:

acromania (heights)
ailuromania (cats)
cynomania (dogs)
gymnomania (nudity)
hedonomania (pleasure)
heliomania (sunbathing)
hippomania (horses)
hypnomania (sleep)
necromania (death)
noctimania (night)
ochlomania (crowds)
ophidiomania (reptiles)
ornithomania (birds)
pharmacomania (medicines)
sitomania (food)
xenomania (foreigners)
zoomania (animals)

ă pat/ā ate/âr care/ä bar/b bib/ch chew/d deed/ĕ pet/ē be/f fit/g gag/h hat/hw what/ ĭ pit/ī pie/îr pier/j judge/k kick/l lid, fatal/m mum/n no, sudden/ng sing/ŏ pot/ō go/

ma·ni·ac (mā′nē-ăk′) *n.* **1.** An insane person; lunatic. **2.** One who has an excessive enthusiasm for something. —**ma′ni·ac′, ma·ni′a·cal** (mə-nī′ə-kəl) *adj.*

man·ic-de·pres·sive (măn′ĭk-dĭ-prĕs′ĭv) *adj.* Of or afflicted with a psychosis in which periods of manic excitation alternate with melancholic depression. —*n.* A person so afflicted.

man·i·cure (măn′ĭ-kyŏŏr′) *n.* Treatment of the hands and fingernails. —*v.* **-cured, -curing. 1.** To care for (the fingernails). **2.** To trim closely. [F, "hand care."] —**man′i·cur′ist** *n.*

man·i·fest (măn′ə-fĕst′) *adj.* Clearly apparent, esp. to the sight; obvious. —*v.* **1.** To show plainly; reveal. **2.** To be evidence of; prove. —*n.* A list of cargo or passengers. [< L *manifestus*, palpable, "grasped by hand."]

man·i·fes·ta·tion (măn′ə-fĕs-tā′shən) *n.* **1.** A demonstration or display. **2.** One of the forms in which someone or something, such as a divine being or an idea, is revealed.

man·i·fes·to (măn′ə-fĕs′tō) *n., pl.* **-toes** or **-tos.** A public declaration of principles or intentions.

man·i·fold (măn′ə-fōld) *adj.* **1.** Of many kinds; varied. **2.** Having many forms. **3.** Consisting of or operating several of one kind. —*n.* **1.** One of many copies. **2.** A pipe having apertures for multiple connections. —*v.* **1.** To make several copies of. **2.** To multiply.

man·i·kin, man·ni·kin (măn′ĭ-kĭn) *n.* **1.** A little man; dwarf. **2.** An anatomical model of the human body, as used in medical study. **3.** A mannequin. [MDu *mannekīn*.]

Ma·nil·a (mə-nĭl′ə). The largest city of the Philippines. Pop. 1,139,000.

ma·nip·u·late (mə-nĭp′yə-lāt′) *v.* **-lated, -lating. 1.** To handle or control skillfully. **2.** To influence or manage shrewdly or deviously. [< L *manipulus*, handful.] —**ma·nip′u·la′tion** *n.* —**ma·nip′u·la′tor** *n.*

Man·i·to·ba (măn′ĭ-tō′bə). A province of C Canada. Pop. 958,000. Cap. Winnipeg.

man·kind. *n.* **1.** (măn′kīnd′, -kīnd′). The human race. **2.** (măn′kīnd′). Men as distinguished from women.

man·ly (măn′lē) *adj.* **-lier, -liest.** Having the admirable qualities attributed to a man. —**man′li·ness** *n.*

man·made (măn′mād′) *adj.* Made by man; not of natural origin.

Mann (män), **Thomas.** 1875–1955. German author.

man·na (măn′ə) *n.* **1.** The food miraculously provided for the Israelites in the wilderness. Exodus 16:14–36. **2.** Something of value received unexpectedly. [Aram *mannā.*]

man·ne·quin (măn′ĭ-kĭn) *n.* **1.** A representation of the human body, used for displaying clothes. **2.** A woman who models clothes. [< MDu *mannekīn*, MANIKIN.]

man·ner (măn′ər) *n.* **1.** A way of doing something. **2.** One's natural bearing or behavior. **3. manners. a.** Social behavior. **b.** Polite social behavior. **4.** A style or method in the arts. **5.** Kind or sort. [< VL **manuāria*, "way of handling."]

man·nered (măn′ərd) *adj.* **1.** Having manners of a specific kind: *ill-mannered.* **2.** Artificial or affected.

man·ner·ism (măn′ər-ĭz′əm) *n.* **1.** A distinctive behavioral trait; idiosyncrasy. **2.** Exaggerated or affected style or habit.

man·ner·ly (măn′ər-lē) *adj.* Polite; well-behaved.

man·ni·kin. Variant of **manikin.**

man·nish (măn′ĭsh) *adj.* Of, befitting, or resembling a man. —**man′nish·ly** *adv.* —**man′nish·ness** *n.*

ma·noeu·vre. *Chiefly Brit.* Variant of **maneuver.**

man-of-war (măn′ə-wôr′) *n., pl.* **men-of-war. 1.** A warship. **2.** See **Portuguese man-of-war.**

man·or (măn′ər) *n.* **1.** The estate of a feudal lord. **2.** Any landed estate. **3.** The main house on any estate; mansion. [< L *manēre*, to dwell, remain.] —**ma·no′ri·al** (mă-nôr′ē-əl, mă-nōr′-) *adj.*

man·pow·er (măn′pou′ər) *n.* **1.** The power of human strength. **2.** The men available to a particular group or required for a particular task.

man·qué (mäN-kā′) *adj.* Unfulfilled; frustrated: *an artist manqué.* [F < It *manco*, lacking, defective.]

man·sard (măn′särd) *n.* A roof having two slopes on all four sides, with the lower slope steeper than the upper. [< F. *Mansart* (1598–1666), French architect.]

manse (măns) *n.* A clergyman's residence. [< L *manēre*, to dwell, remain.]

man·sion (măn′shən) *n.* A large, stately house. [< L *mānsiō*, dwelling.]

man·slaugh·ter (măn′slô′tər) *n.* The unlawful killing of someone without premeditation.

man·tel (măn′təl) *n.* Also **man·tle. 1.** A facing around a fireplace. **2.** A mantelpiece. [< L *mantellum*, MANTLE.]

man·tel·piece (măn′təl-pēs′) *n.* Also **man·tle·piece.** The shelf over a fireplace.

man·til·la (măn-tē′yə, -tĭl′ə) *n.* A scarf, usually of lace, worn over the head and shoulders by women in Spain and Latin America. [< Span *manta*, cape.]

man·tis (măn′tĭs) *n.* A predatory grasshopper-like insect that holds its forelimbs in a praying position. [< Gk, prophet, diviner.]

man·tis·sa (măn-tĭs′ə) *n.* The decimal part of a logarithm written as the sum of an integer and a decimal. [L, a gain.]

man·tle (măn′təl) *n.* **1.** A loose, sleeveless coat worn over outer garments. **2.** Anything that covers, envelops, or conceals. **3.** A device in gas lamps consisting of a sheath of threads that gives off brilliant illumination when heated by the flame. **4.** The layer of the earth between the crust and core. **5.** Variant of **mantel.** —*v.* **-tled, -tling.** To cover with or as with a mantle; cloak. [< L *mantellum*, cloak.]

man·u·al (măn′yŏŏ-əl) *adj.* **1.** Of or operated by the hands. **2.** Employing human rather than mechanical energy: *manual labor.* —*n.* **1.** Any small reference book, esp. one giving instructions. **2.** A keyboard of an organ played with the hands. **3.** Prescribed movements in the handling of a rifle. [< L *manus*, hand.] —**man·u·al·ly** *adv.*

manual alphabet. An alphabet of hand signals used for communication by deaf-mutes.

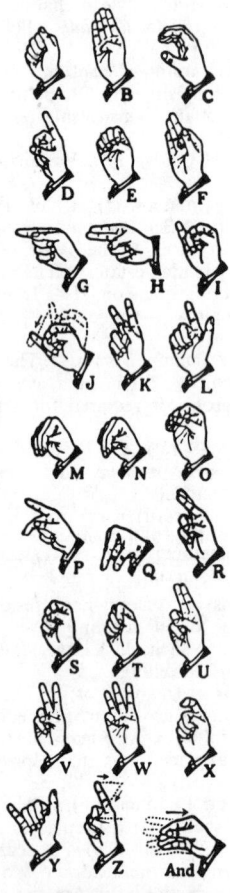

manual alphabet

man·u·fac·ture (măn′yə-făk′chər) *v.* -tured, -turing. **1.** To make or process into a finished product, esp. through a large-scale industrial operation. **2.** To concoct or invent. —*n.* **1.** The act or process of manufacturing. **2.** A manufactured product. [< LL *manūfactus*, handmade.] —**man·u·fac′tur·er** *n.*

man·u·mit (măn′yōō-mĭt′) *v.* -mitted, -mitting. To free from slavery. [< L *manū ēmittere*, to liberate, release from one's hand.] —**man′u·mis′sion** (-mĭsh′ən) *n.*

ma·nure (mə-n/y/ōōr′) *n.* Animal dung or other material used to fertilize soil. —*v.* -nured, -nuring. To apply manure to. [< OF *manoeuvrer*, to till, "work by hand."]

man·u·script (măn′yə-skrĭpt′) *n.* **1.** A book or other composition written by hand. **2.** A typewritten or handwritten version of a book, article, etc., esp. the author's own copy, submitted for publication. **3.** Handwriting as op-

posed to printing. [ML *manūscrīptus*, handwritten.]

man·y (měn′ē) *adj.* **more, most.** Amounting to or consisting of a large, indefinite number: *many friends.* —*n. (takes pl. v.).* A large, indefinite number. —*pron. (takes pl. v.).* A large number of persons or things. [< OE *manig, mænig.* See menegh-.]

Ma·o·ri (mou′rē) *n., pl.* **-ri** or **-ris. 1.** A member of the aboriginal people of New Zealand. **2.** The language of the Maori. —**Ma′o·ri** *adj.*

Mao Tse-tung (mou′tsĭ-tŏŏng′, mou′dzŭ′-dŏŏng′). 1893-1976. Political theorist; leader of the Chinese revolution; head of state (1949-59); party chairman (from 1943). —**Mao′ism′** *n.* —**Mao′ist** *n. & adj.*

Mao Tse-tung

map (măp) *n.* A representation, usually on a plane surface, of a region of the earth or heavens. —*v.* **mapped, mapping. 1.** To make a map of. **2.** To plan, esp. in detail; arrange: *mapping out their vacation.* [< ML *mappa*, napkin, sheet, cloth.] —**map′per** *n.*

ma·ple (mā′pəl) *n.* **1.** Any of various trees with lobed leaves and close-grained, usually hard wood and, in a North American species, sap that is boiled to produce a sweet syrup (**maple syrup**) or sugar (**maple sugar**). **2.** The wood of such a tree. [< OE *mapel(treow)*, maple (tree).]

mar (mär) *v.* **marred, marring.** To damage, deface, or spoil. [< OE *merran, mierran.* See mer-².]

mar. 1. maritime. **2.** married.

Mar. March.

mar·a·bou (măr′ə-bōō′) *n.* **1.** A large, Old World stork having soft down used to trim women's garments. **2.** The down of this bird. [< Ar *murābit*, stork.]

ma·ra·ca (mə-rä′kə) *n.* A percussion instrument consisting of a hollow-gourd rattle. [< Tupi.]

mar·a·schi·no (măr′ə-skē′nō, -shē′nō) *n.* A cordial made from the juice and pits of an Old World cherry. [It.]

maraschino cherry. A maraschino-flavored preserved cherry.

ă pat/ā ate/âr care/ä bar/b bib/ch chew/d deed/ě pet/ē be/f fit/g gag/h hat/hw what/
ĭ pit/ī pie/îr pier/j judge/k kick/l lid, fatal/m mum/n no, sudden/ng sing/ŏ pot/ō go/

mar•a•thon (măr′ə-thŏn′) *n.* **1.** A long-distance race, esp. one on foot. **2.** A contest of endurance. —**mar′a•thon′** *adj.*

ma•raud (mə-rôd′) *v.* To rove in search of booty; raid for plunder. [F *marauder.*] —**ma•raud′er** *n.*

mar•ble (măr′bəl) *n.* **1.** A metamorphic rock, chiefly calcium carbonate, often irregularly colored with impurities. **2. a.** A small ball used in children's games. **b. marbles** *(takes sing. v.).* A game played with such balls. —*adj.* Consisting of or resembling marble. [< Gk *marmaros,* marble, any hard stone.]

mar•bling (măr′blĭng) *n.* A mottling or streaking that resembles marble.

march¹ (märch) *v.* **1.** To walk or cause to walk in a military manner with measured steps at a steady rate. **2.** To advance or proceed with steady movement. **3.** To traverse by marching. —*n.* **1.** The act of marching. **2.** Forward movement. **3.** A regulated pace. **4.** The distance covered by marching. **5.** A musical composition in regularly accented meter, to accompany marching. [OF *marcher, marchier,* to walk, trample.]

march² (märch) *n.* A border region or frontier. [< OF *marche, marc,* borderland.]

March (märch) *n.* The 3rd month of the year. March has 31 days. [< L *Mārtius (mēnsis),* (month) of Mars.]

mar•chion•ess (mär′shən-ĭs, mär′shə-nĕs′) *n.* **1.** The wife or widow of a marquis. **2.** A peeress of the rank of marquis in her own right. [< ML *marchiō,* marquis.]

Mar•di gras (mär′dē grä′). The last day before Lent. [F, "fat Tuesday."]

mare¹ (mâr) *n.* A female horse, zebra, etc. [< OE *mere, mīere.* See marko-.]

ma•re² (mä′rā) *n., pl.* **-ria** (-rē-ə). *Astron.* Any of the large dark areas on the moon or Mars. [< L, sea.]

mar•ga•rine (mär′jə-rĭn) *n.* A butter substitute made with vegetable oils. [F.]

mar•gin (mär′jən) *n.* **1.** An edge and the area immediately adjacent to it; border. **2.** The blank space bordering the printed area on a page. **3.** A limit of a state or process: *the margin of reality.* **4.** A surplus measure or amount: *a margin of safety.* **5.** A measure or degree of difference: *a margin of 500 votes.* [< L *margō (margin-).*] —**mar′gin•al** *adj.*

mar•gi•na•li•a (mär′jə-nā′lē-ə) *pl.n.* Notes in a book margin.

Ma•rie An•toi•nette (mə-rē′ ăn′twə-nĕt′). 1755-1793. Queen of France; wife (1770) of Louis XVI; guillotined.

mar•i•gold (măr′ə-gōld′, mâr′-) *n.* A widely cultivated plant with showy yellow, orange, or reddish flowers. [ME *marygould.*]

mar•i•jua•na, mar•i•hua•na (măr′ə-wä′nə) *n.* **1.** The hemp plant. **2.** The dried flowers and leaves of this plant, esp. when smoked to induce euphoria. [Mex Span *mariguana, marihuana.*]

ma•rim•ba (mə-rĭm′bə) *n.* A large xylophone with resonators.

ma•ri•na (mə-rē′nə) *n.* A boat basin for small pleasure boats. [< L *marīnus,* MARINE.]

mar•i•nade (măr′ə-nād′) *n.* A liquid, as vinegar or wine, in which food is soaked before cooking. [< Span *marino,* "briny," marine.]

mar•i•nate (măr′ə-nāt′) *v.* **-nated, -nating.** To soak (meat or fish) in a marinade. [Var of MARINADE.]

ma•rine (mə-rēn′) *adj.* **1. a.** Of or pertaining to the sea: *marine exploration.* **b.** Native to the sea: *marine life.* **2.** Pertaining to shipping or maritime affairs. **3.** Pertaining to sea navigation: *marine chart.* —*n.* **1.** Shipping in general; maritime interests as represented by ships: *merchant marine.* **2. a.** A soldier serving on a ship. **b. Marine.** A member of the U.S. Marine Corps. [< L *marīnus* < *mare,* sea.]

Marine Corps. A branch of the U.S. Armed Forces composed chiefly of amphibious troops.

mar•i•ner (măr′ə-nər) *n.* A sailor or seaman.

mar•i•o•nette (măr′ē-ə-nĕt′) *n.* A jointed puppet manipulated by strings.

mar•i•tal (măr′ə-təl) *adj.* Of or pertaining to marriage. [< L *marītus,* married, husband.]

mar•i•time (măr′ə-tīm′) *adj.* **1.** Located on or near the sea. **2.** Of or concerned with shipping or navigation. [< L *mare,* sea.]

mar•jo•ram (mär′jər-əm) *n.* An aromatic plant with leaves used as seasoning. [< ML *majorāna.*]

mark¹ (märk) *n.* **1.** A visible trace or impression on something, as a spot, dent, or line. **2.** A written or printed symbol: *a punctuation mark.* **3.** A grade, as in school. **4.** A name, stamp, etc., placed on an article to signify ownership, quality, etc. **5.** A visible indication of some quality, property, etc. **6.** A standard or criterion of quality. **7.** Quality; note; importance. **8.** A target. **9.** That which one wishes to achieve; a goal. **10.** An object or point that serves as a guide. —*v.* **1.** To make a visible impression (on). **2.** To form, distinguish, or separate by making a visible impression on. **3.** To pay attention to. **4.** To characterize; set off. **5.** To grade (school papers). [< OE *mearc,* boundary, landmark, sign. See merg-.] —**mark′er** *n.*

mark² (märk) *n.* See **Deutsche mark, ostmark.**

Mark (märk), **Saint.** Christian apostle; reputed author of the 2nd Gospel of the New Testament.

marked (märkt) *adj.* **1.** Having a mark or marks. **2.** Having a noticeable trait. —**mark′ed•ly** (mär′kĭd-lē) *adv.*

mar•ket (mär′kĭt) *n.* **1.** An open place or building where merchandise is offered for sale. **2.** A store that sells a particular type of merchandise: *a meat market.* **3. a.** A region in which goods can be bought and sold: *the European market.* **b.** A type of buyer or demand: *the college market.* **4.** Demand for goods. —*v.* **1.** To offer for sale. **2.** To sell. **3.** To buy household supplies. [< L *mercārī,* to trade.] —**mar′ket•er, mar′ke•teer′** *n.*

mar•ket•place (mär′kĭt-plās′) *n.* **1.** A public square in which a market is set up. **2.** The world of trade.

mark•ka (mär′kä′) *n., pl.* **-kaa** (-kä′). The basic monetary unit of Finland.

ô paw, for/oi boy/ou out/ŏŏ took/ōō coo/p pop/r run/s sauce/sh shy/t to/th thin/*th* the/
ŭ cut/ûr fur/v van/w wag/y yes/z size/zh vision/ə ago, item, edible, gallop, circus/

marks·man (märks′mən) *n.* One skilled at shooting a gun or other weapon. —**marks′·man·ship′** *n.*

mark·up (märk′ŭp′) *n.* 1. A raise in price. 2. The amount added to the cost of an item when figuring the selling price.

marl (märl) *n.* A loam used as fertilizer. [< LL *marga.*]

mar·lin (mär′lən) *n.* A large marine game fish resembling the swordfish.

mar·line·spike (mär′lən-spīk′) *n.* A metal spike used to separate strands of rope and wire cable in splicing.

Mar·lowe (mär′lō), **Christopher.** 1564–1593. English poet and dramatist.

mar·ma·lade (mär′mə-lād′) *n.* A jellylike preserve made of the pulp and rind of fruits, esp. citrus fruits. [< Gk *melimēlon,* "honey-apple."]

mar·mo·re·al (mär-môr′ē-əl, -mōr′ē-əl) *adj.* Pertaining to or resembling marble. [< L *marmor,* marble.]

mar·mo·set (mär′mə-sĕt′, -zĕt′) *n.* Any of various small, furry, long-tailed tropical American monkeys. [< OF, grotesque figure.]

mar·mot (mär′mət) *n.* A stocky, short-legged burrowing rodent such as the woodchuck. [< ML *mormotāna,* "mountain mouse."]

ma·roon[1] (mə-rōōn′) *v.* 1. To put (a person) ashore on a deserted island or coast. 2. To abandon (a person) with little hope of rescue or escape. [F *marron.*]

ma·roon[2] (mə-rōōn′) *n.* Dark red. [< F *marron,* chestnut.]

mar·quee (mär-kē′) *n.* 1. A large tent, used chiefly for outdoor entertainment. 2. A roof-like structure projecting over an entrance, as to a theater. [F *marquise,* a linen tent pitched atop an officer's tent.]

mar·quis (mär′kwĭs) *n., pl.* **-quis** or **-quises.** Also *chiefly Brit.* **mar·quess.** The title of a nobleman ranking below a duke. [< OF, "count of the march (frontier)."]

mar·riage (măr′ĭj) *n.* 1. The state of being married; wedlock. 2. A wedding. 3. Any close union. —**mar′riage·a·ble** *adj.*

mar·row (măr′ō) *n.* 1. The soft material that fills bone cavities, consisting of fat cells and maturing blood cells, with supporting connective tissue and blood vessels. 2. Spinal marrow; the spinal cord. [< OE *mærg, mærh.* See mozgo-.]

mar·ry (măr′ē) *v.* **-ried, -rying.** 1. To join as husband and wife. 2. To take as husband or wife. 3. To enter into a close relationship. [< L *maritus,* husband.]

Mars (märz) *n.* 1. The Roman god of war. 2. The 4th planet from the sun, having a sidereal period of revolution about the sun of 687 days at a mean distance of 141.6 million miles, a mean radius of approx. 2,090 miles, and a mass approx. 0.15 that of Earth.

Mar·seille (mär-sā′). A city of SE France. Pop. 778,000.

marsh (märsh) *n.* An area of low-lying, wet land; a swamp. [< OE *mersc, merisc.* See mori-.] —**marsh′y** *adj.*

mar·shal (mär′shəl) *n.* 1. In some countries, a

military officer of the highest rank. 2. In the U.S.: **a.** A Federal or city officer who carries out court orders. **b.** The head of a police or fire department. 3. One in charge of a ceremony. —*v.* 1. To arrange or place in order. 2. To guide (a person) ceremoniously; usher. [< OHG *marahscalc,* "keeper of the horses," marshal.]

Mar·shall (mär′shəl). 1. **George Catlett.** 1880–1959. American General of the Army, statesman, and diplomat. 2. **John.** 1755–1835. American jurist, Chief Justice of the U.S. (1801–35).

marsh·mal·low (märsh′mĕl′ō, -măl′ō) *n.* 1. A confection of sweetened paste, formerly made from the root of a mallow. 2. A confection made of corn syrup, gelatin, etc., and dusted with powdered sugar.

marsh marigold. A North American swamp plant with yellow, buttercuplike flowers.

mar·su·pi·al (mär-sōō′pē-əl) *n.* Any of a group of mammals including the kangaroo and the opossum, of which the females have an external pouch in which the newly born young are fed and sheltered. [< Gk *marsupion,* pouch.] —**mar·su′pi·al** *adj.*

mart (märt) *n.* A market. [< MARKET.]

mar·ten (märt′n) *n.* 1. A thick-furred, weasel-like mammal of N regions. 2. The fur of a marten. [< OF *martre.*]

mar·tial (mär′shəl) *adj.* 1. Of, pertaining to, or suggestive of war or warriors. 2. Pertaining to the army or the military profession. [< L *Mārs,* Mars.] —**mar′tial·ism′** *n.* —**mar′tial·ist** *n.* —**mar′tial·ly** *adv.*

martial law. Temporary military rule imposed upon a civilian population, as in time of war.

Mar·tian (mär′shən) *adj.* Of or pertaining to the planet Mars. —*n.* A fictitious inhabitant of the planet Mars.

mar·tin (märt′n) *n.* Any of several birds resembling and closely related to the swallows. [ME.]

mar·ti·net (mär′tə-nĕt′) *n.* A rigid disciplinarian. [< J. *Martinet,* 17th-century French general.]

mar·tin·gale (mär′tən-gāl′) *n.* A part of a harness designed to prevent a horse from throwing back its head. [< *Martigue,* small village in Provence.]

mar·ti·ni (mär-tē′nē) *n., pl.* **-nis.** A cocktail usually made of three parts of gin to one part of dry vermouth.

mar·tyr (mär′tər) *n.* 1. One who chooses to suffer death rather than renounce religious principles. 2. One who makes a great sacrifice for his principles. 3. One who endures great suffering. [< Gk *martus,* witness, witness (of Christ).] —**mar′tyr** *v.* —**mar′tyr·dom** *n.*

mar·vel (mär′vəl) *n.* 1. Something that evokes surprise, admiration, or wonder. 2. A sense of profound wonder or astonishment. —*v.* To feel wonder or astonishment. [< L *mīrābilis,* wonderful.]

mar·vel·ous (mär′vəl-əs) *adj.* Also **mar·vel·lous.** 1. Causing wonder or astonishment. 2. Miraculous. 3. Of the highest kind or quality. —**mar′vel·ous·ly** *adv.*

ă pat/ā ate/âr care/ä bar/b bib/ch chew/d deed/ĕ pet/ē be/f fit/g gag/h hat/hw what/ ĭ pit/ī pie/îr pier/j judge/k kick/l lid, fatal/m mum/n no, sudden/ng sing/ŏ pot/ō go/

Marx (märks), **Karl.** 1818–1883. German philosopher and political economist; founder of Communism. —**Marx'ism'** *n.* —**Marx'ist** *n. & adj.*

Karl Marx

Mar•y (mâr'ē). The mother of Jesus. Matthew 1:18–25.
Mar•y•land (mâr'ə-lənd). A state of the E U.S. Pop. 3,922,000. Cap. Annapolis.
masc. masculine.
mas•car•a (măs-kăr'ə) *n.* A cosmetic used to darken the eyelashes. [Span *máscara,* "mask."]
mas•cot (măs'kŏt, -kət) *n.* A person, animal, or object believed to bring good luck. [F *mascotte.*]
mas•cu•line (măs'kyə-lĭn) *adj.* **1.** Of or pertaining to men or boys; male. **2.** Mannish. **3.** Of, designating, or constituting the gender of words or grammatical forms referring normally to males. —*n.* **1.** The masculine gender. **2.** A word or word form of the masculine gender. [< L *masculus,* male.] —**mas'cu•line•ly** *adv.* —**mas'cu•lin'i•ty** (măs'kyə-lĭn'ə-tē) *n.*
ma•ser (mā'zər) *n.* A device similar to a laser that operates at microwave frequencies.
Mas•er•u (măz'ə-roo'). The capital of Lesotho. Pop. 9,000.
mash (măsh) *n.* **1.** Any fermentable starchy mixture from which alcohol can be distilled. **2.** A mixture of ground grain and nutrients fed to livestock. **3.** Any soft, pulpy mass. —*v.* **1.** To convert (something) into a soft, pulpy mixture. **2.** To crush or grind. [< OE *māsc.*] —**mash'er** *n.*
mask (măsk, mäsk) *n.* **1.** A cover worn on the face to protect or conceal identity. **2.** A mold of a person's face, as a death mask. **3.** A grotesque representation of a face. **4.** Anything that disguises or conceals. **5.** A masque. —*v.* To cover, disguise, or protect with or as with a mask. [F *masque.*]
mas•o•chism (măs'ə-kĭz'əm) *n.* **1.** An abnormal sexual condition in which satisfaction depends on being subjected to abuse or pain. **2.** The deriving of pleasure from being mistreated in some way. [< L. von Sacher-*Masoch* (1836–1895), Austrian novelist.]

—**mas'o•chist** *n.* —**mas'o•chis'tic** (măs'ə-kĭs'tĭk) *adj.* —**mas'o•chis'ti•cal•ly** *adv.*
ma•son (mā'sən) *n.* **1.** One who builds or works with stone or brick. **2. Mason.** A Freemason. [< Frank **makòn,* to make.]
Ma•son•ic (mə-sŏn'ĭk) *adj.* Of or pertaining to Freemasons or Freemasonry.
ma•son•ry (mā'sən-rē) *n., pl.* **-ries. 1.** The trade of a mason. **2.** Stonework or brickwork. **3. Masonry.** Freemasonry.
Ma•so•ra (mə-sôr'ə, -sôr'ə) *n.* The tradition relating to correct textual reading of the Hebrew Scriptures, as embodied in critical notes made by Jewish scholars before the 10th century A.D. —**Mas'o•ret'ic** (măs'ə-rĕt'ĭk) *adj.*
masque (măsk, mäsk) *n.* A dramatic entertainment, usually mythological or allegorical in theme, popular in England in the 16th and early 17th centuries; a mask. [Var of MASK.]
mas•quer•ade (măs'kə-rād') *n.* **1. a.** A costume ball at which masks are worn. **b.** The costume for such a ball. **2.** Any disguise or false outward show. —*v.* **-aded, -ading. 1.** To wear a disguise, as at a masquerade. **2.** To go about as if in disguise; put on a deceptive appearance. [< It *maschera,* mask.] —**mas'quer•ad'er** *n.*
mass (măs) *n.* **1.** A unified body of matter with no specific shape. **2.** Any large but nonspecific amount or number. **3.** The major part of something; majority. **4.** The physical volume or bulk of a solid body. **5.** The measure of a body's resistance to acceleration, different from but proportional to its weight. —**the masses.** The body of common people. —*v.* To gather, form, or assemble into a mass. [< Gk *maza,* barley cake, lump, mass.]
Mass (măs) *n.* In Roman Catholic and some Protestant churches, the celebration of the Eucharist. [< LL *missa,* eucharist.]
Mass. Massachusetts.
Mas•sa•chu•set (măs'ə-choo'sĭt, -zĭt) *n.* Also **Mas•sa•chu•sett. 1.** A member of a large tribe of Algonquian-speaking Indians who lived on or near the coast in Massachusetts. **2.** The language of these Indians.
Mas•sa•chu•setts (măs'ə-choo'sĭts, -zĭts). A state of the NE U.S. Pop. 5,689,000. Cap. Boston.
mas•sa•cre (măs'ə-kər) *n.* **1.** Savage and indiscriminate killing; slaughter. **2.** *Informal.* A severe defeat, as in sports. [< L *mateola,* a kind of mallet.] —**mas'sa•cre** *v.* **(-cred, -cring).**
mas•sage (mə-säzh') *n.* The rubbing or kneading of the body to aid circulation or relax the muscles. [< F *masser,* to massage.] —**mas'sage'** *v.* **(-saged, -saging).**
mass communication. Communication directed at or reaching many people.
mas•seur (mă-sûr') *n.* A man who gives massages professionally. [< F *masser,* to MASSAGE.] —**mas•seuse'** ('-sœz') *fem.n.*
mas•sive (măs'ĭv) *adj.* **1.** Consisting of or making up a large mass; bulky. **2.** Imposing in quantity, scope, degree, intensity, or scale.
mass number. The total number of neutrons and protons in an atomic nucleus.
mass production. The manufacture of goods

in large quantities, often using assembly-line techniques.

mast (măst, mäst) *n.* **1.** A tall vertical spar that rises from the keel of a ship to support the sails and rigging. **2.** Any vertical pole. [< OE *mæst.*]

mas•ter (măs′tər, mäs′-) *n.* **1.** A man having control over others; an employer; owner. **2.** The captain of a merchant ship. **3.** A teacher or tutor. **4.** One highly skilled, as in a trade. **5. Master.** A title preceding the name of a boy too young to be addressed as Mister. **6. a.** A college or university degree granted to a person who has completed at least one year of study beyond the bachelor's degree. **b.** One holding such a degree. —*v.* **1.** To make oneself a master of (an art, craft, or science). **2.** To overcome or subdue. [< L *magister.*]

mas•ter•ful (măs′tər-fəl, mäs′-) *adj.* **1.** Given to playing the master; domineering. **2.** Expert; skillful. —**mas′ter•ful•ly** *adv.*

mas•ter•ly (măs′tər-lē, mäs′-) *adj.* Indicating the knowledge or skill of a master.

mas•ter•mind (măs′tər-mīnd′, mäs′-) *n.* A person who plans and directs a project. —**mas′ter•mind′** *v.*

master of ceremonies. One who acts as host at a formal event or program of varied entertainment.

mas•ter•piece (măs′tər-pēs′, mäs′-) *n.* **1.** An outstanding work of art. **2.** Anything superlative.

master sergeant. A U.S. noncommissioned officer of the next to highest rating.

mas•ter•work (măs′tər-wûrk′, mäs′-) *n.* A masterpiece.

mas•ter•y (măs′tər-ē, mäs′-) *n., pl.* **-ies. 1.** Possession of consummate skill. **2.** The status of master; dominion. **3.** Full command of some subject of study.

mast•head (măst′hěd′, mäst′-) *n.* **1.** The top of a ship's mast. **2.** The listing in a publication of information about its staff and operation.

mas•tic (măs′tĭk) *n.* A pastelike cement. [< Gk *mastikhē,* mastic, "chewing gum."]

mas•ti•cate (măs′tə-kāt′) *v.* **-cated, -cating.** To chew. [< Gk *mastikhān,* to grind the teeth.] —**mas′ti•ca′tion** *n.* —**mas′ti•ca•to′ry** (-tĭ-kə-tôr′ē, -tōr′ē) *adj.*

mas•tiff (măs′tĭf) *n.* A large dog with a short brownish coat. [< L *mānsuētus,* tamed, "accustomed to the hand."]

masto–. *comb. form.* The breast or protuberances resembling a breast or nipple. [< Gk *mastos,* breast.]

mas•to•don (măs′tə-dŏn′) *n.* An extinct elephantlike mammal. [NL, "breast-tooth."]

mas•toid (măs′toid′) *n.* The **mastoid process.**

mas•toid•ec•to•my (măs′toid-ěk′tə-mē) *n., pl.* **-mies.** Removal of part or all of the mastoid process.

mas•toid•i•tis (măs′toid-ī′tĭs) *n.* Inflammation of part or all of the mastoid process.

mastoid process. The rear portion of the temporal bone.

mas•tur•ba•tion (măs′tər-bā′shən) *n.* Excitation of the genital organs, usually to orgasm, by means other than sexual intercourse. [< L *masturbārī,* to masturbate.] —**mas′tur•bate′** *v.* (-bated, -bating).

mat[1] (măt) *n.* **1.** A flat piece of fabric or other material used as a floor covering, table pad, etc. **2.** A floor pad to protect athletes, as in wrestling. **3.** A dense or tangled mass. —*v.* **matted, matting. 1.** To cover, protect, or decorate with a mat. **2.** To form into a mat. [< LL *matta.*]

mat[2] (măt) *n.* **1.** A border placed around a picture to serve as a frame or provide contrast between the picture and frame. **2.** A dull finish, as on paper. **3.** *Ptg.* A matrix. —*adj.* Having a dull finish. [< L *mattus,* dull, vague.]

mat•a•dor (măt′ə-dôr′) *n.* The bullfighter with the role of killing the bull. [Span, "killer."]

match[1] (măch) *n.* **1.** One equal or similar to another. **2.** Two persons or things that harmonize. **3.** A game or contest. **4.** A marriage or arrangement of marriage. —*v.* **1.** To be or make similar or equal to. **2.** To harmonize with. **3.** To place in competition with. **4.** To join in marriage. [< OE *gemæcca,* mate. See **mag–.**] —**match′er** *n.*

match[2] (măch) *n.* A narrow strip of wood, cardboard, or wax coated on one end with a compound that ignites easily by friction. [< ML *myxa,* lamp wick.]

match•book (măch′bŏŏk′) *n.* A small folder containing safety matches.

match•less (măch′lĭs) *adj.* Having no equal; peerless. —**match′less•ly** *adv.*

match•lock (măch′lŏk′) *n.* A musket in which powder is ignited by a match.

match•mak•er (măch′mā′kər) *n.* **1.** One who arranges marriages. **2.** One who arranges athletic competitions.

mate (māt) *n.* **1.** One of a matched pair. **2.** A spouse. **3.** One of a pair of breeding animals. **4.** An associate. **5.** A deck officer on a merchant ship ranking below the master. —*v.* **mated, mating. 1.** To join closely; couple. **2.** To unite in marriage or for breeding. [< MLG *mate, gemate,* companion.]

ma•té (mä′tā′) *n.* A tealike beverage made from the dried leaves of a South American tree.

ma•te•ri•al (mə-tîr′ē-əl) *n.* **1.** The substance out of which a thing is or can be constructed. **2. materials.** Tools or apparatus for the performance of a given task. —*adj.* **1.** Composed of or pertaining to physical substances. **2.** Of or affecting the enjoyment of physical well-being. **3.** Of or concerned with the physical as distinct from the spiritual. **4.** Of importance to an argument; relevant. [< L *māteria,* matter.] —**ma•te′ri•al•ly** *adv.*

ma•te•ri•al•ism (mə-tîr′ē-əl-ĭz′əm) *n.* **1.** The view that matter and material process are the sole constituents of reality. **2.** Preoccupation with money and possessions to the exclusion of spiritual or intellectual things. —**ma•te′ri•al•ist** *adj. & n.* —**ma•te′ri•al•is′tic** *adj.*

ma•te•ri•al•ize (mə-tîr′ē-əl-īz′) *v.* **-ized, -izing. 1.** To assume or cause to assume material or effective form. **2.** To take form or shape. —**ma•te′ri•al•i•za′tion** *n.*

ă pat/ā ate/âr care/ä bar/b bib/ch chew/d deed/ĕ pet/ē be/f fit/g gag/h hat/hw what/ ĭ pit/ī pie/îr pier/j judge/k kick/l lid, fatal/m mum/n no, sudden/ng sing/ŏ pot/ō go/

ma·te·ri·el, ma·té·ri·el (mə-tîr′ē-ĕl′) *n.* The equipment, apparatus, and supplies of an organization, esp. of an army.

ma·ter·nal (mə-tûr′nəl) *adj.* 1. Relating to or characteristic of a mother or motherhood; motherly. 2. Inherited from or related to through one's mother. [< L *māter*, mother.] —**ma·ter′nal·ly** *adv.*

ma·ter·ni·ty (mə-tûr′nə-tē) *n.* The state of being a mother; motherhood.

math (măth) *n.* Mathematics.

math. mathematical; mathematician; mathematics.

math·e·mat·ics (măth′ə-măt′ĭks) *n.* *(takes sing. v.).* The study of number, form, arrangement, and associated relationships, using rigorously defined literal, numerical, and operational symbols. [< Gk *mathēma*, science.] —**math′e·mat′i·cal** *adj.* —**math′e·mat′i·cal·ly** *adv.* —**math′e·ma·ti′cian** (-mə-tĭsh′ən) *n.*

mat·i·nee, mat·i·née (măt′n-ā′) *n.* A dramatic or musical performance given usually in the afternoon. [< L *(tempus) mātūtīnum*, morning (time).]

matri–. *comb. form.* Motherhood. [< L *māter*, mother.]

ma·tri·arch (mā′trē-ärk′) *n.* A woman who rules a family, clan, or tribe. —**ma′tri·ar′chal** *adj.*

ma·tri·ar·chy (mā′trē-är′kē) *n., pl.* **-chies.** A social system in which descent is traced through the mother's side of the family.

ma·tric·u·late (mə-trĭk′yə-lāt′) *v.* **-lated, -lating.** To enroll in a group, esp. in a college or university. [< L *mātrix*, list, womb, source.] —**ma·tric′u·la′tion** *n.*

mat·ri·mo·ny (măt′rə-mō′nē) *n.* The act or state of being married; the sacrament or rite of marriage. [< L *mātrimōnium*, marriage, "motherhood."] —**mat′ri·mo′ni·al** *adj.*

ma·trix (mā′trĭks) *n., pl.* **-trices** (-trə-sēz′, măt′rə-) or **-trixes.** 1. A medium within which something originates, develops, or is contained. 2. *Ptg.* A mold from which metal plates can be cast. [L *mātrix*, womb, pregnant animal.]

ma·tron (mā′trən) *n.* 1. A married woman, esp. a mature woman with dignity and social position. 2. A woman who supervises a public institution, such as a prison. [< L *māter*, mother.] —**ma′tron·li·ness** *n.* —**ma′tron·ly** *adj. & adv.*

matron of honor *pl.* **matrons of honor.** A married woman serving as chief attendant of the bride at a wedding.

Matt. Matthew (New Testament).

mat·ter (măt′ər) *n.* 1. a. That which occupies space, can be perceived by the senses, and constitutes any physical body or the universe as a whole. b. Any entity displaying gravitation and inertia when at rest as well as when in motion. 2. A specific type of substance: *inorganic matter.* 3. The substance of thought or expression. 4. Any subject of concern or action. 5. A difficulty: *What's the matter?* 6. An indefinite quantity: *a matter of a few cents.* 7. Something written or printed. —*v.* To be of importance. [< L *māteria*, matter.]

mat·ter-of-fact (măt′ər-əv-făkt′) *adj.* Pertaining or adhering to facts; literal.

Mat·thew (măth′yōō), **Saint.** Christian apostle; reputed author of 1st Gospel.

mat·ting (măt′ĭng) *n.* A coarsely woven fabric used for covering floors and similar purposes.

mat·tock (măt′ək) *n.* A digging tool with a blade set at right angles to the handle. [< OE *mattuc.*]

mat·tress (măt′rĭs) *n.* A rectangular pad of heavy cloth filled with soft material, used as or on a bed. [< Ar *maṭrah*, place where something is thrown.]

mat·u·rate (măch′ōō-rāt′) *v.* **-rated, -rating.** To mature or ripen. —**mat′u·ra′tion** *n.*

ma·ture (mə-t/y/ōōr′, -chōōr′) *adj.* **-turer, -turest.** 1. Fully grown or developed. 2. Fully aged or ripened. 3. Worked out fully by the mind; perfected. 4. Payable; due: *a mature bond.* —*v.* **-tured, -turing.** To bring or come to full development. [< L *mātūrus.*] —**ma·ture′ly** *adv.* —**ma·tur′i·ty** *n.*

mat·zo (mät′sə) *n., pl.* **-zoth** (-sōth′, -sôt′, -sōs′) or **-zos** (-səz, -səs, -sōz′) or **-zot** (-sōt′). A brittle, flat piece of unleavened bread, eaten esp. during the Passover. [Yid *matse.*]

maud·lin (môd′lĭn) *adj.* Effusively sentimental. —**maud′lin·ly** *adv.*

maul (môl) *n.* A heavy hammer used to drive stakes, piles, or wedges. —*v.* To handle roughly; bruise or tear. [< L *malleus*, hammer.] —**maul′er** *n.*

maun·der (môn′dər, män′-) *v.* 1. To talk incoherently or aimlessly. 2. To move or act aimlessly or vaguely.

Mau·pas·sant (mō-pä-säN′), **Guy de.** 1850–1893. French novelist and short-story writer.

Mau·ri·ta·ni·a (môr′ə-tā′nē-ə). A republic of NW Africa. Pop. 900,000. Cap. Nouakchott. —**Mau′ri·ta′ni·an** *adj. & n.*

Mauritania

Mau·ri·ti·us (mô-rĭsh′ē-əs, -rĭsh′əs). An island nation in the Indian Ocean, formerly a British crown colony. Pop. 734,000. Cap. Port Louis. —**Mau·ri′ti·an** (-rĭsh′ən) *adj. & n.*

mau·so·le·um (mô′sə-lē′əm, mô′zə-) *n., pl.* **-leums** or **-lea** (-lē′ə). A large and stately tomb. [L *mausōlēum.*]

ô paw, for/oi boy/ou out/ŏŏ took/ōō coo/p pop/r run/s sauce/sh shy/t to/th thin/*th* the/
ŭ cut/ûr fur/v van/w wag/y yes/z size/zh vision/ə ago, item, edible, gallop, circus/

mauve (mōv) *n.* Moderate purple or pale violet. [F *mauve*, "mallow(-colored)."]

mav·er·ick (măv'ər-ĭk, măv'rĭk) *n.* 1. An unbranded or orphaned range animal, esp. a calf. 2. a. A nonconformist. b. An independent, as in politics. [< S.A. *Maverick* (1803–1870), Texas cattleman.]

maw (mô) *n.* 1. The stomach, mouth, or gullet of a voracious animal. 2. An opening that gapes. [< OE *maga*.]

mawk·ish (mô'kĭsh) *adj.* Excessively and objectionably sentimental. —**mawk'ish·ly** *adv.*

max. maximum.

max·il·la (măk-sĭl'ə) *n., pl.* -**lae** (-sĭl'ē) or -**las**. One of a pair of bones forming the upper jaw. [L, "lower jaw."] —**max'il·lar** (măk'sə-lər, măk-sĭl'ər), **max'il·lar'y** (-sə-lĕr'ē) *adj.*

max·im (măk'sĭm) *n.* A succinct formulation of some fundamental principle or rule of conduct. [< ML *(prōpositiō) maxima*, "greatest proposition."]

max·i·mal (măk'sə-məl) *adj.* Of or designating a maximum. —**max'i·mal·ly** *adv.*

max·i·mum (măk'sə-məm) *n., pl.* -**mums** or -**ma** (-mə). 1. a. The greatest possible quantity, degree, or number. b. The period during which the highest point or degree is attained. 2. An upper limit stipulated by law or other authority. —*adj.* Having or being the greatest quantity or highest degree that has been or can be attained. [L, "greatest (quantity)."]

may¹ (mā) *v. p.t.* **might.** —Used as an auxiliary to indicate: 1. A requesting or granting of permission: *May I take a swim? You may.* 2. Possibility: *It may rain.* 3. Ability or capacity, with the force of *can: If I may be of service.* 4. Obligation or function, with the force of *must* or *shall: "Congress may determine the time of choosing the electors."* (Constitution). 5. Desire or fervent wish: *Long may he live!* 6. Contingency, purpose, or result: *so that the average man may understand.* [< OE *magan*, to be able. See **magh-**.]

may² (mā) *n. Brit.* The blossoms of the hawthorn. [< MAY.]

May (mā) *n.* The 5th month of the year. May has 31 days. [< L *Maius (mēnsis)*, (the month) of *Maia*, Italic goddess.]

Ma·ya (mä'yə) *n., pl.* -**ya** or -**yas**. 1. A member of a race of Indians in S Mexico and Central America. 2. Their language. —**Ma'ya** *adj.*

Ma·yan (mä'yən) *adj.* Of or pertaining to the Maya. —*n.* 1. A Maya. 2. A family of Central American languages, including the language of the Maya.

May apple. A North American plant with poisonous seeds and foliage, a single white flower, and yellowish fruit.

may·be (mā'bē) *adv.* Perhaps; possibly.

May Day. 1. May 1, marked by the celebration of spring. 2. May 1, regarded in a number of places as an international holiday to celebrate labor organizations.

may·flow·er (mā'flou'ər) *n.* A spring-blooming flower, esp. the arbutus.

may·hem (mā'hĕm', mā'əm) *n. Law.* The offense of willfully maiming or crippling a person. [< OF *mahaignier*, maim.]

may·n't (mā'ənt, mānt). Contraction of *may not.*

may·on·naise (mā'ə-nāz') *n.* A dressing of beaten raw egg yolk, oil, and lemon juice or vinegar. [F.]

may·or (mā'ər, mâr) *n.* The chief magistrate of a city or borough. [< L *mājor*, "greater."] —**may'or·al** *adj.* —**may'or·al·ty** *n.*

May·pole (mā'pōl') *n.* Also **may·pole**. A pole decorated with streamers that May Day celebrators hold while dancing.

maze (māz) *n.* 1. An intricate, usually confusing, network of walled or hedged pathways; a labyrinth. 2. Anything resembling or likened to such a network, as a puzzle. [< OE *ā-masian*.] —**maz'y** *adj.*

ma·zur·ka (mə-zûr'kə, -zŏŏr'kə) *n.* 1. A lively Polish dance. 2. Music for such a dance. [F.]

Mba·bane (əm-bä-bän'). The capital of Swaziland. Pop. 8,400.

MC 1. Marine Corps. 2. Medical Corps. 3. Member of Congress.

m.c. master of ceremonies.

M.C. 1. Master of Ceremonies. 2. Member of Congress.

Mc·Kin·ley (mə-kĭn'lē), **William.** 1843–1901. 25th President of the U.S. (1897–1901).

William McKinley

Md mendelevium.

Md. Maryland.

M.D. Doctor of Medicine (L *Medicinae Doctor*).

mdse. merchandise.

me (mē) *pron.* The objective case of the 1st person pronoun *I,* used as the direct or indirect object of a verb or as the object of a preposition. [< OE *mē, me.* See **me-**.]

Usage: I, rather than *me,* is the grammatically prescribed 1st person pronoun for use after the verb *be: It is I.* But *it is me* (or *it's me*) is acceptable in informal writing and in speech on all levels as a more natural variant.

ME Middle English.

Me. Maine (unofficial).

M.E. 1. mechanical engineer. 2. Middle English. 3. mining engineer.

ă pat/ā ate/âr care/ä bar/b bib/ch chew/d deed/ĕ pèt/ē be/f fit/g gag/h hat/hw what/
ĭ pit/ī pie/îr pier/j judge/k kick/l lid, fatal/m mum/n no, sudden/ng sing/ŏ pot/ō go/

mead¹ (mēd) *n.* An alcoholic beverage made from fermented honey and water. [< OE *medu, meodu.* See **medhu-**.]

mead² (mēd) *n. Archaic.* A meadow. [< OE *mæd.*]

mead•ow (mĕd′ō) *n.* A tract of grassland, as one used for pasture or growing hay. [< OE *mæd,* MEAD².]

mea•ger (mē′gər) *adj.* Also **mea•gre.** 1. Having little flesh; thin; lean. 2. Conspicuously deficient in quantity. 3. Deficient in richness or fertility. [< L *macer,* thin.] —**mea′ger•ly** *adv.* —**mea′ger•ness** *n.*

meal¹ (mēl) *n.* 1. Coarsely ground edible grain. 2. A similar granular substance. [< OE *melu,* flour. See **melə-**.] —**meal′y** *adj.*

meal² (mēl) *n.* The food served and eaten in one sitting. [< OE *mæl,* fixed time, mealtime. See **mē-²**.]

meal•time (mēl′tīm′) *n.* The usual time for eating a meal.

meal•y-mouthed (mē′lē-mouthd′, -moutht′) *adj.* Unwilling to speak simply and directly.

mean¹ (mēn) *v.* **meant, meaning.** 1. a. To be defined as; denote. b. To act as a symbol of; represent. 2. To intend to convey or indicate: *What do you mean by that look?* 3. To have as a purpose or intention. 4. To have as a consequence: *Friction means heat.* 5. To be of a specified importance; matter: *Advice meant little to him.* [< OE *mænan,* to intend, tell, signify. See **mei-no-**.]

mean² (mēn) *adj.* 1. Low in quality or grade. 2. Low in social status. 3. Ignoble; base; petty. 4. Low in value or amount. 5. Miserly. 6. Lacking elevating human qualities, as kindness and good will. 7. *Informal.* Ill-tempered. 8. *Slang.* Hard to cope with. [< OE *gemæne,* "common."] —**mean′ly** *adv.* —**mean′ness** *n.*

mean³ (mēn) *n.* 1. The middle point or state between two extremes. 2. Moderation. 3. *Math.* a. A number that represents a set of numbers in a way determined by a rule involving all members of the set; average. b. The arithmetic mean. 4. **means.** A course of action or instrument by which some act can be accomplished or some end achieved. 5. **means.** Money, property, or other wealth. —**by all means.** Without fail; certainly. —*adj.* Occupying a middle or intermediate position, esp. one between two extremes. [< L *mediānus,* median.]

me•an•der (mē-ăn′dər) *v.* 1. To follow a winding course. 2. To wander aimlessly and idly. [< Gk *Maiandros,* a river in Phrygia noted for its windings.] —**me•an′der•er** *n.*

mean•ing (mē′nĭng) *n.* 1. That which is signified by something; sense; import. 2. That which one wishes to convey. 3. Functional value; efficacy; significance. —**mean′ing•ful** *adj.* —**mean′ing•less** *adj.*

meant (mĕnt). *p.t. & p.p.* of **mean.**

mean•time (mēn′tīm′) *n.* The time between one occurrence and another. —*adv.* Meanwhile.

mean•while (mēn′hwīl′) *n.* The intervening time. —*adv.* In the intervening time.

meas. measurable; measure.

mea•sles (mē′zəlz) *n. (takes sing. v.).* 1. An acute, contagious viral disease, usually involving the eruption of red spots. 2. German measles. [< MDu *māsel,* blemish.]

mea•sly (mēz′lē) *adj.* **-slier, -sliest.** *Slang.* Contemptibly small.

meas•ure (mĕzh′ər) *n.* 1. The dimensions, quantity, or capacity of anything as ascertained by measuring. See tables of measurement on following pages. 2. A reference standard or sample used for the quantitative comparison of properties. 3. A unit specified by a scale, as an inch, or by variable conditions, as a day's march. 4. A device, such as a marked tape, used for measuring. 5. An act of measuring. 6. A criterion. 7. Extent or degree. 8. A limited amount or degree. 9. An action taken as a means to an end. 10. A legislative bill or enactment. 11. Poetic meter. 12. *Mus.* The metrical unit between two bars on the staff; a bar. —**for good measure.** In addition to the required amount. —*v.* **-ured, -uring.** 1. To ascertain or mark off the dimensions, quantity, or capacity of. 2. To have a specified measure. 3. To bring into opposition: *measured her power with that of her rival.* 4. To choose with care; weigh: *measured his words.* [< L *mēnsūra.*] —**meas′ur•a•ble** *adj.* —**meas′ure•ment** *n.* —**meas′ur•er** *n.*

meat (mēt) *n.* 1. The edible flesh of animals, esp. mammals, as distinguished from fish or poultry. 2. The edible portion of fruits, nuts, etc. 3. The essence or principal part of something. 4. *Slang.* Something one enjoys or excels in. [< OE *mete,* food. See **mad-**.] —**meat′i•ness** *n.* —**meat′y** *adj.*

Mec•ca (mĕk′ə). A capital of Saudi Arabia and holy city of Islam. Pop. 200,000.

mec•ca (mĕk′ə) *n.* Often **Mecca.** A place regarded as the center of an activity or interest; a goal to which adherents of a faith or practice aspire.

mech. mechanical; mechanics.

me•chan•ic (mĭ-kăn′ĭk) *n.* A worker skilled in making, using, or repairing machines and tools.

me•chan•i•cal (mĭ-kăn′ĭ-kəl) *adj.* 1. Of or pertaining to machines or tools. 2. Operated or produced by a machine. 3. Acting or performing like a machine. 4. Of or dominated by physical forces. [< Gk *mēkhanē,* contrivance, machine.] —**me•chan′i•cal•ly** *adv.*

mechanical advantage. The ratio of the output force of a machine to the input force.

mechanical engineering. The branch of engineering that encompasses the production of mechanical power and the design, production, and use of machines and tools. —**mechanical engineer.**

me•chan•ics (mĭ-kăn′ĭks) *n. (takes sing. v.).* 1. The analysis of the action of forces on matter or material systems. 2. The design, construction, operation, and application of machinery or mechanical structures.

mech•a•nism (mĕk′ə-nĭz′əm) *n.* 1. a. A machine. b. The arrangement of connected parts in a machine. 2. Any system of parts that interact like those of a machine. 3. An in-

---

ô paw, for/oi boy/ou out/o͞o took/o͞o coo/p pop/r run/s sauce/sh shy/t to/th thin/*th* the/
ŭ cut/ûr fur/v van/w wag/y yes/z size/zh vision/ə ago, item, edible, gallop, circus/

Measurement Units

Length

U.S. Customary Unit	U.S. Equivalents	Metric Equivalents
inch	0.083 foot	2.54 centimeters
foot	⅓ yard, 12 inches	0.3048 meter
yard	3 feet, 36 inches	0.9144 meter
rod	5½ yards, 16½ feet	5.0292 meters
mile (statute, land)	1,760 yards, 5,280 feet	1.609 kilometers
mile (nautical, international)	1.151 statute miles	1.852 kilometers

Area

U.S. Customary Unit	U.S. Equivalents	Metric Equivalents
square inch	0.007 square foot	6.4516 square centimeters
square foot	144 square inches	929.030 square centimeters
square yard	1,296 square inches, 9 square feet	0.836 square meter
acre	43,560 square feet, 4,840 square yards	4,047 square meters
square mile	640 acres	2.590 square kilometers

Volume or Capacity

U.S. Customary Unit	U.S. Equivalents	Metric Equivalents
cubic inch	0.00058 cubic foot	16.387 cubic centimeters
cubic foot	1,728 cubic inches	0.028 cubic meter
cubic yard	27 cubic feet	0.765 cubic meter

U.S. Customary Liquid Measure	U.S. Equivalents	Metric Equivalents
fluid ounce	8 fluid drams, 1.804 cubic inches	29.573 milliliters
pint	16 fluid ounces, 28.875 cubic inches	0.473 liter
quart	2 pints, 57.75 cubic inches	0.946 liter
gallon	4 quarts, 231 cubic inches	3.785 liters
barrel	varies from 31 to 42 gallons, established by law or usage	

U.S. Customary Dry Measure	U.S. Equivalents	Metric Equivalents
pint	½ quart, 33.6 cubic inches	0.551 liter
quart	2 pints, 67.2 cubic inches	1.101 liters
peck	8 quarts, 537.605 cubic inches	8.810 liters
bushel	4 pecks, 2,150.42 cubic inches	35.238 liters

British Imperial Liquid and Dry Measure	U.S. Customary Equivalents	Metric Equivalents
fluid ounce	0.961 U.S. fluid ounce, 1.734 cubic inches	28.412 milliliters
pint	1.032 U.S. dry pints, 1.201 U.S. liquid pints, 34.678 cubic inches	568.26 milliliters
quart	1.032 U.S. dry quarts, 1.201 U.S. liquid quarts, 69.354 cubic inches	1.136 liters
gallon	1.201 U.S. gallons, 277.420 cubic inches	4.546 liters
peck	554.84 cubic inches	0.009 cubic meter
bushel	1.032 U.S. bushels, 2,219.36 cubic inches	0.036 cubic meter

Weight

U.S. Customary Unit (Avoirdupois)	U.S. Equivalents	Metric Equivalents
grain	0.036 dram, 0.002285 ounce	64.79891 milligrams
dram	27.344 grains, 0.0625 ounce	1.772 grams
ounce	16 drams, 437.5 grains	28.350 grams
pound	16 ounces, 7,000 grains	453.59237 grams
ton (short)	2,000 pounds	0.907 metric ton (1,000 kilograms)
ton (long)	1.12 short tons, 2,240 pounds	1.016 metric tons

Apothecary Weight Unit	U.S. Customary Equivalents	Metric Equivalents
scruple	20 grains	1.296 grams
dram	60 grains	3.888 grams
ounce	480 grains, 1.097 avoirdupois ounces	31.103 grams
pound	5,760 grains, 0.823 avoirdupois pound	373.242 grams

strument or process by which something is done or comes into being.

mech·a·nis·tic (měk′ə-nĭs′tĭk) *adj.* Pertaining to mechanics as a branch of physics. —**mech′-a·nis′ti·cal·ly** *adv.*

mech·a·nize (měk′ə-nīz′) *v.* **-nized, -nizing. 1.** To equip with machinery or mechanical devices. **2.** To make automatic or mechanical. —**mech′a·ni·za′tion** *n.*

med. 1. medical; medicine. **2.** medieval. **3.** medium.

med·al (měd′l) *n.* **1.** A piece of metal stamped with a design or inscription commemorating an event or person, often given as an award. **2.** A piece of metal stamped with a religious device. [< L *metallum*, metal.]

me·dal·lion (mə-dăl′yən) *n.* **1.** A large medal. **2.** Something resembling a large medal, such as a decorative design.

med·dle (měd′l) *v.* **-dled, -dling.** To intrude in other people's affairs; interfere. [< L *miscēre*, to mix.] —**med′dler** *n.*

me·di·a. Alternate *pl.* of **medium.**

me·di·al (mē′dē-əl) *adj.* Situated in or extending toward the middle; median. [< L *medius*, middle.]

me·di·an (mē′dē-ən) *adj.* **1.** Of, at, or toward the middle; medial. **2.** Of or lying in the plane that divides a symmetrical organism into right and left halves. **3.** *Stat.* Relating to the middle value in a distribution. —*n.* **1.** A median point, plane, line, or part. **2.** *Stat.* The middle value in a distribution, above and below which lie an equal number of values. **3.** A line that joins a vertex of a triangle to the midpoint of the opposite side. [< L *medius*, middle.]

me·di·ate (mē′dē-āt′) *v.* **-ated, -ating.** To act as an intermediary, esp. to seek to resolve (differences) between two or more conflicting parties. [L *mediāre*, to be in the middle.] —**me′di·a′tion** *n.* —**me′di·a′tor** *n.*

med·ic (měd′ĭk) *n. Informal.* **1.** A physician or surgeon. **2.** A military medical corpsman. [L *medicus*, doctor.]

Med·i·caid (měd′ĭ-kād′) *n.* Also **Med·i·caid.** A program, jointly funded by the states and the federal government, that provides medical aid for people who fall below a certain income level. [MEDIC(AL) + AID.]

med·i·cal (měd′ĭ-kəl) *adj.* **1.** Of or pertaining to the study or practice of medicine. **2.** Requiring medical as distinct from surgical treatment. [< L *medicus*, doctor.]

me·dic·a·ment (mĭ-dĭk′ə-mənt, měd′ĭ-kə-mənt) *n.* An agent that promotes recovery from injury or ailment; medicine.

Med·i·care (měd′ə-kâr′) *n.* Also **med·i·care.** A government program that provides medical care for the aged.

med·i·cate (měd′ə-kāt′) *v.* **-cated, -cating. 1.** To treat medicinally. **2.** To tincture or permeate with a medicinal substance. —**med′i·ca′tive** *adj.*

med·i·ca·tion (měd′ə-kā′shən) *n.* **1.** A medicine. **2.** The act or process of being medicated. **3.** The administration of medicine.

me·dic·i·nal (mə-dĭs′ə-nəl) *adj.* Pertaining to or having the properties of medicine; healing; curative. —**me·dic′i·nal·ly** *adv.*

med·i·cine (měd′ə-sən) *n.* **1. a.** The science of diagnosing, treating, or preventing disease. **b.** The branch of this science encompassing treatment by drugs, diet, exercise, and other nonsurgical means. **2.** Any drug or other agent used to treat disease or injury. [< L *medicina*, the art of a physician.]

medicine man. One believed among preliterate peoples to possess supernatural powers for healing and invoking spirits.

med·i·co (měd′ĭ-kō′) *n., pl.* **-cos.** *Informal.* A doctor or medical student. [< L *medicus*, doctor.]

me·di·e·val (mē′dē-ē′vəl, měd′ē′vəl) *adj.* Also **me·di·ae·val.** Pertaining or belonging to the Middle Ages. [< NL *Medium Aevum*, the Middle Age.] —**me′di·e′val·ly** *adv.*

Medieval Greek. Greek from about A.D. 700 to 1500.

Medieval Latin. Latin as used throughout Europe from about A.D. 700 to 1500.

Me·di·na (mə-dē′nə). A city of NW Saudi Arabia; a sacred center of Islam. Pop. 30,000.

me·di·o·cre (mē′dē-ō′kər) *adj.* Of medium and unimpressive quality. [< L *mediocris*, "halfway up the mountain," in a middle state.] —**me′di·oc′ri·ty** (-ŏk′rə-tē) *n.*

med·i·tate (měd′ə-tāt′) *v.* **-tated, -tating. 1.** To reflect upon; contemplate. **2.** To intend. **3.** To engage in contemplation. [L *meditārī.*] —**med′i·ta′tion** *n.* —**med′i·ta′tive** *adj.*

Med·i·ter·ra·ne·an (měd′ə-tə-rā′nē-ən, -rān′yən) *adj.* **1.** Of, pertaining to, or characteristic of the Mediterranean Sea or the areas that border on it. **2.** Designating languages spoken in the Mediterranean region before the coming of the Indo-Europeans. —*n.* **1.** The Mediterranean Sea. **2.** The Mediterranean languages.

Mediterranean Sea. The world's largest inland sea, bounded by Africa in the S, Asia in the E, and Europe in the N and W.

me·di·um (mē′dē-əm) *n., pl.* **-dia** (-dē-ə) **-ums. 1.** Something occupying a position or having a condition midway between extremes. **2.** An intervening substance through which something is transmitted or carried on. **3.** An agency by means of which something is accomplished, conveyed, or transferred. **4.** A means of mass communication. **5.** *pl.* **-ums** *only.* One thought to have powers of communicating with the spirits of the dead. **6.** An environment in which something functions and thrives. **7.** A means of expression as determined by the materials or creative methods involved. —*adj.* Intermediate in degree, amount, quantity, or quality. [< L *medius*, middle.]

med·ley (měd′lē) *n., pl.* **-leys. 1.** A jumbled assortment; mixture. **2.** A musical arrangement made from various melodies. [< OF *meslee.*]

me·dul·la (mə-dŭl′ə) *n., pl.* **-las** or **-lae** (-ē). **1.** *Anat.* The inner core of certain vertebrate body structures, such as the marrow of bone. **2.** The medulla oblongata. [L, marrow.] —**me·dul′lar** (mə-dŭl′ər), **med·ul·lar′y** (měd′ə-lěr′ē, mə-dŭl′ə-rē) *adj.*

medulla ob·lon·ga·ta (ŏb′lông-gä′tə) *pl.* me-

dulla oblongatas or **medullae oblongatae** (-gä'tē). The nervous tissue at the bottom of the brain that controls respiration, circulation, and certain other bodily functions.

meed (mēd) *n. Archaic.* A merited gift or reward. [< OE *mēd.*]

meek (mēk) *adj.* 1. Humble and patient. 2. Submissive. [< ON *mjūkr,* soft.] —**meek'ly** *adv.* —**meek'ness** *n.*

meer•schaum (mîr'shəm, -shôm) *n.* A tough, compact, usually white mineral, $H_4Mg_2Si_3O_{10}$, used in fashioning tobacco pipes and as a building stone. [G, "sea-foam."]

meet¹ (mēt) *v.* **met, meeting.** 1. To come upon. 2. To be present at the arrival of: *meet a train.* 3. To be introduced (to). 4. To come into conjunction (with); join: *where sea meets sky.* 5. To come into the company of, as for a conference. 6. To come to the notice of (the senses): *more than meets the eye.* 7. To cope or contend effectively with. 8. To satisfy (a demand, need, etc.). 9. To come together: *Let's meet tonight.* —*n.* A meeting or contest. [< OE *mētan.* See **mōd-.**]

meet² (mēt) *adj. Archaic.* Fitting; proper. [< OE *gemǣte.*] —**meet'ly** *adv.*

meet•ing (mēt'ĭng) *n.* 1. A coming together; assembly. 2. A joining. 3. A hostile encounter, as a duel.

mega–. *comb. form.* 1. One million (10^6). 2. Large. [< Gk *megas,* great.]

meg•a•cy•cle (mĕg'ə-sī'kəl) *n.* 1. One million cycles. 2. One million cycles per second.

megalo–. *comb. form.* Largeness or exaggerated size. [< Gk *megas,* great.]

meg•a•lo•ma•ni•a (mĕg'ə-lō-mā'nē-ə, -mān'-yə) *n.* A psychopathological condition marked by fantasies of self-grandeur and omnipotence. —**meg'a•lo•ma'ni•ac** *adj. & n.*

meg•a•lop•o•lis (mĕg'ə-lŏp'ə-lĭs) *n.* A region made up of several large cities and their surrounding areas.

meg•a•phone (mĕg'ə-fōn') *n.* A horn-shaped device used to project the voice.

meg•a•ton (mĕg'ə-tŭn') *n.* A unit of explosive force equal to one million tons of TNT.

me•gil•lah (mə-gĭl'ə) *n. Slang.* A prolix, tediously detailed or embroidered account. [Heb *məgillāh,* "scroll."]

me•grim (mē'grĭm) *n.* 1. A migraine. 2. Often **megrims.** A caprice. 3. **megrims.** Depression. 4. **megrims.** A disease of cattle and horses. [< OF *migraine,* migraine.]

mei•o•sis (mī-ō'sĭs) *n., pl.* **-ses** (-sēz'). The cell division in sexually reproducing organisms that reduces the number of chromosomes in reproductive cells. [< Gk *meiōsis,* diminution.]

Me•kong (mā'kŏng'). A river of SE Asia.

mel•an•cho•li•a (mĕl'ən-kō'lē-ə) *n.* A mental disorder characterized by feelings of dejection and usually by withdrawal.

mel•an•chol•ic (mĕl'ən-kŏl'ĭk) *adj.* 1. Subject to melancholy. 2. Of or afflicted with melancholia. —**mel'an•chol'i•cal•ly** *adv.*

mel•an•chol•y (mĕl'ən-kŏl'ē) *n.* 1. Sadness; gloom. 2. Pensive reflection. —*adj.* 1. Sad; gloomy. 2. Pensive; thoughtful. [< Gk

melankholia, sadness, "(an excess of) black bile."] —**mel'an•chol'i•ness** *n.*

Mel•a•ne•sia (mĕl'ə-nē'zhə, -shə). An island group in the SW Pacific Ocean. —**Mel'a•ne'sian** *adj.*

mé•lange (mā-länzh') *n.* Also **me•lange.** A mixture. [F.]

mel•a•nin (mĕl'ə-nĭn) *n.* A dark pigment found in the skin, retina, and hair. [< Gk *melas,* black.]

mel•a•no•ma (mĕl'ə-nō'mə) *n., pl.* **-mas** or **-mata** (-mə-tə). A dark-pigmented malignant tumor.

Mel•ba toast (mĕl'bə). Very thinly sliced crisp toast. [< Dame Nellie *Melba* (1861–1931), Australian soprano.]

Mel•bourne (mĕl'bərn). A city of SE Australia. Pop. 2,122,000.

meld¹ (mĕld) *v.* To declare or display (a card or combination of cards in a hand) for inclusion in one's score in a game such as pinochle. —*n.* A combination of cards to be declared for a score. [G *melden,* to declare.]

meld² (mĕld) *v.* To be or cause to become blended. [Blend of MELT + WELD.]

me•lee (mā'lā', mā-lā') *n.* Also **mê•lée** (mě-lā'). 1. Hand-to-hand fighting. 2. A brawl. 3. A crowded tumult. [< OF *meslee,* MEDLEY.]

mel•io•rate (mĕl'yə-rāt', mē'lē-ə-) *v.* **-rated, -rating.** To make or become better; improve. [< L *melior,* better.] —**mel'io•ra'tion** *n.*

mel•lif•lu•ous (mə-lĭf'lōō-əs) *adj.* 1. Flowing with honey. 2. Euphoniously smooth and sweet. [< L *mellifluus.*]

mel•low (mĕl'ō) *adj.* 1. a. Soft, sweet, juicy, and full-flavored because of ripeness. b. Suggesting these qualities. 2. Rich and soft in quality. 3. Gently and maturely dignified. 4. Relaxed and at ease. 5. Slightly and pleasantly intoxicated. —*v.* To make or become mellow. [Perh < OE *melu,* meal, "soft and rich."] —**mel'low•ly** *adv.* —**mel'low•ness** *n.*

me•lo•de•on (mə-lō'dē-ən) *n.* A small reed organ.

me•lo•di•ous (mə-lō'dē-əs) *adj.* 1. Tuneful. 2. Agreeable to hear.

mel•o•dra•ma (mĕl'ə-drä'mə, -drăm'ə) *n.* 1. A sentimental dramatic presentation characterized by heavy use of suspense and sensational episodes. 2. Melodramatic behavior or occurrences. [F *mélodrame,* "musical drama."]

mel•o•dra•mat•ic (mĕl'ə-drə-măt'ĭk) *adj.* 1. Having the excitement and emotional appeal of melodrama. 2. Exaggeratedly emotional or sentimental; histrionic.

mel•o•dy (mĕl'ə-dē) *n., pl.* **-dies.** 1. A pleasing succession or arrangement of sounds. 2. Musical quality. 3. *Mus.* a. A sequence of single tones. b. The structure of music with respect to the succession of single tones. c. The leading part in a composition. [< Gk *melōidia,* choral song.] —**me•lod'ic** (mə-lŏd'ĭk) *adj.*

mel•on (mĕl'ən) *n.* Any of several fruits, as a cantaloupe or watermelon, having a hard rind and juicy flesh. [< Gk *mēlo(pepōn),* melon, "apple(-gourd)."]

melt (mĕlt) *v.* 1. To change or be changed from a solid to a liquid state by the application of

---

ô paw, for/oi boy/ou out/ŏŏ took/ōō coo/p pop/r run/s sauce/sh shy/t to/th thin/*th* the/
ŭ cut/ûr fur/v van/w wag/y yes/z size/zh vision/ə ago, item, edible, gallop, circus/

heat, pressure, or both. **2.** To dissolve. **3.** To disappear or cause to disappear gradually. **4.** To pass or merge imperceptibly into something else; blend or cause to blend gradually. **5.** To become softened in feeling; be made gentle. [< OE *meltan*. See **mel-**.]

melting point. The temperature at which a solid and its liquid are in equilibrium, at any fixed pressure.

Mel·ville (mĕl'vĭl), **Herman.** 1819–1891. American novelist.

mem (mĕm) *n.* The 13th letter of the Hebrew alphabet, representing *m*.

mem. **1.** member. **2.** memoir. **3.** memorial.

mem·ber (mĕm'bər) *n.* **1.** A distinct part of a whole. **2.** A part or organ, as of the human body. **3.** One who belongs to a group or organization. **4.** One elected to a political body such as Congress. [< L *membrum.*]

mem·ber·ship (mĕm'bər-shĭp') *n.* **1.** The state of being a member. **2.** The total number of members in a group.

mem·brane (mĕm'brān') *n.* **1.** A thin, pliable layer of animal or plant tissue covering or separating structures or organs. **2.** A thin sheet of natural or synthetic material that is permeable to substances in solution. [L *membrāna*, "skin covering a member of the body."] —**mem'bra·nous** (-brə-nəs) *adj.*

me·men·to (mə-mĕn'tō) *n., pl.* **-tos** or **-toes.** Any reminder of the past; a souvenir. [< L *meminisse*, to remember.]

mem·o (mĕm'ō) *n., pl.* **-os.** A memorandum.

mem·oir (mĕm'wär', -wôr') *n.* **1.** **memoirs.** An autobiography; biography. **2.** A written reminder; memorandum. **3.** The report of the proceedings of a learned society. [< L *memoria*, MEMORY.]

mem·o·ra·bil·i·a (mĕm'ər-ə-bĭl'ē-ə, -bĭl'yə) *pl.n.* Things worthy of remembrance.

mem·o·ra·ble (mĕm'ər-ə-bəl) *adj.* Worth being remembered or noted; remarkable. [< L *memor*, mindful.] —**mem'o·ra·bly** *adv.*

mem·o·ran·dum (mĕm'ə-răn'dəm) *n., pl.* **-dums** or **-da** (-də). **1.** A short note written as a reminder. **2.** A written record or communication, as in a business office.

me·mo·ri·al (mə-môr'ē-əl, mə-mōr'-) *n.* **1.** An established remembrance of a person or event; monument. **2.** A written statement of facts or a petition. —*adj.* Commemorative. —**me·mo'ri·al·ize'** *v.* (-ized, -izing).

mem·o·rize (mĕm'ə-rīz') *v.* **-rized, -rizing.** To commit to memory; learn by heart. —**mem'o·ri·za'tion** (-rĭ-zā'shən) *n.* —**mem'o·riz'er** *n.*

mem·o·ry (mĕm'ər-ē) *n., pl.* **-ries.** **1.** The faculty of retaining and recalling past experience; the ability to remember. **2.** A remembrance; recollection. **3.** All that a person can remember. **4.** Something remembered of a person, thing, or event. **5.** The period of time covered by remembrance or recollection. [< L *memoria.*]

Mem·phis (mĕm'fĭs). A city of SW Tennessee. Pop. 624,000.

men. *pl.* of man.

men·ace (mĕn'ĭs) *n.* **1.** A threat. **2.** A troublesome or annoying person. —*v.* **-aced, -acing.**

To threaten. [< L *minacia*, menace, orig "threatening things."] —**men'ac·ing·ly** *adv.*

mé·nage (mā-näzh') *n.* Also **me·nage.** A household. [< VL *mansiōnāticum*, household.]

me·nag·er·ie (mə-năj'ə-rē, mə-năzh'-) *n.* A collection of live wild animals on exhibition. [F *ménagerie*, orig "the management of domestic animals."]

mend (mĕnd) *v.* **1.** To make right or correct; repair. **2.** To reform or improve. **3.** To improve in health or heal. **4.** To correct errors. —*n.* **1.** The act of mending. **2.** A mended place. [< ME *amenden*, to amend.]

men·da·cious (mĕn-dā'shəs) *adj.* **1.** Lying; untruthful. **2.** False; untrue. [< L *mendāx.*] —**men·dac'i·ty** (-dăs'ə-tē) *n.*

men·de·le·vi·um (mĕn'də-lē'vē-əm) *n.* Symbol **Md** A radioactive element with two isotopes, Md[255] and Md[256]. [< D. *Mendeleev* (1834–1907), Russian chemist.]

Men·dels·sohn (mĕn'dəl-sən), **Felix.** 1809–1847. German composer.

men·di·cant (mĕn'dĭ-kənt) *adj.* Depending upon alms for a living; practicing begging. —*n.* **1.** A beggar. **2.** A mendicant friar. [< L *mendīcāre*, to beg.]

me·ni·al (mē'nē-əl, mēn'yəl) *adj.* **1.** Pertaining to or appropriate for a servant. **2.** Of or pertaining to work regarded as servile. —*n.* A servant, esp. a domestic servant. [< VL *mansiōnāta*, household.] —**me'ni·al·ly** *adv.*

men·in·gi·tis (mĕn'ĭn-jī'tĭs) *n.* Inflammation of any or all of the meninges of the brain and spinal cord, usually caused by a bacterial infection. [< MENING(ES) + -ITIS.]

me·ninx (mē'nĭngks) *n., pl.* **meninges** (mə-nĭn'jēz). Any of the membranes enclosing the brain and spinal cord in vertebrates. [< Gk *mēninx*, membrane.] —**me·nin'ge·al** *adj.*

me·nis·cus (mə-nĭs'kəs) *n., pl.* **menisci** (-nĭs'ī') or **-cuses.** **1.** A crescent-shaped body. **2.** The curved upper surface of a nonturbulent liquid in a container. [< Gk *mēniskos*, crescent.] —**me·nis'cal** (-kəl), **me·nis'coid'** (-koid'), **men'is·coi'dal** (mĕn'ĭs-koid'l) *adj.*

Men·non·ite (mĕn'ən-īt') *n.* A member of an Evangelical Protestant Christian sect opposed to taking oaths, performing military service, etc. [< *Menno* Simons (1492–1559), religious reformer.]

men·o·pause (mĕn'ə-pôz') *n.* The period of cessation of menstruation, occurring usually between the ages of 45 and 50. [< Gk *mēn*, moon + PAUSE.] —**men'o·paus'al** *adj.*

men·ses (mĕn'sēz) *pl.n.* Blood and dead cell debris discharged from the uterus through the vagina by adult women at approximately monthly intervals between puberty and menopause. [L *mēnsēs*, months.]

men·stru·al (mĕn'strōō-əl) *adj.* Relating to menstruation. [< L *mēnstruus*, menstrual, monthly.]

men·stru·ate (mĕn'strōō-āt') *v.* **-ated, -ating.** To undergo menstruation.

men·stru·a·tion (mĕn'strōō-ā'shən) *n.* The process or an instance of discharging the menses.

ă pat/ā ate/âr care/ä bar/b bib/ch chew/d deed/ĕ pet/ē be/f fit/g gag/h hat/hw what/
ĭ pit/ī pie/îr pier/j judge/k kick/l lid, fatal/m mum/n no, sudden/ng sing/ŏ pot/ō go/

men·su·ra·ble (měn'sər-ə-bəl, měn'shər-ə-) *adj.* Capable of being measured. [< L *mēnsūra*, measure.] —**men'su·ra·bil'i·ty** *n.*

men·su·ra·tion (měn'sə-rā'shən, měn'shə-) *n.* The process, act, or art of measuring. —**men'su·ral** *adj.* —**men'su·ra·tive** *adj.*

–ment. *comb. form.* Product, means, action, or state: **measurement**. [< L *-mentum.*]

men·tal (měn'təl) *adj.* **1.** Pertaining to the mind; intellectual. **2.** Done or performed by the mind. [< L *mēns (ment-)*, mind.] —**men'tal·ly** *adv.*

mental deficiency. Subnormal intellectual development.

men·tal·i·ty (měn-tăl'ə-tē) *n., pl.* **-ties. 1.** Intellectual capability or endowment; intelligence. **2.** Mental status or inclination.

mental retardation. Mental deficiency.

men·thol (měn'thôl') *n.* A white, crystalline organic compound, $C_{10}H_{19}OH$, used in perfumes, as a mild anesthetic, and as a flavoring. [< L *mentha*, MINT² + -OL.] —**men'tho·lat'ed** *adj.*

men·tion (měn'shən) *v.* To cite or refer to incidentally. —*n.* An act of mentioning. [< L *mentiō*, remembrance, mention.]

men·tor (měn'tôr', -tər) *n.* A wise and trusted counselor or teacher. [< *Mentor*, a character in Fénelon's *Télémaque* (1699).]

men·u (měn'yōō, măn'yōō) *n.* A list of dishes to be served or available for a meal; bill of fare. [F, menu, list.]

me·ow (mē-ou'). Also **mi·aow, mi·aou.** *n.* The cry of a cat. [Imit.] —**me·ow'** *v.*

mep, m.e.p. mean effective pressure.

me·phi·tis (mə-fī'tĭs) *n.* **1.** An offensive smell; stench. **2.** A poisonous or foul-smelling gas emitted from the earth. [L *mefitis*, stench.] —**me·phit'ic** (-fĭt'ĭk), **me·phit'i·cal** *adj.*

meq. milliequivalent.

mer·can·tile (mûr'kən-tēl', -tīl', -tĭl) *adj.* Of or pertaining to merchants or trade. [< VL *mercātāns*, merchant.]

Mer·ca·tor projection (mər-kā'tər). Also **Mer·ca·tor's projection.** A map projection in which the meridians and parallels appear as straight lines crossing at right angles and areas appear greater farther from the equator. [< G. *Mercator* (1512–1594), Flemish cartographer.]

mer·ce·nar·y (mûr'sə-něr'ē) *adj.* **1.** Motivated solely by a desire for monetary or material gain. **2.** Hired for service in a foreign army. [< L *mercēs*, pay.] —**mer'ce·nar'i·ly** *adv.* —**mer'ce·nar'i·ness** *n.* —**mer'ce·nar'y** *n.*

mer·cer (mûr'sər) *n. Brit.* A dealer in textiles, esp. silks. [< L *merx (merc-)*, merchandise.]

mer·cer·ize (mûr'sə-rīz') *v.* **-ized, -izing.** To treat (cotton thread) with sodium hydroxide, so as to shrink the fiber and increase its color absorption and luster. [< J. *Mercer* (1791–1866), English textile maker.]

mer·chan·dise (mûr'chən-dīz', -dīs'). Also **mer·chan·dize.** *n.* The commodities of commerce; goods that can be bought or sold. —*v.* (mûr'chən-dīz') **-dised, -dising.** To buy and sell (commodities). —**mer'chan·dis'er** *n.*

mer·chant (mûr'chənt) *n.* **1.** One whose occupation is the wholesale purchase and retail sale of goods for profit. **2.** A shopkeeper. [< L *mercāri*, to trade.]

mer·chant·man (mûr'chənt-mən) *n.* A ship used in commerce.

merchant marine. 1. A nation's ships that are engaged in commerce. **2.** The personnel of such ships.

mer·cu·ri·al (mər-kyŏŏr'ē-əl) *n.* A medical or chemical preparation containing mercury. —*adj.* **1.** Containing or caused by the action of the element mercury. **2.** Quick and changeable in character. [< L *Mercurius*, the god Mercury.] —**mer·cu'ri·al·ly** *adv.*

mer·cu·ri·al·ism (mər-kyŏŏr'ē-əl-ĭz'əm) *n.* Poisoning caused by mercury or any of its compounds.

mer·cu·ric (mər-kyŏŏr'ĭk) *adj.* Of or containing bivalent mercury.

Mer·cu·ro·chrome (mər-kyŏŏr'ə-krōm') *n.* A trademark for an organic mercury compound used as an antiseptic.

mer·cu·ry (mûr'kyə-rē) *n.* **1.** *Symbol* **Hg** A silvery-white, poisonous metallic element, liquid at room temperature, used in thermometers, barometers, vapor lamps, and batteries and in the preparation of chemical pesticides. Atomic number 80, atomic weight 200.59. **2. Mercury.** The planet nearest the sun, having a sidereal period of revolution about the sun of 88.0 days at a mean distance of 36.2 million miles, a mean radius of approx. 1,500 miles, and a mass approx. 0.05 that of Earth. **3. Mercury.** Roman god of commerce and science, serving as messenger to the other gods. [ME *Mercurie*, god, planet, and metal.]

mer·cy (mûr'sē) *n., pl.* **-cies. 1.** Compassionate treatment of an offender, enemy, etc.; clemency. **2.** A disposition to be kind and forgiving. **3.** A fortunate occurrence. **4.** Alleviation of distress; relief. [< LL *mercēs*, reward, God's gratuitous compassion.] —**mer'ci·ful** *adj.* —**mer'ci·less** *adj.*

mercy killing. Euthanasia.

mere (mîr) *adj. superl.* **merest.** Being nothing more than what is specified. [L *merus*, clear, pure, unmixed.] —**mere'ly** *adv.*

mer·e·tri·cious (měr'ə-trĭsh'əs) *adj.* Attracting attention in a vulgar manner. [< L *meretrix*, a prostitute.] —**mer'e·tri'cious·ly** *adv.* —**mer'e·tri'cious·ness** *n.*

merge (mûrj) *v.* **merged, merging.** To blend together or cause to be absorbed so as to lose identity. [< L *mergere*, to dive, plunge.] —**mer'gence** *n.*

merg·er (mûr'jər) *n.* The union of two or more commercial interests or corporations.

me·rid·i·an (mə-rĭd'ē-ən) *n.* **1. a.** A great circle on the earth's surface passing through both geophysical poles. **b.** Either half of such a great circle lying between the poles. **2.** A great circle passing through the two poles of the celestial sphere and the observer's zenith. **3.** The highest point or stage of development; zenith. [< L *merīdiēs*, midday.] —**me·rid'i·an** *adj.*

me·ringue (mə-răng') *n.* A dessert topping made of beaten egg whites, sweetened and baked. [F *méringue.*]

ô paw, for/oi boy/ou out/ŏŏ took/ōō coo/p pop/r run/s sauce/sh shy/t to/th thin/*th* the/
ŭ cut/ûr fur/v van/w wag/y yes/z size/zh vision/ə ago, item, edible, gallop, circus/

me·ri·no (mə-rē′nō) *n., pl.* **-nos.** **1.** A sheep of a breed having fine, soft wool. **2.** The wool of such a sheep or fabric made from it. [Span.] —**me·ri′no** *adj.*

mer·it (mĕr′ĭt) *n.* **1.** Value, excellence, or superior quality. **2.** Often **merits.** An aspect of a person's character deserving approval or disapproval. **3. a.** The intrinsic right or wrong of any matter. **b.** The actual facts of a legal matter. —*v.* To earn; deserve; warrant. [< L *merēre* (pp *meritus*), to earn, deserve.] —**mer′it·ed·ly** *adv.*

mer·i·to·ri·ous (mĕr′ə-tôr′ē-əs, -tōr′ē-əs) *adj.* Deserving reward or praise; having merit. —**mer′i·to′ri·ous·ly** *adv.*

Mer·lin (mûr′lən). Magician and prophet of Arthurian legend.

mer·maid (mûr′mād) *n.* A fabled creature of the sea with the head and upper body of a woman and the tail of a fish. [ME *meremaide*, "sea creature."]

mer·ri·ment (mĕr′ĭ-mənt) *n.* Gay conviviality; hilarity.

mer·ry (mĕr′ē) *adj.* **-rier, -riest.** **1.** Full of high-spirited gaiety; jolly. **2.** Marked by fun and gaiety; festive. **3.** Pleasurable; entertaining. [< *mirige*, pleasant. See **mreghu-**.] —**mer′ri·ly** *adv.* —**mer′ri·ness** *n.*

mer·ry-go-round (mĕr′ē-gō-round′) *n.* **1.** A circular revolving platform fitted with seats, often animal-shaped, ridden for amusement. **2.** Any whirl or swift round.

mer·ry·mak·ing (mĕr′ē-mā′kĭng) *n.* **1.** Participation in a revel. **2.** A festivity; revelry. —**mer′ry·mak′er** *n.*

Mer·thi·o·late (mər-thī′ə-lāt′) *n.* A trademark for an organic mercury compound used as an antiseptic.

me·sa (mā′sə) *n.* A flat-topped elevation with clifflike sides, common in the SW U.S. [< L *mēnsa*, table.]

mes·ca·line (mĕs′kə-lēn′) *n.* A psychedelic drug, $C_{11}H_{17}NO_3$. [< Nah *mexcalli*.]

Mes·dames. *pl.* of **Madame** and **Madam.**

mes·en·ter·y (mĕs′ən-tĕr′ē) *n., pl.* **-ies.** Also **mes·en·ter·i·um** (mĕs′ən-tĭr′ē-əm) *pl.* **-ia** (-ē-ə). Any of several peritoneal folds that connect the intestines to the dorsal abdominal wall. [< Gk *mesenterion*, "middle intestine."] —**mes′en·ter′ic** *adj.*

mesh (mĕsh) *n.* **1.** Any of the open spaces in a cord, thread, or wire network. **2.** A net or network. **3.** The engagement of gear teeth. —*v.* **1.** To entangle or ensnare. **2.** To engage or become engaged, as gear teeth. **3.** To coordinate; harmonize. [< MDu *masche*, *maesche*.] —**mesh′y** *adj.*

mesh·work (mĕsh′wûrk′) *n.* Meshes; network.

mes·mer·ize (mĕz′mə-rīz′, mĕs′-) *v.* **-ized, -izing.** To hypnotize. —**mes′mer·ism′** *n.* —**mes′mer·iz′er** *n.*

meso-. *comb. form.* Middle, center, or intermediate. [< Gk *mesos*, middle.]

Mes·o·lith·ic (mĕz′ə-lĭth′ĭk, mĕs′-) *adj.* Pertaining to a period of human culture between the Paleolithic and Neolithic ages, marked by the appearance of the bow and of cutting tools. —*n.* The Mesolithic Age.

Mes·o·po·ta·mi·a (mĕs′ə-pə-tā′mē-ə). The ancient country between the Tigris and Euphrates rivers. —**Mes′o·po·ta′mi·an** *adj. & n.*

Mesopotamia

Mes·o·zo·ic (mĕz′ə-zō′ĭk, mĕs′-) *adj.* Of or belonging to the geologic time, rock systems, or deposits of the era between the Paleozoic and Cenozoic, and including the Cretaceous, Jurassic, and Triassic periods. —*n.* The Mesozoic era.

mes·quite (mĕs-kēt′, mə-skēt′) *n.* A thorny, pod-bearing shrub of SW North America. [< Nah *mizquitl*.]

mess (mĕs) *n.* **1.** A disorderly accumulation of items; jumble. **2.** A confusing state of affairs; muddle; chaos. **3.** A quantity of food: *a mess of fish.* **4. a.** A group of persons who regularly eat meals together. **b.** The meal eaten by such a group. —*v.* **1.** To make disorderly and soiled; clutter. **2.** To bungle or mismanage. **3.** To interfere; meddle. [< L *missus*, "placement," course of a meal.]

mes·sage (mĕs′ĭj) *n.* **1.** A communication transmitted from one person or group to another. **2.** The basic theme or significance of something. [< VL *missāticum, "something sent."]

mes·sen·ger (mĕs′ən-jər) *n.* One who transmits messages or performs errands.

Mes·si·ah (mə-sī′ə) *n.* **1.** The anticipated deliverer and king of the Jews. **2.** Jesus Christ. **3. messiah.** Any expected deliverer or liberator. [Aram *məshīḥa* or Heb *māshiaḥ*.]

Messrs. *pl.* of **Mr.**

mess·y (mĕs′ē) *adj.* **-ier, -iest.** Untidy; dirty; disordered. —**mess′i·ly** *adv.* —**mess′i·ness** *n.*

mes·ti·zo (mĕs-tē′zō) *n., pl.* **-zos** or **-zoes.** A person of mixed European and Indian ancestry. [Span, "mixed."]

met (mĕt). *p.t. & p.p.* of **meet**[1].

met. 1. meteorology. **2.** metropolitan.

meta-. *comb. form.* **1.** *Anat.* Situated behind. **2.** Occurring later. **3.** Beyond; transcending. **4.** Changed or involving change. **5.** Alternating. **6.** *Geol.* Having undergone metamorphic change. [< Gk *meta*, between, with, beside, after.]

me·tab·o·lism (mə-tăb′ə-lĭz′əm) *n.* **1.** The complex of physical and chemical processes involved in the maintenance of life. **2.** The

---

ă pat/ā ate/âr care/ä bar/b **b**ib/ch **ch**ew/d **d**ee**d**/ĕ pet/ē be/f **f**it/g **g**a**g**/h **h**at/hw **wh**at/
ĭ pit/ī pie/îr pier/j **j**udge/k **k**ic**k**/l **l**id, fata**l**/m **m**u**m**/n **n**o, sudde**n**/ng si**ng**/ŏ pot/ō go/

functioning of any specific substance within the living body: *water metabolism; iodine metabolism.* —**met′a•bol′ic** (mĕt′ə-bŏl′ĭk) *adj.* —**me•tab′o•lize′** *v.* (**-lized, -lizing**).

met•a•car•pus (mĕt′ə-kär′pəs) *n.* The part of the hand or forefoot that includes the five bones between the phalanges and carpus.

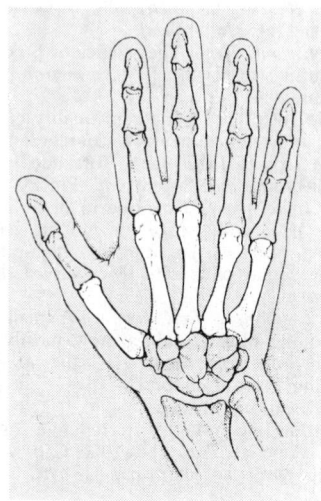

metacarpus

met•al (mĕt′l) *n.* **1.** Any of a category of electropositive elements that are usually whitish, lustrous, and often ductile and malleable with high tensile strength. **2.** An alloy of two or more metallic elements. **3.** An object made of metal. **4.** Basic character; mettle. [< Gk *metallon,* a mine, mineral, metal.] —**me•tal′lic** (mə-tăl′ĭk) *adj.* —**me•tal′li•cal•ly** *adv.*

metall. metallurgical; metallurgy.

met•al•lur•gy (mĕt′l-ûr′jē) *n.* The science or technology of extracting metals from their ores, of purifying metals, and of creating useful objects from metals. [< Gk *metallourgos,* a miner.] —**met′al•lur′gic, met′al•lur′gi•cal** *adj.* —**met′al•lur′gist** *n.*

met•a•mor•phic (mĕt′ə-môr′fĭk) *adj.* Also **met•a•mor•phous** (-môr′fəs). **1.** Of or relating to metamorphosis. **2.** Characteristic of, pertaining to, or changed by metamorphism.

met•a•mor•phism (mĕt′ə-môr′fĭz′əm) *n.* Any alteration in composition, texture, or structure of rock masses, caused by great heat or pressure.

met•a•mor•phose (mĕt′ə-môr′fōz′, -fōs′) *v.* **-phosed, -phosing.** To change or be changed by metamorphosis.

met•a•mor•pho•sis (mĕt′ə-môr′fə-sĭs) *n., pl.* **-ses** (-sēz′). **1.** A transformation, as by magic. **2.** A marked change in appearance, character, etc. **3.** Marked changes in form and mode of life during development to maturity, as in insects. [< Gk *metamorphōsis.*]

met•a•phase (mĕt′ə-fāz′) *n.* The stage of mitosis during which the chromosomes are aligned along the equator of the mitotic spindle.

met•a•phor (mĕt′ə-fôr′, -fər) *n.* A figure of speech in which a term is transferred from the object it ordinarily designates to one it can designate only by implicit comparison or analogy, as in the phrase *evening of life.* [< Gk *metaphora,* transference.] —**met′a•phor′ic** (-fôr′ĭk, -fŏr′ĭk), **met′a•phor′i•cal** *adj.*

met•a•phys•i•cal (mĕt′ə-fĭz′ĭ-kəl) *adj.* **1.** Of or pertaining to metaphysics. **2.** Based on speculative or abstract reasoning. **3.** Abstruse. **4.** Immaterial or imaginary.

met•a•phys•ics (mĕt′ə-fĭz′ĭks) *n. (takes sing. v.).* The systematic investigation of the nature of first principles and problems of ultimate reality. [ML *metaphysica.*] —**met′a•phy•si′cian** (-fə-zĭsh′ən) *n.*

me•tas•ta•sis (mə-tăs′tə-sĭs) *n., pl.* **-ses** (-sēz′). Transmission of disease from an original site to one or more sites elsewhere in the body, as in tuberculosis or cancer. [< LL, transition.] —**me•tas′ta•size′** *v.* (**-sized, -sizing**).

met•a•tar•sus (mĕt′ə-tär′səs) *n., pl.* **-si** (-sī′). The middle part of the foot, composed of the five bones between the toes and tarsus, that forms the instep. —**met′a•tar′sal** *adj. & n.*

mete• (mēt) *v.* **meted, meting.** To deal out; allot. [< OE *metan.* See med-.]

me•tem•psy•cho•sis (mə-tĕm′sĭ-kō′sĭs, mĕt′əm-sĭ-kō′sĭs) *n., pl.* **-ses** (-sēz′). The transmigration of souls. [Gk *metempsukhōsis.*]

me•te•or (mē′tē-ər, -ôr′) *n.* **1.** The luminous trail or streak that appears in the sky when a meteoroid is made incandescent by the earth's atmosphere. **2.** A meteoroid. [< Gk *meteōros,* high in the air.]

me•te•or•ic (mē′tē-ôr′ĭk, -ŏr′ĭk) *adj.* **1.** Of or formed by a meteor or meteors. **2.** Resembling a meteor in speed and brilliance.

me•te•or•ite (mē′tē-ə-rīt′) *n.* The stony or metallic material of a meteoroid that survives passage through the atmosphere and reaches the earth's surface.

me•te•or•oid (mē′tē-ə-roid′) *n.* Any of numerous celestial bodies, ranging in size from specks of dust to asteroids weighing thousands of tons, that appear as meteors when entering the earth's atmosphere.

meteorol. meteorology.

me•te•or•ol•o•gy (mē′tē-ə-rŏl′ə-jē) *n.* The science of the earth's atmosphere, esp. weather conditions. —**me′te•or′o•log′i•cal** (-ôr′ə-lŏj′ĭ-kəl, -ŏr′ə-lŏj′ĭ-kəl) *adj.* —**me′te•or•ol′o•gist** *n.*

me•ter¹ (mē′tər) *n.* Also *chiefly Brit.* **me•tre.** **1.** The measured rhythm characteristic of verse. **2. a.** The division of music into measures or bars. **b.** A specific division of this kind. [< Gk *metron,* measure.]

me•ter² (mē′tər) *n.* Also *chiefly Brit.* **me•tre.** The fundamental metric unit of length, approx. 39.37 inches. [< Gk *metron,* meter, measure.]

me•ter³ (mē′tər) *n.* Any of various devices designed to measure or indicate and record. —*v.* **1.** To measure with a meter. **2.** To imprint with postage by means of a postage meter or other similar device.

ô paw, for/oi boy/ou out/ŏŏ took/ōō coo/p pop/r run/s sauce/sh shy/t to/th thin/*th* the/
ŭ cut/ûr fur/v van/w wag/y yes/z size/zh vision/ə ago, item, edible, gallop, circus/

–meter. *comb. form.* A measuring device: **ba-rometer.**

meth-. *comb. form.* Chemical compounds containing methyl.

meth·a·done hydrochloride (měth′ə-dōn′). An organic compound, $C_{21}H_{27}NO \cdot HCL$, used as an analgesic and in treating heroin addiction.

meth·ane (měth′ān′) *n.* An odorless, colorless, flammable gas, CH_4, that is the major constituent of natural gas, used as a fuel and as a source of hydrogen and a wide variety of organic compounds.

meth·a·nol (měth′ə-nôl′, -nŏl′) *n.* A colorless, flammable liquid, CH_3OH, used as an antifreeze, solvent, fuel, and denaturant for ethanol.

me·thinks (mĭ-thĭngks′) *v. Archaic.* It seems to me.

meth·od (měth′əd) *n.* **1.** A systematic means or manner of procedure. **2.** Orderliness; regularity. [< Gk *methodos,* "a going after."] —**me·thod′i·cal** (mə-thŏd′ĭ-kəl) *adj.*

Meth·od·ist (měth′ə-dĭst) *n.* A Protestant Christian denomination developed from the doctrines of John Wesley concerning free grace and individual responsibility. —**Meth′od·ism′** *n.* —**Meth′od·ist** *adj.*

meth·od·ol·o·gy (měth′ə-dŏl′ə-jē) *n., pl.* **-gies.** **1.** The system of principles and procedures applied in a science or discipline. **2.** The theoretical foundations of a given practical activity. —**meth′od·o·log′i·cal** (měth′ə-də-lŏj′ĭ-kəl) *adj.* —**meth′od·o·log′i·cal·ly** *adv.*

me·thu·se·lah (mě-thōō′zə-lə) *n.* An extremely old man. [< *Methuselah,* Biblical patriarch said to have lived 969 years. Genesis 5:27.]

meth·yl (měth′əl) *n.* The univalent organic radical CH_3. [< Gk *methu,* wine, mead.]

methyl alcohol. Methanol.

meth·yl·at·ed spirit (měth′ə-lā′tĭd). Often **methylated spirits.** A denatured alcohol consisting of a mixture of ethanol and methanol.

me·tic·u·lous (mə-tĭk′yə-ləs) *adj.* Extremely or excessively careful and precise; scrupulous. [L *meticulōsus,* overly concerned, fearful.] —**me·tic′u·los′i·ty** (mə-tĭk′yə-lŏs′ə-tē) *n.*

mé·tier (mā-tyā′) *n.* **1.** An occupation, trade, or profession. **2.** One's specialty. [< VL *misterium.*]

me·tre. *Chiefly Brit.* Variant of **meter.**

met·ric (mět′rĭk) *adj.* Of or using the metric system.

met·ri·cal (mět′rĭ-kəl) *adj.* **1.** Pertaining to versification or measure in music or poetry. **2.** Composed in poetic meter. **3.** Pertaining to measurement. [< Gk *metron,* measure, meter.] —**met′ri·cal·ly** *adv.*

metric system. A decimal system of weights and measures based on the meter as a unit length and the kilogram as a unit mass. Derived units include the liter for liquid volume, the stere for solid volume, and the are for area.

metric ton. A unit of mass equal to 1,000 kilograms.

met·ri·fy (mět′rə-fī′) *v.* **-fied, -fying.** To convert to or adopt the metric system. —**met′ri·ca′tion,**

met′ri·fi·ca′tion *n.*

met·ro·nome (mět′rə-nōm′) *n.* A device that marks time at a steady beat in adjustable intervals. [Gk *metron,* measure + *nomos,* rule, law.] —**met′ro·nom′ic** (mět′rə-nŏm′ĭk) *adj.*

me·trop·o·lis (mə-trŏp′ə-lĭs) *n., pl.* **-lises. 1.** A major city, esp. the capital of a country, state, or. region. **2.** A large urban center of culture, trade, etc. [< Gk *mētropolis.*] —**met′ro·pol′i·tan** (mět′rə-pŏl′ə-tən) *adj.*

–metry. *comb. form.* The science or process of measuring: **optometry.** [< Gk *metron,* meter, measure.]

met·tle (mět′l) *n.* **1.** Inherent quality of character and temperament. **2.** Courage and fortitude; spirit. [ME *metel,* fortitude, metal.]

met·tle·some (mět′l-səm) *adj.* Plucky.

mew[1] (myōō) *v.* To confine in or as if in a cage. [ME *mewe,* cage for molting hawks.]

mew[2] (myōō) *v.* To utter the high-pitched, crying sound of a cat. [ME *mewen* (imit.).] —**mew** *n.*

mews (myōōz) *n. (takes sing. v.).* A small street containing private stables, now mostly converted into apartments. [< the *Mews* at Charing Cross, London.]

Mex. Mexican; Mexico.

Mex·i·co (měk′sĭ-kō′). A republic of SW North America. Pop. 39,643,000. Cap. Mexico City. —**Mex′i·can** (-kən) *adj.*

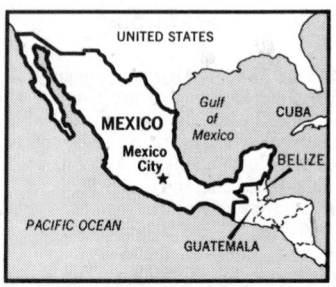

Mexico

Mexico, Gulf of. An inlet of the Atlantic Ocean, surrounded by the U.S., Mexico, and Cuba.

Mexico City. The capital of Mexico. Pop. 3,193,000.

mez·za·nine (měz′ə-nēn′, měz′ə-nēn′) *n.* **1.** A partial story between two main stories of a building. **2.** The lowest balcony in a theater or its first few rows. [< It *mezzano,* middle.]

mez·zo·so·pran·o (mět′sō-sə-prăn′ō, -prä′nō, měd′zō-, měz′ō-) *n., pl.* **-os.** Also **mez·zo. 1.** The range between soprano and contralto. **2.** A woman having such a range.

mfg. manufacturing.

mfr. manufacture; manufacturer.

mg milligram.

Mg magnesium.

M.G. Major General.

mgr. manager.

MH Medal of Honor.

mi. mile.

ă pat/ā ate/âr care/ä bar/b bib/ch chew/d deed/ě pet/ē be/f fit/g gag/h hat/hw what/
ĭ pit/ī pie/îr pier/j judge/k kick/l lid, fatal/m mum/n no, sudden/ng sing/ŏ pot/ō go/

Mi·am·i (mī-ăm'ē, -ăm'ə). A city of SE Florida. Pop. 335,000.

mi·aou, mi·aow. Variants of **meow.**

mi·as·ma (mī-ăz'mə, mē-) n., pl. **-mas** or **-mata** (-mə-tə). 1. A poisonous atmosphere formerly thought to rise from swamps and cause disease. 2. Any noxious atmosphere or influence. [< Gk *miainein,* to pollute.] —**mi·as'mal** (-məl), **mi·as·mat'ic** (mī'əz-măt'ĭk), **mi·as'mic** adj.

Mic. Micah (Old Testament).

mi·ca (mī'kə) n. Any of a group of chemically and physically related mineral silicates, common in igneous and metamorphic rocks. [< L *mica,* grain.]

mice. pl. of **mouse.**

Mich. Michigan.

Mi·chel·an·ge·lo (mī'kəl-ăn'jə-lō', mĭk'əl-). 1475–1564. Italian sculptor, painter, and architect.

Mich·i·gan (mĭsh'ĭ-gən). A state of the north-central U.S. Pop. 8,875,000. Cap. Lansing.

Michigan, Lake. The third largest of the Great Lakes.

mi·cra. Alternate pl. of **micron.**

micro-. comb. form. 1. Small or smaller than. 2. Invisible to the naked eye. 3. *Symbol* μ One-millionth (10⁻⁶). [< Gk *mikros,* small.]

mi·crobe (mī'krōb') n. A minute life form; a microorganism, esp. one that causes disease. —**mi·cro'bi·al** (mī-krō'bē-əl), **mi·cro'bic** adj.

mi·cro·cosm (mī'krə-kŏz'əm) n. A diminutive, representative world; a system analogous to a much larger system in constitution, configuration, or development. [< Gk *mikros kosmos,* small world.] —**mi'cro·cos'mic, mi'cro·cos'mi·cal** adj.

mi·cro·film (mī'krə-fĭlm') n. 1. A film upon which documents are photographed greatly reduced in size. 2. A reproduction on microfilm. —**mi'cro·film'** v.

Mi·cro·groove (mī'krō-grōōv') n. A trademark for a long-playing phonograph record.

mi·crom·e·ter (mī-krŏm'ə-tər) n. Any of various devices for measuring minute distances.

mi·cron (mī'krŏn') n., pl. **-crons** or **-cra** (-krə). Also **mi·kron.** A unit of length equal to one-millionth (10⁻⁶) of a meter. [< Gk *mikros,* small.]

Mi·cro·ne·sia (mī'krō-nē'zhə, -shə). The islands in the Pacific E of the Philippines and N of the equator. —**Mi'cro·ne'sian** adj. & n.

mi·cro·or·gan·ism (mī'krō-ôr'gən-ĭz'əm) n. An organism, as a bacterium or protozoan, of microscopic size.

mi·cro·phone (mī'krə-fōn') n. An instrument that converts acoustical waves into an electric current, usually fed into an amplifier, recorder, or broadcast transmitter.

mi·cro·scope (mī'krə-skōp') n. An instrument that uses a combination of lenses to produce magnified images of small objects, esp. of objects too small to be seen by the unaided eye.

mi·cro·scop·ic (mī'krə-skŏp'ĭk) adj. Also **mi·cro·scop·i·cal** (-ĭ-kəl). 1. Invisible to the naked eye but large enough to be studied under a microscope. 2. Exceedingly small; minute. 3.

Extremely detailed. 4. Of or pertaining to a microscope. —**mi'cro·scop'i·cal·ly** adv.

mi·cro·wave (mī'krə-wāv') n. Any electromagnetic radiation having a wavelength in the approximate range from one millimeter to one meter, the region between infrared and short-wave radio wavelengths.

mid (mĭd) adj. Middle; central.

mid·air (mĭd'âr') n. A point or region in the middle of the air.

mid·day (mĭd'dā') n. The middle of the day; noon. —**mid'day'** adj.

mid·dle (mĭd'l) adj. 1. Equally distant from extremes or limits; central; mean. 2. Intermediate; in-between. 3. Medium; moderate. —n. 1. A middle area or point. 2. The waist. [< OE *middel.* See medhyo-.]

middle age. The time of life between 40 and 60. —**mid'dle-aged'** adj.

Middle Ages. The period in European history between antiquity and the Renaissance, regarded as dating from A.D. 476 to 1453.

Middle America. 1. Mexico and Central America. 2. a. That part of the U.S. middle class thought of as being conservative in values and attitudes. b. The American heartland, thought of as being made up of small towns, small cities, and suburbs.

mid·dle·brow (mĭd'l-brou') n. *Informal.* A person of mediocre culture.

middle class. The members of society occupying an intermediate social and economic position. —**mid'dle-class'** adj.

Middle Dutch. Dutch from about 1150 to 1500.

middle ear. The tympanic membrane together with the malleus, incus, and stapes and the structure that encloses them.

Middle East. The area in Asia and Africa from Libya in the W to Pakistan in the E.

Middle English. English from about 1100 to 1500.

Middle High German. High German from about 1000 to 1500.

Middle Low German. Low German from about 1250 to 1500.

mid·dle·man (mĭd'l-măn') n. An intermediary or go-between, esp. one who buys from producers and sells to retailers or consumers.

mid·dle·weight (mĭd'l-wāt') n. A boxer or wrestler weighing between 147 and 160 pounds.

Middle West. A region of the U.S. from Ohio through Iowa and from the Ohio and Missouri rivers through the Great Lakes. —**Middle Western.** —**Middle Westerner.**

mid·dling (mĭd'lĭng, -lĭn) adj. Of medium size, quality, etc.; fair. —adv. Fairly; moderately.

mid·dy (mĭd'ē) n., pl. **-dies.** 1. *Informal.* A midshipman. 2. Also **middy blouse.** A woman's or child's loose blouse with a sailor collar.

midge (mĭj) n. A small, gnatlike fly. [< OE *mycg.*]

midg·et (mĭj'ĭt) n. 1. An extremely small person. 2. Something very small of its kind. [Dim of MIDGE.] —**midg'et** adj.

mid·night (mĭd'nīt') n. The middle of the night; specifically, twelve o'clock at night.

mid·point (mĭd′point′) *n.* A point or position midway between two extremes.

mid·riff (mĭd′rĭf′) *n.* **1.** The diaphragm. **2.** The outer part of the human body, extending from the chest to the waistline. [< MID + OE *hrif*, belly (see **krep-**).] —**mid′riff** *adj.*

mid·ship·man (mĭd′shĭp′mən, mĭd-shĭp′mən) *n.* A student training to be commissioned as an officer in the U.S. Navy or Coast Guard.

mid·ships (mĭd′shĭps′) *adv.* Amidships.

midst (mĭdst, mĭtst) *n.* **1.** The middle portion or part; center. **2.** The condition of being surrounded by or enveloped in something. —*prep.* Among.

mid·sum·mer (mĭd′sŭm′ər) *n.* **1.** The middle of the summer. **2.** The summer solstice, about June 21.

mid·way (mĭd′wā′) *n.* The area of a fair, carnival, etc., where side shows and other amusements are located. —*adv. & adj.* In the middle; halfway.

Mid·west (mĭd′wĕst′) *n.* The **Middle West.** —**Mid′west′, Mid′west′ern** (-wĕs′tərn) *adj.* —**Mid′west′ern·er** *n.*

mid·wife (mĭd′wīf′) *n.* A woman who assists women in childbirth. [< OE *mid*, with + *wīf*, WIFE.] —**mid′wife′ry** (-wīf′rē, -wĭ′fə-rē) *n.*

mid·win·ter (mĭd′wĭn′tər) *n.* **1.** The middle of the winter. **2.** The winter solstice, about December 22.

mien (mēn) *n.* Manner; appearance; aspect.

miff (mĭf) *v.* To offend; upset.

might[1] (mīt) *n.* **1.** Great or supreme power. **2.** Great physical strength. [< OE *miht*. See **magh-.**]

might[2] (mīt). *p.t.* of **may**[1].

might·y (mī′tē) *adj.* **-ier, -iest. 1.** Powerful. **2.** Great; pre-eminent. —*adv. Informal.* Very. —**might′i·ly** *adv.* —**might′i·ness** *n.*

mi·gnon·ette (mĭn′yən-ĕt′) *n.* A plant cultivated for its small, fragrant greenish flowers. [< F *mignon*, dainty, small.]

mi·graine (mī′grān′) *n.* Severe, recurrent headache, usually affecting only one side of the head. [< LL *hēmicrānia*, pain in half of the head.]

mi·grant (mī′grənt) *n.* **1.** One that migrates. **2.** One who travels from place to place in search of work. —**mi′grant** *adj.*

mi·grate (mī′grāt′) *v.* **-grated, -grating. 1.** To move from one country or region and settle in another. **2.** To move seasonally from one region to another. [L *migrāre.*] —**mi·gra′tion** *n.* —**mi′gra·to′ry** (-grə-tôr′ē, -tōr′ē) *adj.*

mi·ka·do (mĭ-kä′dō) *n., pl.* **-dos.** The emperor of Japan. [Jap, "exalted gate."]

mike (mīk) *n. Informal.* A microphone.

mi·kron. Variant of **micron.**

mil (mĭl) *n.* A unit of length equal to one-thousandth (10⁻³) of an inch. [< L *mille*, thousand.]

mil. military.

mil·age. Variant of **mileage.**

Mi·lan (mĭ-lăn′, -län′). A city of NW Italy. Pop. 1,666,000. —**Mil′an·ese′** (mĭl′ə-nēz′, -nēs′) *adj. & n.*

milch (mĭlch) *adj.* Giving milk: *a milch cow.*

mild (mīld) *adj.* **1.** Gentle or meek in dis-

position or behavior. **2.** Not extreme; moderate. **3.** Not sharp or strong in taste or odor. [< OE *milde.* See **mel-.**] —**mild′ly** *adv.* —**mild′ness** *n.*

mil·dew (mĭl′d/y/ōō′) *n.* A white or grayish coating formed by fungi on plant leaves, cloth, paper, etc. [< OE *mildēaw.*] —**mil′dew** *v.*

mile (mīl) *n.* **1.** A unit of length, equal to 5,280 feet, 1,760 yards, or 1,609.34 meters, used in the U.S. and other English-speaking countries; statute mile. **2.** A nautical mile. **3.** An air mile. [< L *mīle, mīlle,* thousand.]

mile·age (mī′lĭj) *n.* Also **mil·age. 1.** Distance measured or expressed in miles. **2.** Service or wear estimated by or as by miles used or traveled. **3.** An allowance for travel expenses established at a specified rate per mile.

mile·stone (mīl′stōn′) *n.* **1.** A stone marker indicating the distance in miles from a given point. **2.** An important event or turning point.

mi·lieu (mē-lyœ′) *n.* Environment or surroundings. [< OF, midst, center.]

mil·i·tant (mĭl′ə-tənt) *adj.* **1.** Fighting or warring. **2.** Aggressive, esp. in the service of some cause. —*n.* One who is militant. [< L *mīlitāre,* to MILITATE.] —**mil′i·tan·cy** (mĭl′ə-tən-sē) *n.* —**mil′i·tant·ly** *adv.*

mil·i·ta·rism (mĭl′ə-tə-rĭz′əm) *n.* The glorification of a professional military class or policies arising from its predominance in state affairs. —**mil′i·ta·rist** *n.* —**mil′i·ta·ris′tic** *adj.*

mil·i·ta·rize (mĭl′ə-tə-rīz′) *v.* **-rized, -rizing. 1.** To equip or train for war. **2.** To imbue with militarism.

mil·i·tar·y (mĭl′ə-tĕr′ē) *adj.* Of, pertaining to, or associated with soldiers, the armed forces, or warfare. —*n.* —**the military.** The armed forces; soldiers collectively. [< L *miles (mīlit-),* soldier.] —**mil′i·tar′i·ly** *adv.*

mil·i·tate (mĭl′ə-tāt′) *v.* **-tated, -tating.** To have force as evidence. [L *mīlitāre,* to serve as a soldier.]

mi·li·tia (mə-lĭsh′ə) *n.* Those who are not members of the regular armed forces, but who are called to military service in an emergency. —**mi·li′tia·man** *n.*

milk (mĭlk) *n.* **1. a.** A whitish liquid produced by the mammary glands of female mammals for feeding their young. **b.** Cows' milk used as human food. **2.** A milklike liquid, as a plant juice. —*v.* **1.** To draw milk from (a female mammal). **2.** To press or extract something from as by milking. [< OE *milc, meolc.* See **melg-.**] —**milk′er** *n.* —**milk′y** *adj.*

milk fever. A disease affecting dairy cows and occasionally sheep or goats, esp. soon after giving birth.

milk·maid (mĭlk′mād′) *n.* A girl or woman who milks cows.

milk·man (mĭlk′măn′) *n.* A man who sells or delivers milk.

milk of magnesia. A liquid suspension of magnesium hydroxide, $Mg(OH)_2$, used as an antacid and laxative.

milk shake. A whipped beverage made of milk, flavoring, and usually ice cream.

milk·sop (mĭlk′sŏp′) *n.* A man lacking manly qualities; a mollycoddle.

ă pat/ā ate/âr care/ä bar/b̧ bib/ch chew/d deed/ĕ pet/ē be/f fit/g gag/h hat/hw what/
ĭ pit/ī pie/îr pier/j judge/k kick/l lid, fatal/m mum/n no, sudden/ng sing/ŏ pot/ō go/

milk·weed (mĭlk'wēd') *n.* A plant with milky juice and large pods that split open to release downy seeds.

Milky Way. The galaxy in which the solar system is located, visible as a luminous band in the night sky.

mill¹ (mĭl) *n.* **1.** A building or establishment equipped with machinery for grinding grain. **2.** A machine or device for grinding, crushing, cutting, rolling, etc. **3.** A place where materials are processed; a factory. **4.** A place, institution, etc., that turns out something routinely and in large quantities. *—v.* **1.** To grind or process in or as in a mill. **2.** To move with a circular or whirling motion. [< OE *mylen* < Gmc *mulīna* < LL *molīna*.]

mill² (mĭl) *n.* A monetary unit equal to ¹⁄₁₀₀₀ of a U.S. dollar. [< L *millēsimus*, thousandth.]

Mill (mĭl), **John Stuart.** 1806–1873. English economist, philosopher, and political theorist.

mil·len·ni·um (mə-lĕn'ē-əm) *n., pl.* **-ums** or **-lennia** (-lĕn'ē-ə). **1.** A span of one thousand years. **2.** A thousand-year period of holiness during which Christ is to rule on earth. Revelation 20:1–5. **3.** A hoped-for period of prosperity and justice. [< L *mille*, thousand + *annus*, year.] *—mil·len'ni·al adj.*

mill·er (mĭl'ər) *n.* One who operates or owns a mill for grinding grain.

mil·let (mĭl'ĭt) *n.* **1.** A grass cultivated for its edible seed and for hay. **2.** The white seeds of this plant. [< L *milium.*]

milli–. *comb. form.* One-thousandth (10⁻³). [< L *mille*, thousand.]

mil·liard (mĭl'yərd, -yärd', mĭl'ē-ärd') *n. Brit.* A billion.

mil·li·me·ter (mĭl'ĭ-mē'tər) *n.* One-thousandth of a meter.

mil·li·ner (mĭl'ə-nər) *n.* One who makes, trims, designs, or sells women's hats. [< *Milaner*, native of Milan.]

mil·li·ner·y (mĭl'ə-nĕr'ē) *n.* **1.** Merchandise sold by a milliner. **2.** The business of a milliner.

mil·lion (mĭl'yən) *n., pl.* **-lion** or **-lions**. **1.** The cardinal number written 1,000,000. **2.** A million monetary units, as of dollars. **3.** Often **millions.** An indefinitely large number. [< L *mille*, thousand.] *—mil'lion adj.*

Usage: *Million*, preceded by a number or numeral, is used to signify a specific amount: *two million. Millions* is rarely used with a specific number: *many millions; millions of victims of war.*

mil·lion·aire (mĭl'yə-nâr') *n.* A person whose wealth amounts to a million or more in dollars or other currency.

mil·lionth (mĭl'yənth) *n.* **1.** The ordinal number one million in a series. **2.** One of a million equal parts. *—mil'lionth adj.*

mill·pond (mĭl'pŏnd') *n.* A pond formed by a dam to supply power for operating a mill.

mill·stone (mĭl'stōn') *n.* **1.** One of a pair of cylindrical stones used in a mill for grinding grain. **2.** A heavy burden.

mill·stream (mĭl'strēm') *n.* A stream whose flow is used to run a mill.

milque·toast (mĭlk'tōst') *n.* A meek, timid

man. [< Caspar *Milquetoast*, a character in the newspaper cartoon *The Timid Soul.*]

milt (mĭlt) *n.* The sperm of fishes. [Prob < MDu *milte*, milt, spleen.]

Mil·ton (mĭl'tən), **John.** 1608–1674. English poet.

Mil·wau·kee (mĭl-wô'kē). A city of SE Wisconsin. Pop. 717,000.

mime (mīm) *n.* **1.** The art of pantomime. **2.** A performer in pantomime. **3.** A mimic. *—v.* **mimed, miming.** **1.** To mimic; ape. **2.** To act or portray in pantomime. [< Gk *mimos*, imitator.] *—mim'er n.*

mim·e·o·graph (mĭm'ē-ə-grăf', -gräf') *n.* A duplicator that makes copies of written or typed material from a stencil fitted around an inked drum. [< Gk *mimeisthai*, to imitate.] *—mim'e·o·graph' v.*

mi·me·sis (mĭ-mē'sĭs, mī-) *n. Med.* The appearance, often due to hysteria, of symptoms of a disease not actually present. [< Gk *mimeisthai*, to imitate.]

mi·met·ic (mĭ-mĕt'ĭk, mī-) *adj.* Of, pertaining to, or using mimicry; imitative. *—mi·met'i·cal·ly adv.*

mim·ic (mĭm'ĭk) *v.* **-icked, -icking.** **1.** To imitate another's speech, gestures, etc., as in mockery; ape. **2.** To resemble closely; simulate. *—n.* One who mimics others, as for amusement. *—adj.* Of or pertaining to mimicry; imitative. [L *mimicus*, imitative.] *—mim'ick·er n.*

mim·ic·ry (mĭm'ĭk-rē) *n.* The act or practice of mimicking; imitation.

mi·mo·sa (mĭ-mō'sə, -zə) *n.* Any of various plants, shrubs, and trees with compound leaves and ball-like clusters of small flowers. [< MIME.]

min minute (unit of time).

min. **1.** minimum. **2.** mining.

min·a·ret (mĭn'ə-rĕt') *n.* A tall, slender tower on a mosque. [< Ar *manārat*, lamp.]

min·a·to·ry (mĭn'ə-tôr'ē, -tōr'ē) *adj.* Menacing; threatening. [< L *minārī*, to menace.]

mince (mĭns) *v.* **minced, mincing.** **1.** To cut into very small pieces. **2.** To pronounce with forced refinement or restraint. **3.** To walk primly or affectedly. [< L *minuere*, to diminish.] *—minc'er n.*

mince·meat (mĭns'mēt') *n.* A mixture of finely chopped apples, raisins, spices, suet, and sometimes meat, used esp. as pie filling.

mince pie. A pie filled with mincemeat.

mind (mīnd) *n.* **1.** The consciousness that originates in the brain and directs mental and physical behavior. **2.** Memory; recollection. **3.** Conscious thoughts; attention. **4.** Opinion or intentions. **5.** Intellect; intelligence. **6.** One considered with regard to intellectual ability. **7.** Mental or emotional health; sanity. *—v.* **1.** To attend to; heed. **2.** To obey. **3.** To take care of; tend. **4.** To be careful about. **5.** To be concerned or troubled (about); object (to). [< OE *gemynd*, memory, mind. See **men-**.]

mind·ful (mīnd'fəl) *adj.* Attentive; heedful. *—mind'ful·ly adv.* *—mind'ful·ness n.*

mind·less (mīnd'lĭs) *adj.* **1.** Lacking intelligence or sensible intention. **2.** Careless; heedless. *—mind'less·ly adv.* *—mind'less·ness n.*

ô paw, for/oi boy/ou out/ŏŏ took/ōō coo/p pop/r run/s sauce/sh shy/t to/th thin/*th* the/
ŭ cut/ûr fur/v van/w wag/y yes/z size/zh vision/ə ago, item, edible, gallop, circus/

mine¹ (mīn) *n.* **1.** An excavation made in the earth to extract metals, coal, salt, or other minerals. **2.** A natural deposit of ore or minerals. **3.** An abundant supply or source. **4.** A tunnel dug under an enemy emplacement. **5.** An explosive device usually placed in a concealed position and detonated by contact or a time fuse. —*v.* **mined, mining. 1.** To dig from or as from a mine. **2.** To dig a mine (in). **3.** To lay explosive mines in or under. **4.** To undermine. [< VL *mina* < Celt *meini-*, ore.] —**min′er** *n.*

mine² (mīn). The possessive form of the pronoun *I,* used as a predicate adjective or as a substantive: *This nearly was mine. If you can't find your hat, take mine.* —**of mine.** Belonging to me: *a friend of mine.* [< OE *min.* See **me-**.]

min·er·al (mĭn′ər-əl) *n.* **1.** Any naturally occurring, homogeneous inorganic substance having a definite chemical composition and characteristic crystalline structure, color, and hardness. **2. a.** An element, such as gold or silver. **b.** A mixture of inorganic compounds, such as hornblende or granite. **c.** An organic derivative, such as coal or petroleum. **3.** Any substance that is neither animal nor vegetable; inorganic matter. **4.** An ore. —*adj.* **1.** Of or pertaining to minerals: *a mineral deposit.* **2.** Impregnated with minerals: *mineral water.* [< MINE¹.]

min·er·al·o·gy (mĭn′ə-rŏl′ə-jē, -răl′ə-jē) *n.* The scientific study of minerals. [MINERA(L) + -LOGY.] —**min′er·al′o·gist** *n.*

mineral oil. Any of various light hydrocarbon oils, esp. a refined distillate of petroleum used medicinally as a laxative.

mineral water. Water containing dissolved minerals or gases.

Mi·ner·va (mĭ-nûr′və). Roman goddess of wisdom, invention, and the arts.

min·e·stro·ne (mĭn′ə-strō′nē) *n.* An Italian soup containing a variety of vegetables in a broth base. [< It *minestrare,* to serve, dish out.]

min·gle (mĭng′gəl) *v.* **-gled, -gling.** To mix together in close association. [< OE *mengan,* to mix. See **mag-**.] —**min′gler** *n.*

mini-. *comb. form.* Something distinctively smaller or shorter than other members of its class: *miniskirt.*

min·i·a·ture (mĭn′ē-ə-chŏŏr′, mĭn′ə-chŏŏr′, -chər) *n.* **1.** A very small or greatly reduced copy or model. **2.** A small painting executed with great detail. —*adj.* On a small or greatly reduced scale. [It *miniatura,* painting.]

min·im (mĭn′əm) *n.* **1.** A unit of fluid measure: **a.** In the U.S., ¹⁄₆₀ of a fluid dram or 0.00376 cubic inches. **b.** In Great Britain, ¹⁄₂₀ of a scruple or 0.00361 cubic inches. **2.** A very small amount. [< L *minimus,* least.]

min·i·mal (mĭn′ə-məl) *adj.* Least in amount or degree. —**min′i·mal·ly** *adv.*

min·i·mize (mĭn′ə-mīz′) *v.* **-mized, -mizing.** To reduce to or represent as having minimum importance, value, etc. —**min′i·miz′er** *n.*

min·i·mum (mĭn′ə-məm) *n., pl.* **-mums** or **-ma** (-mə). **1.** The least possible quantity or degree. **2.** The lowest amount or degree reached or permitted. **3.** A number not greater than any other in a finite set of numbers. [< L *minimus,* least.] —**min′i·mum** *adj.*

min·ion (mĭn′yən) *n.* **1.** An obsequious follower or subordinate agent. **2.** *Archaic.* A favorite. [F *mignon,* darling.]

min·is·ter (mĭn′ĭ-stər) *n.* **1.** A person serving as an agent for another by carrying out specified orders. **2.** A clergyman; pastor. **3.** A high officer of state appointed to head an executive or administrative department of government. **4.** A diplomat, usually ranking next below an ambassador. —*v.* **1.** To attend to the wants and needs of others. **2.** *Eccles.* To administer or dispense. [< L, attendant, servant.] —**min′is·te′ri·al** (-stîr′ē-əl) *adj.* —**min′is·trant** (-strənt) *adj. & n.* —**min′is·tra′tion** *n.*

min·is·try (mĭn′ĭ-strē) *n., pl.* **-tries. 1.** The act of ministering or serving. **2. a.** The profession of a minister of religion. **b.** The clergy. **c.** The period of service of a minister of religion. **3. a.** A governmental department presided over by a minister. **b.** The building in which it is housed. **c.** The duties or term of a governmental minister.

mink (mĭngk) *n.* **1.** A semiaquatic weasellike mammal with soft, lustrous, brownish fur. **2.** The fur of this animal. [< Scand.]

Minn. Minnesota.

Min·ne·ap·o·lis (mĭn′ē-ăp′ə-lĭs). A city of SE Minnesota. Pop. 434,000.

Min·ne·so·ta (mĭn′ə-sō′tə). A state in the north-central U.S. Pop. 3,805,000. Cap. St. Paul. —**Min′ne·so′tan** (mĭn′ə-sō′tən) *n. & adj.*

min·now (mĭn′ō) *n.* Any of numerous small freshwater fishes often used as bait. [< OE *mynwe.*]

mi·nor (mī′nər) *adj.* **1.** Lesser or smaller in amount, size, or importance. **2.** Lesser in seriousness or danger: *minor difficulties; a minor injury.* **3.** Designating a field of academic specialization requiring fewer credits than a major field. **4.** *Mus.* Of or based on a minor scale. —*n.* **1.** One who has not reached full legal age. **2.** An area of minor study. —*v.* To pursue academic studies in a minor field. [< L, less.]

mi·nor·i·ty (mə-nôr′ə-tē, -nŏr′ə-tē, mī-) *n., pl.* **-ties. 1.** A group of persons or things numbering less than half of a total. **2.** A racial, religious, political, national, or other group regarded as being different from the larger group of which it is part. **3.** The state or period of being under legal age.

minor scale. *Mus.* A diatonic scale having a minor third between the 1st and 3rd tones.

Mi·nos (mī′nəs, -nŏs′). Mythical king of Crete.

Min·o·taur (mĭn′ə-tôr′, mī′nə-tôr′). *Gk. Myth.* A monster having the body of a man and the head of a bull.

Minsk (mĭnsk). Capital of the Byelorussian S.S.R. Pop. 916,000.

min·ster (mĭn′stər) *n. Brit.* A monastery church. [< LL *monastērium,* monastery.]

min·strel (mĭn′strəl) *n.* **1.** A medieval singer who traveled from place to place. **2.** A performer in a minstrel show. [< LL *ministeriālis,* household officer.] —**min′strel·sy** *n.*

ă pat/ā ate/âr care/ä bar/b bib/ch chew/d deed/ĕ pet/ē be/f fit/g gag/h hat/hw what/
ĭ pit/ī pie/îr pier/j judge/k kick/l lid, fatal/m mum/n no, sudden/ng sing/ŏ pot/ō go/

minstrel show. A variety show, formerly popular in the U.S., in which performers, some in black facial make-up, sing, dance, and tell jokes.

mint[1] (mĭnt) *n.* **1.** A place where coins are manufactured by a government. **2.** An abundant amount, esp. of money. —*v.* To produce (money) by stamping metal. —*adj.* In original condition; unused. [< OE *mynet*, money < Gmc *munita* < L *monēta*.] —**mint′age** (mĭn′tĭj) *n.*

mint[2] (mĭnt) *n.* **1.** Any of various related plants, many of which yield an aromatic oil used as flavoring. **2.** A candy flavored with mint. [< OE *minte* < Gmc *minta* < L *mentha*.] —**mint′y** *adj.*

min·u·end (mĭn′yōō-ĕnd′) *n.* The quantity from which another quantity is to be subtracted. [< L *minuere*, to lessen.]

min·u·et (mĭn′yōō-ĕt′) *n.* **1.** A stately dance originated in 17th-century France. **2.** The music for this dance. [< obs F *menuet*, dainty, small.]

mi·nus (mī′nəs) *prep.* **1.** *Math.* Reduced by the subtraction of; less: *Seven minus four equals three.* **2.** *Informal.* Lacking; without. —*adj.* **1.** *Math.* Negative or on the negative part of a scale: *a minus value; minus five degrees.* **2.** Designating one subdivision of a grade less than; slightly less than: *a grade of B minus.* —*n.* **1.** The minus sign (–). **2.** A negative quantity. **3.** A loss, deficiency, or disadvantage. [< L *minus*, less.]

min·us·cule (mĭn′ə-skyōōl′, mĭ-nŭs′kyōōl) *adj.* Very small; tiny; minute. [< L *minusculus*, less.] —**mi·nus′cu·lar** (-kyə-lər) *adj.*

minus sign. The symbol –, used to indicate subtraction or a negative quantity.

min·ute[1] (mĭn′ĭt) *n.* **1. a.** A unit of time equal to 1/60 of an hour, or 60 seconds. **b.** A unit of angular measurement equal to 1/60 of a degree, or 60 seconds. **2.** Any short interval of time; a moment. **3.** A specific point in time. **4. minutes.** An official record of proceedings at a meeting of an organization. [< L *minūtus*, small, MINUTE.]

mi·nute[2] (mī-n/yōōt′, mĭ-) *adj.* **1.** Exceptionally small; tiny. **2.** Insignificant; trifling. **3.** Characterized by close examination. [L *minūtus*, small.] —**min·ute′ly** *adv.* —**min·ute′-ness** *n.*

min·ute·man (mĭn′ĭt-măn′) *n.* Also **Min·ute·man.** A Revolutionary War militiaman or any armed civilian pledged to be ready to fight on a minute's notice.

mi·nu·ti·a (mī-n/y ōō′shē-ə, -shə) *n., pl.* **-tiae** (-shē-ē′). A small or trivial detail.

minx (mĭngks) *n., pl.* **minxes.** A pert, impudent, or flirtatious young girl. [LG *minsk*, hussy.]

Mi·o·cene (mī′ə-sēn′) *adj.* Of or belonging to the geologic time, rock series, or sedimentary deposits of the fourth epoch of the Tertiary period. —*n.* The Miocene epoch. [G *meiōn*, less + -CENE.]

mir·a·cle (mĭr′ə-kəl) *n.* **1.** An event that appears unexplainable by the laws of nature and so is held to be supernatural or an act of God. **2.** A person, thing, or event that excites ad-

miring awe. [< L *mīrārī*, to wonder at.] —**mi·rac·u·lous** (mĭ-răk′yə-ləs) *adj.* —**mi·rac′u·lous·ly** *adv.* —**mi·rac′u·lous·ness** *n.*

mi·rage (mĭ-räzh′) *n.* **1.** An optical phenomenon that creates the illusion of water, often with inverted reflections of distant objects. **2.** Something that is illusory like a mirage. [< L *mirus*, wonder.]

mire (mīr) *n.* **1.** A bog. **2.** Deep, slimy soil or mud. —*v.* **mired, miring. 1.** To cause to sink or become stuck in or as in mire. **2.** To soil with mud. [< ON *mȳrr*, a bog.] —**mir′y** *adj.*

mir·ror (mĭr′ər) *n.* **1.** Any surface capable of reflecting sufficient undiffused light to form a virtual image of an object placed in front of it. **2.** Anything that gives a true picture of something else. —*v.* To reflect in or as in a mirror. [< L *mīrārī*, to wonder at.]

mirth (mûrth) *n.* Rejoicing or enjoyment, esp. when expressed by laughter. [< OE *myrgth*. See **mregh-**.] —**mirth′ful** *adj.* —**mirth′ful·ly** *adv.* —**mirth′ful·ness** *n.*

mis-. *comb. form.* **1.** Error or wrongness. **2.** Badness or impropriety. **3.** Unsuitableness. **4.** Opposite or lack of. **5.** Failure. [< OE (see **mei-**) and < L *minus*, MINUS.]

mis·ad·ven·ture (mĭs′əd-vĕn′chər) *n.* A mishap; misfortune.

mis·al·li·ance (mĭs′ə-lī′əns) *n.* An unsuitable marriage.

mis·an·thrope (mĭs′ən-thrōp′, mĭz′-) *n.* A hater of mankind. [Gk *misanthrōpos*, hating mankind.] —**mis′an·throp′ic** (-thrōp′ĭk) *adj.* —**mis·an′thro·py** (mĭs-ăn′thrə-pē, mĭz-) *n.*

mis·ap·ply (mĭs′ə-plī′) *v.* To apply wrongly. —**mis′ap·pli·ca′tion** (-ăp-lĭ-kā′shən) *n.*

mis·ap·pre·hend (mĭs′ăp-rĭ-hĕnd′) *v.* To fail to interpret correctly; misunderstand. —**mis′ap·pre·hen′sion** (-hĕn′shən) *n.*

mis·ap·pro·pri·ate (mĭs′ə-prō′prē-āt′) *v.* To appropriate dishonestly for one's own use. —**mis′ap·pro′pri·a′tion** *n.*

mis·be·got·ten (mĭs′bĭ-gŏt′n) *adj.* Illegally begotten, esp. illegitimate.

mis·be·have (mĭs′bĭ-hāv′) *v.* To behave badly. —**mis′be·hav′ior** *n.*

misc. miscellaneous.

mis·cal·cu·late (mĭs-kăl′kyə-lāt′) *v.* To calculate wrongly; make a wrong estimate of. —**mis′cal·cu·la′tion** *n.*

mis·call (mĭs-kôl′) *v.* To call by a wrong name.

mis·car·riage (mĭs-kăr′ĭj) *n.* **1. a.** Mismanagement. **b.** Failure. **2.** Premature expulsion of a nonviable fetus from the uterus.

mis·car·ry (mĭs-kăr′ē) *v.* **1.** To go wrong. **2.** To abort.

mis·cast (mĭs-kăst′, -käst′) *v.* To cast in an unsuitable role.

mis·ce·ge·na·tion (mĭs′ĭ-jə-nā′shən, mĭ-sĕj′ə-nā′shən) *n.* The interbreeding of what are presumed to be distinct human races, esp. marriage between white and nonwhite persons. [< L *miscēre*, to mix + *genus*, race.]

mis·cel·la·ne·ous (mĭs′ə-lā′nē-əs) *adj.* Made up of a variety of parts, members, or characteristics. [< L *miscellus*, mixed.] —**mis′cel·la′ne·ous·ly** *adv.*

mis·cel·la·ny (mĭs′ə-lā′nē) *n., pl.* **-nies. 1.** A

collection of various items or ingredients. 2. A collection of diverse literary works.

mis·chance (mĭs-chăns′, -chäns′) *n.* 1. An unfortunate occurrence; mishap. 2. Bad luck.

mis·chief (mĭs′chĭf) *n.* 1. A cause of discomfiture or annoyance. 2. An inclination to play pranks. 3. Injury caused by a specified human agency. [< OF *meschever*, to meet with misfortune.]

mis·chie·vous (mĭs′chə-vəs) *adj.* 1. Playful, teasing, or troublesome. 2. Causing harm or injury. —**mis′chie·vous·ly** *adv.* —**mis′chie·vous·ness** *n.*

mis·ci·ble (mĭs′ə-bəl) *adj.* Capable of being mixed in all proportions. [< L *miscēre*, to mix.] —**mis′ci·bil′i·ty** *n.*

mis·con·ceive (mĭs′kən-sēv′) *v.* To interpret incorrectly; misunderstand. —**mis′con·cep′tion** (-sĕp′shən) *n.*

mis·con·duct (mĭs-kŏn′dŭkt) *n.* 1. Improper behavior; impropriety. 2. Dishonest or bad management. 3. Malfeasance.

mis·con·strue (mĭs′kən-strōō′) *v.* To misinterpret. —**mis′con·struc′tion** (-strŭk′shən) *n.*

mis·count (mĭs-kount′) *v.* To count incorrectly; miscalculate.

mis·cre·ant (mĭs′krē-ənt) *n.* An evildoer. [< OF *mescroire*, to disbelieve.] —**mis′cre·ant** *adj.*

mis·cue (mĭs-kyōō′) *n.* A blunder or mistake. —**mis·cue′** *v.*

mis·deed (mĭs-dēd′) *n.* A wicked deed.

mis·de·mean·or (mĭs′dĭ-mē′nər) *n.* 1. A misdeed. 2. *Law.* An offense of lesser gravity than a felony.

mis·di·rect (mĭs′dĭ-rĕkt′, -dī-rĕkt′) *v.* To direct incorrectly. —**mis′di·rec′tion** *n.*

mise en scène (mēz äN sĕn′). 1. The setting and staging of a play. 2. Any setting or environment. [F, "placing on stage."]

mis·em·ploy (mĭs′ĕm-ploi′) *v.* To put to a wrong use. —**mis′em·ploy′ment** *n.*

mi·ser (mī′zər) *n.* 1. One who hoards money. 2. A greedy or avaricious person. [< L, wretched, unfortunate.] —**mi′ser·li·ness** *n.* —**mi′ser·ly** *adj.*

mis·er·a·ble (mĭz′ər-ə-bəl, mĭz′rə-bəl) *adj.* 1. Very uncomfortable or unhappy; wretched. 2. Causing wretchedness. 3. Wretchedly inadequate or inferior. [< L *miser*, wretched, unfortunate.] —**mis′er·a·bly** *adv.*

mis·er·y (mĭz′ər-ē) *n., pl.* -ies. 1. Prolonged or extreme suffering; wretchedness. 2. An affliction or deprivation.

mis·fea·sance (mĭs-fē′zəns) *n.* The improper and unlawful execution of an act that in itself is lawful and proper. [< OF *mesfaire*, to misdo.] —**mis·fea′sor** *n.*

mis·fire (mĭs-fīr′) *v.* 1. To fail to explode or ignite, as a gun or engine. 2. To fail to achieve an anticipated result. —**mis′fire** *n.*

mis·fit (mĭs′fĭt, mĭs-fĭt′) *n.* 1. A poor fit. 2. A maladjusted person.

mis·for·tune (mĭs-fôr′chən) *n.* 1. Bad fortune. 2. A mishap.

mis·giv·ing (mĭs-gĭv′ĭng) *n.* Often **misgivings.** A feeling of uncertainty or apprehension.

mis·gov·ern (mĭs-gŭv′ərn) *v.* To govern badly. —**mis·gov′ern·ment** *n.*

mis·guide (mĭs-gīd′) *v.* To give misleading direction to; lead astray. —**mis·guid′ance** *n.* —**mis·guid′ed·ly** *adv.* —**mis·guid′er** *n.*

mis·han·dle (mĭs-hăn′dəl) *v.* To deal with clumsily or inefficiently.

mis·hap (mĭs′hăp′, mĭs-hăp′) *n.* An unfortunate accident.

mis·hear (mĭs-hîr′) *v.* To hear wrongly.

mish·mash (mĭsh′măsh′, -mŏsh′) *n.* A hodgepodge. [Redupl of MASH.]

mis·in·form (mĭs′ĭn-fôrm′) *v.* To give wrong or inaccurate information to. —**mis′in·form′ant** (-fôr′mənt) *n.* —**mis′in·for·ma′tion** *n.*

mis·in·ter·pret (mĭs′ĭn-tûr′prĭt) *v.* 1. To explain inaccurately. 2. To err in understanding. —**mis′in·ter′pre·ta′tion** *n.*

mis·judge (mĭs-jŭj′) *v.* To judge or estimate wrongly. —**mis·judg′ment** *n.*

mis·lay (mĭs-lā′) *v.* 1. To lose. 2. To put in a place that is afterward forgotten.

mis·lead (mĭs-lēd′) *v.* 1. To lead in the wrong direction. 2. To lead into error of action or belief.

mis·lead·ing (mĭs-lē′dĭng) *adj.* Deceptive.

mis·man·age (mĭs-măn′ĭj) *v.* To manage badly or carelessly. —**mis·man′age·ment** *n.*

mis·match (mĭs-măch′) *v.* To match unsuitably, esp. in marriage. —**mis′match** *n.*

mis·name (mĭs-nām′) *v.* To call by a wrong name.

mis·no·mer (mĭs-nō′mər) *n.* A name or designation wrongly applied. [< OF *mesnommer*, to misname.]

miso–. *comb. form.* Hating or hatred. [< Gk *misein*, to hate, and *misos*, hatred.]

mi·sog·y·ny (mĭ-sŏj′ə-nē) *n.* Hatred of women. —**mi·sog′y·nist** *n.* —**mi·sog′y·nous** *adj.*

mis·place (mĭs-plās′) *v.* 1. a. To put in a wrong place. b. To lose. 2. To bestow on a wrong object: *misplacing her trust.*

mis·play (mĭs-plā′) *n.* A mistaken action in a game. —**mis·play′** *v.*

mis·print (mĭs-prĭnt′) *v.* To print incorrectly. —**mis′print′** *n.*

mis·pri·sion (mĭs-prĭzh′ən) *n.* Maladministration of public office. [< NF *mesprendre*, to take wrongly.]

mis·pro·nounce (mĭs′prə-nouns′) *v.* To pronounce incorrectly. —**mis′pro·nun′ci·a′tion** (-nŭn′sē-ā′shən) *n.*

mis·quote (mĭs-kwōt′) *v.* To quote incorrectly. —**mis′quo·ta′tion** (-kwō-tā′shən) *n.*

mis·read (mĭs-rēd′) *v.* 1. To read incorrectly. 2. To misinterpret.

mis·rep·re·sent (mĭs′rĕp-rĭ-zĕnt′) *v.* To give an incorrect or dishonest representation of. —**mis′rep·re·sen·ta′tion** *n.*

mis·rule (mĭs-rōōl′) *v.* To misgovern. —**mis·rule′** *n.*

miss¹ (mĭs) *v.* 1. To fail to hit, reach, or otherwise make contact with. 2. To fail to perceive or understand. 3. To fail to achieve or obtain. 4. To fail to attend or perform. 5. To omit. 6. To avoid. 7. To discover or feel the absence of. 8. To misfire. —*n.* 1. A failure to hit or succeed. 2. A misfire. [< OE *missan*. See mei-.]

miss² (mĭs) *n., pl.* **misses.** 1. **Miss.** A title preceding the name of an unmarried woman or girl. **2.** *Informal.* An unmarried woman or girl. [Short for MISTRESS.]

Miss. Mississippi.

mis·sal (mĭs′əl) *n.* A book containing all the prayers and responses necessary for celebrating the Roman Catholic Mass. [< LL *missa*, Mass.]

mis·shape (mĭs-shāp′) *v.* To shape badly; deform. —**mis·shap′en** *adj.*

mis·sile (mĭs′əl) *n.* Any object or weapon fired, thrown, dropped, or otherwise projected at a target. [< L *mittere* (pp *missus*), to let go, send.]

mis·sile·ry (mĭs′əl-rē) *n.* Also **mis·sil·ry.** The science of making and using guided missiles.

miss·ing (mĭs′ĭng) *adj.* Absent; lost; lacking.

mis·sion (mĭsh′ən) *n.* **1.** A body of envoys to a foreign country. **2.** A body of missionaries, their ministry, or the place of its exercise. **3.** A permanent diplomatic office in a foreign country. **4.** A combat assignment. **5.** A function or task. [< L *mittere* (pp *missus*), to let go, send.] —**mis′sion·al** *adj.*

mis·sion·ar·y (mĭsh′ə-nĕr′ē) *n., pl.* **-ies.** One sent to do religious or charitable work in some territory or foreign country. —*adj.* Of or pertaining to church missions or missionaries.

Mis·sis·sip·pi (mĭs′ə-sĭp′ē). **1.** A state of the SE U.S. Pop. 2,217,000. Cap. Jackson. **2.** A river of the C U.S.

Mis·sis·sip·pi·an (mĭs′ə-sĭp′ē-ən) *adj.* Of or belonging to the geologic time, rock system, or sedimentary deposits of the fifth period of the Paleozoic era. —*n.* **1.** The Mississippian period. **2.** A native or inhabitant of Mississippi.

mis·sive (mĭs′ĭv) *n.* A letter or message. [< L *mittere* (pp *missus*), to send.]

Mis·sou·ri (mĭ-zŏŏr′ē, -zŏŏr′ə). **1.** A state of the C U.S. Pop. 4,677,000. Cap. Jefferson City. **2.** A river flowing from Montana to the Mississippi.

mis·spell (mĭs-spĕl′) *v.* To spell incorrectly. —**mis·spell′ing** *n.*

mis·state (mĭs-stāt′) *v.* To state wrongly or falsely. —**mis·state′ment** *n.*

mis·step (mĭs-stĕp′) *n.* **1.** A wrong step. **2.** An instance of wrong or improper conduct.

mist (mĭst) *n.* **1.** A mass of fine droplets of water in the atmosphere. **2.** Water vapor condensed on and clouding the appearance of a surface. **3.** Fine drops of any liquid, as perfume, sprayed into the air. **4.** Something that dims or obscures; a haze. —*v.* To make or become misty or obscured. [< OE. See **meigh-.**]

mis·take (mĭ-stāk′) *n.* **1.** An error or blunder. **2.** A misconception or misunderstanding. [< ON *mistaka*, to take in error.] —**mis·take′** *v.* (**-took, -taken.**)

mis·tak·en (mĭ-stā′kən) *adj.* **1.** Wrong or incorrect, as in opinion, understanding, etc. **2.** Misunderstood. —**mis·tak′en·ly** *adv.*

Mis·ter (mĭs′tər) *n.* A courtesy title preceding a man's surname or title of office: *Mr. Secretary.* [< MASTER.]

mis·tle·toe (mĭs′əl-tō′) *n.* A plant growing as a parasite on trees and having leathery evergreen leaves and waxy white berries. [< OE *mistel*, mistletoe + *tān*, twig < Gmc **tainaz.*]

mis·treat (mĭs-trēt′) *v.* To treat roughly or wrongly; abuse. —**mis·treat′ment** *n.*

mis·tress (mĭs′trĭs) *n.* **1.** A woman in a position of authority, control, or ownership. **2.** A country enjoying hegemony: *mistress of the seas.* **3.** A man's female lover. **4. Mistress.** *Archaic.* Mrs.

mis·tri·al (mĭs-trī′əl, -trīl′) *n. Law.* **1.** A trial that becomes invalid because of basic error in procedure. **2.** An inconclusive trial, as one in which the jurors fail to reach a verdict.

mis·trust (mĭs-trŭst′) *n.* Lack of trust; suspicion. —*v.* To regard without confidence. —**mis·trust′ful** *adj.* —**mis·trust′ing·ly** *adv.*

mist·y (mĭs′tē) *adj.* **-ier, -iest. 1.** Consisting of or resembling mist. **2.** Obscured by or as by mist; vague. —**mist′i·ly** *adv.* —**mist′i·ness** *n.*

mis·un·der·stand (mĭs′ŭn-dər-stănd′) *v.* **1.** To fail to understand. **2.** To understand incorrectly.

mis·un·der·stand·ing (mĭs′ŭn-dər-stăn′dĭng) *n.* **1.** A failure to understand correctly. **2.** A disagreement or quarrel.

mis·use (mĭs-yōōs′) *n.* Improper use; misapplication. —*v.* (mĭs-yōōz′). **1.** To misapply. **2.** To abuse.

mite[1] (mīt) *n.* Any of various small, spiderlike, often parasitic organisms. [< OE *mīte.* See **mai-**[1].]

mite[2] (mīt) *n.* **1.** A very small contribution or amount of money. **2.** A tiny thing or amount. [< MDu *mīte.*]

mi·ter (mī′tər) *n.* Also *chiefly Brit.* **mi·tre. 1.** A hat with peaks in front and back, worn by bishops. **2.** A joint made by beveling each of two surfaces at an angle and fitting them to form a 90° corner. [< Gk *mitra*, headband.]

mit·i·gate (mĭt′ə-gāt′) *v.* **-gated, -gating.** To make or become less harsh or severe; alleviate. [< L *mītis*, gentle, mild.] —**mit′i·ga′tion** *n.* —**mit′i·ga′tor** *n.*

mi·to·sis (mī-tō′sĭs) *n.* **1.** The sequential differentiation and segregation of replicated chromosomes in a cell nucleus that precedes complete cell division. **2.** The sequence of processes by which a cell divides to form two daughter cells having the normal number of chromosomes. [< Gk *mitos*, a thread + -OSIS.] —**mi·tot′ic** (-tŏt′ĭk) *adj.*

mitt (mĭt) *n.* **1.** A large glove worn by baseball catchers and first basemen. **2. mitts.** *Slang.* Hands. [Short for MITTEN.]

mit·ten (mĭt′n) *n.* A covering for the hand that encases the thumb separately and the four fingers together. [< OF *mitaine.*]

mix (mĭks) *v.* **1.** To combine or blend so that the constituent parts are indistinguishable. **2.** To form by blending. **3.** To combine or join: *mix joy with sorrow.* **4.** To crossbreed. **5.** To associate socially. —*n.* A packaged mixture, as of baking ingredients. [< L *miscēre* (pp *mixtus*), to mix.] —**mix′a·ble** *adj.* —**mix′er** *n.*

mix·ture (mĭks′chər) *n.* **1.** Something produced by mixing. **2.** Anything consisting of diverse elements. **3.** The act or process of mixing or being mixed. **4.** Any blend of substances not chemically bound to each other.

mix-up (mĭks′ŭp′) *n.* A state or instance of confusion.

miz·zen, miz·en (mĭz′ən) *n.* A fore-and-aft sail set on the mizzenmast. [< L *medietās,* half.] —**miz′zen** *adj.*

miz·zen·mast, miz·en·mast (mĭz′ən-məst, -mäst′, -mäst′) *n.* The third mast aft on sailing ships carrying three or more masts.

mk. mark.

mkt. market.

ml milliliter.

ML Medieval Latin.

Mlle. Mademoiselle.

mm millimeter.

MM. Messieurs.

Mme. Madame.

Mmes. Mesdames.

Mn manganese.

mne·mon·ic (nĭ-mŏn′ĭk) *adj.* Assisting or designed to aid the memory. [< Gk *mnēmōn,* mindful.] —**mne·mon′i·cal·ly** *adv.*

Mo molybdenum.

mo. month.

Mo. Missouri.

m.o. **1.** mail order. **2.** medical officer. **3.** money order.

moan (mōn) *n.* A low, sustained, mournful sound, as of sorrow or pain. [< OE **mān,* complaint. See **mei-no-.**] —**moan** *v.*

moat (mōt) *n.* A wide, deep ditch, usually filled with water, surrounding a medieval town or fortress. [ME *mote,* orig "mound," "embankment" < OF *mote, motte,* clod, hill, mound, prob < Gaul **mutt(a).*]

mob (mŏb) *n.* **1.** A large, disorderly crowd. **2.** The rabble. **3.** An organized gang of hoodlums. —*v.* **mobbed, mobbing. 1.** To crowd around and jostle or attack. **2.** To crowd into (a place). [< L *mōbile (vulgus),* "the fickle (crowd)."]

mo·bile (mō′bəl, -bēl′, -bīl′) *adj.* **1.** Capable of moving or being moved. **2.** Moving quickly from one condition to another. —*n.* (mō′bēl′). A type of sculpture consisting of parts that move, esp. in response to air currents. [< L *mōbilis.*] —**mo·bil′i·ty** (-bĭl′-ə-tē) *n.*

Mo·bile (mō′bēl′). A city of SW Alabama. Pop. 203,000.

–mobile. *comb. form.* A specialized kind of vehicle: bookmobile. [< AUTOMOBILE.]

mo·bi·lize (mō′bə-līz′) *v.* **-lized, -lizing. 1.** To make mobile or capable of movement. **2.** To assemble and prepare for war or a similar emergency. —**mo′bi·li·za′tion** *n.*

mob·ster (mŏb′stər) *n.* A member of a criminal gang.

moc·ca·sin (mŏk′ə-sĭn) *n.* **1.** A soft leather slipper or shoe. **2.** A snake, the **water moccasin.** [< Algon.]

mo·cha (mō′kə) *n.* **1.** A type of coffee originally produced in Arabia. **2.** Coffee flavoring, often mixed with chocolate. [< *Mocha,* a port of Yemen.] —**mo′cha** *adj.*

mock (mŏk) *v.* **1.** To treat with scorn or contempt; deride. **2. a.** To mimic in sport or derision. **b.** To imitate. —*adj.* Simulated; sham.

[< OF *mocquer,* to deride.] —**mock′er** *n.* —**mock′er·y** *n.* —**mock′ing·ly** *adv.*

mock·ing·bird (mŏk′ĭng-bûrd′) *n.* A gray and white songbird common in the S U.S.

mock·up (mŏk′ŭp′) *n.* Also **mock-up. 1.** A full-sized scale model for study, testing, etc. **2.** A layout of printed matter.

mod. 1. moderate. **2.** modern.

mode (mōd) *n.* **1. a.** A manner, way, or method of doing or acting. **b.** A particular form, variety, or manner. **2.** The current fashion or style. **3.** *Mus.* Any of certain arrangements of the diatonic tones of an octave. [< L *modus,* measure, manner, melody.] —**mo′dal** *adj.*

mod·el (mŏd′l) *n.* **1.** A miniature representation of some existing object. **2.** A preliminary pattern. **3.** A tentative ideational structure used as a testing device. **4.** A type or design. **5.** An example to be emulated. **6.** One who poses for an artist or photographer. **7.** A mannequin. —*v.* **1.** To plan or construct. **2.** To display (clothes) by wearing. **3.** To work as a model. [< L *modulus,* little measure.] —**mod′el** *adj.* —**mod′el·er** *n.*

mod·er·ate (mŏd′ər-ĭt) *adj.* **1.** Not excessive or extreme. **2.** Temperate. **3.** Average; mediocre. **4.** Opposed to radical views or measures. —*n.* One who holds moderate views. —*v.* (mŏd′ə-rāt′) **-ated, -ating. 1.** To make or become less violent, severe, or extreme. **2.** To preside over as a moderator. [< L *moderārī, moderāre,* to reduce, control.] —**mod′er·ate·ly** *adv.* —**mod′er·a′tion** *n.*

mod·er·a·tor (mŏd′ə-rā′tər) *n.* **1.** One that moderates. **2.** A presiding officer, as of a general assembly.

mod·ern (mŏd′ərn) *adj.* Of, pertaining to, or characteristic of recent times or the present. [< LL *modernus.*] —**mod′ern** *n.* —**mod·ern′i·ty** (mŏ-dûr′nə-tē) *n.* —**mod′ern·ly** *adv.*

Modern English. English since the early 16th century.

Modern Greek. Greek since the early 16th century.

mod·ern·ism (mŏd′ər-nĭz′əm) *n.* A theory, practice, or belief that is peculiar to modern times. —**mod′ern·ist** *n.* —**mod′ern·ist′ic** *adj.*

mod·ern·ize (mŏd′ər-nīz′) *v.* **-ized, -izing.** To make or become modern in appearance, style, etc. —**mod′ern·i·za′tion** *n.*

mod·est (mŏd′ĭst) *adj.* **1.** Having or showing a moderate estimation of oneself. **2.** Shy; reserved. **3.** Decent. **4.** Unpretentious. **5.** Moderate; not extreme: *a modest charge.* [< L *modestus,* "keeping due measure."] —**mod′est·ly** *adv.* —**mod′es·ty** *n.*

mod·i·cum (mŏd′ĭ-kəm) *n.* A small or moderate amount. [< L *modicus,* moderate.]

mod·i·fy (mŏd′ə-fī′) *v.* **-fied, -fying. 1.** To change; alter. **2.** To make or become less extreme, severe, or strong. **3.** *Gram.* To qualify or limit the meaning of. [< L *modus,* a measure + *facere,* to do, make.] —**mod′i·fi·ca′tion** *n.* —**mod′i·fi′er** *n.*

mod·ish (mō′dĭsh) *adj.* Stylish; fashionable. [< MODE.] —**mod′ish·ly** *adv.*

mo·diste (mō-dēst′) *n.* One who produces or designs ladies' fashions.

ă pat/ā ate/âr care/ä bar/b **bib**/ch **chew**/d **deed**/ĕ pet/ē be/f **fit**/g **gag**/h **hat**/hw **what**/
ĭ pit/ī pie/îr pier/j **judge**/k **kick**/l lid, fatal/m **mum**/n no, sudden/ng sing/ŏ pot/ō go/

mod·u·late (mŏj′ŏŏ-lāt′, mŏd′yə-) *v.* **-lated, -lating. 1.** To regulate; temper. **2.** To change or vary the pitch, intensity, or tone of. **3.** *Mus.* To pass from one tonality to another by means of harmonic progression. **4.** To vary the frequency, amplitude, phase, or other characteristic of (any carrier wave). [< L *modus*, measure, rhythm.] —**mod′u·la′tion** *n.* —**mod′u·la′tive, mod′u·la·to′ry** *adj.* —**mod′u·la′tor** *n.*

mod·ule (mŏj′ŏŏl, mŏd′yŏŏl) *n.* A standardized unit or component, generally having a defined function in a system. [L *modulus*, a small measure.] —**mod′u·lar** *adj.*

Mog·a·dish·u (mŏg′ə-dĭsh′ŏŏ). The capital of Somalia. Pop. 100,000.

mo·gul (mŏ′gəl) *n.* A very rich or powerful person.

mo·hair (mŏ′hâr′) *n.* **1.** The soft, silky hair of the Angora goat. **2.** A fabric made from this hair. [< Ar *mukhayyar*, "select," cloth of goat's hair.]

Mo·ham·med (mō-hăm′ĭd, -hä′mĭd). A.D. 570?–632. Prophet and founder of Islam.

Mo·hawk (mō′hôk′) *n., pl.* **-hawk** or **-hawks. 1.** A member of an Iroquoian-speaking tribe of North American Indians formerly living in N New York State and SE Canada. **2.** The language of this tribe. —**Mo′hawk′** *adj.*

Mo·he·gan (mō-hē′gən) *n., pl.* **-gan** or **-gans.** A member of a tribe of Algonquian-speaking Indians formerly living in E Connecticut. —**Mo·he′gan** *adj.*

Mo·hi·can. Variant of **Mahican.**

moi·e·ty (moi′ə-tē) *n., pl.* **-ties. 1.** A half. **2.** A part or share of indefinite size. [< L *medietās*, half.]

moil (moil) *v.* To toil or slave. [< OF *moillier*, to moisten, paddle in mud.] —**moil** *n.*

moi·ré (mwä-rā′). Also **moire** (mwär). *n.* **1.** Cloth, esp. silk, that has a watered or wavy pattern. **2.** A watered pattern produced on cloth by engraved rollers. [< MOHAIR.] —**moi·ré′** *adj.*

moist (moist) *adj.* Slightly wet or damp; humid. [< VL *muscidus*, moldy, wet.] —**moist′ly** *adv.* —**moist′ness** *n.*

mois·ten (mois′ən) *v.* To make or become moist. —**mois′ten·er** *n.*

mois·ture (mois′chər) *n.* Diffuse wetness; dampness.

mo·lar (mō′lər) *n.* A tooth with a broad crown for grinding food, located behind the bicuspids. [< L *mola*, millstone.] —**mo′lar** *adj.*

mo·las·ses (mə-lăs′ĭz) *n.* Any of various thick syrups produced in refining sugar. [< LL *mellāceum*, must.]

mold¹ (mōld). Also *chiefly Brit.* **mould.** *n.* **1.** A form or matrix for shaping a fluid or plastic substance. **2.** A frame or model for shaping or forming something. **3.** Something made in or shaped on a mold. **4.** General shape or form: *the oval mold of her face.* **5.** Distinctive shape, character, or type. —*v.* To shape in or on a mold. [< L *modulus*, a small measure.] —**mold′a·ble** *adj.*

mold² (mōld). Also *chiefly Brit.* **mould.** *n.* **1.** Any of various fungous growths formed on the surface of organic matter. **2.** A fungus that

causes mold. —*v.* To become moldy. [< ON *mugla, mygla,* mold.]

mold³ (mōld) *n.* Also *chiefly Brit.* **mould.** Loose soil rich in humus. [< OE *molde.*]

Mol·da·vi·a (mŏl-dā′vē-ə, -vyə). **1.** A historic region of E Rumania. **2.** The Moldavian Soviet Socialist Republic.

Mol·da·vi·an Soviet Socialist Republic (mŏl-dā′vē-ən, -vyən). A republic of the SW Soviet Union. Pop. 3,572,000. Cap. Kishinev. —**Mol·da′vi·an** *n.* & *adj.*

mold·er (mōl′dər) *v.* Also *chiefly Brit.* **mould·er.** To decay or crumble into dust. [Prob < Scand.]

mold·ing (mōl′dĭng) *n.* Also *chiefly Brit.* **mould·ing. 1. a.** Anything that is molded. **b.** The process of shaping in a mold. **2.** An embellishment in strip form used to decorate a surface.

mold·y (mōl′dē) *adj.* **-ier, -iest.** Also *chiefly Brit.* **mould·y. 1.** Covered with or containing mold. **2.** Musty or stale. —**mold′i·ness** *n.*

mole¹ (mōl) *n.* A small congenital growth on the human skin, usually slightly raised and dark and sometimes hairy. [< OE *māl.* See **mai-².**]

mole² (mōl) *n.* A small, burrowing mammal with minute eyes, a narrow snout, and silky fur. [< MDu *mol* and ML *mulus.*]

mole³ (mōl) *n.* The amount of a substance that has a weight in grams numerically equal to the molecular weight of the substance. [< G *Molekulargewicht,* molecular weight.]

mol·e·cule (mŏl′ə-kyŏŏl′) *n.* **1.** A stable configuration of atomic nuclei and electrons bound together by electrostatic and electromagnetic forces, the simplest structural unit that displays the characteristic physical and chemical properties of a compound. **2.** A small particle; tiny bit. [< L *mōlēs,* mass, bulk, burden.] —**mo·lec′u·lar** (mə-lĕk′yə-lər) *adj.*

mole·hill (mōl′hĭl′) *n.* A small mound of loose earth thrown up by a burrowing mole.

mole·skin (mōl′skĭn′) *n.* **1.** The fur of a mole. **2.** A napped cotton fabric.

mo·lest (mə-lĕst′) *v.* **1.** To interfere with or annoy. **2.** To accost and harass sexually. [< L *molestus,* troublesome.] —**mo′les·ta′tion** *n.* —**mo·lest′er** *n.*

Mo·lière (mōl-yâr′). Pen name of Jean-Baptiste Poquelin. 1622–1673. French dramatist.

moll (mŏl) *n. Slang.* A female companion of a gangster.

mol·li·fy (mŏl′ə-fī′) *v.* **-fied, -fying. 1.** To placate; calm. **2.** To soften or ease. [< L *mollificāre,* to make soft.] —**mol′li·fi·ca′tion** (mŏl′ə-fĭ-kā′shən) *n.*

mol·lusk (mŏl′əsk) *n.* Also **mol·lusc.** Any of a large group of soft-bodied, usually shell-bearing invertebrates, including the snails, oysters, clams, etc. [< L *mollis,* soft.]

mol·ly·cod·dle (mŏl′ē-kŏd′l) *n.* A pampered boy or man. —*v.* **-dled, -dling.** To spoil by pampering. —**mol′ly·cod′dler** *n.*

molt (mōlt). Also *chiefly Brit.* **moult.** *v.* To shed an outer covering, as feathers or skin, that is replaced periodically by a new growth. —*n.* The process of molting. [< L *mūtāre*, to change.]

mol·ten (mōlt′n) *adj.* Made liquid and glowing by heat; melted.

mo·lyb·de·num (mə-lĭb′də-nəm) *n. Symbol* **Mo** A hard, gray metallic element used to toughen alloy steels. Atomic number 42, atomic weight 95.94. [< Gk *molubdos*, lead.]

mom (mŏm) *n. Informal.* Mother.

mo·ment (mō′mənt) *n.* 1. A brief interval of time. 2. A specific point in time: *He is reading at the moment.* 3. A particular period of importance or excellence. 4. Importance. [< L *mōmentum,* MOMENTUM.]

mo·men·tar·y (mō′mən-tĕr′ē) *adj.* 1. Lasting only a brief time. 2. Occurring or present at every moment. 3. Short-lived; ephemeral. —**mo′men·tar′i·ly** *adv.* —**mo′men·tar′i·ness** *n.*

mo·ment·ly (mō′mənt-lē) *adv.* From moment to moment.

mo·men·tous (mō-mĕn′təs) *adj.* Of utmost importance or outstanding significance. —**mo·men′tous·ly** *adv.* —**mo·men′tous·ness** *n.*

mo·men·tum (mō-mĕn′təm) *n., pl.* -ta (-tə) or -tums. 1. The product of a body's mass and linear velocity. 2. Impetus. [L *mōmentum,* motion, movement < *movēre,* to move.]

mon (mŏn) *n. Scot.* Man.

Mon. Monday.

Mon·a·co (mŏn′ə-kō′, mə-nä′kō). A principality on the Mediterranean coast of France. Pop. 22,000. Cap. Monaco-Ville.

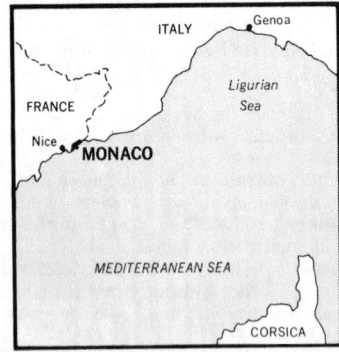

Monaco

mon·arch (mŏn′ərk) *n.* 1. A sovereign, such as a king or emperor. 2. One that presides over or rules. 3. A large orange and black butterfly. [< Gk *monarkhēs.*] —**mon·ar′chic, mon·ar′chi·cal** *adj.*

mon·ar·chism (mŏn′ər-kĭz′əm) *n.* Belief in or advocacy of monarchy. —**mon′ar·chist** (-kĭst) *n. & adj.* —**mon′ar·chis′tic** *adj.*

mon·ar·chy (mŏn′ər-kē) *n., pl.* -chies. 1. Government by a monarch. 2. A state ruled by a monarch.

mon·as·ter·y (mŏn′ə-stĕr′ē) *n., pl.* -ies. The dwelling place of a community of monks. [< Gk *monazein,* to live alone.] —**mon′as·te′ri·al** (-stîr′ē-əl, -stĕr′ē-əl) *adj.*

mo·nas·tic (mə-năs′tĭk) *adj.* Of or pertaining to monasteries or persons living in religious or contemplative seclusion.

mo·nas·ti·cism (mə-năs′tə-sĭz′əm) *n.* The monastic life or system.

mon·au·ral (mŏn-ôr′əl, mō-nôr′əl) *adj.* 1. Designating sound reception by one ear. 2. Monophonic.

Mon·day (mŭn′dē, -dā′) *n.* The 2nd day of the week. [< OE *mōnan dæg,* moon's day.]

Mo·net (mō-nā′), **Claude.** 1840–1926. French painter.

mon·e·tar·y (mŏn′ə-tĕr′ē, mŭn′-) *adj.* 1. Of or pertaining to money. 2. Of or pertaining to a nation's currency or coinage.

mon·ey (mŭn′ē) *n., pl.* -eys or -ies. 1. A commodity that is legally established as an exchangeable equivalent of all other commodities and used as a measure of their comparative market value. 2. The official currency issued by a government. 3. Assets and property that can be converted into actual currency. 4. Pecuniary profit or loss. [< L *monēta,* money, mint.]

mon·eyed (mŭn′ēd) *adj.* Also **mon·ied.** 1. Having a great deal of money. 2. Representing or arising from the possession of money.

mon·ger (mŭng′gər, mŏng′-) *n.* A dealer: *ironmonger.* [< L *mangō,* (fraudulent) dealer.]

Mon·gol (mŏng′gəl, -gŏl′) *n.* 1. A member of one of the nomadic tribes of Mongolia or a native of Mongolia. 2. Any of the languages of Mongolia. 3. A member of the Mongoloid ethnic group. —**Mon′gol** *adj.*

Mon·go·li·a (mŏng-gō′lē-ə, -gŏl′yə, mŏn-). A region of east-central Asia, now consisting of the Mongolian People's Republic (Outer Mongolia) and the Inner Mongolian Autonomous Region of China (Inner Mongolia).

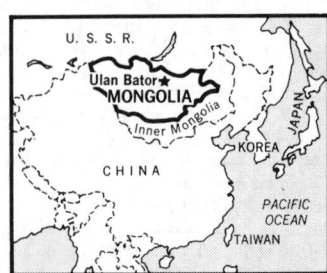

Mongolian People's Republic

Mon·go·li·an (mŏng-gō′lē-ən, -gŏl′yən, mŏn-) *n.* 1. A native of Mongolia. 2. A member of the Mongoloid ethnic division. 3. **a.** The Mongolic subfamily of the Altaic languages. **b.** Any of the Mongolic languages of Mongolia. —**Mon·go′li·an** *adj.*

Mongolian People's Republic. A republic of east-central Asia. Pop. 1,050,000. Cap. Ulan Bator.

Mon·gol·ic (mŏng-gŏl′ĭk, mŏn-) *n.* The Altaic subfamily that includes the various languages of Mongolia. —*adj.* Of or pertaining to the

Mongoloid ethnic division or to the subfamily of Altaic languages spoken in Mongolia.

mon·gol·ism (mŏng'gə-lĭz'əm, mŏn'-) *n.* A congenital idiocy in which a child is born with a short, flattened skull, slanting eyes, and other anomalies. —**mon'gol·oid'** (-loid') *adj.*

Mon·gol·oid (mŏng'gə-loid', mŏn'-) *adj.* **1.** Pertaining to a major ethnic division of the human species having yellowish-brown to white skin color. **2.** Characteristic of or like a Mongol. —**Mon'gol·oid'** *n.*

mon·goose (mŏng'gōōs', mŏn'-) *n., pl.* **-gooses.** Any of various weasellike, chiefly African or Asian mammals noted for their ability to kill venomous snakes. [< Dravid.]

mon·grel (mŭng'grəl, mŏng'-) *n.* A plant or animal, esp. a dog, of mixed breed. [Prob < OE *gemang*, mixture. See mag-.]

mon·ied. Variant of **moneyed.**

mo·nism (mō'nĭz'əm, mŏn'ĭz'əm) *n.* A metaphysical system in which reality is conceived as a unified whole. —**mo'nist** *n. & adj.* —**mo·nis'tic** (mō-nĭs'tĭk, mŏ-) *adj.*

mo·ni·tion (mō-nĭsh'ən, mə-) *n.* A warning or admonition. [< L *monēre*, to warn.]

mon·i·tor (mŏn'ə-tər) *n.* **1.** A student who assists a teacher. **2.** Any device used to record or control a process. —*v.* To check, watch, or keep track of, often by means of an electronic device. [L, one who warns.]

mon·i·to·ry (mŏn'ə-tôr'ē, -tōr'ē) *adj.* Conveying an admonition.

monk (mŭngk) *n.* A member of a religious brotherhood living in a monastery. [< LGk *monakhos*, solitary, monk.]

mon·key (mŭng'kē) *n., pl.* **-keys.** Any member of the primates except man, esp. one of the long-tailed small- to medium-sized species as distinguished from the larger apes and the smaller lemurs. —*v. Informal.* To play or tamper with something.

mon·key·shine (mŭng'kē-shīn') *n.* Often **monkeyshines.** *Slang.* A prank.

monkey wrench. A hand tool with adjustable jaws for turning nuts.

monks·hood (mŭngks'hŏŏd') *n.* Any of several poisonous plants with hood-shaped, usually purplish flowers.

mono-. *comb. form.* **1.** One; single; alone. **2.** The presence of a single atom, radical, or group in a compound. [< Gk *monos*, single, sole, alone.]

mon·o·chro·mat·ic (mŏn'ə-krō-măt'ĭk) *adj.* Also **mon·o·chro·ic** (-krō'ĭk). Of only one color. —**mon'o·chro·mat'i·cal·ly** *adv.*

mon·o·cle (mŏn'ə-kəl) *n.* An eyeglass for one eye. [< LL *monoculus*, one-eyed.]

mon·o·cot·y·le·don (mŏn'ə-kŏt'l-ēd'n) *n.* Also **mon·o·cot** (mŏn'ə-kŏt'). A plant, as a grass, with a single embryonic seed leaf that appears at germination. —**mon'o·cot'y·le'don·ous** *adj.*

mo·noc·u·lar (mō-nŏk'yə-lər, mə-) *adj.* **1.** Of or having one eye. **2.** Adapted for the use of only one eye.

mon·o·dy (mŏn'ə-dē) *n., pl.* **-dies.** An ode or elegy. —**mo·nod'ic** (mə-nŏd'ĭk) *adj.* —**mon'o·dist** (mŏn'ə-dĭst) *n.*

mo·nog·a·my (mə-nŏg'ə-mē) *n.* The custom

or condition of being married to only one person at a time. —**mo·nog'a·mist** *n.* —**mo·nog'a·mous** *adj.* —**mo·nog'a·mous·ly** *adv.*

mon·o·gram (mŏn'ə-grăm') *n.* A design composed of one or more initials of a name. —**mon'o·gram'** *v.* (**-grammed** or **-gramed, -gramming** or **-graming**).

mon·o·graph (mŏn'ə-grăf', -gräf') *n.* A scholarly paper or treatise. —**mo·nog'ra·pher** (mə-nŏg'rə-fər) *n.* —**mon'o·graph'ic** *adj.*

mon·o·lith (mŏn'ə-lĭth') *n.* A large block of stone used in architecture or sculpture.

mon·o·lith·ic (mŏn'ə-lĭth'ĭk) *adj.* **1.** Consisting of a monolith. **2.** Like a monolith; massive and uniform.

mon·o·logue (mŏn'ə-lôg', -lŏg') *n.* **1.** A long speech. **2.** A soliloquy. [< MONO- + (DIA)LOGUE.]

mon·o·ma·ni·a (mŏn'ō-mā'nē-ə, -mān'yə) *n.* **1.** Obsession with one idea. **2.** Obsessive concentration on a single subject. —**mon'o·ma'ni·ac'** (-ăk') *n.*

mon·o·mer (mŏn'ə-mər) *n.* Any molecule that can be chemically bound as a unit of a polymer.

mo·no·mi·al (mō-nō'mē-əl, mō-, mə-) *n.* An algebraic expression consisting of only one term. [MON(O)- + (BIN)OMIAL.] —**mo·no'mi·al** *adj.*

mon·o·nu·cle·o·sis (mŏn'ō-n/y/ōō'klē-ō'sĭs) *n.* An infectious disease characterized by an abnormally large number of leukocytes with single nuclei in the bloodstream. [< MONO- + NUCLE(US) + -OSIS.]

mon·o·phon·ic (mŏn'ə-fŏn'ĭk) *adj. Electronics.* Using one channel to carry or reproduce sounds through audio devices; monaural.

mon·o·plane (mŏn'ə-plān') *n.* An airplane with only one pair of wings.

mo·nop·o·ly (mə-nŏp'ə-lē) *n., pl.* **-lies. 1.** Exclusive ownership or control, as of a given commodity or business activity. **2. a.** A company or group having such control. **b.** A commodity or service thus controlled. [< Gk *monopōlion*, sole selling rights.] —**mo·nop'o·list** *n. & adj.* —**mo·nop'o·lis'tic** *adj.* —**mo·nop'o·li·za'tion** *n.* —**mo·nop'o·lize'** *v.* (**-lized, -lizing**).

mon·o·rail (mŏn'ə-rāl') *n.* A single-rail railway track or system.

mon·o·so·di·um glu·ta·mate (mŏn'ə-sō'dē-əm glōō'tə-māt'). **Sodium glutamate.**

mon·o·syl·la·ble (mŏn'ə-sĭl'ə-bəl) *n.* A word of one syllable. —**mon'o·syl·lab'ic** (-sĭ-lăb'ĭk) *adj.* —**mon'o·syl·lab'i·cal·ly** *adv.*

mon·o·the·ism (mŏn'ə-thē-ĭz'əm) *n.* The doctrine or belief that there is only one God. —**mon'o·the'ist** *n. & adj.* —**mon'o·the·is'tic** *adj.*

mon·o·tone (mŏn'ə-tōn') *n.* A succession of sounds or words uttered in a single tone of voice or sung at a single pitch.

mo·not·o·nous (mə-nŏt'n-əs) *adj.* **1.** Unvarying in inflection or pitch. **2.** Repetitiously dull. —**mo·not'o·nous·ly** *adv.* —**mo·not'o·ny** *n.*

mon·o·va·lent (mŏn'ə-vā'lənt) *adj.* Possessing a valence of 1; univalent.

mon·ox·ide (mŏ-nŏk'sīd', mə-) *n.* An oxide with each molecule containing one oxygen atom.

ô paw, for/oi boy/ou out/ōō took/ōō coo/p pop/r run/s sauce/sh shy/t to/th thin/*th* the/ ŭ cut/ûr fur/v van/w wag/y yes/z size/zh vision/ə ago, item, edible, gallop, circus/

Mon•roe (mən-rō'), **James.** 1758–1831. 5th President of the U.S. (1817–25).

James Monroe

Mon•ro•vi•a (mən-rō'vē-ə). The capital of Liberia. Pop. 80,000.

Mon•si•gnor (mŏn-sēn'yər) n. Also **mon•si•gnor.** A title of certain officials of the Roman Catholic Church.

mon•soon (mŏn-soōn') n. A wind system that influences large climatic regions and reverses direction seasonally, esp. the Asiatic monsoon that produces dry and wet seasons in India and S Asia. [< Ar *mausim,* season, monsoon season.]

mon•ster (mŏn'stər) n. **1.** An animal or plant that is structurally abnormal or grotesquely deformed. **2.** Any very large animal, plant, or object. **3.** One who inspires horror or disgust. —*adj.* Gigantic; huge. [< L *mōnstrum,* prodigy, portent.] —**mon•stros'i•ty** (-strŏs'ə-tē) n. —**mon'strous** *adj.* —**mon'strous•ly** *adv.* —**mon'strous•ness** n.

mon•strance (mŏn'strəns) n. *R.C.Ch.* A receptacle in which the Host is held. [< L *mōnstrum,* portent, MONSTER.]

Mont. Montana.

mon•tage (mŏn-täzh') n. A composite photograph or other artistic composition consisting of several superimposed components.

Mon•tan•a (mŏn-tăn'ə). A state of the W U.S. Pop. 694,000. Cap. Helena. —**Mon•tan'an** *adj. & n.*

Mont Blanc (môN bläN'). The highest mountain in the Alps (15,781 ft.).

Mon•te•vi•de•o (mŏn'tə-vĭ-dā'ō). The capital of Uruguay. Pop. 1,204,000.

Mont•gom•er•y (mŏnt-gŭm'ər-ē, -gŭm'rē, mənt-). The capital of Alabama. Pop. 134,000.

month (mŭnth) n. **1.** One of the 12 divisions of a year as determined by the Gregorian calendar. **2.** Any period extending from a date in one calendar month to the corresponding date in the following month. **3. a.** A period of four weeks. **b.** A period of 30 days. **4.** One twelfth of a tropical year. [< OE *mōnath.* See mē-².]

Usage: The singular *month,* preceded by a numeral (or number) and a hyphen, is used as a compound attributive: *a three-month vacation.* The plural possessive form without a hyphen is also possible: *a three months' vacation.*

month•ly (mŭnth'lē) *adj.* **1.** Of, occurring, coming due, or published every month. **2.** Lasting for a month. —*n., pl.* **-lies.** A monthly publication. —**month'ly** *adv.*

Mont•pe•lier (mŏnt-pēl'yər). The capital of Vermont. Pop. 9,000.

Mon•tre•al (mŏn'trē-ôl', mŭn'-). Canada's largest city. Pop. 1,191,000.

mon•u•ment (mŏn'yə-mənt) n. **1.** A structure erected as a memorial. **2.** A tombstone. **3.** Any place or region officially designated and preserved as having special interest or significance. **4.** Something that commemorates by association. **5.** An exceptional example of something. [< L *monumentum* < *monēre,* to remind, warn.] —**mon'u•men'tal** (-měn'təl) *adj.* —**mon'u•men'tal•ly** *adv.*

moo (moō) v. To emit the deep, bellowing sound made by a cow. [Imit.] —**moo** n.

mooch (moōch) v. *Slang.* **1.** To obtain free of charge, as by begging. **2.** To steal or filch.

mood¹ (moōd) n. **1.** A state of mind or feeling. **2.** Inclination or disposition. [< OE *mōd.* See mē-¹.]

mood² (moōd) n. A set of verb forms used to indicate the speaker's attitude toward the factuality, likelihood, or desirability of the action or condition expressed. [Var of MODE.]

mood•y (moō'dē) *adj.* **-ier, -iest. 1.** Given to changeable emotional states. **2.** Gloomy; uneasy. —**mood'i•ly** *adv.* —**mood'i•ness** n.

moon (moōn) n. **1.** The natural satellite of the earth, varying in distance from the earth between 221,600 and 252,950 miles, having a mean diameter of 2,160 miles, a mass approx. ¹⁄₈₀ that of the earth, and an average period of revolution around the earth of 29 days 12 hours 44 minutes. **2.** Any natural satellite revolving around a planet. **3.** The moon as it appears at a particular time in its cycle of phases: *the full moon.* **4.** A month. **5.** Any disk, globe, or crescent resembling the moon. **6.** Moonlight. —*v.* **1.** To dream or wander about aimlessly. **2.** To exhibit infatuation. [< OE *mōna.* See mē-².]

moon•light (moōn'līt') n. The light of the moon. —**moon'lit'** (-lĭt') *adj.*

moon•shine (moōn'shīn') n. **1.** Moonlight. **2.** *Informal.* Foolish talk. **3.** *Slang.* Illegally distilled whiskey. —**moon'shine'** *adj.* —**moon'shin'er** n.

moon•stone (moōn'stōn') n. A form of feldspar valued as a gem for its pearly translucence.

moon•struck (moōn'strŭk') *adj.* Also **moon•strick•en** (moōn'strĭk'ən). **1.** Afflicted with insanity; crazed. **2.** Distracted with romantic sentiment.

moor¹ (moōr) v. To secure or make fast, as with cables or anchors. [< MLG *mōren.*]

moor² (moōr) n. A broad tract of open, often boggy land. [< OE *mōr.* See mā-.]

Moor (moōr) n. **1.** One of a Moslem people

now living chiefly in N Africa. **2.** One of a
Moslem people who invaded Spain in the 8th
century A.D. —**Moor'ish** *adj.*

moor•ing (mŏŏr'ĭng) *n.* **1.** A place at which a
vessel or aircraft can be moored. **2.** Often
moorings. Elements providing stability or security.

moose (mŏŏs) *n., pl.* **moose.** A very large deer
of N North America, having broad, flattened
antlers. [< Algon.]

moot (mŏŏt) *adj.* **1.** Subject to debate; argu-
able: *a moot question.* **2.** Without legal significance. [< OE *mōt,* moot, assembly.]

mop (mŏp) *n.* A household implement made of
absorbent material attached to a handle and
used for cleaning floors. [Perh < *mappa,*
cloth.] —**mop** *v.* (**mopped, mopping**).

mope (mōp) *v.* **moped, moping. 1.** To be gloomy
or dejected. **2.** To dawdle. [Orig, to move as
in a daze.] —**mop'er** *n.*

mo•ped (mō'pĕd') *n.* A low, two-wheeled, mo-
tor-driven vehicle having two pedals and resembling a bicycle. [MO(TOR) PED(AL).]

mo•raine (mə-rān') *n.* An accumulation of
boulders, stones, or other debris carried and
deposited by a glacier. [F.]

mor•al (môr'əl, mŏr'-) *adj.* **1.** Of or concerned
with the discernment or instruction of what is
good and evil. **2.** Being or acting in accordance
with established standards of good behavior.
3. Arising from conscience. **4.** Having psychological rather than tangible effects. —*n.* **1.** The
principle taught by a story or event. **2. morals.**
Rules or habits of conduct, esp. sexual conduct. [< L *mōs* (*mōr*-), custom.] —**mor'al•ly**
adv.

mo•rale (mə-răl') *n.* The state of mind of an
individual or group with respect to confidence,
cheerfulness, discipline, etc. [< F *moral,*
moral.]

mor•al•ist (môr'ə-lĭst, mŏr'-) *n.* **1.** A teacher or
student of ethics. **2.** One who follows a system
of moral principles rather than an established
religion. —**mor'a•lis'tic** *adj.*

mo•ral•i•ty (mə-răl'ə-tē, mô-) *n.* **1.** The quality
of being moral. **2.** A set of ideas or customs of
a given religion, society, or social class. **3.**
Virtuous conduct.

mor•al•ize (môr'ə-līz', mŏr'-) *v.* **-ized, -izing.** To
think about or discuss moral or ethical issues.
—**mor'al•i•za'tion** *n.* —**mor'al•iz'er** *n.*

mo•rass (mə-răs', mô-) *n.* **1.** An area of low-
lying, soggy ground; a bog or marsh. **2.** Any
difficult or perplexing situation. [< OF
marasc.]

mor•a•to•ri•um (môr'ə-tôr'ē-əm, -tōr'ē-əm,
mŏr'-) *n., pl.* **-ums** or **-toria** (-tôr'ē-ə, -tōr'ē-ə).
1. An authorization to a debtor permitting
temporary suspension of payments. **2.** A de-
ferment or delay of any action. [< L *morārī,*
to delay.]

mo•ray (môr'ā, mŏr'ā, mə-rā') *n.* Any of various often voracious tropical marine eels. [<
Gk *muraina.*]

mor•bid (môr'bĭd) *adj.* **1.** Of, relating to, or
caused by disease. **2.** Characterized by preoccupation with unwholesome matters. **3.**

Gruesome; grisly. [L *morbidus,* diseased.]
—**mor•bid'i•ty** *n.* —**mor'bid•ly** *adv.*

mor•dant (môr'dənt) *adj.* **1.** Bitingly sarcastic.
2. Incisive and trenchant. [< OF *mordre,* to
bite.] —**mor'dan•cy** *n.* —**mor'dant•ly** *adv.*

more (môr, mōr) *adj.* *superl.* **most. 1. a.** *compar.*
of **many.** Greater in number. **b.** *compar. of*
much. Greater in size, amount, extent, or degree. **2.** Additional; extra: *They need more*
food. —*n.* A greater or additional quantity,
number, degree, or amount. —*adv.* **1.** —Used
to form the comparative of many adjectives
and adverbs: *more difficult; more intelligently.*
2. In addition; further; again; longer. —**more**
or less. 1. About; approximately. **2.** To an
undetermined degree. [< OE *māra* (adj), *māre*
(adv and n). See mē-³.]

More (môr, mōr), **Saint** (Sir) **Thomas.** 1478–
1535. English statesman and author.

mo•rel (mə-rĕl', mô-) *n.* An edible mushroom
with a brownish, spongelike cap. [< L *Maur-*
us, Moor.]

more•o•ver (môr-ō'vər, mōr-, môr'ō'vər,
mōr'-) *adv.* Beyond what has been stated;
further; besides.

mo•res (môr'āz, mōr'-, -ēz) *pl.n.* The traditional customs of a social group that come
through general observance to have the force
of law. [< L *mōs,* custom.]

Mor•gan (môr'gən), **J(ohn) P(ierpont).** 1837–
1913. American capitalist and financier.

morgue (môrg) *n.* A place in which the bodies
of persons found dead are temporarily kept.
[< *le Morgue,* the mortuary building in Paris.]

mor•i•bund (môr'ə-bŭnd', mŏr'-) *adj.* At the
point of death; about to die. [< L *morī,* to
die.] —**mor'i•bund'ly** *adv.*

Mor•mon (môr'mən) *n.* A member of the
Church of Jesus Christ of Latter-day Saints.
—**Mor'mon** *adj.* —**Mor'mon•ism'** *n.*

morn (môrn) *n. Poetic.* The morning. [< OE
morgen. See mer-¹.]

morn•ing (môr'nĭng) *n.* The first or early part
of the day, esp. from sunrise to noon. [<
MORN.] —**morn'ing** *adj.*

morn•ing-glo•ry (môr'nĭng-glôr'ē, -glōr'ē) *n.*
Any of various twining vines with funnel-
shaped, variously colored flowers that close
late in the day.

mo•roc•co (mə-rŏk'ō) *n., pl.* **-cos.** A soft,
grainy-textured goatskin leather.

Mo•roc•co (mə-rŏk'ō). A kingdom of NW

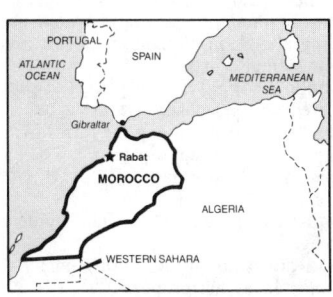

Morocco

ô paw, for/oi boy/ou out/ŏŏ took/ōō coo/p pop/r run/s sauce/sh shy/t to/th thin/*th* the/
ŭ cut/ûr fur/v van/w wag/y yes/z size/zh vision/ə ago, item, edible, gallop, circus/

Africa. Pop. 11,598,000. Cap. Rabat. **—Mo‧roc'can** (mə-rŏk'ən) *adj. & n.*

mo‧ron (môr'ŏn', môr'-) *n.* A mentally retarded person, esp. one having mental age between 7 and 12 years. [< Gk *mōros*, foolish.] **—mo‧ron'ic** (mə-rŏn'ĭk, mô-) *adj.*

mo‧rose (mə-rōs', mô-) *adj.* Sullenly melancholy; gloomy. [L *mōrōsus*, captious, fretful.]

mor‧pheme (môr'fēm') *n.* A linguistic unit that cannot be divided into smaller meaningful parts. [< Gk *morphē*, form.]

Mor‧phe‧us (môr'fē-əs, -fyōōs') *n.* Something that causes sleep. [< *Morpheus*, Ovid's name for the god of dreams.]

—morphic, —morphous. *comb. form.* Possession of (some specified) shape or form: *polymorphic,* **amorphous.** [< Gk *morphē*, form.]

mor‧phine (môr'fēn') *n.* An organic compound, $C_{17}H_{19}NO_3$, extracted from opium, the soluble salts of which are used in medicine as an anesthetic or sedative. [< MORPHEUS.]

mor‧phol‧o‧gy (môr-fŏl'ə-jē) *n.* **1.** The biological study of the form and structure of organisms. **2.** *Ling.* The study of word formation, including the origin and function of inflections and derivations. [< Gk *morphē*, form + -LOGY.] **—mor'pho‧log'i‧cal** (-fə-lŏj'ĭ-kəl) *adj.* **—mor'pho‧log'i‧cal‧ly** *adv.*

mor‧row (môr'ō, mŏr'ō) *n.* **1.** The day following some specified day. **2.** *Archaic.* The morning. [< OE *morgen*, MORN.]

Morse code (môrs). A system of communication used in telegraphy in which letters and numbers are represented by short and long patterns of sounds, flashes of light, written dots and dashes, etc. [< S. *Morse* (1791–1872), American artist and inventor.]

mor‧sel (môr'səl) *n.* **1.** A small piece or bite of food. **2.** A tasty tidbit. [< L *mordēre*, to bite.]

mor‧tal (môrt'l) *adj.* **1.** Liable or subject to death. **2.** Causing death; fatal. **3.** Fought to the death. **4.** Unrelenting; implacable: *a mortal enemy.* **5.** Like the fear of death: *in mortal terror.* **6.** Causing spiritual death: *a mortal sin.* **—n.** A human being. [< L *mors (mort-),* death.] **—mor'tal‧ly** *adv.*

mor‧tal‧i‧ty (môr-tăl'ə-tē) *n., pl.* **-ties. 1.** The condition of being subject to death. **2.** The ratio of deaths to population; death rate.

mor‧tar (môr'tər) *n.* **1.** A receptacle in which substances are crushed or ground with a pestle. **2.** A muzzle-loading cannon used to fire shells in a high trajectory. **3.** A mixture of cement or lime with sand and water, used in building. [< L *mortārium,* a mortar and the substance made in it.]

mort‧gage (môr'gĭj) *n.* **1.** A pledge of property to a creditor as security against a debt. **2.** A contract or deed specifying the terms of such a pledge. **—v.** **-gaged, -gaging.** To pledge (property) by mortgage. [< OF, "dead pledge."]

mort‧ga‧gee (môr'gĭ-jē') *n.* The holder of a mortgage.

mort‧ga‧gor (môr'gĭ-jôr', môr'gĭ-jər) *n.* One who mortgages his property.

mor‧ti‧cian (môr-tĭsh'ən) *n.* A funeral director; undertaker.

mor‧ti‧fy (môr'tə-fī') *v.* **-fied, -fying. 1.** To shame; humiliate. **2.** To discipline (one's body and appetites) by self-denial. **3.** To cause gangrene or become gangrenous. [< LL *mortificāre,* to cause to die.] **—mor'ti‧fi‧ca'tion** (-fĭ-kā'shən) *n.* **—mor'ti‧fy'ing‧ly** *adv.*

mor‧tise (môr'tĭs) *n.* Also **mor‧tice.** A cavity, usually rectangular, in a piece of wood or other material, prepared to receive a tenon of another piece, to join the two. [< OF *mortoise.*]

mor‧tu‧ar‧y (môr'chōō-ĕr'ē) *n., pl.* **-ies.** A place where dead bodies are prepared or kept prior to burial or cremation. [< LL *mortuārius,* of burial.]

mos. months.

mo‧sa‧ic (mō-zā'ĭk) *n.* A picture or decorative design made by setting small colored pieces, such as tile, in mortar. [< Gk *mouseios,* belonging to the Muses.] **—mo‧sa'ic** *adj.*

Mos‧cow (mŏs'kou', -kō). The capital of the Soviet Union. Pop. 7,061,000.

Mo‧ses (mō'zĭz, -zĭs). Hebrew prophet and lawgiver. **—Mo‧sa'ic** (-zā'ĭk) *adj.*

mo‧sey (mō'zē) *v. Informal.* To amble along. [?]

Mos‧lem (mŏz'ləm, mŏs'-) *n.* Also **Mus‧lim** (mŭz'ləm, mŏŏz'-, mŭs'-, mŏŏs'-), *archaic*

A .—	V ...—
B —...	W .——
C —.—.	X —..—
D —..	Y —.——
E .	Z ——..
F ..—.	Á .——.—
G ——.	Ä .—.—
H	É ..—..
I ..	Ñ ——.——
J .———	Ö ———.
K —.—	Ü ..——
L .—..	1 .————
M ——	2 ..———
N —.	3 ...——
O ———	4 ....—
P .——.	5 .....
Q ——.—	6 —....
R .—.	7 ——...
S ...	8 ———..
T —	9 ————.
U ..—	0 —————
, (comma) —.—.——	
. (period) .—.—.—	
? ..——..	
; —.—.—.	
: ———...	
/ —..—.	
- (hyphen) —....—	
apostrophe .————.	
parenthesis —.——.—	
underline ..——.—	

Morse code

ă pat/ā ate/âr care/ä bar/b bib/ch chew/d deed/ĕ pet/ē be/f fit/g gag/h hat/hw what/
ĭ pit/ī pie/îr pier/j judge/k kick/l lid, fatal/m mum/n no, sudden/ng sing/ŏ pot/ō go/

Mus•sul•man (mŭs′əl-mən, mōōs′-). A believer in or adherent of Islam. —**Mos′lem** adj.

mosque (mŏsk) n. A Moslem house of worship.

mos•qui•to (mə-skē′tō) n., pl. **-toes** or **-tos.** Any of various winged insects of which the females suck blood and in some species transmit diseases. [< L musca, fly.]

moss (môs, mŏs) n. Any of various small, green, nonflowering plants often forming a dense, matlike growth. [< OE mos. See **meu-**.] —**moss′i•ness** n. —**moss′y** adj.

most (mōst) adj. **1. a.** superl. of **many.** Greatest in number. **b.** superl. of **much.** Greatest in amount, size, or degree. **2.** In the greatest number of instances: Most fish have fins. —n. **1.** The greatest amount, quantity, or degree; the largest part. **2.** (takes pl. v.). The greatest number (of a group or classification); the majority. —**at (the) most.** Not over; at the absolute limit: four miles at most. —**make the most of.** To use as advantageously as possible. —adv. **1.** In the highest degree, quantity, or extent: most honest; what I need most. **2.** Very: a most impressive book. **3.** Informal. Almost: Most everyone agrees. [< OE mǣst. See **mē-³**.] —**most.** comb. form. Forms the superlative degree of adverbs and adjectives: innermost. [< OE -mǣst, -mest.]

most•ly (mōst′lē) adv. For the most part; almost entirely.

mote (mōt) n. A speck, esp. of dust. [< OE mot.]

mo•tel (mō-tĕl′) n. A hotel for motorists, usually opening directly on a parking area. [Blend of MOTOR and HOTEL.]

mo•tet (mō-tĕt′) n. A polyphonic musical composition based on a sacred text. [< OF mot, phrase, word.]

moth (môth, mŏth) n., pl. **moths** (môthz, mŏthz, môths, mŏths). **1.** Any of various insects related to and resembling the butterflies but generally night-flying and with featherlike antennae. **2.** Also **clothes moth.** A small whitish moth with larvae that feed on wool, fur, etc. [< OE moththe.]

moth ball. 1. A marble-sized ball of naphthalene, stored with clothes to repel moths. **2. moth balls.** Protective storage: warships put into moth balls.

moth•er (mŭth′ər) n. **1.** A female parent. **2.** A creative or environmental source: Necessity is the mother of invention. —adj. **1.** Being a mother: a mother hen. **2.** Characteristic of a mother: mother love. **3.** Native: one's mother tongue. —v. **1.** To give birth to; be the mother of. **2.** To care for; nourish and protect. [< OE mōdor. See **māter-**.] —**moth′er•hood′** n.

moth•er-in-law (mŭth′ər-ĭn-lô′) n., pl. **mothers-in-law.** The mother of one's wife or husband.

moth•er•land (mŭth′ər-lănd′) n. One's native land.

moth•er•ly (mŭth′ər-lē) adj. Of or characteristic of a mother; maternal.

moth•er-of-pearl (mŭth′ər-əv-pûrl′) n. The pearly internal layer of certain mollusk shells, used to make decorative objects.

mo•tif (mō-tēf′) n. Also **mo•tive** (mō′tĭv, mō-

tēv′). A recurrent thematic element used in the development of a musical, artistic, or literary work. [< OF, motive.]

mo•tile (mōt′l, mō′tīl′) adj. Moving or having the power to move spontaneously. [< MOTION.] —**mo•til′i•ty** (mō-tĭl′ə-tē) n.

mo•tion (mō′shən) n. **1.** The action or process of change of position. **2.** A significant movement of a part of the body; a gesture. **3.** A formal proposal put to vote under parliamentary procedures. —v. **1.** To signal to or direct by making a gesture. **2.** To make a gesture signifying something. [< L movēre (pp mōtus), to move.]

mo•tion•less (mō′shən-lĭs) adj. Not moving. —**mo′tion•less•ly** adv.

motion picture. A series of filmed images viewed in sufficiently rapid succession to create the illusion of motion and continuity. —**mo′tion-pic′ture** adj.

mo•ti•vate (mō′tə-vāt′) v. **-vated, -vating.** To stimulate to action; provide with an incentive or motive. —**mo′ti•va′tion** n.

mo•tive (mō′tĭv) n. **1.** An impulse acting as an incitement to action. **2.** Variant of **motif.** —adj. Causing or able to cause motion. [< OF motif, "causing to move."]

mot•ley (mŏt′lē) adj. **1.** Having components of great variety; heterogeneous; varied. **2.** Having or exhibiting many colors; multicolored. [ME motteley.]

mo•tor (mō′tər) n. **1.** Anything that imparts or produces motion. **2.** A device that converts any form of energy into mechanical energy, esp. a device that converts electric current into mechanical power. —adj. **1.** Causing or producing motion. **2.** Driven by or having a motor. **3.** Of or for motor vehicles: motor oil. **4.** Relating to movements of the muscles. —v. To drive or travel in a motor vehicle. [< L movēre (pp mōtus), to move.]

mo•tor•boat (mō′tər-bōt′) n. A boat propelled by an internal-combustion engine.

mo•tor•cade (mō′tər-kād′) n. A procession of automobiles or other motor vehicles. [MOTOR + (CAVAL)CADE.]

mo•tor•car (mō′tər-kär′) n. An automobile.

motor court. A motel.

mo•tor•cy•cle (mō′tər-sī′kəl) n. A vehicle with two wheels in tandem, propelled by an internal-combustion engine. —**mo′tor•cy′clist** (-sī′klĭst) n.

mo•tor•ist (mō′tər-ĭst) n. One who travels in an automobile.

mo•tor•ize (mō′tə-rīz′) v. **-ized, -izing.** To equip with a motor or motors.

mo•tor•man (mō′tər-mən) n. One who drives an electrically powered streetcar, locomotive, or subway train.

motor scooter. A small two-wheeled vehicle powered by a gasoline engine.

mo•tor•ship (mō′tər-shĭp′) n. A ship powered by an internal-combustion engine.

motor vehicle. Any self-propelled land vehicle that does not run on rails.

mot•tle (mŏt′l) v. **-tled, -tling.** To cover (a surface) with spots or streaks of different shades or colors.

ô paw, for/oi boy/ou out/ōo took/ōo coo/p pop/r run/s sauce/sh shy/t to/th thin/th the/
ŭ cut/ûr fur/v van/w wag/y yes/z size/zh vision/ə ago, item, edible, gallop, circus/

mot·to (mŏt'ō) *n., pl.* **-toes** or **-tos.** A brief sentence, phrase, or single word used to express a principle, goal, or ideal; maxim. [It, "a word."]

mould. *Chiefly Brit.* Variant of **mold.**

mould·er. *Chiefly Brit.* Variant of **molder.**

moult. *Chiefly Brit.* Variant of **molt.**

mound (mound) *n.* **1.** A pile or bank of earth, sand, or rocks. **2.** A natural elevation, as a small hill. **3.** The slightly elevated pitcher's area in the center of a baseball diamond. [Perh < Du *mond,* protection.]

mount¹ (mount) *v.* **1.** To climb or ascend. **2.** To get up on: *mount a horse.* **3.** To increase in amount, degree, extent, intensity, or number. **4.** To place in an appropriate setting, as for display, study, etc. **5. a.** To set (guns) in position. **b.** To launch and carry out: *mount an attack.* —*n.* **1.** A horse or other animal on which to ride. **2.** An object to which another is affixed for accessibility, display, or use. [< VL *montâre,* "to climb a mountain."] —**mount'a·ble** *adj.*

mount² (mount) *n.* A mountain or hill. [< L *mōns,* mountain.]

moun·tain (moun'tən) *n.* A natural elevation of the earth's surface having a height greater than that of a hill. [< L *mōns,* mountain.] —**moun'tain** *adj.*

moun·tain·eer (moun'tən-îr') *n.* **1.** An inhabitant of a mountainous area. **2.** One who climbs mountains for sport. —*v.* To climb mountains for sport.

mountain lion. A large, tawny wild cat of mountainous regions of the W Hemisphere.

moun·tain·ous (moun'tən-əs) *adj.* Having many mountains.

moun·te·bank (moun'tə-băngk') *n.* **1.** A hawker of quack medicines. **2.** Any charlatan or trickster. [It *montambanco,* "one who climbs on a bench."]

mount·ing (moun'tĭng) *n.* Something that provides a setting: *a mounting for a gem.*

mourn (môrn, mōrn) *v.* To feel or express sorrow (for or over). [< OE *murnan.* See **smer-¹.**] —**mourn'er** *n.*

mourn·ful (môrn'fəl, mōrn'-) *adj.* **1.** Feeling or expressing grief. **2.** Arousing or suggesting grief. —**mourn'ful·ly** *adv.*

mourn·ing (môr'nĭng, mōr'-) *n.* **1.** The actions or expressions of one who has suffered a bereavement. **2.** Clothes worn as a sign of grief for the dead. **3.** The period during which a death is mourned.

mouse (mous) *n., pl.* **mice** (mīs). Any of various small, usually long-tailed rodents, some of which live in or near human dwellings. —*v.* (mouz) **moused, mousing.** To hunt or catch mice. [< OE *mūs.* See **mū-.**]

mousse (mōōs) *n.* Any of various chilled desserts made with whipped cream, gelatin, and flavoring. [F, "froth."]

mous·tache. *Chiefly Brit.* Variant of **mustache.**

mous·y (mou'sē, -zē) *adj.* **-ier, -iest.** Mouselike in color, features, or shyness: *mousy hair; a mousy person.* —**mous'i·ness** *n.*

mouth (mouth) *n., pl.* **mouths** (mou*th*z). **1.** The body opening and related organs with which food is taken in, chewed, and swallowed and sounds and speech are articulated. **2.** A natural opening, such as the part of a river that empties into a larger body of water or the entrance to a harbor, canyon, etc. **3.** The opening through which any container is filled or emptied. —*v.* (mou*th*). **1.** To utter in a meaninglessly declamatory manner. **2.** To put, take, or move around in the mouth. [< OE *mūth.* See **menth-.**]

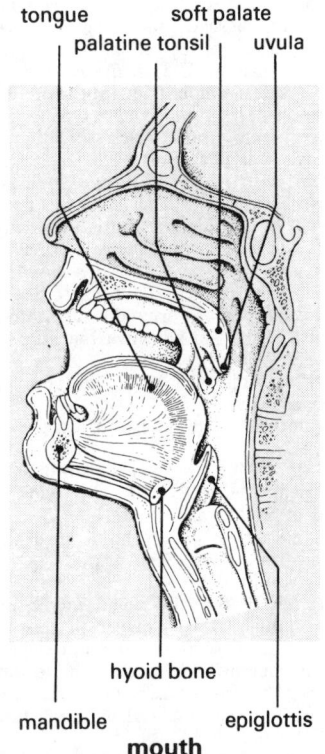

tongue   soft palate
palatine tonsil   uvula

hyoid bone

mandible   epiglottis

mouth

mouth organ. A harmonica.

mouth·piece (mouth'pēs') *n.* **1.** A part of an instrument that functions in or near the mouth. **2.** *Informal.* A spokesman.

mou·ton (mōō'tŏn') *n.* Sheepskin sheared and processed to resemble beaver or seal. [F, "sheep."]

move (mōōv) *v.* **moved, moving. 1.** To change in position from one point to another. **2.** To transfer (a piece) in a board game. **3.** To settle in a new place. **4.** To change hands commercially: *Furs move slowly in summer.* **5.** To affect deeply. **6.** To take some action. **7.** To make a formal motion in parliamentary procedure. **8.** To cause (the bowels) to evacuate. —*n.* **1.** An act of moving. **2.** A change of residence or place of business. **3. a.** The transferring of a piece from one position to another in a board game. **b.** A player's turn to maneuver one of his pieces. **4.** One of a series

---

ă pat/ā ate/âr care/ä bar/b bib/ch chew/d deed/ĕ pet/ē be/f fit/g gag/h hat/hw what/
ĭ pit/ī pie/îr pier/j judge/k kick/l lid, fatal/m mum/n no, sudden/ng sing/ŏ pot/ō go/

of actions undertaken to achieve some end. [< L *movēre*, to move.]

move·ment (mo͞ov'mənt) *n.* **1. a.** An act of moving; a change in position. **b.** A maneuver in which military or naval units are moved toward some tactical or strategic objective. **2.** The activities of a group toward the achievement of a specific goal: *the labor movement.* **3.** Activity, esp. in business or commerce. **4.** An evacuation of the bowels. **5.** *Mus.* A primary section of a composition. **6.** A mechanism that produces or transmits motion, as the works of a watch.

mov·er (mo͞o'vər) *n.* **1.** One that moves. **2.** One whose occupation is transporting furnishings.

mov·ie (mo͞o'vē) *n. Informal.* **1.** A motion picture. **2.** A theater that shows motion pictures. **3. the movies.** A showing of a motion picture. [Short for moving picture.]

mow¹ (mō) *v.* **mowed, mowed** or **mown** (mōn), **mowing. 1.** To cut down (grain, grass, etc.) with a scythe or mechanical device. **2.** To cut (such growth) from. —**mow down.** To fell in great numbers, as in battle. [< OE *māwan.* See mē-⁴.] —**mow'er** (mō'ər) *n.*

mow² (mou) *n.* A place for storing hay or grain. [< OE *mūwa.*]

Mo·zam·bique (mō'zăm-bēk'). A country in SE Africa, formerly an overseas province of Portugal. Pop. 7,376,000. Cap. Lourenço Marques.

Mo·zart (mōt'särt'), **Wolfgang Amadeus.** 1756-1791. Austrian composer.

MP military police; military policeman.

M.P. 1. Member of Parliament. **2.** military police; military policeman.

mph, m.p.h. miles per hour.

Mr. (mĭs'tər) *n., pl.* **Messrs.** The abbreviated form of the title **Mister** when used with a name.

Mrs. (mĭs'ĭz) *n., pl.* **Mmes.** A title of courtesy used in speaking to or of a married woman, preceding her surname.

ms manuscript.

Ms., Ms (mĭz, ĕm'ĕs') *n., pl.* **Mses** or **Mss.** A title of courtesy used before a woman's surname or before her given name and surname without regard to her marital status. [Abbr. of **mistress,** formed by combining and shortening MISS and MRS.]

mss, MSS, mss., MSS. manuscripts.

MST, M.S.T. Mountain Standard Time.

mt., Mt. mount; mountain.

m.t., M.T. Mountain Time.

mtn. mountain.

mu (m/y/o͞o) *n.* The 12th letter of the Greek alphabet, representing *m.*

much (mŭch) *adj.* **more, most.** Great in quantity, degree, or extent: *much rain.* —*n.* **1.** A large quantity or amount. **2.** Anything impressive or important: *not much of a swimmer.* —*adv.* **more, most. 1.** To a great degree; to a large extent: *much better.* **2.** Just about; almost: *much the same.* [< OE *mycel, micel,* great, large, greatly. See meg-.]

mu·ci·lage (myo͞o'sə-lĭj) *n.* A sticky substance used as an adhesive. [< L *mūcus,* MUCUS.] —**mu'ci·lag'i·nous** (-lăj'ə-nəs) *adj.*

muck (mŭk) *n.* **1.** A moist, sticky mixture, esp. of mud and filth. **2.** Moist animal dung. **3.**

Dark, fertile soil containing putrid vegetable matter. [< ON *mykr.*] —**muck'y** *adj.*

muck·rake (mŭk'rāk') *v.* **-raked, -raking.** To search for and expose political or commercial corruption. —**muck'rak'er** *n.*

mu·cous (myo͞o'kəs) *adj.* Also **mu·cose** (-kōs'). Producing or secreting mucus.

mucous membrane. The membrane lining all bodily channels that communicate with the air, the glands of which secrete mucus.

mu·cus (myo͞o'kəs) *n.* The viscous material secreted as a protective lubricant coating by glands in the mucous membrane. [L *mūcus.*]

mud (mŭd) *n.* **1.** Wet, sticky, soft earth. **2.** Slanderous charges; calumny. [ME *mudde.*]

mud·dle (mŭd'l) *v.* **-dled, -dling. 1.** To make turbid; muddy. **2.** To mix confusedly; jumble. **3.** To mix up (the mind), as with alcohol; confuse. **4.** To mismanage or bungle. —*n.* A confusion, jumble, or mess. [Perh < MDu *moddelen,* to make muddy.]

mud·dy (mŭd'ē) *adj.* **-dier, -diest. 1.** Covered, full of, or spattered with mud. **2.** Not clear or pure, as a color or liquid. —*v.* **-died, -dying. 1.** To make muddy or dirty. **2.** To make dull or cloudy. —**mud'di·ness** *n.*

mud·guard (mŭd'gärd') *n.* A shield over a vehicle's wheel.

mud·sling·er (mŭd'slĭng'ər) *n.* One who makes malicious charges against an opponent. —**mud'sling'ing** *n.*

mu·ez·zin (m/y/o͞o-ĕz'ĭn) *n.* A Moslem crier who calls the faithful to prayer, usually from a minaret.

muff¹ (mŭf) *v.* To perform (an act) clumsily; bungle. [?] —**muff** *n.*

muff² (mŭf) *n.* A small cylindrical cover, open at both ends, for keeping the hands warm. [< MDu *moffel.*]

muf·fin (mŭf'ĭn) *n.* A small, cup-shaped bread, usually served hot. [Prob < LG *muffen.*]

muf·fle (mŭf'əl) *v.* **-fled, -fling. 1.** To wrap up snugly for warmth or protection. **2.** To wrap or cover in order to deaden a sound. **3.** To deaden (a sound). [< OF *moufle,* mitten.]

muf·fler (mŭf'lər) *n.* **1.** A heavy scarf worn around the neck. **2.** Any device that absorbs noise, esp. that of an internal-combustion engine.

muf·ti (mŭf'tē) *n.* Civilian dress as distinguished from a uniform.

mug¹ (mŭg) *n.* A cylindrical drinking vessel, often having a handle. [?]

mug² (mŭg). *Slang. n.* **1.** The face of a person. **2.** A grimace. **3.** A hoodlum. —*v.* **mugged, mugging.** To waylay and beat severely, usually with intent to rob. —**mug'ger** *n.*

mug·gy (mŭg'ē) *adj.* **-gier, -giest.** Warm and extremely humid. [< ON *mugga,* to drizzle.] —**mug'gi·ly** *adv.* —**mug'gi·ness** *n.*

mu·lat·to (m/y/o͞o-lăt'ō, -lä'tō) *n., pl.* **-tos** or **-toes.** A person having one white and one Negro parent. [Span *mulato,* young mule, mulatto.] —**mu·lat'to** *adj.*

mul·ber·ry (mŭl'bĕr'ē, -bə-rē) *n.* **1.** A tree bearing sweet reddish or purplish berrylike fruit. **2.** The fruit of such a tree. [< OE *mōrberie.*] —**mul'ber·ry** *adj.*

ô paw, for/oi boy/ou out/o͞o took/o͞o coo/p pop/r run/s sauce/sh shy/t to/th thin/*th* the/
ŭ cut/ûr fur/v van/w wag/y yes/z size/zh vision/ə ago, item, edible, gallop, circus/

mulch (mŭlch) *n.* A protective covering, as of leaves, manure, or hay, placed around plants to prevent evaporation of moisture and freezing of roots. —*v.* To cover with a mulch. [Prob < OE *melisc,* mild, mellow.]

mulct (mŭlkt) *n.* A fine or similar penalty. —*v.* 1. To penalize by fining. 2. To acquire or take away from by trickery or deception. [L *mulcta,* a fine.]

mule¹ (myōol) *n.* 1. The sterile hybrid offspring of a male ass and a female horse. 2. *Informal.* A stubborn person. [< L *mūlus,* mule.]

mule² (myōol) *n.* A slipper that has no strap to fit around the heel. [< L *mulleus (calceus),* "red (shoe)."]

mu·le·teer (myōo'lə-tîr') *n.* A mule driver.

mul·ish (myōo'lĭsh) *adj.* Like a mule; stubborn. —**mul'ish·ness** *n.*

mull¹ (mŭl) *v.* To heat and spice (a beverage, such as wine). [Perh < ME *mul,* dust, meal, powdered spice.]

mull² (mŭl) *v.* To ponder or ruminate on (with *over*). [< ME *mullen,* to pulverize.]

mul·let (mŭl'ĭt) *n.* Any of various widely distributed, chiefly marine food fishes. [< L *mullus,* red mullet.]

mul·li·ga·taw·ny (mŭl'ĭ-gə-tô'nē) *n.* An East Indian meat soup strongly flavored with curry.

multi-. *comb. form.* 1. Many or much. 2. More than one. [< L *multus,* much.]

mul·ti·col·ored (mŭl'tĭ-kŭl'ərd) *adj.* Having many colors.

mul·ti·far·i·ous (mŭl'tə-fâr'ē-əs) *adj.* Having great variety; made up of many parts or kinds. [L *multifārius.*] —**mul'ti·far'i·ous·ness** *n.*

mul·ti·form (mŭl'tə-fôrm') *adj.* Having many forms, shapes, or appearances.

mul·ti·mil·lion·aire (mŭl'tə-mĭl'yə-nâr') *n.* One whose financial assets equal many millions of dollars.

mul·ti·na·tion·al (mŭl'tē-năsh'ə-nəl, -năsh'nəl) *adj.* 1. Having operations, subsidiaries, or investments in more than one country: *a multinational corporation.* 2. Of or in several or many countries: *a multinational research project.* —*n.* A multinational company or corporation.

mul·ti·ple (mŭl'tə-pəl) *adj.* Of or having more than one element, component, etc. —*n.* A quantity into which another can be divided with zero remainder. [< LL *multiplus.*]

mul·ti·ple-choice (mŭl'tə-pəl-chois') *adj.* Offering a number of answers from which the correct one is to be chosen.

multiple sclerosis. A degenerative disease of the central nervous system, in which hardening of tissue occurs.

mul·ti·pli·cand (mŭl'tə-plĭ-kănd') *n.* The number that is or is to be multiplied by another.

mul·ti·pli·ca·tion (mŭl'tə-plĭ-kā'shən) *n.* 1. The act of multiplying or process of being multiplied. 2. The propagation of plants and animals. 3. a. An operation on two real numbers in which the number of times either is taken in summation is determined by the value of the other. b. An extension of this operation to quantities other than real numbers.

multiplication sign. The sign ×, placed between multiplicand and multiplier.

mul·ti·plic·i·ty (mŭl'tə-plĭs'ə-tē) *n.* 1. The state of being various or manifold. 2. A large number.

mul·ti·pli·er (mŭl'tə-plī'ər) *n.* The number by which the multiplicand is multiplied. If 3 is multiplied by 2, 3 is the multiplicand and 2 is the multiplier.

mul·ti·ply (mŭl'tə-plī') *v.* -plied, -plying. 1. To increase in number, amount, or degree. 2. To breed; propagate. 3. To perform multiplication (on). [< L *multiplicāre.*]

mul·ti·stage (mŭl'tə-stāj') *adj.* Functioning by stages.

mul·ti·tude (mŭl'tə-t/y/ōod') *n.* A great, indefinite number. [< L *multus,* many.]

mul·ti·tu·di·nous (mŭl'tə-t/y/ōod'n-əs) *adj.* Very numerous; existing in great numbers.

mum¹ (mŭm) *adj.* Not talking. [Prob < LG.]

mum² (mŭm) *n. Informal.* A chrysanthemum.

mum·ble (mŭm'bəl) *v.* -bled, -bling. To speak or utter indistinctly by lowering the voice or partially closing the mouth. [< MUM¹.] —**mum'ble** *n.* —**mum'bler** *n.*

mum·bo jum·bo (mŭm'bō jŭm'bō). 1. An object believed to have supernatural powers; a fetish. 2. Confusing or meaningless activity; obscure ritual. [Mandingo *mā-mā-gyo-mbō,* "magician who makes the troubled spirits of ancestors go away."]

mum·mer (mŭm'ər) *n.* One who acts or plays in a mask or costume. [< MDu *mommer.*] —**mum'mer·y** *n.*

mum·mi·fy (mŭm'ə-fī') *v.* -fied, -fying. 1. To make into a mummy. 2. To shrivel up like a mummy. —**mum'mi·fi·ca'tion** *n.*

mum·my (mŭm'ē) *n., pl.* -ies. A body embalmed after death, as by the ancient Egyptians. [< Ar *mūmiyā.*]

mumps (mŭmps) *n. (takes sing. v.).* An inflammatory, contagious viral disease of the salivary glands and, sometimes, of the ovaries or testes. [Prob < Scand.]

munch (mŭnch) *v.* To chew steadily with a crunching sound. [ME *monchen.*]

mun·dane (mŭn'dān', mŭn'dān') *adj.* 1. Bound to earth; worldly. 2. Typical of or concerned with the ordinary. [< L *mundus,* the world.] —**mun·dane'ly** *adv.*

Mu·nich (myōo'nĭk). A city of SE West Germany. Pop. 1,193,000.

mu·nic·i·pal (myōo-nĭs'ə-pəl) *adj.* 1. Of or pertaining to a city or its government. 2. Having local self-government: *a municipal borough.* [< L *mūnicipium,* a franchised city.]

mu·nic·i·pal·i·ty (myōo-nĭs'ə-păl'ə-tē) *n., pl.* -ties. A city, town, or other district incorporated for local self-government.

mu·nif·i·cent (myōo-nĭf'ə-sənt) *adj.* Extremely liberal in giving; very generous. [< L *mūnificus,* "present-making," generous.] —**mu·nif'i·cence** *n.* —**mu·nif'i·cent·ly** *adv.*

mu·ni·tions (myōo-nĭsh'ənz) *pl.n.* War materiel. [< L *mūnire,* to defend, fortify.]

mu·ral (myōor'əl) *n.* A picture or decoration, usually very large, applied directly to a wall or ceiling. —*adj.* 1. Of or like a wall. 2. Painted on a wall. [< L *mūrus*, a wall.] —**mu'ral•ist** *n.*

mur•der (mûr'dər) *n.* The unlawful killing of one human being by another, esp. with malice aforethought. —*v.* **1.** To kill (a human being) unlawfully. **2.** To mar or spoil by ineptness: *murder the English language.* [< OE *morthor.*] —**mur'der•er** *n.* —**mur'der•ess** *fem.n.*

mur•der•ous (mûr'dər-əs) *adj.* **1.** Capable of, guilty of, or intending murder. **2.** Characteristic of murder; brutal. **3.** *Informal.* Very difficult or dangerous: *a murderous exam.*

murk (mûrk) *n.* Darkness; gloom. [< OE *mirce*, darkness.]

murk•y (mûr'kē) *adj.* **-ier, -iest.** **1.** Dark or gloomy. **2. a.** Heavy and thick with smoke, mist, etc. **b.** Turbid with sediment: *murky waters.* —**murk'i•ly** *adv.* —**murk'i•ness** *n.*

mur•mur (mûr'mər) *n.* **1.** A low, indistinct, and continuous sound. **2.** An indistinct complaint. **3.** An abnormal sound, as from the heart or lungs. —*v.* To make or utter in a low, continuous, and indistinct sound. [< L.]

Mur•ray River (mûr'ē). A river of SE Australia.

mus. **1.** museum. **2.** music.

mus•cat (mŭs'kăt', -kət) *n.* A sweet white grape used for making wine or raisins. [< LL *muscus*, musk.]

Mus•cat (mŭs'kăt'). The capital of Oman. Pop. 6,000.

Mus•cat and O•man. See Oman.

mus•ca•tel (mŭs'kə-tĕl') *n.* A rich, sweet wine made from muscat grapes.

mus•cle (mŭs'əl) *n.* **1.** A tissue composed of fibers capable of contracting and relaxing to effect bodily movement. **2.** A contractile organ consisting of muscle tissue. **3.** Muscular strength. —*v.* **-cled, -cling.** To force one's way. [< L *mūsculus*, "little mouse," muscle.]

mus•cle-bound (mŭs'əl-bound') *adj.* Having stiff, overdeveloped muscles, as from excessive exercise.

mus•cu•lar (mŭs'kyə-lər) *adj.* **1.** Pertaining to or consisting of muscle or muscles. **2.** Having strong muscles. —**mus'cu•lar'i•ty** (-lär'ə-tē) *n.*

muscular dystrophy. A chronic, noncontagious disease of unknown cause, in which there is gradual but irreversible muscular deterioration.

mus•cu•la•ture (mŭs'kyə-lə-choŏr') *n.* The system of muscles of an animal or a body part.

muse (myooz) *v.* **mused, musing.** To ponder or meditate (on); consider reflectively or at length. [< OF *muser*, to muse, "sniff around."] —**mus'er** *n.*

Muse (myooz) *n.* **1.** *Gk.Myth.* Any of the nine daughters of Zeus, each of whom presided over a different art or science. **2. muse.** The spirit regarded as inspiring a poet; a source of inspiration. [< Gk *Mousa.*]

mu•se•um (myoo-zē'əm) *n.* A building in which works of artistic, historical, and scientific interest are exhibited. [< Gk *mouseion*, "place of the Muses."]

mush (mŭsh) *n.* **1.** Boiled cornmeal. **2.** Anything thick, soft, and pulpy. **3.** *Informal.* Maudlin sentimentality. [Prob var of MASH.]

mush•room (mŭsh'room', -room') *n.* Any of various fleshy fungi having an umbrella-shaped cap borne on a stalk, esp. one that is edible. —*v.* To multiply, grow, or expand rapidly. [< OF *mousseron.*]

mush•y (mŭsh'ē) *adj.* **-ier, -iest.** **1.** Like mush; soft and pulpy. **2.** *Informal.* Excessively sentimental. —**mush'i•ness** *n.*

mu•sic (myoo'zĭk) *n.* **1.** The art of organizing sound so as to elicit an aesthetic response in a listener. **2.** Vocal or instrumental sounds having some degree of rhythm, melody, and harmony. **3.** A musical composition or body of such compositions. **4.** Any aesthetically pleasing or harmonious sound or combination of sounds. [< Gk *mousikē (tekhnē)*, (art) of the Muses.]

mu•si•cal (myoo'zĭ-kəl) *adj.* **1.** Of, pertaining to, or capable of producing music. **2.** Resembling music; melodious. **3.** Set to or accompanied by music. **4.** Devoted to or skilled in music. —*n.* Also **musical comedy.** A play in which dialogue is interspersed with songs and dances. —**mu'si•cal•ly** *adv.*

mu•si•cale (myoo-zĭ-kăl') *n.* A program of music performed at a social gathering.

mu•si•cian (myoo-zĭsh'ən) *n.* One skilled in composing or performing music.

mu•si•col•o•gy (myoo'zĭ-kŏl'ə-jē) *n.* The historic and scientific study of music. —**mu'si•col'o•gist** *n.*

musk (mŭsk) *n.* An odorous substance secreted by an Asian deer or produced synthetically, used in perfumery. [< Pers *mushk.*] —**musk'i•ness** *n.* —**musk'y** *adj.*

mus•kel•lunge (mŭs'kə-lŭnj') *n.* A large North American freshwater game fish similar to the pike. [< Algon.]

mus•ket (mŭs'kĭt) *n.* A smoothbore shoulder gun used in the 17th and 18th centuries. [< It *moschetto.*] —**mus'ket•eer** (mŭs'kĭ-tîr') *n.*

mus•ket•ry (mŭs'kĭ-trē) *n.* **1.** Muskets collectively. **2.** The fire of muskets. **3.** The technique of using small arms.

Mus•kho•ge•an (mŭs-kō'gē-ən) *n.* Also **Mus•ko•ge•an.** A North American Indian language family, including Creek and Seminole. —**Mus•kho'ge•an** *adj.*

musk•mel•on (mŭsk'mĕl'ən) *n.* A melon, as the cantaloupe, having flesh with a musky aroma.

musk ox. A large, shaggy, horned mammal of N Canada and Greenland.

musk•rat (mŭs'krăt') *n.* **1.** An aquatic North American rodent with dense brown fur. **2.** The fur of this rodent.

Mus•lim (mŭz'ləm, moos'-, mooz'-) *n.* **1.** See **Moslem.** **2.** A member of the **Nation of Islam.** —**Mus'lim** *adj.*

mus•lin (mŭz'lĭn) *n.* Any of various sturdy, plain-weave cotton fabrics, used esp. for sheets. [< It *mussolina*, "cloth of Mosul," city in Iraq.]

mus•quash (mŭs'kwäsh', -kwôsh') *n. Chiefly Brit.* The muskrat or its fur. [< Algon.]

muss (mŭs) *v.* To make messy or untidy; rumple. —*n.* A state of disorder; mess. [Perh var of MESS.] —**muss'y** *adj.*

mus•sel (mŭs'əl) *n.* Any of various narrow-shelled bivalve mollusks, esp. an edible marine species. [< L *músculus*, "little mouse," muscle, mussel.]

Mus·so·li·ni (mōōs'sō-lē'nē), **Benito.** 1883–1945. Fascist dictator of Italy (1922–43).

Benito Mussolini

Mus·sul·man (mŭs'əl-mən) *n.*, *pl.* -men or -mans. *Archaic.* A Moslem.

must (mŭst) *v.* —Used as an auxiliary to indicate: **1.** Necessity or obligation: *You must register in order to vote.* **2.** Probability: *It must be midnight.* **3.** Inevitability or certainty: *To each of us, death must come.* —*n.* An absolute requirement; something that should be done without fail. [< OE *mōtan,* to be allowed.]

mus·tache (mŭs'tăsh', mə-stăsh') *n.* Also *chiefly Brit.* **mous·tache.** The hair growing on the upper lip, esp. when cultivated and groomed. [< Gk *mustax,* the upper lip, mustache.]

mus·tang (mŭs'tăng') *n.* A wild horse of the W North American plains. [< Span *mestengo,* stray (animal).]

mus·tard (mŭs'tərd) *n.* **1.** Any of various plants with yellow flowers and often pungent seeds. **2.** A condiment made from powdered mustard seeds. **3.** Dark brownish yellow. [< OF *moustarde.*]

mustard gas. An oily, volatile liquid, (ClCH$_2$CH$_2$)$_2$S, used in warfare as a gaseous blistering agent.

mus·ter (mŭs'tər) *v.* **1.** To summon or assemble (troops). **2.** To gather up: *muster up courage.* —**muster in** (or **out**). To enlist (someone) in, or discharge (someone) from, military service. —*n.* A gathering, esp. of troops, as for inspection. —**pass muster.** To be acceptable. [< L *monstrāre,* to show, indicate.]

must·y (mŭs'tē) *adj.* -ier, -iest. Having a stale or moldy odor. [Var of obs *moisty* < MOIST.]

mu·ta·ble (myōō'tə-bəl) *adj.* **1.** Subject to change. **2.** Prone to frequent change; fickle. [< L *mūtāre,* to change.] —**mu'ta·bil'i·ty** *n.*

mu·tant (myōō'tənt) *n.* An organism differing from the parental strain or strains as a result of mutation. [< L *mūtāre,* to MUTATE.] —**mu'tant** *adj.*

mu·tate (myōō'tāt', myōō-tāt') *v.* -tated, -tating. To undergo or cause to undergo alteration, esp. by mutation. [L *mūtāre.*] —**mu'ta'tive** (myōō'tā'tĭv, myōō-tā'tə-) *adj.*

mu·ta·tion (myōō-tā'shən) *n.* **1.** An alteration or change, as in nature, form, or quality. **2.** *Biol.* Any heritable alteration of an organism.

mute (myōōt) *adj.* **1.** Incapable of producing speech or vocal sound. **2.** Not speaking or spoken; silent. —*n.* **1.** A person incapable of speech, esp. one both deaf and mute. **2.** A device used to muffle or soften the tone of a musical instrument. —*v.* **muted, muting.** To soften the sound, color, or shade of. [< L *mūtus,* silent, dumb.] —**mute'ness** *n.*

mu·ti·late (myōōt'l-āt') *v.* -lated, -lating. **1.** To deprive of a limb or other essential part. **2.** To disfigure by seriously damaging a part. [< L *mutilus,* maimed.] —**mu'ti·la'tion** *n.*

mu·ti·neer (myōōt'n-îr') *n.* One who takes part in a mutiny.

mu·ti·nous (myōōt'n-əs) *adj.* Engaged in or disposed toward mutiny.

mu·ti·ny (myōōt'n-ē) *n., pl.* -nies. Open rebellion against constituted authority, esp. by sailors or soldiers against their officers. [< OF *muete,* revolt, "movement."] —**mu'ti·ny** *v.* (-nied, -nying).

mutt (mŭt) *n. Slang.* A mongrel dog. [Short for *muttonhead.*]

mut·ter (mŭt'ər) *v.* **1.** To speak or utter in low, indistinct tones. **2.** To complain or grumble morosely. —*n.* A low, indistinct uttering or utterance. [ME *muteren.*]

mut·ton (mŭt'n) *n.* The flesh of fully grown sheep. [< ML *multō,* sheep.]

mu·tu·al (myōō'chōō-əl) *adj.* **1.** Having the same feelings each for the other: *mutual enemies.* **2.** Felt or directed for or toward each other: *mutual respect; mutual recriminations.* **3.** Possessed in common: *mutual interests.* [< L *mūtuus,* exchanged, mutual.] —**mu'tu·al'i·ty** (-ăl'ə-tē) *n.* —**mu'tu·al·ly** *adv.*

muz·zle (mŭz'əl) *n.* **1.** The usually projecting jaws and nose of certain animals. **2.** A device fitted over an animal's snout to prevent biting or eating. **3.** The front end of the barrel of a firearm. —*v.* -zled, -zling. **1.** To put a muzzle on (an animal). **2.** To restrain (someone) from expressing opinions. [< LL *mūsum,* snout.]

muz·zle·load·er (mŭz'əl-lō'dər) *n.* A firearm loaded through the muzzle. —**muz'zle·load'ing** *adj.*

mV millivolt.

MV motor vessel.

my (mī). The possessive form of the pronoun *I,* used attributively: *my book.* —*interj.* Expressive of surprise, pleasure, or dismay. [< OE *mīn.* See me-.]

–mycin. *comb. form.* Derivation of a specified

ă pat/ā ate/âr care/ä bar/b bib/ch chew/d deed/ě pet/ē be/f fit/g gag/h hat/hw what/
ĭ pit/ī pie/îr pier/j judge/k kick/l lid, fatal/m mum/n no, sudden/ng sing/ŏ pot/ō go/

substance from bacteria or fungi: **streptomycin.** [< Gk *mukēs,* fungus.]

my·col·o·gy (mī-kŏl′ə-jē) *n.* The botanical study of fungi. [< Gk *mukēs,* fungus + -LOGY.] —**my′co·log′i·cal** (mī′kə-lŏj′ĭ-kəl) *adj.* —**my·col′o·gist** *n.*

my·e·lin (mī′ə-lĭn) *n.* Also **my·e·line** (mī′ə-lĭn, -lēn′). A white, fatty material that encloses some nerve fibers.

my·e·li·tis (mī′ə-lī′tĭs) *n.* Inflammation of the spinal column or bone marrow. [< Gk *muelos,* marrow + -ITIS.]

my·na (mī′nə) *n.* Also **my·nah.** Any of various Asian birds related to the starlings. [< Sk *madana.*]

my·o·pi·a (mī-ō′pē-ə) *n.* **1.** A visual defect in which distant objects appear blurred because their images are focused in front of the retina rather than on it; nearsightedness. **2.** Short-sightedness in thinking or planning. [< Gk *muōps,* myopic, "closing the eyes."] —**my·op′ic** (mī-ŏp′ĭk, -ō′pĭk) *adj.*

my·o·sin (mī′ə-sĭn) *n.* The commonest protein in muscle.

myr·i·ad (mîr′ē-əd) *adj.* Amounting to a very large, indefinite number. —*n.* A vast number. [< Gk *murios,* countless.]

myr·mi·don (mûr′mə-dŏn′, -dən) *n.* A faithful follower who carries out orders without question.

myrrh (mûr) *n.* An aromatic gum resin obtained from several Asian or African trees and shrubs and used in perfume and incense. [< Gk *murrha.*]

myr·tle (mûr′tl) *n.* **1.** An Old World shrub with pink or white flowers and blackish berries. **2.** A trailing vine with evergreen leaves and usually blue flowers. [< Gk *murtos.*]

my·self (mī-sĕlf′) *pron.* A form of the 1st person sing. pronoun: **1.** —Used reflexively: *I hurt myself.* **2.** —Used for emphasis: *I told him so myself.* **3.** —Used to indicate one's normal or proper state: *I am not myself today.* —**by myself. 1.** Alone. **2.** Without help.

mys·te·ri·ous (mī-stîr′ē-əs) *adj.* **1.** Full of mystery; difficult to explain or account for.

2. Implying a mystery. **3.** Enigmatic. —**mys·te′ri·ous·ly** *adv.* —**mys·te′ri·ous·ness** *n.*

mys·ter·y (mĭs′tər-ē) *n., pl.* **-ies. 1.** Anything that arouses curiosity because it is unexplained, inexplicable, or secret. **2.** The quality of being inexplicable or secret. **3.** A piece of fiction dealing with a puzzling crime. **4.** A religious truth revealed through Christ to the elect. **5. mysteries.** Any of certain ancient Mediterranean cults and secret rites to which only initiates were admitted. [< Gk *mustērion,* "secret rites."]

mystery play. A medieval drama based on episodes in the life of Christ.

mys·tic (mĭs′tĭk) *adj.* **1.** Of or pertaining to mystics or mysticism. **2.** Mysterious. —*n.* One who practices a specified form of mysticism. [< Gk *mustikos.*]

mys·ti·cal (mĭs′tĭ-kəl) *adj.* **1.** Of or pertaining to the experience described by mystics. **2.** Spiritually symbolic. —**mys′ti·cal·ly** *adv.*

mys·ti·cism (mĭs′tə-sĭz′əm) *n.* A spiritual discipline aiming at union with the divine through deep meditation or contemplation.

mys·ti·fy (mĭs′tə-fī′) *v.* **-fied, -fying. 1.** To awe or perplex; bewilder. **2.** To make obscure or difficult to comprehend. [< F *mystère,* mystery.] —**mys′ti·fi·ca′tion** *n.* —**mys′ti·fi′er** *n.* —**mys′ti·fy′ing·ly** *adv.*

mys·tique (mĭ-stēk′) *n.* **1.** An attitude of mystical veneration conferring upon a person or thing an awesome and mythical status. **2.** The object of such veneration. [< L *mysticus,* mystic.]

myth (mĭth) *n.* **1.** A traditional story presenting supernatural beings, ancestors, or heroes that serve as primordial types in a primitive view of the world. **2.** Any fictitious or imaginary story, person, or thing. **3.** A notion based more on tradition or convenience than on fact. [< Gk *muthos.*] —**myth′i·cal** *adj.*

myth. mythological; mythology.

my·thol·o·gy (mĭ-thŏl′ə-jē) *n., pl.* **-gies.** A body of myths about the origin and history of a people. —**myth′o·log′i·cal** (mĭth′ə-lŏj′ĭ-kəl) *adj.* —**my·thol′o·gist** *n.*

Nn

n, N (ĕn) *n.* The 14th letter of the English alphabet.

n 1. nano-. **2.** north; northern.

N 1. nitrogen. **2.** north; northern.

n. 1. net. **2.** north; northern. **3.** noun. **4.** number.

N. 1. Norse. **2.** north; northern. **3.** November.

Na sodium (L *natrium*).

NAACP, N.A.A.C.P. National Association for the Advancement of Colored People.

nab (năb) *v.* **nabbed, nabbing.** *Slang.* **1.** To arrest. **2.** To grab. [Prob < Scand.]

na·bob (nā′bŏb′) *n.* A man of wealth or prominence.

na·cre (nā′kər) *n.* Mother-of-pearl. [< Ar *naqqārah,* shell.] —**na′cre·ous** (-krē-əs) *adj.*

Na-De·ne (nä-dā′nē) *n.* Also **Na-Dé·né.** A phylum of North American Indian languages including Athapascan.

na·dir (nā′dər, nā′dîr′) *n.* **1.** A point on the

celestial sphere diametrically opposite the zenith. **2.** The lowest point. [< Ar *nazir (assamt)*, opposite (the zenith).]

nae·vus. Variant of **nevus**.

nag¹ (năg) *v.* **nagged, nagging. 1.** To annoy by constant scolding, complaining, or urging. **2.** To torment with anxiety or discomfort: *nagged by worries.* **3.** To complain or find fault constantly. —*n.* One who nags. [< ON *gnaga*, to bite.] —**nag'ging·ly** *adv.*

nag² (năg) *n.* A horse, esp. an old or worn-out horse. [< MDu *negghe*, horse.]

Na·hua·tl (nä'wät'l) *n., pl.* **-tl** or **-tls. 1.** A member of a group of Mexican and Central American Indian tribes, including the Aztecs. **2.** The language of the Nahuatl.

nai·ad (nā'əd, nā'ăd', nī'-) *n., pl.* **-ades** (-ə-dēz') or **-ads.** *Gk.Myth.* One of the nymphs living in brooks, springs, and fountains.

na·if, na·ïf. Variants of **naive**.

nail (nāl) *n.* **1.** A slim, pointed piece of metal hammered into wood or other material as a fastener. **2.** A fingernail or toenail. —**hit the nail on the head.** To express the sense of something exactly and concisely. —*v.* **1.** To fasten with or as with nails. **2.** To secure or make sure of: *nail down the facts.* **3.** *Informal.* To stop and seize; catch. **4.** *Informal.* To strike; hit. [< OE *nægl.* See **nogh-**.]

Nai·ro·bi (nī-rō'bē). The capital of Kenya. Pop. 267,000.

na·ive, na·ïve (nä-ēv') *adj.* Also **na·if, na·ïf** (nä-ēf'). Lacking worldliness and sophistication; artless; ingenuous. [< OF, ingenuous, natural < L *nātivus*, native.]

na·ive·té, na·ïve·té (nä'ēv-tā') *n.* **1.** The quality of being naive. **2.** A naive statement or action.

na·ked (nā'kĭd) *adj.* **1.** Without clothing on the body; nude. **2.** Without covering, esp. without usual or natural covering. **3.** Without addition, concealment, etc.: *the naked facts.* [< OE *nacod.* See **nogw-**.] —**na'ked·ness** *n.*

N.A.M. National Association of Manufacturers.

Na·mib·i·a (nə-mĭb'ē-ə). A country of SW Africa. Pop. 900,000. Cap. Windhoek.

nam·by-pam·by (năm'bē-păm'bē) *adj.* **1.** Insipidly affected. **2.** Lacking vigor or decisiveness. [< *Namby-Pamby*, a satire on sentimental pastorals, by Henry Carey (died 1743).]

name (nām) *n.* **1.** A word or words by which any entity is designated. **2.** A disparaging designation: *called him names.* **3.** Verbal representation as opposed to reality: *a democracy in name only.* **4.** Reputation; renown. **5.** *Informal.* A famous or outstanding person. —*v.* **named, naming. 1.** To give a name to. **2.** To mention, specify, or identify by name. **3.** To nominate or appoint. —*adj. Informal.* Well-known by a name: *name brands.* [< OE *nama.* See **nomen-**.] —**nam'er** *n.*

name·less (nām'lĭs) *adj.* **1.** Having no name. **2.** Unknown by name. **3.** Inexpressible; indescribable: *nameless horror.*

name·ly (nām'lē) *adv.* That is to say; specifically.

nan·keen (năn-kēn') *n.* Also **nan·kin** (năn-kēn', -kĭn'). A sturdy yellow or buff cotton cloth. [< NANKING.]

Nan·king (năn'kĭng'). A city of E China. Pop. 1,419,000.

nan·ny (năn'ē) *n., pl.* **-nies.** *Chiefly Brit.* A children's nurse. [< baby-talk *nana.*]

nanny goat. A female goat. [< *Nanny*, pet form for Ann.]

nano-. *comb. form.* One-billionth of (a specified unit). [L *nānus*, dwarf.]

na·no·sec·ond (năn'ə-sĕk'ənd, nă'nə-) *n.* One-billionth of a second.

nap¹ (năp) *n.* A brief sleep, often during a period other than one's regular sleeping hours. —*v.* **napped, napping. 1.** To doze or sleep lightly for a brief period. **2.** To be unaware of imminent danger or trouble. [< OE *hnappian.*] —**nap'per** *n.*

nap² (năp) *n.* A soft, fuzzy surface on certain textiles, usually formed by raising fibers from the underlying material. —*v.* **napped, napping.** To form or raise a nap on (fabric or leather). [< MDu *noppe.*] —**nap'less** *adj.*

na·palm (nā'päm') *n.* An incendiary mixture composed of gasoline, thickening agents, and other hydrocarbons.

nape (nāp) *n.* The back of the neck.

naph·tha (năf'thə, năp'-) *n.* A colorless flammable liquid obtained from crude petroleum, used as a solvent and as a raw material for gasoline. [Gk.]

naph·tha·lene (năf'thə-lēn', năp'-) *n.* A white crystalline compound, $C_{10}H_8$, used to manufacture dyes, moth repellents, explosives, and solvents.

nap·kin (năp'kĭn) *n.* **1.** A soft piece of fabric or paper used at table to protect the clothes or wipe the lips. **2.** Any similar cloth or towel. [< L *mappa*, napkin, towel.]

Na·ples (nā'pəlz). A city of SW Italy. Pop. 1,221,000.

Na·po·le·on I (nə-pō'lē-ən, -pōl'yən). Surname, Bonaparte. 1769–1821. Emperor of the French (1804–15). —**Na·po·le·on·ic** (nə-pō'lē-ŏn'ĭk) *adj.*

Napoleon I

nar·cis·sism (när'sə-sĭz'əm) *n.* Excessive admiration of oneself. [< NARCISSUS.] —**nar'cis·**

sist (när'sə-sĭst) n. —nar'cis•sis'tic (när'sə-sĭs'-tĭk) adj.

nar•cis•sus (när-sĭs'əs) n., pl. -suses or -cissi (-sĭs'ī', -sĭs'ē). A widely cultivated plant having grasslike leaves and white or yellow flowers with a cup-shaped or trumpet-shaped central part. [< Gk narkissos.]

Nar•cis•sus (när-sĭs'əs). Gk.Myth. A youth who pined away for love of his own image reflected in a pool and was transformed into a flower.

nar•co•sis (när-kō'sĭs) n. Deep unconsciousness produced by a drug. [Gk narkōsis, a numbing.]

nar•cot•ic (när-kŏt'ĭk) n. Any drug that dulls the senses, induces sleep, and with prolonged use becomes addictive. [< Gk narkōtikos, numbing, narcotic.] —nar•cot'ic adj.

nar•co•tism (när'kə-tĭz'əm) n. Addiction to narcotics such as opium, heroin, or morphine.

nar•co•tize (när'kə-tīz') v. -tized, -tizing. 1. To place under the influence of a narcotic. 2. To lull or induce to sleep.

nard (närd) n. A plant, spikenard, or a fragrant ointment obtained from it. [< Gk nardos.]

nar•es (nâr'ēz) pl.n. Sing. -is (-ĭs). The nostrils. [< L näris, nostril.]

nar•rate (nâr'āt', nă-rāt') v. -rated, -rating. 1. To tell (a story). 2. To give an account or commentary. [L narräre.] —nar•ra'tion n. —nar'ra'tor, nar'ra'ter n.

nar•ra•tive (năr'ə-tĭv) n. 1. A story or description of actual or fictional events. 2. The technique or process of narrating.

nar•row (năr'ō) adj. 1. Of small or limited width, esp. in comparison with length. 2. Limited in area or scope. 3. Barely sufficient or successful: a narrow margin of victory. —v. To make or become narrow or narrower; lessen in width or extent. —n. narrows. A narrow body of water connecting two larger ones. [< OE nearu.] —nar'row•ly adv. —nar'row•ness n.

nar•row-mind•ed (năr'ō-mīn'dĭd) adj. Lacking breadth of view, tolerance, etc.; bigoted. —nar'row-mind'ed•ness n.

nar•whal (när'wəl) n. A whalelike mammal of arctic seas, having a long spiral tusk. [< ON nähvalr, "corpse-whale."]

NASA (năs'ə) National Aeronautics and Space Administration.

na•sal (nā'zəl) adj. 1. Of or pertaining to the nose. 2. Uttered so that the air passes through the nose: a nasal twang. [< L näsus, nose.] —na•sal'i•ty (nā-zăl'ə-tē) n.

nas•cent (năs'ənt, nā'sənt) adj. Coming into existence; in the process of emerging. [< L näscī, to be born.] —nas'cence n.

Nash•ville (năsh'vĭl'). The capital of Tennessee. Pop. 448,000.

Nas•sau (năs'ô'). The capital of the Bahama Islands. Pop. 82,000.

na•stur•tium (nə-stûr'shəm, nă-) n. A plant with showy orange or yellow flowers and pungent leaves and seeds. [L nästurtium, a kind of cress.]

nas•ty (năs'tē) adj. -tier, -tiest. 1. Disgusting to see, smell, or touch; filthy. 2. Malicious; spiteful. 3. Unpleasant: nasty weather. 4. Painful

and dangerous: a nasty accident. [ME.] —nas'ti•ly adv. —nas'ti•ness n.

nat. 1. national. 2. native. 3. natural.

na•tal (nāt'l) adj. 1. Of, relating to, or accompanying birth. 2. Of or pertaining to the time or place of one's birth. [< L näscī (pp nätus), to be born.]

na•tion (nā'shən) n. 1. An aggregation of people organized under a single government. 2. A federation or tribe, esp. one composed of North American Indians. [< L nätiō, "race," "breed."]

na•tion•al (năsh'ən-əl, năsh'nəl) adj. 1. Of, pertaining to, or characteristic of a nation. 2. Of or relating to nationality. —n. A citizen of a particular nation. —na'tion•al•ly adv.

National Guard. The military reserve units controlled by each state of the U.S.

na•tion•al•ism (năsh'ən-əl-ĭz'əm, năsh'nəl-) n. 1. Devotion to the interests of a particular nation. 2. Aspirations for national independence. —na'tion•al•ist adj. & n. —na'tion•al•is'tic adj. —na'tion•al•is'ti•cal•ly adv.

na•tion•al•i•ty (năsh'ə-năl'ə-tē) n., pl. -ties. 1. The status of belonging to a particular nation by origin, birth, or naturalization. 2. A people having common origins or traditions and constituting or considered to constitute a nation. 3. Existence as a politically autonomous entity; the status of a nation. 4. National character.

na•tion•al•ize (năsh'ən-əl-īz', năsh'nəl-) v. -ized, -izing. 1. To convert from private to governmental ownership and control. 2. To make national. —na'tion•al•i•za'tion n.

Nation of Islam. An organization of American Negroes who follow the religious practices of Islam.

na•tion•wide (nā'shən-wīd') adj. Throughout a whole nation.

na•tive (nā'tĭv) adj. 1. Inborn; innate. 2. Being such by birth or origin. 3. One's own because of the place or circumstances of one's birth: his native land. 4. Originating or produced in a certain place; indigenous. —n. 1. One born in or connected with a place by birth. 2. An original inhabitant of a place. 3. One belonging to a people of primitive culture originally occupying a country. [< L nätīvus, born, native.] —na'tive•ly adv.

na•tiv•i•ty (nə-tĭv'ə-tē, nā-) n., pl. -ties. 1. Birth, esp. the conditions or circumstances of one's birth. 2. Nativity. The birth of Jesus. [< L nätīvus, born, NATIVE.]

natl. national.

NATO (nā'tō) North Atlantic Treaty Organization.

nat•ty (năt'ē) adj. -tier, -tiest. Neat, trim, and smart. [Perh < OF net, neat.]

nat•u•ral (năch'ər-əl, năch'rəl) adj. 1. Present in or produced by nature; not artificial. 2. Pertaining to or concerning nature. 3. Produced solely by nature: a natural death. 4. a. Inherent; innate. b. Distinguished by innate qualities or aptitudes. 5. Free from affectation. 6. Consonant with particular circumstances; expected and accepted. 7. Mus. Not sharped or flatted. —n. 1. Informal. One with talent for a particular endeavor. **2.** *Mus.* The sign (♮) placed before a note to cancel a preceding sharp or flat. —**nat'u·ral·ness** *n.*

natural history. The study of natural objects and organisms and their origins and interrelationships.

nat·u·ral·ism (năch'ər-ə-lĭz'əm, năch'rə-) *n.* Conformity to nature; factual or realistic representation, esp. in art and literature. —**nat'u·ral·is'tic** *adj.*

nat·u·ral·ist (năch'ər-ə-lĭst, năch'rə-) *n.* One who studies plants and animals in their natural environment.

nat·u·ral·ize (năch'ər-ə-lĭz', năch'rə-) *v.* **-ized, -izing. 1.** To grant full citizenship to. **2.** To adapt or acclimate (a plant or animal) to life in a new environment. —**nat'u·ral·i·za'tion** *n.*

nat·u·ral·ly (năch'ər-ə-lē, năch'rə-) *adv.* **1.** In a natural manner. **2.** By nature; inherently. **3.** Without a doubt; of course.

natural science. A science, such as biology, chemistry, or physics, based chiefly on objective quantitative hypotheses.

natural selection. 1. The principle that individuals possessing characteristics advantageous for survival in a specific environment constitute an increasing proportion of their species in that environment with each succeeding generation. **2.** The natural phenomenon of such a selective increase leading to new species.

na·ture (nā'chər) *n.* **1.** The intrinsic character of a person or thing. **2.** The order, disposition, and essence of all entities composing the physical universe. **3.** The physical world, including living things, natural phenomena, etc. **4.** The primitive state of existence. **5.** Kind; type: *something of that nature.* **6.** Disposition; temperament: *a sweet nature.* [< L *nātūra,* nature, "birth."] —**na'tured** *adj.*

naught (nôt) *n.* Also **nought. 1.** Nothing. **2.** A cipher; zero. [< OE *nā,* NO¹ + *wiht,* creature, thing.]

naugh·ty (nô'tē) *adj.* **-tier, -tiest.** Disobedient; mischievous: *a naughty child.* [< ME *nauht,* "worthless," naught.] —**naugh'ti·ly** *adv.* —**naugh'ti·ness** *n.*

nau·se·a (nô'zē-ə, -zhə, -sē-ə, -shə) *n.* **1.** A stomach disturbance characterized by a feeling of the need to vomit. **2.** Strong disgust. [< Gk *nausia,* seasickness.]

nau·se·ate (nô'zē-āt', -zhē-āt', -sē-āt', -shē-āt') *v.* **-ated, -ating.** To feel or cause to feel nausea. —**nau'se·a'tion** *n.*

nau·seous (nô'shəs, nô'zē-əs) *adj.* **1.** Causing nausea; sickening. **2.** Nauseated.

naut. nautical.

nau·ti·cal (nô'tĭ-kəl) *adj.* Of or pertaining to ships, seamen, or navigation. [< Gk *naus,* ship.] —**nau'ti·cal·ly** *adv.*

nautical mile. A unit of length used in sea and air navigation, esp. an international and U.S. unit equal to 1,852 meters, or about 6,076 feet.

nau·ti·lus (nô'tə-ləs) *n., pl.* **-luses** or **-li** (-lī'). A tropical marine mollusk with a partitioned spiral shell. [< Gk *nautilos,* sailor.]

nav. 1. naval. **2.** navigation.

Nav·a·ho (năv'ə-hō', nä'və-) *n., pl.* **-ho, -hos,** or **-hoes. 1.** A member of a group of Athapascan-speaking Indians occupying an extensive reservation in parts of New Mexico, Arizona, and Utah. **2.** The language of this group. —**Nav'a·ho'** *adj.*

na·val (nā'vəl) *adj.* Of, pertaining to, or possessing a navy.

nave (nāv) *n.* The central part of a church. [ML *nāvis,* "ship."]

na·vel (nā'vəl) *n.* The mark on the abdomen where the umbilical cord was attached during gestation. [< OE *nafela.* See nobh-.]

nav·i·ga·ble (năv'ə-gə-bəl) *adj.* **1.** Sufficiently deep or wide to provide passage for vessels. **2.** Capable of being steered, as a vessel or aircraft. —**nav'i·ga·bil'i·ty** *n.*

nav·i·gate (năv'ə-gāt') *v.* **-gated, -gating. 1.** To control the course of a ship or aircraft. **2.** To voyage over water in a boat or ship; sail. [L *nāvigāre,* to manage a ship.] —**nav'i·ga'tion** *n.* —**nav'i·ga'tor** *n.*

na·vy (nā'vē) *n., pl.* **-vies. 1.** All of a nation's warships. **2.** Often **Navy.** A nation's entire military organization for sea warfare and defense. [< L *nāvis,* ship.]

nay (nā) *adv.* **1.** No. **2.** And moreover: *He was ill-favored, nay, hideous.* —*n.* A negative vote. [< ON *nei.*]

Naz·a·reth (năz'ə-rĭth). A town in N Israel, site of Jesus' childhood.

Na·zi (nät'sē, năt'-) *n., pl.* **-zis.** A member or supporter of the fascist National Socialist German Workers' Party, brought to power in 1933 under Adolf Hitler. —**Na'zi** *adj.* —**Na'zism', Na'zi·ism'** *n.*

Nb niobium.

N.B. 1. New Brunswick. **2.** nota bene.

N.C. North Carolina.

NCO, N.C.O. noncommissioned officer.

Nd neodymium.

N.D. North Dakota (unofficial).

N. Dak. North Dakota.

N'Dja·me·na (ĕn-jä'mə-nə). **The capital of** Chad. Pop. 135,000.

Ne neon.

NE northeast.

N.E. New England.

NEA, N.E.A. National Education Association.

Ne·an·der·thal (nē-ăn'dər-thôl', -tôl', nä-än'dər-täl') *adj.* **1.** Of, pertaining to, or designating an extinct primitive man of the Stone Age. **2.** Crude, primitive, or boorish.

neap tide (nēp). A tide of lowest range. [< OE *nēp(flōd),* neap (tide).]

near (nîr) *adv.* To, at, or within a short distance or interval in space or time. —*adj.* **1.** Close in time, space, position, or degree. **2.** Closely related; intimate. **3.** Accomplished or missed by a small margin: *a near accident.* **4.** Closer of two or more. —*prep.* Close to; within a short distance or time of. —*v.* To come close or closer to; draw near. [< OE *nēah,* near < Gmc **nēwh-iz.*] —**near'ness** *n.*

near·by (nîr'bī') *adj. & adv.* Not far away; adjacent.

Near East. The countries of the E Mediterranean and the Arabian Peninsula.

near·ly (nîr'lē) *adv.* Almost but not quite.

ă pat/ā ate/âr care/ä bar/b bib/ch chew/d deed/ĕ pet/ē be/f fit/g gag/h hat/hw what/
ĭ pit/ī pie/îr pier/j judge/k kick/l lid, fatal/m mum/n no, sudden/ng sing/ŏ pot/ō go/

near·sight·ed (nîr'sī'tĭd) *adj.* **1.** Afflicted with myopia. **2.** Shortsighted. **—near'sight'ed·ly** *adv.* **—near'sight'ed·ness** *n.*

neat (nēt) *adj.* **1.** In good order or clean condition; tidy. **2.** Orderly in appearance or procedure. **3.** Skillfully executed; adroit. **4.** Simple and smoothly consistent. **5.** Not diluted with other substances: *neat whiskey.* **6.** *Slang.* Stylish; appealing. [< L *nitidus*, elegant, shiny.] **—neat'ly** *adv.* **—neat'ness** *n.*

Nebr. Nebraska.

Ne·bras·ka (nə-brăs'kə). A Midwestern state of the U.S. Pop. 1,484,000. Cap. Lincoln. **—Ne·bras'kan** *adj. & n.*

Neb·u·chad·nez·zar II (nĕb'ə-kəd-nĕz'ər, nĕb'yŏŏ-). King of Babylon (605–562 B.C.).

neb·u·la (nĕb'yə-lə) *n., pl.* **-lae** (-lē', -lī') or **-las.** Any diffuse mass of interstellar dust or gas or both. [< L, cloud.] **—neb'u·lar** *adj.*

neb·u·los·i·ty (nĕb'yə-lŏs'ə-tē) *n., pl.* **-ties.** The quality or condition of being nebulous.

neb·u·lous (nĕb'yə-ləs) *adj.* Lacking definite form or limits; unclearly established. [< L *nebula,* cloud.] **—neb'u·lous·ly** *adv.*

nec·es·sar·i·ly (nĕs'ə-sĕr'ə-lē) *adv.* **1.** By necessity. **2.** Inevitably.

nec·es·sar·y (nĕs'ə-sĕr'ē) *adj.* **1.** Needed for the continuing existence or functioning of something; essential. **2.** Needed to achieve a certain result; requisite. **3.** Required by obligation, compulsion, etc. *—n.* Often **necessaries.** That which is needed. [< L *necesse,* necessary.]

ne·ces·si·tate (nə-sĕs'ə-tāt') *v.* **-tated, -tating.** To make necessary or unavoidable. **—ne·ces'si·ta'tion** *n.*

ne·ces·si·tous (nə-sĕs'ə-təs) *adj.* Needy; indigent. **—ne·ces'si·tous·ly** *adv.*

ne·ces·si·ty (nə-sĕs'ə-tē) *n., pl.* **-ties.** **1.** Something necessary. **2.** The state or fact of being necessary or unavoidable. **3.** Pressing or urgent need.

neck (nĕk) *n.* **1.** The part of the body joining the head to the trunk. **2.** The part of a garment around or near the neck of the wearer. **3.** Any relatively narrow elongation or connecting part: *a neck of land.* **4. a.** The length of the head and neck of a horse: *won the race by a neck.* **b.** *Slang.* Any narrow margin by which a competition is won. *—v. Slang.* To kiss and caress. [< OE *hnecca.*]

neck·er·chief (nĕk'ər-chĭf) *n.* A kerchief worn around the neck.

neck·lace (nĕk'lĭs) *n.* An ornament, such as a string of beads, worn around the neck.

neck·line (nĕk'līn') *n.* The line formed by the edge of a garment at the neck.

neck·tie (nĕk'tī') *n.* A narrow band of fabric worn around the neck and tied in a knot or bow.

nec·ro·man·cy (nĕk'rə-măn'sē) *n.* The art that professes to conjure up and commune with the spirits of the dead in order to predict the future. [< Gk *nekromanteia,* divination by corpses, and < ML *nigromantia,* black magic.] **—nec'ro·man'cer** *n.*

nec·tar (nĕk'tər) *n.* **1.** *Gk.&Rom.Myth.* The drink of the gods. **2.** The undiluted juice of a fruit. **3.** A sweet liquid secreted by flowers. [< Gk *nektar.*]

nec·tar·ine (nĕk'tə-rēn') *n.* A smooth-skinned variety of peach. [< obs *nectarine,* "sweet as nectar."]

née (nā) *adj.* Also **nee.** Born: *Mrs. Mary Parks, née Case.* [< F *naître,* to be born.]

need (nēd) *n.* **1.** A state in which something necessary or desirable is required or wanted. **2.** A wish for something lacking or desired. **3.** Necessity; obligation. **4.** Poverty. *—v.* **1.** —Used with an infinitive to express necessity or obligation: *He needs to study.* **2.** To want urgently; require. **3.** To be in want. [< OE *nēd,* necessity, distress. See nāu-.]

Usage: Need, as an auxiliary verb, is not inflected in the third person singular present tense in negative statements and questions: *He need not come. Need it have happened?*

need·ful (nēd'fəl) *adj.* Necessary; required.

nee·dle (nēd'l) *n.* **1.** A small, slender sewing implement, made of steel, pointed at one end and having an eye at the other to hold thread. **2.** Any of various implements similar in shape and use, as a knitting needle. **3.** A small, pointed stylus used to transmit vibrations from the grooves of a phonograph record. **4.** Any slender pointer or indicator, as on a magnet. **5.** A stiff, narrow leaf, as of a pine. **6.** Any fine, sharp projection. *—v.* **-dled, -dling.** To goad, provoke, or tease. [< OE *nædl.* See snē-[1].]

nee·dle·point (nēd'l-point') *n.* **1.** Decorative needlework on canvas. **2.** A type of lace worked on paper patterns with a needle.

need·less (nēd'lĭs) *adj.* Not needed; unnecessary. **—need'less·ly** *adv.*

nee·dle·work (nēd'l-wûrk') *n.* Work done with a needle, esp. embroidery.

need·n't (nēd'ənt). Contraction of *need not.*

needs (nēdz) *adv.* Necessarily: *He must needs go.*

need·y (nē'dē) *adj.* **-ier, -iest.** Being in need; impoverished. **—need'i·ness** *n.*

ne'er (nâr). *Poetic.* Contraction of *never.*

ne'er-do-well (nâr'dŏŏ-wĕl') *n.* An irresponsible person.

ne·far·i·ous (nĭ-fâr'ē-əs) *adj.* Evil; wicked. [< L *nefas,* sin.] **—ne·far'i·ous·ness** *n.*

neg. negative.

ne·gate (nĭ-gāt') *v.* **-gated, -gating.** **1.** To render ineffective or invalid; nullify. **2.** To rule out; deny. [L *negāre,* to deny.]

ne·ga·tion (nĭ-gā'shən) *n.* **1.** The act of negating. **2.** A denial, contradiction, or negative statement.

neg·a·tive (nĕg'ə-tĭv) *adj.* **1.** Expressing negation, refusal, or denial. **2.** Lacking the quality of being positive or affirmative. **3.** Pertaining to or denoting a quantity less than zero or a quantity, number, angle, velocity, or direction in a sense opposite to another indicated or understood to be positive. **4.** Pertaining to or denoting electric charge of the same sign as that of an electron, designated by the symbol (-). *—n.* **1.** A negative word, statement, or concept. **2.** The side opposing the opinion upheld by the affirmative side in a debate.

ô paw, for/oi boy/ou out/ŏŏ took/ōō coo/p pop/r run/s sauce/sh shy/t to/th thin/*th* the/
ŭ cut/ûr fur/v van/w wag/y yes/z size/zh vision/ə ago, item, edible, gallop, circus/

3. a. An image in which the light areas of the object rendered appear dark and the dark areas appear light. **b.** A film, plate, or other photographic material containing such an image. —*adv.* No. —*v.* **-tived, -tiving. 1.** To refuse to approve; veto. **2.** To deny; contradict. [< L *negāre*, to NEGATE.] —**neg·a·tive·ly** *adv.* —**neg·a·tive·ness, neg·a·tiv·i·ty** *n.*

ne·glect (nĭ-glĕkt′) *v.* **1.** To disregard; ignore. **2.** To fail to care for or give proper attention to. **3.** To fail to do through oversight. —*n.* **1.** The act or an instance of neglecting something. **2.** The state of being neglected. [< L *neglegere*, "not to choose," not to heed.] —**ne·glect′er, ne·glec′tor** *n.*

ne·glect·ful (nĭ-glĕkt′fəl) *adj.* Careless; heedless. —**ne·glect′ful·ly** *adv.*

neg·li·gee (nĕg′lĭ-zhā′) *n.* A woman's dressing gown, often of delicate fabric. [F, "casual," "neglected."]

neg·li·gence (nĕg′lĭ-jəns) *n.* **1.** The state or quality of being negligent. **2.** Any negligent act or failure to act.

neg·li·gent (nĕg′lĭ-jənt) *adj.* **1.** Habitually guilty of neglect. **2.** Extremely careless.

neg·li·gi·ble (nĕg′lĭ-jə-bəl) *adj.* Not worth considering; trifling: *a negligible amount.* [< L *negligere*, to neglect.] —**neg′li·gi·bly** *adv.*

ne·go·tia·ble (nĭ-gō′shə-bəl, -shē-ə-bəl) *adj.* **1.** Capable of being negotiated. **2.** Capable of being legally transferred from one person to another. —**ne·go′tia·bil′i·ty** *n.*

ne·go·ti·ate (nĭ-gō′shē-āt′) *v.* **-ated, -ating. 1.** To confer with another or others in order to come to terms. **2.** To arrange by conferring: *negotiate a contract.* **3.** To transfer ownership of (financial documents) to another party in return for value received. **4.** To succeed in getting across, through, or around: *negotiate a curve.* [< L *negōtium*, business, "lack of leisure."] —**ne·go′ti·a′tion** *n.* —**ne·go′ti·a′tor** *n.*

Ne·gril·lo (nĭ-grĭl′ō, -grē′yō) *n., pl.* **-los** or **-loes.** One of a group of Negroid peoples of Africa who are short in stature.

Ne·gri·to (nĭ-grē′tō) *n., pl.* **-tos** or **-toes. 1.** A Negrillo. **2.** One of various groups of Negroid people of short stature inhabiting parts of Malaysia, the Philippines, and SE Asia.

Ne·gro (nē′grō) *n., pl.* **-groes. 1.** A member of the Negroid ethnic division of the human species, esp. one of various peoples of C and S Africa. **2.** A descendant of these or other Negroid peoples. —*adj.* **1.** Pertaining to or characteristic of a Negro or Negroes. **2.** Negroid.

Ne·groid (nē′groid′) *adj.* **1.** Pertaining to a major ethnic division of the human species having brown to black skin color. **2.** Of or characteristic of Negroes. —**Ne′groid′** *n.*

Neh. Nehemiah.

Neh·ru (nā′rōō), **Jawaharlal.** 1889–1964. Indian nationalist leader; first prime minister (1947–64).

neigh (nā) *v.* To utter the breathy, prolonged cry of a horse. [< OE *hnægan.*] —**neigh** *n.*

neigh·bor (nā′bər). Also *chiefly Brit.* **neigh·bour.** *n.* One living or located near or next to another. —*v.* To lie close to; live or be situated nearby. [< OE *nēah*, near + *gebūr*, dweller (see **bheu-**).]

neigh·bor·hood (nā′bər-hŏŏd′) *n.* **1.** A district considered in regard to its inhabitants or characteristics. **2.** The people who live in a particular vicinity. **3.** *Informal.* Approximate amount: *in the neighborhood of ten dollars.*

neigh·bor·ing (nā′bər-ĭng) *adj.* Living or situated close by.

neigh·bor·ly (nā′bər-lē) *adj.* Of or characteristic of a neighbor; friendly; helpful. —**neigh′bor·li·ness** *n.*

nei·ther (nē′thər, nī′-) *adj.* Not one or the other: *Neither shoe fits.* —*pron.* Not the one nor the other: *Neither of them fits.* —*conj.* Not either; not in either case (with *nor*): *Neither we nor they want it.* [< OE *nā*, no, not + *hwæther*, which of two (see **kwo-**).]

Usage: When all the elements within a *neither... nor* construction are singular, the verb is always singular: *Neither he nor she was told.* When the elements are all plural, the verb is plural. When the elements differ in number, the verb agrees in number with the element to which it is nearer: *Neither my father nor my uncles were included.* When the nearer element is a personal pronoun, the verb agrees with it: *Neither Tom nor I know.* The same rule applies to *either... or* constructions.

nem·e·sis (nĕm′ə-sĭs) *n., pl.* **-ses** (-sēz′). **1.** An inflicter of retribution; avenger. **2.** An unbeatable rival, as in sports. **3.** Retributive justice. [< Gk, retribution.]

neo-, Neo-. *comb. form.* **1.** A new or recent form, development, or type. **2.** A recent formation, modification, or abnormal change. **3.** The most recent subdivision of a series of periods. [< Gk *neos*, new.]

ne·o·clas·si·cism (nē′ō-klăs′ə-sĭz′əm) *n.* A revival of classical aesthetics and forms in art, music, and literature. —**ne′o·clas′sic, ne′o·clas′si·cal** *adj.*

ne·o·dym·i·um (nē′ō-dĭm′ē-əm) *n. Symbol* **Nd** A bright, silvery rare-earth metallic element, used for coloring glass and in some lasers. Atomic number 60, atomic weight 144.24

Ne·o·lith·ic (nē′ə-lĭth′ĭk) *adj.* Of or denoting a period of human culture beginning around 10,000 B.C. in the Middle East and later elsewhere and characterized by the invention of farming and the making of technically advanced stone implements. —*n.* The Neolithic Age.

ne·ol·o·gism (nē-ŏl′ə-jĭz′əm) *n.* A newly coined word or expression.

ne·on (nē′ŏn′) *n. Symbol* **Ne** An inert gaseous element occurring in the atmosphere to the extent of 18 parts per million, used in display and television tubes. Atomic number 10, atomic weight 20.183. [< Gk *neos*, new.]

ne·o·phyte (nē′ə-fīt′) *n.* **1.** A recent convert. **2.** A beginner; novice. [< Gk *neophutos*, "newly planted."]

ne·o·plasm (nē′ə-plăz′əm) *n.* An abnormal new growth of tissue; tumor.

ne·o·prene (nē′ə-prēn′) *n.* A synthetic rubber used in weather-resistant products, adhesives, and shoe soles.

ă pat/ā ate/âr care/ä bar/b **bib**/ch **chew**/d **deed**/ĕ pet/ē be/f fit/g gag/h hat/hw **what**/ ĭ pit/ī pie/îr pier/j **judge**/k **kick**/l lid, fatal/m **mum**/n no, sudden/ng **sing**/ŏ pot/ō go/

Ne•pal (nə-pôl′, -päl′). A kingdom in the Himalayas. Pop. 9,500,000. Cap. Katmandu.

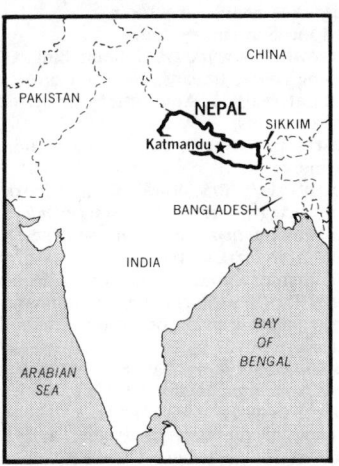

Nepal

Nep•al•ese (nĕp′əl-ēz′) *n., pl.* **-ese.** **1.** A native or resident of Nepal. **2.** The central Indic language of Nepal. **—Nep′al•ese′** *adj.*

ne•pen•the (nĭ-pĕn′thē) *n.* **1.** A drug of ancient times used to remedy grief and pain. **2.** Anything that eases suffering. [Gk *nēpenthes (pharmakon),* "grief-banishing (drug)."]

neph•ew (nĕf′yōō) *n.* The son of one's brother, sister, brother-in-law, or sister-in-law. [< L *nepôs,* nephew, grandson.]

neph•rite (nĕf′rīt′) *n.* A white to dark green variety of jade. [G *Nephrit,* "kidney mineral."]

ne•phri•tis (nə-frī′tĭs) *n.* Any of various acute or chronic inflammations of the kidneys.

nephro–. *comb. form.* The kidney. [< Gk *nephros,* kidney.]

nep•o•tism (nĕp′ə-tĭz′əm) *n.* Favoritism shown to relatives, esp. in filling political positions. [< It *nepotismo,* "favoring of nephews."] **—nep′o•tis′tic, nep′o•tis′ti•cal** *adj.*

Nep•tune (nĕp′t/y/ōōn′) *n.* **1.** Roman god of the sea. **2.** The 8th planet from the sun, having a sidereal period of revolution around the sun of 164.8 years at a mean distance of 2.8 billion miles, a mean radius of 14,000 miles, and a density 17.2 times that of Earth. **—Nep•tu′ni•an** *adj.*

nep•tu•ni•um (nĕp-t/y/ōō′nē-əm) *n. Symbol* **Np** A silvery, metallic, naturally radioactive element. Atomic number 93, longest-lived isotope Np 237.

Ne•ro (nîr′ō). Roman emperor (A.D. 54–68).

nerve (nûrv) *n.* **1.** Any of the bundles of fibers interconnecting the central nervous system and the organs or parts of the body, capable of transmitting both sensory stimuli and motor impulses from one part of the body to another. **2. a.** Forcefulness; stamina. **b.** Strong will; courage. **c.** *Informal.* Brazenness; effrontery. **3. nerves.** Neurological manifestations, such as involuntary trembling, agitation, or hysteria. [L *nervus,* sinew, nerve.]

nerve cell. Any of the cells of nerve tissue consisting of a nucleated portion, and cytoplasmic extensions, the cell body, the dendrites, and axons.

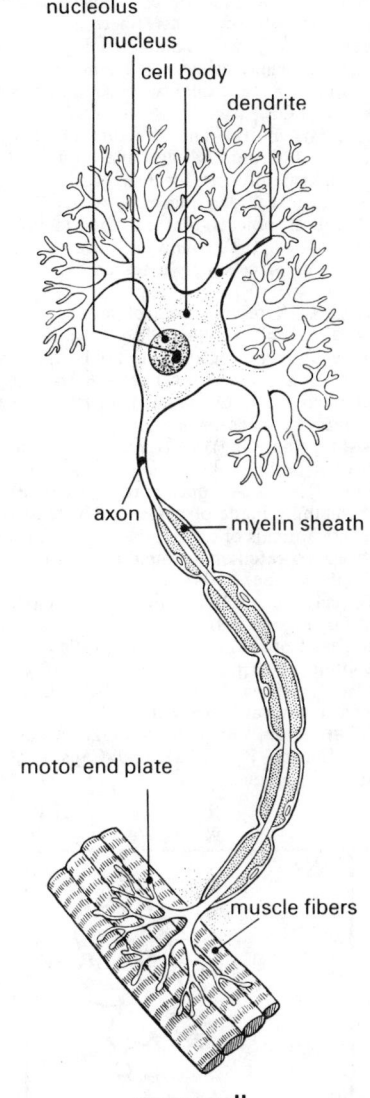

nerve cell

nerve•less (nûrv′lĭs) *adj.* **1.** Listless; inert. **2.** Self-controlled. **—nerve′less•ly** *adv.*

nerve-rack•ing (nûrv′răk′ĭng) *adj.* Also **nerve-wrack•ing.** Intensely distressing.

nerv•ous (nûr′vəs) *adj.* **1.** High-strung; excitable. **2.** Spirited. **3. a.** Of or relating to the nerves or nervous system. **b.** Stemming from or affecting the nerves or nervous system: *a nervous disorder.* **4.** Uneasy; anxious. **—ner′vous•ly** *adv.* **—ner′vous•ness** *n.*

nervous system. A coordinating mechanism in all multicellular animals, except sponges, that regulates internal body functions and responses to external stimuli.
nerv•y (nûr′vē) *adj.* **-ier, -iest.** **1.** Brazen; rude. **2.** Showing fortitude or endurance. **3.** Nervous. **—nerv′i•ly** *adv.* **—nerv′i•ness** *n.*
–ness. *comb. form.* **1.** State, quality, or condition of being: **quietness.** **2.** An instance or example of a state, quality, or condition: **kindness.** [< OE.]
nest (nĕst) *n.* **1. a.** The structure made by a bird for holding its eggs and young. **b.** A similar structure, as for fish or insect eggs. **2.** A snug, secluded place. **3.** A den; haunt. **4.** A set of objects that can be stacked together. **—v.** **1.** To build or occupy a nest. **2.** To fit or place snugly together. [< OE. See nizdo-.]
nest egg. A reserve fund of money.
nes•tle (nĕs′əl) *v.* **-tled, -tling.** **1. a.** To settle snugly and comfortably. **b.** To lie half-sheltered, as a house near trees. **2.** To snuggle contentedly. [< OE *nestlian,* to make a nest. See nizdo-.] **—nes′tler** *n.*
nest•ling (nĕst′lĭng) *n.* A bird too young to leave its nest.
net¹ (nĕt) *n.* **1.** An openwork meshed fabric. **2.** Something made of net, as a device used to capture animals or act as a barrier. **—v.** **netted, netting.** To catch or surround in or as in a net. [< OE *net.* See ned-.]
net² (nĕt) *adj.* **1.** Remaining after all deductions or losses. **2.** Ultimate; final. **—n.** Total gain, as of profit or weight. **—v.** **netted, netting.** To bring in as profit. [ME *net,* neat, clear.]
neth•er (nĕth′ər) *adj.* Lower. [< OE *nither,* down, downward. See ni.]
Neth•er•lands, the (nĕth′ər-ləndz). A country of W Europe. Pop. 12,212,000. Caps. Amsterdam, The Hague.

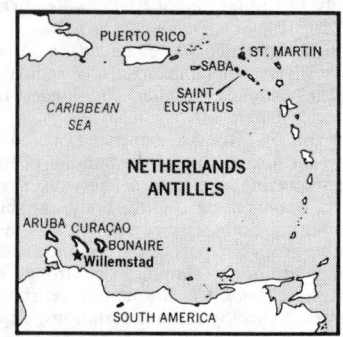

the Netherlands

Netherlands Antilles. An autonomous territory of the Netherlands, consisting of six islands, in the West Indies. Pop. 204,000.
neth•er•most (nĕth′ər-mōst′) *adj.* Lowest.
net•ting (nĕt′ĭng) *n.* A net or network.

net•tle (nĕt′l) *n.* A plant covered with stinging hairs. **—v.** **-tled, -tling.** To irritate; vex. [< OE *netle.* See ned-.] **—net′tler** *n.*
net ton. See ton.
net•work (nĕt′wûrk′) *n.* **1.** Something, as a net, having ropes, threads, etc., that cross at regular intervals. **2.** Any pattern or system that interconnects.
neu•ral (n/y/o͞or′əl) *adj.* Of or pertaining to the nerves.
neu•ral•gia (n/y/o͞o-răl′jə) *n.* Paroxysmal pain along a nerve. **—neu•ral′gic** *adj.*
neu•ras•the•ni•a (n/y/o͞or′əs-thē′nē-ə) *n.* A condition marked by fatigue, loss of energy and memory, and feelings of inadequacy.
neu•ri•tis (n/y/o͞o-rī′tĭs) *n.* Inflammation of a nerve, causing pain, loss of reflexes, and muscular atrophy.
neuro–. *comb. form.* Nerve or nervous system. [< Gk *neuron,* tendon, nerve.]
neu•rol•o•gy (n/y/o͞o-rŏl′ə-jē) *n.* The medical science of the nervous system and its disorders. [L *neurologia* : NEURO- + -LOGY.] **—neu′ro•log′i•cal** (n/y/o͞or′ə-lŏj′ĭ-kəl) *adj.* **—neu•rol′o•gist** *n.*
neu•ron (n/y/o͞or′ŏn′) *n.* A nerve cell. [Gk, sinew, nerve.]
neu•ro•sis (n/y/o͞o-rō′sĭs) *n., pl.* **-ses** (-sēz′). Any of various functional disorders of the mind or emotions, without obvious organic lesion or change, and involving anxiety, phobia, or other abnormal behavior symptoms. **—neu•rot′ic** (-rŏt′ĭk) *adj. & n.*
neut. neuter.
neu•ter (n/y/o͞o′tər) *adj.* **1.** *Gram.* Neither masculine nor feminine in gender. **2. a.** *Biol.* Having no functional sexual organs. **b.** *Bot.* Having no pistils or stamens; asexual. **—n.** **1.** *Gram.* **a.** The neuter gender. **b.** A neuter word. **2. a.** A castrated animal. **b.** A sexually undeveloped or imperfectly developed female insect; worker. **c.** A plant without stamens or pistils. [< L, neither.]
neu•tral (n/y/o͞o′trəl) *adj.* **1.** Not favoring either side in a dispute. **2.** Belonging to neither side nor party. **3.** Indifferent. **4.** *Chem.* Neither acidic nor basic. **5.** Having a net electric charge of zero. **6.** Designating a color with no hue. **—n.** **1.** One that is neutral. **2.** A neutral

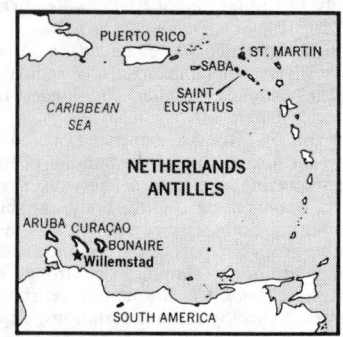

Netherlands Antilles

ă pat/ā ate/âr care/ä bar/b bib/ch chew/d deed/ĕ pet/ē be/f fit/g gag/h hat/hw what/
ĭ pit/ī pie/îr pier/j judge/k kick/l lid, fatal/m mum/n no, sudden/ng sing/ŏ pot/ō go/

color. **3.** The position of gears that are not engaged. —**neu′tral·ly** *adv.*

neu·tral·ism (n/y/ o͞o′trə-lĭz′əm) *n.* A neutral policy in foreign affairs.

neu·tral·i·ty (n/y/ o͞o-trăl′ə-tē) *n.* The quality or state of being neutral, esp. nonparticipation in war.

neu·tral·ize (n/y/ o͞o′trə-līz′) *v.* **-ized, -izing.** To make neutral or ineffective. —**neu′tral·i·za′tion** *n.* —**neu′tral·iz′er** *n.*

neu·tron (n/y/ o͞o′trŏn′) *n. Symbol* **n** *Phys.* An electrically neutral subatomic particle, having a mass 1,839 times that of the electron, stable when bound in an atomic nucleus, and having a mean lifetime of approx. 16.6 minutes as a free particle. [NEUTR(AL) + -ON.]

Nev. Nevada.

Ne·vad·a (nə-văd′ə, -vä′də). A state of the W U.S. Pop. 489,000. Cap. Carson City.

nev·er (nĕv′ər) *adv.* **1.** Not ever; on no occasion. **2.** Not at all; in no way. [< OE *næfre,* "not ever."]

nev·er·more (nĕv′ər-môr′, -mōr′) *adv.* Never again.

nev·er·the·less (nĕv′ər-thə-lĕs′) *adv.* None the less; however.

ne·vus (nē′vəs) *n., pl.* **-vi** (-vī′). Also **nae·vus.** Any congenital growth or mark on the skin, such as a birthmark. [L *naevus.*] —**ne′void′** (nē′void′) *adj.*

new (n/y/ o͞o) *adj.* **1. a.** Not old; recent. **b.** Used for the first time. **2.** Recently become known. **3.** Unfamiliar. **4.** Unaccustomed. **5.** Begun afresh. **6.** Refreshed; rejuvenated. **7.** Different and distinct from what was before. **8. a.** Modern; current. **b.** In the most recent form, period, or development of something: *New Latin.* —*n.* That which is new. —*adv.* Freshly; recently. [< OE *nēowe, nīwe.* See newo-.] —**new′ness** *n.*

New·ark (n/y/ o͞o′ərk). A city of NE New Jersey. Pop. 382,000.

New Bed·ford (bĕd′fərd). A port of SE Massachusetts. Pop. 102,000.

new·born (n/y/ o͞o′bôrn′) *adj.* **1.** Very recently born. **2.** Reborn.

New Bruns·wick (brŭnz′wĭk). A province of SE Canada. Pop. 623,000. Cap. Fredericton.

new·com·er (n/y/ o͞o′kŭm′ər) *n.* One who has lately come to a place or situation.

New Deal. The programs and policies for economic recovery and reform introduced during the 1930's by President Franklin D. Roosevelt. —**New Dealer.**

New Del·hi (dĕl′ē). The capital of the Republic of India. Pop. 295,000.

new·el (n/y/ o͞o′əl) *n.* **1.** The vertical post at the center of a winding staircase. **2.** A post at the bottom or landing of a staircase. [< OF *nouel,* "kernel," newel.]

New England. The NE U.S., comprising Maine, New Hampshire, Vermont, Massachusetts, Connecticut, and Rhode Island. —**New Englander.**

Newf. Newfoundland.

new·fan·gled (n/y/ o͞o′făng′gəld) *adj.* **1.** Novel. **2.** Fond of novelty. [< ME *newefangel,* fond of new things.]

New·found·land (n/y/ o͞o′fən-lənd, -lănd′). **1.** An island off the SE coast of Canada. **2.** A province of Canada, comprising this island and Labrador. Pop. 498,000. Cap. St. John's.

New Greek. Modern Greek.

New Guinea. A large island in the Pacific N of Australia.

New Hamp·shire (hămp′shər, hăm′shər, -shîr′). A state of the NE U.S. Pop. 738,000. Cap. Concord.

New Ha·ven (hā′vən). A city of S Connecticut. Pop. 152,000.

New High German. German.

New Jer·sey (jûr′zē). A state of the E U.S. Pop. 7,168,000. Cap. Trenton.

New Latin. The form of Latin in use, esp. in scientific nomenclature, since the beginning of the Renaissance.

new·ly (n/y/ o͞o′lē) *adv.* **1.** Lately; recently. **2.** Once more; anew. **3.** In a different way.

new·ly·wed (n/y/ o͞o′lē-wĕd′) *n.* Also **new·ly·wed.** One recently married.

New Mexico. A state of the SW U.S. Pop. 1,016,000. Cap. Santa Fe.

new moon. 1. The phase of the moon occurring when it passes between the earth and sun and is invisible or visible only as a narrow crescent at sunset. **2.** The crescent moon.

New Or·le·ans (ôr′lē-ənz, ôr′lənz, ôr-lēnz′). A city of SE Louisiana. Pop. 593,000.

New·port News (n/y/ o͞o′pôrt′ n/y/ o͞oz, -pôrt′). A city in SE Virginia. Pop. 114,000.

news (n/y/ o͞oz) *n. (takes sing. v.).* **1.** Recent events and happenings. **2.** A report about recent events. **3.** New information.

news·boy (n/y/ o͞oz′boi′) *n.* A boy who sells newspapers.

news·cast (n/y/ o͞oz′kăst′, -käst′) *n.* A broadcast of news events.

news·let·ter (n/y/ o͞oz′lĕt′ər) *n.* A news periodical for a special-interest group.

news·pa·per (n/y/ o͞oz′pā′pər) *n.* A typically daily or weekly publication containing news, feature articles, advertising, etc.

news·pa·per·man (n/y/ o͞oz′pā′pər-măn′) *n.* One who owns or is employed on a newspaper.

news·print (n/y/ o͞oz′prĭnt′) *n.* Inexpensive paper used chiefly for printing newspapers.

news·reel (n/y/ o͞oz′rēl′) *n.* A short film of current events.

news·stand (n/y/ o͞oz′stănd′) *n.* An open booth or shop at which newspapers are sold.

news·y (n/y/ o͞o′zē) *adj.* **-ier, -iest.** Full of news. —**news′i·ness** *n.*

newt (n/y/ o͞ot) *n.* Any of several small, semiaquatic salamanders. [< ME *an ewt,* an eft.]

New Test. New Testament.

New Testament. The Gospels, Acts, Pauline and other Epistles, and the Book of Revelation, which together have been viewed by Christians as forming the record of the new dispensation belonging to the Church, as distinct from the Old Testament dispensation shared with Judaism.

new·ton (n/y/ o͞ot′n) *n.* A unit equal to the force required to accelerate a mass of one kilogram one meter per second per second. [< Sir Isaac NEWTON.]

ô paw, for/oi boy/ou out/ o͞o took/ o͞o coo/p pop/r run/s sauce/sh shy/t to/th thin/*th* the/
ŭ cut/ûr fur/v van/w wag/y yes/z size/zh vision/ə ago, item, edible, gallop, circus/

New·ton (n/y/ōot′n), Sir **Isaac**. 1642–1727. English philosopher and scientist.

New·to·ni·an (n/y/ōo-tō′nē-ən) *adj*. Pertaining to or in accordance with the work of Newton, esp. that in mechanics and gravitation.

New World. The W Hemisphere.

new year. The year about to begin or just begun.

New Year's Day. The 1st day of the year, as reckoned according to the Gregorian calendar; January 1.

New York (yôrk). **1.** A state of the NE U.S. Pop. 18,191,000. Cap. Albany. **2.** Also **New York City.** The largest city of the U.S., in SE New York State. Pop. 7,782,000. —**New Yorker.**

New Zea·land (zē′lənd). An insular nation in the S Pacific. Pop. 2,640,000. Cap. Wellington. —**New Zealander.**

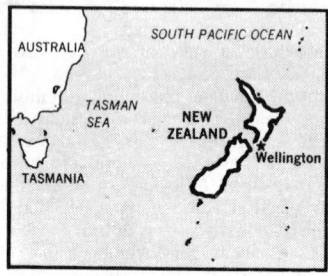

New Zealand

next (nĕkst) *adj.* **1.** Nearest in space; adjacent. **2.** Immediately succeeding. —*adv.* **1.** In the time, order, or place immediately following. **2.** On the first subsequent occasion. —*prep.* Close to; nearest. [< OE *nēahst*, superl of *nēah*, near.]

nex·us (nĕk′səs) *n., pl.* **-us** or **-uses. 1.** A means of connection; link. **2.** A connected series or group. [< L *nectere*, to bind, connect.]

N.F. Norman French.

Nfld. Newfoundland.

NG, N.G. National Guard.

NGk New Greek.

N.H. New Hampshire.

NHG New High German.

Ni nickel.

ni·a·cin (nī′ə-sĭn) *n.* Nicotinic acid.

Nia·mey (nyä-mā′). The capital of Niger. Pop. 30,000.

nib (nĭb) *n.* The point of a pen. [?]

nib·ble (nĭb′əl) *v.* **-bled, -bling. 1.** To bite gently and repeatedly. **2.** To take small or hesitant bites. —*n.* A small bite. [Prob < LG *nibbeln*.]

Nic·a·ra·gua (nĭk′ə-rä′gwə). A republic of Central America. Pop. 1,593,000. Cap. Managua. —**Nic′a·ra′guan** *adj. & n.*

nice (nīs) *adj.* **nicer, nicest. 1.** Pleasing; appealing. **2.** Considerate; well-mannered. **3.** Respectable; virtuous. **4.** Proper; seemly. **5.** Fastidious; exacting. **6. a.** Showing or requiring sensitive discernment. **b.** Done with skill. [< L *nescire*, to be ignorant.] —**nice′ly** *adv.*

ni·ce·ty (nī′sə-tē) *n., pl.* **-ties. 1.** Precision or accuracy. **2.** Fastidiousness. **3.** A subtle point, detail, or distinction. **4.** Often **niceties.** An elegant or dainty thing.

niche (nĭch) *n.* **1.** A recess in a wall, as for holding a statue. **2.** A suitable situation or activity. [< OF *niche*, "nest."]

nick (nĭk) *n.* A shallow notch or indentation on a surface. —**in the nick of time.** Just at the critical moment. —*v.* **1.** To cut a nick in. **2.** To cut short. [ME *nyke.*] —**nick′er** *n.*

nick·el (nĭk′əl) *n.* **1.** *Symbol* **Ni** A silvery, hard, ductile metallic element. It is used in alloys, in corrosion-resistant surfaces and batteries, and for electroplating. Atomic number 28, atomic weight 58.71. **2.** A U.S. coin worth five cents. [< G *Kupfernickel*, "copper-demon."]

nick·el·o·de·on (nĭk′ə-lō′dē-ən) *n.* **1.** An early movie house charging an admission price of five cents. **2.** A juke box.

nickel silver. A silvery, hard, corrosion-resistant, malleable alloy of copper, zinc, and nickel, used in tableware and as a structural material for hospital and restaurant equipment.

nick·name (nĭk′nām′) *n.* **1.** A descriptive appellation added to or replacing one's actual name. **2.** A familiar form of a proper name. —*v.* **-named, -naming.** To call by a nickname. [< ME *an ekename*, an additional name.]

Nic·o·si·a (nĭk′ə-sē′ə). The capital of Cyprus. Pop. 103,000.

nic·o·tine (nĭk′ə-tēn′) *n.* A poisonous alkaloid, $C_5H_4NC_4H_7NCH_3$, derived from the tobacco plant, used in medicine and as an insecticide. [F.]

nic·o·tin·ic acid (nĭk′ə-tĭn′ĭk). A member of the vitamin B complex, C_5H_4NCOOH, occurring in living cells and synthesized for use in treating pellagra.

niece (nēs) *n.* A daughter of one's brother, sister, brother-in-law, or sister-in-law. [< L *neptis.*]

Nie·tzsche (nē′chə, -chē), **Friedrich**. 1844–1900. German philosopher, poet, and critic.

nif·ty (nĭf′tē) *adj.* **-tier, -tiest.** *Slang.* Stylish; pleasing. [Poss < MAGNIFICENT.]

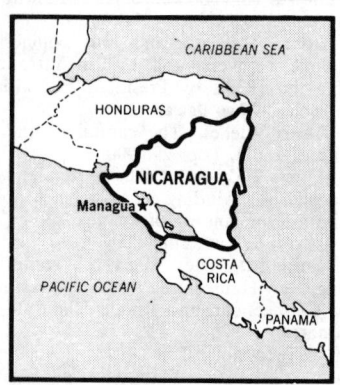

Nicaragua

ă pat/ā ate/âr care/ä bar/b **bib**/ch **chew**/d **deed**/ĕ pet/ē be/f **fit**/g **gag**/h **hat**/hw **what**/ ĭ pit/ī pie/îr pier/j **judge**/k **kick**/l lid, fatal/m **mum**/n no, sudden/ng **sing**/ŏ pot/ō **go**/

Ni·ger (nī′jər). **1.** A republic in west-central Africa. Pop. 3,100,000. Cap. Niamey. **2.** A river in W Africa.

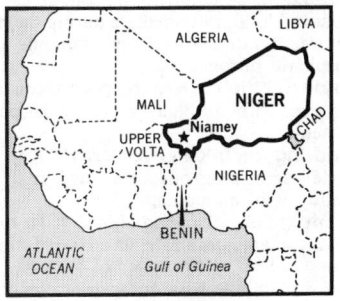

Niger

Ni·ger-Con·go (nī′jər-kŏng′gō) *n.* A large language family of Africa that includes the Mande, Kwa, and Bantu languages.
Ni·ge·ri·a (nī-jîr′ē-ə). A nation of W Africa. Pop. 55,654,000. Cap. Lagos. —**Ni·ge′ri·an** *adj.* & *n.*

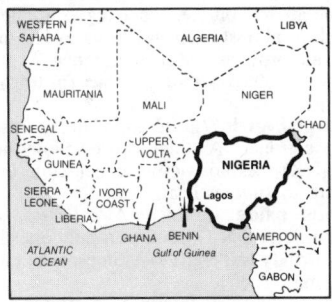

Nigeria

nig·gard (nĭg′ərd) *n.* A stingy, grasping person. —*adj.* Parsimonious. [< Scand.]
nig·gard·ly (nĭg′ərd-lē) *adj.* **-lier, -liest. 1.** Unwilling to part with anything; stingy. **2.** Meager. —**nig′gard·li·ness** *n.* —**nig′gard·ly** *adv.*
nig·gling (nĭg′lĭng) *adj.* **1.** Fussy. **2.** Petty. **3.** Showing or requiring close attention to details. [Prob < Scand.] —**nig′gling·ly** *adv.*
nigh (nī) *adj.* **nigher, nighest** or **next.** Close; near. —*adv.* **1.** Near in time or location. **2.** Nearly; almost —*prep.* Not far from; near to. [< OE *nēah,* NEAR.]
night (nīt) *n.* **1.** The period of darkness between sunset and sunrise. **2.** Darkness. [< OE *niht, neaht.* See nekwt-.] —**night** *adj.*
night blindness. Poor vision in the dark. —**night′-blind′** *adj.*
night·cap (nīt′kăp′) *n.* **1.** A cloth cap worn in bed. **2.** A drink taken just before bedtime.
night·clothes (nīt′klōz′, -klō*th*z′) *pl.n.* Clothes worn in bed.
night·club (nīt′klŭb′) *n.* An establishment that stays open late at night and provides food, drink, and entertainment.

night crawler. An earthworm that emerges from the ground at night.
night·dress (nīt′drĕs′) *n.* A nightgown.
night·fall (nīt′fôl′) *n.* The approach of darkness.
night·gown (nīt′goun′) *n.* A loose gown worn to bed.
night·hawk (nīt′hôk′) *n.* **1.** A night-flying bird related to and resembling the whippoorwill. **2.** *Informal.* One who stays up late at night.
night·in·gale (nīt′n-gāl′, nī′tĭng-) *n.* A brownish Old World songbird that sings at night. [< OE *nihtegale,* "night-singer."]
Night·in·gale (nīt′n-gāl′, nī′tĭng-), **Florence.** 1820–1910. British nurse and hospital reformer.
night·ly (nīt′lē) *adj.* **1.** Nocturnal. **2.** Happening or done every night. —*adv.* On every night.
night·mare (nīt′mâr′) *n.* **1.** A frightening dream. **2.** A horrifying event or condition. [ME *nihtmare,* female incubus.]
night owl. One who stays up late at night.
night·shade (nīt′shād′) *n.* Any of several related, often poisonous plants with variously colored flowers and berries.
night·shirt (nīt′shûrt′) *n.* A long shirt worn as nightclothes.
night·stick (nīt′stĭk′) *n.* A club carried by a policeman.
night·time (nīt′tīm′) *n.* The time between sunset and sunrise.
night watchman. One who acts as a guard at night.
ni·hil·ism (nī′əl-ĭz′əm, nī′hĭl-, nē′-) *n.* Systematic denial of the reality of experience and rejection of all value or meaning attributed to it. [< L *nihil,* nothing.] —**ni′hil·ist** *n.*
nil (nĭl) *n.* Nothing; naught. [< L *nihil.*]
Nile (nīl). A river of E Africa, flowing through Egypt to the Mediterranean.
Ni·lo-Sa·har·an (nī′lō-sə-hâr′ən) *n.* A large language family of Africa, including Chari-Nile and a number of smaller groups. —**Ni′lo-Sa·har′an** *adj.*
nim·ble (nĭm′bəl) *adj.* **-bler, -blest. 1.** Quick and agile; deft. **2.** Cleverly alert; acute. [< OE *nǣmel,* quick to seize or understand, and *numol,* seizing. See nem-.] —**nim′ble·ness** *n.* —**nim′bly** *adv.*
nim·bo·stra·tus (nĭm′bō-strā′təs, -străt′əs) *n.* A low, gray cloud, often dark, that precipitates rain, snow, or sleet.
nim·bus (nĭm′bəs) *n., pl.* **-bi** (-bī′) or **-buses.** A surrounding radiance or circle of light, as in a representation of a holy person. [L, heavy rain, rain cloud.]
Nim·rod (nĭm′rŏd′) *n.* A hunter. [< *Nimrod,* son of Cush, described as a mighty man and hunter. Genesis 10:8.]
nin·com·poop (nĭn′kəm-pōōp′, nĭng′-) *n.* A fool; simpleton. [?]
nine (nīn) *n.* The cardinal number written 9 or in Roman numerals IX. [< OE *nigon.* See newn̥.] —**nine** *adj.* & *pron.*
nine·teen (nīn′tēn′) *n.* The cardinal number written 19 or in Roman numerals XIX. —**nine′teen′** *adj.* & *pron.*

ô paw, for/oi boy/ou out/ŏŏ took/ōō coo/p pop/r run/s sauce/sh shy/t to/th thin/*th* the/
ŭ cut/ûr fur/v van/w wag/y yes/z size/zh vision/ə ago, item, edible, gallop, circus/

nine·teenth (nīn′tēnth′) *n.* **1.** The ordinal number 19 in a series. **2.** One of 19 equal parts. —**nine′teenth′** *adj. & adv.*

nine·ti·eth (nīn′tē-ĭth) *n.* **1.** The ordinal number 90 in a series. **2.** One of 90 equal parts. —**nine′ti·eth** *adj. & adv.*

nine·ty (nīn′tē) *n.* The cardinal number written 90 or in Roman numerals XC or LXXXX. —**nine′ty** *adj. & pron.*

nin·ny (nĭn′ē) *n., pl.* **-nies.** A fool; simpleton. [< INNOCENT.]

ni·non (nē′nŏn′) *n.* A sheer lightweight fabric.

ninth (nīnth) *n.* **1.** The ordinal number 9 in a series. **2.** One of 9 equal parts. —**ninth** *adj. & adv.*

ni·o·bi·um (nī-ō′bē-əm) *n. Symbol* **Nb** A silvery, soft, ductile metallic element, used in steel alloys, arc welding, and superconductivity research. Atomic number 41, atomic weight 92.906.

nip¹ (nĭp) *v.* **nipped, nipping. 1. a.** To squeeze, pinch, or press between two points. **b.** To give a small, sharp bite to. **2.** To clip or sever. **3.** To sting, as cold. **4.** To check growth or development. **5.** *Slang.* **a.** To snatch up hastily. **b.** To steal. —*n.* **1.** A bite or pinch. **2.** A small bit. **3. a.** A stinging quality, as of frosty air. **b.** Severely sharp cold or frost. —**nip and tuck.** Very close; closely contested. [Prob < ON *hnippa.*]

nip² (nĭp) *n.* A small quantity of liquor. —*v.* **nipped, nipping.** To drink (alcoholic liquor) in small portions. [Prob < Du *nippen,* to sip.]

nip·per (nĭp′ər) *n.* **1.** One that nips. **2.** Often **nippers.** A pincerlike device or structure, as pliers or a lobster claw.

nip·ple (nĭp′əl) *n.* **1.** The small conical protuberance near the center of the mammary gland, containing the outlets of the milk ducts. **2.** The rubber cap on a nursing bottle. **3.** Anything resembling or functioning like a nipple, as: **a.** A regulated opening for discharging a liquid, as in a small stopcock. **b.** A pipe threaded on both ends. [< OE *nebb,* a beak < Gmc **nabja-.*]

nip·py (nĭp′ē) *adj.* **-pier, -piest.** Sharp or biting.

nir·va·na (nĭr-vä′nə, nər-) *n.* **1.** Nirvana. The Buddhist state of absolute blessedness, characterized by release from the cycle of reincarnations and attained through the extinction of the self. **2.** Oblivion; bliss. [Sk *nirvāna,* "extinction (of individual existence)."]

Ni·sei (nē-sā′, nē′sā′) *n., pl.* **-sei** or **-seis.** One born in America of immigrant Japanese parents. [Jap, "second generation."]

nit (nĭt) *n.* The egg or young of a parasitic insect, as a louse. [< OE *hnitu,* louse egg.] —**nit′ty** *adj.*

ni·ter (nī′tər) *n.* Also *chiefly Brit.* **ni·tre.** A white, gray, or colorless mineral of potassium nitrate, KNO₃, used in making gunpowder. [< Gk *nitron.*]

ni·trate (nī′trāt′, -trĭt) *n.* A salt or ester of nitric acid. —*v.* **-trated, -trating.** To treat with nitric acid or with a nitrate, usually to change an organic compound into a nitrate. —**ni·tra′tion** *n.*

ni·tric acid (nī′trĭk). A corrosive liquid, HNO₃, used in the production of fertilizers, explosives, and rocket fuels, and in a wide variety of industrial metallurgical processes.

nitric oxide. A colorless, poisonous gas, NO, produced as an intermediate during the manufacture of nitric acid from ammonia or atmospheric nitrogen.

ni·tride (nī′trīd′) *n.* A compound containing nitrogen with another, more electropositive element.

ni·trid·ing (nī′trī′dĭng) *n. Metall.* The case-hardening of a ferrous alloy, such as steel, by heating it in ammonia.

ni·tri·fy (nī′trə-fī′) *v.* **-fied, -fying. 1.** To oxidize into nitric acid, a nitrate, or a related nitrogen compound, as by the action of bacteria. **2.** To treat or combine with nitrogen or compounds containing nitrogen. —**ni′tri·fi·ca′tion** *n.*

nitro-. *comb. form.* A compound containing the univalent group NO₂. [< Gk *nitron.*]

ni·tro·cel·lu·lose (nī′trō-sĕl′yə-lōs′) *n.* A pulpy or cottonlike material derived from cellulose treated with sulfuric and nitric acids and used in the manufacture of explosives and plastics.

ni·tro·gen (nī′trə-jən) *n. Symbol* **N** A nonmetallic element constituting nearly four-fifths of the air by volume, occurring as a colorless, odorless, almost inert gas in various minerals and all proteins. Atomic number 7, atomic weight 14.0067. —**ni·trog′e·nous** (nī-trŏj′ə-nəs) *adj.*

ni·tro·glyc·er·in (nī′trō-glĭs′ər-ĭn) *n.* Also **ni·tro·glyc·er·ine.** A thick, pale-yellow liquid, C₃N₃H₅O₉, explosive on concussion or exposure to sudden heat.

ni·trous oxide (nī′trəs). A colorless, sweet inorganic gas, N₂O, used as a mild anesthetic.

nit·ty-grit·ty (nĭt′ē-grĭt′ē) *n. Slang.* The essence of a matter.

nit·wit (nĭt′wĭt′) *n. Informal.* A stupid or silly person.

nix (nĭks). *Slang. n.* Nothing. —*adv.* No. —*v.* To forbid; veto. [< G *nichts,* nothing.]

Nix·on (nĭk′sən), **Richard Milhous.** Born 1913. 37th President of the United States (1969–74); resigned.

Richard M. Nixon

N.J. New Jersey.
NL New Latin.
NLRB National Labor Relations Board.
nm, n.m. nautical mile.
N.M. New Mexico (unofficial).
N. Mex. New Mexico.
NNE north-northeast.
NNW north-northwest.
no¹ (nō) *adv.* **1.** Not so; opposed to "yes." Used in expressing refusal, denial, or disagreement. **2.** Not by any degree: *no better.* **3.** Not: *whether or no.* —*n., pl.* **noes.** A negative response. [< OE *nā* : *ne,* no (see **ne**) + *ā,* ever (see **aiw-**).]
no² (nō) *adj.* **1.** Not any. **2.** Not at all. [< OE *nān,* NONE.]
No nobelium.
no., No. **1.** north; northern. **2.** number.
No·ah (nō′ə). Biblical patriarch commanded by God to build the ark.

Noah

no·bel·i·um (nō-bĕl′ē-əm) *n.* *Symbol* **No** A synthetic radioactive element produced in trace amounts. Atomic number 102, longest-lived isotope No 254. [< the *Nobel* Institute at Stockholm.]
No·bel Prize (nō-bĕl′). Any of the annual prizes awarded for distinction in literature, medicine, chemistry, physics, and economics, and for the promotion of world peace. [< A. *Nobel* (1833–1896), Swedish chemist whose will set up the Nobel Prize.]
no·ble (nō′bəl) *adj.* **-bler, -blest.** **1.** Of high hereditary rank. **2.** Showing greatness and magnanimity of character; illustrious. **3.** Grand; stately; magnificent. —*n.* A person of noble rank. [< L *nōbilis,* knowable, famous, noble.] —**no·bil′i·ty** (nō-bĭl′ə-tē) *n.* —**no′ble·ness** *n.* —**no′bly** *adv.*
no·ble·man (nō′bəl-mən) *n.* A man of noble rank.
no·bod·y (nō′bŏd′ē, -bə-dē) *pron.* No person; no one. —*n., pl.* **-bodies.** One without fame or influence.
noc·tur·nal (nŏk-tûr′nəl) *adj.* **1.** Of, suitable to, or occurring at night. **2.** Active or functioning by night: *nocturnal animals.* [< L *nox (noct-),* night.] —**noc·tur′nal·ly** *adv.*
noc·turne (nŏk′tûrn′) *n.* A romantic musical composition intended to embody sentiments appropriate to the evening or night.
nod (nŏd) *v.* **nodded, nodding.** **1.** To bow the head briefly, as in a gesture of agreement or in dozing. **2.** To express (greeting, approval, or acknowledgement) by bowing the head. **3.** To be briefly inattentive, as if sleepy. **4.** To sway or bend, as plants in the wind. —*n.* A nodding motion. [ME *nodden.*] —**nod′der** *n.*
node (nōd) *n.* **1.** A knob, knot, protuberance, or swelling: *a lymph node.* **2.** The often enlarged point on a plant stem where a leaf or other organ is attached. [L *nōdus,* a knob, knot.] —**nod′al** *adj.*
nod·ule (nŏj′ool) *n.* A small, knotlike protuberance; a small node. —**nod′u·lar** (nŏj′ōo-lər) *adj.*
No·ël (nō-ĕl′) *n.* **1.** Christmas. **2.** **noël.** A Christmas carol. [< L *nātālis (dies),* "birth-(day) of Christ."]
no-fault (nō′fôlt′) *adj.* Of a system of automobile insurance in which accident victims are compensated by their insurance companies without any assignment of blame.
nog·gin (nŏg′ĭn) *n.* **1.** A small mug or cup. **2.** A unit of liquid measure equal to one-quarter of a pint. **3.** The head. [?]
noise (noiz) *n.* **1.** A sound or sounds, esp. when loud, unexpected, or disagreeable. **2.** An outcry, clamor, or din. **3.** *Phys.* Any disturbance, esp. a random and persistent disturbance, that obscures or reduces the clarity or quality of a signal. —*v.* **noised, noising.** To spread the rumor or report of. [< L *nausea,* seasickness.] —**nois′y** *adj.*
noi·some (noi′səm) *adj.* **1.** Offensive; disgusting. **2.** Harmful or dangerous. [< ME *anoien,* ANNOY + -SOME.] —**noi′some·ly** *adv.*
no·mad (nō′măd) *n.* **1.** One of a people having no fixed abode and moving from place to place. **2.** A wanderer. [< Gk *nomas,* one that wanders about for pasture.] —**no·mad′ic** *adj.*
nom de plume (nŏm′ də ploom′). A pseudonym; pen name. [F, "pen name."]
no·men·cla·ture (nō′mən-klā′chər, nō-mĕn′-klə-chər) *n.* A system of names; systematic naming in an art or science. [L *nōmenclātūra.*]
nom·i·nal (nŏm′ə-nəl) *adj.* **1.** Of or like a name. **2.** In name only. **3.** Insignificant. [< L *nōmen,* name.] —**nom′i·nal·ly** *adv.*
nom·i·nate (nŏm′ə-nāt′) *v.* **-nated, -nating.** **1.** To propose as a candidate. **2.** To designate or appoint to an office, honor, etc. —**nom′i·na′tion** *n.* —**nom′i·nee′** (-nē′) *n.*
nom·i·na·tive (nŏm′ə-nə-tĭv, nŏm′nə-tĭv). *Gram. adj.* Of or designating the case of the subject of a finite verb and of words identified with the subject. —*n.* The nominative case or a word in that case.
-nomy. *comb. form.* The systematization of knowledge about a specified field: **astronomy.** [< Gk *nomos,* law.]
non-. *comb. form.* Not. [< L *nōn,* not.]
non·age (nŏn′ĭj, nō′nĭj) *n.* **1.** Legal minority. **2.** Immaturity.
non·a·ligned (nŏn′ə-līnd′) *adj.* Not in alliance with any power bloc; neutral: *a nonaligned nation.*
nonce (nŏns) *n.* The present or a particular time or occasion: *for the nonce.* [< ME *for then anes,* "for the one (purpose or occasion)."]
non·cha·lant (nŏn′shə-länt′) *adj.* Appearing

casually unconcerned or indifferent. [< OF *nonchaloir,* to be unconcerned.] —**non′cha·lance′** *n.* —**non′cha·lant·ly** *adv.*

non·com·bat·ant (nŏn′kəm-băt′ənt, -kŏm′bə-tənt) *n.* **1.** One in the armed forces whose duties exclude fighting. **2.** A civilian in wartime.

non·com·mis·sioned officer (nŏn′kə-mĭsh′-ənd). An enlisted member of the armed forces appointed to a rank conferring leadership.

non·com·mit·tal (nŏn′kə-mĭt′l) *adj.* Revealing no preference or purpose.

non com·pos men·tis (nŏn kŏm′pəs mĕn′tĭs). Not of sound mind. [L, "not having control of the mind."]

non·con·duc·tor (nŏn′kən-dŭk′tər) *n.* A substance that conducts little or no electricity or heat. —**non′con·duct′ing** *adj.*

non·con·form·ist (nŏn′kən-fôr′mĭst) *n.* One who does not conform to accepted rules, beliefs, or practices. —**non′con·form′i·ty** *n.*

non·co·op·er·a·tion (nŏn′kō-ŏp′ə-rā′shən) *n.* Failure or refusal to cooperate, esp. refusal to perform civil duties.

non·de·nom·i·na·tion·al (nŏn′dĭ-nŏm′ə-nā′shən-əl) *adj.* Not restricted to or associated with a religious denomination.

non·de·script (nŏn′dĭ-skrĭpt′) *adj.* Lacking in distinctive qualities. [< NON- + L *dēscrībere,* DESCRIBE.]

none (nŭn) *pron.* **1.** No one; nobody. **2.** Not any of a specified group. **3.** No part; not any. —*adj.* Not one; no. —*adv.* In no way; not at all. [< OE *nān : ne,* no + *ān,* one.]

Usage: None (pronoun) can take either a singular or a plural verb. A singular verb is used when *none* can logically be construed as singular (when *not one* or *no one* can be substituted for *none*) or when *none* precedes a singular noun. A plural verb is used when *none* applies to more than one (when *not any of a group of persons or things* can be substituted for *none*). When *none* can logically be construed as either singular or plural, either a singular or a plural verb is possible.

non·en·ti·ty (nŏn-ĕn′tə-tē) *n., pl.* **-ties.** An insignificant person or thing.

none·such (nŭn′sŭch′) *n.* A person or thing without equal.

none·the·less (nŭn′*th*ə-lĕs′) *adv.* Nevertheless.

non·ex·ist·ence (nŏn′ĭg-zĭs′təns) *n.* The condition of not existing. —**non′ex·ist′ent** *adj.*

non·fic·tion (nŏn-fĭk′shən) *n.* Prose works other than fiction. —**non·fic′tion·al** *adj.*

no·nil·lion (nō-nĭl′yən) *n.* **1.** The cardinal

Note: Many compounds are formed with *non-.* Normally, *non-* combines with a second element without an intervening hyphen. However, if the second element begins with a capital letter, it is separated with a hyphen: *non-French.*

non′a·ban′don·ment *n.*
non′ab·di·ca′tion *n.*
non′ab·o·li′tion *n.*
non′a·bra′sive *adj.*
non′a·bridg′ment *n.*
non′ab·so·lute *adj.* & *n.*
non′ab·sorb′ent *adj.* & *n.*
non′ab·sorp′tion *n.*
non′ab·stain′er *n.*
non·ab′stract *adj.* & *n.*
non′a·bu′sive *adj.*
non′ac·a·dem′ic *adj.*
non′ac·cel′er·a′tion *n.*
non·ac′cent *n.*
non′ac·cept′ance *n.*
non′ac·ces′so·ry *adj.* & *n.*
non′ac·ci·den′tal *adj.* & *n.*
non′ac·com′mo·dat′ing *adj.*
non′ac·cord′ *n.*
non′ac·cu·mu·la′tion *n.*
non·ac′id *n.* & *adj.*

non′ac·qui·es′cent *adj.*
non′ac·quit′tal *n.*
non·ac′tion *n.*
non·ac′tive *adj.*
non·ac′tu·al *adj.*
non′a·cute′ *adj.*
non′a·dapt′a·ble *adj.*
non′ad·dic′tive *adj.*
non′a·dept′ *adj.*
non′ad·her′ence *n.*
non′ad·he′sive *adj.*
non′ad·ja′cent *adj.*
non′ad·jec·ti′val *adj.*
non′ad·join′ing *adj.*
non′ad·just′a·ble *adj.*
non′ad·min′is·tra′tive *adj.*
non′ad·mis′sion *n.*
non′a·dult′ *adj.* & *n.*
non′ad·vance′ment *n*
non′ad·van·ta′geous *adj.*
non′ad·ven′tur·ous *adj.*
non′ad·ver′bi·al *adj.*

non′aes·thet′ic *adj.*
non′af·fec·ta′tion *n.*
non′af·fil′i·a′tion *n.*
non-Af′ri·can *adj.* &
non′al·co·hol′ic *adj.*
non′a·pol′o·get′ic *adj.*
non′ap·par′ent *adj.*
non′ap·pear′ance *n.*
non′ap·pre′ci·a′tion *n.*
non′ap·proach′a·ble *adj.*
non·a′que·ous *adj.*
non·ar′bi·trar′y *adj.*
non′ar·o·mat′ic *adj.*
non-Ar′y·an *n.* & *adj.*
non-A′sian *n.* & *adj.*
non′as·ser′tive *adj.*
non′as·sim′i·la′tion *n.*
non′ath′lete *n.*
non′a·tom′ic *adj.*
non′at·tach′ment *n.*
non′at·tain′a·ble *adj.*

ă pat/ā ate/âr care/ä bar/b bib/ch chew/d deed/ĕ pet/ē be/f fit/g gag/h hat/hw what/
ĭ pit/ī pie/îr pier/j judge/k kick/l lid, fatal/m mum/n no, sudden/ng sing/ŏ pot/ō go/

number represented by the figure 1 followed by 30 zeros. **2.** In Great Britain, the cardinal number represented by the figure 1 followed by 54 zeros. [< OF, "the ninth power of a million."] —**no•nil'lion** *adj.*

no•nil•lionth (nō-nĭl'yənth) *n.* The ordinal number nonillion in a series. —**no•nil'lionth** *adj.*

non•in•ter•ven•tion (nŏn'ĭn-tər-vĕn'shən) *n.* Failure or refusal to intervene in the affairs of another, esp. in international affairs. —**non'in•ter•ven'tion•ist** *n.* & *adj.*

non•met•al (nŏn-mĕt'l) *n.* Any of a number of elements, such as oxygen or sulfur, that generally occur as negatively charged ions or radicals, form oxides that produce acids, and are poor conductors of heat and of electricity when solid. —**non'me•tal'lic** (nŏn'-mə-tăl'ĭk) *adj.*

non•ob•jec•tive (nŏn'əb-jĕk'tĭv) *adj.* Designating a style of graphic art that does not represent objects.

non•pa•reil (nŏn'pə-rĕl') *adj.* Without rival; matchless; peerless. —*n.* One without equal; a paragon.

non•par•ti•san (nŏn-pär'tə-zən) *adj.* **1.** Not partisan. **2.** Not influenced by the policies of any one political party.

non•plus (nŏn-plŭs') *v.* **-plused** or **-plussed**, **-plusing** or **-plussing.** To perplex; baffle. [L *nōn plūs*, "no more (can be said)."]

non•prof•it (nŏn-prŏf'ĭt) *adj.* Not seeking profit.

non•sec•tar•i•an (nŏn'sĕk-târ'ē-ən) *adj.* Not limited to or associated with any particular religious denomination.

non•sense (nŏn'sĕns', -səns) *n.* **1.** Something that does not make or have sense, esp. meaningless or absurd behavior or language. **2.** Extravagant foolishness or frivolity. —**non•sen'si•cal** (nŏn-sĕn'sĭ-kəl) *adj.*

non se•qui•tur (nŏn sĕk'wĭ-tŏŏr'). An inference that does not follow from established premises. [L, "it does not follow."]

non•skid (nŏn'skĭd') *adj.* Designed to prevent or inhibit skidding.

non•stan•dard (nŏn-stăn'dərd) *adj.* **1.** Not adhering to a standard. **2.** *Ling.* Of or pertaining to usages or varieties of a language that do not conform to those approved by educated native users of the language.

non•stop (nŏn'stŏp') *adj.* Making or having made no stops. —**non'stop'** *adv.*

non•sup•port (nŏn'sə-pôrt', -pōrt') *n.* Failure to provide for the maintenance of one's legal dependents.

non•un•ion (nŏn-yōōn'yən) *adj.* **1. a.** Not be-

non'at•ten'dance *n.*
non'at•trib'u•tive *adj.* & *n.*
non'au•to•mat'ic *adj.*
non'bac•te'ri•al *adj.*
non-Bap'tist *n.*
non•ba'sic *adj.*
non•beau'ty *n.*
non•be'ing *n.*
non•be•liev'er *n.*
non'be•nev'o•lent *adj.*
non-Bib'li•cal *adj.*
non-Brit'ish *adj.*
non•bus'y *adj.*
non-caf•feine' *n.*
non-cak'ing *adj.* & *n.*
non•can'cer•ous *adj.*
non'ca•non'i•cal *adj.*
non'cap•i•tal•is'tic *adj.*
non'car•niv'o•rous *adj.*
non'cat•e•gor'i•cal *adj.*
non-Cath'o•lic *adj.* & *n.*
non'-Cau•ca'sian *adj.* & *n.*
non•ce•les'tial *adj.*
non-cel'lu•lar *adj.*
non-Celt'ic *adj.*
non'cer•e•mo'ni•al *adj.*

non'cer'ti•fied' *adj.*
non-chem'i•cal *adj.* & *n.*
non'-Chi•nese' *adj.* & *n.*
non-Chris'tian *adj.* & *n.*
non-cit'i•zen *n.*
non-civ'i•lized' *adj.*
non'clas•si•fi•ca'tion *n.*
non-cler'i•cal *adj.*
non-clin'i•cal *adj.*
non'co-er'cive *adj.*
non'co•he'sive *adj.*
non'col•laps'i•ble *adj.*
non'col•le'giate *adj.*
non'com'bat•ant *n.*
non'com•bus'ti•ble *adj.* & *n.*
non'com•mer'cial *adj.* & *n.*
non'com•mu'ni•ca•ble *adj.*
non'com'mu•nist *n.* & *adj.*
non'com•pen•sa'tion *n.*
non'com'pe•tent *adj.*
non'com'pe•tent•ly *adv.*
non'com•pet'i•tive *adj.*
non'com•pet'i•tive•ness *n.*

non'com•ple'tion *n.*
non'com•pres'sion *n.*
non'com•pul'sion *n.*
non'con•cur'rence *n.*
non'con•cur'rent *adj.*
non'con•den•sa'tion *n.*
non'con•duc'tive *adj.*
non'con•fi•den'tial *adj.*
non'con•fine'ment *n.*
non'con•flic'tive *adj.*
non'con•form'i•ty *n.*
non'con•ges'tion *n.*
non'-Con•gres'sion•al *adj.*
non'con•nec'tive *adj.* & *n.*
non'con•no'ta•tive *adj.*
non'con'scious *adj.*
non'con•sec'u•tive *adj.*
non'con•sent' *n.*
non'con•ser'va•tive *adj.* & *n.*
non'con•sid'er•a'tion *n.*
non'con•spir'a•tor *n.*
non'con•sult'a•tive *adj.*
non'con•ta'gious *adj.*
non'con•tem'po•rar'y *adj.* & *n.*

ô paw, for/oi boy/ou out/ŏŏ took/ōō cōo/p pop/r run/s sauce/sh shy/t to/th thin/*th* the/ ŭ cut/ûr fur/v van/w wag/y yes/z size/zh vision/ə ago, item, edible, gallop, circus/

longing to a labor union. **b.** Not unionized: *a nonunion shop.* **2.** Not produced by union labor.

non•vi•o•lence (nŏn-vī′ə-ləns) *n.* A social philosophy based on the rejection of violent means to gain objectives. —**non•vi′o•lent** *adj.*

noo•dle (nōōd′l) *n.* A thin strip of food paste, usually made of flour and eggs. [G *Nudel.*]

nook (nōōk) *n.* **1.** A corner, esp. in a room. **2.** A quiet or secluded spot. [Perh < Scand.]

noon (nōōn) *n.* Twelve o'clock in the daytime; midday. [< OE *nōn,* "the ninth hour (after sunrise)."]

noon•day (nōōn′dā′) *n.* Noon.

no one (nō′wŭn′). No person; nobody.

noon•tide (nōōn′tīd′) *n.* Noon.

noon•time (nōōn′tīm′) *n.* Noon.

noose (nōōs) *n.* A loop formed by a running knot in a rope or cord, as in a lasso. [< L *nōdus,* a knot.]

nor (nôr; *unstressed* nər) *conj.* And not; or not; likewise not; not either. —Used: **a.** As a correlative to give continuing negative force: *He never worked nor offered to help.* **b.** For rhetorical effect: *The day was bright, nor were there clouds above.* [< ME *nother,* neither.]

Nor•dic (nôr′dĭk) *adj.* Of, pertaining to, or relating to the Caucasoid ethnic group most predominant in Scandinavia. [< OE *north,* NORTH.] —**Nor′dic** *n.*

Nor•folk (nôr′fək). A port of SE Virginia. Pop. 306,000.

norm (nôrm) *n.* A standard, model, or pattern regarded as typical. [L *norma,* carpenter's square, pattern.]

nor•mal (nôr′məl) *adj.* **1.** Conforming to a usual or typical pattern. **2.** *Math.* Perpendicular. —*n.* **1.** Anything normal; the standard. **2.** The usual state, amount, etc. **3.** A perpendicular. [< L *normālis,* made according to the carpenter's square.] —**nor•mal′i•ty** (-măl′ə-tē), **nor′mal•cy** *n.* —**nor′mal•ly** *adv.*

normal school. A school that trains teachers, chiefly for the elementary grades.

Nor•man (nôr′mən) *n.* **1.** One of a Scandinavian people who conquered Normandy in the 10th century. **2.** One of the people of Normandy who conquered England in 1066. **3.** A native of Normandy. —**Nor′man** *adj.*

Nor•man•dy (nôr′mən-dē). A region of NW France on the English Channel.

Norman French. 1. The dialect of Old French used in medieval Normandy and England. **2.** The form of this dialect used in English court and legal circles from the Norman conquest until the 15th century.

---

non′con•tin′u•ous *adj.*

non•con′tra•band′ *n. & adj.*

non′con•tra•dic′ tion *n.*

non′con•tri•bu′tion *n.*

non′con•trib′u•tor *n.*

non′con•tro•ver′ sial *adj.*

non′con•ver′gence *n.*

non′con•ver′sion *n.*

non′con•vic′tion *n.*

non′co•or′di•na′ tion *n.*

non′cor•po•rate *adj.*

non′cor•rec′tive *adj. & n.*

non′cor′re•lat′ing *adj.*

non′cor•re•la′tion *n.*

non′cos′mic *adj.*

non′cre•a′tive *adj.*

non•cred′i•ble *adj.*

non•crim′i•nal *adj. & n.*

non•cul′pa•ble *adj.*

non•cul′ture *n.*

non•cu′mu•la•tive *adj*

non•cur′rent *adj.*

non′cur•tail′ment *n.*

non•cus′tom•ar′y *adj.*

non′de•cay′ing *adj.*

non′de•cep′tive *adj.*

non′de•liv′er•y *n.*

non′dem•o•crat′ic *adj.*

non′de•part•men′tal *adj.*

non′de•par′ture *n.*

non′de•pen′dence *n.*

non′de•pos′i•tor *n.*

non′de•pre′ci•a′ tion *n.*

non′de•riv′a•tive *adj. & n.*

non′de•rog′a•to′ry *adj.*

non′de•struc′tive *adj.*

non′de•tach′a•ble *adj.*

non′det•ri•men′tal *adj.*

non′de•vel′op•ment *n.*

non′de•vi•a′tion *n.*

non′de•vo′tion•al *adj.*

non′di•a•lec′tal *adj.*

non′di•dac′tic *adj.*

non′dif•fer•en′ti• a′tion *n.*

non′di•gest′i•ble *adj.*

non′di•rec′tion•al *adj.*

non′dis•cern′ment *n.*

non•dis′ci•pli•nar′y *adj.*

non′dis•crim′i•na′ tion *n.*

non′dis•pos′al *n.*

non′dis•rup′tive *adj.*

non′dis•si•dence *n.*

non′dis•tinc′tive *adj.*

non′dis•tri•bu′tion *n.*

non′di•ver′gence *n.*

non′di•ver′si•fi• ca′tion *n.*

non′di•vis′i•ble *adj.*

non•doc′tri•nal *adj.*

non•doc•u•men′ta•ry *adj. & n.*

non•dog•mat′ic *adj.*

non•do•mes′tic *adj. & n.*

non′dra•mat′ic *adj.*

non•dry′ing *adj.*

non′ec•cle′si•as′ti• cal *adj.*

non′ec•lec′tic *adj.*

non′ec•o•nom′ic *adj.*

non•ed′i•ble *adj. & n.*

non′ed•i•to′ri•al *adj.*

non•ed′u•ca•ble *adj.*

non•ed•u•ca′tion•al *adj.*

non′ef•fec′tive *adj.*

non′ef•fer•ves′cent *adj.*

non′ef•fi′cien•cy *n.*

non′e•las′tic *adj.*

non′e•lect′ *n.*

Norse (nôrs) *adj.* Of or pertaining to ancient Scandinavia, its people, or their language. —**Norse** *n.*

Norse·man (nôrs′mən) *n.* Any of the ancient Scandinavians.

north (nôrth) *n.* **1. a.** The direction along a meridian to the left of an observer facing in the direction of the earth's rotation. **b.** The point on a mariner's compass located at 0°. **2.** Often **North. a.** The N or arctic part of the earth. **b.** The N part of any country or region. —**the North:** In the U.S., the states N of Maryland, the Ohio River, and Missouri. —*adj.* **1.** To or from the north. **2. North.** Designating the N part of a country, continent, or other geographical area: *North Korea.* —*adv.* In, from, or toward the north. [< OE. See ner-.]

North America. The northern continent of the W Hemisphere.

North Car·o·li·na (kăr′ə-lī′nə). A state of the S U.S. Pop. 5,082,000. Cap. Raleigh.

North Da·ko·ta (də-kō′tə). A state of the Midwestern U.S. Pop. 618,000. Cap. Bismarck.

north·east (nôrth-ēst′) *n.* **1.** The direction halfway between north and east. **2.** Any area or region lying in this direction. —**the Northeast.** In the U.S., New England, New York, and sometimes Pennsylvania and New Jersey. —*adj.* To, from, or in the northeast. —*adv.* In, from, or toward the northeast. —**north·east′ern** *adj.*

north·east·er (nôrth-ē′stər) *n.* A storm or gale from the northeast.

north·east·er·ly (nôrth-ē′stər-lē) *adj.* **1.** Toward the northeast. **2.** From the northeast. —**north·east′er·ly** *adv.*

north·er (nôr′thər) *n.* A sudden cold gale from the north.

north·er·ly (nôr′thər-lē) *adj.* **1.** Toward the north. **2.** From the north. —**north′er·ly** *adv.*

north·ern (nôr′thərn) *adj.* **1.** Toward, in, or facing the north. **2.** Coming from the north. **3.** Often **Northern.** Of or characteristic of northern regions or the North.

north·ern·er (nôr′thər-nər) *n.* **1.** A native or inhabitant of the north. **2.** Often **Northerner.** A native or inhabitant of the NE U.S.

Northern Hemisphere. The half of the earth north of the equator.

Northern Ireland. A component of the United Kingdom in NE Ireland. Pop. 1,458,000. Cap. Belfast.

northern lights. The aurora borealis.

North Germanic. A branch of Germanic including Danish, Norwegian, and Swedish.

---

non′e·lec′tion *n.*
non′e·lec′tive *adj.*
non′e·lec′tric *adj.*
non′el·e·men′ta·ry *adj.*
non′e·lim′i·na′tion *n.*
non′e·mo′tion·al *adj.*
non′em·pir′i·cal *adj.*
non′en·cy′clo·pe′dic *adj.*
non′en·force′a·ble *adj.*
non-Eng′lish *adj.* & *n.*
non·en′ter·pris·ing *adj.*
non′-E·pis′co·pa′lian *adj.* & *n.*
non·e′qual *adj.* & *n.*
non′e·quiv′a·lent *adj.* & *n.*
non′e·ra′sure *n.*
non′e·rot′ic *adj.*
non·er′u·dite′ *adj.*
non′es·sen′tial *adj.* & *n.*
non′es·thet′ic *adj.*
non′e·ter′nal *adj.*
non·eth′i·cal *adj.*
non′eth·no·log′i·cal *adj.*
non′-Eu·clid′e·an *adj.*
non′-Eu·ro·pe′an *adj.* & *n.*
non′e·vac′u·a′tion *n.*

non′e·va′sion *n.*
non′e·va′sive *adj.*
non′e·vic′tion *n.*
non′ev·o·lu′tion·ar′y *adj.*
non′ex·pan′sive *adj.*
non′ex·pend′a·ble *adj.*
non′ex·per′i·men′tal *adj.*
non′ex·plo′sive *adj.* & *n.*
non·ex′tant *adj.*
non′ex·ter′nal *adj.*
non·ex·tinct′ *adj.*
non′ex·tra·di′tion *n.*
non′ex·tra′ne·ous *adj.*
non·fa·ce′tious *adj.*
non·fac′tu·al *adj.*
non·fan′ta·sy *n.*
non·fas′cist *n.* & *adj.*
non′fas·tid′i·ous *adj.*
non·fa′tal *adj.*
non·fed′er·al *adj.*
non·fer′tile *adj.*
non·fes′tive *adj.*
non·feu′dal *adj.*
non·fig′ur·a·tive *adj.*
non′fi·nan′cial *adj.*
non·fi′nite *adj.* & *n.*
non·fire′proof′ *adj.*
non·for′mal *adj.*
non′for·tu′i·tous *adj.*

non′fra·ter′nal *adj.*
non·fraud′u·lent *adj.*
non·free′dom *n.*
non-French′ *adj.* & *n.*
non·fre′quent *adj.*
non′ful·fill′ment *n.*
non·func′tion·al *adj.*
non′fun·da·men′tal *adj.* & *n.*
non·gas′e·ous *adj.*
non′ge·lat′i·nous *adj.*
non′ge·net′ic *adj.*
non′gov·ern·ment′al *adj.*
non′gre·gar′i·ous *adj.*
non·hab′it·a·ble *adj.*
non·ha·bit′u·al *adj.*
non·haz′ard·ous *adj.*
non·hea′then *n.* & *adj.*
non′he·red′i·tar′y *adj.*
non′he·ret′i·cal *adj.*
non′he·ro′ic *adj.*
non′his·tor′ic *adj.*
non′ho·mo·ge′ne·ous *adj.*
non·hos′tile *adj.*
non·hu′man *adj.*
non·hu′man·ness *n.*
non·hu′mor·ous *adj.*
non′i·den′ti·cal *adj.*
non′i·den′ti·ty *n.*
non′id·i·o·mat′ic *adj.*

ô paw, for/oi boy/ou out/o͝o took/o͞o coo/p pop/r run/s sauce/sh shy/t to/th thin/*th* the/
ŭ cut/ûr fur/v van/w wag/y yes/z size/zh vision/ə ago, item, edible, gallop, circus/

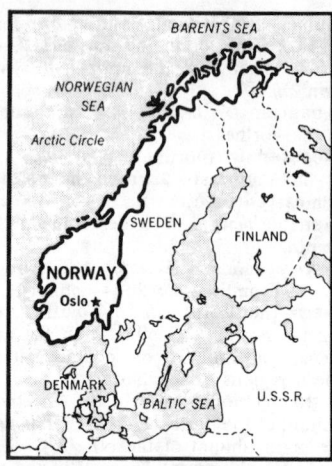

Norway

Idaho. —*adj.* To, from, or in the northwest. —*adv.* In, from, or toward the northwest. —**north·west'ern** *adj.*

north·west·er·ly (nôrth-wĕs'tər-lē) *adj.* **1.** Toward the northwest. **2.** From the northwest. —**north·west'er·ly** *adv.*

Norw. Norway; Norwegian.

Nor·way (nôr'wā'). A kingdom of NW Europe. Pop. 3,708,000. Cap. Oslo.

Nor·we·gian (nôr-wē'jən) *n.* **1.** A native or inhabitant of Norway. **2.** The North Germanic language of the Norwegians. —**Nor·we'gian** *adj.*

nose (nōz) *n.* **1.** The facial part or structure bearing the nostrils and containing the organ

North Korea. The unofficial name for the People's Democratic Republic of Korea. See **Korea.**

North Pole. 1. The northern end of the earth's axis of rotation. **2.** The celestial zenith of this terrestrial point. **3. north pole.** The north-seeking magnetic pole of a magnet.

North Sea. A part of the Atlantic between Great Britain and Denmark.

North Star. The polar star; Polaris.

North Vietnam. The former unofficial name for the Democratic Republic of Vietnam. See **Vietnam.**

north·ward (nôrth'wərd) *adv.* Also **north·wards** (-wərdz). Toward the north. —*adj.* Toward, facing, or in the north. —*n.* **1.** A direction toward the north. **2.** A region in or toward the north. —**north'ward·ly** *adj. & adv.*

north·west (nôrth-wĕst') *n.* **1.** The direction halfway between north and west. **2.** Any area or region lying in this direction. —**the Northwest.** In the U.S.: **1.** Formerly, the area W of the Mississippi and N of the Missouri. **2.** The present states of Washington, Oregon, and

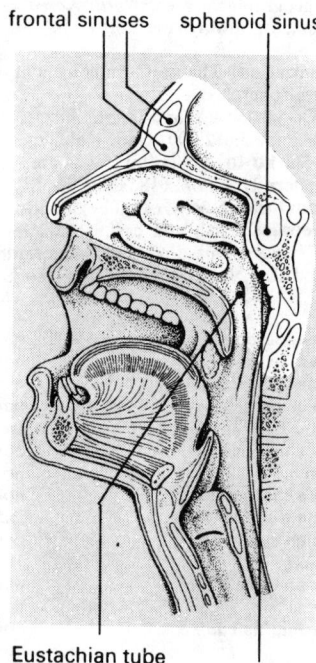

frontal sinuses   sphenoid sinus

Eustachian tube

pharyngeal tonsil

nose

non'i·dol'a·trous *adj.*	non·in'dexed *adj.*	non'in·quir'ing *adj.*
non'im·ag'i·nar'y *adj.*	non'in·dict'ment *n.*	non'in·struc'tion·al *adj.*
non'im·i·ta'tive *adj.*	non'in·di·vid'u·al *adj.*	non'in·stru·men'tal *adj.*
non'im·mune' *adj.*	non'in·duc'tive *adj.*	non'in·tel·lec'tu·al *adj. & n.*
non'im·pair'ment *n.*	non'in·dus'tri·al *adj.*	non'in·tel'li·gent *adj.*
non'im·pe'ri·al *adj.*	non'in·fal'li·ble *adj.*	non'in·ter·change'a·ble *adj.*
non'im·prove'ment *n.*	non'in·flam'ma·ble *adj.*	non'in·tox'i·cant *adj.*
non'im·pul'sive *adj.*	non'in·flec'tion·al *adj.*	non·ir'ri·tant *adj. & n.*
non'in·can·des'cent *adj.*	non'in·form'a·tive *adj.*	non-Jew' *n.*
non'in·clu'sive *adj.*	non·in'ju·ry *n.*	
non·in'crease *n.*		
non'in·de·pend'ent *adj.*		

ă pat/ā ate/âr care/ä bar/b bib/ch chew/d deed/ĕ pet/ē be/f fit/g gag/h hat/hw what/
ĭ pit/ī pie/îr pier/j judge/k kick/l lid, fatal/m mum/n no, sudden/ng sing/ŏ pot/ō go/

of smell and the beginning of the respiratory tract. **2. a.** The sense of smell. **b.** The ability to discover, as if by smell: *a nose for news.* **3.** Anything resembling a nose in shape or position. —*v.* **nosed, nosing. 1.** To find out by or as by smell. **2.** To touch with the nose; nuzzle. **3.** To steer or move forward with care. **4.** To pry curiously. [< OE *nosu.* See **nas-.**]

nose·bleed (nōz′blēd′) *n.* A nasal hemorrhage.

nose cone. The forwardmost section of a rocket or guided missile.

nose dive. 1. A sudden plunge of an aircraft, nose toward the earth. **2.** Any sudden plunge. —**nose′-dive′** (nōz′dīv′) *v.*

nose·gay (nōz′gā′) *n.* A small bunch of flowers.

nose·piece (nōz′pēs′) *n.* A piece of armor serving as a guard for the nose.

nos·tal·gi·a (nŏ-stăl′jə, nə-) *n.* **1.** A longing for things, persons, or situations that are not present. **2.** Homesickness. [< Gk *nostos,* a return + -ALGIA.] —**nos·tal′gic** *adj.*

Nos·tra·da·mus (nŏs′trə-dä′məs, nŏs′trə-dā′məs). 1503–1566. French astrologer; author of prophecies (1555).

nos·tril (nŏs′trəl) *n.* An external opening of the nose. [< OE *nosthyrl,* "nose hole."]

nos·trum (nŏs′trəm) *n.* A quack medicine or remedy. [NL, "our own."]

nos·y, nos·ey (nō′zē) *adj.* **-ier, -iest.** *Informal.* Prying; inquisitive. —**nos′i·ness** *n.*

not (nŏt) *adv.* In no way; to no degree: *I will not go. You may not have any.* [< OE *nāwiht : nā,* no + *wiht,* a man, thing (see **wekti-**).]

no·ta be·ne (nō′tə běn′ē, nō′tä bā′nā). Note well. [L.]

no·ta·ble (nō′tə-bəl) *adj.* Worthy of notice; remarkable; striking. —*n.* A person of note or distinction. [< L *notāre,* to note.] —**no′ta·bil′i·ty** *n.* —**no′ta·bly** *adv.*

no·ta·rize (nō′tə-rīz′) *v.* **-rized, -rizing.** To authenticate or attest to as a notary. —**no′ta·ri·za′tion** *n.*

no·ta·ry (nō′tə-rē) *n., pl.* **-ries.** A notary public. [< L *notārius,* "stenographer."]

notary public *pl.* **notaries public.** A public officer authorized to certify documents, take affidavits, and administer oaths.

no·ta·tion (nō-tā′shən) *n.* **1.** A system of fig-

ures or symbols used to represent numbers, quantities, etc. **2.** The act or process of using such a system. [< L.]

notch (nŏch) *n.* **1.** A V-shaped cut, esp. one used for keeping count. **2.** A narrow pass between mountains. —*v.* **1.** To cut notches in. **2.** To record by or as by making notches. [< OF *ochier,* to notch.] —**notch′y** *adj.*

note (nōt) *n.* **1.** A brief written record or communication. **2.** A formal diplomatic or official communication. **3.** A commentary to a passage in a text. **4. a.** A piece of paper currency. **b.** A certificate issued by a government or bank, often negotiable. **c. A promissory note.** **5.** *Mus.* **a.** A tone of definite pitch. **b.** The symbol of such a tone in musical notation.

Notes		Rests
○	whole	
𝅗𝅥 or 𝅗𝅥	half	
♩ or ♩	quarter	
♫ or ♫♪	8th	
♬ or ♬	16th	
𝅘𝅥𝅲 or 𝅘𝅥𝅲	32nd	
𝅘𝅥𝅳 or 𝅘𝅥𝅳	64th	

note

ô paw, for/oi boy/ou out/ōō took/ōō coo/p pop/r run/s sauce/sh shy/t to/th thin/*th* the/
ŭ cut/ûr fur/v van/w wag/y yes/z size/zh vision/ə ago, item, edible, gallop, circus/

6. A musical call or cry, as of a bird. **7.** An indication of some quality or aspect: *a note of suspicion.* **8.** Importance; consequence. **9.** Notice; observation. —*v.* **noted, noting. 1.** To observe carefully; notice; perceive. **2.** To write down; make a note of. **3.** To make particular mention of; remark. [< L *nota,* mark, sign, cipher.]

note•book (nōt′bŏ͝ok′) *n.* A book of blank pages for notes.

not•ed (nō′tĭd) *adj.* Distinguished by reputation; eminent. —**not′ed•ly** *adv.*

note•wor•thy (nōt′wûr′thē) *adj.* Worthy of notice; remarkable. —**note′wor′thi•ness** *n.*

noth•ing (nŭth′ĭng) *n.* **1.** No thing; not anything. **2.** No significant thing. **3.** No portion. **4.** Insignificance; obscurity. **5.** A person or thing of no consequence. **6.** Absence of anything perceptible; nonexistence. **7.** Zero. —*adv.* In no way or degree; not at all. [< OE *nān,* NONE + *thing,* THING.]

noth•ing•ness (nŭth′ĭng-nĭs) *n.* **1.** The condition or quality of being nothing; nonexistence. **2.** Insignificance.

no•tice (nō′tĭs) *n.* **1.** The act of observing; attention. **2.** An announcement or indication of some event. **3.** A formal announcement of intent to leave a job. **4.** A critical review, as of a play. —*v.* **-ticed, -ticing. 1.** To observe; perceive; be aware of. **2.** To take note of; remark on. [< L *nōtus,* pp of *nōscere,* to get acquainted with.]

no•tice•a•ble (nō′tĭs-ə-bəl) *adj.* **1.** Readily observed; evident. **2.** Worth noticing; significant. —**no′tice•a•bly** *adv.*

no•ti•fy (nō′tə-fī′) *v.* **-fied, -fying. 1.** To give notice to; inform. **2.** To give notice of; proclaim. —**no′ti•fi•ca′tion** (-fĭ-kā′shən) *n.* —**no′ti•fi′er** *n.*

no•tion (nō′shən) *n.* **1.** A general impression or feeling. **2.** A view; conception; theory. **3.** Intention or inclination. **4. notions.** Small items for household and clothing use. [L *nōtiō,* "a becoming acquainted."]

no•to•ri•ous (nō-tôr′ē-əs, -tōr′ē-əs) *adj.* **1.** Known widely and regarded unfavorably; infamous. **2.** Generally known and discussed. [< L *nōtus,* known.] —**no′to•ri′e•ty** (nō′tə-rī′ə-tē) *n.* —**no•to′ri•ous•ly** *adv.*

no-trump (nō′trŭmp′) *n.* **1.** A declaration to play a hand without a trump suit, as in bridge. **2.** A hand so played. —**no′-trump′** *adj.*

---

non′min•is•te′ri•al *adj.*
non•mo′bile *adj.*
non•mor′tal *adj. & n.*
non-Mos′lem *adj. & n.*
non•mo′tile *adj.*
non′mu•nic′i•pal *adj.*
non•mus′cu•lar *adj.*
non•mys′ti•cal *adj.*
non•myth′i•cal *adj.*
non•na′tion•al *adj. & n.*
non•nau′ti•cal *adj.*
non•na′val *adj.*
non′ne•go′tia•ble *adj.*
non-Ne′gro *n. & adj.*
non•neu′tral *adj. & n.*
non•nu′cle•ar *adj.*
non•nu′tri•ent *n. & adj.*
non′o•be′di•ence *n.*
non′o•blig′a•to′ry *adj.*
non′ob•ser′vance *n.*
non′ob•struc′tive *adj.*
non′oc•cu•pa′tion *n.*
non′oc•cur′rence *n.*
non•o′dor•ous *adj.*
non′of•fen′sive *adj.*
non′of•fi′cial *adj.*
non•op′er•a′tive *adj.*
non•op′tion•al *adj.*
non′or•gan′ic *adj.*
non•own′er *n.*
non′pa•cif′ic *adj.*
non′pa•gan *n. & adj.*
non•pa′pal *adj.*
non•par′ *adj.*
non•par′al•lel′ *adj. & n.*
non′par•a•sit′ic *adj.*
non′pa•ren′tal *adj.*
non′pa•rish′ion•er *n.*
non′par•lia•men′ta•ry *adj.*
non′pa•ro′chi•al *adj.*
non•par′tial *adj.*
non•par•tic′i•pant *n.*
non′par•tic′i•pat′ing *adj.*
non′par•tic′i•pa′tion *n.*
non′pa•ter′nal *adj.*
non′path•o•gen′ic *adj.*
non•pay′ment *n.*
non′per•cep′tu•al *adj.*
non′per•form′ance *n.*
non′pe•ri•od′i•cal *adj. & n.*
non•per′ish•a•ble *adj. & n.*
non′per′ma•nent *adj.*
non•per′me•a•ble *adj.*
non′per•pet′u•al *adj.*
non′per•sist′ence *n.*
non′per•sist′ent *adj.*
non′phil•an•throp′ic *adj.*
non′phys′i•cal *adj.*
non′phys•i•o•log′i•cal *adj.*
non•plan′e•tar′y *adj.*
non′po•et′ic *adj.*
non′poi′son•ous *adj.*
non′po•lit′i•cal *adj.*
non•po′rous *adj.*
non•pred′a•to′ry *adj.*
non′pre•dict′a•ble *adj.*
non′pref•er•en′tial *adj.*
non′pres•i•den′tial *adj.*
non•prev′a•lent *adj.*
non•priest′ly *adj.*
non′pro•duc′er *n.*
non′pro•duc′tive *adj.*
non′pro•fes′sion•al *adj. & n.*
non′pro•fi′cien•cy *n.*
non′pro•gres′sive *adj. & n.*
non′pro•lif′ic *adj.*
non′pro•por′tion•al *adj.*
non′pro•pri′e•ty *n.*
non′pro•tec′tion *n.*
non-Prot′es•tant *n. & adj.*
non-psy′chic *adj. & n.*
non•pub′lic *adj.*
non•ra′cial *adj.*
non•rad′i•cal *adj. & n.*
non•ra′tion•al *adj.*

ă pat/ā ate/âr care/ä bar/b bib/ch chew/d deed/ĕ pet/ē be/f fit/g gag/h hat/hw what/
ĭ pit/ī pie/îr pier/j judge/k kick/l lid, fatal/m mum/n no, sudden/ng sing/ŏ pot/ō go/

not·with·stand·ing (nŏt'wĭth-stăn'dĭng, nŏt'wĭth-) *prep.* In spite of. —*adv.* All the same; nevertheless. —*conj.* Although.

Nouak·chott (nwäk'shŏt'). The capital of Mauritania. Pop. 13,000.

nou·gat (nōō'gət) *n.* A confection made from a sweet paste into which nuts are mixed. [< OProv *nogat*, confection of nuts.]

nought. Variant of **naught.**

noun (noun) *n.* A word used to denote or name a person, place, thing, quality, or act. [< L *nōmen*, name.]

nour·ish (nûr'ĭsh) *v.* **1.** To provide with food or other substances necessary for life and growth. **2.** To foster the development of; promote and sustain. [< L *nūtrīre*, to feed.] —**nour'ish·er** *n.* —**nour'ish·ment** *n.*

nou·veau riche (nōō-vō' rēsh') *pl.* **nouveaux riches** (nōō-vō' rēsh'). One who has lately become rich. [F, "new rich."]

Nov. November.

no·va (nō'və) *n., pl.* **-vae** (-vē) or **-vas.** A star that suddenly increases in brightness to several times its normal magnitude and then returns to its original appearance. [< L *novus*, new.]

No·va Sco·tia (nō'və skō'shə). A province of SE Canada. Pop. 763,000. Cap. Halifax. —**Nova Scotian.**

nov·el¹ (nŏv'əl) *n.* A fictional prose narrative of considerable length, typically having a plot unfolded by the actions, speech, and thoughts of the characters. [< L *novellus*, new.] —**nov'el·ist** *n.* —**nov'el·is'tic** *adj.*

nov·el² (nŏv'əl) *adj.* Strikingly new, unusual, or different. [< L *novus*, new.]

nov·el·ette (nŏv'ə-lĕt') *n.* A short novel.

no·vel·la (nō-vĕl'ə) *n., pl.* **-las** or **-le** (-vĕl'ē). A short novel.

nov·el·ty (nŏv'əl-tē) *n., pl.* **-ties.** **1.** Newness; originality. **2.** Something that is novel; a new or unusual thing; an innovation. **3. novelties.** Small mass-produced articles, as trinkets. [< NOVEL².]

No·vem·ber (nō-vĕm'bər) *n.* The 11th month of the year. November has 30 days. [< L *Novembris (mēnsis)*, the ninth (month) (of the Roman calendar).]

no·ve·na (nō-vē'nə) *n., pl.* **-nas** or **-nae** (-nē). *R.C.Ch.* A nine-days' devotion. [< L *novem*, nine.]

nov·ice (nŏv'ĭs) *n.* **1.** One new to any activity; a beginner. **2.** One who has entered a religious

non're·ac'tive *adj.*	non're·sid'u·al *adj.*	non·sen'su·al *adj.*
non're·ceiv'a·ble *adj.* & *n.*	non're·solv'a·ble *adj.*	non·ser'vile *adj.*
non're·cip'ro·cal *adj.* & *n.*	non're·stric'tive *adj.*	non·sex'u·al *adj.*
non'rec·og·ni'tion *n.*	non're·ten'tion *n.*	non'sig·nif'i·cant *adj.*
non'rec·tan'gu·lar *adj.*	non're·ten'tive *adj.*	non·slip'per·y *adj.*
non're·cur'rent *adj.*	non're·tir'ing *adj.*	non·smok'er *n.*
non're·deem'a·ble *adj.*	non're·turn'a·ble *adj.*	non·so'cial *adj.*
non're·gen'er·a'tive *adj.*	non're·vers'i·ble *adj.*	non·so'cial·ist *n.* & *adj.*
non'reg·i·men'tal *adj.*	non're·volt'ing *adj.*	non·sol'vent *n.*
non'reg·is·tra'tion *n.*	non'rhe·tor'i·cal *adj.*	non·spar'ing *adj.*
non're·li'ance *n.*	non·rig'id *adj.*	non·spar'kling *adj.*
non're·lig'ious *adj.*	non·ri'val *n.* & *adj.*	non·spe·cif'ic *adj.*
non're·mu'ner·a'tive *adj.*	non-Ro'man *adj.* & *n.*	non'spec·tac'u·lar *adj.*
non're·new'a·ble *adj.*	non·ru'ral *adj.*	non·spec'u·la'tive *adj.*
non're·pay'a·ble *adj.*	non'sac·ra·men'tal *adj.*	non·spher'i·cal *adj.*
non're·pen'tant *adj.*	non·sa'cred *adj.*	non·spir'i·tu·al *adj.* & *n.*
non're·pet'i·tive *adj.*	non·sal'a·ble *adj.*	non'spon·ta'ne·ous *adj.*
non're·pre·hen'si·bly *adv.*	non·sal'a·ried *adj.*	non·sport'ing *adj.*
non're·pre·sen·ta'tion *n.*	non·sched'uled *adj.*	non·stand'ard·ized' *adj.*
non're·pre·sen'ta·tive *n.* & *adj.*	non'scho·las'tic *adj.*	non·sta'tion·ar'y *adj.*
non're·pro·duc'tive *adj.*	non'sci·en·tif'ic *adj.*	non·stat'u·to'ry *adj.*
non're·sem'bla·nce *n.*	non·scor'ing *adj.*	non'stim·u·la'tion *n.*
non'res·i·den'tial *adj.*	non·sea'son·al *adj.*	non'stra·te'gic *adj.*
	non'sec·re·tar'i·al *adj.*	non·stretch'a·ble *adj.*
	non·sec'u·lar *adj.*	non·stri'at·ed *adj.*
	non'seg·men'tal *adj.*	non·strik'er *n.*
	non'se·lec'tive *adj.*	non·struc'tur·al *adj.*
	non-Sem'ite *n.*	non'sub·mis'sive *adj.*
	non'sen·a·to'ri·al *adj.*	non'sub·scrib'er *n.*
	non·sen'si·tive *adj.*	

order but is on probation before taking final vows. [< L *novus,* new.]

no·vi·ti·ate (nō-vĭsh'ē-ĭt, -āt') *n.* **1.** The period or state of being a novice. **2.** A novice.

No·vo·cain (nō'və-kān') *n.* A trademark for procaine hydrochloride.

No·vo·si·birsk (nō'vō-sĭ-bîrsk'). A city in south-central Siberia. Pop. 1,161,000.

now (nou) *adv.* **1.** At the present time. **2.** At once; immediately. **3.** Very recently. **4.** Very soon. **5.** At this point in a narrative or series of events; then. **6.** Nowadays. **7.** In these circumstances. *—conj.* Since; seeing that. *—n.* The present time or moment: *Now is the time to act.* [< OE *nū.* See nu-.]

NOW (nou). National Organization for Women.

now·a·days (nou'ə-dāz') *adv.* In these days.

no·way (nō'wā') *adv.* Also **no·ways** (-wāz'). Nowise.

no·where (nō'hwâr') *adv.* In, to, or at no place; not anywhere. *—n.* A nonexistent or insignificant place.

no·wise (nō'wīz') *adv.* In no way, manner, or degree.

nox·ious (nŏk'shəs) *adj.* Injurious to health or morals. [< L *noxa,* injury, damage.]

noz·zle (nŏz'əl) *n.* A spout, as the end of a hose, through which gas or liquid is discharged. [< NOSE.]

Np neptunium.

N.P. notary public.

N.S. **1.** Nova Scotia. **2.** not specified.

NT, N.T. New Testament.

nu (n/y/ōō) *n.* The 13th letter of the Greek alphabet, representing *n.*

nu·ance (n/y/ōō-äns', n/y/ōō'äns') *n.* A subtle or slight variation, as in meaning, color, or quality. [< OF *nuer,* to show shades of color.]

nub (nŭb) *n.* **1.** A protuberance or knob. **2.** A small lump. **3.** The gist or point. [< MLG *knobbe,* knob.] *—***nub'by** *adj.*

nu·bile (n/y/ōō'bĭl,-bĭl') *adj.* Ready for marriage; of a marriageable age. [< L *nŭbilis,* marriageable.]

nu·cle·ar (n/y/ōō'klē-ər) *adj.* **1.** Of or involving a nucleus. **2.** Of or involving nuclear energy.

nuclear energy. The energy released by a nuclear reaction, esp. by fission, fusion, or radioactive decay.

nuclear fission. *Phys.* Fission.

nuclear fusion. *Phys.* Fusion.

nuclear physics. The scientific study of the forces, reactions, and internal structures of atomic nuclei.

nuclear reaction. A reaction that alters the energy, composition, or structure of an atomic nucleus.

nuclear reactor. Any of several devices in which a chain reaction is initiated and controlled, with the consequent production of heat, neutrons, and fission products.

nu·cle·ate (n/y/ōō'klē-ĭt) *adj.* Having a nucleus or nuclei. *—v.* (n/y/ōō'klē-āt') **-ated, -ating. 1.** To bring together into or form a nucleus. **2.** To act as a nucleus for. *—***nu'cle·a'tion** *n.* *—***nu'cle·a'tor** *n.*

nu·cle·ic acid (n/y/ōō-klē'ĭk). Any member of either of two groups of complex compounds found in all living cells.

nucleo-. *comb. form.* Nucleus.

nu·cle·o·lus (n/y/ōō-klē'ə-ləs, -klē-ō'ləs) *n., pl.* **-li** (-lī'). A small particle of protein and ribonucleic acid in the nucleus of a cell. *—***nu·cle'o·lar** (-lər) *adj.*

nu·cle·on (n/y/ōō'klē-ŏn') *n.* A proton or neutron, esp. as part of an atomic nucleus. *—***nu'cle·on'ic** *adj.*

nu·cle·us (n/y/ōō'klē-əs) *n., pl.* **-clei** (-klē-ī') or

non'suc·cess' *n.*	non·ther'mal *adj.*	non·u·ni·ver'sal *adj.* & *n.*
non'sup·port'er *n.*	non·think'er *n.*	non·ur'ban *adj.*
non·sur'gi·cal *adj.*	non·tox'ic *adj.*	non·us'er *n.*
non·sus·tain'ing *adj.*	non'tra·di'tion·al *adj.*	non'u·til'i·tar'i·an *adj.*
non'sym·pa·thet'ic *adj.*	non·trag'ic *adj.*	non'va·lid'i·ty *n.*
non'sym'pa·thy *n.*	non·trans·fer'a·ble *adj.*	non·val'ue *n.*
non'sym·phon'ic *adj.*	non'tran·si'tion·al *adj.*	non·vas'cu·lar *adj.*
non'symp·to·mat'ic *adj.*	non'trans·par'ent *adj.*	non·ven'om·ous *adj.*
non·syn'chro·nous *adj.*	non·triv'i·al *adj.*	non·ver'bal *adj.*
non'syn·tac'tic *adj.*	non·truth' *n.*	non·ver'ti·cal *adj.*
non'sys·tem·at'ic *adj.*	non'tu·ber'cu·lar *adj.*	non·vet'er·an *n.*
non·talk'a·tive *adj.*	non·typ'i·cal *adj.*	non'vi·o·la'tion *n.*
non·tech'ni·cal *adj.*	non'ty·po·graph'ic *adj.*	non·vi'o·lence *n.*
non·tem'po·ral *adj.*	non'ty·po·graph'i·cal *adj.*	non·vis'u·al *adj.*
non'ter·ri·to'ri·al *adj.*	non'un·der·stand'a·ble *adj.*	non·vi'tal *adj.*
non·tex'tu·al *adj.*	non'un·der·stand'ing *adj.* & *n.*	non·vo'cal *adj.*
non'the·at'ri·cal *adj.*	non·u'ni·form' *adj.*	non'vo·ca'tion·al *adj.*
non'ther·a·peu'tic *adj.*		non·vol'a·tile *adj.*
		non·vol'un·tar'y *adj.*
		non·vot'er *n.*
		non·white' *n.* & *adj.*
		non·work'er *n.*
		non·yield'ing *adj.*

rare **-uses. 1.** A central thing or part around which other things are grouped; core. **2.** Anything regarded as a basis for development and growth. **3.** A complex, usually spherical, protoplasmic body within a living cell that contains the cell's hereditary material and controls its metabolism, growth, and reproduction. **4.** The positively charged central region of an atom, composed of protons and neutrons and containing all of the mass of the atom. [L, "nut," "kernel."]

nude (n/y/o͞od) *adj.* Without clothing; naked. —*n.* **1.** The nude human figure or a representation of it. **2.** Nude state: *in the nude.* [L *nūdus.*] —**nu′di·ty** *n.*

nudge (nuj) *v.* **nudged, nudging.** To push against gently, esp. to gain attention or give a signal. [Prob < Scand.] —**nudge** *n.*

nud·ism (n/y/o͞o′dĭz′əm) *n.* The doctrine or practice of living in the nude for reasons of health. —**nud′ist** *adj. & n.*

nug·get (nŭg′ĭt) *n.* A small lump, esp. of natural gold.

nui·sance (n/y/o͞o′səns) *n.* A source of inconvenience, annoyance, or vexation; a bother. [< OF.]

null (nŭl) *adj.* **1.** Having no legal force; invalid. **2.** Of no consequence, effect, or value; insignificant. **3.** Amounting to nothing. **4.** Of zero magnitude. [< L *nullus.*] —**null′i·ty** *n.*

nul·li·fy (nŭl′ə-fī′) *v.* **-fied, -fying. 1.** To deprive of legal force; annul. **2.** To make ineffective or useless. —**nul′li·fi·ca′tion** (-fĭ-kā′shən) *n.* —**nul′li·fi′er** *n.*

Num. Numbers.

numb (nŭm) *adj.* **1.** Insensible, as from excessive chill. **2.** Stunned, as from shock. [< OE *niman,* take, seize. See nem-.] —**numb** *v.* —**numb′ly** *adv.* —**numb′ness** *n.*

num·ber (nŭm′bər) *n.* **1. a.** A member of the set of positive integers. **b.** A member of any of the further sets of mathematical objects that can be derived from the positive integers. **2. numbers.** Arithmetic. **3.** A numeral or series of numerals designating a specific object. **4.** A specific quantity composed of equal units. **5.** Quantity of units: *The crowd was small in number.* **6.** A multitude. **7.** One item in a sequence or series. —*v.* **1.** To add up to. **2.** To count or enumerate. **3.** To include in or be one of a group. **4.** To assign a number to. **5.** To limit in number. [< L *numerus.*]

num·ber·less (nŭm′bər-lĭs) *adj.* Countless; innumerable.

nu·mer·a·ble (n/y/o͞o′mər-ə-bəl) *adj.* Capable of being counted.

nu·mer·al (n/y/o͞o′mər-əl) *n.* A symbol used to denote a number. [< L *numerus,* NUMBER.] —**nu′mer·al** *adj.*

nu·mer·ate (n/y/o͞o′mə-rāt′) *v.* **-ated, -ating.** To enumerate; number; reckon.

nu·mer·a·tor (n/y/o͞o′mə-rā′tər) *n.* The expression written above the line in a common fraction.

nu·mer·i·cal (n/y/o͞o-mĕr′ĭ-kəl) *adj.* Also **nu·mer·ic** (n/y/o͞o-mĕr′ĭk). **1.** Pertaining to a number or series of numbers. **2.** Expressed in or counted by numbers. —**nu·mer′i·cal·ly** *adv.*

nu·mer·ol·o·gy (n/y/o͞o′mə-rŏl′ə-jē) *n.* The study of the occult meanings of numbers.

nu·mer·ous (n/y/o͞o′mər-əs) *adj.* **1.** Consisting of many persons or things: *a numerous collection.* **2.** Many: *numerous books.* —**nu′mer·ous·ly** *adv.* —**nu′mer·ous·ness** *n.*

nu·mis·mat·ics (n/y/o͞o′mĭz-măt′ĭks, n/y/o͞o′mĭs-) *n. (takes sing. v.).* The study and collection of money and medals. [< Gk *nomisma,* usage, current coin.] —**nu·mis′ma·tist** *n.*

num·skull (nŭm′skŭl′) *n.* A stupid person; blockhead.

nun[1] (nŭn) *n.* A woman who belongs to a religious order, usually under vows of poverty, chastity, and obedience. [< ML *nonna.*]

nun[2] (no͞on, no͞on) *n.* The 14th letter of the Hebrew alphabet, representing *n.*

nun·ci·o (nŭn′sē-ō′, no͞on′-) *n., pl.* **-os.** An ambassador from the pope. [< L *nūntius,* messenger.]

nun·ner·y (nŭn′ə-rē) *n., pl.* **-ies.** A community of nuns or the buildings in which they live.

nup·tial (nŭp′shəl, -chəl) *adj.* Pertaining to marriage or the wedding ceremony. —*n.* Often **nuptials.** A wedding ceremony. [L *nuptiālis.*] —**nup′tial·ly** *adv.*

nurse (nûrs) *n.* **1.** A person trained to care for the sick. **2.** A woman employed to take care of another's children. —*v.* **nursed, nursing. 1.** To suckle. **2.** To care for or tend (a child or invalid). **3.** To take special care of; foster. **4.** To bear privately in the mind: *nurse a grudge.* **5.** To hold or clasp carefully. [< L *nutrix,* a nurse.] —**nurs′er** *n.*

nurse·maid (nûrs′mād′) *n.* A woman employed to take care of children.

nurs·er·y (nûr′sə-rē, nûrs′rē) *n.,pl.* **-ies. 1.** A room set apart for the use of children. **2.** A place where plants are grown, esp. for sale.

nurs·er·y·man (nûr′sə-rē-mən, nûrs′rē-) *n.* One who owns or works in a nursery for plants.

nursery school. A school for children not old enough to attend kindergarten.

nurs·ling (nûrs′lĭng) *n.* **1.** A nursing infant or young animal. **2.** A carefully nurtured person or thing.

nur·ture (nûr′chər) *n.* **1.** Anything that nourishes; sustenance; food. **2.** The promotion or influencing of development or growth; upbringing; rearing. —*v.* **-tured, -turing. 1.** To nourish. **2.** To train. [< L *nūtrīre,* to feed, suckle.] —**nur′tur·er** *n.*

nut (nŭt) *n.* **1. a.** A fruit or seed with a hard shell and usually a single kernel. **b.** The kernel itself. **2.** *Slang.* An eccentric or deranged person. **3.** A small block of metal or wood having a central, threaded hole, designed to fit around and secure a bolt or screw. [< OE *hnutu.*]

nut·crack·er (nŭt′krăk′ər) *n.* An implement used to crack nuts.

nut·hatch (nŭt′hăch′) *n.* A small, grayish, sharp-billed bird that climbs up and down tree trunks.

nut·meat (nŭt′mēt′) *n.* The edible kernel of a nut.

nut·meg (nŭt′mĕg′) *n.* The hard, aromatic seed of a tropical tree, grated or ground for use as a spice. [< VL *nuce muscāta, "musky nut."]

nu·tri·a (n/y/ōō'trē-ə) *n.* The thick, brownish fur of a beaverlike South American rodent. [Span.]

nu·tri·ent (n/y/ōō'trē-ənt) *n.* A nourishing ingredient or substance. —*adj.* Having nutritive value. [< L *nūtrīre,* to feed, nourish.]

nu·tri·ment (n/y/ōō'trə-mənt) *n.* Anything that nourishes; food. [< L *nūtrīre,* to feed, nourish.] —**nu'tri·men'tal** (-měn'təl) *adj.*

nu·tri·tion (n/y/ōō-trǐsh'ən) *n.* The process of nourishing, esp. the interrelated steps by which a living organism assimilates and uses food. [< L *nūtrīre,* to feed, nourish.] —**nu·tri'tion·al** *adj.* —**nu·tri'tion·al·ly** *adv.*

nu·tri·tion·ist (n/y/ōō-trǐsh'ən-ǐst) *n.* One who specializes in the study of nutrition.

nu·tri·tious (n/y/ōō-trǐsh'əs) *adj.* Aiding growth and development; nourishing.

nu·tri·tive (n/y/ōō'trə-tǐv) *adj.* Promoting nutrition; nourishing.

nuts (nŭts) *adj. Slang.* **1.** Crazy; insane. **2.** Extremely enthusiastic.

nut·shell (nŭt'shěl') *n.* The shell enclosing the kernel of a nut. —**in a nutshell.** In concise or brief form.

nut·ty (nŭt'ē) *adj.* **-tier, -tiest. 1.** Having a flavor like that of nuts. **2.** *Informal.* Eccentric.

nuz·zle (nŭz'əl) *v.* **-zled, -zling. 1.** To rub or push against gently with the nose or snout. **2.** To nestle or cuddle together. [< NOSE.]

NW northwest.

n.wt. net weight.

N.Y. New York.

N.Y.C. New York City.

nyc·ta·lo·pi·a (nǐk'tə-lō'pē-ə) *n.* Vision that is normal in daylight but abnormally weak when the light is dim.

ny·lon (nī'lŏn') *n.* **1.** Any of a family of high-strength, resilient synthetic materials. **2.** Cloth or yarn made from nylon. **3. nylons.** Stockings made of nylon.

nymph (nǐmf) *n.* **1.** *Gk.&Rom.Myth.* Any of numerous female spirits, inhabiting and animistically representing features of nature. **2.** A young stage of an insect that undergoes incomplete metamorphosis. [< Gk *numphē,* nymph, bride.]

nym·pho·ma·ni·a (nǐm'fə-mā'nē-ə, -mān'yə) *n.* Abnormally strong and uncontrollable sexual desire in women. —**nym'pho·ma'ni·ac'** *adj. & n.*

N.Z. New Zealand.

o, O (ō) *n.* **1.** The 15th letter of the English alphabet. **2.** A zero. **3.** Anything shaped like the letter O; a circle.

O 1. ocean. **2.** order. **3.** oxygen.

O. 1. ocean. **2.** Ohio (unofficial). **3.** order.

O (ō). Used before the substantive in prayer or invocation.

o' (ə, ō) *prep.* A reduced form of the preposition *of* used esp. in the phrase *o'clock* but also found in such terms as *will-o'-the-wisp.*

O'. *comb. form.* A descendant of: *O'Connor.*

oaf (ōf) *n.* A stupid or clumsy person. [< ON *alfr,* elf.] —**oaf'ish** *adj.* —**oaf'ish·ly** *adv.* —**oaf'ish·ness** *n.*

oak (ōk) *n.* **1.** Any of various trees having usually lobed leaves and bearing acorns. **2.** The hard, durable wood of such a tree. [< OE *āc* < Gmc *aik-.*] —**oak'en** *adj.*

Oak·land (ōk'lənd). A city of W California. Pop. 368,000.

oa·kum (ō'kəm) *n.* Loose hemp or jute fiber, sometimes treated with tar, used for caulking ships. [< OE *ācumba,* "off-combings."]

oar (ōr, ôr) *n.* **1.** A long, thin pole with a blade at one end, used to row and, occasionally, steer a boat. **2.** One who rows; rower. [< OE *ār* < Gmc *airo.*] —**oared** *adj.*

oar·lock (ôr'lŏk', ōr'-) *n.* A U-shaped device used to hold an oar in place.

oars·man (ôrz'mən, ōrz'-) *n.* One who rows, esp. an expert in rowing.

OAS Organization of American States.

o·a·sis (ō-ā'sǐs) *n., pl.* **-ses** (-sēz'). A fertile or green spot in a desert or waste. [< Gk.]

oat (ōt) *n.* Often **oats. 1.** A cereal grass widely cultivated for its edible seeds. **2.** The seeds of this plant. [< OE *āte.*] —**oat'en** *adj.*

oath (ōth) *n., pl.* **oaths** (ōthz, ōths). **1.** A formal promise to fulfill a pledge, often calling upon God as witness. **2.** A blasphemous use of a sacred name. [< OE *āth.* See oito-.]

oat·meal (ōt'mēl') *n.* **1.** Meal made by rolling or grinding oats. **2.** Porridge made from this.

Ob (ŏb, ôb). A river of W Siberia.

ob-. *comb. form.* Inverse shape or attachment. [< L, to, toward, in front of, on account of, against.]

ob. 1. incidentally (L *obiter*). **2.** obstetric; obstetrics.

Obad. Obadiah (Old Testament).

ob·bli·ga·to (ŏb'lə-gä'tō) *n., pl.* **-tos.** *Mus.* An accompaniment that is an integral, indispensable part of a piece. [< It *obbligare,* to obligate.]

ob·du·rate (ŏb'd/y/ōō-rǐt) *adj.* Hardened against influence or feeling; unyielding. [< L *obdūrāre,* to harden.] —**ob'du·ra·cy** *n.*

o·be·di·ent (ō-bē'dē-ənt) *adj.* Obeying a re-

ă pat/ā ate/âr care/ä bar/b bib/ch chew/d deed/ě pet/ē be/f fit/g gag/h hat/hw what/
ĭ pit/ī pie/îr pier/j judge/k kick/l lid, fatal/m mum/n no, sudden/ng sing/ŏ pot/ō go/

quest, command, etc.; submissive to control; dutiful. [< L *oboedīre*, OBEY.] —**o•be'di•ence** *n.* —**o•be'di•ent•ly** *adv.*

o•bel•sance (ō-bā'səns, ō-bē'-) *n.* **1.** A gesture, as a bow, expressing respect. **2.** An attitude, as deference, associated with this gesture. [< OF *obeir*, to obey.] —**o•bel'sant** *adj.*

ob•e•lisk (ŏb'ə-lĭsk) *n.* A tall, four-sided shaft of stone, usually tapering to a pyramidal point. [< Gk *obeliskos.*]

o•bese (ō-bēs') *adj.* Extremely fat. [L *obēsus*, "grown fat by eating."] —**o•be'si•ty** *n.*

o•bey (ō-bā') *v.* **1.** To carry out the commands of; behave obediently. **2.** To comply with (a command, order, or request). [< L *oboedīre*, "to listen to."] —**o•bey'er** *n.*

ob•fus•cate (ŏb'fə-skāt', ŏb-fŭs'kāt') *v.* -cated, -cating. **1.** To render indistinct or dim; darken. **2.** To confuse or becloud. [LL *obfuscāre*, to darken.] —**ob'fus•ca'tion** *n.*

o•bit (ō'bĭt, ō-bĭt') *n. Informal.* An obituary.

o•bit•u•ar•y (ō-bĭch'ōō-ĕr'ē) *n., pl.* -ies. A notice of a death, usually with a brief biography. [< L *obīre*, to fall, die.]

obj. *Gram.* object; objective.

ob•ject[1] (əb-jĕkt') *v.* **1.** To present a dissenting or opposing argument. **2.** To feel or express disapproval of something. [< L *objicere*, to throw against, oppose.] —**ob•jec'tion** *n.*

ob•ject[2] (ŏb'jĭkt, -jĕkt') *n.* **1.** Anything perceptible by the senses; a material thing. **2.** *Phil.* Anything intelligible or perceptible by the mind. **3.** Anything serving as a focus of attention or action. **4.** The purpose of a specific action. **5.** *Gram.* A noun that receives or is affected by the action of a verb or that follows and is governed by a preposition. [< L *objectus*, "something thrown before or presented to (the mind)."]

ob•jec•tion•a•ble (əb-jĕk'shən-ə-bəl) *adj.* Arousing disapproval; offensive; unpleasant.

ob•jec•tive (əb-jĕk'tĭv) *adj.* **1.** Of or having to do with a material object as distinguished from a mental concept, idea, or belief. **2.** Having actual existence. **3. a.** Uninfluenced by emotion or personal prejudice. **b.** Based on observable phenomena. **4.** *Gram.* Denoting the case of a noun or pronoun serving as the object of a verb or preposition. **5.** Serving as the goal of a course of action. —*n.* **1.** Something worked toward or striven for; a goal. **2.** *Gram.* The objective case or a noun or pronoun in the objective case. **3.** The lens in an optical system that is closest to the object. —**ob•jec'tive•ly** *adv.* —**ob•jec'tive•ness** *n.* —**ob'jec•tiv'i•ty** (ŏb'jĕk-tĭv'ə-tē) *n.*

ob•jet d'art (ŏb-zhē' där') *pl.* **objets d'art** (ŏb-zhē där'). An object valued for its artistry.

obl. **1.** oblique. **2.** oblong.

ob•late (ŏb'lāt', ŏb-lāt') *adj.* Having an equatorial diameter greater than the distance between poles; compressed along or flattened at the poles. [NL *oblatus*, "carried toward," stretched.]

ob•la•tion (ŏb-lā'shən) *n.* The ritual of offering something to a deity. [< L *oblātus*, "one offered."] —**ob•la'tion•al** *adj.*

ob•li•gate (ŏb'lə-gāt') *v.* -gated, -gating. To

bind, compel, or constrain by a legal or moral tie. [L *obligāre*, to OBLIGE.]

ob•li•ga•tion (ŏb'lə-gā'shən) *n.* **1.** The act of binding oneself by a social, legal, or moral tie. **2.** The contract, promise, etc., that compels one to follow a certain course of action. **3.** The constraining power of a law, promise, contract, or sense of duty. **4.** The state, fact, or condition of being indebted for a favor received.

o•blig•a•to•ry (ə-blĭg'ə-tôr'ē, -tōr'ē, ŏb'lĭ-gə-) *adj.* **1.** Legally or morally constraining. **2.** Compulsory. —**o•blig'a•to'ri•ly** *adv.*

o•blige (ə-blīj') *v.* obliged, obliging. **1.** To constrain by physical, legal, or moral means. **2.** To make indebted for a favor. **3.** To do a service or favor for. [< L *obligāre*, to tie to.] —**o•blig'er** *n.* —**o•blig'ing•ly** *adv.*

o•blique (ō-blēk', ə-) *adj.* **1. a.** Slanting or sloping. **b.** Neither parallel nor perpendicular. **2.** Indirect or evasive in action or expression; not straightforward. [< L *oblīquus*.] —**o•blique'ly** *adv.* —**o•bliq'ui•ty** (-blĭk'wə-tē), **o•blique'ness** *n.*

o•blit•er•ate (ə-blĭt'ə-rāt') *v.* -ated, -ating. **1.** To destroy so as to leave no trace. **2.** To wipe out; erase. [L *obliterāre*, "to strike out words."] —**o•blit'er•a'tion** *n.* —**o•blit'er•a'tor** *n.*

o•bliv•i•on (ə-blĭv'ē-ən) *n.* **1.** The state or condition of being completely forgotten. **2.** Forgetfulness. [< L *oblīviscī*, to forget.]

o•bliv•i•ous (ə-blĭv'ē-əs) *adj.* **1.** Lacking all memory of something; forgetful. **2.** Unaware or unmindful. —**o•bliv'i•ous•ly** *adv.* —**o•bliv'i•ous•ness** *n.*

ob•long (ŏb'lông', -lŏng') *adj.* **1.** Having one of two perpendicular dimensions, as length or width, greater than the other; rectangular. **2.** Elongated. —**ob'long'** *n.*

ob•lo•quy (ŏb'lə-kwē) *n., pl.* -quies. **1.** Abusively detractive language or utterance. **2.** Ill repute or discredit. [< L *obloquī*, to speak against.]

ob•nox•ious (ŏb-nŏk'shəs, əb-) *adj.* Highly disagreeable or offensive; odious. [L *obnoxiōsus*, injurious.] —**ob•nox'ious•ly** *adv.* —**ob•nox'ious•ness** *n.*

o•boe (ō'bō) *n.* A woodwind instrument with a conical bore and a double-reed mouthpiece. [< F *hautbois*, "high wood."] —**o'bo•ist** *n.*

obs. obsolete.

ob•scene (ŏb-sēn', əb-) *adj.* **1.** Offensive to accepted standards of decency. **2.** Inciting lustful feelings. **3.** Offensive to the senses. [L *obscēnus*, ill-boding, repulsive.] —**ob•scene'ly** *adv.* —**ob•scen'i•ty** (-sĕn'ə-tē) *n.*

ob•scur•ant•ism (ŏb-skyōōr'ən-tĭz'əm, əb-, ŏb'skyōō-răn'tĭz'əm) *n.* **1.** Deliberate abstruseness. **2.** Opposition to the diffusion of enlightenment. —**ob•scur'ant•ist** *n.* & *adj.*

ob•scure (ŏb-skyōōr', əb-) *adj.* -scurer, -scurest. **1.** Dark; gloomy. **2.** Indistinctly heard or perceived. **3.** Out of sight; hidden. **4.** Inconspicuous. **5.** Difficult to understand. —*v.* -scured, -scuring. **1.** To make indistinct or unclear. **2.** To conceal from view; hide. [< L *obscūrus*.] —**ob•scure'ly** *adv.* —**ob•scu'ri•ty** *n.*

ob•se•qui•ous (ŏb-sē'kwē-əs, əb-) *adj.* Full of

servile compliance; fawning. [< L *obsequī,* to comply with.] —**ob·se′qui·ous·ly** *adv.* —**ob·se′qui·ous·ness** *n.*

ob·se·quy (ŏb′sə-kwē) *n., pl.* -quies. Often obsequies. A funeral rite or ceremony. [< L *obsequium,* compliance, service.]

ob·ser·vance (əb-zûr′vəns) *n.* 1. The act of observing or complying with something prescribed, as a law or custom. 2. The keeping or celebrating of a holiday or other ritual occasion. 3. Observation.

ob·ser·vant (əb-zûr′vənt) *adj.* 1. Quick to perceive or apprehend; alert. 2. Diligent in observing a law, custom, duty, etc.

ob·ser·va·tion (ŏb′zər-vā′shən) *n.* 1. The act or faculty of paying attention or noticing; the fact of being observed. 2. a. The noting and recording of a phenomenon. b. The record of such notation. 3. A comment or remark.

ob·ser·va·to·ry (əb-zûr′və-tôr′ē, -tōr′ē) *n., pl.* -ries. A building equipped for making observations of astronomical, meteorological, or other natural phenomena.

ob·serve (əb-zûrv′) *v.* -served, -serving. 1. To perceive; take notice. 2. To watch attentively. 3. To make a systematic observation of. 4. To say; make a comment. 5. To adhere to or abide by. 6. To keep or pay tribute to (a holiday, rite, etc.). 7. To watch or be present without participating actively. [< L *observāre,* to pay attention to, look to.] —**ob·serv′a·ble** *adj.* —**ob·serv′er** *n.*

ob·sess (əb-sĕs′, ŏb-) *v.* To haunt as a fixed idea. [L *obsidēre* (pp *obsessus*), to sit down before, besiege.] —**ob·ses′sive** *adj.*

ob·ses·sion (əb-sĕsh′ən, ŏb-) *n.* 1. Compulsive preoccupation with a fixed idea or unwanted feeling. 2. An idea or emotion causing such preoccupation. —**ob·ses′sion·al** *adj.*

ob·sid·i·an (ŏb-sĭd′ē-ən) *n.* An acid-resistant, lustrous volcanic glass, usually black or banded. [L *obsidiānus.*]

ob·so·les·cent (ŏb′sə-lĕs′ənt) *adj.* Becoming obsolete. [< L *obsolēscere,* to grow old.] —**ob′so·les′cence** *n.* —**ob′so·les′cent·ly** *adv.*

ob·so·lete (ŏb′sə-lēt′, ŏb′sə-lēt′) *adj.* 1. No longer in use or fashion. 2. No longer useful or functioning. [< L **obsolēre,* to be old or in disuse.] —**ob′so·lete′ly** *adv.*

ob·sta·cle (ŏb′stə-kəl) *n.* One that opposes, stands in the way of, or holds up progress toward some goal. [< L *obstāre,* to hinder.]

ob·ste·tri·cian (ŏb′stə-trĭsh′ən) *n.* A physician specializing in obstetrics.

ob·stet·rics (ŏb-stĕt′rĭks, əb-) *n. (takes sing. or pl. v.).* The branch of medicine concerned with the care of women during pregnancy, childbirth, and the period following delivery. [< L *obstetrīx,* midwife.] —**ob·stet′ric** *adj.*

ob·sti·nate (ŏb′stə-nĭt) *adj.* 1. Stubbornly adhering to an idea or course; inflexible. 2. Difficult to control or subdue. [< L *obstināre,* to persist.] —**ob′sti·na·cy** (-nə-sē), **ob′sti·nate·ness** *n.* —**ob′sti·nate·ly** *adv.*

ob·strep·er·ous (ŏb-strĕp′ər-əs, əb-) *adj.* Noisily defiant; unruly. [< L *obstrepere,* to make noise against.] —**ob·strep′er·ous·ness** *n.*

ob·struct (əb-strŭkt′, ŏb-) *v.* 1. To block (a passage) with obstacles. 2. To impede or retard. 3. To get in the way of; hide, as a view. [< L *obstruere* (pp *obstructus*).] —**ob·struct′er** *n.* —**ob·struc′tor** *n.* —**ob·struc′tive** *adj.*

ob·struc·tion (əb-strŭk′shən, ŏb-) *n.* 1. An obstacle. 2. An act or instance of obstructing. 3. The causing of delay.

ob·struc·tion·ist (əb-strŭk′shən-ĭst, ŏb-) *n.* One who systematically obstructs or interrupts progress. —**ob·struc′tion·ism′** *n.*

ob·tain (əb-tān′, ŏb-) *v.* 1. To succeed in gaining; get or acquire. 2. To be established or accepted: *Certain customs still obtain.* [< L *obtinēre,* attain.] —**ob·tain′a·ble** *adj.*

ob·trude (ŏb-trōōd′, əb-) *v.* -truded, -truding. 1. To force (oneself or one's ideas) upon others. 2. To thrust out; push forward. [L *obtrūdere.*] —**ob·tru′sion** (-trōō′zhən) *n.* —**ob·tru′sive** (-trōō′sĭv) *adj.*

ob·tuse (ŏb-t/y/ōōs′, əb-) *adj.* 1. Not sharp, pointed, or acute; blunt. 2. Slow to apprehend or perceive. [L *obtūsus,* pp of *obtundere,* to blunt.] —**ob·tuse′ly** *adv.* —**ob·tuse′ness** *n.*

obtuse angle. An angle greater than 90° and less than 180°.

ob·verse (ŏb-vûrs′, ŏb′vûrs′) *adj.* 1. Facing the observer. 2. Serving as a counterpart or complement. —*n.* (ŏb′vûrs′, ŏb-vûrs′). 1. The side of a coin or medal that bears the principal stamp or design and, on U.S. coins, the date. 2. A counterpart or complement. [< L *obvertere,* to turn toward.]

ob·vi·ate (ŏb′vē-āt′) *v.* -ated, -ating. To prevent or dispose of effectively; anticipate so as to render unnecessary. [LL *obviare,* "to meet in the way," prevent.] —**ob′vi·a′tion** *n.*

ob·vi·ous (ŏb′vē-əs) *adj.* 1. Easily perceived or understood. 2. Easily seen through; lacking subtlety. [< L *obviam,* in the way.] —**ob′vi·ous·ly** *adv.* —**ob′vi·ous·ness** *n.*

oc·a·ri·na (ŏk′ə-rē′nə) *n.* A small terra-cotta or plastic wind instrument with a mouthpiece, finger holes, and a bulbous shape. [It, "little goose."]

OCAS Organization of Central American States.

occ. occupation.

oc·ca·sion (ə-kā′zhən) *n.* 1. An event or happening, esp. a significant event. 2. The time of an occurrence. 3. A favorable time; opportunity. 4. That which brings on an action. 5. Ground; reason. 6. Need; necessity. —*v.* To provide occasion for. [< L *occāsiō,* "a falling down, happening."]

oc·ca·sion·al (ə-kā′zhən-əl) *adj.* 1. Occurring from time to time. 2. Occurring, used on, or created for a special occasion. —**oc·ca′sion·al·ly** *adv.*

Oc·ci·dent (ŏk′sə-dənt, -dĕnt′) *n.* Europe and the W Hemisphere. [< L *occidēns,* "quarter of the setting sun," west.]

Oc·ci·den·tal (ŏk′sə-dĕn′təl) *adj.* Pertaining to the Occident. —*n.* An inhabitant of the Occident.

oc·clude (ə-klōōd′) *v.* -cluded, -cluding. 1. To close or shut off; obstruct. 2. To make contact at opposing surfaces. 3. *Chem.* To absorb or adsorb. [L *occlūdere.*] —**oc·clu′sion** *n.*

ă pat/ā ate/âr care/ä bar/b **bib**/ch **chew**/d **deed**/ĕ pet/ē be/f **fit**/g **gag**/h **hat**/hw **what**/ ĭ pit/ī pie/îr **pier**/j **judge**/k **kick**/l lid, fatal/m **mum**/n no, sudden/ng sing/ŏ pot/ō go/

oc•cult (ə-kŭlt′, ŏ-kŭlt′, ŏk′ŭlt′) *adj.* **1.** Of or relating to supernatural influences, agencies, or phenomena. **2.** Beyond human comprehension. **3.** Available only to the initiate; secret. [< L *occulere*, to conceal.]

oc•cu•pan•cy (ŏk′yə-pən-sē) *n., pl.* **-cies. 1.** The act of occupying or condition of being occupied; occupation. **2.** The period during which one owns, rents, or uses premises or land.

oc•cu•pant (ŏk′yə-pənt) *n.* **1.** One who occupies a position or place. **2.** A tenant or an owner of premises.

oc•cu•pa•tion (ŏk′yə-pā′shən) *n.* **1.** An activity that serves as one's regular source of livelihood. **2.** The act of occupying or state of being occupied. **3.** The invasion, conquest, and control of a nation or territory by a foreign military force. —**oc′cu•pa′tion•al** *adj.*

occupational therapy. Therapy in which the principal element is some form of productive or creative activity.

oc•cu•py (ŏk′yə-pī′) *v.* **-pied, -pying. 1.** To seize possession of and maintain control over (a place or region). **2.** To fill or take (time or space). **3.** To dwell or reside in. **4.** To hold or fill (an office). **5.** To engage or busy (oneself). [< L *occupāre*, to seize.]

oc•cur (ə-kûr′) *v.* **-curred, -curring. 1.** To take place. **2.** To be found to exist or appear. **3.** To come to mind. [L *occurrere*, to run to meet.]

oc•cur•rence (ə-kûr′əns) *n.* **1.** An act or instance of occurring. **2.** Something that takes place. —**oc•cur′rent** *adj.*

OCD Office of Civil Defense.

o•cean (ō′shən) *n.* **1.** The entire body of salt water that covers about 72% of the earth's surface. **2.** Often **Ocean.** Any of the principal divisions of this body of water, including the Atlantic, Pacific, and Indian oceans, their southern extensions in Antarctica, and the Arctic Ocean. **3.** A great expanse or amount. [< Gk *Ōkeanos,* god of the outer sea encircling the earth.] —**o′ce•an′ic** (ō′shē-ăn′ĭk) *adj.*

o•cean•og•ra•phy (ō′shə-nŏg′rə-fē) *n.* The exploration and scientific study of the ocean. —**o′cean•og′ra•pher** *n.*

oc•e•lot (ŏs′ə-lŏt′, ō′sə-) *n.* A spotted wild cat of the SW U.S. and Central and South America. [< Nah *ocelotl.*]

o•cher (ō′kər) *n.* Also **o•chre. 1.** Any of several earthy mineral oxides of iron mingled with varying amounts of clay and sand, occurring in yellow, brown, or red, and used as pigments. **2.** Moderate orange yellow. [< Gk *ōkhros,* yellow.]

o'clock (ə-klŏk′) *adv.* Of or according to the clock: *three o'clock.* [< *of the clock.*]

OCS Officer Candidate School.

oct. octavo.

Oct. October.

oc•ta•gon (ŏk′tə-gŏn′) *n.* A polygon with eight sides. [< Gk *oktagōnos,* having eight angles.] —**oc′tag′o•nal** (ŏk-tăg′ə-nəl) *adj.*

oc•ta•he•dron (ŏk′tə-hē′drən) *n., pl.* **-drons** or **-dra** (-drə). A polyhedron with eight surfaces. —**oc′ta•he′dral** (-drəl) *adj.*

oc•tane (ŏk′tān′) *n.* **1.** Any of various hydrocarbons with the formula C_8H_{18}. **2.** Also **octane number.** A numerical measure of the antiknock properties of motor fuel, based on the percentage by volume of one particular octane in a standard reference fuel.

oc•tant (ŏk′tənt) *n.* One-eighth of a circle or of an arc of a circle. [< L *octō,* eight.]

oc•tave (ŏk′tĭv, -tāv′) *n.* **1.** The interval of eight diatonic degrees between two musical tones. **2.** Any group or series of eight. [< L *octō,* eight.]

oc•ta•vo (ŏk-tā′vō, -tä′vō) *n., pl.* **-vos. 1.** The page size (from 5×8 to $6 \times 9\frac{1}{2}$ inches) of a book composed of printer's sheets folded into eight leaves. **2.** A book composed of pages of this size. [L (*in*) *octāvō,* "in eighth."]

oc•tet (ŏk-tĕt′) *n.* Also **oc•tette. 1.** A musical composition written for eight voices or instruments. **2.** Any group of eight. [< It *otto,* eight.]

octo– *comb. form.* Eight. [< L *octō,* eight, and < Gk *oktō,* eight.]

Oc•to•ber (ŏk-tō′bər) *n.* The 10th month of the year. October has 31 days. [< L *Octōber,* "eighth month."]

oc•to•ge•nar•i•an (ŏk′tə-jə-nâr′ē-ən) *n.* Someone between eighty and ninety years of age. [< L *octōgintā,* eighty.]

oc•to•pus (ŏk′tə-pəs) *n., pl.* **-puses** or **-pi** (-pī′). A marine mollusk with a rounded, saclike body and eight sucker-bearing tentacles. [< Gk *oktōpous,* eight-footed.]

oc•to•roon (ŏk′tə-rōōn′) *n.* A person who is one-eighth Negro.

oc•u•lar (ŏk′yə-lər) *adj.* **1.** Pertaining to the eye. **2.** Visual. —*n.* The eyepiece of an optical instrument. [< L *oculus,* eye.]

oc•u•list (ŏk′yə-lĭst) *n.* **1.** A physician who treats diseases of the eyes; an ophthalmologist. **2.** An optometrist.

O.D. 1. Doctor of Optometry. **2.** officer of the day. **3.** overdraft. **4.** overdrawn.

odd (ŏd) *adj.* **1. a.** Strange; unusual. **b.** Queer or eccentric in conduct. **2.** In addition to or in excess of what is usual, regular, or approximated: *odd jobs; 40-odd persons.* **3.** Being one of an incomplete pair or sct; extra. **4.** Not divisible by two. [< ON *oddi,* triangle, third, odd number.] —**odd′ly** *adv.*

odd•i•ty (ŏd′ə-tē) *n., pl.* **-ties. 1.** One that is odd. **2.** The state or quality of being odd.

odd•ment (ŏd′mənt) *n.* Something left over.

odds (ŏdz) *pl.n.* **1.** An advantage given to a weaker side in a contest to equalize the chances of the participants. **2.** A ratio expressing the probability of an event or outcome. —**at odds.** In disagreement.

odds and ends. Miscellaneous items.

ode (ōd) *n.* A lyric poem often addressed to some praised object or person and characterized by exalted style. [< Gk *ōidē, aoidē,* song.]

–ode. *comb. form.* A way or path: *cathode.* [< Gk *hodos,* a way.]

O•des•sa (ō-dĕs′ə). A city of the SW Soviet Union. Pop. 735,000.

O•din (ō′dĭn). Supreme god of the Norse pantheon.

ô paw, for/oi boy/ou out/ōō took/ōō coo/p pop/r run/s sauce/sh shy/t to/th thin/*th* the/ ŭ cut/ûr fur/v van/w wag/y yes/z size/zh vision/ə ago, item, edible, gallop, circus/

o·di·ous (ō′dē-əs) *adj.* Offensive; hateful; repugnant. [< L *odium,* ODIUM.] —**o′di·ous·ly** *adv.* —**o′di·ous·ness** *n.*

o·di·um (ō′dē-əm) *n.* **1.** The state or quality of being odious. **2.** Disgrace resulting from hateful conduct. [L, hatred.]

o·dom·e·ter (ō-dŏm′ə-tər) *n.* An instrument that indicates distance traveled by a vehicle. [< Gk *hodos,* road, journey + *metron,* METER.]

o·dor (ō′dər) *n.* Also *chiefly Brit.* **o·dour.** **1.** The property or quality of a thing that stimulates or is perceived by the sense of smell. **2.** Esteem; repute. [< L.] —**o′dor·less** *adj.* —**o′dor·ous** *adj.*

o·dor·if·er·ous (ō′də-rĭf′ər-əs) *adj.* Having or giving off an odor.

O·dys·seus (ō-dĭs′yōōs′, ō-dĭs′ē-əs). The hero of Homer's *Odyssey.*

od·ys·sey (ŏd′ə-sē) *n.* An extended adventurous wandering. [< Homer's *Odyssey,* which recounted the wanderings of Odysseus.]

OE Old English

OED, O.E.D. Oxford English Dictionary.

Oed·i·pus complex (ĕd′ə-pəs, ē′də-). Libidinal feelings in a male child for the mother, often accompanied by hostility to the father. [< *Oedipus,* mythical Greek king who unwittingly killed his father and married his mother.]

OEO Office of Economic Opportunity.

o′er. *Poetic.* Contraction of **over.**

of (ŭv; *unstressed* əv) *prep.* **1.** From. **2.** Owing to. **3.** Away from. **4.** So as to be separated or relieved from: *robbed of his dignity.* **5.** From the total or group comprising. **6.** Composed or made from. **7.** Associated with or adhering to. **8.** Belonging or connected to. **9.** Possessing; having: *a man of honor.* **10.** Containing or carrying. **11.** Specified as; named or called: *a depth of ten feet; the Garden of Eden.* **12.** Centering on or directed toward. **13.** Produced by; issuing from. **14.** Characterized or identified by. **15.** With reference to; about. **16.** Set aside for; taken up by: *a day of rest.* **17.** Before; until: *five minutes of two.* **18.** During or on (a specified time): *of recent years.* [< OE. See apo-.]

off (ŏf, ôf) *adv.* **1.** At or to a distance from a nearer place. **2.** Distant in time. **3.** So as to be unattached, disconnected, or removed. **4.** So as to be smaller, fewer, or less. **5.** So as to be away from work or duty. —*adj.* **1.** More distant or removed. **2.** Not on, attached, or connected. **3.** Not continuing, operating, or functioning. **4.** No longer existing or effective; canceled. **5.** Fewer, smaller, or less. **6.** Inferior. **7.** In a specified condition: *well off.* **8.** In error. **9.** Absent or away from work or duty: *He's off Tuesday.* —*prep.* **1.** So as to be removed or distant from. **2.** Away or relieved from: *off duty.* **3. a.** By consuming: *living off honey.* **b.** With the means provided by: *living off his pension.* **4.** Extending or branching out from: *an artery off the heart.* **5.** Below the usual level of: *off his game.* **6.** Abstaining from. **7.** Seaward of: *a mile off Sandy Hook.* [< OE *of.* See apo-.]

off. office; officer; official.

of·fal (ô′fəl, ŏf′əl) *n.* **1.** Waste parts, esp. of a butchered animal. **2.** Refuse; rubbish. [< MDu *afval,* "that which falls off," refuse.]

off·beat (ôf′bēt′, ŏf′-) *n.* An unaccented beat in a musical measure. —*adj.* (ôf′bēt′, ŏf′-). *Slang.* Unconventional.

off-col·or (ôf′kŭl′ər, ŏf′-) *adj.* **1.** Varying from the expected or required color. **2.** In bad taste: *an off-color joke.* **3.** *Chiefly Brit.* Not in good health.

of·fend (ə-fĕnd′) *v.* **1.** To create anger, resentment, or annoyance in; affront. **2.** To be displeasing or disagreeable (to). **3.** To sin. [< L *offendere,* to strike against.] —**of·fend′er** *n.*

of·fense (ə-fĕns′) *n.* Also *chiefly Brit.* **of·fence.** **1.** The act of offending. **2. a.** Any violation of a moral or social code. **b.** A crime. **3.** (ŏf′ĕns′). The act of attacking or assaulting. —**take offense.** To become displeased or resentful. —**of·fen′sive** *adj.* —**of·fen′sive·ly** *adv.* —**of·fen′sive·ness** *n.*

of·fer (ô′fər, ŏf′ər) *v.* **1.** To present for acceptance or rejection. **2.** To present for sale. **3.** To propose as payment; bid. **4.** To present as an act of worship. **5.** To volunteer. **6.** To provide; furnish; afford. **7.** To produce or introduce on the stage. [< L *offerre.*] —**of′fer** *n.* —**of′fer·er, of′fer·or** *n.*

of·fer·ing (ô′fər-ĭng, ŏf′ər-) *n.* **1.** The act of making an offer. **2.** Something offered. **3.** A presentation made to a deity as an act of worship or sacrifice. **4.** A contribution, esp. at a religious service.

of·fer·to·ry (ô′fər-tôr′ē, -tōr′ē, ŏf′ər-) *n., pl.* **-ries.** **1.** Often **Offertory.** The part of the Eucharistic liturgy at which bread and wine are offered by the celebrant. **2.** The collection of offerings at a church service.

off·hand (ôf′hănd′, ŏf′-) *adv. & adj.* Without preparation or forethought; impromptu.

of·fice (ô′fĭs, ŏf′ĭs) *n.* **1. a.** A place in which services, clerical work, professional duties, etc., are carried out. **b.** The staff working in such a place. **2.** A duty or function assigned to or assumed by someone. **3.** A position of authority given to a person, as in a government or other organization. **4.** A branch of the Federal government of the U.S. ranking just below a department. **5.** A public position: *seek office.* **6.** Often **offices.** A favor. **7.** *Eccles.* A ceremony, usually prescribed by liturgy, esp. a rite for the dead. [< L *officium,* performance of duty.]

of·fice·hold·er (ô′fĭs-hōl′dər, ŏf′ĭs-) *n.* One who holds a public office.

of·fi·cer (ô′fĭ-sər, ŏf′ĭ-) *n.* **1.** One who holds an office of authority or trust in a corporation, government, or other institution. **2.** One holding a commission in the armed forces. **3.** A man licensed in the merchant marine as master, mate, chief engineer, or assistant engineer. **4.** A policeman.

of·fi·cial (ə-fĭsh′əl) *adj.* **1.** Of, pertaining to, or authorized by a proper authority; authoritative. **2.** Formal or ceremonious: *an official banquet.* —*n.* One who holds an office or position. —**of·fi′cial·dom** *n.* —**of·fi′cial·ly** *adv.*

of·fi·cial·ism (ə-fĭsh′ə-lĭz′əm) *n.* Rigid adher-

---

ence to official regulations, forms, and procedures.

of•fi•ci•ant (ə-fĭsh′ē-ənt) *n. Eccles.* The celebrant at a religious service.

of•fi•ci•ate (ə-fĭsh′ē-āt′) *v.* **-ated, -ating.** To perform the duties and functions of an office or position of authority, esp. as a priest or minister at a religious service.

of•fi•cious (ə-fĭsh′əs) *adj.* Excessively forward in offering one's services or advice to others. [< L *officium,* duty, service, OFFICE.] **—of•fi′cious•ly** *adv.* **—of•fi′cious•ness** *n.*

off•ing (ô′fĭng, ŏf′ĭng) *n.* The part of the sea that is visible from the shore. **—in the offing.** In the near or immediate future. [< OFF.]

off•ish (ô′fĭsh, ŏf′ĭsh) *adj.* Inclined to be reserved in manner; aloof. **—off′ish•ness** *n.*

off•set (ôf′sĕt′, ŏf′-) *n.* **1.** Something that balances, counteracts, or compensates. **2.** A ledge or recess in a wall. **3.** A bend in a pipe or bar to allow it to pass around an obstruction. **4.** Printing by indirect image transfer. *—v.* (ôf′sĕt′, ŏf′-) **-set, -setting. 1.** To counterbalance, counteract, or compensate for. **2.** To print by offset. **3.** To make or form an offset in (a wall, bar, or pipe). **—off′set′** *adj.*

off•shoot (ôf′shōōt′, ŏf′-) *n.* Something that branches out or originates from a particular source, as a shoot from a plant stem.

off•shore (ôf′shôr′, -shōr′, ŏf′-) *adj.* **1.** Moving or directed away from the shore. **2.** Located or occurring at a distance from the shore. **—off′shore′** *adv.*

off•spring (ôf′sprĭng′, ŏf′-) *n., pl.* **-spring.** Progeny; young.

off-stage (ôf′stāj′, ŏf′-) *adj. & adv.* Away from the area of a stage visible to the audience.

off-the-rec•ord (ôf′thə-rĕk′ərd, ŏf′-) *adj.* Not intended for publication, not to be repeated. **—off′-the-rec′ord** *adv.*

oft (ôft, ŏft) *adv. Poetic.* Often. [< OE *oft.* See **op-.**]

of•ten (ô′fən, ŏf′ən) *adv.* Frequently; repeatedly. [< OFT.]

of•ten•times (ô′fən-tīmz′, ŏf′ən-) *adv.* Often.

o•gle (ō′gəl, ô′-) *v.* **ogled, ogling. 1.** To stare at. **2.** To stare in an impertinent or amorous manner. [Prob < LG *oegeln.*] **—o′gle** *n.*

o•gre (ō′gər) *n.* **1.** A fabled man-eating giant or monster. **2.** Anyone who is esp. cruel or hideous. [F.] **—o′gress** (ō′grĭs) *fem.n.*

oh (ō) *interj.* Expressive of strong emotion, as surprise, fear, etc. *—n., pl.* **oh's** or **ohs.** The exclamation *oh.*

O•hi•o (ō-hī′ō). A state of the C U.S. Pop. 10,652,000. Cap. Columbus. **—O•hi′o•an** *n.*

Ohio River. A river of the C U.S.

ohm (ōm) *n.* A unit of electrical resistance equal to that of a conductor in which a current of one ampere is produced by a potential of one volt across its terminals. [< G. *Ohm* (1787–1854), German physicist.]

o•ho (ō-hō′) *interj.* Expressive of surprise or mock astonishment.

–old. *comb. form.* Likeness, resemblance, or similarity to: **planetoid.** [< Gk *eidos,* form, shape.]

oil (oil) *n.* **1.** Any of numerous mineral, vege-

table, and synthetic substances and animal and vegetable fats, that are generally slippery, combustible, viscous, liquid or liquefiable at room temperatures, soluble in various organic solvents, such as ether, but not in water, and used in a great variety of products, esp. lubricants and fuels. **2.** Petroleum. **3.** Any substance with an oily consistency. **4.** An **oil color. 5.** An **oil painting. 6.** *Informal.* Insincere flattery. *—v.* **1.** To lubricate, supply, cover, or polish with oil. **2.** To load up with or take on fuel oil. **3.** To become oil by melting. [< L *oleum.*] **—oil** *adj.*

oil•cloth (oil′klôth′, -klŏth′) *n.* A fabric treated with clay, oil, and pigments to make it waterproof.

oil color. A color consisting of pigment ground in oil, usually linseed, used in oil painting.

oil paint. Any paint in which the vehicle is a drying oil.

oil painting. 1. A painting in oil colors. **2.** The art of painting with oil colors.

oil•skin (oil′skĭn′) *n.* **1.** Cloth treated with oil so that it is waterproof. **2.** A garment made of this material.

oil well. A hole dug or drilled in the earth to obtain petroleum.

oil•y (oi′lē) *adj.* **-ier, -iest. 1.** Of, pertaining to, or smeared with oil; greasy. **2.** Unctuous.

oint•ment (oint′mənt) *n.* Any of numerous highly viscous or semisolid substances used on the skin for cosmetic or medical purposes. [< L *unguere,* to anoint.]

O•jib•wa (ō-jĭb′wä′, -wə) *n., pl.* **-wa** or **-was.** Also **O•jib•way** (ō-jĭb′wä′) *pl.* **-way** or **-ways. 1.** A member of a tribe of Algonquian-speaking North American Indians inhabiting regions of the U.S. and Canada around Lake Superior. **2.** The language of this tribe.

O.K., OK, o•kay (ō-kā′) *n., pl.* **O.K.'s** or **OK's** or **okays.** *Informal.* Approval; endorsement; agreement. *—v.* **O.K.'d** or **OK'd** or **okayed, O.K.'ing** or **OK'ing** or **okaying.** To approve or endorse by signing with an O.K.; agree to. *—interj.* Expressive of approval or agreement. **—O.K.** *adj. & adv.*

Usage: O.K. (or *OK*) is especially appropriate to business correspondence and informal speech and writing and is usually inappropriate to expressly formal usage. In written usage, it is generally most acceptable when used as a noun or verb, not as an adjective or adverb.

O•ki•na•wa (ō′kĭ-nä′wə). The largest of the Ryukyu Islands, off the S tip of Japan. Pop. 759,000.

O•kla•ho•ma (ō′klə-hō′mə). A state of the SW U.S. Pop. 2,559,000. Cap. Oklahoma City. **—O′kla•ho′man** *adj. & n.*

Oklahoma City. The capital of Oklahoma. Pop. 366,000.

o•kra (ō′krə) *n.* **1.** A tall plant with edible, mucilaginous green pods. **2.** The pods of this plant, used esp. in soups. [West African native name *nkruma.*]

–ol. *comb. form. Chem.* Alcohol or phenol: **menthol.** [< ALCOHOL.]

old (ōld) *adj.* **older** or **elder, oldest** or **eldest.**

ō paw, for/oi boy/ou out/ōō took/ōō coo/p pop/r run/s sauce/sh shy/t to/th thin/*th* the/
ŭ cut/ûr fur/v van/w wag/y yes/z size/zh vision/ə ago, item, edible, gallop, circus/

1. Having lived or existed for a relatively long time; far advanced in years or life. 2. Made long ago; ancient. 3. Characteristic of an aged person. 4. Mature; sensible. 5. Having a specified age: *She was two years old.* 6. Of an earlier time: *his old classmates.* 7. Worn-out. 8. Dear or cherished through long acquaintance: *good old Harry.* —*n.* Former times; yore: *in days of old.* [< OE *eald, ald.* See al-².] —**old′ness** *n.*

Old Church Sla•von•ic (slə-vŏn′ĭk). The literary language of the oldest Slavic manuscripts (10th or early 11th century).

old•en (ōl′dən) *adj. Archaic & Poetic.* Old.

Old English. English from about 700 to 1150; Anglo-Saxon.

old fashioned. A cocktail made of whiskey, bitters, sugar, and fruit.

old-fash•ioned (ōld′făsh′ənd) *adj.* Outdated.

old fogy. Also **old fogey.** One who is tiresomely conservative or old-fashioned.

Old French. French from about 800 to 1500.

Old High German. High German from about 850 to 1100.

Old Iranian. Iranian before the Christian era.

Old Irish. Irish from 725 to 950.

Old Italian. Italian before 1550.

old-line (ōld′lĭn′) *adj.* 1. Conservative or reactionary. 2. Traditional.

old maid. 1. An unmarried older woman; a spinster. 2. A primly fastidious person.

Old Norse. The North Germanic language from which the modern Scandinavian languages are descended.

Old North French. The northern dialect of Old French.

Old Persian. An ancient form of Persian, recorded in inscriptions from the sixth to the fifth century B.C.

Old Provençal. Provençal before 1550.

Old Prussian. The Baltic language of the Prussians, which became extinct in the 18th century.

Old Saxon. Low German from about 850 to 1250.

old school. Any group committed to traditional ideas or practices. —**old′-school′** *adj.*

Old Spanish. Spanish before 1550.

old•ster (ōld′stər) *n.* An old or elderly person.

Old Testament. 1. The first of the two main divisions of the Christian Bible, containing the Hebrew Scriptures. 2. The covenant of God with Israel as distinguished in Christianity from the dispensation of Christ constituting the New Testament.

old-tim•er (ōld′tī′mər) *n. Informal.* 1. One who has been a resident, member, employee, etc., for a long time. 2. Something very old or antiquated.

Old World. The E Hemisphere, esp. Europe.

old-world (ōld′wûrld′) *adj.* 1. Antique; old-fashioned; quaint. 2. Often **Old-World.** Native or pertaining to the E Hemisphere, or Old World.

o•le•an•der (ō′lē-ăn′dər, ō′lē-ăn′dər) *n.* A poisonous, chiefly tropical shrub with clusters of white or reddish flowers. [ML.]

o•le•ic acid (ō-lē′ĭk). An oily liquid, CH₃(CH₂)₇CH:CH(CH₂)₇COOH, occurring in animal and vegetable oils.

$CH_3(CH_2)_7CH:CH(CH_2)_7COOH$

oleo–. *comb. form.* Oil or pertaining to oil. [< L *oleum,* (olive) oil.]

o•le•o•mar•ga•rine (ō′lē-ō-mär′jə-rĭn, -gə-rĭn, -rēn′) *n.* Margarine.

ol•fac•to•ry (ŏl-făk′tər-ē, -trē, ōl-) *adj.* Of or contributing to the sense of smell. [< L *olfacere,* to smell.]

ol•i•gar•chy (ŏl′ə-gär′kē) *n., pl.* **-chies.** 1. a. Government by the few, esp. by a small faction. b. Those making up such a faction. 2. A state so governed. —**ol′i•garch′** *n.* —**ol′i•gar′chic, ol′i•gar′chi•cal** *adj.*

oligo–. *comb. form.* Few. [< Gk *oligos,* few, little.]

Ol•i•go•cene (ŏl′ĭ-gō-sēn′) *adj.* Of or belonging to the geologic time, rock series, or sedimentary deposits of the third epoch of the Tertiary period. —*n.* The Oligocene epoch.

ol•ive (ŏl′ĭv) *n.* 1. The small, edible ovoid fruit of an Old World tree, pressed to extract a yellowish oil, olive oil, used in cooking. 2. A tree bearing such fruit. 3. Dull yellowish green. [< L *oliva* < Gk *elaia.*] —**ol′ive** *adj.*

O•lym•pi•a (ō-lĭm′pē-ə). The capital of the state of Washington. Pop. 23,000.

O•lym•pic games (ō-lĭm′pĭk). 1. An ancient Greek festival of athletic games and other contests. 2. An international athletic contest held every four years.

O•lym•pus (ō-lĭm′pəs). A mountain of Greece, the abode of the gods in ancient mythology.

—oma. *comb. form.* Tumor: melanoma. [< Gk -ōma, abstract nominal ending.]

O•ma•ha (ō′mə-hô′, -hä′). A city in E Nebraska. Pop. 347,000.

O•man (ō-män′). A sultanate of the E Arabian peninsula. Pop. 750,000. Cap. Muscat.

om•buds•man (ŏm′bŭdz-mən) *n.* A government official who investigates citizens' complaints. [Norw.]

o•me•ga (ō-mĕg′ə, ō-mē′gə, ō-mā′-) *n.* The 24th and final letter of the Greek alphabet, representing long *o.* [Gk *ō mega,* "large o."]

om•e•let (ŏm′lĭt, ŏm′ə-lĭt) *n.* Also **om•e•lette.** A dish consisting of beaten eggs cooked and folded, often around a filling. [< L *lamella,* thin metal plate.]

o•men (ō′mən) *n.* 1. A prophetic sign. 2. Portent: *birds of ill omen.* [L *ōmen.*]

om•i•cron (ŏm′ə-krŏn′, ō′mə-) *n.* The 15th letter of the Greek alphabet, representing *o.* [Gk *o mikron,* "small o."]

om•i•nous (ŏm′ə-nəs) *adj.* 1. Being or pertaining to an evil omen; foreboding; portentous. 2. Menacing; threatening. —**om′i•nous•ly** *adv.* —**om′i•nous•ness** *n.*

o•mit (ō-mĭt′) *v.* **omitted, omitting.** 1. To leave out; fail to include. 2. To neglect; fail (to do). [< L *omittere.*] —**o•mis′sion** (-mĭsh′ən) *n.*

omni–. *comb. form.* All. [< L *omnis,* all.]

om•ni•bus (ŏm′nĭ-bŭs′) *n., pl.* **-buses.** A bus. —*adj.* Including many things or classes; covering many situations at once. [< L, "for all."]

om•nip•o•tent (ŏm-nĭp′ə-tənt) *adj.* Having unlimited power, authority, or force; all-powerful. —*n.* **the Omnipotent.** God. —**om•nip'o•tence** *n.* —**om•nip'o•tent•ly** *adv.*

om•ni•pres•ence (ŏm'nĭ-prĕz'əns) *n.* The fact of being present everywhere. —**om'ni•pres'ent** *adj.*

om•nis•cient (ŏm-nĭsh'ənt) *adj.* Having total knowledge; knowing everything. [ML *omnisciēns.*] —**om•nis'cience** *n.*

om•niv•o•rous (ŏm-nĭv'ər-əs) *adj.* **1.** Eating all kinds of food, including animal and vegetable substances. **2.** Taking in everything available, as with the mind. —**om•niv'o•rous•ly** *adv.* —**om•niv'o•rous•ness** *n.*

on (ŏn, ôn) *prep.* **1.** —Used to indicate: **a.** Position upon. **b.** Contact with. **c.** Location at or along. **d.** Proximity. **e.** Attachment to or suspension from. **2.** —Used to indicate motion or direction toward or against. **3.** —Used to indicate: **a.** Occurrence during: *on July 3rd.* **b.** The occasion of what is stated: *On entering the room, she saw him.* **c.** The exact moment or point of: *every hour on the hour.* **4.** —Used to indicate: **a.** The object affected by an action: *The spotlight fell on the actress.* **b.** The agent or agency performing a specified action: *He cut his foot on the broken glass.* **c.** Something used to perform a stated action: *talk on the telephone.* **5.** —Used to indicate an originating or sustaining source or agency: *live on bread and water.* **6.** —Used to indicate: **a.** The state, condition, or process of: *on leave; on fire.* **b.** The purpose of: *travel on business.* **c.** A means of conveyance: *ride on a train.* **d.** Availability by means of: *beer on tap.* **e.** Association with: *a doctor on the staff.* **f.** The ground or basis for: *on principle.* **g.** Addition or repetition: *error on error.* **7.** Concerning; about: *a book on astronomy.* **8.** In one's possession; with: *I haven't a cent on me.* **9.** At the expense of: *drinks on the house.* —*adv.* **1.** In or into a position of being attached to or covering something. **2.** In the direction of: *He looked on while the ship docked.* **3.** Toward or at a point lying ahead in space or time; forward. **4.** In a continuous course. **5.** In or into action or operation. **6.** In or at the present position: *stay on; hang on.* [< OE *on, an.* See **an¹.**]

ON Old Norse.

–on. *comb. form.* Subatomic particle, unit, or quantum: *photon.* [< (I)ON.]

once (wŭns) *adv.* **1.** One time only: *once a day.* **2.** At one time in the past; formerly. **3.** At any time; ever. —**at once. 1.** Simultaneously. **2.** Immediately. —*conj.* As soon as; when. [< OE *ān,* one.]

once-o•ver (wŭns'ō'vər) *n.* A quick but comprehensive survey or performance.

on•com•ing (ŏn'kŭm'ĭng, ôn'-) *adj.* Approaching.

one (wŭn) *adj.* **1.** Being a single entity or being; single; individual. **2.** Of a single kind or nature; undivided. **3.** Designating an unspecified person or thing. **4.** Single in kind; alike or the same. —*n.* **1.** The cardinal number written 1 or in Roman numerals I. **2.** A single person or thing; unit. —*pron.* **1.** A certain person or thing. **2.** Any person or thing. **3.** A single person or thing among persons or things already mentioned. [< OE *ān.* See **oino-**.]

–one. *comb. form.* An oxygen-containing compound: *acetone.* [< Gk *-ōnē.*]

O'Neill (ō-nēl'), **Eugene.** 1888–1953. American dramatist.

one•ness (wŭn'nĭs) *n.* **1.** The quality or state of being one. **2.** Identity of character, as of several things. **3.** Unison; agreement.

on•er•ous (ŏn'ər-əs, ō'nər-) *adj.* Troublesome or oppressive; burdensome. [< L *onus (oner-),* burden.] —**on'er•ous•ness** *n.*

one•self (wŭn-sĕlf') *pron.* A form of the 3rd person sing. pronoun *one:* **1.** —Used reflexively: *to hurt oneself.* **2.** —Used for emphasis: *to take the initiative oneself.* —**by oneself. 1.** Alone. **2.** Without help.

one-sid•ed (wŭn'sī'dĭd) *adj.* **1.** Partial; biased. **2.** More developed on one side.

one-time (wŭn'tīm') *adj.* Also **one•time.** At or in some past time; former.

one-track (wŭn'trăk') *adj.* Obsessively limited to a single idea: *a one-track mind.*

one-way (wŭn'wā') *adj.* Moving or permitting movement in one direction only.

on•go•ing (ŏn'gō-ĭng, ôn'-) *adj.* Progressing or evolving.

on•ion (ŭn'yən) *n.* **1.** A plant widely cultivated for its pungent edible bulb. **2.** The bulb of this plant. [< OF *oignon.*]

on•ion•skin (ŭn'yən-skĭn') *n.* A thin, strong, translucent paper.

on•look•er (ŏn'lŏŏk'ər, ôn'-) *n.* A spectator.

on•ly (ŏn'lē) *adj.* Alone in kind or class; sole. —*adv.* **1.** Without anyone or anything else; alone. **2. a.** No more than; at least; just. **b.** Merely. **3.** Exclusively; solely. —*conj.* But; except (that). [< OE *ānlīc : ān,* ONE + *-līc,* -LY.]

on•o•mat•o•poe•ia (ŏn'ə-măt'ə-pē'ə) *n.* The formation or use of a word that sounds like its referent, as *buzz* or *cuckoo.* [< Gk *onomatopoiein,* to coin names.] —**on'o•mat'o•poe'ic** (-pē'ĭk) *adj.*

on•rush (ŏn'rŭsh', ôn'-) *n.* **1.** A forward rush. **2.** An assault.

on•set (ŏn'sĕt', ôn'-) *n.* **1.** An onslaught. **2.** A beginning; start.

on•slaught (ŏn'slôt', ôn'-) *n.* A violent attack.

On•tar•i•o (ŏn-târ'ē-ō'). A province of C Canada. Pop. 6,731,000. Cap. Toronto.

Ontario, Lake. The smallest and easternmost of the Great Lakes.

on•to (ŏn'tōō', ôn'-, ŏn'tə, ôn'-) *prep.* **1.** On top of; upon. **2.** *Informal.* Aware of: *I'm onto your schemes.* [ON + TO.]

on•tol•o•gy (ŏn-tŏl'ə-jē) *n.* The systematic study of being. [< Gk *ŏn,* being + -LOGY.] —**on'to•log'i•cal** (ŏn'tə-lŏj'ĭ-kəl) *adj.*

o•nus (ō'nəs) *n.* **1.** A burden, esp. a disagreeable responsibility. **2.** A stigma or blame. [< L, burden.]

on•ward (ŏn'wərd, ôn'-) *adv.* Also **on•wards** (-wərdz). In a direction or toward a position that is ahead; forward. —*adj.* Moving or tending forward.

–onym. *comb. form.* Word or name: *acronym.* [< Gk *onuma, onoma,* name.]

ô paw, for/oi boy/ou out/ŏŏ took/ōō coo/p pop/r run/s sauce/sh shy/t to/th thin/*th* the/
ŭ cut/ûr fur/v van/w wag/y yes/z size/zh vision/ə ago, item, edible, gallop, circus/

on•yx (ŏn′ĭks) *n.* A kind of translucent quartz that occurs in bands of different colors and is used as a gemstone. [< Gk *onux*, claw, fingernail, onyx.]

oo•dles (oō′dəlz) *pl.n. Informal.* A great amount. [Perh < HUDDLE.]

oo•mi•ak. Variant of **umiak.**

oomph (oōmf) *n. Slang.* 1. Spirited vigor. 2. Sex appeal.

ooze¹ (oōz) *v.* **oozed, oozing.** 1. To flow or leak out slowly; exude. 2. To disappear or ebb slowly. [< OE *wôs*, juice. See **wes-²**.] —**ooze** *n.* —**ooz′i•ness** *n.* —**ooz′y** *adj.*

ooze² (oōz) *n.* Soft, thin mud or mudlike sediment, as on the floor of oceans and lakes. [< OE *wāse*. See **weis-**.] —**ooz′y** *adj.*

op., OP. opus.

o•pal (ō′pəl) *n.* A translucent mineral of hydrated silicon dioxide, often used as a gem. [< Sk *úpala*, (precious) stone.] —**o′pal•ine′** (ō′pə-lĭn′, -lēn′) *adj.*

o•pal•es•cence (ō′pə-lĕs′əns) *n.* A milky iridescence like that of an opal. —**o′pal•es′cent** *adj.*

o•paque (ō-pāk′) *adj.* 1. a. Impenetrable by light. b. Not reflecting light; dull. 2. Obtuse; dense. [< L *opācus*, dark.] —**o•pac′i•ty** (-păs′ə-tē), **o•paque′ness** *n.*

op. cit. In the work cited (L *opere citato*).

OPEC (ō′pĕk′) Organization of Petroleum Exporting Countries.

o•pen (ō′pən) *adj.* 1. Affording unobstructed passage or entrance and exit; not shut or closed; spacious. 2. Having no cover; exposed. 3. Not sealed, tied, or folded. 4. Having interspersed gaps, spaces, or intervals. 5. Accessible to all; unrestricted. 6. Susceptible; vulnerable. 7. Available; obtainable. 8. Ready to transact business. 9. Unoccupied. 10. Characterized by lack of pretense; candid; receptive. —*v.* 1. To become or cause to become open; release from a closed position. 2. To remove obstructions from; clear. 3. To spread out or apart. 4. To remove the cover or wrapping from; expose; undo. 5. To begin; initiate; commence. 6. To make available. 7. To make or become more responsive or understanding. 8. To reveal the secrets of. 9. To come into view; become revealed. —*n.* 1. **the open.** The outdoors. 2. A contest with both professional and amateur participants. [< OE. See **upo.**] —**o′pen•er** *n.* —**o′pen•ly** *adv.* —**o′pen•ness** *n.*

o•pen-air (ō′pən-âr′) *adj.* Occurring, done, or existing outdoors.

o•pen•hand•ed (ō′pən-hăn′dĭd) *adj.* Giving freely; generous. —**o′pen•hand′ed•ly** *adv.* —**o′pen•hand′ed•ness** *n.*

o•pen-heart (ō′pən-härt′) *adj.* Involving surgery in which the heart is open while its normal functions are assumed by external apparatus.

o•pen-hearth (ō′pən-härth′) *adj.* Designating a reverberatory furnace used in the production of high-quality steel.

o•pen•ing (ō′pən-ĭng) *n.* 1. The act of becoming open or being made to open. 2. An open space; a hole. 3. The first stage of or occasion

for something. 4. A series of beginning moves in chess. 5. An unfilled job.

o•pen-mind•ed (ō′pən-mīn′dĭd) *adj.* Receptive to new ideas; free from prejudice.

open shop. A business establishment or factory having nonunion employees.

o•pen•work (ō′pən-wûrk′) *n.* Ornamental or structural work containing numerous openings.

op•er•a¹ (ŏp′rə, ŏp′ər-ə) *n.* 1. A form of theatrical presentation in which a dramatic performance is set to music. 2. A work of this kind. [< L, work.] —**op′er•at′ic** (ŏp′ə-răt′ĭk) *adj.* —**op′er•at′i•cal•ly** *adv.*

o•pe•ra². Alternate *pl.* of **opus.**

op•er•a•ble (ŏp′ər-ə-bəl, ŏp′rə-) *adj.* 1. Capable of being used or operated. 2. Capable of being treated by surgery. —**op′er•a•bil′i•ty** *n.*

opera glasses. Small binoculars for use at a theatrical performance.

op•er•ate (ŏp′ə-rāt′) *v.* **-ated, -ating.** 1. To function effectively; work. 2. To bring about a desired effect. 3. To perform surgery. 4. To run; control the functioning of. [L *operāri*, to work, labor.]

op•er•a•tion (ŏp′ə-rā′shən) *n.* 1. The act, process, or way of operating. 2. The state of being operative. 3. A method of productive activity. 4. *Med.* Any procedure for remedying an injury or ailment in a living body, esp. one performed with instruments. 5. *Math.* A process or action, such as addition, subtraction, or transposition, performed in accordance with specific rules of procedure.

op•er•a•tion•al (ŏp′ə-rā′shən-əl) *adj.* 1. Pertaining to an operation or series of operations. 2. Fit for proper functioning.

op•er•a•tive (ŏp′ər-ə-tĭv, ŏp′rə-, ŏp′ə-rā′tĭv) *adj.* 1. Exerting influence or force. 2. Functioning effectively; efficient. 3. In operation. 4. Engaged in or related to physical or mechanical activity. 5. Of, pertaining to, or resulting from a surgical operation. —*n.* 1. A skilled worker. 2. A secret agent.

op•er•a•tor (ŏp′ə-rā′tər) *n.* 1. One who operates a mechanical device: *a telephone operator.* 2. A symbol that represents a mathematical operation. 3. *Informal.* A shrewd and sometimes unscrupulous person.

op•e•ret•ta (ŏp′ə-rĕt′ə) *n.* A theatrical production that has many of the elements of opera but is lighter and more popular in subject and style.

Oph•i•u•chus (ŏf′ē-yoō′kəs, ō′fē-) *n.* A constellation in the equatorial region. [< Gk *ophioukhos*, "serpent-holder."]

oph•thal•mic (ŏf-thăl′mĭk, ŏp-thăl′-) *adj.* Of or pertaining to the eye or eyes; ocular.

ophthalmo–. *comb. form.* The eye or eyeball. [< Gk *ophthalmos*, eye.]

oph•thal•mol•o•gy (ŏf′thăl-mŏl′ə-jē, ŏf′thăl-, ŏp′-) *n.* The medical specialty encompassing the anatomy, functions, pathology, and treatment of the eye. —**oph′thal•mol′o•gist** *n.*

–opia. *comb. form.* A specific visual condition or defect: *myopia.* [< Gk *ōps*, eye.]

o•pi•ate (ō′pē-ĭt, -āt′) *n.* 1. A narcotic containing opium or its derivatives. 2. Any seda-

---

ă pat/ā ate/âr care/ä bar/b bib/ch chew/d deed/ĕ pet/ē be/f fit/g gag/h hat/hw what/ ĭ pit/ī pie/îr pier/j judge/k kick/l lid, fatal/m mum/n no, sudden/ng sing/ŏ pot/ō go/

tive or narcotic drug. **3.** Anything that relaxes or induces sleep or torpor. —*adj.* (ō'pē-ĭt, -āt'). **1.** Consisting of or containing opium. **2.** Causing or producing sleep or sedation. —*v.* (ō'pē-āt') -**ated,** -**ating. 1.** To subject to the action of an opiate. **2.** To dull or deaden as if with a narcotic drug.

o•pine (ō-pīn') *v.* **opined, opining.** To hold or state as an opinion.

o•pin•ion (ə-pĭn'yən) *n.* **1.** A belief, conclusion, or judgment not substantiated by positive knowledge or proof. **2.** An evaluation based on special knowledge. **3.** Prevailing feeling or sentiment: *public opinion.* [< L *opināri,* to think.]

o•pin•ion•at•ed (ə-pĭn'yə-nā'tĭd) *adj.* Holding stubbornly to one's own opinions.

o•pi•um (ō'pē-əm) *n.* **1.** A bitter, yellowish-brown, strongly addictive narcotic prepared from the dried juice of unripe pods of an Old World poppy, containing morphine and other alkaloids. **2.** Something that numbs or stupefies. [< Gk *opion,* poppy juice, opium, dim of *opos,* juice.]

o•pos•sum (ə-pŏs'əm, pŏs'əm) *n.* Also **pos•sum** (pŏs'əm). Any of various furry, mostly tree-dwelling marsupials of the New World and Australia. [< Algon.]

opp. opposite.

op•po•nent (ə-pō'nənt) *n.* One that opposes, as in a battle, controversy, etc.; an adversary.

op•por•tune (ŏp'ər-t/y/o͞on') *adj.* **1.** Suited for a particular purpose. **2.** Occurring at a fitting or advantageous time. [< L *opportūnus,* seasonable.] —**op'por•tune'ly** *adv.*

op•por•tun•ist (ŏp'ər-t/y/o͞o'nĭst) *n.* One who takes advantage of any opportunity, usually with little regard for moral principles. —**op'por•tun'ism'** *n.* —**op'por•tun•is'tic** *adj.*

op•por•tu•ni•ty (ŏp'ər-t/y/o͞o'nə-tē) *n., pl.* -**ties.** A favorable or advantageous combination of circumstances.

op•pose (ə-pōz') *v.* -**posed,** -**posing. 1.** To be in contention or conflict with; resist. **2.** To be against. **3.** To place in opposition; contrast. [< L *oppōnere,* to set against.] —**op•pos'a•ble** *adj.* —**op'po•si'tion** (ŏp'ə-zĭsh'ən) *n.*

op•po•site (ŏp'ə-zĭt) *adj.* **1.** Placed or located directly across from; lying in a corresponding position to: *opposite sides of a building.* **2.** Facing the other way. **3.** Diametrically opposed; altogether different. —*n.* One that is opposite or contrary to another. —*prep.* Across from or facing. —**op'po•site** *adv.*

op•press (ə-prĕs') *v.* **1.** To subjugate or persecute by unjust use of force. **2.** To weigh heavily upon, esp. so as to depress. [< L *opprimere* (pp *oppressus*), to press against.] —**op•pres'sion** *n.* —**op•pres'sor** (ə-prĕs'ər) *n.*

op•pres•sive (ə-prĕs'ĭv) *adj.* **1.** Difficult to bear; harsh. **2.** Physically or mentally distressing. —**op•pres'sive•ness** *n.*

op•pro•bri•ous (ə-prō'brē-əs) *adj.* **1.** Contemptuously scornful. **2.** Shameful; infamous.

op•pro•bri•um (ə-prō'brē-əm) *n.* **1.** Disgrace arising from shameful conduct; ignominy. **2.** Scornful reproach or contempt. **3.** A cause of shame. [L, "a reproach against."]

–opsy. *comb. form.* An examination: **biopsy.** [< Gk *opsis,* sight, appearance.]

opt (ŏpt) *v.* To make a choice. [< L *optāre.*]

opt. 1. optical; optician; optics. **2.** optional.

op•tic (ŏp'tĭk) *adj.* Pertaining to the eye or vision. [< Gk *optos,* visible.]

op•ti•cal (ŏp'tĭ-kəl) *adj.* **1.** Of or pertaining to sight. **2.** Of or pertaining to optics. —**op'ti•cal•ly** *adv.*

op•ti•cian (ŏp-tĭsh'ən) *n.* One who makes or sells lenses and eyeglasses.

op•tics (ŏp'tĭks) *n. (takes sing. v.).* The scientific study of light and vision.

op•ti•mism (ŏp'tə-mĭz'əm) *n.* **1.** A tendency to expect the best possible outcome or to dwell upon the most hopeful aspects of a situation. **2.** *Phil.* The doctrine that this world is the best of all possible worlds. [< L *optimum,* best.] —**op'ti•mist** *n.* —**op'ti•mis'tic** *adj.*

op•ti•mum (ŏp'tə-məm) *n., pl.* -**ma** (-mə) or -**mums.** The best or most favorable condition for a particular situation. [< L *optimus,* best.] —**op'ti•mal** *adj.* —**op'ti•mal•ly** *adv.*

op•tion (ŏp'shən) *n.* **1.** The act of choosing; choice. **2.** The freedom to choose. **3.** The right to buy or sell something within a specified time and at a specified price. [< L *optiō,* choice.] —**op'tion•al** *adj.* —**op'tion•al•ly** *adv.*

op•tom•e•try (ŏp-tŏm'ə-trē) *n.* The profession of examining, measuring, and treating certain visual defects by means of corrective lenses or other methods that do not require license as a physician. [Gk *optos,* visible + -METRY.] —**op•tom'e•trist** *n.*

op•u•lent (ŏp'yə-lənt) *adj.* **1.** Extremely wealthy; rich; affluent. **2.** Abundant; luxuriant. [L *opulentus.*] —**op'u•lence** *n.*

o•pus (ō'pəs) *n., pl.* **opera** (ō'pər-ə, ŏp'ər-ə) or **opuses.** A creative work, esp. a musical composition. [L, work.]

or (ôr; *unstressed* ər) *conj.* —Used to indicate: **1. a.** An alternative. **b.** The second of two alternatives: *either right or wrong.* **2.** A synonymous or equivalent expression: *acrophobia, or fear of great heights.* **3.** Uncertainty or indefiniteness: *two or three.* [< OE *oththe.*]

Usage: When all of the elements connected by *or* are singular, the verb they govern must be singular: *Tom or Jack is coming. Beer or ale or wine is included in the charge.* When the elements are all plural, the verb is plural. When the elements do not agree in number, or when one or more of the elements is a personal pronoun, the verb is governed by the element to which it is nearer: *Tom or his brothers are going.*

–or¹. *comb. form.* One that performs the action expressed by the root verb: **percolator.** [< L.]

–or². *comb. form.* Also *Brit.* -**our.** A state, quality, or activity: **behavior.** [< L, abstract suffix.]

or•a•cle (ôr'ə-kəl, ŏr'-) *n.* **1. a.** A shrine consecrated to a prophetic god. **b.** The priest at such a shrine. **c.** A prophecy made known at such a shrine. **2.** A wise person. [< L *ōrāre,* to speak.] —**o•rac'u•lar** (ô-răk'yə-lər, ō-răk'-) *adj.* —**o•rac'u•lar•ly** *adv.*

o•ral (ôr'əl, ōr'-) *adj.* **1.** Spoken rather than

written. **2.** Of or pertaining to speech. **3.** Of, used in, or taken through the mouth. [< L *ōs (ōr-)*, the mouth.] —**o'ral·ly** *adv.*

o·ral contraceptive. Any of various hormone compounds in pill form, used in specific sequence to prevent ovulation and conception.

or·ange (ôr'ĭnj, ŏr'-) *n.* **1.** A round citrus fruit with a reddish-yellow rind and juicy, sectioned pulp. **2.** An evergreen, white-flowered tree bearing such fruit. **3.** A color between yellow and red. [< Sk *nāranga*, orange, orange tree.] —**or'ange** *adj.*

or·ange·ade (ôr'ĭn-jād', ŏr'-) *n.* A beverage of orange juice, sugar, and water.

o·rang·u·tan (ō-răng'ə-tăn', ə-răng'-) *n.* Also **o·rang·u·tan, o·rang·ou·tan, o·rang·u·tang** (ō-răng'ə-tăng', ə-răng'-). A large, shaggy-haired, long-armed ape of Borneo and Sumatra. [Malay *orang hutan.*]

o·rate (ô-rāt', ō-rāt', ôr'āt', ŏr'āt') *v.* **orated, orating.** To speak publicly in a grandiloquent manner.

o·ra·tion (ô-rā'shən, ō-rā'-) *n.* A formal address or speech, esp. one at an academic celebration, funeral, etc. [< L *ōrāre*, to speak.]

or·a·tor (ôr'ə-tər, ŏr'-) *n.* **1.** One who delivers an oration. **2.** One skilled in the art of public address. —**or'a·tor'i·cal** (ôr'ə-tôr'ĭ-kəl, ŏr'ə-tŏr'-) *adj.* —**or'a·tor'i·cal·ly** *adv.*

or·a·to·ri·o (ôr'ə-tôr'ē-ō', -tôr'ē-ō', ŏr'-) *n., pl.* **-os.** A musical composition for voices and orchestra, telling a sacred story. [< the *Oratory* of St. Philip Neri at Rome.]

or·a·to·ry¹ (ôr'ə-tôr'ē, -tôr'ē, ŏr'-) *n.* **1.** The art of public speaking; rhetoric. **2.** Rhetorical style or skill.

or·a·to·ry² (ôr'ə-tôr'ē, -tôr'ē, ŏr'-) *n., pl.* **-ries.** A small private chapel. [< LL *ōrātōrium (templum)*, (place) of prayer.]

orb (ôrb) *n.* **1.** A sphere. **2.** A heavenly body. **3.** One of a series of concentric transparent spheres revolving about the earth, postulated by medieval astronomers as support for the stars and planets. [< L *orbis*, orb, disk.]

or·bit (ôr'bĭt) *n.* **1.** The path of a celestial body or man-made satellite as it revolves around another body. **2.** The path of any body in a field of force surrounding another body, as the movement of an atomic electron in relation to a nucleus. **3.** A range of activity, experience, or influence. **4.** Either of two bony cavities in the skull containing an eye and its external structures; eye socket. —*v.* **1.** To put into or cause to move in an orbit. **2.** To revolve or move in orbit. [< L *orbis*, ORB.] —**or'bit·al** *adj.*

or·chard (ôr'chərd) *n.* **1.** A tract of land where fruit or nut trees are cultivated. **2.** The trees cultivated in such an area. [< L *hortus*, a garden + OE *geard*, yard.]

or·ches·tra (ôr'kĭ-strə, ôr'kĕs'trə) *n.* **1.** A large group of musicians who play together on various instruments. **2. a.** The section of seats nearest the orchestra pit in a theater. **b.** The entire. main floor of a theater. [< Gk *orkheisthai*, to dance.] —**or·ches'tral** (ôr-kĕs'trəl) *adj.* —**or·ches'tral·ly** *adv.*

or·ches·trate (ôr'kĭ-strāt') *v.* **-trated, -trating.**

To compose or arrange (music) for an orchestra. —**or·ches·tra'tion** *n.*

or·chid (ôr'kĭd) *n.* **1.** Any of numerous chiefly tropical plants with irregularly shaped flowers. **2.** The flower of such a plant. **3.** Light reddish purple. [< Gk *orkhis*, testicle, orchid.]

ord. order.

or·dain (ôr-dān') *v.* **1.** To invest with ministerial or priestly authority; confer holy orders upon. **2.** To order or decree. **3.** To predestine: *by fate ordained.* [< L *ōrdināre*, to arrange in order.]

or·deal (ôr-dēl') *n.* A severely difficult or painful experience. [< OE *ordāl.*]

or·der (ôr'dər) *n.* **1.** A condition of logical or comprehensible arrangement among the separate elements of a group. **2.** The state, condition, or disposition of a thing. **3. a.** The existing structures of a given society. **b.** The condition in which these structures are maintained and preserved by the rule of law. **4.** A sequence, arrangement, or category of successive things. **5.** The established sequence; customary procedure. **6.** A command or direction. **7.** A commission or instruction to buy, sell, or supply something. **8.** A portion of food requested by a customer at a restaurant. **9. a.** Any of several grades of the Christian ministry. **b. orders.** Ordination. **10.** A monastic institution. **11.** An organization of people bound by some common fraternal bond or social aim. **12.** A group of persons upon whom a government or sovereign has formally conferred honor: *the Order of the Garter.* **13.** Degree of quality; distinction; rank. **14.** Approximate size or magnitude. —*v.* **1.** To issue a command or instruction (to). **2.** To request to be supplied with (something). **3.** To put in a systematic arrangement. [< L *ōrdō.*]

or·der·ly (ôr'dər-lē) *adj.* **1.** Tidy; neat. **2.** Peaceful; well-behaved. —*n., pl.* **-lies. 1.** A male hospital attendant. **2.** A soldier assigned to attend upon a superior officer.

or·di·nal (ôrd'n-əl) *adj.* **1.** Of a specified position in a numbered series. **2.** Pertaining to a biological order.

ordinal number. A number indicating position in a series or order. The ordinal numbers are first (1st), second (2nd), third (3rd), etc.

or·di·nance (ôrd'n-əns) *n.* **1.** An authoritative command or order. **2.** A municipal statute or regulation. **3.** A long-established custom. [< L *ōrdināre*, to put in order.]

or·di·nar·i·ly (ôrd'n-ĕr'ə-lē, ôrd'n-ĕr'-) *adv.* Usually; as a general rule.

or·di·nar·y (ôrd'n-ĕr'ē) *adj.* **1.** Commonly encountered; usual; regular; normal. **2.** Average in rank or merit; commonplace. [< L *ōrdō*, order.] —**or'di·nar'i·ness** *n.*

or·di·nate (ôrd'n-ĭt, -āt') *adj.* The plane Cartesian coordinate representing the distance from a specified point to the *x*-axis, measured parallel to the *y*-axis.

or·di·na·tion (ôrd'n-ā'shən) *n. Eccles.* The ceremony during which a person is ordained.

ord·nance (ôrd'nəns) *n.* **1.** Military supplies, esp. weapons, ammunition, etc. **2.** Heavy guns; artillery. [< ORDINANCE.]

ă pat/ā ate/âr care/ä bar/b bib/ch chew/d deed/ĕ pet/ē be/f fit/g gag/h hat/hw what/
ĭ pit/ī pie/îr pier/j judge/k kick/l lid, fatal/m mum/n no, sudden/ng sing/ŏ pot/ō go/

Or·do·vi·cian (ôr'də-vĭsh'ən) adj. Of or belonging to the geologic time, system of rocks, or sedimentary deposits of the second period of the Paleozoic era. —n. The Ordovician period. [< the Ordovices, an ancient Celtic tribe of N Wales.]

or·dure (ôr'jər, ôr'dyŏŏr) n. Excrement; dung. [< L horridus, horrid.]

ore (ôr, ōr) n. A mineral or aggregate of minerals from which a valuable constituent, esp. a metal, can profitably be mined or extracted. [< OE ār, brass. See ayos-.]

Ore. Oregon (unofficial).

Oreg. Oregon.

o·reg·a·no (ə-rĕg'ə-nō', ô-rĕg'-) n. The dried leaves of a type of marjoram, used as seasoning. [< Gk origanon, oregano, marjoram.]

Or·e·gon (ôr'ə-gən, -gŏn', ôr'-). A state of the NW U.S. Pop. 2,091,000. Cap. Salem. —**Or'e·go'ni·an** (ôr'ə-gō'nē-ən, ôr'-) adj. & n.

org. 1. organic. 2. organization; organized.

or·gan (ôr'gən) n. 1. A musical instrument consisting of a keyboard and pipes supplied with wind by means of bellows. 2. A differentiated part of an organism, adapted for a specific function. 3. A medium by means of which some action is performed. 4. An instrument of communication, esp. a periodical publication. [< L organum, implement, instrument.]

or·gan·dy (ôr'gən-dē) n., pl. -dies. Also **or·gan·die.** A transparent crisp fabric of cotton or silk. [F organdi.]

or·gan·elle (ôr'gə-nĕl') n. Biol. A specialized part of a cell that resembles and functions as an organ.

organ grinder. A street musician who plays a hurdy-gurdy.

or·gan·ic (ôr-găn'ĭk) adj. 1. Of or affecting an organ of the body. 2. Of or derived from living organisms. 3. Likened to an organism in organization or development. 4. Of or constituting the essential part of something; constitutional; substantive. 5. Chem. Of or designating carbon compounds. —**or·gan'i·cal·ly** adv.

organic chemistry. The chemistry of carbon compounds.

or·gan·ism (ôr'gə-nĭz'əm) n. Any living being; a plant or animal. —**or'gan·is'mal** (ôr'gə-nĭz'məl), **or'gan·is'mic** adj.

or·gan·ist (ôr'gə-nĭst) n. One who plays the organ.

or·gan·i·za·tion (ôr'gə-nə-zā'shən) n. 1. The act of organizing or the process or state of being organized. 2. Something that has been organized. 3. A number of persons united for some purpose or work. —**or'gan·i·za'tion·al** adj. —**or'gan·i·za'tion·al·ly** adv.

or·gan·ize (ôr'gə-nīz') v. -ized, -izing. 1. To form an orderly, functional, structured whole. 2. To arrange; systematize. 3. To establish as an organization. 4. To induce employees to form or join a union. [< L organum, instrument, ORGAN.] —**or'gan·iz'er** n.

organo-. comb. form. Organ or organic.

or·gan·za (ôr-găn'zə) n. A sheer, stiff fabric of silk or synthetic fibers.

or·gasm (ôr'găz'əm) n. The climax of sexual excitement. [< Gk organ, to swell (with lust), be excited.] —**or·gas'mic, or·gas'tic** adj.

or·gy (ôr'jē) n., pl. -gies. 1. A revel involving unrestrained indulgence, as in drinking or sexual activity. 2. Excessive indulgence in any activity: an orgy of reading. [< Gk orgia.] —**or'gi·as'tic** (-ăs'tĭk) adj.

o·ri·el (ôr'ē-əl, ōr'-) n. A projecting bay window supported from below. [< ML ortolum, upper chamber.]

o·ri·ent (ôr'ē-ənt, -ĕnt', ōr'-) n. 1. The east; eastern regions. 2. Orient. The countries of Asia, esp. of E Asia. 3. In ancient times, the regions east of the Mediterranean. —v. (ôr'ē-ĕnt', ōr'-). 1. To align or position with respect to a specific direction or reference system. 2. To familiarize with or adjust to a situation. [< L oriēns, rising, rising sun, east.] —**o'ri·en·ta'tion** n.

O·ri·en·tal (ôr'ē-ĕn'təl, ōr'-) adj. Of or pertaining to the Orient. —n. An inhabitant of the Orient.

or·i·fice (ôr'ə-fĭs, ŏr'-) n. An opening; mouth; vent. [< LL ōrificium.]

orig. original; originally.

o·ri·ga·mi (ôr'ĭ-gä'mē) n. The Japanese art of folding paper into decorative shapes. [Jap.]

or·i·gin (ôr'ə-jĭn, ŏr'-) n. 1. A source or cause of existence. 2. Ancestry; derivation. 3. A coming into being. 4. Math. The point of intersection of coordinate axes. [< L oriri, to rise.]

o·rig·i·nal (ə-rĭj'ən-əl) adj. 1. Primary; first. 2. Fresh and novel. 3. Creative; inventive. —n. 1. The primary form from which copies are made or varieties arise. 2. An authentic work of art as distinguished from a copy. [< L origō, origin.] —**o·rig'i·nal'i·ty** (ə-rĭj'ə-năl'ə-tē) n. —**o·rig'i·nal·ly** adv.

o·rig·i·nate (ə-rĭj'ə-nāt') v. -nated, -nating. 1. To come or bring into being; begin. —**o·rig'i·na'tion** n. —**o·rig'i·na'tor** n.

O·ri·no·co (ôr'ə-nō'kō, ōr'-). A river of NW South America.

o·ri·ole (ôr'ē-ōl', ōr'-) n. A songbird with bright orange or yellow and black plumage. [< ML oriolus, "golden (bird)."]

O·ri·on (ō-rī'ən) n. A constellation on the celestial equator.

Or·lon (ôr'lŏn') n. A trademark for a synthetic fiber used in a variety of fabrics.

or·mo·lu (ôr'mə-lōō') n. A copper and tin or zinc alloy resembling gold, used for decorative work. [F or molulu, "ground gold."]

or·na·ment (ôr'nə-mənt) n. 1. Something used for decoration or adornment. 2. One who does honor or credit: an ornament to his profession. —v. (ôr'nə-mĕnt'). To decorate; adorn. [< L ōrnāre, to adorn.] —**or'na·men'tal** (-mĕn'təl) adj. —**or'na·men·ta'tion** n.

or·nate (ôr-nāt') adj. 1. Elaborately ornamented. 2. Showy in style; florid. [< L ōrnāre, to adorn.] —**or·nate'ly** adv. —**or·nate'ness** n.

or·ner·y (ôr'nə-rē) adj. -ier, -iest. Ill-tempered; perversely stubborn. [Var of ORDINARY.]

ornitho-. comb. form. Bird or birds. [< Gk ornis (ornith-), bird.]

---

or·ni·thol·o·gy (ôr′nə-thŏl′ə-jē) *n.* The scientific study of birds. —**or′ni·tho·log′i·cal** (ôr′nĭ-thə-lŏj′ĭ-kəl) *adj.* —**or′ni·thol′o·gist** *n.*

o·ro·tund (ôr′ə-tŭnd′, ōr′-) *adj.* 1. Full in sound; sonorous. 2. Pompous; bombastic. [L *ōre rotundō,* "with round mouth."]

or·phan (ôr′fən) *n.* A child whose parents are dead. —*v.* To cause to become an orphan. [< Gk *orphanos,* orphaned.]

or·phan·age (ôr′fə-nĭj) *n.* An institution for the care of orphans.

Or·phe·us (ôr′fē-əs, -fyoōs′). Legendary Thracian poet and musician; reputed founder of a mystery religion. —**Or′phic** (-fĭk) *adj.*

or·ris·root (ôr′ĭs-roōt′, -roōt′, ōr′-) *n.* The fragrant root of an Old World iris, used in perfumes and cosmetics.

orth. orthopedic; orthopedics.

ortho-. *comb. form.* 1. Straight or upright. 2. *Math.* Perpendicular to or at right angles. 3. Correct or standard. 4. *Med.* Correction of maladjustments or deformities. [< Gk *orthos,* straight, correct.]

or·tho·don·tia (ôr′thə-dŏn′shə) *n.* The dental specialty and practice of correcting abnormally aligned or positioned teeth. [ORTHO- + Gk *odous (odont-),* tooth.] —**or′tho·don′tic** *adj.* —**or′tho·don′tist** *n.*

or·tho·dox (ôr′thə-dŏks′) *adj.* 1. Adhering to traditional and established beliefs and practices, esp. in religion. 2. **Orthodox. a.** Of or belonging to Christian churches derived from the church of the Byzantine Empire. **b.** Of or belonging to a branch of Judaism adhering strictly to the ancient Hebrew law. [< Gk *orthodoxos,* having the right opinion.] —**or′tho·dox′y** *n.*

or·thog·o·nal (ôr-thŏg′ə-nəl) *adj.* Pertaining to or composed of right angles. [Gk *orthogōnios.*]

or·thog·ra·phy (ôr-thŏg′rə-fē) *n.* 1. Correct spelling. 2. The study and formulation of systems of spelling. —**or′tho·graph′ic** (-thə-grăf′ĭk) *adj.* —**or′tho·graph′i·cal·ly** *adv.*

or·tho·pe·dics (ôr′thə-pē′dĭks) *n. (takes sing. v.)* The surgical or manipulative treatment of disorders of the skeletal system and associated motor organs. [< ORTHO- + Gk *paideia,* education.] —**or′tho·pe′dic** *adj.* —**or′tho·pe′dist** *n.*

-ory¹. *comb. form.* A place for or something used as: **observatory.** [< L *-ōrius,* adj suffix.]

-ory². *comb. form.* Characterization by, possession of the nature of, or tendency toward: **compensatory.** [< L *-ōrius,* adj suffix.]

Os osmium.

O·sage (ō′sāj′, ō-sāj′) *n., pl.* **Osage** or **Osages.** 1. A member of a tribe of Siouan-speaking North American Indians, formerly inhabiting the region between the Missouri and Arkansas rivers. 2. The language of this tribe. —**O′sage** *adj.*

O·sa·ka (ō-sä′kə). A city of Japan, on Honshu Island. Pop. 3,119,000.

Os·can (ŏs′kən) *n.* 1. One of an ancient people of S Italy. 2. The Italic language of this people. —**Os′can** *adj.*

os·cil·late (ŏs′ə-lāt′) *v.* **-lated, -lating.** 1. To swing back and forth steadily. 2. To waver;

vacillate. 3. *Phys.* To vary between alternate extremes. [L *ōscillāre.*] —**os′cil·la′tion** *n.* —**os′cil·la′tor** *n.* —**os′cil·la·to′ry** (ŏs′ə-lə-tôr′ē, -tōr′ē) *adj.*

os·cil·lo·scope (ō-sĭl′ə-skōp′, ə-sĭl′-) *n.* An electronic instrument that produces a visual display on the screen of a cathode-ray tube corresponding to some external signal. —**os·cil′lo·scop′ic** (-skŏp′ĭk) *adj.*

Os·co-Um·bri·an (ŏs′kō-ŭm′brē-ən) *n.* A subdivision of Italic, consisting of Oscan and Umbrian.

os·cu·late (ŏs′kyə-lāt′) *v.* **-lated, -lating.** To kiss. [L *ōsculārī.*] —**os′cu·la′tion** *n.*

-ose¹. *comb. form.* Possession of or similarity to: **grandiose.** [< L *-ōsus.*]

-ose². *comb. form.* A carbohydrate: **fructose.** [< GLUCOSE.]

o·sier (ō′zhər) *n.* 1. A willow with long, flexible twigs used in basketry. 2. A twig of such a willow. [< ML *ausēria,* willow bed.]

O·si·ris (ō-sī′rĭs). Egyptian fertility god.

-osis. *comb. form.* 1. A condition or process: **osmosis.** 2. A diseased or abnormal condition: **neurosis.** 3. An increase or formation of: **sclerosis.** [< Gk *-ōsis,* abstract noun suffix.]

Os·lo (ŏz′lō, ŏs′lō). The capital of Norway. Pop. 483,000.

os·mi·um (ŏz′mē-əm) *n. Symbol* **Os** A bluishwhite, hard metallic element, used as a platinum hardener and in making pen points, phonograph needles, and instrument pivots. Atomic number 76, atomic weight 190.2. [< Gk *osmē,* odor.]

os·mo·sis (ŏz-mō′sĭs, ŏs-) *n.* 1. The diffusion of fluid through a semipermeable membrane until there is an equal concentration of fluid on either side of the membrane. 2. A gradual process resembling this. [< Gk *ōsmos,* action of pushing.] —**os·mot′ic** (-mŏt′ĭk) *adj.*

os·prey (ŏs′prē, -prā′) *n., pl.* **-preys.** A large fish-eating hawk with blackish and white plumage. [< L *avis praedae,* "bird of prey."]

os·si·fi·ca·tion (ŏs′ə-fĭ-kā′shən) *n.* 1. The natural process of bone formation. 2. **a.** The abnormal hardening or calcification of soft tissue into a bonelike material. **b.** A mass or deposit of such material. 3. A being or becoming set in a rigidly conventional pattern, as of habits or beliefs.

os·si·fy (ŏs′ə-fī′) *v.* **-fied, -fying.** 1. To change into bone. 2. To set into a rigidly conventional pattern. [L *os,* bone + -FY.]

os·ten·si·ble (ŏ-stĕn′sə-bəl) *adj.* Outwardly apparent; seeming; professed. [< L *ostendere,* to show.] —**os·ten′si·bly** *adv.*

os·ten·ta·tion (ŏs′tĕn-tā′shən, ŏs′tən-) *n.* Pretentious display or showiness. [< L *ostendere,* to show.] —**os′ten·ta′tious** *adj.* —**os′ten·ta′tious·ly** *adv.*

osteo-. *comb. form.* Bone or bones. [< Gk *osteon,* bone.]

os·te·op·a·thy (ŏs′tē-ŏp′ə-thē) *n.* A medical therapy that emphasizes manipulative techniques for correcting somatic abnormalities thought to cause disease and inhibit recovery. —**os′te·o·path′** (ŏs′tē-ə-păth′) *n.* —**os′te·o·path′ic** (-ə-păth′ĭk) *adj.*

ă pat/ā ate/âr care/ä bar/b bib/ch chew/d deed/ĕ pet/ē be/f fit/g gag/h hat/hw what/
ĭ pit/ī pie/îr pier/j judge/k kick/l lid, fatal/m mum/n no, sudden/ng sing/ŏ pot/ō go/

ost·mark (ôst′märk′, ŏst′-) n. The basic monetary unit of East Germany.

os·tra·cize (ŏs′trə-sīz′) v. -cized, -cizing. To banish or exclude from a group. [< Gk ostrakon, shell, shard (with which the Athenian citizen voted for ostracism).] —**os′tra·cism′** (-sĭz′əm) n.

os·trich (ŏs′trĭch, ôs′-) n. A very large, long-necked, long-legged, flightless African bird. [< VL *avistrūthius.*]

OT Old Testament.

oth·er (ŭth′ər) adj. 1. Being or designating the remaining or alternate one or ones: *the other ear.* 2. Different or apart from that or those under consideration: *any other man.* 3. Additional; extra: *I have no other shoes.* 4. Alternating: *every other day.* 5. Recently past: *the other day.* —pron. 1. The remaining or alternate one. 2. A different or additional person or thing. —adv. Differently. [< OE ōther. See an².]

oth·er·wise (ŭth′ər-wīz′) adv. 1. In another way; differently. 2. Under other circumstances. 3. In other respects: *an otherwise logical mind.* —adj. Other than supposed; different.

oth·er·world·ly (ŭth′ər-wûrld′lē) adj. Transcending concrete or mundane matters or considerations. —**oth′er·world′li·ness** n.

-otic. comb. form. 1. Affected with or by: **sclerotic.** 2. Having a specific disease: **neurotic.** [< Gk -ōtikos, adj suffix.]

OTS Officer's Training School.

Ot·ta·wa¹ (ŏt′ə-wə, -wä′, -wô′) n., pl. -wa or -was. 1. A group of Algonquian-speaking Indians, originally inhabiting the region of the Ottawa River in Ontario, Canada. 2. A member of this group. 3. The Ojibwa dialect of this group.

Ot·ta·wa² (ŏt′ə-wə, -wä′, -wô′). The capital of Canada. Pop. 281,000.

ot·ter (ŏt′ər) n. 1. A weasellike aquatic mammal with webbed feet and dense, dark-brown fur. 2. The fur of such an animal. [< OE otor. See wed-.]

ot·to·man (ŏt′ə-mən) n., pl. -mans. 1. A low, backless, armless seat or cushioned footstool. 2. A heavy ribbed fabric. [< OTTOMAN.]

Ot·to·man (ŏt′ə-mən) n., pl. -mans. A Turk. —adj. Turkish.

Oua·ga·dou·gou (wä′gə-dōō′gōō). The capital of Upper Volta. Pop. 51,000.

ou·bli·ette (ōō′blē-ĕt′) n. A dungeon entered through a trap door in the ceiling. [< F oublier, to forget.]

ouch (ouch) interj. Expressive of sudden pain.

ought¹ (ôt) v. —Used as an auxiliary verb followed by an infinitive with *to.* Indicates: 1. Obligation: *You ought to work harder than that.* 2. Expediency or prudence: *You ought to wear a raincoat.* 3. Desirability: *You ought to have been there; it was great fun.* 4. Probability: *She ought to finish by next week.* [< OE āhte, 1st & 3rd sing past indicative of āgan, to possess. See ēik-.]

ought². Variant of **aught.**

ounce (ouns) n. 1. a. A U.S. Customary System unit of weight equal to 16 drams or 437.5

grains. b. A unit of apothecary weight equal to 480 grains or 1.097 avoirdupois ounces. 2. a. A U.S. Customary System unit of volume or capacity used in liquid measure, equal to 8 fluid drams or 1.804 cubic inches. b. A British Imperial System unit of volume or capacity used in dry and liquid measure, equal to 1.734 cubic inches. 3. A tiny bit. [< L uncia, a twelfth, ounce.]

our (our) adj. The possessive form of the pronoun *we,* used attributively. [< OE ūre. See nes-.]

-our. Brit. Variant of -or².

ours (ourz). The possessive form of the pronoun *we,* used as a predicate adjective or as a substantive: *This house is ours. Ours is the best.* —**of ours.** Belonging to us: *a friend of ours.*

our·selves (our-sĕlvz′, är-) pron. A form of the 1st person pl. pronoun: 1. —Used reflexively: *We are only deceiving ourselves.* 2. —Used for emphasis: *We did it ourselves.* —**by ourselves.** 1. Alone. 2. Without help.

-ous. comb. form. 1. Possessing or full of: **joyous.** 2. Chem. Occurring with a valence that is lower than that in a comparable -ic system: **ferrous.** [< L -ōsus, -us, adj suffixes.]

oust (oust) v. To evict; force out. [< L obstāre, to hinder.]

oust·er (ous′tər) n. Eviction; expulsion.

out (out) adv. 1. Away or forth from inside. 2. Away from the center or middle. 3. Away from a usual place. 4. To depletion or extinction: *Supplies have run out.* 5. Into being or view: *The moon came out.* 6. Without inhibition; boldly: *Speak out.* 7. Into disuse or an unfashionable status. 8. Baseball. So as to be retired. —adj. 1. Exterior; external. 2. Unable to be used. 3. Informal. Not available for use or consideration. 4. Bare or threadbare. —prep. 1. Through; forth from: *fall out the window.* 2. Beyond or outside of. —n. 1. A person or thing that is out. 2. A means of escape. 3. Baseball. Any play in which a batter or base runner is retired. [< OE ūt. See ud-.]

out-. comb. form. 1. To a surpassing or superior degree. 2. Located outside.

out-and-out (out′n-out′) adj. Complete; thoroughgoing.

out·bid (out-bĭd′) v. To bid higher than (another).

out·board (out′bôrd′, -bōrd′) adj. 1. Situated or attached on the outside of the hull of a vessel: *an outboard motor.* 2. Situated toward or nearer the end of an aircraft wing. —**out′board′** adv.

out·bound (out′bound′) adj. Outward bound; headed outward.

out·break (out′brāk′) n. A sudden eruptive occurrence.

out·build·ing (out′bĭl′dĭng) n. A building separate from but associated with a main building.

out·burst (out′bûrst′) n. A sudden, violent manifestation, as of activity or emotion: *an outburst of hatred.*

out·cast (out′kăst′, -käst′) n. One that has been rejected or excluded, as from society. —**out′cast′** adj.

ô paw, for/oi boy/ou out/ŏŏ took/ōō coo/p pop/r run/s sauce/sh shy/t to/th thin/*th* the/ ŭ cut/ûr fur/v van/w wag/y yes/z size/zh vision/ə ago, item, edible, gallop, circus/

out·class (out-klăs', -kläs') *v.* To surpass decisively.

out·come (out'kŭm') *n.* A natural result; consequence.

out·crop (out'krŏp') *n. Geol.* A portion of bedrock or other stratum protruding through the soil level.

out·cry (out'krī') *n.* 1. A loud cry or clamor. 2. A strong protest.

out·dat·ed (out-dā'tĭd) *adj.* Old-fashioned; obsolete.

out·dis·tance (out-dĭs'təns) *v.* -tanced, -tancing. To go far beyond or surpass, as in a race or competition.

out·do (out-dōō') *v.* To exceed in performance.

out·door (out'dôr', -dōr') *adj.* Located in, done in, or suited to the open air.

out·doors (out-dôrz', -dōrz') *adv.* In or into the open; outside of a house or shelter. —*n.* The open air; the area away from human habitation.

out·er (out'ər) *adj.* 1. Located on the outside; external. 2. Farther from the center or middle.

Outer Mongolia. The Mongolian People's Republic. See **Mongolia.**

out·er·most (out'ər-mōst') *adj.* Farthest out.

out·face (out-fās') *v.* To overcome or defy with bold self-assurance.

out·field (out'fēld') *n.* 1. The area of a baseball field extending beyond the base lines. 2. The members of a baseball team playing in the outfield. —**out'field·er** *n.*

out·fit (out'fĭt') *n.* 1. A set of equipment or clothing, esp. for a special purpose. 2. *Informal.* An association of persons, as a military unit or business organization. —*v.* To provide with an outfit. —**out'fit'ter** *n.*

out·flank (out-flăngk') *v.* To maneuver around the flank of (an opposing force).

out·fox (out-fŏks') *v.* To get the better of by cunning.

out·go (out'gō') *n., pl.* -goes. An expenditure or cost.

out·go·ing (out'gō'ĭng) *adj.* 1. Departing; going out. 2. Friendly and unreserved.

out·grow (out-grō') *v.* 1. To grow too large for. 2. To lose or discard in the course of maturing. 3. To surpass in growth.

out·growth (out'grōth') *n.* 1. A part growing out; an offshoot. 2. A result or consequence.

out·guess (out-gĕs') *v.* 1. To anticipate correctly the actions of. 2. To outwit.

out·house (out'hous') *n.* An enclosed outdoor toilet; a privy.

out·ing (ou'tĭng) *n.* 1. An excursion or pleasure trip. 2. A walk outdoors; an airing.

out·land·ish (out-lăn'dĭsh) *adj.* 1. Foreign and unusual. 2. Conspicuously odd or unconventional; bizarre. [< OE *ūtlandisc.*] —**out·land'ish·ly** *adv.* —**out·land'ish·ness** *n.*

out·last (out-lăst', -läst') *v.* To endure or live longer than.

out·law (out'lô') *n.* 1. A person excluded from normal legal protection and rights. 2. One who lives lawlessly. —*v.* 1. To declare illegal; ban. 2. To deprive of the protection of the law.

out·lay (out'lā') *n.* 1. The spending or disbursing of money. 2. An amount spent.

out·let (out'lĕt', -lĭt) *n.* 1. A passage for escape or exit; vent. 2. A means of releasing emotions, energies, etc. 3. A market for commercial goods. 4. *Elec.* A receptacle that is connected to a power supply and equipped with a socket for a plug.

out·line (out'līn') *n.* 1. A line forming the boundary of an object or figure. 2. Drawing in which objects are depicted in lines without shading. 3. A general description, plan, or summary. —*v.* 1. To draw or show the outline of. 2. To give the main points of; summarize.

out·live (out-lĭv') *v.* To live longer than; outlast; survive.

out·look (out'lŏŏk') *n.* 1. The prospect seen from a viewing place. 2. A point of view; attitude. 3. A probable result; expectation.

out·ly·ing (out'lī'ĭng) *adj.* Distant or remote from a point or center.

out·mod·ed (out-mō'dĭd) *adj.* No longer in use or fashion; obsolete.

out·num·ber (out-nŭm'bər) *v.* To be more numerous than.

out-of-date (out'əv-dāt') *adj.* Outmoded; old-fashioned.

out-of-the-way (out'əv-*th*ə-wā') *adj.* 1. Remote; secluded. 2. Out of the ordinary.

out·pa·tient (out'pā'shənt) *n.* A patient who receives treatment at a hospital or clinic without being hospitalized.

out·play (out-plā') *v.* To play better than (an opponent).

out·post (out'pōst') *n.* 1. A detachment of troops stationed at a distance from a main unit. 2. The station occupied by such troops. 3. An outlying settlement.

out·put (out'pŏŏt') *n.* 1. Production, esp. the amount produced or manufactured during a given span of time. 2. *Technology.* **a.** The energy, power, or work produced by a system. **b.** The information produced by a computer from a specific input.

out·rage (out'rāj') *n.* 1. A viciously violent or grossly offensive act. 2. A severe insult or offense. 3. Resentful anger. —*v.* -raged, -raging. 1. To commit an outrage upon. 2. To rape. 3. To fill with angry resentment. [< OF, "excess," atrocity.]

out·ra·geous (out-rā'jəs) *adj.* 1. Grossly offensive; heinous. 2. Disgraceful; shocking. —**out·ra'geous·ly** *adv.* —**out·ra'geous·ness** *n.*

ou·tré (ōō-trā') *adj.* Outlandishly improper or unconventional. [< F *outrer,* to pass beyond.]

out·reach (out-rēch') *v.* 1. To surpass in reach. 2. To reach out. 3. To outdo by trickery.

out·rig·ger (out'rĭg'ər) *n.* 1. A float attached to the laterally projecting spars of a seagoing canoe, riding parallel on either side to prevent capsizing. 2. A vessel fitted with such a float.

out·right (out'rīt', -rīt') *adv.* 1. Entirely; wholly. 2. Without delay; at once. —*adj.* (out'rīt'). 1. Unqualified: *an outright gift.* 2. Complete or thoroughgoing; out-and-out. 3. *Archaic.* Proceeding straight onward: *"an even, outright, but imperceptible speed"* (R.L. Stevenson).

out•run (out-rŭn') *v.* **1.** To run faster than. **2.** To escape from. **3.** To exceed.

out•sell (out-sĕl') *v.* To surpass in sales or selling.

out•set (out'sĕt') *n.* Beginning; start.

out•shine (out-shīn') *v.* **1.** To shine brighter than. **2.** To surpass.

out•side (out-sīd', out'sīd') *n.* **1.** The outer surface; exterior. **2.** The external or surface aspect. **3.** The space beyond a boundary or limit. **4.** The utmost limit or extent. —*adj.* **1.** Coming from without: *outside agitators.* **2.** External: *an outside door.* **3.** Apart from one's regular occupation. **4.** Maximum: *an outside estimate.* **5.** Slight; remote: *an outside possibility.* —*adv.* On or to the outside. —*prep.* **1.** On or to the outer side of. **2.** Beyond the limits of. **3.** Except. —**outside of.** Outside.

out•sid•er (out-sī'dər) *n.* **1.** A nonmember of a given group. **2.** A contestant given little chance of winning.

out•size (out'sīz') *n.* A very large size. —**out'size', out'sized'** *adj.*

out•skirts (out'skûrts') *pl.n.* The peripheral parts, as of a town.

out•smart (out-smärt') *v.* To outwit.

out•spo•ken (out-spō'kən) *adj.* Frank and direct. —**out•spo'ken•ly** *adv.*

out•spread (out-sprĕd') *adj.* Spread out; extended.

out•stand•ing (out'stăn'dĭng, out-stăn'dĭng) *adj.* **1.** Projecting upward or outward. **2.** Prominent; salient. **3.** Distinguished; excellent. **4.** Not paid, settled, or resolved.

out•sta•tion (out'stā'shən) *n.* A remote station or post.

out•stay (out-stā') *v.* **1.** To stay longer than. **2.** To outdo in staying power.

out•stretch (out-strĕch') *v.* To extend.

out•strip (out-strĭp') *v.* To leave behind; outrun.

out•ward (out'wərd) *adj.* **1.** Heading toward the outside. **2.** Outer; exterior. **3.** Manifest or external. —*adv.* Also **out•wards** (-wərdz). Toward the outside. —**out'ward•ly** *adv.*

out•wear (out-wâr') *v.* **1.** To wear out; exhaust. **2.** To outlast.

out•weigh (out-wā') *v.* **1.** To weigh more than. **2.** To be more significant than.

out•wit (out-wĭt') *v.* To best by cleverness or cunning.

out•work¹ (out-wûrk') *v.* To work better or faster than.

out•work² (out'wûrk') *n.* A minor fortification outside the main defenses.

o•va. *pl.* of ovum.

o•val (ō'vəl) *adj.* Egg-shaped; ellipsoidal or elliptical. [< L *ōvum*, egg.] —**o'val** *n.*

o•va•ry (ō'və-rē) *n., pl.* **-ries. 1.** One of a pair of female reproductive glands that produce ova. **2.** The plant structure at the base of the pistil, in which seeds are produced. —**o•var'i•an** (ō-vâr'ē-ən), **o•var'i•al** *adj.*

o•vate (ō'vāt') *adj.* Oval; egg-shaped.

o•va•tion (ō-vā'shən) *n.* An enthusiastic show of public homage; applause. [< L *ovāre*, to rejoice.]

ov•en (ŭv'ən) *n.* A compartment, as in a stove,

for baking or heating. [< OE *ofen.* See **aukwh-**.]

o•ver (ō'vər) *prep.* **1.** Above. **2.** On or above and across. **3.** On the other side of. **4.** Upon. **5.** Throughout or during. **6.** Along the length of. **7.** In excess of; more than. **8.** While engaged in or partaking of: *a chat over coffee.* **9.** On account of or with reference to: *an argument over methods.* —*adv.* **1.** Above. **2. a.** Across to another or opposite side. **b.** Across the edge or brim. **3.** Across an intervening distance. **4.** To a different opinion or allegiance: *win him over.* **5.** To a different person, condition, or title: *sign over land.* **6.** So as to be completely covered: *The river froze over.* **7.** Through or thoroughly: *think it over.* **8. a.** From an upright position. **b.** From an upward to an inverted or reversed position. **9. a.** Again. **b.** In repetition: *ten times over.* **10.** In addition or excess. —*adj.* **1.** Finished: *The war is over.* **2. a.** Upper; higher. **b.** Covering; outer. **3.** In excess: *His estimate was fifty dollars over.* —*interj.* Used in radio conversations to mark the end of a transmission by one speaker. [< OE *ofer.* See **uper.**]

over–. *comb. form.* **1.** Superiority of rank or power. **2.** Location above or across a specified position. **3.** Passage beyond or above a limit. **4.** Movement or transferal to a lower or inferior position. **5.** Quantity in excess of what is normal or desirable.

o•ver•act (ō'vər-ăkt') *v.* To act with unnecessary exaggeration.

o•ver•age (ō'vər-āj') *adj.* Beyond the proper or normal age.

o•ver•all (ō'vər-ôl') *adj.* Comprehensive.

o•ver•alls (ō'vər-ôlz') *pl.n.* Coarse, loose-fitting trousers with a bib front and shoulder straps.

o•ver•arm (ō'vər-ärm') *adj.* Executed with the arm raised above the shoulder: *an overarm throw of the ball.*

o•ver•awe (ō'vər-ô') *v.* To subdue by inspiring awe.

o•ver•bal•ance (ō'vər-băl'əns) *v.* **1.** To outweigh. **2.** To throw off balance.

o•ver•bear (ō'vər-bâr') *v.* **1.** To crush or press down upon. **2.** To prevail over; dominate.

o•ver•bear•ing (ō'vər-bâr'ĭng) *adj.* Domineering; arrogant. —**o'ver•bear'ing•ly** *adv.*

o•ver•blown¹ (ō'vər-blōn') *adj.* **1.** Blown down or over. **2.** Blown up with conceit.

o•ver•blown² (ō'vər-blōn') *adj.* Past the stage of full bloom.

o•ver•board (ō'vər-bôrd', -bōrd') *adv.* Over the side of a boat or ship.

o•ver•cast (ō'vər-kăst', -kăst', ō'vər-kăst', -kăst') *adj.* Clouded; gloomy; dark.

o•ver•charge (ō'vər-chärj') *v.* **1.** To charge (a person) too high a price for something. **2.** To fill too full. —**o'ver•charge'** *n.*

o•ver•cloud (ō'vər-kloud') *v.* To cover or become covered with clouds or gloom.

o•ver•coat (ō'vər-kōt') *n.* A heavy outdoor coat.

o•ver•come (ō'vər-kŭm') *v.* **1.** To conquer; defeat. **2.** To surmount; prevail over. **3.** To overpower or exhaust.

ô paw, for/oi boy/ou out/o͞o took/o͞o coo/p pop/r run/s sauce/sh shy/t to/th thin/*th* the/
ŭ cut/ûr fur/v van/w wag/y yes/z size/zh vision/ə ago, item, edible, gallop, circus/

o·ver·do (ō'vər-dōō') *v.* **1.** To exaggerate. **2.** To do too much. **3.** To wear oneself out. **4.** To cook too much or too long.

o·ver·draft (ō'vər-drăft', -dräft') *n.* An amount overdrawn on a bank account.

o·ver·draw (ō'vər-drô') *v.* **1.** To draw against (an account) in excess of credit. **2.** To exaggerate or overstate.

o·ver·drive (ō'vər-drīv') *n.* A gearing mechanism of an automobile that increases the ratio of drive shaft to engine speed in a given speed range.

o·ver·flow (ō'vər-flō') *v.* **1.** To flow over the top, brim, or banks (of). **2.** To inundate; flood. **3.** To be filled beyond capacity. **4.** To be superabundant. —*n.* (ō'vər-flō'). **1.** A flood. **2.** An excess; surplus. **3.** An outlet through which excess liquid can escape.

o·ver·glaze (ō'vər-glāz') *n.* An outer glaze in ceramics.

o·ver·grown (ō'vər-grōn') *adj.* **1.** Covered with growth. **2.** Grown beyond normal size. —o'ver·growth' *n.*

o·ver·hand (ō'vər-hănd') *adj.* Thrown, struck, or executed with the hand brought down from above. —o'ver·hand' *adv.*

o·ver·hang (ō'vər-hăng') *v.* **1.** To project or extend over, out, or beyond. **2.** To threaten or menace; loom over. —*n.* (ō'vər-hăng'). **1.** A projecting part, as of a roof or rock face. **2.** The amount of projection.

o·ver·haul (ō'vər-hôl', ō'vər-hôl') *v.* **1.** To examine or dismantle for needed repairs. **2.** To fix; renovate. —*n.* (ō'vər-hôl'). A repair job; renovation.

o·ver·head (ō'vər-hĕd') *adj.* **1.** Located or functioning above the level of the head. **2.** Of or pertaining to operating expenses. —*n.* (ō'vər-hĕd'). **1.** The operating expenses of a business. **2.** The top surface in an enclosed space of a ship. —*adv.* (ō'vər-hĕd'). Over or above the level of the head.

o·ver·hear (ō'vər-hîr') *v.* To hear without being noticed or addressed by the speaker.

o·ver·joyed (ō'vər-joid') *adj.* Filled with joy; delighted.

o·ver·kill (ō'vər-kĭl') *n.* Nuclear destructive capacity exceeding the amount needed to destroy an enemy.

o·ver·land (ō'vər-lănd', -lənd) *adj.* Traversing land: *an overland trip.* —o'ver·land' *adv.*

o·ver·lap (ō'vər-lăp') *v.* -lapped, -lapping. **1.** To

o'ver·a·bound' *v.*	o'ver·ea'ger *adj.*	o'ver·fat'ten *v.*
o'ver·a·bun'dance *n.*	o'ver·ear'nest *adj.*	o'ver·fed' *adj.*
o'ver·a·bun'dant *adj.*	o'ver·ear'nest·ly *adv.*	o'ver·feed' *v.*
o'ver·ac'tive *adj.*	o'ver·eas'y *adj.*	o'ver·fem'i·nine *adj.*
o'ver·anx'ious *adj.*	o'ver·eat' *v.*	o'ver·fierce' *adj.*
o'ver·at·tached' *adj.*	o'ver·ed'u·cate' *v.*	o'ver·fill' *v.*
o'ver·care'ful *adj.*	o'ver·e·lab'o·rate *adj.*	o'ver·fond'ness *n.*
o'ver·cau'tious *adj.*	o'ver·el'e·gant *adj.*	o'ver·frank' *adj.*
o'ver·cau'tious·ly *adv.*	o'ver·em·bel'lish *v.*	o'ver·free'ly *adv.*
o'ver·cau'tious·ness *n.*	o'ver·e·mo'tion·al *adj.*	o'ver·fre'quent *adj.*
o'ver·chill' *v.*	o'ver·em'pha·sis *n.*	o'ver·full' *adj.*
o'ver·con'fi·dence *n.*	o'ver·em'pha·size' *v.*	o'ver·full'ness *n.*
o'ver·con'fi·dent *adj.*	o'ver·em·phat'ic *adj.*	o'ver·fur'nish *v.*
o'ver·con'fi·dent·ly *adv.*	o'ver·en·thu'si·as'tic *adj.*	o'ver·gen'er·al·ize' *v.*
o'ver·cook' *v.*	o'ver·es'ti·mate' *v.*	o'ver·gen'er·ous *adj.*
o'ver·cool' *adj.*	o'ver·ex·cit'a·ble *adj.*	o'ver·gift'ed *adj.*
o'ver·cour'te·ous *adj.*	o'ver·ex·cite' *v.*	o'ver·glad' *adj.*
o'ver·crit'i·cal *adj.*	o'ver·ex·cite'ment *n.*	o'ver·gra'cious *adj.*
o'ver·crowd' *v.*	o'ver·ex·ert' *v.*	o'ver·grate'ful *adj.*
o'ver·dar'ing *adj.*	o'ver·ex·er'tion *n.*	o'ver·greas'y *adj.*
o'ver·dec'o·rate' *v.*	o'ver·ex·pand' *v.*	o'ver·hard' *adj.*
o'ver·de·mand' *v.*	o'ver·ex·pan'sion *n.*	o'ver·hard'en *v.*
o'ver·de·vot'ed *adj.*	o'ver·ex·pect'ant *adj.*	o'ver·harsh' *adj.*
o'ver·de·vo'tion *n.*	o'ver·ex·u'ber·ant *adj.*	o'ver·hast'y *adj.*
o'ver·dil'i·gence *n.*	o'ver·faith'ful *adj.*	o'ver·help'ful *adj.*
o'ver·dil'i·gent *adj.*	o'ver·fa·mil'iar *adj.*	o'ver·hon'est *adj.*
o'ver·dis'ci·pline *v.*	o'ver·fan'ci·ful *adj.*	o'ver·i·de'al·ism' *n.*
o'ver·dose' *n.*	o'ver·fas·tid'i·ous *adj.*	o'ver·im·ag'i·na·tive *adj.*
o'ver·dra·mat'ic *adj.*		o'ver·im·press' *v.*
o'ver·drink' *v.*		o'ver·in·clined' *adj.*
		o'ver·in·dulge' *v.*
		o'ver·in·dul'gence *n.*
		o'ver·in·dul'gent *adj.*
		o'ver·in·flate' *v.*
		o'ver·in·fla'tion *n.*

ă pat/ā ate/âr care/ä bar/b bib/ch chew/d deed/ĕ pet/ē be/f fit/g gag/h hat/hw what/
ĭ pit/ī pie/îr pier/j judge/k kick/l lid, fatal/m mum/n no, sudden/ng sing/ŏ pot/ō go/

extend over and cover part of. **2.** To coincide partly. —**o'ver·lap'** *n.*

o·ver·lay (ō'vər-lā') *v.* **1.** To lay or spread over or upon. **2.** To cover or embellish the surface of: *overlay wood with silver.* —**o'ver·lay'** *n.*

o·ver·leap (ō'vər-lēp') *v.* **1.** To leap across or over. **2.** To pass over; omit.

o·ver·lie (ō'vər-lī') *v.* To lie over or upon.

o·ver·look (ō'vər-lŏŏk') *v.* **1.** To look over from a higher place. **2.** To afford a view over. **3.** To miss, ignore, or disregard. **4.** To inspect or examine. **5.** To supervise.

o·ver·lord (ō'vər-lôrd') *n.* A lord having supremacy over other lords.

o·ver·ly (ō'vər-lē) *adv.* Excessively; too.

o·ver·mas·ter (ō'vər-măs'tər, -mäs'tər) *v.* To overpower; overcome.

o·ver·match (ō'vər-măch') *v.* **1.** To be more than the match of; defeat. **2.** To match with a superior opponent.

o·ver·night (ō'vər-nīt') *adj.* **1.** Lasting or remaining for a night. **2.** For use on a short journey. —*adv.* (ō'vər-nīt'). **1.** On or during the night. **2.** Suddenly: *The political situation changed overnight.*

o·ver·pass (ō'vər-păs', -päs') *n.* A roadway or bridge that crosses above another thoroughfare.

o·ver·play (ō'vər-plā') *v.* **1.** To play (a role) in an exaggerated manner; overact. **2.** To overestimate the strength of (one's position): *overplay one's hand.*

o·ver·pow·er (ō'vər-pou'ər) *v.* **1.** To vanquish by superior force; subdue. **2.** To overwhelm.

o·ver·reach (ō'vər-rēch') *v.* **1.** To reach or extend over or beyond. **2.** To miss by reaching too far or attempting too much: *overreach a goal.* **3.** To defeat (oneself) by going too far. —**o'ver·reach'er** *n.*

o·ver·ride (ō'vər-rīd') *v.* **1.** To ride across. **2.** To trample upon. **3.** To prevail over. **4.** To declare null and void; set aside.

o·ver·rule (ō'vər-rōōl') *v.* **1.** To disallow or rule against. **2.** To invalidate; reverse. **3.** To prevail over.

o·ver·run (ō'vər-rŭn') *v.* **1.** To attack and defeat conclusively. **2. a.** To spread or swarm over destructively. **b.** To infest. **3.** To spread swiftly throughout. **4.** To overflow. **5.** To go beyond.

o·ver·seas (ō'vər-sēz', ō'vər-sēz') *adv.* Beyond the sea; abroad. —**o'ver·seas'** *adj.*

---

o'ver·in'flu·en'tial *adj.*

o'ver·in·sist'ence *n.*

o'ver·in·sist'ent *adj.*

o'ver·in·sure' *v.*

o'ver·in'tel·lec'tu·al *adj.*

o'ver·in·tense' *adj.*

o'ver·in'ter·est *n.*

o'ver·in·vest' *v.*

o'ver·jeal'ous *adj.*

o'ver·keen' *adj.*

o'ver·kind' *adj.*

o'ver·large' *adj.*

o'ver·late' *adj.*

o'ver·lav'ish *adj.*

o'ver·lax' *adj.*

o'ver·lib'er·al *adj.*

o'ver·live'ly *adj.*

o'ver·load' *v.*

o'ver·long' *adj. & adv.*

o'ver·loud' *adj.*

o'ver·loy'al *adj.*

o'ver·mag'ni·fy' *v.*

o'ver·man'y *adj.*

o'ver·ma·ture' *adj.*

o'ver·meek' *adj.*

o'ver·mer'ci·ful *adj.*

o'ver·might'y *adj.*

o'ver·mix' *v.*

o'ver·mod'est *adj.*

o'ver·moist' *adj.*

o'ver·mois'ten *v.*

o'ver·mort'gage *v.*

o'ver·near' *adj.*

o'ver·neat' *adj.*

o'ver·neg·lect' *v.*

o'ver·ner'vous *adj.*

o'ver·nour'ish *v.*

o'ver·o·bese' *adj.*

o'ver·o·blige' *v.*

o'ver·ob·se'qui·ous *adj.*

o'ver·of·fi'cious *adj.*

o'ver·op'ti·mis'tic *adj.*

o'ver·or·nate' *adj.*

o'ver·par·tic'u·lar *adj.*

o'ver·pas'sion·ate *adj.*

o'ver·pas'sion·ate·ly *adv.*

o'ver·pa'tri·ot'ic *adj.*

o'ver·pes'si·mis'tic *adj.*

o'ver·plain' *adj.*

o'ver·pol'ish *v.*

o'ver·pop'u·lar *adj.*

o'ver·pop'u·la'tion *n.*

o'ver·pop'u·lous *adj.*

o'ver·pre·cise' *adj.*

o'ver·press' *v.*

o'ver·print'ed *adj.*

o'ver·pro·cras'ti·na'tion *n.*

o'ver·pro·duc'tive *adj.*

o'ver·pro·lif'ic *adj.*

o'ver·prom'i·nent *adj.*

o'ver·prompt' *adj.*

o'ver·proud' *adj.*

o'ver·pro·vide' *v.*

o'ver·pro·voke' *v.*

o'ver·pub'lic *adj.*

o'ver·pun'ish *v.*

o'ver·pun'ish·ment *n.*

o'ver·quan'ti·ty *n.*

o'ver·quick' *adj.*

o'ver·qui'et *adj.*

o'ver·ra'tion·al *adj.*

o'ver·re·act' *v.*

o'ver·re·ac'tion *n.*

o'ver·read'y *adj.*

o'ver·re·al·is'tic *adj.*

o'ver·re·fined' *adj.*

o'ver·re·fine'ment *n.*

o'ver·re·flec'tive *adj.*

o'ver·re·li'ant *adj.*

o'ver·re·lig'ious *adj.*

o'ver·re·served' *adj.*

o'ver·re·strain' *v.*

o'ver·rich' *adj.*

o'ver·rife' *adj.*

o'ver·right'eous *adj.*

o'ver·right'eous·ness *n.*

o'ver·rig'id *adj.*

o'ver·rig'or·ous *adj.*

o'ver·ripe' *adj.*

o'ver·rip'en *v.*

o'ver·rough' *adj.*

o'ver·rude' *adj.*

o'ver·sad' *adj.*

o'ver·sale' *n.*

ô paw, for/oi boy/ou out/ŏŏ took/ōō coo/p pop/r run/s sauce/sh shy/t to/th thin/*th* the/
ŭ cut/ûr fur/v van/w wag/y yes/z size/zh vision/ə ago, item, edible, gallop, circus/

o·ver·see (ō'vər-sē') *v.* **1.** To supervise. **2.** To inspect.

o·ver·se·er (ō'vər-sē'ər) *n.* A supervisor or foreman.

o·ver·sexed (ō'vər-sĕkst') *adj.* Obsessed with sex.

o·ver·shad·ow (ō'vər-shăd'ō) *v.* **1.** To cast a shadow over. **2.** To make insignificant by comparison.

o·ver·shoe (ō'vər-shōō') *n.* An article of footwear worn over shoes as protection from water or snow.

o·ver·shoot (ō'vər-shōōt') *v.* **1.** To shoot over or beyond. **2.** To miss by shooting or flying over and beyond. **3.** To exceed.

o·ver·shot (ō'vər-shŏt') *adj.* **1.** Having an upper part projecting beyond the lower: *an overshot jaw.* **2.** Designating a water wheel turned by a stream at the top of its circumference.

o·ver·sight (ō'vər-sīt') *n.* **1.** An unintentional omission or mistake. **2.** Watchful care or management; supervision.

o·ver·sleep (ō'vər-slēp') *v.* To sleep beyond one's usual time for waking.

o·ver·state (ō'vər-stāt') *v.* To exaggerate. —**o'ver·state'ment** *n.*

o·ver·stay (ō'vər-stā') *v.* To stay beyond the set limits or expected duration of.

o·ver·step (ō'vər-stĕp') *v.* To go beyond; transgress.

o·ver·stuffed (ō'vər-stŭft') *adj.* **1.** Excessively stuffed. **2.** Thickly upholstered.

o·ver·sub·scribe (ō'vər-səb-skrīb') *v.* To subscribe for in excess of available supply or accommodation.

o·vert (ō-vûrt', ō'vûrt') *adj.* Not concealed or hidden; open. [< OF, pp of *ovrir*, to open.] —**o·vert'ly** *adv.*

o·ver·take (ō'vər-tāk') *v.* To catch up with.

o·ver·throw (ō'vər-thrō') *v.* **1.** To overturn. **2.** To bring about the downfall of, esp. by force or concerted action. **3.** To throw something over and beyond. —**o'ver·throw'** *n.*

o·ver·time (ō'vər-tīm') *n.* Time beyond an established limit, esp. working hours in addition to those of the regular schedule. —**o'ver·time'** *adv. & adj.*

o·ver·tone (ō'vər-tōn') *n.* **1.** One of the series of higher tones produced by a fundamental tone. **2.** An implication or suggestion.

o·ver·top (ō'vər-tŏp') *v.* **1.** To tower above. **2.** To surpass in importance.

---

o'ver·salt' *v.*
o'ver·salt'y *adj.*
o'ver·sat'u·rate' *v.*
o'ver·sat'u·ra'tion *n.*
o'ver·scent'ed *adj.*
o'ver·scru'pu·lous *adj.*
o'ver·scru'pu·lous·ness *n.*
o'ver·sea'son *v.*
o'ver·sea'soned *adj.*
o'ver·se·cure' *adj.*
o'ver·sell' *v.*
o'ver·sen'si·tive *adj.*
o'ver·sen'ti·men'tal *adj.*
o'ver·se'ri·ous *adj.*
o'ver·se·vere' *adj.*
o'ver·sharp' *adj.*
o'ver·short' *adj.*
o'ver·short'en *v.*
o'ver·shrink' *v.*
o'ver·si'lent *adj.*
o'ver·sim·ple *adj.*
o'ver·sim·plic'i·ty *n.*
o'ver·sim'pli·fi·ca'tion *n.*
o'ver·sim'pli·fy' *v.*
o'ver·skep'ti·cal *adj.*
o'ver·slow' *adj.*
o'ver·small' *adj.*
o'ver·smooth' *adj.*
o'ver·soak' *v.*
o'ver·soft' *adj.*

o'ver·sol'emn *adj.*
o'ver·so·lic'i·tous *adj.*
o'ver·so·phis'ti·cat'ed *adj.*
o'ver·so·phis'ti·ca'tion *n.*
o'ver·spar'ing *adj.*
o'ver·spar'ing·ly *adv.*
o'ver·spe'cial·i·za'tion *n.*
o'ver·spe'cial·ize' *v.*
o'ver·spec'u·late' *v.*
o'ver·spec'u·la'tion *n.*
o'ver·spec'u·la'tive *adj.*
o'ver·spent' *adj.*
o'ver·stim'u·late' *v.*
o'ver·stim'u·la'tion *n.*
o'ver·stock' *v.*
o'ver·strain' *v.*
o'ver·stress' *v.*
o'ver·stretch' *v.*
o'ver·striv'ing *adj. & n.*
o'ver·sub·scrip'tion *n.*
o'ver·sub'tle *adj.*
o'ver·sub'tle·ty *n.*
o'ver·suf·fi'cient *adj.*
o'ver·su'per·sti'tious *adj.*
o'ver·sure' *adj.*

o'ver·sus·pi'cious *adj.*
o'ver·sus·pi'cious·ly *adv.*
o'ver·sweet' *adj.*
o'ver·sys'tem·at'ic *adj.*
o'ver·talk'a·tive *adj.*
o'ver·talk'a·tive·ness *n.*
o'ver·tax' *v.*
o'ver·tax·a'tion *n.*
o'ver·teach' *v.*
o'ver·tech'ni·cal *adj.*
o'ver·te·na'cious *adj.*
o'ver·ten'der *adj.*
o'ver·ten'der·ness *n.*
o'ver·tense' *adj.*
o'ver·ten'sion *n.*
o'ver·thick' *adj.*
o'ver·thin' *adj.*
o'ver·thought'ful *adj.*
o'ver·thrift'y *adj.*
o'ver·tight' *adj.*
o'ver·tire' *v.*
o'ver·train' *v.*
o'ver·truth'ful *adj.*
o'ver·use' *v.*
o'ver·val'u·a·ble *adj.*
o'ver·va·ri'e·ty *n.*
o'ver·ve'he·ment *adj.*
o'ver·ven'ti·late' *v.*
o'ver·ven'tur·ous *adj.*

ă pat/ā ate/âr care/ä bar/b bib/ch chew/d deed/ĕ pet/ē be/f fit/g gag/h hat/hw what/
ĭ pit/ī pie/îr pier/j judge/k kick/l lid, fatal/m mum/n no, sudden/ng sing/ŏ pot/ō go/

o·ver·ture (ō'vər-chŏŏr') *n.* **1.** An instrumental introduction to an extended musical work, as an opera. **2.** Any introductory section or part. **3.** An offer or proposal. [< L *apertūra*, an opening.]

o·ver·turn (ō'vər-tûrn') *v.* **1.** To capsize; upset. **2.** To overthrow; defeat.

o·ver·view (ō'vər-vyōō') *n.* A comprehensive view; survey.

o·ver·ween·ing (ō'vər-wē'nĭng) *adj.* **1.** Arrogant; overbearing. **2.** Excessive; immoderate.

o·ver·weigh (ō'vər-wā') *v.* **1.** To outweigh. **2.** To oppress.

o·ver·whelm (ō'vər-hwĕlm') *v.* **1.** To submerge; engulf. **2.** To overcome; overpower. **3.** To upset; overthrow. —**o'ver·whelm'ing** *adj.*

o·ver·wrought (ō'vər-rôt') *adj.* **1.** Excessively nervous. **2.** Extremely elaborate.

ovi–. *comb. form.* Egg or ovum. [< L *ōvum*, egg.]

Ov·id (ŏv'ĭd). 43 B.C.–A.D. 17? Roman poet.

o·vip·a·rous (ō-vĭp'ər-əs) *adj.* Producing eggs that hatch outside the body. —**o'vi·par'i·ty** (ō'və-păr'ə-tē) *n.* —**o·vip'a·rous·ly** *adv.*

o·void (ō'void') *adj.* Egg-shaped. [< OV(I)- + -OID.] —**o'void'** *n.*

o·vu·late (ō'vyə-lāt') *v.* **-lated, -lating.** To produce or discharge ova. —**o'vu·la'tion** *n.*

o·vule (ō'vyōōl) *n.* A minute plant structure that after fertilization becomes a seed. [< L *ōvum*, egg.]

o·vum (ō'vəm) *n., pl.* **ova** (ō'və). A female reproductive cell; an egg. [< L *ōvum*, egg.]

owe (ō) *v.* **owed, owing. 1.** To have to pay or repay. **2.** To be morally obligated to: *I owe him an apology.* **3.** To be in debt to. **4.** To be obliged for. **5.** To bear (a feeling) toward a person: *He owes them a grudge.* **6.** *Obs.* To own; have. —**owing to.** Because of. [< OE *āgan,* to possess. See **ēik-**.]

owl (oul) *n.* A usually night-flying bird of prey with a large head, a short, hooked bill, and a disklike face. [< OE *ūle.*] —**owl'ish** *adj.*

owl·et (ou'lĭt) *n.* A young or small owl.

own (ōn) *adj.* Of or belonging to oneself. —Used as an intensive adjective: *my own book.* —*n.* That which belongs to one: *It is my own.* —*v.* **1.** To have or possess. **2.** To acknowledge, admit, or confess. [< OE *āgen.* See **ēik-**.] —**own'er** *n.* —**own'er·ship'** *n.*

ox (ŏks) *n., pl.* **oxen** (ŏk'sən). **1.** An adult castrated bull. **2.** Any of various bovine mammals. [< OE *oxa.*]

ox·al·ic acid (ŏk-săl'ĭk). A poisonous, crystalline organic acid, $C_2H_2O_4·2H_2O$, used as a cleansing agent and bleach.

ox·bow (ŏks'bō') *n.* **1.** A U-shaped collar for a draft ox. **2.** A U-shaped bend in a river.

ox·ford (ŏks'fərd) *n.* A low shoe that laces over the instep. [< OXFORD, England.]

Ox·ford (ŏks'fərd). A city of S England; site of Oxford University. Pop. 109,000. —**Ox·o'ni·an** (ŏk-sō'nē-ən) *adj.*

ox·i·dant (ŏk'sə-dənt) *n.* A chemical reagent that oxidizes.

ox·i·da·tion (ŏk'sə-dā'shən) *n.* **1.** The combination of a substance with oxygen. **2.** A reaction in which the atoms in an element lose electrons and its valence is correspondingly increased. —**ox'i·da'tive** (ŏk'sə-dā'tĭv) *adj.* —**ox'i·da'tive·ly** *adv.*

ox·ide (ŏk'sīd') *n.* A binary compound of an element or radical with oxygen. [< OXYGEN.] —**ox·id'ic** (ŏk-sĭd'ĭk) *adj.*

ox·i·dize (ŏk'sə-dīz') *v.* **-dized, -dizing. 1.** To combine with oxygen. **2.** To increase the positive charge or valence of (an element) by removing electrons. **3.** To coat with oxide. [< OXIDE.] —**ox'i·di·za'tion** *n.*

ox·i·diz·er (ŏk'sə-dī'zər) *n.* Any substance that oxidizes or induces another substance to oxidize.

oxy–. *comb. form. Chem.* Containing oxygen.

ox·y·a·cet·y·lene (ŏk'sē-ə-sĕt'l-ĭn, -ə-sĕt'l-ēn') *adj.* Containing a mixture of acetylene and oxygen, as commonly used in metal welding and cutting torches.

ox·y·gen (ŏk'sĭ-jən) *n. Symbol* **O** A colorless, odorless, tasteless gaseous element constituting 21% of the atmosphere by volume, required for nearly all combustion and combustive processes. Atomic number 8, atomic

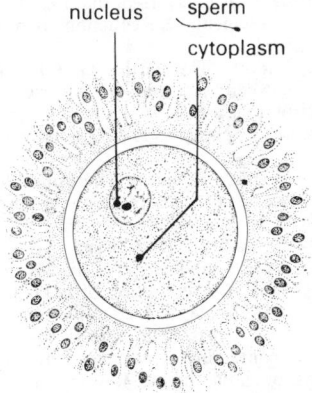

ovum
Human ovum, enlarged
126 diameters

nucleus   sperm

cytoplasm

o'ver·vig'or·ous *adj.*	o'ver·will'ing *adj.*	o'ver·youth'ful *adj.*
o'ver·vi'o·lent *adj.*	o'ver·wise' *adj.*	o'ver·zeal' *n.*
o'ver·warm' *v.*	o'ver·wor'ry *v.*	o'ver·zeal'ous *adj.*
o'ver·warmed' *adj.*	o'ver·write' *v.*	o'ver·zeal'ous·ly *adv.*
o'ver·weak' *adj.*	o'ver·writ'ten *adj.*	o'ver·zeal'ous·ness
o'ver·wet' *adj.*	o'ver·young' *adj.*	*n.*

ŏ paw, for/oi boy/ou out/ŏŏ took/ōō coo/p pop/r run/s sauce/sh shy/t to/th thin/*th* the/
ŭ cut/ûr fur/v van/w wag/y yes/z size/zh vision/ə ago, item, edible, gallop, circus/

weight 15.9994. [F *oxygène,* "acid-former" : Gk *oxus,* sharp + -GEN.] —**ox′y•gen′ic** (ŏk′sĭ-jĕn′ĭk), **ox•yg′e•nous** (ŏk-sĭj′ə-nəs) *adj.*

ox•y•gen•ate (ŏk′sĭ-jə-nāt′) *v.* **-ated, -ating.** To treat, combine, or infuse with oxygen. —**ox′y•gen•a′tion** *n.*

oxygen mask. A masklike device covering the mouth and nose through which oxygen is supplied from a tank or other source.

oxygen tent. A canopy placed over the head and shoulders to provide oxygen therapy.

ox•y•mo•ron (ŏk′sē-môr′ŏn′, -mōr′ŏn′) *n., pl.* **-mora** (-môr′ə, -mōr′ə). A rhetorical figure in which an epigrammatic effect is created by a paradoxical conjunction of terms. [< Gk *oxumōros,* "sharp-foolish."]

oys•ter (oi′stər) *n.* Any of several often edible bivalve mollusks with an irregularly shaped shell. [< Gk *ostreon.*]

oz ounce.

oz ap apothecaries' ounce.

O•zark Mountains (ō′zärk). A range of low mountains in the south-central U.S.

o•zone (ō′zōn) *n.* **1.** A blue, gaseous, powerfully oxidizing form of oxygen, O_3, derived from O_2 by electric discharge or exposure to ultraviolet radiation. **2.** *Informal.* Fresh, pure air. [< Gk *ozein,* to smell, reek.]

Pp

p, P (pē) *n.* The 16th letter of the English alphabet.

p **1.** pico-. **2.** proton.

P phosphorous.

p. **1.** page. **2.** participle. **3.** past. **4.** per. **5.** pint. **6.** population. **7.** president.

P. president.

pa (pä) *n. Informal.* Father.

Pa protactinium.

PA public-address system.

Pa. Pennsylvania.

p.a. per annum.

P.A. power of attorney.

pab•u•lum (păb′yə-ləm) *n.* Food; nourishment. [L *pābulum,* food, fodder.]

Pac. Pacific.

pace (pās) *n.* **1.** A step made in walking. **2.** The distance spanned by a step taken as a unit of measurement. **3.** Rate of movement or progress. **4.** A manner of walking or running. **5.** A horse's gait in which both feet on one side move together. —*v.* **paced, pacing. 1.** To walk or cover at a slow pace. **2.** To measure by paces. **3.** To set or regulate the rate of speed for. **4.** To train (a horse) in a particular gait, esp. the pace. [< L *passus,* a step, "stretch of the leg."] —**pac′er** *n.*

pace•mak•er (pās′mā′kər) *n.* **1.** One who sets the pace in a race. **2.** A leader in any field. **3. a.** A mass of specialized muscle fibers of the heart that regulate the heartbeat. **b.** Any of several usually miniaturized and surgically implanted electronic devices used to regulate the heartbeat.

pace•set•ter (pās′sĕt′ər) *n.* A pacemaker. —**pace′set′ting** *adj.*

pach•y•derm (păk′ĭ-dûrm′) *n.* A large, thick-skinned mammal, as the elephant or rhinoceros. [< Gk *pakhudermos,* thick-skinned.]

pach•y•san•dra (păk′ĭ-săn′drə) *n.* A low-growing plant with evergreen leaves, cultivated as a ground cover. [NL, "with thick stamens."]

pa•cif•ic (pə-sĭf′ĭk) *adj.* **1.** Tending to diminish conflict. **2.** Peaceful; tranquil. [< L *pāx,* peace + -FIC.] —**pa•cif′i•cal•ly** *adv.*

pac•i•fi•ca•tion (păs′ə-fĭ-kā′shən) *n.* **1.** Placation; appeasement. **2.** Reduction to peaceful submission.

Pacific Ocean. The earth's largest body of water, between Asia and the Americas.

pac•i•fi•er (păs′ə-fī′ər) *n.* **1.** One that pacifies. **2.** A rubber or plastic nipple for a baby to suck on.

pac•i•fism (păs′ə-fĭz′əm) *n.* Opposition to war or violence as a means of resolving disputes. —**pac′i•fist** *n.* & *adj.*

pac•i•fy (păs′ə-fī′) *v.* **-fied, -fying. 1.** To calm; appease. **2.** To subdue. [< L *pācificāre.*]

pack (păk) *n.* **1.** A collection of items tied up or wrapped; bundle. **2.** A container carried on the back of a person or animal. **3.** A small package containing a standard number of identical or similar items. **4.** A deck of playing cards. **5.** A large amount; heap. **6. a.** A group of animals, as wolves, that run together. **b.** A gang or band of people. **7.** A compacted mass of ice floes. **8.** *Med.* **a.** The swathing of a patient in hot, cold, wet, or dry sheets or blankets. **b.** The sheets or blankets so used. **c.** A material, as gauze, therapeutically inserted into a cavity or wound. **9.** A folded cloth filled with crushed ice and applied to sore or swollen parts of the body. —*v.* **1.** To combine into a bundle. **2. a.** To put into a protective receptacle. **b.** To stow luggage or belongings. **3.** To crowd together. **4.** To fill up tight; cram. **5.** *Med.* To apply a pack. **6.** To compact firmly. **7.** *Informal.* To carry: *pack a pistol.* **8.** To send or be sent off peremptorily.

ă pat/ā ate/âr care/ä bar/b bib/ch chew/d deed/ĕ pet/ē be/f fit/g gag/h hat/hw what/ ĭ pit/ī pie/îr pier/j judge/k kick/l lid, fatal/m mum/n no, sudden/ng sing/ŏ pot/ō go/

9. To rig (a voting panel) to be fraudulently favorable: *pack the jury.* [ME.]

pack•age (păk′ĭj) *n.* **1.** A parcel or bundle. **2.** A configuration of several related items offered for sale. *—v.* **-aged, -aging.** To put or make into a package.

pack•er (păk′ər) *n.* One that packs, esp. a wholesaler of meat products.

pack•et (păk′ĭt) *n.* **1.** A small package or bundle. **2.** A regularly scheduled passenger and cargo boat.

pack•ing (păk′ĭng) *n.* **1.** The processing and packaging of food products. **2.** Material used to prevent leakage or seepage.

pact (păkt) *n.* A treaty or compact. [< L *pactum.*]

pad¹ (păd) *n.* **1.** A cushion or something functioning as a cushion. **2.** A number of sheets of paper, stacked and glued together at one end. **3.** A broad, floating leaf, as of a water lily. **4.** The cushionlike flesh on the underpart of the foot of an animal. *—v.* **padded, padding.** To line or stuff with padding. [Akin to Flem *pad.*]

pad² (păd) *v.* **padded, padding.** To move or walk about quietly on foot. [Prob < MDu *paden,* to walk along a path.]

pad•ding (păd′ĭng) *n.* **1.** Material used as stuffing, filling, or lining. **2.** Unnecessary matter added to a text to make it longer.

pad•dle¹ (păd′l) *n.* **1.** An oar for a canoe. **2.** An implement or part resembling this. **3.** A ping-pong racket. **4.** A board of a paddle wheel. *—v.* **-dled, -dling. 1.** To row or swim with or as with a paddle. **2.** To stir or beat with a paddle. **3.** To spank. [ME *padell.*] *—pad′dler n.*

pad•dle² (păd′l) *v.* **-dled, -dling. 1.** To dabble or wade about in shallow water. **2.** To toddle. [?]

paddle wheel. A wheel with paddles on its rim, used to propel a ship.

pad•dock (păd′ək) *n.* A fenced area in which horses are kept, as for grazing or for preparation and display before a race. [< OE *pearroc* < Gmc *parruk.*]

pad•dy (păd′ē) *n., pl.* **-dies.** An irrigated or flooded field where rice is grown. [Malay *padi.*]

paddy wagon. A police van for taking suspects into custody.

pad•lock (păd′lŏk′) *n.* A lock with a U-shaped bar that can be passed through the staple of a hasp and then snapped shut. [ME *padlok.*] *—pad′lock′ v.*

pae•an (pē′ən) *n.* A song of joyful praise or exultation. [L *paeān.*]

pa•gan (pā′gən) *n.* One who is not a Christian, Moslem, or Jew. [< L *pāgānus,* country-dweller.] *—pa′gan adj. —pa′gan•ism′ n.*

page¹ (pāj) *n.* **1.** An errand boy or messenger. **2.** A youth in knightly or ceremonial attendance at court. *—v.* **paged, paging.** To summon by calling the name of. [Prob < Gk *paidion,* child.]

page² (pāj) *n.* A leaf of a book or manuscript or one side of it. *—v.* **paged, paging. 1.** To number the pages of; paginate. **2.** To thumb through. [< L *pāgina.*]

pag•eant (păj′ənt) *n.* An elaborate and color-

ful public spectacle. [< ML *pāgina,* scene of a play < L, PAGE².] *—pag′eant•ry (-ən-trē) n.*

pag•i•na•tion (păj′ə-nā′shən) *n.* **1.** The numbering of pages. **2.** The arrangement and number of pages in a book.

pa•go•da (pə-gō′də) *n.* A many-storied Buddhist tower. [< Dravid.]

paid (pād). *p.t. & p.p.* of **pay.**

pail (pāl) *n.* A cylindrical vessel with a handle; bucket. [< ML *pagella,* a measure.]

pain (pān) *n.* **1.** An unpleasant sensation arising from injury, disease, or emotional disorder. **2.** Suffering or distress. **3. pains.** Trouble; effort. **4.** Penalty: *pain of death. —v.* To cause or suffer pain. [< Gk *poinē,* penalty.] *—pain′-ful adj. —pain′ful•ly adv.*

Paine (pān), **Thomas.** 1737–1809. Political leader in the American Revolution.

pain•kill•er (pān′kĭl′ər) *n.* Something that relieves pain. *—pain′kill′ing adj.*

pain•less (pān′lĭs) *adj.* Free from pain. *—pain′less•ly adv. —pain′less•ness n.*

pains•tak•ing (pānz′tā′kĭng) *adj.* Taking pains; careful. *—pains′tak′ing•ly adv.*

paint (pānt) *n.* **1. a.** A mixture of a pigment in a liquid, used as a decorative or protective coating. **b.** The dry film formed by such a mixture applied to a surface. **2.** A cosmetic. *—v.* **1.** To represent with or as with paints. **2.** To coat with paint. **3.** To apply cosmetics. **4.** To practice the art of painting pictures. [< L *pingere.*] *—paint′er n.*

paint•ing (pān′tĭng) *n.* **1.** The art or occupation of working with paint. **2.** A painted picture.

pair (pâr) *n., pl.* **pairs** or *informal* **pair. 1.** Two corresponding persons or items, similar in form or function. **2.** Something composed of two corresponding parts. **3.** Two associated persons or animals considered together. *—v.* **1.** To arrange in sets of two. **2.** To form a pair or pairs. [< L *paria,* equal things.]

pais•ley (pāz′lē) *adj.* Having a colorful, swirled pattern of curved shapes. [< *Paisley,* Scotland.]

pa•ja•mas (pə-jä′məz, -jăm′əz) *pl.n.* A loose-fitting garment consisting of trousers and a jacket, for sleeping or lounging. [Hindi *pāe-jāma.*]

Pak•i•stan (păk′ĭ-stăn′, pä′kĭ-stăn′). A repub-

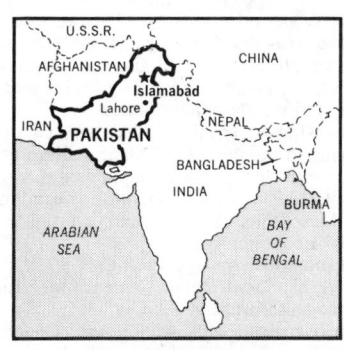

Pakistan

lic in southern Asia. Pop. 112,600,000. Cap. Islamabad. —**Pak'i•stan'i** *adj.* & *n.*

pal (păl) *n. Informal.* A friend; chum. [< Sk *bhrātar-,* brother.]

pal•ace (păl'ĭs) *n.* **1.** The official residence of a royal person. **2.** Any splendid residence; mansion. [< L *palātium.*]

pal•a•din (păl'ə-dĭn) *n.* **1.** Any of the 12 peers of Charlemagne's court. **2.** A paragon of chivalry; knightly champion. [< L *palātium,* PALACE.]

pal•an•quin (păl'ən-kēn') *n.* A covered litter, carried on poles on the shoulders of two or four men.

pal•at•a•ble (păl'ĭt-ə-bəl) *adj.* **1.** Acceptable to the taste. **2.** Acceptable to the mind or sensibilities: *a palatable solution to the problem.* [< PALATE.]

pal•ate (păl'ĭt) *n.* **1.** The roof of the mouth, consisting of the **hard palate** and the **soft palate**. **2.** The sense of taste. [< L *palātum.*] —**pal'a•tal** *adj.*

pa•la•tial (pə-lā'shəl) *adj.* **1.** Of or suitable for a palace. **2.** Spacious and ornate.

pa•lat•i•nate (pə-lăt'n-āt', -ĭt) *n.* The territory of a palatine.

pal•a•tine¹ (păl'ə-tīn') *n.* **1.** A title of various administrative officials of the late Roman and Byzantine empires. **2.** A feudal lord delegated with royal powers. —*adj.* **1.** Belonging to or fit for a palace. **2.** Of or designating a palatine or palatinate. [< L *palātium,* a PALACE.]

pal•a•tine² (păl'ə-tīn') *adj.* **1.** Pertaining to the palate. **2.** Designating either of the two bones that make up the hard palate. —*n.* Either of these bones.

pa•lav•er (pə-lăv'ər, -lä'vər) *n.* Long and idle chatter or cajolery. [< LL *parabola,* speech, parable.] —**pa•lav'er** *v.*

pale¹ (pāl) *n.* **1.** A stake or picket. **2.** The area enclosed by a fence or boundary. [< L *pālus.*]

pale² (pāl) *adj.* **paler, palest. 1.** Pallid; wan. **2.** Of a low intensity of color; light. **3.** Of a low intensity of light; dim. **4.** Feeble; weak. —*v.* **paled, paling.** To make or become pale. [< L *pallēre,* to be pale.] —**pale'ness** *n.*

paleo-. *comb. form.* Ancient or prehistoric. [< Gk *palaios,* ancient.]

Pa•le•o•cene (pā'lē-ə-sēn') *adj.* Of or belonging to the geologic time, rock series, or sedimentary deposits of the first epoch of the Tertiary period. —*n.* The Paleocene epoch.

pa•le•og•ra•phy (pā'lē-ŏg'rə-fē) *n.* The study and interpretation of ancient documents. —**pa'le•og'ra•pher** *n.* —**pa'le•o•graph'ic** (-ə-grăf'ĭk), **pa'le•o•graph'i•cal** *adj.*

Pa•le•o•lith•ic (pā'lē-ə-lĭth'ĭk) *adj.* Of or belonging to the period of human culture beginning with the earliest chipped stone tools, about 750,000 years ago, until the beginning of the Mesolithic, about 15,000 years ago. —*n.* The Paleolithic Age.

pa•le•on•tol•o•gy (pā'lē-ŏn-tŏl'ə-jē) *n.* The study of fossils and ancient life forms. —**pa'le•on•tol'o•gist** *n.*

Pa•le•o•zo•ic (pā'lē-ə-zō'ĭk) *adj.* Of or belonging to the geologic time, rock series, or sedimentary deposits of the era preceding the Mesozoic, divided into seven periods from the Cambrian to the Permian. —*n.* The Paleozoic era.

Pa•ler•mo (pä-lĕr'mō). The capital of Sicily. Pop. 623,000.

Pal•es•tine (păl'ĭ-stīn'). **1.** The land between the Mediterranean Sea and the Jordan River that was occupied by the Hebrews in Biblical times. **2.** This territory, occupied today by Israel. —**Pal'es•tin'i•an** (păl'ĭ-stĭn'ē-ən) *n.*

pal•ette (păl'ĭt) *n.* **1.** A board, typically with a hole for the thumb, upon which an artist mixes colors. **2.** The range of colors on a palette. [< L *pāla,* spade, shovel.]

Pa•li (pä'lē) *n.* An ancient Indic language.

pal•imp•sest (păl'ĭmp-sĕst') *n.* Vellum or parchment that has been written upon several times, often with remnants of earlier, imperfectly erased writing still visible. [< Gk *palimpsēstos,* rubbed again.]

pal•in•drome (păl'ĭn-drōm') *n.* A word, verse, or sentence that reads the same backward and forward, as *A man, a plan, a canal, Panama!* [Gk *palindromos,* running back again.]

pal•ing (pā'lĭng) *n.* **1.** A pale; picket. **2.** Pointed sticks used in making fences. **3.** A fence of pales.

pal•i•node (păl'ə-nōd') *n.* A poem of retraction or recantation. [< Gk *palinōidia.*]

pal•i•sade (păl'ə-sād') *n.* **1.** A fence of pales forming a fortification. **2.** A line of steep cliffs, usually along a river.

pall¹ (pôl) *n.* **1.** A cloth covering for a coffin or bier. **2.** A coffin. **3.** Something that covers with darkness or gloom. [< L *pallium,* a cover, cloak.]

pall² (pôl) *v.* **1.** To make or become insipid, boring, or wearisome. **2.** To cloy; satiate. [< ME *appallen,* appall.]

pal•la•di•um (pə-lā'dē-əm) *n. Symbol* **Pd** A soft, ductile, steel-white, tarnish-resistant metallic element alloyed for use in electric contacts, jewelry, nonmagnetic watch parts, and surgical instruments. Atomic number 46, atomic weight 106.4.

Pal•las (păl'əs) *n.* The second-largest asteroid of the solar system, approx. 300 miles in diameter. [< P. *Pallas* (died 1811), German naturalist.]

pall•bear•er (pôl'bâr'ər) *n.* One of the persons carrying or attending the coffin at a funeral.

pal•let (păl'ĭt) *n.* A narrow, hard bed or straw-filled mattress. [< L *palea,* chaff.]

pal•li•ate (păl'ē-āt') *v.* **-ated, -ating. 1.** To extenuate; excuse. **2.** To alleviate without curing. [< L *pallium,* cloak.] —**pal'li•a'tion** *n.* —**pal'li•a'tive** (-ā'tĭv, -ə-tĭv) *adj.* & *n.*

pal•lid (păl'ĭd) *adj.* Pale in color or complexion; wan. [< L *pallēre,* to be pale.]

pal•lor (păl'ər) *n.* Extreme or unnatural paleness.

palm¹ (päm) *n.* The inner surface of the hand, extending from the wrist to the base of the fingers. —*v.* **1.** To conceal in the palm of the hand. **2.** To pick up furtively. —**palm off.** To dispose of fraudulently. [< L *palma,* palm of the hand, palm tree.]

palm² (päm) *n.* **1.** Any of various chiefly trop-

ă pat/ā ate/âr care/ä bar/b bib/ch chew/d deed/ĕ pet/ē be/f fit/g gag/h hat/hw what/
ĭ pit/ī pie/îr pier/j judge/k kick/l lid, fatal/m mum/n no, sudden/ng sing/ŏ pot/ō go/

ical trees usually having an unbranched trunk
with a crown of large featherlike or fanlike
leaves. **2. a.** An emblem of victory. **b.** Triumph; victory. [< OE < L *palma,* PALM.]
pal•mate (păl′māt, păl′-, pä′māt′) *adj.* Also
pal•mat•ed (păl′mā′tĭd, päl′-, pä′mā′-). Resembling a hand with the fingers extended.
palm•er (pä′mər) *n.* Formerly, a person who
wore two crossed palm leaves as a token of
having visited the Holy Land.
pal•met•to (păl-mĕt′ō) *n., pl.* **-tos** or **-toes.** Any
of several small palms with fan-shaped leaves.
palm•is•try (pä′mĭ-strē) *n.* The practice or art
of telling fortunes from the lines, marks, and
patterns on the palms of the hands. —**palm′ist,**
palm′is•ter (pä′mĭ-stər) *n.*
Palm Sunday. The Sunday before Easter,
commemorating Christ's triumphal entry into
Jerusalem.
palm•y (pä′mē) *adj.* **-ier, -iest. 1.** Of or covered
with palm trees. **2.** Prosperous; flourishing.
pal•o•mi•no (păl′ə-mē′nō) *n., pl.* **-nos.** A horse
with a light tan coat and a whitish mane and
tail. [< Span, dove-colored.]
pal•pa•ble (păl′pə-bəl) *adj.* **1.** Capable of being felt; tangible. **2.** Easily perceived; obvious.
[< L *palpāre,* to touch.] —**pal′pa•bil′i•ty** *n.*
—**pal′pa•bly** *adv.*
pal•pate (păl′pāt′) *v.* **-pated, -pating.** *Med.* To
examine by touching. [L *palpāre,* to touch.]
pal•pi•tate (păl′pə-tāt′) *v.* **-tated, -tating.** To
shake, quiver, or throb. [< L *palpāre,* to
touch.] —**pal′pi•ta′tion** *n.*
pal•sy (pôl′zē) *n., pl.* **-sies. 1.** Paralysis. **2.** A
condition marked by loss of power to feel or to
control movement in any part of the body.
3. a. A weakening or debilitating influence.
b. An enfeebled condition or debilitated state
thought to result from such an influence. [<
L *paralysis,* paralysis.] —**pal′sied** *adj.*
pal•ter (pôl′tər) *v.* **1.** To talk or act insincerely;
equivocate. **2.** To quibble. [?]
pal•try (pôl′trē) *adj.* **-trier, -triest. 1.** Petty; trifling. **2.** Worthless; trashy. **3.** Contemptible;
vile. [?] —**pal′tri•ly** *adv.*
pam•pas (păm′pəz) *pl.n. Sing.* **-pa** (-pə). A
nearly treeless grassland area of South America, chiefly in C Argentina and Uruguay. [<
Amer Span *pampa.*]
pam•per (păm′pər) *v.* To treat with excessive
indulgence; coddle; cater to. [ME *pamperen.*]
—**pam′per•er** *n.*
pam•phlet (păm′flĭt) *n.* A short essay or treatise, usually on a current topic, published
without a binding. [< *Pamphilus,* a popular
short Latin poem of the 12th century.]
—**pam′phle•teer′** (-flə-tîr′) *n.*
pan (păn) *n.* **1.** A shallow, wide, open container
for holding liquids, cooking, etc. **2.** A similar
container or object. —*v.* **panned, panning. 1.** To
wash (gravel, sand, etc.) in a pan to separate
precious metal. **2.** *Informal.* To criticize harshly. —**pan out.** *Informal.* To turn out well; be
successful. [< OE *panne* < Gmc **panna.*]
pan-. *comb. form.* All. [< Gk *pas (pant-),* all.]
pan•a•ce•a (păn′ə-sē′ə) *n.* A remedy for all
diseases, evils, or difficulties; cure-all. [< Gk
panakēs, all-healing.]

pa•nache (pə-năsh′, -näsh′) *n.* **1.** A bunch of
feathers or a plume, esp. on a helmet. **2.** Dash;
swagger; verve. [< L *pinna,* feather.]
Pan•a•ma (păn′ə-mä′). **1.** A republic of Central America. Pop. 1,076,000. **2.** Also **Panama
City.** Its capital. Pop. 273,000. —**Pan′a•ma′ni•an**
(păn′ə-mä′nē-ən) *adj. & n.*

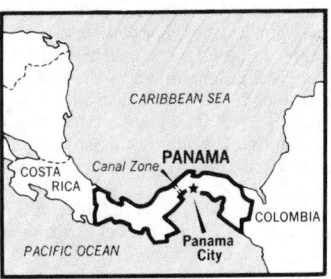

Panama

Panama, Isthmus of. An isthmus connecting
North and South America and separating the
Pacific from the Caribbean.
Panama Canal. A ship canal across the Isthmus of Panama, connecting the Caribbean
with the Pacific.
Pan-A•mer•i•can (păn′ə-mĕr′ə-kən) *adj.* Of or
pertaining to North, South, and Central America collectively.
pan•a•tel•a (păn′ə-tĕl′ə) *n.* A long, slender
cigar. [< Amer Span, a long thin biscuit.]
pan•cake (păn′kāk′) *n.* A thin cake made of
batter, cooked on a hot, greased skillet.
pan•chro•mat•ic (păn′krō-măt′ĭk) *adj.* Sensitive to all colors, as film.
pan•cre•as (păng′krē-əs, păn′-) *n.* A long,
soft, irregularly shaped gland that secretes
pancreatic juice into the duodenum and, in the
islands of Langerhans, produces insulin. [Gk
pankreas, "all-flesh."] —**pan′cre•at′ic** (-ăt′ĭk)
adj.
pancreatic juice. A clear, alkaline secretion of
the pancreas containing enzymes that aid in
the digestion of proteins, carbohydrates, and
fats.
pan•da (păn′də) *n.* **1.** Also **giant panda.** A
bearlike black and white mammal of the
mountains of China and Tibet. **2.** Also **lesser
panda.** A related raccoonlike mammal. [F.]
pan•dem•ic (păn-dĕm′ĭk) *adj.* Prevalent over
a wide geographic area, as a disease. [< Gk
pandēmos, of all the people.]
pan•de•mo•ni•um (păn′də-mō′nē-əm) *n.* Wild
uproar or noise. [< *Pandæmonium,* capital of
Hell in Milton's *Paradise Lost.*]
pan•der (păn′dər) *n.* Also **pan•der•er** (păn′dər-
ər). A go-between in sexual intrigues; pimp;
procurer. —*v.* **1.** To act as a pander. **2.** To
cater to the vices or weaknesses of others. [<
Pandare, character in Chaucer's *Troilus and
Criseyde.*]
Pan•do•ra (păn-dôr′ə, -dōr′ə). *Gk.Myth.* The
first woman; opened a box containing all the
ills that could plague mankind.

ô paw, for/oi boy/ou out/o͞o took/o͞o coo/p pop/r run/s sauce/sh shy/t to/th thin/*th* the/
ŭ cut/ûr fur/v van/w wag/y yes/z size/zh vision/ə ago, item, edible, gallop, circus/

pane (pān) *n.* A sheet of glass in a window or door. [ME, piece of cloth, section.]

pan•e•gyr•ic (păn'ə-jĭr'ĭk, -jī'rĭk) *n.* Elaborate praise expressed formally; an encomium. [< Gk *(logos) panêgurikos,* "(speech) for a public festival."] —**pan'e•gyr'i•cal** *adj.*

pan•el (păn'əl) *n.* **1.** A flat, usually rectangular, raised, recessed or framed piece forming a part of a surface in which it is set. **2.** A board containing instruments or controls. **3.** A group of people gathered or selected to discuss an issue, make a judgment, etc. —*v.* **-eled** or **-elled, -eling** or **-elling.** To cover, furnish, or decorate with panels. [< OF, piece of parchment on which names of a jury were written.]

pan•el•ing (păn'əl-ĭng) *n.* Panels, esp. decorative panels.

pan•el•ist (păn'əl-ĭst) *n.* A member of a panel.

panel truck. A small delivery truck with a fully enclosed body.

pang (păng) *n.* A sudden, sharp feeling of pain or distress.

pan•han•dle[1] (păn'hănd'l) *n.* A narrow strip of territory projecting from a larger, broader area to which it belongs.

pan•han•dle[2] (păn'hănd'l) *v.* **-dled, -dling.** *Informal.* To beg, esp. on the streets. —**pan'han'dler** *n.*

pan•ic (păn'ĭk) *n.* A sudden, overpowering, often contagious terror. —*v.* **-icked, -icking.** To affect or be affected with panic. [< Gk *panikos,* of Pan (god who aroused terror in lonely places).] —**pan'ick•y** *adv.*

pan•i•cle (păn'ĭ-kəl) *n.* A loosely and irregularly branched flower cluster. [< L *pānus,* tuft.] —**pan'i•cled** *adj.*

pan•nier (păn'yər, păn'ē-ər) *n.* **1.** A large wicker basket, esp. one carried on the back. **2.** A part of a skirt or overskirt puffed out at the hips. [< L *pānārium,* breadbasket.]

pan•o•ply (păn'ə-plē) *n., pl.* **-plies. 1.** The complete arms and armor of a warrior. **2.** Any magnificent, shining array. [< PAN- + Gk *hoplon,* weapon.]

pan•o•ram•a (păn'ə-răm'ə, -rä'mə) *n.* **1.** An unlimited view over a wide area. **2.** A picture or representation of a continuous scene or series of events. [PAN- + Gk *horâma,* sight.] —**pan'o•ram'ic** *adj.* —**pan'o•ram'i•cal•ly** *adv.*

pan•sy (păn'zē) *n., pl.* **-sies.** A garden plant having variously colored flowers with rounded, velvety petals. [< F *pensée,* "thought."]

pant (pănt) *v.* **1.** To breathe rapidly in short gasps, as after exertion. **2.** To utter hurriedly or breathlessly. —*n.* A short, labored breath; gasp. [< VL **phantasiāre,* to gasp with horror.] —**pant'ing•ly** *adv.*

pan•ta•loons (păn'tə-lōōnz') *pl.n.* Trousers. [< OIt *Pantalone,* orig a nickname for a Venetian.]

pan•the•ism (păn'thē-ĭz'əm) *n.* The doctrine identifying the Deity with the various forces and workings of nature. —**pan'the•ist** *n.* —**pan'the•is'tic, pan'the•is'ti•cal** *adj.*

pan•the•on (păn'thē-ŏn', -ən) *n.* **1.** A temple dedicated to all gods. **2.** A public building commemorating and dedicated to the great persons of a nation. **3.** All the gods of a people. [< PAN- + Gk *theos,* god.]

pan•ther (păn'thər) *n.* A large wild cat, esp. a leopard or a mountain lion. [< Gk *panthêr.*]

pant•ies (păn'tēz) *pl.n. Informal.* A pair of women's or children's underpants.

pan•to•mime (păn'tə-mīm') *n.* **1.** A type of theatrical performance in which the actors use motions and gestures rather than speech. **2.** Such motions or gestures used for expressive communication. —*v.* **-mimed, -miming.** To express or act in pantomime. [L *pantomīmus,* "the complete mime."]

pan•try (păn'trē) *n., pl.* **-tries.** A small room or closet, usually off a kitchen, where food, china, silver, linens, etc., are stored. [< OF *panetier,* servant in charge of the bread.]

pants (pănts) *pl.n.* **1.** A pair of trousers. **2.** A pair of underpants. [Short for PANTALOONS.]

pant•suit (pănt'sōōt') *n.* Also **pants suit.** A woman's suit having trousers instead of a skirt.

pant•y•hose (păn'tē-hōz') *n., pl.* **pantyhose.** A garment consisting of stretchable stockings and underpants in one piece.

pap (păp) *n.* Soft or semiliquid food, as for infants. [Prob < L *pappa,* baby talk for food.]

pa•pa (pä'pə, pə-pä') *n. Informal.* Father. [< OF.]

pa•pa•cy (pā'pə-sē) *n., pl.* **-cies. 1.** The office and jurisdiction of a pope. **2.** The period of time during which a pope is in office. **3.** Papacy. The system of church government headed by the pope.

pa•pal (pā'pəl) *adj.* Of or pertaining to the pope or the papacy. —**pa'pal•ly** *adv.*

pa•paw (pô'pô') *n.* Also **paw•paw. 1.** A North American tree, with fleshy, edible fruit. **2.** The fruit of this tree. [Prob < Span *papaya,* papaya.]

pa•pa•ya (pə-pä'yə) *n.* The large, yellow, edible fruit of a tropical American tree. [< Cariban.]

pa•per (pā'pər) *n.* **1.** A thin sheet material made of cellulose pulp, derived mainly from wood and rags, and used chiefly for writing, printing, drawing, wrapping, and covering walls. **2.** A single sheet or leaf of this material. **3.** An official document. **4.** An essay, report, or scholarly dissertation. **5.** A newspaper. **6. papers.** Documents establishing the identity of the bearer. —*v.* To cover with wallpaper. —*adj.* Made of paper. [< Gk *papuros,* PAPYRUS.] —**pa'per•er** *n.* —**pa'per•y** *adj.*

pa•per•back (pā'pər-băk') *n.* A book having a flexible paper binding.

pa•per•weight (pā'pər-wāt') *n.* A small heavy object placed on top of loose papers to keep them in place.

pa•per•work (pā'pər-wûrk') *n.* Also **paper work.** Work involving the handling of reports, letters, forms, etc.

pa•pier-mâ•ché (pā'pər-mə-shā') *n.* A material made from paper pulp mixed with glue or paste, that can be molded into various shapes when wet. [F, "chewed paper."]

pa•pil•la (pə-pĭl'ə) *n., pl.* **-pillae** (-pĭl'ē). A small, nipplelike projection, as on the tongue. [< L. nipple.] —**pap'il•lar'y**

pa·poose (pă-pōōs′, pə-) *n.* A North American Indian infant or young child. [Algon *papoos.*]

pa·pri·ka (pă-prē′kə, pə-, păp′rĭ-kə) *n.* A mild, powdered seasoning made from sweet red peppers. [Hung.]

Pap test (păp). A test in which a smear of a bodily secretion, esp. from the cervix or vagina, is immediately fixed and examined to detect cancer in an early stage or to evaluate hormonal condition. [< G. *Papanicolaou* (1883–1962), American scientist.]

pa·py·rus (pə-pī′rəs) *n., pl.* **-ruses** or **-ri** (-rī′). **1.** A tall, grasslike water plant of N Africa. **2.** Paper made from the pith or stems of this plant. [< Gk *papuros.*]

par (pär) *n.* **1.** An accepted average; normal standard: *up to par.* **2.** An equal status, level, or footing: *on a par.* **3. a.** The established face value of the monetary unit of a country. **b.** The face value of a stock, bond, etc. **4.** *Golf.* The number of strokes considered necessary to complete a hole or course in expert play. [L, equal.] —**par** *adj.*

par. **1.** paragraph. **2.** parallel. **3.** parish.

para-. *comb. form.* **1.** Alongside; beside. **2.** Beyond. **3.** Resembling or similar to. **4.** Subsidiary to. **5.** Isomeric to or polymeric to. [< Gk *para,* beside, for.]

par·a·ble (păr′ə-bəl) *n.* A simple story illustrating a moral or religious lesson. [< Gk *parabolē,* comparison.]

pa·rab·o·la (pə-răb′ə-lə) *n.* A plane curve formed by the locus of points equidistant from a fixed line and a fixed point not on the line. [< Gk *parabolē,* juxtaposition, parallelism.] —**par′a·bol′ic** (păr′ə-bŏl′ĭk) *adj.*

par·a·chute (păr′ə-shōōt′) *n.* An umbrella-shaped apparatus used to retard free fall from an aircraft. —*v.* **-chuted, -chuting.** To drop or descend by means of a parachute. —**par′a·chut′ist** *n.*

Par·a·clete (păr′ə-klēt′) *n.* The Holy Ghost. [< Gk *Paraklētos,* "the Comforter."]

pa·rade (pə-rād′) *n.* **1.** A public procession held on a festive or ceremonial occasion. **2.** A ceremonial review of troops. —*v.* **-raded, -rading.** **1.** To march in or as in a parade. **2.** To exhibit ostentatiously; flaunt. [< VL *parāta,* "a making ready."] —**pa·rad′er** *n.*

par·a·digm (păr′ə-dĭm, -dīm′) *n.* **1.** A list of all the inflectional forms of a word taken as an illustrative example. **2.** An example or model. [< Gk *paradeiknunai,* to compare, exhibit.]

par·a·dise (păr′ə-dīs′, -dīz′) *n.* **1. Paradise. a.** Heaven, the abode of righteous souls after death. **b.** Eden. **2.** Any place of ideal beauty or loveliness. [< Gk *paradeisos,* garden, park, paradise.]

par·a·dox (păr′ə-dŏks′) *n.* **1.** A seemingly contradictory statement that may nonetheless be true. **2.** A person or situation having contradictory aspects. [< Gk *paradoxos,* incredible, conflicting with expectation.] —**par′a·dox′i·cal** *adj.* —**par′a·dox′i·cal·ly** *adv.*

par·af·fin (păr′ə-fĭn) *n.* **1.** A waxy, white or colorless, solid hydrocarbon mixture used to make candles, wax paper, lubricants, and seal-

ing materials. **2.** *Brit.* Kerosene. [< L *parum,* too little + *affinis,* neighboring.]

par·a·gon (păr′ə-gŏn′, -gən) *n.* A model or pattern of excellence; peerless example: *the paragon of virtue.* [< Gk *parakonan,* to sharpen against, compare.]

par·a·graph (păr′ə-grăf′, -gräf′) *n.* **1.** A distinct division of a written work or composition, begun on a new line and indented. **2.** A mark (¶) used to indicate a new paragraph. —*v.* To divide or arrange in paragraphs. [< Gk *paragraphein,* to write beside.]

Par·a·guay (păr′ə-gwī′, -gwā′). A republic of C South America. Pop. 1,817,000. Cap. Asunción. —**Par′a·guay′an** (păr′ə-gwī′ən, -gwä′ən) *adj. & n.*

Paraguay

par·a·keet (păr′ə-kēt′) *n.* A small parrot with a long, pointed tail. [OF *paroquet.*]

par·al·lax (păr′ə-lăks′) *n.* An apparent change in the direction of an object, caused by a change in the viewer's position. [< Gk *parallassein,* to change.]

par·al·lel (păr′ə-lĕl′) *adj.* **1.** Being an equal distance at every point so as never to intersect. **2.** Having comparable parts, analogous aspects, or readily recognized similarities. In a parallel relationship or manner. —*n.* **1.** A surface or line that is equidistant from another. **2.** One of a set of parallel geometric figures, usually lines. **3. a.** Anything that closely resembles or is analogous to something else. **b.** A comparison indicating likeness or analogy. **4.** Any of the imaginary lines of the earth's surface parallel to the equator, representing a given latitude. —*v.* **-leled** or **-lelled, -leling** or **-lelling.** **1.** To extend parallel to. **2.** To be similar or analogous to. [< Gk *parallēlos.*] —**par′al·lel·ism′** *n.*

par·al·lel·o·gram (păr′ə-lĕl′ə-grăm′) *n.* A four-sided plane figure with opposite sides parallel.

pa·ral·y·sis (pə-răl′ə-sĭs) *n., pl.* **-ses** (-sēz′). **1.** Loss or impairment of the ability to move or have sensation in a bodily part. **2.** A stoppage or crippling of activity. [< Gk *paraluein,* to loosen, disable.] —**par′a·lyt′ic** (păr′ə-lĭt′ĭk) *adj. & n.*

par·a·lyze (păr′ə-līz′) *v.* **-lyzed, -lyzing.** **1.** To affect with paralysis. **2.** To make inoperative or powerless. —**par′a·lyz′er** *n.*

par·a·me·ci·um (păr′ə-mē′shē-əm, -sē-əm) *n., pl.* **-cia** (-shē-ə, -sē-ə) or **-ums.** A usually oval, aquatic protozoan that moves by means of cilia. [< Gk *paramēkēs*, oblong.]

par·a·med·ic (păr′ə-mĕd′ĭk) *n.* A person who assists a medical professional, as a nurse or corpsman. [PARA- + MEDIC]

par·a·mil·i·tar·y (păr′ə-mĭl′ə-tĕr′e) *adj.* Designating forces organized after a military pattern, as an auxiliary military force.

pa·ram·e·ter (pə-răm′ə-tər) *n.* A variable or an arbitrary constant appearing in a mathematical expression, each value of which restricts or determines the specific form of the expression. —**par′a·met′ric** (păr′ə-mĕt′rĭk) *adj.*

par·a·mount (păr′ə-mount′) *adj.* Of chief rank or importance; primary; foremost. [NF *paramont*, "superior."] —**par′a·mount′ly** *adv.*

par·a·mour (păr′ə-mo͞or′) *n.* A lover, esp. in an adulterous relationship. [< OF *par amour*, "by love."]

Pa·ra·ná (păr′ə-nä′). A river of E South America.

par·a·noi·a (păr′ə-noi′ə) *n.* A chronic psychosis characterized by well-rationalized delusions of persecution or of grandeur. [< Gk, madness.] —**par′a·noi′ac** (-noi′ăk, -noi′ĭk) *n.* —**par′a·noid′** (păr′ə-noid′) *adj.*

par·a·pet (păr′ə-pĭt, -pĕt′) *n.* 1. A low wall or railing along the edge of a roof, balcony, etc. 2. An embankment protecting soldiers from enemy fire. [< It *parapetto*, chest-high wall.]

par·a·pher·na·lia (păr′ə-fər-nāl′yə, -fə-nāl′yə) *n. (takes sing. or pl. v.).* 1. Personal belongings. 2. The articles used in some activity; equipment; gear. [< Gk *parapherna*, a woman's property beyond her dowry.]

par·a·phrase (păr′ə-frāz′) *n.* A restatement of a passage in other words, often to clarify the meaning. [< Gk *paraphrazein*, to paraphrase.] —**par′a·phrase′** *v.* —**par′a·phras′er** *n.*

par·a·ple·gi·a (păr′ə-plē′jē-ə, -jə) *n.* Complete paralysis of the lower half of the body. [< Gk *paraplēssein*, to strike on one side.] —**par′a·ple′gic** (-plē′jĭk) *adj. & n.*

par·a·pro·fes·sion·al (păr′ə-prə-fĕsh′ə-nəl) *n.* A worker who is not a member of a given profession but who assists a professional. [PARA- (alongside) + PROFESSIONAL.]

par·a·site (păr′ə-sīt′) *n.* 1. An often harmful organism that lives on or in a different organism. 2. A person who habitually takes advantage of the generosity of others without making any useful return. [< Gk *parasitos*, "fellow guest."] —**par′a·sit′ic** (-sĭt′ĭk) *adj.* —**par′a·sit·ism′** (-sĭt-ĭz′əm) *n.*

par·a·sol (păr′ə-sôl′, -sŏl′) *n.* A light, usually small umbrella carried as protection from the sun. [< OIt *parasole*.]

par·a·sym·pa·thet·ic nervous system (păr′ə-sĭm′pə-thĕt′ĭk). The part of the autonomic nervous system that, in general, inhibits or opposes the physiological effects of the sympathetic nervous system.

par·a·troops (păr′ə-tro͞ops′) *pl.n.* Infantry trained and equipped to parachute. —**par′a·troop′er** *n.*

par·boil (pär′boil′) *v.* To cook partially by boiling for a brief period. [ME *parboilen*, "to boil thoroughly."]

par·cel (pär′səl) *n.* 1. Something wrapped up or packaged; bundle; package. 2. A portion or plot of land, usually a division of a larger area. —*v.* -celed or -celled, -celing or -celling. To divide into portions and distribute. [< *particula*, portion, particle.]

parcel post. The branch of the postal service that handles and delivers parcels.

parch (pärch) *v.* 1. To make very dry, esp. by the action of heat. 2. To make thirsty. [ME *parchen*.]

parch·ment (pärch′mənt) *n.* 1. The skin of a sheep or goat, prepared for writing upon. 2. A written text on this material. [< VL *particamīnum*.]

par·don (pärd′n) *v.* 1. To release (a person) from punishment. 2. To pass over (an offense) without punishment. 3. To make courteous allowance for; excuse. —*n.* 1. The act of forgiving. 2. *Law.* **a.** An exemption from the penalties of an offense or crime. **b.** The official document declaring such an exemption. [< LL *perdōnāre*, to give wholeheartedly.] —**par′don·a·ble** *adj.* —**par′don·a·bly** *adv.*

pare (pâr) *v.* **pared, paring.** 1. To remove the outer skin of; peel. 2. To reduce little by little. [< L *parāre*, to prepare.]

par·e·gor·ic (păr′ə-gôr′ĭk, -gŏr′ĭk) *n.* Camphorated tincture of opium, taken chiefly for the relief of diarrhea. [< Gk *parēgoros*, encouraging, soothing.]

paren. parenthesis.

par·ent (pâr′ənt) *n.* 1. A father or mother. 2. A forefather; ancestor; progenitor. 3. The source or cause of something; origin. [< L *parere*, to give birth.] —**pa·ren′tal** (pə-rĕnt′l) *adj.* —**par′ent·hood′** *n.*

par·ent·age (pâr′ən-tĭj) *n.* Descent from parents or ancestors; lineage; origin.

pa·ren·the·sis (pə-rĕn′thə-sĭs) *n., pl.* **-ses** (-sēz′). Either of the upright curved lines, ( ), used to mark off explanatory or qualifying remarks. [< Gk, "a putting in beside."]

par·en·thet·i·cal (păr′ən-thĕt′ĭ-kəl) *adj.* Also **par·en·thet·ic** (-thĕt′ĭk). Contained, or as if contained, in parentheses; qualifying or explanatory. —**par′en·thet′i·cal·ly** *adv.*

pa·re·sis (pə-rē′sĭs, păr′ə-sĭs) *n.* Slight or partial paralysis. [< Gk, act of letting go.] —**pa·ret′ic** (-rĕt′ĭk) *n. & adj.*

par ex·cel·lence (pär ĕk-sə-läns′). The highest degree or epitome of something; preeminently.

par·fait (pär-fā′) *n.* A dessert made of cream, eggs, and sugar, or different flavors of ice cream, served in a tall glass. [< L *perfectus*, perfect.]

pa·ri·ah (pə-rī′ə) *n.* 1. A member of a low caste in S India. 2. A social outcast. [Tamil *paraiyan*, drummer.]

pa·ri·e·tal bone (pə-rī′ə-təl). Either of the two large bones that make up the top and sides of the skull.

par·i·mu·tu·el (păr′ĭ-myo͞o′cho͞o-əl) *n., pl.* **-els.** A system of betting on races whereby the winners divide the net amount bet in proportion to the sums they have wagered. [F *pari mutuel*, mutual stake.]

ă pat/ā ate/âr care/ä bar/b bib/ch chew/d deed/ĕ pet/ē be/f fit/g gag/h hat/hw what/ ĭ pit/ī pie/îr pier/j judge/k kick/l lid, fatal/m mum/n no, sudden/ng sing/ŏ pot/ō go/

Par·is¹ (păr'ĭs). *Gk.Myth.* The prince of Troy whose abduction of Helen provoked the Trojan War.

Par·is² (păr'ĭs). The capital of France, in the NW. Pop. 2,790,000. —**Pa·ri'sian** (pə-rĭzh'ən, -rē'zhən) *adj. & n.*

par·ish (păr'ĭsh) *n.* **1.** An administrative. part of a diocese that has its own church. **2.** A civil district in Louisiana, corresponding to a county in other states. **3.** Members of a parish; the community of parishioners. [< LGk *paroikos,* Christian.]

pa·rish·ion·er (pə-rĭsh'ən-ər) *n.* A member of a parish.

par·i·ty (păr'ə-tē) *n., pl.* **-ties. 1.** Equality, as in amount, status, or value. **2.** The equivalent in value of a sum of money expressed in terms of a different currency. **3.** A level for farm-product prices, maintained by governmental support. [< L *pâr,* equal.]

park (pärk) *n.* **1.** An expanse of enclosed grounds for recreational use. **2.** A stadium or enclosed playing field: *ball park.* —*v.* **1.** To put or leave (a vehicle) for a time in a certain location. **2.** To place, put, set, or leave (something) somewhere. [< OF *parc,* enclosure.]

par·ka (pär'kə) *n.* A hooded fur jacket. [< Russ, pelt of a reindeer.]

parking lot. An area for parking motor vehicles.

Par·kin·son's disease (pär'kĭn-sənz). A progressive nervous disease of the later years, characterized by muscular tremor, slowing of movement, partial facial paralysis, and impaired motor control. [< J. *Parkinson* (1755–1824), English surgeon.]

park·way (pärk'wā') *n.* A broad landscaped highway.

Parl. Parliament.

par·lance (pär'ləns) *n.* Manner of speaking; language, style, or idiom: *legal parlance.* [< ML *parabolare,* to parley.]

par·lay (pär'lā, -lē) *v.* To bet (an original wager and its winnings) on a subsequent event. —*n.* A bet comprising the sum of an original wager plus its winnings. [< It *parolo,* a set of dice.]

par·ley (pär'lē) *n., pl.* **-leys.** A discussion or conference, esp. between enemies. [< LL *parabola,* discourse, parable.] —**par'ley** *v.*

par·lia·ment (pär'lə-mənt) *n.* **1.** A legislative body. **2. Parliament.** The legislative body of various countries, esp. that of the United Kingdom. [< OF *parler,* to talk.] —**par·lia·men'ta·ry** (-měn'tə-rē) *adj.*

par·lia·men·tar·i·an (pär'lə-měn-târ'ē-ən) *n.* An expert in parliamentary procedures, rules, or debate.

par·lor (pär'lər) *n.* Also chiefly *Brit.* **par·lour. 1.** A room for the entertainment of visitors. **2.** A room designed for some special function or business: *beauty parlor.* [< OF *parleur,* room used for conversation.]

par·lous (pär'ləs) *adj. Archaic.* Perilous; dangerous. [< PERIL.] —**par'lous·ly** *adv.*

Par·me·san (pär'mə-zän', -zăn', -zən) *n.* A hard, dry Italian cheese usually served grated as a garnish. [< *Parma,* Italy.]

pa·ro·chi·al (pə-rō'kē-əl) *adj.* **1.** Of, pertaining to, supported by, or located in a parish. **2.** Narrow; provincial: *parochial attitudes.* [< LL *parochia,* parish.] —**pa·ro'chi·al·ly** *adv.*

parochial school. A school supported by a church parish.

par·o·dy (păr'ə-dē) *n., pl.* **-dies. 1.** A satirical imitation of a work of literature or music. **2.** A travesty: *a parody of justice.* [< Gk *parōidia,* "mock-song."] —**par'o·dy** *v.* **(-died, -dying).**

pa·role (pə-rōl') *n.* The release of a prisoner before his term has expired on condition of good behavior. —*v.* **-roled, -roling.** To release (a prisoner) on parole. [F, word of honor.] —**pa·rol'ee'** *n.*

pa·rot·id gland (pə-rŏt'ĭd). Either of the salivary glands located ahead of and below each ear.

–parous. *comb. form.* Giving birth to or bearing: *viviparous.* [< L *parere,* to give birth to.]

par·ox·ysm (păr'ək-sĭz'əm) *n.* **1.** A sudden outburst: *a paroxysm of laughter.* **2. a.** A crisis in or recurrent intensification of a disease. **b.** A spasm or fit; convulsion. [< Gk *paroxusmos,* irritation, paroxysm.] —**par'ox·ys'mal** (păr'ək-sĭz'məl) *adj.*

par·quet (pär-kā') *n.* **1.** The main floor of a theater; the orchestra. **2.** A floor of parquetry. —*v.* **-queted** (-kād'), **-queting** (-kā'ĭng). To make (a floor) of parquetry. [< OF *parc,* enclosure, PARK.]

par·quet·ry (pär'kĭ-trē) *n., pl.* **-ries.** Wood worked into an inlaid mosaic, used esp. for floors.

par·rot (păr'ət) *n.* **1.** Any of various chiefly tropical birds having a short, hooked bill, brightly colored plumage, and sometimes the ability to mimic human speech. **2.** One who mindlessly imitates words or actions of another. —*v.* To repeat or imitate without meaning or understanding. [< OF *paroquet,* PARAKEET.] —**par'rot·er** *n.*

par·ry (păr'ē) *v.* **-ried, -rying. 1.** To deflect or ward off. **2.** To avoid or evade: *He skillfully parried her questions.* [< F *parer,* to defend, parry.]

parse (pärs) *v.* **parsed, parsing.** To describe the form, function, and syntactical relationship of each part of a sentence. [< L *pars,* part.]

par·si·mo·ny (pär'sə-mō'nē) *n.* Unusual or excessive frugality; extreme economy; stinginess. [< L *parcere,* to spare.] —**par'si·mo'ni·ous** *adj.*

pars·ley (pärs'lē) *n.* A plant with much-divided, curled leaves used as a seasoning and garnish. [< Gk *petroselinon,* rock parsley.]

pars·nip (pärs'nĭp) *n.* **1.** A plant cultivated for its long edible root. **2.** The root of this plant. [< L *pastinâca,* parsnip, carrot.]

par·son (pär'sən) *n.* A clergyman in charge of a parish. [< L *persôna (ecclêsiae),* "person (of the church)."]

par·son·age (pär'sən-ĭj) *n.* The official residence of a parson, as provided by his church.

part (pärt) *n.* **1.** A portion, division, or segment of a whole. **2.** An essential component: *a machine part.* **3.** A role. **4.** One's share in responsibility or obligation; duty. **5.** Often **parts.** A region, land, or territory: *foreign parts.*

6. The line where the hair on the head is parted. **7.** One of the melodic lines in concerted music or in harmony. **—for one's part.** So far as one is concerned. **—for the most part.** Generally; mostly. **—in part.** To some extent; partly. **—take part in.** To join in; participate. **—v. 1.** To divide into separate parts. **2.** To separate by coming between; keep apart. **3.** To comb (the hair) away from a dividing line on the scalp. **4.** To go away from one another; separate. **5.** To leave; depart. **—part with.** To give up; relinquish. **—adv.** Partially; in part: *part yellow.* **—adj.** Not full or complete; partial: *a part owner.* [< L *pars (part-).*]

part. participle.

par•take (pär-tāk′) *v.* -took, -taken, -taking. **1.** To take part; participate. **2.** To take or be given part or portion. [Back-formation < partaker < *part taker.*] **—par•tak′er** *n.*

par•the•no•gen•e•sis (pär′thə-nō-jĕn′ə-sĭs) *n.* Reproduction of organisms without conjunction of gametes of opposite sexes. [< Gk *parthenos,* virgin, girl + -GENESIS.]

par•tial (pär′shəl) *adj.* **1.** Not total; incomplete. **2.** Biased; prejudiced. **3.** Especially fond. [< L *pars (part-),* PART.] **—par′ti•al′i•ty** (pär′shē-ăl′ə-tē) *n.* **—par′tial•ly** *adv.*

par•tic•i•pant (pär-tĭs′ə-pənt) *n.* One who participates or takes part in something.

par•tic•i•pate (pär-tĭs′ə-pāt′) *v.* -pated, -pating. To take part; join or share with others. [< L *particeps,* a partaker.] **—par•tic′i•pa′tion** *n.*

par•ti•ci•ple (pär′tə-sĭp′əl) *n.* A form of a verb that is used with an auxiliary verb to indicate certain tenses and that can also function independently as an adjective. [< L *particeps,* partaker.] **—par′ti•cip′i•al** *adj.*

par•ti•cle (pär′tĭ-kəl) *n.* **1.** A very small piece or part; speck. **2.** A very small amount: *not a particle of difference.* **3.** One of a class of words, such as prepositions or conjunctions. [< L *pars,* PART.]

par•ti-col•ored (pär′tē-kŭl′ərd) *adj.* Having different parts or sections colored differently. [< OF *parti,* striped.]

par•tic•u•lar (pər-tĭk′yə-lər) *adj.* **1.** Pertaining to a single person, group, or thing; not general or universal. **2.** Separate and distinct from others; specific. **3.** Worthy of note; exceptional; special. **4.** Especially concerned with details or niceties; fussy. **—n.** An individual item, fact, or detail. **—in particular.** Particularly; especially. [< L *particula,* detail, particle.] **—par•tic′u•lar′i•ty** (-lăr′ə-tē) *n.* **—par•tic′u•lar•ly** *adv.*

par•tic•u•lar•ize (pər-tĭk′yə-lə-rīz′) *v.* -ized, -izing. **1.** To state or enumerate in detail; itemize. **2.** To give particulars.

par•tic•u•late (pər-tĭk′yə-lĭt, -lāt′) *adj.* Of, pertaining to, or formed of separate particles.

part•ing (pär′tĭng) *n.* **1.** The act of separating or dividing. **2.** A departure or leave-taking. **—adj.** Done, given, or said on departing or separating.

par•ti•san (pär′tə-zən) *n.* **1.** A militant supporter of a party, cause, faction, person, or idea. **2.** A guerrilla. [< L *pars,* PART.] **—par′ti•san** *adj.* **—par′ti•san•ship′** *n.*

par•ti•ta (pär-tē′tə) *n. Mus.* A composition similar to a suite. [< L *partire,* to divide.]

par•ti•tion (pär-tĭsh′ən) *n.* **1.** The act or process of dividing something into parts. **2.** Something that separates, such as a partial wall dividing a larger area. **—v. 1.** To divide into parts or sections. **2.** To divide or separate by means of a partition.

par•ti•tive (pär′tə-tĭv) *Gram. adj.* Indicating a part as distinct from a whole. **—n.** A partitive word or construction.

part•ly (pärt′lē) *adv.* In part; in some degree; not completely.

part•ner (pärt′nər) *n.* A person associated with another in some common activity, esp.: **a.** A member of a business partnership. **b.** Either of two persons dancing together. **c.** One of two players on the same side in a game or sport. [< L *partītiō,* partition.] **—part′ner•ship′** *n.*

part of speech. One of the traditional classifications of words according to their functions in context, such as noun, verb, etc.

par•took (pär-tŏŏk′). *p.t.* of partake.

par•tridge (pär′trĭj) *n.* Any of several plump-bodied game birds. [< Gk *perdix.*]

part-time (pärt′tīm′) *adj.* For or during less than the customary time: *a part-time job.* **—part′-time′** *adv.*

par•tu•ri•tion (pär′t/y/ŏŏ-rĭsh′ən, pär′chŏŏ-) *n.* The act of giving birth; childbirth. [< L *parturire,* to be in labor.]

par•ty (pär′tē) *n., pl.* -ties. **1.** A social gathering for pleasure or entertainment. **2.** A group of persons participating in some common activity. **3.** A political group organized to promote its principles and candidates for public office. **4.** A person or group involved in a legal proceeding. **5.** A participant or accessory. [< OF *partir,* to divide.] **—par′ty** *adj.*

party line. 1. A telephone circuit used by two or more subscribers. **2.** The official policies of a political party to which loyal members are expected to adhere.

par•ve•nu (pär′və-n/y/ŏŏ′) *n.* One who has suddenly risen above his social and economic class; an upstart. [< F *parvenir,* to arrive.]

Pas•a•de•na (păs′ə-dē′nə). A city in SW California. Pop. 116,000.

pas•chal (păs′kəl) *adj.* Of or pertaining to the Passover or to Easter. [< LL *pascha,* Passover, Easter.]

pa•sha (pä′shə, păsh′ə) *n.* A former Turkish title of honor placed after the name.

Pash•to (pŭsh′tō) *n.* An Iranian language that is a major language of Afghanistan.

pas•qui•nade (păs′kwə-nād′) *n.* A lampoon posted in a public place. [< It *pasquinata.*]

pass (păs, päs) *v.* **1.** To go by without stopping. **2.** To move on or ahead; proceed. **3.** To run; extend: *The river passes through our land.* **4.** To cause to move: *pass one's hand over the fabric.* **5.** To hand over to someone else: *pass the bread.* **6.** To move past in time; elapse. **7.** To be communicated, exchanged, transferred, or conveyed. **8.** To allow to go by or elapse; spend. **9.** To come to an end; be terminated. **10.** To happen; take place. **11.** To be allowed to happen without challenge: *Let a*

pass. / pasteurization

remark pass. **12.** To undergo (an examination or trial) with favorable results. **13. a.** To approve; adopt: *The legislature passed the bill.* **b.** To be sanctioned, ratified, or approved (by). **14.** To pronounce; utter: *pass judgment.* **15.** To be accepted as something different. **16.** To transfer (a ball or puck) to a teammate. **17.** To decline to bid in a card game. **18.** To discharge; void (bodily waste). **—come to pass.** To happen. **—pass away.** To die. **—pass for.** To be accepted as being something one is not. **—pass out. 1.** To distribute. **2.** To faint. **—pass up.** To reject; let go by. **—***n.* **1.** The act of passing; passage. **2. a.** A narrow passage between mountains. **3. a.** A permit, ticket, or authorization to come and go at will or without charge. **b.** Written leave of absence from military duty. **4.** A sweep or run by an aircraft over an area or target. **5.** A critical condition or situation; predicament. **6.** A sexual invitation or overture. **7.** A motion of the hand or the waving of a wand for magic. [< L *passus,* step, pace, pp of *pandere,* to stretch out.] **—pass′less** *adj.*

pass. **1.** passenger. **2.** passive.

pass•a•ble (păs′ə-bəl, päs′-) *adj.* **1.** Capable of being passed, traversed, or crossed. **2.** Satisfactory but not outstanding. **—pass′a•bly** *adv.*

pas•sage (păs′ij) *n.* **1.** The act or process of passing: **a.** Movement; transit. **b.** The process of elapsing. **c.** Transition. **d.** The enactment of a legislative measure. **2.** A journey. **3. a.** The right to travel, esp. on a ship: *to book passage.* **b.** The price paid for this. **4.** A path, channel, or duct through, over, or along which something may pass. **5.** A segment of a literary work or musical composition.

pas•sage•way (păs′ij-wā′) *n.* A corridor.

pass•book (păs′b͞ook′, päs′-) *n.* A bankbook.

pas•sé (pă-sā′) *adj.* **1.** Out-of-date; old-fashioned. **2.** Past one's prime. [< F *passer,* to pass.]

pas•sen•ger (păs′ən-jər) *n.* A person traveling in a train, airplane, ship, bus, or other conveyance. [< OF *passager,* passing.]

pas•ser-by (păs′ər-bī′, päs′-) *n., pl.* **passers-by.** One who passes by, often by chance.

pas•sim (păs′ĭm) *adv.* Throughout; here and there, as occurrence of a word or passage in a text. [L, here and there.]

pass•ing (păs′ĭng, päs′-) *adj.* **1.** Of brief duration; transitory. **2.** Cursory; superficial; casual. **3.** Satisfactory: *a passing mark.* **—***n.* **1.** The act of one that passes. **2.** Death.

pas•sion (păsh′ən) *n.* **1.** Any powerful emotion or appetite, such as love, joy, hatred, anger, or greed. **2. a.** Ardent adoring love. **b.** Strong sexual desire; lust. **c.** The object of such love or desire. **3. a.** Boundless enthusiasm. **b.** The object of such enthusiasm. **4.** An outburst of emotion, esp. of anger. **5. Passion.** The sufferings of Christ in the period following the Last Supper and including the Crucifixion. [< L *pati* (pp *passus*), to suffer.]

pas•sion•ate (păsh′ən-ĭt) *adj.* **1.** Capable of or having intense feelings. **2.** Ardent; fervent. **—pas′sion•ate•ly** *adv.*

pas•sive (păs′ĭv) *adj.* **1.** Not active but acted upon. **2.** Accepting without resistance; submissive. **3.** Not participating, acting, or operating; inert. **4.** Denoting a verb form or voice used to indicate that the subject is the object of the action. **—***n.* **1.** The passive voice. **2.** A verb or construction in this voice. [< L *passivus,* capable of suffering.] **—pas′sive•ly** *adv.* **—pas•siv′i•ty, pas′sive•ness** *n.*

Pass•o•ver (păs′ō′vər, päs′-) *n.* A Jewish festival commemorating the exodus from Egypt. [< the phrase *pass over.*]

pass•port (păs′pôrt′, -pōrt′, päs′-) *n.* An official governmental document that certifies the identity and citizenship of a person traveling abroad. [F *passeport,* permission to pass through a port.]

pass•word (păs′wûrd′, päs′-) *n.* A secret word or phrase which indicates that the speaker is to be admitted.

past (păst, päst) *adj.* **1.** No longer current; gone by; over. **2.** Having existed or occurred in an earlier time; bygone. **3.** Just gone by or elapsed. **4.** Having served formerly in some official capacity. **5.** Denoting a verb tense or form used to express an action or condition prior to the time it is expressed. **—***n.* **1.** The time before the present. **2.** Former background, career, experiences, and activities. **3. a.** The past tense. **b.** A verb form in the past tense. **—***adv.* So as to pass by or go beyond: *He waved as he walked past.* **—***prep.* **1.** By and beyond: *walk past the theater.* **2.** Beyond in position, time, extent, or amount. [ME, pp of *passen,* to pass.]

pas•ta (päs′tə) *n.* **1.** Paste or dough made of flour and water, as in macaroni and ravioli. **2.** A prepared dish of pasta. [< LL, paste.]

paste[1] (pāst) *n.* **1.** A smooth viscous adhesive, made of flour and water or starch and water. **2.** Any similar soft, moist, smooth substance: *toothpaste.* **3.** A smooth dough used in making pastry. **4.** A hard, brilliant glass used in making artificial gems. **—***v.* **pasted, pasting.** To cause to adhere by applying paste. [< Gk *pastē,* barley porridge.]

paste[2] (pāst) *Slang.* *v.* **pasted, pasting.** To hit with a hard blow; punch. **—***n.* A hard blow. [Var of BASTE[3].]

paste•board (pāst′bôrd′, -bōrd′) *n.* A thin, firm material made of sheets of paper pasted together.

pas•tel (pă-stĕl′) *n.* **1.** A crayon made of a paste of ground and mixed pigment, chalk, water, and gum. **2.** A picture drawn with this type of crayon. **3.** The art or process of drawing with such crayons. **4.** A soft, delicate hue. [< LL *pastellus,* woad dye, crayon.] **—pas•tel′** *adj.* **—pas•tel′ist, pas•tel′list** *n.*

pas•tern (păs′tərn) *n.* The part of a horse's foot between the fetlock and hoof. [< LL *pāstōria,* a sheep's hobble.]

Pas•teur (pă-stûr′), **Louis.** 1822–1895. French chemist.

pas•teur•i•za•tion (păs′chər-ə-zā′shən, päs′tər-) *n.* The process of destroying most disease-producing microorganisms and limiting fermentation in milk, beer, and other liquids by partial or complete sterilization. [< L.

ô paw, for/oi boy/ou out/o͝o took/o͞o coo/p pop/r run/s sauce/sh shy/t to/th thin/*th* the/
ŭ cut/ûr fur/v van/w wag/y yes/z size/zh vision/ə ago, item, edible, gallop, circus/

PASTEUR.] —**pas·teur·ize**′ (păs′chə-rīz′, păs′tə-) *v.* (**-ized, -izing**).
pas·tille (pă-stēl′) *n.* A small tablet or lozenge. [< L *pāstillus*, little loaf, roll.]
pas·time (păs′tīm′, päs′-) *n.* An activity that occupies one's time pleasantly.
pas·tor (păs′tər, päs′-) *n.* A Christian minister in charge of a congregation. [< L *pāstor*, shepherd.]
pas·tor·al (păs′tər-əl, päs′-) *adj.* **1.** Of or pertaining to shepherds. **2. a.** Of or pertaining to the country or country life; rural. **b.** Having the qualities of idealized country life, as simplicity and a leisurely pace. **3.** Of or pertaining to a pastor or his duties. —*n.* A literary or other artistic work that portrays rural life, usually in an idealized manner. [< L *pāstor*, shepherd, PASTOR.]
pas·tor·ate (păs′tər-ĭt, päs′-) *n.* The office, rank, or jurisdiction of a pastor.
past participle. A verb form indicating past or completed action or time.
pas·tra·mi (pə-strä′mē) *n.* A highly seasoned smoked cut of beef, usually from the breast or shoulder. [Yidd.]
pas·try (pās′trē) *n., pl.* **-tries. 1.** A baked paste of flour, water, and shortening, used for the crusts of pies, tarts, etc. **2.** Baked foods, such as pies or tarts, made with this paste. [< PASTE.]
past tense. A verb tense used to express an action or condition that occurred in or during the past.
pas·ture (păs′chər, päs′-) *n.* Also **pas·tur·age** (păs′chər-ĭj, päs′-). **1.** Grass or other plants eaten by grazing animals. **2.** Land used for grazing. —*v.* **-tured, -turing. 1.** To put in a pasture. **2.** To graze. [< L *pāscere* (pp *pāstus*), to pasture, feed.] —**pas′tur·er** *n.*
past·y (pā′stē) *adj.* **-ier, -iest. 1.** Resembling paste in color or consistency. **2.** Pale and lifeless-looking.
pat[1] (păt) *v.* **patted, patting.** To tap gently with the open hand or with something flat. —*n.* **1.** A light stroke or tap. **2.** The sound made by such a stroke or tap. **3.** A small mass: *a pat of butter.* [ME *patte* (prob imit).]
pat[2] (păt) *adj.* **1.** Timely; opportune; fitting: *a pat answer.* **2.** Facile; glib. **3.** Needing no change; exactly right. —*adv.* **1.** Without changing position; steadfastly. **2.** Perfectly; precisely; aptly. [Prob < PAT.]
pat. patent.
patch (păch) *n.* **1.** A small piece of material affixed to another to conceal or reinforce a weakened or worn area. **2.** *Mil.* A small cloth badge affixed to a sleeve to indicate the unit to which one belongs. **3. a.** A dressing for a wound. **b.** A small shield of cloth worn over an injured eye. **4.** A small piece of land. **5.** A small piece or part of anything: *a patch of blue sky.* —*v.* To put a patch or patches on. —**patch up.** To settle; make up: *patched up a quarrel.* [< OF *pece, pieche,* piece.]
patch test. A test for allergic sensitivity made by applying a suspected allergen to the skin by a small surgical pad.
patch·work (păch′wûrk′) *n.* **1.** Needlework

consisting of varicolored patches of material sewed together, as in a quilt. **2.** A collection of miscellaneous parts; jumble.
pate (pāt) *n.* The head, esp. the top of the head. [ME.]
pâ·té (pä-tā′) *n.* A seasoned meat paste. [< OF *paste,* paste.]
pa·tel·la (pə-tĕl′ə) *n., pl.* **-tellae** (-tĕl′ē). A flat, triangular bone located at the front of the knee joint. [L, dim of *patina,* plate.] —**pa·tel′lar, pa·tel′late** (pə-tĕl′ĭt, -āt′) *adj.*
pat·ent (păt′ənt) *n.* A grant made by a government to an inventor, assuring him the sole right to make, use, and sell his invention over a certain period of time. —*adj.* **1.** Open to general inspection; unsealed: *letters patent.* **2.** (păt′ənt). Obvious; plain. **3.** Protected by a patent. **4.** Of or pertaining to patents: *patent law.* —*v.* To obtain a patent on. [< ML (*litterae*) *patentes,* "open (letters)."]
pat·ent·ee (păt′n-tē′) *n.* One who has been granted a patent.
patent leather. Black leather finished to a hard, glossy surface. [Made by a once-patented process.]
pa·ter·nal (pə-tûr′nəl) *adj.* **1.** Of, pertaining to, or characteristic of a father; fatherly. **2.** Inherited from a father. **3.** On the father's side of a family. [< L *pater,* father.]
pa·ter·nal·ism (pə-tûr′nəl-ĭz′əm) *n.* A practice of treating or governing people in a fatherly manner, esp. by providing for their needs without giving them responsibility. —**pa·ter′nal·is′tic** (-ĭs′tĭk) *adj.*
pa·ter·ni·ty (pə-tûr′nə-tē) *n.* The fact or condition of being a father; fatherhood.
Pat·er·son (păt′ər-sən). A city in NE New Jersey. Pop. 144,000.
path (păth, päth) *n., pl.* **paths** (păthz, päthz, päths, päths). **1.** A trodden track or way. **2.** Any road, way, or track. **3.** The route or course along which something moves. **4.** A course of action or conduct. [< OE *pæth.*]
path. pathological; pathology.
pa·thet·ic (pə-thĕt′ĭk) *adj.* Arousing pity, sympathy, or tenderness. [< Gk *pathos,* passion, suffering.] —**pa·thet′i·cal·ly** *adv.*
path·find·er (păth′fīn′dər, päth′-) *n.* One who discovers a way through or into unexplored regions.
patho-. *comb. form.* Disease or suffering. [< Gk *pathos,* emotion, suffering.]
path·o·gen (păth′ə-jən) *n.* Any agent that causes disease, esp. a microorganism such as a bacterium or fungus.
path·o·gen·ic (păth′ə-jĕn′ĭk) *adj.* Capable of causing disease.
pathol. pathological; pathology.
pa·thol·o·gy (pă-thŏl′ə-jē) *n., pl.* **-gies. 1.** The scientific study of disease. **2.** The anatomic or functional manifestations of disease. —**path′o·log′i·cal** *adj.* —**path′o·log′i·cal·ly** *adv.* —**pa·thol′o·gist** *n.*
pa·thos (pā′thŏs′, -thôs′) *n.* A quality in something or someone that arouses feelings of pity, sympathy, tenderness, or sorrow in another. [Gk, passion, suffering.]
path·way (păth′wā′, päth′-) *n.* A path.

–pathy. *comb. form.* Feeling; perception: te-lepathy. [< Gk *pathos,* suffering.]

pa·tience (pā'shəns) *n.* The capacity of calm endurance.

pa·tient (pā'shənt) *adj.* 1. Capable of bearing affliction with calmness. 2. Capable of bearing delay and waiting for the right moment. 3. Persevering; constant. —*n.* One under medical treatment. [< L *patiēns,* pres part of *patī,* to suffer.] —**pa'tient·ly** *adv.*

pat·i·na (păt'ə-nə) *n.* A thin layer of corrosion, usually brown or green, that appears on copper or bronze as a result of oxidation. [It.]

pat·i·o (păt'ē-ō', pä'tē-ō') *n., pl.* **-os.** 1. An inner, roofless courtyard. 2. A space for dining or recreation, adjacent to a house. [Span.]

pat·ois (păt'wä') *n., pl.* **patois** (păt'wäz'). 1. A nonstandard regional dialect. 2. The special jargon of a group. [< OF.]

patri–. *comb. form.* Father. [< L *pater,* father, and Gk *patēr,* father.]

pa·tri·arch (pā'trē-ärk') *n.* 1. The paternal leader of a family or tribe. 2. One of the founders of the Israelites. 3. An ecclesiastical dignitary, esp. in Eastern churches. 4. A venerable old man. —**pa'tri·ar'chal** *adj.*

pa·tri·cian (pə-trĭsh'ən) *n.* A person of high rank; an aristocrat. [< L *patres,* "fathers," senators.] —**pa·tri'cian** *adj.*

Pat·rick (păt'rĭk), **Saint.** A.D. 389?–461? Patron saint and apostle of Ireland.

pat·ri·mo·ny (păt'rə-mō'nē) *n., pl.* **-nies.** An inheritance, esp. from one's father. —**pat'ri·mo'ni·al** (-mō'nē-əl) *adj.*

pa·tri·ot (pā'trē-ət, -ŏt') *n.* One who loves and defends his country. [< Gk *patris,* fatherland.] —**pa'tri·ot'ic** (-ŏt'ĭk) *adj.* —**pa'tri·ot'i·cal·ly** *adv.* —**pa'tri·ot·ism'** (-ə-tĭz'əm) *n.*

pa·trol (pə-trōl') *n.* 1. The action of moving about an area for observation or security. 2. A person or group performing such an action. 3. A military unit sent out to reconnoiter. —*v.* **-trolled, -trolling.** To engage in a patrol. [< OF *patouiller,* to paw or paddle around in mud.] —**pa·trol'ler** *n.*

pa·trol·man (pə-trōl'mən) *n.* A policeman or guard who patrols an assigned area.

patrol wagon. A police truck used to convey prisoners.

pa·tron (pā'trən) *n.* 1. One who supports or protects; benefactor. 2. A regular customer. [< L *patrōnus,* defender, advocate < *pater,* father.] —**pa'tron·ess** *fem.n.*

pa·tron·age (pā'trə-nĭj, păt'rə-) *n.* 1. Support from a patron. 2. The trade of customers. 3. Customers; clientele. 4. The action of distributing governmental positions.

pa·tron·ize (pā'trə-nīz', păt'rə-) *v.* **-ized, -izing.** 1. To act as a patron to. 2. To treat condescendingly. —**pa'tron·iz'er** *n.*

pat·ro·nym·ic (păt'rə-nĭm'ĭk) *n.* A name received from a paternal ancestor, esp. one formed by a prefix or suffix. [< LL *patrōnymicus,* "derived from the name of a father."] —**pat'ro·nym'ic** *adj.*

pat·sy (păt'sē) *n., pl.* **-sies.** *Slang.* One who is cheated or victimized. [?]

pat·ter¹ (păt'ər) *v.* To make a quick succession of light taps. —*n.* A succession of quick, light taps. [Freq of PAT¹.]

pat·ter² (păt'ər) *v.* To chatter glibly or mumble mechanically. —*n.* 1. The jargon of a particular group; cant. 2. Glib, rapid speech. [ME *patren.*] —**pat'ter·er** *n.*

pat·tern (păt'ərn) *n.* 1. An ideal worthy of imitation. 2. A model to be followed in making things. 3. A sample. 4. Any artistic or decorative design. 5. A composite of traits or characteristics. —*v.* To make by following a pattern. [< ML *patrōnus,* patron, "something to be imitated," pattern.]

pat·ty (păt'ē) *n., pl.* **-ties.** 1. A small, flattened cake of chopped food. 2. A small pie. [< OF *paste,* paste.]

pau·ci·ty (pô'sə-tē) *n.* Smallness of number or quantity. [< L *paucus,* little, few.]

Paul (pôl), **Saint.** A.D. 5?–67?! Christian apostle. —**Paul'ine** (pô'līn') *adj.*

paunch (pônch, pänch) *n.* The belly, esp. a potbelly. [< L *pantex.*] —**paunch'y** *adj.*

pau·per (pô'pər) *n.* A very poor person, esp. one living on charity. [L, poor.] —**pau'per·ism'** (-pə-rĭz'əm) *n.* —**pau'per·i·za'tion** *n.* —**pau'per·ize'** *v.* (-ized, -izing).

pause (pôz) *v.* **paused, pausing.** To cease action for a time; linger or hesitate. —*n.* 1. A temporary stop. 2. A hesitation. 3. A reason for hesitation: *give one pause.* [< Gk *pausis,* a stopping.]

pave (pāv) *v.* **paved, paving.** To cover with a hard, smooth surface that will bear travel. —**pave the way.** To make progress or development easier. [< L *pavīre,* to strike, stamp.] —**pav'er** *n.*

pave·ment (pāv'mənt) *n.* 1. A hard, paved surface. 2. The material used for such a surface.

pa·vil·ion (pə-vĭl'yən) *n.* 1. An ornate tent. 2. A temporary, often open structure, used at parks or fairs for amusement or shelter. 3. An annex of a building. [< L *pāpiliō,* butterfly, tent.]

pav·ing (pā'vĭng) *n.* Pavement.

Pav·lov (păv'lôf', păv'lŏv'), **Ivan Petrovich.** 1849–1936. Russian physiologist.

paw (pô) *n.* 1. The clawed foot of an animal, as a dog or cat. 2. *Informal.* A human hand. —*v.* 1. To strike, touch, or scrape with a paw or forefoot. 2. To handle clumsily or rudely. [< OF *poue* < Gmc **pauta.*]

pawl (pôl) *n.* A hinged or pivoted device fit into a notch of a ratchet wheel to impart forward or prevent backward motion. [Du *pal.*]

pawn¹ (pôn) *n.* 1. Something given as security for a loan. 2. The condition of being held as security. —*v.* 1. To give as security for money borrowed. 2. To risk; hazard; stake: *pawn one's honor.* [< OF *pan.*]

pawn² (pôn) *n.* 1. A chessman of lowest value. 2. One used to further the purposes of another. [< ML *pedō,* a foot soldier.]

pawn·bro·ker (pôn'brō'kər) *n.* One who lends money for personal property left as security.

Paw·nee (pô-nē') *n., pl.* **-nee** or **-nees.** 1. A confederation of four Caddoan-speaking

North American Plains Indian tribes in the region of Kansas and Nebraska. **2.** The language or a member of this confederation.

pawn·shop (pôn'shŏp') *n.* The shop of a pawnbroker.

paw·paw. Variant of **papaw.**

pay (pā) *v.* **paid, paying 1.** To recompense for goods or services. **2.** To discharge (a debt or obligation). **3.** To requite. **4.** To yield as recompense. **5.** To be profitable or worthwhile. **6.** To give or bestow. **7.** To make (a visit or call). —**pay out. 1.** To expend or hand out (money). **2.** *p.t.* **payed out.** *Naut.* To let out (a line or cable) by slackening. —**pay up.** To pay in full. —*adj.* **1.** Requiring payment to operate. **2.** Yielding valuable metal in mining: *pay streak.* —*n.* **1.** Salary; wages. **2.** Recompense or reward. **3.** Paid employment. [< ML *pācāre,* to satisfy, pay.] —**pay'a·ble** *adj.* —**pay·ee'** (pā-ē') *n.* —**pay'er** *n.*

pay·check (pā'chĕk') *n.* A check to an employee in payment of his salary or wages.

pay dirt. Earth, ore, or gravel with a rich enough metal content to make mining profitable.

pay·load (pā'lōd') *n.* The significant part of a transported burden or cargo.

pay·mas·ter (pā'măs'tər, -mäs'tər) *n.* One in charge of paying wages.

pay·ment (pā'mənt) *n.* **1.** The act of paying. **2.** That which is paid.

pay off. 1. a. To pay the full amount owed. **b.** To requite. **2.** To pay the due wages and discharge. **3.** To bribe. **4.** To be profitable.

pay·off (pā'ôf', -ŏf') *n.* **1.** Full payment of a salary or wages. **2.** The climax of a sequence of events. **3.** A bribe.

pay·roll (pā'rōl') *n.* Also **pay roll. 1.** A list of employees and the wages due to each. **2.** The total sum of all these wages.

pay station. A coin-operated telephone.

Pb lead (L *plumbum*).

p.c. 1. after meals (L *post cibum*). **2.** per cent. **3.** petty cash. **4.** post card.

pct. per cent.

Pd palladium.

pd. paid.

p.d. per diem.

P.D. Police Department.

pe (pā) *n.* The 17th letter of the Hebrew alphabet, representing *p(ph).*

pea (pē) *n.* **1.** A vine cultivated for its round, edible green seeds enclosed in green pods. **2.** A seed of this plant. **3.** Any of several similar or related plants. [< Gk *pison,* a pea.]

peace (pēs) *n.* **1.** The absence of war or other hostilities. **2.** An agreement to end hostilities. **3.** Freedom from quarrels and disagreement. **4.** Public security. **5.** Calm; serenity: *peace of mind.* [< L *pāx.*] —**peace'a·ble** (pē'sə-bəl) *adj.* —**peace'ful** *adj.* —**peace'ful·ly** *adv.*

peace·mak·er (pēs'mā'kər) *n.* One who makes peace, esp. by settling disputes.

peace officer. A law officer, such as a sheriff, responsible for maintaining civil peace.

Peace River. A river of W Canada.

peace·time (pēs'tīm') *n.* A time of absence of war. —**peace'time'** *adj.*

peach (pēch) *n.* **1.** A sweet, juicy fruit with downy reddish or yellowish skin. **2.** A tree bearing such fruit. **3.** Light yellowish pink. [< L *persicum (mālum),* "Persian (apple)."]

pea·cock (pē'kŏk') *n.* The male of a large Asian bird, the **peafowl,** having brilliant blue or green plumage and long tail feathers with eyelike spots. [< L *pāvō,* peacock + COCK.]

pea green. Strong yellow green to moderate yellowish green. —**pea'-green'** *adj.*

peak (pēk) *n.* **1.** A pointed extremity. **2. a.** The pointed summit of a mountain. **b.** A mountain. **3.** The point of greatest development, value, or intensity. **4.** The highest value attained by a varying quantity. —*v.* **1.** To be formed into a peak or peaks. **2.** To achieve a maximum. [Prob < ME *pike,* summit.]

peak·ed (pē'kid) *adj.* Sickly, pale, or emaciated. —**peak'ed·ness** *n.*

peal (pēl) *n.* **1.** A ringing of bells. **2.** A set of tuned bells. **3.** A loud sound or series of sounds. —*v.* To ring or resound. [< ME *appel,* an appeal.]

pea·nut (pē'nŭt') *n.* **1.** A pealike vine bearing brittle-shelled pods that ripen underground. **2.** The pod or edible, nutlike seed of this vine.

pear (pâr) *n.* **1.** An edible fruit with a rounded base and a tapering stem end. **2.** A tree bearing such fruit. [< L *pirus,* pear tree, and *pirum,* pear.]

pearl (pûrl) *n.* **1.** A smooth, often rounded, lustrous deposit formed in the shells of certain oysters and other mollusks and valued as a gem. **2.** Mother-of-pearl. **3.** Something likened to a pearl in value. [< L *perna,* ham, sea-mussel.] —**pearl, pearl'y** *adj.*

peas·ant (pĕz'ənt) *n.* **1.** A member of the agricultural class, including farmers, laborers, etc. **2.** A countryman; rustic. **3.** An ill-bred person. [< ML *pāgēnsis,* "inhabitant of a district," peasant.] —**peas'ant·ry** *n.*

peat (pēt) *n.* Partially carbonized moss or other matter, found in bogs and used as fuel. [< ML *peta.*] —**peat'y** *adj.*

peb·ble (pĕb'əl) *n.* **1.** A small stone eroded smooth. **2. a.** Clear, colorless quartz; rock crystal. **b.** A lens made of such quartz. **3.** A crinkled surface, as on leather or paper. —*v.* **-bled, -bling. 1.** To pave or pelt with pebbles. **2.** To impart a rough, grainy surface to (leather or paper). [< OE *papol-,* pebble.] —**peb'bly** *adj.*

pe·can (pĭ-kän', -kăn') *n.* **1.** A smooth-shelled, oval, edible nut. **2.** A tree bearing such nuts. [< Algon.]

pec·ca·dil·lo (pĕk'ə-dĭl'ō) *n., pl.* **-loes** or **-los.** A minor offense. [< L *peccāre,* to sin.]

pec·ca·ry (pĕk'ə-rē) *n., pl.* **-ries.** A piglike tropical American mammal with long, dark bristles. [< Cariban *pakira.*]

pec·ca·vi (pĕ-kä'vī, -kä'vē) *n., pl.* **-vis.** A confession of sin. [L, "I have sinned."]

peck¹ (pĕk) *v.* **1.** To strike or form by striking with or as with the beak. **2.** To pick up with the beak. **3.** To kiss briefly and casually. —*n.* **1.** A stroke or mark made with the beak. **2.** A light, quick kiss. [ME *pecken.*]

peck² (pĕk) *n.* **1.** A U.S. Customary System

ă pat/ā ate/âr care/ä bar/b bib/ch chew/d deed/ĕ pet/ē be/f fit/g gag/h hat/hw what/
i pit/ī pie/îr pier/j judge/k kick/l lid, fatal/m mum/n no, sudden/ng sing/ŏ pot/ō go/

unit of volume or capacity, used in dry measure, equal to 8 quarts or 537.605 cubic inches. **2.** A corresponding British Imperial System unit, used in dry and liquid measure, equal to 554.84 cubic inches. [< NF *pek.*]

pec•tin (pĕk′tĭn) *n.* Any of a group of complex colloidal substances of high molecular weight found in ripe fruits, such as apples, and used to jell various foods, drugs, and cosmetics. [< Gk *pēktikos*, coagulating.] —**pec′tic, pec′tin•ous** *adj.*

pec•to•ral (pĕk′tər-əl) *adj.* Of or pertaining to the breast or chest: *a pectoral muscle.* [< L *pectus (pector-),* breast.]

pec•u•late (pĕk′yə-lāt′) *v.* **-lated, -lating.** To embezzle. [< L *peculium,* "wealth in cattle."] —**pec′u•la′tion** *n.* —**pec′u•la′tor** *n.*

pe•cu•liar (pĭ-kyōol′yər) *adj.* **1.** Unusual or eccentric; odd. **2.** Distinct and particular. **3. a.** Exclusive. **b.** Belonging distinctively to one person or group. [< L *peculiāris,* individual, peculiar, of private property.] —**pe•cu′li•ar′i•ty** (pĭ-kyōo′lē-ăr′ə-tē) *n.* —**pe•cu′liar•ly** *adv.*

pe•cu•ni•ar•y (pĭ-kyōo′nē-ĕr′ē) *adj.* Of or pertaining to money. [< L *pecūnia,* "wealth in cattle," money.]

–ped, –pede. *comb. form.* Foot or feet: biped, centipede. [L *pēs (ped-),* foot.]

ped•a•gogue (pĕd′ə-gŏg′, -gôg′) *n.* A schoolteacher. [< Gk *paidagōgos,* teacher, trainer (of boys).]

ped•a•go•gy (pĕd′ə-gō′jē, -gŏj′ē) *n.* The art, profession, or study of teaching. —**ped′a•gog′ic** (pĕd′ə-gŏj′ĭk, -gō′jĭk), **ped′a•gog′i•cal** (-ĭ-kəl) *adj.* —**ped′a•gog′i•cal•ly** *adv.*

ped•al (pĕd′l) *n.* **1.** A lever operated by the foot on various musical instruments, such as the piano, organ, or harp. **2.** A lever worked by the foot. —*adj.* Of or pertaining to a foot or footlike part: *the pedal extremities.* —*v.* **-aled** or **-alled, -aling** or **-alling. 1.** To use or operate a pedal or pedals. **2.** To ride a bicycle. [< L *pedālis,* of the foot.]

ped•ant (pĕd′ənt) *n.* **1.** One who stresses trivial details of learning. **2.** One who parades learning. **3.** *Archaic.* A schoolmaster. [< It *pedante.*] —**pe•dan′tic** (pə-dăn′tĭk) *adj.* —**ped′ant•ry** (pĕd′n-trē) *n.*

ped•dle (pĕd′l) *v.* **-dled, -dling.** To travel about selling (wares). [< ME *pedlere,* a peddler.] —**ped′dler** *n.*

–pede. Variant of **-ped.**

ped•er•as•ty (pĕd′ə-răs′tē) *n.* Sexual relations between a man and a boy. [< Gk *paiderastēs,* "a lover of boys."] —**ped′er•ast′** *n.*

ped•es•tal (pĕd′ə-stəl) *n.* **1.** A support or base, as for a column or statue. **2.** A position of esteem. [< OIt *pie di stallo,* "foot of a stall."]

pe•des•tri•an (pə-dĕs′trē-ən) *n.* One traveling on foot. —*adj.* **1.** Going or performed on foot. **2.** Commonplace; undistinguished. [< L *pedester,* going on foot, prosaic.]

pedi–. *comb. form.* Foot. [< L *pēs (ped-),* foot.]

pe•di•at•rics (pē′dē-ăt′rĭks) *n.* (*takes sing. v.*). The branch of medicine that deals with the care of infants and children and the treatment of their diseases. —**pe′di•at′ric** *adj.*

ped•i•cure (pĕd′ĭ-kyōor′) *n.* Cosmetic care or

treatment of the feet and toenails. —*v.* **-cured, -curing.** To give a pedicure to.

ped•i•form (pĕd′ə-fôrm′) *adj.* Shaped like a foot.

ped•i•gree (pĕd′ə-grē′) *n.* **1.** Ancestry; lineage. **2.** A list or record of ancestors or descent, as of a purebred animal. [< OF *pie de grue,* "crane's foot" < the claw-shaped marks used in pedigrees.] —**ped′i•greed′** *adj.*

ped•i•ment (pĕd′ə-mənt) *n.* A wide, low-pitched gable surmounting the façade of a building in the Classical style. [Prob < a var of PYRAMID.]

pe•dom•e•ter (pĭ-dŏm′ə-tər) *n.* An instrument that gauges the approximate distance traveled on foot by registering the number of steps taken. [< PEDI- + -METER.]

peek (pēk) *v.* **1.** To glance quickly. **2.** To peer furtively. —*n.* A furtive or brief look.

peek•a•boo (pēk′ə-bōo′) *n.* A child's game in which one suddenly exposes the face, exclaiming "peekaboo!"

peel (pēl) *n.* Skin or rind, esp. of a fruit. —*v.* **1.** To strip or cut away the skin, rind, or bark from; pare. **2.** To strip away; pull off (an outer covering). **3.** To come off in thin strips or pieces. [< OF *peler.*] —**peel′er** *n.*

peel•ing (pē′lĭng) *n.* A peeled-off piece or strip of skin or rind.

peen (pēn) *n.* The end of a hammerhead opposite the flat striking surface, often wedge-shaped or ball-shaped. [?]

peep[1] (pēp) *v.* To utter a short, high-pitched sound, as of a baby bird. —*n.* **1.** A weak, shrill sound. **2.** Any slight utterance.

peep[2] (pēp) *v.* **1.** To peek furtively, as through a small aperture. **2.** To become visible gradually. —*n.* **1.** A quick or furtive look. **2.** A first glimpse or appearance.

peep•hole (pēp′hōl′) *n.* A small hole through which one may peep.

peer[1] (pîr) *v.* **1.** To look intently. **2.** To be partially visible. [Perh contraction of APPEAR.]

peer[2] (pîr) *n.* **1.** One who has equal standing with another. **2.** A member of the British peerage; a duke, marquis, earl, viscount, or baron. [< OF *per,* equal.] —**peer′age** *n.* —**peer′ess** *fem.n.*

peer•less (pîr′lĭs) *adj.* Without peer; unmatched. —**peer′less•ly** *adv.*

peeve (pēv) *v.* **peeved, peeving.** To annoy or vex. —*n.* **1.** A vexation; grievance. **2.** A resentful mood. [Back-formation < PEEVISH.]

pee•vish (pē′vĭsh) *adj.* Querulous; irritable. [Perh < F *pervers,* perverse.] —**pee′vish•ly** *adv.* —**pee′vish•ness** *n.*

pee•wee (pē′wē) *n.* One that is noticeably small. —**pee′wee** *adj.*

peg (pĕg) *n.* **1.** A small cylindrical pin, as of wood, used to fasten things. **2.** A projection used as a support or as a boundary marker. **3.** A degree or notch. **4.** A pretext or occasion for. —*v.* **pegged, pegging. 1.** To put or insert a peg into. **2.** To mark with pegs. **3.** To stabilize prices. **4.** To throw. **5.** To work steadily. [ME *pegge.*]

peg leg. *Informal.* An artificial leg.

pei•gnoir (pān-wär′, pĕn-) *n.* A woman's

loose-fitting dressing gown. [F, "garment worn while combing the hair."]

pe·jor·a·tive (pĭ-jôr'ə-tĭv, -jŏr'ə-tĭv, pĕj'ə-rā'tĭv, pē'jə-) *adj.* Tending to make or become worse; disparaging; downgrading. —*n.* A pejorative word. [< L *pējor*, worse.] —**pe·jor'a·tive·ly** *adv.*

Pe·king (pē'kĭng'). The capital of the People's Republic of China. Pop. 5,420,000.

Pe·king·ese (pē'kĭng-ēz', -ēs') *n., pl.* -ese. Also **Pe·kin·ese** (pē'kə-nēz', -nēs'). 1. A resident or native of Peking, China. 2. (pē'kə-nēz', -nēs'). A small, short-legged, long-haired dog with a flat nose. —**Pe'king·ese'** *adj.*

pe·koe (pē'kō, pĕk'ō) *n.* Black tea made from relatively small leaves. [Chin (Amoy) *peh ho.*]

pel·age (pĕl'ĭj) *n.* The hairy, furry, or woolly coat of an animal. [< L *pilus*, hair.]

pe·lag·ic (pə-lăj'ĭk) *adj.* Of open oceans or seas. [< Gk *pelagos*, sea.]

pelf (pĕlf) *n.* Wealth or riches. [< OF *pelfre*, booty.]

pel·i·can (pĕl'ĭ-kən) *n.* A large, web-footed bird with a large pouch under the lower bill, used for catching fish. [< Gk *pelekan, pelekinos.*]

pel·la·gra (pə-lăg'rə, -lā'grə, -lä'grə) *n.* A chronic niacin deficiency disease, marked by skin eruptions and digestive and nervous disturbances. [< L *pellis*, skin + Gk *agra*, seizure.] —**pel·lag'rous** *adj.*

pel·let (pĕl'ĭt) *n.* 1. A small, solid or densely packed ball or mass, as of medicine. 2. A bullet or piece of small shot. —*v.* To strike with pellets. [< L *pila*, ball, pill.]

pell-mell (pĕl'mĕl') *adv.* Also **pell·mell.** 1. In a confused manner. 2. In disorderly haste; headlong. [F *pêle-mêle.*]

pel·lu·cid (pə-lōō'sĭd) *adj.* 1. Admitting the maximum passage of light; transparent; translucent. 2. Clear. [< L *pellūcēre*, to shine through.] —**pel·lu'cid·ly** *adv.*

pelt¹ (pĕlt) *n.* An animal skin, esp. with the fur or hair still on it. [ME.]

pelt² (pĕlt) *v.* To strike repeatedly with or as with blows or missiles. [ME *pelten.*]

pel·vis (pĕl'vĭs) *n., pl.* -vises or -ves (-vēz'). A

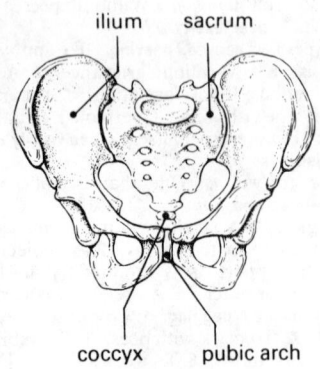

ilium   sacrum

coccyx   pubic arch

pelvis
Male pelvis

basin-shaped skeletal structure that rests on the lower limbs and supports the spinal column. [< L *pelvis*, basin.] —**pel'vic** *adj.*

pem·mi·can (pĕm'ĭ-kən) *n.* A food prepared from dried meat pounded into paste and mixed with fat. [< Algon.]

pen¹ (pĕn) *n.* An instrument for writing or drawing with ink. —*v.* **penned, penning.** To write. [< L *penna*, feather.]

pen² (pĕn) *n.* A small fenced enclosure, as for animals. —*v.* **penned** or **pent, penning.** To confine in or as in a pen. [< OE *penn.* See **bend-.**]

pen. peninsula.

pe·nal (pē'nəl) *adj.* Of or pertaining to punishment, esp. for breaking the law. [< L *poena*, penalty.] —**pe'nal·ly** *adv.*

pe·nal·ize (pē'nəl-īz', pĕn'əl-) *v.* -ized, -izing. To subject to a penalty.

pen·al·ty (pĕn'əl-tē) *n., pl.* -ties. 1. A punishment for a crime or offense. 2. Something required as a forfeit for an offense. 3. A punishment, handicap, or disadvantage imposed for some action.

pen·ance (pĕn'əns) *n.* 1. An act of contrition. 2. *Eccles.* A sacrament that includes contrition, confession to a priest, acceptance of punishment, and absolution. [< L *paenitēns*, penitent.]

pe·na·tes (pə-nä'tēz, -nā'tēz) *pl.n.* See **lares and penates.**

pence. *Brit.* Alternate *pl.* of **penny:** *twopence.*

pen·chant (pĕn'chənt) *n.* A strong inclination or liking. [< F *pencher*, to incline.]

pen·cil (pĕn'səl) *n.* A writing implement consisting of a thin rod of graphite or similar substance encased in wood or held in a plastic or metal mechanical device. —*v.* -ciled or -cilled, -ciling or -cilling. To write, draw, or mark with a pencil. [< L *pēnicillus*, a brush, pencil.] —**pen'cil·er** *n.*

pen·dant (pĕn'dənt) *n.* Something suspended from something else, esp. an ornament. [< L *pendēre*, to hang.]

pen·dent (pĕn'dənt) *adj.* Also **pen·dant.** Hanging down; dangling; suspended. [< L *pendēre*, to hang.] —**pen'dent·ly** *adv.*

pend·ing (pĕn'dĭng) *adj.* 1. Not yet decided or settled. 2. Impending. —*prep.* 1. During. 2. While awaiting; until. [< OF *pendant*, "hanging."]

pen·du·lar (pĕn'jōō-lər, pĕn'dyə-) *adj.* Of or resembling the motion of a pendulum; swinging back and forth.

pen·du·lous (pĕn'jōō-ləs, pĕn'dyə-) *adj.* Hanging loosely. [< L *pendēre*, to hang.]

pen·du·lum (pĕn'jōō-ləm, pĕn'dyə-, pĕn'də-) *n.* A mass suspended so that it is free to swing in a vertical plane under the influence of gravitational force only. [< L *pendēre*, to hang.]

Pe·nel·o·pe (pə-nĕl'ə-pē). The faithful wife of Odysseus in Homer's *Odyssey.*

pe·nes. Alternate *pl.* of **penis.**

pen·e·tra·ble (pĕn'ə-trə-bəl) *adj.* Capable of being penetrated. —**pen'e·tra·bil'i·ty** *n.*

pen·e·trate (pĕn'ə-trāt') *v.* -trated, -trating. 1. To enter into; pierce. 2. To permeate. 3. To

---

ă pat/ā ate/âr care/ä bar/b bib/ch chew/d deed/ĕ pet/ē be/f fit/g gag/h hat/hw what/
ĭ pit/ī pie/îr pier/j judge/k kick/l lid, fatal/m mum/n no, sudden/ng sing/ŏ pot/ō go/

grasp the meaning of; understand. **4.** To see through. **5.** To affect deeply. [< L *penus,* the interior of a house.] —**pen·e·tra'tion** (pĕn'ə-trā'shən) *n.*

pen·e·trat·ing (pĕn'ə-trā'tĭng) *adj.* **1.** Piercing. **2.** Keenly perceptive; discerning: *penetrating insight.* —**pen'e·trat'ing·ly** *adv.*

pen·e·tra·tive (pĕn'ə-trā'tĭv) *adj.* Capable of penetrating; piercing.

pen·guin (pĕn'gwĭn, pĕng'gwĭn) *n.* A flightless sea bird of cool regions of the S Hemisphere, having flipperlike wings and webbed feet. [Perh < W *pen gwyn.*]

pen·i·cil·lin (pĕn'ə-sĭl'ĭn) *n.* Any of several antibiotic compounds obtained from certain molds or produced synthetically, and used to treat a wide variety of diseases and infections.

pen·in·su·la (pə-nĭn's/y/ə-lə) *n.* A long projection of land into water. [L *pēninsula.*] —**pen·in'su·lar** *adj.*

pe·nis (pē'nĭs) *n., pl.* **-nises** or **-nes** (-nēz'). The male organ of copulation, esp. in higher vertebrates. [L *pēnis,* tail, penis.]

pen·i·tent (pĕn'ə-tənt) *adj.* Repentant of misdeeds or sins. [< L *paenitēre,* to repent.] —**pen'i·tence** *n.* —**pen'i·ten'tial** (pĕn'ə-tĕn'shəl) *adj.* —**pen'i·tent·ly** *adv.*

pen·i·ten·tia·ry (pĕn'ə-tĕn'shə-rē) *n., pl.* **-ries.** A prison for those convicted of major crimes. —*adj.* Of, pertaining to, or incurring imprisonment in a penitentiary. [< L *paenitēns,* penitent.]

pen·knife (pĕn'nīf') *n.* A small pocketknife.

pen·man (pĕn'mən) *n.* **1.** A copyist. **2.** An expert in penmanship. **3.** An author.

pen·man·ship (pĕn'mən-shĭp') *n.* The skill or style of handwriting.

Penn (pĕn), **William.** 1644–1718. English Quaker leader; founder of Pennsylvania (1681).

Penn., Penna. Pennsylvania (unofficial).

pen name. A literary pseudonym.

pen·nant (pĕn'ənt) *n.* **1.** A long narrow flag, as one used for signaling. **2.** Such a flag as a symbol of championship. [Blend of PENDANT and PENNON.]

pen·ni·less (pĕn'ē-lĭs, -ə-lĭs) *adj.* Without money. —**pen'ni·less·ness** *n.*

pen·non (pĕn'ən) *n.* A long, narrow banner borne on a lance. [< OF *penne,* feather, wing.]

Penn·syl·va·nia (pĕn'səl-vān'yə, -vā'nē-ə). A state of the E U.S. Pop. 11,794,000. Cap. Harrisburg.

Penn·syl·va·nian (pĕn'səl-vān'yən, -vā'nē-ən) *adj.* **1.** Of or pertaining to the state of Pennsylvania. **2.** Of or belonging to the geologic time, system of rocks, or sedimentary deposits of the sixth period of the Paleozoic era. —*n.* **1.** A native of Pennsylvania. **2.** The Pennsylvanian period.

pen·ny (pĕn'ē) *n., pl.* **-nies. 1.** A coin of the U.S. and Canada, the cent. **2.** *pl.* **-nies** or **pence** (pĕns). **a.** A subdivision of the pound of the United Kingdom. After 1971, it will equal ¹/₁₀₀ of the pound. **b.** A subdivision of the pound of Gambia, the Republic of Ireland, Jamaica, Malawi, Malta, Nigeria, Rhodesia, and various dependent territories of the United Kingdom. [< OE *penig, penning* < Gmc **panninga.*]

pen·ny·roy·al (pĕn'ē-roi'əl) *n.* An aromatic plant with hairy leaves and small bluish flowers.

pen·ny·weight (pĕn'ē-wāt') *n.* A unit of troy weight equal to ¹/₂₀ of a troy ounce or approx. 1.555 grams.

pe·nol·o·gy (pē-nŏl'ə-jē) *n.* The theory and practice of prison management and criminal rehabilitation. [L *poena,* penalty + -LOGY.]

pen·sion (pĕn'shən) *n.* A sum of money paid regularly, esp. as a retirement benefit. —*v.* To give a pension to. [< L *pēnsiō,* payment.] —**pen'sion·er** *n.*

pen·sive (pĕn'sĭv) *adj.* Wistfully or sadly thoughtful. [< OF *penser,* to think.] —**pen'sive·ly** *adv.* —**pen'sive·ness** *n.*

pent (pĕnt). Alternate *p.t. & p.p.* of **pen².** —*adj.* Penned or shut up; closely confined.

penta-. *comb. form.* Five. [< Gk *pente,* five.]

pen·ta·cle (pĕn'tə-kəl) *n.* A five-pointed star formed by five straight lines connecting the vertices of a pentagon.

pen·ta·gon (pĕn'tə-gŏn') *n.* A polygon having five sides. —**pen·tag'o·nal** (pĕn-tăg'ə-nəl) *adj.*

pen·tam·e·ter (pĕn-tăm'ə-tər) *n.* A line of verse composed of five metrical feet.

Pen·ta·teuch (pĕn'tə-t/y/ook') *n.* The first five books of the Bible: Genesis, Exodus, Leviticus, Numbers, and Deuteronomy. See **Bible.** —**Pen'ta·teuch'al** *adj.*

Pen·te·cost (pĕn'tĭ-kôst', -kŏst') *n.* A church festival occurring on the 7th Sunday after Easter, to celebrate the descent of the Holy Ghost upon the disciples; Whitsunday. [< Gk *pentēkostē (hēmera),* the 50th day (after the Resurrection).] —**Pen'te·cos'tal** *adj.*

pent·house (pĕnt'hous') *n.* An apartment situated on the roof of a building. [< ML *appenticium,* appendage.]

pe·nul·ti·mate (pĭ-nŭl'tə-mĭt) *adj.* Next to last. [< L *paenultimus,* last but one.]

pe·nu·ri·ous (pə-n/y/oor'ē-əs) *adj.* Miserly; stingy. —**pe·nu'ri·ous·ness** *n.*

pen·u·ry (pĕn'yə-rē) *n.* Extreme poverty. [< L *paenūria,* scarcity.]

Pe·nu·ti·an (pə-noo'tē-ən, -shən) *n.* A family or phylum of North American Indian languages of Pacific coastal areas.

pe·on (pē'ŏn', pē'ən) *n.* **1.** A laborer of Latin America or the SW U.S. **2.** One bound in servitude to a creditor. [< ML *pedo,* a foot soldier.] —**pe'on·age** (-ə-nĭj) *n.*

pe·o·ny (pē'ə-nē) *n., pl.* **-nies.** A garden plant with large pink, red, or white flowers. [< Gk *paiōnia.*]

peo·ple (pē'pəl) *n., pl.* **-ple. 1.** *pl.* **-ples** (only form for sense 1). A body of persons of the same country, culture, etc. **2. a.** The mass of ordinary persons; populace. **b.** The electorate. **3.** Persons loyal to a superior. **4.** One's relatives. **5.** Human beings. —*v.* **-pled, -pling.** To populate. [< L *populus.*]

pep (pĕp) *Informal. n.* Energy; vim. —*v.* **pepped, pepping. —pep up.** To invigorate. [Short for PEPPER.] —**pep'py** *adj.*

pep·per (pĕp'ər) *n.* **1. a.** The small, pungent

berry of a tropical Asian vine, used ground or whole as a condiment. **b.** The vine itself. **2. a.** The podlike or bell-shaped fruit of several related bushy plants, having a mild to pungent flavor and used as a vegetable or condiment. **b.** A plant bearing such fruit. —*v.* **1.** To season or sprinkle with or as with pepper. **2.** To pelt with numerous small missiles. [< Gk *peperi* < Sk *pippalī*, berry.]

pep•per•corn (pĕp′ər-kôrn′) *n.* A dried berry of the pepper vine.

pep•per•mint (pĕp′ər-mĭnt′) *n.* **1.** An aromatic plant yielding a pungent oil. **2.** A candy with this flavoring.

pep•per•y (pĕp′ə-rē) *adj.* -ier, -iest. **1.** Of, like, or containing pepper; pungent. **2.** Sharp-tempered; touchy. **3.** Vivid; fiery: *a peppery speech.* —**pep′per•i•ness** *n.*

pep•sin (pĕp′sĭn) *n.* A digestive enzyme found in gastric juice. [< Gk *pepsis*, digestion.]

pep•tic (pĕp′tĭk) *adj.* **1. a.** Of or assisting digestion: *peptic secretion.* **b.** Of or associated with the action of digestive secretions: *peptic ulcer.* **2.** Of or involving pepsin. [< Gk *peptein*, to digest.]

per (pûr) *prep.* **1.** Through; by means of. **2.** To, for, or by each. **3.** According to. [L.]

per-. *comb. form.* *Chem.* A compound that includes an element in its highest oxidation state. [< L *per*, through, by, away.]

per. period.

per•ad•ven•ture (pûr′əd-vĕn′chər, pĕr′-) *adv.* *Archaic.* Perhaps.

per•am•bu•late (pə-răm′byə-lāt′) *v.* -lated, -lating. To walk about; stroll. [L *perambulāre.*] —**per•am′bu•la′tion** *n.*

per•am•bu•la•tor (pə-răm′byə-lā′tər) *n.* *Chiefly Brit.* A baby carriage.

per an•num (ăn′əm). By the year; annually. [L.]

per•cale (pər-kāl′) *n.* A close-woven cotton fabric used esp. to make sheets. [< Pers *pargālah.*]

per cap•i•ta (kăp′ə-tə). Per person. [L, "by heads."]

per•ceive (pər-sēv′) *v.* -ceived, -ceiving. **1.** To become aware of through the senses. **2.** To observe; detect. **3.** To achieve understanding of. [< L *percipere*, "to seize wholly."]

per cent. Also **per•cent** (pər-sĕnt′). Per hundred; for or out of each hundred. [< L *per centum*, by the hundred.]

per•cent•age (pər-sĕn′tĭj) *n.* **1.** A fraction or ratio with 100 fixed and understood as the denominator. **2.** A proportion or share in relation to a whole.

per•cen•tile (pər-sĕn′tīl′) *n.* *Stat.* A number that divides the range of a set of data so that a given percentage lies below this number.

per•cept (pûr′sĕpt′) *n.* An impression in the mind of something perceived by the senses. [Back-formation < PERCEPTION.]

per•cep•ti•ble (pər-sĕp′tə-bəl) *adj.* Capable of being perceived. —**per•cep′ti•bly** *adv.*

per•cep•tion (pər-sĕp′shən) *n.* **1.** The act or result of perceiving. **2.** Awareness; discernment; insight. [< L *percipere*, PERCEIVE.]

per•cep•tive (pər-sĕp′tĭv) *adj.* **1.** Of or per-

taining to perception. **2.** Having the ability to perceive; discerning.

per•cep•tu•al (pər-sĕp′chōō-əl) *adj.* Of, based on, or involving perception. —**per•cep′tu•al•ly** *adv.*

perch¹ (pûrch) *n.* **1.** A rod or branch serving as a roost for a bird. **2.** A place for resting or sitting. —*v.* To alight or rest on a perch. [< L *pertica*, stick.]

perch² (pûrch) *n., pl.* **perch** or **perches.** **1.** A freshwater food fish. **2.** Any of various related or similar fishes. [< Gk *perkē.*]

per•chance (pər-chăns′, -chäns′) *adv.* Perhaps.

per•co•late (pûr′kə-lāt′) *v.* -lated, -lating. **1.** To cause (fluid) to pass through a porous substance; filter. **2.** To pass or ooze through. **3.** To make (coffee) in a percolator. [L *percōlāre.*] —**per′co•la′tion** *n.*

per•co•la•tor (pûr′kə-lā′tər) *n.* A coffeepot in which boiling water is forced up through a center tube to filter through ground coffee.

per•cus•sion (pər-kŭsh′ən) *n.* **1.** The striking together of two bodies, esp. when noise is produced. **2.** The act of detonating a cap in a firearm. **3.** Musical percussion instruments collectively. [< L *percutere* (pp *percussus*), to strike hard.]

percussion instrument. A musical instrument in which sound is produced by striking.

per di•em (dē′əm, dī′əm). Per day. [L.]

per•di•tion (pər-dĭsh′ən) *n.* **1.** Eternal damnation. **2.** Hell. [< L *perdere*, to destroy, lose.]

per•e•gri•nate (pĕr′ə-grə-nāt′) *v.* -nated, -nating. To travel from place to place. [L *peregrinārī*, to travel in foreign lands.] —**per′e•gri•na′tion** *n.*

per•emp•to•ry (pə-rĕmp′tə-rē) *adj.* **1.** *Law.* Precluding further debate or action. **2.** Not admitting denial; imperative. **3.** Expressing a command; urgent. **4.** Dictatorial; imperious. [LL *peremptōrius*, "precluding debate," decisive.] —**per•emp′to•ri•ly** *adv.*

per•en•ni•al (pə-rĕn′ē-əl) *adj.* **1.** Lasting through a year or many years. **2. a.** Everlasting; perpetual. **b.** Continually recurring. **3.** *Bot.* Having a life span of more than two years. —*n.* A perennial plant. [< L *perennis.*] —**per•en′ni•al•ly** *adv.*

perf. **1.** perfect. **2.** perforated.

per•fect (pûr′fĭkt) *adj.* **1.** Without defect; flawless. **2.** Accurate; exact. **3.** Complete; utter. **4.** Excellent in all respects. **5.** *Gram.* Of, pertaining to, or constituting a verb tense expressing completed past action. —*n.* *Gram.* **1.** The perfect tense. **2.** A verb or verb form in this tense. —*v.* (pər-fĕkt′). To bring to perfection. [< L *perficere*, to complete.] —**per•fect′er** *n.* —**per′fect•ly** *adv.*

per•fec•tion (pər-fĕk′shən) *n.* **1.** The state or quality of being perfect. **2.** The act of perfecting. **3.** A person or thing that perfectly embodies something.

per•fec•tion•ism (pər-fĕk′shə-nĭz′əm) *n.* A propensity for setting extremely high standards and being displeased with anything less. —**per•fec′tion•ist** *n.*

per•fi•dy (pûr′fə-dē) *n., pl.* -dies. Deliberate breach of faith; treachery. [< L *perfidus*,

---

ă pat/ā ate/âr care/ä bar/b **bib**/ch **chew**/d **deed**/ĕ pet/ē be/f fit/g **gag**/h hat/hw **what**/
ĭ pit/ī pie/îr pier/j **judge**/k **kick**/l lid, fatal/m **mum**/n no, sudden/ng **sing**/ŏ pot/ō go/

treacherous.] —per•fid′i•ous (pər-fĭd′ē-əs) *adj.*
per•fo•rate (pûr′fə-rāt′) *v.* -rated, -rating. 1. To
pierce, punch, or bore a hole or holes in. 2. To
pierce or stamp with rows of holes to allow
easy separation. [L *perforāre.*] —per′fo•ra′tion
n. —per′fo•ra′tor *n.*
per•force (pər-fôrs′, -fōrs′) *adv.* By necessity.
per•form (pər-fôrm′) *v.* 1. To carry out (an
action); function. 2. To fulfill, as a duty or
obligation. 3. To give a public presentation, as
of a dramatic work or musical composition.
[< OF *parfornir.*] —per•form′er *n.*
per•form•ance (pər-fôr′məns) *n.* 1. The act or
manner of performing. 2. A presentation before an audience. 3. A deed; feat.
per•fume (pûr′fyōōm′, pər-fyōōm′) *n.* 1. A
fragrant volatile liquid, as one distilled from
flowers. 2. Any pleasing odor. —*v.* (pər-
fyōōm′) -fumed, -fuming. To impart a pleasant
odor to. [< OIt *parfumare,* to smoke through.]
per•fum•er•y (pər-fyōō′mə-rē) *n., pl.* -ies. 1.
Perfumes in general. 2. An establishment that
makes or sells perfume.
per•func•to•ry (pər-fŭngk′tə-rē) *adj.* Done or
acting routinely and with little interest or care.
[< L *perfungī,* "to get through with."] —per•
func′to•ri•ly *adv.* —per•func′to•ri•ness *n.*
per•go•la (pûr′gə-lə) *n.* An arbor or passageway with a roof of latticework. [< L *pergula.*]
per•haps (pər-hăps′) *adv.* Maybe; possibly.
[PER + HAP (chance).]
peri-. *comb. form.* 1. About, around, encircling,
or enclosing. 2. Close at hand; adjacent. [<
Gk *peri,* about, near, around.]
Per•i•cles (pĕr′ə-klēz′). 495?-429 B.C. Athenian statesman, orator, and general.

Pericles

per•i•gee (pĕr′ə-jē) *n.* The point nearest the
earth in the orbit of the moon or a satellite.
[< Gk *perigeios,* near the earth.]
per•i•he•li•on (pĕr′ə-hē′lē-ən, -hēl′yən) *n., pl.*
-helia (-hē′lē-ə, -hēl′yə). The point nearest the
sun in the orbit of a planet or other body.
per•il (pĕr′əl) *n.* 1. A condition of imminent
danger. 2. Something that endangers. [< L
periculum, trial, danger.] —per′il•ous *adj.*
—per′il•ous•ly *adv.*
pe•rim•e•ter (pə-rĭm′ə-tər) *n.* 1. A closed

curve bounding a plane area. 2. The length of
such a boundary.
pe•ri•od (pîr′ē-əd) *n.* 1. An interval of time
characterized by the occurrence or prevalence
of certain conditions or events. 2. A unit of
geologic time longer than an epoch and shorter than an era. 3. An interval regarded as a
developmental phase; stage. 4. Any of various
arbitrary temporal units, as of an academic
day. 5. An instance of menstruation. 6. A
point or portion of time at which something is
ended; completion. 7. A punctuation mark (.)
indicating a full stop and placed esp. at the
end of sentences. —*adj.* Of a certain historical
age or time: *a period piece.* [< Gk *periodos,*
circuit, rhetorical period.]
pe•ri•od•ic (pîr′ē-ŏd′ĭk) *adj.* 1. Having periods
or repeated cycles. 2. Happening or appearing
at regular intervals. 3. Taking place now and
then; intermittent. —pe•ri•od′i•cal•ly *adv.*
—pe′ri•o•dic′i•ty (-ə-dĭs′ə-tē) *n.*
pe•ri•od•i•cal (pîr′ē-ŏd′ĭ-kəl) *adj.* 1. Periodic.
2. a. Published at regular intervals of more
than one day. b. Of or pertaining to a publication issued at such intervals. —*n.* A periodical publication.
pe•ri•o•don•tal (pĕr′ē-ō-dŏnt′l) *adj.* Of or designating tissue and structures that surround
and support the teeth.
per•i•pa•tet•ic (pĕr′ə-pə-tĕt′ĭk) *adj.* 1. Walking about from place to place. 2. Carried on
while walking about. [< Gk *peripatein,* to
walk about while teaching.]
pe•riph•er•al (pə-rĭf′ər-əl) *adj.* 1. Of or on the
periphery. 2. Relatively unimportant. —pe•
riph′er•al•ly *adv.*
pe•riph•er•y (pə-rĭf′ə-rē) *n., pl.* -ies. 1. The
outermost region within a precise boundary.
2. The region immediately beyond a precise
boundary. 3. A zone constituting an imprecise
boundary. 4. Perimeter. [< Gk *peripherein,* to
carry around.]
per•i•scope (pĕr′ə-skōp′) *n.* Any of various
optical instruments that permit observation
from a position displaced from a direct line of
sight.
per•ish (pĕr′ĭsh) *v.* 1. To die, esp. in a violent
or untimely manner. 2. To disappear gradually. [< L *perīre,* to pass away.]
per•ish•a•ble (pĕr′ĭsh-ə-bəl) *adj.* Easily destroyed or spoiled. —per′ish•a•bly *adv.*
per•i•stal•sis (pĕr′ə-stôl′sĭs, -stăl′sĭs) *n., pl.* -ses
(-sēz′). Wavelike muscular contractions that
propel contained matter along the tubular organs, as in the alimentary canal. [< Gk *per-
istellein,* to wrap around.] —per′i•stal′tic
(-stôl′tĭk, -stăl′tĭk) *adj.*
per•i•to•ne•um (pĕr′ə-tə-nē′əm) *n., pl.* -nea
(-nē′ə). Also per•i•to•nae•um. The membrane
lining the walls of the abdominal cavity. [<
Gk *peritonaios,* stretched across.] —per′i•to•
ne′al *adj.*
per•i•to•ni•tis (pĕr′ə-tə-nī′tĭs) *n.* Inflammation
of the peritoneum.
per•i•wig (pĕr′ĭ-wĭg′) *n.* A wig. [< OF *per-
ruque.*]
per•i•win•kle¹ (pĕr′ĭ-wĭng′kəl) *n.* A small, edible marine snail with a cone-shaped shell.

[Prob < L *pīna*, a mussel + OE *-wincel*, snail shell (see weng-).]

per·i·win·kle² (pĕr'ĭ-wĭng'kəl) *n.* A trailing blue-flowered myrtle. [< L *pervinca*.]

per·jure (pûr'jər) *v.* -jured, -juring. To testify falsely and deliberately under oath. [< L *perjūrāre*.] —**per'jur·er** *n.* —**per'ju·ry** *n.*

perk (pûrk) *v.* **1.** To raise, as the head, smartly and quickly. **2.** To make or become vigorous and lively again (with *up*). [< NF *perquer*, to perch.] —**perk'i·ness** *n.* —**perk'y** *adj.*

perm. permanent.

per·ma·frost (pûr'mə-frôst', -frŏst') *n.* Permanently frozen subsoil in frigid areas.

per·ma·nent (pûr'mə-nənt) *adj.* Fixed and lasting. —*n.* A long-lasting hair setting. [< L *permanēre*, to remain throughout.] —**per'ma·nence** *n.* —**per'ma·nen·cy** *n.* —**per'ma·nent·ly** *adv.*

per·me·a·ble (pûr'mē-ə-bəl) *adj.* Capable of being permeated. —**per'me·a·bly** *adv.*

per·me·ate (pûr'mē-āt') *v.* -ated, -ating. **1.** To pervade. **2.** To pass through the openings or interstices of. [L *permeāre*.] —**per'me·a'tion** *n.*

Per·mi·an (pûr'mē-ən, pĕr'-) *adj.* Of or belonging to the geologic time, system of rocks, or sedimentary deposits of the seventh and last period of the Paleozoic era. —*n.* The Permian period. [< *Perm*, former Russian province.]

per·mis·si·ble (pər-mĭs'ə-bəl) *adj.* That can be permitted; allowable.

per·mis·sion (pər-mĭsh'ən) *n.* Consent, esp. formal consent.

per·mis·sive (pər-mĭs'ĭv) *adj.* **1.** Granting permission. **2.** Lenient; tolerant.

per·mit (pər-mĭt') *v.* -mitted, -mitting. **1.** To allow; consent to. **2.** To afford opportunity to. —*n.* (pûr'mĭt, pər-mĭt'). A document granting permission. [L *permittere*.]

per·mu·ta·tion (pûr'myōō-tā'shən) *n.* **1.** A transformation. **2.** The act of altering a given set of objects in a group. **3.** *Math.* An ordered arrangement of all or some of the elements of a set.

per·ni·cious (pər-nĭsh'əs) *adj.* Destructive or deadly. [< L *perniciēs*, destruction.]

per·o·ra·tion (pĕr'ə-rā'shən) *n.* The formal recapitulation at the end of a speech. [< L *perōrāre*, to harangue at length.]

per·ox·ide (pə-rŏk'sīd') *n.* **1. Hydrogen peroxide. 2.** Any compound containing oxygen that yields hydrogen peroxide with an acid, such as sodium peroxide, Na_2O_2.

per·pen·dic·u·lar (pûr'pən-dĭk'yə-lər) *adj.* **1.** Intersecting at or forming right angles. **2.** At right angles to the horizontal; vertical. [< L *perpendiculum*, plumb line.] —**per'pen·dic'u·lar** *n.* —**per'pen·dic'u·lar·ly** *adv.*

per·pe·trate (pûr'pə-trāt') *v.* -trated, -trating. **1.** To be guilty of; commit. **2.** To carry out; perform. [L *perpetrāre*, to accomplish.] —**per'pe·tra'tion** *n.* —**per'pe·tra'tor** (-trā'tər) *n.*

per·pet·u·al (pər-pĕch'ōō-əl) *adj.* **1.** Lasting for eternity. **2.** Lasting for an indefinitely long duration. **3.** Ceaselessly repeated. [< L *perpetuus*, continuous, permanent.] —**per·pet'u·al·ly** *adv.* —**per·pet'u·al·ness** *n.*

per·pet·u·ate (pər-pĕch'ōō-āt') *v.* -ated, -ating.

1. To make perpetual. **2.** To prolong the existence of. —**per·pet'u·a'tion** *n.*

per·pe·tu·i·ty (pûr'pə-t/y/ōō'ə-tē) *n., pl.* -ties. The qua.ity or condition of being perpetual.

per·plex (pər-plĕks') *v.* To confuse or puzzle; bewilder. [< L *perplexus*, intricate.] —**per·plex'i·ty** *n.*

per·qui·site (pûr'kwə-zĭt) *n.* **1.** A payment or profit received in addition to a regular wage or salary. **2.** Something claimed as an exclusive right. [< L *perquīrere*, to search for.]

Pers. Persia; Persian.

per se (sā', sē'). In or by itself; intrinsically. [L *per sē*.]

per·se·cute (pûr'sə-kyōōt') *v.* -cuted, -cuting. **1.** To oppress or harass with ill-treatment. **2.** To annoy persistently. [< L *persequī*, to pursue.] —**per'se·cu'tion** *n.* —**per'se·cu'tor** (-kyōō'tər) *n.*

per·se·vere (pûr'sə-vîr') *v.* -vered, -vering. To persist in or remain constant to a purpose, idea, or task in the face of obstacles. [< L *persevērus*, very serious.] —**per'se·ver'ance** *n.*

Per·sia (pûr'zhə). The former name for Iran.

Per·sian (pûr'zhən) *n.* **1.** A native or inhabitant of ancient Persia or modern Iran. **2.** The Iranian language of the Persians. —**Per'sian** *adj.*

Persian Gulf. An inlet of the Arabian Sea between the Arabian Peninsula and Iran.

Persian lamb. The glossy, tightly curled fur of a young lamb of the karakul sheep.

per·sim·mon (pər-sĭm'ən) *n.* **1.** A tree with hard wood and orange-red, edible fruit. **2.** The fruit of such a tree. [< Algon.]

per·sist (pər-sĭst', -zĭst') *v.* **1.** To hold firmly and steadfastly to some purpose or undertaking, despite obstacles. **2.** To continue in existence. [L *persistere*.] —**per·sist'ence** *n.* —**per·sist'ent** *adj.* —**per·sist'ent·ly** *adv.*

per·snick·e·ty (pər-snĭk'ə-tē) *adj.* Fastidious.

per·son (pûr'sən) *n.* **1.** A human being. **2.** The living body of a human being. **3.** The personality of a human being; self. **4.** Any of three groups of pronouns with corresponding verb inflections that distinguish between the speaker (first person), the individual addressed (second person), and the individual or thing spoken of (third person). [< L *persōna*, mask.]

per·son·a·ble (pûr'sən-ə-bəl) *adj.* Pleasing in appearance or personality.

per·son·age (pûr'sən-ĭj) *n.* A person of distinction.

per·son·al (pûr'sən-əl) *adj.* **1.** Of or pertaining to a particular person; private. **2.** Done in person: *a personal appearance.* **3.** Of or pertaining to the body of a human being. **4.** Pertaining to an individual, esp. in an offensive way: *a highly personal remark.* **5.** *Law.* Pertaining to a person's movable property. **6.** Indicating grammatical person. —*n.* A personal item or notice in a newspaper. —**per'son·al·ly** *adv.*

per·son·al·i·ty (pûr'sən-ăl'ə-tē) *n., pl.* -ties. **1.** The state or quality of being a person. **2.** The totality of distinctive traits of an individual. **3.** The personal traits that make one socially appealing. **4.** A person of renown.

ă pat/ā ate/âr care/ä bar/b bib/ch chew/d deed/ĕ pet/ē be/f fit/g gag/h hat/hw what/
ĭ pit/ī pie/îr pier/j judge/k kick/l lid, fatal/m mum/n no, sudden/ng sing/ŏ pot/ō go/

per·son·al·ize (pûr′sən-əl-īz′) v. -ized, -izing. **1.** To make personal. **2.** To mark with one's name or initials.

per·so·na non gra·ta (pər-sō′nə nŏn grä′tə, grăt′ə). A person who is not acceptable or welcome. [L, "unacceptable person."]

per·son·i·fy (pər-sŏn′ə-fī′) v. -fied, -fying. **1.** To think of or represent (an inanimate object or abstraction) as a person. **2.** To be the embodiment or perfect example of. —**per·son′i·fi·ca′tion** (-fĭ-kā′shən) n.

per·son·nel (pûr′sən-ĕl′) n. **1.** The body of persons employed by or active in an organization. **2.** An administrative div'sion concerned with this body of persons.

per·spec·tive (pər-spĕk′tĭv) n. **1.** Any of various techniques for representing three-dimensional objects and depth relationships on a two-dimensional surface. **2.** The relationship of aspects of a subject to each other and to a whole: *a perspective of history.* **3.** Point of view. [< L *perspicere,* to see through or into.]

per·spi·cac·i·ty (pûr′spĭ-kăs′ə-tē) n. Acuteness of perception or understanding. [< L *perspicere,* to see through.] —**per′spi·ca′cious** (-kā′shəs) *adj.* —**per′spi·ca′cious·ly** *adv.*

per·spic·u·ous (pər-spĭk′yōō-əs) *adj.* Clearly expressed or presented; lucid. [< L *perspicere,* to see through.] —**per′spi·cu′i·ty** (pûr′spĭ-kyōō′ə-tē), **per·spic′u·ous·ness** n.

per·spi·ra·tion (pûr′spə-rā′shən) n. **1.** The saline moisture excreted through the pores of the skin by the sweat glands; sweat. **2.** The act or process of perspiring.

per·spire (pər-spīr′) v. -spired, -spiring. To excrete perspiration through the pores of the skin. [< L *perspīrāre,* breathe through.]

per·suade (pər-swād′) v. -suaded, -suading. **1.** To cause (someone) to do something by means of argument, reasoning, or entreaty. **2.** To make (someone) believe something. [L *persuādēre.*] —**per·suad′a·ble** *adj.* —**per·suad′er** n. —**per·sua′sive** *adj.*

per·sua·sion (pər-swā′zhən) n. **1.** The act of persuading or the state of being persuaded. **2.** The ability to persuade. **3.** A body of religious beliefs: *worshipers of various persuasions.*

pert (pûrt) *adj.* **1.** Impudently bold. **2.** High-spirited. **3.** Jaunty: *a pert little hat.* [< OF *apert,* straightforward, open.]

pert. pertaining.

per·tain (pər-tān′) v. **1.** To have reference; relate. **2.** To belong as an adjunct or accessory. **3.** To be suitable. [< L *pertinēre,* to relate to, to reach to.]

Perth (pûrth). A city of W Australia. Pop. 465,000.

per·ti·na·cious (pûr′tə-nā′shəs) *adj.* **1.** Holding firmly to some purpose or opinion. **2.** Stubbornly persistent. [< L *pertināx.*] —**per′ti·nac′i·ty** (-năs′ə-tē) n.

per·ti·nent (pûr′tə-nənt) *adj.* Relating to a specific matter; apposite: *a pertinent fact.* [< L *pertinēre,* to reach, concern.] —**per′ti·nence, per′ti·nen·cy** n. —**per′ti·nent·ly** *adv.*

per·turb (pər-tûrb′) v. To disturb greatly; make uneasy or anxious. [< L *perturbāre.*] —**per·tur·ba′tion** (pûr′tər-bā′shən) n.

Pe·ru (pə-rōō′). A republic in W South America. Pop. 10,365,000. Cap. Lima. —**Pe·ru′vi·an** *adj. & n.*

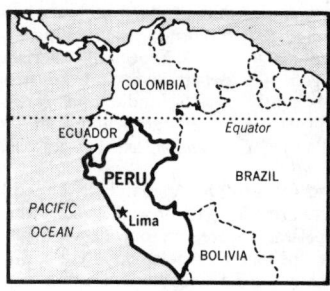

Peru

pe·ruse (pə-rōōz′) v. -rused, -rusing. To read or examine, esp. with great care. [ME *perusen,* to use up.] —**pe·rus′al** n. —**pe·rus′er** n.

per·vade (pər-vād′) v. -vaded, -vading. To spread throughout; permeate. [L *pervādere.*] —**per·va′sive** (-vā′sĭv, -zĭv) *adj.*

per·verse (pər-vûrs′) *adj.* **1.** Directed away from what is right or good. **2.** Obstinately persisting in an error or fault. **3.** Cranky; peevish. [< L *pervertere,* to PERVERT.] —**per·verse′ly** *adv.* —**per·ver′si·ty** n.

per·ver·sion (pər-vûr′zhən, -shən) n. **1.** The act of perverting or the state of being perverted. **2.** A deviant sexual practice.

per·vert (pər-vûrt′) v. **1.** To corrupt or debase. **2.** To misuse. **3.** To interpret incorrectly. —*n.* (pûr′vûrt′). One who practices sexual perversion. [< L *pervertere,* to turn the wrong way, turn around.] —**per·vert′ed** *adj.*

pe·se·ta (pə-sā′tə) n. The basic monetary unit of Spain.

pes·ky (pĕs′kē) *adj.* -kier, -kiest. Annoying. [Prob < PEST.] —**pes′ki·ness** n.

pe·so (pĕ′sō) n., *pl.* -sos. The basic monetary unit of Argentina, Bolivia, Colombia, Cuba, the Dominican Republic, Mexico, the Philippines, and Uruguay. [Span, "weight."]

pes·si·mism (pĕs′ə-mĭz′əm) n. **1.** A tendency to take the gloomiest possible view of a situation. **2.** The belief that the evil in the world outweighs the good. [< L *pessimus,* worst.] —**pes′si·mist** n. —**pes′si·mis′tic** *adj.*

pest (pĕst) n. **1.** An annoying person or thing; nuisance. **2.** An injurious plant or animal. [< L *pestis.*]

pes·ter (pĕs′tər) v. To harass with petty annoyances; bother. [Prob < OF *espestrer,* to tie up (an animal), impede.] —**pes′ter·er** n.

pes·ti·cide (pĕs′tə-sīd′) n. A chemical used to kill pests, esp. insects and rodents.

pes·tif·er·ous (pĕs-tĭf′ər-əs) *adj.* **1.** Producing or breeding infectious disease. **2.** Bothersome.

pes·ti·lence (pĕs′tə-ləns) n. A fatal epidemic disease, esp. bubonic plague.

pes·ti·lent (pĕs′tə-lənt) *adj.* Also **pes·ti·len·tial** (pĕs′tə-lĕn′shəl). **1.** Tending to cause death. **2.** Likely to cause an epidemic disease. [< L *pestis,* plague, PEST.]

ô paw, for/oi boy/ou out/ŏŏ took/ōō coo/p pop/r run/s sauce/sh shy/t to/th thin/*th* the/
ŭ cut/ûr fur/v van/w wag/y yes/z size/zh vision/ə ago, item, edible, gallop, circus/

pes·tle (pĕs′əl, pĕs′təl) *n.* A club-shaped hand tool for grinding or mashing substances in a mortar. [< L *pistillum*.]

pet (pĕt) *n.* **1.** An animal kept for amusement or companionship. **2.** Any object of the affections. **3.** A favorite: *teacher's pet.* —*adj.* **1.** Kept as a pet. **2.** Especially cherished or indulged. —*v.* **petted, petting. 1.** To stroke or caress gently. **2.** To fondle and caress. [?]

pet·al (pĕt′l) *n.* A separate segment of a flower corolla. [< Gk *petalon*, leaf.] —**pet′aled, pet′-alled** *adj.*

pe·tard (pĭ-tärd′) *n.* A small bell-shaped bomb used to breach a gate or wall. —**hoist with one's own petard.** Injured by one's own cleverness.

pe·ter (pē′tər) *v.* —**peter out. 1.** To diminish gradually. **2.** To become exhausted.

Pe·ter I (pē′tər). Called "Peter the Great." 1672–1725. Czar of Russia (1682–1725).

Pe·ter (pē′tər), **Saint.** Died A.D. 67? The chief of the Apostles; traditionally regarded as first bishop of Rome.

Saint Peter

pe·tite (pə-tēt′) *adj.* Small, slender, and trim, as a girl or woman. [F.]

pe·ti·tion (pə-tĭsh′ən) *n.* **1.** A solemn request; an entreaty. **2.** A formal document containing such a request. —*v.* **1.** To address a petition to. **2.** To request formally. **3.** To make an entreaty: *petition for retrial.* [< L *petere*, to seek, demand.] —**pe·ti′tion·er** *n.*

Pe·trarch (pē′trärk′). 1304–1374. Italian poet.

pet·rel (pĕt′rəl) *n.* Any of various small, blackish sea birds.

pet·ri·fy (pĕt′rə-fī′) *v.* **-fied, -fying. 1.** To convert (wood or other organic matter) into a stony replica by structural impregnation with dissolved minerals. **2.** To cause to become stonelike; deaden. **3.** To stun or paralyze with terror. [< L *petra*, stone + *facere*, to make.]

pet·ro·chem·i·cal (pĕt′rō-kĕm′ĭ-kəl) *n.* Any chemical derived from petroleum or natural gas. —**pet′ro·chem′i·cal** *adj.*

pet·ro·dol·lar (pĕt′rō-dŏl′ər) *n.* A unit of hard currency, as a dollar, held by oil-exporting countries.

pet·rol (pĕt′rəl) *n. Chiefly Brit.* Gasoline. [< PETROLEUM.]

pet·ro·la·tum (pĕt′rə-lā′təm, -lä′təm) *n.* A colorless-to-amber gelatinous semisolid, obtained from petroleum and used in lubricants and medicinal ointments.

pe·tro·le·um (pə-trō′lē-əm) *n.* A natural, yellow-to-black, thick, flammable liquid hydrocarbon mixture found principally beneath the earth's surface and processed for fractions including natural gas, gasoline, naphtha, kerosene, fuel and lubricating oils, paraffin wax, and asphalt. [< Gk *petros*, stone + L *oleum*, oil.]

pet·ti·coat (pĕt′ē-kōt′) *n.* A skirt, esp. a woman's slip or underskirt. [< ME *pety*, small, petty + *cote*, coat.]

pet·ti·fog·ger (pĕt′ē-fŏg′ər, -fôg′ər) *n.* A petty, quibbling, unscrupulous lawyer.

pet·tish (pĕt′ĭsh) *adj.* Ill-tempered; petulant.

pet·ty (pĕt′ē) *adj.* **-tier, -tiest. 1.** Small, trivial, or insignificant in quantity or quality. **2.** Of contemptibly narrow mind or views. **3.** Spiteful; mean. [< OF *petit*, small.] —**pet′ti·ly** *adv.* —**pet′ti·ness** *n.*

petty officer. A naval noncommissioned officer.

pet·u·lant (pĕch′ōō-lənt) *adj.* Unreasonably irritable; peevish. [< L *petulāre*, to jab at.] —**pet′u·lance** *n.* —**pet′u·lant·ly** *adv.*

pe·tu·nia (pə-t/y/ōōn′yə) *n.* A cultivated plant with funnel-shaped variously colored flowers. [< Tupi *petyn*, *petyma*.]

pew (pyōō) *n.* A bench for the congregation in a church. [< L *podium*, podium, balcony.]

pe·wee (pē′wē) *n.* A small, brownish North American bird. [Imit.]

pew·ter (pyōō′tər) *n.* An alloy of tin with various amounts of antimony, copper, and lead, used for kitchen utensils and tableware. [< OF *peltre*, tin.] —**pew′ter** *adj.*

pe·yo·te (pā-ō′tē) *n.* A hallucinatory drug derived from a species of cactus. [< Nah.]

Pfc, Pfc. private first class.

P.G. postgraduate.

pH A measure of the acidity or alkalinity of a solution, numerically equal to 7 for neutral solutions, increasing with increasing alkalinity and decreasing with increasing acidity. [P(otential of) h(ydrogen).]

pha·lanx (fā′lăngks′) *n., pl.* **-lanxes** or **phalanges** (fə-lăn′jēz, fā-). **1.** A formation of foot soldiers carrying overlapping shields and long spears, used by Alexander the Great. **2.** Any close-knit or compact group. **3.** *pl.* **phalanges.** Any bone of a finger or toe. [< Gk, wooden beam, line of battle.]

phal·a·rope (făl′ə-rōp′) *n.* Any of several small wading birds with lobed toes that enable them to swim. [< Gk *phalaros*, having a white spot + *pous*, foot.]

phal·lus (făl′əs) *n., pl.* **phalli** (făl′ī′) or **-luses. 1.** The penis. **2.** A representation of the penis and testes as a symbol of generative power. [< Gk *phallos*.] —**phal′lic** *adj.*

phan·tasm (făn′tăz′əm) *n.* A phantom. [< Gk *phantasma*, apparition, specter.]

phan·tas·ma·go·ri·a (făn-tăz′mə-gôr′ē-ə,

ă pat/ā ate/âr care/ä bar/b bib/ch chew/d deed/ĕ pet/ē be/f fit/g gag/h hat/hw what/ ĭ pit/ī pie/îr pier/j judge/k kick/l lid, fatal/m mum/n no, sudden/ng sing/ŏ pot/ō go/

-gôr′ē-ə) *n.* A fantastic sequence of haphazardly associative imagery, as in dreams.

phan·tom (făn′təm) *n.* **1.** Something apparently seen, heard, or sensed, but having no physical reality; ghost; specter. **2.** An illusory mental image. [< Gk *phantasma,* PHANTASM.] —**phan′tom** *adj.*

Phar·aoh (fâr′ō, fā′rō) *n.* A king of ancient Egypt.

phar·i·see (făr′ə-sē) *n.* **1. Pharisee.** A member of an ancient Jewish sect that emphasized strict interpretation and observance of the Mosaic law. **2.** A hypocritically self-righteous person. [< Aram *perīshayyā.*] —**phar′i·sa′ic** (-sā′ĭk) *adj.*

pharm. pharmaceutical; pharmacist; pharmacy.

phar·ma·ceu·ti·cal (fär′mə-sōō′tĭ-kəl) *adj.* Pertaining to pharmacy or pharmacists. —*n.* A pharmaceutical product or preparation.

phar·ma·cist (fär′mə-sĭst) *n.* A person trained in pharmacy; druggist.

pharmaco-. *comb. form.* Drugs. [< Gk *pharmakon,* drug, poison, potion.]

phar·ma·col·o·gy (fär′mə-kŏl′ə-jē) *n.* The science of drugs, including their composition, uses, and effects.

phar·ma·co·poe·ia (fär′mə-kə-pē′ə) *n., pl.* -**ias.** **1.** A book listing medicinal drugs together with articles on their preparation and use. **2.** A collection or stock of drugs.

phar·ma·cy (fär′mə-sē) *n., pl.* -**cies.** **1.** The art of preparing and dispensing drugs. **2.** A drugstore. [< Gk *pharmakon,* drug.]

phar·ynx (făr′ĭngks) *n., pl.* **pharynges** (fə-rĭn′jēz) or -**ynxes.** The section of the digestive tract that extends from the nasal cavities to the larynx, there becoming continuous with the esophagus. [< Gk *pharunx,* throat, pharynx.] —**pha·ryn′ge·al** (fə-rĭn′jē-əl, făr′ĭn-jē′əl) *adj.*

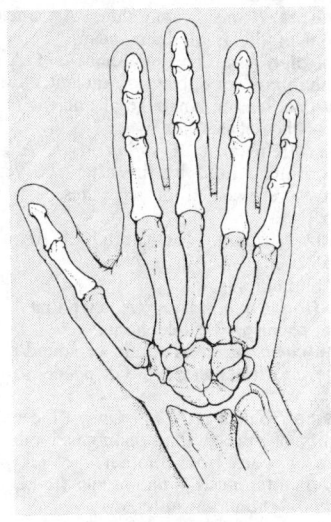

phalanx
Phalanges of the hand

phase (fāz) *n.* **1.** One of a sequence of apparent forms. **2.** A distinct stage of development. **3.** A temporary pattern of behavior: *a passing phase.* **4.** One of the cyclically recurring apparent forms of the moon or a planet. —*v.* **phased, phasing.** —**phase out.** To eliminate by one stage at a time. [< Gk *phasis,* appearance, phase of the moon.]

Ph.D. Doctor of Philosophy (L *Philosophiae Doctor*).

pheas·ant (fĕz′ənt) *n.* Any of various long-tailed, often brightly colored chickenlike birds. [< Gk *phasianos,* "the Phasian (bird)," of the Phasis River in the Caucasus.]

pheno-. *comb. form. Chem.* **1.** Showing or displaying. **2.** A compound derived from, containing, or related to benzene. [< Gk *phainein,* to show.]

phe·no·bar·bi·tal (fē′nō-bär′bə-tôl′) *n.* A white, shiny, crystalline compound, $C_{12}H_{12}N_2O_3$, used in medicine as a sedative and hypnotic.

phe·nol (fē′nôl′, -nôl′) *n.* A caustic, poisonous, white, crystalline compound, C_6H_5OH, derived from benzene and used in various resins, plastics, disinfectants, and pharmaceuticals.

phe·nom·e·nal (fĭ-nŏm′ə-nəl) *adj.* **1.** Pertaining to a phenomenon or phenomena. **2.** Extraordinary; outstanding.

phe·nom·e·non (fĭ-nŏm′ə-nŏn′) *n., pl.* -**na** (-nə). **1.** Any occurrence or fact that is directly perceptible. **2.** Also *pl.* -**nons. a.** An unusual fact or occurrence. **b.** A person outstanding for some extreme quality or achievement. [< Gk *phainesthai,* to appear.]

phe·no·type (fē′nə-tīp′) *n.* **1.** The environmentally and genetically determined observable appearance of an organism. **2.** An individual or group of organisms exhibiting a particular phenotype. —**phe′no·typ′ic** (-tĭp′ĭk) *adj.*

phi (fī) *n.* The 21st letter of the Greek alphabet, representing *ph.*

phi·al (fī′əl) *n.* A small bottle; a vial. [< Gk *phialē,* broad vessel.]

Phi Be·ta Kap·pa (fī′ bā′tə kăp′ə). An honorary fraternity whose members are chosen on the basis of high academic standing. [< Gk *philosophia biou kubernētēs,* "philosophy, the guide of life."]

phil. philosophy.

Phil. Philippians (New Testament).

Phil·a·del·phi·a (fĭl′ə-dĕl′fē-ə). A city in SE Pennsylvania. Pop. 1,928,000. [Gk, "brotherly love."] —**Phil′a·del′phi·an** *adj. & n.*

phi·lan·der (fĭ-lăn′dər) *v.* To engage in love affairs frivolously; flirt. [< Gk *philandros,* "loving men," "loving one's husband."] —**phi·lan′der·er** *n.*

phi·lan·thro·py (fĭ-lăn′thrə-pē) *n., pl.* -**pies. 1.** The effort to increase the well-being of mankind, as by charitable donations. **2.** Love of mankind in general. **3.** A charitable action or institution. [< Gk *philanthrōpos,* "lover of mankind."] —**phil′an·throp′ic** (fĭl′ən-thrŏp′ĭk) *adj.* —**phi·lan′thro·pist** *n.*

phi·lat·e·ly (fĭ-lăt′l-ē) *n.* The collection and study of postage stamps and related materials.

[< F *philatélie.*] —**phil•a•tel′ic** (fĭl′ə-tĕl′ĭk) *adj.*
—**phi•lat′e•list** *n.*
-phile, –phil. *comb. form.* One having love,
strong affinity, or preference for: **Anglophile.**
[< Gk *philos,* beloved, dear, loving.]
Philem. Philemon (New Testament).
phil•har•mon•ic (fĭl′här-mŏn′ĭk, fĭl′ər-) *adj.*
Pertaining to a symphony orchestra. —*n.* Also
Phil•har•mon•ic. A symphony orchestra or the
group that supports it. [< It *filarmonico.*]
–philia. *comb. form.* Tendency toward or attraction to: **hemophilia.** [< Gk *philos,* loving.]
Phil•ip•pines, Republic of the (fĭl′ə-pēnz′,
fĭl′ə-pēnz′). A republic consisting of the
Philippine Islands, a group of islands in the W
Pacific. Pop. 27,088,000. Cap. Quezon City.

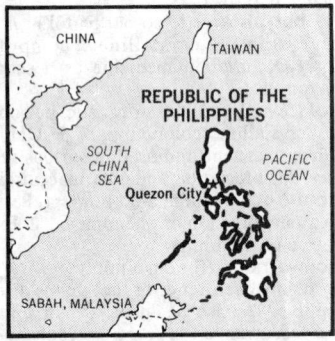

Republic of the Philippines

Phi•lis•tine (fĭ-lĭs′tĭn, -tēn′, fĭl′ĭ-stēn′) *n.* **1.**
One of an ancient people of SW Palestine.
2. One who is annoyingly indifferent to artistic
and cultural values. —*adj.* **1.** Of or pertaining
to the ancient Philistines. **2.** Often **philistine.**
Boorish; barbarous: "*Interpretation amounts to
the philistine refusal to leave the work of art
alone.*" (Susan Sontag). [< Heb *pelesheth,*
"land of the Philistines."]
philo–. *comb. form.* Love. [< Gk *philos,* loving.]
phil•o•den•dron (fĭl′ə-dĕn′drən) *n., pl.* -drons
or -dra (-drə). Any of various climbing tropical American plants often cultivated as house
plants. [< Gk *philodendros,* "tree-loving."]
phi•lol•o•gy (fĭ-lŏl′ə-jē) *n.* **1.** Historical linguistics. **2.** Literary study or classical scholarship. [< Gk *philologos,* loving reason or learning.] —**phi•lol′o•gist** *n.*
philos. philosopher; philosophy.
phi•los•o•pher (fĭ-lŏs′ə-fər) *n.* **1.** A specialist
in philosophy. **2.** One who lives by a
particular philosophy. **3.** One who is calm and
rational under any circumstances. [< Gk
philosophos, "loving wisdom."]
phi•los•o•phize (fĭ-lŏs′ə-fīz′) *v.* -phized, -phiz-
ing. To speculate in a philosophical manner.
phi•los•o•phy (fĭ-lŏs′ə-fē) *n., pl.* -phies. **1. a.**
Speculative inquiry concerning the source and
nature of human knowledge. **b.** Any system of
ideas based on such thinking. **2.** *Archaic.* The
investigation of natural phenomena: *natural*

philosophy. **3.** The sciences and liberal arts,
excluding medicine, law, and theology: *Doctor
of Philosophy.* **4.** A basic theory concerning a
particular subject: *philosophy of education.* **5.**
The set of values of an individual, culture, etc.
—**phil•o•soph′i•cal** (fĭl′ə-sŏf′ĭ-kəl) *adj.* —**phil′o•
soph′i•cal•ly** *adv.*
–philous. *comb. form.* A love of or fondness
for: **photophilous.** [< Gk *philos,* beloved, loving.]
phil•ter (fĭl′tər) *n.* Also **phil•tre.** **1.** A love potion. **2.** Any magic potion or charm. [< Gk
philtron, "love charm."]
phle•bi•tis (flĭ-bī′tĭs) *n.* Inflammation of a
vein.
phlebo–. *comb. form.* A vein. [< Gk *phleps
(phleb-),* blood vessel, vein.]
phle•bot•o•my (flĭ-bŏt′ə-mē) *n., pl.* -mies. The
therapeutic practice of opening a vein to draw
blood.
phlegm (flĕm) *n.* Stringy, thick mucus produced in the respiratory tract. [< Gk *phlegma,*
flame, inflammation, phlegm.]
phleg•mat•ic (flĕg-măt′ĭk) *adj.* Having or suggesting a calm, sluggish temperament; unemotional. [< Gk *phlegma,* PHLEGM.]
phlox (flŏks) *n., pl.* **phlox** or **phloxes.** A plant
with clusters of white, red, or purple flowers.
[< Gk, wallflower, flame.]
Phnom Penh (pə-nôm′ pĕn′). The capital of
Cambodia. Pop. 403,000.
–phobe. *comb. form.* One who fears or is
averse to something: **xenophobe.** [< Gk
phobos, fear.]
pho•bi•a (fō′bē-ə) *n.* **1.** A persistent, illogical
fear of a specific thing or situation. **2.** Any
strong fear or aversion. —**pho′bic** (-bĭk) *adj.*
–phobia. *comb. form.* Persistent, abnormal, or
intense fear: **claustrophobia.** [< Gk *phobos,*
fear, flight.]
phoe•be (fē′bē) *n.* A small, grayish North
American bird.
Phoe•ni•cia (fĭ-nĭsh′ə, -nē′shə). An ancient
kingdom of the E Mediterranean.
Phoe•ni•cian (fĭ-nĭsh′ən, -nē′shən) *n.* **1.** A native, inhabitant, or subject of ancient Phoenicia. **2.** The Semitic language of ancient Phoenicia. —**Phoe•ni′cian** *adj.*
phoe•nix (fē′nĭks) *n. Egyptian Myth.* A bird
that consumed itself by fire after 500 years,
and rose renewed from its ashes. [< Gk
phoinix.]
Phoe•nix (fē′nĭks). The capital of Arizona.
Pop. 580,000.
phon. phonetics.
phone (fōn). *Informal. n.* A telephone. —*v.*
phoned, phoning. To telephone.
–phone. *comb. form.* A sound or sound-emit-
ting device: **telephone.** [< Gk *phōnē,* sound,
voice.]
pho•neme (fō′nēm′) *n. Ling.* One of the smallest units of speech that distinguish one utterance or word from another. [< Gk *phō-
nēma,* an utterance.] —**pho•ne′mic** (fə-nē′mĭk,
fō-) *adj.* —**pho•ne′mi•cal•ly** *adv.*
pho•net•ic (fə-nĕt′ĭk) *adj.* **1.** Pertaining to
phonetics. **2.** Representing the sounds of
speech with a set of distinct symbols, each

ă pat/ā ate/âr care/ä bar/b bib/ch chew/d deed/ĕ pet/ē be/f fit/g gag/h hat/hw what/
ĭ pit/ī pie/îr pier/j judge/k kick/l lid, fatal/m mum/n no, sudden/ng sing/ŏ pot/ō go/

denoting a single sound: *phonetic alphabet.* [< Gk *phōnein*, to sound, speak.]

pho·net·ics (fə-nĕt'ĭks) *n.* *(takes sing. v.).* The branch of linguistics dealing with the study of the sounds of speech.

phono–. *comb. form.* Sound or voice. [Gk *phōnē*, sound, voice.]

pho·no·graph (fō'nə-grăf', -gräf') *n.* A machine that reproduces sound from a disc. —**pho'no·graph'ic** *adj.*

pho·ny (fō'nē) *adj.* **-nier, -niest.** Not genuine; spurious; fake. [?] —**pho'ni·ly** *adv.* —**pho'ni·ness** *n.* —**pho'ny** *n.*

–phony. *comb. form.* Sound of a specified kind: telephony. [< Gk *phōnē*, sound.]

–phore. *comb. form.* A bearer or producer of: semaphore. [< Gk *pherein*, to bear.]

phos·phate (fŏs'fāt') *n.* **1.** A salt or ester of phosphoric acid. **2.** A fertilizer containing phosphorus compounds. [< PHOSPHORUS.] —**phos'phat'ic** (fŏs'făt'ĭk) *adj.*

phos·phor (fŏs'fər, -fôr') *n.* **1.** Any substance that can be stimulated to emit light by incident radiation. **2.** Something exhibiting phosphorescence. [< PHOSPHORUS.]

phos·pho·res·cence (fŏs'fə-rĕs'əns) *n.* **1.** Persistent emission of light following exposure to and removal of incident radiation. **2.** Organically generated light emission. —**phos'pho·resce'** *v.* **(-resced, -rescing).** —**phos'pho·res'cent** *adj.*

phos·phor·ic acid (fŏs-fôr'ĭk, -fŏr'ĭk). A clear colorless liquid, H_3PO_4, used in fertilizers, soaps, and detergents.

phos·pho·rus (fŏs'fər-əs) *n.* **1.** *Symbol* P A highly reactive, poisonous, nonmetallic element used in safety matches, pyrotechnics, incendiary shells, fertilizers, glass, and steel. Atomic number 15, atomic weight 30.9738. **2.** Any phosphorescent substance. [< Gk *phōsphoros,* "light-bearing."]

pho·to (fō'tō) *n., pl.* **-tos.** A photograph.

photo–. *comb. form.* **1.** Light. **2.** Photographic. [Gk *phōs (phōt-),* light.]

pho·to·cell (fō'tō-sĕl') *n.* A photoelectric cell.

pho·to·cop·y (fō'tō-kŏp'ē) *v.* **-ied, -ying.** To make a photographic reproduction of. —*n., pl.* **-ies.** A photographic reproduction. —**pho'to·cop'i·er** *n.*

pho·to·e·lec·tric (fō'tō-ĭ-lĕk'trĭk) *adj.* Pertaining to electric effects, esp. increased electrical conduction, caused by illumination.

photoelectric cell. An electronic device having an electrical output that varies in response to incident radiation, esp. to visible light.

pho·to·en·grave (fō'tō-ĕn-grāv') *v.* **-graved, -graving.** To reproduce by photoengraving. —**pho'to·en·grav'er** *n.*

pho·to·en·grav·ing (fō'tō-ĕn-grā'vĭng) *n.* **1.** The process of reproducing graphic material by transferring the image photographically to a plate or other surface in etched relief for printing. **2.** A reproduction made by this method.

photo finish. A race so closely contested that the winner must be determined by a photograph taken of the finish.

pho·to·flash (fō'tō-flăsh') *n.* A flash bulb.

pho·to·flood (fō'tō-flŭd') *n.* An electric lamp that produces a bright continuous light for photographic illumination.

pho·to·gen·ic (fō'tə-jĕn'ĭk) *adj.* Attractive as a subject for photography. —**pho'to·gen'i·cal·ly** *adv.*

pho·to·graph (fō'tə-grăf', -gräf') *n.* An image, esp. a positive print, recorded by a camera and reproduced on a photosensitive surface. —*v.* **1.** To take a photograph of. **2.** To be the subject for photographs.

pho·to·graph·ic (fō'tə-grăf'ĭk) *adj.* **1.** Pertaining to photography or a photograph. **2.** Used in photography. **3.** Like a photograph in accuracy or detail. —**pho'to·graph'i·cal·ly** *adv.*

pho·tog·ra·phy (fə-tŏg'rə-fē) *n.* **1.** The process of rendering optical images on photosensitive surfaces. **2.** The art, practice, or occupation of taking and printing photographs. **3.** A body of photographs. —**pho·tog'ra·pher** *n.*

pho·to·me·chan·i·cal (fō'tō-mĭ-kăn'ĭ-kəl) *adj.* Of or designating any of various methods by which plates are prepared for printing by means of photography.

pho·to·mi·cro·graph (fō'tō-mī'krə-grăf', -gräf') *n.* A photograph made through a microscope.

pho·ton (fō'tŏn') *n.* The quantum of electromagnetic energy, generally regarded as a discrete particle having zero mass, no electric charge, and an indefinitely long lifetime. [PHOT(O)- + -ON.] —**pho'ton'ic** *adj.*

pho·to·play (fō'tō-plā') *n.* A play filmed or arranged for filming as a motion picture.

pho·to·re·cep·tion (fō'tō-rĭ-sĕp'shən) *n.* The detection or perception of visible light; vision. —**pho'to·re·cep'tive** *adj.*

pho·to·re·cep·tor (fō'tō-rĭ-sĕp'tər) *n.* A photoreceptive nerve.

pho·to·sen·si·tive (fō'tō-sĕn'sə-tĭv) *adj.* Sensitive to light.

pho·to·sen·si·tize (fō'tō-sĕn'sə-tīz') *v.* **-tized, -tizing.** To make sensitive to light.

Pho·to·stat (fō'tə-stăt') *n.* **1.** A trademark for a device used to make photographic copies of written, printed, or graphic material. **2.** Often **photostat.** A copy made by Photostat. —*v.* **-stated** or **-statted, -stating** or **-statting.** Often **photostat.** To make a copy of by Photostat.

pho·to·syn·the·sis (fō'tō-sĭn'thə-sĭs) *v.* The process by which chlorophyll-containing cells in green plants use the energy of light to synthesize carbohydrates from carbon dioxide and water. —**pho'to·syn'the·size'** (-sĭn'thə-sīz') *v.* **(-sized, -sizing).** —**pho'to·syn·thet'ic** (-sĭn-thĕt'ĭk) *adj.* —**pho'to·syn·thet'i·cal·ly** *adv.*

phr. phrase.

phrase (frāz) *n.* **1.** Any sequence of words intended to have meaning. **2.** A brief, cogent expression. **3.** *Gram.* Two or more words in sequence that form a syntactic unit or group of syntactic units, less completely predicated than a sentence. **4.** A segment of a musical composition, usually consisting of several measures. —*v.* **phrased, phrasing. 1.** To express orally or in writing. **2.** *Mus.* To render in phrases. [< Gk *phrasis,* speech, style of speech.] —**phras'al** *adj.*

ō **paw,** for/oi **boy**/ou **out**/oo **took**/ōō **coo**/p **pop**/r **run**/s **sauce**/sh **shy**/t **to**/th **thin**/*th* **the**/ ŭ **cut**/ûr **fur**/v **van**/w **wag**/y **yes**/z **size**/zh **vision**/ə **ago, item, edible, gallop, circus/**

phra·se·ol·o·gy (frā'zē-ŏl'ə-jē) *n., pl.* **-gies.** The way in which words and phrases are used; style.

phre·net·ic, phre·net·i·cal. Variants of **frenetic.**

—phrenia. *comb. form.* Mental disorder: **schizophrenia.** [< Gk *phrēn,* mind.]

phren·ic (frĕn'ĭk, frē'nĭk) *adj.* Pertaining to the mind.

phreno—. *comb. form.* **1.** The mind. **2.** The diaphragm. [< Gk *phrēn,* diaphragm, mind.]

phre·nol·o·gy (frĭ-nŏl'ə-jē) *n.* The practice of studying character and mental capacity from the conformation of the human skull. **—phrenol'o·gist** *n.*

phy·lac·ter·y (fĭ-lăk'tə-rē) *n., pl.* **-ies.** *Judaism.* Either of two small leather boxes containing quotations from the Hebrew Scriptures. One is strapped to the forehead and the other to the left arm by observant Jewish men during morning worship, except on the Sabbath and holidays. [< Gk *phulaktērion,* safeguard.]

—phyll. *comb. form.* Leaf: **chlorophyll.** [< Gk *phullon,* leaf.]

phy·lum (fī'ləm) *n., pl.* **-la** (-lə). **1.** One of the broad categories, esp. of the animal kingdom, used in the classification of organisms. **2.** A large division of genetically related families of languages or linguistic stocks. [< Gk *phulon,* tribe, class, race.]

phys. **1.** physical. **2.** physician. **3.** physicist; physics.

phys·ic (fĭz'ĭk) *n.* **1.** Any medicine or drug. **2.** A cathartic. *—v.* **-icked, -icking.** To act upon as a cathartic. [< L *physica,* natural medicine or science, physics.]

phys·i·cal (fĭz'ĭ-kəl) *adj.* **1.** Of or pertaining to the body, as distinguished from the mind or spirit. **2.** Of or pertaining to material things. **3.** Of or pertaining to matter and energy or the sciences dealing with them, esp. physics. *—n.* A medical examination. [< L *physica,* natural medicine.] **—phys'i·cal·ly** *adv.*

physical education. Education in the care and development of the human body, stressing athletics.

physical geography. The study of the structure and phenomena of the earth's surface.

physical science. Any of the sciences, such as physics, chemistry, astronomy, and geology, that analyzes the nature and properties of energy and nonliving matter.

physical therapy. The treatment of disease and injury by mechanical means such as exercise, heat, light, and massage.

phy·si·cian (fĭ-zĭsh'ən) *n.* A medical doctor. [< OF *fisique,* medicine, physic.]

phy·si·cian·ly (fĭ-zĭsh'ən-lē) *adj.* Characteristic of a physician.

phys·i·cist (fĭz'ə-sĭst) *n.* A scientist who specializes in physics.

phys·ics (fĭz'ĭks) *n. (takes sing. v.).* The science of matter and energy and of interactions between the two. [Pl of PHYSIC.]

physio—. *comb. form.* **1.** Natural or nature. **2.** Physical. [< Gk *phusis,* nature.]

phys·i·og·no·my (fĭz'ē-ŏg'nə-mē, -ŏn'ə-mē) *n., pl.* **-mies.** Facial features, esp. when re-garded as revealing character. [< PHYSIO- + Gk *gnōmōn,* "judge."]

physiol. physiological; physiology.

phys·i·ol·o·gy (fĭz'ē-ŏl'ə-jē) *n.* **1.** The biological science of life processes, activities, and functions. **2.** The vital processes of an organism. **—phys'i·o·log'i·cal** (-ə-lŏj'ĭ-kəl) *adj.* **—phys'i·ol'o·gist** *n.*

phys·i·o·ther·a·py (fĭz'ē-ō-thĕr'ə-pē) *n.* **Physical therapy.**

phy·sique (fĭ-zēk') *n.* The body, considered with reference to its proportions, muscular development, and appearance. [< F, "physical."]

pi (pī) *n., pl.* **pis.** **1.** The 16th letter of the Greek alphabet, representing *p.* **2.** *Symbol* ρ *Math.* A transcendental number, approx. 3.14159, representing the ratio of the circumference to the diameter of a circle.

pi·a·nis·si·mo (pē'ə-nĭs'ə-mō') *adv. Mus.* Very softly or quietly. [It, superl of PIANO².] **—pi'a·nis'si·mo'** *adj.*

pi·an·ist (pē-ăn'ĭst, pē'ə-nĭst) *n.* One who plays the piano.

pi·an·o¹ (pē-ăn'ō) *n., pl.* **-os.** A musical keyboard instrument with hammers that strike wire strings. [It, short for PIANOFORTE.]

pi·a·no² (pē-ä'nō) *adv. Mus.* Softly; quietly. [It.] **—pi·a'no** *adj.*

pi·an·o·for·te (pē-ăn'ō-fôr'tā, -fôr'tē, -fôrt') *n.* A piano. [< It *piano e forte,* soft and loud.]

pi·as·ter (pē-ăs'tər, -ä'stər) *n.* Also **pi·as·tre.** The basic monetary unit of South Vietnam.

pi·az·za (pē-ăz'ə, -ä'zə) *n., pl.* **-zas.** A verandah; porch.

pi·ca (pī'kə) *n.* A printer's unit of type size, equal to 12 points or about ⅙ inch. [Prob < ML *pica,* almanac.]

pic·a·resque (pĭk'ə-rĕsk', pē'kə-) *adj.* Of or involving clever rogues or adventurers. [< Span *picaro,* rogue.]

Pi·cas·so (pĭ-kä'sō, pē-), **Pablo.** Born 1881. Spanish painter and sculptor, resident in France.

pic·a·yune (pĭk'ē-yōōn') *adj.* **1.** Of little value or importance. **2.** Petty; mean. [< F *picaillon,* small copper coin.]

pic·ca·lil·li (pĭk'ə-lĭl'ē) *n., pl.* **-lis.** A pickled relish made of chopped vegetables. [Perh blend of PICKLE and CHILI.]

pic·co·lo (pĭk'ə-lō') *n., pl.* **-los.** A small flute pitched an octave above a regular flute. [< It *piccolo,* small.]

pick¹ (pĭk) *v.* **1.** To select from a group. **2.** To gather in; harvest. **3. a.** To remove the outer covering of; pluck. **b.** To tear off bit by bit. **4.** To poke at with the fingers. **5.** To break up or detach with a pointed instrument. **6.** To pierce with a sharp instrument. **7.** To steal the contents of. **8.** To open (a lock) without the use of a key. **9.** To make (one's way) carefully. **10.** To provoke: *pick a fight.* **—pick off.** To shoot after singling out. **—pick on.** To tease or bully. *—n.* **1.** The act of selecting; choice. **2.** The best or choicest part. [Prob < VL **piccāre,* to prick, pierce.] **—pick'er** *n.*

pick² (pĭk) *n.* **1.** A tool for breaking hard surfaces, consisting of a curved bar sharpened

at both ends and fitted to a long handle.
2. *Mus.* A plectrum. [ME *pik.*]

pick·ax, pick·axe (pĭk′ăks′) *n.* A pick, esp.
with one end of the head pointed and the
other end with a chisel edge. [< OF *picois.*]

pick·er·el (pĭk′ər-əl, pĭk′rəl) *n., pl.* -el or -els. A
North American freshwater fish related to the
pike. [< PIKE².]

pick·et (pĭk′ĭt) *n.* **1.** A pointed stake driven
into the ground to support a fence, secure a
tent, tether an animal, etc. **2.** A soldier or
group of soldiers on guard against enemy
approach. **3. a.** A worker on strike, stationed
outside a place of employment to express
grievance or protest. **b.** Any protester. —*v.*
1. To enclose, secure, tether, etc., with pickets.
2. To guard with pickets. **3.** To post a picket or
pickets. **4.** To act as a picket. [< OF *piquer,*
to prick, pierce.] —**pick′et·er** *n.*

pick·ing (pĭk′ĭng) *n.* **1.** The act of one that
picks. **2. pickings.** Something that is or may be
picked. **3.** Often **pickings. a.** Leftovers. **b.** A
share of spoils.

pick·le (pĭk′əl) *n.* **1.** A food, esp. a cucumber,
preserved in a solution of brine or vinegar.
2. A solution of brine or vinegar for preserving
and flavoring food. **3.** *Informal.* An embarrassing or difficult situation. —*v.* **-led, -ling.** To
preserve or flavor in a solution of brine or
vinegar. [ME *pekille.*]

pick·pock·et (pĭk′pŏk′ĭt) *n.* One who steals
from pockets.

pick up. 1. To take or lift up. **2.** To take on
(passengers, freight, etc.). **3.** To fetch or acquire. **4.** To accelerate.

pick·up (pĭk′ŭp′) *n.* **1.** The action or process of
picking up. **2.** Capacity for acceleration. **3.**
One that is picked up. **4.** A light truck with an
open body and low sides. **5.** A device that
converts the oscillations of a phonograph
needle into electrical impulses.

pick·y (pĭk′ē) *adj.* **-ier, -iest.** Excessively meticulous.

pic·nic (pĭk′nĭk) *n.* **1.** A meal eaten outdoors
on an excursion. **2.** *Slang.* An easy task. —*v.*
-nicked, -nicking. To go on a picnic. [F *pique-
nique.*] —**pic′nick·er** *n.*

pico-. *comb. form.* One trillionth, 10⁻¹²: *pico-
second,* one-trillionth of a second. [Span *pico,*
small quantity, peak.]

pi·cot (pē′kō, pē-kō′) *n.* A small loop forming
an ornamental edging, as on ribbon. [F,
"small point."]

pic·to·ri·al (pĭk-tôr′ē-əl, -tōr′ē-əl) *adj.* **1.** Of,
characterized by, or composed of pictures.
2. Illustrated by pictures.

pic·ture (pĭk′chər) *n.* **1.** A visual representation or image painted, drawn, photographed,
or otherwise rendered on a flat surface. **2.** A
vivid verbal description. **3.** One that bears a
striking resemblance to another. **4.** One that
typifies or embodies an emotion, state of
mind, or mood. **5.** The chief circumstances of;
a situation. **6.** A motion picture. —*v.* **-tured,
-turing. 1.** To make a visible representation or
picture of. **2.** To visualize. **3.** To describe vividly in words. [< L *pingere* (pp *pictus*), to
paint.] —**pic′tur·er** *n.*

pic·tur·esque (pĭk′chə-rĕsk′) *adj.* **1.** Of, suggesting, or suitable for a picture. **2.** Unusually
or quaintly attractive; charming. **3.** Strikingly
expressive or vivid. —**pic′tur·esque·ly** *adv.*

pid·dling (pĭd′lĭng) *adj.* Trifling; trivial.

pidg·in (pĭj′ən) *n.* A simplified mixture of two
or more languages, used for communication
between groups speaking different languages.

Pidgin English. A pidgin based on English
and used as a trade language in Far Eastern
ports. [A pidgin corruption of *business
English.*]

pie (pī) *n.* A baked pastry shell filled with fruit,
meat, etc., and often covered with a pastry
crust. [ME.]

pie·bald (pī′bôld′) *adj.* Having spotted or
patchy markings: *a piebald horse.*

piece (pēs) *n.* **1.** A unit or element of a larger
quantity or class; portion. **2.** An artistic, musical, or literary work. **3.** An instance; specimen. **4.** One's mind: *speak one's piece.* **5.** A
coin or counter. **6.** A figure used in a game.
7. A firearm, esp. a rifle. **8.** A short or manageable distance: *down the road a piece.* —*v.*
pieced, piecing. 1. To mend by adding a piece
to. **2.** To join the pieces of. [< Gaul *pettia.*]

pièce de ré·sis·tance (pyĕs də rā-zē-stäNs′).
1. The principal dish of a meal. **2.** An outstanding accomplishment. [F.]

piece·meal (pēs′mēl′) *adv.* Piece by piece.
—*adj.* Made piece by piece.

piece·work (pēs′wûrk′) *n.* Work paid for by
the piece.

pied (pīd) *adj.* Having spots or patches of
different colors.

pier (pîr) *n.* **1.** A platform extending from a
shore over water, used to secure, protect, and
provide access to ships or boats. **2.** A support
for the spans of a bridge. **3.** *Archit.* Any of
various vertical supporting structures. [< L
podium, raised platform, podium.]

pierce (pîrs) *v.* **pierced, piercing. 1.** To cut or
pass through with or as with a sharp instrument; stab. **2.** To perforate. **3.** To penetrate
through. [< L *pertundere* (pp *pertūsus*), to
pierce through.] —**pierc′ing·ly** *adv.*

Pierce (pîrs), **Franklin.** 1804–1869. 14th President of the U.S. (1853–57).

Franklin Pierce

Pierre (pîr). The capital of South Dakota. Pop. 10,000.

pi•e•ty (pī'ə-tē) *n., pl.* **-ties. 1.** Devotion and reverence, esp. to God and family. **2.** A pious act or thought. [< L *pius,* PIOUS.]

pif•fle (pĭf'əl) *n.* Foolish or futile talk or ideas; nonsense. [?]

pig (pĭg) *n.* **1.** A hoofed mammal with short legs, bristly hair, and a blunt snout used for digging, esp. one of a kind raised for meat. **2.** A person regarded as being piglike, greedy, or gross. **3.** An oblong block of metal, chiefly iron or lead, poured from a smelting furnace. [Prob < OE **picga.*]

pi•geon (pĭj'ən) *n.* **1.** Any of various related birds with a deep-chested body, a small head, and short legs, esp. a common, often domesticated species. **2.** *Slang.* One easily swindled; a dupe. [< L *pīpiō,* squab, young chirping bird.]

pi•geon•hole (pĭj'ən-hōl') *n.* A small compartment, as in a desk. —*v.* **-holed, -holing. 1.** To place or file in a pigeonhole. **2.** To categorize. **3.** To put aside and ignore.

pi•geon-toed (pĭj'ən-tōd') *adj.* Having the toes turned inward.

pig•gish (pĭg'ĭsh) *adj.* Like a pig; greedy.

pig•gy•back (pĭg'ē-băk') *adv.* **1.** On the shoulders or back. **2.** By a method of transportation in which truck trailers are carried on trains. —**pig'gy•back'** *adj.*

pig•head•ed (pĭg'hĕd'ĭd) *adj.* Stubborn.

pig iron. Crude iron cast in blocks or pigs.

pig•ment (pĭg'mənt) *n.* **1.** A coloring substance or matter. **2.** A substance, such as chlorophyll or hemoglobin, that produces a characteristic color in plant or animal tissue. [L *pigmentum* < *pingere,* to paint.]

pig•men•ta•tion (pĭg'mən-tā'shən) *n. Biol.* **1.** Coloration of tissues by pigment. **2.** Deposition of pigment by cells.

pig•my. Variant of **pygmy.**

Pig•my. Variant of **Pygmy.**

pig•pen (pĭg'pĕn') *n.* **1.** A pen for pigs. **2.** A dirty place.

pig•skin (pĭg'skĭn') *n.* **1.** The skin of a pig or leather made from it. **2.** A football.

pig•sty (pĭg'stī') *n., pl.* **-sties.** A shelter where pigs are kept.

pig•tail (pĭg'tāl') *n.* A braid of hair.

pike¹ (pīk) *n.* A long spear formerly used by infantry. [< VL **piccāre,* to pierce.]

pike² (pīk) *n., pl.* **pike** or **pikes.** A narrow-bodied freshwater game and food fish with a long snout. [ME.]

pike³ (pīk) *n.* A turnpike.

pike⁴ (pīk) *n.* A spike or sharp point. [< OE *pīc.*]

pik•er (pī'kər) *n. Slang.* A stingy, petty person. [?]

pi•las•ter (pĭ-lăs'tər) *n.* A rectangular column set into a wall, often as an ornament. [< ML *pilastrum.*]

Pi•late (pī'lĭt), **Pontius.** Roman procurator of Judea (A.D. 26?–36?); assumed to have authorized the execution of Jesus.

pil•chard (pĭl'chərd) *n.* Any of various small marine fishes related to the herrings. [?]

pile¹ (pīl) *n.* **1.** A quantity of objects in a heap.

2. A large accumulation or quantity. **3.** A funeral pyre. **4.** A large building or complex of buildings. **5.** A nuclear reactor. —*v.* **piled, piling. 1.** To stack in or form a pile. **2.** To load with a pile. [< L *pīla,* PILLAR.]

pile² (pīl) *n.* A heavy beam driven into the earth as a support for a structure. [< L *pīlum,* heavy javelin, pestle.]

pile³ (pīl) *n.* Cut or uncut loops of yarn forming the surface of certain fabrics, as velvet, plush, etc. [< L *pilus,* hair.] —**piled** *adj.*

piles (pīlz) *pl.n.* Hemorrhoids. [< L *pila,* ball.]

pil•fer (pĭl'fər) *v.* To steal; filch. [< OF *pelfre,* booty.] —**pil'fer•age** (-ĭj) *n.* —**pil'fer•er** *n.*

pil•grim (pĭl'grĭm, -grəm) *n.* **1.** One who goes on a pilgrimage. **2.** Any traveler. **3. Pilgrim.** One of the English Puritans who migrated to New England (1620). [< L *peregrīnus,* a foreigner.]

pil•grim•age (pĭl'grə-mĭj) *n.* **1.** A journey to a sacred place or shrine. **2.** A long journey or search.

pill (pĭl) *n.* **1.** A small pellet or tablet of medicine. **2. the Pill.** An oral contraceptive. **3.** Anything distasteful but necessary. **4.** *Slang.* An ill-natured person. [< L *pila,* ball.]

pil•lage (pĭl'ĭj) *v.* **-laged, -laging. 1.** To plunder. **2.** To take as spoils. —*n.* **1.** The act of pillaging. **2.** Spoils. [< OF *piller,* to tear up, plunder.] —**pil'lag•er** *n.*

pil•lar (pĭl'ər) *n.* **1.** A slender, freestanding vertical support; a column. **2.** One occupying a central or responsible position. [< L *pīla,* pillar.]

pill•box (pĭl'bŏks') *n.* **1.** A small box for pills. **2.** A roofed concrete emplacement for a weapon.

pil•lion (pĭl'yən) *n.* A seat for an extra rider behind the saddle on a horse or motorcycle. [< L *pellis,* skin, hide.]

pil•lo•ry (pĭl'ə-rē) *n., pl.* **-ries.** A wooden framework with holes for the head and hands, in which offenders were formerly locked to be exposed to public scorn as punishment. —*v.* **-ried, -rying. 1.** To put in a pillory. **2.** To expose to ridicule and abuse. [Prob < L *pila,* PILLAR.]

pil•low (pĭl'ō) *n.* **1.** A cloth case stuffed with something soft and used to cushion the head during sleep. **2.** A decorative cushion. —*v.* **1.** To rest (one's head) on or as on a pillow. **2.** To act as a pillow for. [< L *pulvīnus,* pillow.] —**pil'low•y** *adj.*

pil•low•case (pĭl'ō-kās') *n.* A removable pillow covering.

pi•lot (pī'lət) *n.* **1.** One who operates or is licensed to operate an aircraft. **2. a.** One who is licensed to conduct ships into and out of port. **b.** The helmsman of a ship. **3.** One who guides or directs. —*v.* **1.** To serve as the pilot of. **2.** To steer or control the course of. —*adj.* Serving as a tentative model for future development. [< It *pilota.*]

pi•lot•house (pī'lət-hous') *n.* An enclosed area on the deck or bridge of a vessel from which the vessel is controlled.

pilot light. A small flame kept burning in order to ignite a burner, as in a stove.

ă pat/ā ate/âr care/ä bar/b bib/ch chew/d deed/ĕ pet/ē be/f fit/g gag/h hat/hw what/
ĭ pit/ī pie/îr pier/j judge/k kick/l lid, fatal/m mum/n no, sudden/ng sing/ŏ pot/ō go/

pi·men·to (pĭ-mĕn'tō) *n., pl.* **-tos.** Also **pi·mien·to** (pĭ-mĕn'tō, -myĕn'-). A mild-flavored red pepper. [< LL *pigmentum*, plant juice, pigment.]

pimp (pĭmp) *n.* A procurer; pander. —*v.* To serve as a pimp. [?]

pim·per·nel (pĭm'pər-nĕl', -nəl) *n.* A plant with red, purple, or white flowers that close in bad weather. [< VL *piperīnella.*]

pim·ple (pĭm'pəl) *n.* A small swelling of the skin, sometimes containing pus. [ME *pinple.*] —**pim'pled, pim'ply** *adj.*

pin (pĭn) *n.* **1.** A short, straight, stiff piece of wire with a blunt head and a sharp point, used for fastening. **2.** Anything resembling a pin in shape or use, as a hairpin. **3.** An ornament fastened to the clothing with a clasp. **4.** A slender, cylindrical piece of wood or metal for holding, fastening, or supporting. **5.** One of the wooden clubs at which the ball is aimed in bowling. **6.** *Golf.* The pole bearing a pennant to mark a hole. **7. pins.** The legs. —*v.* **pinned, pinning. 1.** To fasten or secure with or as with a pin or pins. **2.** To place in a position of trusting dependence: *pinned his hopes on his victory.* **3.** To hold fast; immobilize. **4.** To oblige (someone) to make a definite response. —**pin on.** To attribute (a wrongdoing or crime). [< OE *pinn.*] —**pin'ner** *n.*

pin·a·fore (pĭn'ə-fôr', -fōr') *n.* A sleeveless garment similar to an apron.

pince-nez (păns'nā', pĭns'-) *n., pl.* **-nez** (-nāz', -nā'). Eyeglasses clipped to the nose. [F, "pinch-nose."]

pin·cers (pĭn'sərz) *n.* Also **pin·chers** (pĭn'chərz). *(often takes sing. v.).* **1.** A grasping tool having a pair of jaws and handles pivoted together to work in opposition. **2.** A jointed, clawlike grasping part, as of a lobster. [< OF *pincier*, to PINCH.]

pinch (pĭnch) *v.* **1.** To squeeze between the thumb and a finger, the jaws of a tool, etc. **2.** To squeeze or bind (a part of the body) painfully. **3.** To wither or shrivel. **4.** To be miserly. **5.** *Slang.* To steal. **6.** *Slang.* To arrest. —*n.* **1.** The act of pinching. **2.** An amount that can be held between thumb and forefinger. **3.** A difficult or straitened circumstance. **4.** Any emergency. [< OF *pincier.*]

pinch-hit (pĭnch'hĭt') *v.* To substitute for another, esp. to bat in place of another in a baseball game. —**pinch hitter.**

pin·cush·ion (pĭn'kŏŏsh'ən) *n.* A cushion in which pins are stuck when not in use.

pine[1] (pīn) *n.* **1.** Any of various cone-bearing evergreen trees with clustered, needle-shaped leaves. **2.** The wood of such a tree. [< L *pīnus.*]

pine[2] (pīn) *v.* **pined, pining. 1.** To suffer intense longing or yearning. **2.** To wither away from longing or grief. [< Gk *poinē*, payment, punishment.]

pin·e·al body (pĭn'ē-əl, pī'-). A small gland-like body of uncertain function located in the brain.

pine·ap·ple (pīn'ăp-əl) *n.* **1.** A tropical American plant with swordlike leaves and a large, fleshy, edible fruit. **2.** The fruit of this plant.

3. *Slang.* A small hand grenade. [< PINE + APPLE.]

pin·feath·er (pĭn'fĕth'ər) *n.* A feather still enclosed in its horny sheath and just emerging through the skin.

ping (pĭng) *n.* A brief, high-pitched sound, as that made by a bullet striking metal. [Imit.] —**ping** *v.*

pin·hole (pĭn'hōl') *n.* A tiny puncture made by or as if by a pin.

pin·ion[1] (pĭn'yən) *n.* A bird's wing. —*v.* **1.** To restrain or immobilize by binding the wings or arms. **2.** To fix in one place. [< L *pinna, penna*, a feather, wing.]

pin·ion[2] (pĭn'yən) *n.* A small cogwheel that engages or is engaged by a larger cogwheel or a rack. [< L *pecten*, a comb.]

pink[1] (pĭngk) *n.* **1.** Any of various plants related to the carnation, often cultivated for their fragrant flowers. **2.** Light red. **3.** The highest degree of excellence: *in the pink of health.* **4.** *Slang.* A pinko. [Poss short for *pink eye*, "small eye."] —**pink, pink'ish** *adj.*

pink[2] (pĭngk) *v.* **1.** To stab lightly. **2.** To decorate with a perforated pattern. [ME *pynken.*]

pink·eye (pĭngk'ī') *n.* Also **pink eye.** Acute contagious conjunctivitis. [Part trans of obs Du *pinck oog(en)*, "small eye(s)."]

pink·ie (pĭng'kē) *n.* Also **pink·y** *pl.* **-ies.** The little finger. [< Du *pink*, little finger.]

pink·o (pĭng'kō) *n., pl.* **-os.** *Slang.* One in sympathy with Communist doctrine.

pin·nace (pĭn'ĭs) *n.* **1.** A small sailing boat. **2.** A ship's boat. [< VL **pīnācea (nāvis)*, "(ship) of pine-wood."]

pin·na·cle (pĭn'ə-kəl) *n.* **1.** A small turret or spire on a roof or buttress. **2.** Any tall, pointed formation. **3.** The highest point; summit. [< LL *pinnāculum*, "little wing."]

pin·nate (pĭn'āt') *adj.* Featherlike, as compound leaves with leaflets along each side of a stalk. [L *pinnātus*, feathered.]

pi·noch·le (pē'nŭk'əl, -nŏk'əl) *n.* A card game for two to four persons, played with a deck of 48 cards. [Earlier *binuochle.*]

pi·ñon (pĭn'yōn', -yən) *n.* Also **pin·yon.** Any pine tree bearing edible, nutlike seeds. [< Span, pine nut, pine cone.]

pin·point (pĭn'point') *n.* An extremely small thing or spot; particle. —*v.* **1.** To pierce. **2.** To locate and identify precisely.

pin·prick (pĭn'prĭk') *n.* **1.** A slight puncture made by or as if by a pin. **2.** A minor annoyance.

pins and needles. A tingling felt in a part of the body that has been numbed from lack of circulation.

pin·stripe (pĭn'strīp') *n.* **1.** A thin stripe on a fabric. **2.** A thinly striped fabric.

pint (pīnt) *n.* **1.** A U.S. Customary System unit of volume or capacity, used in liquid measure, equal to 16 fluid ounces or 28.875 cubic inches. **2.** A U.S. Customary System unit of volume or capacity, used in dry measure, equal to $1/2$ quart or 33.6 cubic inches. **3.** A British Imperial System unit of volume or capacity, used in dry and liquid measure, equal to 34.678 cubic inches. **4.** A container

ŏ paw, for/oi boy/ou out/ŏŏ took/ōō coo/p pop/r run/s sauce/sh shy/t to/th thin/*th* the/
ŭ cut/ûr fur/v van/w wag/y yes/z size/zh vision/ə ago, item, edible, gallop, circus/

with such a capacity or the amount it will hold. [< OF *pinte*.]

pin·to (pǐn'tō) *n., pl.* **-tos** or **-toes.** A horse with irregular spots or markings. [< obs Span, "painted."]

pin·up (pǐn'ǔp') *n.* A picture to be pinned up on a wall, esp. a photograph of a sexually attractive girl. —*adj.* Pertaining to or suitable for a pinup.

pin·wale (pǐn'wāl') *n.* A corduroy having narrow ribs or wales. —**pin'wale'** *adj.*

pin·wheel (pǐn'hwēl') *n.* **1.** A toy consisting of colored vanes pinned to the end of a stick in such a way that they turn when blown upon. **2.** A firework that forms a rotating wheel of colored flames.

pin·yon. Variant of **piñon.**

pi·o·neer (pī'ə-nîr') *n.* **1.** One who ventures into unknown or unclaimed territory to settle. **2.** An innovator in any field. [OF *pionier*, orig "a foot soldier sent out to clear the way."] —**pi'o·neer'** *v.*

pi·ous (pī'əs) *adj.* **1.** Reverently observant of religion; devout. **2.** Solemnly hypocritical. **3.** Devotional. **4.** High-minded. **5.** Commendable; worthy. [L *pius*.] —**pi'ous·ly** *adv.* —**pi'ous·ness** *n.*

pip¹ (pǐp) *n.* A small fruit seed, as of an orange. [Short for PIPPIN.]

pip² (pǐp) *n.* A dot indicating a unit of numerical value on dice or dominoes. [Earlier *peepe*.]

pip³ (pǐp) *n.* A short, high-pitched radio signal. [Var of PEEP.]

pip⁴ (pǐp) *n.* **1.** A disease of birds. **2.** *Slang.* Any minor or imaginary human ailment. [Prob < L *pituita*, phlegm.]

pipe (pīp) *n.* **1.** Any hollow cylinder or tubular conveyance for a fluid or gas. **2.** A tube of wood or clay with a mouthpiece at one end and a small bowl at the other, used for smoking. **3. a.** A tubular part or organ. **b. pipes.** *Informal.* The human respiratory system. **4. a.** A tubular wind instrument, such as a flute. **b.** Any of the tubes in an organ. **5. pipes. a.** A small wind instrument, consisting of tubes of different lengths bound together: *pipes of Pan.* **b.** A bagpipe. —*v.* **piped, piping. 1.** To convey (liquid or gas) by means of pipes. **2.** To play (a tune) on pipes. **3.** To make a shrill or whistling noise. [< Gmc *pīpa* < L *pīpāre*, to chirp.]

pipe·line (pīp'līn') *n.* **1.** A conduit of pipe for the conveyance of water or petroleum products. **2.** A channel by which secret information is transmitted. **3.** A line of supply.

pipe organ. An organ whose sound is made by pipes.

pip·er (pī'pər) *n.* One who plays pipes.

pip·ing (pī'pǐng) *n.* **1.** The act of playing pipes. **2.** A rounded strip of cloth used for trimming seams of fabric.

pip·pin (pǐp'ǐn) *n.* Any of several varieties of apple. [< OF *pepin*, seed, seedling apple.]

pip-squeak (pǐp'skwēk') *n.* A small or insignificant person.

pi·quant (pē'kənt, -känt', pē-känt') *adj.* **1.** Pleasantly pungent. **2.** Appealingly provocative. [< OF *piquer*, to pierce.] —**pi'quan·cy** *n.*

pique (pēk) *n.* Resentment or vexation arising from wounded pride or vanity. —*v.* **piqued, piquing. 1.** To cause such resentment. **2.** To provoke; arouse. [< OF *piquer*, to pierce.]

pi·qué (pǐ-kā', pē-) *n.* A fabric with various patterns of wales. [F, "quilting."]

pi·ra·nha (pǐ-rän'/y/ə, -răn'/y/ə) *n.* Also **pi·ra·ña.** A sharp-toothed tropical American freshwater fish that often attacks and destroys living animals. [< Tupi, "toothed fish."]

pi·rate (pī'rǐt) *n.* **1.** One who robs at sea or plunders the land from the sea. **2.** One who makes use of the copyrighted or patented work of another without permission or illicitly. [< Gk *peiratēs*, "attacker."] —**pi'ra·cy** *n.* —**pi'rate** *v.* (**-rated, -rating**).

pir·ou·ette (pǐr'ōō-ĕt') *n. Ballet.* A full turn on the tip of the toe or on the ball of the foot. [< OF *pirouet*, a spinning top.] —**pir'ou·ette'** *v.* (**-etted, -etting**).

pis·ca·to·ri·al (pǐs'kə-tôr'ē-əl, -tōr'ē-əl) *adj.* Of or pertaining to fishing. [< L *piscis*, fish.]

Pi·sces (pī'sēz) *n.* **1.** A constellation in the equatorial region of the N Hemisphere. **2.** The 12th sign of the zodiac. [< L *piscis*, fish.]

pis·mire (pǐs'mīr', pǐz'-) *n.* An ant. [ME *pissemyre*.]

pis·ta·chi·o (pǐ-stăsh'ē-ō', -stä'shē-ō') *n., pl.* **-os. 1.** A tree bearing hard-shelled, edible nuts with a green kernel. **2.** Also **pistachio nut.** The nut of this tree. [< Pers *pistah*.]

pis·til (pǐs'tǐl) *n.* The seed-bearing reproductive organ of a flower. [< L *pistillum*, pestle.]

pis·tol (pǐs'təl) *n.* A firearm designed to be held and fired with one hand. [< Czech *pištala*, "pipe."]

pis·ton (pǐs'tən) *n.* A solid cylinder or disk that fits snugly into a larger cylinder and moves back and forth under fluid pressure. [< OIt *pistone*, a large pestle.]

pit¹ (pǐt) *n.* **1.** A relatively deep hole in the ground. **2.** A trap; pitfall. **3.** Hell. **4.** An enclosed space in which animals are placed for fighting. **5. a.** A natural depression in the surface of the body. **b.** A small indentation in the skin left by disease or injury; pockmark. **6.** The musician's section directly in front of the stage of a theater. **7.** *Bot.* A thin-walled spot or depression in the wall of some plant cells. —*v.* **pitted, pitting. 1.** To make cavities, depressions, or scars in. **2.** To place in contest against another. [< Gmc *putti* < L *puteus*, a pit, well.]

pit² (pǐt) *n.* The single, hard-shelled seed of certain fruits, as a peach or cherry; stone. —*v.* **pitted, pitting.** To extract pits from (fruit). [< Gmc *pithan*, pit, pith.]

pit·a·pat (pǐt'ə-pät') *v.* **-patted, -patting.** To make a repeated tapping sound. —*n.* A series of quick steps, taps, or beats. [Imit.]

pitch¹ (pǐch) *n.* Any of various thick, dark, sticky substances, as those obtained from the distillation residue of coal tar, wood tar, or petroleum, used for waterproofing, roofing, caulking, and paving. [< L *pix*.]

pitch² (pǐch) *v.* **1.** To throw in a specific, intended direction; hurl. **2.** *Baseball.* To throw (the ball) from the mound to the batter. **3.** To put up or in position; establish. **4.** To set firmly; implant. **5.** To fix the level of. **6.** To plunge; fall, esp. forward. **7.** To dip bow and stern alternately, as a ship in rough seas. **—pitch in.** *Informal.* **1.** To set to work vigorously. **2.** To help; cooperate. —*n.* **1.** An act or instance of pitching. **2. a.** Any downward slant. **b.** The degree of such a slant. **3.** A point or stage of development. **4.** The subjective quality of a complex sound, as a musical tone, that is dependent mostly on frequency. **5. a.** The distance traveled by a screw in a single revolution. **b.** The distance between two corresponding points on adjacent screw threads or gear teeth. **6.** *Slang.* A set talk designed to persuade. [< OE *pician, to PICK.]

pitch·black (pĭch′blăk′) *adj.* Extremely black.

pitch·blende (pĭch′blĕnd′) *n.* A brownish-black mineral, the principal ore of uranium.

pitch-dark (pĭch′därk′) *adj.* Extremely dark.

pitch·er[1] (pĭch′ər) *n.* One that pitches in a baseball game.

pitch·er[2] (pĭch′ər) *n.* **1.** A vessel for liquids, with a handle and a lip or spout for pouring. **2.** *Bot.* A pitcherlike part such as the leaf of a pitcher plant. [< ML *bicārius*, goblet.]

pitch·fork (pĭch′fôrk′) *n.* A large fork with widely spaced prongs for pitching hay and breaking ground. [< PICK + FORK.]

pitch·man (pĭch′mən) *n.* A peddler or vender.

pit·e·ous (pĭt′ē-əs) *adj.* Exciting pity; pathetic.

pit·fall (pĭt′fôl′) *n.* **1.** A trap made by digging a hole in the ground and concealing its opening. **2.** A danger or difficulty.

pith (pĭth) *n.* **1.** The soft, spongelike central substance in the stems of many plants. **2.** The essential or central part of anything. **3.** Force; strength. [< OE *pitha* < Gmc *pithan*.]

pith·y (pĭth′ē) *adj.* **-i·er, -i·est. 1.** Of or resembling pith. **2.** Precisely meaningful.

pit·i·a·ble (pĭt′ē-ə-bəl) *adj.* Arousing or deserving of pity. **—pit′i·a·bly** *adv.*

pit·i·ful (pĭt′i-fəl) *adj.* **1.** Arousing pity; pathetic. **2.** So inferior or insignificant as to be contemptible. **—pit′i·ful·ly** *adv.*

pit·i·less (pĭt′ĭ-lĭs) *adj.* Having no pity; without mercy. **—pit′i·less·ness** *n.*

pi·ton (pē′tŏn′) *n.* A metal spike having a ring through which to pass a rope, used in mountain climbing as a hold. [< OF, "nail."]

pit·tance (pĭt′əns) *n.* **1.** A meager amount, esp. of money. **2.** A very small salary. [< VL *pietantia*, pious donation, portion.]

pit·ter-pat·ter (pĭt′ər-păt′ər) *n.* A rapid series of light, tapping sounds. [Imit.] **—pit′ter-pat′ter** *adv.*

Pitts·burgh (pĭts′bûrg′). A city in SW Pennsylvania. Pop. 513,000.

pi·tu·i·tar·y (pĭ-t/y/o͞o′ə-tĕr′ē) *n., pl.* **-ies.** The pituitary gland. [< L *pituita*, phlegm.] **—pi·tu′i·tar′y** *adj.*

pituitary gland. A small, oval endocrine gland attached to the base of the vertebrate brain, the secretions of which control the other endocrine glands and influence growth, metabolism, and maturation.

pit·y (pĭt′ē) *n., pl.* **-ies. 1. a.** Sorrow or grief aroused by the misfortune of another. **b.** Con-

descending sympathy. **2.** A regrettable or disagreeable fact or necessity. —*v.* **-ied, -ying.** To feel pity (for). [< L *pius*, pious.] **—pit′y·ing·ly** *adv.*

piv·ot (pĭv′ət) *n.* **1.** A short rod or shaft about which a related part rotates or swings. **2.** One that determines the direction or effect of something. **3.** The act of turning on or as if on a pivot. —*v.* To turn or cause to turn on or as if on a pivot. [< OF.] **—piv′ot·al** *adj.*

pix. Variant of **pyx.**

pix·y (pĭk′sē) *n., pl.* **-ies.** Also **pix·ie.** A fairylike or elfin creature. [?]

Pi·zar·ro (pĭ-zär′ō), **Francisco.** 1470?–1541. Spanish explorer; conqueror of Peru.

piz·za (pēt′sə) *n.* An Italian baked dish having a pielike crust covered usually with a spiced mixture of tomatoes and cheese.

piz·zazz (pĭ-zăz′) *n. Slang.* Flamboyance; zest; flair. [Expr.]

piz·ze·ri·a (pēt′sə-rē′ə) *n.* A place where pizzas are made and sold.

piz·zi·ca·to (pĭt′sĭ-kä′tō) *adj.* Played by plucking the strings of an instrument. [It.] **—piz′zi·ca′to** *adv.* & *n.*

pk. **1.** pack. **2.** park. **3.** peak. **4.** peck.

pkg. package.

pkt. packet.

pl. plural.

Pl. Place.

plac·ard (plăk′ärd′, -ərd) *n.* **1.** A poster for public display. **2.** A nameplate, as on the door of a house. —*v.* **1.** To announce on a placard. **2.** To post placards on or in. [< OF *plaquart*, plate.] **—plac′ard·er** *n.*

pla·cate (plā′kāt′, plăk′āt′) *v.* **-cated, -cating.** To allay the anger of; appease. [L *plācāre*.] **—pla·ca′tion** (plā-kā′shən) *n.*

place (plās) *n.* **1.** A portion of space; an area with or without definite boundaries. **2.** An area occupied by or set aside for someone or something. **3.** A definite location. **4. Place.** A public square or thoroughfare in a town. **5.** A table setting. **6.** A position regarded as possessed by someone or something else; stead: *I was chosen in his place.* **7.** A relative position in a series; standing: *fourth place.* —*v.* **placed, placing. 1.** To put in some particular position; set. **2.** To appoint to a post. **3.** To rank (someone or something) in an order or sequence. **4.** To make: *place a telephone call.* **5.** To request formally: *place an order.* **6.** To finish in second place or among the first three finishers in a race. [< L *platea*, "broad street," space.]

pla·ce·bo (plə-sē′bō) *n., pl.* **-bos** or **-boes. 1.** A substance containing no medication and given merely to humor a patient. **2.** An inactive substance used as a control in an experiment. [< L *placēre*, to please.]

place·ment (plās′mənt) *n.* **1.** The act of placing or arranging. **2.** The act or business of finding jobs, lodgings, or other positions for applicants.

pla·cen·ta (plə-sĕn′tə) *n., pl.* **-tas** or **-tae** (-tē). A vascular, membranous organ that develops in female mammals during pregnancy, lining the uterine wall and partially enveloping the fetus,

---

to which it is attached by the umbilical cord. [< L, flat cake.] —pla•cen′tal *adj.*

plac•er (plăs′ər) *n.* **1.** A glacial or alluvial deposit of sand or gravel containing eroded particles of valuable minerals. **2.** A place where such a deposit is washed to extract its mineral content. [< L *platea,* "broad road," PLACE.]

plac•id (plăs′ĭd) *adj.* **1.** Outwardly calm or composed. **2.** Self-satisfied. [< L *placêre,* to please.] —plac′id•ly *adv.*

plack•et (plăk′ĭt) *n.* A slit in a garment. [< PLACARD.]

pla•gia•rize (plā′jə-rīz′) *v.* -rized, -rizing. To steal and use (the ideas or writings of another) as one's own. [< L *plagium,* kidnaping.] —pla′gia•rism′ *n.* —pla′gia•riz′er *n.*

plague (plāg) *n.* **1.** A pestilence, affliction, or calamity. **2.** Any cause for annoyance; a nuisance. **3.** A highly infectious, usually fatal, epidemic disease, esp. the bubonic plague. —*v.* **plagued, plaguing.** To harass, pester, or annoy. [< L *plāga,* a stroke, wound.]

plaid (plăd) *n.* **1.** A rectangular woolen scarf of a checked or tartan pattern worn over one shoulder by Scottish Highlanders. **2.** Cloth with a tartan or checked pattern. —*adj.* Having a tartan or checked pattern. [Scot Gael *plaide.*] —plaid′ed *adj.*

plain (plān) *adj.* **1.** Free from obstructions; open to view; clear. **2.** Easily understood; clearly evident. **3.** Uncomplicated; simple. **4.** Straightforward. **5.** Not mixed with other substances; pure. **6.** Common in rank or station; ordinary. **7.** Not pretentious; unsophisticated; simple. **8.** Unattractive. **9.** Sheer; unqualified: *plain terror.* —*n.* An extensive, level, treeless land region, such as a valley floor or a plateau summit. —*adv.* In a clear or intelligible manner. [< L *plānus,* flat, clear.] —plain′ly *adv.* —plain′ness *n.*

plain-clothes man (plān′klōz′). Also **plain-clothes-man** (plān′klōz′mən). A member of a police force who wears civilian clothes on duty.

Plains Indian. A member of any of the tribes of North American Indians that once inhabited the plains of the C U.S. and Canada.

plaint (plānt) *n.* **1.** A complaint. **2.** Lamentation. [< L *plangere,* to strike (one's breast), lament.]

plain-tiff (plān′tĭf) *n. Law.* The party that institutes a suit in a court.

plain-tive (plān′tĭv) *adj.* Expressing sorrow; mournful. —plain′tive•ly *adv.*

plait (plāt, plăt) *n.* A braid, esp. of hair. —*v.* To braid. [< L *plicāre,* to fold.]

plan (plăn) *n.* **1.** A detailed scheme or method for the accomplishment of an object. **2.** A proposed or tentative project or goal. **3.** An outline or sketch, esp. a drawing or diagram made to scale. —*v.* **planned, planning.** **1.** To formulate, draw up, or make a plan or plans. **2.** To intend. [< L *plānus,* flat, and *planta,* sole of the foot.] —plan′ner *n.*

pla•nar (plā′nər) *adj.* **1.** Of or in a plane. **2.** Flat. —pla•nar′i•ty (plə-nâr′ə-tē) *n.*

plane¹ (plān) *n.* **1.** A surface containing all the straight lines connecting any two points on it.

2. Any flat or level surface. **3.** A level of development. **4.** An airplane. **5.** A supporting surface of an airplane. [< L *plānus,* flat.] —plane′ness *n.*

plane² (plān) *n.* A carpenter's tool for smoothing and leveling wood. —*v.* **planed, planing.** To smooth or finish with or as with a plane. [< L *plānus,* level.] —plan′er *n.*

plane³ (plān) *n.* Also **plane tree.** A sycamore or related tree with maplelike leaves and ball-like fruit clusters.

plan•et (plăn′ət) *n.* A nonluminous celestial body illuminated by light from a star around which it revolves. [< Gk *planētos,* wandering planet.] —plan′e•tar′y *adj.*

plan•e•tar•i•um (plăn′ə-târ′ē-əm) *n., pl.* -iums or -ia (-ē-ə). **1.** An apparatus or model representing the solar system. **2.** A device for projecting images of celestial bodies in their courses, on the inner surface of a hemispherical dome. **3.** A building or room containing such a device. [PLANET + -ARIUM.]

plan•e•toid (plăn′ə-toid′) *n.* An asteroid.

plank (plăngk) *n.* **1.** A thick piece of lumber. **2.** One of the articles of a political platform. —*v.* **1.** To cover with planks. **2.** To bake or broil and serve (fish or meat) on a board. **3.** To put or set down with force. [< L *planca.*] —plank′less *adj.*

plank•ing (plăng′kĭng) *n.* **1.** Planks collectively. **2.** A covering of planks.

plank•ton (plăngk′tən) *n.* Usually minute plants and animals floating in bodies of water. [< Gk, "wanderer."] —plank•ton′ic (plăngk-tŏn′ĭk) *adj.*

plant (plănt, plänt) *n.* **1.** An organism characteristically having cellulose cell walls, growing by synthesis of inorganic substances, and lacking the power of locomotion. **2.** A plant without a permanent woody stem, as distinguished from a tree or shrub. **3.** A factory. **4.** The buildings, equipment, and fixtures of any institution. —*v.* **1.** To place in the ground to grow. **2.** To sow or supply with or as if with seeds or plants. **3.** To fix or set firmly in position. **4.** To establish. **5.** To implant in the mind. **6.** To place for the purpose of spying or deception. [< L *plantāre,* to plant.]

plan•tain¹ (plăn′tən) *n.* A weedy plant with a dense spike of small, greenish or whitish flowers. [< L *plantāgō.*]

plan•tain² (plăn′tən) *n.* A bananalike tropical plant or its fruit. [< L *platanus,* plane tree.]

plan•ta•tion (plăn-tā′shən) *n.* **1.** A group of cultivated trees or plants. **2.** A large estate or farm on which crops are worked by resident workers.

plant•er (plăn′tər) *n.* **1.** One that plants. **2.** A decorative plant container.

plaque (plăk) *n.* **1.** An ornamented or engraved plate, slab, or disk used for decoration or on a monument for information. **2.** A small ornament or a badge of membership. [< OF, metal plate, coin.]

plash (plăsh) *v.* To splash. [< MDu *plasschen* (imit).]

-plasm. *comb. form. Biol.* Cell-forming material: **protoplasm.** [< PLASMA.]

---

plas·ma (plăz'mə) *n.* Also **plasm** (plăz'əm). **1.** The clear, yellowish fluid portion of blood, lymph, or intramuscular fluid in which cells are suspended. **2.** The fluid portion of milk from which the curd has been separated; whey. **3.** A highly ionized gas composed of ions, electrons, and neutral particles. [< LL, a form, mold.] —**plas·mat·ic** (plăz-măt'ĭk), **plas'·mic** *adj.*

plas·ter (plăs'tər, pläs'-) *n.* **1.** A paste that hardens to a smooth solid and is used for coating walls and ceilings. **2. plaster of Paris. 3.** A pastelike mixture applied to a part of the body for healing or cosmetic purposes. —*v.* **1.** To cover with or as if with plaster. **2.** To cover conspicuously or to excess. [< Gk *emplassein,* to daub on, plaster.] —**plas'ter·er** *n.*

plaster of Paris. Any of a group of gypsum cements, essentially partially hydrated calcium sulfate, $CaSo_4 \cdot 1/2 H_2O$, a powder that hardens into a solid when mixed with water.

plas·tic (plăs'tĭk) *adj.* **1.** Capable of being shaped or formed; pliable. **2.** Pertaining to or dealing with shaping or modeling. **3.** Made of a plastic or plastics. —*n.* Any of various complex organic compounds produced by polymerization. They can be molded, extruded, or cast into various shapes and films, or drawn into filaments used as textile fibers. [< Gk *plassein,* to mold.] —**plas·tic'i·ty** *n.*

plastic surgery. Surgery to remodel, repair, or restore injured or defective tissue or body parts. —**plastic surgeon.**

plate (plāt) *n.* **1.** A smooth, flat, relatively thin, rigid body of uniform thickness. **2. a.** A sheet of hammered, rolled, or cast metal. **b.** A flat piece of metal on which something is engraved. **3. a.** A sheet of material converted into a printing surface, such as an electrotype. **b.** An impression taken from such a surface. **c.** A full-page book illustration, often in color. **4.** A sheet of glass or metal upon which a photographic image can be recorded. **5.** A thin metallic or plastic support fitted to the gums to anchor artificial teeth. **6.** *Baseball.* Home base or plate, usually a flat piece of heavy rubber. **7.** A shallow dish from which food is served or eaten. **8.** Food and service for one person at a meal. **9.** Household articles covered with a precious metal. —*v.* **1.** To cover with a thin layer of metal. **2.** To armor. [< Gk *platus,* broad, flat.] —**plat'ed** *adj.*

pla·teau (plă-tō') *n., pl.* **-teaus** or **-teaux** (-tōz'). **1.** An elevated, level expanse of land. **2.** A leveling off. [< Gk *platus,* broad, flat.]

plat·en (plăt'n) *n.* **1.** One of the two flat members in a printing press that holds the paper against the inked type. **2.** The roller on a typewriter. [Earlier *plattin* < OF *plate,* plate.]

plat·form (plăt'fôrm') *n.* **1.** Any horizontal surface raised above the level of the adjacent area. **2.** A formal declaration of the policy of a group, such as a political party. [OF *plateforme,* "flat form."]

plat·ing (plā'tĭng) *n.* **1.** A thin layer or coating of metal, such as gold or silver. **2.** A covering or layer of metal plates.

plat·i·num (plăt'ə-nəm) *n. Symbol* **Pt** A silver-white, corrosive-resistant, metallic element used in electrical components, jewelry, dentistry, electroplating, and as a catalyst. Atomic number 78, atomic weight 195.09. [< Span *plata,* silver, plate.]

plat·i·tude (plăt'ə-t/y/ōōd') *n.* A trite remark, statement, or idea. [F, "flatness."] —**plat'i·tu'di·nous** *adj.* —**plat'i·tu'di·nous·ly** *adv.*

Pla·to (plā'tō). 427?–347 B.C. Greek philosopher.

Pla·ton·ic (plə-tŏn'ĭk, plā-) *adj.* **1.** Of or characteristic of Plato or his philosophy. **2.** Often **platonic.** Transcending physical desire; spiritual. —**Pla·ton'i·cal·ly** *adv.*

pla·toon (plə-tōōn') *n.* **1.** A subdivision of a military company usually consisting of two or more squads. **2.** A body of persons working together. [F *peloton,* "little ball," group of soldiers.]

plat·ter (plăt'ər) *n.* **1.** A large, shallow dish or plate. **2.** A meal served on such a dish. [< OF *plate,* plate.]

plat·y·pus (plăt'ĭ-pəs) *n., pl.* **-puses.** A semi-aquatic, egg-laying, Australian mammal with webbed feet and a snout resembling a duck's bill. [< Gk *platupous,* "flat-footed."]

plau·dit (plô'dĭt) *n.* An expression of praise. [< L *plaudere,* to applaud.]

plau·si·ble (plô'zə-bəl) *adj.* Apparently valid or likely. [Orig "deserving applause" < L *plaudere,* to applaud.] —**plau'si·bil'i·ty, plau'si·ble·ness** *n.* —**plau'si·bly** *adv.*

play (plā) *v.* **1.** To occupy oneself in amusement, sport, etc. **2.** To take part in (a game or sport). **3.** To act or perform in jest. **4.** To toy; trifle. **5.** To act in a specified way: *play fair.* **6.** To act or perform (a role). **7.** To perform (on a musical instrument). **8.** To be performed: *Othello is playing next week.* **9.** To move lightly or irregularly: *The breeze played on the water.* **10.** To pretend to be. **11.** To compete against in a game. **12. a.** To occupy (a position) in a game: *He plays first base.* **b.** To employ (a player) in a game or position. **c.** To use (a card, piece, etc.) in a game. **13.** To manipulate: *He played his two opponents against each other.* **14.** To bet or wager. **15.** To cause (a record, radio, etc.) to emit sounds. —**play down.** To minimize the importance of. —**play on** (or **upon**). To take advantage of (another's feelings). —**play up.** *Informal.* To emphasize or publicize. —**play up to.** *Informal.* To curry favor with. —*n.* **1. a.** A literary work written for the stage. **b.** The performance of such a work. **2.** Activity engaged in for enjoyment or recreation. **3.** Fun: *It was done in play.* **4.** The act or manner of playing a game or sport. **5.** A method of dealing with people generally: *fair play.* **6.** A move in a game: *It's your play.* **7.** *Sports.* Legitimate use: *The ball was in play.* **8.** Action or use: *the play of the imagination.* **9.** Free movement, as of mechanical parts. —**make a play for.** To attempt to attract or obtain. [< OE *plegan* < Gmc *plegan,* to exercise oneself.] —**play'a·ble** *adj.* —**play'ing·ly** *adv.*

play-act (plā'ăkt') *v.* **1.** To play a pretended role. **2.** To behave in an artificial manner.

play·bill (plā′bĭl′) *n.* A program for a theatrical performance.

play·boy (plā′boi′) *n.* A wealthy man devoted to the pleasures of nightclubs, sports, and female company.

play·er (plā′ər) *n.* 1. One who participates in a game or sport. 2. An actor. 3. One who plays a musical instrument.

play·ful (plā′fəl) *adj.* 1. Full of fun; sportive. 2. Humorous; jesting. —**play′ful·ly** *adv.* —**play′ful·ness** *n.*

play·go·er (plā′gō′ər) *n.* One who attends the theater.

play·ground (plā′ground′) *n.* An outdoor area set aside for recreation and play.

playing card. A card marked with its rank and suit belonging to any of several decks used in playing various games.

play·mate (plā′māt′) *n.* A companion in play.

play-off (plā′ôf′, -ŏf′) *n. Sports.* A final game or series of games played to determine a championship.

play·pen (plā′pěn′) *n.* A portable enclosure in which a baby can be left to play.

play·thing (plā′thĭng′) *n.* A toy.

play·wright (plā′rīt′) *n.* One who writes plays.

pla·za (plä′zə, plăz′ə) *n.* A public square or similar open area in a town or city. [< L *platea*, broad street, courtyard.]

plea (plē) *n.* 1. An appeal or entreaty. 2. An excuse; pretext. 3. *Law.* The answer of the accused to a charge or indictment. [< OF *plaid*, legal action, agreement.]

plead (plēd) *v.* **pleaded** or **pled, pleading.** 1. To appeal earnestly; implore. 2. To argue for or against something. 3. To submit as an excuse or defense: *plead illness.* 4. To put forward a plea of a specific nature in a court of law. 5. To argue or present (a case) in a court. [< OF *plaidier*.] —**plead′er** *n.*

pleas·ant (plěz′ənt) *adj.* 1. Giving or affording mild pleasure; agreeable. 2. Pleasing in manner, appearance, etc. [< L *placēre*, to please.] —**pleas′ant·ly** *adv.* —**pleas′ant·ness** *n.*

pleas·ant·ry (plěz′ən-trē) *n., pl.* **-ries.** A jesting or friendly remark.

please (plēz) *v.* **pleased, pleasing.** 1. To make glad; give enjoyment or satisfaction to. 2. To be the will or desire of: *may it please the court.* 3. To be willing to. Used to introduce or indicate a politely intended request: *Please read it now.* 4. To like; wish: *Do whatever you please.* [< L *placēre*.] —**pleas′er** *n.*

pleas·ing (plē′zĭng) *adj.* Agreeable; gratifying.

pleas·ur·a·ble (plězh′ər-ə-bəl) *adj.* Giving pleasure; gratifying. —**pleas′ur·a·bly** *adv.*

pleas·ure (plězh′ər) *n.* 1. Enjoyment; satisfaction. 2. A source of enjoyment. 3. One's preference, wish, or choice: *What is your pleasure?* [< OF *plaisir*, to please.]

pleat (plēt) *n.* A fold in cloth made by doubling the material upon itself. [< PLAIT.] —**pleat** *v.*

ple·be·ian (plĭ-bē′ən) *adj.* Common; vulgar. —*n.* Someone who is common or crude. [< L *plēbs*, common people.]

pleb·i·scite (plěb′ə-sīt′, -sĭt) *n.* A vote in which the entire people is called to accept or refuse a political proposal. [< L *plēbiscītum*, people's decree.]

plec·trum (plěk′trəm) *n., pl.* **-trums** or **-tra** (-trə) Also **plec·tron** (plěk′trŏn′). A small, thin piece of metal, plastic, etc., used to play a stringed instrument. [< Gk *plēktron*.]

pled (plěd). Alternate *p.t. & p.p.* of **plead.**

pledge (plěj) *n.* 1. A formal promise. 2. Something given or held as security in a loan, contract, etc. 3. One who has promised to join a fraternity, club, etc. —*v.* **pledged, pledging.** 1. To promise solemnly. 2. To bind by or as by a pledge. 3. To deposit as security. 4. To promise to join (a fraternity, club, etc.). [< LL *plebium*.] —**pledg′er** *n.*

-plegia. *comb. form.* A form of paralysis: **paraplegia.** [< Gk *plēgē*, a stroke, blow.]

Plei·a·des (plē′ə-dēz′) *pl.n.* An open star cluster in the constellation Taurus, consisting of several hundred stars, of which six are visible to the naked eye.

Pleis·to·cene (plī′stə-sēn′) *adj.* Of or belonging to the geologic time, rock series, or sedimentary deposits of the earlier of the two epochs of the Quaternary period. —*n.* The Pleistocene epoch. [Gk *pleistos*, most + -CENE.]

ple·na·ry (plē′nə-rē, plěn′ə-) *adj.* 1. Full; absolute: *a diplomat with plenary powers.* 2. Fully attended by qualified members. [< L *plēnus*, full.] —**ple′na·ri·ly** *adv.*

plen·i·po·ten·ti·ar·y (plěn′ə-pə-těn′shē-ěr′ē, -shə-rē) *adj.* Invested with full powers. —*n., pl.* **-ies.** A diplomatic agent, as an ambassador, fully authorized to represent his government. [< LL *plēnipotens*.]

plen·i·tude (plěn′ə-t/y/ood′) *n.* 1. Abundance; copiousness. 2. The condition of being full or complete. [< L *plēnus*, full.]

plen·te·ous (plěn′tē-əs) *adj.* 1. Abundant; copious. 2. Producing or yielding in abundance. —**plen′te·ous·ness** *n.*

plen·ti·ful (plěn′tĭ-fəl) *adj.* 1. Existing in great quantity; abundant. 2. Providing an abundance. —**plen′ti·ful·ly** *adv.*

plen·ty (plěn′tē) *n.* 1. A large quantity or amount; abundance: *goods in plenty.* 2. A condition of general abundance or prosperity. [< L *plēnus*, full.]

pleth·o·ra (plěth′ər-ə) *n.* Superabundance; excess. [< Gk *plēthōra*, fullness.]

pleu·ri·sy (ploor′ə-sē) *n.* Inflammation of the membranous sacs that enclose the lungs. [< Gk *pleura*, side, rib.]

plex·us (plěk′səs) *n., pl.* **-us** or **-uses.** A structure in the form of a network, esp. of nerves, blood vessels, or lymphatics. [< L, pp of *plectere*, to plait.]

pli·a·ble (plī′ə-bəl) *adj.* 1. Easily bent or shaped; flexible. 2. Easily influenced or persuaded; tractable. —**pli′a·bil′i·ty** *n.*

pli·ant (plī′ənt) *adj.* 1. Easily bent or flexed; supple. 2. Receptive to change; adaptable. [< L *plicāre*, to fold.] —**pli′an·cy** (-ən-sē) *n.*

pli·ers (plī′ərz) *pl.n.* Any of variously shaped tools having a pair of pivoted jaws, used for holding, bending, etc.

plight¹ (plīt) *n.* A condition or situation of

difficulty or adversity. [< OF *pleit, ploit,* "a fold."]

plight² (plīt) *v.* To promise or bind by a solemn pledge, esp. to betroth. [< OE *pliht,* peril < Gmc **plegan,* to risk, pledge.]

plinth (plĭnth) *n.* A block or slab upon which a pedestal, column, or statue is placed. [< Gk *plinthos,* brick, square stone block.]

Pli·o·cene (plī′ə-sēn′) *adj.* Of or belonging to the geologic time, rock series, or sedimentary deposits of the last of the five epochs of the Tertiary period. —*n.* The Pliocene epoch. [< Gk *pleiōn,* more + -CENE.]

plod (plŏd) *v.* **plodded, plodding. 1.** To walk heavily or laboriously; trudge. **2.** To work perseveringly or monotonously. [Imit.] —**plod′der** *n.* —**plod′ding·ly** *adv.*

–ploid. *comb. form.* A specific multiple of a set of chromosomes: **haploid.** [< Gk *-ploos,* -fold.]

plop (plŏp) *v.* **plopped, plopping. 1.** To fall with a sound like that of an object falling into water. **2.** To drop or sink heavily. [Imit.] —**plop** *n.*

plot (plŏt) *n.* **1.** A small piece of ground. **2.** The series of events constituting an outline of the action of a narrative or drama. **3.** A secret plan; scheme. —*v.* **plotted, plotting. 1.** To represent graphically, as on a chart. **2.** To plan secretly; scheme; conspire. [< OE *plot,* piece of ground, and OF *complote,* secret plan.] —**plot′ter** *n.*

plov·er (plŭv′ər, plō′vər) *n.* Any of various relatively small, short-billed wading birds. [< VL **ploviārius,* "rain-bird."]

plow (plou) Also *chiefly Brit.* **plough.** *n.* **1.** A farm implement used for breaking up soil and cutting furrows. **2.** Any implement of similar function, as a snowplow. —*v.* **1.** To break and turn up (earth) with a plow. **2.** To make (one's) way forcefully: *plowed through the crowd.* [< OE *plōg, plōh,* plowland.]

plow·share (plou′shâr′) *n.* The cutting blade of a plow.

ploy (ploi) *n.* A stratagem to obtain an advantage over one's opponent. [< EMPLOY.]

pluck (plŭk) *v.* **1.** To pull off or out; pick. **2.** To pull the hair or feathers from. **3.** To sound (the strings of an instrument) by pulling and releasing them. —*n.* **1.** The act of plucking. **2.** Resourceful courage; spirit. [< VL **piluccāre,* to remove the hair.]

pluck·y (plŭk′ē) *adj.* **-ier, -iest.** Courageous in trying circumstances. —**pluck′i·ly** *adv.*

plug (plŭg) *n.* **1.** An object used to stop a hole. **2. a.** A fitting, commonly with metal prongs for insertion in a fixed socket, used to make electric connections. **b.** A **spark plug. 3.** A fireplug. **4.** A portion of chewing tobacco. **5.** *Informal.* A favorable public mention of a product, business, etc. —*v.* **plugged, plugging. 1.** To fill (a hole) tightly with or as with a plug. **2.** To connect to a socket by means of a plug. **3.** *Slang.* To hit with a bullet. **4.** *Informal.* To make favorable public mention of (a product, business, etc.). **5.** *Informal.* To work doggedly at some activity. [MDu *plugge.*]

plum (plŭm) *n.* **1.** A smooth-skinned, fleshy fruit with a hard-shelled pit. **2.** A tree bearing such fruit. **3.** Something especially desirable, as a good position. [< OE *plūme* < Gmc < L *prūnum.*]

plum·age (plōō′mĭj) *n.* The feathers of a bird. [< OE *plume,* plume.]

plumb (plŭm) *n.* **1.** A weight suspended from the end of a line, used to determine water depth. **2.** Such a device used to establish a true vertical. —*adj.* **1.** Exactly vertical. **2.** *Informal.* Utter; sheer: *a plumb fool.* —*v.* **1.** To test the alignment or angle of with a plumb. **2.** To determine the depth of; sound. [< L *plumbum,* lead.] —**plumb** *adv.* —**plumb′a·ble** *adj.*

plumb bob. A usually conical weight attached to a plumb line.

plumb·er (plŭm′ər) *n.* One who installs and repairs pipes and plumbing. [< LL *plumbār- ius,* lead worker.]

plumb·ing (plŭm′ĭng) *n.* **1.** The pipes and fixtures of a water or sewage system. **2.** The trade of a plumber.

plumb line. A line from which a weight is suspended to determine verticality or depth.

plume (plōōm) *n.* **1.** A feather, esp. a large or showy one. **2.** A featherlike form: *a plume of smoke.* —*v.* **plumed, pluming. 1.** To decorate with or as with plumes. **2.** To pride or congratulate (oneself). [< L *plūma.*]

plum·met (plŭm′ĭt) *v.* To drop straight down; plunge. [< L *plumbum,* lead.]

plump¹ (plŭmp) *adj.* Well-rounded and full in form; chubby. —*v.* To make well-rounded: *plump up a pillow.* [MLG, thick, blunt, dull.] —**plump′ly** *adv.* —**plump′ness** *n.*

plump² (plŭmp) *v.* **1.** To drop abruptly or heavily. **2.** To give full support or praise. —*n.* **1.** A heavy or abrupt fall. **2.** The sound of this. —*adv.* **1.** With a heavy impact. **2.** Straight down or ahead. [MLG *plumpen,* to plunge into water.]

plun·der (plŭn′dər) *v.* To rob of goods, esp. by force; pillage. —*n.* Property stolen by fraud or force; booty. [MDu *plunderen* or Fris *plun- derje,* "to rob (of household goods)."] —**plun′- der·a·ble** *adj.* —**plun′der·er** *n.*

plunge (plŭnj) *v.* **plunged, plunging. 1.** To thrust or throw oneself forcefully into a substance or place. **2.** To enter or cast suddenly into a given state, situation, or activity. **3.** To descend steeply or suddenly. [< VL **plumb- icāre,* to sound with a plumb.] —**plunge** *n.*

plung·er (plŭn′jər) *n.* **1.** A machine part that operates with a repeated thrusting or plunging movement. **2.** A device consisting of a rubber suction cup at the end of a stick, used to unclog drains and pipes.

plunk (plŭngk) *v.* **1.** To pluck (the strings of a musical instrument). **2.** To drop heavily or abruptly. **3.** To emit a hollow, twanging sound. —*n.* A hollow, twanging sound. [Imit.] —**plunk′er** *n.*

plu·per·fect (plōō-pûr′fĭkt) *Gram. adj.* Of or designating a verb tense used to express action completed prior to a specified or implied past time. —*n.* **1.** The pluperfect tense. **2.** A verb or form in this tense. [< L *(tempus praeter-*

ô paw, for/oi boy/ou out/ōō took/ōō coo/p pop/r run/s sauce/sh shy/t to/th thin/*th* the/
ŭ cut/ûr fur/v van/w wag/y yes/z size/zh vision/ə ago, item, edible, gallop, circus/

itum) plŭs quam perfectum, "(past tense) more than perfect."]

plu·ral (ploor′əl) *Gram. adj.* Of or relating to a form that designates more than one of the things specified. —*n.* **1.** The plural number or form. **2.** A word or term in this form. [< L *plūs (plŭr-),* more.] —**plu′ral·ly** *adv.*

Usage: Terms made up of single letters or numbers, or groups of letters or numbers, are made plural by the addition of *'s* or *s,* as *two R's* (or *Rs*), *two 6's* (or *6s*), *GI's* (or *GIs*), *the 1930's* (or *1930s*). The *'s* form is usually used for lower-case letters: *two t's.* Plurals of surnames of one syllable ending in *s* are formed by adding *es: Joneses.* Plurals of given names ending in *y* preceded by a consonant are formed by adding *s: the three Marys.*

plu·ral·i·ty (ploo-răl′ə-tē) *n., pl.* **-ties. 1.** In a contest of more than two alternatives, the number of votes cast for the winning alternative, if this number is not more than one half of the total votes cast. **2.** The number by which the vote of a winning candidate exceeds that of his closest opponent.

plus (plŭs) *prep.* **1.** Added to. **2.** Increased by; along with: *earnings plus dividends.* —*adj.* **1.** Positive, as on a scale or in polarity. **2.** Being in addition to what is expected or specified. —*n.* **1.** The symbol +, used to indicate addition or a positive quantity. **2.** A favorable factor. [L *plŭs,* more.]

plush (plŭsh) *n.* A fabric with a thick, deep pile. —*adj.* Luxurious. [< OF *peluchier,* to pluck.] —**plush′ly** *adv.*

Plu·to (ploo′tō) *n.* **1.** The 9th and farthest planet from the sun, having a sidereal period of revolution about the sun of 248.4 years, 2.8 billion miles distant at perihelion and 4.6 billion miles at aphelion, and a diameter approx. half that of the earth. **2.** Roman god of the dead.

plu·toc·ra·cy (ploo-tŏk′rə-sē) *n., pl.* **-cies. 1.** Government by the wealthy. **2.** A wealthy class that controls a government. [< Gk *ploutos,* wealth + -CRACY.] —**plu′to·crat′** (-tə-krăt′) *n.* —**plu′to·crat′ic** *adj.*

plu·ton·ic (ploo-tŏn′ĭk) *adj. Geol.* Of deep igneous or magmatic origin: *plutonic water.*

plu·to·ni·um (ploo-tō′nē-əm) *n. Symbol* **Pu** A naturally radioactive, silvery metallic element, used as a reactor fuel and in nuclear weapons. Atomic number 94, longest-lived isotope Pu 244. [< PLUTO.]

ply[1] (plī) *n., pl.* **plies. 1.** A layer, as of doubled-over cloth. **2.** One of the layers or strands of which something, as plywood, rope, or yarn, is composed. [< L *plicāre,* to fold.]

ply[2] (plī) *v.* **plied, plying. 1.** To use diligently, as a tool or weapon. **2.** To engage in, as a trade; work diligently. **3.** To traverse or sail over regularly. **4.** To continue supplying: *ply guests with food.* [< APPLY.]

ply·wood (plī′wood′) *n.* A material made of layers of wood glued tightly together. [PLY[1] + WOOD.]

Pm promethium.

PM postmaster.

P.M. 1. postmaster. **2.** post meridiem. **3.** post-

mortem examination. **4.** prime minister.

p.n. promissory note.

pneu·mat·ic (n/y/oo-măt′ĭk) *adj.* Of, operated by, or filled with air or another gas. [< Gk *pneuma,* wind, spirit.]

pneu·mo·nia (n/y/oo-mōn′yə) *n.* An acute or chronic disease marked by inflammation of the lungs and caused by viruses, bacteria, and physical and chemical agents. [< Gk *pneumonia,* var of *pleumonia,* disease of the lungs.]

Po polonium.

Po (pō). A river of N Italy.

P.O. 1. petty officer. **2.** postal (money) order. **3.** post office.

poach[1] (pōch) *v.* To cook in boiling or simmering liquid. [< OF *pochier (des œufs),* "to put (egg yolks) in pockets."]

poach[2] (pōch) *v.* **1.** To trespass on another's property in order to take fish or game. **2.** To take (fish or game) in a forbidden area. [OF *pochier,* to trample, poach into.] —**poach′er** *n.*

pock (pŏk) *n.* **1.** A pustule caused by smallpox or a similar eruptive disease. **2.** A mark or scar left in the skin by such a pustule; pockmark. [< OE *pocc.* See beu-.]

pock·et (pŏk′ĭt) *n.* **1.** A pouch or piece of material sewn onto a garment with one edge open. **2.** Any receptacle or cavity. **3.** Financial means. **4.** A small isolated or protected area or group. —*adj.* **1.** Suitable for or capable of being carried in a pocket. **2.** Tiny; miniature. —*v.* **1.** To place in or as in a pocket. **2.** To take possession of for oneself, esp. dishonestly. [< OF *poche,* pocket.]

pock·et·book (pŏk′ĭt-book′) *n.* **1.** A wallet; billfold. **2.** A handbag; purse. **3.** Financial resources. **4.** A pocket-sized, usually paper-bound book.

pock·et·knife (pŏk′ĭt-nīf′) *n.* A small knife with a blade or blades folding into the handle.

pock·mark (pŏk′märk′) *n.* A pitlike scar left on the skin by smallpox or another eruptive disease. —**pock′marked′** *adj.*

pod (pŏd) *n.* **1.** A seed vessel, as of a pea or bean, that splits open. **2.** A housing that encloses an externally mounted part of an aircraft. [Prob var of COD.]

po·di·a·try (pə-dī′ə-trē) *n.* The study and treatment of foot ailments. [Gk *pous (pod-),* foot + -IATRY.] —**po·di′a·trist** *n.*

po·di·um (pō′dē-əm) *n., pl.* **-dia** (-dē-ə) or **-ums.** An elevated platform for an orchestra conductor, lecturer, etc. [< Gk *podion,* "small foot," base.]

P.O.E. port of entry.

Poe (pō), **Edgar Allan.** 1809–1849. American poet and critic.

po·em (pō′əm, -ĭm) *n.* A verbal composition having the suggestive power to engage the feelings and imagination, typically through the highly structured patterning and movement of sound, rhythm, and meaning characteristic of verse. [< Gk *poiēma,* "created thing," work, poem.]

po·e·sy (pō′ə-zē, -sē) *n. Archaic.* Poetry.

po·et (pō′ĭt) *n.* A writer of poems. [< Gk *poiētēs,* "maker," poet.]

po·et·as·ter (pō′ĭt-ăs′tər) *n.* An inferior poet.

ă pat/ā ate/âr care/ä bar/b bib/ch chew/d deed/ĕ pet/ē be/f fit/g gag/h hat/hw what/
ĭ pit/ī pie/îr pier/j judge/k kick/l lid, fatal/m mum/n no, sudden/ng sing/ŏ pot/ō go/

po·et·ic (pō-ĕt′ĭk) *adj.* Also **po·et·i·cal** (-ĭ-kəl). Of, pertaining to, or characteristic of poetry or poets. —**po·et′i·cal·ly** *adv.*

po·et·ry (pō′ĭ-trē) *n.* 1. The art or work of a poet. 2. Verse as distinguished from prose. 3. The quality characteristic of the poetic experience.

po·grom (pō′grəm, pō-grŏm′) *n.* An organized massacre of a minority group, esp. Jews. [Russ, "like thunder," devastation.]

poign·ant (poin′yənt, poi′nənt) *adj.* 1. Keenly distressing to the mind or feelings: *poignant anxiety.* 2. Affecting; touching: *poignant sentiment.* [< L *pungere*, to prick, pierce.] —**poign′an·cy** *n.* —**poign′ant·ly** *adv.*

poin·set·ti·a (poin-sĕt′ē-ə) *n.* A tropical American shrub with showy, usually scarlet petallike leaves beneath the small yellow flowers. [< J.R. *Poinsett* (1799–1851), U.S. minister to Mexico.]

point (point) *n.* 1. The sharp or tapered end of something. 2. A tapering extension of land projecting into water. 3. A dimensionless geometric object having no property but location. 4. A position or place. 5. A specified or distinct degree or condition. 6. A specific moment in time. 7. An important, essential, or primary factor or idea. 8. A purpose; reason. 9. An individual item or element. 10. A distinctive characteristic or quality. 11. A single unit, as in counting, rating, or measuring. 12. An electrical contact, esp. one in the distributor of an automobile engine. 13. A unit equal to one dollar, used to quote or state the current prices of stocks, commodities, etc. —*v.* 1. To direct or aim. 2. To bring to notice: *pointed out the landmarks.* 3. To indicate the position or direction of with or as with the finger. 4. To give emphasis to; stress: *pointed up the difference.* [< L *punctus,* pp of *pungere,* to pierce, prick.]

point-blank (point′blăngk′) *adj.* 1. a. So close to a target that a weapon can be aimed directly at it: *pointblank range.* b. Close enough so that missing the target is unlikely. 2. Straightforward; blunt. —*adv.* 1. With a straight aim: *fired pointblank.* 2. Without hesitation or equivocation: *answer pointblank.*

point·ed (poin′tĭd) *adj.* 1. Having a point. 2. Pertinent; incisive. 3. Obviously making reference to something or someone. 4. Conspicuous; marked: *a pointed lack of interest.* —**point′ed·ly** *adv.* —**point′ed·ness** *n.*

point·er (poin′tər) *n.* 1. An indicator on a watch, balance, etc. 2. A long stick for indicating objects on a chart, blackboard, etc. 3. A hunting dog with a short, smooth coat. 4. A suggestion; piece of advice.

point·less (point′lĭs) *adj.* Meaningless; irrelevant. —**point′less·ly** *adv.*

point of view. 1. The position from which something is observed or considered. 2. One's manner of viewing things; attitude.

poise (poiz) *v.* **poised, poising.** To balance or be balanced. —*n.* 1. Balance; stability. 2. a. Composure. b. Dignity of manner. [< OF *poiser,* to weigh.]

poi·son (poi′zən) *n.* Any substance that causes injury or death, esp. by chemical means. —*v.* 1. To give poison to; kill or harm with poison. 2. To make poisonous. 3. To have a harmful influence on; corrupt or ruin. [< L *pōtiō,* potion.] —**poi′son·ous** *adj.*

poison ivy. A North American plant having leaflets in groups of three and causing a rash on contact.

poke (pōk) *v.* **poked, poking.** 1. To push or jab, as with a finger or stick. 2. To make (a hole or pathway) by or as by prodding or thrusting. 3. To thrust forward; appear. 4. To pry or meddle. 5. To search curiously; rummage. —*n.* A push, thrust, or jab. [< MDu and MLG *poken,* to strike, thrust.]

pok·er[1] (pō′kər) *n.* A metal rod used to stir a fire.

pok·er[2] (pō′kər) *n.* Any of various card games played by two or more players who bet on the value of their hands. [?]

po·key (pō′kē) *n., pl.* **-keys.** *Slang.* Jail. [< POKY.]

pok·y (pō′kē) *adj.* **-ier, -iest.** Dawdling; slow. [< POKE.] —**pok′i·ness** *n.*

Pol. Poland; Polish.

Po·land (pō′lənd). A republic of C Europe. Pop. 31,340,000. Cap. Warsaw.

Poland

po·lar (pō′lər) *adj.* 1. Of, measured from, or referred to a pole or poles. 2. Of or near the North or South Pole. 3. Occupying or characterized by opposite extremes.

polar bear. A large white bear of Arctic regions.

polar cap. 1. A high-altitude icecap. 2. The polar regions of ice.

Po·lar·is (pō-lăr′ĭs, -lâr′ĭs) *n.* A star at the end of the handle of the Little Dipper and almost at the N celestial pole. [NL *(Stella) Polāris,* polar (star).]

po·lar·i·ty (pō-lăr′ə-tē, pō-lâr′-) *n., pl.* **-ties.** 1. Intrinsic polar separation, alignment, or orientation, esp. of a physical property. 2. The manifestation of two opposing tendencies. 3. An indicated polar extreme.

po·lar·ize (pō′lə-rīz′) *v.* **-ized, -izing.** 1. To impart polarity to. 2. To cause to concentrate about two opposing positions. 3. To acquire polarity. —**po′lar·i·za′tion** *n.*

pole¹ (pōl) *n.* **1.** Either axial extremity of any axis through a sphere. **2.** The **North Pole** or the **South Pole**. **3.** A magnetic pole. **4.** Either of two oppositely charged terminals, as in an electric cell or battery. **5.** Either of two opposing forces. [< Gk *polos,* axis of the sphere.]

pole² (pōl) *n.* A long, slender piece of wood or other material. [< L *pālus,* stake.]

Pole (pōl) *n.* A native of Poland.

pole•cat (pōl'kăt') *n.* **1.** A weasellike Old World mammal. **2.** A skunk.

po•lem•ic (pə-lĕm'ĭk) *n.* **1.** A controversy, argument, or refutation. **2. polemics.** The art or practice of argumentation or controversy. [< Gk *polemos,* war.] —**po•lem'ic, po•lem'i•cal** *adj.*

pole•star (pōl'stär') *n.* **1.** Polaris. **2.** A guiding principle.

pole vault. *Sports.* A field event in which the contestant vaults over a high crossbar with the aid of a long pole. —**pole'-vault'er** (pōl'vôlt'ər) *n.*

po•lice (pə-lēs') *n., pl.* **-lice. 1. a.** A governmental department established to maintain order, enforce the law, and prevent and detect crime. **b.** *(takes pl. v.).* The members of such a department. **2.** Any group of persons resembling the police force of a community in function: *campus police.* **3.** Soldiers assigned to a specified maintenance duty: *kitchen police.* —*v.* **-liced, -licing. 1.** To control or keep in order with or as with police. **2.** To make (a military area) neat and orderly. [< Gk *polis,* city.]

po•lice•man (pə-lēs'mən) *n.* A member of a police department.

pol•i•cy¹ (pŏl'ə-sē) *n., pl.* **-cies. 1.** A method or course of action adopted by a government, business organization, etc., designed to influence and determine decisions. **2.** A guiding principle or procedure. **3.** Shrewdness; sagacity. [< Gk *politeia,* citizenship.]

pol•i•cy² (pŏl'ə-sē) *n., pl.* **-cies.** A written contract or certificate of insurance. [< Gk *apodeixis,* "a showing or making known."]

po•li•o (pō'lē-ō') *n.* Poliomyelitis.

po•li•o•my•e•li•tis (pō'lē-ō-mī'ə-lī'tĭs) *n.* An infectious viral disease occurring mainly in children and in its acute forms attacking the central nervous system and producing paralysis, muscular atrophy, and often death. [Gk *polios,* gray + MYELITIS.]

pol•ish (pŏl'ĭsh) *v.* **1.** To make smooth or shiny, as by abrasion or rubbing. **2.** To remove flaws from; perfect; refine. —*n.* **1.** Smoothness or shininess of surface. **2.** A substance used to shine a surface. **3.** Elegance of style or manners. [< L *polīre.*] —**pol'ish•er** *n.*

Po•lish (pō'lĭsh) *adj.* Of or pertaining to Poland, its inhabitants, or their language. —*n.* The Slavic language of Poland.

polit. political; politics.

po•lite (pə-līt') *adj.* **-liter, -litest. 1.** Marked by consideration and correct manners; courteous. **2.** Refined; cultivated. [< L *politus,* "polished."] —**po•lite'ly** *adv.* —**po•lite'ness** *n.*

pol•i•tic (pŏl'ə-tĭk) *adj.* **1.** Shrewd and tactful. **2.** Prudent; judicious.

po•lit•i•cal (pə-lĭt'ĭ-kəl) *adj.* **1.** Of or pertain-

ing to government or politics. **2.** Characteristic of political parties or politicians. [< Gk *politikos,* of a citizen.] —**po•lit'i•cal•ly** *adv.*

pol•i•ti•cian (pŏl'ə-tĭsh'ən) *n.* **1.** One actively involved in politics, esp. party politics. **2.** One who holds or seeks a political office.

pol•i•tick (pŏl'ə-tĭk) *v.* To engage in or talk politics.

pol•i•tics (pŏl'ə-tĭks) *n. (takes sing. v.).* **1.** The art or science of political government. **2.** The policies or affairs of a government. **3. a.** The conducting of or engaging in political affairs, often professionally. **b.** The profession of a person so involved. **4.** *(takes pl. v.).* Political opinions or principles.

pol•i•ty (pŏl'ə-tē) *n., pl.* **-ties.** Any organized society, as a nation, having one specific form of government. [< Gk *politēs,* citizen.]

Polk (pōk), **James Knox.** 1795–1849. 11th President of the U.S. (1845–49).

James K. Polk

pol•ka (pōl'kə, pō'kə) *n.* **1.** A lively round dance performed by couples. **2.** Music for this dance. [< Pol *polka,* Polish woman.]

polka dot. A pattern or fabric with uniform dots. [Perh < *poke a dot.*]

poll (pōl) *n.* **1. a.** The casting and registering of votes in an election. **b.** The number of votes cast or recorded. **c.** Often **polls.** The place where votes are cast and registered. **2.** A canvassing of persons to analyze public opinion on a particular question. —*v.* **1. a.** To receive (a given number of votes). **b.** To receive or record the votes of. **2.** To canvass (persons) to survey public opinion. **3.** To cut off; trim; clip. [ME *pol, polle,* head.] —**poll'er** *n.*

pol•len (pŏl'ən) *n.* The powderlike material produced by the anthers of flowering plants and functioning as the male element in fertilization. [< L, flour, dust.]

pollen count. The average number of pollen grains, usually of ragweed, in a cubic yard or other standard volume of air over a 24-hour period at a specified time and place, used to estimate the possible severity of hay-fever attacks.

ă pat/ā ate/âr care/ä bar/b bib/ch chew/d deed/ĕ pet/ē be/f fit/g gag/h hat/hw what/
ĭ pit/ī pie/îr pier/j judge/k kick/l lid, fatal/m mum/n no, sudden/ng sing/ŏ pot/ō go/

pol·li·nate (pŏl′ə-nāt′) *v.* -nated, -nating. To fertilize by transferring pollen to a stigma of (a plant or flower). —**pol′li·na′tion** *n.*

pol·li·wog (pŏl′ē-wŏg′, -wôg′) *n.* Also **pol·ly·wog.** A tadpole. [< POLL + WIGGLE.]

pol·lut·ant (pə-lōot′nt) *n.* Anything that pollutes, esp. any gaseous, chemical, or organic waste that contaminates air, soil, or water.

pol·lute (pə-lōot′) *v.* -luted, -luting. To make impure or unclean; contaminate. [< L *polluere.*] —**pol·lu′tion** *n.*

Pol·lux (pŏl′əks) *n.* A bright star in the constellation Gemini.

po·lo (pō′lō) *n.* A game played by two teams on horseback, equipped with long-handled mallets for driving a wooden ball. [Akin to Tibetan *bo-lo.*]

Po·lo (pō′lō), **Marco.** 1254?–1324? Venetian traveler to the court of Kublai Khan.

po·lo·ni·um (pə-lō′nē-əm) *n.* *Symbol* **Po** A naturally radioactive metallic element, occurring in minute quantities as a product of radium disintegration and produced by bombarding bismuth or lead with neutrons. Atomic number 84, longest-lived isotope Po 210. [< L *Polōnia,* Poland.]

pol·ter·geist (pōl′tər-gīst′) *n.* A ghost that manifests itself by noises and rappings. [G.]

pol·troon (pŏl-trōon′) *n.* *Archaic.* A coward. [< OIt *poltrone,* "foal."]

poly-. *comb. form.* **1.** More than one; many. **2.** More than usual. [< Gk *polus,* much, many.]

pol·y·clin·ic (pŏl′ē-klĭn′ĭk) *n.* A clinic that treats all types of diseases and injuries.

pol·y·es·ter (pŏl′ē-ĕs′tər) *n.* Any of numerous synthetic resins. [POLY(MER) + ESTER.]

pol·y·eth·yl·ene (pŏl′ē-ĕth′ə-lēn′) *n.* A synthetic resin, used esp. in the form of films and sheets. [POLY(MER) + ETHYLENE.]

po·lyg·a·my (pə-lĭg′ə-mē) *n.* The practice of having more than one wife or husband at one time. —**po·lyg′a·mist** (-mĭst) *n.* —**po·lyg′a·mous** (-məs) *adj.*

pol·y·glot (pŏl′ē-glŏt′) *n.* One with a reading, writing, or speaking knowledge of several languages. [< Gk *poluglōttos.*]

pol·y·gon (pŏl′ē-gŏn′) *n.* A closed plane figure bounded by three or more line segments. [< Gk *polugōnos,* "having many angles."] —**po·lyg′o·nal** (pə-lĭg′ə-nəl) *adj.*

pol·y·graph (pŏl′ē-grăf′, -gräf′) *n.* An instrument that records changes in such physiological processes as heartbeat, blood pressure, and respiration, and is sometimes used in lie detection. [Gk *polugraphos,* "writing a lot."]

pol·y·he·dron (pŏl′ē-hē′drən) *n.,* *pl.* -drons or -dra (-drə). A solid bounded by polygons. —**pol′y·he′dral** *adj.*

pol·y·mer (pŏl′ə-mər) *n.* Any of numerous natural and synthetic compounds of usually high molecular weight consisting of repeated linked units, each a relatively light and simple molecule. —**pol′y·mer′ic** (-mĕr′ĭk) *adj.*

pol·y·mer·ize (pŏl′ə-mə-rīz′, pə-lĭm′ə-) *v.* -ized, -izing. To unite two or more monomers to form a polymer. —**po·lym′er·i·za′tion** (pə-lĭm′ər-ə-zā′shən, pŏl′ə-mər-) *n.*

Pol·y·ne·sia (pŏl′ə-nē′zhə, -shə). A scattered group of islands of the E and SE Pacific. —**Pol′y·ne′sian** *adj. & n.*

pol·y·no·mi·al (pŏl′ē-nō′mē-əl) *adj.* Of, pertaining to, or consisting of more than two names or terms. —*n.* An algebraic function of two or more summed terms, each term consisting of a constant multiplier and one or more variables raised, in general, to integral powers. [POLY- + (BI)NOMIAL.]

pol·yp (pŏl′ĭp) *n.* **1.** An organism, as a coral, with a cylindrical body and a mouth opening surrounded by tentacles. **2.** A pathological growth protruding from the mucous lining of an organ. [< Gk *polupous,* "many-footed."]

po·lyph·o·ny (pə-lĭf′ə-nē) *n.* The simultaneous combination of two or more independent melodic parts. [Gk *poluphōnia,* variety of tones.] —**pol′y·phon′ic** (pŏl′ē-fŏn′ĭk) *adj.*

pol·y·sty·rene (pŏl′ē-stī′rēn′) *n.* A hard, rigid, dimensionally stable, clear thermoplastic polymer.

pol·y·syl·la·ble (pŏl′ē-sĭl′ə-bəl) *n.* A word of more than three syllables. —**pol′y·syl·lab′ic** (-sĭ-lăb′ĭk) *adj.*

pol·y·tech·nic (pŏl′ē-tĕk′nĭk) *adj.* Of or involving many arts or sciences.

pol·y·the·ism (pŏl′ē-thē-ĭz′əm) *n.* The worship of or belief in more than one god. —**pol′y·the·ist** *n.* —**pol′y·the·is′tic** *adj.*

pol·y·un·sat·u·rat·ed (pŏl′ē-ŭn-săch′ə-rā′tĭd) *adj.* Pertaining to long-chain carbon compounds, esp. fats, having many unsaturated bonds.

pol·y·vi·nyl chloride (pŏl′ē-vī′nəl). A common thermoplastic resin, used in a wide variety of manufactured products.

po·made (pə-mād′, -măd′, pō-) *n.* A perfumed hair ointment. [< It *pomata,* hair ointment orig apple-scented.]

pome·gran·ate (pŏm′grăn′ĭt, pŭm′-) *n.* **1.** A fruit with a tough, reddish rind and many seeds enclosed in juicy, red pulp. **2.** A tree bearing such fruit. [< OF *pome grenate,* "many-seeded apple."]

pom·mel (pŭm′əl, pŏm′-) *n.* **1.** A knob on the hilt of a sword. **2.** The upper front part of a saddle. —*v.* To beat; pummel. [< VL *pōmellum,* rounded knob.]

pomp (pŏmp) *n.* **1.** Magnificent display; splendor. **2.** Ostentatious display. [< Gk *pompē,* "a sending," solemn procession.]

pom·pa·no (pŏm′pə-nō′, pŭm′-) *n.,* *pl.* -no or -nos. A food fish of tropical and temperate Atlantic waters. [Span *pámpano,* name of a fish.]

pom·pon (pŏm′pŏn′) *n.* Also **pom·pom** (-pŏm′). **1.** A tuft or ball of material worn as decoration. **2.** A small, buttonlike chrysanthemum. [F.]

pom·pous (pŏm′pəs) *adj.* **1.** Self-important; pretentious. **2.** Characterized by pomp or stately display. —**pom·pos′i·ty** (pŏm′pŏs′ə-tē), **pom′pous·ness** *n.* —**pom′pous·ly** *adv.*

pon·cho (pŏn′chō) *n.,* *pl.* -chos. **1.** A blanket-like cloak with a center hole for the head. **2.** A similar garment used as a raincoat. [Amer Span.]

ô paw, for/oi boy/ou out/ŏŏ took/ōō coo/p pop/r run/s sauce/sh shy/t to/th thin/*th* the/ ŭ cut/ûr fur/v van/w wag/y yes/z size/zh vision/ə ago, item, edible, gallop, circus/

pond (pŏnd) *n.* A still body of water, smaller than a lake. [< OE *pund-*, enclosure.]

pon·der (pŏn′dər) *v.* 1. To consider carefully. 2. To meditate; reflect. [< L *ponderāre*, to weigh, ponder.] —**pon′der·er** *n.*

pon·der·ous (pŏn′dər-əs) *adj.* 1. Having great weight; massive; unwieldy. 2. Lacking fluency; dull. [< L *pondus* (*ponder-*), weight.]

pone (pōn) *n.* A cornmeal patty usually made without milk or eggs. [< Algon.]

pon·gee (pŏn-jē′, pŏn′jē) *n.* A soft, thin silk cloth. [Mand Chin *pen³ chi¹*, "(made by) one's own loom."]

pon·iard (pŏn′yərd) *n.* A dagger. [F *poignard.*]

pons (pŏnz) *n., pl.* **pontes** (pŏn′tēz). Any slender tissue joining two parts of an organ. [L *pōns*, bridge.]

pon·tiff (pŏn′tĭf) *n.* 1. The pope. 2. A bishop. [< L *pontifex*, Roman high priest.]

pon·tif·i·cal (pŏn-tĭf′ĭ-kəl) *adj.* Of or pertaining to a pope or bishop. —*n.* **pontificals.** The vestments and insignia of a pontiff.

pon·toon (pŏn-tōōn′) *n.* 1. A flat-bottomed boat or other structure used to support a floating bridge. 2. A float on a seaplane. [< L *pontō*, boat bridge.]

po·ny (pō′nē) *n., pl.* **-nies.** A small horse. [< L *pullus*, foal.]

pooch (pōōch) *n. Slang.* A dog. [?]

poo·dle (pōōd′l) *n.* A dog with thick, curly hair. [G *Pudel(hund)*, "poodle (dog)."]

pooh (pōō) *interj.* Expressive of disdain.

pooh-pooh (pōō′pōō′) *v. Informal.* To express contempt or disdain for.

pool¹ (pōōl) *n.* 1. A small pond. 2. A puddle of any liquid. 3. A deep place in a river or stream. [< OE *pōl* < Gmc **pōla-.*]

pool² (pōōl) *n.* 1. In certain gambling games, the total amount staked by all players. 2. Any grouping of resources for the common advantage of the participants. 3. An agreement between competing business concerns to establish certain controls for common profit. 4. Any of several games played on a six-pocket billiard table. —*v.* To combine (money, funds, or interests) for mutual benefit. [F *poule*, stakes, target.]

poop¹ (pōōp) *n.* 1. The stern superstructure of a ship. 2. A poop deck. [< L *puppis.*]

poop² (pōōp) *v. Slang.* To become or cause to become fatigued; tire. [?]

poop deck. The aftermost deck of a ship.

poor (pōōr) *adj.* 1. a. Having little or no wealth. b. Destitute. 2. Inferior; inadequate; inefficient. 3. a. Lacking desirable elements or constituents. b. Undernourished; lean. 4. Lacking in value. 5. a. Humble. b. Pitiable. [< L *pauper.*] —**poor′ly** *adv.*

poor·house (pōōr′hous′) *n.* A publicly supported establishment for paupers.

pop¹ (pŏp) *v.* **popped, popping.** 1. To make or cause to make a short, sharp, explosive sound. 2. To burst open with such a sound. 3. To appear abruptly. 4. To open the eyes wide suddenly. 5. To put or thrust suddenly: *popped the cooky into her mouth.* 6. To fire (a pistol or other firearm). —*n.* 1. A sudden sharp, explosive sound. 2. A shot with a firearm. 3. A

nonalcoholic carbonated beverage. [ME *poppen.*]

pop² (pŏp) *n. Informal.* Father.

pop³ (pŏp) *adj. Informal.* 1. Pertaining to or specializing in popular music. 2. Suggestive of pop art.

pop. 1. popular. 2. population.

pop art. A form of art that depicts objects of everyday life and adapts techniques of commercial art.

pop·corn (pŏp′kôrn′) *n.* 1. A variety of corn with hard kernels that burst to form white puffs when heated. 2. The edible popped kernels of popcorn. [< *popped corn.*]

pope (pōp) *n.* 1. Often **Pope.** The bishop of Rome and head of the Roman Catholic Church. 2. *E.O.Ch.* A priest. [< Gk *pappas*, title of bishops.]

Pope (pōp), **Alexander.** 1688–1744. English poet and satirist.

pop·eyed (pŏp′īd′) *adj.* Having bulging eyes.

pop·gun (pŏp′gŭn′) *n.* A toy gun operating by compressed air to fire corks or pellets.

pop·in·jay (pŏp′ĭn-jā′) *n.* A vain, supercilious person. [< OF *papegai*, a parrot.]

pop·lar (pŏp′lər) *n.* Any of several trees with triangular leaves and soft wood. [< L *pōpulus.*]

pop·lin (pŏp′lĭn) *n.* A ribbed fabric used in making clothing and upholstery. [< It *papalino*, papal.]

pop·o·ver (pŏp′ō′vər) *n.* A light, puffy, hollow muffin made with eggs, milk, and flour.

pop·py (pŏp′ē) *n., pl.* **-pies.** Any of various plants with showy red, orange, or white flowers and milky juice. [< L *papāver.*]

pop·py·cock (pŏp′ē-kŏk′) *n.* Senseless talk. [Du dial *pappekak*, "soft dung."]

pop·u·lace (pŏp′yə-lĭs) *n.* 1. The common people; masses. 2. A population. [< L *populus*, people.]

pop·u·lar (pŏp′yə-lər) *adj.* 1. Widely liked or appreciated. 2. Of, representing, or carried on by the people at large. 3. Accepted by or suited to the people in general. [L *populāris*, of the people.] —**pop′u·lar′i·ty** (-lăr′ə-tē) *n.* —**pop′u·lar·ly** *adv.*

pop·u·lar·ize (pŏp′yə-lə-rīz′) *v.* **-ized, -izing.** To make popular.

pop·u·late (pŏp′yə-lāt′) *v.* **-lated, -lating.** 1. To supply with inhabitants. 2. To inhabit. [< L *populus*, people.]

pop·u·la·tion (pŏp′yə-lā′shən) *n.* 1. The people or total number of people inhabiting a specified area. 2. *Stat.* The entire set of individuals, items, or scores from which a sample is drawn.

pop·u·lous (pŏp′yə-ləs) *adj.* Thickly settled or populated. —**pop′u·lous·ness** *n.*

p.o.r. pay on return.

por·ce·lain (pôrs′lĭn, pôrs′-, pôr′sə-lĭn, pôr′sə-) *n.* 1. A hard, white, translucent ceramic. 2. An object made of this material. [< OF *pourcelaine.*]

porch (pôrch, pōrch) *n.* 1. A platform, usually with a separate roof, at an entrance to a house. 2. A gallery or room attached to the outside of a building. [< L *porticus*, PORTICO.]

ă pat/ā ate/âr care/ä bar/b **bib**/ch **chew**/d **deed**/ĕ pet/ē be/f fit/g **gag**/h **hat**/hw **what**/
ĭ pit/ī pie/îr pier/j **judge**/k **kick**/l lid, fatal/m **mum**/n no, sudden/ng **sing**/ŏ pot/ō go/

por•cine (pôr'sīn') *adj.* Of or like swine or a pig. [< L *porcus*, pig.]

por•cu•pine (pôr'kyə-pīn') *n.* A rodent having the back covered with long, sharp spines. [< OF *porc espin*, "spiny pig."]

pore¹ (pôr, pōr) *v.* **pored, poring.** **1.** To read or study attentively. **2.** To ponder. [ME *pouren.*]

pore² (pôr, pōr) *n.* A minute opening, as in an animal's skin or a plant leaf, esp. for the passage of fluid. [< Gk *poros*, passage.]

por•gy (pôr'gē) *n., pl.* **-gies.** A deep-bodied marine food fish. [< Gk *phagros.*]

pork (pôrk, pōrk) *n.* The flesh of a pig, used as

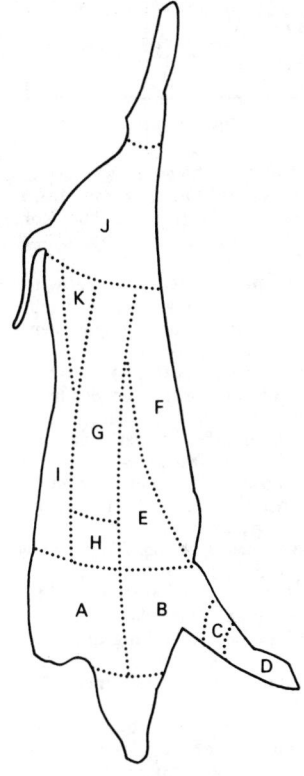

pork
A. Boston butt
B. Picnic ham
C. Hock
D. Foot
E. Spareribs
F. Bacon
G. Center loin
H. Rib chops
I. Fatback for salt pork
J. Ham
K. Tenderloin

food. [< L *porcus*, pig.]

pork•er (pôr'kər, pōr'-) *n.* A fattened young pig.

por•no (pôr'nō) *n.,pl.* **-nos.** *Slang.* **1.** Pornography. **2.** A pornographic motion picture, book, etc. —**por'no** *adj.*

por•nog•ra•phy (pôr-nŏg'rə-fē) *n.* Written or graphic material intended to excite lascivious feeling. [< Gk *pornographos*, writing about prostitutes.] —**por'no•graph'ic** (pôr'nə-grăf'ĭk) *adj.* —**por'no•graph'i•cal•ly** *adv.*

po•ros•i•ty (pə-rŏs'ə-tē, pô-) *n., pl.* **-ties.** **1.** The state or property of being porous. **2.** A porous structure or part.

po•rous (pôr'əs, pōr'-) *adj.* **1.** Having or full of pores. **2.** Admitting the passage of gas or liquid through pores or interstices. —**po'rous•ly** *adv.* —**po'rous•ness** *n.*

por•phy•ry (pôr'fə-rē) *n., pl.* **-ries.** Rock containing relatively large, conspicuous crystals, esp. feldspar, in a fine-grained igneous matrix. [< L *porphyrītēs*, purple-colored stone.]

por•poise (pôr'pəs) *n.* A marine mammal related to the whales but smaller, usually having a blunt snout. [< VL **porcopiscis*, "pig fish."]

por•ridge (pôr'ĭj, pŏr'-) *n.* Boiled oatmeal, usually eaten with milk. [Var of POTTAGE.]

por•rin•ger (pôr'ĭn-jər, pŏr'-) *n.* A shallow cup or bowl with a handle. [< OF *potage*, pottage.]

port¹ (pôrt, pōrt) *n.* **1.** A town having a harbor. **2.** A harbor or waterfront district. [< L *portus*, house door, port.]

port² (pôrt, pōrt) *n.* The left-hand side of a ship or aircraft facing forward. —*adj.* Of, pertaining to, or on the port. —*v.* To turn or shift (the helm of a vessel) to the left. [?]

port³ (pôrt, pōrt) *n.* **1.** A porthole. **2.** An opening for the passage of steam or fluid. [< L *porta*, gate.]

port⁴ (pôrt, pōrt) *n.* A rich, sweet fortified wine. [< Port *o porto*, "the port."]

port⁵ (pôrt, pōrt) *v.* To carry (a rifle, sword, etc.) diagonally across the body, with the muzzle or blade near the left shoulder. [< OF *porter*, to bear.]

Port. Portugal; Portuguese.

port•a•ble (pôr'tə-bəl, pōr'-) *adj.* **1.** Capable of being carried. **2.** Easily moved. [< L *portāre*, to carry.] —**port'a•bil'i•ty** *n.*

port•age (pôr'tĭj, pōr'-, pôr-täzh') *n.* **1.** The carrying of boats and supplies overland between two waterways. **2.** A route by which this is done. —*v.* **-aged, -aging.** To transport by portage. [< L *portāre*, to carry.]

por•tal (pôrt'l, pōrt'l) *n.* A doorway or entrance. [< L *porta*, a gate.]

Port-au-Prince (pôrt'ō-prĭns', pōrt'-). The capital of Haiti. Pop. 250,000.

port•cul•lis (pôrt-kŭl'ĭs, pōrt-) *n.* A grating suspended in the gateway of a fortified place. [< OF *porte coleīce.*]

porte-co•chère, porte-co•chere (pôrt'kō-shâr', pōrt'-) *n.* A projecting roof at a building entrance, providing shelter for those getting in and out of vehicles. [F *porte cochère*, "coach-door."]

por•tend (pôr-tĕnd', pōr-) *v.* To serve as an omen of. [< L *portendere.*]

por•tent (pôr'tĕnt', pōr'-) *n.* **1.** An indication of something about to occur; an omen. **2.**

Something amazing; a prodigy. [< L *portendere*, to PORTEND.]

por·ten·tous (pôr-těn′təs, pōr-) *adj.* **1.** Of the nature of or constituting a portent. **2.** Exciting wonder and awe; prodigious. —**por·ten′tous·ly** *adv.* —**por·ten′tous·ness** *n.*

por·ter[1] (pôr′tər, pōr′-) *n.* **1.** One employed to carry luggage. **2.** A railroad employee who waits on passengers. [< L *portāre*, to carry.]

por·ter[2] (pôr′tər, pōr′-) *n. Chiefly Brit.* A gatekeeper; doorman. [< L *porta*, a gate.]

por·ter[3] (pôr′tər, pōr′-) *n.* A dark beer. [Short for *porter's beer.*]

por·ter·house (pôr′tər-hous′, pōr′-) *n.* A cut of beef having a T-bone and a sizable piece of tenderloin.

port·fo·li·o (pōrt-fō′lē-ō′, pōrt′-) *n., pl.* **-os.** **1.** A portable case for holding papers, drawings, etc. **2.** The office or post of a minister of state. **3.** An itemized list of investments or securities. [It *portafoglio.*]

port·hole (pōrt′hōl′, pōrt′-) *n.* A small, usually circular window in a ship's side.

por·ti·co (pôr′tĭ-kō′, pōr′-) *n., pl.* **-coes** or **-cos.** A porch or walkway with a roof supported by columns. [< L *porticus*, porch.]

por·tière, por·tiere (pôr-tyâr′, pōr-) *n.* A heavy curtain hung across a doorway. [< F *porte*, door.]

por·tion (pôr′shən, pōr′-) *n.* **1.** A section or quantity within a larger thing; a part of a whole. **2.** A part that is allotted to a person or group. **3.** One's lot or fate. —*v.* **1.** To divide into parts or shares (with *out*). **2.** To provide with a share or inheritance. [< L *portiō.*]

Port·land (pōrt′lənd, pōrt′-). A city of NW Oregon. Pop. 375,000.

Portland cement. A hydraulic cement made from a mixture of limestone and clay. [< *Portland*, England.]

Port Lou·is (lōō′ĭs, lōō′ē, lōō-ē′). The capital of Mauritius. Pop. 128,000.

port·ly (pōrt′lē, pōrt′-) *adj.* **-lier, -liest.** Comfortably stout. [< OF *porter*, to bear.]

port·man·teau (pôrt-măn′tō, pōrt-, pôrt′măn-tō′, pōrt′-) *n., pl.* **-teaus** or **-teaux** (-tōz). *Chiefly Brit.* A large leather suitcase with two hinged compartments. [< OF *portemanteau*, "coatcarrier."]

port of call. A port where ships dock in the course of voyages to load or unload cargo, obtain supplies, etc.

port of entry. A place where travelers or goods can enter or leave a country under official supervision.

Port-of-Spain (pōrt′əv-spān′, pōrt′-). The capital of Trinidad and Tobago. Pop. 94,000.

Por·to-No·vo (pōr′tō-nō′vō). The capital of Benin. Pop. 80,000.

por·trait (pōr′trĭt, -trāt′, pōr′-) *n.* A painting, photograph, etc., esp. one showing the face. [< OF *portraire*, portray.]

por·trait·ist (pōr′trə-tĭst, pōr-) *n.* One who makes portraits.

por·trai·ture (pōr′trĭ-chōōr′, pōr′-) *n.* The practice or art of making portraits.

por·tray (pôr-trā′, pōr-) *v.* **1.** To depict pictorially. **2.** To describe in words. **3.** To represent

dramatically. [< L *prōtrahere*, to draw forth, reveal.] —**por·tray′al** *n.*

Por·tu·gal (pōr′chə-gəl, pōr′-). A republic of SW Europe. Pop. 8,889,000. Cap. Lisbon.

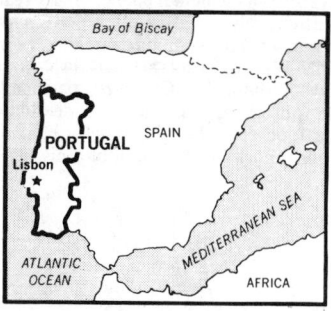

Portugal

Por·tu·guese (pōr′chə-gēz′, -gēs′, pōr′-; pôr′chə-gēz′, -gēs′, pōr′-) *n., pl.* **-guese.** **1.** A native or inhabitant of Portugal. **2.** The Romance language of Portugal and Brazil. —**Por′tu·guese′** *adj.*

Portuguese man-of-war. A chiefly tropical marine organism having a bluish, bladderlike float and numerous long stinging tentacles.

pos. **1.** position. **2.** positive.

pose[1] (pōz) *v.* **posed, posing.** **1.** To assume or hold a particular position or posture, as in sitting for a portrait. **2.** To place in a specific position. **3.** To affect a particular attitude. **4.** To propound or assert. —*n.* **1.** A bodily attitude or position, esp. one assumed in modeling. **2.** An affected attitude of mind or body. [< LL *pausāre*, to cease.]

pose[2] (pōz) *v.* **posed, posing.** To puzzle with a difficult question. [< OF *opposer*, to oppose.]

Po·sei·don (pō-sī′dən). Greek god of the sea.

pos·er[1] (pō′zər) *n.* One who poses.

pos·er[2] (pō′zər) *n.* A baffling question.

po·seur (pō-zœr′) *n.* One who affects a particular attitude to impress others. [< OF *poser*, POSE[1].]

posh (pŏsh) *adj. Informal.* Fashionable.

pos·it (pŏz′ĭt) *v.* To put forward as a truth; postulate. [L *pōnere* (pp *positus*), to place.]

po·si·tion (pə-zĭsh′ən) *n.* **1.** A place or location. **2.** The appropriate place. **3. a.** The way in which something is placed. **b.** The arrangement of bodily parts; posture. **4.** A point of view. **5.** A situation relative to circumstances. **6.** Status; rank. **7.** A post of employment. —*v.* To place. [< L *pōnere* (pp *positus*), to place.] —**po·si′tion·al** *adj.*

pos·i·tive (pŏz′ə-tĭv) *adj.* **1.** Characterized by or displaying affirmation. **2.** Explicitly expressed. **3.** Admitting of no doubt; irrefutable. **4.** Confident. **5.** Overconfident; dogmatic. **6.** Concerned with practical matters. **7.** Real, not fictitious. **8. a.** Of or being a quantity greater than zero. **b.** Of or being the opposite of something negative. **c.** Of or having electric charge of a sign opposite to that of an electron. **9.** *Photog.* Having the areas of light and

---

dark in their original and normal relationship, as in a print made from a negative. **10.** *Gram.* Of, pertaining to, or denoting the simple uncompared degree of an adjective or adverb. —*n.* **1.** That which is positive. **2.** *Photog.* An image in which the lights and darks appear as they do in nature. **3.** *Gram.* The uncompared degree of an adjective or adverb. [< L *pōnere* (pp *positus*), to place.] —**pos′i·tive·ly** *adv.* —**pos′i·tive·ness** *n.*

pos·i·tron (pŏz′ə-trŏn′) *n.* The antiparticle of the electron.

poss. possessive.

pos·se (pŏs′ē) *n.* A body of men summoned to aid a peace officer. [< ML *posse*, power.]

pos·sess (pə-zĕs′) *v.* **1.** To have as property; own. **2.** To have as an attribute. **3.** To have knowledge of. **4.** To exert influence or control over; dominate. [< L *possidere,* "to sit as master," and L *possidēre,* to own, possess.] —**pos·ses′sor** *n.*

pos·sessed (pə-zĕst′) *adj.* **1.** Owning or having. **2.** Controlled by or as by a spirit or other force. **3.** Calm; collected.

pos·ses·sion (pə-zĕsh′ən) *n.* **1.** The act or fact of possessing. **2.** The state of being possessed. **3.** That which is owned or possessed. **4.** Self-control. **5.** The state of being dominated.

pos·ses·sive (pə-zĕs′ĭv) *adj.* **1.** Of or pertaining to ownership or possession. **2.** Having a desire to control or dominate. **3.** *Gram.* Of, pertaining to, or designating a noun or pronoun case that expresses belonging or other similar relation. —*n. Gram.* **1.** The possessive case. **2.** A possessive form or construction. —**po·ses′sive·ly** *adv.* —**pos·ses′sive·ness** *n.*

Usage: Possessive forms are made in English in the following ways: **1.** By adding an apostrophe *s* (*'s*): **a.** To the singular of most nouns, proper names, and irregular plurals: *the boy's chair, Bill's car, the men's hats.* **b.** To monosyllabic singular nouns and proper names ending in a sibilant: *the boss's car, Marx's philosophy.* **2.** By adding an apostrophe (') alone: **a.** To regular plurals: *the girls' dresses, the ladies' furs.* **b.** To certain expressions with *sake: for appearance' sake, for goodness' sake.* **c.** To plurals of proper nouns: *the Joneses' house.* **d.** To proper nouns when a sibilant occurs before the last syllable: *Moses' law, Xerxes' palace.* **e.** To ancient or classical names: *Achilles' heel.* When a singular noun or a proper name ending in a sibilant has two or more syllables, the possessive may be formed by the apostrophe alone or by *'s: Dickens'* or *Dickens's* and *witness'* or *witness's.*

pos·si·ble (pŏs′ə-bəl) *adj.* **1.** Capable of happening, existing, or being true. **2.** Capable of occurring or being done. **3.** Potential. **4.** That may or may not occur. [< L *posse,* to be able.] —**pos′si·bil′i·ty** *n.* —**pos′si·bly** *adv.*

pos·sum (pŏs′əm) *n.* An opossum. —**play possum.** To pretend to be dead, asleep, or unaware.

post¹ (pōst) *n.* **1.** A stake set upright in the ground to serve as a marker or support. **2.** Anything resembling this. —*v.* **1.** To fasten up (an announcement) in a place of public view.

2. To announce by or as by posters. **3.** To publish (a name) on a list. [< L *postis.*]

post² (pōst) *n.* **1.** A military base where troops are stationed. **2.** An assigned position or station, as of a sentry. **3.** A position of employment, esp. an appointive public office. **4.** A trading post. —*v.* **1.** To assign to a position or station. **2.** To put forward; present: *post bail.* [< L *positum,* neut pp of *pōnere,* to place.]

post³ (pōst) *n.* **1.** A rider on a mail route; courier. **2.** *Brit.* **a.** The mail. **b.** A post office. —*v.* **1.** To travel quickly; hasten. **2.** To mail (a letter). **3.** To inform of the latest news. [< L *posita,* fem pp of *pōnere,* to place.]

post-. *comb. form.* **1.** After in time; later; subsequent to. **2.** After in position; behind; posterior to. [< L *post,* behind, after.]

post·age (pō′stĭj) *n.* The charge for mailing an item.

postage stamp. A small engraved adhesive label affixed to items of mail as evidence of the payment of postage.

post·al (pōst′l) *adj.* Of or pertaining to the post office or mail service. —**post′al·ly** *adv.*

postal card. A card printed with a postage stamp for sending messages at low rates; post card.

post card. Also **post·card.** **1.** An unofficial card, usually bearing a picture on one side, with space for an address, postage stamp, and short message. **2.** A postal card.

post·date (pōst-dāt′) *v.* **1.** To put a date on (a check, letter, or document) that is later than the actual date. **2.** To occur later than; follow in time.

post·er (pō′stər) *n.* A large placard, bill, or announcement posted to advertise or publicize something.

pos·te·ri·or (pŏ-stîr′ē-ər, pō-) *adj.* **1.** Located behind a part or toward the rear of a structure. **2.** Following in time; later. —*n.* The buttocks. [< L *posterus,* coming after, next.]

pos·ter·i·ty (pŏ-stĕr′ə-tē) *n.* **1.** Future generations. **2.** All of a person's descendants. [< L *posterus,* next.]

pos·tern (pō′stərn, pŏs′tərn) *n.* A small rear gate, esp. in a fort or castle. [< LL *postera,* back door.]

poster paint. Opaque water-color paint in bright colors.

Post Exchange, post exchange. A store on a military base that sells to military personnel and their families.

post·grad·u·ate (pōst-grăj′ōō-ĭt, -āt′) *adj.* Of, pertaining to, or pursuing studies beyond the bachelor's degree. —*n.* A person engaged in such study.

post·haste (pōst′hāst′) *adv.* With great speed; hastily; rapidly.

post·hu·mous (pŏs′chōō-məs) *adj.* **1.** Occurring or continuing after one's death. **2.** Born after the death of the father. [L *posthumus.*] —**post′hu·mous·ly** *adv.*

post·hyp·not·ic suggestion (pōst′hĭp-nŏt′ĭk). A suggestion made to a hypnotized person specifying an action to be performed in a subsequent waking state.

pos·til·ion (pō-stĭl′yən, pō-) *n.* Also **pos·til·lion.**

ô paw, for/oi boy/ou out/ŏŏ took/ōō coo/p pop/r run/s sauce/sh shy/t to/th thin/*th* the/
ŭ cut/ûr fur/v van/w wag/y yes/z size/zh vision/ə ago, item, edible, gallop, circus/

One who rides and guides the near horse of a pair or of one of the pairs drawing a coach. [< It *posta*, post (mail).]

post·man (pōst'mən) *n.* A mailman.

post·mark (pōst'märk') *n.* An official mark stamped on mail that cancels the postage stamp and records the date and place of mailing. —**post'mark'** *v.*

post·mas·ter (pōst'măs'tər, -mäs'tər) *n.* A government official in charge of the operations of a local post office.

postmaster general *pl.* **postmasters general.** The executive head of a national postal service.

post·me·rid·i·an (pōst'mə-rĭd'ē-ən) *adj.* Of or taking place in the afternoon.

post me·rid·i·em (pōst' mə-rĭd'ē-əm). After noon. [L *post merīdiem*, after midday.]

post-mor·tem (pōst-môr'təm) *adj.* After death. —*n.* **1.** A post-mortem examination, esp. an autopsy. **2.** *Informal.* An analysis or review of some completed event. [L *post mortem*, after death.]

post·na·tal (pōst-nāt'l) *adj.* After birth.

post office. 1. The public department responsible for the transportation and delivery of the mails. **2.** Any local office where mail is sorted, stamps sold, etc.

post·op·er·a·tive (pōst-ŏp'ər-ə-tĭv, -ŏp'rə-tĭv, -ŏp'ə-rā'tĭv) *adj.* After surgery. —**post·op'er·a·tive·ly** *adv.*

post·or·bi·tal (pōst-ôr'bĭ-təl) *adj.* Located behind the eye socket: *a postorbital bone.*

post·paid (pōst'pād') *adj.* With the postage paid in advance.

post·pone (pōst-pōn', pōs-pōn') *v.* **-poned, -poning.** To delay until a future time; put off. [L *postpōnere*, to place after.] —**post·pone'ment** *n.* —**post·pon'er** *n.*

post·script (pōst'skrĭpt', pōs'skrĭpt') *n.* A message appended at the end of a letter after the writer's signature. [< L *postscrībere*, to write after.]

pos·tu·late (pŏs'chŏŏ-lāt') *v.* **-lated, -lating. 1.** To assume the truth or reality of with no proof, esp. as a basis of an argument. **2.** To assume as a premise or axiom; take for granted. —*n.* (pŏs'chŏŏ-lĭt, -lāt'). Something assumed without proof as being self-evident or generally accepted. [L *postulāre*, to request, demand.] —**pos'tu·la'tion** *n.*

pos·ture (pŏs'chər) *n.* **1.** A position or attitude of the body. **2.** A characteristic way of bearing one's body; carriage. **3.** The present condition of something: *a nation's military posture.* —*v.* **-tured, -turing.** To assume an exaggerated or unnatural pose. [< L *positūra*, position.] —**pos'tur·al** *adj.*

post·war (pōst'wôr') *adj.* Occurring after a war.

po·sy (pō'zē) *n., pl.* **-sies.** A flower or bunch of flowers. [Var of POESY.]

pot (pŏt) *n.* **1.** A round, fairly deep vessel or container, as for cooking. **2.** The amount such a vessel will hold; potful. **3.** A container in which plants are grown. **4.** *Card Games.* The total amount staked by all the players in one hand. **5.** *Slang.* Marijuana. —**go to pot.** *Infor-*

mal. To deteriorate. —*v.* **potted, potting. 1.** To place or plant in a pot. **2.** To cook in a pot. [< OE *pott* < VL **pottus.*]

pot. potential.

po·ta·ble (pō'tə-bəl) *adj.* Fit to drink. [< L *pōtāre*, to drink.]

pot·ash (pŏt'ăsh') *n.* **1.** Potassium carbonate. **2.** Potassium hydroxide. **3.** Any of several compounds containing potassium, esp. soluble basic compounds.

po·tas·si·um (pə-tăs'ē-əm) *n.* *Symbol* K A soft, silver-white, light, highly reactive metallic element found in, or converted to, a wide variety of salts used in fertilizers and soaps. Atomic number 19, atomic weight 39.102. [< POTASH.]

potassium bromide. A white crystalline solid or powder, KBr, used as a sedative and in photographic emulsions.

potassium carbonate. A transparent, white, granular powder, K_2CO_3, used in making glass, pigments, ceramics, and soaps.

potassium hydroxide. A caustic solid, KOH, used as a bleach and in the manufacture of liquid detergents and soaps.

potassium nitrate. A transparent white crystalline compound, KNO_3, used to pickle meat and in the manufacture of explosives, matches, and fertilizers.

po·ta·to (pə-tā'tō) *n., pl.* **-toes. 1.** The starchy, edible tuber of a widely cultivated plant. **2.** The plant itself. [< Arawakan *batata.*]

potato chip. A thin slice of potato fried in deep fat until crisp and then salted.

pot·bel·ly (pŏt'bĕl'ē) *n., pl.* **-lies.** A protruding abdominal region. —**pot'bel'lied** *adj.*

pot·boil·er (pŏt'boi'lər) *n.* A literary or artistic work of poor quality, produced as quickly as possible for profit.

pot cheese. Cottage cheese.

po·tent (pōt'nt) *adj.* **1.** Possessing great strength; powerful. **2.** Cogent; convincing. **3.** Producing strong effects, as medicines or alcoholic beverages. **4.** Able to perform sexually, as a male. [< L *potēns.*] —**po'ten·cy** *n.*

po·ten·tate (pōt'n-tāt') *n.* One who has the power and position to rule over others; monarch. [< L *potēns*, POTENT.]

po·ten·tial (pə-tĕn'shəl) *adj.* Possible but not yet realized; latent. —*n.* **1.** The inherent ability or capacity for growth, development, or coming into being. **2.** The potential energy possessed by a unit charge by virtue of its location in an electric field; voltage. [< L *potēns*, POTENT.] —**po·ten'ti·al'i·ty** *n.* —**po·ten'tial·ly** *adv.*

potential energy. The energy derived from position, rather than motion, with respect to a field of force.

poth·er (pŏth'ər) *n.* **1.** A commotion; disturbance. **2.** A fuss. [?]

pot·hold·er (pŏt'hōl'dər) *n.* A cloth pad for holding hot cooking utensils.

pot·hole (pŏt'hōl') *n.* A deep hole or pit, esp. in a road.

pot·hook (pŏt'hŏŏk') *n.* A bent or hooked piece of iron for hanging a pot or kettle over a fire or for lifting hot pots or stove lids.

ă pat/ā ate/âr care/ä bar/b bib/ch chew/d deed/ĕ pet/ē be/f fit/g gag/h hat/hw what/
ĭ pit/ī pie/îr pier/j judge/k kick/l lid, fatal/m mum/n no, sudden/ng sing/ŏ pot/ō go/

potion / ppd.

po•tion (pō'shən) *n.* A liquid dose, esp. of medicinal, magic, or poisonous content. [< L *pōtāre,* to drink.]

pot•luck (pŏt'lŭk') *n.* Whatever food happens to be available to a guest.

Po•to•mac (pə-tō'mək). A river of the E U.S.

pot•pie (pŏt'pī') *n.* **1.** A mixture of meat or poultry and vegetables covered with a pastry crust and baked in a deep dish. **2.** A meat or poultry stew with dumplings.

pot•pour•ri (pō'pŏo-rē') *n.* **1.** A combination of various incongruous elements. **2.** A fragrant mixture of dried flower petals and spices. [F *pot pourri,* "rotten pot."]

pot roast. A cut of beef that is browned and then cooked in a covered pot.

pot•sherd (pŏt'shûrd') *n.* A fragment of broken pottery, esp. one found in an archaeological excavation.

pot shot. **1.** A shot aimed to kill, without regard for sporting rules. **2.** A shot fired at an animal or person within easy range.

pot•tage (pŏt'ĭj) *n.* A thick soup or stew of vegetables and sometimes meat. [< OF *potage.*]

pot•ted (pŏt'ĭd) *adj.* **1.** Grown in a pot, as a plant. **2.** *Slang.* Intoxicated.

pot•ter¹ (pŏt'ər) *n.* One who makes earthenware pots, dishes, or other vessels.

pot•ter². *Chiefly Brit.* Variant of **putter.**

pot•ter•y (pŏt'ə-rē) *n., pl.* **-ies.** **1.** Ware, such as vases, pots, etc., shaped from moist clay and hardened by heat. **2.** The craft or occupation of a potter. **3.** The establishment in which this craft is pursued.

pouch (pouch) *n.* **1.** A small flexible receptacle, esp. for carrying loose pipe tobacco. **2.** A mailbag, esp. one for diplomatic dispatches. **3.** A saclike structure, as the external abdominal pocket in which marsupials carry their young. [< OF *pouche.*]

poul•tice (pōl'tĭs) *n.* A moist, soft mass of bread, meal, clay, or other adhesive substance spread on cloth, and applied to warm, moisten, or stimulate an aching or inflamed part of the body. [< ML *pultēs,* pulp, thick paste.]

poul•try (pōl'trē) *n.* Domestic fowls, as chickens, turkeys, or ducks, raised for flesh or eggs. [< OF *poule,* hen, chicken.]

pounce (pouns) *v.* **pounced, pouncing.** To spring or swoop with intent to seize someone or something. —*n.* The act of pouncing. [Prob < OF *poinçon,* pointed tool.]

pound¹ (pound) *n., pl.* **pound** or **pounds.** **1.** The fundamental unit of weight in the U.S. Customary and British Imperial Systems, equal to 16 ounces or 7,000 grains; avoirdupois pound. **2.** An apothecary unit of weight, equal to 0.823 of the avoirdupois pound. **3.** Also **pound sterling. a.** The basic monetary unit of the United Kingdom, originally equal to 20 shillings or 240 pence, but after 1971 equal to 100 new pence. **b.** The basic monetary unit of Gambia, Ireland, Malawi, Malta, Nigeria, Rhodesia, and of various dependent territories of the United Kingdom. **4. a.** The basic monetary unit of Lebanon, Libya, Sudan, Syria, and the United Arab Republic. **b.** The basic monetary

unit of Cyprus. **c.** The basic monetary unit of Israel. [< OE *pund* < L *pondō.*]

pound² (pound) *v.* **1.** To strike heavily; hammer or thump. **2.** To beat to a powder or pulp; pulverize or crush. [< OE *pūnian.*]

pound³ (pound) *n.* A public enclosure for confining stray animals. [< OE *pund-.*]

pound cake. A rich cake containing eggs and originally made with a pound each of flour, butter, and sugar.

pour (pôr, pōr) *v.* **1.** To flow or cause to flow in a stream or flood. **2.** To rain hard or heavily. **3.** To go forth in large numbers. [ME *pouren.*]

pout (pout) *v.* **1.** To protrude the lips in displeasure. **2.** To show displeasure or disappointment; sulk. [ME *pouten.*] —**pout** *n.*

pov•er•ty (pŏv'ər-tē) *n.* **1.** The state or condition of being poor. **2.** Deficiency in amount; scantiness. [< L *pauper,* poor.]

pov•er•ty-strick•en (pŏv'ər-tē-strĭk'ən) *adj.* Poor; destitute.

POW, P.O.W. prisoner of war.

pow•der (pou'dər) *n.* **1.** A substance consisting of ground, pulverized particles. **2.** Any of various preparations in this form, as certain cosmetics and medicines. **3.** Gunpowder or a similar explosive substance. —*v.* **1.** To reduce to powder; pulverize. **2.** To apply powder to. [< L *pulvis (pulver-).*] —**pow'der•er** *n.*

powder puff. A soft pad for applying powder to the skin.

powder room. A lavatory for women.

pow•der•y (pou'də-rē) *adj.* Composed of or similar to powder.

pow•er (pou'ər) *n.* **1.** The ability or capacity to act or perform effectively. **2.** Often **powers.** A specific capacity, faculty, or aptitude: *powers of concentration.* **3.** Strength or force capable of being exerted; might. **4.** The ability or capacity to exercise control; authority. **5.** A nation having influence over other nations. **6.** *Math.* An exponent. **7.** A measure of the magnification of an optical instrument. —*v.* To supply with power, esp. mechanical power. [< OF *povoir.*]

pow•er•boat (pou'ər-bōt') *n.* A motorboat.

pow•er•ful (pou'ər-fəl) *adj.* **1.** Having or capable of exerting power. **2.** Effective or potent, as medicine. —**pow'er•ful•ly** *adv.*

pow•er•house (pou'ər-hous') *n.* **1.** A station for the generating of electricity. **2.** One who possesses great force or energy.

pow•er•less (pou'ər-lĭs) *adj.* **1.** Lacking strength or power; helpless; ineffectual. **2.** Lacking legal or other authority.

power of attorney. A legal instrument authorizing one to act as another's attorney or agent.

pow•wow (pou'wou') *n. Informal.* A conference or gathering. [< Algon.]

pox (pŏks) *n.* **1.** Any disease characterized by purulent skin eruptions, such as chicken pox or smallpox. **2.** Syphilis. **3.** *Archaic.* Misfortune and calamity. [< POCK.]

pp. **1.** pages. **2.** past participle. **3.** *Mus.* pianissimo.

P.P. parcel post.

ppd. **1.** postpaid. **2.** prepaid.

ô paw, for/oi boy/ou out/ŏŏ took/ōō coo/p pop/r run/s sauce/sh shy/t to/th thin/*th* the/
ŭ cut/ûr fur/v van/w wag/y yes/z size/zh vision/ə ago, item, edible, gallop, circus/

P.P.S. additional postscript *(L post postscriptum).*
p.q. previous question.
P.Q. Province of Quebec.
Pr praseodymium.
PR public relations.
pr. 1. pair. 2. present. 3. price. 4. pronoun.
P.R. 1. proportional representation. 2. public relations. 3. Puerto Rico.
prac•ti•ca•ble (prăk′tǐ-kə-bəl) *adj.* 1. Capable of being effected, done, or executed; feasible. 2. Capable of being used for a specified purpose. —**prac′ti•ca•bil′i•ty** *n.*
prac•ti•cal (prăk′tǐ-kəl) *adj.* 1. Acquired through practice or action, rather than theory or speculation. 2. Capable of being used or put into effect. 3. Designed to serve a purpose; useful. 4. Level-headed, efficient, and unspeculative. 5. Being actually so in almost every respect; virtual. [< Gk *prattein, prassein,* to practice.] —**prac′ti•cal′i•ty** (prăk′tǐ-kǎl′ə-tē) *n.*
practical joke. A mischievous trick played on a person.
prac•ti•cal•ly (prăk′tǐk-lē) *adj.* 1. In a way that is practical. 2. In every important respect; virtually. 3. Almost.
prac•tice (prăk′tǐs) *v.* -ticed, -ticing. Also *chiefly Brit.* **prac•tise.** 1. To do or perform (something) habitually or customarily. 2. To exercise or perform (something) repeatedly in order to acquire a skill. 3. To work at (a profession). —*n.* Also *chiefly Brit.* **prac•tise.** 1. A habitual or customary action or way of doing something. 2. **a.** Repeated performance of an activity in order to learn or perfect a skill. **b.** Proficiency gained through repeated exercise: *out of practice.* 3. The act of doing something; performance. 4. The exercise of an occupation or profession. 5. The business of a professional person. 6. **practices.** Questionable or unacceptable actions. [< LL *practicus,* practical.]
prac•ticed (prăk′tǐst) *adj.* Proficient; skilled.
prac•ti•tion•er (prăk-tǐsh′ən-ər) *n.* One who practices an occupation, profession, or technique.
prae•tor (prē′tər) *n.* A high elected Roman magistrate ranking below a consul. [L, "leader," "chief."]
prag•mat•ic (prăg-măt′ǐk) *adj.* 1. Dealing with facts or actual occurrences; practical. 2. Emphasizing the practical outcome of events and historical phenomena. [L *pragmaticus,* skilled in affairs.] —**prag•mat′i•cal•ly** *adv.*
prag•ma•tism (prăg′mə-tiz′əm) *n.* A method used in the conduct of affairs based on practical means and expedients. —**prag′ma•tist** *n.*
Prague (präg). The capital of Czechoslovakia. Pop. 1,021,000.
prai•rie (prâr′ē) *n.* An extensive area of flat or rolling grassland, esp. the plains of C North America. [< L *prātum,* meadow.]
prairie dog. A burrowing rodent of C North America.
prairie schooner. A canvas-covered wagon used by pioneers crossing the North American prairies.

prairie state. Any of the states in the Midwestern and W U.S. prairie regions.
praise (prāz) *n.* 1. An expression of warm approval or admiration. 2. The extolling of a deity, ruler, or hero. —*v.* **praised, praising.** 1. To express warm approval of or admiration for; commend; applaud. 2. To extol or exalt; worship. [< LL *pretiāre,* to prize, praise.]
praise•wor•thy (prāz′wûr′thē) *adj.* Meriting praise; highly commendable.
pram (prăm) *n.* *Chiefly Brit.* A perambulator.
prance (prăns, präns) *v.* **pranced, prancing.** 1. To spring forward on the hind legs, as a horse. 2. To walk or move about in a lively manner; caper; strut. —*n.* An act of prancing; caper. [ME *praunncen.*] —**pranc′er** *n.*
prank (prăngk) *n.* A mischievous trick; practical joke. [?]
prank•ster (prăngk′stər) *n.* One who plays tricks or pranks.
pra•se•o•dym•i•um (prā′zē-ō-dǐm′ē-əm, prā′sē-) *n.* *Symbol* **Pr** A soft, silvery, malleable, ductile rare-earth element, used to color glass yellow and in metallic alloys. Atomic number 59, atomic weight 140.907. [< Gk *prasios,* "leek-green" + DIDYMIUM.]
prate (prāt) *v.* **prated, prating.** To talk idly at great length; chatter. [ME *praten.*]
prat•tle (prăt′l) *v.* -tled, -tling. To talk idly or meaninglessly; babble. —*n.* Childish or meaningless sounds; babble. [Freq of PRATE.]
prawn (prôn) *n.* An edible crustacean related to and resembling the shrimps. [ME *prayne.*]
pray (prā) *v.* 1. To utter or address a prayer to a deity or other object of worship. 2. To ask (someone) imploringly; beseech: *Pray, be careful.* [< L *precārī,* to entreat.]
prayer (prâr) *n.* 1. A reverent petition made to a deity or other object of worship. 2. The act of making such a petition. 3. A specially worded or spontaneously expressed appeal to God. 4. Often **prayers.** A religious service in which praying predominates. [< L *precārī,* to entreat, PRAY.]
prayer•ful (prâr′fəl) *adj.* Inclined to pray frequently; devout. —**prayer′ful•ly** *adv.*
pre—. *comb. form.* 1. An earlier or prior time. 2. Preliminary or preparatory work or activity. 3. A location in front of or anterior to. [< L *prae,* before, in front.]
preach (prēch) *v.* 1. To deliver (a sermon). 2. To advocate earnestly. 3. To give moral advice, esp. in a tiresome manner. [< L *praedicāre,* to proclaim.] —**preach′er** *n.*
pre•am•ble (prē′ăm′bəl) *n.* An introduction to a formal document, explaining its purpose. [< LL *praeambulus,* walking in front.]
pre•ar•range (prē′ə-rānj′) *v.* To arrange in advance. —**pre′ar•range′ment** *n.*
Pre•cam•bri•an (prē-kăm′brē-ən) *adj.* Of or belonging to the oldest and largest division of geologic time, preceding the Cambrian and characterized by the appearance of primitive forms of life. —*n.* The Precambrian era.
pre•car•i•ous (prǐ-kâr′ē-əs) *adj.* 1. Dangerously lacking in stability. 2. Subject to chance or unknown conditions. [< L *precārius,* dependent on prayer.] —**pre•car′i•ous•ly** *adv.*

ă pat/ā ate/âr care/ä bar/b bib/ch chew/d deed/ĕ pet/ē be/f fit/g gag/h hat/hw what/
ĭ pit/ī pie/îr pier/j judge/k kick/l lid, fatal/m mum/n no, sudden/ng sing/ŏ pot/ō go/

pre·cau·tion (prĭ-kô'shən) *n.* An action taken in advance to protect against possible failure or danger. **—pre·cau'tion·ar'y** (-shə-nĕr'ē) *adj.*

pre·cede (prĭ-sēd') *v.* **-ceded, -ceding.** To come before in time, place, or rank. [< L *praecēdere.*] **—pre·ced'a·ble** *adj.*

pre·ced·ence (prĭ-sēd'əns, prĕs'ə-dəns) *n.* The act, state, or right of preceding; priority.

prec·e·dent (prĕs'ə-dənt) *n.* **1.** An act or instance that can be used as an example in dealing with subsequent similar cases. **2.** Convention or custom. **—adj.** (prĭ-sēd'ənt). Preceding; prior. [< L *praecēdere,* **PRECEDE.**]

pre·ced·ing (prĭ-sē'dĭng) *adj.* Existing or coming before; previous.

pre·cept (prē'sĕpt') *n.* A rule or principle imposing a standard of action or conduct. [< L *praecipere* (pp *praeceptus*), to take beforehand, warn, teach.]

pre·cep·tor (prĭ-sĕp'tər, prē'sĕp'tər) *n.* A teacher; instructor.

pre·cinct (prē'sĭngkt) *n.* **1.** A subdivision of a city patrolled by a unit of the police force. **2.** An election district. **3.** Often **precincts.** A place or enclosure marked off by definite limits. **4. precincts.** Neighborhood; environs. [< ML *praecinctum,* "enclosure."]

‣**pre·cious** (prĕsh'əs) *adj.* **1.** Of high cost or worth; valuable. **2.** Dear; beloved. **3.** Affectedly dainty or overrefined. [< L *pretium,* price.] **—pre'cious·ly** *adv.*

prec·i·pice (prĕs'ə-pĭs) *n.* An extremely steep or overhanging mass of rock, as the face of a cliff. [< L *praecipitāre,* to throw headlong.]

pre·cip·i·tate (prĭ-sĭp'ə-tāt') *v.* **-tated, -tating. 1.** To hurl downward. **2.** To cause to happen before anticipated or required. **3.** *Meteorol.* To condense and fall. **4.** To separate from a solution as a precipitate. **—adj.** (prĭ-sĭp'ə-tĭt, -tāt'). **1.** Speeding headlong; moving rapidly and heedlessly. **2.** Acting with excessive haste or impulse. **—n.** (prĭ-sĭp'ə-tāt', -tĭt). A solid separated from a solution. [L *praecipitāre,* to throw headlong.] **—pre·cip'i·tate·ly** *adv.*

pre·cip·i·ta·tion (prĭ-sĭp'ə-tā'shən) *n.* **1.** Abrupt or impulsive haste. **2.** Any form of rain or snow. **3.** The production of a precipitate.

pre·cip·i·tous (prĭ-sĭp'ə-təs) *adj.* **1.** Like a precipice; extremely steep. **2.** Precipitate. **—pre·cip'i·tous·ly** *adv.* **—pre·cip'i·tous·ness** *n.*

pré·cis (prā'sē, prā-sē') *n., pl.* **-cis** (-sēz, -sēz'). A concise summary; an abstract. [F, "precise."]

pre·cise (prĭ-sīs') *adj.* **1.** Clearly expressed or delineated; definite. **2.** Exactly corresponding to what is indicated; correct. **3.** Strictly distinguished from others; very: *at that precise moment.* **4.** Conforming strictly to rule. [< L *praecisus,* shortened.] **—pre·cise'ly** *adv.* **—pre·cise'ness** *n.*

pre·ci·sion (prĭ-sĭzh'ən) *n.* The state or quality of being precise. **—adj.** Used or intended for precise measurement: *a precision tool.*

pre·clude (prĭ-klōōd') *v.* **-cluded, -cluding. 1.** To make impossible; prevent. **2.** To exclude; debar. [L *praeclūdere.*]

pre·co·cious (prĭ-kō'shəs) *adj.* Early in development or maturity, esp. in mental aptitude. [< L *praecox,* "ripening before its time."] **—pre·co'cious·ness, pre·coc'i·ty** (-kŏs'ə-tē) *n.*

pre·cog·ni·tion (prē'kŏg-nĭsh'ən) *n.* Knowledge of something in advance of its occurrence. [< L *praecognōscere,* to know before.]

pre·con·ceive (prē'kən-sēv') *v.* To form an opinion of (something) beforehand. **—pre'·con·cep'tion** (-sĕp'shən) *n.*

pre·con·di·tion (prē'kən-dĭsh'ən) *n.* A prerequisite. **—v.** To condition, train, or accustom in advance.

pre·cur·sor (prĭ-kûr'sər, prē'kûr'sər) *n.* **1.** A forerunner; harbinger. **2.** One that precedes another; predecessor. [< L *praecurrere,* to run before.]

pred. predicate.

pre·da·cious, pre·da·ceous (prĭ-dā'shəs) *adj.* Living by seizing prey; predatory. [< L *praedārī,* to plunder.]

pre·date (prē-dāt') *v.* **1.** To mark with an earlier date than the actual one. **2.** To precede in time; antedate.

pred·a·tor (prĕd'ə-tər, -tôr') *n.* **1.** An animal that preys upon others. **2.** One that preys, destroys, or devours.

pred·a·to·ry (prĕd'ə-tôr'ē, -tōr'ē) *adj.* **1.** Characterized by plundering or pillaging. **2.** Preying on other animals. [< L *praedārī,* to plunder.] **—pred'a·to'ri·ness** *n.*

pre·de·cease (prē'dĭ-sēs') *v.* To die before (some other person).

pred·e·ces·sor (prĕd'ə-sĕs'ər, prē'də-) *n.* One who precedes another in time, esp. in an office or position. [< LL *praedecessor.*]

pre·des·ti·na·tion (prē-dĕs'tə-nā'shən) *n.* **1.** The act whereby God is believed to have foreordained all things. **2.** The doctrine asserting this.

pre·des·tine (prē-dĕs'tĭn) *v.* To decide or decree in advance; foreordain.

pre·de·ter·mine (prē'dĭ-tûr'mĭn) *v.* To determine or decide in advance. **—pre'de·ter'mi·na'tion** *n.*

pre·dic·a·ment (prĭ-dĭk'ə-mənt) *n.* A troublesome, embarrassing, or ludicrous situation. [< LL *praedicāmentum,* something predicated, condition.]

pred·i·cate (prĕd'ə-kāt') *v.* **-cated, -cating. 1.** To base or establish (a concept, statement, or action): *predicate an argument on the facts.* **2.** To affirm as an attribute or quality of something. **—n.** (prĕd'ĭ-kĭt). The part of a sentence or clause that expresses something about the subject. **—adj.** (prĕd'ĭ-kĭt). Of or belonging to the predicate of a sentence or clause. [LL *praedicāre,* to proclaim.] **—pred'i·ca'tion** (-ĭ-kā'shən) *n.* **—pred'i·ca'tive** *adj.*

predicate adjective. *Gram.* An adjective that follows certain verbs and describes the subject of the verb. In the sentence *The man is good,* the predicate adjective is *good.*

predicate nominative. *Gram.* A noun, or a pronoun in the subject form, that follows certain verbs, and is identified with the subject of the verb. In the sentence *It is I,* the predicate nominative is *I.*

pre·dict (prĭ-dĭkt') *v.* To foretell; prophesy. [L

praedīcere.] —pre·dict'a·ble adj. —pre·dic'tion (-dĭk'shən) n. —pre·dic'tor n.

pre·di·lec·tion (prĕd'ə-lĕk'shən, prē'də-) n. A preference or partiality. [< ML praedīligere, to prefer.]

pre·dis·pose (prē'dĭs-pōz') v. To make (someone) inclined to something in advance; put into a certain mood. —pre'dis·po·si'tion n.

pre·dom·i·nant (prĭ-dŏm'ə-nənt) adj. 1. Having greatest importance or authority. 2. Most common or conspicuous; prevalent. —pre·dom'i·nance n. —pre·dom'i·nant·ly adv.

pre·dom·i·nate (prĭ-dŏm'ə-nāt') v. 1. To be most numerous, important, or outstanding. 2. To have authority, power, or controlling influence; prevail. —pre·dom'i·nate·ly (-nĭt-lē) adv. —pre·dom'i·na'tion n.

pre·em·i·nent (prē-ĕm'ə-nənt) adj. Also pre·em·i·nent. Superior to all others; outstanding. —pre-em'i·nence n. —pre-em'i·nent·ly adv.

pre-empt (prē-ĕmpt') v. Also pre·empt. 1. To gain possession of by prior right, esp. to settle on (public land) so as to obtain the right to buy before others. 2. To appropriate, seize, or act for oneself before others. [< ML praeemere, to buy beforehand.] —pre-emp'tion n. —pre-emp'tive adj. —pre-emp'tive·ly adv.

preen (prēn) v. 1. To smooth or clean (feathers) with the beak. 2. To adorn (oneself) carefully; primp. [Poss < OF poroindre, to anoint before.] —preen'er n.

pref. 1. preface. 2. preference; preferred. 3. prefix.

pre·fab·ri·cate (prē-făb'rĭ-kāt') v. To construct in standard sections that can be easily shipped and assembled.

pref·ace (prĕf'ĭs) n. An introduction to a book, speech, etc. —v. -aced, -acing. To introduce by or provide with a preface. [< L praefārī, to say beforehand.] —pref'ac·er n. —pref'a·to·ry (-ə-tôr'ē, -tōr'ē) adj.

pre·fect (prē'fĕkt') n. Also prae·fect. A high administrative official. [< L praefectus, overseer, chief.] —pre'fec'ture (-fĕk'chər) n.

pre·fer (prĭ-fûr') v. -ferred, -ferring. 1. To value more highly; like better. 2. To file before a court: prefer charges. [< L praeferre, to hold or set before.] —pre·fer'rer n.

pref·er·a·ble (prĕf'ər-ə-bəl) adj. More desirable; preferred. —pref'er·a·bly adv.

pref·er·ence (prĕf'ər-əns) n. 1. The selecting of or right to select someone or something over another or others. 2. That which is preferred. 3. An advantage given to one over others. —pref'er·en'tial (-ə-rĕn'shəl) adj.

pre·fix (prē-fĭks') n. Gram. An affix put before a word, changing or modifying the meaning. —v. (prē-fĭks'). 1. (also prē'fĭks'). To put or fix before. 2. To add as a prefix. —pre'fix·al adj. —pre'fix'al·ly adv.

preg·nant (prĕg'nənt) adj. 1. Carrying a developing fetus within the uterus. 2. Creative; inventive. 3. Fraught with significance or implication. 4. Filled; charged; fraught. [< L̄ praegnāns, praegnās.] —preg'nan·cy n.

pre·hen·sile (prĭ-hĕn'sĭl) adj. Adapted for seizing or holding, esp. by wrapping around: a prehensile tail. [< L prehendere, to seize.]

pre·his·tor·ic (prē'hĭs-tôr'ĭk, -tŏr'ĭk) adj. Of the era before recorded history.

pre·judge (prē-jŭj') v. To judge beforehand without possessing adequate evidence.

prej·u·dice (prĕj'ə-dĭs) n. 1. A preconceived preference; bias. 2. Irrational hatred of a particular group, race, or religion. 3. Detriment or injury. —v. -diced, -dicing. 1. To cause to judge prematurely; bias. 2. To affect injuriously or detrimentally. [< L praejūdicium.] —prej'u·di'cial (-dĭsh'əl) adj.

prel·ate (prĕl'ĭt) n. A high-ranking clergyman, as a bishop. [< ML praelātus.] —prel'a·cy (-ə-sē) n.

pre·lim·i·nar·y (prĭ-lĭm'ə-nĕr'ē) adj. Prior to the main action or business; introductory; prefatory. —n., pl. -ies. Something antecedent or preparatory. [< ML praelīmināris.]

pre·lit·er·ate (prē-lĭt'ər-ĭt) adj. Of or pertaining to any culture not having a written language.

prel·ude (prĕl'yōōd', prē'lōōd') n. 1. A preliminary part; preface. 2. A piece or movement serving as an introduction to a musical composition. [< L praelūdere, to play beforehand.]

prem. premium.

pre·ma·ture (prē'mə-chŏor', -t/y/ŏor') adj. Occurring, born, or done prior to the customary or correct time; too early. —pre'ma·ture'ly adv. —pre'ma·ture'ness n.

pre·med·i·cal (prē'mĕd'ĭ-kəl) adj. Of or involving preparation for the study of medicine.

pre·med·i·tate (prē-mĕd'ə-tāt') v. To plan, arrange, or plot in advance. —pre·med'i·ta'tion n. —pre·med'i·ta'tor n.

pre·mier (prē'mē-ər, prĭ-mîr') adj. First in status or importance; chief. —n. (prĭ-mîr'). A prime minister. [< L primus, first.]

pre·mière (prĭ-mîr') n. The first public presentation of a movie, play, etc. [< F premier, first, chief, premier.]

prem·ise (prĕm'ĭs) n. 1. A proposition upon which an argument is based or from which a conclusion is drawn. 2. premises. Land and the buildings on it. [< ML praemissa (prōpositiō), "(proposition) put before."]

pre·mi·um (prē'mē-əm) n. 1. A prize awarded, esp. as an inducement to buy. 2. A sum of money paid in addition to a regular amount. 3. The amount paid, often in installments, for an insurance policy. 4. An unusual or high value: put a premium on hard work. [L praemium, "that which is obtained before others."]

pre·mo·lar (prē-mō'lər) n. Any of eight bicuspid teeth located in pairs between the canines and molars.

pre·mo·ni·tion (prē'mə-nĭsh'ən, prĕm'ə-) n. 1. A warning in advance; forewarning. 2. A presentiment of the future; foreboding. [< L praemonēre, to warn beforehand.] —pre·mon'i·to'ry (-mŏn'ə-tôr'ē, -tōr'ē) adj.

pre·na·tal (prē-nāt'l) adj. Existing or taking place prior to birth.

pre·oc·cu·py (prē-ŏk'yə-pī') v. 1. To occupy the mind of completely; engross. 2. To occupy in advance or before another. —pre·oc'cu·pa'tion (-pā'shən) n.

pre•or•dain (prē′ôr-dān′) v. To decree or ordain in advance; foreordain.

prep•a•ra•tion (prĕp′ə-rā′shən) n. 1. The act or process of preparing. 2. Readiness. 3. Often **preparations.** Preliminary measures. 4. A substance, as a medicine, prepared for a particular purpose.

pre•par•a•to•ry (prĭ-păr′ə-tôr′ē, -tōr′ē, prĭ-pâr′-) adj. Serving to make ready or prepare; introductory.

pre•pare (prĭ-pâr′) v. -pared, -paring. 1. To make or get ready. 2. To put together or make by combining various elements or ingredients. 3. To fit out; equip. [< L praeparāre, to prepare in advance.] —**pre•par′er** n.

pre•par•ed•ness (prĭ-pâr′ĭd-nĭs) n. The state of being prepared, esp. military readiness for war.

pre•pay (prē-pā′) v. To pay or pay for beforehand. —**pre•pay′ment** n.

pre•pon•der•ate (prĭ-pŏn′də-rāt′) v. -ated, -ating. To be greater in power, force, quantity, importance, etc.; predominate. [L praeponderāre, to exceed in weight.] —**pre•pon′der•ance** (-dər-əns) n. —**pre•pon′der•ant** adj.

prep•o•si•tion (prĕp′ə-zĭsh′ən) n. A word that indicates the relation of a substantive to a verb, an adjective, or another substantive. [< L praepōnere (pp praepositus), to place in front.] —**prep′o•si′tion•al** adj.

pre•pos•sess (prē′pə-zĕs′) v. 1. To influence beforehand; prejudice; bias. 2. To impress favorably in advance.

pre•pos•sess•ing (prē′pə-zĕs′ĭng) adj. Impressing favorably; pleasing.

pre•pos•ter•ous (prĭ-pŏs′tər-əs) adj. Contrary to nature, reason, or common sense; absurd. [L praeposterus, "inverted," perverted, absurd.]

pre•puce (prē′pyoōs′) n. 1. The loose fold of skin that covers the glans of the penis. 2. A similar structure covering the glans of the clitoris. [< L praepūtium.]

pre•req•ui•site (prē-rĕk′wə-zĭt) adj. Required as a prior condition to something. —n. That which is prerequisite.

pre•rog•a•tive (prĭ-rŏg′ə-tĭv) n. An exclusive right or privilege. [< L praerogātivus, asked to vote first.]

pres. 1. present (time). 2. president.

Pres. President.

pres•age (prĕs′ĭj) n. 1. An omen; portent. 2. A presentiment; foreboding. —v. **pre•sage** (prĭ-sāj′) -saged, -saging. 1. To indicate or warn of in advance; portend. 2. To foretell or predict. [< L praesāgīre, to perceive beforehand.]

pres•by•ter (prĕz′bə-tər, prĕs′-) n. Eccles. 1. In various hierarchical churches, a priest. 2. In the Presbyterian Church, an elder. [< Gk presbuteros, a priest, "elder."]

Pres•by•te•ri•an (prĕz′bə-tîr′ē-ən, prĕs′-) adj. Of or pertaining to a Protestant church governed by presbyters and traditionally Calvinist in doctrine. —n. A member or adherent of a Presbyterian Church. —**Pres′by•te′ri•an•ism′** n.

pre•sci•ence (prē′shē-əns, prĕsh′ē-) n. Knowledge of actions or events before they occur. —**pre′sci•ent** adj.

pre•scribe (prĭ-skrīb′) v. -scribed, -scribing. 1. To set down as a rule or guide. 2. To order or recommend a remedy or treatment. [< L praescribere, to write at the beginning, prescribe.] —**pre•scrip′tive** (-skrĭp′tĭv) adj.

pre•scrip•tion (prĭ-skrĭp′shən) n. 1. The act of prescribing. 2. a. A written instruction by a physician for the preparation and administration of a medicine. b. A prescribed medicine.

pres•ence (prĕz′əns) n. 1. The state or fact of being present. 2. Immediate proximity: in the presence of ladies. 3. A manner of carrying oneself; bearing.

pres•ent[1] (prĕz′ənt) n. 1. A moment or period in time intermediate between past and future; now. 2. The present tense. —adj. 1. Being or occurring at the present time. 2. Being at hand. 3. Denoting a verb tense or form that expresses current time. [< L praeesse, to be before one, be present.]

pre•sent[2] (prĭ-zĕnt′) v. 1. To introduce. 2. To bring before the public: present a play. 3. a. To make a gift or award of. b. To make a gift to; bestow formally. 4. To offer formally: present one's credentials. 5. To offer for consideration. 6. To salute with or aim (a weapon). —n. **pres•ent** (prĕz′ənt). Something presented; a gift. [< L praesēns, present, being at hand.]

pre•sent•a•ble (prĭ-zĕn′tə-bəl) adj. 1. Capable of being given, displayed, or offered. 2. Fit for introduction to others. —**pre•sent′a•bly** adv.

pres•en•ta•tion (prĕz′ən-tā′shən, prē′zən-) n. 1. The act of presenting. 2. A performance, as of a drama.

pres•ent-day (prĕz′ənt-dā′) adj. Current.

pre•sen•ti•ment (prĭ-zĕn′tə-mənt) n. A sense of something about to occur; premonition. [< L praesentīre, to perceive beforehand.]

pres•ent•ly (prĕz′ənt-lē) adv. 1. In a short time; soon; directly. 2. At this time or period; now.

pre•serv•a•tive (prĭ-zûr′və-tĭv) adj. Tending to preserve. —n. Something used to preserve, esp. a chemical used in foods to inhibit spoilage.

pre•serve (prĭ-zûrv′) v. -served, -serving. 1. To protect from injury, peril, or other adversity. 2. To keep or maintain intact. 3. To treat or prepare so as to prevent decay. —n. 1. Often **preserves.** Fruit cooked with sugar to protect against decay. 2. An area maintained for the protection of wildlife or natural resources. [< ML praeservāre, "to guard beforehand."] —**pres′er•va′tion** (prĕz′ər-vā′shən) n.

pre•side (prĭ-zīd′) v. -sided, -siding. 1. To act as chairman or president. 2. To possess or exercise authority or control. [< L praesidēre, "to sit in front of," superintend.]

pres•i•dent (prĕz′ə-dənt, -dĕnt′) n. 1. One chosen to preside over an assembly or meeting. 2. Often **President.** The chief executive of a republic, esp. of the U.S. 3. The chief officer of a branch of government, a corporation, a university, etc. [< L praesidēre, PRESIDE.] —**pres′i•den•cy** n. —**pres′i•den′tial** adj.

press (prĕs) v. 1. To exert steady weight or force (against). 2. To squeeze the juice from. 3. To iron (clothing). 4. To clasp or embrace closely. 5. To entreat insistently; urge on;

spur. **6.** To distress by constraining circumstances: *pressed for time.* **7.** To put forward
importunately or insistently. **8.** To advance
eagerly; push forward; crowd. —*n.* **1.** Any of
various machines or devices that apply pressure. **2.** A **printing press. 3.** A printing or publishing establishment. **4.** Printed matter as a
whole, esp. newspapers and periodicals. **5.** A
crowding or pushing forward; crush. **6.** The
pressure or urgency of business or affairs.
7. The set of proper creases in a garment. [<
L *premere* (pp *pressus*), to press.]
press conference. An interview held for
newsmen by a political figure or celebrity.
press•ing (prĕs′ĭng) *adj.* Demanding immediate attention; urgent. —**press′ing•ly** *adv.*
press•man (prĕs′mən, -măn′) *n.* **1.** A printing
press operator. **2.** *Brit.* A newspaperman.
pres•sure (prĕsh′ər) *n.* **1. a.** The act of pressing. **b.** The condition of being pressed. **2.** The
application of continuous force. **3.** Force applied over a surface measured as force per unit
of area. **4.** A compelling influence. **5.** Urgent
claim or demand: *the pressure of business.* —*v.*
-sured, -suring. To force, as by overpowering
influence or persuasion.
pres•sur•ize (prĕsh′ə-rīz′) *v.* **-ized, -izing. 1.** To
maintain normal air pressure in (an aircraft,
submarine, etc.). **2.** To put under a greater
than normal pressure. —**pres′sur•i•za′tion** *n.*
pres•ti•dig•i•ta•tion (prĕs′tə-dĭj′ĭ-tā′shən) *n.*
Sleight of hand. [< F *prestidigitateur*, juggler.]
—**pres′ti•dig′i•ta•tor** *n.*
pres•tige (prĕ-stēzh′, -stēj′) *n.* Prominence or
influential status achieved through success,
renown, or wealth. [< L *praestigiae*, "juggler's
tricks," illusions.] —**pres•tig′ious** (prĕ-stĭj′əs,
-stē′jəs) *adj.* —**pres•tig′ious•ly** *adv.*
pres•to (prĕs′tō) *adv.* **1.** *Mus.* In rapid tempo.
2. Suddenly; at once. [< L *praestus*, ready.]
—**pres′to** *adj.*
pre•sume (prĭ-zōōm′) *v.* **-sumed, -suming. 1.** To
assume; take for granted. **2.** To venture; dare.
3. To take unwarranted advantage of something. [< L *praesūmere*, "to take in advance,"
presuppose.] —**pre•sum′a•ble** *adj.* —**pre•sum′-
ab•ly** *adv.*
pre•sump•tion (prĭ-zŭmp′shən) *n.* **1.** Behavior
or language that is boldly arrogant or offensive; effrontery. **2.** Acceptance or belief based
on reasonable evidence; an assumption or
supposition. [< L *praesūmere*, PRESUME.]
—**pre•sump′tive** *adj.*
pre•sump•tu•ous (prĭ-zŭmp′chōō-əs) *adj.* Excessively forward or confident; arrogant.
—**pre•sump′tu•ous•ly** *adv.* —**pre•sump′tu•ous•
ness** *n.*
pre•sup•pose (prē′sə-pōz′) *v.* **1.** To assume or
suppose in advance. **2.** To require or involve
necessarily as an antecedent condition.
—**pre′sup•po•si′tion** (-sŭp-ə-zĭsh′ən) *n.*
pre•tend (prĭ-tĕnd′) *v.* **1.** To make believe. **2.**
To claim or allege insincerely or falsely; profess. **3.** To take upon oneself; venture. **4.** To
put forward a claim. [< L *praetendere*, "to
stretch forth," hold out as a pretext.] —**pre•
tend′ed•ly** *adv.*
pre•tend•er (prĭ-tĕn′dər) *n.* **1.** One who pre-

tends; a hypocrite or dissembler. **2.** A claimant to a throne.
pre•tense (prē′tĕns′, prĭ-tĕns′) *n.* Also *chiefly
Brit.* **pre•tence. 1.** A false appearance or action
intended to deceive. **2.** A false reason or excuse; pretext. **3.** A claim asserted without
foundation.
pre•ten•sion (prĭ-tĕn′shən) *n.* **1.** A claim to
something. **2.** Pretentiousness.
pre•ten•tious (prĭ-tĕn′shəs) *adj.* **1.** Claiming or
demanding a position of distinction or merit.
2. Making an extravagant outer show; ostentatious. —**pre•ten′tious•ness** *n.*
pret•er•it, pret•er•ite (prĕt′ər-ĭt) *adj.* Denoting the verb tense that expresses a past or
completed action. —*n.* **1.** The past tense. **2.** A
verb in this tense. [< L *praeteritus*, gone by,
past.]
pre•ter•nat•u•ral (prē′tər-năch′ər-əl) *adj.* **1.**
Transcending the normal course of nature;
abnormal; exceptional. **2.** Supernatural. [< L
praeter nātūram, beyond nature.]
pre•test (prē′tĕst′) *n.* **1.** A test given in advance
of an action, use, or experiment. **2.** The condition existing before an experiment. —*v.*
(prē-tĕst′). To subject to a pretest.
pre•text (prē′tĕkst′) *n.* An ostensible or professed purpose; pretense; excuse. [L *praetex-
tus*, outward show, pretense.]
Pre•to•ri•a (prĭ-tôr′ē-ə, -tōr′ē-ə). The administrative capital of the Republic of South Africa.
Pop. 423,000.
pret•ti•fy (prĭt′ĭ-fī′) *v.* **-fied, -fying.** To make
pretty. —**pret′ti•fi′er** *n.*
pret•ty (prĭt′ē) *adj.* **-tier, -tiest. 1.** Pleasing or
attractive. **2.** Excellent; fine; good. Often used
ironically: *a pretty mess.* **3.** *Informal.* Considerable in size or extent: *a pretty penny.* —*adv.*
To a fair degree; somewhat; moderately: *a
pretty good student.* —*v.* **-tied, -tying.** *Informal.*
To make pretty. [< OE *prætt*, trick, wile <
Gmc *pratt-.*] —**pret′ti•ly** *adv.*
pret•zel (prĕt′səl) *n.* A glazed biscuit, salted on
the outside, usually baked in the form of a
loose knot or stick. [< OHG *brezitella.*]
pre•vail (prĭ-vāl′) *v.* **1.** To triumph; be victorious. **2.** To prove superior in strength or
influence. **3.** To be most common or frequent;
be predominant. **4.** To be in force, use, or
effect; be current. **5.** To persuade. [< L *praevalēre*, to be more powerful.]
pre•vail•ing (prĭ-vā′lĭng) *adj.* **1.** Most frequent
or common; predominant. **2.** Generally current; widespread; prevalent.
prev•a•lent (prĕv′ə-lənt) *adj.* Widely or commonly occurring or existing; generally accepted or practiced. [< L *praevalēre*, to PREVAIL.]
—**prev′a•lence** *n.* —**prev′a•lent•ly** *adv.*
pre•var•i•cate (prĭ-văr′ə-kāt′) *v.* **-cated, -cating.**
To stray from or evade the truth; equivocate.
[L *praevāricārī*, to walk crookedly, deviate.]
—**pre•var′i•ca′tion** *n.* —**pre•var′i•ca′tor** *n.*
pre•vent (prĭ-vĕnt′) *v.* **1.** To keep from happening; avert; thwart. **2.** To keep (someone)
from doing something; hinder; impede: *He
kept him from his work.* [< L *praevenīre*, to
come before, anticipate.] —**pre•vent′a•ble, pre•
vent′i•ble** *adj.* —**pre•ven′tion** *n.*

ă pat/ā ate/âr care/ä bar/b bib/ch chew/d deed/ĕ pet/ē be/f fit/g gag/h hat/hw what/
ĭ pit/ī pie/îr pier/j judge/k kick/l lid, fatal/m mum/n no, sudden/ng sing/ŏ pot/ō go/

pre·ven·tive (prĭ-věn′tĭv) *adj.* Also **pre·ven·ta·tive** (-tə-tĭv). 1. Designed or used to prevent or ward off; precautionary. 2. Preventing illness or disease; prophylactic. —**pre·ven′tive** *n.*

pre·view (prē′vyōō′) *n.* Also **pre·vue.** 1. An advance showing of a motion picture or play. 2. An advance showing of several scenes advertising a forthcoming motion picture.

pre·vi·ous (prē′vē-əs) *adj.* Existing or occurring prior to something else in time or order; antecedent. —**previous to.** Prior to; before. [L *praevius*, going before, leading the way.] —**pre′vi·ous·ly** *adv.*

pre·war (prē′wôr′) *adj.* Existing or occurring before a war.

prey (prā) *n.* 1. An animal hunted or caught for food. 2. A victim. 3. The act of seizing animals to devour: *bird of prey.* —*v.* 1. To feed by seizing as prey. 2. To victimize. 3. To plunder or pillage. 4. To exert a wearing effect: *prey upon one's mind.* [L < *praeda* "booty," prey.]

price (prīs) *n.* 1. The sum of money or goods asked or given for something. 2. The cost at which something is obtained. 3. Value or worth. —*v.* **priced, pricing.** 1. To fix or establish a price for. 2. To find out the price of. [< L *pretium*, price, value, reward.]

price·less (prīs′lĭs) *adj.* Of inestimable worth; invaluable. —**price′less·ly** *adv.*

prick (prĭk) *n.* 1. a. An instance of pricking. b. The sensation of being pricked. 2. A small mark or puncture made by a pointed object. 3. Something that pricks, as a thorn or bee sting. —*v.* 1. To puncture lightly. 2. To sting. 3. To incite; impel. 4. To outline by means of small punctures. 5. *Archaic.* To ride at a gallop: *"A gentle knight was pricking on the plain"* (Spenser). —**prick up one's ears.** To listen with attentive interest. [< OE *prica*, pricked mark, puncture < Gmc *prikk-.*]

prick·le (prĭk′əl) *n.* 1. A small, sharp spine or thorn. 2. A slight stinging sensation. —*v.* **-led, -ling.** 1. To prick as with a thorn. 2. To tingle. —**prick′li·ness** *n.* —**prick′ly** *adj.*

prickly heat. A skin disease caused by inflammation of the sweat glands.

prickly pear. 1. A cactus bearing egg-shaped, often edible fruit. 2. The fruit of such a cactus.

pride (prīd) *n.* 1. Self-respect. 2. Elation or satisfaction over one's achievements or possessions. 3. a. A cause or source of pride. b. The prime; flower: *the flush and pride of youth.* 4. Conceit, arrogance, or disdain. 5. A group of lions. —*v.* **prided, priding.** To esteem (oneself) for: *I pride myself on my garden.* [< OE *prŭt, prŭd*, PROUD.] —**pride′ful** *adj.*

prie·dieu (prē-dyœ′) *n., pl.* **-dieus.** A low desk with space for a book above and with a foot piece below for kneeling in prayer. [F *prie-Dieu*, "pray God."]

pri·er (prī′ər) *n.* Also **pry·er.** One who pries.

priest (prēst) *n.* In the Roman Catholic, Eastern Orthodox, Anglican, Armenian, and separated Catholic hierarchies, a member of the second grade of clergy ranking below a bishop but above a deacon and having authority to pronounce absolution and administer all sac-

raments save that of ordination. [< Gk *presbuteros*, "elder."] —**priest′ess** *fem.n.* —**priest′hood′** *n.* —**priest′li·ness** *n.* —**priest′ly** *adj.*

prig (prĭg) *n.* A person regarded as overprecise and smugly narrow-minded. [?] —**prig′gish** *adj.* —**prig′gish·ly** *adv.*

prim (prĭm) *adj.* **primmer, primmest.** Precise, neat, or proper to the point of affectation. [?]

prim. 1. primary. 2. primitive.

pri·ma·cy (prī′mə-sē) *n., pl.* **-cies.** 1. The state of being first or foremost. 2. The office or rank of an ecclesiastical primate.

pri·ma don·na (prē′mə dŏn′ə, prĭm′ə). 1. The leading female soloist in an opera company. 2. A temperamental or conceited performer. [It, "first lady."]

pri·ma fa·cie (prī′mə fā′shē, fā′shə). At first sight. [L *prīmā faciē*, "on first appearance."] —**pri′ma-fa′cie** *adj.*

pri·mal (prī′məl) *adj.* 1. Original; archetypal. 2. Fundamental; primary. [< L *primus*, first.]

pri·ma·ri·ly (prī-měr′ə-lē, prī′měr′ə-lē) *adv.* 1. At first; originally. 2. Chiefly; principally.

pri·ma·ry (prī′měr′ē, -mə-rē) *adj.* 1. Occurring first in time, sequence, or importance. 2. Primal. 3. Fundamental. 4. Immediate; direct. 5. Of or being a fundamental or generative part. —*n., pl.* **-ries.** 1. Something that is first in time, order, or importance. 2. A preliminary election in which the registered voters of a political party nominate candidates for office. [< L *primus*, first.]

primary school. A school usually comprising the first three or four grades of elementary school and sometimes kindergarten.

pri·mate (prī′māt) *n.* 1. One of the group of mammals that includes the monkeys, apes, and man. 2. A bishop of highest rank in a province or country. [< L *primus*, first.] —**pri·ma′tial** (prī-mā′shəl) *adj.*

prime (prīm) *adj.* 1. First in quality, degree, or sequence. 2. Designating a **prime number.** —*n.* 1. The earliest stage of something. 2. Springtime. 3. The period of ideal or peak condition. 4. A mark (′) written above and to the right of a letter in order to distinguish it from the same letter already in use or to designate a related quantity or thing, as feet, minutes of angle, or minutes of time. 5. *Math.* A **prime number.** —*v.* **primed, priming.** 1. To make ready; prepare. 2. To load for firing. 3. To prepare for operation, as by pouring water into a pump. [< L *primus*, first.]

prime meridian. The zero meridian from which longitude E and W is measured and which passes through Greenwich, England.

prime minister. 1. A chief minister appointed by a ruler. 2. The chief executive in various kinds of parliamentary democracy.

prime number. A number that has itself and unity as its only factors.

prim·er¹ (prĭm′ər) *n.* 1. An elementary textbook. 2. A basic handbook of any subject. [< L *prīmārius*, basic, primary.]

prim·er² (prī′mər) *n.* 1. A device for detonating an explosive charge. 2. Someone or something that primes. 3. An undercoat of paint or size used to prime a surface.

ô paw, for/oi boy/ou out/ŏŏ took/ōō coo/p pop/r run/s sauce/sh shy/t to/th thin/*th* the/
ŭ cut/ûr fur/v van/w wag/y yes/z size/zh vision/ə ago, item, edible, gallop, circus/

pri·me·val (prī-mē′vəl) *adj.* Belonging to the earliest ages. [< L *primaevus,* in the first period of life.] —**pri·me′val·ly** *adv.*

prim·i·tive (prĭm′ə-tĭv) *adj.* **1.** Of or pertaining to an early or original stage or state of development, evolution, etc. **2.** Crude or unsophisticated. **3.** Of or pertaining to early stages in the evolution of human culture. [< L *primitivus,* first of its kind.] —**prim′i·tive** *n.* —**prim′i·tive·ly** *adv.*

pri·mo·gen·i·tor (prī′mō-jĕn′ə-tər) *n.* The earliest ancestor. [ML.]

pri·mo·gen·i·ture (prī′mō-jĕn′ə-chŏŏr′) *n.* **1.** The state of being the eldest child of the same parents. **2.** The right of the eldest son to inherit his parents' entire estate. [ML *prīmōgenitūra.*]

pri·mor·di·al (prī-môr′dē-əl) *adj.* Primary, primeval, original, or fundamental. —*n.* A basic principle. [< L *prīmōrdius.*] —**pri·mor′di·al·ly** *adv.*

primp (prĭmp) *v.* To dress or groom oneself with finicky attention to detail. [Akin to PRIM.]

prim·rose (prĭm′rōz′) *n.* A plant with clustered, variously colored flowers. [< ML *prīma rosa,* "first (or earliest) rose."]

primrose path. A way of life of worldly ease or pleasure.

prin. principal.

prince (prĭns) *n.* **1. a.** A male member of a royal family. **b.** *Archaic.* A hereditary ruler. **2.** An outstanding man: *a merchant prince.* [< L *princeps,* first in rank, sovereign, ruler.] —**prince′li·ness** *n.* —**prince′ly** *adj.*

Prince Edward Island. A province of SE Canada. Pop. 108,000. Cap. Charlottetown.

prince·ling (prĭns′lĭng) *n.* A petty prince.

prin·cess (prĭn′sĭs, -sĕs′, prĭn-sĕs′) *n.* **1.** A female member of a royal family other than the monarch. **2.** The consort of a prince.

prin·ci·pal (prĭn′sə-pəl) *adj.* First or foremost in importance; chief. —*n.* **1.** The head of a school. **2.** A main participant. **3.** A leading person, as in a play. **4. a.** Capital, as distinguished from the revenue from it. **b.** A sum of money owed as a debt, upon which interest is calculated. **5. a.** A person who empowers another to act as his representative. **b.** The person having prime responsibility for an obligation, as distinguished from one who acts as his agent. [< L *princeps,* first one in rank, PRINCE.] —**prin′ci·pal·ly** *adv.*

prin·ci·pal·i·ty (prĭn′sə-păl′ə-tē) *n., pl.* **-ties.** A territory ruled by a prince or from which a prince derives his title.

principal parts. In traditional grammars of inflected languages, the primary forms of a verb from which all other forms can be derived. In English, the principal parts are generally considered to be the present infinitive *(play, eat),* the past tense *(played, ate),* the past participle *(played, eaten),* and the present participle *(playing, eating).*

prin·ci·ple (prĭn′sə-pəl) *n.* **1.** A basic truth, law, or assumption. **2.** An ethical code or standard. **3.** A fixed policy or mode of action. **4.** A basic quality determining intrinsic nature

or characteristic behavior. **5.** A basic source. [< L *principium* < *princeps,* first.]

prin·ci·pled (prĭn′sə-pəld) *adj.* Motivated by or based on ethical principles.

print (prĭnt) *n.* **1.** A mark or impression made by pressure. **2.** Something marked with an impression. **3. a.** Lettering or other impressions produced in ink. **b.** The state or form of matter so produced. **4.** A design or picture reproduced by printing. **5.** A photographic copy. **6.** A fabric with a stamped dyed pattern. —*v.* **1.** To press as a mark onto a surface. **2.** To produce by means of pressed type on a paper surface. **3.** To publish. **4.** To write in characters similar to those commonly used in print. **5.** To produce (a positive photograph) by passing light through a negative onto sensitized paper. [< OF *preindre,* to press.] —**print′er** *n.*

print. printing.

print·a·ble (prĭn′tə-bəl) *adj.* **1.** Capable of being printed or of producing a print. **2.** Fit for publication.

print·ing (prĭn′tĭng) *n.* **1.** The process, art, or business of producing printed material. **2.** All the copies of a publication that are printed at one time. **3.** Written characters resembling those appearing in print.

printing press. A machine that transfers lettering or images by contact with various forms of inked surface onto paper or similar material.

pri·or[1] (prī′ər) *adj.* **1.** Preceding in time or order. **2.** Preceding in importance. [L.] —**pri·or·i·ty** (-ôr′ə-tē, -ŏr′ə-tē) *n.*

pri·or[2] (prī′ər) *n.* A monastic officer in charge of a priory. [< L, former, superior.] —**pri′or·ess** *fem.n.*

pri·or·y (prī′ə-rē) *n., pl.* **-ies.** A religious house governed by a prior or prioress.

prism (prĭz′əm) *n.* **1.** *Geom.* A polyhedron having parallel, congruent polygons as bases and parallelograms as sides. **2.** A homogeneous transparent solid, usually with triangular bases and rectangular sides, used to produce or analyze a continuous spectrum. **3.** A cut-glass object, such as a pendant of a chandelier. [< Gk *prisma,* "a thing sawed," prism.] —**pris·mat′ic** (-măt′ĭk) *adj.*

pris·on (prĭz′ən) *n.* A place of confinement for persons convicted or accused of crimes. [< L *prehendere,* to seize.]

pris·on·er (prĭz′ə-nər, prĭz′nər) *n.* A person held in custody, captivity, or a condition of forcible restraint.

pris·sy (prĭs′ē) *adj.* **-sier, -siest.** Finicky, fussy, and prudish. [Blend of PRIM and SISSY.] —**pris′si·ly** *adv.* —**pris′si·ness** *n.*

pris·tine (prĭs′tēn′, prĭ-stēn′) *adj.* **1.** Primitive or original. **2.** Remaining in a pure and uncorrupted state. [L *prīstinus,* original.]

prith·ee (prĭth′ē, prĭth′ē) *interj. Archaic.* Please. [< (I) *pray thee.*]

pri·va·cy (prī′və-sē) *n., pl.* **-cies. 1.** The condition of being secluded. **2.** Secrecy.

pri·vate (prī′vĭt) *adj.* **1.** Secluded from the sight, presence, or intrusion of others. **2.** Of or confined to one person; personal. **3.** Not available for public use or participation. **4.** Belonging to a particular person or persons. **5.** Not holding an official or public position. **6.** Intimate; secret. *—n.* An enlisted man ranking below private first class in the Army or Marine Corps. **—in private.** Secretly; confidentially. [< L *prīvātus,* not in public life.] **—pri′vate·ly** *adv.* **—pri′vate·ness** *n.*

pri·va·teer (prī′və-tîr′) *n.* **1.** A ship privately owned and manned but authorized to attack and capture enemy vessels. **2.** The commander or one of the crew of such a ship.

private first class. An enlisted man ranking below corporal and above private in the Army or Marine Corps.

pri·va·tion (prī-vā′shən) *n.* **1.** Lack of the basic necessities or comforts of life. **2.** The condition resulting from such lack. [< L *prīvāre,* to deprive.]

priv·et (prĭv′ĭt) *n.* A shrub with small, dark-green leaves, widely used for hedges. [?]

priv·i·lege (prĭv′ə-lĭj) *n.* A special immunity, right, or benefit enjoyed by an individual or class. *—v.* **-leged, -leging.** To grant a privilege to. [< L *prīvilēgium,* law affecting an individual, prerogative.]

priv·i·leged (prĭv′ə-lĭjd) *adj.* Enjoying a privilege or having privileges.

privileged communication. A confidential communication that one cannot be made to divulge.

priv·y (prĭv′ē) *adj.* **1.** Made a participant in a secret: *privy to the plan.* **2.** Belonging to a person, as the British sovereign, in his private rather than his official capacity: *Privy Council.* *—n. pl.* **-ies.** A latrine or outhouse. [< L *prīvātus,* PRIVATE.] **—priv′i·ly** *adv.*

prize¹ (prīz) *n.* **1.** Something offered or won as an award in a competition or game of chance. **2.** Anything worth striving for. *—adj.* **1.** Offered or given as a prize. **2.** Given a prize. **3.** Outstanding; first-class. *—v.* **prized, prizing.** To value highly; esteem. [ME *pris,* value, price.]

prize² (prīz) *n.* Something, as an enemy ship, seized during wartime. [< VL **prensa,* "something seized."]

prize³ (prīz) *v.* **prized, prizing.** To pry. [< PRIZE².]

prize fight. Also **prize·fight** (prīz′fīt′). A professional boxing match. **—prize′fight′er** *n.* **—prize′fight′ing.** *n.*

pro¹ (prō) *n., pl.* **pros. 1.** An argument in favor of something. **2.** One who takes the affirmative side in debate. *—adv.* In favor of. *—adj.* Favoring; supporting. [< L *prō,* for.]

pro² (prō) *n., pl.* **pros.** *Informal.* A professional or expert.

pro–. *comb. form.* **1.** Favor or support. **2.** Acting as. [< L *prō,* before, in front of, according to, for.]

prob. 1. probable; probably. **2.** problem.

prob·a·bil·i·ty (prŏb′ə-bĭl′ə-tē) *n., pl.* **-ties. 1.** The quality or condition of being probable; likelihood. **2.** A probable situation, condition, or event. **3.** A number expressing the likelihood of occurrence of a specific event. **—in all probability.** Most probably; very likely.

prob·a·ble (prŏb′ə-bəl) *adj.* **1.** Likely to happen or to be true. **2.** Apparently true; plausible. [< L *probābilis,* provable, laudable.] **—prob′a·bly** *adv.*

pro·bate (prō′bāt′) *n.* Legal establishment of the validity of a will. [< L *probāre,* to examine, demonstrate as good, PROVE.] **—pro′bate′** *v.* **(-bated, -bating).**

pro·ba·tion (prō-bā′shən) *n.* **1.** A trial period. **2.** The action of granting a convicted offender provisional freedom on the promise of good behavior. [< L *probāre,* to try, PROVE.] **—pro·ba′tion·al, pro·ba′tion·ar′y** *adj.*

pro·ba·tion·er (prō-bā′shən-ər) *n.* A person on probation.

pro·ba·tive (prō′bə-tĭv) *adj.* Serving to test, try, or prove.

probe (prōb) *n.* **1.** A slender instrument used to explore a wound or body cavity. **2.** A penetrating investigation. [< L *probāre,* to test, PROVE.] **—probe** *v.* **(probed, probing).**

pro·bi·ty (prō′bə-tē) *n.* Integrity; uprightness. [< L *probus,* good, virtuous.]

prob·lem (prŏb′ləm) *n.* **1.** A question or situation that presents uncertainty or difficulty. **2.** A source of trouble or annoyance. **3.** A question put forward for consideration or solution. [< Gk *problēma,* "thing thrown forward," projection, problem.]

prob·lem·at·i·cal (prŏb′lə-măt′ĭ-kəl) *adj.* Also **prob·lem·at·ic** (-ĭk). **1.** Difficult to solve. **2.** Open to doubt; debatable.

pro·bos·cis (prō-bŏs′ĭs) *n., pl.* **-cises** or **-boscides** (-bŏs′ə-dēz′). A long, flexible snout, as an elephant's trunk. [< Gk *pro-,* in front + *boskein,* to feed.]

pro·caine hydrochloride (prō′kān′). A white crystalline powder, $C_{13}H_{20}O_2N_2 \cdot HCl$, used as a local anesthetic in medicine and dentistry.

pro·ce·dure (prə-sē′jər) *n.* **1.** A manner of proceeding. **2.** A series of steps or course of action. **3.** A set of established forms for conducting business or public affairs. **—pro·ce′dur·al** *adj.*

pro·ceed (prō-sēd′, prə-) *v.* **1.** To advance or continue. **2.** To undertake and carry on some action. **3.** To move on in an orderly manner. **4.** To issue forth; originate. **5.** To take legal action. [< L *prōcēdere.*] **—pro·ceed′er** *n.*

pro·ceed·ing (prō-sē′dĭng, prə-) *n.* **1.** A procedure. **2.** A transaction. **3. a. proceedings.** Events or doings. **b.** Minutes, as of a meeting. **c.** Legal action.

pro·ceeds (prō′sēdz′) *pl.n.* The amount of money derived from a commercial venture; profits.

proc·ess (prŏs′ĕs′, prō′sĕs′) *n.* **1.** A system of operations in the production of something. **2.** A series of actions, changes, or functions that bring about a particular result. **3.** Ongoing movement; progression. **4. a.** A court summons or writ. **b.** The entire course of a judicial proceeding. **5.** *Biol.* A part extending or projecting from an organ or organism; an appendage. **6.** Any of various photo-mechanical or photoengraving methods. *—v.* **1.** To put through the steps of a prescribed procedure. **2.** To prepare or convert by subjecting to some special process. [< L *prōc-essus*, pp of *prōcēdere*, to PROCEED.] —**proc'-es'sor, proc'es'ser** *n.*

pro·ces·sion (prə-sĕsh'ən) *n.* **1.** A group of persons moving along in an orderly and formal manner. **2.** Any continuous and orderly course.

pro·ces·sion·al (prə-sĕsh'ən-əl) *n.* A hymn sung when the clergy enter a church at the beginning of the service.

pro·claim (prō-klām', prə-) *v.* To announce officially and publicly; declare. [< L *prō-clāmāre.*] —**pro·claim'er** *n.* —**proc'la·ma'tion** (prŏk'lə-mā'shən) *n.*

pro·cliv·i·ty (prō-klĭv'ə-tē) *n., pl.* -ties. A natural propensity. [< L *prōclīvus,* sloping forward.]

pro·cras·ti·nate (prō-krăs'tə-nāt', prə-) *v.* -nated, -nating. To put off doing something until a future time. [L *prōcrāstināre,* "to put forward until tomorrow."] —**pro·cras'ti·na'tion** *n.* —**pro·cras'ti·na'tor** *n.*

pro·cre·ate (prō'krē-āt') *v.* -ated, -ating. To beget or reproduce. —**pro'cre·ant** *adj.* —**pro'-cre·a'tion** *n.* —**pro'cre·a'tive** *adj.* —**pro'cre·a'tor** (-ā'tər) *n.*

pro·crus·te·an (prō-krŭs'tē-ən) *adj.* Forcing conformity by ruthless or arbitrary means. [< *Procrustes,* a Greek giant who stretched or shortened captives to fit one of his iron beds.]

proc·tol·o·gy (prŏk-tŏl'ə-jē) *n.* The physiology and pathology of the rectum and anus. [Gk *prōktos,* anus + -LOGY.] —**proc·tol'o·gist** *n.*

proc·tor (prŏk'tər) *n.* An examination supervisor. [< PROCURATOR.] —**proc'tor** *v.* —**proc·to'ri·al** (-tôr'ē-əl, -tŏr'ē-əl) *adj.*

proc·u·ra·tor (prŏk'yə-rā'tər) *n.* An administrator of a minor Roman province. [< L *prōcūrāre,* to take care of, PROCURE.]

pro·cure (prō-kyŏor', prə-) *v.* -cured, -curing. **1.** To obtain; acquire. **2.** To bring about; effect. **3.** To obtain (a woman) to serve as a prostitute. [< L *prōcūrāre,* to take care of, manage for someone else.] —**pro·cur'er** *n.* —**pro·cur'ess** *fem.n.* —**pro·cure'ment** *n.*

Pro·cy·on (prō'sē-ŏn') *n.* A double star in the constellation Canis Minor; Dog Star. [< Gk *Prokuōn,* "before the dog star."]

prod (prŏd) *v.* prodded, prodding. **1.** To jab or poke. **2.** To urge; goad. [Perh blend of POKE and *brod,* var of BRAD.] —**prod** *n.*

prod. **1.** produce. **2.** produced. **3.** product.

prod·i·gal (prŏd'ĭ-gəl) *adj.* **1.** Recklessly wasteful; extravagant. **2.** Profuse in giving. **3.** Profuse; lavish. [< L *prōdigere,* to drive away, squander.] —**prod'i·gal** *n.* —**prod'i·gal'i·ty** (-găl'ə-tē) *n.*

pro·di·gious (prə-dĭj'əs) *adj.* **1.** Enormous. **2.** Extraordinary; marvelous. [< L *prōdigium,* omen, PRODIGY.] —**pro·di'gious·ly** *adv.* —**pro·di'gious·ness** *n.*

prod·i·gy (prŏd'ə-jē) *n., pl.* -gies. **1.** A person with exceptional talents or powers. **2.** A marvel. [L *prōdigium,* prophetic sign, marvel.]

pro·duce (prə-d/y/ōōs', prō-) *v.* -duced, -ducing. **1.** To bring forth; yield. **2.** To manufacture. **3.** To cause or give rise to. **4.** To bring forward; exhibit. —*n.* (prŏd'yōōs, prō'dyōōs).

Something produced; a product, esp. farm products, as fruits and vegetables. [L *prōdūcere,* to lead or bring forth.] —**pro·duc'er** *n.* —**pro·duc'i·ble** *adj.*

prod·uct (prŏd'əkt) *n.* **1.** Anything produced by labor. **2.** The result obtained by performing multiplication.

pro·duc·tion (prə-dŭk'shən, prō-) *n.* **1.** The act or process of producing. **2.** The creation of value by producing goods and services. **3.** A product. **4.** The total number of products; output. **5.** A public performance. —**pro·duc'tive** *adj.* —**pro·duc'tive·ly** *adv.* —**pro·duc·tiv'i·ty** *n.*

pro·em (prō'ĕm') *n.* A short introduction; preface. [< Gk *prooimion.*]

prof (prŏf) *n. Informal.* A professor.

Prof. professor.

pro·fane (prō-fān', prə-) *adj.* **1.** Blasphemous. **2.** Nonreligious; secular. **3.** Impure. [< L *profānus,* "before (i.e., outside) the temple," not sacred.] —**prof'a·na'tion** (prŏf'ə-nā'shən) *n.* —**pro·fane'** *v.* (-faned, -faning). —**pro·fan'i·ty** (-făn'ə-tē) *n.*

pro·fess (prə-fĕs', prō-) *v.* **1.** To affirm. **2.** To make a pretense of. **3.** To claim skill in or knowledge of. **4.** To affirm belief in. [L *prō-fitēri* (pp *professus*), to declare publicly.] —**pro·fessed'** *adj.* —**pro·fess'ed·ly** *adv.*

pro·fes·sion (prə-fĕsh'ən) *n.* **1.** An occupation or vocation requiring advanced study in a specialized field. **2.** The body of qualified persons of one specific field. **3.** The act or an instance of professing; declaration. **4.** An avowal of faith. [< L *professiō,* declaration, confession < *prōfitēri,* PROFESS.]

pro·fes·sion·al (prə-fĕsh'ən-əl) *adj.* **1.** Of, related to, or suitable for a profession. **2.** Engaged in one of the learned professions, as law. **3.** Participating for pay in a sport. —*n.* **1.** A person following a profession. **2.** One who earns his livelihood as an athlete. **3.** One who has an assured competence in a particular field or occupation. —**pro·fes'sion·al·ly** *adv.*

pro·fes·sion·al·ism (prə-fĕsh'ən-ə-lĭz'əm) *n.* **1.** Professional status, methods, character, or standards. **2.** The use of professional players in organized athletics.

pro·fes·sor (prə-fĕs'ər) *n.* **1.** A teacher of the highest rank in an institution of higher learning. **2.** A teacher or instructor. —**pro'fes·so'ri·al** *adj.* —**pro·fes'sor·ship'** *n.*

prof·fer (prŏf'ər) *v.* To offer or tender. [< OF *proffrir.*] —**prof'fer** *n.*

pro·fi·cien·cy (prə-fĭsh'ən-sē) *n., pl.* -cies. The state or quality of being proficient; skill; competence.

pro·fi·cient (prə-fĭsh'ənt) *adj.* Performing in a given art, skill, or branch of learning with expert correctness and facility; adept. —*n.* An expert. [< L *prōficere,* to make progress.] —**pro·fi'cien·cy** *n.* —**pro·fi'cient·ly** *adv.*

pro·file (prō'fīl') *n.* **1.** A side view of the human head. **2.** An outline of any object. **3.** A biographical sketch. [< It *profilare,* to draw in outline.]

prof·it (prŏf'ĭt) *n.* **1.** A gain or return; benefit. **2.** The return received on a business under-

---

ă pặt/ā ate/âr care/ä bar/b bib/ch chew/d deed/ĕ pet/ē be/f fit/g gag/h hat/hw what/ ĭ pit/ī pie/îr pier/j judge/k kick/l lid, fatal/m mum/n no, sudden/ng sing/ŏ pot/ō go/

taking after costs have been met. —*v.* **1.** To make a gain or profit. **2.** To be advantageous; benefit. [< L *prōficere*, to go forward, make progress.] —**prof′it•a•bil′i•ty** *n.* —**prof′it•a•ble** *adj.* —**prof′it•a•bly** *adv.*

prof•i•teer (prŏf′ə-tîr′) *n.* One who makes excessive profits on commodities in short supply. —**prof′i•teer′** *v.*

prof•li•gate (prŏf′lĭ-gĭt, -gāt′) *adj.* **1.** Dissolute. **2.** Recklessly extravagant. —*n.* A wastrel. [< L *prōflīgāre*, to strike down, destroy.] —**prof′li•ga•cy** (-lĭ-gə-sē) *n.*

pro for•ma (prō fôr′mə). As a matter of form. [L.]

pro•found (prə-found′, prō-) *adj.* **1.** Extended to or coming from a great depth; deep. **2.** Coming as if from the depths of one's being: *profound contempt.* **3.** Thoroughgoing. **4.** Penetrating beyond what is superficial or obvious. **5.** Absolute; complete: *a profound silence.* [< L *profundus.*] —**pro•found′ly** *adv.* —**pro•fun′di•ty** (-fŭn′də-tē) *n.*

pro•fuse (prə-fyōōs′, prō-) *adj.* Copious or abundant. [< L *prōfundere*, to pour forth.] —**pro•fuse′ly** *adv.* —**pro•fu′sion** (-fyōō′zhən), **pro•fuse′ness** *n.*

pro•gen•i•tor (prō-jĕn′ə-tər) *n.* **1.** A direct ancestor. **2.** An originator of a line of descent. [< L *prōgignere*, to beget.]

prog•e•ny (prŏj′ə-nē) *n.* Children or descendants; offspring. [< L *prōgignere*, to beget.]

prog•no•sis (prŏg-nō′sĭs) *n., pl.* **-ses** (-sēz′). **1.** A prediction of the probable course and outcome of a disease. **2.** The likelihood of recovery from a disease. [< Gk *prognōskein*, to foreknow, predict.]

prog•nos•tic (prŏg-nŏs′tĭk) *n.* **1.** A portent; omen. **2.** A prophecy. [< Gk *prognōskein*, to predict.] —**prog•nos′tic** *adj.*

prog•nos•ti•cate (prŏg-nŏs′tĭ-kāt′) *v.* **-cated, -cating.** To predict on the basis of present indications. —**prog•nos′ti•ca′tion** *n.* —**prog•nos′ti•ca′tor** *n.*

pro•gram (prō′grăm′, -grəm) *n.* Also *chiefly Brit.* **pro•gramme.** **1.** A listing of the order of events for some public presentation. **2.** Any organized list of procedures; schedule. **3.** Instructions coded for a computer. —*v.* **-grammed** or **-gramed, -gramming** or **-graming.** **1.** To include in a program. **2.** To provide (a computer) with a set of instructions. [< Gk *programma*, public notice.] —**pro′gram•mat′ic** (-grə-măt′ĭk) *adj.* —**pro′gram′mer** *n.*

prog•ress (prŏg′rĕs′, -rəs) *n.* **1.** Movement toward a goal. **2.** Development; unfolding. **3.** Steady improvement. —*v.* **pro•gress** (prə-grĕs′). **1.** To advance; proceed. **2.** To improve. [< L *prōgredī*, to go forward.]

pro•gres•sion (prə-grĕsh′ən) *n.* **1.** Progress. **2.** Advance. **3.** A sequence. **4.** A series of numbers or quantities, each derived from the one preceding by some consistent operation. —**pro•gres′sion•al** *adj.*

pro•gres•sive (prə-grĕs′ĭv) *adj.* **1.** Moving forward; ongoing. **2.** Proceeding in steps or by stages. **3.** Promoting or favoring political reform. **4.** *Gram.* Designating a verb form that expresses an action or condition in progress.

—*n.* A partisan of reform in politics, education, or other fields.

pro•hib•it (prō-hĭb′ĭt) *v.* **1.** To forbid by authority. **2.** To prevent or debar. [< L *prōhibēre*, to hold in front, hinder.]

pro•hi•bi•tion (prō′ə-bĭsh′ən) *n.* **1.** The act of prohibiting. **2.** A ban on the manufacture and sale of alcoholic beverages.

pro•hib•i•tive (prō-hĭb′ə-tĭv) *adj.* **1.** Prohibiting. **2.** Discouraging purchase or use.

proj•ect (prŏj′ĕkt′, -ĭkt) *n.* **1.** A plan; scheme. **2.** An undertaking requiring concerted effort. —*v.* **pro•ject** (prə-jĕkt′). **1.** To protrude. **2.** To throw forward. **3.** To direct one's voice so as to be heard clearly at a distance. **4.** To form a plan or intention for. **5.** To cause (an image) to appear upon a surface. [< L *prōjicere*, to throw forth.] —**pro•jec′tion** (prə-jĕk′shən) *n.*

pro•jec•tile (prə-jĕk′təl, -tīl′) *n.* **1.** A fired, thrown, or otherwise projected object, as a bullet. **2.** A self-propelling missile, as a rocket. [< L *prōjicere*, to throw forth, PROJECT.]

pro•jec•tor (prə-jĕk′tər) *n.* A device for projecting an image onto a screen.

pro•le•tar•i•an (prō′lə-târ′ē-ən) *n.* A member of the proletariat. [< L *prōlētārius*, Roman citizen of the lowest class.]

pro•le•tar•i•at (prō′lə-târ′ē-it) *n.* The class of industrial wage earners.

pro•lif•er•ate (prō-lĭf′ə-rāt′) *v.* **-ated, -ating.** To reproduce or increase rapidly and repeatedly. [< ML *prōlifer*, producing offspring.] —**pro•lif′er•a′tion** *n.*

pro•lif•ic (prō-lĭf′ĭk) *adj.* **1.** Producing offspring in abundance. **2.** Producing abundant works or results. [< ML *prōlificus.*] —**pro•lif′i•cal•ly** *adv.*

pro•lix (prō-lĭks′, prō′lĭks) *adj.* Wordy; verbose. [< L *prōlixus*, "poured forth," extended.] —**pro•lix′i•ty** *n.* —**pro•lix′ly** *adv.*

pro•logue (prō′lôg′, -lŏg′) *n.* An introduction, as to a play. [< Gk *prologos*, (speaker of) a prologue.]

pro•long (prə-lông′, -lŏng′) *v.* **1.** To lengthen in duration; protract. **2.** To lengthen in extent; elongate. —**pro′lon•ga′tion** (-gā′shən) *n.*

prom (prŏm) *n.* A formal dance held for a high-school or college class. [Short for PROMENADE.]

prom•e•nade (prŏm′ə-nād′, -näd′) *n.* **1.** A leisurely walk; stroll. **2.** A public place for such walking. **3.** A formal march by the guests at the opening of a ball. —*v.* **-naded, -nading.** To go on a leisurely walk. [< LL *prōmināre*, to drive forward.]

pro•me•thi•um (prə-mē′thē-əm) *n. Symbol* **Pm** A radioactive rare-earth element. Atomic number 61, longest-lived isotope Pm 145. [NL.]

prom•i•nence (prŏm′ə-nəns) *n.* **1.** The condition or quality of being prominent. **2.** Something prominent; a projection.

prom•i•nent (prŏm′ə-nənt) *adj.* **1.** Projecting outward. **2.** Immediately noticeable; conspicuous. **3.** Widely known; eminent. [< L *prōminēre*, to jut out.] —**prom′i•nent•ly** *adv.*

pro•mis•cu•ous (prə-mĭs′kyōō-əs) *adj.* **1.** Consisting of diverse and unrelated parts or

---

ô paw, for/oi boy/ou out/ōō took/ōō coo/p pop/r run/s sauce/sh shy/t to/th thin/*th* the/ ŭ cut/ûr fur/v van/w wag/y yes/z size/zh vision/ə ago, item, edible, gallop, circus/

individuals; confused. **2.** Indiscriminate, esp. in sexual relations. **3.** Casual; random. [L *prōmiscuus,* mixed.] —**prom·is·cu·i·ty** (prŏm'ĭ-skyōō'ə-tē, prō'mĭ-), —**pro·mis'cu·ous·ness** *n.* —**pro·mis'cu·ous·ly** *adv.*

prom·ise (prŏm'ĭs) *n.* **1.** A declaration assuring that one will or will not do something. **2.** Something promised. **3.** Indication of future excellence or success. —*v.* **-ised, -ising. 1.** To pledge or offer assurance. **2.** To make a promise of. **3.** To afford a basis for expecting. [< L *prōmittere,* "to send forth," promise.]

Promised Land. 1. The land of Canaan. Genesis 12:7. **2. promised land.** Any place of anticipated happiness.

prom·is·ing (prŏm'ĭ-sĭng) *adj.* Likely to develop in a desirable manner. —**prom'is·ing·ly** *adv.*

prom·is·so·ry note (prŏm'ĭ-sôr'ē, -sōr'ē). A written promise to pay a specified sum of money at a stated time or on demand.

prom·on·to·ry (prŏm'ən-tôr'ē, -tōr'ē) *n., pl.* **-ries.** A high ridge of land or rock jutting out into a sea or other expanse of water. [< L *prōmunturium.*]

pro·mote (prə-mōt') *v.* **-moted, -moting. 1.** To raise in position or rank. **2.** To contribute to the progress or growth of; further. **3.** To urge the adoption of; advocate. **4.** To attempt to sell or popularize. [< L *prōmovēre* (pp *prōmōtus*), to move forward, advance.] —**pro·mo'tion** *n.* —**pro·mo'tion·al** *adj.*

pro·mot·er (prə-mō'tər) *n.* **1.** An active supporter; advocate. **2.** A finance and publicity organizer.

prompt (prŏmpt) *adj.* **1.** On time; punctual. **2.** Done without delay. —*v.* **1.** To press into action; incite. **2.** To give rise to; inspire. **3.** To assist with a reminder; remind. **4.** To give a cue to, as in the theater. [< L *promptus,* "brought to light," "visible," at hand, prompt.] —**prompt'er** *n.* —**promp'ti·tude', prompt'ness** *n.* —**prompt'ly** *adv.*

prom·ul·gate (prŏm'əl-gāt', prō-mŭl'gāt') *v.* **-gated, -gating.** To make known or put into effect by public declaration. [L *prōmulgāre.*] —**prom'ul·ga'tion** (prŏm'əl-gā'shən, prō'-məl-) *n.* —**prom'ul·ga'tor** *n.*

pron. 1. pronoun. **2.** pronunciation.

pro·na·tal·ism (prō-nāt'l-ĭz'əm) *n.* Any policy that encourages childbearing. [PRO- + NATAL + -ISM.] — **pro·na'tal·ist** *adj.* & *n.*

prone (prōn) *adj.* **1.** Lying with the front or face downward. **2.** Tending: *prone to mischief.* [< L *prōnus,* "bending."] —**prone'ness** *n.*

prong (prông, prŏng) *n.* **1.** A sharply pointed part, as a tine of a fork. **2.** Any slender projection. [ME *pronge,* forked instrument.]

pro·noun (prō'noun') *n.* One of a class of words that function as substitutes for nouns. [< L *prōnōmen.*]

pro·nounce (prə-nouns') *v.* **-nounced, -nouncing. 1.** To articulate (a word or speech sound). **2.** To state officially and formally; declare. [< L *prōnuntiāre,* to speak in public, declare.] —**pro·nounce'a·ble** *adj.* —**pro·nun'ci·a'tion** (-nŭn'sē-ā'shən) *n.*

pro·nounced (prə-nounst') *adj.* Distinct;

strongly marked.

pro·nounce·ment (prə-nouns'mənt) *n.* A formal declaration or statement.

pron·to (prŏn'tō) *adv. Informal.* Without delay; quickly. [< L *promptus,* PROMPT.]

proof (prōōf) *n.* **1.** The evidence establishing the validity of a given assertion. **2.** Conclusive demonstration of something. **3.** The proving of something. **4.** The alcoholic strength of a liquor. **5.** A trial sheet of printed material on which corrections are made before publication. **6.** A photographer's trial print. —*adj.* **1.** Fully resistant: *proof against fire.* **2.** Of standard alcoholic strength. [< L *probāre,* to test, prove.]

–proof. *comb. form.* Impervious to or able to resist: *shockproof.*

proof·read (prōōf'rēd') *v.* To read (copy or a printer's proof) against the original manuscript for corrections. —**proof'read'er** *n.*

prop[1] (prŏp) *n.* A support or stay. [ME *proppe.*] —**prop** *v.* **(propped, propping).**

prop[2] (prŏp) *n.* A stage property.

prop[3] (prŏp) *n. Informal.* A propeller.

prop. 1. property. **2.** proposition. **3.** proprietary; proprietor.

prop·a·gan·da (prŏp'ə-găn'də) *n.* **1.** The systematic propagation of a given doctrine. **2.** Material disseminated by the proselytizers of a doctrine. [< L *prōpāgāre,* to PROPAGATE.] —**prop'a·gan'dist** *n.* —**prop'a·gan'dize'** *v.* **(-dized, -dizing).**

prop·a·gate (prŏp'ə-gāt') *v.* **-gated, -gating. 1.** To produce or cause to produce offspring; reproduce; breed. **2.** To move through a medium. [L *prōpāgāre.*] —**prop'a·ga'tion** *n.*

pro·pane (prō'pān') *n.* A colorless gas, C_3H_8, found in natural gas and petroleum, used as a fuel.

pro·pel (prə-pĕl') *v.* **-pelled, -pelling.** To cause to move or sustain in motion. [< L *prōpellere.*]

pro·pel·lant (prə-pĕl'ənt) *n.* Also **pro·pel·lent.** Something that propels, as an explosive charge or a rocket fuel.

pro·pel·ler (prə-pĕl'ər) *n.* Also **pro·pel·lor.** A device for propelling aircraft or boats, esp. one having radiating blades mounted on a revolving power-driven shaft.

pro·pen·si·ty (prə-pĕn'sə-tē) *n., pl.* **-ties.** An innate inclination; tendency; bent. [< L *prōpendēre,* to be inclined or favorable.]

prop·er (prŏp'ər) *adj.* **1.** Suitable; fitting. **2.** Out-and-out; thorough: *a proper whipping.* **3.** Worthy of the name. **4.** Meeting a requisite standard. **5. a.** Within the strict limitation of a term: *France proper.* **b.** Rigorously correct; exact. **6.** Seemly; decorous. [< L *proprius,* one's own, personal, particular.] —**prop'er·ly** *adv.* —**prop'er·ness** *n.*

proper fraction. A numerical fraction in which the numerator is less than the denominator.

proper noun. Also **proper name.** A noun designating by name a being or thing without a limiting modifier.

prop·er·ty (prŏp'ər-tē) *n., pl.* **-ties. 1.** Ownership. **2.** A possession or possessions. **3.** Any article, except costumes and scenery, used as

---

ă pat/ā ate/âr care/ä bar/b bib/ch chew/d deed/ĕ pet/ē be/f fit/g gag/h hat/hw what/ ĭ pit/ī pie/îr pier/j judge/k kick/l lid, fatal/m mum/n no, sudden/ng sing/ŏ pot/ō go/

PROOFREADERS' MARKS

Instruction	Mark in Margin	Mark in Type	Corrected Type
Delete	*℘*	the ~~good~~ word	the word
Insert indicated material	good	the⌄word	the good word
Let it stand	*stet*	the ~~good~~ word	the good word
Make capital	*cap*	the w̲o̲r̲d	the Word
Make lower case	*lc*	/The Word	the Word
Set in small capitals	*sc*	See w̲o̲r̲d̲.	See WORD.
Set in italic type	*ital*	The word is w̲o̲r̲d̲.	The word is *word*.
Set in roman type	*rom*	the (word)	the word
Set in boldface type	*bf*	the entry word	the entry **word**
Set in lightface type	*lf*	the entry (**word**)	the entry word
Transpose	*tr*	the word good	the good word
Close up space	⌒	the wo rd	the word
Delete and close up space	⌒℘	the woord	the word
Spell out	*sp*	②words	two words
Insert: space	#	theword	the word
period	⊙	This is the word⌄	This is the word.
comma	⌃	words⌄words, words	words, words, words
hyphen	⌒=⌒/⌒=⌒	word⌄for⌄word test	word-for-word test
colon	⊙	The following words⌄	The following words:
semicolon	⌃;	Scan the words⌄skim the words.	Scan the words; skim the words.
apostrophe	⌄	Johns words	John's words
quotation marks	⌄/⌄/	the word word	the word "word"
parentheses	(/)/	The word⌄word⌄is in parentheses.	The word (word) is in parentheses.
brackets	[/]/	He read from the Word ⌄the Bible⌄.	He read from the Word [the Bible].
en dash	⅟N	1964⌄1972	1964–1972
em dash	⅟M/⅟M/	The dictionary⌄how often it is needed⌄belongs in every home.	The dictionary—how often it is needed—belongs in every home.
superior type	⌄2	2 = 4	$2^2 = 4$
inferior type	⌃2	H⌄O	H_2O
asterisk	⌄*	word⌄	word*

ô paw, for/oi boy/ou out/o͞o took/o͞o coo/p pop/r run/s sauce/sh shy/t to/th thin/*th* the/
ŭ cut/ûr fur/v van/w wag/y yes/z size/zh vision/ə ago, item, edible, gallop, circus/

PROOFREADERS' MARKS

Instruction	Mark in Margin	Mark in Type	Corrected Type
dagger	†	a word∧	a word†
double dagger	‡	words and words∧	words and words‡
section symbol	§	∧Book Reviews	§Book Reviews
virgule	/	either∧or	either/or
Start paragraph	¶	"Where is it?" ∧"It's on the shelf."	"Where is it?" "It's on the shelf."
Run in	*run in*	The entry word is printed in boldface. The pronunciation follows.	The entry word is printed in boldface. The pronunciation follows.
Turn right side up	↻	the word	the word
Move left	⊏	⊏ the word	the word
Move right	⊐	the word	the word
Move up	⊓	the word	the word
Move down	⊔	the word	the word
Align	‖	the word the word the word	the word the word the word
Straighten line	=	the word	the word
Wrong font	*wf*	the word	the word
Broken type	✗	the word	the word

part of a play. **4.** A characteristic trait or quality. [< L *proprius*, own, PROPER.]
pro·phase (prō'fāz') *n.* The first stage of cell division by mitosis.
proph·e·cy (prŏf'ə-sē) *n., pl.* **-cies. 1.** A prediction. **2.** The inspired utterance of a prophet.
proph·e·sy (prŏf'ə-sī') *v.* **-sied, -sying. 1.** To reveal by divine inspiration. **2.** To predict. —**proph'e·si'er** *n.*
proph·et (prŏf'ĭt) *n.* **1.** One who speaks by divine inspiration. **2.** A predictor. **3. The Prophets.** The prophetic writings of the Hebrew Scriptures. [< Gk *prophētēs*, "one who speaks beforehand," proclaimer.] —**proph'et·ess** *fem.n.*
pro·phet·ic (prə-fĕt'ĭk) *adj.* Of or belonging to a prophet or prophecy.
pro·phy·lac·tic (prō'fə-lăk'tĭk, prŏf'ə-) *adj.* Acting against or to prevent something, esp. disease. —*n.* A prophylactic medicine, device, or measure, esp. a condom. [< Gk *prophulassein*, to stand on guard before (a place), take precautions against.]
pro·pin·qui·ty (prō-pĭng'kwə-tē) *n.* **1.** Nearness; proximity. **2.** Kinship. [< L *propinquus*, near.]
pro·pi·ti·ate (prō-pĭsh'ē-āt') *v.* **-ated, -ating.** To

conciliate; appease. [< L *propitius*, PRO-PITIOUS.] —pro•pi′ti•a′tion *n.* —pro•pi′ti•a•to′ry (-ə-tôr′ē, -tōr′ē) *adj.*

pro•pi•tious (prə-pĭsh′əs) *adj.* Presenting favorable circumstances; auspicious. [< L *propitius*, favorable, kind.]

pro•po•nent (prə-pō′nənt) *n.* One who argues in support of something; an advocate. [< L *prōpōnere*, to PROPOSE.]

pro•por•tion (prə-pôr′shən, -pōr′shən) *n.* **1.** A part considered in relation to the whole. **2.** A relationship between things or variable quantities. **3.** A relation between quantities such that if one varies, another varies as a multiple of the first; ratio. **4.** Harmonious relation; balance. **5.** Often **proportions.** Dimensions; size. —*v.* **1.** To adjust so that proper relations between parts are attained. **2.** To form with symmetry. [< L *prō portiōne*, "for (its or his) share," proportionally.] —pro•por′tion•al *adj.* —pro•por′tion•al′i•ty (-shə-năl′ə-tē) *n.* —pro•por′tion•al•ly *adv.* —pro•por′tion•ate *adj.*

pro•pose (prə-pōz′) *v.* **-posed, -posing. 1.** To put forward for consideration; suggest. **2.** To present or nominate (a person) for a position, office, etc. **3.** To purpose; intend. **4.** To make an offer, esp. of marriage. [< L *prōpōnere* (pp *prōpositus*), to put or set forth, declare.] —pro•pos′al *n.* —pro•pos′er *n.*

prop•o•si•tion (prŏp′ə-zĭsh′ən) *n.* **1.** A plan or scheme suggested for acceptance. **2.** *Informal.* A matter requiring special handling. **3.** A subject for discussion or analysis. [<L *prōpōnere*, PROPOSE.]

pro•pound (prə-pound′) *v.* To put forward for consideration or debate. [< L *prōpōnere*, to PROPOSE.] —pro•pound′er *n.*

pro•pri•e•tar•y (prə-prī′ə-tĕr′ē) *adj.* **1.** Of or characteristic of a proprietor or proprietors. **2.** Exclusively owned; private. [< L *proprietās*, property, propriety.]

pro•pri•e•tor (prə-prī′ə-tər) *n.* An owner. [Var of PROPRIETARY.] —pro•pri′e•tor•ship′ *n.* —pro•pri′e•tress *fem.n.*

pro•pri•e•ty (prə-prī′ə-tē) *n., pl.* **-ties. 1.** The quality of being proper; appropriateness. **2.** Conformity to prevailing customs and usages. [< L *proprius*, PROPER.]

pro•pul•sion (prə-pŭl′shən) *n.* **1.** The process of propelling. **2.** A driving force. [< L *prōpellere* (pp *prōpulsus*), to drive forward, PROPEL.] —pro•pul′sive *adj.*

pro ra•ta (prō rä′tə, rāt′ə, rä′tə). In proportion. [L *pro rata (parte)*, according to the calculated (share).]

pro•rate (prō-rāt′, prō′rāt′) *v.* **-rated, -rating.** To divide, distribute, or assess proportionately. [< PRO RATA.] —pro•ra′tion *n.*

pro•rogue (prō-rōg′) *v.* **-rogued, -roguing.** To discontinue a session of (a legislative body). [< L *prōrogāre*, "to ask publicly," defer.] —pro′ro•ga′tion *n.*

pros. prosody.

pro•sa•ic (prō-zā′ĭk) *adj.* **1.** Matter-of-fact; straightforward. **2.** Dull; ordinary. [< L *prōsa*, PROSE.] —pro•sa′i•cal•ly *adv.*

pro•sce•ni•um (prō-sē′nē-əm) *n., pl.* **-nia** (-nē-ə). The area located between the curtain and orchestra in a theater. [< Gk *proskēnion.*]

pro•scribe (prō-skrīb′) *v.* **-scribed, -scribing. 1.** To outlaw. **2.** To prohibit; forbid. [L *prōscribere*, to publish in writing, proscribe.] —pro•scrip′tion (-skrĭp′shən) *n.*

prose (prōz) *n.* Ordinary speech or writing as distinguished from verse. [< L *prōsa (ōrātiō)*, "straightforward discourse."]

pros•e•cute (prŏs′ə-kyōot′) *v.* **-cuted, -cuting. 1.** To pursue or persist in so as to complete. **2.** To initiate and conduct court action against. [< L *prōsequī*, to follow up or forward.] —pros′e•cu′tion *n.* —pros′e•cu′tor *n.*

pros•e•lyte (prŏs′ə-līt′) *n.* A new convert to a religion or doctrine. [< Gk *prosēlutos*, "one who comes to a place," stranger, religious convert.]

pros•e•lyt•ize (prŏs′ə-lə-tīz′) *v.* **-ized, -izing.** To convert from one doctrine to another. —pros′e•lyt•iz′er *n.*

pros•o•dy (prŏs′ə-dē) *n.* The study of the metrical structures of verse. [< Gk *prosōidia*, accompanied song, modulation of voice.] —pro•sod′ic (prō-sŏd′ĭk) *adj.*

pros•pect (prŏs′pĕkt′) *n.* **1.** Something expected; a possibility. **2. prospects.** Chances for success. **3.** A potential customer or candidate. **4.** The direction in which something faces; an outlook. **5.** A scene; view. —*v.* To explore for mineral deposits. [< L *prōspectus*, pp of *prōspicere*, to look forward, foresee.] —pros′-pec′tor *n.*

pro•spec•tive (prə-spĕk′tĭv) *adj.* Expected. —pro•spec′tive•ly *adv.*

pro•spec•tus (prə-spĕk′təs) *n., pl.* **-tuses.** A formal summary of a proposed commercial venture. [L, PROSPECT.]

pros•per (prŏs′pər) *v.* To be successful; thrive. [< L *prosperus*, fortunate.]

pros•per•i•ty (prŏs-pĕr′ə-tē) *n.* Financial success or well-being.

pros•per•ous (prŏs′pər-əs) *adj.* **1.** Flourishing or wealthy. **2.** Propitious; favorable.

pros•tate (prŏs′tāt′) *n.* A gland in male mammals composed of muscular and glandular tissue that surrounds the urethra at the bladder. [< Gk *prostatēs*, "one that stands before (the bladder)."]

pros•the•sis (prŏs-thē′sĭs) *n., pl.* **-ses** (-sēz′). An artificial replacement for a limb, tooth, or other part of the body. [< Gk, attachment, addition.] —pros•thet′ic (-thĕt′ĭk) *adj.* —pros•thet′i•cal•ly *adv.*

pros•thet•ics (prŏs-thĕt′ĭks) *n. (takes sing. v.).* Prosthetic surgery or dentistry.

pros•ti•tute (prŏs′tə-t/yōot′) *n.* A whore. —*v.* **-tuted, -tuting. 1.** To offer (oneself or another) for sexual hire. **2.** To sell (one's talents) to an unworthy cause. [< L *prōstituere*, to expose publicly, prostitute.] —pros′ti•tu′tion *n.*

pros•trate (prŏs′trāt′) *v.* **-trated, -trating. 1.** To put or throw down in a posture of adoration or submission. **2.** To lay low; overcome. —*adj.* **1.** Lying face down. **2.** Exhausted; incapacitated. [< L *prōsternere*, to throw down, prostrate.] —pros•tra′tion *n.*

Prot. Protestant.

pro•tac•tin•i•um (prō′tăk-tĭn′ē-əm) *n. Symbol*

protagonist / provincial

Pa A rare radioactive element chemically similar to uranium. Atomic number 91, longest-lived isotope Pa 231. [< PROT(O)- + ACTINIUM.]

pro·tag·o·nist (prō-tăg′ə-nĭst) *n.* **1.** A leading character in a drama or story. **2.** Any leading figure. [< PROT(O)- + Gk *agōnistēs*, actor.]

pro·tect (prə-tĕkt′) *v.* To keep from harm or injury; guard. [L *prōtegere* (pp *prōtectus*), to cover in front, protect.] —**pro·tec′tion** *n.* —**pro·tec′tive** *adj.* —**pro·tec′tor** *n.*

pro·tec·tor·ate (prə-tĕk′tər-ĭt) *n.* **1.** A relationship of partial control assumed by a superior power over a dependent country or region. **2.** The dependent country.

pro·té·gé (prō′tə-zhā′) *n.* One whose welfare or career is promoted by an influential person. [< L *prōtegere*, PROTECT.]

pro·tein (prō′tēn, -tē-ĭn) *n.* Any of a group of complex organic compounds that contain amino acids as their basic structural units, occur in all living matter, and are essential for the growth and repair of animal tissue. [F *protéine*, "primary substance."]

pro·test (prə-tĕst′, prō-tĕst′, prō′tĕst′) *v.* **1.** To object (to). **2.** To promise or affirm solemnly. —*n.* (prō′tĕst′). **1.** The act of protesting. **2.** A strong or solemn objection. [< L *prōtestārī*, to declare in public, testify.] —**prot′es·ta′tion** (prŏt′ĭs-tā′shən, prō′tĭs-) *n.* —**pro·test′er** *n.*

Prot·es·tant (prŏt′ĭs-tənt) *n.* Any Christian belonging to a sect descending from those that seceded from the Church of Rome at the time of the Reformation. [< L *prōtestārī*, to PROTEST.] —**Prot′es·tant·ism′** *n.*

Protestant Episcopal Church. A church body in the U.S. originally associated with the Church of England, but a separate entity since 1789.

proto-. *comb. form.* **1.** The earliest form or the first in rank or time. **2.** Proto-. The earliest reconstructed form of a language: *Proto-Indo-European.* [< Gk *prōtos*, first.]

pro·to·col (prō′tə-kôl′, -kŏl′, -kōl′) *n.* **1.** The forms of ceremony and etiquette observed by diplomats and heads of state. **2.** The first copy of a treaty prior to ratification. **3.** Any preliminary draft or record. [< Gk *prōtokollon*, first sheet glued to a papyrus roll, bearing a table of contents.]

pro·ton (prō′tŏn′) *n. Symbol* **p** A stable, positively charged subatomic particle having a mass 1,836 times that of the electron. [< Gk *prōtos*, first.]

pro·to·plasm (prō′tə-plăz′əm) *n.* A complex, jellylike colloidal substance constituting the living matter of plant and animal cells. —**pro′to·plas′mic, pro′to·plas′mal, pro′to·plas·mat′ic** (-plăz-măt′ĭk) *adj.*

pro·to·type (prō′tə-tīp′) *n.* An original form or model.

pro·to·zo·an (prō′tə-zō′ən) *n., pl.* **-ans** or **-zoa** (-zō′ə). Any of numerous single-celled, usually microscopic organisms belonging to a group that includes the most primitive forms of animal life. [< PROTO- + Gk *zōion*, animal.] —**pro′to·zo′an, pro′to·zo′ic** (-zō′ĭk) *adj.*

pro·tract (prō-trăkt′) *v.* To draw out; prolong.

[L *prōtrahere*, to drag out, lengthen.] —**pro·trac′tion** *n.*

pro·trac·tor (prō-trăk′tər) *n.* A semicircular instrument for measuring and constructing angles.

pro·trude (prō-trōōd′) *v.* **-truded, -truding.** To push or jut outward; project. [L *prōtrūdere.*] —**pro·tru′sion** *n.*

pro·tu·ber·ance (prō-t/y/ōō′bər-əns) *n.* A bulge or swelling. [< LL *prōtūberāre*, to bulge out.] —**pro·tu′ber·ant** *adj.*

proud (proud) *adj.* **1.** Feeling pleasurable satisfaction. **2.** Occasioning pride; gratifying. **3.** Marked by exacting self-respect. **4.** Having excessive self-esteem; haughty; arrogant. **5.** Of great dignity; honored. **6.** Majestic; magnificent. **7.** Spirited. [< LL *prōde*, advantageous.] —**proud′ly** *adv.*

prov. **1.** province; provincial. **2.** provisional. **3.** provost.

Prov. **1.** Provençal. **2.** Proverbs (Old Testament).

prove (prōōv) *v.* **proved, proved** or **proven** (prōō′vən), **proving.** **1.** To establish the truth or validity of by presentation of argument or evidence. **2.** To determine the quality of by testing; try out. **3.** To be shown to be; turn out. [< L *probāre*, to test, demonstrate as good.] —**prov′a·ble** *adj.* —**prov′er** *n.*

prov·e·nance (prŏv′ə-nəns, -näns′) *n.* Place of origin; derivation. [< L *prōvenīre*, to come forth.]

Pro·ven·çal (prō′vən-säl′, prŏv′ən-) *n.* **1.** A native or inhabitant of Provence, France. **2.** The Romance language of Provence, esp. the literary language of the troubadours. —**Pro′ven·çal′** *adj.*

Pro·vence (prô-väns′). A region of SE France.

prov·en·der (prŏv′ən-dər) *n.* **1.** Dry food for livestock. **2.** Food or provisions. [< LL *praebenda*, support, subsistence.]

pro·ve·nience (prə-vēn′yəns, -vē′nē-əns) *n.* Origin; source. [< L *prōvenīre*, to come forth.]

prov·erb (prŏv′ûrb′) *n.* A short, popular saying expressing a well-known truth or fact. [< L *prōverbium*, "set of words put forth."] —**pro·ver′bi·al** (prə-vûr′bē-əl) *adj.*

pro·vide (prə-vīd′) *v.* **-vided, -viding.** **1.** To furnish; supply. **2.** To make ready; prepare. **3.** To make available; afford. **4.** To set down as a stipulation. [< L *prōvidēre*, to foresee.] —**pro·vid′er** *n.*

prov·i·dence (prŏv′ə-dəns, -dĕns′) *n.* **1.** Foresight. **2.** Economy. **3.** Divine direction. **4. Providence.** God.

Prov·i·dence (prŏv′ə-dəns, -dĕns′). The capital of Rhode Island. Pop. 177,000.

prov·i·dent (prŏv′ə-dənt, -dĕnt′) *adj.* **1.** Providing for future needs. **2.** Frugal; economical. —**prov′i·dent·ly** *adv.*

prov·i·den·tial (prŏv′ə-dĕn′shəl) *adj.* **1.** Of or resulting from divine providence. **2.** Fortunate; opportune. —**prov′i·den′tial·ly** *adv.*

prov·ince (prŏv′ĭns) *n.* **1.** A territory governed as an administrative or political unit of a country or empire. **2.** A comprehensive area of interest; sphere. [< L *prōvincia.*]

pro·vin·cial (prə-vĭn′shəl) *adj.* **1.** Of or per-

pat/ā ate/âr care/ä bar/b **bib**/ch **chew**/d **deed**/ĕ pet/ē be/f **fit**/g **gag**/h **hat**/hw **what**/
ĭ pit/ī pie/îr pier/j **judge**/k **kick**/l lid, fatal/m **mum**/n no, sudden/ng **sing**/ŏ pot/ō go/

taining to a province. **2.** Limited in perspective; narrow. —**pro•vin′cial•ism′** *n.*

pro•vi•sion (prə-vĭzh′ən) *n.* **1.** The act of supplying or fitting out. **2.** That which is provided. **3.** A preparatory measure. **4. provisions.** A stock of necessary supplies, esp. food. **5.** A stipulation or qualification. —*v.* To supply with provisions. [< L *prōvīsus,* pp of *prōvidēre,* to PROVIDE.]

pro•vi•sion•al (prə-vĭzh′ən-əl) *adj.* Provided for the time being, pending permanent arrangements. —**pro•vi′sion•al•ly** *adv.*

pro•vi•so (prə-vī′zō) *n., pl.* **-sos** or **-soes.** A qualifying clause or stipulation. [< L *prō-videre,* to PROVIDE.]

prov•o•ca•tion (prŏv′ə-kā′shən) *n.* **1.** The act of provoking or inciting. **2.** A cause of irritation.

pro•voc•a•tive (prə-vŏk′ə-tĭv) *adj.* Exciting; stimulating. —**pro•voc′a•tive•ly** *adv.*

pro•voke (prə-vōk′) *v.* **-voked, -voking. 1.** To incite to anger or resentment. **2.** To incite to action; arouse. **3.** To bring on by inciting: *provoke a fight.* [< L *prōvocāre,* to call forth, challenge.] —**pro•vok′ing•ly** *adv.*

pro•vost (prō′vōst′, prŏv′əst, prō′vəst) *n.* A chief officer, as in some colleges. [< L *prae-positus,* "(one) placed before (others)," president.]

prow (prou) *n.* The forward part of a ship's hull. [F *proue.*]

prow•ess (prou′ĭs) *n.* Superior skill, strength, or courage. [< OF *prod, prud,* gallant, proud.]

prowl (proul) *v.* To roam about furtively, as in search of prey. [ME *prollen.*] —**prowl** *n.* —**prowl′er** *n.*

prowl car. A squad car.

prox•im•i•ty (prŏk-sĭm′ə-tē) *n.* Nearness; closeness. [< L *proximus,* nearest.]

prox•y (prŏk′sē) *n., pl.* **-ies. 1.** A person authorized to act for another; agent. **2.** The written authorization for such action. [< L *prōcūrātiō,* a caring for.]

prude (prōōd) *n.* One who is overconcerned with being or seeming to be modest or proper. [< OF *preudefemme,* virtuous woman.] —**prud′ish** *adj.* —**prud′ish•ness** *n.*

pru•dence (prōōd′əns) *n.* **1.** The state, quality, or fact of being prudent; discretion. **2.** Careful management; economy. —**pru•den′tial** *adj.* —**pru•den′tial•ly** *adv.*

pru•dent (prōōd′ənt) *adj.* **1.** Wise in handling practical matters. **2.** Provident. **3.** Careful about one's conduct. [< L *prūdēns,* foreseeing, wise < *prōvidens,* provident.] —**pru′dent•ly** *adv.*

prud•er•y (prōō′də-rē) *n., pl.* **-ies. 1.** Excessive regard for propriety, modesty, or morality. **2.** An instance of prudish behavior. [< PRUDE.]

prune[1] (prōōn) *n.* A partially dried plum. [< L *prūnum,* plum.]

prune[2] (prōōn) *v.* **pruned, pruning. 1.** To cut branches, stems, etc., from (a plant) to improve shape or growth. **2.** To remove as superfluous. **3.** To reduce; retrench. [< VL *prō-rotundiāre,* to cut round in front.] —**prun′er** *n.*

pru•ri•ent (prōōr′ē-ənt) *adj.* Obsessively in-

terested in matters of a sexual nature. [< L *prūrīre,* to itch, be lascivious.] —**pru′ri•ence** *n.*

Prus•sia (prŭsh′ə). A former German kingdom and state in N and C Germany. —**Prus′sian** *adj. & n.*

pry[1] (prī) *v.* **pried, prying.** To look closely, curiously, or inquisitively; snoop. [ME *prien.*] —**pry** *n.* —**pry′ing•ly** *adv.*

pry[2] (prī) *v.* **pried, prying. 1.** To raise, move, or force open with a lever. **2.** To obtain with difficulty. —*n., pl.* **pries. 1.** Something used to apply leverage, such as a crowbar. **2.** Leverage. [Var of PRIZE[3].]

pry•er. Variant of prier.

Ps. Psalm; Psalms (Old Testament).

p.s. postscript.

P.S. 1. postscript. **2.** public school.

Psa. Psalm; Psalms (Old Testament).

psalm (säm) *n.* **1.** A sacred song; hymn. **2.** Often **Psalm.** Any of the sacred songs or hymns collected in the Old Testament Book of Psalms. [< Gk *psalmos,* song sung to the harp, psalm.] —**psalm′ist** *n.*

pseud. pseudonym.

pseu•do (sōō′dō) *adj.* Counterfeit; fake.

pseudo-. *comb. form.* **1.** Lack of authenticity; sham. **2.** Deceptive similarity. [< Gk *pseudēs,* false.]

pseu•do•nym (sōō′də-nĭm′) *n.* A fictitious name assumed by an author; pen name.

psf, p.s.f. pounds per square foot.

pshaw (shô) *interj.* Expressive of impatience, irritation, or disbelief.

psi (psī, sī) *n.* The 23rd letter of the Greek alphabet, representing *ps.*

psi, p.s.i. pounds per square inch.

pso•ri•a•sis (sə-rī′ə-sĭs) *n.* A chronic, noncontagious skin disease characterized by inflammation and white, scaly patches. [< Gk *psōrian,* to have the itch.]

PST, P.S.T. Pacific Standard Time.

psych (sīk) *n. Informal.* Psychology.

psych. psychologist; psychology.

psy•che (sī′kē) *n.* **1.** The soul or spirit as distinguished from the body. **2.** The mind functioning as the center of thought, feeling, and behavior. [Gk *psukhē,* breath, life, soul.]

psych•e•del•ic (sī′kə-dĕl′ĭk) *adj.* Of or generating hallucinations, distortions of perception, and, occasionally, states resembling psychosis. [< PSYCHE + Gk *dēlos,* clear, visible.]

psy•chi•a•try (sĭ-kī′ə-trē, sī-) *n.* The medical study, diagnosis, treatment, and prevention of mental illness. [PSYCH(O)- + -IATRY.] —**psy′-chi•at′ric** (sī′kē-ăt′rĭk) *adj.* —**psy•chi′a•trist** *n.*

psy•chic (sī′kĭk) *adj.* Also **psy•chi•cal** (-kĭ-kəl). **1.** Pertaining to the human mind or psyche. **2.** Pertaining to extraordinary, esp. extrasensory and nonphysical, mental processes, such as extrasensory perception and mental telepathy. —*n.* **1.** An individual apparently unresponsive to psychic forces. **2.** A medium. [< Gk *psukhē,* soul, life, PSYCHE.] —**psy′chi•cal•ly** *adv.*

psy•cho (sī′kō) *n., pl.* **-chos.** *Slang.* A psychopath.

psycho-. *comb. form.* The mind or mental processes. [< Gk *psukhē,* breath, life, PSYCHE.]

psy·cho·a·nal·y·sis (sī'kō-ə-năl'ə-sĭs) *n.* **1.** The analytic technique originated by Sigmund Freud to investigate mental processes. **2.** The theory of human psychology founded by Freud. **3.** Any psychiatric therapy incorporating such an analytic technique in such a theoretical framework. —**psy'cho·an'a·lyst** (-ăn'ə-lĭst) *n.* —**psy'cho·an'a·lyt'ic** (-ăn'ə-lĭt'ĭk), **psy'cho·an'a·lyt'i·cal** *adj.* —**psy'cho·an'a·lyt'i·cal·ly** *adv.* —**psy'cho·an'a·lyze** *v.* (-lyzed, -lyzing).

psychol. psychologist; psychology.

psy·cho·log·i·cal (sī'kə-lŏj'ĭ-kəl) *adj.* **1.** Pertaining to psychology. **2.** Of or involving the mind or emotions. —**psy'cho·log'i·cal·ly** *adv.*

psy·chol·o·gy (sī-kŏl'ə-jē) *n., pl.* **-gies. 1.** The science of mental processes and behavior. **2.** The emotional and behavioral characteristics of an individual, group, or activity: *the psychology of war.* **3.** Subtle tactical action or argument. —**psy·chol'o·gist** *n.*

psy·cho·path (sī'kə-păth') *n.* A person with a personality disorder, esp. one manifested in aggressively antisocial behavior. —**psy'cho·path'ic** *adj.*

psy·cho·sis (sī-kō'sĭs) *n., pl.* **-ses** (-sēz'). Any severe mental disorder, with or without organic damage, characterized by deterioration of normal intellectual and social functioning and by partial or complete withdrawal from reality.

psy·cho·so·mat·ic (sī'kō-sō-măt'ĭk) *adj.* Both physiological and psychological.

psy·cho·ther·a·py (sī'kō-thĕr'ə-pē) *n.* The psychological treatment of mental, emotional, and nervous disorders. —**psy'cho·ther'a·pist** *n.*

psy·chot·ic (sī-kŏt'ĭk) *n.* One afflicted with a psychosis. —*adj.* Of or caused by psychosis. —**psy·chot'i·cal·ly** *adv.*

Pt platinum.

pt. 1. part. **2.** payment. **3.** pint. **4.** point. **5.** port.

p.t. pro tempore.

P.T. 1. Pacific Time. **2.** physical therapy. **3.** physical training.

PTA, P.T.A. Parent-Teachers Association.

ptar·mi·gan (tär'mĭ-gən) *n., pl.* **-gan** or **-gans.** A grouselike bird of northern regions. [Var of Scot Gael *tarmachan.*]

PT boat. A fast, lightly armed vessel used to torpedo enemy shipping. [< patrol torpedo boat.]

ptero–. *comb. form.* Feather, wing, or winglike part. [< Gk *pteron,* feather, wing.]

pter·o·dac·tyl (tĕr'ə-dăk'tĭl) *n.* An extinct flying reptile.

ptg. printing.

Ptol·e·my (tŏl'ə-mē). Greek astronomer of the 2nd century A.D. —**Ptol'e·ma'ic** (tŏl'ə-mā'ĭk) *adj.*

pto·maine (tō'mān', tō-mān') *n.* Also **pto·main.** Any of various basic nitrogenous materials, some poisonous, produced by the putrefaction and decomposition of protein. [Gk *ptōma,* "fall, fallen body," corpse.]

pty. proprietary.

Pu plutonium.

pub (pŭb) *n.* A tavern; bar. [Short for PUBLIC HOUSE.]

pub. 1. public. **2.** publication. **3.** published; publisher.

pu·ber·ty (pyōō'bər-tē) *n.* The stage of maturation in which the individual becomes physiologically capable of sexual reproduction. [< L *pūber,* adult.]

pu·bic (pyōō'bĭk) *adj.* Of or in the region of the lower part of the abdomen.

publ. 1. public. **2.** publication. **3.** published; publisher.

pub·lic (pŭb'lĭk) *adj.* **1.** Of, concerning, or affecting the community or the people. **2.** Maintained for, used by, or open to the people or community: *a public park.* **3.** Serving or acting on behalf of the people or community: *public office.* **4.** Open to general knowledge; widely known. —*n.* **1.** The community or the people as a whole. **2.** A group of people sharing a common interest. [< L *populus,* people.] —**pub'lic·ly** *adv.*

pub·li·can (pŭb'lĭ-kən) *n.* **1.** *Chiefly Brit.* The keeper of a public house. **2.** A tax collector in the ancient Roman Empire.

pub·li·ca·tion (pŭb'lĭ-kā'shən) *n.* **1.** The act or process of publishing. **2.** Published material. [< L *pūblicāre,* to make public.]

public domain. The status of being unprotected by patent or copyright.

public house. *Chiefly Brit.* A licensed tavern or bar.

pub·li·cist (pŭb'lə-sĭst) *n.* One who publicizes, esp. a press or publicity agent.

pub·lic·i·ty (pŭ-blĭs'ə-tē) *n.* **1.** Information that attracts public notice. **2.** Public interest or notice.

pub·li·cize (pŭb'lə-sīz') *v.* **-cized, -cizing.** To give publicity to.

public relations. The activities undertaken by an organization to promote a favorable relationship with the public.

public school. 1. In the U.S., a tax-supported school. **2.** In Great Britain, a private secondary boarding school.

pub·lic-spir·i·ted (pŭb'lĭk-spîr'ĭ-tĭd) *adj.* Motivated by devotion to public welfare.

pub·lish (pŭb'lĭsh) *v.* **1.** To prepare and issue (printed material) for public distribution or sale. **2.** To announce to the public. [< L *pūblicāre,* to make public.] —**pub'lish·a·ble** *adj.* —**pub'lish·er** *n.*

Puc·ci·ni (pōōt-chē'nē), **Giacomo.** 1858–1924. Italian composer of operas.

puce (pyōōs) *n.* Deep red to dark grayish purple. [F *(couleur) puce,* "flea (color)."] —**puce** *adj.*

puck (pŭk) *n.* A hard rubber disk used in ice hockey. [< POKE.]

Puck (pŭk) *n.* A mischievous sprite. [< OE *pūca.*] —**puck'ish** *adj.*

puck·a. Variant of **pukka.**

puck·er (pŭk'ər) *v.* To gather into wrinkles or folds. —*n.* A wrinkle or wrinkled part. [Perh < POCKET.]

pud·ding (pōōd'ĭng) *n.* A soft dessert usually containing flour or a cereal product. [< OF *boudin.*]

pud·dle (pŭd'l) *n.* A small pool of liquid, as of muddy water. [< OE *pudd,* ditch.]

ă pat/ā ate/âr care/ä bar/b **bib**/ch **chew**/d **deed**/ĕ pet/ē be/f fit/g **gag**/h **hat**/hw **what**/ ĭ pit/ī pie/îr **pier**/j **judge**/k **kick**/l lid, fatal/m **mum**/n no, sudden/ng sing/ŏ pot/ō go/

pud•dling (pŭd′lĭng) *n.* The purification of impure metal, esp. pig iron, by agitation of a molten bath of the metal in an oxidizing atmosphere.

pudg•y (pŭj′ē) *adj.* **-ier, -iest.** Short and fat; chubby. [Prob < Scot *pud,* belly.]

pueb•lo (pwĕb′lō) *n., pl.* **-los. 1.** A flat-roofed community dwelling, up to five stories high, of Indian tribes of the SW U.S. **2. Pueblo.** A member of a tribe, as the Hopi, inhabiting such dwellings. [Span, "people."]

pu•er•ile (pyōō′ər-ĭl, pyōōr′ĭl, -ĭl′, pwĕr′ĭl, -ĭl′) *adj.* Immature; childish. [< L *puer,* child, boy.] **—pu′er•il′i•ty** *n.*

Puer•to Ri•co (pwĕr′tō rē′kō, pōr′-). An island in the Caribbean; a self-governing U.S. Commonwealth. Pop. 2,584,000. Cap. San Juan. **—Puerto Rican.**

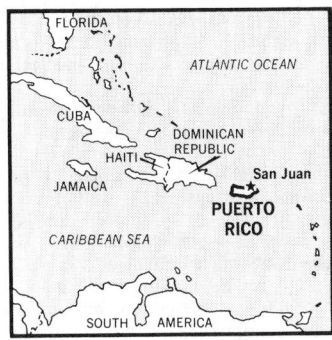

Puerto Rico

puff (pŭf) *n.* **1. a.** A short, forceful discharge, as of smoke or air. **b.** A short, sibilant sound produced by a puff. **2.** A swelling or rounded protuberance. **3.** A light, inflated pastry. **4.** A soft pad for applying cosmetic powder. **5.** An approving or flattering recommendation. —*v.* **1.** To blow in puffs. **2.** To breathe forcefully and rapidly. **3.** To emit clouds of smoke, vapor, etc. **4.** To swell or seem to swell. **5.** To fill with pride or conceit. **6.** To praise exaggeratedly. [< OE *pyffan.*] **—puff′er** *n.* **—puff′i•ness** *n.* **—puff′y** *adj.*

puff•ball (pŭf′bôl′) *n.* A ball-shaped fungus that releases dustlike spores when broken open.

puf•fin (pŭf′ĭn) *n.* A black and white northern sea bird with a flattened, brightly colored bill. [ME *poffoun.*]

pug (pŭg) *n.* **1.** A small, short-haired dog with a square, flat muzzle. **2.** A short, turned-up nose. [?]

pu•gi•lism (pyōō′jə-lĭz′əm) *n.* Boxing. [< L *pugil,* fighter.] **—pu′gi•list** *n.* **—pu′gi•lis′tic** *adj.*

pug•na•cious (pŭg-nā′shəs) *adj.* Eager to fight; aggressive by nature. [< L *pugnus,* fist.] **—pug•nac′i•ty** (pŭg-năs′ə-tē) *n.*

puis•sance (pwĭs′əns, pyōō′ə-səns, pyōō-ĭs′-əns) *n.* Power; might. [< L *posse,* to be powerful.] **—puis′sant** *adj.* **—puis′sant•ly** *adv.*

puke (pyōōk) *v.* **puked, puking.** To vomit.

puk•ka (pŭk′ə) *adj.* Also **puck•a. 1.** Genuine; authentic. **2.** Superior; first-class. [Hindi *pakkā,* cooked, ripe, firm.]

pul•chri•tude (pŭl′krĭ-t/y/ōōd′) *n.* Physical beauty. [< L *pulcher,* beautiful.]

pule (pyōōl) *v.* **puled, puling.** To whine; whimper. **—pul′er** *n.*

pull (pōōl) *v.* **1.** To apply force so as to draw something toward the force. **2.** To move. **3.** To extract. **4.** To tug; jerk. **5.** To rip or tear. **6.** To stretch. **7.** To strain. **8.** *Informal.* To attract. **9.** *Informal.* To perform, esp. with skill. **10.** To draw (a knife or gun). **11.** To produce (an impression) from type. —*n.* **1.** The action or process of pulling. **2.** Force exerted in pulling. **3.** Something used for pulling. **4.** *Slang.* Special influence. **5.** *Informal.* Ability to attract; appeal. [< OE *pullian.*]

pul•let (pōōl′ĭt) *n.* A young hen. [< L *pullus,* young of an animal, chicken.]

pul•ley (pōōl′ē) *n., pl.* **-leys. 1.** A simple machine used esp. for lifting weight, consisting essentially of a wheel with a grooved rim in which a pulled rope or chain is run. **2.** A wheel turned by or driving a belt. [Prob < Gk *polos,* pole, pivot.]

Pull•man (pōōl′mən) *n.* Also **Pullman car.** A railroad parlor car or sleeping car. [< G.M. *Pullman* (1831–1897), American industrialist.]

pull•o•ver (pōōl′ō′vər) *n.* A garment, as a sweater, put on by being drawn over the head.

pul•mo•nar•y (pōōl′mə-nĕr′ē, pŭl′-) *adj.* Of or involving the lungs. [< L *pulmō,* lung.]

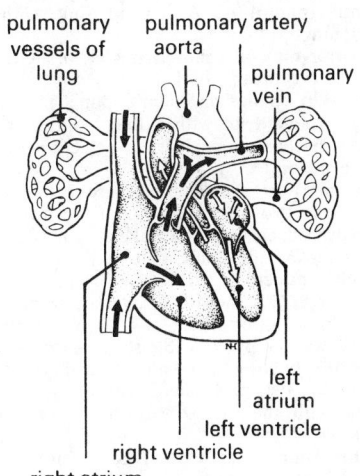

pulmonary
Pulmonary circulation

pulp (pŭlp) *n.* **1.** A soft, moist mass. **2.** The soft, moist part of fruit. **3.** A moist mixture of ground wood, rags, etc., used to make paper. **4.** The soft inner structure of a tooth, consisting of nerve and blood vessels. **5.** A magazine with lurid subject matter, usually printed on rough paper. [L *pulpa,* solid flesh, pulp.] **—pulp′y** *adj.*

ô paw, for/oi boy/ou out/ōō took/ōō coo/p pop/r run/s sauce/sh shy/t to/th thin/*th* the/
ŭ cut/ûr fur/v van/w wag/y yes/z size/zh vision/ə ago, item, edible, gallop, circus/

pul·pit (pŏŏl′pĭt, pŭl′-) *n.* An elevated platform or lectern, as one used in conducting a religious service. [< L *pulpitum,* scaffold, platform.]

pul·sar (pŭl′sär′) *n. Astron.* Any of several very short-period variable Galactic radio sources.

pul·sate (pŭl′sāt′) *v.* -sated, -sating. To expand and contract rhythmically. —**pul·sa′tion** *n.*

pulse (pŭls) *n.* 1. The rhythmical throbbing of arteries produced by the regular contractions of the heart. 2. *Electronics.* A transient amplification or intensification of a characteristic of a system. —*v.* pulsed, pulsing. To pulsate. [< L *pulsus,* pp of *pellere,* to push, beat.]

pul·ver·ize (pŭl′və-rīz′) *v.* -ized, -izing. To crush or grind to a powder or dust. [< L *pulvis* (*pulver-*), dust.]

pu·ma (pyŏŏ′mə) *n.* The mountain lion. [< Quechua.]

pum·ice (pŭm′ĭs) *n.* A porous, lightweight volcanic rock used as an abrasive and polish. [< L *pūmex.*]

pum·mel (pŭm′əl) *v.* -meled or -melled, -meling or -melling. To beat; pommel.

pump¹ (pŭmp) *n.* A machine or device for transferring a liquid or gas from a source or container through tubes or pipes to another container or receiver. —*v.* 1. To propel, eject, or insert with or as with a pump. 2. To question closely or persistently: *pump a witness.* 3. To move up and down in the manner of a pump handle. [< MLG *pumpe* or MDu *pompe.*] —**pump′er** *n.*

pump² (pŭmp) *n.* A low-cut shoe without fastenings. [?]

pump·per·nick·el (pŭm′pər-nĭk′əl) *n.* A dark, coarse rye bread. [G.]

pump·kin (pŭmp′kĭn, pŭm′-, pŭng′-) *n.* 1. A large, round fruit with a thick, orange rind. 2. A vine bearing such fruit. [< Gk *pepōn,* a large melon.]

pun (pŭn) *n.* A humorous use of a word involving two interpretations of the meaning. —*v.* punned, punning. To make a pun. [Perh < It *puntiglio,* fine point, quibble.]

punch¹ (pŭnch) *n.* 1. A tool for piercing or stamping. 2. A tool for forcing a pin, bolt, or rivet in or out of a hole. —*v.* To perforate or mark with a punch. [Short for PUNCHEON.]

punch² (pŭnch) *v.* 1. To hit with a sharp blow, as of the fist. 2. To herd (cattle). —*n.* 1. A blow with the fist. 2. Vigor or drive. [ME *punchen.*]

punch³ (pŭnch) *n.* A beverage of fruit juices, often with a wine or liquor base. [Perh < Hindi *pānch.*]

pun·cheon (pŭn′chən) *n.* 1. A short, wooden upright used in structural framing. 2. A piece of broad, roughly dressed timber. [< L *pungere,* to prick.]

punch line. The climax of a joke or humorous story.

punc·til·i·o (pŭngk-tĭl′ē-ō′) *n.* Precise observance of formalities. [It *punctiglio,* PUN.]

punc·til·i·ous (pŭngk-tĭl′ē-əs) *adj.* 1. Attentive to details of formal conduct. 2. Precise; scrupulous. —**punc·til′i·ous·ly** *adv.*

punc·tu·al (pŭngk′chŏŏ-əl) *adj.* Acting or arriving at the time appointed; prompt. [ML *punctuālis,* "to the point."] —**punc·tu·al′i·ty** *n.* —**punc′tu·al·ly** *adv.*

punc·tu·ate (pŭngk′chŏŏ-āt′) *v.* -ated, -ating. 1. To provide (a text) with punctuation. 2. To interrupt periodically. 3. To emphasize. [< L *punctum,* pricked mark, point.]

punc·tu·a·tion (pŭngk′chŏŏ-ā′shən) *n.* 1. The use of standard marks in writing and printing to separate units and clarify meaning. 2. The marks so used.

punc·ture (pŭngk′chər) *v.* -tured, -turing. 1. To pierce with or as with a sharp or pointed object. 2. To deflate by or as by piercing. —*n.* 1. An act or instance of puncturing. 2. A hole made by a sharp or pointed object. [L *punctūra,* a pricking, puncture.]

pun·dit (pŭn′dĭt) *n.* A learned person. [< Sk *paṇḍita.*]

pun·gent (pŭn′jənt) *adj.* 1. Sharp and acrid to taste or smell. 2. Penetrating; biting; caustic. [< L *pungere,* to prick, sting.] —**pun′gen·cy** *n.* —**pun′gent·ly** *adv.*

Pu·nic (pyŏŏ′nĭk) *adj.* Of or pertaining to ancient Carthage. [< L *Poenus,* a Carthaginian.]

pun·ish (pŭn′ĭsh) *v.* 1. To subject to penalty for a crime or offense. 2. To inflict a penalty for (an offense). 3. To injure; hurt. [< L *pūnīre, poenīre.*] —**pun′ish·a·ble** *adj.*

pun·ish·ment (pŭn′ĭsh-mənt) *n.* 1. a. An act of punishing. b. The condition of being punished. 2. A penalty imposed for wrongdoing. 3. Rough handling.

pu·ni·tive (pyŏŏ′nə-tĭv) *adj.* Inflicting or aiming to inflict punishment. —**pu′ni·tive·ly** *adv.*

punk¹ (pŭngk) *n.* Dry, decayed wood or fungi, used as tinder. [?]

punk² (pŭngk) *n. Slang.* 1. An inexperienced youth. 2. A young ruffian. —*adj.* Of poor quality. [Earlier *punck.*]

punt¹ (pŭnt) *n.* An open, flat-bottomed boat propelled by a pole. —*v.* To propel (a boat) with a pole. [< L *pontō,* floating bridge, pontoon.] —**punt′er** *n.*

punt² (pŭnt) *n.* A kick in which a football is dropped and kicked before touching the ground. —*v.* To kick by means of a punt. [Prob dial *bunt, punt,* to push, kick.]

pu·ny (pyŏŏ′nē) *adj.* -nier, -niest. Of inferior size, strength, or significance; weak. [OF *puisne,* "born afterward."] —**pu′ni·ly** *adv.* —**pu′ni·ness** *n.*

pup (pŭp) *n.* 1. A young dog; puppy. 2. A young seal or similar animal. [Back-formation < PUPPY.]

pu·pa (pyŏŏ′pə) *n., pl.* -pae (-pē′) or -pas. An inactive stage in the life cycle of an insect, between the larval and adult forms. [< L *pūpa,* girl, doll.] —**pu′pal** *adj.*

pu·pil¹ (pyŏŏ′pəl) *n.* A student supervised by a teacher. [< L *pūpus,* boy.]

pu·pil² (pyŏŏ′pəl) *n.* The apparently black circular aperture in the center of the iris of the eye. [< L *pūpilla,* "little orphan girl," pupil.]

pup·pet (pŭp′ĭt) *n.* 1. A small figure of a person or animal, moved by strings or by the

---

ă pat/ā ate/âr care/ä bar/b bib/ch chew/d deed/ĕ pet/ē be/f fit/g gag/h hat/hw what/
ĭ pit/ī pie/îr pier/j judge/k kick/l lid, fatal/m mum/n no, sudden/ng sing/ŏ pot/ō go/

hand. **2.** One whose behavior is controlled by others. [< L *pŭpa*, girl, doll.]

pup•py (pŭp'ē) *n., pl.* **-pies.** A young dog. [< L *pŭpa*, doll.]

pur•blind (pûr'blīnd') *adj.* **1.** Nearly or partly blind. **2.** Slow in understanding or discerning. [ME *pureblind*, orig "totally blind" : PURE + BLIND.] **—pur'blind'ness** *n.*

pur•chase (pûr'chĭs) *v.* **-chased, -chasing.** To obtain in exchange for money or its equivalent; buy. **—n. 1.** That which is bought. **2.** The act or an instance of buying. **3.** A secure hold. [< OF *purchacier*, to pursue, seek to obtain.] **—pur'chas•er** *n.*

pure (pyŏŏr) *adj.* **purer, purest. 1.** Having a uniform composition; not mixed. **2.** Free from adulterants or impurities. **3.** Free from contaminants; clean. **4.** Complete; utter. **5.** Without faults; perfect; sinless. **6.** Chaste; virgin. **7.** Theoretical rather than applied: *pure science.* [< L *pūrus*, clean.] **—pure'ly** *adv.*

pure•bred (pyŏŏr'brĕd') *adj.* Of a strain established through constant breeding of unmixed stock.

pu•rée (pyŏŏ-rā', pyŏŏr'ā) *v.* **-réed, -réeing.** To rub (food) through a strainer. **—n.** Food so prepared. [< OF *purer*, to purify, strain.]

pur•ga•tion (pûr-gā'shən) *n.* The act of purging or purifying.

pur•ga•tive (pûr'gə-tĭv) *adj.* Tending to cleanse or purge, esp. tending to cause evacuation of the bowels. **—n.** A purgative agent or medicine.

pur•ga•to•ry (pûr'gə-tôr'ē, -tōr'ē) *n., pl.* **-ries. 1.** *R.C.Ch.* A state in which the souls of those who have died in grace must expiate their sins. **2.** Any place of expiation or remorse. [< L *purgāre*, to PURGE.] **—pur'ga•to'ri•al** (-tôr'ē-əl, -tōr'ē-əl) *adj.*

purge (pûrj) *v.* **purged, purging. 1.** To purify. **2.** To rid of sin or guilt. **3.** To rid (a nation, political party, etc.) of persons considered undesirable. **4.** To cause evacuation of the bowels. **—n. 1.** The act or process of purging. **2.** That which purges. [< L *purgāre*, to cleanse.] **—purg'er** *n.*

pu•ri•fy (pyŏŏr'ə-fī') *v.* **-fied, -fying.** To make or become clean or pure. **—pu'ri•fi•ca'tion** *n.* **—pu•rif'i•ca•to'ry** (pyŏŏ-rĭf'ĭ-kə-tôr'ē, -tōr'ē) *adj.* **—pu'ri•fi'er** *n.*

pur•ism (pyŏŏr'ĭz'əm) *n.* Strict observance of traditional correctness, esp. of language. **—pur'ist** *n.*

pu•ri•tan (pyŏŏr'ə-tən) *n.* **1.** Puritan. A member of the 16th- and 17th-century English Protestant group advocating simplification of the ceremonies of the Church of England. **2.** One who advocates strict religious and moral discipline. [< LL *pūritās*, purity.] **—pu'ri•tan'i•cal** *adj.* **—pu'ri•tan'i•cal•ly** *adv.*

pu•ri•ty (pyŏŏr'ə-tē) *n.* The quality or condition of being pure.

purl¹ (pûrl) *v.* To flow or ripple with a murmuring sound. **—n.** The sound made by rippling water. [Norw *purla*.]

purl² (pûrl) *v.* To knit with an inverted stitch. **—n.** An inverted knitting stitch. [Earlier *pyrle*.]

pur•lieu (pûrl'yŏŏ, pûr'lŏŏ) *n.* **1.** Any outlying area. **2.** purlieus. Outskirts; environs. [< NF *puralée*, perambulation.]

pur•loin (pər-loin', pûr'loin') *v.* To steal; filch. [< NF *purloigner*, "to put far away."]

pur•ple (pûr'pəl) *n.* **1.** A bluish red color. **2.** Cloth of this color, worn as a symbol of royalty or high office. **—adj. 1.** Of the color purple. **2.** Elaborate: *purple prose.* [< Gk *porphura*, shellfish yielding a purple dye, purple dye.] **—pur'plish** *adj.*

pur•port (pər-pôrt', -pōrt', pûr'pôrt', -pōrt') *v.* **1.** To claim or profess as the meaning. **2.** To have or give the impression, often falsely, of being. **—n.** (pûr'pôrt', -pōrt'). An apparent meaning or significance. [< ML *prōportāre*, to carry forth.] **—pur•port'ed•ly** (pər-pôr'tĭd-lē, pər-pōr'-) *adv.*

pur•pose (pûr'pəs) *n.* **1.** A result or effect that is intended or desired; intention. **2.** Determination; resolution. **—on purpose.** Intentionally. **—v. -posed, -posing.** To resolve to perform or accomplish. [< L *prōpōnere* (pp *prōpositus*), to PROPOSE.] **—pur'pose•ful** *adj.* **—pur'pose•ly** *adv.*

purr (pûr) *n.* **1.** The low, vibrant sound made by a cat to express contentment. **2.** A similar sound. **—purr** *v.*

purse (pûrs) *n.* **1.** A small bag or pouch for carrying money. **2.** A woman's handbag. **3.** Available wealth or resources. **4.** A sum of money offered as a present or prize. **—v. pursed, pursing.** To pucker. [< Gk *bursa*, leather, hide.]

purs•er (pûr'sər) *n.* The officer in charge of money matters on board a ship. [< PURSE.]

pur•su•ance (pər-soo'əns) *n.* A carrying out or putting into effect.

pur•su•ant (pər-soo'ənt) *adj.* **—pursuant to.** In accordance with.

pur•sue (pər-soo') *v.* **-sued, -suing. 1.** To follow in an effort to overtake; chase. **2.** To strive to accomplish. **3.** To follow. **4.** To engage in (a vocation, hobby, etc.). [< L *prōsequi*.] **—pur•su'a•ble** *adj.* **—pur•su'er** *n.*

pur•suit (pər-soot') *n.* **1.** The act or an instance of pursuing. **2.** Any vocation, hobby, etc.

pu•ru•lence (pyŏŏr'ə-ləns, pyŏŏr'yə-) *n.* **1.** The condition of secreting or containing pus. **2.** Pus.

pu•ru•lent (pyŏŏr'ə-lənt, pyŏŏr'yə-) *adj.* Containing or secreting pus. [L *pūrulentus*.] **—pu'ru•lent•ly** *adv.*

pur•vey (pər-vā', pûr'vā') *v.* To supply (food, information, etc.); furnish. [< L *prōvidēre*, to foresee, PROVIDE.] **—pur•vey'or** *n.*

pur•vey•ance (pər-vā'əns) *n.* Procurement of supplies.

pur•view (pûr'vyŏŏ) *n.* **1.** The range of function, power, or competence. **2.** Range of vision or comprehension. [< OF *porveeir*, to provide.]

pus (pŭs) *n.* A viscous, yellowish-white fluid formed in infected tissue, consisting chiefly of leukocytes, cellular debris, and liquefied tissue elements. [L *pūs*.]

Pu•san (poo'sän'). A port of SE South Korea. Pop. 1,391,000.

ŏ paw, for/oi boy/ou out/oo took/oo coo/p pop/r run/s sauce/sh shy/t to/th thin/*th* the/
ŭ cut/ûr fur/v van/w wag/y yes/z size/zh vision/ə ago, item, edible, gallop, circus/

push (pŏŏsh) *v.* **1.** To exert force against (an object) to move it. **2.** To thrust; shove. **3.** To press or urge forward. **4.** *Slang.* To promote or sell (a product). *—n.* **1.** The act of pushing; a thrust. **2.** A vigorous effort; drive. **3.** A provocation to action. [< L *pellere* (pp *pulsus*), to push, beat.] —push'er *n.*

push·cart (pŏŏsh'kärt') *n.* A light cart pushed by hand.

Push·kin (pŏŏsh'kĭn), **Aleksandr Sergeyevich.** 1799–1837. Russian poet.

push·o·ver (pŏŏsh'ō'vər) *n.* **1.** Anything easily accomplished. **2.** A person or group easily defeated or taken advantage of.

Push·tu (pŭsh'tōō) *n.* Pashto.

push·y (pŏŏsh'ē) *adj.* **-ier, -iest.** *Informal.* Disagreeably forward or aggressive. —push'i·ly *adv.* —push'i·ness *n.*

pu·sil·lan·i·mous (pyōō'sə-lăn'ə-məs) *adj.* Cowardly; faint-hearted. [< L *pūsillus,* weak + *animus,* mind.] —pu'sil·la·nim'i·ty (-lə-nĭm'-ə-tē) *n.* —pu'sil·lan'i·mous·ly *adv.*

puss¹ (pŏŏs) *n. Informal.* A cat.

puss² (pŏŏs) *n. Slang.* The face. [Ir *bus,* lip, mouth.]

puss·y¹ (pŏŏs'ē) *n., pl.* **-ies.** *Informal.* A cat.

pus·sy² (pŭs'ē) *adj.* **-sier, -siest.** Resembling or containing pus.

puss·y·foot (pŏŏs'ē-fŏŏt') *v.* **1.** To move stealthily or cautiously. **2.** *Slang.* To avoid committing oneself.

pussy willow. A shrub with silky catkins.

pus·tule (pŭs'chōōl, pŭs'tyōōl) *n.* A slight, inflamed elevation of the skin filled with pus. [< L *pustula,* a blister.]

put (pŏŏt) *v.* **put, putting. 1.** To place in a specified location; set. **2.** To cause to be in a specified condition. **3.** To subject. **4.** To assign; attribute. **5.** To estimate. **6.** To impose or levy. **7.** To hurl with an overhand pushing motion: *put the shot.* **8.** To bring up for consideration. **9.** To express; state. **10.** To adapt. **11.** To apply. **12.** To proceed. —put across. To state so as to be understood or accepted. —put down. **1.** To record. **2.** To repress. **3.** *Slang.* To reject. —put forth. To grow: *The plant put forth leaves.* —put off. **1.** To postpone. **2.** To discard. —put on. **1.** To clothe oneself with. **2.** To apply. **3.** To pretend. —put out. **1.** To extinguish. **2.** *Baseball.* To retire (a runner). **3.** To inconvenience. —put up. **1.** To erect. **2.** To preserve. **3.** To provide (funds). **4.** To provide lodgings for. **5.** To incite to some action. —put upon. To impose on. —put up with. To endure. [< OE *pūtian,* to push, thrust.]

pu·ta·tive (pyōō'tə-tĭv) *adj.* Generally regarded as such; reputed. [< L *putāre,* to compute, consider.] —pu'ta·tive·ly *adv.*

pu·tre·fy (pyōō'trə-fī') *v.* **-fied, -fying. 1.** To decompose; decay. **2.** To become gangrenous. [< L *putrefacere.*] —pu'tre·fac'tion *n.* —pu'tre·fac'tive *adj.*

pu·trid (pyōō'trĭd) *adj.* **1.** Decayed; rotten. **2.** Proceeding from, pertaining to, or displaying putrefaction. **3.** Corrupt. **4.** Vile. [L *putridus.*] —pu·trid'i·ty, pu'trid·ness *n.*

putsch (pŏŏch) *n.* A suddenly effected attempt by a group to overthrow a government. [G.]

putt (pŭt) *n.* A golf stroke made in an effort to place the ball into the hole. [Var of PUT.] —putt *v.* **(putted, putting).**

put·tee (pŭ-tē', pŭt'ē) *n.* **1.** A strip of cloth wound around the lower leg. **2.** A gaiter covering the lower leg. [Hindi *paṭṭī.*]

put·ter¹ (pŭt'ər) *n. Golf.* **1.** A short, stiff-shafted club used for putting. **2.** A golfer who is putting.

put·ter² (pŭt'ər) *v.* Also *chiefly Brit.* **pot·ter** (pŏt'ər). To move about or act aimlessly. [< OE *potian,* to push, kick.]

putting green. *Golf.* The area at the end of a fairway in which the hole is placed.

put·ty (pŭt'ē) *n., pl.* **-ties. 1.** A doughlike cement made by mixing whiting and linseed oil, used to fill holes in woodwork and secure panes of glass. **2.** A fine lime cement used as a finishing on plaster. [< OF *potee,* contents of a pot, a potful.]

puz·zle (pŭz'əl) *v.* **-zled, -zling. 1.** To bewilder; perplex. **2.** To clarify or solve by reasoning or study (with *out*). **3.** To ponder over a problem. *—n.* **1.** Something that puzzles. **2.** A toy, game, or device that tests ingenuity. **3.** Perplexity; bewilderment. [?] —puz'zler *n.* —puz'zle·ment *n.*

pvt., Pvt. private.

pwt. pennyweight.

PX post exchange; Post Exchange.

Pyg·ma·lion (pĭg-māl'yən, -mā'lē-ən). *Gk.Myth.* A sculptor who fell in love with his statue of a woman.

pyg·my (pĭg'mē) *n., pl.* **-mies.** Also **pig·my. 1.** One of unusually small size or significance. **2. Pygmy.** A member of any of several African and Asian peoples with a hereditary stature of from four to five feet. *—adj.* **1.** Unusually or atypically small. **2. Pygmy.** Of or pertaining to the Pygmies. [< Gk *pugmē,* fist, the length from the elbow to the knuckles.]

py·lon (pī'lŏn') *n.* **1.** A monumental gateway in the form of a pair of truncated pyramids, as the entrance to an Egyptian temple. **2.** A tower marking a turning point in an air race. **3.** A steel tower supporting high-tension wires. [< Gk *pulē,* a gate.]

py·lo·rus (pī-lôr'əs, -lōr'əs, pĭ-) *n.* The passage connecting the stomach and duodenum. [< Gk *pulōros,* "a gatekeeper."]

pyo-. *comb. form.* Pus. [< Gk *puon,* pus.]

Pyong·yang (pyŭng'yäng'). The capital of North Korea. Pop. 940,000.

py·or·rhe·a, py·or·rhoe·a (pī'ə-rē'ə) *n.* **1.** A discharge of pus. **2.** Inflammation of the gum and tooth sockets leading to loosening of the teeth. [< PYO- + -RRHEA.]

pyr·a·mid (pĭr'ə-mĭd) *n.* **1.** A polyhedron with a polygonal base and triangular faces meeting in a common vertex. **2.** A pyramidal monument. *—v.* **1.** To place or build in the shape of a pyramid. **2.** To increase rapidly and on a widening base. [< Gk *puramis.*] —py·ram'i·dal (pĭ-răm'ə-dəl) *adj.*

pyre (pīr) *n.* A combustible heap, esp. for burning a corpse. [< Gk *pur,* fire.]

Pyr·e·nees (pĭr'ə-nēz'). A mountain range between France and Spain.

---

py•rite (pī′rīt′) *n.* A yellow to brown, widely occurring mineral, FeS_2, used as a source of iron and sulfur. [L *pyrītēs*, pyrites.]

py•ri•tes (pī-rī′tēz, pə-) *n., pl.* **-tes.** Any of various natural metallic sulfides, esp. of iron. [< Gk *purītēs (lithos)*, "fire (stone)."]

pyro–. *comb. form.* Fire. [< Gk *pur*, fire.]

py•ro•ma•ni•a (pī′rō-mā′nē-ə, -mān′yə) *n.* The uncontrollable impulse to start fires. —**py′ro•ma′ni•ac′** (-mā′nē-ăk′) *adj. & n.*

py•ro•tech•nics (pī′rə-tĕk′nĭks, pîr′ə-) *n.* **1.** A display of fireworks. **2.** A brilliant display, as of rhetoric or wit.

Py•thag•o•ras (pĭ-thăg′ər-əs). Greek philosopher of the 6th century B.C. —**Py•thag′o•re′an** (-ə-rē′ən) *adj.*

Pythagorean theorem. The theorem that the sum of the squares of the lengths of the sides of a right triangle is equal to the square of the length of the hypotenuse.

py•thon (pī′thŏn′, -thən) *n.* A large, nonvenomous Old World snake that coils around and crushes its prey. [< *Python*, Greek mythological serpent or dragon.]

pyx (pĭks) *n.* Also **pix.** A container in which the Eucharist is carried to the sick.

Qq

q, Q (kyōō) *n.* The 17th letter of the English alphabet.

q. **1.** quart. **2.** question.

qb quarterback.

Q.E.D. which was to be demonstrated or proved (L *quod erat demonstrandum*).

QM quartermaster.

qoph (kōf) *n.* The 19th letter of the Hebrew alphabet, representing *q*.

qq.v. which (things) see (NL *quae vide*).

qr. quarter.

qt quart.

q.t. *Slang.* Quiet; in secret.

qto. quarto.

qty. quantity.

qua (kwā, kwä) *adv.* In the function or character of. [L *quā*, abl of *qui*, who.]

quack¹ (kwăk) *n.* The hoarse sound uttered by a duck. —**quack** *v.*

quack² (kwăk) *n.* **1.** One who pretends to have medical knowledge. **2.** A charlatan. [Short for QUACKSALVER.] —**quack** *adj.* —**quack′er•y** *n.*

quack•sal•ver (kwăk′săl′vər) *n.* *Archaic.* A charlatan; quack. [< MDu *quacsalven*, to cure with home remedies.]

quad¹ (kwŏd) *n.* *Informal.* A quadrangle.

quad² (kwŏd) *n.* Shortened form of **quadruplet.**

quad•ran•gle (kwŏd′răng′gəl) *n.* **1.** A plane figure consisting of four points, no three of which are collinear, connected by straight lines. **2.** A rectangular area bordered by buildings. [< L *quadriangulus*, having four angles.]

quad•rant (kwŏd′rənt) *n.* **1. a.** A circular arc subtending a central angle of 90°. **b.** The plane area bounded by two perpendicular radii and the arc they subtend. **2.** An early instrument for measuring altitudes, consisting of a 90° graduated arc with a movable radius for measuring angles. [< L *quadrāns*, fourth part, quarter.]

quad•ra•phon•ic (kwŏd′rə-fŏn′ĭk) *adj.* Of or for an extension of stereophonic sound reproduction in which two additional channels are used at the rear of the listening space, reproducing signals that are independent of or derived from the front channels. [Prob < QUADR(I)- + PHONIC.]

quad•rat•ic (kwŏ-drăt′ĭk) *adj.* Of or containing mathematical quantities of the second degree and no higher. —**quad•rat′ic** *n.*

quad•ren•ni•al (kwŏ-drĕn′ē-əl) *adj.* **1.** Happening once in four years. **2.** Lasting for four years.

quad•ren•ni•um (kwŏ-drĕn′ē-əm) *n., pl.* **-ums** or **quadrennia** (-drĕn′ē-ə). A period of four years. [L *quadriennium*.]

quadri–. *comb. form.* Four. [L.]

quad•ri•cen•ten•ni•al (kwŏd′rī-sĕn-tĕn′ē-əl) *n.* A 400th anniversary. —**quad′ri•cen•ten′ni•al** *adj.*

quad•ri•lat•er•al (kwŏd′rə-lăt′ər-əl) *n.* A four-sided polygon. —*adj.* Having four sides.

qua•drille (kwŏ-drĭl′, kwə-, kə-) *n.* A square dance composed of five figures and performed by four couples. [F, orig "one of the four divisions of an army."]

quad•ril•lion (kwŏ-drĭl′yən) *n.* **1.** The cardinal number represented by 1 followed by 15 zeros. **2.** In British usage, the cardinal number represented by 1 followed by 24 zeros. [< QUADR(I)- + (M)ILLION.] —**quad•ril′lion** *adj.*

quad•ril•lionth (kwŏ-drĭl′yənth) *n.* The ordinal number quadrillion in a series. —**quad•ril′lionth** *adj. & adv.*

quad•ri•par•tite (kwŏd′rə-pär′tīt′) *adj.* **1.** Consisting of four parts. **2.** Involving four participants.

quadru–. *comb. form.* Four. [L.]

quad•ru•ped (kwŏd′rōō-pĕd′) *n.* A four-footed animal.

quad•ru•ple (kwŏ-drōō′pəl, -drŭp′əl, kwŏd′-rōō-pəl) *adj.* **1.** Having four parts. **2.** Multi-

---

ô paw, for/oi boy/ou out/ōō took/ōō coo/p pop/r run/s sauce/sh shy/t to/th thin/*th* the/
ŭ cut/ûr fur/v van/w wag/y yes/z size/zh vision/ə ago, item, edible, gallop, circus/

plied by four. —*n.* A number or amount four times as many or as much as another. —*v.* -pled, -pling. To multiply or increase by four. [< L *quadruplus.*]

quad•ru•plet (kwŏ-drŭp′lĭt, -drōō′plĭt, kwŏd′-rōō-plĭt) *n.* 1. A group or combination of four. 2. One of four offspring born in a single birth.

quad•ru•pli•cate (kwŏ-drōō′plĭ-kĭt) *adj.* 1. Multiplied by four; quadruple. 2. Fourth in a group or set. —*n.* One of a set or group of four. —*v.* (kwŏ-drōō′plĭ-kāt′) -cated, -cating. To multiply four times. —**quad•ru′pli•ca′tion** *n.*

quaff (kwŏf, kwăf, kwôf) *v.* To drink heartily. [Perh imit.] —**quaff** *n.* —**quaff′er** *n.*

quag•mire (kwăg′mīr′, kwŏg′-) *n.* A bog having a surface that yields when stepped on.

qua•hog (kwō′hôg′, -hŏg′, kwō′-, kō′-) *n.* A hard-shelled, edible clam of the North American Atlantic coast. [< Algon.]

quail[1] (kwāl) *n., pl.* quail or quails. Any of various small, short-tailed chickenlike birds. [< ML *quaccula.*]

quail[2] (kwāl) *v.* To lose courage; cower. [Perh < L *coāgulāre,* to curdle, COAGULATE.]

quaint (kwānt) *adj.* 1. Agreeably curious and old-fashioned. 2. Unfamiliar or unusual; strange. [< OF *cointe,* expert, elegant.] —**quaint′ly** *adv.* —**quaint′ness** *n.*

quake (kwāk) *v.* quaked, quaking. 1. To shake or tremble. 2. To shiver, as with cold or emotion. —*n.* 1. An instance of quaking. 2. An earthquake. [< OE *cwacian* < Gmc **kwei-,* to shake.] —**quak′y** *adj.*

Quak•er (kwā′kər) *n.* A member of the Society of Friends.

qual•i•fi•ca•tion (kwŏl′ə-fĭ-kā′shən) *n.* 1. The act of qualifying or condition of being qualified. 2. A quality or ability that suits a person to a specific position or task.

qual•i•fy (kwŏl′ə-fī′) *v.* -fied, -fying. 1. To describe; characterize. 2. To make competent or suitable for an office, position, etc. 3. To give legal power to. 4. To limit or restrict. 5. To make less harsh. 6. To modify the meaning of (a word or phrase). [< ML *quālificāre,* to attribute a quality to.]

qual•i•ta•tive (kwŏl′ə-tā′tĭv) *adj.* Of or pertaining to quality or qualities. —**qual′i•ta′tive•ly** *adv.*

qual•i•ty (kwŏl′ə-tē) *n., pl.* -ties. 1. A characteristic or attribute; a property. 2. The natural or essential character of something. 3. Degree of excellence. 4. High social position. [< L *quālis,* of what kind.]

qualm (kwäm, kwôm) *n.* 1. A sudden feeling of sickness, nausea, etc. 2. Doubt or misgiving; uneasiness. 3. A pang of conscience. [?]

quan•da•ry (kwŏn′drē, -də-rē) *n., pl.* -ries. A state of uncertainty or perplexity. [?]

quan•ti•ta•tive (kwŏn′tə-tā′tĭv) *adj.* Of or pertaining to number or quantity. —**quan′ti•ta′tive•ly** *adv.*

quan•ti•ty (kwŏn′tə-tē) *n., pl.* -ties. 1. A number or amount of anything, either specified or indefinite. 2. A sufficient or considerable amount or number: *sell books in quantity.* [< L *quantus,* how great.]

quan•tum (kwŏn′təm) *n., pl.* -ta (-tə). 1. Quan-

tity or amount. 2. An indivisible unit of energy. [< L *quantus,* how great.]

quar•an•tine (kwôr′ən-tēn′, kwŏr′-) *n.* 1. a. A period of time during which one suspected of carrying a contagious disease is detained. b. A place for such detention. 2. Enforced isolation or restriction of free movement imposed to prevent the spread of a contagious disease. —*v.* -tined, -tining. To place in quarantine. [It *quarantina (giorni),* forty days.]

quark (kwôrk) *n.* Any of three hypothetical subatomic particles with fractional electric charges, proposed as the fundamental units of matter.

quar•rel (kwôr′əl, kwŏr′-) *n.* 1. An angry dispute or argument. 2. A cause for a dispute. —*v.* -reled or -relled, -reling or -relling. 1. To engage in a quarrel. 2. To find fault. [< L *queri,* to complain.] —**quar′rel•some** *adj.*

quar•ry[1] (kwôr′ē, kwŏr′ē) *n., pl.* -ries. 1. A hunted animal. 2. Any object of pursuit. [ME *querre,* entrails of a beast given to the hounds.]

quar•ry[2] (kwôr′ē, kwŏr′ē) *n., pl.* -ries. An open excavation from which stone is obtained. —*v.* -ried, -rying. To obtain (stone) from a quarry. [< OF *quarre,* "square stone."]

quart (kwôrt) *n.* 1. A U.S. Customary System unit of volume or capacity, used in liquid measure, equal to two pints or 57.75 cubic inches. 2. A corresponding U.S. Customary System unit, used in dry measure, equal to two pints or 67.2 cubic inches. 3. A corresponding British Imperial System unit, used in liquid and dry measure, equal to 1.201 U.S. liquid quarts, 1.032 U.S. dry quarts, or 69.354 cubic inches. [< L *quārtus,* fourth (part of a gallon).]

quar•ter (kwôr′tər) *n.* 1. One of four equal parts of something. 2. A coin equal to one-fourth of the dollar of the U.S. and Canada. 3. Mercy; clemency. 4. Either side of a horse's hoof. 5. quarters. A place of residence; lodgings. 6. A district of a city. —*v.* 1. To divide into four equal or equivalent parts. 2. To dismember (a human body). 3. To furnish with lodgings. —*adj.* 1. Being one of four equal or equivalent parts. 2. Being one-fourth of a standard or usual value. [< L *quārtus,* fourth.]

quar•ter•back (kwôr′tər-băk′) *n.* The backfield football player who usually calls the signals.

quar•ter•deck (kwôr′tər-dĕk′) *n.* The after part of a ship's upper deck.

quar•ter•ly (kwôr′tər-lē) *adj.* 1. Made up of four parts. 2. Being one of four parts. 3. Occurring at regular intervals of three months. —*n., pl.* -lies. A quarterly publication. —*adv.* In or by quarters.

quar•ter•mas•ter (kwôr′tər-măs′tər, -mäs′tər) *n.* 1. A military officer responsible for the food, clothing, and equipment of troops. 2. A naval petty officer responsible for the navigation of a ship. [< QUARTER (residence).]

quarter note. *Mus.* A note having one-fourth the time value of a whole note.

quar•ter•staff (kwôr′tər-stăf′, -stäf′) *n.* A long wooden staff formerly used as a weapon.

quar•tet (kwôr-tĕt′) *n.* Also quar•tette. 1. a. A

ă pat/ā ate/âr care/ä bar/b **bib**/ch **chew**/d **deed**/ĕ pet/ē be/f fit/g gag/h hat/hw **what**/. ĭ pit/ī pie/îr pier/j **judge**/k **kick**/l lid, fatal/m **mum**/n no, sudden/ng sing/ŏ pot/ō go/

musical composition for four instruments.
b. A group of four performing musicians.
2. Any set of four persons or things. [L
quártus, fourth.]
quar•to (kwôr'tō) *n., pl.* **-tos. 1.** The page size
obtained by folding a whole sheet into four
leaves. **2.** A book composed of such pages. [L
(in) quárto, in quarter.]
quartz (kwôrts) *n.* A hard, crystalline, vitreous
mineral silicon dioxide, SiO_2, found worldwide
as a component of sandstone and granite or as
pure crystals. [G.]
qua•sar (kwā'zär', -sär', -zər, -sər) *n.* A **quasi-
stellar object.**
quash¹ (kwŏsh) *v. Law.* To set aside or annul.
[< LL *cassáre*.]
quash² (kwŏsh) *v.* To put down or suppress
completely. [< L *quatere* (pp *quassus*), to
shake, shatter.]
qua•si (kwā'zī', -sī', kwä'zē, -sē) *adv.* To some
degree; almost or somewhat. —*adj.* Resembling but not being: *a quasi-victory.* [L <
quánsei, as if.]
qua•si-stel•lar object (kwā'zī'stĕl'ər, kwä'sī'-,
kwä'zē-, kwä'sē-). *Astron.* A member of any of
several classes of starlike objects having exceptionally large red shifts and apparently immense speeds, energies, and distances from
earth.
Qua•ter•nar•y (kwŏt'ər-nĕr'ē, kwə-tûr'nə-rē)
adj. Of or belonging to the geologic time,
system of rocks, or sedimentary deposits of the
second period of the Cenozoic era, including
the Pleistocene and Holocene epochs. —*n.*
The Quaternary period. [< L *quaternárius*,
consisting of four.]
quat•rain (kwŏt'rān', kwŏ-trān') *n.* A typically
rhyming four-line stanza. [< L *quattuor*,
four.]
qua•ver (kwā'vər) *v.* **1.** To quiver; tremble.
2. To speak in a quivering voice. [< ME
quaven, to tremble.] —**qua'ver** *n.*
quay (kē) *n.* A wharf. [< Gaul *caio*, rampart,
retaining wall.]
Que. Quebec.
quea•sy (kwē'zē) *adj.* **-sier, -siest. 1.** Nauseated.
2. Uneasy. [ME *coysy*, perh orig "wounded."]
—**quea'si•ness** *n.*
Que•bec (kwĭ-bĕk'). **1.** A province of E Canada. Pop. 5,657,000. **2.** The capital of this
province. Pop. 331,000.
Quech•ua (kĕch'wə, -wä') *n., pl.* **-ua** or **-uas.
1.** A member of a tribe of South American
Indians formerly living chiefly in Peru, Bolivia, and Ecuador. **2.** The language of this tribe.
queen (kwēn) *n.* **1.** The wife or widow of a
king. **2.** A female monarch. **3.** A woman who
is eminent or supreme in a given domain.
4. The most powerful chessman. **5.** A playing
card bearing the figure of a queen. **6.** The
fertile female in a colony of bees, ants, etc. [<
OE *cwēn*, woman, wife, queen. See **gwen-**.]
—**queen'li•ness** *n.* —**queen'ly** *adj.*
Queens (kwēnz). A borough of New York
City. Pop. 1,810,000.
queer (kwîr) *adj.* **1.** Deviating from the expected or normal; strange; peculiar. **2.** Eccentric. —*v. Slang.* To ruin or thwart. [Perh < G

quer, perverse, cross.] —**queer'ly** *adv.*
quell (kwĕl) *v.* **1.** To put down forcibly. **2.** To
pacify. [< OE *cwellan*, to destroy. See **gwel-²**.]
quench (kwĕnch) *v.* **1.** To put out; extinguish.
2. To suppress; squelch. **3.** To slake; satisfy.
4. To cool (hot metal) by thrusting in water or
other liquid. [< OE *ācwencan*.]
quer•u•lous (kwĕr'ə-ləs, kwĕr'yə-) *adj.* **1.** Giv-
en to complaining or fretting. **2.** Expressing a
complaint. [< L *querī*, to complain.]
que•ry (kwîr'ē) *n., pl.* **-ries. 1.** A question. **2.** A
notation calling attention to an item to ques-
tion its accuracy. —*v.* **-ried, -rying.** To question. [< L *quaerere*, to seek, ask.]
quest (kwĕst) *n.* **1.** An act or instance of seeking; a search. **2.** An expedition undertaken by
a medieval knight: *the quest for the Holy Grail.*
[< L *quaerere*, to seek.]
ques•tion (kwĕs'chən) *n.* **1.** An expression of
inquiry that invites or calls for a reply; an
interrogative sentence or phrase. **2.** A controversial subject or point. **3.** A difficult matter;
problem: *a question of ethics.* **4.** A proposal or
subject under discussion. **5.** Uncertainty;
doubt: *no question about it.* **6.** Possibility: *out
of the question.* —*v.* **1.** To put a question to;
ask questions. **2.** To interrogate, as a witness.
3. To express doubt about; dispute. [< L
quaerere (pp *quaestus*), to seek, ask.]
ques•tion•a•ble (kwĕs'chən-ə-bəl) *adj.*
1. Open to doubt; uncertain. **2.** Of dubious
morality or respectability.
question mark. A punctuation symbol (?)
written at the end of a sentence or phrase to
indicate a direct question.
ques•tion•naire (kwĕs'chə-nâr') *n.* A printed
form containing a set of questions, esp. one
used in a survey.
quet•zal (kĕt-säl') *n.* **1.** A long-tailed Central
American bird with brilliant green and red
plumage. **2.** *pl.* **-zales** (-sä'läs). The basic monetary unit of Guatemala. [< Nah *quetzall*,
large brilliant tail feather.]
Quet•zal•co•a•tl (kĕt-säl'kō-ät'l). The plumed
serpent god of the Toltecs and Aztecs.

Quetzalcoatl
Aztec pictorial manuscript

queue (kyōō) *n.* **1.** A line of people or vehicles awaiting a turn, as at a ticket window. **2.** A braid of hair worn hanging down the back of the neck. —*v.* **queued, queuing.** To wait in a queue. [F, tail, pigtail, line.]

Que·zon City (kā′sôn′). The capital of the Philippines. Pop. 398,000.

quib·ble (kwĭb′əl) *v.* **-bled, -bling.** To make petty distinctions or raise objections to unimportant details. [Perh < obs *quib*, pun.] —**quib′ble** *n.* —**quib′bler** *n.*

quick (kwĭk) *adj.* **1.** Moving or functioning rapidly; speedy. **2.** Occurring or achieved in a brief space of time. **3.** Understanding, perceiving, or learning with speed; alert; keen. **4.** Hasty or sharp in reacting. —*n.* **1.** Sensitive exposed flesh, as under the fingernails. **2.** The most sensitive aspect of the emotions: *cut to the quick.* **3.** The living: *the quick and the dead.* [< OE *cwic*, living, alive. See **gwei-.**] —**quick′ adv.** —**quick′ly** *adv.* —**quick′ness** *n.*

Usage: Quick (adverb) is used frequently in speech and written dialogue: *Come quick!* In other written contexts, *quickly* is much more common.

quick·en (kwĭk′ən) *v.* **1.** To make or become more rapid; accelerate. **2.** To revive; come to life. **3.** To excite and stimulate.

quick·ie (kwĭk′ē) *n. Informal.* Something made or done hastily.

quick·sand (kwĭk′sănd′) *n.* A bed of loose sand mixed with water forming a soft, shifting mass that yields easily to pressure and tends to suck down any object resting on its surface.

quick·sil·ver (kwĭk′sĭl′vər) *n.* The element mercury.

quick·step (kwĭk′stĕp′) *n.* A march for accompanying military quick time.

quick-tem·pered (kwĭk′tĕm′pərd) *adj.* Easily aroused to anger.

quick time. A military marching pace of 120 steps per minute.

quick-wit·ted (kwĭk′wĭt′ĭd) *adj.* Mentally alert and sharp.

quid[1] (kwĭd) *n.* A cut of something to be chewed, such as tobacco. [< OE *cwidu.*]

quid[2] (kwĭd) *n., pl.* **quid** or **quids.** *Brit. Slang.* A pound sterling. [?]

quid pro quo (kwĭd′ prō kwō′). An equal exchange or substitution. [L, "something for something."]

qui·es·cent (kwī-ĕs′ənt, kwē-) *adj.* Inactive or still; dormant. [< L *quiēscere,* to be quiet.] —**qui·es′cence** *n.* —**qui·es′cent·ly** *adv.*

qui·et (kwī′ĭt) *adj.* **1.** Silent; hushed. **2.** Still. **3.** Untroubled; peaceful. **4.** Unobtrusive; restrained. —*n.* Tranquillity; repose. —*v.* To become or cause to become quiet or calm. [< L *quiēs,* quiet.] —**qui′et·ly** *adv.* —**qui′et·ness** *n.*

qui·e·tude (kwī′ə-t/y/ōōd′) *n.* A condition of tranquillity.

qui·e·tus (kwī-ē′təs) *n., pl.* **-tuses. 1.** Death. **2.** A final discharge, as of a debt. [< L *quiētus,* at rest, quiet.]

quill (kwĭl) *n.* **1.** The hollow main shaft of a feather. **2.** A large, stiff feather. **3.** A writing pen made from such a feather. **4.** A sharp, hollow spine, as of a porcupine. [ME *quille.*]

quilt (kwĭlt) *n.* A padded coverlet for a bed. [< L *culcita,* sack filled with feathers.]

quince (kwĭns) *n.* **1.** An applelike, aromatic fruit used chiefly for preserves. **2.** A tree bearing such fruit. [< L *cotōneum, cydōneum.*]

qui·nine (kwī′nīn′) *n.* A bitter alkaloid, $C_{20}H_{24}N_2O_2$·$3H_2O$, used to treat malaria. [< Span *quina,* cinchona bark + **-INE.**]

quin·sy (kwĭn′zē) *n.* Acute inflammation of the tonsils and the surrounding tissue, often leading to the formation of an abscess. [< Gk *kunanchē,* dog quinsy, sore throat.]

quint (kwĭnt) *n.* Shortened form of **quintuplet.**

quin·tes·sence (kwĭn-tĕs′əns) *n.* **1.** The pure, highly concentrated essence of something. **2.** The purest or most typical instance. [< ML *quinta essentia,* fifth essence.]

quin·tet (kwĭn-tĕt′) *n.* **1.** A group of five, esp. of musicians. **2.** A musical composition for five voices or instruments. [< L *quintus,* fifth.]

quin·til·lion (kwĭn-tĭl′yən) *n.* **1.** The cardinal number represented by 1 followed by 18 zeros. **2.** In British usage, the cardinal number represented by 1 followed by 30 zeros. [L *quintus,* fifth + (M)ILLION.] —**quin·til′lion** *adj.*

quin·til·lionth (kwĭn-tĭl′yənth) *n.* The ordinal number quintillion in a series. —**quin·til′lionth** *adj.*

quin·tu·ple (kwĭn-t/y/ōō′pəl, -tŭp′əl, kwĭn′-tōō-pəl) *adj.* **1.** Having five parts. **2.** Multiplied by five. —*n.* A number or amount five times as many or as much as another. —*v.* **-pled, -pling.** To multiply or increase by five. [< LL *quintuplex.*]

quin·tu·plet (kwĭn-tŭp′lĭt, -t/y/ōō′plĭt, kwĭn′-tōō-plĭt) *n.* **1.** A group of five. **2.** One of five offspring born in a single birth.

quip (kwĭp) *n.* A witty or sarcastic remark. —*v.* **quipped, quipping.** To make quips. [Perh < L *quippe,* indeed, certainly.]

quire (kwīr) *n.* A set of 24 or sometimes 25 sheets of paper of the same size and stock. [< OF *quaer,* set of four sheets.]

quirk (kwûrk) *n.* **1.** A sudden sharp turn or twist. **2.** A peculiarity of behavior or action. [?] —**quirk′i·ness** *n.*

quirt (kwûrt) *n.* A riding whip with a short handle and a lash of rawhide. [Perh < Span *cuerda,* whip, chord.]

quis·ling (kwĭz′lĭng) *n.* A traitor who serves as the puppet of the enemy occupying his country. [< V. *Quisling* (1887–1945), head of the State Council of Norway during the German occupation (1940–45).]

quit (kwĭt) *v.* **quit** or **quitted, quitting. 1.** To end one's involvement in; leave abruptly. **2.** To give up; relinquish. **3.** To stop. **4.** To conduct (oneself) in a specified way. —*n.* —**call it quits.** To stop. [< ML *quiētāre,* to set free, quit, discharge.] —**quit′ter** *n.*

quite (kwīt) *adv.* **1.** Entirely; completely. **2.** Actually; really. **3.** Somewhat; rather. —**quite a** (or **an**). **1.** Considerable; notable. **2.** Extraordinary; impressive. [< L *quiētus,* freed, quiet.]

Qui·to (kē′tō). The capital of Ecuador. Pop. 348,000.

quits (kwĭts) *adj.* Even (with someone) by

ă pat/ā ate/âr care/ä bar/b bib/ch chew/d deed/ĕ pet/ē be/f fit/g gag/h hat/hw what/
ĭ pit/ī pie/îr pier/j judge/k kick/l lid, fatal/m mum/n no, sudden/ng sing/ŏ pot/ō go/

payment or requital. [< ML *quittus,* discharged, var of *quiētus,* freed.]

quit·tance (kwĭt′ns) *n.* **1.** Release from a debt. **2.** Something given as recompense. [< OF *quiter,* to discharge a debt, quit.]

quit·ter (kwĭt′ər) *n.* One who gives up easily.

quiv·er¹ (kwĭv′ər) *v.* To shake or cause to shake with a rapid slight agitating motion; tremble; vibrate. —*n.* The act of quivering. [ME *quiveren.*]

quiv·er² (kwĭv′ər) *n.* A portable case for arrows. [Prob < ML *cucurum.*]

quix·ot·ic (kwĭk-sŏt′ĭk) *adj.* Idealistic without regard to practicality. [< DON QUIXOTE.]

quiz (kwĭz) *v.* **quizzed, quizzing. 1.** To question closely; interrogate. **2.** To test the knowledge of by posing questions. —*n., pl.* **quizzes. 1.** A questioning or inquiry. **2.** A short oral or written test. [?] —**quiz′zer** *n.*

quiz·zi·cal (kwĭz′ĭ-kəl) *adj.* **1.** Suggesting puzzlement. **2.** Teasing; mocking.

quoin (koin, kwoin) *n.* **1. a.** An exterior angle of a wall or other masonry. **b.** A stone serving to form such an angle; cornerstone. **2.** A keystone. [Var of COIN.]

quoit (kwoit, koit) *n.* **1. quoits.** A game in which flat rings are pitched at a stake. **2.** One of the rings used in this game. [ME *coite.*]

quon·dam (kwŏn′dəm, -dăm′) *adj.* That once was; former. [L, formerly.]

quo·rum (kwôr′əm, kwōr′-) *n.* The minimum number of members of an organization who must be present for the valid transaction of business. [< L, gen pl of *quī,* who.]

quot. quotation.

quo·ta (kwō′tə) *n.* **1. a.** An allotment. **b.** A production assignment. **2.** The maximum number of persons who may be admitted, as to a nation, group, or institution. [< L *quotus,* of what number.]

quo·ta·tion (kwō-tā′shən) *n.* **1.** The act of quoting. **2.** A passage that is quoted. **3.** The quoting of current prices and bids for securities and goods. —**quo·ta′tion·al** *adj.* —**quo·ta′tion·al·ly** *adv.*

quotation mark. Either of a pair of punctuation marks used to mark the beginning and end of a passage attributed to another and repeated word for word. They usually appear in the form (" "). Single quotation marks (' ') are usually reserved to set off a quotation within a quotation.

quote (kwōt) *v.* **quoted, quoting. 1.** To repeat or copy the words of (another), usually with acknowledgment. **2.** To cite or refer to for illustration or proof. **3.** To state (a price) for securities, goods, or services. —*n.* A quotation. [ME *coten,* to mark with numbers < L *quot,* how many.] —**quot′er** *n.*

quoth (kwōth) *v. Archaic.* Uttered; said: *"Quoth the raven 'Nevermore!'"* (Poe). [< OE *cwethan,* to say. See **gwet-.**]

quo·tid·i·an (kwō-tĭd′ē-ən) *adj.* **1.** Recurring daily. **2.** Commonplace. [< L *quotīdiē,* each day.]

quo·tient (kwō′shənt) *n.* The quantity resulting from division of one quantity by another. [< L *quotiēns,* how many times.]

q.v. which see (L *quod vide*).

qy. query.

Rr

r, R (är) *n.* The 18th letter of the English alphabet.

r 1. radius. **2.** *Elec.* resistance.

R 1. radius. **2.** Republican. **3.** *Elec.* resistance.

r. 1. right. **2.** rod (unit of length).

R. 1. railroad; railway. **2.** Republican. **3.** right. **4.** river. **5.** road.

Ra (rä). Egyptian sun god and supreme deity.

Ra radium.

Ra·bat (rä-bät′). The capital of Morocco. Pop. 227,000.

rab·bet (răb′ĭt) *n.* A groove along or near the edge of a piece of wood that allows another piece to fit into it to form a joint. —*v.* **1.** To cut a rabbet in. **2.** To join by a rabbet. [< OF *rabat,* a beating down.]

rab·bi (răb′ī) *n.* **1.** The ordained spiritual leader of a Jewish congregation. **2.** Formerly, a person authorized to interpret Jewish law. [Heb *rabbī,* my master.] —**rab·bin′i·cal** (rə-bĭn′ĭk-əl) *adj.*

rab·bin·ate (răb′ĭn-āt′) *n.* The office or function of a rabbi.

rab·bit (răb′ĭt) *n.* **1.** A long-eared, short-tailed, burrowing mammal with soft fur. **2.** The fur of a rabbit. [ME *rabet.*]

rabbit fever. A disease, tularemia.

rab·ble (răb′əl) *n.* **1.** A mob. **2.** Any group regarded contemptuously. [?]

rab·ble-rous·er (răb′əl-rou′zər) *n.* A demagogue.

Rab·e·lais (răb′ə-lā), **François.** 1494?–1553. French humanist and satirist. —**Rab′e·lai′si·an** (-lā′zē-ən) *adj.*

rab·id (răb′ĭd) *adj.* **1.** Of or afflicted with rabies. **2.** Fanatical. **3.** Raging: *rabid thirst.* [L *rabidus,* raving.] —**ra·bid′i·ty** (rə-bĭd′ə-tē, rā-), **rab′id·ness** *n.* —**rab′id·ly** *adv.*

ra·bies (rā′bēz) *n.* An acute, infectious, often fatal, viral disease of most warm-blooded animals, esp. wolves, cats, and dogs, that attacks the central nervous system and is transmitted by the bite of infected animals. [< L *rabiēs*, rage.]

rac•coon (ră-kōōn') *n.* 1. A North American mammal with a bushy, black-ringed tail. 2. The fur of this animal. [< Algon.]

race¹ (rās) *n.* 1. A local geographic or global human population distinguished by genetically transmitted physical characteristics. 2. Any group of people more or less distinct, as on the basis of nationality. 3. A subspecies, breed, or strain of plants or animals. [F, group of people, generation.]

race² (rās) *n.* 1. A competition of speed. 2. Any contest for supremacy: *the Presidential race.* 3. Steady or rapid onward movement. 4. a. A strong current of water. b. The channel of such a current. —*v.* raced, racing. 1. To compete in a race. 2. To rush. 3. To cause an engine to run swiftly or too swiftly. [< ON *rās.*] —**rac'er** *n.*

race•course (rās'kôrs') *n.* A racetrack.

race•horse (rās'hôrs') *n.* A horse bred and trained to race.

ra•ceme (rā-sēm', rə-) *n.* A flower cluster with stalked flowers arranged singly along a stem. [L *racēmus,* stalk of a cluster of grapes, bunch of berries.]

race•track (rās'trăk') *n.* A course laid out for racing.

Rach•ma•ni•noff (răKH-mä'nĭ-nôf), **Sergei.** 1873–1943. Russian composer and pianist.

ra•cial (rā'shəl) *adj.* 1. Pertaining to or typical of an ethnic group or groups. 2. Arising from or based upon differences between ethnic groups. —**ra'cial•ly** *adv.*

Ra•cine (rá-sēn'), **Jean.** 1639–1699. French playwright.

ra•cism (rā'sĭz'əm) *n.* The notion that one's own ethnic stock is superior. —**rac'ist, ra'cial•ist** *n. & adj.*

rack (răk) *n.* 1. A framework or stand in which to hold or display various articles. 2. A toothed bar that meshes with another toothed structure, such as a pinion or gearwheel. 3. A framelike instrument of torture. 4. A state or cause of torment. —*v.* 1. To torture by means of the rack. 2. To torment. 3. To strain with great effort: *rack one's brain.* [Prob < MDu *rec,* framework.] —**rack'er** *n.*

rack•et¹ (răk'ĭt) *n.* Also **rac•quet.** A light bat with a nearly elliptical hoop strung with a network of catgut, nylon, or silk, used in various ball games. [< dial Ar *râḥet,* palm of the hand.]

rack•et² (răk'ĭt) *n.* 1. A clamor; uproar. 2. a. A business that obtains money through fraud or extortion. b. An illegal or dishonest practice. [?]

rack•et•eer (răk'ə-tîr') *n.* One engaged in an illegal business.

rack•et•y (răk'ĭt-ē) *adj.* Noisy.

rac•on•teur (răk'ŏn-tûr') *n.* One who recounts stories and anecdotes with skill and wit. [< OF *raconter,* to tell.]

rac•y (rā'sē) *adj.* **-ier, -iest.** 1. Piquant or pungent. 2. Risqué; ribald. [< RACE (lineage, hence kind, type).] —**rac'i•ness** *n.*

rad. 1. radical. 2. radius.

ra•dar (rā'där) *n.* 1. A method of detecting distant objects and determining their position, velocity, or other characteristics by analysis of very high frequency radio waves reflected from their surfaces. 2. The equipment used in such detection. [Ra(dio) d(etecting) a(nd) r(anging).]

ra•di•al (rā'dē-əl) *adj.* 1. Of or arranged like rays or radii. 2. Radiating from or converging to a common center. [< L *radius,* rod, ray.]

ra•di•ant (rā'dē-ənt) *adj.* 1. Emitting heat or light. 2. Consisting of or emitted as radiation: *radiant heat.* 3. a. Bright. b. Glowing. [< L *radiāre,* to RADIATE.] —**ra'di•ance** *n.* —**ra'di•ant•ly** *adv.*

radiant energy. Energy transferred by radiation, esp. by an electromagnetic wave.

ra•di•ate (rā'dē-āt') *v.* **-ated, -ating.** 1. To emit radiation. 2. To issue or emerge in rays. 3. To spread out or converge radially, as the spokes of a wheel. 4. To manifest in a glowing manner: *He radiated confidence.* [< L *radiāre,* emit beams.] —**ra'di•a'tive** *adj.*

ra•di•a•tion (rā'dē-ā'shən) *n.* 1. The act or process of radiating. 2. The emission and propagation of waves or particles, such as light, sound, radiant heat, or particles emitted by radioactivity.

radiation sickness. Illness induced by ionizing radiation, ranging in severity of effects from nausea to death.

ra•di•a•tor (rā'dē-ā'tər) *n.* 1. A heating device for the circulation of steam or hot water. 2. A cooling device, as in automotive engines. 3. Something that emits radiation.

rad•i•cal (răd'ĭ-kəl) *adj.* 1. Fundamental; basic. 2. Carried to the farthest limit; extreme; sweeping: *radical social change.* 3. Favoring revolutionary changes, as in politics. —*n.* 1. One who advocates political and social revolution. 2. *Math.* The root of a quantity as indicated by the **radical sign.** 3. An atom or group of atoms with at least one unpaired electron. [< LL *rādīcālis,* having roots.] —**rad'i•cal•ly** *adv.* —**rad'i•cal•ness** *n.*

rad•i•cal•ism (răd'ĭ-kəl-ĭz'əm) *n.* 1. The quality of being radical. 2. The doctrines or practices of political radicals.

rad•i•cal•ize (răd'ĭ-kə-līz') *v.* **-ized, -izing.** To make radical or more radical. —**rad'i•cal•i•za'tion** *n.*

radical sign. The sign √ placed before a quantity, indicating extraction of the root designated by a raised integral index.

ra•di•i. *pl.* of **radius.**

ra•di•o (rā'dē-ō) *n., pl.* **-os.** 1. The use of electromagnetic waves in the approximate frequency range from 10 kilocycles/second to 300,000 megacycles/second to transmit or receive electric signals without wires connecting the points of transmission and reception. 2. Communication of audible signals, such as music, encoded in electromagnetic waves so transmitted and received. 3. Transmission of programs for the public by this means; radio broadcast. 4. The equipment used for transmitting or receiving radio signals. —*adj.* 1. Of or sent by radio. 2. Of or using oscillations of

---

ă pat/ā ate/år care/ä bar/b bib/ch chew/d deed/ĕ pet/ē be/f fit/g gag/h hat/hw what/ ĭ pit/ī pie/îr pier/j judge/k kick/l lid, fatal/m mum/n no, sudden/ng sing/ŏ pot/ō go/

radio frequency. —*v.* To transmit a message to, or communicate with, by radio. [Short for RADIOTELEGRAPHY.]

radio–. *comb. form.* Emission and propagation of radiation.

radioactive decay. A progressive decrease in the number of radioactive atoms in a substance by spontaneous nuclear disintegration or transformation.

ra·di·o·ac·tiv·i·ty (rā′dē-ō-ăk′tĭv′ə-tē) *n.* **1.** The spontaneous emission of radiation, either directly from unstable atomic nuclei or as a consequence of a nuclear reaction. **2.** Broadly, the radiation so emitted, including alpha particles, nucleons, electrons, and gamma rays. —**ra′di·o·ac′tive** (rā′dē-ō-ăk′tĭv) *adj.* —**ra′di·o·ac′tive·ly** *adv.*

radio astronomy. The study of celestial objects and phenomena by observation and analysis of emitted or reflected radio-frequency waves.

ra·di·o·broad·cast (rā′dē-ō-brôd′kăst′, -kăst′) *v.* To broadcast by radio. —**ra′di·o·broad′cast′er** *n.*

ra·di·o·chem·is·try (rā′dē-ō-kĕm′ĭs-trē) *n.* The chemistry of radioactive materials. —**ra′di·o·chem′i·cal** *adj.*

radio frequency. Any frequency in the range within which radio waves may be transmitted, from about 10 kilocycles/second to about 300,000 megacycles/second.

ra·di·o·gram (rā′dē-ō-grăm′) *n.* A message transmitted by wireless telegraphy.

ra·di·o·graph (rā′dē-ō-grăf′, -gräf′) *n.* An image produced on a radiosensitive surface, such as a photographic film, by radiation other than visible light, esp. by x rays. —*v.* To make a radiograph of. —**ra′di·o·graph′ic** *adj.* —**ra′di·og′ra·phy** (-ŏg′rə-fē) *n.*

ra·di·o·i·so·tope (rā′dē-ō-ī′sə-tōp′) *n.* A radioactive isotope.

ra·di·ol·o·gy (rā′dē-ŏl′ə-jē) *n.* The use of ionizing radiation for medical diagnosis, esp. of x rays in medical radiography and for radiotherapy. —**ra′di·o·log′i·cal** (-ə-lŏj′ĭ-kəl) *adj.* —**ra′di·ol′o·gist** *n.*

ra·di·o·man (rā′dē-ō-măn′) *n.* A radio technician or operator.

ra·di·os·co·py (rā′dē-ŏs′kə-pē) *n.* The examination of the inner structure of optically opaque objects by x rays or other penetrating radiation. —**ra′di·o·scop′ic** (-ō-skŏp′ĭk), **ra′di·o·scop′i·cal** *adj.*

ra·di·o·sen·si·tive (rā′dē-ō-sĕn′sə-tĭv) *adj.* Sensitive to radiation.

ra·di·o·te·leg·ra·phy (rā′dē-ō-tə-lĕg′rə-fē) *n.* Wireless telegraphy, in which messages are sent by radio. [RADI(ATE) + TELEGRAPHY.] —**ra′di·o·tel′e·graph′ic** *adj.*

ra·di·o·tel·e·phone (rā′dē-ō-tĕl′ə-fōn′) *n.* A telephone in which communication is established by radio. —**ra′di·o·tel′e·phon′ic** (-ə-fŏn′ĭk) *adj.*

radio telescope. A sensitive, directional radio-antenna system used to detect and analyze radio waves of extraterrestrial origin.

ra·di·o·ther·a·py (rā′dē-ō-thĕr′ə-pē) *n.* The treatment of disease with radiation.

radio wave. A radio-frequency electromagnetic wave.

rad·ish (răd′ĭsh) *n.* **1.** A plant cultivated for its pungent, edible root. **2.** The root of this plant, eaten raw as an appetizer and in salads. [< L *rādix (rādīc-),* root.]

ra·di·um (rā′dē-əm) *n. Symbol* **Ra** A rare brilliant-white, luminescent, highly radioactive metallic element, used in radiotherapy, as a neutron source, and as a constituent of luminescent paints. Atomic number 88, longest-lived isotope Ra 226. [< L *radius,* ray.]

radium therapy. The use of radium in radiotherapy, esp. in treating cancer.

ra·di·us (rā′dē-əs) *n., pl.* **-dii** (-dē-ī′) or **-uses.** **1. a.** A line segment that joins the center of a circle with any point on its circumference. **b.** A line segment that joins the center of a sphere with any point on its surface. **c.** A line segment that joins the center of a regular polygon to any of its vertices. **2.** A measure of range of activity or influence. **3.** The shorter and thicker of the two forearm bones, located on the lateral side of the ulna. [L *radius,* spoke of a wheel, ray.]

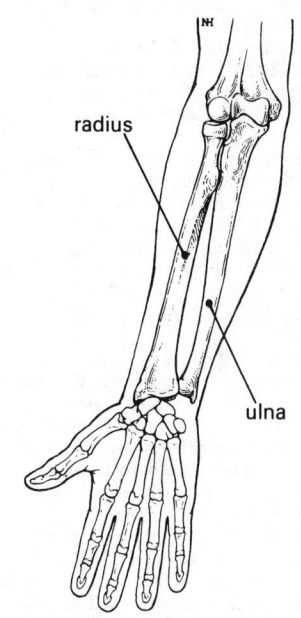

radius
ulna

radius

ra·don (rā′dŏn) *n. Symbol* **Rn** A colorless, radioactive, inert gaseous element formed by disintegration of radium and used in radiotherapy. Atomic number 86, atomic weight 222. [< RADIUM.]

RAF Royal Air Force.

raf·fi·a (răf′ē-ə) *n.* A fiber from the leaves of an African palm, used for mats, baskets, etc. [Malagasy *rafia, rofia.*]

raff·ish (răf′ĭsh) *adj.* **1.** Vulgar; showy. **2.** Rak-

ish. [Prob < dial *raff*, trash.] —**raff'ish•ly** *adv.*
—**raff'ish•ness** *n.*

raf•fle (răf'əl) *n.* A lottery in which a number
of persons buy chances on a prize. —*v.* **-fled,
-fling.** To dispose of in a raffle. [< OF, act of
snatching.] —**raf'fler** *n.*

raft¹ (răft, räft) *n.* A flat structure, typically
made of planks, logs, or barrels, that floats on
water and is used for transport or as a platform for swimmers. [< ON *raptr*, beam,
rafter.]

raft² (răft, räft) *n. Informal.* A great number or
amount. [Perh < Scand.]

raft•er (răf'tər, räf'-) *n.* One of the sloping
beams that support a pitched roof. [< OE
ræfter. See *rep-*.]

rag¹ (răg) *n.* A scrap of cloth. [< ON *rögg*,
tuft.]

rag² (răg) *v.* **ragged, ragging.** *Slang.* **1.** To taunt.
2. To scold. [?]

rag•a•muf•fin (răg'ə-mŭf'ĭn) *n.* A dirty or unkempt child. [< *Ragamoffyn*, demon in *Piers
Plowman* (1393).]

rage (rāj) *n.* **1.** Violent anger. **2.** A fad; craze.
—*v.* **raged, raging. 1.** To speak or act furiously.
2. To move with great violence or intensity.
3. To spread or prevail unchecked. [< L
rabere, to rave.]

rag•ged (răg'ĭd) *adj.* **1.** Tattered. **2.** Dressed in
tattered clothes. **3.** Having a rough surface or
edges. **4.** Imperfect; sloppy: *a ragged performance.* [< RAG.] —**rag'ged•ly** *adv.* —**rag'ged•
ness** *n.*

rag•lan (răg'lən) *n.* A loose coat, jacket, or
sweater with slanted shoulder seams and with
the sleeves extending in one piece to the neckline. [< Field Marshal Lord *Raglan* (1788–
1855), British soldier.] —**rag'lan** *adj.*

ra•gout (ră-gōō') *n.* A meat and vegetable
stew. [< F *ragoûter*, to renew the taste.]

rag•tag (răg'tăg') *n.* Rabble; riffraff. [RAG +
TAG.]

rag•time (răg'tīm') *n.* A style of jazz characterized by elaborately syncopated rhythm in
the melody. [Perh < *ragged time.*]

rag•weed (răg'wēd') *n.* A weedy plant whose
pollen is one of the chief causes of hay fever.

raid (rād) *n.* A small-scale surprise attack. —*v.*
To make a raid on. [< OE *rād*, ride, road. See
reidh-.] —**raid'er** *n.*

rail¹ (rāl) *n.* **1.** A horizontal bar supported by
vertical posts, as in a fence. **2.** A railing or
balustrade. **3.** A bar used as a track for railroad cars and similar vehicles. **4.** The railroad:
It was transported by rail. —*v.* To supply or
enclose with a rail or rails. [< OF *reille*, bar.]

rail² (rāl) *n.* A brownish, short-winged marsh
bird. [< OProv *rasclar*, to scrape, make a
scraping noise.]

rail³ (rāl) *v.* To use bitter or abusive language.
[< LL *ragere*, to neigh, roar.]

rail•ing (rā'lĭng) *n.* A banister, fence, etc.,
made of rails.

rail•ler•y (rā'lər-ē) *n., pl.* **-ies.** Good-natured
teasing or ridicule. [< RAIL³.]

rail•road (rāl'rōd') *n.* **1.** A road composed of
parallel steel rails supported by ties and providing a track for trains. **2.** An entire system

of such track, together with the land, stations,
and rolling stock belonging to it. —*v.* **1.** To
transport by railroad. **2.** To rush through
quickly in order to prevent careful consideration: *railroad a law through Congress.*

rail•way (rāl'wā') *n.* **1.** A railroad. **2.** A track
providing a runway for wheeled equipment.

rai•ment (rā'mənt) *n.* Clothing. [< OF *araie*,
an array.]

rain (rān) *n.* **1. a.** Water condensed from atmospheric vapor, falling to earth in drops.
b. Rainy weather. **2.** The rapid falling of anything in this manner. —*v.* To fall or release as
or like rain. [< OF *regn, rên.* See reg-².]
—**rain'i•ness** *n.* —**rain'y** *adj.*

rain•bow (rān'bō') *n.* **1.** An arc of spectral
colors appearing in the sky opposite the sun as
a result of the refractive dispersion of sunlight
in drops of rain or mist. **2.** Any similar arc or
graded display of colors.

rain•coat (rān'kōt') *n.* A waterproof or water-
resistant coat.

rain•fall (rān'fôl') *n.* **1.** A shower of rain. **2.**
The quantity of water, expressed in inches,
precipitated as rain, snow, hail, or sleet in a
specified area and time interval.

rain•storm (rān'stôrm') *n.* A storm accompanied by rain.

rain•wat•er (rān'wô'tər, -wŏt'ər) *n.* Water precipitated as rain.

raise (rāz) *v.* **raised, raising. 1.** To elevate; lift.
2. To make erect. **3.** To build. **4.** To cause to
arise or appear: *raise from the dead.* **5.** To
increase in size, worth, degree, etc. **6.** To improve in rank or status. **7.** To breed or rear.
8. To utter (a cry, shout, etc.). **9.** To arouse or
stir up. **10.** To collect: *raise money.* **11.** To
cause (dough) to puff up. **12.** To end (a siege).
—*n.* **1.** An act of raising or increasing. **2.** An
increase in salary. [< ON *reisa.*]

rai•sin (rā'zən) *n.* A sweet dried grape. [<
OF, grape.]

rai•son d'ê•tre (rĕ-zôN' dĕ'tr). Reason for
being. [F.]

ra•jah, ra•ja (rä'jə) *n.* A prince in India.
[Hindi *rājā.*]

rake¹ (rāk) *n.* A long-handled implement with
a row of projecting teeth at its head, used to
gather leaves and grass. —*v.* **raked, raking.
1.** To gather, move, or loosen with or as with a
rake. **2.** To aim heavy gunfire along the length
of. [< OE *raca, racu.* See reg-¹.]

rake² (rāk) *n.* A profligate man; roué.

rake³ (rāk) *n.* Inclination from the vertical or
from the horizontal. [?]

rake-off (rāk'ôf') *n.* A share of the profits of an
enterprise, esp. one accepted as a bribe.

rak•ish¹ (rā'kĭsh) *adj.* **1.** *Naut.* Having a trim,
streamlined appearance. **2.** Gay and showy;
jaunty. —**rak'ish•ly** *adv.*

rak•ish² (rā'kĭsh) *adj.* Debauched; libertine.

Ra•leigh (rô'lē). The capital of North Carolina. Pop. 94,000.

Ra•leigh (rô'lē), Sir **Walter.** 1552?–1618. English courtier, navigator, colonizer, and writer.

ral•ly¹ (răl'ē) *v.* **-lied, -lying. 1.** To call or join
together for a common purpose. **2.** To reas-
semble. **3.** To recover (one's strength). —*n., pl.*

-lies. **1.** A mass assembly, esp. to inspire enthusiasm for a cause. **2.** A reassembling. **3.** A notable rise in market prices and active trading after a decline. [< OF *ralier*, to ally again.] —**ral′li•er** *n.*

ral•ly² (răl′ē) *v.* -lied, -lying. To banter; tease. [< OF *railler*, to RAIL³.] —**ral′li•er** *n.*

ram (răm) *n.* **1.** A male sheep. **2.** Ram. A constellation and sign of the zodiac, Aries. **3.** Any of several devices used to drive, batter, or crush by forceful impact. —*v.* **rammed, ramming.** **1.** To strike or drive against with a heavy impact. **2.** To force into place. **3.** To cram; stuff. [< OE *ramm* < Gmc *ramma-.*]

ram•ble (răm′bəl) *v.* -bled, -bling. **1.** To walk or wander aimlessly. **2.** To follow an irregularly winding course. **3.** To speak or write with many digressions. —*n.* A leisurely stroll. [< ME *romen*, to roam.]

ram•bler (răm′blər) *n.* **1.** One who rambles. **2.** A climbing rose with numerous small flowers.

ram•bunc•tious (răm-bŭngk′shəs) *adj.* Boisterous. [< L *robustus*, oaken, strong.]

ram•ie (răm′ē) *n.* A textile fiber obtained from the stems of an Asian plant. [Malay *rami*.]

ram•i•fy (răm′ə-fī′) *v.* -fied, -fying. To divide into branchlike parts; branch out. [< L *rāmus*, branch.] —**ram′i•fi•ca′tion** *n.*

ram•jet (răm′jĕt′) *n.* A jet engine that propels aircraft by igniting fuel with air taken and compressed by the engine in a fashion that produces greater exhaust than intake velocity.

ramp (rămp) *n.* An inclined passage connecting different levels, as of a building or road. [< F *ramper*, to slope, creep.]

ram•page (răm′pāj) *n.* A course of violent, frenzied behavior. —*v.* (răm-pāj′) -paged, -paging. To move about wildly or violently. [Scot.] —**ram•pag′er** *n.*

ram•pant (răm′pənt) *adj.* **1.** Extending unchecked; unrestrained. **2.** *Heraldry.* Rearing on the left hind leg with the forelegs elevated, the right above the left, and usually with the head in profile. [< OF *ramper*, to climb.]

ram•part (răm′pärt) *n.* **1.** A fortification consisting of an embankment, often with a parapet. **2.** Anything that serves to protect. [< OF *ramparer*, to fortify.]

ram•rod (răm′rŏd′) *n.* **1.** A metal rod used to force the charge into a muzzleloading firearm. **2.** A rod used to clean the barrel of a firearm. —*adj.* Like a rod in stiffness.

ram•shack•le (răm′shăk′əl) *adj.* Shoddily constructed; rickety. [< ME *ransaken*, to ransack.]

ran (răn). *p.t.* of **run**.

ranch (rănch) *n.* A large farm, as in the W U.S., esp. for raising cattle, sheep, or horses. —*v.* To work on or manage a ranch. [< OF *ranger*, to put in a line.] —**ranch′er** *n.*

ran•cid (răn′sĭd) *adj.* Having the disagreeable odor or taste of decomposed oils or fats; rank. [< L *rancēre*, to stink.] —**ran′cid•ness** *n.*

ran•cor (răng′kər) *n.* Deep-seated ill will. [< L *rancēre*, to stink.] —**ran′cor•ous** *adj.*

rand (rănd, ränd) *n.* The basic monetary unit of the Republic of South Africa.

ran•dom (răn′dəm) *adj.* Having no specific pattern or objective; haphazard. —**at random.** Without definite method or purpose. [< OF *randon*, haphazard.] —**ran′dom•ly** *adv.*

rang (răng). *p.t.* of **ring**.

range (rānj) *n.* **1. a.** The extent of perception, knowledge, experience, or ability. **b.** The area, sphere, or scope of activity or occurrence. **2.** The extent of variation: *price range.* **3.** The maximum distance that a ship or other vehicle can travel before exhausting its fuel supply. **4.** A place for shooting at targets. **5.** Open land on which livestock wander and graze. **6.** The act of roaming. **7.** An extended series of mountains. **8.** A type of cooking stove. —*v.* **ranged, ranging.** **1.** To arrange in order, esp. in rows or lines. **2.** To classify. **3.** To roam through; explore. **4.** To roam freely. **5.** To extend in a particular direction. **6.** To vary within limits. [< OF, range, rank.]

rang•er (rān′jər) *n.* **1.** A wanderer or rover. **2.** One of an armed troop who patrols a specific region. **3.** A warden employed to patrol a forest.

Ran•goon (răng-gōōn′). The capital of Burma. Pop. 1,530,000.

rang•y (rān′jē) *adj.* -ier, -iest. Slender and long-limbed. —**rang′i•ness** *n.*

rank¹ (răngk) *n.* **1.** Relative position or status in a group. **2.** Official position. **3.** Eminent position. **4.** A row, line, or series. **5.** A line of soldiers or military vehicles standing side by side in close order. **6. ranks. a.** The armed forces. **b.** Enlisted men. —*v.* **1.** To place in or form a row or rows. **2.** To classify. **3.** To hold a particular rank. **4.** To take precedence over. [OF *ranc, renc*, rank, range.]

rank² (răngk) *adj.* **1.** Growing profusely or with excessive vigor. **2.** Strong and offensive in odor or flavor. [< OE *ranc*, haughty, full-grown.] —**rank′ly** *adv.* —**rank′ness** *n.*

rank•ing (răngk′ĭng) *adj.* Of the highest rank.

ran•kle (răng′kəl) *v.* -kled, -kling. **1.** To cause irritation or resentment. **2.** To become sore or inflamed. [< OF *rancle, draoncle*, ulcer, festering sore.]

ran•sack (răn′săk′) *v.* **1.** To search thoroughly. **2.** To pillage. [< ON *rannsaka*, search a house.] —**ran′sack′er** *n.*

ran•som (răn′səm) *n.* **1.** The release of a person in return for payment. **2.** The price demanded or paid. [< L *redemptiō*, redemption.] —**ran′som** *v.* —**ran′som•er** *n.*

rant (rănt) *v.* To speak or declaim in a vehement manner; rave. [Prob < Du *ranten*.] —**rant′er** *n.*

rap (răp) *v.* **rapped, rapping.** **1.** To strike quickly and lightly. **2.** To utter sharply. **3.** *Slang.* To talk. —*n.* **1.** A knock. **2.** A reprimand. **3.** *Slang.* A talk. —**beat the rap.** *Slang.* To escape legal punishment. [ME *rappen*.]

ra•pa•cious (rə-pā′shəs) *adj.* **1.** Taking by force; plundering. **2.** Greedy; ravenous. **3.** Subsisting on prey. [< L *rapere*, to seize.] —**ra•pa′cious•ly** *adv.* —**ra•pa′cious•ness, ra•pac′i•ty** (rə-păs′ə-tē) *n.*

rape¹ (rāp) *n.* **1.** The crime of forcing a female to submit to sexual intercourse. **2.** The act of

rape² (răp) *n.* A plant with oil-rich seeds used as animal feed. [< L *răpa, răpum,* turnip.]

carrying off by force. **3.** Profanation. [< L *rapere,* to seize.] —**rape** *v.* (**raped, raping**). —**rap′ist** *n.*

Raph·a·el (răf′ē-əl, rä′fē-). 1483–1520. Italian painter.

rap·id (răp′ĭd) *adj.* Very fast; swift. —*n.* Often **rapids.** An extremely fast-moving part of a river. [L *rapidus,* hurrying, seizing.] —**ra·pid′i·ty** (rə-pĭd′ə-tē), **rap′id·ness** *n.* —**rap′id·ly** *adv.*

ra·pi·er (rā′pē-ər, rāp′yər) *n.* **1.** A long, slender, two-edged sword used in the 16th and 17th centuries. **2.** An 18th-century, lighter, sharp-pointed sword, used only for thrusting. [F *rapière.*]

rap·ine (răp′ĭn) *n.* Pillage. [< L *rapere,* to RAPE.]

rap·pel (ră-pĕl′) *n.* The method of descending from a steep height by means of a double rope passed under one thigh and over the opposite shoulder. [F, "recall."] —**rap·pel** *v.* (**-pelled, -pelling**).

rap·port (ră-pôr′, -pōr′) *n.* Relationship, esp. one of mutual trust or understanding. [< F *rapporter,* to bring back, yield.]

rap·proche·ment (ră-prôsh-män′) *n.* **1.** A re-establishing of cordial relations. **2.** The state of cordial relations. [< F *rapprocher,* to bring together.]

rap·scal·lion (răp-skăl′yən) *n.* A rascal; scamp. [< RASCAL.]

rapt (răpt) *adj.* Deeply absorbed; engrossed. [< L *raptus,* "seized."]

rap·ture (răp′chər) *n.* A state of ecstasy. [< L *raptus,* RAPT.] —**rap′tur·ous** *adj.*

ra·ra a·vis (râr′ə ā′vĭs) *pl.* **rara avises** or **rarae aves** (râr′ē ā′vēz). A rare or unique person or thing. [L, "rare bird."]

rare¹ (râr) *adj.* **rarer, rarest. 1.** Unusual. **2.** Special. **3.** Thin in density; rarefied: *the rare air of the high altitudes.* [< L *rārus,* loose, thin, scarce.] —**rare′ly** *adv.* —**rare′ness, rar′i·ty** *n.*

rare² (râr) *adj.* **rarer, rarest.** Cooked a short time to retain juice and redness: *rare meat.* [< OE *hrēr,* soft-boiled.] —**rare′ness** *n.*

rare·bit (râr′bĭt) *n.* Welsh rabbit. [Var of (WELSH) RABBIT.]

rare-earth element (râr′ûrth′). Any of the related series of metallic elements of atomic number 57 through 71.

rar·e·fied (râr′ə-fīd′) *adj.* Elevated in character or style; esoteric.

rar·e·fy (râr′ə-fī′) *v.* **-fied, -fying. 1.** To make or become thin or less dense. **2.** To purify or refine. —**rar′e·fac′tion** *n.*

rar·ing (râr′ĭng) *adj. Informal.* Full of eagerness. [< REAR².]

ras·cal (răs′kəl) *n.* **1.** An unscrupulous or dishonest person. **2.** One who is playfully mischievous. [Perh < OF *rasque, rasche,* mud, filth.] —**ras′cal·ly** *adj.*

rash¹ (răsh) *adj.* Acting without forethought or due caution; hasty. [ME *rasch,* nimble, quick.] —**rash′ly** *adv.* —**rash′ness** *n.*

rash² (răsh) *n.* **1.** A skin eruption. **2.** A wide recurrence of something within a given period. [Poss < VL *rasciāre,* to scrape.]

rash·er (răsh′ər) *n.* A thin slice of bacon to be fried or broiled. [?]

rasp (răsp, räsp) *v.* **1.** To file or scrape with a rasp. **2.** To speak in a grating voice. **3.** To grate upon (nerves or feelings). —*n.* A file having abrasive, pointed projections. [< OHG *raspōn.*] —**rasp′er** *n.* —**rasp′ing·ly** *adv.* —**rasp′y** *adj.*

rasp·ber·ry (răz′bĕr′ē, -bə-rē, räz′-) *n.* **1.** The sweet, usually red berry of a prickly woody plant. **2.** A plant bearing such berries. [< earlier *raspis.*]

Ras·pu·tin (răs-pyōō′tĭn), **Grigori.** 1871?–1916. Russian mystic monk; favorite of the imperial family.

rat (răt) *n.* **1.** Any of various long-tailed, often destructive rodents resembling but larger than a mouse. **2.** A sneaky person, esp. one who betrays his associates. —*v.* **ratted, ratting. 1.** To hunt for or catch rats. **2.** *Slang.* To desert or betray one's comrades: *rat on a friend.* [< OE *ræt* < Gmc **ratt-.*] —**rat′ter** *n.*

ratch·et (răch′ĭt) *n.* A mechanism consisting of a pawl, or hinged catch, that engages the sloping teeth of a wheel or bar, permitting motion in one direction only. [< OF *rocquet,* head of a lance.]

rate¹ (rāt) *n.* **1.** A measured quantity within the limits of a fixed quantity of something else. **2.** A quantitative measure of a part to a whole; proportion. **3. a.** A charge or payment. **b.** A cost per unit. **4.** Level of quality. —**at any rate. 1.** Whatever the case may be. **2.** At least. —*v.* **rated, rating. 1.** To calculate the value of. **2.** To classify or be classified. **3.** To regard. **4.** To deserve. **5.** To have importance or status. [< ML *rata,* calculated, fixed.]

rate² (rāt) *v.* **rated, rating.** To scold. [Perh < ON *hrata.*]

rath·er (răth′ər, rä′thər) *adv.* **1.** Preferably. **2.** With more reason. **3.** With more accuracy. **4.** Somewhat. **5.** On the contrary. **6.** *Chiefly Brit.* Most certainly. Used as an emphatic reply. [< OE *hræth,* early.]

rat·i·fy (răt′ə-fī′) *v.* **-fied, -fying.** To give formal sanction to; approve and so make valid. [< ML *ratificāre.*] —**rat′i·fi·ca′tion** *n.*

rat·ing (rā′tĭng) *n.* **1.** A place assigned on a scale; a standing or rank. **2.** A classification according to specialty or proficiency.

ra·tio (rā′shō, rā′shē-ō′) *n., pl.* **-tios. 1.** Relation in degree or number between two similar things; rate. **2.** *Math.* The relative size of two quantities expressed as the quotient of one divided by the other. [L *ratiō,* computation.]

ra·ti·oc·i·nate (răsh′ē-ŏs′ə-nāt′) *v.* **-nated, -nating.** To reason methodically and logically. [< L *ratiō,* RATIO.] —**ra′ti·oc′i·na′tion** *n.* —**ra′ti·oc′i·na′tive** *adj.* —**ra′ti·oc′i·na′tor** *n.*

ra·tion (răsh′ən, rā′shən) *n.* **1.** A fixed portion, esp. an amount of food allotted to persons in military service or to civilians in times of scarcity. **2. rations.** *Mil.* Food. —*v.* **1.** To supply with rations. **2.** To restrict to limited allotments. [< L *ratiō (ratiōn-),* RATIO.]

ra·tion·al (răsh′ən-əl) *adj.* **1.** Having or exercising the ability to reason. **2.** Of sound mind. **3.** Manifesting or based upon reason;

logical. **4.** *Math.* Expressible as a ratio of two integers. [< L *ratiō*, reason, RATIO.] —**ra′tion·al′i·ty** *n.* —**ra′tion·al·ly** *adv.*

ra·tion·ale (răsh′ə-năl′) *n.* **1** The fundamental reasons for something. **2.** An exposition of principles or reasons.

ra·tion·al·ism (răsh′ən-əl-ĭz′əm) *n.* The theory that the exercise of reason provides the only valid basis for action or belief. —**ra′tion·al·ist** *n.* —**ra′tion·al·is′tic** *adj.* —**ra′tion·al·is′ti·cal·ly** *adv.*

ra·tion·al·ize (răsh′ən-əl-īz′) *v.* **-ized, -izing. 1.** To make conformable to reason. **2.** To interpret from a rational standpoint. **3.** To devise self-satisfying but incorrect reasons for (one's behavior). —**ra′tion·al·i·za′tion** (-ə-zā′shən) *n.*

rat·line (răt′lĭn) *n.* Also **rat·lin.** *Naut.* Any of the small ropes fastened horizontally to the shrouds of a ship and forming a ladder for going aloft. [?]

rats·bane (răts′bān′) *n.* Rat poison.

rat·tan (ră-tăn′) *n.* The long, tough, slender stems of a climbing tropical palm, used for wickerwork, canes, etc. [Malay *rotan.*]

rat·tle (răt′l) *v.* **-tled, -tling. 1.** To make or cause to emit a quick succession of short, sharp sounds. **2.** To move with such sounds. **3.** To talk or utter rapidly and at length: *rattle off a list.* **4.** *Informal.* To fluster; unnerve. —*n.* **1.** Short, percussive sounds produced in rapid succession. **2.** A device for producing these sounds, such as a baby's toy. **3.** The series of horny structures at the end of a rattlesnake's tail. [< MLG *rattelen.*]

rat·tler (răt′lər) *n.* A rattlesnake.

rat·tle·snake (răt′l-snāk′) *n.* A venomous New World snake with a series of loose, horny segments at the end of the tail.

rat·tle·trap (răt′l-trăp′) *n.* A rickety, worn-out vehicle.

rat·ty (răt′ē) *adj.* **-tier, -tiest. 1.** Of or characteristic of rats. **2.** *Slang.* Disreputable; dilapidated.

rau·cous (rô′kəs) *adj.* Rough-sounding; harsh. [L *raucus,* hoarse, harsh.] —**rau′cous·ly** *adv.* —**rau′cous·ness** *n.*

rav·age (răv′ĭj) *v.* **-aged, -aging.** To destroy or despoil. —*n.* **1.** The act of ravaging. **2.** Grievous damage. [< OF *ravir,* to ravish.] —**rav′ag·er** *n.*

rave (răv) *v.* **raved, raving. 1.** To speak or utter wildly, irrationally, or incoherently. **2.** To roar; rage. **3.** To speak with wild enthusiasm. —*n.* **1.** The state or act of raving. **2.** *Informal.* An extravagantly enthusiastic opinion or review. [< ONF *raver.*]

rav·el (răv′əl) *v.* **-eled** or **-elled, -eling** or **-elling. 1.** To separate the fibers or threads of (cloth); unravel; fray. **2.** To tangle or become confused. —*n.* **1.** A raveling. **2.** A loose thread. **3.** A tangle. [< Du *rafelen,* to unravel.]

Ra·vel (rə-vĕl′, ră-), **Maurice.** 1875–1937. French composer and pianist.

ra·ven (rā′vən) *n.* A large crowlike bird with a croaking cry. —*adj.* Black and shiny. [< OE *hræfn.* See **ker-**[2].]

rav·en·ing (răv′ən-ĭng) *adj.* Predatory; voracious. [< OF *raviner,* to ravage.]

rav·en·ous (răv′ən-əs) *adj.* **1.** Extremely hungry. **2.** Predatory. **3.** Greedy for gratification. [< OF *raviner,* to ravage.] —**rav′en·ous·ly** *adv.*

ra·vine (rə-vēn′) *n.* A deep, narrow cleft or gorge in the earth's surface, esp. one worn by water. [F, mountain torrent.]

ra·vi·o·li (ră′vē-ō′lē) *pl.n. (takes sing.* or *pl. v.).* Small casings of pasta with various fillings, as chopped meat or cheese. [< It *rava,* turnip.]

rav·ish (răv′ĭsh) *v.* **1.** To seize and carry away by force. **2.** To rape. **3.** To enrapture. [< L *rapere,* seize.] —**rav′ish·er** *n.* —**rav′ish·ment** *n.*

rav·ish·ing (răv′ĭsh-ĭng) *adj.* Entrancing.

raw (rô) *adj.* **1.** Uncooked. **2.** In a natural condition; not subjected to manufacturing or refining. **3.** Untrained. **4.** Having subcutaneous tissue exposed: *a raw wound.* **5.** Penetratingly damp. **6.** Cruel and unfair. **7.** Outspoken; crude. [< OE *hrēaw.* See **kreu-**[1].] —**raw′ly** *adv.* —**raw′ness** *n.*

raw·boned (rô′bōnd′) *adj.* Having a lean, gaunt frame with prominent bones.

raw·hide (rô′hīd′) *n.* **1.** The untanned hide of cattle. **2.** A whip or rope made of such hide.

ray[1] (rā) *n.* **1.** A thin line or narrow beam of radiation, esp. of visible light. **2.** A trace; hint: *a ray of hope.* **3.** A straight line extending from a point. **4.** A part or structure having this form. [< L *radius.*]

ray[2] (rā) *n.* A marine fish with a broad, flattened body and a long, narrow tail. [< L *raia.*]

ray·on (rā′ŏn) *n.* **1.** A synthetic fiber produced by forcing a cellulose solution through a plate with fine holes and solidifying the resulting filaments. **2.** Fabric made from such fibers. [< RAY[1].]

raze (rāz) *v.* **razed, razing. 1.** To tear down or demolish. **2.** To scrape or shave off. [< L *rādere* (pp *rāsus*), to scrape.]

ra·zor (rā′zər) *n.* A sharp-edged cutting instrument used esp. for shaving. [< OF *raser,* to scrape, raze.]

razz (răz) *v. Slang.* To deride or tease.

Rb rubidium.

r.b.i. *Baseball.* run or runs batted in.

R.C. 1. Red Cross. **2.** Roman Catholic.

R.C.Ch. Roman Catholic Church.

rcpt. receipt.

rd rod (unit of length).

rd. 1. road. **2.** round.

R.D. rural delivery.

re (rē) *prep.* Concerning; in reference to; in the case of. [< L *rēs,* thing.]

Re rhenium.

re-. *comb. form.* **1.** Restoration to a previous condition. **2.** Repetition of a previous action. [< L.]

reach (rēch) *v.* **1.** To stretch out or extend (a bodily part). **2.** To touch, take hold of, or try to grasp (something) by extending a bodily part, esp. the hand. **3.** To get to or arrive at. **4.** To succeed in communicating with. **5.** To extend or carry as far as. **6.** To aggregate or amount to. —*n.* **1.** The act or power of stretching or thrusting out. **2.** The extent or distance something can reach. **3.** An unbroken expanse. [< OE *ræcan.* See **reig-**.]

ô paw, for/oi boy/ou out/ o͞o took/ o͞o coo/p pop/r run/s sauce/sh shy/t to/th thin/*th* the/
ŭ cut/ûr fur/v van/w wag/y yes/z size/zh vision/ə ago, item, edible, gallop, circus/

re·act (rē-ăkt′) v. **1.** To act in response or opposition to some former act or state. **2.** To be affected or influenced by circumstances or events. **3.** To undergo chemical change.

re·ac·tant (rē-ăk′tənt) n. A substance participating in a chemical reaction.

re·ac·tion (rē-ăk′shən) n. **1.** A response to a stimulus or the state resulting from such a response. **2.** A reverse or opposing action. **3.** Opposition to progress or liberalism. **4.** A chemical change or transformation. **5.** A nuclear reaction.

re·ac·tion·ar·y (rē-ăk′shə-nĕr′ē) adj. Characterized by reaction, esp. opposing progress or liberalism. —n., pl. -ies. An opponent of progress or liberalism.

re·ac·tive (rē-ăk′tĭv) adj. **1.** Tending to be responsive or to react to a stimulus. **2.** Characterized by reaction.

re·ac·tor (rē-ăk′tər) n. **1.** One that reacts. **2.** A nuclear reactor.

read (rēd) v. read (rĕd), **reading. 1.** To comprehend the meaning of (something written or printed). **2.** To utter or render aloud (something written or printed). **3.** To ascertain the intent or mood of: He read her mind. **4.** To derive a special meaning from or ascribe a special significance to: read improper motives into his actions. **5.** To foretell or predict. **6.** To comprehend (a signal, message, etc.). **7.** To study. **8.** To learn by reading. **9.** To indicate or register: The dial reads 0°. **10.** To have a particular wording. **11.** To contain a specific meaning. [< OE rǣdan, advise, explain, read.] —read′a·bil′i·ty, read′a·ble·ness n. —read′a·ble adj. —read′er n.

read·i·ly (rĕd′ə-lē) adv. **1.** Promptly. **2.** Willingly. **3.** Easily.

read·ing (rē′dĭng) n. **1.** The act or practice of a reader. **2.** Written or printed material. **3.** A public recitation of literary or other written material. **4.** A personal interpretation or appraisal. **5.** The specific form of a particular passage in a text. **6.** Information indicated, as by a gauge.

read·y (rĕd′ē) adj. -ier, -iest. **1.** Prepared or available for service or action. **2.** Mentally disposed; willing. **3.** Prompt in apprehending or reacting. [< OE rǣde. See reidh-.] —read′i·ness n.

read·y-made (rĕd′ē-mād′) adj. Made to a set pattern; not custom-made.

read·y-wit·ted (rĕd′ē-wĭt′ĭd) adj. Quick-witted. —read′y·wit′ted·ly adv.

re·a·gent (rē-ā′jənt) n. Any substance used in a chemical reaction to detect, measure, exam-

---

Note: Many compounds may be formed with re-. In forming compounds re- is normally joined with the following element without space or hyphen: reopen. If the second element begins with e, it is preferable to separate it with a hyphen. However, such compounds may often be found written solid: reenter; reexamine.

re′a·ban′don v.	re′ap·pear′ance n.	re′at·tain′ v.
re′ab·sorb′ v.	re′ap·ply′ v.	re′at·tempt′ v.
re′ab·sorp′tion n.	re′ap·point′ v.	re′a·vow′ v.
re′ac·cept′ v.	re′ap·point′ment n.	re′a·wake′ v.
re′ac·com′mo·date′ v.	re′ap·por′tion v.	re′a·wak′en v.
re′ac·com′pa·ny v.	re′ap·por′tion·ment n.	re·bill′ v.
re′ac·cuse′ v.	re·ar′gue v.	re·bind′ v.
re′ac·quire′ v.	re·ar′gu·ment n.	re·bloom′ v.
re·ac′ti·vate′ v.	re·arm′ v.	re·blos′som v.
re′a·dapt′ v.	re·ar′ma·ment n.	re·boil′ v.
re′ad·dress′ v.	re·ar·range′ v.	re·broad′cast′ v. & n.
re′ad·journ′ v.	re·ar·range′ment n.	re·build′ v.
re′ad·journ′ment n.	re′as·cend′ v.	re·bur′y v.
re′ad·just′ v.	re′as·cent′ n.	re·car′ry v.
re′ad·just′ment n.	re′as·sem′ble v.	re·cast′ v. & n.
re′ad·mis′sion n.	re′as·sem′bly n.	re·cel′e·brate′ v.
re′ad·mit′ v.	re′as·sert′ v.	re·chal′lenge v.
re′a·dopt′ v.	re′as·ser′tion n.	re·charge′ v.
re′a·dorn′ v.	re′as·sign′ v.	re·char′ter v.
re′ad·vance′ v.	re′as·sim′i·late′ v.	re·check′ v.
re′af·firm′ v.	re′as·sim′i·la′tion n.	re·choose′ v.
re′a·lign′ v.	re′as·so′ci·ate′ v.	re·chris′ten v.
re′a·lign′ment n.	re′as·sume′ v.	re·cir′cle v.
re·an′i·mate′ v.	re′as·sump′tion n.	re·cir′cu·late′ v.
re′an·nex′ v.	re′at·tach′ v.	re·clasp′ v.
re′a·noint′ v.	re′at·tack′ v.	re·clean′ v.
re′ap·pear′ v.		re·clothe′ v.

ă pat/ā ate/âr care/ä bar/b bib/ch chew/d deed/ĕ pet/ē be/f fit/g gag/h hat/hw what/
ĭ pit/ī pie/îr pier/j judge/k kick/l lid, fatal/m mum/n no, sudden/ng sing/ŏ pot/ō go/

ine, or produce other substances. [RE- +
AGENT.]

re·al (rē'əl, rēl) *adj.* **1.** Being or occurring in
fact or actuality. **2.** Genuine; authentic. **3.**
Opt. Pertaining to an image formed by light
rays that converge in space. **4.** *Law.* Of or
pertaining to stationary or fixed property, as
buildings or land. —*adv. Informal.* Very: *I'm
real sorry.* [< LL *reālis*, actual, real < L *rēs*,
thing.]

real estate. Landed property including all
inherent natural resources and any man-made
improvements established thereon; realty.
—**re'al·es·tate'** *adj.*

re·al·ism (rē'ə-lĭz'əm) *n.* **1.** Inclination toward
literal truth and pragmatism. **2.** Artistic representation felt to be accurate. —**re'al·ist** *n.*
—**re'al·is'tic** *adj.* —**re'al·is'ti·cal·ly** *adv.*

re·al·i·ty (rē-ăl'ə-tē) *n., pl.* **-ties. 1.** The quality
or state of being actual or true. **2.** The totality
of all things possessing actuality, existence, or
essence.

re·al·ize (rē'ə-līz') *v.* **-ized, -izing. 1.** To comprehend completely or correctly. **2.** To make
real or actualize (a plan, ambition, etc.). **3.** To
obtain or achieve, esp. from a commercial
transaction. —**re'al·iz'a·ble** *adj.* —**re'al·i·za'tion**
(-lə-zā'shən) *n.* —**re'al·iz'er** *n.*

re·al·ly (rē'ə-lē, rē'lē) *adv.* **1.** In reality. **2.**
Truly.

realm (rĕlm) *n.* **1.** A kingdom. **2.** Any field,
sphere, or province. [< L *regimen*, system of
government.]

Re·al·tor (rē'əl-tər, -tôr') *n.* Also **re·al·tor.** A
real-estate agent affiliated with the National
Association of Real Estate Boards. [<
REALTY.]

re·al·ty (rē'əl-tē) *n., pl.* **-ties. Real estate.** [REAL
+ -TY.]

ream¹ (rēm) *n.* **1.** A quantity of paper, 500
sheets or, in a printer's ream, 516. **2.** Often
reams. Very much: *reams of verse.* [< Ar
rizmah, bundle.]

ream² (rēm) *v.* **1.** To form, taper, or enlarge (a
hole) with or as with a reamer. **2.** To remove
(material) by reaming. [Perh < OE *rȳman*, to
widen.]

ream·er (rē'mər) *n.* Any of various tools used
to shape or enlarge holes.

reap (rēp) *v.* **1.** To harvest by cutting with or as
with a scythe, sickle, etc. **2.** To obtain as a
result of effort; receive as reward or punishment. [< OE *rīpan.* See rei-¹.]

reap·er (rē'pər) *n.* **1.** One who reaps. **2.** A
machine for harvesting.

rear¹ (rîr) *n.* The back or hind part. —**bring up**

re·coin' *v.*	re'de·scend' *v.*	re'-en·gage' *v.*
re·coin'age *n.*	re'de·scent' *n.*	re'-en·gage'ment *n.*
re'·col·lect' *v.*	re'de·scribe' *v.*	re'-en·grave' *v.*
re·col'o·nize' *v.*	re'de·ter'mine *v.*	re'-en·list' *v.*
re·col'or *v.*	re'de·vel'op *v.*	re'-en·list'ment *v.*
re'com·bine' *v.*	re'di·gest' *v.*	re'-en·slave' *v.*
re'com·mence' *v.*	re'dis·cov'er *v.*	re-en'ter *v.*
re'com·mis'sion *n.*	re'dis·cov'er·y *n.*	re'-e·rect' *v.*
re'com·pose' *v.*	re'dis·solve' *v.*	re'-es·tab'lish *v.*
re'con·dense' *v.*	re'dis·till' *v.*	re'-es·tab'lish·ment
re'con·duct' *v.*	re'dis·trib'ute *v.*	*n.*
re'con·firm' *v.*	re'di·vide' *v.*	re'-e·val'u·ate' *v.*
re·con'quer *v.*	re'di·vi'sion *n.*	re'-e·val'u·a'tion
re·con'quest *n.*	re·do' *v.*	*n.*
re·con'se·crate' *v.*	re·dou'ble *v.*	re'-ex·am'i·na'tion
re·con'sol'i·date' *v.*	re'draft' *n.*	*n.*
re·con'sti·tute *v.*	re·draw' *v.*	re'-ex·am'ine *v.*
re·con'sti·tu'tion *n.*	re·drive' *v.*	re'-ex·change' *v.*
re'con·vene' *v.*	re·dry' *v.*	re'-ex·hib'it *v.*
re'con·vert' *v.*	re·dye' *v.*	re'-ex·pel' *v.*
re'con·vey' *v.*	re-ech'o *n. & v.*	re'-ex·pe'ri·ence *v.*
re·cop'y *v.*	re-ed'it *v.*	re'ex·port' *v.*
re'cor·o·na'tion *n.*	re-ed'u·cate' *v.*	re·face' *v.*
re·cross' *v.*	re'-e·lect' *v.*	re·fash'ion *v.*
re·crown' *v.*	re'-e·lec'tion *n.*	re·fas'ten *v.*
re'crys·tal·li·za'	re-el'e·vate' *v.*	re·fer'ti·lize' *v.*
tion *n.*	re'-em·bark' *v.*	re·fire' *v.*
re·crys'tal·lize' *v.*	re'-em·bod'y *v.*	re'flow' *v.*
re·cul'ti·vate' *v.*	re'-em·brace' *v.*	re·flow'er *v.*
re'cy'cle *v.*	re'-e·merge' *v.*	re·fold' *v.*
re'ded·i·ca'tion *n.*	re'-e·mer'gence *n.*	re·forge' *v.*
re'de·feat' *v. & n.*	re-em'i·grate' *v.*	re·for'mu·late' *v.*
re'de·fine' *v.*	re'-en·act' *v.*	re·for·ti·fi·ca'
re'de·liv'er *v.*	re'-en·act'ment *n.*	tion *n.*
re'de·mand' *v.*	re'-en·cour'age *v.*	re·for'ti·fy' *v.*
re·dem'on·strate' *v.*	re'-en·cour'age·ment	re·frame' *v.*
re'de·ny' *v.*	*n.*	re·freeze' *v.*
re'de·pos'it *v. & n.*	re'-en·dow' *v.*	re·fu'el *v.*

the rear. To be last in a line. —*adj.* Of or located in the rear. [Short for ARREAR.]

rear² (rîr) *v.* **1.** To care for during the early stages of life; bring up. **2.** To lift upright. **3.** To build. **4.** To rise on the hind legs, as a horse. [< OE *rǣran,* to raise < Gmc *raizjan.*] —**rear′er** *n.*

rear admiral. A naval officer ranking next below a vice admiral.

rear guard. A detachment of troops that protects the rear of a military force. —**rear′guard′** (rîr′gärd′) *adj.*

rear·most (rîr′mōst′) *adj.* Farthest in the rear; in the last position.

rear·ward (rîr′wərd) *adj.* Directed toward or situated at the rear. —*adv.* Also **rear·wards** (-wərdz). Toward, to, or at the rear.

rea·son (rē′zən) *n.* **1.** The basis or motive for an action, decision, or conviction. **2.** An underlying fact or cause that provides logical sense for a premise or occurrence. **3.** The capacity for rational thought, inference, or discrimination. —**stand to reason.** To be logical or likely. —*v.* **1.** To use the faculty of reason; think logically. **2.** To talk or argue logically and persuasively. **3.** To determine or conclude by logical thinking. [< L *ratiō,* calculation, judgment.] —**rea′son·er** *n.* —**rea′son·ing** *n.*

rea·son·a·ble (rē′zən-ə-bəl) *adj.* **1.** Capable of reasoning; rational. **2.** In accordance with reason or sound thinking. **3.** Not excessive or extreme. —**rea′son·a·bil′i·ty, rea′son·a·ble·ness** *n.* —**rea′son·a·bly** *adv.*

re·as·sure (rē′ə-shŏŏr′) *v.* **1.** To restore confidence to. **2.** To assure again. —**re′as·sur′ance** *n.* —**re′as·sur′ing·ly** *adv.*

re·bate (rē′bāt′) *n.* A deduction from an amount to be paid or a return of part of an amount paid. —*v.* (rē′bāt′, rĭ-bāt′) **-bated, -bating.** To deduct or return (an amount) from a payment or bill. [< OF *rabattre,* to beat down again, reduce.] —**re′bat′er** (rē′bā′tər, rĭ-bā′tər)· *n.*

re·bel (rĭ-bĕl′) *v.* **-belled, -belling. 1.** To refuse allegiance to and oppose by force an established government or ruling authority. **2.** To resist or defy any authority or generally accepted convention. —*n.* **reb·el** (rĕb′əl). **1.** One who rebels or is in rebellion. **2. Rebel.** A Confederate soldier in the Civil War. —*adj.* Of or pertaining to rebels. [< L *rebellāre,* to make war again.]

re·bel·lion (rĭ-bĕl′yən) *n.* **1.** An uprising intended to change or overthrow an existing government or ruling authority. **2.** An act or show of defiance of any authority or established convention.

re·bel·lious (rĭ-bĕl′yəs) *adj.* **1.** Participating in or tending toward rebellion. **2.** Resisting control; unruly. —**re·bel′lious·ly** *adv.* —**re·bel′lious·ness** *n.*

---

re·fur′nish *v.*	re′in·fect′ *v.*	re′in·vest′ment *n.*
re·gath′er *v.*	re′in·fec′tion *n.*	re′in·vig′or·ate′
re·gear′ *v.*	re′in·flame′ *v.*	*v.*
re·ger′mi·nate′ *v.*	re′in·form′ *v.*	re′in·vig′or·a′
re′ger·mi·na′tion *n.*	re′in·fuse′ *v.*	tion *n.*
re·gild′ *v.*	re′in·hab′it *v.*	re′in·vite′ *v.*
re·glaze′ *v.*	re′in·oc′u·late′ *v.*	re′in·volve′ *v.*
re·glue′ *v.*	re′in·oc′u·la′tion	re·is′sue *n.* & *v.*
re·grade′ *v.*	*n.*	re·judge′ *v.*
re·graft′ *v.*	re′in·scribe′ *v.*	re·kin′dle *v.*
re·grant′ *v.*	re′in·sert′ *v.*	re·la′bel *v.*
re·group′ *v.*	re′in·ser′tion·*n.*	re·lace′ *v.*
re·han′dle *v.*	re′in·spect′ *v.*	re·launch′ *v.*
re·hear′ing *n.*	re′in·spec′tion *n.*	re·learn′ *v.*
re·heat′ *v.*	re′in·spire′ *v.*	re·light′ *v.*
re·heel′ *v.*	re′in·stall′ *v.*	re·line′ *v.*
re·hire′ *v.*	re′in·stal·la′tion	re·liq′ui·date′ *v.*
re·ig·nite′ *v.*	*n.*	re′liq·ui·da′tion
re′im·plant′ *v.*	re′in·struct′ *v.*	*n.*
re′im·port′ *v.*	re′in·sure′ *v.*	re·load′ *n.* & *v.*
re′im·pose′ *v.*	re′in′te·grate′ *v.*	re·loan′ *n.* & *v.*
re′im·po·si′tion *n.*	re′in·te·gra′tion	re·lo′cate *v.*
re′im·preg′nate *v.*	*n.*	re′lo·ca′tion *n.*
re′im·press′ *v.*	re′in·ter′ *v.*	re·make′ *v.* & *n.*
re′im·print′ *v.*	re′in·ter′ro·gate′	re′man·u·fac′ture
re′im·pris′on *v.*	*v.*	*v.*
re′im·pris′on·ment	re′in·tro·duce′ *v.*	re·mar′ry *v.*
n.	re′in·tro·duc′tion	re′match′ *n.*
re′in·au′gu·rate′	*n.*	re·meas′ure *v.*
v.	re′in·vent′ *v.*	re·melt′ *v.*
re′in·cite′ *v.*	re′in·vest′ *v.*	re·merge′ *v.*
re′in·cor′po·rate′	re′in·ves′ti·gate′	re·mi′grate *v.*
v.	*v.*	re′mi·gra′tion *n.*
re′in·cur′ *v.*	re′in·ves·ti·ga′	re·mil′i·ta·rize′ *v.*
re′in·duce′ *v.*	tion *n.*	re·mix′ *v.*

ă pat/ā ate/âr care/ä bar/b bib/ch chew/d deed/ĕ pet/ē be/f fit/g gag/h hat/hw what/
ĭ pit/ī pie/îr pier/j judge/k kick/l lid, fatal/m mum/n no, sudden/ng sing/ŏ pot/ō go/

re•birth (rē-bûrth′, rē′bûrth′) *n.* **1.** A second or new birth. **2.** A renaissance; revival.

re•born (rē-bôrn′) *adj.* Born again; spiritually revived or regenerated.

re•bound (rē′bound′, rĭ-) *v.* **1.** To spring or bounce back after hitting or colliding with something. **2.** To recover, as from depression or disappointment. —**re′bound′** (rē′bound′, rĭ-bound′) *n.*

re•buff (rĭ-bŭf′) *n.* **1.** A blunt or abrupt repulse or refusal. **2.** Any abrupt setback to progress or action. —*v.* **1.** To refuse bluntly or contemptuously; snub. **2.** To repel or drive back. [< It *ribuffo,* reprimand.]

re•buke (rĭ-byōōk′) *v.* **-buked, -buking.** To criticize sharply; reprimand. —*n.* A sharp reproof. [< ONF *rebuker.*]

re•bus (rē′bəs) *n., pl.* **-buses.** A riddle composed of pictures that suggest the sound of the words or syllables they represent. [L *rēbus,* by things.]

re•but (rĭ-bŭt′) *v.* **-butted, -butting.** To refute, esp. by offering opposing evidence or arguments, as in a legal case. [< OF *rebuter.*] —**re•but′tal** *n.*

rec. 1. receipt. **2.** recipe. **3.** record; recording. **4.** recreation.

re•cal•ci•trant (rĭ-kăl′sə-trənt) *adj.* Stubbornly resistant to authority or guidance. [< L *recalcitrāre,* to kick back.] —**re•cal′ci•trance, re•cal′ci•tran•cy** *n.*

re•call (rĭ-kôl′) *v.* **1.** To call back; ask or order to return. **2.** To remember or recollect. **3.** To cancel; take back. **4.** To bring back; restore. —*n.* (rĭ-kôl′, rē′kôl′). **1.** The act of recalling. **2.** The ability to remember information or experiences. **3. a.** The procedure by which a public official can be removed from office by popular vote. **b.** The right to employ this procedure. —**re•call′a•ble** *adj.*

re•call•ment (rĭ-kôl′mənt) *n.* Recall.

re•cant (rĭ-kănt′) *v.* To make a formal retraction or disavowal of (a previously held statement, position, or belief). [L *recantāre.*] —**re′can•ta′tion** (rē′kăn-tā′shən) *n.* —**re•cant′er** *n.* —**re•cant′ing•ly** *adv.*

re•cap[1] (rē-kăp′) *v.* · To restore (a used automobile tire) to usable condition by bonding new rubber onto the worn tread and lateral surface. —*n.* (rē′kăp′). A tire thus reconditioned.

re•cap[2] (rē′kăp′) *v.* **-capped, -capping.** To summarize. —*n.* A summary. [Short for RECAPITULATE.]

re•ca•pit•u•late (rē′kə-pĭch′ōō-lāt′) *v.* **-lated, -lating.** To repeat in concise form; summarize. [LL *recapitulāre.*] —**re′ca•pit′u•la′tion** *n.* —**re•ca•pit′u•la′tive** *adj.*

re•cap•ture (rē-kăp′chər) *v.* **1.** To capture again; retake or recover. **2.** To recall: *an attempt to recapture the past.*

recd. received.

re′mod·i·fi·ca′ tion *n.*	re·plunge′ *v.*	re·shape′ *v.*
re·mod′i·fy′ *v.*	re·pol′ish *v.* & *n.*	re·sharp′en *v.*
re·mold′ *v.*	re·pop′u·late′ *v.*	re·ship′ *v.*
re·mount′ *v.* & *n.*	re′pop·u·la′tion *n.*	re·ship′ment *n.*
re·name′ *v.*	re·pour′ *v.*	re·shuf′fle *v.*
re·nav′i·gate′ *v.*	re′-press′ *v.*	re·sift′ *v.*
re·nom′i·nate′ *v.*	re′print′ *n.*	re·sol′der *v.*
re′nom·i·na′tion *n.*	re·proc′ess *v.*	re·sole′ *v.*
re·no′ti·fy′ *v.*	re′pro·claim′ *v.*	re′so·lid′i·fy′ *v.*
re·num′ber *v.*	re′pub·li·ca′tion *n.*	re·sow′ *v.*
re′ob·tain′ *v.*	re·pub′lish *v.*	re·spell′ *v.*
re′ob·tain′a·ble *adj.*	re·pur′chase *v.*	re·spread′ *v.*
re′oc·cu·pa′tion *n.*	re·pu′ri·fy′ *v.*	re·stack′ *v.*
re·oc′cu·py′ *v.*	re′pur·sue′ *v.*	re·state′ *v.*
re′oc·cur′ *v.*	re·ra′di·ate′ *v.*	re·state′ment *n.*
re′oc·cur′rence *n.*	re·read′ *v.*	re·stip′u·late′ *v.*
re·o′pen *v.*	re′re·cord′ *v.*	re′stip·u·la′tion *n.*
re′op·pose′ *v.*	re·rise′ *v.*	re·stock′ *v.*
re′or·dain′ *v.*	re·roll′ *v.*	re·strength′en *v.*
re′or·di·na′tion *n.*	re·route′ *v.*	re·string′ *v.*
re·o′ri·ent′ *v.*	re·sad′dle *v.*	re·strive′ *v.*
re·pac′i·fy′ *v.*	re·sail′ *v.*	re·stud′y *n.* & *v.*
re·pack′ *v.*	re′sale *n.*	re′sub·ject′ *v.*
re·pack′age *v.*	re·sa·lute′ *v.*	re′sub·jec′tion *n.*
re·paint′ *v.* & *n.*	re·seal′ *v.*	re·sum′mon *v.*
re·pa′per *v.*	re·seat′ *v.*	re·sum′mons *n.*
re·pass′ *v.*	re·seed′ *v.*	re′sup·ply′ *v.*
re·pave′ *v.*	re·seek′ *v.*	re′sur·vey′ *v.* & *n.*
re·pe′nal·ize′ *v.*	re·seg′re·gate′ *v.*	re·teach′ *v.*
re·plant′ *v.*	re·seize′ *v.*	re·tell′ *v.*
re·play′ *v.*	re·sei′zure *n.*	re·test′ *v.*
re′play *n.*	re·sell′ *v.*	re·tie′ *v.*
re·pledge′ *v.*	re·set′ *v.* & *n.*	re′trans·late′ *v.*
	re·set′tle *v.*	re·trav′erse *v.*
	re·set′tle·ment *n.*	re·type′ *v.*

ô paw, for/oi boy/ou **out**/ŏŏ took/ōō coo/p **pop**/r run/s sauce/sh **shy**/t to/th **thin**/*th* the/ ŭ cut/ûr **fur**/v van/w **wag**/y yes/z size/zh vision/ə ago, item, edible, gallop, circus/

re·cede (rĭ-sēd') *v.* **-ceded, -ceding. 1.** To move back or away; retreat. **2.** To slope backward. **3.** To become or seem to become more distant. [L *recēdere,* to go back.]

re·ceipt (rĭ-sēt') *n.* **1.** The act of receiving or fact of being received. **2.** Often **receipts.** The amount of something received: *cash receipts.* **3.** A written acknowledgment that something specified has been received. **4.** *Regional.* A recipe. —*v.* **1.** To mark (a bill) as paid. **2.** To give a receipt for. [< L *recipere* (pp *receptus*), to take, RECEIVE.]

re·ceiv·a·ble (rĭ-sē'və-bəl) *adj.* **1.** Suitable for being received; acceptable as payment. **2.** Awaiting or requiring payment; due or collectable: *accounts receivable.* ·

re·ceive (rĭ-sēv') *v.* **-ceived, -ceiving. 1.** To take or acquire (something given, offered, or transmitted); get. **2.** To meet with; experience. **3.** To take in, hold, or contain. **4.** To admit or welcome (members, guests, etc.). **5.** To regard in a specified manner: *theories well received.* [< L *recipere,* to take back, regain.]

re·ceiv·er (rĭ-sē'vər) *n.* **1.** One that receives something; a recipient; receptacle. **2.** A person appointed by a court to take into custody the property or funds of others pending litigation. **3.** A device, as a radio, television set, or telephone, that receives incoming signals and converts them to perceptible forms.

re·ceiv·er·ship (rĭ-sē'vər-shĭp') *n. Law.* **1.** The office or functions of a receiver. **2.** The state of being held by a receiver.

re·cent (rē'sənt) *adj.* **1.** Of, belonging to, or occurring at a time immediately prior to the present. **2.** Modern; new. [L *recēns,* fresh, new.] —**re'cent·ly** *adv.*

re·cep·ta·cle (rĭ-sĕp'tə-kəl) *n.* **1.** A container. **2.** *Elec.* A fitting connected to a power supply and equipped to receive a plug. [< L *receptāre,* to take again.]

re·cep·tion (rĭ-sĕp'shən) *n.* **1.** The act or process of receiving or being received. **2.** A welcome, greeting, or acceptance. **3.** A formal· social function. **4. a.** The receiving of electromagnetic signals. **b.** The condition or quality of received signals.

re·cep·tion·ist (rĭ-sĕp'shə-nĭst) *n.* One employed to receive callers and answer the telephone.

re·cep·tive (rĭ-sĕp'tĭv) *adj.* **1.** Able or willing to receive favorably. **2.** Capable of or qualified for receiving. —**re·cep'tive·ly** *adv.* —**re'cep·tiv'i·ty, re·cep'tive·ness** *n.*

re·cep·tor (rĭ-sĕp'tər) *n.* A nerve ending specialized to sense or receive stimuli.

re·cess (rē'sĕs', rĭ-sĕs') *n.* **1. a.** A cessation of customary activities. **b.** The period of such cessation. **2.** A remote or secret place. **3.** An indentation or small hollow. —*v.* **1.** To place in a recess. **2.** To make a recess in. **3.** To suspend for a recess. [< L *recēdere,* to RECEDE.]

re·ces·sion (rĭ-sĕsh'ən) *n.* **1.** The act of withdrawing. **2.** The filing out of clergy and choir members after a church service. **3.** A moderate and temporary decline in economic activity.

re·ces·sion·al (rĭ-sĕsh'ən-əl) *n.* A hymn that accompanies the exit of the clergy and choir after a church service.

re·ces·sive (rĭ-sĕs'ĭv) *adj.* **1.** Tending to go backward or recede. **2.** *Genetics.* Incapable of being manifested when occurring with a dominant form of a gene.

recip. reciprocal; reciprocity.

rec·i·pe (rĕs'ə-pē') *n.* A formula for preparing something, esp. in cooking or pharmacology. [< L *recipere,* to RECEIVE.]

re·cip·i·ent (rĭ-sĭp'ē-ənt) *n.* One that receives.

re·cip·ro·cal (rĭ-sĭp'rə-kəl) *adj.* **1.** Concerning each of two or more persons or things. **2.** Mutual. **3.** Interchangeable. —*n.* **1.** One that is reciprocal to another; a converse or complement. **2.** *Math.* Either of a pair of quantities whose product is unity. [L *reciprocus,* alternating, returning.] —**re·cip'ro·cal·ly** *adv.*

re·cip·ro·cate (rĭ-sĭp'rə-kāt') *v.* **-cated, -cating. 1.** To give or take mutually; interchange. **2.** To show or feel in response or return. **3.** To make a return for something given or done. **4.** To be equivalent. —**re·cip'ro·ca'tion** *n.* —**re·cip'ro·ca'tive** *adj.*

rec·i·proc·i·ty (rĕs'ə-prŏs'ə-tē) *n.* **1.** A reciprocal condition or relationship. **2.** A commercial policy or trade agreement between two or more parties.

re·cit·al (rĭ-sīt'l) *n.* **1.** A public reading of memorized materials. **2.** A narration. **3.** A performance of music or dance, esp. by one performer.

rec·i·ta·tion (rĕs'ə-tā'shən) *n.* **1. a.** The act of reciting. **b.** The material recited. **2. a.** The oral delivery of prepared lessons by a pupil. **b.** The class period within which this occurs.

rec·i·ta·tive (rĕs'ə-tə-tēv') *n.* **1.** A musical style used in opera or oratorio, in which the text is declaimed in the rhythm of natural speech. **2.** A passage rendered in this form.

re·cite (rĭ-sīt') *v.* **-cited, -citing. 1.** To repeat or utter aloud something rehearsed or memorized, esp. publicly. **2.** To relate in detail. **3.** To enumerate or list. [< L *recitāre,* to cite again.] —**re·cit'er** *n.*

reck·less (rĕk'lĭs) *adj.* **1. a.** Careless. **b.** Headstrong; rash. **2.** Uncontrolled; wild. [< OE

re·u'ni·fy' *v.*	re·var'nish *v.*	re·voice' *v.*
re'u·ni·fi·ca'tion *n.*	re'ver·i·fi·ca' tion *n.*	re·warm' *v.*
re·use' *v.*	re·ver'i·fy' *v.*	re·wash' *v.*
re·u'til·ize' *v.*	re·vin'di·cate' *v.*	re·weigh' *v.*
re·ut'ter *v.*	re·vin'di·ca'tion *n.*	re·wind' *v.*
re·val'ue *v.*	re·vis'it *v.*	re·wire' *v.*
		re·work' *v.*

ă pat/ā ate/âr care/ä bar/b bib/ch chew/d deed/ĕ pet/ē be/f fit/g gag/h hat/hw what/ ĭ pit/ī pie/îr pier/j judge/k kick/l lid, fatal/m mum/n no, sudden/ng sing/ŏ pot/ō go/

rĕcelēas. See reg-[1].] —**reck′less•ly** *adv.* —**reck′-less•ness** *n.*

reck•on (rĕk′ən) *v.* **1.** To count or compute. **2.** To regard as. **3.** *Informal.* To think or assume. [< OE *gerecenian,* to enumerate. See reg-[1].] —**reck′on•er** *n.*

reck•on•ing (rĕk′ən-ĭng) *n.* **1.** The act of counting. **2.** The settlement of an account. **3.** The calculated position of a ship, aircraft, etc.

re•claim (rĭ-klām′) *v.* **1.** To make (marsh land or desert) suitable for cultivation or habitation. **2.** To procure (usable substances) from refuse or waste products. **3.** To reform. —**re•claim′a•ble** *adj.* —**rec′la•ma′tion** (rĕk′lə-mā′shən) *n.*

re•cline (rĭ-klīn′) *v.* **-clined, -clining.** To assume or cause to assume a leaning or prone position. [< L *-reclīnāre,* to bend back.] —**re•clin′er** *n.*

re•cluse (rĕk′loōs′, rĭ-kloōs′) *n.* One who lives in solitude and seclusion; a hermit. [< L *reclūdere,* to close off.]

rec•og•ni•tion (rĕk′əg-nĭsh′ən) *n.* **1.** The act of recognizing or state of being recognized. **2.** An awareness that something perceived has been perceived before. **3.** An acknowledgment.

re•cog•ni•zance (rĭ-kŏg′nə-zəns, -kŏn′ə-zəns) *n.* An obligation of record entered into before a court with the condition to perform a particular act, as to appear in court. —**re•cog′ni•zant** *adj.*

rec•og•nize (rĕk′əg-nīz′) *v.* **-nized, -nizing. 1.** To know or be aware that something perceived has been perceived before. **2.** To identify from past experience or knowledge. **3.** To acknowledge the validity of. **4.** To acknowledge as a speaker. **5.** To acknowledge or accept the national status of as a new government. **6.** To admit the acquaintance of. [< L *recognōscere,* to know again.] —**rec′og•niz′a•ble** *adj.* —**rec′og•niz′a•bly** *adv.*

re•coil (rĭ-koil′) *v.* **1.** To spring back, as a gun upon firing. **2.** To shrink back in fear or repugnance. —**re′coil′** (rē′koil′, rĭ-koil′) *n.*

rec•ol•lect (rĕk′ə-lĕkt′) *v.* To recall to mind; remember. [< L *recolligere,* to gather again.] —**rec′ol•lec′tion** *n.*

rec•om•mend (rĕk′ə-mĕnd′) *v.* **1.** To commend to the attention of another as reputable, worthy, or desirable. **2.** To make attractive or acceptable. **3.** To entrust. **4.** To counsel or advise. —**rec′om•mend′a•ble** *adj.* —**rec′om•men•da′tion** *n.*

rec•om•pense (rĕk′əm-pĕns′) *v.* **-pensed, -pensing.** To award compensation to or for. —*n.* **1.** Amends made for damage or loss. **2.** Payment in return for services. [< LL *recompensāre.*]

rec•on•cile (rĕk′ən-sīl′) *v.* **-ciled, -ciling. 1.** To re-establish friendship between. **2.** To settle, as a dispute. **3.** To bring to acquiescence: *reconcile oneself to defeat.* **4.** To make compatible or consistent. [< L *reconciliāre.*] —**rec′on•cil′a•ble** *adj.* —**rec′on•cil′i•a′tion** (-sĭl′ē-ā′shən) *n.*

rec•on•dite (rĕk′ən-dīt′, rĭ-kŏn′dĭt′) *adj.* **1.** Not easily understood; abstruse. **2.** Concealed; hidden. [< L *recondere,* to hide, put up again.]

re•con•nais•sance (rĭ-kŏn′ə-səns, -zəns) *n.* A preliminary survey of a region to examine its terrain or to determine the disposition of military forces.

re•con•noi•ter (rē′kə-noi′tər, rĕk′ə-) *v.* To make a preliminary inspection (of).

re•con•sid•er (rē′kən-sĭd′ər) *v.* To consider again, esp. with intent to modify a previous decision. —**re′con•sid′er•a′tion** *n.*

re•con•struct (rē′kən-strŭkt′) *v.* To construct again.

re•con•struc•tion (rē′kən-strŭk′shən) *n.* **1.** The act or result of reconstructing. **2. Reconstruction.** The period (1865–77) during which the Confederate states were forced to change politically and socially as prerequisite to full readmission to the Union.

rec•ord (rĕk′ərd) *n.* **1.** A written account of events or facts. **2.** Something on which such an account is made. **3.** Information on a particular subject collected and preserved: *the coldest day on record.* **4.** The known history of performance. **5.** The best performance known, as in a sport. **6.** A disk structurally coded to reproduce sound; phonograph record. —*v.* **re•cord** (rĭ-kôrd′). **1.** To set down for preservation in a record. **2.** To register or indicate. **3.** To register (sound) in permanent form on a record or a tape. —*adj.* **rec•ord** (rĕk′ərd). Establishing a record: *a record crowd.* [< L *recordāri,* to remember.]

re•cord•er (rĭ-kôr′dər) *n.* **1.** One that records. **2.** A horizontal flute usually of wood.

re•cord•ing (rĭ-kôr′dĭng) *n.* Sound recorded on a phonograph record or magnetic tape or wire.

re•count (rē-kount′) *v.* To count again. —*n.* (rē′kount′, rē-kount′). An additional count, esp. of votes in an election.

re•count (rĭ-kount′) *v.* **1.** To narrate the facts or particulars of. **2.** To enumerate.

re•coup (rĭ-koōp′) *v.* **1.** To receive an equivalent for. **2.** To reimburse. **3.** To regain. [< OF *recouper,* to cut back.]

re•course (rē′kôrs′, -kôrs′, rĭ-kôrs′, -kôrs′) *n.* **1.** A turning or applying to a person or thing for aid or security. **2.** One that is turned to for such aid or security.

re•cov•er (rĭ-kŭv′ər) *v.* **1.** To get back; regain. **2.** To regain a normal or usual condition or state. **3.** To receive a favorable judgment in a lawsuit. [< L *recuperāre,* to RECUPERATE.] —**re•cov′er•a•ble** *adj.* —**re•cov′er•y** *n.*

rec•re•ant (rĕk′rē-ənt) *adj.* **1.** Unfaithful. **2.** Craven or cowardly. —*n.* **1.** A disloyal person. **2.** A coward. [< OF *recroire,* to yield, surrender.] —**rec′re•ant•ly** *adv.*

re•cre•ate (rē′krē-āt′) *v.* To create anew.

rec•re•a•tion (rĕk′rē-ā′shən) *n.* Refreshment of one's mind or body after labor through diverting activity; play. —**rec′re•a′tion•al** *adj.*

re•crim•i•nate (rĭ-krĭm′ə-nāt′) *v.* **-nated, -nating.** To counter one accusation with another. —**re•crim′i•na′tion** *n.*

re•cruit (rĭ-kroōt′) *v.* **1.** To engage for military service. **2.** To enroll as a supporter. **3.** To replenish. **4.** To renew or restore (health or vitality). —*n.* A newly engaged member of a

---

ŏ p**aw,** for/oi b**oy**/ou **out**/oō t**ook**/oō c**oo**/p p**op**/r r**un**/s s**auce**/sh sh**y**/t t**o**/th th**in**/*th* **the**/
ŭ c**ut**/ûr f**ur**/v v**an**/w **wag**/y y**es**/z s**ize**/zh vi**sion**/ə **ago, item, edible, gallop, circus**/

military force or an organization. [< L *recrescere*, to grow again.] —re•cruit′er *n.* —re•cruit′ment *n.*

rect. **1.** receipt. **2.** rectangle. **3.** rector; rectory.

rec•tan•gle (rĕk′tăng′gəl) *n.* A parallelogram with a right angle. [< L *rectus*, right + *angulus*, ANGLE.] —rec•tan′gu•lar *adj.*

rec•ti•fy (rĕk′tə-fī′) *v.* -fied, -fying. To set right; correct. [< L *rectus*, straight + *facere*, to make.] —rec′ti•fi•ca′tion *n.* —rec′ti•fi′er *n.*

rec•ti•lin•e•ar (rĕk′tə-lĭn′ē-ər) *adj.* Of, moving in, or bounded by a straight line or lines.

rec•ti•tude (rĕk′tə-t/y/ōōd′) *n.* **1.** Moral uprightness. **2.** Sound intellectual judgment. [< L *rectus*, straight.]

rec•to (rĕk′tō) *n., pl.* **-tos.** A right-hand page. [< L *rectus*, right, straight.]

rec•tor (rĕk′tər) *n.* **1.** A clergyman in charge of a parish. **2.** The principal of certain schools, colleges, and universities. **3.** A priest serving as head of a seminary or university. [L *rector*, governor.] —rec′tor•ate (-ĭt) *n.* —rec•to′ri•al (-tôr′ē-əl, -tōr′-) *adj.*

rec•to•ry (rĕk′tə-rē) *n., pl.* **-ries.** A rector's dwelling.

rec•tum (rĕk′təm) *n., pl.* **-tums** or **-ta** (-tə). The portion of the large intestine extending from the sigmoid flexure to the anal canal. [NL *rectum (intestinum)*, straight (intestine).] —rec′tal *adj.*

re•cum•bent (rĭ-kŭm′bənt) *adj.* Lying down; reclining. [< L *recumbere*, to lie down.]

re•cu•per•ate (rĭ-k/y/ōō′pə-rāt′) *v.* -ated, -ating. **1.** To return to health or strength; recover. **2.** To recover or regain. [L *recuperare*.] —re•cu′per•a′tion *n.*

re•cur (rĭ-kûr′) *v.* -curred, -curring. To happen, come up, or show up again or repeatedly; return. [L *recurrere*, run back.] —re•cur′rence *n.* —re•cur′rent *adj.* —re•cur′rent•ly *adv.*

re•cy•cle (rē-sī′kəl) *v.* -cled, -cling. **1.** To start a different cycle in. **2. a.** To extract useful materials from (garbage, waste, etc.). **b.** To extract and reuse (useful substances found in garbage, waste, etc.).

red (rĕd) *n.* **1.** Any of a group of colors whose hue resembles that of blood. **2.** A pigment or dye having or giving this hue. **3.** Something that has this hue. **4.** Often **Red.** A communist or revolutionary activist. —*adj.* **redder, reddest.** **1.** Having a color resembling that of blood. **2.** Having a coppery skin tone. **3.** Having a ruddy or flushed complexion. **4.** Often **Red.** **a.** Revolutionary. **b.** Of, pertaining to, or aroused by revolution or revolutionaries. **c.** Composed of or directed by Communists. [< OE *rēad.* See reudh-.] —red′ness *n.*

red-blood•ed (rĕd′blŭd′ĭd) *adj.* Strong or virile. —red′-blood′ed•ness *n.*

red•coat (rĕd′kōt′) *n.* A British soldier during the American Revolution and the War of 1812.

Red Cross. Officially, Red Cross Society. An international organization, formed for the care of the wounded, sick, and homeless.

red•den (rĕd′n) *v.* To make or become red.

red•dish (rĕd′ĭsh) *adj.* Mixed or tinged with red. —red′dish•ness *n.*

re•deem (rĭ-dēm′) *v.* **1.** To recover ownership of by paying a specified sum. **2.** To pay off, as a promissory note. **3.** To turn in (coupons, certificates, etc.) and receive something in exchange. **4.** To fulfill (an oath or promise). **5.** To cash. **6.** To rescue or ransom. **7.** To save from sin. [< L *redimere*, to buy back.] —re•deem′a•ble *adj.* —re•deem′er *n.*

re•demp•tion (rĭ-dĕmp′shən) *n.* The act of redeeming or the condition of being redeemed.

red-hand•ed (rĕd′hăn′dĭd) *adj. & adv.* In the act of committing, or having just committed, a crime. —red′-hand′ed•ly *adv.*

red•head (rĕd′hĕd′) *n.* A person with red hair.

red herring. Something that draws attention away from the matter at hand. [< the use of red herring to distract hunting dogs from the scent.]

red-hot (rĕd′hŏt′) *adj.* **1.** Glowing hot; very hot. **2.** New; very recent.

re•dis•trict (rē-dĭs′trĭkt) *v.* To divide again, as into administrative or election districts.

red-let•ter (rĕd′lĕt′ər) *adj.* Memorably happy: *a red-letter day.*

red•o•lent (rĕd′ə-lənt) *adj.* **1.** Emitting fragrance; pleasantly odorous. **2.** Smelling: *boatyards redolent of tar.* [< L *redolēre*, to emit an odor.] —red′o•lence, red′o•len•cy *n.* —red′o•lent•ly *adv.*

re•doubt (rĭ-dout′) *n.* A defensive fortification. [< ML *reductus*, concealed place.]

re•doubt•a•ble (rĭ-dou′tə-bəl) *adj.* **1.** Awesome; formidable. **2.** Worthy of respect or honor. [< OF *redouter*, to dread.]

re•dound (rĭ-dound′) *v.* **1.** To have an effect or consequence. **2.** To contribute; accrue. [< L *redundāre*, to overflow.]

re•dress (rĭ-drĕs′) *v.* **1.** To set right; remedy or rectify. **2.** To make amends to or for. —*n.* (rĭ-drĕs′, rē′drĕs). **1.** Satisfaction for wrong done. **2.** Correction.

Red River. A river of the SW U.S.

Red Sea. A body of water separating the Arabian Peninsula from Africa and connected with the Mediterranean by the Suez Canal.

red shift. **1.** An apparent increase in the wavelength of radiation emitted by a receding celestial body. **2.** A similar increase in wavelength resulting from loss of energy by radiation moving against a gravitational field.

red•skin (rĕd′skĭn′) *n. Informal.* A North American Indian.

red tape. Impedimental use of official forms and procedures.

re•duce (rĭ-d/y/ōōs′) *v.* -duced, -ducing. **1.** To lessen in extent, amount, etc.; diminish or become diminished. **2.** To gain control of; conquer. **3.** To put in order systematically. **4.** To separate into orderly components by analysis. **5.** To bring to a certain state. **6.** To pulverize. **7.** *Chem.* **a.** To decrease the valence of (an atom) by adding electrons. **b.** To deoxidize. **c.** To add hydrogen to. **8.** To lose weight, as by dieting. [< L *redūcere*, bring back.] —re•duc′i•ble *adj.* —re•duc′i•bly *adv.* —re•duc′tion (-dŭk′shən) *n.* —re•duc′tive *adj.*

re•dun•dant (rĭ-dŭn′dənt) *adj.* **1.** Exceeding what is necessary or natural. **2.** Needlessly repetitive. [< L *redundāre*, to overflow.] —re‧dun′dan‧cy *n.* —re‧dun′dant‧ly *adv.*

redupl. reduplicate; reduplication; reduplicative.

re‧du‧pli‧ca‧tion (rĭ-d/y/ōō′plə-kā′shən) *n.* A doubling of an initial syllable or a whole word to form a new word. —re‧du′pli‧cate′ *v.*

red‧wood (rĕd′wŏŏd′) *n.* **1.** A very tall evergreen tree of coastal California. **2.** The soft, reddish wood of this tree.

reed (rēd) *n.* **1. a.** Any of various tall hollow-stemmed swamp or marsh grasses. **b.** The stalk of such a grass. **2. a.** A strip of cane or metal set into certain musical instruments to produce tone by vibration. **b.** An instrument fitted with a reed. [< OE *hrēod.* See kreut-.] —reed′i‧ness *n.* —reed′y *adj.*

reef¹ (rēf) *n.* A strip or ridge of rocks, sand, or coral that rises to or near the surface of a body of water. [< MDu *rif*, ridge.]

reef² (rēf) *n. Naut.* A portion of a sail rolled and tied down to lessen the area exposed to the wind. —*v.* To reduce the size of (a sail) by tucking in a part. [< ON *rif*, ridge, rib.]

reef‧er (rē′fər) *n. Slang.* A marijuana cigarette.

reek (rēk) *v.* **1.** To smoke, steam, or fume. **2.** To emit or be pervaded by something unpleasant. **3.** To give off or become permeated with a strong and unpleasant odor. —*n.* **1.** A stench. **2.** Vapor; steam. [< OE *rēocan.* See reug-.] —reek′er *n.* —reek′y *adj.*

reel¹ (rēl) *n.* **1.** A cylinder, spool, or frame that turns on an axis and is used for winding rope, tape, etc. **2.** Such a device on a fishing rod to let out or wind up the line. **3.** The quantity of something wound on one reel. —*v.* **1.** To wind on a reel. **2.** To recover by winding on a reel: *reel in the marlin.* **3.** To recite fluently: *reel off the names.* [< OE *hrēol.*]

reel² (rēl) *v.* **1.** To throw or be thrown off balance; fall back. **2.** To stagger, lurch, or sway. **3.** To go round and round in a whirling motion. **4.** To feel dizzy.

reel³ (rēl) *n.* A fast dance of Scottish origin.

re‧en‧try (rē-ĕn′trē) *n., pl.* **-tries.** Also **re‧en‧try.** **1.** A second or subsequent entry. **2.** The return of a missile or spacecraft into the earth's atmosphere.

reeve (rēv) *v.* **reeved** or **rove, reeving.** *Naut.* To pass (a rope) through a hole. [?]

ref. **1.** reference; referred. **2.** refining. **3.** reformation; reformed.

re‧fec‧tion (rĭ-fĕk′shən) *n.* **1.** Refreshment with food and drink. **2.** A light meal or repast. [< L *reficere*, to refresh.]

re‧fec‧to‧ry (rĭ-fĕk′tə-rē) *n., pl.* **-ries.** A room where meals are served.

re‧fer (rĭ-fûr′) *v.* **-ferred, -ferring. 1.** To turn or direct to a source for help or information. **2.** To assign or attribute to. **3.** To submit (a matter in dispute) to an authority for decision or examination. **4.** To direct the attention of. **5.** To pertain. **6.** To allude or make reference. [< L *referre*, refer to, carry back.] —ref′er‧a‧ble (rĕf′ər-ə-bəl, rĭ-fûr′-) *adj.* —re‧fer′ral *n.* —re‧fer′rer *n.*

ref‧e‧ree (rĕf′ə-rē′) *n.* **1.** One to whom something is referred, esp. in a court of law; an

arbitrator. **2.** An official supervising a game; an umpire. —*v.* **-reed, -reeing.** To act as referee.

ref‧er‧ence (rĕf′ər-əns, rĕf′rəns) *n.* **1.** An act of referring. **2.** One that is referred to. **3.** The state of being related or referred: *with reference to; in reference to.* **4.** An allusion. **5.** A note in a publication referring the reader to another passage or source. **6.** A statement attesting to personal qualifications of one seeking employment.

ref‧er‧en‧dum (rĕf′ə-rĕn′dəm) *n., pl.* **-dums** or **-da** (-də). **1.** The submission of a proposed public measure or actual statute to a direct popular vote. **2.** Such a vote.

ref‧er‧ent (rĕf′ər-ənt, rĭ-fûr′ənt) *n.* **1.** Something that refers, esp. a linguistic item in its capacity of referring to a meaning. **2.** Something referred to.

re‧fill (rē-fĭl′) *v.* To fill again. —*n.* (rē′fĭl′). **1.** A replacement for the used contents of a container. **2.** A second or subsequent filling.

re‧fine (rĭ-fīn′) *v.* **-fined, -fining. 1.** To reduce to a pure state; become pure; purify. **2.** To free from coarse characteristics. **3.** To improve. —re‧fin′er *n.*

re‧fined (rĭ-fīnd′) *adj.* **1.** Free from coarseness or vulgarity. **2.** Free of impurities. **3.** Precise to a fine degree; subtle; exact.

re‧fine‧ment (rĭ-fīn′mənt) *n.* **1. a.** An act of refining. **b.** The state of being refined. **2.** An improvement. **3.** Fineness of thought or expression. **4.** A keen or precise phrasing.

re‧fin‧er‧y (rĭ-fī′nə-rē) *n., pl.* **-ies.** An industrial plant for purifying a crude substance, such as petroleum or ore.

refl. **1.** reflection. **2.** reflexive.

re‧flect (rĭ-flĕkt′) *v.* **1.** To throw or bend back (heat, light, or sound) from a surface. **2.** To mirror or become mirrored. **3.** To manifest as a result of one's actions. **4.** To think or consider seriously. **5.** To bring blame or reproach. [< L *reflectere*, to bend back.] —re‧flec′tion *n.* —re‧flec′tive *adj.* —re‧flec′tive‧ly *adv.*

re‧flec‧tor (rĭ-flĕk′tər) *n.* **1.** That which reflects. **2.** A surface that reflects radiation.

re‧flex (rē′flĕks′) *adj.* **1.** Turned, thrown, or bent backward. **2.** *Physiol.* Designating an involuntary action or response, as a sneeze, blink, or hiccup. —*n.* (rē′flĕks′). **1.** Reflection or an image produced by reflection. **2.** An unlearned, involuntary, or instinctive response to a stimulus.

re‧flex‧ive (rĭ-flĕk′sĭv) *adj. Gram.* **1.** Designating a verb having an identical subject and direct object, as *dressed* in *She dressed herself.* **2.** Designating the pronoun used as the direct object in the preceding example. —re‧flex′ive *n.* —re‧flex′ive‧ly *adv.* —re‧flex′ive‧ness *n.*

re‧for‧est (rē-fôr′ĭst, -fŏr′ĭst) *v.* To replant with forest trees. —re′for‧es‧ta′tion *n.*

re‧form (rē-fôrm′) *v.* To form again.

re‧form (rĭ-fôrm′) *v.* **1.** To improve, as by alteration. **2.** To abolish malpractice in. **3.** To give up or cause to abandon immoral practices. —*n.* **1.** A change for the better. **2.** A movement that attempts to improve social and political conditions without revolutionary change. **3.** Moral improvement. —re·for′ma·tive *adj.* —re·formed′ *adj.* —re·form′er *n.*

ref·or·ma·tion (rĕf′ər-mā′shən) *n.* **1.** The act of reforming or state of being reformed. **2. Reformation.** A 16th-century movement resulting in the separation of the Protestant churches from the Roman Catholic Church.

re·for·ma·to·ry (rĭ-fôr′mə-tôr′ē, -tôr′ē) *n., pl.* **-ries.** A penal institution for juvenile and first offenders.

re·fract (rĭ-frăkt′) *v.* To deflect by refraction. [L *refringere* (pp *refractus*), to break off.]

re·frac·tion (rĭ-frăk′shən) *n.* The deflection of a propagating wave, as of light or sound, at the boundary between two mediums with different characteristics. —re·frac′tive *adj.* —re·frac′tive·ness, re′frac·tiv′i·ty *n.*

re·frac·to·ry (rĭ-frăk′tə-rē) *adj.* **1.** Obstinate; unmanageable. **2.** Difficult to melt or work; resistant to heat. —*n., pl.* **-ries.** A material that does not significantly deform or change chemically at high temperatures.

re·frain¹ (rĭ-frān′) *v.* To hold oneself back; forbear: *Kindly refrain from singing.* [< L *refrēnāre*, hold back, bridle.]

re·frain² (rĭ-frān′) *n.* A phrase or verse repeated at intervals throughout a song or poem. [< OF *refraindre*, echo, to break off.]

re·fresh (rĭ-frĕsh′) *v.* **1.** To revive or become revived, as with rest, food, or drink. **2.** To make cool, clean, or damp; freshen. **3.** To renew by stimulation: *refresh one's memory.* —re·fresh′er *n.* & *adj.* —re·fresh′ing *adj.*

re·fresh·ment (rĭ-frĕsh′mənt) *n.* **1.** The act of refreshing or state of being refreshed. **2.** Something that refreshes. **3. refreshments.** A light meal or snack.

re·frig·er·ant (rĭ-frĭj′ər-ənt) *adj.* Cooling or freezing; refrigerating. —*n.* A substance used to produce refrigeration, either as the working substance of a refrigerator or by direct absorption of heat.

re·frig·er·ate (rĭ-frĭj′ə-rāt′) *v.* **-ated, -ating. 1.** To cool or chill (a substance). **2.** To preserve (food) by chilling. —re·frig′er·a′tion *n.*

re·frig·er·a·tor (rĭ-frĭj′ə-rā′tər) *n.* An apparatus for refrigerating and freezing food.

ref·uge (rĕf′yo͞oj) *n.* **1.** Protection or shelter, as from danger or hardship. **2.** A haven or sanctuary. **3.** Anything to which one may turn for help, relief, or escape. [< L *refugere*, flee back.]

ref·u·gee (rĕf′yo͞o-jē′) *n.* One who flees to find refuge, esp. one who escapes from political persecution.

re·ful·gent (rĭ-fŭl′jənt) *adj.* Shining radiantly; brilliant. [< L *refulgēre*, to flash back.] —re·ful′gence *n.* —re·ful′gent·ly *adv.*

re·fund (rĭ-fŭnd′, rē′fŭnd′) *v.* To return or repay; give back; reimburse. —*n.* (rē′fŭnd′). **1.** A repayment of funds. **2.** The amount repaid. —re·fund′er *n.*

re·fur·bish (rē-fûr′bĭsh) *v.* To make clean, bright, or fresh again; renovate.

re·fuse¹ (rĭ-fyo͞oz′) *v.* **-fused, -fusing.** To decline to do, accept, give, or allow. [< L *refundere*, to pour back.] —re·fus′al *n.*

ref·use² (rĕf′yo͞os) *n.* Anything discarded or

rejected as useless or worthless; trash; rubbish.

re·fute (rĭ-fyo͞ot′) *v.* **-futed, -futing.** To prove to be false or erroneous; disprove. [L *refutāre*, rebut, drive back.] —re·fut′a·ble *adj.* —ref′u·ta′tion (rĕf′yo͞o-tā′shən) *n.* —re·fut′er *n.*

reg. 1. regent. **2.** regiment. **3.** region. **4.** register; registered. **5.** registrar. **6.** registry. **7.** regular. **8.** regulation.

re·gain (rē-gān′) *v.* **1.** To get back again. **2.** To reach again. —re·gain′er *n.*

re·gal (rē′gəl) *adj.* Of or pertaining to a king; royal. [< L *rēx*, king.] —re′gal·ly *adv.*

re·gale (rĭ-gāl′) *v.* **-galed, -galing. 1.** To delight or entertain; give pleasure to. **2.** To entertain sumptuously. —re·gale′ment *n.*

re·ga·lia (rĭ-gāl′yə, -gā′lē-ə) *pl.n. (often takes sing. v.).* **1.** The emblems and symbols of royalty. **2.** The rights and privileges of royalty. **3.** The distinguishing symbols of any rank, office, etc.

re·gard (rĭ-gärd′) *v.* **1.** To observe closely. **2.** To look upon or consider in a particular way. **3.** To have great affection or admiration for. **4.** To relate, concern, or refer to. **5.** To take into account. **6.** To pay attention. —*n.* **1.** A look or gaze. **2.** Careful thought or attention; concern. **3.** Respect, affection, or esteem. **4. regards.** Good wishes: *send one's regards.* **5.** Reference or relation: *in regard to this case.* **6.** A particular point: *I agree in this regard.* [< OF *reguarder*, to look at, regard.]

re·gard·ing (rĭ-gär′dĭng) *prep.* In reference to; with respect to; concerning.

re·gard·less (rĭ-gärd′lĭs) *adj.* In spite of everything; anyway.

re·gat·ta (rĭ-gä′tə, -găt′ə) *n.* A boat race or an organized series of boat races. [It *regata*, gondola race.]

regd. registered.

re·gen·cy (rē′jən-sē) *n., pl.* **-cies. 1.** The office, area of jurisdiction, or government of a regent or regents. **2.** The period during which a regent governs.

re·gen·er·ate (rĭ-jĕn′ə-rāt′) *v.* **-ated, -ating. 1.** To reform spiritually or morally. **2.** To form, construct, or create anew. —*adj.* (rĭ-jĕn′ər-ĭt). **1.** Spiritually or morally revitalized. **2.** Restored; refreshed; renewed. —re·gen′er·a′tion *n.* —re·gen′er·a′tive *adj.* —re·gen′er·a′tor *n.*

re·gent (rē′jənt) *n.* **1.** One who rules during the absence or disability of a sovereign. **2.** One acting as a ruler or governor. **3.** One serving on a board that governs an educational institution in the U.S. [< L *regere*, to rule.] —re′gent *adj.*

reg·i·cide (rĕj′ə-sīd′) *n.* **1.** The killing of a king. **2.** One who kills a king. [L *rēx*, king.] —reg′i·ci′dal (-sīd′l) *adj.*

re·gime (rā-zhēm′, rĭ-) *n.* **1.** A system of management of government; an administration. **2.** A regimen. [< L *regere*, to rule.]

reg·i·men (rĕj′ə-mən, -mĕn′) *n.* **1.** Governmental rule or control. **2.** A systematic procedure of therapy.

reg·i·ment (rĕj′ə-mənt) *n.* A military unit of ground troops, consisting of several battalions. —*v.* (rĕj′ə-mĕnt′). **1.** To organize; systematize. **2.** To force uniformity and discipline upon.

ă pat/ā ate/âr care/ä bar/b **bib**/ch **chew**/d **deed**/ĕ pet/ē be/f **fit**/g **gag**/h **hat**/hw **what**/ĭ pit/ī **pie**/îr **pier**/j **judge**/k **kick**/l lid, fatal/m **mum**/n **no**, sudden/ng **sing**/ŏ pot/ō **go**/

[< L *regere*, to rule.] —reg′i•men′tal *adj.*
—reg′i•men•ta′tion *n.*

Re•gi•na (rĭ-jī′nə). The capital of Saskatchewan, Canada. Pop. 112,000.

re•gion (rē′jən) *n.* **1.** Any large, usually continuous segment of a surface or space; an area. **2.** An area of the body: *the abdominal region.* [< L *regiō*, direction, boundary.]

re•gion•al (rē′jən-əl) *adj.* **1.** Of, pertaining to, or characteristic of a large geographic region. **2.** Of, pertaining to, or characteristic of a particular region. —re′gion•al•ly *adv.*

reg•is•ter (rĕj′ĭ-stər) *n.* **1. a.** A formal or official recording of items, names, or actions. **b.** A book for such entries. **2.** A device that automatically registers a quantity or number. **3.** An adjustable device through which heated or cooled air is released into a room. **4.** A part of the range of a voice or instrument that is similar in timbre. —*v.* **1.** To enter in a register; enroll. **2.** To indicate, as on a scale. **3.** To show (emotion). **4.** To cause (mail) to be officially recorded by payment of a fee. **5.** To have one's name officially placed on a list of eligible voters. [< LL *regesta*, list.]

registered nurse. A graduate trained nurse who has passed a state registration examination.

reg•is•trar (rĕj′ĭ-strär′, rĕj′ĭ-strär′) *n.* One who keeps records, esp. in a college or university.

reg•is•tra•tion (rĕj′ĭ-strā′shən) *n.* **1.** A registering, as of voters or students. **2.** The number of persons registered; enrollment.

reg•is•try (rĕj′ĭ-strē) *n., pl.* **-tries. 1.** Registration. **2.** A place where registers are kept.

re•gress (rĭ-grĕs′) *v.* To go back; return to a previous condition or state. —*n.* (rē′grĕs′). Return or withdrawal. [< L *regredī*, to go back.] —re•gres′sive *adj.*

re•gres•sion (rĭ-grĕsh′ən) *n.* **1.** Reversion; retrogression. **2.** Relapse to a less perfect or developed state.

re•gret (rĭ-grĕt′) *v.* **-gretted, -gretting. 1.** To feel sorry, disappointed, or distressed about. **2.** To mourn. —*n.* **1.** Distress over a desire unfulfilled or an action performed or not performed. **2.** An expression of grief or disappointment. **3. regrets.** A courteous declining to accept an invitation. [< OF *regreter*, to lament.] —re•gret′ful *adj.* —re•gret′ful•ly *adv.* —re•gret′ta•ble *adj.*

regt. regiment.

reg•u•lar (rĕg′yə-lər) *adj.* **1.** Customary, usual, or normal. **2.** Orderly or symmetrical. **3.** Conforming to set procedure, principle, or discipline. **4.** Methodical; well-ordered. **5.** Occurring at fixed intervals; periodic. **6.** Constant; not varying. **7.** Proper. **8.** Complete; thorough: *a regular villain.* **9.** *Gram.* Belonging to a standard mode of inflection or conjugation. **10.** Belonging to a religious order and bound by its rules. **11.** *Geom.* **a.** Having equal sides and equal angles. **b.** Having faces that are congruent regular polygons and congruent polyhedral angles. **12.** Belonging to or constituting the permanent army of a nation. —*n.* A soldier belonging to a regular army. [< L *rēgulāris*, containing rules.] —reg′u•lar′i•ty

(-lăr′ə-tē) *n.* —reg′u•lar•ize′ (-lə-rīz′) *v.* (-ized, -izing). —reg′u•lar•ly *adv.*

reg•u•late (rĕg′yə-lāt′) *v.* **-lated, -lating. 1.** To control or direct according to a rule. **2.** To adjust in conformity to a specification or requirement. **3.** To adjust for accurate and proper functioning. —reg′u•la′tive, reg′u•la•to′ry (-lə-tôr′ē, -tōr′ē) *adj.* —reg′u•la′tor *n.*

reg•u•la•tion (rĕg′yə-lā′shən) *n.* **1.** A principle, rule, or law designed to govern behavior. **2.** A governmental order having the force of law. —*adj.* Prescribed in accordance with a rule.

re•gur•gi•tate (rē-gûr′jə-tāt′) *v.* **-tated, -tating.** To pour back, esp. to cast up (partially digested food); vomit. [ML *regurgitāre.*] —re•gur′gi•ta′tion *n.*

re•ha•bil•i•tate (rē′hə-bĭl′ə-tāt′) *v.* **-tated, -tating. 1.** To restore to good condition, as through education and therapy. **2.** To reinstate the good name of. **3.** To restore the former rank, privileges, or rights of. —re′ha•bil′i•ta′tion *n.* —re′ha•bil′i•ta′tive *adj.*

re•hash (rē-hăsh′) *v.* To repeat or rework (old material). —re′hash′ (rē′hăsh′) *n.*

re•hear•ing (rē-hîr′ĭng) *n. Law.* A second or new consideration of a case.

re•hears•al (rĭ-hûr′səl) *n.* **1.** The act or process of rehearsing. **2.** A verbal repetition or recital.

re•hearse (rĭ-hûrs′) *v.* **-hearsed, -hearsing. 1.** To practice in preparation for a public performance. **2.** To perfect or cause to perfect (an action) by repetition. **3.** To retell. [< OF *rehercer*, to repeat.] —re•hears′er *n.*

Reich (rīk) *n.* Formerly, the territory or government of a German empire or republic. [< OHG *rīhhi*, realm.]

reign (rān) *n.* **1.** The exercise of sovereign power. **2.** The term during which sovereignty is held. **3.** Dominance or widespread influence. —*v.* **1.** To rule with sovereign power. **2.** To be prevalent. [< L *rēx*, a king.]

re•im•burse (rē′ĭm-bûrs′) *v.* **-bursed, -bursing. 1.** To repay. **2.** To compensate for money spent or losses incurred. —re′im•burse′ment *n.*

rein (rān) *n.* **1.** Often **reins.** Two narrow leather straps attached to the bit of a bridle and used by a rider to control a horse. **2.** Any means of restraint, check, or guidance. —**give (free) rein to.** To release from restraints. —*v.* **1.** To check or hold back. **2.** To guide or control. [< L *retinēre*, to RETAIN.]

re•in•car•nate (rē′ĭn-kär′nāt′) *v.* **-nated, -nating.** To be reborn in another body. —re′in•car•na′tion *n.*

rein•deer (rān′dîr′) *n.* A large deer of arctic regions, domesticated in the Old World. [< ON *hreindȳri.*]

re•in•force (rē′ĭn-fôrs′, -fōrs′) *v.* **-forced,-forcing. 1.** To strengthen; support. **2.** To strengthen with additional troops or equipment. —re′in•force′ment *n.*

re•in•state (rē′ĭn-stāt′) *v.* **-stated, -stating.** To restore to a previous condition or position. —re′in•state′ment *n.*

re•it•er•ate (rē-ĭt′ə-rāt′) *v.* **-ated, -ating.** To say over again. [L *reiterāre.*] —re•it′er•a′tion *n.*

re•ject (rĭ-jĕkt′) *v.* **1.** To refuse to accept, recognize, or make use of; repudiate. **2.** To refuse to grant; deny. **3.** To discard as defective or useless; throw away. —*n.* (rē′jĕkt). One that has been rejected. [< L *rejicere*, to throw back.] —**re·jec′tion** *n.*

re·joice (rĭ-jois′) *v.* **-joiced, -joicing. 1.** To feel or be joyful. **2.** To fill with joy. —**re·joic′er** *n.*

re·join¹ (rē′join′) *v.* To come or join together again.

re·join² (rĭ-join′) *v.* To respond; answer. [< OF *rejoindre.*]

re·join·der (rĭ-join′dər) *n.* An answer, esp. in response to a reply.

re·ju·ve·nate (rĭ-jōō′və-nāt′) *v.* **-nated, -nating.** To restore the youthful vigor or appearance of. —**re·ju′ve·na′tion** *n.*

rel. 1. relating. **2.** relative. **3.** released. **4.** religion; religious.

re·lapse (rĭ-lăps′) *v.* **-lapsed, -lapsing.** To fall back or revert to a former state, esp. to regress after partial recovery from illness. —*n.* (rē′lăps, rĭ-lăps′). The act or result of relapsing. [< L *relābī*, to slide back.]

re·late (rĭ-lāt′) *v.* **-lated, -lating. 1.** To narrate or tell. **2.** To bring into logical or natural association. **3.** To have relation or reference to. **4.** To interact with others meaningfully. [L *relātus.*] —**re·lat′er** *n.*

re·lat·ed (rĭ-lā′tĭd) *adj.* Connected, as by kinship, marriage, or common origin.

re·la·tion (rĭ-lā′shən) *n.* **1.** A logical or natural association between two or more things; relevance of one to another; connection. **2.** Connection by blood or marriage; kinship. **3.** A relative. **4.** The mode in which a person or thing is connected with another. **5. relations.** Business or diplomatic connections or associations. **6.** Reference; regard. **7.** A narration; account. —**re·la′tion·al** *adj.*

re·la·tion·ship (rĭ-lā′shən-shĭp′) *n.* **1.** The condition or fact of being related. **2.** Kinship.

rel·a·tive (rĕl′ə-tĭv) *adj.* **1.** Relevant; connected; related. **2.** Considered in comparison to or relationship with something else. **3.** Dependent upon something else for significance; not absolute. **4.** *Gram.* Referring to or qualifying an antecedent. —*n.* **1.** One related by kinship. **2.** One that is relative. **3.** A relative term. [< L *relātus.*] —**rel′a·tive·ly** *adv.*

relative clause. A dependent clause introduced by a relative pronoun. In *He who hesitates is lost,* the relative clause is *who hesitates.*

relative pronoun. A pronoun that introduces a relative clause and has reference to an antecedent.

rel·a·tiv·i·ty (rĕl′ə-tĭv′ə-tē) *n.* **1.** The quality or state of being relative. **2.** *Phys.* **a. Special relativity. b. General relativity.**

re·lax (rĭ-lăks′) *v.* **1.** To make or become lax or loose. **2.** To make or become less severe. **3.** To slacken. **4.** To relieve from strain. **5.** To take one's ease; rest. **6.** To become less formal or tense. —**re·lax′er** *n.*

re·lax·a·tion (rē′lăk·sā′shən) *n.* **1.** The act of relaxing or state of being relaxed. **2.** Recreation. **3.** The lengthening of inactive muscle or muscle fibers. —**re·lax′ant** *adj. & n.*

re·lay (rē′lā, rĭ-lā′) *n.* **1.** A fresh team or crew to relieve others in work, a journey, etc. **2.** The

act of relaying. **3.** A race between two teams, in which each team member runs a set part of the total race. **4.** A device that responds to a small current or voltage change by activating switches or other devices in an electric circuit. —*v.* **1.** To pass or send along from one group or station to another: *relay a message.* **2.** To supply with fresh relays. [< OF *relaier*, to relay, leave behind.]

re·lease (rĭ-lēs′) *v.* **-leased, -leasing. 1.** To set free, as from confinement or bondage; liberate. **2.** To free; unfasten. **3.** To allow performance, sale, publication, or circulation of. **4.** To relinquish, as a right or claim. —*n.* **1.** The act of releasing or state of being released. **2.** A device or catch for locking or releasing a mechanism. [< L *relaxāre*, to relax.] —**re·leas′er** *n.*

rel·e·gate (rĕl′ə-gāt′) *v.* **-gated, -gating. 1.** To consign, esp. to an obscure place, position, or condition. **2.** To assign to a particular category. **3.** To refer for decision or performance. **4.** To banish; exile. [L *relēgāre*, to send away.] —**rel′e·ga′tion** *n.*

re·lent (rĭ-lĕnt′) *v.* To become softened or gentler in attitude or determination; abate. [< ML **relentāre.*]

re·lent·less (rĭ-lĕnt′lĭs) *adj.* **1.** Unyielding; pitiless. **2.** Steady and persistent. —**re·lent′less·ly** *adv.* —**re·lent′less·ness** *n.*

rel·e·vant (rĕl′ə-vənt) *adj.* Related to the matter at hand; pertinent. [< L *relevāre*, to lift up, RELIEVE.] —**rel′e·vance, rel′e·van·cy** *n.* —**rel′e·vant·ly** *adv.*

re·li·a·ble (rĭ-lī′ə-bəl) *adj.* Able to be relied upon; dependable. —**re·li′a·bil′i·ty, re·li′a·ble·ness** *n.* —**re·li′a·bly** *adv.*

re·li·ance (rĭ-lī′əns) *n.* **1.** The act of relying. **2.** Confidence; dependence; trust. **3.** One depended on. —**re·li′ant** *adj.*

rel·ic (rĕl′ĭk) *n.* **1.** Something that has survived the passage of time, esp., an object or custom whose original cultural environment has disappeared. **2.** A keepsake. **3.** An object of religious veneration. **4. relics.** Remains. [< L *relinquere*, to RELINQUISH.]

re·lief (rĭ-lēf′) *n.* **1.** Ease from or lessening of pain or discomfort. **2.** Anything that lessens pain, anxiety, etc. **3.** Assistance given to the needy or aged. **4.** The projection of figures or forms from a flat background, as in sculpture. **5.** The variations in elevation of any area of the earth's surface.

re·lieve (rĭ-lēv′) *v.* **-lieved, -lieving. 1.** To lessen or alleviate; ease. **2.** To free from pain, anxiety, etc. **3.** To aid. **4.** To free from a specified duty by providing a substitute. **5.** To make less unpleasant or monotonous. **6.** To make distinct through contrast. [< L *relevāre*, to raise again.] —**re·liev′er** *n.*

re·lig·ion (rĭ-lĭj′ən) *n.* **1. a.** An organized system of beliefs and rituals centering on a supernatural being or beings. **b.** Adherence to such a system. **2.** A belief upheld or pursued with zeal and devotion. [< L *religiō*, bond between man and the gods.] —**re·lig′ious** *adj.*

re·lin·quish (rĭ-lĭng′kwĭsh) *v.* **1.** To retire from; leave; abandon. **2.** To put aside or desist from. **3.** To surrender; renounce. **4.** To release. [< L *relinquere*, to leave behind.] —**re•lin′quish•er** *n.* —**re•lin′quish•ment** *n.*

rel•ish (rĕl′ĭsh) *n.* **1.** An appetite for something; appreciation. **2.** Pleasure; zest. **3.** A spicy or savory condiment served with other food. **4.** The flavor of a food, esp. when appetizing. —*v.* **1.** To take pleasure in. **2.** To like the flavor of. [< L *relaxāre*, to loosen, relax.] —**rel′ish•a•ble** *adj.*

re•live (rē-lĭv′) *v.* To undergo again, as an experience.

re•luc•tant (rĭ-lŭk′tənt) *adj.* Unwilling; averse. [< L *reluctārī*, to struggle against.] —**re•luc′tance, re•luc′tan•cy** (-tən-sē) *n.* —**re•luc′tant•ly** *adv.*

re•ly (rĭ-lī′) *v.* **-lied, -lying.** —**rely on** (or **upon**). **1.** To depend. **2.** To trust confidently. [< L *religāre*, to bind back.]

re•main (rĭ-mān′) *v.* **1.** To continue without change of condition, quality, or place. **2.** To stay or be left over after the removal, departure, or destruction of others. **3.** To be left as still to be dealt with: *A cure remains to be found.* **4.** To endure or persist. [< L *remanēre*, to stay behind.]

re•main•der (rĭ-mān′dər) *n.* **1.** Something left over after other parts have been taken away. **2. a.** In division, the dividend minus the product of the divisor and quotient. **b.** In subtraction, the difference between the minuend and subtrahend.

re•mains (rĭ-mānz′) *pl.n.* **1.** All that is left after other parts have been taken away. **2.** A corpse.

re•mand (rĭ-mănd′) *v.* To send or order back, as someone in custody to prison, to another court, etc. [< LL *remandāre*, to send back word.] —**re•mand′ment** *n.*

re•mark (rĭ-märk′) *v.* **1.** To say or write briefly and casually as a comment. **2.** To take notice of; observe. —*n.* **1.** The act of noticing or observing; mention. **2.** A casual comment.

re•mark•a•ble (rĭ-mär′kə-bəl) *adj.* **1.** Worthy of notice. **2.** Extraordinary; uncommon. —**re•mark′a•bly** *adv.*

Rem•brandt (rĕm′brănt). 1606–1669. Dutch painter and graphic artist.

re•me•di•al (rĭ-mē′dē-əl) *adj.* **1.** Supplying a remedy. **2.** Intended to correct something, esp. study or reading habits. —**re•me′di•al•ly** *adv.*

rem•e•dy (rĕm′ə-dē) *n., pl.* **-dies.** **1.** Something, as medicine or therapy, that relieves pain, cures disease, or corrects a disorder. **2.** Something that corrects any evil, fault, or error. —*v.* **-died, -dying.** **1.** To relieve or cure. **2.** To counteract or rectify. [< L *remedium*, medicine.]

re•mem•ber (rĭ-mĕm′bər) *v.* **1.** To recall to the mind; think of again. **2.** To retain in the mind. **3.** To keep (someone) in mind. **4.** To mention (someone) to another as sending greetings. [< LL *rememorārī*, to remember again.] —**re•mem′ber•a•ble** *adj.* —**re•mem′ber•er** *n.*

re•mem•brance (rĭ-mĕm′brəns) *n.* **1.** The act of remembering or state of being remembered. **2.** A memorial. **3.** The length of time over which one's memory extends. **4.** Something

remembered. **5.** A memento or souvenir. **6.** **remembrances.** Greetings.

re•mind (rĭ-mīnd′) *v.* To cause (someone) to remember. [RE- + MIND.] —**re•mind′er** *n.*

rem•i•nisce (rĕm′ə-nĭs′) *v.* **-nisced, -niscing.** To recollect and tell of past experiences or events.

rem•i•nis•cence (rĕm′ə-nĭs′əns) *n.* **1.** The act or process of recalling the past. **2.** A memory. **3.** Often **reminiscences.** A narration of past experiences.

rem•i•nis•cent (rĕm′ə-nĭs′ənt) *adj.* **1.** Having the quality of or containing reminiscence. **2.** Tending to recall or talk of the past. [< L *reminiscī*, to recollect.]

re•miss (rĭ-mĭs′) *adj.* Lax in attending to duty; negligent. [< L *remissus*, slack.] —**re•miss′ness** *n.*

re•mis•sion (rĭ-mĭsh′ən) *n.* The act of remitting or condition of being remitted.

re•mit (rĭ-mĭt′) *v.* **-mitted, -mitting.** **1.** To send (money). **2. a.** To cancel (a penalty or punishment). **b.** To pardon; forgive. **3.** To relax; slacken. **4.** To diminish; abate. [< L *remittere*, to send back, release.]

re•mit•tance (rĭ-mĭt′əns) *n.* Money or credit sent to someone.

rem•nant (rĕm′nənt) *n.* **1.** Something left over; a remainder. **2.** A surviving trace or vestige. [< OF *remanoir, remaindre*, to remain.]

re•mod•el (rē-mŏd′l) *v.* To remake with a new structure; renovate. —**re•mod′el•er** *n.*

re•mon•strance (rĭ-mŏn′strəns) *n.* The act or an instance of remonstrating.

re•mon•strate (rĭ-mŏn′strāt′) *v.* **-strated, -strating.** To say or plead in protest, objection, or reproof. [ML *remōnstrāre*, to demonstrate.] —**re′mon•stra′tion** (rē′mŏn-strā′shən, rĕm′ən-) *n.* —**re•mon′stra•tive** (-strə-tĭv) *adj.*

re•morse (rĭ-môrs′) *n.* Moral anguish arising from repentance for past misdeeds; bitter regret. [< L *remorsus*, a biting back.] —**re•morse′ful** *adj.* —**re•morse′ful•ly** *adv.*

re•morse•less (rĭ-môrs′lĭs) *adj.* Having no pity or compassion; merciless.

re•mote (rĭ-mōt′) *adj.* **-moter, -motest.** **1.** Located far away. **2.** Distant in time. **3.** Barely discernible; slight. **4.** Distantly related: *a remote descendant.* **5.** Distant in manner; aloof. [L *remōtus*, pp of *removēre*, to move back.] —**re•mote′ly** *adv.* —**re•mote′ness** *n.*

re•move (rĭ-mōōv′) *v.* **-moved, -moving.** **1.** To move from a position occupied; convey from one place to another. **2.** To take away; extract; do away with. **3.** To dismiss from office. **4.** To change one's residence; move. —*n.* **1.** The act of removing. **2.** Distance or degree away or apart. [< L *removēre*, to move back.] —**re•mov′a•ble** *adj.* —**re•mov′al** *n.*

re•mu•ner•ate (rĭ-myōō′nə-rāt′) *v.* **-ated, -ating.** To pay (a person) for goods provided, services rendered, or losses incurred. [L *remūnerāre*.] —**re•mu′ner•a′tion** *n.* —**re•mu′ner•a′tive** *adj.*

ren•ais•sance (rĕn′ə-säns′, -zäns′) *n.* **1.** A rebirth; revival. **2. Renaissance. a.** The humanistic revival of art, literature, and learning in Europe. **b.** The period of this revival, roughly from the 14th through the 16th century. **3.** Often **Renaissance.** Any similar period of re-

---

ô paw, for/oi boy/ou out/ŏŏ took/ōō coo/p pop/r run/s sauce/sh shy/t to/th thin/*th* the/
ŭ cut/ûr fur/v van/w wag/y yes/z size/zh vision/ə ago, item, edible, gallop, circus/

vived intellectual or artistic achievement. [<
L *renasci*, to be born again.]

re·nal (rē'nəl) *adj.* Of, pertaining to, or in the region of the kidneys. [< L *rēnēs*, kidneys.]

re·nas·cence (rĭ-năs'əns, -nā'səns) *n.* A rebirth; renaissance.

rend (rĕnd) *v.* **rent** or **rended, rending. 1.** To tear apart or into pieces violently; split. **2.** To remove forcibly. **3.** To penetrate and disturb as if by tearing. [< OE *rendan*. See **rendh-**.] —**rend'er** *n.*

ren·der (rĕn'dər) *v.* **1.** To submit: *render a bill.* **2.** To give or make available: *render assistance.* **3.** To give what is due. **4.** To represent in a verbal or artistic form. **5.** To translate. **6.** To cause to become; make: *renders me helpless.* **7.** To liquefy (fat) by heating. [< OF *rendre*, to give back.] —**ren'der·er** *n.*

ren·dez·vous (rän'dā-vōō', rän'də-) *n., pl.* **-vous** (-vōōz'). **1.** A prearranged meeting place. **2.** The meeting itself. **3.** A popular gathering place. —*v.* To meet together at a specified time and place. [< OF *rendez vous*, "present yourselves."]

ren·di·tion (rĕn-dĭsh'ən) *n.* The act or result of rendering, as: **a.** An interpretation or performance of a musical score or dramatic piece. **b.** A translation.

ren·e·gade (rĕn'ə-gād') *n.* **1.** One who rejects his religion or allegiance for another. **2.** An outlaw. [< ML *renegāre*, to deny.]

re·nege (rĭ-nĭg', -nĕg', -nēg') *v.* **-neged, -neging.** To fail to carry out a promise or commitment. [ML *renegāre*, to deny.] —**re·neg'er** *n.*

re·new (rĭ-n/y/ōō') *v.* **1.** To make new or as if new again; restore. **2.** To take up again; resume. **3.** To grant or obtain for the extension of: *renew a contract.* **4.** To replenish. [RE- + NEW.] —**re·new'a·ble** *adj.* —**re·new'al** *n.*

ren·net (rĕn'ĭt) *n.* An extract from the lining of a calf's stomach, used to curdle milk in making cheese or junket. [< OE *rynet*.]

ren·nin (rĕn'ĭn) *n.* A milk-coagulating enzyme produced from rennet. [RENN(ET) + -IN.]

Re·noir (rĕn'wär'), **Pierre Auguste.** 1841–1919. French painter.

re·nounce (rĭ-nouns') *v.* **-nounced, -nouncing. 1.** To give up (a title or activity), esp. by formal announcement. **2.** To reject; disown. [< L *renūntiāre*, to bring back word, protest against.] —**re·nounce'ment** *n.*

ren·o·vate (rĕn'ə-vāt') *v.* **-vated, -vating.** To restore to an earlier condition. [L *renovāre*.] —**ren'o·va'tion** *n.* —**ren'o·va'tor** *n.*

re·nown (rĭ-noun') *n.* The quality of being widely honored and acclaimed. [< OF *renomer*, to name again, make famous.] —**re·nowned'** *adj.*

rent¹ (rĕnt) *n.* Periodic payment made by one in return for the right to use the property of another. —*v.* **1.** To pay for and obtain use of (another's property). **2.** To be for rent. [< VL *rendere*, to render.]

rent² (rĕnt). Alternate *p.t.* & *p.p.* of **rend.** —*n.* An opening made by rending; rip.

rent·al (rĕnt'l) *n.* **1.** An amount paid out or taken in as rent. **2.** An act of renting. **3.** Property rented.

re·nun·ci·a·tion (rĭ-nŭn'sē-ā'shən) *n.* The act or practice of renouncing.

re·or·der (rē-ôr'dər) *v.* **1.** To rearrange. **2.** To order (the same goods) again.

re·or·gan·ize (rē-ôr'gə-nīz') *v.* **-ized, -izing.** To organize again or anew. —**re·or'gan·i·za'tion** *n.*

rep (rĕp) *n.* A ribbed or corded fabric. [F *reps*.]

rep. 1. repair. **2.** report. **3.** reporter. **4.** representative. **5.** republic.

Rep. 1. representative. **2.** republic. **3.** Republican (Party).

re·pair¹ (rĭ-pâr') *v.* To restore to sound condition after damage or injury. —*n.* **1.** The work or act of repairing. **2.** General condition after use or repairing: *in good repair.* **3.** Often **repairs.** An instance of repairing. [< L *reparāre*.] —**re·pair'a·ble** *adj.* —**re·pair'er** *n.*

re·pair² (rĭ-pâr') *v.* To betake oneself. [< OF *repairer*, to return.]

rep·a·ra·tion (rĕp'ə-rā'shən) *n.* **1.** The act or process of making amends. **2.** Something done or paid to make up for. **3. reparations.** Compensation required from a defeated nation for damage or injury during a war. [< L *reparāre*, REPAIR.] —**re·par'a·tive** (rĭ-păr'ə-tĭv), **re·par'a·to'ry** (-tôr'ē, -tōr'ē) *adj.*

rep·ar·tee (rĕp'ər-tē', -ər-tā', -är-tē', -är-tā') *n.* **1.** A swift, witty reply. **2.** Conversation characterized by such replies. [< F *repartir*, to reply readily.]

re·past (rĭ-păst', -päst') *n.* A meal, or the food eaten or provided at a meal. [< LL *repascere*, to feed again.]

re·pay (rĭ-pā') *v.* **1.** To pay back (money). **2.** To pay (someone) back, either in return or in requital. **3.** To make or do in return: *repay a call.* —**re·pay'a·ble** *adj.* —**re·pay'ment** *n.*

re·peal (rĭ-pēl') *v.* To withdraw or annul officially or formally. [< OF *rapeler*.] —**re·peal'** *n.* —**re·peal'er** *n.*

re·peat (rĭ-pēt') *v.* **1.** To say or do (something) again. **2.** To manifest or express in the same way or words: *History repeats itself.* —*n.* **1.** The act of repeating. **2.** Something repeated. [< L *repetere*, to go back to, seek again.] —**re·peat'er** *n.*

re·peat·ed (rĭ-pē'tĭd) *adj.* Said, done, or occurring again and again. —**re·peat'ed·ly** *adv.*

re·pel (rĭ-pĕl') *v.* **-pelled, -pelling. 1.** To drive back; ward off or keep away. **2.** To cause aversion or distaste in. **3.** To be incapable of absorbing or mixing with. **4.** To present an opposing force to: *Electric charges of the same sign repel one another.* [< L *repellere*.]

re·pel·lent (rĭ-pĕl'ənt) *adj.* **1.** Serving or tending to repel. **2.** Resistant to some substance. —*n.* **1.** A substance used to repel insects. **2.** A substance for making a surface resistant to something.

re·pent (rĭ-pĕnt') *v.* **1.** To feel regret for (what one has done or failed to do). **2.** To feel contrition for one's sins and to abjure sinful ways. [< OF *repentir*.] —**re·pen'tance** *n.* —**re·pen'tant** *adj.* —**re·pent'er** *n.*

re·per·cus·sion (rē'pər-kŭsh'ən) *n.* **1.** An indirect effect produced by an event or action. **2.** A reciprocal action. [< L *repercutere*, to cause to rebound.] —**re'per·cus'sive** *adj.*

ă pat/ā ate/âr care/ä bar/b **bib**/ch **chew**/d **deed**/ĕ pet/ē be/f fit/g gag/h hat/hw what/
ĭ pit/ī pie/îr pier/j **judge**/k **kick**/l lid, fatal/m **mum**/n no, sudden/ng sing/ŏ pot/ō go/

rep·er·toire (rĕp′ər-twär, -twôr) *n.* Also **rep·er·to·ry** (-tôr′ē, -tōr′ē). **1.** The stock of songs, plays, etc., that a person or group is prepared to perform. **2.** The skills or accomplishments of a person or group. [< LL *repertōrium*, repertory.]

rep·er·to·ry (rĕp′ər-tôr′ē, -tōr′ē) *n., pl.* **-ries. 1.** A repertoire. **2.** A theatrical company that presents plays from a specified repertoire. [< L *reperīre*, to find out, find again.]

rep·e·ti·tion (rĕp′ə-tĭsh′ən) *n.* **1.** The act of repeating. **2.** Something repeated.

rep·e·ti·tious (rĕp′ə-tĭsh′əs) *adj.* Characterized by repetition, esp. needless repetition. —**rep′e·ti′tious·ly** *adv.* —**rep′e·ti′tious·ness** *n.*

re·pet·i·tive (rĭ-pĕt′ə-tĭv) *adj.* Characterized by repetition. —**re·pet′i·tive·ly** *adv.* —**re·pet′i·tive·ness** *n.*

re·phrase (rē-frāz′) *v.* To state in a new or different way.

repl. replacement.

re·place (rĭ-plās′) *v.* **1.** To put back in place. **2.** To take or fill the place of. —**re·place′a·ble** *adj.* —**re·place′ment** *n.* —**re·plac′er** *n.*

re·play (rē-plā′) *v.* To play (a record, video tape, etc.) again. —**re′play′** *n.*

re·plen·ish (rĭ-plĕn′ĭsh) *v.* To fill or make complete again. [< OF *replenir*.] —**re·plen′ish·er** *n.* —**re·plen′ish·ment** *n.*

re·plete (rĭ-plēt′) *adj.* Plentifully supplied; abounding. [< L *replēre*, to refill.]

rep·li·ca (rĕp′lĭ-kə) *n.* A copy or close reproduction. [< It *replicare*, to repeat.]

re·ply (rĭ-plī′) *v.* **-plied, -plying.** To say or give as an answer. —*n., pl.* **-plies.** An answer; response. [< OF *replier*, to fold back, reply.] —**re·pli′er** *n.*

re·port (rĭ-pôrt′) *n.* **1.** An account that is prepared or presented, usually in formal or organized form. **2.** Rumor. **3.** Reputation. **4.** An explosive noise. —*v.* **1.** To make or present an account of (something). **2.** To relate or tell about; present. **3.** To complain about or make known to the proper authorities. **4.** To serve as a reporter. **5.** To present oneself: *report for duty.* [< L *reportāre*, "to carry back."] —**re·port′a·ble** *adj.*

re·port·ed·ly (rĭ-pôr′tĭd-lē, rĭ-pōr′-) *adv.* By report; supposedly.

re·port·er (rĭ-pôr′tər, rĭ-pōr′-) *n.* A person who reports, esp. a writer of news stories.

re·pose¹ (rĭ-pōz′) *n.* **1. a.** The act of resting; a rest. **b.** The state of being at rest; relaxation. **2.** Calmness; tranquillity. —*v.* **-posed, -posing. 1.** To lie at rest; relax. **2.** To lie supported by something. [< LL *repausāre*.]

re·pose² (rĭ-pōz′) *v.* **-posed, -posing.** To place, as faith or trust in. [< RE- + POSE.]

re·pos·i·to·ry (rĭ-pŏz′ə-tôr′ē, -tōr′ē) *n., pl.* **-ries.** A place where things can be put for safekeeping. [< L *repōnere* (pp *repositus*), to put back.]

re·pos·sess (rē′pə-zĕs′) *v.* To regain possession of (property). —**re′pos·ses′sion** *n.*

rep·re·hend (rĕp′rĭ-hĕnd′) *v.* To reprove; censure. [< L *reprehendere*, to rebuke, hold back.]

rep·re·hen·si·ble (rĕp′rĭ-hĕn′sə-bəl) *adj.* De-serving of rebuke or censure; blameworthy. [< L *reprehendere*, to REPREHEND.] —**rep′re·hen′si·bly** *adv.*

rep·re·sent (rĕp′rĭ-zĕnt′) *v.* **1.** To stand for; symbolize. **2.** To depict; portray. **3.** To serve as the authorized delegate or agent for. **4.** To serve as an example of. [< L *repraesentāre*, show, bring back.]

rep·re·sen·ta·tion (rĕp′rĭ-zĕn-tā′shən, rĕp′rĭ-zən-) *n.* **1.** The act of representing or state of being represented. **2.** That which represents. **3.** The right of being represented by delegates in a legislative body.

rep·re·sen·ta·tive (rĕp′rĭ-zĕn′tə-tĭv) *n.* **1.** A person or thing serving as an example or type. **2.** One who serves as a delegate, esp. a member of a governmental body, usually legislative. —*adj.* **1.** Of or pertaining to government by representation. **2.** Exemplary of others in the same class; typical.

re·press (rĭ-prĕs′) *v.* **1.** To hold back; restrain. **2.** To suppress; quell. **3.** To force (memories, ideas, or fears) into the subconscious mind. [< L *reprimere*, to press back.] —**re·pres′sion** *n.* —**re·pres′sive** *adj.*

re·prieve (rĭ-prēv′) *v.* **-prieved, -prieving.** To postpone the punishment of. —*n.* The postponement of a punishment. [< L *reprehendere*, to hold back, REPREHEND.]

rep·ri·mand (rĕp′rə-mănd′, -mänd′) *v.* To rebuke or censure severely. —*n.* A severe or formal rebuke. [< L *reprimere*, to REPRESS.]

re·pri·sal (rĭ-prī′zəl) *n.* Retaliation for an injury with the intent of inflicting at least as much injury in return. [< L *reprehensus*, pp of *reprehendere*, to REPREHEND.]

re·proach (rĭ-prōch′) *v.* To blame for something; rebuke. —*n.* **1.** Rebuke; blame. **2.** Disgrace; shame. [< VL *repropiāre*, bring back near.] —**re·proach′a·ble** *adj.*

re·proach·ful (rĭ-prōch′fəl) *adj.* Expressing reproach or blame. —**re·proach′ful·ly** *adv.*

rep·ro·bate (rĕp′rə-bāt′) *n.* A morally unprincipled person. [< LL *reprobāre*, to reprove.]

re·pro·duce (rē′prə-d/y/ōōs′) *v.* **-duced, -ducing. 1.** To produce a counterpart, image, or copy of. **2.** To produce offspring. **3.** To produce again or anew; re-create. **4.** To undergo copying. —**re′pro·duc′tion** (-dŭk′shən) *n.* —**re′pro·duc′tive** (-dŭk′tĭv) *adj.*

re·proof (rĭ-prōōf′) *n.* An act or expression of reproving.

re·prove (rĭ-prōōv′) *v.* **-proved, -proving. 1.** To rebuke; scold. **2.** To find fault with. [< LL *reprobāre*.] —**re·prov′ing·ly** *adv.*

rept. **1.** receipt. **2.** report.

rep·tile (rĕp′tĭl, -tīl′) *n.* Any of various cold-blooded vertebrates covered with scales or horny plates, as a lizard, snake, or turtle. [< L *repere*, to creep.] —**rep·til′i·an** (-tĭl′ē-ən, -tĭl′yən) *adj. & n.*

re·pub·lic (rĭ-pŭb′lĭk) *n.* **1.** Any political order that is not a monarchy. **2.** A constitutional form of government, esp. a democratic one. [< L *rēspūblica*, "public matter."]

re·pub·li·can (rĭ-pŭb′lĭ-kən) *adj.* **1.** Of, pertaining to, or characteristic of a republic. **2.** **Republican.** Of, pertaining to, characteristic of, or belonging to the Republican Party of the U.S. —*n.* **1.** One who favors a republican form of government. **2. Republican.** A member of the Republican Party of the U.S.

Republican Party. One of the two major political parties of the U.S.

re•pu•di•ate (rĭ-pyōō′dē-āt′) *v.* **-ated, -ating. 1.** To reject the validity of. **2.** To refuse to recognize, acknowledge, or pay. [L *repudiāre,* to reject, cast off.] —**re•pu′di•a′tion** *n.*

re•pug•nant (rĭ-pŭg′nənt) *adj.* Offensive; distasteful; repulsive. [< L *repugnāre,* to fight against.] —**re•pug′nance** *n.*

re•pulse (rĭ-pŭls′) *v.* **-pulsed, -pulsing. 1.** To drive back; repel. **2.** To repel with rudeness, coldness, or denial. —*n.* **1.** The act of repulsing or state of being repulsed. **2.** Rejection; refusal. [L *repulsus,* pp of *repellere,* to REPEL.]

re•pul•sion (rĭ-pŭl′shən) *n.* **1.** The act of repulsing or condition of being repulsed. **2.** Extreme aversion or dislike.

re•pul•sive (rĭ-pŭl′sĭv) *adj.* **1.** Causing extreme dislike or aversion; disgusting. **2.** Tending to repel or drive off. —**re•pul′sive•ly** *adv.* —**re•pul′sive•ness** *n.*

rep•u•ta•ble (rĕp′yə-tə-bəl) *adj.* Having a good reputation; honorable. —**rep′u•ta•bly** *adv.*

rep•u•ta•tion (rĕp′yə-tā′shən) *n.* **1.** The general estimation in which one is held by the public. **2.** The state of being held in high repute. **3.** A specific character or trait ascribed to one: *a reputation for courtesy.* [< L *reputāre,* to consider, REPUTE.]

re•pute (rĭ-pyōōt′) *v.* **-puted, -puting.** To assign a reputation to: *He was reputed to be honest.* —*n.* **1.** Reputation. **2.** A good reputation. [< L *reputāre,* to count over, consider.]

re•put•ed (rĭ-pyōō′tĭd) *adj.* Generally considered or supposed. —**re•put′ed•ly** *adv.*

req. **1.** require; required. **2.** requisition.

re•quest (rĭ-kwĕst′) *v.* **1.** To ask for. **2.** To ask (a person) to do something. —*n.* **1.** An expressed desire; the act of asking. **2.** That which is asked for. [< L *requīrere,* to seek again, REQUIRE.]

re•qui•em (rĕk′wē-əm, rē′kwē-) *n.* **1. Requiem. R.C.Ch.** A mass for a deceased person. **2.** A hymn, composition, or service for the dead. [< L *requiēs,* rest, "after-rest."]

re•quire (rĭ-kwīr′) *v.* **-quired, -quiring. 1.** To have use for as a necessity; need. **2.** To demand; insist upon. [< L *requīrere,* to seek again, inquire.] —**re•quire′ment** *n.*

req•ui•site (rĕk′wə-zĭt) *adj.* Required; absolutely needed. —*n.* A necessity; something absolutely essential. —**req′ui•site•ly** *adv.*

req•ui•si•tion (rĕk′kwə-zĭsh′ən) *n.* A formal written request for something needed. —*v.* To demand, as for military needs.

re•quite (rĭ-kwīt′) *v.* **-quited, -quiting. 1.** To make repayment or return for. **2.** To avenge. [RE- + obs *quite,* to repay, var of QUIT.] —**re•qui′tal** *n.* —**re•quit′er** *n.*

re•run (rē′rŭn′) *n.* A repetition of a recorded performance, as a television program.

res. **1.** research. **2.** reserve. **3.** residence. **4.** resolution.

re•scind (rĭ-sĭnd′) *v.* To void; repeal. [L *rē-*

scindere, to cut off, abolish.] —**re•scind′a•ble** *adj.* —**re•scis′sion** (-sĭzh′ən) *n.*

res•cue (rĕs′kyōō) *v.* **-cued, -cuing.** To save, as from danger. —*n.* An act of saving; deliverance. [< VL **reexcutere,* to drive away, shake off.] —**res′cu•er** *n.*

re•search (rĭ-sûrch′, rē′sûrch) *n.* Scholarly or scientific investigation or inquiry. [< OF *recercher,* to seek out, search again.] —**re•search′** *v.* —**re•search′er** *n.*

re•sec•tion (rĭ-sĕk′shən) *n.* The surgical removal of part of an organ or structure.

re•sem•blance (rĭ-zĕm′bləns) *n.* The condition or quality of resembling something.

re•sem•ble (rĭ-zĕm′bəl) *v.* **-bled, -bling.** To have a similarity to. [< OF *resembler.*]

re•sent (rĭ-zĕnt′) *v.* To feel indignantly aggrieved at (an act, situation, or person). [Obs *resentir,* to feel strongly.] —**re•sent′ful** *adj.* —**re•sent′ful•ly** *adv.* —**re•sent′ment** *n.*

res•er•va•tion (rĕz′ər-vā′shən) *n.* **1.** The act of reserving. **2.** A limiting qualification, condition, or exception. **3.** A tract of land set apart by the Federal government for a special purpose. **4.** An arrangement by which accommodations are secured in advance.

re•serve (rĭ-zûrv′) *v.* **-served, -serving. 1.** To save for future use. **2.** To set apart for a particular person or use. **3.** To retain: *I reserve the right to disagree.* —*n.* **1.** Something saved for future use. **2.** The state of being set aside or saved: *funds held in reserve.* **3.** Reticence; discretion. **4.** A reservation of public land. **5.** Often **reserves.** The part of a country's armed forces subject to call in an emergency. [< L *reservāre,* to keep back.]

re•served (rĭ-zûrvd′) *adj.* **1.** Held in reserve. **2.** Characterized by self-restraint or reticence.

re•serv•ist (rĭ-zûr′vĭst) *n.* A member of a military reserve.

res•er•voir (rĕz′ər-vwär′, -vwôr′, -vôr′) *n.* **1.** A body of water stored in a natural or artificial lake. **2.** A chamber for storing a fluid.

resh (rĕsh) *n.* The 20th letter of the Hebrew alphabet, representing *r.*

re•side (rĭ-zīd′) *v.* **-sided, -siding. 1.** To live in a place. **2.** To be inherently present; exist (with *in*). [< L *residēre,* "to sit back," "remain sitting."] —**re•sid′er** *n.*

res•i•dence (rĕz′ə-dəns, -dĕns′) *n.* **1.** The place in which one lives; a dwelling. **2.** The act or a period of residing somewhere.

res•i•den•cy (rĕz′ə-dən-sē, -dĕn′sē) *n., pl.* **-cies.** The period during which a physician receives specialized clinical training.

res•i•dent (rĕz′ə-dənt, -dĕnt′) *n.* **1.** One who makes his home in a particular place. **2.** A physician serving his period of residency.

res•i•den•tial (rĕz′ə-dĕn′shəl) *adj.* Of, characterized by, suitable for, or limited to dwellings.

re•sid•u•al (rĭ-zĭj′ōō-əl) *adj.* Remaining as a residue.

res•i•due (rĕz′ə-d/y/ōō′) *n.* Matter remaining after completion of a process such as evaporation, combustion, distillation, or filtration. [< L *residēre,* RESIDE.]

re•sign (rĭ-zīn′) *v.* **1.** To give over or submit

(oneself). **2.** To give up (a position); quit. **3.** To relinquish (a privilege, right, or claim). [< L *resignāre*, to unseal, resign.]

res•ig•na•tion (rĕz'ĭg-nā'shən) *n.* **1.** The act of resigning. **2.** A written or oral statement that one is resigning a position or office. **3.** Acceptance; submission.

re•signed (rĭ-zīnd') *adj.* Feeling or marked by resignation; acquiescent. **—re•sign'ed•ly** (rĭ-zī'nĭd-lē) *adv.*

re•sil•ience (rĭ-zĭl'yəns) *n.* Also **re•sil•ien•cy** (-yən-sē). **1.** The ability to recover quickly, as from illness; buoyancy. **2.** The property of a material that enables it to resume an original shape after being bent, stretched, etc. [< L *resilīre*, to leap back.] **—re•sil'ient** *adj.*

res•in (rĕz'ĭn) *n.* **1.** A plant substance, as rosin or amber, used in lacquers, varnishes, adhesives, etc. **2.** Any of numerous physically similar polymerized synthetics or chemically modified natural resins used in making plastics. [< Gk *rhētinē*.] **—res'in•ous** (rĕz'ə-nəs) *adj.*

re•sist (rĭ-zĭst') *v.* **1.** To strive or work against; fight off. **2.** To withstand. [< L *resistere*, to stand back, resist.] **—re•sist'er** *n.*

re•sis•tance (rĭ-zĭs'təns) *n.* **1.** The act of resisting or capacity to resist. **2.** Any force that tends to oppose or retard motion. **3.** The opposition to electric current characteristic of a medium, substance, or circuit element.

re•sis•tor (rĭ-zĭs'tər) *n.* An electric circuit element used to provide resistance.

res•o•lute (rĕz'ə-lōōt') *adj.* Characterized by firmness or determination. [< L *resolvere*, to RESOLVE.] **—res'o•lute'ly** *adv.*

res•o•lu•tion (rĕz'ə-lōō'shən) *n.* **1.** The state or quality of being resolute. **2.** A course of action determined or decided upon. **3.** A formal statement of a decision put before or adopted by an assembly. **4.** The action of separating something into its constituent parts.

re•solve (rĭ-zŏlv') *v.* **-solved, -solving. 1.** To make a firm decision about. **2.** To cause (a person) to reach a decision. **3.** To decide or express by formal vote. **4.** To separate (something) into constituent parts. **5.** To find a solution to. *—n.* **1.** Firmness of purpose; resolution. **2.** A determination or decision. [< L *resolvere*, to release, resolve.] **—re•solv'a•ble** *adj.* **—re•solv'er** *n.*

re•solved (rĭ-zŏlvd') *adj.* Firmly determined; resolute.

res•o•nance (rĕz'ə-nəns) *n.* **1.** The enhancement of the response of an electric or mechanical system to a periodic driving force when the driving frequency is equal to the natural undamped frequency of the system. **2.** The intensification and prolongation of a tone by sympathetic vibration. [< L *resonāre*, to RESOUND.] **—res'o•nant** *adj.*

res•o•nate (rĕz'ə-nāt') *v.* **-nated, -nating. 1.** To exhibit resonance or resonant effects. **2.** To resound. **—res'o•na'tor** *n.*

re•sort (rĭ-zôrt') *v.* To seek assistance or relief; have recourse: *resorted to censorship. —n.* **1.** A place frequented by people for relaxation or recreation. **2.** A person or thing turned to for

aid or relief: *a last resort.* [< OF *resortir*, to come out again, to resort.]

re•sound (rĭ-zound') *v.* **1.** To be filled with sound; reverberate. **2.** To sound loudly; ring. [< L *resonāre*, to sound again, echo.] **—re•sound'ing** *adj.* **—re•sound'ing•ly** *adv.*

re•source (rē'sôrs', rĭ-sôrs') *n.* **1.** An available supply that can be drawn upon when needed. **2.** An ability to deal with a situation effectively. **3.** Often **resources.** Available capital; assets. [< L *resurgere*, to rise or surge again.]

re•source•ful (rĭ-sôrs'fəl) *adj.* Readily able to act effectively. **—re•source'ful•ness** *n.*

resp. respective; respectively.

re•spect (rĭ-spĕkt') *v.* **1.** To feel or show esteem for. **2.** To show consideration for. **3.** To relate or refer to; concern. *—n.* **1.** A feeling of deferential regard. **2.** The state of being regarded with esteem. **3.** A particular aspect, feature, or detail. **4.** Relation; reference. **5. respects.** Polite expressions of deference: *pay one's respects.* [L *respectus,* pp of *respicere,* to regard, look back.] **—re•spect'ful** *adj.* **—re•spect'ful•ly** *adv.* **—re•spect'ful•ness** *n.*

re•spect•a•ble (rĭ-spĕk'tə-bəl) *adj.* **1.** Meriting respect; worthy. **2.** Proper or conventional in conduct. **3.** Of moderately good quality. **—re•spect'a•bil'i•ty** *n.* **—re•spect'a•bly** *adv.*

re•spect•ing (rĭ-spĕk'tĭng) *prep.* In relation to; concerning.

re•spec•tive (rĭ-spĕk'tĭv) *adj.* Pertaining to two or more persons or things regarded individually: *They took their respective seats.*

re•spec•tive•ly (rĭ-spĕk'tĭv-lē) *adv.* Singly in the order designated or mentioned.

res•pi•ra•ble (rĕs'pər-ə-bəl, rĭ-spīr'-) *adj.* **1.** Fit for breathing. **2.** Capable of breathing. **—res'pi•ra•bil'i•ty** *n.*

res•pi•ra•tion (rĕs'pə-rā'shən) *n.* **1.** The act or process of inhaling and exhaling. **2.** The metabolic process by which an organism assimilates oxygen and releases carbon dioxide and other products. **—res'pi•ra•to'ry** (rĕs'pər-ə-tôr'ē, -tōr'ē, rĭ-spīr'ə-) *adj.*

res•pi•ra•tor (rĕs'pə-rā'tər) *n.* **1.** An apparatus used in administering artificial respiration. **2.** A screenlike device worn over the mouth or nose, or both, to protect the respiratory tract.

re•spire (rĭ-spīr') *v.* **-spired, -spiring. 1.** To inhale and exhale. **2.** To undergo the metabolic process of respiration. [< L *respīrāre,* to breathe again.]

res•pite (rĕs'pĭt) *n.* A temporary cessation or postponement, usually of something disagreeable. [< L *respectus,* a looking back, a refuge.]

re•splend•ent (rĭ-splĕn'dənt) *adj.* Having splendor; brilliant. [< L *resplendēre,* to shine brightly.] **—re•splen'dence** *n.*

re•spond (rĭ-spŏnd') *v.* **1.** To reply; answer. **2.** To act in return or in answer. **3.** To react positively or cooperatively. [L *respondēre,* "to promise in return."]

re•sponse (rĭ-spŏns') *n.* **1.** A reply or answer. **2.** A reaction to a stimulus.

re•spon•si•bil•i•ty (rĭ-spŏn'sə-bĭl'ə-tē) *n., pl.* **-ties. 1.** The state or fact of being responsible. **2.** A person or thing that one is answerable for; a duty or obligation.

re·spon·si·ble (rĭ-spŏn′sə-bəl) *adj.* **1.** Involving personal ability to act without superior authority: *a responsible position.* **2.** Being the source or cause of something (with *for*). **3.** Able to be trusted or depended upon; reliable. **4.** Accountable; answerable (with *to*). [< L *respondēre,* to RESPOND.] —**re·spon′si·bly** *adv.*

re·spon·sive (rĭ-spŏn′sĭv) *adj.* Readily reacting to suggestions, appeals, etc. —**re·spon′sive·ly** *adv.* —**re·spon′sive·ness** *n.*

rest¹ (rĕst) *n.* **1.** The act or state of ceasing from work, activity, or motion. **2.** Ease or refreshment resulting from sleep or the cessation of an activity. **3.** Sleep. **4.** *Mus.* An interval of silence. —*v.* **1.** To refresh (oneself) by rest. **2.** To sleep. **3.** To be, become, or remain temporarily still, quiet, or inactive. **4. a.** To be supported: *rests against the wall.* **b.** To place or lay: *rest it against the wall.* **5.** To be imposed as a responsibility or burden. **6.** To depend or rely. [< OE *reste* < Gmc **rast-.*] —**rest′er** *n.*

rest² (rĕst) *n.* **1.** That which is left over; remainder. **2.** Those remaining: *The rest are coming later.* —*v.* To be or continue to be: *rest easy.* [< OF *rester,* to remain.]

res·tau·rant (rĕs′tər-ənt, -tə-ränt′) *n.* A place where meals are served to the public. [F, "restorative."]

res·tau·ra·teur (rĕs′tər-ə-tûr′) *n.* The manager of a restaurant.

rest·ful (rĕst′fəl) *adj.* Affording tranquillity.

res·ti·tu·tion (rĕs′tə-t/y/ōō′shən) *n.* **1.** The act of restoring to the rightful owner something taken away, lost, or surrendered. **2.** The act of compensating for loss, damage, or injury; indemnification.

res·tive (rĕs′tĭv) *adj.* **1.** Impatient or nervous under restriction or delay; restless. **2.** Difficult to control; unruly. [< L *restāre,* to keep back.] —**res′tive·ly** *adv.* —**res′tive·ness** *n.*

rest·less (rĕst′lĭs) *adj.* **1.** Without quiet or rest: *a restless night.* **2.** Incapable of or opposed to resting or relaxing: *a restless child.* —**rest′less·ly** *adv.* —**rest′less·ness** *n.*

res·to·ra·tion (rĕs′tə-rā′shən) *n.* **1.** The act of restoring or state of being restored. **2.** That which has been restored, such as a renovated building.

re·stor·a·tive (rĭ-stôr′ə-tĭv, rĭ-stōr′-) *adj.* Tending to restore something, such as health. —*n.* Something that restores.

re·store (rĭ-stôr′, -stōr′) *v.* **-stored, -storing. 1.** To bring back into existence or use. **2.** To bring back to a previous, normal condition. **3.** To put (someone) back in a prior position. **4.** To give or bring back; make restitution of. [< L *restaurāre.*] —**re·stor′er** *n.*

re·strain (rĭ-strān′) *v.* **1.** To control; check. **2.** To limit or restrict. [< L *restringere,* to bind back, RESTRICT.]

re·straint (rĭ-strānt′) *n.* **1.** The act of restraining. **2.** Any influence that restrains. **3.** An instrument or means of restraining. **4.** Control of feelings; constraint.

re·strict (rĭ-strĭkt′) *v.* To hold down or keep within limits. [L *restringere* (pp *restrictus*), to bind back.] —**re·stric′tive** *adj.*

re·stric·tion (rĭ-strĭk′shən) *n.* **1.** The act of limiting or restricting or state of being limited or restricted. **2.** That which restrains or restricts; a limitation.

re·sult (rĭ-zŭlt′) *v.* **1.** To occur or exist as a consequence of a particular cause. **2.** To end in a particular way. —*n.* The consequence of a particular action, operation, or course; outcome. [< L *resultāre,* to leap back, rebound.]

re·sul·tant (rĭ-zŭl′tənt) *adj.* Issuing or following as a consequence or result.

re·sume (rĭ-zōōm′) *v.* **-sumed, -suming. 1.** To begin again; continue after interruption. **2.** To occupy or take again. [< L *resūmere,* to take up again.] —**re·sump′tion** (-zŭmp′shən) *n.*

rés·u·mé (rĕz′ōō-mā′, rĕz′ōō-mā′) *n.* A summary, esp. a summary of experience submitted with a job application. [< OF *resumer,* resume.]

re·sur·gent (rĭ-sûr′jənt) *adj.* Rising or tending to rise again. —**re·sur′gence** *n.*

res·ur·rect (rĕz′ə-rĕkt′) *v.* **1.** To bring back to life. **2.** To bring back into practice, notice, or use.

res·ur·rec·tion (rĕz′ə-rĕk′shən) *n.* **1.** A returning to life. **2.** A returning to practice, notice, or use. **3. the Resurrection.** The rising again of Christ on the third day after the Crucifixion. [< L *resurgere,* to rise again.]

re·sus·ci·tate (rĭ-sŭs′ə-tāt′) *v.* **-tated, -tating.** To return to life or consciousness; revive. [L *resuscitāre.*] —**re·sus′ci·ta′tion** *n.*

re·tail (rē′tāl′) *n.* The sale of commodities in small quantities to the consumer. —*v.* To sell at retail. [< OF *retailler,* to cut up.] —**re′tail** *adj.* —**re′tail′er** *n.*

re·tain (rĭ-tān′) *v.* **1.** To keep in one's possession. **2.** To continue to practice, employ, etc. **3.** To keep in a particular place, condition, or position. **4.** To hire (a lawyer) by the payment of a fee. **5.** To keep in one's service or pay. **6.** To keep in mind; remember. [< L *retinēre.*] —**re·tain′ment** *n.*

re·tain·er (rĭ-tā′nər) *n.* **1.** A person or thing that retains. **2.** One who served in a noble household as an attendant. **3.** The fee paid to engage the services of a lawyer, consultant, etc.

re·tal·i·ate (rĭ-tăl′ē-āt′) *v.* **-ated, -ating.** To return like for like, esp. to return evil for evil. [L *retaliāre,* repay in kind.] —**re·tal′i·a′tion** *n.* —**re·tal′i·a·to′ry** (-ē-ə-tôr′ē, -tōr′ē) *adj.*

re·tard (rĭ-tärd′) *v.* To impede or delay. [< L *retardāre.*]

re·tar·date (rĭ-tär′dāt′, -dĭt) *n.* A mentally retarded person.

re·tar·da·tion (rē′tär-dā′shən) *n.* **1.** The act of retarding or condition of being retarded. **2. a.** That which retards; a delay or hindrance. **b.** The amount or time of delay or hindrance. **3. Mental deficiency.**

re·tard·ed (rĭ-tär′dĭd) *adj.* Slow or deficient in mental or emotional development.

retch (rĕch) *v.* To vomit or attempt to vomit. [< OE *hrǣcan,* to cough up phlegm. See ker-².]

re·ten·tion (rĭ-tĕn′shən) *n.* **1.** The act of retaining or condition of being retained. **2.** The capacity to remember. —**re·ten′tive** *adj.*

ă pat/ā ate/âr care/ä bar/b **bib**/ch **chew**/d **deed**/ĕ pet/ē be/f fit/g gag/h hat/hw **what**/ ĭ pit/ī pie/îr pier/j **judge**/k **kick**/l lid, fatal/m **mum**/n no, sudden/ng sing/ŏ pot/ō go/

ret·i·cent (rĕt′ə-sənt) *adj.* Not inclined to speak; uncommunicative. [< L *reticēre,* to keep silent.] —**ret′i·cence** *n.*

ret·i·na (rĕt′n-ə) *n., pl.* **-nas** or **-nae** (-n-ē′). A delicate multilayer light-sensitive membrane lining the inner eyeball and connected by the optic nerve to the brain. [< ML *retina.*] —**ret′i·nal** *adj.*

ret·i·nue (rĕt′n-/y͞oo′) *n.* The attendants accompanying a person of rank. [< OF *retenir,* to retain.]

re·tire (rĭ-tīr′) *v.* **-tired, -tiring. 1.** To go away; depart, as for rest or seclusion. **2.** To go to bed. **3.** To withdraw from business or public life. **4.** To remove from active service: *retire an old career officer.* **5.** To withdraw troops. **6.** To take out of circulation: *retire bonds.* **7.** *Baseball.* To put out (a batter). [< OF *retirer,* to draw back.] —**re·tire′ment** *n.*

re·tired (rĭ-tīrd′) *adj.* Withdrawn from business or public life.

re·tir·ing (rĭ-tī′rĭng) *adj.* Shy and modest; reticent. —**re·tir′ing·ly** *adv.*

re·tort[1] (rĭ-tôrt′) *v.* **1.** To reply, esp. to answer in a quick, direct manner. **2.** To present a counterargument. **3.** To return in kind; pay back. —*n.* A quick, incisive reply. [L *retorquēre* (pp *retortus*), to bend back.]

re·tort[2] (rĭ-tôrt′, rē′tôrt′) *n.* A closed laboratory vessel with an outlet tube, used for distillation, sublimation, or decomposition by heat. [< L *retortus,* "bent back."]

re·touch (rē-tŭch′) *v.* To add new details or touches to (a photograph, painting, etc.) for correction or improvement.

re·trace (rē-trās′) *v.* To go back over: *retraced his steps.* —**re·trace′a·ble** *adj.*

re·tract (rĭ-trăkt′) *v.* **1.** To take back or disavow (a statement, offer, etc.). **2.** To draw back or in: *The turtle retracted its head.* [< L *retrahere* (pp *retractus*), to draw back.] —**re·tract′a·ble** *adj.* —**re·trac′tion** *n.*

re·trac·tile (rĭ-trăk′tĭl) *adj.* Capable of being drawn back or in: *retractile claws.*

re·tread (rē′trĕd′) *n.* A worn automobile tire fitted with a new tread.

re·treat (rĭ-trēt′) *n.* **1.** The act of going backward or withdrawing. **2.** A quiet, private, or secure place; refuge. **3.** A period of seclusion or solitude. **4.** The withdrawal of a military force from a dangerous position or from an enemy attack. —*v.* To withdraw; go back. [< L *retrahere,* to RETRACT.]

re·trench (rĭ-trĕnch′) *v.* **1.** To cut down; reduce. **2.** To curtail expenses; economize. [< OF *retrenchier.*] —**re·trench′ment** *n.*

ret·ri·bu·tion (rĕt′rə-by͞oo′shən) *n.* Something given or demanded in repayment, esp. punishment. [< L *retribuere,* to pay back.] —**re·trib′u·tive** (rĭ-trĭb′yə-tĭv), **re·trib′u·to·ry** (-tôr′ē, -tōr′ē) *adj.*

re·trieve (rĭ-trēv′) *v.* **-trieved, -trieving. 1.** To get back; regain. **2.** To find and carry back; fetch. **3.** To find and bring back game. [< OF *retrover,* to find again.] —**re·triev′a·ble** *adj.* —**re·triev′al** *n.*

re·triev·er (rĭ-trē′vər) *n.* A dog bred or trained to retrieve game.

retro–. *comb. form.* **1.** Backward or back. **2.** Situated behind. [< L *retrō,* backward, behind.]

ret·ro·ac·tive (rĕt′rō-ăk′tĭv) *adj.* Influencing or applying to a period prior to enactment. [< L *retroagere,* to drive back.]

ret·ro·grade (rĕt′rə-grād′) *adj.* **1.** Moving or tending backward. **2.** Reverting to an earlier or inferior condition. [< L *retrōgradus.*]

ret·ro·gress (rĕt′rə-grĕs′, rĕt′rə-grĕs′) *v.* To return to an earlier, inferior, or less complex condition. [L *retrogradī* (pp *retrōgressus*), to go backward.] —**ret′ro·gres′sion** *n.* —**ret′ro·gres′sive** *adj.*

ret·ro·rock·et (rĕt′rō-rŏk′ĭt) *n.* A rocket engine used to retard, arrest, or reverse motion.

ret·ro·spect (rĕt′rə-spĕkt′) *n.* A review or contemplation of things in the past. [< L *retrōspicere,* to look back at.] —**ret′ro·spec′tive** *adj.* —**ret′ro·spec′tive·ly** *adv.*

re·turn (rĭ-tûrn′) *v.* **1.** To go or come back, as to an earlier condition or place. **2.** To answer; respond. **3.** To send, put, or carry back. **4.** To give in reciprocation: *She returned his praise.* **5.** To yield (profit or interest). **6.** To deliver (a verdict). **7.** To re-elect, as to a legislative body. —*n.* **1.** The act of going, coming, bringing, or sending back. **2. a.** Something brought or sent back. **b.** Something that goes or comes back. **3.** Often **returns.** A profit or yield, as from investments. **4.** Often **returns.** A report on the vote in an election. —*adj.* **1.** Of or for coming back: *the return voyage.* **2.** Given, sent, or done in reciprocation or exchange: *a return visit.* [< VL *retornāre,* to turn back.] —**re·turn′a·ble** *adj.*

re·un·ion (rē-y͞oon′yən) *n.* **1.** The act of reuniting or state of being reunited. **2.** A gathering of the members of a group who have been separated.

re·u·nite (rē′y͞oo-nīt′) *v.* To bring or come together again.

rev (rĕv). *Informal. n.* A revolution, as of a motor. —*v.* **revved, revving.** To increase the speed of a motor.

rev. 1. revenue. **2.** reverse; reversed. **3.** review; reviewed. **4.** revise; revision. **5.** revolution. **6.** revolving.

Rev. 1. Revelation (New Testament). **2.** reverend (title).

re·vamp (rē-vămp′) *v.* **1.** To reconstruct or restore. **2.** To vamp (a shoe or boot) anew.

re·veal (rĭ-vēl′) *v.* **1.** To divulge or disclose; make known. **2.** To bring to view; expose. [< L *revēlāre,* to unveil, reveal.]

rev·eil·le (rĕv′ə-lē) *n.* The sounding of a bugle in the morning to awaken soldiers. [< OF *reveiller,* to rouse.]

rev·el (rĕv′əl) *v.* **-eled** or **-elled, -eling** or **-elling. 1.** To take great pleasure or delight (with *in*). **2.** To engage in uproarious festivities. —*n.* Often **revels.** A noisy festivity. [< OF *reveler,* to make noise, "rebel."] —**rev′el·er** *n.*

rev·e·la·tion (rĕv′ə-lā′shən) *n.* **1.** Something revealed. **2.** An act of revealing. **3.** A manifestation of divine will or truth. **4. Revelation.** The last book in the New Testament, attributed to Saint John.

ŏ paw, for/oi boy/ou out/o͞o took/o͞o coo/p pop/r run/s sauce/sh shy/t to/th thin/*th* the/
ŭ cut/ûr fur/v van/w wag/y yes/z size/zh vision/ə ago, item, edible, gallop, circus/

rev·el·ry (rĕv′əl-rē) *n., pl.* **-ries.** Boisterous merrymaking.

re·venge (rĭ-vĕnj′) *v.* **-venged, -venging.** To inflict punishment in return for (injury or insult); avenge. —*n.* **1.** Vengeance; retaliation. **2.** The act of taking vengeance. **3.** A desire for revenge. [< LL *revindicāre,* to avenge.] —**re·venge′ful** *adj.*

rev·e·nue (rĕv′ə-n/yo͞o) *n.* **1.** The income of a government. **2.** Yield from property or investment. [< OF *revenir,* to return.]

re·ver·ber·ate (rĭ-vûr′bə-rāt′) *v.* **-ated, -ating.** To re-echo; resound. [L *reverberāre,* to cause to rebound.] —**re·ver′ber·a′tion** *n.*

re·vere (rĭ-vîr′) *v.* **-vered, -vering.** To regard with awe, great respect, or devotion. [L *reverēri.*] —**re·ver′er** *n.*

Re·vere (rĭ-vîr′), **Paul.** 1735–1818. American silversmith and Revolutionary patriot.

rev·er·ence (rĕv′ər-əns) *n.* **1.** A feeling of profound awe and respect. **2.** An act of showing respect. **3.** The state of being revered. **4.** Reverence. A title of respect for a clergyman: *Your Reverence.*

rev·er·end (rĕv′ər-ənd) *adj.* **1.** Deserving of reverence. **2.** Often **Reverend.** Designating a member of the clergy. [< L *reverēri,* REVERE.]

rev·er·ent (rĕv′ər-ənt) *adj.* Feeling or expressing reverence. —**rev′er·ent·ly** *adv.*

rev·er·en·tial (rĕv′ə-rĕn′shəl) *adj.* Expressing reverence; reverent.

rev·er·ie (rĕv′ər-ē) *n.* **1.** Abstracted musing; daydreaming. **2.** A daydream. [< OF *rever,* to dream.]

re·ver·sal (rĭ-vûr′səl) *n.* **1.** An act or instance of reversing. **2.** The state of being reversed.

re·verse (rĭ-vûrs′) *adj.* **1.** Turned backward in position, direction, or order. **2.** Causing backward movement: *a reverse gear.* —*n.* **1.** The opposite or contrary of something. **2.** The back or rear of something, as of a coin. **3.** A change in fortune from better to worse. **4.** A mechanism for reversing movement, as a gear in an automobile. —*v.* **-versed, -versing. 1.** To turn to the opposite direction or tendency. **2.** To exchange the positions of; transpose. **3.** *Law.* To revoke or annul (a decision or decree). **4.** To turn or move in the opposite direction. [< L *reversus,* pp of *revertere,* REVERT.] —**re·vers′er** *n.*

re·vers·i·ble (rĭ-vûr′sə-bəl) *adj.* Capable of being reversed. —**re·vers′i·bil′i·ty, re·vers′i·ble·ness** *n.* —**re·vers′i·bly** *adv.*

re·vert (rĭ-vûrt′) *v.* To return to a former condition, practice, or belief. [< L *revertere,* to turn back.] —**re·ver′sion** (-vûr′zhən) *n.*

re·view (rĭ-vyo͞o′) *v.* **1.** To look over or study (material) again. **2.** To look back on. **3.** To examine with an eye to criticism or correction. **4.** To write or give a critical report on (a new work or performance). **5.** To subject to a military inspection. —*n.* **1.** A re-examination or reconsideration. **2.** A retrospective survey. **3.** A restudying of subject matter. **4.** An inspection or examination for the purpose of evaluating. **5.** A report or essay giving a critical estimate of a work or performance. [OF *revoir,* to see again, look over.] —**re·view′er** *n.*

re·vile (rĭ-vīl′) *v.* **-viled, -viling.** To denounce with abusive language. [< OF *reviler.*]

re·vise (rĭ-vīz′) *v.* **-vised, -vising. 1.** To prepare a newly edited version of (a text). **2.** To change or modify. [L *revisere,* to look back.] —**re·vi′sion** (-vĭzh′ən) *n.*

Revised Standard Version. A modern translation of the Bible existing in both Protestant and Catholic editions.

re·vi·tal·ize (rē-vīt′l-īz′) *v.* **-ized, -izing.** To impart new life or vigor to; restore the vitality of. —**re·vi′tal·i·za′tion** *n.*

re·viv·al (rĭ-vī′vəl) *n.* **1.** The act of reviving or condition of being revived. **2.** A restoration to use, acceptance, or vigor. **3.** A new presentation of an old play or motion picture. **4.** A meeting or series of meetings for the purpose of reawakening religious faith.

re·vive (rĭ-vīv′) *v.* **-vived, -viving. 1.** To bring or come back to life or consciousness. **2.** To impart or regain vigor or spirit. **3.** To restore to use. [< LL *revivere.*]

re·viv·i·fy (rē-vĭv′ə-fī′) *v.* **-fied, -fying.** To impart new life to. —**re·viv′i·fi·ca′tion** *n.*

re·voke (rĭ-vōk′) *v.* **-voked, -voking.** To annul by recalling or withdrawing; cancel; rescind: *revoke a license.* [< L *revocāre,* to call back.] —**re·vok′er** *n.*

re·volt (rĭ-vōlt′) *v.* **1.** To institute or take part in a rebellion against authority. **2.** To fill or be filled with disgust or abhorrence. —*n.* An uprising against authority; rebellion. [< L *revolvere,* to roll back, REVOLVE.]

re·volt·ing (rĭ-vōl′tĭng) *adj.* Causing disgust; repulsive. —**re·volt′ing·ly** *adv.*

rev·o·lu·tion (rĕv′ə-lo͞o′shən) *n.* **1. a.** Orbital motion about a point, esp. as distinguished from axial rotation. **b.** A turning or rotational motion about an axis. **c.** A single complete cycle of such orbital or axial motion. **2.** A momentous change in any situation. **3.** A sudden political overthrow brought about from within a given system. [< L *revolvere,* REVOLVE.]

rev·o·lu·tion·ar·y (rĕv′ə-lo͞o′shə-nĕr′ē) *adj.* Of, pertaining to, or bringing about a revolution. —*n., pl.* **-ies.** A militant in the struggle for revolution.

Revolutionary War. The American Revolution.

rev·o·lu·tion·ize (rĕv′ə-lo͞o′shə-nīz′) *v.* **-ized, -izing.** To bring about a radical change in; alter drastically.

re·volve (rĭ-vŏlv′) *v.* **-volved, -volving. 1.** To orbit a central point. **2.** To turn on an axis; rotate. **3.** To recur in cycles or at periodic intervals. [< L *revolvere,* to roll back.] —**re·volv′a·ble** *adj.*

re·volv·er (rĭ-vŏl′vər) *n.* A pistol having a revolving cylinder with several cartridge chambers.

re·vue (rĭ-vyo͞o′) *n.* A show consisting of skits, songs, and dances, often of a satirical nature. [< OF *revoir,* to REVIEW.]

re·vul·sion (rĭ-vŭl′shən) *n.* A sudden and strong change or reaction in feeling, esp. a feeling of violent disgust or loathing. [< L *revellere* (pp *revulsus*), to pull back or away.]

re·ward (rĭ-wôrd′) *n.* **1.** Something given or

---

received in recompense. **2.** Money offered for some special service, as for the return of something lost. —*v.* **1.** To bestow a reward on. **2.** To give a reward in return for. [< NF *rewarder,* "to look at."]

re•word (rē-wûrd') *v.* To state or express again in different words.

re•write (rē-rīt') *v.* To write again, esp. in a different form. —**re•writ'er** *n.*

Rey•kja•vík (rā'kyə-vēk'). The capital of Iceland. Pop. 75,000.

RF radio frequency.

RFD. rural free delivery.

Rh rhodium.

r.h. right hand.

rhap•so•dize (răp'sə-dīz') *v.* -dized, -dizing. To express oneself in a rhapsodic manner.

rhap•so•dy (răp'sə-dē) *n., pl.* -dies. **1.** Exalted or excessively enthusiastic expression of feeling in speech or writing. **2.** *Mus.* A composition that is free or irregular in form. [< Gk *rhapsōidos,* "weaver of songs," rhapsodist.] —**rhap•sod'ic** (-sŏd'ĭk) *adj.* —**rhap'so•dist** *n.*

rhe•a (rē'ə) *n.* A large South American bird resembling the ostrich.

rhe•ni•um (rē'nē-əm) *n. Symbol* **Re** A rare dense, silvery-white metallic element with a very high melting point, used for electrical contacts and with tungsten for high-temperature thermocouples. Atomic number 75, atomic weight 186.2. [< L *Rhēnus,* the Rhine.]

rhe•o•stat (rē'ə-stăt') *n.* A variable electrical resistor used to regulate current. [Gk *rheos,* current + -STAT.]

rhet•o•ric (rĕt'ər-ĭk) *n.* The art of effective expression in speech or writing. [< Gk *rhētorikē,* rhetorical.]

rhe•tor•i•cal (rĭ-tôr'ĭ-kəl, rĭ-tōr'-) *adj.* Concerned primarily with style or effect.

rhetorical question. A question to which no answer is expected or to which only one answer can be made.

rheum (rōōm) *n.* A watery or thin mucous discharge from the eyes or nose. [< Gk *rheuma,* stream, humor of the body, rheum.] —**rheum'y** *adj.*

rheu•mat•ic (rōō-măt'ĭk) *adj.* Of, pertaining to, or afflicted with rheumatism. —*n.* A person afflicted with rheumatism.

rheumatic fever. A severe infectious disease occurring chiefly in children and frequently resulting in permanent damage to the valves of the heart.

rheu•ma•tism (rōō'mə-tĭz'əm) *n.* **1.** Any of several pathological conditions of the muscles, tendons, joints, bones, or nerves, characterized by discomfort and disability. **2. Rheumatoid arthritis.** [< Gk *rheuma,* stream, flux, RHEUM.]

rheu•ma•toid arthritis (rōō'mə-toid'). A chronic disease marked by stiffness and inflammation of the joints.

Rh factor. Any of several substances on the surface of red blood cells that induce antigenic reactions with Rh negative blood cells. [First discovered in the blood of the *rhesus monkey,* a brownish monkey of India.]

Rhine (rīn). A river of W Europe.

rhine•stone (rīn'stōn') *n.* A colorless artificial gem of paste or glass. [Trans of F *caillou du Rhin.*]

rhi•noc•er•os (rī-nŏs'ər-əs) *n.* A large, thick-skinned African or Asian mammal with one or two upright horns on the snout. [< Gk *rhinokerōs,* "nose-horned."]

rhi•zome (rī'zōm') *n.* A rootlike plant stem sending out roots from its lower surface and leaves or shoots from its upper surface. [< Gk *rhizōma,* mass of roots of a tree.]

Rh negative. Lacking an Rh factor.

rho (rō) *n.* The 17th letter of the Greek alphabet, representing *r(rh).*

Rhode Island (rōd). A state of the NE U.S. Pop. 950,000. Cap. Providence.

Rho•de•sia (rō-dē'zhə). A self-governing British protectorate in central-south Africa. In 1965 it unilaterally declared its independence. Pop. 3,849,000. Cap. Salisbury. —**Rho•de'sian** *adj. & n.*

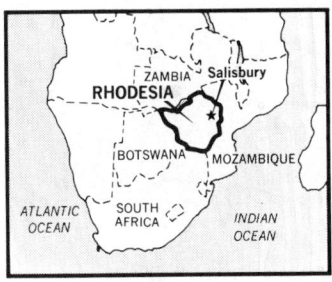

Rhodesia

rho•di•um (rō'dē-əm) *n. Symbol* **Rh** A hard, durable, silvery-white metallic element that is used to form high-temperature alloys with platinum and is plated on other metals to produce a durable corrosion-resistant coating. Atomic number 45, atomic weight 102.905. [< Gk *rhodon,* rose (color).]

rho•do•den•dron (rō'də-dĕn'drən) *n.* A shrub with evergreen leaves and clusters of variously colored flowers. [< Gk, "rose tree."]

rhom•bus (rŏm'bəs) *n., pl.* -buses or -bi (-bī'). An equilateral parallelogram. [< Gk *rhombos,* magic wheel, rhombus.] —**rhom'bic** (-bĭk) *adj.*

Rhône (rōn). A river of W Europe.

Rh positive. Containing an Rh factor.

rhu•barb (rōō'bärb') *n.* **1.** A plant with large leaves and long, fleshy, edible leafstalks. **2.** *Slang.* A quarrel. [Prob < ML *rha barbarum,* barbarian rhubarb.]

rhyme (rīm). Also **rime.** *n.* **1.** Correspondence of terminal sounds of words or lines of verse. **2.** A rhyming poem or verse: *nursery rhyme.* **3.** A word that corresponds with another in terminal sound. —*v.* **rhymed, rhyming. 1.** To form a rhyme; correspond in sound. **2.** To make use of rhymes in composing verse. **3.** To use (a word or words) as a rhyme or rhymes. [< L *rhythmus,* rhythm.]

rhythm (rĭth'əm) *n.* **1. a.** Any kind of movement characterized by the regular recurrence of strong and weak elements: *the rhythm of the tides.* **b.** The pattern of this, as in verse. **2.** The element of music that derives mainly from the relative duration and intensity of sounds. [< Gk *rhuthmos*, recurring motion, measure, rhythm.] —**rhyth′mi•cal** (-mĭ-kəl), **rhyth′mic** *adj.* —**rhyth′mi•cal•ly** *adv.*

rhythm method. A birth-control method dependent on continence during ovulation.

R.I. Rhode Island.

ri•al (rē-ôl′, -äl′) *n.* **1.** The basic monetary unit of Iran. **2.** Variant of **riyal.**

rib (rĭb) *n.* **1.** One of a series of long, curved, paired bones extending from the spine to or toward the breastbone. **2.** A part or piece similar to a rib and serving to shape or support. **3.** A raised ridge, as in fabric. —*v.* **ribbed, ribbing. 1.** To shape or support with a rib or ribs. **2.** To make with ridges. **3.** *Slang.* To tease. [< OE. See **rebh-.**]

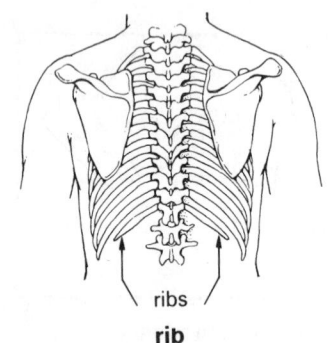

ribs

rib

rib•ald (rĭb′əld) *adj.* Pertaining to or indulging in vulgar, lewd humor. —*n.* A ribald person. [< OF *riber*, to be wanton.] —**rib′ald•ry** (-əl-drĕ) *n.*

rib•bon (rĭb′ən) *n.* **1.** A narrow strip or band of fine fabric, such as satin or velvet, finished at the edges and used for trimming or tying. **2. ribbons.** Tattered or ragged strips: *torn to ribbons.* **3.** An inked strip of cloth, as for a typewriter. [< MDu *ringhband*, necklace.]

ri•bo•fla•vin (rī′bō-flā′vĭn) *n.* A crystalline orange-yellow pigment, $C_{17}H_{20}O_6N_4$, the principal growth-promoting factor in the vitamin B_2 complex, found in milk, leafy vegetables, fresh meat, and egg yolks.

ri•bo•nu•cle•ic acid (rī′bō-n/y/ōō-klē′ĭk). A universal polymeric constituent of all living cells, consisting of a single-stranded chain of alternating units, the structure and sequence of which are determinants of protein synthesis. [RIBO(SE) + NUCLEIC ACID.]

ri•bose (rī′bōs′) *n.* A sugar, $C_5H_{10}O_5$, occurring as a component of nucleic acids. [< G *Ribon(säure)*, acid from which ribose is obtained.]

ri•bo•some (rī′bə-sōm) *n.* A cytoplasmic particle that contains RNA and acts in protein synthesis.

rice (rīs) *n.* **1.** A cereal grass cultivated extensively in warm climates. **2.** The starchy edible seed of this grass. —*v.* **riced, ricing.** To

sieve (food) to the consistency of rice. [< Gk *oruzon, oruza.*] —**ric′er** *n.*

rich (rĭch) *adj.* **1.** Possessing great wealth. **2.** Of great worth; valuable. **3.** Elaborate or sumptuous. **4.** Plentiful; abundant. **5.** Abounding in natural resources. **6.** Producing or yielding much. **7.** Containing a large proportion of tasty ingredients. **8.** Pleasing and satisfying to the senses. —*n.* **the rich.** Wealthy people collectively. [< OF *riche*, powerful, and OE *rice*.] —**rich′ly** *adv.* —**rich′ness** *n.*

Ri•che•lieu (rē-shə-lyœ′), **Duc de.** 1585–1642. French cardinal and statesman.

rich•es (rĭch′ĭz) *pl.n.* Abundant wealth.

Rich•mond (rĭch′mənd). **1.** The capital of Virginia. Pop. 250,000. **2.** A borough of New York City, coextensive with Staten Island.

rick•ets (rĭk′ĭts) *n.* A deficiency disease resulting from a lack of vitamin D and from insufficient exposure to sunlight, characterized by defective bone growth. [< Gk *rakhitis*, a disease of the spine.]

rick•et•y (rĭk′ĭt-ē) *adj.* **-ier, -iest. 1.** Likely to break or fall apart; shaky. **2.** Of or having rickets. —**rick′et•i•ness** *n.*

ric•o•chet (rĭk′ə-shā′, -shĕt′) *v.* **-cheted** (-shād′) or **-chetted** (-shĕt′ĭd), **-cheting** (-shā′ĭng) or **-chetting** (-shĕt′ĭng). To rebound at least once from a surface. [F.] —**ric′o•chet′** *n.*

rid (rĭd) *v.* **rid** or **ridded, ridding.** To free from something objectionable or undesirable. [< ON *rythja* < Gmc **rudjan*.]

rid•dance (rĭd′əns) *n.* —**good riddance.** A welcome removal of or deliverance from something. [RID + -ANCE.]

rid•den (rĭd′n). *p.p.* of **ride.** —*adj.* Dominated by: *grief-ridden.*

rid•dle¹ (rĭd′l) *v.* **-dled, -dling.** To pierce with numerous holes; perforate: *riddle with bullets.* [< OE *hriddel, hridder*, sieve.]

rid•dle² (rĭd′l) *n.* A question or problem requiring a clever answer or solution. [< OE *rǣdelse.*]

ride (rīd) *v.* **rode, ridden, riding. 1.** To sit on and be conveyed by an animal. **2.** To be conveyed in a vehicle. **3.** To travel over a surface: *This car rides well.* **4.** To float or move on or as on water. **5.** To sit on and drive. **6.** To be supported or carried upon. **7.** To take part in or do by riding: *rode his last race.* **8.** To cause to be carried: *rode him out of town.* **9.** To tease or ridicule. —*n.* **1.** An excursion or journey by any means of conveyance. **2.** In amusement parks, any of various structures in which persons ride for excitement. [< OE *ridan.* See **reidh-.**]

rid•er (rī′dər) *n.* **1.** One who rides. **2.** A clause, usually having little relevance to the main issue, added to a legislative bill. **3.** An amendment or addition to a document or record.

ridge (rĭj) *n.* **1.** The long, narrow crest of something. **2.** A long, narrow land elevation. **3.** The horizontal line formed by the juncture of two sloping planes. **4.** Any narrow raised strip. —*v.* **ridged, ridging.** To mark with, form into, or provide with ridges. [< OE *hrycg.* See **sker-².**]

rid•i•cule (rĭd′ə-kyōōl′) *n.* Words or actions

intended to evoke contemptuous laughter at a person or thing. —*v.* **-culed, -culing.** To engage in ridicule. [< L *ridiculus,* RIDICULOUS.]

ri·dic·u·lous (rĭ-dĭk′yə-ləs) *adj.* Deserving or inspiring ridicule; absurd or preposterous. [L *ridiculōsus, ridiculus,* laughable.] —**ri·dic′u·lous·ly** *adv.* —**ri·dic′u·lous·ness** *n.*

ri·el (rē-ĕl′) *n.* The basic monetary unit of Cambodia.

rife (rīf) *adj.* **rifer, rifest.** **1.** Widespread; prevalent. **2.** Abundant. **3.** Abounding: *a department rife with incompetents.* [< OE *rȳfe.*]

riff·raff (rĭf′răf′) *n.* Worthless or disreputable persons. [< OF *rif et raf.*]

ri·fle¹ (rī′fəl) *n.* A firearm with a rifled bore, designed to be fired from the shoulder. —*v.* **-fled, -fling.** To cut spiral grooves within (a gun barrel). [< OF *rifler,* to file.]

ri·fle² (rī′fəl) *v.* **-fled, -fling.** **1.** To search with intent to steal. **2.** To rob: *rifle a safe.* [< OF *rifler,* to scratch, file, plunder.] —**ri′fler** *n.*

rift (rĭft) *n.* **1. a.** *Geol.* A fault. **b.** A narrow fissure in rock. **2.** A break in friendly relations. [< Scand.]

rig (rĭg) *v.* **rigged, rigging.** **1.** To fit out; equip. **2.** To equip (a ship) with rigging. **3.** To make in a makeshift manner. **4.** To manipulate dishonestly for personal gain. —*n.* **1.** The arrangement of masts, spars, and sails on a sailing vessel: *a square rig.* **2.** A vehicle with one or more horses harnessed to it. **3.** The special apparatus used for drilling oil wells. [Prob < Scand.]

Ri·ga (rē′gə). The capital of Latvia. Pop. 733,000.

rig·a·ma·role. Variant of **rigmarole.**

rig·ging (rĭg′ĭng) *n.* The system of ropes, chains, and tackle used to support and control the masts, sails, and yards of a sailing vessel.

right (rīt) *adj.* **1.** In accordance with justice, law, or morality; fitting; proper. **2.** In accordance with fact or truth. **3.** Most appropriate, desirable, or convenient: *the right time to act.* **4.** Sound or normal: *in one's right mind.* **5.** Intended to be worn facing outward: *the right side of cloth.* **6. a.** Of, pertaining to, or toward that side of the human body in which the liver is normally located. **b.** Of, pertaining to, or toward the corresponding side of something relative to the observer's point of view. **7.** Often **Right.** Of or tending toward conservative or reactionary political policies or views. —*n.* **1.** That which is just, morally good, legal, proper, or fitting. **2.** The right-hand side. **3.** **the Right.** A political group whose policies are conservative or reactionary. **4.** That which is due to anyone by law, tradition, or nature. **5.** A just or legal claim or title. —*adv.* **1.** Directly; straight: *right to the heart of the matter.* **2.** Properly; correctly: *The suit doesn't fit right.* **3.** Exactly; just: *happened right there.* **4.** Immediately: *She will be right down.* **5.** Completely: *The bullet went right through him.* **6.** According to law, morality, or justice. **7.** On or toward the right side or direction. **8.** Extremely: *answered right well.* **9.** —Used in certain titles: *the Right Reverend.* —*v.* **1.** To restore to or regain an upright or proper posi-

tion or order. **2.** To redress: *right a wrong.* [< OE *riht.* See reg-¹.] —**right′ness** *n.*

right angle. A 90° angle.

right·eous (rī′chəs) *adj.* Meeting the standards of what is right and just. [< OE *rihtwīs.*] —**right′eous·ly** *adv.* —**right′eous·ness** *n.*

right·ful (rīt′fəl) *adj.* **1.** Right or proper; just. **2.** Having or held by a just or proper claim. —**right′ful·ly** *adv.* —**right′ful·ness** *n.*

right-hand (rīt′hănd′) *adj.* **1.** Located on or directed toward the right side. **2.** Of, for, or done by the right hand. **3.** Helpful; reliable: *my right-hand man.*

right-hand·ed (rīt′hăn′dĭd) *adj.* **1.** Using the right hand more easily than the left. **2.** Made to be used by the right hand.

right·ly (rīt′lē) *adv.* **1.** With correctness. **2.** Properly; suitably.

right of way. **1.** *Law.* **a.** The right to pass over property owned by another. **b.** The path or thoroughfare on which such passage is made. **2.** The strip of land over which highways, railroads, etc., are built. **3.** The customary or legal right of a person, vessel, or vehicle to pass in front of another.

right on *Slang.* Expressive of encouragement, approval, support, etc.

right triangle. A triangle containing a 90° angle.

rig·id (rĭj′ĭd) *adj.* **1.** Not bending; stiff; inflexible. **2.** Not moving; fixed. **3.** Harsh; severe. [< L *rigēre,* to be stiff.] —**ri·gid′i·ty** *n.*

rig·ma·role (rĭg′mə-rōl) *n.* Also **rig·a·ma·role** (-ə-mə-rōl). **1.** Confused or incoherent discourse; nonsense. **2.** A complicated and petty set of procedures. [< ME *Ragmane rolle,* scroll used in a medieval game.]

rig·or (rĭg′ər) *n.* **1.** Strictness or severity, as in temperament, action, or judgment. **2.** A harsh or trying circumstance; hardship. **3.** Strict precision; accuracy. [< L *rigēre,* to be stiff.] —**rig′or·ous** *adj.* —**rig′or·ous·ly** *adv.*

rig·or mor·tis (rĭg′ər môr′tĭs). Muscular stiffening following death. [L, "the stiffness of death."]

rile (rīl) *v.* **riled, riling.** **1.** To vex; anger. **2.** To stir up (liquid); roil. [Var of ROIL.]

rill (rĭl) *n.* A small brook; rivulet. [Du *ril* or LG *rille.*]

rim (rĭm) *n.* **1.** The border or edge of an object. **2.** The circular outer part of a wheel, furthest from the axle, around which a tire is fitted. —*v.* **rimmed, rimming.** To furnish with a rim. [< OE *rima* < Gmc *rimō.*]

rime. Variant of **rhyme.**

rind (rīnd) *n.* A tough outer covering, as the skin of some fruits or the coating on cheese. [< OE *rinde.* See rendh-.]

ring¹ (rĭng) *n.* **1.** A circular object, form, or arrangement with a vacant circular center. **2.** A small circular band, generally of precious metal, worn on a finger. **3.** Any circular band used for carrying, holding, or containing something. **4. a.** An area in which prize fights, exhibitions, etc., are held. **b. the ring.** The sport of prize fighting. **5.** An exclusive group of persons acting privately or illegally. —*v.* **1.** To surround with a ring; encircle. **2.** To move in a

---

ô paw, for/oi boy/ou out/ŏŏ took/ōō coo/p pop/r run/s sauce/sh shy/t to/th thin/*th* the/
ŭ cut/ûr fur/v van/w wag/y yes/z size/zh vision/ə ago, item, edible, gallop, circus/

spiral or circular course. [< OE *hring.* See sker-².]

ring² (rĭng) *v.* **rang, rung, ringing. 1.** To give forth a clear, resonant sound when caused to vibrate. **2.** To cause (a bell, chimes, etc.) to sound. **3.** To sound a bell in order to summon someone. **4.** To have a character suggestive of a particular quality: *a perception that rings true.* **5.** To resound. **6.** To hear a persistent humming or buzzing: *ears ringing from the blast.* **7.** To call (someone) on the telephone. —*n.* **1.** The sound created by a bell or other sonorous, vibrating object. **2.** A telephone call. **3.** A particular quality: *a suspicious ring.* [< OE *hringan.* See ker-².]

ring·let (rĭng′lĭt) *n.* A long, spirally curled lock of hair.

ring·side (rĭng′sīd′) *n.* The seats immediately outside an arena or ring, as at a prize fight.

ring·worm (rĭng′wûrm′) *n.* A contagious skin disease caused by a fungus and characterized by ring-shaped itching patches.

rink (rĭngk) *n.* **1.** An area surfaced with smooth ice for skating. **2.** A smooth floor suited for roller-skating. [< OF *renc,* row, range.]

rinse (rĭns) *v.* **rinsed, rinsing. 1.** To wash lightly. **2.** To remove (soap, dirt, etc.) with water. —*n.* **1. a.** The act of washing lightly. **b.** The water or solution used in this process. **2.** A cosmetic solution used in conditioning or tinting the hair. [Prob < L *recēns,* fresh, recent.]

Ri·o de Ja·nei·ro (rē′ō dĭ jə-nâr′ō, zhə-nâr′ō). A city of SE Brazil. Pop. 3,223,000.

Ri·o Grande (rē′ō grănd). A river forming much of the U.S.-Mexican border.

ri·ot (rī′ət) *n.* **1.** A wild or turbulent disturbance created by a large number of people. **2.** A profusion, as of colors. —**run riot. 1.** To move or act with wild abandon. **2.** To grow abundantly. —*v.* **1.** To take part in a riot. **2.** To engage in uncontrolled revelry. [< OF *ruihoter,* to quarrel.] —**ri′ot·er** *n.* —**ri′ot·ous** *adj.* —**ri′ot·ous·ly** *adv.* —**ri′ot·ous·ness** *n.*

rip (rĭp) *v.* **ripped, ripping. 1.** To tear or become torn apart. **2.** To remove by pulling or tearing roughly. **3.** To move quickly or violently. **4.** To attack or censure: *ripped into his opponent's record.* —*n.* A torn or split place. [Prob < Flem *rippen.*] —**rip′per** *n.*

rip·cord (rĭp′kôrd′) *n.* A cord pulled to release the pack of a parachute.

ripe (rīp) *adj.* **1.** Fully developed; mature: *ripe fruit.* **2.** Sufficiently advanced; opportune: *The time is ripe.* [< OE *rīpe.* See rei-¹.]

rip·en (rī′pən) *v.* To become or make ripe.

rip off. *Slang.* 1. To steal from; rob: *rip off a store.* **2.** To steal: *rip off merchandise.* **3.** To exploit or swindle.

rip-off (rĭp′ôf′, -ŏf′) *n. Slang.* **1.** A theft. **2.** One who steals; a thief. **3.** An act of exploitation; a swindle.

rip·ple (rĭp′əl) *v.* **-pled, -pling. 1.** To form small waves on the surface. **2.** To rise and fall gently in tone or volume. —*n.* **1.** A slight wave or undulation. **2.** An indistinct vibrating sound. [Perh freq of RIP.]

rip·saw (rĭp′sô′) *n.* A coarse-toothed saw for cutting wood along the grain.

rise (rīz) *v.* **rose, risen** (rĭz′ən), **rising. 1.** To assume a standing position. **2.** To get out of bed. **3.** To move from a lower to a higher position. **4.** To increase in amount, value, or size. **5.** To appear above the horizon. **6.** To extend upward. **7.** To originate. **8.** To puff up or swell up, as dough. **9.** To increase in intensity, force, or pitch. **10.** To meet a demand or challenge. **11.** To return to life. **12.** To rebel. —*n.* **1.** The act of rising; an ascent. **2.** The degree of elevation; upward slope. **3.** An increase in height, as of the level of water. **4.** An origin or beginning. **5.** Occasion or opportunity: *give rise to doubt.* **6.** An increase in price, worth, quantity, or degree. **7.** An increase in intensity, volume, or pitch. **8.** Elevation in social status, prosperity, or importance. [< OE *rīsan* < Gmc.]

ris·er (rī′zər) *n.* A person who rises, esp. from sleep: *a late riser.*

ris·i·ble (rĭz′ə-bəl) *adj.* **1.** Inclined to laugh. **2.** Causing laughter; ludicrous; laughable. [< L *rīdēre* (pp *rīsus*), to laugh.]

risk (rĭsk) *n.* **1.** The possibility of suffering harm or loss; danger. **2.** A person considered with respect to the possibility of loss to an insurer: *a poor risk.* —*v.* **1.** To expose to a chance of loss or damage. **2.** To incur the risk of. [< VL *resecum,* risk at sea, danger, "that which cuts."] —**risk′y** *adj.*

ris·qué (rĭs-kā′) *adj.* Suggestive of or bordering on indelicacy or impropriety. [< F *risquer,* to risk.]

rite (rīt) *n.* **1.** The prescribed form for conducting a religious or other solemn ceremony. **2.** A ceremonial act or series of acts: *fertility rites.* [< L *rītus.*]

rit·u·al (rĭch′ōō-əl) *n.* **1.** The prescribed form for conducting a solemn ceremony. **2.** A body of ceremonies or rites. [< L *rītus,* RITE.] —**rit′u·al** *adj.* —**rit′u·al·ly** *adv.*

ri·val (rī′vəl) *n.* **1.** A person who pursues the same object as another; competitor. **2.** One that equals or almost equals another in some respect. —*adj.* Acting as or being a rival; competing. —*v.* **1.** To attempt to equal or surpass. **2.** To be the equal of; be a match for. [< L *rīvālis,* "one using the same brook as another," rival.] —**ri′val·ry** *n.*

rive (rīv) *v.* **rived, rived** or **riven** (rĭv′ən), **riving. 1.** To rend or tear apart. **2.** To cleave or split asunder. [< ON *rīfa.*]

riv·er (rĭv′ər) *n.* A large natural stream of water emptying into an ocean, lake, or other body of water. [< L *rīpārius,* on a bank.]

riv·er·side (rĭv′ər-sīd′) *n.* The bank of a river. —*adj.* On or near the bank of a river.

riv·et (rĭv′ĭt) *n.* A metal bolt or pin, having a head on one end, used to fasten metal plates or other objects together by inserting the shank through a hole in each piece and forming the plain end into a new head. —*v.* **1.** To fasten or secure with a rivet. **2.** To engross or hold (the attention). [< OF *river,* to fix.]

riv·u·let (rĭv′yə-lĭt) *n.* A small brook or stream. [< L *rīvus,* brook, stream.]

Ri·yadh (rē-yäd′). A capital of Saudi Arabia. Pop. 300,000.

ă pat/ā ate/âr care/ä bar/b bib/ch chew/d deed/ĕ pet/ē be/f fit/g gag/h hat/hw what/
ĭ pit/ī pie/îr pier/j judge/k kick/l lid, fatal/m mum/n no, sudden/ng sing/ŏ pot/ō go/

ri•yal (rē-ôl′, -äl′) *n.* 1. Also **ri•al.** The basic monetary unit of Saudi Arabia. 2. The basic monetary unit of Yemen.

rm. 1. ream. 2. room.

Rn radon.

R.N. 1. registered nurse. 2. Royal Navy.

RNA ribonucleic acid.

ro. rood (measure).

roach¹ (rōch) *n.* A cockroach.

roach² (rōch) *n.* A European freshwater fish. [< OF *roche.*]

road (rōd) *n.* 1. An open way for the passage of vehicles, persons, and animals. 2. A way or course toward the achievement of something. [< OE *rād*, riding, journey. See **reidh-.**]

road•bed (rōd′bĕd′) *n.* The foundation laid for railroad tracks or a road.

road•run•ner (rōd′rŭn′ər) *n.* A swift-running, long-tailed, crested bird of SW North America.

road•side (rōd′sīd′) *n.* The area on the side of a road. —**road′side′** *adj.*

road•ster (rōd′stər) *n.* An open automobile having a single seat for two or three people.

road•way (rōd′wā′) *n.* A road, esp. the part over which vehicles travel.

roam (rōm) *v.* To move or travel (through) without purpose or plan. [ME *romen.*]

roan (rōn) *adj.* Having a brownish coat sprinkled with white or gray, as a horse. —*n.* A roan horse or other animal. [< OSpan *roano.*]

roar (rôr) *v.* 1. To utter a loud, deep, prolonged sound. 2. To utter or express with a roar. 3. To laugh loudly or excitedly. —*n.* 1. A loud, deep sound, cry, or noise. 2. A loud burst of laughter. [< OE *rārian.*]

roast (rōst) *v.* 1. To cook with dry heat. 2. To expose to great or excessive heat. 3. To heat (ores) in a furnace in order to dehydrate, purify, or oxidize. 4. *Informal.* To criticize or ridicule harshly. —*n.* 1. Something roasted. 2. A cut of meat suitable or prepared for roasting. —*adj.* Roasted. [< OF *rostir.*] —**roast′er** *n.*

rob (rŏb) *v.* **robbed, robbing.** 1. To steal (from). 2. To deprive of something. [< OF *rober.*] —**rob′ber** *n.*

rob•ber•y (rŏb′ər-ē) *n., pl.* **-ies.** 1. The act of robbing. 2. An instance of this.

robe (rōb) *n.* 1. A long, loose, flowing outer garment, esp. one worn on formal occasions. 2. A dressing gown or bathrobe. 3. A blanket or covering: *a lap robe.* —*v.* **robed, robing.** To dress in a robe or robes. [< VL **rauba,* "clothes taken away as booty," robe.]

Robes•pierre (rōbz′pē-âr), **Maximilien de.** 1758–1794. French revolutionary leader.

rob•in (rŏb′ĭn) *n.* 1. A North American songbird with a rust-red breast and a dark back. 2. A small Old World bird with an orange breast and a brown back. [< *Robin,* given name.]

Rob•in Hood (rŏb′ĭn hood). One who takes from the rich to give to the poor. [< *Robin Hood,* legendary 12th-century English outlaw.]

ro•bot (rō′bət, rŏb′ət) *n.* 1. A manlike mechanical device capable of performing human tasks. 2. A person who works mechanically

without original thought. 3. Any machine or device that works automatically. [Czech.]

ro•bust (rō-bŭst′, rō′bŭst) *adj.* Full of health and strength; vigorous; hardy. [L *robustus,* oaken.] —**ro•bust′ly** *adv.* —**ro•bust′ness** *n.*

Roch•es•ter (rŏch′ĕs-tər). A city in W New York State. Pop. 319,000.

rock¹ (rŏk) *n.* 1. Any relatively hard naturally formed mass of mineral or petrified matter; stone. 2. A support, foundation, or source of strength. —**on the rocks.** 1. In a state of ruin. 2. Served over ice cubes without water or mix. [< VL **rocca.*]

rock² (rŏk) *v.* 1. To move or sway back and forth or from side to side, esp. gently or rhythmically. 2. To shake violently, as from a blow or shock. —*n.* 1. A rocking motion. 2. Rock 'n' roll. [< OE *roccian.*]

rock-and-roll. Variant of **rock 'n' roll.**

rock-bound (rŏk′bound′) *adj.* Hemmed in by or bordered with rocks.

Rock•e•fel•ler (rŏk′ə-fĕl′ər), **John D(avison).** 1839–1937. American capitalist.

rock•er (rŏk′ər) *n.* 1. A rocking chair. 2. One of the two curved pieces upon which a cradle or rocking chair rocks. —**off one's rocker.** *Slang.* Out of one's mind; crazy.

rock•et (rŏk′ĭt) *n.* 1. **a.** Any device propelled by ejection of matter, esp. by the high-velocity ejection of gaseous combustion products. **b.** An engine that propels in this manner; a rocket engine. 2. A rocket-propelled explosive weapon. —*v.* To move swiftly, as a rocket. [It *rocchetta,* rocket, small distaff.]

rock•et•ry (rŏk′ĭt-rē) *n.* The science and technology of rocket design, construction, and flight.

Rock•ies (rŏk′ēz). *Informal.* The Rocky Mountains.

rocking chair. A chair mounted on rockers or springs.

rocking horse. A toy horse large enough for a child to ride, mounted upon rockers or springs.

rock 'n' roll (rŏk′ ən rōl′). Also **rock-and-roll** (rŏk′ən-rōl′). Popular music combining elements of rhythm and blues with country and western music and having a heavily accented beat. —**rock 'n' roll** *adj.*

rock-ribbed (rŏk′rĭbd′) *adj.* 1. Having rocks or rock outcroppings. 2. Stern and unyielding.

rock salt. Common salt, essentially sodium chloride, occurring in large solid masses.

rock•y¹ (rŏk′ē) *adj.* **-ier, -iest.** 1. Consisting of or abounding in rocks. 2. Marked by hazards or difficulties.

rock•y² (rŏk′ē) *adj.* **-ier, -iest.** 1. Unsteady; shaky. 2. Weak, dizzy, or nauseated.

Rock•y Mountains (rŏk′ē). The major mountain system of North America, extending from Mexico to Alaska.

ro•co•co (rə-kō′kō, rō′kə-kō′) *n.* A style of architecture and decoration characterized by elaborate, profuse designs intended to produce a delicate effect. [< F *rocaille,* rockwork.] —**ro•co′co** *adj.*

rod (rŏd) *n.* 1. A straight, thin piece or bar of metal, wood, or other material. 2. A stick or bundle of sticks used for chastisement. 3. A

ô paw, for/oi boy/ou out/oo took/oo coo/p pop/r run/s sauce/sh shy/t to/th thin/*th* the/
ŭ cut/ûr fur/v van/w wag/y yes/z size/zh vision/ə ago, item, edible, gallop, circus/

scepter or staff symbolizing power or authority; wand. **4.** A metal bar in a machine: *a piston rod.* **5.** A linear measure equal to 5.5 yards, 16.5 feet, or 5.03 meters. **6.** *Slang.* A pistol or revolver. [< OE *rodd.* See **rĕt-**.]
rode (rōd). *p.t.* of **ride.**
ro•dent (rōd′ənt) *n.* Any of various related mammals, as a mouse, rat, squirrel, or beaver, having teeth adapted for gnawing. [< L *rōdere,* to gnaw.]
ro•de•o (rō′dē-ō′, rō-dā′ō) *n., pl.* **-os. 1.** A cattle roundup. **2.** A public exhibition of cowboy skills, including riding broncos, lassoing, etc. [< Span *rodear,* to surround.]
Ro•din (rō-dăn′), **Auguste.** 1840–1917. French sculptor.
roe[1] (rō) *n.* The eggs or egg-laden ovary of a fish. [< MLG or MDu *roge.*]
roe[2] (rō) *n.* Also **roe deer.** A small Old World deer with short antlers. [< OE *rā.* See **rei-**[2].]
roe•buck (rō′bŭk′) *n.* A male roe deer.
roent•gen (rĕnt′gən, rŭnt′-) *n.* An obsolete unit of radiation dosage, equal to the quantity of ionizing radiation that will produce a standard amount of electricity in one cubic centimeter of dry air at 0°C and standard atmospheric pressure. [< W. *Roentgen* (1845–1923), German physicist.]
Roentgen ray. X ray.
Rog•er (rŏj′ər) *interj.* Also **rog•er.** Used in radio communications to indicate message received.
rogue (rōg) *n.* **1.** An unprincipled person; a scoundrel or rascal. **2.** A playfully mischievous person; scamp. [Orig "beggar," prob < L *rogāre,* to ask, beg.] **—ro′guer•y** *n.*
roil (roil) *v.* **1.** To make (a liquid) muddy or cloudy by stirring up sediment. **2.** To displease; irritate; vex. [?]
roist•er (rois′tər) *v.* **1.** To engage in boisterous merrymaking. **2.** To behave in a blustering manner; swagger. [Prob < OF *rustre,* churl, boor.] **—roist′er•er** *n.*
Ro•land (rō′lənd). Legendary paladin and nephew of Charlemagne.
role (rōl) *n.* Also **rôle. 1.** A character or part played by an actor. **2.** A function or position. [< OF *rolle,* roll (on which a part is written).]
roll (rōl) *v.* **1.** To move by turning over and over. **2.** To move on wheels. **3.** To gain momentum. **4.** To go by; elapse. **5.** To turn over and over: *roll in the mud.* **6.** To advance with a rising and falling motion, as waves. **7.** To move or rock from side to side, as a ship. **8.** To make a deep, prolonged, surging sound, as thunder. **9.** To rotate: *roll one's eyes.* **10.** To pronounce or utter with a trill: *roll one's "r's".* **11.** To wrap (something) round and round upon itself or around something else. **12.** To envelop or enfold in a covering. **13.** To spread, compress, or flatten by applying pressure with a roller. **14.** To throw (dice) in craps or other games. **—roll in.** To arrive in large numbers; pour in. **—roll out.** To unroll and spread out. **—roll up.** *Informal.* To arrive in a vehicle. **—n. 1.** An instance of rolling. **2.** A quantity of something rolled up in the form of a cylinder. **3.** A piece of parchment or paper that can be

or is rolled up; scroll. **4.** A list of names of persons belonging to a given group. **5. a.** A small rounded portion of bread. **b.** Any food that is prepared by rolling up: *an egg roll.* **6.** A rolling, swaying, or rocking motion. **7.** A deep reverberation or rumble. **8.** A rapid succession of short sounds: *the roll of a drum.* [< L *rota,* wheel.]
roll call. The reading aloud of a list of names to determine who is absent.
roll•er (rō′lər) *n.* **1.** A small, spokeless wheel, as that of a roller skate or caster. **2.** An elongated cylinder upon which something is wound. **3.** Any of various cylindrical devices used for leveling, crushing, or curling. **4.** A heavy wave that breaks on the coast.
roller coaster. A sharply banked railway with small open cars, operated in amusement parks.
roller skate. A skate having four small wheels instead of a runner. **—roll′er-skate′** *v.* (**-skated,** **-skating).**
rol•lick (rŏl′ĭk) *v.* To behave or move in a carefree manner; romp. [Prob a blend of ROMP or ROLL and FROLIC.] **—rol′lick•ing** *adj.*
rolling pin. A smooth cylinder, usually of wood, used for rolling out dough.
rolling stock. A railroad's wheeled vehicles.
ro•ly-po•ly (rō′lē-pō′lē) *adj.* Short and plump; pudgy. [Perh < ROLL + POLL.]
rom. roman (type).
Rom. 1. Roman. **2.** Romance (language). **3.** Romans (New Testament).
ro•maine (rō-mān′) *n.* A type of lettuce with long leaves forming a head. [< F *Romain,* Roman.]
Ro•man (rō′mən) *adj.* **1.** Of or characteristic of Rome and its people, esp. ancient Rome. **2.** Of or pertaining to the Roman Catholic Church. **3. roman.** Designating the most common style of type, with letters having serifs and vertical lines thicker than horizontal lines. **—n.** A native, resident, or citizen of Rome, esp. ancient Rome.
Roman Catholic. 1. Of or pertaining to the Roman Catholic Church. **2.** A member of the Roman Catholic Church.
Roman Catholic Church. The Christian church that is characterized by a hierarchic structure of bishops and priests, with the pope as head of the episcopal college. **—Roman Catholicism.**
ro•mance (rō-măns′, rō′măns) *n.* **1.** A long medieval narrative in prose or verse, telling of the adventures of chivalric heroes. **2.** Any long, fictitious tale of heroes and extraordinary or mysterious events. **3.** The quality of adventure and idealized exploits found in such tales. **4.** A novel or story dealing with a love affair. **5.** A love affair. [< VL *Rōmānicē,* in the Roman manner.]
Ro•mance (rō-măns′, rō′măns) *n.* The languages that developed from Vulgar Latin, the principal ones being French, Italian, Portuguese, Rumanian, and Spanish. **—Ro•mance′** *adj.*
Roman Empire. The empire of the ancient Romans from 27 B.C. to A.D. 395.
Ro•man•esque (rō′mən-ĕsk′) *adj.* Designating

ă pat/ā ate/âr care/ä bar/b bib/ch chew/d deed/ĕ pet/ē be/f fit/g gag/h hat/hw what/
ĭ pit/ī pie/îr pier/j judge/k kick/l lid, fatal/m mum/n no, sudden/ng sing/ŏ pot/ō go/

a transitional style of European architecture prevalent from the 9th to the 12th century. [< ROMAN.] —Ro′man•esque′ *n.*

Ro•ma•ni•a. Variant of **Rumania.**

Ro•ma•ni•an. Variant of **Rumanian.**

Roman numeral. One of the letters employed in the ancient Roman system of numeration, still used in certain formal contexts.

I	1
II	2
III	3
IV	4
V	5
VI	6
VII	7
VIII	8
IX	9
X	10
XI	11
XII	12
XIII	13
XIV	14
XV	15
XVI	16
XVII	17
XVIII	18
XIX	19
XX	20
XXI	21
XXIX	29
XXX	30
XL	40
XLVIII	48
IL	49
L	50
LX	60
XC	90
XCVIII	98
IC	99
C	100
CI	101
CC	200
D	500
DC	600
CM	900
M	1,000
MDCLXVI	1666
MCMLXX	1970

Roman numeral

ro•man•tic (rō-măn′tĭk) *adj.* **1.** Of, pertaining to, or characteristic of romance. **2.** Given to thoughts or feelings of romance. **3.** Conducive to romance. **4.** Imaginative but impractical: *romantic notions.* **5.** Not based on fact; imaginary. **6.** Of or characteristic of romanticism in the arts. —*n.* A romantic person. —**ro•man′ti•cal•ly** *adv.*

ro•man•ti•cism (rō-măn′tə-sĭz′əm) *n.* A literary movement originating toward the end of the 18th century that sought to assert the validity of subjective experience and escape from the prevailing subordination to classical forms. —**ro•man′ti•cist** *n.*

ro•man•ti•cize (rō-măn′tə-sīz′) *v.* **-cized, -cizing. 1.** To interpret romantically. **2.** To think in a romantic way.

Rom•a•ny (rŏm′ə-nē, rō′mə-) *n., pl.* **-ny** or **-nies. 1.** A Gypsy. **2.** The Indic language spoken by the Gypsies; Gypsy. —**Rom′a•ny** *adj.*

Rome (rōm). **1.** The capital of Italy and site of Vatican City; formerly the capital of the Roman Empire. Pop. 2,445,000. **2.** The ancient Roman kingdom, republic, and empire.

Ro•me•o (rō′mē-ō) *n., pl.* **-os.** One given over to courtship or lovemaking. [< *Romeo,* lover in Shakespeare's *Romeo and Juliet.*]

romp (rŏmp) *v.* **1.** To play or frolic boisterously. **2.** *Slang.* To win a race easily. —*n.* **1.** Lively, merry play; frolic. **2.** *Slang.* An easy win.

romp•er (rŏm′pər) *n.* **1.** One who romps, esp. a small child. **2. rompers.** A loose-fitting sports or play outfit with short bloomers.

roof (roof, ro͝of) *n.* **1.** The exterior top covering of a building. **2.** The top covering of anything: *the roof of a car.* **3.** The upper part of the mouth. —*v.* To cover with a roof. [< OE *hrōf.* See krapo-.]

roof garden. 1. A garden on the roof of a building. **2.** A restaurant on the roof of a building.

roof•ing (roo′fĭng, ro͝of′ĭng) *n.* Materials used in building a roof.

rook¹ (ro͝ok) *n.* A crowlike Old World bird. —*v. Slang.* To swindle. [< OE *hrōc.*]

rook² (ro͝ok) *n.* A chess piece that may move in a straight line over any number of empty squares; castle. [< Pers *rukh.*]

rook•er•y (ro͝ok′ər-ē) *n., pl.* **-ies.** A breeding place of rooks or certain animals, as seals.

rook•ie (ro͝ok′ē) *n. Slang.* **1.** An untrained recruit. **2.** A novice player in baseball or football. [Var of RECRUIT.]

room (room, ro͝om) *n.* **1.** Space: *This desk takes up too much room.* **2. a.** An area of a building set off by walls or partitions. **b.** The people present in such an area: *The whole room laughed.* **3. rooms.** Living quarters. **4.** Suitable opportunity: *room for error.* —*v.* To occupy a room; live or lodge. [< OE *rūm.* See rewə-.]

room•er (roo′mər, ro͝om′ər) *n.* A lodger.

room•ette (roo-mĕt′, ro͝om-ĕt′) *n.* A small private compartment in a railroad sleeping car.

room•ful (room′fo͝ol′, ro͝om′-) *n., pl.* **-fuls. 1.** As much or as many as a room will hold. **2.** The number of people in a room.

rooming house. A house where lodgers can rent rooms.

room•mate (room′māt′, ro͝om′-) *n.* A person with whom one shares a room or apartment.

room•y (roo′mē, ro͝om′ē) *adj.* **-ier, -iest.** Having plenty of room; spacious; large. —**room′i•ly** *adv.* —**room′i•ness** *n.*

ô paw, for/oi boy/ou out/o͝o took/o͞o coo/p pop/r run/s sauce/sh shy/t to/th thin/*th* the/
ŭ cut/ûr fur/v van/w wag/y yes/z size/zh vision/ə ago, item, edible, gallop, circus/

Roo·se·velt (rō′zə-vĕlt, rōz′vĕlt, -vəlt). **1.** Franklin Delano. 1882–1945. 32nd President of the U.S. (1933–45). **2.** Theodore. 1858–1919. 26th President of the U.S. (1901–09).

Franklin Delano Roosevelt

Theodore Roosevelt

roost (rōost) n. **1.** A perch on which domestic fowls or other birds rest. **2.** A place with such perches. **—rule the roost.** To be in charge. —v. To rest or sleep on a perch or roost. [< OE *hrōst.*]

roost·er (rōos′tər) n. The adult male of the common domestic fowl.

root¹ (rōot, rŏot) n. **1.** The usually underground portion of a plant that serves as support and absorbs and stores food. **2.** The embedded part of an organ or structure such as a hair, tooth, or nerve. **3.** An essential element; core. **4.** A primary source; origin. **5.** *Ling.* **a.** In etymology, a word or word element from which other words are formed. **b.** In morphology, a base to which prefixes and suffixes may be added. **6.** A number that when multiplied by itself an indicated number of times equals a specified number. **—take root. 1.** To put forth roots and begin to grow. **2.** To become firmly fixed or established. —v. **1.** To put forth roots. **2.** To implant or become fixed by or as by roots. **3.** To pull up by or as by the roots. [< OE *rōt* < ON.]

root² (rōot, rŏot) v. To dig with or as with the snout or nose. [< OE *wrōtan.* See **wrŏd-.**]

root³ (rōot, rŏot) v. To support a contestant or team; cheer (with *for*). [Perh < ROOT².] **—root′er** n.

root beer. A carbonated soft drink made from extracts of the roots of several plants.

root·stock (rōot′stŏk′, rŏot′-) n. A rootlike stem; a rhizome.

rope (rōp) n. A flexible, heavy cord of twisted hemp or other fiber. **—know the ropes.** To be experienced with the details of an operation. —v. **roped, roping. 1.** To tie or fasten with rope. **2.** To enclose with a rope. **3.** To lasso. **4.** *Informal.* To entice or deceive. [< OE *rāp.* See **rei-¹.**]

Roque·fort cheese (rōk′fərt). A French cheese made from goat's and ewe's milk and containing a blue mold. [< *Roquefort,* village in S France.]

Ror·schach test (rôr′shäk, -shäкн, rōr′-). A psychological test of personality in which a subject's interpretations of ten standard abstract designs are analyzed as a measure of emotional and intellectual functioning and integration. [< H. *Rorschach* (1884–1922), Swiss psychiatrist.]

ro·sa·ry (rō′zə-rē) n., pl. **-ries.** A string of beads on which prayers are counted. [< ML *rosārium.*]

rose¹ (rōz) n. **1.** Any of various usually prickly shrubs or vines with compound leaves and showy, often fragrant flowers. **2.** The flower of such a plant. **3.** Dark pink. **4.** Something resembling a rose in form. [< L *rosa.*]

rose² (rōz). p.t. of **rise.**

ro·sé (rō-zā′) n. A light, pink table wine. [F, "pink."]

ro·se·ate (rō′zē-ĭt, -āt′) adj. **1.** Rose-colored. **2.** Cheerful; optimistic; rosy.

rose-col·ored (rōz′kŭl′ərd) adj. **1.** Having the color rose. **2.** Seeing or seen overoptimistically.

rose fever. A spring or early summer hay fever.

rose·mar·y (rōz′mâr′ē) n., pl. **-ies.** An aromatic shrub with grayish-green leaves used as seasoning. [< L *rōs marīnus,* "sea dew."]

ro·sette (rō-zĕt′) n. An ornament or badge made of ribbon or silk gathered and tufted to resemble a rose. [F, "small rose."]

rose water. A fragrant preparation made by steeping or distilling rose petals in water, used in cosmetics and cookery.

rose·wood (rōz'wŏŏd') *n.* The hard, dark or reddish wood of a tropical tree.

Rosh Ha·sha·nah (rŏsh hə-shä'nə, rōsh). Also **Rosh Ha·sha·na, Rosh Ha·sho·na** (hə-shō'nə), **Rosh Ha·sho·nah.** The Jewish New Year, celebrated in September or early October. [Heb *rōsh hashānāh,* beginning of the year.]

ros·in (rŏz'ĭn) *n.* A brown or yellowish resin derived from the sap of pine trees and used to increase friction on the bows of certain stringed instruments and in varnishes and other products. [< RESIN.]

ros·ter (rŏs'tər) *n.* A list of names, esp. of officers and men enrolled for military duty. [Du *rooster,* gridiron, list.]

Ros·tov (rŏs'tŏv). A Soviet city on the Don. Pop. 789,000.

ros·trum (rŏs'trəm) *n., pl.* **-trums** or **-tra.** (-trə). A dais or platform for public speaking. [L, beak, ship's prow.]

ros·y (rō'zē) *adj.* **-ier, -iest.** 1. Having the characteristic pink or red color of a rose. 2. Bright; cheery; optimistic. 3. Flushed with a healthy glow. —**ros'i·ly** *adv.* —**ros'i·ness** *n.*

rot (rŏt) *v.* **rotted, rotting.** 1. To decompose; decay. 2. To disappear or fall by decaying. —*n.* 1. The process of rotting. 2. Anything rotting or rotten. 3. Pointless talk. [< OE *rotian* < Gmc *rutjan.*]

ro·ta·ry (rō'tə-rē) *adj.* Of or involving rotation, esp. axial rotation.

ro·tate (rō'tāt') *v.* **-tated, -tating.** 1. To turn or spin on an axis. 2. To alternate in sequence. [L *rotāre,* to revolve.] —**ro'ta·tor** *n.* —**ro'ta·to·ry** (rō'tə-tôr'ē, -tôr'ē) *adj.*

ro·ta·tion (rō-tā'shən) *n.* 1. Motion in which the path of every point in the moving object is a circle or circular arc centered on a specified axis, esp. on an internal axis. 2. A single complete cycle of such motion; revolution. 3. Uniform sequential variation; alternation. —**ro·ta'tion·al** *adj.*

ROTC Reserve Officers' Training Corps.

rote (rōt) *n.* A memorizing process using routine or repetition without full comprehension: *learn by rote.* [ME.]

ro·tis·se·rie (rō-tĭs'ə-rē) *n.* A cooking device equipped with a rotating spit for roasting. [< OF *rostir,* to roast.]

ro·to·gra·vure (rō'tə-grə-vyŏŏr', -grā'vyər) *n.* 1. A process in which letters and pictures are printed from an etched copper cylinder in a rotary press. 2. Material thus printed. [L *rota,* wheel + GRAVURE.]

ro·tor (rō'tər) *n.* A rotating part of an electrical or mechanical device. [Short for ROTATOR.]

rot·ten (rŏt'n) *adj.* 1. Decayed; decomposed. 2. Putrid; stinking. 3. Made unsound by or as by rot. 4. Very bad; wretched. [< ON *rotinn* < Gmc *ruteno-,* akin to *rutjan,* to ROT.] —**rot'ten·ly** *adv.* —**rot'ten·ness** *n.*

Rot·ter·dam (rŏt'ər-dăm). A city of the Netherlands. Pop. 732,000.

ro·tund (rō-tŭnd') *adj.* Rounded; plump. [L *rotundus,* round.] —**ro·tun'di·ty** *n.*

ro·tun·da (rō-tŭn'də) *n.* 1. A circular building or hall, esp. one with a dome. 2. A large room with a high ceiling. [< L *rotundus,* round.]

rou·ble, ru·ble (rōō'bəl) *n.* The basic monetary unit of the Soviet Union.

rou·é (rōō-ā') *n.* A lecherous and dissipated man. [F, "broken on the wheel," completely tired.]

rouge (rōōzh) *n.* 1. A red or pink cosmetic for coloring the cheeks or lips. 2. A reddish powder used to polish metals or glass. —*v.* **rouged, rouging.** To color with rouge. [< L *rubeus,* red.]

rough (rŭf) *adj.* 1. Having an uneven surface; not smooth. 2. Coarse; shaggy. 3. Turbulent; agitated: *rough waters.* 4. Not gentle or careful; violent: *rough handling.* 5. Rude; unmannerly; uncouth. 6. *Informal.* Difficult or unpleasant: *a rough time.* 7. In a crude or unpolished state. 8. Not perfected, elaborated, or completed: *a rough drawing.* —*n.* 1. The part of a golf course left unmowed and uncultivated. 2. Something in an unfinished or hastily worked-out state. —**in the rough.** In a crude or unfinished state. —*v.* 1. To make rough; roughen. 2. To treat roughly or with physical violence. 3. To prepare or indicate in a rough or unfinished form: *rough in the illustrations.* —**rough it.** To get along without the usual comforts. [< OE *rūh.* See ruk-.] —**rough'ly** *adv.* —**rough'ness** *n.*

rough·age (rŭf'ĭj) *n.* The relatively coarse, indigestible parts of certain foods.

rough·en (rŭf'ən) *v.* To make or become rough.

rough·hew (rŭf'hyōō') *v.* 1. To hew or shape roughly, without finishing. 2. To make in rough form.

rough·house (rŭf'hous') *n.* Rowdy, uproarious play or behavior. —*v.* **-housed, -housing.** To engage in roughhouse.

rough·neck (rŭf'nĕk') *n.* A pugnacious fellow; a rowdy.

rough·shod (rŭf'shŏd') *adj.* —**ride roughshod over.** To treat inconsiderately or arrogantly.

rou·lette (rōō-lĕt') *n.* A gambling game played with a rotating disk having numbered slots in which a small ball will come to rest. [< L *rota,* a wheel.]

Rou·ma·ni·a. See Rumania.

Rou·ma·ni·an. Variant of Rumanian.

round (round) *adj.* 1. Spherical; globular; ball-shaped. 2. Circular. 3. Curved. 4. Complete; full: *a round dozen.* 5. Expressed or designated as a whole number or integer; not fractional. 6. Approximate; not exact: *a round estimate.* —*n.* 1. Something round, as a circle, disk, globe, or ring. 2. A cut of beef between the rump and shank. 3. A complete course, succession, or series: *a round of parties.* 4. Often **rounds.** A course of customary or prescribed actions, duties, or places. 5. A single distribution, as of drinks. 6. A single outburst of applause. 7. **a.** A single shot or volley. **b.** Ammunition for a single shot; a cartridge. 8. A period of play or action in various sports. 9. *Mus.* A musical form in which the same melody is repeated by successive overlapping voices. —*v.* 1. To make or become round. 2. To make or become plump. 3. To bring to completion or perfection. 4. To go or pass around. **5.** To make a turn about or to the other side of. **6.** To encompass; surround. —*adv.* **1.** Around. **2.** Throughout: *the year round.* —*prep.* Around. [< L *rotundus.*] —**round'ness** *n.*

round•a•bout (round'ə-bout') *adj.* Indirect; circuitous.

roun•de•lay (roun'də-lā') *n.* A poem or song with a regularly recurring refrain. [< OF *rondel,* "small circle."]

round•house (round'hous') *n.* **1.** A circular building for housing and switching locomotives. **2.** *Slang.* A punch or swing delivered with a sweeping sidearm movement.

round•ly (round'lē) *adv.* **1.** In the form of a circle or sphere. **2.** Vigorously; bluntly. **3.** Fully; thoroughly.

round robin. A tournament in which each contestant is matched against every other contestant.

round-shoul•dered (round'shōl'dərd) *adj.* Having the shoulders and upper back rounded: *a round-shouldered man.*

round-the-clock (round'thə-klŏk') *adj.* Throughout the entire day; continuous.

round trip. A trip from one place to another and back; two-way trip. —**round'-trip'** *adj.*

round up. **1.** To seek out and bring together; gather. **2.** To herd (cattle) together.

round•up (round'ŭp') *n.* **1.** The herding together of cattle. **2.** A gathering up of persons under suspicion by the police. **3.** A summing up; summation; résumé.

rouse (rouz) *v.* **roused, rousing.** **1.** To bring out of a state of slumber or apathy. **2.** To excite, as to anger or action; spur. [< ME *rowsen,* to shake feathers or body.] —**rous'er** *n.*

Rous•seau (rōō-sō'), **Jean Jacques.** 1712–1778. French philosopher and social reformer.

roust•a•bout (roust'ə-bout') *n.* A laborer employed for transient or unskilled jobs, as on a wharf or in a circus or oil field. [< ROUSE + ABOUT.]

rout (rout) *n.* **1.** A disorderly retreat or flight following defeat. **2.** An overwhelming defeat. —*v.* **1.** To put to disorderly flight or retreat. **2.** To defeat overwhelmingly. [< L *rumpere* (pp *ruptus*), to break.]

route (rōōt, rout) *n.* **1.** A road, course, or way for travel from one place to another. **2.** A fixed course or territory assigned to a salesman or deliveryman. —*v.* **1.** To send along; forward. **2.** To schedule or dispatch on a certain route. [< VL *rupta (via),* "broken or beaten (way)."]

rou•tine (rōō-tēn') *n.* **1.** A prescribed and detailed method of procedure. **2.** A set of customary and often mechanically performed activities. —*adj.* **1.** Habitual; regular. **2.** Lacking in interest or originality. [< ROUTE.] —**rou•tine'ly** *adv.*

rove[1] (rōv) *v.* **roved, roving.** To wander about at random, esp. over a wide area; roam. [Prob < Scand.]

rove[2] (rov). Alternate *p.t.* & *p.p.* of **reeve.**

rov•er (rō'vər) *n.* **1.** One who roves; wanderer; nomad. **2.** A pirate or pirate vessel. [Sense 2 < MDu *rōven,* to rob.]

row[1] (rō) *n.* **1.** A horizontal linear arrangement or array. **2.** A line of adjacent seats, as in a theater. [< OE *rāw, rǣw.* See rei-[1].]

row[2] (rō) *v.* **rowed, rowing. 1.** To propel (a boat) with or as with oars. **2.** To travel or carry in a rowboat. —*n.* A trip or excursion in a rowboat. [< OE *rōwan.* See erə-.] —**row'er** *n.*

row[3] (rou) *n.* A boisterous disturbance or quarrel; brawl. —*v.* To take part in a row. [?]

row•an (rou'ən) *n.* A small tree with white flowers and orange-red berries. [< Scand.]

row•boat (rō'bōt') *n.* A small boat propelled by oars.

row•dy (rou'dē) *n., pl.* **-dies.** A rough, disorderly person. —*adj.* **-dier, -diest.** Disorderly; rough. [Prob < ROW[3].]

row•el (rou'əl) *n.* A sharp-toothed wheel inserted into the end of a spur. [< L *rota,* a wheel.]

roy•al (roi'əl) *adj.* **1.** Of or pertaining to a king, queen, or other monarch. **2.** Befitting a king; stately. [< L *rēgālis,* regal.] —**roy'al•ly** *adv.*

royal blue. Deep to strong blue.

roy•al•ist (roi'əl-ĭst) *n.* A supporter of a king or monarchy.

roy•al•ty (roi'əl-tē) *n., pl.* **-ties. 1.** Monarchs and their families collectively. **2.** The power, status, or authority of monarchs. **3.** Royal quality or bearing. **4. a.** A share paid to an author or composer out of the proceeds resulting from the sale or performance of his work. **b.** A share paid to an inventor for the right to use his invention.

r.p.m. revolutions per minute.

r.p.s. revolutions per second.

rpt. report.

RR railroad.

–rrhea. *comb. form.* A flow or discharge: **pyor-rhea.** [< Gk *rhein,* to flow.]

R.S. 1. recording secretary. **2.** right side. **3.** Royal Society.

R.S.V. Revised Standard Version (of the Bible).

r.s.v.p. répondez s'il vous plaît (English *please reply*).

rt. right.

rte. route.

Ru ruthenium.

rub (rŭb) *v.* **rubbed, rubbing. 1.** To apply pressure and friction to (a surface). **2.** To apply firmly and with friction upon a surface. **3.** To contact or cause to contact repeatedly and with friction; scrape. **4.** To become or cause to become chafed or irritated. **5.** To remove or erase (with *out* or *off*). —*n.* **1.** The act of rubbing. **2.** An obstacle or difficulty. [ME *rubben.*]

rub•ber[1] (rŭb'ər) *n.* **1.** Any of numerous elastic materials of varying chemical composition, some natural and others synthetic. **2.** Often **rubbers.** A low overshoe made of rubber.

rub•ber[2] (rŭb'ər) *n.* A series of games of which two out of three must be won to terminate the play. [?]

rub•ber•ize (rŭb'ər-īz') *v.* **-ized, -izing.** To coat, treat, or impregnate with rubber.

rub•ber•y (rŭb'ər-ē) *adj.* Of or like rubber; elastic; resilient.

ă pat/ā ate/âr care/ä bar/b bib/ch chew/d deed/ĕ pet/ē be/f fit/g gag/h hat/hw what/
ĭ pit/ī pie/îr pier/j judge/k kick/l lid, fatal/m mum/n no, sudden/ng sing/ŏ pot/ō go/

rub·bish (rŭb'ĭsh) *n.* **1.** Refuse; garbage; litter. **2.** Worthless material. **3.** Nonsense. [< NF *robel,* RUBBLE.]

rub·ble (rŭb'əl) *n.* **1.** Fragments of stone or brick used in masonry. **2.** The debris remaining after severe destruction: *reduce to rubble.* [< NF *robel,* "rubbings."]

rub·down (rŭb'doun') *n.* A vigorous massage of the body.

rube (rōōb) *n. Slang.* An unsophisticated country fellow.

ru·bel·la (rōō-bĕl'ə) *n.* **German measles.** [< L *rubellus,* reddish.]

Ru·bens (rōō'bənz), **Peter Paul.** 1577–1640. Flemish painter.

ru·bi·cund (rōō'bə-kənd) *adj.* Inclined to a healthy rosiness; ruddy. [L *rubicundus.*]

ru·bid·i·um (rōō-bĭd'ē-əm) *n. Symbol* **Rb** A soft silvery-white, highly reactive alkali element used in photoelectric cells and in the manufacture of vacuum tubes. Atomic number 37, atomic weight 85.47. [< L *rubidus,* red.]

ru·ble. Variant of **rouble.**

ru·bric (rōō'brĭk) *n.* **1.** A title, heading, or initial letter, usually written in red. **2.** A title or heading of a statute or chapter in a code of law. **3.** A direction in a missal, hymnal, or other liturgical book. [< L *rubrica (terra),* "red earth."]

ru·by (rōō'bē) *n., pl.* **-bies. 1.** A deep-red, translucent corundum, highly valued as a precious stone. **2.** A dark red. [< L *rubeus,* red.]

ruck·us (rŭk'əs) *n. Informal.* A noisy disturbance; commotion.

rud·der (rŭd'ər) *n.* A vertically hinged plate mounted at the rear of a vessel or aircraft, used for directing or altering its course. [< OE *rōther,* steering oar. See **erə-**.]

rud·dy (rŭd'ē) *adj.* **-dier, -diest. 1.** Having a healthy, reddish color. **2.** Reddish; rosy. [< OE *rudu,* red color. See **reudh-**.] **—rud'di·ly** *adv.* **—rud'di·ness** *n.*

rude (rōōd) *adj.* **ruder, rudest. 1.** Impolite; uncivil; discourteous. **2.** Formed without skill or precision; makeshift; crude. [< L *rudis,* rough, raw.] **—rude'ly** *adv.* **—rude'ness** *n.*

ru·di·ment (rōō'də-mənt) *n.* Often **rudiments. 1.** A fundamental element, principle, or skill. **2.** Something in an incipient or incompletely developed form. [< L *rudis,* RUDE.] **—ru'di·men'ta·ry** (-mĕn'tər-ē) *adj.*

rue[1] (rōō) *v.* **rued, ruing.** To feel remorse or sorrow for; regret; repent. [< OE *hrēowan,* to make penitent, distress. See **kreu-**[2].]

rue[2] (rōō) *n.* A strong-smelling Old World plant formerly used in medicine. [< Gk *rhutē.*]

rue·ful (rōō'fəl) *adj.* **1.** Inspiring pity or compassion. **2.** Expressive of a bitter, faintly sardonic compassion; wry. **—rue'ful·ly** *adv.*

ruff (rŭf) *n.* **1.** A stiffly starched frilled collar worn in the 16th and 17th centuries. **2.** A collarlike projecting growth, as of feathers or fur. [Short for RUFFLE.]

ruf·fi·an (rŭf'ē-ən, rŭf'yən) *n.* A tough or rowdy fellow. [< It *ruffiano,* pander, "filthy or scabby person."]

ruf·fle (rŭf'əl) *n.* **1.** A strip of frilled or closely pleated fabric used for trimming or decoration. **2.** A slight disturbance. *—v.* **-fled, -fling. 1.** To disturb the smoothness of; ripple. **2.** To pleat or gather (fabric) into a ruffle. **3.** To erect (the feathers). **4.** To discompose; fluster. **5.** To flip through (the pages of a book). [ME *ruffelen,* to roughen, disarrange.]

rug (rŭg) *n.* A piece of heavy fabric or animal skin used as a floor covering. [Prob < Swed *rugg,* ruffled hair.]

Rug·by football (rŭg'bē). A British form of football. [< *Rugby* School, Warwickshire, England.]

rug·ged (rŭg'ĭd) *adj.* **1.** Having a rough, irregular surface. **2.** Marked with furrows or wrinkles. **3.** Hard; trying; severe. **4.** Vigorously healthy; hardy. [< Scand.] **—rug'ged·ness** *n.*

Ruhr (rōōr). A river of West Germany.

ru·in (rōō'ĭn) *n.* **1. a.** Total destruction or disintegration. **b.** The cause of such destruction. **2.** Often **ruins.** The remains of something destroyed. *—v.* **1.** To reduce to ruin. **2.** To harm irreparably. **3.** To reduce to poverty or bankruptcy. [< L *ruina,* "fall."] **—ru'in·a'tion** *n.* **—ru'in·ous** *adj.* **—ru'in·ous·ly** *adv.*

rule (rōōl) *n.* **1.** Governing power. **2.** An authoritative direction for conduct or procedure. **3.** Something that generally prevails or obtains. **4.** A standard method or procedure. **5.** A straight-edge; ruler. *—v.* **ruled, ruling. 1.** To exercise control (over); govern. **2.** To dominate; hold sway over. **3.** To decide judicially; decree. **4.** To mark with straight parallel lines. **—rule out.** To exclude. [< L *rēgula,* straight stick, ruler, rule, pattern.]

rul·er (rōō'lər) *n.* **1.** One who rules or governs, as a sovereign. **2.** A straight-edged strip for drawing straight lines and measuring lengths.

rul·ing (rōō'lĭng) *adj.* Exercising control; governing. *—n.* **1.** The act of governing or controlling. **2.** An authoritative or official decision.

rum (rŭm) *n.* An alcoholic liquor distilled from fermented molasses or sugar cane.

Ru·ma·ni·a (rōō-mā'nē-ə, -nyə). Also **Ro·ma·ni·a** (rō-), **Rou·ma·ni·a** (rōō-). A country of SE Europe. Pop. 18,927,000. Cap. Bucharest.

Ru·ma·ni·an (rōō-mā'nē-ən, -mān'yən) *n.* Also **Ro·ma·ni·an** (rō-mā'nē-ən, -nyən), **Rou·ma·ni·an** (rōō-mā'nē-ən, -nyən). **1.** An inhab-

Rumania

itant or native of Rumania. **2.** The Romance language of the Rumanian people. —**Ru•ma′ni•an** *adj.*

rum•ba (rŭm′bə) *n.* A rhythmical dance that originated among Cuban Negroes. [< Amer Span *rumbo,* carousel.]

rum•ble (rŭm′bəl) *v.* **-bled, -bling. 1.** To make a continuous deep, heavy, reverberating sound. **2.** To move or proceed with such a sound. —*n.* A continuous deep, heavy, rolling sound. [ME *romblen.*] —**rum′bly** *adj.*

ru•mi•nant (rōo′mə-nənt) *n.* Any of a group of hoofed, cud-chewing mammals, including cattle, sheep, goats, and deer. —*adj.* **1.** Chewing cud. **2.** Meditative; contemplative. [< L *rūmināre,* to RUMINATE.]

ru•mi•nate (rōo′mə-nāt′) *v.* **-nated, -nating. 1.** To chew cud. **2.** To meditate at length; muse. [L *rūmināre.*] —**ru′mi•na′tion** *n.*

rum•mage (rŭm′ĭj) *v.* **-maged, -maging. 1.** To discover by searching thoroughly. **2.** To make an energetic, hasty search. [Orig "arrangement of cargo in a ship's hold," odds and ends.] —**rum′mag•er** *n.*

rummage sale. A sale of secondhand miscellaneous objects.

rum•my (rŭm′ē) *n.* A card game in which the object is to obtain sets of three or more cards of the same denomination or suit. [?]

ru•mor (rōo′mər). Also *chiefly Brit.* **ru•mour.** *n.* Unverified information of uncertain origin. —*v.* To spread rumor. [< L *rūmor.*]

rump (rŭmp) *n.* **1. a.** The often fleshy hind part of an animal. **b.** A cut of beef or veal from this part. **2.** The last or inferior part of something. [< Scand.]

rum•ple (rŭm′pəl) *v.* **-pled, -pling.** To wrinkle or form into folds or creases. [< MDu *rumpelen.*] —**rum′ple** *n.* —**rum′ply** *adj.*

rum•pus (rŭm′pəs) *n.* A noisy clamor. [?]

rum•run•ner (rŭm′rŭn′ər) *n.* One who illegally transports liquor across a border.

run (rŭn) *v.* **ran, run, running. I.** To move or cause to move rapidly. **1.** To move on foot at a pace faster than the walk. **2.** To retreat rapidly; flee. **3.** To move without hindrance or restraint. **4.** To make a short, quick trip. **5.** To swim in large numbers, as in migrating. **6. a.** To hurry; hasten. **b.** To have frequent recourse to someone or something. **II.** To compete or cause to compete. **7.** To take part in a race. **8.** To compete for elected office. **9.** To finish a race in a specified position. **III.** To move or cause to move in a specified way. **10.** To move freely, as by rolling or sliding. **11.** To be in operation. **12.** To go regularly. **13.** To sail or steer before the wind or on an indicated course. **IV.** To flow or cause to flow. **14.** To flow in a steady stream. **15.** To melt and flow. **16.** To flow and spread. **17.** To be wet with: *streets running with blood.* **18.** To overflow. **19.** To discharge; drain. **20.** To surge, as waves. **V.** To extend in space. **21.** To extend, stretch, or reach. **22.** To spread or climb, as vines. **23.** To spread rapidly. **24.** To be valid in a given area: *The writ runs only to the county line.* **25.** To unravel along a line. **VI.** To extend in time. **26.** To continue. **27.** To

pass. **28.** To persist or recur. **29.** *Law.* **a.** To be effective. **b.** To be concurrent with: *Fishing tickets run with the ownership of land.* **30. a.** To accumulate or accrue. **b.** To become payable. **31.** To be expressed in a given way. **32.** To tend or incline. **33.** To be channeled. **34.** To vary or range in quality, price, size, proportion, etc. **35.** To come into or out of a specified condition. —*n.* **I. 1. a.** A pace faster than the walk. **b.** A gait faster than the canter. **2.** An act of running. **3. a.** A distance covered by or as by running. **b.** The time taken to cover it. **4.** A quick trip or visit. **5.** *Baseball.* **a.** The process of scoring a point by running from home plate around the bases and back to home plate. **b.** The point so scored. **6.** A shoaling or migrating of fish prior to spawning. **7.** Unrestricted freedom or use of: *the run of the library.* **II. 8. a.** A journey between points on a scheduled route. **b.** The time taken to cover this distance. **9.** A continuous period of operation by a machine, factory, etc. **III. 10.** A movement or flow, as of fluid or sand. **11.** A pipe or channel through which something flows: *a mill run.* **IV. 12.** A continuous length or extent of something. **13.** The direction, configuration, or lie of something: *the run of the grain in leather.* **14.** An outdoor enclosure for domestic animals or poultry. **15.** A length of torn or unraveled stitches in a knitted fabric. **V. 16.** An unbroken series or sequence. **17.** An unbroken sequence of theatrical performances. **18.** A series of unexpected and urgent demands by customers: *a run on a bank.* **19. a.** In certain games, a continuous set or sequence, as of playing cards in one suit. **b.** A successful sequence of shots or points. **20.** A sustained state or condition: *a run of good luck.* **21.** A trend or tendency. **22.** An average type, group, or category; majority: *the broad run of voters.* —**in the long run.** In the final analysis or outcome. —**on the run. 1.** In hiding. **2.** Hurrying busily from place to place. [< OE *rinnan.* See er-¹.]

run•a•bout (rŭn′ə-bout′) *n.* A small open automobile, wagon, or motorboat.

run•a•round (rŭn′ə-round′) *n.* Deception in the form of evasive excuses.

run•a•way (rŭn′ə-wā′) *n.* **1.** One that runs away. **2.** An act of running away. **3.** *Informal.* An easy victory. —*adj.* **1.** Escaping or having escaped from captivity or control. **2.** Of or done by running away. **3.** Easily won, as a race.

run down. 1. a. To slow down and stop because of a failure of motive power. **b.** To exhaust or wear out. **2.** To pursue and capture. **3.** To hit with a moving vehicle. **4.** To disparage; decry. **5.** To give a brief or summary account of.

run-down (rŭn′doun′) *n.* A summary or résumé. —*adj.* **1.** In poor condition. **2.** Unwound and not running.

rune (rōon) *n.* **1.** One of the letters of an alphabet used by ancient Germanic peoples. **2.** A poem written in runic characters. **3.** Magic. [< ON *rūn,* secret writing, rune.] —**run′ic** *adj.*

ă pat/ā ate/âr care/ä bar/b bib/ch chew/d deed/ĕ pet/ē be/f fit/g gag/h hat/hw what/ ĭ pit/ī pie/îr pier/j judge/k kick/l lid, fatal/m mum/n no, sudden/ng sing/ŏ pot/ō go/

rung¹ (rŭng) *n.* **1.** A bar forming a step of a ladder. **2.** A crosspiece supporting the legs or back of a chair. **3.** A spoke in a wheel. [< OE *hrung*.]

rung² (rŭng). *p.p.* of **ring**.

run in. 1. To insert or include as something extra. **2.** *Slang.* To take into legal custody.

run-in (rŭn′ĭn′) *n.* A quarrel or fight.

run•let (rŭn′lĭt) *n.* A rivulet. [Dim of RUN (stream).]

run•nel (rŭn′əl) *n.* A narrow channel or rivulet. [< OE *rinnan*, to RUN.]

run•ner (rŭn′ər) *n.* **1.** One who or that which runs, as a messenger or errand boy. **2.** A device in or on which something slides or moves, as the blade of a skate. **3.** A long narrow carpet or tablecloth. **4.** A creeping stem that roots at intervals along its length.

run•ner-up (rŭn′ər-ŭp′) *n.* One that takes second place.

running gear. 1. The working parts of an automobile or other vehicle. **2.** The part of a ship's rigging that comprises the ropes with which sails are raised or lowered, booms are operated, etc.

run•ny (rŭn′ē) *adj.* **-nier, -niest.** Inclined to run.

run-off (rŭn′ôf′, -ŏf′) *n.* An extra competition held to break a tie.

runt (rŭnt) *n.* **1.** An undersized animal, esp. the smallest of a litter. **2.** An undersized person. [Poss < Du *rund*, small ox.] —**runt′i•ness** *n.* —**runt′y** *adj.*

run through. 1. To pierce. **2.** To use up

f u th a r k

g w h n i j e

p z s t b e

m l ng o d

basic Germanic
runic alphabet

ð ȝ

edh yogh

two later runes
used in English

rune

(money) quickly. **3.** To examine or rehearse quickly.

run-through (rŭn′thrōō′) *n.* A complete but rapid review or rehearsal of something.

run•way (rŭn′wā′) *n.* **1.** A path, channel, or track over which something runs. **2.** A narrow walkway extending from a stage into an auditorium. **3.** A strip on which aircraft take off and land.

ru•pee (rōō-pē′, rōō′pē) *n.* **1.** The basic monetary unit of Ceylon and Mauritius. **2.** The basic monetary unit of India. **3.** The basic monetary unit of Nepal. **4.** The basic monetary unit of Pakistan.

ru•pi•ah (rōō-pē′ä) *n., pl.* **-ah** or **-ahs.** The basic monetary unit of Indonesia.

rup•ture (rŭp′chər) *n.* **1.** A breaking open or bursting. **2.** A tear in bodily tissue. [< L *rumpere* (pp *ruptus*), to break.] —**rup′ture** *v.* **(-tured, -turing).**

ru•ral (rōōr′əl) *adj.* Of or pertaining to the country as opposed to the city; rustic. [< L *rūs (rūr-)*, country.] —**ru′ral•ly** *adv.*

ruse (rōōz) *n.* A trick; artifice; strategem. [< OF *ruser*, to repulse, detour.]

rush¹ (rŭsh) *v.* **1.** To move or act swiftly. **2.** To attack; charge. **3.** To perform with great haste. —*n.* **1.** A sudden forward motion. **2.** General haste or busyness. **3.** A sudden onslaught. **4.** A great flurry of activity or press of business. [< L *recusāre*, to object to.] —**rush′er** *n.*

rush² (rŭsh) *n.* A grasslike marsh plant with hollow or pithy stems. [< OE *rysc.* See **rezg-**.]

Russ. Russia; Russian.

rus•set (rŭs′ĭt) *n.* **1.** Moderate to strong brown. **2.** A reddish-brown homespun cloth. **3.** A winter apple with a reddish-brown skin. [< L *russus*, red.] —**rus′set** *adj.*

Rus•sia (rŭsh′ə). **1.** The name commonly applied to the **Union of Soviet Socialist Republics.** **2.** The **Russian Soviet Federated Socialist Republic.**

Rus•sian (rŭsh′ən) *n.* **1.** A native or inhabitant of Russia. **2.** One of Russian descent. **3.** The Slavic language of the Russian people. —**Rus′sian** *adj.*

Russian dressing. Mayonnaise with chili sauce, chopped pickles, and pimientos.

Russian Orthodox Church. 1. An independent branch of the Eastern Orthodox Church in the Soviet Union headed by the Patriarch of Moscow. **2.** A branch of this church outside the Soviet Union.

Russian Soviet Federated Socialist Republic. The largest republic of the Soviet Union, in Europe and Asia. Pop. 130,090,000. Cap. Moscow.

rust (rŭst) *n.* **1.** Any of various reddish oxides formed on iron by low-temperature oxidation in the presence of water. **2.** A stain or coating resembling iron dust. **3.** A plant disease caused by parasitic fungi, characterized by brownish spots on leaves and stems. **4.** Reddish brown. —*v.* **1.** To corrode. **2.** To deteriorate through inactivity. **3.** To become the color of rust. [< OE *rūst.* See **reudh-**.] —**rust′i•ness** *n.* —**rust′y** *adj.*

ô paw, for/oi boy/ou out/ŏŏ took/ōō coo/p pop/r run/s sauce/sh shy/t to/th thin/*th* the/
ŭ cut/ûr fur/v van/w wag/y yes/z size/zh vision/ə ago, item, edible, gallop, circus/

rus•tic (rŭs′tĭk) *adj.* **1.** Typical of country life. **2.** Unsophisticated; bucolic. **3.** Made of rough tree branches: *rustic furniture.* —*n.* **1.** A country person. **2.** A simpleton. [< L *rūs,* country.] —**rus′ti•cal•ly** *adv.* —**rus•tic′i•ty** (-tĭs′ə-tē) *n.*

rus•ti•cate (rŭs′tĭ-kāt′) *v.* -cated, -cating. To go to or live in the country. —**rus′ti•ca′tion** *n.* —**rus′ti•ca′tor** *n.*

rus•tle¹ (rŭs′əl) *v.* -tled, -tling. **1.** To move with soft whispering sounds. **2.** To cause to make such sounds. [ME *rustelen.*] —**rus′tle** *n.*. —**rus′tler** *n.* —**rus′tling•ly** *adv.*

rus•tle² (rŭs′əl) *v.* -tled, -tling. **1.** To steal cattle. **2.** *Informal.* To forage. [Prob < RUSTLE.] —**rus′tler** *n.*

rut¹ (rŭt) *n.* **1.** A sunken track or groove made by the passage of wheels. **2.** A fixed routine of thought or action. [OF *route,* way, route.]

rut² (rŭt) *n.* A condition of sexual excitement and reproductive activity in male mammals, as deer. —*v.* **rutted, rutting.** To be in rut. [< L *rūgire,* to roar.]

ru•ta•ba•ga (rōō′tə-bā′gə) *n.* A turniplike plant with a thick, bulbous, edible root. [Swed (dial) *rotabagge,* "baggy root."]

ru•the•ni•um (rōō-thē′nē-əm) *n. Symbol* **Ru** A hard white acid-resistant metallic element used to harden platinum and palladium and in nonmagnetic wear-resistant alloys. Atomic number 44, atomic weight 101.07. [< ML *Ruthenia,* Russia.]

ruth•less (rōōth′lĭs) *adj.* Having no compassion or pity; merciless. [< OE *hrēowan,* to rue + -LESS.] —**ruth′less•ly** *adv.* —**ruth′less•ness** *n.*

Rwan•da (rwän′dä, rōō-än′-). A republic of east-central Africa. Pop. 3,000,000. Cap. Kigali.

Rwanda

Rwy., Ry. railway.

–ry. Variant of **-ery.**

rye (rī) *n.* **1.** A widely cultivated cereal grass. **2.** The grain of this plant, used in making flour and whiskey. **3.** Whiskey made from rye. [< OE *ryge.* See **wrughyo-.**]

Ryu•kyu Islands (ryōō′kyōō′). A group of islands in the Pacific between Kyushu, Japan, and Taiwan.

Ss

s, S (ĕs) *n.* **1.** The 19th letter of the English alphabet. **2. S** Anything shaped like the letter S.

s 1. second. **2.** south; southern. **3.** stere.

S 1. small. **2.** south; southern. **3.** sulfur.

s. 1. small. **2.** son. **3.** south; southern. **4.** substantive.

S. 1. Saturday. **2.** school. **3.** sea. **4.** September. **5.** south; southern. **6.** Sunday.

–s¹. *comb. form.* Indicates the plural form: *toys.* [< OE *-as.*]

–s². *comb. form.* Indicates the 3rd person sing. form of the present indicative: *She sleeps.* [< OE *-es, -as.*]

–s³. *comb. form.* Used in the formation of certain adverbs from nouns and adjectives: *unawares.*

–'s¹. *comb. form.* Indicates the possessive case: *men's.* [< OE *-es.*]

–'s². **1.** Contraction of **is:** *She's here.* **2.** Contraction of **has:** *He's been eating.* **3.** Contraction of **us:** *Let's go.*

Sab•bath (săb′əth) *n.* **1.** The 7th day of the week, Saturday, observed as the day of rest and worship by Jews and some Christian sects. **2.** The 1st day of the week, Sunday, observed as the day of rest by most Christian churches. [< Heb *shâbhath,* to rest.]

sa•ber (sā′bər) *n.* Also *chiefly Brit.* **sa•bre.** **1.** A heavy cavalry sword with a one-edged, slightly curved blade. **2.** A two-edged sword used in fencing. [< MHG *sabel, sebel.*]

Sa•bin vaccine (sā′bĭn). A live attenuated virus taken orally to immunize against poliomyelitis. [< A. *Sabin* (born 1906), American physician.]

sa•ble (sā′bəl) *n.* **1.** A weasellike mammal of N Eurasia, having soft, dark fur. **2.** The valuable fur of this animal. **3. a.** The color black. **b. sables.** Black garments worn in mourning. [< ML *sabelum.*] —**sa′ble** *adj.*

sab•o•tage (săb′ə-täzh′) *n.* **1.** The damaging of property or procedure so as to obstruct productivity or normal functioning. **2.** Any underhanded effort to defeat or do harm to an endeavor; deliberate subversion. [< F *sabo-*

ter, "to clatter shoes," work clumsily.] —**sab'-o•tage'** *v.* (-taged, -taging).

sab•o•teur (săb'ə-tûr') *n.* One who commits sabotage.

sa•bra (sä'brə, -brä) *n.* A native-born Israeli. [Heb *Şabēr.*]

sa•bre. *Chiefly Brit.* Variant of **saber.**

sac (săk) *n.* A pouchlike plant or animal structure. [< L *saccus,* a sack.]

SAC Strategic Air Command.

sac•cha•rin (săk'ə-rĭn) *n.* An extremely sweet crystalline powder, $C_7H_5NO_3S$, used as a calorie-free sweetener. [< Gk *sakkharon,* sugar.]

sac•cha•rine (săk'ə-rĭn, -rīn') *adj.* 1. Of, relating to, or of the nature of sugar or saccharin; sweet. 2. Having a cloyingly sweet attitude, tone, or character.

sac•er•do•tal (săs'ər-dōt'l, săk'-) *adj.* Of or pertaining to priests or the priesthood; priestly. [< L *sacerdōs,* a priest.]

sa•chem (sā'chəm) *n.* The chief of a tribe or confederation among some North American Indians. [< Algon.]

sa•chet (să-shā') *n.* A small bag containing perfumed powder, used to scent clothes. [< OF, a small bag.]

sack[1] (săk) *n.* 1. A large bag of strong, coarse material. 2. A similar but smaller container, often of paper or plastic. 3. A short, loose-fitting coat or dress. 4. *Slang.* Dismissal from employment: *get the sack.* 5. *Slang.* A bed. —*v.* 1. To place in a sack. 2. *Slang.* To discharge from employment. [< Gk *sakkos.*]

sack[2] (săk) *v.* To loot or pillage. [< OF *(mettre a) sac,* (to put in) a sack, plunder.] —**sack** *n.*

sack•cloth (săk'klôth') *n.* 1. A rough cloth. 2. Garments made of this cloth, worn as a symbol of mourning or penitence.

sack•ing (săk'ĭng) *n.* Stout woven cloth used for making sacks.

sac•ra•ment (săk'rə-mənt) *n.* 1. Any of the rites of the Christian church considered to have been instituted by Christ, as the Eucharist, baptism, etc. 2. **Sacrament.** The consecrated elements of the Eucharist. [< L *sacrāre,* to consecrate.] —**sac'ra•men'tal** (-měn'təl) *adj.* —**sac'ra•men'tal•ly** *adv.*

Sac•ra•men•to (săk'rə-měn'tō). The capital of California. Pop. 258,000.

sa•cred (sā'krĭd) *adj.* 1. Dedicated to or set apart for worship. 2. Made or declared holy. 3. Dedicated or devoted exclusively to a single use or person. 4. Worthy of reverence or respect. 5. Of or pertaining to religious as opposed to secular things; not secular or profane. [< L *sacer,* dedicated, holy, sacred.] —**sa'cred•ly** *adv.* —**sa'cred•ness** *n.*

sac•ri•fice (săk'rə-fis) *n.* 1. The offering of something to a deity. 2. a. The forfeiture of something highly valued for the sake of someone or something considered to have a greater value or claim. b. Something so forfeited. 3. a. A relinquishing of something at less than its presumed value. b. A loss so sustained. —*v.* -**ficed, -ficing.** 1. To offer as a sacrifice. 2. To forfeit something for something considered to have a greater value or claim. 3. To sell or give

away at a loss. [< L *sacrificium.*] —**sac'ri•fic'er** *n.* —**sac'ri•fi'cial** (-fĭsh'əl) *adj.* —**sac'ri•fi'cial•ly** *adv.*

sac•ri•lege (săk'rə-lĭj) *n.* The misuse, theft, desecration, or profanation of anything regarded as sacred. [< L *sacrilegus,* one who steals sacred things.] —**sac'ri•le'gious** (-lē'jəs) *adj.* —**sac'ri•le'gious•ness** *n.*

sac•ris•tan (săk'rĭs-tən) *n.* 1. A person in charge of a sacristy. 2. A sexton. [< ML *sacrista,* "one in charge of sacred vessels."]

sac•ris•ty (săk'rĭs-tē) *n., pl.* -ties. A room in a church housing the sacred vessels and vestments; vestry.

sac•ro•sanct (săk'rō-săngkt') *adj.* Regarded as inviolably sacred. [L *sacrōsanctus,* consecrated with religious ceremonies.]

sa•crum (sā'krəm) *n., pl.* -cra (-krə). A triangular bone that forms the posterior section of the pelvis. [< LL *(os) sacrum,* "sacred bone."]

sad (săd) *adj.* **sadder, saddest.** 1. Sorrowful; unhappy. 2. Causing or expressing sorrow. 3. Deplorable; sorry. [< OE *sæd,* sated, weary. See sā-.] —**sad'ly** *adv.* —**sad'ness** *n.*

sad•den (săd'n) *v.* To make or become sad.

sad•dle (săd'l) *n.* 1. A leather seat for a rider, secured on an animal's back by a girth. 2. A cut of meat, as lamb, including the backbone. —**in the saddle.** In a position of control. —*v.* -**dled, -dling.** 1. To put a saddle on (a horse). 2. To load or burden; encumber. [< OE *sadol.* See sed-.]

sad•dle•bow (săd'l-bō') *n.* The arched upper front part of a saddle; pommel.

saddle horse. A horse bred or schooled for riding.

saddle shoe. A flat casual shoe, usually white, having a band of leather in a contrasting color across the instep.

Sad•du•cee (săj'ōō-sē, săd'yōō-) *n.* An ancient Jewish priestly sect that opposed the Pharisees. —**Sad'du•ce'an** (-sē'ən) *adj.*

sa•de, sa•dhe (sä'də, -dē) *n.* Also **tsa•de** (tsä'də, -dē). The 18th letter of the Hebrew alphabet, representing *ş.*

sad•i•ron (săd'ī'ərn) *n.* A heavy flatiron with a removable handle. [SAD (in the dial sense of "heavy") + IRON.]

sa•dism (sā'dĭz'əm, săd'ĭz'əm) *n.* 1. The association of sexual satisfaction with the infliction of pain on others. 2. Broadly, delight in cruelty. [< D.A.F. de *Sade* (1740–1814), who expounded principles of anarchic sexual violence.] —**sa'dist** *n.* —**sa•dis'tic** (sə-dĭs'tĭk) *adj.* —**sa•dis'ti•cal•ly** *adv.*

sa•fa•ri (sə-fä'rē) *n.* An overland expedition, esp. for hunting or exploration in Africa. [Ar *safarīy,* a journey.]

safe (sāf) *adj.* **safer, safest.** 1. Not apt to cause or incur danger or harm. 2. Unhurt: *safe and sound.* 3. Free from hazard; sure: *a safe bet.* 4. Affording protection: *a safe place.* 5. *Baseball.* Having reached a base without being put out. —*n.* A metal container or enclosure for storing valuables; strongbox. [< L *salvus,* healthy, uninjured, safe.] —**safe'ly** *adv.*

safe-con•duct (sāf'kŏn'dŭkt) *n.* A document

assuring unmolested passage, as through enemy lines.

safe·guard (sāf′gärd′) *n.* A precautionary measure or device. —*v.* To insure the safety of; protect.

safe·keep·ing (sāf′kē′pĭng) *n.* Protection; care.

safe·ty (sāf′tē) *n., pl.* **-ties.** 1. Freedom from danger or injury. 2. Any of various protective devices. 3. *Football.* **a.** A play in which the offensive team downs the ball behind its own goal line. **b.** A defensive back closest to his own goal line.

safety match. A match that can be lighted only by being struck against a chemically prepared friction surface.

safety pin. A pin in the form of a clasp, having a sheath to cover and hold the point.

saf·fron (săf′rən) *n.* 1. The dried orange-yellow stigmas of a kind of crocus, used to color and flavor food and as a dye. 2. Orange-yellow. [< Ar *za′farān*.] —**saf′fron** *adj.*

sag (săg) *v.* **sagged, sagging.** 1. To sink or bend downward, as from pressure or slackness. 2. To droop. [Perh < Scand.] —**sag** *n.*

sa·ga (sä′gə) *n.* 1. An Icelandic prose narrative of the 12th and 13th centuries. 2. A long heroic narrative. [ON, a story, legend.]

sa·ga·cious (sə-gā′shəs) *adj.* Shrewd and wise. [< L *sagāx.*] —**sa·gac′i·ty** (-găs′ə-tē) *n.*

sage[1] (sāj) *n.* A venerable wise man. —*adj.* **sager, sagest.** Judicious; wise. [< L *sapere,* to be sensible, be wise.] —**sage′ly** *adv.*

sage[2] (sāj) *n.* 1. An aromatic plant with grayish-green leaves used as seasoning. 2. Sagebrush. [< L *salvia,* "the healing plant."]

sage·brush (sāj′brŭsh′) *n.* An aromatic shrub of arid regions of W North America.

sag·it·tal (săj′ə-təl) *adj.* 1. Of or like an arrow or arrowhead. 2. Relating to the suture uniting the two parietal bones of the skull. [< L *sagitta,* arrow.] —**sag′it·tal·ly** *adv.*

Sag·it·ta·ri·us (săj′ə-târ′ē-əs) *n.* 1. A constellation in the S Hemisphere. 2. The 9th sign of the zodiac. [< L *sagittārius,* an archer, Sagittarius.]

sa·go (sā′gō) *n.* A powdery starch obtained from the trunks of an Asian palm. [Malay *sagu.*]

sa·gua·ro (sə-gwär′ō, sə-wär′ō) *n., pl.* **-ros.** Also **sa·hua·ro** (sə-wär′ō). A very large branching cactus of SW North America. [Mex Span.]

Sa·har·a (sə-hâr′ə, -hä′rə). A desert of N Africa.

sa·hib (sä′ĭb) *n.* A title of respect for Europeans in colonial India, equivalent to *master* or *sir.* [Hindi *ṣāhib,* master, lord.]

said (sĕd). *p.t.* & *p.p.* of **say.** —*adj.* Aforementioned.

Sai·gon (sī-gŏn′). Officially, Ho Chi Minh City. A port of Vietnam. Pop. 1,707,000.

sail (sāl) *n.* 1. A length of shaped fabric that catches the wind and propels or aids in maneuvering a vessel. 2. A sailing ship. 3. A trip in a sailing craft. 4. Something resembling a sail. —*v.* 1. To move across the surface of water by means of a sail. 2. To travel by water

in a vessel. 3. To start out on a voyage. 4. To operate a sailing craft; navigate or manage (a vessel). 5. To glide through the air; soar. [< OE *segl* < Gmc **seglam.*]

sail·boat (sāl′bōt′) *n.* A small boat propelled by a sail or sails.

sail·fish (sāl′fĭsh′) *n.* A large marine fish with a large dorsal fin and a spearlike projection from the upper jaw.

sail·or (sā′lər) *n.* 1. One who serves in a navy or earns his living working on a ship. 2. A straw hat with a flat top and brim.

saint (sānt) *n.* 1. *Theol.* **a.** A person officially entitled to public veneration for extreme holiness. **b.** A human soul inhabiting heaven. 2. A very holy or unselfish person. [< L *sanctus,* sacred.] —**saint′dom** *n.* —**saint′hood′** *n.*

saint·ly (sānt′lē) *adj.* **-lier, -liest.** Of or befitting a saint. —**saint′li·ness** *n.*

Saint-Saëns (săn-säns′), **Camille.** 1835–1921. French composer.

saith (sĕth, sā′əth). *Archaic.* 3rd person sing. present indicative of **say.**

sake[1] (sāk) *n.* 1. Purpose; motive: *for the sake of argument.* 2. Advantage, benefit, or welfare. [< OE *sacu,* lawsuit. See **sāg-.**]

sa·ke[2] (sä′kē) *n.* Also **sa·ki.** A Japanese liquor made from fermented rice.

sa·laam (sə-läm′) *n.* An Oriental obeisance performed by bowing low while placing the right palm on the forehead. [Ar *salām,* "peace."] —**sa·laam′** *v.*

sa·la·cious (sə-lā′shəs) *adj.* Lewd; bawdy. [< L *salāx,* fond of leaping, lustful.] —**sa·la′-cious·ly** *adv.* —**sa·la′cious·ness, sa·lac′i·ty** (sə-lăs′ə-tē) *n.*

sal·ad (săl′əd) *n.* A dish usually consisting of raw green vegetables tossed with a dressing. [< VL **salāre,* to salt.]

sal·a·man·der (săl′ə-măn′dər) *n.* 1. A small, lizardlike amphibian. 2. A portable stove used to heat or dry buildings under construction. [< Gk *salamandra.*]

sa·la·mi (sə-lä′mē) *n.* A highly spiced and salted sausage. [< It *salame,* "salted pork."]

sal·a·ried (săl′ə-rēd) *adj.* Earning or yielding a regular salary.

sal·a·ry (săl′ə-rē, săl′rē) *n., pl.* **-ries.** A fixed compensation for services, paid on a regular basis. [< L *salārium,* orig "money given to Roman soldiers to buy salt."]

sale (sāl) *n.* 1. The exchange of property or ownership for money. 2. Demand; ready market. 3. Availability for purchase: *on sale.* 4. An auction. 5. A special disposal of goods at lowered prices. [< OE *sala* < ON.] —**sal′a·ble, sale′a·ble** *adj.*

Sa·lem (sā′ləm). The capital of Oregon. Pop. 68,000.

sales·man (sālz′mən) *n.* A man employed to sell merchandise, insurance, etc. —**sales′man·ship′** *n.* —**sales′wom′an** *fem.n.*

sal·i·cyl·ic acid (săl′ə-sĭl′ĭk). A white crystalline acid, $C_7H_6O_3$, used in making aspirin. [< L *salix,* willow.]

sa·li·ent (sā′lē-ənt) *adj.* 1. Projecting or jutting beyond a line. 2. Striking; conspicuous. [< L *salīre,* to leap, jump.] —**sa′li·ence, sa′li·en·cy** *n.*

sa•line (sā'lēn', -līn') *adj.* Of or containing salt. [< L *săl*, salt.] —**sa•lin'i•ty** (sə-lĭn'ə-tē) *n.*
Salis•bur•y (sôlz'bĕr-ē, -brē). The capital of Rhodesia. Pop. 314,000.
Sa•lish (sā'lĭsh) *n.* Also **Sa•lish•an** (sā'lĭsh-ən, săl'ĭsh-). **1.** A family of languages spoken by North American Indian tribes in the NW U.S. and British Columbia. **2.** The Indians speaking languages of this family. —**Sa'lish•an** *adj.*
sa•li•va (sə-lī'və) *n.* The watery, tasteless liquid mixture of salivary and oral mucous gland secretions that lubricates chewed food, moistens the oral walls, and functions in the digestion of starches. [L *salīva.*] —**sal'i•var'y** (săl'ə-vĕr'ē) *adj.*
salivary gland. A gland that secretes saliva, esp. any of three pairs of large glands the secretions of which enter the mouth and mingle in saliva.
sal•i•vate (săl'ə-vāt') *v.* **-vated, -vating.** To secrete or produce saliva. —**sal'i•va'tion** *n.*
Salk vaccine (sôlk). A killed-virus vaccine used to immunize actively against poliomyelitis. [< J. *Salk* (born 1914), American microbiologist.]
sal•low (săl'ō) *adj.* Of a sickly yellowish hue or complexion. [< OE *salo.* See **sal-²**.] —**sal'low•ly** *adv.* —**sal'low•ness** *n.*
sal•ly (săl'ē) *n., pl.* **-lies. 1.** A sudden assault from a defensive position. **2.** A quick witticism; quip. **3.** A short excursion; jaunt. [< L *salīre*, to leap.] —**sal'ly** *v.* (**-lied, -lying**).
salm•on (săm'ən) *n., pl.* **-on** or **-ons. 1.** Any of various food and game fishes of northern waters, usually having pinkish flesh. **2.** Yellowish pink to reddish orange. [< L *salmō.*] —**salm'on** *adj.*
sa•lon (sə-lŏn') *n.* **1.** An elegant drawing room. **2.** An assemblage of persons, usually of social or intellectual distinction, who frequent such a room. **3.** A shop offering something related to fashion: *beauty salon.* [< It *sala*, a hall, room.]
sa•loon (sə-lōōn') *n.* **1.** A barroom. **2.** A large lounge or ballroom on a ship. [F *salon*, salon.]
sal soda. A hydrated sodium carbonate used as a general cleanser.
salt (sôlt) *n.* **1.** A colorless or white crystalline solid, chiefly sodium chloride, extensively used as a food seasoning and preservative. **2.** A chemical compound formed by replacing all or part of the hydrogen ions of an acid with one or more metallic ions. **3. salts.** Any of various mineral salts used as a laxative or cathartic. **4.** An element that gives flavor or zest. **5.** Wit or pungency of expression. **6.** *Informal.* A veteran sailor. —*adj.* **1.** Tasting of salt. **2.** Preserved in salt. —*v.* To season, cure, or feed with salt. [< OE *sealt.* See **sal-¹**.] —**salt'i•ness** *n.* —**salt'y** *adj.*
salt•cel•lar (sôlt'sĕl'ər) *n.* A small dish or shaker for salt. [Var of ME *salt saler.*]
sal•tine (sôl-tēn') *n.* A thin salted cracker.
Salt Lake City. The capital of Utah. Pop. 177,000.
salt lick. A deposit or block of exposed salt that animals lick.
salt marsh. Low coastal grassland frequently overflowed by the tide.

salt•pe•ter (sôlt'pē'tər) *n.* Also *chiefly Brit.* **salt•pe•tre. 1.** Potassium nitrate. **2.** Sodium nitrate. [< ML *salpetra*, prob "salt rock."]
salt•shak•er (sôlt'shā'kər) *n.* A container for sprinkling table salt.
salt•wat•er (sôlt'wô'tər, -wŏt'ər) *adj.* Consisting of or inhabiting salt water.
sa•lu•bri•ous (sə-lōō'brē-əs) *adj.* Conducive to health or well-being. [< L *salūs*, health.] —**sa•lu'bri•ous•ly** *adv.*
sal•u•tar•y (săl'yə-tĕr'ē) *adj.* **1.** Beneficially corrective; remedial. **2.** Wholesome. [< L *salūs*, health.]
sal•u•ta•tion (săl'yə-tā'shən) *n.* An expression of greeting, good will, or courtesy. [< L *salūtāre*, to SALUTE.]
sa•lute (sə-lōōt') *v.* **-luted, -luting. 1.** To greet. **2.** To recognize (a military superior) with a prescribed gesture. **3.** To honor formally. —*n.* **1.** A greeting. **2.** A prescribed military display of honor or greeting. [< L *salūtāre*, to preserve, salute, wish health to.]
sal•vage (săl'vĭj) *v.* **1.** The rescue of a ship. **2.** Compensation given to those who voluntarily aid in such a rescue. **3. a.** The saving of any imperiled property from loss. **b.** The property so saved. —*v.* **-vaging, -vages.** To save from loss or destruction. [< F, the act of saving.] —**sal'vage•a•ble** *adj.*
sal•va•tion (săl-vā'shən) *n.* **1.** Preservation or deliverance from evil or difficulty. **2.** A means or cause of such deliverance. **3.** Deliverance from the power or penalty of sin; redemption. [< LL *salvāre*, to save.]
salve (săv, säv) *n.* An analgesic or medicinal ointment. —*v.* **salved, salving. 1.** To dress (a wound or sore) with salve. **2.** To soothe; ease. [< OE *salf, sealf.* See **selp-**.]
sal•ver (săl'vər) *n.* A serving platter or tray. [< F *salve*, a tray for presenting food (to the king).]
sal•vo (săl'vō) *n., pl.* **-vos** or **-voes.** A simultaneous firing of guns. [< It *salva*, salute, volley.]
sa•mar•i•um (sə-mâr'ē-əm) *n. Symbol* **Sm** A silvery or pale-gray metallic rare-earth element used in laser materials, in infrared absorbing glass, and as a neutron absorber. Atomic number 62, atomic weight 150.35.
same (sām) *adj.* **1.** Being the very one; not different; identical. **2.** Similar or corresponding. —*pron.* **1.** A person, thing, or event identical with or similar to another. **2.** An aforesaid person or thing. —*adv.* In like or identical manner. [< ON *samr.*] —**same'ness** *n.*
sa•mekh (sä'mĕk) *n.* Also **sa•mech, sa•mek.** The 15th letter of the Hebrew alphabet, representing *s.*
Sa•mo•a (sə-mō'ə). An island group in the South Pacific. —**Sa•mo'an** *adj.*
sam•o•var (săm'ə-vär') *n.* A metal urn with a spigot, used to boil water for tea. [Russ, "self-boiler."]
Sam•o•yed (săm'ə-yĕd') *n.* Also **Sam•o•yede. 1.** A member of a Ural-Altaic people inhabiting the tundra lands of the NE European Soviet Union and NW Siberia. **2.** A branch of the Uralic family of languages including four

---

ô paw, for/oi boy/ou out/ŏŏ took/ōō coo/p pop/r run/s sauce/sh shy/t to/th thin/*th* the/
ŭ cut/ûr fur/v van/w wag/y yes/z size/zh vision/ə ago, item, edible, gallop, circus/

languages spoken by the Samoyed tribes inhabiting this region. —**Sam'o•yed'ic** *adj.*

sam•pan (săm'păn') *n.* Any of various flat-bottomed skiffs used in the Orient. [Chin *san¹ pan³* (obs).]

sam•ple (săm'pəl) *n.* A portion, piece, or segment regarded as representative of a whole. —*v.* **-pled, -pling.** To take a sample of, esp. to test or examine by a sample. [< OF *essample,* example.]

sam•pler (săm'plər) *n.* **1.** One employed to appraise samples. **2.** A piece of cloth embroidered with various designs.

sam•u•rai (săm'ŏŏ-rī') *n., pl.* **-rai** or **-rais.** The military aristocracy of feudal Japan, or one of its members.

San•a (sä-nä'). Also **Sa•n'a.** The capital of Yemen. Pop. 135,000.

San An•to•ni•o (săn' ăn-tō'nē-ō). A city of Texas. Pop. 588,000.

san•a•to•ri•um (săn'ə-tôr'ē-əm, -tōr'ē-əm) *n.* **1.** An institution for the treatment of chronic diseases. **2.** A sanitarium. [< L *sānus,* healthy, sane.]

sanc•ti•fy (săngk'tə-fī') *v.* **-fied, -fying. 1.** To reserve for sacred use; consecrate. **2.** To make holy; purify. [< LL *sanctificāre.*] —**sanc'ti•fi•ca'tion** *n.* —**sanc'ti•fi'er** *n.*

sanc•ti•mo•ni•ous (săngk'tə-mō'nē-əs) *adj.* Making a pretense of piety. [< L *sanctus,* sacred.] —**sanc'ti•mo'ni•ous•ly** *adv.* —**sanc'ti•mo'ni•ous•ness** *n.*

sanc•tion (săngk'shən) *n.* **1.** Authoritative permission or approval. **2.** A penalty intended to enforce compliance or conformity. **3.** A coercive measure adopted usually by several nations against a nation violating international law. —*v.* To authorize, approve, or encourage. [< L *sanctus,* sacred.]

sanc•ti•ty (săngk'tə-tē) *n., pl.* **-ties. 1.** Saintliness or godliness. **2.** Sacredness or inviolability: *the sanctity of a church.* [< L *sanctus,* sacred.]

sanc•tu•ar•y (săngk'chŏŏ-ĕr'ē) *n., pl.* **-ies. 1.** A consecrated place, as of a house of worship. **2.** A place of refuge, asylum, or protection. [< L *sanctus,* sacred.]

sanc•tum (săngk'təm) *n., pl.* **-tums** or **-ta** (-tə). A private room or study. [< L *sanctus,* sacred.]

sand (sănd) *n.* Loose, granular, gritty particles of worn or disintegrated rock, finer than gravel and coarser than dust. —*v.* **1.** To polish or scour with sand or sandpaper. **2.** To fill up (a harbor) with sand. [< OE.] —**sand'er** *n.* —**sand'i•ness** *n.* —**sand'y** *adj.*

san•dal (săn'dəl) *n.* **1.** A shoe consisting of a sole fastened to the foot by thongs or straps. **2.** A light slipper or low-cut shoe. [< Gk *sandalon.*]

san•dal•wood (săn'dəl-wŏŏd') *n.* **1.** An Asian tree with aromatic wood used for carving and in perfumery. **2.** The wood of this tree. [< Gk *sandanon.*]

sand•bar (sănd'bär') *n.* A ridge or shoal of sand in a river, off a shore, etc.

sand•blast (sănd'blăst', -bläst') *n.* A blast of air carrying sand at high velocity, as for cleaning stone or metal surfaces. —**sand'blast'** *v.* —**sand'blast'er** *n.*

sand•box (sănd'bŏks') *n.* A low, sand-filled box in which children play.

sand•cast (sănd'kăst', -käst') *v.* To make (a casting of something) by pouring molten metal into a sand mold.

sand•hog (sănd'hôg', -hŏg') *n.* A laborer who works under compressed air, as in underwater tunnel-building.

San Di•e•go (săn' dē-ā'gō). A city in S California. Pop. 676,000.

sand-lot (sănd'lŏt') *adj.* Designating a game played by amateurs, esp. children, usually in a vacant lot: *sand-lot baseball.*

sand•man (sănd'măn') *n.* A mysterious character of folklore who causes children to sleep by sprinkling sand in their eyes.

sand•pa•per (sănd'pā'pər) *n.* Heavy paper coated on one side with a particulate abrasive, used for smoothing. —**sand'pa'per** *v.*

sand•pi•per (sănd'pī'pər) *n.* Any of various small, slender-billed shore birds.

sand•stone (sănd'stōn') *n.* Variously colored sedimentary rock composed predominantly of sandlike quartz.

sand•storm (sănd'stôrm') *n.* A strong wind carrying clouds of sand.

sand•wich (sănd'wĭch, săn'-) *n.* Two or more slices of bread with meat, cheese, or other filling placed between them. [< the Fourth Earl of *Sandwich* (1718–92).]

sane (sān) *adj.* **saner, sanest. 1.** Of sound mind. **2.** Having sound judgment; reasonable; rational. [L *sānus,* sound, whole, healthy.] —**sane'ly** *adv.* —**sane'ness** *n.*

San Fran•cis•co (săn' frən-sĭs'kō). A city of N California. Pop. 704,000.

sang (săng). *p.t.* of **sing.**

sang-froid (säɴ-frwä') *n.* Composure; imperturbability. [F, "cold blood."]

san•gui•nar•y (săng'gwə-nĕr'ē) *adj.* **1.** Bloody. **2.** Bloodthirsty. [L *sanguinārius,* of blood.] —**san'gui•nar'i•ly** *adv.*

san•guine (săng'gwĭn) *adj.* **1.** Ruddy, as the complexion. **2.** Eagerly optimistic; cheerful. [< L *sanguis,* blood.] —**san'guine•ly** *adv.* —**san'guine•ness** *n.*

san•i•tar•i•um (săn'ə-târ'ē-əm) *n.* **1.** A health resort. **2.** A sanatorium. [< L *sānitās,* health, sanity.]

san•i•tar•y (săn'ə-tĕr'ē) *adj.* **1.** Of or used to preserve health. **2.** Clean; hygienic. [< L *sānitās,* health, sanity.]

san•i•ta•tion (săn'ə-tā'shən) *n.* **1.** The formulation and application of public health measures. **2.** The disposal of sewage and garbage.

san•i•tize (săn'ə-tīz') *v.* **-tized, -tizing.** To make sanitary.

san•i•ty (săn'ə-tē) *n.* Soundness of mind or reason. [< L *sānus,* healthy, SANE.]

San Jo•se (săn' hō-zā'). A city of W California. Pop. 204,000.

San Jo•sé (sän' hō-zā'). The capital of Costa Rica. Pop. 114,000.

San Juan (sän' hwän'). The capital of Puerto Rico. Pop. 452,000.

sank (săngk). *p.t.* of **sink.**

ă pat/ā ate/âr care/ä bar/b bib/ch chew/d deed/ĕ pet/ē be/f fit/g gag/h hat/hw what/
ĭ pit/ī pie/îr pier/j judge/k kick/l lid, fatal/m mum/n no, sudden/ng sing/ŏ pot/ō ·go/

San Ma•ri•no (săn′ mə-rē′nō). **1.** A republic in the Apennines of Italy. Pop. 17,000. **2.** The capital of this republic.

San Marino

sans (sănz) *prep.* Without. [< L *sine.*]
San Sal•va•dor (săn′ săl′və-dôr). The capital of El Salvador. Pop. 281,000.
San•skrit (săn′skrĭt′) *n.* An ancient Indic language of India, now used only for sacred or scholarly writings.
San•ta Claus (săn′tə klôz′). The personification of the spirit of Christmas as a fat old man with a white beard and a red suit. [< MDu *Sint Nicolaes,* Saint Nicholas, the patron saint of children.]
San•ta Fe (săn′tə fā′). The capital of New Mexico. Pop. 39,000.
San•ta Is•a•bel (săn′tə ĭz′ə-bĕl′). The capital of Equatorial Guinea. Pop. 20,000.
San•ti•a•go (săn-tyä′gō). The capital of Chile. Pop. 1,907,000.
San•to Do•min•go (săn′tō dō-mĕng′gō). The capital of the Dominican Republic. Pop. 478,000.
São Pau•lo (souɴ pou′lōō). A city of SE Brazil. Pop. 3,825,000.
sap¹ (săp) *n.* **1.** The watery fluid that circulates through plant tissue. **2.** A similar juice or fluid. **3.** Health and energy; vitality. **4.** *Slang.* A dupe; fool. [< OE *sæp.* See **sab-**.]
sap² (săp) *v.* **sapped, sapping. 1.** To undermine the foundations of. **2.** To deplete or weaken gradually. [< OF *sappe,* "an undermining."]
sa•pi•ent (sā′pē-ənt) *adj.* Having wisdom; discerning. [< L *sapere,* to taste, to have good taste.] **—sa′pi•ence** *n.* **—sa′pi•ent•ly** *adv.*
sap•ling (săp′lĭng) *n.* A young tree.
sap•phire (săf′ĭr) *n.* **1.** Any of several relatively pure forms of corundum, esp. a blue form used as a gemstone. **2.** A corundum gem. **3.** The blue color of a gem sapphire. [< Gk *sappheiros.*]
sap•py (săp′ē) *adj.* **-pier, -piest. 1.** Full of sap; juicy. **2.** Vital; vigorous. **3.** *Slang.* Silly or foolish. **—sap′pi•ness** *n.*
sap•suck•er (săp′sŭk′ər) *n.* A small North American woodpecker that drills into trees to drink the sap.

sar•a•band (săr′ə-bănd′) *n.* **1.** A stately dance of the 17th and 18th centuries. **2.** Music for this dance. [< Span *zarabanda.*]
Sar•a•cen (săr′ə-sən) *n.* **1.** Any Moslem, esp. of the time of the Crusades. **2.** An Arab.
sa•ra•pe. Variant of **serape.**
sar•casm (sär′kăz′əm) *n.* **1.** A mocking remark utilizing statements opposite or irrelevant to the underlying meaning. **2.** The use of such remarks. [< Gk *sarkazein,* "to tear flesh," bite the lips in rage.] **—sar•cas′tic** (-kăs′tĭk) *adj.*
sar•coph•a•gus (sär-kŏf′ə-gəs) *n., pl.* **-gi** (-jī′). A stone coffin. [L *sarcophagus (lapis),* "flesh-eating (stone)."]
sar•dine (sär-dēn′) *n.* A small herring or similar fish, often canned in oil. [< Gk *sardinos.*]
Sar•din•i•a (sär-dĭn′ē-ə). An Italian island in the W Mediterranean. **—Sar•din′i•an** *adj. & n.*
sar•don•ic (sär-dŏn′ĭk) *adj.* Scornful; cynical. [< L *Sardonius (risus),* bitter (laugh).] **—sar•don′i•cal•ly** *adv.*
sarge (särj) *n. Informal.* Sergeant.
sa•ri (sär′ē) *n., pl.* **-ris.** A lightweight garment worn chiefly by women of India and Pakistan. [Hindi *sārī.*]
sa•rong (sə-rông′, -rŏng′) *n.* A brightly colored cloth garment worn by both men and women of the Malay Archipelago and the Pacific islands. [Malay, *sarong,* sheath.]
sar•sa•pa•ril•la (săs′pə-rĭl′ə, sär′sə-pə-rĭl′ə) *n.* **1.** The dried roots of a tropical American plant, used as a flavoring. **2.** A soft drink flavored with sarsaparilla. [Span *zarzaparrilla.*]
sar•to•ri•al (sär-tôr′ē-əl, -tōr′ē-əl) *adj.* **1.** Pertaining to tailors or tailoring. **2.** Pertaining to clothing, esp. men's. [< L *sartor,* a tailor.]
sash¹ (săsh) *n.* A band or ribbon worn about the waist or over the shoulder. [< Ar *shāsh,* muslin.]
sash² (săsh) *n.* A frame in which the panes of a window or door are set. [< F *châssis,* a frame, chassis.]
sa•shay (să-shā′) *v. Informal.* To strut or flounce. [< F *chasser,* to chase.]
Sas•katch•e•wan (săs-kăch′ə-wän′, -wən). A province of W Canada. Pop. 953,000. Cap. Regina.
sass (săs). *Informal. n.* Impertinence; back talk. *—v.* To talk back to. [Back-formation < SASSY.]
sas•sa•fras (săs′ə-frăs′) *n.* **1.** A North American tree with irregularly lobed leaves and aromatic bark. **2.** The dried root bark of this tree, used as flavoring. [< Span *sasafrás.*]
sas•sy (săs′ē) *adj.* **-sier, -siest.** *Informal.* Impudent; saucy. [Var of SAUCY.]
sat (săt). *p.t. & p.p.* of **sit.**
SAT Scholastic Aptitude Test.
Sat. Saturday.
Sa•tan (sāt′n) *n.* The Devil. [< Heb *śāṭān,* devil, adversary.]
sa•tan•ic (sə-tăn′ĭk) *adj.* Also **sa•tan•i•cal** (-ĭ-kəl). **1.** Pertaining to or suggestive of Satan. **2.** Profoundly cruel or evil.
satch•el (săch′əl) *n.* A small valise or bag. [< L *saccus,* a bag, SACK.]
sate¹ (sāt) *v.* **sated, sating. 1.** To indulge (an

ô paw, for/oi boy/ou out/ōō took/ōō coo/p pop/r run/s sauce/sh shy/t to/th thin/*th* the/
ŭ cut/ûr fur/v van/w wag/y yes/z size/zh vision/ə ago, item, edible, gallop, circus/

appetite) fully. **2.** To indulge to excess; glut. [Prob < OE *sadian*. See **să-**.]

sate² (săt, sāt). *Archaic. p.t.* of **sit**.

sa·teen (să-tēn') *n.* A cotton fabric with a satin finish. [Var of SATIN.]

sat·el·lite (săt'l-īt') *n.* **1.** A relatively small body, natural or artificial, orbiting a planet. **2.** One who attends a dignitary. **3.** A nation dominated politically by another. [< L *satelles*, an attendant, escort.]

sa·ti·ate (sā'shē-āt') *v.* **-ated, -ating. 1.** To satisfy fully. **2.** To gratify to excess. [< L *satis*, sufficient, enough.] **—sa'ti·a'tion** *n.*

sa·ti·e·ty (sə-tī'ə-tē) *n.* The condition of being satiated.

sat·in (săt'n) *n.* A smooth, close-woven fabric with a glossy face. [Prob < Ar *Zaytūn*, Ar form of Chin *Tseutung*, former name of *Tsinkiang*, city in S China.] **—sat'in·y** *adj.*

sat·ire (săt'īr) *n.* **1.** A literary work in which irony, derision, or wit is used to expose folly or wickedness. **2.** The use of derisive wit to attack folly or wickedness. [< L *satira*, satire, medley, mixture.] **—sa·tir'i·cal** (sə-tîr'ĭ-kəl), **sa·tir'ic** *adj.* **—sat'i·rist** (săt'ə-rĭst) *n.*

sat·i·rize (săt'ə-rīz') *v.* **-rized, -rizing.** To ridicule by means of satire.

sat·is·fac·tion (săt'ĭs-făk'shən) *n.* **1.** Fulfillment or gratification of a desire, need, etc. **2.** Pleasure derived from gratification. **3.** Reparation in the form of penance. **4.** Compensation for injury or loss.

sat·is·fac·to·ry (săt'ĭs-făk'tə-rē) *adj.* Giving satisfaction; adequate. **—sat'is·fac'to·ri·ly** *adv.*

sat·is·fy (săt'ĭs-fī') *v.* **-fied, -fying. 1.** To gratify or fulfill a need, desire, etc. **2.** To relieve of doubt or question; assure. **3.** To fulfill or discharge an obligation. **4.** To conform to the requirements of. **5.** To give satisfaction. [< L *satisfacere*.] **—sat'is·fi'er** *n.*

sa·trap (sā'trăp, săt'răp) *n.* A subordinate ruler. [< OPers *khshathrapāvan*, "protector of the country."]

sat·u·rate (săch'ə-rāt') *v.* **-rated, -rating. 1.** To soak thoroughly. **2.** To fill to capacity. [L *saturāre*, to fill, satiate.] **—sat'u·ra·ble** (săch'ər-ə-bəl) *adj.* **—sat'u·ra'tion** *n.*

Sat·ur·day (săt'ər-dē, -dā') *n.* The 7th day of the week. [< OE *sæternesdæg*, "Saturn's day."]

Sat·urn (săt'ərn) *n.* The 6th planet from the sun, having a diameter of 74,000 miles, a mass 95 times that of Earth, and an orbital period of 29.5 years at a mean distance of about 886,000,000 miles. [< L *Sāturnus*, Roman deity.]

sat·ur·nine (săt'ər-nīn') *adj.* **1.** Morose and sardonic. **2.** Pertaining to or resembling lead or produced by the absorption of lead.

sat·yr (săt'ər, sā'tər) *n.* **1.** *Gk.Myth.* A woodland god often with the ears, legs, and horns of a goat. **2.** A lecher. [< Gk *saturos*.]

sat·y·ri·a·sis (săt'ə-rī'ə-sĭs) *n.* Excessive, often uncontrollable sexual desire in men.

sauce (sôs) *n.* **1.** A soft or liquid dressing served as an accompaniment to food. **2.** Stewed or puréed fruit. **3.** *Informal.* Impudence. **—v.** **sauced, saucing. 1.** To add zest to.

2. *Informal.* To be impudent to. [< L *salsus*, salted.]

sauce·pan (sôs'păn') *n.* A long-handled cooking pan.

sau·cer (sô'sər) *n.* A small, shallow dish for holding a cup. [ME, sauce dish.]

sau·cy (sô'sē) *adj.* **-cier, -ciest. 1.** Impudent. **2.** Piquant; pert. **—sau'ci·ly** *adv.*

Sa·u·di A·ra·bi·a (sä-ōō'dē ə-rā'bē-ə). A kingdom of the Arabian peninsula. Pop. 6,000,000. Caps. Riyadh and Mecca.

Saudi Arabia

sauer·kraut (sour'krout') *n.* Shredded cabbage that is salted and fermented in its own juice. [G.]

Saul (sôl). 1st king of Israel.

sau·na (sou'nə) *n.* A heat and bath treatment in which one is subjected to heat produced usually by running water over heated rocks. [Finn.]

saun·ter (sôn'tər) *v.* To stroll. **—n.** A leisurely pace; stroll. [Prob ME *santeren*, to muse.]

-saur, -saurus. *comb. form.* Lizard: **bronto-saur.** [< Gk *sauros*, lizard.]

sau·sage (sô'sĭj) *n.* Finely chopped and seasoned meat, stuffed into a prepared casing. [< LL *salsicius*, prepared by salting.]

sau·té (sō-tā', sô-) *v.* **-téed, -téing.** To fry lightly in fat. [F, "tossed in a pan."]

sau·terne, sau·ternes (sō-tûrn', sô-) *n.* A delicate, sweet white dessert wine. [< *Sauternes*, commune in SW France.]

sav·age (săv'ĭj) *adj.* **1.** Not domesticated or cultivated; wild. **2.** Not civilized; primitive. **3.** Ferocious; fierce. **—n.** **1.** A primitive or uncivilized person. **2.** A brutal person. **3.** A rude person. [< L *silvāticus*, of the woods, wild.] **—sav'age·ly** *adv.* **—sav'age·ry** *n.*

Sa·van·nah (sə-văn'ə). A city of Georgia. Pop. 149,000.

sa·vant (sə-vänt', săv'ənt) *n.* A learned man. [< L *sapere*, to be sensible, be wise.]

save¹ (sāv) *v.* **saved, saving. 1.** To rescue from danger. **2.** To preserve or safeguard. **3.** To keep for future use; store. **4.** To prevent waste. **5.** To avoid fatigue, wear, or damage; spare. **6.** To redeem from sin. [< L *salvus*, safe.] **—sav'er** *n.*

save² (sāv) *prep.* With the exception of; ex-

ă pat/ā ate/âr care/ä bar/b bib/ch chew/d deed/ĕ pet/ē be/f fit/g gag/h hat/hw what/
ĭ pit/ī pie/îr pier/j judge/k kick/l lid, fatal/m mum/n no, sudden/ng sing/ŏ pot/ō go/

cept. —*conj.* Except; but. [< L *salvō,* without injury or prejudice to.]
sav•ing (sā'vǐng) *adj.* **1.** Serving to save. **2.** Redeeming. **3.** Economical. —*n.* **1.** The act or condition of being saved. **2.** A reduction, as in expenditure. **3.** That which is saved. **4. savings.** Sums of money saved. —*prep.* With the exception of. —*conj.* Except; save.
sav•ior (sāv'yər) *n.* Also **sav•iour.** One who saves or preserves. —**the Saviour.** Christ.
sa•voir-faire (să-vwár-fâr') *n.* Experienced social skill or tact. [F, "to know how to do."]
sa•vor (sā'vər). Also *chiefly Brit.* **sa•vour.** *n.* **1.** Taste or aroma. **2.** A specific taste, smell, or quality. —*v.* **1.** To have a particular savor. **2.** To taste with zest; relish. [< L *sapor,* taste, savor.] —**sa'vor•i•ness** *n.* —**sa'vor•y** *adj.*
sav•vy (săv'ē) *v.* **-vied, -vying.** *Slang.* To understand. [< Span *sabe (usted),* (you) know.]
saw[1] (sô) *n.* A cutting tool having a thin metal blade or disk with a sharp-toothed edge. —*v.* **sawed, sawed** or **sawn, sawing.** To cut with or as if with a saw. [< OE *sagu, sage.* See **sek-.**]
saw[2] (sô) *n.* A saying discredited through long repetition. [< OE *sagu,* speech, talk. See **sekw-**[1].]
saw[3] (sô). *p.t.* of **see.**
saw•buck (sô'bŭk') *n.* **1.** A sawhorse, esp. one with X-shaped legs projecting above the crossbar. **2.** *Slang.* A ten-dollar bill.
saw•dust (sô'dŭst') *n.* The small waste particles resulting from sawing.
saw•horse (sô'hôrs') *n.* A rack or trestle used to support wood being sawed.
saw•mill (sô'mǐl') *n.* A mill where logs are cut into lumber.
sawn (sôn). Alternate *p.p.* of **saw.**
saw•yer (sô'yər) *n.* One employed to saw wood, as in a sawmill.
sax (săks) *n.* *Informal.* A saxophone.
Sax•on (săk'sən) *n.* **1.** A member of a Germanic tribal group that invaded England in the 5th century and with the Angles and Jutes formed the Anglo-Saxon peoples. **2.** The Germanic language or dialect spoken by any Saxon people. —**Sax'on** *adj.*
sax•o•phone (săk'sə-fōn') *n.* A wind instrument having a single-reed mouthpiece, a usually curved conical metal bore, and finger keys, and made in a variety of sizes. [Invented (1846) by Adolphe *Sax.*] —**sax'o•phon'ist** (-fō'nǐst) *n.*
say (sā) *v.* **said, saying. 1.** To utter aloud; pronounce; speak. **2.** To express in words. **3.** To state with assurance. **4.** To recite. **5.** To allege. **6.** To estimate or suppose. —**that is to say.** In other words. —*n.* **1.** A positive assurance. **2.** One's chance to speak. **3.** Authority. —*adv.* **1.** Approximately. **2.** For instance. [< OE *secgan.* See **sekw-**[1].]
say•ing (sā'ǐng) *n.* An often repeated expression.
Sb antimony (L *stibium*).
sb. substantive.
Sc scandium.
sc. 1. scene. **2.** sculpsit.
s.c. *Ptg.* small capitals.
S.C. South Carolina.

scab (skăb) *n.* **1.** The crustlike exudate that covers a healing wound. **2.** *Informal.* A worker who refuses membership in a labor union or who works while others are on strike. —*v.* **scabbed, scabbing. 1. a.** To form a scab. **b.** To become covered with a scab. **2.** *Informal.* To work as a scab. [< ON *skabb.*]
scab•bard (skăb'ərd) *n.* A sheath for a dagger, sword, etc. [< NF *escaubers* (pl).]
scab•by (skăb'ē) *adj.* **-bier, -biest. 1.** Having, consisting of, or covered with scabs or something resembling scabs. **2.** Afflicted with scabies. —**scab'bi•ly** *adv.* —**scab'bi•ness** *n.*
sca•bies (skā'bēz') *n. (takes sing. v.).* A contagious skin disease caused by a mite and characterized by intense itching. [L *scabiēs,* roughness, scurf.]
scab•rous (skăb'rəs, skā'brəs) *adj.* Rough or harsh. [< L *scaber,* rough, scurfy.]
scads (skădz) *pl.n.* *Informal.* A large number. [?]
scaf•fold (skăf'əld, -ōld') *n.* **1.** A temporary platform for supporting workers. **2.** A platform for the execution of condemned prisoners. [< OF *chafaud.*]
scaf•fold•ing (skăf'əl-dǐng, skăf'ōl'-) *n.* **1.** A system of scaffolds. **2.** The materials for scaffolds.
scal•a•wag (skăl'ə-wăg') *n.* *Informal.* A rascal.
scald[1] (skôld) *v.* **1.** To burn with or as if with hot liquid or steam. **2.** To subject to or treat with boiling water. **3.** To heat (a liquid) almost to the boiling point. —*n.* An injury caused by scalding. [< LL *excaldāre,* to wash in hot water.]
scald[2]. Variant of **scall.**
scale[1] (skāl) *n.* **1.** One of the small, platelike structures forming the external covering of fishes, reptiles, etc. **2.** A similar structure or part. **3.** A dry, thin flake of epidermis shed from the skin. **4.** A small, thin piece of anything. **5.** Also **scale insect.** A destructive insect that forms and remains under waxy scales on plants. **6.** A flaky oxide film formed on a metal. —*v.* **scaled, scaling. 1.** To clear or strip of scale or scales. **2.** To remove or come off in layers or scales. **3.** To cover with scales or become covered with encrustation. [< OF *escale,* "shell," "husk" < Gmc.] —**scal'y** *adj.*
scale[2] (skāl) *n.* **1.** A system of ordered marks at fixed intervals used in measurement. **2.** A progressive classification, as of size, amount, importance, or rank. **3.** A relative level or degree. **4.** *Mus.* An ascending or descending series of tones proceeding by a specified scheme of intervals. —*v.* **scaled, scaling. 1.** To climb up with or as if with a ladder, rope, etc. **2.** To reproduce in accordance with a scale. **3.** To adjust according to a proportion. [< L *scālae,* stairs.]
scale[3] (skāl) *n.* Often **scales.** Any instrument or machine for weighing. [< ON *skāl,* bowl, scale of a balance.]
sca•lene (skā'lēn', skā-lēn') *adj.* Having three unequal sides. [< Gk *skalēnos,* uneven.]
Scales (skālz) *pl.n.* The constellation and sign of the zodiac Libra.
scall (skôl) *n.* Also **scald** (skôld). A scaly

eruption of the skin or scalp. [< ON *skalli*, baldhead.]

scal·lion (skăl'yən) *n*. A young onion before the bulb enlarges. [< L *Ascalōnia (caepa)*, (onion) of Ascalon, port in S Palestine.]

scal·lop (skŏl'əp, skăl'-) *n*. 1. A bivalve marine mollusk with a fan-shaped, ridged shell. 2. The edible muscle of a scallop. 3. One of a series of curved projections forming an ornamental border. —*v*. 1. To border with scallops. 2. Also **es·cal·lop** (ĕ-skŏl'əp, ĕ-skăl'-). To bake in a casserole with milk or a sauce and often with bread crumbs. [< OF *escalope*, shell.] —**scal'lop·er** *n*.

scalp (skălp) *n*. The skin covering the top of the head. —*v*. 1. To cut or tear the scalp from; deprive of the scalp. 2. *Informal*. To sell at a price higher than the established value. [Prob < Scand.] —**scalp'er** *n*.

scal·pel (skăl'pəl, skăl-pĕl') *n*. A small straight surgical knife with a very thin, sharp blade. [< L *scalpere*, to cut, scratch.]

scamp (skămp) *n*. A rogue; rascal. [< obs *scamp*, to slip away, bolt.]

scam·per (skăm'pər) *v*. To run nimbly. —*n*. A hasty run or departure. [Flem *scamperen*, to decamp.] —**scam'per·er** *n*.

scam·pi (skăm'pē) *pl.n*. Large shrimps used in Italian cooking. [It.]

scan (skăn) *v*. **scanned, scanning**. 1. To examine closely. 2. To inspect or look over quickly. 3. To analyze (verse) into metrical patterns. —*n*. An act or instance of scanning. [< LL *scandere*, "to analyze the rising and falling rhythm in verses."] —**scan'ner** *n*.

Scand. Scandinavia; Scandinavian.

scan·dal (skăn'dəl) *n*. 1. Public disgrace. 2. Outrage; shame. 3. Malicious gossip. [< Gk *skandalon*, trap, snare, stumbling block.] —**scan'dal·ous** *adj*. —**scan'dal·ous·ly** *adv*.

scan·dal·ize (skăn'də-līz') *v*. **-ized, -izing**. To shock or outrage the propriety of.

Scan·di·na·vi·a (skăn'də-nā'vē-ə, -nāv'yə). 1. The NW European countries of Norway, Sweden, and Denmark. 2. These countries and Iceland considered as a linguistic and cultural unit. 3. These countries, Iceland, and Finland.

Scan·di·na·vi·an (skăn'də-nā'vē-ən, -nāv'yən) *n*. 1. A native or inhabitant of Scandinavia. 2. A branch of Germanic including Norwegian, Swedish, Danish, and Icelandic. —**Scan'di·na'vi·an** *adj*.

scan·di·um (skăn'dē-əm) *n*. *Symbol* **Sc** A silvery-white, very lightweight metallic element found in various rare minerals. Atomic number 21, atomic weight 44.956. [< L *Scandia*, ancient name for Scandinavia.]

scan·sion (skăn'shən) *n*. The analysis of verse into metrical patterns. [LL *scansiō*.]

scant (skănt) *adj*. 1. Barely enough; meager; inadequate. 2. Being just short of a specific measure. —*v*. 1. To skimp. 2. To limit, as in amount; stint. [< ON *skammr*, short.]

scant·ling (skănt'lĭng, -lĭn) *n*. A small piece of timber, esp. one used as an upright in a building frame. [Prob < VL *scandilia*, measure, scale.]

scant·y (skăn'tē) *adj*. **-ier, -iest**. Deficient in extent or degree; skimpy. —**scant'i·ly** *adv*. —**scant'i·ness** *n*.

scape·goat (skāp'gōt') *n*. One bearing blame for others. [(E)SCAPE + GOAT.]

scape·grace (skāp'grās') *n*. An incorrigible rascal. [(E)SCAPE + GRACE.]

scap·u·la (skăp'yə-lə) *n., pl*. **-las** or **-lae** (-lē'). Either of two large, flat, triangular bones forming the back part of the shoulder. [L, shoulder blade, shoulder.] —**scap'u·lar** *adj*.

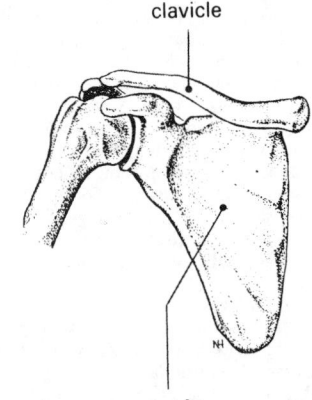

clavicle

scapula

scar (skär) *n*. 1. A mark left on the skin following the healing of a surface injury or wound. 2. Any sign remaining as evidence of injury, damage, or an injurious mental or physical condition. —*v*. **scarred, scarring**. To mark or become marked with a scar. [< Gk *eskhara*, hearth, scab caused by burning.] —**scar'less** *adj*.

scar·ab (skăr'əb) *n*. Also **scar·a·bae·us** (skăr'ə-bē'əs) *pl*. **-uses** or **-baei** (-bē'ī'). 1. Any of numerous often large beetles, esp. one regarded as sacred by the ancient Egyptians. 2. A representation of a scarab beetle. [< L *scarabaeus*.]

scarce (skârs) *adj*. **scarcer, scarcest**. 1. Infrequently seen or found. 2. Not plentiful or abundant. [< VL **excarpsus*, "picked," "choice."] —**scar'ci·ty** *n*.

scarce·ly (skârs'lē) *adv*. 1. By a small margin; just; barely. 2. Almost not; hardly. 3. Assuredly not.
   Usage: Scarcely has a negative sense, and is therefore not preceded by another negative in standard usage: *He could scarcely hear* (not *couldn't scarcely*). Scarcely is preferably followed by *when* or (less often) *before*, rather than by *than*, in constructions such as: *Scarcely had he entered when the telephone rang.*

scare (skâr) *v*. **scared, scaring**. To startle; frighten. —*n*. 1. A fright. 2. Panic. [< ON *skjarr*, shy, timid.]

scare·crow (skâr'krō') *n*. A crude figure set up in a cultivated area to scare birds away.

scarf (skärf) *n., pl*. **scarfs** or **scarves** (skärvz). 1. A rectangular or triangular piece of cloth,

---

ă pat/ā ate/âr care/ä bar/b bib/ch chew/d deed/ě pet/ē be/f fit/g gag/h hat/hw what/ ĭ pit/ī pie/îr pier/j judge/k kick/l lid, fatal/m mum/n no, sudden/ng sing/ŏ pot/ō go/

worn about the neck or head. **2.** A runner, as for a bureau. [< OF *escherpe*, orig "pilgrim's wallet suspended from the neck."]

Scar·lat·ti (skär-lät′ē), **Domenico.** 1683–1757. Italian harpsichordist and composer.

scar·let (skär′lĭt) *n.* Strong to vivid red or reddish orange. [< Pers *säqirlaṭ*, silk material dyed red.]

scarlet fever. An acute contagious disease caused by a bacterium, occurring predominantly among children and characterized by a scarlet skin eruption and high fever.

scar·y (skâr′ē) *adj.* **-ier, -iest.** *Informal.* **1.** Frightening. **2.** Easily scared.

scat (skăt) *v.* **scatted, scatting.** *Informal.* To leave hastily. [Poss short for SCATTER.]

scath·ing (skā′thĭng) *adj.* Extremely severe or harsh. [< ON *skadha*, to harm.]

scat·ter (skăt′ər) *v.* **1.** To disperse. **2.** To distribute loosely by or as if by sprinkling or strewing. [Poss < SHATTER.] —**scat′ter·er** *n.*

scat·ter·brain (skăt′ər-brān′) *n.* A flighty or disorganized person. —**scat′ter·brained′** *adj.*

scat·ter·ing (skăt′ər-ĭng) *n.* **1. a.** The act or process of scattering. **b.** The state of being scattered. **2.** A sparse distribution. —*adj.* Placed at intervals or occurring irregularly.

scav·enge (skăv′ĭnj) *v.* **-enged, -enging. 1.** To act as a scavenger. **2.** To search through for salvageable material.

scav·en·ger (skăv′ĭn-jər) *n.* **1.** An animal that feeds on dead flesh or other decaying matter. **2.** One who scavenges. [< ME *skawager*, collector of tolls.]

sce·nar·i·o (sĭ-nâr′ē-ō′, sĭ-när′-) *n., pl.* **-os.** A script or an outline of the plot of a motion picture. [It, "scenery."] —**sce·nar′ist** *n.*

scene (sēn) *n.* **1.** A prospect; view. **2.** The setting of some action. **3.** A subdivision of an act of a play. **4.** A unit of continuous related action in a film. **5.** The scenery for a dramatic presentation. **6.** A display of temper. [< Gk *skēnē*, "tent."]

scen·er·y (sē′nə-rē) *n.* **1.** The landscape. **2.** The painted backdrops on a theatrical stage. [It *scenario*, SCENARIO.] —**sce′nic** *adj.*

scent (sĕnt) *n.* **1.** A distinctive odor. **2.** A perfume. **3.** The trail of a hunted animal or fugitive. —*v.* **1.** To smell; hunt by smell. **2.** To fill with an odor. [< L *sentire*, to feel.]

scep·ter (sĕp′tər) *n.* Also *chiefly Brit.* **scep·tre.** A staff held by a sovereign as an emblem of authority. [< Gk *skēptron*, "staff," "stick."]

scep·tic. Variant of **skeptic.**

sch. school.

sched·ule (skĕj′ōōl, -ōō-əl, skĕj′əl) *n.* **1.** A list of items. **2.** A program. **3.** A timetable. **4.** A production plan. —*v.* **-uled, -uling. 1.** To enter on a schedule. **2.** To make up a schedule for. **3.** To plan for a certain time. [< L *scheda*, papyrus leaf.]

sche·mat·ic (skē-măt′ĭk) *adj.* Pertaining to or in the form of a scheme; diagrammatic. —*n.* A structural or procedural diagram, esp. of an electrical or mechanical system.

scheme (skēm) *n.* **1.** A systematic plan or design. **2.** A secret plan; plot; intrigue. —*v.* **schemed, scheming. 1.** To contrive a scheme

for. **2.** To plot. [< Gk *skhēma*, form, figure.]

scher·zo (skĕr′tsō) *n., pl.* **-zos.** *Mus.* A lively movement commonly in ³/₄ time. [It, joke.]

Schick test (shĭk). An intracutaneous skin test of susceptibility to diphtheria. [< B. *Schick* (1877–1967), American pediatrician.]

Schil·ler (shĭl′ər), **Friedrich von.** 1759–1805. German poet.

schil·ling (shĭl′ĭng) *n.* The basic monetary unit of Austria. [G.]

schism (sĭz′əm, skĭz′-) *n.* A separation or division into factions, esp. within a Christian church. [< Gk *skhisma*, a split, division.] —**schis·mat′ic** (sĭz-măt′ĭk, skĭz-) *adj.* —**schis·mat′i·cal·ly** *adv.*

schist (shĭst) *n.* Also **shist.** A metamorphic rock consisting of laminated, often flaky, parallel layers. [< L *(lapis) schistos*, "fissile (stone)."] —**schis′tose′** (shĭs′tōs′), **schis′tous** (shĭs′təs) *adj.*

schizo–. *comb. form.* Division, split, or cleavage. [< Gk *skhizein*, to split.]

schiz·oid (skĭt′soid′) *adj.* Of or resembling schizophrenia. —*n.* A schizophrenic. [SCHIZ(O)- + -OID.]

schiz·o·phre·ni·a (skĭt′sə-frē′nē-ə, -frĕn′ē-ə) *n.* Any of a group of psychotic reactions characterized by withdrawal from reality with highly variable accompanying affective, behavioral, and intellectual disturbances. —**schiz′o·phren′ic** (-frĕn′ĭk) *adj. & n.*

schnapps (shnäps, shnăps) *n.* Any of various strong liquors. [G *Schnaps*.]

schnit·zel (shnĭt′səl) *n.* A thin cutlet of veal fried lightly in butter. [< G *Schnitz*, slice.]

schol·ar (skŏl′ər) *n.* **1.** A learned person. **2.** A pupil or student. [< LL *scholāris*, of a school.] —**schol′ar·li·ness** *n.* —**schol′ar·ly** *adj.*

schol·ar·ship (skŏl′ər-shĭp′) *n.* **1.** The knowledge or discipline of a scholar. **2.** A grant-in-aid awarded to a student.

scho·las·tic (skə-lăs′tĭk) *adj.* Of or pertaining to schools or scholarship. [< Gk *skholē*, school.] —**scho·las′ti·cal·ly** *adv.*

school¹ (skōōl) *n.* **1.** An institution for instruction and learning. **2.** The student body of an educational institution. **3.** The process of being educated. **4.** A group of persons under some common influence or sharing a unifying belief. —*v.* **1.** To instruct. **2.** To train; discipline. [< Gk *skholē*, leisure (devoted to learning), lecture, school.]

school² (skōōl) *n.* A group of fish or other aquatic animals swimming together. [< MDu *schōle*, troop, group.]

school·boy (skōōl′boi′) *n.* A boy attending school.

school·child (skōōl′chīld′) *n.* A child attending school.

school·girl (skōōl′gûrl′) *n.* A girl attending school.

school·house (skōōl′hous′) *n.* A building used as a school.

school·marm (skōōl′märm′) *n. Informal.* A woman schoolteacher, esp. an old-fashioned disciplinarian.

school·mas·ter (skōōl′măs′tər, -mäs′tər) *n.* A male teacher.

ō paw, for/oi boy/ou out/ōō took/ōō coo/p pop/r run/s sauce/sh shy/t to/th thin/*th* the/ ŭ cut/ûr fur/v van/w wag/y yes/z size/zh vision/ə ago, item, edible, gallop, circus/

school•mate (sko͞ol'māt') *n.* A school companion.

school•mis•tress (sko͞ol'mĭs'trĭs) *n.* A woman teacher.

school•room (sko͞ol'ro͞om', -ro͞om') *n.* A classroom.

school•teach•er (sko͞ol'tē'chər) *n.* One who teaches in a school below the college level.

schoo•ner (sko͞o'nər) *n.* 1. A fore-and-aft-rigged ship with two or more masts, the mainmast being taller than the foremast. 2. A large beer glass, generally holding a pint or more. [Earlier *scooner*.]

Scho•pen•hau•er (shō'pən-hou'ər), **Arthur.** 1788–1860. German philosopher.

Schu•bert (sho͞o'bərt), **Franz.** 1797–1828. Austrian composer.

Schu•mann (sho͞o'män), **Robert.** 1810–1856. German composer.

schwa (shwä, shvä) *n.* A symbol (ə) for an indeterminate vowel sound, in English occurring in many unstressed syllables. [< Heb *shəwā'*.]

Schwei•tzer (shwīt'sər, shvīt'sər), **Albert.** 1875–1965. French missionary doctor in Africa.

sci. science.

sci•at•i•ca (sī-ăt'ĭ-kə) *n.* Chronic neuralgic pain in the area of the hip or thigh. [< ML *sciatica (passiō)*, "(suffering) in the hip."]

sci•ence (sī'əns) *n.* 1. The observation, identification, description, experimental investigation, and theoretical explanation of natural phenomena. 2. Any methodological activity, discipline, or study. 3. Any activity that appears to require study and method. 4. Knowledge, esp. knowledge gained through experience. [< L *sciēns*, pres part of *scīre*, to know.] —**sci'en•tif'ic** (sī'ən-tĭf'ĭc) *adj.* —**sci'en•tif'i•cal•ly** *adv.*

science fiction. Fiction based on elements of scientific discovery and prediction.

sci•en•tist (sī'ən-tĭst) *n.* A person having expert knowledge of one or more sciences.

scim•i•tar (sĭm'ə-tər, -tär') *n.* A curved Oriental sword. [< Pers *šimšīr*.]

scin•til•la (sĭn-tĭl'ə) *n.* A minute amount; trace. [L, spark.]

scin•til•late (sĭn'tə-lāt') *v.* -lated, -lating. To throw off sparks; flash and sparkle. [< L *scintilla*, spark.] —**scin'til•la'tion** *n.*

sci•on (sī'ən) *n.* 1. A descendant or heir. 2. A detached plant shoot used in grafting. [< OF *ciun, cion*.]

sci•roc•co. Variant of **sirocco**.

scis•sors (sĭz'ərz) *n. (takes sing. or pl. v.).* A cutting implement of two blades, joined by a swivel pin that allows the cutting edges to be opened and closed. [< LL *cīsōrium*, cutting instrument.]

scissors kick. A swimming kick in which one leg is swung forward, the other bent back at the knee, and then both straightened and snapped together.

scle•ra (sklîr'ə) *n.* The tough, fibrous tissue that covers all of the eyeball except the cornea.

scle•ro•sis (sklə-rō'sĭs) *n., pl.* -ses (-sēz'). A thickening or hardening of a body part, esp.

from tissue overgrowth or disease. [< Gk *sklēros*, hard.] —**scle•rot'ic** (-rŏt'ĭk) *adj.*

scoff (skôf, skŏf) *v.* To mock at or scorn. —*n.* An expression of scorn; a jeer. [Prob < Scand.] —**scoff'er** *n.*

scold (skōld) *v.* To reprimand harshly. —*n.* One who persistently rails against others. [< ME, ribald or abusive person.]

scold•ing (skōl'dĭng) *n.* A sharp reprimand.

sconce¹ (skŏns) *n.* A small fort. [< It *scanso*, defense.]

sconce² (skŏns) *n.* A decorative wall bracket for candles or lights. [< OF *esconse*, lantern, hiding place.]

scone (skōn, skŏn) *n.* A round, soft, doughy pastry. [Short for Du *schoonbrood*, fine white bread.]

scoop (sko͞op) *n.* 1. A small, shovellike utensil. 2. The bucket or shovel of a steam shovel or dredge. 3. The amount taken with one scoop. 4. *Slang.* An exclusive news story acquired by luck or initiative. —*v.* 1. To take up with or as with a scoop. 2. To hollow out. 3. *Slang.* To outmaneuver in acquiring a news story. [< MLG and MDu *schōpe*.]

scoot (sko͞ot) *v.* To go speedily. —*n.* A darting or scurrying off. [Prob < Scand.]

scoot•er (sko͞o'tər) *n.* A child's vehicle consisting of a long footboard between two small end wheels.

scope (skōp) *n.* 1. The range of one's perceptions, thoughts, or actions. 2. Breadth or opportunity to function. 3. The area covered by a given activity or subject. [< Gk *skopos*, watcher, goal, aim.]

–scope. *comb. form.* An instrument for observing or detecting: **microscope**. [< Gk *skopein*, to see.]

sco•pol•a•mine (skō-pŏl'ə-mēn', -mĭn) *n.* A thick, syrupy, colorless alkaloid, $C_{17}H_{21}NO_4$, used as a sedative and truth serum.

scor•bu•tic (skôr-byo͞o'tĭk) *adj.* Also **scor•bu•ti•cal** (-tĭ-kəl). Related to, resembling, or afflicted with scurvy. [< LL *scorbūtus*, scurvy.]

scorch (skôrch) *v.* 1. To burn the surface of. 2. To wither or parch. —*n.* 1. A slight or surface burn. 2. A discoloration caused by heat. [ME *scorchen*.] —**scorch'ing•ly** *adv.*

score (skôr, skōr) *n.* 1. A notch or incision. 2. A record of points made in a competitive event. 3. A result of a test or examination. 4. A debt. 5. A reason; account. 6. A group of 20 items. 7. The written form of a musical composition. 8. The music composed for a stage show or film. —*v.* scored, scoring. 1. To mark with lines or notches. 2. To gain (a point) in a game or contest. 3. To record the score in a contest. 4. To achieve; win. 5. To evaluate and assign a grade to. 6. *Mus.* **a.** To orchestrate. **b.** To arrange for a specific instrument. [< ON *skor*, notch, twenty.]

scorn (skôrn) *n.* 1. Contempt or disdain. 2. Derision. —*v.* To consider or treat as contemptible; disdain. [< OF *escharnir*.] —**scorn'ful** *adj.* —**scorn'ful•ly** *adv.*

scor•pi•on (skôr'pē-ən) *n.* 1. An arachnid with a segmented body and a tail tipped with a venomous sting. 2. **Scorpion.** The constellation

---

ă pat/ā ate/âr care/ä bar/b bib/ch chew/d deed/ĕ pet/ē be/f fit/g gag/h hat/hw what/
ĭ pit/ī pie/îr pier/j judge/k kick/l lid, fatal/m mum/n no, sudden/ng sing/ŏ pot/ō go/

and sign of the zodiac Scorpius. [< Gk *skorpios.*]

Scor•pi•us (skôr'pē-əs) *n.* Also **Scor•pi•o** (skôr'pē-ō'). **1.** A constellation in the S Hemisphere. **2.** The 8th sign of the zodiac. [< L *scorpiō*, scorpion.]

Scot (skŏt) *n.* **1.** A native or inhabitant of Scotland. **2.** A member of the ancient Gaelic tribe that migrated to N Great Britain from Ireland in about the 6th century A.D.

Scot. Scotch; Scotland; Scottish.

scotch (skŏch) *v.* **1.** To cut or scratch. **2.** To cripple. **3.** To put an end to; stifle. [< NF *escocher*, to cut a notch.]

Scotch (skŏch) *n.* **1.** The people of Scotland. **2.** Any of the English dialects spoken in Scotland. **3.** Scotch whisky. [Contraction of SCOTTISH.] —**Scotch** *adj.*

Scotch•man (skŏch'mən) *n.* A Scot.

Scotch whisky. A smoky-flavored whiskey distilled in Scotland from malted barley, the malt having been dried°over a peat fire.

scot-free (skŏt'frē') *adj.* Free from obligation or penalty. [< ME *scot*, tax.]

Scot•land (skŏt'lənd). A constituent country of the United Kingdom, located in N Great Britain. Pop. 5,178,000. Cap. Edinburgh.

Scotland Yard. The headquarters of the London Metropolitan Police.

Scots•man (skŏts'mən) *n.* A Scot.

Scott (skŏt), Sir **Walter.** 1771–1832. Scottish poet and historical novelist.

Scot•tie (skŏt'ē) *n.* A Scotsman.

Scot•tish (skŏt'ĭsh) *n.* **1.** A dialect of English spoken by the Lowlanders of Scotland. **2.** The people of Scotland. —**Scot'tish** *adj.*

Scottish Gaelic. The Gaelic language of the Scottish Highlanders.

scoun•drel (skoun'drəl) *n.* A villain. [?]

scour¹ (skour) *v.* **1.** To clean by scrubbing vigorously, as with an abrasive. **2.** To scrub something in order to clean it. [< LL *excūrāre*, to clean out.]

scour² (skour) *v.* **1.** To search through or over thoroughly. **2.** To move swiftly. [Prob < ON *skŷra*, to rush in.]

scourge (skûrj) *n.* **1.** A whip used to inflict punishment. **2.** Any means of inflicting punishment. **3.** A cause of affliction, as pestilence or war. —*v.* **scourged, scourging. 1.** To flog. **2.** To chastise severely; excoriate. **3.** To devastate; ravage. [< OF *escorgier*, to whip.] —**scourg'er** *n.*

scout¹ (skout) *n.* **1.** One dispatched to gather information. **2.** A watchman or sentinel. —*v.* **1.** To reconnoiter. **2.** To observe and evaluate. [< OF *escoute*, "listener," spy.]

scout² (skout) *v.* **1.** To reject contemptuously. **2.** To scoff. [< Scand.]

scow (skou) *n.* A flat-bottomed boat with square ends. [Du *schouw*.]

scowl (skoul) *n.* An angry frown. —*v.* To form a scowl. [Prob < Scand.]

scrab•ble (skrăb'əl) *v.* **-bled, -bling. 1.** To grope about frenetically with the hands. **2.** To struggle. **3.** To scribble. **4.** To make or obtain by scraping together. [< MDu *schrabben*, to scrape.] —**scrab'ble** *n.*

scrag•gly (skrăg'lē) *adj.* **-glier, -gliest.** Ragged or irregular; unkempt.

scram (skrăm) *v.* **scrammed, scramming.** *Slang.* To leave a scene at once. [Short for SCRAMBLE.]

scram•ble (skrăm'bəl) *v.* **-bled, -bling. 1.** To move or climb hurriedly. **2.** To compete frantically. **3.** To mix confusedly. **4.** To fry (eggs) with the yolks and whites mixed together. **5.** *Electronics.* To distort (a signal) so as to render it unintelligible without a special receiver. [Blend of obs *scamble*, to struggle for, and *cramble*, to crawl.] —**scram'ble** *n.* —**scram'bler** *n.*

scrap¹ (skrăp) *n.* **1.** A fragment or shred. **2.** **scraps.** Leftover food. **3.** Construction material left over or discarded as refuse. —*v.* **scrapped, scrapping. 1.** To break down into parts for disposal or salvage. **2.** To discard as worthless. [< ON *skrap*, trifles, remains.]

scrap² (skrăp) *v.* **scrapped, scrapping.** To fight or quarrel. —*n.* A quarrel. [Perh var of SCRAPE.] —**scrap'per** *n.* —**scrap'py** *adj.*

scrap•book (skrăp'bŏŏk') *n.* A book with blank pages for mounting pictures or other mementos.

scrape (skrāp) *v.* **scraped, scraping. 1.** To rub (a surface) with considerable pressure. **2.** To draw (a hard or abrasive object) forcefully over a surface. **3.** To abrade, smooth, injure, or remove by this procedure. **4.** To come into abrasive contact. **5.** To rub or move with a grating noise. **6.** To amass or produce with difficulty: *He scraped together the money.* —*n.* **1.** The act or result of scraping. **2. a.** A predicament. **b.** A scuffle. [< ON *skrapa.*] —**scrap'er** *n.*

scratch (skrăch) *v.* **1.** To make a shallow cut or mark with something sharp. **2.** To use the nails or claws to dig, scrape, or wound. **3.** To rub (the skin) to relieve itching. **4.** To strike out or cancel (a word, name, or passage) by or as if by drawing lines through. —*n.* A mark or wound produced by scratching. —**from scratch.** From the beginning. —*adj.* **1.** Done by chance. **2.** Assembled at random. **3.** Used for hasty jottings: *scratch paper.* [Blend of obs *scrat* and *cratch.*] —**scratch'y** *adj.*

scrawl (skrôl) *v.* To write hastily or illegibly. —*n.* Irregular or illegible handwriting. [Blend of SPRAWL and CRAWL.] —**scrawl'y** *adj.*

scraw•ny (skrô'nē) *adj.* **-nier, -niest.** Gaunt and bony; skinny. [?] —**scraw'ni•ness** *n.*

scream (skrēm) *v.* **1.** To cry out loudly and shrilly, as from pain or fear. **2.** To have a blatantly arresting effect. —*n.* A loud piercing sound. [< ON *skrǽma.*]

screech (skrēch) *n.* **1.** A shriek. **2.** A sound resembling this. [< ON *skrǽkja.*] —**screech** *v.*

screen (skrēn) *n.* **1.** Something that serves to divide, conceal, or protect, as a movable room partition. **2.** A coarse sieve. **3.** A window insertion of framed mesh used to keep out insects. **4. a.** The white or silver surface upon which a picture is projected for viewing. **b.** The motion-picture industry. —*v.* **1.** To provide with a screen. **2.** To conceal or protect. **3.** To separate with or as if with a sieve. **4.** To show on a screen, as a motion picture. [< MDu *scherm,* "shield," "protection."]

screen•play (skrĕn'plā') *n.* The script for a motion picture.

screw (skrōō) *n.* **1.** A metal pin with incised thread or threads, having a broad slotted head so that it can be driven as a fastener by turning it with a screwdriver. **2.** A propeller. —*v.* **1.** To fasten, tighten, adjust, or attach by or as if by means of a screw. **2.** To turn or twist. **3.** To become attached by means of screw threads. [< L *scrōfa,* sow (prob because screw threads coil like a sow's tail).]

screw•ball (skrōō'bôl') *n.* **1.** *Baseball.* A pitched ball curving in the direction opposite to a normal curve. **2.** *Slang.* An eccentric or irrational person.

screw•driv•er (skrōō'drī'vər) *n.* **1.** A tool used for turning screws. **2.** A cocktail of vodka and orange juice.

scrib•ble (skrĭb'əl) *v.* **-bled, -bling.** To write hurriedly and carelessly. [< L *scrībere,* to write.] —**scrib'ble** *n.* —**scrib'bler** *n.*

scribe (skrīb) *n.* **1.** A public clerk. **2.** A professional copyist of manuscripts. **3.** A writer. [< L *scrībere,* to write.]

scrim•mage (skrĭm'ĭj) *n. Football.* **1.** The contest between two teams from the time the ball is snapped back until it becomes out of play. **2.** A team's practice session. —**line of scrimmage.** *Football.* An imaginary line across the field on which the ball rests and at which the teams line up for a new play. [< var of SKIRMISH.]

scrimp (skrĭmp) *v.* To economize severely. [Perh < Scand.] —**scrimp'y** *adj.*

scrip¹ (skrĭp) *n.* Paper money issued for temporary and often emergency use. [Var of SCRIPT.]

scrip² (skrĭp) *n.* A certificate entitling the holder to a fractional share of stock or of other property. [Short for *subscription (receipt).*]

script (skrĭpt) *n.* **1.** Handwriting as distinguished from print. **2.** Cursive writing. **3.** The text of a play, broadcast, or motion picture. [< L *scrīptus,* pp of *scrībere,* to write.]

Script. Scriptural; Scriptures.

Scrip•ture (skrĭp'chər) *n.* Often **Scriptures. 1.** A sacred writing or book, esp. the Bible. **2.** A passage from such a writing. [< L *scrīptūra,* act of writing.] —**Scrip'tur•al** *adj.*

scriv•en•er (skrĭv'nər) *n. Archaic.* **1.** A professional copyist; scribe. **2.** A notary. [< L *scrība,* scribe.]

scrod (skrŏd) *n.* A young cod or haddock. [Obs Du *schrood,* slice, shred.]

scroll (skrōl) *n.* **1.** A roll of parchment, papyrus, etc., used esp. for writing a document. **2.** Ornamentation resembling a partially rolled scroll of paper. [< OF *escroue,* strip of parchment.]

Scrooge (skrōōj) *n.* A mean, miserly person. [< the character in Dickens' *Christmas Carol.*]

scro•tum (skrō'təm) *n., pl.* **-ta** (-tə) or **-tums.** The external sac of skin enclosing the testes. [L *scrōtum.*] —**scro'tal** (skrōt'l) *adj.*

scrounge (skrounj) *v.* **scrounged, scrounging. 1.** To forage about in an effort to acquire (something) at no cost. **2.** To wheedle. [Var of dial *scrunge,* to steal.] —**scroung'er** *n.*

scrub¹ (skrŭb) *v.* **scrubbed, scrubbing. 1.** To rub hard, as with a brush, soap, and water, in order to clean. **2.** To clean by hard rubbing. [< MLG or MDu *schrobben, schrubben.*] —**scrub** *n.* —**scrub'ber** *n.*

scrub² (skrŭb) *n.* **1.** A growth of stunted trees or shrubs. **2.** A stunted or inferior domestic animal, tree, etc. [< SHRUB.] —**scrub** *adj.* —**scrub'by** *adj.*

scruff (skrŭf) *n.* The back of the neck; nape. [Var of obs *scuff.*]

scrump•tious (skrŭmp'shəs) *adj. Slang.* Splendid; delectable. [Perh var of SUMPTUOUS.]

scru•ple (skrōō'pəl) *n.* **1.** Ethical objection to certain actions; principle; dictate of conscience. **2.** A unit of apothecary weight equal to 20 grains. [< L *scrūpulus,* small sharp stone, scruple.]

scru•pu•lous (skrōō'pyə-ləs) *adj.* **1.** Having scruples; principled. **2.** Very conscientious and exacting. —**scru'pu•lous•ly** *adv.* —**scru'pu•lous•ness** *n.*

scru•ti•nize (skrōōt'n-īz') *v.* **-nized, -nizing.** To examine or observe with great care.

scru•ti•ny (skrōōt'n-ē) *n., pl.* **-nies.** A close, careful examination or study. [< L *scrūtārī,* to search, examine.]

scu•ba (skōō'bə) *n.* An apparatus containing compressed air and used for free-swimming underwater breathing. [S(elf)-c(ontained) u(nderwater) b(reathing) a(pparatus).]

scud (skŭd) *v.* **scudded, scudding.** To run or skim along swiftly and easily. —*n.* Wind-driven clouds or mist.

scuff (skŭf) *v.* **1.** To scrape the feet while walking. **2.** To scrape and roughen the surface of (shoes). —*n.* **1.** The sound or act of scuffing. **2.** A spot left as a result of scuffing. [Prob < Scand.]

scuf•fle (skŭf'əl) *v.* **-fled, -fling. 1.** To fight confusedly at close quarters. **2.** To shuffle. —*n.* A disorderly struggle at close quarters. [Prob < Scand.] —**scuf'fler** *n.*

scull (skŭl) *n.* **1.** A long oar twisted from side to side over the stern of a boat to propel it. **2.** One of a pair of short-handled oars used by a single rower. —*v.* To propel (a boat) with a scull or sculls. [ME *sculle.*]

scul•ler•y (skŭl'ə-rē) *n., pl.* **-ies.** A room adjoining the kitchen where dishwashing and other chores are done. [< OF *escuelier,* keeper of dishes.]

sculp•sit (skŭlp'sĭt). He (or she) sculptured (it). [L.]

sculpt (skŭlpt) *v.* To sculpture.

sculp•tor (skŭlp'tər) *n.* One who sculptures, esp. an artist who works in stone or metal. —**sculp'tress** *fem.n.*

sculp•ture (skŭlp'chər) *n.* **1.** The art or practice of shaping figures or designs in the round or in relief, as by carving wood, chiseling marble, modeling clay, or casting in metal. **2.** A work or formation created in this manner. —*v.* **-tured, -turing. 1.** To fashion into a three-dimensional figure. **2.** To represent in sculpture. [< L *sculpere* (pp *sculptus*), to carve.]

ă pat/ā ate/âr care/ä bar/b bib/ch chew/d deed/ĕ pet/ē be/f fit/g gag/h hat/hw what/
ĭ pit/ī pie/îr pier/j judge/k kick/l lid, fatal/m mum/n no, sudden/ng sing/ŏ pot/ō go/

scum (skŭm) *n.* **1.** A filmy layer of impure matter on the surface of a liquid or body of water. **2.** Any refuse or worthless matter. **3.** An element of society regarded as being vile or worthless. [< MDu *schūm*.]

scup•per (skŭp′ər) *n.* An opening in the side of a ship at deck level to allow water to run off. [ME *skopper*.]

scurf (skûrf) *n.* Scaly or shredded dry skin, such as dandruff. —**scurf′i•ness** *n.* —**scurf′y** *adj.*

scur•ri•lous (skûr′ə-ləs) *adj.* Vulgar; abusive; obscene. [< L *scurrīlis*, buffoonlike, jeering.]

scur•ry (skûr′ē) *v.* -**ried,** -**rying.** **1.** To scamper. **2.** To flurry or swirl about.

scur•vy (skûr′vē) *n.* A disease caused by deficiency of vitamin C, characterized by spongy and bleeding gums, bleeding under the skin, and extreme weakness. —*adj.* -**vier,** -**viest.** Mean; worthless. [< SCURF.]

scut•tle[1] (skŭt′l) *n.* A small hatch, esp. in the deck or side of a ship. —*v.* -**tled,** -**tling.** To sink (a ship) by cutting or opening a hole in the hull. [< OF *escoutille*.]

scut•tle[2] (skŭt′l) *n.* A pail for carrying coal. [< L *scutella*, salver.]

scut•tle[3] (skŭt′l) *v.* -**tled,** -**tling.** To run hastily; scurry. [< SCUD.]

scut•tle•butt (skŭt′l-bŭt′) *n. Slang.* Gossip; rumor.

scythe (sīth) *n.* An implement with a long, curved single-edged blade, used for mowing or reaping. [< OE *sīthe.* See sek-.] —**scythe** *v.* (**scythed, scything**).

s.d. Indefinitely (L *sine die*).

S.D. **1.** special delivery. **2.** South Dakota (unofficial).

S.Dak. South Dakota.

Se selenium.

SE southeast; southeastern.

sea (sē) *n.* **1. a.** The continuous body of salt water covering most of the earth's surface, esp. this body regarded as a geophysical entity distinct from the earth and sky. **b.** A tract of water within an ocean. **c.** A relatively large body of salt water completely or partly land-locked. **d.** A body of fresh water. **2.** The condition of the ocean's surface: *a high sea.* **3.** Something that suggests the sea in its overwhelming sweep or vastness. [< OE *sǣ* < Gmc *saiwa-*.]

sea anemone. A marine organism with a flexible, cylindrical body and numerous tentacles.

sea•board (sē′bôrd′, -bōrd′) *n.* **1.** The seacoast. **2.** The land near the sea.

sea•coast (sē′kōst′) *n.* Land bordering the sea.

sea•far•er (sē′fâr′ər) *n.* A sailor.

sea•far•ing (sē′fâr′ĭng) *n.* The occupation of a sailor. —*adj.* Following a life at sea.

sea•food (sē′fōōd′) *n.* Edible fish or shellfish from the sea.

sea•go•ing (sē′gō′ĭng) *adj.* **1.** Made or used for ocean voyages. **2.** Seafaring.

sea horse. A small marine fish with a horse-like head and a body covered with bony plates.

seal[1] (sēl) *n.* **1. a.** A die or signet having a raised or incised emblem, used to stamp an impression upon a substance such as wax or lead. **b.** The impression made. **c.** The design or emblem itself. **d.** A small disk or wafer bearing such an imprint and affixed to a document to prove authenticity or seal it shut. **2.** Something (as a commercial hallmark) that serves similarly to authenticate, confirm, or attest. —*v.* **1.** To affix a seal to so as to prove authenticity or attest to accuracy, quality, etc. **2.** To close with or as with a seal; make fast. **3.** To establish or determine irrevocably. [< L *signum*, sign.] —**seal′er** *n.*

seal[2] (sēl) *n.* **1.** An aquatic mammal with a torpedo-shaped body and limbs in the form of flippers. **2.** Also **seal•skin** (sēl′skĭn′). The pelt or fur of a seal. —*v.* To hunt seals. [< OE *seolh.*] —**seal′er** *n.*

sea level. The level of the ocean's surface, esp. the mean level halfway between high and low tide.

sea lion. A brown seal of Pacific waters.

seam (sēm) *n.* **1. a.** A line formed by sewing together two pieces of material. **b.** A similar line, ridge, or groove. **2.** Any line across a surface, as a fissure or wrinkle. **3.** A thin layer or stratum, as of coal. —*v.* **1.** To join with or as with a seam. **2.** To mark with a wrinkle, scar, or other seamlike line. [< OE *sēam.* See syū-.] —**seam′er** *n.* —**seam′less** *adj.*

sea•man (sē′mən) *n.* **1.** A sailor. **2.** *U.S. Navy.* An enlisted man ranking below petty officer.

sea•man•ship (sē′mən-shĭp′) *n.* Skill in managing or navigating a boat or ship.

seam•stress (sēm′strĭs) *n.* A woman who makes her living by sewing.

seam•y (sē′mē) *adj.* -**ier,** -**iest.** **1.** Having or showing a seam. **2.** Rough and raw; sordid.

sé•ance (sā′äns′) *n.* A meeting of persons to receive spiritualistic messages. [F, "a sitting."]

sea•plane (sē′plān′) *n.* An aircraft equipped to land on or take off from a body of water.

sea•port (sē′pôrt′, -pōrt′) *n.* A port with facilities for seagoing ships.

sear (sîr) *v.* **1.** To make or become withered; dry up. **2.** To char, scorch, or burn the surface of. [< OE *sēar*, withered. See saus-.]

search (sûrch) *v.* **1.** To make a thorough examination of in order to find something; explore. **2.** To make a careful investigation of; probe. **3.** To make a thorough check of; scrutinize. [< OF *cerchier*, "to go around."] —**search** *n.* —**search′er** *n.*

search•light (sûrch′līt′) *n.* **1.** An apparatus for projecting a bright beam of light. **2.** The beam so projected.

sea•shell (sē′shĕl′) *n.* The shell of a marine mollusk.

sea•shore (sē′shôr′, -shōr′) *n.* Land by the sea.

sea•sick•ness (sē′sĭk′nĭs) *n.* Nausea and other malaise provoked by the motion of a vessel at sea. —**sea′sick′** *adj.*

sea•side (sē′sīd′) *n.* The seashore.

sea•son (sē′zən) *n.* **1. a.** One of the four equal divisions of the year, spring, summer, autumn, and winter. **b.** The two divisions of the year, rainy and dry, in tropical climates. **2.** A recurrent period characterized by certain occupations, festivities, or crops. —*v.* **1.** To improve or enhance the flavor of (food) by adding spices, herbs, etc. **2.** To add zest or interest to. **3.** To accustom; inure. **4.** To make or become usable, as by aging or drying. [< L *satiō,* act of sowing.] —**sea′son·al** *adj.*

sea·son·a·ble (sē′zə-nə-bəl) *adj.* **1.** In keeping with the season. **2.** Occurring at the proper time; timely. —**sea′son·a·bly** *adv.*

sea·son·ing (sē′zə-nĭng) *n.* Anything used to flavor food.

seat (sēt) *n.* **1.** Something that may be sat upon, as a chair. **2.** A place in which one may sit. **3.** The part of something on which one rests in sitting. **4.** The buttocks. **5. a.** The place where anything is located or based. **b.** A center of authority; capital. **6.** Membership, as in a legislative body. —*v.* **1.** To place in or on a seat. **2.** To have or provide seats for. **3.** To install in a position of authority or eminence. [< ON *sæti.*]

seat belt. A safety strap attached to the seat of a passenger vehicle.

SEATO (sē′tō) Southeast Asia Treaty Organization.

Se·at·tle (sē-ăt′l). A city in W Washington. Pop. 524,000.

sea urchin. A marine organism with a spiny globular shell.

sea·ward (sē′wərd) *adv.* Also **sea·wards** (-wərdz). Toward the sea. —**sea′ward** *adj.*

sea·way (sē′wā′) *n.* An inland waterway for ocean shipping.

sea·weed (sē′wēd′) *n.* Any of various large or branching marine algae.

sea·wor·thy (sē′wûr′thē) *adj.* Designating a vessel that is fit to sail.

se·ba·ceous (sĭ-bā′shəs) *adj.* Of or secreting fat. [< L *sēbum,* tallow + -ACEOUS.]

sec, sec. **1.** second[1]. **2.** secretary. **3.** sector.

se·cant (sē′kənt, -kănt′) *n.* A straight line intersecting a curve at two or more points. [F *(ligne) secante,* "cutting (line)."]

se·cede (sĭ-sēd′, sē′-) *v.* **-ceded, -ceding.** To withdraw formally from membership in an organization or alliance. [L *sēcēdere,* to go away.]

se·ces·sion (sĭ-sĕsh′ən) *n.* The act of seceding.

se·clude (sĭ-klōōd′) *v.* **-cluded, -cluding. 1.** To set apart from others; isolate. **2.** To screen from view. [< L *sēclūdere.*] —**se·clu′sion** (-klōō′zhən) *n.*

sec·ond[1] (sĕk′ənd) *n.* **1.** A unit of time equal to $1/60$ of a minute. **2.** A moment. **3.** *Geom.* A unit of angular measure equal to $1/60$ of a minute of arc. [< ML *(pars minūta) secunda,* "second (small part)."]

sec·ond[2] (sĕk′ənd) *adj.* **1.** Next after the first. **2.** Inferior to another; subordinate. —*n.* **1.** The ordinal number two in a series. **2.** One that is next after the first. **3.** The forward gears in an automobile transmission having the second highest ratio. **4.** Often **seconds.** Merchandise of inferior quality. **5.** The official attendant of a contestant in a duel or boxing match. —*v.* **1.** To attend as an aide or assistant. **2.** To promote or encourage. **3.** To

endorse (a motion or nomination). [< L *secundus,* following, coming next.] —**sec′ond, sec′-ond·ly** *adv.*

sec·on·dar·y (sĕk′ən-dĕr′ē) *adj.* **1. a.** One step removed from the first; not primary. **b.** Inferior; minor. **2.** Derived from what is original: *a secondary source.* **3.** Of or relating to education between elementary school and college. —*n., pl.* **-ies.** One that acts in an auxiliary or subordinate capacity.

sec·ond-class (sĕk′ənd-klăs′, -kläs′) *adj.* **1.** In the rank or class next below the first or best. **2.** Inferior. —**sec′ond-class′** *adv.*

sec·ond-guess (sĕk′ənd-gĕs′) *v.* **1.** To criticize (a decision) after the outcome is known; reconsider from hindsight. **2.** To outguess.

sec·ond·hand (sĕk′ənd-hănd′) *adj.* **1.** Previously used; not new. **2.** Dealing in used merchandise. **3.** Not original; borrowed. —*adv.* Indirectly.

second person. A set of grammatical forms used in referring to the person addressed.

se·cre·cy (sē′krə-sē) *n.* **1.** The quality or condition of being secret. **2.** The ability to keep or habit of keeping secrets.

se·cret (sē′krĭt) *adj.* **1.** Concealed from general knowledge or view; kept hidden. **2.** Operating covertly: *a secret agent.* **3.** Beyond ordinary understanding; mysterious. —*n.* **1.** Something kept hidden from others. **2.** Something beyond understanding or explanation; a mystery. [< L *sēcrētus,* separate, out of the way, secret.] —**se′cret·ly** *adv.*

sec·re·tar·i·at (sĕk′rə-târ′ē-ĭt) *n.* **1.** The department administered by a governmental secretary. **2.** The position of a governmental secretary.

sec·re·tar·y (sĕk′rə-tĕr′ē) *n., pl.* **-ies. 1.** One employed to handle correspondence and do clerical work. **2.** An officer, as of a corporation, in charge of correspondence or records. **3.** An official in charge of a governmental department. **4.** A writing desk. [< ML *sēcrētārius,* confidential officer, secretary < L *sēcrētus,* SECRET.] —**sec′re·tar′i·al** (-târ′ē-əl) *adj.*

se·crete[1] (sĭ-krēt′) *v.* **-creted, -creting.** To generate and separate out (a substance) from cells or bodily fluids. [< L *sēcernere,* to separate.] —**se·cre′tion** *n.* —**se·cre′to·ry** (-krē′tə-rē) *adj.*

se·crete[2] (sĭ-krēt′) *v.* **-creted, -creting.** To conceal; cache. [< SECRET.]

se·cre·tive (sē′krə-tĭv, sĭ-krē′tĭv) *adj.* Closemouthed. —**se′cre·tive·ness** *n.*

sect (sĕkt) *n.* **1.** A group of people forming a distinct unit within a larger group and united by common beliefs, interests, etc. **2.** A schismatic religious body. **3.** A religious denomination. [< L *secta,* "following."]

—**sect.** *comb. form.* Cut or divide: **bisect.** [< L *secāre,* to cut.]

sec·tar·i·an (sĕk-târ′ē-ən) *adj.* **1.** Of or pertaining to a sect or sects. **2.** Adhering to a sect. **3.** Narrow-minded. —*n.* **1.** A member of a sect. **2.** One characterized by a narrow or factional viewpoint.

sec·tion (sĕk′shən) *n.* **1.** A component part or subdivision of something; a portion. **2.** The representation of a solid object as it would appear if cut by an intersecting plane, so that the internal structure is displayed. —*v.* To separate or divide into parts. [< L *secāre*, to cut.]

–section. *comb. form.* The act or process of dividing or cutting: **vivisection.**

sec•tion•al (sĕk'shən-əl) *adj.* **1.** Of or pertaining to a particular district. **2.** Composed of or divided into component sections.

sec•tor (sĕk'tər, -tôr') *n.* **1.** The portion of a circle bounded by two radii and one of the intercepted arcs. **2.** A division of a military position for which one unit is responsible. [< L *secāre*, to cut.]

sec•u•lar (sĕk'yə-lər) *adj.* **1.** Temporal rather than spiritual. **2.** Not pertaining to religion or a religious body. **3.** Not under monastic vows: *secular clergy.* [< L *saeculum*, generation, age.] —**sec'u•lar•ly** *adv.*

se•cure (sĭ-kyŏor') *adj.* **-curer, -curest. 1.** Free from danger; safe. **2.** Free from fear or doubt. **3.** Not likely to fail or give way; stable. **4.** Assured; certain. —*v.* **-cured, -curing. 1.** To guard from danger or risk of loss. **2.** To make firm; fasten. **3.** To make certain; guarantee. **4.** To acquire. [L *secūrus,* "without care."] —**se•cure'ly** *adv.* —**se•cure'ness** *n.*

se•cu•ri•ty (sĭ-kyŏor'ə-tē) *n., pl.* **-ties. 1.** Safety. **2.** Confidence. **3.** Anything that gives or assures safety. **4.** Something deposited as assurance of the fulfillment of an obligation. **5. securities.** Written evidence of ownership, as stocks, bonds, notes, etc.

secy. secretary.

se•dan (sĭ-dăn') *n.* **1.** A closed automobile having a front and rear seat. **2.** An enclosed chair carried on poles by two men.

se•date¹ (sĭ-dāt') *adj.* Serenely deliberate in character or manner. [< L *sēdāre*, to settle, calm, compose.] —**se•date'ly** *adv.* —**se•date'-ness** *n.*

se•date² (sĭ-dāt') *v.* **-dated, -dating.** To administer a sedative to. —**se•da'tion** *n.*

sed•a•tive (sĕd'ə-tĭv) *adj.* Having a soothing, calming, or tranquilizing effect. —*n.* A sedative agent or drug.

sed•en•tar•y (sĕd'n-tĕr'ē) *adj.* Characterized by much sitting: *a sedentary job.*

Se•der (sā'dər) *n., pl.* **Seders** or **Sedarim** (sĭ-där'ĭm). *Judaism.* The feast commemorating the departure of the Israelites from Egypt, celebrated on the eves of the first and second days of Passover or only on the eve of the first day. [Heb *sēdher,* "order."]

sedge (sĕj) *n.* Any of various grasslike plants growing chiefly in wet places. [< OE *secg.*]

sed•i•ment (sĕd'ə-mənt) *n.* Material that settles to the bottom of a liquid. [< L *sedēre*, to sit, settle.] —**sed'i•men•ta'tion** *n.*

sed•i•men•ta•ry (sĕd'ə-mĕn'tə-rē, -mĕn'trē) *adj.* **1.** Of or resembling sediment. **2.** Pertaining to rocks formed from sediment.

se•di•tion (sĭ-dĭsh'ən) *n.* Conduct or language inciting to rebellion against the authority of the state. [< L *sēditiō,* "a going apart," separation.] —**se•di'tious** *adj.*

se•duce (sĭ-d/y/ōos') *v.* **-duced, -ducing. 1.** To entice into wrongful behavior; corrupt. **2.** To

induce to have sexual intercourse. [< L *sēdūcere,* to lead away.] —**se•duc'er** *n.* —**se•duc'tion** (-dŭk'shən) *n.* —**se•duc'tive** *adj.*

sed•u•lous (sĕj'ŏo-ləs) *adj.* Diligent; industrious. [< L *sē doiō,* "without guile."]

see¹ (sē) *v.* **saw, seen, seeing. 1.** To perceive with the eye; have the power of sight. **2.** To understand; comprehend. **3.** To regard; view; imagine. **4.** To foresee. **5.** To know through experience; undergo. **6.** To find out; ascertain. **7.** To take note of. **8.** To meet; visit socially or for consultation. **9.** To escort: *see someone to the door.* **10.** To make sure: *See that it gets done.* [< OE *sēon.* See **sekw-².**]

see² (sē) *n.* The official seat, center of authority, jurisdiction, or office of a bishop. [< L *sēdes,* "seat," "residence."]

seed (sēd) *n.,pl.* **seeds** or **seed. 1.** A fertilized plant ovule containing an embryo capable of developing a new plant. **2.** Seeds collectively. **3.** A source or germ. **4.** Offspring. **5.** Ancestry. —*v.* **1.** To plant seeds in. **2.** To remove seeds from. [<OE *sæd* See **sē-.**]

seed•ling (sēd'lĭng) *n.* A young, newly developing plant.

seed money. Money needed or provided to start a new project.

seed•y (sē'dē) *adj.* **-ier, -iest. 1.** Having many seeds. **2.** Worn and shabby. **3.** Somewhat disreputable; squalid. —**seed'i•ness** *n.*

see•ing (sē'ĭng) *conj.* Inasmuch as.

seek (sēk) *v.* **sought, seeking. 1.** To search for. **2.** To endeavor to obtain or reach. **3.** To try; attempt. [< OE *sēcan.* See **sāg-.**] —**seek'er** *n.*

seem (sēm) *v.* **1.** To give the impression of being; appear. **2.** To appear to one's own mind. **3.** To be evident. **4.** To appear to exist. [< ON *sœma,* to conform to, honor.]

seem•ing (sē'mĭng) *adj.* Apparent; ostensible. —**seem'ing•ly** *adv.* —**seem'ing•ness** *n.*

seem•ly (sēm'lē) *adj.* **-lier, -liest. 1.** Proper; suitable. **2.** Of pleasing appearance. [< ON *sœmr,* fitting.] —**seem'li•ness** *n.*

seen (sēn). *p.p.* of **see.**

seep (sēp) *v.* **1.** To pass slowly through small openings. **2.** To enter, depart, or become diffused gradually. —**seep'age** *n.*

seer (sē'ər) *n.* **1.** A prophet. **2.** A clairvoyant.

see•saw (sē'sô') *n.* **1.** A long plank balanced on a central fulcrum so that with a person riding on either end, one end goes up as the other goes down. **2.** A back-and-forth or up-and-down movement.] [Redupl of SAW¹.] —**see'saw'** *v.*

seethe (sēth) *v.* **seethed, seething. 1.** To churn and foam as if boiling. **2.** To be violently agitated. [< OE *sēothan.* See **seu-¹.**]

seg•ment (sĕg'mənt) *n.* A part into which something can be divided; a subdivision or section. —*v.* (sĕg-mĕnt'). To divide or become divided into segments. [< L *secāre,* to cut.] —**seg'men'tal** *adj.* —**seg'men•ta'tion** *n.*

seg•re•gate (sĕg'rə-gāt') *v.* **-gated, -gating. 1.** To separate or isolate from others or from a main body or group. **2.** To impose the separation of (a race or class) from the rest of society. [L *sēgregāre,* "to separate from the flock."] —**seg're•ga'tion** *n.*

ô paw, for/oi boy/ou out/ŏo took/ōo coo/p pop/r run/s sauce/sh shy/t to/th thin/*th* the/
ŭ cut/ûr fur/v van/w wag/y yes/z size/zh vision/ə ago, item, edible, gallop, circus/

seg·re·ga·tion·ist (sĕg'rə-gā'shən-ĭst) *n.* One who advocates or practices a policy of racial segregation.

seign·ior (sān'yôr) *n.* A feudal landlord. [< L *senior,* older.] —**sei·gnio'ri·al** *adj.*

seine (sān) *n.* A large fishing net with weights at the lower edge and floats at the top. —*v.* **seined, seining.** To fish or catch with a seine. [< Gk *sagēnē.*]

Seine (sĕn). A river of N France.

seis·mic (sīz'mĭk) *adj.* Of or caused by an earthquake. [SEISM(O)- + -IC.] —**seis'mi·cal·ly** *adv.*

seismo–. *comb. form.* Earthquake. [< Gk *seismos,* earthquake.]

seis·mo·graph (sīz'mə-grăf', -gräf') *n.* An instrument for automatically detecting and recording the intensity, direction, and duration of any movement of the ground. —**seis·mog'ra·pher** (sīz-mŏg'rə-fər) *n.* —**seis'mo·graph'ic** *adj.* —**seis·mog'ra·phy** *n.*

seize (sēz) *v.* **seized, seizing.** 1. To grasp suddenly and forcibly. 2. To have a sudden effect upon; overwhelm. 3. To take into legal custody; confiscate. [< OF *seisir.*]

sei·zure (sē'zhər) *n.* 1. The act of seizing or state of being seized. 2. A sudden paroxysm, as an epileptic convulsion.

sel. select; selected.

sel·dom (sĕl'dəm) *adv.* Not often; infrequently. [< OE *seldan* < Gmc **seldo-.*] —**sel'dom·ness** *n.*

se·lect (sĭ-lĕkt') *v.* To choose from among several; make a choice. —*adj.* Also **se·lect·ed** (sĭ-lĕk'tĭd). 1. Chosen; picked out. 2. Of special value or quality. [L *sēligere* (pp *sēlectus*), to choose out.] —**se·lec'tive** *adj.* —**se·lec'tiv·i·ty** *n.* —**se·lec'tor** *n.*

se·lec·tion (sĭ-lĕk'shən) *n.* 1. a. The act of selecting or fact of being selected; choice. b. That which is selected. 2. A literary or musical text chosen for reading or performance. 3. A process that promotes the continued existence of certain organisms in competition with others.

selective service. Compulsory military service according to stipulated requirements for induction.

se·lect·man (sĭ-lĕkt'mən) *n.* One of a board of town officers of New England communities.

se·le·ni·um (sĭ-lē'nē-əm) *n. Symbol* **Se** A non-metallic element resembling sulfur, used as a semiconductor and in xerography. Atomic number 34, atomic weight 78.96. [< Gk *selēnē,* moon.]

self (sĕlf) *n., pl.* **selves** (sĕlvz). 1. The total being of one person; the individual. 2. Individuality. 3. One's own interests, welfare, or advantage. —*pron.* Myself, yourself, himself, or herself. [< OE *self, silf.* See **seu-².**]

self–. *comb. form.* Forms hyphenated compounds indicating: 1. Oneself or itself. 2. Of, to, toward, in, on, with, by, for, or from the self, oneself, or itself. 3. Autonomous, automatic, or automatically.

self-ad·dressed (sĕlf'ə-drĕst') *adj.* Addressed to oneself.

self-cen·tered (sĕlf'sĕn'tərd) *adj.* Engrossed in oneself and one's affairs. —**self'-cen'tered·ly** *adv.* —**self'-cen'tered·ness** *n.*

self-con·fi·dence (sĕlf'kŏn'fə-dəns) *n.* Confidence in oneself or one's abilities. —**self'-con'fi·dent** *adj.* —**self'-con'fi·dent·ly** *adv.*

self-con·scious (sĕlf'kŏn'shəs) *adj.* 1. Excessively conscious of one's appearance or manner. 2. Not natural; stilted. —**self'-con'scious·ly** *adv.* —**self'-con'scious·ness** *n.*

self-con·tained (sĕlf'kən-tānd') *adj.* 1. Self-sufficient. 2. Keeping to oneself; reserved.

self-con·trol (sĕlf'kən-trōl') *n.* Control of one's emotions, desires, or actions by one's own will. —**self'-con·trolled'** *adj.*

self-de·fense (sĕlf'dĭ-fĕns') *n.* 1. Defense against attack on oneself, one's property, or one's reputation. 2. *Law.* The right to protect oneself against violence or threatened violence with whatever means are reasonably necessary.

self-de·ni·al (sĕlf'dĭ-nī'əl) *n.* Sacrifice of one's own comfort or gratification. —**self'-de·ny'ing** *adj.* —**self'-de·ny'ing·ly** *adv.*

self-de·ter·mi·na·tion (sĕlf'dĭ-tûr'mə-nā'shən) *n.* 1. Determination of one's own fate or course of action without compulsion. 2. Freedom of a people or area to determine its own political status.

self-ef·fac·ing (sĕlf'ĭ-fā'sĭng) *adj.* Not drawing attention to oneself; modest. —**self'-ef·face'ment** *n.*

self-ev·i·dent (sĕlf'ĕv'ə-dənt) *adj.* Requiring no proof or explanation.

self-ex·plan·a·to·ry (sĕlf'ĭk-splăn'ə-tôr'ē, -tōr'ē) *adj.* Needing no explanation.

self-ex·pres·sion (sĕlf'ĭk-sprĕsh'ən) *n.* Expression of one's own personality, as through speech or art.

self-gov·ern·ment (sĕlf'gŭv'ərn-mənt) *n.* 1. Political independence; autonomy. 2. Democracy. —**self'-gov'ern·ing** *adj.*

self-im·por·tance (sĕlf'ĭm-pôr'təns) *n.* Excessively high opinion of one's own importance; conceit. —**self'-im·por'tant** *adj.*

self-in·ter·est (sĕlf'ĭn'trĭst, -ĭn'tər-ĭst) *n.* Personal advantage or interest; selfish motive or gain. —**self'-in'ter·est·ed** *adj.*

self·ish (sĕl'fĭsh) *adj.* Concerned chiefly or only with oneself, without regard for the well-being of others; egotistic. —**self'ish·ly** *adv.* —**self'ish·ness** *n.*

self-knowl·edge (sĕlf'nŏl'ĭj) *n.* Knowledge of one's own nature; insight into oneself.

self·less (sĕlf'lĭs) *adj.* Without concern for oneself; unselfish. —**self'less·ly** *adv.* —**self'less·ness** *n.*

self-made (sĕlf'mād') *adj.* 1. Having achieved success unaided. 2. Made by oneself or itself.

self-pos·ses·sion (sĕlf'pə-zĕsh'ən) *n.* Full command of one's faculties, feelings, and behavior; poise. —**self'-pos·sessed'** *adj.*

self-re·li·ance (sĕlf'rĭ-lī'əns) *n.* Reliance upon one's own capabilities or resources. —**self'-re·li'ant** *adj.* —**self'-re·li'ant·ly** *adv.*

self-re·spect (sĕlf'rĭ-spĕkt') *n.* Due respect for oneself, one's character, and one's conduct. —**self'-re·spect'ing** *adj.*

self-right·eous (sĕlf'rī'chəs) *adj.* Piously sure

of one's righteousness. —**self'-right'eous•ly** *adv.*
—**self'-right'eous•ness** *n.*

self•same (sĕlf'sām') *adj.* The very same; identical.

self-seek•ing (sĕlf'sē'kĭng) *adj.* Pursuing or seeking only for oneself. —**self'-seek'er** *n.*

self-styled (sĕlf'stīld') *adj.* As characterized by oneself.

self-suf•fi•cient (sĕlf'sə-fĭsh'ənt) *adj.* Also **self-suf•fic•ing** (-fī'sĭng). Able to provide for oneself without help; not dependent. —**self'-suf•fi'cien•cy** *n.*

self-will (sĕlf'wĭl') *n.* Willfulness, esp. in satisfying one's own desires. —**self'-willed'** *adj.*

self-wind•ing (sĕlf'wīn'dĭng) *adj.* Winding automatically.

sell (sĕl) *v.* **sold, selling. 1.** To exchange for money or its equivalent. **2.** To offer for sale, as for one's livelihood: *He sells textiles.* **3.** To be sold or be on sale. **4.** To attract prospective buyers: *an item that sells well.* **5.** To convince: *They sold him on the idea.* [< OE *sellan,* to give, betray, sell. See **sel-**[1].] —**sell'er** *n.*

sell out. 1. To sell all one's goods or possessions. **2.** *Slang.* To betray one's cause or colleagues. —**sell'out'** *n.*

selt•zer (sĕlt'sər) *n.* **1.** A natural effervescent spring water of high mineral content. **2.** Such water artificially prepared and containing carbon dioxide. [G *Selterser (Wasser),* "(water) of Nieder Selters," a district near Wiesbaden, West Germany.]

sel•vage (sĕl'vĭj) *n.* Also **sel•vedge.** The edge of a fabric woven so that it will not ravel. [< SELF + EDGE.]

selves. *pl.* of **self.**

se•man•tic (sə-măn'tĭk) *adj.* Pertaining to meaning, esp. in language. [Gk *sēmantikos,* significant.]

se•man•tics (sə-măn'tĭks) *n.* (takes sing. v.). The study or science of meaning in language forms, esp. with regard to its historical change.

sem•a•phore (sĕm'ə-fôr', -fōr') *n.* Any visual signaling apparatus with flags, lights, or mechanically moving arms. [Gk *sēma,* sign + -PHORE.]

sem•blance (sĕm'bləns) *n.* **1.** An outward or token appearance. **2.** A representation; resemblance. **3.** The barest trace. [< OF *sembler,* to resemble, seem.]

se•men (sē'mən) *n.* A viscous whitish secretion of the male reproductive organs, the transporting medium for spermatozoa; sperm. [< L *sēmen,* "seed."]

se•mes•ter (sə-mĕs'tər) *n.* One of two divisions of 15 to 18 weeks each of an academic year. [< L (*cursus*) *sēmēstris,* "(period) of six months."]

semi-. *comb. form.* **1.** Partly or partially. **2.** Half of. **3.** Occurring twice within a particular period of time. [L *sēmi-.*]

sem•i•an•nu•al (sĕm'ē-ăn'yōō-əl, sĕm'ī-) *adj.* Happening or issued twice a year.

sem•i•cir•cle (sĕm'ī-sûr'kəl) *n.* A half of a circle as divided by a diameter. —**sem'i•cir'cu•lar** (-sûr'kyə-lər) *adj.*

semicircular canal. Any of the three looped, fluid-containing tubes in the inner ear that

function in maintaining the sense of balance and orientation.

sem•i•co•lon (sĕm'ī-kō'lən) *n.* A mark of punctuation (;) indicating a degree of separation intermediate between the comma and the period.

sem•i•con•duc•tor (sĕm'ē-kən-dŭk'tər, sĕm'ī-) *n.* Any of various solid crystalline substances, such as germanium or silicon, having electrical conductivity greater than insulators but less than good conductors.

sem•i•fi•nal (sĕm'ē-fī'nəl, sĕm'ī-) *adj.* Immediately preceding the final, as in a series of competitions.

sem•i•month•ly (sĕm'ē-mŭnth'lē, sĕm'ī-) *adj.* Occurring or issued twice a month. See Usage note at **bimonthly.** —*adv.* Twice monthly.

sem•i•nal (sĕm'ə-nəl) *adj.* Of, relating to, or containing semen.

sem•i•nar (sĕm'ə-när') *n.* **1.** A small group of advanced college students engaged in original research under the guidance of a professor. **2.** A course of study so pursued. [< L *sēminārium,* seed plot, nursery.]

sem•i•nar•y (sĕm'ə-nĕr'ē) *n., pl.* **-ies.** A school, esp. a theological school for the training of priests, ministers, or rabbis. [< L *sēminārium,* garden, seed plot, nursery.] —**sem'i•nar'i•an** (sĕm'ə-nâr'ē-ən) *n.*

Sem•i•nole (sĕm'ə-nōl') *n., pl.* **-nole** or **-noles. 1.** A member of a tribe of Muskhogean-speaking North American Indians, now living chiefly in Oklahoma and Florida. **2.** The language of this tribe.

sem•i•per•me•a•ble (sĕm'ē-pûr'mē-ə-bəl, sĕm'ī-) *adj.* **1.** Partially permeable. **2.** Pertaining to a membrane that is permeable to some molecules in a solution but not to all.

sem•i•pre•cious (sĕm'ē-prĕsh'əs, sĕm'ī-) *adj.* Of less value than precious stones, as a topaz.

sem•i•pri•vate (sĕm'ē-prī'vĭt, sĕm'ī-) *adj.* Shared with other occupants.

sem•i•skilled (sĕm'ē-skĭld', sĕm'ī-) *adj.* Possessing minimal skills.

sem•i•sol•id (sĕm'ē-sŏl'ĭd, sĕm'ī-) *adj.* Intermediate in properties, esp. in rigidity, between solids and liquids. —*n.* A semisolid substance.

Sem•ite (sĕm'īt') *n.* Also **Shem•ite** (shĕm'īt'). A member of any of a group of Caucasoid peoples, chiefly Jews and Arabs, of the E Mediterranean area.

Se•mit•ic (sə-mĭt'ĭk) *adj.* **1.** Of or pertaining to the Semites, esp. Jewish or Arabic. **2.** Pertaining to a subfamily of Afro-Asiatic, including Arabic, Hebrew, and Aramaic. —*n.* **1.** The Semitic subfamily of languages. **2.** Any one of these languages.

Sem•i•to-Ha•mit•ic (sĕm'ə-tō'hă-mĭt'ĭk) *n.* Afro-Asiatic. —**Sem'i•to'-Ha•mit'ic** *adj.*

sem•i•vow•el (sĕm'ī-vou'əl) *n.* A letter or vocal sound having the sound of a vowel but used as a consonant, as *y* and *w.*

sem•i•week•ly (sĕm'ē-wēk'lē, sĕm'ī-) *adj.* Issued or happening twice a week. See Usage note at **bimonthly.** —*adv.* Twice weekly.

sem•i•year•ly (sĕm'ē-yîr'lē, sĕm'ī-) *adj.* Happening or issued twice a year or once every

---

ô paw, for/oi boy/ou out/ōō took/ōō coo/p pop/r run/s sauce/sh shy/t to/th thin/*th* the/
ŭ cut/ûr fur/v van/w wag/y yes/z size/zh vision/ə ago, item, edible, gallop, circus/

half year. See Usage note at **bimonthly.** —*adv.* Every half year.

sen., Sen. 1. senate; senator. 2. senior.

Sen·ate (sĕn'ĭt) *n.* 1. **senate.** A legislative and deliberative assembly. 2. The upper house of Congress in the U.S. 3. The upper house in the bicameral legislature of many U.S. states. 4. The upper legislative house in Canada, France, and other countries. [< L *senātus.*]

sen·a·tor (sĕn'ə-tər) *n.* Also **Sen·a·tor.** A member of a senate. —**sen'a·to'ri·al** (-tôr'ē-əl, -tōr'ē-əl) *adj.*

send (sĕnd) *v.* **sent, sending.** 1. To cause to be conveyed by an intermediary to a destination. 2. a. To direct to go on a mission. b. To enable to go. 3. To command or request to go. 4. To cause to depart. 5. To emit. 6. To direct or propel with force. 7. To cause to take place or befall. 8. To put into some state or condition. —**send for.** 1. To order. 2. To summon. [< OE *sendan.* See **sent-.**] —**send'er** *n.*

send·off (sĕnd'ôf', -ŏf') *n.* 1. A demonstration of good wishes for one about to leave on a journey or begin a new undertaking. 2. A start given to someone or something.

Sen·e·gal (sĕn'ə-gôl'). A republic in W Africa. Pop. 3,100,000. Cap. Dakar.

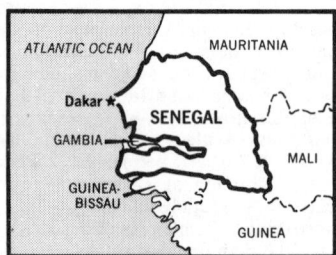

Senegal

Senegal River. A river of W Africa.

se·nile (sē'nīl', sĕn'īl') *adj.* 1. Characteristic of or proceeding from old age. 2. Mentally and physically deteriorating with old age. [< L *senex,* old.] —**se·nil'i·ty** (sĭ-nĭl'ə-tē) *n.*

sen·ior (sēn'yər) *adj.* 1. Of or designating the older of two, esp. the older of two persons having the same name. 2. Above others in rank or length of service. 3. Pertaining to the fourth and last year of high school or college. —*n.* 1. A senior person. 2. A student in his fourth year of high school or college. [< L *senex,* old.]

senior high school. A high school usually including grades 10, 11, and 12.

sen·ior·i·ty (sēn-yôr'ə-tē, -yŏr'ə-tē) *n., pl.* **-ties.** 1. The state of being older or higher in rank. 2. Precedence of position, esp. by reason of longer service.

sen·na (sĕn'ə) *n.* 1. A plant with compound leaves and yellow flowers. 2. The dried leaves of such a plant, used as a cathartic. [< Ar *sanā'.*]

sen·sa·tion (sĕn-sā'shən, sən-) *n.* 1. a. A perception associated with stimulation of a sense

organ or with a specific bodily condition. b. The faculty to feel or perceive. 2. A state of heightened interest or emotion. 3. a. A condition of intense public interest and excitement. b. An event or object causing such public excitement. —**sen'sa'tion·al** *adj.*

sen·sa·tion·al·ism (sĕn'sā'shən-əl-ĭz'əm, sən-) *n.* The use of sensational matter or methods in writing, art, politics, etc. —**sen'sa'tion·al·ist** *n.*

sense (sĕns) *n.* 1. Any of the functions of hearing, sight, smell, touch, and taste. 2. The faculty of external or self-perception exemplified by these functions. 3. **senses.** The faculties of sensation as means of providing physical gratification and pleasure. 4. A feeling or perception either through the senses or the intellect. 5. Correct judgment. 6. a. Import; point. b. Lexical meaning. —*v.* **sensed, sensing.** 1. To become aware of; perceive. 2. To understand. 3. To detect something automatically: *sense radioactivity.* [< L *sentīre,* to perceive by the senses, to feel.]

sense·less (sĕns'lĭs) *adj.* 1. Without sense or meaning; meaningless. 2. Foolish; lacking sense. 3. Unconscious.

sen·si·bil·i·ty (sĕn'sə-bĭl'ə-tē) *n., pl.* **-ties.** 1. The ability to feel or perceive. 2. Keen perception. 3. Delicate sensitivity to. 4. The aptness of plant organisms and instruments to be affected by environment.

sen·si·ble (sĕn'sə-bəl) *adj.* 1. Perceptible by the senses or mind. 2. Readily perceived; appreciable. 3. Able to feel or perceive. 4. Cognizant; aware. 5. Acting with or showing good sense: *a sensible choice.* —**sen'si·bly** *adv.*

sen·si·tive (sĕn'sə-tĭv) *adj.* 1. Capable of perceiving with a sense or senses. 2. Responsive to external conditions or stimulation. 3. Susceptible to the feelings of others. 4. Quick to take offense; touchy. 5. a. Easily irritated. b. Easily altered. 6. Registering very slight differences or changes of condition. —**sen'si·tive·ly** *adv.* —**sen'si·tiv'i·ty, sen'si·tive·ness** *n.*

sen·si·tize (sĕn'sə-tīz') *v.* **-tized, -tizing.** To make or become more sensitive. —**sen'si·ti·za'tion** *n.*

sen·sor (sĕn'sər, -sôr') *n.* A device, such as a photoelectric cell, that receives and responds to a signal or stimulus.

sen·so·ry (sĕn'sər-ē) *adj.* Pertaining to senses.

sen·su·al (sĕn'shoo-əl) *adj.* 1. Of or affecting the senses. 2. a. Pertaining to the gratification of the physical appetites. b. Suggesting sexuality. c. Carnal rather than intellectual. 3. Sensory. —**sen'su·al·ist** *n.* —**sen'su·al'i·ty, sen'su·al·ness** *n.* —**sen'su·al·ly** *adv.*

sen·su·ous (sĕn'shoo-əs) *adj.* 1. Pertaining to, derived from, or appealing to the senses. 2. Highly appreciative of the pleasures of sensation. —**sen'su·ous·ly** *adv.* —**sen'su·ous·ness** *n.*

sent (sĕnt). *p.t.* & *p.p.* of **send.**

sen·tence (sĕn'təns) *n.* 1. A grammatical unit comprising a word or group of words that usually consists of at least one subject and a finite verb or verb phrase. 2. a. A court judgment, esp. a decision of the penalty to be given a convicted person. b. The penalty meted out.

ă pat/ā ate/âr care/ä bar/b bib/ch chew/d deed/ĕ pet/ē be/f fit/g gag/h hat/hw what/
ĭ pit/ī pie/îr pier/j judge/k kick/l lid, fatal/m mum/n no, sudden/ng sing/ŏ pot/ō go/

—v. **-tenced, -tencing.** To pass sentence upon (a convicted person). [< L *sententia,* a way of thinking < *sentire,* to feel.] **—sen·ten'tial** (sĕn-tĕn'shəl) *adj.* **—sen'ten'tial·ly** *adv.*

sen·ten·tious (sĕn-tĕn'shəs) *adj.* **1.** Terse and energetic in expression. **2. a.** Fond of aphoristic utterances. **b.** Given to pompous moralizing. [< L *sententia,* opinion, SENTENCE.] **—sen·ten'tious·ly** *adv.*

sen·ti·ent (sĕn'chĭ-ənt) *adj.* **1.** Having sense perception. **2.** Experiencing sensation. [< L *sentire,* to feel.] **—sen'ti·ent·ly** *adv.*

sen·ti·ment (sĕn'tə-mənt) *n.* **1. a.** A cast of mind regarding something. **b.** An opinion; view. **2.** A thought or attitude based on emotion instead of reason. **3.** The emotional import of something. [< L *sentire,* to feel.]

sen·ti·men·tal (sĕn'tə-mĕnt'l) *adj.* **1. a.** Characterized by or swayed by sentiment. **b.** Extravagantly emotional. **2.** Appealing to the sentiments, esp. to romantic feelings. **—sen'ti·men'tal·ism', sen'ti·men·tal'i·ty** *n.* **—sen'ti·men'tal·ize** *v.* **(-ized, -izing). —sen'ti·men'tal·ly** *adv.*

sen·ti·nel (sĕnt'n-əl) *n.* One that keeps guard; a sentry. [< It *sentinella.*]

sen·try (sĕn'trē) *n., pl.* **-tries. 1.** A guard, esp. a soldier posted to prevent the passage of unauthorized persons. **2.** The duty of a sentry. [Perh short for obs *centrinell,* var of SENTINEL.]

Seoul (sōl). The capital of South Korea. Pop. 3,376,000.

se·pal (sē'pəl) *n.* One of the leaflike segments of a flower calyx. [< Gk *skepē,* covering + (PET)AL.]

sep·a·ra·ble (sĕp'ər-ə-bəl, sĕp'rə-) *adj.* Capable of being separated.

sep·a·rate (sĕp'ə-rāt') *v.* **-rated, -rating. 1. a.** To set, keep, or come apart; divide or become divided; disunite. **b.** To sort. **2.** To differentiate between; distinguish. **3.** To remove from a mixture or combination; isolate. **4.** To part, as a married couple, by decree. **5.** To part company; disperse. *—adj.* (sĕp'ər-ĭt, sĕp'rĭt). **1.** Set apart from the rest; not connected. **2.** Existing as an entity; independent. **3.** Dissimilar; distinct. **4.** Not shared; individual. [< L *sēparāre.*] **—sep'a·rate·ly** *adv.* **—sep'a·rate·ness** *n.*

sep·a·ra·tion (sĕp'ə-rā'shən) *n.* **1. a.** The act or process of separating. **b.** The state of being separated. **2.** The place where a division occurs.

sep·a·ra·tist (sĕp'ər-ə-tĭst, sĕp'rə-, sĕp'ə-rā'-tĭst) *n.* Also **sep·a·ra·tion·ist** (sĕp'ə-rā'shən-ĭst). One who advocates separation, esp. from an established church. **—sep'a·ra·tism'** *n.*

sep·a·ra·tor (sĕp'ə-rā'tər) *n.* **1.** One that separates. **2.** A device for separating cream from milk.

se·pi·a (sē'pē-ə) *n.* **1.** A dark-brown pigment or color. **2.** Dark yellowish brown. [< L *sēpia,* cuttlefish (pigment).]

sep·sis (sĕp'sĭs) *n.* The presence of pathogenic organisms, or their toxins, in the blood or tissues. [< Gk *sēpein,* to make rotten.]

Sept. September.

Sep·tem·ber (sĕp-tĕm'bər) *n.* The 9th month of the year. September has 30 days. [< L

September, the 7th month (of the Roman calendar).]

septi-. *comb. form.* Seven. [< L *septem,* seven.]

sep·tic (sĕp'tĭk) *adj.* **1.** Pertaining to sepsis. **2.** Causing sepsis; putrefactive.

sep·ti·ce·mi·a (sĕp'tĭ-sē'mē-ə) *n.* A systemic disease caused by pathogenic organisms or their toxins in the bloodstream. [< L *sēpticus,* septic + -EMIA.]

septic tank. A sewage-disposal tank in which waste material is decomposed by certain bacteria.

sep·til·lion (sĕp-tĭl'yən) *n.* **1.** The cardinal number represented by 1 followed by 24 zeros. **2.** In British usage, the cardinal number represented by 1 followed by 42 zeros. **—sep·til'lion** *adj.*

sep·til·lionth (sĕp-tĭl'yənth) *n.* **1.** The ordinal number septillion in a series. **2.** One of a septillion equal parts. **—sep·til'lionth** *adj.* & *adv.*

Sep·tu·a·gint (sĕp'chōō-ə-jĭnt', sĕp'tōō-) *n.* A Greek translation of the Old Testament dating from the 3rd century B.C. [L *septuāgintā,* seventy, "the Seventy" < the 70 or 72 Jewish scholars who are traditionally recognized as having done the translation.]

sep·tu·ple (sĕp't/y/ōō-pəl, sĕp-t/y/ōō'pəl) *adj.* **1.** Consisting of or containing seven. **2.** Multiplied by seven. *—v.* **-pled, -pling.** To multiply by seven.

sep·ul·cher (sĕp'əl-kər). Also chiefly Brit. **sep·ul·chre.** *n.* A burial vault. *—v.* To inter. [< L *sepulchrum* < *sepelīre,* to bury.] **—se·pul'chral** (sə-pŭl'krəl) *adj.*

seq. the following (L *sequēns*).

se·quel (sē'kwĕl) *n.* **1.** Something that follows; a continuation. **2.** A literary work continuing the narrative of an earlier work. **3.** A consequence. [< L *sēqui,* to follow.]

se·quence (sē'kwəns) *n.* **1.** A following of one thing after another; succession. **2.** An order of succession; arrangement. **3.** A related or continuous series. [< L *sequī,* to follow.] **—se·quen'tial** (sĭ-kwĕn'shəl) *adj.* **—se·quen'ti·al'i·ty** *n.* **—se·quen'tial·ly** *adv.*

se·ques·ter (sĭ-kwĕs'tər) *v.* **1.** To remove or set apart; segregate. **2.** To withdraw into seclusion. [< L, depository.]

se·ques·trate (sĭ-kwĕs'trāt') *v.* **-trated, -trating.** To sequester. **—se'ques·tra'tion** *n.*

se·quin (sē'kwĭn) *n.* A small, shiny ornamental disk, often sewn on cloth. [< Ar *sikkah,* coin die.]

se·quoi·a (sĭ-kwoi'ə) *n.* A very tall, massive evergreen tree of the mountains of California. [< *Sequoya* (died 1843), American Indian scholar.]

ser. **1.** serial. **2.** series. **3.** sermon.

se·ra. Alternate *pl.* of **serum.**

se·ra·glio (sĭ-răl'yō, -räl'yō) *n., pl.* **-glios. 1.** A large harem. **2.** A sultan's palace. [Prob < Turk *serai,* a palace.]

se·ra·pe (sə-rä'pē) *n.* Also **sa·ra·pe.** A woolen poncho worn by Latin-American men.

ser·aph (sĕr'əf) *n., pl.* **-aphs** or **-aphim** (-ə-fĭm) or **-aphin** (-ə-fĭn). A celestial being or angel.

ô paw, for/oi boy/ou out/ŏŏ took/ōō coo/p pop/r run/s sauce/sh shy/t to/th thin/*th* the/
ŭ cut/ûr fur/v van/w wag/y yes/z size/zh vision/ə ago, item, edible, gallop, circus/

[< Heb *sărăph*.] —**se·raph'ic** (sĭ-răf'ĭk) *adj.*

Serb (sûrb) *n.* A Serbian.

Ser·bi·a (sûr'bē-ə). A constituent republic of Yugoslavia, in the E part of the country.

Ser·bi·an (sûr'bē-ən) *n.* **1.** A member of a southern Slavic people that is the dominant ethnic group of Serbia and adjacent republics of Yugoslavia. **2.** A Serbo-Croatian. —*adj.* **1.** Of Serbia or the Serbians. **2.** Serbo-Croatian.

Ser·bo-Cro·a·tian (sûr'bō-krō-ā'shən) *n.* **1.** The Slavic language of the Serbs and Croats of Yugoslavia. **2.** A speaker of this language. —**Ser'bo-Cro·a'tian** *adj.*

sere (sîr) *adj.* Withered; dry. [< OE *sēar*. See **saus-**.]

ser·e·nade (sĕr'ə-nād', sĕr'ə-nād') *n.* An honorific musical performance, esp. one given by a lover for his sweetheart. —*v.* (sĕr'ə-nād') -**naded, -nading.** To perform a serenade (for). [< L *serēnus*, SERENE.] —**ser'e·nad'er** *n.*

ser·en·dip·i·ty (sĕr'ən-dĭp'ə-tē) *n.* The faculty of making fortunate and unexpected discoveries by accident. [< the fairy tale *The Three Princes of Serendip*.] —**ser'en·dip'i·tous** *adj.*

se·rene (sĭ-rēn') *adj.* **1.** Unruffled; tranquil; dignified. **2.** Unclouded; bright. [L *serēnus*.] —**se·rene'ly** *adv.* —**se·ren'i·ty** (sĭ-rĕn'ə-tē) *n.*

serf (sûrf) *n.* **1.** A member of the lowest feudal class, bound to the land and owned by a lord. **2.** A slave. [< L *servus*, slave.] —**serf'dom** *n.*

serge (sûrj) *n.* A cloth of worsted or worsted and wool, often used for suits. [< L *sēricus*, of Seres (a people).]

ser·geant (sär'jənt) *n.* **1. a.** Any of several ranks of noncommissioned officers in the U.S. Army, Air Force, or Marine Corps. **b.** One holding any of these ranks. **2.** Also *chiefly Brit.* **ser·jeant. a.** The rank of police officer next below a captain, lieutenant, or inspector. **b.** One holding this rank. [< L *servus*, slave.] —**ser'gean·cy, ser'geant·ship'** *n.*

sergeant at arms. An officer appointed to keep order within an organization, as in a legislative body.

sergeant first class. A noncommissioned officer next below master sergeant in the U.S. Army.

sergeant major. 1. A noncommissioned officer serving as chief administrative assistant of a headquarters unit of the U.S. Army, Air Force, or Marine Corps. **2.** *Brit.* A noncommissioned officer of the highest rank.

se·ri·al (sîr'ē-əl) *adj.* **1.** Of, forming, or arranged in a series. **2.** Published or produced in installments. —*n.* A work published or produced in installments. [< SERIES.] —**se'ri·al·ize'** *v.* (-ized, -izing.) —**se'ri·al·ly** *adv.*

se·ries (sîr'ēz) *n., pl.* -**ries. 1. a.** A group of events related by order of occurrence. **b.** A group of thematically connected works or performances. **2.** A group of related objects. [L *seriēs* < *serere*, to join.]

ser·if (sĕr'ĭf) *n.* Also *chiefly Brit.* **cer·iph.** *Ptg.* A fine line finishing off the main strokes of a letter. [Perh < L *scribere*, to write.]

se·ri·ous (sîr'ē-əs) *adj.* **1.** Grave in character, quality, or mien; sober. **2.** Sincere; earnest.

3. Concerned with important rather than trivial matters. **4.** Difficult. **5.** Causing anxiety; critical. [< L *sērius*.] —**se'ri·ous·ly** *adv.* —**se'ri·ous·ness** *n.*

ser·jeant. *Chiefly Brit.* Variant of **sergeant.**

ser·mon (sûr'mən) *n.* **1.** A religious discourse delivered as part of a church service. **2.** A lengthy and tedious reproof or exhortation. [< L *sermō*, a discourse.]

se·rous (sîr'əs) *adj.* Containing, secreting, or resembling serum.

ser·pent (sûr'pənt) *n.* A snake. [< L *serpēns*, "crawling thing."]

ser·pen·tine (sûr'pən-tēn', -tīn') *adj.* Snakelike, as in form, movement, or insinuating slyness.

ser·rate (sĕr'āt', -ĭt) *adj.* Also **ser·rat·ed** (-rā'tĭd). Edged with notched, toothlike projections. [< L *serra*, saw.] —**ser·ra'tion** *n.*

ser·ried (sĕr'ēd) *adj.* Pressed together in rows; in close order. [< OF *serrer*, to crowd.]

se·rum (sîr'əm) *n., pl.* -**rums** or **sera** (sîr'ə). **1.** The clear yellowish fluid obtained upon separating whole blood into its solid and liquid components. **2.** The fluid from the tissues of immunized animals, used esp. as an antitoxin. [L, whey, serum.]

serv. service.

ser·vant (sûr'vənt) *n.* One employed to perform domestic or other services.

serve (sûrv) *v.* **served, serving. 1.** To work for; be a servant to. **2.** To act in a particular capacity. **3.** To place food before; wait on. **4.** To provide goods and services for. **5.** To be of assistance to. **6.** To spend or complete (time), as in prison or in elective office. **7.** To undergo military service for. **8.** To requite: *Punish her; it will serve her right.* **9.** To meet a need; satisfy. **10.** To be used by or of use to. **11.** To give homage to. **12.** To present (a legal writ or summons). **13.** To put (a ball) in play, as in tennis. —*n.* The right, manner, or act of serving in many games played on a court. [< L *servīre* < *servus*, slave.] —**serv'er** *n.*

serv·ice (sûr'vĭs) *n.* **1.** The occupation or duties of a servant. **2.** The act or means of serving. **3.** A government department and its employees: *civil service.* **4.** The armed forces of a nation, or any branch thereof. **5.** Duties performed as an occupation. **6.** Installation, maintenance, or repairs provided or guaranteed by a dealer or manufacturer. **7.** A set of dishes or utensils: *a tea service.* **8.** A serve in a game. —*adj.* **1.** Useful. **2.** Reserved for employees, deliveries, etc.: *a service elevator.* —*v.* -**iced, -icing. 1.** To adjust; repair; maintain. **2.** To provide services to. [< L *servus*, slave.]

serv·ice·a·ble (sûr'vĭs-ə-bəl) *adj.* **1.** Ready for service; usable. **2.** Able to give good service; durable. —**serv'ice·a·bil'i·ty, serv'ice·a·ble·ness** *n.* —**serv'ice·a·bly** *adv.*

serv·ice·man (sûr'vĭs-măn', -mən) *n.* **1.** A member of the armed forces. **2.** Also **service man.** One whose work is the maintenance and repair of equipment.

ser·vile (sûr'vəl, -vīl') *adj.* Slavish in character or attitude; submissive. [< L *servus*, slave.] —**ser·vil'i·ty** (sər-vĭl'ə-tē) *n.*

ser·vi·tor (sûr′və-tər, -tôr′) *n.* An attendant; servant. [< L *servīre*, to SERVE.]

ser·vi·tude (sûr′və-t/y/ōōd′) *n.* Submission to a master; slavery. [< L *servus*, slave.]

ses·a·me (sĕs′ə-mē) *n.* 1. An Asian plant bearing small, edible, oil-rich seeds. 2. The seeds of this plant. [< Gk *sēsamē* < Sem.]

ses·sion (sĕsh′ən) *n.* 1. a. A meeting of a legislative or judicial body. b. A series of such meetings. c. The duration of such a series of meetings. 2. The part of a year or of a day during which a school holds classes. [< L *sessus*, pp of *sedēre*, to sit.] —**ses′sion·al** *adj.* —**ses′sion·al·ly** *adv.*

set¹ (sĕt) *v.* **set, setting.** 1. To put in a specified position or state. 2. To put into a stable position; fix. 3. To restore to a proper and normal state. 4. To adjust, as for proper functioning. 5. To arrange tableware upon a (table) preparatory to eating. 6. To apply curlers and clips to (one's hair) in order to style. 7. To arrange (type) into words and sentences preparatory to printing; compose. 8. To prescribe, establish, or assign. 9. To put forth as a model to be emulated. 10. To put in a mounting; mount. 11. To cause to sit. 12. To sit on eggs, as a hen. 13. To affix (a price or value). 14. To disappear below the horizon, as the sun. 15. To diminish or decline; wane. 16. To become fixed; harden or congeal. —**set about.** To start or begin doing. —**set aside.** 1. To separate and reserve for a special purpose. 2. To annul. —**set forth.** 1. To utter or express. 2. To embark on a journey. —**set out.** To begin any procedure or progress; start. —*adj.* 1. Fixed or established. 2. Stereotyped. 3. Fixed and rigid; unflinching. 4. Unyielding; firm. 5. Ready: *get set.* —*n.* 1. The act or process of setting. 2. The condition resulting from setting. [< OE *settan*, to cause to sit, place. See sed-.]

set² (sĕt) *n.* 1. A group of persons or things connected by or collected for their similar appearance, interest, importance, etc.: *a chess set.* 2. A group of circumstances, situations, etc., joined to be treated as a whole. 3. A group of books published as a unit. 4. a. The scenery constructed for a theatrical performance. b. The enclosure in which a motion picture is being filmed; studio. 5. The receiving apparatus assembled to operate a radio or television. 6. *Math.* Any collection of distinct elements. 7. In tennis and other games, a group of games constituting one division or unit of a match. [< L *secta*, SECT.]

set·back (sĕt′băk′) *n.* An unanticipated or sudden check in progress; a reverse.

set·tee (sĕt-tē′) *n.* 1. A wooden bench with a high back. 2. A small sofa.

set·ter (sĕt′ər) *n.* A long-haired dog of a breed originally trained to hunt game.

set·ting (sĕt′ĭng) *n.* 1. The act of a person or thing that sets. 2. The context in which a situation is set. 3. A jewelry mounting. 4. The scenery for a theatrical performance. 5. The descent of the sun or other celestial body below the horizon.

set·tle (sĕt′l) *v.* **-tled, -tling.** 1. To put into order;

place; arrange or fix definitely as desired. 2. To establish residence in. 3. To restore calmness or comfort to. 4. a. To come or cause to come to rest, sink, or become compact. b. To cause (a liquid) to become clear by forming a sediment. 5. To stabilize; assure. 6. a. To make compensation for (a claim). b. To pay (a debt). 7. To decide by mutual agreement. [< OE *setl*, seat. See sed-.] —**set′-tler** *n.*

set·tle·ment (sĕt′l-mənt) *n.* 1. The act or process of settling. 2. a. Establishment in a new business or region. b. A newly colonized region. 3. A small community. 4. An understanding reached, as in financial matters. 5. A welfare center providing community services in an underprivileged area.

sev·en (sĕv′ən) *n.* The cardinal number written 7 or in Roman numerals VII. [< OE *seofon*. See septm.] —**sev′en** *adj. & pron.*

sev·en·teen (sĕv′ən-tēn′, sĕv′ən-tēn′) *n.* The cardinal number written 17 or in Roman numerals XVII. —**sev′en·teen′** *adj. & pron.*

sev·en·teenth (sĕv′ən-tēnth′, sĕv′ən-tēnth′) *n.* 1. The ordinal number 17 in a series. 2. One of 17 equal parts. —**sev′en·teenth′** *adj. & adv.*

sev·enth (sĕv′ənth) *n.* 1. The ordinal number 7 in a series. 2. One of 7 equal parts. —**sev′enth** *adj. & adv.*

sev·en·ti·eth (sĕv′ən-tē-ĭth) *n.* 1. The ordinal number 70 in a series. 2. One of 70 equal parts. —**sev′en·ti·eth** *adj. & adv.*

sev·en·ty (sĕv′ən-tē) *n.* The cardinal number written 70 or in Roman numerals LXX. —**sev′en·ty** *adj. & pron.*

sev·er (sĕv′ər) *v.* 1. To divide or separate into parts; keep apart. 2. To cut or become cut into two or more parts. 3. To break off (a relationship); dissolve. [< L *sēparāre*, to SEPARATE.]

sev·er·al (sĕv′ər-əl) *adj.* 1. Being of a number more than two or three, but not many; of an indefinitely small number. 2. Single; distinct. —*n.* Several ones; a few. [< L *sēparāre*, to SEPARATE.] —**sev′er·al·ly** *adv.*

sev·er·ance (sĕv′ər-əns) *n.* 1. a. The act or process of severing. b. The condition of being severed. 2. Extra pay given an employee upon leaving a job.

se·vere (sə-vîr′) *adj.* **-verer, -verest.** 1. Unsparing and harsh in treating others; stern; strict. 2. Maintained rigidly; accurate. 3. Austere in appearance or temperament; grave; forbidding. 4. Extremely plain; conservatively presented. 5. Causing intense pain or distress; violent; sharp. 6. Extremely difficult to perform or accomplish; rigorous; trying. [< L *sevērus.*] —**se·vere′ly** *adv.* —**se·ver′i·ty** (-vĕr′ə-tē), **se·vere′ness** *n.*

Se·ville (sə-vĭl′). A city of SW Spain. Pop. 532,000.

sew (sō) *v.* **sewed, sewn** or **sewed, sewing.** 1. To make, repair, or fasten with a needle and thread or a sewing machine. 2. To furnish with stitches for the purpose of closing, fastening, etc. [< OE *seowian.* See syū-.]

sew·age (sōō′ĭj) *n.* Waste carried off with ground water in sewers or drains.

sew·er (sōō′ər) *n.* An artificial, usually under-

ô paw, for/oi boy/ou out/ōō took/ōō coo/p pop/r run/s sauce/sh shy/t to/th thin/*th* the/
ŭ cut/ûr fur/v van/w wag/y yes/z size/zh vision/ə ago, item, edible, gallop, circus/

ground conduit for carrying off sewage or rainwater. [< VL *exaquāria.*]

sew•er•age (sōō'ər-ĭj) *n.* **1.** A system of sewers. **2.** The removal of waste materials by means of sewers. **3.** Sewage.

sew•ing (sō'ĭng) *n.* **1.** The act of one who sews. **2.** The article upon which one sews; needlework.

sewing machine. A machine for sewing.

sewn (sōn). *p.p.* of **sew.**

sex (sĕks) *n.* **1. a.** The property or quality by which organisms are classified according to their reproductive functions. **b.** Either of two divisions, designated *male* and *female,* of this classification. **2.** Males or females collectively. **3.** The sexual urge or instinct as it manifests itself in behavior. **4.** Sexual intercourse. [< L *sexus.*]

sex-. *comb. form.* Six. [< L *sex,* six.]

sex•ism (sĕk'sĭz'əm) *n.* Discrimination by members of one sex against the other, esp. by males against females, based on the assumption that one sex is superior. —**sex'ist** *adj. & n.*

sex•less (sĕks'lĭs) *adj.* **1.** Lacking sexual characteristics; asexual; neuter. **2.** Arousing or exhibiting no sexual interest or desire. —**sex'less•ly** *adv.* —**sex'less•ness** *n.*

sex reversal. The natural, artificial, or pathological functional transformation from one sex to another.

sex•tant (sĕks'tənt) *n.* A navigational instrument used for measuring the altitudes of celestial bodies.

sex•tet (sĕks-tĕt') *n.* **1. a.** A group of six musicians. **b.** A musical composition for six performers. **2.** A group of six.

sex•tile (sĕks'tīl') *adj.* Designating the position of two celestial bodies when they are 60° apart. [L *sextīlis,* one sixth (of a circle).]

sex•til•lion (sĕks-tĭl'yən) *n.* **1.** The cardinal number represented by 1 followed by 21 zeros. **2.** In British usage, the cardinal number represented by 1 followed by 36 zeros. [< SEX- + (M)ILLION.] —**sex•til'lion** *adj.*

sex•til•lionth (sĕks-tĭl'yənth) *n.* **1.** The ordinal number sextillion in a series. **2.** One of sextillion equal parts. —**sex•til'lionth** *adj. & adv.*

sex•ton (sĕks'tən) *n.* One responsible for the care and upkeep of church property. [< ML *sacristānus.*]

sex•tu•ple (sĕks-t/y/ōō'pəl, -tŭp'əl, sĕks'-tōō-pəl) *adj.* **1.** Having six parts. **2.** Multiplied by six. —*n.* A number or amount six times as many or as much as another. —*v.* **-pled, -pling.** To multiply or increase by six. [Prob SEX- + (QUIN)TUPLE.]

sex•tu•plet (sĕks-tŭp'lĭt, -t/y/ōō'plĭt, sĕks'-tōō-plĭt) *n.* One of six offspring delivered at one birth.

sex•u•al (sĕk'shōō-əl) *adj.* **1.** Of or involving sex, the sexes, or the sex organs and their functions. **2.** Having a sex or sexual organs. **3.** Implying or symbolizing erotic desires or activity. **4.** Pertaining to or designating reproduction involving the union of male and female gametes. —**sex'u•al•ly** *adv.*

sexual intercourse. Coitus, esp. between humans.

sex•u•al•i•ty (sĕk'shōō-ăl'ə-tē) *n.* **1.** The condition of being characterized and distinguished by sex. **2.** Concern or preoccupation with sex. **3.** The quality of possessing a sexual character or potency.

sex•y (sĕk'sē) *adj.* **-ier, -iest.** *Slang.* Arousing or intending to arouse sexual desire or interest. —**sex'i•ness** *n.*

Sfc. sergeant first class.

S.G. solicitor general.

sgd. signed.

Sgt. sergeant.

sh (sh) *interj.* Used to urge silence.

sh. 1. share (capital stock). **2.** sheet. **3.** shilling.

shab•by (shăb'ē) *adj.* **-bier, -biest. 1.** Threadbare; worn-out. **2.** Wearing worn garments; seedy. **3.** Dilapidated; deteriorated. **4.** Despicable; mean. **5.** Unfair. [< OE *sceabb,* a scab. See **skep-**.] —**shab'bi•ly** *adv.* —**shab'bi•ness** *n.*

shack (shăk) *n.* A small, crudely built cabin. [< Aztec *xacalli,* thatched cabin.]

shack•le (shăk'əl) *n.* **1.** A metal fastening, usually one of a pair, for encircling the ankle or wrist of a prisoner or captive; fetter; manacle. **2.** Anything that confines or restrains. —*v.* **-led, -ling.** To put shackles on; fetter. [< OE *sceacel,* fetter < Gmc **skakulo-.*] —**shack'ler** *n.*

shad (shăd) *n., pl.* **shad** or **shads.** A food fish that swims up streams from marine waters to spawn. [< OE *sceadd.*]

shade (shād) *n.* **1. a.** Diminished or partial light; comparative darkness or obscurity. **b.** An area or space of such partial darkness or obscurity. **2.** Cover or shelter from the sun or its rays. **3. shades.** *Slang.* Sunglasses. **4.** The degree to which a color is mixed with black or otherwise darkened. **5.** A slight variation; nuance. **6.** A small amount; trace. —*v.* **shaded, shading. 1.** To screen from light or heat. **2.** To obscure or darken. **3.** To represent or produce degrees of darkness in (a picture). **4.** To change or vary by slight degrees. [< OE *sceadu, scead.* See **skot-**.]

shad•ing (shā'dĭng) *n.* The lines or other marks used to fill in outlines of a sketch, engraving, etc., to represent gradations of colors or darkness.

shad•ow (shăd'ō) *n.* **1.** A partially or totally unilluminated area, caused by an object blocking rays of light. **2.** The outline of an object that casts a shadow. **3.** Gloom or an influence that causes such feeling. **4.** A shaded area in a picture. **5.** A phantom; ghost. **6.** A faint indication. **7.** A remnant. **8.** A slight trace. —*v.* **1.** To cast a shadow upon; shade. **2.** To make gloomy or dark. **3.** To represent vaguely or mysteriously. **4.** To darken in a painting; shade in. **5.** To follow after, esp. in secret. [< OE *sceaduwe < sceadu,* SHADE.] —**shad'ow•er** *n.* —**shad'ow•i•ness** *n.* —**shad'ow•y** *adj.*

shad•y (shā'dē) *adj.* **-ier, -iest. 1.** Full of shade; shaded. **2.** Hidden. **3.** Of dubious character or honesty; questionable.

shaft¹ (shăft, shäft) *n.* **1.** The long, narrow stem or body of a spear or arrow. **2.** A spear or arrow. **3.** Something suggestive of a missile in appearance. **4.** The handle of any of various

---

ă pat/ā ate/âr care/ä bar/b bib/ch chew/d deed/ĕ pet/ē be/f fit/g gag/h hat/hw what/ ĭ pit/ī pie/îr pier/j judge/k kick/l lid, fatal/m mum/n no, sudden/ng sing/ŏ pot/ō go/

tools or implements. **5.** A long, generally cylindrical bar, esp. one that rotates and transmits power. [< OE *sceaft.* See **skep-**.]
shaft² (shăft, shäft) *n.* A long, narrow passage, duct, or conduit. [Prob < MLG *schacht.*]
shag (shăg) *n.* **1.** A tangle or mass, esp. of rough, matted hair. **2.** A coarse, long nap, as on some woolen cloth. [< OE *sceacga* < Gmc **skag-.*]
shag•gy (shăg'ē) *adj.* **-gier, -giest. 1.** Having long, rough hair or wool. **2.** Bushy and matted. **3.** Poorly groomed. **—shag'gi•ness** *n.*
shah (shä) *n.* The monarch of certain lands of the Middle East, esp. Iran. [Pers *shāh.*]
shake (shāk) *v.* **shook, shaken** (shā'kən), **shaking. 1.** To move or cause to move to and fro with short jerky movements. **2.** To vibrate or rock; tremble. **3.** To cause to stagger; waver; unsettle. **4.** To remove or dislodge by or as by jerky movements. **5.** To brandish or wave: *shake one's fist.* **6.** To clasp (hands or another's hand) in greeting or leave-taking or as a sign of agreement. **—shake up.** To unnerve; disturb or agitate. **—n. 1.** An act of shaking. **2.** A beverage mixed by shaking: *a milk shake.* **—get a fair (or good) shake.** *Slang.* To be treated with fairness. [< OE *sceacan* < Gmc **skakan.*] **—shak'a•ble, shake'a•ble** *adj.* **—shak'-er** *n.*
shake•down (shāk'doun') *n. Informal.* An extortion of money by blackmail or other means.
Shak•er (shā'kər) *n.* A member of a sect practicing communal living and observing celibacy.
Shake•speare (shāk'spîr), **William.** Also **Shak•spere.** 1564–1616. English dramatist and poet. **—Shake•spear'e•an** *adj.*
shake•up (shāk'ŭp') *n.* A thorough or drastic reorganization, as in a business or government.
shak•y (shā'kē) *adj.* **-ier, -iest. 1.** Trembling or quivering. **2.** Unsteady; weak. **3.** Wavering; insecure. **—shak'i•ly** *adv.* **—shak'i•ness** *n.*
shale (shāl) *n.* A rock composed of layers of claylike, fine-grained sediments. [Prob < OE *sc(e)alu,* shell.]
shall (shăl) *v.* past **should. —**Used as an auxiliary followed by a simple infinitive to indicate (often with future reference) willingness, intention, obligation, compulsion, permission, or necessity. *Shall* is rarely used in speech outside of questions with subject *I* or *we.* See Usage note at **will². [< OE *sceal.* See **skel-².**]
shal•lot (shə-lŏt') *n.* **1.** An onionlike plant with an edible bulb divided into sections. **2.** The bulb of this plant. [< L *Ascalōnia (caepa).* See **scallion.**]
shal•low (shăl'ō) *adj.* **1.** Measuring little from bottom to top or surface; not deep. **2.** Lacking depth, as in intellect or significance. **—n.** A shallow part of a body of water. [ME *schalowe.*] **—shal'low•ness** *n.*
shalt (shălt). *Archaic.* 2nd person sing. present tense of **shall.**
sham (shăm) *n.* **1.** Something false or empty purporting to be genuine. **2.** A person who assumes a false character. **—adj.** Not genuine; counterfeit. **--v. shammed, shamming.** To

assume a false appearance or character; feign. [Poss var of SHAME.]
sham•ble (shăm'bəl) *v.* **-bled, -bling.** To walk in an awkward, lazy, or unsteady manner, shuffling the feet. [< earlier *shamble,* ungainly.] **—sham'ble** *n.*
sham•bles (shăm'bəlz) *n. (takes sing. v.).* A scene or condition of complete disorder or ruin. [< earlier *shamble,* table for display or sale of meat.]
shame (shām) *n.* **1.** A painful emotion caused by a strong sense of guilt, unworthiness, or disgrace. **2.** Capacity for such a feeling: *Have you no shame?* **3.** A person or thing that brings dishonor or disgrace. **4.** A condition of dishonor or disgrace. **5.** A great disappointment. **—v. shamed, shaming. 1.** To cause to feel shame. **2.** To bring dishonor or disgrace upon. **3.** To force by making ashamed: *shamed into an apology.* [< OE *sceamu* < Gmc **skamō.*]
shame•faced (shām'fāst') *adj.* **1.** Indicative of shame: *a shamefaced explanation.* **2.** Modest; shy. [< OE *sceamu,* SHAME + *fæst,* FAST (firm).] **—shame'fac'ed•ly** (-fā'sĭd-lē) *adv.* **—shame'fac'ed•ness** *n.*
shame•ful (shām'fəl) *adj.* Bringing or deserving shame; disgraceful. **—shame'ful•ly** *adv.* **—shame'ful•ness** *n.*
shame•less (shām'lĭs) *adj.* Without shame; impudent; brazen. **—shame'less•ly** *adv.* **—shame'less•ness** *n.*
sham•poo (shăm-pōō') *n.* **1.** Any of various preparations used to wash the hair and scalp. **2.** Any of various cleaning agents for rugs or upholstery. **3.** The act or process of washing or cleaning with shampoo. [Hindi *champo.*] **—sham•poo'** *v.*
sham•rock (shăm'rŏk') *n.* A plant, as a clover, having leaves with three leaflets, considered the national emblem of Ireland. [Ir *seamrog.*]
shang•hai (shăng-hī') *v.* To kidnap (a man) for compulsory service aboard a ship, esp. after rendering him insensible. [< SHANGHAI.]
Shang•hai (shăng-hī'). A city of E China. Pop. 7,000,000.
shank (shăngk) *n.* **1.** The part of the leg between the knee and the ankle or a corresponding part. **2.** A cut of meat from the leg of a steer or lamb. **3.** The section of a tool or instrument connecting the functioning part and handle. [< OE *sceanca.* See **skeng-**.]
shan't, sha'nt (shănt, shänt). Contractions of *shall not.*
shan•tung (shăn'tŭng') *n.* A plain-woven fabric with an irregular texture, originally of silk. [< *Shantung,* province of E China.]
shan•ty (shăn'tē) *n., pl.* **-ties.** A roughly built or ramshackle cabin; shack. [Perh < Ir *sean tig,* "old house."]
shape (shāp) *n.* **1.** The outline or characteristic surface configuration of a thing; contour; form. **2.** The contour of a person's body; figure. **3.** Developed or definite form. **4.** Any form or condition in which something may exist or appear. **—v. shaped, shaping. 1.** To give a particular form to. **2.** To take a definite form; develop. [< OE *(ge)sceap.* See **skep-**.]
shape•less (shāp'lĭs) *adj.* **1.** Having no dis-

tinct shape. **2.** Lacking symmetrical or attractive form. **—shape′less·ness** *n.*

shape·ly (shāp′lē) *adj.* **-lier, -liest.** Having a pleasing shape; well-proportioned. **—shape′li·ness** *n.*

shard (shärd) *n.* A fragment of a brittle substance, as of glass or metal. [< OE *sceard.* See **sker-¹.**]

share¹ (shâr) *n.* **1.** A part or portion belonging to a person or group. **2.** An equitable or full portion. **3.** Any of the equal parts into which the capital stock of a corporation or company is divided. **—v. shared, sharing. 1.** To divide and parcel out in shares; apportion. **2.** To have, use, or experience in common. **3.** To participate; join: *share in an effort.* [< OE *scearu,* division or fork of the body, tonsure. See **sker-¹.**] **—shar′er** *n.*

share² (shâr) *n.* A plowshare. [< OE *scēar.* See **sker-¹.**]

share·crop·per (shâr′krŏp′ər) *n.* A tenant farmer who gives a share of his crop to the landlord in lieu of rent.

share·hold·er (shâr′hōl′dər) *n.* A person who owns a share or shares of stock.

shark (shärk) *n.* **1.** Any of various often large and voracious marine fishes with tough skin and small, toothlike scales. **2.** A ruthless, greedy, or dishonest person. [?]

shark·skin (shärk′skĭn′) *n.* **1.** A shark's skin or leather made from it. **2.** A plain-woven, smooth-textured fabric.

sharp (shärp) *adj.* **1.** Having a thin, keen edge or a fine, acute point. **2.** Not rounded or blunt; pointed: *a sharp nose.* **3.** Abrupt; sudden. **4.** Clear or marked; distinct. **5.** Shrewd; astute. **6.** Artful; underhand. **7.** Alert. **8.** Harsh; biting. **9.** Sudden and shrill. **10.** Angular; not rounded. **11.** *Mus.* **a.** Being one half step higher than the corresponding natural key. **b.** Being below the intended pitch. **12.** *Slang.* Attractive or stylish. **—adv. 1.** In a sharp manner. **2.** Punctually; exactly. **3.** *Mus.* Above the proper pitch. **—n.** *Mus.* **1.** A sign (#) affixed to a note to indicate that it is to be raised by a half step. **2.** A note that is raised by a half step. **—v.** *Mus.* **1.** To raise (a note) a half step. **2.** To sing or play above the proper pitch. [< OE *scearp.* See **sker-¹.**] **—sharp′ly** *adv.* **—sharp′ness** *n.*

sharp·en (shär′pən) *v.* To make or grow sharp or sharper. **—sharp′en·er** *n.*

sharp·shoot·er (shärp′shōō′tər) *n.* An expert marksman.

shat·ter (shăt′ər) *v.* To break or burst suddenly into pieces, as with a violent blow. [< OE *sceaterian.* See **skhed-.**]

shave (shāv) *v.* **shaved, shaved** or **shaven** (shā′-vən), **shaving. 1.** To remove (the beard or other body hair) from with a razor. **2.** To remove thin slices from. **3.** To cut or scrape into thin slices. **4.** To come close to or graze in passing. **—n.** The act, process, or result of shaving. **—close shave.** A narrow escape. [< OE *sceafan.* See **skep-.**]

shav·er (shā′vər) *n.* **1.** An electric or mechanical device used to shave. **2.** *Informal.* A small boy.

shav·ing (shā′vĭng) *n.* **1.** A thin slice; sliver. **2.** The action of one that shaves.

Shaw (shô), **George Bernard.** 1856–1950. Irish-born English dramatist, critic, and essayist.

shawl (shôl) *n.* A piece of cloth worn by women as a covering for the head, neck, and shoulders. [< Pers *shāl.*]

she (shē) *pron.* The 3rd person sing. pronoun in the nominative case, feminine gender. **1.** —Used to represent the female person last mentioned. **2.** —Used traditionally of certain objects and institutions, such as ships and nations. **—n.** A female animal or person: *Is the cat a she?* [< OE *sēo.* See **so-.**]

sheaf (shēf) *n., pl.* **sheaves** (shēvz). **1.** A bundle of cut stalks, esp. of grain. **2.** Any collection of articles held or bound together. [< OE *scēaf.* See **skeup-.**]

shear (shîr) *v.* **sheared, sheared** or **shorn, shearing. 1.** To remove (fleece, hair, etc.) by cutting or clipping with a sharp instrument. **2.** To remove the hair or fleece from. **3.** To cut with or as with shears. **4.** To strip or deprive of. [< OE *sceran.* See **sker-¹.**]

shears (shîrz) *pl.n.* **1.** Large-sized scissors. **2.** Any of various other implements or machines that cut with scissorlike action. [< OE *scēara,* scissors. See **sker-¹.**]

sheath (shēth) *n., pl.* **sheaths** (shē*th*z, shēths). **1.** A case for the blade of a knife, sword, etc. **2.** A part or covering resembling this. **3.** A close-fitting dress. [< OE *scēath.*]

sheathe (shē*th*) *v.* **sheathed, sheathing.** To insert into or provide with a sheath.

sheaves. *pl.* of **sheaf.**

shed¹ (shĕd) *v.* **shed, shedding. 1.** To pour forth or cause to pour forth: *shed tears.* **2.** To diffuse or radiate: *shed light.* **3.** To repel without allowing penetration: *A duck's feathers shed water.* **4.** To lose, drop, or cast off, as a covering, by a natural process. **—shed blood.** To take life; kill. [< OE *scēadan,* to divide. See **skei-.**]

shed² (shĕd) *n.* A small structure for storage or shelter. [Perh < SHADE.]

she'd (shēd). **1.** Contraction of *she had.* **2.** Contraction of *she would.*

sheen (shēn) *n.* Glistening brightness; shininess. [< OE *scīene,* beautiful, bright. See **keu-.**]

sheep (shēp) *n., pl.* **sheep. 1.** A hoofed, thick-fleeced mammal widely domesticated for wool and meat. **2.** One who is meek and submissive. [< OE *scēap* < Gmc **skæpa.*]

sheep·ish (shēp′ĭsh) *adj.* Embarrassed, as by consciousness of a fault: *a sheepish grin.* **—sheep′ish·ly** *adv.* **—sheep′ish·ness** *n.*

sheep·skin (shēp′skĭn′) *n.* **1.** The skin of a sheep. **2.** A diploma.

sheer¹ (shîr) *v.* To swerve or deviate from a course. [Perh var of SHEAR.]

sheer² (shîr) *adj.* **1.** Thin, fine, and transparent, as a fabric. **2.** Undiluted; pure: *sheer happiness.* **3.** Perpendicular or nearly perpendicular; steep. [Perh < ME *schir,* bright, shining.] **—sheer′ly** *adv.* **—sheer′ness** *n.*

sheet¹ (shēt) *n.* **1.** A rectangular piece of linen

ă pat/ā ate/âr care/ä bar/b bib/ch chew/d deed/ĕ pet/ē be/f fit/g gag/h hat/hw what/
ĭ pit/ī pie/îr pier/j judge/k kick/l lid, fatal/m mum/n no, sudden/ng sing/ŏ pot/ō go/

or similar material serving as a basic article of bedding. **2.** A broad, thin, usually rectangular mass or piece of any material, as paper, metal, glass, etc. [< OE *scēte.*]

sheet² (shēt) *n. Naut.* A rope attached to one or both of the lower corners of a sail. [< OE *scēata,* corner of a sail.]

sheik (shēk, shāk) *n.* The leader of an Arab family, village, or tribe.

shelf (shĕlf) *n., pl.* **shelves** (shĕlvz). **1.** A flat, usually rectangular structure of a rigid material fixed at right angles to a wall or other surface and used to hold objects. **2.** Anything resembling such an object, as a balcony or a ledge of rock. [ME *shelfe.*]

shell (shĕl) *n.* **1.** A hard or brittle outer covering, as of a mollusk, egg, or nut. **2.** Anything resembling or having the form of such a covering, as: **a.** A framework or exterior, as of a building. **b.** A thin layer of pastry. **c.** A long, narrow racing boat propelled by oarsmen. **3.** A projectile or piece of ammunition. —*v.* **1.** To remove from a shell, pod, etc. **2.** To fire shells at; bombard. **3.** *Informal.* To pay: *shell out five dollars.* [< OE *scell, scill.* See **skel-¹.**]

shel·lac (shə-lăk') *n.* **1.** A purified lac formed into thin yellow or orange flakes, often bleached white, and widely used in varnishes, paints, stains, inks, and sealing wax. **2.** A thin varnish made by dissolving flake shellac in denatured alcohol. —*v.* **-lacked, -lacking. 1.** To apply shellac. **2.** *Slang.* To defeat decisively. [SHEL(L) + LAC (lacquer).]

Shel·ley (shĕl'ē), **Percy Bysshe.** 1792–1822. English poet.

shell·fish (shĕl'fĭsh') *n., pl.* **-fish** or **-fishes.** An aquatic animal, as a mollusk or crustacean, with a shell or shell-like covering.

shell shock. Combat fatigue. —**shell'-shocked'** *adj.*

shel·ter (shĕl'tər) *n.* **1.** Something that provides cover or protection, as from the weather. **2.** The state of being covered or protected. —*v.* To provide cover or protection for. [?]

shelve (shĕlv) *v.* **shelved, shelving. 1.** To place on a shelf or shelves. **2.** To put aside; postpone.

shelves. *pl.* of **shelf.**

Shem·ite. Variant of **Semite.**

Shen·yang (shŭn'yäng'). A city of NE China. Pop. 2,411,000.

shep·herd (shĕp'ərd) *n.* One that herds or tends sheep. —*v.* To herd, guard, or care for as or in the manner of a shepherd. [< OE *scēap,* SHEEP + *hirde,* HERD (herdsman).] —**shep'herd·ess** *fem.n.*

sher·bet (shûr'bĭt) *n.* A sweet-flavored water ice to which milk, egg white, or gelatin has been added. [< Ar *sharbah,* drink.]

sher·iff (shĕr'ĭf) *n.* The chief law-enforcement officer in a county. [< OE *scīr,* SHIRE + *gerēfa,* officer.]

Sher·pa (shûr'pə) *n., pl.* **-pa** or **-pas.** A member of a Tibetan people living in N Nepal.

sher·ry (shĕr'ē) *n., pl.* **-ries. 1.** An amber-colored fortified Spanish wine ranging from very dry to sweet. **2.** Any similar wine. [Earlier *sherris,* "wine of Jerez," city in Spain.]

shib·bo·leth (shĭb'ə-lĭth, -lĕth') *n.* A slogan or saying, esp. one distinctive of a particular group. [Heb *shibbōleth,* an ear of corn, stream.]

shield (shēld) *n.* **1.** An article of protective armor made of leather, metal, or wood, carried on the forearm. **2.** A similar protective plate or covering. **3.** Something resembling a shield in shape. —*v.* **1.** To protect or defend with or as if with a shield. **2.** To cover up; conceal. [< OE *scild, sceld.* See **skel-¹.**]

shift (shĭft) *v.* **1.** To move or transfer (something) from one place or position to another. **2.** To change gears. **3.** To change position, direction, etc. **4.** To provide for one's needs. —*n.* **1.** A change, transference, or displacement. **2.** A change of direction or form. **3. a.** A change of workers. **b.** The working period of such a group: *the night shift.* **4.** A dodge, evasion, or trick. **5.** A chemise. [< OE *sciftan,* to arrange < Gmc *skip-.*]

shift·less (shĭft'lĭs) *adj.* Showing a lack of ambition, purpose, or resourcefulness. —**shift'less·ly** *adv.* —**shift'less·ness** *n.*

shift·y (shĭf'tē) *adj.* **-ier, -iest. 1.** Tricky; crafty. **2.** Suggesting craft or guile. —**shift'i·ness** *n.*

Shi·ko·ku (shĭ-kō'kōō). The smallest of the major islands of Japan, between SW Honshu and E Kyushu.

shil·le·lagh (shə-lā'lē, -lə) *n.* A club or cudgel. [< *Shillelagh,* town in Ireland.]

shil·ling (shĭl'ĭng) *n.* **1.** The basic monetary unit of Kenya, the Somali Republic, Tanzania, and Uganda. **2.** A subdivision of the pound of the United Kingdom, Gambia, Republic of Ireland, Malawi, Malta, Nigeria, Rhodesia, and various dependent territories of the United Kingdom, such as Bermuda. [< OE *scilling* < Gmc *skillingaz.*]

shil·ly-shal·ly (shĭl'ē-shăl'ē) *v.* **-lied, -lying.** To put off acting; hesitate or waver. [Short for *to stand* (or *go), shill I? shall I?* redupl of *shall I?*] —**shil'ly-shal'li·er** *n.*

shim (shĭm) *n.* A thin, often tapered piece of material used to fill a space between parts or to level a structure. [?]

shim·mer (shĭm'ər) *v.* To shine with a soft, tremulous light. —*n.* A glimmering or tremulous light. [< OE *scimerian, scimrian.* See **skī-.**] —**shim'mer·y** *adj.*

shim·my (shĭm'ē) *n., pl.* **-mies. 1.** Abnormal vibration or wobbling, as in an automobile chassis. **2.** *Regional.* A chemise. —*v.* **-mied, -mying.** To vibrate or wobble. [Short for *shimmy-shake,* "to shake one's chemise."]

shin¹ (shĭn) *n.* The front part of the leg below the knee and above the ankle. —*v.* **shinned, shinning.** To climb (a rope, pole, etc.) by gripping and pulling alternately with the hands and legs. [< OE *scinu.* See **skei-.**]

shin² (shēn) *n.* The 22nd letter of the Hebrew alphabet, representing *sh.*

shin·dig (shĭn'dĭg') *n. Slang.* A festive party or celebration.

shine (shīn) *v.* **shone** or **shined, shining. 1.** To emit light; be radiant. **2.** To reflect light; glint or glisten. **3.** To distinguish oneself in some sphere; excel. **4.** To aim the beam or glow of.

ô paw, for/oi boy/ou out/ōō took/ōō coo/p pop/r run/s sauce/sh shy/t to/th thin/*th* the/
ŭ cut/ûr fur/v van/w wag/y yes/z size/zh vision/ə ago, item, edible, gallop, circus/

5. To make glossy or bright by polishing. —*n.* **1.** Brightness; radiance. **2.** The act or an instance of polishing shoes. **3.** Fair weather: *rain or shine.* —**take a shine to.** To like spontaneously. [< OE *scīnan.* See **skī-**.]

shin·er (shī′nər) *n.* **1.** A black eye. **2.** A small, silvery fish.

shin·gle¹ (shǐng′gəl) *n.* **1.** A thin oblong piece of wood, asbestos, etc., laid in overlapping rows to cover the roofs or sides of houses. **2.** A small signboard, as one indicating a doctor's office. —*v.* **-gled, -gling.** To cover (a roof or building) with shingles. [< L *scindula.*] —**shin′gler** *n.*

shin·gle² (shǐng′gəl) *n.* **1.** Beach gravel consisting of large smooth pebbles. **2.** A beach covered with such gravel. [Prob < MLG *singele,* outermost wall.]

shin·ny (shǐn′ē) *v.* **-nied, -nying.** To climb by shinning.

Shin·to (shǐn′tō) *n.* Also **Shin·to·ism** (-ĭz′əm). The aboriginal religion of Japan, marked by the veneration of nature spirits and ancestors. —**Shin′to·ist** *n.*

shin·y (shī′nē) *adj.* **-ier, -iest.** Bright; glistening. —**shin′i·ness** *n.*

ship (shǐp) *n.* **1.** Any large vessel adapted for deep-water navigation. **2.** A ship's company. **3.** An airplane. —*v.* **shipped, shipping. 1.** To place or take on board a ship. **2.** To send or cause to be transported. **3.** To take in (water) over the side. [< OE *scip* < Gmc **skipam.*]

–ship. *comb. form.* **1.** The quality or condition of: **friendship. 2.** The status, rank, or office of: **professorship. 3.** The art or functioning of: **penmanship.** [< OE *-scipe.* See **skep-**.]

ship·board (shǐp′bôrd′, -bōrd′) *n.* A ship. —**on shipboard.** On board a ship.

ship·build·ing (shǐp′bĭl′dĭng) *n.* The business of constructing ships. —**ship′build′er** *n.*

ship·mate (shǐp′māt′) *n.* A fellow sailor.

ship·ment (shǐp′mənt) *n.* **1.** The act of sending or transporting goods. **2.** The goods or cargo transported.

ship·ping (shǐp′ĭng) *n.* **1.** The act or business of transporting goods. **2.** The body of ships belonging to one port or country.

ship·shape (shǐp′shāp′) *adj.* Neatly arranged; orderly; tidy.

ship·wreck (shǐp′rĕk′) *n.* **1.** The remains of a wrecked ship. **2.** The destruction of a ship, as by storm or collision. —*v.* To cause to suffer shipwreck. [SHIP + OE *wræc,* thing driven by the sea.]

ship·yard (shǐp′yärd′) *n.* An area where ships are built or repaired.

shire (shīr) *n.* One of the counties of Great Britain. [< OE *scīr,* official charge, province, shire.]

shirk (shûrk) *v.* To put off or avoid (work or duty). [Prob < G *Schurke,* scoundrel.] —**shirk′er** *n.*

shirr (shûr) *v.* **1.** To gather (cloth) into parallel rows. **2.** To bake (eggs) in molds. —*n.* A decorative gathering of cloth into parallel rows. [?]

shirt (shûrt) *n.* **1.** A garment for the upper part of the body, typically having a collar, sleeves,

and a front opening. **2.** An undershirt. [< OE *scyrte.* See **sker-¹**.]

shish ke·bab (shǐsh′ kə-bŏb′). Pieces of seasoned meat roasted and served with condiments on skewers. [Turk *sıs kebabı.*]

shist. Variant of **schist.**

Shi·va (shē′və). Hindu god of destruction and reproduction.

shiv·er¹ (shǐv′ər) *v.* To shudder or shake, as from cold. [ME *shiveren.*] —**shiv′er** *n.*

shiv·er² (shǐv′ər) *v.* To break suddenly into fragments or splinters; shatter. [< ME *scivre,* fragment.]

shoal¹ (shōl) *n.* **1.** A shallow. **2.** A sandy elevation of the bottom of a body of water, constituting a hazard to navigation. [< OE *sceald,* shallow < Gmc **skaldaz.*]

shoal² (shōl) *n.* **1.** A large group. **2.** A school of fish. —*v.* To form a shoal; school. [Prob < MDu or MLG *schōle,* school of fish.]

shoat (shōt) *n.* Also **shote.** A young pig. [ME *shote.*]

shock¹ (shŏk) *n.* **1.** A violent collision or impact. **2. a.** Something that jars the mind or emotions as if with a violent, unexpected blow. **b.** The disturbance of function or equilibrium caused by such a blow. **3.** A severe offense to one's sense of propriety or decency. **4.** A massive physiological reaction to bodily trauma, usually characterized by loss of blood pressure and depression of vital processes. **5.** The sensation and muscular spasm caused by an electric current passing through a bodily part. —*v.* **1.** To strike with great surprise and agitation. **2.** To strike with disgust; offend. **3.** To induce shock in (a person). **4.** To subject to an electric shock. [< OF *choquer,* to strike (with fear).]

shock² (shŏk) *n.* A number of sheaves of grain stacked upright in a field for drying. [ME *shokke.*]

shock³ (shŏk) *n.* A thick, heavy mass: *a shock of hair.* [Perh < SHOCK².]

shock·ing (shŏk′ĭng) *adj.* **1.** Highly disturbing emotionally. **2.** Highly offensive; distasteful. —**shock′ing·ly** *adv.*

shock wave. A large-amplitude compression wave, such as that produced by an explosion, caused by supersonic motion of a body in a medium.

shod·dy (shŏd′ē) *adj.* **-dier, -diest. 1.** Made of or containing inferior material. **2.** Imitative; ersatz. **3.** Shabby. [?] —**shod′di·ly** *adv.* —**shod′di·ness** *n.*

shoe (shōō) *n.* **1.** A durable covering for the human foot. **2.** A horseshoe. **3.** The outer covering, casing, or tread of a pneumatic rubber tire. **4.** The part of a brake that presses against the wheel or drum to retard its motion. —*v.* **shod** (shŏd), **shod** or **shodden** (shŏd′n), **shoeing.** To furnish or fit with shoes. [< OE *scōh* < Gmc **skōhaz.*]

shoe·horn (shōō′hôrn′) *n.* A curved implement used to help slip a shoe on the foot.

shoe·lace (shōō′lās′) *n.* A string or cord used for lacing and fastening shoes.

shoe·mak·er (shōō′mā′kər) *n.* One who makes or repairs shoes.

ă pat/ā ate/âr care/ä bar/b bib/ch chew/d deed/ĕ pet/ē be/f fit/g gag/h hat/hw what/
ĭ pit/ī pie/îr pier/j judge/k kick/l lid, fatal/m mum/n no, sudden/ng sing/ŏ pot/ō go/

shoe·tree (shōō'trē') *n.* A foot-shaped form inserted into a shoe to preserve its shape.

shone (shōn). *p.t.* & *p.p.* of **shine.**

shoo (shōō) *interj.* Used to scare away something. —*v.* To drive or scare away, as by crying "shoo." [ME *schowe* (imit.).]

shook (shŏŏk). *p.t.* of **shake.**

shoot (shōōt) *v.* **shot, shooting. 1.** To hit, wound, or kill with a missile. **2.** To fire or let fly (a missile) from a weapon. **3.** To discharge (a weapon); go off. **4.** To move or send forth swiftly. **5.** To pass over or through swiftly: *shoot the rapids.* **6.** To record on film. **7.** To project or cause to project or protrude. **8.** To put forth; begin to grow; sprout. **9.** To move or propel (a marble or ball) toward a goal. —*n.* **1.** A newly sprouting plant growth or part. **2.** A skeet tournament, hunt, etc. [< OE *scēotan.* See **skeud-.**] —**shoot'er** *n.*

shooting star. A briefly visible meteor.

shop (shŏp) *n.* **1.** A small retail store. **2.** A business or industrial establishment. **3.** A workshop. —*v.* **shopped, shopping.** To visit stores for the purpose of inspecting and buying merchandise. [< OE *sceoppa,* booth, stall < Gmc *skupp-.*] —**shop'per** *n.*

shop·keep·er (shŏp'kē'pər) *n.* An owner or manager of a shop.

shop·lift·er (shŏp'lĭf'tər) *n.* One who steals goods on display in a store. —**shop'lift'ing** *n.*

shop·worn (shŏp'wôrn', -wōrn') *adj.* **1.** Soiled, faded, etc., from being on display in a store. **2.** Trite; hackneyed.

shore¹ (shôr, shōr) *n.* The land along the edge of an ocean, sea, lake, or river. [< MDu and MLG *schore.*]

shore² (shôr, shōr) *v.* **shored, shoring.** To prop up, as with an inclined timber. [< MDu *schōren.*]

shore·line (shôr'līn', shōr'-) *n.* The line marking the edge of a body of water.

shorn (shôrn, shōrn). Alternate *p.p.* of **shear.**

short (shôrt) *adj.* **1.** Having little length. **2.** Having little height. **3.** Having a small extent in time. **4.** Not attaining that which is required. **5.** Lacking in length or amount. **6.** Rudely brief; curt. **7.** Containing shortening; crisp, as pastry. **8.** Designating a particular pronunciation of the letters for vowel sounds, as the sound of (ă) in *pan.* —*adv.* **1.** Abruptly; quickly. **2.** Concisely. **3.** Without getting to. **4.** Without owning what one is selling: *sell short.* —*n.* **1.** Anything that is short. **2. shorts.** Short drawers or trousers. **3.** A **short circuit.** —*v.* To cause a short circuit in. [< OE *scort.* See **sker-¹.**] —**short'ness** *n.*

short·age (shôr'tĭj) *n.* A deficiency in amount.

short·cake (shôrt'kāk') *n.* A cake made of biscuit dough, split and filled with fruit.

short·change (shôrt'chānj') *v.* To give (someone) less than what is due.

short circuit. A low-resistance connection, often unintended, between two points in an electric circuit.

short·cir·cuit (shôrt'sûr'kĭt) *v.* To cause or have a short circuit.

short·com·ing (shôrt'kŭm'ĭng) *n.* A deficiency or flaw.

short cut. 1. A more direct route than the customary one. **2.** Any means of saving time or effort.

short·en (shôrt'n) *v.* To make or become short or shorter. —**short'en·er** *n.*

short·en·ing (shôrt'n-ĭng, shôrt'nĭng) *n.* A fat, as butter or lard, used to make pastry light or flaky.

short·fall (shôrt'fôl) *n.* **1.** A shortage. **2.** The amount by which a supply falls short. **3.** A monetary deficit. [SHORT + FALL.]

short·hand (shôrt'hănd') *n.* A system of rapid handwriting employing symbols to represent words, phrases, and letters; stenography.

short-lived (shôrt'lĭvd', -līvd') *adj.* Living or lasting only a short time.

short·ly (shôrt'lē) *adv.* **1.** In a short time; soon. **2.** In a few words; concisely.

short·sight·ed (shôrt'sī'tĭd) *adj.* **1.** Nearsighted; myopic. **2.** Lacking foresight. —**short'sight'ed·ness** *n.*

short·stop (shôrt'stŏp') *n. Baseball.* The field position or player between second and third bases.

short story. A short prose fiction aiming at unity of characterization, theme, and effect.

short-tem·pered (shôrt'tĕm'pərd) *adj.* Easily angered.

short ton. A unit of weight, the ton.

short wave. An electromagnetic wave with a wavelength of 80 meters or less. —**short'-wave'** (shôrt'wāv') *adj.*

Sho·sho·ne (shō-shō'nē) *n., pl.* **-ne** or **-nes.** Also **Sho·sho·ni. 1.** A member of a tribe of Uto-Aztecan-speaking North American Indians, formerly occupying parts of the W U.S. **2.** The language of this tribe.

Sho·sho·ne·an (shō-shō'nē-ən) *n.* An Indian linguistic group in W North America, comprising most of the Uto-Aztecan languages found in the U.S. —**Sho·sho'ne·an** *adj.*

shot¹ (shŏt) *n.* **1.** The firing or discharge of a weapon. **2.** *pl.* **shots** or **shot.** A pellet, bullet, etc., fired from various firearms. **3.** A throw, hit, or drive in any of several games. **4.** One who shoots: *a good shot.* **5.** Scope; range. **6.** An attempt, guess, or opportunity. **7.** The heavy metal ball put for distance in the shotput. **8.** A photograph or single cinematic view. **9.** A hypodermic injection. **10.** A drink of liquor, esp. a jigger. [< OE *scot.* See **skeud-.**]

shot² (shŏt). *p.t.* & *p.p.* of **shoot.**

shote. Variant of **shoat.**

shot·gun (shŏt'gŭn') *n.* A firearm that fires a charge of pellets through a smooth bore.

shot-put (shŏt'pŏŏt') *n.* An athletic event in which the contestants attempt to throw or put a shot as far as possible. —**shot'-put'ter** *n.*

should (shŏŏd). *p.t.* of **shall,** used as an auxiliary expressing obligation, necessity, anticipation, contingency, or uncertainty. [< OE *sceolde.* See **skel-².**]

Usage: In sentences expressing simple conditions (contingency of one clause on another clause or phrase), both *would* and *should* are employed, but *would* is much more frequent in American usage: *If I had known that, I would* (or *should*) *have made a different reply. We*

ŏ paw, for/oi boy/ou out/ōō took/ōō coo/p pop/r run/s sauce/sh shy/t to/th thin/*th* the/
ŭ cut/ûr fur/v van/w wag/y yes/z size/zh vision/ə ago, item, edible, gallop, circus/

would (or *should*) *not have succeeded without your assistance.* Either *would* or *should* (indicating condition, not obligation) is acceptable on all levels of usage in the preceding examples. *Would* is employed in such constructions in all three grammatical persons, whereas *should* is limited to the first person. Either *would* or *should* is possible in the first person, as an auxiliary, with *like, be inclined, be glad, prefer,* and related verbs: *I would* (or *should*) *like to call your attention to an oversight.*

shoul•der (shōl′dər) *n.* **1. a.** The part of the body between the neck and the upper arm or forelimb. **b.** The joint connecting the arm with the trunk. **2. shoulders.** The two shoulders and the area of the back between them. **3.** The edge or ridge on either side of a roadway. —*v.* **1.** To carry on or as on the shoulders. **2.** To push with or as with the shoulder. [< OE *sculdor* < Gmc *skuldra-.*]

shoulder blade. Either of two flat bones forming the back of the shoulders.

should•n't (shŏŏd′ənt). Contraction of *should not.*

shouldst (shŏŏdst). Also **should•est** (shŏŏd′ĭst). *Archaic.* 2nd person sing. past tense of **shall.**

shout (shout) *n.* A loud cry, often expressing strong emotion or a command. [ME *shouten.*] —**shout** *v.* —**shout′er** *n.*

shove (shŭv) *v.* **shoved, shoving.** To prod or give thrust to; push roughly or rudely. —*n.* The act of shoving, esp. a rude push. [< OE *scūfan.* See **skeubh-.**] —**shov′er** *n.*

shov•el (shŭv′əl) *n.* **1.** A tool with a handle and a scoop for picking up dirt, snow, etc. **2.** A large mechanical device for heavy digging or excavation. —*v.* **-eled** or **-elled, -eling** or **-elling. 1.** To dig or move with a shovel. **2.** To convey in a rough way, as with a shovel. [< OE *scofl.* See **skeubh-.**]

show (shō) *v.* **showed, shown** or **showed, showing. 1.** To cause or allow to be seen; display. **2.** To conduct; guide. **3.** To point out; demonstrate. **4.** To manifest; reveal. **5.** To grant; confer. **6.** To instruct. **7.** To be visible or evident. **8.** To finish third in a horse race. —*n.* **1.** A display; demonstration. **2.** An appearance; semblance. **3.** A spectacle. **4.** A public exhibition or entertainment. **5.** Third place in a horse race. [< OE *scēawian,* to look at, see. See **keu-.**]

show bill. An advertising poster.

show•case (shō′kās′) *n.* A display case or cabinet, as in a store or museum.

show•down (shō′doun′) *n.* An event or circumstance that forces an issue to a conclusion.

show•er (shou′ər) *n.* **1.** A brief fall of rain. **2.** An outpouring: *a shower of abuse.* **3.** A party held to honor and present gifts to someone. **4.** A bath in which water is sprayed on the bather. —*v.* **1.** To sprinkle; spray. **2.** To bestow abundantly. **3.** To fall or pour down in a shower. **4.** To bathe by taking a shower. [< OE *scūr.* See **kēwero-.**]

show•ing (shō′ĭng) *n.* **1.** The presenting or displaying of something. **2.** A show. **3.** Performance: *a poor showing.*

show•man (shō′mən) *n.* **1.** A theatrical pro-

ducer. **2.** A person having a flair for doing things dramatically. —**show′man•ship′** *n.*

shown (shōn). Alternate *p.p.* of **show.**

show off. To behave in an impudent and exhibitionistic manner.

show•off (shō′ôf′, -ŏf′) *n.* An exhibitionist.

show place. A place that is exhibited for its beauty, historical interest, etc.

show room. A room in which merchandise is on display.

show•y (shō′ē) *adj.* **-ier, -iest.** Making a conspicuous display; ostentatious; gaudy. —**show′i•ly** *adv.* —**show′i•ness** *n.*

shpt. shipment.

shr. share (capital stock).

shrank (shrăngk). Alternate *p.t.* of **shrink.**

shrap•nel (shrăp′nəl) *n., pl.* **-nel. 1. a.** A projectile containing metal balls, fused to explode in the air above enemy troops. **b.** The metal balls in such a weapon. **2.** Shell fragments from any high-explosive shell. [< Gen. Henry *Shrapnel* (1761–1842), British artillery officer.]

shred (shrĕd) *n.* **1.** A long, irregular strip cut or torn off. **2.** A small amount; particle. —*v.* **shredded** or **shred, shredding.** To cut or tear into shreds. [< OE *scrēade.* See **skeru-.**] —**shred′der** *n.*

Shreve•port (shrĕv′pôrt′, -pōrt′). A city of NW Louisiana. Pop. 178,000.

shrew (shrōō) *n.* **1.** A very small mouselike mammal with a pointed nose. **2.** A woman who constantly nags or scolds. [< OE *scrēawa.* See **skeru-.**] —**shrew′ish** *adj.*

shrewd (shrōōd) *adj.* **1.** Having keen insight; discerning; astute. **2.** Artful; cunning. [< SHREW.] —**shrewd′ly** *adv.* —**shrewd′ness** *n.*

shriek (shrēk) *n.* A shrill outcry; screech. —*v.* To utter such a cry. [Prob < ON *skrækja.*]

shrike (shrīk) *n.* A predatory bird with a hooked bill, often impaling its prey on thorns. [Prob < OE *scrīc,* thrush.]

shrill (shrĭl) *adj.* High-pitched and piercing: *a shrill whistle.* [Prob < Scand.] —**shrill′ness** *n.* —**shril′ly** *adv.*

shrimp (shrĭmp) *n.* **1.** A small, often edible marine crustacean. **2.** *Slang.* A diminutive or unimportant person. [ME *shrimpe,* pigmy, shrimp.]

shrine (shrīn) *n.* **1.** A container for sacred relics. **2.** The tomb of a saint. **3.** A site hallowed by a venerated object or its associations. [< L *scrīnium,* box, bookcase.]

shrink (shrĭngk) *v.* **shrank** or **shrunk, shrunk** or **shrunken, shrinking. 1.** To draw together or contract from heat, moisture, or cold. **2.** To diminish in amount or value; dwindle. **3.** To draw back; recoil. **4.** To be reluctant to do or say something. [< OE *scrincan.* See **sker-².**] —**shrink′age** *n.*

shrive (shrīv) *v.* **shrove** (shrōv) or **shrived, shriven** (shrĭv′ən) or **shrived, shriving.** To confess and give absolution to (a penitent). [< OE *scrīfan* < Gmc *skrīban,* to write, "prescribe (penance)."]

shriv•el (shrĭv′əl) *v.* **-eled** or **-elled, -eling** or **-elling. 1.** To shrink and wrinkle, often in drying. **2.** To cause to become shriveled. [Poss < ON *skrīfla,* to wrinkle.]

ă pat/ā ate/âr care/ä bar/b bib/ch chew/d deed/ĕ pet/ē be/f fit/g gag/h hat/hw what/
ĭ pit/ī pie/îr pier/j judge/k kick/l lid, fatal/m mum/n no, sudden/ng sing/ŏ pot/ō go/

shroud (shroud) *n.* **1.** A cloth used to wrap a body for burial. **2.** Something that conceals, protects, or screens. —*v.* To envelop; screen; hide. [< OE *scrūd.* See skeru-.]

Shrove•tide (shrōv'tīd') *n.* The three days preceding Ash Wednesday. [< ME *schrof-,* "shriving" + TIDE (time).]

shrub (shrŭb) *n.* A many-stemmed woody plant of relatively low height. [< OE *scrybb.* See sker-¹.] —**shrub'by** *adj.*

shrub•ber•y (shrŭb'ə-rē) *n., pl.* **-ies.** A group or planting of shrubs.

shrug (shrŭg) *v.* **shrugged, shrugging.** To raise (the shoulders) as a gesture of doubt, disdain, or indifference. —**shrug off.** To minimize the importance of. —*n.* The expressive gesture so made. [Perh < Scand.]

shrunk (shrŭngk). Alternate *p.t. & p.p.* of **shrink.**

shrunken (shrŭng'kən). Alternate *p.p.* of **shrink.**

shtg. shortage.

shuck (shŭk) *n.* A husk, shell, etc. —**not worth shucks.** Of little value; worthless. —*v.* To remove the husk or shell from. [?]

shucks (shŭks) *interj.* Expressive of disappointment, disgust, or annoyance. [< SHUCK.]

shud•der (shŭd'ər) *v.* To tremble or shiver convulsively, as from fear or aversion. —*n.* A convulsive shiver, as from fear, aversion, or cold; a tremor. [< MLG *schōderen.*] —**shud'der•ing•ly** *adv.*

shuf•fle (shŭf'əl) *v.* **-fled, -fling.** **1.** To move with a shambling, idle gait. **2.** To mix together (playing cards, dominoes, etc.) to change their order. **3.** To mix together in a disordered, haphazard fashion. —*n.* **1.** A shuffling gait or movement. **2.** The mixing of cards, dominoes, etc. [Prob < LG *schüffeln,* to walk clumsily, shuffle cards.] —**shuf'fler** *n.*

shuf•fle•board (shŭf'əl-bôrd', -bōrd') *n.* A game in which disks are pushed along a smooth, level surface toward numbered squares with a pronged cue. [Var of earlier *shove-board.*]

shun (shŭn) *v.* **shunned, shunning.** To avoid (a person, group, or thing) deliberately and consistently; keep away from. [< OE *scunian,* to avoid, be afraid, abhor.] —**shun'ner** *n.*

shunt (shŭnt) *v.* **1.** To turn or move (something) aside or onto another course. **2.** To shift or switch (a train or car) from one track to another. **3.** To divert by means of a shunt. —*n.* **1.** The act of shunting. **2.** A railroad switch. **3.** A low resistance alternative path for a portion of an electric current. [Perh < ME *shunnen,* shun.]

shush (shŭsh) *interj.* Used to express a demand for silence. —*v.* To demand silence from by saying "shush."

shut (shŭt) *v.* **shut, shutting.** **1.** To move (a door, lid, valve, etc.) into closed position. **2.** To block passage or access to; close. **3.** To move or become moved to a closed position. —**shut off.** **1.** To turn off. **2.** To isolate. **3.** To cease operating automatically. —**shut up.** **1.** To silence (a person). **2.** To be or become silenced. [< OE *scyttan.*]

shut•down (shŭt'doun') *n.* A temporary closing of an industrial plant.

shut•eye (shŭt'ī') *n.* *Slang.* Sleep.

shut-in (shŭt'ĭn') *n.* An invalid.

shut out. 1. To keep out. **2.** *Sports.* To prevent (the opposing team) from scoring.

shut•out (shŭt'out') *n.* A game in which one side does not score.

shut•ter (shŭt'ər) *n.* **1.** A hinged cover or screen for a window. **2.** A device that opens and shuts the lens aperture of a camera. —*v.* To furnish or close with a shutter.

shut•tle (shŭt'l) *n.* **1.** A device used in weaving to carry the thread back and forth. **2.** A device for holding the thread in tatting, in a sewing machine, etc. **3.** A train, bus, or plane making short, frequent trips between two points. —*v.* **-tled, -tling.** To move back and forth by shuttle: *shuttle between New York and Boston.* [< OE *scytel,* dart, missile. See skeud-.]

shut•tle•cock (shŭt'l-kŏk') *n.* A small rounded piece of cork, plastic, etc., with a crown of feathers, used in badminton. [SHUTTLE + COCK (bird).]

shy¹ (shī) *adj.* **shier** or **shyer, shiest** or **shyest.** **1.** Easily startled; timid. **2.** Bashful; reserved. **3.** Distrustful; wary; cautious. **4.** *Informal.* Short; lacking. —*v.* **shied, shying.** **1.** To move suddenly, as if startled. **2.** To draw back, as from fear or caution. [< OE *scēoh* < Gmc *skiuhwaz.*] —**shi'er, shy'er** *n.* —**shy'ly, shi'ly** *adv.* —**shy'ness** *n.*

shy² (shī) *v.* **shied, shying.** To throw (something) with a swift sideways motion. [Prob < SHY.]

shy•ster (shī'stər) *n.* *Slang.* An unethical or unscrupulous lawyer. [Poss < *Scheuster,* an unscrupulous 19th-century New York lawyer.]

Si silicon.

Si•am. The former name for **Thailand.**

Si•a•mese (sī'ə-mēz', -mēs') *adj.* Thai. —*n., pl.* **-mese.** Thai.

Siamese twins. Twins born with their bodies joined together.

Si•be•li•us (sĭ-bā'lē-əs, -bāl'yəs), **Jean.** 1865–1957. Finnish composer.

Si•be•ri•a (sī-bîr'ē-ə). A large region of the Soviet Union in Asia. —**Si•be'ri•an** *adj. & n.*

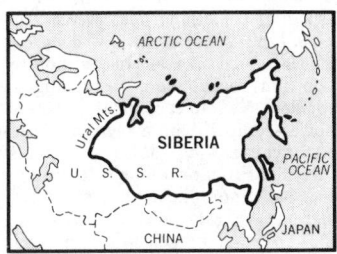

Siberia

sib•i•lant (sĭb'ə-lənt) *adj.* Producing a hissing sound. —*n.* A speech sound that suggests hissing, as (s), (sh), (z), or (zh). [< L *sibilāre,* to hiss, whistle.]

ô paw, for/oi boy/ou out/ōō took/ōō coo/p pop/r run/s sauce/sh shy/t to/th thin/*th* the/
ŭ cut/ûr fur/v van/w wag/y yes/z size/zh vision/ə ago, item, edible, gallop, circus/

sib·ling (sĭb′lĭng) *n.* An offspring of the same parents; a brother or sister. [< OE *sibb,* kin + -LING.]

sic[1] (sĭk, sēk) *adv.* Thus; so. Used in written texts to indicate that a surprising quotation is not a mistake and is to be read as it stands. [L *sic.*]

sic[2] (sĭk) *v.* **sicced, siccing.** Also **sick.** 1. To urge to attack or chase. 2. To set upon or chase. [Dial var of SEEK.]

Sic·i·ly (sĭs′ə-lē). An Italian island in the Mediterranean. Pop. 4,712,000. Cap. Palermo. **—Si·cil′ian** *adj.* & *n.*

sick[1] (sĭk) *adj.* 1. a. Ailing; ill; unwell. b. Violently nauseated. 2. Of or for sick persons. 3. a. Mentally ill or disturbed. b. Morbid or unwholesome: *a sick joke.* 4. a. Deeply distressed; chagrined; upset. b. Disgusted; revolted. c. Weary; tired: *sick of it all.* [< OE *sēoc* < Gmc **siukaz.*] **—sick′ish** *adj.* **—sick′-ness** *n.*

sick[2]. Variant of sic[2].

sick·bay (sĭk′bā′) *n.* The hospital and dispensary of a ship.

sick·bed (sĭk′bĕd′) *n.* A sick person's bed.

sick·en (sĭk′ən) *v.* To make or become sick.

sick·en·ing (sĭk′ə-nĭng) *adj.* 1. Causing sickness or nausea. 2. Revolting or disgusting; loathsome. **—sick′en·ing·ly** *adv.*

sick·le (sĭk′əl) *n.* An implement having a semicircular blade attached to a short handle, for cutting grain or tall grass. [< L *sēcula.*]

sick leave. Time off from work with pay allowed an employee because of sickness.

sick·ly (sĭk′lē) *adj.* **-lier, -liest.** 1. Prone to sickness; ailing. 2. Of, caused by, or associated with sickness: *a sickly pallor.* 3. Nauseating; sickening

side (sīd) *n.* 1. A surface of an object, esp. a surface joining a top and a bottom. 2. Either of the two surfaces of a flat object, such as a piece of paper. 3. The left or right half in reference to a vertical axis, as of the body. 4. The space immediately next to someone or something: *stood at her side.* 5. An area separated from another by some intervening line, barrier, or other feature: *on this side of the Atlantic.* 6. One of two or more opposing groups, teams, or sets of opinions. 7. A distinct aspect of something: *the cruel side of her nature.* 8. Line of descent: *my aunt on my mother's side.* **—on the side.** In addition to the main portion, occupation, or arrangement. **—side by side.** Next to each other. **—take sides.** To associate oneself with a faction, contested opinion, or cause. *—adj.* 1. Located on a side: *a side door.* 2. From or to one side; oblique: *a side view.* 3. Minor; incidental; secondary: *a side interest.* *—v.* **sided, siding. —side with** (or **against**). To align oneself with (or against). [< OE *side.*]

side·board (sīd′bôrd′, -bōrd′) *n.* A piece of dining-room furniture for holding linens and tableware.

side·burns (sīd′bûrnz′) *pl.n.* Growths of hair down the sides of the face in front of the ears. [Var of *burnsides* < A. Burnside (1824–81), U.S. military leader.]

side·car (sīd′kär′) *n.* A one-wheeled car for a single passenger, attached to the side of a motorcycle.

side·kick (sīd′kĭk′) *n. Slang.* A close friend or associate.

side·line (sīd′lĭn′) *n.* Also **side line.** 1. a. A line along either side of a playing field, marking its limits. b. **sidelines.** The space outside such limits, occupied by spectators and inactive players. 2. A subsidiary line of merchandise. 3. An activity pursued in addition to one's regular occupation. *—v.* **-lined, -lining.** To keep from active participation, as in athletic contests.

side·long (sīd′lông′, -lŏng′) *adj.* Directed to one side; sideways: *a sidelong glance.*

si·de·re·al (sī-dîr′ē-əl) *adj.* Relative to the stars. [< L *sīdus,* constellation.]

side·sad·dle (sīd′săd′l) *n.* A woman's saddle enabling her to sit with both legs on one side of the horse. *—adv.* On a sidesaddle.

side·step (sīd′stĕp′) *v.* **-stepped, -stepping.** 1. To step out of the way of. 2. To evade; skirt. **—side′step′per** *n.*

side stroke. A stroke in which a person swims on one side and thrusts his arms forward alternately while performing a scissors kick.

side·swipe (sīd′swīp′) *v.* **-swiped, -swiping.** To strike along the side in passing.

side·track (sīd′trăk′) *v.* 1. To switch from a main track to a siding. 2. To divert from a main issue or course. *—n.* A railroad siding.

side·walk (sīd′wôk′) *n.* A walk or raised path along the side of a road for pedestrians.

side·ways (sīd′wāz′) *adv.* 1. Toward or from one side. 2. With one side forward. *—adj.* Toward or from one side.

sid·ing (sī′dĭng) *n.* 1. A short section of railroad track connected by switches with a main track. 2. Material used for surfacing a frame building.

si·dle (sīd′l) *v.* **-dled, -dling.** To move sideways; edge along furtively or indirectly. [Backformation < SIDELONG.]

siege (sēj) *n.* 1. The surrounding and blockading of a town or fortress by an army bent on capturing it. 2. A prolonged period, as of illness. [< OF, "seat."]

si·er·ra (sē-ĕr′ə) *n.* A rugged range of mountains having an irregular or serrated profile. [Span, "a saw."]

Si·er·ra Le·one (sē-ĕr′ə lē-ōn′). A country of W Africa. Pop. 2,183,000. Cap. Freetown.

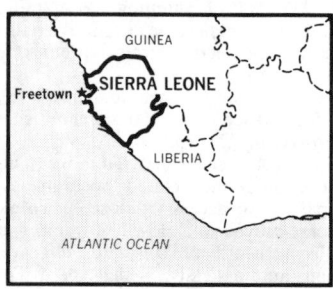

Sierra Leone

Si•er•ra Ne•vad•a (sē-ĕr′ə nə-vä′də, -văd′ə). A mountain range in E California.

si•es•ta (sē-ĕs′tə) *n.* A rest, usually taken after the midday meal. [< L *sexta (hora)*, 6th (hour after sunrise), noon.]

sieve (sĭv) *n.* A utensil of wire mesh or closely perforated metal, used for straining or sifting. [< OE *sife* < Gmc **sib-*.]

sift (sĭft) *v.* 1. To put through a sieve to separate fine particles from coarse ones. 2. To examine closely and carefully: *sift the evidence.* [< OE *siftan* < Gmc **sib-*.] —**sift′er** *n.*

sig. 1. signal. 2. signature.

sigh (sī) *v.* To exhale audibly in a long, deep breath, as in sorrow, weariness, or relief. —*n.* The act or sound of sighing. [Prob < OE *sican* < Gmc **sik-*.]

sight (sīt) *n.* 1. The ability to see. 2. The act or fact of seeing. 3. The field of one's vision. 4. Something that is seen. 5. Something worth seeing: *the sights of London.* 6. *Informal.* Something unsightly: *Her hair was a sight.* 7. A device used to assist in aiming, as on a gun. —*v.* 1. To see or observe within one's field of vision: *sight land.* 2. To take aim with (a firearm). [< OE *sihth*, eyesight, thing seen. See sekw-[2].]

sight•ed (sī′tĭd) *adj.* Having sight; not blind.

sight•less (sīt′lĭs) *adj.* 1. Blind. 2. Invisible.

sight•ly (sīt′lē) *adj.* -lier, -liest. Pleasing to the eye; handsome. —**sight′li•ness** *n.*

sight-read (sīt′rēd′) *v.* To read or perform, as music, without preparation or prior acquaintance. —**sight′-read′er** *n.*

sight•see•ing (sīt′sē′ĭng) *n.* The act or pastime of touring places of interest. —*adj.* Used or engaged in seeing sights. —**sight′se′er** *n.*

sig•ma (sĭg′mə) *n.* The 18th letter of the Greek alphabet, representing *s.*

sig•moid flex•ure (sĭg′moid′; flĕk′shər). *Anat.* An S-shaped bend in the colon between the descending section and the rectum.

sign (sīn) *n.* 1. Something that suggests a fact, condition, or quality not immediately evident; an indication. 2. An action or gesture used to convey an idea, desire, information, or a command. 3. A board, poster, or placard displayed to advertise or convey information. 4. A conventional figure or device that stands for a word, phrase, or operation. 5. A trace or vestige: *no sign of life.* —*v.* 1. To affix one's signature to. 2. To write (one's name). 3. To approve (a document) by affixing one's signature. 4. To hire by written contract. 5. To relinquish or transfer title to by signature. —**sign off.** *Broadcasting.* To cease transmission. —**sign up.** To volunteer one's services; enlist. [< L *signum*, distinctive mark or figure, seal, signal.] —**sign′er** *n.*

sig•nal (sĭg′nəl) *n.* 1. A sign or other indicator serving as a means of communication. 2. a. A fluctuating quantity, such as voltage or current strength, the variations of which represent information. b. Information so represented. —*adj.* 1. Out of the ordinary; remarkable; conspicuous: *a signal feat.* 2. Used or acting as a signal: *a signal flare.* —*v.* -naled or -nalled, -naling or -nalling. 1. To make a signal or

signals (to). 2. To relate or make known by signals. [< L *signum*, SIGN.]

sig•nal•ize (sĭg′nə-līz′) *v.* -ized, -izing. 1. To make remarkable or conspicuous. 2. To point out particularly.

sig•na•to•ry (sĭg′nə-tôr′ē, -tōr′ē) *adj.* Bound by signed agreement. —*n., pl.* **-ries.** A person or nation that has signed a treaty or other document.

sig•na•ture (sĭg′nə-choor′) *n.* 1. The name of a person as written by himself. 2. *Mus.* A sign used to indicate key or tempo. [< L *signāre*, to mark with a sign.]

sign•board (sīn′bôrd′, -bōrd′) *n.* A board bearing a sign.

sig•net (sĭg′nĭt) *n.* A small seal used to authenticate a document. [< OF *signe*, sign.]

sig•nif•i•cance (sĭg-nĭf′ĭ-kəns) *n.* 1. Importance; consequence. 2. Meaning; import.

sig•nif•i•cant (sĭg-nĭf′ĭ-kənt) *adj.* 1. Having a meaning; meaningful. 2. Full of meaning: *a significant glance.* 3. Important; notable.

sig•ni•fy (sĭg′nə-fī′) *v.* -fied, -fying. 1. To serve as a sign of; betoken; denote. 2. To make known; communicate.

sign language. A system of communication by means of hand gestures.

sign•post (sīn′pōst′) *n.* A post supporting a sign.

Sikh (sēk) *n.* An adherent of Sikhism. —*adj.* Of or pertaining to the Sikhs. [Hindi.]

Sikh•ism (sē′kĭz′əm) *n.* The doctrines and practices of a monotheistic Hindu religious sect founded in the 16th century.

Sik•kim (sĭk′ĭm). A kingdom between India and China. Pop. 162,000. Cap. Gangtok.

Sikkim

si•lage (sī′lĭj) *n.* Fodder made from green plants stored and fermented in a silo.

si•lence (sī′ləns) *n.* 1. The condition or quality of being silent. 2. The absence of sound; stillness. 3. Refusal or failure to speak out. —*v.* -lenced, -lencing. 1. To make silent or bring to silence. 2. To suppress: *silence all criticism.*

si•lenc•er (sī′lən-sər) *n.* A device for muffling the sound of a firearm.

si•lent (sī′lənt) *adj.* 1. Making no sound or noise; quiet. 2. Not disposed to speak; taciturn. 3. Unable to speak; mute. 4. Not voiced or expressed; tacit. 5. Having no phonetic value; unpronounced, as the *b* in *subtle.* 6. Having no soundtrack: *silent motion pictures.*

[< L *silēre*, to be silent.] —**si′lent•ly** *adv.*

sil•hou•ette (sĭl′ōō-ĕt′) *n.* A representation of the outline of something, usually filled in with black or another solid color. —*v.* **-etted, -etting.** To cause to be seen as a silhouette; outline. [< Étienne de *Silhouette* (1709–67), French official.]

sil•i•ca (sĭl′ĭ-kə) *n.* A white or colorless crystalline compound, SiO_2, occurring abundantly as quartz, sand, flint, agate, and many other minerals. [< L *silex (silic-)*, flint.]

sil•i•cate (sĭl′ĭ-kāt′, -kĭt) *n.* Any of numerous compounds containing silicon, oxygen, and a metallic or organic radical.

si•li•ceous (sĭ-lĭsh′əs) *adj.* Containing, resembling, or consisting of silica.

sil•i•con (sĭl′ĭ-kən, -kŏn′) *n. Symbol* **Si** A nonmetallic element occurring extensively in the earth's crust in silica and silicates, and used in glass, semiconducting devices, concrete, brick, refractories, pottery, and silicones. Atomic number 14, atomic weight 28.086. [< SILICA.]

silicon carbide. A bluish-black crystalline compound, SiC, one of the hardest known substances, used as an abrasive and heat-refractory material.

silicon dioxide. Silica.

sil•i•cone (sĭl′ĭ-kōn′) *n.* Any of a group of materials based on the structural unit R_2SiO, where R is an organic group, used in adhesives, lubricants, protective coatings, paints, and electrical insulation. [< SILICA.]

sil•i•co•sis (sĭl′ĭ-kō′sĭs) *n.* A disease of the lungs caused by long-term inhalation of silica dust and resulting in a chronic shortness of breath.

silk (sĭlk) *n.* **1.** The fine, lustrous fiber produced by a silkworm to form its cocoon. **2.** Thread or fabric made from this fiber. **3.** Fibers or material resembling silk. [< OE *sioloc, seoluc*.] —**silk′en** *adj.* —**silk′y** *adj.*

silk•worm (sĭlk′wûrm′) *n.* The larva of an Asian moth whose cocoons are the source of commercial silk.

sill (sĭl) *n.* The horizontal member that bears the upright portion of a frame, esp. the base of a window. [< OE *sylle*, threshold, sill. See **swel-³**.]

sil•ly (sĭl′ē) *adj.* **-lier, -liest.** Showing a lack of good sense; foolish; stupid. [< OE *gesǣlig*, happy. See **sel-²**.] —**sil′li•ness** *n.*

si•lo (sī′lō) *n., pl.* **-los. 1.** A tall, cylindrical structure or a pit in which fodder is stored. **2.** A sunken shelter for storing and launching missiles. [< Gk *siros*, pit for keeping grain in.]

silt (sĭlt) *n.* Fine mineral particles deposited as sediment in rivers and lakes. —*v.* To fill or become filled with silt. [Prob < Scand.]

Si•lu•ri•an (sĭ-lŏŏr′ē-ən, sī-) *adj.* Of or belonging to the geologic time, system of rocks, or sedimentary deposits of the third period of the Paleozoic era. —*n.* The Silurian period.

sil•van. Variant of **sylvan.**

sil•ver (sĭl′vər) *n.* **1.** *Symbol* **Ag** A lustrous white, ductile, malleable metallic element, highly valued for jewelry and tableware and widely used in coinage, photography, dental and soldering alloys, and electrical contacts.

Atomic number 47, atomic weight 107.87. **2.** Coins made of this metal. **3.** Tableware made of this metal. **4.** A lustrous medium-gray color. —*adj.* **1.** Made of, containing, or pertaining to silver. **2.** Having a lustrous medium-gray color. **3.** Of or designating a 25th anniversary. —*v.* To cover, plate, or adorn with silver. [< OE *siolfor, seolfor* < Gmc *silubhra-*.]

sil•ver•fish (sĭl′vər-fĭsh′) *n.* A silvery, wingless insect found in human dwellings.

silver iodide. A pale-yellow, odorless powder, AgI, that darkens on exposure to light and is used in artificial rainmaking and in photography.

silver nitrate. A poisonous, colorless crystalline compound, $AgNO_3$, that becomes grayish black when exposed to light in the presence of organic matter and is used in photography, manufacturing, and medicine.

sil•ver•smith (sĭl′vər-smĭth′) *n.* One who makes, repairs, or replates articles of silver.

sil•ver•ware (sĭl′vər-wâr′) *n.* Articles made of or plated with silver, esp. tableware.

sil•ver•y (sĭl′və-rē) *adj.* **1.** Containing or coated with silver. **2.** Like silver in luster; shining; glittering. —**sil′ver•i•ness** *n.*

sim•i•an (sĭm′ē-ən) *adj.* Pertaining to or characteristic of apes or monkeys. —*n.* An ape or monkey. [< L *sīmia*, ape.]

sim•i•lar (sĭm′ə-lər) *adj.* **1.** Showing some resemblance; related in appearance or nature; alike though not identical. **2.** *Geom.* Having corresponding angles equal and corresponding line segments proportional. [< L *similis*, like.] —**sim′i•lar′i•ty** *n.* —**sim′i•lar•ly** *adv.*

Usage: Similar is an adjective only, and is not employed adverbially in standard usage: *The heating mechanism is similar to that of a drier* or *works like that* (or *similarly to that*) *of a drier,* but not *works similar to that of a drier.*

sim•i•le (sĭm′ə-lē) *n.* A figure of speech in which two essentially unlike things are compared. [< L *similis*, SIMILAR.]

si•mil•i•tude (sĭ-mĭl′ə-t/y/ōōd′) *n.* Similarity.

sim•mer (sĭm′ər) *v.* **1.** To cook below or just at the boiling point. **2.** To be filled with barely controlled anger or resentment; seethe. —**simmer down.** To become calm after excitement or anger. —*n.* The state of simmering. [< ME *simperen* (imit.).]

si•mon•ize (sī′mə-nīz′) *v.* **-ized, -izing.** To clean and polish (an automobile) with wax.

si•mon-pure (sī′mən-pyŏŏr′) *adj.* Genuine; real.

sim•o•ny (sĭm′ə-nē, sī′mə-) *n.* The buying or selling of ecclesiastical pardons, offices, or emoluments.

sim•per (sĭm′pər) *v.* To smile in a silly or self-conscious manner. [< Scand.] —**sim′per** *n.* —**sim′per•er** *n.*

sim•ple (sĭm′pəl) *adj.* **-pler, -plest. 1.** Consisting of one thing or part only; not compound. **2.** Not involved or complicated; easy. **3.** Without additions or modifications; bare; mere. **4.** Without embellishment; not ornate or luxurious. **5.** Not affected; unassuming or unpretentious. **6.** Not guileful or deceitful; sincere;

7. Humble or lowly in condition or rank. **8.** Ordinary or common. **9.** Having little sense or intellect; silly. [< L *simplus.*]

sim·ple-mind·ed (sĭm′pəl-mīn′dĭd) *adj.* **1.** Not sophisticated; artless. **2.** Stupid or silly. **3.** Mentally defective.

sim·ple·ton (sĭm′pəl-tən) *n.* A silly or stupid person; a fool.

sim·plic·i·ty (sĭm-plĭs′ə-tē) *n., pl.* **-ties.** The state or quality of being simple; absence of complexity, intricacy, or artificiality.

sim·pli·fy (sĭm′plə-fī′) *v.* **-fied, -fying.** To make simple or simpler; render less complex or intricate. —**sim′pli·fi·ca′tion** *n.*

sim·ply (sĭm′plē) *adv.* **1.** In a simple manner; plainly. **2.** Merely; only. **3.** Absolutely; altogether.

sim·u·late (sĭm′yə-lāt′) *v.* **-lated, -lating. 1.** To have or take on the appearance of; imitate. **2.** To make a pretense of; feign. [< L *similis,* SIMILAR.] —**sim′u·la′tion** *n.* —**sim′u·la′tive** *adj.* —**sim′u·la′tor** *n.*

si·mul·ta·ne·ous (sī′məl-tā′nē-əs, sĭm′əl-) *adj.* Happening, existing, or done at the same time. [< L *simul,* at the same time.] —**si′mul·ta′ne·ous·ness, si′mul·ta·ne′i·ty** (-tə-nē′ə-tē) *n.* —**si′mul·ta′ne·ous·ly** *adv.*

Usage: Simultaneous is an adjective only. Its use as an adverb, for *simultaneously,* is not standard: *The referendum was conducted simultaneously* (not *simultaneous*) *with the general election.*

sin¹ (sĭn) *n.* **1.** A transgression of a religious or moral law, esp. when deliberate. **2.** Any offense, violation, fault, or error. —*v.* **sinned, sinning.** To commit a sinful act; do wrong. [< OE *synn.* See es-.]

sin² (sēn) *n.* The 21st letter of the Hebrew alphabet, representing *s.*

since (sĭns) *adv.* **1.** From then until now. **2.** Between then and now. **3.** At some past time; before now; ago: *long since forgotten.* —*prep.* **1.** During the time after. **2.** Continuously throughout the time following. —*conj.* **1.** During the time after which. **2.** Continuously from the time when. **3.** As a result of the fact that; inasmuch as. [< OE *siththan,* "after that."]

sin·cere (sĭn-sîr′) *adj.* **-cerer, -cerest. 1.** Not feigned or affected; true. **2.** Presenting no false appearance; not hypocritical; honest. [< L *sincērus,* clean, pure, genuine, honest.] —**sin·cere′ly** *adv.* —**sin·cer′i·ty** (-sĕr′ə-tē, -sîr′-) *n.*

si·ne·cure (sī′nə-kyŏŏr′, sĭn′ə-) *n.* An office, commission, or charge that requires no work yet provides compensation. [ML (*beneficium*) *sine cūrā,* (benefice) without cure (of souls).] —**si′ne·cur·ist** *n.*

sin·ew (sĭn′yŏŏ) *n.* **1.** A tendon. **2.** Vigorous strength; muscular power. [< OE *sinu, seonu.* See snēu-.] —**sin′ew·y** *adj.*

sin·ful (sĭn′fəl) *adj.* Marked by or full of sin; wicked. —**sin′ful·ly** *adv.* —**sin′ful·ness** *n.*

sing (sĭng) *v.* **sang** or **sung, sung, singing. 1.** To utter a series of words or sounds in musical tones. **2.** To render in tones with musical inflections of the voice. **3.** To proclaim or extol, esp. in verse. **4.** To bring to a specified state by singing: *She sang him to sleep.* **5.** *Slang.* To

give information or evidence against someone. —*n.* A gathering of people for group singing. [< OE *singan.* See sengwh-.] —**sing′er** *n.*

sing. singular.

Sin·ga·pore (sĭng′gə-pôr′, -pōr′, sĭng′ə-). **1.** A country on an island off the S tip of the Malay Peninsula. **2.** The capital of this country. Pop. 1,775,000.

Singapore

singe (sĭnj) *v.* **singed, singeing. 1.** To burn superficially. **2.** To burn off the feathers or bristles of by subjecting briefly to flame. [< OE *sengan.* See senk-.]

Sin·gha·lese (sĭng′gə-lēz′, -lēs′) *n., pl.* **-lese.** Also **Sin·ha·lese** (sĭn′hə-). **1.** A people constituting the major portion of the population of Ceylon. **2.** The Indic language of these people. —**Sin′gha·lese′** *adj.*

sin·gle (sĭng′gəl) *adj.* **1.** One only; lone; sole; solitary. **2.** Consisting of one form, part, or element. **3.** Separate; individual: *every single one.* **4.** Intended or designed to accommodate one person: *a single bed.* **5.** Unmarried. **6.** One-against-one; man-to-man: *single combat.* —*n.* **1.** A separate unit; individual. **2.** An accommodation for one person. **3.** A one-dollar bill. **4. singles.** A tennis match between two players. —*v.* **-gled, -gling.** To separate or distinguish from among others (with *out*). [< L *singulus.*] —**sin′gle·ness** *n.*

sin·gle-breast·ed (sĭng′gəl-brĕs′tĭd) *adj.* Closing with a narrow overlap and a single row of fasteners: *a single-breasted coat.*

single file. A line of people, animals, or things standing or moving one behind the other.

sin·gle-hand·ed (sĭng′gəl-hăn′dĭd) *adj.* **1.** Working or done without help; unassisted. **2.** Having or using only one hand. —**sin′gle-hand′ed·ly** *adv.*

sin·gle-mind·ed (sĭng′gəl-mīn′dĭd) *adj.* Having one overriding aim or purpose. —**sin′gle-mind′ed·ness** *n.*

sin·gle-space (sĭng′gəl-spās′) *v.* To type (copy) without leaving a blank line between lines.

sin·gle·ton (sĭng′gəl-tən) *n.* A playing card that is the only one of its suit in a player's hand.

sin·gly (sĭng′glē) *adv.* **1.** Without company or help; alone. **2.** One by one; individually.

sing·song (sĭng′sông′, -sŏng′) *n.* Monotonous regularity of rhythm and rhyme. —**sing′song** *adj.*

sin·gu·lar (sĭng′gyə-lər) *adj.* **1.** Being only one; separate; individual. **2.** Exceptional; extraordinary. **3.** *Gram.* Denoting a single person or thing. —*n. Gram.* The singular number or the form denoting it. —**sin′gu·lar′i·ty** *n.* —**sin′gu·lar·ly** *adv.*

Sin·ha·lese. Variant of **Singhalese.**

sin·is·ter (sĭn′ĭ-stər) *adj.* **1.** Suggesting an evil force or motive. **2.** Presaging trouble; ominous. [< L, left, on the left, evil, unlucky.] —**sin′is·ter·ly** *adv.*

sink (sĭngk) *v.* **sank** or **sunk, sunk** or **sunken, sinking. 1.** To submerge beneath the surface or descend to the bottom of a liquid or soft substance. **2.** To descend slowly or in stages. **3.** To force into the ground. **4.** To dig or drill (a mine or well) in the earth. **5.** To pass into a worsened physical condition; approach death. **6.** To become weaker, quieter, or less forceful. **7.** To diminish or decline. **8.** To penetrate the mind; become understood: *The facts sank in finally.* **9.** To invest. **10.** To get the ball into the hole or basket, as in golf, pool, or basketball. —*n.* A water basin fixed to a wall or floor and having a drainpipe and generally a piped supply of water. [< OE *sincan.* See **sengw-.**] —**sink′a·ble** *adj.*

Usage: As the past tense, *sank* is now preferable to the alternative form *sunk,* esp. in formal usage: *The bow sank beneath the water. Sunk* (not *sank*) is the past participle: *They have sunk both destroyers. The skiff may have sunk.*

sink·er (sĭng′kər) *n.* **1.** One that sinks. **2.** A weight used for sinking fishing lines, nets, etc.

sinking fund. A fund accumulated to pay off a public or corporate debt.

sin·ner (sĭn′ər) *n.* One who sins.

Sino-. *comb. form.* Chinese.

Sin·o-Ti·bet·an (sī′nō-tĭ-bĕt′n, sĭn′ō-) *n.* A linguistic group that includes Tibeto-Burman. —**Sin′o-Ti·bet′an** *adj.*

sin·u·ous (sĭn′yōō-əs) *adj.* Having many curves or turns; winding. [< L *sinus,* a bend, curve, fold.] —**sin′u·os′i·ty** (-ŏs′ə-tē) *n.*

si·nus (sī′nəs) *n.* **1.** A depression or cavity formed by a bending or curving. **2.** Any of various air-filled cavities in the skull, esp. one communicating with the nostrils. [L *sinus,* a bend, curve, fold, hollow.]

Si·on. Variant of **Zion.**

Siou·an (sōō′ən) *n.* A large North American Indian language family spoken from Lake Michigan to the Rocky Mountains and southward to Arkansas. —**Siou′an** *adj.*

Sioux (sōō) *n., pl.* **Sioux. 1.** A member of or any of the various groups of Siouan-speaking North American Indian peoples formerly occupying parts of C North America. **2.** The language of one of the Sioux groups. —**Sioux** *adj.*

sip (sĭp) *v.* **sipped, sipping.** To drink delicately and in small quantities. —*n.* **1.** The act of

sipping. **2.** A small quantity of liquid sipped. [ME *sippen.*]

si·phon (sī′fən). Also **sy·phon.** *n.* A pipe or tube having an inverted U shape and filled until atmospheric pressure is sufficient to force a liquid from a reservoir into one end of the tube over a barrier higher than the reservoir and out the other end. —*v.* To draw off with or as if with a siphon. [< Gk *siphōn,* pipe, tube.] —**si′phon·al, si·phon′ic** (sī-fŏn′ĭk) *adj.*

sir (sûr) *n.* **1.** Often **Sir.** A respectful form of address used instead of a man's name. **2. Sir.** A title of honor used before the name of baronets and knights. [< SIRE.]

sire (sīr) *n.* **1.** A father or forefather. **2.** The male parent of an animal, as a horse. **3.** *Archaic.* A title and form of address used esp. in addressing a king. —*v.* **sired, siring.** To beget. [< L *senior,* older.]

si·ren (sī′rən) *n.* **1.** Often **Siren.** *Gk.Myth.* One of a group of sea nymphs whose singing lured mariners to destruction on the rocks surrounding their island. **2.** A device producing a loud, penetrating whistle, wailing, or other sound as a signal or warning.

Sir·i·us (sīr′ē-əs) *n.* A star in the constellation Canis Major, the brightest star in the sky.

sir·loin (sûr′loin′) *n.* A cut of beef from the upper part of the loin. [< OF *surlonge.*]

si·roc·co (sə-rŏk′ō) *n., pl.* **-cos.** Also **sci·roc·co** (shə-). A hot, humid wind originating in the Sahara Desert and blowing into S Europe. [< Ar *sharq, sharuq,* "east (wind)."]

sir·up. Variant of **syrup.**

sis (sĭs) *n. Informal.* Sister.

si·sal (sī′zəl, -səl) *n.* A cordage fiber obtained from the leaves of a Mexican plant. [< *Sisal,* town in Yucatán, Mexico.]

sis·sy (sĭs′ē) *n., pl.* **-sies.** An effeminate boy or man. [< SIS.]

sis·ter (sĭs′tər) *n.* **1.** A female having the same mother and father as another. **2.** A female who shares a common ancestry, allegiance, character, or purpose with another. **3. Sister.** A member of a religious order of women; a nun. —*adj.* Related by or as by sisterhood. [< OE *sweostor.* See **swesor-.**] —**sis′ter·ly** *adj.*

sis·ter·hood (sĭs′tər-hōōd′) *n.* **1.** The state or relationship of being a sister or sisters. **2.** A women's auxiliary organization, esp. in a church or synagogue.

sis·ter-in-law (sĭs′tər-ĭn-lô′) *n., pl.* **sisters-in-law. 1.** The sister of one's spouse. **2.** The wife of one's brother. **3.** The wife of the brother of one's spouse.

Sis·y·phus (sĭs′ĭ-fəs). *Gk.Myth.* A king of Corinth condemned forever to roll a stone up a hill in Hades only to have it roll down again on nearing the top.

sit (sĭt) *v.* **sat, sitting. 1.** To rest with the body supported upon the buttocks or hindquarters. **2.** To perch, as a bird. **3.** To rest on and cover eggs for hatching. **4.** To maintain a seated position on (a horse). **5.** To be situated; lie. **6.** To pose for an artist or photographer. **7.** To be in session. **8.** To remain inactive or unused. **9.** To baby-sit. **10.** To cause to sit; seat. [<OE *sittan.* See **sed-.**] —**sit′ter** *n.*

ă pat/ā ate/âr care/ä bar/b bib/ch chew/d deed/ĕ pet/ē be/f fit/g gag/h hat/hw what/
ĭ pit/ī pie/îr pier/j judge/k kick/l lid, fatal/m mum/n no, sudden/ng sing/ŏ pot/ō go/

si•tar (sĭ-tär′) *n.* A Hindu stringed instrument.
sit•com (sĭt′kŏm) *n.* Also **sit-com**. *Informal.* A situation comedy. **—sit′com′** *adj.*
site (sīt) *n.* The place or plot of land where something was, is, or is to be located. [< L *situs,* place.]
sit•ting (sĭt′ĭng) *n.* **1.** The act or position of one that sits. **2.** A period during which one is seated, as when posing for a portrait. **3.** A term or session, as of a legislature.
Sit•ting Bull (sĭt′ĭng bool). 1834?–1890. American Indian leader; chief of the Dakota; leader in Sioux war (1876–77).

Sitting Bull

sitting room. A small living room.
sit•u•ate (sĭch′oō-āt′) *v.* -ated, -ating. To place in a certain spot or position; locate. [< L *situs,* place, SITE.]
sit•u•a•tion (sĭch′oō-ā′shən) *n.* **1.** A location; position. **2.** A state of affairs. **3.** A position of employment. **—sit′u•a′tion•al** *adj.*
situation comedy. A humorous television series with a continuing cast of characters.
six (sĭks) *n.* The cardinal number written 6 or in Roman numerals VI. [< OE *sex, six.* See **sweks.**] **—six** *adj. & pron.*
six•teen (sĭk′stēn′) *n.* The cardinal number written 16 or in Roman numerals XVI. **—six′teen′** *adj. & pron.*
six•teenth (sĭk′stēnth′) *n.* **1.** The ordinal number 16 in a series. **2.** One of 16 equal parts. **—six′teenth′** *adj. & adv.*
sixth (sĭksth) *n.* **1.** The ordinal number 6 in a series. **2.** One of 6 equal parts. **—sixth** *adj. & adv.*
six•ti•eth (sĭk′stē-ĭth) *n.* **1.** The ordinal number 60 in a series. **2.** One of 60 equal parts. **—six′ti•eth** *adj. & adv.*
six•ty (sĭk′stē) *n.* The cardinal number written 60 or in Roman numerals LX. **—six′ty** *adj. & pron.*
siz•a•ble (sī′zə-bəl) *adj.* Also **size•a•ble.** Of considerable size; fairly large. **—siz′a•bly** *adv.*

size¹ (sīz) *n.* **1.** The physical dimensions, magnitude, or extent of something. **2.** Any of a series of graduated categories of dimension whereby manufactured articles are classified. **3.** Actual state of affairs: *That's about the size of it.* **—v. sized, sizing.** To arrange according to size. [ME *syse,* fixed amount, assize.]
size² (sīz) *n.* A gelatinous or glutinous substance used as a glaze or filler for porous materials such as paper, cloth, or wall surfaces. **—v. sized, sizing.** To treat or coat with size. [Prob < SIZE¹.]
siz•ing (sī′zĭng) *n.* **1.** A glaze or filler, size. **2.** The treatment of a surface with size.
siz•zle (sĭz′əl) *v.* -zled, -zling. To make the hissing sound characteristic of frying fat. [Imit.] **—siz′zle** *n.*
S.J. Society of Jesus.
skate¹ (skāt) *n.* **1. a.** A bladelike metal runner fixed to a shoe, enabling the wearer to glide easily over ice. **b.** A shoe having such a runner or runners. **2.** A roller skate. [< ONF *escace,* stilt.] **—skate** *v.* **(skated, skating). —skat′er** *n.*
skate² (skāt) *n.* A marine fish having a flattened body with fins forming winglike extensions. [< ON *skata.*]
skeet (skēt) *n.* A kind of trapshooting in which clay targets are used to simulate birds in flight.
skein (skān) *n.* A length of thread or yarn wound in a loose, elongated coil. [< OF *escaigne.*]
skel•e•ton (skĕl′ə-tən) *n.* **1. a.** The internal vertebrate structure composed of bone and cartilage that protects and supports the soft organs, tissues, and parts. **b.** The hard external supporting and protecting structure in many invertebrates and certain vertebrates, such as turtles. **2.** Any supporting structure or framework. **3.** An outline or sketch. [< Gk *skeletos,* dried up, withered.] **—skel′e•tal** *adj.* **—skel′e•tal•ly** *adv.*
skeleton key. A key with a slender bit that can open different locks.
skep•tic (skĕp′tĭk) *n.* Also **scep•tic. 1.** One who habitually questions assertions or generally accepted conclusions. **2.** One inclined to skepticism in religious matters. **3.** An adherent of any philosophical school of skepticism. [< Gk *skeptesthai,* to examine, consider.]
skep•ti•cal (skĕp′tĭ-kəl) *adj.* Doubting; questioning; disbelieving. **—skep′ti•cal•ly** *adv.*
skep•ti•cism (skĕp′tə-sĭz′əm) *n.* **1.** A doubting or questioning attitude or state of mind. **2.** The philosophical doctrine that absolute knowledge is impossible. **3.** Doubt or disbelief of religious tenets.
sketch (skĕch) *n.* **1.** A rough preliminary drawing or painting. **2.** A brief outline. **3.** A brief, light, or informal short story, play, etc. **—v.** To make a sketch (of). [< It *schizzare,* to sketch.] **—sketch′er** *n.*
sketch•y (skĕch′ē) *adj.* -ier, -iest. **1.** Resembling a sketch. **2.** Incomplete; slight; superficial. **—sketch′i•ness** *n.*
skew (skyoō) *v.* To turn or place at an angle; slant. **—adj.** Placed or turned to one side; slanting; oblique. [< ONF *eskuer.*]
skew•er (skyoō′ər) *n.* A long pin used to

secure or suspend meat during cooking; a spit. [Var of dial *skiver*.]

ski (skē, shē) *n., pl.* **skis** or **ski.** One of a pair of long, flat runners attached to a boot for gliding or traveling over snow. —*v.* To travel on skis, esp. as a sport. [< ON *skīth,* ski, snowshoe.] —**ski′er** *n.*

skid (skĭd) *n.* **1.** The act of sliding or slipping over a surface. **2.** A plank or log, usually one of a pair, used for sliding or rolling heavy objects. **3.** A runner in the landing gear of certain aircraft. —*v.* **skidded, skidding. 1.** To slip or slide sideways because of loss of traction, as a vehicle. **2.** To slide without revolving, as a wheel. [?]

skiff (skĭf) *n.* A small, flat-bottomed open boat. [< It *schifo.*]

skill (skĭl) *n.* **1.** Proficiency; expertness. **2.** An art, trade, or technique, esp. one requiring use of the hands or body. [< ON *skil.*] —**skilled** *adj.*

skil·let (skĭl′ĭt) *n.* A frying pan. [Prob < Scand.]

skill·ful (skĭl′fəl) *adj.* **1.** Possessing or exercising skill. **2.** Characterized by or requiring skill. —**skill′ful·ly** *adv.* —**skill′ful·ness** *n.*

skim (skĭm) *v.* **skimmed, skimming. 1.** To remove (floating matter) from (a liquid). **2.** To glide quickly and lightly over. **3.** To read or glance through quickly or superficially. [< OF *escume,* foam.]

skim milk. Milk from which the cream has been removed.

skimp (skĭmp) *v.* **1.** To do hastily, carelessly, or with poor material. **2.** To be extremely sparing with; scrimp. [Poss a var of SCRIMP.]

skimp·y (skĭm′pē) *adj.* **-ier, -iest. 1.** Inadequate in size, fullness, or amount; scanty. **2.** Unduly thrifty; stingy; niggardly.

skin (skĭn) *n.* **1.** The membranous tissue forming the external covering of the animal body. **2.** An animal pelt. **3.** An outer layer or covering, as the rind of fruit. **4.** A liquid container made of animal skin. —*v.* **skinned, skinning. 1.** To remove skin from; flay or peel. **2.** To bruise, cut, or injure the skin or surface of. [< ON *skinn.*]

skin diving. Underwater swimming in which the diver is equipped with a snorkel or other breathing device. —**skin′-dive′** (skĭn′dīv′) *v.* —**skin diver.**

skin·flint (skĭn′flĭnt) *n.* A miser.

skin·ny (skĭn′ē) *adj.* **-nier, -niest.** Very thin.

skin·ny-dip (skĭn′ē-dĭp′) *v.* **-dipped, -dipping.** *Informal.* To swim in the nude. —**skin′ny-dip′per** *n.*

skip (skĭp) *v.* **skipped, skipping. 1.** To leap or spring lightly (over). **2.** To ricochet. **3.** To pass from point to point omitting what intervenes. **4.** To pass over, omit, or disregard. **5.** To be promoted beyond (the next grade or level). **6.** *Informal.* To leave hastily: *skip town.* —*n.* **1.** A gait in which hops and steps alternate. **2.** A passing over or omission. [ME *skippen.*] —**skip′per** *n.*

skip·per (skĭp′ər) *n.* The master of a ship. [< MDu *schip,* ship.]

skir·mish (skûr′mĭsh) *n.* **1.** A minor encounter between small bodies of troops. **2.** Any minor or preliminary conflict. [< OF *eskermir,* to fight with the sword.] —**skir′mish** *v.*

skirt (skûrt) *n.* **1.** That part of a garment, such as a dress, that hangs from the waist down. **2.** A separate garment hanging from the waist. —*v.* **1.** To lie along; bound. **2.** To pass around rather than across or through. **3.** To avoid (a subject) by circumlocution. [< ON *skyrta,* shirt.]

skit (skĭt) *n.* A short, usually comic theatrical sketch. [?]

skit·ter (skĭt′ər) *v.* To skip, glide, or move lightly or rapidly along a surface. [Prob < dial *skite,* to run rapidly, shoot about.]

skit·tish (skĭt′ĭsh) *adj.* **1.** Excitable or nervous. **2.** Shy, coy, or timid. **3.** Undependable or fickle. [ME.] —**skit′tish·ness** *n.*

skiv·vy (skĭv′ē) *n., pl.* **-vies.** *Slang.* **1.** Also **skivvy shirt.** A man's cotton knit undershirt. **2. skivvies.** A man's underwear consisting of shirt and shorts. [?]

Skr., Skt. Sanskrit.

skulk (skŭlk) *v.* To move about stealthily. [< Scand.] —**skulk′er** *n.*

skull (skŭl) *n.* The bony framework of the head. [ME *skulle.*]

occipital   temporal

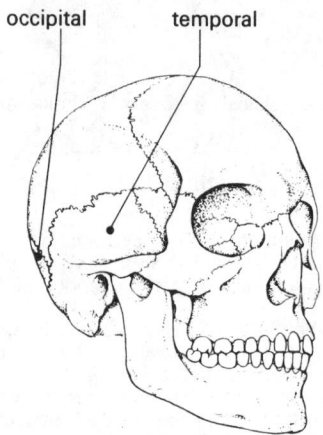

skull

skull and crossbones. A representation of the human skull above two long crossed bones, a symbol of death once used by pirates and now used as a warning label on poisons.

skull·cap (skŭl′kăp′) *n.* A close-fitting, brimless cap.

skull·dug·ger·y (skŭl-dŭg′ə-rē) *n.* Also **skul·dug·ger·y.** Crafty deception or trickery. [?]

skunk (skŭngk) *n.* **1.** A New World mammal having black and white fur and ejecting a malodorous secretion. **2.** *Slang.* A despicable person. [< Algon.]

sky (skī) *n., pl.* **skies. 1.** The upper atmosphere, appearing as a hemisphere above the earth. **2.** The celestial or heavenly regions. [< ON *skȳ,* cloud < Gmc **skewja-.*]

ă pat/ā ate/âr care/ä bar/b **bib**/ch **chew**/d **deed**/ĕ pet/ē be/f fit/g gag/h hat/hw **what**/ ĭ pit/ī pie/îr **pier**/j **judge**/k **kick**/l lid, fatal/m **mum**/n no, sudden/ng sing/ŏ pot/ō go/

sky·jack (skĭ'jăk') v. -jacked, -jacking. *Informal.* To hijack (an airplane), as through the use or threat of force. —**sky'jack'er** n.

sky·lark (skĭ'lärk') n. An Old World bird that sings while in flight. —v. To indulge in frolic.

sky·light (skĭ'līt') n. An overhead window admitting daylight.

sky·line (skĭ'līn') n. 1. The horizon. 2. The outline of a group of buildings seen against the sky.

sky·rock·et (skĭ'rŏk'ĭt) n. A firework that ascends high into the air, where it explodes in a cascade of flares and sparks. —v. To rise rapidly or suddenly, as in amount, position, reputation, etc.

sky·scrap·er (skĭ'skrā'pər) n. A very tall building.

sky·ward (skĭ'wərd) adv. Also **sky·wards** (-wərdz). Toward the sky. —**sky'ward** adj.

slab (slăb) n. A broad, flat, somewhat thick piece, as of cake, stone, or cheese. [ME slabbe.]

slack (slăk) adj. 1. Slow; dull; sluggish. 2. Not busy: *a slack business season.* 3. Not tense or taut; loose. 4. Careless; negligent. —v. To slacken. —n. 1. A loose or slack part or portion of something. 2. A lack of tension; looseness. 3. A period of little activity; a lull. 4. **slacks.** Trousers for casual wear. [< OE slæc. See **slēg-**.] —**slack'ness** n.

slack·en (slăk'ən) v. 1. To slow down. 2. To loosen. 3. To make or become less vigorous or intense.

slack·er (slăk'ər) n. One who shirks work or responsibility.

slag (slăg) n. 1. The vitreous mass left as a residue by the smelting of metallic ore. 2. Volcanic refuse. [MLG slagge.]

slain (slān). *p.p.* of **slay**.

slake (slāk) v. **slaked, slaking. 1.** To quench, as thirst. **2.** To combine (lime) chemically with water or moist air. [< OE slacian, to loose < slæc, SLACK.]

sla·lom (slä'ləm) n. A skiing race along a downhill zigzag course. [Norw. "sloping path."]

slam¹ (slăm) v. **slammed, slamming. 1.** To shut with force and loud noise. **2.** To put, throw, or strike with great force so as to produce a loud noise. —n. **1.** A forceful closing that produces a loud noise. **2.** The noise so produced. [Perh < Scand.]

slam² (slăm) n. In bridge, the winning of all the tricks, **grand slam,** or all but one, **little slam.** [?]

slan·der (slăn'dər) n. The utterance of defamatory statements injurious to the reputation or well-being of a person. —v. To utter damaging reports about. [< L scandalum, scandal.] —**slan'der·er** n. —**slan'der·ous** adj. —**slan'der·ous·ly** adv.

slang (slăng) n. Nonstandard vocabulary consisting typically of arbitrary and often ephemeral coinages and figures of speech. [?] —**slang'i·ness** n. —**slang'y** adj.

slant (slănt, slänt) v. **1.** To incline; slope. **2.** To present so as to conform with a particular bias. —n. **1.** A sloping direction, plane, or course;

incline. **2.** A bias or point of view. [< ME slenten.] —**slant'ing·ly** adv.

slap (slăp) n. **1.** A smacking blow made with the open hand. **2.** An insult; rebuff. —v. **slapped, slapping.** To strike with a flat object, as the palm of the hand. [LG slapp.]

slap·dash (slăp'dăsh') adj. Hasty; careless. —adv. Recklessly; haphazardly.

slap·stick (slăp'stĭk') n. Comedy characterized by loud and boisterous farce.

slash (slăsh) v. **1.** To cut or lash with violent sweeping strokes. **2.** To make a gash or gashes in. **3.** To reduce or curtail drastically. —n. **1.** A sweeping stroke made with a sharp instrument. **2.** A cut or other injury made by such a stroke; a gash. **3.** *Ptg.* A virgule. [ME slaschen.] —**slash'er** n.

slat (slăt) n. A narrow strip of metal or wood. [< OF esclater, to splinter.]

slate (slāt) n. **1.** A fine-grained rock that splits into thin, smooth-surfaced layers. **2.** A piece of this material cut for use as roofing material or a writing surface. **3.** A list of the candidates of a political party running for various offices. —v. **slated, slating. 1.** To cover with slate. **2.** To designate; schedule: *slated to arrive at noon.* [< OF esclat, fragment, splinter.]

slat·tern (slăt'ərn) n. A woman untidy or slovenly in person or habits. [Perh < dial slatter, to spill awkwardly.]

slaugh·ter (slô'tər) n. **1.** The killing of animals for food. **2.** The killing of a large number of persons; carnage; massacre. —v. **1.** To kill (animals) for food; butcher. **2.** To kill (persons) in large numbers; massacre. [ME.]

slaugh·ter·house (slô'tər-hous') n. A place where animals are butchered.

Slav (släv) n. A member of one of the Slavic-speaking peoples of eastern Europe.

Slav. Slavic.

slave (slāv) n. **1.** One bound in servitude as an instrument of labor. **2.** One completely under the domination of a specified person or influence. —v. **slaved, slaving.** To work like a slave; drudge. [< ML Sclavus, Slav.]

slave driver. 1. A severely exacting employer or supervisor. **2.** An overseer of slaves at work.

slav·er (slăv'ər) v. To slobber. —n. Saliva drooling from the mouth. [Prob < ON slafra.]

slav·er·y (slā'və-rē, slāv'rē) n. Bondage to a master or household.

Slav·ic (slä'vĭk) adj. Of or pertaining to the Slavs or their languages. —n. A branch of Indo-European including Czech, Bulgarian, Polish, Russian, and Serbo-Croatian.

slav·ish (slā'vĭsh) adj. **1.** Of or like a slave; servile. **2.** Of or like the institution of slavery; oppressive. **3.** Blindly dependent on or imitative. —**slav'ish·ly** adv. —**slav'ish·ness** n.

slaw (slô) n. Coleslaw.

slay (slā) v. **slew, slain, slaying.** To kill by violent means. [< OE slēan. See **slak-**.] —**slay'er** n.

sld. 1. sailed. **2.** sealed.

slea·zy (slē'zē) adj. **-zier, -ziest. 1.** Flimsy or thin, as fabric. **2.** Cheap; shoddy. [?] —**slea'zi·ly** adv. —**slea'zi·ness** n.

sled (slĕd) *n.* A vehicle mounted on runners, used for moving over ice and snow. —*v.* **sledded, sledding.** To ride or use a sled. [ME *sledde.*] —**sled'der** *n.*

sledge (slĕj) *n.* A vehicle on low runners used for transporting loads across ice and snow. [< MDu *sleedse.*]

sledge•ham•mer (slĕj'hăm'ər) *n.* A long, heavy hammer, often wielded with both hands. [< OE *slecg.* See **slak-.**]

sleek (slēk) *adj.* **1.** Smooth and lustrous as if polished; glossy. **2.** Well-groomed and neatly tailored in appearance. —*v.* **1.** To make lustrous or smooth; polish. **2.** To gloss over; conceal. [Var of SLICK.] —**sleek'ness** *n.*

sleep (slēp) *n.* **1.** A natural, periodically recurring state of rest, characterized by relative physical and nervous inactivity, unconsciousness, and lessened responsiveness to external stimuli. **2.** Any similar condition of inactivity, as unconsciousness or hibernation. —*v.* **slept, sleeping. 1.** To be in the state of sleep or fall asleep. **2.** To pass or get rid of by sleeping: *He went home to sleep it off.* [< OE *slǣp.*]

sleep•er (slē'pər) *n.* **1.** A person or animal that sleeps. **2.** A sleeping car on a railroad train. **3.** *Brit.* A heavy beam used as a support for rails in a railroad track.

sleeping bag. A warmly lined zippered bag in which one may sleep outdoors.

sleeping car. A railroad car having accommodations for sleeping.

sleeping pill. A sedative, esp. a barbiturate, in the form of a pill or capsule.

sleeping sickness. Any of various often fatal diseases of man and animals in tropical Africa, characterized by fever and lethargy.

sleep•less (slēp'lĭs) *adj.* Without sleep; wakeful; restless. —**sleep'less•ness** *n.*

sleep•walk•ing (slēp'wô'kĭng) *n.* The act of walking in one's sleep. —**sleep'walk'er** *n.*

sleep•y (slē'pē) *adj.* **-ier, -iest. 1.** Ready for or needing sleep; drowsy. **2.** Quiet: *a sleepy town.* —**sleep'i•ly** *adv.* —**sleep'i•ness** *n.*

sleep•y•head (slē'pē-hĕd') *n. Informal.* A sleepy person.

sleet (slēt) *n.* **1.** Partially frozen rain. **2.** A mixture of rain and snow. —*v.* To shower sleet. [< OE **slēte.*] —**sleet'y** *adj.*

sleeve (slēv) *n.* **1.** The part of a garment that covers the arm. **2.** Any encasement or shell into which a piece of equipment fits. [< OE *slīf, slēf.* See **sleubh-.**] —**sleeve'less** *adj.*

sleigh (slā) *n.* .A light vehicle mounted on runners for use on snow or ice, and usually drawn by a horse. [< MDu *slēde.*]

sleight of hand. 1. Tricks or feats performed by jugglers or magicians so quickly that their manner of execution cannot be observed. **2.** Skill in performing such feats.

slen•der (slĕn'dər) *adj.* **1.** Gracefully slim. **2.** Meager; inadequate. **3.** Slight; feeble: *a slender chance.* [ME *slendre.*] —**slen'der•ly** *adv.*

slen•der•ize (slĕn'də-rīz') *v.* **-ized, -izing.** To make or become slender.

slept (slĕpt) *p.t.* & *p.p.* of **sleep.**

sleuth (slōōth) *n. Informal.* A detective. [< ME, track of an animal.]

slew[1] (slōō) *n.* Also **slue.** *Informal.* A large amount or number; a lot. [Ir Gael *sluagh.*]

slew[2] (slōō). *p.t.* of **slay.**

slice (slīs) *n.* **1.** A thin, broad piece cut from a larger object. **2.** A portion or share. **3.** A stroke that causes a ball to curve off course. —*v.* **sliced, slicing. 1.** To cut or divide into slices. **2.** To cut or remove from a larger piece. **3.** To hit (a ball) with a slice. [< OF *esclicier,* to reduce to splinters < Gmc **slītjan.*] —**slice'a•ble** *adj.* —**slic'er** *n.*

slick (slĭk) *adj.* **1.** Smooth, glossy, and slippery, as if covered with oil or ice. **2.** Deftly executed; adroit; facile. **3.** Shrewd; wily. **4.** Superficially attractive but without depth. —*n.* A smooth or slippery surface or area. —*v.* **1.** To make smooth, glossy, or oily. **2.** *Informal.* To make neat, trim, or tidy; spruce. [ME *slike.*]

slick•er (slĭk'ər) *n.* **1.** A glossy raincoat, esp. one made of oilskin. **2.** *Informal.* A stylish city dweller; a dude.

slide (slīd) *v.* **slid** (slĭd), **slid** or **slidden** (slĭd'n), **sliding. 1.** To move or cause to move in smooth, continuous contact with a surface. **2.** *Baseball.* To drop down and skid into a base to avoid being tagged out. —*n.* **1.** A sliding movement or action. **2.** A playground apparatus for children to slide upon. **3.** An image on a transparent plate for projection on a screen. **4.** A small glass plate for mounting specimens to be examined under a microscope. **5.** An avalanche. [< OE *slīdan.* See **sleidh-.**] —**slid'er** *n.*

slide rule. A device consisting essentially of two scaled rules mounted to slide along each other so that computations can be performed mechanically.

slight (slīt) *adj.* **1.** Small in size, degree, or amount; meager. **2.** Of small importance or consideration. **3.** Slender or frail; delicate. —*v.* **1.** To treat with disrespect. **2.** To do negligently; shirk. **3.** To treat as unimportant. —*n.* An act of pointed disrespect or discourtesy. [ME.] —**slight'ness** *n.*

slight•ly (slīt'lē) *adv.* To a small degree or extent; somewhat.

slim (slĭm) *adj.* **slimmer, slimmest. 1.** Small in girth or thickness; slender. **2.** Small in quality or amount; scant; meager. —*v.* **slimmed, slimming.** To make or become slim. [Du, small, inferior.] —**slim'ly** *adv.* —**slim'ness** *n.*

slime (slīm) *n.* A moist, sticky substance or coating. [< OE *slīm.* See **lei-.**] —**slim'y** *adj.*

sling (slĭng) *n.* **1.** A weapon consisting of a looped strap in which a stone is whirled and then let fly. **2.** A looped rope, strap, or chain for supporting, cradling, or hoisting something, esp. a band suspended from the neck to support an injured arm or hand. —*v.* **slung, slinging.** To hurl with or as if from a sling; fling. [ME.] —**sling'er** *n.*

sling•shot (slĭng'shŏt') *n.* A Y-shaped stick with an elastic strap attached to the prongs, used for flinging small stones.

slink (slĭngk) *v.* **slunk, slinking.** To move in a quiet, furtive manner. [< OE *slincan.* See **slenk-.**]

ă pat/ā ate/âr care/ä bar/b bib/ch chew/d deed/ĕ pet/ē be/f fit/g gag/h hat/hw what/
ĭ pit/ī pie/îr pier/j judge/k kick/l lid, fatal/m mum/n no, sudden/ng sing/ŏ pot/ō go/

slip¹ (slĭp) v. **slipped, slipping. 1.** To move quietly and stealthily. **2.** To slide accidentally; lose one's balance. **3.** To slide out of place or from one's grasp. **4.** To get away (from); escape unnoticed. **5.** *Informal.* To decline in ability, strength, or keenness. **6.** *Informal.* To decline; fall off. **7.** To place or insert smoothly and quietly. **8.** To put on or remove (clothing) easily or quickly. —**let slip.** To say inadvertently. —**slip up.** *Informal.* To make a mistake; err. —n. **1.** The act of slipping. **2.** A slight error or oversight. **3.** A docking place for a ship between two piers. **4.** A woman's undergarment of various lengths. **5.** A pillowcase. [ME *slippen,* to slip, slip away.]

slip² (slĭp) n. **1.** A plant part removed for grafting or planting. **2.** A youthful, slender person: *a slip of a girl.* **3.** A small piece of paper. [ME *slippe,* a strip.]

slip·cov·er (slĭp′kŭv′ər) n. A fitted, removable cover for a piece of upholstered furniture.

slip·knot (slĭp′nŏt′) n. A knot made with a loop so that it slips along the rope around which it is tied.

slip·o·ver (slĭp′ō′vər) adj. Designed to be put on or taken off over the head. —n. A slipover garment, such as a sweater.

slip·page (slĭp′ĭj) n. **1.** A slipping. **2.** Loss of motion or power due to slipping.

slip·per (slĭp′ər) n. A light, low shoe, worn mainly indoors, that may be slipped on and off easily.

slip·per·y (slĭp′ə-rē) adj. **-ier, -iest. 1.** Causing or tending to cause sliding or slipping. **2.** Elusive; evasive. [< OE *slipor.* See lei-.]

slip·shod (slĭp′shŏd′) adj. Poorly made or done; careless.

slip-up (slĭp′ŭp′) n. *Informal.* An error or oversight.

slit (slĭt) n. A long, narrow cut or opening. —v. **slit, slitting. 1.** To make a long, narrow incision in. **2.** To cut lengthwise into strips; split. [ME *slitte.*]

slith·er (slĭth′ər) v. To slip and slide, as on a loose or uneven surface. [< OE *slīdan,* to SLIDE.] —**slith′er·y** adj.

sliv·er (slĭv′ər) n. A slender piece cut, split, or broken off; a splinter. [< ME *slyven,* to cleave, split.]

slob (slŏb) n. *Informal.* A crude, slovenly person. [Ir *slab,* mud.]

slob·ber (slŏb′ər) v. **1.** To drool; slaver. **2.** To spill (liquid or food) from the mouth while eating or drinking. —n. Saliva running from the mouth; drivel. [ME *sloberen.*]

sloe (slō) n. The blackish, plumlike fruit of the blackthorn. [< OE *slāh.*]

slog (slŏg) v. **slogged, slogging.** To walk with a slow, plodding gait. [?]

slo·gan (slō′gən) n. **1.** The motto of a political party, school, or other group. **2.** An often repeated word or phrase used in advertising or promotion. [< Gael *sluagh-ghairm.*]

sloop (slōōp) n. A single-masted, fore-and-aft-rigged sailing boat. [Du *sloep.*]

slop (slŏp) n. **1.** Liquid spilled or splashed. **2.** Soft mud or slush. **3.** Unappetizing, watery food or soup. **4.** Refuse used as animal feed.

—v. **slopped, slopping.** To spill or splash. [ME *sloppe,* a muddy place.]

slope (slōp) v. **sloped, sloping.** To incline upward or downward. —n. **1.** Any inclined line, surface, plane, position, or direction. **2.** A stretch of ground forming a natural or artificial incline: *ski slope.* [< ME, sloping.]

slop·py (slŏp′ē) adj. **-pier, -piest. 1.** Of, like, or covered with slop; splashy; muddy. **2.** *Informal.* Untidy; messy. **3.** *Informal.* Careless; slipshod. —**slop′pi·ly** adv. —**slop′pi·ness** n.

slosh (slŏsh) v. To splash or flounder, as in water or another liquid. —n. Slush. [Var of SLUSH.] —**slosh′y** adj.

slot (slŏt) n. A long narrow groove or opening. [ME, hollow between the breasts.]

sloth (slŏth, slôth, slōth) n. **1.** Laziness; indolence; sluggishness. **2.** A slow-moving, tree-dwelling, tropical American mammal. [ME *slowthe* < *slow,* slow.] —**sloth′ful** adj.

slot machine. A coin-operated vending or gambling machine.

slouch (slouch) n. **1.** A drooping posture or gait. **2.** A lazy or inept person. [?] —**slouch** v.

slough¹ (slōō, slou) n. **1.** A mud hollow. **2.** A swamp. **3.** A state of dejection or despondency. [< OE *slōh.*]

slough² (slŭf) n. **1.** *Med.* Dead tissue separated from a living structure. **2.** Any outer layer or covering that is shed. —v. To cast off or shed, as dead skin. [ME *slouh.*] —**slough′y** adj.

Slo·vak (slō′văk′, -väk′) n. **1.** Any of a Slavic people living in Slovakia. **2.** The Slavic language of these people, closely related to Czech. —adj. Of or pertaining to Slovakia, the Slovaks, or their language.

Slo·vak·i·a (slō-vä′kē-ə). The E region and a former province of Czechoslovakia.

slov·en (slŭv′ən) n. A habitually unwashed and untidy person. [ME *sloveyn.*]

Slo·vene (slō′vēn′) n. The Slavic language of NW Yugoslavia. —**Slo′vene′** adj.

slov·en·ly (slŭv′ən-lē) adj. **-lier, -liest. 1.** Untidy; messy. **2.** Careless; slipshod. —**slov′en·li·ness** n.

slow (slō) adj. **1.** Moving or proceeding at a low speed. **2. a.** Taking a long or inordinate time. **b.** Gradual. **3. a.** Registering behind the correct time. **b.** Tardy. **4.** Not precipitate. **5.** Sluggish; inactive. **6.** Boring. **7.** Dull; stupid. —v. **1.** To make or become slow or slower. **2.** To delay; retard. [< OE *slāw* < Gmc **slǣwaz.*] —**slow, slow′ly** adv. —**slow′ness** n.

sludge (slŭj) n. **1.** Mire or ooze, as on a river bed. **2.** Material precipitated by the treatment of sewage. —**sludg′y** adj.

slue. Variant of **slew¹.**

slug¹ (slŭg) n. **1. a.** A lump of metal. **b.** A bullet. **2.** A shot of liquor. **3.** A metal disk for use in a slot machine. [Prob < SLUG².]

slug² (slŭg) n. **1.** A land mollusk related to the snails but having no shell. **2.** A sluggard. [Prob < Scand.]

slug³ (slŭg) v. **slugged, slugging.** To strike hard and heavily. [Perh < SLUG¹.] —**slug′ger** n.

slug·gard (slŭg′ərd) n. A slothful person. [Prob < Scand.]

slug·gish (slŭg′ĭsh) adj. **1.** Slow; inactive. **2.**

Lazy or dull. [ME.] **—slug'gish•ly** *adv.* **—slug'gish•ness** *n.*

sluice (slōōs) *n.* **1.** A man-made channel for water with a gate to regulate the flow. **2.** The gate used in this way. **3.** Any artificial channel for carrying off excess water. **4.** An inclined trough, as for floating logs or separating gold ore. **—v. sluiced, sluicing. 1.** To wash with a sudden flow of water; flush. **2.** To draw off or let out by a sluice. **3.** To send (logs) down a sluice. [< L *excludere*, to shut out, EXCLUDE.]

slum (slŭm) *n.* A squalid and overcrowded district inhabited by the poor. **—v. slummed, slumming.** To visit a slum. [?]

slum•ber (slŭm'bər) *v.* **1.** To sleep or doze. **2.** To be dormant or sluggish. **—n.** Sleep. [ME *slumberen.*] **—slum'ber•er** *n.*

slum•ber•ous (slŭm'bər-əs) *adj.* **1.** Sleepy; drowsy. **2.** Quiet; inactive.

slump (slŭmp) *v.* **1.** To decline or sink suddenly; collapse. **2.** To droop or slouch. [Prob < Scand.] **—slump** *n.*

slung (slŭng). *p.t.* & *p.p.* of **sling**.

slunk (slŭngk). *p.t.* & *p.p.* of **slink**.

slur (slûr) *v.* **slurred, slurring. 1.** To pass over lightly or carelessly. **2.** To pronounce indistinctly. **3.** To disparage; calumniate. **4.** To glide over (a series of musical notes) smoothly without a break. **—n. 1.** A disparaging remark; aspersion. **2.** *Mus.* A curved line connecting notes on a score to indicate that they are to be played or sung legato. [< ME *sloor.*]

slurp (slûrp) *v.* To eat or drink noisily. [< MDu *slorpen.*]

slush (slŭsh) *n.* **1.** Partially melted snow or ice. **2.** Soft mud; mire. [Perh < Scand.] **—slush'i•ness** *n.* **—slush'y** *adj.*

slut (slŭt) *n.* **1.** A slovenly woman. **2.** A whorish woman. [ME *slutte.*] **—slut'tish** *adj.*

sly (slī) *adj.* **slier** or **slyer, sliest** or **slyest. 1.** Stealthily clever; cunning. **2.** Secretive or underhand. **3.** Roguish; arch. [< ON *slægr*, cunning, clever.] **—sly'ly** *adv.* **—sly'ness** *n.*

Sm samarium.

sm. small.

smack¹ (smăk) *v.* **1.** To compress and open (the lips) with a sharp sound expressive of relish. **2.** To kiss or slap noisily. **—n. 1.** The sound produced by smacking the lips. **2.** A noisy kiss. **3.** A sharp blow or loud slap. **—adv. 1.** With a smack: *fell smack on her head.* **2.** Directly; completely: *smack against the rules.* [< MLG or MDu *smacken.*]

smack² (smăk) *n.* **1.** A savor or hint. **2.** A smattering. **—v. 1.** To taste of: *cheese that smacks of mold.* **2.** To be distinctly suggestive of. [< OE *smæc.* See **smeg-**.]

smack³ (smăk) *n.* A sloop-rigged fishing vessel with a well for live fish. [< MDu *smacke.*]

small (smôl) *adj.* **1.** Little. **2.** Trifling or trivial. **3.** Limited in operation or scope. **4.** Of low or minor status. **5.** Unpretentious; modest. **6.** Petty or mean. **7.** Diluted; weak: *small beer.* **8.** Soft; low: *a small voice.* **—adv. 1.** In small pieces: *Cut it up small.* **2.** Softly and timidly: *sing small.* **—n.** Something smaller than the rest: *the small of the back.* [< OE *smæl.* See **mēlo-**.] **—small'ness** *n.*

small capital. A smaller letter having the form of a capital letter: SMALL CAPITALS.

small intestine. The part of the intestine between the outlet of the stomach and the large intestine.

small•pox (smôl'pŏks') *n.* An acute, highly infectious viral disease, characterized by chills, high fever, headache, and backache, with subsequent eruption of pimples that form pockmarks.

small talk. Casual or trivial conversation.

smar•my (smär'mē) *adj.* **-mier, -miest.** Marked by an exaggerated or insincere earnestness; smug and self-righteous. [?]

smart (smärt) *v.* **1.** To cause or feel a stinging pain. **2.** To feel or suffer distress. **—n.** A stinging pain. **—adj. 1. a.** Mentally alert; bright. **b.** Clever or skillful. **2.** Impertinently witty: *a smart reply.* **3.** Sharp and quick: *a smart pace.* **4.** Shrewd: *a smart lawyer.* **5.** Stylish or fashionable. [< OE *smeortan.* See **smerd-**.] **—smart'ly** *adv.* **—smart'ness** *n.*

smart al•eck (ăl'ĭk). *Informal.* A pretentiously clever person.

smart•en (smärt'n) *v.* To make or become smart.

smash (smăsh) *v.* **1.** To break or be broken into pieces. **2.** To throw or move violently so as to shatter or crush. **3.** To destroy completely; wreck. **—n. 1.** The act or sound of smashing. **2. a.** Collapse; ruin. **b.** Bankruptcy. **3.** A collision or crash. **4.** A violent overhand stroke in tennis. [Perh blend of SMACK and CRASH.] **—smash'er** *n.*

smat•ter•ing (smăt'ər-ĭng) *n.* Fragmented or superficial knowledge.

smear (smîr) *v.* **1.** To daub with a sticky or greasy substance. **2.** To smudge or soil. **3.** To sully; vilify. **—n. 1.** A smudge or blot. **2.** Vilification; slander. [< OE *smierwan, smerian.* See **smer-²**.]

smell (smĕl) *v.* **smelled** or **smelt, smelling. 1.** To perceive by means of the olfactory nerves. **2.** To sense the presence of by or as if by the olfactory nerves. **3.** To have or emit an odor. **4.** To stink. **—n. 1.** The olfactory sense. **2.** Odor; scent. **3.** The act or an instance of smelling. [ME *smellen.*]

smell•y (smĕl'ē) *adj.* **-ier, -iest.** *Informal.* Having an unpleasant odor.

smelt¹ (smĕlt) *v.* To melt or fuse (ores), separating the metallic constituents. [Du or LG *smelten.*]

smelt² (smĕlt) *n.* A small silvery, narrow-bodied food fish. [< OE.]

smelt³ (smĕlt). Alternate *p.t.* & *p.p.* of **smell**.

smelt•er (smĕl'tər) *n.* **1.** A worker who smelts ore. **2.** Also **smelt•er•y** (-tə-rē) A smelting works.

smi•lax (smī'lăks') *n.* A climbing vine with glossy leaves, used for decoration. [< Gk.]

smile (smīl) *n.* A facial expression indicative of pleasure, affection, or amusement and formed by an upward curving of the corners of the mouth. **—v. smiled, smiling. 1.** To have or form a smile. **2.** To express favor or approval. **3.** To express with a smile. [Perh < Scand.]

smirch (smûrch) *v.* **1.** To soil, stain, or dirty.

2. To dishonor or disgrace. [ME *smorchen.*] —**smirch** *n.*

smirk (smûrk) *v.* To smile in an obnoxiously arch or simpering manner. [< OE *smearcian,* to smile. See smei-.] —**smirk** *n.*

smite (smīt) *v.* smote, smitten (smĭt′n) or smit (smĭt) or smote, smiting. **1. a.** To inflict a heavy blow on. **b.** To kill by striking. **2.** To afflict: *smitten with cholera.* [< OE *smitan.* See smē-.] —**smit′er** *n.*

smith (smĭth) *n.* One who works in metals, esp. a blacksmith. [< OE. See smi-.]

Smith, Adam. 1723–1790. Scottish political economist and philosopher.

smith•er•eens (smĭth′ə-rēnz′) *pl.n.* Splintered pieces; bits. [< Ir *smiodar,* small fragment.]

smith•y (smĭth′ē, smĭth′ē) *n., pl.* -ies. A blacksmith's shop. [< ON *smidhja.*]

smock (smŏk) *n.* A loose outer garment worn to protect the clothes while working. —*v.* To decorate (fabric) with small, regularly spaced stitches forming a gathered pattern. [< OE *smoc.*]

smog (smŏg, smôg) *n.* Fog that has become mixed and polluted with smoke. [Blend of SMOKE and FOG.] —**smog′gy** *adj.*

smoke (smōk) *n.* **1.** The vapor made up of small particles of matter in the air, resulting from the incomplete combustion of material such as wood or coal. **2.** Any cloud of fine particles. **3.** The act of smoking tobacco. **4.** *Informal.* A cigarette. —*v.* smoked, smoking. **1.** To emit smoke. **2.** To emit smoke excessively. **3.** To draw in and exhale the smoke of tobacco or the like. **4.** To preserve (meat or fish) by exposure to smoke. **5.** To fumigate or discolor with smoke. [< OE *smoca.* See smeug-.] —**smok′i•ness** *n.* —**smok′y** *adj.*

smoke•house (smōk′hous′) *n.* A structure in which meat or fish is cured with smoke.

smok•er (smō′kər) *n.* **1.** One that smokes. **2.** A railroad car in which smoking is permitted.

smoke•stack (smōk′stăk′) *n.* A large vertical pipe through which smoke, gases, etc., are discharged, as from a factory.

smol•der (smōl′dər). Also **smoul•der.** *v.* **1.** To burn with little smoke and no flame. **2.** To burn or exist inwardly. —*n.* Thick smoke resulting from a slow fire. [ME *smolderen.*]

smooth (smōōth) *adj.* **1.** Not irregular or rough; even. **2.** Having a fine consistency or texture. **3.** Having an even or gentle motion. **4.** Agreeable; mild. —*v.* **1.** To make or become smooth. **2.** To rid of hindrances, difficulties, etc. **3.** To soothe or tranquilize. [< OE *smōth.*] —**smooth′er** *n.* —**smooth′ly** *adv.* —**smooth′ness** *n.*

smooth•bore (smōōth′bôr′, -bōr′) *adj.* Having no rifling within the barrel, as a firearm. —*n.* Also **smooth bore.** A firearm having no rifling.

smor•gas•bord (smôr′gəs-bôrd′, -bōrd′) *n.* A meal consisting of a number of dishes served buffet-style. [Swed *smörgàsbord.*]

smote (smōt). *p.t.* & alternate *p.p.* of smite.

smoth•er (smŭth′ər) *v.* **1.** To suffocate. **2.** To suppress. **3.** To cook or cover (a foodstuff) under a thick mass of another foodstuff. —*n.* A dense cloud of smoke or dust or a welter of

spume. [< OE *smorian,* to suffocate, smother.] —**smoth′er•y** *adj.*

smoul•der. Variant of smolder.

smudge (smŭj) *v.* smudged, smudging. To smear or blur. —*n.* **1.** A blotch or smear. **2.** A smoky fire used against insects or frost. [ME *smogen.*] —**smudg′y** *adj.*

smug (smŭg) *adj.* smugger, smuggest. Complacent or self-satisfied. [Prob < LG *smuck,* neat, smooth.] —**smug′ly** *adv.* —**smug′ness** *n.*

smug•gle (smŭg′əl) *v.* -gled, -gling. **1.** To import or export without paying lawful customs charges or duties. **2.** To convey illicitly or by stealth. [< LG *smuggeln* and Du *smokkelen.*] —**smug′gler** *n.*

smut (smŭt) *n.* **1.** A smudge or something that smudges. **2.** Obscenity. **3.** A plant disease caused by fungi and characterized by black, powdery masses. [Perh < LG *smutt.*] —**smut′-ti•ness** *n.* —**smut′ty** *adj.*

smutch (smŭch) *n.* A stain or smudge. [Perh related to SMUDGE.]

Sn tin (L *stannum*).

snack (snăk) *n.* A light meal. [ME *snake,* a snatch with the teeth, bite.]

snaf•fle (snăf′əl) *n.* A jointed bit for a horse. [?]

snag (snăg) **1.** A sharp or jagged projection. **2.** An unforeseen or hidden obstacle. —*v.* snagged, snagging. **1.** To get caught by or as by a snag. **2.** To snatch. [Prob < Scand.] —**snag′gy** *adj.*

snail (snāl) *n.* A mollusk with a spirally coiled shell into which the head and body can be withdrawn. [< OE *snœgel.* See sneg-.]

snake (snāk) *n.* Any of various legless, long-bodied, sometimes venomous reptiles. —*v.* snaked, snaking. To move, crawl, or drag with a snakelike motion. [< OE *snaca.* See sneg-.] —**snak′i•ly** *adv.* —**snak′y** *adj.*

Snake River. A river of the NW U.S.

snap (snăp) *v.* snapped, snapping. **1.** To make or cause to make a sharp cracking sound. **2.** To break suddenly with a sharp sound. **3.** To give way abruptly. **4.** To bite or seize with a snatching motion. **5.** To speak abruptly or sharply. **6.** To move smartly. **7.** To flash or sparkle. **8.** *Football.* To pass the ball so as to initiate a play. **9.** To open or close with a click. —*n.* **1.** A sharp cracking sound. **2.** A sudden breaking or release of something under pressure. **3.** A clasp, catch, or other fastening device. **4.** A thin, crisp cooky. **5.** Briskness; energy. **6.** A spell of cold weather. **7.** The passing of the ball that initiates each play in football. [Prob < MLG or MDu *snappen,* to seize, speak hastily.] —**snap′pish** *adj.* —**snap′py** *adj.*

snap•drag•on (snăp′drăg′ən) *n.* A cultivated plant with showy clusters of two-lipped flowers.

snap•per (snăp′ər) *n.* **1.** One that snaps. **2.** Any of various marine food fishes.

snap•shot (snăp′shŏt′) *n.* A casual photograph taken with a small camera.

snare¹ (snâr) *n.* **1.** A trap consisting of a noose for capturing birds and other small animals. **2.** Anything that entangles the unwary. **3.** A

ô paw, for/oi boy/ou out/ōō took/ōō coo/p pop/r run/s sauce/sh shy/t to/th thin/*th* the/
ŭ cut/ûr fur/v van/w wag/y yes/z size/zh vision/ə ago, item, edible, gallop, circus/

surgical instrument with a wire loop controlled by a mechanism in the handle, used to remove growths, such as tumors and polyps. [< ON *snara*.] —snare v. (snared, snaring).

snare² (snâr) *n.* Any of the wires or cords stretched across the lower skin of a drum to increase reverberation. [Prob Du *snaar*, string.]

snarl¹ (snärl) *v.* 1. To growl with bared teeth. 2. To speak angrily or threateningly. [< MLG *snarren*.] —snarl *n.* —snarl'y *adj.*

snarl² (snärl) *n.* A tangle. [Prob < SNARE¹.] —snarl *v.* —snarl'y *adj.*

snatch (snăch) *v.* 1. To try to grasp or seize. 2. To seize or grab. —*n.* 1. The act of snatching. 2. A brief period. 3. A small part: *a snatch of song.* [ME *snacchen*, make a sudden gesture.] —snatch'er *n.*

sneak (snēk) *v.* sneaked or *nonstandard* snuck, sneaking. To move, give, or take in a stealthy way. —*n.* 1. A cowardly or underhand person. 2. A stealthy move. [Of dial origin.] —sneak'i·ness *n.* —sneak'y *adj.*

sneak·er (snē'kər) *n.* A canvas shoe with a soft rubber sole.

sneer (snir) *n.* A slight raising of one corner of the upper lip, expressive of contempt. —sneer *v.* —sneer'er *n.* —sneer'ful *adj.*

sneeze (snēz) *v.* sneezed, sneezing. To expel air forcibly from the mouth and nose in an explosive, spasmodic, involuntary action. [< OE *fnēosan.* See pneu-.] —sneeze *n.*

snick·er (snĭk'ər) *n.* Also snig·ger (snĭg'ər). A snide, partly stifled laugh. [Imit.] —snick'er *v.* —snick'er·ing·ly *adv.*

snide (snīd) *adj.* 1. Slyly derogatory or sarcastic. 2. Mean. [?]

sniff (snĭf) *v.* sniffed, sniffing. 1. To inhale a short, audible breath through the nose. 2. To indicate contempt or disdain. 3. To detect by or as if by sniffing. [ME *sniffen.*] —sniff *n.* —sniff'er *n.* —sniff'ing·ly *adv.*

snif·fle (snĭf'əl) *v.* -fled, -fling. To snuffle or whimper. [Freq of SNIFF.] —snif'fle *n.*

snif·ter (snĭf'tər) *n.* A pear-shaped brandy glass. [< dial *snifter*, to sniff.]

snip (snĭp) *v.* snipped, snipping. To cut or clip with short, quick strokes. —*n.* 1. A stroke of the scissors. 2. A small piece clipped off. [LG or Du *snippen*, to snap.]

snipe (snīp) *n., pl.* snipe or snipes. A long-billed, brownish wading bird. —*v.* sniped, sniping. To shoot at an enemy from a concealed place. [ME.]

snip·er (snī'pər) *n.* A rifleman detailed to pick off enemy soldiers from a concealed position.

snip·pet (snĭp'ĭt) *n.* A tidbit or morsel. [< SNIP.]

snitch (snĭch) *v. Slang.* 1. To steal. 2. To turn informer. [?] —snitch'er *n.*

sniv·el (snĭv'əl) *v.* -eled or -elled, -eling or -elling. 1. To whine tearfully. 2. To run at the nose. [< OE *snyflan.* See snē-².] —sniv'el *n.*

snob (snŏb) *n.* One who is convinced of and flaunts his social or other superiority. [?] —snob'ber·y *n.* —snob'bish *adj.* —snob'bish·ly *adv.* —snob'bish·ness *n.*

snoop (snōōp) *v.* To pry furtively. —*n. Infor-*

mal. One who pries or meddles. [Du *snoepen*, to eat on the sly.] —snoop'er *n.* —snoop'y *adj.*

snooze (snōōz) *v.* snoozed, snoozing. To doze. [?] —snooze *n.*

snore (snôr, snōr) *v.* snored, snoring. To make snorting sounds while sleeping. [ME *snoren*, to snort.] —snore *n.* —snor'er *n.*

snor·kel (snôr'kəl) *n.* 1. A retractable vertical tube in a submarine, containing air-intake and exhaust pipes that permit extended periods of submergence. 2. A breathing apparatus used by skin divers, consisting of a long tube held in the mouth. [G *Schnorchel*.]

snort (snôrt) *v.* 1. To exhale or inhale forcibly and noisily through the nostrils in the manner of a horse. 2. To laugh or express contempt with or as if with a snort. [ME *snorten*.] —snort *n.* —snort'er *n.*

snout (snout) *n.* An animal's projecting nose or facial part. [ME *snoute.*]

snow (snō) *n.* 1. Solid precipitation in the form of white or translucent ice crystals. 2. A falling of snow; snowstorm. —*v.* 1. To fall as snow. 2. To cover or close off with snow. [< OE *snāw.* See sneigwh-.] —snow'y *adj.*

snow·ball (snō'bôl') *n.* 1. A mass of soft, wet snow packed into a ball. 2. A shrub with rounded clusters of white flowers. —*v.* 1. To throw snowballs. 2. To grow rapidly in significance, importance, or size.

snow·bound (snō'bound') *adj.* Confined in one place by heavy snow.

snow·drift (snō'drĭft') *n.* Snow banked up by the wind.

snow·fall (snō'fôl') *n.* 1. The amount of snow that falls during a given period or in a specified area. 2. A fall of snow.

snow·mo·bile (snō'mō-bēl') *n.* A small motor vehicle with skilike runners, used for driving in or traveling on snow.

snow·plow (snō'plou') *n.* Any plowlike device for snow removal.

snow·shoe (snō'shōō') *n.* A racket-shaped frame worn under the shoe to facilitate walking on deep snow. —snow'shoe' *v.*

snow·storm (snō'stôrm') *n.* A storm marked by heavy snowfall.

snub (snŭb) *v.* snubbed, snubbing. To treat with scorn. [< ON *snubba.*] —snub *n.*

snub-nosed (snŭb'nōzd') *adj.* Having a short, turned-up nose.

snuck (snŭk). *Nonstandard. p.t. & p.p.* of sneak.

snuff¹ (snŭf) *v.* 1. To inhale through the nose; sniff. 2. To smell. 3. To use snuff. —*n.* 1. Finely pulverized tobacco for snorting up the nostrils. 2. A sniff. [Prob < MDu *snuffen.*]

snuff² (snŭf) *v.* 1. To cut off the charred end of (a candle). 2. To extinguish (a candle). [ME *snoffe.*]

snuf·fle (snŭf'əl) *v.* -fled, -fling. 1. To breathe or sniff noisily. 2. To sniffle. [Prob < LG or Du *snuffelen.*] —snuf'fle *n.*

snug (snŭg) *adj.* snugger, snuggest. 1. Cozy. 2. Close-fitting, compact, or tight. [Perh < Scand.] —snug, snug'ly *adv.* —snug'ness *n.*

snug·gle (snŭg'əl) *v.* -gled, -gling. To nestle or cuddle.

so (sō) *adv.* 1. In the manner expressed or

indicated. **2.** To the degree expressed. **3.** To an evident degree. **4.** Therefore; consequently. **5.** Thereabouts: *ten dollars or so.* **6.** Likewise; also. **7.** Then. **8.** Indeed. —*adj.* True; factual. —*conj.* For that reason or with the consequence that: *He agreed, so they went ahead with plans.* —**so that.** With the purpose or result that. [< OE *swā.* See **swo-.**]

So. south; southern.

s.o. **1.** seller's option. **2.** strikeout.

soak (sōk) *v.* **1.** To wet or saturate, as by immersing for a period of time. **2.** To absorb. **3.** To be immersed. **4.** To permeate; seep. **5.** *Slang.* To overcharge. —*n.* **1.** The act or process of soaking. **2.** Liquid in which something is soaked. **3.** *Slang.* A drunkard. [< OE *socian.* See **seu-⁴.**] —**soak'er** *n.*

soap (sōp) *n.* A cleansing agent made from an alkali acting on natural oils and fats. —*v.* To treat or cover with soap. [< OE *sāpe* < Gmc **saip-*, "dripping thing."] —**soap'i•ly** *adv.* —**soap'i•ness** *n.* —**soap'y** *adj.*

soap opera. A daytime radio or television serial drama.

soap•stone (sōp'stōn') *n.* Steatite.

soar (sôr, sōr) *v.* To rise, fly upward, or glide high in the air. [< VL **exaurāre.*]

sob (sŏb) *v.* **sobbed, sobbing.** To weep convulsively. [ME *sobben,* to catch breath.] —**sob** *n.* —**sob'bing•ly** *adv.*

so•ber (sō'bər) *adj.* **1.** Abstemious or temperate. **2.** Not drunk. **3.** Serious or grave. **4.** Plain or subdued. **5.** Without frivolity, excess, or exaggeration. **6.** Rational and impartial. —*v.* To make or become sober. [< L *sōbrius.*] —**so'ber•ly** *adv.* —**so'ber•ness** *n.*

so•bri•e•ty (sō-brī'ə-tē) *n.* **1.** Seriousness, gravity, or solemnity. **2.** Absence of alcoholic intoxication.

so•bri•quet (sō'brĭ-kā', -kĕt', sō'brĭ-kā', -kĕt') *n.* A nickname. [F.]

soc. **1.** socialist. **2.** society.

so-called (sō'kōld') *adj.* Thus (but often wrongly thus) designated: *our so-called allies.*

soc•cer (sŏk'ər) *n.* A kind of football in which two teams maneuver a round ball mainly by kicking in attempts to score points. [Short var of ASSOCIATION (football).]

so•cia•ble (sō'shə-bəl) *adj.* Friendly; companionable; convivial. [< L *socius,* partner, sharer.] —**so'cia•bil'i•ty** (sō'shə-bĭl'ə-tē) *n.* —**so'cia•ble•ness** *n.* —**so'cia•bly** *adv.*

so•cial (sō'shəl) *adj.* **1.** Living together in communities or organized groups. **2.** Of or pertaining to human society or its class and individual interrelationships. **3.** Of or pertaining to fashionable society. **4.** Sociable or convivial. —*n.* A social gathering: *church social.* [< L *socius,* companion, partner.] —**so'cial•ly** *adv.*

so•cial•ism (sō'shə-lĭz'əm) *n.* A system or theory of social organization in which the producers possess both political power and production and distribution means. —**so'cial•ist** *n.* & *adj.* —**so'cial•is'tic** *adj.*

so•cial•ize (sō'shə-līz') *v.* **-ized, -izing.** **1.** To place under public ownership or control. **2.** To convert or adapt to social needs. **3.** To take part in social activities. —**so'cial•i•za'tion** *n.* —**so'cial•iz'er** *n.*

social security. A U.S. governmental system providing people with economic assistance for unemployment, disability, or old age.

so•ci•e•ty (sə-sī'ə-tē) *n., pl.* **-ties. 1. a.** The totality of human interrelationships. **b.** A given human group distinguished by participation in characteristic economic and political relationships and a common culture. **2.** The fashionable social class. **3.** Companionship; company. [< L *societās,* fellowship, union, society.] —**so•ci'e•tal** (-təl) *adj.*

Society of Friends. A Christian sect founded in about 1650 in England. It rejects ritual, formal sacraments, a priesthood, and violence.

socio-. *comb. form.* **1.** Society. **2.** Social. [< L *socius,* a sharing.]

so•ci•ol•o•gy (sō'sē-ŏl'ə-jē, sō'shē-) *n.* The study of human social structures and relationships. —**so'ci•o•log'ic** (-ə-lŏj'ĭk), **so'ci•o•log'i•cal** *adj.* —**so'ci•ol'o•gist** *n.*

sock¹ (sŏk) *n.* **1.** *pl.* **socks** or **sox.** A short stocking. **2.** *pl.* **socks. a.** A light shoe worn in the comedy of antiquity. **b.** Comic drama; comedy. [< OE *socc,* a kind of light shoe < L *soccus.*]

sock² (sŏk) *v. Slang.* To hit forcefully; punch. [?] —**sock** *n.*

sock•et (sŏk'ĭt) *n.* **1.** A cavity that acts as the receptacle for an inserted part. **2. a.** The hollow part of a joint that receives the end of a bone. **b.** A hollow into which a part, such as the eye, fits. [ME *soket.*]

Soc•ra•tes (sŏk'rə-tēz'). 470?–399 B.C. Greek philosopher and teacher. —**So•crat'ic** (sō-krăt'ĭk) *adj.*

sod (sŏd) *n.* Grass-covered surface soil held together by matted roots. —*v.* **sodded, sodding.** To cover with sod. [ME.]

so•da (sō'də) *n.* **1.** Any of various carbonates or bicarbonates of sodium. **2.** Carbonated water or a soft drink containing it. [ML.]

soda pop. *Informal.* A soft drink; soda.

sod•den (sŏd'n) *adj.* **1.** Thoroughly soaked; saturated. **2.** Bloated and dull, as from drink. [ME *soden,* pp of *sethen,* to seethe.] —**sod'den•ly** *adv.* —**sod'den•ness** *n.*

so•di•um (sō'dē-əm) *n. Symbol* **Na** A soft, light, extremely malleable silver-white metallic element, used esp. in the production of many industrially important compounds. Atomic number 11, atomic weight 22.99. [< SOD(A) + -IUM.]

sodium bicarbonate. A white crystalline compound, $NaHCO_3$, used in making effervescent salts and beverages, artificial mineral water, baking soda, and pharmaceuticals, and in fire extinguishers; bicarbonate of soda.

sodium borate. A crystalline compound, $Na_2B_4O_7 \cdot 10H_2O_2$, used in the manufacture of glass, detergents, and pharmaceuticals.

sodium carbonate. A white powdery compound, Na_2CO_3, used to manufacture various sodium compounds, ceramics, detergents, and soap.

sodium chloride. A colorless crystalline compound, NaCl, used to manufacture chemicals

---

ô paw, for/oi boy/ou out/ŏŏ took/ōō coo/p pop/r run/s sauce/sh shy/t to/th thin/*th* the/
ŭ cut/ûr fur/v van/w wag/y yes/z size/zh vision/ə ago, item, edible, gallop, circus/

and as a food preservative and seasoning.

sodium glutamate. A white crystalline compound, $C_5H_8O_4NaM$, having a meatlike taste, used in cooking.

sodium hydroxide. A strongly alkaline compound, $NaOH$, used to manufacture chemicals and soaps and in petroleum refining.

sodium peroxide. A yellowish-white powder, Na_2O_2, employed as an oxidizing and bleaching agent.

sod•om•y (sŏd'ə-mē) *n.* Anal copulation of one male with another.

so•fa (sō'fə) *n.* A long upholstered couch with a back and arms. [< Ar *suffah*, a cushioned dais.]

So•fi•a (sō-fē-ə, sō-fē'ə). The capital of Bulgaria. Pop. 747,000.

soft (sôft, sŏft) *adj.* **1. a.** Offering little resistance; not hard. **b.** Yielding readily; not firm. **2.** Flabby. **3. a.** Smooth or fine. **b.** Bland. **4.** Not loud. **5.** Subdued. **6.** Not sharp. **7.** Gentle; mild. **8. a.** Compassionate. **b.** Affectionate; tender. **9.** Easy: *a soft job.* **10.** Having low dissolved mineral content. —*adv.* Softly; gently. [< OE *sōfte, sēfte* < Gmc *samfti-.*] —**soft'ly** *adv.* —**soft'ness** *n.*

soft•ball (sôft'bôl', sŏft'-) *n.* **1.** A variation of baseball played with a larger, softer ball. **2.** The ball used.

soft drink. A nonalcoholic, usually carbonated beverage.

soft drug. A drug, such as marijuana, that is considered to be less damaging to the health than a hard drug.

sof•ten (sôf'ən, sŏf'-) *v.* To make or become soft or softer. —**sof'ten•er** *n.*

soft palate. The movable fold of muscular fibers suspended from the rear of the hard palate that closes off the nasal cavity from the oral cavity during swallowing.

soft•ware (sôft'wâr', sŏft'-) *n.* **1.** Written or printed data, as programs, essential to the operation of computers. **2.** Documents, as manuals, containing information on the operation and maintenance of computers.

sog•gy (sŏg'ē) *adj.* **-gier, -giest. 1.** Sodden; soaked. **2.** Humid; sultry. —**sog'gi•ly** *adv.* —**sog'gi•ness** *n.*

soil¹ (soil) *n.* **1.** The loose top layer of the earth's surface. **2.** Country; region: *native soil.* [< L *solium*, seat.]

soil² (soil) *v.* **1.** To make or become dirty; begrime. **2.** To disgrace; tarnish. **3.** To pollute; defile. —*n.* **1.** A stain or defilement. **2.** Human excrement used as fertilizer. [< VL *suculāre.*]

soi•ree (swä-rā') *n.* Also **soi•rée.** An evening party. [< F *soir*, evening.]

so•journ (sō'jûrn, sō-jûrn') *v.* To stay for a time; reside temporarily. [< OF *sojorner.*] —**so'journ** *n.* —**so'journ•er** *n.*

sol (sōl) *n.* The basic monetary unit of Peru.

sol•ace (sŏl'ĭs) *n.* **1.** Comfort in distress; consolation. **2.** That which furnishes comfort or consolation. [< L *sōlāri*, to comfort, console.] —**sol'ace** *v.* **(-aced, -acing).**

so•lar (sō'lər) *adj.* **1.** Of or proceeding from the sun. **2.** Utilizing or operated by energy derived

from the sun: *solar battery.* **3.** Determined or measured with respect to the sun. [< L *sōl*, sun.]

so•lar•i•um (sō-lâr'ē-əm) *n., pl.* **-laria** (-lâr'ē-ə) or **-iums.** A room, gallery, etc., exposed to the sun, as in a sanitarium. [L *sōlārium*, sundial, terrace, balcony.]

solar plexus. 1. The large network of nerves located behind the stomach. **2.** *Informal.* The pit of the stomach.

solar system. The sun together with the nine planets and all other celestial bodies that orbit the sun.

sold (sōld). *p.t.* & *p.p.* of **sell.**

sol•der (sŏd'ər, sôd'-) *n.* **1.** Any of various fusible alloys, usually tin and lead, used to join metallic parts. **2.** Anything that joins or cements. —*v.* To join or repair with or as with solder. [< L *solidāre*, to make solid.]

sol•dier (sōl'jər) *n.* **1.** One who serves in an army. **2.** An enlisted man as distinguished from a commissioned officer. **3.** A sexually undeveloped form of certain ants and termites, having the jaws specialized to serve as fighting weapons. —*v.* To be or serve as a soldier. [< OF *soulde*, pay.] —**sol'dier•ly** *adj.*

sol•dier•y (sōl'jə-rē) *n., pl.* **-ies. 1.** A body of soldiers. **2.** The military profession.

sole¹ (sōl) *n.* **1.** The undersurface of the foot. **2.** The undersurface of a shoe or boot. —*v.* **soled, soling.** To furnish (a shoe or boot) with a sole. [< L *solum*, bottom, ground, sole of the foot.]

sole² (sōl) *adj.* Single; only. [< L *sōlus*, alone, single.] —**sole'ly** *adv.*

sole³ (sōl) *n., pl.* **sole** or **soles.** A marine flatfish valued as food. [< OF, sole (fish), SOLE¹, from the shape of the fish.]

sol•e•cism (sŏl'ə-sĭz'əm, sō'lə-) *n.* **1.** A nonstandard usage or grammatical construction. **2.** A violation of etiquette. [< Gk *soloikos*, speaking incorrectly.]

sol•emn (sŏl'əm) *adj.* **1.** Deeply earnest; grave. **2.** Performed with full ceremony: *a Solemn High Mass.* **3.** Gloomy; somber. [< L *sollemnis*, stated, established, appointed.] —**so•lem'ni•ty** (sə-lĕm'nə-tē), **sol'emn•ness** —**sol'emn•ly** *adv.*

sol•em•nize (sŏl'əm-nīz') *v.* **-nized, -nizing. 1.** To observe with formal ceremonies or rites. **2.** To perform with formal ceremony: *solemnize a marriage.* —**sol'em•ni•za'tion** *n.*

so•lic•it (sə-lĭs'ĭt) *v.* **1.** To seek to obtain: *solicit votes.* **2.** To entreat; importune. **3.** To entice; tempt. [< L *sollicitāre*, to disturb, agitate.] —**so•lic'i•ta'tion** *n.*

so•lic•i•tor (sə-lĭs'ə-tər) *n.* **1.** One who solicits contributions, subscriptions, etc. **2.** The chief law officer of a city or government department. **3.** *Brit.* A lawyer who is not a member of the bar and who may be heard only in the lower courts.

so•lic•i•tous (sə-lĭs'ə-təs) *adj.* **1.** Concerned; attentive. **2.** Eager. [L *sollicitus*, thoroughly moved, agitated.] —**so•lic'i•tous•ly** *adv.* —**so•lic'i•tous•ness** *n.*

so•lic•i•tude (sə-lĭs'ə-t/y/ōōd') *n.* The state of being solicitous; concern.

sol•id (sŏl'ĭd) *adj.* **1.** Not liquid or gaseous. **2.** Not hollowed out. **3.** Being the same substance throughout. **4.** Of or pertaining to three-dimensional geometric figures or bodies. **5.** Without breaks; continuous. **6.** Well-made. **7.** Forceful; hearty. **8.** Substantial. **9.** Sound; concrete. **10.** Upstanding and dependable. —*n.* **1.** A solid substance. **2.** A geometric figure having three dimensions. [< L *solidus.*] —**so•lid'i•ty** (sə-lĭd'ə-tē), **sol'id•ness** *n.* —**sol'id•ly** *adv.*

sol•i•dar•i•ty (sŏl'ə-dăr'ə-tē) *n.* Unity of purpose, interest, or sympathy.

so•lid•i•fy (sə-lĭd'ə-fī') *v.* **-fied, -fying.** To make or become solid. —**so•lid'i•fi•ca'tion** *n.*

sol•id-state (sŏl'ĭd-stāt') *adj.* **1.** Of or involving the physical properties of solid materials, esp. the electromagnetic, thermodynamic, and structural properties of crystalline solids. **2.** Based on or using semiconducting materials.

so•lil•o•quize (sə-lĭl'ə-kwīz') *v.* **-quized, -quizing.** To utter a soliloquy.

so•lil•o•quy (sə-lĭl'ə-kwē) *n., pl.* **-quies. 1.** A dramatic discourse in which a character expresses his thoughts verbally without addressing a listener. **2.** The act of talking to oneself. [LL *sōliloquium.*]

sol•ip•sism (sŏl'əp-sĭz'əm, sō'ləp-) *n.* The theory that the self is the only reality. [L *solus,* alone + *ipse,* self + -ISM.] —**sol'ip•sist** *n.* —**sol'ip•sis'tic** *adj.*

sol•i•taire (sŏl'ə-târ') *n.* **1.** A gemstone set alone, as in a ring. **2.** A card game played by one person. [< L *sōlitārius,* solitary.]

sol•i•tar•y (sŏl'ə-tĕr'ē) *adj.* **1.** Existing or living alone. **2.** Happening or done alone. **3.** Secluded. **4.** Lonely. **5.** Single; sole. [L *solus,* alone.] —**sol'i•tar'i•ness** *n.*

sol•i•tude (sŏl'ə-t/y/ōōd') *n.* **1.** The state of being alone. **2.** A lonely or secluded place. [< L *sōlus,* alone.]

soln solution.

so•lo (sō'lō) *n., pl.* **-los. 1.** A musical composition for an individual voice or instrument, with or without accompaniment. **2.** Any performance accomplished by a single individual. —*v.* To perform alone, esp. to fly an airplane without an instructor. [< L *sōlus,* alone.] —**so'lo** *adj. & adv.* —**so'lo•ist** *n.*

Sol•o•mon (sŏl'ə-mən) King of Israel in the 10th century B.C.; noted for his wisdom.

so long. *Informal.* Good-by.

sol•stice (sŏl'stəs, sōl'-) *n.* Either of two times of the year when the sun has no apparent northward or southward motion. [< L *sōlstitium.*] —**sol•sti'tial** (-stĭsh'əl) *adj.*

sol•u•ble (sŏl'yə-bəl) *adj.* **1.** Capable of being dissolved, esp. easily dissolved. **2.** Capable of being solved. [< L *solvere,* to loosen.] —**sol'u•bil'i•ty** *n.* —**sol'u•bly** *adv.*

sol•ute (sŏl'yōōt', sō'lōōt') *n.* A substance dissolved in another substance, usually the component of a solution present in the lesser amount. —*adj.* In solution; dissolved. [L *solūtus,* pp of *solvere,* to loosen.]

so•lu•tion (sə-lōō'shən) *n.* **1.** A spontaneously forming homogeneous mixture of two or more substances, retaining its constitution in sub-division to molecular volumes and having various possible proportions of the constituents. **2.** The process of forming such a mixture. **3.** The state of being dissolved. **4.** The method or process of solving a problem. **5.** The answer to or disposition of a problem. [< L *solūtus.* See **solute.**]

solv•a•ble (sŏl'və-bəl) *adj.* Capable of being solved. —**solv'a•bil'i•ty** *n.*

solve (sŏlv) *v.* **solved, solving.** To find a solution to (a problem). [< L *solvere,* to loosen.]

sol•vent (sŏl'vənt) *adj.* **1.** Able to meet financial obligations. **2.** Capable of dissolving another substance. —*n. Chem.* **1.** The component of a solution that is present in excess or that undergoes no change of state. **2.** A liquid capable of dissolving another substance. [< L *solvere,* to loosen.] —**sol'ven•cy** *n.*

So•ma•li•a (sō-mä'lē-ə). A republic of E Africa. Pop. about 2,000,000. Cap. Mogadishu.

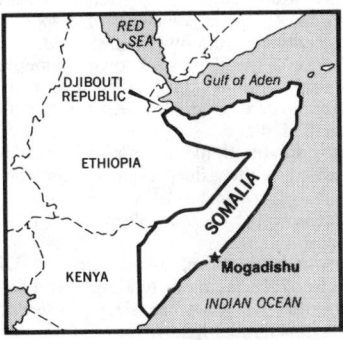

Somalia

so•mat•ic (sə-măt'ĭk) *adj.* Of or pertaining to the body, esp. as distinguished from a bodily part, the mind, or the environment. [< Gk *sōma,* body.]

som•ber (sŏm'bər) *adj.* Also **som•bre. 1.** Dark; gloomy. **2.** Melancholy; dismal. [< VL **subombrāre,* to shade.] —**som'ber•ly** *adv.*

som•bre•ro (sŏm-brâr'ō) *n., pl.* **-ros.** A broad-brimmed Spanish or Mexican hat. [< VL **subombrāre,* to shade.]

some (sŭm) *adj.* **1.** Being an unspecified number or part: *Some laws are bad.* **2.** Being unknown or unspecified by name: *Some fool laughed.* **3.** *Informal.* Remarkable: *He is some skier.* —*pron.* **1.** An unspecified number or portion. **2.** An indefinite additional quantity: *three and some.* —*adv.* **1.** Approximately: *some 40 people.* **2.** *Informal.* Somewhat. [< OE *sum,* one, a certain one. See **sem-**[1].]

-some[1]. *comb. form.* Being or tending to be: *burdensome.* [< OE *-sum.*]

-some[2]. *comb. form.* Body: *chromosome.* [< Gk *sōma,* body.]

-some[3]. *comb. form.* A group of. Used with numerals: *threesome.* [< SOME.]

some•bod•y (sŭm'bŏd'ē, -bŭd'ē, -bə-dē) *pron.* An unspecified person; someone. —*n. Informal.* A person of importance.

some•day (sŭm'dā') *adv.* At a future time.

some•how (sŭm'hou') *adv.* In a way not specified or known.

some•one (sŭm'wŭn', -wən) *pron.* Some person; somebody.

some•place (sŭm'plās') *adv. Informal.* Somewhere.

som•er•sault (sŭm'ər-sôlt') *n.* An acrobatic stunt in which the body rolls in a complete circle, heels over head. [< OProv *sobresaut.] —**som'er•sault'** *v.*

some•thing (sŭm'thĭng) *pron.* An unspecified thing. —*n.* An important person or thing.

some•time (sŭm'tīm') *adv.* At an indefinite time. —*adj.* **1.** Having been at some prior time; former. **2.** *Nonstandard.* Occasional.

some•times (sŭm'tīmz') *adv.* Upon occasion; now and then.

some•way (sŭm'wā') *adv.* Also **some•ways** (-wāz'). *Informal.* Somehow.

some•what (sŭm'hwät, sŭm-hwät') *adv.* To some extent; rather. —*n.* Some amount, part, or degree: *He is somewhat of a fool.*

some•where (sŭm'hwĕr') *adv.* **1.** At, in, or to a place not specified or known; someplace. **2.** At or to some unspecified point in time, amount, or degree. —*n.* An unknown or unspecified place.

som•nam•bu•lism (sŏm-năm'byə-lĭz'əm) *n.* Walking while asleep or in a sleeplike condition. —**som•nam'bu•list** *n.*

somni–. *comb. form.* Sleep. [< L *somnus,* sleep.]

som•no•lent (sŏm'nə-lənt) *adj.* **1.** Drowsy; sleepy. **2.** Inducing or tending to induce sleep; soporific. [< L *somnus,* sleep.] —**som'no•lence** *n.* —**som'no•lent•ly** *adv.*

son (sŭn) *n.* **1.** A male offspring. **2.** Any male descendant. **3. the Son.** The second person of the Trinity, Christ. [< OE *sunu.* See seu-[3].]

so•nar (sō'när') *n.* A system using transmitted and reflected acoustic waves to detect and locate submerged objects. [So(und) na(vigation) r(anging).]

so•na•ta (sə-nä'tä) *n. Mus.* An instrumental composition consisting of three or four movements. [It.]

song (sông, sŏng) *n.* **1.** Sound produced by singing. **2.** A brief musical composition for singing. **3.** The act of singing. **4.** A lyric poem or ballad. [< OE *sang.* See sengwh-.] —**song'ful** *adj.* —**song'ful•ly** *adv.*

song•bird (sông'bûrd', sŏng'-) *n.* A bird with a melodious song or call.

song•ster (sông'stər, sŏng'-) *n.* One that sings.

son•ic (sŏn'ĭk) *adj.* Of or relating to sound or its speed of propagation. [< L *sonus,* sound.]

sonic boom. A loud, transient explosive sound caused by the shock wave preceding an aircraft traveling at supersonic speeds.

son-in-law (sŭn'ĭn-lô') *n., pl.* **sons-in-law** (sŭnz'-). The husband of one's daughter.

son•net (sŏn'ĭt) *n.* A 14-line poetic form embodying the statement and resolution of a single theme. [< OProv *sonet.*]

so•no•rous (sə-nôr'əs, sə-nōr'-, sŏn'ər-) *adj.* **1.** Producing sound. **2.** Producing a full, rich sound when struck, as a gong. **3.** Impressive. [< It *sonāre,* to sound.] —**so•nor'i•ty** *n.*

soon (sōōn) *adv.* **1.** In the near future. **2.** Promptly. **3.** Early. **4.** Readily. [< OE *sōna* < Gmc **sænô.*]
   Usage: No sooner is preferably followed by *than,* rather than by *when,* as in the following typical example: *No sooner had she come than the maid knocked.*

soot (sōōt, sŭt, sōōt) *n.* A fine dispersion of black particles, chiefly carbon, produced by the incomplete combustion of fuels. [< OE *sōt.* See sed-.] —**soot'y** *adj.*

sooth (sōōth) *n. Archaic.* Truth. [< OE *sōth.* See es-.]

soothe (sōōth) *v.* **soothed, soothing. 1.** To calm; mollify; placate. **2.** To ease or relieve the pain of. [< OE *sōth,* truth, sooth.] —**sooth'er** *n.*

sooth•say•er (sōōth'sā'ər) *n.* One who foretells events.

sop (sŏp) *v.* **sopped, sopping. 1.** To dip, soak, or steep in a liquid; saturate. **2.** To take up by absorption. —*n.* **1.** A bit of food soaked in a liquid. **2.** something yielded to placate; a bribe. [< OE *sopp,* dipped bread.]

soph. sophomore.

soph•ism (sŏf'ĭz'əm) *n.* **1.** A plausible but fallacious argument. **2.** Any deceptive or fallacious argumentation. [< Gk *sophisma,* acquired skill, clever device.]

soph•ist (sŏf'ĭst) *n.* One skillful in devious argumentation. [< Gk *sophistēs,* expert, deviser.]

so•phis•tic (sə-fĭs'tĭk) *adj.* Also **so•phis•ti•cal** (-tĭ-kəl). **1.** Of or characteristic of sophists. **2.** Specious; fallacious.

so•phis•ti•cat•ed (sə-fĭs'tĭ-kā'tĭd) *adj.* **1.** Lacking natural simplicity or naiveté. **2.** Complex or complicated. **3.** Suitable for the tastes of sophisticates. [< Gk *sophistēs,* SOPHIST.] —**so•phis'ti•cate** (-kĭt) *n.* —**so•phis'ti•ca'tion** *n.*

soph•is•try (sŏf'əs-trē) *n., pl.* **-tries.** Plausible but misleading or fallacious argumentation.

Soph•o•cles (sŏf'ə-klēz'). 496?–406 b.c. Athenian tragic poet. —**Soph'o•cle'an** *adj.*

soph•o•more (sŏf'ə-môr') *n.* A second-year student in a four-year American college or high school. [Prob < earlier *sophumer,* arguments.]

so•po•rif•ic (sŏp'ə-rĭf'ĭk) *adj.* **1.** Inducing sleep. **2.** Drowsy. [< L *sopor,* sleep.] —**so'po•rif'ic** *n.*

so•pran•o (sə-prăn'ō, -prä'nō) *n., pl.* **-os. 1.** The highest natural human voice, found in some women and boys. **2.** A singer having such a voice. **3.** A part for such a voice. [< It *sopra,* above.] —**so•pran'o** *adj.*

sor•cer•y (sôr'sər-ē) *n.* Black magic; witchcraft. [< VL **sortiārius,* caster of lots.] —**sor'cer•er** *n.* —**sor'cer•ess** *fem.n.*

sor•did (sôr'dĭd) *adj.* **1.** Filthy; foul. **2.** Squalid; wretched. **3.** Vile; base. **4.** Grasping; selfish. [< L *sordidus.*] —**sor'did•ly** *adv.* —**sor'did•ness** *n.*

sore (sôr, sōr) *adj.* **sorer, sorest. 1.** Painful; tender. **2.** Feeling physical pain; hurting. **3.** Causing sorrow or distress; grievous. —*n.* An open skin lesion, wound, or ulcer. [< OE *sār.* See sai-.] —**sore'ly** *adv.* —**sore'ness** *n.*

sor•ghum (sôr'gəm, sōr'-) *n.* A cereal grass

cultivated for grain, forage, or as a source of syrup. [< VL *syricum (grānum),* "Syrian (grain)."]

so•ror•i•ty (sə-rôr′ə-tē, sə-rōr′-) *n., pl.* **-ties.** A social club for female students, as at a college. [< L *soror,* sister.]

sor•rel¹ (sôr′əl) *n.* Any of several plants with acid-tasting leaves. [< OF *sur,* sour.]

sor•rel² (sôr′əl) *n.* **1.** Yellowish or reddish brown. **2.** A horse of this color. [< OF *sor,* red-brown.] —**sor′rel** *adj.*

sor•row (sŏr′ō, sôr′ō) *n.* **1.** Mental suffering because of injury or loss. **2.** A misfortune. **3.** Grief. —*v.* To feel or display sorrow; grieve. [< OE *sorh, sorg,* anxiety, sorrow. See **swergh-.**] —**sor′row•ful** *adj.* —**sor′row•ful•ly** *adv.* —**sor′row•ful•ness** *n.*

sor•ry (sŏr′ē, sôr′ē) *adj.* **-rier, -riest. 1.** Feeling or expressing sympathy or regret. **2.** Poor; paltry. **3.** Grievous; sad. [< OE *sārig,* painful, sad. See **sai-.**] —**sor′ri•ness** *n.*

sort (sôrt) *n.* **1.** A group or collection of similar persons or things; class; kind. **2.** Type; quality. **3.** Manner; style. —*v.* To arrange according to class, kind, or size; classify. [Prob < L *sors (sort-),* lot, fortune.]

Usage: Sort (noun), in written usage, usually takes a singular modifier and verb: *This sort of problem is not new.* In the plural: *These sorts of problems are not new.* An alternative form, *these sort of problems are,* is more common to speech. *All sort of problems* (for *all sorts*) has less standing.

sor•tie (sôr′tē) *n.* **1.** A sally by besieged forces upon the besiegers. **2.** A single flight of an airplane on a combat mission. [F, "a going out."]

so-so (sō′sō′) *adv.* Indifferently; passably.

sot (sŏt) *n.* A chronic drunkard. [< ML *sottus.*] —**sot′tish** *adj.* —**sot′tish•ly** *adv.*

So•tho (sō′thō) *n.* A group of Bantu languages spoken in Lesotho, Botswana, and South Africa.

sou•brette (soo-brĕt′) *n.* A lady's maid in comedies or comic opera. [< Prov *soubret,* conceited.]

souf•flé (soo-flā′) *n.* A light, fluffy baked dish made with egg yolks and beaten egg whites. [< F *souffler,* to puff up.]

sough (sŭf, sou) *v.* To make a soft murmuring or rustling sound. [< OE *swōgan.*] —**sough** *n.*

sought (sôt). *p.t. & p.p.* of **seek.**

soul (sōl) *n.* **1.** An immaterial entity said to be the animating and vital principle in man. **2.** A person: *a trusting soul.* **3.** The vital core of something. **4.** An inspiring leader: *the soul of our enterprise.* [< OE *sāwol* < Gmc *saiwalō.*] —**soul′less** *adj.* —**soul′less•ness** *n.*

soul•ful (sōl′fəl) *adj.* Full of or expressing deep feeling. —**soul′ful•ly** *adv.* —**soul′ful•ness** *n.*

sound¹ (sound) *n.* **1.** A vibratory disturbance, with frequency in the approximate range between 20 and 20,000 cycles per second, capable of being heard. **2. a.** The sensation stimulated in the organs of hearing by such a disturbance. **b.** Such sensations collectively. **3.** An articulation made by the vocal apparatus. **4.** Audible material recorded, as for a motion picture. —*v.* **1.** To make or cause to make a sound. **2.** To seem to be. **3.** To summon, announce, or signal by a sound: *sound a warning.* [< L *sonus.*]

sound² (sound) *adj.* **1.** In good condition. **2.** Healthy. **3.** Solid; unshakable. **4.** Reliable. **5.** Sensible and correct. **6.** Thorough; complete. **7.** Unbroken; undisturbed: *a sound sleep.* **8.** Upright; honorable. [< OE *gesund.* See **swento-.**] —**sound′ly** *adv.* —**sound′ness** *n.*

sound³ (sound) *n.* **1.** A body of water larger than a strait or channel, connecting larger bodies of water. **2.** A long, wide ocean inlet. [< OE *sund,* swimming.]

sound⁴ (sound) *v.* **1.** To measure the depth of (water). **2.** To try to learn the opinions of a person. **3.** To dive swiftly downward, as a whale. [< OF *sonde,* a sounding line.] —**sound′er** *n.*

sound effects. Imitative sounds produced artificially for theatrical purposes.

sound•ing (soun′dĭng) *n.* **1.** The act of one that sounds. **2.** A measured depth of water.

sounding board. 1. A thin board that acts to reinforce the sound in a musical instrument, as a violin or piano. **2.** One whose reactions serve as a test of the effectiveness or acceptability of one's ideas.

sound•proof (sound′proof′) *adj.* Not penetrable by audible sound. —*v.* To make soundproof.

sound•track (sound′trăk′) *n.* The narrow strip at one side of a motion-picture film that carries the sound recording.

soup (soop) *n.* A liquid food prepared from meat, fish, or vegetable stock, often with various other ingredients added. —*v.* —**soup up.** *Slang.* To add greater speed potential to (an engine). [< OF *soupe.*]

sour (sour) *adj.* **1.** Having a sharp or acid taste. **2.** Spoiled; rank. **3.** Bad-tempered; disagreeable. —*v.* To make or become sour. [< OE *sūr.* See **sūro-.**] —**sour′ly** *adv.* —**sour′ness** *n.*

source (sôrs, sōrs) *n.* **1.** A point of origin. **2.** The beginning of a stream of water. **3.** One that supplies information. [< OF *sourdre,* to rise.]

sour•puss (sour′poos′) *n. Slang.* A gloomy or sullen person.

sour salt. Crystals of citric acid used in cooking.

souse (sous) *v.* **soused, sousing. 1.** To plunge into a liquid. **2.** To drench. **3.** To steep in a mixture, as in pickling. **4.** *Slang.* To make intoxicated. —*n.* **1.** The act or process of sousing. **2.** Food steeped in pickle, as pigs' feet. **3.** *Slang.* A drunkard. [ME *sousen,* to souse, to pickle.]

south (south) *n.* **1. a.** The direction along a meridian to the right of an observer facing in the direction of the earth's rotation. **b.** The point on the mariner's compass 180° clockwise from north. **2.** Often **South. a.** The S part of the earth. **b.** The S part of any country or region. —**the South.** In the U.S., the states S of Pennsylvania and the Ohio River and E of the Mississippi. —*adj.* **1.** To or from the south. **2. South.** Designating the S part of a country,

---

continent, or other geographical area: *South America.* —*adv.* In, from, or toward the south. [< OE *sūth.* See **sâwel-**.]

South Africa, Republic of. A country in the extreme S of Africa. Pop. 17,474,000. Caps. Pretoria and Cape Town.

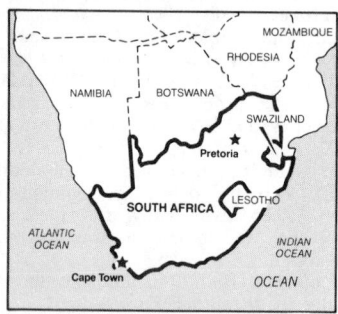

South Africa

South African. 1. A native of the Republic of South Africa, esp. one of European descent; an Afrikaner. **2.** Of or pertaining to South Africa or its inhabitants.

South African Dutch. 1. See **Boer. 2.** Afrikaans.

South America. The southern of the two continents of the W Hemisphere. —**South American.**

South·amp·ton (south-hămp'tən, sou-thămp'-). A city and major seaport in England. Pop. 210,000.

South Bend. A city of N Indiana. Pop. 132,000.

south·bound (south'bound') *adj.* Going toward the south.

South Carolina. A state of the SE U.S. Pop. 2,591,000. Cap. Columbia. —**South Car·o·lin·i·an** (-lĭn'ē-ən).

South China Sea. A section of the Pacific SE of China.

South Dakota. A Middle Western state of the U.S. Pop. 666,000. Cap. Pierre. —**South Dakotan.**

South·down (south'doun') *n.* Any of a breed of small, hornless sheep of English origin, having dense, short, fine-textured wool. [< SOUTH DOWNS.]

South Downs. A range of hills extending W to E in SE England.

south·east (south-ēst') *n.* **1.** The direction halfway between south and east. **2.** Any area or region lying in this direction. —*adj.* To, from, or in the southeast. —*adv.* From or toward the southeast. —**south·east'ern** *adj.*

Southeast Asia. A region generally considered to include Indochina, Malaysia, Indonesia, and the Philippines.

south·east·er (south-ē'stər) *n.* A storm or gale blowing from the southeast.

south·east·er·ly (south-ē'stər-lē) *adj.* **1.** Toward the southeast. **2.** From the southeast. —**south·east'er·ly** *adv.*

south·er (sou'thər) *n.* A strong wind coming

from the south.

south·er·ly (sŭth'ər-lē) *adj.* **1.** Toward the south. **2.** From the south. —**south'er·ly** *adv.*

south·ern (sŭth'ərn) *adj.* **1.** Toward, in, or facing the south. **2.** Coming from the south. **3.** Often **Southern.** Of or characteristic of southern regions or the South.

Southern Cross. A constellation, Crux.

south·ern·er (sŭth'ər-nər) *n.* **1.** A native or inhabitant of the South. **2.** Often **Southerner.** A native or inhabitant of the S U.S.

Southern Hemisphere. The half of the earth south of the equator.

southern lights. The aurora australis.

south·ern·most (sŭth'ərn-mōst') *adj.* Farthest south.

south·ern·wood (sŭth'ərn-wŏod') *n.* An aromatic woody plant native to Europe, having finely divided grayish foliage.

Southern Yemen. A former name for the People's Democratic Republic of Yemen.

South Korea. The unofficial name for the Republic of Korea. See **Korea.**

south·paw (south'pô') *n. Informal.* A left-handed player, especially a left-handed baseball pitcher. —*adj. Informal.* Left-handed.

South Pole. 1. The southern end of the earth's axis of rotation. **2.** The celestial zenith of the heavens as viewed from the south terrestrial pole. **3. south pole.** The south-seeking magnetic pole of a magnet.

South Sea Islands. The islands of the South Pacific.

South Seas. The South Pacific.

South Vietnam. The unofficial name for the former Republic of Vietnam. See **Vietnam.**

south·ward (south'wərd) *adv.* Also **south·wards** (south'wərdz). Toward the south. —*adj.* Toward, facing, or in the south. —**south'ward·ly** *adj. & adv.*

south·west (south-wĕst') *n.* **1.** The direction halfway between south and west. **2.** Any area or region lying in this direction. —**the Southwest.** A region of the SW U.S. including New Mexico, Texas, Arizona, California, Nevada, Utah, and Colorado. —*adj.* To, from, or in the southwest. —*adv.* In, from, or toward southwest. —**south·west'ern** *adj.*

south·west·er (south-wĕs'tər) *n.* Also **sou·west·er** (sou-wĕs'tər). **1.** A storm or strong wind from the southwest. **2.** A sailor's waterproof hat with a broad brim to protect the neck.

south·west·er·ly (south-wĕs'tər-lē) *adj.* **1.** Toward the southwest. **2.** From the southwest. —**south·west'er·ly** *adv.*

Sou·tine (sōō-tēn'), **Chaim.** 1894–1943. Lithuanian painter.

sou·ve·nir (sōō'və-nîr') *n.* Something serving as a remembrance; a memento. [< L *subvenīre,* to come to aid, come to mind.]

sov. sovereign.

sov·er·eign (sŏv'ər-ən) *n.* **1.** The chief of state in a monarchy. **2.** A British gold coin worth one pound. —*adj.* **1.** Paramount; supreme. **2.** Having supreme rank or power. **3.** Independent: *a sovereign state.* **4.** Unsurpassed; excellent. [< VL *superānus.*]

---

sov•er•eign•ty (sŏv'ər-ən-tē) *n.* **1.** Supremacy of authority or rule. **2.** Royal rank, authority, or power. **3.** Complete independence and self-government.

so•vi•et (sō'vē-ĕt', sō-vyĕt', sŏv'ē-ĕt) *n.* In the Soviet Union, one of the popularly elected legislative assemblies. —*adj.* **1.** Of or pertaining to a soviet. **2. Soviet.** Of or pertaining to the U.S.S.R. [Russ *sovet*, "council."]

Soviet Union. See **Union of Soviet Socialist Republics.**

sow[1] (sō) *v.* **sowed, sown** (sōn) or **sowed, sowing. 1.** To scatter (seed) over the ground for growing. **2.** To strew with seed. **3.** To propagate. [< OE *sāwan.* See **sē-**.] —**sow'er** *n.*

sow[2] (sou) *n.* An adult female pig. [< OE *sugu.* See **su-**.]

sox. Alternate *pl.* of **sock**[1].

soy (soi) *n.* **1.** The soybean. **2.** Also **soy sauce.** A brown, salty liquid condiment made from fermented soybeans. [Jap *shō-yu.*]

soy•bean (soi'bēn') *n.* An Asian bean cultivated for its nutritious seeds.

SP shore patrol; shore police.

sp. 1. special. **2.** species. **3.** spelling.

Sp. Spain; Spanish.

spa (spä) *n.* **1.** A mineral spring. **2.** A resort area with such a spring. [< *Spa*, town in Belgium.]

space (spās) *n.* **1. a.** A set of elements or points satisfying specified geometric conditions. **b.** The three-dimensional field of everyday experience or its infinite extension. **2.** The expanse in which the solar system, stars, and galaxies exist; the universe. **3.** Broadly, the distance between two points or the area or volume between specified boundaries. **4.** A particular area. **5. a.** A period or interval of time. **b.** A little while: *for a space.* —*v.* **spaced, spacing.** To organize or arrange with spaces between. [< L *spatium*, space, distance.]

space•craft (spās'krăft, -kräft) *n.,pl.* -**craft.** A vehicle designed to be launched into space.

space•ship (spās'shĭp) *n.* A spacecraft.

space shuttle. A space vehicle designed to transport astronauts to and from between Earth and an orbiting space station.

space station. A large manned satellite designed for permanent orbit around Earth.

space suit. A protective pressure suit having an independent air supply and other devices designed to permit the wearer relatively free movement in space.

space-time (spās'tīm') *n.* The four-dimensional continuum of one temporal and three spatial coordinates, in which any event or physical object is located.

spa•cial. Variant of **spatial.**

spa•cious (spā'shəs) *adj.* **1.** Having much space; extensive. **2.** Vast in range or scope. —**spa'cious•ly** *adv.* —**spa'cious•ness** *n.*

spade[1] (spād) *n.* A digging tool having a thick handle and a flat blade. —*v.* **spaded, spading.** To dig with a spade. [< OE *spadu.* See **sphē-**.]

spade[2] (spād) *n.* Any of a suit of playing cards marked with a symbol in the shape of an inverted heart with a short stalk. [It *spada*, "broad sword."]

spa•ghet•ti (spə-gĕt'ē) *n.* An Italian pasta consisting of long strings of flour paste. [< It *spago*, string.]

Spain (spān). A country of W Europe. Pop. 30,903,000. Cap. Madrid.

Spain

spait. Variant of **spate.**

spake (spāk). *Archaic. p.t.* of **speak.**

span[1] (spăn) *n.* **1.** The extent or measure of space between two points or extremities. **2.** Something that extends over or across. **3.** *Archaic.* A unit of measure equal to the length of the fully extended hand from the tip of the thumb to the tip of the little finger, generally considered as nine inches. **4.** A period of time: *a life span.* —*v.* **spanned, spanning. 1.** To measure by or as by the fully extended hand. **2.** To reach or extend over or from one side to the other. [< OE. See **spen-**.]

span[2] (spăn) *n.* A pair of animals, such as oxen, matched in size, strength, or color. [MDu *spannen.*]

span[3] (spăn). *Archaic. p.t.* & *p.p.* of **spin.**

Span. Spanish.

span•gle (spăng'gəl) *n.* A small piece of bright, shiny metal used on a garment for decoration. —*v.* **-gled, -gling.** To adorn with or as with spangles. [< MDu *spange*, ornament, clasp.] —**span'gly** *adv.*

Span•iard (spăn'yərd) *n.* A native or inhabitant of Spain.

span•iel (spăn'yəl) *n.* A dog with drooping ears, short legs, and a silky, wavy coat. [< OF *espaignol*, "Spanish."]

Span•ish (spăn'ĭsh) *n.* **1.** The Romance language of Spain and Spanish America. **2. the Spanish.** The inhabitants of Spain. —**Span'ish** *adj.*

Spanish America. The parts of the W Hemisphere inhabited mostly by Spanish-speaking people.

Span•ish-A•mer•i•can (spăn'ĭsh-ə-mĕr'ĭ-kən) *n.* **1.** A native or inhabitant of a country of Spanish America. **2.** A person of Spanish descent who lives in the U.S. —**Span'ish-A•mer'i•can** *adj.*

Spanish moss. A plant of the SE U.S. and tropical America that grows on trees in long, threadlike tangled masses.

spank (spăngk) *v.* To slap on the buttocks with the open hand. —*n.* A slap on the buttocks.

ŏ paw, for/oi boy/ou out/ōō took/ōō coo/p pop/r run/s sauce/sh shy/t to/th thin/*th* the/
ŭ cut/ûr fur/v van/w wag/y yes/z size/zh vision/ə ago, item, edible, gallop, circus/

spank•ing (spăng′kĭng) *adj.* **1.** *Informal.* Exceptional of its kind in size, quality, or, esp., smartness. **2.** Bright; fast: *a spanking pace.* [?]

spar¹ (spär) *n.* A wooden or metal pole used to support sail rigging. [< ON *sperra,* beam.]

spar² (spär) *v.* **sparred, sparring. 1.** To go through the motions of boxing. **2.** To bandy words about in argument. [< OE *sperran,* to strike.]

spare (spâr) *v.* **spared, sparing. 1. a.** To treat mercifully. **b.** To refrain from harming or destroying. **2.** To save or relieve (one) from pain, trouble, etc. **3.** To use frugally. **4.** To do without. —*adj.* **sparer, sparest. 1. a.** Ready when needed. **b.** Extra: *spare cash.* **c.** Unoccupied: *spare time.* **2. a.** Without excess; meager. **b.** Thin or lean. —*n.* **1.** A replacement, as a tire, reserved for future use. **2.** The knocking down of all ten bowling pins with two successive rolls of the ball. [< OE *sparian* < Gmc **sparōjan.*] —**spare′ness** *n.*

spare•ribs (spâr′rĭbz′) *pl.n.* A cut of pork consisting usually of the lower ribs with the meat closely trimmed. [Inverted var of LG *ribbespêr.*]

spar•ing (spâr′ĭng) *adj.* Thrifty; frugal.

spark¹ (spärk) *n.* **1.** An incandescent particle, as one thrown off from a burning substance or resulting from friction; ember. **2. a.** A flash of light, esp. a flash produced by electric discharge. **b.** A short pulse or flow of electric current. **3.** Something, as a quality or factor, with latent potential; seed: *the spark of genius.* —*v.* **1.** To give off sparks. **2.** To set in motion; activate; ignite. [< OE *spearca, spœrca.*]

spark² (spärk) *n.* **1.** A young dandy. **2.** A suitor. —*v.* To court or woo.

spar•kle (spär′kəl) *v.* **-kled, -kling. 1.** To give off or reflect flashes of light; glitter. **2.** To effervesce. —*n.* **1.** A small spark or gleaming particle. **2.** Animation; vivacity. **3.** Effervescence. [< SPARK.] —**spar′kler** *n.*

spark plug. A device in an internal-combustion-engine cylinder that ignites the fuel mixture by means of an electric spark.

spar•row (spăr′ō) *n.* Any of various small birds with grayish or brownish plumage. [< OE *spearwa.* See **sper-³.**]

sparse (spärs) *adj.* **sparser, sparsest.** Growing or settled at widely spaced intervals; not dense or crowded. [L *sparsus,* pp of *spargere,* to strew, scatter.] —**spar′si•ty** (spär′sə-tē) *n.*

Spar•ta (spär′tə). A city-state of ancient Greece, renowned for military prowess and austerity.

Spar•tan (spärt′n) *adj.* **1.** Of or pertaining to Sparta or its people. **2.** Resembling the Spartans; austere. —*n.* **1.** A citizen of Sparta. **2.** Someone of Spartan character.

spasm (spăz′əm) *n.* **1.** A sudden, involuntary muscular contraction. **2.** Any sudden burst of activity, emotion, etc. [< Gk *spasmos* < *span,* to draw, pull.]

spas•mod•ic (spăz-mŏd′ĭk) *adj.* **1.** Pertaining to, affected by, or having the character of a spasm; convulsive. **2.** Happening intermittently; fitful. —**spas•mod′i•cal•ly** *adv.*

spas•tic (spăs′tĭk) *adj.* Continuously con- vulsing or contracting. —*n.* A person suffering from chronic spasms. [< Gk *spastikos* < *span,* to draw, pull.] —**spas′ti•cal•ly** *adv.*

spat¹ (spăt). *p.t.* & *p.p.* of **spit¹.**

spat² (spăt) *n.* A gaiter covering the upper shoe and ankle. [Short for earlier *spatterdash.*]

spat³ (spăt) *n.* A brief, petty quarrel. [?] —**spat** *v.* **(spatted, spatting).**

spate, spait (spāt) *n.* A sudden flood, rush, or outpouring. [ME *spate.*]

spa•tial (spā′shəl) *adj.* Also **spa•cial.** Of or involving space.

spat•ter (spăt′ər) *v.* **1.** To scatter in drops or small splashes. **2.** To splash. **3.** To fall with a splash or a splashing sound. —*n.* **1.** The act of spattering. **2.** A spot or stain of something spattered. **3.** A spattering sound.

spat•u•la (spăch′ə-lə) *n.* A small flat-bladed implement used to spread or mix plaster, paint, etc. [< Gk *spathē,* blade, broad sword.]

spav•in (spăv′ən) *n.* A disease affecting the hock joint of horses. [< OF *espavin.*] —**spav′-ined** *adj.*

spawn (spôn) *n.* **1.** The eggs of aquatic animals such as oysters, fish, or frogs. **2.** Offspring produced in large numbers. —*v.* **1.** To produce spawn. **2.** To produce offspring in large numbers. **3.** To bring forth. [< NF *espaundre,* to shed roe.]

spay (spā) *v.* To remove the ovaries of (a female animal). [< OF *espeer,* to cut with a sword.]

S.P.C.A. Society for the Prevention of Cruelty to Animals.

speak (spēk) *v.* **spoke, spoken, speaking. 1.** To utter words; talk. **2.** To express oneself. **3.** To deliver an address or lecture; make a speech. **4.** To converse in or be able to converse in (a language). [< OE *specan.* See **spreg-.**]

speak•eas•y (spēk′ē′zē) *n., pl.* **-ies.** *Slang.* A place for the illegal sale of alcoholic drinks.

speak•er (spē′kər) *n.* **1. a.** One who speaks. **b.** A spokesman. **2.** One who delivers a public speech. **3.** The presiding officer of a legislative assembly.

spear (spîr) *n.* **1.** A sharply pointed weapon with a long shaft. **2.** A sharp, barbed shaft for spearing fish. **3.** A slender stalk, as of asparagus. —*v.* To pierce or stab with or as with a spear. [< OE *spere.* See **sper-¹.**]

spear•mint (spîr′mĭnt′) *n.* A common mint widely used as flavoring.

spec. **1.** special. **2.** specification.

spe•cial (spĕsh′əl) *adj.* **1.** Surpassing what is common or usual; exceptional. **2.** Distinct among others of a kind. **3.** Peculiar to a specific person or thing. **4.** Having a specific function, application, etc. **5.** Esteemed: *special friends.* **6.** Additional; extra. —*n.* **1.** Something arranged or designed for a particular service or occasion. **2.** A featured attraction such as a reduced price: *a special on lamb chops.* **3.** A single television production of unusual importance. [< L *speciālis,* special, of a particular kind.] —**spe′cial•ly** *adv.*

spe•cial•ist (spĕsh′ə-lĭst) *n.* One who has devoted himself to a particular branch of study or research.

spe•cial•ize (spĕsh'ə-līz') v. -ized, -izing. 1. To train or employ oneself in a special study or activity. 2. To adapt to a specific environment or function. —**spe'cial•i•za'tion** n.

special relativity. The physical theory of space and time developed by Albert Einstein.

spe•cial•ty (spĕsh'əl-tē) n., pl. -ties. 1. A special pursuit, occupation, service, etc. 2. An aspect of medicine to which physicians confine their practice after certification of special knowledge by examination. 3. A special feature or characteristic.

spe•cie (spē'shē, -sē) n. Coined money; coin. [L (in) specie, (in) kind.]

spe•cies (spē'shēz, -sēz) n., pl. **species.** 1. Kind; type; sort. 2. a. A category of similar, closely related organisms capable of interbreeding. b. A member of such a category. [L speciēs, a seeing, likeness, kind, species.]

specif. specifically.

spe•cif•ic (spə-sĭf'ĭk) adj. 1. Explicitly set forth; definite. 2. Pertaining to, characterizing, or distinguishing a species. 3. Special, distinctive, or unique, as a quality or attribute. —n. 1. A distinct quality, statement, attribute, etc. 2. A remedy intended for a particular disorder. [< L speciēs, kind, SPECIES.] —**spe•cif'i•cal•ly** adv.

spec•i•fi•ca•tion (spĕs'ə-fĭ-kā'shən) n. 1. Often **specifications.** A detailed description of materials, dimensions, and workmanship for something to be built, installed, or manufactured. 2. A specified item.

specific gravity. The ratio of the mass of a solid or liquid to the mass of an equal volume of distilled water at 4°C, or of a gas to an equal volume of air or hydrogen under prescribed conditions of temperature and pressure.

spec•i•fy (spĕs'ə-fī') v. -fied, -fying. 1. To state explicitly. 2. To include in a specification.

spec•i•men (spĕs'ə-mən) n. An individual, item, or part representative of a class or whole; example. [L, mark, token.]

spe•cious (spē'shəs) adj. Seemingly fair, attractive, sound, or true, but actually not so; deceptive. [< L speciōsus, good-looking.] —**spe'cious•ly** adv. —**spe'cious•ness** n.

speck (spĕk) n. 1. A small spot, mark, or discoloration. 2. A small bit or particle. —v. To mark with specks. [< OE specca.]

speck•le (spĕk'əl) n. A speck or small spot, esp. a natural marking. —v. -led, -ling. To mark or cover with or as with speckles. [MDu spekkel.]

spec•ta•cle (spĕk'tə-kəl) n. 1. A public performance or display. 2. A marvel or curiosity. 3. **spectacles.** A pair of eyeglasses. [< L spectāre, to look at.]

spec•tac•u•lar (spĕk-tăk'yə-lər) adj. Of the nature of a spectacle; unusual or sensational.

spec•ta•tor (spĕk'tā-tər) n. One who views an event; an observer or onlooker. [< L spectāre, look at.]

spec•ter (spĕk'tər) n. Also chiefly Brit. **spec•tre.** A phantom; apparition. [< L spectrum, appearance, image.]

spec•tral (spĕk'trəl) adj. 1. Of or resembling a

specter. 2. Of, pertaining to, or produced by a spectrum.

spectro–. comb. form. Spectrum.

spec•tro•scope (spĕk'trə-skōp') n. Phys. Any of various instruments for resolving and observing or recording spectra. —**spec'tro•scop'ic** (-skōp'ĭk), **spec'tro•scop'i•cal** adj. —**spec'tro•scop'i•cal•ly** adv.

spec•trum (spĕk'trəm) n., pl. **-tra** (-trə) or **-trums.** 1. The distribution of a characteristic of a physical system or phenomenon, esp. the distribution of energy emitted by a radiant source, as by an incandescent body, arranged in order of wavelengths. 2. A broad sequence or range of related qualities, ideas, etc. [L, appearance, image, form.]

spec•u•late (spĕk'yə-lāt') v. -lated, -lating. 1. To meditate on a given subject; reflect. 2. To engage in risky business transactions on the chance of great profit. [L speculārī, to spy out, watch, observe.] —**spec'u•la'tion** n. —**spec'u•la•tive** (-lə-tĭv, -lā'tĭv) adj.

speech (spēch) n. 1. The faculty or act of speaking. 2. Conversation; vocal communication. 3. A talk or public address. 4. A person's habitual manner of speaking. 5. The language or dialect of a nation or region. [< OE spēc, sprǣc. See spreg-.]

speech•less (spēch'lĭs) adj. 1. Lacking the faculty of speech. 2. Temporarily unable to speak. —**speech'less•ly** adv.

speed (spēd) n. 1. Rate of motion. 2. A rate of performance; swiftness of action. 3. Rapid movement. 4. A gear in a motor vehicle. 5. a. The sensitivity of a film, plate, or paper to light. b. The capacity of a lens to accumulate light. c. The time in which a camera shutter exposes film. —v. **sped** (spĕd) or **speeded, speeding.** 1. To move rapidly. 2. To accelerate; increase the speed of. 3. To drive at a high or illegal rate of speed. 4. To help to succeed; aid. [< OE spēd, success, prosperity. See spēi-.] —**speed'y** adj.

speed•ing (spē'dĭng) adj. Moving with speed. —n. The act of driving faster than is allowed by law.

speed•om•e•ter (spē-dŏm'ə-tər, spī-) n. An instrument for indicating speed or distance traveled.

speed•way (spēd'wā') n. 1. A course for automobile racing. 2. A road designed for fast-moving traffic.

speed•well (spēd'wĕl') n. A low-growing plant with small blue flowers.

spell¹ (spĕl) v. **spelled** or **spelt, spelling.** 1. To name or write in order the letters constituting (a word or part of a word). 2. To mean; signify. [< OF espeller, to read out.]

spell² (spĕl) n. 1. An incantational word or formula. 2. Compelling attraction; fascination. 3. A bewitched state. [< OE, story, fable. See spel-².]

spell³ (spĕl) n. 1. A short, indefinite period of time. 2. Informal. A period of weather of a particular kind. 3. A short turn of work. 4. Informal. A period of illness or indisposition. —v. To relieve (someone) from work temporarily. [< OE spelian, to substitute.]

ô paw, for/oi boy/ou out/ŏŏ took/ōō coo/p pop/r run/s sauce/sh shy/t to/th thin/*th* the/ ŭ cut/ûr fur/v van/w wag/y yes/z size/zh vision/ə ago, item, edible, gallop, circus/

spell•bind (spĕl'bīnd') *v.* To hold under or as if under a spell; enchant.

spell•bind•er (spĕl'bīn'dər) *n.* One who holds others spellbound.

spell•bound (spĕl'bound') *adj.* Entranced; fascinated.

spell•er (spĕl'ər) *n.* 1. One who spells words. 2. A textbook to teach spelling.

spell•ing (spĕl'ĭng) *n.* 1. The forming of words with letters. 2. The way in which a word is spelled.

spelt (spĕlt). Alternate *p.t.* & *p.p.* of **spell**[1].

spe•lun•ker (spĭ-lŭng'kər, spē'lŭng-kər) *n.* One who explores and studies caves. [< Gk *spēlunx*, cave.]

spend (spĕnd) *v.* **spent, spending.** 1. To pay out (money). 2. To exhaust; wear out. 3. To pass (time). 4. To waste; squander. [< L *expendere*, to EXPEND, and < OF *despendre*, to dispend.] —**spend'er** *n.*

spending money. Cash for small personal needs.

spend•thrift (spĕnd'thrĭft') *n.* One who spends money wastefully. —*adj.* Wasteful or extravagant.

spent (spĕnt). *p.t.* & *p.p.* of **spend.** —*adj.* 1. Consumed; used up; expended. 2. Passed; over with. 3. Depleted of energy or strength; exhausted.

sperm (spûrm) *n.* 1. A male gamete or reproductive cell; spermatozoon. 2. The male fluid of fertilization; semen. [< Gk *sperma*.] —**sper•mat'ic** (spûr-măt'ĭk) *adj.*

spermato–. *comb. form.* 1. Sperm. 2. Seed.

sper•ma•to•gen•e•sis (spûr-măt'ə-jĕn'ə-sĭs, spûr'mə-tə-) *n.* The generation of sperm.

sper•ma•to•zo•on (spûr-măt'ə-zō'ŏn, spûr'mə-tə-zō'ŏn) *n., pl.* **-zoa** (-zō'ə). The fertilizing gamete of a male animal, usually a long nucleated cell with a thin, motile tail.

spew (spyōō) *v.* 1. To vomit. 2. To force out in a stream; eject. [< OE *spīwan* and *spīowan*. See **spyeu-**.]

sphe•noid (sfē'noid') *n.* The **sphenoid bone.** —*adj.* Also **sphe•noid•al** (sfē-noid'l). 1. Wedge-shaped. 2. Of or pertaining to the sphenoid bone.

sphenoid bone. A compound bone situated at the base of the skull.

sphere (sfîr) *n.* 1. A three-dimensional surface, all points of which are equidistant from a fixed point. 2. A spherical object or figure. 3. A planet, star, or other heavenly body. 4. The sky, appearing as a hemisphere to an observer. 5. The environment in which one exists or acts; range. [< Gk *sphaira*.] —**spher'i•cal** (sfîr'ĭ-kəl, sfĕr'-) *adj.* —**spher'i•cal•ly** *adv.* —**sphe•ric'i•ty** (sfîr-ĭs'ə-tē) *n.*

–sphere. *comb. form.* The shape of a sphere: **bathysphere.**

sphinc•ter (sfĭngk'tər) *n.* A ringlike muscle that normally maintains constriction of a bodily passage or orifice and relaxes as required by normal physiological functioning. [< Gk *sphinktēr*, that which binds tight.]

sphinx (sfĭnks) *n., pl.* **sphinxes** or **sphinges** (sfĭn'jēz'). 1. An ancient Egyptian figure with the body of a lion and the head of a man, ram,

or hawk. 2. *Gk.Myth.* A winged monster that destroyed all who could not answer its riddle. 3. Any mysterious or enigmatic person. [< Gk *Sphinx*.]

spice (spīs) *n.* 1. An aromatic or pungent plant substance, as cinnamon or pepper, used as flavoring. 2. Something that adds zest or flavor. [< LL *speciēs*, goods, spices.] —**spice** *v.* **(spiced, spicing).** —**spic'i•ly** *adv.* —**spic'i•ness** *n.* —**spic'y** *adj.*

spick-and-span (spĭk'ən-spăn') *adj.* 1. Neat and clean. 2. Brand-new. [Short for obs *spick and spannew.*]

spic•ule (spĭk'yōōl) *n.* A small needlelike structure or part. [L *spīculum.*] —**spic'u•lar,** **spic'u•late** (-yə-lĭt, -lāt') *adj.*

spi•der (spī'dər) *n.* 1. Any of various eight-legged arachnids that have a body divided into two parts and that spin webs to trap insects. 2. A long-handled frying pan, often with short legs. [< OE *spīthra.*] —**spi'der•y** *adj.*

spig•ot (spĭg'ət) *n.* 1. A faucet. 2. The vent plug of a cask. [ME.]

spike[1] (spīk) *n.* 1. A heavy nail. 2. A sharp-pointed projection. —*v.* **spiked, spiking.** 1. To secure or provide with a spike. 2. To impale, pierce, or injure with a spike. 3. To put an end to; thwart; block. 4. *Slang.* To add alcoholic liquor to. [ME *spyk.*]

spike[2] (spīk) *n.* 1. An ear of grain. 2. A long cluster of stalkless or nearly stalkless flowers. [< L *spīca*, point, ear of grain.]

spike•nard (spīk'närd') *n.* An aromatic plant from which a fragrant ointment was obtained in ancient times.

spill (spĭl) *v.* **spilled** or **spilt** (spĭlt), **spilling.** 1. To cause or allow to run or fall out of a container. 2. To shed (blood). 3. To cause to fall. —*n.* 1. An act of spilling. 2. The amount spilled. 3. A fall, as from a horse. [< OE *spillan*, to destroy, spill (blood). See **spel-**[1].]

spill•way (spĭl'wā') *n.* A channel for reservoir overflow.

spin (spĭn) *v.* **spun, spinning.** 1. To draw out and twist fibers into thread. 2. To form thread or yarn in this manner. 3. To form (a thread, web, etc.) by extruding a viscous substance. 4. To relate, esp. imaginatively: *spin a story.* 5. To twirl. 6. To rotate rapidly; whirl. —*n.* 1. A swift whirling motion. 2. A state of mental confusion. 3. A short excursion in a vehicle. 4. The flight condition of an aircraft in a nose-down, spiraling, stalled descent. [< OE *spinnan.* See **spen-**.] —**spin'ner** *n.*

spin•ach (spĭn'ĭch) *n.* A plant cultivated for its dark-green edible leaves. [< Ar *isfānākh.*]

spi•nal (spī'nəl) *adj.* 1. Of, pertaining to, or situated near the spine or spinal cord. 2. Resembling a spine or spiny part. —*n.* A spinal anesthetic. —**spi'nal•ly** *adv.*

spinal canal. The canal formed by the successive openings in the vertebrae through which the spinal cord and its membranes pass.

spinal column. The columnar assemblage of vertebrae extending from the cranium to the coccyx or the end of the tail, encasing the spinal cord and forming the supporting axis of the body; the backbone.

ă pat/ā ate/âr care/ä bar/b bib/ch chew/d deed/ĕ pet/ē be/f fit/g gag/h hat/hw what/
ĭ pit/ī pie/îr pier/j judge/k kick/l lid, fatal/m mum/n no, sudden/ng sing/ŏ pot/ō go/

spinal cord. The part of the central nervous system contained within the spinal canal.

spin·dle (spĭnd′l) *n.* **1.** A stick or rod used in spinning for twisting or winding thread. **2.** Any of various slender mechanical parts that revolve or serve as axes for larger revolving parts, as in a lock or axle. —*v.* **-dled, -dling. 1.** To perforate on or as on the spike of a spindle. **2.** To grow into a thin, elongated, or weakly form. [< OE *spinel,* rod of a spinning wheel. See **spen-**.]

spin·dly (spĭnd′lē) *adj.* **-dlier, -dliest.** Also **spind·ling** (-lĭng). Long, thin, and often weak.

spine (spīn) *n.* **1.** The spinal column of a vertebrate. **2.** A sharp-pointed projecting plant or animal part; a thorn, prickle, or quill. [< L *spina,* thorn, prickle, spine.] —**spin′y** *adj.*

spine·less (spīn′lĭs) *adj.* **1.** Lacking a spine or spines. **2.** Lacking in courage or will power. —**spine′less·ness** *n.*

spin·et (spĭn′ĭt) *n.* A small piano or harpsichord. [< It *spinetta.*]

spin·ning (spĭn′ĭng) *n.* The process of making fibrous material into yarn or thread. —*adj.* Of, for, or used in spinning.

spinning jenny. An early form of spinning machine having several spindles.

spinning wheel. An apparatus for making yarn or thread, consisting of a foot- or hand-driven wheel and a single spindle.

spin-off (spĭn′ôf′, -ŏf′) *n.* An object, product, etc., derived from a larger, more or less unrelated enterprise.

spin·ster (spĭn′stər) *n.* A woman who has remained single beyond the conventional age for marrying. [ME *spinnester,* "one who spins."] —**spin′ster·hood′** *n.*

spi·ral (spī′rəl) *n.* **1.** The path in a plane of a point moving around a fixed center at an increasing or decreasing distance. **2.** The path of a point moving parallel to and about a central axis; helix. **3.** Something having the form of such a curve. **4.** A continuously accelerating increase or decrease. —*adj.* **1.** Of or resembling a spiral. **2.** Coiling in a constantly changing plane; helical. **3.** Circling around to form a series of constantly changing planes, as a spring. —*v.* **-raled** or **-ralled, -raling** or **-ralling. 1.** To take a spiral form or course. **2.** To rise or fall with steady acceleration. [< L *spira,* coil.] —**spi′ral·ly** *adv.*

spire¹ (spīr) *n.* **1.** The top part or point of something that tapers upward. **2.** A pointed formation or structure, as a steeple. [< OE *spir,* slender stalk. See **spei-**.]

spire² (spīr) *n.* A spiral, esp. a single turn of a spiral; whorl. [< Gk *speira.*]

spir·it (spĭr′ĭt) *n.* **1.** The vital principle or animating force within living beings; the soul. **2. Spirit.** The Holy Ghost. **3.** A supernatural being. **4.** An individual. **5.** Mood or emotional state. **6.** Vivacity and courage. **7.** Loyalty or dedication. **8.** The real sense or significance of something. **9.** Often **spirits.** An alcohol solution of an essential or volatile substance. **10. spirits.** An alcoholic beverage. —*v.* To carry off mysteriously or secretly. [< L *spiritus,* breath, breath of a god, inspiration.]

spir·it·ed (spĭr′ĭ-tĭd) *adj.* Energetic; vigorous.

spir·it·less (spĭr′ĭt-lĭs) *adj.* Lacking energy or enthusiasm. —**spir′it·less·ly** *adv.*

spir·i·tu·al (spĭr′ĭ-chōō-əl) *adj.* **1.** Of, relating to, or consisting of spirit; not tangible or material. **2.** Sacred. **3.** Ecclesiastical. —*n.* A religious folk song of American Negro origin. —**spir′i·tu·al′i·ty** *n.* —**spir′i·tu·al·ly** *adv.*

spir·i·tu·al·ism (spĭr′ĭ-chōō-ə-lĭz′əm, -chə-lĭz′-əm) *n.* The belief that the dead communicate with the living. —**spir′i·tu·al·ist** *n.* —**spir′i·tu·al·is′tic** *adj.*

spir·i·tu·ous (spĭr′ĭ-chōō-əs) *adj.* Having the nature of or containing alcohol.

spi·ro·chete (spī′rə-kēt′) *n.* Any of various slender, twisted microorganisms, including those causing syphilis and other diseases. [< L *spira,* coil + Gk *khaitē,* long hair.] —**spi′ro·che′tal** *adj.*

spi·roid (spī′roid) *adj.* Having resemblance to a spiral.

spit¹ (spĭt) *n.* **1.** Saliva, esp. when expectorated; spittle. **2.** The act of spitting. —*v.* **spat** or **spit, spitting. 1.** To eject from the mouth. **2.** To eject as if by spitting. [< OE *spittan.* See **spyeu-**.]

spit² (spĭt) *n.* **1.** A pointed rod on which meat is impaled for broiling. **2.** A narrow point of land extending into a body of water. [< OE *spitu.* See **spei-**.]

spite (spīt) *n.* Malicious ill will prompting an urge to hurt or humiliate. —**in spite of.** Regardless of; despite. —*v.* **spited, spiting.** To treat with malice. [ME, insult, ill will.]

spite·ful (spīt′fəl) *adj.* Filled with spite; vindictive. —**spite′ful·ly** *adv.*

spit·tle (spĭt′l) *n.* Spit; saliva. [< OE *spātl.* See **spyeu-**.]

spit·toon (spĭ-tōōn′) *n.* A bowl-shaped vessel for spit. [< SPIT¹.]

splash (splăsh) *v.* **1.** To dash or scatter (a liquid) about in masses. **2.** To dash liquid upon. **3.** To fall into or move through liquid with the sound of splashing. —*n.* **1.** The act or sound of splashing. **2.** A flying mass of liquid. **3.** A marking produced by or as if by scattered liquid. [Var of PLASH.] —**splash′er** *n.*

splash·down (splăsh′doun′) *n.* The landing of a missile or spacecraft on water.

splat¹ (splăt) *n.* A slat of wood, as one in the middle of a chair back. [?]

splat² (splăt) *n.* A slapping noise. [?]

splat·ter (splăt′ər) *v.* To spatter with splashes of liquid. —*n.* A splash of liquid. [Perh a blend of SPLASH and SPATTER.]

splay (splā) *adj.* **1.** Spread or turned out. **2.** Clumsy or clumsily formed; awkward. —*v.* **1.** To spread out or apart. **2.** To slant or slope. [< ME *displayen,* to display.]

splay·foot (splā′fŏŏt′) *n.* A deformity characterized by abnormally flat and turned-out feet. —**splay′foot′ed** *adj.*

spleen (splēn) *n.* **1.** A visceral organ composed of a white pulp of lymphatic nodules and tissue and a red pulp of venous tissue, functioning as a blood filter and to store blood. **2.** Ill temper. [< Gk *splēn.*]

splen·did (splĕn′dĭd) *adj.* **1.** Brilliant; radiant.

---

2. Magnificent; grand. **3.** Very satisfying; praiseworthy. [< L *splendēre*, to shine.] —**splen'did•ly** *adv.*

splen•dor (splĕn'dər) *n.* Also *Brit.* **splen•dour. 1.** Great light or luster; brilliance. **2.** Magnificence; grandeur.

splice (splīs) *v.* **spliced, splicing. 1.** To join (pieces of material) at the ends. **2.** To join (pieces of wood) by overlapping and binding at the ends. —*n.* A joint made by splicing. [Prob < MDu *splissen*.] —**splic'er** *n.*

splint (splĭnt) *n.* **1.** A rigid device used to prevent motion of a joint or the ends of a fractured bone. **2.** A thin, flexible wooden strip, as used in making baskets. [ME, small strip of metal, splint.]

splin•ter (splĭn'tər) *n.* A sharp, slender piece, as of wood, bone, glass, etc., split or broken off from a main body. —*v.* To split or break into splinters. [< MDu.] —**splin'ter•y** *adj.*

split (splĭt) *v.* **split, splitting. 1.** To divide, esp. into lengthwise sections. **2.** To break, burst, or rip apart with force. **3.** To disunite. **4.** To divide and share. **5.** To separate into layers or sections. —*n.* **1.** The act or result of splitting. **2.** A breach or rupture in a group. —*adj.* **1.** Divided or separated. **2.** Fissured longitudinally; cleft. [Du *splitten*.]

split•ting (splĭt'ĭng) *adj.* **1.** Acute; piercing. **2.** Very severe, as a headache.

splotch (splŏch) *n.* An irregularly shaped stain, spot, or blotch. [Perh a blend of SPOT and BLOTCH.] —**splotch** *v.* —**splotch'y** *adj.*

splurge (splûrj) *n.* An extravagant expense or luxury. [?] —**splurge** *v.* (**splurged, splurging**).

splut•ter (splŭt'ər) *v.* **1.** To make a spitting sound. **2.** To speak hastily and incoherently. —*n.* A spluttering noise. [Perh var of SPUTTER.] —**splut'ter•er** *n.*

spoil (spoil) *v.* **spoiled** or **spoilt** (spoilt), **spoiling. 1.** To damage. **2.** To impair the completeness, perfection, or unity of. **3.** To disrupt; disturb. **4.** To overindulge so as to harm the character. **5.** *Obs.* To plunder; pillage. **6.** To become tainted or rotten; decay, as food. —*n.* **spoils. 1.** Goods or property seized by force; plunder. **2.** Political patronage enjoyed by a successful party or candidate. [< L *spolium*, hide torn from an animal, booty.] —**spoil'age** *n.* —**spoil'er** *n.*

Spo•kane (spō-kǎn') A city of E Washington. Pop. 182,000.

spoke[1] (spōk) *n.* **1.** One of the rods that connect the hub and rim of a wheel. **2.** A rung of a ladder. [< OE *spāca*. See spei-.]

spoke[2] (spōk). *p.t.* & *archaic p.p.* of **speak**.

spo•ken (spō'kən). *p.p.* of **speak**.

spokes•man (spōks'mən) *n.* One who speaks on behalf of others. [< obs *spoke*, "speaking" + MAN.]

spo•li•a•tion (spō'lē-ā'shən) *n.* The act of despoiling or plundering. [< L *spoliāre*, to despoil.] —**spo'li•a'tor** *n.*

sponge (spŭnj) *n.* **1.** A primitive marine animal with a porous skeleton. **2.** The absorbent, fibrous skeletal part of such an animal, used for bathing, cleaning, etc. **3.** A substance having spongelike qualities. **4.** A gauze pad used

to absorb blood and other fluids, as in surgery. —*v.* **sponged, sponging. 1.** To wipe or clean with a sponge. **2.** *Informal.* To live by relying on another's generosity. [< Gk *sphongos*, sponge.] —**spong'er** *n.* —**spon'gy** *adj.*

spon•sor (spŏn'sər) *n.* **1.** One who vouches or assumes responsibility for a person or thing. **2.** A godparent. **3.** A business enterprise that pays for a radio or television program, usually in return for advertising time. [< L *spondēre*, to make a solemn pledge.] —**spon'sor** *v.* —**spon'sor•ship'** *n.*

spon•ta•ne•ous (spŏn-tā'nē-əs) *adj.* **1.** Happening or arising without external cause. **2.** Voluntary; unpremeditated. **3.** Natural and unstudied in manner or behavior. [< L *sponte*, of one's own accord, out of free will.] —**spon'ta•ne'i•ty** (-tə-nē'ə-tē), **spon•ta'ne•ous•ness** *n.* —**spon•ta'ne•ous•ly** *adv.*

spontaneous combustion. Ignition in a thermally isolated substance, as oily rags or hay, caused by a localized heat-increasing reaction between the oxidant and fuel.

spoof (spoof) *n.* **1.** A hoax. **2.** A light parody. [< *spoof*, a card game characterized by nonsense and hoaxing.] —**spoof** *v.*

spook (spook). *Informal. n.* A ghost; specter. —*v.* **1.** To haunt. **2.** To frighten; startle. [< MDu *spoocke*.] —**spook'y** *adj.*

spool (spool) *n.* A small cylinder upon which wire, thread, or string is wound. [< MDu *spoele*.]

spoon (spoon) *n.* **1.** A utensil consisting of a shallow bowl on a handle, used in preparing or eating food. **2.** A shiny, curved metallic fishing lure. —*v.* To lift, scoop up, or carry with or as with a spoon. [< OE *spōn*, chip of wood. See sphē-.]

spoon•er•ism (spoo'nə-rĭz'əm) *n.* An unintentional transposition of sounds in spoken language, as *Let me sew you to your sheet* for *Let me show you to your seat.* [< W.A. *Spooner* (1844–1930), English clergyman noted for such slips.]

spoor (spoor) *n.* The track or trail of an animal. [< MDu.]

spo•rad•ic (spô-rǎd'ĭk, spō-) *adj.* Occurring at irregular intervals. [< Gk *sporas*, scattered, dispersed.] —**spo•rad'i•cal•ly** *adv.*

spore (spôr, spōr) *n.* A usually single-celled reproductive structure or resting stage, as of a fern, fungus, or bacterium. [< Gk *spora*, a sowing, seed.]

sport (spôrt, spōrt) *n.* **1.** An active pastime or diversion. **2.** A specific diversion, as athletics or hunting. **3.** Light mockery. **4.** One known for the manner of his acceptance of rules or a difficult situation: *a poor sport.* **5.** *Informal.* One who lives a gay, extravagant life. **6.** *Archaic.* Amorous dalliance; lovemaking. —*v.* **1.** To play; frolic. **2.** To joke or trifle. **3.** To display or show off. —*adj.* Of, relating to, or appropriate for sports. [ME *sporten*, to amuse, divert.]

spor•tive (spôr'tĭv, spōr'-) *adj.* **1.** Full of fun; frisky. **2.** Of or interested in sports.

sports•man (spôrts'mən, spōrts'-) *n.* **1.** A participant in sports. **2.** One who abides by rules and accepts victory or defeat graciously. **—sports'wom'an** *fem.n.*

sports•man•ship (spôrts'mən-shĭp', spôrts'-) *n.* The qualities and conduct befitting a sportsman.

sports•wear (spôrts'wâr', spôrts'-) *n.* Clothes for casual wear.

sport•y (spôr'tē, spôr'-) *adj.* -ier, -iest. *Informal.* 1. Appropriate to sport. 2. Casual in style, as clothes. 3. Gay; carefree.

spot (spŏt) *n.* 1. A particular place of relatively small and definite limits. 2. A mark on a surface differing sharply in color from the surroundings, esp. a stain or blot. 3. A position; location. 4. *Informal.* A situation, esp. a difficult one. 5. A blot on one's reputation. *—v.* **spotted, spotting.** 1. To mark or become marked with a spot or spots. 2. To detect; locate; discern. [ME.] **—spot'less** *adj.*

spot•light (spŏt'lĭt') *n.* 1. A strong beam of light that illuminates only a small area, as on a stage. 2. A lamp that produces such a light. 3. Public notoriety.

spot•ter (spŏt'ər) *n.* One that looks for and reports something, as a military lookout.

spot•ty (spŏt'ē) *adj.* -tier, -tiest. 1. Having or marked with spots. 2. Lacking consistency; uneven. **—spot'ti•ness** *n.*

spouse (spous, spouz) *n.* One's husband or wife. [< L *spōnsus,* betrothed (person), betrothal.]

spout (spout) *v.* 1. To gush forth or discharge in a rapid stream or in spurts. 2. To speak volubly and pompously. *—n.* 1. A pipe through which liquid is released. 2. A continuous stream of liquid. [ME *spouten.*]

spp. species (plural).

sprain (sprān) *n.* 1. A painful wrenching or laceration of the ligaments of a joint. 2. The resulting condition. *—v.* To cause a sprain in (a muscle or joint). [Perh < OF *espraindre,* to squeeze out, strain.]

sprang (sprăng). *p.t.* of **spring.**

sprat (sprăt) *n.* A small herring or similar fish. [< OE *sprott.*]

sprawl (sprôl) *v.* 1. To sit or lie with the limbs spread out awkwardly. 2. To spread out awkwardly, as handwriting. [< OE *sprēawlian.* See *sper-².*] **—sprawl** *n.* **—sprawl'er** *n.*

spray¹ (sprā) *n.* 1. Liquid moving in a mass of dispersed droplets, as from a wave. 2. a. A fine jet of liquid discharged from a pressurized container. b. Such a pressurized container; an atomizer. *—v.* 1. To disperse (a liquid) in a spray. 2. To apply a spray to (a surface). [< MDu *spraeyen,* to sprinkle.] **—spray'er** *n.*

spray² (sprā) *n.* A small leafy or flowery branch. [< OE *sprǣg.*]

spread (sprĕd) *v.* 1. To open or be extended more fully; stretch. 2. To separate or become separated more widely; move farther apart. 3. To distribute over a surface in a layer; apply. 4. To extend or cause to extend over a considerable area; distribute widely. 5. To become or cause to become widely known; disseminate. *—n.* 1. The act of spreading. 2. An open area of land; expanse. 3. The extent or limit to which something is or can be spread; a

range. 4. A cloth covering for a bed, table, or other piece of furniture. 5. *Informal.* An abundant meal laid out on a table. 6. A food to be spread on bread or crackers. 7. Printed matter running across two or more columns in a magazine, newspaper, etc. [< OE *sprǣdan.* See *sper-².*] **—spread'er** *n.*

spree (sprē) *n.* 1. A gay, lively outing. 2. A drinking bout. 3. An overindulgence in some activity. [Perh Scot *spreath,* cattle taken as booty, raid, plunder.]

sprig (sprĭg) *n.* A small twig or shoot. [ME *sprigg.*]

spright•ly (sprīt'lē) *adj.* -lier, -liest. Animated; full of life. [< SPRITE.] **—spright'li•ness** *n.*

spring (sprĭng) *v.* **sprang** or **sprung, sprung, springing.** 1. To move upward or forward suddenly; leap. 2. To emerge suddenly. 3. To shift position suddenly. 4. To arise from a source; develop. 5. To be or become warped or bent, as wood. 6. To actuate: *spring a trap.* 7. To present suddenly: *spring a surprise. —n.* 1. An elastic device, as a coil of wire, that regains its original shape after being compressed or extended. 2. Elasticity; resilience. 3. The act of springing. 4. A natural fountain or flow of water. 5. A source or origin. 6. The season between winter and summer. [< OE *springan.* See *spergh-*.] **—spring'y** *adj.*

spring•board (sprĭng'bôrd', -bôrd') *n.* A flexible board used by gymnasts, divers, etc.

Spring•field (sprĭng'fēld'). 1. The capital of Illinois. Pop. 90,000. 2. A city in SW Massachusetts. Pop. 162,000.

spring•time (sprĭng'tīm') *n.* The season of spring.

sprin•kle (sprĭng'kəl) *v.* -kled, -kling. To scatter or release in drops or small particles, as water. *—n.* A light rainfall. [ME *sprenklen.*] **—sprin'kler** *n.*

sprint (sprĭnt) *n.* A short race run at top speed. *—v.* To run at top speed. [< Scand.] **—sprint'er** *n.*

sprite (sprīt) *n.* A small or elusive supernatural being; an elf or pixie. [< L *spīritus,* SPIRIT.]

sprock•et (sprŏk'ĭt) *n.* Any of various toothlike projections arranged on a wheel rim to engage the links of a chain. [?]

sprout (sprout) *v.* To begin to grow; produce or appear as a bud, shoot, or new growth. *—n.* A young plant growth, as a bud or shoot. [< OE *sprūtan.* See *sper-².*]

spruce¹ (sprōōs) *n.* 1. A cone-bearing evergreen tree with short, pointed needles and soft wood. 2. The wood of such a tree. [Short for earlier *Spruce fir,* "Prussian fir."]

spruce² (sprōōs) *adj.* **sprucer, sprucest.** Having a neat or dapper appearance. *—v.* **spruced, sprucing.** To make or become spruce: *He spruced himself up for the evening.*

sprue (sprōō) *n.* A chronic, chiefly tropical disease characterized by diarrhea, emaciation, and anemia. [Du *spruw.*]

sprung (sprŭng). *p.p. & alternate p.t.* of **spring.**

spry (sprī) *adj.* **sprier** or **spryer, spriest** or **spryest.** Active; nimble; lively. [Perh < Scand.]

spud (spŭd) *n. Slang.* A potato. [ME *spudde,* short knife.]

---

spume (spyo͞om) *n.* Foam or froth on a liquid. [< L *spūma*.]

spun (spŭn). *p.t.* & *p.p.* of **spin**.

spunk (spŭngk) *n. Informal.* Spirit; mettle. [Scot Gael *spong*, tinder, sponge.] —**spunk′i-ness** *n.* —**spunk′y** *adj.*

spur (spûr) *n.* 1. One of a pair of spiked devices attached to a rider's heels and used to urge the horse forward. 2. An incentive or goad. 3. A narrow pointed projection, as on the back of a bird's leg or on certain flowers. 4. A lateral ridge projecting from a mountain or mountain range. —*v.* **spurred, spurring.** 1. To urge (a horse) on by the use of spurs. 2. To incite; stimulate. [< OE *spora, spura.* See **spher-**.] —**spurred** *adj.*

spurge (spûrj) *n.* Any of various plants with milky juice and small flowers. [< OF *espurge*, "purge."]

spu-ri-ous (spyo͞or′ē-əs) *adj.* Lacking authenticity; counterfeit; false. [< L *spurius*, illegitimate.] —**spu′ri-ous-ly** *adv.*

spurn (spûrn) *v.* To reject or refuse disdainfully; scorn. [< OE *spurnan, spornan.* See **spher-**.] —**spurn′er** *n.*

spurt (spûrt) *n.* 1. A sudden and forcible gush, as of water. 2. Any sudden burst of activity. —*v.* 1. To burst forth. 2. To force out in a burst; squirt. [< OE *spryttan*, to sprout. See **sper-²**.]

sput-nik (spŭt′nĭk, spo͞ot′-) *n.* Any of the artificial Earth satellites launched by the U.S.S.R. [Russ *sputnik (zemlyi)*, "fellow traveler (of Earth)."]

sput-ter (spŭt′ər) *v.* 1. a. To spit out small particles in short bursts. b. To make the sporadic coughing noise characteristic of such activity. 2. To stammer. [< Du *sputteren*.] —**sput′ter** *n.* —**sput′ter-er** *n.*

spu-tum (spyo͞o′təm) *n., pl.* **-ta** (-tə). Expectorated matter, including saliva, substances from the respiratory tract, and foreign material. [< L *spuere*, to spit.]

spy (spī) *n., pl.* **spies.** 1. A clandestine agent employed to obtain intelligence. 2. One who secretly watches another or others. —*v.* **spied, spying.** 1. To keep under surveillance with hostile intent. 2. To catch sight of; see. 3. To investigate; pry: *spying into their activities.* [< OF *espier*, to spy, watch.]

spy-glass (spī′glăs′, -gläs′) *n.* A small telescope.

sq. 1. squadron. 2. square.

squab (skwŏb) *n.* A young pigeon. [Prob < Scand.]

squab-ble (skwŏb′əl) *n.* A trivial quarrel. [Prob < Scand.] —**squab′ble** *v.* (-bled, -bling).

squad (skwŏd) *n.* 1. A small group of persons organized for a specific purpose. 2. *Mil.* The smallest unit of personnel. [< OSpan *escuadra*, "square," "square formation (of troops)."]

squad car. A police patrol car connected by radiotelephone with headquarters.

squad-ron (skwŏd′rən) *n.* 1. A group of naval vessels constituting two or more divisions of a fleet. 2. An armored cavalry unit. 3. The basic air force tactical unit, consisting of two or

more flights. [It *squadrone*, "square formation (of troops)."]

squal-id (skwŏl′ĭd) *adj.* 1. Having a dirty or wretched appearance. 2. Morally repulsive; sordid. [< L *squālus*, scabby, filthy.] —**squal′id-ly** *adv.* —**squal′id-ness** *n.*

squall¹ (skwôl) *n.* A loud, harsh outcry. [Prob < Scand.] —**squall** *v.*

squall² (skwôl) *n.* A brief, sudden, and violent windstorm, often with rain or snow. [Prob < Scand.] —**squall′y** *adj.*

squal-or (skwŏl′ər) *n.* The state or quality of being squalid.

squan-der (skwŏn′dər) *v.* To spend wastefully or extravagantly. [?]

square (skwâr) *n.* 1. A rectangle having four equal sides. 2. Anything with this form. 3. An instrument for drawing or testing right angles. 4. The product of a number or quantity multiplied by itself. 5. Any of the quadrilateral spaces on a checkerboard. 6. a. An open area at the intersection of two or more streets. b. A rectangular space enclosed by streets; a block. 7. *Slang.* One characterized by rigid conventionality. —*adj.* squarer, squarest. 1. Having four equal sides and four right angles. 2. Forming a right angle. 3. a. Expressed in units measuring area: *square feet.* b. Having a specified length in each of two equal dimensions. 4. Of more or less quadrate dimensions. 5. Honest; direct. 6. Just; equitable. 7. Paid-up; settled. 8. *Slang.* Rigidly conventional. —*v.* **squared, squaring.** 1. To cut to a square or rectangular shape. 2. To bring into balance; settle: *square a debt.* 3. To raise (a number or quantity) to the second power. 4. To agree or conform. [< VL *exquadrāre*, to square.] —**square′ly** *adv.*

square dance. A dance in which sets of four couples form squares.

square rig. A sailing-ship rig with rectangular sails set approx. at right angles to the keel line from horizontal yards. —**square′-rigged** *adj.*

square root. A divisor of a quantity that when squared gives the quantity.

squash¹ (skwŏsh, skwôsh) *n.* 1. A fleshy fruit related to the pumpkins and gourds, eaten as a vegetable. 2. A plant bearing such fruit. [< Algon.]

squash² (skwŏsh, skwôsh) *v.* 1. To beat or flatten to a pulp; crush. 2. To be crushed or flattened. 3. To suppress; quash. —*n.* 1. The impact or sound of a soft body dropping against a surface. 2. A crush of people; a crowd. 3. A game played in a walled court with a racket and a hard rubber ball. [< VL *exquassāre*, "to break to pieces."]

squat (skwŏt) *v.* **squatted** or **squat, squatting.** 1. To sit on one's heels. 2. To settle on unoccupied land without legal claim. 3. To occupy a given piece of public land in order to acquire title to it. —*adj.* squatter, squattest. Short and thick; low and broad. —*n.* The act or posture of squatting. [< OF *esquatir*, to flatten.] —**squat′ter** *n.*

squaw (skwô) *n.* A North American Indian woman. [< Algon.]

squawk (skwôk) *n.* 1. A loud screech. 2. A

ă pat/ā ate/âr care/ä bar/b bib/ch chew/d deed/ĕ pet/ē be/f fit/g gag/h hat/hw what/ ĭ pit/ī pie/îr pier/j judge/k kick/l lid, fatal/m mum/n no, sudden/ng sing/ŏ pot/ō go/

loud or insistent protest. [Perh blend of SQUALL and SQUEAK.] —squawk v.
squeak (skwēk) v. To utter, speak in, or make a brief thin, shrill cry or sound. [Prob < Scand.] —squeak n. —squeak'y adj.
squeal (skwēl) v. 1. To make a loud, shrill cry or sound. 2. Slang. To turn informer. —n. A loud, shrill cry or sound. [Prob < Scand.] —squeal'er n.
squeam•ish (skwē'mĭsh) adj. 1. a. Easily nauseated or sickened. b. Nauseated. 2. Easily disgusted. 3. Excessively fastidious. [< OE swima, dizziness. See swei-.] —squeam'ish•ly adv. —squeam'ish•ness n.
squeeze (skwēz) v. **squeezed, squeezing.** 1. To press hard upon or together; compress. 2. To exert pressure. 3. To extract from by applying pressure: squeeze juice from a lemon. 4. To force by pressure; cram. —n. 1. An act or instance of squeezing. 2. An amount squeezed. [< OE cwȳsan, to press.]
squelch (skwĕlch) v. 1. To suppress completely. 2. To silence, as with a crushing remark. —n. A crushing reply. [Imit.]
squid (skwĭd) n., pl. squids or squid. A marine mollusk with a long body and ten arms surrounding the mouth. [?]
squint (skwĭnt) v. 1. a. To look with the eyes partly open. b. To close (the eyes) partly. 2. To glance to the side. [< ME asquint, with a sidelong glance.] —squint n.
squire (skwīr) n. 1. A young nobleman attendant upon a knight. 2. An English country gentleman. 3. A judge or other local dignitary. 4. A man who attends or escorts a woman. —v. squired, squiring. To attend as a squire or escort. [< OF esquier, "shield-bearer."]
squirm (skwûrm) v. 1. To twist about in a wriggling motion; writhe. 2. To feel or show signs of humiliation or embarrassment.
squir•rel (skwûr'əl, skwĭr'əl) n. 1. Any of various tree-climbing rodents with gray or reddish-brown fur and a long bushy tail. 2. The fur of a squirrel. [< Gk skiouros, "shadow-tail."]
squirt (skwûrt) v. To eject liquid in a thin swift stream. —n. 1. a. A device used to squirt. b. The stream squirted. 2. Informal. An insignificant but arrogant person. [ME squirten.]
Sr strontium.
sr. senior.
Sri Lan•ka (srē läng'kə). An insular nation off the SE coast of India. Pop. 12,510,000. Cap. Colombo.
SSE south-southeast.
S.S.R. Soviet Socialist Republic.
SSW south-southwest.
–st. Variant of -est².
St. 1. saint. 2. strait. 3. street.
sta. station.
stab (stăb) v. stabbed, stabbing. 1. To pierce or wound with or as with a pointed weapon. 2. To lunge with or as with a pointed weapon. —n. 1. A thrust made with a pointed weapon. 2. A wound inflicted by stabbing. 3. An attempt. [< ME stabbe, wound by stabbing.]
sta•bi•lize (stā'bə-līz') v. -lized, -lizing. 1. To make, hold, or become stable. 2. To maintain

the stability of. —sta'bi•li•za'tion n. —sta'bi•liz'er n.
sta•ble¹ (stā'bəl) adj. -bler, -blest. 1. Resistant to sudden change. 2. Maintaining equilibrium. 3. Enduring. [< L stabilis, standing firm.] —sta•bil'i•ty (stə-bĭl'ə-tē) n.
sta•ble² (stā'bəl) n. 1. A building for the shelter and feeding of domestic animals, esp. horses. 2. All of the racehorses belonging to a single owner. [< L stabulum, "standing place," enclosure, stable.]
stack (stăk) n. 1. A large conical pile of straw. 2. A pile arranged in layers. 3. A large quantity. 4. A chimney or vertical exhaust pipe. 5. **stacks.** The area of a library in which books are shelved. —v. 1. To arrange in a stack; to pile. 2. To prearrange the order of (playing cards) so as to cheat. [< ON stakkr.]
sta•di•um (stā'dē-əm) n. A large, often unroofed structure in which athletic events are held. [< Gk spadion, racetrack.]
staff (stăf) n. 1. pl. **staffs** or **staves** (stāvz). A rod or stick carried as a weapon, an aid in walking, etc. 2. pl. **staffs. a.** A group of assistants to an executive or military commander. b. The personnel of an enterprise. 3. pl. **staves.** The set of lines on which music is written. —v. To provide with a staff of employees. [< OE stæf, stick, rod. See stebh-.]
staff sergeant. 1. A noncommissioned army officer ranking next below a sergeant first class. 2. A noncommissioned air force officer ranking next below a technical sergeant. 3. A noncommissioned marine officer ranking next below a gunnery sergeant.
stag (stăg) n. 1. An adult male deer. 2. A man who attends a social affair without escorting a woman. —adj. For or attended by men only. [< OE stagga. See stegh-.]
stage (stāj) n. 1. Any raised platform, as a workmen's scaffold. 2. a. The raised platform upon which theatrical performances are presented. b. Any area in which actors perform. c. The acting profession. 3. The scene or set-

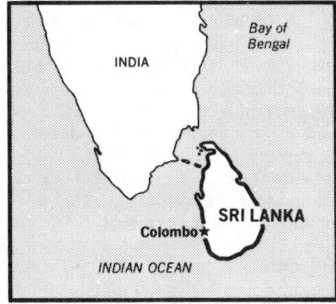

Sri Lanka

ting of an event. 4. A leg of a journey. 5. A step in development. —v. staged, staging. 1. To present or perform on or as if on a stage. 2. To arrange and carry out: stage an invasion. [< VL *staticum, "standing place," position.]
stage•coach (stāj'kōch') n. A horse-drawn

vehicle formerly used to transport mail and passengers.

stage-struck (stāj'strŭk') *adj.* Enthralled with hopes of becoming an actor.

stag•ger (stăg'ər) *v.* **1.** To move or cause to move unsteadily; totter. **2.** To overwhelm with emotion or surprise. **3.** To arrange in alternating or overlapping time periods. —*n.* **1.** The act of staggering; a tottering or reeling motion. **2. staggers** *(takes sing. v.).* A disease of animals, esp. horses, characterized by staggering and falling. [< ON *staka,* to push, cause to stumble.] —**stag'ger•er** *n.*

stag•ing (stā'jĭng) *n.* The process of producing and directing a stage play.

stag•nant (stăg'nənt) *adj.* **1.** Not moving or flowing. **2.** Foul from standing still. **3.** Inactive; sluggish. [< L *stagnum,* pond, swamp.]

stag•nate (stăg'nāt') *v.* -nated, -nating. To lie inactive; fail to progress or develop. —**stag'-na'tion** *n.*

staid (stād) *adj.* Reserved and colorless; grave; sober. [< *staid,* obs pp of STAY.]

stain (stān) *v.* **1.** To discolor or spot. **2.** To corrupt or disgrace. **3.** To color, as wood, with a penetrating dye. —*n.* **1.** A spot or smudge of foreign matter. **2.** A blemish upon one's name; stigma. **3.** A dye. [< VL *distingere,* to deprive of color.] —**stain'er** *n.*

stain•less (stān'lĭs) *adj.* **1.** Without stain or blemish. **2.** Resistant to corrosion.

stainless steel. Any of various steels alloyed with sufficient chromium to resist corrosion, oxidation, or rusting.

stair (stâr) *n.* **1.** Often **stairs.** A flight of steps; a staircase. **2.** One of a flight of steps. [< OE *stæger.* See steigh-.]

stair•case (stâr'kās') *n.* A flight of steps and its supporting structure.

stair•way (stâr'wā') *n.* A flight of stairs.

stake¹ (stāk) *n.* **1.** A pointed piece of wood or metal for driving into the ground, as a marker, a fence pole, or a tent peg. **2.** A vertical post to which an offender is bound for execution by burning. —*v.* staked, staking. **1.** To indicate the limits of with or as if with stakes: *stake out a claim.* **2.** To attach or support with stakes. **3.** To tie to a stake. [< OE *staca.* See steg-².]

stake² (stāk) *n.* **1.** Often **stakes. a.** Money or property risked in a wager or gambling game. **b.** The prize in a contest or race. **2.** A share or interest in any enterprise. —*v.* staked, staking. **1.** To gamble or risk. **2.** To finance.

sta•lac•tite (stə-lăk'tīt', stăl'ək-) *n.* A cylindrical or conical deposit projecting downward from the roof of a cavern. [< Gk *stalaktos,* dripping.]

sta•lag•mite (stə-lăg'mīt', stăl'əg-) *n.* A cylindrical or conical deposit projecting upward from the floor of a cavern. [< Gk *stalagmos,* dripping.]

stale (stāl) *adj.* staler, stalest. **1.** Having lost freshness or palatability. **2.** Lacking in originality. **3.** Impaired in strength. —*v.* staled, staling. To make or become stale. [Prob < OF *estale,* not moving, slack.]

stale•mate (stāl'māt') *n.* **1.** *Chess.* A drawing position in which only the king can move and although not in check can move only into check. **2.** A deadlock. —**stale'mate'** *v.* (-mated, -mating).

Sta•lin (stä'lĭn), **Joseph.** 1879–1953. General secretary of the Communist Party of the Soviet Union (1922–53); premier (1941–53). —**Sta'-lin•ism'** *n.* —**Sta'lin•ist** *adj. & n.*

Joseph Stalin

stalk¹ (stôk) *n.* **1.** A stem of a plant or plant part. **2.** A similar supporting structure. [Prob < Scand.]

stalk² (stôk) *v.* **1.** To walk with a stiff, haughty gait. **2.** To move menacingly. **3.** To track (game). [< OE *stealcian,* to walk cautiously. See ster-⁴.] —**stalk'er** *n.*

stall (stôl) *n.* **1.** A compartment for one domestic animal in a barn or shed. **2.** Any small compartment or booth. —*v.* **1.** To bring or come to a standstill accidentally: *stall an engine.* **2.** To employ delaying tactics: *stall for time.* [< OE *steall,* standing place, stable.]

stal•lion (stăl'yən) *n.* An uncastrated adult male horse. [< Frank **stal,* stable.]

stal•wart (stôl'wərt) *adj.* **1.** Having physical strength; sturdy. **2.** Resolute; uncompromising. [< OE *stælwierthe,* serviceable.]

sta•men (stā'mən) *n.* The pollen-producing reproductive organ of a flower. [L *stāmen,* thread of the warp, stamen.]

stam•i•na (stăm'ə-nə) *n.* Physical or moral power of endurance. [< L *stāmen,* thread of the warp, thread of human life.]

stam•mer (stăm'ər) *v.* To intrude involuntary pauses and sometimes syllabic repetitions into one's speaking; falter. [< OE *stamerian* < Gmc **stam-.*] —**stam'mer** *n.* —**stam'mer•er** *n.*

stamp (stămp) *v.* **1.** To bring the foot down upon (a surface or object) forcibly. **2.** To thrust the foot forcibly downward. **3.** To imprint or impress with a mark. **4.** To affix an adhesive stamp to. **5.** To form or cut out with a mold, form, or die. **6.** To characterize or identify. —*n.* **1.** The act of stamping. **2.** A mark or seal indicating ownership, approval, etc. **3.** A small piece of gummed paper, as used for postage. **4.** Any identifying mark.

5. a. An implement used to impress, cut out, or shape. **b.** The impression or shape thus formed. [< OE *stampian, to pound, stamp. See stebh-.]

stam•pede (stăm'pēd') *n.* A sudden headlong rush, as of startled animals. —*v.* **-peded, -ped-ing.** To participate in or cause a stampede. [< Span *estampar,* to pound, stamp.]

stance (stăns) *n.* The posture of a standing person. [< VL *stantia,* a standing.]

stanch (stänch, stănch) *v.* To check the flow of blood, as from a wound. [< L *stāre,* to stand.]

stan•chion (stăn'chən, -shən) *n.* An upright pole or post. [< OF *estanche,* a stay, prop.]

stand (stănd) *v.* **stood, standing. 1.** To take, cause to take, or maintain an upright position on the feet. **2.** To assume an erect position in a specified manner: *stand straight.* **3.** To measure or equal a specified height. **4.** To remain stable or intact. **5.** To remain unchanged; stagnate. **6.** To withstand. **7.** To tolerate; endure. **8.** To rank. **9.** To undergo: *stand trial.* —*n.* **1.** The act of standing. **2.** A halt; standstill. **3.** A stop on a performance tour. **4.** The place where a person stands, as a witness box in a courtroom. **5.** A counter for the display of goods. **6.** A small rack or prop for holding various articles. **7. stands.** Bleachers, as at a stadium. **8.** A parking space reserved for taxis. **9.** A group or growth of tall plants or trees. [< OE *standan.* See stā-.]

stan•dard (stăn'dərd) *n.* **1.** A flag, banner, or ensign. **2.** An acknowledged measure of comparison for quantitative or qualitative value; criterion; norm. **3.** The commodity or commodities, such as gold, used to back a monetary system. **4.** A degree or level or excellence. **5.** A pedestal or stand. [Prob < Frank *standhard,* "standing firmly."] —**stan'dard** *adj.*

stan•dard•ize (stăn'dər-dīz') *v.* **-ized, -izing.** To make, cause, or adapt to fit a standard. —**stan'dard•i•za'tion** *n.*

standard time. The time in any of 24 time zones, usually the mean solar time at the central meridian of each zone.

stand•by (stănd'bī') *n., pl.* **-bys. 1.** One that can be depended upon. **2.** One ready to serve as a substitute.

stand-in (stănd'ĭn') *n.* A substitute, as for an actor.

stand•ing (stăn'dĭng) *n.* **1.** Status with respect to credit, rank, etc. **2.** Length of time. —*adj.* **1.** Remaining upright. **2.** Performed from an upright position: *standing jumps.* **3.** Permanent. **4.** Stationary. **5.** Stagnant.

stand•off•ish (stănd-ôf'ĭsh, -ŏf'ĭsh) *adj.* Unsociable; aloof.

stand•pipe (stănd'pīp') *n.* A large vertical pipe into which water is pumped in order to produce a desired pressure.

stand•point (stănd'point') *n.* A position from which things are considered; point of view.

stand•still (stănd'stĭl') *n.* A halt: *came to a standstill.*

stank (stăngk). *p.t.* of **stink.**

stan•za (stăn'zə) *n.* One of the divisions of a poem having two or more lines. [It, "a stopping or standing."]

sta•pes (stā'pēz') *n., pl.* **-pes** or **stapedes** (stə-pē'dēz'). One of three small bones located in the middle ear. [< ML *stapēs.*]

staph•y•lo•coc•cus (stăf'ə-lō-kŏk'əs) *n., pl.* **-cocci** (-kŏk'sī'). Any of various spherical parasitic bacteria occurring in grapelike clusters and causing boils, septicemia, and other infections. [< Gk *staphulē,* bunch of grapes + *kokkos,* a berry.]

sta•ple¹ (stā'pəl) *n.* **1.** A major commodity or product. **2.** A major part or element. **3.** Raw material. **4.** The fiber of cotton, wool, etc. [ME, market town, trade center.]

sta•ple² (stā'pəl) *n.* **1.** A U-shaped metal loop with pointed ends, driven into a surface to hold a bolt, hook, etc., or to hold wiring in place. **2.** A thin piece of wire having the shape of a square bracket, used as a fastening for papers. [< OE *stapol,* post, pillar.] —**sta'ple** *v.* **(-pled, -pling).** —**sta'pler** *n.*

star (stär) *n.* **1.** *Astron.* A celestial object consisting of a self-luminous, self-containing mass of gas. **2.** Any of the celestial bodies visible at night from Earth as relatively stationary, usually twinkling points of light. **3.** Anything regarded as resembling such a body. **4.** A graphic design with radiating points, esp. one with five points. **5. a.** A superior performer. **b.** A leading actor or actress. **6.** An asterisk. **7. stars.** *Astrol.* **a.** The constellations of the zodiac believed to influence personal destiny. **b.** Loosely, the planets in relation to them. —*v.* **starred, starring. 1.** To ornament with stars. **2.** To mark with an asterisk. **3.** To play the leading role in a theatrical production. [< OE *steorra.* See ster-³.] —**star'ry** *adj.*

star•board (stär'bərd) *n.* The right-hand side of a ship or aircraft as one faces forward. [< OE *stēorbord,* "rudder side."] —**star'board** *adj. & adv.*

starch (stärch) *n.* **1.** A carbohydrate, $(C_6H_{10}O_5)_n$, found chiefly in the seeds, fruits, tubers, and roots of plants, as corn, potatoes, or wheat, and commonly prepared as a white, tasteless powder. **2.** Any of various substances, including natural starch, used to stiffen fabrics. **3.** A food having a high starch content. —*v.* To stiffen with starch. [< OE *stercan,* to stiffen. See ster-¹.] —**starch'y** *adj.*

stare (stâr) *v.* **stared, staring.** To fix with a steady, often wide-eyed gaze. [< OE *starian.* See ster-¹.] —**stare** *n.*

star•fish (stär'fĭsh') *n.* A marine animal having a star-shaped form with five radiating arms.

stark (stärk) *adj.* **1.** Bare; blunt. **2.** Utter; extreme. **3.** Harsh in appearance; grim. —*adv.* Utterly; absolutely: *stark raving mad.* [< OE *stearc,* hard, stern, severe, cruel. See ster-¹.]

stark naked. Completely naked. [< ME *stert naked,* "naked to the tail."]

star•let (stär'lĭt) *n.* A young actress publicized as a future star.

star•light (stär'līt') *n.* The light given by the stars.

star•ling (stär'lĭng) *n.* An Old World bird with dark plumage, widely naturalized in North America. [< OE *stær,* starling (see **storos**) + -LING.]

ô paw, for/oi boy/ou out/ŏŏ took/ōō coo/p pop/r run/s sauce/sh shy/t to/th thin/*th* the/
ŭ cut/ûr fur/v van/w wag/y yes/z size/zh vision/ə ago, item, edible, gallop, circus/

Stars and Stripes, The. The flag of the U.S.
Star-Span•gled Banner, The (stär'spăng'-gəld). **1.** The flag of the U.S. **2.** The national anthem of the U.S.

start (stärt) *v.* **1.** To commence; begin. **2.** To set in motion, operation, or activity. **3.** To establish: *start a business.* **4.** To move suddenly and involuntarily. —*n.* **1. a.** A beginning. **b.** A place or time of beginning. **2.** A position of advantage, as in a race. **3.** A sudden, involuntary movement. [< OE *styrtan*, to leap up. See ster-¹.] —**start'er** *n.*

star•tle (stär'təl) *v.* **-tled, -tling. 1.** To cause to make a quick, involuntary movement, as in fright. **2.** To become startled. [< OE *steartlian*, to kick, struggle. See ster-¹.]

starve (stärv) *v.* **starved, starving. 1.** To die or cause to die from hunger. **2.** To suffer or cause to suffer from or as from hunger. [< OE *steorfan*, to die. See ster-¹.] —**star•va'tion** *n.*

stash (stăsh) *v.* To store away in a secret place. [?]

–stasis. *comb. form.* A stable state or a balance: homeostasis. [< Gk *stasis*, a standing, standstill.]

–stat. *comb. form.* Stationary or making stationary: thermostat. [< Gk *-statēs*, one that causes to stand.]

stat. statute.

state (stāt) *n.* **1.** A condition of being with regard to a set of circumstances. **2.** A condition of being in a stage or form, as of structure, growth, or development. **3.** A mental or emotional condition. **4. a.** The supreme public power within a sovereign political entity. **b.** The sphere of supreme civil power within a given polity: *matters of state.* **5.** A specific mode of government: *a welfare state.* **6.** A body politic, esp. one constituting a nation: *the states of eastern Europe.* **7.** One of the internally autonomous political units composing a federation under a sovereign government: *New York State.* —*v.* **stated, stating.** To set forth in words; declare. [< L *status*, manner of standing, condition, position, attitude.] —**state'hood'** *n.*

state•ly (stāt'lē) *adj.* **-lier, -liest. 1.** Dignified; formal. **2.** Majestic; lofty. —**state'li•ness** *n.*

state•ment (stāt'mənt) *n.* **1.** The act of stating. **2.** Something stated; an account. **3.** An abstract of a financial account.

Stat•en Island (stăt'n). An island in the bay of New York.

state•room (stāt'room') *n.* A private room on a ship or train.

state•side (stāt'sīd') *adj.* Of or in the continental U.S. —**state'side'** *adv.*

states•man (stāts'mən) *n.* **1.** One who is a leader in public affairs. **2.** A political leader regarded as a promoter of the public good. —**states'man•like'** *adj.* —**states'man•ship'** *n.*

stat•ic (stăt'ĭk) *adj.* **1.** Having no motion; quiescent. **2.** Of or produced by random radio noise. —*n.* Random noise produced in a radio or television receiver. [< Gk *statikos*, causing to stand.] —**stat'i•cal•ly** *adv.*

static electricity. 1. An accumulation of electric charge on an insulated body. **2.** Electric

discharge resulting from such accumulation.

sta•tion (stā'shən) *n.* **1.** The position where a person or thing stands or is placed. **2.** The place from which a service is provided or operations directed: *a police station.* **3.** A transportation depot. **4.** Social position; status. **5.** An establishmen for radio or television transmission. —*v.* To assign to a position; to post. [< L *statiō*, a standing.]

sta•tion•ar•y (stā'shə-nĕr'ē) *adj.* **1.** Fixed in a position; not moving. **2.** Remaining in a fixed condition. [< L *statiō*, a standstill, STATION.]

sta•tion•er (stā'shən-ər) *n.* One who sells stationery.

sta•tion•er•y (stā'shə-nĕr'ē) *n.* **1.** Writing materials and office supplies. **2.** A store that sells stationery and related items.

station wagon. An automobile having an extended interior with a luggage platform and a hinged rear wall that can be let down.

sta•tis•tic (stə-tĭs'tĭk) *n.* Any numerical datum. —**sta•tis'ti•cal** *adj.*

sta•tis•tics (stə-tĭs'tĭks) *n.* **1.** *(takes sing. v.)* The mathematics of the collection, organization, and interpretation of numerical data, esp. the analysis of population characteristics by inference from sampling. **2.** *(takes pl. v.)* A collection of numerical data. [G *Statistik*, orig "political science dealing with state affairs."] —**stat'is•ti'cian** (stăt'ə-stĭsh'ən) *n.*

stat•u•ar•y (stăch'ōō-ĕr'ē) *n.* Statues collectively.

stat•ue (stăch'ōō) *n.* A form or likeness sculpted, modeled, carved, or cast in a material such as stone, clay, wood, or bronze. [< L *statuere*, to set up, erect.]

stat•u•esque (stăch'ōō-ĕsk') *adj.* Suggestive of a statue, as in proportion, grace, or dignity.

stat•u•ette (stăch'ōō-ĕt') *n.* A small statue.

stat•ure (stăch'ər) *n.* **1.** Natural height in an upright position, esp. of a person. **2.** A level achieved; status; caliber. [< L *statūra.*]

stat•us (stā'təs, stăt'əs) *n.* **1.** The legal condition of a person or thing. **2.** A relative position, esp. social standing. **3.** High standing. **4.** A state of affairs; position, posture, condition. [L, manner of standing, posture, condition.]

sta•tus quo (stā'təs kwō', stăt'əs). The existing state of affairs. [L, "state in which."]

stat•ute (stăch'ōōt) *n.* **1.** A law enacted by a legislative body. **2.** A decree or edict. **3.** An established rule, as of a corporation. [< L *statuere*, to set up, decree.]

statute mile. The standard mile, 5,280 feet.

stat•u•to•ry (stăch'ə-tôr'ē, -tōr'ē) *adj.* Enacted, regulated, or defined by statute.

staunch (stônch, stänch) *adj.* **1.** Firm and steadfast; true. **2.** Having a strong construction or constitution. [< OF *estanchier*, stanch.] —**staunch'ly** *adv.* —**staunch'ness** *n.*

stave (stāv) *n.* **1.** A narrow strip of wood forming part of the sides of a barrel, tub, etc. **2.** A staff or cudgel. **3.** A stanza. —*v.* **staved** or **stove, staving. 1.** To break in the staves of. **2.** To break or smash a hole in. **3.** To ward or keep off: *He staved off hunger.* [Back-formation < STAVES.]

staves. Alternate *pl.* of **staff.**

---

stay¹ (stā) *v.* **1.** To remain or cause to remain. **2.** To stop; halt. **3.** To pause; wait. **4.** To hold on; endure. **5.** To postpone. **6.** To keep up, as in a race. —*n.* **1.** The action of halting. **2.** A sojourn or visit. **3.** A postponement. [< L *stāre,* to stand.]

stay² (stā) *v.* To support or prop up. —*n.* **1.** A support or brace. **2.** A strip of bone, plastic, or metal, used to stiffen a garment or part, as a shirt collar. **3. stays.** A corset. [< OF *estaie,* support.]

stay³ (stā) *n.* A heavy rope or cable used as a support, as for a ship's mast. —*v.* To brace or support with a stay or stays. [< OE *stæg.* See **stāk-**.]

St. Ber•nard (sănt bər-närd′). A large dog of a breed used by monks of the hospice of St. Bernard in the Swiss Alps to help travelers.

St. Croix (sănt′ kroi′). The largest island of the Virgin Islands of the U.S.

std. standard.

stead (stĕd) *n.* **1.** The place or function properly occupied by another. **2.** Advantage; avail: *stand one in good stead.* [< OE *stede.* See **stā-**.]

stead•fast (stĕd′făst′) *adj.* **1.** Fixed or unchanging. **2.** Firmly loyal or constant. [< OE *stedefæst,* fixed in one place.] —**stead′fast′ly** *adv.* —**stead′fast′ness** *n.*

stead•y (stĕd′ē) *adj.* **-ier, -iest. 1.** Firm in position or place. **2.** Unfaltering; sure. **3.** Having a continuous movement or quality. **4.** Calm; controlled. **5.** Reliable. —*v.* **-ied, -ying.** To make or become steady. [< STEAD, place.] —**stead′i•ly** *adv.* —**stead′i•ness** *n.*

steak (stāk) *n.* A slice of meat, usually beef, cooked by broiling or frying. [< ON *steikja,* to roast on a spit.]

steal (stēl) *v.* **stole, stolen, stealing. 1.** To take without right or permission, generally in a surreptitious way. **2.** To get or effect secretly or artfully. **3.** To move or happen stealthily or unobtrusively. **4.** *Baseball.* To gain (a base) without a hit, error, or wild pitch. —*n.* **1.** The act of stealing; theft. **2.** *Slang.* A bargain. [< OE *stelan.* See **ster-⁴**.]

stealth (stĕlth) *n.* The quality or state of being secret, sly, or surreptitious. —**stealth′i•ly** *adv.* —**stealth′i•ness** *n.* —**stealth′y** *adj.*

steam (stēm) *n.* **1. a.** The vapor phase of water. **b.** The mist of cooling water vapor. **2.** Power; energy. —*v.* **1.** To produce or emit steam. **2.** To move or be powered by steam. **3.** To expose to steam, as in cooking. [< OE *stēam* < Gmc **stauma.*] —**steam′y** *adj.*

steam•boat (stēm′bōt′) *n.* A steamship.

steam engine. An engine that converts the heat energy of pressurized steam into mechanical energy.

steam•er (stē′mər) *n.* **1.** A steamship. **2.** A container in which something is steamed.

steam•rol•ler (stēm′rō′lər) *n.* A steam-driven machine used chiefly for rolling road surfaces flat. —*v.* To overwhelm or crush.

steam•ship (stēm′shĭp′) *n.* A large vessel propelled by steam-driven screws or propellers.

steam shovel. A steam-driven machine for digging.

ste•a•tite (stē′ə-tīt′) *n.* A massive, white-to-green talc used in paints, ceramics, and insulation. [< Gk *steatitis,* "tallow stone."]

steed (stēd) *n.* A horse, esp. a spirited mount. [< OE *stēda,* stallion.]

steel (stēl) *n.* **1.** Any of various generally hard, strong, durable, malleable alloys of iron and carbon, often with other constituents. **2.** A quality suggestive of steel, esp. a hard, unflinching character. —*adj.* **1.** Made of or with steel. **2.** Resembling the properties of steel. —*v.* To make hard, strong, or obdurate. [< OE *stēli.* See **stāk-**.] —**steel′y** *adj.*

steel wool. Fine fibers of woven or matted steel used esp. for scouring.

steep¹ (stēp) *adj.* **1.** Having a sharp inclination; nearly perpendicular; precipitous. **2.** Excessive; exorbitant: *a steep price.* [< OE *stēap,* lofty, deep, projecting. See **steu-**.] —**steep′ly** *adv.* —**steep′ness** *n.*

steep² (stēp) *v.* **1.** To soak or be soaked in liquid in order to cleanse, soften, or extract some property from. **2.** To saturate. [ME *stepen.*] —**steep′er** *n.*

steep•en (stē′pən) *v.* To make or become steeper.

stee•ple (stē′pəl) *n.* **1.** A tall tower forming the superstructure of a building, such as a church, and usually surmounted by a spire. **2.** A spire. [< OE *stȳpel.* See **steu-**.]

stee•ple•chase (stē′pəl-chās′) *n.* A horse race across open country or over a course provided artificially with obstacles.

stee•ple•jack (stē′pəl-jăk′) *n.* A worker on steeples or other very high structures.

steer¹ (stîr) *v.* **1.** To guide (a vessel or vehicle) by means of a rudder, wheel, paddle, etc. **2.** To direct the course of. **3.** To move in a set course. **4.** To allow of being steered or guided: *The boat steers easily.* [< OE *stīeran.* See **stā-**.]

steer² (stîr) *n.* A young ox, esp. one raised for beef. [< OE *stēor.*]

steer•age (stîr′ĭj) *n.* **1.** The action of steering. **2.** The section of a passenger ship providing the cheapest accommodations for passengers.

steg•o•saur (stĕg′ə-sôr′) *n.* Also **steg•o•sau•rus** (stĕg′ə-sôr′əs). A dinosaur with a double row of upright bony plates along the back. [< Gk *stegos,* roof, "ridge of plates" + -SAUR.]

stein (stīn) *n.* An earthenware mug, esp. one for beer. [G.]

Stein•beck (stīn′bĕk), **John.** 1902–1968. American novelist.

stel•lar (stĕl′ər) *adj.* Of or relating to stars or a star performer. [< L *stella,* star.]

stem¹ (stĕm) *n.* **1.** The main axis of a plant or a slender supporting or connecting plant part; a stalk. **2. a.** Something similar to a plant stem. **b.** A stemlike part, as of a pipe, wine glass, etc. **3.** The main part of a word to which affixes are added. **4.** The prow of a vessel. —*v.* **stemmed, stemming. 1.** To derive or develop (from). **2.** To make headway against (a tide, current, or comparable force). [< OE *stemn, stefn,* stem, tree trunk. See **stā-**.] —**stem′less** *adj.*

stem² (stĕm) *v.* **stemmed, stemming.** To stop or hold back, by or as if by damming. [< ON *stemma.*]

stemmed (stĕmd) *adj.* **1.** Having the stems removed. **2.** Provided with a stem.

stem·ware (stĕm'wâr') *n.* Glassware mounted on a stem.

stench (stĕnch) *n.* A strong and foul odor. [< OE *stenc* < Gmc *stenkw-*.]

sten·cil (stĕn'səl) *n.* A sheet of material in which a desired lettering or design has been cut so that when ink or paint is passed over the sheet the pattern will be reproduced on the surface placed below. —*v.* -ciled or -cilled, -ciling or -cilling. To mark or produce with a stencil. [< OF *estenceler*, "to cause to sparkle."]

sten·o (stĕn'ō) *n., pl.* -os. **1.** A stenographer. **2.** Stenography.

steno, stenog. stenographer; stenography.

ste·nog·ra·pher (stə-nŏg'rə-fər) *n.* A person employed to take and transcribe dictation.

ste·nog·ra·phy (stə-nŏg'rə-fē) *n.* The art or process of writing in shorthand. [< Gk *stenos*, narrow + -GRAPHY.] —**sten'o·graph'ic** (stĕn'-ə-grăf'ĭk) *adj.*

sten·to·ri·an (stĕn-tôr'ē-ən, stĕn-tōr'-) *adj.* Extremely loud. [Gk *Stentōr*, name of a loud-voiced herald in the *Iliad*.]

step (stĕp) *n.* **1. a.** The single complete movement of raising one foot and putting it down in another spot in the act of walking. **b.** A manner of walking. **c.** The rhythm or pace of another or others, as in a march. **d.** The sound of a tread. **2. a.** The distance traversed by moving one foot ahead of the other. **b.** A very short distance. **c.** steps. Course: *followed in his father's steps.* **3. a.** A rest for the foot in ascending or descending. **b.** steps. Stairs. **4. a.** One of a series of actions taken toward some end. **b.** A stage in a process. **5.** A degree in progress or a grade or rank in a scale. —**in step.** **1.** Moving in rhythm. **2.** *Informal.* In conformity with one's environment. —*v.* **stepped, stepping.** **1.** To put or press the foot down (on). **2.** To shift or move slightly: *step back.* **3.** To walk a short distance to a specified place: *step over.* **4.** To move with the feet in a particular manner: *step lively.* **5.** To measure by pacing: *step off ten yards.* —**step up.** **1.** To increase. **2.** To advance; put oneself forward. [< OE *stæpe, stepe.* See stebh-.]

step-. *comb. form.* Relationship through the previous marriage of a spouse or through the remarriage of a parent, rather than by blood. [< OE *stēop-*.]

step·broth·er (stĕp'brŭth'ər) *n.* The son of one's stepparent by a previous marriage.

step·child (stĕp'chīld') *n.* The child of one's spouse by a former marriage.

step·daugh·ter (stĕp'dô'tər) *n.* The daughter of one's spouse by a former marriage.

step·fa·ther (stĕp'fä'thər) *n.* The husband of one's mother by a later marriage.

step·lad·der (stĕp'lăd'ər) *n.* A portable ladder with a hinged supporting frame and usually topped with a small platform.

step·moth·er (stĕp'mŭth'ər) *n.* The wife of one's father by a later marriage.

step·par·ent (stĕp'pâr'ənt) *n.* A stepfather or a stepmother.

steppe (stĕp) *n.* A vast semiarid plain, as found in SE Europe and Siberia. [Russ *step'*.]

step·ping·stone (stĕp'ĭng-stōn') *n.* **1.** A stone that provides a place to step. **2.** An advantageous position for advancement toward some goal.

step·sis·ter (stĕp'sĭs'tər) *n.* The daughter of one's stepparent by a previous marriage.

step·son (stĕp'sŭn') *n.* The son of one's spouse by a former marriage.

–ster. *comb. form.* **1.** One who does: teamster. **2.** One who is associated with: gangster. **3.** One who is given to making: prankster. **4.** One who is: youngster. [< OE *-estre* < Gmc *-strjōn*, agent-noun suffix.]

ster. sterling.

stere (stîr) *n.* A unit of volume equal to one cubic meter. [< Gk *stereos*, solid, hard.]

ste·re·o (stĕr'ē-ō', stîr'-) *n., pl.* -os. **1. a.** A stereophonic sound-reproduction system. **b.** Stereophonic sound. **2.** A stereoscopic system or photograph. —**ste're·o'** *adj.*

stereo-. *comb. form.* Solid, firm, or three-dimensional. [< Gk *stereos*, solid, hard.]

ster·e·o·phon·ic (stĕr'ē-ō-fŏn'ĭk, -fō'nĭk, stîr'-) *adj.* Having or rendering the illusion of having a natural distribution of sources of sound. —**ster'e·o·phon'i·cal·ly** *adv.*

ster·e·o·scope (stĕr'ē-ə-skōp', stîr'-) *n.* An optical instrument used to impart a three-dimensional effect to two photographs of the same scene taken at slightly different angles and viewed through two eyepieces. —**ster'e·o·scop'ic** (-skŏp'ĭk) *adj.*

ster·e·o·type (stĕr'ē-ə-tīp', stîr'-) *n.* **1.** A metal printing plate cast from a matrix that is molded from a raised printing surface, such as type. **2.** A conventional and usually oversimplified conception or belief. **3.** One considered typical of an unvarying pattern or manner. —**ster'e·o·typ'er** *n.*

ster·e·o·typed (stĕr'ē-ə-tīpt', stîr'-) *adj.* **1.** Printed or reproduced from stereotype plates. **2.** Not individualized; unoriginal; conventional.

ster·ile (stĕr'əl) *adj.* **1.** Incapable of reproducing sexually. **2.** Incapable of producing fruit, vegetation, etc. **3.** Free from bacteria or other microorganisms. **4.** Not productive or effective. [< L *sterilis*, unfruitful.] —**ste·ril'i·ty** (stə-rĭl'ə-tē) *n.*

ster·il·ize (stĕr'ə-līz') *v.* -ized, -izing. To render sterile. —**ster'il·i·za'tion** (-lə-zā'shən, -lĭ-zā'shən) *n.* —**ster'il·iz'er** *n.*

ster·ling (stûr'lĭng) *n.* **1.** British money, esp. the pound as the basic monetary unit. **2.** Sterling silver. —*adj.* **1.** Consisting of or relating to British money. **2.** Made of sterling silver. **3.** Of the highest quality. [ME, "small star" (stamped on silver pennies).]

sterling silver. An alloy of 92.5% silver with copper or another metal.

stern¹ (stûrn) *adj.* **1.** Firm or unyielding. **2.** Grave or severe in manner or appearance. **3.** Inexorable; relentless. [< OE *stierne.* See ster-¹.] —**stern'ly** *adv.*

stern² (stûrn) *n.* The rear part of a ship or boat. [ME *sterne.*]

---

ster·num (stûr'nəm) *n., pl.* **-na** (-nə) or **-nums.** A long flat bone forming the midventral support of most of the ribs. [< Gk *sternon,* breast, breastbone.]

steth·o·scope (stĕth'ə-skōp') *n.* An instrument used for listening to sounds produced within the body. [< Gk *stēthos,* chest, breast + -SCOPE.] **—steth'o·scop'ic** (-skŏp'ĭk) *adj.*

ste·ve·dore (stē'və-dôr', -dōr') *n.* A person employed in loading or unloading ships. [< Span *estivar,* to stow, pack.]

Ste·ven·son (stē'vən-sən). **1. Adlai Ewing.** 1900–1965. American statesman; twice Democratic candidate for President (1952 and 1956). **2. Robert Louis.** 1850–1894. Scottish poet and novelist.

stew (st/y/o͞o) *v.* **1.** To cook (food) by simmering or boiling slowly. **2.** *Informal.* To worry; fret. —*n.* **1.** A dish cooked by stewing, esp. a mixture of meat or fish and vegetables. **2.** *Informal.* Mental agitation. [ME *stewen,* orig "to bathe in hot water."]

stew·ard (st/y/o͞o'ərd) *n.* **1.** One who manages another's property, finances, or other affairs. **2.** One in charge of the household affairs of a hotel, resort, etc. **3.** An officer on a ship in charge of provisions and dining arrangements. **4.** A male member of the staff of a ship or airplane who waits on the passengers. [< OE *stigweard,* "keeper of the hall."] **—stew'ard·ess** *fem.n.*

stg. sterling.

stick (stĭk) *n.* **1.** A long, slender piece of wood, esp. a branch or stem from a tree or shrub. **2.** Any of various sticklike implements, as a cane or baton. **3.** Something having the shape of a stick. **4.** *sticks. Informal.* An area far from a city or town. **5.** *Informal.* A stiff, spiritless, or boring person. —*v.* **stuck, sticking. 1.** To pierce, puncture, or penetrate with a pointed instrument. **2.** To fasten or attach. **3.** To fix or impale on a pointed object. **4.** To adhere (to); cling. **5.** To be or become fixed or embedded in place. **6.** To be at or come to a standstill; become fixed or obstructed. **7.** To put, thrust, or poke into a specified place or position. **8.** To put responsibility on; burden: *stuck with paying the bill.* **9.** To persist, endure, or persevere. **10.** To remain in a vicinity; linger: *Stick around a while.* **11.** To extend, project, or protrude. [< OE *sticca,* a stick, and < OE *stician,* to pierce, stab. See **steig-.**]

stick·er (stĭk'ər) *n.* **1.** A person or thing that sticks. **2.** A gummed or adhesive label or patch.

stick·ler (stĭk'lər) *n.* **1.** A person who insists on something unyieldingly. **2.** Anything puzzling or difficult. [< OE *stihtan,* to order, arrange.]

stick·y (stĭk'ē) *adj.* **-ier, -iest. 1.** Adhering or sticking to a surface; adhesive. **2.** Warm and humid; muggy. **3.** *Informal.* Painful or difficult. **—stick'i·ly** *adv.* **—stick'i·ness** *n.*

stiff (stĭf) *adj.* **1.** Difficult to bend or stretch; not flexible. **2.** Not moving or operating easily; not limber. **3.** Excessively formal, awkward, or constrained. **4.** Not liquid, loose, or fluid. **5.** Having a strong, swift, steady force or movement. **6.** Potent or strong: *a stiff drink.*

7. Difficult; arduous. **8.** Harsh or severe. —*adv.* **1.** In a stiff manner. **2.** Completely: *bored stiff.* [< OE *stíf.* See **steip-.**] **—stiff'ly** *adv.* **—stiff'ness** *n.*

stiff·en (stĭf'ən) *v.* To make or become stiff or stiffer. **—stiff'en·er** *n.*

stiff-necked (stĭf'nĕkt') *adj.* Stubborn; unyielding.

sti·fle (stī'fəl) *v.* **-fled, -fling. 1.** To kill by preventing respiration; smother or suffocate. **2.** To interrupt or cut off (the voice or breath). **3.** To keep or hold back; suppress. [< OF *estouffer,* to choke, smother.] **—sti'fler** *n.*

stig·ma (stĭg'mə) *n., pl.* **stigmata** (stĭg-mä'tə, stĭg'mə-tə). **1.** A mark or token of disgrace or reproach. **2.** Usually *pl.* **stigmas.** The tip of a flower pistil, upon which pollen is deposited. **3. stigmata.** Marks or sores corresponding to and resembling the crucifixion wounds of Jesus. [< Gk, tattoo mark.] **—stig·mat'ic** (stĭg-mǎt'ĭk) *adj.*

stig·ma·tize (stĭg'mə-tīz') *v.* **-tized, -tizing. 1.** To characterize as disgraceful or ignominious. **2.** To brand or mark with a stigma or stigmata.

stile (stīl) *n.* A set or series of steps for getting over a fence or wall. [< OE *stigel.*]

sti·let·to (stĭ-lĕt'ō) *n., pl.* **-tos** or **-toes.** A small dagger with a slender, tapering blade. [< It *stilo,* dagger.]

still[1] (stĭl) *adj.* **1.** Free from sound; silent. **2.** Low in sound; subdued. **3.** Without movement. **4.** Free from disturbance. **5.** Pertaining to a single or static photograph as opposed to a motion picture. —*n.* **1.** Silence; calm. **2.** A still photograph, esp. one from a motion picture. —*adv.* **1.** Without movement. **2.** Now as before: *He is still sick.* **3.** In increasing amount or degree: *still further complaints.* **4.** Nevertheless; all the same. —*conj.* Nevertheless: *It was difficult, still he tried.* —*v.* **1.** To make or become still. **2.** To allay; calm. [< OE *stille.* See **stel-.**] **—still'ness** *n.*

still[2] (stĭl) *n.* An apparatus for distilling liquids, particularly alcohols. [< ME *distillen,* distill.]

still·birth (stĭl'bûrth') *n.* The birth of a dead child or fetus. **—still'born'** (stĭl'bôrn', -bōrn') *adj.*

still life *pl.* **still lifes.** A painting or picture of inanimate objects. **—still'-life'** *adj.*

stilt (stĭlt) *n.* **1.** Either of a pair of long, slender poles, each equipped with a raised footrest to permit walking elevated above the ground. **2.** Any of various tall posts or pillars used as support, as for a building. [ME *stilte,* stilt, crutch.]

stilt·ed (stĭl'tĭd) *adj.* Stiffly or artificially formal; pompous. **—stilt'ed·ly** *adv.*

stim·u·late (stĭm'yə-lāt') *v.* **-lated, -lating.** To rouse to activity or heightened action; excite. [L *stimulāre,* to goad on.] **—stim'u·lant** (-lənt) *adj. & n.* **—stim'u·la'tion** *n.*

stim·u·lus (stĭm'yə-ləs) *n., pl.* **-li** (-lī', -lē'). **1.** Anything causing or regarded as causing a response. **2.** Something that rouses to action; an incentive. [L *stimulus,* a goad.] **—stim'u·la'tive** (-lā'tĭv) *adj. & n.*

sting (stĭng) *v.* **stung, stinging. 1.** To pierce with or as with a sharp-pointed structure or organ.

2. To cause pain by or as by pricking with a sharp point. 3. To cause to suffer keenly. —*n.* 1. The act of stinging. 2. The wound or pain caused by or as by stinging. 3. A sharp, piercing organ or part, as of certain insects. [< OE *stingan.* See stegh-.] —**sting'er** *n.*

stin•gy (stĭn'jē) *adj.* -gier, -giest. 1. Giving or spending reluctantly. 2. Scanty or meager. [Perh < OE *stingan,* to STING.] —**stin'gi•ly** *adv.* —**stin'gi•ness** *n.*

stink (stĭngk) *v.* stank or stunk, stunk, stinking. 1. To emit or cause to emit a strong foul odor. 2. To be highly offensive. —*n.* A strong offensive odor. [< OE *stincan* < Gmc **stinkwan.*] —**stink'er** *n.*

stint (stĭnt) *v.* 1. To restrict or limit; be sparing with. 2. To subsist on a meager allowance; be frugal. —*n.* 1. A duty to be performed within a given period of time. 2. A limitation or restriction. [< OE *styntan,* to blunt, dull. See steu-.] —**stint'er** *n.*

sti•pend (stī'pĕnd', -pənd) *n.* A fixed or regular payment, as a salary or allowance. [< L *stipendium,* tax, tribute.]

stip•ple (stĭp'əl) *v.* -pled, -pling. To draw, engrave, or paint in dots or short touches. —*n.* 1. The method of painting, drawing, or engraving by stippling. 2. The effect produced by stippling. [< MDu *stip,* dot, point.]

stip•u•late (stĭp'yə-lāt') *v.* -lated, -lating. 1. To specify as a condition of an agreement; require by contract. 2. To guarantee in an agreement. [L *stipulāri,* to bargain, demand.] —**stip'u•la'tion** *n.* —**stip'u•la'tor** *n.*

stir (stûr) *v.* stirred, stirring. 1. To mix a liquid by passing an implement through it in circular motions. 2. To change or alter the placement of slightly; disarrange. 3. To move briskly or vigorously. 4. To rouse (someone) from sleep or indifference. 5. To incite or instigate: *stir up trouble.* 6. To move or affect strongly. —*n.* 1. An act of stirring; a mixing or poking movement. 2. A disturbance or commotion. 3. An excited reaction; a ferment. [< OE *styrian,* to move, excite. See twer-.] —**stir'rer** *n.*

stir•ring (stûr'ĭng) *adj.* 1. Rousing; exciting. 2. Active; lively. —**stir'ring•ly** *adv.*

stir•rup (stûr'əp, stĭr'-) *n.* 1. A flat-based loop or ring hung from either side of a horse's saddle to support the rider's foot. 2. Any similar device in which something is supported. [< OE *stigrāp.*]

stitch (stĭch) *n.* 1. A single complete movement of a threaded needle in sewing or surgical suturing. 2. A single loop of yarn around a knitting needle or similar implement. 3. A sudden sharp pain in the side. 4. *Informal.* An article of clothing: *not a stitch on.* 5. *Informal.* The least part; a bit: *He didn't do a stitch of work.* —*v.* 1. To fasten, join, or ornament with stitches. 2. To sew. [< OE *stice,* a sting, prick. See steig-.] —**stitch'er** *n.*

St. John (sănt jŏn'). An island of the Virgin Islands of the U.S.

St. Johns (sănt jŏnz'). The capital of Antigua.

stk. stock.

St. Law•rence River (sănt lôr'əns). A river of SE Canada.

St. Lou•is (sănt lōō'ĭs). A city of E Missouri. Pop. 608,000.

stoat (stōt) *n. Chiefly Brit.* The ermine, esp. in its brown color phase.

stock (stŏk) *n.* 1. A supply accumulated for future use. 2. The total merchandise kept on hand by a commercial establishment. 3. Domestic animals; livestock. 4. a. The capital that a corporation raises through the sale of shares entitling the holder to dividends and other rights of ownership. b. A certificate that shows such ownership. 5. a. The original progenitor of a family line or group of descendants. b. Ancestry or lineage. c. A group, as of organisms or languages, descended from a common ancestor. 6. The raw material out of which something is made. 7. Broth used as a base for soup, gravy, or sauces. 8. A supporting structure, block, or frame. 9. stocks. A pillory. 10. A theatrical activity, esp. one outside a main theatrical center. —*v.* 1. To provide with stock or a stock. 2. To keep for future sale or use. 3. To put forth or sprout new shoots. —*adj.* 1. Kept regularly available for sale or use. 2. Commonplace: *a stock answer.* [< OE *stocc,* tree trunk. See steu-.]

stock•ade (stŏk'ād') *n.* A barrier or enclosure made of strong posts driven upright side by side in the ground, used for protection or imprisonment. [< Span *estaca,* stake < Gmc.]

stock•bro•ker (stŏk'brō'kər) *n.* One who acts as an agent in the buying and selling of securities.

stock car. 1. An automobile of a standard make, modified for racing. 2. A railroad car carrying livestock.

stock exchange. 1. A place where stocks, bonds, or other securities are bought and sold. 2. An association of stockbrokers.

stock•hold•er (stŏk'hōl'dər) *n.* One who owns stock in a company.

Stock•holm (stŏk'hōlm). The capital of Sweden. Pop. 794,000.

stock•ing (stŏk'ĭng) *n.* A close-fitting covering for the foot and leg. [< dial *stock,* stocking.]

stock market. 1. A stock exchange. 2. The business transacted at a stock exchange.

stock•pile (stŏk'pīl') *n.* Also **stock pile.** A supply of material stored for future use. —*v.* -piled, -piling. To accumulate a stockpile of.

stock•y (stŏk'ē) *adj.* -ier, -iest. Solidly built; thickset. —**stock'i•ness** *n.*

stock•yard (stŏk'yärd') *n.* A large enclosed yard in which livestock is kept until being slaughtered or shipped elsewhere.

stodg•y (stŏj'ē) *adj.* -ier, -iest. 1. a. Dull, narrow, and commonplace. b. Prim or pompous; stuffy. 2. Heavy. [< earlier *stodge,* to cram, gorge.] —**stodg'i•ly** *adv.* —**stodg'i•ness** *n.*

sto•ic (stō'ĭk) *n.* One seemingly indifferent to or unaffected by joy, grief, pleasure, or pain. —*adj.* Also **sto•i•cal** (-ĭ-kəl). Indifferent to or unaffected by pleasure or pain; impassive. [< Gk *Stōïkos,* a member of a school of philosophy that held that all occurrences were the unavoidable result of divine will.] —**sto'i•cal•ly** *adv.* —**sto'i•cism'** (stō'ĭ-sĭz'əm) *n.*

ă pat/ā ate/âr care/ä bar/b bib/ch chew/d deed/ĕ pet/ē be/f fit/g gag/h hat/hw what/
ĭ pit/ī pie/îr pier/j judge/k kick/l lid, fatal/m mum/n no, sudden/ng sing/ŏ pot/ō go/

stoke (stōk) *v.* **stoked, stoking. 1.** To stir up (a fire or furnace). **2.** To tend a fire or furnace. [< MDu *stoken,* to poke.] —**stok′er** *n.*

stole¹ (stōl) *n.* **1.** A long scarf worn by some clergymen while officiating. **2.** A women's long scarf worn about the shoulders. [< OE *stol,* a long robe < L *stola.*]

stole² (stōl). *p.t.* of **steal.**

sto·len (stō′lən). *p.p.* of **steal.**

stol·id (stŏl′ĭd) *adj.* Having or showing little emotion; impassive. [L *stolidus.*] —**sto·lid′i·ty** (stə-lĭd′ə-tē) *n.* —**stol′id·ly** *adv.*

stom·ach (stŭm′ək) *n.* **1.** A large, saclike digestive organ of the alimentary canal, located in vertebrates between the esophagus and small intestine. **2.** *Informal.* The abdomen or belly. **3.** An appetite for food. **4.** Any desire or inclination. —*v.* **1.** To bear; tolerate; endure. **2.** To digest. [< Gk *stomakhos,* throat, mouth, gullet.]

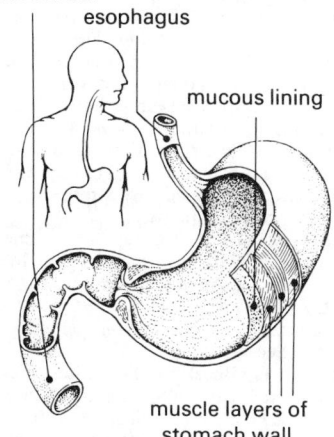

duodenum
esophagus
mucous lining
muscle layers of stomach wall

stomach

stom·ach·er (stŭm′ə-kər) *n.* An embroidered or jeweled garment formerly worn over the chest and stomach, esp. by women.

stomp (stŏmp, stŏmp) *v.* To tread or trample heavily (on). [Var of STAMP.]

stone (stōn) *n.* **1.** Concreted earthy or mineral matter; rock. **2.** Such material used for construction. **3.** A small piece of rock. **4.** A piece of rock shaped for a particular purpose, as a gravestone or millstone. **5.** A gem or precious stone. **6.** A seed with a hard covering, as of a cherry or plum. **7.** *Path.* A mineral concretion in a hollow organ, as in the kidney. **8.** *pl.* **stone.** A unit of weight in Britain, 14 pounds avoirdupois. —*adv.* Utterly; completely: *stone-blind.* —*v.* **stoned, stoning. 1.** To hurl or throw stones at; pelt or kill with stones. **2.** To remove the stones or pits from. [< OE *stān.* See **stei-.**] —**stone** *adj.*

Stone Age. The early period of human culture characterized by the use of stone tools.

stoned (stōnd) *adj. Slang.* Intoxicated; drunk.

stone·wall (stōn′wôl′) *v.* **-walled, -walling. 1.** *Cricket.* To play defensively. **2.** *Informal.* To refuse to answer or cooperate (with).

ston·y (stō′nē) *adj.* **-ier, -iest.** Also **ston·ey. 1.** Covered with or full of stones. **2.** Hard as a stone. **3.** Hard-hearted; unemotional. **4.** Emotionally numbing: *stony fear.*

stood (stŏŏd). *p.t.* & *p.p.* of **stand.**

stooge (stŏŏj) *n.* **1.** One who allows himself to be used for another's profit. **2.** One placed to spy or inform on others.

stool (stŏŏl) *n.* **1.** A backless and armless single seat supported on legs or a pedestal. **2.** A low bench or support for the feet. **3.** A bowel movement. [< OE *stōl.*]

stool pigeon. 1. A pigeon used as a decoy. **2.** An informer, esp. for the police.

stoop¹ (stŏŏp) *v.* **1.** To bend from the waist or middle of the back. **2.** To lower or debase oneself. —*n.* The act of stooping. [< OE *stūpian.* See **steu-.**]

stoop² (stŏŏp) *n.* A small porch, platform, or staircase leading to the entrance of a house or building. [Du *stoep,* front verandah.]

stop (stŏp) *v.* **stopped, stopping. 1.** To close (an opening) by covering, filling in, or plugging up. **2.** To adjust a vibrating medium to produce a desired musical pitch. **3.** To obstruct or block passage on. **4.** To prevent the flow or passage of. **5.** To cause to halt, cease, or desist. **6.** To desist from; cease; come to a halt. **7.** To visit briefly; stay. —*n.* **1.** The act of stopping or condition of being stopped. **2.** A finish; an end. **3.** A stay or visit. **4.** A place stopped at. **5.** A device or means that obstructs, blocks, etc. **6.** An order given to a bank to withhold payment on a check. **7.** A mark of punctuation, esp. a period. **8.** *Mus.* A tuned set of pipes, as in an organ. [< Gmc *stoppōn,* to plug up < LL *stuppāre,* to stop up with a tow.]

stop·gap (stŏp′găp′) *n.* A temporary expedient.

stop·page (stŏp′ĭj) *n.* The act of stopping or condition of being stopped; a halt.

stop·per (stŏp′ər) *n.* Any device inserted to close an opening. —**stop′per** *v.*

stop·watch (stŏp′wŏch′) *n.* A timepiece with a sweep hand operated by an external trigger to measure duration of time.

stor·age (stôr′ĭj, stōr′-) *n.* **1.** The act of storing goods. **2.** A space for storing goods. **3.** The price charged for storing goods.

storage battery. *Elec.* A group of rechargeable cells acting as a unit.

store (stôr, stōr) *n.* **1.** A place where merchandise is offered for sale; a shop. **2.** A stock or supply reserved for future use. **3.** A warehouse or storehouse. **4.** An abundance. —*v.* **stored, storing. 1.** To put away for future use. **2.** To stock with something. **3.** To deposit or receive in a warehouse for safekeeping. [< L *instaurāre,* to restore.]

store·house (stôr′hous′, stōr′-) *n.* **1.** A warehouse. **2.** An abundant source or supply.

store·room (stôr′rŏŏm′, -rŏŏm′, stōr′-) *n.* A room in which things are stored.

sto·rey. *Chiefly Brit.* Variant of **story².**

sto•ried (stôr′ĕd, stōr′-) *adj.* Celebrated in history or story.

stork (stôrk) *n.* A large wading bird with long legs and a long bill. [< OE *storc.* See ster-[1].]

storm (stôrm) *n.* 1. An atmospheric disturbance manifested in strong winds accompanied by rain, snow, or other precipitation, and often by thunder and lightning. 2. A violent, sudden attack. —*v.* 1. To rain, snow, hail, or otherwise precipitate violently: *It stormed last night.* 2. To rant and rage. 3. To try to capture by a violent, sudden attack. [< OE. See twer-.] —**storm′y** *adj.*

sto•ry[1] (stôr′ē, stōr′ē) *n., pl.* -ries. 1. The narrating or relating of an event or series of events, either true or fictitious. 2. A tale. 3. A short fictional literary composition: *short story.* 4. The plot of a novel, play, etc. 5. A statement or allegation of facts. 6. An anecdote. 7. A lie. [< Gk *historia.*]

sto•ry[2] (stôr′ē, stōr′ē) *n., pl.* -ries. Also *chiefly Brit.* **sto•rey.** A complete horizontal division of a building, comprising the area between two adjacent levels. [< ML *historia,* orig a row of windows with pictures on them < STORY.]

stoup (stoōp) *n.* A basin for holy water in a church. [< ON *staup,* vessel.]

stout (stout) *adj.* 1. Determined, bold, or brave. 2. Strong; sturdy; solid. 3. Bulky in figure; corpulent. —*n.* Strong, very dark beer or ale. [< OF *estout* < Gmc.] —**stout′ly** *adv.* —**stout′ness** *n.*

stout•heart•ed (stout′här′tĭd) *adj.* Brave; courageous. —**stout′heart′ed•ness** *n.*

stove[1] (stōv) *n.* An apparatus in which electricity or a fuel is used to furnish heat, as for cooking or comfort. [< MLG or MDu.]

stove[2] (stōv) Alternate *p.t.* & *p.p.* of **stave.**

stove•pipe (stōv′pīp′) *n.* 1. A pipe used to conduct smoke from a stove into a chimney flue. 2. A man's tall silk hat.

stow (stō) *v.* 1. To place, arrange, or store away. 2. To fill by packing tightly. [< OE *stōw,* a place.]

stow•a•way (stō′ə-wā′) *n.* One who hides aboard a ship or other conveyance in order to obtain free passage.

St. Paul (sānt pôl′). The capital of Minnesota. Pop. 309,000.

St. Pe•ters•burg (sānt pē′tərz-bûrg′). 1. A former name for Leningrad. 2. A city of W Florida. Pop. 181,000.

stra•bis•mus (strə-bĭz′məs) *n.* A visual defect in which one eye cannot focus with the other on an objective because of imbalance of the eye muscles. [< Gk *strabizein,* to squint.]

strad•dle (străd′l) *v.* -dled, -dling. 1. To sit astride (of). 2. To appear to favor both sides of (an issue). [< STRIDE.] —**strad′dle** *n.*

strafe (strāf, sträf) *v.* strafed, strafing. To attack with machine-gun fire from low-flying aircraft. [< G *strafen,* to punish.]

strag•gle (străg′əl) *v.* -gled, -gling. 1. To stray or fall behind. 2. To spread out in a scattered or irregular group. [ME *straglen.*] —**strag′gler** *n.* —**strag′gly** *adj.*

straight (strāt) *adj.* 1. Extending continuously in the same direction without curving. 2. Having

no irregularities. 3. Upright. 4. Direct and candid. 5. Uninterrupted. 6. Accurate; true. 7. Unmodified or unaltered. 8. Undiluted. 9. *Slang.* a. Conventional and law-abiding. b. Not being a criminal, drug user, homosexual, etc. —*adv.* In a straight course or manner. —*n.* 1. The straight part of a racecourse between the winning post and the last turn. 2. A straight line, piece or position. 3. In poker, a sequence of five consecutive cards. [ME *streight,* pp of *strecchen* to stretch.] —**straight′ly** *adv.* —**straight′ness** *n.*

straight•edge (strāt′ĕj′) *n.* A rigid flat rectangular bar with a straight edge for testing or drawing straight lines.

straight•en (strāt′n) *v.* To make or become straight. —**straight′en•er** *n.*

straight•for•ward (strāt-fôr′wərd) *adj.* 1. Proceeding in a straight course. 2. Honest; candid. —*adv.* Also **straight•for•wards** (-wərdz). In a straightforward course or manner. —**straight•for′ward•ness** *n.*

straight jacket. Variant of **strait jacket.**

strain[1] (strān) *v.* 1. To pull, draw, or stretch tight. 2. To exert, tax, or be taxed to the utmost. 3. To injure or become injured by overexertion. 4. To stretch beyond the proper point or limit. 5. To strive hard. 6. To filter; pass through a strainer. —*n.* 1. a. The act of straining. b. The state of being strained. 2. A great effort, exertion, or tension. 3. *Phys.* A deformation produced by stress. [< L *stringere,* to draw tight, tie.]

strain[2] (strān) *n.* 1. A group of the same ancestry or species having shared distinctive characteristics. 2. Ancestry; lineage. 3. A kind; sort. 4. A streak; trace. 5. The tone or tenor of something. [< OE *strēon,* generation, offspring. See ster-[2].]

strain•er (strā′nər) *n.* 1. A filter, sieve, colander, etc., used to separate liquids from solids. 2. One that strains.

strait (strāt) *n.* 1. A narrow passage of water joining two larger bodies of water. 2. Often **straits.** A position of difficulty or need. —*adj. Archaic.* 1. Narrow or constricted. 2. Strict, rigid, or righteous. [< L *strictus,* pp of *stringere,* to draw tight.]

strait•en (strāt′n) *v.* 1. To make narrow; restrict. 2. To bring into difficulty or distress: in *straitened circumstances.*

strait jacket. Also **straight jacket.** A jacketlike garment used to bind the arms tightly as a means of restraining a violent patient or prisoner.

strait-laced (strāt′lāst′) *adj.* Prudish.

strand[1] (strănd) *n.* A shore; beach. —*v.* 1. To drive or be driven aground, as a ship. 2. To leave or be left in a difficult or helpless position. [< OE.]

strand[2] (strănd) *n.* 1. Each of the fibers or filaments that are twisted together to form a rope, cable, etc. 2. A string of beads, pearls, etc. [ME *strond.*]

strange (strānj) *adj.* **stranger, strangest.** 1. Previously unknown; unfamiliar. 2. Unusual; extraordinary. 3. Peculiar; queer. 4. Not of one's own or a particular locality or kind;

ă pat/ā ate/âr care/ä bar/b bib/ch chew/d deed/ĕ pet/ē be/f fit/g gag/h hat/hw what/
ĭ pit/ī pie/îr pier/j judge/k kick/l lid, fatal/m mum/n no, sudden/ng sing/ŏ pot/ō go/

exotic. **5.** Lacking experience. [< L *extrā-neus*, foreign, strange.] —**strange'ly** *adv.* —**strange'ness** *n.*

stran•ger (strān'jər) *n.* **1.** One who is neither friend nor acquaintance. **2.** A foreigner, newcomer, or outsider.

stran•gle (străng'gəl) *v.* **-gled, -gling. 1. a.** To kill by choking or suffocating. **b.** To smother. **2.** To suppress or stifle. **3.** To restrict. [< L *strangulāre*, STRANGULATE.] —**stran'gler** *n.*

stran•gu•late (străng'gyə-lāt') *v.* **-lated, -lating. 1.** To strangle. **2.** *Path.* To constrict so as to cut off the flow of blood or other fluid. [L *strangulāre*.] —**stran'gu•la'tion** *n.*

strap (străp) *n.* A long, narrow strip of leather or other similar material, esp. one with a buckle for binding or securing objects. —*v.* **strapped, strapping.** To fasten or secure with a strap. [Var of STROP.]

strap•less (străp'lĭs) *adj.* Without a strap or straps. —*n.* A strapless garment.

strap•ping (străp'ĭng) *adj.* Tall and sturdy.

stra•ta. *pl.* of **stratum.** See Usage note at **stratum.**

strat•a•gem (străt'ə-jəm) *n.* **1.** A trick or artifice designed to deceive or surprise an enemy. **2.** A deception. [< Gk *stratēgēma*, "act of a general."]

strat•e•gy (străt'ə-jē) *n., pl.* **-gies. 1.** The science or art of military command as applied to the overall planning and conduct of combat operations. **2.** A plan of action resulting from the practice of this science. [< Gk *stratēgos*, general.] —**stra•te'gic** (strə-tē'jĭk) *adj.* —**strat'-e•gist** *n.*

strat•i•fy (străt'ə-fī') *v.* **-fied, -fying.** To form strata. —**strat'i•fi•ca'tion** *n.*

stra•to•cu•mu•lus (străt'ō-kyōōm'yə-ləs) *n., pl.* **-li** (-lī'). A low-lying cloud occurring in extensive horizontal layers with massive rounded summits.

strat•o•sphere (străt'ə-sfîr') *n.* The part of the atmosphere above the troposphere. —**strat'o•spher'ic** (-sfîr'ĭk, -sfĕr'ĭk) *adj.*

stra•tum (strā'təm, strä'-, străt'əm) *n., pl.* **-ta** (-tə) or *rare* **-tums. 1.** A horizontal layer of any material, esp. one of several parallel layers arranged one on top of another. **2.** A level in a hierarchy. [< L *strātus*, stretched out, pp of *sternere*, to stretch out.] —**stra'tal** *adj.*

Usage: Strata is standard as a plural form but not as a singular: *All strata of society are represented. Each stratum is accounted for. Stratas* (plural) is not a standard form.

stra•tus (strā'təs, străt'əs) *n., pl.* **-ti** (-tī'). A low-altitude cloud typically resembling a horizontal layer of fog.

Strauss (strous), **Johann.** 1825–1899. Austrian composer.

Stra•vin•sky (strə-vĭn'skē), **Igor.** Born 1882. Russian-born American composer.

straw (strô) *n.* **1.** A stalk or stalks of threshed grain. **2.** A slender tube used for sucking up a liquid. **3.** Something of minimal value. —*adj.* **1.** Pertaining to, used for, or like straw. **2.** Made of straw. [< OE *strēaw*. See ster-[2].]

straw•ber•ry (strô'bĕr'ē, -bə-rē) *n.* **1.** The red, fleshy, edible fruit of a low-growing plant with white flowers. **2.** The plant itself. [< STRAW + BERRY.]

straw vote. An unofficial vote or poll.

stray (strā) *v.* **1. a.** To wander beyond established limits; roam. **b.** To become lost. **2.** To wander about or meander. **3.** To go astray; err. **4.** To digress. —*n.* One that has strayed, esp. a lost domestic animal. —*adj.* **1. a.** Straying or having strayed; out of place. **b.** Lost. **2.** Scattered or separate. [< VL *estragāre*.] —**stray'er** *n.*

streak (strēk) *n.* **1.** A line, mark, or smear differentiated by color or texture from its surroundings. **2.** A trait. **3.** A brief stretch of time: *a streak of good luck.* —*v.* **1.** To mark with or form a streak or streaks. **2.** To move at high speed; rush. [< OE *strica*. See streig-.] —**streak'i•ness** *n.* —**streak'y** *adj.*

stream (strēm) *n.* **1. a.** A body of running water. **b.** A steady current in such a body. **2.** A course or drift, as of opinion or history. —*v.* **1.** To flow in or as in a stream. **2.** To pour forth or emit. **3.** To move in large numbers. **4.** To extend, wave, or float outward. **5.** To give forth a continuous stream of light rays or beams; shine. [< OE *strēam.* See sreu-.] —**stream'y** *adj.*

stream•er (strē'mər) *n.* **1.** A long narrow flag or banner. **2.** A long narrow strip of material. **3.** A ray of light extending upward. **4.** A newspaper headline that runs across a full page.

stream•lined (strēm'līnd') *adj.* Also **stream•line** (-līn'). **1.** Designed or arranged to offer the least resistance to fluid flow. **2.** Improved in efficiency; modernized. —**stream'line'** *v.* (-lined, -lining).

street (strēt) *n.* **1.** A public way or thoroughfare, as in a city or town. **2.** The people living along such a roadway. [< OE *strǣt* < Gmc **strāta* < L *strātus*, pp of *sternere*, to extend.]

street•car (strēt'cär') *n.* A public passenger car operated on rails along the streets of a city.

street•walk•er (strēt'wô'kər) *n.* A prostitute.

strength (strĕngkth, strĕngth) *n.* **1.** The state, quality, or property of being strong; physical power; muscularity. **2.** The power of resisting force or stress; durability; impregnability. **3.** Power or capability. **4.** A source of power or force. **5.** Moral courage or power. **6.** Effective or binding force: *the strength of an argument.* **7.** Degree of concentration, distillation, or saturation; potency. **8.** Intensity. **9.** A concentration of available force or personnel. [< OE *strengthu.*]

strength•en (strĕngk'thən, strĕng'-) *v.* To make or become strong or stronger. —**strength'en•er** *n.*

stren•u•ous (strĕn'yōō-əs) *adj.* **1.** Requiring great effort, energy, or exertion. **2.** Vigorously active; energetic. [L *strēnuus*, brisk, nimble.] —**stren'u•ous•ly** *adv.* —**stren'u•ous•ness** *n.*

strepto–. *comb. form.* A twisted chain. [< Gk *streptos*, twisted.]

strep•to•coc•cus (strĕp'tə-kŏk'əs) *n., pl.* **-ci** (-sī'). Any of various rounded bacteria occurring in pairs or chains and often causing disease.

strep•to•my•cin (strĕp'tə-mī'sən) *n.* An :anti-

ō paw, for/oi boy/ou out/ōō took/ōō coo/p pop/r run/s sauce/sh shy/t to/th thin/*th* the/ ŭ cut/ûr fur/v van/w wag/y yes/z size/zh vision/ə ago, item, edible, gallop, circus/

biotic, $C_{21}H_{39}N_7O_{12}$, produced from mold cultures and used medicinally to combat various bacteria.

stress (strĕs) *n.* **1.** Importance, significance, or emphasis placed upon something. **2. a.** The emphasis placed upon the sound or syllable spoken loudest in a given word or phrase. **b.** A syllable receiving such emphasis. **3.** *Mus.* An accent. **4.** *Phys.* A force that tends to deform a body. **5.** A mentally or emotionally disruptive influence; distress. —*v.* **1.** To place emphasis on; accent. **2.** To subject to pressure or strain. **3.** To subject to mechanical pressure or force. [< L *strictus,* strict.]

–stress. *comb. form.* A feminine agent: **seamstress.** [-ST(ER) + -ESS.]

stretch (strĕch) *v.* **1. a.** To lengthen, widen, or distend by pulling. **b.** To become lengthened, widened, or distended. **2.** To cause to extend across a given space. **3.** To make taut; tighten. **4.** To reach or put forth; extend: *He stretched out his hand.* **5.** To extend (oneself) at full length in a prone position. **6.** To flex one's muscles. **7.** To strain. **8.** To cause to suffice; make do with. **9.** To extend the limits of credulity, conscience, etc. **10.** To prolong. —*n.* **1.** The act of stretching or state of being stretched. **2.** The extent to which something can be stretched; elasticity. **3.** A continuous or unbroken length, area, or expanse. **4.** A straight section of a racecourse or track leading to the finish line. **5.** A continuous period of time. —*adj.* Capable of being stretched; elastic: *a stretch sock.* [< OE *streccan,* to spread out < Gmc *strakkjan.*] —**stretch'a•ble** *adj.* —**stretch'y** *adj.*

stretch•er (strĕch'ər) *n.* **1.** One that stretches. **2.** A canvas-covered frame used to transport the sick, wounded, or dead.

strew (strōō) *v.* **strewn** (strōōn) or **strewed, strewing.** **1.** To spread here and there; scatter; sprinkle. **2.** To cover (a surface) with things scattered or sprinkled. **3.** To be or become dispersed over (a surface). [< OE *strēowian.* See ster-².]

stri•a (strī'ə) *n., pl.* **striae** (strī'ē'). **1.** A thin, narrow groove or channel. **2.** A thin line or band. [L, furrow, channel.] —**stri'at'ed** (-ā'tĭd) *adj.* —**stri•a'tion** *n.*

strick•en (strĭk'ən). Alternate *p.p.* of **strike.** —*adj.* **1.** Struck or wounded, as by a projectile. **2.** Afflicted with something overwhelming, such as a disease, emotion, etc.

strict (strĭkt) *adj.* **1.** Precise; accurate; exact. **2.** Complete; absolute. **3.** Kept within narrow and specific limits; stringent. **4.** Imposing an exacting discipline. **5.** Rigidly conforming; devout: *a strict Catholic.* [L *strictus,* tight, narrow < *stringere,* to draw tight, tighten.] —**strict'ly** *adv.* —**strict'ness** *n.*

stric•ture (strĭk'chər) *n.* **1.** Something that restrains, limits, or restricts. **2.** An adverse criticism; censure. **3.** *Path.* An abnormal narrowing of a duct or passage. [< L *strictus,* STRICT.]

stride (strīd) *v.* **strode, stridden** (strĭd'n), **striding.** To walk vigorously with long steps. —*n.* **1.** The act of striding. **2.** A long step. **3.** A char-

acteristic motion or manner of striding or running. **4.** A step forward; an advance. [< OE *strīdan* < Gmc.] —**strid'er** *n.*

stri•dent (strīd'ənt) *adj.* Loud and harsh; shrill. [< L *strīdēre,* to make a harsh sound.]

strife (strīf) *n.* **1.** Violent dissension; bitter conflict. **2.** A struggle between rivals. [< OF *estrif.*]

strike (strīk) *v.* **struck, struck** or **stricken, striking.** **1. a.** To hit sharply, as with the hand, fist, or a weapon. **b.** To inflict (a blow). **2.** To collide (with) or crash into. **3.** To attack or begin an attack. **4.** To afflict suddenly with a disease. **5.** To impress by stamping or printing. **6.** To produce by hitting some agent, as a key on a musical instrument. **7.** To indicate by a percussive sound: *The clock struck nine.* **8.** To produce (a flame or spark) by friction. **9.** To eliminate: *struck out the error.* **10.** To come upon; discover. **11.** To reach; fall upon. **12.** To impress abruptly or freshly: *strikes me as a good idea.* **13.** To cause (an emotion) to penetrate deeply. **14. a.** To make or conclude (a bargain). **b.** To achieve (a balance). **15.** To fall into or assume (a pose). **16.** To proceed, esp. in a new direction; set out; head. **17.** To engage in a strike against an employer. —*n.* **1.** An act of striking. **2.** An attack. **3.** A cessation of work by employees in support of demands made upon their employer, as for higher pay. **4.** *Baseball.* A pitched ball that is counted against the batter, typically one swung at and missed or one taken and judged to have been in the strike zone. **5.** *Bowling.* The knocking down of all the pins with one ball. [< OE *strican,* to stroke, rub. See streig-.] —**strik'er** *n.*

strike out. *Baseball.* To retire (a batter) or be retired by the recording of three strikes.

strike•out (strīk'out') *n.* The act or an instance of striking out.

strike zone. *Baseball.* The area over the plate between the batter's armpits and knees.

strik•ing (strī'kĭng) *adj.* Impressing the mind or senses with immediacy; prominent.

string (strĭng) *n.* **1.** A cord usually made of fiber, thicker than thread, used for fastening or lacing. **2.** Anything shaped into a long, thin line. **3.** A set of objects threaded together: *a string of beads.* **4.** *Mus.* **a.** A stretched cord that is struck, plucked, or bowed to produce tones. **b.** **strings.** Instruments having such strings, esp. the instruments of the violin family. —*v.* **strung, stringing.** **1.** To furnish with string or strings. **2.** To thread on a string. **3.** To arrange in a series. **4.** To fasten, tie, or hang with a string. **5.** To stretch out. [< OE *streng.*] —**string'i•ness** *n.* —**string'y** *adj.*

string bean. **1.** A narrow, green, edible bean pod. **2.** A plant bearing such pods.

strin•gent (strĭn'jənt) *adj.* **1.** Imposing rigorous standards of performance; severe. **2.** Constricted; tight. [< L *stringere,* to tighten.] —**strin'gen•cy** *n.* —**strin'gent•ly** *adv.*

strip¹ (strĭp) *v.* **stripped, stripping.** **1.** To undress. **2.** To deprive of honors, rank, etc. **3.** To remove all excess detail from. **4.** To dismantle piece by piece. **5.** To denude; bare. [< OE

ă pat/ā ate/âr care/ä bar/b bib/ch chew/d deed/ĕ pet/ē be/f fit/g gag/h hat/hw what/
ĭ pit/ī pie/îr pier/j judge/k kick/l lid, fatal/m mum/n no, sudden/ng sing/ŏ pot/ō go/

(be)striepan, to plunder < Gmc **straupjan.*]
strip² (strĭp) *n.* **1.** A long, narrow piece, usually of uniform width: *a strip of paper.* **2.** An airstrip. [Perh var of STRIPE.]
stripe (strīp) *n.* **1.** A long, narrow band distinguished, as by color or texture, from the surrounding material or surface. **2.** A strip of cloth worn on a uniform to indicate rank, awards, etc.; a chevron. **3.** Sort; kind. —*v.* **striped, striping.** To mark with a stripe or stripes. [< MDu *stripe.*] —**striped** (strĭpt, strī'-pĭd) *adj.*
strip·ling (strĭp'lĭng) *n.* A youth. [ME, prob "slender as a strip."]
strive (strīv) *v.* **strove, striven** (strĭv'ən) or **strived, striving. 1.** To exert much effort or energy. **2.** To struggle; contend. [< OF *estriver.*] —**striv'er** *n.*
strob·o·scope (strŏ'bə-skōp') *n.* Any of various instruments used to make moving objects appear stationary by intermittent illumination or observation. [Gk *strobos,* a whirling round + -SCOPE.] —**strob'o·scop'ic** (-skŏp'ĭk) *adj.* —**strob'o·scop'i·cal·ly** *adv.*
strode (strōd). *p.t.* of **stride.**
stroke (strōk) *n.* **1.** An impact; blow; strike. **2.** An act of striking. **3.** An event having a powerful immediate effect: *a stroke of luck.* **4.** Apoplexy. **5.** An inspired idea or act: *a stroke of genius.* **6.** A single completed movement, as in swimming or rowing. **7.** The member of a rowing crew who sets the tempo of the oarsmen. **8.** Any of a series of movements of a piston from one end of the limit of its motion to the other. **9.** A single mark made by a pen or other marking implement. **10.** A light caressing movement. —*v.* **stroked, stroking. 1.** To rub lightly, as with the hand; caress. **2.** To set the pace for (a rowing crew). [< OE **strāc.* See streig-.]
stroll (strōl) *v.* To walk at a leisurely pace. [Perh < G dial *strollen.*] —**stroll** *n.*
stroll·er (strō'lər) *n.* **1.** One who strolls. **2.** A light four-wheeled chair for transporting small children.
strong (strông) *adj.* **1. a.** Having great physical strength; muscular. **b.** Powerful; forceful. **2.** In sound health; thriving. **3.** Capable of enduring; solid. **4.** Having a specified number of units or members. **5. a.** Persuasive and effective. **b.** Emphatic. **6.** Extreme; drastic. **7.** Intense in degree or quality. [< OE *strang.*] —**strong'ly** *adv.*
strong·box (strông'bŏks') *n.* A stoutly made box or safe in which valuables are deposited.
strong·hold (strông'hōld') *n.* **1.** A fortress. **2.** An area of predominance.
stron·ti·um (strŏn'chē-əm, -tē-əm) *n. Symbol* **Sr** A soft, silvery, easily oxidized metallic element used in pyrotechnic compounds and various alloys. Atomic number 38, atomic weight 87.62. [< *Strontian,* mining village in Scotland.]
strop (strŏp) *n.* A flexible strip of leather or canvas used for sharpening a razor. —*v.* **stropped, stropping.** To sharpen on a strop. [< Gk *strophos,* twisted cord.]
stro·phe (strō'fē, strō'fē') *n.* A stanza of a

poem. [Gk *strophē,* a turning.] —**stroph'ic** *adj.*
strove (strōv). *p.t.* of **strive.**
struck (strŭk). *p.t. & p.p.* of **strike.**
struc·ture (strŭk'chər) *n.* **1.** A complex entity. **2. a.** Organization; arrangement. **b.** Constitution; make-up. **3.** Something constructed, esp. a building or part. —*v.* **-tured, -turing.** To construct or give structure to. [< L *struere* (pp *structus*), to construct.] —**struc'tur·al** *adj.* —**struc'tur·al·ly** *adv.*
stru·del (strōōd'l) *n.* A rolled sheet of dough filled with fruit or cheese and baked. [G.]
strug·gle (strŭg'əl) *v.* **-gled, -gling. 1.** To exert muscular energy, as against a material force or mass; wrestle. **2.** To be strenuously engaged with a problem, task, etc. **3. a.** To contend against. **b.** To compete with. —*n.* **1.** An act of struggling. **2.** Strenuous effort. **3.** Combat; strife. [ME *struglen.*] —**strug'gler** *n.*
strum (strŭm) *v.* **strummed, strumming.** To play idly on (a stringed musical instrument) by plucking the strings with the fingers. [Perh blend of STRING and THRUM.]
strum·pet (strŭm'pĭt) *n.* A whore.
strung (strŭng). *p.t. & p.p.* of **string.**
strut (strŭt) *v.* **strutted, strutting.** To walk with pompous bearing; swagger. —*n.* **1.** A stiff, self-important gait. **2.** A bar or rod used to strengthen a framework by resisting longitudinal thrust. [< OE *strūtian,* to stand out stiffly. See ster-¹.] —**strut'ter** *n.* —**strut'ting·ly** *adv.*
strych·nine (strĭk'nīn', -nən, -nēn') *n.* An extremely poisonous white crystalline alkaloid, $C_{21}H_{22}N_2O_2$. [< Gk *strukhnos,* a kind of plant.]
St. Thom·as (sănt' tŏm'əs). The second-largest of the Virgin Islands of the U.S.
stub (stŭb) *n.* **1.** The short blunt end remaining after something has been cut, broken off, or worn down. **2. a.** The part of a check or receipt retained as a record. **b.** The part of a ticket returned as a voucher of payment. —*v.* **stubbed, stubbing.** To strike (one's toe or foot) against something. [< OE *stybb.* See steu-.]
stub·ble (stŭb'əl) *n.* **1.** Short, stiff stalks, as of grain, left on a field after harvesting. **2.** Anything resembling stubble. [< L *stipula,* straw.] —**stub'bly** *adj.*
stub·born (stŭb'ərn) *adj.* **1.** Unduly determined to exert one's will; obstinate. **2.** Persistent. **3.** Difficult to handle or work. [ME *stoborne.*] —**stub'born·ness** *n.*
stub·by (stŭb'ē) *adj.* **-bier, -biest.** Short and stocky. —**stub'bi·ness** *n.*
stuc·co (stŭk'ō) *n., pl.* **-coes** or **-cos.** A plaster or cement finish for walls. —*v.* To finish or decorate with stucco. [< OHG *stukki,* fragment, covering.]
stuck (stŭk). *p.t. & p.p.* of **stick.**
stuck-up (stŭk'ŭp') *adj. Informal.* Snobbish; conceited.
stud¹ (stŭd) *n.* **1.** An upright post in the framework of a wall for supporting sheets of lath, wallboard, etc. **2.** A small knob, nail head, etc., fixed in and slightly projecting from a surface. **3.** A small ornamental button, as on a dress shirt. —*v.* **studded, studding.** To provide

---

ŏ paw, for/oi boy/ou out/ŏŏ took/ōō coo/p pop/r run/s sauce/sh shy/t to/th thin/*th* the/
ŭ cut/ûr fur/v van/w wag/y yes/z size/zh vision/ə ago, item, edible, gallop, circus/

with or construct with a stud or studs. [< OE *studu*, post, prop.]

stud² (stŭd) *n.* **1.** A stallion or other male animal kept for breeding. **2.** A group of such animals. [< OE *stōd*, stable for breeding.]

stud. student.

stu•dent (st/y/ōō'dənt) *n.* One who studies, esp. at a school.

stud•ied (stŭd'ēd) *adj.* Carefully contrived; deliberate; lacking spontaneity.

stu•di•o (st/y/ōō'dē-ō) *n., pl.* **-os.** **1.** An artist's workroom. **2.** An establishment where an art is taught or studied. **3.** A room or building for motion-picture, television, or radio productions. [< L *studium*, study.]

stu•di•ous (st/y/ōō'dē-əs) *adj.* **1.** Devoted to study. **2.** Earnest; diligent. —**stu'di•ous•ly** *adv.*

stud•y (stŭd'ē) *n., pl.* **-ies.** **1.** The act or process of studying; the pursuit of knowledge. **2.** A branch of knowledge. **3.** A work on a particular subject. **4.** A room intended or equipped for studying. —*v.* **-ied, -ying.** **1.** To apply one's mind purposefully to the acquisition of knowledge or understanding of (any subject). **2.** To take (a course) at a school. **3.** To inquire into; investigate. **4.** To examine closely; contemplate. [< L *studium* < *studēre*, to be eager, study.] —**stud'i•er** *n.*

stuff (stŭf) *n.* **1.** The material out of which something is made or formed; substance. **2.** The basic elements of; essence. **3.** Material not specifically identified. **4.** Woven material, esp. woolens. —*v.* **1. a.** To pack tightly; fill up; cram. **b.** To block or obstruct. **2.** To fill with an appropriate stuffing. **3.** To eat to excess. [< LL *stuppāre*, to plug up.]

stuff•ing (stŭf'ĭng) *n.* Material used to stuff or fill, esp. padding put in cushions or food put in a cavity of meat or vegetables.

stuff•y (stŭf'ē) *adj.* **-ier, -iest.** **1.** Lacking sufficient ventilation. **2.** Blocked: *a stuffy nose.* **3.** Formal; straitlaced. —**stuff'i•ness** *n.*

stul•ti•fy (stŭl'tə-fī') *v.* **-fied, -fying.** **1.** To render useless or ineffectual. **2.** To cause to appear stupid, ridiculous, etc. [< L *stultus*, foolish + *facere*, to make.] —**stul'ti•fi•ca'tion** *n.*

stum•ble (stŭm'bəl) *v.* **-bled, -bling.** **1. a.** To trip and almost fall. **b.** To proceed unsteadily or falteringly. **2.** To make a mistake; blunder. **3.** To come upon accidentally or unexpectedly. [ME *stumblen.*] —**stum'ble** *n.* —**stum'bler** *n.* —**stum'bling•ly** *adv.*

stumbling block. An obstacle or impediment.

stump (stŭmp) *n.* **1.** The part of a tree trunk remaining rooted after the tree has been felled. **2.** A part, as of a limb, remaining after the main part has been cut away. —*v.* **1.** To traverse (a district) making political speeches. **2.** To bring to a halt; perplex. [< MLG.] —**stump'er** *n.* —**stump'y** *adj.*

stun (stŭn) *v.* **stunned, stunning.** **1.** To daze or render senseless, as by a blow. **2.** To stupefy, as with the emotional impact of an experience. [< VL *extonāre*.]

stung (stŭng). *p.t. & p.p.* of **sting**.

stunk (stŭngk). *p.p.* & alternate *p.t.* of **stink**.

stun•ning (stŭn'ĭng) *adj.* **1.** Causing loss of consciousness or emotional shock. **2.** *Informal.*

Of a strikingly attractive appearance.

stunt¹ (stŭnt) *v.* To check the growth or development of; dwarf. [Perh < ME *stont*, short in duration.] —**stunt'ed•ness** *n.*

stunt² (stŭnt) *n.* **1.** A feat displaying unusual skill or daring. **2.** Something of an unusual nature: *publicity stunt.* [?]

stu•pe•fy (st/y/ōō'pə-fī') *v.* **-fied, -fying.** **1.** To dull the senses of. **2.** To amaze; astonish. [< L *stupefacere.*] —**stu'pe•fa'cient** (-fā'shənt) *adj. & n.* —**stu'pe•fac'tion** *n.*

stu•pen•dous (st/y/ōō-pĕn'dəs) *adj.* **1.** Of astounding force, volume, degree, or excellence. **2.** Of tremendous size; huge. [< L *stupēre*, to be stunned.] —**stu•pen'dous•ly** *adv.*

stu•pid (st/y/ōō'pĭd) *adj.* **1.** Slow to apprehend; dull; obtuse. **2.** Showing a lack of sense or intelligence. **3.** Uninteresting; trite: *a stupid job.* [< L *stupēre*, to be stunned.] —**stu•pid'i•ty** *n.* —**stu'pid•ly** *adv.*

stu•por (st/y/ōō'pər) *n.* **1.** A state of reduced sensibility; lethargy. **2.** Mental confusion; daze. [< L *stupēre*, to be stunned.] —**stu'por•ous** *adj.*

stur•dy (stûr'dē) *adj.* **-dier, -diest.** Substantially built; durable; strong. [< OF *estourir*, to stun, daze.] —**stur'di•ly** *adv.* —**stur'di•ness** *n.*

stur•geon (stûr'jən) *n.* A large food fish whose roe is valued as caviar. [< VL *sturiō* < Gmc *strujōn.*]

stut•ter (stŭt'ər) *v.* To speak with a spasmodic hesitation, prolongation, or repetition of sounds. —*n.* The act or habit of stuttering. [< ME *stutten.*] —**stut'ter•er** *n.* —**stut'ter•ing•ly** *adv.*

Stutt•gart (stŭt'gärt). A city of SW West Germany. Pop. 632,000.

St. Vi•tus' dance (sānt' vī'təs-ĭz). Also **St. Vi•tus's dance.** *Path.* Chorea. [< St. *Vitus*, 3rd-century Christian martyr, venerated by sufferers of the disease.]

sty¹ (stī) *n., pl.* **sties.** An enclosure for pigs. [< OE *stī*, *stig* < Gmc *stijam.*]

sty² (stī) *n., pl.* **sties** or **styes.** Inflammation of a sebaceous gland of an eyelid. [< OE *stīgan*, to rise. See **steigh-.**]

style (stīl) *n.* **1.** The way in which something is said or done. **2.** The combination of distinctive features of literary or artistic expression characterizing a particular person, school, etc. **3.** Sort; kind; type: *a style of furniture.* **4.** Individuality expressed in one's actions and tastes. **5.** An elegant mode of existence: *live in style.* **6.** The fashion of the moment. **7.** A customary manner of presenting printed material, including usage, punctuation, spelling, typography, and arrangement. **8.** The slender stalk of a flower pistil. —*v.* **styled, styling.** **1.** To call or name; designate. **2.** To design: *style hair.* [< L *stilus*, writing instrument, style.] —**styl'er** *n.*

styl•ish (stī'lĭsh) *adj.* In step with current fashion; modish; smart; elegant. —**styl'ish•ly** *adv.* —**styl'ish•ness** *n.*

styl•ist (stī'lĭst) *n.* One who cultivates an artful style, esp. a writer.

sty•lis•tic (stī-lĭs'tĭk) *adj.* Of or relating to style, esp. literary style. —**sty•lis'ti•cal•ly** *adv.*

---

styl·ize (stī′līz′) v. **-ized, -izing.** To subordinate verisimilitude to principles of design in the representation of.

sty·lus (stī′ləs) n., pl. **-luses** or **-li** (-lī′). **1.** A sharp, pointed instrument used for writing, marking, or engraving. **2.** A phonograph needle. [L *stilus*, STYLE.]

sty·mie (stī′mē) v. **-mied, -mieing** or **-mying.** To block; thwart. [?]

styp·tic (stĭp′tĭk) adj. **1.** Contracting the tissues or blood vessels; astringent. **2.** Tending to check bleeding. —n. A styptic drug or substance. [< Gk *stuphein*, to contract.]

sty·rene (stī′rēn′) n. A colorless oily liquid, C_8H_8, the monomer for polystyrene.

suave (swäv, swāv) adj. Smoothly gracious in social manner; urbane. [< L *suāvis*, delightful.] **—suave′ly** adv. **—suav′i·ty, suave′ness** n.

sub (sŭb) n. Informal. **1.** A submarine. **2.** A substitute. —v. **subbed, subbing.** To act as a substitute.

sub-. comb. form. **1.** Under or beneath. **2.** Inferior in rank. **3.** Somewhat short of or less than. **4.** Forming a subordinate or constituent part of a whole. [< L *sub*, under, from below.]

sub. subscription.

sub·al·tern (sŭb′ôl′tərn) n. A subordinate. [LL *subalternus*.]

sub·a·tom·ic (sŭb′ə-tŏm′ĭk) adj. **1.** Pertaining to the constituents of the atom. **2.** Participating in reactions characteristic of these constituents.

sub·com·mit·tee (sŭb′kə-mĭt′ē) n. A subordinate committee composed of members appointed from the main committee.

sub·con·scious (sŭb′kŏn′shəs) adj. Not wholly conscious but capable of being made conscious. **—sub′con′scious·ly** adv.

sub·con·ti·nent (sŭb′kŏn′tə-nənt) n. A large land mass on a continent, but in some geographic respect independent of it, as India or S Africa.

sub·con·tract (sŭb′kŏn′trăkt′) n. A contract that assigns some of the obligations of a prior contract to another party. **—sub′con′tract′** v.

sub·cu·ta·ne·ous (sŭb′kyōo-tā′nē-əs) adj. Just beneath the skin. **—sub′cu·ta′ne·ous·ly** adv.

sub·di·vide (sŭb′də-vīd′) v. **-vided, -viding.** To divide into smaller parts. **—sub′di·vi′sion** (-vĭzh′ən) n.

sub·due (səb-d/y/ōo′) v. **-dued, -duing. 1.** To conquer and subjugate. **2.** To quiet or bring under control. **3.** To make less intense. [< L *subdūcere*, to lead away, withdraw.]

sub·e·qua·to·ri·al (sŭb′ē-kwə-tôr′ē-əl, -tōr′ē-əl, sŭb′ĕk-wə-) adj. Belonging to a region adjacent to the equatorial area.

sub·group (sŭb′grōop′) n. A subordinate group.

subj. 1. subject. **2.** subjunctive.

sub·ja·cent (sŭb′jā′sənt) adj. **1.** Located beneath or below. **2.** Lying at a lower level but not directly beneath. [< L *subjacēre*, to lie under.]

sub·ject (sŭb′jĭkt) adj. **1.** Under the power or authority of another. **2.** Prone; disposed: *subject to colds.* **3.** Liable to incur or receive:

subject to misinterpretation. **4.** Contingent or dependent: *subject to rules.* —n. **1.** One who owes allegiance to a government or ruler. **2.** A person or thing concerning which something is said or done. **3.** A course or area of study. **4.** One that experiences or is subjected to something. **5.** *Gram.* A word or phrase in a sentence that denotes the doer of the action or the receiver of the action in passive constructions. —v. (səb-jĕkt′). **1.** To subjugate; subdue. **2.** To submit to the authority of. **3.** To cause to experience or undergo. [< L *subicere*, to bring under.] **—sub·jec′tion** (-jĕk′shən) n.

sub·jec·tive (səb-jĕk′tĭv) adj. **1.** Proceeding from or taking place within an individual's mind. **2.** Particular to a given individual; personal. **—sub·jec′tive·ly** adv. **—sub·jec′tive·ness, sub′jec·tiv′i·ty** n.

subject matter. Matter under consideration in a written work or speech.

sub·join (sŭb-join′) v. To add at the end; append.

sub·ju·gate (sŭb′jə-gāt′) v. **-gated, -gating.** To bring under dominion; conquer. [< L *subjugāre*, to place under a yoke.] **—sub′ju·ga′tion** n. **—sub′ju·ga′tor** n.

sub·junc·tive (sŭb-jŭngk′tĭv) adj. Designating a verb form or set of forms used in English to express a contingent or hypothetical action. [< L *subjungere*, subjoin.] **—sub·junc′tive** n.

sub·let (sŭb′lĕt′) v. **-let, -letting.** To rent (property one holds by lease) to another.

sub·li·mate (sŭb′lə-māt′) v. **-mated, -mating. 1.** To modify the natural expression of (an instinctual impulse) in a socially acceptable manner. **2.** To transform directly from the solid to the gaseous or from the gaseous to the solid state. [L *sublīmāre*, to raise.] **—sub′li·ma′tion** n.

sub·lime (sə-blīm′) adj. **1.** Exalted; lofty. **2.** Inspiring awe; impressive; moving. [L *sublīmis*.] **—sub·lime′ly** adv. **—sub·lim′i·ty** (sə-blĭm′ə-tē), **sub·lime′ness** n.

sub·lim·i·nal (sŭb-lĭm′ə-nəl) adj. Below the threshold of conscious perception. [SUB- + L *limen*, threshold.] **—sub·lim′i·nal·ly** adv.

sub·ma·chine gun (sŭb′mə-shēn′). A lightweight automatic or semiautomatic gun fired from the shoulder or hip.

sub·ma·rine (sŭb′mə-rēn′, sŭb′mə-rēn′) adj. Beneath the surface of the water; undersea. —n. A ship capable of operating submerged.

sub·merge (səb-mûrj′) v. **-merged, -merging. 1.** To place or go under or as if under water or other liquid. **2.** To cover with water. [L *submergere*.] **—sub·mer′gence** n. **—sub·mer′gi·ble** adj. **—sub·mer′gi·bil′i·ty** n.

sub·merse (səb-mûrs′) v. **-mersed, -mersing.** To submerge. **—sub·mers′i·bil′i·ty** n. **—sub·mers′i·ble** adj. **—sub·mer′sion** n.

sub·mi·cro·scop·ic (sŭb′mī′krə-skŏp′ĭk) adj. Too small to be resolved by an optical microscope.

sub·min·i·a·ture (sŭb′mĭn′ē-ə-chŏor′, -chər) adj. Smaller than miniature; exceedingly small. **—sub′min′i·a·tur·ize′** (-chə-rīz′) v. **(-ized, -izing).**

---

sub•mit (səb-mǐt′) *v.* **-mitted, -mitting. 1.** To yield or surrender (oneself) to the will or authority of another; give in. **2.** To commit (something) to the consideration of another. **3.** To offer as a proposition or contention: *I submit that the terms are unreasonable.* **4.** To allow oneself to be subjected to; acquiesce. [< L *submittere,* to place under.] —**sub•mis′sion** *n.* —**sub•mis′sive** *adj.*

sub•nor•mal (sŭb′nôr′məl) *adj.* Less than normal; below the average.

sub•or•di•nate (sə-bôr′də-nǐt) *adj.* **1.** Belonging to a lower or inferior class or rank. **2.** Subject to the authority or control of another. **3.** *Gram.* Dependent on another clause. —*n.* One that is subordinate. —*v.* (sə-bôr′də-nāt′) **-nated, -nating. 1.** To put in a lower or inferior rank or class. **2.** To make subservient. [< ML *subôrdināre,* to put in a lower rank.] —**sub•or′di•na′tion** *n.*

sub•orn (sə-bôrn′) *v.* To induce (a person) to commit a wrong or unlawful act, as perjury. [L *subôrnāre.*] —**sub′or•na′tion** *n.*

sub•poe•na (sə-pē′nə). Also **sub•pe•na.** *n.* A legal writ requiring appearance in court to give testimony. —*v.* To serve or summon with such a writ. [< L *sub poenā,* under penalty (first words in the writ).]

sub ro•sa (sŭb rō′zə). In secret; privately.

sub•scribe (səb-scrīb′) *v.* **-scribed, -scribing. 1.** To sign (one's name). **2.** To sign one's name to in testimony or consent: *subscribe a will.* **3.** To pledge or contribute (a sum of money). **4.** To express concurrence or approval (with *to*). **5.** To receive and pay for a certain number of issues of a periodical (with *to*). [< L *subscrībere.*] —**sub•scrib′er** *n.*

sub•script (sŭb′skrǐpt′) *adj.* Written beneath. —*n.* A character or symbol written next to and slightly below a letter or number. [L *subscriptus,* pp of *subscrībere,* SUBSCRIBE.]

sub•scrip•tion (səb-skrǐp′shən) *n.* **1.** The signing of one's name, as to a document. **2.** A purchase made by signed order, as for the issues of a periodical or a series of theatrical performances.

sub•se•quent (sŭb′sə-kwənt) *adj.* Following in time or order; succeeding. [< L *subsequī,* to follow close after.] —**sub′se•quent•ly** *adv.*

sub•ser•vi•ent (səb-sûr′vē-ənt) *adj.* **1.** Subordinate in capacity or function. **2.** Servile. —**sub•ser′vi•ent•ly** *adv.* —**sub•ser′vi•ence** *n.*

sub•set (sŭb′sĕt′) *n.* A mathematical set contained within a set.

sub•side (səb-sīd′) *v.* **-sided, -siding. 1.** To sink to a lower or normal level. **2.** To become less agitated or active; abate. [L *subsidere,* to sink down.] —**sub•si′dence** *n.*

sub•sid•i•ar•y (səb-sǐd′ē-ăr′ē) *adj.* **1.** Serving to assist or supplement. **2.** Secondary in importance. —*n., pl.* **-ies. 1.** One that is subsidiary. **2.** A company having more than half of its stock owned by another company. [< L *subsidium,* support, SUBSIDY.]

sub•si•dize (sŭb′sə-dīz′) *v.* **-dized, -dizing.** To assist or support with a subsidy.

sub•si•dy (sŭb′sə-dē) *n., pl.* **-dies.** Monetary assistance, as that granted by a government to a private commercial enterprise. [< L *subsidium,* reserve troops, support, help.]

sub•sist (səb-sǐst′) *v.* **1.** To exist. **2.** To be sustained, nourished, etc.; live. [L *subsistere,* to stand still, stand up.]

sub•sis•tence (səb-sǐs′təns) *n.* The act, state, or a means of subsisting.

sub•soil (sŭb′soil′) *n.* The layer of earth beneath the surface soil.

sub•son•ic (sŭb′sŏn′ǐk) *adj.* **1.** Of less than audible frequency. **2.** Having a speed less than that of sound in a designated medium.

sub•stance (sŭb′stəns) *n.* **1. a.** Matter. **b.** Material of a specified, esp. complex, constitution. **2.** The essence of what is said or written; gist. **3.** That which is solid or real; reality as opposed to appearance. **4.** Density; body. **5.** Material possessions; wealth. [< L *substāre,* to be present, stand up.]

sub•stan•dard (sŭb′stăn′dərd) *adj.* Failing to meet a standard; below standard.

sub•stan•tial (səb-stăn′shəl) *adj.* **1.** Of or having substance; material. **2.** Not imaginary; real. **3.** Solidly built; strong. **4.** Ample; sustaining. **5.** Considerable in amount, extent, etc. [< L *substantia,* substance.] —**sub•stan′tial•ly** *adv.*

sub•stan•ti•ate (səb-stăn′shē-āt′) *v.* **-ated, -ating.** To support with proof or evidence; verify. —**sub•stan′ti•a′tion** *n.*

sub•stan•tive (sŭb′stən-tǐv) *adj.* Of substantial amount; considerable. —*n.* A word or group of words functioning as a noun. —**sub′stan•ti′val** (-tī′vəl) *adj.*

sub•sta•tion (sŭb′stā′shən) *n.* A branch station, as of a post office.

sub•sti•tute (sŭb′stə-t/y/ōot′) *n.* One that takes the place of another; a replacement. —*v.* **-tuted, -tuting. 1.** To put or use (a person or thing) in place of another. **2.** To take the place of another. [< L *substituere.*] —**sub′sti•tut′a•bil′i•ty** *n.* —**sub′sti•tu′tion** *n.*

sub•stra•tum (sŭb′strā′təm, -străt′əm) *n., pl.* **-ta** (-tə) or **-tums.** An underlying layer. —**sub′stra′tive** *adj.*

sub•sume (sŭb-s/y/ōōm′) *v.* **-sumed, -suming.** To place in a more comprehensive category. —**sub•sum′a•ble** *adj.*

sub•tend (səb-tĕnd′) *v. Geom.* To be opposite to and delimit. [L *subtendere,* to extend beneath.]

sub•ter•fuge (sŭb′tər-fyōōj′) *n.* An evasive tactic or a trick. [< L *subterfugere,* to flee secretly.]

sub•ter•ra•ne•an (sŭb′tə-rā′nē-ən) *adj.* **1.** Situated beneath the earth's surface; underground. **2.** Hidden; secret. [< L *subterrāneus.*] —**sub′ter•ra′ne•an•ly** *adv.*

sub•ti•tle (sŭb′tīt′l) *n.* **1.** A secondary and usually explanatory title, as of a literary work. **2.** A printed narration or portion of dialogue shown on the screen during or between the scenes of a motion picture.

sub•tle (sŭt′l) *adj.* **-tler, -tlest. 1.** So slight as to be difficult to detect or analyze; elusive. **2.** Not immediately obvious; abstruse. **3.** Able to make fine distinctions; keen. **4.** Characterized by skill or ingenuity. **5.** Characterized by craft

or slyness. [< L *subtīlis*, thin, fine.] —**sub'tle•ty**, **sub'tle•ness** *n.* —**sub'tly** *adv.*
sub•tract (səb-trăkt') *v.* **1.** To take away; deduct. **2.** To find the arithmetic difference between two quantities. [L *substrahere*, to draw away.] —**sub•trac'tion** *n.*
sub•tra•hend (sŭb'trə-hĕnd') *n.* A quantity to be subtracted from another.
sub•trop•i•cal (sŭb'trŏp'ĭ-kəl) *adj.* Of or being the geographical areas adjacent to the tropics. **sub•trop•ics** (sŭb'trŏp'ĭks) *pl.n.* Subtropical regions.
sub•urb (sŭb'ərb') *n.* **1.** A usually residential community outlying a city. **2.** **the suburbs.** The perimeter of country around a major city; environs. [< L *sub-*, near + *urbs*, city.] —**sub•ur'ban** (sə-bûr'bən) *adj.*
sub•ur•ban•ite (sə-bûr'bə-nīt') *n.* One who lives in a suburb.
sub•ur•bi•a (sə-bûr'bē-ə) *n.* Suburbs or suburbanites collectively.
sub•ver•sive (səb-vûr'sĭv, -zĭv) *adj.* Intended or serving to subvert. —*n.* One who advocates subversive means or policies.
sub•vert (səb-vûrt') *v.* **1.** To destroy completely; ruin. **2.** To undermine the character, morals, or allegiance of; corrupt. **3.** To overthrow completely. [< L *subvertere*, to turn upside down.] —**sub•ver'sion** (-vûr'zhən, -shən) *n.* —**sub•vert'er** *n.*
sub•way (sŭb'wā') *n.* An underground urban railroad, usually operated by electricity.
suc•ceed (sək-sēd') *v.* **1.** To follow or come next in time or order; replace, esp. in an office or position. **2.** To accomplish something desired or attempted. [< L *succēdere*, to follow closely, go after.] —**suc•ceed'er** *n.*
suc•cess (sək-sĕs') *n.* **1.** The achievement of something desired or attempted. **2.** The gaining of fame or prosperity. **3.** One that succeeds. [L *successus*, pp of *succēdere*, SUCCEED.] —**suc•cess'ful** *adj.* —**suc•cess'ful•ly** *adv.*
suc•ces•sion (sək-sĕsh'ən) *n.* **1.** The act or process of following in order or sequence. **2.** A group of persons or things following in order; sequence. **3.** The sequence, right, or act of succeeding to a title, throne, dignity, or estate. —**suc•ces'sion•al** *adj.*
suc•ces•sive (sək-sĕs'ĭv) *adj.* Following in uninterrupted order or sequence. —**suc•ces'sive•ly** *adv.*
suc•ces•sor (sək-sĕs'ər) *n.* One that succeeds another.
suc•cinct (sək-sĭngkt') *adj.* Clearly expressed in few words; concise; terse. [L *succinctus*, girdled, concise.] —**suc•cinct'ly** *adv.* —**suc•cinct'ness** *n.*
suc•cor (sŭk'ər) *n.* Also *Brit.* **suc•cour.** Assistance or help in time of distress; relief. [< L *succurrere*, to run to the aid of, run under.] —**suc'cor** *v.*
suc•co•tash (sŭk'ə-tăsh') *n.* Corn kernels and lima beans cooked together. [< Algon.]
Suc•coth (sook'ŏt, -əs) *n.* Also **Suk•koth.** A Jewish harvest festival. [Heb *sukkôth*, "(feast of) booths."]
suc•cu•lent (sŭk'yə-lənt) *adj.* **1.** Full of juice; juicy. **2.** Having thick, fleshy leaves or stems.

—*n.* A succulent plant, as a cactus. [< L *succus*, juice.] —**suc'cu•lence**, **suc'cu•len•cy** *n.* —**suc'cu•lent•ly** *adv.*
suc•cumb (sə-kŭm') *v.* **1.** To yield or submit to an overpowering force. **2.** To die. [< L *succumbere*, to lie down under.]
such (sŭch) *adj.* **1.** Of this or that kind. **2.** Being the same as that which has been mentioned or implied. **3.** Being the same in quality or kind: *pins, needles, and other such trivia.* **4.** Of so great a degree or quality. —**such as.** **1.** For example. **2.** Of the stated or implied kind or degree. Such a one or ones. —*pron.* **1.** To such an extent or degree. **2.** Very. [< OE *swylc, swelc.* See **swo-**.]
suck (sŭk) *v.* **1.** To draw (liquid) into the mouth by inhalation. **2. a.** To draw in by establishing a partial vacuum. **b.** To draw in by or as by suction. **3.** To draw nourishment through or from with the mouth. —*n.* The act of sucking. [< OE *sūcan.* See **seu-⁴**.]
suck•er (sŭk'ər) *n.* **1.** One that sucks. **2.** *Slang.* One who is easily deceived; a dupe. **3.** A lollipop. **4.** A structure or part adapted for clinging by suction. **5.** A shoot arising from the base of a tree trunk or shrub.
suck•le (sŭk'əl) *v.* **-led, -ling.** **1.** To feed at the breast or udder. **2.** To rear; nourish.
suck•ling (sŭk'lĭng) *n.* A young unweaned mammal.
su•cre (soo'krā) *n.* The basic monetary unit of Ecuador.
Su•cre (soo'krā). A capital of Bolivia. Pop. 541,000.
su•crose (soo'krōs') *n.* A sugar, $C_{12}H_{22}O_{11}$, found in sugar cane, sugar beets, etc., and used widely as a sweetener. [F *sucre*, sugar + -OSE.]
suc•tion (sŭk'shən) *n.* **1.** The act or process of sucking. **2.** A force that causes a fluid or solid to be drawn into an interior space or to adhere to a surface. —*adj.* **1.** Creating suction. **2.** Operating by suction. [< L *sūgere* (pp *sūctus*), to suck.]
Su•dan (soo-dăn'). A region lying across Africa, S of the Sahara and N of the equator. —**Su•da•nese'** ('-də-nēz', -nēs') *adj. & n.*
Su•dan, Republic of the (soo-dăn'). A country in NE Africa. Pop. 13,011,000. Cap. Khartoum. —**Su•dan'ic** *adj. & n.*

Republic of the Sudan

sud•den (sŭd′n) *adj.* **1.** Happening without warning; unforeseen. **2.** Characterized by hastiness; rash. **3.** Characterized by rapidity; quick; swift. [< L *subitus.*] —**sud′den•ly** *adv.* —**sud′den•ness** *n.*

suds (sŭdz) *pl.n.* **1.** Soapy water. **2.** Foam; lather. [Orig, dregs, muddy water.] —**suds′y** *adj.*

sue (sōō) *v.* **sued, suing. 1.** To institute legal proceedings; bring suit against (a person) for redress of grievances. **2.** To make an appeal or entreaty. [ME *sewen,* to pursue, prosecute.]

suede (swād) *n.* Also **suède.** **1.** Leather with a soft napped surface. **2.** Fabric resembling this. [< F *(gants) de suède,* "(gloves) of Sweden."]

su•et (sōō′ĭt) *n.* Hard fat of cattle and sheep, used in cooking and making tallow. [< L *sēbum,* tallow, suet.]

Su•ez Canal (sōō-ĕz′, sōō′ĕz). A waterway in NE Egypt, connecting the Mediterranean and Gulf of Suez.

suf. suffix.

suff. 1. sufficient. **2.** suffix.

suf•fer (sŭf′ər) *v.* **1.** To feel pain or distress. **2.** To experience or sustain (an injury, loss, disadvantage, etc.). **3.** To endure or bear; stand. **4.** To permit; allow. [< L *sufferre,* to sustain, "to bear up."] —**suf′fer•a•ble** *adj.* —**suf′fer•er** *n.* —**suf′fer•ing•ly** *adv.*

suf•fer•ance (sŭf′ər-əns, sŭf′rəns) *n.* Sanction or permission implied or given by failure to prohibit; tacit assent.

suf•fer•ing (sŭf′ər-ĭng, sŭf′rĭng) *n.* The act or condition of one who suffers.

suf•fice (sə-fĭs′) *v.* **-ficed, -ficing. 1.** To meet present needs or requirements; be sufficient or adequate for. **2.** To be capable or competent. [< L *sufficere,* to put under, substitute, suffice.] —**suf•fic′er** *n.*

suf•fi•cient (sə-fĭsh′ənt) *adj.* As much as is needed; enough. [< L *sufficere,* SUFFICE.] —**suf•fi′cien•cy** *n.* —**suf•fi′cient•ly** *adv.*

suf•fix (sŭf′ĭks) *n. Gram.* An affix added to the end of a word or stem, serving to form a new word or an inflectional ending. [< L *suffigere,* to affix, fasten beneath.]

suf•fo•cate (sŭf′ə-kāt′) *v.* **-cated, -cating. 1.** To kill or destroy by cutting off from oxygen. **2.** To impair the respiration of. **3.** To cause discomfort by or as by cutting off the supply of air. **4.** To die from suffocation. [L *suffocāre.*] —**suf′fo•ca′tion** *n.*

suf•frage (sŭf′rĭj) *n.* **1.** The right or privilege of voting; franchise. **2.** The exercise of such a right. [< ML *suffrāgium,* vote, support, prayer.]

suf•fra•gette (sŭf′rə-jĕt′) *n.* A female advocate of suffrage for women.

suf•fuse (sə-fyōōz′) *v.* **-fused, -fusing.** To spread through or over, as with color or light. [L *suffundere* (pp *suffūsus*), to pour underneath or into.] —**suf•fu′sion** *n.*

sug•ar (shōōg′ər) *n.* Any of a class of water-soluble crystalline carbohydrates having a characteristically sweet taste. —*v.* To coat or sweeten with sugar. [< Ar *sukkar.*]

sugar beet. A beet with white roots from which sugar is obtained.

sugar cane. A tall grass of warm regions, having thick stems that are a major commercial source of sugar.

sug•ar•plum (shōōg′ər-plŭm′) *n.* A small piece of candy.

sug•ar•y (shōōg′ə-rē) *adj.* **-ier, -iest. 1.** Containing or tasting like sugar. **2.** Deceitfully or cloyingly sweet.

sug•gest (səg-jĕst′, sə-jĕst′) *v.* **1.** To offer for consideration or action; propose. **2.** To bring or call to mind by association; evoke. **3.** To make evident indirectly; imply. [L *suggerere,* to carry or put underneath, furnish, suggest.]

sug•ges•tion (səg-jĕs′chən, sə-jĕs′-) *n.* **1.** The act of suggesting. **2.** Something suggested. **3.** A trace; touch.

sug•ges•tive (səg-jĕs′tĭv, sə-jĕs′-) *adj.* **1.** Tending to suggest thoughts or ideas. **2.** Tending to suggest something improper or indecent. —**sug•ges′tive•ly** *adv.* —**sug•ges′tive•ness** *n.*

su•i•cide (s/y/ōō′ə-sīd′) *n.* **1.** The act or an instance of intentionally killing oneself. **2.** One who commits suicide. [< L *suī,* of oneself + -CIDE.] —**su′i•ci′dal** *adj.*

su•i gen•e•ris (s/y/ōō′ī jĕn′ər-ĭs). Unique. [L, "of one's own kind."]

suit (sōōt) *n.* **1.** A set of outer garments consisting of a coat and trousers or skirt. **2.** Any of the four sets of playing cards that constitute a deck. **3.** Any proceeding in a court of law to recover a right or claim. —*v.* **1.** To meet the requirements of. **2.** To be or make appropriate; adapt. **3.** To please; satisfy. [< VL **sequita,* pursuit.]

suit•a•ble (s/y/ōō′tə-bəl) *adj.* Appropriate to a given purpose or occasion. —**suit′a•bil′i•ty** (-bĭl′ə-tē) *n.* —**suit′a•bly** *adv.*

suit•case (s/y/ōōt′kās′) *n.* A rectangular, flat piece of luggage.

suite (swēt) *n.* **1.** A staff of attendants; retinue. **2.** A series of connected rooms used as a living unit. **3.** (*also* sōōt). A set of matched furniture pieces. **4.** An instrumental composition consisting of a succession of short pieces. [< OF *sieute,* following, retinue.]

suit•ing (sōō′tĭng) *n.* Fabric from which suits are made.

suit•or (sōō′tər) *n.* A man in the process of courting a woman. [< L *sequī,* to follow.]

Suk•koth. Variant of **Succoth.**

sulf-. *comb. form.* Sulfur. [< SULFUR.]

sul•fa drug (sŭl′fə). Any of a group of synthetic organic compounds, such as sulfanilamide, capable of inhibiting bacterial growth and activity.

sul•fa•nil•a•mide (sŭl′fə-nĭl′ə-mīd′) *n.* A white, odorless compound, $C_6H_8N_2SO_2$, used to treat various bacterial infections.

sul•fate (sŭl′fāt′) *n.* A chemical compound containing the bivalent group SO_4.

sul•fide (sŭl′fīd′) *n.* A compound of bivalent sulfur with an electropositive element or group.

sul•fur (sŭl′fər) *n.* Also **sul•phur.** *Symbol* **S** A pale-yellow nonmetallic element used in gunpowder, rubber vulcanization, the manufacture of insecticides and pharmaceuticals, and in the preparation of industrial chemicals.

Atomic number 16, atomic weight 32.064. [< L *sulfur, sulphur.*]

sulfur dioxide. A colorless, extremely irritating gas or liquid, SO_2, used to manufacture sulfuric acid.

sul•fu•ric (sŭl′fyoor′ĭk) *adj.* Of or containing sulfur.

sulfuric acid. A highly corrosive, dense oily liquid, H_2SO_4, used to manufacture fertilizers, paints, detergents, and explosives.

sul•fur•ous (sŭl′fə-rəs, sŭl′fyoor′əs) *adj.* Of, relating to, derived from, or containing sulfur.

sulk (sŭlk) *v.* To be sullenly aloof or withdrawn. —*n.* A mood or display of sulking. [Back-formation < SULKY[1].]

sulk•y[1] (sŭl′kē) *adj.* -ier, -iest. Sullenly aloof or withdrawn. [Perh < obs *sulke*, sluggish.] —**sulk′i•ly** *adv.* —**sulk′i•ness** *n.*

sulk•y[2] (sŭl′kē) *n., pl.* -ies. A light two-wheeled vehicle accommodating one person and drawn by one horse. [< SULKY.]

sul•len (sŭl′ən) *adj.* 1. Showing a brooding ill humor or resentment; morose; sulky. 2. Gloomy or somber in tone, color, etc. [< NF *solein*, alone, sullen.] —**sul′len•ly** *adv.* —**sul′-len•ness** *n.*

sul•ly (sŭl′ē) *v.* -lied, -lying. 1. To mar the cleanness or luster of. 2. To defile; taint. [Prob < OF *souiller*, to soil.]

sul•phur. Variant of sulfur.

sul•tan (sŭl′tən) *n.* A Moslem ruler. [< Ar *sulṭān*, ruler.] —**sul′tan•ate** (-āt′) *n.*

sul•tan•a (sŭl-tăn′ə, -tä′nə) *n.* The wife, mother, sister, or daughter of a sultan.

sul•try (sŭl′trē) *adj.* -trier, -triest. 1. Very hot and humid. 2. Extremely hot; torrid. [< SWELTER.] —**sul′tri•ness** *n.*

sum (sŭm) *n.* 1. The amount obtained as a result of adding. 2. The whole amount or number; aggregate: *the sum of our knowledge.* 3. An amount of money. 4. An arithmetic problem. 5. A summary: *in sum.* —*v.* summed, summing. To give a brief review; summarize. [< L (*res*) *summa,* the highest thing, sum, total.]

su•mac (soo′măk′, shoo′-) *n.* Also **su•mach.** Any of various shrubs or small trees with compound leaves and pointed clusters of small, usually red, hairy fruits. [< Ar *summaq,* sumac tree.]

Su•ma•tra (soo-mä′trə). The second-largest island of Indonesia.

sum•ma•rize (sŭm′ə-rīz′) *v.* -rized, -rizing. To make a summary of; restate briefly. —**sum′-ma•ri•za′tion** *n.*

sum•ma•ry (sŭm′ə-rē) *adj.* 1. Presenting the substance in a condensed form; concise. 2. Performed speedily and without ceremony: *summary justice.* —*n., pl.* -ries. A condensation of the substance of a work. [< L *summa,* SUM.] —**sum•ma′ri•ly** (sə-măr′ə-lē, sŭm′ər-ə-lē) *adv.*

sum•ma•tion (sə-mā′shən) *n.* A summing up, esp. a concluding statement containing a summary of the principal points of a case before a court of law.

sum•mer (sŭm′ər) *n.* The usually warmest season of the year, occurring between spring and autumn. [< OE *sumor.* See **sem-[2].**] —**sum′mer, sum′mer•y** *adj.*

sum•mer•time (sŭm′ər-tīm′) *n.* The summer season.

sum•mit (sŭm′ĭt) *n.* The highest point or part; the top, esp. of a mountain. [< L *summus,* highest, topmost.]

sum•mon (sŭm′ən) *v.* 1. To call together; convene. 2. To send for; request to appear. 3. To order (a person) to appear in court. 4. To call forth; muster: *summoned up a smile.* [< L *summonēre,* to remind secretly.]

sum•mons (sŭm′ənz) *n., pl.* -monses. 1. A call or order to appear or come. 2. A notice summoning a defendant to report to a court.

sump•tu•ous (sŭmp′choo-əs) *adj.* Of a size or splendor suggesting great expense; lavish. [< L *sumptus,* expense.] —**sump′tu•ous•ly** *adv.* —**sump′tu•ous•ness** *n.*

sun (sŭn) *n.* 1. The central star of the solar system, having a mean distance from Earth of about 93 million miles, a diameter of approx. 864,000 miles, and a mass about 330,000 times that of Earth. 2. Any star that is the center of a planetary system. 3. The radiant energy, esp. heat and visible light, emitted by the sun; sunshine. —*v.* sunned, sunning. To expose to or bask in the sun's rays. [< OE *sunne.* See **sāwel-.**]

Sun. Sunday.

sun•bathe (sŭn′bāth′) *v.* To expose the body to the sun. —**sun′-bath′er** *n.*

sun•burn (sŭn′bûrn′) *n.* An inflammation or blistering of the skin caused by overexposure to sunlight. —*v.* To afflict with or be subjected to a sunburn.

sun•dae (sŭn′dē, -dā′) *n.* A dish of ice cream topped with syrup, fruits, nuts, and whipped cream. [?]

Sun•day (sŭn′dē, -dā′) *n.* The first day of the week and the Christian Sabbath. [< OE *sunnandæg,* "day of the sun."]

sun•der (sŭn′dər) *v.* To break apart; divide. [< OE *syndrian, sundrian.* See **sen-.**]

sun•di•al (sŭn′dī′əl) *n.* An instrument that indicates local apparent solar time by measuring the hour angle of the sun with a pointer that casts a shadow on a calibrated dial.

sun•down (sŭn′doun′) *n.* The time of sunset.

sun•dries (sŭn′drēz) *pl.n.* Miscellaneous articles. [< SUNDRY.]

sun•dry (sŭn′drē) *adj.* Various; miscellaneous. [< OE *syndrig,* apart, separate. See **sen-.**]

sun•fish (sŭn′fĭsh′) *n.* 1. Any of various flat-bodied North American freshwater fishes. 2. A large marine fish with a rounded body.

sun•flow•er (sŭn′flou′ər) *n.* A tall plant bearing large, yellow-rayed flowers and oil-rich, edible seeds.

sung (sŭng). *p.p.* & alternate *p.t.* of **sing.**

sun•glass•es (sŭn′glăs′ĭz, -glä′sĭz) *pl.n.* Eyeglasses with tinted lenses to protect the eyes from the sun's glare.

sunk (sŭngk). *p.p.* & alternate *p.t.* of **sink.** See Usage note at **sink.**

sunk•en (sŭng′kən). Alternate *p.p.* of **sink.** —*adj.* 1. Depressed, fallen in, or hollowed. 2. Submerged. 3. Below the surrounding level.

ô paw, for/oi boy/ou out/oo took/oo coo/p pop/r run/s sauce/sh shy/t to/th thin/*th* the/
ŭ cut/ûr fur/v van/w wag/y yes/z size/zh vision/ə ago, item, edible, gallop, circus/

sun·light (sŭn'lĭt') *n.* The light of the sun; sunshine.

sun·lit (sŭn'lĭt') *adj.* Illuminated by the sun.

sun·ny (sŭn'ē) *adj.* **-nier, -niest. 1.** Exposed to or abounding in sunshine. **2.** Cheerful; genial.

sun·rise (sŭn'rīz') *n.* The first appearance of the sun above the E horizon.

sun·set (sŭn'sĕt') *n.* The disappearance of the sun below the W horizon.

sun·shine (sŭn'shīn') *n.* The light of the sun; the direct rays from the sun.

sun·spot (sŭn'spŏt') *n.* Any of the relatively dark spots that appear in groups on the surface of the sun.

sun·stroke (sŭn'strōk') *n.* Heat stroke caused by exposure to the sun and characterized by a rise in temperature, convulsions, and coma. —**sun'struck'** (-strŭk') *adj.*

sun tan. Also **sun·tan** (sŭn'tăn'). A tan color on the skin from exposure to the sun. —**sun'-tanned'** *adj.*

sun·up (sŭn'ŭp') *n.* The time of sunrise.

Sun Yat-sen (sōōn' yät'sĕn'). 1866–1925. Founder of the Republic of China (1911).

sup (sŭp) *v.* **supped, supping.** To eat the evening meal; dine. [< OF *soup*, piece of bread dipped in broth, soup.]

sup. 1. above (L *supra*). **2.** superior. **3.** *Gram.* superlative. **4.** supplement. **5.** supply.

su·per (sōō'pər) *n. Informal.* A superintendent in an apartment or office building. —*adj. Slang.* Ideal; first-rate.

super–. *comb. form.* **1.** Placement above, over, or outside. **2.** Superiority in size, quality, number, or degree. **3.** A degree exceeding a norm. **4.** *Chem.* Presence of an ingredient in a high proportion. [< L *super*, above, over.]

super. 1. superintendent. **2.** superior.

su·per·a·bun·dant (sōō'pər-ə-bŭn'dənt) *adj.* Abundant to excess; more than ample. —**su'-per·a·bun'dance** *n.*

su·per·an·nu·at·ed (sōō'pər-ăn'yōō-ā'tĭd) *adj.* **1.** Retired or discharged because of age or infirmity. **2.** Obsolete; antiquated. [< ML *superannuāri*, to be too old.]

su·perb (sōō-pûrb', sə-) *adj.* **1.** Of unusually high quality. **2.** Majestic; imposing. [< L *superbus*, superior, proud, arrogant.]

su·per·charge (sōō'pər-chärj') *v.* To increase the power of (an engine). —**su'per·charg'er** *n.*

su·per·cil·i·ar·y (sōō'pər-sĭl'ē-ĕr'ē) *adj.* **1.** Pertaining to the eyebrow. **2.** Located over the eyebrow. [< L *supercilium*, eyebrow.]

su·per·cil·i·ous (sōō'pər-sĭl'ē-əs) *adj.* Characterized by haughty scorn; disdainful; arrogant. [< L *supercilium*, "upper eyelid," eyebrow, pride.] —**su'per·cil'i·ous·ly** *adv.* —**su'-per·cil'i·ous·ness** *n.*

su·per·con·duc·tiv·i·ty (sōō'pər-kŏn'dŭk'tĭv'ə-tē) *n.* The flow of electric current without resistance in certain metals and alloys at temperatures near absolute zero. —**su'per·con·duc'tor** *n.*

su·per·e·go (sōō'pər-ē'gō, -ĕg'ō) *n.* The division of the psyche that develops by the incorporation of the perceived moral standards of the community, is mainly unconscious, and includes the conscience.

su·per·e·rog·a·to·ry (sōō'pər-ə-rŏg'ə-tôr'ē, -tōr'ē) *adj.* Superfluous; unnecessary.

su·per·fi·cial (sōō'pər-fĭsh'əl) *adj.* **1.** Of or being on or near the surface. **2.** Concerned with or comprehending only what is apparent or obvious. **3. a.** Apparent rather than actual or substantial. **b.** Trivial. [< L *superficiēs*, surface.] —**su'per·fi'ci·al'i·ty, su'per·fi'cial·ness** *n.* —**su'per·fi'cial·ly** *adv.*

su·per·flu·id (sōō'pər-flōō'ĭd) *n.* A fluid exhibiting frictionless flow at temperatures close to absolute zero. —**su'per·flu·id'i·ty** *n.*

su·per·flu·i·ty (sōō'pər-flōō'ə-tē) *n., pl.* **-ties. 1.** The quality or condition of being superfluous. **2.** Something that is superfluous.

su·per·flu·ous (sōō-pûr'flōō-əs) *adj.* Beyond what is required or sufficient; extra. [< L *superfluere*, to overflow.] —**su·per'flu·ous·ly** *adv.* —**su·per'flu·ous·ness** *n.*

su·per·high·way (sōō'pər-hī'wā') *n.* A broad highway for high-speed traffic.

su·per·hu·man (sōō'pər-hyōō'mən) *adj.* **1.** Divine; supernatural. **2.** Beyond ordinary or normal human ability, power, or experience.

su·per·im·pose (sōō'pər-ĭm-pōz') *v.* To lay or place upon or over something else. —**su'per·im'po·si'tion** *n.*

su·per·in·tend (sōō'pər-ĭn-tĕnd') *v.* To have charge of; exercise supervision over; manage. [LL *superintendere*, to oversee.] —**su'per·in·ten'dence** *n.*

su·per·in·ten·dent (sōō'pər-ĭn-tĕn'dənt) *n.* One who supervises or is in charge of some undertaking, building, etc.

su·pe·ri·or (sə-pîr'ē-ər) *adj.* **1.** Higher in rank, station, or authority. **2.** Of a higher nature or kind. **3.** Of great value or excellence. **4.** Greater in number or amount. **5.** Haughty. **6.** *Ptg.* Set above the main line of type. —*n.* **1.** One who surpasses another in rank or quality. **2.** The head of a monastery, convent, etc. **3.** *Ptg.* A superior character. [< L *superus*, situated above, upper.] —**su·pe'ri·or'i·ty** (-pîr'ē-ôr'ə-tē, -ŏr'ə-tē) *n.*

Superior, Lake. The largest of the Great Lakes.

su·per·la·tive (sōō-pûr'lə-tĭv) *adj.* **1.** Of the highest order, quality, or degree. **2.** *Gram.* Expressing the extreme degree of comparison of an adjective or adverb. —*n.* **1.** The highest degree; acme. **2.** *Gram.* **a.** The superlative degree. **b.** An adjective or adverb expressing the superlative degree. [< LL *superlātīvus.*] —**su·per'la·tive·ly** *adv.* —**su·per'la·tive·ness** *n.*

su·per·man (sōō'pər-măn') *n.* A man with more than human powers.

su·per·mar·ket (sōō'pər-mär'kĭt) *n.* A large self-service retail food and household-goods store.

su·per·nal (sōō-pûr'nəl) *adj.* **1.** Celestial; heavenly. **2.** Exalted. [< L *supernus.*]

su·per·nat·u·ral (sōō'pər-năch'ər-əl) *adj.* **1.** Not attributable to natural forces. **2.** Attributable to divine power. —*n.* That which is supernatural. —**su'per·nat'u·ral·ly** *adj.* —**su'-per·nat'u·ral·ness** *n.*

su·per·no·va (sōō'pər-nō'və) *n., pl.* **-vae** (-vē'). The explosion of most of the material in a star,

---

ă pat/ā ate/âr care/ä bar/b bib/ch chew/d deed/ĕ pet/ē be/f fit/g gag/h hat/hw what/ ĭ pit/ī pie/îr pier/j judge/k kick/l lid, fatal/m mum/n no, sudden/ng sing/ŏ pot/ō go/

resulting in an extremely bright, short-lived object that emits vast amounts of energy.

su•per•nu•mer•ar•y (sōō′pər-n/y/ōō′mər-är′ē) *n., pl.* **-ries. 1.** Someone or something in excess of the regular, necessary, or usual number. **2.** *Theater.* A performer without a speaking part. —*su′per•nu′mer•ar•y adj.*

su•per•pow•er (sōō′pər-pou′ər) *n.* A powerful and influential nation, esp. a nuclear power that dominates its satellites and allies in an international power bloc.

su•per•sat•u•rate (sōō′pər-săch′ər-āt′) *v.* **-rated, -rating.** To cause (a chemical solution) to be more highly concentrated than is normally possible under given conditions of temperature and pressure.

su•per•scribe (sōō′pər-skrīb′) *v.* **-scribed, -scribing.** To write (something) on the outside or upper part of, as on a letter, envelope, etc. [L *superscribere,* to write over.]

su•per•script (sōō′pər-skrĭpt′) *adj.* Written above, as a diacritical mark. —*n.* A character printed or written above and immediately to one side of another; 2 is the superscript in x^2. [L *superscriptus,* pp of *superscribere,* SUPERSCRIBE.]

su•per•sede (sōō′pər-sēd′) *v.* **-seded, -seding. 1.** To take the place of; replace or succeed. **2.** To cause to be set aside or displaced. [< L *supersedēre,* to sit above, desist from.]

su•per•son•ic (sōō′pər-sŏn′ĭk) *adj.* Of, at, or caused by a speed greater than the speed of sound in a specified medium.

su•per•sti•tion (sōō′pər-stĭsh′ən) *n.* **1.** A belief that some action not logically related to a course of events influences its outcome. **2.** Any belief, practice, or rite unreasoningly upheld by faith in magic, chance, or dogma. [< L *superstitiō,* excessive fear, superstition.] —*su′per•sti′tious adj.*

su•per•struc•ture (sōō′pər-strŭk′chər) *n.* **1.** Any structure built on top of something else. **2.** That part of a building above the foundation.

su•per•vise (sōō′pər-vīz′) *v.* **-vised, -vising.** To direct and inspect the performance of (workers or work); oversee. [ML *supervidēre,* to look over.] —*su′per•vi′sion* (-vĭzh′ən) *n.* —*su′per•vi′sor n.* —*su′per•vi•so•ry* (-vī′zə-rē) *adj.*

su•pine (sōō′pīn′, sōō′pīn′) *adj.* **1.** Lying on the back or having the face upward. **2.** Indisposed to act; lethargic; passive. [L *supinus.*]

sup•per (sŭp′ər) *n.* An evening meal, esp. a light one. [< SUP.]

suppl. supplement; supplementary.

sup•plant (sə-plănt′) *v.* To take the place of; supersede or displace. [< L *supplantāre,* to trip up one's heel.] —*sup•plant′er n.*

sup•ple (sŭp′əl) *adj.* **-pler, -plest. 1.** Readily bent; pliant. **2.** Moving and bending with agility; limber. **3.** Compliant or adaptable. [< L *supplex,* beseeching, submissive.] —*sup′ple•ness n.*

sup•ple•ment (sŭp′lə-mənt) *n.* **1.** Something added to complete a thing or make up for a deficiency. **2.** A section added to a newspaper, book, or document to give further information. —*v.* (sŭp′lə-mĕnt′). To provide or form a supplement to. [< L *supplēre,* to complete, SUPPLY.] —*sup′ple•men′ta•ry* (-tə-rĕ, -trē), *sup′ple•men′tal adj.*

sup•pli•ant (sŭp′lĭ-ənt) *adj.* Asking humbly and earnestly; beseeching. —*n.* One who supplicates. [< L *supplicāre,* SUPPLICATE.]

sup•pli•cant (sŭp′lĭ-kənt) *n.* A suppliant.

sup•pli•cate (sŭp′lĭ-kāt′) *v.* **-cated, -cating. 1.** To ask for humbly or earnestly, as by praying. **2.** To make a humble entreaty to; beseech. [< L *supplicāre,* to kneel down, beg humbly.] —*sup′pli•ca′tion n.*

sup•ply (sə-plī′) *v.* **-plied, -plying. 1.** To make available for use; provide. **2.** To furnish or equip with what is needed or lacking. **3.** To fill sufficiently; satisfy: *supply a need.* —*n., pl.* **-plies. 1.** The act of supplying. **2.** An amount available for a given use; stock. **3.** Often **supplies.** Materials or provisions stored and dispensed when needed. **4.** *Econ.* The amount of a commodity available for meeting a demand or for purchase at a given price. [< L *supplēre,* to fill up, complete.] —*sup•pli′er n.*

sup•port (sə-pôrt′, -pōrt′) *v.* **1.** To bear the weight of, esp. from below. **2.** To hold in position; prevent from falling. **3.** To be capable of bearing; withstand. **4.** To provide for or maintain by supplying with money or other necessities. **5.** To corroborate or substantiate. **6.** To aid the cause of by approving, favoring, or advocating. **7.** To endure; tolerate. **8.** To act in a subordinate role to (a leading actor). —*n.* **1.** The act of supporting. **2.** Someone or something that supports. **3.** Maintenance or subsistence. [< L *supportāre,* to carry, convey.] —*sup•port′er n.* —*sup•por′tive adj.*

sup•pose (sə-pōz′) *v.* **-posed, -posing. 1.** To assume to be true for argument's sake. **2.** To believe probable; be inclined to think. **3.** To consider as a suggestion: *Suppose we dine together.* **4.** To expect or require: *He is supposed to come at 8:00.* [< L *suppōnere* (pp *suppositus*), to put under, substitute.]

sup•po•si•tion (sŭp′ə-zĭsh′ən) *n.* **1.** The act of supposing. **2.** An unproven statement or assumption.

sup•pos•i•to•ry (sə-pŏz′ə-tôr′ē, -tōr′ē) *n., pl.* **-ries.** A solid medication designed to melt within a bodily cavity other than the mouth. [< L *suppositōrius,* "placed under."]

sup•press (sə-prĕs′) *v.* **1.** To put an end to forcibly; subdue; crush. **2.** To curtail or prohibit the activities of. **3.** To keep from being revealed, published, or circulated. **4.** To hold back, as an impulse; check. [< L *supprimere,* to press down.] —*sup•pres′sion n.* —*sup•pres′sive adj.*

sup•pu•rate (sŭp′yə-rāt′) *v.* **-rated, -rating.** To form pus, as a wound. [L *suppūrāre.*] —*sup′pu•ra′tion n.*

su•prem•a•cy (sə-prĕm′ə-sē) *n., pl.* **-cies. 1.** The condition or quality of being supreme. **2.** Supreme power or authority.

su•preme (sə-prĕm′) *adj.* **1.** Greatest in power, authority, or rank. **2.** Greatest in importance or degree. **3.** Ultimate; final. [L *suprēmus,* superl of *superus,* situated above, upper.] —*su•preme′ly adv.*

ô paw, for/oi boy/ou out/ōō took/ōō coo/p pop/r run/s sauce/sh shy/t to/th thin/*th* the/ ŭ cut/ûr fur/v van/w wag/y yes/z size/zh vision/ə ago, item, edible, gallop, circus/

Supreme Court. 1. The highest Federal court in the U.S. 2. The highest court in a state within the U.S.

Supreme Soviet. The legislature of the Soviet Union.

supt., **Supt.** superintendent.

sur-. *comb. form.* 1. Over, beyond, or above. 2. Excessively; extremely. [< L *super*, above, over.]

Su·ra·ba·ya (sōōr'ə-bī'ə). A city of NE Java. Pop. 1,008,000.

su·rah (sōōr'ə) *n.* A soft twilled fabric of silk, rayon, etc. [< *Surat*, republic of India.]

sur·cease (sûr'sēs', sər-sēs') *n.* A ceasing; end.

sur·charge (sûr'chärj') *n.* 1. An additional sum added to the usual amount or cost. 2. A new value or denomination printed over a postage stamp. —*v.* 1. To overcharge (a person). 2. To print a surcharge on (a postage stamp).

sur·cin·gle (sûr'sĭng'gəl) *n.* A girth that binds a saddle, pack, or blanket to the body of a horse. [< OF *sur-*, over + *cengle*, belt.]

sur·coat (sûr'kōt') *n.* 1. A loose outer coat or gown. 2. A tunic worn in the Middle Ages by a knight over his armor.

sure (shōōr) *adj.* **surer, surest.** 1. Incapable of being doubted. 2. Having no doubt; certain; confident. 3. Not liable to fail; thoroughly dependable. 4. a. Bound to happen; inevitable. b. Destined: *sure to succeed.* —**make sure.** To establish without doubt; make certain. —**to be sure.** Indeed; certainly. —*adv. Informal.* Surely; indeed; undoubtedly. —**for sure.** Certainly; unquestionably: *We'll win for sure.* [< L *sēcūrus*, "free from care," safe.]

sure-fire (shōōr'fīr') *adj. Informal.* Bound to be successful or perform as expected: *a sure-fire plan.*

sure-foot·ed (shōōr'fŏŏt'ĭd) *adj.* Not liable to stumble or fall.

sure·ly (shōōr'lē) *adv.* 1. Firmly and with confidence. 2. Undoubtedly; certainly.

sure·ty (shōōr'ə-tē) *n., pl.* **-ties.** 1. Confidence in one's abilities; poise. 2. A certainty. 3. A guarantee against loss, damage, or default. 4. A guarantor.

surf (sûrf) *n.* The mass of foamy water caused by the breaking of the sea against the shore. —*v.* To engage in surfing. [?]

sur·face (sûr'fəs) *n.* 1. a. The outer or the topmost boundary of an object. b. A material layer constituting such a boundary. 2. The superficial or outward appearance of anything. —*v.* **-faced, -facing.** 1. To give a surface to by smoothing or leveling. 2. To rise to the surface. 3. To emerge after concealment. [< F *sur*, above + FACE.] —**sur'face** *adj.*

surf·board (sûrf'bôrd', -bôrd') *n.* The narrow, somewhat rounded board used by surfers for riding waves into shore.

sur·feit (sûr'fĭt) *v.* To feed or supply to fullness or excess; satiate. —*n.* 1. Overindulgence in food or drink. 2. The result of such overindulgence; satiety. 3. An excessive amount. [< VL *superficere*, to overdo.]

surf·er (sûr'fər) *n.* One who engages in surfing.

surf·ing (sûr'fĭng) *n.* A sport in which one

attempts to ride a surfboard toward the shore.

surg. surgeon; surgery; surgical.

surge (sûrj) *v.* **surged, surging.** 1. To move in a billowing or swelling manner. 2. To move forward in great numbers. 3. To increase suddenly. —*n.* 1. A heavy, billowing, or swelling motion like that of great waves. 2. A sudden increase or onrush: *a surge of joy.* [< L *surgere*, "to lead straight up," rise.]

sur·geon (sûr'jən) *n.* A physician specializing in surgery.

sur·ger·y (sûr'jə-rē) *n., pl.* **-ies.** 1. The medical diagnosis and treatment of injury, deformity, and disease by manual and instrumental operations. 2. A surgical operating room or laboratory. [< Gk *kheirurgos*, working by hand.] —**sur'gi·cal** *adj.*

Su·ri·nam (sōōr'ə-năm). A territory of the Netherlands, in N South America. Pop. 362,000. Cap. Paramaribo.

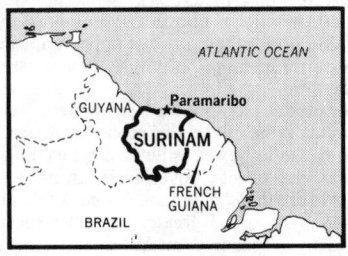

Surinam

sur·ly (sûr'lē) *adj.* **-lier, -liest.** Sullenly rude and ill-humored; brazenly uncivil; gruff. [Earlier *sirly*, orig "lordly" < SIR.] —**sur'li·ness** *n.*

sur·mise (sər-mīz') *v.* **-mised, -mising.** To infer (something) without sufficiently conclusive evidence. —*n.* A guess; conjecture. [< LL *supermittere*, to throw upon.]

sur·mount (sər-mount') *v.* 1. To overcome (an obstacle). 2. To ascend to the top of and cross over. 3. To place something above; to top. 4. To be above or on top of.

sur·name (sûr'nām') *n.* One's family name as distinguished from his given name.

sur·pass (sər-păs', -päs') *v.* 1. To go beyond the limit, powers, or extent of; transcend. 2. To be or go beyond in quantity, degree, amount, etc.

sur·plice (sûr'plĭs) *n.* A loose-fitting white gown worn over a cassock by some clergymen. [< ML *superpellicium.*]

sur·plus (sûr'pləs) *adj.* Being in excess of what is needed or required. —*n.* A quantity in excess of what is needed. [< ML *superplūs.*]

sur·prise (sər-prīz') *v.* **-prised, -prising.** 1. To encounter suddenly or unexpectedly; take or catch (a person) unawares. 2. To attack or capture suddenly and without warning. 3. To cause to feel astonishment or amazement. —*n.* 1. The act of surprising. 2. A feeling of amazement or wonder. 3. An unexpected encounter, event, or gift. [< OF *surprendre*, "to overtake."] —**sur·pris'er** *n.*

---

sur•re•al•ism (sə-rē'əl-ĭz'əm) *n.* A literary and artistic movement that attempts to express the workings of the subconscious mind. —**sur•re'al•ist** *adj.* & *n.* —**sur•re'al•is'tic** *adj.*

sur•ren•der (sə-rĕn'dər) *v.* 1. To relinquish possession or control of to another because of demand or compulsion. 2. To give oneself up, as to an enemy. [< OF *surrendre.*] —**sur•ren'der** *n.*

sur•rep•ti•tious (sûr'əp-tĭsh'əs) *adj.* Performed, made, or acquired by secret, clandestine, or stealthy means. [< L *surripere,* to seize secretly.] —**sur'rep•ti'tious•ly** *adv.*

sur•rey (sûr'ē) *n., pl.* **-reys.** A horse-drawn four-wheeled vehicle with two seats. [< *Surrey,* county in England.]

sur•ro•gate (sûr'ə-gĭt, -gāt') *n.* 1. One that is substituted for another; a substitute. 2. A judge having jurisdiction over the probate of wills and settlement of estates. [L *subrogāre,* to substitute.]

sur•round (sə-round') *v.* 1. To enclose on all sides; encircle; ring. 2. To confine on all sides so as to bar escape. [< LL *superundāre.*]

sur•round•ings (sə-roun'dĭngz) *pl.n.* External circumstances, conditions, and objects; environment.

sur•tax (sûr'tăks') *n.* An additional tax.

sur•veil•lance (sər-vā'ləns) *n.* Close observation of a person or group, esp. of one under suspicion. [< F *surveiller,* to watch over.]

sur•vey (sər-vā', sûr'vā') *v.* 1. To examine or look at in a comprehensive way. 2. To determine the boundaries, area, or elevations of by measuring angles and distances. —*n.* (sûr'vā'). 1. A detailed inspection or investigation. 2. A general or comprehensive view. 3. a. The process of surveying. b. A report on or map of that which is surveyed. [< ML *supervidēre,* to look over.] —**sur•vey'al** *n.* —**sur•vey'or** *n.*

sur•vey•ing (sər-vā'ĭng) *n.* The measurement of dimensional relationships, as of horizontal distances, elevations, directions, and angles, on the earth's surface.

sur•vive (sər-vīv') *v.* **-vived, -viving.** 1. To remain alive or in existence; continue life or activity. 2. To live longer than; outlive. [< LL *supervivere.*] —**sur•viv'al** *n.* —**sur•vi'vor** *n.*

sus•cep•ti•ble (sə-sĕp'tə-bəl) *adj.* 1. Readily subject to an influence or agency. 2. Liable to be stricken with or by: *susceptible to colds.* 3. Especially sensitive or impressionable. [< L *suscipere,* to take up, receive.] —**sus•cep'ti•bil'i•ty** *n.* —**sus•cep'ti•ble** *adj.*

sus•pect (sə-spĕkt') *v.* 1. To have suspicion; mistrust. 2. To surmise to be probable; imagine. 3. To think (a person) guilty without proof. —*n.* (sŭs'pĕkt'). One who is suspected, esp. of committing a crime. —*adj.* (sŭs'pĕkt'). Open to or viewed with suspicion. [< L *suspicere,* to look up at, watch.]

sus•pend (sə-spĕnd') *v.* 1. To bar for a period from a privilege, office, or position. 2. To interrupt or stop temporarily. 3. a. To hold in abeyance: *suspend judgment.* b. To render ineffective temporarily: *suspend a sentence.* 4. To hang so as to allow free movement. 5. To support or keep from falling without apparent

attachment. 6. To fail to make payments or meet obligations. [< L *suspendēre,* to hang up.]

sus•pend•er (sə-spĕn'dər) *n.* 1. One of a pair of straps worn over the shoulders to support trousers. 2. *Brit.* A garter.

sus•pense (sə-spĕns') *n.* 1. The condition of being suspended; suspension. 2. A state of uncertainty. 3. Anxiety or apprehension. —**sus•pense'ful** *adj.*

sus•pen•sion (sə-spĕn'shən) *n.* 1. The act of suspending or condition of being suspended, as temporary abrogation or postponement. 2. A device from which something is suspended. 3. A relatively coarse, noncolloidal dispersion of solid particles in a liquid.

sus•pi•cion (sə-spĭsh'ən) *n.* 1. The act or an instance of suspecting something without proof. 2. A minute amount; hint; trace. [< L *suspicere,* to look at secretly, SUSPECT.]

sus•pi•cious (sə-spĭsh'əs) *adj.* 1. Arousing or open to suspicion; questionable. 2. Tending to suspect; distrustful. —**sus•pi'cious•ly** *adv.*

sus•tain (sə-stān') *v.* 1. To maintain; prolong. 2. To supply with necessities or nourishment; provide for. 3. To keep from falling or sinking. 4. To support or encourage. 5. To endure or withstand. 6. To suffer (loss or injury). 7. To affirm the validity or justice of. 8. To prove or confirm. [< L *sustinēre,* to hold up.] —**sus•tain'a•ble** *adj.*

sus•te•nance (sŭs'tə-nəns) *n.* 1. The act of sustaining or condition of being sustained. 2. The supporting of life or health; maintenance. 3. Nourishment; food. 4. Means of support. [< OF *sustenir,* sustain.]

su•tra (sōō'trə) *n.* Also **sut•ta** (sōō'tə). Any of various aphoristic discourses or narratives traditional in Buddhism and Hinduism. [Sk *sūtra,* thread, string, collection of rules.]

sut•tee (sŭ'tē', sŭt'ē') *n.* The act or practice of a Hindu widow cremating herself on her husband's funeral pyre.

su•ture (sōō'chər) *n.* 1. a. The process of joining by or as if by sewing. b. The material used in this procedure, as thread, gut, etc. c. The line so formed. 2. The line of junction or an immovable joint between two bones of the skull. —*v.* **-tured, -turing.** To join surgically by means of sutures; sew up. [< L *sūtūra,* a sewing together, seam.]

su•ze•rain (sōō'zə-rən, -rān') *n.* 1. A feudal lord to whom fealty was due. 2. A nation that controls another nation politically. [F.] —**su'ze•rain** *adj.* —**su'ze•rain•ty** *n.*

svelte (svĕlt) *adj.* **svelter, sveltest.** Slender; willowy; lithe. [< It *svelto,* "stretched," slender.]

Sverd•lovsk (sfĕrd'lôfsk'). A city of the Soviet Union, in the W Russian S.F.S.R. Pop. 1,026,000.

sw short wave; short-wave.

SW southwest.

Sw. Swedish.

swab (swŏb). Also **swob.** *n.* 1. Absorbent material attached to the end of a stick or wire and used for cleansing or applying medicine. 2. A mop for cleaning decks. 3. A sailor. —*v.*

ô paw, for/oi boy/ou out/ōō took/ōō coo/p pop/r run/s sauce/sh shy/t to/th thin/*th* the/
ŭ cut/ûr fur/v van/w wag/y yes/z size/zh vision/ə ago, item, edible, gallop, circus/

swabbed, swabbing. To clean or treat with a swab. [Prob < MDu *swabbe*, mop.]

swad·dle (swŏd'l) *v.* **-dled, -dling. 1.** To wrap in bandages; swathe. **2.** To wrap (a baby) in strips of linen or other cloth. [< OE *swæthel*, swaddling clothes.]

swag (swăg) *n.* Goods or property obtained forcibly or illicitly. [Prob < Scand.]

swage (swāj) *n.* A tool used in bending or shaping cold metal. [< OF *souaige*.] —**swage** *v.* (**swaged, swaging**).

swag·ger (swăg'ər) *v.* **1.** To walk with an insolent air; strut. **2.** To brag; bluster. [Prob < SWAG.] —**swag'ger** *n.* —**swag'ger·er** *n.*

swagger stick. A short cane carried by military officers.

Swa·hi·li (swä-hē'lē) *n.* A Bantu language of E and C Africa, widely used as a lingua franca. —**Swa·hi'li·an** *adj.*

swain (swān) *n.* **1.** A country youth, esp. a young shepherd. **2.** A lover. [< ON *sveinn*, a boy, herdsman.]

swal·low¹ (swä'lō) *v.* **1.** To cause to pass from the mouth into the stomach; ingest. **2.** To consume or devour. **3.** To ingest reluctantly. **4. a.** To bear humbly; tolerate: *swallow an insult*. **b.** To believe without question. **5. a.** To suppress: *swallow one's feelings*. **b.** To take back; retract: *swallow one's words*. —*n.* **1.** The act of swallowing. **2.** The amount or matter that can be swallowed at one time. [< OE *swelgan*. See **swel-¹**.]

swal·low² (swä'lō) *n.* Any of various birds with narrow, pointed wings and a usually notched or forked tail. [< OE *swealwe* < Gmc **swalwi*.]

swal·low·tail (swä'lō-tāl') *n.* **1.** Something resembling or suggestive of the deeply forked tail of a swallow. **2.** A man's fitted formal coat with a long, divided back part. **3.** Any of various butterflies with a taillike extension at the end of each hind wing.

swam (swăm). *p.t.* of **swim.**

swa·mi (swä'mē) *n.* **1.** A Hindu religious teacher. **2.** A spiritualist seer.

swamp (swämp, swômp) *n.* Land saturated with water; marsh. —*v.* **1.** To drench in or deluge with water. **2.** To overwhelm. **3.** To sink by filling with water. —**swamp'i·ness** *n.* —**swamp'y** *adj.*

swan (swän) *n.* A large, usually white aquatic bird with webbed feet and a long slender neck. [< OE *swan, suan*. See **swen-**.]

swang (swăng). *Rare. p.t.* of **swing.**

swank (swăngk) *adj.* Also **swank·y** (swăng'kē), **-ier, -iest. 1.** Imposingly fashionable or elegant. **2.** Ostentatious; pretentious. —*n.* **1.** Smartness; elegance. **2.** Swagger; pretentiousness. [< MHG *swanken*, to swing, swag.] —**swank'i·ly** *adv.* —**swank'i·ness** *n.*

swan's-down (swänz'doun') *n.* Also **swans·down. 1.** The down of a swan. **2.** A soft woolen or cotton fabric.

swap (swäp). Also **swop.** *v.* **swapped, swapping.** *Informal.* To trade one thing for another; exchange. [ME *swappen*, to strike, hit.] —**swap** *n.* —**swap'per** *n.*

sward (swôrd) *n.* Land covered with grassy

turf. [< OE *sweard*, skin of the body, rind of bacon.]

sware (swâr). *Archaic. p.t.* of **swear.**

swarm (swôrm) *n.* **1.** A large number of insects or other small organisms, esp. when in motion. **2.** A throng of persons or animals. —*v.* **1.** To move in a swarm. **2.** To leave a beehive to form a new colony. **3.** To move or congregate in great numbers; throng. **4.** To be overrun or filled. [< OE *swearm*. See **swer-²**.]

swarth·y (swôr'thē) *adj.* **-ier, -iest.** Having a dark or sunburned complexion. [< OE *sweart*. See **swordo-**.] —**swarth'i·ness** *n.*

swash (swäsh, swôsh) *n.* A splash or splashing sound. [Prob imit.] —**swash** *v.*

swash·buck·ler (swäsh'bŭk'lər) *n.* A flamboyant swordsman or daredevil. —**swash'buck'ling** *adj.*

swas·ti·ka (swäs'tĭ-kə, swä-stē'kə) *n.* **1.** An ancient symbol formed by a cross with the ends of the arms bent at right angles. **2.** The emblem of Nazi Germany. [Sk *svastika*, a sign of good luck.]

swat (swät) *v.* **swatted, swatting.** To deal a sharp blow to; slap. [Var of SQUAT.] —**swat** *n.* —**swat'ter** *n.*

swath (swäth, swôth) *n.* Also **swathe** (swäth, swôth). **1.** The width of the stroke of a scythe or mowing machine. **2. a.** A path made in mowing. **b.** A row of mown grass or grain. [< OE *swæth*, track, trace < Gmc **swath-*.]

swathe (swäth) *v.* **swathed, swathing.** To wrap or bind with or as with bandages. [< OE *swathian*, to wrap up.]

sway (swā) *v.* **1.** To swing or cause to swing from side to side. **2.** To bend; swerve. **3.** To vacillate. **4.** To persuade; exert influence on. **5.** *Archaic.* To rule or govern. —*n.* **1.** A gentle swinging from side to side. **2.** Power; influence. **3.** Dominion; sovereign power. [Prob < ON *sveigja*, to bend, yield.]

Swa·zi·land (swä'zĭ-lănd'). A kingdom in SE Africa. Pop. 400,000. Cap. Mbabane.

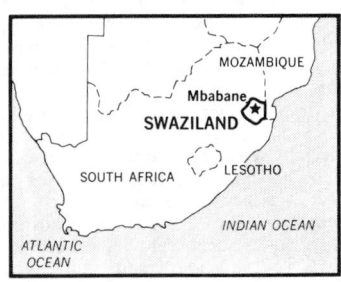

Swaziland

swear (swâr) *v.* **swore, sworn, swearing. 1.** To make a solemn declaration or promise. **2.** To curse or blaspheme. **3.** To assert under oath. **4.** To pledge with a solemn oath; vow. **5.** To administer a legal oath to. **6.** To affirm earnestly and with great conviction. [< OE *swerian*. See **swer-¹**.] —**swear'er** *n.*

sweat (swĕt) *v.* **sweated** or **sweat, sweating. 1.**

To excrete perspiration through the pores in the skin; perspire. **2.** To exude in or become moist with surface droplets. **3.** To condense atmospheric moisture. **4.** *Informal.* To work or cause to work long and hard. **5.** *Informal.* To worry or suffer. —*n.* **1.** Perspiration. **2.** Any condensation of moisture on a surface. **3.** Strenuous exercise or labor. [< OE *swǣtan.* See **sweid**-.] —**sweat'y** *adj.*

sweat•er (swĕt'ər) *n.* A knitted or crocheted garment worn on the upper part of the body.

sweat gland. Any of the numerous small, tubular glands that in man are found everywhere in the skin and that secrete perspiration externally through pores.

Swed. Swedish.

Swede (swēd) *n.* **1.** A native or inhabitant of Sweden. **2.** A person of Swedish descent.

Swe•den (swēd'n). A kingdom in NW Europe. Pop. 7,495,000. Cap. Stockholm.

Sweden

Swed•ish (swē'dĭsh) *adj.* Of or pertaining to Sweden, the Swedes, or their language. —*n.* The Germanic language of Sweden.

sweep (swēp) *v.* **swept, sweeping. 1.** To clean or clear with or as with a broom. **2.** To brush. **3.** To move, remove, or clear, as by wind or rain. **4.** To move or unbalance emotionally. **5.** To traverse with speed or intensity. **6.** To encompass in a wide curve. —*n.* **1.** A clearing or removal with or as with a broom. **2.** The motion of sweeping: *a sweep of the arm.* **3.** An encompassed range or scope. **4.** A reach or extent. **5.** Any curve or contour. [< OE *swāpan,* to sweep. See **swei**-.] —**sweep'er** *n.*

sweep•ing (swē'pĭng) *adj.* Extending over a great area; wide-ranging. —*n.* **1.** The action of one who sweeps. **2. sweepings.** That which is swept up; debris; litter.

sweep•stakes (swēp'stāks') *n., pl.* **-stakes.** Also **sweep•stake** (-stāk'). A lottery in which the participants' contributions form a fund to be awarded as a prize to the winner or winners.

sweet (swēt) *adj.* **1.** Having a sugary taste. **2.** Pleasing to the senses, feelings, or mind. **3.** Having a pleasing disposition. **4.** Not saline; fresh: *sweet water.* **5.** Not spoiled, sour, or decaying. —*n.* **1.** Something that is sweet or contains sugar. **2.** A dear or beloved person. [< OE *swēte.* See **swād**-.] —**sweet'ly** *adv.* —**sweet'ness** *n.*

sweet•bread (swēt'brĕd') *n.* The thymus gland of an animal, used for food.

sweet•bri•er (swēt'brī'ər) *n.* Also **sweet•bri•ar.** A rose with prickly stems and fragrant pink flowers.

sweet•en (swēt'n) *v.* **1.** To make sweet or sweeter by the addition of sugar. **2.** To make pleasurable or gratifying. **3.** To make bearable; alleviate. —**sweet'en•er** *n.*

sweet•en•ing (swēt'n-ĭng) *n.* **1.** The act or process of making sweet. **2.** Something used to sweeten.

sweet•heart (swēt'härt') *n.* One who is loved by another.

sweet•meat (swēt'mēt') *n.* A candy.

sweet pea. A climbing plant cultivated for its variously colored, fragrant flowers.

sweet potato. 1. The thick, sweetish, orange-colored, edible root of a tropical vine. **2.** The vine itself.

swell (swĕl) *v.* **swelled, swelled** or **swollen, swelling. 1.** To increase in size or volume as a result of internal pressure; expand; protrude. **2.** To increase in force, number, or intensity. **3.** To fill or become filled with an emotion, as pride. —*n.* **1.** A bulge or protuberance. **2.** A long wave that moves continuously without breaking. **3.** *Informal.* One who is always fashionably dressed. —*adj. Informal.* **1.** Fashionably elegant; stylish. **2.** Fine; excellent. [< OE *swellan* < Gmc **swaljan.*]

swell•ing (swĕl'ĭng) *n.* **1.** The act of swelling or expanding. **2.** Something that is swollen, esp. an abnormally swollen bodily part.

swel•ter (swĕl'tər) *v.* To be affected by oppressive heat; feel faint from the heat. [< OE *sweltan,* to die. See **swel-²**.]

swel•ter•ing (swĕl'tər-ĭng) *adj.* Oppressively hot and humid.

swept (swĕpt). *p.t. & p.p.* of **sweep.**

swerve (swûrv) *v.* **swerved, swerving.** To turn abruptly aside from a straight course. [< OE *sweorfan,* to file away, scour, polish. See **swerbh**-.] —**swerve** *n.*

swift (swĭft) *adj.* **1.** Moving or able to move with speed; fast; fleet. **2.** Coming, occurring, or accomplished quickly. —*n.* A dark-colored, narrow-winged, swallowlike bird. [< OE. See **swei**-.] —**swift'ly** *adv.* —**swift'ness** *n.*

Swift (swĭft), **Jonathan.** 1667–1745. English satirist.

swig (swĭg) *n. Informal.* A large swallow or draft, as of a liquid; a gulp. [?] —**swig** *v.* **(swigged, swigging).**

swill (swĭl) *v.* **swilled, swilling.** To drink eagerly, greedily, or to excess. —*n.* **1.** A mixture of liquid and solid food fed to animals. **2.** Garbage; refuse. [< OE *swilian,* to wash out.] —**swill'er** *n.*

swim¹ (swĭm) *v.* **swam, swum, swimming. 1.** To

propel oneself through water by bodily movements. **2.** To swim across (a body of water). —*n.* **1.** The act of one that swims. **2.** A period or instance of swimming. [< OE *swimman.*] —**swim′mer** *n.*

swim² (swĭm) *v.* **swam, swum, swimming.** To be dizzy; feel faint or giddy: *my head is swimming.* [< OE *swima,* dizziness. See **swei-.**]

swin•dle (swĭnd′l) *v.* **-dled, -dling.** To cheat or defraud (someone) of money or property. —*n.* The act or an instance of swindling; a fraud. [< G *schwindeln,* to be dizzy, swindle, cheat.] —**swin′dler** *n.*

swine (swīn) *n., pl.* **swine. 1.** Often *pl.* A pig or related animal. **2.** A contemptible, vicious, or greedy person. [< OE *swīn.* See **su-.**] —**swin′-ish** *adj.*

swing (swĭng) *v.* **swung, swinging. 1.** To move rhythmically back and forth. **2.** To ride on a swing. **3.** To move, walk, or run with a free-swaying motion. **4.** To turn in place, as on a hinge or other pivot. **5.** To move with a swinging motion; brandish. **6.** *Slang.* To be executed by hanging. **7.** *Slang.* To manipulate or manage successfully. —*n.* **1.** A rhythmic back-and-forth movement. **2.** A sweeping blow or stroke. **3.** The manner in which a person or thing swings something, as a baseball bat or golf club. **4.** A seat suspended from above for the enjoyment of those who sit and swing thereon. **5.** A type of dance music based on jazz but employing a larger band and simpler harmonic and rhythmic patterns. —**in full swing.** In action to the maximum speed, capacity, or ability. [< OE *swingan,* to whip, strike, fling oneself. See **sweng-.**]

swing•er (swĭng′ər) *n. Slang.* One who participates actively in youthful fads.

swipe (swīp) *n.* A heavy, sweeping blow. —*v.* **swiped, swiping. 1.** To hit with a sweeping blow. **2.** *Slang.* To steal; filch.

swirl (swûrl) *v.* To rotate or spin in or as in a whirlpool or eddy. —*n.* **1.** The motion of whirling or spinning. **2.** Something that swirls; a whirlpool or eddy. [ME *swyrl,* eddy, whirlpool.] —**swirl′y** *adj.*

swish (swĭsh) *v.* **1.** To move with a whistle or hiss. **2.** To rustle, as certain fabrics. —*n.* **1.** A sharp sibilant or rustling sound. **2.** A movement making such a sound. [Prob imit.]

swiss (swĭs) *n.* Also **Swiss.** A crisp, sheer cotton cloth used for curtains, light garments, etc. [< Swiss.]

Swiss (swĭs) *adj.* Of or pertaining to Switzerland, its inhabitants, or its culture. —*n., pl.* **Swiss.** A native or inhabitant of Switzerland.

Swiss cheese. A firm white or pale-yellow cheese with many large holes.

switch (swĭch) *n.* **1.** A slender flexible rod, stick, twig, etc., used for whipping. **2.** A flailing or lashing, as with a slender rod. **3.** A device used to break or open an electrical circuit. **4.** A device used to transfer rolling stock from one track to another. **5.** A shift, as of opinion. —*v.* **1.** To whip with or as with a switch. **2.** To shift, transfer, or change: *switch the conversation.* **3.** To cause (an electric current or appliance) to begin or cease operation:

switch off the radio. [Perh < MDu *swijch,* bough, twig.] —**switch′er** *n.*

switch•board (swĭch′bôrd′, -bōrd′) *n.* A panel containing control switches and other apparatus for operating electric circuits.

switch•man (swĭch′mən) *n.* One who operates railroad switches.

Swit•zer•land (swĭt′sər-lənd). A federal republic in C Europe. Pop. 5,429,000. Cap. Bern.

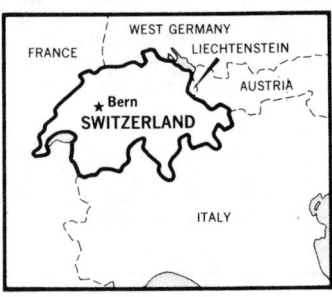

Switzerland

swiv•el (swĭv′əl) *n.* A link, pivot, or other fastening that permits free turning of attached parts. —*v.* **-eled** or **-elled, -eling** or **-elling.** To turn or rotate on or as on a swivel. [Perh < OE *swīfan,* to revolve. See **swei-.**]

swob. Variant of **swab.**

swol•len (swōl′ən). Alternate *p.p.* of **swell.**

swoon (swōōn) *v.* To faint. —*n.* A fainting spell. [< OE *swōgan,* to suffocate, choke.]

swoop (swōōp) *v.* To make a sudden sweeping movement, as a bird descending upon its prey. —*n.* A swift, sudden descent. [< OE *swāpan,* to swing, sweep, drive. See **swei-.**]

swop. Variant of **swap.**

sword (sôrd) *n.* A weapon having a long blade for cutting or thrusting, often worn ceremonially as a symbol of power or authority. —**at swords′ points.** Ready for combat; antagonistic. [< OE. See **swer-³.**]

sword•fish (sôrd′fĭsh′) *n.* A large marine game and food fish with a long, swordlike extension of the upper jaw.

sword•play (sôrd′plā′) *n.* The action or art of using a sword; fencing.

swords•man (sôrdz′mən) *n.* **1.** A person skilled in the use of the sword. **2.** A person armed with a sword, as a fencer or soldier. —**swords′man•ship′** *n.*

swore (swôr). *p.t.* of **swear.**

sworn (swôrn). *p.p.* of **swear.**

swum (swŭm). *p.p.* & *archaic p.t.* of **swim.**

swung (swŭng). *p.t.* & *p.p.* of **swing.**

syb•a•rite (sĭb′ər-īt) *n.* Also **Syb•a•rite.** A person devoted to pleasure and luxury. [L *Sybarita,* native of Sybaris, ancient Greek city.] —**syb′a•rit′ic** (-ə-rĭt′ĭk) *adj.*

syc•a•more (sĭk′ə-môr′, -mōr′) *n.* **1.** A large North American tree with maplelike leaves, ball-like seed clusters, and patchy bark. **2.** An Old World tree related to the maples. [< Gk *sukamoros.*]

syc•o•phant (sĭk′ə-fənt) *n.* One who attempts

---

to win favor or advance himself by flattering persons of influence; a servile self-seeker. [< Gk *sukophantēs*, "fig-shower," "accuser."] —syc'o•phan•cy *n.*

Syd•ney (sĭd'nē). A city of SE Australia. Pop. 2,300,000.

syl., syll. 1. syllable. 2. syllabus.

syl•lab•i•cate (sĭ-lăb'ə-kāt') *v.* -cated, -cating. Also **syl•lab•i•fy** (-fī'), -fied, -fying. To divide into syllables. —syl•lab'i•ca'tion *n.*

syl•la•ble (sĭl'ə-bəl) *n.* A single uninterrupted sound forming part of a word or, in some cases, an entire word. [< Gk *sullabē*, "a gathering (of letters)."] —syl•lab'ic (sĭ-lăb'ĭk) *adj.*

syl•la•bus (sĭl'ə-bəs) *n., pl.* -buses or -bi (-bī'). An outline of the main subjects covered in a course of study. [< Gk *sittuba*, book title, label, table of contents.]

syl•lo•gism (sĭl'ə-jĭz'əm) *n.* A form of deductive reasoning consisting of a major premise and a minor premise that, taken together, lead to a conclusion. [< Gk *sullogismos*, "a reckoning together."] —syl'lo•gis'tic (-jĭs'tĭk) *adj.* —syl'lo•gis'ti•cal•ly *adv.*

sylph (sĭlf) *n.* 1. Any of a class of elemental beings believed to inhabit the air. 2. A slim, graceful woman or girl. [NL *sylphus*.]

syl•van (sĭl'vən) *adj.* 1. Of, pertaining to, or characteristic of woods or forest regions. 2. Abounding in trees; wooded. [< L *silva, sylva*, forest.]

sym–. Variant of **syn–.**

sym. 1. symbol. 2. symphony.

sym•bol (sĭm'bəl) *n.* 1. Something that represents something else by association, resemblance, or convention. 2. A sign used to represent an operation, element, quantity, quality, or relation, as in mathematics or music. [L *symbolum*, sign, token.] —sym•bol'ic (-bŏl'ĭk) *adj.* —sym•bol'i•cal•ly *adv.*

sym•bol•ism (sĭm'bə-lĭz'əm) *n.* The representation of things by means of symbols.

sym•bol•ize (sĭm'bə-līz') *v.* -ized, -izing. 1. To be or serve as a symbol of. 2. To represent by a symbol or symbols.

sym•me•try (sĭm'ə-trē) *n.* 1. A relationship of characteristic correspondence, equivalence, or identity among constituents of a system or between different systems. 2. Exact correspondence of form and constituent configuration on opposite sides of a dividing line or plane or about a center or axis. [< Gk *summetros*, "of like measure," symmetrical.] —sym•met'ri•cal (sĭ-mĕt'rĭ-kəl) *adj.*

sym•pa•thet•ic (sĭm'pə-thĕt'ĭk) *adj.* 1. Of, expressing, feeling, or resulting from sympathy. 2. In agreement; favorable; inclined. —sym'pa•thet'i•cal•ly *adv.*

sympathetic nervous system. The part of the autonomic nervous system whose stimulation increases the blood pressure, heart rate, and respiration rate, and, in general, prepares an organism for vigorous activity, as in response to danger.

sym•pa•thize (sĭm'pə-thīz') *v.* -thized, -thizing. 1. To feel or express compassion; commiserate (with *with*). 2. To share or understand an-

other's feelings or ideas (with *with*). —sym'pa•thiz'er *n.*

sym•pa•thy (sĭm'pə-thē) *n., pl.* -thies. 1. Mutual understanding between persons. 2. A feeling or expression of pity or sorrow for the distress of another; compassion. 3. Favor; agreement; approval: *in sympathy with one's ideas.* [< Gk *sumpathēs*, affected by like feelings.]

sym•pho•ny (sĭm'fə-nē) *n., pl.* -nies. 1. *Mus.* A long orchestral composition, usually consisting of three or four related movements. 2. A **symphony orchestra.** [< Gk *sumphōnos*, harmonious.] —sym•phon'ic (-fŏn'ĭk) *adj.*

symphony orchestra. A large orchestra composed of string, wind, and percussion sections.

sym•po•si•um (sĭm-pō'zē-əm) *n., pl.* -ums or -sia (-zē-ə). 1. A conference for discussion of some topic. 2. A collection of writings on a particular topic. [< Gk *sumposion*, drinking party.]

symp•tom (sĭm'təm, sĭmp'-) *n.* 1. A circumstance or phenomenon regarded as an indication of a certain condition. 2. A phenomenon experienced by an individual as a departure from normal function, sensation, or appearance, generally indicating disorder or disease. [< Gk *sumptōma*, occurrence, phenomenon.] —symp'to•mat'ic *adj.*

syn–, sym–. *comb. form.* 1. Together or with. 2. Same, alike, similar, or at the same time. 3. Union or fusion. [< Gk *sun, xun*, together, with.]

syn. synonym; synonymous; synonymy.

syn•a•gogue (sĭn'ə-gŏg') *n.* A building or place of meeting for Jewish worship and religious instruction. [< Gk *sunagōgē*, assembly.]

syn•apse (sĭn'ăps) *n.* The point at which a nerve impulse passes between neurons. [< Gk *sunapsis*, point of contact.]

syn•chro•nize (sĭn'krə-nīz', sĭng'-) *v.* -nized, -nizing. 1. To occur at the same time; be simultaneous. 2. To cause to operate with exact coincidence in time or rate. —syn'chro•ni•za'tion *n.* —syn'chro•niz'er *n.*

syn•chro•nous (sĭn'krə-nəs, sĭng'-) *adj.* Occurring at the same time; simultaneous. [< Gk *sunkhronos*.] —syn'chro•nous•ly *adv.*

syn•cline (sĭn'klīn') *n.* A low, troughlike area in bedrock, in which rocks incline together from opposite sides.

syn•co•pate (sĭn'kə-pāt', sĭng'-) *v.* -pated, -pating. To modify (musical rhythm) by syncopation. [< Gk *sunkopē*, a cutting off.]

syn•co•pa•tion (sĭn'kə-pā'shən, sĭng'-) *n. Mus.* A shift in which a normally weak beat is stressed.

syn•cre•tism (sĭn'krə-tĭz'əm, sĭng'-) *n.* The attempt or tendency to combine or reconcile differing beliefs, as in philosophy or religion. [< Gk *sunkrētismos*, union.] —syn'cre•tis'tic, syn•cret'ic (-krĕt'ĭk) *adj.*

synd. syndicate.

syn•di•cate (sĭn'dĭ-kĭt) *n.* 1. An association of people formed to carry out a large business undertaking. 2. An agency that sells articles for simultaneous publication in a number of newspapers or periodicals. [< Gk *sundikos*,

---

ô paw, for/oi boy/ou out/ŏŏ took/ōō coo/p pop/r run/s sauce/sh shy/t to/th thin/*th* the/
ŭ cut/ûr fur/v van/w wag/y yes/z size/zh vision/ə ago, item, edible, gallop, circus/

SYMBOLS AND SIGNS

+ plus

− minus

± plus or minus

∓ minus or plus

× multiplied by

÷ divided by

= equal to

≠ or ≑ not equal to

≈ or ≐ nearly equal to

≡ identical with

≢ not identical with

⇆ equivalent

∼ difference

≅ congruent to

> greater than

≯ not greater than

< less than

≮ not less than

≧ or ≥ greater than
      or equal to

≦ or ≤ less than
      or equal to

| | absolute value

∪ logical sum or union

∩ logical product
    or intersection

⊂ is contained in

∈ is a member of;
    permittivity; mean error

: is to; ratio

∷ as; proportion

≐ approaches

⟶ approaches limit of

∝ varies as

∥ parallel

⊥ perpendicular

∠ angle

∟ right angle

△ triangle

□ square

▭ rectangle

▱ parallelogram

○ circle

⌒ arc of circle

⊥ equilateral

≜ equiangular

√ radical; root; square root

∛ cube root

∜ fourth root

Σ sum

! or ∟ factorial product

∞ infinity

∫ integral

ƒ function

∂ or δ differential; variation

π pi

∴ therefore

∵ because

‾ vinculum (above letter)

( ) parentheses

[ ] brackets

{ } braces

° degree

′ minute

″ second

△ increment

ω angular frequency;
    solid angle

Ω ohm

μΩ microhm

MΩ megohm

Φ magnetic flux

ă pat/ā ate/âr care/ä bar/b bib/ch chew/d deed/ĕ pet/ē be/f fit/g gag/h hat/hw what/
ĭ pit/ī pie/îr pier/j judge/k kick/l lid, fatal/m mum/n no, sudden/ng sing/ŏ pot/ō go/

Ψ dielectric flux; electrostatic flux

ρ resistivity

Λ equivalent conductivity

ℛ reluctance

→ direction of flow

⇌ electric current

◯ benzene ring

→ yields

⇌ reversible reaction

↓ precipitate

↑ gas

‰ salinity

☉ or ☼ sun

● or ◉ new moon

☽ first quarter

◯ or ☺ full moon

☾ last quarter

☿ Mercury

♀ Venus

⊖ or ⊕ Earth

♂ Mars

♃ Jupiter

♄ Saturn

♅ Uranus

♆ Neptune

♇ Pluto

♈ Aries

♉ Taurus

♊ Gemini

♋ Cancer

♌ Leo

♍ Virgo

♎ Libra

♏ Scorpius

♐ Sagittarius

♑ Capricornus

♒ Aquarius

♓ Pisces

☌ conjunction

☍ opposition

△ trine

□ quadrature

✳ sextile

☊ dragon's head, ascending node

☋ dragon's tail, descending node

🌧 rain

✳ snow

⊠ snow on ground

← floating ice crystals

▲ hail

△ sleet

∨ frostwork

⊔ hoarfrost

≡ fog

∞ haze; dust haze

⊤ thunder

< sheet lightning

⊙ solar corona

⊕ solar halo

⟨ thunderstorm

\ direction

◯ or ⊙ or ① annual

⊙⊙ or ② biennial

♃ perennial

♂ or ♂ male

♀ female

□ male (in charts)

◯ female (in charts)

℞ take (from Latin *Recipe*)

ĀĀ or Ā or āā of each (doctor's prescription)

℔ pound

ô paw, for/oi boy/ou out/ŏŏ took/ōō coo/p pop/r run/s sauce/sh shy/t·to/th thin/*th* the/
ŭ cut/ûr fur/v van/w wag/y yes/z size/zh vision/ə ago, item, edible, gallop, circus/

3	ounce
3	dram
𝄐	scruple
ʄ3	fluid ounce
ʄ3	fluid dram
ℳ	minim
&	or & and; ampersand
℔	per
#	number
/	virgule; slash; solidus; shilling
©	copyright
%	per cent
℅	care of
℀	account of
@	at

*	asterisk
†	dagger
‡	double dagger
§	section
☞	index
´	acute
`	grave
~	tilde
^	circumflex
¯	macron
˘	breve
¨	dieresis
¸	cedilla
∧	caret

public advocate.] —**syn′di•cate′** (sĭn′dĭ-kāt′) v. (-cated, -cating).

syn•drome (sĭn′drōm′) n. A group of signs and symptoms that collectively indicate a disease or disorder. [< Gk *sundromē*, a running together, concurrence (of symptoms).]

syn•er•gism (sĭn′ər-jĭz′əm) n. Also **syn•er•gy** (-ər-jē). The action of two or more substances, organs, or organisms to achieve an effect of which each is individually incapable. [< Gk *sunergos*, working together.]

syn•od (sĭn′əd) n. 1. A council or assembly of churches. 2. Any council or assembly. [< Gk *sunodos*, meeting.]

syn•o•nym (sĭn′ə-nĭm′) n. A word having a meaning similar to that of another. [< Gk *sunōnumon*.]

syn•op•sis (sĭ-nŏp′sĭs) n., pl. -ses (-sēz′). A brief statement or outline of a subject. [< Gk

Syria

sunopsis, a viewing all together, general view.]

syn•tax (sĭn′tăks′) n. The way in which words are put together to form phrases and sentences. [< Gk *suntassein*, to put together, arrange in order.] —**syn•tac′tic** (-tăk′tĭk), **syn•tac′ti•cal** adj.

syn•the•sis (sĭn′thə-sĭs) n., pl. -ses (-sēz′). The combining of separate elements or substances to form a coherent whole. [< Gk, a putting together.] —**syn′the•size′** (-sīz′) v. (-sized, -sizing).

syn•thet•ic (sĭn-thĕt′ĭk) adj. Also **syn•thet•i•cal** (-ĭ-kəl). 1. Of, pertaining to, involving, or produced by synthesis. 2. Not genuine; artificial. [< Gk *suntithenai*, to put together.] —**syn•thet′i•cal•ly** adv.

syph•i•lis (sĭf′ə-lĭs) n. A chronic infectious venereal disease transmitted by direct contact, usually in sexual intercourse, and sometimes progressing from its local phase through three stages to systemic infection. —**syph′i•lit′ic** (-lĭt′ĭk) adj. & n.

sy•phon. Variant of **siphon.**

Syr•a•cuse (sĭr′ə-kyōōz′, -kyōōs′). A city of C New York State. Pop. 216,000.

Syr•i•a (sĭr′ē-ə). A country on the E Mediterranean coast. Pop. 5,067,000. Cap. Damascus. —**Syr′i•an** adj. & n.

syr•inge (sə-rĭnj′, sĭr′ĭnj) n. A medical instrument used to inject fluids into the body or draw them from it. [< Gk *surinx*, shepherd's pipe.]

syr•up (sûr′əp, sĭr′-) n. Also **sir•up.** A thick, sweet, sticky liquid, as a sugar solution or boiled plant sap. [< Ar *sharāb*, beverage, syrup.] —**syr′up•y** adj.

sys•tem (sĭs′təm) n. 1. A group of interrelated elements forming a collective entity. 2. The human body regarded as a functional physiological unit. 3. A network, as for communications, travel, or distribution. **4.** A set of inter-related ideas, principles, rules, procedures, laws, etc. **5.** A social, economic, or political organizational form. **6.** The state or condition of harmonious, orderly interaction. [< Gk *sustēma,* a composite whole.] —sys'tem•at'ic *adj.* —sys'tem•at'i•cal•ly *adv.*

sys•tem•a•tize (sĭs'tə-mə-tīz') *v.* -tized, -tizing. To formulate into or reduce to a system. —sys'tem•a•ti•za'tion *n.*

sys•tem•ic (sĭ-stĕm'ĭk) *adj.* **1.** Pertaining to a system or systems. **2.** Of or affecting the entire body. —sys•tem'i•cal•ly *adv.*

sys•to•le (sĭs'tə-lē) *n.* The rhythmic contraction of the heart, esp. of the ventricles. [Gk *sustolē,* contraction.] —sys•tol'ic (-tŏl'ĭk) *adj.*

Tt

t, T (tē) *n.* **1.** The 20th letter of the English alphabet. **2. T** Anything shaped like the letter **T.** —**to a T.** Perfectly; precisely.

t 1. ton. **2.** troy.

T temperature.

t. 1. teaspoon. **2.** *Gram.* tense. **3.** time. **4.** *Gram.* transitive.

T. 1. tablespoon. **2.** territory. **3.** Testament. **4.** time. **5.** transit.

Ta tantalum.

tab (tăb) *n.* **1.** A projection, flap, or short strip attached to an object to facilitate opening, handling, or identification. **2.** A bill or check, as in a restaurant. [?]

tab•by (tăb'ē) *n., pl.* -bies. **1.** A black and grayish striped or mottled domestic cat. **2.** A female domestic cat. [F *tabis.*]

tab•er•na•cle (tăb'ər-năk'əl) *n.* Often **Tabernacle. 1.** The portable sanctuary in which the Jews carried the ark of the covenant through the desert. **2.** A receptacle on a church altar containing the consecrated elements of the Eucharist. [< L *taberna,* hut.]

ta•ble (tā'bəl) *n.* **1.** An article of furniture having a flat horizontal surface supported by vertical legs. **2.** An orderly display of data, usually arranged in rows and columns. **3.** An abbreviated list, as of contents; a synopsis. **4.** A slab or tablet, as of stone, bearing an inscription or device. —*v.* -bled, -bling. **1.** To put or place on a table. **2.** To postpone consideration of; shelve. [< L *tabula,* board, list.]

tab•leau (tăb'lō', tă-blō') *n., pl.* -leaux (tăb'lōz', tă-blōz') or -leaus. **1.** A vivid or graphic description. **2.** A scene presented on stage by costumed actors who remain silent and motionless as if in a picture. [F.]

ta•ble•cloth (tā'bəl-klôth', -klŏth') *n.* A cloth to cover a table.

ta•ble d'hôte (tā'bəl dōt') *pl.* **tables d'hôte** (tā'bəl dōt'). A full meal served in a restaurant at a fixed price. [F, "table of (the) host."]

ta•ble•land (tā'bəl-lănd') *n.* A plateau.

ta•ble•spoon (tā'bəl-spōōn') *n.* **1.** A large spoon used for serving food. **2.** A household cooking measure, three teaspoons or four liquid drams.

tab•let (tăb'lĭt) *n.* **1.** A slab or plaque, as of stone or ivory, bearing an inscription. **2.** A pad of writing paper glued together along one edge. **3.** A small flat pellet of oral medication. [< OF *table,* table.]

table tennis. A game similar to tennis, played on a table with wooden paddles and a small Celluloid ball.

ta•ble•ware (tā'bəl-wâr') *n.* Dishes, glassware, etc., used in setting a table for a meal.

tab•loid (tăb'loid') *n.* A newspaper of small format giving the news in condensed form, usually with illustrated, often sensational material. [< TABL(ET) + -OID.]

ta•boo, ta•bu (tə-bōō', tă-) *n., pl.* -boos. **1.** A prohibition excluding something from use, approach, or mention because of its sacred and inviolable nature. **2.** A ban attached to something by social custom. —*adj.* Excluded or forbidden from use, approach, or mention. —*v.* To place under taboo.

ta•bor (tā'bər) *n.* A small drum used to accompany a fife. [< OF *tabour.*]

tab•u•lar (tăb'yə-lər) *adj.* Organized as a table or list. —tab'u•lar•ly *adv.*

tab•u•late (tăb'yə-lāt') *v.* -lated, -lating. To arrange in tabular form; condense and list. —tab'u•la'tion *n.* —tab'u•la'tor *n.*

ta•chom•e•ter (tə-kŏm'ə-tər) *n.* An instrument used to determine speed, esp. rotational speed. [Gk *takhos,* speed + -METER.]

tac•it (tăs'ĭt) *adj.* **1.** Not spoken: *tacit consent.* **2.** Implied by or inferred from actions or statements. [< L *tacēre,* to be silent.]

tac•i•turn (tăs'ə-tûrn') *adj.* Habitually untalkative; laconic; uncommunicative. [< L *taciturnus,* silent, tacit.] —tac'i•tur'ni•ty (-tûr'nə-tē) *n.*

tack (tăk) *n.* **1.** A short, light nail with a sharp point and a flat head. **2.** The position of a vessel relative to the trim of its sails. **3.** A course of action. —*v.* **1.** To fasten or attach with a tack. **2.** To append; add (with *on*). **3.** To change the course of a vessel. [< OF *tache,* nail, fastening.]

tack•le (tăk'əl) *n.* **1.** The equipment used in a sport or occupation, esp. in fishing; gear. **2.** (*also* tā'kəl). A system of ropes and blocks for raising and lowering weights. **3.** *Football.* **a.** A lineman stationed between guard and end. **b.** The seizing and throwing to the ground of an opposing player. —*v.* **-led, -ling. 1.** To take on; come to grips with: *tackle a problem.* **2.** *Football.* To seize and throw (an opposing player) to the ground. [Prob < MLG *taken,* to seize.] —**tack′ler** *n.*

tack•y¹ (tăk′ē) *adj.* **-ier, -iest.** Slightly adhesive or gummy to the touch; sticky. [< TACK.] —**tack′i•ness** *n.*

tack•y² (tăk′ē) *adj.* **-ier, -iest.** *Informal.* **1.** Run-down; shabby. **2.** Lacking style; dowdy. [< dial *tacky,* an inferior horse.] —**tack′i•ness** *n.*

Ta•co•ma (tə-kō′mə). A city of W Washington. Pop. 152,000.

tact (tăkt) *n.* The ability to appreciate the delicacy of ⁀ situation and do or say the most fitting thing. [< L *tactus,* sense of touch.] —**tact′ful** *adj.* —**tact′less** *adj.*

tac•tics (tăk′tĭks) *n.* *(takes sing. v.).* The technique or science ɨf securing strategic objectives, esp. the art of deploying and directing one's forces against an enemy. [< Gk *(ta) taktika,* "(the) matters of arrangement."] —**tac′ti•cal** *adj.* —**tac′ti′cian** *n.*

tac•tile (tăk′təl, -tīl′) *adj.* Of, pertaining to, or perceptible to the sense of touch. [< L *tactus,* sense of touch.]

tad•pole (tăd′pōl′) *n.* The aquatic larval stage of a frog or toad, having a tail and external gills. [ME *taddepol,* "toad head."]

Ta•dzhik Soviet Socialist Republic (tä′jĭk, -jĕk′). A republic of the south-central Soviet Union. Pop. 2,900,000. Cap. Dushanbe.

taf•fe•ta (tăf′ə-tə) *n.* A glossy, plain-woven fabric of silk, rayon, or nylon. [< Pers *tăftah,* "woven."]

taf•fy (tăf′ē) *n.* A sweet, chewy candy made of molasses or brown sugar.

Taft (tăft), **William Howard.** 1857–1930. 27th President of the U.S. (1909–13).

William Howard Taft
Photographed during a
1908 speech in Wisconsin

tag¹ (tăg) *n.* **1.** A strip of paper, metal, etc., attached to something for purposes of identification, classification, or labeling. **2.** A plastic or metal tip on shoelaces. **3.** A designation or epithet. —*v.* **tagged, tagging. 1.** To label or identify with a tag. **2.** To follow closely. [Prob < Scand.] —**tag′ger** *n.*

tag² (tăg) *n.* **1.** A children's game in which one

player pursues the others until he can touch one of them. **2.** *Baseball.* The act of touching a runner to retire him. —*v.* **tagged, tagging. 1.** To touch (another player) in the game of tag. **2.** *Baseball.* To touch (a runner) with the ball in order to retire him. —**tag′ger** *n.*

Ta•ga•log (tə-gä′lôg′) *n., pl.* **-log** or **-logs. 1.** A member of a people native to the Philippines. **2.** The language of the Austronesian family spoken by this people.

Ta•gus (tā′gəs). A river of Spain and Portugal.

Ta•hi•ti (tə-hē′tē). An island of Polynesia, in the SE Pacific.

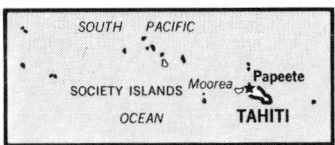

Tahiti

Ta•hi•tian (tə-hē′shən, -hē′tē-ən) *n.* **1.** A native or inhabitant of Tahiti. **2.** The Polynesian language of Tahiti. —**Ta•hi′tian** *adj.*

Tai (tī) *n.* A family of languages spoken in SE Asia and S China, including Thai and other languages.

tai•ga (tī-gä′) *n.* The evergreen forest of Siberia and of similar regions elsewhere in Eurasia and North America. [Russ *taiga.*]

tail (tāl) *n.* **1.** The hind part of an animal, esp. when elongated and extending beyond the main part of the body. **2.** Anything resembling an animal's tail. **3.** The bottom, rear, or hindmost part of anything. **4. a.** The rear of an aircraft. **b.** An assembly of stabilizing planes and control surfaces in this region. **5. tails.** The reverse of a coin: *heads or tails.* **6. tails.** A formal evening costume worn by men. —*v. Informal.* To follow and keep under surveillance. —*adj.* **1.** Posterior; hindmost. **2.** Coming from behind: *a tail wind.* [< OE *tægel.* See **dek-.**]

tail•light (tāl′līt′) *n.* A light mounted on the rear end of a vehicle.

tai•lor (tā′lər) *n.* One who makes, repairs, and alters garments. —*v.* **1.** To make (a garment). **2.** To make, alter, or adapt for a particular purpose. [< VL **tāliātor,* "cutter."]

tai•lor-made (tā′lər-mād′) *adj.* Made or as if made to order.

tail•spin (tāl′spĭn′) *n.* **1.** The descent of an aircraft in a nose-down spiraling motion. **2.** A sudden precipitous decline or slump.

taint (tānt) *v.* **1.** To affect slightly with something undesirable. **2.** To make poisonous or rotten; infect or spoil. —*n.* **1.** A moral defect considered as a stain or spot. **2.** An infecting touch, influence, or tinge. [< L *tingere,* to dip in liquid, dye.]

Tai•pei (tī′pā′). The capital of the Republic of China, on Taiwan. Pop. 1,028,000.

Tai•wan (tī′wän′). An island off the SE coast of China, constituting along with smaller islands the Republic of China.

ă pat/ā ate/âr care/ä bar/b bib/ch chew/d deed/ĕ pet/ē be/f fit/g gag/h hat/hw what/ ĭ pit/ī pie/îr pier/j judge/k kick/l lid, fatal/m mum/n no, sudden/ng sing/ŏ pot/ō go/

Ta·iz (tä-ĭz'). A former capital of the Yemen Arab Republic. Pop. 80,000.

take (tāk) v. **took, taken** (tā'kən), **taking. 1.** To get possession of; capture; seize. **2.** To grasp with the hands. **3.** To carry with one to another place. **4.** To lead or convey to another place. **5.** To remove from a place. **6.** To charm; captivate. **7.** To eat, drink, consume, or inhale. **8.** To assume upon oneself; commit oneself to. **9.** *Gram.* To govern: *Intransitive verbs take no direct object.* **10.** To select; pick out; choose. **11.** To use as a means of conveyance or transportation. **12.** To occupy: *take a seat.* **13.** To require: *It takes money to do that.* **14.** To determine through measurement or observation. **15.** To write down: *take notes.* **16.** To make by photography: *take a picture.* **17.** To accept (something owed, offered, or given). **18.** To endure: *take criticism.* **19.** To follow (advice, a suggestion, etc.). **20.** To indulge in; do; perform: *take a step.* **21.** To allow to come in; admit. **22.** To interpret or react to in a certain manner: *take literally.* **23.** To subtract. **24.** To commit oneself to the study of: *take a course.* **25.** To have the intended effect; work. **26.** To become: *take sick.* **27.** To set out for; make one's way; go. **—take aback.** To bewilder; astonish; nonplus. **—take after. 1.** To pursue; chase. **2.** To resemble. **—take down. 1.** To bring to a lower position from a higher. **2.** To dismantle; take apart. **3.** To put down in writing. **—take for.** To consider or suppose to be. **—take in. 1.** To grant admittance to. **2.** To make smaller or shorter. **3.** To include or comprise. **4.** To deceive; swindle. **5.** To look at thoroughly; view. **—take it. 1.** To understand; assume: *as I take it.* **2.** *Informal.* To endure abuse, criticism, etc. **—take on. 1.** To hire. **2.** To undertake. **3.** To oppose in competition. **—take out. 1.** To extract; remove. **2.** *Informal.* To escort, as on a date. **—take over.** To assume the control or management of. **—take place.** To happen. **—take to. 1.** To go to, as for safety. **2.** To develop as a habit or steady practice. **3.** To become fond of. **—take up. 1.** To raise up; lift. **2.** To reduce in size; shorten or tighten. **3.** To accept, as an option, bet, or challenge. **4.** To begin again; resume. **5.** To use up, consume, or occupy (space, time, etc.). **6.** To develop an interest in. **—take up with.** *Informal.* To develop a friendship or association with. *—n.* **1. a.** The act or process of taking. **b.** That which is taken. **2.** The amount of money collected as admission to a sporting event. [< OE *tacan* < ON *taka.*]

take off. 1. To remove, as clothing. **2.** To deduct. **3.** *Slang.* To leave; depart. **4.** To leave the ground, as an airplane.

take·off (tāk'ôf', -ŏf') n. **1.** The act of leaving the ground. **2.** *Informal.* An amusing imitative caricature or burlesque.

tak·er (tā'kər) n. A person who takes or takes up something, as a wager.

tak·ing (tā'kĭng) adj. Fetching; winning. *—n.* **1.** The act of a person or thing that takes. **2. takings.** Receipts, esp. of money.

talc (tălk) n. A fine-grained mineral used in making talcum powder. [< Ar *talq.*]

tal·cum powder (tăl'kəm). A fine powder made from purified talc, for use on the skin.

tale (tāl) n. **1.** A recital of events or happenings. **2.** A malicious story; piece of gossip. **3.** A deliberate lie; falsehood. [< OE *talu,* discourse, narrative. See del-².]

tale·bear·er (tāl'bâr'ər) n. One who spreads malicious stories or gossip.

tal·ent (tăl'ənt) n. **1.** A natural or acquired ability; aptitude. **2.** Natural endowment or ability of a superior quality. **3.** A variable unit of weight and money used in ancient times. [< L *talentum,* unit of weight or money.]

ta·ler (tä'lər) n. Also **tha·ler.** Any of numerous silver coins formerly used in certain Germanic countries. [G.]

tal·is·man (tăl'ĭs-mən, tăl'ĭz-) n. An object marked with magical signs and believed to confer on its bearer supernatural powers or protection. [< LGk *telesma,* completion, consecrated object.]

talk (tôk) v. **1.** To articulate words. **2.** To converse by means of spoken language. **3.** To speak (an idiom). **4.** To gossip. **5.** To parley or negotiate. **6.** To consult or confer. **—talk back.** To make an impertinent reply. **—talk down to.** To address someone with insulting condescension. **—talk (someone) into.** To persuade. **—talk (someone) out of.** To dissuade. **—talk over.** To discuss. *—n.* **1.** The act of talking; conversation. **2.** An informal speech. **3.** Any hearsay, rumor, or speculation concerning something: *talk of war.* **4.** Any subject of conversation. **5.** A conference. [< OE *talian,* to reckon, tell, relate. See del-².] **—talk'er** n.

talk·a·tive (tô'kə-tĭv) adj. Having an inclination to talk; loquacious.

talk·ing-to (tô'kĭng-tōō') n., pl. **-tos.** *Informal.* A scolding.

tall (tôl) adj. **1.** Having greater than ordinary height. **2.** Having a stated height: *six feet tall.* **3.** *Informal.* Fanciful; boastful: *tall tales.* [ME, seemly, handsome, valiant.]

Tal·la·has·see (tăl'ə-hăs'ē). The capital of Florida. Pop. 72,000.

tal·low (tăl'ō) n. Whitish, tasteless solid or hard fat obtained from cattle, sheep, etc., and used in edibles or to make candles, leather dressing, soap, and lubricants. [< MLG *talg,* talch.] **—tal'low·y** adj.

tal·ly (tăl'ē) n., pl. **-lies. 1.** A stick on which notches are made to keep a count or score. **2.** A reckoning or score. *—v.* **-lied, -lying. 1.** To reckon or count. **2.** To correspond; agree. [< L *tālea,* twig, cutting, stick.]

tal·ly·ho (tăl'ē-hō') interj. Used to urge hounds in fox hunting. [Prob < OF *thialau,* cry used to urge hounds.]

Tal·mud (tăl'mōōd', täl'məd) n. The collection of ancient Rabbinic writings constituting the basis of religious authority for traditional Judaism. [Heb *talmūd,* learning, instruction.]

tal·on (tăl'ən) n. The claw of a bird of prey or other predatory animal. [< L *tālus,* ankle.]

ta·ma·le (tə-mä'lē) n. A Mexican dish of fried chopped meat and crushed peppers, wrapped in corn husks and steamed. [< Nah *tamalli.*]

ô paw, for/oi boy/ou out/ŏŏ took/ōŏ coo/p pop/r run/s sauce/sh shy/t to/th thin/*th* the/
ŭ cut/ûr fur/v van/w wag/y yes/z size/zh vision/ə ago, item, edible, gallop, circus/

tam·a·rack (tăm′ə-răk′) *n.* An American larch tree. [< Algon.]

tam·a·rind (tăm′ə-rĭnd′) *n.* **1.** A tropical tree with pulpy, acid-flavored pods. **2.** The fruit of this tree. [< Ar *tamr hindī*, "date of India."]

tam·a·risk (tăm′ə-rĭsk′) *n.* A shrub or small tree with small, scalelike leaves and clusters of pink flowers. [< L *tamarix*.]

tam·bou·rine (tăm′bə-rēn′) *n.* A musical instrument consisting of a small drumhead with jingling disks fitted into the rim. [F *tambourin*.]

tame (tām) *adj.* **tamer, tamest.** **1.** Brought from wildness into a domesticated state. **2.** Gentle; docile. **3.** Insipid; flat. —*v.* **tamed, taming.** **1.** To domesticate. **2.** To subdue or curb. [< OE *tam*. See dema-².]

Tam·er·lane (tăm′ər-lān′). 1336?–1405. Islamic conqueror of much of C Asia and E Europe.

Tam·il (tăm′əl, tŭm′-) *n.* **1.** A member of a Dravidian people of S India and Ceylon. **2.** The language spoken by this people. —**Tam′il** *adj.*

tam-o'-shan·ter (tăm′ə-shăn′tər) *n.* A tight-fitting Scottish cap, sometimes having a pompon, tassel, or feather in the center. [< the hero of Burns's poem *Tam o'Shanter*.]

tamp (tămp) *v.* To pack down tightly by a succession of blows or taps.

Tam·pa (tăm′pə). A city of W Florida. Pop. 302,000.

tam·per (tăm′pər) *v.* —**tamper with.** **1.** To interfere in a harmful manner. **2.** To meddle rashly or foolishly. **3.** To engage in underhand dealings. [Orig "to prepare (clay) by mixing," var of TEMPER.] —**tam′per·er** *n.*

tan (tăn) *v.* **tanned, tanning.** **1.** To convert (hide) into leather, as by treating with tannin. **2.** To make or become brown by exposure to the sun. **3.** *Informal.* To thrash; beat. —*n.* **1.** A light brown. **2.** The brown color sun rays impart to the skin. —*adj.* **tanner, tannest.** **1.** Of the color tan. **2.** Having a sun tan. [< ML *tannāre*.]

tan·a·ger (tăn′ĭ-jər) *n.* Any of various New World birds often having brightly colored plumage. [< Port *tangará*.]

Ta·nan·a·rive (tə-năn′ə-rēv′). The capital of the Malagasy Republic. Pop. 299,000.

tan·bark (tăn′bärk′) *n.* **1.** Tree bark used as a source of tannin. **2.** Shredded bark used to cover circus arenas, racetracks, etc.

tan·dem (tăn′dəm) *n.* **1.** A two-wheeled carriage drawn by horses harnessed one behind the other. **2.** A bicycle built for two. —*adv.* One behind the other. [L, "exactly then," at length.] —**tan′dem** *adj.*

tang (tăng) *n.* **1.** A sharp, often acrid taste, flavor, or odor. **2.** A projection by which a tool is attached to its handle. [Prob < ON *tangi*, a sting, point.] —**tang′y** *adj.*

tan·ge·lo (tăn′jə-lō′) *n., pl.* **-los.** A citrus fruit that is a cross between a grapefruit and a tangerine. [Blend of TANGE(RINE) and *pomelo*, a grapefruit.]

tan·gent (tăn′jənt) *adj.* Making contact at a single point or along a line; touching but not intersecting. —*n.* **1.** A line, curve, or surface touching but not intersecting another line, curve, or surface. **2.** A sudden digression or change of course. [< L *tangere*, to touch.]

—**tan·gen′tial** (-jĕn′shəl) *adj.* —**tan·gen′ti·al′i·ty** (-shē-ăl′ə-tē) *n.* —**tan·gen′tial·ly** *adv.*

tan·ger·ine (tăn′jə-rēn′) *n.* A citrus fruit with easily peeled deep-orange skin. [Short for *tangerine orange*, "orange of Tangier."]

tan·gi·ble (tăn′jə-bəl) *adj.* **1.** Discernible by the touch; palpable. **2.** Real; concrete: *tangible evidence.* —*n.* **1.** Something palpable or concrete. **2. tangibles.** Material assets. [< L *tangere*, to touch.] —**tan′gi·bil′i·ty, tan′gi·ble·ness** *n.* —**tan′gi·bly** *adv.*

Tan·gier (tăn-jîr′). A city and port in N Morocco. Pop. 142,000.

tan·gle (tăng′gəl) *v.* **-gled, -gling.** **1.** To intertwine in a confused mass; snarl. **2.** To be or become entangled. —*n.* **1.** A confused, intertwined mass. **2.** A jumbled or confused state or condition. [Prob < Scand.]

tan·go (tăng′gō) *n., pl.* **-gos.** A Latin-American ballroom dance. [Amer Span.] —**tan′go** *v.*

tank (tăngk) *n.* **1.** A large container for fluids. **2.** An enclosed, heavily armored combat vehicle mounted with cannon and guns and moving on caterpillar treads. [Perh < Sk *taḍāga*, pond.]

tank·ard (tăng′kərd) *n.* A large drinking cup having a single handle and often a hinged cover. [ME.]

tank·er (tăng′kər) *n.* A ship, plane, or truck constructed to transport oil or other liquids in bulk.

tan·ner (tăn′ər) *n.* One who tans hides.

tan·ner·y (tăn′ər-ē) *n., pl.* **-ies.** A place where hides are tanned.

tan·nic acid (tăn′ĭk). A lustrous yellowish to light-brown powdered, flaked, or spongy mass having the approximate composition $C_{76}H_{52}O_{46}$, used in tanning and as an astringent and styptic. [< TANNIN.]

tan·nin (tăn′ən) *n.* Tannic acid or some compound having similar uses. [< F *tanner*, to tan.]

Ta·no·an (tä′nō-ən) *n.* A language family of several Indian peoples of New Mexico and NE Arizona. —**Ta′no·an** *adj.*

tan·sy (tăn′zē) *n., pl.* **-sies.** A pungently aromatic plant with buttonlike yellow flowers. [Perh < ML *athanasia*, an elixir of life.]

tan·ta·lize (tăn′tə-līz′) *v.* **-lized, -lizing.** To tease or torment by exposing to view but keeping out of reach something much desired. [< *Tantalus*, Greek mythological king who was punished thus.] —**tan′ta·li·za′tion** *n.* —**tan′ta·liz′er** *n.*

tan·ta·lum (tăn′tə-ləm) *n.* *Symbol* Ta A very hard, heavy, gray metallic element used to make electric-light-bulb filaments, lightning arresters, nuclear reactor parts, and some surgical instruments. Atomic number 73, atomic weight 180.948. [< *Tantalus*.]

tan·ta·mount (tăn′tə-mount′) *adj.* Equivalent in effect or value. [< NF *tant amunter*, to amount to so much.]

tan·trum (tăn′trəm) *n.* A fit of bad temper. [?]

Tan·za·ni·a (tăn′zə-nē′ə, tăn-zä′nē-ə). A republic of E Africa. Pop. 10,514,000. Cap. Dar
es Salaam.

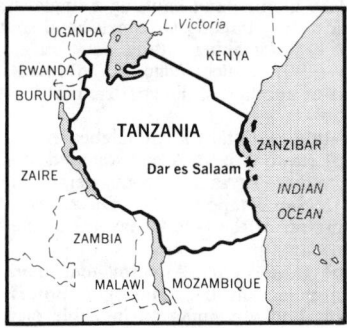

Tanzania

Tao·ism (tou′ĭz′əm, dou′-) *n.* A principal philosophy and religious system of China based
upon the teachings of Lao-tse in the 6th century B.C. [< Mand Chin *tao⁴*, "the Way."]
tap¹ (tăp) *v.* **tapped, tapping. 1.** To strike gently;
rap. **2.** To repair (shoe heels or toes) by applying a tap. —*n.* **1.** A gentle but audible
blow. **2.** A metal plate attached to the toe or
heel of a shoe. [< OF *taper.*]
tap² (tăp) *n.* **1.** A faucet; spigot. **2.** Liquor
drawn from a tap. **3.** A tool for cutting an
internal screw thread. **4.** A makeshift terminal
in an electric circuit. —*v.* **tapped, tapping. 1.** To
furnish with a spigot or tap. **2.** To pierce in
order to draw off liquid. **3.** To draw (liquid)
from a vessel or container. **4.** To open outlets
from: *tap a water main.* **5. a.** To wiretap. **b.** To
establish an electric connection in (a power
line). **6.** To cut screw threads in. [< OE *tæppa*
< Gmc **tap-.*]
tape (tăp) *n.* **1.** A narrow strip of woven fabric.
2. Any continuous narrow, flexible strip, as
adhesive tape. **3.** A string stretched across a
finish line. **4.** A **tape recording.** —*v.* **taped,
taping. 1.** To bind or wrap with tape. **2.** To
measure with a tape measure. **3.** To tape-
record. [< OE *tæppa, tæppe.*]
tape measure. A tape marked off in a linear
scale, as inches, and used for taking measurements.
ta·per (tā′pər) *n.* **1.** A slender candle or waxed
wick. **2.** A gradual decrease in thickness or
width of an elongated object. —*v.* **1.** To make
or become gradually narrower toward one
end. **2.** To become gradually smaller; slacken
off. [< OE *tapor, tapur.*] —**ta′per·ing·ly** *adv.*
tape recorder. A device for recording and
playing back sound on magnetic tape.
tape recording. 1. Magnetized recording tape.
2. The sound recorded on a magnetic tape.
—**tape′-re·cord′** *v.*
tap·es·try (tăp′ĭ-strē) *n., pl.* **-tries.** A heavy
textile with a varicolored design woven across
the warp, used esp. for a wall hanging. [< Gk
tapēs, carpet.]
tape·worm (tăp′wûrm′) *n.* A long, ribbonlike

worm that lives as a parasite in the intestines
of vertebrates, including man.
tap·i·o·ca (tăp′ē-ō′kə) *n.* A beady starch obtained from cassava root and used for thickening puddings, soups, etc. [< Tupi *tipioca,*
"residue."]
ta·pir (tā′pər, tə-pîr′) *n.* A tropical American
or Asian mammal with a heavy body, short
legs, and a fleshy proboscis.
tap·room (tăp′rōōm′, -rŏŏm′) *n.* A barroom.
tap·root (tăp′rōōt′, -rŏŏt′) *n.* The often stout
main root of a plant, growing straight downward from the stem.
taps (tăps) *n. (takes sing. v.).* A military bugle
call blown as an order to put out lights and at
military funerals and memorial services. [<
TAP¹.]
tar¹ (tär) *n.* A dark, oily, viscid mixture, consisting mainly of hydrocarbons, produced by
the destructive distillation of organic substances such as wood, coal, or peat. —*v.* **tarred,
tarring.** To coat with tar. [< OE *teru.* See
deru-.]
tar² (tär) *n. Informal.* A sailor. [Short for
TARPAULIN.]
ta·ran·tu·la (tə-răn′chŏŏ-lə) *n.* Any of various
large, hairy, chiefly tropical spiders capable of
inflicting a painful bite. [< It *tarantola.*]
tar·dy (tär′dē) *adj.* **-dier, -diest. 1. a.** Late. **b.**
Dilatory. **2.** Slow; sluggish. [< L *tardus,*
slow.] —**tar′di·ly** *adv.* —**tar′di·ness** *n.*
tare¹ (târ) *n.* Any of several weeds that grow in
grain fields. [ME, seed of the vetch.]
tare² (târ) *n.* The weight of a container or
wrapper that is deducted from the gross weight
to obtain net weight. [< Ar *ṭarḥah,* thing
thrown away.]
tar·get (tär′gĭt) *n.* **1.** An object with a marked
surface that is shot at to test accuracy. **2.**
Anything aimed at or fired at. **3.** An object of
criticism or attack. **4.** A desired goal. [< OF
targe, light shield.]
tar·iff (tăr′ĭf) *n.* **1. a.** A list or system of duties
imposed on imported or exported goods. **b.** A
duty of this kind. **2.** Any schedule of rates or
fees. [< Turk *ta′rifa.*]
tar·nish (tär′nĭsh) *v.* **1.** To make or become
dull or discolored. **2.** To sully or taint. [OF
ternir.] —**tar′nish** *n,* —**tar′nish·a·ble** *adj.*
ta·ro (tär′ō, tăr′ō) *n., pl.* **-ros.** A tropical plant
with broad leaves and a large, starchy, edible
root. [Tahitian and Maori.]
tar·ot (tăr′ō) *n.* Any of a set of playing cards
used in fortunetelling. [< It *tarocco.*]
tar·pau·lin (tär-pô′lĭn, tär′pə-lĭn) *n.* Waterproof canvas used for covering and protecting.
[Earlier *tarpawling.*]
tar·pon (tär′pən) *n., pl.* **-pon** or **-pons.** A large,
silvery game fish of Atlantic coastal waters. [?]
tar·ra·gon (tăr′ə-gŏn′, -gən) *n.* An aromatic
herb with leaves used as seasoning. [< Ar
tarkhūn.]
tar·ry (tăr′ē) *v.* **-ried, -rying. 1.** To delay or be
late; linger. **2.** To stay temporarily; sojourn.
[ME *tarien.*] —**tar′ri·er** *n.*
tart¹ (tärt) *adj.* **1.** Agreeably pungent or sour.
2. Caustic; cutting. [< OE *teart,* sharp, severe.] —**tart′ly** *adv.* —**tart′ness** *n.*

ô paw, for/oi boy/ou out/ŏŏ took/ōō coo/p pop/r run/s sauce/sh shy/t to/th thin/*th* the/
ŭ cut/ûr fur/v van/w wag/y yes/z size/zh vision/ə ago, item, edible, gallop, circus/

tart² (tärt) *n.* **1.** A small open pie with a sweet filling. **2.** A whore. [< L *torta*, round bread, "twisted."]

tar·tan (tärt'n) *n.* Any of numerous textile patterns of Scottish origin consisting of stripes of varying widths and colors crossed at right angles against a solid background. [Prob < OF *tertaine*, a kind of fabric.] —**tar'tan** *adj.*

tar·tar¹ (tär'tər) *n.* **1.** A reddish acid material found in the juice of grapes and deposited on the sides of casks during wine-making. **2.** A hard, yellowish deposit on the teeth. [< MGk *tartaron.*] —**tar·tar'ic** (-tär'ĭc) *adj.*

tar·tar² (tär'tər) *n.* Also **Tar·tar.** A ferocious or violent-tempered person. [< TATAR.]

Tar·tar. Variant of **Tatar.**

Tash·kent (täsh-kĕnt'). The capital of the Uzbek S.S.R. Pop. 1,385,000.

task (tăsk, täsk) *n.* **1.** A piece of assigned work. **2.** A difficult or tedious undertaking. [ME *taske*, tax, work imposed, task.]

task·mas·ter (tăsk'măs'tər, täsk'mäs'tər) *n.* One who imposes heavy work on another.

tas·sel (tăs'əl) *n.* **1.** A pendent ornament consisting of a bunch of loose threads or cords bound at one end. **2.** Something resembling a tassel, as the pollen-bearing flower cluster of a corn plant. —*v.* **-seled** or **-selled, -seling** or **-selling. 1.** To fringe or decorate with tassels. **2.** To put forth a tassellike inflorescence. [< OF.]

taste (tāst) *v.* **tasted, tasting. 1.** To distinguish the flavor of by taking into the mouth. **2.** To eat or drink a small quantity of. **3.** To experience, esp. for the first time. **4.** To have a distinct flavor. —*n.* **1. a.** The sense that distinguishes the sweet, sour, salty, and bitter qualities of dissolved substances in contact with the taste buds on the tongue. **b.** A sensation of such a quality, or a combination of such qualities, perceived with this sense. **2.** The act of tasting. **3.** A small quantity eaten or tasted. **4.** A limited or first experience. **5.** A personal preference or inclination. **6.** Discernment of what is aesthetically excellent or appropriate. **7.** The sense of what is proper in a given social situation. [< L *taxāre*, to touch.] —**tast'er** *n.*

taste bud. Any of numerous nests of cells distributed over the tongue that are primarily responsible for the sense of taste.

taste·ful (tāst'fəl) *adj.* Having or exhibiting good taste. —**taste'ful·ly** *adv.*

taste·less (tāst'lĭs) *adj.* **1.** Lacking flavor; insipid. **2.** Having or exhibiting poor taste.

tast·y (tā'stē) *adj.* **-ier, -iest.** Having a pleasing flavor; savory. —**tast'i·ness** *n.*

tat (tăt) *v.* **tatted, tatting.** To make tatting or produce by tatting. —**tat'ter** *n.*

Ta·tar (tä'tər) *n.* Also **Tar·tar. 1.** A member of one of the Mongolian peoples who invaded much of C and W Asia and E Europe in the 13th century. **2.** Any of the Turkic languages of the Tatars. —**Ta'tar** *adj.*

tat·ter (tăt'ər) *n.* **1.** A torn and hanging piece of cloth; shred. **2. tatters.** Torn and ragged clothing; rags. —*v.* To make or become ragged. [< ON *tōturr.*]

tat·ter·de·mal·ion (tăt'ər-də-mā'lē-ən, -măl'-ē-ən) *n.* A person wearing tattered clothing; ragamuffin. [< TATTER.]

tat·ting (tăt'ĭng) *n.* **1.** Handmade lace fashioned by looping and knotting a single strand of heavy-duty thread on a small hand shuttle. **2.** The art of making tatting.

tat·tle (tăt'l) *v.* **-tled, -tling. 1.** To reveal the secrets of another. **2.** To chatter; prate. —**tat'-tler** *n.*

tat·tle·tale (tăt'l-tāl') *n.* A talebearer.

tat·too¹ (tă-tōo') *n.* **1.** A call sounded to summon soldiers or sailors to quarters at night. **2.** A rhythmic tapping. [< Du *taptoe*, "the shutting off of the taps (at taverns at the end of the day).")

tat·too² (tă-tōo') *n.* A permanent mark or design made on the skin by a process of pricking and ingraining an indelible pigment or by raising scars. —*v.* To mark (the skin) with a tattoo or tattoos. [Of Polynesian origin.] —**tat·too'er** *n.*

tau (tou, tô) *n.* The 19th letter of the Greek alphabet, representing *t.*

taught (tôt). *p.t.* & *p.p.* of **teach.**

taunt (tônt) *v.* To jeer or challenge mockingly. —*n.* A scornful jeer or challenge. [Perh < L *temptāre*, TEMPT.] —**taunt'er** *n.*

taupe (tōp) *n.* Brownish gray. [< L *talpa*, mole.] —**taupe** *adj.*

Tau·rus (tôr'əs) *n.* **1.** A constellation in the N Hemisphere. **2.** The 2nd sign of the zodiac. [< L, bull.]

taut (tôt) *adj.* **1.** Tight; not slack. **2.** Strained; tense. **3.** Trim; tidy. [< OE *togian*, to pull. See **deuk-.**] —**taut'ness** *n.*

tau·tol·o·gy (tô-tŏl'ə-jē) *n., pl.* **-gies. 1. a.** Needless repetition of the same sense in different words; redundancy. **b.** An instance of such repetition. **2.** A statement composed of simpler statements in a fashion that makes it true whether the simpler statements are true or false, as *Either it will rain tomorrow or it will not rain tomorrow.* [< Gk *tautologos*, repeating the same ideas.] —**tau'to·log'i·cal** (tô'tə-lŏj'ĭ-kəl) *adj.* —**tau'to·log'i·cal·ly** *adv.*

tav (tăf, tôf) *n.* Also **taw.** The 23rd letter of the Hebrew alphabet, representing *t(th).*

tav·ern (tăv'ərn) *n.* **1.** A saloon; bar. **2.** A public house or inn. [< L *taberna*, hut, inn.]

taw·dry (tô'drē) *adj.* **-drier, -driest.** Gaudy and cheap; vulgarly ornamental.

taw·ny (tô'nē) *n.* Light brown to brownish orange. [< OF *tane*, tanned.] —**taw'ny** *adj.*

tax (tăks) *n.* **1.** A contribution for the support of a government required of persons, groups, or businesses within the domain of that government. **2.** A burdensome or excessive demand; a strain. —*v.* **1.** To place a tax on. **2.** To make difficult or excessive demands upon. **3.** To make a charge against; accuse. [< L *taxāre* < *tangere*, to touch.] —**tax'a·ble** *adj.* —**tax·a'tion** *n.* —**tax'er** *n.*

tax·i (tăk'sē) *n., pl.* **-is** or **-ies.** A taxicab. —*v.* **-ied, -iing** or **-ying. 1.** To be transported by taxi. **2.** To move slowly on the ground or water before takeoff or after landing. [Short for TAXICAB.]

tax·i·cab (tăk'sē-kăb') *n.* An automobile that carries passengers for a fare. [< F *taxe*, charge + CAB.]

tax·i·der·my (tăk'sə-dûr'mē) *n.* The art or process of stuffing and mounting animal skins in lifelike form. [< TAXO- + -DERM + -Y.] —**tax'i·der'mist** *n.*

tax·ing (tăk'sĭng) *adj.* Burdensome.

taxo–. *comb. form.* Arrangement or order. [< Gk *taxis*, arrangement, order.]

tax·on·o·my (tăk-sŏn'ə-mē) *n.* The science, laws, or principles of classification, esp. the classification of organisms in categories based on common characteristics. —**tax'o·nom'ic** (-sə-nŏm'ĭk) *adj.* —**tax'o·nom'i·cal·ly** *adv.* —**tax·on'o·mist** *n.*

tax shelter. Any financial operation, such as the acquisition of expenses, that reduces taxes on current earnings.

Tay·lor (tā'lər), **Zachary.** 1784–1850. 12th President of the U.S. (1849–50).

Zachary Taylor

Tb terbium.

TB tuberculosis.

Tbi·li·si (tə-bē-lē'sē). The capital of the Georgian S.S.R. Pop. 889,000.

tbs., tbsp. tablespoon.

Tc technetium.

Tchai·kov·sky (chī-kôf'skē, -kŏf'skē), **Peter Ilyich.** 1840–1893. Russian composer.

TD touchdown.

Te tellurium.

tea (tē) *n.* 1. An Asian shrub with evergreen leaves. 2. The dried, processed leaves of this shrub, steeped in boiling water to make a beverage. 3. The beverage thus prepared. 4. A similar beverage. 5. An afternoon refreshment or social gathering at which tea is taken. [< Ancient Chin *d'a.*]

tea bag. A small porous sac holding tea leaves to make an individual serving of tea.

teach (tēch) *v.* **taught, teaching.** 1. To impart knowledge or skill to; give instruction. 2. To instruct in. 3. To cause to learn by example or experience. 4. To advocate or expound. [< OE *tæcan.* See deik-.]

teach·er (tē'chər) *n.* One who teaches, esp. a person hired by a school to teach.

teach·ing (tē'chĭng) *n.* 1. The occupation of teachers. 2. A precept or doctrine.

teak (tēk) *n.* 1. An Asian tree with hard, durable, yellowish-brown wood. 2. The wood of this tree. [Port *teca.*]

teal (tēl) *n.* Any of several small wild ducks. [ME *tele.*]

team (tēm) *n.* 1. Two or more harnessed draft animals. 2. A group of players in a game. 3. Any group organized to work together. —*v.* 1. To harness together to form a team. 2. To form a team. [< OE *tēam*, offspring, brood, team of animals. See deuk-.]

team·mate (tēm'māt') *n.* A fellow member of a team.

team·ster (tēm'stər) *n.* 1. One who drives a team. 2. A truck driver.

tear¹ (târ) *v.* **tore, torn, tearing.** 1. To pull apart or into pieces; rend. 2. To make (an opening) by ripping. 3. To lacerate. 4. To extract or separate forcefully; wrench. 5. To divide; disunite. 6. To rush headlong. —*n.* A rip or rent. [< OE *teran.* See der-².]

tear² (tîr) *n.* 1. A drop of the clear saline liquid that lubricates the surface between the eyeball and eyelid. 2. A drop of any liquid or hardened fluid. 3. **tears.** The act of weeping: *left in tears.* [< OE *tēar, tehher.* See dakru-.] —**tear'ful** *adj.* —**tear'ful·ly** *adv.*

tear·drop (tîr'drŏp') *n.* 1. A single tear. 2. An object having the shape of a tear.

tear gas (tîr). Any of various agents that on dispersal irritate the eyes and cause blinding tears.

tease (tēz) *v.* **teased, teasing.** 1. To annoy; vex. 2. To make fun of. 3. To coax. 4. To disentangle and dress the fibers of (wool). 5. To raise the nap of (cloth). —*n.* 1. One given to playful mocking. 2. A coquettish woman. [< OE *tæsan*, to pull, tear < Gmc *taisan.*] —**teas'er** *n.* —**teas'ing·ly** *adv.*

tea·sel (tē'zəl) *n.* Also **tea·zel, tea·zle.** 1. A plant with thistlelike flowers surrounded by stiff bristles. 2. The flower head of such a plant, used to raise a nap on fabrics. [< OE *tæsel* < Gmc *taisilā.*]

tea·spoon (tē'spōon') *n.* 1. The common small spoon used esp. with tea, coffee, and desserts. 2. A household cooking measure, 1/3 tablespoon or 1 1/3 drams.

teat (tĕt, tĭt) *n.* A mammary gland or nipple. [< Gmc *titta*, TIT.]

tech. technical.

tech·ne·ti·um (tĕk'nē'shē-əm) *n. Symbol* **Tc** A silvery-gray, radioactive metallic element, used as a tracer and to eliminate corrosion in steel. Atomic number 43, longest-lived isotope Tc 97. [< Gk *tekhnētos*, artificial.]

tech·ni·cal (tĕk'nĭ-kəl) *adj.* 1. Of, pertaining to, or derived from technique. 2. Specialized. 3. **a.** Abstract or theoretical. **b.** Scientific. 4. Formal rather than practical. 5. Technological. [< Gk *tekhnikos*, of art or skill.] —**tech'ni·cal·ly** *adv.* —**tech'ni·cal·ness** *n.*

tech·ni·cal·i·ty (tĕk'nĭ-kăl'ə-tē) *n., pl.* **-ties.** 1. The condition or quality of being technical. 2. Something meaningful or relevant in principle only.

ô paw, for/oi boy/ou out/ŏŏ took/ōō coo/p pop/r run/s sauce/sh shy/t to/th thin/*th* the/
ŭ cut/ûr fur/v van/w wag/y yes/z size/zh vision/ə ago, item, edible, gallop, circus/

tech·ni·cian (těk′nĭsh′ən) *n.* An expert in a technique or technology.

tech·nique (těk-nēk′) *n.* 1. The systematic procedure by which a task is accomplished. 2. Also **tech·nic** (těk′nĭk). The degree of skill shown in any performance. [F, "technical."]

tech·nol·o·gy (těk-nŏl′ə-jē) *n., pl.* **-gies.** 1. The application of science, esp. in industry or commerce. 2. The methods and materials thus used. [Gk *tekhnē*, skill, art + -LOGY.] **—tech′·no·log′i·cal** (-nə-lŏj′ĭ-kəl) *adj.* **—tech′no·log′i·cal·ly** *adv.* **—tech·nol′o·gist** *n.*

ted·dy bear (těd′ē). A child's toy bear.

te·di·ous (tē′dē-əs) *adj.* Tiresome by reason of length or slowness; boring. [L *taedium,* TEDIUM.] **—te′di·ous·ly** *adv.* **—te′di·ous·ness** *n.*

te·di·um (tē′dē-əm) *n.* Boredom; tediousness. [L *taedium* < *taedēre,* to bore, weary.]

tee (tē) *n.* 1. A small peg with a concave top for holding a golf ball for an initial drive. 2. The place from which a player makes his first stroke in golf. *—v.* **teed, teeing.** To place (a golf ball) on a tee. **—tee off.** 1. To drive a golf ball from the tee. 2. *Slang.* To start. [Earlier *teaz.*]

teem (tēm) *v.* To abound or swarm. [< OE *tīeman,* to breed. See **deuk-**.]

teem·ing (tē′mĭng) *adj.* Abounding in or swarming with.

-teen. *comb. form.* Used in the names of the cardinal numbers **thirteen** through **nineteen.** [< OE *-tēne, -tŷne.*]

tee·ter (tē′tər) *v.* 1. To totter. 2. To seesaw; vacillate. [Prob < ON *titra,* to tremble.]

teeth. *pl.* of **tooth.**

teethe (tēth) *v.* **teethed, teething.** To grow teeth; cut one's teeth in infancy.

tee·to·tal·er (tē′tōt′l-ər) *n.* One who abstains completely from alcoholic liquors. [*Tee,* first letter in TOTAL + total (abstinence).]

Te·gu·ci·gal·pa (tä-gōō′sē-gäl′pä). The capital of Honduras. Pop. 168,000.

Te·he·ran (tē′ə-răn′, -rän′). The capital of Iran. Pop. 2,317,000.

tel. 1. telegram; telegraph. 2. telephone.

Tel A·viv (těl′ ə-vēv′). A city of W Israel. Pop. 394,000.

tele-. *comb. form.* 1. Distance. 2. Television. [< Gk *tēle,* at a distance, far off.]

tel·e·cast (těl′ə-kăst′, -käst′) *v.* **-cast** or **-casted, -casting.** To broadcast by television. *—n.* A television broadcast.

tel·e·com·mu·ni·ca·tion (těl′ə-kə-myōō′nĭ-kā′shən) *n.* Often **telecommunications.** The science and technology of communication by electrical or electronic means.

tel·e·gram (těl′ə-grăm′) *n.* A communication transmitted by telegraph.

tel·e·graph (těl′ə-grăf′, -gräf′) *n.* 1. Any communications system that transmits and receives unmodulated electric impulses, esp. one in which the transmission and reception stations are connected by wires. 2. A telegram. *—v.* To transmit (a message) by telegraph. **—tel′e·graph′ic** *adj.* **—tel′e·graph′i·cal·ly** *adv.* **—te·leg′ra·phy** (tə-lěg′rə-fē) *n.*

Tel·e·gu (těl′ə-gōō′) *n.* A Dravidian language spoken in SE India.

tel·e·ki·ne·sis (těl′ə-kĭ-nē′sĭs, -kĭ-nē′sĭs) *n.* The movement of, or ability to move, objects by scientifically unknown or inexplicable means, as by the exercise of mystical powers.

te·lem·e·try (tə-lěm′ə-trē) *n.* The science and technology of automatic acquisition and transmission of data from remote sources.

te·lep·a·thy (tə-lěp′ə-thē) *n.* Communication by scientifically unknown means. **—tel′e·path′ic** (těl′ə-păth′ĭk) *adj.*

tel·e·phone (těl′ə-fōn′) *n.* 1. An electrical or electronic device that transmits voice or other acoustic signals to remote locations. 2. A system of such devices together with connecting and supporting equipment. *—v.* **-phoned, -phoning.** To communicate, or communicate with, by telephone. **—tel′e·phon′er** *n.* **—tel′e·phon′ic** (-fŏn′ĭk) *adj.*

te·leph·o·ny (tə-lěf′ə-nē) *n.* The electrical transmission of sound between distant stations.

tel·e·pho·to (těl′ə-fō′tō) *adj.* Of or pertaining to a photographic lens or lens system used to produce a large image of a distant object.

tel·e·scope (těl′ə-skōp′) *n.* 1. An arrangement of lenses or mirrors or both that gathers light, permitting direct observation or photographic recording of distant objects. 2. Any of various devices used to detect and observe distant objects by their emission or reflection of radiant energy. *—v.* **-scoped, -scoping.** 1. To slide inward or outward in overlapping sections, as the cylindrical sections of a small hand telescope. 2. To crush or compress inward. 3. To make shorter or more precise; condense. [< Gk *teleskopos,* farseeing.] **—tel′e·scop′ic** (-skŏp′ĭk) *adj.*

tel·e·type·writ·er (těl′ə-tīp′rī′tər) *n.* An electromechanical typewriter that either transmits or receives messages coded in electrical signals.

tel·e·vise (těl′ə-vīz′) *v.* **-vised, -vising.** To broadcast (a program) by television.

tel·e·vi·sion (těl′ə-vĭzh′ən) *n.* 1. The transmission and reception of images of moving and stationary objects, generally with accompanying sound, by electronic means. 2. The receiving apparatus used in this process. 3. The industry of broadcasting television programs.

tell (těl) *v.* **told, telling.** 1. To narrate; recount. 2. To express with words. 3. To notify; inform. 4. To command; order. 5. To discern; identify. 6. To have an effect or impact: *In this game every move tells.* [< OE *tellan.* See **del-².**] **—tell′a·ble** *adj.*

tell·er (těl′ər) *n.* A bank employee who receives and pays out money.

tell·ing (těl′ĭng) *adj.* 1. Having force or effect. 2. Revealing. **—tell′ing·ly** *adv.*

tell·tale (těl′tāl′) *n.* 1. A talebearer. 2. A sign; token. 3. Any of various devices that indicate or register information. *—adj.* Serving to indicate, reveal, or betray.

tel·lu·ri·um (tě-lŏŏr′ē-əm) *n. Symbol* **Te** A brittle, silvery-white metallic element used to alloy stainless steel and lead, in ceramics, and in thermoelectric devices. Atomic number 52, atomic weight 127.60. [< L *tellūs,* earth.]

Tell (tĕl), **William.** Legendary Swiss independence hero.

te•mer•i•ty (tə-mĕr'ə-tē) *n.* Rashness; foolish boldness. [< L *temere*, blindly, rashly.]

temp. 1. in the time of (L *tempore*). 2. temperature. 3. temporary.

tem•per (tĕm'pər) *v.* 1. To modify; moderate. 2. To bring to a specified consistency, as by blending, kneading, etc. 3. To harden or toughen (a metal), as by alternate heating and cooling. —*n.* 1. A state of mind or emotions; mood; disposition. 2. Equanimity; composure. 3. **a.** Irascibility. **b.** An outburst of rage: *a fit of temper.* 4. The condition or degree of being tempered. [< L *temperāre*, "to mingle in due proportion."]

tem•per•a (tĕm'pər-ə) *n.* 1. A painting medium in which pigment is mixed with water-soluble glutinous materials such as size or egg yolk. 2. Painting done with this medium. [< It *temperare*, to mingle, temper.]

tem•per•a•ment (tĕm'prə-mənt, tĕm'pər-ə-) *n.* 1. The manner of thinking, behaving, and reacting characteristic of a specific individual. 2. Excessive irritability or sensitiveness. [< L *temperāmentum*, "a mixing (of the humors)."] —**tem'per•a•men'tal** *adj.* —**tem'per•a•men'tal•ly** *adv.*

tem•per•ance (tĕm'pər-əns, tĕm'prəns) *n.* 1. Moderation or self-restraint. 2. Total abstinence from alcoholic liquors.

tem•per•ate (tĕm'pər-ĭt, tĕm'prĭt) *adj.* 1. Exercising moderation and self-restraint. 2. Moderate; mild. 3. Neither hot nor cold in climate. [< L *temperāre*, to moderate, TEMPER.] —**tem'per•ate•ly** *adv.*

Temperate Zone. Either of two middle latitude zones of the earth lying between 23¹/₂° and 66¹/₂° N and S.

tem•per•a•ture (tĕm'pər-ə-chŏŏr', tĕm'prə-) *n.* 1. The degree of hotness or coldness of a body or environment. 2. A bodily temperature above normal, caused by illness; fever. [< L *temperāre*, to mix, TEMPER.]

tem•pered (tĕm'pərd) *adj.* 1. Having a specified temper or disposition. 2. Moderated: *justice tempered with clemency.*

tem•pest (tĕm'pĭst) *n.* A violent storm. [< L *tempestās*, storm, weather, season.] —**tem•pes'tu•ous** (-pĕs'chŏŏ-əs) *adj.*

tem•plate (tĕm'plĭt) *n.* Also **tem•plet.** A pattern or gauge used as a guide in making something accurately. [< F *templet.*]

tem•ple¹ (tĕm'pəl) *n.* A building or place dedicated to the worship or the presence of a deity. [< L *templum*, sanctuary.]

tem•ple² (tĕm'pəl) *n.* The flat region on either side of the forehead. [< L *tempus*, temple of the head.]

tem•po (tĕm'pō) *n., pl.* **-pos.** 1. The relative speed at which music is to be played. 2. A characteristic rate of activity; pace. [It, "time."]

tem•po•ral¹ (tĕm'pər-əl, tĕm'prəl) *adj.* 1. Pertaining to or limited by time. 2. Secular as distinguished from ecclesiastical. [< L *tempus*, time.] —**tem'po•ral•ly** *adv.*

tem•po•ral² (tĕm'pər-əl, tĕm'prəl) *adj.* Of, per-

taining to, or near the temples of the skull. [< L *tempus*, TEMPLE².]

tem•po•rar•y (tĕm'pə-rĕr'ē) *adj.* Lasting, used, or enjoyed for a limited time; not permanent. [< L *tempus*, time.] —**tem'po•rar'i•ly** *adv.*

tem•po•rize (tĕm'pə-rīz') *v.* **-rized, -rizing.** To compromise or act evasively in order to gain time or postpone a decision. [< L *tempus*, time.] —**tem'po•ri•za'tion** *n.*

tempt (tĕmpt) *v.* 1. To entice (someone) to commit an unwise or immoral act. 2. To be attractive to. 3. To provoke or risk provoking. 4. To incline or dispose strongly. [< L *temptāre*, to try, touch, tempt.] —**tempt•a'tion** *n.* —**tempt'er** *n.* —**tempt'ress** (tĕmp'trĭs) *fem.n.*

ten (tĕn) *n.* The cardinal number written 10 or in Roman numerals X. [< OE *tīen, tȳn.* See **dekm̥-.**] —**ten** *adj. & pron.*

ten. tenor.

ten•a•ble (tĕn'ə-bəl) *adj.* Defensible or logical. [< L *tenēre*, to hold.] —**ten'a•bil'i•ty, ten'a•ble•ness** *n.* —**ten'a•bly** *adv.*

te•na•cious (tə-nā'shəs) *adj.* 1. Persistent; stubborn. 2. Cohesive or adhesive. 3. Tending to retain; retentive. [< L *tenēre*, to hold.] —**te•nac'i•ty** (-năs'ə-tē) *n.*

ten•an•cy (tĕn'ən-sē) *n., pl.* **-cies.** 1. The possession or occupancy of lands or tenements by lease or rent. 2. The period of a tenant's occupancy or possession.

ten•ant (tĕn'ənt) *n.* 1. One who temporarily holds or occupies property owned by another. 2. An occupant or inhabitant. [< L *tenēre*, to hold.]

Ten Commandments. The ten injunctions received by Moses.

tend¹ (tĕnd) *v.* 1. To move or extend in a certain direction. 2. To be likely. 3. To be disposed or inclined. [< L *tendere*, to stretch, direct one's course, be inclined.]

tend² (tĕnd) *v.* 1. To look after. 2. To serve at: *tend bar.* [< ME *attenden*, attend.]

ten•den•cy (tĕn'dən-sē) *n., pl.* **-cies.** 1. A demonstrated inclination to think, act, or behave in a certain way; propensity. 2. The drift or purport of a literary work. [< L *tendere*, to stretch, TEND.]

ten•der¹ (tĕn'dər) *adj.* 1. Delicate; soft; fragile. 2. Young and vulnerable. 3. Frail; weakly delicate. 4. Sensitive or sore. 5. Gentle and loving. [< L *tener*, tender, delicate.] —**ten'der•ly** *adv.* —**ten'der•ness** *n.*

ten•der² (tĕn'dər) *n.* 1. A formal offer or bid. 2. Money: *legal tender.* —*v.* To offer formally. [< L *tendere*, to stretch.]

tend•er³ (tĕn'dər) *n.* 1. One who tends something. 2. *Naut.* A vessel attendant on another vessel or vessels. 3. A railroad car attached to the locomotive, carrying fuel and water.

ten•der•foot (tĕn'dər-fŏŏt') *n., pl.* **-foots** or **-feet.** A greenhorn; novice.

ten•der•heart•ed (tĕn'dər-här'tĭd) *adj.* Compassionate.

ten•der•iz•er (tĕn'də-rī'zər) *n.* A substance applied to meat to make it tender.

ten•der•loin (tĕn'dər-loin') *n.* The tenderest part of a loin of beef, pork, etc.

ten•don (tĕn'dən) *n.* A band of tough, inelastic

ŏ paw, for/oi boy/ou out/ŏŏ took/ōō coo/p pop/r run/s sauce/sh shy/t to/th thin/*th* the/
ŭ cut/ûr fur/v van/w wag/y yes/z size/zh vision/ə ago, item, edible, gallop, circus/

fibrous tissue that connects a muscle with its bony attachment. [< L *tendere*, to stretch.]

ten·dril (těn′drəl) *n.* **1.** A slender, coiling extension by which a climbing plant clings to a support. **2.** Something resembling this. [< OF *tendron*, cartilage, young shoot.]

ten·e·ment (těn′ə-mənt) *n.* **1.** A building to live in, esp. one intended for rent. **2.** A cheap apartment house whose facilities and maintenance barely meet minimum standards. [< ML *tenementum*, feudal holding, house.]

ten·et (těn′ĭt) *n.* A fundamental principle or dogma. [< L *tenēre*, to hold.]

Tenn. Tennessee.

Ten·nes·see (těn′ə-sē′). A state of the SE U.S. Pop. 3,924,000. Cap. Nashville.

ten·nis (těn′ĭs) *n.* A game played with rackets and a light ball by two players *(singles)* or two pairs of players *(doubles)* on a court divided by a net. [ME *tennys.*]

Ten·ny·son (těn′ə-sən), **Alfred Lord.** 1809–1892. English poet.

ten·on (těn′ən) *n.* A projection on the end of a piece of wood shaped for insertion into a mortise. [< L *tenēre*, to hold.]

ten·or (těn′ər) *n.* **1.** Flow of meaning; gist; purport. **2. a.** *Law.* The exact meaning or actual wording of a document as distinct from its effect. **b.** An exact copy or transcript of a document. **3. a.** The highest natural adult male voice. **b.** A part for this voice. **c.** One who sings this part. [< L, uninterrupted course, a holding on.]

ten·pin (těn′pĭn′) *n.* **1.** A bowling pin used in playing tenpins. **2. tenpins.** A game, bowling.

tense¹ (těns) *adj.* **tenser, tensest. 1.** Taut; strained. **2.** Nerveracking; suspenseful: *a tense situation.* —*v.* **tensed, tensing.** To make or become tense. [L *tensus*, pp of *tendere*, to stretch out.] —**tense′ness** *n.*

tense² (těns) *n.* Any of the inflected forms of a verb that indicate the time and continuance or completion of the action or state. [< L *tempus*, time.]

ten·sile (těn′səl, -sīl′) *adj.* Of or involving a force that produces stretching. [< L *tensus*, "stretched," TENSE.]

ten·sion (těn′shən) *n.* **1.** The act of stretching or the condition of being stretched. **2.** A force tending to produce elongation or extension. **3. a.** Mental strain. **b.** A strained relation between persons or groups. **c.** Uneasy suspense. [< L *tensus*, TENSE.] —**ten′sion·al** *adj.*

tent (těnt) *n.* A portable shelter, as of canvas stretched over a supporting framework of poles, ropes, and pegs. [< L *tendere*, to stretch.]

ten·ta·cle (těn′tə-kəl) *n.* A flexible, unjointed, projecting appendage, as of an octopus or sea anemone. [< L *temptāre*, to touch, feel, TEMPT.] —**ten·tac′u·lar** (-tăk′yə-lər) *adj.*

ten·ta·tive (těn′tə-tĭv) *adj.* **1.** Of an experimental nature. **2.** Uncertain. [< L *temptāre*, to feel, try, TEMPT.] —**ten′ta·tive·ly** *adv.*

ten·ter·hook (těn′tər-hŏok′) *n.* A hooked nail for securing cloth on a drying framework. —**on tenterhooks.** In a state of suspense or anxiety.

tenth (těnth) *n.* **1.** The ordinal number 10 in a series. **2.** One of 10 equal parts. —**tenth** *adj.* & *adv.*

ten·u·ous (těn′yōō-əs) *adj.* **1.** Slender or thin; rarefied. **2.** Unsubstantial; flimsy. [< L *tenuis*, thin, rare, fine.] —**ten′u·ous·ly** *adv.* —**ten′u·ous·ness** *n.*

ten·ure (těn′yər, -yōor′) *n.* **1.** The holding of something, as an office; occupation. **2.** The terms under which something is held. **3. a.** The period of holding. **b.** Permanence of position. [< L *tenēre*, to hold.]

te·pee (tē′pē) *n.* A cone-shaped tent of skins or bark used by North American Indians.

tep·id (těp′ĭd) *adj.* Moderately warm; lukewarm. [< L *tepēre*, to be lukewarm.]

te·qui·la (tə-kē′lə) *n.* An alcoholic liquor distilled from a fleshy-leaved Central American plant. [< *Tequila*, district in Mexico.]

ter. territorial; territory.

tera–. Indicates a trillion (10¹²): *terahertz.* [< Gk *teras*, monster.]

ter·bi·um (tûr′bē-əm) *n. Symbol* Tb A soft, silvery-gray metallic rare-earth element, used in electronics and as a laser material. Atomic number 65, atomic weight 158.924. [< *Ytterby*, a village in Sweden.]

ter·cen·te·nar·y (tûr′sĕn-tĕn′ə-rē, tûr-sĕn′tə-nĕr′ē) *n., pl.* **-ies.** Also **ter·cen·ten·ni·al** (tûr′sĕn-tĕn′ē-əl). A 300th anniversary or its celebration. —**ter′cen·te′nar·y** *adj.*

term (tûrm) *n.* **1. a.** A limited period of time. **b.** An assigned period for a person to serve. **2. a.** A point of time beginning or ending a period. **b.** A deadline, as for making a payment. **c.** The end of a normal gestation period. **3. a.** A word having a precise meaning. **b. terms.** Language or manner of expression employed: *no uncertain terms.* **4. terms. a.** Conditions or stipulations: *peace terms.* **b.** The relation between two persons or groups: *on speaking terms.* **5.** *Math.* Each of the quantities connected by addition or subtraction signs in an equation or series. —*v.* To designate; call. [< L *terminus*, boundary line, boundary, limit.] —**term′ly** *adv.*

ter·ma·gant (tûr′mə-gənt) *n.* A shrew. [ME *Termagaunt*, imaginary Moslem deity who appeared as such a character in mystery plays.]

ter·mi·nal (tûr′mə-nəl) *adj.* **1.** Pertaining to, situated at, or forming the end or boundary of something. **2.** Concluding; final. **3.** Pertaining to or occurring in a term or each term. —*n.* **1.** A terminating point, limit, or part. **2.** A point at which a connection to an electrical component is normally made. **3.** A railroad or bus station, esp. a terminus. [< L *terminus*, boundary, TERMINUS.] —**ter′mi·nal·ly** *adv.*

ter·mi·nate (tûr′mə-nāt′) *v.* **-nated, -nating.** To end or conclude. [< L *terminus*, TERMINUS.] —**ter′mi·na′tion** *n.* —**ter′mi·na′tive** *adj.*

ter·mi·nol·o·gy (tûr′mə-nŏl′ə-jē) *n., pl.* **-gies.** The technical terms of a particular trade, science, or art; nomenclature. [< L *terminus*, limit + -LOGY.] —**ter′mi·no·log′i·cal** (-nə-lŏj′ĭ-kəl) *adj.* —**ter′mi·no·log′i·cal·ly** *adv.* —**ter′mi·nol′o·gist** *n.*

ter·mi·nus (tûr′mə-nəs) *n., pl.* **-nuses** or **-ni**

(-nĭ'). **1.** The end of something. **2. a.** A terminal on a transportation line. **b.** The last stop on such a line. [L, boundary line, boundary, limit.]

ter•mite (tûr'mīt') *n.* Any of various superficially antlike social insects that feed on and destroy wood. [< L *tarmes*, wood-eating worm.]

tern (tûrn) *n.* Any of various sea birds related to and resembling the gulls but usually smaller and with a forked tail. [< Scand.]

ter•na•ry (tûr'nə-rē) *adj.* **1.** Composed of three or arranged in threes. **2.** *Math.* **a.** Having the base three. **b.** Involving three variables. [< L *ternī*, three each.]

terp•si•cho•re•an (tûrp'sĭk-ə-rē'ən, tûrp'sə-kôr'ē-ən, -kōr'ē-ən) *adj.* Pertaining to dancing. [< *Terpsichore*, Greek muse of dancing.]

terr. territorial; territory.

ter•race (tĕr'ĭs) *n.* **1.** A porch or balcony. **2.** An open area adjacent to a house; patio. **3.** A raised bank of earth having vertical or sloping sides and a flat top. **4.** A row of buildings erected on raised ground or on a sloping site. [< L *terra*, earth.]

ter•ra cot•ta (tĕr'ə kŏt'ə). A hard ceramic clay used in pottery and construction. [It, "cooked earth."] —**ter'ra-cot'ta** *adj.*

ter•ra fir•ma (tĕr'ə fûr'mə). Dry land. [L, "firm land."]

ter•rain (tə-rān', tĕ-) *n.* **1.** A tract of land; ground. **2.** The character of land. [< L *terra*, earth.]

ter•ra•pin (tĕr'ə-pən) *n.* Any of various aquatic North American turtles. [< Algon.]

ter•rar•i•um (tə-râr'ē-əm) *n., pl.* **-ums** or **-ia** (-ē-ə). A closed container in which small plants are grown or small animals, as turtles or lizards, are kept. [< L *terra*, earth + -ARIUM.]

ter•res•tri•al (tə-rĕs'trē-əl) *adj.* **1.** Pertaining to the earth or its inhabitants. **2.** Of, pertaining to, or composed of land as distinct from water or air. **3.** Living or growing on land. [< L *terra*, earth.]

terre-verte (tĕr'vĕrt') *n.* An olive-green pigment. [F, "green earth."]

ter•ri•ble (tĕr'ə-bəl) *adj.* **1.** Causing terror or fear; dreadful. **2.** Eliciting awe. **3.** Intense; severe. **4.** Unpleasant; disagreeable. [< L *terrēre*, to frighten.] —**ter'ri•ble•ness** *n.* —**ter'ri•bly** *adv.*

ter•ri•er (tĕr'ē-ər) *n.* Any of various usually small, active dogs originally bred for hunting burrowing animals. [< F *terrier*, burrow.]

ter•ri•fic (tə-rĭf'ĭk) *adj.* **1.** Terrifying or frightful. **2.** Splendid; magnificent. **3.** Awesome; astounding: *a terrific speed.* [< L *terrēre*, to frighten + -FIC.] —**ter•rif'i•cal•ly** *adv.*

ter•ri•fy (tĕr'ə-fī') *v.* **-fied, -fying.** To fill with terror. —**ter'ri•fy'ing•ly** *adv.*

ter•ri•to•ri•al (tĕr'ə-tôr'ē-əl, -tōr'ē-əl) *adj.* **1.** Of or pertaining to a territory or to its powers of jurisdiction. **2.** Pertaining or restricted to a particular territory; regional; local.

territorial waters. Inland and coastal waters under the jurisdiction of a state.

ter•ri•to•ry (tĕr'ə-tôr'ē, -tōr'ē) *n., pl.* **-ries. 1.** A region. **2.** The land and waters under the juris-

diction of a state. **3. Territory. a.** A part of the U.S. not admitted as a state. **b.** A part of Canada or Australia not accorded statehood or provincial status. **4.** The area for which a person is responsible. **5.** A sphere of action or interest; province. [< L *terra*, land.]

ter•ror (tĕr'ər) *n.* **1.** Intense, overpowering fear. **2.** A terrifying object or occurrence. **3.** A policy of violence aiming to achieve or maintain supremacy. [< L *terrēre*, to frighten.]

ter•ror•ism (tĕr'ər-ĭz'əm) *n.* The political use of terror and intimidation. —**ter'ror•ist** *n.* & *adj.*

ter•ror•ize (tĕr'ər-īz') *v.* **-ized, -izing. 1.** To fill with terror. **2.** To coerce by intimidation.

ter•ry (tĕr'ē) *n., pl.* **-ries. 1.** Any of the uncut loops that form the pile of a fabric. **2.** A looped pile fabric used for bath towels and robes. [?]

terse (tûrs) *adj.* **terser, tersest.** Effectively concise. [< L *tersus*, pp of *tergēre*, to wipe off, polish.] —**terse'ly** *adv.* —**terse'ness** *n.*

ter•ti•ar•y (tûr'shē-ĕr'ē) *adj.* **1.** Third in place, order, degree, or rank. **2. Tertiary.** Of or belonging to the geologic time, system of rocks, and sedimentary deposits of the first period of the Cenozoic era. —*n.* The Tertiary period. [< L *tertius*, third.]

tes•sel•late (tĕs'ə-lāt') *v.* **-lated, -lating.** To form into a mosaic pattern, as by using small squares of stone or glass. [< L *tessella*, a small cube.] —**tes'sel•la'tion** *n.*

test (tĕst) *n.* **1.** A means of examination, trial, or proof. **2.** A series of questions or problems designed to determine knowledge or intelligence. **3.** A criterion; standard. [< L *testum*, earthen vessel.] —**test** *v.* —**test'er** *n.*

test. 1. testator. **2.** testimony.

Test. Testament.

tes•ta•ment (tĕs'tə-mənt) *n.* **1. a.** A document providing for the disposition of personal property after death. **b.** A will. **2. a.** Any proof that serves as evidence of something. **b.** A statement of belief. **3. Testament. a.** Either of the two main divisions of the Bible, the Old Testament and the New Testament. **b.** The New Testament. [< L *testis*, witness.]

tes•tate (tĕs'tāt') *adj.* Having made a legally valid will before death. [< L *testārī*, to make a will.]

tes•ta•tor (tĕs'tā'tər, tĕs-tā'tər) *n.* One who has made a legally valid will before death.

tes•ti•cle (tĕs'tĭ-kəl) *n.* A testis.

tes•ti•fy (tĕs'tə-fī') *v.* **-fied, -fying. 1.** To make a declaration of fact under oath. **2.** To make a serious or solemn statement in support of an argument or asserted fact. **3.** To declare publicly; make known. [< L *testificārī*.]

tes•ti•mo•ni•al (tĕs'tə-mō'nē-əl) *n.* **1.** A formal statement testifying to a particular fact. **2.** A written affirmation of another's character or worth. **3.** Something given as a tribute for a person's achievement. —**tes'ti•mo'ni•al** *adj.*

tes•ti•mo•ny (tĕs'tə-mō'nē) *n., pl.* **-nies. 1.** A declaration or affirmation of fact or truth. **2.** Any evidence in support of a fact or assertion; proof. **3.** The collective testimony in a legal case. **4.** A public declaration regarding a

---

ô paw, for/oi boy/ou out/ŏŏ took/ōō coo/p pop/r run/s sauce/sh shy/t to/th thin/*th* the/
ŭ cut/ûr fur/v van/w wag/y yes/z size/zh vision/ə ago, item, edible, gallop, circus/

religious experience. [< L *testis*, witness.]

tes•tis (těs′tĭs) *n., pl.* **-tes** (-tēz′). The male reproductive gland. [L, "witness" (to virility).]

test tube. A cylindrical clear glass tube usually open at one end and rounded at the other, used in laboratory experimentation.

tes•ty (těs′tē) *adj.* **-tier, -tiest. 1.** Irritable; touchy; peevish. **2.** Characterized by irritability, impatience, or exasperation: *a testy remark.* [ME *testif*, headstrong.] **—tes′ti•ly** *adv.* **—tes′ti•ness** *n.*

tet•a•nus (tět′n-əs) *n.* An acute, often fatal infectious disease caused by a bacillus and characterized by rigidity and spasmodic contraction of the voluntary muscles. [< Gk *tetanos*, "stretched."]

tête-à-tête (tāt′ə-tāt′) *adv.* Together without a third person; in privacy. **—n.** A private conversation between two people. **—adj.** For or between two only; private. [F, "head to head."]

teth (tět, těs) *n.* The 9th letter of the Hebrew alphabet, representing *ṭ*.

teth•er (tět*h*′ər) *n.* **1.** A rope or chain for an animal, allowing it a short radius to move about. **2.** The range or scope of one's resources or abilities. **—v.** To restrict with a tether. [< ON *tjōthr.*]

tetra–. *comb. form.* Four. [Gk.]

tet•ra•he•dron (tět′rə-hē′drən) *n., pl.* **-drons** or **-dra** (-drə). A polyhedron with four faces. [< Gk *tetraedros*, four-faced.] **—tet′ra•he′dral** (-drəl) *adj.*

te•tram•e•ter (tě-trăm′ə-tər) *n.* A line of verse consisting of four metrical feet.

Teu•ton (t/y/ōōt′n) *n.* **1. Teutons.** An ancient people, probably of Germanic or Celtic origin, who lived in N Europe until about 100 B.C. **2.** One of the peoples speaking a Germanic language, esp. a German.

Teu•ton•ic (t/y/ōō-tŏn′ĭk) *adj.* **1.** Of or relating to the Teutons. **2.** Of or relating to the Germanic languages. **—n.** The Germanic languages.

Tex. Texas.

Tex•as (těk′səs). A state of the south-central U.S. Pop. 11,197,000. Cap. Austin. **—Tex′an** *adj. & n.*

text (těkst) *n.* **1.** The wording or words of something written or printed. **2.** The body of a printed work as distinct from a preface, footnote, or appendix. **3.** A Scriptural passage to be read and expounded upon in a sermon. **4.** The subject matter of a discourse. **5.** A textbook. [< L *textus*, literary composition, "woven thing."] **—tex′tu•al** (těks′chōō-əl) *adj.*

text•book (těkst′bŏŏk′) *n.* A book used for the study of a particular subject.

tex•tile (těks′tīl′, -tĭl) *n.* **1.** Cloth; fabric, esp. a woven or knitted one. **2.** Fiber or yarn used for making fabric. **—adj.** Pertaining to textiles or their manufacture. [< L *textus*, "woven thing."]

tex•ture (těks′chər) *n.* **1.** The appearance of a fabric resulting from the woven arrangement of its yarns or fibers. **2.** The composition or structure of a substance; grain. [< L *textus*, woven thing.] **—tex′tur•al** *adj.*

–th¹. *comb. form.* **1.** The act or result of the act expressed in the verb root: *spilth.* **2.** The quality suggested by the adjective root: **width.** [< OE *-thu, -tho.*]

–th², –eth. *comb. form.* Ordinal numbers: **millionth.** [< OE *-tha, -the.*]

–th³. Variant of **-eth¹.**

Th thorium.

Thack•er•ay (thăk′ə-rē, thăk′rē), **William Makepeace.** 1811–1863. English novelist.

Thai (tī) *n., pl.* **Thai. 1.** A native or citizen of Thailand. **2.** The official language of Thailand, a member of the Tai family; Siamese. **—Thai** *adj.*

Thai•land (tī′lănd′). A kingdom of SE Asia. Pop. 26,258,000. Cap. Bangkok.

Thailand

thal•a•mus (thăl′ə-məs) *n., pl.* **-mi** (-mī′). A large mass of gray matter that relays sensory stimuli to the cerebral cortex. [< Gk *thalamos*, inner chamber.] **—tha•lam′ic** (thə-lăm′ĭk) *adj.*

tha•ler. Variant of **taler.**

thal•li•um (thăl′ē-əm) *n. Symbol* **Tl** A soft, malleable, highly toxic metallic element, used in rodent and ant poisons, photocells, and low-melting glass. Atomic number 81, atomic weight 204.37. [< L *thallus*, green shoot + -IUM.]

Thames (těmz). A river of S England.

than (th*ă*n) *conj.* **1. —**Used in comparative statements to introduce the second element of a comparison or inequality. **2. —**Used in statements of preference to introduce the rejected alternative: *I would rather dance than eat.* **3. —**Used with the sense of "beyond" with adverbs of degree or quantity: *Read more than the first page.* [< OE *thanne, thænne.* See **to-.**]

Usage: In sentences involving comparison, the case of the word following *than* is governed by its function in the clause introduced by *than: He speaks better than I do.* This is true also of elliptical clauses in which the unexpressed words are clearly indicated: *He is a better speaker than I* (that is, *than I am*). *The students disliked no one more than her* (that is,

---

ă pat/ā ate/âr care/ä bar/b **bib**/ch **chew**/d **deed**/ĕ pet/ē be/f **fit**/g **gag**/h **hat**/hw **what**/
ĭ pit/ī pie/îr **pier**/j **judge**/k **kick**/l **lid**, fatal/m **mum**/n **no**, sudden/ng **sing**/ŏ pot/ō go/

than they disliked her). In the first example, *I* is construed as the subject of an unexpressed verb; in the second, *her* is construed as an object. See Usage note at **different.**
thane (thān) *n.* Also **thegn. 1.** In Anglo-Saxon England, a freeman granted land by the king in return for military service. **2.** A feudal lord in Scotland. [< OE *thegen.*]
thank (thăngk) *v.* To express gratitude to. [< OE *thancian.* See **tong-.**]
thank•ful (thăngk′fəl) *adj.* Grateful. —**thank′-ful•ly** *adv.* —**thank′ful•ness** *n.*
thank•less (thăngk′lĭs) *adj.* **1.** Not feeling or showing gratitude; ungrateful. **2.** Not apt to be appreciated: *a thankless task.*
thanks (thăngks) *pl.n.* An acknowledgment of a favor, gift, etc. —**thanks to.** On account of; because of. —*interj.* Expressive of gratitude.
thanks•giv•ing (thăngks′gĭv′ĭng) *n.* An act of giving thanks; an expression of gratitude, esp. to God.
Thanksgiving Day. A U.S. national holiday set apart for giving thanks to God, celebrated on the fourth Thursday of November.
that (thăt; *unstressed* thət) *adj., pl.* **those** (thōz). **1.** Being the one singled out, implied, or understood. **2.** Being the one further removed or less obvious. —*pron., pl.* **those. 1. a.** The one designated, implied, mentioned, or understood. **b.** The further or less immediate one. **2.** —Used as a relative pronoun to introduce a clause. **3.** Something: *There is that about him which mystifies me.* —*adv.* To such an extent: *Is it that complicated?* —*conj.* **1.** —Used chiefly to introduce a subordinate clause stating a fact, wish, consequence, or reason: *We supposed that you were lost.* **2.** —Used to introduce an elliptical exclamation of desire: *Oh, that I were rich!* [< OE *thæt.* See **to-.**]
thatch (thăch) *n.* Plant stalks or foliage, as reeds or palm fronds, used for roofing. —*v.* To cover with or as if with thatch. [< OE *theccan,* to thatch, cover. See **steg-¹.**]
thaw (thô) *v.* **1.** To change from a frozen solid to a liquid by gradual warming. **2.** To become warm enough to melt snow and ice. **3.** To become less reserved. —*n.* **1.** The process of thawing. **2.** A period during which ice and snow melt. [< OE *thāwian.* See **tā-.**]
the¹ (thē *before a vowel; thə before a consonant*). The definite article, functioning as an adjective before singular or plural nouns and noun phrases that denote particular specified persons or things and before certain nouns and adjectives with generic force. [< OE *thē.* See **to-.**]
the² (thē *before a vowel; thə before a consonant*) *adv.* To that extent; by that much: *the sooner the better.* [< OE *thē,* THE and *thæt,* THAT.]
the•a•ter (thē′ə-tər) *n.* Also **the•a•tre. 1.** A building for the presentation of motion pictures and dramatic performances. **2.** Any similar place with tiers of seats. **3.** Dramatic literature or performance. **4.** A place that is the setting for dramatic events. [< Gk *theatron.*]
the•at•ri•cal (thē-ăt′rĭ-kəl) *adj.* **1.** Of, relating to, or suitable for the theater. **2.** Affectedly dramatic. —**the•at′ri•cal′i•ty** *n.*

thee (thē) *pron. Archaic & Poetic.* The objective case of the 2nd person pronoun *thou.*
theft (thĕft) *n.* The act or an instance of stealing; larceny. [< OE *thēofth* < Gmc *thiufith.*]
thegn. Variant of **thane.**
their (thâr). The possessive form of the pronoun *they,* used attributively: *their books.* [< ON *theirra.*]
theirs (thârz). The possessive form of the pronoun *they,* used as a predicate adjective or as a substantive: *The choice ought to be theirs. Theirs is better than ours.* —**of theirs.** Belonging to them: *a friend of theirs.*
the•ism (thē′ĭz′əm) *n.* Belief in the existence of a god or gods. [THE(O)- + -ISM.] —**the′ist** *n.* —**the•is′tic** *adj.* —**the•is′ti•cal•ly** *adv.*
them (thĕm) *pron.* The objective case of the 3rd person pl. pronoun *they,* used as the direct or indirect object of a verb or as the object of a preposition. [< ON *theim* and OE *thǣm.* See **to-.**]
the•mat•ic (thĭ-măt′ĭk) *adj.* Of, constituting, or relating to a theme or themes. —**the•mat′i•cal•ly** *adv.*
theme (thēm) *n.* **1.** A topic of discourse or discussion. **2.** The subject of an artistic work. **3.** A short written composition. **4.** *Mus.* A melody forming the basis of variations or other development in a composition. [< Gk *thema,* "thing placed," proposition.]
them•selves (thĕm′sĕlvz′, thəm′-) *pron.* A form of the 3rd person pl. pronoun: **1.** —Used reflexively: *They have only themselves to blame.* **2.** —Used for emphasis: *They did it themselves.* —**by themselves. 1.** Alone. **2.** Without help.
then (thĕn) *adv.* **1.** At that time in the past. **2.** Next in time, space, or order. **3.** At another time in the future. **4.** In that case; accordingly. **5.** In addition; besides. **6.** Yet; on the other hand. —*n.* A particular time or moment. —*adj.* Being so at that time. [< OE *thanne, thænne.* See **to-.**]
thence (thĕns, thĕns) *adv.* **1.** From that place. **2.** From that time; thenceforth. **3.** From that circumstance or source. [< OE *thanon,* from there. See **to-.**]
thence•forth (thĕns-fôrth′, thĕns-) *adv.* From that time forward; thereafter.
thence•for•ward (thĕns-fôr′wərd, thĕns-) *adv.* Also **thence•for•wards** (-wərdz). **1.** Thenceforth. **2.** From that time or place onward.
theo-. *comb. form.* A god or gods. [< Gk *theos,* god.]
the•oc•ra•cy (thē-ŏk′rə-sē) *n., pl.* **-cies. 1.** Government by a god regarded as the ruling power or by officials claiming divine sanction. **2.** A state so governed. —**the′o•crat′ic** *adj.* —**the′o•crat′i•cal•ly** *adv.*
theol. theological; theology.
the•ol•o•gy (thē-ŏl′ə-jē) *n., pl.* **-gies. 1.** The study of the nature of God and religious truth. **2.** An organized body of opinions concerning God and man's relationship to God. —**the′o•lo′gi•an** *n.* —**the′o•log′i•cal** (-lŏg′ĭ-kəl) *adj.* —**the′o•log′i•cal•ly** *adv.*
the•o•rem (thē′ə-rəm, thîr′əm) *n.* **1.** An idea that is demonstrably true or is assumed to be

so. 2. *Math*. A proposition that is proven or to be proved. [< Gk *theōrein*, to observe.]
the•o•rize (thē'ə-rīz') *v.* -rized, -rizing. 1. To formulate or analyze theories. 2. To speculate. —**the'o•rist** *n.* —**the'o•riz'er** *n.*
the•o•ry (thē'ə-rē, thîr'ē) *n., pl.* -ries. 1. a. Systematically organized knowledge applicable in a relatively wide variety of circumstances, esp. a system of assumptions, accepted principles, and rules of procedure devised to analyze, predict, or otherwise explain a specified set of phenomena. b. Such knowledge or such a system distinguished from experiment or practice. 2. Abstract reasoning; speculation. 3. Broadly, hypothesis or supposition. [< Gk *theōria*, contemplation, theory.] —**the'o•ret'i•cal** (-rĕt'ĭ-kəl) *adj.* —**the'-o•ret'i•cal•ly** *adv.*
the•os•o•phy (thē-ŏs'ə-fē) *n.* Religious speculation dealing with the mystical apprehension of God. —**the'o•soph'i•cal** (-ə-sŏf'ĭ-kəl) *adj.* —**the•os'o•phist** *n.*
ther•a•peu•tic (thĕr'ə-pyōō'tĭk) *adj.* Having healing or curative powers. [< Gk *therapeuein*, to administer to (medically).] —**ther'a•peu'-ti•cal•ly** *adv.*
ther•a•peu•tics (thĕr'ə-pyōō'tĭks) *n. (takes sing. v.).* The medical treatment of disease.
ther•a•py (thĕr'ə-pē) *n., pl.* -pies. The treatment of illness or disability. [< Gk *theraps*, attendant.] —**ther'a•pist** *n.*
there (thâr) *adv.* 1. At or in that place. 2. To, into, or toward that place; thither. 3. At a point of action or time. —*n.* That place. —*interj.* Expressive of an emotion, as relief or satisfaction. [< OE *thær, thēr.* See **to-**.]
Usage: There frequently precedes a linking verb such as *be, seem,* or *appear* in beginning a sentence or clause: *There has been much trouble.* The number of the verb is governed by the subject, which in such constructions follows the verb: *There is a garage across the street. There seem to be many good candidates.* But a singular verb is also possible before a compound subject whose parts are joined by a conjunction or conjunctions, especially when the parts are singular: *There is much pain and toil involved.* When the first element of such a subject is singular, a singular verb is also possible even though the other elements are plural: *There was* (or *were*) *a man and two children in the car.*
there•a•bout (thâr'ə-bout') *adv.* Also **there•a•bouts** (-bouts'). Approximately.
there•af•ter (thâr'ăf'tər, -äf'tər) *adv.* From a specified time onward; from then on.
there•at (thâr'ăt') *adv.* 1. At a specified place. 2. At such time. 3. By reason of that.
there•by (thâr'bī') *adv.* 1. By that means; as a result. 2. In a specified connection or relation wherein.
there•for (thâr'fôr') *adv.* For that, this, or it.
there•fore (thâr'fôr', -fōr') *adv. & conj.* For that reason; consequently; hence.
there•from (thâr'frŏm', -frŭm') *adv.* From that, this, or it.
there•in (thâr'ĭn', thâr'ĭn') *adv.* In that place or context.

there•in•af•ter (thâr'ĭn-ăf'tər, -äf'tər) *adv.* In a later or subsequent portion.
there•of (thâr'ŏv', -ŭv') *adv.* 1. Of or concerning this, that, or it. 2. From a stated cause or origin.
there•on (thâr'ŏn', -ôn') *adv.* 1. On or upon this, that, or it. 2. Following that immediately.
there•to (thâr'tōō') *adv.* 1. To that, this, or it. 2. *Archaic.* Furthermore.
there•to•fore (thâr'tə-fôr', -fōr') *adv.* Until or prior to a specified time.
there•un•to (thâr'ŭn-tōō') *adv.* To that, this, or it.
there•up•on (thâr'ə-pŏn', -ə-pôn') *adv.* 1. Upon this, that, or it. 2. Directly following that.
there•with (thâr'wĭth', -wĭth') *adv.* 1. With that, this, or it. 2. Immediately thereafter.
there•with•al (thâr'wĭth-ôl') *adv.* 1. With all that, this, or it; besides. 2. *Obs.* Therewith; with that, this, or it.
ther•mal (thûr'məl) *adj.* Also **ther•mic** (-mĭk). Of, pertaining to, using, producing, or caused by heat. [< Gk *thermē*, heat.] —**ther'mal•ly** *adv.*
thermo–. *comb. form.* Pertaining to or caused by heat. [< Gk *thermē*, heat < *thermos*, hot.]
ther•mo•cou•ple (thûr'mə-kŭp'əl) *n.* A device consisting of two dissimilar metals joined at two points, the potential difference between the two junctions being a measure of their difference in temperature.
ther•mo•dy•nam•ics (thûr'mō-dī-năm'ĭks) *n. (takes sing. v.).* The physics of the relationships between heat and other forms of energy. —**ther'mo•dy•nam'ic** *adj.*
ther•mom•e•ter (thər-mŏm'ə-tər) *n.* An instrument for measuring temperature. —**ther'-mo•met'ric** (thûr'mō-mĕt'rĭk), **ther'mo•met'ri•cal** *adj.* —**ther•mom'e•try** *n.*
ther•mo•nu•cle•ar (thûr'mō-n/y/ōō'klē-ər) *adj.* 1. Of or derived from the fusion of atomic nuclei at high temperatures. 2. Pertaining to atomic weapons based on fusion.
ther•mo•plas•tic (thûr'mə-plăs'tĭk) *adj.* Becoming soft when heated and hardening when cooled. —*n.* A thermoplastic material.
ther•mos bottle (thûr'məs). A commercially produced heat-insulated flask.
ther•mo•set•ting (thûr'mō-sĕt'ĭng) *adj.* Permanently hardening or solidifying on being heated, as certain synthetic resins.
ther•mo•stat (thûr'mə-stăt') *n.* A device that automatically responds to temperature changes and activates switches controlling equipment such as furnaces, refrigerators, and air conditioners.
the•sau•rus (thĭ-sôr'əs) *n., pl.* -sauri (-sôr'ī') or -ruses. A book of selected words, esp. a book of synonyms and antonyms. [L *thēsaurus*, treasure.]
these. *pl. of* **this.**
the•sis (thē'sĭs) *n., pl.* -ses (-sēz'). 1. A proposition maintained by argument. 2. A dissertation resulting from original research, esp. as a requirement for an academic degree. [< Gk, a placing, a laying down, position.]
Thes•pi•an (thĕs'pē-ən) *adj.* Also **thes•pi•an.** Of or pertaining to drama; dramatic. —*n.* An

actor or actress. [< *Thespis*, Greek poet of the 6th cent. B.C.]

Thess. Thessalonians (New Testament).

the•ta (thā'tə, thē'-) *n.* The 8th letter in the Greek alphabet, representing *th.*

thew (thyōō) *n.* 1. A well-developed sinew or muscle. 2. **thews.** Muscular power or strength. [< OE *thēaw*, usage, custom, characteristic.]

they (*thā*) *pron.* The 3rd person pl. pronoun in the nominative case, used to represent the persons or things last mentioned. [< ON *their* and OE *thā.* See to-.]

they'd (*thād*). Contraction of *they had* or *they would.*

they'll (*thāl*). Contraction of *they will.*

they're (*thâr*). Contraction of *they are.*

they've (*thāv*). Contraction of *they have.*

thi•a•mine (thī'ə-mĭn, -mēn') *n.* A B-complex vitamin, $C_{12}H_{17}ClN_4OS$, occurring in the bran coat of grains, in yeast, and in meat, that is necessary for carbohydrate metabolism, maintenance of normal nerve function, and the prevention of beriberi. [< Gk *theion*, sulfur + (VIT)AMIN.]

thick (thĭk) *adj.* 1. Relatively great in depth or in extent from one surface to the opposite; not thin. 2. Measuring in this dimension. 3. Thickset. 4. Dense; concentrated. 5. Having a viscous consistency; not transparent or fluid. 6. Having a great number of; abounding. 7. Indistinctly articulated. 8. Pronounced; heavy. 9. Lacking mental agility; stupid. 10. *Informal.* Very friendly; intimate. 11. *Informal.* Excessive. —*n.* 1. The thickset part of something. 2. The most active or intense part. [< OE *thicce.* See tegu-.] —**thick'ly** *adv.* —**thick'ness** *n.*

thick•en (thĭk'ən) *v.* To make or become thick or thicker. —**thick'en•er** *n.*

thick•en•ing (thĭk'ən-ĭng) *n.* 1. The act or process of making or becoming thick. 2. Any material used to thicken liquid.

thick•et (thĭk'ĭt) *n.* A dense growth of shrubs or underbrush. [< OE *thiccet* < *thicce*, THICK.]

thick•set (thĭk'sĕt') *adj.* 1. Having a short, stocky body; stout. 2. Positioned or placed closely together.

thief (thēf) *n., pl.* **thieves** (thēvz). One who steals. [< OE *thiof, thēof* < Gmc **thiuf.*]

thieve (thēv) *v.* **thieved, thieving.** To take by theft; steal. —**thiev'er•y** *n.*

thigh (thī) *n.* The portion of the leg between the hip and the knee. [< OE *thēoh.* See teuə-.]

thigh•bone (thī'bōn') *n.* The femur.

thim•ble (thĭm'bəl) *n.* A small cuplike guard worn to protect the finger that pushes the needle in sewing. [< OE *thӯmel* < *thūma*, THUMB.]

thim•ble•ful (thĭm'bəl-fəl) *n.* A very small quantity.

Thim•phu (thĭm'pōō'). The capital of Bhutan.

thin (thĭn) *adj.* **thinner, thinnest.** 1. Having a relatively small distance between opposite sides or surfaces. 2. Not great in diameter or cross section; fine. 3. Lean or slender. 4. Not dense or concentrated; sparse. 5. Not rich or heavy in consistency. 6. Lacking force or sub-

stance; flimsy. —*v.* **thinned, thinning.** To become or make thin or thinner. [< OE *thynne.* See ten-.] —**thin'ly** *adv.* —**thin'ness** *n.*

thine (thīn). 1. The possessive form of the pronoun *thee*, used as a predicate adjective or as a substantive. 2. —Used instead of *thy* before an initial vowel or *h: thine enemy.* [OE *thīn.* See tu-.]

thing (thĭng) *n.* 1. Something that exists; an entity. 2. A tangible object. 3. An inanimate object. 4. A creature. 5. **things.** Possessions; belongings. 6. An article of clothing. 7. An act, deed, or work. 8. A thought or notion. 9. A piece of information. 10. A matter to be dealt with. 11. A turn of events. 12. **things.** The general state of affairs; conditions. [< OE, creature, thing, deed, assembly.]

think (thĭngk) *v.* **thought, thinking.** 1. To have as a thought; formulate in the mind. 2. To ponder. 3. To reason. 4. To believe; suppose. 5. To remember; call to mind. 6. To visualize; imagine. 7. To devise or invent. 8. To consider. [< OE *thencan.* See tong-.] —**think'er** *n.*

think•a•ble (thĭng'kə-bəl) *adj.* Fit to be considered; possible. —**think'a•bly** *adv.*

thin•ner (thĭn'ər) *n.* A liquid, such as turpentine, mixed with paint to reduce viscosity.

thin-skinned (thĭn'skĭnd') *adj.* 1. Having a thin rind or skin. 2. Excessively sensitive.

thi•on•ic (thī-ŏn'ĭk) *adj.* Of, containing, or derived from sulfur. [< Gk *theion*, sulfur.]

third (thûrd) *n.* 1. The ordinal number 3 in a series. 2. One of 3 equal parts. 3. The gear next higher after second in an automobile transmission. —*adj.* 1. Being number 3 in a series; next after second. 2. Being one of 3 equal parts. —*adv.* Also **third•ly** (thûrd'lē). In the 3rd place, rank, or order. [< OE *thridda.* See trei-.]

third person. A set of grammatical forms used in referring to a person or thing other than the speaker or the one spoken to.

Third World. Also **third world.** The underdeveloped or developing countries of Africa, Asia, and Latin America, esp. those not allied with any superpower.

thirst (thûrst) *n.* 1. a. A sensation of dryness in the mouth related to a desire to drink. b. The desire to drink. 2. An insistent desire; craving. —*v.* 1. To feel a need to drink. 2. To have a strong craving. [< OE *thurst.* See ters-.] —**thirst'i•ly** *adv.* —**thirst'y** *adj.*

thir•teen (thûr'tēn') *n.* The cardinal number written 13 or in Roman numerals XIII. [< OE *thrēotīne.* See trei-.] —**thir'teen'** *adj. & pron.*

thir•teenth (thûr'tēnth') *n.* 1. The ordinal number 13 in a series. 2. One of 13 equal parts. —**thir'teenth'** *adj. & adv.*

thir•ti•eth (thûr'tē-ĭth) *n.* 1. The ordinal number 30 in a series. 2. One of 30 equal parts. —**thir'ti•eth** *adj. & adv.*

thir•ty (thûr'tē) *n.* The cardinal number written 30 or in Roman numerals XXX. [< OE *thrītig.* See trei-.] —**thir'ty** *adj. & pron.*

this (thĭs) *pron., pl.* **these** (thēz). 1. The person or thing present, nearby, or just mentioned. 2. What is about to be said. 3. The one that is nearer than another or the one compared with

---

ō paw, for/oi boy/ou out/ŏŏ took/ōō coo/p pop/r run/s sauce/sh shy/t to/th thin/*th* the/
ŭ cut/ûr fur/v van/w wag/y yes/z size/zh vision/ə ago, item, edible, gallop, circus/

the other. **4.** The present occasion or time. —*adj., pl.* **these. 1.** Being just mentioned or present. **2.** Being nearer than another or compared with another. **3.** Being about to be stated or described. —*adv.* To this extent. [< OE *thes* or *thēs.* See **to-**.]

this•tle (thĭs′əl) *n.* Any of various prickly plants with usually purplish flowers. [< OE *thistel* < Gmc **thistilaz.*]

this•tle•down (thĭs′əl-doun′) *n.* The silky down attached to the seeds of a thistle.

thith•er (thĭth′ər, thĭth′-) *adv.* To or toward that place; there. —*adj.* Being on the more distant side. [< OE *thider.* See **to-**.]

thith•er•ward (thĭth′ər-wərd, thĭth′-) *adv.* In that direction; thither.

thole pin (thōl). A peg set in pairs in the gunwale of a boat to serve as an oarlock. [< OE *tholl.*]

thong (thông, thŏng) *n.* A strip of leather used for binding or lashing. [< OE *thwong, thwang.* See **twengh-**.]

tho•rax (thôr′ăks′, thôr′-) *n., pl.* **-raxes** or **thoraces** (thôr′ə-sēz′, thôr′-, thô-rā′-). The part of the body between the neck and the diaphragm, partially encased by the ribs; the chest. [< Gk *thōrax,* breastplate, chest covering.] —**tho•rac′ic** (thə-răs′ĭk) *adj.*

tho•ri•um (thôr′ē-əm, thōr′-) *n. Symbol* **Th** A silvery-white metallic element used in magnesium alloys. Atomic number 90, atomic weight 232.038. [< *Thor,* Norse god of thunder.]

thorn (thôrn) *n.* **1.** A sharp, woody spine protruding from a plant stem. **2.** Any of various shrubs, trees, or plants bearing such spines. **3.** One that causes pain or discomfort. [< OE, thorn, thornbush. See **stern-**.] —**thorn′y** *adj.*

thor•ough (thûr′ō) *adj.* **1.** Fully done; finished. **2.** Completely as described; absolute. **3.** Painstakingly careful. [< OE *thurh,* THROUGH.] —**thor′ough•ly** *adv.* —**thor′ough•ness** *n.*

thor•ough•bred (thûr′ō-brĕd′, thûr′ə-) *adj.* Bred of pure or pedigreed stock. —*n.* **1.** A purebred or pedigreed animal. **2. Thoroughbred.** Any of a breed of horse originating from a cross of Arabian stallions with English mares.

thor•ough•fare (thûr′ō-fâr′, thûr′ə-) *n.* A main road or public highway.

thor•ough•go•ing (thûr′ō-gō′ĭng, thûr′ə-) *adj.* **1.** Very thorough. **2.** Absolute.

those. *pl.* of **that.**

thou (thou) *pron. Archaic & Poetic.* The 2nd person sing. in the nominative case, equivalent to *you.* [< OE *thū.* See **tu-**.]

though (thō) *conj.* **1.** Despite the fact that; although. **2.** Conceding or supposing that. **3.** However; yet. —*adv.* However; nevertheless. [< ON *thō.*]

thought (thôt). *p.t. & p.p.* of **think.** —*n.* **1.** The act or process of thinking. **2.** An idea. **3.** The power to reason or imagine. **4.** Consideration; concern. **5.** Expectation. **6.** A trifle; a bit. [< OE *thōht.* See **tong-**.]

thought•ful (thôt′fəl) *adj.* **1.** Contemplative; meditative. **2.** Well thought-out. **3.** Considerate. —**thought′ful•ly** *adv.* —**thought′ful•ness** *n.*

thought•less (thôt′lĭs) *adj.* **1.** Careless; unthinking. **2.** Reckless. **3.** Inconsiderate. —**thought′less•ly** *adv.* —**thought′less•ness** *n.*

thou•sand (thou′zənd) *n.* The cardinal number written 1,000 or in Roman numerals M. [< OE *thūsend.* See **teuə-**.] —**thou′sand** *adj. & pron.*

thou•sandth (thou′zəndth, -zənth) *n.* **1.** The ordinal number 1,000 in a series. **2.** One of 1,000 equal parts. —**thou′sandth** *adj. & adv.*

thrall (thrôl) *n.* **1.** A slave, serf, or bondman. **2.** Servitude; bondage. [< OE *thrǽl* < ON *thrǽll.*] —**thrall′dom** (-dəm), **thral′dom** *n.*

thrash (thrăsh) *v.* **1.** To beat or flog with or as with a flail. **2.** To defeat utterly. **3.** To move wildly or violently. [Orig a var of THRESH.] —**thrash′er** *n.*

thrash•er (thrăsh′ər) *n.* A long-tailed New World songbird often having a spotted breast.

thrash•ing (thrăsh′ĭng) *n.* A whipping.

thread (thrĕd) *n.* **1.** A fine cord of a fibrous material made of filaments twisted together. **2.** Anything suggestive of the fineness of thread. **3.** Anything suggestive of the continuousness and sequence of thread. **4.** A helical or spiral ridge on a screw, nut, or bolt. —*v.* **1.** To pass one end of a thread through the eye of (a needle or the various hooks and holes on a sewing machine). **2.** To pass cautiously through. **3.** To machine a thread on (a screw, nut, or bolt). [< OE *thrǽd.* See **ter-**².] —**thread′er** *n.*

thread•bare (thrĕd′bâr′) *adj.* **1.** Having the nap worn down so threads show through; frayed or shabby. **2.** Hackneyed; trite.

thread•y (thrĕd′ē) *adj.* **-ier, -iest. 1.** Consisting of or resembling thread; fibrous; filamentous. **2.** *Med.* Weak and shallow, as a pulse.

threat (thrĕt) *n.* **1.** An expression of an intention to inflict pain, injury, evil, etc. **2.** One regarded as a possible danger. [< OE *thrēat,* oppression, use of force, threat. See **treud-**.]

threat•en (thrĕt′n) *v.* **1.** To express a threat against. **2.** To serve as a threat to. **3.** To portend. —**threat′en•ing•ly** *adv.*

three (thrē) *n.* The cardinal number written 3 or in Roman numerals III. [< OE *thrēo.* See **trei-**.] —**three** *adj. & pron.*

three-di•men•sion•al (thrē′dĭ-mĕn′shən-əl) *adj.* **1.** Of, having, or existing in three dimensions. **2.** Having or appearing to have extension in depth.

three•score (thrē′skôr′, -skōr′) *adj.* Sixty; three times twenty. —**three′score′** *n.*

three•some (thrē′səm) *n.* A group of three.

thren•o•dy (thrĕn′ə-dē) *n., pl.* **-dies.** A song of lamentation. [< Gk *thrēnos,* dirge, lament + *ōidē,* song, ODE.]

thresh (thrĕsh) *v.* **1.** To beat (cereal plants), as with a flail, to remove the grain or seeds. **2.** *Rare.* To thrash. [< OE *therscan.* See **ter-**².] —**thresh′er** *n.*

thresh•old (thrĕsh′ōld′, thrĕsh′hōld′) *n.* **1.** The piece of wood or stone placed beneath a door. **2.** An entrance. **3.** The intensity below which a stimulus produces no response. [< OE *therscold, threscold.* See **ter-**².]

threw (thrōō). *p.t.* of **throw.**

thrice (thrīs) *adv.* Three times. [< OE *thriga, thriwa.* See **trei-**.]

thrift (thrĭft) *n.* Wise economy in the management of money; frugality. [< ON, prosperity.] —**thrift′i•ly** *adv.* —**thrift′y** *adj.*

thrill (thrĭl) *v.* 1. To feel or cause to feel a sudden intense sensation. 2. To quiver or vibrate or cause to quiver or vibrate. —*n.* 1. A quivering or trembling. 2. That which produces great excitement. [< OE *thyrlian,* to pierce < *thyrl,* hole.] —**thrill′er** *n.*

thrive (thrīv) *v.* **throve** or **thrived, thrived** or **thriven, thriving.** 1. To prosper. 2. To grow vigorously; flourish. [< ON *thrīfask,* "to grasp for oneself."] —**thriv′er** *n.*

throat (thrōt) *n.* 1. The portion of the digestive tract lying between the rear of the mouth and the esophagus. 2. The anterior portion of the neck. [< OE *throte, throtu* < Gmc **thrut-*.]

throat•y (thrō′tē) *adj.* **-ier, -iest.** Uttered or sounding as if uttered deep in the throat. —**throat′i•ly** *adv.* —**throat′i•ness** *n.*

throb (thrŏb) *v.* **throbbed, throbbing.** 1. To beat rapidly or violently; pound. 2. To vibrate, pulsate, or sound with a steady, pronounced rhythm. —*n.* The act of throbbing.

throe (thrō) *n.* 1. Often **throes.** A violent pang or spasm of pain. 2. **throes.** A condition of agonizing struggle or effort. [< OE *thrawe,* paroxysm.]

throm•bo•sis (thrŏm-bō′sĭs) *n., pl.* **-ses** (-sēz′). The formation, presence, or development of a thrombus.

throm•bus (thrŏm′bəs) *n., pl.* **-bi** (-bī′). A blood clot blocking a blood vessel or formed in a heart cavity. [< Gk *thrombos,* lump, clot.]

throne (thrōn) *n.* 1. The chair occupied by a sovereign, bishop, or other exalted personage on ceremonial occasions. 2. Sovereign power or rank. [< Gk *thronos.*]

throng (thrŏng) *n.* A large group of people or things crowded together; a multitude. —*v.* 1. To crowd into. 2. To move in a throng. [< OE *thrang,* prob < Gmc **thring-,* to press, crowd.]

throt•tle (thrŏt′l) *n.* 1. **a.** A valve in an internal-combustion engine that regulates the amount of vaporized fuel entering the cylinders. **b.** A similar valve in a steam engine regulating the amount of steam. 2. A lever or pedal controlling this valve. —*v.* **-tled, -tling.** 1. To regulate the speed of (an engine) with a throttle. 2. To strangle; choke. 3. To suppress. [Perh < THROAT.] —**throt′tler** *n.*

through (thrōō) *prep.* 1. In one side and out another side of. 2. In the midst of. 3. By way of. 4. By the means or agency of. 5. Here and there in; around. 6. From the beginning to the end of. 7. Done or finished with. —*adv.* 1. From one end or side to another end or side. 2. From beginning to end. 3. To a conclusion. 4. Out into the open. —*adj.* 1. Passing or extending from one end, side, or surface to another. 2. Allowing continuous passage; unobstructed. 3. Finished; done. [< OE *thurh, thuruh.* See **ter-¹**.]

through•out (thrōō-out′) *prep.* In, to, through, or during every part of. —*adv.* 1. Everywhere.

2. During the entire duration or extent.

through•way. Variant of **thruway.**

throve (thrōv). *p.t.* of **thrive.**

throw (thrō) *v.* **threw, thrown** (thrōn), **throwing.** 1. To propel through the air with a swift motion of the arm; cast. 2. To hurl. 3. To perplex. 4. To put on or off casually. 5. To put quickly into use or place. 6. To put into a specified condition. 7. To move (a controlling lever or switch). —**throw away.** To discard. —**throw off.** 1. To cast out; to reject; spurn. 2. To rid oneself of; evade. —**throw out.** To reject or discard. —**throw up.** 1. To abandon. 2. To vomit. —*n.* 1. The act of throwing; a cast. 2. The distance, height, or direction of something thrown. 3. A light coverlet. [< OE *thrāwan,* to turn, twist. See **ter-²**.] —**throw′er** *n.*

throw back. To revert to a type or stage in one's ancestral past.

throw•back (thrō′băk′) *n.* A reversion to a former type or ancestral characteristic.

thrum (thrŭm) *v.* **thrummed, thrumming.** To play (a stringed instrument) idly or monotonously; strum. [Imit.]

thrush (thrŭsh) *n.* Any of various songbirds usually having brownish upper plumage and a spotted breast. [< OE *thrysce.* See **trozdos-**.]

thrust (thrŭst) *v.* 1. To push or drive forcibly. 2. To stab; pierce. 3. To force into a specified condition or situation. 4. To interject. —*n.* 1. A forceful shove or push. 2. **a.** A driving force or pressure. **b.** The forward-directed force developed in a jet or rocket engine as a reaction to the rearward ejection of fuel gases. 3. A stab. 4. Outward or lateral stress in a structure. [< ON *thrȳsta,* to thrust, compress.]

thru•way (thrōō′wā′) *n.* Also **through•way.** An expressway.

thud (thŭd) *n.* 1. A dull sound. 2. A blow or fall causing such a sound. —*v.* **thudded, thudding.** To make such a sound. [< OE *thyddan* (imit).] —**thud′ding•ly** *adv.*

thug (thŭg) *n.* A ruffian; hoodlum. [Hindi *thag,* cheat, thief.]

thu•li•um (thōō′lē-əm) *n. Symbol* **Tm** A bright silvery rare-earth element, one isotope of which is used in small portable medical x-ray units. Atomic number 69, atomic weight 168.934.

thumb (thŭm) *n.* 1. The short first digit of the hand, opposable to each of the other four digits. 2. The part of a glove or mitten that covers the thumb. —**all thumbs.** Clumsy. —**thumbs down.** Expressive of refusal or disapproval. —**under the thumb of.** Under the influence or power of. —*v.* 1. To disarrange, soil, or wear by handling. 2. *Informal.* To hitchhike. [< OE *thūma.* See **teuə-**.]

thumb index. A series of indentations in the front edge of a reference book, each labeled to indicate a section of the book.

thumb•nail (thŭm′nāl′) *n.* 1. The nail of the thumb. —*adj.* 1. Of the size of a thumbnail. 2. Brief.

thumb•screw (thŭm′skrōō′) *n.* 1. A screw designed that it can be turned with the thumb and fingers. 2. An instrument of torture used to compress the thumb.

ŏ paw, for/oi boy/ou out/ŏŏ took/ōō coo/p pop/r run/s sauce/sh shy/t to/th thin/*th* the/
ŭ cut/ûr fur/v van/w wag/y yes/z size/zh vision/ə ago, item, edible, gallop, circus/

thumb•tack (thŭm'tăk') *n.* A tack with a smooth head that can be pressed into place with the thumb. —*v.* To affix with a thumbtack.

thump (thŭmp) *n.* 1. A blow with a blunt instrument. 2. The muffled sound produced by such a blow. —*v.* 1. To strike with a blunt or dull instrument so as to produce a muffled sound. 2. To pound. [Imit.]

thun•der (thŭn'dər) *n.* 1. The explosive sound emitted as a result of the electrical discharge of lightning. 2. Any similar sound. —*v.* 1. To produce thunder. 2. To produce sounds like thunder. 3. To utter loudly. [< OE *thunor.* See steno-.] —**thun'der•er** *n.*

thun•der•bolt (thŭn'dər-bōlt') *n.* The discharge of lightning that accompanies thunder.

thun•der•clap (thŭn'dər-klăp') *n.* A single sharp crash of thunder.

thun•der•cloud (thŭn'dər-kloud') *n.* A large, dark cloud charged with electricity and producing thunder and lightning.

thun•der•head (thŭn'dər-hĕd') *n.* The upper portion of a thundercloud.

thun•der•ous (thŭn'dər-əs) *adj.* 1. Producing thunder or a similar sound. 2. Loud and unrestrained. —**thun'der•ous•ly** *adv.*

thun•der•show•er (thŭn'dər-shou'ər) *n.* A brief rainstorm accompanied by thunder and lightning.

thun•der•stone (thŭn'dər-stōn') *n.* Any of various mineral concretions formerly supposed to be thunderbolts.

thun•der•storm (thŭn'dər-stôrm') *n.* An electrical storm accompanied by heavy rain.

thun•der•struck (thŭn'dər-strŭk') *adj.* Astonished; amazed.

Thurs•day (thûrz'dē, -dā') *n.* The 5th day of the week. [< OE *thunresdæg,* "day of Thor" (Old Norse god of thunder).]

thus (*thŭs*) *adv.* 1. In a manner previously stated or to be stated. 2. To a stated degree or extent; so. 3. Therefore; consequently. [< OE. See to-.]

Usage: Except when it is used to provide intentional humor, *thusly* is not an acceptable variant of *thus,* which is itself an adverb.

thwack (thwăk) *v.* To strike or hit with something flat; whack. [Imit.] —**thwack** *n.*

thwart (thwôrt) *v.* 1. To prevent from taking place; frustrate. 2. To oppose directly. —*n.* A seat across a boat, on which the oarsman sits. —*adj.* Extending across something. —*adv.* Athwart. [< ON *thverr,* transverse.]

thy (*thī*). *Archaic & Poetic.* The possessive form of the pronoun *thee,* used attributively. [< OE *thin.* See tu-.]

thyme (tīm) *n.* An aromatic plant with leaves used as seasoning. [< Gk *thumon.*]

thy•mus (thī'məs) *n.* A ductless glandlike structure, situated near the throat, that plays some part in building resistance to disease but is usually vestigial in adults. [< Gk *thumos.*] —**thy'mic** *adj.*

thy•roid (thī'roid') *adj.* Of or relating to the thyroid gland. —*n.* 1. The thyroid gland. 2. A dried and powdered preparation of the thyroid gland of certain domestic animals, used in

medicine. [< Gk *thuroidēs,* shaped like a door or oblong shield.]

thyroid gland. A two-lobed endocrine gland found in all vertebrates, located in front of and on either side of the trachea in humans, and producing a hormone that regulates metabolism.

thy•self (*thī*-sĕlf') *pron. Archaic & Poetic.* Yourself. —Used as the reflexive or emphatic form of *thee* or *thou.*

Ti titanium.

ti•ar•a (tē-ăr'ə, -âr'ə, -är'ə) *n.* 1. The triple crown worn by the pope. 2. A woman's ornamental headpiece worn on formal occasions. [< Gk, a kind of Persian headdress.]

Ti•ber (tī'bər). A river of C Italy.

Ti•bet (tĭ-bĕt'). A former state in S Asia, now a region of S China. Pop. 1,270,000. Cap. Lhasa.

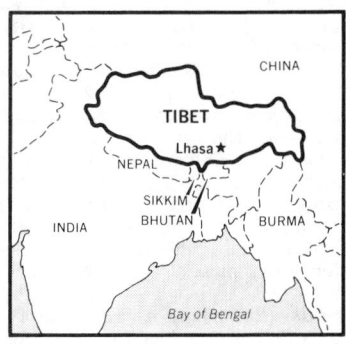

Tibet

Ti•bet•an (tĭ-bĕt'n) *adj.* Of or pertaining to Tibet, its people, or their language or culture. —*n.* 1. One of the Mongoloid people of Tibet. 2. The Tibeto-Burman language of Tibet.

Ti•bet•o-Bur•man (tĭ-bĕt'ō-bûr'mən) *n.* A language family including Tibetan and Burmese, usually classed as a subgroup of Sino-Tibetan. —**Ti•bet'o-Bur'man** *adj.*

tib•i•a (tĭb'ē-ə) *n., pl.* **-iae** (-ē-ē') or **-ias.** The inner and larger of the two bones of the lower leg from the knee to the ankle. [L *tibia,* shinbone, pipe.] —**tib'i•al** *adj.*

tic (tĭk) *n.* A spasmodic muscular contraction, usually in the face or extremities. [F.]

tick¹ (tĭk) *n.* 1. The recurring clicking sound made by a machine, esp. by a clock. 2. A light mark used to check off or call attention to an item. [ME *tek.*] —**tick** *v.*

tick² (tĭk) *n.* Any of various bloodsucking parasitic arachnids or louselike insects, many of which transmit diseases. [< OE *ticia.* See deigh-.]

tick³ (tĭk) *n.* 1. The cloth case of a mattress or pillow. 2. Ticking. [< Gk *thēkē,* cover, case.]

tick•er (tĭk'ər) *n.* A telegraphic printing or display device that receives and records stock-market quotations.

ticker tape. The paper strip on which a ticker prints.

tick•et (tĭk'ĭt) *n.* 1. A paper slip or card indicating that its holder has paid for admission. **2.** A certificate or license. **3.** An identifying tag; a label. **4.** A list of candidates endorsed by a political party. **5.** A summons, esp. for a traffic violation. —*v.* **1.** To provide with a ticket. **2.** To attach a tag to; label. [Obs F *etiquet,* ticket, label.]

tick•ing (tĭk′ĭng) *n.* A strong, tightly woven fabric used to make ticks.

tick•le (tĭk′əl) *v.* **-led, -ling. 1.** To feel a tingling sensation. **2.** To touch (the body) lightly causing laughter or twitching movements. **3.** To tease or excite pleasurably. —*n.* The act or sensation of tickling. [< ME *ticken,* to touch lightly.] —**tick′ler** *n.*

tick•lish (tĭk′lĭsh) *adj.* **1.** Sensitive to tickling. **2.** Easily offended or upset. **3.** Requiring skillful handling. —**tick′lish•ly** *adv.*

tid•al (tīd′l) *adj.* **1.** Having tides: *a tidal river.* **2.** Scheduled by the time of high tide: *a tidal ship.* —**tid′al•ly** *adv.*

tidal wave. 1. An unusual rise or incursion of water along the seashore. **2.** Loosely, a tsunami.

tid•bit (tĭd′bĭt′) *n.* A choice morsel.

tide (tīd) *n.* **1. a.** The periodic variation in the surface level of the oceans and of bays, gulfs, inlets, etc., caused by the gravitational attraction of the moon and sun. **b.** A specific occurrence of such a variation. **c.** The waters in such a variation. **2.** A tendency regarded as alternating and inexorable. **3.** A time or season: *eventide; Christmastide.* —*v.* **tided, tiding. 1.** To rise and fall like the tide. **2.** To drift with the tide. —**tide over.** To support through a difficult period. [< OE *tīd,* season, time. See dā-.]

tide•land (tīd′lănd′) *n.* Coastal land submerged during high tide.

tide•wa•ter (tīd′wô′tər, -wŏt′ər) *n.* **1.** Water that inundates land at flood tide. **2.** Water affected by the tides, esp. tidal streams. **3.** Low coastal land drained by tidal streams.

tid•ings (tī′dĭngz) *pl.n.* Information; news. [Perh < ON *tidhendi,* events.]

ti•dy (tī′dē) *adj.* **-dier, -diest. 1.** Orderly and neat. **2.** *Informal.* Considerable. —*v.* **-died, -dying.** To put in order. —*n., pl.* **-dies.** A fancy protective covering for the arms or headrest of a chair. [ME, timely, seasonable < TIDE.] —**ti′di•ly** *adv.* —**ti′di•ness** *n.*

tie (tī) *v.* **tied, tying. 1.** To fasten or secure with a cord, rope, etc. **2.** To draw together and knot with strings or laces. **3.** To make (a knot or bow). **4.** To bring together; unite. **5.** To equal (an opponent or his score) in a contest. —*n.* **1.** A cord, string, etc., by which something is tied. **2.** That which unites; a bond. **3.** A necktie. **4.** A beam or rod that joins and supports parts. **5.** One of the timbers laid across a railroad bed to support the tracks. **6.** An equality of scores, votes, or performance in a contest. [< OE *tigan.* See deuk-.]

Tien•tsin (tĭn′tsĭn′). A city of NE China. Pop. 3,320,000.

tier (tîr) *n.* One of a series of rows placed one above another. [< OF *tire,* sequence, rank.]

Ti•er•ra del Fu•e•go (tĭ-ĕr′ə dĕl f/y/ōō-ā′gō).

1. A group of islands at the extreme S tip of South America. **2.** The main island of this group.

tiff (tĭf) *n.* **1.** A fit of irritation. **2.** A petty quarrel. [?] —**tiff** *v.*

Tif•lis (tĭf′lĭs). The former Russian name for Tbilisi.

ti•ger (tī′gər) *n.* A large carnivorous Asian cat having a tawny coat with black stripes. [< Gk *tigris.*] —**ti′gress** *fem.n.*

tight (tīt) *adj.* **1.** Of such a close construction, texture, or organization as to be impermeable, esp. by water or air. **2.** Fastened, held, or closed securely. **3.** Compact. **4.** Drawn out; taut. **5.** Snug, often uncomfortably so. **6.** Constricted. **7.** Stingy. **8.** Difficult to deal with or get out of: *a tight spot.* **9.** Closely contested. **10.** *Slang.* Drunk. —*adv.* **1.** Firmly; securely. **2.** Soundly: *sleep tight.* [< ON *thēttr,* watertight, dense.] —**tight′ly** *adv.* —**tight′ness** *n.*

tight•en (tīt′n) *v.* To make or become tight or tighter. —**tight′en•er** *n.*

tight•fist•ed (tīt′fĭs′tĭd) *adj.* Stingy.

tight•lipped (tīt′lĭpt′) *adj.* **1.** Having the lips pressed together. **2.** Reticent.

tight•rope (tīt′rōp′) *n.* A tightly stretched rope or wire on which acrobats perform.

tights (tīts) *pl.n.* A snug stretchable garment covering the body from the waist down.

tight•wad (tīt′wŏd′) *n.* *Slang.* A stingy person.

Ti•gris (tī′grĭs). A river of SW Asia.

til•de (tĭl′də) *n.* A diacritical mark (˜) used in Spanish and Portuguese to indicate certain nasal sounds, as in *cañon.*

tile (tīl) *n.* **1.** A slab of baked clay, plastic, etc., laid to cover walls, floors, and roofs. **2.** A length of clay or concrete pipe used in sewers and drains. **3.** A marked playing piece, as in mahjong. —*v.* **tiled, tiling.** To cover or provide with tiles. [< L *tegere,* to cover.]

till¹ (tĭl) *v.* To prepare (land) for the raising of crops by plowing, harrowing, and fertilizing. [< OE *tilian,* to work at, cultivate < Gmc **tilōjan.*] —**till′a•ble** *adj.*

till² (tĭl) *prep.* Until. —*conj.* Until. [< OE *til,* prob < Gmc **tilam,* fixed point.]

Usage: Till and until are generally interchangeable, and each is appropriate to the highest level of usage. *'Til* is a rare variant form of *until; 'till* is nonstandard.

till³ (tĭl) *n.* A drawer or compartment for money, esp. in a store. [ME *tylle.*]

till•age (tĭl′ĭj) *n.* **1.** The cultivation of land. **2.** Tilled land.

till•er¹ (tĭl′ər) *n.* One that tills land.

till•er² (tĭl′ər) *n.* A lever used to turn a boat's rudder. [< L *tēla,* web, warp of a fabric, weaver's beam.]

tilt (tĭlt) *v.* **1.** To slope or cause to slope, as by raising one end; incline; tip. **2.** To thrust (a lance) in a joust. —*n.* **1.** A slant; slope. **2.** A joust. **3.** A verbal duel. [Perh < Scand.]

tilth (tĭlth) *n.* Tillage.

Tim. Timothy (New Testament).

tim•ber (tĭm′bər) *n.* **1.** Trees or wooded land considered as a source of wood. **2. a.** Wood as a building material. **b.** A dressed piece of

---

wood, esp. a beam in a structure. **c.** A rib in a ship's frame. —*interj.* Used to warn of a falling tree. [< OE, building. See **dema-¹.**]

tim·ber·line (tĭm′bər-līn′) *n.* Also **timber line.** The limit of altitude in mountainous regions beyond which trees do not grow.

tim·bre (tĭm′bər, tăm′-) *n.* The quality of a sound that distinguishes it from others of the same pitch and volume. [< Gk *tumpanon.*]

time (tīm) *n.* **1.** A nonspatial continuum in which events occur in apparently irreversible succession. **2.** An interval separating two points on this continuum, measured essentially in terms of occurrences or a regularly recurring event. **3.** A number, as of years, days, or minutes, representing such an interval. **4.** A similar number representing a specific point, as the present, as reckoned from an arbitrary past point on the continuum. **5.** A system by which such intervals are measured or such numbers reckoned. **6.** Often **times.** A span of years; era. **7.** One's heyday. **8.** A suitable or opportune moment. **9.** A designated moment or period: *harvest time.* **10.** One of several instances. **11.** An occasion. **12.** *Informal.* A prison sentence. **13.** The rate of speed of a measured activity. **14.** The characteristic beat of musical rhythm. —*adj.* **1.** Of or relating to time. **2.** Constructed to operate at a particular moment: *time bomb.* **3.** Of or relating to installment buying. —*v.* **timed, timing. 1.** To set the time for (an event or occasion). **2.** To adjust to keep accurate time. **3.** To regulate for orderly sequence of movements or events. **4.** To record, set, or maintain the speed, duration, or tempo of. [< OE *tīma.* See **dā-.**] —**tim′er** *n.*

time clock. A device that records the arrival and departure times of employees.

time-hon·ored (tīm′ŏn′ərd) *adj.* Honored because of age or age-old observance.

time·keep·er (tīm′kē′pər) *n.* One who keeps track of time, as in a sports event.

time·less (tīm′lĭs) *adj.* **1.** Unending. **2.** Unaffected by time. —**time′less·ly** *adv.*

time·ly (tīm′lē) *adj.* **-lier, -liest.** Occurring at a suitable or opportune time; well-timed.

time·piece (tīm′pēs′) *n.* An instrument that measures, registers, or records time.

times (tīmz) *prep.* Multiplied by: *Five times two is ten.*

time·ta·ble (tīm′tā′bəl) *n.* A table listing the scheduled arrival and departure times of trains, buses, etc.

time·worn (tīm′wôrn′, -wōrn′) *adj.* **1.** Showing the effects of long use or wear. **2.** Used too often; trite.

tim·id (tĭm′ĭd) *adj.* **1.** Hesitant or fearful. **2.** Shy. [< L *timēre,* to fear.] —**ti·mid′i·ty, tim′id·ness** *n.* —**tim′id·ly** *adv.*

tim·ing (tī′mĭng) *n.* The regulating of occurrence, pace, or coordination to achieve the most desirable effects.

tim·or·ous (tĭm′ər-əs) *adj.* Apprehensive; timid. [< L *timēre,* to fear.] —**tim′or·ous·ly** *adv.* —**tim′or·ous·ness** *n.*

tim·o·thy (tĭm′ə-thē) *n.* A grass with narrow, cylindrical flower spikes, widely cultivated for hay. [< *Timothy* Hanson, 18th-century American farmer.]

tim·pa·ni (tĭm′pə-nē) *pl.n.* Also **tym·pa·ni.** A set of kettle-drums. [< L *tympanum,* tympanum.] —**tim′pa·nist** *n.*

tim·pa·num. Variant of **tympanum.**

tin (tĭn) *n.* **1.** *Symbol* **Sn** A malleable, silvery metallic element used to coat other metals to prevent corrosion and in numerous alloys, such as soft solder, pewter, type metal, and bronze. Atomic number 50, atomic weight 118.69. **2.** A tin container or box. —*v.* **tinned, tinning. 1.** To plate or coat with tin. **2.** To preserve or pack in tins; can. [< OE < Gmc *tinam.*]

tinc·ture (tĭngk′chər) *n.* **1.** A dyeing substance; pigment. **2.** A trace; vestige. **3.** An alcohol solution of a nonvolatile medicine: *tincture of iodine.* [< L *tinctūra,* a dyeing.]

tin·der (tĭn′dər) *n.* Readily combustible material used to kindle fires. [< OE *tynder* < Gmc *tund-.*]

tin·der·box (tĭn′dər-bŏks′) *n.* A metal box for holding tinder.

tine (tīn) *n.* A pointed part or prong, as of a fork or an antler. [< OE *tind* < Gmc *tind-,* point.]

tin·foil (tĭn′foil′) *n.* Also **tin foil.** A thin, pliable sheet of tin or tin-lead alloy.

tinge (tĭnj) *v.* **tinged** (tĭnjd), **tingeing** or **tinging. 1.** To color slightly; tint. **2.** To affect slightly, as with a contrasting quality. —*n.* A faint trace of color, flavor, etc. [< L *tingere,* to moisten, plunge, dye.]

tin·gle (tĭng′gəl) *v.* **-gled, -gling.** To have a prickling, stinging sensation as from cold or excitement. [ME *tinglen,* orig. to be affected with a ringing sound in the ears.] —**tin′gle** *n.* —**tin′gler** *n.* —**tin′gly** *adj.*

tink·er (tĭng′kər) *n.* **1.** A traveling mender of metal household utensils. **2.** One who is clumsy at his work; a bungler. —*v.* **1.** To work as a tinker. **2.** To play with machine parts experimentally. [ME *tynkere.*]

tin·kle (tĭng′kəl) *v.* **-kled, -kling.** To make or cause to make light metallic sounds, as of a small bell. —*n.* A light metallic sound.

tin·ny (tĭn′ē) *adj.* **-nier, -niest. 1.** Of, containing, or yielding tin. **2.** Having a thin metallic sound. **3.** Tasting or smelling of tin.

tin·sel (tĭn′səl) *n.* **1.** Very thin sheets, strips, or threads of a glittering material used as decoration. **2.** Anything superficially showy but basically valueless. [< OF *estincelle,* a spark.]

tin·smith (tĭn′smĭth′) *n.* One who works with light metal, as tin.

tint (tĭnt) *n.* **1.** A shade of a color, esp. a pale or delicate variation. **2.** A slight coloration. —*v.* To imbue with a tint; color. [< L *tinctus,* a dipping or dyeing.] —**tint′er** *n.*

tin·tin·nab·u·la·tion (tĭn′tĭ-năb′yə-lā′shən) *n.* The ringing or sounding of bells. [< L *tinnīre,* to ring.]

tin·type (tĭn′tīp′) *n.* A ferrotype.

ti·ny (tī′nē) *adj.* **-nier, -niest.** Extremely small. [< ME *tine.*] —**ti′ni·ness** *n.*

-tion. *comb. form.* Action or process involved with: *adsorption.* [< L *-tiō (-tiōn).*]

ă pat/ā ate/âr care/ä bar/b **b**ib/ch **ch**ew/d **d**eed/ĕ pet/ē be/f fit/g gag/h hat/hw **wh**at/
ĭ pit/ī pie/îr pier/j **j**udge/k kick/l lid, fatal/m mum/n no, sudden/ng sing/ŏ pot/ō go/

tip¹ (tĭp) *n.* 1. The end or extremity of something. 2. A piece meant to be fitted to the end of something. —*v.* **tipped, tipping.** 1. To furnish with a tip. 2. To cover, decorate, or remove the tip of. [Prob < ON *typpi.*]

tip² (tĭp) *v.* **tipped, tipping.** 1. To knock over or upset; topple over. 2. To slant; tilt. —*n.* A slant or tilt. [ME *tipen.*]

tip³ (tĭp) *v.* **tipped, tipping.** To strike gently; tap. [ME *tippen.*] —**tip** *n.*

tip⁴ (tĭp) *n.* 1. A sum of money given for services rendered; gratuity. 2. Useful information; a helpful hint. [Orig "to pass to" < TIP³.] —**tip** *v.* (**tipped, tipping**). —**tip'per** *n.*

ti•pi. Variant of **tepee.**

tip•pet (tĭp'ĭt) *n.* A covering for the shoulders, as a cape or scarf. [ME *tipet.*]

tip•ple (tĭp'əl) *v.* **-pled, -pling.** To drink alcoholic liquor, esp. habitually or intemperately. [Back-formation < *tippler*, a bartender.] —**tip'pler** *n.*

tip•ster (tĭp'stər) *n. Informal.* One who sells tips to bettors or speculators.

tip•sy (tĭp'sē) *adj.* **-sier, -siest.** Slightly drunk. [< TIP².] —**tip'si•ness** *n.*

tip•toe (tĭp'tō') *v.* To walk or move on or as on the tips of one's toes. —*n.* The tip of a toe. —*adv.* On tiptoe.

tip•top (tĭp'tŏp') *n.* The highest point; summit. —*adj.* Excellent; first-rate.

ti•rade (tī'rād', tĭ-rād') *n.* A long violent or harshly censorious speech; a diatribe. [F, "a stretching."]

Ti•ra•na (tĭ-rä'nə). The capital of Albania. Pop. 153,000.

tire¹ (tīr) *v.* **tired, tiring.** 1. To make or become weary or fatigued. 2. To make or become bored; lose interest. [< OE *tēorian.*]

tire² (tīr) *n.* Also *Brit.* **tyre.** 1. A solid or air-filled covering for a wheel, typically of rubber, fitted around the wheel's rim to absorb shock and provide traction. 2. A hoop of iron or heavy rubber fitted about the rim of a wheel. [Prob < TIRE.]

tired (tīrd) *adj.* 1. a. Fatigued. b. Impatient; bored. 2. Hackneyed.

tire•less (tīr'lĭs) *adj.* Untiring; indefatigable. —**tire'less•ly** *adv.* —**tire'less•ness** *n.*

tire•some (tīr'səm) *adj.* Causing fatigue or boredom; tedious. —**tire'some•ly** *adv.*

'tis (tĭz). *Archaic & Poetic.* Contraction of *it is.*

ti•sane (tĭ-zăn', -zän') *n.* A herbal infusion or similar preparation, drunk as a beverage or for its mildly medicinal effect. [< L *ptisana*, barley.]

tis•sue (tĭsh'ōō) *n.* 1. *Biol.* a. A group of cells that are similar in form or function. b. Cellular matter in general. 2. A soft, absorbent piece of paper used as a handkerchief. 3. A thin, translucent paper used for packing, wrapping, etc. 4. A fine sheer cloth, as gauze. 5. A web; network. [< L *texere*, to weave.]

tit¹ (tĭt) *n.* Any of various small Old World birds related to and resembling the New World chickadees. [Short for TITMOUSE.]

tit² (tĭt) *n.* A teat. [< OE *titt* < Gmc *titta.*]

Tit. Titus (New Testament).

ti•tan (tīt'n) *n.* A person of colossal size or strength. [< *Titan*, one of a family of Greek gods.]

ti•tan•ic (tī-tăn'ĭk) *adj.* Having great stature, strength, or power.

ti•ta•ni•um (tī-tā'nē-əm, tĭ-) *n. Symbol* **Ti** A strong, low-density, highly corrosion-resistant, lustrous white metallic element used in alloys requiring low weight, strength, and high-temperature stability. Atomic number 22, atomic weight 47.90.

tithe (tīth) *n.* 1. A tenth part of one's annual income, paid for the support of a church. 2. A tenth part. [< OE *tēotha, teogetha*, tenth.] —**tithe** *v.* (**tithed, tithing**). —**tith'er** (tī'thər) *n.*

tit•il•late (tĭt'ə-lāt') *v.* **-lated, -lating.** 1. To tickle. 2. To excite agreeably. [L *tītillāre.*] —**tit'il•la'tion** *n.* —**tit'il•la'tive** *adj.*

ti•tle (tīt'l) *n.* 1. An identifying name given to a book, painting, etc. 2. A claim or right, esp. a legal right to ownership. 3. a. A formal appellation, as of rank or office. b. Such an appellation used to indicate nobility. 4. *Law.* a. Just cause of possession or control. b. The evidence of such means. c. The instrument constituting this evidence, such as a deed. 5. *Sports.* A championship. —*v.* **-tled, -tling.** To give a title to. [< L *titulus*, superscription, label, title.]

ti•tled (tīt'əld) *adj.* Having a title, esp. of nobility.

tit•mouse (tĭt'mous') *n., pl.* **-mice** (-mīs'). A small grayish, crested North American bird. [Perh dial *tit*, small object + MOUSE.]

tit•ter (tĭt'ər) *v.* To utter a restrained, nervous giggle. [Imit.] —**tit'ter** *n.*

tit•tle (tĭt'l) *n.* The tiniest bit; an iota. [< L *titulus*, TITLE.]

tit•u•lar (tĭch'ōō-lər) *adj.* 1. Of, relating to, or constituting a title. 2. Existing as such in name only; nominal.

tiz•zy (tĭz'ē) *n., pl.* **-zies.** *Slang.* A state of nervous confusion; a dither. [?]

tk. truck.

TKO technical knockout.

tkt. ticket.

Tl thallium.

Tm thulium.

tn. 1. town. 2. train.

tnpk. turnpike.

TNT Trinitrotoluene.

to (tōō; *unstressed* tə) *prep.* 1. In a direction toward. 2. In the direction of. 3. Reaching as far as. 4. Toward or reaching the state of. 5. To the extent of. 6. In contact with: *cheek to cheek.* 7. In front of: *face to face.* 8. Through and including; until: *from three to five.* 9. For the attention, benefit, or possession of. 10. For the purpose of; for: *to that end.* 11. For or of: *the belt to this dress.* 12. Concerning or regarding: *deaf to her pleas.* 13. In relation to: *parallel to the road.* 14. With the resulting condition of: *torn to shreds.* 15. As an accompaniment for. 16. With regard to. 17. Composing or constituting; in: *two pints to the quart.* 18. In accord with: *not to my liking.* 19. As compared with: *a score of four to three.* 20. Before: *ten to five.* 21. In honor of: *a toast to his success.* —*adv.* 1. Into a shut or closed

---

ô paw, for/oi boy/ou out/ōō took/ōō coo/p pop/r run/s sauce/sh shy/t to/th thin/*th* the/
ŭ cut/ûr fur/v van/w wag/y yes/z size/zh vision/ə ago, item, edible, gallop, circus/

position: *slammed the door to.* **2.** Into consciousness: *He came to.* **3.** Into a state of application to the action or work at hand: *to fall to.* **4.** *Naut.* Turned into the wind. [< OE *tō, te.* See **de-**.]

t.o. turnover.

toad (tōd) *n.* A froglike, mostly land-dwelling amphibian with rough, warty skin. [< OE *tādige.*]

toad•stool (tōd'stōōl') *n.* An inedible or poisonous mushroom.

toad•y (tō'dē) *n., pl.* **-ies.** A servile flatterer; a sycophant. —**toad'y** *v.* (**-ied, -ying**).

toast[1] (tōst) *v.* **1.** To heat and brown (bread, rolls, etc.). **2.** To warm thoroughly: *toast one's feet.* —*n.* Sliced bread heated and browned. [< L *torrēre* (pp *tostus*), to dry, parch.]

toast[2] (tōst) *n.* **1.** A person or thing in whose honor persons drink. **2.** The act of proposing the honor of a person or thing as a toast. —*v.* To drink to or propose as a toast.

toast•er (tō'stər) *n.* An electrical appliance used to toast bread.

to•bac•co (tə-băk'ō) *n., pl.* **-cos** or **-coes.** **1.** A plant native to tropical America, having broad leaves used chiefly for smoking. **2.** The leaves of this plant processed for use in cigarettes, cigars, pipes, etc. **3.** Such products collectively. [Prob < Ar *tabāq,* euphoria-causing herb.]

to•bac•co•nist (tə-băk'ə-nĭst) *n.* A dealer in tobacco.

To•ba•go (tə-bā'gō). See **Trinidad and Tobago.**

to•bog•gan (tə-bŏg'ən) *n.* A long, runnerless sled constructed of thin boards curled upward at the front. —*v.* **1.** To ride on a toboggan. **2.** To decline or fall rapidly. [< Algon.] —**to•bog'gan•ist** *n.*

To•char•i•an (tō-kâr'ē-ən, -kär'ē-ən) *n.* Also **To•khar•i•an.** **1.** A people of possible European origin living in Asia until about the 10th century A.D. **2.** An Indo-European language with eastern and western dialects, *Tocharian A* and *B* respectively, known from documents of the 7th century A.D.

toc•sin (tŏk'sĭn) *n.* **1.** An alarm sounded on a bell. **2.** A warning; omen. [< OProv *tocar,* to strike (a bell), touch + *senh,* bell.]

to•day (tə-dā'). Also **to-day.** *adv.* **1.** During or on the present day. **2.** During or at the present time. —*n.* The present day, time, or age. [< OE *tōdæge,* on this day : TO + *dæge,* dat of *dæg,* DAY.]

tod•dle (tŏd'l) *v.* **-dled, -dling.** To walk with short, unsteady steps, as a small child. [?] —**tod'dle** *n.* —**tod'dler** *n.*

tod•dy (tŏd'ē) *n., pl.* **-dies.** A drink consisting of liquor with hot water, sugar, and spices. [< Hindi *tārī,* sap of a palm.]

to-do (tə-dōō') *n. Informal.* Commotion or bustle; a stir.

toe (tō) *n.* **1.** One of the digits of the foot. **2.** The forward part of something worn on the foot. **3.** Anything suggestive of a toe in form, function, or location. —*v.* **toed, toeing.** To touch, kick, follow, or trace with the toe. [< OE *tā* < Gmc **taihwō.*]

tof•fee (tŏf'ē, tô'fē) *n.* Also **tof•fy** *pl.* **-fies.** A

candy of brown sugar and butter. [Var of TAFFY.]

to•ga (tō'gə) *n.* A draped one-piece outer garment worn in public by citizens of ancient Rome. [L < *tegere,* to cover.]

to•geth•er (tə-gĕth'ər) *adv.* **1.** In or into a single group or place. **2.** Against or in relationship to one another. **3.** Regarded collectively; in total. **4.** Simultaneously. **5.** In harmony, accord, or cooperation. [< OE *tōgædere.* See **ghedh-**.]

To•go (tō'gō). A republic of W Africa. Pop. 1,500,000. Cap. Lomé.

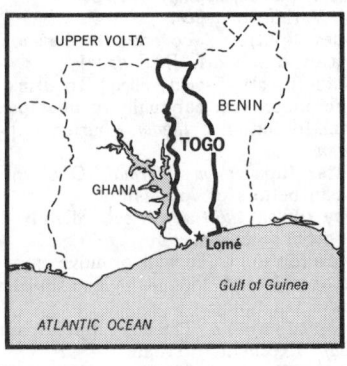

Togo

togs (tŏgz) *pl.n.* Clothes: *gardening togs.* [Short for cant *togman.*]

toil[1] (toil) *v.* **1.** To labor continuously and untiringly; work strenuously. **2.** To proceed with difficulty. —*n.* Exhausting labor or effort. [< L *tudiculāre,* to stir about.]

toil[2] (toil) *n.* Often **toils.** An entrapment: *in the toils of despair.* [< L *tēla,* a net.]

toi•let (toi'lĭt) *n.* **1.** A disposal apparatus used for urination and defecation. **2.** A room or booth containing such an apparatus. **3.** The act or process of grooming and dressing oneself. [F *toilette,* lavatory.]

toi•let•ry (toi'lĭ-trē) *n., pl.* **-ries.** Any article or cosmetic used in dressing or grooming oneself.

toi•lette (twä-lĕt') *n.* **1.** The act or process of dressing or grooming oneself. **2.** A person's dress or style of dress. [F, TOILET.]

to•ken (tō'kən) *n.* **1.** Something that serves as an indication or representation; a sign; symbol. **2.** Something that tangibly signifies authority, validity, etc. **3.** A keepsake. **4.** A piece of stamped metal used as a substitute for currency. —*adj.* Done as an indication or pledge: *a token payment.* [< OE *tācen.* See **deik-**.]

to•ken•ism (tō'kə-nĭz'əm) *n.* The policy of making only a superficial effort or symbolic gesture toward the accomplishment of a goal, such as racial integration.

To•khar•i•an. Variant of **Tocharian.**

To•ky•o (tō'kē-ō). The capital of Japan. Pop. 8,527,000.

told (tōld). *p.t.* & *p.p.* of **tell.**

ă pat/ā ate/âr care/ä bar/b bib/ch chew/d deed/ĕ pet/ē be/f fit/g gag/h hat/hw what/
ĭ pit/ī pie/îr pier/j judge/k kick/l lid, fatal/m mum/n no, sudden/ng sing/ŏ pot/ō go/

To•le•do (tə-lē′dō). A city of NW Ohio. Pop. 363,000.

tol•er•a•ble (tŏl′ər-ə-bəl) *adj.* 1. Able to be tolerated; endurable. 2. Adequate; passable. —**tol′er•a•bly** *adv.*

tol•er•ance (tŏl′ər-əns) *n.* 1. The capacity for or practice of recognizing and respecting the opinions, practices, or behavior of others. 2. Leeway for variation, as from a standard. 3. The capacity to endure hardship, pain, etc. —**tol′er•ant** *adj.* —**tol′er•ant•ly** *adv.*

tol•er•ate (tŏl′ə-rāt′) *v.* -ated, -ating. 1. To allow without prohibiting or opposing; permit. 2. To recognize and respect, as the opinions, practices, or behavior of others, whether agreeing with them or not. 3. To put up with; endure. [L *tolerāre*, to bear, tolerate.] —**tol′er•a′tion** *n.* —**tol′er•a′tive** *adj.* —**tol′er•a′tor** *n.*

toll¹ (tōl) *n.* 1. A fixed tax for a privilege, as passage across a bridge. 2. A charge for a service, as a long-distance telephone call. 3. A quantity of people or things destroyed or adversely affected, as in a disaster. [< Gk *telōnēs*, a tax collector.]

toll² (tōl) *v.* 1. To sound (a bell) slowly at regular intervals. 2. To announce or summon by tolling. 3. To sound in slowly repeated single tones. —*n.* The sound of a tolling bell. [ME *tollen.*]

toll•gate (tōl′gāt′) *n.* A gate barring passage of vehicles until a toll is paid.

Tol•stoi (tōl′stoi′, tŏl′-), Count **Lev Nikolaye-vich.** English name, Leo Tolstoy. 1828–1910. Russian novelist.

Tol•tec (tōl′tĕk′, tŏl′-) *n.* One of an ancient Nahuatl people of C and S Mexico. —**Tol′tec′** *adj.*

tom (tŏm) *n.* A male animal, as a cat or turkey.

tom•a•hawk (tŏm′ə-hôk′) *n.* A light ax used as a tool or weapon by North American Indians. —*v.* To strike with a tomahawk. [< Algon.]

to•ma•to (tə-mā′tō, -mä′tō) *n., pl.* -toes. 1. A fleshy, smooth-skinned reddish fruit eaten in salads or as a vegetable. 2. A plant bearing such fruit. [< Nah *tomatl.*]

tomb (tōōm) *n.* 1. A vault or chamber for the dead. 2. Any place of burial. [< Gk *tombos*, sepulchral mound.]

tom•boy (tŏm′boi′) *n.* A girl who behaves like a spirited boy. —**tom′boy′ish** *adj.*

tomb•stone (tōōm′stōn′) *n.* A stone marking a grave.

tom•cat (tŏm′kăt′) *n.* A male cat.

tome (tōm) *n.* A book, esp. a large or scholarly one. [< L *tomus*, cut, tome, roll of paper.]

tom•fool•er•y (tŏm′fōō′lə-rē) *n.* 1. Foolish behavior. 2. Nonsense.

to•mor•row (tə-môr′ō, -mŏr′ō). Also **to-mor•row.** *n.* 1. The day following today. 2. The near future. —*adv.* On or for the day following today. [< TO (at, on) + OE *morgenne*, dat of *morgen*, MORROW.]

tom•tit (tŏm′tĭt′) *n. Brit.* A tit or other small bird.

tom-tom (tŏm′tŏm′) *n.* Any of various small-headed drums that are beaten with the hands. [Hindi *ṭamṭam.*]

–tomy. *comb. form.* A cutting of (a specified part or tissue): lobotomy. [< Gk *tomos*, a cutting.]

ton (tŭn) *n.* 1. a. A U.S. Customary System unit of weight equal to 2,240 pounds; long ton. b. A U.S. Customary System unit of weight equal to 2,000 pounds; short ton; net ton. 2. Loosely, a very large quantity of anything. [ME *tonne*, a measure of wine, tun.]

to•nal•i•ty (tō-năl′ə-tē) *n., pl.* -ties. *Mus.* The arrangement of the tones of a composition in relation to a tonic.

tone (tōn) *n.* 1. a. A sound of distinct pitch, quality, and duration. b. Quality of sound. 2. *Mus.* The largest interval between adjacent notes of a diatonic scale. 3. The pitch of a word or phrase. 4. Manner of expression: *an angry tone of voice.* 5. A general quality or atmosphere: *the tone of the debate.* 6. a. A color or shade of color. b. Quality of color. 7. a. The tension in resting muscles. b. Normal tissue firmness. —*v.* **toned, toning.** 1. To give a particular tone or inflection to. 2. To soften or change the color of. 3. To harmonize in color. [< L *tonus*, a stretching, tone, sound.] —**to′nal** *adj.* —**to′nal•ly** *adv.*

tongs (tôngz, tŏngz) *n. (often takes sing. v.).* A grasping device consisting of two arms joined at one end by a pivot or hinge. [< OE *tange* (sing). See denk-.]

tongue (tŭng) *n.* 1. The fleshy, movable muscular organ in the mouth that functions in tasting, speech, and as an aid in chewing and swallowing. 2. The tongue of an animal, as a cow, used as food. 3. Anything resembling a tongue in form or function. 4. A spoken language. 5. Quality of utterance: *her sharp tongue.* [< OE *tunge.* See dṇghū.]

tongue-tied (tŭng′tīd′) *adj.·* Speechless or confused in expression, as from shyness, embarrassment, or astonishment.

ton•ic (tŏn′ĭk) *n.* 1. Anything that invigorates, refreshes, or restores. 2. *Mus.* The primary tone of a diatonic scale. —*adj.* 1. Producing or stimulating physical or mental vigor. 2. *Mus.* Pertaining to or based on the tonic. [< Gk *tonos*, a stretching, tone.]

to•night (tə-nīt′). Also **to-night.** *adv.* On or during the present or coming night. —*n.* This night or the night of this day.

ton•nage (tŭn′ĭj) *n.* 1. The number of tons of water a ship displaces afloat. 2. The capacity of a merchant ship in units of 100 cubic feet. 3. A charge per ton on cargo. 4. The total shipping of a country or port, figured in tons. 5. Weight, measured in tons.

ton•neau (tŭn-ō′) *n.* The rear seating compartment of an early type of automobile. [F, "barrel," "cask."]

ton•sil (tŏn′səl) *n.* A mass of lymphoid tissue, esp. either of two such masses, embedded in the lateral walls of the aperture between the mouth and pharynx. [L *tonsillae.*] —**ton′sil•ar** *adj.*

ton•sil•lec•to•my (tŏn′sə-lĕk′tə-mē) *n., pl.* -mies. The surgical removal of a tonsil.

ton•sil•li•tis (tŏn′sə-lī′tĭs) *n.* Tonsil inflammation.

ton•so•ri•al (tŏn-sôr′ē-əl, -sōr′ē-əl) *adj.* Of or

ô paw, for/oi boy/ou out/ŏŏ took/ōō coo/p pop/r run/s sauce/sh shy/t to/th thin/*th* the/ ŭ cut/ûr fur/v van/w wag/y yes/z size/zh vision/ə ago, item, edible, gallop, circus/

pertaining to a barber or barbering. [< L *tonsor,* a barber.]

ton•sure (tŏn′shər) *n.* **1.** The act of shaving the head, esp. as a preliminary to becoming a member of a monastic order. **2.** The part of a monk's head so shaven. [< L *tonsūra,* a shearing.]

too (to͞o) *adv.* **1.** In addition; also; as well. **2.** More than sufficient; excessively. **3.** Very; extremely; immensely. **4.** *Informal.* Indeed; so. [ME *to,* in addition to, to.]
Usage: The phrase *not too* is employed, principally informally, in the approximate sense of *not very: Ratification of the treaty is not considered too likely.*

took (to͞ok). *p.t.* of **take.**

tool (to͞ol) *n.* **1.** An instrument, as a hammer, used or worked by hand. **2. a.** A machine, as a lathe, used to cut and shape machinery parts. **b.** The cutting part of such a machine. **3.** Anything used in the performance of an operation; an instrument. **4.** Anything necessary to the carrying out of one's occupation: *tools of the trade.* **5.** A dupe. —*v.* **1.** To form or work with a tool or tools. **2.** To furnish tools or machinery for (a factory). [< OE *tōl* < Gmc **tōwlam.*]

toot (to͞ot) *v.* **1.** To sound (a horn or whistle) in short blasts. **2.** To sound (a blast or series of blasts) on a horn or whistle. —*n.* The act or sound of tooting. [Prob < MDu *tūten* (imit.).]

tooth (to͞oth) *n., pl.* **teeth** (tēth). **1.** One of a set of hard, bonelike structures rooted in sockets in the jaws, typically composed of a core of soft pulp surrounded by a layer of hard dentine that is coated with cement or enamel at the crown, and used to seize, hold, or masticate. **2.** A structure or projection resembling a tooth in shape or function, as on a comb, gear, or saw. [< OE *tōth.* See dent-.] —**toothed** *adj.*

tooth•paste (to͞oth′pāst′) *n.* A paste dentifrice.

tooth•pick (to͞oth′pĭk′) *n.* A small piece of wood or other material, for removing food particles from between the teeth.

tooth•some (to͞oth′səm) *adj.* Delicious; savory. —**tooth′some•ness** *n.*

top¹ (tŏp) *n.* **1.** The uppermost part, point, surface, or end of something. **2.** A lid or cap. **3. a.** The highest rank or position. **b.** The highest degree or pitch; acme; zenith. —*adj.* Of, pertaining to, at, or forming the top. —*v.* **topped, topping. 1.** To remove the top from. **2.** To furnish with, form, or serve as a top. **3.** To reach the top of. **4.** To go over the top of. **5.** To exceed or surpass. [< OE *topp.*]

top² (tŏp) *n.* A toy consisting of a symmetrical rigid body spun on a pointed end about the axis of symmetry.

to•paz (tō′păz′) *n.* **1.** A colorless, blue, yellow, brown, or pink mineral, often found in association with granitic rocks and valued as a gemstone. **2.** Any of various yellow gemstones, esp. a yellow variety of sapphire. **3.** A light-yellow variety of quartz. [< Gk *topazos.*]

top•coat (tŏp′kōt′) *n.* A lightweight overcoat.

tope (tōp) *v.* **toped, toping.** To drink (alcoholic liquors) habitually and excessively. —**top′er** *n.*

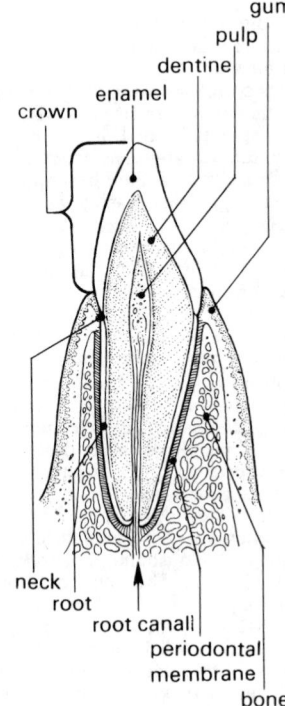

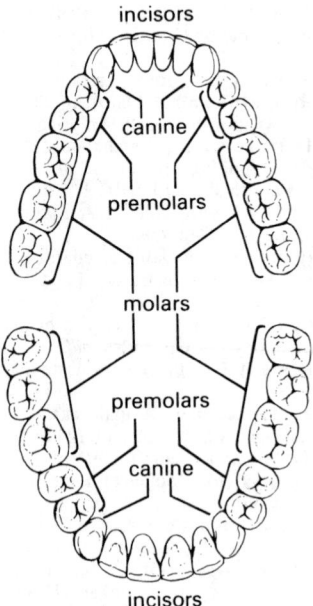

tooth
Above: Cross section of a human incisor
Below: The upper and lower teeth of an adult human

ă pat/ā ate/âr care/ä bar/b bib/ch chew/d deed/ĕ pet/ē be/f fit/g gag/h hat/hw what/
ĭ pit/ī pie/îr pier/j judge/k kick/l lid, fatal/m mum/n no, sudden/ng sing/ŏ pot/ō go/

To•pe•ka (tə-pē′kə). The capital of Kansas. Pop. 119,000.

top•flight (tŏp′flīt′) *adj.* First-rate; superior: *a topflight athlete.*

top-heav•y (tŏp′hĕv′ē) *adj.* Likely to topple because overloaded at the top.

top•ic (tŏp′ĭk) *n.* **1.** A subject treated in a speech, essay, or portion of a discourse; theme. **2.** A subject of discussion or conversation. **3.** A subdivision of a theme, thesis, or outline. [< Aristotle's *Topics.*]

top•i•cal (tŏp′ĭ-kəl) *adj.* **1.** Pertaining or belonging to a particular location or place; local. **2.** Contemporary. **3.** Of or pertaining to a particular topic. **4.** *Med.* Applied or pertaining to a local part of the body.

top•knot (tŏp′nŏt′) *n.* **1.** A crest of hair or feathers on the crown of the head. **2.** Any decorative ribbon, bow, etc., worn as a headdress.

top•most (tŏp′mōst′) *adj.* Highest; uppermost.

top•notch (tŏp′nŏch′) *adj. Informal.* First-rate; excellent.

topo–. *comb. form.* Place or region. [< Gk *topos,* a place.]

topog. topography.

to•pog•ra•phy (tə-pŏg′rə-fē) *n., pl.* **-phies. 1.** The art of graphically representing on a map the exact physical configuration of a place or region. **2.** The features of a place or region. —**to•pog′ra•pher** *n.* —**top′o•graph′ic** (tŏp′ə-grăf′-ĭk), **top′o•graph′i•cal** *adj.*

top•ping (tŏp′ĭng) *n.* A sauce, frosting, or garnish for food.

top•ple (tŏp′əl) *v.* **-pled, -pling. 1.** To push over; overturn. **2.** To totter and fall. [Freq of TOP.]

tops (tŏps) *adj. Slang.* First-rate; excellent.

top•sail (tŏp′səl, -sāl′) *n.* A square sail set above the lowest sail on the mast of a square-rigged ship.

top•se•cret (tŏp′sē′krĭt) *adj.* Designating information of the highest level of security classification.

top•soil (tŏp′soil′) *n.* The surface layer of soil.

top•sy-tur•vy (tŏp′sē-tûr′vē) *adv.* **1.** Upside-down. **2.** In a state of utter disorder or confusion. —*adj.* In a disordered condition.

toque (tōk) *n.* A small brimless, close-fitting woman's hat. [< Span *toca.*]

to•rah (tôr′ə, tōr′ə) *n.* **1.** The body of Jewish literature and oral tradition as a whole. **2. Torah. a.** The Pentateuch. **b.** A scroll on which the Pentateuch is written, used in a synagogue during services. [Heb *tôrāh,* a law, instruction.]

torch (tôrch) *n.* **1.** A portable light produced by the flame of an inflammable material wound about the end of a stick of wood. **2.** A portable apparatus that produces a very hot flame by the combustion of gases, as used in welding. **3.** Anything that serves to illuminate or guide. **4.** *Brit.* A flashlight. [< L *torquēs,* a twisted necklace, wreath.]

tore (tôr, tōr). *p.t.* of **tear¹.**

tor•e•a•dor (tôr′ē-ə-dôr′) *n.* A bullfighter. [< Span *torear,* to fight bulls.]

tor•ment (tôr′mĕnt′) *n.* **1.** Great pain or anguish. **2.** A source of harassment or pain. —*v.*

(tôr-mĕnt′, tôr′mĕnt′). **1.** To cause to undergo great pain or anguish. **2.** To agitate or upset greatly. **3.** To annoy or harass. [< L *tormentum,* **torquementum,* a twisted rope.] —**tor•ment′ing•ly** *adv.* —**tor•men′tor** *n.*

torn (tôrn, tōrn). *p.p.* of **tear¹.**

tor•na•do (tôr-nā′dō) *n., pl.* **-does** or **-dos.** A rotating column of air usually accompanied by a funnel-shaped downward extension of a cloud and having a vortex several hundred yards in diameter whirling at speeds of up to 300 miles per hour. [Var of Span *tronada,* thunderstorm.]

To•ron•to (tə-rŏn′tō). The capital of Ontario. Pop. 665,000.

tor•pe•do (tôr-pē′dō) *n., pl.* **-does. 1.** A cigar-shaped, self-propelled underwater projectile launched from a plane, ship, or submarine and designed to detonate on contact with or in the vicinity of a target. **2.** Any of various submarine explosive devices, esp. a submarine mine. **3.** Any of various devices that contain explosives. —*v.* To attack or destroy with or as with a torpedo or torpedoes. [< L *torpēdō,* stiffness, numbness.]

tor•pid (tôr′pĭd) *adj.* In a sluggish, benumbed, or lethargic state of inactivity. [< L *torpēre,* to be stiff.] —**tor′pid•ly** *adv.*

tor•por (tôr′pər) *n.* **1.** A condition of inactivity or insensibility. **2.** Lethargy; apathy. [< L *torpēre,* to be stiff.]

torque (tôrk) *n.* The tendency of a force to produce rotation about an axis. [< L *torquēre,* to twist.]

tor•rent (tôr′ənt, tŏr′-) *n.* **1.** A turbulent, swift-flowing stream. **2.** A raging flood; deluge. **3.** Any turbulent or overwhelming flow. [< L *torrēns,* a burning, a torrent.] —**tor•ren′tial** (tô-rĕn′shəl, tə-) *adj.*

tor•rid (tôr′ĭd, tŏr′-) *adj.* **1.** Parched with the heat of the sun. **2.** Scorching. **3.** Passionate. [< L *torrēre,* to dry, parch.]

Torrid Zone. The region of the earth's surface between the tropics of Cancer and Capricorn.

tor•sion (tôr′shən) *n.* **1.** A twisting or turning. **2.** The stress caused when one end of an object is twisted in one direction and the other end is held motionless. [< LL *torsus,* "twisted."]

tor•so (tôr′sō) *n., pl.* **-sos** or **-si** (-sē′). The trunk of the human body. [It, a stalk, trunk of a statue.]

tort (tôrt) *n. Law.* Any wrongful act, not involving breach of contract, for which a civil suit can be brought. [< L *tortum,* twisted, distorted.]

tor•til•la (tôr-tē′yə) *n.* A thin unleavened pancake characteristic of Mexican cookery. [< Span *torta,* a round cake.]

tor•toise (tôr′təs) *n.* A turtle, esp. a land turtle. [< OF *tortue.*]

tor•toise•shell (tôr′təs-shĕl′) *n.* **1.** The translucent brownish outer covering of certain sea turtles, used to make combs, jewelry, etc. **2.** A domestic cat with brown, black, and yellowish fur.

tor•tu•ous (tôr′chōō-əs) *adj.* **1.** Winding; twisting. **2.** Devious; deceitful. **3.** Complex. [< L *tortus,* a twist, pp of *torquēre,* to twist.]

ô paw, for/oi boy/ou out/ŏŏ took/ōō coo/p pop/r run/s sauce/sh shy/t to/th thin/*th* the/
ŭ cut/ûr fur/v van/w wag/y yes/z size/zh vision/ə ago, item, edible, gallop, circus/

tor·ture (tôr′chər) *n.* **1.** The infliction of severe pain as a means of punishment or coercion. **2.** Pain or mental anguish. —*v.* **-tured, -turing. 1.** To subject (a person or animal) to torture. **2.** To afflict with great pain or anguish. [< LL *tortūra,* a twisting, torment.] —**tor′tur·er** *n.*

To·ry (tôr′ē, tōr′ē) *n., pl.* **-ries. 1.** A member of the Conservative Party in Great Britain. **2.** An American who during the American Revolution favored the British side. —**To′ry** *adj.*

toss (tôs, tŏs) *v.* **1.** To throw or be thrown to and fro. **2.** To throw lightly. **3.** To move or lift (the head) with rapidity. **4.** To flip a coin to decide something. **5.** To move oneself about vigorously. —*n.* **1.** An act of tossing. **2.** A rapid lift, as of the head. [?]

toss·up (tôs′ŭp′, tŏs′-) *n. Informal.* An even chance or choice.

tot (tŏt) *n.* **1.** A small child. **2.** A small amount of something, as of liquor. [?]

to·tal (tōt′l) *n.* **1.** The amount or quantity obtained by addition. **2.** A whole quantity; an entirety. —*adj.* **1.** Constituting or pertaining to the whole. **2.** Complete; utter; absolute. —*v.* **-taled** or **-talled, -taling** or **-talling. 1.** To determine the sum or total of. **2.** To amount to. [< L *tōtus,* whole.] —**to′tal·ly** *adv.*

to·tal·i·tar·i·an (tō-tăl′ə-târ′ē-ən) *adj.* Of, pertaining to, or designating a polity based on monolithic unity and authoritarianism. —**to· tal′i·tar′i·an·ism′** *n.*

to·tal·i·ty (tō-tăl′ə-tē) *n., pl.* **-ties. 1.** The state or condition of being total. **2.** The aggregate amount; a sum.

tote (tōt) *v.* **toted, toting.** To haul; carry.

to·tem (tō′təm) *n.* **1.** An animal, plant, or natural object serving among certain primitive peoples as the emblem of a clan or family. **2.** A representation of this. —**to·tem′ic** (tō-tĕm′ĭk) *adj.*

totem pole. A post carved and painted with a series of totemic symbols, as among certain Indian peoples of the NW coast of North America.

tot·ter (tŏt′ər) *v.* **1.** To sway as if about to fall. **2.** To walk unsteadily. [< MDu *touteren,* to stagger.] —**tot′ter·er** *n.*

tou·can (tōō′kăn′, -kän′) *n.* A tropical American bird with brightly colored plumage and a very large bill. [< Tupi *tucana.*]

touch (tŭch) *v.* **1.** To cause or permit a part of the body to come in contact with so as to feel. **2.** To be or come into contact. **3.** To tap or nudge lightly. **4.** To partake of: *didn't touch her food.* **5.** To move by handling. **6.** To adjoin; border. **7.** To come up to; equal. **8.** To treat of a subject, as in a lecture. **9.** To be pertinent to. **10.** To have an effect upon; act on; change. **11.** To move to tender response. —*n.* **1.** The act or an instance of touching. **2.** The physiological sense by which bodily contact is registered. **3.** The sensation from a specific contact. **4.** A mark or effect left by a specific contact. **5.** A small amount; tinge; trace. **6.** A mild tap or stroke. **7.** A facility; knack. **8.** A characteristic manner of doing something. **9.** The state of being in contact with a specified or unspecified reality: *getting*

out of touch. [< VL **toccāre,* to strike, ring a bell, touch.] —**touch′a·ble** *adj.*

touch and go. A precarious state of affairs. —**touch′-and-go′** *adj.*

touch·down (tŭch′doun′) *n.* **1.** *Football.* A play worth six points, accomplished by carrying or passing the ball across the opponent's goal line. **2.** The contact, or moment of contact, of a landing aircraft or spacecraft with the landing surface.

tou·ché (tōō-shā′) *interj.* Expressive of concession to an opponent for a point well made, as in an argument. [F, "touched."]

touch·ing (tŭch′ĭng) *adj.* Eliciting a tender reaction. —**touch′ing·ly** *adv.*

touch·stone (tŭch′stōn′) *n.* A criterion; standard.

touch·y (tŭch′ē) *adj.* **-ier, -iest. 1.** Oversensitive; irritable. **2.** Precarious; risky.

tough (tŭf) *adj.* **1.** Strong and resilient. **2.** Hard to cut or chew. **3.** Physically rugged. **4.** Severe; harsh. **5.** Aggressive; pugnacious. **6.** Difficult; demanding. **7.** Having a determined will. **8.** *Informal.* Unfortunate; too bad. —*n.* A hoodlum. [< OE *tōh.* See **denk-**.] —**tough′ly** *adv.* —**tough′ness** *n.*

tough·en (tŭf′ən) *v.* To make or become tough. —**tough′en·er** *n.*

tough-mind·ed (tŭf′mīn′dĭd) *adj.* Not sentimental or timorous.

tou·pee (tōō-pā′) *n.* A hair piece worn to cover a bald spot. [< OF *top, toup,* top, summit.]

tour (tōōr) *n.* **1.** A comprehensive trip with visits to places of established interest. **2.** A brief trip to or through a place for the purpose of seeing it. **3.** A journey to fulfill a round of engagements in several places: *a concert tour.* **4.** A period of duty at a single place or job. —*v.* To go on a tour; make a tour of. [< L *tornus,* tool for drawing a circle, lathe.]

tour·ism (tōōr′ĭz′əm) *n.* The business of providing tours and services for tourists.

tour·ist (tōōr′ĭst) *n.* A person who is traveling for pleasure.

tourist class. A grade of travel accommodations less luxurious than first class.

tour·ma·line (tōōr′mə-lĭn, -lēn′) *n.* A mineral valued, esp. in its green, clear, and blue varieties, as a gemstone. [F.]

tour·na·ment (tōōr′nə-mənt, tûr′-) *n.* **1.** A contest composed of a series of elimination games or trials. **2.** A medieval jousting match. [< OF *torneier,* "to turn around."]

tour·ney (tōōr′nē, tûr′-) *n., pl.* **-neys.** A tournament. [< OF *torneier,* "to turn around."]

tour·ni·quet (tōōr′nĭ-kĭt, -kā′, tûr′-) *n.* Any device used to stop temporarily the flow of blood through a large artery in a limb, esp. a cloth band tightened around a limb. [F, "a turning instrument."]

tou·sle (tou′zəl) *v.* **-sled, -sling.** To disarrange or rumple; dishevel. [ME *touselen.*]

tout (tout) *v.* **1.** To obtain and deal in information regarding horse races. **2.** To publicize as being of great worth. [< OE *tūtian* < Gmc **tūt-,* to stick out, protrude.] —**tout** *n.*

tow¹ (tō) *v.* To draw or pull along behind by a chain or line. —*n.* **1.** An act of towing or the

condition of being towed. **2.** Something being towed, as a barge. [< OE *togian.* See **deuk-.**] **tow²** (tō) *n.* Coarse broken flax or hemp fiber prepared for spinning. [ME *towe.*]
to•ward (tôrd, tōrd, tə-wôrd′) *prep.* Also **to• wards** (tôrdz, tōrdz, tə-wôrdz′). **1.** In the direction of. **2.** In a position facing. **3.** Somewhat before in time. **4.** With regard to. **5.** In furtherance of. **6.** By way of achieving. [< OE *tōweard,* coming, favorable, future : TO + -WARD.]
tow•el (tou′əl) *n.* An absorbent cloth or paper used for wiping or drying. [< OF *toaille.*]
tow•el•ing (tou′əl-ĭng) *n.* Any of various fabrics used for making towels.
tow•er (tou′ər) *n.* **1.** A tall building or part of a building. **2.** A tall framework or structure used for observation, signaling, etc. —*v.* To rise to a conspicuous height. [< Gk *turris.*]
tow•er•ing (tou′ər-ĭng) *adj.* **1.** Of imposing height. **2.** Outstanding. **3.** Awesomely intense. —**tow′er•ing•ly** *adv.*
tow•head (tō′hĕd′) *n.* One having white-blond hair. [< TOW².] —**tow′head′ed** *adj.*
tow•hee (tō′hē, tō-hē′) *n.* A North American bird with black, white, and rust-colored plumage. [Imit.]
town (toun) *n.* **1.** A population center, often incorporated, larger than a village and smaller than a city. **2.** *Informal.* A city. [< OE *tūn,* enclosed place, homestead, village.]
town•ship (toun′shĭp′) *n.* **1.** A subdivision of a county in most Northeastern and Midwestern states. **2.** A public land surveying unit of 36 square miles.
towns•man (tounz′mən) *n.* **1.** A resident of a town. **2.** A fellow resident of one's town.
towns•peo•ple (tounz′pē′pəl) *pl.n.* The inhabitants or citizens of a town or city.
tow•path (tō′păth′, -päth′) *n.* A path along a canal or river used by animals towing boats.
tox-. *comb. form.* Poison. [< L *toxicum,* poison.]
tox•e•mi•a (tŏk-sē′mē-ə) *n.* A condition in which toxins produced locally by body cells are contained in the blood. [< TOX- + -EMIA.]
tox•ic (tŏk′sĭk) *adj.* **1.** Of or pertaining to a toxin. **2.** Harmful; deadly; poisonous. [< L *toxicum,* poisons for arrows.] —**tox′i•cal•ly** *adv.* —**tox•ic′i•ty** (-sĭs′ə-tē) *n.*
tox•i•col•o•gy (tŏk′sĭ-kŏl′ə-jē) *n.* The study of poisons and the treatment of poisoning. —**tox′- i•co•log′i•cal** (-kə-lŏj′ĭ-kəl) *adj.* —**tox′i•co•log′i• cal•ly** *adv.* —**tox′i•col′o•gist** *n.*
tox•in (tŏk′sĭn) *n.* A substance, having a protein structure, secreted by certain organisms and capable of causing poisoning when introduced into the body tissues but also capable of inducing a counteragent or antitoxin. [TOX- + -IN.]
toy (toi) *n.* **1.** An object for children to play with. **2.** Something of little importance; a trinket. **3.** A small ornament. —*v.* To amuse oneself idly; trifle (with *with*). —*adj.* **1.** Designed as a toy. **2.** Miniature. [ME *toye,* dallying, amorous sport.]
tp. township.
tpk. turnpike

tr. **1.** transitive. **2.** translated; translation; translator. **3.** transpose; transposition. **4.** treasurer.
trace¹ (trās) *n.* **1.** A visible mark or sign of the former presence or passage of some person, thing, or event. **2.** A barely perceivable indication of something; a touch. **3.** A minute quantity. —*v.* **traced, tracing.** **1.** To follow the trail of. **2.** To ascertain the successive stages in the development of. **3.** To locate or discover, as a cause. **4.** To delineate or sketch (a figure). **5.** To form (letters) with special care. **6.** To copy by following lines seen through transparent paper. [< VL *tractiāre,* to drag.] —**trace′a•ble** *adj.* —**trac′er** *n.*
trace² (trās) *n.* One of two side straps or chains connecting a harnessed draft animal to a vehicle. [< L *tractus,* a dragging.]
trac•er•y (trā′sə-rē) *n., pl.* **-ies.** Ornamental work of interlaced and ramified lines.
tra•che•a (trā′kē-ə) *n., pl.* **-cheae** (-kē-ē′) or **-as.** A thin-walled tube of cartilaginous and membranous tissue descending from the larynx to the bronchi and carrying air to the lungs. [< Gk *(artēria) trakheia,* "rough (artery)."] —**tra′- che•al** *adj.*
tra•che•ot•o•my (trā′kē-ŏt′ə-mē) *n., pl.* **-mies.** The act or procedure of cutting into the trachea through the neck.
track (trăk) *n.* **1.** A mark, as a footprint, left by the passage of something; a trace. **2.** A path, route, or course; trail. **3. a.** A road or course, as of cinder, laid out for racing. **b.** Athletic competition on such a course. **4.** A set of parallel rails upon which a train or trolley runs. —*v.* **1.** To follow the footprints or traces of; trail. **2.** To carry on the shoes and deposit as tracks. **3.** To observe or monitor, as by radar. [ME *trak,* trace, trail, footprints.] —**track′a•ble** *adj.* —**track′er** *n.*
tract¹ (trăkt) *n.* **1.** An expanse of land. **2.** A system of organs and tissues that together perform one specialized function: *the alimentary tract.* [L *tractus,* "a drawing," course, tract.]
tract² (trăkt) *n.* A propaganda pamphlet, esp. one put out by a religious or political group. [< L *tractātus,* a discussion, treatise.]
tract•a•ble (trăk′tə-bəl) *adj.* **1.** Easily controlled; governable. **2.** Easily worked; malleable. [< L *tractāre,* to pull violently, take in hand, manage.] —**tract′a•bly** *adv.*
trac•tion (trăk′shən) *n.* **1.** The act of drawing or pulling or condition of being drawn or pulled. **2.** Adhesive friction, as of a wheel on a track. **3.** The pulling power of a railroad engine. [< L *trahere,* to draw, pull.]
trac•tor (trăk′tər) *n.* **1.** An automotive vehicle designed for pulling machinery. **2.** A truck having a cab and no body, used for pulling large vehicles. [< L *trahere,* to pull.]
trade (trād) *n.* **1.** An occupation, esp. one requiring skill; a craft. **2.** The business of buying and selling commodities; commerce. **3.** The persons associated with a specified business or industry. **4.** An exchange of one thing for another. —*v.* **traded, trading.** **1.** To engage in buying and selling. **2.** To exchange

one thing for another. **3.** To shop regularly at a given store. [< MLG, a track, path.]

trade·mark (trād'märk') *n.* A name, symbol, or other device identifying a product, legally restricted to the use of the owner or manufacturer. —*v.* **1.** To label (a product) with a trademark. **2.** To register as a trademark.

trade name. 1. The name by which a commodity, service, process, etc., is known to the trade. **2.** The name under which a business firm operates.

trad·er (trā'dər) *n.* **1.** One who trades; a dealer. **2.** A ship employed in foreign trade.

trades·man (trādz'mən) *n.* **1.** One engaged in retail trade, esp. a shopkeeper. **2.** A skilled worker; craftsman.

trade wind. A system of winds occupying most of the tropics, blowing northeasterly in the N Hemisphere and southeasterly in the S Hemisphere.

trading post. A station or store in a sparsely settled area established by traders to barter supplies for local products.

tra·di·tion (trə-dĭsh'ən) *n.* **1.** The passing down of elements of a culture from generation to generation, esp. orally. **2. a.** A cultural custom or usage. **b.** A set of such customs and usages viewed as a coherent body of precedents. **3.** Any time-honored set of practices. [< L *trādere*, to hand over.] —**tra·di'tion·al** *adj.* —**tra·di'tion·al·ly** *adv.*

tra·duce (trə-d/y/ōōs') *v.* **-duced, -ducing.** To speak falsely or maliciously of; slander. [L *trādūcere*, to lead across, make public.] —**tra·duce'ment** *n.* —**tra·duc'er** *n.*

traf·fic (trăf'ĭk) *n.* **1. a.** The commercial exchange of goods; trade. **b.** The quantity of goods traded. **2. a.** The passage of persons, vehicles, or messages through routes of transportation or communication. **b.** The amount, as of vehicles, in transit. **3.** Connections; dealings. —*v.* **-ficked, -ficking.** To carry on trade in. [< L *trafficare*, to trade.] —**traf'fick·er** *n.*

tra·ge·di·an (trə-jē'dē-ən) *n.* An actor of tragic roles. —**tra·ge'di·enne'** (-dē-ĕn') *fem.n.*

trag·e·dy (trăj'ə-dē) *n., pl.* **-dies. 1.** A dramatic or literary work depicting a protagonist engaged in a morally significant struggle ending in ruin or profound unhappiness. **2.** Any dramatic, disastrous event. [< Gk *tragōidia*, "goat-song."]

trag·ic (trăj'ĭk) *adj.* Also **trag·i·cal** (trăj'ĭ-kəl). **1.** Pertaining to, in the style of, or having the character of tragedy. **2.** Calamitous; disastrous. —**trag'i·cal·ly** *adv.*

trag·i·com·e·dy (trăj'ĭ-kŏm'ə-dē) *n., pl.* **-dies.** A drama that combines elements of both tragedy and comedy. —**trag'i·com'ic** *adj.*

trail (trāl) *v.* **1.** To drag or allow to drag or stream behind, as along the ground. **2.** To follow the traces or scent of; track. **3.** To lag behind (an opponent). **4.** To extend or grow along the ground or over a surface. **5.** To drift in a tenuous stream, as smoke. **6.** To become gradually fainter: *Her voice trailed off.* —*n.* **1.** Something that trails, esp. something that hangs loose and long. **2. a.** A mark, trace, or path left by a moving body. **b.** The scent of a

person or animal. **c.** A path or beaten track. [Prob < VL *tragulāre*, to drag.]

trail·er (trā'lər) *n.* **1.** One that trails. **2.** A large transport vehicle hauled by a truck or tractor. **3.** A van drawn by a truck or automobile and used as a home.

train (trān) *n.* **1.** Something that follows or is drawn along behind, as the part of a gown that trails. **2.** A staff of followers; retinue. **3.** A long line of moving persons, animals, or vehicles. **4.** A string of connected railroad cars. **5.** An orderly succession of related events or thoughts. —*v.* **1.** To coach in or accustom to some mode of behavior or performance. **2.** To make or become proficient with specialized instruction and practice. **3.** To prepare physically, as with a regimen. **4.** To cause (a plant or one's hair) to take a desired course or shape. **5.** To focus (on); aim. [< OF *trahiner*, to drag.] —**train'a·ble** *adj.* —**train·ee'** *n.* —**train'er** *n.* —**train'ing** *n.*

train·man (trān'mən) *n.* A member of the operating crew on a railroad train.

traipse (trāps) *v.* **traipsed, traipsing.** *Informal.* To walk about idly. [?]

trait (trāt) *n.* A distinguishing feature, as of character. [< L *tractus,* a pulling, a drawing.]

trai·tor (trā'tər) *n.* One who betrays his country, a cause, or a trust, esp. one who has committed treason. [< L *trādere,* to hand over, betray.] —**trai'tor·ous** *adj.*

tra·jec·to·ry (trə-jĕk'tə-rē) *n., pl.* **-ries.** The path of a moving particle or body, esp. such a path in three dimensions. [< L *trājicere,* to throw across.]

tram (trăm) *n.* **1.** *Chiefly Brit.* A streetcar. **2.** An open wagon or car run on tracks in a coal mine. [Perh < Scand.]

tram·mel (trăm'əl) *n.* Often **trammels.** Something that restricts activity or free movement; a hindrance. —*v.* **-meled** or **-melled, -meling** or **-melling. 1.** To confine or hinder. **2.** To entrap. [< LL *tremaculum.*]

tramp (trămp) *v.* **1.** To walk with a firm, heavy step. **2.** To traverse on foot. **3.** To tread down; trample. —*n.* **1.** The sound of heavy walking or marching. **2.** A walking trip. **3.** One who travels aimlessly about as a vagrant. **4.** An immoral woman. **5.** A cargo vessel that has no regular schedule but takes on freight wherever it can be found and discharges it wherever required. [ME *trampen.*] —**tramp'er** *n.*

tram·ple (trăm'pəl) *v.* **-pled, -pling. 1.** To tread heavily so as to injure or destroy. **2.** To treat harshly, as if tramping upon. —*n.* The action or sound of treading underfoot. [< ME *trampen,* to TRAMP.] —**tram'pler** *n.*

trance (trăns) *n.* **1.** A hypnotic, cataleptic, or ecstatic state. **2.** A state of detachment from one's physical surroundings, as in contemplation. **3.** A dazed state. [< OF *transir,* "to pass (from life to death)," depart.]

tran·quil (trăng'kwəl) *adj.* **-quiler** or **-quiller, -quilest** or **-quillest.** Free from agitation; calm. [L *tranquillus.*] —**tran'quil·ly** *adv.* —**tran·quil'li·ty** *n.* —**tran·quil'i·ty** *n.*

tran·quil·ize (trăng'kwə-līz') *v.* **-ized, -izing.** Also **tran·quil·lize.** To make or become tranquil.

tranquilizer / translate

tran•quil•iz•er (trăn'kwə-līz'ər) n. A tranquilizing drug.

trans–. comb. form. 1. Across or over. 2. Beyond or above. 3. From one place to another. 4. Transferring or transporting. 5. Changing. 6. Having a greater atomic number. [< L trāns, across, over, beyond, through, through and through.]

trans. 1. transaction. 2. transitive. 3. translated; translation; translator. 4. transportation.

trans•act (trăn-săkt', -zăkt') v. To carry out or conduct (business or affairs).

trans•ac•tion (trăn-săk'shən, -zăk'shən) n. 1. The act of transacting or fact of being transacted. 2. Something transacted. 3. transactions. The proceedings, as of a convention.

trans•at•lan•tic (trăns'ət-lăn'tĭk, trănz'ət-) adj. 1. On the other side of the Atlantic. 2. Spanning or crossing the Atlantic.

tran•scend (trăn-sĕnd') v. 1. To exist above and independent of. 2. To rise above; surpass; exceed. [< L transcendere, "to climb over."] —**tran•scen'dent** adj.

tran•scen•den•tal (trăn'sĕn-dĕnt'l) adj. 1. Of or pertaining to transcendentalism. 2. Rising above common thought or ideas; mystical.

tran•scen•den•tal•ism (trăn'sən-dĕnt'l-ĭz'əm) n. Phil. The belief or doctrine that knowledge of reality is derived from intuitive sources rather than objective experience. —**tran'scen•den'tal•ist** n.

trans•con•ti•nen•tal (trăns'kŏn'tə-nĕn'təl, trănz'-) adj. Spanning or crossing a continent.

tran•scribe (trăn-skrīb') v. -scribed, -scribing. 1. To write or type a copy of; write out fully, as from shorthand notes. 2. To adapt or arrange (a musical composition). 3. To record for broadcasting at a later date. [L transcribere, to copy, "write over."]

tran•script (trăn'skrĭpt') n. Something transcribed; a written or printed copy.

tran•scrip•tion (trăn-skrĭp'shən) n. 1. The act or process of transcribing. 2. Something transcribed, esp.: a. An adaptation of a musical composition. b. A recorded radio or television program.

tran•sept (trăn'sĕpt') n. Either of the two lateral arms of a cruciform church. [< TRANS- + L septum, partition.]

trans•fer (trăns-fûr', trăns'fər) v. -ferred, -ferring. 1. To convey, shift, or change from one person or place to another. 2. To make over the possession or title of to another. 3. To convey (a drawing or design) from one surface to another. 4. To change from one train, airplane, or bus to another. —n. 1. Also **trans•fer•al** (trăns-fûr'əl), **trans•fer•ral**. The conveyance of something from one person or place to another. 2. Also **trans•fer•al**, **trans•fer•ral**. Any person or thing that has or has been transferred. 3. A ticket entitling a passenger to change from one carrier to another. 4. Law. The conveyance of title or property from one person to another. [< L trānsferre, to bear across.] —**trans•fer'a•bil'i•ty** n. —**trans•fer'a•ble** adj. —**trans•fer'ence** n.

trans•fig•ure (trăns-fĭg'yər) v. -ured, -uring. 1. To change radically the figure or appearance

of. 2. To exalt; glorify. —**trans'fig•u•ra'tion** n.

trans•fix (trăns-fĭks') v. 1. To pierce through with or as with a pointed weapon; impale. 2. To render motionless, as with terror.

trans•form (trăns-fôrm') v. 1. To change markedly in form or appearance. 2. To change the nature, function, or condition of; convert or be converted. —**trans'for•ma'tion** n.

trans•form•er (trăns-fôr'mər) n. 1. One that transforms. 2. A device used to transfer electric energy, usually that of an alternating current, from one circuit to another, often with a change in voltage, current, or other electric characteristic.

trans•fuse (trăns-fyo͞oz') v. -fused, -fusing. 1. To transfer (liquid) from one vessel to another. 2. To permeate; instill. 3. To administer a transfusion of or to. [< L trānsfundere, "to pour over."] —**trans•fus'er** n.

trans•fu•sion (trăns-fyo͞o'zhən) n. 1. The act or process of transfusing. 2. The direct injection of whole blood, plasma, or another solution into the blood stream.

trans•gress (trăns-grĕs', trănz-) v. 1. To go beyond or over (a limit or boundary). 2. To act in violation of (a law, commandment, etc.); sin. [L trānsgredī, to step across.] —**trans•gres'sion** n. —**trans•gres'sor** n.

tran•ship. Variant of transship.

tran•sient (trăn'shənt, -zhənt, -zē-ənt) adj. 1. Passing away with time; transitory. 2. Passing through from one place to another; stopping only briefly. —n. One that is transient, esp. a person making a brief stay at a hotel. [< L transīre, to go over.] —**tran'sience, tran'sien•cy** n. —**tran'sient•ly** adv.

tran•sis•tor (trăn-zĭs'tər, trăn-sĭs'-) n. 1. A three-terminal semiconductor device used for amplification, switching, etc. 2. A radio equipped with transistors. [TRAN(SFER) + (RE)SISTOR.]

tran•sit (trăn'sĭt, -zĭt) n. 1. a. The act of passing over, across, or through. b. The conveyance of persons or goods from one place to another, esp. on a local public transportation system. 2. A surveying instrument that measures horizontal and vertical angles. [< L transīre, to go across.]

tran•si•tion (trăn-zĭsh'ən, -sĭsh'ən) n. The process or an instance of changing or passing from one form, state, subject, or place to another. —**tran•si'tion•al** adj.

tran•si•tive (trăn'sə-tĭv, trăn'zə-) adj. Gram. Designating a verb or verb construction that requires a direct object to complete its meaning. [LL transitīvus, passing over (as from the subject to the object).]

tran•si•to•ry (trăn'sə-tôr'ē, -tôr'ē, trăn'zə-) adj. Existing or occurring only briefly; short-lived. [< L transitus, TRANSIT.]

transl. translated; translation.

trans•late (trăns-lāt', trănz-, trăns'lāt', trănz'-) v. -lated, -lating. 1. To express or admit of being expressed in another language. 2. To put in simpler terms; explain. 3. To convey from one form or style to another. 4. Phys. To move from one place to another without rotation. [< L translātus, "carried across."] —**trans•**

ô paw, for/oi boy/ou out/o͞o took/o͞o coo/p pop/r run/s sauce/sh shy/t to/th thin/th the/ ŭ cut/ûr fur/v van/w wag/y yes/z size/zh vision/ə ago, item, edible, gallop, circus/

lat'a•ble *adj.* —**trans•la'tion** *n.* —**trans•la'tor** *n.*

trans•lit•er•ate (trăns-lĭt′ə-rāt′, trănz-) *v.* -ated, -ating. To represent (letters or words) in the characters of another alphabet. [TRANS- + L *littera,* LETTER + -ATE.] —**trans•lit'er•a'tion** *n.*

trans•lu•cent (trăns-lōō′sənt, trănz-) *adj.* Transmitting light but causing sufficient diffusion to eliminate perception of distinct images. [< L *translūcēre,* to shine through.] —**trans•lu'cence, trans•lu'cen•cy** *n.*

trans•mi•grate (trăns-mī′grāt′, trănz-) *v.* -grated, -grating. *Theol.* To pass into another body after death. —**trans'mi•gra'tion** *n.*

trans•mis•sion (trăns-mĭsh′ən, trănz-) *n.* 1. The act or process of transmitting. 2. Something transmitted. 3. a. An assembly of gears that links an engine to a driving axle. b. A system of gears. 4. The sending of a signal, as by radio.

trans•mit (trăns-mĭt′, trănz-) *v.* -mitted, -mitting. 1. To send from one person, thing, or place to another. 2. To cause to spread, as an infection. 3. To impart by heredity. 4. To send (a signal), as by radio. 5. To convey (force or energy) from one part of a mechanism to another. [< L *transmittere,* to send across.] —**trans•mis'si•ble, trans•mit'ta•ble** *adj.* —**trans•mit'tal** *n.*

trans•mit•ter (trăns-mĭt′ər, trănz-) *n.* 1. One that transmits. 2. Any of various electrical or electronic devices used to originate signals, as in radio or telegraphy.

trans•mute (trăns-myōōt′, trănz-) *v.* -muted, -muting. To change from one form, nature, substance, or state into another; transform. [< L *transmūtāre.*] —**trans•mut'a•ble** *adj.* —**trans'mu•ta'tion** *n.*

trans•o•ce•an•ic (trăns′ō-shē-ăn′ĭk, trănz′-) *adj.* 1. Situated beyond the ocean. 2. Spanning or crossing the ocean.

tran•som (trăn′səm) *n.* 1. A small hinged window above a door or another window. 2. A horizontal dividing piece in a window. [ME *traunson,* crossbeam, lintel.]

transp. transportation.

trans•pa•cif•ic (trăns′pə-sĭf′ĭk) *adj.* 1. Crossing the Pacific Ocean. 2. Situated beyond the Pacific Ocean.

trans•par•ent (trăns-pâr′ənt, -păr′ənt) *adj.* 1. Capable of transmitting light so that objects or images can be seen as if there were no intervening material. 2. Of such texture that objects can be seen on the other side; sheer. 3. Easily detected; flimsy: *transparent lies.* 4. Guileless; candid; open. [< ML *trānspārēre,* to be seen through.] —**trans•par'en•cy** *n.* —**trans•par'ent•ly** *adv.*

tran•spire (trăn-spīr′) *v.* -spired, -spiring. 1. To give off vapor containing waste products through pores. 2. To become known; come to light. 3. To happen; occur. [< L *trāns-,* out + *spīrāre,* to breathe.] —**tran'spi•ra'tion** *n.*
Usage: Transpire, in the sense of happen or occur, is widely employed but still disputed.

trans•plant (trăns-plănt′, -plänt′) *v.* 1. To uproot and replant (a growing plant). 2. To transfer from one place or residence to another. 3. To transfer (tissue or an organ) from

one body, or body part, to another. —**trans'-plant'** *n.* —**trans'plan•ta'tion** *n.*

trans•port (trăns-pôrt′, -pōrt′) *v.* 1. To carry from one place to another. 2. To move to strong emotion; enrapture. 3. To send abroad to a penal colony. —*n.* (trăns′pôrt′, -pōrt′). 1. The act of transporting; conveyance. 2. Rapture. 3. A ship used to transport troops or military equipment. 4. A vehicle, as an aircraft, used to transport passengers or freight. [< L *trānsportāre.*] —**trans'por•ta'tion** *n.*

trans•pose (trăns-pōz′) *v.* -posed, -posing. 1. To reverse or transfer the order or place of; interchange. 2. *Mus.* To write or perform (a composition) in a key other than the original. —**trans'po•si'tion** *n.*

trans•ship (trăns-shĭp′) *v.* -shipped, -shipping. Also **tran•ship.** To transfer (cargo) from one vessel or vehicle to another for reshipment. —**trans•ship'ment** *n.*

tran•sub•stan•ti•a•tion (trăn′səb-stăn′shē-ā′shən) *n.* The doctrine that the bread and wine of the Eucharist are transformed into the true presence of Christ, although their appearance remains the same.

trans•verse (trăns-vûrs′, trănz-, trăns′vûrs′, trănz′-) *adj.* Situated or lying across; crosswise. [< L *trānsvertere,* to turn or direct across.] —**trans•verse'** *n.* —**trans•verse'ly** *adv.*

trap (trăp) *n.* 1. A device for catching and holding animals. 2. A stratagem for betraying, tricking, or exposing an unsuspecting person. 3. a. A receptacle for collecting waste or other materials. b. A device for sealing a passage against the escape of gases, as in a drainpipe. 4. *Golf.* A land hazard or bunker. 5. A light two-wheeled carriage. 6. Often **traps.** Percussion instruments. —*v.* **trapped, trapping.** 1. To catch in or as in a trap. 2. To trap fur-bearing animals, esp. as a business. [< OE *træppe.* See der-1.] —**trap'per** *n.*

trap door. A hinged or sliding door in a floor or roof.

tra•peze (tră-pēz′) *n.* A short horizontal bar suspended from two parallel ropes, used for acrobatics. [< Gk *trapeza,* "four-footed," table.]

trap•e•zoid (trăp′ə-zoid′) *n.* A quadrilateral having two parallel sides. [< Gk *trapeza,* table + -OID.] —**trap'e•zoi'dal** *adj.*

trap•pings (trăp′ĭngz) *pl.n.* Ornamental coverings or dress, esp. for a horse.

trap•shoot•ing (trăp′shōō′tĭng) *n.* The sport of shooting at clay disks hurled into the air from traps.

trash (trăsh) *n.* 1. Worthless or discarded material or objects; refuse. 2. Cheap or empty expressions or ideas. 3. An ignorant or contemptible person. [?] —**trash'y** *adj.*

trau•ma (trou′mə, trô′-) *n., pl.* **-mas** or **-mata** (-mə-tə). 1. *Path.* A wound, esp. one produced by sudden physical injury. 2. An emotional shock that creates substantial and lasting psychological damage. [Gk, wound, hurt.] —**trau•mat'ic** (-măt′ĭk) *adj.* —**trau•mat'i•cal•ly** *adv.* —**trau'ma•tize'** *v.* (-tized, -tizing).

tra•vail (trə-vāl′, trăv′āl′) *n.* 1. Strenuous exertion; toil. 2. Tribulation or agony; anguish.

ă pat/ā ate/âr care/ä bar/b bib/ch chew/d deed/ĕ pet/ē be/f fit/g gag/h hat/hw what/
ĭ pit/ī pie/îr pier/j judge/k kick/l lid, fatal/m mum/n no, sudden/ng sing/ŏ pot/ō go/

3. The labor of childbirth. —*v*. **1.** To toil.
2. To be in the labor of childbirth. [< VL
tripālium, torture instrument (made of three
stakes).]
trav•el (trăv′əl) *v.* -eled or -elled, -eling or -elling.
1. To go from one place to another; journey
(through). **2.** To journey from one place to
another as a salesman. **3.** To be transmitted;
move, as light. **4.** To associate: *travel in
wealthy circles.* **5.** To move swiftly. **6.** *Basketball.* To walk or run illegally while holding the
ball. —*n.* **1.** The act or process of traveling.
2. travels. A series of journeys. [ME *travailen*,
to toil, make a (toilsome) journey.] —**trav′el•er**,
trav′el•ler *n.*
trav•e•logue (trăv′ə-lôg′, -lŏg′) *n.* Also **trav•
e•log.** A lecture on travel, illustrated by slides
or films.
trav•erse (trăv′ərs, trə-vûrs′) *v.* -ersed, -ersing.
1. To travel across, over, or through. **2.** To
move forward and backward over. **3.** To turn
laterally; swivel. **4.** To extend across; cross.
—*n.* One lying across something else, esp. a
structural crosspiece. —*adj.* Lying or extending across. [< L *trānsversus*, transverse.]
—**tra•vers′al** (trə-vûr′səl) *n.*
trav•er•tine (trăv′ər-tēn′, -tĭn) *n.* A light-colored, porous calcium carbonate deposited
from solution in ground or surface waters. [<
L *(lapis) Tīburtīnus*, "(stone) of Tibur."]
trav•es•ty (trăv′ĭ-stē) *n., pl.* -ties. A grotesque
imitation with intent to ridicule. —*v.* -tied,
-tying. To make a travesty on or of. [< It
travestire, "to disguise."]
trawl (trôl) *n.* **1.** A large, tapered fishing net
towed along the sea bottom. **2.** A multiple
fishing line. —*v.* To fish or catch (fish) with a
trawl. [Perh < Du *tragel*, dragnet.]
trawl•er (trô′lər) *n.* A boat used for trawling.
tray (trā) *n.* A flat, shallow receptacle of wood,
metal, etc., with a raised edge or rim, used for
carrying, holding, or displaying articles. [<
OE *trig, trēg.* See **deru-**.]
treach•er•ous (trĕch′ər-əs) *adj.* **1.** Betraying a
trust; disloyal. **2. a.** Not dependable. **b.** Not to
be trusted; deceptive; dangerous.
treach•er•y (trĕch′ə-rē) *n., pl.* -ies. Willful be-
trayal of trust; perfidy; treason. [< OF *trich-
ier*, to trick.]
trea•cle (trē′kəl) *n. Brit.* Molasses. [ME
triacle, antidote for poison.]
tread (trĕd) *v.* **trod, trodden** or **trod, treading.**
1. To walk on, over, or along. **2.** To press
beneath the foot; trample. **3.** To walk; dance.
—*n.* **1.** The act, manner, or sound of treading.
2. The horizontal part of a step in a staircase.
3. The grooved face of an automobile tire.
4. The part of the sole of a shoe that touches
the ground. [< OE *tredan.* See **der-1**.]
tread•le (trĕd′l) *n.* A pedal or lever operated
by the foot, as in a sewing machine.
tread•mill (trĕd′mĭl′) *n.* **1.** A mechanism operated by walking on the moving steps of a
wheel or treading an endless sloping belt. **2.** A
monotonous routine.
treas. treasurer; treasury.
trea•son (trē′zən) *n.* Violation of allegiance
toward one's sovereign or country. [< L *trā-*

ditiō, a handing over.] —**trea′son•a•ble** *adj.*
—**trea′son•ous** *adj.*
treas•ure (trĕzh′ər) *n.* **1.** Accumulated, stored,
or cached wealth in the form of valuables, as
jewels. **2.** One considered especially precious
or valuable. —*v.* -ured, -uring. **1.** To accumulate; hoard. **2.** To value highly. [< Gk *thēsau-
ros.*] —**treas′ur•a•ble** *adj.*
treas•ur•er (trĕzh′ər-ər) *n.* One in charge of
funds or revenues, esp. a financial officer for a
government or society.
treas•ure-trove (trĕzh′ər-trōv′) *n.* **1.** Any treasure found hidden and not claimed by its
owner. **2.** A discovery of great value. [NF
tresor trove, "discovered treasure."]
treas•ur•y (trĕzh′ə-rē) *n., pl.* -ies. **1.** A place
where treasure is kept or stored. **2.** A place
where private or public funds are received,
kept, managed, and disbursed. **3. Treasury.** A
governmental department in charge of public
revenue.
treat (trēt) *v.* **1.** To act or behave in a specified
manner toward. **2.** To regard or consider in a
certain way. **3.** To deal with in a specified
manner or style, esp. in art or literature. **4.** To
entertain at one's own expense. **5.** To subject
to a process. **6.** To give medical aid to. —*n.*
1. Something generously paid for by someone
else. **2.** The act of providing a treat. **3.** A
special delight or pleasure. [< L *tractāre*, to
drag, handle, treat.] —**treat′er** *n.*
trea•tise (trē′tĭs) *n.* A formal, systematic account in writing of some subject.
treat•ment (trēt′mənt) *n.* **1.** The act or manner
of treating something. **2.** The application of
remedies with the aim of effecting a cure;
therapy.
trea•ty (trē′tē) *n., pl.* -ties. **1. a.** A formal agreement between two or more states containing
terms of trade, peace, etc.; a pact. **b.** A document embodying this. **2.** Any contract or
agreement. [< L *tractāre*, TREAT.]
treb•le (trĕb′əl) *adj.* **1.** Triple. **2.** *Mus.* Of, having, or performing the highest part, voice, or
range. **3.** High-pitched; shrill. —*n.* **1.** *Mus.*
The highest part, voice, instrument, performer,
or range; soprano. **2.** A high, shrill sound or
voice. —*v.* -led, -ling. To triple. [< L *triplus*,
TRIPLE.] —**treb′ly** *adv.*
treble clef. *Mus.* A symbol centered on the
second line of the staff to indicate the position
of G above middle C.
tree (trē) *n.* **1.** A usually tall woody plant with
a single main stem or trunk. **2.** Something
suggestive of a tree: *a clothes tree.* **3.** A diagram showing a family lineage; family tree.
—*v.* **treed, treeing.** To force to climb a tree in
evasion of pursuit. [< OE *trēow.* See **deru-**.]
tre•foil (trē′foil′, trĕf′oil′) *n.* **1.** A plant, as a
clover, having compound leaves with three
leaflets. **2.** Any ornament resembling the
leaves of such a plant. [< L *trifolium*, three-
leaved grass.]
trek (trĕk) *v.* **trekked, trekking.** To make a slow
or arduous journey. —*n.* **1.** An arduous journey. **2.** A migration. [< MDu *trekken*, to pull,
draw, travel.] —**trek′ker** *n.*
trel•lis (trĕl′ĭs) *n.* An open latticework used for

training creeping plants. [< L *trilix*, triple-twilled.]

trem•ble (trĕm′bəl) *v.* **-bled, -bling. 1.** To shake involuntarily, as from fear, cold, etc.; quake; shiver; quiver. **2.** To feel or express fear or anxiety. —*n.* The act or state of trembling. [< L *tremulus*, TREMULOUS.] —**trem′bler** *n.* —**trem′bling•ly** *adv.*

tre•men•dous (trĭ-mĕn′dəs) *adj.* **1.** Capable of making one tremble; terrible. **2. a.** Extremely large; enormous. **b.** Marvelous; wonderful. [< L *tremere*, to tremble.] —**tre•men′dous•ly** *adv.* —**tre•men′dous•ness** *n.*

trem•o•lo (trĕm′ə-lō′) *n., pl.* **-los.** *Mus.* A tremulous effect produced by the rapid repetition of a single tone or the rapid alternation of two tones. [It, "tremulous."]

trem•or (trĕm′ər) *n.* **1.** A quick shaking or vibrating movement. **2.** An involuntary trembling motion of the body; a nervous quiver or shiver. [< L *tremere*, to tremble.]

trem•u•lous (trĕm′yə-ləs) *adj.* **1.** Vibrating or quivering; trembling. **2.** Timid; fearful. [L *tremulus* < *tremere*, to tremble.]

trench (trĕnch) *n.* **1.** A deep furrow. **2.** A ditch, esp. one embanked with its own soil and used for concealment and protection in warfare. —*v.* **1.** To cut trenches in. **2.** To fortify with trenches. **3.** To verge or encroach. [< OF *trenchier*, to cut, dig.]

trench•ant (trĕn′chənt) *adj.* **1.** Keen; incisive. **2.** Forceful; effective. **3.** Distinct; sharply defined. [< OF *trenchier*, to cut.] —**trench′an•cy** *n.* —**trench′ant•ly** *adv.*

trench coat. A loose-fitting, belted raincoat having many pockets and flaps.

trench•er (trĕn′chər) *n.* A wooden board or plate on which food is cut or served. [< OF *trenchier*, to cut.]

trench fever. An acute infectious relapsing fever caused by a microorganism transmitted by lice.

trench foot. Frostbite of the feet, often afflicting soldiers obliged to stand in cold water over long periods of time.

trench mouth. An oral disease characterized by pain, foul odor, and the formation of a gray film over the diseased area.

trend (trĕnd) *n.* **1.** A direction of movement; a flow. **2.** A general tendency. —*v.* **1.** To move in a specified direction. **2.** To tend. [< OE *trendan*, to turn < Gmc **trand-*.]

tren•dy (trĕn′dē) *adj.* **-ier, -iest.** *Informal.* According to the latest fad or fashion; modish and unconventional. —**trend′i•ness** *n.*

Tren•ton (trĕn′tən). The capital of New Jersey. Pop. 105,000.

tre•pan (trĭ-păn′) *n.* A trephine. —*v.* **-panned, -panning.** To trephine. [< Gk *trupanon*, auger, borer.] —**trep′a•na′tion** (trĕp′ə-nā′shən, trĭ-păn′ā′shən) *n.* —**tre•pan′ner** *n.*

tre•phine (trĭ-fīn′, -fēn′) *n.* A surgical instrument having circular, sawlike edges, used to cut out disks of bone, usually from the skull. —*v.* **-phined, -phining.** To operate on with or extract by means of a trephine. [< L *tres fines*, three ends.] —**treph′i•na′tion** (trĕf′ə-nā′shən, trĭ-fī′-, trĭ-fē′-) *n.*

trep•i•da•tion (trĕp′ə-dā′shən) *n.* **1.** A state of alarm or dread; apprehension. **2.** A trembling. [< L *trepidus*, alarmed.]

tres•pass (trĕs′pəs, -păs′) *v.* **1.** To commit an offense or sin; err; transgress. **2.** To infringe upon the privacy or attention of another. **3.** To invade the property or rights of another without his consent. —*n.* **1.** A transgression. **2.** The act of trespassing. [< ML *transpassāre*, to pass across.] —**tres′pass•er** *n.*

tress (trĕs) *n.* A lock of hair. [< OF *tresse.*]

tres•tle (trĕs′əl) *n.* **1.** A horizontal bar held up by two pairs of divergent legs and used as a support. **2.** A framework consisting of vertical, slanted supports and horizontal crosspieces supporting a bridge. [< L *transtrum*, crossbeam.]

trey (trā) *n.* A card, die, or domino with three pips; a three. [< L *trēs*, three.]

tri-. *comb. form.* **1.** Three. **2.** Every three or every third. [L and Gk, three.]

tri•ad (trī′ăd′, -əd) *n.* A group of three persons or things; trinity. [< Gk *trias.*] —**tri•ad′ic** *adj.*

tri•al (trī′əl, trīl) *n.* **1.** The examination of evidence and applicable law to determine the issue of specified charges or claims. **2.** The act or process of testing and trying by use and experience. **3.** An effort or attempt. **4.** A state of pain or anguish. **5.** A test of patience or endurance. —*adj.* **1.** Of or pertaining to a trial or trials. **2.** Made, done, or used during the course of a test or tests. [< OF *trier*, try.]

tri•an•gle (trī′ăng′gəl) *n.* **1.** The plane figure formed by connecting three points not in a straight line by straight line segments. **2.** Something having the shape of this figure. [< L *triangulus*, three-angled.] —**tri•an′gu•lar** *adj.*

tri•an•gu•late (trī-ăng′gyə-lāt′) *v.* **-lated, -lating.** To measure by using trigonometry. —**tri•an′gu•la′tion** *n.*

Tri•as•sic (trī-ăs′ĭk) *adj.* Of or belonging to the geologic time, rock systems, and sedimentary deposits of the first period of the Mesozoic era. —*n.* The Triassic period. [< LL *trias*, triad.]

tribe (trīb) *n.* **1.** A social organization or division comprising several local villages, bands, lineages, or other groups and sharing a common ancestry, language, culture, and name. **2.** A group having a common distinguishing characteristic. [< L *tribus*, division of the Roman people.] —**trib′al** *adj.*

tribes•man (trībz′mən) *n.* A member of a tribe.

trib•u•la•tion (trĭb′yə-lā′shən) *n.* **1.** Great affliction or distress. **2.** That which causes such distress. [< LL *trībulāre*, to oppress.]

tri•bu•nal (trī-byōō′nəl, trĭ-) *n.* **1.** A seat or court of justice. **2.** One having the power of determining. [< L *tribūnus*, TRIBUNE.]

trib•une (trĭb′yōōn, trī-byōōn′) *n.* **1.** An official of ancient Rome chosen by the common people to protect their rights. **2.** A protector or champion of the people. [< L *tribūnus*, "head of the tribe."] —**trib′u•nar′y** (trĭb′yə-nĕr′ē) *adj.*

trib•u•tar•y (trĭb′yə-tĕr′ē) *adj.* **1.** Contributory; subsidiary. **2.** Having the nature of or paying tribute. —*n., pl.* **-ries. 1.** One that pays tribute.

2. A stream or river flowing into a larger stream or river.

trib•ute (trĭb′yōōt) *n.* **1.** A gift or other acknowledgment of gratitude, respect, or admiration. **2. a.** A sum of money paid by one ruler or nation to another as acknowledgment of submission or as the price for protection by that nation. **b.** A forced levy. [< L *tribuere,* to distribute (as among the Roman tribes) < *tribus,* TRIBE.]

trice (trīs) *n.* A very short period of time; a moment; an instant: *in a trice.* [< ME *at a tryse,* immediately.]

tri•ceps (trī′sĕps′) *n.* A large muscle running along the back of the upper arm and serving to extend the forearm. [L, three-headed.]

tri•cer•a•tops (trī-sĕr′ə-tŏps′) *n.* A horned plant-eating dinosaur with a bony plate covering the neck. [< TRI- + Gk *keras,* horn + *ōps,* eye, face.]

trich•i•no•sis (trĭk′ə-nō′sĭs) *n.* A disease characterized by intestinal disorders, fever, muscular swelling, pain, and insomnia, and caused by eating inadequately cooked pork infested with parasitic worms. [< NL *trichina,* a parasitic worm + -OSIS.]

trick (trĭk) *n.* **1.** A device or action designed to achieve an end by deceptive or fraudulent means; stratagem. **2.** A practical joke; prank. **3.** A childish act or performance. **4.** A peculiar trait; mannerism. **5.** The quality necessary to accomplish something easily. **6.** A feat of magic. **7.** A clever act. **8.** *Card Games.* All the cards played in a single round. —*v.* **1.** To swindle or cheat; deceive. **2.** To ornament or adorn. [Perh < L *tricae,* trifles, tricks.] —**trick** *adj.* —**trick′er** *n.*

trick•er•y (trĭk′ə-rē) *n., pl.* -**ies.** **1.** The practice or use of tricks; artifice; deception by stratagem. **2.** A trick used to deceive.

trick•ish (trĭk′ĭsh) *adj.* Characterized by or tending to use tricks or trickery. —**trick′ish•ly** *adv.* —**trick′ish•ness** *n.*

trick•le (trĭk′əl) *v.* -**led,** -**ling.** **1.** To flow or fall in drops or in a thin, intermittent stream; drip steadily. **2.** To proceed slowly or bit by bit. —*n.* **1.** The act or condition of trickling. **2.** Any slow, small, or irregular quantity of trickling. [ME *triklen.*]

trick•ster (trĭk′stər) *n.* One who tricks; a cheater; deceiver.

trick•y (trĭk′ē) *adj.* -**ier,** -**iest.** **1.** Crafty; sly; wily. **2.** Requiring caution or skill. —**trick′i•ly** *adv.* —**trick′i•ness** *n.*

tri•col•or (trī′kŭl′ər) *n.* A flag with three stripes of different colors, esp. the French flag. —*adj.* Having three colors.

tri•cot (trē′kō) *n.* A knitted fabric. [< F *tricoter,* to knit.]

tri•cy•cle (trī′sĭk′əl, -sĭ-kəl) *n.* A vehicle with three wheels usually propelled by pedals.

tri•dent (trīd′ənt) *n.* A long, three-pronged weapon. [L *tridēns,* three-toothed.]

tried (trīd) *adj.* Thoroughly tested and proved to be good or trustworthy.

tri•en•ni•al (trī-ĕn′ē-əl) *adj.* **1.** Occurring every third year. **2.** Lasting three years. —*n.* A third anniversary.

tri•fle (trī′fəl) *n.* **1.** Something of slight importance or very little value. **2.** A small amount; a little. —**a trifle.** Very little; somewhat: *"A couple of the very youngest children dragged the tempo a trifle . . ."* (J.D. Salinger). —*v.* -**fled,** -**fling. 1.** To deal with something as if it were of little significance or value. **2.** To jest. **3.** To play or toy with something; handle things idly. **4.** To waste. [< OF *truffle,* trickery.] —**tri′fler** (trī′flər) *n.*

tri•fling (trī′flĭng) *adj.* **1.** Of slight importance; insignificant. **2.** Frivolous.

tri•fo•cal (trī-fō′kəl) *adj.* Having three focal lengths. —*pl.n.* **trifocals.** Eyeglasses having trifocal lenses.

trig (trĭg) *adj.* **1.** Trim; neat; tidy. **2.** Firm; strong. [< ON *tryggr,* active.]

trig. trigonometry.

trig•ger (trĭg′ər) *n.* **1.** The lever pressed by the finger to discharge a firearm. **2.** A device used to release or activate a mechanism. **3.** A stimulus. —*v.* To initiate; activate; set off. [< MDu *trecken,* to pull, travel.]

trig•o•nom•e•try (trĭg′ə-nŏm′ə-trē) *n.* The study of the relations between the sides and angles of triangles. [< Gk *trigōnon,* triangle + -METRY.] —**trig′o•no•met′ric** (-nə-mĕt′rĭk) *adj.*

trill (trĭl) *n.* **1.** A fluttering or tremulous sound, as that made by certain birds; warble. **2.** *Mus.* The rapid alternation of two tones either a whole or a half tone apart. **3.** *Phon.* **a.** A rapid vibration of one speech organ against another. **b.** A speech sound pronounced with such a vibration. —*v.* **1.** To sound, sing, play with, or give forth a trill. **2.** *Phon.* To articulate with a trill. [It *trillo.*]

tril•lion (trĭl′yən) *n.* **1.** The cardinal number represented by 1 followed by 12 zeros. **2.** In Great Britain, the cardinal number represented by 1 followed by 18 zeros. [< TRI- + (M)ILLION.] —**tril′lion** *adj.*

tril•lionth (trĭl′yənth) *n.* **1.** The ordinal number one trillion in a series. **2.** One of a trillion equal parts. —**tril′lionth** *adj. & adv.*

tril•o•gy (trĭl′ə-jē) *n., pl.* -**gies.** A group of three dramatic or literary works related in subject or theme. [< TRI- + -LOGY.]

trim (trĭm) *v.* **trimmed, trimming. 1.** To make neat or tidy by clipping, smoothing, or pruning. **2.** To rid of excess or remove by cutting. **3.** To ornament; decorate. **4. a.** To adjust (the sails and yards) so that they receive the wind properly. **b.** To balance (a ship) by shifting its cargo or contents. **5.** To balance (an airplane) in flight. —*n.* **1.** State of order or appearance; condition. **2.** Ornamentation. **3.** Excised or rejected material. **4. a.** The readiness of a vessel for sailing. **b.** The balance of a ship. —*adj.* **trimmer, trimmest. 1.** In good or neat order. **2.** Having lines of neat and pleasing simplicity. [Perh < OE *trymian,* to strengthen, arrange.] —**trim′ly** *adv.* —**trim′mer** *n.* —**trim′ness** *n.*

trim•ming (trĭm′ĭng) *n.* **1.** That which is added as decoration; an ornament. **2. trimmings.** Accessories; extras. **3.** That which is trimmed.

trine (trīn) *adj.* Threefold; triple. [< L *trīnī,* three each.]

Trin·i·dad and To·ba·go (trĭn′ə-dăd′; tə-bā′-gō). A state comprising the islands of Trinidad and Tobago, off the coast of Venezuela. Pop. 932,000. Cap. Port-of-Spain.

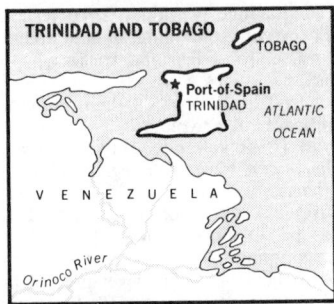

Trinidad and Tobago

tri·ni·tro·tol·u·ene (trī′nī′trō-tŏl′yōō-ēn′) *n.* A yellow crystalline compound, $C_7H_5N_3O_6$, used mainly as a high explosive.
trin·i·ty (trĭn′ə-tē) *n., pl.* **-ties.** 1. Any three parts in union; a triad. 2. **Trinity.** The Godhead of orthodox Christian belief, constituted by the persons of the Father, Son, and Holy Ghost.
trin·ket (trĭng′kĭt) *n.* 1. Any small ornament, as a piece of jewelry. 2. A trivial thing. [?]
tri·o (trē′ō) *n., pl.* **-os.** 1. A group of three. 2. *Mus.* **a.** A composition for three performers. **b.** The people who perform this composition. [It.]
trip (trĭp) *n.* 1. A going from one place to another; journey. 2. *Slang.* An extended hallucination induced by a hallucinogen, as LSD. 3. A stumble or fall caused by an obstacle or loss of balance. 4. **a.** A device for tripping a mechanism. **b.** The action of such a device. —*v.* **tripped, tripping.** 1. To stumble or cause to stumble; make a false step. 2. To move quickly or nimbly with light, rapid steps; skip. 3. To make or catch in a mistake; err. 4. To release or be released, as a catch, trigger, etc. [< MDu *trippen,* to hop.]
tri·par·tite (trī-pär′tīt′) *adj.* 1. Composed of or divided into three parts. 2. Relating to or executed by three parties.
tripe (trīp) *n.* 1. The light-colored, rubbery lining of the stomach of cattle or other ruminants, used as food. 2. *Informal.* Anything with no value; rubbish. [< OF.]
trip·le (trĭp′əl) *adj.* 1. Consisting of three parts. 2. Thrice multiplied. —*n.* 1. A quantity three times as great as another. 2. A group or set of three; triad. —*v.* **-led, -ling.** 1. To make or become three times as great in number or amount. 2. *Baseball.* To make a three-base hit. [< L *triplus.*] —**trip′ly** *adv.*
trip·let (trĭp′lĭt) *n.* 1. A group or set of three of one kind. 2. One of three children born at one birth.
trip·lex (trĭp′lĕks′, trī′plĕks′) *adj.* Triple.

trip·li·cate (trĭp′lĭ-kĭt) *adj.* Made with three identical copies. —*n.* One of a set of three identical objects. —*v.* (trĭp′lĭ-kāt′) **-cated, -cating.** 1. To triple. 2. To make three identical copies of. —**trip′li·ca′tion** *n.*
tri·pod (trī′pŏd′) *n.* A three-legged utensil, stool, or stand used for support. [< Gk *tripous,* three-footed.]
Trip·o·li (trĭp′ə-lē). The capital of Libya. Pop. 162,000.
trip·tych (trĭp′tĭk) *n.* A three-paneled picture. [Gk *triptukhos,* threefold.]
tri·sect (trī′sĕkt′, trī-sĕkt′) *v.* To divide into three equal parts.
trit. triturate.
trite (trīt) *adj.* **triter, tritest.** Overused and commonplace; lacking interest or originality. [L *tritus,* pp of *terere,* to rub (away).] —**trite′ly** *adv.* —**trite′ness** *n.*
trit·i·um (trĭt′ē-əm, trĭsh′ē-) *n.* A rare radioactive hydrogen isotope with atomic mass 3 and half-life 12.5 years. [< Gk *tritos,* third.]
tri·umph (trī′əmf) *v.* 1. To be victorious; win; prevail. 2. To rejoice over a victory. —*n.* 1. The instance or fact of being victorious; success. 2. Exultation derived from victory. [< L *triumphus.*] —**tri·um′phal** *adj.* —**tri·um′phant** *adj.* —**tri·um′phant·ly** *adv.*
tri·um·vir (trī-ŭm′vər) *n., pl.* **-virs** or **-viri** (-və-rī′). One of three men sharing civil authority, as in ancient Rome. [L.] —**tri·um′vi·ral** *adj.* —**tri·um′vi·rate** *n.*
tri·une (trī′yōōn′) *adj.* Being three in one. —*n.* A trinity.
triv·et (trĭv′ĭt) *n.* 1. A three-legged stand. 2. A metal stand with short feet, used under a hot dish. [< L *tripēs,* "three-footed."]
triv·i·a (trĭv′ē-ə) *pl.n. (takes sing. or pl. v.).* Insignificant or inessential matters; trivialities; trifles. [NL, "that which comes from the street."]
triv·i·al (trĭv′ē-əl) *adj.* 1. Of little importance or significance; trifling. 2. Ordinary; commonplace. —**triv′i·al·i·ty** *n.* —**triv′i·al·ly** *adv.*
tro·che (trō′kē) *n.* A small circular medicinal lozenge; pastille. [< Gk *trokhos,* wheel.]
trod (trŏd). *p.t.* & alternate *p.p.* of **tread.**
trod·den (trŏd′n). *p.p.* of **tread.**
Tro·jan (trō′jən) *n.* A native or inhabitant of ancient Troy. —*adj.* Of or pertaining to ancient Troy or its residents.
Trojan War. The prehistoric ten-year war waged against Troy by the confederated Greeks, ending in the burning of Troy.
troll¹ (trōl) *v.* 1. To fish by trailing a baited line from behind a slowly moving boat. 2. To sing in succession the parts of (a round). 3. To sing heartily. —*n.* 1. The act of trolling for fish. 2. A lure used for trolling. [ME *trollen,* to ramble, roll.] —**troll′er** *n.*
troll² (trōl) *n.* A supernatural creature of Scandinavian folklore. [< ON, monster, demon.]
trol·ley (trŏl′ē) *n., pl.* **-leys.** Also **trol·ly** *pl.* **-lies.** 1. An electric car; a streetcar. 2. A wheeled carriage or basket suspended from an overhead track. 3. A device that collects electric current and transmits it to the motor of an electric vehicle. [Prob < TROLL¹.]

ă pat/ā ate/âr care/ä bar/b bib/ch chew/d deed/ĕ pet/ē be/f fit/g gag/h hat/hw what/
ĭ pit/ī pie/îr pier/j judge/k kick/l lid, fatal/m mum/n no, sudden/ng sing/ŏ pot/ō go/

trolley bus. An electric bus that is powered by electricity from an overhead wire.

trol•lop (trŏl'əp) *n.* **1.** A slovenly, untidy woman. **2.** A loose woman; strumpet.

trom•bone (trŏm-bōn', trəm-, trŏm'bōn') *n.* A low-pitched brass musical instrument related to the trumpet. [< It.] —**trom•bon'ist** *n.*

-tron. *comb. form.* **1.** Vacuum tube: *dynatron.* **2.** Device for manipulating subatomic particles: **cyclotron.** [Gk, suffix denoting instrument.]

troop (trōōp) *n.* **1.** A group or company of people, animals, or things. **2.** A group of soldiers. **3. troops.** Military units; soldiers. —*v.* To move or go as a throng. [< F *troupeau,* herd.]

troop•er (trōō'pər) *n.* **1. a.** A cavalryman. **b.** A cavalry horse. **2.** A mounted policeman. **3.** A state policeman.

troop•ship (trōōp'shĭp') *n.* A transport ship designed for carrying troops.

trop. tropic; tropical.

trope (trōp) *n.* The figurative use of a word or expression. [< Gk *tropos,* a turn, way, manner.]

tro•phy (trō'fē) *n., pl.* **-phies.** A prize or memento received as a symbol of victory. [< Gk *tropaios,* of turning, of defeat.]

trop•ic (trŏp'ĭk) *n.* **1.** Two parallels of latitude 23 degrees 27 minutes N and S of the equator that are the boundaries of the Torrid Zone. **2. tropics.** The region of the earth's surface lying between these latitudes; the Torrid Zone. —*adj.* Of or relating to the tropics; tropical. [ME *tropik,* solstice point at which the sun "turns."]

trop•i•cal (trŏp'ĭ-kəl) *adj.* **1.** Of, indigenous to, or characteristic of the tropics. **2.** Hot and humid; sultry; torrid. —**trop'i•cal•ly** *adv.*

tropical year. The time interval between two successive passages of the sun through the vernal equinox; the calendar year.

tropic of Cancer. The parallel of latitude 23 degrees 27 minutes N of the equator, the northern boundary of the Torrid Zone.

tropic of Capricorn. The parallel of latitude 23 degrees 27 minutes S of the equator, the southern boundary of the Torrid Zone.

tro•pism (trō'pĭz'əm) *n.* Responsive growth or movement of an organism toward or away from an external stimulus. [< Gk *tropos,* turn.]

tro•po•sphere (trō'pə-sfîr', trŏp'ə-) *n.* The lowest region of the earth's atmosphere, characterized by decreasing temperature with increasing altitude. [< Gk *tropos,* a turn, change + SPHERE.]

trot (trŏt) *n.* **1.** A gait of a four-footed animal in which diagonal pairs of legs move forward together. **2.** A gait faster than a walk; a jog. —*v.* **trotted, trotting. 1.** To go or move at a trot. **2.** To proceed rapidly; hurry. [< OF *troter.*] —**trot'ter** *n.*

troth (trôth, trŏth, trōth) *n.* **1.** Good faith; fidelity. **2.** One's pledged fidelity; betrothal. [< OE *trēowth,* TRUTH.]

Trots•ky (trŏt'skē), **Leon.** 1879–1940. Russian revolutionary leader.

trou•ba•dour (trōō'bə-dôr', -dōr', -dōōr') *n.* One of a class of lyric poets of the 12th and 13th centuries, attached to the courts of Provence and N Italy, who composed songs. [< OProv *trobador.*]

troub•le (trŭb'əl) *n.* **1.** A state of distress, affliction, danger, or need. **2.** Something that contributes to such a state. **3.** Exertion; effort; pains. **4.** A condition of pain, disease, or malfunction: *heart trouble.* —*v.* **-led, -ling. 1.** To agitate; stir up. **2.** To afflict with pain or discomfort. **3.** To perturb. **4.** To inconvenience; bother. **5.** To take pains. [< L *turbidus,* TURBID.] —**troub'le•some** *adj.*

troub•le•mak•er (trŭb'əl-mā'kər) *n.* One who habitually stirs up trouble.

troub•le•shoot•er (trŭb'əl-shōō'tər) *n.* One who locates and eliminates sources of trouble.

trough (trôf, trŏf) *n.* **1.** A long, narrow, generally shallow receptacle, esp. one for holding water or feed for animals. **2.** A gutter under the eaves of a roof. **3.** A long, narrow depression, as between waves or ridges. [< OE *trog.* See deru-.]

trounce (trouns) *v.* **trounced, trouncing. 1.** To thrash; beat. **2.** To defeat decisively. [?]

troupe (trōōp) *n.* A company or group, esp. of touring actors, singers, or dancers. [F, troop.] —**troup'er** *n.*

trou•sers (trou'zərz) *pl.n.* Also **trow•sers.** A garment covering the body from the waist to the ankles, divided into sections to fit each leg separately, worn esp. by men and boys. [< Scot Gael *triubhas.*]

trous•seau (trōō'sō, trōō-sō') *n., pl.* **-seaux** (-sōz, -sōz') or **-seaus.** The special wardrobe a bride assembles for her marriage. [< OF *trusse,* a bundle.]

trout (trout) *n., pl.* **trout** or **trouts.** Any of various chiefly freshwater food and game fishes related to the salmon. [< LL *tructa.*]

trow (trō) *v. Archaic.* To think; suppose. [< OE *trēowian* and *trūwian.*]

trow•el (trou'əl) *n.* **1.** A flat-bladed hand tool used for shaping substances such as cement or mortar. **2.** A small gardening implement with a scoop-shaped blade. [< L *trua,* stirring spoon, ladle.]

troy (troi) *adj.* Of or expressed in troy weight. [Prob < *Troyes,* France.]

Troy (troi). An ancient city in NW Asia Minor.

troy weight. A system of units of weight in which the grain is the same as in the avoirdupois system and the pound contains 12 ounces.

tru•ant (trōō'ənt) *n.* **1.** One who is absent without permission, esp. from school. **2.** One who shirks his work or duty. —*adj.* **1.** Absent without permission. **2.** Idle, lazy, or neglectful. [< OF, idle rogue.] —**tru'an•cy** *n.*

truce (trōōs) *n.* A temporary cessation of hostilities by agreement of the contending forces; an armistice. [< OE *trēow,* faith, pledge. See deru-.]

truck¹ (trŭk) *n.* **1.** Any of various heavy automotive vehicles designed for transporting loads. **2.** A two-wheeled barrow for moving heavy objects by hand. **3.** One of the swiveling frames of wheels under each end of a railroad car, trolley car, etc. —*v.* 1. To transport by truck. 2. To drive a truck. [Perh < L *trochus,* a wheel.]

truck² (trŭk) *v.* 1. To exchange; barter. 2. To have dealings; traffic. —*n.* 1. Trade goods. 2. Garden produce raised for the market. 3. Barter; exchange. 4. Dealings; business. [< OF *troquer.*]

truck•age (trŭk′ĭj) *n.* 1. Transportation of goods by truck. 2. A charge for this.

truck•le (trŭk′əl) *n.* 1. A small wheel or roller; caster. 2. A trundle bed. —*v.* -led, -ling. To be servile; yield weakly. [< L *trochlea,* system of pulleys.] —**truck′ler** *n.*

truck•load (trŭk′lōd′) *n.* The quantity or weight that a truck carries.

truc•u•lent (trŭk′yə-lənt) *adj.* 1. Savage and cruel; fierce. 2. Pugnacious; defiant. [L *truculentus.*] —**truc′u•lence** *n.* —**truc′u•lent•ly** *adv.*

trudge (trŭj) *v.* trudged, trudging. To walk in a heavy-footed way; plod. —*n.* A long, tedious walk. [?] —**trudg′er** *n.*

true (trōō) *adj.* truer, truest. 1. Consistent with fact or reality; not false or erroneous. 2. Exactly conforming to a rule, standard, or pattern. 3. Reliable; accurate. 4. Real; genuine. 5. Faithful; loyal. 6. Fundamental; essential: *his true motive.* 7. Rightful; legitimate. 8. Determined with reference to the earth's axis, not the magnetic poles: *true north.* —*adv.* 1. Rightly; truthfully. 2. Unswervingly; exactly. 3. So as to conform to an ancestral type or stock: *breed true.* —*v.* trued, truing or trueing. To adjust so as to conform with a standard. —*n.* 1. Truth. 2. Proper alignment or adjustment. [< OE *trēowe,* loyal, trustworthy. See deru-.] —**true′ness** *n.*

true•blue (trōō′blōō′) *n.* Also **true blue.** One of unswerving loyalty. —**true′-blue′** *adj.*

true•love (trōō′lŭv′) *n.* One's beloved; a sweetheart.

truf•fle (trŭf′əl) *n.* An underground fungus esteemed as a food delicacy. [< L *tūber,* tuber, truffle.]

tru•ism (trōō′ĭz′əm) *n.* A statement of an obvious truth.

tru•ly (trōō′lē) *adv.* 1. Sincerely; genuinely. 2. Truthfully; accurately. 3. Indeed: *truly ugly.*

Tru•man (trōō′mən), **Harry S** Born 1884–1972. 33rd President of the U.S. (1945–53).

trump (trŭmp) *n.* 1. A suit the cards of which are declared as outranking all other cards for the duration of a hand. 2. A card of such a suit. —*v.* To play a trump card. —**trump up.** To devise fraudulently. [Var of TRIUMPH.]

trump•er•y (trŭm′pə-rē) *n., pl.* -ies. 1. Showy but worthless finery. 2. Nonsense. 3. Deception. [< OF *tromper,* to cheat.]

trum•pet (trŭm′pĭt) *n.* 1. A soprano brass wind instrument consisting of a long metal tube ending in a flared bell. 2. Something shaped or sounding like a trumpet. —*v.* 1. To play a trumpet. 2. To give forth a resounding call. [< OF *trompe.*]

trum•pet•er (trŭm′pĭt-ər) *n.* 1. A trumpet player. 2. One who announces something, as on a trumpet; herald.

trun•cate (trŭng′kāt′) *v.* -cated, -cating. To shorten by or as by cutting; lop. [< L *truncus,* torso, TRUNK.] —**trun′ca′tion** *n.*

trun•cheon (trŭn′chən) *n.* A short stick carried by policemen; billy. [< L *truncus,* torso, TRUNK.]

trun•dle (trŭnd′l) *v.* -dled, -dling. To push or propel on wheels or rollers. [< OE *trendel,* circle.] —**trun′dler** *n.*

trundle bed. A low bed on casters that can be rolled under another bed when not in use.

trunk (trŭngk) *n.* 1. The main woody stem of a tree. 2. The human body excluding the head and limbs; torso. 3. A main body, apart from tributaries or appendages. 4. A large packing case or box that clasps shut, used as luggage or for storage. 5. A covered compartment of an automobile, used for luggage and storage. 6. A proboscis, esp. the long, prehensile proboscis of an elephant. 7. **trunks.** Men's shorts worn for swimming or athletics. —*adj.* Of or designating the main body or line of a system. [< L *truncus.*]

trunk line. 1. A direct line between two telephone switchboards. 2. The main line of a communication or transportation system.

truss (trŭs) *n.* 1. A supportive device worn to prevent enlargement of a hernia or the return of a reduced hernia. 2. A wooden or metal framework used to support a roof, bridge, or similar structure. —*v.* 1. To tie up or bind. 2. To bind or skewer the wings or legs of (a fowl) before cooking. 3. To support or brace with a truss. [< OF *trousser,* to tie in a bundle.] —**truss′er** *n.*

trust (trŭst) *n.* 1. Firm reliance; confident belief; faith. 2. The person or thing in which confidence is placed. 3. Custody; care. 4. One committed into the care of another; charge. 5. The condition and resulting obligation of having confidence placed in one. 6. Reliance on something in the future; hope. 7. A legal title to property held by one party for the benefit of another. 8. A combination of firms for the purpose of reducing competition. —*v.*

Harry S Truman

---

1. To rely; depend; have confidence in. **2.** To be confident; hope. **3.** To expect with assurance; assume. **4.** To believe. **5.** To entrust. **6.** To grant discretion to confidently. **7.** To extend credit to. —*adj.* Maintained in trust. [Prob < ON *traust,* confidence, firmness.] —**trust′er** *n.*

trus•tee (trŭs′tē′) *n.* **1.** A person or agent holding legal title to property in order to administer it for a beneficiary. **2.** A member of a board that directs the funds and policy of an institution. —**trus•tee′ship′** *n.*

trust•ful (trŭst′fəl) *adj.* Full of trust. —**trust′-ful•ly** *adv.* —**trust′ful•ness** *n.*

trust•wor•thy (trŭst′wûr′thē) *adj.* Dependable; reliable. —**trust′wor′thi•ness** *n.*

trust•y (trŭs′tē) *adj.* **-ier, -iest.** Dependable; faithful. —*n., pl.* **-ies.** A trusted person, esp. a convict granted special privileges.

truth (trōoth) *n., pl.* **truths** (trōothz, trōoths). **1.** Conformity to knowledge, fact, actuality, or logic. **2.** Fidelity to an original or standard. **3.** Reality; actuality. **4.** A statement proven to be or accepted as true. **5.** Sincerity; integrity. [< OE *trēowth, trīewth.*]

truth•ful (trōoth′fəl) *adj.* **1.** Honest. **2.** Corresponding to reality. —**truth′ful•ly** *adv.* —**truth′-ful•ness** *n.*

try (trī) *v.* **tried, trying. 1.** To test in order to determine strength, effect, etc. **2. a.** To examine or hear (evidence or a case) by judicial process. **b.** To put (an accused person) on trial. **3.** To subject to great strain or hardship; tax. **4.** To melt (fat) to separate out impurities; render. **5.** To make an effort (to do something); attempt. **6.** To smooth, fit, or align accurately. —*n., pl.* **tries.** An attempt; effort. [ME *trien,* to separate, pick out, sift.]

Usage: Try and is common in speech for *try to,* esp. in such established combinations as *try and stop me* (defiance) and *try and get some rest* (exhortation). In most contexts, however, it is usually not interchangeable with *try to* unless the level is expressly informal.

try•ing (trī′ĭng) *adj.* Causing severe strain or distress. —**try′ing•ly** *adv.*

try•out (trī′out′) *n.* A test to ascertain the qualifications of applicants, as for a theatrical role.

tryst (trĭst) *n.* **1.** An agreement between lovers to meet. **2.** The meeting or meeting place so arranged. [Perh < Scand.]

tsa•de. Variant of sade.

tsar. Variant of czar.

tset•se fly (tsĕt′sē, tsēt′sē). A bloodsucking African fly that transmits microorganisms causing diseases such as sleeping sickness.

Tshi. Variant of Twi.

T-shirt (tē′shûrt′) *n.* A short-sleeved, collarless shirt worn by men.

tsp. teaspoon; teaspoonful.

tsu•na•mi (tsōo-nä′mē) *n.* A very large ocean wave caused by an underwater earthquake or volcanic eruption. [Jap.]

tub (tŭb) *n.* **1.** A round, open, flat-bottomed vessel used for packing, storing, or washing. **2.** A bathtub. [< MDu and MLG *tubbe.*]

tu•ba (t/y/ōo′bə) *n.* A large brass musical

wind instrument with a bass pitch and several valves. [< L, a trumpet.]

tub•by (tŭb′ē) *adj.* **-bier, -biest.** Short and fat.

tube (t/y/ōob) *n.* **1.** A hollow cylinder that conveys a fluid or functions as a passage. **2.** A flexible cylindrical container sealed at one end and having a screw cap at the other, for pigments, toothpaste, etc. **3.** An electron tube or vacuum tube. **4.** A subway. [< L *tubus.*]

tu•ber (t/y/ōo′bər) *n.* **1.** A swollen, usually underground stem, as a potato, bearing buds from which new plants sprout. **2.** A swelling; tubercle. [L *tūber,* a lump, swelling, tumor.] —**tu′ber•ous** *adj.*

tu•ber•cle (t/y/ōo′bər-kəl) *n.* **1.** A small, rounded prominence or process, such as a wartlike excrescence on the roots of some leguminous plants or a knoblike process in the skin or on a bone. **2.** The characteristic lesion of tuberculosis. [< L *tūber,* a lump, TUBER.]

tubercle bacillus. A rod-shaped bacterium that causes tuberculosis.

tu•ber•cu•lar (t/y/ōo-bûr′kyə-lər) *adj.* **1.** Of or covered with tubercles. **2.** Of or afflicted with tuberculosis.

tu•ber•cu•late (t/y/ōo-bûr′kyə-lĭt) *adj.* **1.** Having tubercles. **2.** Tubercular.

tu•ber•cu•lin (t/y/ōo-bûr′kyə-lĭn) *n.* A substance derived from tubercle bacilli, used in the diagnosis and treatment of tuberculosis.

tu•ber•cu•loid (t/y/ōo-bûr′kyə-loid′) *adj.* **1.** Resembling tuberculosis. **2.** Resembling a tubercle.

tu•ber•cu•lo•sis (t/y/ōo-bûr′kyə-lō′sĭs) *n.* **1.** A communicable disease of man and animals, caused by a microorganism and manifesting itself in bodily lesions, esp. of the lung. **2.** Tuberculosis of the lungs. —**tu•ber′cu•lous** *adj.*

tube•rose (t/y/ōob′rōz′, t/y/ōo′bə-rōz′, -rōs′) *n.* A tuber-bearing plant native to Mexico, cultivated for its fragrant white flowers. [< L *tūberōsus,* full of lumps.]

tu•bu•lar (t/y/ōo′byə-lər) *adj.* Having the form of a tube. —**tu′bu•lar•ly** *adv.*

tuck (tŭk) *v.* **1.** To make one or more folds in. **2.** To thrust or turn in the end or edge of (a shirt, blanket, etc.) in order to secure. **3.** To put in an out-of-the-way and snug place. **4.** To draw in; contract. —*n.* A flattened pleat or fold, esp. a very narrow one stitched in place. [< OE *tūcian,* to punish, torment.]

tuck•er (tŭk′ər) *v.* To weary; exhaust. [Freq of TUCK.]

Tuc•son (tōo′sŏn′). A city of S Arizona. Pop. 213,000.

-tude. *comb. form.* A condition or state of being: **exactitude.** [< L *-tūdō.*]

Tues•day (t/y/ōoz′dē, -dā′) *n.* The 3rd day of the week. [< OE *tīwesdæg,* "day of Tiu," Germanic god of war.]

tu•fa (t/y/ōo′fə) *n.* The calcareous and siliceous rock deposits of springs, lakes, or ground water. [< L *tōphus, tōfus.*] —**tu•fa′ceous** (-fā′shəs) *adj.*

tuft (tŭft) *n.* A cluster of yarn, hair, grass, etc., held or growing close together. [< OF *toffe.*]

tug (tŭg) *v.* **tugged, tugging. 1.** To pull at vigorously. **2.** To move by pulling with great effort or exertion. —*n.* **1.** A strong pull or pulling force. **2.** A tugboat. [< OE *tēon.* See **deuk-.**] —**tug'ger** *n.*

tug·boat (tŭg'bōt') *n.* A powerful small boat designed for towing larger vessels.

tug of war. A contest in which two teams tug on opposite ends of a rope, each trying to pull the other across a dividing line.

tu·i·tion (t/y/ōō-ĭsh'ən) *n.* **1.** A fee for instruction, esp. at a formal institution of learning. **2.** Instruction; teaching. [< L *tuitiō,* protection, a watching.]

tu·la·re·mi·a (t/y/ōō'lə-rē'mē-ə) *n.* An infectious disease transmitted from infected rodents to man and characterized by fever and swelling of the lymph nodes. [< *Tulare,* a county in California + -EMIA.]

tu·lip (t/y/ōō'lĭp) *n.* A bulb-bearing plant widely cultivated for its showy, variously colored flowers. [NL *Tulipa.*]

tulip tree. A tall tree with tuliplike green and orange flowers and soft yellowish, easily worked wood.

tulle (tōōl) *n.* A fine starched net of silk, rayon, or nylon, used for veils, gowns, etc. [< *Tulle,* city in central France.]

Tul·sa (tŭl'sə). A city of NE Oklahoma. Pop. 262,000.

tum·ble (tŭm'bəl) *v.* -bled, -bling. **1.** To perform acrobatic feats, such as somersaults. **2.** To fall or roll end over end. **3.** To spill or roll out in confusion or disorder. **4.** To pitch headlong; fall. **5.** To drop: *Prices tumbled.* **6.** To cause to fall; bring down. —*n.* **1.** An act of tumbling; a fall. **2.** A condition of confusion or disorder. [< OE *tumbian.*]

tum·ble-down (tŭm'bəl-doun') *adj.* Dilapidated; rickety.

tum·bler (tŭm'blər) *n.* **1.** An acrobat or gymnast. **2.** A drinking glass having no handle or stem. **3.** The part in a lock that releases the bolt when moved by a key.

tum·ble·weed (tŭm'bəl-wēd') *n.* A densely branched plant that when withered breaks off and is rolled about by the wind.

tum·bling (tŭm'blĭng) *n.* The skill or practice of gymnastic falling, rolling, or somersaulting.

tum·brel, tum·bril (tŭm'brəl) *n.* A two-wheeled cart, esp. one that can be tilted to dump a load. [< OF *tomberel,* a dumpcart.]

tu·mid (t/y/ōō'mĭd) *adj.* **1.** Swollen; distended. **2.** Overblown; bombastic. [< L *tumēre,* to swell.] —**tu·mid'i·ty** *n.*

tum·my (tŭm'ē) *n., pl.* -mies. *Informal.* The stomach. [Baby-talk var of STOMACH.]

tu·mor (t/y/ōō'mər) *n.* A circumscribed, non-inflammatory growth arising from existing tissue but growing independently and serving no physiological function. [< L *tumēre,* to swell.]

tu·mult (t/y/ōō'məlt) *n.* **1.** The din and commotion of a general crowd. **2.** Agitation of the mind or emotions. [< L *tumultus.*] —**tu·mul'tu·ous** (tə-mŭl'chōō-əs) *adj.*

tun (tŭn) *n.* A large cask. [< OE *tunne,* cask, vat < ML *tunna.*]

tu·na (t/y/ōō'nə) *n., pl.* -na or -nas. **1.** Any of various often large marine food fishes. **2.** Also **tuna fish.** The canned or commercially processed flesh of such a fish. [< L *thunnus,* tunny.]

tun·dra (tŭn'drə) *n.* A treeless area of arctic regions, having a permanently frozen subsoil and low-growing vegetation such as lichens, mosses, and stunted shrubs. [< Lapp *tundar.*]

tune (t/y/ōōn) *n.* **1.** A melody, esp. an easily remembered one. **2. a.** Correct musical pitch. **b.** The state of being properly in agreement or adjustment with respect to pitch. **3.** Concord or agreement; harmony: *in tune with the times.* **4.** *Electronics.* Adjustment of a receiver or circuit for maximum response to a given signal or frequency. —*v.* tuned, tuning. **1.** To put into tune. **2.** To adjust for maximum performance. **3.** To adjust a radio or television receiver to receive signals at a particular frequency. [< TONE.] —**tun'a·ble** *adj.*

tune·ful (t/y/ōōn'fəl) *adj.* Melodious; musical. —**tune'ful·ly** *adv.* —**tune'ful·ness** *n.*

tune·less (t/y/ōōn'lĭs) *adj.* Deficient in melody; unmusical. —**tune'less·ly** *adv.*

tun·er (t/y/ōō'nər) *n.* **1.** One that tunes: *a piano tuner.* **2.** An electronic device used to select signals at a specific radio frequency for amplification and conversion to sound.

tune-up (t/y/ōōn'ŭp') *n.* An adjustment of a motor or engine to put it in efficient working order.

tung·sten (tŭng'stən) *n. Symbol* **W** A hard, brittle, corrosion-resistant gray to white metallic element used in high-temperature structural materials and electrical elements, notably lamp filaments requiring thermally compatible glass-to-metal seals. Atomic number 74, atomic weight 183.85. [Swed, "heavy stone."]

Tun·gus (tōōng-gōōz') *n., pl.* -guses or -gus. **1.** A Mongoloid people inhabiting E Siberia. **2.** The Tungusic language of this people.

Tun·gus·ic (tōōng-gōō'zĭk) *n.* A subgroup of Altaic, including Tungus and Manchu, spoken in E Siberia and N Manchuria. —*adj.* Of or pertaining to the Tungus peoples or to Tungusic.

tu·nic (t/y/ōō'nĭk) *n.* **1.** A loose-fitting garment extending to the knees, worn by men and women esp. in ancient Greece and Rome. **2.** A long plain sleeved or sleeveless blouse worn over a skirt by women. [L *tunica,* a sheath, tunic.]

tuning fork. A small two-pronged instrument that when struck produces a sound of fixed pitch.

Tu·nis (t/y/ōō'nĭs). **1.** The capital of Tunisia. Pop. 714,000. **2.** A former kingdom on the N coast of Africa.

Tu·ni·sia (t/y/ōō-nē'zhə, -nĭzh'ə, -nĭsh'ə). A republic in N Africa. Pop. 4,030,000. Cap. Tunis. —**Tu·ni'sian** *adj. & n.*

tun·nel (tŭn'əl) *n.* An underground or underwater passage. —*v.* -neled or -nelled, -neling or -nelling. **1.** To make a tunnel under or through. **2.** To dig in the form of a tunnel. [< ML *tunna, tonna,* TUN.]

tun·ny (tŭn'ē) *n., pl.* -nies. *Chiefly Brit.* The tuna. [< Gk *thunnos.*]

Tu·pi (tōō'pē, tōō-pē') *n., pl.* -pi or -pis. **1.** A member of any of a group of peoples formerly living along the coast of Brazil and in the Amazon River valley. **2.** The language of these peoples.

Tu•pi•an (tōō′pē-ən, tōō-pē′ən) *adj.* Of or pertaining to the Tupi. —*n.* A major division of Tupi-Guarani that includes Tupi.

Tu•pi-Gua•ra•ni (tōō-pē′gwär′ən-ē′, tōō′pē′-) *n.* A family of languages, of which the chief divisions are Tupian and Guarani, spread throughout large areas of coastal Brazil and NE South America. —**Tu•pi′-Gua•ra•ni′, Tu•pi′-Gua′ra•ni′an** *adj.*

tur•ban (tûr′bən) *n.* A headdress of Moslem origin, consisting of a long scarf of linen, cotton, or silk wound around the head or a cap. [< Pers *dulband.*]

tur•bid (tûr′bĭd) *adj.* 1. Having sediment or foreign particles stirred up or suspended: *turbid water.* **2.** Heavy, dark, or dense, as smoke. **3.** In turmoil; muddled: *turbid feelings.* [< L *turba,* turmoil, uproar.]

tur•bine (tûr′bĭn, -bīn′) *n.* Any of various machines in which the kinetic energy of a moving fluid is converted to useful rotational power by the interaction of the fluid with a series of vanes arrayed about the circumference of a wheel or cylinder. [< L *turbō (turbin-),* a spinning thing, top, whirlwind.]

turbo–. *comb. form.* Turbine.

tur•bo•jet (tûr′bō-jĕt′) *n.* A jet engine having a turbine-driven compressor.

tur•bo•prop (tûr′bō-prŏp′) *n.* A turbojet engine used to drive an external propeller.

tur•bo•ram•jet (tûr′bō-răm′jĕt′) *n.* A turbojet engine that at high speeds compresses air taken in as a ramjet and increases exhaust velocities with an afterburner.

tur•bot (tûr′bət) *n., pl.* -bot or -bots. A European flatfish esteemed as food. [< OF.]

tur•bu•lent (tûr′byə-lənt) *adj.* 1. Violently agitated or disturbed; stormy: *turbulent waters.* **2.** Causing unrest or disturbance; unruly: *turbulent troops.* [< L *turba,* confusion.] —**tur′bu•lence** *n.* —**tur′bu•lent•ly** *adv.*

tu•reen (t/y/ōō-rēn′) *n.* A broad, deep dish

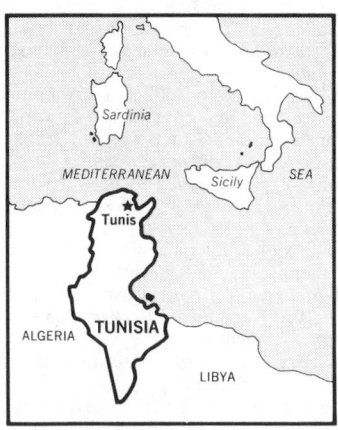

Tunisia

with a cover, used for serving soups, stews, etc. [< F *terrine,* "earthen vessel."]

turf (tûrf) *n.* 1. Surface earth containing a dense growth of grass and its matted roots. **2.** A piece cut from this. —**the turf. 1.** A racetrack. **2.** The sport or business of racing horses. [< OE.] —**turf′y** *adj.*

tur•gid (tûr′jĭd) *adj.* 1. Swollen; bloated. **2.** Overornate in style or language; grandiloquent. [L *turgēre,* to be swollen, to swell.]

Tu•rin (t/y/ōō′-rĭn). A city of NW Italy. Pop. 1,117,000.

Turk (tûrk) *n.* 1. A native or inhabitant of Turkey. **2.** A person speaking a Turkic language. **3.** A Moslem. **4.** Formerly, an Ottoman. **5.** A brutal or tyrannical person. **6.** Turkic.

Turk. Turkey; Turkish.

tur•key (tûr′kē) *n., pl.* -keys. 1. A large, widely domesticated North American bird with a bare wattled head and neck. **2.** The edible flesh of such a bird. —**talk turkey.** To discuss in a straightforward and direct manner.

Tur•key (tûr′kē). A republic mainly in Asia Minor and partly in SE Europe. Pop. 31,391,000. Cap. Ankara.

Turkey

Tur•kic (tûr′kĭk) *n.* A subdivision of Altaic including Turkish. —*adj.* 1. Of or pertaining to the Turks. **2.** Of or pertaining to Turkic.

Turk•ish (tûr′kĭsh) *adj.* 1. Of or relating to Turkey or the Turks. **2.** Of or relating to the Turkic language of Turkey. —*n.* The Turkic language of Turkey.

Turk•men Soviet Socialist Republic (tûrk′-mĕn, -mən). A republic of the Soviet Union in C Asia. Pop. 2,158,000. Cap. Ashkhabad.

tur•moil (tûr′moil) *n.* Utter confusion; extreme agitation. [?]

turn (tûrn) *v.* 1. To move around an axis or center; rotate; revolve. **2.** To shape (something) on a lathe. **3.** To give distinctive form to: *turn a phrase.* **4.** To change the position of so as to show another side of. **5.** To injure by twisting: *turn an ankle.* **6.** To upset; be or become nauseated. **7. a.** To change the direction or course of: *turn the car left.* **b.** To direct or change one's way or course. **8.** To make a course around or about: *turn the corner.* **9.** To set in a specified way or direction. **10.** To direct (the attention, interest, etc.) toward or away from something: *turn to music.* **11.** To antagonize or become antagonistic. **12.** To send, drive, or let go: *turn the* *dog loose.* **13.** To change; transform or become transformed. **14.** To become: *She turns twelve today.* **15.** To have recourse to a person or thing for help. **16.** To depend upon for success or failure; rely. **17.** To change color. **18.** To make or become sour; ferment. **—turn down. 1.** To diminish, as the volume of. **2.** To reject or refuse. **—turn in. 1.** To turn or go into. **2.** To hand in; give over. **3.** To go to bed. **—turn off. 1.** To stop the operation of. **2.** To leave a path or road at a point and enter another. **3.** *Slang.* To affect with dislike or displeasure. **—turn on. 1.** To cause to begin the operation of: *turn on the light.* **2.** *Slang.* **a.** To affect with great pleasure. **b.** To smoke or ingest a drug. **—turn tail.** To run away; flee. **—turn up. 1.** To increase, as the volume of. **2.** To find or be found. **3.** To arrive; appear. **—***n.* **1.** The act of turning or condition of being turned; a rotation; revolution. **2.** A change of direction: *a right turn.* **3.** A departure or deviation, as in a trend: *a turn of events.* **4.** A chance or opportunity to do something accorded individuals in scheduled order. **5.** Natural inclination: *a speculative turn of mind.* **6.** A deed or action: *did her a good turn.* **7.** A short excursion: *a turn in the park.* **8.** A single wind or convolution, as of wire upon a spool. **9.** A rendering or fashioning: *an interesting turn of phrase.* **10.** A momentary shock or scare. **—at every turn.** In every place; at every moment. **—in turn.** In the proper order or sequence. **—take turns.** To take part or do in order, one after another. **—to a turn.** Perfectly: *The roast was done to a turn.* [< L *tornāre,* to turn in a lathe, round off.]

turn•a•bout (tûrn'ə-bout') *n.* A shift or change in opinion or allegiance.

turn•coat (tûrn'kōt') *n.* One who traitorously switches allegiance.

turning point. A point at which a crucial decision must be made; decisive moment.

tur•nip (tûr'nĭp) *n.* **1.** A cultivated plant with a large, edible yellow or white root. **2.** The root of this plant. [Earlier *turnepe.*]

turn out. 1. To shut off, as a light. **2.** To arrive or assemble. **3.** To produce; make. **4.** To result; end up.

turn•out (tûrn'out') *n.* **1.** The act of turning out. **2.** The number of people at a gathering; attendance. **3.** An outfit.

turn over. 1. To bring the bottom to the top or vice versa. **2.** To think about; consider. **3.** To transfer to another.

turn•o•ver (tûrn'ō'vər) *n.* **1.** The act of turning over; an upset. **2.** An abrupt change; reversal. **3.** A small filled pastry with half the crust turned back over the other half. **4.** The number of times a particular stock of goods is sold and restocked during a given period. **5.** The amount of business transacted during a given period. **6.** The number of workers hired by an establishment to replace those who have left. **—***adj.* Capable of being folded over.

turn•pike (tûrn'pīk') *n.* A road, esp. a wide highway with tollgates. [ME *turnepike,* a revolving barrier used to block a road.]

turn•stile (tûrn'stīl') *n.* A device used to con-

trol passage from one area to another, typically consisting of revolving horizontal arms projecting from a central post.

turn•ta•ble (tûrn'tā'bəl) *n.* A circular rotating platform, used for turning locomotives, phonograph records, etc.

tur•pen•tine (tûr'pən-tīn') *n.* A thin, volatile oil, $C_{10}H_{16}$, obtained from the wood or exudate of certain pine trees and used as a paint thinner, solvent, and medicinally as a liniment. [< L *terebinthus.*]

tur•pi•tude (tûr'pə-t/y/ōōd') *n.* Baseness; depravity. [< L *turpis,* ugly, vile.]

tur•quoise (tûr'kwoiz', -koiz') *n.* **1.** A blue to blue-green mineral of aluminum and copper, esteemed as a gemstone. **2.** Light to brilliant bluish green. [< OF (*pierre*) *turqueise,* "Turkish (stone)."]

tur•ret (tûr'ĭt) *n.* **1.** A small tower-shaped projection on a building. **2.** A projecting armored structure, usually rotating horizontally, containing mounted guns and their gunners, as on a warship or tank. **3.** An attachment for a lathe, consisting of a rotating cylindrical block holding various cutting tools. [< OF *tour,* a TOWER.] **—tur'ret•ed** *adj.*

tur•tle[1] (tûrt'l) *n.* Any of various reptiles having beaklike jaws and the body enclosed in a bony or leathery shell. [Perh var of F *tortue,* tortoise.]

tur•tle[2] (tûrt'l) *n. Archaic.* A turtledove. [< L *turtur.*]

tur•tle•dove (tûrt'l-dŭv') *n.* An Old World dove with a soft, purring voice.

tusk (tŭsk) *n.* A long pointed tooth, as of an elephant or walrus, extending outside of the mouth. [< OE *tūx, tūsc.*]

tus•sle (tŭs'əl) *v.* **-sled, -sling.** To struggle; scuffle. [ME *tussillen.*] **—tus'sle** *n.*

tus•sock (tŭs'ək) *n.* A clump or tuft, as of grass.

tu•te•lage (t/y/ōō'tə-lĭj) *n.* **1.** The function or capacity of a guardian; guardianship. **2.** The act or capacity of a tutor; instruction. **3.** The state of being under a guardian or tutor. [< L *tūtor,* TUTOR.] **—tu'te•lar'y** (-lĕr'ē) *adj.*

tu•tor (t/y/ōō'tər) *n.* **1.** A private instructor. **2.** *Law.* The guardian of a minor and his property. **—***v.* To act as a tutor to. [< L *tūtor,* a guardian, tutor.] **—tu•to'ri•al** (-tôr'ē-əl, -tōr'-ē-əl) *adj.*

tut•ti-frut•ti (tōō'tē-frōō'tē) *n.* A confection, esp. ice cream, containing a variety of chopped candied fruits. [It, "all fruits."]

tux•e•do (tŭk-sē'dō) *n., pl.* **-dos.** A man's suit, usually black, designed to be worn for semiformal occasions. [< *Tuxedo* Park, New York.]

TV television.

TVA Tennessee Valley Authority.

twad•dle (twŏd'l) *n.* Foolish, trivial, or idle talk. [Prob < Scand.] **—twad'dle** *v.* (-dled, -dling). **—twad'dler** *n.*

twain (twān) *n. Poetic.* A set of two. [< OE *twēgen,* two. See dwō.]

twang (twăng) *v.* **1.** To emit or cause to emit a sharp, vibrating sound, as the string of a musical instrument when plucked. **2.** To utter

---

with a twang. —*n.* **1.** A sharp, vibrating sound, as that of a plucked string. **2.** An excessively nasal tone of voice. [Imit.] —**twang′y** *adj.*

tweak (twĕk) *v.* To pinch or twist sharply. [Prob < OE *twiccian* < Gmc **twik-.*] —**tweak** *n.* —**tweak′y** *adj.*

tweed (twĕd) *n.* **1.** A rough-textured woolen fabric made in any of various twill weaves. **2. tweeds.** Clothing made of this fabric. [< TWILL.] —**tweed′y** *adj.*

tweet (twĕt) *n.* A chirping sound, as of a small bird. [Imit.] —**tweet** *v.*

tweet·er (twē′tər) *n.* A loud-speaker designed to reproduce high-pitched sounds in a high-fidelity audio system.

tweez·ers (twē′zərz) *pl.n.* Any small, usually metal, pincerlike tool used for plucking or handling small objects. [Orig "a set or case of small instruments."]

twelfth (twĕlfth) *n.* **1.** The ordinal number 12 in a series. **2.** One of 12 equal parts. —**twelfth** *adj. & adv.*

twelve (twĕlv) *n.* The cardinal number written 12 or in Roman numerals XII. [< OE *twelf.* See **dwŏ.**] —**twelve** *adj. & pron.*

twelve·month (twĕlv′mŭnth′) *n.* A year.

twen·ti·eth (twĕn′tē-ĭth) *n.* **1.** The ordinal number 20 in a series. **2.** One of 20 equal parts. —**twen′ti·eth** *adj. & adv.*

twen·ty (twĕn′tē) *n.* The cardinal number written 20 or in Roman numerals XX. [< OE *twēntig.* See **dwŏ.**] —**twen′ty** *adj. & pron.*

Twi (chwē, chē). Also **Tshi.** A language spoken in W Africa.

twice (twīs) *adv.* **1.** In two cases or on two occasions; two times. **2.** In doubled degree or amount. [< OE *twige, twiga,* twice. See **dwŏ.**]

twid·dle (twĭd′l) *v.* **-dled, -dling. 1.** To turn over or around idly or lightly. **2.** To trifle with something. [Prob a blend of TWIRL and FID-DLE.] —**twid′dler** *n.*

twig (twĭg) *n.* A small slender branch. [< OE *twigge.* See **dwŏ.**] —**twig′gy** *adj.*

twi·light (twī′līt′) *n.* **1.** The time interval during which the sun is at a small angle below the horizon. **2.** The illumination of the atmosphere during this interval, esp. after a sunset. **3.** A period or condition of decline. [ME, "light between (night and day)," half-light.]

twill (twĭl) *n.* A fabric with parallel diagonal ribs. [< OE *twilic,* "two-threaded."] —**twilled** *adj.*

twin (twĭn) *n.* **1.** One of two offspring born at the same birth. **2.** One of two identical or similar things. **3. Twins.** The constellation and sign of the zodiac Gemini. —*adj.* **1.** Born at the same birth. **2.** Being one of two identical or similar things. **3.** Consisting of two identical or similar parts. [< OE *getwinn.* See **dwŏ.**]

twine (twīn) *v.* **twined, twining. 1.** To twist together; intertwine. **2.** To form by twisting. **3.** To encircle or coil about. **4.** To go in a winding course; twist about. —*n.* A strong string or cord formed of two or more threads twisted together. [< OE *twin,* a rope of two strands. See **dwŏ.**] —**twin′er** *n.*

twinge (twĭnj) *n.* A sharp and sudden physical,

mental, or emotional pain. [< OE *twengan.* See **twengh-.**]

twin·kle (twĭng′kəl) *v.* **-kled, -kling. 1.** To shine with slight, intermittent gleams; sparkle. **2.** To be bright or sparkling: *Her eyes twinkle.* —*n.* **1.** A slight, intermittent gleam of light. **2.** A sparkle of delight in the eye. **3.** A brief interval; a twinkling. [< OE **twincan,* to wink < Gmc **twink-.*] —**twin′kler** *n.*

twin·kling (twĭng′klĭng) *n.* A brief interval; an instant.

twirl (twûrl) *v.* To rotate or revolve briskly; spin. [Poss a blend of TRILL or TWIST and WHIRL.] —**twirl** *n.*

twist (twĭst) *v.* **1.** To entwine (two or more threads) so as to produce a single strand. **2.** To coil (vines, rope, etc.) about something. **3. a.** To impart a coiling or spiral shape to. **b.** To assume a spiral shape. **4. a.** To turn or open by turning. **b.** To break by turning: *twist off a dead branch.* **5.** To wrench or sprain: *twist one's wrist.* **6.** To distort the intended meaning of. **7.** To move in a winding course. **8.** To rotate or revolve. —*n.* **1.** Something twisted or formed by winding. **2.** The act of twisting or condition of being twisted; a spin or twirl. **3.** A spiral curve or turn. **4.** A sprain or wrench, as of a muscle. **5.** An unexpected change in a process or a departure from a pattern. [< OE *-twist,* a rope.] —**twist′a·ble** *adj.* —**twist′er** *n.*

twit (twĭt) *v.* **twitted, twitting.** To taunt or tease, esp. for embarrassing mistakes or faults. [< OE *æt,* AT + *witan,* to reproach, ascribe to (see **weid-**).]

twitch (twĭch) *v.* To move or cause to move jerkily or spasmodically. —*n.* **1.** A sudden involuntary muscular movement: *a twitch in the eye.* **2.** A sudden pulling; a jerk. [ME *twicchen.*]

twit·ter (twĭt′ər) *v.* To make tremulous chirping sounds. —*n.* A tremulous chirping sound. [ME *twiteren.*] —**twit′ter·y** *adj.*

two (tōō) *n.* The cardinal number written 2 or in Roman numerals II. —**in two.** So as to be in two separate units. [< OE *twā, tū.* See **dwŏ.**] —**two** *adj. & pron.*

two-faced (tōō′fāst′) *adj.* **1.** Having two faces or surfaces. **2.** Hypocritical or double-dealing; deceitful.

two-ply (tōō′plī′) *adj.* **1.** Made of two inter-woven layers. **2.** Consisting of two thicknesses or strands: *two-ply yarn.*

two·some (tōō′səm) *n.* Two people together; a pair or couple; a duo.

two-way (tōō′wā′) *adj.* **1.** Affording passage in two directions. **2.** Permitting communication in two directions, as a radio. **3.** Involving mutual action or responsibility.

–ty[1]. *comb. form.* A condition or quality: **reality.** [< L *-tās.*]

–ty[2]. *comb. form.* A multiple of ten: **sixty.** [< OE *-tig.*]

ty·coon (tī-kōōn′) *n.* A wealthy and powerful businessman or industrialist; magnate. [Jap *taikun,* a military title.]

tyke (tīk) *n.* A small child, esp. a mischievous one. [< ON *tík,* a bitch.]

ô paw, for/oi boy/ou out/ōō took/ōō coo/p pop/r run/s sauce/sh shy/t to/th thin/*th* the/ ŭ cut/ûr fur/v van/w wag/y yes/z size/zh vision/ə ago, item, edible, gallop, circus/

Ty·ler (tī'lər), **John.** 1790–1862. 10th President of the U.S. (1841–45).

John Tyler

tym·pa·ni. Variant of **timpani.**

tym·pan·ic membrane (tĭm-păn'ĭk). The thin, semitransparent, oval-shaped membrane separating the middle ear from the external ear.

tym·pa·num (tĭm'pə-nəm) *n., pl.* **-na** (-nə) or **-nums.** Also **tim·pa·num.** The eardrum or the middle part of the ear that the eardrum separates from the outer part. [< Gk *tumpanon,* a drum.]

tym·pa·ny (tĭm'pə-nē) *n.* Variant of **timpani.**

typ. typographer; typographical.

type (tīp) *n.* **1.** A group or category of persons or things sharing common traits or characteristics that distinguish them as an identifiable class. **2.** One belonging to such a group or category. **3.** An example or model; embodiment. **4. a.** A small block of metal bearing a raised character that when inked and pressed upon paper leaves a printed impression. **b.** Such pieces collectively. **5.** Printed or typewritten characters; print. —*v.* **typed, typing.** **1.** To typewrite. **2.** To classify according to a particular type. **3.** To represent or typify. [< Gk *tupos,* a blow, impression.]
Usage: Type (noun) is followed by *of* in constructions such as *that type of leather.* The variant form omitting *of, that type leather,* is not standard usage.

–type. *comb. form.* **1.** Type or representative form: **prototype.** **2.** Stamping or printing type or photographic process: **Linotype.**

type·face (tīp'fās') *n. Ptg.* The size and style of the characters on type.

type foundry. A factory where type metal is cast. —**type founder.**

type·set·ter (tīp'sĕt'ər) *n.* **1.** One who sets type; compositor. **2.** A machine used for setting type. —**type'set'ting** *n.*

type·write (tīp'rīt') *v.* To write (something) with a typewriter; type.

type·writ·er (tīp'rī'tər) *n.* A manually operated keyboard machine that prints characters by means of a set of metal hammers bearing raised, inked type that strike the paper.

ty·phoid (tī'foid') *n.* An acute, highly infectious disease caused by a bacillus transmitted by contaminated food or water and characterized by red rashes, high fever, bronchitis, and intestinal hemorrhaging.

ty·phoon (tī-fōōn') *n.* A severe tropical hurricane occurring in the western Pacific or the China Sea. [Cant *tai fung,* "great wind."]

ty·phus (tī'fəs) *n.* Any of several forms of an infectious disease caused by microorganisms and characterized generally by severe headache, sustained high fever, depression, delirium, and red rashes. [< Gk *tuphos,* (fever-causing) delusion.] —**ty'phous** (-fəs) *adj.*

typ·i·cal (tĭp'ĭ-kəl) *adj.* **1.** Exhibiting the traits or characteristics peculiar to a kind, group, or category. **2.** Pertaining to a representative specimen; characteristic. **3.** Constituting or serving as a type. [< Gk *tupikos,* impressionable < *tupos,* impression, TYPE.] —**typ'i·cal·ly** *adv.* —**typ'i·cal·ness** *n.*

typ·i·fy (tĭp'ə-fī') *v.* **-fied, -fying. 1.** To serve as a typical example of. **2.** To represent by an image, form, or model; symbolize. —**typ'i·fi·ca'tion** *n.* —**typ'i·fi'er** *n.*

typ·ist (tī'pĭst) *n.* One who operates a typewriter.

typo., typog. typographer; typographical; typography.

ty·pog·ra·pher (tī-pŏg'rə-fər) *n.* A printer or compositor.

typographical error. A mistake in printing, typing, or writing.

ty·pog·ra·phy (tī-pŏg'rə-fē) *n.* **1.** The composition of printed material from movable type. **2.** The arrangement and appearance of such matter. —**ty'po·graph'i·cal** (tī'pə-grăf'ĭ-kəl), **ty'po·graph'ic** *adj.*

ty·ran·ni·cal (tī-răn'ĭ-kəl, tī-) *adj.* Also **ty·ran·nic** (-răn'ĭk). Of, pertaining to, or characteristic of a tyrant; despotic. —**ty·ran'ni·cal·ly** *adv.* —**ty·ran'ni·cal·ness** *n.*

tyr·an·nize (tĭr'ə-nīz') *v.* **-nized, -nizing. 1.** To rule as a tyrant. **2.** To treat tyrannically. —**tyr'an·niz'er** *n.*

ty·ran·no·saur (tī-răn'ə-sôr', tī-) *n.* Also **ty·ran·no·saur·us** (tī-răn'ə-sôr'əs, tī-). A carnivorous dinosaur with small forelimbs and a large head. [< Gk *turannos,* TYRANT + -SAUR.]

tyr·an·nous (tĭr'ə-nəs) *adj.* Characterized by tyranny; despotic; cruel; tyrannical. —**tyr'an·nous·ly** *adv.*

tyr·an·ny (tĭr'ə-nē) *n., pl.* **-nies. 1.** A government in which a single ruler is vested with absolute power. **2.** Absolute power, esp. when exercised unjustly or cruelly. **3.** A tyrannical act.

ty·rant (tī'rənt) *n.* **1.** A ruler who exercises power in a harsh, cruel manner; an oppressor. **2.** Any tyrannical or despotic person. [< Gk *turannos.*]

tyre. *Brit.* Variant of **tire**[2].

Tyre (tīr). The capital of ancient Phoenicia.

ty·ro (tī'rō) *n., pl.* **-ros.** An inexperienced person; a beginner. [< L *tīrō,* a young soldier, recruit.]

tzar. Variant of **czar.**

ă pat/ā ate/âr care/ä bar/b bib/ch chew/d deed/ĕ pet/ē be/f fit/g gag/h hat/hw what/
ĭ pit/ī pie/îr pier/j judge/k kick/l lid, fatal/m mum/n no, sudden/ng sing/ŏ pot/ō go/

747

Uu

u, U (yōō) n. 1. The 21st letter of the English alphabet. 2. U Anything shaped like the letter U.
U uranium.
U. 1. university. 2. upper.
UAR United Arab Republic.
UAW United Automobile Workers.
u•biq•ui•tous (yōō-bĭk'wə-təs) adj. Being or seeming to be everywhere at the same time. [< L ubīque, everywhere.] —u•biq'ui•tous•ly adv. —u•biq'ui•ty n.
ud•der (ŭd'ər) n. The baglike mammary organ of cows, sheep, and goats. [< OE ūder. See eudh-.]
UFO unidentified flying object.
U•gan•da (yōō-găn'də, ōō-gän'dä). A country in east-central Africa. Pop. 7,190,000. Cap. Kampala.

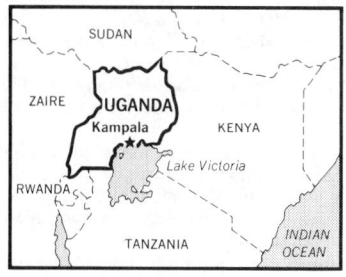

Uganda

ug•ly (ŭg'lē) adj. -lier, -liest. 1. Displeasing to the eye; unsightly. 2. Repulsive or offensive in any way; objectionable. [< ON uggr, fear.] —ug'li•ness n.
U•gric (/y/ōō'grĭk) n. A branch of Finno-Ugric, including Hungarian. —U'gric adj.
uhf ultrahigh frequency.
U.K. United Kingdom.
u•kase (yōō-kās', -kāz', yōō'kās', -kāz') n. 1. A decree of the czar in imperial Russia. 2. Any authoritative decree; an edict. [< Russ ukaz, decree.]
U•krain•i•an (yōō-krā'nē-ən) n. 1. An inhabitant or native of the Ukraine. 2. A Slavic language of the Ukraine, similar to but distinct from Russian. —U•krain'i•an adj.
Ukrainian Soviet Socialist Republic. Also U•kraine (yōō-krān', yōō-krīn', yōō'krān). A republic of the SW Soviet Union. Pop. 47,136,000. Cap. Kiev.
u•ku•le•le (/y/ōō'kə-lā'lē) n. A small four-stringed guitar popularized in Hawaii. [Hawaiian 'ukulele, "jumping little flea."]
U•lan Ba•tor (ōō'län bä'tôr). The capital of the Mongolian People's Republic. Pop. 250,000.
–ular. comb. form. A relationship or resemblance: tubular. [< L -ulus.]
ul•cer (ŭl'sər) n. An inflammatory lesion on the skin or an internal mucous surface of the body. [< L ulcus (ulcer-), a sore, ulcer.]
ul•cer•ate (ŭl'sə-rāt') v. -ated, -ating. To affect or become affected with or as with an ulcer. —ul'cer•a'tive (ŭl'sə-rā'tĭv, ŭl'sər-ə-tĭv), ul'cer• ous adj.
ul•na (ŭl'nə) n., pl. -nae (-nē') or -nas. The bone extending from the elbow to the wrist on the side opposite the thumb. [< L, elbow, arm.] —ul'nar adj.
ul•ster (ŭl'stər) n. A loose, long overcoat. [< Ulster, province of the Republic of Ireland.]
ult. 1. ultimate; ultimately. 2. ultimo.
ul•te•ri•or (ŭl'tîr'ē-ər) adj. 1. Lying beyond or outside the area of immediate interest. 2. Lying beyond what is evident or avowed: an ulterior motive. 3. Occurring later; subsequent. [L, farther.] —ul'te'ri•or•ly adv.
ul•ti•mate (ŭl'tə-mĭt) adj. 1. Final; conclusive. 2. Representing the furthest possible extent of analysis or division into parts: ultimate particle. 3. Fundamental; elemental. 4. Maximum. 5. Farthest; most remote. —n. 1. The basic or fundamental fact. 2. A conclusive result; conclusion. 3. The maximum. [< L ultimus, farthest, last.] —ul'ti•mate•ly adv.
ul•ti•ma•tum (ŭl'tə-mā'təm, -mä'təm) n., pl. -tums or -ta (-tə). A statement of terms that expresses or implies the threat of serious penalties if the terms are not accepted. [< L ultimātus, last.]
ul•ti•mo (ŭl'tə-mō') adv. In or of the month before the present one. [L ultimo (mense), in last (month).]
ul•tra (ŭl'trə) adj. Extreme. —n. An extremist.
ultra–. comb. form. 1. A surpassing of a specified limit or range. 2. An exceeding of what is common, moderate, or proper. [< L ultrā, beyond.]
ul•tra•con•ser•va•tive (ŭl'trə-kən-sûr'və-tĭv) adj. Extremely conservative; reactionary. —ul'tra•con•ser'va•tive n.
ul•tra•high frequency (ŭl'trə-hī'). A band of radio frequencies from 300 to 3,000 megacycles per second.
ul•tra•ma•rine (ŭl'trə-mə-rēn') n. 1. A blue pigment. 2. Vivid or strong blue to purplish blue. [ML ultrāmarīnus, "(coming from) beyond the sea."]

ô paw, for/oi boy/ou out/ōō took/ōō coo/p pop/r run/s sauce/sh shy/t to/th thin/th the/
ŭ cut/ûr fur/v van/w wag/y yes/z size/zh vision/ə ago, item, edible, gallop, circus/

ul·tra·mod·ern (ŭl'trə-mŏd'ərn) *adj.* Extremely modern in style.

ul·tra·son·ic (ŭl'trə-sŏn'ĭk) *adj.* Pertaining to acoustic frequencies above the range audible to the human ear, approx. above 20,000 cycles per second.

ul·tra·vi·o·let (ŭl'trə-vī'ə-lĭt) *adj.* Pertaining to the range of radiation wavelengths from just beyond the violet in the visible spectrum to the border of the x-ray region. —**ul'tra·vi'o·let** *n.*

ul·u·late (ŭl'yə-lāt', yōōl'-) *v.* -lated, -lating. To howl, hoot, wail, or lament loudly. [L *ululāre,* to howl.] —**ul'u·la'tion** *n.*

U·lys·ses. Latin name for **Odysseus.**

um·bel (ŭm'bəl) *n.* A flat-topped or rounded flower cluster in which the individual flower stalks arise from about the same point. [< L *umbella,* an umbrella.]

um·ber (ŭm'bər) *n.* **1.** A natural brown earth composed of iron oxide, silica, alumina, lime, and manganese oxides and used as pigment. **2.** Any of the shades of brown produced by umber in its various states. —*adj.* Having a brownish hue. [< OF *terre d'Umbre,* "earth of Umbria."]

um·bil·i·cal (ŭm'bĭl'ĭ-kəl) *adj.* **1.** Of or resembling an umbilicus. **2.** Pertaining to or located near the central area of the abdomen.

umbilical cord. The flexible, cordlike structure connecting the fetus at the navel with the placenta and containing two arteries and one vein that nourish the fetus and remove its wastes.

um·bil·i·cus (ŭm'bĭl'ĭ-kəs, ŭm'bə-lī'kəs) *n.* The navel. [L *umbilīcus.*]

um·bra (ŭm'brə) *n., pl.* -brae (-brē). **1.** A dark area; specifically, the blackest part of a shadow from which all light is cut off. **2.** The shadow region over an area of the earth where a solar eclipse is total. [L *umbra,* shadow.]

um·brage (ŭm'brĭj) *n.* **1.** Offense: *take umbrage.* **2.** *Archaic.* Shade or foliage. [< L *umbrāticus,* of a shadow.]

um·brel·la (ŭm'brĕl'ə) *n.* A device for protection from the weather consisting of a collapsible canopy mounted on a central rod. [< L *umbra,* shade.]

Um·bri·a (ŭm'brē-ə). A region of C Italy.

Um·bri·an (ŭm'brē-ən) *n.* **1.** An inhabitant or native of ancient or modern Umbria. **2.** The extinct Italic language of ancient Umbria. —**Um'bri·an** *adj.*

u·mi·ak (ōō'mē-ăk') *n.* Also **oo·mi·ak.** An open Eskimo boat made of skins stretched on a wooden frame.

um·laut (ōōm'lout') *n. Ling.* **1.** A change in a vowel sound caused by partial assimilation to a vowel or semivowel originally occurring in the following syllable. **2.** A vowel sound changed in this manner, such as the German *ä, ö,* or *ü.* **3.** The diacritical mark (¨) placed over a vowel to indicate an umlaut. [G.]

um·pire (ŭm'pīr') *n.* **1.** A person appointed to rule on plays in various sports. **2.** A person empowered to settle a dispute. **3.** A judge. [< ME *(a) noumpere,* (an) umpire.] —**um'pire'** *v.* (-pired, -piring).

ump·teen (ŭmp-tēn', ŭm-) *adj. Informal.* Large but indefinite in number. —**ump·teenth'** *adj.*

UMW United Mine Workers.

un–1. *comb. form.* Not or contrary to. [< OE *un-.* See **ne.**]

un–2. *comb. form.* **1.** Reversal of an action. **2.** Deprivation. **3.** Release or removal from. **4.** Intensified action. [< OE *ond-, and-,* against. See **anti.**]

UN United Nations.

un·a·ble (ŭn-ā'bəl) *adj.* **1.** Not able; incapable. **2.** Incompetent.

un·a·bridged (ŭn'ə-brĭjd') *adj.* Not condensed: *an unabridged edition.*

un·ac·com·pa·nied (ŭn'ə-kŭm'pə-nēd) *adj.* Not accompanied, esp. without instrumental accompaniment.

un·ac·count·a·ble (ŭn'ə-koun'tə-bəl) *adj.* **1.** Inexplicable; mysterious. **2.** Not responsible. —**un'ac·count'a·bly** *adv.*

un·ac·cus·tomed (ŭn'ə-kŭs'təmd) *adj.* **1.** Not used to. **2.** Unfamiliar or unusual.

un·a·dorned (ŭn'ə-dôrnd') *adj.* Without embellishment or artificiality; simple.

un·a·dul·ter·at·ed (ŭn'ə-dŭl'tə-rā'tĭd) *adj.* Not mixed or diluted; pure.

un·ad·vised (ŭn'əd-vīzd') *adj.* **1.** Having received no advice. **2.** Ill-advised; rash; imprudent. —**un'ad·vis'ed·ly** (-vī'zĭd-lē) *adv.*

un·af·fect·ed (ŭn'ə-fĕk'tĭd) *adj.* **1.** Not changed or affected. **2.** Natural; sincere; genuine. —**un'af·fect'ed·ly** *adv.*

un·al·ien·a·ble (ŭn-āl'yə-nə-bəl) *adj. Archaic.* Inalienable.

un-A·mer·i·can (ŭn'ə-měr'ĭ-kən) *adj.* Considered subversive to the institutions or interests of the U.S.

u·nan·i·mous (yōō-năn'ə-məs) *adj.* **1.** Sharing the same opinions or views. **2.** Based on complete assent or agreement. [L *ūnanimus,* "of one mind."] —**u'na·nim'i·ty** (-nə-nĭm'ə-tē) *n.* —**u·nan'i·mous·ly** *adv.*

un·armed (ŭn'ärmd') *adj.* Lacking weapons or armor.

un·as·sail·a·ble (ŭn'ə-sā'lə-bəl) *adj.* **1.** Undeniable; unquestionable. **2.** Impregnable. —**un'as·sail'a·bly** *adv.*

un·as·sum·ing (ŭn'ə-sōō'mĭng) *adj.* Not pretentious; modest. —**un'as·sum'ing·ly** *adv.*

un·at·tached (ŭn'ə-tăcht') *adj.* **1.** Not attached. **2.** Not engaged or married.

un·at·test·ed (ŭn'ə-tĕs'tĭd) *adj.* Not attested.

un·a·void·a·ble (ŭn'ə-voi'də-bəl) *adj.* Not able to be avoided; inevitable. —**un'a·void'a·bil'i·ty** *n.* —**un'a·void'a·bly** *adv.*

un·a·ware (ŭn'ə-wâr') *adj.* Not aware or cognizant.

un·a·wares (ŭn'ə-wârz') *adv.* **1.** By surprise; unexpectedly. **2.** Without forethought or plan.

un·bal·anced (ŭn'băl'ənst) *adj.* **1.** Not in proper balance. **2. a.** Mentally deranged. **b.** Not of sound judgment; irrational. **3.** Not adjusted so that debit and credit correspond.

un·bar (ŭn'bär') *v.* -barred, -barring. To open.

un·bear·a·ble (ŭn'bâr'ə-bəl) *adj.* Unendurable; intolerable. —**un'bear'a·bly** *adv.*

un·beat·a·ble (ŭn'bē'tə-bəl) *adj.* Impossible to surpass or defeat. —**un'beat'a·bly** *adv.*

---

un•beat•en (ŭn'bēt'n) *adj.* **1.** Undefeated. **2.** Not traversed; untrod. **3.** Not beaten or pounded.

un•be•com•ing (ŭn'bĭ-kŭm'ĭng) *adj.* **1.** Not appropriate or attractive. **2.** Not seemly; indecorous. —**un'be•com'ing•ly** *adv.*

un•be•known (ŭn'bĭ-nŏn') *adj.* Occurring or existing without the knowledge of; unknown.

un•be•lief (ŭn'bĭ-lēf') *n.* Lack of religious belief. —**un'be•liev'er** *n.*

un•be•liev•a•ble (ŭn'bĭ-lē'və-bəl) *adj.* Not to be believed; incredible. —**un'be•liev'a•bly** *adv.*

un•bend (ŭn'bĕnd') *v.* **1.** To release from tension. **2.** *Naut.* To untie or loosen. **3.** To make or become less tense.

un•bend•ing (ŭn'bĕn'dĭng) *adj.* Resolute; uncompromising.

un•bi•ased (ŭn'bī'əst) *adj.* Without bias; impartial. —**un'bi'ased•ly** *adv.*

un•bid•den (ŭn'bĭd'n) *adj.* Not invited.

un•bind (ŭn'bīnd') *v.* **1.** To untie or unfasten. **2.** To release.

un•blessed (ŭn'blĕst') *adj.* **1.** Not blessed. **2.** Unholy; evil.

un•blush•ing (ŭn'blŭsh'ĭng) *adj.* **1.** Without shame or remorse. **2.** Not blushing.

un•bolt (ŭn'bōlt') *v.* To release the bolts of (a door or gate); unlock.

un•born (ŭn'bôrn') *adj.* Not yet born.

un•bos•om (ŭn'bo͝oz'əm, -bo͞o'zəm) *v.* **1.** To confide or disclose. **2.** To reveal one's thoughts or feelings.

un•bound•ed (ŭn'boun'dĭd) *adj.* Having no limits. —**un'bound'ed•ly** *adv.*

un•bowed (ŭn'boud') *adj.* **1.** Not bowed. **2.** Not subdued.

un•bri•dled (ŭn'brī'dəld) *adj.* **1.** Not fitted with a bridle. **2.** Unrestrained; uncontrolled. —**un'bri'dled•ly** *adv.*

un•bro•ken (ŭn'brō'kən) *adj.* **1.** Not broken; intact. **2.** Not violated or breached. **3.** Uninterrupted; continuous. **4.** Not tamed or broken to harness.

un•buck•le (ŭn'bŭk'əl) *v.* To loosen or undo the buckle of.

un•bur•den (ŭn'bûrd'n) *v.* To free or relieve, as from a burden: *unburden one's mind.*

un•but•ton (ŭn'bŭt'n) *v.* To unfasten the buttons of.

un•can•ny (ŭn'kăn'ē) *adj.* **-nier, -niest.** **1.** Inexplicable; strange. **2.** So keen as to seem preternatural: *uncanny insight.* —**un'can'ni•ly** *adv.*

Note: Many compounds are formed with *un-*. Normally *un-* combines with a second element without an intervening hyphen. However, if the second element begins with a capital letter, it is separated with a hyphen: *un-American.*

un'ac•cept'a•ble *adj.*
un'ac•quaint'ed *adj.*
un'a•fraid' *adj.*
un'aid'ed *adj.*
un'an•nounced' *adj.*
un'a•shamed' *adj.*
un'au'thor•ized' *adj.*
un'bap'tized *adj.*
un'bleached' *adj.*
un'break'a•ble *adj.*
un'called'-for *adj.*
un'cared'-for *adj.*
un'chal'lenged *adj.*
un'checked' *adj.*
un'claimed' *adj.*
un'clear' *adj.*
un'clut'tered *adj.*
un'con•test'ed *adj.*
un'con•vinced' *adj.*
un'cov'ered *adj.*
un'dam'aged *adj.*
un'damped' *adj.*
un'de•fined' *adj.*
un'de•vel'oped *adj.*
un'dig'ni•fied' *adj.*
un'ed'u•cat'ed *adj.*
un'e•mo'tion•al *adj.*
un'end'ing *adj.*
un'fal'ter•ing *adj.*
un'fath'omed *adj.*
un'fin'ished *adj.*

un'flag'ging *adj.*
un'fore•seen' *adj.*
un'for•giv'a•ble *adj.*
un'grace'ful *adj.*
un'ham'pered *adj.*
un'harmed' *adj.*
un'heat'ed *adj.*
un'i•den'ti•fied' *adj.*
un'im•por'tant *adj.*
un'in•sured' *adj.*
un'in•vit'ed *adj.*
un'la'beled *adj.*
un'leav'ened *adj.*
un'li'censed *adj.*
un'list'ed *adj.*
un'loved' *adj.*
un'marked' *adj.*
un'mar'ried *adj.*
un'mer'it•ed *adj.*
un'named' *adj.*
un'no'ticed *adj.*
un'num'bered *adj.*
un'ob•struct'ed *adj.*
un'o'pened *adj.*
un'par'don•a•ble *adj.*
un'pa'tri•ot'ic *adj.*
un'pol'ished *adj.*
un'polled' *adj.*
un'pol•lut'ed *adj.*
un'prej'u•diced *adj.*
un'pressed' *adj.*

un'proc'essed *adj.*
un'pro•tect'ed *adj.*
un'prov'en *adj.*
un'pro•voked' *adj.*
un'pub'lished *adj.*
un'ques'tion•ing *adj.*
un'rea'son•ing *adj.*
un're•cord'ed *adj.*
un'reg'is•tered *adj.*
un're•port'ed *adj.*
un're•quit'ed *adj.*
un'ro•man'tic *adj.*
un'salt'ed *adj.*
un'san'i•tar'y *adj.*
un'sat'u•rat'ed *adj.*
un'sched'uled *adj.*
un'sea'soned *adj.*
un'shaved' *adj.*
un'signed' *adj.*
un'sink'a•ble *adj.*
un'so•lic'it•ed *adj.*
un'spoiled' *adj.*
un'suit'ed *adj.*
un'sure' *adj.*
un'sus•pect'ing *adj.*
un'tal'ent•ed *adj.*
un'trained' *adj.*
un'tried' *adj.*
un'var'y•ing *adj.*
un'want'ed *adj.*
un'wed' *adj.*
un'wel'come *adj.*
un'yield'ing *adj.*

---

un•cap (ŭn′kăp′) *v.* To remove the cap or covering of.

un•ceas•ing (ŭn′sē′sĭng) *adj.* Continuous. —**un′ceas′ing•ly** *adv.*

un•cer•e•mo•ni•ous (ŭn′sĕr′ə-mō′nē-əs) *adj.* Without the due formalities; abrupt. —**un′cer′e•mo′ni•ous•ly** *adv.*

un•cer•tain (ŭn′sûrt′n) *adj.* 1. Not known or established. 2. Vague; undecided. 3. Subject to change; variable. 4. Unsteady; fitful. 5. Not sure. —**un′cer′tain•ly** *adv.*

un•cer•tain•ty (ŭn′sûrt′n-tē) *n., pl.* -ties. 1. Lack of certainty. 2. Something that is uncertain.

un•chain (ŭn′chān′) *v.* To set free.

un•char•i•ta•ble (ŭn′chăr′ə-tə-bəl) *adj.* Not generous; unkind. —**un′char′i•ta•ble•ness** *n.* —**un′char′i•ta•bly** *adv.*

un•chaste (ŭn′chāst′) *adj.* Not chaste or modest. —**un′chaste′ly** *adv.*

un•chris•tian (ŭn′krĭs′chən) *adj.* 1. Not Christian. 2. Not in accordance with the Christian spirit.

un•cial (ŭn′shəl, -shē-əl) *adj.* Of or pertaining to a script with rounded capital letters found in Greek and Latin manuscripts of the 4th to the 8th centuries A.D. [LL *unciāles (litterae),* "(letters) of an inch long."] —**un′cial** *n.*

un•cir•cum•cised (ŭn′sûr′kəm-sīzd′) *adj.* 1. Not circumcised. 2. Not Jewish; Gentile.

un•civ•il (ŭn′sĭv′əl) *adj.* 1. Impolite; rude. 2. Uncivilized; barbarous. —**un′civ′il•ly** *adv.*

un•civ•i•lized (ŭn′sĭv′ə-līzd′) *adj.* Not civilized.

un•clad (ŭn′klăd′) *adj.* Naked.

un•clasp (ŭn′klăsp′, -kläsp′) *v.* 1. To release or loosen the clasp of. 2. To release from a clasp or embrace.

un•cle (ŭng′kəl) *n.* 1. The brother of one's mother or father. 2. The husband of one's aunt. —*interj. Slang.* Expressive of surrender: *They beat him until he cried uncle.* [< L *avunculus,* maternal uncle.]

un•clean (ŭn′klēn′) *adj.* 1. Foul or dirty. 2. Morally defiled. 3. Ceremonially impure. —**un′clean′ly** (ŭn′klēn′lē) *adv.*

un•clean•ly (ŭn′klĕn′lē) *adj.* -lier, -liest. Unclean. —**un′clean′li•ness** (ŭn′klĕn′lē-nĭs) *n.*

un•clench (ŭn′klĕnch′) *v.* To loosen from a clenched position; relax.

Uncle Sam. A personification of the U.S. Government, represented as a tall, thin man with a white beard, dressed in red, white, and blue. [< *U.S.* (for United States).]

un•close (ŭn′klōz′) *v.* To open.

un•clothe (ŭn′klōth′) *v.* To remove the clothing or cover from.

un•coil (ŭn′koil′) *v.* To unwind.

un•com•fort•a•ble (ŭn′kŭmf′tə-bəl, -kŭm′fər-tə-bəl) *adj.* 1. Experiencing discomfort; uneasy. 2. Causing discomfort. —**un′com′fort•a•ble•ness** *n.* —**un′com′fort•a•bly** *adv.*

un•com•mit•ted (ŭn′kə-mĭt′ĭd) *adj.* Not pledged to a specific cause or course of action.

un•com•mon (ŭn′kŏm′ən) *adj.* 1. Not common; unusual; rare. 2. Wonderful; remarkable. —**un′com′mon•ly** *adv.*

un•com•mu•ni•ca•tive (ŭn′kə-myōō′nĭ-kā′tĭv,

-nĭ-kə-tĭv) *adj.* Not disposed to be communicative; reserved.

un•com•pro•mis•ing (ŭn′kŏm′prə-mī′zĭng) *adj.* Not granting concessions; inflexible.

un•con•cern (ŭn′kən-sûrn′) *n.* 1. Lack of interest; indifference. 2. Lack of worry or apprehensiveness.

un•con•cerned (ŭn′kən-sûrnd′) *adj.* 1. Not interested; indifferent. 2. Not anxious or apprehensive; unworried. —**un′con•cern′ed•ly** (-kən-sûr′nĭd-lē) *adv.*

un•con•di•tion•al (ŭn′kən-dĭsh′ən-əl) *adj.* Without conditions or limitations; absolute. —**un′con•di′tion•al•ly** *adv.*

un•con•di•tioned (ŭn′kən-dĭsh′ənd) *adj.* 1. Unconditional; unrestricted. 2. Not the result of conditioning.

un•con•quer•a•ble (ŭn′kŏng′kər-ə-bəl) *adj.* Incapable of being overcome or defeated.

un•con•scion•a•ble (ŭn′kŏn′shən-ə-bəl) *adj.* 1. Not governed or restrained by conscience. 2. Unreasonable; immoderate; excessive. —**un′con′scion•a•bly** *adv.*

un•con•scious (ŭn′kŏn′shəs) *adj.* 1. Without conscious awareness, esp. psychological rather than physiological, and unavailable for direct conscious scrutiny. 2. Temporarily lacking consciousness. 3. Without conscious control; involuntary. —*n.* The division of the psyche not subject to direct conscious observation but inferred from its effects on conscious processes and behavior. —**un′con′scious•ly** *adv.* —**un′con′scious•ness** *n.*

un•con•sti•tu•tion•al (ŭn′kŏn-stə-t/y/ōō′shən-əl) *adj.* Not in accord with the principles set forth in the constitution of a country. —**un′con•sti•tu′tion•al′i•ty** *n.* —**un′con•sti•tu′tion•al•ly** *adv.*

un•con•trol•la•ble (ŭn′kən-trō′lə-bəl) *adj.* Not able to be controlled or governed. —**un′con•trol′la•bly** *adv.*

un•con•ven•tion•al (ŭn′kən-vĕn′shən-əl) *adj.* Not adhering to convention. —**un′con•ven′tion•al′i•ty** *n.* —**un′con•ven′tion•al•ly** *adv.*

un•cork (ŭn′kôrk′) *v.* 1. To draw the cork from. 2. To free from a constrained state.

un•count•ed (ŭn′koun′tĭd) *adj.* Unable to be counted; innumerable.

un•coup•le (ŭn′kŭp′əl) *v.* To disconnect: *uncouple railroad cars.*

un•couth (ŭn′kōōth′) *adj.* 1. Crude or unrefined. 2. Awkward or ungraceful. [< OE *un-,* not + *cūth,* known (see gnō-).]

un•cov•er (ŭn′kŭv′ər) *v.* 1. To remove the cover from. 2. To disclose; reveal. 3. To bare (the head) in respect or reverence.

un•cross (ŭn′krôs′, -krŏs′) *v.* To move (one's legs) from a crossed position.

unc•tion (ŭngk′shən) *n.* 1. The act of anointing as part of a ceremonial or healing ritual. 2. An ointment or oil; salve. 3. Something that serves to soothe or restore; balm. 4. Affected or exaggerated earnestness. [< L *unguere,* to anoint.]

unc•tu•ous (ŭngk′chōō-əs) *adj.* 1. Greasy. 2. Containing or composed of oil or fat. 3. Characterized by affected or insincere earnestness: *unctuous flattery.* [< L *unctum,* ointment.]

ă pat/ā ate/âr care/ä bar/b bib/ch chew/d deed/ĕ pet/ē be/f fit/g gag/h hat/hw what/ ĭ pit/ī pie/îr pier/j judge/k kick/l lid, fatal/m mum/n no, sudden/ng sing/ŏ pot/ō go/

—**unc′tu•ous•ly** *adv.* —**unc′tu•ous•ness, unc′tu•os′l•ty** (-ŏs′ə-tē) *n.*

un•cut (ŭn′kŭt′) *adj.* **1.** Not cut. **2.** *Bookbinding.* Having the page edge not slit or trimmed. **3.** Not ground to a specific shape: *uncut diamonds.* **4.** Unabridged.

un•daunt•ed (ŭn′dôn′tĭd, -dän′tĭd) *adj.* Not discouraged or disheartened; resolute; fearless. —**un′daunt′ed•ly** *adv.*

un•de•cld•ed (ŭn′dĭ-sī′dĭd) *adj.* **1.** Not yet determined or settled; open. **2.** Not having reached a decision; uncommitted.

un•de•mon•stra•tive (ŭn′dĭ-mŏn′strə-tĭv) *adj.* Not disposed to expressions of feeling; reserved. —**un′de•mon′stra•tive•ness** *n.*

un•de•ni•a•ble (ŭn′dĭ-nī′ə-bəl) *adj.* **1.** Not able to be denied; irrefutable. **2.** Unquestionably good; excellent. —**un′de•ni′a•bly** *adv.*

un•der (ŭn′dər) *prep.* **1.** In a lower position or place than. **2.** Beneath the surface of. **3.** Beneath the guise of: *under a false name.* **4.** Less than; smaller than. **5.** Less than the required amount or degree of: *under voting age.* **6.** Inferior to. **7.** Subject to the authority of. **8.** Undergoing or receiving the effects of: *under intensive care.* **9.** Subject to the obligation of: *under contract.* **10.** Within the group or classification of: *listed under biology.* **11.** In the process of: *under discussion.* **12.** Because of: *under these conditions.* —*adv.* **1.** In or into a place below or beneath. **2.** In or into a subordinate or inferior condition or position. **3.** So as to be covered or enveloped by. **4.** So as to be less than the required amount or degree. —*adj.* **1.** Located or moving on a lower level. **2.** Lower in rank. **3.** Substandard. **4.** Lower in strength or intensity; held in restraint or check. [< OE. See ṇdher-.]

under-. *comb. form.* **1.** Location below or under. **2.** Inferiority in rank or importance. **3.** Degree, rate, or quantity that is lower or less than normal or proper. **4.** Secrecy or treachery.

un•der•a•chieve (ŭn′dər-ə-chēv′) *v.* To perform below the expected level, as indicated by tests of intelligence, aptitude, or ability, esp. in school. —**un′der•a•chiev′er** *n.*

un•der•act (ŭn′dər-ăkt′) *v.* To perform (a role) weakly or in an understated way.

un•der•age (ŭn′dər-āj′) *adj.* Below the customary, required, or legal age.

un•der•arm¹ (ŭn′dər-ärm′) *adj.* Located, placed, or used under the arm. —*n.* The armpit.

un•der•arm² (ŭn′dər-ärm′) *adj.* Executed with the hand kept below the level of the shoulder; underhand: *an underarm pitch.*

un•der•bid (ŭn′dər-bĭd′) *v.* **1.** To bid lower than (a competitor). **2.** *Bridge.* To bid less than the full value of (one's hand).

un•der•brush (ŭn′dər-brŭsh′) *n.* Small trees, shrubs, etc., growing beneath taller trees.

un•der•car•riage (ŭn′dər-kăr′ĭj) *n.* **1.** A supporting framework, as for the body of an automobile. **2.** The landing gear of an aircraft.

un•der•charge (ŭn′dər-chärj′) *v.* **1.** To charge less than is customary or required. **2.** To load (a firearm) with an insufficient charge. —*n.*

(ŭn′dər-chärj′). An insufficient or improper charge.

un•der•class•man (ŭn′dər-klăs′mən, -kläs′-mən) *n.* A student in the freshman or sophomore class at a secondary school or college.

un•der•clothes (ŭn′dər-klōz′, -klōᵗʰz′) *pl.n.* Also **un•der•cloth•ing** (-klō′thĭng). Underwear.

un•der•coat (ŭn′dər-kōt′) *n.* **1.** A coat worn beneath another. **2.** Short hairs or fur concealed by the longer outer hairs of an animal's coat. **3.** A coat of sealing material applied to a surface before the top coat is applied.

un•der•cov•er (ŭn′dər-kŭv′ər) *adj.* Performed or occurring in secret.

un•der•cur•rent (ŭn′dər-kûr′ənt) *n.* **1.** A current, as of air or water, below another current or surface. **2.** An underlying tendency or force, often contrary to what is superficially evident.

un•der•cut (ŭn′dər-kŭt′) *v.* **1.** To make a cut under or below. **2.** To sell at a lower price or work for lower wages than (a competitor). **3.** *Sports.* **a.** To impart backspin to (a ball) by striking downward as well as forward, as in golf. **b.** To cut or slice (a ball) with an underarm stroke, as in tennis. —**un′der•cut′** *n.*

un•der•de•vel•oped (ŭn′dər-dĭ-vĕl′əpt) *adj.* **1.** Not adequately or normally developed; immature. **2.** Economically backward; having a potential but not yet self-sufficient.

un•der•dog (ŭn′dər-dôg′, -dŏg′) *n.* **1.** One who is expected to lose a contest or struggle. **2.** One who is at a disadvantage.

un•der•done (ŭn′dər-dŭn′) *adj.* Insufficiently cooked.

un•der•draw•ers (ŭn′dər-drôrz′) *pl.n.* Shorts worn as undergarments; underpants.

un•der•es•ti•mate (ŭn′dər-ĕs′tə-māt′) *v.* To estimate too low the quantity, degree, or worth of. —**un′der•es′ti•ma′tion** *n.*

un•der•ex•pose (ŭn′dər-ĭk-spōz′) *v.* To expose (film) to light for too short a time. —**un′der•ex•po′sure** (-spō′zhər) *n.*

un•der•feed (ŭn′dər-fēd′) *v.* To feed insufficiently.

un•der•foot (ŭn′dər-fŏŏt′) *adv.* **1.** Below or under the foot or feet; directly below. **2.** In the way.

un•der•gar•ment (ŭn′dər-gär′mənt) *n.* A garment worn under outer garments.

un•der•gird (ŭn′dər-gûrd′) *v.* To gird or support from beneath.

un•der•go (ŭn′dər-gō′) *v.* **1.** To experience; be subjected to. **2.** To endure; suffer.

un•der•grad•u•ate (ŭn′dər-grăj′ŏŏ-ĭt) *n.* A college or university student who has not yet received a degree.

un•der•ground (ŭn′dər-ground′) *adj.* **1.** Below the surface of the earth. **2.** Hidden; clandestine. —*n.* (ŭn′dər-ground′). **1.** A clandestine subversive organization. **2.** *Brit.* A subway system. —*adv.* (ŭn′dər-ground′). **1.** Below the surface of the earth. **2.** In secret; stealthily; furtively.

un•der•growth (ŭn′dər-grōth′) *n.* Low-growing plants, shrubs, etc., beneath trees in a forest.

un•der•hand (ŭn′dər-hănd′) *adj.* **1.** Deceitful;

sneaky; base. **2.** Underarm. —*adv.* **1.** With an underhand movement. **2.** Slyly; secretly.

un·der·hand·ed (ŭn′dər-hăn′dĭd) *adj.* Underhand. —**un′der·hand′ed·ly** *adv.* —**un′der·hand′-ed·ness** *n.*

un·der·lie (ŭn′dər-lī′) *v.* **1.** To be located under or below. **2.** To be the support or basis of; account for.

un·der·line (ŭn′dər-līn′, ŭn′dər-līn′) *v.* **1.** To draw a line under; underscore. **2.** To emphasize. —**un′der·line′** *n.*

un·der·ling (ŭn′dər-lĭng) *n.* A subordinate; lackey.

un·der·ly·ing (ŭn′dər-lī′ĭng) *adj.* **1.** Lying under or beneath something. **2.** Basic; fundamental. **3.** Implicit; hidden.

un·der·mine (ŭn′dər-mīn′) *v.* **1.** To dig a mine or tunnel beneath. **2.** To weaken by wearing away; subvert.

un·der·most (ŭn′dər-mōst′) *adj.* Lowest in position, rank, or place. —*adv.* Lowest.

un·der·neath (ŭn′dər-nēth′) *adv.* **1.** In a place beneath; below. **2.** On the lower face or underside. —*prep.* **1.** Under; below; beneath. **2.** Under the power or control of. —*adj.* Lower; under. —*n.* The part or side below or under. [< UNDER + OE *neothan*, below (see **ni**).]

un·der·nour·ish (ŭn′dər-nûr′ĭsh) *v.* To provide with insufficient nourishment. —**un′der·nour′ish·ment** *n.*

un·der·pants (ŭn′dər-pănts′) *pl.n.* An undergarment worn over the loins; drawers; shorts.

un·der·pass (ŭn′dər-păs′, -päs′) *n.* A section of road that passes under another road or a railroad.

un·der·pay (ŭn′dər-pā′) *v.* To pay insufficiently.

un·der·play (ŭn′dər-plā′, ŭn′dər-plā′) *v.* To act (a role) subtly or with restraint.

un·der·priv·i·leged (ŭn′dər-prĭv′ə-lĭjd) *adj.* Socially or economically deprived.

un·der·pro·duc·tion (ŭn′dər-prə-dŭk′shən) *n.* **1.** Production below full capacity. **2.** Production below demand.

un·der·rate (ŭn′dər-rāt′) *v.* To rate too low; underestimate.

un·der·score (ŭn′dər-skôr′, -skōr′) *v.* **1.** To underline. **2.** To emphasize or stress. —**un′der·score′** *n.*

un·der·sea (ŭn′dər-sē′) *adj.* Pertaining to, existing, or created for use beneath the surface of the sea.

un·der·sec·re·tar·y (ŭn′dər-sĕk′rə-tĕr′ē) *n.* An official directly subordinate to a Cabinet member.

un·der·sell (ŭn′dər-sĕl′) *v.* To sell for a lower price than.

un·der·shirt (ŭn′dər-shûrt′) *n.* An undergarment worn next to the skin under a shirt.

un·der·shot (ŭn′dər-shŏt′) *adj.* **1.** Driven by water passing from below, as a water wheel. **2.** Projecting from below.

un·der·side (ŭn′dər-sīd′) *n.* The side or surface that is underneath; bottom side.

un·der·signed (ŭn′dər-sīnd′) *n.* The person or persons who have signed at the bottom of a document.

un·der·sized (ŭn′dər-sīzd′) *adj.* Also **un·der·size** (-sīz′). Being of subnormal or insufficient size.

un·der·slung (ŭn′dər-slŭng′) *adj.* Having springs attached to the axles from below, as a vehicle.

un·der·staffed (ŭn′dər-stăft′) *adj.* Having too small a staff.

un·der·stand (ŭn′dər-stănd′) *v.* -stood, -standing. **1.** To perceive and comprehend the nature and significance of; know. **2.** To know thoroughly. **3.** To grasp or comprehend. **4.** To be tolerant or sympathetic toward. **5.** To learn indirectly, as by hearsay; gather. **6.** To conclude; infer. **7.** To accept as an agreed fact: *It is understood that the fee is five dollars.* [< OE *understandan*. See **stā-**.] —**un′der·stand′a·ble** *adj.* —**un′der·stand′a·bly** *adv.*

un·der·stand·ing (ŭn′dər-stăn′dĭng) *n.* **1.** The quality of comprehension; discernment. **2.** The faculty by which one understands; intelligence. **3.** Individual or specified judgment or opinion; interpretation. **4. a.** A compact implicit between two or more persons or groups. **b.** The matter implicit in such a compact. **5.** A reconciliation of differences. —*adj.* **1.** Characterized by comprehension or good sense. **2.** Compassionate and sympathetic.

un·der·state (ŭn′dər-stāt′) *v.* **1.** To state with less completeness or truth than seems warranted by the facts. **2.** To express with restraint or lack of emphasis. **3.** To state (a number, quantity, etc.) that is too low. —**un′-der·state′ment** *n.*

un·der·stood (ŭn′dər-stood′) *adj.* **1.** Agreed upon. **2.** Not expressed in writing; implied.

un·der·stud·y (ŭn′dər-stŭd′ē) *v.* **1.** To study or know (a role) so as to be able to replace the regular actor. **2.** To act as an understudy to. —*n., pl.* -ies. An actor trained to do the work of another.

un·der·take (ŭn′dər-tāk′) *v.* **1.** To take upon oneself; decide or agree to do. **2.** To pledge or commit oneself.

un·der·tak·er (ŭn′dər-tā′kər) *n.* One whose business it is to arrange for the burial or cremation of the dead.

un·der·tak·ing (ŭn′dər-tā′kĭng) *n.* **1.** An enterprise or venture. **2.** A guaranty, engagement, or promise. **3.** The occupation of an undertaker.

un·der-the-count·er (ŭn′dər-*th*ə-koun′tər) *adj.* Transacted or sold illicitly.

un·der·tone (ŭn′dər-tōn′) *n.* **1.** A speech tone of low pitch or volume. **2.** A pale or subdued color. **3.** An implied tendency or meaning; undercurrent.

un·der·tow (ŭn′dər-tō′) *n.* The seaward pull of receding waves breaking on a shore.

un·der·val·ue (ŭn′dər-văl′yōō) *v.* **1.** To assign too low a value to; underestimate. **2.** To have too little regard or esteem for.

un·der·wa·ter (ŭn′dər-wô′tər, -wŏt′ər) *adj.* Occurring, used, or performed beneath the surface of water. —**un′der·wa′ter** *adv.*

under way. 1. In motion or operation; started. **2.** Already in progress; afoot. **3.** Not anchored and not moored to a fixed object.

ă pat/ā ate/âr care/ä bar/b bib/ch chew/d deed/ĕ pet/ē be/f fit/g gag/h hat/hw what/ ĭ pit/ī pie/îr pier/j judge/k kick/l lid, fatal/m mum/n no, sudden/ng sing/ŏ pot/ō go/

un•der•wear (ŭn'dər-wâr') *n.* Clothing worn under the outer clothes and next to the skin; underclothes.

un•der•weight (ŭn'dər-wāt') *adj.* Weighing less than is normal.

un•der•world (ŭn'dər-wûrld') *n.* **1.** The world of the dead, conceived to be below the surface of the earth. **2.** The part of society engaged in and organized for the purpose of crime and vice.

un•der•write (ŭn'dər-rīt') *v.* **1.** To subscribe, esp. to endorse (a document). **2.** To assume financial responsibility for (an enterprise). **3. a.** To sign an insurance policy, thus assuming liability in case of specified losses. **b.** To insure. **c.** To insure against losses totaling (a given amount). **4.** To agree to buy (the stock in a new enterprise not yet sold publicly) at a fixed time and price. **—un'der•writ'er** *n.*

un•de•sir•a•ble (ŭn'dĭ-zīr'ə-bəl) *adj.* Not desirable; objectionable.

un•dies (ŭn'dēz) *pl.n. Informal.* Underwear.

un•do (ŭn'dōō') *v.* **1.** To reverse; cancel; annul. **2.** To untie or loosen. **3.** To open; unwrap. **4.** To ruin or destroy.

un•do•ing (ŭn'dōō'ĭng) *n.* **1.** The act of reversing or annulling; cancellation. **2.** The act of unfastening or loosening. **3. a.** The act of bringing to ruin. **b.** The cause of ruin.

un•doubt•ed (ŭn'dou'tĭd) *adj.* Accepted as beyond question; undisputed. **—un•doubt'ed•ly** *adv.*

un•dress (ŭn'drĕs') *v.* To remove the clothing of; disrobe; strip. —*n.* **1.** Informal attire. **2.** Nakedness.

un•due (ŭn'd/y/ōō') *adj.* **1.** Exceeding what is appropriate or normal; excessive. **2.** Not just, proper, or legal. **3.** Not yet payable or due.

un•du•lant (ŭn'jōō-lənt, ŭn'd/y/ə-) *adj.* Undulating.

un•du•late (ŭn'jōō-lāt', ŭn'd/y/ə-) *v.* -lated, -lating. **1.** To move or cause to move in a wavelike motion. **2.** To have a wavelike appearance or form. [< L *unda*, wave.]

un•du•la•tion (ŭn'jōō-lā'shən, ŭn'd/y/ə-) *n.* **1.** A wavelike movement, outline, appearance, or form. **2.** One of a series of waves or wavelike segments; a pulsation.

un•du•ly (ŭn'd/y/ōō'lē) *adv.* **1.** Excessively; immoderately. **2.** In disregard of a legal or moral precept.

un•dy•ing (ŭn'dī'ĭng) *adj.* Endless; everlasting; immortal.

un•earned (ŭn'ûrnd') *adj.* **1.** Not gained by work or service. **2.** Not deserved.

un•earth (ŭn'ûrth') *v.* **1.** To dig up; uproot. **2.** To bring to public notice; uncover.

un•earth•ly (ŭn'ûrth'lē) *adj.* **1.** Not of the earth; supernatural. **2.** Frighteningly weird and unaccountable. **3.** Outlandish.

un•eas•y (ŭn'ē'zē) *adj.* **1.** Lacking ease, comfort, or a sense of security. **2.** Affording no ease; difficult. **3.** Awkward or unsure in manner; constrained. **—un'eas'i•ly** *adv.* **—un'eas'i•ness** *n.*

un•em•ployed (ŭn'ĭm-ploid') *adj.* Out of work; without a job. **—un'em•ploy'ment** *n.*

un•e•qual (ŭn'ē'kwəl) *adj.* **1.** Not equal. **2.** Asymmetric. **3.** Irregular. **4.** Inadequate. **—un'e'qual•ly** *adv.*

un•e•qualed (ŭn'ē'kwəld) *adj.* Also **un•e•qualled.** Not equaled; unrivaled.

un•e•quiv•o•cal (ŭn'ĭ-kwĭv'ə-kəl) *adj.* Admitting of no doubt or misunderstanding; clear. **—un'e•quiv'o•cal•ly** *adv.*

un•err•ing (ŭn'ûr'ĭng, -ĕr'ĭng) *adj.* Consistently accurate; without error. **—un'err'ing•ly** *adv.*

un•e•ven (ŭn'ē'vən) *adj.* **1.** Not equal, as in size, length, or quality. **2.** Not consistent or uniform. **3.** Not smooth or level. **4.** Not straight or parallel. **—un'e'ven•ly** *adv.* **—un'e'ven•ness** *n.*

un•e•vent•ful (ŭn'ĭ-vĕnt'fəl) *adj.* Lacking in significant events; without incident.

un•ex•am•pled (ŭn'ĭg-zăm'pəld, -zăm'pəld) *adj.* Without precedent; unparalleled.

un•ex•cep•tion•a•ble (ŭn'ĭk-sĕp'shən-ə-bəl) *adj.* Beyond the least reasonable objection; irreproachable. **—un'ex•cep'tion•a•bly** *adv.*

un•ex•cep•tion•al (ŭn'ĭk-sĕp'shən-əl) *adj.* **1.** Not varying from a norm; usual. **2.** Not subject to exceptions; absolute.

Usage: Unexceptional is often confused with *unexceptionable,* for which it can only be substituted loosely. When the desired meaning is "not open to objection," the term is *unexceptionable.*

un•ex•pect•ed (ŭn'ĭk-spĕk'tĭd) *adj.* Coming without warning; unforeseen. **—un'ex•pect'ed•ly** *adv.* **—un'ex•pect'ed•ness** *n.*

un•fail•ing (ŭn'fā'lĭng) *adj.* **1.** Inexhaustible. **2.** Constant; unflagging. **3.** Infallible. **—un'fail'ing•ly** *adv.* **—un'fail'ing•ness** *n.*

un•fair (ŭn'fâr') *adj.* **1.** Not just; biased. **2.** Unethical: *unfair practices.* **—un'fair'ly** *adv.* **—un'fair'ness** *n.*

un•faith•ful (ŭn'fāth'fəl) *adj.* **1.** Not adhering to a pledge or contract; disloyal. **2.** Not justly representing or reflecting an original; inaccurate. **—un'faith'ful•ly** *adv.* **—un'faith'ful•ness** *n.*

un•fa•mil•iar (ŭn'fə-mĭl'yər) *adj.* **1.** Not within one's knowledge; strange. **2.** Not acquainted; not conversant. **—un'fa•mil'i•ar'i•ty** (-mĭl'yăr'ə-tē, -mĭl'ē-ăr'ə-tē) *n.*

un•fas•ten (ŭn'făs'ən, -fä'sən) *v.* To separate the connected parts of; become loosened or separated.

un•fa•vor•a•ble (ŭn'fā'vər-ə-bəl, -fā'vrə-bəl) *adj.* **1.** Not propitious. **2.** Adverse; opposed. **—un'fa'vor•a•bly** *adv.*

un•feel•ing (ŭn'fē'lĭng) *adj.* **1.** Having no sensation; insentient. **2.** Not sympathetic; callous. **—un'feel'ing•ly** *adv.*

un•feigned (ŭn'fānd') *adj.* Not simulated; genuine.

un•fit (ŭn'fĭt') *adj.* **1.** Inappropriate. **2.** Unqualified. **3.** Not in good health. **—un'fit'ly** *adv.* **—un'fit'ness** *n.*

un•fix (ŭn'fĭks') *v.* **1.** To detach or unfasten. **2.** To unsettle; disturb.

un•fledged (ŭn'flĕjd') *adj.* **1.** Immature with plumage insufficiently developed for flight. **2.** Inexperienced, immature, or untried.

un•flinch•ing (ŭn'flĭn'chĭng) *adj.* Not betraying fear or indecision; resolute. **—un'flinch'ing•ly** *adv.*

ô paw, for/oi boy/ou out/ŏŏ took/ōō coo/p pop/r run/s sauce/sh shy/t to/th thin/*th* the/ ŭ cut/ûr fur/v van/w wag/y yes/z size/zh vision/ə ago, item, edible, gallop, circus/

un•fold (ŭn′fōld′) *v.* 1. To open and spread out; extend. 2. To disclose to view. 3. To reveal or be revealed gradually.

un•for•get•ta•ble (ŭn′fər-gĕt′ə-bəl) *adj.* Earning a permanent place in the memory; memorable. —**un′for•get′ta•bly** *adv.*

un•formed (ŭn′fôrmd′) *adj.* 1. Having no definite shape or structure; unorganized. 2. Not yet developed to maturity.

un•for•tu•nate (ŭn′fôr′chə-nĭt) *adj.* 1. Unlucky. 2. Causing misfortune; disastrous. 3. Regrettable; deplorable. —*n.* A victim of bad luck, disaster, poverty, etc. —**un′for′tu•nate•ly** *adv.* —**un′for′tu•nate•ness** *n.*

un•found•ed (ŭn′foun′dĭd) *adj.* Not based on fact or sound observation; groundless.

un•fre•quent•ed (ŭn′frĭ-kwĕn′tĭd, ŭn′frē′- kwən-tĭd) *adj.* Receiving few or no visitors.

un•friend•ly (ŭn′frĕnd′lē) *adj.* 1. Not disposed to friendship; hostile. 2. Indicating a bad prospect; unfavorable. —**un′friend′li•ness** *n.*

un•frock (ŭn′frŏk′) *v.* To strip of priestly privileges and functions.

un•furl (ŭn′fûrl′) *v.* To spread or open out; unroll.

un•fur•nished (ŭn′fûr′nĭsht) *adj.* Not containing or provided with furniture.

un•gain•ly (ŭn′gān′lē) *adj.* -lier, -liest. Awkward; clumsy. —**un′gain′li•ness** *n.*

un•glued (ŭn-glōōd′) *adj.* Loosened or separated. —**come unglued.** *Slang.* To become upset and lose one's composure, as in a crisis.

un•god•ly (ŭn′gŏd′lē) *adj.* -lier, -liest. 1. Not revering God. 2. Sinful; wicked. 3. *Informal.* Outrageous. —**un′god′li•ness** *n.*

un•gov•ern•a•ble (ŭn′gŭv′ər-nə-bəl) *adj.* Not able to be governed; uncontrollable; unruly.

un•gra•cious (ŭn′grā′shəs) *adj.* 1. Discourteous; rude. 2. Unacceptable; unattractive. —**un′gra′cious•ly** *adv.*

un•grate•ful (ŭn′grāt′fəl) *adj.* 1. Without a feeling of gratitude or appreciation. 2. Disagreeable; repellent.

un•guard•ed (ŭn′gär′dĭd) *adj.* 1. Unprotected. 2. Without discretion; imprudent.

un•guent (ŭng′gwənt) *n.* A salve; ointment. [< L *unguere,* to anoint.]

un•gu•late (ŭng′gyə-lĭt, -lāt′) *adj.* Having hoofs. —*n.* A hoofed mammal. [< L *ungula,* hoof.]

un•hand (ŭn′hănd′) *v.* To remove one's hands from; let go.

un•hap•py (ŭn′hăp′ē) *adj.* 1. Not happy; sad. 2. Unlucky. 3. Not suitable or tactful; inappropriate. —**un′hap′pi•ly** (-hăp′ə-lē) *adv.* —**un′- hap′pi•ness** *n.*

un•har•ness (ŭn′här′nĭs) *v.* 1. To remove the harness from. 2. To release, as energy.

un•health•y (ŭn′hĕl′thē) *adj.* 1. In ill health; sick. 2. Symptomatic of ill health. 3. Likely to cause illness. 4. Harmful to morals; corruptive. —**un′health′i•ness** *n.*

un•heard (ŭn′hûrd′) *adj.* 1. Not heard. 2. Not given a hearing.

un•heard-of (ŭn′hûrd′ŭv′, -ŏv′) *adj.* 1. Not previously known. 2. Without precedent.

un•hinge (ŭn′hĭnj′) *v.* 1. To remove from hinges. 2. To unbalance (the mind).

un•hitch (ŭn′hĭch′) *v.* To unfasten.

un•ho•ly (ŭn′hō′lē) *adj.* 1. Not hallowed or consecrated. 2. Wicked; immoral. 3. *Informal.* Outrageous.

un•hook (ŭn′hŏŏk′) *v.* 1. To remove from a hook. 2. To unfasten the hooks of.

un•horse (ŭn′hôrs′) *v.* -horsed, -horsing. To cause to fall from a horse.

uni–. *comb. form.* Single. [< L *ūnus,* one.]

u•ni•cam•er•al (yōō′nĭ-kăm′ər-əl) *adj.* Consisting of a single legislative chamber.

u•ni•cel•lu•lar (yōō′nĭ-sĕl′yə-lər) *adj.* Consisting of a single cell; one-celled: *unicellular organisms.*

u•ni•corn (yōō′nə-kôrn′) *n.* A fabled creature usually represented as a horse with a single spiraled horn on its forehead. [< UNI- + L *cornū,* horn.]

u•ni•di•rec•tion•al (yōō′nĭ-dĭ-rĕk′shən-əl, -dī-rĕk′shən-əl) *adj.* Having, operating, or moving in one direction only.

u•ni•form (yōō′nə-fôrm′) *adj.* 1. Unchanging; consistent. 2. Being the same everywhere; identical. —*n.* A distinctive outfit intended to identify those who wear it as members of a specific group. [< L *ūniformis,* of one form.] —**u′ni•for′mi•ty,** **u′ni•form′ness** *n.* —**u′ni•form′ly** *adv.*

u•ni•fy (yōō′nə-fī′) *v.* -fied, -fying. To make into a unit; unite; consolidate. [< UNI- + L *facere,* to make.] —**u′ni•fi•ca′tion** *n.* —**u′ni•fi′er** *n.*

u•ni•lat•er•al (yōō′nĭ-lăt′ər-əl) *adj.* 1. Of, on, pertaining to, involving, or affecting only one side. 2. Having only one side. —**u′ni•lat′er•al•ly** *adv.*

un•im•peach•a•ble (ŭn′ĭm-pē′chə-bəl) *adj.* Beyond doubt or reproach; unquestionable. —**un′im•peach′a•bly** *adv.*

un•in•hib•i•ted (ŭn′ĭn-hĭb′ə-tĭd) *adj.* Free from inhibition. —**un′in•hib′i•ted•ly** *adv.*

un•in•tel•li•gent (ŭn′ĭn-tĕl′ə-jənt) *adj.* 1. Lacking intelligence; stupid. 2. Uneducated; ignorant. —**un′in•tel′li•gent•ly** *adv.*

un•in•ten•tion•al (ŭn′ĭn-tĕn′shən-əl) *adj.* Not intentional; not done or said on purpose. —**un′in•ten′tion•al•ly** *adv.*

un•in•ter•est•ed (ŭn-ĭn′trĭs-tĭd, -ĭn′tə-rĕs′tĭd) *adj.* Not paying attention; indifferent.

un•ion (yōōn′yən) *n.* 1. The act of uniting or state of being united. 2. A combination so formed; an alliance or confederation. 3. The state of matrimony; marriage. 4. An organization of wage earners formed for the purpose of serving their class interests with respect to wages and working conditions. 5. A coupling device for connecting parts, as pipes or rods. 6. A device on a flag signifying the union of two or more sovereignties. —**the Union.** The United States of America, esp. during the Civil War. —*adj.* 1. Of or pertaining to a union, esp. a labor union. 2. **Union.** Supporting the Federal government during the Civil War. [< L *ūnus,* one.]

un•ion•ize (yōōn′yə-nīz′) *v.* -ized, -izing. To organize (into) a labor union.

union jack. 1. Any flag consisting entirely of a union. 2. Often **Union Jack.** The flag of the United Kingdom.

Union of Soviet Socialist Republics. A country of 15 constituent republics in N Eurasia; Soviet Union; Russia. Pop. 241,748,000. Cap. Moscow.

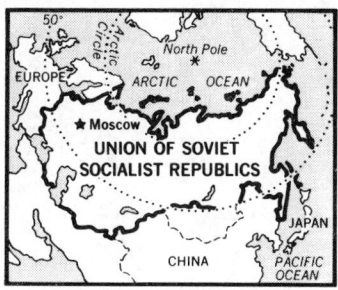

**Union of Soviet
Socialist Republics**

union shop A business or industrial establishment whose employees are required to be union members or agree to join the union within a specified time after being hired.
u·nique (yōō-nēk') *adj.* 1. Being the only one of its kind; solitary; sole; single. 2. Being without an equal or equivalent; unparalleled. [< L *ūnicus*, only, sole.] —**u·nique'ly** *adv.* —**u·nique'ness** *n.*
Usage: Unique, in careful usage, is not preceded by adverbs that qualify it with respect to degree. By definition, *unique* cannot strictly be said to vary in degree or intensity. Therefore, constructions such as *rather* (or *somewhat* or *very*) *unique* and *more* (or *most*) *unique* are rendered more appropriately by substituting for *unique* less special terms, such as *unusual, rare,* or *remarkable.*
u·ni·sex (yōō'nĭ-sĕks') *n.* The elimination of gender distinctions, as in dress. —*adj.* Not distinguished or distinguishable on the basis of gender: *unisex hair styles.*
u·ni·son (yōō'nə-sən, -zən) *n.* 1. a. Identity of musical pitch. b. The combination of musical parts at the same pitch or in octaves. 2. Any speaking of the same words simultaneously by two or more speakers. 3. Agreement; concord. [< ML *ūnisonus*, of the same sound.]
u·nit (yōō'nĭt) *n.* 1. Anything regarded as an elementary structural or functional constituent of a whole. 2. a. A mechanical part or module. b. An entire apparatus. 3. A precisely specified quantity in terms of which the magnitudes of other quantities of the same kind can be stated. [Back-formation < UNITY.]
U·ni·tar·i·an (yōō'nə-târ'ē-ən) *n.* A member of a Christian denomination that rejects the doctrine of the Trinity and emphasizes freedom and tolerance in religious belief. [< L *ūnitās*, unity.] —**U'ni·tar'i·an·ism'** *n.*
u·nite (yōō-nīt') *v.* **united, uniting.** 1. To bring together so as to form a whole. 2. To combine (people) in interest, attitude, or action. 3. To become joined, formed, or combined into a unit. [< L *ūnus*, one.]

United Arab Emirates. A federation in E Arabia. Pop. 179,000. Cap. Abu Dhabi.
United Kingdom. In full, United Kingdom of Great Britain and Northern Ireland. A kingdom of W Europe, consisting of England, Scotland, Wales, and Northern Ireland. Pop. 54,068,000. Cap. London.

United Kingdom

United Nations. An international organization of 144 independent countries, with headquarters in New York City.
United States of America. A North American republic composed of 50 states. Pop. 200,000,000. Cap. Washington. See map on following page.
u·ni·ty (yōō'nə-tē) *n., pl.* **-ties.** 1. The state of being one; singleness. 2. Oneness of mind; agreement; concord. 3. An ordering of all elements in a work of art so that each contributes to a unified aesthetic effect. 4. Singleness of purpose or action; continuity. 5. The number 1. [< L *ūnus*, one.]
univ. 1. universal. 2. university.
Univ. university.
u·ni·va·lent (yōō'nĭ-vā'lənt) *adj.* 1. Having valence 1. 2. Having only one valence.
u·ni·valve (yōō'nĭ-vălv') *n.* A mollusk, as a snail, having a single shell. —**u'ni·valve'** *adj.*
u·ni·ver·sal (yōō'nə-vûr'səl) *adj.* 1. Extending to or affecting the entire world; worldwide. 2. Including or affecting all members of a class or group. 3. Applicable to all purposes, conditions, or situations. 4. Of or pertaining to the universe or cosmos; cosmic. 5. Comprising all or many subjects: *a universal genius.* —**u'ni·ver·sal'i·ty** *n.* —**u'ni·ver'sal·ly** *adv.*
universal joint. A joint that allows parts of a machine limited movement in any direction while transmitting rotary motion.
u·ni·verse (yōō'nə-vûrs') *n.* All existing things regarded as a collective entity. [< L *ūniversus*, whole, entire, "turned into one."]
u·ni·ver·si·ty (yōō'nə-vûr'sə-tē) *n., pl.* **-ties.** An institution for higher learning comprising a graduate school, professional schools, and an undergraduate division. [< LL *ūniversitās*, a society, guild.]

ô paw, fôr/oi boy/ou out/ŏŏ took/ōō coo/p pop/r run/s sauce/sh shy/t to/th thin/*th* the/
ŭ cut/ûr fur/v van/w wag/y yes/z size/zh vision/ə ago, item, edible, gallop, circus/

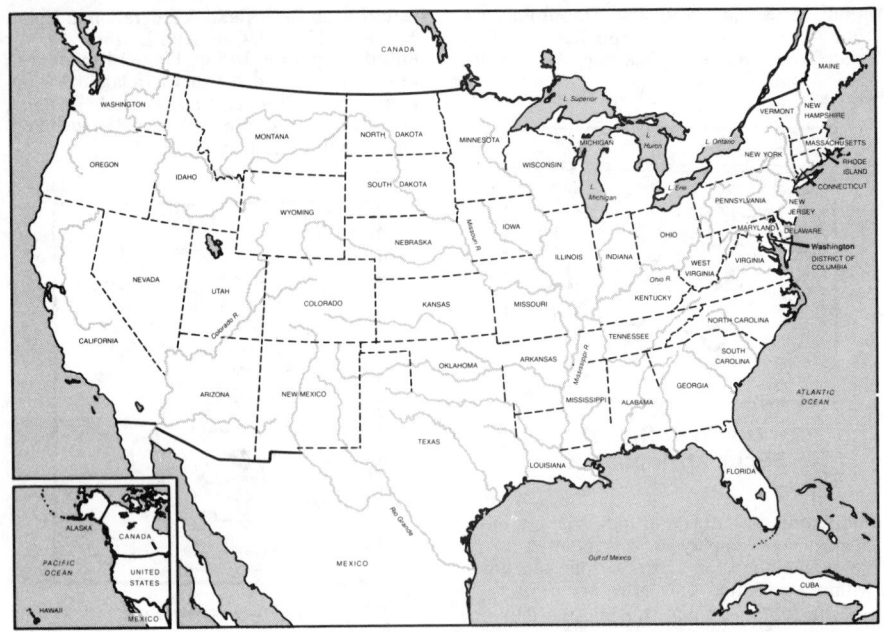

United States of America

un·just (ŭn'jŭst') *adj.* Violating principles of justice or fairness; unfair. —**un'just'ly** *adv.*

un·kempt (ŭn'kĕmpt') *adj.* 1. Not combed: *unkempt hair.* 2. Untidy; messy. [< UN-¹ + OE *cemban,* to comb.]

un·kind (ŭn'kīnd') *adj.* Lacking kindness; unsympathetic. —**un'kind'ly** *adv.*

un·know·ing (ŭn'nō'ĭng) *adj.* Not knowing; unaware. —**un'know'ing·ly** *adv.*

un·known (ŭn'nōn') *adj.* 1. Not known; unfamiliar; strange. 2. Not identified or ascertained. —*n.* 1. One that is unknown. 2. A quantity of unknown numerical value.

un·lace (ŭn'lās') *v.* To loosen or undo the lace or laces of.

un·latch (ŭn'lăch') *v.* To unfasten or open by releasing a latch.

un·law·ful (ŭn'lô'fəl) *adj.* Not lawful; in violation of law; illegal. —**un'law'ful·ly** *adv.* —**un'law'ful·ness** *n.*

un·learn (ŭn'lûrn') *v.* To put (something learned) out of the mind; forget.

un·learn·ed. *adj.* 1. (ŭn'lûr'nĭd). Not educated; ignorant or illiterate. 2. (ŭn'lûrnd'). Not acquired by training or studying.

un·leash (ŭn'lēsh') *v.* To release or loose from or as from a leash.

un·less (ŭn-lĕs') *conj.* Except on the condition that; except under the circumstances that. [< ME *(up)on less than,* "on a less condition than."]

un·let·tered (ŭn'lĕt'ərd) *adj.* Not educated; illiterate.

un·like (ŭn'līk') *adj.* Not alike; different; dissimilar. —*prep.* 1. Different from; not like. 2. Not typical of.

un·like·ly (ŭn'līk'lē) *adj.* 1. Not likely; improbable. 2. Likely to fail. —**un'like'li·hood'**, **un'like'li·ness** *n.*

un·lim·ber (ŭn'lĭm'bər) *v.* To prepare for action.

un·lim·it·ed (ŭn'lĭm'ĭ-tĭd) *adj.* Having no limits, bounds, or qualifications.

un·load (ŭn'lōd') *v.* 1. a. To remove the load or cargo from. b. To discharge (a cargo or load). 2. To remove the charge from (a firearm). 3. To dispose of, esp. by selling in great quantity; dump.

un·lock (ŭn'lŏk') *v.* 1. To undo (a lock). 2. To undo the lock of.

un·looked-for (ŭn'lŏŏkt'fôr') *adj.* Not looked for or expected.

un·loose (ŭn'lŏŏs') *v.* 1. To let loose or unfasten; release; set free. 2. To relax; ease, as a hold.

un·loos·en (ŭn'lŏŏ'sən) *v.* To unloose.

un·luck·y (ŭn'lŭk'ē) *adj.* Marked by or bringing bad luck; unfortunate.

un·man·ly (ŭn'măn'lē) *adj.* 1. Weak; cowardly. 2. Effeminate. —**un'man'li·ness** *n.*

un·manned (ŭn'mănd') *adj.* Operated without a crew on board.

un·man·ner·ly (ŭn'măn'ər-lē) *adj.* Rude; illmannered. —**un'man'ner·li·ness** *n.*

un·mar·ried (ŭn'măr'ēd) *adj.* Not married.

un·mask (ŭn'măsk', -mäsk') *v.* 1. To remove a mask from. 2. To disclose the true character of; expose.

un·men·tion·a·ble (ŭn'mĕn'shən-ə-bəl) *adj.* Not fit for polite conversation.

un·mer·ci·ful (ŭn'mûr'sĭ-fəl) *adj.* Having no mercy; merciless.

un·mind·ful (ŭn'mīnd'fəl) *adj.* Careless; forgetful; oblivious: *unmindful of the time.*

ă pat/ā ate/âr care/ä bar/b bib/ch chew/d deed/ĕ pet/ē be/f fit/g gag/h hat/hw what/
ĭ pit/ī pie/îr pier/j judge/k kick/l lid, fatal/m mum/n no, sudden/ng sing/ŏ pot/ō go/

un·mis·tak·a·ble (ŭn'mĭ-stā'kə-bəl) *adj.* Obvious; evident. —**un'mis·tak'a·bly** *adv.*
un·mit·i·gat·ed (ŭn'mĭt'ə-gā'tĭd) *adj.* **1.** Not diminished in intensity or severity; unrelieved. **2.** Absolute; out-and-out.
un·nat·u·ral (ŭn'năch'ər-əl) *adj.* **1.** Violating natural law. **2.** Deviating from a behavioral, ethical, or social norm. **3.** Contrived or constrained; artificial.
un·nec·es·sar·y (ŭn'nĕs'ə-sĕr'ē) *adj.* Not necessary; needless. —**un'nec·es·sar'i·ly** (-sâr'ə-lē) *adv.* —**un'nec'es·sar'i·ness** *n.*
un·nerve (ŭn'nûrv') *v.* **-nerved, -nerving.** To deprive of composure, energy, or firmness.
un·ob·tru·sive (ŭn'əb-trōō'sĭv) *adj.* Not readily noticeable; inconspicuous.
un·oc·cu·pied (ŭn'ŏk'yə-pīd') *adj.* Not occupied; vacant.
un·of·fi·cial (ŭn'ə-fĭsh'əl) *adj.* **1.** Not official. **2.** Not acting officially. —**un'of·fi'cial·ly** *adv.*
un·or·gan·ized (ŭn'ôr'gə-nīzd') *adj.* **1.** Lacking order, system, or unity. **2.** Not unionized.
un·or·tho·dox (ŭn'ôr'thə-dŏks') *adj.* Not orthodox; unconventional.
un·pack (ŭn'păk') *v.* **1.** To remove the contents of (a suitcase). **2.** To remove from a container or from packaging.
un·paid (ŭn'pād') *adj.* **1.** Not yet paid. **2.** Serving without pay.
un·par·al·leled (ŭn'păr'ə-lĕld') *adj.* Without parallel; unequaled.
un·pin (ŭn'pĭn') *v.* **1.** To remove a pin from. **2.** To unfasten by removing pins.
un·pleas·ant (ŭn'plĕz'ənt) *adj.* Not pleasing; offensive; disagreeable. —**un'pleas'ant·ness** *n.*
un·plug (ŭn'plŭg') *v.* **1.** To remove a plug or stopper from. **2.** To disconnect from a source of electric power.
un·pop·u·lar (ŭn'pŏp'yə-lər) *adj.* Lacking general approval or acceptance. —**un'pop'u·lar'i·ty** (-lăr'ə-tē) *n.*
un·prec·e·dent·ed (ŭn'prĕs'ə-dĕn'tĭd) *adj.* Without precedent.
un·pre·dict·a·ble (ŭn'prĭ-dĭk'tə-bəl) *adj.* Not predictable. —**un'pre·dict'a·bly** *adv.*
un·pre·pared (ŭn'prĭ-pârd') *adj.* **1.** Having made no preparations. **2.** Not equipped to meet a contingency. **3.** Impromptu.
un·pre·ten·tious (ŭn'prĭ-tĕn'shəs) *adj.* Lacking pretention; modest.
un·prin·ci·pled (ŭn'prĭn'sə-pəld) *adj.* Lacking principles or moral scruples; unscrupulous: *unprincipled behavior.*
un·print·a·ble (ŭn'prĭn'tə-bəl) *adj.* Not suitable for publication.
un·pro·duc·tive (ŭn'prə-dŭk'tĭv) *adj.* Producing or yielding little or nothing.
un·pro·fes·sion·al (ŭn'prə-fĕsh'ən-əl) *adj.* **1.** Not a qualified member of a professional group. **2.** Not conforming to the standards of a profession. —**un'pro·fes'sion·al·ly** *adv.*
un·prof·it·a·ble (ŭn'prŏf'ĭ-tə-bəl) *adj.* **1.** Yielding no profit. **2.** Serving no purpose; useless. —**un'prof'it·a·bly** *adv.*
un·qual·i·fied (ŭn'kwŏl'ə-fīd') *adj.* **1.** Lacking the proper or required qualifications. **2.** Without reservations.
un·ques·tion·a·ble (ŭn'kwĕs'chən-ə-bəl) *adj.*

Beyond question or doubt; indisputable. —**un'ques'tion·a·bly** *adv.*
un·ques·tioned (ŭn'kwĕs'chənd) *adj.* Not questioned or doubted; unquestionable.
un·quote (ŭn'kwōt') *v.* To close (a quotation). Used by a speaker to indicate the termination of a quotation.
un·rav·el (ŭn'răv'əl) *v.* **1.** To separate (entangled threads). **2.** To solve; clear up (something mysterious or baffling).
un·read (ŭn'rĕd') *adj.* **1.** Not read, studied, or perused. **2.** Having read little; ignorant.
un·read·a·ble (ŭn'rē'də-bəl) *adj.* **1.** Illegible. **2.** Incomprehensible; obscure.
un·read·y (ŭn'rĕd'ē) *adj.* **1.** Not ready or prepared. **2.** Slow to see or respond. —**un'read'i·ly** *adv.* —**un'read'i·ness** *n.*
un·re·al (ŭn'rē'əl, -rēl') *adj.* Not real or substantial; imaginary; artificial; illusory.
un·rea·son·a·ble (ŭn'rē'zə-nə-bəl) *adj.* **1.** Not governed by or predicated upon reason. **2.** Exorbitant; immoderate.
un·re·hearsed (ŭn'rĭ-hûrst') *adj.* Not rehearsed; extemporaneous.
un·re·lent·ing (ŭn'rĭ-lĕn'tĭng) *adj.* **1.** Not relenting; inexorable. **2.** Not diminishing in intensity, speed, or effort.
un·re·li·a·ble (ŭn'rĭ-lī'ə-bəl) *adj.* Not reliable. —**un're·li'a·bil'i·ty** *n.* —**un're·li'a·bly** *adv.*
un·re·mit·ting (ŭn'rĭ-mĭt'ĭng) *adj.* Never slackening; incessant; persistent.
un·re·served (ŭn'rĭ-zûrvd') *adj.* **1.** Not reserved for a particular person: *an unreserved seat.* **2.** Given without reservation; unqualified. **3.** Not reserved in manner; open; candid. —**un're·serv'ed·ly** (-zûr'vĭd-lē) *adv.*
un·rest (ŭn'rĕst') *n.* Uneasiness; disquiet: *social unrest.*
un·re·strained (ŭn'rĭ-strānd') *adj.* **1.** Not restrained; immoderate; uncontrolled. **2.** Not constrained; natural.
un·ripe (ŭn'rīp') *adj.* Not ripe; immature.
un·ri·valed (ŭn'rī'vəld) *adj.* Unequaled; supreme.
un·roll (ŭn'rōl') *v.* **1.** To unwind and open out (something rolled up). **2.** To become unrolled.
un·ruf·fled (ŭn'rŭf'əld) *adj.* Not ruffled or agitated; calm.
un·ru·ly (ŭn'rōō'lē) *adj.* **-lier, -liest.** Difficult or impossible to govern; not amenable to discipline. —**un'ru'li·ness** *n.*
un·sad·dle (ŭn'săd'l) *v.* To remove the saddle from.
un·safe (ŭn'sāf') *adj.* Not safe; involving danger or risk; dangerous.
un·sat·is·fac·to·ry (ŭn'săt'ĭs-făk'tə-rē) *adj.* Not satisfactory; not meeting the necessary requirements.
un·sa·vor·y (ŭn'sā'və-rē) *adj.* **1.** Tasteless. **2.** Having an unpleasant taste. **3.** Socially objectionable or undesirable.
un·scathed (ŭn'skāthd') *adj.* Unharmed; uninjured.
un·schooled (ŭn'skōōld') *adj.* Not schooled; uninstructed.
un·sci·en·tif·ic (ŭn'sī-ən-tĭf'ĭk) *adj.* Not scientific, esp. lacking in method or objectivity. —**un'sci·en·tif'i·cal·ly** *adv.*

un•scram•ble (ŭn'skrăm'bəl) *v.* To disentangle; straighten out; resolve.

un•screw (ŭn'skrōō') *v.* **1.** To take out the screws from. **2.** To loosen, adjust, or detach by rotating.

un•scru•pu•lous (ŭn'skrōō'pyə-ləs) *adj.* Without scruples; contemptuous of what is right or honorable. —**un'scru'pu•lous•ly** *adv.*

un•seal (ŭn'sēl') *v.* To break or remove the seal of.

un•sea•son•a•ble (ŭn'sē'zə-nə-bəl) *adj.* **1.** Not characteristic of the time of year. **2.** Poorly timed. —**un'sea'son•a•bly** *adv.*

un•seat (ŭn'sēt') *v.* **1.** To remove from a seat, esp. from a saddle. **2.** To dislodge from a position or office.

un•seem•ly (ŭn'sēm'lē) *adj.* Not in good taste; indecorous; unbecoming.

un•seen (ŭn'sēn') *adj.* Not directly evident; invisible.

un•sel•fish (ŭn'sĕl'fĭsh) *adj.* Not selfish; generous. —**un'sel'fish•ly** *adv.* —**un'sel'fish•ness** *n.*

un•set•tle (ŭn'sĕt'l) *v.* To disrupt; disturb.

un•set•tled (ŭn'sĕt'əld) *adj.* **1.** Disordered; disturbed. **2.** Not determined or resolved. **3.** Not paid or adjusted. **4.** Unpopulated. **5.** Not fixed or established, as in a residence.

un•shack•le (ŭn'shăk'əl) *v.* To release from or as from confinement or shackles; set free.

un•sheathe (ŭn'shē*th*') *v.* To draw from a sheath or scabbard.

un•sight•ly (ŭn'sīt'lē) *adj.* Unpleasant or offensive to look at; unattractive. —**un'sight'li•ness** *n.*

un•skilled (ŭn'skĭld') *adj.* **1.** Lacking skill or technical training. **2.** Requiring no training or skill.

un•skill•ful (ŭn'skĭl'fəl) *adj.* Lacking skill or proficiency; inexpert. —**un'skill'ful•ly** *adv.*

un•snap (ŭn'snăp') *v.* To undo the snaps of; unfasten.

un•snarl (ŭn'snärl') *v.* To free of snarls; disentangle.

un•so•cia•ble (ŭn'sō'shə-bəl) *adj.* Not disposed to seek the company of others; not companionable. —**un'so'cia•bil'i•ty** *n.*

un•so•phis•ti•cat•ed (ŭn'sə-fĭs'tĭ-kā'tĭd) *adj.* Not sophisticated.

un•sound (ŭn'sound') *adj.* **1.** Not dependably strong or solid. **2.** Not physically healthy; diseased. **3.** Not logically founded; fallacious; invalid. —**un'sound'ly** *adv.*

un•spar•ing (ŭn'spâr'ĭng) *adj.* **1.** Not frugal; lavish. **2.** Unmerciful; severe. —**un'spar'ing•ly** *adv.* —**un'spar'ing•ness** *n.*

un•speak•a•ble (ŭn'spē'kə-bəl) *adj.* **1.** Beyond description; inexpressible. **2.** Inexpressibly bad or objectionable. —**un'speak'a•bly** *adv.*

un•sta•ble (ŭn'stā'bəl) *adj.* **1.** Lacking stability or firmness. **2. a.** Of fickle temperament; irresponsible; flighty. **b.** Psychologically maladjusted. **3.** Decomposing or decaying readily. —**un'sta'ble•ness** *n.*

un•stead•y (ŭn'stĕd'ē) *adj.* **1.** Not securely in place; unstable. **2.** Fluctuating; inconstant. **3.** Wavering; uneven; erratic.

un•stop (ŭn'stŏp') *v.* To remove a stopper or obstruction from; open.

un•stressed (ŭn'strĕst') *adj.* **1.** Not stressed or having the weakest stress, as a speech segment. **2.** Not emphasized.

un•strung (ŭn'strŭng') *adj.* **1.** Having the strings loosened or removed. **2.** Emotionally upset; unnerved.

un•suc•cess•ful (ŭn'sək-sĕs'fəl) *adj.* Not succeeding; without success. —**un'suc•cess'ful•ly** *adv.* —**un'suc•cess'ful•ness** *n.*

un•suit•a•ble (ŭn'sōō'tə-bəl) *adj.* Not suitable; inappropriate. —**un'suit'a•bil'i•ty** *n.*

un•sung (ŭn'sŭng') *adj.* **1.** Not sung. **2.** Not honored or praised in song; uncelebrated: *unsung heroes.*

un•sure (ŭn'shōōr') *adj.* Lacking confidence or assurance; uncertain.

un•tan•gle (ŭn'tăng'gəl) *v.* **1.** To disentangle. **2.** To clarify; resolve.

un•ten•a•ble (ŭn'tĕn'ə-bəl) *adj.* **1.** Indefensible. **2.** Not suitable for occupation.

un•think•a•ble (ŭn'thĭng'kə-bəl) *adj.* Not thinkable; inconceivable; out of the question.

un•think•ing (ŭn'thĭng'kĭng) *adj.* Not thinking or mindful; inattentive.

un•ti•dy (ŭn'tī'dē) *adj.* Not neat and tidy; slovenly. —**un'ti'di•ly** *adv.* —**un'ti'di•ness** *n.*

un•tie (ŭn'tī') *v.* **1.** To undo or loosen (a knot). **2.** To free from something that binds or restrains.

un•til (ŭn-tĭl') *prep.* **1.** Up to the time of. **2.** Before a specified time: *not until Friday.* —*conj.* **1.** Up to the time that. **2.** Before. **3.** To the point or extent that. —See Usage note at **till.** [ME, to, toward, up to, till.]

un•time•ly (ŭn'tīm'lē) *adj.* **1.** Occurring or done at an inappropriate time; inopportune. **2.** Occurring too soon; premature. —**un'time'ly** *adv.* —**un'time'li•ness** *n.*

un•tir•ing (ŭn'tīr'ĭng) *adj.* **1.** Not tiring. **2.** Not ceasing despite fatigue; indefatigable. —**un'-tir'ing•ly** *adv.*

un•to (ŭn'tōō) *prep. Poetic & Archaic.* To.

un•told (ŭn'tōld') *adj.* **1.** Not told or revealed. **2.** Beyond description or enumeration.

un•touch•a•ble (ŭn'tŭch'ə-bəl) *adj.* **1.** Not to be touched. **2.** Out of reach; unobtainable. —*n.* A Hindu of the lowest caste, whose touch is considered to defile those of higher castes.

un•to•ward (ŭn'tôrd', -tōrd') *adj.* **1.** Unfavorable; unpropitious. **2.** Hard to control; refractory.

un•true (ŭn'trōō') *adj.* **1.** Contrary to fact; false. **2.** Disloyal; unfaithful.

un•truth (ŭn'trōōth') *n.* **1.** A lie. **2.** Falsity. —**un'truth'ful** *adj.* —**un'truth'ful•ness** *n.*

un•tu•tored (ŭn't/y/ōō'tərd) *adj.* Having had no formal education.

un•twist (ŭn'twĭst') *v.* To loosen or separate (that which is twisted together) by turning in the opposite direction.

un•used (ŭn'yōōzd') *adj.* **1.** Not in use. **2.** Never having been used. **3.** (ŭn'yōōst'). Not accustomed: *unused to city traffic.*

un•u•su•al (ŭn'yōō'zhōō-əl) *adj.* Not usual, common, or ordinary.

un•ut•ter•a•ble (ŭn'ŭt'ər-ə-bəl) *adj.* Not capable of being expressed; too profound for oral expression. —**un'ut'ter•a•bly** *adv.*

---

un·var·nished (ŭn'vär'nĭsht) *adj.* **1.** Not varnished. **2.** Stated without any effort to soften or disguise: *the unvarnished truth.*
un·veil (ŭn'vāl') *v.* **1.** To remove a veil from. **2.** To disclose; reveal.
un·voiced (ŭn'voist') *adj.* **1.** Not expressed or uttered. **2.** *Phon.* Voiceless.
un·war·rant·ed (ŭn'wôr'ən-tĭd, ŭn'wŏr'-) *adj.* Having no justification; groundless.
un·war·y (ŭn'wâr'ē) *adj.* Not alert to danger or deception; not cautious.
un·well (ŭn'wĕl') *adj.* Not well; ailing; ill.
un·whole·some (ŭn'hōl'səm) *adj.* Injurious to physical, mental, or moral health. —**un'whole·some·ly** *adv.* —**un'whole·some·ness** *n.*
un·wield·y (ŭn'wēl'dē) *adj.* **-ier, -iest.** Difficult to carry or manage because of bulk or shape.
un·will·ing (ŭn'wĭl'ĭng) *adj.* **1.** Hesitant; loath. **2.** Done, given, or said reluctantly. —**un'will'ing·ly** *adv.* —**un'will'ing·ness** *n.*
un·wind (ŭn'wīnd') *v.* **1.** To unroll; uncoil. **2.** To become unrolled or uncoiled.
un·wise (ŭn'wīz') *adj.* Lacking wisdom; foolish or imprudent. —**un'wise'ly** *adv.*
un·wit·ting (ŭn'wĭt'ĭng) *adj.* **1.** Not knowing; unaware. **2.** Not intended; unintentional. [< UN-¹ + OE *witan*, to know (see weid-).] —**un'wit'ting·ly** *adv.*
un·wont·ed (ŭn'wôn'tĭd, -wōn'tĭd, -wŭn'tĭd) *adj.* Not habitual or ordinary; unusual.
un·wor·thy (ŭn'wûr'thē) *adj.* **1.** Insufficient in worth; undeserving: *unworthy of the award.* **2.** Not suiting or befitting. —**un'wor'thi·ness** *n.*
un·wrap (ŭn'răp') *v.* To remove the wrappings from; open.
un·writ·ten (ŭn'rĭt'n) *adj.* **1.** Not written or recorded. **2.** Not formulated; operating through custom; traditional.
un·zip (ŭn'zĭp') *v.* To open or unfasten (a zipper).
up (ŭp) *adv.* **1.** From a lower to a higher position. **2.** In or toward a higher position. **3.** From a reclining to an upright position. **4. a.** Above a surface. **b.** Above the horizon. **5.** Into view or consideration. **6.** In or toward a position conventionally regarded as higher. **7.** To or at a higher price. **8.** So as to advance, increase, or improve. **9.** With or to a greater pitch or volume. **10.** Into a state of excitement or turbulence. **11.** So as to detach or unearth: *pulling up weeds.* **12.** To a stop. **13.** Apart; into pieces: *tore it up.* **14.** To windward. **15.** Each; apiece: *The score was eight up.* **16.** Completely; entirely. **17.** —Used as an intensifier: *cleaning up.* —*adj.* **1.** High or relatively high. **2. a.** Standing; erect. **b.** Out of bed. **3.** Moving or directed upward: *an up elevator.* **4.** Actively functioning: *up and around.* **5.** Rising toward the flood level. **6.** Marked by agitation or acceleration: *The winds are up.* **7.** *Informal.* Going on: *What's up?* **8.** Being considered; under study: *a contract up for renewal.* **9.** Running as a candidate. **10.** Charged; on trial. **11.** Finished; over: *His time was up.* **12.** *Informal.* Well-informed: *not up on sports.* **13.** Being ahead of the opponent: *up two holes in a golf match.* **14.** *Baseball.* At bat. **15.** As a bet; at stake. —*prep.* **1.** From a lower to or toward a

higher point on. **2.** Toward or at a point farther along: *up the road.* **3.** In a direction toward the source of: *up the Hudson.* **4.** Against: *up the wind.* —*n.* **1.** A rise or ascent. **2.** An upward movement or trend. —*v.* **upped, upping. 1.** To increase or improve. **2.** To raise. **3.** *Informal.* To act suddenly or unexpectedly: *upped and went home.* [< OE *ŭp* and *uppe*. See **upo.**]
up-. *comb. form.* **1.** Up. **2.** Upper.
up-and-com·ing (ŭp'ən-kŭm'ĭng) *adj.* Marked for future success; promising.
up·beat (ŭp'bēt') *n. Mus.* An unaccented beat, esp. the last beat of a measure.
up·braid (ŭp'brād') *v.* To reprove sharply; scold or chide vehemently; censure. [< OE *ŭpbrēdan*, "to throw up against," reproach.] —**up'braid'er** *n.*
up·bring·ing (ŭp'brĭng'ĭng) *n.* The rearing and training received during childhood.
up·com·ing (ŭp'kŭm'ĭng) *adj.* About to take place; approaching.
up·coun·try (ŭp'kŭn'trē) *n.* The interior of a country. —*adj.* (ŭp'kŭn'trē). Located, originating from, or characteristic of the upcountry. —**up'coun'try** *adv.*
up·date (ŭp'dāt') *v.* To bring up to date.
up·draft (ŭp'drăft', -dräft') *n.* An upward current of air.
up·end (ŭp'ĕnd') *v.* **1.** To stand, set, or turn on one end. **2.** To overturn or overthrow.
up·grade (ŭp'grād') *v.* To raise to a higher grade or standard. —*n.* An incline leading uphill.
up·heav·al (ŭp'hē'vəl) *n.* **1.** The process or an instance of being heaved upward. **2.** A sudden and violent disruption. **3.** A lifting of the earth's crust.
up·hill (ŭp'hĭl') *adj.* **1.** Going up a hill or slope. **2.** Prolonged and laborious. —*n.* (ŭp'hĭl'). An upward incline. —*adv.* (ŭp'hĭl'). Toward higher ground; upward.
up·hold (ŭp-hōld') *v.* **1.** To hold aloft. **2.** To prevent from falling; support. **3.** To maintain or affirm in the face of a challenge.
up·hol·ster (ŭp-hōl'stər) *v.* To furnish (chairs, sofas, etc.) with stuffing, springs, cushions, and covering fabric. [< ME *upholdester*, one who upholds or repairs.] —**up·hol'ster·er** *n.*
up·hol·ster·y (ŭp-hōl'stər-ē, -strē) *n., pl.* **-ies. 1.** The materials used in upholstering. **2.** The business of upholstering.
UPI, U.P.I. United Press International.
up·keep (ŭp'kēp') *n.* **1.** Maintenance in proper condition. **2.** The cost of such maintenance.
up·land (ŭp'lənd, -lănd') *n.* The higher parts of a region or tract of land. —**up'land** *adj.*
up·lift (ŭp-lĭft') *v.* **1.** To raise up or aloft; elevate. **2.** To raise to a higher social, intellectual, or moral level. —*n.* (ŭp'lĭft'). **1.** The act, process, or result of lifting up. **2.** A movement to improve social, moral, or intellectual standards.
up·on (ə-pŏn', ə-pôn') *prep.* On.
up·per (ŭp'ər) *adj.* **1.** Higher in place, position, or rank. **2.** **Upper.** *Geol. & Archaeol.* Being a later division of the period named. —*n.* That part of a shoe above the sole.

up·per-case (ŭp′ər-kās′) *adj.* Pertaining to or printed in capital letters.
up·per-class (ŭp′ər-klăs′, -kläs′) *adj.* **1.** Pertaining to an upper social class. **2.** Of or characteristic of the junior and senior classes in a school or college.
upper crust. *Informal.* The highest social class or group.
up·per·cut (ŭp′ər-kŭt′) *n. Boxing.* A short swinging blow directed upward, as to the opponent's chin. —**up′per·cut′** *v.*
upper hand. A position of control or advantage.
up·per·most (ŭp′ər-mōst′) *adj.* Highest in position, place, rank, or influence; foremost. —*adv.* In the first or highest rank, position, or place; first.
Upper Vol·ta (vŏl′tə). A republic of W Africa. Pop. 4,600,000. Cap. Ouagadougou.

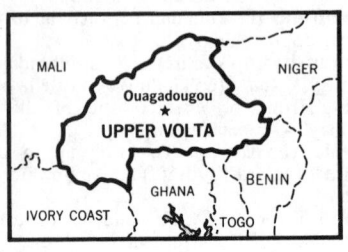

Upper Volta

up·pi·ty (ŭp′ə-tē) *adj. Informal.* Tending to be snobbish or arrogant. [< UP.]
up·raise (ŭp-rāz′) *v.* To raise or lift up; elevate.
up·right (ŭp′rīt′) *adj.* **1. a.** In a vertical position, direction, or stance. **b.** Erect in posture or carriage. **2.** Morally respectable; honorable. —*n.* Something standing upright, as a beam. —**up′right′ness** *n.*
upright piano. A piano having vertically mounted strings.
up·ris·ing (ŭp′rī′zĭng) *n.* **1.** The act of rising or rising up. **2.** A revolt; insurrection.
up·roar (ŭp′rôr′, -rōr′) *n.* A condition of noisy excitement and confusion; a tumult. [< MDu *op*, up + *roer*, motion.]
up·roar·i·ous (ŭp′rôr′ē-əs, ŭp′rōr′-) *adj.* **1.** Causing or accompanied by an uproar. **2.** Boisterous. —**up′roar′i·ous·ly** *adv.*
up·root (ŭp-rōōt′, -rŏŏt′) *v.* **1.** To tear or remove (a plant and its roots) from the ground. **2.** To destroy completely; eradicate. **3.** To force to leave an accustomed or native location. —**up·root′er** *n.*
up·set (ŭp-sĕt′) *v.* **-set, -setting. 1.** To overturn or capsize; tip over. **2.** To disturb the usual or normal functioning of. **3.** To distress or perturb mentally or emotionally. **4.** To defeat unexpectedly. —*n.* (ŭp′sĕt′). **1. a.** An act of upsetting. **b.** The condition of being upset. **2.** A disturbance, disorder, or agitation. **3.** A game or contest in which the favorite is defeated. —*adj.* (ŭp-sĕt′). **1.** Overturned; capsized. **2.** Disordered; disturbed. **3.** Distressed;

distraught; agitated. [Orig "to set up," "erect."] —**up·set′ter** *n.*
up·shot (ŭp′shŏt′) *n.* The final result; outcome. [Orig the last shot in an archery contest.]
up·side-down (ŭp′sīd′doun′) *adj.* **1.** Overturned completely so that the upper side is down. **2.** In great disorder or confusion; topsy-turvy. —*adv.* Also **upside down. 1.** With the upper and lower parts reversed in position. **2.** In or into great disorder. [< ME *up so doun,* "up as if down."]
up·si·lon (ŭp′sə-lŏn′) *n.* The 20th letter of the Greek alphabet, representing *u* (sometimes *y*).
up·stage (ŭp′stāj′) *adj.* Pertaining to the rear of a stage. —*adv.* Toward, to, on, or at the back part of a stage. —*v.* (ŭp′stāj′). **1.** To distract audience attention from (another actor). **2.** To steal the show from.
up·stairs (ŭp′stârz′) *adv.* In, on, or to an upper floor; up the stairs. —*adj.* (ŭp′stârz′). Of or pertaining to an upper floor or floors. —*n.* (ŭp′stârz′). *(takes sing. or pl. v.).* A floor above the ground level.
up·stand·ing (ŭp′stăn′dĭng, ŭp′-) *adj.* **1.** Standing erect or upright. **2.** Morally upright; honest.
up·start (ŭp′stärt′) *n.* One of humble origin who attains sudden wealth or prominence, esp. one having an exaggerated sense of his own importance or ability.
up·state (ŭp′stāt′) *adj.* Designating that part of a state lying inland or farther north of a large city. —**up′state′** *adv.*
up·stream (ŭp′strēm′) *adv.* In, at, or toward the source of a stream or current.
up·surge (ŭp′sûrj′) *n.* A rapid upward swell or rise.
up·swing (ŭp′swĭng′) *n.* An upward swing or trend; an increase.
up·take (ŭp′tāk′) *n.* **1.** A passage for drawing up smoke or air. **2.** Understanding; comprehension: *quick on the uptake.*
up tight. Also **up·tight** (ŭp′tīt′). *Slang.* Tense; nervous.
up-to-date (ŭp′tə-dāt′) *adj.* Informed of or reflecting the latest improvement, facts, or style; modern.
up·town (ŭp′toun′) *adv.* In or toward the upper part of a city. —*n.* The upper part of a city. —**up′town′** *adj.*
up·turn (ŭp′tûrn′) *n.* An upward movement, curve, or trend.
up·ward (ŭp′wərd) *adv.* Also **up·wards** (-wərdz). In, to, or toward a higher place, level, or position. —**upward** or **upwards** of. More than; in excess of. —*adj.* Ascending.
U·ral-Al·ta·ic (yŏŏr′əl-ăl-tā′ĭk) *n.* A hypothetical group of languages including Uralic and Altaic. —**U′ral-Al·ta′ic** *adj.*
U·ral·ic (yŏŏ-răl′ĭk) *n.* A family of languages including Finno-Ugric and Samoyed. —**U·ral′-ic** *adj.*
U·ral Mountains (yŏŏr′əl). A mountain system of the Soviet Union, constituting the traditional boundary between Europe and Asia.
u·ra·ni·um (yŏŏ-rā′nē-əm) *n. Symbol* **U** A heavy, silvery-white radioactive metallic ele-

---

ă pat/ā ate/âr care/ä bar/b bib/ch chew/d deed/ĕ pet/ē be/f fit/g gag/h hat/hw what/
ĭ pit/ī pie/îr pier/j judge/k kick/l lid, fatal/m mum/n no, sudden/ng sing/ŏ pot/ō go/

ment used in research, nuclear fuels, and nuclear weapons. Atomic number 92, atomic weight 238.03. [< URANUS.]

U•ra•nus (yŏŏr'rə-nəs, yŏŏ-rā'nəs) *n.* The 7th planet from the sun, revolving about it every 84.02 years at a distance of approx. 1,790,000,000 miles. It has an equatorial diameter of 30,000 miles, a mass 14.6 times that of Earth, and five satellites. [< Gk *Ouranos,* "heaven," god of the sky.] —**U•ra'ni•an** (yŏŏ-rā'nē-ən, -rān'yən) *adj.*

u•ra•ri. Variant of **curare.**

ur•ban (ûr'bən) *adj.* **1.** Pertaining to, located in, or constituting a city. **2.** Characteristic of the city or city life. [< L *urbs,* city.]

ur•bane (ûr'bān') *adj.* Having the refined manners of polite society; suave. [< L *urbānus,* characteristic of city life.] —**ur'bane'ly** *adv.* —**ur'ban'i•ty** (-bǎn'ə-tē) *n.*

ur•ban•ize (ûr'bə-nīz') *v.* **-ized, -izing.** To cause to become urban in nature or character. —**ur'ban•i•za'tion** *n.*

ur•chin (ûr'chĭn) *n.* **1.** A small, mischievous boy; a scamp. **2.** See **sea urchin.** [< L *hēr,* hedgehog.]

Ur•du (ŏŏr'dŏŏ, ûr'-) *n.* **1.** A Hindustani language spoken in West Pakistan. **2.** Hindustani.

-ure. *comb. form.* **1.** An act or process: **erasure.** **2.** A function or office or a body performing a function: **legislature.** [< L *-ūra.*]

u•re•a (yŏŏ-rē'ə) *n.* A white crystalline or powdery compound, CON_2H_4, found in mammalian urine and other body fluids. [< URINE.]

u•re•mi•a (yŏŏ-rē'mē-ə) *n.* An excess of urea in the blood, characterized by headache, nausea, vomiting, and coma.

u•re•ter (yŏŏ-rē'tər) *n.* The long, narrow duct that conveys urine from the kidney to the urinary bladder. [< Gk *ouron,* urine.]

u•re•thra (yŏŏ-rē'thrə) *n., pl.* **-thras** or **-thrae** (-thrē). The canal through which urine is discharged and which serves as the male genital duct. [< Gk *ouron,* urine.] —**u•re'thral** *adj.*

urge (ûrj) *v.* **urged, urging. 1.** To drive onward forcefully; impel; spur. **2.** To entreat earnestly and repeatedly; plead with; exhort. **3.** To advocate persistently; press emphatically. —*n.* An irresistible or impelling force, influence, or instinct. [L *urgēre,* to push, press.]

ur•gent (ûr'jənt) *adj.* **1.** Compelling immediate action; pressing: *a crisis of an urgent nature.* **2.** Conveying a sense of pressing importance or necessity. [< L *urgēre,* to push, press, URGE.] —**ur'gen•cy** *n.* —**ur'gent•ly** *adv.*

-urgy. *comb. form.* A technology: **metallurgy.** [< Gk *ergon,* work.]

u•ric (yŏŏr'ĭk) *adj.* Of, in, or obtained from urine.

u•ri•nal (yŏŏr'ə-nəl) *n.* **1.** An upright wall fixture used by men for urinating. **2.** A place containing such a fixture or fixtures.

u•ri•nal•y•sis (yŏŏr'ə-nǎl'ə-sĭs) *n.* The chemical analysis of urine.

u•ri•nar•y (yŏŏr'ə-nĕr'ē) *adj.* Pertaining to urine, its production, function, or excretion.

urinary bladder. A muscular membrane-lined sac situated in the anterior part of the pelvic cavity and used as a urine reservoir prior to excretion.

u•ri•nate (yŏŏr'ə-nāt') *v.* **-nated, -nating.** To excrete urine.

u•rine (yŏŏr'ĭn) *n.* The fluid and dissolved substances secreted by the kidneys, stored in the bladder, and excreted from the body through the urethra. [< L *ūrīna.*]

urn (ûrn) *n.* **1.** A vase with a pedestal, used esp. as a receptacle for the ashes of the cremated dead. **2.** A closed metal vessel with a spigot, used for warming or serving tea or coffee; a samovar. [< L *urna.*]

Ur•sa Major (ûr'sə). A constellation in the region of the N celestial pole, containing the Big Dipper. [< L *ursus,* bear.]

Ursa Minor. A constellation having the shape of a ladle with Polaris at the tip of its handle.

ur•sine (ûr'sīn') *adj.* Of or characteristic of a bear. [< L *ursus,* bear.]

ur•ti•car•i•a (ûr'tĭ-kâr'ē-ə) *n.* A skin condition having various causes, characterized by intensely itching welts. [< L *urtīca,* nettle.]

U•ru•guay (yŏŏr'ə-gwā, -gwī'). A republic of SE South America. Pop. 2,590,000. Cap. Montevideo.

Uruguay

us (ŭs) *pron.* The objective case of the 1st person pl. pronoun *we,* used as the direct or indirect object of a verb or as the object of a preposition. [< OE *ūs.* See **nes-.**]

US, U.S. United States.

USA, U.S.A. 1. United States Army. **2.** United States of America.

us•a•ble (yŏŏ'zə-bəl) *adj.* Also **use•a•ble. 1.** Capable of being used. **2.** In a fit condition for use. —**us'a•ble•ness** *n.*

USAF, U.S.A.F. United States Air Force.

us•age (yŏŏ'sĭj, -zĭj) *n.* **1.** The act or manner of using; use or employment. **2.** Customary practice; habitual use. **3.** The actual way in which a language or its elements are used, interrelated, or pronounced.

USCG, U.S.C.G. United States Coast Guard.

USDA, U.S.D.A. United States Department of Agriculture.

use (yŏŏz) *v.* **used, using. 1.** To bring or put into service; employ for some purpose. **2.** To consume or expend. **3.** *Informal.* To exploit for one's own advantage. —Used as an auxiliary in the past tense to express former prac-

---

ô paw, for/oi boy/ou out/ŏŏ took/ŏŏ coo/p pop/r run/s sauce/sh shy/t to/th thin/*th* the/ ŭ cut/ûr fur/v van/w wag/y yes/z size/zh vision/ə ago, item, edible, gallop, circus/

tice, fact, or state: *I used to go; he didn't use to.*
—used to. Accustomed to. *—n.* (yσ̄σs). **1. a.**
The act of using. **b.** The condition or fact of
being used. **2.** The manner of using; usage.
3. a. The permission to use or privilege of using
something: *have use of the car.* **b.** The power or
ability to use something: *lose the use of one
arm.* **4.** The need or occasion to use: *Do you
have any use for this book?* **5.** The quality of
being suitable or adaptable to an end; usefulness. **6.** The goal, object, or purpose for which
something is used. **—have no use for. 1.** To
have no need of. **2.** To have no tolerance for;
dislike. **—in use.** Being used; occupied. [< L
ūti (pp *ūsus*).] **—us′er** *n.*

used (yσ̄σzd) *adj.* Not new; secondhand.

use·ful (yσ̄σs′fəl) *adj.* Capable of being used
advantageously or beneficially. **—use′ful·ly**
adv. **—use′ful·ness** *n.*

use·less (yσ̄σs′lĭs) *adj.* Having no beneficial
purpose or use; of little or no worth. **—use′·
less·ly** *adv.* **—use′less·ness** *n.*

ush·er (ŭsh′ər) *n.* **1.** An official doorkeeper, as
in a courtroom or legislative chamber. **2.** One
who escorts people to their seats in a theater,
church, stadium, etc. **3.** A male attendant at a
wedding. *—v.* **1.** To escort; lead or conduct.
2. To precede and introduce; be a forerunner
of. [< L *ōstiārius,* doorkeeper.]

USIA United States Information Agency.

U.S.M. United States Mail.

USMC, U.S.M.C. United States Marine Corps.

USN, U.S.N. United States Navy.

USO, U.S.O. United Service Organizations.

U.S.S. United States Ship.

U.S.S.R. Union of Soviet Socialist Republics.

u·su·al (yσ̄σ′zhσ̄σ-əl) *adj.* **1.** Such as is commonly or frequently encountered or used; ordinary; normal. **2.** Habitual or customary. [<
L *ūsus,* use, custom.] **—u′su·al·ly** *adv.* **—u′su·
al·ness** *n.*

u·surp (yσ̄σ-sûrp′, -zûrp′) *v.* To seize and hold
by force and without legal right or authority.
[< L *ūsūrpāre,* to take into use.] **—u′sur·pa′tion**
n. **—u·surp′er** *n.*

u·su·ry (yσ̄σ′zhə-rē) *n., pl.* **-ries. 1.** The lending
of money at an exorbitant rate of interest.
2. Such an excessive rate of interest. [< L
ūsūra, use of money lent, interest.] **—u′su·rer** *n.*
—u·su′ri·ous (yσ̄σ-zhσ̄σr′ē-əs) *adj.*

U·tah (yσ̄σ′tô, -tä) A state of the W U.S. Pop.
1,059,000. Cap. Salt Lake City.

u·ten·sil (yσ̄σ-tĕn′səl) *n.* Any instrument or
container, esp. one used domestically, as in a

kitchen or on a farm. [< L *ūtēnsilia,* "things
for use."]

u·ter·us (yσ̄σ′tər-əs) *n.* A pear-shaped muscular organ located in the pelvic cavity of
female mammals that holds the fertilized
ovum during the development of the fetus and
is the principal agent in its expulsion at birth.
[L.] **—u′ter·ine** (-ĭn, -tə-rīn′) *adj.*

u·til·i·tar·i·an (yσ̄σ-tĭl′ə-târ′ē-ən) *adj.* **1.** Pertaining to or associated with utility. **2.** Stressing utility over aesthetic qualities.

u·til·i·ty (yσ̄σ-tĭl′ə-tē) *n., pl.* **-ties. 1.** Usefulness.
2. A public service, such as gas, electricity,
water, or transportation. [< L *ūtī,* to USE.]

u·til·ize (yσ̄σ′tə-līz′) *v.* **-ized, -izing.** To put to
use for a certain purpose. **—u′til·i·za′tion** *n.*

ut·most (ŭt′mōst′) *adj.* **1.** Being or situated at
the farthest limit or point. **2.** Of the highest or
greatest degree, amount, or intensity. *—n.*
The greatest possible amount, degree, or extent; maximum. [< OE *ūtemest,* outermost.]

U·to-Az·tec·an (yσ̄σ′tō-ăz′tĕk′ən) *n.* **1.** A large
language family of North and Central Amer-
ican Indians, including Nahuatl. **2.** A tribe
speaking a Uto-Aztecan language. **3.** A member of such a tribe. **—U′to-Az′tec′an** *adj.*

u·to·pi·a (yσ̄σ-tō′pē-ə) *n.* **1.** Any condition,
place, or situation of social or political perfection. **2.** Any idealistic goal or concept for
social and political reform. [NL, "no-place."]
—u·to′pi·an *adj.*

ut·ter¹ (ŭt′ər) *v.* **1.** To express audibly; pronounce; say. **2.** To give forth as a sound: *utter
a sigh.* [< MDu *ūteren,* to drive away, announce, speak.] **—ut′ter·er** *n.*

ut·ter² (ŭt′ər) *adj.* Complete; absolute; entire.
[< OE *ūtera, ūttra,* outer, external. See ud-.]
—ut′ter·ly *adv.*

ut·ter·ance (ŭt′ər-əns) *n.* **1.** The act of uttering. **2.** Something that is uttered or expressed.

ut·ter·most (ŭt′ər-mōst′) *adj.* **1.** Utmost. **2.**
Outermost. *—n.* Utmost.

U-turn (yσ̄σ′tûrn′) *n.* A turn, as by a vehicle,
completely reversing the direction of travel.

u·vu·la (yσ̄σ′vyə-lə) *n.* The small, conical,
fleshy mass of tissue suspended from the center of the soft palate above the back of the
tongue. [< LL, "small grape."] **—u′vu·lar** *adj.*

ux·o·ri·ous (ŭk′sôr′ē-əs, ŭk′sōr′-, ŭg′zôr′-, ŭg′-
zōr′-) *adj.* Excessively submissive or devoted
to one's wife. [< L *uxor,* wife.]

Uz·bek Soviet Socialist Republic (σ̄σz′bĕk,
ŭz′-). A republic of the Soviet Union, in C
Asia. Pop. 11,963,000. Cap. Tashkent.

ă pat/ā ate/âr care/ä bar/b bib/ch chew/d deed/ĕ pet/ē be/f fit/g gag/h hat/hw what/
ĭ pit/ī pie/îr pier/j judge/k kick/l lid, fatal/m mum/n no, sudden/ng sing/ŏ pot/ō go/

Vv

v, V (vē) *n.* **1.** The 22nd letter of the English alphabet. **2.** Anything shaped like the letter **V**.
v The Roman numeral for five.
V 1. vanadium. **2.** velocity. **3.** volt. **4.** volume. **5.** The Roman numeral for five.
v. 1. verb. **2.** verse. **3.** version. **4.** versus. **5.** vide. **6.** voice. **7.** volume (book).
V. 1. vice (in titles). **2.** village.
VA Veterans' Administration.
Va. Virginia.
va•can•cy (vā′kən-sē) *n., pl.* **-cies. 1.** The state or condition of being vacant. **2.** A position, office, or accommodation that is unfilled or unoccupied.
va•cant (vā′kənt) *adj.* **1.** Containing nothing; empty. **2.** Not occupied. **3.** Expressionless; blank: *a vacant stare.* [< L *vacāre*, to be empty.] **—va′cant•ly** *adv.*
va•cate (vā′kāt′) *v.* **-cated, -cating.** To cease to occupy or hold; give up; leave. [L *vacāre*, to be empty.] **—va′cat•a•ble** *adj.*
va•ca•tion (vā-kā′shən) *n.* An interval of time devoted to rest or relaxation from work, study, etc. **—v.** To take or spend a vacation. [< L *vacātiō*, freedom, release from occupation.] **—va•ca′tion•er** *n.*
vac•ci•nate (văk′sə-nāt′) *v.* **-nated, -nating.** To inoculate with a vaccine to produce immunity against one of various diseases. **—vac′ci•na′tion** *n.* **—vac′ci•na′tor** *n.*
vac•cine (văk-sēn′) *n.* A suspension of attenuated or killed microorganisms, as of viruses or bacteria, incapable of inducing severe infection but capable, when inoculated, of counteracting the unmodified species. [F *(virus) vaccine,* (virus) of cowpox.]
vac•il•late (văs′ə-lāt′) *v.* **-lated, -lating. 1.** To sway to and fro; oscillate. **2.** To swing indecisively from one course of action or opinion to another; waver. [L *vacillāre*, to waver.] **—vac′il•la′tion** *n.* **—vac′il•la′tor** *n.*
va•cu•i•ty (vă-kyoo′ə-tē) *n., pl.* **-ties. 1.** Emptiness. **2.** An empty space; vacuum. **3.** Emptiness of mind. [< L *vacuus*, empty.]
vac•u•ous (văk′yoo-əs) *adj.* **1.** Devoid of matter; empty. **2.** Stupid; dull; inane. [L *vacuus*, empty.] **—vac′u•ous•ness** *n.*
vac•u•um (văk′yoo-əm, -yoom) *n., pl.* **-ums** or **vacua** (vak′yoo-ə). **1.** A space empty or relatively empty of matter. **2.** A state of emptiness; a void. **—v.** To clean with a vacuum cleaner. [< L *vacuus*, empty.] **—vac′u•um** *adj.*
vacuum cleaner. An electrical appliance that draws light dirt from surfaces by suction.
vacuum tube. An electron tube having an internal vacuum sufficiently high to permit electrons to move with low interaction with any remaining gas molecules.
Va•duz (fä-doots′). The capital of Liechtenstein. Pop. 4,000.
vag•a•bond (văg′ə-bŏnd′) *n.* A person who wanders from place to place with no apparent means of support. [< L *vagus*, wandering, undecided, VAGUE.] **—vag′a•bond′** *adj.*
va•gar•y (vā′gə-rē, və-gâr′ē) *n., pl.* **-ies. 1.** A whimsical notion or action. **2.** Often **vagaries.** An unpredictable change or fluctuation: *vagaries of weather.* [< L *vagārī*, to wander.]
va•gi•na (və-jī′nə) *n., pl.* **-nas** or **-nae** (-nē). The passage leading from the external genital orifice to the uterus in female mammals. [L *vāgīna*, sheath.] **—vag′i•nal** (văj′ə-nəl) *adj.*
va•grant (vā′grənt) *n.* A person who wanders from place to place and ekes out a living by begging or stealing; a tramp; vagabond. **—adj. 1.** Wandering from place to place; roving. **2.** Moving in a random fashion; not fixed in place. [Prob < L *vagus*, wandering, undecided, VAGUE.] **—va′gran•cy** *n.*
vague (văg) *adj.* **vaguer, vaguest. 1.** Not clearly expressed or outlined; inexplicit. **2.** Lacking definite shape, form, or character. **3.** Indistinctly felt, perceived, understood, or recalled. [< L *vagus*, wandering, undecided, vague.] **—vague′ly** *adv.* **—vague′ness** *n.*
vain (vān) *adj.* **1.** Unsuccessful; futile; fruitless. **2.** Lacking substance or worth; hollow. **3.** Showing undue preoccupation with one's appearance or accomplishments; conceited. **—in vain. 1.** To no avail. **2.** Irreverently. [< L *vānus*, empty.] **—vain′ly** *adv.*
vain•glo•ry (vān′glôr′ē, -glōr′ē) *n., pl.* **-ries. 1.** Excessive vanity. **2.** Vain and ostentatious display. **—vain•glo′ri•ous** *adj.*
val.
val•ance (văl′əns) *n.* A short ornamental drapery hung across the top of a window or along a bed, shelf, etc. [ME *valaunce.*]
vale (vāl) *n.* A valley; dale. [< L *vallis.*]
val•e•dic•to•ri•an (văl′ə-dĭk-tôr′ē-ən, -tōr′ē-ən) *n.* A student, usually of the highest scholastic standing, who delivers the valedictory at commencement.
val•e•dic•to•ry (văl′ə-dĭk′tə-rē) *n., pl.* **-ries.** A farewell address, esp. one delivered by a valedictorian. [< L *valedīcere*, to say farewell.]
va•lence (vā′ləns) *n.* Also **va•len•cy** (vā′lən-sē) *pl.* **-cies. 1.** *Chem.* The capacity of an atom or group of atoms to combine in specific proportions with other atoms or groups of atoms. **2.** An integer used to represent this capacity. [< L *valēre*, to be strong.]

ô paw, for/oi boy/ou out/ŏŏ took/ōō coo/p pop/r run/s sauce/sh shy/t to/th thin/*th* the/
ŭ cut/ûr fur/v van/w wag/y yes/z size/zh vision/ə ago, item, edible, gallop, circus/

Va•len•ci•a (və-lĕn'shĕ-ə, -shə). A city of E Spain. Pop. 583,000.

val•en•tine (văl'ən-tīn') n. 1. A greeting card sent on Saint Valentine's Day, February 14. 2. A person singled out as one's sweetheart on Saint Valentine's Day.

val•et (văl'ĭt, vă-lā') n. 1. A man's personal attendant. 2. A hotel employee who performs personal services for patrons. [< OF vaslet, orig "young nobleman," "squire."]

val•e•tu•di•nar•i•an (văl'ə-t/y/ōōd'n-âr'e-ən) n. A person constantly and morbidly concerned with his health. [L valētūdinārius, in poor health.] —val'e•tu'di•nar'i•an•ism' n.

Val•hal•la (văl-hăl'ə) n. Also **Wal•hal•la** (văl-, wŏl-). Norse Myth. The hall in which the souls of slain warriors were received by Odin.

val•iant (văl'yənt) adj. Possessing, showing, or acting with valor; brave; courageous; stouthearted. [< L valēre, to be strong.] —val'ian•cy n. —val'iant•ly adv.

val•id (văl'ĭd) adj. 1. Well-grounded; sound; supportable: a valid objection. 2. Having legal force: a valid passport. [< L validus, strong, effective.] —va•lid'i•ty (və-lĭd'ə-tē) n.

val•i•date (văl'ə-dāt') v. -dated, -dating. 1. To declare or make legally valid. 2. To substantiate; verify. —val'i•da'tion n.

va•lise (və-lēs') n. A small piece of hand luggage. [< ML valisia.]

Val•let•ta (və-lĕt'ə). The capital of Malta. Pop. 18,000.

val•ley (văl'ē) n., pl. -leys. 1. An elongated lowland between ranges of mountains or hills. 2. The land area drained by a river system. [< L vallis.]

val•or (văl'ər) n. Also chiefly Brit. **val•our**. Courage and boldness; bravery. [< L valēre, to be strong, be of value.] —val'or•ous adj.

val•u•a•ble (văl'yōō-ə-bəl, văl'yə-) adj. 1. Having high monetary or material value. 2. Having useful or admirable qualities or characteristics. —n. Often **valuables**. A valuable personal possession, as a piece of jewelry.

val•u•a•tion (văl'yōō-ā'shən) n. 1. The act of assessing the value or price of something; an appraisal. 2. The assessed value or price of something.

val•ue (văl'yōō) n. 1. An amount considered a suitable equivalent for something else; a fair return for goods or services. 2. Monetary or material worth. 3. Worth in usefulness or importance to the possessor; merit. 4. A principle, standard, or quality considered worthwhile or desirable. 5. Precise meaning. 6. An assigned or calculated numerical quantity. 7. Mus. The relative duration of a tone or rest. 8. The relative darkness or lightness of a color in a picture. —v. -ued, -uing. 1. To determine or estimate the value of; appraise. 2. To prize; esteem. 3. To rate according to relative estimate of worth or desirability; evaluate. [< L valēre, to be strong, be of value.]

valve (vălv) n. 1. A membranous bodily structure that retards or prevents the return flow of a bodily fluid. 2. a. Any of various devices that regulate gas or liquid flow by opening, closing, or obstructing its passage, as through piping.

b. The control element of such a device. c. A device in a brass wind instrument that permits rapid variation of tube length to produce changes in pitch. 3. A paired or separable structure or part, as of a seed pod or mollusk shell. [< L valva, the leaf of a door.]

va•moose (vă-mōōs', və-) v. -moosed, -moosing. Slang. To leave or go away hastily. [Span vamos, "let's go."]

vamp¹ (vămp) n. The part of a boot or shoe covering the instep and sometimes the toe. —v. 1. To provide with a new vamp. 2. To refurbish. 3. To improvise. [< OF avantpie.]

vamp² (vămp). Informal. n. An unscrupulously seductive woman. —v. To play the vamp; seduce and exploit. [Short for VAMPIRE.]

vam•pire (văm'pīr') n. 1. In folklore, one that rises from the grave by night to suck the blood of sleeping persons. 2. One who preys upon others, esp. an extortionist or exploiter. 3. Also **vampire bat**. Any of various tropical bats thought to feed on the blood of living mammals. [< Hung vampir.]

vam•pir•ism (văm'pī-rĭz'əm) n. 1. Belief in the vampires of folklore. 2. The practice of a vampire; bloodsucking.

van¹ (văn) n. 1. A covered truck or wagon for transporting goods or livestock. 2. Brit. A closed railroad car for baggage or freight. [Short for CARAVAN.]

van² (văn) n. The vanguard. [Short for VANGUARD.]

va•na•di•um (və-nā'dē-əm) n. Symbol **V** A bright, white, soft, ductile metallic element, used in rust-resistant high-speed tools, as a carbon stabilizer in some steels, and as a catalyst. Atomic number 23, atomic weight 50.942. [< ON Vanadīs, name of Freya, goddess of love and beauty.]

Van Al•len belt (văn ăl'ən). Either of two zones of high-intensity radiation trapped in the earth's magnetic field, beginning at an altitude of approx. 800 kilometers and extending thousands of kilometers into space. [< J. Van Allen (born 1914), American physicist.]

Van Bu•ren (văn byōōr'ən), Martin. 1782–

Martin Van Buren

1862. 8th President of the U.S. (1837–41).

Van•cou•ver (văn-koo'vər). A city of S,W British Columbia, Canada. Pop. 385,000.

van•dal (vănd'l) n. One who willfully or maliciously defaces or destroys public or private property. [< VANDAL.] —**van'dal•ism'** n.

Van•dal (vănd'l) n. A member of a Germanic people that sacked Rome in A.D. 455. [L *Vandalus,* "wanderer" < Gmc.]

Van de Graaff generator (văn' də grăf'). An electrostatic generator in which electric charge is either removed from or transferred to a large, hollow spherical electrode by a rapidly moving belt. [< R. *Van de Graaff* (1901–67), American physicist.]

Van•dyke beard (văn-dīk'). A short pointed beard. [< Sir Anthony *Vandyke* (1599–1641), Flemish painter.]

vane (văn) n. 1. A device that pivots on an elevated vertical spindle to indicate wind direction. 2. One of several surfaces radially mounted along an axis that is turned by or used to turn a fluid. [< OE *fana,* banner. See pan-.]

van Gogh (văn gō', gôKH'), **Vincent.** 1853–1890. Dutch painter.

van•guard (văn'gärd') n. 1. The foremost position in an army or fleet; van. 2. The leading position in a trend or movement. [< OF *avant-garde.*]

va•nil•la (və-nĭl'ə) n. 1. A flavoring obtained from the narrow, beanlike pods of a tropical American orchid. 2. An orchid bearing such pods. [Span *vainilla,* "little sheath."]

van•ish (văn'ĭsh) v. 1. To disappear or become invisible, esp. quickly. 2. To pass out of existence. [< L *ēvānēscere.*]

van•i•ty (văn'ə-tē) n., pl. **-ties.** 1. Excessive pride; conceit. 2. Futility; worthlessness. 3. Something vain, futile, or worthless. 4. A case for cosmetics. [< L *vānus,* empty, vain.]

van•quish (văng'kwĭsh, văn'-) v. 1. To defeat; subjugate. 2. To overcome; suppress. [< L *vincere.*] —**van'quish•er** n.

van•tage (văn'tĭj) n. 1. a. An advantage in a competition. b. Something providing superiority or advantage. 2. A commanding view or outlook. [< OF *avantage,* advantage.]

vap•id (văp'ĭd) adj. Insipid; flat; stale. [< L *vapidus.*] —**vap'id•ly** adv. —**vap'id•ness** n.

va•por (vā'pər) n. Also chiefly Brit. **va•pour.** 1. Any barely visible or cloudy diffused matter, as mist, fumes, or smoke, suspended in the air. 2. The gaseous state of any substance that is liquid or solid under ordinary conditions. 3. vapors. Archaic. Depression or hysteria. [< L, steam.]

va•por•ize (vā'pə-rīz') v. **-ized, -izing.** To convert or be converted into vapor, esp. by heating. —**va'por•i•za'tion** n. —**va'por•iz'er** n.

va•por•ous (vā'pər-əs) adj. 1. Pertaining to or resembling vapor. 2. a. Volatile. b. Giving off vapors. 3. Insubstantial, vague, or ethereal. 4. Extravagantly fanciful. —**va'por•ous•ly** adv. —**va'por•ous•ness** n.

var. 1. variable. 2. variant. 3. variation. 4. variety. 5. various.

var•i•a•ble (vâr'ē-ə-bəl) adj. 1. a. Subject to

variation; changeable. b. Inconstant; fickle. 2. *Math.* Having no fixed quantitative value. —n. 1. Anything that varies or is prone to variation. 2. *Math.* A quantity capable of assuming any of a set of values. —**var'i•a•bil'i•ty,** **var'i•a•ble•ness** n. —**var'i•a•bly** adv.

var•i•ance (vâr'ē-əns) n. 1. a. The act of varying. b. Variation; difference. 2. A difference of opinion; dispute. 3. A license to engage in an act contrary to a usual rule.

var•i•ant (vâr'ē-ənt) adj. 1. Exhibiting variation; differing. 2. Tending to vary; variable. 3. Deviant. —n. Something exhibiting slight variation in form from another, as a different spelling of the same word.

var•i•a•tion (vâr'ē-ā'shən) n. 1. The act, process, or result of varying; change or deviation. 2. The extent or degree of such change. 3. Something that is slightly different from another of the same type. 4. A musical form that is an altered version of a given theme, diverging from it by melodic ornamentation and changes in harmony, rhythm, or key.

var•i•col•ored (vâr'ĭ-kŭl'ərd) adj. Having a variety of colors; variegated.

var•i•cose (văr'ə-kōs') adj. Designating blood or lymph vessels that are abnormally dilated, knotted, and tortuous. [< L *varix,* swollen vein.]

var•ied (vâr'ēd) adj. 1. Marked by variety. 2. Modified or altered. 3. Varicolored. —**var'ied•ly** adv.

var•i•e•gate (vâr'ē-ə-gāt') v. **-gated, -gating.** 1. To impart a variety of colors to. 2. To give variety to; diversify. —**var'i•e•ga'tion** n.

va•ri•e•ty (və-rī'ə-tē) n., pl. **-ties.** 1. The condition or quality of being various or varied; diversity. 2. A number of varied things, esp. of a particular group; an assortment. 3. A different kind, sort, or form of something of the same general classification. 4. An organism, esp. a plant, belonging to a naturally occurring or selectively bred subdivision of a species. [< L *varius,* VARIOUS.]

var•i•ous (vâr'ē-əs) adj. 1. a. Of diverse kinds. b. Unlike; different. 2. More than one; several. 3. Many-sided; versatile. 4. Having a variegated nature or appearance. 5. Individual and separate: *The various reports all agreed.* [L *varius,* speckled, changeable.] —**var'i•ous•ly** adv. —**var'i•ous•ness** n.

Usage: Various sometimes appears as a plural collective pronoun followed by *of* rather than by a noun, but the usage is not standard: *He spoke to various of the members. Various* has its proper function as an adjective in *He spoke to various members.*

var•let (vär'lĭt) n. Archaic. 1. An attendant. 2. A rascal; knave. [OF *vaslet, valet,* VALET.]

var•mint (vär'mənt) n. Regional. An animal or person considered objectionable or troublesome. [Var of VERMIN.]

var•nish (vär'nĭsh) n. 1. An oil-based liquid covering used to coat a surface with a hard, glossy, thin film. 2. a. The smooth coating or gloss resulting from the application of varnish. b. Something resembling varnish. 3. Outward show; gloss. [< OF *vernis.*] —**var'nish** v.

ô paw, for/oi boy/ou out/oo took/oo coo/p pop/r run/s sauce/sh shy/t to/th thin/*th* the/
ŭ cut/ûr fur/v van/w wag/y yes/z size/zh vision/ə ago, item, edible, gallop, circus/

var•si•ty (vär′sə-tē) *n., pl.* **-ties.** 1. The principal team representing a university, college, or school, as in sports. 2. *Brit. Slang.* A university. [Short for UNIVERSITY.] **—var′si•ty** *adj.*

var•y (vâr′ē) *v.* **-ied, -ying.** 1. To cause or undergo change; modify or alter. 2. To give variety to; diversify. 3. To deviate; diverge; differ. [< L *varius,* speckled, changeable.]

vas•cu•lar (văs′kyə-lər) *adj.* Of or containing vessels for the circulation of fluids such as blood, lymph, or sap. [< L *văs,* vessel.]

vase (vās, văz, väz) *n.* A tall open vessel used chiefly for holding and displaying flowers. [< L *văs,* vessel.]

Vas•e•line (văs′ə-lēn′, -lĭn) *n.* A trademark for a petroleum jelly used primarily as a vehicle for ointments and as a protective coating for metals. [< G *Wasser,* water.]

vas•o•mo•tor (văs′ō-mō′tər, vā′sō-) *adj.* Causing or regulating constriction or dilation of blood vessels.

vas•sal (văs′əl) *n.* 1. One who holds land from a feudal lord and receives protection in return for homage and allegiance. 2. One subservient to another; a subordinate or dependent. [< ML *vassus,* servant, valet.]

vas•sal•age (văs′ə-lĭj) *n.* 1. The condition of being a vassal. 2. The service, homage, and fealty required of a vassal. 3. Subordination or subjection: *"Am I the man to reproach Coleridge with this vassalage to opium?"* (De Quincey). 4. A fief.

vast (văst, väst) *adj.* 1. Very great in size, amount, or quantity. 2. Very great in area or extent; immense. [L *vastus,* immense, vast.] **—vast′ly** *adv.* **—vast′ness** *n.*

vat (văt) *n.* A large tub or barrel used to store or hold liquids. [< OE *fæt.* See **ped-²**.]

vat•ic (văt′ĭk) *adj.* Prophetic; oracular. [< L *vātēs,* prophet.]

Vat•i•can (văt′ĭ-kən) *n.* 1. **the Vatican.** The official residence of the pope in Vatican City. 2. The papal government.

Vatican City. A sovereign papal state in Rome, Italy. Pop. 900.

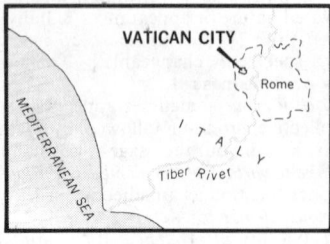

Vatican City

vau. Variant of **vav.**

vaude•ville (vôd′vĭl, vōd′-, vô′də-vĭl′) *n.* Stage entertainment offering a variety of short acts. [< OF *vaudevire.*]

vault¹ (vôlt) *n.* 1. An arched structure forming a ceiling or roof. 2. A room with arched walls and ceiling, esp. when underground, as a storeroom. 3. A compartment for the safekeeping of valuables. 4. A burial chamber. *—v.* To construct or cover with a vault. [< VL **volvita,* a turn, vault.]

vault² (vôlt) *v.* To jump or leap over, esp. with the aid of a support, as the hands or a pole. *—n.* The act of vaulting; a leap. [< L *volvere,* to turn.] **—vault′er** *n.*

vaunt (vônt, vänt) *v.* To boast; brag. [< L *vānus,* empty, vain.] **—vaunt** *n.*

vav (väv, vôv) *n.* Also **vau, waw.** The 6th letter of the Hebrew alphabet, representing *w.*

vb. verb.

V.C. Vietcong.

VD venereal disease.

veal (vēl) *n.* The meat of a calf. [< L *vitulus,* calf, "yearling."]

vec•tor (věk′tər) *n.* 1. *Math.* A quantity completely specified by a magnitude and a direction. 2. An organism that transmits microorganisms that cause disease. [L, carrier.] **—vec•to′ri•al** (věk-tôr′ē-əl, -tōr′ē-əl) *adj.*

Ve•da (vā′də, vē′-) *n.* Any of the oldest sacred writings of Hinduism. [Sk *veda,* "knowledge."] **—Ve′dic** *adj.*

Ve•dan•ta (vĭ-dän′tə, -dăn′tə) *n.* The Hindu doctrine that all reality is a single principle, Brahman, and that the believer's goal is to transcend the limitations of self-identity and realize his unity with Brahman. [Sk *vedanta,* "complete knowledge of the Veda."] **—Ve•dan′tic** *adj.*

veer (vîr) *v.* To turn aside from a course or direction; swerve; shift. [< VL **virāre.*] **—veer** *n.* **—veer′ing•ly** *adv.*

Ve•ga (vē′gə, vā′-) *n.* The brightest star in the constellation Lyra. [ML.]

veg•e•ta•ble (věj′tə-bəl, věj′ə-tə-) *n.* 1. **a.** A plant cultivated for an edible part, as roots, stems, leaves, or flowers. **b.** The edible part of such a plant. 2. A plant as distinguished from an animal or mineral. 3. A person who leads a passive or inert existence. *—adj.* 1. Of, pertaining to, or derived from plants. 2. Suggestive of inactivity. [< L *vegetus,* lively.]

veg•e•tar•i•an (věj′ə-târ′ē-ən) *n.* One who practices or advocates vegetarianism. **—veg′e•tar′i•an** *adj.*

veg•e•tar•i•an•ism (věj′ə-târ′ē-ə-nĭz′əm) *n.* 1. The practice of eating only vegetables and plant products. 2. The practice of not eating meat.

veg•e•tate (věj′ə-tāt′) *v.* **-tated, -tating.** 1. To grow or sprout as a plant does. 2. To lead a passive or inert existence. [LL *vegetāre,* to grow.]

veg•e•ta•tion (věj′ə-tā′shən) *n.* 1. The act or process of vegetating. 2. Plant life collectively.

veg•e•ta•tive (věj′ə-tā′tĭv) *adj.* 1. Of, pertaining to, or characteristic of plants or plant growth. 2. *Biol.* **a.** Of, pertaining to, or capable of growth. **b.** Of, pertaining to, or functioning in processes such as growth or nutrition rather than sexual reproduction.

ve•he•ment (vē′ə-mənt) *adj.* 1. Forceful; intense; ardent. 2. Strong; violent. [< L *vehemēns.*] **—ve′he•mence** *n.* **—ve′he•ment•ly** *adv.*

ve•hi•cle (vē′ĭ-kəl) *n.* 1. Any device for carrying passengers, goods, or equipment; a con-

veyance. **2.** A medium through which something is expressed or conveyed. **3.** A substance used as the medium in which active ingredients are applied or administered. [< L *vehere,* to carry.] —**ve·hic'u·lar** (vē-hĭk'yə-lər) *adj.*
veil (vāl) *n.* **1.** A piece of cloth, often transparent, worn by women over the head or face. **2.** The life or vows of a nun: *take the veil.* **3.** Anything that conceals, separates, or screens: *a veil of secrecy.* —*v.* To cover with or as with a veil. [< L *vēlum,* covering, veil.]
veil·ing (vā'lĭng) *n.* **1.** A veil. **2.** Gauzy material used for veils.
vein (vān) *n.* **1.** A vessel that transports blood toward the heart. **2.** Loosely, any blood vessel. **3.** One of the branching structures forming the framework of a leaf or an insect's wing. **4.** A regularly shaped and lengthy occurrence of an ore; a lode. **5.** A long, wavy strip of color, as in marble. **6.** Any fissure, crack, or cleft. **7.** Inherent character or quality; a strain or streak. **8.** Style or mode of expression: *talk in a serious vein.* —*v.* To form or mark with veins. [< L *vēna,* vein.]
Ve·láz·quez (və-läs'kĭs, -käs, və-läs'-), **Diego.** 1599–1660. Spanish painter.
veldt (fĕlt, vĕlt) *n.* Also **veld.** Any of the open grasslands of S Africa. [Afrik *veld.*]
vel·le·i·ty (vĕ-lē'ə-tē) *n., pl.* **-ties. 1.** The lowest level of volition. **2.** A mere wish. [< L *velle,* to wish.]
vel·lum (vĕl'əm) *n.* **1.** A fine parchment made from the skins of calf, lamb, or kid and used for the pages and binding of fine books. **2.** A paper resembling vellum. [< OF *veel,* calf, veal.]
ve·loc·i·pede (və-lŏs'ə-pēd') *n.* A tricycle. [F *vélocipède,* "swift-footed."]
ve·loc·i·ty (və-lŏs'ə-tē) *n., pl.* **-ties. 1.** Rapidity or speed. **2.** *Phys.* A vector quantity, the magnitude of which is a body's speed and the direction of which is the body's direction of motion. [< L *vēlōx,* fast.]
ve·lours, ve·lour (və-lŏor') *n., pl.* **-lours** (-lŏor'). A closely napped, velvetlike fabric. [< L *villus,* shaggy hair, wool.]
ve·lum (vē'ləm) *n., pl.* **-la** (-lə). A covering or partition of thin membranous tissue. [< L *vēlum,* veil, covering, sail.]
vel·vet (vĕl'vĭt) *n.* **1. a.** A fabric of silk or a synthetic fiber such as rayon, having a smooth, dense pile and a plain back. **b.** Anything resembling this fabric. **2.** Smoothness; softness. **3.** The soft covering on the newly developing antlers of deer. —*adj.* Made of, covered with, or resembling velvet. [< L *villus,* shaggy hair, wool.] —**vel'vet·y** *adj.*
vel·vet·een (vĕl'və-tēn') *n.* A velvetlike fabric made of cotton.
ve·nal (vē'nəl) *adj.* Open or susceptible to bribery; corrupt or corruptible. [< L *vēnum,* sale.] —**ve·nal'i·ty** (-năl'ə-tē) *n.* —**ve'nal·ly** *adv.*
vend (vĕnd) *v.* To sell, esp. as a vender. [< L *vēndere.*]
vend·ee (vĕn-dē') *n.* A buyer.
ven·der (vĕn'dər) *n.* Also **ven·dor. 1.** One who vends; a peddler. **2.** A vending machine.

ven·det·ta (vĕn-dĕt'ə) *n.* A hereditary blood feud between two families. [< L *vindicāre,* to revenge, VINDICATE.]
vending machine. A coin-operated machine that dispenses small articles.
ve·neer (və-nîr') *n.* **1.** A thin finishing or surface layer bonded to an inferior substratum. **2.** Surface show; gloss. —*v.* To overlay with a veneer. [< G *furniren,* to furnish, veneer.]
ven·er·a·ble (vĕn'ər-ə-bəl) *adj.* **1.** Worthy of reverence or respect by virtue of dignity, position, or age. **2.** Commanding reverence by association: *venerable relics.* [< L *venerāri,* VENERATE.] —**ven'er·a·bil'i·ty** *n.*
ven·er·ate (vĕn'ə-rāt') *v.* **-ated, -ating.** To regard with respect and reverence. [L *venerāri.*] —**ven'er·a'tion** *n.* —**ven'er·a'tor** *n.*
ve·ne·re·al (və-nîr'ē-əl) *adj.* **1.** Pertaining to sexual intercourse. **2.** Transmitted by sexual intercourse. **3.** Pertaining to the genitals. [< L *venus,* love, lust.]
Venetian blind. A window blind consisting of adjustable horizontal or sometimes vertical slats that can be set at a desired angle to regulate the amount of light admitted.
Ven·e·zue·la (vĕn'ə-zwā'lə, -zwē'lə). A republic in N South America. Pop. 8,722,000. Cap. Caracas.

Venezuela

venge·ance (vĕn'jəns) *n.* Retaliation for a wrong or injury; retribution. [< L *vindicāre,* to revenge, VINDICATE.]
venge·ful (vĕnj'fəl) *adj.* Desiring vengeance; vindictive. —**venge'ful·ness** *n.*
ve·ni·al (vē'nē-əl, vēn'yəl) *adj.* Easily excused or forgiven; pardonable: *a venial offense.* [< L *venia,* forgiveness.]
Ven·ice (vĕn'ĭs). A city of NE Italy. Pop. 360,000. —**Ve·ne'tian** (və-nē'shən) *adj.* & *n.*
ven·i·son (vĕn'ə-sən, -zən) *n.* The flesh of a deer used for food. [< L *vēnātiō,* hunting, game.]
ven·om (vĕn'əm) *n.* **1.** A poisonous secretion of some animals, as certain snakes or spiders, usually transmitted by a bite or sting. **2.** Malice; evil; spite. [< L *venēnum.*]
ven·om·ous (vĕn'ə-məs) *adj.* **1.** Secreting venom: *a venomous snake.* **2.** Full of or containing venom. **3.** Malicious; malignant.
ve·nous (vē'nəs) *adj.* **1.** Of or pertaining to a vein or veins. **2.** Returning to the heart through the great veins.

ô paw, for/oi boy/ou out/ŏŏ took/ōō coo/p pop/r run/s sauce/sh shy/t to/th thin/*th* the/
ŭ cut/ûr fur/v van/w wag/y yes/z size/zh vision/ə ago, item, edible, gallop, circus/

vent¹ (vĕnt) *n.* **1.** A means of escaping; an outlet or exit. **2.** An opening for the passage or escape of liquids or gases. —*v.* **1.** To give expression to. **2.** To discharge through a vent. **3.** To provide with a vent. [< OF *esventer*, to let out air.] —**vent'er** *n.*

vent² (vĕnt) *n.* A slit at the bottom of a seam in a skirt or jacket: *side vents.* [< OF *fente*, slit.]

ven•ti•late (vĕnt'l-āt') *v.* **-lated, -lating.** **1.** To admit fresh air into in order to replace stale air. **2.** To provide with a vent or a similar means of airing. **3.** To vent: *ventilate one's grievances.* **4.** To expose to public discussion. [< L *ventilāre*, to fan.] —**ven'ti•la'tion** *n.* —**ven'ti•la'tor** *n.* —**ven'ti•la•to'ry** (vĕnt'l-ə-tôr'ē, -tôr'ē) *adj.*

ven•tral (vĕn'trəl) *adj.* **1.** Of, on, or near the belly; abdominal. **2.** Pertaining to the anterior aspect of the human body or the lower surface of the body of an animal. [< L *venter*, the belly.]

ven•tri•cle (vĕn'trĭ-kəl) *n.* A small anatomical cavity or chamber, as of the brain or heart, esp.: **a.** The chamber on the left side of the heart that receives blood from the left atrium and contracts to drive it into the aorta. **b.** The chamber on the right side of the heart that receives blood from the right atrium and sends it to the lungs. [< L *venter*, belly, womb.] —**ven•tric'u•lar** (vĕn-trĭk'yə-lər) *adj.*

ven•tril•o•quism (vĕn-trĭl'ə-kwĭz'əm) *n.* Also **ven•tril•o•quy** (-kwē) *pl.* **-quies.** A method of producing vocal sounds so that they seem to originate in a source other than the speaker. [< LL *ventriloquus*, "speaking from the belly."] —**ven•tril'o•quist** (-ə-kwĭst) *n.*

ven•ture (vĕn'chər) *n.* **1.** A speculative or risky undertaking. **2.** Something at hazard in such an undertaking; stake. —*v.* **-tured, -turing.** **1.** To hazard; stake. **2.** To brave the dangers of. **3.** To express at the risk of denial, criticism, or censure. [< ME *aventure*, adventure.] —**ven'tur•er** *n.*

ven•ture•some (vĕn'chər-səm) *adj.* **1.** Daring; bold. **2.** Hazardous.·

ven•tur•ous (vĕn'chər-əs) *adj.* Venturesome. —**ven'tur•ous•ly** *adv.*

ven•ue (vĕn'yōō) *n.* **1.** The locality where a crime is committed or a cause of action occurs. **2.** The locality from which a jury must be called and in which a trial must be held. [ME, arrival, assault.]

Ve•nus (vē'nəs) *n.* **1.** The second planet from the sun, having an average radius of 3,800 miles, a mass 0.816 times that of the earth, and a period of revolution about the sun of 224.7 days at a mean distance of approx. 67.2 million miles. **2.** Roman goddess of love.

ver. version.

ve•ra•cious (və-rā'shəs) *adj.* **1.** Honest; truthful. **2.** Accurate; precise. [< L *vērāx*, truth.] —**ve•ra'cious•ly** *adv.* —**ve•ra'cious•ness** *n.*

ve•rac•i•ty (və-răs'ə-tē) *n.*, *pl.* **-ties.** **1.** Habitual adherence to the truth. **2.** Conformity to fact; accuracy. **3.** Something true.

ve•ran•dah, ve•ran•da (və-răn'də) *n.* A roofed porch or balcony. [Hindi.]

verb (vûrb) *n.* Any of a class of words func-

tioning to express existence, action, or occurrence. [< L *verbum*, word.]

ver•bal (vûr'bəl) *adj.* **1.** Of, pertaining to, or associated with words. **2.** Concerned with words rather than the ideas they represent. **3.** Expressed in speech; unwritten: *a verbal contract.* **4.** Literal; word for word: *a verbal translation.* **5.** Having the nature or function of a verb. —*n.* A verb or verb phrase functioning as a noun, adjective, or adverb. [< L *verbum*, word, VERB.] —**ver'bal•ly** *adv.*

ver•bal•ize (vûr'bə-līz') *v.* **-ized, -izing.** To express (oneself) in words. —**ver'bal•i•za'tion** *n.*

ver•ba•tim (vûr-bā'tĭm) *adj.* Literal; word for word. [< L *verbum*, word, VERB.] —**ver•ba'tim** *adv.*

ver•be•na (vər-bē'nə) *n.* Any of various plants cultivated for their clusters of variously colored, sometimes fragrant flowers. [< L *verbēnae*, sacred boughs of olive or myrtle.]

ver•bi•age (vûr'bē-ĭj) *n.* **1.** Excess of words; wordiness. **2.** Wording; diction. [< L *verbum*, word, VERB.]

ver•bose (vər-bōs') *adj.* Characterized by dull and windy speech; wordy; prolix. [< L *verbum*, word, VERB.] —**ver•bose'ly** *adv.* —**ver•bose'ness, ver•bos'i•ty** (-bŏs'ə-tē) *n.*

ver•bo•ten (fĕr-bōt'n) *adj.* Forbidden, as by arbitrary or dictatorial authority. [G.]

ver•dant (vûr'dənt) *adj.* **1.** Green with plant growth. **2.** Inexperienced or unsophisticated; green. [< OF *verd*, green.] —**ver'dant•ly** *adv.*

Ver•di (vâr'dē), **Giuseppe.** 1813–1901. Italian composer of operas.

ver•dict (vûr'dĭkt) *n.* **1.** The decision reached by a jury at the conclusion of a legal proceeding. **2.** A conclusion or judgment. [< OF *voirdit*, "true saying."]

ver•di•gris (vûr'də-grēs, -grĭs) *n.* A green patina or crust of copper sulfate or copper chloride formed on copper, brass, and bronze exposed to air or sea water for long periods of time. [< OF *vert-de-Grice*, "green of Greece."]

ver•dure (vûr'jər) *n.* The fresh greenness of flourishing vegetation. [< OF *verd*, green.]

verge¹ (vûrj) *n.* **1.** The extreme edge, rim, or margin of something. **2.** A brink or threshold. **3.** A staff carried as an emblem of authority or office. —*v.* **verged, verging.** To approach, come near, or border upon. [< L *virga*, rod, strip.]

verge² (vûrj) *v.* **verged, verging.** **1.** To slope or incline. **2.** To be in the process of becoming something else. [L *vergere*, to tend toward.]

verg•er (vûr'jər) *n. Chiefly Brit.* **1.** One who carries the verge before a dignitary in a procession. **2.** A person who has charge of the interior of a church.

ver•i•fy (vĕr'ə-fī') *v.* **-fied, -fying.** **1.** To prove the truth of; substantiate. **2.** To test the truth or accuracy of, as by comparison. [< L *vērus*, true + *facere*, to make.] —**ver'i•fi'a•ble** *adj.* —**ver'i•fi•ca'tion** (-fə-kā'shən) *n.*

ver•i•ly (vĕr'ə-lē) *adv. Archaic.* **1.** In truth; of a certainty. **2.** Assuredly. [< ME *verray*, true, very.]

ver•i•si•mil•i•tude (vĕr'ə-sĭm-ĭl'ə-t/y/ōōd') *n.* **1.** The quality of appearing to be true or real; likelihood. **2.** Something that has the appear-

ance of being true or real. [L *vērisimilitūdō*.]
ver·i·ta·ble (vĕr'ə-tə-bəl) *adj.* Unquestionable; actual; true. [< OF.] —**ver'i·ta·bly** *adv.*
ver·i·ty (vĕr'ə-tē) *n., pl.* **-ties.** 1. The condition or quality of being true. 2. A true statement or principle. [< L *vērus,* true.]
ver·meil (vûr'mĭl) *n.* 1. Vermilion. 2. Gilded metal, such as silver, bronze, or copper. [< LL *vermiculus.*]
vermi-. *comb. form.* Worm. [< L *vermis,* worm.]
ver·mi·cel·li (vûr'mə-chĕl'ē, -sĕl'ē) *n.* A very thin spaghettilike pasta. [It, "little worms."]
ver·mi·form (vûr'mə-fôrm') *adj.* Resembling or having the shape of a worm.
vermiform appendix. A wormlike vestigial organ of the cecum found in man and some other mammals.

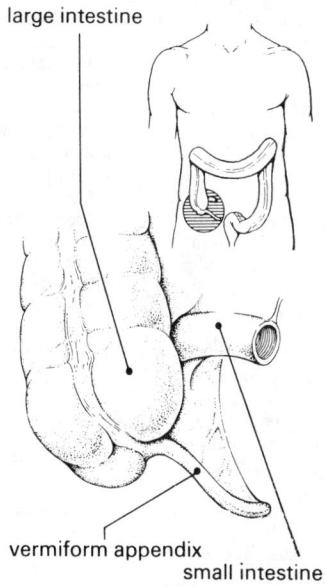

large intestine

vermiform appendix

small intestine

vermiform appendix

ver·mi·fuge (vûr'mə-fyōōj') *n.* Any agent that expels or destroys intestinal worms.
ver·mil·ion (vər-mĭl'yən) *n.* Also **ver·mil·lion.** Vivid red to reddish orange. [< OF *vermeillon.*]
ver·min (vûr'mĭn) *n., pl.* **vermin.** Any of various small destructive or obnoxious animals, as cockroaches or rats. [< L *vermis,* worm.] —**ver'min·ous** *adj.*
Ver·mont (vər-mŏnt'). A state of the NE U.S. Pop. 445,000. Cap. Montpelier.
ver·mouth (vər-mōōth') *n.* A fortified wine flavored with aromatic herbs. [< G *Wermut,* wormwood.]
ver·nac·u·lar (vər-năk'yə-lər) *n.* 1. The normal spoken language of a country or region as distinct from literary or learned language. 2. The idiom of a particular trade or profession: *legal vernacular.* [< L *vernāculus,* domestic.] —**ver·nac'u·lar** *adj.*

ver·nal (vûr'nəl) *adj.* Of, pertaining to, or occurring in the spring. [< L *vernus,* of spring.] —**ver'nal·ly** *adv.*
vernal equinox. 1. The point at which the ecliptic intersects the celestial equator, the sun having a northerly motion. 2. The moment at which the sun passes through this point, about March 21, marking the beginning of spring.
ver·ni·er (vûr'nē-ər) *n.* A small scale attached to a main scale to indicate fractional parts of the subdivisions of the larger scale. [< P. *Vernier* (1580–1637), French mathematician.]
ver·sa·tile (vûr'sə-təl) *adj.* 1. Skillfully adaptable; having a generalized aptitude. 2. Having varied uses or functions. [< L *vertere,* to turn.] —**ver'sa·til'i·ty** *n.*
verse (vûrs) *n.* 1. a. A line of poetry. b. A stanza. 2. Poetry. 3. A specific type of metrical composition: *blank verse.* 4. One of the numbered subdivisions of a chapter in the Bible. [< L *versus,* "a turning of the plow," furrow, line.]
versed (vûrst) *adj.* Knowledgeable, practiced, or skilled.
ver·si·cle (vûr'sĭ-kəl) *n.* A short verse or sentence spoken or chanted by a priest and followed by a response from the congregation.
ver·si·fy (vûr'sə-fī') *v.* **-fied, -fying.** To write verses or put into verse. —**ver'si·fi·ca'tion** *n.* —**ver'si·fi'er** *n.*
ver·sion (vûr'zhən, -shən) *n.* 1. A description, narration, or account related from a specific or subjective viewpoint. 2. A translation. Often used to designate one of the various Christian revisions of the Bible as translated into the vernacular. 3. A variation of any prototype; variant. 4. An adaptation into another medium or style. [< L *vertere,* to turn, change.] —**ver'sion·al** *adj.*
vers li·bre (vĕr lē'br'). Free verse. [F.]
ver·so (vûr'sō) *n., pl.* **-sos.** 1. *Ptg.* A left-hand page of a book or the reverse side of a leaf. 2. The back of a coin or medal. [L *versō (folio),* "(the page) being turned."]
ver·sus (vûr'səs) *prep.* 1. Against: *the plaintiff versus the defendant.* 2. As an alternative to; in contrast with: *death versus dishonor.* [< L *vertere,* to turn.]
vert. vertical.
ver·te·bra (vûr'tə-brə) *n., pl.* **-brae** (-brē) or **-bras.** Any of the bones or cartilaginous segments forming the spinal column. [L, joint, vertebra, "something to turn on."] —**ver'te·bral** *adj.*
ver·te·brate (vûr'tə-brāt', -brĭt) *adj.* 1. Having a backbone or spinal column. 2. Of or characteristic of vertebrates. —*n.* Any of a group of animals having a backbone, including the fishes, amphibians, reptiles, birds, and mammals.
ver·tex (vûr'tĕks') *n., pl.* **-texes** or **-tices** (-tə-sēz'). 1. The highest point of anything; apex; summit. 2. a. The point at which sides of an angle intersect. b. The point on a triangle opposite to and farthest away from its base. c. A point on a polyhedron common to three or more sides. [L, whirl, crown of the head.]

ver•ti•cal (vûr′tĭ-kəl) *adj.* **1. a.** At right angles to the horizon. **b.** Extending perpendicularly from a plane. **2.** Of or at the vertex or highest point; directly overhead. —*n.* **1.** A vertical line, plane, circle, etc. **2.** A vertical position. [< L *vertex*, VERTEX.] —**ver′ti•cal′i•ty, ver′ti•cal•ness** *n.* —**ver′ti•cal•ly** *adv.*

ver•tig•i•nous (vər-tĭj′ə-nəs) *adj.* **1.** Revolving; whirling; rotary. **2.** Affected by vertigo; dizzy. **3.** Tending to produce vertigo. [< L *vertīgō,* VERTIGO.] —**ver•tig′i•nous•ly** *adv.*

ver•ti•go (vûr′tĭ-gō′) *n., pl.* **-goes** or **vertigines** (vər-tĭj′ə-nēz′). Severe dizziness. [L *vertīgō,* "a whirling."]

verve (vûrv) *n.* Vitality; liveliness; vivacity. [< OF, fancy, fanciful expression.]

ver•y (vĕr′ē) *adv.* **1.** Extremely; exceedingly: *very happy.* **2.** Truly: *the very best way.* **3.** Precisely: *the very same one.* —*adj.* **1.** Absolute; utter: *the very end.* **2.** Identical; selfsame. **3.** —Used as an intensive to emphasize the importance of the thing described: *The very mountains crumbled.* **4.** Particular; precise. **5.** Mere: *The very mention of the name was frightening.* **6.** Actual: *caught in the very act.* [< L *vērus,* true.]

Usage: Very (adverb) is sometimes employed to qualify directly a past participle used predicatively in passive constructions: *He was very tired* (or *very discouraged*). This usage is generally acceptable when the participle is felt to have the nature of a true adjective, as in the foregoing. When the participle remains essentially a verb form, it is preferable to replace *very* with *very much, much, greatly,* or a like term: *much disliked; greatly inconvenienced.*

very high frequency. A band of radio frequencies between 30 and 300 megacycles per second.

very low frequency. A band of radio frequencies between 3 and 30 kilocycles per second.

ves•i•cant (vĕs′ĭ-kənt) *n.* A blistering agent, as mustard gas, used in chemical warfare. —*adj.* Causing blisters.

ves•i•cle (vĕs′ĭ-kəl) *n.* **1.** A small bladderlike cell or cavity. **2.** A blister. [< L *vēsīca,* bladder.] —**ve•sic′u•lar** (və-sĭk′yə-lər) *adj.*

ves•per (vĕs′pər) *n.* **1.** A bell used to summon persons to vespers. **2.** *Archaic.* Evening. **3. Vesper.** The evening star. —*adj.* Of or pertaining to the evening or vespers.

ves•pers (vĕs′pərz) *pl.n.* Also **Ves•pers.** A worship service held in the late afternoon or evening. [< L *vesper,* evening, evening star.]

Ves•puc•ci (vĕs-pōōt′chē), **Amerigo.** 1451–1512. Italian navigator for whom America was named.

ves•sel (vĕs′əl) *n.* **1.** A container or receptacle. **2.** A craft larger than a rowboat, designed to navigate on water. **3.** ′A bodily duct, canal, etc., for containing or circulating a bodily fluid. [< L *vās,* vessel.]

vest (vĕst) *n.* **1.** A sleeveless garment, buttoning in front, worn typically under a suit coat. **2.** *Chiefly Brit.* An undershirt. —*v.* **1.** To clothe, as with ecclesiastical vestments. **2.** To place (authority or ownership) in the control

of. **3.** To place (authority or power). [< L *vestis,* garment.]

Ves•ta (vĕs′tə). Roman goddess of the hearth.

ves•tal (vĕs′təl) *adj.* **1.** Pertaining to or sacred to Vesta. **2.** Pertaining to or characteristic of the priestesses of Vesta; chaste. —*n.* Also **vestal virgin.** One of the six virgin priestesses who tended the sacred fire in the temple of Vesta.

ves•ti•bule (vĕs′tə-byōōl′) *n.* **1.** A small entrance hall or lobby. **2.** An enclosed area at the end of a railroad passenger car. **3.** Any body cavity, chamber, or channel that serves as an approach or entrance to another cavity. [< L *vestibulum.*] —**ves•tib′u•lar** (vĕ-stĭb′yə-lər) *adj.*

ves•tige (vĕs′tĭj) *n.* A visible trace or sign of something that exists or appears no more. [< L *vestīgium,* footprint, trace.]

ves•tig•i•al (vĕ-stĭj′ē-əl) *adj.* **1.** Of, pertaining to, or constituting a vestige. **2.** Occurring or persisting as a rudimentary or degenerate bodily structure. —**ves•tig′i•al•ly** *adv.*

vest•ment (vĕst′mənt) *n.* **1.** An official or ceremonial gown. **2.** Any of the robes worn by clergymen or other assistants at ecclesiastical ceremonies. [< L *vestis,* garment.]

ves•try (vĕs′trē) *n., pl.* **-tries. 1.** A room in a church where vestments and sacred objects are stored. **2.** A meeting room in a church. **3.** A committee that administers the temporal affairs of an Episcopal parish. [ME *vestrie.*]

ves•try•man (vĕs′trē-mən) *n.* A member of a vestry.

ves•ture (vĕs′chər) *n.* **1.** Clothing; apparel. **2.** Something that covers or cloaks. [< L *vestire,* to clothe.]

Ve•su•vi•us (və-sōō′vē-əs). An active volcano in SW Italy near Naples.

vet (vĕt) *n. Informal.* **1.** A veterinarian. **2.** A veteran.

vet. **1.** veteran. **2.** veterinarian; veterinary.

vetch (vĕch) *n.* A climbing or twining plant with featherlike leaves and usually purplish flowers. [< L *vicia.*]

vet•er•an (vĕt′ər-ən, vĕt′rən) *n.* **1.** One of long experience in a given activity. **2.** A former member of the armed forces. **3.** An old soldier. [< L *vetus (veter-),* old.] —**vet′er•an** *adj.*

vet•er•i•nar•i•an (vĕt′ər-ə-nâr′ē-ən, vĕt′rə-) *n.* One trained and authorized to treat animals medically.

vet•er•i•nar•y (vĕt′ər-ə-nĕr′ē, vĕt′rə-) *adj.* Of or pertaining to the diagnosis and treatment of diseases and injuries of animals. —*n., pl.* **-ies.** A veterinarian. [< L *veterinus,* of cattle.]

ve•to (vē′tō) *n., pl.* **-toes. 1.** The vested power or constitutional right of a branch of government, esp. of a chief executive, to reject a bill passed by a legislative body and thus prevent or delay its enactment into law. **2.** The exercise of this right. **3.** The official document communicating the rejection and the reasons for it. **4.** Any authoritative prohibition or rejection of a proposed or intended act. [L *vetō,* I forbid.] —**ve′to** *v.* —**ve′to′er** *n.*

vex (vĕks) *v.* **1.** To irritate or annoy; bother. **2.** To perplex. **3.** To debate at length. **4.** To

---

ă pat/ā ate/âr care/ä bar/b bib/ch chew/d deed/ĕ pet/ē be/f fit/g gag/h hat/hw what/
ĭ pit/ī pie/îr pier/j judge/k kick/l lid, fatal/m mum/n no, sudden/ng sing/ŏ pot/ō go/

agitate. [< L *vexāre*.] —**vex•a'tion** *n.* —**vex•a'tious** *adj.* —**vex•a'tious•ly** *adv.*
vhf, VHF very high frequency.
VI, V.I. Virgin Islands.
vi•a (vī'ə, vē'ə) *prep.* By way of. [< L, road, way.]
vi•a•ble (vī'ə-bəl) *adj.* **1.** Capable of living or developing under normal or favorable conditions. **2.** Capable of actualization; practicable. [< OF *vie*, life.] —**vi'a•bil'i•ty** *n.*
vi•a•duct (vī'ə-dŭkt') *n.* A series of spans or arches used to carry a road or railroad over a wide valley or other roads. [L *via*, road, way + (AQUE)DUCT.]
vi•al (vī'əl) *n.* A small container for liquids. [ME *viole*.]
vi•ands (vī'əndz) *pl.n.* Food; victuals. [< L *vivere*, to live.]
vi•at•i•cum (vī-ăt'ĭ-kəm, vē-) *n., pl.* **-ca** (-kə) or **-cums.** The Eucharist as given to a dying person or one in danger of death. [< L *viāticus*, of a road or journey.]
vi•brant (vī'brənt) *adj.* **1.** Exhibiting, characterized by, or resulting from vibration; vibrating. **2.** Pulsing with energy or activity. —**vi'bran•cy** *n.* —**vi'brant•ly** *adv.*
vi•brate (vī'brāt') *v.* **-brated, -brating. 1.** To move or cause to move back and forth rapidly. **2.** To produce a sound; resonate. [L *vibrāre*.] —**vi•bra'tion** (vī-brā'shən) *n.* —**vi•bra'tion•al** *adj.* —**vi'bra'tor** *n.* —**vi'bra•to'ry** *adj.*
vi•bra•to (vĭ-brä'tō, vē-) *n.* A tremulous or pulsating effect produced in a musical tone by minute and rapid variations in pitch. [< L *vibrāre*, VIBRATE.]
vic. 1. vicar. **2.** vicinity.
vic•ar (vĭk'ər) *n.* **1.** An Anglican priest of a parish. **2.** A substitute; deputy. [< L *vicārius*, a substitute.] —**vi•car'i•al** (vī-kâr'ē-əl) *adj.*
vic•ar•age (vĭk'ər-ĭj) *n.* The residence or benefice of a vicar.
vicar general *pl.* **vicars general.** An administrative deputy to a Roman Catholic bishop.
vi•car•i•ous (vī-kâr'ē-əs, vĭ-) *adj.* **1.** Performed or endured by one person substituting for another. **2.** Experienced through sympathetic participation in the experience of another. [< L *vicis*, change, turn, office.] —**vi•car'i•ous•ly** *adv.* —**vi•car'i•ous•ness** *n.*
vice¹ (vīs) *n.* **1.** An immoral practice or habit. **2.** Depravity; corruption. **3.** A flaw or blemish. [< L *vitium*, blemish, offense, vice.]
vice² Variant of **vise.**
vice³ (vīs) *adj.* Substituting for; deputy: *vice chairman.* —*prep.* Replacing or succeeding. [< L *vicis*, change.]
vice-. *comb. form.* One substituting for another. [< L *vice*, in place of, vice.]
vice admiral. A naval officer ranking next below an admiral.
vice president. 1. An officer ranking next below a president, usually empowered to assume the president's duties under such conditions as absence, illness, or death. **2.** A deputy of a president, as in a corporation. —**vice'-pres'i•den•cy** *n.* —**vice'-pres•i•den'tial** *adj.*
vice•re•gal (vīs-rē'gəl) *adj.* Of or pertaining to a viceroy. —**vice•re'gal•ly** *adv.*

vice•roy (vīs'roi') *n.* A governor of a country, province, or colony, ruling as the representative of a sovereign. —**vice'roy'al•ty** *n.*
vi•ce ver•sa (vī'sĕ vûr'sə, vīs', vī'sə). Conversely. [L, "the position being changed."]
vi•chy•ssoise (vĭsh'ē-swäz', vē'shē-) *n.* A creamy potato soup flavored with leeks or onions and usually served cold. [F, "(cream) of *Vichy*," city in C France.]
vic•i•nage (vĭs'ə-nĭj) *n.* Neighborhood or vicinity. [< L *vīcīnus*, neighbor.]
vic•i•nal (vĭs'ə-nəl) *adj.* Restricted to a limited area; local. [< L *vīcīnus*, neighbor.]
vi•cin•i•ty (vī-sĭn'ə-tē) *n., pl.* **-ties. 1.** The state of being near in space or relationship; proximity. **2.** A neighborhood; locality. [< L *vīcīnus*, neighbor.]
vi•cious (vĭsh'əs) *adj.* **1.** Depraved; debased. **2.** Malicious; reprobate; evil. **3.** Failing to meet a standard or criterion; defective. **4.** Impure; foul. **5.** Characterized by a tendency to worsen. [< L *vitium*, VICE¹.] —**vi'cious•ly** *adv.* —**vi'cious•ness** *n.*
vi•cis•si•tude (vĭ-sĭs'ə-t/y/ood') *n.* **1.** The quality of being changeable; mutability. **2.** *vicissitudes.* Sudden changes or alterations. [< L *vicissim*, in turn.]
vic•tim (vĭk'tĭm) *n.* **1.** A living being slain and offered as a sacrifice to a deity. **2.** One who is harmed or killed, as by accident. **3.** A person who is tricked, swindled, or injured. [L *victima*.]
vic•tim•ize (vĭk'tə-mīz') *v.* **-ized, -izing.** To make a victim of. —**vic'tim•i•za'tion** *n.*
vic•tor (vĭk'tər) *n.* **1.** One who defeats or vanquishes an adversary. **2.** A winner. [< L *vincere*, to conquer.]
vic•to•ri•a (vĭk-tôr'ē-ə, -tōr'ē-ə) *n.* A low four-wheeled carriage for two with a folding top and an elevated driver's seat in front. [< Queen VICTORIA.]
Vic•to•ri•a¹ (vĭk-tôr'ē-ə, -tōr'ē-ə). 1819–1901. Queen of the United Kingdom of Great Brit-

Victoria¹
Photographed in 1876

ain and Ireland (1837–1901); Empress of India (1876–1901).

Vic·to·ri·a² (vĭk-tôr′ē-ə, -tōr′ē-ə). **1.** The capital of British Columbia, Canada. Pop. 55,000. **2.** The capital of Hong Kong. Pop. 1,005,000.

Vic·to·ri·a, Lake (vĭk-tôr′ē-ə, -tōr′ē-ə). The largest lake in Africa.

Vic·to·ri·an (vĭk-tôr′ē-ən, -tôr′ē-ən) *adj.* **1.** Pertaining or belonging to the period of Queen Victoria's reign. **2.** Exhibiting qualities associated with the time of Queen Victoria, as prudishness and stuffiness. **3.** Being in the highly ornamented, massive style of architecture and furnishings popular in 19th-century England. —**Vic·to′ri·an** *n.* —**Vic·to′ri·an·ism′** *n.*

vic·to·ri·ous (vĭk-tôr′ē-əs, -tôr′ē-əs) *adj.* **1.** Triumphant; conquering. **2.** Expressing a sense of victory or fulfillment. —**vic·to′ri·ous·ly** *adv.* —**vic·to′ri·ous·ness** *n.*

vic·to·ry (vĭk′tə-rē) *n., pl.* **-ries. 1.** Final and complete defeat of the enemy in a military engagement. **2.** Any successful struggle against an opponent or obstacle. [< L *victus*, sustenance.]

vict·ual (vĭt′l) *n.* **1.** Food fit for human consumption. **2.** victuals. Food; provisions. —*v.* **1.** To provide with food. **2.** To lay in food supplies. [< L *victus*, sustenance.]

vict·ual·er (vĭt′l-ər) *n.* **1.** A supplier of victuals, as to an army or ship. **2.** An innkeeper.

vi·cu·ña (və-kōōn′yə, -k/y/ōō′nə, vī-) *n.* Also **vi·cu·na. 1.** A South American mammal, related to the llama, having fine, silky fleece. **2. a.** The fleece of this animal. **b.** Fabric made from this fleece. [< Quechua *wikuña.*]

vi·de (vī′dē) *v.* See. Used to direct a reader's attention: *vide page 64.* [< L *vidēre*, to see.]

vi·de·li·cet (vĭ-dĕl′ə-sĭt) *adv.* That is; namely. [L *vidēlicet*, it is easy (permissible) to see.]

vid·e·o (vĭd′ē-ō′) *adj.* Pertaining to television, esp. to televised images. —*n.* **1.** The visual portion of a televised broadcast. **2.** Television. [< L *vidēre*, to see.]

vie (vī) *v.* **vied, vying.** To strive; contend; compete. [< OF *envier*, to challenge, bid.]

Vi·en·na (vē-ĕn′ə). The capital of Austria. Pop. 1,628,000. —**Vi′en·nese′** (vē′ə-nēz′, -nēs′) *adj.*

Vien·tiane (vyăN-tyàn′). The administrative capital of Laos. Pop. 100,000.

Vi·et·cong (vē-ĕt′kŏng′, vyĕt′-) *n., pl.* **Vietcong.** Also **Vi·et Cong. 1.** A Vietnamese supporting the National Liberation Front of South Vietnam. **2.** The Front itself, esp. its armed forces. —**Vi·et′cong′** *adj.*

Vi·et·minh (vē-ĕt′mĭn′, vyĕt′-) *n., pl.* **Vietminh.** Also **Vi·et Minh. 1.** The Vietnamese national independence front (1941–54) led by Ho Chi Minh. **2.** A member or members of this front, esp. of its armed forces. —**Vi·et′minh′** *adj.*

Viet·nam (vē-ĕt′näm′, -năm′, vyĕt′-). A country of SE Asia, divided from 1954 to 1975 into the Democratic Republic of Vietnam (North Vietnam), pop. 21,340,000, cap. Hanoi, and the Republic of Vietnam (South Vietnam), pop. 16,543,000, cap. Saigon. In 1975 the country was reunified under the government of the Democratic Republic of Vietnam.

Vi·et·nam·ese (vē-ĕt′nə-mēz′, -mēs′, vyĕt′-) *n.*

1. A native of Vietnam. **2.** The language of Vietnam. —**Vi·et′nam·ese′** *adj.*

view (vyōō) *n.* **1.** An examination or inspection. **2.** A systematic survey; coverage. **3. views.** Thoughts or opinions. **4.** The field of vision. **5.** A prospect or vista. **6.** An aspect, as from a given vantage point. **7.** An aim; intention. **8.** Expectation; chance: *no view of success.* —*v.* **1.** To see; behold. **2. a.** To examine; inspect. **b.** To survey or consider. [< L *vidēre*, to see.] —**view′er** *n.*

view·point (vyōō′point′) *n.* A point of view.

vig·il (vĭj′əl) *n.* **1.** A watch kept during normal sleeping hours. **2.** The eve of a religious festival as observed by devotional watching. **3. vigils.** Ritual devotions observed on the eve of a holy day. [< L, alert.]

vig·i·lance (vĭj′ə-ləns) *n.* Watchfulness.

vig·i·lant (vĭj′ə-lənt) *adj.* On the alert; watchful. [< L *vigilāre*, to be alert.] —**vig′i·lant·ly** *adv.* —**vig′i·lant·ness** *n.*

vig·i·lan·te (vĭj′ə-lăn′tē) *n.* A member of an unauthorized group exercising police power, esp. in the 19th-century South.

vi·gnette (vĭn-yĕt′) *n.* **1.** An unenclosed decorative design placed at the beginning or end of a book or chapter. **2.** An unbordered portrait that shades off into the surrounding ground. **3.** A brief literary sketch. —*v.* **-gnetted, -gnetting.** To soften the edges of (a picture) in vignette style. [< OF, "young vine."]

vig·or (vĭg′ər) *n.* Also chiefly *Brit.* **vig·our. 1.** Active physical or mental strength. **2.** Effectiveness or force. [< L *vigēre*, to be lively or vigorous.]

vig·or·ous (vĭg′ər-əs) *adj.* **1.** Robust; hardy. **2.** Energetic; forceful. —**vig′or·ous·ly** *adv.* —**vig′or·ous·ness** *n.*

vi·king (vī′kĭng) *n.* Also **Vi·king.** One of the Scandinavian mariners and marauders of the 8th through the 10th century. [ON *vīkingr.*]

vil. village.

vile (vīl) *adj.* **viler, vilest. 1.** Wretched; base. **2.** Depraved; ignoble. **3.** Loathsome; disgusting. **4.** Unpleasant or objectionable. [< L *vilis.*] —**vile′ly** *adv.* —**vile′ness** *n.*

vil·i·fy (vĭl′ə-fī′) *v.* **-fied, -fying.** To defame; denigrate. [< L *vīlis*, VILE + *facere*, to make.] —**vil′i·fi·ca′tion** *n.* —**vil′i·fi′er** *n.*

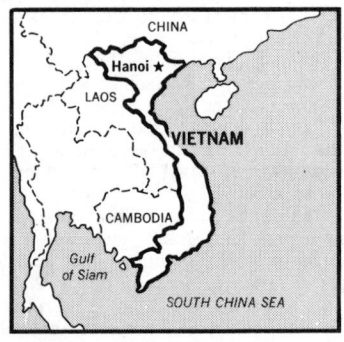

Vietnam

---

vil•la (vĭl′ə) *n.* **1.** A resort or country estate. **2.** *Brit.* A middle-class house in the suburbs. [< L *villa,* country home.]

vil•lage (vĭl′ĭj) *n.* **1.** A rural settlement ranking in size between a hamlet and a town. **2.** An incorporated municipality smaller than a town. **3.** The inhabitants of a village. [< L *villa,* VILLA.] —**vil′lage** *adj.*

vil•lag•er (vĭl′ĭ-jər) *n.* An inhabitant of a village.

vil•lain (vĭl′ən) *n.* **1.** One of wicked deeds; scoundrel. **2.** Variant of **villein.** [< OF *vilain,* "feudal serf."]

vil•lain•ous (vĭl′ə-nəs) *adj.* **1.** Viciously wicked or criminal. **2.** Obnoxious. —**vil′lain•ous•ly** *adv.* —**vil′lain•ous•ness** *n.*

vil•lain•y (vĭl′ə-nē) *n., pl.* **-ies. 1.** Viciousness of conduct or action. **2.** Baseness of mind or character. **3.** A treacherous or vicious act.

vil•lein (vĭl′ən) *n.* Also **vil•lain.** One of a class of feudal serfs who held the legal status of freemen in their dealings with all persons except their lord. [< VILLAIN.]

Vil•lon (vē-yôN′), **François.** 1431–1463? French poet.

Vil•ni•us (vĭl′nē-əs, vēl′-). The capital of Lithuania. Pop. 372,000.

vim (vĭm) *n.* Ebullient vitality and energy. [< L *vis,* power.]

Vin•ci, Leonardo da. See **Leonardo da Vinci.**

vin•di•ca•ble (vĭn′dĭ-kə-bəl) *adj.* Capable of being vindicated; justifiable.

vin•di•cate (vĭn′dĭ-kāt′) *v.* **-cated, -cating. 1.** To clear of accusation, blame, etc., with supporting proof. **2.** To justify: *vindicate one's claim.* [L *vindicāre,* to claim, defend, revenge.] —**vin′di•ca′tion** *n.*

vin•dic•tive (vĭn-dĭk′tĭv) *adj.* **1.** Disposed to seek revenge; revengeful. **2.** Unforgiving; bitter; spiteful. —**vin•dic′tive•ly** *adv.* —**vin•dic′tive•ness** *n.*

vine (vīn) *n.* **1.** A plant having a stem supported by climbing, twining, or creeping along a surface. **2.** A grapevine or grapevines collectively. [< L *vīnum,* wine.]

vin•e•gar (vĭn′ĭ-gər) *n.* An impure dilute solution of acetic acid obtained by fermentation beyond the alcohol stage and used as a condiment and preservative. [< OF *vin,* wine + *aigre,* sour.]

vin•e•gar•y (vĭn′ĭ-gə-rē) *adj.* **1.** Having the nature of vinegar; sour; acid. **2.** Sour in disposition or speech.

vine•yard (vĭn′yərd) *n.* Ground planted with cultivated grapevines.

vin•tage (vĭn′tĭj) *n.* **1.** The yield of wine or grapes from a particular vineyard or district during one season. **2.** Wine, usually of high quality, identified as to year and vineyard or district of origin. **3.** The year in which or place where a particular wine was bottled. **4.** The harvesting of a grape crop or the initial stages of wine-making. **5.** A year or period of origin: *a car of 1942 vintage.* —*adj.* **1.** Venerable; classic. **2.** Old or outmoded. [< L *vindēmia,* grape gathering.]

vint•ner (vĭnt′nər) *n.* A wine merchant. [< L *vinētum,* vineyard.]

vi•nyl (vī′nəl) *n.* Any of various plastics, typically tough, flexible, and shiny, often used for coverings and clothing. —**vi′nyl** *adj.*

vi•o•la (vē-ō′lə, vī-) *n.* A stringed musical instrument of the violin family, slightly larger than a violin, tuned a fifth lower, and having a deeper, more sonorous tone. [It.]

vi•o•late (vī′ə-lāt′) *v.* **-lated, -lating. 1.** To break (a law or regulation) intentionally or unintentionally. **2.** To injure the person or property of, esp. to rape. **3.** To profane; desecrate. [< L *violāre* < *vis,* force.] —**vi′o•la•ble** *adj.* —**vi′o•la•bly** *adv.* —**vi′o•la′tion** *n.* —**vi′o•la′tive** *adj.* —**vi′o•la′tor** *n.*

vi•o•lence (vī′ə-ləns) *n.* **1.** Physical force exerted, as for violating, damaging, or abusing. **2.** An act of violent action or behavior. **3.** Intensity or severity: *the violence of a hurricane.* **4.** Fanaticism.

vi•o•lent (vī′ə-lənt) *adj.* **1.** Displaying extreme physical or emotional force. **2.** Extreme; severe: *violent contrast.* **3.** Severe; harsh. **4.** Caused by unexpected force or injury rather than by natural causes: *a violent death.* [< L *violentus.*] —**vi′o•lent•ly** *adv.*

vi•o•let (vī′ə-lĭt) *n.* **1.** Any of various low-growing plants with spurred, irregular flowers that are usually purplish-blue but sometimes yellow or white. **2.** Any of several similar plants. **3.** Any of a group of colors, reddish blue in hue. [< L *viola.*] —**vi′o•let** *adj.*

vi•o•lin (vī′ə-lĭn′) *n.* A stringed instrument played with a bow, having four strings tuned at intervals of a fifth and an unfretted fingerboard. [< VIOLA.]

vi•o•lin•ist (vī′ə-lĭn′ĭst) *n.* One who plays the violin.

vi•o•list (vē-ō′lĭst) *n.* A person who plays the viola.

vi•o•lon•cel•list (vē′ə-lən-chĕl′ĭst) *n.* A cellist.

vi•o•lon•cel•lo (vē′ə-lən-chĕl′ō) *n., pl.* **-los.** A cello. [< VIOLONE.]

vio•lo•ne (vyō-lō′nä) *n.* A double bass. [< VIOLA.]

VIP *Informal.* very important person.

vi•per (vī′pər) *n.* **1.** Any of various venomous Old World snakes. **2.** Any of various other venomous or supposedly venomous snakes. **3.** A malicious person. [< L *vipera,* snake.]

vi•ra•go (vĭ-rä′gō, -rä′gō, vī-) *n., pl.* **-goes** or **-gos.** A noisy, domineering woman; a scold. [L *virāgō.*]

vi•ral (vī′rəl) *adj.* Of, pertaining to, or caused by a virus.

vir•e•o (vĭr′ē-ō′) *n., pl.* **-os.** Any of several small grayish or greenish New World birds. [L.]

Vir•gil (vûr′jəl). 70–19 B.C. Latin poet.

vir•gin (vûr′jĭn) *n.* **1.** One who has not experienced sexual intercourse. **2.** A chaste or unmarried woman. **3. the Virgin.** Mary, the mother of Jesus. —*adj.* **1.** Chaste. **2.** In a pure or natural state: *virgin snow.* [< L *virgō.*] —**vir•gin′i•ty** *n.*

vir•gin•al (vûr′jə-nəl) *adj.* **1.** Chaste; pure. **2.** Remaining in a state of virginity. **3.** Untouched or unsullied.

Vir•gin•ia (vər-jĭn′yə). A state of the SE U.S.

Pop. 4,648,000. Cap. Richmond. —**Vir•gin'ian** *adj. & n.*

Virginia creeper. A North American climbing vine with compound leaves and bluish-black berries.

Virginia reel. A country dance in which couples perform various figures to the instructions called out by a leader.

Virgin Islands. An island group E of Puerto Rico in the Caribbean, divided into: **a.** The British Virgin Islands, a British colony. Pop. 9,000. **b.** The Virgin Islands of the U.S., including the islands of St. Thomas, St. John, and St. Croix. Pop. 32,000. Cap. Charlotte Amalie on St. Thomas.

Virgin Mary. The mother of Jesus.

Vir•go (vûr'gō) *n.* **1.** A constellation in the region of the celestial equator. **2.** The sixth sign of the zodiac. [L *virgō*, VIRGIN.]

vir•gu•late (vûr'gyə-lĭt, -lāt') *adj.* Shaped like a small rod. [< L *virgula*, small rod.]

vir•gule (vûr'gyōōl) *n.* A diagonal mark (/) used esp. to separate alternatives, as in *and/or*, or to represent the word *per*, as in *miles/hour.* [< L *virgula*, small rod.]

vir•ile (vĭr'əl) *adj.* **1.** Having masculine strength, vigor, force, etc. **2.** Pertaining to male sexual functions. [< L *vir*, man.] —**vi•ril'i•ty** (və-rĭl'ə-tē) *n.*

vi•rol•o•gy (vĭ-rŏl'ə-jē) *n.* The study of viruses and viral diseases. —**vi•rol'o•gist** *n.*

vir•tu•al (vûr'chōō-əl) *adj.* Existing in essence or effect though not in actual fact or form. [< L *virtūs*, capacity, VIRTUE.]

virtual image. An image from which rays of reflected or refracted light appear to diverge, as from an image seen in a plane mirror.

vir•tu•al•ly (vûr'chōō-ə-lē) *adv.* Essentially; practically.

vir•tue (vûr'chōō) *n.* **1.** Moral excellence, righteousness, and responsibility; goodness. **2.** Conformity to standard morality or mores; rectitude. **3.** Chastity. **4.** A particular beneficial or efficacious quality; an advantage. —**by** (or **in**) **virtue of.** On the grounds or basis of; by reason of. [< L *virtūs*, manliness, strength, capacity.] —**vir'tu•ous** *adj.* —**vir'tu•ous•ly** *adv.* —**vir'tu•ous•ness** *n.*

vir•tu•os•i•ty (vûr'chōō-ŏs'ə-tē) *n., pl.* **-ties.** The technical skill, fluency, or style exhibited by a virtuoso.

vir•tu•o•so (vûr'chōō-ō'sō) *n., pl.* **-sos** or **-si** (-sē). **1.** A musician with masterly ability, technique, or personal style. **2.** One with masterly skill or technique in any field, esp. in the arts. [< L *virtūs*, VIRTUE.]

vir•u•lent (vîr'/y/ə-lənt) *adj.* **1.** Extremely poisonous or harmful, as a disease or microorganism. **2.** Bitterly hostile or antagonistic; venomously spiteful; full of hate. **3.** Intensely irritating, obnoxious, or harsh: *virulent anti-rationalism.* [< L *virus*, VIRUS.] —**vir'u•lence** (-ləns) *n.* —**vir'u•lent•ly** *adv.*

vi•rus (vī'rəs) *n., pl.* **-ruses. 1.** Any of various submicroscopic disease-causing agents consisting essentially of a core of a nucleic acid surrounded by a protein coat, having the ability to reproduce only inside a living cell. **2.**

Any specific disease-causing agent. [L *virus*, poison, slime.]

vis. 1. visibility. **2.** visual.

vi•sa (vē'zə) *n.* An official authorization appended to a passport, permitting entry into and travel within a particular country or region. [< L *visa*, "things seen."]

vis•age (vĭz'ĭj) *n.* The face or facial expression of a person. [< OF *vis*, face.]

vis-à-vis (vē'zə-vē') *adv.* Face to face. —*prep.* Compared with; in relation to. [F, "face to face."] —**vis'-à-vis'** *adj.*

vis•cer•a (vĭs'ər-ə) *pl.n. Sing.* **viscus** (vĭs'kəs). **1.** The internal organs of the body, esp. those contained within the abdominal and thoracic cavities. **2.** Broadly, the intestines. [< L *viscus*, body organ.]

vis•cer•al (vĭs'ər-əl) *adj.* **1.** Of, in, or affecting the viscera. **2.** Intensely emotional.

vis•cid (vĭs'ĭd) *adj.* **1.** Thick and adhesive: *a viscid fluid.* **2.** Covered with a sticky coating. [< L *viscum*, mistletoe, birdlime.] —**vis•cid'i•ty** *n.* —**vis'cid•ly** *adv.*

vis•cose (vĭs'kōs') *n.* A thick, golden-brown viscous solution derived from cellulose, used in the manufacture of rayon and cellophane. [< LL *viscōsus*, VISCOUS.]

vis•cos•i•ty (vĭs-kŏs'ə-tē) *n., pl.* **-ties.** The condition, property, or degree of being viscous.

vis•count (vī'kount') *n.* A peer ranking below an earl and above a baron. [< VICE³ + ML *comes*, count.]

vis•cous (vĭs'kəs) *adj.* **1.** Having relatively high resistance to flow. **2.** Viscid. [< LL *viscōsus*.] —**vis'cous•ly** *adv.* —**vis'cous•ness** *n.*

vis•cus. *Sing.* of **viscera.**

vise (vīs) *n.* Also **vice.** A clamping device, usually consisting of two jaws closed by a screw or lever, used, as in carpentry, to hold work in position. [< L *vītis*, (winding) vine.]

Vish•nu (vĭsh'nōō) *n. Hinduism.* Second member of the trinity including also Brahma and Shiva.

vis•i•bil•i•ty (vĭz'ə-bĭl'ə-tē) *n., pl.* **-ties. 1.** The fact, state, or degree of being visible. **2.** The greatest distance under given weather conditions to which it is possible to see without instrumental assistance.

vis•i•ble (vĭz'ə-bəl) *adj.* **1.** Capable of being seen; perceptible to the eye. **2.** Manifest; apparent. [< L *visus*, sight, VISION.] —**vis'i•ble•ness** *n.* —**vis'i•bly** *adv.*

vi•sion (vĭzh'ən) *n.* **1.** The faculty of sight. **2.** Intelligent foresight. **3.** A mental image produced through the imagination. **4.** Something perceived through unusual means, as a supernatural sight. **5.** Something of extraordinary beauty. [< L *visus*, pp of *vidēre*, to see.]

vi•sion•ar•y (vĭzh'ən-ĕr'ē) *adj.* **1.** Characterized by vision or foresight. **2.** Having the nature of a vision. **3.** Not practicable; utopian. —*n., pl.* **-ies. 1.** One who has visions. **2.** One given to impractical ideas.

vis•it (vĭz'ĭt) *v.* **1.** To go or come to see for reasons of business, duty, or pleasure. **2.** To stay with as a guest. **3.** To afflict; assail. **4.** To inflict punishment; avenge. **5.** To pay a call. **6.** To converse or chat. —*n.* **1.** An act or

---

ă pat/ā ate/âr care/ä bar/b bib/ch chew/d deed/ĕ pet/ē be/f fit/g gag/h hat/hw what/
ĭ pit/ī pie/îr pier/j judge/k kick/l lid, fatal/m mum/n no, sudden/ng sing/ŏ pot/ō go/

instance of visiting. **2.** A stay or sojourn as a guest. [< L *visāre*, to view < *visus*, sight, VISION.] —**vis'it•a•ble** *adj.*

vis•i•ta•tion (vĭz'ə-tā'shən) *n.* **1.** An official visit. **2.** A visit of affliction or blessing, regarded as being ordained by God. —**vis'i• ta'tion•al** *adj.*

vis•i•tor (vĭz'ə-tər) *n.* One who pays a visit; a guest.

vi•sor (vī'zər, vĭz'ər) *n.* Also **vi•zor.** **1.** A piece projecting from the front of a cap or the windshield of a vehicle to shade the eyes. **2.** The front piece of a helmet, capable of being raised and lowered. [< L *visus*, sight, VISION.]

vis•ta (vĭs'tə) *n.* **1.** A distant view seen through a passage or opening. **2.** A comprehensive awareness of a series of events. [< L *vidēre*, to see.]

Vis•tu•la (vĭs'chŏo-lə). A river of Poland.

vis•u•al (vĭzh'ŏo-əl) *adj.* **1.** Of or involving the sense of sight. **2.** Capable of being seen by the eye; visible. **3.** Done, maintained, or executed by the sight only. **4.** Designating instruction involving sight: *visual aids.* [< L *visus*, VISION.] —**vis'u•al•ly** *adv.*

vis•u•al•ize (vĭzh'ŏo-ə-līz') *v.* **-ized, -izing.** To form a mental image or vision of. —**vis'u• al•i•za'tion** *n.* —**vis'u•al•iz'er** *n.*

vi•ta (vī'tə, vē'-) *n.* An outline of one's personal history and experience, as one submitted when applying for a job.

vi•tal (vī'təl, vīt'l) *adj.* **1.** Of or characteristic of life. **2.** Necessary to the continuation of life. **3.** Full of life; vigorous; animated. **4.** Essential. **5.** Concerned with data pertinent to lives. [< L *vita*, life.] —**vi'tal•ly** *adv.*

vi•tal•i•ty (vī-tăl'ə-tē) *n., pl.* **-ties. 1.** That which distinguishes the living from the nonliving. **2.** The capacity to live, grow, develop, or survive. **3.** Vigor; energy.

vi•tal•ize (vīt'l-īz') *v.* **-ized, -izing.** To endow with life or vigor. —**vi'tal•i•za'tion** *n.* —**vi'tal• iz'er** *n.*

vi•tals (vī'təlz) *pl.n.* **1.** Any bodily parts or organs regarded as vital. **2.** Essential elements.

vi•ta•min (vī'tə-mən) *n.* Also *rare* **vi•ta•mine** (-mēn, -mĭn). Any of various relatively complex organic substances occurring naturally in plant and animal tissue and essential in small amounts for metabolic processes. [< L *vita*, life + AMINE.]

vitamin A. A vitamin or mixture of vitamins occurring principally in fish-liver oils and some yellow and dark-green vegetables, functioning in normal cell growth and development and responsible in deficiency for night blindness and degeneration of mucous membranes.

vitamin B. 1. Vitamin B complex. **2.** A member of the vitamin B complex.

vitamin B₁₂. A complex, cobalt-containing compound found in liver and widely used to treat some forms of anemia.

vitamin B complex. A group of vitamins important for growth, occurring chiefly in yeast, liver, eggs, and some vegetables.

vitamin C. Ascorbic acid.

vitamin D. Any of several chemically similar compounds obtained from milk, fish, and eggs, required for normal bone growth and used to treat rickets in children.

vitamin K. Any of several natural and synthetic substances essential for the promotion of blood clotting and prevention of hemorrhage.

vi•ti•ate (vĭsh'ē-āt') *v.* **-ated, -ating. 1.** To impair the value or quality of; spoil. **2.** To debase; pervert. **3.** To invalidate or render legally ineffective. [< L *vitium*, defect, fault.] —**vi'ti• a'tion** *n.* —**vi'ti•a'tor** *n.*

vit•re•ous (vĭt'rē-əs) *adj.* **1.** Of or resembling glass; glassy. **2.** Obtained or made from glass. [< L *vitrum*, glass.]

vit•ri•fy (vĭt'rə-fī') *v.* **-fied, -fying.** To change into glass or a similar substance. [< L *vitrum*, glass + -FY.] —**vit'ri•fi'a•ble** *adj.*

vit•ri•ol (vĭt'rē-ōl') *n.* **1. a.** Sulfuric acid. **b.** Any of various salts of sulfuric acid. **2.** Vituperative feeling or utterance. [< L *vitrum*, glass.]

vit•ri•ol•ic (vĭt'rē-ŏl'ĭk) *adj.* **1.** Of or derived from vitriol. **2.** Bitterly scathing; caustic.

vit•tles (vĭt'lz) *pl.n.* Nonstandard. Victuals.

vi•tu•per•ate (vī-t/y/ŏo'pə-rāt', vĭ-) *v.* **-ated, -ating.** To rail against abusively; revile; berate. [L *vituperāre*.] —**vi•tu'per•a'tion** *n.* —**vi•tu'per• a•tive** (-pər-ə-tĭv) *adj.*

vi•va•ce (vē-vä'chā) *adv. Mus.* Lively; vivaciously; briskly. [It.] —**vi•va'ce** *adj.*

vi•va•cious (vī-vä'shəs, vĭ-) *adj.* Animated; lively; spirited. [L *vivāx*, lively.] —**vi•va'cious• ly** *adv.* —**vi•vac'i•ty** (-văs'ə-tē) *n.*

viv•id (vĭv'ĭd) *adj.* **1.** Perceived as bright and distinct; brilliant; intense. **2.** Full of the vigor and freshness of immediate experience. **3.** Evoking lifelike images within the mind. [L *vividus*, full of life, lifelike.] —**viv'id•ly** *adv.* —**viv'id•ness** *n.*

viv•i•fy (vĭv'ə-fī') *v.* **-fied, -fying. 1.** To impart life to; animate. **2.** To make more lively or intense. [< L *vivus*, alive + *facere*, to do.] —**viv'i•fi•ca'tion** *n.* —**viv'i•fi'er** *n.*

vi•vip•a•rous (vī-vĭp'ər-əs) *adj.* Giving birth to offspring that develop within the mother's body rather than hatching from eggs. [< L *vivus*, alive + -PAROUS.]

viv•i•sec•tion (vĭv'ə-sĕk'shən) *n.* The act of cutting into or dissecting the body of a living animal, esp. for scientific research. —**viv'i•sect'** (-sĕkt') *v.*

vix•en (vĭk'sən) *n.* **1.** A female fox. **2.** A quarrelsome, shrewish woman. [< OE *fyxe*, she-fox. See puk-.]

viz. videlicet.

viz•ard (vĭz'ərd) *n.* **1.** A visor. **2.** A mask.

vi•zier (vĭ-zîr', vĭz'yər) *n.* Also **vi•zir** (vĭ-zîr'). A high officer in a Moslem government, esp. in the old Turkish Empire.

vi•zor. Variant of visor.

V.M.D. Doctor of Veterinary Medicine (L *Veterinariae Medicinae Doctor*).

voc. vocative.

vocab. vocabulary.

vo•cab•u•lar•y (vō-kăb'yə-lĕr'ē) *n., pl.* **-ies. 1.** A list of words and phrases, usually arranged alphabetically and defined or translated; a

---

ô paw, for/oi boy/ou out/ŏŏ took/ōō coo/p pop/r run/s sauce/sh shy/t to/th thin/*th* the/
ŭ cut/ûr fur/v van/w wag/y yes/z size/zh vision/ə ago, item, edible, gallop, circus/

lexicon. **2.** All the words of a language. **3.** The sum of words used by a particular person, profession, etc. [< L *vocābulum*, an appellation, name.]

vo•cal (vō′kəl) *adj.* **1.** Of or pertaining to the voice. **2.** Uttered by the voice. **3.** Capable of emitting sound or speech. **4.** Full of voices; resounding with speech. **5.** Outspoken. —*n.* **1.** A vocal sound. **2.** A popular piece of music for a singer. [< L *vōx*, voice.] —**vo′cal•ly** *adv.*

vocal cords. The lower of two pairs of bands or folds in the larynx that vibrate when pulled together and when air is passed up from the lungs, thereby producing vocal sounds.

vo•cal•ic (vō-kăl′ĭk) *adj.* Pertaining to or having the nature of a vowel.

vo•cal•ist (vō′kə-lĭst) *n.* A singer.

vo•cal•ize (vō′kə-līz′) *v.* -ized, -izing. To make vocal; articulate or sing.

vo•ca•tion (vō-kā′shən) *n.* **1.** A profession, esp. one for which one is specially suited or trained. **2.** An urge to undertake a certain kind of work. [< L *vōcātiō*, a calling, summoning.] —**vo•ca′tion•al** *adj.*

voc•a•tive (vŏk′ə-tĭv) *adj. Gram.* Pertaining to or designating a case used to indicate the one being addressed. —*n.* **1.** The vocative case. **2.** A word in this case. [< L *vōcāre*, to call.]

vo•cif•er•ate (vō-sĭf′ə-rāt′) *v.* -ated, -ating. To cry out vehemently; clamor. [< L *vōx*, voice + *ferre*, to bear.] —**vo•cif′er•a′tion** *n.*

vo•cif•er•ous (vō-sĭf′ər-əs) *adj.* Making an outcry; clamorous. —**vo•cif′er•ous•ly** *adv.*

vod•ka (vŏd′kə) *n.* A colorless alcoholic liquor distilled from wheat, potatoes, etc. [< Russ *voda*, water.]

vogue (vōg) *n.* **1.** The prevailing fashion, practice, or style. **2.** Popular acceptance; popularity. [F, fashion, "rowing."]

voice (vois) *n.* **1.** The sound or sounds produced by the vocal organs of a vertebrate. **2.** The specified quality, condition, or timbre of vocal sound. **3.** A medium or agency of expression. **4.** *Gram.* A verb form indicating the relation between the subject and the action expressed by the verb. **5.** The expiration of air through vibrating vocal cords, used in the production of vowels and voiced consonants. **6.** Musical tone produced by the vibration of vocal cords. **7.** Any of the melodic parts for a musical composition. —*v.* **voiced, voicing.** To express or utter; give voice to. [< L *vōx*.]

voiced (voist) *adj.* **1.** Having a voice or a specified kind of voice. **2.** Expressed by voice. **3.** *Phon.* Uttered with vibration of the vocal cords, as the consonant *d.*

voice•less (vois′lĭs) *adj.* **1.** Having no voice. **2.** *Phon.* Uttered without vibration of the vocal cords, as the consonant *t.*

voice-o•ver (vois′ō′vər) *n.* In motion pictures and television, the voice of a narrator who does not appear on camera.

void (void) *adj.* **1.** Containing no matter; empty. **2.** Unoccupied. **3.** Devoid; lacking: *void of understanding.* **4.** Ineffective; useless. **5.** Having no legal force or validity; null. —*n.* **1.** Something void; empty space. **2.** A feeling of emptiness, loneliness, or loss. —*v.* **1.** To

invalidate; annul. **2. a.** To empty. **b.** To evacuate (body wastes). **3.** To leave; vacate. [< L *vocāre*, to be empty.] —**void′er** *n.*

voile (voil) *n.* A sheer fabric used for making dresses, curtains, etc. [< L *vēlum*, cloth, veil.]

vol. 1. volume. **2.** volunteer.

vol•a•tile (vŏl′ə-tĭl) *adj.* **1.** Evaporating readily at normal temperatures and pressures. **2.** Capable of being readily vaporized. **3.** Changeable. **4.** Lighthearted. [< L *volāre*, to fly.] —**vol′a•til′i•ty** *n.*

vol•a•til•ize (vŏl′ə-tə-līz′) *v.* -ized, -izing. **1.** To make or become volatile. **2.** To evaporate or cause to evaporate.

vol•ca•no (vŏl-kā′nō) *n., pl.* -noes or -nos. **1.** A vent in the earth's crust through which molten lava and gases are ejected. **2.** A mountain formed by the materials so ejected. [< L *Volcānus*, VULCAN.] —**vol•can′ic** (-kăn′ĭk) *adj.* —**vol•can′i•cal•ly** *adv.*

vole (vōl) *n.* Any of various rodents resembling rats or mice but having a shorter tail. [Earlier *volemouse*, "field mouse."]

Vol•ga (vŏl′gə). A river of the W Soviet Union.

Vol•go•grad (vŏl′gə-grăd′). A city of the SW Russian S.F.S.R. Pop. 818,000.

vo•li•tion (və-lĭsh′ən) *n.* **1.** A conscious choice; decision. **2.** The power of choosing; the will. [< L *velle*, to wish.] —**vo•li′tion•al** *adj.* —**vo•li′tion•al•ly** *adv.*

vol•ley (vŏl′ē) *n., pl.* -leys. **1. a.** The simultaneous discharge of a number of missiles. **b.** The missiles thus discharged. **2.** A bursting forth of a number of things simultaneously. —*v.* To discharge in or as in a volley. [< L *volāre*, to fly.] —**vol′ley•er** *n.*

vol•ley•ball (vŏl′ē-bôl′) *n.* **1.** A court game in which a score is made by grounding a ball on the opposing team's side of a high net. **2.** The large ball used in this game.

volt (vōlt) *n.* A unit of electric potential and electromotive force, equal to the difference of electric potential between two points on a conducting wire carrying a constant current of one ampere when the power dissipated between the points is one watt. [< Count A. *Volta* (1745–1827), Italian physicist.]

volt•age (vōl′tĭj) *n.* Electromotive force or potential difference.

vol•ta•ic (vŏl-tā′ĭk) *adj.* Of or involving electricity produced by chemical action.

Vol•taire (vŏl-târ′, vōl-). Pen name of François Marie Arouet. 1694–1778. French poet, dramatist, satirist, and historian.

volt•me•ter (vōlt′mē′tər) *n.* An instrument for measuring potential differences in volts.

vol•u•ble (vŏl′yə-bəl) *adj.* Characterized by ready, fluent speech; garrulous. [< L *volū-bilis.*] —**vol′u•bil′i•ty** *n.* —**vol′u•bly** *adv.*

vol•ume (vŏl′yōom, -yəm) *n.* **1.** A collection of written or printed sheets bound together; a book. **2.** One book of a set. **3.** The measure of a three-dimensional object or region of space. **4.** A large amount. **5. a.** The loudness of a sound. **b.** A control for adjusting loudness. [< L *volvere*, to roll, turn.]

vol•u•met•ric (vŏl′yə-mĕt′rĭk) *adj.* Pertaining to measurement of volume.

ă pat/ā ate/âr care/ä bar/b bib/ch chew/d deed/ĕ pet/ē be/f fit/g gag/h hat/hw what/
ĭ pit/ī pie/îr pier/j judge/k kick/l lid, fatal/m mum/n no, sudden/ng sing/ŏ pot/ō go/

vo•lu•mi•nous (və-lōō′mə-nəs) *adj.* **1.** Having great volume, fullness, size, or number. **2.** Filling or capable of filling volumes. **3.** Having many coils; winding.

vol•un•tar•y (vŏl′ən-tĕr′ē) *adj.* **1.** Arising from one's own free will. **2.** Acting by choice and without constraint or guarantee of reward. **3.** Normally controlled by individual volition. **4.** Not accidental; intentional. [< L *voluntās,* will, free will.] —**vol′un•tar′i•ly** *adv.*

vol•un•teer (vŏl′ən-tîr′) *n.* One who performs or gives services of his own free will. —*v.* **1.** To give or offer to give on one's own initiative. **2.** To enter into or offer to enter into an undertaking of one's own free will. —**vol′un•teer′** *adj.*

vo•lup•tu•ar•y (və-lŭp′chōō-ĕr′ē) *n., pl.* -**ies.** One given to luxury and sensual pleasures. [< L *voluptās,* pleasure.]

vo•lup•tu•ous (və-lŭp′chōō-əs) *adj.* **1.** Consisting of, devoted to, or characterized by sensual pleasures. **2.** Full and appealing in form. [< L *voluptās,* pleasure.] —**vo•lup′tu•ous•ness** *n.*

vo•lute (və-lōōt′) *n.* A spiral, scroll-like formation or decoration. [< L *volūta,* scroll.]

vom•it (vŏm′ĭt) *v.* **1.** To eject part or all of the contents of the stomach through the mouth. **2.** To eject or discharge in a gush. —*n.* Matter ejected from the stomach. [< L *vomere.*]

voo•doo (vōō′dōō) *n.* A religious cult of African origin characterized by a belief in sorcery and fetishes and rituals in which participants communicate by trance with ancestors, saints, or animistic deities. —**voo′doo** *adj.* —**voo′doo•ism′** *n.*

vo•ra•cious (vô-rā′shəs, vō-, və-) *adj.* **1.** Greedy for food; ravenous. **2.** Too eager; insatiable. [< L *vorāre,* to devour.] —**vo•ra′ci•ty** (vô-răs′ə-tē, vō-, və-), **vo•ra′cious•ness** *n.*

Vo•ro•nezh (vŏ-rô′nĭsh). A city of the W Russian S.F.S.R. Pop. 576,000.

–vorous. *comb. form.* Eating or feeding on: *herbivorous.* [< L *vorāre,* to devour.]

vor•tex (vôr′tĕks) *n., pl.* -**texes** or -**tices** (-tə-sēz′). **1.** Fluid flow involving rotation about an axis. **2.** A situation that draws into its center all surrounding it. [L *vortex, vertex.*]

vo•ta•ry (vō′tə-rē) *n., pl.* -**ries. 1.** One bound by religious vows. **2.** A devotee. [< L *vovēre,* to vow.]

vote (vōt) *n.* **1.** A formal expression of preference for a candidate or a proposed resolution. **2.** That by which such a preference is made known. **3.** A group of voters: *the labor vote.* **4.** The result of an election, referendum, etc. **5.** Suffrage. —*v.* **voted, voting. 1.** To express preference by a vote. **2.** To bring into existence or make available by vote. **3.** To declare or pronounce by general consent. [L *vōtum,* vow.] —**vot′er** *n.*

vo•tive (vō′tĭv) *adj.* Given or dedicated in fulfillment of a vow or pledge. [< L *vōtum,* vow.]

vouch (vouch) *v.* **1.** To substantiate by supplying evidence; verify. **2.** To function or serve as a guarantee; furnish supporting evidence: *He vouched for her courage.* [< L *vōcāre,* to call.]

vouch•er (vou′chər) *n.* **1.** One who vouches. **2.** A document serving as proof that the terms of a transaction have been met.

vouch•safe (vouch′sāf′) *v.* -**safed, -safing.** To condescend to grant or bestow; deign. [ME *vouchen sauf,* "to warrant as safe."]

vow (vou) *n.* **1.** An earnest promise or pledge that binds one to a specified act or mode of behavior. **2.** A formal declaration. —*v.* **1.** To promise or pledge solemnly; make a vow. **2.** To declare formally. [< L *vōtum,* pp of *vovēre,* to pledge, promise.] —**vow′er** *n.*

vow•el (vou′əl) *n.* **1.** A speech sound created by the relatively free passage of breath through the larynx and oral cavity. **2.** A letter that represents such a sound. [< L *(littera) vōcālis,* "sounding (letter)."]

voy•age (voi′ĭj) *n.* A long journey, esp. one across a sea or ocean. —*v.* -**aged, -aging.** To make a voyage; travel. [< L *via,* road, way.] —**voy′ag•er** *n.*

vo•yeur (vwä-yûr′) *n.* One who derives sexual gratification by secretly observing the sex organs or sexual acts of others. [< OF, "one who sees."] —**vo•yeur′ism′** *n.* —**vo′yeur•is′tic** (vwä′yə-rĭs′tĭk) *adj.*

V.P. vice president.

vs. versus.

v.s. vide supra.

Vt. Vermont.

VTOL vertical takeoff and landing.

Vul. Vulgate.

Vul•can (vŭl′kən). Roman god of fire and craftsmanship. [L *Vulcānus, Volcānus.*]

vul•can•ize (vŭl′kə-nīz′) *v.* -**ized, -izing. 1.** To modify the properties of rubber by treatment with sulfur or other additives in the presence of heat and pressure. **2.** To treat (other substances) similarly. [< VULCAN.] —**vul′can•i•za′tion** *n.* —**vul′can•iz′er** *n.*

Vulg. Vulgate.

vul•gar (vŭl′gər) *adj.* **1.** Of or associated with the common people. **2.** Vernacular. **3.** Ill-bred; boorish. **4.** Obscene; offensive; coarse. [< L *vulgus,* the common people.] —**vul′gar•ly** *adv.* —**vul′gar•ness** *n.*

vul•gar•i•an (vŭl′gâr′ē-ən) *n.* A vulgar person, esp. one who makes a display of his money.

vul•gar•ism (vŭl′gə-rĭz′əm) *n.* **1.** Vulgarity. **2.** A word or expression used mainly by uncultivated people.

vul•gar•i•ty (vŭl′găr′ə-tē) *n., pl.* -**ties. 1.** The condition or quality of being vulgar. **2.** Something that offends good taste or propriety.

vul•gar•ize (vŭl′gə-rīz′) *v.* -**ized, -izing. 1.** To render vulgar; debase; cheapen. **2.** To popularize. —**vul′gar•i•za′tion** *n.*

Vulgar Latin. The common speech of ancient Rome, differing from literary or standard Latin and forming the basis for the development of the Romance languages.

vul•ner•a•ble (vŭl′nər-ə-bəl) *adj.* **1.** Susceptible to injury; unprotected from danger. **2.** Susceptible to attack; insufficiently defended. **3.** *Bridge.* In a position to receive greater penalties. [< L *vulnerāre,* to wound.] —**vul′ner•a•bil′i•ty** *n.* —**vul′ner•a•bly** *adv.*

vul•pine (vŭl′pĭn, -pīn′) *adj.* **1.** Resembling or

characteristic of a fox. 2. Clever; devious; cunning. [< L *vulpēs,* fox.]
vul•ture (vŭl'chər) *n.* Any of various large birds characteristically having dark plumage, a naked head and neck, and feeding on carrion. [< L *vultur.*]

vul•va (vŭl'və) *n., pl.* **-vae** (-vē). The external female genitalia. [L *vulva, volva,* womb, covering.]
vv. verses.
v.v. vice versa.
vy•ing (vī'ĭng) *adj.* Competing; contending.

w, W (dŭb'əl-yōō, -yōō) *n.* 1. The 23rd letter of the English alphabet. 2. Anything shaped like the letter **W**.
w 1. west; western. 2. width.
W 1. tungsten. 2. watt. 3. west; western. 4. *Broadcasting.* A letter prefixed to the call letters of some U.S. radio and TV stations.
w. west; western.
W. 1. Wednesday. 2. Welsh. 3. west; western.
Wac (wăk) *n.* A member of the Women's Army Corps of the U.S. Army.
wack•y (wăk'ē) *adj.* **-ier, -iest.** Also **whack•y.** *Slang.* Highly irrational or erratic. [Prob < WHACK.] —**wack'i•ness** *n.*
wad (wŏd) *n.* 1. A small mass of soft material. 2. A compressed ball, roll, or lump, as of tobacco. 3. A disk, as of felt, to keep the powder and shot in place in a shotgun cartridge. 4. *Informal.* **a.** A large amount. **b.** A sizable roll of paper money. —*v.* **wadded, wadding.** 1. To compress into a wad. 2. To pad or plug with wadding. 3. To hold (shot or powder) in place with a wad. [?]
wad•ding (wŏd'ĭng) *n.* 1. A wad or wads collectively. 2. A soft layer of fibrous cotton or wool used for padding or stuffing.
wad•dle (wŏd'l) *v.* **-dled, -dling.** To walk with short steps that tilt the body from side to side, as a duck does. —*n.* A waddling gait. [Prob freq of WADE.] —**wad'dler** *n.*
wade (wād) *v.* **waded, wading.** 1. To walk in or through water or something that similarly impedes movement. 2. To make one's way arduously. —*n.* The act of wading. [< OE *wadan,* to go, wade. See **wādh-.**]
wad•er (wā'dər) *n.* 1. One that wades. 2. A long-legged bird that frequents shallow water. 3. **waders.** Waterproof hip boots or trousers worn esp. by fishermen or hunters.
wa•di (wä'dē) *n.* In N Africa and SW Asia, a valley or gully that remains dry except during the rainy season. [Ar *wādī.*]
wa•fer (wā'fər) *n.* 1. A small, thin, crisp cake, biscuit, or candy. 2. A small disk. [< MLG *wāfel.*]
waf•fle¹ (wŏf'əl) *n.* A crisp batter cake baked in a waffle iron. [Du *wafel.*]
waf•fle² (wŏf'əl) *v.* **-fled, -fling.** *Informal.* To speak or write evasively. —*n. Informal.* Vague or misleading language. [Prob imit.]

waffle iron. An appliance with hinged metal plates that impress a grid pattern into waffle batter.
waft (wäft, wăft) *v.* To carry or cause to go gently and smoothly through the air or over water. —*n.* 1. Something, as an odor, carried through the air. 2. A light breeze. 3. A waving. [< MDu *wachten,* to watch, guard.]
wag¹ (wăg) *v.* **wagged, wagging.** To move briskly and repeatedly from side to side, to and fro, or up and down. —*n.* The act or motion of wagging. [< OE *wagian,* to totter.]
wag² (wăg) *n.* One who jests. [?]
wage (wāj) *n.* 1. Often **wages.** Payment for services. 2. **wages** *(takes sing. or pl. v.).* Recompense; requital. —*v.* **waged, waging.** To engage in (a war or campaign). [ME, a pledge, wage, soldier's pay.]
wa•ger (wā'jər) *n.* A bet. —*v.* To bet. [< ONF *wage,* a pledge, wage.]
wag•gish (wăg'ĭsh) *adj.* Playfully humorous.
wag•gle (wăg'əl) *v.* **-gled, -gling.** To move with short, quick motions. —*n.* A waggling motion. [Freq of WAG.] —**wag'gly** *adj.*
Wag•ner (väg'nər), **Richard.** 1813–1883. German poet and composer. —**Wag•ne'ri•an** *adj.*
wag•on (wăg'ən) *n.* 1. A 4-wheeled, usually horse-drawn vehicle having a large rectangular body. 2. **a.** A station wagon. **b.** A police patrol wagon. 3. A child's low four-wheeled cart. —**on the wagon.** *Slang.* Abstaining from liquor. [< MDu *wagen, waghen.*]
wag•on•er (wăg'ə-nər) *n.* A wagon driver.
wag•on•ette (wăg'ə-nĕt') *n.* A light wagon with two facing seats behind the driver's seat.
wa•gon-lit (vȧ-gôN-lē') *n., pl.* **wagons-lits** (vȧ-gôN-lē'). A railroad sleeping car. [F.]
waif (wāf) *n.* 1. **a.** A forsaken or orphaned child. **b.** A stray young animal. 2. Something found and unclaimed. [ME *waife,* property without owner.]
wail (wāl) *v.* 1. To grieve or protest audibly; to lament. 2. To make a high-pitched mournful sound. —*n.* 1. A high-pitched mournful cry. 2. Any similar sound. [Prob < ON *veila,* to moan, lament.] —**wail'er** *n.*
wail•ful (wāl'fəl) *adj.* Mournful.
wain (wān) *n.* A large open farm wagon. [< OE *wægen.*]

wain•scot (wān′skət, -skŏt′, -skōt′) *n.* Wall paneling, esp. on the lower part of an interior wall. —*v.* **-scoted** or **-scotted, -scoting** or **-scotting.** To line or panel (a room or wall) with wainscot. [< MDu *wagenschot,* perh "timber for wagons."]

wain•scot•ing (wān′skə-tĭng, -skŏt′ĭng, -skō′-tĭng) *n.* Also **wain•scot•ting.** 1. A wainscoted wall or walls. 2. Material for a wainscot.

wain•wright (wān′rīt′) *n.* A builder and repairer of wagons.

waist (wāst) *n.* 1. The part of the human trunk between the bottom of the rib cage and the pelvis. 2. a. The part of a garment from the shoulders to the waistline. b. A blouse. c. A child's undershirt. 3. The middle section or part of something. [< OE *wæst,* growth, size of body. See aug-.]

waist•coat (wĕs′kĭt, wāst′kōt′) *n.* *Chiefly Brit.* A vest.

waist•line (wāst′līn′) *n.* 1. a. The place at which the circumference of the waist is smallest. b. The measurement of this circumference. 2. The line at which the skirt and bodice of a dress join.

wait (wāt) *v.* 1. To remain inactive in anticipation. 2. To delay; postpone. 3. To serve as a waiter or waitress. 4. To attend, as a clerk or servant: *He waited on her.* —*n.* The act of waiting or the time spent waiting. [ME *waiten,* to watch, lie in wait, wait.]

wait•er (wā′tər) *n.* 1. A man who waits on table. 2. A tray.

wait•ress (wā′trĭs) *n.* A woman or girl who waits on table.

waive (wāv) *v.* **waived, waiving.** 1. To relinquish or give up (a claim or right) voluntarily. 2. To put aside or off for the time. [ME *weiven,* to outlaw, abandon, relinquish.}

waiv•er (wā′vər) *n.* 1. The intentional relinquishment of a right, claim, or privilege. 2. A document that evidences such an act.

Wa•kash•an (wŏ′kə-shăn′, wä-kăsh′ən) *n.* A family of North American Indian languages spoken by certain tribes of Washington and British Columbia. —**Wa′kash•an** *adj.*

wake¹ (wāk) *v.* **woke, waked** or *chiefly Brit. & regional* **woke** or **woken, waking.** 1. To awaken: *He woke up with a start.* 2. To keep watch or guard, esp. over a corpse. 3. To remain awake. 4. To make aware of; alert. —*n.* 1. A watch, esp. over the body of a deceased person before burial. 2. The condition of being awake. [< OE *wacian,* to be awake, and **wacan,* to rouse. See weg-.]

Usage: The verbs *wake, waken, awake,* and *awaken* are alike in meaning but differentiated in usage. Each has transitive and intransitive senses, but *awake* is used largely intransitively and *waken* transitively. In the passive voice, *awaken* and *waken* are the more frequent. In figurative usage, *awake* and *awaken* are the more prevalent: *He awoke to the danger. His suspicions were awakened. Wake* is frequently used with *up;* the others do not take a preposition. The preferred past participle of *wake* is *waked,* not *woke* or *woken.* The preferred past participle of *awake* is *awaked,* not *awoke.*

wake² (wāk) *n.* 1. The track of turbulence left by something moving through water. 2. The track or course left behind anything. [Prob < ON *vök,* a hole or crack in ice.]

wake•ful (wāk′fəl) *adj.* 1. a. Not sleeping. b. Sleepless. 2. Alert. —**wake′ful•ness** *n.*

wak•en (wā′kən) *v.* 1. To rouse from sleep; awake. 2. To rouse from an inactive state. —See Usage note at **wake.** [< OE *wæcnian.*]

wale (wāl) *n.* 1. A welt on the skin. 2. a. One of the ribs or ridges in the surface of a fabric. b. The texture of a fabric. —*v.* **waled, waling.** To mark (the skin) with wales. [< OE *walu,* a ridge of earth or stone, weal.]

Wales (wālz). A principality comprising part of the United Kingdom located in W Great Britain. Pop. 2,676,000.

Wal•hal•la. Variant of **Valhalla.**

walk (wôk) *v.* 1. To go, cause to go, or lead around on foot. 2. To pass over, on, or through on foot. 3. To conduct oneself in a particular manner. 4. *Baseball.* To go to first base after the pitcher has thrown four balls. —*n.* 1. a. The act or an instance of walking. b. A relatively slow gait in which the feet are lifted alternately. 2. a. Walking pace. b. The characteristic way in which one walks. 3. The distance to be covered in walking. 4. A place on which one may walk. [< OE *wealcan,* to roll, toss, and *wealcian,* to roll up, muffle up.] —**walk′er** *n.*

walk•ie-talk•ie (wô′kē-tô′kē) *n.* A portable sending and receiving radio set.

walk-in (wôk′ĭn′) *adj.* Large enough to admit entrance, as a closet. —**walk′-in′** *n.*

walking stick. A cane used as an aid in walking.

walk-on (wôk′ŏn′, -ôn′) *n.* A minor role in a theatrical production.

walk•out (wôk′out′) *n.* A strike of workmen.

walk•up (wôk′ŭp′) *n.* 1. A building with no elevator. 2. An apartment in such a building.

wall (wôl) *n.* 1. A vertical construction forming an inner partition or exterior siding of a building. 2. A continuous structure forming a rampart and built for defensive purposes. 3. Something resembling a wall in appearance, function, or construction. —*v.* 1. To enclose, surround, or fortify with or as if with a wall. 2. To separate with or as if with a wall. [< OE *weall* < L *vallum,* palisade, wall.]

wal•la•by (wŏl′ə-bē) *n., pl.* **-bies.** Any of various Australian marsupials related to and resembling the kangaroos but generally smaller.

wall•board (wôl′bôrd′, -bōrd′) *n.* A structural material used as a substitute for plaster or wood panels.

wal•let (wŏl′ĭt) *n.* A small, flat folding case for holding paper money, cards, photographs, etc. [ME *walet,* a pilgrim's knapsack or provisions bag.]

wall•eye (wôl′ī′) *n.* 1. An eye in which the cornea is white or opaque. 2. An eye abnormally turned away from the center of the face. 3. Also **walleyed pike.** A North American freshwater food and game fish with large, conspicuous eyes. [Back-formation < WALL-EYED.]

---

wall·eyed (wôl'īd') *adj.* Having a walleye. [< ON *vagleygr.*]

wall·flow·er (wôl'flou'ər) *n.* **1.** A cultivated plant with fragrant yellowish or brownish flowers. **2.** *Informal.* One who does not participate in social activity because of shyness or unpopularity.

Wal·loon (wŏ-lōōn') *n.* **1.** One of a French-speaking people of Celtic descent inhabiting SE Belgium and adjacent regions of France. **2.** The French dialect of this people. —**Wal·loon'** *adj.*

wal·lop (wŏl'əp) *v.* **1.** To beat soundly; thrash. **2.** To strike with a hard blow. —*n.* **1.** A severe blow. **2.** The ability to strike such a blow. [< ME *walopen,* to gallop.]

wal·lop·ing (wŏl'ə-pĭng) *adj. Informal.* Very large; huge.

wal·low (wŏl'ō) *v.* **1.** To roll the body about in or as in water, snow, or mud. **2.** To luxuriate; revel. —*n.* A place where animals go to wallow. [< OE *wealwian.* See **wel-³.**]

wall·pa·per (wôl'pā'pər) *n.* Paper printed with designs used as a wall covering. —*v.* To cover with wallpaper.

wal·nut (wôl'nŭt', -nət) *n.* **1.** An edible nut with a hard, corrugated shell. **2.** A tree bearing such nuts. **3.** The hard, dark wood of such a tree. [< OE *wealhhnutu,* "Gaulish nut."]

wal·rus (wôl'rəs, wŏl'-) *n., pl.* **-ruses** or **-rus.** A large Arctic marine mammal with tough, wrinkled skin and large tusks. [< Scand.]

waltz (wôlts) *n.* A dance in triple time with a strong accent on the first beat. —*v.* **1.** To dance the waltz (with). **2.** To move briskly and with ease. [< MHG *walzen,* to roll, turn, dance.] —**waltz'er** *n.*

wam·pum (wŏm'pəm, wôm'-) *n.* Small beads made from polished shells, formerly used by North American Indians as currency and as jewelry. [< Algon.]

wan (wŏn) *adj.* **1.** Unnaturally pale. **2.** Languid; melancholy. [< OE *wann,* dusky, dark, livid.] —**wan'ly** *adv.* —**wan'ness** *n.*

wand (wŏnd) *n.* **1.** A slender rod carried as a symbol of office in a procession. **2.** A musician's baton. **3.** A rod used by a magician, diviner, or conjurer. [< ON *vöndr.*]

wan·der (wŏn'dər) *v.* **1.** To roam aimlessly. **2.** To go by an indirect route or at no set pace. **3.** To go astray. **4.** To think or express oneself incoherently. [< OE *wandrian.* See **wendh-.**] —**wan'der·er** *n.*

wandering Jew. A trailing plant often with variegated foliage, popular as a house plant.

wan·der·lust (wŏn'dər-lŭst') *n.* A strong impulse to travel. [G.]

wane (wān) *v.* **waned, waning. 1.** To decrease gradually; dwindle; decline. **2.** To show decreasing illuminated area from full moon to new moon. **3.** To approach an end. —*n.* **1.** The act or process of waning. **2.** A period of waning, esp. the period of the decrease of the moon's illuminated visible surface. [< OE *wanian,* to lessen. See **eu-.**]

wan·gle (wăng'gəl) *v.* **-gled, -gling. 1.** To make, achieve, or get by contrivance. **2.** To manipulate or juggle. **3.** To use tricky or fraudulent methods. [Orig "to manipulate or devise a substitute for."] —**wan'gler** *n.*

Wan·kel engine (väng'kəl, wäng'-). A rotary internal-combustion engine in which a triangular rotor turning in a specially shaped housing performs the functions alloted to the pistons of a conventional engine. [< Felix *Wankel* (born 1902), German engineer.]

want (wŏnt, wônt) *v.* **1.** To fail to have; lack. **2.** To desire; wish for: *He wants to leave.* **3.** To need or require. **4. a.** To request the presence of. **b.** To seek with intent to capture. —*n.* **1.** The condition or quality of lacking a usual or necessary amount. **2.** Pressing need. **3.** Something needed. **4.** A fault. [< ON *vanta,* to be lacking.]

want·ing (wŏn'tĭng, wôn'-) *adj.* **1.** Absent; lacking. **2.** Not up to standards or expectations. —*prep.* **1.** Without. **2.** Minus; less.

wan·ton (wŏn'tən) *adj.* **1.** Immoral or unchaste; lewd. **2.** Maliciously cruel. **3.** Freely extravagant. **4.** Luxuriant. —*n.* A wanton person, esp. an immoral woman. [ME *wantowen,* lacking discipline, lewd.] —**wan'ton·ly** *adv.* —**wan'ton·ness** *n.*

wap·i·ti (wŏp'ə-tē) *n.* A large North American deer with many-branched antlers; an elk. [< Algon.]

war (wôr) *n.* **1. a.** A state of open, armed conflict between nations, states, or parties. **b.** The period of such conflict. **2.** Any condition of active antagonism. **3.** Military science; strategy. —*v.* **warred, warring. 1.** To wage war. **2.** To be in a state of hostility. [< OHG *werra,* confusion, strife.]

War Between the States. The Civil War.

war·ble (wôr'bəl) *v.* **-bled, -bling.** To sing with trills, runs, or other melodic embellishments. —*n.* The act of warbling. [< ONF *werble,* a warbling, melody.]

war·bler (wôr'blər) *n.* **1.** Any of various small, often yellowish New World birds. **2.** Any of various small brownish or grayish Old World birds.

war bonnet. A feathered ceremonial headdress used by some North American Plains Indians, consisting of a cap or band and a trailing extension decorated with erect feathers.

war cry. 1. A cry uttered by combatants as they attack. **2.** A slogan used to rally people to a cause.

ward (wôrd) *n.* **1.** A division of a city for administrative and representative purposes. **2.** A division in a hospital. **3.** A division of a prison. **4.** *Law.* A child or incompetent person placed under the care or protection of a guardian or court. **5.** The state of being under guard. **6.** The act of guarding. **7.** A means of protection. —*v.* To turn aside; parry; avert; repel: *ward off a blow.* [< OE *weard,* a watching over. See **wer-⁴.**]

-ward, -wards *comb. form.* Direction toward: skyward, westwards. [< OE *-weard.* See **wer-³.**]

war·den (wôrd'n) *n.* **1.** The chief administrative official of a prison. **2.** An official charged with the enforcement of certain laws and regulations, as an air-raid warden. [< ONF *warder,* to guard.]

ă pat/ā ate/âr care/ä bar/b bib/ch chew/d deed/ĕ pet/ē be/f fit/g gag/h hat/hw what/ ĭ pit/ī pie/îr pier/j judge/k kick/l lid, fatal/m mum/n no, sudden/ng sing/ŏ pot/ō go/

ward•er (wôr′dər) *n.* A guard, porter, or watchman of a gate or tower. [< ONF *warder,* to guard, keep.]

ward•robe (wôrd′rōb′) *n.* **1.** A tall cabinet, closet, or small room designed to hold clothes. **2.** Garments collectively, esp. all the articles of clothing belonging to one person. [< ONF *warderobe.*]

ward•ship (wôrd′shĭp′) *n.* **1.** The state of being in the charge of a guardian. **2.** Guardianship.

–ware. *comb. form.* **1.** Articles of the same general kind: *glassware.* **2.** Pottery or ceramics: *earthenware.*

ware•house (wâr′hous′) *n.* A place in which goods or merchandise is stored.

wares (wârz) *pl.n.* Articles of commerce; goods. [< OE *waru* (sing).]

war•fare (wôr′fâr′) *n.* **1.** The waging of war. **2.** Conflict of any kind. [ME *werrefare,* a going to war.]

war•head (wôr′hĕd′) *n.* A part of the system in the forward part of a projectile, as a guided missile, that contains the explosive charge.

war-horse (wôr′hôrs′) *n.* **1.** A horse used in combat. **2.** One who has been through many struggles.

war•like (wôr′līk′) *adj.* **1.** Belligerent; hostile. **2.** Of or pertaining to war.

war•lock (wôr′lŏk′) *n.* A male witch, sorcerer, or wizard. [< OE *wǣrloga,* "oath-breaker."]

war•lord (wôr′lôrd′) *n.* A military commander exercising civil power in a given region, often in defiance of the national government.

warm (wôrm) *adj.* **1.** Moderately hot. **2.** Having the natural heat of living beings. **3.** Preserving or imparting heat. **4.** Having a sensation of unusually high bodily heat, as from exercise. **5.** Marked by enthusiasm. **6.** Sympathetic; cordial. **7.** Loving; passionate. **8.** Quick to be aroused; fiery. **9.** Recently made: *a warm trail.* **10.** Close to discovering something. —*v.* To increase slightly in temperature; make or become warm. —**warm up.** To make or become ready for operation, as an engine. [< OE *wearm.*] —**warm′ly** *adv.*

warm-blood•ed (wôrm′blŭd′ĭd) *adj.* Maintaining a relatively constant, warm body temperature independent of environmental temperature, as a mammal.

warm-heart•ed (wôrm′här′tĭd) *adj.* Friendly; sympathetic. —**warm′-heart′ed•ly** *adv.*

war•mon•ger (wôr′mŭng′gər, -mŏng′ər) *n.* One who advocates or attempts to stir up war.

warmth (wôrmth) *n.* **1.** The state, sensation, or quality of moderate heat. **2.** Excitement or intensity, as of love or passion; ardor; zeal. [< OE **wiermthu.*]

warn (wôrn) *v.* **1.** To make aware of potential danger; caution. **2.** To admonish as to action or manners. **3.** To notify (a person) to go or stay away. **4.** To notify in advance. [< OE *wearnian,* to take heed, warn. See **wer-⁵.**]

warn•ing (wôr′nĭng) *n.* **1.** An intimation or sign of impending danger. **2. a.** Advice to beware. **b.** Counsel to desist from a given course of action. —*adj.* Acting or serving as a warning. —**warn′ing•ly** *adv.*

warp (wôrp) *v.* **1.** To twist or become twisted

out of shape. **2.** To pervert; corrupt. **3.** *Naut.* To move (a vessel) by hauling on a line fastened to a piling, anchor, or pier. —*n.* **1.** The state of being twisted or bent out of shape. **2.** A distortion or twist. **3.** The threads that run lengthwise in a fabric, crossed at right angles by the woof. [< OE *weorpan,* to throw (away). See **wer-³.**] —**warp′er** *n.*

war paint. Pigments applied to the face or body by certain tribes preparatory to going to war.

war•path (wôr′păth′, -päth′) *n.* **1.** The route taken by a party of North American Indians on the attack. **2.** A hostile course or mood: *on the warpath.*

war•rant (wôr′ənt, wŏr′-) *n.* **1.** Authorization or certification. **2.** Justification for some action; grounds. **3.** Evidence; proof. **4.** A writ or other order that serves as authorization for something, esp. a judicial writ authorizing a search, seizure, or arrest. —*v.* **1.** To guarantee or attest to the quality or accuracy of. **2.** To vouch for. **3. a.** To guarantee (a product). **b.** To guarantee (a purchaser) indemnification against damage or loss. **4.** To guarantee the security of. **5.** To call for; deserve. **6.** To authorize or empower. [Prob < OHG *werenti,* "the one protecting."]

war•ran•ty (wôr′ən-tē, wŏr′-) *n., pl.* **-ties: 1.** Official authorization, sanction, or warrant. **2.** Justification for an act or course of action. **3.** A legally binding guarantee.

war•ren (wôr′ən, wŏr′-) *n.* **1.** An area where rabbits live in burrows. **2.** Any overcrowded place of habitation. [< ONF *warenne.*]

war•ri•or (wôr′ē-ər, -yər, wŏr′-) *n.* One engaged or experienced in battle.

War•saw (wôr′sô). The capital of Poland. Pop. 1,241,000.

war•ship (wôr′shĭp′) *n.* A ship equipped for use in battle.

wart (wôrt) *n.* **1.** A small, hard growth on the outer skin, caused by a virus and occurring typically on the hands or feet. **2.** Any similar protuberance, as on a plant. [< OE *wearte.* See **wart-¹.**] —**wart′y** *adj.*

wart hog. An African hog with curved tusks and wartlike protuberances on the face.

war•time (wôr′tīm′) *n.* A time of war.

war•y (wâr′ē) *adj.* **-ier, -iest. 1.** On one's guard; cautious; watchful. **2.** Characterized by caution. [< OE *wǣr.* See **wer-⁴.**] —**war′i•ness** *n.*

was (wŏz, wŭz; *unstressed* wəz). 1st and 3rd person sing. past indicative of **be.** See Usage note at **were.** [< OE *wæs.* See **wes-³.**]

wash (wŏsh, wôsh) *v.* **1.** To cleanse, using water or other liquid, usually with soap, detergent, etc., by immersing, dipping, rubbing, or scrubbing. **2.** To cleanse oneself. **3.** To rid of corruption; purify. **4.** To make moist or wet. **5.** To flow over, against, or past: *shores washed by ocean tides.* **6.** To sweep or carry away: *The rain had washed them away.* **7.** To erode or destroy by moving water: *The roads were washed out.* **8.** To coat with a watery layer of paint or other coloring substance. **9.** To remove particulate constituents from (an ore) by immersion in or agitation with water. **10.** *Brit.*

Informal. To hold up under examination: *Your excuse won't wash!* —*n.* **1.** The act or process of washing or cleansing. **2.** A quantity of articles washed or intended for washing. **3.** Waste liquid; swill. **4.** Any preparation or product used in washing or coating. **5.** A light tint or hue: *a wash of red sunset.* **6. a.** The rush or surge of water or waves. **b.** The sound of this. **7.** The removal or erosion of soil, subsoil, etc., by the action of moving water. **8.** *Western U.S.* The dry bed of a stream. [< OE *wæscan, wacsan.* See wed-.]

Wash. Washington.

wash·a·ble (wŏsh'ə-bəl, wôsh'-) *adj.* Capable of being washed without injury.

wash-and-wear (wŏsh'ən-wâr', wôsh'-) *adj.* Treated so as to require little or no ironing.

wash·board (wŏsh'bôrd', -bōrd', wôsh'-) *n.* A board with a corrugated surface upon which clothes can be rubbed in the process of laundering.

wash·cloth (wŏsh'klôth', -klŏth', wôsh'-) *n.* A small, usually square cloth used for washing the face or body.

washed-out (wŏsht'out', wôsht'-) *adj.* **1.** Pale; faded. **2.** *Informal.* Exhausted.

wash·er (wŏsh'ər, wôsh'-) *n.* **1.** One that washes. **2.** A small perforated disk, as of metal, rubber, or plastic, placed beneath a nut or at an axle bearing to relieve friction, prevent leakage, or distribute pressure. **3.** A machine or apparatus for washing.

wash·er·wom·an (wŏsh'ər-wŏŏm'ən, wô'-shər-) *n.* A laundress.

wash·ing (wŏsh'ĭng, wôsh'-) *n.* **1.** A quantity of articles washed at one time: *the week's washing.* **2.** The residue after an ore or other material has been washed.

washing soda. A hydrated sodium carbonate, used as a general cleanser.

Wash·ing·ton (wŏsh'ĭng-tən, wôsh'-). **1.** A state of the NW U.S. Pop. 3,409,000. Cap. Olympia. **2.** The capital of the U.S., a city coextensive with the District of Columbia. Pop. 757,000.

Wash·ing·ton (wŏsh'ĭng-tən, wôsh'-). **1.** Booker T(aliaferro). 1856–1915. American Negro educator. **2.** George. 1732–1799. 1st President of the U.S. (1789–97).

wash·out (wŏsh'out', wôsh'-) *n.* **1. a.** The erosion, as of a roadbed, by a transient stream of water. **b.** A channel produced by washout. **2.** A total failure.

wash·room (wŏsh'rŏŏm', -rŏŏm', wôsh'-) *n.* A bathroom or lavatory, esp. in a public place.

wash·stand (wŏsh'stănd', wôsh'-) *n.* **1.** A stand designed to hold a basin and pitcher of water for washing. **2.** A bathroom sink.

wash·tub (wŏsh'tŭb', wôsh'-) *n.* A tub used for washing clothes.

wash·y (wŏsh'ē, wôsh'ē) *adj.* -ier, -iest. **1.** Watery; diluted. **2.** Lacking intensity or strength. —**wash'i·ness** *n.*

was·n't (wŏz'ənt, wŭz'-). Contraction of *was not.*

wasp (wŏsp, wôsp) *n.* Any of various insects having a slender body with a narrow midsection and often inflicting a painful sting. [<

OE *wæsp, wæps.* See wopsā.] —**wasp'y** *adj.*

wasp·ish (wŏs'pĭsh, wôs'-) *adj.* **1.** Suggestive of a wasp. **2.** Easily irritated or annoyed. —**wasp'ish·ly** *adv.* —**wasp'ish·ness** *n.*

wasp waist. A very slender or tightly corseted woman's waist. —**wasp'-waist'ed** (wŏsp'wās'tĭd, wôsp'-) *adj.*

was·sail (wŏs'əl, wăs'-, wŏ-sāl') *n.* **1. a.** A toast formerly given in drinking someone's health. **b.** The drink used in such toasting. **2.** A festivity characterized by much drinking. —*v.* To drink to the health of. [< ON *ves heill,* be in good health.]

Was·ser·mann test (wä'sər-mən). A diagnostic blood test for syphilis. [< A. von *Wassermann* (1866–1925), German bacteriologist.]

wast (wŏst). *Archaic.* 2nd person sing. *p.t.* of be.

wast·age (wā'stĭj) *n.* Loss by deterioration, wear, destruction, etc.

waste (wāst) *v.* wasted, wasting. **1.** To consume thoughtlessly or carelessly. **2.** To weaken or become weak. **3.** To fail to take advantage of:

Booker T. Washington

George Washington

waste an opportunity. —*n.* **1.** The act of wasting or condition of being wasted. **2.** A desert or wilderness. **3.** A useless or worthless by-product of a process. **4.** The undigested residue of food eliminated from the body. —*adj.* **1.** Discarded as worthless or useless: *waste paper.* **2.** Used as a container for refuse: *a waste can.* **3.** Not cultivated or inhabited. **4.** Excreted from the body as useless. [< L *vāstāre,* to make empty.]

waste•ful (wāst′fəl) *adj.* Characterized by heedless wasting; extravagant. —**waste′ful•ly** *adv.* —**waste′ful•ness** *n.*

waste•land (wāst′lănd′) *n.* Uncultivated or desolate land.

wast•rel (wā′strəl) *n.* **1.** One who wastes. **2.** An idler or loafer.

watch (wŏch) *v.* **1.** To look or observe carefully and continuously. **2.** To look and wait expectantly or in anticipation: *watch for an opportunity.* **3.** To be on the lookout or alert; guard. **4.** To stay alert as a devotional or religious exercise; keep vigil. **5.** To observe the course of mentally. **6.** To tend, as flocks. —**watch out.** To be careful or on the alert. —*n.* **1.** The act of watching. **2.** Formerly, any of the periods into which the night was divided. **3.** A period of close observation. **4.** A person or group of persons serving, esp. at night, to guard or protect. **5.** The post or period of duty of a guard, sentinel, or watchman. **6.** A small, portable timepiece, esp. one worn on the wrist or carried in the pocket. **7.** A vigil. **8.** A period of assignment to duty on a ship. [< OE *wæccan,* to be or stay awake, keep vigil. See **weg-**.]

watch•dog (wŏch′dôg′, -dŏg′) *n.* A dog trained to guard property.

watch•ful (wŏch′fəl) *adj.* Alert; vigilant. —**watch′ful•ly** *adv.* —**watch′ful•ness** *n.*

watch•man (wŏch′mən) *n.* A man employed to stand guard or keep watch.

watch•tow•er (wŏch′tou′ər) *n.* An observation tower for a guard.

watch•word (wŏch′wûrd′) *n.* **1.** A password. **2.** A rallying cry; slogan.

wa•ter (wô′tər, wŏt′ər) *n.* **1.** A clear, colorless, nearly odorless and tasteless liquid, H₂O, essential for most plant and animal life and the most widely used of all solvents. **2.** Any of various forms of water, as rain. **3.** Any body of water, as a sea, lake, river, or stream. **4.** An aqueous solution of a substance. —*v.* **-tered, -tering. 1.** To pour water upon; make wet. **2.** To supply with drinking water. **3.** To dilute by or as by adding water. **4.** To produce or discharge fluid, as from the eyes. **5.** To treat so as to produce a wavy surface effect, as on silk. [< OE *wæter.* See **wed-**.]

Water Bearer. The constellation and sign of the zodiac Aquarius.

water buffalo. An African or Asian buffalo with large, spreading horns, often domesticated as a draft animal.

Wa•ter•bur•y (wô′tər-bĕr′ē, wŏt′ər-). A city of west-central Connecticut. Pop. 142,000.

water closet. A room or booth containing a toilet and often a sink.

water color. 1. A paint composed of a water-soluble pigment. **2.** A work done in water colors. **3.** The art of using water colors.

water cooler. A device for cooling, storing, and dispensing drinking water.

wa•ter•course (wô′tər-kôrs′, -kōrs′, wŏt′ər-) *n.* **1.** A waterway. **2.** The bed or channel of a waterway.

wa•ter•cress (wô′tər-krĕs′, wŏt′ər-) *n.* A plant growing in freshwater ponds and streams and having pungent edible leaves.

wa•ter•fall (wô′tər-fôl′, wŏt′ər-) *n.* A steep descent of water from a height.

wa•ter•fowl (wô′tər-foul′, wŏt′ər-) *n.* **1.** A swimming bird, as a duck or goose. **2.** Such birds collectively.

wa•ter•front (wô′tər-frŭnt′, wŏt′ər-) *n.* Improved or unimproved land abutting on a body of water.

Wa•ter•gate (wô′tər-gāt′, wŏt′ər-) *n. Informal.* A scandal that involves officials violating public or corporate trust through acts of abuse of power. [< *Watergate,* a building complex in Washington, D.C.]

watering place. A health resort featuring water activities or mineral springs.

water lily. Any of various aquatic plants with broad floating leaves and showy, variously colored flowers.

water line. Any of several lines marked on the hull of a ship, indicating the depth to which the ship sinks under various loads.

wa•ter•logged (wô′tər-lôgd′, -lŏgd′, wŏt′ər-) *adj.* Soaked or saturated with water.

water main. A principal pipe in a system of pipes for conveying water.

wa•ter•mark (wô′tər-märk′, wŏt′ər-) *n.* **1.** A mark showing the height to which water has risen. **2.** A translucent design impressed on paper during manufacture and visible when the paper is held to the light.

wa•ter•mel•on (wô′tər-mĕl′ən, wŏt′ər-) *n.* A large melon with a hard green rind and watery, reddish flesh.

water moccasin. A venomous snake of swampy regions of the S U.S.

wa•ter•pow•er (wô′tər-pou′ər, wŏt′ər-) *n.* **1.** The energy of running or falling water as used for driving machinery, esp. for generating electricity. **2.** A source of such power.

wa•ter•proof (wô′tər-prōōf′, wŏt′ər-) *adj.* Impenetrable to or unaffected by water. —*n. Chiefly Brit.* A raincoat or other waterproof garment. —*v.* To make waterproof.

wa•ter•re•pel•lent (wô′tər-rĭ-pĕl′ənt, wŏt′ər-) *adj.* Repelling water but not waterproof.

wa•ter•re•sis•tant (wô′tər-rĭ-zĭs′tənt, wŏt′ər-) *adj.* Resistant to wetting but not waterproof.

wa•ter•shed (wô′tər-shĕd′, wŏt′ər-) *n.* **1.** A ridge of high land dividing two areas that are drained by different river systems. **2.** The region draining into a body of water.

wa•ter•ski (wô′tər-skē′, wŏt′ər-) *v.* To ski on water while being towed by a power boat. —*n.* A broad ski used in water-skiing.

wa•ter•spout (wô′tər-spout′, wŏt′ər-) *n.* **1.** A tornado or lesser whirlwind occurring over water and resulting in a whirling column of

---

ŏ paw, for/oi boy/ou out/ŏŏ took/ōō coo/p pop/r run/s sauce/sh shy/t to/th thin/*th* the/ ŭ cut/ûr fur/v van/w wag/y yes/z size/zh vision/ə ago, item, edible, gallop, circus/

spray and mist. **2.** A pipe from which water is discharged.

water system. 1. A river and all its tributaries. **2. a.** The water available for a community or region. **b.** The sources and delivery system of such water.

water table. The surface in a permeable body of rock of a zone saturated with water.

wa·ter·tight (wô'tər-tīt', wŏt'ər-) *adj.* **1.** Permitting neither entry nor escape of water. **2.** Having no flaws or loopholes.

water tower. A standpipe or tank used as a reservoir or for maintaining equal pressure on a water system.

wa·ter·way (wô'tər-wā', wŏt'ər-) *n.* A body of water used for travel or transport, esp. a river or canal.

water wheel. A wheel propelled by falling or running water, primarily for use as a source of power.

wa·ter·works (wô'tər-wûrks', wŏt'ər-) *pl.n.* **1.** The water system of a city. **2.** A single unit, as a pumping station, within such a system.

wa·ter·y (wô'tə-rē, wŏt'ə-) *adj.* **-ier, -iest. 1.** Wet; moist. **2.** Resembling or suggestive of water; liquid. **3.** Diluted. **4.** Without force; insipid: *watery prose.*

watt (wŏt) *n.* A unit of power equal to one joule per second. [< J. *Watt* (1736–1819), Scottish engineer.]

wat·tage (wŏt'ĭj) *n.* An amount of power, esp. electric power, expressed in watts.

wat·tle (wŏt'l) *n.* **1. a.** Poles intertwined with twigs, reeds, or branches for use in construction, as of walls or fences. **b.** Materials thus used. **2.** A fleshy fold of skin hanging from the neck or throat, as of certain birds. [< OE *watel, watul.*]

wave (wāv) *v.* **waved, waving. 1. a.** To move or cause to move back and forth or up and down in the air. **b.** To signal by such a movement, esp. with the hand. **2.** To curve or curl. —*n.* **1.** A ridge or swell moving along the surface of a body of water. **2.** Often **waves.** The sea or seas. **3.** A moving curve or succession of curves in or upon a surface: *waves of wheat in the wind.* **4.** A curve or curl, as in the hair. **5.** A movement up and down or back and forth. **6.** A surge. **7.** A persistent meteorological condition: *cold wave.* **8.** *Phys.* A disturbance or oscillation propagated from point to point in a medium or in space. [< OE *wafian*, to move back and forth, esp. with the hands, and < OE *wǣg*, motion, wave.] —**wav'er** *n.*

Wave (wāv) *n.* A member of the WAVES.

wave·form (wāv'fôrm') *n.* The mathematical representation of a wave, esp. a graph of deviation at a fixed point versus time.

wave front. A surface of a propagating wave that is the locus of all points having identical phase.

wave·length (wāv'lĕngth') *n.* In a periodic wave, the distance between two points of corresponding phase in consecutive cycles.

wa·ver (wā'vər) *v.* **1.** To swing or move back and forth; sway. **2.** To show irresolution or indecision. **3.** To falter. **4.** To tremble or quaver, as a voice. **5.** To flicker or flash, as light. [ME *waveren*, to wander, fluctuate.] —**wa'ver** *n.* —**wa'ver·ing·ly** *adv.*

WAVES (wāvz). The women's reserve of the U.S. Navy. [W(omen) A(ccepted for) V(olunteer) E(mergency) S(ervice).]

wa·vy (wā'vē) *adj.* **-vier, -viest. 1.** Having or rising in waves: *a wavy sea.* **2.** Proceeding in a wavelike motion. **3.** Having curls, curves, or undulations. —**wa'vi·ness** *n.*

waw. Variant of **vav.**

wax¹ (wăks) *n.* **1.** Any of various natural unctuous, viscous or solid heat-sensitive substances, as beeswax, consisting essentially of heavy hydrocarbons or fats. **2.** A waxy substance found in the ears. —*v.* To coat or treat with wax. [< OE *weax, wæx,* beeswax. See **wokso-.**] —**wax'en, wax'y** *adj.*

wax² (wăks) *v.* **1.** To become gradually larger, more numerous, stronger, or more intense. **2.** To increase in illumination or progress toward being full. Used of the moon. **3.** To grow or become: *The seas wax calm.* [< OE *weaxan.* See **aug-.**]

wax bean. A variety of string bean with yellow pods.

wax·wing (wăks'wĭng') *n.* A crested bird with mostly brown plumage and waxy red tips on the wing feathers.

wax·works (wăks'wûrks') *pl.n.* An exhibition of wax figures.

way (wā) *n.* **1.** A road or path. **2.** Room to proceed: *clear the way.* **3.** A course or route. **4.** Travel along a route. **5.** A manner of doing something. **6.** A mode of living or conduct. **7.** Freedom to do as one prefers. **8.** Distance: *a long way off.* **9.** A specific direction. **10.** An aspect of something. **11.** An individual manner of behaving. **12.** A condition, as of health: *in a bad way.* **13.** A home or neighborhood. —**by the way.** Incidentally. —**by way of. 1.** By route of. **2.** As a means of. —**have a way with.** To have the ability to handle. —**under way.** Making progress. —*adv.* Also **'way.** *Informal.* **1.** At a great distance; far: *way off yonder.* **2.** Away: *go way.* [< OE *weg,* a road, path. See **wegh-.**]

way·far·er (wā'fâr'ər) *n.* One who travels, esp. by foot. —**way'far'ing** *adj. & n.*

way·lay (wā'lā') *v.* **-laid** (-lād'), **-laying. 1.** To lie in wait for and assail from ambush. **2.** To accost or intercept. —**way'lay'er** *n.*

way-out (wā'out') *adj. Informal.* Strange or unconventional.

-ways. *comb. form.* Manner, direction, or position: **sideways.**

way·side (wā'sīd') *n.* The side or edge of a road.

way·ward (wā'wərd) *adj.* **1.** Wanting one's own way in spite of the advice or wishes of another; willful. **2.** Erratic; unpredictable. [< ME *awayward,* turned away.] —**way'ward·ly** *adv.* —**way'ward·ness** *n.*

we (wē) *pron.* The 1st person pl. pronoun in the nominative case, used to represent the speaker and one or more others that share in the action of the verb. [< OE *wē,* we. See **we-.**]

weak (wēk) *adj.* **1.** Lacking physical strength.

ă pat/ā ate/âr care/ä bar/b **bib**/ch **chew**/d **deed**/ĕ pet/ē be/f fit/g gag/h **hat**/hw **what**/ ĭ pit/ī pie/îr pier/j **judge**/k **kick**/l lid, fatal/m **mum**/n no, sudden/ng sing/ŏ pot/ō go/

2. Liable to fail under pressure; lacking resistance. 3. Lacking strength of character or will. 4. Lacking the proper or full strength of some component. 5. Unsound. 6. Lacking capacity or capability. 7. Lacking authority or power to rule. [< ON *veikr,* pliant, flexible.] —**weak′ly** *adj.* & *adv.*

weak•en (wē′kən) *v.* To make or become weak or weaker. —**weak′en•er** *n.*

weak•fish (wēk′fĭsh′) *n.* A marine food and game fish of North Atlantic waters.

weak•ling (wēk′lĭng) *n.* A person of weak constitution or character.

weak•ness (wēk′nĭs) *n.* 1. The state of being weak. 2. A defect or failing. 3. A special fondness.

weal¹ (wēl) *n.* Prosperity; well-being. [< OE *weola,* wealth, well-being.]

weal² (wēl) *n.* A welt. [Var of WALE.]

wealth (wĕlth) *n.* 1. A great quantity of valuable material possessions or resources; riches. 2. A profusion or abundance. 3. All goods and resources having economic value. [< WEAL¹.]

wealth•y (wĕl′thē) *adj.* **-ier, -iest.** Prosperous; affluent. —**wealth′i•ness** *n.*

wean (wēn) *v.* 1. To cause (a young mammal) to give up suckling and accept other food. 2. To detach (a person) from that to which he is accustomed or devoted. [< OE *wenian,* to accustom, train, wean. See **wen-.**]

weap•on (wĕp′ən) *n.* 1. Any instrument or possession used in combat. 2. Any means employed to get the better of another. [< OE *wǣpen* < Gmc **wēpnam.*]

weap•on•ry (wĕp′ən-rē) *n.* Weapons collectively.

wear (wâr) *v.* **wore, worn, wearing.** 1. To be clothed in. 2. To have on one's person. 3. To affect or exhibit: *wear a smile.* 4. To bear or maintain in a particular manner: *wears her hair long.* 5. To impair or consume by or as by long or hard use, friction, or exposure to elements. 6. To produce by constant use or exposure: *wore a hole in the steps.* 7. To fatigue; weary. 8. To react to use or strain in a specified way. 9. To pass gradually or tediously: *The hours wore on endlessly.* —**wear off.** 1. To diminish gradually. 2. To become effaced; rub off. —**wear out.** 1. To make or become unusable through heavy use. 2. To use up. 3. To exhaust. —*n.* 1. The act of wearing or state of being worn; use. 2. Clothing, esp. of a particular kind: *footwear.* 3. Gradual impairment or diminution from use or attrition. [< OE *werian,* wear, carry. See **wes-¹.**] —**wear′-er** *n.*

wea•ri•some (wîr′ē-səm) *adj.* Causing mental or physical fatigue. —**wea′ri•some•ness** *n.*

wea•ry (wîr′ē) *adj.* **-rier, -riest.** 1. Tired; fatigued. 2. Expressive of fatigue or resignation. —*v.* **-ried, -rying.** To make or become weary. [< OE *wērig* < Gmc **wōriga.*] —**wear′i•ly** *adv.* —**wear′i•ness** *n.*

wea•sel (wē′zəl) *n.* Any of various carnivorous mammals with a long, slender body, short legs, and a long tail. —*v.* To be evasive; equivocate. [< OE *weosule, wesle.*]

weath•er (wĕth′ər) *n.* 1. The state of the atmosphere at a given time and place, described by temperature, moisture, wind velocity, and pressure. 2. Unpleasant or destructive atmospheric conditions, esp. high winds and heavy rain on the seas and in the air. —**under the weather.** *Informal.* Ill; indisposed. —*v.* 1. To expose to or withstand the action of the weather. 2. To show the effects of exposure to the weather. 3. To pass through safely; survive. [< OE *weder.* See **wē-.**]

weath•er-beat•en (wĕth′ər-bēt′n) *adj.* 1. Worn by exposure to the weather. 2. Tanned and leathery from being outdoors.

weath•er•board (wĕth′ər-bôrd′, -bōrd′) *n.* Clapboard; siding.

weath•er-bound (wĕth′ər-bound′) *adj.* Delayed, halted, or kept indoors by bad weather.

weath•er•cock (wĕth′ər-kŏk′) *n.* 1. A weather vane, esp. in the form of a rooster. 2. One that is fickle.

weath•er•ing (wĕth′ər-ĭng) *n.* Chemical or mechanical processes by which rocks exposed to the weather decay to soil.

weath•er•man (wĕth′ər-măn′) *n.* One who predicts or reports weather conditions.

weath•er•proof (wĕth′ər-prōōf′) *adj.* Able to withstand exposure to weather without damage. —*v.* To render weatherproof.

weath•er-strip (wĕth′ər-strĭp′) *v.* To fit or equip with weather stripping.

weather stripping. A narrow piece of material installed around doors and windows to protect an interior from external extremes of temperature.

weather vane. A vane for indicating wind direction.

weave (wēv) *v.* **wove, woven, weaving.** 1. a. To make (cloth) by interlacing the threads of the weft and warp on a loom. b. To interlace (yarns) into cloth. 2. To construct by interlacing or interweaving the materials of: *weave a basket.* 3. To interweave or combine (elements) into a whole: *wove the incidents into a story.* 4. To run (something) in and out through some material or composition. 5. To spin, as a web. 6. *p.t.* **weaved.** To make or move in (a course) by winding in and out or shuttling from side to side. —*n.* The pattern, method of weaving, or construction of a fabric: *a twill weave.* [< OE *wefan.* See **webh-.**] —**weav′er** *n.*

web (wĕb) *n.* 1. A textile fabric, esp. one woven on a loom. 2. A latticed or woven structure. 3. A structure of threadlike strands spun by spiders or certain insect larvae. 4. Something intricately constructed, esp. something that ensnares. 5. A complex network. 6. A fold of skin or membranous tissue, as that connecting the toes of certain water birds. 7. A metal sheet or plate connecting the heavier sections or ribs of any structural element. —*v.* **webbed, webbing.** 1. To provide with a web. 2. To cover or envelop with or as with a web. 3. To ensnare or entrap in a web. [< OE *webb.* See **webh-.**] —**webbed** *adj.*

web•bing (wĕb′ĭng) *n.* Sturdy woven strips of fabric used for seat belts, upholstering, etc.

ō paw, for/oi boy/ou out/ōō took/ōō coo/p pop/r run/s sauce/sh shy/t to/th thin/*th* the/ ŭ cut/ûr fur/v van/w wag/y yes/z size/zh vision/ə ago, item, edible, gallop, circus/

web-foot·ed (wĕb'fŏŏt'ĭd) *adj.* Having feet with webbed toes.

Web·ster (wĕb'stər). **1. Daniel.** 1782–1852. American statesman and diplomat. **2. Noah.** 1758–1843. American lexicographer.

wed (wĕd) *v.* **wedded, wed** or **wedded, wedding. 1.** To take as husband or wife; marry. **2.** To perform the marriage ceremony for. **3.** To unite. [< OE *weddian*, to engage (to do something), marry. See **wadh-**.]

we'd (wĕd). Contraction of *we had, we should,* and *we would.*

Wed. Wednesday.

wed·ding (wĕd'ĭng) *n.* **1.** The ceremony or celebration of a marriage. **2.** The anniversary of a marriage. **3.** A joining or uniting.

wedge (wĕj) *n.* **1.** A piece of metal or wood tapered for insertion in a narrow crevice and used for splitting, tightening, securing, or levering. **2.** Anything in the shape of a wedge. **3.** Something that tends to divide or split associations of people. —*v.* **wedged, wedging. 1.** To split or force apart with or as with a wedge. **2.** To fix in place with a wedge. **3.** To crowd or force into a limited space. [< OE *wecg*, a wedge, ingot of metal.]

wed·lock (wĕd'lŏk') *n.* The state of being married. [< OE *wedlāc*, "pledge-giving," marriage vow.]

Wednes·day (wĕnz'dē, -dā') *n.* The 4th day of the week. [< OE *Wōdnesdæg*, "day of Woden," a Teutonic god.]

wee (wē) *adj.* **weer, weest. 1.** Very small. **2.** Very early: *the wee hours.* [< OE *wǣge*, a weight.]

weed¹ (wēd) *n.* A plant considered troublesome or useless, esp. one growing abundantly in cultivated ground. —*v.* **1.** To remove weeds from. **2.** To eliminate as unsuitable or unwanted: *weed out unqualified applicants.* [< OE *wēod* < Gmc **wiudha*.] —**weed'er** *n.*

weed² (wēd) *n.* **1.** A token of mourning. **2. weeds.** A widow's mourning clothes. [< OE *wǣd* and *wǣde*, a garment.]

weed·y (wē'dē) *adj.* **-ier, -iest. 1.** Full of weeds. **2.** Resembling a weed; weedlike. **3.** Spindly. —**weed'i·ly** *adv.* —**weed'i·ness** *n.*

week (wēk) *n.* **1. a.** A period of seven days. **b.** A seven-day calendar period, esp. one starting with Sunday and continuing through Saturday. **2.** A week designated by an event occurring within it: *graduation week.* [< OE *wice, wicu.* See **weik-¹.**]

week·day (wēk'dā') *n.* **1.** Any day of the week except Sunday. **2.** Any day exclusive of the days of the weekend.

week·end (wēk'ĕnd') *n.* The end of the week; usually, the period from Friday evening through Sunday evening.

week·ly (wēk'lē) *adv.* **1.** Once a week. **2.** Every week. **3.** By the week. —*adj.* **1.** Of or pertaining to a week. **2.** Occurring once a week or each week. **3.** Computed by the week. —*n., pl.* **-lies.** A publication issued once a week.

ween (wēn) *v. Archaic.* To think; suppose. [< OE *wēnan.*]

weep (wēp) *v.* **wept, weeping. 1.** To mourn; grieve (with *for*). **2.** To shed (tears). **3.** To emit drops of moisture. [< OE *wēpan.* See **wāb-.**] —**weep'er** *n.*

weep·ing (wē'pĭng) *adj.* **1.** Tearful. **2.** Having slender, drooping branches.

wee·vil (wē'vəl) *n.* Any of numerous destructive beetles characteristically having a downward-curving snout. [< OE *wifel*, a beetle.]

weft (wĕft) *n.* **1.** The horizontal threads interlaced through the warp in a woven fabric; woof. **2.** Woven fabric. [< OE *wefta, weft.*]

weigh¹ (wā) *v.* **1.** To determine the weight of by or as by using a scale or balance. **2.** To measure off an amount equal in weight to. **3.** To determine mentally the worth or significance of; ponder. **4.** To burden (with *down*). **5.** To be a burden. **6.** To have or be of a specific weight. **7.** To carry weight; be considered important. **8.** *Naut.* To raise anchor. [< OE *wegan*, to carry, balance in the scale, weigh. See **wegh-.**] —**weigh'er** *n.*

weigh² (wā) *n.* —**under weigh.** In progress. [Var of WAY.]

weight (wāt) *n.* **1.** A measure of the heaviness or mass of an object. **2.** The gravitational force exerted on an object, equal to the product of the object's mass and the local value of gravitational acceleration. **3. a.** A unit measure of this force. **b.** A system of such measures. **4.** Any object used principally to exert a force by virtue of its gravitational attraction to the earth, esp.: **a.** A solid used as a standard in weighing. **b.** An object used to hold something down. **c.** A dumbbell or other object used in weightlifting. **5.** Burden; oppressiveness: *the weight of responsibilities.* **6.** The greatest part or stress; preponderance. **7.** Influence; importance. —*v.* **1.** To add heaviness or weight to. **2.** To load down; burden. [< OE *wiht, gewiht.* See **wegh-.**]

weight·less (wāt'lĭs) *adj.* **1.** Having little or no weight. **2.** Experiencing little or no gravitational force. —**weight'less·ness** *n.*

weight·lift·ing (wāt'lĭf'tĭng) *n.* The lifting of heavy weights as an exercise or in athletic competition.

weight·y (wā'tē) *adj.* **-ier, -iest. 1.** Heavy. **2.** Burdensome. **3.** Of great consequence. **4.** Carrying weight; efficacious. **5.** Solemn. —**weight'i·ly** *adv.* —**weight'i·ness** *n.*

weir (wîr) *n.* **1.** A fence or wattle placed in a stream to catch or retain fish. **2.** A dam placed across a river or canal to raise or divert the water or regulate the flow. [< OE *wer.*]

weird (wîrd) *adj.* **1.** Suggestive of or concerned with the supernatural. **2.** Of an odd and inexplicable character. [< OE *wyrd*, fate, destiny. See **wer-³.**] —**weird'ness** *n.*

wel·come (wĕl'kəm) *adj.* **1.** Received with pleasure and hospitality. **2.** Gratifying. **3.** Cordially permitted or invited, as to do or enjoy. —*n.* A cordial greeting to or reception of an arriving person. —*v.* **-comed, -coming. 1.** To greet or entertain cordially or hospitably. **2.** To receive or accept gladly. —*interj.* Expressive of cordial greeting or reception. [< OE *wilcuma*, a welcome guest, and *wilcume*, the greeting of welcome. See **gwā-.**]

weld (wĕld) *v.* **1.** To join (metals) by applying

heat, sometimes with pressure. **2.** To bring together as a unit. —*n.* A union or joint produced by welding. [Var of WELL (to surge).] —**weld′er** *n.*

wel•fare (wĕl′fâr′) *n.* **1.** Health, happiness, and general well-being. **2.** Work on behalf of the poor. **3.** Public relief. [< ME *wel faren*, to fare well.]

welfare state. A state that assumes primary responsibility for the welfare of its citizens.

wel•kin (wĕl′kĭn) *n. Archaic.* The vault of heaven; sky. [< OE *wolcen*, sky.]

well¹ (wĕl) *n.* **1.** A deep hole or shaft dug or drilled to obtain water, oil, gas, or brine. **2.** Something resembling this in shape or function, as an inkwell. **3.** An opening cut vertically through the floors of a building, as for stairs or ventilation. **4.** A spring or fountain. **5.** A source to be drawn upon. —*v.* **1.** To rise to the surface, ready to flow. **2.** To surge from some inner source. [< OE *wælla, wiella.* See **wel-³**.]

well² (wĕl) *adv.* **better, best. 1.** Satisfactorily. **2.** With skill: *sing well.* **3.** In a comfortable or affluent manner: *live well.* **4.** Advantageously: *married well.* **5.** With reason or propriety; properly: *I can't very well say no.* **6.** Prudently: *You would do well to say nothing.* **7.** On close or familiar terms: *I know him well.* **8.** Favorably: *speak well of him.* **9.** Thoroughly: *well cooked.* **10.** Entirely: *well worth seeing.* **11.** Far: *well in advance.* —**as well. 1.** In addition; also. **2.** With equal or better effect: *I might as well go.* —**as well as. 1.** In addition to. **2.** As satisfactorily as. —*adj.* **1.** In a satisfactory state: *All is well.* **2. a.** In good health. **b.** Cured or healed. **3. a.** Advisable; prudent. **b.** Fortunate; good. —*interj.* **1.** Expressive of surprise. **2.** Used to introduce a remark or cover a pause. [< OE *wel.* See **wel-²**.]

we'll (wĕl). Contraction of *we will* and *we shall.*

well-be•ing (wĕl′bē′ĭng) *n.* The state of being healthy, happy, or prosperous; welfare.

well-born (wĕl′bôrn′) *adj.* Of good lineage or stock.

well-bred (wĕl′brĕd′) *adj.* Of good upbringing; polite; refined.

well-dis•posed (wĕl′dĭs-pôzd′) *adj.* Disposed to be kindly or sympathetic.

well-done (wĕl′dŭn′) *adj.* **1.** Cooked all the way through. **2.** Properly accomplished.

well-found•ed (wĕl′foun′dĭd) *adj.* Based on sound judgment, reasoning, or evidence.

well-groomed (wĕl′grōōmd′) *adj.* **1.** Attentive to details of dress. **2.** Carefully tended.

well-ground•ed (wĕl′groun′dĭd) *adj.* **1.** Adequately versed in a subject. **2.** Having a sound basis.

Wel•ling•ton (wĕl′ĭng-tən). The capital of New Zealand on North Island. Pop. 127,000.

well-mean•ing (wĕl′mē′nĭng) *adj.* Having or prompted by good intentions.

well-nigh (wĕl′nī′) *adv.* Nearly; almost.

well-off (wĕl′ôf′, -ŏf′) *adj.* **1.** In fortunate circumstances. **2.** Wealthy.

well-timed (wĕl′tīmd′) *adj.* Occurring or done at an opportune time.

well-to-do (wĕl′tə-dōō′) *adj.* Affluent.

well-turned (wĕl′tûrnd′) *adj.* **1.** Shapely. **2.** Aptly expressed.

well-wish•er (wĕl′wĭsh′ər) *n.* One who wishes another well.

well-worn (wĕl′wôrn′, -wōrn′) *adj.* **1.** Showing signs of much wear. **2.** Trite; hackneyed.

welsh (wĕlsh, wĕlch) *v. Slang.* **1.** To swindle a person by not paying a debt or wager. **2.** To fail to fulfill an obligation. [?] —**welsh′er** *n.*

Welsh (wĕlsh) *n.* **1. the Welsh** *(takes pl. v.).* The people of Wales. **2.** The Celtic language of Wales. —**Welsh** *adj.* —**Welsh′man** *n.*

Welsh rabbit. Also **Welsh rarebit.** A dish made of melted cheese, served hot over toast or crackers.

welt (wĕlt) *n.* **1.** A strip of leather or other material stitched into a shoe between the sole and upper. **2.** A tape or covered cord sewn into a seam as reinforcement or trimming. **3.** A ridge or bump raised on the skin by a blow or an allergic disorder. —*v.* **1.** To reinforce or trim with a welt. **2.** To beat severely. [ME *welte, walt.*]

wel•ter (wĕl′tər) *v.* **1.** To writhe, roll, or wallow. **2.** To lie soaked in blood. **3.** To roll and surge, as the sea. —*n.* **1.** Turbulence; tossing. **2. a.** Confusion; turmoil. **b.** A confused mass. [ME *welteren.*]

wel•ter•weight (wĕl′tər-wāt′) *n.* A boxer or wrestler who weighs between 136 and 147 pounds.

wen (wĕn) *n.* A cyst containing sebaceous matter. [< OE *wenn.*]

wench (wĕnch) *n. Archaic.* A young woman or girl. [< OE *wencel*, child, maid.]

wend (wĕnd) *v.* To proceed on or along: *wend one's way.* [< OE *wendan*, to turn away, direct, happen. See **wendh-**.]

went (wĕnt). *p.t.* of **go.** [< ME *wenden*, to wend.]

wept (wĕpt). *p.t.* & *p.p.* of **weep.**

were (wûr). **1.** Pl. & 2nd person sing. of the past indicative of **be. 2.** Past subjunctive of **be.** [< OE *wǣre* (sing), *wǣron* (pl). See **wes-³**.]

Usage: Were, as a past subjunctive form, occurs principally in clauses expressing conditions that are clearly hypothetical or contrary to fact, as in *if I were you.* Often such clauses are introduced by *if, as if,* or *as though.* Sometimes they express a wish or desire. When the clause expresses a mere condition that is neither purely hypothetical nor contrary to fact, however, *was* is the choice. It is also the choice in indirect questions. In each of the following, *was* (not *were*) is proper: *He said that if Smith was elected, he would resign. I peered out to see whether the way was clear. He inquired whether I was satisfied with the outcome.*

we're (wîr). Contraction of *we are.*

wer•en't (wûrnt, wûr′ənt). Contraction of *were not.*

were•wolf (wîr′wŏōlf′, wûr′-, wâr′-) *n.* Also **wer•wolf.** A person capable of assuming the form of a wolf. [< OE *wer(e)wulf* : *wer*, a man + *wulf*, a WOLF.]

wert (wûrt). *Archaic.* 2nd person sing. past indicative and past subjunctive of **be.**

Wes·ley (wĕs'lē, wĕz'-), **John.** 1703–1791. English theologian; founder of Methodism.
west (wĕst) *n.* **1. a.** The direction opposite that of the earth's rotation. **b.** The point on the mariner's compass 270° clockwise from north, directly opposite east. **2.** Often **West. a.** The W part of any country or region. **b.** The W part of the world, esp. Europe and the W Hemisphere; the Occident. **—the West.** In the U.S.: **1.** Formerly, the region lying W of the Alleghenies. **2.** The region W of the Mississippi. *—adj.* **1.** To or from the west. **2. West.** Designating the W part of a country, continent, or other geographic area: *West Germany. —adv.* In, from, or toward the west. [< OE. See **wespero-.**]
West Berlin. The W zone of Berlin, associated politically and economically with West Germany. Pop. 2,200,000.
west·er·ly (wĕs'tər-lē) *adj.* **1.** Toward the west. **2.** From the west. **—west'er·ly** *adv.*
west·ern (wĕs'tərn) *adj.* **1.** Toward, in, or facing the west. **2.** Coming from the west. **3.** Often **Western.** Of or characteristic of western regions or the West, esp. Europe and the W Hemisphere; Occidental. *—n.* Often **Western.** A film dealing with frontier or cowboy life.
west·ern·er (wĕs'tər-nər) *n.* **1.** A native or inhabitant of the west. **2.** Often **Westerner.** A native or inhabitant of the W U.S.
Western Hemisphere. The half of the earth that includes North and South America.
west·ern·ize (wĕs'tər-nīz') *v.* **-ized, -izing.** To convert to the ways of Western civilization.
Western Samoa. A nation in the S Pacific. Pop. 122,000. Cap. Apia.
West Germanic. A subdivision of Germanic.
West Germany. The unofficial name for the German Federal Republic. See **Germany.**
West In·dies (ĭn'dēz). An island chain between the SE U.S. and N South America, separating the Caribbean from the Atlantic and including the Bahamas, the Greater Antilles, and the Lesser Antilles. **—West Indian.**
West Virginia. A state of the east-central U.S. Pop. 1,744,000. Cap. Charleston.
west·ward (wĕst'wərd) *adv.* Also **west·wards** (-wərdz), **west·ward·ly** (-wərd-lē). Toward the west. *—adj.* Toward or in the west.
wet (wĕt) *adj.* **wetter, wettest. 1.** Covered or saturated with a liquid, esp. water; moistened; damp. **2.** Not yet dry or firm: *wet plaster.* **3.** Rainy. **4.** Allowing alcoholic beverages to be produced and sold: *a wet county. —n.* **1.** Moisture. **2.** Rainy or snowy weather. *—v.* **wetted, wetting.** To make or become wet. [< OE wǣt, wēt. See wed-.]
wet·back (wĕt'băk') *n.* A Mexican laborer who illegally crosses the U.S. border.
wet blanket. *Informal.* One that discourages enjoyment, enthusiasm, etc.
weth·er (wĕth'ər) *n.* A castrated male sheep. [< OE.]
wet nurse. A woman who suckles another woman's child.
we've (wēv). Contraction of *we have.*
whack (hwăk) *v.* To strike with a sharp blow; slap. *—n.* **1.** A sharp, swift blow. **2.** The

sound made by such a blow. **—have** (or **take**) **a whack at.** To attempt; try out. **—out of whack.** Not functioning correctly. [Perh var of THWACK.]
whack·y. Variant of **wacky.**
whale¹ (hwāl) *n.* **1.** Any of various often very large marine mammals having a generally fishlike form. **2.** A superlative example of a thing specified: *a whale of a game. —v.* **whaled, whaling.** To hunt whales. [< OE *hwæl.* See skwalo-.]
whale² (hwāl) *v.* **whaled, whaling.** To thrash; flog. [?]
whale·boat (hwāl'bōt') *n.* A long rowboat, pointed at both ends and formerly used in whaling.
whale·bone (hwāl'bōn') *n.* **1.** The elastic, hornlike material forming plates or strips in the upper jaw of certain whales. **2.** An object made of this material, as a corset stay.
whal·er (hwā'lər) *n.* **1.** One who hunts or processes whales. **2.** A whaling ship.
whal·ing (hwā'lĭng) *n.* The hunting, killing, and processing of whales.
wham (hwăm) *n.* **1.** A forceful, resounding blow. **2.** The sound of such a blow. *—v.* **whammed, whamming.** To strike or smash into with resounding impact.
wham·my (hwăm'ē) *n., pl.* **-mies.** *Slang.* A supernatural spell; hex. [Perh < WHAM.]
wharf (hwôrf) *n., pl.* **wharves** (hwôrvz) or **wharfs.** A landing place at which vessels may tie up and load or unload. [< OE *hwearf.* See kwerp-.]
wharf·age (hwôr'fĭj) *n.* **1.** The use of a wharf or wharves. **2.** The charges for this.
what (hwŏt, hwŭt; *unstressed* hwət) *pron.* **1. a.** Which thing or which particular one of many. **b.** Which kind, character, or designation. **c.** A person or thing of how much value or significance: *What are possessions to a dying man?* **2. a.** That which or the thing that. **b.** Whatever thing that: *come what may.* **3. a.** *Nonstandard.* Which, who, or that: *It's the poor what gets the blame.* **b.** *Informal.* Something: *I'll tell you what. —adj.* **1.** Which one or ones of many. **2.** Whatever: *repaired what damage had been done.* **3.** How great: *What a fool! —adv.* **1.** How: *What does it matter?* **2.** Why (with *for*): *What are you hurrying for? —interj.* **1.** Expressive of surprise or incredulity. **2.** *Brit. Informal.* Expressive of agreement: *A fine evening, what?* [< OE *hwæt.* See kwo-.]
  Usage: What (relative pronoun), used as the subject of a clause, can be either singular or plural in construction, depending on the sense involved. It is construed as singular when it is the equivalent of *that which* or *a* (or *the*) *thing that,* and plural when it stands for *things that* or *those which.* The number of the verb or verbs governed by *what* depends on how it is construed: *He is involved in what seems to be an outright fraud. They are making what appear to be signs of welcome.*
what·ev·er (hwŏt-ĕv'ər, hwŭt-) *pron.* **1.** Everything or anything that. **2.** What amount that. **3.** No matter what. **4.** *Informal.* What. *—adj.* **1.** Of any number or kind; any. **2.** All of

---

ă pat/ā ate/âr care/ä bar/b bib/ch chew/d deed/ĕ pet/ē be/f fit/g gag/h hat/hw what/
ĭ pit/ī pie/îr pier/j judge/k kick/l lid, fatal/m mum/n no, sudden/ng sing/ŏ pot/ō go/

3. No matter what. **4.** Of any kind at all.
what•not (hwŏt'nŏt', hwŭt'-) *n.* A set of open
shelves for ornaments.
what•so•ev•er (hwŏt'sō-ĕv'ər, hwŭt'-) *pron.*
Whatever. —**what'so•ev'er** *adj.*
wheat (hwēt) *n.* **1.** A cereal grass widely cultivated for its commercially important grain.
2. The grain of such a plant, ground to produce flour. [< OE *hwǣte.* See **kweit-.**]
wheat germ. The vitamin-rich embryo of the
wheat kernel, separated before milling for use
as a cereal or food supplement.
whee•dle (hwēd'l) *v.* **-dled, -dling.** To persuade,
attempt to persuade, or obtain by flattery or
guile; cajole. [Perh < G *wedeln,* "to wag the
tail."] —**whee'dler** *n.*
wheel (hwēl) *n.* **1.** A solid disk or rigid circular
ring connected by spokes to a hub, designed to
turn around an axle passed through the center.
2. Anything resembling such a device in appearance or movement. **3.** A medieval instrument to which a victim was bound for torture.
4. The steering device on a vehicle. **5.** *Informal.* A bicycle. **6. wheels.** Forces that provide energy, movement, or direction: *the
wheels of commerce.* **7.** The act or process of
turning. **8.** *Slang.* One with a great deal of
power or influence. —*v.* **1.** To roll or move on
or as on a wheel or wheels. **2.** To revolve;
rotate. **3.** To turn or whirl around; pivot. [<
OE *hwēol.* See **kwel-.**]
wheel•bar•row (hwēl'băr'ō) *n.* A one- or two-
wheeled vehicle with handles, used to convey
small loads.
wheel•base (hwēl'bās') *n.* The distance from
front to rear axle in a motor vehicle.
wheel•chair (hwēl'châr') *n.* Also **wheel chair.** A
chair mounted on large wheels for the use of
the sick or disabled.
wheel•er-deal•er (hwē'lər-dē'lər) *n. Informal.*
A sharp operator.
wheel house. A pilothouse.
wheel•wright (hwēl'rīt') *n.* One whose trade is
the building and repairing of wheels.
wheeze (hwēz) *v.* **wheezed, wheezing.** To
breathe with difficulty, producing a hoarse
whistling sound. —*n.* **1.** A wheezing sound.
2. An old joke. [Prob < ON *hvǣsa,* to hiss.]
wheez•y (hwē'zē) *adj.* **-ier, -iest.** Given to
wheezing. —**wheez'i•ness** *n.*
whelk (hwĕlk) *n.* Any of various large, sometimes edible marine snails. [< OE *weoloc.*]
whelm (hwĕlm) *v.* To overwhelm. [< OE
hwelman, to turn over.]
whelp (hwĕlp) *n.* **1.** A young offspring of a
dog, wolf, etc. **2. a.** A mere child or youth.
b. An impudent young fellow. —*v.* To give
birth to whelps. [< OE *hwelp.*]
when (hwĕn) *adv.* **1.** At what time. **2.** At which
time. —*conj.* **1.** At the time that. **2.** As soon
as. **3.** Whenever. **4.** While. **5.** Whereas. **6.**
Considering that; since. —*pron.* What or
which time. —*n.* The time or date. [< OE
hwanne, hwenne. See **kwo-.**]
whence (hwĕns) *adv.* **1.** From where. **2.** From
what origin or source. **3.** Out of which. —*conj.*
By reason of which; from which; wherefore.
[< OE *hwanon.* See **kwo-.**]

Usage: Whence contains the sense of *from;*
consequently, the construction *from whence* is
redundant, though it has literary precedent,
and *whence* is preferably used alone.
when•ev•er (hwĕn-ĕv'ər) *adv.* **1.** At whatever
time. **2.** When. —*conj.* **1.** At whatever time
that. **2.** Every time that.
when•so•ev•er (hwĕn'sō-ĕv'ər) *adv.* At whatever time at all; whenever. —*conj.* Whenever.
where (hwâr) *adv.* **1.** At or in what place. **2.** In
what situation or position. **3.** From what place
or source. **4.** To what place. —*conj.* **1.** At
what or which place. **2. a.** In a place in which.
b. Wherever. **3. a.** To a place in which. **b.** To
any place or situation in which. —*pron.*
Which place. —*n.* The place or occasion. [<
OE *hwǣr.* See **kwo-.**]
Usage: Where is used with *from* to indicate
motion from a place: *Where did they come
from?* A preposition is not needed to indicate
direction or motion to a place in a construction such as *Where did they go?* (*go to* is
redundant); nor is a preposition used to indicate location or position of rest in *Where are
they?* (not *Where are they at?*).
where•a•bouts (hwâr'ə-bouts') *adv.* About
where; in, at, or near what location. —*n.* The
approximate location of someone or something.
where•as (hwâr-ăz') *conj.* **1.** It being the fact
that; inasmuch as. **2.** While at the same time.
3. While on the contrary.
where•at (hwâr-ăt') *adv.* **1.** At which place.
2. Whereupon.
where•by (hwâr-bī') *adv.* **1.** In accordance
with or by means of which. **2.** By what means;
how.
where•fore (hwâr'fôr', -fōr') *adv. Archaic.* For
what purpose or reason; why. —*conj. Archaic.*
For which reason. —*n.* A purpose or cause:
whys and wherefores.
where•from (hwâr'frŏm', -frŭm') *adv. Archaic.*
Whence.
where•in (hwâr-ĭn') *adv.* **1.** In what; how. **2.** In
which thing, place, or situation.
where•of (hwâr-ŏv', -ŭv') *adv.* **1.** Of what or
which. **2.** Of whom.
where•on (hwâr-ŏn', -ôn') *adv. Archaic.* On
which or what.
where•so•ev•er (hwâr'sō-ĕv'ər) *conj.* In, to, or
from whatever place at all.
where•to (hwâr'tōō') *adv.* **1.** To what place or
end. **2.** To which.
where•up•on (hwâr'ə-pŏn', -pôn') *adv.*
1. *Archaic.* Upon what. **2.** On top of which.
3. At which time; after which.
wher•ev•er (hwâr-ĕv'ər) *adv.* **1.** In or to whatever place. **2.** Where. —*conj.* In or to whichever place or situation.
where•with (hwâr'wĭth', -wĭth') *adv.* With
what or which. —*pron. Archaic.* The thing or
things with which.
where•with•al (hwâr'wĭth-ôl', -wĭth-ôl') *adv.*
Archaic. Wherewith. —*pron. Archaic.* Wherewith. —*n.* The necessary means.
wher•ry (hwĕr'ē) *n., pl.* **-ries.** A light, swift
rowboat. [ME *whery.*]
whet (hwĕt) *v.* **whetted, whetting. 1.** To sharpen

(a knife or other tool); hone. **2.** To stimulate; heighten. [< OE *hwettan.* See kwed-.] —whet'ter *n.*

wheth·er (hwĕth'ər) *conj.* **1.** If it is so that. **2.** If it happens that; in case. **3.** Either. [< OE *hwæther.* See kwo-.]

whet·stone (hwĕt'stōn') *n.* A stone for honing tools.

whew (hw/y/ōō) *interj.* Expressive of relief, amazement, etc. [ME *whewe.*]

whey (hwā) *n.* The watery part of milk that separates from the curds, as in the process of making cheese. [< OE *hwæg* < Gmc *khwuja-.*] —whey'ey *adj.*

which (hwĭch) *pron.* **1.** What particular one or ones. **2.** The particular one or ones. **3.** The thing, animal, group of people, or event previously designated or implied. **4.** *Archaic.* The person designated or implied. **5.** Whichever. **6.** A thing or circumstance that. —*adj.* **1.** What particular one or ones. **2.** Any one or any number of; whichever. **3.** Being the one or ones previously designated. [< OE *hwilc, hwelc.* See kwo-.]

which·ev·er (hwĭch-ĕv'ər) *pron.* **1.** Any one or ones. **2.** No matter which. —*adj.* **1.** Any one or any number of a group. **2.** No matter what.

which·so·ev·er (hwĭch'sō-ĕv'ər) *pron.* Whichever. —which'so·ev'er *adj.*

whick·er (hwĭk'ər) *v.* To whinny. [Imit.] —whick'er *n.*

whiff (hwĭf) *n.* **1.** A slight, gentle gust of air; a waft. **2.** A brief, passing odor carried in the air. **3.** An inhalation of air, perfume, smoke, etc. —*v.* **1.** To be carried in brief gusts; convey in whiffs. **2.** To draw in or breathe out air, smoke, etc. Smell; sniff.

whif·fle·tree (hwĭf'əl-trē) *n.* The pivoted horizontal crossbar to which the harness traces of a draft animal are attached.

Whig (hwĭg) *n.* **1.** In England, a member of a political party of the 18th and 19th centuries, opposed to the Tories. **2.** In the American Revolution, one who supported the war against England. **3.** In the U.S., a political party (1834–55) formed to oppose the Democratic Party. [Prob short for *Whiggamore,* a 17th-century Scottish insurgent.]

while (hwīl) *n.* **1.** A period of time: *stay for a while.* **2.** The time or effort taken in doing something. —*conj.* **1.** As long as. **2.** Although. **3.** Whereas; and. —*v.* whiled, whiling. To spend (time) idly or pleasantly: *while the time away.* [< OE *hwīl.* See kweyə-.]

whi·lom (hwī'ləm) *adj.* Former; having once been: *the whilom Miss Smith.* —*adv. Archaic.* Formerly. [< OE *hwīlum.*]

whilst (hwīlst) *conj. Chiefly Brit.* While.

whim (hwĭm) *n.* **1.** A sudden or capricious idea; a passing fancy. **2.** Arbitrary thought or impulse. [Short for earlier *whim-wham.*]

whim·per (hwĭm'pər) *v.* **1.** To cry or sob with soft intermittent sounds; whine. **2.** To complain. —*n.* A whine. [Dial *whimp* (imit.]

whim·si·cal (hwĭm'zĭ-kəl) *adj.* **1.** Capricious; playful; arbitrary. **2.** Unusual; fantastic; odd. —whim'si·cal·ly *adv.*

whim·sy (hwĭm'zē) *n., pl.* -sies. Also whim·sey

pl. -seys. **1.** An odd or capricious idea. **2.** Anything quaint, fanciful, or odd. [Prob < WHIM.]

whine (hwīn) *v.* whined, whining. **1.** To utter a plaintive, high-pitched sound, as in pain, fear, complaint, etc. **2.** To complain in an annoying fashion. **3.** To produce a sustained noise of relatively high pitch. [< OE *hwīnan.* See kwei-.] —whine *n.* —whin'y *adj.*

whin·ny (hwĭn'ē) *v.* -nied, -nying. To neigh, esp. softly. [Prob < WHINE.] —whin'ny *n.*

whip (hwĭp) *v.* whipped or whipt, whipping. **1.** To strike with repeated strokes, as of a strap; lash; beat. **2. a.** To punish in this manner; flog; thrash. **b.** To reprove severely. **3.** To drive or force by flogging, lashing, etc. **4.** To move in a manner similar to a whip; thrash about. **5.** To beat (cream or eggs) into a froth or foam. **6.** To move or remove in a sudden, rapid manner: *whipped off his cap.* **7.** To dart about. **8.** To wrap or bind (a robe) with twine to prevent unraveling. **9.** To defeat; outdo; beat. —*n.* **1.** A flexible instrument, as a rod or thong, used in whipping. **2.** A whipping or lashing motion or stroke; whiplash. **3.** A blow made by or as by whipping. **4.** A member of a legislative body charged by his party with enforcing party discipline and insuring attendance. **5.** A dish made of sugar and stiffly beaten egg whites or cream, often with fruit. [Perh < MDu *wippen,* to vacillate, swing.] —whip'per *n.*

whip·cord (hwĭp'kôrd') *n.* **1.** A ribbed worsted fabric. **2.** A strong twisted or braided cord. **3.** Catgut.

whip·lash (hwĭp'lăsh') *n.* **1.** The lash of a whip. **2.** An injury caused by an abrupt jerking motion of the head, either backward or forward. —whip'lash' *adj.*

whip·per·snap·per (hwĭp'ər-snăp'ər) *n.* An insignificant and pretentious person.

whip·pet (hwĭp'ĭt) *n.* A swift-running dog resembling the greyhound but smaller. [?]

whip·poor·will (hwĭp'ər-wĭl', hwĭp'ər-wĭl') *n.* Also whip-poor-will. A brownish night-flying North American bird having a call of which its name is imitative.

whip·saw (hwĭp'sô') *n.* A narrow two-man crosscut saw.

whipt (hwĭpt). Alternate *p.t. & p.p.* of whip.

whir (hwûr) *v.* whirred, whirring. To move so as to produce a vibrating or buzzing sound. —*n.* **1.** A sound of buzzing or vibration. **2.** A bustle; hurry. [< Scand.]

whirl (hwûrl) *v.* **1.** To revolve or spin rapidly. **2.** To turn aside or away rapidly; wheel. **3.** To have the sensation of spinning; reel. **4.** To move or drive rapidly. **5.** To move or drive in a circular or curving course, esp. at high speed. —*n.* **1.** The act of whirling. **2.** One that whirls or is whirled. **3.** A state of confusion; tumult. [< ON *hvirfla.*] —whirl'er *n.*

whirl·i·gig (hwûr'lĭ-gĭg') *n.* **1.** Any of various spinning toys. **2.** A carousel or merry-go-round. **3.** Something that continuously whirls.

whirl·pool (hwûrl'pōōl') *n.* Water in rapid rotating movement.

whirl·wind (hwûrl'wĭnd') *n.* **1.** A column of air

rotating around a more or less vertical axis and moving forward. **2.** Anything moving forward or whirling with violence and force. **whirl•y•bird** (hwûr'lē-bûrd') *n. Slang.* A helicopter.

whisk (hwĭsk) *v.* **1.** To move or cause to move with quick light, sweeping motions. **2.** To whip (eggs or cream). —*n.* **1.** A quick light, sweeping motion. **2.** A small broom. **3.** A small bunch, as of twigs or hair. **4.** A kitchen utensil for whipping. [< Scand.]

whisk•broom (hwĭsk'brōōm', -brŏŏm') *n.* A small short-handled broom used esp. to brush clothes.

whisk•er (hwĭs'kər) *n.* **1. whiskers. a.** The unshaven hair on a man's face; the beard. **b.** *Informal.* The mustache. **2.** One hair from the beard. **3.** One of the bristles or long hairs growing near the mouth of certain animals. [< WHISK.]

whis•key (hwĭs'kē) *n., pl.* **-keys.** Also **whis•ky** *pl.* **-kies.** An alcoholic liquor distilled from grain, such as corn, rye, or barley, and containing approx. 40 to 50% ethyl alcohol by volume. [< Ir Gael *uisce beathadh,* "water of life."] —**whis'key** *adj.*
Usage: Whiskey is the usual American spelling, esp. with reference to U.S. and Irish liquor. *Whisky* is the spelling used in *Scotch whisky* and *Canadian whisky.*

whis•per (hwĭs'pər) *v.* **1.** To speak softly, without full voice. **2.** To tell secretly or privately. **3.** To make a soft rustling sound, as leaves. —*n.* **1.** Speech produced by whispering. **2.** Something whispered. **3.** A rumor or hint. [< OE *hwisprian.* See **kwei-.**]

whist (hwĭst) *n.* A game played with 52 cards by two teams of two players each. [?]

whis•tle (hwĭs'əl) *v.* **-tled, -tling. 1.** To produce a clear musical sound by forcing air through the teeth or an aperture formed by pursing the lips. **2.** To produce a similar high-pitched sound. —*n.* **1.** A device for making whistling sounds by means of the breath, air, or steam. **2.** A sound produced by such a device or by whistling through the lips. [< OE *hwistlian.* See **kwei-.**]

whis•tler (hwĭs'lər) *n.* **1.** One that whistles. **2.** *Phys.* An electromagnetic wave of audio frequency produced by atmospheric disturbances such as lightning, having a characteristically decreasing frequency responsible for a whistling sound of descending pitch in detection equipment.

whit (hwĭt) *n.* A particle; least bit; iota. [Var of ME *wight,* thing.]

white (hwīt) *n.* **1.** An achromatic color of maximum lightness. **2.** The white or nearly white part of something, as: **a.** The albumen of an egg. **b.** The white part of an eyeball. **3.** Something or somebody white or nearly white, as: **a. whites.** A white outfit: *tennis whites.* **b.** A white pigment. **c.** A Caucasoid. —*adj.* **whiter, whitest. 1.** Being of the color white. **2.** Pale; weakly colored; almost colorless. **3. a.** Having the comparatively pale complexion typical of Caucasoids. **b.** Of, pertaining to, characteristic of, or dominated by

Caucasians. **4.** Not written or printed upon; blank. **5.** Unsullied; pure. **6.** Incandescent: *white heat.* [< OE *hwīt,* white, white of an egg. See **kweit-.**]

white ant. A termite.

white blood cell. A leukocyte.

white•cap (hwīt'kăp') *n.* A wave with a crest of foam.

white-col•lar (hwīt'kŏl'ər) *adj.* Of or pertaining to workers, salaried or professional, whose work usually does not involve manual labor and who are expected to dress with some degree of formality.

white elephant. 1. A rare whitish form of the Asian elephant, often regarded with special veneration locally. **2.** A rare and expensive possession that is financially a burden to maintain. **3.** An article no longer wanted by its owner.

white feather. A sign of cowardice.

white•fish (hwīt'fĭsh') *n.* Any of various silvery freshwater food fishes.

white flag. A white cloth or flag signaling surrender or truce.

White House, The. 1. The executive mansion of the President of the U.S. in Washington, D.C. **2.** The supreme executive authority of the U.S. Government.

white lead. A heavy white poisonous compound of lead, used in paint pigments.

whit•en (hwīt'n) *v.* To make or become white. —**whit'en•er** *n.*

white•ness (hwīt'nĭs) *n.* The condition or quality of being white.

white slave. A woman held unwillingly for purposes of prostitution.

white squall. A sudden squall occurring in tropical or subtropical waters, characterized by the absence of a dark cloud and the presence of white-capped waves or broken water.

white•wall (hwīt'wôl') *n.* A vehicular tire having a white band on the visible side.

white•wash (hwīt'wŏsh', -wôsh') *n.* **1.** A mixture of lime and water, often with whiting added, used to whiten walls, concrete, etc. **2.** A concealing or glossing over of flaws or failures. —*v.* **1.** To paint or coat with or as with whitewash. **2.** To gloss over (a flaw).

whith•er (hwĭth'ər) *adv.* **1.** To what place, result, or condition. **2.** To which specified place, position, etc. **3.** To whatever place, result, or condition. [< OE *hwider.* See **kwo-.**]

whith•er•so•ev•er (hwĭth'ər-sō-ĕv'ər) *adv.* To whatever place.

whit•ing¹ (hwī'tĭng) *n.* A pure white ground chalk used in paints, ink, and putty.

whit•ing² (hwī'tĭng) *n.* Any of several marine food fishes. [< MDu *wijting.*]

whit•ish (hwī'tĭsh) *adj.* Somewhat or almost white. —**whit'ish•ness** *n.*

whit•low (hwĭt'lō) *n.* Any inflammation of the area around the nail of a finger or toe.

Whit•man (hwĭt'mən), **Walt.** 1819–1892. American poet.

Whit•ney, Mount (hwĭt'nē). The highest elevation (14,495 ft.) in the U.S., excluding Alaska, in E California.

Whit•sun•day (hwĭt'sən-dē, -dā') *n.* Pentecost.

ō paw, for/oi boy/ou out/ŏŏ took/ōō coo/p pop/r run/s sauce/sh shy/t to/th thin/*th* the/
ŭ cut/ûr fur/v van/w wag/y yes/z size/zh vision/ə ago, item, edible, gallop, circus/

[< OE *hwīta sunnandæg,* "white Sunday."]
whit•tle (hwĭt′l) *v.* -tled, -tling. **1.** To cut small bits or pare shavings from (a piece of wood). **2.** To fashion or shape in this way. **3.** To reduce or eliminate gradually by or as by whittling: *He whittled down his expenditures.* [< OE *thwītan.* See twei-.] —**whit′tler** *n.*
whiz (hwĭz) *v.* **whizzed, whizzing.** Also **whizz.** **1.** To make a whirring, buzzing, or hissing sound, as of something rushing through air. **2.** To rush past. —*n., pl.* **whizzes. 1.** The sound or passage of something that whizzes. **2.** *Slang.* One who has remarkable skill. [Imit.]
who (hōō) *pron.* The interrogative pronoun in the nominative case. **1.** What or which person or persons. **2.** That. **3.** The person or persons that; whoever. [Who, whose, whom < OE *hwā, hwæs, hwæm.* See kwo-.]
Usage: The distinction between *who* and *whoever,* nominative forms, and *whom* and *whomever,* the corresponding objective forms, is carefully observed in formal usage, esp. in writing. In speech, however, *who* frequently occurs in examples such as the following, in which *whom* is the grammatical choice: *Who did you meet? He wants to know who he should speak to. Who* (or *whoever*) is always the choice when it functions as the subject of a clause: *He saw a girl who he thinks may fit the role. Who shall I say is calling? Choose whoever seems most suitable.*
who•ev•er (hōō-ěv′ər) *pron.* **1.** Anyone that. **2.** No matter who. **3.** Who: *Whoever did it?*
whole (hōl) *adj.* **1.** Containing all component parts; complete: *a whole formal wardrobe.* **2.** Not divided or disjoined. **3.** Sound; healthy. **4.** Constituting the full amount, extent, or duration: *cried the whole trip home.* **5.** *Math.* Integral; not fractional. —*n.* **1.** All of the component parts or elements of a thing. **2.** A complete entity or system. —**on the whole.** In general. [< OE *hāl,* sound, unharmed. See kailo-.] —**whole′ness** *n.*
whole•heart•ed (hōl′här′tĭd) *adj.* Without reservation: *wholehearted cooperation.* —**whole′-heart′ed•ly** *adv.* —**whole′heart′ed•ness** *n.*
whole note. *Mus.* A note having the value of four quarter notes.
whole number. An integer.
whole•sale (hōl′sāl′) *n.* The sale of goods in large quantities, as for resale by a retailer. —*adj.* **1.** Pertaining to or engaged in the sale of goods at wholesale. **2.** Sold in large bulk or quantity, usually at a lower cost. **3.** Made or accomplished extensively and indiscriminately: *wholesale destruction.* —*adv.* **1.** In large bulk or quantity. **2.** Extensively and indiscriminately. [< the phrase *by (the) whole sale.*] —**whole′sal′er** *n.*
whole•some (hōl′səm) *adj.* Conducive to mental or physical well-being; healthy. —**whole′some•ly** *adv.* —**whole′some•ness** *n.*
whole-wheat (hōl′hwēt′) *adj.* Made from the entire grain of wheat.
whol•ly (hō′lē, hōl′lē) *adv.* **1.** Entirely. **2.** Exclusively.
whom (hōōm). The objective case of *who.* See Usage note at **who.**

whom•ev•er (hōōm-ěv′ər). The objective case of *whoever.*
whom•so•ev•er (hōōm′sō-ěv′ər). The objective case of *whosoever.*
whoop (hōōp, hwōōp) *n.* **1.** A loud or hooting cry, as of exultation or excitement. **2.** The gasp characteristic of whooping cough. —**whoop** *v.* —**whoop′er** *n.*
whooping cough. An infectious disease involving catarrh of the respiratory passages and characterized by spasms of coughing interspersed with deep, noisy inspiration.
whoosh (hwōōsh, hwŏŏsh) *v.* To make a gushing or rushing sound. —*n.* A whooshing sound. [Imit.]
whop•per (hwŏp′ər) *n. Informal.* **1.** Something exceptionally big or remarkable. **2.** A gross untruth. —**whop′ping** *adj.*
whore (hôr, hōr) *n.* One who engages in sexual intercourse for money. [< OE *hōre.* See kā-.]
whore•house (hôr′hous′, hōr′-) *n.* A brothel.
whorl (hwôrl, hwûrl) *n.* **1.** An arrangement of three or more radiating parts, as leaves or petals. **2.** A coil or convolution, as one of the circular ridges of a fingerprint or a turn of a spiral shell. [ME *whorle.*] —**whorled** *adj.*
whose (hōōz). The possessive form of the pronoun *who* and, less commonly, *which.*
Usage: Whose, as the possessive form of a relative pronoun, can refer to both persons and things: *the boy whose arm was broken; the book whose cover was soiled.*
who•so (hōō′sō) *pron.* Whoever.
who•so•ev•er (hōō′sō-ěv′ər) *pron.* Whoever.
whse. warehouse.
whsle. wholesale.
why (hwī) *adv.* **1.** For what purpose, reason, or cause. **2.** For which; because of which. —*n.* The cause or intention: *whys and wherefores.* [< OE *hwȳ.* See kwo-.]
Wich•i•ta[1] (wĭch′ə-tô′) *n., pl.* **-ta** or **-tas. 1.** A confederacy of Caddoan-speaking North American Indians, formerly living between the Arkansas River and C Texas. **2.** A member of this confederacy. **3.** The language of these Indians.
Wich•i•ta[2] (wĭch′ə-tô). A city of S Kansas. Pop. 255,000.
wick (wĭk) *n.* A cord of fibers, as in a candle, that draws up fuel to the flame by capillary attraction. [< OE *wēoce.*]
wick•ed (wĭk′ĭd) *adj.* **1.** Vicious; depraved. **2.** Harmful. [< OE *wicca,* wizard. See weik-[2].] —**wick′ed•ly** *adv.* —**wick′ed•ness** *n.*
wick•er (wĭk′ər) *n.* Also **wick•er•work** (-wûrk). Flexible twigs or shoots, as of a willow, interwoven to make baskets, furniture, etc. [< Scand.] —**wick′er** *adj.*
wick•et (wĭk′ĭt) *n.* **1.** A small door or gate. **2.** *Cricket.* Either of the two sets of three upright sticks that forms the target of the player hurling the ball. **3.** *Croquet.* A small arch, usually made of wire, through which one tries to direct the ball. [< ONF *wiket.*]
wide (wīd) *adj.* **wider, widest. 1.** Extending over a large area from side to side; broad. **2.** Having a specified extent from side to side. **3.** Having great range or scope: *a wide selec-*

tion. **4.** Fully open: *wide eyes.* **5.** Landing or located away from a desired goal. —*adv.* **1.** Over a large area; extensively. **2.** To the full extent; completely. [< OE *wīd.* See **wi-.**] —**wide′ly** *adv.* —**wide′ness** *n.*

wide-a•wake (wīd′ə-wāk′) *adj.* **1.** Completely awake. **2.** Alert.

wide-eyed (wīd′īd′) *adj.* With the eyes completely opened, as in wonder.

wid•en (wīd′n) *v.* To make or become wide or wider. —**wid′en•er** *n.*

wide•spread (wīd′sprĕd′) *adj.* Occurring or accepted widely.

wid•geon (wĭj′ən) *n.* Also *Brit.* **wi•geon.** A wild duck with brownish plumage and a light head patch. [?]

wid•ow (wĭd′ō) *n.* A woman whose husband has died and who has not remarried. [< OE *widuwe.* See **weidh-.**]

wid•ow•er (wĭd′ō-ər) *n.* A man whose wife has died and who has not remarried.

width (wĭdth, wĭth) *n.* **1.** The state of being wide. **2.** The measurement of the extent of something from side to side. **3.** Something having a specified width.

wield (wēld) *v.* **1.** To handle (a weapon, tool, etc.). **2.** To exercise (power or influence). [< OE *wealdan* and *wieldan.* See **wal-.**]

wife (wīf) *n., pl.* **wives** (wīvz). A woman married to a man. [< OE *wīf* < Gmc **wīf,* woman.] —**wife′ly** *adj.*

wig (wĭg) *n.* A piece of artificial or human hair worn on the head as personal adornment, part of a costume, or to conceal baldness. [Short for PERIWIG.]

wi•geon. *Brit.* Variant of **widgeon.**

wig•gle (wĭg′əl) *v.* **-gled, -gling.** To move or cause to move with short irregular motions from side to side. [ME *wiglen.*] —**wig′gler** *n.*

wig•wam (wĭg′wŏm′) *n.* A North American Indian dwelling, commonly having an arched or conical framework overlaid with bark or hides. [< Algon.]

wild (wīld) *adj.* **1.** Occurring, growing, or living in a natural state; not domesticated, cultivated, or tamed. **2.** Lacking discipline, restraint, or control. **3.** Full of intense, ungovernable emotion: *wild with jealousy.* **4.** Furiously disturbed or turbulent; stormy. **5.** *Card Games.* Having an arbitrary equivalence or value determined by the holder's needs. —*n.* An uninhabited or uncultivated region. [< OE *wilde.* See **welt-.**] —**wild, wild′ly** *adv.* —**wild′-ness** *n.*

wild•cat (wīld′kăt′) *n.* **1.** A lynx, bobcat, or other small to medium-sized wild cat. **2.** An oil well drilled in an area not known to yield oil. —*adj.* **1.** Risky or unsound, esp. financially. **2.** Done without official sanction: *a wildcat strike.*

wil•de•beest (wĭl′də-bēst′, vĭl′-) *n.* The gnu.

wil•der•ness (wĭl′dər-nĭs) *n.* An unsettled, uncultivated region left in its natural condition. [< OE *wildēor,* wild beast.]

wild-eyed (wīld′īd′) *adj.* Glaring in or as in anger, terror, or madness.

wild•fire (wīld′fīr′) *n.* A raging fire that travels and spreads rapidly.

wild•fowl (wīld′foul′) *n.* A bird, as a duck or goose, hunted as game.

wild-goose chase (wīld′gōōs′). A hopeless pursuit of an unattainable or imaginary object.

wild•life (wīld′līf′) *n.* Animals living in a natural, undomesticated state.

wile (wīl) *n.* **1.** A deceitful stratagem or trick. **2.** A disarming or seductive manner, device, or procedure. **3.** Trickery. —*v.* **wiled, wiling.** To entice; lure. [ME *wil.*]

wil•ful. Variant of **willful.**

will¹ (wĭl) *n.* **1.** The mental faculty by which one deliberately chooses or decides upon a course of action; volition. **2.** Deliberate intention or wish: *against his will.* **3.** Free discretion; inclination: *wandered about at will.* **4.** Bearing or attitude toward others; disposition: *full of good will.* **5.** Determination: *the will to win.* **6.** A legal declaration of how a person wishes his possessions to be disposed of after his death. —*v.* **1.** To decide upon; choose; determine. **2.** To bequeath; grant in a legal will. [< OE *will, willa.* See **wel-².**]

will² (wĭl) *v.* past **would,** present **will.** **1.** —Used as an auxiliary followed by a simple infinitive to indicate (often with future reference) willingness, intention, likelihood, requirement, habitual action, or ability. *Will* is used more commonly than *shall* in all persons except (a) in questions with subject *I* or *we,* (b) in formulaic contexts requiring the special prescriptive force of *shall,* and (c) in formal prose as a stylistic device expressing various shades of meaning. **2.** To wish: *Do what you will.* [< OE *wyllan.* See **wel-².**]

Usage: On all but an expressly formal level, *will* often occurs in all three grammatical persons, including the first, in expressing simple futurity (unstressed intention or normal expectation). *Will,* in all three persons, is now also used more often than *shall* to express any of the forms of emphatic futurity.

willed (wĭld) *adj.* Having a will of a specified kind: *weak-willed.*

will•ful (wĭl′fəl) *adj.* Also **wil•ful.** **1.** Said or done in accordance with one's will; deliberate. **2.** Inclined to impose one's will; obstinate. —**will′ful•ly** *adv.* —**will′ful•ness** *n.*

Wil•liam I (wĭl′yəm). Called the Conqueror. 1027–1087. King of England (1066–87).

William II. 1859–1941. Emperor of Germany and king of Prussia (1888–1918).

will•ing (wĭl′ĭng) *adj.* **1.** Of or resulting from the process of choosing. **2.** Disposed to accept or tolerate; acquiescent. **3.** Acting or ready to act gladly; compliant. —**will′ing•ly** *adv.* —**will′ing•ness** *n.*

will-o'-the-wisp (wĭl′ə-thə-wĭsp′) *n.* **1.** A phosphorescent light that hovers over swampy ground at night, possibly caused by spontaneous combustion of gases emitted by rotting organic matter. **2.** A delusive or misleading goal. [?]

wil•low (wĭl′ō) *n.* **1.** Any of various trees or shrubs usually having narrow leaves and slender, flexible twigs. **2.** The wood of such a tree. [< OE *welig.*]

wil•low•y (wĭl′ō-ē) *adj.* **-ier, -iest.** Resembling

or suggestive of a willow tree, as in suppleness, slenderness, etc.

will power. The ability to carry out one's decisions, wishes, or plans; strength of mind.

wil•ly-nil•ly (wĭl′ē-nĭl′ē) *adv.* Whether desired or not. [Var of *will I nill I*, "be I willing, be I unwilling."]

Wil•ming•ton (wĭl′mĭng-tən). A city of N Delaware. Pop. 96,000.

Wil•son (wĭl′sən), **(Thomas) Woodrow.** 1856–1924. 28th President of the U.S. (1913–21).

Woodrow Wilson

wilt¹ (wĭlt) *v.* **1.** To lose or cause to lose freshness; make or become limp or drooping. **2.** To weaken. [Var of dial *wilk, welk.*]

wilt² (wĭlt). *Archaic.* 2nd person sing. present tense of **will.**

wi•ly (wī′lē) *adj.* **-lier, -liest.** Full of wiles; guileful; calculating. —**wil′i•ness** *n.*

wim•ple (wĭm′pəl) *n.* A cloth framing the face and drawn into folds beneath the chin, worn by women in medieval times and as part of certain nuns' habits. [< OE *wimpel.*]

win (wĭn) *v.* **won, winning. 1.** To achieve victory over others in a competition. **2.** To finish first in a race. **3.** To receive as a prize or reward for performance. **4.** To succeed in gaining the support of. —*n.* A victory, esp. in a competition. [< OE *winnan,* to strive. See **wen-**.] —**win′ner** *n.*

wince (wĭns) *v.* **winced, wincing.** To shrink or start involuntarily, as in pain or distress. —*n.* A wincing movement or gesture. [ME *wincen,* to kick, wince.] —**winc′er** *n.*

winch (wĭnch) *n.* **1.** A stationary hoisting machine having a drum around which a rope or chain winds as the load is lifted. **2.** The crank used to give motion to a grindstone or similar device. [< OE *wince,* a pulley. See **weng-**.]

wind¹ (wĭnd) *n.* **1.** Moving air, esp. natural and perceptible movement of air parallel to or along the ground. **2. a.** A movement or current of air blowing from one of the four cardinal points of the compass. **b.** The direction from which such currents come. **3. winds.** The wind instruments in an orchestra or band. **4.** Gas produced in the body during digestion. **5.** Respiration; breath, esp. normal or adequate breathing. **6.** Utterance empty of meaning. —**get wind of.** To receive hints of. —*v.* To cause to be out of or short of breath. [< OE. See **wē-**.]

wind² (wĭnd) *v.* **wound, winding. 1.** To wrap (something) around an object or center once or repeatedly. **2.** To turn in a series of circular motions, as a crank or handle. **3.** To coil the spring of (a clock or other mechanism) by turning a stem. **4.** To move in or as in a bending or coiling course. **5.** To be coiled or spiraled about something. —*n.* A single turn, twist, or curve. [< OE *windan.* See **wendh-**.]

wind•burn (wĭnd′bûrn′) *n.* Skin irritation caused by exposure to wind.

wind•ed (wĭn′dĭd) *adj.* **1.** Having breath or respiratory power: *short-winded.* **2.** Out of breath.

wind•fall (wĭnd′fôl′) *n.* **1.** Something that has been blown down by the wind, as a ripened fruit. **2.** A sudden and unexpected piece of good fortune or personal gain.

wind•flow•er (wĭnd′flou′ər) *n.* An anemone.

Wind•hoek (vĭnt′ho͝ok′). The capital of Namibia. Pop. 61,260.

wind•ing (wĭn′dĭng) *adj.* **1.** Twisting or turning; sinuous. **2.** Spiral.

wind instrument (wĭnd). Any musical instrument sounded by wind, esp. by the breath, as a clarinet, trumpet, or harmonica.

wind•lass (wĭnd′ləs) *n.* Any of numerous hauling or lifting machines consisting essentially of a drum or cylinder wound with rope and turned by a crank. [< ON *vindāss.*]

wind•mill (wĭnd′mĭl′) *n.* A mill that runs on the energy generated by a wheel of adjustable blades or slats rotated by the wind.

win•dow (wĭn′dō) *n.* **1.** An opening constructed in a wall to admit light or air, usually framed and spanned with glass. **2.** A pane of glass; windowpane. **3.** Any opening that resembles a window in function or appearance. [< ON *vindauga,* "wind eye."]

win•dow•pane (wĭn′dō-pān′) *n.* A plate of glass in a window.

win•dow-shop (wĭn′dō-shŏp′) *v.* To look at merchandise in the windows or showcases of stores without purchasing anything. —**win′dow-shop′per** *n.*

win•dow•sill (wĭn′dō-sĭl′) *n.* The horizontal ledge at the base of a window opening.

wind•pipe (wĭnd′pīp′) *n.* The trachea.

wind•shield (wĭnd′shēld′) *n.* A framed pane of glass or other transparent shielding located in front of the occupants of a vehicle to protect them from the wind.

wind•sock (wĭnd′sŏk′) *n.* A large, tapered, open-ended sleeve that indicates the direction of the wind blowing through it.

Wind•sor (wĭn′zər). A city of SE Ontario. Pop. 193,000.

wind•swept (wĭnd′swĕpt′) *adj.* Exposed to or moved by the force of wind.

wind up (wīnd). To come or bring to an end.
wind-up (wīnd'ŭp') *n.* **1.** The act of bringing something to a conclusion. **2.** The concluding part of an action, presentation, speech, etc.
wind•ward (wīnd'wərd) *n.* The direction from which the wind blows. —*adj.* **1.** Of or moving toward the quarter from which the wind blows. **2.** Of or on the side exposed to the wind or prevailing winds. —**wind'ward** *adv.*
wind•y (wīn'dē) *adj.* **-ier, -iest. 1.** Characterized by or abounding in wind. **2.** Resembling wind in swiftness or force. **3. a.** Characterized by lack of substance; empty. **b.** Characterized by or given to prolonged talk. —**wind'i•ly** *adv.* —**wind'i•ness** *n.*
wine (wīn) *n.* The fermented juice of grapes or sometimes other fruits or plants. [< OE *win* < Gmc **wina-* < L *vīnum.*]
wing (wĭng) *n.* **1.** One of a pair of specialized organs of flight, as of a bird, bat, or insect. **2.** A structure or part resembling a wing. **3.** An airfoil whose principal function is providing lift, esp. either of two such airfoils positioned on each side of the fuselage. **4.** *Theater.* The unseen backstage area on either side of a stage. **5.** A structure attached to the side of a house, building, or fortification. **6.** A section of a party, legislature, or community holding distinct political views. **7.** Either of the forward positions played near the sideline, as in hockey. **8.** A unit of military aircraft. —**under one's wing.** Under one's protection. —*v.* **1.** To fly. **2.** To wound superficially, as in the wing or arm. [< ON *vængr,* bird's wing.] —**winged** *adj.*
wing•span (wĭng'spăn') *n.* The linear distance from wing tip to wing tip of an aircraft or bird.
wing•spread (wĭng'sprĕd') *n.* The distance between the tips of the extended wings, as of an airplane, bird, or insect.
wink (wĭngk) *v.* **1.** To close and open (the eyelid of one eye) deliberately, as to convey a message, signal, or suggestion. **2.** To shine fitfully; twinkle. —*n.* **1. a.** The act of winking. **b.** The time required for a wink. **2.** A gleam; twinkle. —**wink at.** To pretend not to see: *winked at corruption.* [< OE *wincian,* to close one's eyes. See **weng-.**]
win•kle (wĭng'kəl) *n.* A snail, the periwinkle.
win•ning (wĭn'ĭng) *adj.* **1.** Successful; victorious. **2.** Charming: *a winning personality.* —*n.* **1.** The act of one that wins. **2. winnings.** That which has been won, esp. money.
Win•ni•peg (wĭn'ə-pĕg). The capital of Manitoba. Pop. 476,000.
win•now (wĭn'ō) *v.* **1.** To separate the chaff from (grain) by means of a current of air. **2.** To separate (a desirable or undesirable part); sort or eliminate. [< OE *windwian* < *wind,* WIND¹.]
win•some (wĭn'səm) *adj.* Pleasant; charming. [< OE *wynsum.*] —**win'some•ly** *adv.* —**win'some•ness** *n.*
win•ter (wĭn'tər) *n.* The usually coldest season of the year, occurring between autumn and spring. —*adj.* **1.** Pertaining to, characteristic of, or occurring in winter. **2. a.** Capable of being stored for use during the winter: *winter*

squash. **b.** Planted in the autumn and harvested in the spring or summer: *winter wheat.* [< OE. See **wed-.**] —**win'try, win'ter•y** *adj.*
win•ter•green (wĭn'tər-grēn') *n.* **1.** A low-growing plant with aromatic evergreen leaves and spicy red berries. **2.** An oil or flavoring obtained from this plant.
win•ter•ize (wĭn'tə-rīz') *v.* **-ized, -izing.** To prepare or equip for winter weather.
win•ter•time (wĭn'tər-tīm') *n.* The winter season.
wipe (wīp) *v.* **wiped, wiping. 1.** To rub, as with a cloth or paper, in order to clean or dry. **2.** To remove by rubbing; brush. —**wipe out.** To destroy; annihilate. [< OE *wīpian.* See **weip-.**] —**wipe** *n.*
wip•er (wī'pər) *n.* A device designed for wiping, as for a windshield.
wire (wīr) *n.* **1.** A usually pliable metallic strand or rod, sometimes clad and often electrically insulated, used chiefly for structural support or to conduct electricity. **2.** A group of such strands bundled or twisted together; a cable. **3.** The telegraph service. **4.** A telegram. **5.** An open telephone connection. **6.** The finish line of a racetrack. —*adj.* Made of or like wire. —*v.* **wired, wiring. 1.** To connect or provide with a wire or wires. **2.** To send by telegraph: *wire congratulations.* **3.** To send a telegram to. [< OE *wīr.* See **wei-¹.**]
wire-haired (wīr'hârd') *adj.* Having a coat of stiff, wiry hair.
wire•less (wīr'lĭs) *n.* **1.** A radio telegraph or telephone system. **2.** *Brit.* Radio.
wire•tap (wīr'tăp') *n.* A concealed listening or recording device connected to a communications circuit. —*v.* To monitor (a telephone line) by means of a wiretap.
wir•ing (wīr'ĭng) *n.* A system of electric wires.
wir•y (wīr'ē) *adj.* **-ier, -iest. 1.** Wirelike; kinky: *wiry hair.* **2.** Slender but tough: *a wiry physique.* —**wir'i•ness** *n.*
Wis•con•sin (wĭs-kŏn'sən). A state of the north-central U.S. Pop. 4,418,000. Cap. Madison.
wis•dom (wĭz'dəm) *n.* **1.** Understanding of what is true, right, or lasting. **2.** Common sense; good judgment. [< OE *wisdōm.* See **weid-.**]
wisdom tooth. One of four molars, the last on each side of both jaws, usually erupting much later than the others.
wise¹ (wīz) *adj.* **wiser, wisest. 1.** Having wisdom; judicious. **2.** Prudent; sensible. **3.** Shrewd: *a wise move.* **4.** Having knowledge or information. **5.** *Slang.* Arrogant. [< OE *wis.* See **weid-.**] —**wise'ly** *adv.*
wise² (wīz) *n.* Method or manner of doing: *in no wise.* [< OE *wise, wis,* manner, condition. See **weid-.**]
-wise. *comb. form.* Used to form adverbs from nouns or adjectives to indicate: **1.** Manner, direction, or position: **clockwise. 2.** *Informal.* With reference to: *taxwise.* See Usage note. [< OE *wise,* WISE².]
Usage: The practice of attaching *-wise* to nouns, in the sense of *with reference to,* has become so closely associated with commercial

jargon in the minds of many writers and speakers that it is dubious usage on any higher level.

wise•crack (wīz'krăk') *n. Slang.* A flippant, commonly sardonic remark.

wish (wĭsh) *n.* **1.** A desire for some specific thing. **2.** An expression of such a desire. **3.** Something desired. *—v.* **1.** To have or feel a desire; want: *I wish to know.* **2.** To desire (a person or thing) to be in a specified state or condition: *I wish this rug were green.* **3.** To express wishes for; bid: *wished her good night.* **4.** To 'call or invoke upon: *I wish him luck.* **5.** To express a wish. [< OE *wўscan.* See **wen-**.] —**wish'ful** *adj.* —**wish'ful•ly** *adv.*

wish•bone (wĭsh'bōn') *n.* The forked bone in front of the breastbone of most birds.

wishful thinking. Erroneous identification of one's own wishes with reality.

wish•y-wash•y (wĭsh'ē-wŏsh'ē, -wô'shē) *adj.* **-ier, -iest.** Lacking in strength or purpose; indecisive. [Redupl of *washy* < WASH.]

wisp (wĭsp) *n.* **1.** A small bunch or bundle, as of hair. **2.** Someone or something thin, frail, or slight. **3.** A faint streak, as of smoke or clouds. [ME.] —**wisp'y** *adj.*

wis•ter•i•a (wĭ-stîr'ē-ə) *n.* Also **wis•tar•i•a** (wĭ-stâr'ē-ə). A climbing woody vine with drooping clusters of purplish or white flowers. [< C. *Wistar* or *Wister* (1761–1818), American anatomist.]

wist•ful (wĭst'fəl) *adj.* Full of a melancholy yearning; wishful. —**wist'ful•ly** *adv.* —**wist'ful•ness** *n.*

wit (wĭt) *n.* **1.** Often **wits.** Understanding; intelligence; resourcefulness. **2. a.** The ability to perceive and express in an ingeniously humorous manner the relationship or similarity between seemingly incongruous or disparate things. **b.** One noted for this ability. [< OE. See **weid-**.]

witch (wĭch) *n.* **1.** A woman who practices sorcery or is believed to have dealings with the devil. **2.** An ugly, vicious old woman. [< OE *wicce* (fem), witch, and *wicca* (masc), wizard. See **weik-²**.]

witch•craft (wĭch'krăft', -kräft') *n.* Black magic; sorcery.

witch doctor. A medicine man among primitive peoples.

witch hazel. 1. A North American shrub with yellow flowers that bloom in late autumn or winter. **2.** An astringent liniment obtained from this shrub.

with (wĭth, wĭth) *prep.* **1.** Accompanying. **2.** Next to. **3.** Having as a possession, attribute, or characteristic. **4.** In a manner characterized by. **5.** In the charge or keeping of. **6.** In the opinion or estimation of. **7.** In support of. **8.** Of the same opinion or belief as. **9.** In the same group as; among. **10.** In the membership or employment of. **11.** By the means or agency of. **12.** In spite of. **13.** In the same direction as. **14.** At the same time as. **15.** In regard to. **16.** In comparison or contrast to. **17.** Having received. **18.** And; plus; added to. **19.** In opposition to; against. **20.** As a result or consequence of. **21.** To; onto. **22.** So as to be

separated from. **23.** In the course of. **24.** In proportion to. **25.** In relationship to. **26.** As well as. [< OE, against or in opposition to, together with. See **wi-**.]

with•al (wĭth-ôl') *adv.* **1.** Besides; in addition. **2.** Despite that; nevertheless. **3.** *Archaic.* Therewith. [< WITH + ALL.]

with•draw (wĭth-drô', wĭth-) *v.* **-drew** (-drōō'), **-drawn** (-drôn'), **-drawing. 1.** To take back or away; remove. **2.** To move or draw back; retreat. **3.** To remove oneself from activity or a social or emotional environment.

with•draw•al (wĭth-drô'əl, wĭth-) *n.* **1.** The act or process of withdrawing. **2.** The act or physiological effect of terminating use of an addictive drug.

with•drawn (wĭth-drôn', wĭth-) *adj.* Shy.

withe (wĭth, wĭth, wĭth) *n.* A tough, supple twig, as of willow, used for binding things together. [< OE *withthe.*]

with•er (wĭth'ər) *v.* **1.** To dry up or shrivel from or as from loss of moisture. **2.** To lose freshness; fade; droop. **3.** To cause to feel belittled: *withered her with a glance.* [ME *widderen.*]

with•ers (wĭth'ərz) *pl.n.* The high point of the back of a horse or other animal, between the shoulder blades.

with•hold (wĭth-hōld', wĭth-) *v.* **-held** (-hĕld'), **-holding.** To refrain from giving, granting, or permitting; forbear.

withholding tax. A portion of an employee's wages or salary withheld by his employer as partial payment of his income tax.

with•in (wĭth-ĭn', wĭth-) *adv.* **1.** Inside. **2.** Indoors. **3.** Inside the body or mind; inwardly. *—prep.* **1.** Inside. **2.** Inside the limits or extent of. **3.** Inside the fixed limits of: *within one's rights.* **4.** In the scope or sphere of.

with•it (wĭth'ĭt', wĭth'-) *adj. Slang.* Up-to-date; hip.

with•out (wĭth-out', wĭth-) *adv.* **1.** In or on the outside. **2.** Outdoors. *—prep.* **1.** Not having; lacking. **2. a.** With no or none of. **b.** Not accompanied by. **3.** Free from. **4.** At, on, to, or toward the outside or exterior of. **5.** With neglect or avoidance of.

with•stand (wĭth-stănd', wĭth-) *v.* **-stood** (-stōōd'), **-standing.** To oppose (something) with force; resist or endure successfully.

wit•ness (wĭt'nĭs) *n.* **1.** One who has seen or heard something. **2.** Something that serves as evidence; a sign. **3.** *Law.* **a.** One who is called upon to testify before a court. **b.** One who is called upon to be present at a transaction in order to attest to what took place. *—v.* **1.** To be present at; see. **2.** To serve as or furnish evidence of. **3.** To testify. **4.** To be the setting or site of. **5.** To attest to the authenticity of by signing one's name. [< OE *wit,* knowledge, WIT.] —**wit'ness•er** *n.*

wit•ti•cism (wĭt'ĭ-sĭz'əm) *n.* A witty remark or saying. [< WITTY.]

wit•ting•ly (wĭt'ĭng-lē) *adv.* Intentionally; deliberately.

wit•ty (wĭt'ē) *adj.* **-tier, -tiest.** Having or showing wit; cleverly humorous. —**wit'ti•ly** *adv.* —**wit'ti•ness** *n.*

wives. *pl.* of **wife.**

---

wiz•ard (wĭz'ərd) *n.* **1.** A sorcerer or magician. **2.** A brilliantly skillful person. [< WISE¹.]
wiz•ard•ry (wĭz'ər-drē) *n.* Sorcery.
wiz•ened (wĭz'ənd) *adj.* Shriveled; withered. [< OE *wisnian,* to dry up. See **wei-².**]
wk. **1.** week. **2.** work.
wkly. weekly.
WNW west-northwest.
WO warrant officer.
woad (wōd) *n.* **1.** An Old World plant with leaves that yield a blue dye. **2.** The dye obtained from this plant. [< OE *wād.*]
wob•ble (wŏb'əl) *v.* **-bled, -bling. 1.** To move or cause to move erratically from side to side. **2.** To waver or vacillate. [Perh < LG *wabbeln.*] **—wob'ble** *n.* **—wob'bly** *adj.*
woe (wō) *n.* **1.** Deep sorrow; grief. **2.** Misfortune. [< OE *wā* (interj). See **wai.**]
woe•be•gone (wō'bĭ-gôn', -gŏn') *adj.* Mournful or sorrowful in appearance. [< WOE + ME *be-,* about + *gon,* to GO.]
woe•ful (wō'fəl) *adj.* **1.** Afflicted with woe; mournful. **2.** Pitiful or deplorable.
woke (wōk). *Chiefly Brit. & Regional. p.t.* of **wake.**
wok•en (wō'kən). *Chiefly Brit. & Regional.* Alternate *p.p.* of **wake.**
wolf (wŏŏlf) *n., pl.* **wolves** (wŏŏlvz). **1.** A carnivorous mammal, chiefly of northern regions, related to and resembling the dogs. **2.** *Slang.* A man given to avid amatory pursuit of women. *—v.* To eat voraciously: *wolfed down the hamburger.* [< OE *wulf.* See **wlkwo-.**]
wolf•hound (wŏŏlf'hound') *n.* A large dog originally trained to hunt wolves.
wolf•ram (wŏŏl'frəm) *n.* Tungsten. [G.]
wol•ver•ine (wŏŏl'və-rēn') *n.* A carnivorous mammal of northern regions, having dark fur and a bushy tail. [< WOLF.]
wom•an (wŏŏm'ən) *n., pl.* **women** (wĭm'ĭn). **1.** An adult female human being. **2.** Women collectively. **3.** A mistress; paramour. [< OE *wíf,* WIFE + *man,* person, MAN.]
wom•an•hood (wŏŏm'ən-hŏŏd') *n.* **1.** The state of being a woman. **2.** Womankind.
wom•an•ish (wŏŏm'ə-nĭsh) *adj.* Characteristic of a woman; womanlike.
wom•an•kind (wŏŏm'ən-kīnd') *n.* Female human beings collectively; women.
wom•an•ly (wŏŏm'ən-lē) *adj.* **-lier, -liest.** Having the becoming qualities of a woman. **—wom'an•li•ness** *n.*
womb (wŏŏm) *n.* **1.** The uterus. **2.** A place where something is generated. [< OE *wamb* < Gmc **wambō.*]
wom•bat (wŏm'băt') *n.* An Australian marsupial, resembling a small bear.
wom•en. *pl.* of **woman.**
wom•en•folk (wĭm'ĭn-fōk') *pl.n.* **1.** Women collectively. **2.** A particular group of women.
won¹ (wŏn) *n., pl.* **won. 1.** The basic monetary unit of South Korea. **2.** The basic monetary unit of North Korea.
won² (wŭn). *p.t. & p.p.* of **win.**
won•der (wŭn'dər) *n.* **1. a.** That which arouses awe or admiration; a marvel. **b.** The emotion thus aroused. **2.** A feeling of puzzlement or doubt. *—v.* **1.** To have a feeling of awe or admiration. **2.** To be filled with curiosity or doubt. **3.** To have doubts or curiosity about. [< OE *wundor* < Gmc **wundar-.*]
won•der•ful (wŭn'dər-fəl) *adj.* **1.** Capable of exciting wonder; marvelous. **2.** Admirable; excellent. **—won'der•ful•ly** *adv.*
won•der•land (wŭn'dər-lănd') *n.* **1.** A marvelous imaginary realm. **2.** A marvelous real place or scene.
won•drous (wŭn'drəs) *adj.* Wonderful.
wont (wônt, wŏnt, wŭnt) *adj.* **1.** Accustomed: *The poor man is wont to complain.* **2.** Apt or likely. *—n.* Usage or custom. [< OE *wunian,* to dwell. See **wen-.**]
won't (wônt). Contraction of *will not.*
wont•ed (wôn'tĭd, wŏn'-, wŭn'-) *adj.* Accustomed; usual.
woo (wŏŏ) *v.* **1.** To seek the affection of, esp. with intent to marry. **2.** To seek to achieve. **3.** To entreat or importune. [< OE *wōgian.*]
wood (wŏŏd) *n.* **1. a.** The tough, fibrous supporting and water-conducting substance lying beneath the bark of trees and shrubs. **b.** Such a substance used for various purposes, as building material or fuel. **2.** Often **woods.** A dense growth of trees; a forest. **3.** A wooden object. *—adj.* **1.** Wooden. **2.** Associated with, used on, or containing wood. **3.** Growing or living in woods. *—v.* **1.** To cover with trees. **2.** To gather or be supplied with wood. [< OE *wudu.* See **widhu-.**]
wood alcohol. Methanol.
wood•bine (wŏŏd'bīn') *n.* Any of various climbing vines, esp. an Old World honeysuckle. [< OE *wudu,* WOOD + *bindan,* to BIND.]
wood•carv•ing (wŏŏd'kär'vĭng) *n.* **1.** The art of carving in wood. **2.** An object carved from wood. **—wood'carv'er** *n.*
wood•chuck (wŏŏd'chŭk') *n.* A common North American rodent, with a short-legged, heavy-set body; a ground hog. [< Algon.]
wood•cock (wŏŏd'kŏk') *n.* A short-legged, long-billed game bird.
wood•craft (wŏŏd'krăft', -kräft') *n.* **1.** Skill in matters pertaining to the woods, as hunting or camping. **2.** The art of working with wood.
wood•cut (wŏŏd'kŭt') *n.* **1.** A piece of wood with an engraved design for printing. **2.** A print made from such a piece of wood.
wood•cut•ter (wŏŏd'kŭt'ər) *n.* One who cuts wood or trees.
wood•ed (wŏŏd'ĭd) *adj.* Having trees or woods.
wood•en (wŏŏd'n) *adj.* **1.** Made or consisting of wood. **2.** Without life; lifeless. **3.** Clumsy.
wood•land (wŏŏd'lənd, -lănd') *n.* Land covered with trees.
wood•peck•er (wŏŏd'pĕk'ər) *n.* Any of various birds that cling to and climb trees and have a chisellike bill for drilling through bark and wood.
woods•man (wŏŏdz'mən) *n.* One who works or lives in the woods or is versed in woodcraft.
wood•wind (wŏŏd'wĭnd') *n.* Any of a group of musical wind instruments that includes the bassoon, clarinet, flute, oboe, and sometimes the saxophone. **—wood'wind'** *adj.*

ō paw, for/oi boy/ou out/ŏŏ took/ōō coo/p pop/r run/s sauce/sh shy/t to/th thin/*th* the/
ŭ cut/ûr fur/v van/w wag/y yes/z size/zh vision/ə ago, item, edible, gallop, circus/

wood•work (wŏŏd'wûrk') *n.* Something made of wood, esp. wooden interior fittings.
wood•y (wŏŏd'ē) *adj.* -ier, -iest. 1. Consisting of or containing wood. 2. Suggestive of wood. 3. Wooded.
woof (wŏŏf, wōōf) *n.* 1. The threads in a woven fabric at right angles to the warp threads. 2. The texture of a fabric. [< OE *wefan,* to weave.]
woof•er (wŏŏf'ər) *n.* A loud-speaker designed to reproduce bass frequencies. [< *woof,* the gruff bark of a dog.]
wool (wŏŏl) *n.* 1. The dense, soft, often curly hair of a sheep and some other animals, valued as a textile fabric. 2. A material or garment made of wool. 3. A covering or substance suggestive of the texture of wool. [< OE *wull.* See **wel-**¹.] —**wool** *adj.*
wool•en (wŏŏl'ən). Also **wool•len.** *adj.* Pertaining to or consisting of wool. —*n.* Often **woolens.** Fabric or clothing made from wool.
wool•gath•er•ing (wŏŏl'gǎth'ər-ĭng) *n.* Absent-minded indulgence in fanciful daydreams.
wool•ly (wŏŏl'ē) *adj.* -lier, -liest. Also **wool•y.** 1. a. Pertaining to, consisting of, or covered with wool. b. Resembling wool. 2. Blurry; fuzzy. 3. Rough and generally lawless: *wild and woolly.* —*n., pl.* -lies. Also **wool•y.** A garment, esp. an undergarment, made of wool.
wooz•y (wŏŏ'zē, wōōz'ē) *adj.* -ier, -iest. 1. Dazed; confused. 2. Dizzy or queasy. [Perh var of OOZY.] —**wooz'i•ness** *n.*
Worces•ter (wŏŏs'tər). A city of C Massachusetts. Pop. 187,000.
word (wûrd) *n.* 1. A sound or a combination of sounds, or its representation in writing or printing, that symbolizes and communicates a meaning. 2. An utterance, remark, or comment. 3. **words.** A discourse or talk; speech. 4. **words.** Lyrics; text. 5. An assurance or promise. 6. a. A command or direction. b. A verbal signal. 7. a. News. b. Rumor. 8. **words.** A dispute or argument. 9. **Word.** The Scriptures or Gospel: *the Word of God.* —**in a word.** In short. —**in so many words.** Exactly. —**word for word.** In the same words. —*v.* To express in words. [< OE. See **wer-**².]
word•ing (wûr'dĭng) *n.* The style of expressing in words.
word square. A group of words arranged in a square that read the same vertically and horizontally.
Words•worth (wûrdz'wûrth'), **William.** 1770–1850. English poet.
word•y (wûr'dē) *adj.* -ier, -iest. Expressed in or using more words than are necessary. —**word'i•ly** *adv.* —**word'i•ness** *n.*
wore (wôr, wōr). *p.t.* of **wear.**
work (wûrk) *n.* 1. Effort directed toward the production or accomplishment of something; toil; labor. 2. Employment. 3. A trade, craft, business, or profession. 4. A duty or task. 5. Something that has been produced as a result of effort. 6. **works.** The output of an artist or artisan considered as a whole. 7. **works.** Engineering structures. 8. Any material being processed during manufacture. 9. **works**

(takes sing. v.). A factory, plant, or similar building or system of buildings. 10. **works.** Machinery. 11. The manner or style of working. 12. *Phys.* The transfer of energy to a body by the application of force. —*v.* 1. To labor or toil. 2. To be employed; have a job. 3. To function or operate. 4. To prove successful. 5. To have an influence, result, or effect, as on a person. 6. To change into a specified state, esp. gradually or by repeated movement. 7. To force a passage or way. 8. To move or contort from emotion or pain. 9. To be processed. 10. To ferment. 11. To undergo small motions that result in friction and wear. 12. To cause or effect; bring about. 13. To handle or use. 14. To form or shape; mold. 15. To solve (an arithmetic problem). 16. To make productive; cultivate. 17. To make or force to work. 18. To excite, rouse, or provoke. 19. To influence or persuade. —**work up.** 1. To make one's or its way up. 2. To arouse or excite. 3. To develop. [< OE *weorc, act, deed, work.* See **werg-**.]
—**work.** *comb. form.* 1. A product composed of a (specified) material: **paperwork.** 2. Work produced in a (specified) way or of a (specified) kind: **piecework.** 3. Work performed in a (specified) place: **housework.**
work•a•ble (wûr'kə-bəl) *adj.* 1. Capable of being worked. 2. Practicable or feasible.
work•a•day (wûrk'ə-dā') *adj.* 1. Pertaining or appropriate to working days. 2. Mundane; commonplace.
work•bench (wûrk'bĕnch') *n.* A sturdy table, as one used by a machinist or carpenter.
work•book (wûrk'bŏŏk') *n.* 1. A booklet of problems and exercises in which a student may write. 2. A manual of operating instructions. 3. A book in which a record of work is kept.
work•day (wûrk'dā') *n.* 1. A day on which work is done. 2. The part of the day during which one works.
work•er (wûr'kər) *n.* 1. One that works. 2. One who works for wages. 3. A sterile female of certain social insects, as the ant or bee, that performs specialized work.
work•horse (wûrk'hôrs') *n.* 1. A horse used for labor rather than racing or riding. 2. One who works tirelessly.
work•house (wûrk'hous') *n.* 1. A prison in which limited sentences are served at manual labor. 2. A former British public institution for the indigent.
work•ing (wûr'kĭng) *adj.* 1. Employed. 2. Of, used for, or spent in work. 3. Sufficient or large enough for using. 4. Capable of being used as the basis of further work.
work•man (wûrk'mən) *n.* A man who performs some form of labor.
work•man•like (wûrk'mən-līk') *adj.* Characteristic of a skilled workman or craftsman.
work•man•ship (wûrk'mən-shĭp') *n.* 1. The art, skill, or technique of a workman. 2. The quality of such art, skill, or technique.
work out. 1. To come or make its way out. 2. To exhaust (a mine, soil, etc.). 3. To solve. 4. To formulate or develop. 5. To have a spec-

---

ified end or result. **6.** To perform exercises.

work•out (wûrk'out') *n.* **1.** A period of exercise or practice, esp. in athletics. **2.** An exhausting task.

work•room (wûrk'rōōm', -rōōm') *n.* A room where work is done.

work•shop (wûrk'shŏp') *n.* **1.** An area, room, or establishment in which manual work is done. **2.** A regularly scheduled seminar in some specialized field.

work•ta•ble (wûrk'tā'bəl) *n.* A table designed for a specific task or activity.

world (wûrld) *n.* **1.** The earth. **2.** The universe. **3.** The earth and its inhabitants collectively. **4.** The human race. **5.** The public. **6.** Often **World.** A particular part of the earth. **7.** Any sphere, realm, domain, or kingdom. **8.** An individual way of life or state of being. **9.** The secular life. **10.** A large amount; much. **11.** A planet or other celestial body. [< OE *world, weorold.* See **wiros.**]

world•ly (wûrld'lē) *adj.* **-lier, -liest. 1.** Not spiritual or religious; secular. **2.** Sophisticated or cosmopolitan; worldly-wise. **—world'li•ness** *n.*

world•ly-wise (wûrld'lē-wīz') *adj.* Experienced in the ways of the world; sophisticated.

World War I. A war fought from 1914 to 1918, in which Great Britain, France, Russia, the U.S., and other allies defeated Germany, Austria-Hungary, Turkey, and Bulgaria.

World War II. A war fought from 1939 to 1945, in which Great Britain, France, the Soviet Union, the U.S., and other allies defeated Germany, Italy, and Japan.

world•wide (wûrld'wīd') *adj.* Reaching or extending throughout the world; universal.

worm (wûrm) *n.* **1.** Any of various invertebrates, as an earthworm or tapeworm, having a long, flexible rounded or flattened body. **2.** Any of various insect larvae having a long, soft body. **3.** A contemptible person. **4.** An insidiously tormenting force: *"The worm of conscience still begnaw thy soul!"* (Shakespeare). **5. worms.** Intestinal infestation with worms. **—v. 1.** To make (one's way) with or as with the sinuous crawling motion of a worm. **2.** To elicit by devious means. **3.** To cure of intestinal worms. [< OE *wyrm,* worm, serpent. See **wer-³.**] **—worm'y** *adj.*

worm•wood (wûrm'wŏŏd') *n.* An aromatic plant yielding a bitter extract used in making absinthe. [< OE *wermōd* < Gmc **wer-mōd-.*]

worn (wôrn, wōrn) *p.p.* of **wear. —adj. 1.** Affected or impaired by wear or use. **2.** Exhausted; spent. **3.** Trite; hackneyed.

worn-out (wôrn'out', wōrn'-) *adj.* **1.** Worn or used until no longer usable. **2.** Thoroughly exhausted; spent.

wor•ri•some (wûr'ē-səm) *adj.* **1.** Causing worry or anxiety. **2.** Tending to worry.

wor•ry (wûr'ē) *v.* **-ried, -rying. 1.** To feel uneasy about some uncertain or threatening matter. **2.** To cause to feel anxious, distressed, or troubled. **3. a.** To grasp and tug at repeatedly. **b.** To touch, press, or handle idly. **—n., pl. -ries. 1.** Mental uneasiness or anxiety. **2.** A source of nagging concern. [< OE *wyrgan,* to strangle. See **wer-³.**] **—wor'ri•er** *n.*

wor•ry•wart (wûr'ē-wôrt') *n. Informal.* One who tends to worry excessively and needlessly.

worse (wûrs). **1.** *compar.* of **bad. 2.** *compar.* of **ill. —adj. 1.** More inferior, as in quality, condition, or effect. **2.** More severe or unfavorable. **—n.** Something that is worse. **—adv.** In a worse way. [< OE *wyrsa.* See **wers-.**]

wors•en (wûr'sən) *v.* To make or become worse.

wor•ship (wûr'shĭp) *n.* **1. a.** The reverent love accorded a deity, idol, or sacred object. **b.** A set of ceremonies or prayers by which this love is expressed. **2.** Ardent devotion. **3.** Often **Worship.** *Chiefly Brit.* A title of honor used in addressing magistrates, mayors, etc. **—v. -shiped** or **-shipped, -shiping** or **-shipping. 1.** To honor and love as a deity. **2.** To love devotedly. **3.** To participate in religious rites of worship. [< OE *weorth,* **WORTH** + **-SHIP.**] **—wor'ship•er** *n.*

wor•ship•ful (wûr'shĭp-fəl) *adj.* Given to or expressive of worship; reverent.

worst (wûrst). **1.** *superl.* of **bad. 2.** *superl.* of **ill. —adj. 1.** Most inferior, as in quality, condition, or effect. **2.** Most severe or unfavorable. **—n.** Something that is worst. **—adv.** In the worst manner or degree. **—v.** To gain the advantage over; defeat.

wor•sted (wŏŏs'tĭd, wûr'stĭd) *n.* **1.** Firm-textured, compactly twisted woolen yarn made from long-staple fibers. **2.** Fabric made from such yarn. [< *Worthstede* (now Worstead), a village in England.]

—wort *comb. form.* A plant: **liverwort.** [< OE *wyrt,* plant, herb.]

worth (wûrth) *n.* **1.** The quality of something that renders it desirable or valuable. **2.** The material value of something. **3.** The quantity of something that can be purchased for a specific sum. **4.** The quality within a person that renders him deserving of respect. **—adj. 1.** Equal in value to something specified. **2.** Deserving of; meriting. [< OE *weorth.*]

worth•less (wûrth'lĭs) *adj.* Without worth, use, or value. **—worth'less•ness** *n.*

worth•while (wûrth'hwīl') *adj.* Sufficiently valuable or important to justify the expenditure of time or effort.

wor•thy (wûr'thē) *adj.* **-thier, -thiest. 1.** Having worth, merit, or value. **2.** Honorable; admirable. **3.** Deserving: *worthy of acclaim.* **—n., pl. -thies.** A worthy person. **—wor'thi•ly** *adv.* **—wor'thi•ness** *n.*

would (wŏŏd). *p.t.* of **will².** See Usage note at **should.**

would-be (wŏŏd'bē') *adj.* Desiring or pretending to be.

would•n't (wŏŏd'ənt). Contraction of *would not.*

wouldst, would•est (wŏŏdst; wŏŏd'ĭst). *Archaic.* 2nd person sing. past tense of **will².**

wound¹ (wŏŏnd) *n.* An injury, esp. one in which the skin is torn, pierced, or cut. **—v.** To inflict a wound or wounds upon. [< OE *wund.* See **wā-.**]

wound² (wound). *p.t.* & *p.p.* of **wind².**

wove (wōv). *p.t.* & *rare p.p.* of **weave.**

wo•ven (wō'vən). *p.p.* of **weave.**

ô paw, for/oi boy/ou out/ŏŏ took/ōō coo/p pop/r run/s sauce/sh shy/t to/th thin/*th* the/
ŭ cut/ûr fur/v van/w wag/y yes/z size/zh vision/ə ago, item, edible, gallop, circus/

wow (wou) *interj.* Expressive of wonder, amazement, etc.

w.p.m. words per minute.

wrack (răk) *n.* 1. Damage or destruction by violent means: *bring to wrack and ruin.* 2. Seaweed forming a tangled mass. [< OE *wrǣc,* punishment, vengeance, and MDu *wrak,* wreckage, wrecked ship.]

wraith (rāth) *n.* An apparition. [?]

wran•gle (răng'gəl) *v.* **-gled, -gling.** 1. To dispute noisily or angrily; quarrel. 2. To win or obtain by argument. 3. *Western U.S.* To herd horses or other livestock. —*n.* An angry, noisy dispute. [ME *wranglen.*] —**wran'gler** *n.*

wrap (răp) *v.* **wrapped** or **wrapt** (răpt)**, wrapping.** 1. To arrange or fold about in order to cover or protect. 2. To cover or envelop, as with paper. 3. To clasp, fold, or coil about or around something. 4. To immerse in some condition: *wrapped in thought.* —*n.* 1. A garment to be wrapped or folded about a person. 2. A wrapping or wrapper. [ME *wrappen.*]

wrap•per (răp'ər) *n.* 1. One that wraps. 2. The paper or other material in which something is wrapped. 3. A loose robe or negligee.

wrap•ping (răp'ĭng) *n.* Also **wrap•pings** (-ĭngz). The material in which something is wrapped.

wrap up. 1. To work out and complete the details of: *wrap up a business deal.* 2. To summarize.

wrap-up (răp'ŭp') *n.* A brief summary.

wrath (răth, räth) *n.* 1. Violent, resentful anger; rage. 2. a. A manifestation of anger. b. Divine retribution. [< OE *wrǣth,* angry. See **wer-³.**] —**wrath'ful** *adj.* —**wrath'ful•ly** *adv.*

wreak (rēk) *v.* 1. To inflict (vengeance or punishment). 2. To express or gratify (anger, malevolence, or resentment). [< OE *wrecan,* to drive, expel, vent. See **wreg-.**]

wreath (rēth) *n., pl.* **wreaths** (rēthz). 1. A ring or circlet of flowers or leaves. 2. Something resembling this: *a wreath of smoke.* [< OE *writha.* See **wer-³.**]

wreathe (rēth) *v.* **wreathed, wreathing.** 1. To twist or entwine into a wreath. 2. To crown or decorate with or as with a wreath. 3. To curl or spiral. 4. To assume the form of a wreath. [< WREATH.]

wreck (rĕk) *v.* 1. To destroy accidentally, as by collision. 2. To tear down or dismantle. 3. To bring to a state of ruin. —*n.* 1. The action of wrecking or condition of being wrecked. 2. The remains of something that has been wrecked or ruined. 3. Something in a disorderly or worn-out state. [< Scand.]

wreck•age (rĕk'ĭj) *n.* 1. The act of wrecking or condition of being wrecked. 2. The debris of anything wrecked.

wreck•er (rĕk'ər) *n.* 1. a. A member of a wrecking or demolition crew. b. One who destroys or ruins. 2. A vehicle or ship employed in recovering or removing a wreck.

wren (rĕn) *n.* A small, brownish bird usually holding the tail upright. [< OE *wrenna* < Gmc **wrendila-.*]

wrench (rĕnch) *n.* 1. A sudden, forcible twist or turn. 2. An injury produced by twisting or straining. 3. Any of various tools with fixed or

adjustable jaws for gripping a nut, bolt, etc., and a long handle for effective leverage. —*v.* 1. a. To twist or turn suddenly and forcibly. b. To twist and sprain. 2. To pull forcibly. [< OE *wrencan,* to twist. See **wer-³.**]

wrest (rĕst) *v.* 1. To obtain by or as by pulling with violent twisting movements. 2. To usurp: *wrest power.* [< OE *wrǣstan,* to twist. See **wer-³.**] —**wrest'er** *n.*

wres•tle (rĕs'əl) *v.* **-tled, -tling.** 1. To contend by grappling and attempting to throw one's opponent, esp. under certain contest rules. 2. To contend; struggle to master. 3. To wrestle with. —*n.* An act of wrestling, esp. a wrestling match. [< OE *wrǣstlian.* See **wer-³.**] —**wres'tler** *n.*

wres•tling (rĕs'lĭng) *n.* A gymnastic contest between two competitors who attempt to throw each other by grappling.

wretch (rĕch) *n.* 1. A miserable or unfortunate person. 2. A base or despicable person. [< OE *wrecca,* wretch, exile. See **wreg-.**]

wretch•ed (rĕch'ĭd) *adj.* 1. Attended by misery and woes. 2. Of a poor or depressing character: *a wretched building.* 3. Contemptible. 4. Inferior in performance or quality. —**wretch'ed•ly** *adv.* —**wretch'ed•ness** *n.*

wrig•gle (rĭg'əl) *v.* **-gled, -gling.** 1. To turn or twist the body with sinuous motions. 2. To proceed with sinuous motions. 3. To insinuate or extricate oneself by sly or subtle means. —*n.* The action or movement of wriggling. [< MLG *wriggeln.*] —**wrig'gly** *adj.*

wrig•gler (rĭg'lər) *n.* The larva of a mosquito.

Wright (rīt). 1. Frank Lloyd. 1869–1959. American architect. 2. Orville. 1871–1948. American aviation pioneer and inventor; with his brother, Wilbur (1867–1912), made first powered flights in heavier-than-air craft (1903).

wring (rĭng) *v.* **wrung, wringing.** 1. a. To twist and squeeze. b. To compress to extract liquid. 2. To extract (liquid) by twisting or compressing. 3. To twist forcibly: *wring one's neck.* 4. To cause distress to: *wring one's heart.* 5. To obtain by applying force or pressure to. [< OE *wringan.* See **wer-³.**]

wring•er (rĭng'ər) *n.* One that wrings, esp. a device in which laundry is pressed or spun to extract water.

wrin•kle¹ (rĭng'kəl) *n.* A small furrow, ridge, or crease on a normally smooth surface. —*v.* **-kled, -kling.** 1. To make a wrinkle or wrinkles in. 2. To become wrinkled. [< OE *gewrinclian,* to wind. See **wer-³.**] —**wrin'kly** *adj.*

wrin•kle² (rĭng'kəl) *n. Informal* An ingenious new method; innovation. [< WRINKLE.]

wrist (rĭst) *n.* 1. The junction between the hand and forearm. 2. The system of bones forming this junction. [< OE. See **wer-³.**]

writ (rĭt) *n.* A written order issued by a court, commanding the person to whom it is addressed to perform or cease performing some specified act. [< OE < Gmc **writan,* to scratch.]

write (rīt) *v.* **wrote, written, writing.** 1. To form (letters, words, symbols, etc.) on a surface with a pen, pencil, or other tool. 2. To compose, esp. as an author or musician. 3. To relate or

---

ă pat/ā ate/âr care/ä bar/b bib/ch chew/d deed/ĕ pet/ē be/f fit/g gag/h hat/hw what/
ĭ pit/ī pie/îr pier/j judge/k kick/l lid, fatal/m mum/n no, sudden/ng sing/ŏ pot/ō go/

communicate by writing. —**write down.** To put into writing. —**write off.** 1. To cancel from accounts as a loss. 2. To consider as a failure. [< OE *writan* < Gmc **writan,* to tear, scratch.]

writ•er (rī'tər) *n.* 1. One who has written (something specified): *the writer of the note.* 2. An author.

write-up (rīt'ŭp') *n.* A published account, review, or notice.

writhe (rīth) *v.* **writhed, writhing.** To twist or squirm, as in pain. [< OE *wrīthan.* See wer-³.]

writ•ing (rī'tĭng) *n.* 1. Written form: *Put it in writing.* 2. Something written. 3. Any written work, esp. a literary composition. 4. The activity, art, or occupation of a writer.

writ•ten (rīt'n). *p.p.* of **write.**

wrnt. warrant.

wrong (rông, rŏng) *adj.* 1. Not correct; erroneous. 2. Contrary to conscience, morality, or law. 3. Not required, intended, or wanted: *take a wrong turn.* 4. Not fitting or suitable; improper. 5. Not in accordance with an established method or procedure. 6. Out of order; amiss; awry. —*adv.* 1. In a wrong manner; erroneously. 2. Immorally or unjustly. —*n.* 1. That which is wrong; an unjust, injurious, or immoral act. 2. The condition of being mistaken or to blame: *in the wrong.* —*v.* 1. To treat unjustly or dishonorably. 2. To discredit unjustly; malign. [< Scand.] —**wrong'ly** *adv.*

wrong•do•er (rông'dōō'ər, rŏng'-) *n.* One who does wrong. —**wrong'do'ing** *n.*

wrong•ful (rông'fəl, rŏng'-) *adj.* 1. Wrong; injurious; unjust. 2. Contrary to law; illegal. —**wrong'ful•ly** *adv.* —**wrong'ful•ness** *n.*

wrote (rōt). *p.t.* of **write.**

wroth (rôth) *adj. Archaic.* Wrathful; angry.

wrought (rôt) *adj.* 1. Put together: *carefully wrought.* 2. Shaped by hammering with tools: *wrought iron.* —**wrought up.** Agitated; excited. [< the archaic pt and pp of WORK.]

wrought iron. A very pure easily welded or forged iron containing about 0.2% carbon. —**wrought'-iron'** *adj.*

wrung (rŭng). *p.t.* & *p.p.* of **wring.**

wry (rī) *adj.* **wrier** or **wryer, wriest** or **wryest.** 1. Twisted, as facial features. 2. Temporarily twisted in an expression of distaste or displeasure: *a wry face.* 3. Dryly humorous, often with a touch of irony. [< OE *wrīgian,* to proceed, turn. See wer-³.] —**wry'ly** *adv.*

WSW west-southwest.

wt. weight.

Wu•han (wōō'hän'). A city of E China. Pop. 2,226,000.

W.Va. West Virginia.

W.W.I World War I.

W.W.II World War II.

Wyc•liffe (wĭk'lĭf), **John.** 1320?–1384. English theologian and religious reformer.

Wy•o•ming (wī-ō'mĭng). A state of the W U.S. Pop. 332,000. Cap. Cheyenne.

XxYyZz

x, X (ĕks) *n.* 1. The 24th letter of the English alphabet. 2. Anything shaped like the letter **X.**

x Any unknown or unnamed factor, thing, or person.

X. 1. A symbol for Christ or Christian. 2. A symbol placed on a map or diagram to mark the location or position of a point.

x-ax•is (ĕks'ăk'sĭs) *n., pl.* **x-axes** (-sēz). The horizontal axis of a two-dimensional Cartesian coordinate system.

X-chro•mo•some (ĕks'krō'mə-sōm') *n.* The sex chromosome associated with female characteristics, occurring paired in the female and single in the male sex-chromosome pair.

Xe xenon.

xe•non (zē'nŏn') *n. Symbol* **Xe** A colorless, odorless, highly unreactive gaseous element found in minute quantities in the atmosphere. Atomic number 54, atomic weight 131.30. [< Gk *xenos,* stranger.]

xen•o•phobe (zĕn'ə-fōb') *n.* One unduly fearful or contemptuous of strangers or foreigners. [< Gk *xenos,* stranger + -PHOBE.] —**xen'o•pho'bi•a** *n.* —**xen'o•pho'bic** *adj.*

xe•rog•ra•phy (zĭ-rŏg'rə-fē) *n.* A dry photographic or photocopying process that transfers images by means of electric charges. [< Gk *xēros,* dry + -GRAPHY.] —**xer'o•graph'ic** (zîr'ə-grăf'ĭk) *adj.*

Xer•ox (zîr'ŏks) *n.* A trademark for a photocopying process or machine using xerography. —*v.* To reproduce by means of a Xerox machine. [< XEROGRAPHY.]

Xerx•es I (zûrk'sēz). 519?–465 B.C. King of Persia (486–465 B.C.).

Xho•sa (kō'sä) *n., pl.* **-sa** or **-sas.** Also **Xo•sa.** One of a Bantu people of the Republic of South Africa.

xi (zī, sī) *n.* The 14th letter in the Greek alphabet, representing *x.*

X•mas (krĭs'məs, ĕks'məs) *n. Informal.* Christmas.

   Usage: Xmas occurs principally in commercial writing and is now chiefly appropriate to that level.

x-ra•di•a•tion (ĕks'rā'dē-ā'shən) *n.* 1. Treatment with or exposure to x rays. 2. Radiation composed of x rays.

ô paw, for/oi boy/ou out/ŏŏ took/ōō coo/p pop/r run/s sauce/sh shy/t to/th thin/*th* the/ ŭ cut/ûr fur/v van/w wag/y yes/z size/zh vision/ə ago, item, edible, gallop, circus/

x ray. 1. a. A relatively high-energy photon with a very short wavelength. **b.** Often **x rays.** A stream of such photons. **2.** Also **X ray.** A photograph taken with x rays. —**x'-ray'** *adj.*
x-ray (ĕks'rā') *v.* To examine or photograph by means of x rays.

xy·lo·phone (zī'lə-fōn') *n.* A musical percussion instrument consisting of a mounted row of wooden bars graduated in length to sound a chromatic scale, played with two small mallets. [< Gk *xulon*, wood + -PHONE.] —**xy'lo·phon'ist** *n.*

y, Y (wī) *n.* **1.** The 25th letter of the English alphabet. **2. Y.** Anything shaped like the letter **Y.**
y ordinate.
Y yttrium.
y. year.
–y¹, –ey. *comb. form.* **1.** The existence or possession of what is expressed in the root: **cloudy.** **2.** A relationship to what is expressed in the root: **watery.** [< OE *-ig, -ǣg* < Gmc **-iga.*]
–y². *comb. form.* **1.** A condition or quality: **jealousy.** **2.** An activity, products dealt with, or a place of business: **cookery.** [< L *-ia.*]
–y³, –ey. *comb. form.* **1.** Smallness: **doggy.** **2.** Endearment: **daddy.** [ME *-ie.*]
yacht (yät) *n.* A small sailing or mechanically propelled vessel, used for pleasure cruises or racing. —*v.* To race, sail, or cruise in a yacht. [< obs Du *jaght(schip),* "chasing (ship)."]
yachts·man (yäts'mən) *n.* One who owns or sails a yacht. —**yachts'man·ship'** *n.*
ya·hoo (yä'hōō, yä'-) *n.* A crude or brutish person. [< the *Yahoos,* a race of human beings in Swift's *Gulliver's Travels.*]
Yah·weh (yä'wĕ). Also **Jah·weh.** A name for God, commonly rendered Jehovah.
yak (yăk) *n.* A long-haired bovine mammal of the mountains of C Asia. [Tibetan *gyag.*]
yam (yăm) *n.* **1.** The starchy, edible root of a tropical vine. **2.** A sweet potato with reddish flesh. [Port *inhame,* "edible."]
Yang·tze (yăng'tsē'). A river of C China.
yank (yăngk) *v.* To pull or extract suddenly; jerk. —*n.* A sudden vigorous pull; a jerk. [?]
Yank (yăngk) *n. Informal.* Yankee.
Yan·kee (yăng'kē) *n.* **1.** A native or inhabitant of New England. **2.** A native or inhabitant of a N state. **3.** A native or inhabitant of the U.S. [Poss < the Du name *Janke.*] —**Yan'kee** *adj.*
Ya·oun·dé (yä-ōōn-dā'). The capital of Cameroon. Pop. 178,000.
yap (yăp) *v.* **yapped, yapping. 1.** To bark sharply or shrilly; yelp. **2.** *Slang.* To talk noisily or stupidly; jabber. —*n.* A sharp, shrill bark; yelp. [Imit.] —**yap'per** *n.*
yard¹ (yärd) *n.* **1.** A measure of length equal to 3 feet or 0.9144 meter. **2.** A long spar slung at right angles to a mast to support a sail. [< OE *gerd, gierd,* staff, measuring rod. See **ghasto-.**]
yard² (yärd) *n.* **1.** A tract of ground adjacent to a building. **2.** An enclosed area used for a specific purpose: *shipyard.* **3.** An area where railroad trains are made up and cars are switched, stored, or serviced. [< OE *geard,* enclosure, residence. See **gher-².**]
yard·age (yär'dĭj) *n.* The amount or length of something measured in yards.
yard·arm (yärd'ärm') *n.* Either end of a yard of a square sail.
yard·stick (yärd'stĭk') *n.* **1.** A measuring stick

one yard in length. **2.** Any standard used in comparison or judgment.
yar·mul·ke (yä'məl-kə) *n.* Also **yar·mel·ke.** A skullcap worn by male Jews. [Yidd.]
yarn (yärn) *n.* **1.** A continuous strand of twisted threads of wool, cotton, etc., used in weaving or knitting. **2.** *Informal.* A long story or tale. [< OE *gearn.* See **gher-¹.**]
yaw (yô) *v.* **1.** To deviate from the intended course, as a ship. **2.** To turn about the vertical axis. —*n.* The action or extent of yawing. [?]
yawl (yôl) *n.* A two-masted fore-and-aft-rigged sailing vessel with a smaller mast aft of the mainmast and tiller. [MLG *jolle.*]
yawn (yôn) *v.* **1.** To open the mouth wide with a deep inspiration, from drowsiness or boredom. **2.** To open wide; gape. —*n.* An act of yawning. [< OE *geonian.* See **ghēi-.**]
yaws (yôz) *pl.n.* An infectious tropical skin disease characterized by multiple red pimples. [Cariban.]
y-ax·is (wī'ăk'sĭs) *n., pl.* **y-axes** (-sēz). The vertical axis of a two-dimensional Cartesian coordinate system.
Yb ytterbium.
Y-chro·mo·some (wī'krō'mə-sōm') *n.* The sex chromosome associated with male characteristics, occurring with one X-chromosome in the male sex-chromosome pair.
y·clept (ĭ-klĕpt') *adj. Archaic.* Known as; named; called. [< OE *cleopian,* to speak, call.]
yd yard (measurement).
ye¹ (thē) *adj. Archaic.* The. [Incorrect transcription of the runic letter thorn as *th.*]
ye² (yē) *pron. Poetic & Archaic.* You (plural). [< OE *gē.* See **yu-.**]
yea (yā) *adv.* Yes; aye. —*n.* **1.** An affirmative vote. **2.** One who votes affirmatively. [< OE *gēa,* yes.]
yeah (yĕ'ə, yă'ə, yā'ə) *adv. Informal.* Yes. [Var of YEA.]
year (yîr) *n.* **1.** The period of time as measured by the Gregorian calendar in which the earth completes a single revolution around the sun, consisting of 365 days, 5 hours, 49 minutes, and 12 seconds of mean solar time divided into 12 months, 52 weeks, and 365 or 366 days. **2.** A period of time, usually shorter than 12 months, devoted to some special activity: *the school year.* **3. years. a.** Age, esp. old age. **b.** A long time. [< OE *gēar.* See **yēro-.**]
year·book (yîr'bŏŏk') *n.* A book published every year, containing information about the previous year.
year·ling (yîr'lĭng) *n.* An animal that is one year old or in its second year.
year·ly (yîr'lē) *adj.* Occurring once a year or every year; annual. —*adv.* Once a year.
yearn (yûrn) *v.* To have a strong or deep desire. [< OE *giernan,* to desire. See **gher-⁵.**]

ă pat/ā ate/âr care/ä bar/b bib/ch chew/d deed/ĕ pet/ē be/f fit/g gag/h hat/hw what/
ĭ pit/ī pie/îr pier/j judge/k kick/l lid, fatal/m mum/n no, sudden/ng sing/ŏ pot/ō go/

yearn•ing (yûr′nĭng) *n.* A deep longing.

yeast (yēst) *n.* **1.** Any of various unicellular fungi capable of fermenting carbohydrates. **2.** Froth produced by and containing yeast cells, formed in the production of alcoholic beverages. **3.** A commercial preparation containing yeast cells, used esp. as a leavening agent. [< OE *gist, gyst.* See **yes-.**]

yell (yĕl) *v.* To cry out loudly, as in pain, fright, surprise, or enthusiasm. *—n.* A loud cry; a shout. [< OE *giellan,* to sound, shout. See **ghel-**¹.]

yel•low (yĕl′ō) *n.* **1.** Any of a group of colors of a hue resembling that of ripe lemons. **2.** The yolk of an egg. *—adj.* **1.** Of the color yellow. **2.** Having yellowish skin. **3.** *Slang.* Cowardly. **4.** Distorting or exaggerating news sensationally: *yellow journalism.* *—v.* To make or become yellow. [< OE *geolu.* See **ghel-**².] **—yel′low•ish** *adj.*

yellow fever. An acute infectious viral disease of subtropical and tropical New World areas, transmitted by a mosquito.

yellow jacket. A small wasp with yellow and black markings.

Yellow Sea. An arm of the Pacific between China and Korea.

yelp (yĕlp) *v.* To utter a sharp, short bark or cry. *—n.* A sharp, short cry or bark. [< OE *gielpan,* to boast, exult. See **ghel-**¹.]

Yem•en (yĕm′ən, yä′mən). **1.** Officially, Yemen Arab Republic. A country of S Arabia, at the S entrance to the Red Sea. Pop. 5,237,900. Cap. Sana. **2.** Or **Southern Yemen.** Officially, People's Democratic Republic of Yemen. A country of S Arabia. Pop. 1,555,000. Cap. Aden.

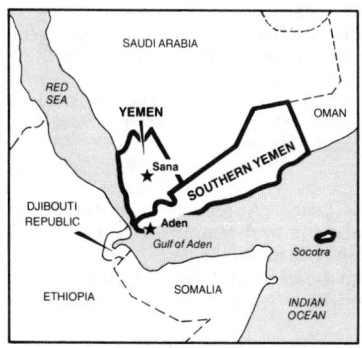

**Yemen
Southern Yemen**

yen¹ (yĕn) *n. Informal.* A yearning; a longing. [Cant *yan.*]

yen² (yĕn) *n., pl.* **yen.** The basic monetary unit of Japan.

yeo•man (yō′mən) *n.* **1.** A member of a former class of lesser freeholder farmers, below the gentry, in England. **2.** A petty officer performing chiefly clerical duties in the U.S. Navy. [Perh < YOUNG + MAN.]

Ye•re•van (yĭ-ryĭ-vän′). The capital of the Armenian S.S.R. Pop. 767,000.

yes (yĕs) *adv.* It is so; as you say or ask. Expressive of affirmation, agreement, or consent. *—n.* An affirmative reply or vote. [< OE *gēa,* YEA + *sīe,* "may it be" (see **es-**).]

yes•ter•day (yĕs′tər-dā′, -dē) *n.* **1.** The day before the present day. **2.** Time recently past. *—adv.* **1.** On the day before the present day. **2.** A short while ago.

yet (yĕt) *adv.* **1.** At this time; now. **2.** Thus far. **3.** In the time remaining; still. **4.** Besides; in addition. **5.** Even; still more: *a yet sadder tale.* **6.** Nevertheless: *young yet wise.* **7.** At some future time; eventually. *—conj.* Nevertheless; and despite this. [< OE *gīet.*]

Usage: Yet, as an adverb of time in the sense *up to the present, thus far,* or in the phrase *as yet,* occurs with a perfect tense rather than with the simple past: *They have not started yet.*

yew (yōō) *n.* **1.** An evergreen tree or shrub with poisonous flat, dark-green needles and scarlet berries. **2.** The hard, fine-grained wood of a yew. [< OE *ēow, īw.*]

Yid•dish (yĭd′ĭsh) *n.* A language derived from High German dialects and Hebrew and some Slavic languages.

yield (yēld) *v.* **1.** To give forth by a natural process; produce. **2.** To furnish or give in return: *an investment that yields 6%.* **3.** To relinquish or concede. **4.** To surrender; submit. **5.** To give way, as to pressure, force, or persuasion. *—n.* **1.** The amount yielded. **2.** The profit obtained from investment; a return. [< OE *gieldan,* to yield, pay.]

-yl. *comb. form. Chem.* A radical: **ethyl.** [< Gk *hulē,* wood, matter.]

yod (yōd, yōōd) *n.* Also **yodh.** The 10th letter of the Hebrew alphabet, representing *y.*

yo•ga (yō′gə) *n.* **1.** A Hindu discipline aimed at training the consciousness for a state of perfect spiritual insight. **2.** A system of exercises practiced as part of this discipline.

yo•gurt (yō′gərt, -gŏŏrt′) *n.* Also **yo•ghurt.** A custardlike food prepared from milk curdled by bacteria. [Turk *yoğurt.*]

yoke (yōk) *n.* **1.** A crossbar with two U-shaped pieces that encircle the necks of a pair of draft animals. **2.** *pl.* **yoke.** A pair of draft animals joined by such a device. **3.** A fitted part of a garment, as at the shoulders, to which another part is attached. **4.** Any form or symbol of subjugation or bondage. *—v.* **yoked, yoking.** **1.** To fit or join with or as with a yoke. **2.** To harness (a draft animal) to something. [< OE *geoc.* See **yeug-.**]

Yo•ko•ha•ma (yō′kə-hä′mə). A city of Japan in C Honshu. Pop. 1,619,000.

yolk (yōk) *n.* The yellow inner mass of nutritive material in the egg of a bird or reptile. [< OE *geolu,* YELLOW.]

Yom Kip•pur (yŏm′ kĭp′ər, yōm′ kĭ-pŏŏr′). The holiest Jewish holiday, observed by fasting and prayer for the atonement of sins.

yon•der (yŏn′dər) *adj.* Being at an indicated distance, usually within sight. *—adv.* Over there. [< OE *geond.*]

yore (yôr, yōr) *n.* Time long past: *days of yore.* [< OE *gēara,* formerly, once.]

you (yōō) *pron.* The 2nd person sing. or pl. in

the nominative or objective case, used to represent the person or persons addressed by the speaker. [< OE *ēow*. See **yu-**.]
you'd (yōōd). Contraction of *you had* or *you would.*
you'll (yōōl). Contraction of *you will* or *you shall.*
young (yŭng) *adj.* **1.** In the early period of life or development; not old. **2.** Vigorous or fresh. —*n.* **1.** Young persons collectively; youth. **2.** Offspring. [< OE *geong*. See **yeu-**.]
young•ster (yŭng'stər) *n.* A young person.
Youngs•town (yŭngz'toun). A city of NE Ohio. Pop. 165,000.
your (yōōr, yôr, yŏr; *unstressed* yər). The possessive form of the pronoun *you,* used attributively. [< OE *ēower*. See **yu-**.]
you're (yōōr; *unstressed* yər). Contraction of *you are.*
yours (yōōrz, yôrz, yŏrz). The possessive form of the pronoun *you,* used as a predicate adjective, a substantive, and in the complimentary closing of letters: *This hat is yours. I like yours better. Yours very truly.* —**of yours.** Belonging to you: *a friend of yours.*
your•self (yōōr-sĕlf', yôr-, yər-) *pron., pl.* **-selves.** A form of the 2nd person pronoun. **1.** Used reflexively: *Did you hurt yourself?* **2.** Used for emphasis: *Do it yourself.* **3.** Used to indicate one's normal or proper state: *You are not yourself today.* —**by yourself. 1.** Alone. **2.** Without help.
youth (yōōth) *n., pl.* **youths** (yōōths, yōōthz). **1.** The condition or quality of being young. **2.** An early period of development or existence. **3. a.** Young people collectively. **b.** A young man. [< OE *geoguth*. See **yeu-**.]
youth•ful (yōōth'fəl) *adj.* **1.** Possessing youth. **2.** Vigorous; active. **3.** Of or belonging to youth. **4.** In an early stage of development; new. —**youth'ful•ness** *n.*
you've (yōōv). Contraction of *you have.*
yowl (youl) *v.* To howl; wail. —*n.* A howl; a wail. [ME *youlen.*]
yr. 1. year. **2.** your.

yt•ter•bi•um (ĭ-tûr'bē-əm) *n. Symbol* **Yb** A soft, bright, silvery rare-earth element used as an x-ray source for portable irradiation devices, in some laser materials, and in some special alloys. Atomic number 70, atomic weight 173.04. [< *Ytterby,* town in Sweden.] —**yt•ter'bic** (ĭ-tûr'bĭk) *adj.*
yt•tri•um (ĭt'rē-əm) *n. Symbol* **Y** A silvery metallic element used to increase the strength of magnesium and aluminum alloys. Atomic number 39, atomic weight 88.905. [< *Ytterby,* town in Sweden.]
yu•an (yü'än') *n.* **1.** The basic monetary unit of China. **2.** The basic monetary unit of Taiwan.
yuc•ca (yŭk'ə) *n.* Any of various tall New World plants with a large cluster of white flowers. [Span *yuca.*]
Yu•go•sla•vi•a (yōō'gō-slä'vĭ-ə). A republic of SE Europe. Pop. 19,279,000. Cap. Belgrade. —**Yu'go•slav'** *n.* —**Yu'go•sla'vi•an** *adj. & n.*

Yugoslavia

Yu•kon River (yōō'kŏn). A river of NW North America.
Yule (yōōl) *n.* Christmas. [< OE *gēol,* originally a twelve-day heathen feast < Gmc **jehwla-.*]
Yule•tide (yōōl'tīd') *n.* The Christmas season.
yum•my (yŭm'ē) *adj.* **-mier, -miest.** *Informal.* Delightful; delicious.

z, Z (zē) *n.* The 26th letter of the English alphabet.
z. 1. zero. **2.** zone.
zaire (zä-îr') *n.* The basic monetary unit of Zaire. [Native word in Zaire.]
Zaire (zä-îr'). Formerly **Democratic Republic of**

the **Congo.** A republic and former Belgian colony in west-central Africa. Pop. 21,638,000. Cap. Kinshasa.
Zam•be•zi (zăm-bē'zē). A river of S Africa.
Zam•bi•a (zăm'bē-ə). A republic in south-

Zaire

Zambia

ă pat/ā ate/âr care/ä bar/b bib/ch chew/d deed/ĕ pet/ē be/f fit/g gag/h hat/hw what/
ĭ pit/ī pie/îr pier/j judge/k kick/l lid, fatal/m mum/n no, sudden/ng sing/ŏ pot/ō go/

central Africa. Pop. 3,733,000. Cap. Lusaka.

za•ny (zā'nē) *n., pl.* **-nies.** A clown; buffoon. —*adj.* **-nier, -niest. 1.** Clownish; droll. **2.** Silly; absurd. [It *zani*, buffoon.]

Za•ra•thus•tra (zär'ə-thōōs'trə, zä'rä-thōōs'-trä). Zoroaster.

za•yin (zä'yĭn) *n.* The 7th letter of the Hebrew alphabet, representing *z*.

zeal (zēl) *n.* Enthusiastic and diligent devotion, as to a cause. [< Gk *zēlos*.]

zeal•ot (zĕl'ət) *n.* One who is fanatically committed, as to a cause.

zeal•ous (zĕl'əs) *adj.* Filled with zeal; enthusiastic; fervent. —**zeal'ous•ly** *adv.*

ze•bra (zē'brə) *n.* A horselike African mammal with conspicuous dark and whitish stripes. [< OSpan. wild ass.]

ze•bu (zē'byōō') *n.* A domesticated Asian or African bovine mammal with a prominent hump and a large dewlap.

zed (zĕd) *n. Chiefly Brit.* The letter *z*.

Zeit•geist (tsīt'gīst') *n.* The spirit and outlook characteristic of a period or generation. [G, "time spirit."]

Zen (zĕn) *n.* A school of Buddhism that asserts that enlightenment can be attained through meditation, self-contemplation, and intuition rather than through the scriptures.

Zend-A•ves•ta (zĕnd'ə-vĕs'tə) *n.* Also **Zend** (zĕnd). The sacred writings of the Zoroastrian religion.

ze•nith (zē'nĭth) *n.* **1.** The point on the celestial sphere that is directly above the observer. **2.** The highest point above the observer's horizon attained by a celestial body. **3.** Any culmination or high point. [< Ar *samt*, road.] —**ze'nith•al** (-nə-thəl) *adj.*

Zeph. Zephaniah (Old Testament).

zeph•yr (zĕf'ər) *n.* **1.** The west wind. **2.** A gentle breeze. **3.** Any of various light, soft fabrics or yarns. [< Gk *zephuros*.]

zep•pe•lin (zĕp'ə-lĭn) *n.* Also **Zep•pe•lin.** A rigid airship having a long, cylindrical body supported by internal gas cells. [< Count Ferdinand von *Zeppelin* (1838–1917), German military leader.]

ze•ro (zîr'ō, zē'rō) *n., pl.* **-ros** or **-roes. 1.** The numerical symbol "0"; a cipher; naught. **2.** *Math.* **a.** An element of a set that when added to any other element in the set produces a sum identical with the element to which it is added. **b.** A cardinal number indicating the absence of any or all units under consideration. **c.** An ordinal number indicating an initial point or origin. **3.** The temperature indicated by the numeral 0 on a thermometer. **4.** A nonentity; nobody. **5.** The lowest point. **6.** Nothing; nil. —*v.* **-roed, -roing.** —**zero in. 1.** To aim or concentrate firepower on an exact target location. **2.** To converge intently; move near; close in. [< Ar *şifr*, zero, CIPHER.]

zero hour. The scheduled time for the start of an operation or action, esp. a concerted military attack.

zero population growth. The limiting of population increase to the number of live births needed to replace the existing population, estimated at 2.11 children per family.

zest (zĕst) *n.* **1.** Piquancy; charm. **2.** Spirited enjoyment; gusto. [Obs F, orange or lemon peel.] —**zest'ful** *adj.*

ze•ta (zā'tə, zē'-) *n.* The 6th letter of the Greek alphabet, representing *z*.

Zeus (zōōs). Supreme god of the Greek pantheon.

zig•zag (zĭg'zăg') *n.* **1.** A line or course that proceeds by sharp turns in alternating directions. **2.** One of a series of such turns. **3.** Something exhibiting one or a series of sharp turns, as a road or design. —*adj.* Having or moving in a zigzag. —*adv.* In a zigzag manner or pattern. —*v.* **-zagged, -zagging.** To form into or move in a zigzag.

zinc (zĭngk) *n. Symbol* **Zn** A bluish-white, lustrous metallic element used to form a wide variety of alloys, including brass, bronze, and various solders, and in galvanizing iron and other metals. Atomic number 30, atomic weight 65.37. [G *Zink*.]

zinc ointment. A salve consisting of about 20% zinc oxide with beeswax or paraffin and petrolatum.

zinc oxide. An amorphous white or yellowish powder, ZnO, used as a pigment and in pharmaceuticals and cosmetics.

zing (zĭng) *n.* A brief high-pitched humming or buzzing sound. [Imit.] —**zing** *v.*

zin•ni•a (zĭn'ē-ə) *n.* A widely cultivated plant with showy, variously colored flowers. [< J. *Zinn* (1727–1759), German botanist.]

Zi•on (zī'ən) *n.* Also **Si•on** (sī'ən). **1. a.** The Jewish people; Israel. **b.** The Jewish homeland as a symbol of Judaism. **2.** A place or religious community regarded as a city of God. **3.** A utopia. [< Heb *Şīyōn*.]

Zi•on•ism (zī'ən-ĭz'əm) *n.* **1.** A plan or movement of the Jewish people to return to Palestine. **2.** A movement for the re-establishment of a Jewish national homeland and state in Palestine. —**Zi'on•ist** *adj. & n.*

zip (zĭp) *n.* **1.** A brief sharp, hissing sound. **2.** Alacrity; vim. —*v.* **zipped, zipping. 1.** To move or act swiftly. **2.** To fasten or unfasten with a zipper. [Imit.]

zip gun. A crude homemade pistol.

zip•per (zĭp'ər) *n.* A fastening device consisting of rows of teeth on adjacent edges of an opening that are interlocked by a sliding tab.

zir•con (zûr'kŏn') *n.* A brown to colorless mineral, essentially ZrSiO₄, that is heated, cut, and polished to form a brilliant blue-white gem. [< Pers *zargūn*, gold-colored.]

zir•co•ni•um (zûr-kō'nē-əm) *n. Symbol* **Zr** A lustrous, grayish-white, strong, ductile metallic element used chiefly in ceramic and refractory compounds, as an alloying agent, and in nuclear reactors. Atomic number 40, atomic weight 91.22. [< ZIRCON.]

zith•er (zĭth'ər) *n.* Also **zith•ern** (-ərn). A musical instrument constructed of a flat sounding box with about 30 to 40 strings stretched over it and played with the finger tips or a plectrum. [< Gk *kithara*, an ancient musical instrument.] —**zith'er•ist** *n.*

zlo•ty (zlô'tē) *n., pl.* **-tys** or **-ty.** The basic monetary unit of Poland.

Zn zinc.

zo•di•ac (zō'dē-ăk') *n.* **1.** A band of the celestial sphere, extending about 8° to either side of the ecliptic, that represents the path of the principal planets, the moon, and the sun. **2.** *Astrol.* This band divided into 12 equal parts called signs each bearing the name of the constellation for which it was named. **3.** A diagram or figure representing the zodiac. [< Gk *zōidiakos (kuklos),* "(circle) of carved figures."] —**zo•di'a•cal** (zō-dī'ə-kəl) *adj.*

-zoic. *comb. form.* A specific geological division: **Mesozoic.** [< Gk *zōion,* animal.]

Zo•la (zō-lä'), **Emile.** 1840–1902. French novelist.

Zom•ba (zŏm'bə). A former interim capital of Malawi. Pop. 20,000.

zom•bie (zŏm'bē) *n.* Also **zom•bi** *pl.* **-bis. 1.** A voodoo snake god. **2. a.** A spell that according to voodoo belief can reanimate a dead body. **b.** A corpse revived in this way. **3.** One who looks or behaves like an automaton.

zo•nal (zō'nəl) *adj.* Also **zo•na•ry** (zō'nər-ē). **1.** Of or associated with a zone or zones. **2.** Divided into zones. —**zo'nal•ly** *adv.*

zone (zōn) *n.* **1.** An area, region, or division distinguished from adjacent parts by some distinctive feature or character. **2.** Any of the five regions of the surface of the earth that are loosely divided according to prevailing climate and latitude, including the Torrid Zone, the N and S Temperate Zones, and the N and S Frigid Zones. **3.** Any section or division of an area or territory. [< Gk *zōnē.*]

zoo (zōō) *n.* Also **zoological garden.** A park or institution in which living animals are kept and exhibited to the public. [Short for zoological garden.]

zoo-. *comb. form.* Animals or animal forms. [< Gk *zōion,* living being, animal.]

zool. zoological; zoology.

zo•o•log•i•cal (zō'ə-lŏj'ĭ-kəl) *adj.* Also **zo•o•log•ic** (-ə-lŏj'ĭk). Of or pertaining to animal life or the science of zoology. —**zo'o•log'i•cal•ly** *adv.*

zo•ol•o•gy (zō-ŏl'ə-jē) *n.* The biological science of animals. —**zo•ol'o•gist** *n.*

zoom (zōōm) *v.* **1.** To move with a buzzing sound. **2.** To climb suddenly and sharply in an airplane. **3.** To move about rapidly; swoop. [Imit.] —**zoom** *n.*

-zoon. *comb. form.* An individual animal or organic unit: **spermatozoon.** [< Gk *zōion, zōon,* living being, animal.]

Zo•ro•as•ter (zôr'ō-ăs'tər). Persian prophet of the 6th century B.C. —**Zo'ro•as'tri•an** *adj. & n.* —**Zo'ro•as'tri•an•ism'** (-trē-ən-īz'əm) *n.*

zounds (zoundz) *interj.* Expressive of anger, surprise, or indignation. [Euphemism for *God's wounds.*]

Zr zirconium.

zuc•chi•ni (zōō-kē'nē) *n., pl.* **-ni.** A narrow, green-skinned variety of squash. [< It *zucca,* gourd.]

Zu•lu (zōō'lōō) *n., pl.* **-lu** or **-lus. 1.** A member of a large Bantu nation of SE Africa. **2.** The Bantu language of this people. —**Zu'lu** *adj.*

Zu•ñi (zōō'n/y/ē, sōō'-) *n., pl.* **-ñi** or **-ñis. 1.** A member of a pueblo-dwelling tribe of North American Indians of W New Mexico. **2.** The language used by this tribe.

Zu•ñi•an (zōōn'yē-ən, sōōn'yē-) *n.* A distinct language family made up of Zuñi alone.

zy•go•mat•ic bone (zī'gə-măt'ĭk). A small quadrangular bone in vertebrates on the side of the face below the eye.

zy•gote (zī'gōt') *n.* **1.** The cell formed by the union of two gametes. **2.** The organism that develops from such a cell. [Gk *zugōtos,* joined, yoked.] —**zy•got'ic** (zī-gŏt'ĭk) *adj.*

ă pat/ā ate/âr̗ care/ä bar/b bib/ch chew/d deed/ĕ pet/ē be/f fit/g gag/h hat/hw what/ ĭ pit/ī pie/îr pier/j judge/k kick/l lid, fatal/m mum/n no, sudden/ng sing/ŏ pot/ō go/

zodiac

APPENDIX OF
INDO-EUROPEAN ROOTS

Some of the etymologies in the main body of the Dictionary make cross-references in bold-face type to entries in this Appendix, which is drawn from the fully explained Appendix in the hard-bound edition of *The American Heritage Dictionary*.

The Appendix selectively represents the prehistoric ancestry of the English language. English, together with most of the languages of Europe and a number of others (see the chart on pages 362–3), is descended from a reconstructed language called *Indo-European*. This language probably belongs to the neolithic period, but the culture in which it was spoken has not been archaeologically identified. The linguistic reconstruction, however, based on 150 years of scholarly work, is firm and intricate.

The fundamental relationship of Indo-European to English is hereditary. Thus, the Indo-European word (or root) for "field" was **agro-;* this, in the Germanic branch of the family (to which English belongs), changed to **akraz*, which in Old English changed to *æcer*, becoming ACRE in Modern English. This word is thus part of the *native* vocabulary, which has been in unbroken use, though with regularly changing phonetic forms, for at least 6,000 years. This Appendix lists a selection of such native words. The histories of the English words that have been borrowed from other Indo-European languages, chiefly from Ger-

manic and Romance and from Latin and Greek, are not traced here

Each boldface entry is an Indo-European root, followed by its meaning. If the meaning is enclosed in quotation marks, it is to be taken as an approximate abstraction rather than a precise meaning. Next, usually, comes a Germanic descendant of the root, then an Old English descendant of the Germanic form. Meanings are given to these only if they differ markedly from that of the root. Following the Old English word is the Modern English form in SMALL CAPITALS. Each of these is a cross-reference to the etymology of the word in the main body of the Dictionary.

Homographic roots are given superscript numbers. When one of these numbers differs from the number given in the hard-bound edition of *The American Heritage Dictionary* (abbreviated AHD), the latter is given in brackets at the end of the entry.

An asterisk is placed before every unattested form (one that is not found in documents but has been reconstructed) except for the entry forms. Technical terms have been used as sparingly as possible in this Appendix. An o-grade form is one in which an *e* has changed to an *o*, and a zero-grade form is one in which an *e* has dropped out or an *ā* or an *ē* has been reduced to *ə* (schwa).

---

abel-. Apple. Gmc **aplu-*, **apal-*, in OE *æppel:* APPLE.

ad-. To, near, at. Gmc **at* in OE *æt:* AT.

agh-¹. To be depressed or afraid. Gmc **ag-* in OE *eglan*, to afflict: AIL.

agh-². A day. Gmc **dagaz* (initial *d-* obscure) in: **a.** OE *dæg:* DAY; **b.** OE *dagian*, to dawn: DAWN.

agro-. Field. Gmc **akraz* in OE *æcer:* ACRE.

agwesī. Ax. Gmc **akwesi* in OE *æx:* AX.

ais-. To wish. Gmc **aiskōn* in OE *āscian*, *ācsian:* ASK.

aiw-. Life, long life, eternity. Gmc **aiwi* in: **a.** OE *ā*, ever: NO¹; **b.** OE *æfre*, ever: EVER.

ak-. Sharp. **1.** Gmc **akjō* in OE *ecg*, sharp side: EDGE. **2.** Gmc **ahuz* in OE *ēar*, *æhher*, ear of grain: EAR².

akwā-. Water. Gmc **ahwjō*, **aujō*, "thing on

the water," in OE *īegland (land*, LAND*):* ISLAND.

al-¹. Beyond. Gmc **aljaz* in OE *elles:* ELSE.

al-². To grow. Gmc **alda-*, "grown," in OE *eald*, old: OLD. [AHD *al-³*.]

alu-. Intoxication. Gmc **aluth-* in OE *ealu*, ale: ALE.

ambhi. Around. Reduced form **bhi* in Gmc **bi* in OE *bī*, *bi*, *be:* BY.

an¹. On. Gmc **ana* in OE *an*, on: ON.

an². Demonstrative particle. Gmc **antharaz* in OE *ōther:* OTHER.

ank-. Also **ang-.** To bend. **1.** Gmc **ank-* in OE *anclēow* (and ON **ankula*): ANKLE. **2.** Gmc **ang-* in OE *angul*, fishhook: ANGLE¹.

anti. Against or in front of; also, an end. **1.** Gmc **andi-* in OE *and-:* UN-². **2.** Gmc **andjō* in OE *ende*, end: END.

apo-. Also **ap-.** Off, away. **1.** Gmc **af* in:

a. OE *of,* off: OF, OFF; **b.** OE *ebba,* low tide: EBB. **2.** Gmc **aftar-* in OE *æfter:* AFTER. **3.** Variant **ĕp-* in Gmc **eben-,* "the after or later time," in OE *æfen,* evening: EVENING.

apsā. Aspen. Gmc **aspōn* in OE *æspe:* ASPEN.

arkw-. Bow and arrow. Gmc **arhwō* in OE *arwe, earh:* ARROW.

as-. To burn. Gmc **askōn-* in OE *æsce:* ASH[1].

aug-. To increase. **1.** Gmc **aukan* in OE *ēacan,* to increase: EKE. **2.** Variant forms **wogs-, *wegs-,* in Gmc **wahsan* in: **a.** OE *weaxan,* to grow: WAX[2]; **b.** OE **wæst,* growth, size: WAIST. [AHD *aug-[1].*]

aukwh-. Also aukw-. Cooking pot. Gmc **uhwna-* in **ufna-* in OE *ofen:* OVEN.

awes-. Also aus-. To shine. **1.** Gmc **aust-* in OE *ēast:* EAST. **2.** Gmc **austrōn-,* dawn goddess worshiped at the vernal equinox, in OE *ēastre:* EASTER.

ayer-. Day, morning. **1.** Gmc **airiz* in OE *ēr,* before: EARLY, ERE. **2.** Gmc **airistaz* in OE *ǣrest,* earliest: ERST.

ayos-. A metal. Variant **ayes-* in Gmc **aiz* in OE *ār,* brass: ORE.

bend-. Protruding point. Gmc **pannja,* "structure of stakes," in OE *penn:* PEN[2].

beu-. Also bheu-. To swell. **1.** Gmc **puk-* in OE *pocc,* pustule: POCK. **2.** Form **bheu-* in: **a.** OE *bōsm:* BOSOM; **b.** OE *bȳle:* BOIL[2]. [AHD *beu-[1].*]

bhā-[1]. To shine. Gmc **baukna-,* beacon, signal, in: **a.** OE *bēacen:* BEACON; **b.** OE *bēcnan:* BECKON.

bhā-[2]. To speak. Gmc **banwan,* "to speak publicly," in OE *bannan,* to summon (and ON *banna,* to prohibit): BAN.

bha-bhā-. Broad bean. Variant **bha-un-* in Gmc **baunō* in OE *bēan:* BEAN.

bhad-. Good. Gmc comparative **batizō* in OE *betera:* BETTER.

bhāghu-. Elbow. Gmc **bōguz* in OE *bōg:* BOUGH.

bhāgo-. Beech tree. **1.** Gmc **bōkō,* "beech staff for carving runes on," in OE *bōc:* BOOK. **2.** Gmc **bōkjo* in OE *bēce:* BEECH.

bhar-. Projection, bristle. **1.** O-grade form **bhor-* in Gmc **barsaz,* "spiny fish," in OE *bærs:* BASS[1]. **2.** Zero-grade form **bhr̥-* in Gmc **bursti-* in OE *byrst:* BRISTLE.

bhardhā. Beard. Gmc **bardaz* in OE *beard:* BEARD.

bhares-. Also bhars-. Barley. Gmc **barz-* in OE *bære:* BARLEY.

bhau-. To strike. Gmc **bautan* in OE *bēatan:* BEAT.

bhē-. To warm. Zero-grade form **bhə-* in: **a.** Gmc **batham* in OE *bæth:* BATH; **b.** Gmc **bakan* in OE *bacan:* BAKE.

bhedh-[1]. To dig. Gmc **badjam,* "garden plot, sleeping place," in OE *bedd:* BED.

bhedh-[2]. To bend. **1.** Gmc **bidjan* in OE *biddan,* to pray: BID. **2.** Gmc **bidam* in OE *gebed,* prayer: BEAD.

bhei-[1]. Bee. Gmc **bīōn-* in OE *bēo:* BEE.

bhei-[2]. To strike. Gmc **bhi-li-* in OE *bile,* bird's beak: BILL[2].

bheid-. To split. **1.** Gmc **bitiz* in OE *bite, a* bite: BIT[2]. **2.** Gmc **bītō* in OE *bita,* piece bitten off: BIT[1]. **3.** Gmc **bītan,* to bite, in: **a.** OE *bītan:* BITE; **b.** OE *biter,* "biting": BITTER. **4.** Gmc **bait-,* boat (< "split planking"),

in OE *bāt* (and ON *bātr*): BOAT.

bheidh-. To persuade, compel. **1.** Gmc **bīdan,* "to trust, to await trustingly, to stay," in OE *bīdan:* BIDE. **2.** Gmc **baidjan* in OE *bǣdan,* to compel: BAD.

bhel-[1]. To shine, flash; shining white; fire. **1.** Gmc **blaikjan* in OE *blǣcan:* BLEACH. **2.** Gmc **blas-* in OE *blǣse,* torch: BLAZE[1]. **3.** Gmc **blend-,* "dazzle, blind," in OE *blind:* BLIND. **4.** Gmc **blisk-* in OE *blyscan:* BLUSH. **5.** Variant **bhleg-* in Gmc **blakaz,* "burned," in OE *blæc:* BLACK.

bhel-[2]. To blow, swell; a round object. Zero-grade form **bhl̥-* in Gmc **bul-* in OE *bolla:* BOWL[1].

bhel-[3]. To thrive, bloom. Extended form **bhlē-.* **1.** O-grade form **bhlō-* in Gmc **blō-s-* in OE *blōstma:* BLOSSOM. **2.** Zero-grade form **bhlə-* in Gmc **bladaz* in OE *blæd,* leaf: BLADE.

bhel-[4]. To yell. Gmc **bell-* in: **a.** OE *belle:* BELL; **b.** OE **belgan:* BELLOW.

bheld-. To strike. Zero-grade form **bhld-* in Gmc **bult-* in OE *bolt,* heavy arrow: BOLT[1].

bhelgh-. To swell. **1.** Gmc **balgiz* in OE *belig,* bellows: BELLY. **2.** Gmc **bolgstraz* in OE *bolster:* BOLSTER.

bhen-. To strike. Gmc **banōn* in OE *bana:* BANE.

bhendh-. To bind. **1.** Gmc **bindan* in OE *bindan:* BIND. **2.** O-grade form **bhondh-* in Gmc **band-* in OE *bendan:* BEND. **3.** Celtic **benna* in OE *binne,* basket: BIN.

bher-[1]. To carry. **1.** Gmc **beran* in OE *beran:* BEAR[1]. **2.** Gmc **bērō* in OE *bēr:* BIER. **3.** Gmc **barwōn* in OE *bearwe,* basket: BARROW. **4.** Gmc **bur-* in OE *byrthen:* BURDEN. **5.** Compound root **bhrenk-* in Gmc **brengan* in OE *bringan:* BRING.

bher-[2]. To bore. Gmc **borōn* in OE *borian:* BORE[1].

bher-[3]. Brown. **1.** Variant **bhrū-* in Gmc **brūnaz* in OE *brūn:* BROWN. **2.** Redupl form **bhibhru-* in OE *beofor:* BEAVER. **3.** Gmc **berō* in OE *bera:* BEAR[2].

bherdh-. To cut. Zero-grade form **bhrdh-* in Gmc **burd-* in OE *bord:* BOARD.

bhereg-. To shine; white. **1.** Gmc **berhtaz* in OE *beorht:* BRIGHT. **2.** Gmc **berkjōn,* "the white tree," in OE *birce:* BIRCH.

bherək-. To shine, glitter, hence to move jerkily. Variant **bhrek-.* **1.** Gmc **bregdan* in OE *bregdan:* BRAID. **2.** Gmc **brigdil-* in OE *brīdel:* BRIDLE.

bherg-. To growl. Gmc **berk-* in OE *beorcan:* BARK[1].

bhergh-[1]. To hide, protect. **1.** Zero-grade form **bhrgh-* in: **a.** Gmc **burgjan* in OE *byrgan:* BURY; **b.** Gmc **burgisli-* in OE *byrgels* (pl): BURIAL. **2.** Gmc **borgēn* in OE *borgian:* BORROW.

bhergh-[2]. High; hill. Zero-grade form **bhrgh-* in Gmc **burgs,* hill-fort, in OE *burg:* BOROUGH, BURG.

bheu-. To be, exist, dwell. **1.** Extended form **bhwī-* in Gmc **biju* in OE *bēon:* BE. **2.** Zero-grade form **bhu-* in Gmc **buthla,* dwelling, in OE *bold:* BUILD. **3.** Lengthened form **bhū-* in Gmc **būram* in OE *būr,* a dwelling, and *gebūr,* dweller: BOWER; NEIGHBOR.

bheudh-. To be or make aware. **1.** Gmc **bi-*

udan, to proclaim, in OE *bēodan:* BID. **2.** Gmc **budōn-* in OE *boda,* messenger: BODE[1]. **3.** Gmc **budilaz,* herald, in OE *bydel:* BEADLE.

bheug-. To swell; curved objects. **1.** Gmc **bugōn-* in OE *boga:* BOW[3]. **2.** Gmc **būgan* in OE *būgan,* to bend: BOW[2], BUXOM. [AHD *bheug-3.*]

bhlē-1. To howl. Gmc **blē-t-* in OE *blǣtan:* BLEAT.

bhlē-2. To blow, swell. Gmc **blē-.* **1.** OE *blāwan:* BLOW[1]. **2.** OE *blǣdre:* BLADDER. **3.** OE *blǣst:* BLAST.

bhoso-. Naked. Gmc **bazaz* in OE *bær:* BARE.

bhrāter-. Brother. Gmc **brōthar-* in OE *brōthor:* BROTHER.

bhreg-. To break. Gmc **brekan* in OE *brecan:* BREAK.

bhrem-. To project. Gmc **brema* in: **a.** OE *brōm:* BROOM; **b.** OE *brǣmbel:* BRAMBLE. [AHD *bhrem-2.*]

bhres-. To burst. Gmc **brest-* in OE *berstan:* BURST.

bhreu-1. To break up. **1.** Gmc **briutan* in OE **brytel:* BRITTLE. **2.** Gmc **briuthan* in OE *brēothan,* to deteriorate: BROTHEL.

bhreu-2. To boil, burn; also to brew, cook. **1.** Gmc **breuwan* in OE *brēowan:* BREW. **2.** Gmc **braudam* in OE *brēad:* BREAD. **3.** Gmc **brudam* in OE *broth:* BROTH. **4.** Variant **bhrē-* in: **a.** Gmc **brōd-,* "a warming, hatching, rearing of young," in OE *brōd:* BROOD; **b.** Gmc **brōdjan,* "to rear," in OE *brēdan:* BREED; **c.** Gmc **brēthaz,* "warm air," in OE *brǣth:* BREATH. **5.** Gmc **brenw-* in OE *beornan, byrnan,* and *bærnan:* BURN. **6.** Gmc **brandaz* in OE *brand,* piece of burning wood: BRAND.

bhreus-1. To swell. Gmc **briustam* in OE *brēost:* BREAST.

bhreus-2. To break. Gmc **brūsjan* in OE *brȳsan:* BRUISE.

bhrū-. Eyebrow. Gmc **brūs* in OE *brū:* BROW.

bhudh-. Bottom. OE *botm:* BOTTOM.

bhugo-. Male animal. Gmc **bukkaz* in OE *buc, bucca:* BUCK[1].

dā-. To divide. Variant **dī-.* **1.** Gmc **tīdiz,* "division of time," in: **a.** OE **tīd:* TIDE; **b.** OE *tīdan,* to happen: BETIDE. **2.** Gmc **tīmo* in OE *tīma:* TIME.

dail-. To divide. **1.** Gmc **dailiz* in OE *dǣlan:* DEAL[1]. **2.** Gmc **dailaz* in OE *dāl,* share: DOLE.

dakru-. A tear. Gmc **tahr-* in OE *tēar:* TEAR[2].

de-. Demonstrative stem. Gmc **tō* in OE *tō:* TO.

deigh-. Insect. Gmc **tik-* in OE *ticia:* TICK[2].

deik-. To show. Variant *deig-.* **1.** Gmc **taikjan* in OE *tǣcan:* TEACH. **2.** Gmc **taiknam* in OE *tācen:* TOKEN.

dek-. "Fringe, tail." Gmc **taglaz* in OE *tægel:* TAIL. [AHD *dek-2.*]

dekm. Ten. Gmc **tehun* in OE *tīen:* TEN.

del-1. Long. Prob form **dlon-gho-* in Gmc **langaz* in: **a.** OE *long:* LONG[1]; **b.** OE *langian,* "to grow longer, yearn": LONG[2].

del-2. To recount. **1.** Gmc **taljan* in OE *tellan:* TELL. **2.** Gmc **talō* in OE *talu:* TALE. **3.** OE *talian:* TALK.

demə-1. To build. Gmc **timram,* building material, in OE *timber:* TIMBER.

demə-2. To constrain, break in (horses), tame. O-grade form **dom-* in Gmc **tamaz* in OE

tam: TAME.

denk-. To bite. **1.** Gmc **tanhuz,* tenacious, in OE *tōh:* TOUGH. **2.** Gmc **tanguz* in OE *tange:* TONGS.

dent-. Tooth. O-grade form **dont-* in Gmc **tanthuz* in OE *tōth:* TOOTH.

der-1. To run, walk, step. **1.** Gmc **tred-* in OE *tredan:* TREAD. **2.** Gmc **trep-,* "something into which one steps, snare," in OE *træppe:* TRAP.

der-2. To split. Gmc **teran* in OE *teran:* TEAR[1].

deru-. To be firm, solid; also "wood, tree." **1.** Variant **drew-* in: **a.** Gmc **trewam* in OE *trēow:* TREE; **b.** Gmc **triuwō* in OE *trēow,* faith: TRUCE. **2.** Variant **dreu-* in Gmc **triuwaz* in OE *trēowe:* TRUE. **3.** Variant **drou-* in Gmc **traujam* in OE *trig,* wooden board: TRAY. **4.** Form **dru-ko-* in Gmc **trugaz* in OE *trog:* TROUGH. **5.** Variant **derw-* in Gmc **terw-,* resin, pitch, in OE *teru:* TAR[1].

deuk-. To lead. **1.** Gmc **tiuhan* in OE *tēon:* TUG. **2.** Zero-grade form **duk-* in Gmc **tugōn* in OE *togian:* TOW[1], TAUT. **3.** O-grade form **douk-* in: **a.** OE *tigan:* TIE; **b.** Gmc **tauhmjan,* to beget, in OE *tīeman:* TEEM; **c.** Gmc **tauhmaz,* descendant, family, in OE *tēam:* TEAM.

dhē-. To set, put. **1.** O-grade form **dhō-* in: **a.** Gmc **dōn* in OE *dōn:* DO; **b.** Gmc **dōmaz* in OE *dōm:* DOOM; **c.** Gmc **domjan* in OE *dēman:* DEEM. **2.** Gmc **dēdiz* in OE *dǣd:* DEED. [AHD *dhē-1.*]

dheigh-. To knead. **1.** Gmc **daigjōn* in OE *dǣge,* bread kneader: DAIRY. **2.** Gmc **-dīg-* in OE *hlǣfdige,* "bread kneader, mistress of a household" (*hlǣf,* LOAF): LADY. **3.** O-grade form **dhoigh-* in Gmc **daigaz* in OE *dāg:* DOUGH.

dhel-. A hollow. **1.** Gmc **daljō* in OE *dell:* DELL. **2.** Gmc **dalam* in OE *dæl:* DALE.

dhelbh-. To dig. Gmc **delban* in OE *delfan:* DELVE.

dher-1. To make muddy; darkness. **1.** Gmc **derk-* in OE *deorc:* DARK. **2.** Zero-grade form **dhr̥-* in: **a.** Gmc **drah-sta-* in OE *drōs:* DROSS; **b.** Gmc **drab-* in OE *dreflian:* DRIVEL.

dher-2. To drone, buzz. Gmc **drēn-,* male honeybee, in OE *drān:* DRONE[1]. [AHD *dher-3.*]

dhers-. To be bold. Gmc **ders-* and **durs-* in OE *durran:* DARE.

dheu-1. "To rise in a cloud as dust"; hence also dark colors, breath, confused perceptions, etc. **1.** Extended form **dheus-* possibly in: **a.** Gmc **dus-* in OE *dysig:* DIZZY; **b.** Gmc **diuzam,* "breathing animal," in OE *dēor:* DEER. **2.** Extended form **dhwens-* in Gmc **duns-* in OE *dūst:* DUST. **3.** Extended form **dhus-* in Gmc **duskaz* in OE *dox:* DUSK. **4.** Extended form **dhoubh-* in: **a.** Gmc **daubaz* in OE *dēaf:* DEAF; **b.** Gmc **dūbōn,* "dark-colored bird," in OE *dūfe:* DOVE[1]. **5.** Zero-grade form **dhu-* in Gmc **dumbaz* in OE *dumb:* DUMB. **6.** Extended form **dhwel-* in Gmc **dwelan* in OE *dwellan,* to deceive: DWELL.

dheu-2. To flow. Gmc **dauwaz* in OE *dēaw:* DEW.

dheu-3. To die. **1.** O-grade form **dhou-* in Gmc **daudaz* in OE *dēad:* DEAD. **2.** Extended zero-grade form **dhwī-* in Gmc **dwīnan* in OE *dwīnan:* DWINDLE.

dheub-. Deep. **1.** Gmc **diupaz* in OE *dēop:*

DEEP. 2. Gmc *duppjan* in OE *dyppan:* DIP. 3. Gmc *dubjan* in OE *dȳfan* and *dufan:* DIVE.

dheubh-. Wedge. Gmc *dub-* in OE *dubbian:* DUB¹.

dhīgw-. To fix. Gmc *dīk-* in OE *dīc:* DIKE, DITCH.

dhragh-. To drag. Gmc *dragan* in: **a.** OE *dragan* (and ON *draga*): DRAG, DRAW; **b.** OE *dræge:* DRAY.

dhreg-. To draw. Variant of **dhragh-.** 1. Gmc *drinkan* in OE *drincan:* DRINK. 2. Gmc *drankjan* in OE *drencan:* DRENCH.

dhreibh-. To drive. Gmc *drīban* in OE *drīfan:* DRIVE.

dhreu-. To fall, drip. 1. Extended form *dhreus-* in Gmc *driusan* in OE *drēosan:* DRIZZLE. 2. O-grade form *dhrous-* in: **a.** Gmc *drauzaz* in OE *drēor:* DREARY; **b.** Gmc *drusjan* in OE *drūsian:* DROWSE. 3. Extended zero-grade form *dhrub-* in Gmc *drupan* in OE *dropa:* DROP.

dhreugh-. To deceive. Gmc *draugma-* in OE *drēam:* DREAM.

dhughəter. Daughter. Gmc *dohtēr* in OE *dohtor:* DAUGHTER.

dhwen-. To make noise. Gmc *duniz* in OE *dyne:* DIN.

dhwer-. Door. Zero-grade form *dhur-* in Gmc *durunz* and *duram* in OE *dor:* DOOR.

dn̥ghū. Tongue. Gmc *tungōn* in OE *tunge:* TONGUE.

dwō. Two. 1. Gmc *twai*, two, in: **a.** OE *twā, tu:* TWO; **b.** OE *twēgen:* TWAIN; **c.** Gmc *twalif-*, "two left (over from ten)," in OE *twelf:* TWELVE. 2. Forms *dwis* and *dwi-* in: **a.** Gmc *twiyes* in OE *twige:* TWICE; **b.** Gmc *twēgentig*, "twice ten," in OE *twēntig:* TWENTY; **c.** Gmc *twīhna*, "double thread," in OE *twīn:* TWINE; **d.** Gmc *twisnaz* in OE *getwinn:* TWIN; **e.** Gmc *twiga*, fork, in OE *twigge:* TWIG.

ed-. To eat. Gmc *itan* in OE *etan:* EAT.

eg. I. Gmc *eg* in OE *ic:* I.

eik-. To possess. 1. Gmc *aigan* in OE *āgan:* OUGHT¹, OWE. 2. Gmc *aiganaz* in OE *āgen:* OWN.

eis-. Ice. Gmc *īs-* in OE *īs:* ICE. [AHD *eis-².*]

el-¹. Elbow. O-grade form *ol-* in Gmc *alinobogōn-* in OE *elnboga:* ELBOW.

el-². Red, brown. 1. Gmc *elmo-* in OE *elm:* ELM. 2. Gmc *aliza* in OE *aler:* ALDER.

en. In. Gmc *in* in OE *in, inn:* IN, INN.

er-¹. To set in motion. 1. O-grade form *or-* in Gmc *arnja-* in OE *eornost:* EARNEST¹. 2. Variant root *rei-*, to flow, in zero-grade form *ri-* in Gmc *rinwan* in OE *rinnan:* RUN.

er-². Earth. Gmc *erthō* in OE *eorthe:* EARTH. [AHD *er-³.*]

erə-. To row. Form *rē-* in: **a.** Gmc *rō-* in OE *rōwan:* ROW²; **b.** Gmc *rōthra* in OE *rōther:* RUDDER. [AHD *erə-¹.*]

es-. To be. 1. Gmc *izmi* in OE *eam:* AM. 2. Stem *sī-* in Gmc *sijai-* in OE *sie:* YES. 3. Form *sont-* in: **a.** Gmc *santhaz* in OE *sōth:* SOOTH; **b.** Zero-grade form *sn̥t-* in Gmc *sunjō*, sin (< a formula of repentance, "it is true, the sin is real") in OE *synn:* SIN¹.

esen-. Harvest. O-grade form *osn-* in Gmc *aznōn*, to do harvest work, serve as a laborer, in OE *earnian:* EARN.

eu-. Lacking. Extended form *wə-* in Gmc *wanēn* in OE *wanian:* WANE. [AHD *eu-².*]

eudh-. Udder. Zero-grade form *ūdh-* in Gmc *ūthr-* in OE *ūder:* UDDER.

gal-¹. Bald. Gmc *kalwaz* in OE *calu*, bald: CALLOW.

gal-². To call, shout. Gmc *klat-* in OE *clatrian:* CLATTER.

gel-¹. To form into a ball. Gmc *klūd-* in OE *clott*, lump: CLOT.

gel-². Bright. Extended form *glei-* in Gmc *klai-* in OE *clǣne:* CLEAN.

gel-³. Cold. 1. Gmc *kaliz* in OE *ciele:* CHILL. 2. Gmc *kaldaz* in OE *ceald:* COLD. 3. Gmc *kōl-* in OE *cōl:* COOL.

gembh-. Tooth. O-grade form *gombh-* in Gmc *kambaz* in OE *comb, camb:* COMB.

genə-. To give birth. Zero-grade form *gn̥-*. 1. Gmc *kunjam* in OE *cynn:* KIN. 2. Gmc *kuningaz*, "son of the royal kin," in OE *cyning:* KING. 3. Gmc *kundjaz* in OE *cynd, gecynd*, birth, nature: KIND². 4. Gmc *kundiz* in OE *gecynde*, natural: KIND¹.

genu-¹. Knee. Variant *gneu-* in: **a.** Gmc *kniwam* in OE *cnēo:* KNEE; **b.** Gmc *kniwljan* in OE *cnēowlian:* KNEEL.

genu-². Chin. Form *genw-* in Gmc *kinnuz* in OE *cinn:* CHIN.

geph-. Jaw. Gmc *kabal-* in OE *ceafl:* JOWL¹.

ger-¹. To gather. Extended form *grem-* in Gmc *kram-* in OE *crammian:* CRAM.

ger-². To cry hoarsely. 1. Gmc *krē-* in: **a.** OE *crāwe:* CROW¹; **b.** OE *crāwan:* CROW²; **c.** OE *cracian:* CRACK. 2. Gmc *kranu-* in OE *cran:* CRANE. [AHD *ger-⁴.*]

gerebh-. To scratch. Variant *grebh-* in: **a.** Gmc *krabb-* in OE *crabba:* CRAB¹; **b.** Gmc *kerban* in OE *ceorfan:* CARVE.

geulo-. A glowing coal. Gmc *kolam* in OE *col:* COAL.

geus-. To choose. Gmc *kiusan* in OE *cēosan:* CHOOSE.

ghabh-. Also **ghebh-.** To give. Gmc *giban* in OE *giefan:* GIVE.

ghaido-. Goat. Gmc *gaitaz* in OE *gāt:* GOAT.

ghalgh-. Branch, rod. Gmc *galgōn* in OE *gealga:* GALLOWS.

ghans-. Goose. 1. Gmc *gans-* in OE *gōs:* GOOSE. 2. Gmc *ganr-* in OE *gandra:* GANDER. 3. Gmc *ganōtōn* in OE *ganot:* GANNET.

ghasto-. Rod. Gmc *gazdaz* in OE *gierd:* YARD¹.

ghē-. To let go. Gmc *gēn* in OE *gān:* GO.

ghedh-. To unite, join, fit. 1. Form *ghōdh-* in Gmc *gōdaz*, "fitting, suitable," in OE *gōd:* GOOD. 2. Gmc *gadurī* in OE *tōgædere:* TOGETHER. 3. Gmc *gadurōn* in OE *gaderian:* GATHER.

ghēi-. To yawn. Form *ghi-n-ā-* in Gmc *ginōn* in OE *geonian:* YAWN.

gheis-. Fear, amazement. O-grade form *ghois-* in Gmc *gaistaz* in OE *gāst:* GHOST.

ghel-¹. To call. 1. Gmc *gel-* in: **a.** OE *giellan:* YELL; **b.** OE *gielpan:* YELP.

ghel-². To shine. 1. Gmc *gelwaz* in OE *geolu:* YELLOW. 2. Zero-grade form *ghl̥-* in Gmc *gultham* in OE *gold:* GOLD.

ghend-. Also **ghed-.** To seize. Gmc *getan* in: **a.** OE *begietan:* BEGET; **b.** OE *forgietan:* FORGET.

ghengh-. To go. Gmc *gang-* in OE *gang:* GANG.

gher-¹. Gut, entrail. Gmc *garnō*, string, in OE

gearn: YARN.

gher-². To enclose. **1.** Zero-grade form *ghr̥- in Gmc *gurdjan in: **a.** OE *gyrdan: GIRD; **b.** OE gyrdel: GIRDLE. **2.** O-grade form *ghor- in Gmc *gardaz, "enclosure," in OE geard: YARD².

gher-³. To call out. Form *ghrēd- in Gmc *grōtjan in OE grētan: GREET.

gher-⁴. Gray. Gmc *grēwaz in OE grǣg: GRAY.

gher-⁵. To want. Gmc *gernjan in OE giernan: YEARN. [AHD gher-⁶.]

ghēu-. To yawn. Gmc *gō-ma- in OE gōma: GUM².

gheu(ə)-. To invoke (as a god). Zero-grade form *ghu- in: **a.** Gmc *gudam in OE god: GOD; **b.** Gmc *gud-igaz, "possessed by a god," in OE gydig: GIDDY.

ghrē-. To grow, become green. **1.** O-grade form *ghrō- in: **a.** Gmc *grōwan in OE grōwan: GROW; **b.** Gmc *grōnjaz in OE grēne: GREEN. **2.** Zero-grade form *ghrə- in Gmc *grasam in OE græs: GRASS.

ghrebh-. To dig, bury. **1.** O-grade form *ghrobh- in: **a.** Gmc *graban in OE grafan: GRAVE³; **b.** Gmc *graba in OE græf: GRAVE¹. **2.** Gmc *grubjan in OE *grybban: GRUB. [AHD ghrebh-².]

ghrelb-. To grip. **1.** Gmc *grip- in OE gripe and gripa: GRIP¹. **2.** Gmc *grīpan in OE grīpan: GRIPE. **3.** O-grade form *ghroib- in Gmc *graipjan in OE grāpian: GROPE.

ghrem-. Angry. Gmc *grimmaz in OE grim: GRIM.

ghren-. Also **gwhren-.** To grind. **1.** Gmc *grindan in OE grindan: GRIND. **2.** Gmc *grinst- in OE grist: GRIST.

ghrēu-. To grind. **1.** Gmc *griut- in OE grēot: GRIT. **2.** Gmc *grautaz, "coarsely ground," in OE grēat: GREAT.

gleubh-. To split. **1.** Gmc *kliuban in OE clēofan: CLEAVE¹. **2.** Gmc *klub- in OE clufu: CLOVE².

gnō-. To know. **1.** Extended form *gnōw- in Gmc *knōw- in OE gecnāwan: KNOW. **2.** Zero-grade form *gnə- in: **a.** Gmc *kunnan in OE cunnan: CAN¹, CON², CUNNING; **b.** Gmc *kunth- in OE cūth: UNCOUTH.

gras-. To devour. Gmc *krasjōn in OE cresse: CRESS.

greut-. To compress. Gmc *krūdan in OE crūdan: CROWD.

grə-no-. Grain. Gmc *kornam in OE corn: CORN¹.

gwā-. To come. **1.** Gmc *kuman in OE cuman: COME. **2.** Gmc *kuma- in OE wilcuma: WEL-COME.

gwei-. To live. Zero-grade form *gwi- in Gmc *kwikwaz in OE cwic, living: QUICK.

gwel-¹. To swallow. Gmc *kel- in OE ceolu: JOWL². [AHD gwel-⁵.]

gwel-². To pierce. **1.** O-grade form *gwol- in Gmc *kwaljan in OE cwellan: QUELL. **2.** Zero-grade form *gwl̥- in Gmc *kuljan in OE *cyllan: KILL.

gwen-. Woman. Lengthened form *gwēn- in Gmc *kwēniz in OE cwēn: QUEEN.

gwet-. To speak. Gmc *kwithan in OE cwethan: BEQUEATH, QUOTH. [AHD gwet-².]

gwou-. Cow. Form *gwōu-s in Gmc kōuz in OE cū: COW¹.

gyeu-. To chew. Gmc *kewwan in OE cēowan: CHEW.

gzhyes. Yesterday. Gmc *ges-ter- in OE geostran: YESTER-.

kā-. To like, desire. Gmc *hōraz in OE hōre: WHORE.

kād-. Hatred. Zero-grade form *kəd- in Gmc *hatōn in OE hatian: HATE.

kadh-. To cover. **1.** Gmc *hattuz in OE hætt: HAT. **2.** Form *kōdh- in: **a.** Gmc *hōda in OE hōd: HOOD¹; **b.** Gmc *hōdjan in OE hēdan: HEED.

kagh-. To catch; fence. Gmc *hagjō in OE hecg: HEDGE.

kaghlo-. Hail. Gmc *haglaz in OE hagol: HAIL¹.

kai-. Heat. **1.** Gmc *haitaz in OE hāt: HOT. **2.** Gmc *haiti- in OE hǣtu: HEAT.

kailo-. Whole, uninjured. **1.** Gmc *hailaz in OE hāl: HALE¹, WHOLE. **2.** Gmc *hailithō in OE hǣlth: HEALTH. **3.** Gmc *hailjan in OE hǣlan: HEAL. **4.** Gmc *hailagaz in OE hālig: HOLY. **5.** Gmc *hailagōn in OE hālgian: HALLOW.

kaito-. Forest. **1.** Gmc *haithiz in OE hǣth: HEATH. **2.** Gmc *haithinaz in OE hǣthen: HEATHEN.

kan-. To sing. Gmc *hannī in OE hen: HEN.

kap-. To grasp. **1.** Gmc *habēn in OE habban: HAVE. **2.** Gmc *habukaz in OE heafoc: HAWK¹. **3.** Gmc *hafigaz, "having weight," in OE hefig: HEAVY. **4.** Gmc *hafjan in OE hebban: HEAVE.

kapho-. Hoof. Form *kāp-o- in Gmc *hōfaz in OE hōf: HOOF.

kaput. Head. Gmc *haubidam in OE hēafod: HEAD.

kar-. Hard. O-grade form *kor- in Gmc *harduz in OE hard: HARD. [AHD kar-¹.]

kas-. Gray. Gmc *hasōn- in OE hara: HARE.

kau-. To hew. **1.** Gmc *hawwan in OE hēawan: HEW. **2.** Gmc *haujam in OE hīeg: HAY. [AHD kau-².]

keg-. Hook. Gmc *hōka- in OE hōc: HOOK.

kē-. To sharpen. O-grade form *kō- in Gmc *hainō in OE hān, stone: HONE.

kei-¹. To lie; home. O-grade form *koi- in Gmc *haima in OE hām: HOME.

kei-². Color adjective. **1.** O-grade form *koi- in Gmc *hairaz in OE hār: HOARFROST. **2.** Zero-grade form *ki- in Gmc *hiwan in OE hēo: HUE¹.

kel-¹. Warm. Form *klē- in Gmc *hlēwaz in OE hlēo: LEE.

kel-². To strike. Extended o-grade form *kold- in Gmc *haltōn in OE healtian: HALT².

kel-³. To shout. Form *klā- in Gmc *hlō- in OE hlōwan: LOW².

kel-⁴. To cover. **1.** Gmc *haljō, "concealed place," in OE hell: HELL. **2.** Gmc *hallō in OE heall: HALL. **3.** Zero-grade form *kl̥- in Gmc *hul- in: **a.** OE hulu: HULL; **b.** OE hol: HOLE; **c.** OE holh: HOLLOW.

kel-⁵. To prick. Gmc *hulin in OE holen: HOLLY. [AHD kel-⁹.]

kel-⁶. Hill. Zero-grade form *kl̥- in Gmc *hul-ni- in OE hyll: HILL. [AHD kel-⁸.]

kelb-. To help. Gmc *helpan in OE helpan: HELP.

kelp-. To hold. O-grade form *kolp- in: **a.** Gmc *halb- in OE helma: HELM; **b.** Gmc *half- in OE hælftre: HALTER.

kem-¹. Hornless. Gmc *hinthjō in OE hind: HIND².

kem-². To compress. Gmc *hamjan in OE *hemm,* a doubling over: HEM¹.

kenəko-. Yellow. Gmc *hunagam in OE *hunig:* HONEY.

kenk-¹. Heel. 1. Gmc *hanha in OE *hōh:* HOCK¹. 2. Gmc *hanhila in OE *hēla:* HEEL¹. [AHD *kenk-³.*]

kenk-². To be hungry. Zero-grade form *kn̥k- in Gmc *hungruz in OE *hungor:* HUNGER.

ker-¹. Horn, head. 1. Zero-grade form *kr̥- in: a. Gmc *hurnaz in OE *horn:* HORN; b. Gmc *hurznuta in OE *hyrnet:* HORNET. 2. Extended form *keru- in Gmc *herutaz in OE *heorot:* HART.

ker-². "Loud noise, bird's cry." Zero-grade form *kr̥-. 1. Gmc *hring- in OE *hringan:* RING². 2. Gmc *hraik- in OE *hrǣcan:* RETCH. 3. Gmc *hraban in OE *hræfn:* RAVEN.

ker-³. Heat, fire. Gmc *herthō in OE *heorth:* HEARTH. [AHD *ker-⁴.*]

kerd-. Heart. Gmc *hertōn- in OE *heorte:* HEART. [AHD *kerd-¹.*]

kerdh-. Herd. Gmc *herdō in OE *heord:* HERD.

kerp-. To harvest. Variant *karp- in Gmc *harbistaz in OE *hærfest:* HARVEST.

kert-. To entwine. Zero-grade form *kr̥t- in Gmc *hurdiz,* wicker frame, hurdle, in OE *hyrdel:* HURDLE.

keu-. To observe, see, hear. O-grade form *kou-. 1. Extended form *kous- in Gmc *hausjan in: a. OE *hieran:* HEAR; b. OE *heorcian:* HARK, HEARKEN. 2. Variant *skou- in: a. Gmc *skauwon, to look at, in OE *scēawian:* SHOW; b. Gmc *skauniz, bright, in OE *scīene:* SHEEN. [AHD *keu-¹.*]

kēwero-. North (wind). Gmc *skūra-, wind, storm, in OE *scūr:* SHOWER.

klēg-. To sound, cry out. Variant *klak- in Gmc *hlahjan in OE *hliehhan:* LAUGH.

klei-. To lean. 1. Zero-grade form *kli- in: a. Gmc *hlid-, "that which bends over," in OE *hlid:* LID; b. Gmc *hlinēn in OE *hleonian:* LEAN¹. 2. O-grade form *kloi- in Gmc *hlaidr- in OE *hlǣdder:* LADDER.

kleng-. To bend. 1. Gmc *hlink- in OE *hlinc:* LINKS. 2. Gmc *hlank- in OE *hlanc:* LANK.

kleu-. To hear. Zero-grade form *klu-. 1. Gmc *hlusinōn in OE *hlysnan:* LISTEN. 2. Lengthened form *klū- in Gmc *hlūdaz in OE *hlūd:* LOUD. [AHD *kleu-¹.*]

ko-. "This." Variant *ki- in Gmc *hi- in: a. OE *he:* HE¹; b. OE *him:* HIM; c. OE *his:* HIS; d. OE *hire:* HER; e. OE *hit:* IT; f. OE *hēr:* HERE; g. OE *heonane:* HENCE; h. OE *hider:* HITHER.

konk-. To hang. Gmc *hanhan in OE *hangian* and *hon* (and ON *hanga):* HANG.

kormo-. Pain. Gmc *harmaz in OE *hearm:* HARM.

koselo-. Hazel. Gmc *haselaz in OE *hæsel:* HAZEL.

krapo-. Roof. Gmc *hrōfam in OE *hrōf:* ROOF.

krep-. Body. Gmc *hrifiz in OE *hrif:* MIDRIFF.

kreu-¹. Raw flesh. Form *krēw- in Gmc *hrēawaz in OE *hrēaw:* RAW.

kreu-². To strike. Gmc *hrewwan in OE *hrēowan:* RUE¹.

kreut-. Reed. Gmc *hriuda- in OE *hrēod:* REED.

kus-. A kiss. Gmc *kussjan in OE *cyssan:* KISS.

kwed-. To sharpen. Gmc *hwatjan in OE *hwettan:* WHET.

kwei-. To hiss. Gmc *hwī-n- and *hwis- in: a. OE *hwīnan:* WHINE; b. OE *hwisprian:* WHISPER; c. OE *hwistlian:* WHISTLE. [AHD *kwei-⁴.*]

kweit-. White. 1. Gmc *hwītaz in OE *hwīt:* WHITE. 2. Gmc *hwaitjaz in OE *hwǣte:* WHEAT.

kwel-. To revolve. Redupl form *kwe-kwel-o- in OE *hwēol:* WHEEL. [AHD *kwel-¹.*]

kwerp-. To turn oneself. Gmc *hwarb- in OE *hwearf,* wharf (< "place where people move about"): WHARF.

kwetwer-. Four. O-grade form *kwetwor- prob in Gmc *petwor- in: a. OE *fēower:* FOUR; b. OE *fēowertig:* FORTY.

kweyə-. Cozy, quiet. Variant *kwī- in Gmc *hwīlō in OE *hwīl:* WHILE.

kwo-. Stem of relative and interrogative pronouns. 1. Gmc *hwas, *hwasa, *hwam, in OE *hwā, hwæs, hwǣm:* WHO, WHOSE, WHOM. 2. Gmc *hwat in OE *hwæt:* WHAT. 3. Gmc *hwī in OE *hwȳ:* WHY. 4. Gmc *hwa-līk- in OE *hwelc:* WHICH. 5. Gmc *hwō- in OE *hū:* HOW. 6. Gmc *hwan- in OE *hwenne* and *hwanon:* WHEN and WHENCE. 7. Gmc *hwithrē in OE *hwider:* WHITHER. 8. Gmc *hwar- in OE *hwǣr:* WHERE. 9. Gmc *hwatharaz in: a. OE *hwæther:* NEITHER, WHETHER; b. Gmc *aiwo gihwatharaz,* "ever each of two," in OE *ǣghwæther:* EITHER.

kwon-. Dog. Zero-grade form *kwn̥- in Gmc *hundaz in OE *hund:* HOUND.

lab-. To lick. Gmc *lapjan in OE *lapian:* LAP³.

las-. To be eager or wanton. 1. Gmc *lustuz in OE *lust:* LUST. 2. Gmc *lustjan in OE *lystan:* LISTLESS.

leb-. Lip. Gmc *lep- in OE *lippa:* LIP. [AHD *leb-².*]

legh-. To lie, lay. 1. Gmc *ligjan in OE *licgan:* LIE¹. 2. Gmc *lagjan in OE *lecgan:* LAY¹.

legwh-. Light. Gmc *līhtaz in OE *līht:* LIGHT².

lei-. Slimy. Gmc *lī- in: a. OE *slīm:* SLIME; b. OE *slipor:* SLIPPERY.

lēi-. To let go. 1. Form *lēd- in Gmc *lētan in OE *lǣtan:* LET¹. 2. Form *lǝd- in: a. Gmc *lataz in OE *læt, lætra, latost:* LATE, LATTER, LAST¹; b. Gmc *latjan in OE *lettan:* LET². [AHD *lēi-².*]

leigh-. To lick. Zero-grade form *lig- in Gmc *likkōn in OE *liccian:* LICK.

leikw-. To leave. O-grade form *loikw- in Gmc *laihwnjan in OE *lǣnan:* LEND.

leip-. To stick, adhere; fat. 1. Gmc *lībam, "continuance," in OE *līf:* LIFE. 2. Gmc *libēn, "to continue," in OE *libban:* LIVE¹. 3. Gmc *laibjan in OE *lǣfan:* LEAVE¹. 4. Gmc *librō in OE *lifer:* LIVER.

leis-. Track, furrow. O-grade form *lois-. 1. Gmc *laist-, "footprint," in OE *lāst:* LAST³. 2. Gmc *laistjan, "to follow a track," in OE *lǣstan:* LAST². 3. Gmc *laizō in OE *lār:* LORE. 4. Gmc *liznōn in OE *leornian:* LEARN.

leit-. To detest. 1. Gmc *laithaz in OE *lāth:* LOATH. 2. Gmc *laithōn in OE *lāthian:* LOATHE.

leith-. To go forth. O-grade form *loit-. 1. Gmc *laidjan in OE *lǣdan:* LEAD¹. 2. Variant *loid- in Gmc *laidō in OE *lād,* course: LOAD, LODE, LIVELIHOOD.

lem-. Broken. Gmc *lamōn- in OE *lama:* LAME. [AHD *lem-¹.*]

lendh-. Open land. Gmc *landam in OE *land:*

LAND. [AHD *lendh-²*.]

lento-. Flexible. Gmc **linthjaz* in OE *līthe:* LITHE.

lep-. To be flat; palm. Form **lōp-* in Gmc **galōfō* in OE *glōf:* GLOVE. [AHD *lep-²*.]

letro-. Leather. Gmc **lethram* in OE *lether-:* LEATHER.

leu-. To cut apart. **1.** Gmc **lausaz* in OE *los:* LOSE, LOSS. **2.** Gmc **ferliusan* in OE *forlēosan:* FORLORN. [AHD *leu-¹*.]

leubh-. To care; love. **1.** O-grade form **loubh-* in Gmc **galaubjan* in OE *gelēfan, belēfan:* BELIEVE. **2.** Zero-grade form **lubh-* in Gmc **lubō* in OE *lufu:* LOVE.

leud-. Small. Gmc **lūt-* in OE *lȳtel:* LITTLE.

leugh-. To lie. Gmc **liugan* in OE *lēogan:* LIE².

leuk-. Light. Gmc **liuhtam* in OE *līht:* LIGHT¹.

leup-. To break off. Gmc **laubaz* in OE *lēaf:* LEAF.

lou-. To wash. **1.** Gmc **laugō* in OE *lēag:* LYE. **2.** OE *lēathor:* LATHER.

lus-. Louse. Gmc **lus-* in OE *lūs:* LOUSE.

mā-. Damp. Gmc **mōra-* in OE *mōr:* MOOR². [AHD *mā-³*.]

mad-. Moist (as food). Gmc **mati-* in OE *mete:* MEAT.

mag-. Also **mak-.** To knead, fit. **1.** Gmc **makōn* in OE *macian:* MAKE. **2.** Gmc **ga-mak-ōn*, "fitted together with (another), spouse," in OE *gemæcca:* MATCH¹. **3.** Gmc **mangjan*, to mix, in: **a.** OE *mengan:* MINGLE; **b.** OE *gemang:* AMONG, MONGREL.

magh-. To be able. **1.** Gmc **mag-* in OE *magan:* MAY¹. **2.** Gmc **mah-ti-* in OE *miht:* MIGHT¹. **3.** Gmc **mag-ena* in OE *mægen:* MAIN. [AHD *magh-¹*.]

maghu-. Young person. Form **magho-* in Gmc **magadin-* in OE *mægden:* MAIDEN.

mai-¹. To cut. **1.** Gmc **ā-mait-jon*, "the biter," in OE *æmette:* ANT. **2.** Gmc **mītōn-* in OE *mīte:* MITE¹.

mai-². To soil. Gmc **mail-*, a blemish, in OE *māl:* MOLE¹.

man-. Man. Extended form **manu-* in Gmc **manna-* in OE *mann:* MAN. [AHD *man-¹*.]

marko-. Horse. Gmc feminine **marhjōn* in OE *mere:* MARE¹.

māter-. Mother. Gmc **mōthar-* in OE *mōdor:* MOTHER.

me-. First person singular pronoun. **1.** Gmc **mē-* in OE *mē:* ME. **2.** Possessive form **mei-no-* in Gmc **mīn-* in OE *mīn:* MINE², MY. [AHD *me-¹*.]

mē-¹. Mind, disposition. O-grade form **mō-* in Gmc **mōthaz* in OE *mōd:* MOOD¹.

mē-². To measure. **1.** Gmc **mǣlaz*, "appointed time," in OE *mǣl:* MEAL². **2.** Extended form **mēn-* in: **a.** Gmc **mǣnon* in OE *mōna:* MOON; **b.** Gmc **mǣnōth-* in OE *mōnath:* MONTH.

mē-³. Big. **1.** Gmc comparative **maizōn-* in OE *māra* and *māre:* MORE. **2.** Gmc superlative **maista-* in OE *mǣst:* MOST.

mē-⁴. To cut down grass. Gmc **mǣ-* in OE *māwan:* MOW¹.

med-. To take appropriate measures. Gmc **metan* in OE *metan:* METE.

medhu-. Honey; mead. Gmc **medu-* in OE *meodu:* MEAD¹.

medhyo-. Middle. Gmc **middila-* in OE *middel:* MIDDLE.

meg-. Great. Gmc **mik-* in OE *mycel:* MUCH.

mei-. To change, exchange. **1.** O-grade form **moi-* in Gmc **ga-maid-az*, "changed for the worse, abnormal," in OE *gemād:* MAD. **2.** Form **mit-to-*, "changed, wrongly," in **a.** Gmc **missa-* in OE *mis-:* MIS-; **b.** Gmc **missjan* in OE *missan:* MISS¹. [AHD *mei-¹*.]

meigh-. To urinate. Gmc **mih-*, urine, rain, in OE *mist:* MIST.

mei-no-. Opinion, intention. **1.** Gmc **main-*, complaint, in OE *mān:* MOAN. **2.** Gmc **main-jan*, to intend, in OE *mænan:* MEAN¹.

mel-. Soft. **1.** Extended form **meld-* in: **a.** Gmc **meltan* in OE *meltan:* MELT; **b.** Gmc **malta-* in OE *mealt:* MALT. **2.** Extended form **meldh-* in Gmc **mildja-* in OE *milde:* MILD. [AHD *mel-¹*.]

melə-. To crush, grind. Gmc **mel-wa-*, flour, in OE *melu:* MEAL¹.

melg-. To milk. Gmc **meluk-* in OE *milc:* MILK.

mēlo-. Also **smēlo-.** Small animal. Zero-grade form **smalo* in Gmc **smal-* in OE *smæl:* SMALL.

men-. To think. Zero-grade form **mn̥-* in Gmc **ga-mundi-* in OE *gemynd:* MIND. [AHD *men-¹*.]

menegh-. Copious. Gmc **managa-* in OE *manig:* MANY.

menth-. To chew. Form **mn̥tho-* in Gmc **muntha-* in OE *mūth:* MOUTH.

mer-¹. To flicker. Gmc **murgana-* in OE *morgen:* MORN.

mer-². To trouble. Gmc **marzjan* in OE *merran:* MAR. [AHD *mer-⁴*.]

merg-. Boundary. Gmc **mark-* in OE *mearc:* MARK¹.

meu-. Damp. Gmc **meus-* in OE *mos:* MOSS.

mōd-. To meet. Gmc **mōtjan* in OE *mētan:* MEET¹.

mon-. Neck. Gmc **manō* in OE *manu:* MANE.

mori-. Body of water. Gmc **mariska-* in OE *mersc:* MARSH.

mozgo-. Marrow. Gmc **mazgā-* in OE *mærg:* MARROW.

mregh-mo-. Brain. Gmc **brag-na-* in OE *brægen:* BRAIN.

mreghu-. Short. Zero-grade form **mr̥ghu-* in: **a.** Gmc **murja-*, short, pleasant, in OE *mirige:* MERRY; **b.** Gmc **murgithō* in OE *myrgth:* MIRTH.

mū-. Mouse. Gmc **mūs-* in OE *mūs:* MOUSE. [AHD *mū-¹*.]

nas-. Nose. Gmc **nasō* in OE *nosu:* NOSE.

nāu-. To be exhausted. Zero-grade form **nəu-* in Gmc **naudi-* in OE *nēod, nēd:* NEED. [AHD *nāu-¹*.]

n̥dher-. Under. Gmc **under-* in OE *under:* UNDER.

ne-. Not. **1.** Gmc **ne-* in OE *ne:* NO¹. **2.** Zero-grade form **n̥-* in Gmc **un-* in OE *un-:* UN-¹.

ned-. To bind, tie. O-grade form **nod-* in: **a.** Gmc **nati-* in OE *net:* NET¹; **b.** Gmc *nat-ilō* in OE *netle:* NETTLE.

nek-. To attain. O-grade form **nok-* in Gmc **ga-nah-* in OE *genōg:* ENOUGH. [AHD *nek-²*.]

nekwt-. Night. O-grade form **nokwt-* in Gmc **naht-* in OE *niht:* NIGHT.

nem-. To take. Form **nem-* in: **a.** OE *niman:* NUMB; **b.** OE *næmel* and *numol:* NIMBLE. [AHD *nem-²*.]

ner-. Under, on the left; north. Zero-grade

form *nr̥ in Gmc *north-* in OE *north:* NORTH. [AHD *ner-¹.*]

nes-. Personal pronoun. Zero-grade form *ns̥-* in: **a.** Gmc *uns* in OE *ūs:* US; **b.** Gmc *unsara-* in OE *ūre:* OUR. [AHD *nes-².*]

nētr-. Snake. Gmc *nēthrō-* in OE *nædre:* ADDER.

newn̥. Nine. Gmc *niwun* in OE *nigon:* NINE.

newo-. New. Gmc *neuja-* in OE *nēowe:* NEW.

ni. Down. **1.** Gmc *nith-* in OE *nithan, neothan:* BENEATH, UNDERNEATH. **2.** Gmc *nitheraz* in OE *nither:* NETHER.

nizdo-. Bird's nest. **1.** Gmc *nist-* in OE *nest:* NEST. **2.** Gmc *nistilōn* in OE *nestlian:* NESTLE.

nobh-. Navel. Gmc *nabalō* in OE *nafela:* NAVEL.

nogh-. Nail. Gmc *nagla-* in OE *nægl:* NAIL.

nogw-. Naked. Gmc *nakweda-* in OE *nacod:* NAKED.

nomen-. Name. Gmc *namōn-* in OE *nama:* NAME.

nu-. Now. Gmc *neuja-* in OE *nū:* NOW.

ōg-. Fruit. Zero-grade form *əg-* in Gmc *akran-* in OE *æcern:* ACORN.

oino-. One. **1.** Gmc *ainaz* in OE *ān:* A, AN, ONE. **2.** Gmc *ain-lif-,* "one left (beyond ten)," in OE *endleofan:* ELEVEN. **3.** Gmc *ainigaz* in OE *ænig:* ANY.

olto-. An oath. Gmc *aithaz* in OE *āth:* OATH.

oktō. Eight. Gmc *ahtō* in OE *eahta:* EIGHT.

okw-. To see. Gmc *augōn-* in OE *ēage:* EYE.

ous-. Ear. Gmc *auzan-* in OE *ēare:* EAR¹.

owi-. Sheep. Gmc *awi-* in OE *ēowu:* EWE.

pā-. To feed. **1.** Gmc *fōdram* in OE *fōdor:* FODDER. **2.** Extended form *pāt-* in: **a.** Gmc *fōd-* in OE *fōda:* FOOD; **b.** Gmc *fōdjan* in OE *fēdan:* FEED; **c.** Gmc *fōstra-* in OE *fōstor:* FOSTER.

pag-. To fasten. Form *pa-n-g-* in Gmc *fangiz* in OE *fang:* FANG.

pan-. Fabric. Gmc *fanōn-* in OE *fana:* VANE.

past-. Solid, firm. **1.** Gmc *fastuz* in OE *fæst:* FAST¹. **2.** Gmc *fastinōn* in OE *fastnian:* FASTEN. **3.** Gmc *fasten,* to hold fast, in OE *fæstan:* FAST².

ped-¹. Foot. **1.** Lengthened o-grade form *pōd-* in Gmc *fōt-* in OE *fōt:* FOOT. **2.** Gmc *feterō* in OE *feter:* FETTER.

ped-². Container. O-grade form *pod-* in Gmc *fatam* in OE *fæt:* VAT.

pelg-¹. Also **peik-.** To cut. Gmc *fīhala* in OE *fēol:* FILE².

pelg-². Also **peik-.** Evil-minded. **1.** Zero-grade form *pig-* in Gmc *fikala-* in OE *ficol:* FICKLE. **2.** O-grade form *poik-* in: **a.** Gmc *gafaihaz* in OE *gefāh:* FOE; **b.** Gmc *faigjaz* in OE *fæge:* FEY.

peisk-. Fish. Gmc *fiska-* in OE *fisc:* FISH.

pel-¹. To thrust. Extended form *peld-* in: **a.** Gmc *falt-* in OE *anfealt:* ANVIL; **b.** Gmc *feltaz,* "compressed wool," in OE *felt:* FELT¹. [AHD *pel-⁶.*]

pel-². Pale. Variant *pal-* in Gmc *falwaz* in OE *fealo:* FALLOW DEER.

pel-³. To fold. Extended form *pelt-* in: **a.** Gmc *falthan* in OE *faldan:* FOLD¹; **b.** Gmc *-falthaz* in OE *-feald:* -FOLD.

pel-⁴. Skin. Gmc *fel-men-* in OE *filmen,* membrane: FILM.

pel-⁵. Also **pela-.** To fill. Zero-grade form *plə-* in: **a.** Gmc *fullaz* in OE *full:* FULL¹; **b.** Gmc

pfull-jan in OE *fyllan:* FILL. [AHD *pel-⁸.*]

pela-. Flat; to spread. **1.** Gmc *felthuz* in OE *feld:* FIELD. **2.** Variant *plā-* in Gmc *flōruz* in OE *flōr:* FLOOR. [AHD *pelə-¹.*]

penkwe. Five. **1.** Gmc *fimfti* in OE *fīf:* FIVE. **2.** Gmc *fimftehun* in OE *fīftēne:* FIFTEEN. **3.** Gmc *fimfton* in OE *fīfta:* FIFTH. **4.** Gmc *fimftig* in OE *fīftig:* FIFTY. **5.** Gmc *fingwraz,* "one of five," in OE *finger:* FINGER. **6.** Form *pn̥ksti-* in Gmc *fūstiz* in OE *fȳst:* FIST.

pent-. To tread, go. Gmc *finthan* in OE *findan:* FIND.

per¹. "Forward, through, before." **1.** Gmc *ferra* in OE *feor:* FAR. **2.** Zero-grade form *pr-* in: **a.** Gmc *for* in OE *for:* FOR; **b.** Gmc *furth-* in OE *forth:* FORTH; **c.** Gmc *furthera-* in OE *furthor:* FURTHER; **d.** Gmc *furma-* in OE *forma:* FORMER; FOREMOST; **e.** Gmc *furista-* in OE *fyrst:* FIRST. **3.** Variant *para* in Gmc *fora* in: **a.** OE *fore:* FORE; **b.** OE *beforan:* BEFORE. **4.** Variant *pro* in: **a.** Gmc *fram* in OE *from:* FROM; **b.** Gmc *framjan,* "to come forward," in OE *framian:* FRAME.

per-². To lead, pass over. **1.** O-grade form *por-* in Gmc *faran* in OE *faran:* FARE. **2.** Zero-grade form *pr-* in Gmc *furdu-* in OE *ford:* FORD.

per-³. To risk. Gmc *fēraz,* "danger," in OE *fǣr:* FEAR. [AHD *per-⁵.*]

perk-. To dig out. Zero-grade form *prk-* in Gmc *furh-* in OE *furh:* FURROW. [AHD *perk-³.*]

perkwu-. Oak. Zero-grade form *prkw-* in Gmc *furhu-* in OE *fyrh:* FIR.

pet-¹. To fly. Gmc *fethrō* in OE *fether:* FEATHER.

pet-². To spread. O-grade form *pot-* in Gmc *fathmaz* in OE *fæthm:* FATHOM.

peya-. To be fat. Form *poid-* in Gmc *faitaz* in OE *fǣtt:* FAT.

peter. Father. Gmc *fadar* in OE *fæder:* FATHER.

phol-. To fall. **1.** Gmc *fallan* in OE *feallan:* FALL. **2.** Gmc *falljan,* "to cause to fall," in OE *fellan:* FELL¹.

plat-. To spread. Variant *plad-* in Gmc *flat-jam* in OE *flett,* floor: FLAT².

plek-. To plait. O-grade form *plok-* in Gmc *flahsam* in OE *fleax:* FLAX.

plēk-. Also **pleik-.** To tear. **1.** Form *plak-* in Gmc *flahan* in OE *flēan:* FLAY. **2.** Gmc *flaiskaz,* "piece of torn flesh," in OE *flæsc:* FLESH.

pleu-. To flow. **1.** Extended form *pleuk-* in: **a.** Gmc *fliugan* in OE *flēogan:* FLY¹; **b.** Gmc *fliugjō* in OE *flēoge:* FLY²; **c.** Zero-grade form *pluk-* in Gmc *flug-ti-* in OE *flyht* and *flyht:* FLIGHT¹, FLIGHT²; **d.** Gmc *fluglaz, fuglaz,* in OE *fugol:* FOWL. **2.** Extended form *pleud-* in: **a.** Gmc *fliutan* in OE *flēotan:* FLEET¹; **b.** Zero-grade form *plud-* in Gmc *flut-* in OE *flotian* and *floterian:* FLOAT, FLUTTER. **4.** Forms *plōu-, plō-,* in: **a.** Gmc *flōwēn* in OE *flōwan:* FLOW; **b.** Gmc *flōdu* in OE *flōd:* FLOOD.

pleus-. Fleece. Gmc *fliusaz* in OE *flēos:* FLEECE.

plou-. Flea. Extended form *plouk-* in Gmc *flauhaz* in OE *flēah:* FLEA.

pneu-. To breathe. Gmc *fniu-* in OE *fnēosan:* SNEEZE.

pōl-. To feel. Gmc *fōljan* in OE *fēlan:* FEEL.

pōu-. Few, little. **1.** Variant *pau-* in Gmc *fawaz* in OE *fēawe:* FEW. **2.** Variant *pu-lo-,* "young of an animal," in Gmc *fulō* in OE *fola:* FOAL.

preu-. To hop. Zero-grade form *pru-* in Gmc *fru-* in OE *frogga:* FROG.

preus-. To freeze. **1.** Gmc *friusan* in OE *frēosan:* FREEZE. **2.** Zero-grade form *prus-* in Gmc *frustaz* in OE *frost:* FROST.

prī-. To love. Extended form *priy-.* **1.** Gmc *frijaz* in OE *frēo:* FREE. **2.** Gmc *frijand-* in OE *frēond:* FRIEND. **3.** Gmc *frije-dagaz* in OE *frigedæg:* FRIDAY.

pu-. To rot. Form *pū-lo-.* **1.** Gmc *fūlaz* in OE *fūl:* FOUL. **2.** Gmc *fūlithō* in OE *fylth:* FILTH. [AHD *pu-².*]

puk-. Bushy-haired. **1.** Gmc *fuhsaz* in OE *fox:* FOX. **2.** Gmc *fuhson* in OE *fyxe:* VIXEN. [AHD *puk-².*]

pūr-. Fire. Gmc *fūri-* in OE *fȳr:* FIRE.

pūro-. Grain. OE *fyrs:* FURZE.

rebh-. To roof over. Gmc *reb-jōn,* "covering of the chest cavity," in OE *rib:* RIB.

reg-¹. To move in a straight line. **1.** Gmc *rehtaz* in OE *riht:* RIGHT. **2.** O-grade form *rog-* in: **a.** Gmc *rakō* in OE *raca:* RAKE¹; **b.** Gmc *rak-inaz* in OE *gerecenian:* RECKON; **c.** Lengthened form *rōg-* in Gmc *rōkja-* in OE *rēcelēas:* RECKLESS.

reg-². Moist. Variant *rek-* in Gmc *regnaz* in OE *rēn:* RAIN.

rei-¹. To scratch, cut. **1.** Form *roig-* in Gmc *raigwa* in OE *rāw:* ROW. **2.** Form *reipp-* in Gmc *raipaz* in OE *rāp:* ROPE. **3.** Form *reib-* in: **a.** Gmc *rīpja-* in OE *ripe:* RIPE; **b.** Gmc *ripjan* in OE *ripan:* REAP.

rei-². Flecked. O-grade form *roi-* in Gmc *raihaz* in OE *rā:* ROE².

reidh-. To ride. **1.** Gmc *rīdan* in OE *rīdan:* RIDE. **2.** O-grade form *roidh-* in: **a.** Gmc *raid-* in OE *rād:* RAID, ROAD; **b.** Gmc *raid-ja* in OE *rǣde:* READY.

reig-. To reach. O-grade form *roidh-* in Gmc *raikjan* in OE *rǣcan:* REACH. [AHD *reig-².*]

rendh-. To tear up. **1.** Gmc *randjan* in OE *rendan:* REND. **2.** Gmc *rind-* in OE *rinde:* RIND.

rēp-. Stake, beam. Variant *rap-* in Gmc *raftra-* in OE *ræfter:* RAFTER. [AHD *rēp-².*]

rēt-. Post. O-grade form *rōt-* in Gmc *rodd-* in OE *rodd:* ROD.

reudh-. Red, ruddy. **1.** O-grade form *roudh-* in Gmc *raudaz* in OE *rēad:* RED. **2.** Zero-grade form *rudh-* in: **a.** Gmc *rudō* in OE *rudu:* RUDDY; **b.** Gmc *rūst-* in OE *rūst:* RUST.

reug-. To belch, smoke. Gmc *riukan* in OE *rēocan:* REEK.

rewə-. To open; space. Variant *rū-* in Gmc *rūmaz* in OE *rūm:* ROOM.

rezg-. To plait. Gmc *ruski-* in OE *rysc:* RUSH².

ruk-. Rough. Form *rūk-* in Gmc *rūhwaz* in OE *rūh:* ROUGH. [AHD *ruk-².*]

sā-. To satisfy. Zero-grade form *sə-.* **1.** Gmc *sadaz* in OE *sæd,* sated: SAD. **2.** Gmc *sadōn* in OE *sadian:* SATE¹.

sab-. Juice. Gmc *sapam* in OE *sæp:* SAP¹.

sāg-. To seek out. **1.** Gmc *sōkjan* in OE *sēcan:* SEEK. **2.** Gmc *sakō* in OE *sacu:* SAKE¹. **3.** Gmc *sakan* in OE *forsacan:* FORSAKE.

sai-. Suffering. **1.** Gmc *sairaz* in OE *sār:* SORE. **2.** Gmc *sairig-* in OE *sārig:* SORRY.

sal-¹. Salt. Gmc *saltam* in OE *sealt:* SALT.

sal-². Dirty. Gmc *salwaz* in OE *salo:* SALLOW.

saus-. Dry. Gmc *sausaz* in OE *sēar:* SEAR, SERE.

sāwel-. Sun. Variants *swen-,* *sun-.* **1.** Gmc *sunnōn* in OE *sunne:* SUN. **2.** Gmc *sunthaz* in OE *sūth:* SOUTH.

sē-. To sow. **1.** Gmc *sējan* in OE *sāwan:* SOW¹. **2.** Gmc *sēdiz* in OE *sǣd:* SEED. [AHD *sē-¹.*]

sed-. To sit. **1.** Gmc *sitan* in OE *sittan:* SIT. **2.** Gmc *setlaz* in OE *setl:* SETTLE. **3.** O-grade form *sod-* in: **a.** Gmc *satjan* in OE *settan:* SET¹; **b.** Gmc *sadulaz* in OE *sadol:* SADDLE; **c.** Lengthened form *sōd-* in Gmc *sōtam* in OE *sōt:* SOOT. [AHD *sed-¹.*]

sek-. To cut. **1.** Gmc *segithō* in OE *sīthe:* SCYTHE. **2.** O-grade form *sok-* in Gmc *sagō* in OE *sagu:* SAW¹.

sekw-¹. To say. O-grade form *sokw-.* **1.** Gmc *sawjan* in OE *secgan:* SAY. **2.** Gmc *sagō* in OE *sagu:* SAW². [AHD *sekw-³.*]

sekw-². To see. **1.** Gmc *sehwan* in OE *sēon:* SEE¹. **2.** Gmc *sih-th* in OE *sihth:* SIGHT.

sel-¹. To take. Gmc *saljan,* "to sell" (< "cause to take"), in OE *sellan:* SELL. [AHD *sel-³.*]

sel-². Of good mood. Gmc *sēl-* in OE *gesǣlig:* SILLY.

selp-. Fat. Gmc *salb-* in OE *salf:* SALVE.

sem-¹. Form *smm-o-* in Gmc *sumaz* in OE *sum:* SOME.

sem-². Summer. Form *smm-* in Gmc *sumaraz* in OE *sumor:* SUMMER. [AHD *sem-³.*]

sen-. Separated. Zero-grade form *sṇ-.* **1.** Gmc *sundro* in OE *sunder:* ASUNDER. **2.** Gmc *sundrōn* in OE *syndrian:* SUNDER. **3.** Gmc *sundriga-* in OE *syndrig:* SUNDRY. [AHD *sen-².*]

sendhro-. Crystalline deposit. Gmc *sendra-* in OE *sinder:* CINDER.

sengw-. To sink. Gmc *sinkwan* in OE *sincan:* SINK.

sengwh-. To sing. **1.** Gmc *singan* in OE *singan:* SING. **2.** O-grade form *songwh-* in Gmc *sangwaz* in OE *sang:* SONG.

senk-. To burn. O-grade form *sonk-* in Gmc *sangjan* in OE *sengan:* SINGE.

sent-. To go. O-grade form *sont-* in Gmc *sandjan* in OE *sendan:* SEND.

septṃ. Seven. Gmc *sibum* in OE *seofon:* SEVEN.

seu-¹. To seethe. Gmc *siuthan* in OE *sēothan:* SEETHE.

seu-². Third person and reflexive pronoun. Form *sel-bho-* in Gmc *selbaz* in OE *self:* SELF.

seu-³. To give birth. Gmc *sunuz* in OE *sunu:* SON.

seu-⁴. To take liquid. Form *sūg-.* **1.** Gmc *sūk-* in OE *sūcan:* SUCK. **2.** Gmc *suk-* in OE *socian:* SOAK.

skei-. To cut. **1.** Gmc *ski-nōn-* in OE *scinu:* SHIN. **2.** Extended form *skeit-* in Gmc *skaith-* in OE *scēadan:* SHED¹.

skel-¹. To cut. **1.** Gmc *skaljō,* "piece cut off," in OE *scell:* SHELL. **2.** Gmc *skelduz* in OE *scield:* SHIELD.

skel-². To be under an obligation. O-grade form *skol-* in Gmc *skal-,* "I owe, I ought," in OE *sceal, sceolde:* SHALL, SHOULD.

skeng-. Crooked. Gmc *skankō in OE *sceanca:* SHANK.

skep-. "To cut, scrape." **1.** Gmc *skap- in: **a.** OE *gesceap:* SHAPE; **b.** OE *-scipe:* -SHIP. **2.** Gmc *skaftaz in OE *sceaft:* SHAFT[1]. **3.** Gmc *skabb- in OE *sceabb:* SHABBY. **4.** Gmc *skab- in OE *sceafan:* SHAVE.

sker-[1]. To cut. **1.** Gmc *skeran in OE *sceran:* SHEAR. **2.** Gmc *skar- in: **a.** OE *scēar:* SHARE[2]; **b.** OE *scearu:* SHARE[1]. **3.** Gmc *skēr- in OE *scēara:* SHEARS. **4.** Gmc *skardaz in OE *sceard:* SHARD. **5.** Extended form *skerd- in Gmc *skurtaz in: **a.** OE *scort:* SHORT; **b.** OE *scyrte:* SHIRT. **6.** Extended form *skerbh- in Gmc *skarpaz in OE *scearp:* SHARP. **7.** Gmc *skrub- in OE *scrybb:* SHRUB.

sker-[2]. To turn, bend. **1.** Form *skreng- in Gmc *skrink- in OE *scrincan:* SHRINK. **2.** Form *skrengh- in Gmc *hringaz in OE *hring:* RING[1]. **3.** Form *kreuk- in Gmc *hrugjaz in OE *hrycg:* RIDGE. [AHD *sker-[3].]

skeru-. To cut. Variant *skreu-. **1.** Gmc *skraw- in OE *scrēawa:* SHREW. **2.** Gmc *skraud- in OE *scrēade:* SHRED. **3.** Gmc *skrūd-, "piece of cloth," in OE *scrūd:* SHROUD.

skeu-. Also **keu-.** To cover. **1.** Zero-grade form *ku- in: **a.** Gmc *husōn- in OE *hosa:* HOSE; **b.** Gmc *huzdam in OE *hord:* HOARD; **c.** Gmc *hūdiz in OE *hȳd:* HIDE[2]. **2.** Gmc *hūdjan in OE *hȳdan:* HIDE[1].

skeubh-. To shove. **1.** Gmc *skiuban in OE *scūfan:* SHOVE. **2.** Gmc *skub-ilōn- in OE *scofl:* SHOVEL.

skeud-. To shoot, chase, throw. **1.** Gmc *skiutan in OE *scēotan:* SHOOT. **2.** Gmc *skutaz in OE *scot:* SHOT[1]. **3.** Gmc *skuttjan in OE *scytel:* SHUTTLE.

skeup-. Cluster. Gmc *skauf- in OE *scēaf:* SHEAF.

skhed-. To split, scatter. Form *skod- in Gmc *skat- in OE *sceaterian:* SHATTER.

skī-. To gleam. **1.** Gmc *skīnan in OE *scīnan:* SHINE. **2.** Gmc *skim- in OE *scimerian:* SHIMMER.

skot-. Shade. Gmc *skadwaz in OE *sceadu:* SHADE.

skwalo-. Big fish. Variant *kwal- in Gmc *hwaliz in OE *hwæl:* WHALE.

slagw-. Also **lagw-.** To seize. Gmc *lakkjan in OE *læccan:* LATCH.

slak-. To strike. **1.** Gmc *slahan in OE *slēan:* SLAY. **2.** Gmc *slagja- in OE *slecg:* SLEDGEHAMMER.

slēg-. To be slack. Zero-grade form *sləg- in Gmc *slak- in OE *slæc:* SLACK.

sleidh-. Slippery. Gmc *slīdan in OE *slīdan:* SLIDE.

slenk-. To wind. Variant *sleng- in Gmc *slinkjan in OE *slincan:* SLINK.

sleubh-. To slide. Gmc *sliub- in OE *slēf:* SLEEVE.

smē-. To smear. Extended root *smeid- in Gmc *smītan in OE *smītan:* SMITE.

smeg-. To taste. Gmc *smak- in OE *smæc:* SMACK[2].

smei-. To smile. Gmc *smer- in OE *smearcian:* SMIRK.

smer-[1]. To remember. Zero-grade form *mr- in Gmc *murnōn in OE *murnan:* MOURN.

smer-[2]. Grease. Gmc *smerwjan in OE *smeri-an:* SMEAR. [AHD *smer-[3].]

smerd-. Pain. Gmc *smertan in OE *smeortan:* SMART.

smeug-. Smoke. Gmc *smuk- in OE *smoca:* SMOKE.

smi-. To cut (as with a sharp instrument). Gmc *smithaz in OE *smith:* SMITH.

snē-[1]. Also **ne-.** To spin, sew. Gmc *nēthlō in OE *nǣdl:* NEEDLE.

snē-[2]. "Nose." Gmc *snuf- in OE *snyflan:* SNIVEL.

sneg-. To creep; creeping thing. O-grade form *snog-. **1.** Gmc *snag-ila- in OE *snægel:* SNAIL. **2.** Gmc *snakan- in OE *snaca:* SNAKE.

sneigwh-. Snow. O-grade form *snoigwh- in Gmc *snaiwaz in OE *snāw:* SNOW.

snēu-. Sinew. Variant *senw- in Gmc *senawō in OE *sinu:* SINEW.

so-. This. Form *syā in Gmc *sō in OE *sēo:* SHE.

spei-. Sharp point. **1.** Gmc *spituz in OE *spitu:* SPIT[2]. **2.** Gmc *spī-ra- in OE *spīr:* SPIRE[1]. **3.** O-grade form *spoig- in Gmc *spaikōn- in OE *spāca:* SPOKE[1].

spēi-. To thrive. O-grade form *spōi- in Gmc *spōdiz in OE *spēd:* SPEED.

spel-[1]. To split, break off. Gmc *spilthjan in OE *spillan:* SPILL.

spel-[2]. To recite. Gmc *spellam in OE *spell:* SPELL[2]. [AHD *spel-[3].]

spen-. To draw, stretch, spin. **1.** Gmc *spinnan in OE *spinnan:* SPIN. **2.** Gmc *spin-ilōn in OE *spinel:* SPINDLE. **3.** O-grade form *spon- in Gmc *spanno- in OE *span:* SPAN[1].

sper-[1]. Spear. Gmc *speru- in OE *spere:* SPEAR.

sper-[2]. To strew. Zero-grade form *spr-. **1.** Gmc *spr- in OE *sprēawlian:* SPRAWL. **2.** Form *spreut- in Gmc *sprūt- in: **a.** OE *sprūtan:* SPROUT; **b.** OE *spryttan:* SPURT. **3.** Form *spreit- in Gmc *spraidjan in OE *sprǣdan:* SPREAD. [AHD *sper-[4].]

sper-[3]. Sparrow. O-grade form *spor- in Gmc *sparwan- in OE *spearwa:* SPARROW.

spergh-. To move, spring. Form *sprengh- in Gmc *springan in OE *springan:* SPRING.

sphē-. Long, flat piece of wood. **1.** Gmc *spēnu- in OE *spōn:* SPOON. **2.** Form *spə-dh- in Gmc *spadan in OE *spadu:* SPADE[1].

spher-. Ankle. **1.** Gmc *spurōn in OE *spora:* SPUR. **2.** Gmc *spurnōn in OE *spurnan,* to kick: SPURN.

sping-. Also **ping-.** Gmc *finki- in OE *finc:* FINCH.

splei-. To split. Gmc *flī- in OE *flint:* FLINT.

spoimo-. Foam. Variant *poimo- in Gmc *faimaz in OE *fām:* FOAM.

spreg-. To speak. Gmc *sprek-, spek-, in: **a.** OE *specan:* SPEAK; **b.** OE *sprǣc:* SPEECH.

spyeu-. To spit. **1.** Gmc *spit- in OE *spittan:* SPIT[1]. **2.** Gmc *spiu- in OE *spīwan:* SPEW. **3.** Gmc *spāt- in OE *spātl:* SPITTLE.

sreu-. To flow. O-grade form *srou- in Gmc *straumaz in OE *strēam:* STREAM.

stā-. To stand. Zero-grade form *stə-. **1.** Gmc *standan in: **a.** OE *standan:* STAND; **b.** OE *understandan:* UNDERSTAND. **2.** Gmc *stamniz in OE *stemn:* STEM[1]. **3.** Gmc *stadiz in OE *stede:* STEAD. **4.** Variant *steu- in Gmc *stiurjan in OE *stīeran:* STEER[1].

stāk-. To stand. Zero-grade form *stək-. **1.** Gmc *staga- in OE *stæg:* STAY[3]. **2.** Gmc *stahla- in OE stēli: STEEL.

stebh-. Post; to place firmly on. **1.** Gmc *stab- in OE stæf: STAFF. **2.** Form *steb- in: **a.** Gmc *stap- in OE stæpe: STEP; **b.** Gmc *stamp- in OE *stampian: STAMP.

steg-¹. To cover. Variant o-grade form *tog- in Gmc *thakjan in OE theccan: THATCH.

steg-². Stick. O-grade form *stog- in Gmc *stak- in OE staca: STAKE¹.

stegh-. To prick. **1.** Form *stengh- in Gmc *stengjan in OE stingan: STING. **2.** O-grade form *stogh- in Gmc *stag- in OE stagga: STAG.

stei-. Stone. O-grade form *stoi- in Gmc *stainaz in OE stān: STONE.

steig-. To stick. Zero-grade form *stig-. **1.** Gmc *stik- in OE sticca and stician: STICK. **2.** Gmc *stikiz in OE stice: STITCH.

steigh-. To stride, step. **1.** Gmc *stīgan in OE stīgan: STY². **2.** O-grade form *stoigh- in Gmc *staigri in OE stǣger: STAIR.

steip-. To compress. Gmc *stīfaz in OE stīf: STIFF.

stel-. To put, stand. Gmc *stilli- in OE stille: STILL. [AHD stel-¹.]

stenǝ-. To thunder. Zero-grade form *stnǝ- in Gmc *thunaraz in OE thunor: THUNDER.

ster-¹. Stiff. **1.** O-grade form *stor- in: **a.** Gmc *staren in OE starian: STARE; **b.** Gmc *starkaz in OE stearc: STARK; **c.** Gmc *starkjan in OE stercan: STARCH. **2.** Zero-grade form *str- in: **a.** Gmc *sturkaz in OE storc: STORK; **b.** Gmc *strūt- in OE strūtian: STRUT. **3.** Extended form *sterd- in Gmc *stert- in: **a.** OE styrtan: START; **b.** OE steartlian: STARTLE. **4.** Gmc *sterban in OE steorfan: STARVE. **5.** Gmc *sternjaz in OE stierne: STERN¹.

ster-². To spread. **1.** Form *streu- in Gmc *striw- in OE strēon: STRAIN². **2.** Form *strou- in: **a.** Gmc *strawjan in OE strēowian: STREW; **b.** Gmc *strāwam in OE strēaw: STRAW.

ster-³. Star. Gmc *sterrōn- in OE steorra: STAR.

ster-⁴. To steal. **1.** Gmc *stelan in OE stelan: STEAL. **2.** Gmc *stalkōjan in OE stealcian: STALK².

stern-. A thorny plant. Form *tr̥-nu- in Gmc *thurnu- in OE thorn: THORN.

steu-. To push, stick, beat. **1.** Extended forms *steup-, *steub-, in: **a.** Gmc *staup- in OE stēap: STEEP¹; **b.** Gmc *staupilaz in OE stȳpel: STEEPLE; **c.** Gmc *stūp- in OE stūpian: STOOP¹; **d.** Gmc *stubb- in OE stybb: STUB. **2.** Extended form *steud- in Gmc *stuntjan in OE styntan: STINT. **3.** Extended form *steug- in Gmc *stukkaz in OE stocc: STOCK.

storos. Starling. Gmc *staraz in OE stær: STARLING.

streig-. To stroke, rub, press. **1.** Gmc *strīkan in OE strīcan: STRIKE. **2.** Gmc *strikōn- in OE strica: STREAK. **3.** O-grade form *stroig- in Gmc *straik- in OE strāc: STROKE.

su-. Pig. **1.** Gmc *swīnam in OE swīn: SWINE. **2.** Celtic *sukko- in OE hogg: HOG. **3.** Lengthened form *sū- in Gmc *sū- in OE sugu: SOW². [AHD su-¹.]

sūro-. Sour. Gmc *sūraz in OE sūr: SOUR.

swād-. Sweet. Gmc *swōtja- in OE swēte: SWEET.

swei-. To bend, turn. **1.** Gmc *swīp- in: **a.** OE swāpan: SWEEP, SWOOP; **b.** OE swift: SWIFT. **2.** Gmc *swīf- in OE swīfan: SWIVEL. **3.** Gmc

*swīm- in OE swīma: SQUEAMISH, SWIM². [AHD swei-².]

sweid-. To sweat. O-grade form *swoid- in Gmc *swaidjan in OE swǣtan: SWEAT. [AHD sweid-².]

sweks. Six. Gmc *seks in OE six: SIX.

swel-¹. To eat, drink. Gmc *swelgan in OE swelgan: SWALLOW¹.

swel-². To shine, burn. Gmc *swiltan in OE sweltan: SWELTER.

swel-³. Post. Gmc *suljō- in OE sylle: SILL.

swen-. To sound. O-grade form *swon- in Gmc *swanaz in OE swan: SWAN.

sweng-. To swing. Gmc *swingan in OE swingan: SWING.

swento-. Healthy. Form *sunto- in Gmc *sunth- in OE gesund: SOUND².

swer-¹. To talk. O-grade form *swor- in: **a.** Gmc *swarjan in OE swerian: SWEAR; **b.** Gmc *andswaru, "a swearing against," in OE andswaru: ANSWER.

swer-². To buzz. O-grade form *swor- in Gmc *swarmaz in OE swearm: SWARM.

swer-³. To pierce. Gmc *swerdam in OE sword: SWORD. [AHD swer-⁴.]

swerbh-. To turn, wipe off. Gmc *swerb- in OE sweorfan: SWERVE.

swergh-. To worry. Gmc *sorg- in OE sorh: SORROW.

swesor-. Sister. Form *swesr̥- in Gmc *swistr- in OE sweostor: SISTER.

swo-. So. **1.** Gmc *swa- in OE swā: SO. **2.** Gmc *swa-līk- in OE swylc: SUCH.

swordo-. Black, dirty. Gmc *swartaz in OE sweart: SWARTHY.

syū-. To bind, sew. **1.** Gmc *siwjan in OE seowian: SEW. **2.** Form *sū- in Gmc *saumaz in OE sēam: SEAM.

tā-. To melt. Gmc *thāwōn in OE thāwian: THAW.

tegu-. Thick. Gmc *thiku- in OE thicce: THICK.

ten-. To stretch. Zero-grade form *tn̥- in Gmc *thunniz in OE thynne: THIN.

ter-¹. To pass through. Zero-grade form *tr̥- in Gmc *thurh in OE thurh: THROUGH. [AHD ter-³.]

ter-². To rub, turn. **1.** Gmc *thersk- in: **a.** OE therscan: THRESH; **b.** OE therscold: THRESHOLD. **2.** Form *trē- in: **a.** Gmc *thrēw- in thrāwan: THROW; **b.** Gmc *thrēdu- in thrǣd: THREAD.

ters-. To dry. Zero-grade form *tr̥s- in Gmc *thurs- in OE thurst: THIRST.

teuǝ-. To swell. **1.** Form *teuk- in Gmc *thiuham in OE thēoh: THIGH. **2.** Form *teus- in Gmc *thus-hundi-, "swollen hundred," in OE thūsend: THOUSAND. **3.** Form *tum- in OE thūma: THUMB.

to-. Demonstrative pronoun. **1.** Gmc *thē- in OE thē: THE. **2.** Gmc *thasi- in OE thes: THIS. **3.** Gmc *thana- in OE thanne: THAN, THEN. **4.** Gmc *thanana- in OE thanon: THENCE. **5.** Gmc *thar in OE thēr: THERE. **6.** Gmc *thathro in OE thider: THITHER. **7.** Gmc *thai in OE thā (and ON their): THEY. **8.** Gmc *thaim in OE thǣm (and ON theim): THEM. **9.** Gmc *that in OE thæt: THAT. **10.** Gmc *thus- in OE thus: THUS.

tong-. To think, feel. **1.** Gmc *thankōn in: **a.** OE thancian: THANK; **b.** OE thencan: THINK. **2.** Gmc *thauht- in OE thōht: THOUGHT.

trei-. Three. **1.** Gmc *thrijiz in OE *thrēo*, *thriga, thrītig,* and *thrēotīne:* THREE, THRICE, THIRTY, THIRTEEN. **2.** Gmc *thrithjaz in OE *thridda:* THIRD.

treud-. To squeeze. Gmc *thriut- in OE *thrēat:* THREAT.

trozdos-. Thrush. Gmc *thruskjōn- in OE *thrysce:* THRUSH.

tu-. You, thou. **1.** Form *tū in Gmc *thū in OE *thū:* THOU. **2.** Form *twei-no- in Gmc *thūnaz in OE *thīn:* THINE, THY.

twei-. To agitate, toss. Extended form *tweid- in Gmc *thwīt- in OE *thwītan:* WHITTLE.

twengh-. To press in on. **1.** Gmc *thwang- in OE *thwang:* THONG. **2.** Gmc *twangjan in OE *twengan:* TWINGE.

twer-. To whirl. Variant *stur-. **1.** Gmc *sturmaz in OE *storm:* STORM. **2.** Gmc *sturjan in OE *styrian:* STIR. [AHD twer-¹.]

ud-. Up, out. **1.** Gmc *ūt- in OE *ūt:* OUT. **2.** Gmc *ūt-era- in OE *ūtera:* UTTER². **3.** Gmc *bi-ūtana in OE *būtan:* BUT, ABOUT.

uper. Over. Gmc *uberi in OE *ofer:* OVER.

upo. Under, up from under, over. **1.** Gmc *upp- in OE *up, uppe:* UP. **2.** Gmc *upanaz in OE *open:* OPEN. **3.** Gmc *bi-ufana in OE *abufan:* ABOVE. **4.** Gmc *ubilaz, "excessive," in OE *yfel:* EVIL. **5.** Gmc *obaswa, "that which is above," in OE *yfes:* EAVES.

wā-. To wound. Zero-grade form *wn̥- in Gmc *wundaz in OE *wund:* WOUND¹. [AHD wā-².]

wāb-. To cry. Gmc *wōpjan in OE *wēpan:* WEEP.

wadh-. A pledge. Gmc *wadi- in OE *weddian:* WED.

wādh-. To go. Gmc *wathan in OE *wadan:* WADE.

wai. Alas. Gmc *wai in OE *wā:* WOE.

wal-. To be strong. Form *woldh- in Gmc *waldan in OE *wieldan:* WIELD.

we-. We. Gmc *wīz in OE *wē:* WE.

wē-. To blow. **1.** Gmc *wedram in OE *weder:* WEATHER. **2.** Gmc *windaz in OE *wind:* WIND¹.

webh-. To weave. **1.** Gmc *weban in OE *wefan:* WEAVE. **2.** O-grade form *wobh- in Gmc *wabjam in OE *webb:* WEB.

wed-. Water; wet. **1.** O-grade form *wod- in: **a.** Gmc *watar- in OE *wæter:* WATER; **b.** Gmc *wat-skan in OE *wæscan:* WASH. **2.** Form *wēd- in Gmc *wēd- in OE *wæt:* WET. **3.** Form *wend- in Gmc *wintruz in OE *winter:* WINTER. **4.** Form *ud-ro- in Gmc *otraz in OE *otor:* OTTER. [AHD wed-¹.]

weg-. To be lively. O-grade form *wog-. **1.** Gmc *waken in OE *wacian and *wacan:* WAKE¹. **2.** Gmc *wakjan in OE *wæccan:* WATCH. [AHD weg-².]

wegh-. To go, transport. **1.** Gmc *wigan in OE *wegan:* WEIGH¹. **2.** Gmc *wihti- in OE *wiht:* WEIGHT. **3.** Gmc *wegaz in OE *weg:* WAY.

wei-¹. To twist. Gmc *wī-ra- in OE *wīr:* WIRE.

wei-². To wither. Gmc *wis- in OE *wisnian:* WIZENED. [AHD wei-³.]

weid-. To see. **1.** Gmc *wītan in OE *wītan:* TWIT. **2.** Gmc *wissaz in: **a.** OE *wīs:* WISE¹; **b.** OE *wīsdōm:* WISDOM. **3.** Gmc *wissōn- in OE *wīse:* WISE². **4.** Zero-grade form *wid- in: **a.** Gmc *wit- in OE *wit:* WIT; **b.** Gmc *witan in OE *witan:* UNWITTING.

weidh-. To separate. Zero-grade form *widh- in Gmc *widewaz in OE *widuwe:* WIDOW.

weik-¹. To wind. Variant *weig-. Gmc *wikōn-, "a series," in OE *wice:* WEEK. [AHD weik-⁴.]

weik-². "Divination, sorcery." Gmc *wikk- in OE *wicce and *wicca:* WICKED, WITCH.

weip-. To vacillate. Variant *weib- in Gmc *wīpjan, "to move back and forth," in OE *wīpian:* WIPE.

weis-. To flow. Gmc *wisōn in OE *wāse:* OOZE². [AHD weis-¹.]

wekti-. Thing. Gmc *wihti- in OE *wiht:* NOT.

wel-¹. Wool. Gmc *wullō in OE *wull:* WOOL. [AHD wel-⁵.]

wel-². To wish, will. **1.** Gmc *wel- in OE *wel:* WELL². **2.** Gmc *wiljōn- in OE *will:* WILL¹. **3.** Gmc *willjan in OE *wyllan:* WILL².

wel-³. To turn, roll. **1.** O-grade form *wol- in Gmc *wall- in OE *wælla:* WELL¹. **2.** Form *welw- in Gmc *walwōn in OE *wealwian:* WALLOW.

welt-. Wild. Gmc *wilthigaz in OE *wilde:* WILD.

wen-. To desire, strive for. **1.** Gmc *winnan in OE *winnan:* WIN. **2.** Zero-grade form *wn̥- in: **a.** Gmc *wunēn in OE *wunian:* WONT; **b.** Gmc *wunsk- in OE *wȳscan:* WISH. **3.** Gmc *wanjan in OE *wenian:* WEAN.

wendh-. To turn, wind. **1.** Gmc *windan in OE *windan:* WIND². **2.** Gmc *wandjan in OE *wendan:* WEND. **3.** Gmc *wandrōn in OE *wandrian:* WANDER.

weng-. To bend, curve. **1.** Gmc *wink- in OE *wincian:* WINK. **2.** Gmc *winkja in OE *wince:* WINCH. **3.** Gmc *winkil- in OE -wincel:* PERIWINKLE¹.

wer-¹. High, raised spot. Gmc *wartōn- in OE *wearte:* WART.

wer-². To speak. Zero-grade form *wr̥- in Gmc *wurdam in OE *word:* WORD. [AHD wer-⁶.]

wer-³. To turn, bend. **1.** Form *wert- in: **a.** Gmc *warth- in OE -weard: -WARD; **b.** Gmc *wurth-, "that which befalls one," in OE *wyrd:* WEIRD. **2.** Form *wreit- in Gmc *wrīth- in: **a.** OE *writha:* WREATH; **b.** OE *wrīthan:* WRITHE; **c.** OE *wrāth:* WRATH. **3.** Form *wergh- in Gmc *wurgjan in OE *wyrgan:* WORRY; **b.** Gmc *wreng- in OE *wringan:* WRING. **4.** Root *werg- in Gmc *wrankjan in: **a.** OE *wrencan:* WRENCH; **b.** OE *gewrinclian:* WRINKLE. **5.** Form *wreik-. **a.** Gmc *wrīg- in OE *wrīgian:* WRY; **b.** Gmc *wristiz in OE *wrist:* WRIST. **6.** Form *wrizd- in Gmc *wraistjan in OE *wrǣstan and *wrǣstlian:* WREST, WRESTLE. **7.** Form *werb- in Gmc *werp- in OE *weorpan:* WARP. **8.** Form *wermi- in Gmc *wurmiz in OE *wyrm:* WORM.

wer-⁴. To watch out for. O-grade form *wor-. **1.** Gmc *waraz in: **a.** OE *wær:* WARY; **b.** OE *gewær:* AWARE. **2.** Gmc *wardaz in OE *weard:* WARD.

wer-⁵. To cover. O-grade form *wor- in Gmc *war-n- in OE *wearnian:* WARN.

werg-. To do. Gmc *werkam in OE *weorc:* WORK. [AHD werg-¹.]

wers-. To confuse. Gmc *wersizōn- in OE *wyrsa:* WORSE.

wes-¹. To clothe. O-grade form *wos- in Gmc *wazjan in OE *werian:* WEAR. [AHD wes-⁴.]

wes-². Wet. Gmc *wōs- in OE *wōs:* OOZE¹.

wes-³. To delay; "to be." O-grade form *wos- in Gmc *wos- in OE *wæs, *wǣre, *wǣron:* WAS, WERE.

wespero-. Evening, night. Gmc *west- in OE

west, WEST.

wi-. Apart, in half. **1.** Gmc **widaz* in OE *wid:* WIDE. **2.** Gmc **withrō* in OE *with:* WITH.

wldhu-. Tree. Gmc **widu-* in OE *wudu:* WOOD.

wlros. Man. Gmc **weraldh-,* "life or age of man," in OE *weorold:* WORLD.

w|kwo-. Wolf. Variant **wlpo-* in Gmc **wulfaz* in OE *wulf:* WOLF.

wokso-. Wax. Gmc **wahsam* in OE *wæx:* WAX.

wopsā. Wasp. Variant **wospā* in Gmc **wosp-* in OE *wæsp:* WASP.

wreg-. To shove, drive. **1.** Gmc **wrekan* in OE *wrecan:* WREAK. **2.** O-grade form **wrog-* in Gmc **wrakjō,* "one pursued," in OE *wrecca:*

wrōd-. To root, gnaw. Gmc **wrōt-* in OE *wrōtan:* ROOT[2].

wrughyo-. Rye. Gmc **rugi-* in OE *ryge:* RYE.

yeg-. Ice. Gmc **jekilaz* in OE *gicel:* ICICLE.

yēro-. Year. Gmc **jēram* in OE *gēar:* YEAR.

yes-. To bubble. Gmc **jest-* in OE *gist,* yeast : YEAST.

yeu-. Young. **1.** Gmc **juwungaz* in OE *geong:* YOUNG. **2.** Gmc **jugunth-* in OE *geoguth:* YOUTH. [AHD *yeu-².*]

yeug-. To join. Zero-grade form **yug-* in Gmc **yukam* in OE *geoc:* YOKE.

yu-. You. Gmc **jūz* and **iww-* in OE *gē, ēow, ēower:* YE[2], YOU, YOUR. [AHD *yu-¹.*]

PICTURE CREDITS

The following list of credits includes the names of many of the organizations and individuals who helped secure illustrations for this Dictionary. The editors wish to thank all of them—as well as others not specifically mentioned—for their invaluable assistance. The credits are arranged alphabetically by entry word, which is printed in boldface type. Unless we have indicated to the contrary, all maps were supplied by Francis & Shaw, Inc., and all human anatomy drawings were supplied by Neil Hardy.

abacus From the Collection of the IBM Corp.; **John Adams** U.S. Bureau of Engraving; **John Quincy Adams** The New-York Historical Society, New York City; **Apollo** Vatican Museum, Photo Alinari; **Chester A. Arthur** U.S. Bureau of Engraving; **Athena** British Museum (Leonard Von Matt); **Augustus** Leonard Von Matt; **bacteria** Prepared from materials in Frobisher's *Fundamentals of Microbiology,* 8th Edition, W.B. Saunders Co., Philadelphia, Pa., 1968; **beef** Jean Erdoes; **Simón Bolívar** Sr. Alfredo Boulton, Caracas; **Brahma** The Metropolitan Museum of Art, Eggleston Fund, 1927; **Braille alphabet** Phoebe McGuire; **Leonid Brezhnev** Pictorial Parade; **James Buchanan** Brown Brothers; **Buddha** Photo Giraudon; **Julius Caesar** Photo Alinari; **Winston Churchill** © Karsh, Ottawa; **Grover Cleveland** Library of Congress; **comet** Yerkes Observatory Photograph; **compass** E.S. Ritchie & Sons, Inc.; **Calvin Coolidge** Library of Congress; **currency** Fundamental Photographs, courtesy American Numismatic Society; **Charles Darwin** Radio Times Hulton Picture Library; **Jefferson Davis** National Archives, Brady Collection; **Charles De Gaulle** French Embassy, Press & Information Division; **Frederick Douglass** Library of Congress; **eclipse** John G. Kirk, Kitt Peak National Observatory; **Albert Einstein** Ernst Haas, © 1966 Magnum Photos; **Dwight David Eisenhower** Burt Glinn, © 1966 Magnum Photos; **Elizabeth I** Detail from National Portrait Gallery, London; **Millard Fillmore** Culver Pic-

tures, Inc.; **fish** Francis & Shaw, Inc.; **flag** (International Code) Phoebe McGuire; **flower** Matthew Kalmenoff; **Benjamin Franklin** Historical Society of Pa.; **Sigmund Freud** Culver Pictures, Inc.; **galaxy** California Institute of Technology—Mount Wilson and Palomar Observatories—(diagrams) After E.P. Hubble from *Sourcebook of Space Sciences* by Samuel Glasstone, © 1965, by Litton Educational Publishing, Inc., by permission of Van Nostrand Reinhold Company; **Mahatma Gandhi** Information Service of India; **James A. Garfield** U.S. Bureau of Engraving; **Geronimo** National Archives; **gill¹** Neil Hardy; **Ulysses S. Grant** The GAF Historical Photo Collection; **Johann Gutenberg** Culver Pictures, Inc.; **Dag Hammarskjöld** United Nations; **Warren G. Harding** Library of Congress; **Benjamin Harrison** U.S. Bureau of Engraving; **William Henry Harrison** The Metropolitan Museum of Art, Gift of I.N. Phelps Stokes, Edward S. Hawes, Alice Mary Hawes, Marion Augusta Hawes, 1937; **Rutherford B. Hayes** Culver Pictures, Inc.; **Adolf Hitler** Wide World Photos; **Ho Chi Minh** Eastfoto; **Herbert Hoover** Fabian Bachrach; **Table of Indo-European Languages** Phoebe McGuire; **Andrew Jackson** The New-York Historical Society, New York City; **Thomas Jefferson** The New-York Historical Society, New York City; **Andrew Johnson** Library of Congress; **Lyndon Baines Johnson** Gerry Cranham, Rapho-Guillumette; **John F. Kennedy** Ted Spiegel, Rapho-Guillumette; **Martin Luther King, Jr.** Wide World Photos;

lamb Cal Sacks; **Lenin** Tass, from Sovfoto; **Abraham Lincoln** Library of Congress; **Lin Piao** Wide World Photos; **Martin Luther** Uffizi Gallery, Florence, Photo Alinari; **James Madison** U.S. Bureau of Engraving; **manual alphabet** Gallaudet College, Washington, D.C.; **Mao Tse-tung** Eastfoto; **Karl Marx** Sovfoto; **William McKinley** Library of Congress; **James Monroe** The Metropolitan Museum of Art, Bequest of Seth Low, 1929; **Benito Mussolini** United Press International Photo; **Napoleon I** Samuel H. Kress Collection, National Gallery of Art, Washington, D.C.; **Richard M. Nixon** United Press International Photo; **Noah** Pierpont Morgan Library; **note** Cal Sacks; **Pericles** British Museum; **Saint Peter** Vatican Grottoes, Leonard Von Matt; **Franklin Pierce** Library of Congress; **James K. Polk** U.S. Bureau of Engraving; **pork** Cal Sacks; **Quetzalcoatl** Bibliothèque Nationale; **Franklin Delano Roosevelt** Franklin D. Roosevelt Library; **Theodore Roosevelt** The White House Collection; **rune** Alice Koeth; **Sitting Bull** National Archives; **Joseph Stalin** Sovfoto; **William Howard Taft** Library of Congress; **Zachary Taylor** U.S. Bureau of Engraving; **Harry S Truman** Wide World Photos; **John Tyler** The White House Collection; **Martin Van Buren** Library of Congress; **Victoria**[1] Radio Times Hulton Picture Library; **Booker T. Washington** Chicago American's Morgue; **George Washington** Pennsylvania Academy of Fine Arts; **Woodrow Wilson** The White House Collection; **zodiac** Zodiac design adapted from zodiac drawn by Hans Holbein and Albrecht Dürer, reproduced with the permission of Charles Scribner's Sons from *Shakespeare's Globe Playhouse* by Irwin Smith, © 1956 Charles Scribner's Sons.

Roget's
THESAURUS

Editors' Preface

PETER MARK ROGET (1779–1869) was a British lexicographer and physician. *Roget's Thesaurus*, a standard reference work for over a century, represents his highly personal view of how the English language reflects the structure of the universe. In some ways, that view is dated today; but the complex structure and breadth of the thesaurus still prove surprisingly helpful to the modern user.

For most users, the key to the synonyms in the body of the book lies in the alphabetical listing in the index. The uniqueness of Roget's original plan of classification provides the user with access to related words and requires nothing more than a near-synonym to help locate the word sought. *Roget's Thesaurus* is more than simply a synonym dictionary—both in the lists following individual headwords and in the grouping of headwords under the various sections, it is a diverse collection of associated and related words and phrases.

For example, suppose you are looking for a synonym for *lull:* a check in the index yields the reference number, 403; turning to that entry provides the synonyms *silence, stillness, quiet, hush, peace.*

But, suppose you are trying to find a verb meaning 'to feel very dissatisfied' and the synonyms listed under *discontent* are not "strong" enough for your purpose. A brief check of the related, contiguous headwords will lead you to the entry for *regret* which provides the synonyms *lament, deplore, bemoan, bewail, rue.*

This edition of *Roget's Thesaurus* has a number of other special features. Dictionaries of synonyms, unless they are of considerable size, rarely provide alphabetical listings of all the words in the book. In this edition, you will find every word listed in the index.

Larger books may provide more synonyms, but the user of a thesaurus is rarely looking for a rare or unusual word: he wants an equivalent word that is part of everyday language. This edition is the only abridged *Roget's Thesaurus* available. While retaining the original structure and all the 1,000 headwords, all antiquated words and phrases have been removed. In addition, the book has been modernized to include the most current usage and the newest developments in language.

It is the Editors' sincere opinion that this volume will serve the user in a great many situations in which a larger, more comprehensive work would prove confusing or misleading. Certainly, its handy size is sure to prove convenient for any writer who wishes to use the English language more expressively and precisely.

Laurence Urdang
Editor in Chief
Mark Boyer
Managing Editor

In this abridgment, many duplications have been omitted to save space. For maximum usefulness, the user should look through other associated parts of speech for the word he is seeking, for adjectives and verbs can yield nouns and adverbs, and vice versa. For example, adverbs can be formed by adding *-ly* to some adjectives and nouns by adding *-ness* to some adjectives.

Caution: If the word selected is not completely familiar, check its meaning and usage in this volume's dictionary before risking its use in an incorrect or unidiomatic context.

Plan of Classification
(following the original Roget plan)

Tabular Synopsis of Categories

Class I. ABSTRACT RELATIONS

I. EXISTENCE

1. existence	2. nonexistence
3. substantiality	4. unsubstantiality
5. intrinsicality	6. extrinsicality
7. state	8. circumstance

II. RELATION

9. relation	10. nonrelation
11. consanguinity	
12. correlation	
13. identity	14. contrariety
15. difference	
16. uniformity	16a. lack of uniformity
17. similarity	18. dissimilarity
19. imitation	20. nonimitation
20a. variation	
21. copy	22. prototype
23. agreement	24. disagreement

III. QUANTITY

25. quantity	26. degree
27. equality	28. inequality
29. mean	
30. compensation	
31. greatness	32. smallness
33. superiority	34. inferiority
35. increase	36. decrease
37. addition	38. deduction
39. adjunct	40. remainder
	40a. decrement
41. mixture	42. simpleness
43. junction	44. disjunction
45. link	
46. coherence	47. incoherence
48. combination	49. decomposition
50. whole	51. part
52. completeness	53. incompleteness
54. composition	55. exclusion
56. component	57. extraneousness

IV. ORDER

58. order	59. disorder
60. arrangement	61. derangement
62. precedence	63. sequence
64. precursor	65. sequel
66. beginning	67. end
68. middle	
69. continuity	70. discontinuity
71. term	
72. assemblage	73. dispersion
74. focus	
75. class	
76. inclusion	77. exclusion
78. generality	79. specialty
80. regulation	81. multiformity
82. conformity	83. unconformity

V. NUMBER

84. number	
85. numeration	
86. list	
87. unity	88. accompaniment
89. duality	
90. duplication	91. bisection
92. triality	
93. triplication	94. trisection
95. quaternity	

1

96. quadruplication	97. quadrisection
98. five, etc.	99. quinquesection
100. plurality	100a. fraction
	101. zero
102. multitude	103. fewness
104. repetition	
105. infinity	

VI. TIME

106. time	107. absence of time
108. period	109. course
110. durability	111. transience
112. perpetuity	113. instantaneousness
114. chronometry	115. anachronism
116. antecedence	117. posteriority
118. present time	119. different time
120. contemporaneousness	
121. the future	122. the past
123. newness	124. oldness
125. morning; noon	126. evening; midnight
127. youth	128. age
129. infant	130. veteran

131. adolescence

132. earliness	133. lateness
134. opportuneness	135. inopportuneness
136. frequency	137. infrequency
138. regularity	139. irregularity

VII. CHANGE

140. change	141. permanence
142. cessation	143. continuance
144. conversion	
	145. reversion
146. revolution	
147. substitution	148. interchange
149. changeableness	150. stability
151. present events	152. future events

VIII. CAUSATION

153. cause	154. effect
155. attribution	156. chance
157. power	158. impotence
159. strength	160. weakness
161. production	162. destruction
163. reproduction	
164. producer	165. destroyer
166. parentage	167. posterity
168. productiveness	169. unproductiveness
170. agency	
171. energy	172. inertness
173. violence	174. moderation
175. influence	175a. absence of influence
176. tendency	
177. liability	
178. concurrence	179. counteraction

Class II. SPACE
I. SPACE IN GENERAL

180. space (indefinite)	180a. inextension
	181. region (definite)
	182. place
183. situation	
184. location	185. displacement
186. presence	187. absence
188. inhabitant	189. habitation
190. contents	191. receptacle

II. DIMENSIONS

192. size	193. littleness
194. expansion	195. contraction
196. distance	197. nearness
198. interval	199. contiguity
200. length	201. shortness

202. breadth, thickness	203. narrowness, thinness
204. layer	205. filament
206. height	207. lowness
208. depth	209. shallowness
210. summit	211. base
212. verticality	213. horizontality
214. suspension	215. support
216. parallelism	217. obliquity
218. inversion	
219. crossing	
220. exteriority	221. interiority
222. centrality	
223. covering	224. lining
225. dress	226. undress
227. environment	228. interspersion
229. circumscription	
230. outline	
231. edge	
232. enclosure	
233. limit	
234. front	235. rear
236. side	237. opposition
238. right	239. left

III. FORM

240. form	241. formlessness
242. symmetry	243. distortion
244. angularity	
245. curvature	246. straightness
247. circularity	248. convolution
249. rotundity	
250. convexity	252. concavity
251. flatness	
253. sharpness	254. bluntness
255. smoothness	256. roughness
257. notch	
258. fold	
259. furrow	
260. opening	261. closure
262. perforator	263. stopper

IV. MOTION

264. motion	265. rest
266. journey	267. navigation
268. traveler	269. mariner, flier
270. transference	
271. carrier	
272. vehicle	273. ship
274. velocity	275. slowness
276. impulse	277. recoil
278. direction	279. deviation
280. precedence	281. sequence
282. progression	283. regression
284. propulsion	285. traction
286. approach	287. recession
288. attraction	289. repulsion
290. convergence	291. divergence
292. arrival	293. departure
294. ingress	295. egress
296. reception	297. ejection
298. eating	299. excretion
300. insertion	301. extraction
302. passage	
303. infringement	304. shortcoming
305. ascent	306. descent
307. elevation	308. depression
309. leap	310. plunge
311. circular motion	
312. rotation	313. evolution
314. oscillation	
315. agitation	

3

Class III. MATTER
I. MATTER IN GENERAL

316. materiality
318. world
319. gravity

317. immateriality

320. levity

II. INORGANIC MATTER

321. density
323. hardness
325. elasticity
327. tenacity
329. structure
330. granularity
331. friction
333. fluidity
335. liquefaction
337. water
339. moisture
341. ocean
343. gulf, lake
345. marsh
347. stream
348. river
350. conduit
352. semiliquidity
354. pulpiness

322. thinness
324. softness
326. inelasticity
328. brittleness

332. lubrication
334. gaseity
336. vaporization
338. air
340. dryness
342. land
344. plain
346. island

349. wind
351. air-pipe
353. bubble, cloud
355. unctuousness
356. oil
356a. resin

III. ORGANIC MATTER

357. animate matter
359. life

364. animality
366. animal
368. zoology
370. ranching
372. mankind
373. man
375. sensibility
377. pleasure
379. touch
380. sensations of touch
382. heat
384. calefaction
386. furnace
388. fuel
389. thermometer
390. taste
392. pungency
393. condiment
394. savoriness
396. sweetness
398. odor
400. fragrance
402. sound
404. loudness
406. snap
408. resonance

410. stridency
411. cry
413. melody, concord
415. music
416. musician
417. musical instruments
418. hearing
420. light

358. inanimate matter
360. death
361. killing
362. corpse
363. interment
365. vegetation
367. vegetable
369. botany
371. agriculture

374. woman
376. insensibility
378. pain

381. numbness
383. cold
385. refrigeration
387. refrigerator

391. tastelessness

395. unsavoriness
397. sourness
399. inordorousness
401. fetor
403. silence
405. faintness
407. roll
408a. nonresonance
409. sibilation

412. ululation
414. discord

419. deafness
421. darkness

422. dimness

4

423. luminary	424. shade
425. transparency	426. opacity
	427. semitransparency
428. color	429. colorlessness
430. whiteness	431. blackness
432. gray	433. brown
434. red	435. green
436. yellow	437. purple
438. blue	439. orange
440. variegation	
441. vision	442. blindness
	443. dimsightedness
444. spectator	
445. optical instruments	
446. visibility	447. invisibility
448. appearance	449. disappearance

Class IV. INTELLECT
I. FORMATION OF IDEAS

450. intellect	450a. absence of intellect
451. thought	452. absence of thought
453. idea	454. topic
455. curiosity	456. incuriosity
457. attention	458. inattention
459. care	460. neglect
461. inquiry	462. answer
463. experiment	
464. comparison	
465. discrimination	465a. indiscrimination
466. measurement	
467. evidence	468. counter-evidence

469. qualification

470. possibility	471. impossibility
472. probability	473. improbability
474. certainty	475. uncertainty
476. reasoning	477. intuition, sophistry
478. demonstration	479. confutation
480. judgment	481. misjudgment
480a. discovery	
482. overestimation	483. underestimation
484. belief	485. disbelief, doubt
486. credulity	487. incredulity
488. assent	489. dissent
490. knowledge	491. ignorance
492. scholar	493. ignoramus
494. truth	495. error
496. maxim	497. absurdity
498. intelligence, wisdom	499. imbecility, folly
500. sage	501. fool
502. sanity	503. insanity
	504. madman
505. memory	506. oblivion
507. expectation	508. nonexpectation
	509. disappointment
510. foresight	
511. prediction	
512. omen	
513. oracle	
514. supposition	
515. imagination	

II. COMMUNICATION OF IDEAS

516. meaning	517. meaninglessness
518. intelligibility	519. unintelligibility

520. equivocalness

521. figure of speech	
522. interpretation	523. misinterpretation
524. interpreter	
525. manifestation	526. latency
527. information	528. concealment
529. disclosure	530. ambush
531. publication	

532. news	533. secret
534. messenger	
535. affirmation	536. negation, denial
537. teaching	538. misteaching
	539. learning
540. teacher	541. learner

542. school

543. veracity	544. falsehood
	545. deception
	546. untruth
547. dupe	548. deceiver
	549. exaggeration
550. indication	
551. record	552. obliteration
553. recorder	
554. representation	555. misrepresentation
556. painting	
557. sculpture	
558. engraving	
559. artist	
560. language	
561. letter	
562. word	563. neology
564. nomenclature	565. misnomer
566. phrase	
567. grammar	568. solecism
569. style	
570. perspicuity	571. obscurity
572. conciseness	573. diffuseness
574. vigor	575. feebleness
576. plainness	577. ornament
578. elegance	579. inelegance
580. voice	581. muteness
582. speech	583. inarticulateness
584. loquacity	585. taciturnity
586. public address	587. response
588. conversation	589. soliloquy
590. writing	591. printing
592. correspondence	593. book
594. description	
595. dissertation	
596. compendium	
597. poetry	598. prose
599. the drama	

Class V. VOLITION
I. INDIVIDUAL VOLITION

600. will	601. necessity
602. willingness	603. unwillingness
604. resolution	605. irresolution
604a. perseverance	
606. obstinacy	607. recantation
	608. caprice
609. choice	
	609a. neutrality; absence of choice
	610. rejection
611. predetermination	612. impulse
613. habit	614. disuse
615. motive	615a. absence of motive
	616. dissuasion
617. plea	
618. good	619. evil
620. intention	621. chance
622. pursuit	623. avoidance
	624. relinquishment
625. business	
626. plan	
627. method	
628. mid-course	629. circuit
630. requirement	
631. instrumentality	
632. means	
633. instrument	

634. substitute
635. materials
636. store
637. provision

638. waste

639. sufficiency

640. insufficiency
642. importance
644. utility
646. expedience
648. goodness
650. perfection
652. cleanness
654. health
656. salubrity
658. improvement
660. restoration
662. remedy
664. safety
666. refuge
668. warning
669. alarm
670. preservation
671. escape
672. deliverance
673. preparation
675. essay
676. undertaking
677. use

641. redundance
643. unimportance
645. inutility
647. inexpedience
649. badness
651. imperfection
653. uncleanness
655. disease
657. insalubrity
659. deterioration
661. relapse
663. bane
665. danger
667. pitfall

674. nonpreparation

678. disuse
679. misuse

680. action
682. activity
684. haste
686. exertion
688. fatigue
690. agent
691. workshop
692. conduct
693. direction
694. director
695. advice
696. council
697. precept
698. skill
700. expert
702. cunning
704. difficulty
706. hindrance
708. opposition
710. opponent
712. party
713. discord
715. defiance
716. attack
718. retaliation
720. contention
722. warfare
724. mediation
725. submission
726. combatant
727. arms
728. arena
729. completion
731. success
733. trophy
734. prosperity

681. inaction
683. inactivity
685. leisure
687. repose
689. refreshment

699. unskillfulness
701. bungler
703. artlessness
705. facility
707. aid
709. cooperation
711. auxiliary

714. concord

717. defense
719. resistance
721. peace
723. pacification

730. noncompletion
732. failure

735. adversity

736. mediocrity

II. INTERSOCIAL VOLITION

737. authority
739. severity
741. command
742. disobedience

738. laxity
740. lenience

743. obedience

744. compulsion
745. master
747. scepter
748. freedom
750. liberation

746. servant

749. subjection
751. restraint
752. prison

753. keeper
755. commission

754. prisoner
756. abrogation
757. resignation

758. consignee
759. deputy
760. permission
762. consent
763. offer
765. request
767. petitioner
768. promise
769. compact
770. conditions
771. security
772. observance

761. prohibition

764. refusal
766. deprecation

773. nonobservance

774. compromise

775. acquisition
777. possession
778. participation
779. possessor
780. property
781. retention
783. transfer
784. giving
786. apportionment
787. lending
789. taking
791. stealing
792. thief
793. booty
794. barter
795. purchase
797. merchant
798. merchandise
799. market
800. money
801. treasurer
802. treasury
803. wealth
805. credit
807. payment
809. expenditure
811. accounts
812. price
814. dearness
816. liberality
818. prodigality

776. loss
777a. exemption

782. relinquishment

785. receiving

788. borrowing
790. restitution

796. sale

804. poverty
806. debt
808. nonpayment
810. receipt

813. discount
815. cheapness
817. economy
819. parsimony

Class VI. AFFECTIONS
I. AFFECTIONS IN GENERAL

820. affections
821. feelings
822. sensibility
824. excitation
825. excitability

823. insensibility

826. inexcitability

II. PERSONAL AFFECTIONS

827. pleasure
829. pleasurableness
831. content

834. relief
836. cheerfulness
838. rejoicing
840. amusement
842. wit

828. pain
830. painfulness
832. discontent
833. regret
835. aggravation
837. dejection
839. lamentation
841. weariness
843. dullness

8

844. humorist
845. beauty
847. ornament

850. taste
852. fashion

858. hope

861. courage
863. rashness
865. desire

866. indifference

870. wonder
872. prodigy
873. repute
875. nobility
877. title
878. pride
880. vanity
882. ostentation
883. celebration
884. boasting
885. insolence
887. blusterer

846. ugliness
848. blemish
849. simplicity
851. vulgarity

853. ridiculousness
854. fop
855. affectation
856. ridicule
857. laughing-stock
859. hopelessness
860. fear
862. cowardice
864. caution
867. dislike

868. fastidiousness
869. satiety
871. expectance

874. disrepute
876. commonalty

879. humility
881. modesty

886. servility

III. SYMPATHETIC AFFECTIONS

888. friendship
890. friend
892. sociality
894. courtesy
896. congratulations
897. love
899. favorite

902. endearment
903. marriage

906. benevolence

910. philanthropy
912. benefactor
914. pity
915. condolence
916. gratitude
918. forgiveness

889. enmity
891. enemy
893. seclusion, exclusion
895. discourtesy

898. hate

900. resentment
901. irascibility
901a. sullenness

904. celibacy
905. divorce
907. malevolence
908. malediction
909. threat
911. misanthropy
913. evildoer
914a. pitilessness

917. ingratitude
919. revenge
920. jealousy
921. envy

IV. MORAL AFFECTIONS

922. right
924. claim
926. duty

928. respect

931. approbation
933. flattery
935. flatterer
937. vindication
939. probity

942. disinterestedness

923. wrong
925. unrightfulness
927. dereliction of duty
927a. exemption
929. disrespect
930. contempt
932. disapprobation
934. detraction
936. detractor
938. accusation
940. improbity
941. knave
943. selfishness

944. virtue
946. innocence
948. good man
950. penitence
952. atonement
953. temperance

955. asceticism
956. fasting
958. sobriety
960. purity

963. legality
965. jurisdiction
966. tribunal
967. judge
968. lawyer
969. lawsuit
970. acquittal

973. reward

945. vice
947. guilt
949. bad man
951. impenitence

954. intemperance
954a. sensualist

957. gluttony
959. drunkenness
961. impurity
962. libertine
964. illegality

971. condemnation
972. punishment
974. penalty
975. scourge

V. RELIGIOUS AFFECTIONS

976. deity
977. angel
979. fabulous spirit
981. heaven
983. theology
983a. orthodoxy
985. revelation
987. piety

990. worship

995. churchdom
996. clergy
998. rite
999. canonicals
1000. temple

978. devil
980. demon
982. hell

984. heterodoxy
986. religious writings
988. impiety
989. irreligion
991. idolatry
992. sorcery
993. spell
994. sorcerer

997. laity

Thesaurus

Class I

Words Expressing Abstract Relations

I. Existence

1 existence *n* being, entity, subsistence, reality, actuality, presence, fact, matter of fact, truth, science of existence: ontology.

v exist, be, subsist, live, breathe; occur, happen, take place; consist in, lie in; endure, remain, abide, survive, last, stay, continue.

adj existent, extant; prevalent, current, afloat; real, actual, true, positive, absolute; substantial, substantive; well founded, well grounded.

adv actually, in fact, in reality.

2 nonexistence *n* inexistence; insubstantiality, nonentity; blank, *tabula rasa*, void, emptiness, nothingness; potential, possibility; annihilation, extinction, obliteration, total destruction.

v not exist; pass away, perish, die, die out, disappear, dissolve; annihilate, destroy, obliterate, wipe off the face of the earth; nullify, void; take away, remove.

adj nonexistent, inexistent; blank, void, empty; unreal, baseless, unsubstantial, intangible, ineffable, spiritual, spectral; unborn, uncreated, unbegotten, unconceived; potential, possible; exhausted, gone, lost, departed, extinct, defunct; fabulous, visionary, imaginative, ideal, conceptual, abstract.

3 substantiality *n* materiality, corporality, tangibility, material existence, bodiliness, matter, stuff; creature, being, person, body, flesh and blood, substance; thing, object, article.

adj substantive, substantial, corporeal, material, bodily, physical, concrete, tangible, palpable, corporal, materialistic.

4 unsubstantiality *n* nothingness; nothing, naught, nil, nullity, zero; shadow, phantom, apparition, dream, illusion; fallacy, inanity, frivolity; hollowness, blank, void; flimsiness, thinness, slightness.

v vanish, evaporate, fade, dissolve, melt away, disappear.

adj unsubstantial, baseless, groundless, ungrounded, without foundation, fallacious, erroneous, untenable; insignificant, slight, thin, trifling, frivolous; imaginary, visionary, dreamy, shadowy, ethereal, airy, immaterial, spectral, illusory, incorporeal, intangible, bodiless, abstract; vacant, vacuous, empty, blank, hollow.

5 intrinsicality *n* ego, essence, quintessence, gist, pith, marrow, sap, lifeblood, backbone, heart, soul, core; principle, nature, constitution, construction, character, type, quality; habit, temper, temperament, personality, spirit, humor, grain, moods, features, peculiarities, aspects, idiosyncrasies, tendencies, bents; inbeing, inherence, essentiality.

v be intrinsic, be inherent.

adj intrinsic, inherent, implanted, innate, inborn, inbred, ingrained; essential, fundamental, basic, normal; inherited, congenital, hereditary, indigenous, in the blood, in the genes; instinctive, instinctual, internal, personal, subjective; characteristic, peculiar, idiosyncratic; fixed, set in one's ways, invariable, unchangeable, incurable, ineradicable.

adv intrinsically, at bottom, in effect, practically, virtually, substantially.

6 extrinsicality *n* extraneousness, externals.

adj extrinsic, extraneous, external, adventitious; collateral, accidental, incidental, objective.

adv extrinsically.

7 state *n* condition, case, circumstances, situation, status, surroundings, pass, plight, pickle; mood, temper, frame; constitution, structure, form, phase, frame, fabric, stamp, set, fit, mold; mode, style, fashion, light, complexion, character; tone, tenor, turn.

v be in a state.

8 circumstance *n* situation, phase, position, condition, posture, attitude, place, point; footing, standing, status; occasion, happening, event, juncture, conjunction; predicament, exigency, emergency, crisis, pinch, plight, pass; climax, apex, turning point.

adj circumstantial, conditional, provisional; contingent, incidental, adventitious; critical, climactic.

adv under the circumstances, under the conditions; thus, in such wise; accordingly, that being the case, since, seeing that, as matters stand; conditionally, provided, if, in case; if so, if it so happen, in the event of, provisionally, unless.

II. Absolute Relation

9 relation *n* connection, concern, bearing, reference; correlation, analogy; similarity, affinity, homogeneity, alliance, association, nearness; approximation, relationship; comparison, ratio, proportion; link, tie, bond.

v relate to, refer to; bear upon, regard, concern, touch, affect, have to do with, pertain to, appertain to, belong to; bring into relation with, associate, connect, parallel; link, bind, tie.

adj relative, relative to, relating to, referable to, with reference to; belonging to; related, connected, associated, affiliated, allied; in the same category, relevant.

adv as regards, about, concerning, with relation to, with reference to, with regard to, with respect to, in connection with, under the head of, in the matter of.

10 [absence of relation] **non-relation** *n* irrelation, dissociation, lack of connection; disconnection, disjunction; inconsequence, irreconcilability, disagreement, heterogeneity; independence.

v have no relation to, have no bearing upon, have nothing to do with, have no connection with.

adj unrelated, irrespective, unallied, unconnected, disconnected, heterogeneous, independent; adrift, insular, isolated; extraneous, strange, alien, foreign, outlandish, exotic; irrelevant, inapplicable, not pertinent, beside the mark, off base; remote, farfetched, out-of-the-way, forced, detached, distanced; incidental, parenthetical.

adv parenthetically, by the way, by the by; incidentally.

11 [relations of kindred] **consanguinity** *n* relationship, kindred, blood; parentage, paternity, maternity, lineage, heritage; filiation, affiliation, connection, alliance, tie; family, blood relation, ties of blood, kinsman, kinfolk, kith and kin, relation, relative, one's own, one's own flesh and blood; fraternity, sorority, brotherhood, sisterhood; race, stock, generation.

v be related to, claim relationship with.

adj related, akin, consanguineous, allied, affiliated, connected; kindred, familial.

12 [double or reciprocal relation] **correlation** *n* correspondence, reciprocity, reciprocation, interdependence, mutuality, interchange, exchange.

v reciprocate, alternate, interchange, interact, interdepend; interchange, exchange; correlate, correspond, relate.

adj reciprocal, mutual, correlative, corresponding, analogous, complementary; equivalent, interchangeable, alternate.

adv reciprocally.

13 identity *n* sameness, exactness, equality, correspondence, parallelism, unity, convertibility, resemblance, similarity; self, oneself, name, personality; facsimile, duplicate, replica, copy, reproduction.

v be identical, coincide, coalesce.

adj identical, self, the same, selfsame; coincident, coinciding, coalescent, indistinguishable; one, equal, equivalent.

adv identically.

14 contrariety *n* contrast, foil, antithesis, oppositeness, opposition, contradiction, antipathy, antagonism; the reverse, the inverse, the converse, inversion, subversion, reversal, the opposite, antipodes.

v be contrary, contrast with, differ from, oppose; invert, revert, turn upside down; contradict, contravene; antagonize.

adj contrary, opposite, counter, converse, reverse; opposed, antithetical, contrasted, antipodean, antagonistic, opposing; conflicting, inconsistent, contradictory; negative, hostile.

15 difference *n* discrepancy, disparity, dissimilarity, inconsistency, variance, variation, diversity, imbalance, disagreement, inequality, inequity, divergence, contrast, contrariety; discrimination, distinction, nice distinction, shade, nuance, subtlety.

v differ, vary; diversify, modify, change, alter; contrast, mismatch; discriminate, distinguish.

adj different, diverse, heterogeneous, unlike, divergent, altered, changed, deviant, deviating, variant, varied, modified; diversified, various, divers, miscellaneous, manifold; other, another, not the same, unequal, unmatched, wide apart; distinctive, characteristic, discriminative.

16 uniformity *n* homogeneity, permanence, continuity, consistency, stability, accordance, standardization, conformity, agreement; regularity, constancy, evenness, sameness; monotony, routine, invariability.

v be uniform, accord with; conform to, assimilate; level, smooth, even.

adj uniform, homogeneous, of a piece, consistent; consistent, regular, constant, even, level; invariable, unchanging, unvarying, unvaried, unchanged, constant, regular; undiversified, solid, plain, dreary, monotonous, routine.

adv uniformly; always, invariably, without exception; ever, forever.

16a lack of uniformity *n* diversity, irregularity, unevenness, inconsistency, nonconformity, heterogeneity.

adj diversified, varied, irregular, inconsistent, motley, patchwork, uneven, rough; multifarious, of various kinds.

17 similarity *n* resemblance, likeness, similitude, semblance, affinity, approximation, parallelism; agreement, correspondence, analogy; brotherhood, family likeness; repetition, sameness, uniformity, identity; the like, fellow, match, pair, mate, twin, double, counterpart; alter ego, chip off the old block, birds of a feather, like two peas in a pod; simile, parallel, type, image, representation.

v be similar, resemble, look like, bear a resemblance, take after, approximate, parallel, match, rhyme with.

adj similar, resembling, like, alike; twin; analogous, parallel, of a piece; allied to, akin to, corresponding; approximate, much the same, near, close, something like; imitative, mock, pseudo, simulating, representing, representative; exact, true, lifelike, faithful, true to life, identical.

adv as if, so to speak; as it were, as if it were; quasi, just as.

18 dissimilarity *n* dissimilitude, unlikeness, difference; diversity, disparity, divergence; novelty, originality, uniqueness.

v be unlike, differ from, bear no resemblance; vary, diversify, differentiate.

adj dissimilar, unlike, different, disparate; unique, new, novel, unprecedented, unmatched, unequaled; diversified.

19 imitation *n* copying; copy, duplication, reproduction, replica; mocking, mimicry, aping; simulation, impersonation, representation, semblance, approximation, paraphrase, parody; plagiarism, forgery.

v imitate, copy, mirror, reflect, impersonate, duplicate, reproduce, simulate, counterfeit; mock, take off, mimic, ape, personate, parody, caricature, travesty; follow, emulate, pattern after, model oneself on, parallel, follow, take after.

adj imitative, modeled after, modeled on, based on; fake, phony, counterfeit, false, imitation, mock; duplicate, second hand.

adv literally, word for word, to the letter.

20 nonimitation *n* originality, uniqueness.

adj unimitated, uncopied; unmatched, unparalleled; inimitable, original, unique, special, one of a kind, rare, exceptional.

20a variation *n* alteration, change, modification; divergence, deviation, aberration, innovation.

v vary, change; deviate, diverge, alternate, modify.

adj varied, modified, diversified, altered, changed.

21 [result of imitation] **copy** *n* facsimile, counterpart, effigy, form, likeness, similitude, semblance, cast, mold, model, representation, image, portrait; reflexion, shadow, echo; transcript, transcription, reproduction, imitation, carbon, ditto, stencil, duplicate, reprint, transfer, replica; parody, caricature, burlesque, travesty, paraphrase; counterfeit, forgery, deception.

adj faithful, lifelike, exact, similar.

22 [thing copied] **prototype** *n* original, model, pattern, precedent, standard; type, archetype, exemplar, paradigm, module, example; text, copy, design; die, mold; matrix, mint, seal, punch, intaglio, negative, plate, stamp.

v be an example, set an example.

23 agreement *n* unanimity, harmony, accord, accordance, concord, union, unity, understanding, settlement, treaty, pact; uniformity, conformity, consistency, congruity, logic, correspondence, parallelism, apposition; consent, assent, concurrence, cooperation.

v agree, accord, harmonize; correspond, tally, (*informal*) jibe; meet, suit, fit, befit, square with, dovetail, match; adapt, fit, accommodate, adjust.

adj agreeing, accordant, correspondent, congenial, harmonious; reconcilable, comfortable, compatible, congruous, consistent, logical, consonant, commensurate; in accordance with, in harmony with, in keeping with; apt, apposite, pat, pertinent; agreeable, happy, felicitous.

24 disagreement *n* discord, dissonance, dissidence, disunion, discrepancy, nonconformity, incongruity, dissension, conflict, opposition, antagonism, difference; disparity, disproportion, mismatch, variance, divergence, inequity, inequality.

v disagree, clash, jar, argue, quarrel, dispute.

adj disagreeing, discordant, dissonant, inharmonious; at variance, hostile, conflicting, antagonistic, clashing, disputing, factious, dissenting, irreconcilable, incompatible, inconsisterĺ with; incongruous, disproportionate, disparate, divergent; disagreeable, uncongenial, mismatched; out of joint, out of step, out of tune.

III. Simple Quantity

25 [absolute quantity] **quantity** *n* size, mass, volume, amount, measure, measurement, substance, strength; mouthful, spoonful, handful; stock, batch, lot, dose.

adj quantitative, some, any, more or less.

26 [relative quantity] **degree** *n* grade, extent, measure, amount, ratio, standard, height, pitch; reach, range, scope, rate, caliber; gradation, shade, tint; tenor, tone, compass; sphere, station, rank, standing; point, mark, stage, level; intensity, strength.

adj comparative, gradual, shading off.

adv by degrees, gradually, step by step, bit by bit, little by little, inch by inch, drop by drop; in some degree, to some extent; up to a point.

27 [sameness of quantity or degree] **equality** *n* parity, symmetry, balance, counterbalance; evenness, monotony, level; equivalence, equipose, equilibrium; par, even keel, quits; identity, similarity; tie, dead heat, draw, drawn game; neck and neck race; match, peer, equal, mate, fellow, brother; equivalent.

v equal, match, reach, keep pace with, run abreast; come up to; balance, even the score; equalize, level, trim, adjust; strike a balance; restore equilibrium.

adj equal, even, level, monotonous, coequal, symmetrical, balanced; on a par with, on a level with, on an equal footing with, up to the mark; equivalent, tantamount, synonymous, quits, even, much the same, all one, one and the same; drawn, half and half, six of one and half a dozen of another.

adv equally, to all intents and purposes.

28 [difference of quantity or degree] **inequality** *n* disparity, dissimilarity, difference, odds; unevenness, imbalance; inferiority, shortcoming, deficiency, imperfection, inadequacy; mediocrity; superiority.

v be unequal, have the advantage, turn the scale, turn the tide; topple, overmatch; not come up to, fall short of, not come up to snuff.

adj unequal, uneven, imbalanced; disparate, partial, inferior, insufficient, deficient, inadequate, mediocre, short.

29 **mean** *n* medium, average, balance, middle, midpoint, center, median, golden mean; compromise, neutrality.

v split the difference, take the average, move to the center.

adj mean, intermediate, middle, average, standard, normal, neutral; mediocre, middle class, bourgeois, commonplace, run of the mill, egalitarian.

adv on the average, in the long run.

30 **compensation** *n* equation; indemnification, requital; compromise, measure for measure, tit for tat, eye for an eye, retaliation, equalization; setoff, off-set, counterpoise, ballast; indemnity, equivalent, *quid pro quo*, amends, reparation.

v compensate, indemnify, recompense, remunerate; counterbalance, counterpoise, countervail, offset, counteract, balance, balance out, make up for, square, even out, equalize; cover, neutralize, nullify; redeem, atone, make amends.

adj compensatory, compensating, equivalent, equal.

adv but, however, yet, still, notwithstanding, nevertheless, although, though, nonetheless; howbeit, albeit; at all events, at any rate, be that as it may, even so, on the other hand, at the same time.

31 **greatness** *n* magnitude, size, bulk, dimensions, vastness; multitude; enormousness, immensity, might, strength, intensity, fullness; importance, distinction, eminence, renown; quantity, store, volume, mass, bulk, heap; abundance, sufficiency.

v be great, soar, tower, rise above, transcend; enlarge, increase, expand.

adj great, large, considerable, big, huge, mammoth, gigantic, ample, abundant, sufficient; full, intense, strong; widespread, extensive, wholesale; goodly, noble, precious, mighty; utter, uttermost, arch, profound, intense, consummate; extraordinary, important, unsurpassed, supreme; complete, total; vast, immense, enormous, extreme, inordinate, excessive, extravagant, exorbitant, outrageous, monstrous; towering, stupendous, prodigious, marvelous; unlimited, infinite; absolute, positive, stark, decided, unequivocal, essential, perfect; remarkable, notable, noteworthy.

adv [in a positive degree] truly; decidedly, unequivocally, absolutely, essentially, fundamentally, downright; [in a complete degree] entirely, completely, totally, wholly; abundantly, fully, amply, widely; [in a great or high degree] greatly, much, indeed, very, very much, most, pretty, pretty well, enough, in so, in a great measure, to a large extent; richly, on a large scale; ever so much; mightily, powerfully; extremely, exceedingly, intensely, exquisitely, consummately, acutely, indefinitely, immeasurably, beyond compare, beyond measure, beyond all bounds, incalculably, infinitely; [in a supreme degree] pre-eminently, superlatively, supremely, incomparably; [in a too great degree] immoderately, inordinately, exorbitantly, excessively, enormously, preposterously, monstrously, out of all proportion, with a vengeance; [in a marked degree] particularly, remarkably, singularly, curiously, uncommonly, unusually, peculiarly, notably, signally, strikingly, pointedly, mainly, chiefly; famously, egregiously, prominently, glaringly, emphatically, strangely, wonderfully, amazingly, surprisingly, astonishingly, incredibly, marvelously, stupendously; [in a violent degree] violently, furiously, severely, desperately, tremendously, extravagantly; [in a painful degree] painfully, sadly, sorely, bitterly, piteously, grievously, miserably, cruelly, woefully, lamentably, shockingly, frightfully, fearfully, dreadfully, terribly, horribly.

32 **smallness** *n* littleness, tininess, diminutiveness; slenderness, thinness, paltriness, slightness; paucity, fewness, sparseness, scarcity; unimportance, triviality, inconsequentiality, pettiness, insignificance; meanness, sordidness, selfishness, narrow-mindedness; small quantity, modicum, atom, particle, molecule, point, speck, dot, dab, mote, jot, iota; minutiae, details, *soupçon*, scintilla, granule; drop, droplet, drizzle, sprinkling, dash, smack, tinge; dole, scrap, shred, splinter; mite, bit, morsel, crumb, seed; snippet, snatch, slip; chip, sliver; nutshell, thimbleful, spoonful, handful, mouthful; fragment, fraction, drop in the ocean; trifle.

v be small.

adj small, little, tiny, diminutive, petite, miniature, minuscule, minute, microscopic, infinitesimal, fine; unimportant, trivial, minor, secondary, trifling, inconsequential, petty, paltry, insignificant; slender, thin, slight, scanty, meager, insufficient; few, sparse, scarce; low, so-so, middling, tolerable, inconsiderable, inappreciable; mean, sordid, selfish, narrow, narrow-minded, illiberal, ungenerous; feeble, weak, faint.

adv [in a small degree] to a small extent; a wee bit; slightly, imperceptibly, faintly; miserably, wretchedly; insufficiently, imperfectly; passably, pretty well, well enough; [in a certain or limited degree] partially, in part, to a certain degree; some, rather, to some degree; simply, only, purely, merely, at the least; ever so little; almost, nearly, well nigh, short of, not quite, all but, near the mark; scarcely, hardly, barely, only just, no more than; [in an uncertain degree] about, thereabouts, somewhere about; [in no degree] noway, nowise, not at all, not in the least, not a bit, not a jot, not a whit, in no respect, by no means, on no account.

33 superiority *n* supremacy, pre-eminence, ascendancy, transcendence; excellence, greatness, nobility, eminence, worthiness, preponderance, predominance, prevalence, advantage; majority; quality; high caliber.

v be superior, exceed, excel, transcend, outdo, outweigh, outrival, outrank; pass, surpass; top, cap, outstrip, eclipse, predominate, prevail; take precedence, come first.

adj superior, greater, major, higher, exceeding; supreme, greatest, utmost, paramount, pre-eminent, foremost, crowning; first-rate, important, excellent, unrivaled, matchless, priceless, unparalleled, unequaled, unsurpassed, inimitable, incomparable, superlative, beyond compare, transcendent.

adv beyond, more, over, over and above, at its height; [in a superior or supreme degree] eminently, pre-eminently, prominently, surpassingly, superlatively, supremely, above all, to crown all, *par excellence;* principally, especially, particularly, peculiarly.

34 inferiority *n* low quality, deficiency, imperfection, shortcoming, inadequacy; mediocrity, commonalty, commonness, poorness, meanness; minority, subordination, subjection.

v be inferior, fall short of, come short of, not come up to, not pass muster; want, lack.

adj inferior, minor, less, lesser, deficient; poor, indifferent, mean, base, bad, shabby, paltry, humble, imperfect, mediocre, common, commonplace, second-rate; poorer; secondary, minor, subordinate, lower; diminished, reduced, unimportant.

adv less, subpar; short of, under.

35 increase *n* growth, augmentation, enlargement, extension, expansion, addition, increment, accretion, aggrandizement; development, rise, ascent.

v increase, grow, dilate, enlarge, expand, multiply; augment, add to, enlarge, greaten; extend, spread out, prolong; advance, rise, sprout, ascend; raise, exalt, deepen, heighten, intensify, magnify, redouble; aggrandize.

adj increasing, growing; additional, incremental; developmental.

36 decrease *n* diminution, abatement, decline, reduction, wane, falling-off, contraction, dwindling, shrinking, lessening, ebb, ebbing; subtraction, abridgment, shortening; depreciation, deterioration.

v decrease, lessen, abate, fall off, decline, contract, shrink, dwindle, wane, ebb, subside; diminish, deteriorate, depreciate, languish, decay; abridge, shorten, subtract.

adj decreased, decreasing, on the wane.

37 addition *n* increment, increase, enlargement, aggrandizement, accession; supplement, adjunct, attachment, addendum; annexation, interposition, insertion; uniting, joining.

v add, annex, affix, subjoin, tack on, append, attach, join, supplement, increase, augment, make an addition to; accrue, accumulate, pile up; total, sum, add up; reinforce.

adj additional, supplemental, supplementary; extra, accessory, auxiliary.

adv in addition, more, plus; and, also, likewise, too, further, furthermore, besides, to boot, etc., and so on, and so forth; over and above, moreover; with, as well as, together with, along with, in conjunction with.

38 deduction *n* subtraction, retrenchment, withdrawal, removal; mutilation, amputation, curtailment; shortening, abbreviation; decrease, cutback.

v deduct, subtract, retrench, withdraw, remove; take from, take away; shorten, abbreviate, cut back, pare down, reduce, decrease, diminish, curtail, eliminate, deprive of; mutilate, amputate, cut off, cut away, excise; pare, thin, thin out, prune, scrape, file.

adj subtracted, subtracting; removable, reducible; deductible.

adv less, short of; minus, without, excepting, except, with the exception of, save, exclusive of.

39 [thing added] **adjunct** *n* addition, affix, suffix, appendage, annex, augmentation, increment, reinforcement, accessory, accompaniment, sequel; addendum, complement, supplement, appendix, attachment; rider, offshoot, episode, corollary.

adj additional.

40 [thing remaining] **remainder** *n* residue, remains, remnant, leftover, excess, superfluity, balance, surplus, rest, relic; leavings, odds and ends, residuum, dregs, refuse, crumbs, stubble, ruins, skeleton, stump.

v remain, survive, be left; be left over.

adj remaining, left, left over, residual; over, odd, spare, unused; superfluous; surviving.

40a [thing deducted] **decrement** *n* discount, defect, loss, deduction.

41 mixture *n* admixture, mix, combination, mingling, amalgamation, junction; infusion, suffusion, transfusion; infiltration, interlarding, interpolation; adulteration, thing mixed; tinge, tincture, touch, dash, sprinkling, spice, seasoning, infusion, compounds; alloy, amalgam, mélange, pastiche, miscellany, medley, patchwork, hotchpotch, gallimaufry, conglomeration, jumble, potpourri, farrago; cross, hybrid, mongrel.

v mix, join; combine, blend, mingle, commingle, confuse, jumble, unite, compound, amalgamate, adulterate; interlard, interlace, intertwine, interweave, interpolate; conjoin, associate, consort; instill, imbue, infuse, suffuse, transfuse, infiltrate, dash, tinge, tincture, season, blend, cross.

adj mixed, composite, half-and-half, hybrid, cross, mongrel, heterogeneous; motley, variegated, miscellaneous, promiscuous, indiscriminate.

adv among, amongst, amid, amidst, with; in the midst of.

42 [freedom from mixture] **simpleness** *n* purity, homogeneity; elimination, sifting, purification.

v simplify; sift, winnow, eliminate, strain, clean, purify; disentangle.

adj simple, uniform, homogeneous, single, pure, clear; unmixed, unadulterated, elemental, elementary, basic.

43 junction *n* joining, union; connection, conjunction, annexation, attachment; coupling, marriage, wedlock; confluence, communication, concatenation; meeting, assemblage, assembly, reunion; joint, joining, juncture, pivot, hinge, articulation; seam, stitch, linkage, link.

v join, unite, connect, link up, link; associate; put together, piece together, bind together; attach, fix, affix, fasten, bind, secure, clinch, twist, tie, string, strap, sew, lace, stitch, hem, knit, button, buckle, hitch, lash, splice, gird, tether, picket, moor, harness, leash; chain; fetter, lock, hook, couple, link, yoke, bracket; marry, wed, bridge over, span; pin, bolt, clasp, clamp, screw, rivet; solder, weld, fuse; entwine, interlace, intertwine, interweave; entangle.

adj joined, joint; corporate, compact; firm, fast, close, tight, taut, secure, set, inseparable, indissoluble.

adv jointly, in conjunction with; fast, firmly; intimately.

44 disjunction *n* disconnection, disunion, disengagement, dissociation, discontinuity; isolation, insularity, insulation, separateness; dispersion; separation, parting; detachment, segregation; divorce; division, subdivision, break, fracture, rupture; dismemberment, dislocation, severance; fissure, breach, rent, split, rift, crack, cut, slit, incision.

v disjoin, disconnect, disengage, disunite, dissociate, divorce, part, detach, separate, disentangle, cut off, rescind, discontinue; segregate, set apart, keep apart, isolate, insulate; cut adrift, loose, set free, liberate; divide, subdivide, sever, dissever, cut, saw, snip, chop, ax, cleave, rive, rend, slit, split, splinter, chip, crack, snap, break, tear, burst, rend; wrench, rupture, shatter; hack, hew, slash, slice, cut up, carve, dissect, tear to pieces; disband, disperse, dislocate, break up, apportion, divide; part, part company, separate, leave.

adj disjoined, discontinuous, disjunctive; isolated, insular; separate, apart, asunder, loose, adrift, free; unattached, unconnected.

adv separately, one by one, severally, apart, adrift, asunder.

45 link *n* connective, connection, vinculum, copula, tie, bond, bridge; junction, bracket.

v link, bond, join, connect, conjoin, fasten, pin, bind, tie; bridge, span.

46 coherence *n* cohesion, cohesiveness, adherence, adhesion, adhesiveness; connection, union, conglomeration, aggregation, consolidation; stickiness, inseparability.

v cohere, adhere, stick, cling, cleave, hold, take hold, clasp, hug; hang together, stay together; glue, cement, paste, solder, weld; consolidate, solidify, agglomerate.

adj cohesive, adhesive, adhering, sticky; tenacious, tough; united, unified, inseparable, inextricable, (*informal*) together, (*informal*) tight.

47 incoherence *n* looseness, laxity, relaxation, nonadhesion; loosening, disjunction, disconnection; disagreement, inconsistency, incongruity.

v loosen, make loose, slacken, relax; detach, disjoin.

adj nonadhesive, noncohesive, detached, loose, slack, lax, relaxed, segregated, unconsolidated; inconsistent, incongruous, illogical, absurd, rambling.

48 combination *n* mixture; junction; union, unification, synthesis, incorporation, amalgamation, coalescence, fusion, blend, blending, mix, centralization; compound, alloy, amalgam, composition, composite.

v combine, unite, incorporate, amalgamate, absorb, blend, mix, merge, fuse, marry, consolidate, coalesce, centralize, cement, harden, solidify.

adj combined, unified.

49 decomposition *n* analysis, dissection, dissolution, breaking down; disjunction; corruption, decay, rot, putrefaction.

v decompose, analyze, dissolve; resolve into its elements, dissect, disperse, crumble; decay, rot, turn.

adj decomposed.

50 [principal part] whole *n* totality, entirety, total, sum, aggregate; unity, completeness, integrity, indivisibility; bulk, mass, lump; body, trunk.

v form a whole, integrate, embody, amass, aggregate, assemble; amount to, come to, add up to.

adj whole, total, full, entire, undiminished, undivided, integral, complete, unimpaired, unbroken, faultless, sound, intact; indivisible, indissoluble.

adv wholly, altogether; totally, completely, entirely, all, all in all, wholesale, in a body, collectively, in the main, on the whole.

51 part *n* division, portion, piece, fragment, fraction, lump, bit, component, constituent, ingredient, element, section, segment, subdivision; member, limb, branch, bough, offshoot, ramification; compartment, department, class.

v part, divide, break, disjoin; partition, apportion, allot.

adj fractional, fragmentary, sectional; divided, split up.

adv partly, in part, partially; piecemeal, bit by bit, by installments, in dribs and drabs, in drips and snatches; in detail.

52 completeness *n* wholeness, entirety, totality, solidarity, fullness, intactness, unity, perfection; thoroughness.

v complete, accomplish, fulfill, finish; fill, charge, load, replenish; fill up, fill in; saturate.

adj complete, entire, whole, full, intact, undivided, one, perfect, fulfilled; full, good, absolute, thorough, solid; exhaustive, radical, sweeping, thoroughgoing; consummate, unmitigated, sheer, unqualified, unconditional; brimming, brimful, chock-full, saturated, crammed, replete, fraught.

adv completely, altogether, outright, wholly, totally, quite, utterly; fully, thoroughly, in all aspects, in every respect, out and out, to all intents and purposes; throughout, from first to last, from beginning to end, from top to bottom, from head to foot, every whit, every inch.

53 incompleteness *n* deficiency, shortcoming, insufficiency, imperfection; immaturity; noncompletion.

[part wanting] defect, deficit, omission, interval, break; discontinuity, missing link.

v be incomplete, fall short of; lack; neglect.

adj incomplete, imperfect, unfinished, uncompleted; defective, deficient, wanting, lacking, failing, short, short of; meager, lame, limp, perfunctory, sketchy, crude, immature; in progress, in preparation, going on, ongoing, proceeding.

adv incompletely.

54 composition *n* constitution, make-up, form; combination, compilation, incorporation, inclusion, synthesis.

v be composed of, be made up of, consist of; include, contain, hold, comprehend, take in, admit, embrace, embody; compose, constitute, form, make.

adj constituting.

55 exclusion *n* omission, exception, rejection, repudiation; exile, seclusion, segregation, separation, elimination, prohibition; restraint, keeping out.

v exclude, bar, leave out, shut out, keep out; reject, repudiate, blackball, throw out, lay aside, put aside, set aside; relegate, segregate, separate, seclude, banish, exile; pass over, omit, eliminate, weed out, winnow.

adj exclusive, not included in; inadmissible.

56 component *n* component part, integral part, element, constituent, ingredient; contents, feature, member, part; personnel.

v enter into, be part of, form part of; merge in, share in, participate; belong to, appertain to; form, make, constitute.

adj inclusive, comprehensive.

57 extraneousness n extrinsicality, externality; super-fluousness; foreign body, foreign substance; intrusion.

v be extraneous, be unnecessary.

adj extraneous, foreign, alien, extrinsic, external; not germane, nonessential, superfluous; excluded.

IV. Order

58 order n regularity, uniformity, arrangement, harmony, symmetry; course, routine, method, methodology; disposition, array, arrangement, system, economy, discipline, orderliness; gradation, progression, series, sequence, continuity; rank, place, grade, class, degree.

v order, regulate, manage, adjust, arrange, systematize, standardize, rank.

adj orderly, regular, systematic, methodical; in order, neat, tidy, well-regulated, well-organized, organized, uniform, symmetrical, businesslike, shipshape.

adv in order, methodically, in turn, in its turn; step by step, at regular intervals, systematically.

59 disorder n derangement, disarray, untidiness, irregularity, anomaly; anarchy, anarchism, disunion, discord; confusion, jumble, mess, muddle, hash, hodgepodge, chaos; perplexity, labyrinth, wilderness, jungle; raveling, entanglement, complication, convolution; turmoil, ferment, agitation, trouble, row, disturbance, convulsion, tumult, uproar, riot, rumpus, ruckus, scramble, fracas, melee, pandemonium.

v disorder, put out of order, derange, ruffle, rumble; confuse, jumble, mess up.

adj disorderly, out of order, out of place, irregular, desultory; anomalous, disorganized, straggling, unsystematic, untidy, slovenly, messy; indiscriminate, chaotic, confused, deranged; anarchic, inverted, convoluted, topsy-turvy; complex, complicated, perplexed, involved, raveled, entangled, knotted, tangled; troublesome, problematical; riotous, violent, turbulent, tumultuous.

adv irregularly, helter skelter; at cross purposes, (informal) after the flood.

60 [reduction to order] **arrangement** n plan, method, organization; preparation, groundwork, planning; sorting, disposal, disposition, distribution, assortment, allotment, apportionment, graduation, groupings; analysis, classification, division, ordering, systematization.

v arrange, dispose, place, form; set out, marshal, range, array, rank, group, parcel out, allot, apportion, assign, dole out, distribute; sort, sift, put into shape; plan, prepare, organize, lay the groundwork; classify, divide, file, register, catalog, record, tabulate, index, graduate, rank; regulate, systematize, coordinate, organize, settle, fix; unravel, disentangle, straighten out.

adj arranged, ordered; methodical, orderly, regular, systematic.

61 [subversion of order] **derangement** n disorder, mess, disarray, disorganization; discomposure, disturbance, dislocation, perturbation, interruption.

v derange, disarrange, discompose, displace, misplace; mislay, disorder, disorganize; embroil, disconcert, convulse, unsettle, disturb, confuse, trouble, perturb, jumble, muddle, fumble; unhinge, dislocate, throw out of gear, throw out of whack; invert, turn upside down, turn topsy-turvy; complicate, confound, tangle, entangle; litter, scatter, mix.

62 precedence n coming before, the lead, superiority; precursor, antecedence; importance, consequence; priority, preference.

v precede, come before, forerun, come first; head, lead the way, usher in, introduce; set the fashion, influence, establish; have precedence, take precedence; place before, prefix, preface.

adj preceding, precedent, antecedent, anterior, prior, before; former, foregoing; preliminary, prefatory, introductory; preparatory.

adv before; in advance.

63 sequence n coming after, following, succession, order, series; posteriority; continuation; order of succession; outcome, consequence, result, sequel.

v succeed, come after, follow, ensue; replace.

adj succeeding, following; consequent, subsequent; proximate, next; sequential, consecutive.

adv after, subsequently; behind.

64 precursor n antecedent, precedent, predecessor, forerunner, pioneer, leader, bellwether; herald, harbinger; prelude, preamble, preface, prolong, proem, prefix, foreword, introduction; heading, frontispiece, groundwork; preparation.

adj prefatory, introductory, preliminary, precursory.

65 sequel n continuation, extension, supplement, outgrowth, offshoot, result, consequence, inference, deduction; result, consequence, aftermath, outcome, effect; conclusion, end, culmination, dénouement, finale, finish; appendage, suffix, epilog, postscript, tag, train, trail, wake; afterthought, afterpiece, second thoughts.

66 beginning n commencement, opening, outset, start, initiation, inauguration; introduction, prelude; outbreak, onset, brunt; initiative, first move; origin, cause, source, bud, germ, genesis, birth, nativity, cradle; starting point, first step, square one; title page, head, heading; rudiments, basics, elements.

v begin, commence, open, start, initiate, inaugurate; conceive; set out, embark, depart; usher in, lead the way, take the lead, take the initiative, head, stand at the head, launch, set in motion, get going, take the first step, break ground; burst forth, break out; begin at the beginning, start again, start over, make a fresh start; originate, conceive, think up.

adj initial, introductory, inaugural; incipient; embryonic, rudimental, primal, essential, natal, nascent; first, foremost, leading; maiden, virgin.

adv first, in the first place, first and foremost; in the bud, in its infancy; from the beginning.

67 end n close, termination, conclusion, finale, finish, last word; consummation, climax, apex, dénouement; goal, destination; expiration, death, finality; limit, extreme, extremity; break up, last stage, final stage, turning point, death blow.

v end, close, finish, terminate, conclude; expire, die, come to a close, draw to a close, run its course, run out, pass away; bring to an end, put an end to, make an end of, wrap up; get through, complete, consummate; stop, desist, call it quits.

adj final, terminal, concluding; conclusive, crowning, definitive, last, ultimate, consummate; ended, settled, decided, over, concluded, played out.

adv finally, at last, once and for all, over and done with.

68 middle n center, midpoint, midst; mean, midcourse, middle ground, compromise; core, kernel, heart, nucleus, nub; equidistance, bisection; equator, diaphragm, midriff.

adj middle, medial, mean, mid, median, midmost; intermediate, equidistant, central, halfway.

adv midway, halfway, in the middle.

69 [uninterrupted sequence] **continuity** n continuousness, consecutiveness, progression, constant flow, succession, train, series, chain, string, scale, gradation; round, suite; procession, column, retinue;

pedigree, genealogy, lineage; rank, file, line, row, range, tier.

v follow in a line; arrange in a series, string together, file, thread, graduate, tabulate.

adj continuous, progressive, successive, serial, consecutive, unbroken, uninterrupted, gradual; linear, in a line; perennial, constant.

adv continuously, in succession, consecutively; gradually, step by step, in a column.

70 [interrupted sequence] **discontinuity** *n* disjunction, disconnectedness; interruption, break, fracture, fault, flaw, crack, cut; gap, interval, caesura, pause, (*informal*) breather, rest, intermission, parenthesis, episode.

v alternate; discontinue, break, interrupt, intervene; pause, rest, take a breather, stop; break in upon, interpose; disconnect.

adj discontinuous, disconnected, unconnected, broken, interrupted; fitful, spasmodic, desultory, intermittent, irregular; alternate, recurrent, periodic.

adv at intervals, in snatches, by fits and starts.

71 term *n* rank, station, stage, step, phase; scale, grade, degree, status, position, place, point, mark, period, limit; stand, standing, footing.

72 assemblage *n* collection, levee, gathering, ingathering, muster; concourse, conflux, congregation; meeting, reunion; assembly, congress, convention, conclave, council; miscellany, compilation, menagerie; crowd, throng, mob, flood, rush, rash, deluge, press, crush, horde, body, tribe, crew, gang, squad, band, party, swarm, flock, bevy; company, troop, regiment, squadron, army; host, multitude, populace, clan, brotherhood, sisterhood, association; group, cluster, clump, batch, pack, assortment; accumulation, heap, lump, pile, mass, conglomeration, conglomerate, aggregation, aggregate; quantity.

v assemble, come together, collect, gather, muster; meet, unite, join, rejoin; cluster, flock, swarm, surge, stream, herd, crowd, throng, associate; congregate, concentrate, huddle; bring together, draw together, place together, lump together; convene, invoke; compile, group, assemble, unite; amass, accumulate, store.

adj assembled; closely packed, dense, crowded, teeming, swarming, populous.

73 dispersion *n* divergence, spreading, radiation, dissemination, diffusion, dissipation, distribution, apportionment, division.

v disperse, scatter, sow, disseminate, diffuse, shed, spread, dispense, disband, distribute, apportion, divide; break up, dispel, cast forth, strew, cast, sprinkle; issue, deal out, dole out.

adj dispersed, spread, scattered, strewn, diffuse, diffusive; sparse, widespread, broadcast; adrift, stray, disheveled.

74 [place of meeting] **focus** *n* center, gathering place, haunt, rendezvous, rallying point, headquarters, club, retreat.

v focus, bring to a point, bring to a focus; center on, bring out, clarify, elucidate.

75 class *n* division, subdivision, category, heading, order, section; department, province, domain; type, kind, sort, genus, species, variety, family, race, tribe, caste, clan, breed, sect.

76 inclusion *n* admission, acceptance into, incorporation, comprehension, reception.

v include, comprise, comprehend, contain, admit, embrace, receive, accept; inclose, circumscribe, encircle, encompass, embody, incorporate; number among, count among, fall under.

adj inclusive, comprehensive, extensive, all-embracing, compendious, sweeping; including, incorporating.

77 exclusion *n* (see 55).

78 generality *n* universality, catholicity, miscellany, miscellaneousness; generalization, simplification, oversimplification; prevalence, common run.

v be general, be universal, prevail, be true for everyone; render general, generalize, universalize; make a generalization, abstract, simplify.

adj general, universal, catholic, common, ecumenical, egalitarian, worldwide; prevalent, prevailing, rife, current; generic, collective, all-encompassing, comprehensive, all-inclusive, broad, widespread.

79 specialty *n* speciality, skill, ability, talent; individuality, singularity, distinctive feature, particularity, personality, characteristic, mannerism, idiosyncrasy, nonconformity; particulars, details, items; special feature.

v specify, particularize, individualize, specialize; designate, determine, single out, isolate, differentiate; be specific, come to the point, detail, get down to particulars.

adj special, particular, especial, individual, specific, proper, personal, original, private, respective, definite, certain, endemic, peculiar, characteristic, marked, appropriate, exclusive, singular, exceptional, idiomatic, unique.

adv specially, especially, in particular; each, apiece, severally, respectively, each to each, each to his own; in detail.

80 regulation *n* regularity, uniformity, constancy, clockwork, precision, exactness; routine, custom, formula, rule, form, procedure; standard, model, precedent, prototype; conformity, convention; nature, law, principle; normal state, ordinary condition, normalcy; hard and fast law.

adj regular, uniform, constant, steady; customary, conventional, formal, formulaic, procedural.

81 multiformity *n* variety, diversity.

adj multifold, multifarious, manifold, many-sided; heterogeneous, motley, mosaic; indiscriminate, irregular, diversified, diverse; of every description, all manner of kinds.

82 conformity *n* observance, compliance, assent; conventionality, customariness, agreement; example, instance, specimen, sample, illustration, exemplification, case in point.

v conform to, accommodate oneself to, adapt to; be regular, conform, follow the rules, obey the rules, go by the rules, comply, assent, agree, yield, give in, accept, harmonize; illustrate, stand as an example, embody.

adj conformable to rule, adaptable, agreeable, compliant, malleable; conventional, customary, standard, ordinary, common, habitual, usual, natural, normal, typical; formal, orthodox, strict, rigid, uncompromising; exemplary, illustrative.

adv by rule, in conformity with, in accordance with, in keeping with, consistent with; for the sake of conformity, as a matter of course, for form's sake; invariably, uniformly.

83 unconformity *n* nonconformity, unconventionality, nonobservance, informality; anomaly, variation, inconsistency, irregularity, incongruity, oddity, eccentricity, peculiarity, aberration, abnormality, exception; violation of custom, infraction, infringement; individuality, originality, mannerism, idiosyncrasy, quirk.

v be unconformable.

adj unconformable, unconventional; unnatural, odd, eccentric, peculiar, aberrant, abnormal, exceptional; anomalous, inconsistent, irregular, incongruous, arbitrary, whimsical, wanton; unusual, uncustomary, uncommon, rare, singular, unique, extraordinary; queer, quaint, strange; original, fan-

tastic, newfangled, bizarre, outlandish, exotic, esoteric.

adv unless, except, save, beside.

V. Number

84 number *n* numeral, symbol, figure, cipher, digit,
integer, round number, whole number, fraction;
sum, total, product.

adj numeral; prime, fractional, decimal; positive,
negative.

85 numeration *n* numbering; tallying, enumeration,
reckoning, computation, calculation; arithmetic,
calculus, algebra; statistics, poll, census, roll call;
arithmetic operations.

v number, count, tell, tally, enumerate, add up,
sum, reckon, compute, calculate, take account;
muster, poll, recite; add, subtract, multiply, divide.

adj numeral, numerical; arithmetical, analytic,
algebraic, statistical, numerable, computable, calculable.

86 list *n* catalog, index, listing, inventory, schedule,
register, record, ledger, tally, file, table, calendar;
directory, gazette, atlas, dictionary, thesaurus; roll,
checklist.

87 unity *n* oneness, singleness, singularity, individuality; unification, unison, uniformity.

v unite, join, combine; isolate, insulate, seclude.

adj one, sole, single, solitary, lone; individual,
apart, alone; unaccompanied, unattended, single-
handed, solo; singular, odd, unique; isolated, insular.

adv singly.

88 accompaniment *n* association, partnership, company; accessory, adjunct, concomitant, attachment,
complement, attendant, fellow, associate, coexistence.

v accompany, join, escort, convoy, wait on;
coexist with, consort with; associate with, couple
with.

adj accompanying, fellow, twin, joint; associated
with, coupled with; accessory, concomitant, attendant.

adv with, together with, along with, in company
with, hand in hand, side by side; therewith, herewith.

89 duality *n* dualism, doubleness, polarity, biformity,
duplexity; two, deuce, couple, brace, pair, twins.

v pair, mate, couple, bracket, pair off, yoke.

adj two, twain; dual, twin, two-sided, binary,
binomial, duplex; coupled, both.

90 duplication *n* doubling, reduplication; iteration,
repetition; renewal.

duplicate, double, copy, carbon, facsimile.

v double; redouble, reduplicate; repeat, renew;
duplicate.

adj double; doubled, duplicated; twin, duplicate,
second.

adv twice, once more, over again.

91 bisection *n* halving, bifurcation, twofold division,
forking, dichotomy, (*informal*) fifty-fifty split.

v bisect, divide in two, halve, divide, split, cut in
two, cleave, fork, bifurcate; split down the middle,
(*informal*) go halves.

adj bisected, cloven, cleft, halved; bipartite;
bifurcated; semi-, demi-, hemi-.

92 triality *n* trinity; three, triad, triplet, trio.

adj three, threefold, triform, tertiary.

93 triplication *n* tripling; triplicity.

v triple, treble, cube.

adj triple, treble; threefold, triplicate; third.

adv three times, thrice; in the third place,
thirdly; triply, trebly.

94 trisection *n* tripartition, threefold division, third,
third part.

v trisect, divide into three parts.

95 quaternity *n* four, tetrad, quartet, quarter.

v square, reduce to a square.

adj four, fourfold, quadrilateral.

96 quadruplication *n* quadrupling, multiplying by
four.

v multiply by four, quadruplicate.

adj four, fourfold, quadruple; fourth.

adv four times, in the fourth place, fourthly.

97 quadrisection *n* quartering, quadripartition, fourfold division; fourth part, quarter.

v quarter, divide into four parts.

adj quartered, quadripartite.

98 five, etc. *n* five; six, half a dozen; seven; eight;
nine; ten, decade; eleven; twelve, dozen; thirteen,
baker's dozen, long dozen; twenty, score; twenty-
five, quarter of a hundred; fifty, half a hundred;
hundred, century, centenary; thousand.

99 quinquesection *n* fivefold division.

adj quinquepartite.

100 [more than one] **plurality** *n* two or more, couple,
few, several; majority, multitude.

adj plural, more than one, upwards of, some,
several, many, numerous.

100a [less than one] **fraction** *n* fractional part, segment, subdivision, part, portion.

101 zero *n* nothing, naught, (*informal*) zip; none,
shutout; nobody.

102 multitude *n* multitudinous, multiplicity, profusion,
mass, quantity, volume, abundance, amplitude,
enormity; numbers, array, scores, droves, host,
throng, collection; mob, crowd, assemblage.

v be numerous, swarm with, teem with, crowd,
swarm, outnumber, multiply; people, populate.

adj multitudinous, manifold, profuse, multiple,
teeming, populous, crowded, thick; many, several,
sundry, various, numerous; endless, infinite.

103 fewness *n* paucity, scarcity, sparseness, scantiness;
small number, small quantity; infrequency.

diminution of number: reduction, weeding, elimination.

v render few, reduce, diminish, weed, thin,
eliminate, eradicate.

adj few, not many, scanty, scarce, sparse, rare,
few and far between, limited, meager; sporadic,
occasional, infrequent; reduced, diminished, pared
back.

104 repetition *n* iteration, reiteration, recapitulation,
restatement; sameness, monotony, harping, recurrence, tautology; redundance; rhythm, beat, echo,
reverberation; reappearance, reproduction, duplication.

v repeat, iterate, reiterate, recapitulate, restate,
rehash, go over again, harp on, hammer; reproduce, duplicate, echo; recur, revert, return, reap-
pear; resume, return to, go back to; rehearse, go
over the same ground.

adj repeated, repetitious, recurrent, recurring,
frequent, incessant, never-ending, unceasing; repetitive, redundant, tautological; rhythmic, reverberant, reverberating; monotonous, harping, iterative; habitual.

adv repeatedly, often, again, anew, afresh, over
again, once more; over and over, again and again,
year after year; ditto, encore.

120

105 infinity *n* infinitude, infiniteness, perpetuity, endlessness, boundlessness, inexhaustibility, immeasurability, limitlessness, vastness, expanse.

v be infinite, have no limits, know no bounds, go on forever.

adj infinite, countless, numberless, limitless, boundless, measureless, unlimited, interminable, inexhaustible, incalculable; immense, vast, endless, perpetual; incomprehensible; eternal, perfect, omnipotent, absolute.

adv infinitely, *ad infinitum*.

VI. Time

106 time *n* duration, extent; period, interval, spell, term, space, span, season, stage; course; interim, interlude; interregnum, intermission; respite, break, timeout; era, epoch, season, age, year, date.

v time, measure, pace; continue, last, endure, go on, remain, persist, stand; pass time, spend time, while away the time, waste time, kill time, fill up the time.

adj permanent, lasting, durable; timely.

adv while, whilst, during, in the course of, for the time being, in due time; meantime, meanwhile, in the meantime, in the interim; till, until, up to, yet; the whole time, all the time, throughout, for good, (*informal*) for keeps.

107 absence of time *n* no time; outside time.

adv never, at no time; on no occasion, nevermore.

108 [definite duration or period of time] **period** *n* interval, age, era, eon, epoch, term, time; year, decade, century, millennium; lifetime, generation.

109 [indefinite duration] **course** *n* march of time, course of time, flux, passing time.

v elapse, lapse, flow, run, proceed, advance, pass, flit, fly, slip, slide, drag, creep, crawl; run its course; expire, go by, pass by.

adv in due time, in due course, in due season, in time.

110 [long duration] **durability** *n* permanence, persistence, continuance, lastingness, standing, stability; survival, longevity; protraction, prolongation.

v last, remain, stand, endure, abide, continue, persist; tarry, drag on, drag out, prolong, protract, eke out, draw out, lengthen; outlive, outlast, survive.

adj permanent, durable, lasting, longstanding, stable, immutable, invariable, constant; enduring, abiding, perpetual; lingering, protracted, prolonged, spun-out.

adv long, for a long time, ever so long; long ago; all day long, all the livelong day.

111 [short duration] **transience** *n* impermanence, evanescence, ephemerality, transitoriness, mortality; suddenness, swiftness, changeableness, vicissitude, uncertainty.

v be transient, flit, pass away, fly, gallop, vanish, fade, evaporate, melt.

adj transient, transitory, evanescent, ephemeral, fleeting, flitting, flying, passing; impermanent, temporal, temporary, provisional, short-lived; perishable, precarious, vulnerable, mortal; brief, quick, brisk; sudden, momentary, instantaneous.

adv temporarily, for the moment, for a time; awhile, soon; briefly.

112 [endless duration] **perpetuity** *n* eternity, timelessness, everlastingness, endlessness, infinity; constancy, endurance, durability, ceaselessness.

v last forever, endure, go on forever; perpetuate, immortalize, eternalize.

adj perpetual, eternal, timeless, everlasting, endless; unceasing, ceaseless, interminable, neverending, continuous, incessant, uninterrupted; unfading, imperishable, unvulnerable, immortal.

adv perpetually, always, ever, evermore, forever; constantly, continuously.

113 [point of time] **instantaneousness** *n* suddenness, abruptness; moment, instant, second, twinkling, trice, flash, crack, burst.

v be instantaneous, twinkle, flash.

adj instantaneous, momentary, sudden, instant, abrupt.

adv instantaneously, in no time, (*informal*) in two shakes (of a lamb's tail), presto, suddenly, like a shot, in a moment, all of a sudden, in a jiffy; immediately, on the spur of the moment, on a moment's notice.

114 [estimation, measurement and record of time] **chronometry** *n* chronology, timetable; almanac, calendar, register, chronicle, log, annal(s), journal, diary; clock, watch, stopwatch, timepiece, chronometer.

v fix the time, mark the time; date, register, chronicle; measure time, mark time, beat time.

adj chronological.

115 [false estimate of time] **anachronism** *n* misdate, misplacement, chronological error; disregard of time.

v misdate, antedate, postdate, anticipate; take no note of time.

adj misdated; undated, overdue; anachronistic, out of place, misplaced.

116 antecedence *n* priority, anteriority, precedence, preexistence; antecedent, predecessor, precursor, forerunner.

v precede, antedate, come before; go before, lead, forerun; dawn, presage, herald, break the ground.

adj antecedent, prior, previous, anterior, preceding, pre-existent; former, foregoing, aforementioned; precursory, introductory.

adv before, prior to; earlier, previously, ere, already, yet, beforehand.

117 posteriority *n* succession, sequence; subsequence, following, continuance; successor, sequel, follower; future, futurity.

v follow after, come after, go after, succeed, be subsequent to.

adj posterior, subsequent, following, after, later, succeeding, successive, ensuing, resulting; posthumous.

adv subsequently, after, afterwards, since, later; next, close upon, thereafter, thereupon; ultimately.

118 present time *n* the present juncture, the present day; the times, the time being, right now.

adj present, actual, instant, current, existing.

adv at this time, at this moment; at the present time, now, at present, nowadays.

119 different time *n* other time; another time.

adv at that time, at that instant; then, on that occasion; when, whenever, whensoever; at some other time, at a different time, at some time or other.

120 contemporaneousness *n* simultaneousness, synchronism, simultaneity, coincidence, concurrence, coexistence, concomitance.

v coexist, concur, accompany, go side by side, keep pace with; synchronize.

adj simultaneous, coincident, concurrent, concomitant, coexisting; contemporary, contemporaneous, coeval.

adv simultaneously, concurrently, together, at the same time.

121 the future *n* futurity, hereafter, time to come, tomorrow, morrow; millennium, doomsday, day of judgment, crack of doom, flood; advent, eventuality; destiny, fate; heritage, heirs, posterity; prospect, expectation, anticipation.

v look forward, anticipate, expect, foresee; approach, await, threaten, impend, come near, draw near, come on.

adj future, to come; coming, impending, near, close at hand, in prospect; eventual, ulterior.

adv prospectively, hereafter, in future, in course of time, tomorrow; eventually, ultimately, sooner or later; henceforth, from this time; soon, early, on the eve of, on the point of, on the brink of.

122 the past *n* past time, days of old, days of yore, days gone by, yesterday, yesteryear, former times, ancient times; retrospection, memory; antiquity, history, time immemorial, remote past; ancestry, lineage, forbears; heritage.

v run its course, pass away, pass, lapse, blow over.

adj past, gone, gone by, passed away, bygone, elapsed, lapsed, expired, extinct, forgotten, irrecoverable, obsolete; former, pristine, late; foregoing, last, latter, recent; looking back, retrospective; retroactive.

adv formerly, of old, of yore, ago, over; long ago, years ago, a long while back, some time ago; lately, of late; retrospectively, ere now, before now, hitherto, heretofore; already, yet, up to this time.

123 newness *n* novelty, recentness, freshness; immaturity, greenness, youth, juvenility; innovation, uniqueness, originality; renovation, restoration; modernity, modernism, stylishness, fashionableness, newfangledness, fashion, faddishness, the latest thing, futurism, trendiness.

v renew, renovate, restore; modernize.

adj new, novel, recent, fresh; green, immature, unripe, young, youthful, untried, untested, virgin, virginal; modern, late, new, newfangled, stylish, fashionable, faddish, trendy, brand-new, up-to-date; renovated, restored, spick and span.

adv newly, afresh, anew, lately, just now, of late.

124 oldness *n* age, antiquity; maturity, ripeness; decline, decay, old age, senility, superannuation; archaism, antiquarianism, relic, thing of the past; tradition, custom, common law.

v be old, have had its day, have seen its day; become old, age, fade.

adj old, ancient, antique; time-honored, venerable, traditional, vintage, of long standing; elderly, aged, hoary, decayed, senile, decrepit; primeval, primitive, aboriginal, primordial, antediluvian, prehistoric, archaic; traditional, prescriptive, customary, immemorial, inveterate, rooted; antiquated, outdated, outmoded, of other times; out of date, obsolete, out-of-fashion, out-of-style, gone by, stale, old-fashioned, timeworn, crumbling, ramshackle, run-down, wasted.

125 morning. noon *n* morning, morn, dawn, daybreak, sunrise, sunup, forenoon, break of day, peep of day, prime of day, morningtide, matins, cockcrow, first blush, antemeridian, A.M.

noon, midday, noonday, noontide, meridian, prime, height, noontime.

spring, springtime; summer, summertime, midsummer.

126 evening. midnight *n* evening, eve, eventide, dusk, vespers, nightfall, sundown, sunset, twilight, curfew, bedtime; afternoon, post meridian, P.M.

midnight, end of the day, close of the day, witching hour, dead of night.

autumn, fall, harvest time; winter.

127 youth *n* juvenility, infancy, childhood, boyhood, girlhood; minority, tender years, young years, formative years, next generation, tender age; cradle, nursery; puberty.

adj young, youthful, juvenile, green, callow, budding, immature, developing, underage, formative; younger, junior.

128 age *n* old age, advanced age, senility, years, gray hairs, declining years, golden years, mature years, decrepitude, anility, superannuation, longevity, ripe age, ripe old age; maturity, seniority, eldership.

adj aged, old, advanced, gray, elderly; senile, decline, failing, waning, ripe, overripe, mellow, venerable, wrinkled, wizened; older, elder, eldest.

129 infant *n* baby, babe, babe in arms, nursling, little one, tot, toddler, chick, kid, lamb, cherub; youth, youngster, child, minor; girl, lass, maiden, miss, schoolgirl; boy, lad, stripling, master, schoolboy.

adj infantile, infantlike, puerile, girlish, boyish, childish, babyish; newborn, young.

130 veteran *n* old man, old woman, patriarch, matriarch, grandmother, grandfather, grandsire, seer, graybeard, forefather, elder.

adj aged, old.

131 adolescence *n* majority, adulthood, manhood, womanhood, maturity, ripeness, fullness, puberty, pubescence; teenage years, prepubescence.

v come of age, grow up, attain majority.

adj adolescent, teenage, pubescent, of age, grown up, full grown, adult, womanly, manly, marriageable, nubile.

132 earliness *n* punctuality, promptitude, speediness, readiness, expedition, alacrity, quickness, haste; suddenness; prematurity, precocity, precipitation, anticipation.

v be early, be beforehand; anticipate, forestall, steal a march on, get a head start; bespeak, secure, engage, pre-engage; accelerate, expedite, quicken, hasten, make haste, make time, hurry.

adj early, timely, punctual, on time, prompt; premature, precipitate, precocious, anticipatory; sudden, instantaneous, immediate, expeditious; unexpected.

adv early, soon, anon, betimes, before long; punctually, to the minute, on time, on the dot; beforehand, prematurely, precipitately, too soon, hastily, in anticipation, unexpectedly; suddenly, instantaneously, at short notice, on the spur of the moment; at once, on the spot, on the instant, at sight, straight, offhand, straightway; forthwith, summarily, immediately, shortly, quickly, speedily; presently, by and by, directly.

133 lateness *n* tardiness, slowness, sloth, tarrying, dilly-dallying, loitering; delay, procrastination, postponement, adjournment, retardation, protraction, prolongation; respite, reprieve, suspension, moratorium, stop, stay.

v be late, tarry, wait, stay, bide, take time, linger, loiter, dawdle, shilly-shally, dilly-dally; put off, defer, delay, lay over, suspend; retard, postpone, adjourn; procrastinate, prolong, protract, drag out, draw out, lengthen, table, shelve, stall.

adj late, tardy, slow, dilatory, backward, unpunctual; delayed, overdue, belated.

adv late; backward, at the eleventh hour, at length, at last; ultimately, behind time; too late; slowly, leisurely, deliberately, at one's leisure, on one's own time.

134 opportuneness *n* timeliness, opportunity, occasion, suitable time, proper time, suitability, high time; crisis, turn, juncture; turning point, given time; nick of time, golden opportunity; clear stage, open field.

v be opportune, be suitable; seize the opportunity, seize the time, seize the day, *carpe diem*, use the occasion; suit the occasion, be expeditious, strike while the iron is hot.

adj opportune, timely, well-timed, seasonable, suitable, appropriate; providential, lucky, fortunate, happy, favorable, fortuitous, propitious, auspicious.

adv opportunely, in due time, in the nick of time, just in time, now or never; by the way, by the by, speaking of, while on the subject; on the spot, on the spur of the moment, since the occasion presents itself.

135 inopportuneness *n* untimeliness, unseasonableness, improper time, unsuitable time; (*informal*) bad timing; intrusion; anachronism.

v be ill timed, mistime, intrude, break in upon, (*informal*) butt in; lose an opportunity, waste an occasion, (*informal*) blow one's chance, let the opportunity slip by; waste time.

adj inopportune, untimely, unpropitious, unseasonable, unsuitable, inauspicious, unfavorable, unfortunate, unsuited, untoward, unlucky; ill-timed, mistimed, poorly timed; unpunctual, premature.

136 frequency *n* repetition, recurrence, iteration, reiteration.

v recur, repeat, reiterate; keep on, continue; attend regularly, visit often, patronize.

adj frequent, oft-repeated, recurring, incessant, constant, continual, perpetual; habitual, customary.

adv often, oft, oftentimes, frequently, repeatedly, day after day; daily, hourly, every day; perpetually, continually, constantly, incessantly, at all times; commonly, habitually, customarily; sometimes, occasionally, at times, now and then, every once in a while, from time to time.

137 infrequency *n* rarity, rare occurrence; long shot, surprise, (*informal*) mindblower.

v be rare, be infrequent.

adj infrequent, occasional, sporadic, rare, uncommon, unusual, unheard of, unprecedented; few, scant, scarce.

adv infrequently, rarely, seldom, scarcely, hardly; not often, hardly ever.

138 regularity [of recurrence] *n* periodicity, intermittence; beat, pulse, pulsation, rhythm; alternation, oscillation, vibration; bout, round, turn, revolution, rotation, rpm; cycle, period, routine; punctuality, regularity, steadiness.

v recur, revolve, return, come in its turn, come round again; beat, pulsate, alternate.

adj regular, periodic, periodical; serial, recurrent, cyclical, cyclic, recurring, rhythmical, rhythmic; intermittent, alternate, every other; regular, steady, punctual, continual, constant, regular as clockwork.

adv regularly, periodically, serially, cyclically; intermittently, alternately; by turns, in turn, in rotation, off and on, round and round.

139 irregularity [of recurrence] *n* uncertainty, unpredictability, haphazardness, fitfulness, capriciousness.

v be irregular, be haphazard.

adj irregular, uncertain, unpredictable, haphazard, fitful, capricious, flickering; spasmodic, sporadic.

adv irregularly, fitfully, capriciously, by fits and starts.

VII. Change

140 change *n* alteration, modulation, modification, variation, mutation, permutation, qualification, deviation, turn, shift, innovation; diversion, break; transformation, transfiguration, transmutation, metamorphosis; conversion, revolution, inversion, reversal; displacement, transference, transposition; changeableness.

v change, alter, vary, modulate, qualify, diversify, tamper with, play with, experiment with; turn, shift, veer, tack, swerve, warp, deviate, turn aside; turn, take a turn, (*informal*) hang a turn; modify, revamp, transform, transfigure, transmute, metamorphose, convert; innovate, restructure, give a new turn to, recast, redesign, remodel.

adj changed, newfangled; changeable, variable, transformable; innovative.

141 permanence *n* stability, invariability, unalterability, immutability, constancy; endurance, durability, persistence; maintenance, preservation, conservation; obstinacy, immovability, inflexibility, immobility, rigidity.

v endure, bide, abide, stay, remain, last, persist, stand, stand fast; maintain, keep, keep up, preserve; subsist, live, outlive, survive.

adj permanent, lasting, unchanged, unchanging, fixed, stable, invariable, constant; enduring, durable, abiding, everlasting; intact, inviolate; persistent.

adv permanently, for good, for good and all.

142 cessation *n* discontinuation, discontinuance, halt, stoppage, termination, suspension, interruption, stopping; pause, rest, lull, respite, truce, break; interregnum, abeyance; completion, end, finish; stop, death.

v cease, discontinue, terminate, desist, stay; break off, leave off, hold, stop, pull up, stop short, halt, pause, rest; suspend, interrupt, delay, cut short, arrest, bring to a standstill; complete, end, finish, close up shop; wear away, go out, die out, pass away, die.

143 continuance [in action] *n* continuation, continuity, protraction, prolongation, maintenance, perpetuation; persistence, perseverance, repetition.

v continue, persist, go on, keep on, hold on; abide, keep, pursue, stick to; maintain course, carry on, keep up; sustain, uphold, hold up, keep going, maintain, preserve, perpetuate, prolong.

adj continuing, uninterrupted, unvarying; continuous, persistent, perpetual.

144 conversion *n* transformation, transmutation, reduction, change, changeover, resolution, assimilation; passage, transit, transition, shifting, flux; growth, progress, development; chemistry, alchemy.

v be converted into, become, turn into, lapse, shift; pass into, grow into, ripen into, merge into; melt, grow, ripen, mature, mellow; convert into, resolve into; make, render, mold, form, model, remodel, remake, do over, reform, reorganize; assimilate, bring into, reduce to.

adj convertible, transmutable, changeable.

145 reversion *n* return, revulsion, reverting, returning; alternation, rotation; inversion; recoil, reaction, reflex, repercussion, rebound, boomerang, ricochet, backlash, repulse; retrospection, retrogression, retrogradation, falling back; restoration, going back; turning point, turn of the tide.

v revert, return, turn back, reverse; relapse, regress, fall back; recoil, rebound; retreat; restore; undo, unmake; turn the tide.

146 [sudden or violent change] **revolution** *n* revolt, rebellion, overthrow, overturn, coup, *coup d'etat*, rising, uprising, mutiny, counterrevolution; break up, destruction, subversion, clean sweep; spasm, convulsion, throe, revulsion.

v revolt, rebel, rise, rise up; revolutionize, re-model, recast, change.

adj revolutionary, rebellious; new.

147 substitution *n* replacement, supplanting, commutation, exchange, change, shift.

substitute, expedient, makeshift, stopgap, equivalent, double, alternative, representative.

v substitute, put in the place of, change, exchange, interchange; replace, supplant, supersede, take the place of, stand for, represent, pinch hit, substitute for, sub; redeem, commute, alternate.

adv instead, in place of, in lieu of.

148 [double or mutual change] **interchange** *n* exchange, commutation, permutation, transposition; reciprocation, reciprocity, intercourse; barter, swap, trade; interchangeability; retaliation, reprisal, requital, retort, crossfire.

v interchange, exchange, barter, trade, swap, bandy, transpose, commute, reciprocate; give and take, battle with words; retort, requite, retaliate.

adj interchangeable, all-purpose, multi-purpose; reciprocal; mutual.

adv in exchange, vice versa, turn and turn about.

149 changeableness *n* mutability, inconstancy, volatility, instability; malleability, adaptability, versatility, mobility; vacillation, irresolution, indecision, capriciousness, oscillation, alternation, fluctuation, vicissitude; restlessness, fidgetiness, disquiet, disquietude; unrest, agitation.

v fluctuate, oscillate, vary, waver, flounder, shuffle, hem and haw, vacillate, tremble, alternate.

adj changeable, mutable, variable, malleable, adaptable, adjustable, versatile, mobile, transformable, convertible; inconstant, unsteady, unstable, unreliable, vacillating, oscillating, fluctuating; volatile, fitful, fickle, capricious, mercurial, indecisive, irresolute, flighty, impulsive, fanciful, erratic, wayward, wanton; restless, fidgety, tremulous, agitated; unfixed, unsettled.

150 stability *n* immutability, unchangeableness, constancy; firmness, fixity, solidity, steadiness, soundness, balance, stabilization, equilibrium, quiescence; immobility, immovability, fixedness; steadfastness, reliability, resolution, determination, obstinacy, stubbornness, pertinacity, tenacity, doggedness, will, pluck, resoluteness; permanence, endurance, perseverance, durability; continuity, uniformity, changelessness.

v be firm, stick fast, stand firm; settle, establish, fix, set, stabilize; retain, keep hold; make sure, fasten, make solid.

adj stable, fixed, rigid, firm, steady, established, strong, sturdy, immovable, invariable, unvarying, permanent, unchangeable, unchanging, unalterable, immutable; enduring, constant, durable, lasting, abiding, secure, fast, perpetual; unwavering, steadfast, staunch, reliable, steady, solid, sound, balanced; resolute, obstinate, dogged, willful, stubborn, pertinacious, tenacious.

151 present events *n* event, occurrence, incident, affair, eventuality, happening, proceeding, transaction, fact; phenomenon; circumstance, situation, particular; adventure, episode, thrill; crisis, pass, emergency, contingency, impasse; things, doings, affairs, matters, issues; the world, life, the times.

v happen, occur, take place, come to pass, come about, come round; fall out, turn out, befall, chance, prove, eventuate; turn up, crop up, arise, arrive, issue, ensue, start, hold; take its course, pass off; experience, meet with, meet up with, fall to, be one's lot, be one's fortune, find, encounter, undergo, go through, live through, endure, put up with.

adj happening, going on, doing, current; eventful, stirring, bustling, busy, full of incident.

adv eventually, finally; as things go, in the course of things, as it happens.

152 future events *n* destiny, luck, lot, chance, fortune, karma, doom, end; future, futurity, next world, hereafter; prospects, expectations, tomorrow.

v impend, hang over, hover, threaten, loom, await, come on, approach; foreordain, preordain; destine, predestine, doom, have in store for.

adj impending, destined; coming, in store, to come, at hand, near, close by, imminent, brewing, forthcoming; in the wind, in the cards, in prospect, looming, on the horizon.

adv in time, in the long run, in good time, in its own sweet time, eventually.

VIII. Causation

153 cause *n* origin, source, principle, element; prime mover, first cause; author, producer, creator; mainspring, agent, catalyst; groundwork, foundation, support; spring, fountain, well, fount, font; genesis, descent, remote cause, influence; pivot, hinge, axis, turning point; egg, germ, embryo, root, nucleus, seed; causality, causation, origination, production.

v cause, originate, give rise to, occasion, sow the seeds of, kindle, bring to pass, bring about; produce, create, set up, develop; found, broach, institute; induce, evoke, elicit, draw, provoke; determine, decide; conduce to, contribute, have a hand in, influence, effect.

adj causal, generative, productive, formative, creative; primal, primary, original, embryonic.

adv because.

154 effect *n* consequence, issue, derivation, upshot, outgrowth, development, fruit, crop, harvest, product, outcome, end, conclusion; offspring, offshoot; complications, concomitants, side effects.

v be the effect of, be due to, be owing to; originate in, originate from, rise from, spring from, proceed from, emanate from, come from, grow from, issue from, flow from, result from; depend upon, hinge upon.

adj owing to, resulting from, due to, derivable from, caused by; derived from, evolved from; derivative, hereditary.

adv consequently, as a consequence, necessarily.

155 [assignment of cause] **attribution** *n* theory, ascription, assignment, rationale, reference to, accounting for; imputation, derivation; explanation, interpretation, reason why.

v attribute to, ascribe to, impute to, refer to, point to, trace to, assign to; account for, derive from; theorize, speculate.

adj attributed, attributable, referable, due to, owing to.

adv hence, thence, therefore, *ergo*, for, since, on account of, because; why? wherefore? whence? how come? how so?

156 [absence of assignable cause] **chance** *n* fortune, fate, accident, hap, hazard, luck, fluke, (*informal*) freak; gamble, lottery, tossup, fifty-fifty chance, throw of the dice, heads or tails; probability, possibility, contingency, odds; speculation, gaming, gambling.

v chance, hap, turn up; fall to one's lot; stumble on, light on; take one's chances.

adj chancy, causal, fortuitous, accidental, (*informal*) iffy, adventitious, haphazard, random, indeterminate, flukey, (*informal*) freaky.

adv by chance, by accident; at random; perchance, as chance will have it.

157 power *n* potency, strength, puissance, might, force, energy, vigor; control, command, dominion, authority, rule, sway, ascendancy, sovereignty, omnipotence; ability, capability, capacity, facility, competence, competency, efficacy; validity, cogency.

v be powerful, control, command, rule; confer power, empower, invest, endow; arm, strengthen, authorize; compel, force.

adj powerful, potent, strong, mighty, energetic; able, capable, competent, efficacious, equal to, up to, effective, efficient, adequate; omnipotent, almighty; influential, forceful.

adv powerfully.

prep by virtue of, by dint of.

158 impotence *n* inability, incapability, incapacity, infirmity, debility, disability; inefficacy, inefficiency, incompetence, ineptitude, feebleness, weakness, frailty, powerlessness; helplessness, prostration, paralysis, collapse, exhaustion; decrepitude, senility; sexual failure, barrenness.

v be impotent; collapse, faint, swoon, drop; render powerless, disable, disarm, incapacitate, disqualify, invalidate; cramp, tie the hands, paralyze, muzzle, cripple, maim, lame, hamstring, throttle, strangle, tie up in knots; unman, unnerve, enervate; shatter, exhaust, weaken; emasculate.

adj impotent, powerless, incapable, unable, incompetent, ineffective, inefficient, ineffectual, inept, unfit, unfitted, unqualified; disabled, incapacitated, crippled, paralyzed, paralytic; decrepit, senile, exhausted, worn out, used up, limp, spent; weak, frail, infirm, feeble, helpless; harmless; sterile, barren, frigid; emasculated, inadequate, inoperative; futile, fruitless, bootless, vain.

159 strength *n* power, force, might, vigor, health, stoutness, hardiness, lustihood, stamina, energy, potency, capacity; spring, bounce, tone, elasticity, tension; virility, vitality, nerve, verve; strengthening, invigoration, refreshment.

v strengthen, invigorate, brace, nerve, fortify, sustain, harden, steel; vivify, revivify, refresh, reinforce, restore.

adj strong, mighty, vigorous, forceful, hard, stout, robust, sturdy, hardy, powerful, potent, puissant; irresistible, invincible, indomitable, unconquerable, impregnable, inextinguishable, incontestable; able-bodied, athletic, muscular, sinewy, strapping, gigantic, Herculean.

adv strongly, by force.

160 weakness *n* debility, relaxation, languor, enervation; impotence, infirmity, fragility, flaccidity; frailty, delicacy, softness; senility, decrepitude.

v be weak, drop, crumble, give way, teeter, totter, tremble, shake, halt, limp, fade, languish, decline, flag, fail; weaken, enfeeble, cramp, debilitate, shake, enervate, unnerve; relax; dilute, water down.

adj weak, feeble, infirm, sickly; languid, faint, dull, slack, spent; limp, flaccid, powerless, impotent; relaxed, unstrung, unnerved; frail, fragile, delicate, flimsy; rickety, drooping, teetering, tottering, withered, shaky, shattered; palsied, decrepit, lame; decayed, rotten, worn, seedy, wasted, laid low.

161 production *n* creation, formation, fabrication, construction, manufacture; building, architecture, erection; organization, establishment; workmanship, craftsmanship, performance; achievement, product, end result; flowering, fructification, fruition, fulfillment; gestation, evolution, development, growth; genesis, generation, procreation; authorship, publication, works, *oeuvre*.

v produce, perform, operate, do, make, form, construct, fabricate, frame, contrive, manufacture; build, raise, rear, erect, put up; set up, establish, constitute, compose, organize, institute; achieve, accomplish, fulfill; bud, flower, blossom, bloom,

bear fruit, bring forth; propagate, beget, generate, procreate, engender; breed, hatch, develop, bring up; induce, cause.

adj productive, constructive, formative, creative; generative; prolific, blooming.

162 [nonproduction] **destruction** *n* waste, dissolution, breaking up, disruption; consumption; fall, downfall, ruin, perdition; breakdown, wreck, wrack, havoc, mess, chaos, cataclysm; desolation, extinction, annihilation; demolition; overthrow, subversion, suppression; dilapidation, devastation, road to ruin.

v perish, fall, tumble, topple, fall to pieces, break up, crumble, go to the dogs, go to wrack and ruin; destroy, do away with, demolish, tear up, overturn, overthrow, wipe out, (*informal*) waste; upset, subvert, undo; waste, squander, dissipate, dispel, dissolve; smash, squash, squelch, shatter, crumble, batter, crush, pull to pieces; fell, sink, scuttle, wreck, swamp, ruin, raze, level, expunge, erase, sweep away, lay waste, ravage, gut; disorganize, dismantle, take apart; devour, devastate, desolate, sap, exterminate, extinguish, stamp out, trample out, crush out, eradicate.

adj destructive, subversive, ruinous, incendiary, deadly, lethal, fatal; destroyed, wiped out, extinct.

163 reproduction *n* renovation, restoration, renewal, revival, regeneration, revivification, resuscitation, reanimation, resurrection; reappearance; generation, childbirth.

v reproduce, renovate, restore, renew, revive, regenerate, revivify, resuscitate, breathe new life into, reanimate, refashion, resurrect, bring back to life; give birth to, multiply, people the world.

adj reproductive; regenerative, restorative; renascent, reappearing, resurgent.

164 producer *n* originator, inventor, author, founder, generator, mover, creator, maker, architect; backer, angel.

165 destroyer *n* spoiler, waster, ravager, wrecker, killer, assassin, executioner; cankerworm, bane; iconoclast, rebel, pessimist, cynic, nihilist, misanthrope.

166 parentage *n* family, ancestry, lineage, genealogy; procreator, progenitor.

paternity: fatherhood, fathership; father, dad, pop, sire, papa, (*informal*) old man; grandfather, grandsire.

maternity: motherhood; mother, mom, ma, mamma, mummy, mum, (*informal*) old lady; grandmother.

adj parental, familial, ancestral, lineal, paternal, maternal; patriarchal, matriarchal.

167 posterity *n* progeny, breed, issue, offspring, brood, litter, family, children, grandchildren, heirs; child, son, daughter; descendant, heir, scion, (*informal*) chip off the old block; heredity.

adj filial.

168 productiveness *n* fecundity, fertility, fruitfulness, productivity; multiplication, propagation, procreation; creativity, inventiveness, originality.

v make productive, fructify, fulfill; procreate, generate, conceive, impregnate, fertilize; teem, multiply, produce, reproduce.

adj productive, prolific, fruitful, copious; teeming, fertile, fecund; procreative, generative, lifegiving.

169 unproductiveness *n* infertility, sterility, barrenness, unfruitfulness, impotence; unprofitableness, wastefulness.

v be unproductive, do nothing, produce nothing, come to nothing.

adj unproductive, unfruitful, infertile, barren, sterile, arid; unprofitable, useless.

170 agency *n* operation, force, working, function, office, maintenance, exercise, work, play; causation, instigation, instrumentality, influence.

v operate, work, do; act, perform, play, support, sustain, maintain, take effect, quicken, strike; come into play, have free play; bring to bear upon, influence.

adj operative, efficient, efficacious, effectual, practical; at work, on foot, in operation, in force, in play, in action.

adv through the agency of, by means of.

171 energy *n* force, power, strength, intensity, vigor, zeal, dynamism, pep, fire, spirit, ebullience, life; activity, agitation, exertion, effervescence, ferment, fermentation, ebullition, bustle.

v give energy, energize, stimulate, kindle, excite, inflame, exert; strengthen, invigorate; sharpen, intensify.

adj energetic, strong, forcible, potent, forceful, active, powerful, intense, vigorous, zealous, dynamic, ebullient, spirited, animated, keen, vivid, sharp, acute, incisive, trenchant, biting; invigorating, rousing, stimulating; energized.

172 inertness *n* inertia, inactivity, torpor, languor, dullness, immobility, passivity, passiveness, lifelessness; quiescence, latency; inexcitability, sloth, indolence, irresolution, indecisiveness, cowardice, spinelessness.

v be inert, be inactive.

adj inert, inactive, immobile, unmoving, motionless, lifeless, passive, dead; sluggish, dull, heavy, flat, slack, tame, slow, blunt, torpid, languid; latent, dormant, sleeping, smoldering, quiescent.

adv in suspense, in abeyance.

173 violence *n* vehemence, fury, ferocity, impetuosity, boisterousness, turbulence, ebullition, effervescence, intensity, severity, acuteness; energy, force, might; fit, paroxysm, orgasm, spasm, convulsion, throe; exacerbation, exasperation, hysterics, excitability, passion; outbreak, outburst, uproar, riot, explosion, blow-up, blast, eruption; turmoil, disorder, ferment, agitation, storm, tempest; destruction, brutality, fighting, combat, warfare, hostilities; injury, wrong, outrage, injustice.

v be violent, ferment, effervesce; romp, rampage, run wild, run riot, rush, tear, run headlong, run amuck, go wild, kick up a row, (*informal*) flip out, go berserk; bluster, rage, roar, riot, storm, boil, boil over, fume, foam; explode, go off, detonate, thunder, blow up, flare, burst; render violent, sharpen, stir up, quicken, excite, incite, urge, lash, whip up, stimulate; irritate, inflame, kindle, accelerate, aggravate, exasperate, exacerbate, convulse, infuriate, madden, fan the fire, whip into a frenzy.

adj violent, vehement, acute, sharp; rough, rude, bluff, boisterous, brusque, abrupt, wild, impetuous, rampant; disorderly, turbulent, blustering, raging, riotous, tumultuous, obstreperous; raving, frenzied, (*informal*) freaked, mad, unhinged, insane; desperate, furious, frantic, hysterical; savage, fierce, ferocious, physical, brutal, combative; uncontrollable, ungovernable, irrepressible, excited; spasmodic, convulsive, orgasmic; explosive, volcanic, stormy.

adv violently; by storm, by force.

174 moderation *n* temperateness, temperance, reasonableness, judiciousness, deliberateness, fairness; gentleness, mildness, calmness, peacefulness; quiet, calm, composure; lenity, lenience; relaxation, assuagement, tranquilization, pacification, mitigation; measure, middle ground, middle of the road.

v moderate, ally, meliorate, calm, pacify, assuage, lull, smooth, compose, still, calm, quiet, hush, sober, mitigate, soften, mollify, temper, qualify, alleviate, appease, lessen, abate, diminish; slake, curb, tame; arbitrate, referee, umpire, regulate.

adj moderate, temperate, reasonable, judicious, deliberate, fair, gentle, mild, calm, cool, sober, measured, unruffled, quiet, tranquil, still, peaceful, pacific; unexciting, even, smooth, bland, palliative; lenient, relaxed, easy going.

adv moderately, in moderation, within reason.

175 influence *n* importance, weight, pressure, preponderance, prevalence, sway; predominance, ascendancy; dominance, reign, rule, authority, power, control, capability, input, (*informal*) say, persuasion, play, leverage, vantage ground; patronage, protection, auspices.

v be influential, have a say, have input, carry weight, affect, sway, impress, bias, direct, control; move, activate, incite, impel, rouse, arouse, induce, persuade; dominate, predominate, outweigh, override, prevail.

adj influential, important, weighty; prevalent, rife, rampant, dominant, predominant; potent, powerful, effective, authoritative.

175a absence of influence *n* impotence, powerlessness; unimportance, irrelevancy.

adj uninfluential, unpersuasive, weak, impotent, (*informal*) wishy-washy.

176 tendency *n* aptness, aptitude, disposition, predisposition, proclivity, proneness, propensity, susceptibility, inclination, leaning, bias, drift, trend, bent, turn; quality, nature, temperament; idiosyncrasy, cast, vein, mood, humor.

v tend, contribute, conduce, lead, dispose, incline, verge, bend to, gravitate toward, lean, drift, tend, affect; promote, influence.

adj tending, leaning; conducive, working toward, in a fair way to; liable, likely; influential, instrumental, useful, subsidiary, subservient.

177 liability *n* susceptibility, penchant, vulnerability, predilection, propensity, tendency; drawback, hindrance, obstacle, difficulty, impediment; responsibility, obligation, debt, debit, indebtedness, pledge.

v be liable, incur, lay oneself open to, run the risk of, stand a chance, expose oneself to.

adj liable, subject, exposed, likely, open, in danger of; obliged, responsible, accountable, answerable; contingent, incidental, possible.

178 concurrence *n* accordance, accord, agreement, consent, assent; cooperation, collaboration, partnership, alliance, concert, union.

v concur, conduce, conspire, contribute; agree, unite, combine, hang together, pull together, cooperate, collaborate; keep pace with, run parallel, go hand in hand with.

adj concurrent, cooperative, collaborative, joint, allied with, of one mind, at one with, in concert with.

179 counteraction *n* opposition, antagonism, contrariety, polarity; clashing, collision, interference, resistance, friction; reaction, response, counterblast, counter maneuver; neutralization, check, curb, hindrance; repression, restraint.

v counteract, run counter to, clash, cross, interfere with, conflict with; jostle, run up against, oppose, antagonize, withstand, resist, hinder, impede, check, curb, repress, restrain; recoil, react; neutralize, nullify, cancel out, undercut, undermine, undo; counterpoise, offset, balance out, compensate.

adj counteracting, antagonistic, conflicting, contrary, reactionary.

adv although.

prep in spite of, against.

194

Class II

Words Relating to Space

I. Space in General

180 [indefinite space] **space** *n* extension, extent, expanse, span, stretch, scope, range, latitude, spread, proportions, sweep, capacity, play, swing, expansion; elbowroom, room, breathing space, leeway; open space(s), free space, waste, desert, wild, wilderness; unlimited space, wide world, heavens, universe, solar system, outer space, abyss, the void, infinity.

adj spacious, roomy, extensive, expansive, capacious, ample; widespread, vast, worldwide, boundless, limitless, unlimited, infinite.

adv extensively, far and wide, right and left, from the four corners of the world, all over, from pole to pole, under the sun, on the face of the earth, from all points of the compass, to the four winds.

180a inextension *n* nonextension, point, atom.

181 [definite space] **region** *n* sphere, ground, soil, area, realm, quarter, orb, hemisphere, circuit, circle; domain, tract, territory, country, county, province; clime, climate, zone, meridian, latitude.

adj regional, provincial, territorial.

182 [limited space] **place** *n* spot, point; niche, nook, hole, pigeonhole; locality; locale, situation.

adv somewhere, in some place, here and there, in various places.

183 situation *n* position, locality, locale, latitude and longitude, location; footing, standing, standpoint; aspect, attitude, posture, perspective, pose; place, site, station, post, predicament, whereabouts; bearings, direction; topography, geography; map, chart.

v be situated, be located, lie, have its seat in; situate, locate.

adj situated, located; local, topical, topographical.

adv here and there, hereabouts, thereabouts, in such and such a place.

184 location *n* place, situation; establishment, settlement, installation; anchorage, mooring, encampment.

v locate, place, situate, put, lay, set, make a place for, seat; station, lodge, quarter, house, post, install; establish, fix, settle, root; graft, plant; inhabit, domesticate, colonize, take root, establish roots, come to rest, settle down, take up quarters, locate oneself, relocate; squat, perch, bivouac, burrow, get a footing, encamp.

adj located, placed, ensconced, rooted, settled, moored.

185 displacement *n* dislocation, misplacement, derangement, transposition; ejection, expulsion, banishment, removal, exile.

v displace, dislodge, disestablish; misplace, disturb, disorder, unsettle, derange, confuse; transpose, set aside, transfer, remove, unload, empty, eject, expel, banish, exile; vacate, depart, leave.

adj displaced; unplaced, unhoused, unsettled, unestablished; homeless, out of place, misplaced, out of its element.

186 presence *n* attendance, company; occupancy, occupation; ubiquity, omnipresence, permeation, pervasion, pervasiveness, diffusion, dispersion; nearness, vicinity, proximity, closeness.

v be present; look on, attend, stand by, remain, find oneself; occupy, inhabit, dwell, stay, sojourn, live, abide, lodge, nestle, roost, perch, tenant; fill, pervade, permeate, run through.

adj present, attending; occupying, inhabiting, resident, moored; ubiquitous, omnipresent, pervasive, diffused; near, close, in proximity.

adv here, there, and everywhere; in presence of.

187 absence *n* nonappearance, nonattendance, absenteeism, nonresidence; emptiness, void, vacuum, vacancy, vacuity.

v be absent; keep away, play truant, absent oneself, stay away.

adj absent, not present, away, out, not here, not in, not present, off, wanting, lacking, missing, nonexistent; vacant, empty, void, vacuous, devoid.

adv without, minus, nowhere, sans; elsewhere.

188 inhabitant *n* resident, dweller, occupant; tenant, inmate, boarder, lodger; native, townsman, villager, citizen; population, community, society, state, people, race, nation.

v inhabit, live, reside, dwell.

adj indigenous, native, domestic.

189 habitation *n* abode, residence, domicile, lodging, dwelling, address, habitation, housing, quarters; home, homestead, motherland, fatherland, country; nest, lair, den, cave, hole, hiding place, cell, hive, haunt, habitat, perch, roost, retreat, (*informal*) pad, (*informal*) crashpad.

v inhabit, take up one's abode.

190 [things contained] **contents** *n* stuffing, cargo, lading, freight, shipment, haul, load, bale, burden.

v load, lade, ship, haul, charge, fill, stuff.

191 receptacle *n* container, holder, repository, vessel, receiver, depository, reservoir; storage areas; bulk containers; liquid containers; wrapping.

II. Dimensions

192 size *n* proportions, dimensions, magnitude, bulk, volume; largeness, greatness; expanse, amplitude, mass; capacity, tonnage; corpulence, obesity, plumpness; hugeness, enormousness, immensity; monstrosity, enormity; giant, monster, mammoth, behemoth, leviathan, elephant; lump, bulk, block, mass, clod, thumper, whopper, strapper, (*informal*) mother, mountain, mound, heap.

v be large; become large, expand.

adj sizable, large, big, great, considerable, bulky, voluminous, ample, massive, massy; capacious, comprehensive, spacious; mighty, towering, magnificent; corpulent; stout, fat, plump, obese, portly; full-grown, stalwart, brawny; hulky, unwieldy, bulky, lumpish, whopping, thundering, thumping; overgrown; huge, immense, enormous, mighty, vast, amplitudinous, stupendous; monstrous, gigantic, colossal.

193 littleness *n* smallness, diminutiveness, tininess; epitome; microcosm; vanishing point.

v be little; become little, decrease.

adj little, small, minute, diminutive, microscopic, submicroscopic; tiny, puny, wee, miniature, pigmy, dwarf, undersized, underdeveloped, dwarfish, stunted, dumpy, squat; imperceptible, invisible, infinitesimal.

194 expansion *n* increase, enlargement, extension, growth, development; augmentation, aggrandizement, increment, amplification; spreading, swelling, distention, puffiness, dropsy.

v expand, widen, enlarge, extend, grow, increase, swell, fill out; dilate, stretch, spread; bud, sprout, shoot, germinate, open, burst forth; outgrow, overrun; spread, extend, aggrandize; distend, develop, amplify, spread out, magnify; inflate, puff up, blow up, stuff, pad, cram, fatten; exaggerate.

adj expanded, larger; swollen, expansive, widespread, overgrown, exaggerated, bloated, fat, turgid, tumid, dropsical; pot-bellied, chubby, corpulent, obese, heavy; full-blown, full-grown.

195 contraction *n* reduction, diminution; decrease, lessening, shrinking; collapse, emancipation, attenuation, atrophy; condensation, compression, compactness, compendium, squeezing.

v contract, become small, lessen, decrease, dwindle, shrink, narrow, shrivel, collapse, wither, wizen, fall away, waste, wane, ebb, decay, deteriorate; diminish, contract, draw in, constrict, condense, compress, squeeze, crush, crumple up, pinch, squash, cramp; pare, reduce, attenuate, scrape, file, grind, chip, shave, shear, cut down; circumscribe, limit, restrain, confine.

adj contracting, astringent; shrunk, shrunken, contracted; wizened, stunted, waning; compact.

196 distance *n* remoteness, farness, background, offing, far cry to, horizon, elongation; interval, remove, gap, span, reach, range; outpost, outskirts, foreign parts.

v be distant; extend to, stretch to, reach to, spread to; range.

adj distant, far off, far away, remote, far, afar, outlying, removed, at a distance, away, yonder, yon; inaccessible, out of the way, unapproachable.

adv far off, far away, afar, away, a long way off.

197 nearness *n* closeness, propinquity, proximity, proximation; vicinity, neighborhood, contiguity; short distance, earshot, close quarters, stone's throw, gunshot, hair's breadth; approach, access.

v be near, adjoin, neighbor, border upon, touch, stand next to; approximate, come close to, resemble; converge, crowd.

adj near, nigh, close, neighboring, adjoining, adjacent, bordering; proximate, approximate; at hand, handy; intimate.

adv near, nigh, hard by, close to, close upon, within reach, at one's fingertips.

198 interval *n* separation, space, break, gap, caesura, interspace, interstice, distance, hiatus, skip, division, opening; pause, recess, interim, respite, interlude, interregnum, interruption, term, spell, period; cleft, crevice, chink, cranny, crack, slit, fissure, rift, flaw, breach, rent, gash, cut, leak; ditch, dike, gorge, ravine, abyss, gulf.

v gape, open; intervene, interrupt.

199 contiguity *n* contact, contiguousness, proximity, apposition, juxtaposition, touching, abutment, meeting.

v be contiguous, join, adjoin, abut on, border, touch, meet, graze, adhere; coincide, coexist.

adj contiguous, touching, in contact, end to end; close, near.

200 length *n* distance, extent, longitude, span, reach, range; lengthiness, elongation, size; duration, continuance, term, period.

v be long, stretch out, sprawl; extend to, reach to, stretch to; lengthen, stretch, elongate, extend; prolong, protract, draw out, spin out.

adj long, lengthy, extended, outstretched; lengthened, interminable; linear, lineal, longitudinal; tall, stringy, protracted, lanky.

adv lengthwise, at length, longitudinally.

201 shortness *n* brevity, littleness; shortening, abridgment, abbreviation, conciseness, condensation; retrenchment, curtailment, reduction.

v be short; shorten, abridge, abbreviate, condense, compact, compress, epitomize; retrench, cut short, reduce, pare down, clip back, cut back, prune, shear, shave, crop, chop up, hackup, truncate.

adj short, brief, curt; compendious, compact, compressed, condensed; stubby, stunted, stumpy, squat, dumpy; concise, pointed; curtailed, cut back, reduced, shortened, abbreviated, abridged.

202 breadth. thickness *n* breadth, width, latitude, amplitude, extent, diameter.

thickness, density, denseness, heaviness, bulk, body.

v be broad; expand, widen.

be thick; thicken.

adj broad, wide, ample, extended, expansive, large; outspread, outstretched.

thick, dense, heavy, bulky, solid, compact; dumpy, squat, thickset.

203 narrowness. thinness *n* narrowness, slenderness, exiguity, closeness, straitness, scantiness, slightness, slimness.

thinness, slenderness, slimness, leanness, lankness, meagerness, skinniness.

v be narrow; narrow, taper.

be thin; thin, slenderize, slim; dilute, water down.

adj narrow, close, slender, thin, fine, threadlike, slim, delicate; restricted, confined, limited; thin, emaciated, lean, skinny, meager, gaunt, spindly, lanky, scrawny, haggard, pinched, skeletal, wasted; frail, unsound, fragile; weak, shrill, faint, feeble; watery, waterish, diluted, unsubstantial.

204 layer *n* stratum, substratum, bed, zone, floor, stage, story, tier, slab, tablet, board, sheet, platter; scale, coat, peel, membrane, film, leaf, slice.

v slice, shave, pare, peel; plate, coat, veneer; cover; layer.

adj layered, stratified, tiered; scaly, filmy, membranous, flaky.

205 filament *n* thread, fiber, strand, hair, cilia, tendril, gossamer, wire, strand, vein.

adj fibrous, threadlike, wiry, stringy, ropy; capillary.

206 height *n* altitude, stature, elevation, tallness; prominence, eminence, pre-eminence, loftiness, sublimity; top, peak, pinnacle, acme, summit, zenith, culmination.

v tower, soar, hover, cap, command; mount, bestride, surmount, overhang; heighten, elevate, raise up, rise up.

adj high, tall, elevated, towering, skyscraping, gigantic, huge, colossal; distinguished, prominent, eminent, pre-eminent, exalted, lofty, sublime; overhanging, overlying.

207 lowness *n* depression, debasement, prostration; flatness, proneness; lowlands, flatlands.

v be low; lie low, lie flat, crouch, slouch, wallow, grovel; underlie; lower, depress.

adj low, flat, level, low-lying; crouched, squat, prone, supine, prostrate, depressed; groveling, abject, sordid, mean, base, lowly, degraded, debased, ignoble, vile.

adv under, beneath, underneath, below, down, downward; underfoot, underground; downstairs, belowstairs.

208 depth *n* deepness, profundity, obscurity; depression, bottom, unfathomable space; pit, hollow, shaft, well, crater, chasm, abyss, bottomless pit; central part, midst, middle, bosom, womb, base, heart, core; soundings, draft, submersion, dive.

v deepen, hollow, plunge, sink, dig, excavate; sound, have the lead, take soundings.

adj deep, deep-seated, profound, mysterious, obscure, unfathomable; sunk, buried, submerged; bottomless, soundless, fathomless, unfathomed, abysmal, yawning, gaping.

adv beyond one's depth, out of one's depth, over one's head.

209 shallowness *n* superficiality, banality, triviality, frivolity, flimsiness, emptiness, vacancy; shallow, shoal, sand bar.

adj shallow, superficial, slight, cursory, trivial, banal, trashy, flimsy, substanceless, empty, vacuous, vacant; skin-deep, ankle-deep, knee-deep.

210 summit *n* top, peak, apex, pinnacle, vertex, acme, culmination, zenith; height, pitch, maximum, climax; crowning point, turning point, watershed.

v culminate, climax, crown, top.

adj highest, top, topmost, uppermost, tiptop; capital, head, polar; supreme, supernal.

211 base *n* bottom, stand, rest, pedestal, dado, understructure, substructure, foot, basis, foundation, ground, groundwork; principle, touchstone, fundamental part, element, ingredient; bottom, nadir, foot, sole, heel.

adj bottom, undermost, nethermost; fundamental, basic, elemental; based on, founded on, grounded on, built on; base, vile, venal.

212 verticality *n* perpendicularity, erectness; wall, precipice, cliff.

v be vertical, stand up straight, stand upright, stand erect, stand straight and tall.

adj vertical, upright, erect, perpendicular, straight, bolt upright, plumb.

adv vertically, on end, endwise.

213 horizontality *n* flatness; level, plane, stratum; horizon; recumbency, lying down, reclination, proneness, supination, prostration.

v be horizontal, lie. recline, lie down, lie flat, sprawl; render horizontal, flatten, level, prostrate, knock down, floor, fell.

adj horizontal, level, even, plane, flat, smooth; prone, supine, prostrate.

adv horizontally, on one's back.

214 suspension *n* hanging down, free swinging; pendant, tail, train, flap, pendulum.

v suspend, hang, swing, dangle; flap, trail, flow; depend.

adj suspended, pendent, hanging, swinging, dangling, pendulous; dependent.

215 support *n* foundation, base, basis, ground, footing, hold; supporter, prop, brace, stay, rib, truss, stalk, stilts, splint; bar, rod, boom, outrigger; staff, stick, crutch; bracket, ledge, shelf, trestle, buttress.

v support, bear, carry, hold, sustain, shoulder, bolster; shore up, hold up, prop up, brace; help, aid, maintain, sustain; base, found, ground.

adj supporting, supported; fundamental.

216 parallelism *n* coextension; comparison, affinity, correspondence, semblance, likeness, resemblance, analogy, equation.

v parallel, compare, relate, associate, connect, correspond to, equate.

adj parallel, coextensive, collateral, aligned, equal; like, similar, allied, corresponding, correlative, analogous, equivalent.

217 obliquity *n* incline, inclination, slope, slant, leaning, tilt, list, bend, curve; acclivity, rise, ascent, grade, rising ground, hill, bank; declivity, decline, downhill, dip, fall; steepness.

v be oblique, slope, slant, lean, incline, stoop, decline, descend; bend, careen, slouch, sidle; render oblique, sway, bias, slant, warp, incline, bend, crook, tilt, distort.

adj oblique, inclined; sloping, tilted; askew, asquint, awry, crooked; uphill, rising, ascending; downhill, falling, descending; declining, declivitous; steep, abrupt, sharp, precipitous; diagonal, transverse.

adv obliquely, on one side; askew, askance, edgewise, at an angle; sidelong, sideways, slantwise.

218 inversion *n* subversion, reversion, contraposition, transposition, transposal, conversion; contrariety, contradiction, opposition, polarity, antithesis; reversal, overturn, somersault, turn of the tide, revulsion, revolution.

v be inverted, turn about, wheel about, go about, turn over, go over, tilt over; invert, subvert, reverse, overturn, upturn, upset, turn topsy-turvy; transpose.

adj inverted, inside out, wrong side out, upside down, topsy-turvy; inverse, reverse, obverse, opposite.

adv inversely.

219 crossing *n* intersection, grade crossing, crossroad, interchange; network, reticulation; net, netting, network, web, mesh, wicker, lace; mat, matting, plait, trellis, lattice, grating, grille, gridiron, tracery, fretwork, filigree; knot, entanglement.

v cross, intersect, interlace, intertwine, interweave, interlink, crisscross; twine, intwine, weave, twist, wreathe; dovetail, splice, link, link up; mat, plait, plat, braid; tangle, entangle, ravel; net, knot, twist.

adj crossing; crossed, matted, transverse; weaved, woven, intertwined, interlaced.

220 exteriority *n* outside, exterior; surface, superficies; covering, skin, face, appearance, facade, aspect, facet.

v be exterior, lie around, encircle.

adj exterior, external, outer, outside, outward, superficial; outlying, extraneous, foreign, extrinsic.

adv externally, out, over, outwards.

221 interiority *n* interior, inside, inner part, center, interspace; subsoil, substratum, contents, substance, pith, marrow, backbone, heart, bowels, belly, guts, lap, womb; recesses, innermost recesses, hollows, nook, niche, cave.

v be interior, be inside; inclose, circumscribe; intern; embed, insert.

adj interior, internal, inside, inner, inward, inmost, innermost; deepseated, inlaid, embedded, ingrained, innate, inherent, intrinsic, inborn; private, secret, intimate, confidential; home, domestic.

adv internally; inward, within, indoors, withindoors.

222 centrality *n* center, middle, midst; core, kernel, nucleus, heart, pole, axis, pivot, navel, nub, hub; centralization; center of gravity.

v be central; centralize, concentrate; focus on, bring into focus, get to the heart of.

adj central, middle, pivotal, focal, concentric; middlemost.

adv centrally; middle, midst.

223 covering *n* cover; canopy, awning, tent, marquee; umbrella, parasol, sunshade; shade, screen, shield; roof, ceiling, thatch, shed; top, lid; ·bandage, wrappings; coverlet, blanket, sheet, quilt, tarpaulin; skin, fleece, fur, hide; clothing, mask; peel, crust, bark, rind; veneer, coating, facing, varnish.

v cover, superimpose, overlay, overspread; wrap, encase, face, case, veneer, paper; conceal, cover over.

adj covered, clothed, wrapped; protected.

224 lining *n* inner coating, coating; filling, stuffing, padding, wadding.

v line, stuff, wad, pad, fill; coat, incrust, face, cover.

adj lined.

225 dress *n* clothing, covering, raiment, drapery, costume, attire, garb, apparel, wardrobe, outfit, clothes; equipment, livery, gear, rigging, trappings, togs, accouterments; uniforms, regimentals, suit.

v dress, clothe, drape, robe, array, fit out, deck out, garb, rig out, apparel; equip, harness, outfit, uniform; cover, wrap, wrap up, sheathe, swathe, swaddle.

adj dressed, clothed, clad, invested.

226 undress *n* nudity, nakedness, bareness, dishabille.

v undress, uncover, divest, expose, disrobe, strip, bare, doff, peel, take off, put off, lay open.

adj undressed, nude, naked, bare, stark-naked, exposed, in the buff, *au naturel*, in the altogether, in one's birthday suit; undressed, unclad, undraped, disrobed.

227 environment *n* environs, surroundings, outskirts, suburbs, purlieus, precincts, neighborhood.

v environ, surround, encompass, compass, inclose, enclose, circle, encircle, gird, twine round, hem in.

adj surrounding, circumjacent.

adv around, about; without; on every side, on all sides, right and left, every which way.

228 interspersion *n* interjacence, interlocation, interpenetration, permeation; interjection, interpolation, interlineation, intercalation; intervention, interference, interposition, intrusion; insinuation; insertion.

v intervene, come between, get between, interpenetrate; intersperse, permeate, introduce, throw in, work in, interpose, interject, interpolate, insert; interfere, intrude, obtrude.

adj intervening, interjacent; parenthetical, episodic; intrusive.

adv between, betwixt, among, amid, amongst; in the thick of, betwixt and between; parenthetically.

229 circumscription *n* limitation, enclosure; confinement, restraint.

v circumscribe, limit, bound, confine, inclose; surround, hedge in, fence in, wall in; imprison, restrain; enfold, bury, incase.

adj circumscribed, confined, restrained, imprisoned; buried in, immersed in, embosomed, embedded.

230 outline *n* circumference, perimeter, periphery; circuit, lines, contour, profile, silhouette.

v outline, draw, sketch, trace, profile.

231 edge *n* frame, fringe, trimming, trim, edging, skirting, hem; verge, brink, brim, lip, margin, border, skirt, rim, mouth; threshold, door, porch, portal; coast, shore.

v edge, skirt, border; trim, hem.

232 enclosure *n* envelope, case, wrapper; girdle; pen, fence, fold, cote, corral, stockyard, paddock, yard, pound, compound; fence, pale, paling, balustrade, rail, railing; hedge; wall, barrier, barricade; gate, gateway, door, doorway; boundary, border.

v enclose, circumscribe.

233 limit *n* boundary, bounds, extent, confine, term, pale, verge; termination, terminus; frontier, marches, outer edges, unknown; boundary line, border, edge; turning point, flood gate.

v limit, restrain, restrict, confine, check, hinder, bound, circumscribe, define.

adj limited, definite; terminal.

adv thus far, only so far, thus far and no further.

234 front *n* forefront, foreground, lead; face, frontage, facade, frontispiece, proscenium; vanguard, front rank, first rank, head of the column, advanced guard.

v front, face, confront; be in front, stand in front; come to the front.

adj fore, foremost; front, frontal, anterior, forward.

adv before, in front, in advance; ahead, right ahead, in the foreground; in the lead.

235 rear *n* back, background, rearguard, rear rank; distance, hinterland; rump, buttocks, posterior, rear, backside, hindquarters; wake, train; reverse, other side of the coin, (*informal*) flipside.

v be behind, bring up the rear; rear, bring up, nurture, raise; elevate, lift, loft, lift up, hold up; build, put up, erect.

adj rear, back, hindmost; posterior.

adv behind, in the rear, in the background, at the heels; after, aft, rearward.

236 side *n* laterality, flank, quarter, lee, hand; cheek, jowl, shoulder; profile, lee side, broadside.

v be on the side; be side by side, cheek to cheek; flank, skirt, outflank, sidle.

adj sidelong, lateral; flanking, skirting; flanked.

adv sideways, sidelong; broadside, on one side, abreast, alongside, beside, side by side, cheek by jowl; laterally.

237 opposition *n* opposite, contraposition, opposite side, opposite poles, polarity, antithesis, reverse, inverse; counterpart, companion piece, complement.

v be opposite; stand as opposites, oppose.

adj opposite, reverse, inverse, converse; antipodal, antithetical, countering, opposing; fronting, facing, diametrically opposite; complementary.

adv over, over the way, over against; poles apart; face to face.

238 right *n* right hand, right side; offside, starboard.

adj right-handed, dextral.

239 left *n* left hand, left side; near side, port.

adj left-handed, sinistral.

III. Form

240 form *n* shape, outline, mold, appearance, cast, cut, configuration; make, formation, frame, construction, cut, set, build, trim; mold, model, pattern; posture, attitude, convention, rule, formality, formula, ceremony, conformity.

v form, shape, figure, fashion, carve, cut, chisel, hew, cast; shape, model, mold, fashion, cast, construct, build; stamp, cast, type.

adj formal, ceremonial, ceremonious, conventional; regular, set, fixed, stiff, rigid.

241 formlessness *n* shapelessness, amorphism, asymmetry; disorder, chaos; misproportion, deformity, disfigurement, defacement, mutilation, truncation.

v deface, disfigure, deform, mutilate, truncate.

adj formless, shapeless, amorphous, asymmetrical, unformed, unshaped, unfashioned, unshapely, misshapen, out of proportion, disordered, chaotic; rough, rude, coarse, barbarous, rugged.

242 [regularity of form] symmetry *n* shapeliness, finish, comeliness, gracefulness, grace, beauty; proportion, uniformity, parallelism; regularity, evenness, balance, order, harmony, agreement.

adj symmetrical, shapely, well set, finished; beautiful, lovely; classic, classical, formal, chaste, severe; regular, uniform, balanced, harmonious, ordered; even, parallel, equal.

243 [irregularity of form] distortion *n* contortion, warp, buckle, screw, twist; crookedness, obliquity; deformity, malformation, misproportion, disfigurement, monstrosity, ugliness; asymmetry.

v distort, contort, warp, buckle, screw, twist, wrest; writhe, grimace, make faces; deform, disfigure, misshape.

adj distorted, out of shape, irregular, unsymmetrical, awry, askew, crooked; not true, not straight, uneven; misshapen, ill-made, ill-fashioned, ill-proportioned, malformed, deformed.

244 angularity *n* bifurcation, bend, fork, crook, notch, angle; elbow, knee, knuckle, crotch; right angle, acute angle, obtuse angle; corner, nook, niche, recess.

v angle, tilt, bend, fork, bifurcate.

adj angular, bent, crooked, jagged, serrated; forked, bifurcate, cornered, V-shaped, hooked; akimbo.

245 curvature *n* curve, incurvature, bend; flexure, bending, crook, hook; deflection, turn, deviation, detour, sweep, curl, winding; curve, arc, arch, arcade, vault, bow, crescent, half-moon, horseshoe, loop; parabola, hyperbola.

v be curved, sweep, sag; deviate, turn; render curved, bend, curve, deflect, inflect, crook; turn, round, arch, arch over, bow, curl, coil, recurve.

adj curved, bowed, vaulted, hooked, arched, arced; circular, nonlinear, semi-circular, rounded, crescent, crescent-shaped, lunar, demi-lune.

246 straightness *n* directness; inflexibility, stiffness; straight line, direct line, bee line.

v be straight, go straight; render straight, straighten, rectify, correct, right; put right, put straight, unbend, unfold, uncurl, unravel.

adj straight, even, true, unbent, direct, rectilinear, linear, not curved, uncurved; square, erect, perpendicular, vertical, upright; candid, forthright, definite, reliable, plain, blunt, frank, sure, positive, irrefutable, certain, unequivocal, inescapable; honest, honorable, fair, just, equitable, impartial, aboveboard, reputable, scrupulous, worthy, lawful, licit, conscientious, decent, ethical; correct, sound, sane, accurate, true; sober, conventional, provincial, (*informal*) unhip, (*informal*) square, (*informal*) not with it.

247 [simple circularity] **circularity** *n* roundness, rotundity; circle, ring, hoop, areola; bracelet, armlet; eye, loop, wheel, cycle, orb, orbit; zone, belt, cord, band, sash, girdle, circuit; wreath, garland, crown, corona, coronet; necklace, collar; ellipse, oval.

v round; go around, encircle, circle.

adj round, rounded, circular, oval, elliptic, elliptical, egg-shaped.

248 [complex circularity] **convolution** *n* involution, winding, wave, undulation, sinuosity, meandering, twist, twirl; coil, roll, curl, buckle, spiral, corkscrew, worm, tendril; serpent, snake, eel; maze, labyrinth.

v wind, twine, entwine, twirl, wave, undulate, meander, turn; twist, coil, roll; wrinkle, curl, frizz, frizzle; wring, contort.

adj convoluted, winding, twisted; wavy, undulating, circling, snaky, serpentine; involved, intricate, complex, complicated, labyrinthine, tortuous, mazy; spiral, coiled.

adv in and out, round and round.

249 rotundity *n* roundness, cylindricality, sphericity, globularity; cylinder, barrel, drum; roll, roller, rolling pin; sphere, globe, ball, spheroid, globule; bulb, pellet, pill, marble, pea, knob, pommel.

v sphere, form into a sphere, roll into a ball, round.

adj rotund, round, circular, ball-shaped; cylindrical, spherical, globular; egg-shaped, pear-shaped, ovoid.

250 convexity *n* prominence, projection, swelling, bulge, protuberance, protrusion; hump, hunch, bunch; knob, node, nodule, bump, clump; pimple, pustule, pock, growth, polyp, blister, boil; nipple, teat, pap, breast; nose, beak, snout, nozzle; peg, button, stud, ridge; cupola, dome, arch; relief, high

relief, low relief; hill, mountain, cape, ness, promontory, headland; jetty, ledge, spur.

v project, bulge, protrude, jut out, stand out, stick out, stick up, start up, shoot up, swell up; raise; emboss.

adj convex, prominent, protuberant; bossed, nodular, bunchy, hummocky, bulbous, swollen, swelling, bloated, bowed, arched, bellied; salient, in relief, raised.

251 flatness *n* smoothness, evenness; plane, level; plate, platter, table, tablet, slab.

v flatten, level, even off.

adj flat, plane, even, smooth; level, smooth, horizontal; flat as a pancake.

252 concavity *n* depression, dip, hollow, indentation, dent, cavity, dint, dimple; excavation, pit, trough; cup, basin, crater; valley, vale, dale, dell, glade, grove, glen, cave, cavern.

v render concave, depress, hollow, scoop, scoop out, gouge, dig, delve, excavate, mine, stave in, tunnel.

adj concave, hollow, hollowed out; indented, dented, sunken, cupped; cavernous, rounded inward, incurved.

253 sharpness *n* acuteness, pointedness; point, spike, spine, needle, pin, prick, prickle, spur, barb, thorn; knife edge, cutting edge, razor edge.

v be sharp, taper to a point; sharpen, point, whet, barb, strop, grind, whittle.

adj sharp, keen, acute, trenchant; pointed, peaked, conical, spiked, spiky, tapering; studded, prickly, barbed, spiny, thorny, bristling, thistly; craggy, snaggy; cutting, sharp edged, razor sharp.

254 bluntness *n* dullness; obtuseness, roughness.

v be blunt; render blunt, dull, take off the point, round the edge.

adj blunt, dull, obtuse, dimwitted; rough, gruff; rounded, round, unsharpened, unpointed.

255 smoothness *n* polish, gloss; lubrication, lubricity.

v smooth, plane, file, scrape, shave, sand, sandpaper; level, press, flatten, roll; iron, steam press; polish, burnish, rub, wax, sleek, buff, glaze; lubricate, oil, grease.

adj smooth, polished, glossy, shiny, sleek, silken, silky; even, level, sanded; soft, downy, velvety; slippery, glassy, oily.

256 roughness *n* asperity, irregularity, corrugation, nodulation; grain, texture, pile, nap.

v roughen, rough up, crinkle, ruffle, rumple, crumple.

adj rough, uneven, irregular, rugged, scabrous, knotted, craggy, gnarled; shaggy, coarse, hairy, bristly, hirsute; scraggly, prickly, bushy; unpolished, unsmooth, rough-hewn, textured; downy, velvety, fluffy, woolly.

adv against the grain.

257 notch *n* dent, nick, cut, scratch, indentation; saw, tooth, scallop.

v notch, nick, cut, scratch, indent, jag, scarify, scallop.

adj notched, toothed, serrated.

258 fold *n* plait, ply, crease, pleat, tuck; wrinkle, ripple, rimple, pucker, ruffle.

v fold, double, plait, crumple, crease, pleat, wrinkle, crinkle, ripple, curl, rumple, frizzle, rimple, ruffle, pucker, corrugate; tuck, hem, gather.

adj folded.

259 furrow *n* groove, rut, scratch, streak, cut, crack, score, incision, slit; channel, gutter, trench, gully, ditch, dike, moat, trough; ravine, valley.

v furrow, dig, plow; channel, flute, groove, incise, cut, engrave, etch, seam, cleave, score; wrinkle, knit, pucker.

adj furrowed, ribbed, striated, fluted.

260 opening *n* hole, gap, aperture, orifice, perforation, pinhole, peephole, keyhole; slot, slit, rift, breach, cleft, chasm, fissure, rent; outlet, inlet, vent, portal, porch, gate, hatch, door, doorway, gateway; way, path, channel, passage.

v open, ope, gape, yawn; perforate, pierce, tap, bore, drill; mine, tunnel, dig to daylight; impale, spike, spear, gore, spit, stab, puncture, lance, stick, prick, riddle; uncover, unclose, lay bare, expose, bare, reveal; lay open, cut open, rip open, throw open.

adj open, unclosed, uncovered, exposed; ajar, wide-open, gaping, yawning; perforated, porous, reticulated, permeable; accessible, available, public.

261 closure *n* blockade, shutting up, obstruction, stoppage, clogging, sealing, plugging; contraction; constipation; culmination; cessation, completion, termination, windup; lid, top, cap, stopper, plug, barrier.

v close, plug, block up, stop up, fill up, cork up, cork, button up, stuff up, shut up, dam up; blockade, obstruct, hinder; bar, bolt, stop, seal, choke, throttle, shut.

adj closed, shut, unopened; unpierced, impervious, impermeable; impenetrable, impassable, pathless; tight, snug, airtight, unventilated, watertight, hermetically sealed.

262 perforator *n* piercer, borer, auger, drill, awl, scoop, corkscrew, probe, lancet, scalpel, needle, pin, stiletto, puncher, hole puncher, gouge: knife, spear, bayonet.

263 stopper *n* lid, cap, cover; cork, spike, stopcock, pin, plug, tap, faucet, valve, spigot, rammer, ramrod; wadding, stuffing, padding, stopping, bandage, tourniquet.

IV. Motion

264 motion *n* movement, action, activity, move, going; progress, locomotion; mobilization, mobility, movableness, motive power; unrest, restlessness; stream, flow, flux, run, course, stir; rate, pace, step, tread, stride, gait; velocity, speed.

v move, go, hie, budge, stir, pass, flit; hover around, hover about; shift, slide, glide, roll, roll on, flow, drift, stream, run, sweep along; wander, meander, browse, stroll, walk, perambulate; dodge, keep on one's toes, keep moving, hit the road, (*informal*) truck; move, impel, propel; mobilize.

adj moving, in motion, traveling, on the road; transitional, shifting, mobile, movable; mercurial, restless, unquiet, nomadic, transient.

adv under way; on the move, on the go, on the march.

265 rest *n* quiescence, stillness, quietude, calm, calmness, tranquillity, repose, serenity, peace, silence; pause, lull, cessation; stagnation, immobility, fixity.

v rest, be still, stand still, lie still, stand immobile, keep quiet, repose; remain, stay, pause, wait, mark time, hold, halt, stop short, cease, desist, discontinue, stop; stagnate, be inactive, immobilize; dwell, settle, settle down, establish roots; alight, arrive; stand fast, stand firm, stick fast; quell, becalm, hush, stay, lull, lull to sleep, tranquilize.

adj restful, quiescent, still, calm, tranquil, peaceful, undisturbed, unruffled, serene, silent; motionless, fixed, stationary; unmoved, stable, at rest, at a standstill, stock-still, sleeping, dormant, inactive, stagnant.

266 [locomotion by land] **journey** *n* traveling, travel, excursion, tour, trip, expedition, jaunt, pilgrimage; wayfaring, roving, gadding about, (*informal*) bumming around, nomadism, vagabondism; migration, immigration, moving; walk, promenade, constitutional, stroll, peregrination, perambulation, march, stroll, saunter, jaunt, outing, hike, airing; horsemanship, horseback riding; drive, driving, motoring, ride, spin; cycling, biking; procession, cavalcade, caravan, file, cortege, column.

v journey, travel, tour, take a trip; flit, take wing, (*informal*) hit the road, rove, ramble, roam, prowl, (*informal*) bum, (*informal*) bum around, range, traverse, scour the country, wander, meander, saunter, gad about, move, migrate, immigrate.

adj journeying, traveling, on the road; itinerant, peripatetic, rambling, roving, gadding, flitting, vagrant, nomadic, migratory, wayfaring.

267 [locomotion by water or air] **navigation** *n* voyage, sail, cruise, passage, boat ride; aquatics, boating, yachting, sailing, shipping.

flight, air travel, flying, gliding; aeronautics, aviation.

v navigate; sail, put to sea, embark, shove off, spread the sails, make sail, take oar; go boating, cruise, float, drift, coast; row, paddle, pull, scull, punt, steam; ride the waves.

fly, take off, take wing, take to the skies; aviate, soar, glide, fly over, plane, jet.

adj sailing, nautical, naval, maritime, seagoing, seafaring, ocean-going; afloat; navigable.

flying, jetting; aloft, in flight; aviational, aeronautical, aerial.

268 traveler *n* wayfarer, journeyer, rover, rambler, wanderer, free spirit, nomad, vagabond, bohemian, gypsy, itinerant, vagrant, tramp, hobo, straggler. waif; pilgrim, palmer, seeker, quester; voyager, passenger, tourist, sightseer, excursionist, vacationer, globe-trotter, jet-setter; immigrant, emigrant, refugee, fugitive; pedestrian, walker, cyclist, biker, rider, horsewoman, horseman, equestrian, driver.

269 mariner, flier *n* mariner, sailor, seaman, seafaring man, sea dog; pilot, skipper, captain, commander, helmsman, steersman; crew, hands, mates; navigator.

flier, airman, aviator, aviatrix, pilot, skipper; astronaut, cosmonaut, spaceman.

270 transference *n* transfer, move, shift, transit, transition, passage, transmission, transport, transplantation, transposition; removal, relegation, deportation, extradition.

v transfer, transmit, transport, convey, carry, bear, pass; move, shift, conduct, convey, bring, fetch, reach; send, delegate, consign, turn over, hand over, deliver; transpose, transplant, displace, remove, relegate, deport, extradite; shovel, ladle.

adj transferable, transmittable, transmissible, transportable, movable, portable.

271 carrier *n* porter, bearer, messenger, runner, courier; postman, letter carrier; conductor, conveyor, transporter; freighter, ship, barge; train, locomotive; truck, vehicle, carriage; beast of burden.

272 vehicle *n* conveyance, carriage, transportation, rig; car, motorcar, automobile, (*informal*) wheels, truck, wagon, cart, coach, chaise, buggy; bicycle, bike, motorcycle, motorscooter; train, sleeping car, cattle car, boxcar.

273 ship *n* vessel, boat, liner, freighter, steamer, schooner, sailboat, motorboat, merchant ship, barge, tugboat, tanker, trawler, yacht, cruiser, yawl, ketch, brig, brigantine, square-rigger, sloop, cutter, launch; navy, fleet.

airplane, plane, jet, jumbo jet, aircraft, glider, helicopter, dirigible, blimp, balloon, spaceship, capsule, module, space station.

287

274 **velocity** n rapidity, quickness, swiftness, celerity, speed, alacrity; acceleration, pickup; spurt, rush, dash, race, flying, flight.

v move quickly, speed, hie, hasten, post, scamper, run, race, shoot, tear, whisk, sweep, rush, dash, dash off; bolt, bound, spring, dart, flit; hurry, hasten, haste, accelerate, (*informal*) turn on the juice, quicken, speed up, take off like a shot.

adj fast, speedy, swift, rapid, quick, brisk, fleet; nimble, agile, expeditious, light-footed, fast as a bullet, quick as lightning.

adv swiftly, apace, at full speed, at full gallop, posthaste.

275 **slowness** n languor, sluggishness, slackness, sloth, indolence; deliberateness, moderation, leisureliness; tardiness.

v move slowly, creep, crawl, lag, drawl, linger, loiter, saunter, trail, drag, dawdle; plod, trudge, lumber; grovel, sneak, steal, worm one's way, inch; waddle, wobble, shuffle, hobble, limp, shamble, amble, traipse, slouch, mince, mince steps, halt; flag, totter, teeter, stagger; retard, hinder, impede, obstruct; slacken, check, relax, moderate; brake, curb, slow, put on the brakes.

adj slow, slack, late, tardy; gentle, easy, unhurried, deliberate, gradual, moderate, leisurely; languid, sluggish, indolent, lazy; tedious, humdrum, dull, boring; dense, stupid.

adv slowly, leisurely; at half speed, at a snail's pace; gradually, little by little, step by step, inch by inch, bit by bit, one step at a time.

276 **impulse** n impetus, implosion, push, thrust, shove; propulsion; sudden impulse, yearning, craving; reaction, response, reflex; collision, clash, encounter, shock, bump, crash; impact; blow, stroke, knock, rap, tap, slap, smack, pat, dab; hit, whack, thwack, slam, punch, belt, kick, thump, cut, thrust, lunge.

v impel, push, urge, thrust, shove, heave, prod, shoulder, jostle, hustle, hurtle, jog, jolt; start, give a start to, set going, get going, drive; run against, bump against, butt against; collide with, run into, bang into, butt; strike, knock, bang, hit, thump, beat, slam, dash, punch, thwack, whack; batter, pelt, buffet, butt; hit, rap, slap, tap, pat, dab.

277 **recoil** n reflex, rebound, ricochet, boomerang, backfire, backlash; snap, elasticity; reverberation, resonance; reaction, response, rebuff, repulse, revulsion.

v recoil, rebound, ricochet, boomerang, snap back, spring back, fly back; react, respond; reverberate, echo, quiver.

adj reactionary; elastic, backfiring.

278 **direction** n bearing, course, set, drift, tenor, trend, tendency, inclination; tack, aim, determination, intention; points of the compass, cardinal points; line, path, road, range, line of march; alignment.

v direct, point, aim; tend toward, point toward, conduct to, go to; bend, tend, verge, incline, determine; steer for, make for, aim at, level at, set one's sights on, take aim, hold a course for, be bound for.

adj direct, straight; bound for; undeviating, unswerving.

adv toward, on the road to; hither, thither, whither; directly, straight, straightforward, point-blank, on a line with.

279 **deviation** n diversion, digression, departure from, aberration; divergence, zigzag, detour, circuit; warp, refraction; swerving.

v deviate, alter one's course, turn, bend, curve, swerve, heel, bear off; divert, deflect, shift, shunt, draw aside, crook, warp; stray, straggle, digress, ramble, rove, drift, go astray, go adrift; wander,

wind, twist, meander; veer, turn aside, change direction, steer clear of, dodge.

adj deviating, errant, aberrant; discursive, desultory, loose, rambling, digressive, stray, erratic, undirected; circuitous, indirect, zigzag, roundabout, crooked.

adv astray, roundabout, wide of the mark; circuitously.

280 [going before] **precedence** n priority; leading, heading, the lead, van, vanguard; precursor, coming beforehand.

v precede, go before, forerun; usher in, introduce, herald; head, take the lead, lead the way; take precedence, have priority, come first, come before.

adv in advance, before, ahead, in the vanguard, in front.

281 [going after] **sequence** n coming after, following, sequel; shadow, dangler, train.

v follow, come in sequence, go after; attend, be attendant on, follow in the steps of, follow in the wake of, trail, shadow; pursue; lag, fall behind.

adj following; sequential.

adv behind, after; in the rear.

282 [motion forward] **progression** n progress, improvement, proceeding, advance, advancement, headway; growth, rise, increase, development.

v proceed, advance, progress, get on, get along, gain ground, press onward, forge ahead, make headway, make progress, make strides, stride forward; grow, develop, increase, improve.

adj advancing; progressive, advanced.

adv forward, onward; forth, on, ahead.

283 [motion backward] **regression** n retrogression, retreat, recession, retirement, withdrawal; reflux, backwater, return, recoil; backsliding; deterioration, decrease, fall.

v regress, recede, return, revert, retreat, back out, back down, turn back, fall back, drop out, retire, withdraw; lose ground, drop off, fall behind; ebb, shrink, shy.

adj retrograde, retrogressive; regressive, refluent, reflex.

adv backwards; aboutface.

284 **propulsion** n propulsive force, impulse, push, projection, thrust, drive, impulsion, impetus; throw, fling, toss, shot, discharge.

v propel, project, throw, fling, cast, pitch, chuck, toss, heave, hurl; drive, sling, push, shove; send off, fire off, discharge, shoot, launch, let fly; put in motion, set in motion, start, get going, impel; expel.

adj propulsive.

285 **traction** n drawing, hauling, pulling, towing, towage; yank, tug, drag, jerk.

v draw, pull, haul, lug, drag, tug, tow, trail, train, take in tow; wrench, jerk, yank.

adj tractile; in tow.

286 [motion towards] **approach** n access, advent, advance; nearness, approximation.

v approach, near, draw near, move towards, get close to; gain on, get closer to; pursue, trail.

adj approaching; approximate; impending, imminent.

287 [motion from] **recession** n retirement, withdrawal; flight, removal, retreat; regression, return, falling back, regress; reaction, reversal, recoil; departure, leave-taking.

v recede, move back, go back, move away from, retire, withdraw; drift, abate, fade, wane, ebb, subside, drift away, fall back, shrink; react, revert, relapse, recoil, regress; run away, fly, avoid.

288

288 attraction *n* attractiveness, inclination, affinity; pull, magnetism, gravity.

v attract, draw, drag, pull, magnetize, exert force; interest, invite, engage, fascinate, lure, allure, charm, decoy, bait.

adj attractive, attracting, enticing, seductive, alluring; have pull, magnetic, gravitational.

289 repulsion *n* aversion, antipathy, dislike; repulse, rebuff.

v repel, push back, drive away, chase away, rebuff, beat back; repulse, revolt, offend, sicken, disgust, displease, irritate.

adj repulsive, repellent, averse, repelling.

290 convergence *n* confluence, conflux, concurrence, concourse, congress, coming together, meeting, joining.

v converge, concur, come together, meet, join, unite; gather together, concentrate, center.

adj convergent, confluent, concurrent.

291 divergence *n* division, radiation, spread, severance, separation, refraction, deflection; ramification, furcation, branching, forking, detachment; deviation, aberration, disparity, difference, variance, heterogeneity.

v diverge, ramify, radiate, branch off, fork, spread, swerve, scatter, disperse; divide, separate, part, sever; vary, deviate, dissent, disagree.

adj divergent, radial, radiant, centrifugal.

292 arrival *n* advent, coming; reaching, attainment, landing, debarkation, disembarkation; reception, welcome, welcoming.

v arrive, get to, come to, reach a point, attain, complete; light, alight, dismount; land, disembark, debark, deplane, detrain.

293 departure *n* embarkation; outset, start, starting point, place of departure, point of departure; removal, exit; exodus, flight; leavetaking, valediction, *adieu*, farewell, goodbye.

v depart, go away, take one's leave, start, set out, leave, retire, quit, withdraw, absent, go, (*informal*) split, take off, (*informal*) cut out, move off, move out, ship out, pack it up; vacate, evacuate, abandon; sally, set forth, set forward, go forth; embark, set sail, put out to sea, shove off, get under way, enplane, entrain.

294 [motion into] **ingress** *n* entrance, entry; influx, intrusion, inroad, incursion, invasion, irruption, penetration, infiltration; insinuation, insertion.

v enter, come in, pour in, flow in; burst in, break in, invade, intrude; penetrate, infiltrate, insinuate oneself.

adj incoming, inbound.

295 [motion out of] **egress** *n* exit, issue; emergence, emanation; outbreak, outburst, eruption; evacuation, leakage, percolation, oozing, drainage, drain; outpouring, gush, effluence, effusion, discharge.

v emerge, emanate, issue; pass out of, come out of, pour out of, flow out of; exude, leak, ooze, drain, drip, trickle, dribble; gush, gush out, pour out, spout, flow out, discharge; escape, find vent.

adj outgoing, outward, outbound.

296 [motion into, actively] **reception** *n* admission, admittance, entry, entree; importation, introduction, initiation, induction, absorption; ingestion, eating, drinking; suction, sucking; insertion, injection.

v give entrance to, admit, introduce, usher, initiate, induct; receive, import, bring in, ingest, absorb, imbibe.

297 [motion out of, actively] **ejection** *n* rejection, expulsion, eviction, dislodgment, banishment, exile; emission, effusion, discharge, evacuation, regurgitation, elimination.

v reject, eject, expel, evict, dislodge, banish, exile; push aside, push away, turn away, brush aside; empty, drain, clear out, clean out, purge, void, evacuate; vomit, spew, regurgitate, throw up, (*informal*) puke, retch, (*informal*) barf, belch out, burp out; discharge, eliminate, discard, get rid of, do away with, cast off, cut adrift, turn out, throw out, oust.

298 eating *n* dining, supping, taking nourishment; ingestion, chewing, mastication; imbibition, drinking, food, nourishment, nutrition, nutriment, sustenance, subsistence, provender, provisions, rations, keep, board, fare; drink, beverage, potion, draught.

v eat, feed, breakfast, lunch, dine, sup, break bread; taste, devour, wolf, swallow, gulp, bolt, gulp down, fall to, dig in; chew, masticate, bite, bite into, chomp, munch, crunch, gnaw, nibble, peck at; live on, live off, fatten, feast on.

drink, drink up, drink one's fill, quaff, (*informal*) down, chug, empty, sip.

adj eatable, edible, digestible; drinkable, potable; nutritious, nutritive.

299 excretion *n* discharge, emanation, exhalation, secretion, effusion, perspiration, sweat; evacuation, elimination, urination; hemorrhage, bleeding.

v excrete; emanate, exhale; secrete, perspire, sweat; eliminate, evacuate; urinate.

300 [forcible ingress] **insertion** *n* implantation, injection, inoculation, infusion, importation, insinuation, interpolation; immersion, submersion, dip, plunge.

v insert, introduce, put in; inject, infuse, instill, inoculate, impregnate, imbue; graft, ingraft, implant, plant, bud; thrust in, stick in, shove in, ram in, stuff in, tuck in, press in, drive in; immerse, merge; dip, plunge.

301 [egress] **extraction** *n* removal, elimination, extrication, eradication, extirpation, extermination, ejection; wrench, squeezing, pulling.

v extract, draw, draw out, take out, pull out, tear out, rip out, pluck out; wring from, wrench, pull; root out, weed out, rake out, eradicate, uproot, pull up, extirpate; evolve, elicit, draw forth; extricate, remove, eliminate; squeeze out.

302 [motion through] **passage** *n* transmission; permeation, penetration, infiltration; ingress, egress; voyage, trip, tour, excursion, journey; way, route, channel, avenue, road, path, way, thoroughfare, conduit.

v pass, pass through; penetrate, permeate, thread, go through, cut across; ford, traverse, cross; go, move, proceed; leave, go away, depart.

303 [motion beyond] **infringement** *n* transgression, trespass, encroachment, infraction.

v infringe, transgress, trespass, encroach; surpass, go beyond, shoot ahead of, overrun; overstep, overreach, overshoot; outstrip, outrun, outride, outdo; exceed, surmount, transcend, soar.

adv beyond the mark, ahead.

304 [motion short of] **shortcoming** *n* failure, falling short; default, defalcation; incompleteness, imperfection, deficiency, insufficiency, noncompletion.

v fall short, come up short, come short of, not reach; want, lack; fail, break down, collapse, come to nothing; fall through, cave in.

adj deficient, lacking, insufficient; incomplete, imperfect.

305 ascent *n* ascension; rising, rise, upgrowth; leap, jump; acclivity, hill, grade.

v ascend, rise, mount, climb upward, climb, arise; clamber, mount, scale, go up, get up; tower, soar, hover, surmount, scale the heights.

adj ascendant; rising, acclivitous.

306 descent *n* declension, inclination, declination, slope, declivity, grade, decline, drop, cliff, precipice, dip, hill; fall, falling, descending, sinking; downfall, tumble, slip, tilt, trip, lurch.

v descend, go down, drop down, come down, drop, fall, gravitate, slip, slide, settle; decline, set, sink, droop, wilt, slump; dismount, alight, get down; swoop down, stoop, stumble, trip, stumble, lurch, pitch, topple, tilt, sprawl.

adj declivitous, sloping, precipitous, steep; descending.

307 elevation *n* raising; erection, lift; upheaval; sublimation, exaltation; prominence, height.

v elevate, heighten, raise, lift, lift up, erect; set up, tilt up, rear, hoist, heave; uplift, upraise, uprear; exalt, enhance, advance; take up, drag up, fish up, drag, dredge.

adj elevated, stilted, rampant.

308 depression *n* lowering; dip, concavity; upset, overturn, overthrow; prostration, abasement, debasement, degradation; bow, curtsy, genuflection, kowtow, obeisance.

v depress, lower, let down, take down, cast down, let drop, let fall; sink, debase, bring low, abase, degrade, reduce; overthrow, overturn, upset, prostrate, level, fell; bow, curtsy, genuflect, kowtow, kneel, bend over, make obeisance.

adj depressed; at a low ebb; prostrate, horizontal.

309 leap *n* jump, hop, spring, bound, vault; dance, caper, frisk, buck.

v leap, jump, hop, spring, bound, vault, hurtle, hurdle; dance, caper, trip, skip, frisk, bob, flounce, start; trip the light fantastic, dance all night.

adj leaping; frisky, lively, springy.

310 plunge *n* dip, dash, rush, dive, leap; ducking, dunking, submersion, immersion.

v plunge, immerse, submerge, douse, souse, dunk, dip; dash, rush, hasten, hurry; dive, leap, jump; descend, drop, fall, hurtle over.

311 circular motion *n* circulation, circularity; turn, excursion; circumvention, circumnavigation, circling; turning; coil, corkscrew, spiral; full circle, full turn, turn, circuit, lap.

v turn, bend, wheel, turn a circle, turn around, make a U-turn, put about, make a complete circle; circle, go around, circuit, circumnavigate; whisk, twirl, twist.

adj circuitous, roundabout; circular.

312 rotation *n* revolution, gyration, circulation, roll; spinning, pirouette, convolution; whir, whirl, eddy, vortex, whirlpool, maelstrom; cyclone, tornado.

v rotate, turn, spin, revolve, wheel, whirl, twirl, spin around; pivot, swivel, circle around.

adj rotating, rotary, gyratory, revolving.

313 evolution *n* evolvement, unfolding, development.

v evolve, unfold, unfurl, unroll, unwind, develop.

adj evolutionary, evolutional.

314 [motion to and fro] **oscillation** *n* vibration, pulsation, undulation; pulse, beat, (*informal*) vibes; ripple, wave; alternation, coming and going, ebb and flow, ups and downs, flux and reflux; fluctuation, vacillation, irresolution.

v oscillate, vibrate, vacillate, swing, fluctuate, vary; undulate, wave; pulsate, beat, throb, ripple; reel, quake, quiver, quaver, shake; roll, toss, pitch; flounder, stagger, totter.

adj oscillating; undulatory; pulsating.

adv to and fro, up and down, back and forth, seesaw, zigzag, in and out, from side to side.

315 [irregular motion] **agitation** *n* stir, ripple, tremor, shake, jog, jolt, jar, jerk, shock, quiver, quaver, twitter, flicker, flutter; disquiet, perturbation, commotion, turbulence, turmoil, tumult; hubbub, bustle, fuss, ado, racket, fits; spasm, throe, throb, palpitation, convulsion, fit; disturbance, disorder, restlessness, hypertension; ferment, fermentation, ebullition, effervescence, hurly-burly; tempest, storm, groundswell, whirlpool, vortex; whirlwind, tornado, cyclone, twister.

v be agitated, shake, tremble, quiver, quaver, quake, shiver, twitter, writhe, toss, shuffle, tumble, stagger, bob, reel, sway; waggle, wriggle, dance, prance, stumble, shamble, flounder, totter, teeter, flounce, flop; throb, pulsate, beat, palpitate, go pit-a-pat; flutter, flicker, bicker, bustle; ferment, effervesce, foam, boil, bubble, simmer; agitate, shake, convulse, toss, tumble, bandy, flap, whisk, jerk, hitch, jolt, joggle, jostle, buffet, hustle, disturb, stir, shake up, churn, jounce, wallop, whip.

adj agitated, shaking, pulsating, tremulous, convulsive, jerky, shaky, throbbing.

adv by fits and starts; in convulsions, in fits.

Class III

Words Relating to Matter

I. Matter in General

316 materiality *n* corporeality, substantiality, flesh and blood, physicality; matter, body, substance, brute matter, physical elements, material; object, article, thing, materials.

science of matter: physics, natural philosophy, physical science, materialism.

materialist, physicist.

v materialize, embody, body in.

adj material, bodily, corporeal, physical, somatic; sensible, tangible, palpable, touchable, substantial, unspiritual, materialistic.

317 immateriality *n* incorporeality, insubstantiality, spirituality, ineffability.

adj immaterial, incorporeal, unsubstantial, intangible, ineffable, untouchable, bodiless, unreal, unearthly, spiritual, psychical, otherworldly.

318 world *n* creation, nature, universe, solar system, galaxy, globe, earth, wide world, sphere, macrocosm; heavens, firmament, vault, celestial spaces, space, sky; heavenly bodies, planets, asteroids, comets, meteors, constellations.

adj worldly, mundane, terrestrial, earthly, sublunary; cosmic, celestial, heavenly, astral, solar, lunar.

adv in all creation, on the face of the earth, under the sun, here below.

319 gravity *n* gravitation, weight, heaviness, pull, pressure, load, burden.

v gravitate, weigh, pull, press, encumber, load, be heavy.

adj weighty, heavy, heavy as lead, ponderous, lumpish, cumbersome, burdensome, cumbrous, massive, unwieldy, like a ton of bricks.

320 levity *n* lightness, buoyancy, volatility; ferment, leaven, yeast.

v be light, float, swim, waft; lighten, leaven.

adj light, subtle, airy, weightless, ethereal, volatile, buoyant, feathery.

II. Inorganic Matter

321 density *n* solidity, solidness, impenetrability, impermeability; condensation, solidification, consolidation, concretion, coagulation, petrification, hardening, crystallization, thickening; solid body, mass, block, knot, lump, conglomerate.

v be dense; solidify, condense, consolidate, coagulate, congeal, set, cohere, crystallize, petrify, harden; condense, compress, thicken.

adj dense, solid, compact, close, thick, substantial, massive; impenetrable, impermeable, coherent, cohesive; indivisible, indissoluble, insoluble.

322 thinness *n* rarity, tenuity; rarefaction, expansion, dilation, inflation.

v thin, rarefy, expand, dilate, inflate.

adj thin, rare, fine, tenuous, compressible, flimsy, slight, light; unsubstantial.

323 hardness *n* rigidity, firmness, inflexibility, temper; induration, petrification, ossification, crystallization.

v harden, stiffen, cement, petrify, temper, ossify.

adj hard, solid, firm, inflexible, rigid, resistant, adamantine, impenetrable, strong, hard as a rock, hard as nails, tough.

324 softness *n* pliability, flexibility, pliancy, malleability, ductility, tractility, plasticity, flaccidity, elasticity; mollification, softening.

v soften, mollify, mash, knead, temper, bend, yield, give, relent, relax.

adj soft, tender, supple, pliant, pliable, flexible, limber, plastic, ductile, tractile, tractable, plastic, malleable, moldable, impressible, elastic; flabby, limp, flimsy, flaccid, doughy, mushy, squishy, waxy, soft as butter.

325 elasticity *n* springiness, spring, resilience, resiliency, give.

v be elastic, spring, give, bend, stretch; spring back, recoil.

adj elastic, tensile, springy, resilient, buoyant, rubbery.

326 inelasticity *n* want of elasticity, flaccidity, limpness, softness, mushiness.

adj inelastic, flaccid, limp.

327 tenacity *n* toughness, strength, cohesiveness, cohesion; stubbornness, obstinacy, grit.

adj tenacious, cohesive, tough, strong, resistant, gristly, stringy, gummy, adhesive, sticky, viscous, glutinous; stubborn, obstinate.

328 brittleness *n* fragility, frailty, breakability.

v be brittle; break, crack, snap, split, shiver, splinter, crumble, burst, fly, fly to pieces, shatter, give way.

adj brittle, fragile, breakable, frangible, delicate, frail, splintery, crisp.

329 structure *n* organization, constitution, anatomy, frame, framework, mold, form, architecture, construction, texture; tissue, grain, web, surface; coarseness; fineness.

adj structural, organizational, anatomical, anatomic, architectural, textural; fine, delicate, subtle, gossamery, filmy; coarse, homespun, rough, woolly.

330 granularity *n* pulverulence, sandiness, graininess, friability; powder, dust, sand, grit, grain, particle, crumb, fine powder.

reduction to powder; pulverization, granulation, disintegration, abrasion, attenuation, filing.

tools for pulverization: mill, grater, rasp, file, mortar and pestle, grinder, grindstone.

v grind, pulverize, granulate, grate, scrape, file, abrade, rasp, pound, beat, crush, crumble, disintegrate.

adj granular, powdery, mealy, floury, branny, dusty, sandy, arenose, gritty, crumbly.

331 friction *n* attrition, rubbing, abrasion, elbow-grease.

v rub, scratch, scrape, scrub, fray, rasp, curry, scour, polish, rub out, erase, grind.

332 [absence or prevention of friction] **lubrication** *n* anointment, oiling, greasing, coating, lathering.

v lubricate, oil, grease, lather; anoint.

333 fluidity *n* liquidity, liquefaction, solubility, fluency.

v be fluid, flow, run, pour, stream; liquefy.

adj fluid, liquid, watery, serous, sappy, juicy, soluble; fluent, unstable.

334 gaseity *n* gaseousness, vaporousness, volatility.

adj gaseous, vaporous, airy, etheric, voluble, evaporable; flatulent, windy.

335 liquefaction *n* liquefying, deliquescence, melting, thawing, solubleness, dissolution.

v liquefy, melt, thaw, dissolve.

adj deliquescent, soluble, dissolvable, solvent.

336 vaporization *n* atomization, steaming, boiling, distillation, gasification, evaporation.

v vaporize, atomize, distill, evaporate, gasify, boil, steam.

adj vapory, vaporous, volatile, evaporable, gaseous.

337 water *n* liquid, serum, lymph, fluid, aqua.

v add water, water, wet, moisten, dip, immerse, submerge, plunge, douse, dunk, drown, soak, steep, wash, sprinkle, splash, souse, drench; dilute; deluge, inundate.

adj watery, aqueous, liquid, fluid, wet, moist, humid, soggy, sodden, rheumy, hydrous, juicy, lush, succulent; waterish, adulterated, transparent, thin, weak, tasteless, insipid, vapid, flat, feeble, dull.

338 air *n* atmosphere, stratosphere, the open, open air, blue sky, sky; weather, climate, clime; ventilation, current, breath of air, wind, breeze.

v air, ventilate, fan, aerate, freshen, refresh, cool.

adj airy, open, exposed, breezy, windy; flatulent; effervescent; atmospheric, aerial, ethereal, aeriform.

adv in the open air, out in the open, out of doors, in the wide open spaces, under the stars.

339 moisture *n* dampness, humidity, dankness, dew, wetness, condensation; perspiration.

v moisten, sponge, damp, bedew, wet, soak, saturate, sodden, sop, drench; perspire.

adj moist, damp, watery, humid, dank, dewy, muggy, juicy, wet; soggy, mushy, marshy, muddy.

340 dryness *n* drought, aridity; dessication, drainage, evaporation.

v dry, dry up, soak up, sponge, swab, wipe; drain, parch, evaporate.

adj dry, arid, parched, juiceless, sapless, dry as a bone.

341 ocean *n* sea, main, deep, brine, salt water, waters, high seas, waves, billows, great waters, tides.

adj oceanic, marine, maritime, seagoing, oceanographic.

342 land *n* earth, ground, dry land, mother earth, *terra firma*; continent, inlands, interior, shore, coast, terrain, dirt, soil, rock, chalk; real estate, lands, grounds, acres, acreage.

v land, alight, arrive, disembark, come ashore, go ashore, tie up, set foot on dry land.

adj earthy, terrestrial, earthly, alluvial, landed, territorial, continental.

adv ashore, on land, on dry land.

343 gulf. lake *n* gulf, bay, inlet, estuary, bayou, arm, fjord, firth, lagoon, cove, mouth, natural harbor, sound, straits.

lake, loch, lough, mere, tarn, basin, reservoir, lagoon, pond, pool.

344 plain *n* plateau, champaign, grassland, pasture, pasturage, meadow, flat, moor, heath, tundra, prairie, lowland, steppe, field, desert, basin, fields, grounds.

345 marsh *n* swamp, morass, moss, fen, bog, quagmire, slough, wash, mud.

adj marshy, swampy, boggy, quaggy, soft, muddy, sloppy, squashy.

346 island *n* isle, islet, atoll, reef, ait, key, bar, holm, ridge, eyot, archipelago.

adj insular, sea-girt.

347 [fluid in motion] **stream** *n* stream, etc. (of water, see **348**); (of air, see **349**).

v flow, etc. (see **348**); blow, etc. (see **349**).

348 [water in motion] **river** *n* running water, jet, spurt, squirt, spout, splash, rush, gush, torrent; fall, cascade, inundation, deluge; rain, rainfall, storm; trickle, drizzle, shower; stream, course, flux, flow, flowing, current, tide, race; spring, rill, rivulet, stream, river, tributary; rapids, flood, whirlpool, maelstrom, vortex, eddy; wave, billow, surge, swell, ripple, surf, breaker, white caps, rough seas, rolling seas, choppy seas; irrigation, pump, hose.

v flow, run, gush, pour, spout, roll, jet, well, issue; drop, drip, dribble, drizzle, trickle, stream, overflow, inundate, deluge, flow over, splash, swash; gurgle, murmur, babble, bubble, sputter, spurt, regurgitate; ooze, flow out, squeeze; rain, rain hard, rain cats and dogs, rain in torrents, rain in buckets; flow into, open into, drain into; pour, pour out, shower down, irrigate, drench, spill.

adj fluent, tidal, streamy, showery, rainy, trickly, drizzly, bubbly.

349 [air in motion] **wind** *n* draft, air, breath of air, puff, whiff, zephyr, drift, blow; fresh wind, stiff breeze, keen blast, trade wind, gust, blast, breeze, squall, gale, storm, tempest, hurricane, whirlwind, tornado, twister, cyclone, monsoon.

v blow, waft, blow hard, blow great guns, stream, gust, blast, storm; respire, breathe, pant, puff, gasp, wheeze, cough; fan, ventilate, inflate, pump, blow up.

adj windy, drafty, breezy, stormy, tempestuous, cyclonic.

350 [channel for the passage of water] **conduit** *n* channel, duct, aqueduct, canal, trough, gutter, dike, main, gully, moat, ditch, drain, sewer, culvert, sough, siphon, pipe, tube, hose, funnel, tunnel, artery, spout, floodgate, watergate, sluice, lock, valve.

351 [channel for the passage of air] **air-pipe** *n* tube, shaft, flue, chimney, funnel, vent, hole, windpipe, duct.

352 semiliquidity *n* viscosity, adhesiveness, stickiness, glutinosity, pastiness.

v thicken, mash, squash, churn, beat up, blend.

adj semiliquid, semifluid; milky, muddy, creamy, slushy, starchy, gummy, gluey, sticky, slimy, oozy, thick, succulent, viscous, viscid, glutinous, adhesive, clammy.

353 [mixture of air and water] **bubble. cloud** *n* bubble, foam, froth, head, lather, suds, spray, surf, yeast; effervescence, fermentation, bubbling, boiling, gurgling, foaming.

cloud, vapor, fog, mist, haze, steam; nebula, nebulosity, cloudiness, opacity, dimness.

v bubble, boil, foam, froth, gurgle, lather, effervesce, ferment, fizzle.

cloud, fog, mist, steam, shadow, darken, cast over, steam up.

adj bubbly, foamy, frothy; effervescent. cloudy, foggy, misty, hazy, steamy.

354 pulpiness *n* pulp, paste, dough, curd; fleshiness, fattiness, sponginess.

v pulp, mash, squeeze, juice, squash.

adj pulpy, pasty, doughy, fleshy, meaty, fatty.

355 unctuousness *n* unctuosity, oiliness, greasiness, lubricity; lubrication, ointment, grease, oil, anointment.

v oil, grease, lubricate.

adj unctuous, oily, greasy, oleaginous, slippery, slimy, slick.

356 oil *n* fat, butter, cream, grease, tallow, suet, lard, dripping, blubber; soap, wax; petroleum, gasoline, kerosene, propane, naphtha; vegetable oil, salad oil, olive oil, linseed oil; ointment, unguent, liniment, salve, balm.

356a resin *n* rosin, gum, wax, amber, ambergris, bitumen, pitch, tar, asphalt; varnish, lacquer, shellac, mastic, sealing wax, putty.

v resin, rosin; varnish, shellac, lacquer, overlay.

adj resinous, gummy, waxy.

III. Organic Matter

357 animate matter *n* nature, natural world, animated nature, living beings, organisms, organic remains, animal life, plant life, fauna, flora; protoplasm, cell.

science of living beings: biology, natural history, zoology, botany, anatomy, physiology, organic chemistry.

naturalist, biologist, zoologist, botanist.

adj animate, organic.

358 inanimate matter *n* mineral world, mineral kingdom, inorganic matter, brute matter.

science of the mineral kingdom: mineralogy, geology, metallurgy.

adj inanimate, inorganic, mineral.

359 life *n* existence, being; animation, vigor, vivacity, vitality, energy, vital spark, vital flame, lifeblood, spirit, soul; respiration, breath, breath of life; nourishment, nutriment, staff of life.

v be alive, live, breathe, respire, exist, subsist; be born, come into the world, see the light; quicken, revive, come to; give birth to, bring to life, vitalize; vivify, reanimate; keep alive, (*informal*) keep going, (*informal*) hang in there.

adj alive, live, vigorous, vivacious, vital, energetic, lively, alive and kicking, active.

360 death *n* decease, demise, expiration, passing, dissolution, departure, release, rest, quietus, fall; end, cessation, loss of life, extinction, dying, mortality, doom, finale, stop; last breath, final gasp, death rattle, death agonies, hand of death, dying day, *rigor mortis;* decay, fatality, natural causes, death blow.

v die, decease, pass away, pass on, perish, expire, depart, dissolve; cease, end, vanish, disappear; fail, subside, fade, sink, fall, decline, wither, decay; be taken, yield, give in, breathe one's last, end one's days, depart this life, be no more, drop off, pop off, drop dead, drop down dead, break one's neck, give up the ghost, shuffle off the mortal coil, go the way of all flesh, turn to dust, (*informal*) kick the bucket, (*informal*) go out like a light, (*informal*) croak.

adj dead, lifeless, extinct, defunct, late, gone, no more, dead and gone, dead as a door nail; deadly, fatal, lethal.

361 [destruction of life; violent death] **killing** *n* murder, homicide, assassination, slaughter, bloodshed, carnage, butchery, massacre, holocaust; suffocation, strangulation, garrote, hanging, electrocution, gassing, drawing and quartering; suicide, regicide, parricide, matricide, fratricide, infanticide; death blow, finishing stroke, *coup de grace,* execution; suicide; slaughtering, hunting, coursing, shooting, fishing; butcher, slayer, murderer, executioner, assassin, cutthroat, thug, guerilla, saboteur, garroter.

v kill, put to death, murder, slaughter, butcher, massacre, execute, behead, decapitate, guillotine, dispatch, (*informal*) waste; (*informal*) wipe out, strangle, garrote, hang, throttle, choke, stifle, suffocate, smother, asphyxiate, drown, gas, electrocute, stab, bayonet, cut, cut to pieces, cut to ribbons, mutilate, run through, put to the sword, shoot, gun down, do away with, (*informal*) blow away; hunt, spear; cut off, nip in the bud, cut down, give no quarter, decimate; commit suicide, destroy oneself, blow one's brains out, put an end to oneself.

adj murderous, homicidal, bloodthirsty, bloody, gory; mortal, fatal, lethal, deadly, deathly; suicidal.

362 corpse *n* body, remains, carcass, corpse, cadaver, empty vessel, bones, skeleton, relics, mortal remains, mortal coil, clay, dust, ashes, earth, carrion, fodder, food for worms, shade, ghost.

adj corpselike, cadaverous.

363 interment *n* burial, sepulture, entombment, inhumation; cremation; funeral, funeral rites, obsequies, wake; knell, death bell, dirge, elegy; shroud, winding sheet, grave clothes; coffin, shell, sarcophagous, urn, pall, bier, catafalque, hearse; grave, pit, sepulchre, tomb, vault, crypt, catacomb, mausoleum, cemetery, burial ground, mortuary, graveyard, charnel house, morgue; monument, gravestone, tombstone, headstone, *memento mori;* exhumation, disinterment, autopsy, post mortem examination.

v inter, bury, lay in the grave, lay to rest, lay in the ground, consign to the grave, entomb; lay out, mummify, embalm; cremate; exhume, disinter, unearth.

adj burial, funereal, funeral, mortuary, sepulchral, cinerary.

364 animality *n* corporality, animal life, living being, flesh, flesh and blood; physique, strength, vigor, vitality.

adj animalistic, bodily, corporeal, fleshly.

365 vegetation *n* vegetable life, growth, plant life.

adj vegetative; rank, dense, lush, fecund.

366 animal *n* animal kingdom, brute creation, fauna; beast, brute, creature, living thing, creeping thing, dumb animal; mammal, quadruped, bird, reptile, fish, crustacean, shellfish, mollusk, worm, insect; flocks and herds, wild animals, domestic animals, livestock, game, beasts of the field, fowls of the air.

adj animal, animalistic, zoological.

367 vegetable *n* vegetable kingdom, flora, plant life, flowerage, herbage, shrubbery, foliage, leafage, leaves, foliation, verdure, greens; tree, shrub, bush, creeper, herb, fruit, grass.

v vegetate, germinate, shoot, sprout, shoot up, grow, swell, spring up, develop, increase, flourish, blossom, bloom.

adj vegetable, vegetal, vegetative, leguminous, herbal, herbaceous, botanic, verdant.

368 [science of animals] **zoology** *n* morphology, zoography, embryology, anatomy; comparative anatomy, animal physiology, comparative physiology, anthropology, ornithology, icthyology, paleontology, entomology.

adj zoological.

369 [science of plants] **botany** *n* phytology, vegetable physiology, dendrology; flora, botanic garden.

adj botanical, herbal, horticultural.

370 [management of animals] **ranching** *n* breeding, raising; taming, domestication; veterinary science.

v ranch, raise, breed; tame, domesticate, train, housebreak; cage, bridle, restrain.

adj bred; tame, domestic, domesticated, housebroken.

371 [management of plants] **agriculture** *n* farming, cultivation, husbandry, tillage; agronomy, agrobiology, agrology, agronomics; gardening, horticulture, floriculture, landscaping, arboriculture; forestry.

v cultivate, till, till the soil, work the land, farm, garden, sow, seed, plant, reap, mow, cut; plow, plough, harrow, rake, weed, hoe, lop; garden, landscape.

adj agricultural, agrarian; arable, fertile.

372 mankind *n* human race, man, woman, humankind, human species, humanity, mortality, people, human being, person, personage, individual, creature, fellow creature, fellow man, mortal, body, soul, somebody, someone, one, party, head, hand, heart.

people, persons, folk, public, society, community, group, general public, society of men, civilization, commonwealth, commonweal, body politic, human community, population, millions, multitudes.

adj human, mortal, personal, individual; social, national, civic, public; cosmopolitan, humanitarian.

373 man *n* male, manhood, masculinity, he, him; gentleman, sir, mister, Mr., master, swain, fellow, chap, boy.

male animal: cock, drake, gander, dog, boar, stag, hart, buck, stallion, tomcat, billygoat, ram, bull, ox; gelding, steer.

adj male, masculine, manly.

374 woman *n* female, womanhood, femininity, she, her; lady, gentlewoman, madam, madame, miss, (*informal*) ma'am, Ms., Mrs., matron, girl.

female animal: hen, bitch, sow, doe, roe, mare, nannygoat, ewe, cow.

adj female, feminine, womanly.

375 sensibility *n* sensation, sensitiveness, feeling, responsiveness, impressibility; sensation, impression, touch; consciousness.

v be sensible, be sensitive to, feel, touch, perceive; render sensible, sharpen, cultivate, stir, excite, sensitize; cause sensation, impress, excite an impression, stir.

adj sensitive, sensible, sensuous; perceptive, sentient, responsive, susceptible, conscious, aware, alive, acute, sharp, keen, vivid, lively.

adv to the quick.

376 insensibility *n* lack of feeling, obtuseness, paralysis, numbness, anesthesia; insusceptibility, unresponsiveness, unconsciousness.

v be insensible; render insensible, blunt, pall, numb, benumb, paralyze, deaden, freeze, anesthetize; cloy, stuff, satiate, drown; stupefy, stun.

adj insensible, senseless, unsusceptible, unresponsive, insensitive, numb, hard, dead; dull, dense, thick, obtuse, unperceptive; anesthetic, paralytic.

377 pleasure *n* bodily pleasure, sensuality, sensuousness, physical gratification, sex, sexuality, sensual delight, ecstasy, orgasm, climax; titillation, teasing; comfort, ease, relish, delight, joy, luxury, luxuriousness, pleasure, lap of luxury.

v feel pleasure, receive pleasure, enjoy, relish, revel in, bask in, swim in, luxuriate, feast on, wallow in, gloat over, (*informal*) dig, (*informal*) get off on, (*informal*) be turned on, (*informal*) get into; give pleasure, (*informal*) turn on, thrill, excite.

adj pleasurable, sensual, sensuous, sexual, voluptuous, luxurious, ecstatic, orgasmic, climactic; agreeable, comfortable, cordial, delightful, joyful; palatable, sweet, tasty; fragrant; melodious, lovely.

adv in comfort, in ecstasy, on a bed of roses.

378 pain *n* suffering, dolor, ache, aching, smart, shoot, shooting, twinge, twitch, gripe, grip, hurt, cut, sore, soreness, tenderness, discomfort, malaise, disease; spasm, cramp, crick, stitch, convulsion, throe, throb, pang; torment, torture, rack, anguish, agony.

v feel pain, suffer, undergo pain, ache, smart, bleed, tingle, shoot, twinge, twitch, writhe, wince, hurt; inflict pain, hurt, chafe, sting, bite, gnaw, gripe, pinch, tweak, grate, gall, fret, prick, pierce, wring, convulse; torment, torture, wrack, agonize.

adj painful, dolorous, sore, tender, raw, uncomfortable; convulsive, torturous.

379 touch *n* contact, feeling, tactility, palpability, impact, feel, sensation; manipulation, handling, rubbing, massaging, fondling, fingering, kneading, stroking, brushing, grazing over.

v touch, feel, handle, finger, fondle, thumb, paw, grab, rub, massage, knead, stroke, brush, manipulate, run the fingers over, graze over.

adj tactual, tactile, palpable.

380 sensations of touch *n* itching, tickling, titillation, scratching, pricking, stinging.

v itch, tingle, creep, thrill, prick, scratch, sting.

adj itching; ticklish, scratchy, itchy.

381 numbness *n* physical insensibility, lack of feeling, deadness.

v benumb, anesthetize, deaden, dull, drug.

adj numb, dull, benumbed, insensible, unfeeling, frozen, drugged, dead, deadened, dulled.

382 heat *n* warmth, caloricity, caloric, temperature; glow, flush, warmth, intensity, ardor, passion, fever, fervor, zeal; fire, spark, flame, blaze.

v be hot, glow, flush, sweat, swelter, smoke, stew, simmer, seethe, boil, burn, broil, blaze, flame; smolder, parch, fume, pant; heat, warm, thaw, defrost; stimulate, stir, animate, arouse.

adj hot, warm, mild, genial, tepid, lukewarm, unfrozen; heated, torrid, sultry, burning, fiery; sunny, tropical, suffocating, stifling, sweltering, oppressive, reeking, baking; fiery, incandescent, ebullient, glowing, smoking, blazing, on fire, afire, in flames, aflame, ablaze; ardent, fervent, fervid, angry, furious, vehement, intense, excited, excitable, irascible, animated, violent, passionate.

383 cold *n* coldness, iciness, frigidity, chilliness, coolness.

v be cold, shiver, quake, shake, tremble, shudder, quiver; chill, freeze, refrigerate.

adj cold, chilly, chill, cool, frigid, gelid, frozen, freezing, bitter, bitter cold, numbing, nipping, cutting, shivering, bleak, raw, frost-bitten, icy, glacial, frosty, wintry, hibernal, arctic, polar; impassionate, unemotional, apathetic, unresponsive, unsympathetic, stoical, unfeeling, indifferent, cold-blooded, heartless, imperturbable; polite, formal, reserved, hostile; deliberate, depressing, dispiriting, disheartening.

adv coldly, bitterly.

384 calefaction *n* heating, melting, fusion, liquefaction, combustion; cauterization; calcination; incineration, cremation; carbonization.

v heat, warm, chafe; fire, set fire to, set on fire, kindle, light, ignite, rekindle; melt, thaw, fuse, liquefy; burn, inflame, roast, broil, toast, cook, fry,

grill, singe, parch, bake, scorch; brand, cauterize, sear, burn in; boil, digest, stew, saute, cook, scald, parboil, simmer; take fire, catch fire.

adj heated, warmed, fired, burnt, scorched; molten; flammable, combustible, volcanic.

385 refrigeration *n* cooling, congelation, glaciation, icing; solidification, hardening.

v refrigerate, keep cold, chill, ice, congeal, freeze; cool, fan, refresh; benumb, starve, pinch, nip, cut, pierce, bite; quench, put out, stamp out, extinguish.

adj cooled, frozen, chilled; incombustible, inflammable, fireproof.

386 furnace *n* oven, stove, range; hearth, heater, kiln, oil burner, space heater, blast furnace, forge, fire place, fiery furnace.

387 refrigerator *n* ice box, fridge, ice chest, frigidaire, cold storage, freezer, ice house.

388 fuel *n* firing, combustible; coal, hard coal, anthracite, bituminous coal, soft coal, carbon, coke, charcoal; wood, firewood, kindling, brushwood, log, cinder, ember, ash; turf, peat, fuel oil, fossil fuel, petroleum, gasoline, kerosene; gas, natural gas, propane; electricity; nuclear power; solar energy; waterpower; windpower.

v fuel, feed, stoke, fire; power.

adj carbonaceous; combustible, flammable, burnable.

389 thermometer *n* thermometograph, thermoscope, thermostat, telethermometer, pyrometer, calorimeter, glass, mercury.

390 taste *n* flavor, savor, sensation, gusto, relish; smack, smatch, tang, aftertaste; morsel, bit, sip.

v taste, flavor, savor, smatch, smack; tickle the palate, tickle the tastebuds; smack the lips.

adj tasty, savory, flavory, flavorful, flavored; palatable, digestible, (*informal*) edible.

391 tastelessness *n* insipidity, blandness, flatness, unsavoriness.

v be tasteless.

adj tasteless, insipid, bland, flat, weak, mild, vapid, wishy-washy, (*informal*) plastic, pasty.

392 pungency *n* piquancy, poignancy, tang, bite, nip, sharpness, acridity, bitterness, hotness, sourness, unsavoriness.

v be pungent; make pungent, season, spice, salt, pepper, pickle, brine, devil, smoke, curry.

adj pungent, strong, full-flavored, seasoned, highly seasoned, spiced; sharp, biting, nippy, acrid, bitter, sour, stinging, spicy, salty, peppery, piquant, hot; unsavory.

393 condiment *n* seasoning, flavoring, sauce, spice, relish; salt, pepper.

v season.

394 savoriness *n* flavor, flavorfulness, taste, tastiness, relish, piquancy, zest, tang, delectability, palatability.

v be savory, tickle the palate, taste good, taste great; savor, enjoy, appreciate, relish, like, taste.

adj savory, good, tasty, palatable, nice, dainty, delectable, flavorful, appetizing, delicate, delicious, exquisite, rich, luscious, full-flavored, pungent, ambrosial.

395 unsavoriness *n* tastelessness, flavorlessness, blandness; acridness, sourness.

v be unsavory, be unpalatable, taste bad, sicken, disgust, pall, nauseate, turn the stomach, make one sick.

adj unsavory, tasteless, flavorless, bland, flat; bad tasting, ill-flavored, acrid, bitter, sour, unpalatable, inedible, offensive, repulsive, nasty, vile, sickening, nauseous, loathsome, unpleasant, awful.

396 sweetness *n* sugariness, saccharinity, syrupiness, stickiness.

v sweeten, sugar, candy.

adj sweet, sugary, syrupy, honeyed, saccharine, candied, sticky, gooey, luscious, lush, cloying; sweetened.

397 sourness *n* acridity, tartness, sharpness, vinegariness, acerbity, acidity.

v sour, acidify, acerbate, curdle, acidulate, ferment, spoil.

adj sour, acid, bitter, tart, sharp, vinegary, acidulous, astringent, acerbic, acrid; fermented, rancid, bad, spoiled, turned, curdled, gone bad, styptic, hard, rough.

398 odor *n* smell, scent; effluvium; exhalation, emanation; fume, essence, redolence.

v have an odor, smell, smell of, give out a smell; smell, scent, sniff, snuff, inhale.

adj odorous, odoriferous, smelly, strong smelling, redolent, pungent.

399 inodorousness *n* absence of smell, odorlessness.

v be inodorous, not smell, have no odor, be odorless.

adj odorless, scentless, unsmelling.

400 fragrance *n* aroma, redolence, perfume, sweet smell, sweet scent, smell.

v be fragrant, smell sweet, have a perfume, scent, perfume.

adj fragrant, aromatic, redolent, spicy, scented, perfumed, sweet scented, sweet smelling, odoriferous, odorific.

401 fetor *n* bad smell, bad odor, foul smell, offensive smell, stink, stench, fume, foulness, fetidness, rancidity, rankness, fustiness, mustiness.

v have a bad smell, smell bad, smell rotten, smell, stink, reek.

adj fetid, strong smelling, bad, strong, fulsome, offensive, rank, rancid, noisome, mephitic, miasmic, musty, fusty, foul, rotten, putrid, reeking, stinking, stinky, suffocating, nauseating, nauseous, (*informal*) gross.

402 sound *n* noise, tone, pitch, sound vibrations, strain, sonority, sonorousness, twang, intonation, cadence; audibility, resonance, voice.

science of sound: acoustics, phonology, phonetics, electronic sound reproduction.

v sound, make a noise; give out sound, emit sound; resound, echo.

adj sounding, sonorous, resonant, audible, distinct.

403 silence *n* stillness, quiet, peace, hush, lull, quiescence, dead silence; muteness, speechlessness, taciturnity.

v silence, still, hush, stifle, muffle, stop, muzzle, gag; be silent, hold one's tongue, shut up, keep quiet, be still.

adj silent, quiet, still, calm, noiseless, soundless, hushed, quiescent; mute, speechless, taciturn; solemn, soft, deathlike, awful, silent as the grave.

adv silently.

404 loudness *n* loud noise, power, resonance, thunderousness, roaring, vociferousness, clamorousness; din, clang, clangor, clamor, noise, roar, uproar, hubbub, boom, racket, outcry; blast, peal, swell, flourish of trumpets; boom; thunder, explosion.

v be loud, peal, swell, clang, boom, thunder, fulminate, roar, resound, bellow, scream, holler, shout; ring in the ears, pierce the ears, split the eardrums, stun, deafen; shake, awake.

adj loud, noisy, vociferous, resounding, clamorous, deafening, stentorian, boisterous, tumul-tuous, sonorous, deep, full, powerful, thundering, ear-splitting, piercing, uproarious, obstreperous, shrill, sharp.

adv loudly, noisily, at the top of one's voice, at the top of one's lungs, aloud.

405 faintness *n* faint sound, whisper, breath, undertone, murmur, hum; inaudibility; hoarseness.

v whisper, breathe, murmur, hum, mutter, speak softly, speak in low tones.

adj faint, whispered, indistinct, dim, inaudible, barely audible, low, stifled, muffled, murmured, muted; gentle, soft, languid, floating, flowing; hoarse, husky.

406 [sudden and violent sounds] **snap** *n* rap, thud, burst, explosion, detonation, discharge, firing, salvo, pop, bang, blast.

v rap, snap, tap, knock, click, clash, crack, crackle, crash, beat.

407 [repeated and protracted sounds] **roll** *n* drumming, tapping, rumbling, grumbling; dingdong, whirring, droning; ratatat, rubadub, pitapat; quaver, quiver, clutter, racket; peal of bells; reverberation.

v roll, drum, rumble, grumble, rattle, clatter, patter, clack; hum, trill, shake; chime, peal, toll; tick, beat.

408 resonance *n* ring, ringing, chime, clang, clangor, boom, roll, roar, rumble, thunder, vibrato, timbre, twang, vibration, reverberation, tintinnabulation, booming, quaver, dingdong, echoing, sonorousness.

v resound, reverberate, re-echo; ring, jingle, chink, clink; gurgle, echo, ring in the ear.

adj resonant, resounding, reverberant, reverberating; deep-toned, deep-sounding.

408a nonresonance *n* dead sound, thud, thump, muffled drums, cracked bell; damper, mute, muffler.

v sound dead, thud, thump; muffle, dampen, mute.

adj nonresonant, dampened, muted, muffled, deadened; dead.

409 [hissing sounds] **sibilation** *n* hissing, wheezing, buzzing, zipping, whooshing; high note.

v hiss, buzz, whiz, wheeze, whoosh, zip, rustle, whistle, fizzle; squash, sneeze.

adj sibilant; hissing, wheezy.

410 [harsh sounds] **stridency** *n* discord, dissonance, harshness, raucousness, atonality, clashing, grinding, grating, rasping, sharpness, creaking, shrillness.

v creak, grate, jar, jangle, clank, clink, grind, grate; scream, yelp.

adj strident, sharp, high, acute, shrill, atonal, unharmonious, unmusical, dissonant, discordant, cacophonous; piercing, ear-piercing, cracked; creaking, harsh, coarse, hoarse, rough, gruff, grating, jarring, guttural, squawking, acute, scratching, croaking, rasping, sour, clashing.

411 cry *n* shout, scream, yell, shriek, roar, howl, wail; exclamation, outcry, clamor, vociferation; hubbub, hullabaloo, chorus, hue and cry; entreaty, appeal, solicitation, plea, plaint, prayer, crying, weeping, wailing, sobbing, lament, whimper, whimpering, tears, moaning.

v cry, roar, shout, bawl, brawl, hoop, whoop, yell, bellow, howl, scream, screech, shriek, squeak, squeal, whine, whimper, wail, weep, sob, moan, lament; cheer, hoot; grumble, groan, complain; vociferate, raise one's voice, sing out, cry out, yell out, exclaim, holler, shout at the top of one's lungs.

adj crying, clamorous; vociferous; solicitous; stentorian.

412 [animal sounds] **ululation** *n* howling, crying, belling, screeching, singing, growling, purring.

v cry, roar, bellow, bark, yelp, yap, growl, snarl, howl, bay, grunt, snort, neigh, bray, mew, purr, caterwaul, bleat, low, moo, squeak, oink, baa, crow, croak, screech, caw, coo, gobble, quack, cackle, gaggle, chuck, cluck, clack, chirp, chirrup, twitter, cuckoo, hum, buzz, hiss, blatter.

413 melody. concord *n* melodiousness, tunefulness, sweet sounds, mellifluence, musicalness, euphony; timbre, tone color, pitch; tune, song, aria, theme, measure, plainsong, canticle, strain, lay.

harmony, harmoniousness; rhythm, meter; symphony, euphony, consonance, attunement, modulation, syncopation; counterpoint, polyphony; concordance, pleasing combination.

v harmonize, chime, symphonize, blend; tune, accord.

adj melodious, musical, tuneful, melodic, lyrical, euphonious, singing, ringing, sweet-sounding, euphonic, mellifluous, dulcet, mellow, clear, sweet, rich, soft, silvery, agreeable, pleasing.

concordant, harmonious, agreeing, symphonious, suiting, congenial, blending, synchronized, consistent, in rapport, in unison, confluent, conjoined, symmetrical, proportionate, consonant, compatible.

414 discord *n* dissonance, atonality; harshness; racket, noise, inharmoniousness.

v be discordant; jar, grate.

adj discordant, dissonant, atonal, harsh; out of tune, tuneless, unmelodious, inharmonious, unmusical; jarring, grating, cacophonous, screeching.

415 music *n* sweet sounds, pleasing sounds, harmonious sounds, melody, song, tune, strain, air, harmony; classical music, popular music, folk music, jazz, electronic music; orchestral music, instrumental music, symphonic music, chamber music; ragtime, reggae, swing, bebop, bop, barrelhouse, rock; pop music, vocal music, choral music, solo, duet, duo, sonata, trio, quartet, quintet, sextet, septet, octet.

v make music, perform; compose.

adj musical, lyrical; instrumental, orchestral, symphonic, vocal, choral, operatic.

416 musician [performance of music] *n* artist, performer, concert artist, player, soloist, instrumentalist, vocalist, accompanist, singer, minstrel; symphony orchestra, orchestra, chamber orchestra, band, rock and roll band, group, combo, ensemble, chamber group, quartet, trio; chorus, choir, vocal group.

v make music, play, perform, strike up, concertize, execute, accompany, present the music, solo, improvise, play the notes; sing, croon, warble, vocalize, spin a melody.

adj musical, instrumental, vocal, choral, operatic; lyrical, harmonious, brilliant, sharp, incisive.

417 musical instruments *n* orchestra, band, brass band, marching band, military band, ensemble, group; strings, plucked instruments, bowed instruments, hammered instruments; woodwinds, winds, tubed instruments, reed instruments, brass instruments; percussion; synthesizer.

418 hearing *n* audition, auscultation, listening, perception, audibility, ear; regarding, attending, heeding.

hearer, auditor, listener; eavesdropper.

v hear, listen, attend, lend an ear, bend an ear, (*informal*) tune in, give a hearing to, give audience to, prick up one's ears, be all ears; overhear, eavesdrop; heed, regard.

adj hearing, auditory, auricular.

419 deafness *n* hardness of hearing, inaudibility.

v be deaf, not hear; turn a deaf ear to, plug up one's ears; deafen, stun, split the eardrums.

adj deaf, stone-deaf, hard of hearing; deafened, stunned; unheeding, inattentive.

420 light *n* ray, beam, stream, gleam, streak; sunbeam, moonbeam, aurora, dawn, sunrise, daybreak, day, daylight, light of day, sunshine, broad daylight, glow, glint, glimmering; sun, moon; flush, halo, glory, aureole; spark, scintilla, scintillation, flash, blaze, coruscation; flame, lightening, flare; luster, sheen, shimmer, reflection, refraction; brightness, brilliancy, splendor, effulgence, radiance, illumination, radiation; luminosity, lucidity.

science of light: optics, photography, radioactivity.

v shine, glow, glitter, glisten, gleam, beam, flare, flare up, glare, flash, glimmer, shimmer, flicker, sparkle, scintillate, coruscate, flash, blaze; light, reflect, dazzle, bedazzle, daze, radiate; lighten, enlighten, light, irradiate, shed light upon, cast light upon, illuminate, illumine, kindle, fire.

adj luminous, lucent; light, bright, vivid, splendid, resplendent, lustrous, shiny, radiant; sheeny, glossy, glassy, sunny, burnished; cloudless, clear, unclouded; effulgent, blazing, ablaze, phosphorescent, aglow; iridescent.

421 darkness *n* blackness; obscurity, doom, murkiness, murk; duskiness, dusk, dimness; night, midnight, dead of night; shade, shadow, umbra, penumbra; obscuration, adumbration, extinction, eclipse, total eclipse.

v be dark; darken, obscure, shade, dim, shadow, overcast, cloud, becloud; extinguish, put out, blow out, snuff out.

adj dark, obscure, black, pitch black, nocturnal, overcast, cloudy, darkened; dingy, lurid, murky, gloomy, oppressive; shadowy, shady, umbrageous.

422 dimness *n* duskiness, shadowiness, gloominess, cloudiness, mist, mistiness, haze, haziness, fogginess, paleness, shade, nebulosity, gray, grayness.

v be dim, grow dim, darken, obscure, adumbrate, becloud, cloud, shadow, shade, eclipse, cloud over; blur, dull, fade, pale; glimmer, twinkle, flutter, flicker, waver.

adj dim, dull, dingy, lackluster, darkish, darkened, gray, dark, faint, pale, cloudy, misty, murky, overcast, nebulous, shadowy, umbrageous, blurry, hazy, opaque, foggy, bleary, gloomy, lurid, leaden.

423 [source of light] **luminary** *n* natural light, sun, moon, stars, flame, fire, spark, phosphorescence; artificial light, lamp, gas lamp, oil lamp, kerosene lamp, electric light, lantern, torch, candle, taper, light bulb.

v light, illuminate.

adj self-luminous; phosphorescent, radiant.

424 shade *n* cover, awning, umbrella, parasol, sunshade; screen, curtain, shutter, blind, gauze, veil, mantle, mask, sunglasses, (*informal*) shades; cloud, mist, fog, shadow.

v shade, veil, cover, screen, curtain, veil, draw a curtain, pull the shade, cast a shadow.

adj shady, shadowy, cloudy.

425 transparency *n* transparence, transluscence, diaphanousness, clearness, lucidity, limpidity, thinness, sheerness, gauziness, flimsiness.

v be transparent, transmit light.

adj transparent, pellucid, lucid, diaphanous, translucent, limpid, clear, crystalline, see-through, sheer, gauzy, flimsy.

426 opacity *n* opaqueness, darkness, cloudiness, filminess, haziness, mistiness, nontransparency.

v be opaque, obstruct the passage of light.

adj opaque, impervious to light, impenetrable to light, dim, filmy, thick, smoky, misty, smoggy, shady, murky, cloudy, hazy, obscure, clouded, foggy, unclear, frosted, nontransparent, nontranslucent.

427 semitransparency n opalescence, milkiness, pearliness; film, mist.

v let in partial light.

adj semitransparent, semipellucid, semiopaque, opalescent, pearly, nacreous, milky.

428 color n hue, tint, tinge, dye, complexion, shade, tincture, cast, coloration, tone, key; primary color, secondary color, complementary color; coloring; spectrum, prism, spectroscope; pigment, paint, dye, wash, stain.

v color, dye, tinge, stain, tint, paint, wash; illuminate, emblazon.

adj colored, dyed, tinted; prismatic, chromatic; bright, vivid, intense, deep, rich, gorgeous; fresh, unfaded; gaudy, florid, garish, showy, flashy, glaring; mellow, harmonious, pearly, sweet, delicate, tender, refined; dull, gray.

429 [absence of color] colorlessness n neutral tint, black and white, chiaroscuro, monochrome; etiolation, pallor, paleness, discoloration.

v lose color, fade, turn pale, become colorless, pale; deprive of color, bleach, wash out, blanch, tarnish, etiolate, tone down, whiten.

adj uncolored, colorless, hueless, pale, pallid, faint, dull, dun, wan, sallow, dingy, ashy, gray, ashen, lackluster; discolored; light-colored, fair, blond, white.

430 whiteness n milkiness, frostiness, silveriness, pearliness; etiolation, albification, decoloration, colorlessness; albinism.

v whiten, bleach, blanch, etiolate, whitewash.

adj white, snowy, frosted, snow-white, milk-white, milky, chalky, pearly, ivory, silver, silvery, opaline, whitish, albinistic, etiolated, bleached, blanched, fair, light, wan, pallid, pale, lackluster, colorless, anemic, sallow, faint.

431 blackness n darkness, swarthiness, lividness; ink, ebony, coal, charcoal, pitch; obscurity.

v black, blacken, darken; blot, smutch, smut, smirch.

adj black, sable, somber, livid, dark, inky, ebony, pitchy, swarthy, sooty, dingy, dusky, murky; jet-black, pitch-black, black as coal, coal-black, kohl-black, black as night.

432 gray n grayness, neutral tint, silver, salt and pepper, dove color.

adj gray, iron-gray, silver, silvery, silverish, grayish, dun, drab, ashy, ashen, dove-colored, dapple-gray; grizzly, grizzled, hoary.

433 brown n brownness, beige, khaki.

adj brown, bay, dapple, auburn, nutbrown, chocolate, chestnut, cinnamon, russet, tawny, tan, brunette, mahogany, khaki, beige, ocher, sepia, hazel, brownish, coffee, cocoa, rust, roan, sorrel.

434 red n redness; blush, color.

v redden, blush, flush, get red in the face, turn color.

adj red, reddish, scarlet, crimson, blood red, bloody, cherry-colored, vermilion, carmine, maroon, pink, hot pink, rosy, ruby, salmon, wine-colored; red-faced, blushing, embarrassed, red as a beet, red as a lobster, flushed, burning, fuming, flaming, inflamed; ruddy, glowing, blooming, warm, hot.

435 green n greenness, verdure, blue and yellow.

adj green, greenish, verdant, olive, pea-green, emerald, apple, Kelly green, blue-green, aquamarine, sea-green; grassy, verdurous; fresh, new, recent, young, innocent, naive, raw, unseasoned,

immature, inexperienced, ignorant; sickly, wan, pale, livid; jealous, envious.

436 yellow n yellowness, jaundice.

v yellow, age, turn color, dry up.

adj yellow, yellowish, gold, golden, ocher, lemon, citrine, saffron, aureate, creamy, straw-colored, flaxen, blond, tawny, sallow; sordid, cheap; cowardly, (informal) chicken, craven, lily-livered, contemptible, despicable, mean, cringing, groveling; jaundiced.

437 purple n blue and red.

adj purple, purplish, lavender, lilac, magenta, orchid, violet, plum-colored, mauve.

438 blue n blueness.

adj blue, bluish, azure, marine blue, navy, aquamarine, greenish blue, sapphire, turquoise, cobalt, baby blue; depressed, down in the dumps, (informal) in the pits, (informal) down, low.

439 orange n red and yellow; flame.

adj orange, orangy, orangish, brass, copper, apricot, tangerine, gold, flame-colored.

440 variegation n striation, spottiness, streakiness, iridescence, play of colors.

v variegate, diversify, streak, stripe, checker, speckle, bespeckle, fleck, dapple; dot, striate, tattoo, inlay; embroider, quilt.

adj variegated, multi-colored, many-colored, kaleidoscopic; iridescent, prismatic, opaline, nacreous, pearly; pied, piebald, mottled; dappled, salt and pepper, marbled, flecked, speckled, spotty, studded, freckled, flecky, spotted, diversified; striped, veined, lined, striated, streaked, brindled, banded, checked, checkered, plaid, mosaic, inlaid.

441 vision n sight, optics, eyesight; view, look, glance, ken, glimpse, peep, peek, gaze, stare, leer; contemplation, regard, survey; point of view, outlook, viewpoint, perspective, standpoint; perspicacity, discernment, perception, penetration.

v see, behold, discern, perceive, have in sight, descry, sight, make out, discover, distinguish, recognize, spy, espy, catch a glimpse of, command a view of, witness; envision, contemplate; look, view, eye, survey, scan, inspect, run the eye over, glance around; observe, watch, watch for, peep, peer, peek, pry, take a peep, leer, ogle, glare.

adj visual, ocular, optic; clear-sighted, eagle-eyed, discerning; visionary, farsighted.

adv on sight, at first sight, at a glance.

442 blindness n sightlessness; cataract; ignorance.

v be blind, not see; grope in the dark; blind, hoodwink, dazzle; screen, hide, mask.

adj blind, eyeless, sightless, unseeing, dark, purblind, stone-blind; dimsighted, undiscerning, ignorant.

adv blindly, blindfold, darkly.

443 [imperfect vision] dimsightedness n nearsightedness, farsightedness, purblindness, presbyopia, myopia, astigmatism, color blindness, cataract, ophthalmia; squint, cross-eye, strabismus, lazy eye, cockeye, swivel eye, goggle-eyes.

fallacies of vision: refraction, distortion, illusion, mirage, phantasm, vision, specter, apparition, ghost; mirror, lens.

v be dimsighted, see double, wink, blink, squint, look askance, screw up the eyes.

adj dimsighted, purblind, myopic, astigmatic, nearsighted, farsighted, colorblind; blear-eyed, goggle-eyed, cockeyed, cross-eyed.

444 spectator n beholder, observer, looker-on, onlooker, witness, eyewitness, bystander, passerby; sightseer, audience, crowd; spy, sentinel.

v witness, behold, look on.

459

445 optical instruments *n* lens, magnifying glass, microscope; spectacles, monocle, eyeglasses, glasses, contact lens, goggles, pince-nez; telescope, lorgnette, binoculars, spyglass, opera glasses; mirror, looking glass, reflector; prism, kaleidoscope, stereoscope.

446 visibility *n* perceptibility, discernibleness, distinctness, clearness, clarity, perceivability, conspicuousness, definition, sharp outline; appearance, manifestation.

v be visible, appear, open to the view, present itself, show itself, reveal itself, peep up, show up, turn up, start up, pop up, crop up; glimmer, loom; burst forth, burst upon the view, come into sight, come into view, come forth, come forward, attract attention.

adj visible, perceptible, discernible, perceivable, apparent, obvious, manifest, plain, clear, distinct, definite, well-defined, outlined, well-marked; recognizable, palpable, glaring, conspicuous, in full view, in full sight, in front of one's nose, under one's nose, before one's eyes.

447 invisibility *n* indistinctness, imperceptibility, invisibleness, indefiniteness; mystery, obscurity, delitescence, haziness, cloudiness; concealment; latency.

v be invisible; be hidden; escape notice; render invisible, conceal, hide.

adj invisible, imperceptible; not in sight, out of sight, out of view, unseen; inconspicuous, covert; dim, faint, mysterious, dark, obscure, confused, indistinct, indistinguishable, shadowy, indefinite, undefined, unmarked, blurry, blurred, unfocused, out of focus, misty, veiled; concealed, hidden.

448 appearance *n* phenomenon, sight, show, scene, view; prospect, vista, perspective, lookout, outlook, bird's-eye view, scenery, landscape, picture, tableau; display, exposure; pageant, spectacle; aspect, phase, seeming, shape, form, manifestation, guise, look, complexion, color, image, mien, air, cast, carriage, comportment, demeanor; presence; feature, trait, lines, outline, contour, face, countenance, physiognomy, visage, profile, outsides.

v appear, be visible, seem, look, show, present; figure, cut a figure; present to the view.

adj apparent, seeming, ostensible.

adv apparently, to all appearance, ostensibly, seemingly, on the face of it, at first sight, to the eye.

449 disappearance *n* evanescence, eclipse; departure, exit; loss.

v disappear, vanish, dissolve, melt, melt away, fade, pass, pass out, go, depart, leave no trace, be gone.

adj disappearing, evanescent; departed, left; missing, lost, vanished.

Class IV

Words Relating to
Intellectual Faculties

I. Formation of Ideas

450 intellect *n* rationality, mind, understanding, reason, faculties, judgment, sense, common sense, wits, brains, (*informal*) smarts; brain, head, pate, (*informal*) noodle, skull, (*informal*) upstairs.

v intellectualize, reason, understand, realize, ruminate; note, notice, mark, be aware of, take cognizance of.

adj intellectual, mental, cerebral, rational, sensical, commonsensical.

450a absence of intellect *n* want of intellect; inanity, imbecility, brutishness, brute instinct.

adj unintellectual, unintelligent, unrational, nonrational, empty-headed.

451 thought *n* abstraction, concept, conception, opinion, judgment, belief, idea, notion, tenet, conviction, speculation, consideration, contemplation; meditation, pondering, reflection, musing, cogitation, thinking; intention, design, purpose, intent; anticipation, expectation; consideration, attention, care, regard; trifle, mote.

v think, cogitate, meditate, reflect, muse, ponder, ruminate, contemplate; consider, regard, suppose, look upon, judge, esteem, deem, count, account; bear in mind, recollect, recall, remember; intend, mean, design, purpose; believe, suppose; anticipate, expect.

adj thoughtful, contemplative, meditative, reflective, pensive, deliberate; lost in thought, absorbed, engrossed in; careful, heedful, mindful, regardful, considerate, attentive; discreet, prudent, wary, cautious, circumspect.

452 absence of thought *n* incogitancy, vacancy of mind, thoughtlessness, fatuity, vacuity, emptiness; inattention.

v not think, make the mind a blank, (*informal*) turn off the brain, (*informal*) tune out.

adj vacant, unoccupied, empty; unthinking, inattentive, absent, (*informal*) turned off, (*informal*) tuned out; thoughtless, inconsiderate, unmindful, unheedful, imprudent; unreflective.

453 idea *n* thought, conception, theory, notion; observation, impression, apprehension, perception, brainstorm, brainchild, fancy, (*informal*) flash; opinion, view, belief, sentiment, judgment, supposition; plan, object, objective, aim.

adj ideational.

454 topic *n* subject, theme, thesis, subject-matter, food for thought; business, affair, argument.

adj topical, thematic.

adv under consideration, in question.

455 curiosity *n* interest, inquisitiveness, inquiring mind, thirst for knowledge; spying, prying, meddlesomeness.

spy, eavesdropper, gossip.

v be curious, take an interest in, stare, gape, spy, pry.

adj curious, inquisitive, inquiring, prying, spying, peeping, meddlesome, interested.

456 incuriosity *n* lack of interest, incuriousness, indifference, unconcern.

v have no curiosity, take no interest in.

adj incurious, uninquisitive, uninquiring, uninterested, indifferent, impassive, bored, apathetic.

457 attention *n* attending to, attentiveness, intentiveness, care, consideration, observation, heed, regard, mindfulness, notice, watchfulness, alertness; study, scrutiny; civility, courtesy, respect, politeness.

v be attentive, attend, observe, look, see, notice, remark, regard, pay attention, heed; examine, study, scrutinize.

adj attentive, observant, mindful, heedful, thoughtful, alive, alert, awake, on the watch, wary, circumspect, watchful, careful; polite, courteous, respectful, deferential.

458 inattention *n* inattentiveness, inconsideration, heedlessness, unmindfulness, disregard, unconcern.

v be inattentive, overlook, disregard, pay no attention to, gloss over.

adj inattentive, unobservant, unmindful, unheeding, thoughtless, blind to, deaf to, napping, asleep, lost.

459 care *n* heed, caution, prudence, pains, anxiety, regard, attention, vigilance, carefulness, solicitude, circumspection, alertness, watchfulness, wakefulness; accuracy, exactness.

v be careful, take care.

adj careful, cautious, circumspect, watchful, vigilant, guarded, wary, prudent, tactful; painstaking, meticulous, discerning, exact, thorough, concerned, scrupulous, particular, finical, conscientious, attentive, heedful, thoughtful.

460 neglect *n* disregard, dereliction, negligence, remissness, carelessness, failure, omission, default, inattention, heedlessness, recklessness.

v neglect, disregard, ignore, slight, overlook, omit, be remiss, be negligent.

adj neglectful, disregardful, remiss, careless, negligent, unmindful, inattentive, indifferent, heedless, inconsiderate, thoughtless, imprudent; unwary, unguarded; neglecting, neglected, unheeded, uncared for, unobserved, unnoticed, unattended to.

461 inquiry *n* investigation, examination, study, scrutiny, exploration, research, search, pursuit; inquiring, questioning, interrogation; query, question.

inquirer, investigator, inquisitor, inspector.

v inquire, ask, question, interrogate, query, investigate, examine, seek, search, look for, study, consider.

adj inquiring, inquisitive, curious, scrutinizing, questioning, exploring; inquisitorial, exploratory, interrogative.

462 answer *n* reply, response, retort, rejoinder; discovery, solution; rationale.

v answer, reply, respond, rebut, retort, rejoin; explain, interpret, discover, solve; satisfy, set at rest, atone for.

adj responsive; answerable, discoverable, soluble.

463 experiment *n* test, trial, examination, proof, assay, procedure; experimentation, research, investigation, analysis.

experimenter, analyzer, adventurer.

v experiment, try, test, examine, analyze, prove, assay, essay.

adj experimental, probative, analytic.

464 comparison *n* collation, association, relating, likening, correlation, comparative relation, setting side by side, juxtaposition.

v compare, collate, confront, place side by side, pit one against another, juxtapose, relate, correlate.

adj comparative, metaphorical, compared with; comparable.

465 discrimination *n* distinction, differentiation, diagnosis; appreciation, estimation, discernment, critique, judgment; nicety, refinement, taste.

v discriminate, distinguish, set apart, differentiate.

adj discriminating, critical, distinguishing, discriminative, discriminatory, choosy, picky; discerning, perceptive; tasteful, refined.

465a indiscrimination *n* indistinction, indistinctness, lack of discernment.

v be indiscriminate, not discriminate, confound, confuse.

adj indiscriminate, miscellaneous, undiscriminating.

466 measurement *n* survey, valuation, appraisement, assessment, estimate, estimation, reckoning, gauging; measure, standard, rule, gauge, scale.

v measure, survey, assess, rate, value, appraise, estimate.

adj measurable.

467 [on one side] **evidence** *n* facts, indication, sign, signal; ground, grounds, proof, testimony; information, deposition, affidavit, exhibit, citation, reference, confirmation, corroboration.

v be evident, evince, show, tell, cite, signal, indicate, imply, argue, bespeak; give evidence, testify, depose, witness.

adj evident, evidential, indicative, inferential, referential, corroborative, confirmatory.

468 counter-evidence *n* disproof, refutation, rebuttal, conflicting evidence, negation.

v rebut, refute, check, weaken, contravene, contradict, deny.

adj countervailing, contradictory, conflicting, unsupportive, uncorroborative.

469 qualification *n* modification, limitation, mitigation, narrowing, restriction, coloring, allowance, consideration, extenuation, extenuating circumstances, condition, proviso, exception.

v qualify, modify, limit, mitigate, restrain, narrow, restrict, color, allow, allow for, make allowance for, consider, extenuate, except, make an exception, take into account, take into consideration.

adj qualified, qualifying, provided, conditional, extenuating, mitigating, admitting, supposing, with the proviso, provided that.

470 possibility *n* feasibility, practicality, likelihood, potentiality; contingency, chance.

v be possible, stand a chance, admit of, (*informal*) could be.

adj possible, imaginable, conceivable, credible, feasible, practical, performable, achievable, within reach, within the bounds of possibility, potential.

adv possibly, perhaps, perchance, peradventure, maybe.

471 impossibility *n* impracticality, unfeasibility, hopelessness.

v be impossible, have no chance.

adj impossible, not possible, inconceivable, incredible, unimaginable, unreasonable, unfeasible, impractical, unobtainable, unperformable, unachievable, beyond the bounds of reason, absurd, (*informal*) fat chance, (*informal*) no way.

472 probability *n* likelihood, likeliness, plausibility, tendency, prospect, good chance, reasonable chance, expectation.

v be probable, point to, tend, imply, bid fair.

adj probable, likely, plausible, reasonable, presumable, well-founded, hopeful.

adv probably, in all probability, in all likelihood, most likely, presumably.

473 improbability *n* unlikelihood, bare possibility, implausibility, doubtfulness, questionableness.

v be improbable, not have much of a chance.

adj improbable, unlikely, implausible, doubtful, questionable, beyond all reasonable expectation.

474 certainty *n* fact, truth; infallibility, reliability, unquestionableness, inevitability, certitude, assurance, confidence, conviction.

v be certain, stand to reason, render certain, clinch, make sure; know.

adj certain, confident, sure, assured, convinced, satisfied, indubitable, indisputable, unquestionable, undeniable, incontestable, unimpeachable, irrefutable, unquestioned, incontrovertible, absolute, positive, plain, patent, obvious, clear; sure, inevitable, infallible, unfailing; fixed, agreed upon, settled, prescribed, determined, determinate, constant, stated, given; definite, particular, special, especial; reliable, trustworthy, dependable, trusty.

adv certainly, for certain, no doubt, doubtless, undoubtedly, (*informal*) sure enough.

475 uncertainty *n* insecurity, instability, unreliability, fallibility, danger; incertitude, doubt, doubtfulness, ambiguity, vagueness, questionableness, dubiousness; haziness, fogginess, obscurity; undependability, changeableness, variability, capriciousness, irregularity, fitfulness, chanciness.

v be uncertain, hesitate, flounder, waver; render uncertain, pose, puzzle, perplex, confuse, confound, bewilder; doubt, question.

adj uncertain, insecure, precarious, unsure, doubtful, unpredictable, problematical, unstable, unreliable, unsafe, fallible, perilous, dangerous; unassured, undecided, indeterminate, undetermined, unfixed, unsettled, indefinite, ambiguous, questionable, dubious; doubtful, vague, indistinct; undependable, changeable, variable, capricious, unsteady, irregular, fitful, desultory, chance, (*informal*) chancy.

476 reasoning *n* ratiocination, rationalism, dialectics; discussion, comment, argumentation, debate, disputation.

logic, induction, deduction, chain of thought, analysis, synthesis, syllogistic reasoning.

argument, case, proposition, terms, premises, postulate, data; inference, *argumentum ad hominem, paralipsis, a priori, a posteriori, reductio ad absurdum*, enthymeme, dilemma, on the horns of a dilemma.

reasoner, logician, dialectician, disputant, wrangler, arguer, debater, polemicist, casuist, rationalist.

arguments, reasons, pros and cons.

v to reason, discuss, argue, debate, dispute, wrangle; deduce, induce, infer, analyze, synthesize, postulate, propose, contend, demonstrate.

adj reasoning, rationalistic, dialectical, dialectic, argumentative, disputatious; logical, inductive, deductive, analytical, synthetic, syllogistic, inferential; demonstrable.

477 [the absence of reasoning] **intuition.**

[false reasoning] **sophistry** *n* intuition, instinct, hunch, presentiment; insight, discernment, inspiration.

casuistry, jesuitry, perversion, equivocation, evasion, chicanery, quiddity, speciousness, (*informal*) bull, (*informal*) malarkey, bunk; false statement; fallacy, sophism.

sophist.

v intuit; reason falsely, pervert, quibble, equivocate, evade, mislead, gloss over, cavil, refine, subtilize, misrepresent, fence, beg the question.

adj intuitive, instinctive, instinctual, sophistical, equivocal, evasive, specious, fallacious, illogical, unsound, false, incorrect, untenable; inconsequential, weak, feeble, poor, flimsy, vague, nonsensical, absurd, foolish, frivolous, pettifogging, trifling, quibbling, nit-picking, subtle, over-refined.

adv intuitively, by intuition; illogically.

478 demonstration *n* proof, conclusiveness, example, verification, explanation.

v demonstrate, prove, establish, verify; evince, show, explain.

adj demonstrative, demonstrable, probative, conclusive, convincing; demonstrated, proven, proved, shown.

479 confutation *n* refutation, answer, disproof, invalidation, exposure.

v confute, refute, disprove, expose the error, overturn, invalidate.

adj confutable, refutable.

480 judgment *n* verdict, decree, decision, determination, conclusion, result, upshot, deduction, inference, assessment, opinion, estimate, criticism, critique; understanding, discrimination, discernment, perspicacity, sagacity, wisdom, intelligence, prudence, brains, taste, penetration, discretion, common sense.

judge, assessor, reviewer, critic, commentator; connoisseur.

v judge, estimate, consider, regard, esteem, appreciate, appraise, reckon, value; decide, determine, conclude, form an opinion, pass judgment; criticize, rate, rank; try, pass sentence upon, rule.

adj judicious, judicial, judgmental, determinate, conclusive; critical, discriminating, penetrating, perspicacious.

480a discovery *n* detection, determination, disclosure, trove, find.

v discover, learn of, ascertain, unearth, uncover, determine, ferret out, flush out, dig up; find out, detect, espy, descry, discern, see, notice, hit upon, stumble onto.

481 misjudgment *n* miscalculation, miscomputation, misconception, misinterpretation, misapprehension.

v misjudge, misconjecture, misconceive, misunderstand, misconstrue, misinterpret; overestimate, underestimate.

adj misjudging, ill-judging, wrongheaded, (*informal*) off base, wrong, in error.

482 overestimation *n* exaggeration, overvaluation, optimism; miscalculation.

v overestimate, overrate, overprize, overpraise, exaggerate, magnify, attach too much importance to, set too high a value on; miscalculate.

adj overestimated, overrated, inflated, pompous, pretentious.

483 underestimation *n* undervaluation, depreciation, detraction; modesty, self-depreciation; pessimism.

v underestimate, undervalue, underrate, depreciate, disparage, detract, slight, minimize, make light of, make little of, disregard.

adj underestimating, depreciating, depreciative, deprecatory; underestimated, depreciated, unvalued, unprized; modest, pessimistic.

484 belief *n* opinion, view, tenet, doctrine, dogma, creed; certainty, conviction, assurance, confidence, persuasion, believing, trust, reliance; credence, credit, acceptance, faith, assent.

v believe, credit, give credence to, accept, have faith in, give assent, accept; know, see, realize, assume, presume; think, opine, hold, conceive, consider; rely on, put one's trust on, have confidence in.

adj certain, sure, assured, positive, cocksure, satisfied, confident, convinced, secure; believing, trusting, confiding, credulous; believed, accredited, trusted, accepted; believable, credible, trustworthy.

485 disbelief. doubt *n* disbelief, incredulity; dissent, change of mind, retraction.

uncertainty, irresolution, hesitation, hesitancy, vacillation, misgiving, suspense; scruple, qualm, mistrust, distrust, suspicion, skepticism.

unbeliever, nonbeliever; skeptic.

v disbelieve, discredit, dissent, doubt, distrust, mistrust, suspect, have qualms; hesitate, waver, demur.

adj unbelieving, incredulous, doubtful, disputable, questionable, suspicious; uncertain, unsure; doubting, hesitating, hesitant, wavering, irresolute, dubious, skeptical.

486 credulity *n* credulousness, gullibility, infatuation, superstition, self-deception, self-delusion.

gull, dupe, (*informal*) sucker.

v be credulous, swallow.

adj credulous, believing, trusting, unsuspecting, gullible; simple, silly, childish, stupid; infatuated, superstitious.

487 incredulity *n* incredulousness, caution, wariness, suspicion, doubt, skepticism, disbelief.

nonbeliever, skeptic, heretic.

v be incredulous, distrust, doubt, suspect.

adj incredulous, cautious, wary; suspicious, dubious, doubtful, skeptical, unbelieving.

488 assent *n* acknowledgment, agreement, concurrence, acquiescence, consent, allowance, approval, concord, accord, approbation.

v assent, acquiesce, accede, concur, agree, fall in, acknowledge, admit, yield, allow; own, avow, confess.

adj assenting, agreeing, concurring, consenting, of one accord, of the same mind; agreed, acquiescent.

489 dissent *n* difference, discordance, dissension, disagreement, dissatisfaction; opposition, protest; nonconformity, separation.

dissenter, protester, rebel, radical, dissident, nonconformist.

v dissent, differ, disagree, protest, contradict; repudiate.

adj dissenting, negative; dissident, contradictory, disagreeing, opposing; nonconformist.

490 knowledge *n* enlightenment, erudition, wisdom, science, letters, information, learning, scholarship, lore; understanding, discernment, perception, apprehension, comprehension, judgment.

v know, be aware of; understand, discern, perceive, realize, fathom, apprehend, comprehend, (*informal*) dig; (*informal*) be hip; learn, discover.

adj knowing, aware of, cognizant of, acquainted with, privy to; discerning, perceptive, (*informal*) sharp, shrewd; knowledgeable, educated, enlightened, erudite, wise, instructed, learned, well-educated, bookish, well-read; known, recognized, received.

491 ignorance *n* illiteracy, unenlightenment, unawareness, unlearnedness, unacquaintance, unconsciousness, inexperience, darkness, blindness, incomprehension, simplicity, stupidity.

v be ignorant, know nothing, have no idea, be blind to.

adj ignorant, illiterate, unlettered, uneducated, uninstructed, untaught, untutored, uninformed, unenlightened, nescient; shallow, superficial; stupid, dumb, thick, dull.

492 scholar *n* savant, wise man, sage, academician, thinker, intellectual, bibliomaniac, bookworm, pedant; student, pupil, disciple, learner.

493 ignoramus *n* illiterate, know-nothing, blockhead, numskull, dullard, simpleton, dunce, ass, fool, bonehead, duffer, dolt, turkey, twerp, idiot, imbecile, cretin, moron, dimwit, (*informal*) jerk.

494 truth *n* fact, reality, verity, veracity; accuracy, precision, exactness.

v be true, be the case, have a true ring.

adj true, factual, actual, real, authentic, genuine, veracious, truthful, veritable; pure, natural; accurate, exact, faithful, correct, precise; agreeing; right, proper; legitimate, rightful; to the point, (*informal*) right on, (*informal*) where it's at, (*informal*) on target.

495 error *n* fallacy, misconception, misapprehension, misunderstanding, misinterpretation, misjudgment; aberration, inexactness, laxity; mistake, fault, blunder, slip, oversight, flaw, stumble, bungle; delusion, false impression.

v err, be in error, mistake, blunder, slip, go astray, trip up; misconceive, misapprehend, misunderstand, misinterpret, miscalculate, misjudge.

adj erroneous, in error, fallacious, mistaken, incorrect, inaccurate, false, wrong, untrue, (*informal*) off base, (*informal*) off the mark.

496 maxim *n* proverb, aphorism, dictum, saying, adage, apothegm, motto, epigram, *mot juste*, truism, words of wisdom, axiom.

adj proverbial, aphoristic, axiomatic, truistic, (*informal*) corny, trite.

adv as they say, as the saying goes.

497 absurdity *n* nonsense, imbecility, foolishness, silliness, inanity, stupidity; farce, rhapsody, farrago, blunder, bathos; inconsistency, paradox, *non sequitur*, jargon, extravagance, exaggeration.

v be absurd, talk nonsense, play the fool.

adj absurd, nonsensical, ridiculous, silly, preposterous, foolish, inane, asinine, stupid, senseless, unreasonable, irrational, incongruous, self-contradictory, paradoxical; farcical, rhapsodic, bathetic, extravagant, exaggerated, bombastic, fantastic, meaningless.

498 intelligence. wisdom *n* intelligence, intellect, mind, capacity, understanding, discernment, reason, acumen, aptitude, penetration, brains, (*informal*) smarts; knowledge, news, information, tidings.

discretion, reasonableness, judgment, discernment, insight, sense, common sense, sagacity, insight, understanding, prudence; knowledge, information, learning, sapience, erudition, enlightenment.

v be intelligent; understand, discern, reason; be wise, discriminate.

adj intelligent, understanding, intellectual, quick, bright; astute, clever, sharp, alert, bright, apt, discerning, canny, shrewd, nimble, penetrating, piercing, on the ball.

wise, discerning, judicious, sage, sapient, sensible, sound, penetrating, sagacious, intelligent, perspicacious, profound, rational, prudent, cautious, politic, reasonable, thoughtful, reflective; learned, educated, erudite, schooled.

499 imbecility. folly *n* imbecility, want of intelligence, incompetence, incapacity, vacancy, dull understanding, meanness, simplicity, shallowness, stolidity, hebetude, puerility, fatuity, silliness, foolishness, driveling, stupidity, idiocy.

frivolity, irrationality, trifling, ineptitude, silliness, eccentricity, extravagance; rashness.

v be imbecilic.

be foolish, trifle, drivel, dote, ramble.

adj imbecile, imbecilic, idiotic, fatuous, driveling; vacant, mindless, witless, brainless, weak-headed, addle-brained, muddle-headed, dull-witted, feebleminded, half-witted, dull, shallow, stolid, dim-witted, thick-skulled; shallow, weak, wanting, soft, sappy, stupid, obtuse, blunt, stolid, doltish, thick as a brick, asinine; childish, childlike, infantile, puerile, simple.

foolish, silly, senseless, irrational, insensate, nonsensical, inept, frivolous, trifling; eccentric, crazed, rash, thoughtless, giddy, obstinate, bigoted, narrow-minded; foolish, unwise, injudicious, improper, unreasonable, ridiculous; stupid, asinine; ill-conceived, ill-advised, ill-judged, inexpedient, extravagant, frivolous, trivial, useless.

500 sage *n* wise man, master mind, thinker, philosopher, oracle, luminary, man of learning, expert, authority.

501 fool *n* simpleton, dolt, dunce, blockhead, nincompoop, ninny, numskull, ignoramus, booby, sap, dunderhead, dunderpate, idiot, natural, oaf, lout, loon, dullard; jester, buffoon, droll, zany, harlequin, clown; imbecile, moron, idiot, cretin.

502 sanity *n* soundness, mental balance, rationality, reason, sense, clearheadedness, lucidity, coherence, normality, sobriety, (*informal*) good head.

v be sane, (*informal*) have one's act together.

adj sane, rational, reasonable, sensible, clear-headed, level-headed, logical, sober, lucid, self-possessed, (*informal*) together.

503 insanity *n* disorder, imbalance, derangement, dementia, lunacy, madness, craziness, aberration; frenzy, raving, incoherence, delirium, delusion; (*informal*) oddity, eccentricity, twist, mania.

v be insane, become insane, lose one's senses, go mad, rave, rant, (*informal*) lose it.

adj insane, deranged, demented, lunatic, crazed, crazy, maniacal, mad, touched, cracked, unhinged, unsettled, daft, frenzied, possessed, delirious, far gone, wild, flighty, distracted, frantic, mad as a hatter, (*informal*) crackers, (*informal*) zonkers, (*informal*) nuts, (*informal*) zonko, (*informal*) weird, (*informal*) bananas, (*informal*) kaput.

504 madman *n* lunatic, maniac, bedlamite, raver, (*informal*) nut, (*informal*) weirdo, (*informal*) crazy; dreamer, romantic, rhapsodist, enthusiast, visionary, seer, fanatic.

505 memory *n* retention, retentiveness, remembrance, recollection, reminiscence, retrospect; recognition; reminder, hint, suggestion, keepsake, souvenir, memento, token, memorial.

v remember, recall, recollect, call up, call to mind, bring to mind, think back upon, haunt one's thoughts, (*informal*) flash on; remind, suggest, hint, prompt, summon up, reminisce; retain, keep in mind, bear in mind, memorize, engrave in the mind, learn by heart; keep the memory alive.

adj reminiscent (of), mindful (of); fresh, alive, vivid; unforgotten, enduring, indelible, memorable, never to be forgotten, unforgettable, stirring, eventful.

506 oblivion *n* forgetfulness, short memory, slippery memory, untrustworthy memory, obliteration of the past, amnesia.

v forget, be forgetful, have a short memory, lose sight of, sink into oblivion; unlearn, efface from the memory, think no more of, consign to oblivion, banish from one's thoughts.

adj oblivious, forgetful, heedless, deaf to the past, insensible; out of mind, unremembered, forgotten, past recollection, buried, sunk into oblivion.

507 expectation *n* expectancy, anticipation, prospect, reckoning, calculation; suspense, waiting; hope, trust, assurance, confidence, reliance, presumption.

v expect, look for, look out for, look forward to, anticipate, await, hope for, wait for, foresee, prepare for, count on, rely on; predict, prognosticate, forecast.

adj expectant, watchful, vigilant, open-eyed, on tenterhooks, on one's toes, ready, in readiness, prepared, (*informal*) all set for; foreseen, long expected, prospective, in view, in sight, on the horizon, impending.

adv expectantly, on the watch, on edge, with bated breath.

508 nonexpectation *n* unforeseen occurrence, surprise, shock, blow, wonder, bolt out of the blue, astonishment; miscalculation, false expectation.

v not expect, be taken by surprise, catch unawares; burst upon, come out of nowhere, drop from the clouds; surprise, startle, stun, stagger, throw off one's guard, astonish.

adj nonexpectant, surprised, unwarned, unaware, off one's guard; unanticipated, unexpected, unlooked for, unforeseen; unheard of, startling; sudden.

adv unexpectedly, abruptly, suddenly, without warning.

509 [failure of expectation] **disappointment** *n* failure, defeat, frustration, unfulfillment, blighted hope,

vain expectation, disillusion, (*informal*) comedown.

v be disappointed; disappoint, dash one's hopes, dash one's expectations, balk, jilt, tantalize; dumfound, disillusion, let down.

adj disappointed; disgruntled, disconcerted, aghast.

510 foresight *n* prudence, forethought, prevision, anticipation, precaution; forecast; prescience, foreknowledge, prospect.

v look forward to, look ahead, look beyond; look into the future; see one's future, catch the lay of the land; anticipate, expect, assume, surmise, predict, forewarn.

adj anticipatory, prescient; farsighted, prudent, provident; prospective, expectant.

511 prediction *n* prophecy, forecast, augury, prognostication, foretoken, portent, divination, soothsaying, presage.

v predict, foretell, prophesy, foresee, forecast, presage, augur, prognosticate, foretoken, portend, divine.

adj prophetic, oracular, portentous, premonitory.

512 omen *n* portent, foreboding, augury, sign, harbinger; sign of the times, symbol, warning.

513 oracle *n* prophet, prophetess, seer, soothsayer, augur, fortune-teller, witch, sibyl, necromancer, sorcerer, clairvoyant, interpreter.

514 supposition *n* assumption, presumption, condition, hypothesis, theory, postulate, proposition, thesis, theorem; conjecture, suggestion, guess, guesswork, suspicion, inkling, speculation.

v suppose, conjecture, surmise, suspect, guess, divine; theorize, speculate, presume, presuppose, assume, predicate; believe, take for granted; propound, put forth, propose, advance, hazard a suggestion, suggest.

adj assumed, given; conjectural, hypothetical, presumptive, theoretical, speculative, suggestive.

515 imagination *n* imaginativeness, fancy, invention, inspiration, creativity, originality, fiction, vision, fantasy, illusion, ideality, castles in the air, dreaming, dream, golden dreams; mental image, conception, idea, notion, thought, conceit, fancy, whim, figment, romance, vision, dream, chimera, shadow, illusion, phantasm, supposition, delusion; verve, vivacity, liveliness, animation.

v imagine, fancy, conceive, dream, idealize; create, originate, think up, devise, invent, coin, fabricate.

adj imaginative, fanciful, original, inventive, creative, visionary, ideal, unreal, illusory, unsubstantial, dreamy, dreamlike, romantic, fantastic, fabulous, chimerical, fantastical; vivacious, lively, animated; imaginable, conceivable, possible, believable; imagined.

II. Communication of Ideas

516 [idea to be conveyed] **meaning** *n* tenor, spirit, gist, trend, idea, purport, significance, signification, sense, import, denotation, connotation, interpretation; intent, intention, aim, object, purpose, design.

thing signified: matter, subject matter, substance, gist, argument.

v mean, signify, denote, connote, express, import, purport; convey, imply, indicate, point to, allude to, touch on, drive at, involve; declare, affirm, state; intend, aim, design, purpose.

adj meaning; meaningful, pointed, poignant, significant, expressive.

517 meaninglessness *n* unmeaningness, absence of meaning, senselessness, emptiness, empty words,

518

rhetoric, platitude, nonsense, jargon, gibberish, jabber, rant, bombast, (*informal*) hot air; inanity, rigmarole, absurdity, ambiguity.

v mean nothing, jabber, rant, say nothing.

adj meaningless, senseless, nonsensical, inexpressive, vague, trivial, insignificant.

518 intelligibility *n* comprehensibility, clarity, clearness, lucidity, coherence, explicitness, perspicuity, precision, plain-speaking.

v be intelligible; render intelligible, clear up, simplify, elucidate, explain; understand, comprehend, take in, catch on, grasp, follow, master.

adj intelligible, understandable, comprehensible, clear, clear as day, lucid, luminous, transparent; plain, distinct, pointed, clear-cut, obvious, explicit, precise; graphic, illustrative, expressive.

519 unintelligibility *n* incomprehensibility, vagueness, obscurity, ambiguity, uncertainty, confusion.

v be unintelligible; render unintelligible, conceal, darken, confuse, perplex, mystify, bewilder.

adj unintelligible, incomprehensible, indecipherable, unfathomable, inexplicable, inscrutable, insoluble, impenetrable; puzzling, enigmatic, obscure, muddy, dim, nebulous, mysterious, (*informal*) strange, (*informal*) weird; inexpressible, incommunicable, ineffable, unutterable.

520 equivocalness *n* ambiguity, uncertainty, questionableness, dubiousness, indeterminateness; double-meaning, word-play, double entendre, pun, play on words, conundrum, riddle, quibble; equivocation, duplicity, prevarication, white lie.

v be equivocal; have two meanings; equivocate, prevaricate.

adj equivocal, ambiguous, uncertain, doubtful, questionable, dubious, indeterminate; duplicitous, enigmatic, double-edged, deceptive, misleading.

521 figure of speech *n* phrase, expression, euphemism, manner of speaking, colloquialism, idiom, image; metaphor, simile, imagery, poetic device, poetics, figures of beauty.

v employ figures of speech; image, speak prettily.

adj figurative, idiomatic, colloquial, colorful, imagistic, poetic, expressive, allusive.

522 interpretation *n* definition, explanation, explication, elucidation, translation; exegesis, exposition, comment, commentary, gloss; solution, answer, meaning.

v interpret, define, explain, explicate, elucidate, translate, shed light on, cast light on, decipher, decode, unravel, disentangle, gloss, annotate, expound, comment upon; construe, understand.

adj explanatory, expository, exegetical, interpretative, interpretive; interpretable, explicable, intelligible.

adv in explanation, that is to say, namely.

523 misinterpretation *n* misapprehension, misconception, misunderstanding, misreading, misconstruction, mistake; misrepresentation, perversion, exaggeration, false coloration, falsification, travesty.

v misinterpret, misapprehend, misconceive, misunderstand, misread, misconstrue, misapply, mistake; misrepresent, pervert, misstate, garble, falsify, distort, travesty, stretch the meaning, twist the meaning.

524 interpreter *n* translator, explainer, expounder, expositor, commentator, annotator, guide, critic; spokesman, speaker, representative.

525 manifestation *n* indication, expression, exposition, demonstration, showing, display, exhibition, declaration; materialization; openness, candor.

v make manifest, show, display, reveal, disclose, open, exhibit, evince, evidence, demonstrate, declare, express, make known; appear, be plain, come to light, materialize; indicate, point out.

adj manifest, evident, obvious, apparent, plain, clear, distinct, patent, open, palpable, visible, unmistakable, conspicuous, explicit; unreserved, downright, frank, plain spoken; barefaced, bold; manifested.

adv manifestly, openly, plainly, above board, in broad daylight, in plain sight.

526 latency *n* dormancy, latentness, quiescence, obscurity, darkness, hidden meaning, obscure meaning, undercurrent, suggestion, concealment; potentiality.

v be latent, lurk, smolder, underlie.

adj latent, dormant; lurking, secret, cryptic, veiled, hidden; potential; implied, implicit; allusive.

527 information *n* enlightenment, knowledge, news, data, facts, circumstances, situations, intelligence, advice; communication, notification, announcement, record; hint, suggestion, innuendo, inkling, whisper, insinuation.

informant, authority, intelligencer, reporter; informer, eavesdropper, detective, newsmonger; messenger.

guide, guidebook, handbook, manual, map, chart.

v inform, tell, acquaint with, impart to, make acquainted with, apprize, advise, enlighten; communicate, make known, express, mention, let fall, intimate, hint, insinuate, allude to, suggest; announce, report, give an account, disclose; know, learn, find out, get the scent of.

adj informed, communicated, reported, advised, apprized of, acquainted with, enlightened, published, (*informal*) filled in; declarative, expository, communicative.

528 concealment *n* hiding, secretion, ensconcing, sheltering, covering, burying, screening; keeping secret, secrecy, hiding, disguising, veiling, camouflaging, obscuring, dissembling, obfuscation, evasiveness; reticence, reserve, reservation, suppression, silence, secretiveness.

v conceal, hide, secrete, cover, put away, ensconce, bury, screen, shelter, keep out of sight, stow away; keep secret, hide, disguise, veil, cloak, mask, camouflage, obscure, obfuscate, dissemble, be evasive.

adj concealed, hidden, secret, private, privy, confidential, in secret, close, undercover, in hiding, in disguise, covert, mysterious; furtive, stealthy, surreptitious, secretive, evasive, clandestine; reserved, reticent, suppressed, uncommunicative.

adv secretly, in secret, in private, behind closed doors, on the sly; confidentially; stealthily.

529 disclosure *n* revelation, divulgence, exposition, exposure; expose, uncovering, muckraking; acknowledgment, avowal, confession.

v disclose, discover, uncover, lay open, expose, bring to light, unmask; reveal, make known, divulge, show, tell, unveil, unmask, communicate; let slip, let drop, betray, blurt out; acknowledge, allow, concede, grant, admit, own up, confess.

adj disclosed, revealed.

530 [means of concealment] **ambush** *n* ambuscade, lurking place, trap, snare, pitfall; hiding place, secret place, recess, hole, cubbyhole; screen, cover, shade, blinker, veil, curtain, cloak, cloud; mask, visor, disguise, masquerade.

v ambush, lie in wait for, set a trap for.

531 publication *n* issuance, distribution; announcement, proclamation, promulgation, propagation, pronouncement, declaration, disclosure, divulgence, advertisement, publicity; edition.

v publish, issue, distribute, print; make public, make known, announce, proclaim, promulgate, propagate, circulate, spread, disseminate, declare, disclose, divulge, advertise, publicize, get into print.

adj published; current, public, in circulation, in print, in black and white.

532 news *n* information, intelligence, tidings, report, rumor, scuttlebutt, hearsay, gossip, (*informal*) the word; news story, headlines, copy.

reporter, newsmonger, talebearer, gossip, tattler, informer.

v transpire, make news, make headlines; be rumored.

adj in the news, in the headlines, current, in circulation, in print.

533 secret *n* mystery; problem, question, difficulty, a confidence; unintelligibility.

adj secret, hidden, concealed, unrevealed, unknown, mysterious; reticent, secretive; private.

534 messenger *n* envoy, emissary, representative, intermediary, go-between, delegate, courier, runner, errand boy; intelligencer, reporter, newsmonger, spokesman, informant; forerunner, harbinger, herald, precursor.

535 affirmation *n* statement, profession, pronouncement, deposition, assertion, declaration; confirmation, ratification, endorsement; swearing, oath, affidavit; emphasis, dogmatism.

v affirm, state, assert, aver, avow, maintain, declare, swear, asseverate, depose, testify, say, pronounce; establish, confirm, ratify, approve, endorse, assent, acknowledge; swear, emphasize.

adj affirmative, declaratory, declarative, positive, assertive, emphatic, dogmatic; confirmative, corroborative, affirming, acquiescent.

536 negation. denial *n* nullification, invalidation.

disputation, confutation, contradiction, qualification; repudiation, rejection, abjuration, disavowal, disclaimer, recantation, retraction, rebuttal.

v negate, nullify, cancel, invalidate, deny, dispute, controvert, contravene, oppose, gainsay, contradict, rebut; reject, renounce, abjure, disclaim, disavow; recant, revoke; refuse, repudiate, disown.

adj contradictory; negative.

537 teaching *n* instruction, education, pedagogy, pedagogics, edification, tutelage, tutorship; guidance, direction, preparation, schooling, learning, discipline; lesson, lecture, disquisition, discourse, explanation, harangue, homily, sermon, lore; doctrine, dogma, tenet, principle, rule, maxim, article of faith, creed, credo, belief, opinion.

v teach, instruct, edify, educate, inform, enlighten, prepare, discipline, train, drill, tutor, prime, coach, guide, direct, school, indoctrinate, inculcate, infuse, instill, imbue; expound, interpret, lecture, discourse, hold forth, sermonize, moralize.

adj educational, scholastic, academic, pedagogic, pedagogical, didactic; edifying, instructive.

538 misteaching *n* misinformation, misdirection, misguidance, perversion, sophistry, error.

v misteach, misinform, misinstruct, misdirect, misguide, pervert, mislead, misrepresent, confuse, bewilder, lie.

539 learning *n* acquisition of knowledge, acquirements, attainment, mental cultivation, scholarship, erudition, study, inquiry, questioning, search, pursuit of knowledge.

apprenticeship, tutelage, matriculation.

v learn, acquire, gain knowledge, memorize, master, study, grind, cram, (*informal*) hook, read, peruse, pore over, wade through, ingest, burn the midnight oil, (*informal*) pull an all-nighter.

adj studious, industrious; scholarly, scholastic, well-read, learned, erudite.

540 teacher *n* instructor, tutor, lecturer, professor, don, master, schoolmaster, guide, counselor, adviser, mentor; preacher, missionary, propagandist.

541 learner *n* scholar, student, pupil, apprentice, novice, neophyte, beginner; disciple, acolyte, follower.

542 school *n* academy, educational institution, college, university, institute, seminary, place of learning.

schoolbook, textbook, text, primer, grammar, reader, workbook.

adj scholastic, academic, collegiate.

543 veracity *n* truthfulness, frankness, truth, sincerity, candor, honesty, probity, fidelity, accuracy.

v speak the truth, (*informal*) level with, (*informal*) be straight with.

adj veracious, true, truthful, sincere, honest, honorable, candid, frank, open, straightforward, honest, scrupulous, punctilious, trustworthy.

544 falsehood *n* falsification, lie, fib, untruth, distortion, deception, misrepresentation, fabrication, fiction, sham; untruthfulness, lying, prevarication, duplicity, double dealing, deceitfulness, equivocation, dissembling, cunning, guile, insincerity, dishonesty, inaccuracy.

v lie, fib, falsify, prevaricate, misrepresent, deceive, (*informal*) come on to, doctor, feign, pretend, play false, dissemble; counterfeit, fabricate.

adj false, untrue, wrong, mistaken, incorrect, erroneous; untruthful, lying, mendacious, dishonest, deceitful, treacherous, faithless, insincere, hypocritical, disingenuous, unfaithful, cunning, perfidious, two-faced, recreant; deceptive, misleading, fallacious, spurious, fraudulent, bogus, phony, sham, counterfeit.

545 deception *n* deceiving, guiling, falseness, untruthfulness; artifice, sham, cheat, imposture, deceit, treachery, subterfuge, stratagem, ruse, hoax, fraud, trick, wile, snare, trap, illusion, delusion.

v deceive, mislead, lead astray, take in, delude, cheat, cozen, dupe, gull, fool, bamboozle, hoodwink, (*informal*) con, trick, double-cross, defraud, outwit; entrap, ensnare, betray.

adj deceptive, misleading, delusive, illusory, fallacious, specious, untrue, false, deceitful; tricky, cunning, insidious.

546 untruth *n* falsehood, fib, lie, fiction, story, tale, tall tale, fabrication, fable, forgery, invention.

v make believe, pretend, feign, sham, fib, lie.

adj untrue, false, trumped up, unfounded, invented, fictitious, fabulous.

547 dupe *n* gull, pigeon, laughingstock, greenhorn, fool, sucker, puppet, (*informal*) nebbish.

v be deceived, be the dupe of, fall into a trap, go for the bait, bite, swallow.

adj credulous, gullible, unsuspecting, trusting.

548 deceiver *n* dissembler, hypocrite, sophist, liar, (*informal*) fast talker, storyteller, (*informal*) faker, (*informal*) phony, fraud, (*informal*) four-flusher, (*informal*) shyster, confidence man, con man, cheat, swindler, imposter, pretender, humbug, adventurer, adventuress, serpent, snake in the grass.

549 exaggeration *n* overstatement, hyperbole, extravagance, coloring, coloration, embroidery; yarn, tale, (*informal*) shaggy dog story, (*informal*) fish story; tempest in a teacup, much ado about nothing, puffery, rant.

v exaggerate, magnify, amplify, expand, overestimate, overstate; heighten, color, embroider, puff up, fill out.

adj exaggerated, overwrought, bombastic, magniloquent, hyperbolic, fabulous, extravagant, preposterous.

550 [means of communication] **indication** *n* symbolism, semiology; sign, symbol, index, indicator, pointer, note, token, symptom; type, mark, figure, emblem, insigne, cipher, device, representation; signal, beacon, alarm; feature, trait, characteristic, peculiarity, quality, earmark, cast; gesture, gesticulation, motion, cue, hint, clue, scent.

v indicate, denote, betoken, designate, signify, represent, stand for, typify, symbolize; note, mark, stamp; label, ticket; make a sign, signalize, signal, gesture, gesticulate; sign, seal, attest, underline, underscore, call attention to.

adj indicative, indicatory; connotative, denotative, typical, representative, symbolic, symbolical, characteristic, significant, emblematic.

551 record *n* trace, vestige, relic, remains; monument, achievement; account, chronicles, annals, history, note, register, memorandum, document, diary, log, journal, ledger.

v record, set down, place in the record, chronicle, enter, register, list, enroll; commemorate, celebrate.

552 [suppression of sign] **obliteration** *n* erasure, cancelation, deletion, blot, effacement, extinction.

v obliterate, efface, expunge, erase, cancel, delete, blot out, rub out, strike out, wipe out, leave no trace.

adj obliterated, erased, blotted out; unrecorded.

553 recorder *n* notary, clerk, registrar, register, secretary, scribe, bookkeeper; annalist, historian, historiographer, chronicler, biographer, journalist, antiquarian, memorialist.

554 representation *n* depiction, imitation, illustration, delineation, expression, imagery, portraiture, figuration.

v represent, delineate, depict, portray, picture, figure, describe, trace, copy, illustrate, symbolize; personate, personify, mimic.

adj representative, imitative, illustrative, figurative, symbolic, descriptive.

555 misrepresentation *n* distortion, exaggeration, misfiguration, falsification; bad likeness, caricature.

v misrepresent, distort, overdraw, exaggerate, falsify, caricature, daub.

556 painting *n* fine art, picture, depiction, representation, pictorialization, delineation, design, drawing, likeness, copy, imitation, fake, image.
art gallery, picture gallery, studio.

v paint, design, limn, draw, sketch, pencil, color; depict, represent.

adj pictorial, picturesque.

557 sculpture *n* carving, modeling, statuary; ceramics, potting.
statue, statuette, bust; cast, mold.

v sculpt, fashion, cast, mold, model, chisel, carve, cut, shape, form, figure, hew.

558 engraving *n* etching, chiseling, incising, plate engraving, photoengraving.

v engrave, grave, carve, incise, chisel, hatch, etch, stipple, print.

559 artist *n* painter, drawer, sketcher, designer, draftsman, cartoonist, caricaturist, sculptor, engraver.

560 language *n* speech, phraseology, style, expression, diction, jargon, dialect, terminology, vernacular, lingo, tongue.
literature, letters, *belles lettres*, humanities, classics, dead language.

linguist.

v express, say, express by words.

adj lingual, linguistic; dialectic, vernacular, current, colloquial, slangy, polyglot, literary.

561 letter *n* character, hieroglyph, symbol, alphabet, consonant, vowel.
syllable, monosyllable, dissyllable, polysyllable.
spelling, orthography; phonetics; cipher, code; monogram, anagram.

v spell.

adj literal; alphabetical; syllabic; phonetic.

562 word *n* term, symbol, name, part of speech.
dictionary, vocabulary, lexicon, index, thesaurus, glossary.
etymology, derivation, philology, terminology, lexicography.

adj literal, verbal.

563 neology *n* neologism, new-fangled expression, *(informal)* hip expression, barbarism, corruption.
neologist, word coiner.

v coin words.

adj neologic, neological; colloquial, slang, *(informal)* hip, cant, barbarous.

564 nomenclature *n* naming; name, appellation, designation, epithet, nickname, *(informal)* moniker, *(informal)* handle, label, title, head, heading; style, proper name, surname, namesake.

v name, call, term, designate, denominate, style, entitle, dub, christen, baptize, nickname, characterize, specify, label.

adj titular, nominal.

565 misnomer *n* misnaming, malapropism; sobriquet, nickname, assumed name, alias, pen name, stage name, pseudonym, *nom de plume, nom de guerre*.

v misname, miscall, misterm; take an assumed name.

adj misnamed; *soi-disant*, self-styled; so-called.

566 phrase *n* expression, set phrase, turn of speech, idiom, tag phrase, figure of speech, euphemism, motto; phraseology.

v phrase, express, put into words, find the right words, arrange in words, voice, vocalize.

567 grammar *n* rules of language, usage, forms, style, formal features, constructions, parts of speech; accidence, syntax, inflection, case, declension, conjugation; grammar book, primer, rulebook.
grammarian.

adj grammatical, syntactic, syntactical.

568 solecism *n* ungrammatical usage, bad grammar, faulty grammar, error, slip, inconsistency, impropriety.

v solecize.

adj ungrammatical, incorrect, inaccurate, faulty, inconsistent, improper.

569 style *n* diction, phraseology, wording; composition, mode of expression, choice of words, command of language, mode, manner, method, approach; kind, form, appearance, character, touch, characteristic, mark, signature, imprint, *(informal)* name.

v style, compose, express by words; write.

adj stylistic; characteristic; expressive.

570 perspicuity *n* clearness, clarity, lucidity, plainness, plain-speaking, distinctness, explicitness, exactness, intelligibility.

adj perspicuous, pellucid, clear, lucid, intelligible, plain, distinct, explicit, exact, definite, unequivocal.

571 obscurity *n* unintelligibility, involution, confusion, indistinctness, indefiniteness, ambiguity, vagueness, inexactness, impenetrability.

adj obscure, involved, confused, unintelligible, impenetrable, indefinite, vague, inexact, hidden, dark.

572 conciseness *n* brevity, summary, abridgment, terseness, pithiness, compression, tightness.

v be concise, condense, abridge, abstract, compress, tighten; come to the point.

adj concise, brief, compendious, short, terse, laconic, pithy, trenchant, succinct, compact, tight.

adv concisely, briefly, summarily, in short.

573 diffuseness *n* long-windedness, verbosity, wordiness, verbiage, looseness, exuberance, redundancy, profuseness, richness.

v be diffuse, enlarge, amplify, expand, inflate; meander, digress, ramble, run on and on.

adj diffuse, profuse, wordy, verbose, copious, exuberant; lengthy, long-winded, protracted, prolix, diffusive, roundabout; digressive, discursive, loose.

574 vigor *n* power, force, boldness, spirit, verve, heart, ardor, enthusiasm, raciness, glow, fire, warmth; loftiness, elevation, gravity, sublimity; eloquence, strong language.

adj vigorous, nervous, powerful, forcible, forceful, trenchant, biting, incisive, impressive; spirited, lively, glowing, sparkling, racy, bold, pungent, pithy; lofty, elevated, sublime, grand, weighty; eloquent, vehement, impassioned, passionate.

575 feebleness *n* weakness, enervation, frailty, faintness.

adj feeble, tame, weak, meager, vapid, insipid; trashy, poor, dull, dry, languid; prosy, prosaic, slight; careless, loose, slip-shod, wishy-washy, sloppy, slovenly; puerile, childish.

576 plainness *n* simplicity, homeliness, restraint, severity.

v speak plainly, speak directly, come straight to the point, be straightforward, not beat around the bush.

adj plain, simple, homely, homey, unadorned, unvarnished, neat, homespun; severe, chaste, pure.

adv in plain terms, in plain English; point-blank.

577 ornament *n* floridness, ornateness, elegance, grandiloquence, magniloquence, rhetorical flourish, declamation, rhetoric, flourish, fancy talk, (*informal*) big words; pretention, inflation, bombast, fustian, rant, fine writing, fine speaking.

v ornament, overcharge, talk big, talk fancy.

adj ornate, ornamented, beautified, florid, rich, flowery, fancy; euphuistic, euphemistic; sonorous, high sounding; inflated, swelling, turgid, pompous, pedantic, stilted, high-flown, sententious, rhetorical, declamatory, grandiose, grandiloquent, magniloquent, bombastic, flashy.

578 elegance *n* taste, good taste, propriety, correctness; lucidity, purity, grace, ease; gracefulness, euphony, gentility, cultivation, polish, refinement.

purist, classicist.

adj elegant, polished, classic, classical, fine, tasteful, proper, correct; chaste, pure, graceful, easy, readable, fluent, flowing, unaffected, natural, mellifluous, euphonious, felicitous, neat, well put.

579 inelegance *n* tastelessness, vulgarity, impropriety; bad diction, awkwardness, stiffness, turgidity, abruptness; barbarism, solecism, slang, mannerism, affectation, formality.

adj inelegant, graceless, ungraceful, harsh, abrupt, dry, stiff, cramped, formal, forced, labored, awkward, ponderous, turgid, artificial, mannered, affected, euphuistic; tasteless, barbarous, uncouth, rude, crude, vulgar.

580 voice *n* vocality, intonation, articulation, enunciation, distinctness, clearness, delivery; accent, accentuation, emphasis, stress; utterance, vocalization.

v voice, speak, utter; articulate, enunciate, vocalize, intone, pronounce, accent, accentuate, deliver.

adj vocal, oral; articulate, distinct, euphonious, melodious.

581 muteness *n* dumbness, silence, speechlessness; aphasia.

v be mute, be silent, be dumb; silence, muzzle, muffle, suppress, smother, gag, strike dumb, dumfound.

adj mute, silent, dumb, mum, tongue-tied; voiceless, speechless.

582 speech *n* talk, parlance, locution, conversation, parley, communication, prattle; talk, oration, address, discourse, lecture, recitation, sermon, harangue, tirade; oratory, eloquence, rhetoric, declamation.

speaker, spokesman, mouthpiece, orator, rhetorician.

v speak, utter, talk, voice, converse, communicate, pronounce, say, articulate; declaim, harangue, stump, spout, rant, lecture, sermonize, discourse, expatiate, soliloquize, address.

adj oral; talkative, conversational; declamatory.

583 [imperfect speech] inarticulateness *n* stammering, hesitation, muttering, mumbling, stuttering; reticence, taciturnity; speech impediment, aphasia.

v be inarticulate, stammer, hesitate, mutter, mumble, slur one's words, garble, sputter, hem and haw, whisper, croak, crack.

adj inarticulate, tongue-tied, speechless, voiceless, hesitant, reticent, taciturn.

584 loquacity *n* loquaciousness, volubility, talkativeness, verbosity, garrulity, volubility; chatter, jabber, prattle, twaddle.

talker, chatterer, chatterbox, babbler, ranter.

v be loquacious, talk a mile a minute, pour forth, prate, chatter, babble, gab, run off at the mouth, jabber, jaw, gush.

adj loquacious, voluble, talkative, verbose, wordy, garrulous, chatty, chattering, glib, fluent, effusive.

585 taciturnity *n* silence, muteness, reserve, reticence, uncommunicativeness.

v be silent, keep silence, keep quiet, hold one's tongue, say nothing.

adj taciturn, silent, mute, mum, reserved, reticent, guarded, uncommunicative, close-mouthed, quiet.

586 public address *n* allocution, speech, formal speech, address, invocation.

v speak to, address; invoke, hail, salute; lecture, pronounce.

587 response *n* answer (see **462**).

588 conversation *n* interlocution, colloquy, confabulation, talk, (*informal*) rap, discourse, verbal interchange, dialog, oral communication; chat, chit, chit-chat, small talk, table talk, idle talk, prattle, gossip; conference, parley, interview, audience, *tête-à-tête*, council, congress; palaver, debate, discussion.

v converse, confabulate, talk together, hold a conversation, carry on a conversation, engage in a discussion; bandy words, chat, chit-chat, gossip, tattle, prate; discourse with, confer with; talk it over, (*infomal*) rap, (*informal*) chew the fat.

adj conversational, conversable; chatty, gossipy.

589 soliloquy *n* monolog, apostrophe, aside.

v soliloquize, talk to oneself, think out loud, apostrophize.

590 writing *n* chirography, penmanship, calligraphy, hand, script, longhand, shorthand, stenography; handwriting, signature, mark, hand; manuscript, MS., document, script, writ, author's copy, copy, original; composition, authorship, work, opus, book, volume, tome, publication, article, poetry, verse, literature.

writer, author, scribe, scrivener, clerk, copyist, secretary.

v write, pen, copy, transcribe; print, scribble, scrawl, scratch; compose, draw out, write down, set down, put pen to paper, take up the pen, take pen in hand.

adj written, in writing, in black and white.

591 printing *n* lettering, typography; type; composition, print, letterpress, text, matter; copy, impression, proof.

printer, compositor, reader, proofreader, copyeditor.

v print, compose; go to press, publish, bring out, issue.

adj typographical, printed.

592 correspondence *n* letter, epistle, missive, note, post card; communication, dispatch, bulletin, circular.

v correspond, communicate, write to, send a letter.

adj epistolary; in touch with, in communication with.

593 book *n* booklet; writing, work, volume, tome, opus, tract, treatise, brochure, handbook; novel, story; script, libretto; publication.

writer, author, essayist, editor; bookseller, publisher; librarian, bibliophile, bookworm.

594 description *n* narration, account, recounting, telling, recital, relation, statement, report, record; delineation, portrayal, characterization, representation, depiction, sketch, vignette.

v describe, set forth, narrate, account, recount, recite, rehearse, tell, relate, detail; picture, delineate, portray, characterize, limn, represent, depict.

595 dissertation *n* treatise, essay, thesis, theme, tract, discourse, disquisition, investigation, study, discussion, exposition; commentary, critique, criticism, review, article.

commentator, critic, essayist, reviewer.

v discuss a subject, treat, examine, comment, criticize, explain.

596 compendium *n* abstract, précis, epitome, analysis, digest, compendium, brief, abridgment, abbreviation, condensation, summary; draft, note, synopsis, outline, syllabus, contents, prospectus; compilation, collection, album, anthology; extracts, cuttings, fragments, pieces; list, inventory, survey.

v abridge, abstract, précis, epitomize, summarize; abbreviate, shorten, condense, compress; compile, collect, note; list, inventory, survey.

adj compendious, synoptic, analytic, analytical.

597 poetry *n* poetics; verse, poesy, versification, rhyming, rhymes, making verses, metrics; doggerel.

poet, laureate, bard, troubadour, minstrel, versifier, rhymer, sonneteer, rhapsodist, poetaster.

v poeticize, sing, versify, rhyme, make verses, compose.

adj poetic, poetical, rhythmic, metrical, lyrical, tuneful, musical; beautiful, lovely, tender, sensitive.

598 prose *n* writing, fiction, imaginative writing, narrative prose.

v write prose.

adj prosy, unpoetic, rhymeless; prosaic, dull, flat, matter-of-fact, unimaginative, commonplace, humdrum, pedestrian, trite, hackneyed, mediocre, stock, ordinary; fictional.

599 the drama *n* the stage, the theater; theatricals, dramaturgy, playwriting; play, drama, stage-play, opera.

performance, acting, representation, impersonation, stage business, actor, actress, player, performer, thespian.

theater, playhouse, operahouse, amphitheater.

dramatist, playwriter, playwright.

v dramatize, act, play, perform, personate, act a part, put on the stage, enact.

adj dramatic, theatrical, histrionic, stagy.

Class V

Words Relating to Voluntary Powers

I. Individual Volition

600 will *n* volition, free will, freedom; choice, wish, desire, pleasure, disposition, inclination; intent, purpose, option; determination, resolution, resoluteness, decision, forcefulness; force of will, will power, self-control.

v will, see fit, think fit, decide, decree, determine, direct, command, bid.

adj willful, voluntary, volitional, intentional; free, optional, discretionary; autocratic, obdurate, adamant.

adv willfully, voluntarily, at will; of one's own accord, intentionally, deliberately.

601 necessity *n* obligation, compulsion, subjection; fate, destiny, fatality; inevitability, inevitableness, unavoidability, unavoidableness, irresistibility; requirement, requisite, demand; instinct, impulse.

v be obligated, be obliged, be fated; necessitate, compel, subject; require.

adj necessary, essential, requisite, needful; inevitable, unavoidable, ineluctable, irresistible, inexorable; compulsory; involuntary, instinctive, automatic, blind, mechanical.

adv necessarily, of necessity, willy nilly.

602 willingness *n* disposition, inclination, leaning, propensity, frame of mind, liking, humor, mood, vein, bent, penchant, aptitude; geniality, cordiality, good will; alacrity, readiness, eagerness, enthusiasm; assent, compliance, agreement.

v be willing, incline, lean to, mind, hold to, cling to; desire; acquiesce, assent, comply; find one's way to, give it a shot, (*informal*) take a swing at, (*informal*) lay into.

adj willing, fain, favorable, content, well disposed; ready, earnest, eager, desirous; genial, cordial.

adv willingly, freely, with pleasure, with all one's heart, graciously.

603 unwillingness *n* indisposition, disinclination, reluctance, dislike; aversion, indifference, slowness, lack of readiness, obstinacy; scrupulousness, hesitation, qualm, shrinking, holding back, recoil; averseness, dissent, refusal.

v be unwilling, dislike; demur, hesitate, shrink from, swerve, recoil; dissent, refuse.

adj unwilling, loath, reluctant, averse; laggard, backward, slow, slack, indifferent; scrupulous, hesitant.

adj unwillingly, grudgingly, against one's will, under protest.

604 resolution *n* determination, will, decision, strength of mind, resolve, firmness, energy, manliness, vigor, resoluteness; pluck, zeal, devotion;

self-control, self-command, self-possession, self-reliance, self-restraint, self-denial; tenacity, perseverance, obstinacy, (*informal*) gumption.

v be resolute, resolve, will, determine, decide, make a resolution, conclude, fix, bring to a crisis, take a decisive step; stand firm, insist upon, make a point of, not give an inch.

adj resolute, firm, steadfast, resolved, purposeful, fixed, inflexible, bold, game, indomitable, relentless, tenacious, gritty, stern, irrevocable, obstinate.

adv resolutely, in earnest, earnestly, manfully.

604a perseverance *n* persistence, tenacity, resolution, doggedness, determination, steadfastness, indefatigability, pluck, stamina, backbone.

v persevere, persist, continue, keep on, last, stick it out, hang in there.

adj persevering, constant, steady, steadfast, persistent, tenacious, resolute, dogged, indefatigable, indomitable, staunch, true, game, (*informal*) tough.

605 irresolution *n* indecision, indetermination, instability, uncertainty; hesitation, hesitancy, vacillation, oscillation, changeableness, fluctuation, fickleness, weakness, frailty, timidity, cowardice.

v be irresolute, dawdle, dilly-dally, shilly-shally, hesitate, falter, waver, vacillate, change, fluctuate, blow hot and cold.

adj irresolute, indecisive, indeterminate, unstable, uncertain; hesitant, changeable, capricious, fickle, frail, feeble, weak, timid, (*informal*) soft, cowardly.

606 obstinacy *n* doggedness, persistence, pertinacity, resolution, intractability, firmness, immovability, inflexibility, obduracy, willfulness, perversity, stubbornness, mulishness; uncontrollability, wildness.

fixed idea, *idée fixe*, fanaticism, zealotry, infatuation, monomania; bigotry, intolerance, dogmatism.

bigot, dogmatist, zealot, fanatic.

v be obstinate, persist, die hard, fight, stick to an idea.

adj obstinate, dogged, persistent, pertinacious, resolute, intractable, firm, refractory, headstrong, willful, inflexible, immovable, perverse, stubborn, mulish, pig-headed; wayward, unruly, incorrigible, uncontrollable, wild; fanatic, zealous, monomaniacal; intolerant, dogmatic, arbitrary.

607 recantation *n* tergiversation, renunciation, abjuration, retraction, defection, apostasy, disavowal, revocation, reversal.

turncoat, apostate, renegade, deserter.

v recant, change one's mind, abjure, retract, renounce, disavow, revoke, defect, change sides.

adj changeful, irresolute, slippery, timeserving.

608 caprice *n* fancy, humor, whim, quirk, freak, fad, vagary, prank.

v be capricious.

adj capricious, erratic, eccentric, fitful, inconsistent, fanciful, whimsical, crotchety, freakish, wayward, wanton; contrary, captious, unreasonable, arbitrary, fickle; frivolous.

609 choice *n* selection, decision, pick, choosing, election, option, alternative, preference, predilection, desire.

v choose, select, elect, make a choice, prefer, pick, cull, decide.

adj optional, discretional, preferential.

609a neutrality. absence of choice *n* neutrality, indifference; indecision, irresolution.

no choice, first come first served.

v be neutral, have no preference, waive, abstain. take what's offered.

adj neutral, indifferent; indecisive, irresolute.

610 rejection *n* refusal, repudiation, renunciation; exclusion, elimination.

v reject, refuse, repudiate, decline, deny, rebuff, repel, renounce; discard, throw away, exclude, eliminate; jettison.

611 predetermination *n* premeditation, predeliberation, foregone conclusion; resolve, intention; fate, predestination, destiny.

v predetermine, predestine, premeditate, resolve beforehand, calculate.

adj aforethought; foregone.

adv advisedly, deliberately, intentionally.

612 impulse *n* sudden thought, flash, spurt, inspiration, improvisation.

v improvise, extemporize; flash on, hit on, come up with, pull out of a hat, pull out of the air; say what comes to mind.

adj impulsive, impromptu, spontaneous; extemporaneous.

adv extempore, extemporaneously; impromptu, offhand, impulsively.

613 habit *n* addiction, disposition, tendency, bent, wont; custom, prescription, practice, way, usage, wont, manner; prevalence, observance; conventionalism, conventionality, mode, fashion, vogue, conformity; rule, precedent, routine, rut, groove.

v habituate, inure, harden, season; accustom, familiarize; acclimate, accommodate; cling to, adhere to, acquire a habit, fall into a rut; be habitual, come into use, become a habit, take root.

adj habitual, customary, prescriptive, usual, general, ordinary, common, frequent, everyday, familiar, trite, commonplace, conventional, regular, set, stock, fixed, permanent; prevalent, current, fashionable; addictive.

adv habitually, as usual, as things go, as the world goes; as a rule, for the most part, generally.

614 disuse *n* desuetude, disusage, lack of practice.

v be unaccustomed, break a habit; disuse.

adj unaccustomed; unusual, original.

615 motive *n* reason, ground, principle, mainspring, purpose, cause, occasion, influence, impulse, instigation, spur, stimulus, incitement, incentive, inducement, consideration, temptation, motivation; intention, ulterior motive.

v motivate, induce, move, inspire, put up to, prompt, stimulate, spur, excite, arouse, rouse, incite, instigate; influence, sway, incline, dispose, lead, persuade, prevail upon, enlist, engage, invite, court, tempt, charm.

adj suasive, persuasive, seductive, attractive, provocative.

615a absence of motive *n* caprice, chance, absence of design.

v have no motive.

adj capricious, without rhyme or reason.

adv capriciously.

616 dissuasion *n* expostulation, remonstrance, deprecation, discouragement, damper, restraint, curb, check.

v dissuade, cry out against, remonstrate, expostulate, warn, disincline, indispose, shake, discourage, dishearten, disenchant; deter, hold back, restrain, repel, turn aside, wean from, damp, cool, chill, blunt.

adj dissuasive.

617 [ostensible motive, ground, or reason] **plea** *n* pretext, allegation, excuse; pretense, shallow excuse, lame excuse, makeshift.

v plead, allege, excuse, make a pretext of, pretend.

618

adj ostensible, alleged.

adv ostensibly, under the pretense of.

618 good *n* benefit, interest, service, behalf, advantage, improvement, gain, boot, profit, harvest; boon, blessing, good luck, prize, good fortune, windfall, godsend; prosperity, happiness, goodness.

v benefit, serve, profit, advantage.

adj commendable; useful, good, beneficial, advantageous.

619 evil *n* ill, harm, hurt, mischief, nuisance; damage, loss; disadvantage, drawback; disaster, accident, casualty, mishap, misfortune; calamity, catastrophe, tragedy, ruin, destruction, adversity; mental suffering, pain, anguish; outrage, wrong, injury, foul play.

v be in trouble; harm, hurt, injure, ruin, destroy, torture.

adj evil, hurtful, injurious, harmful; disastrous, catastrophic, cataclysmic, tragic, ruinous.

620 intention *n* intent, purpose, project, undertaking, design, ambition, contemplation, view, proposal, meaning; object, aim, end, destination, mark, point, goal, target, prey, quarry, game; decision, determination, resolve, resolution, settled purpose.

v intend, mean, design, purpose, propose, contemplate, plan, expect, mediate, calculate, project, aim for, aim at, aspire at.

adj intentional, advised, express, determinate, bound for, bent upon, in view, in prospect.

adv intentionally, advisedly, wittingly, knowingly, purposely, on purpose, by design, pointedly; deliberately.

621 [absence of design] **chance** *n* destiny, lot, fate, luck, good luck, turn, (*informal*) break, (*informal*) jinx, fortune; speculation, venture, stake, shot in the dark, fluke; wager, gambling, betting.

gambler, gamester, adventurer.

v chance, chance it, tempt fate, speculate, risk, venture, hazard, stake, wager, bet, place a bet, gamble, play for.

adj unintentional, accidental, random; fortuitous, lucky; speculative, venturesome.

adv unintentionally, unwittingly.

622 pursuit *n* pursuance, enterprise, undertaking, business, adventure, essay, quest, search.

v pursue, prosecute, follow, do, engage in, undertake, endeavor, seek, aim at, fish for, press on, go after, chase.

adj in quest of, in pursuit of.

623 avoidance *n* evasion, flight, escape, retreat, recoil, departure; abstention, abstinence, forbearance, inaction.

avoider, shirker, quitter, truant; fugitive, refugee, runaway, deserter.

v avoid, shun, steer clear of, keep clear of, evade, elude, shirk, fly from, turn away from; abstain, refrain, eschew, leave alone, not get involved; shrink, hold back, retire, recoil, flinch, blink, shy, dodge, beat a retreat, turn tail, run for one's life, head for the hills, take flight, beat it out; desert, sneak off, shuffle off, slink away, steal away, slip, sneak, bolt, abscond.

adj elusive, evasive, escapist, fugitive.

624 relinquishment *n* surrender, resignation, yielding, waiver, waiving, abdication, leaving, desertion, withdrawal, secession, abandonment, renunciation.

v relinquish, surrender, give up, resign, yield, cede, waive, forswear, forgo, abdicate, leave, forsake, desert, renounce, quit, abandon, let go, resign, (*informal*) throw in the towel, call it quits, (*informal*) hang it up.

625 business *n* occupation, trade, craft, profession, calling, employment, vocation, pursuit; affair, matter, concern, transaction, undertaking; function, duty, office, position, part, role, capacity.

v employ oneself, undertake, turn one's hand to; be at work on, be engaged in, be occupied with.

adj businesslike; workaday, professional, official, functional; busy.

626 plan *n* scheme, plot, stratagem, policy, procedure, project, formula, method, system, organization, design, contrivance, device; drawing, sketch, draft, map, chart, diagram, representation; intrigue, cabal, conspiracy.

planner, designer, organizer, schemer, strategist, intriguer.

v plan, arrange, frame, scheme, plot, design, devise, contrive, invent, concoct, hatch; project, forecast; systematize, organize, cast, recast, lay groundwork.

adj procedural, formulaic, methodological, systematic, organizational; conspiratorial; strategic.

627 [path] **method** *n* road, procedure, way, means, manner, fashion, technique, process, course, route, track, beat, tack; door, gateway, channel, passage, avenue, means of access, approach.

adv how, in what way, in what manner; by what mode; one way or another, after this fashion.

628 mid-course *n* middle way, middle course, mean, golden mean; compromise, (*informal*) six of one and half a dozen of another, half measures, neutrality.

v steer a middle course, go straight; compromise, go half way, make a compromise.

adj moderate, midway; neutral, impartial.

629 circuit *n* roundabout way, digression, detour, loop, winding.

v go round about, make a circuit, detour, wind around, circle around; deviate, digress.

adj circuitous, indirect, roundabout; zigzag.

adv in a roundabout way, by an indirect course, indirectly.

630 requirement *n* requisite, requisition, need, necessity, wants, claim, demand, prerequisite; mandate, order, command, directive, injunction, change, claim, precept.

v require, need, call for, have occasion for, necessitate, obligate; demand, request, need, order, enjoin, direct, ask.

adj requisite, necessary, essential, indispensable, needful; urgent, exigent, instant, crying.

adv of necessity.

631 instrumentality *n* mediation, intervention, medium, intermedium, vehicle, hand; aid; subservience.

go-between, intermediary, minister.

v mediate, minister, intervene; be instrumental, aid.

adj instrumental, useful, serviceable; intermediary, intermediate.

adv through, by, whereby, thereby, by the agency of, by dint of, by means of.

632 means *n* resources, wherewithal, way, ways and means, know how, ability; agency, method, approach; capital, provisions.

v have the means, find the means, possess the means.

adj instrumental.

adv by means of; herewith, therewith; wherewithal.

633 instrument *n* tool, implement, utensil, machinery, equipment.

adj instrumental; mechanical.

634 substitute *n* deputy, alternate, understudy, stand-in, proxy, (*informal*) sub, replacement.

v to substitute for, sub.

635 materials *n* raw materials, resources, stuff, stock, staples, supplies.

636 store *n* stock, fund, mine, supply, reserve, reservoir, (*informal*) stash; accumulation, hoard, storing, storage.

v store, put aside, lay away; store up, put up, hoard away, accumulate, amass, garner; reserve, husband, (*informal*) stash, hold back.

adj in store, in reserve, spare.

637 provision *n* supply, grist, resources, store, provender, stock, food; catering, providing, purveying, purveyance, supplying.

v make provision, provide, lay in, lay in a stock, lay in a store; supply, furnish, purvey, provision, cater, stock, store, replenish.

638 waste *n* consumption, expenditure, dissipation, diminution, decline, emaciation, exhaustion, loss, destruction, decay, impairment; misuse, prodigality, wasting; ruin, devastation, spoilation, desolation.

v waste, consume, spend, throw out, expend, squander, misuse, misspend, dissipate; destroy, wear away, erode, eat away, reduce, wear down, exhaust, enfeeble, wear out.

adj wasteful, prodigal, spendthrift; destructive; wasted, gone to waste.

639 sufficiency *n* adequacy, enough, competence.

v be sufficient, suffice, do, just do, satisfy; have enough.

adj sufficient, enough, adequate, ample, up to the mark, competent, commensurate, satisfactory.

adv sufficiently, amply.

640 insufficiency *n* inadequacy, incompetence, incompleteness, deficiency, imperfection, shortcoming; paucity, scarcity, dearth; dole, pittance; emptiness, poorness, depletion, flaccidity.

v be insufficient, not suffice, not do, fall short of, (*informal*) not cut it; want, lack, need, require, be in want.

adj insufficient, inadequate, too little, not enough, incomplete, deficient, imperfect, wanting, short, scarce, meager, poor, thin, sparse, scant; incompetent, perfunctory.

641 redundance *n* superfluity, superabundance, too much, too many, exuberance, profuseness, profusion, plenty, repletion, plethora, congestion, surfeit, overdose, overflow; excess, surplus; repetition, verbosity.

v superabound, overabound, swarm, overflow, run over, run riot, overrun, overdose, overload, overdo, overwhelm; supersaturate, gorge, glut, load, drench, inundate, deluge, flood; choke, cloy, suffocate, pile on, lay on thick, lavish.

adj redundant, exuberant, inordinate, superabundant, excessive, overmuch, replete, profuse, lavish; exorbitant, extravagant, overweening, (*informal*) much; superfluous, unnecessary, needless, over and above, spare, duplicate; repetitious, verbose.

adv over and above, over much, out of proportion, beyond bounds, over one's head.

642 importance *n* consequence, substance, weight, moment, prominence, consideration, significance, import, concern, emphasis, interest, momentousness, weightiness; gravity, seriousness, solemnity; pressure, urgency, stress.

v be important, deserve consideration, be worthy of notice, merit attention; attach importance, ascribe importance, value, care for, set store by; import, signify, matter, boot, carry weight; accentuate, emphasize, lay stress on; mark, underline, underscore.

adj important, consequential, weighty, momentous, prominent, considerable, significant, notable, salient; grave, serious, earnest, grand, solemn, impressive, commanding, imposing; urgent, pressing, critical, crucial, paramount, essential, vital, prime, primary, principal, all-important, capital, foremost, of vital importance; superior, considerable; significant, telling, trenchant, emphatic.

643 unimportance *n* insignificance, immateriality, triviality, paltriness, indifference, nothing, trifling; trumpery, trash, rubbish, frippery, chaff, bauble, trifle.

v be unimportant, not matter, matter little, signify little; make light of.

adj unimportant, of little account, of small importance, immaterial, unessential, nonessential, inconsequential, insignificant, inconsiderable, so-so; commonplace, ordinary, uneventful, mere, common; trifling, trivial, slight, slender, light, flimsy, shallow; frivolous, petty, niggling, piddling; poor, paltry, pitiful, sorry, mean, meager, shabby, beggarly, worthless, cheap, tawdry, trashy, gimmicky; unworthy of consideration, unworthy of notice; useless, of no account.

644 utility *n* usefulness, efficacy, helpfulness, service, use, stead, avail, help, aid; applicability, value, worth, productiveness.

v be useful, avail, serve, perform, help, aid, benefit; act a part, discharge a function, stand one in good stead.

adj useful, serviceable, functional, advantageous, valuable, productive, profitable, helpful, effectual, effective, efficacious, beneficial, salutary; applicable, available, practical, practicable, workable.

645 inutility *n* uselessness, inefficacy, ineptitude, inaptitude, inadequacy, inefficiency, unfruitfulness, futility, worthlessness, hopelessness.

v be useless, be of no help.

adj useless, unavailing, futile, inutile, fruitless, vain, ineffectual, profitless, bootless, valueless, worthless, hopeless; unserviceable, unusable, inoperative.

646 expedience *n* expediency, fitness, utility, suitability, profitability, advisability, propriety, appropriateness, desirability; opportunism, pragmatism, realism.

v be expedient, suit, befit, suit the occasion.

adj expedient, advantageous, opportune, fit, suitable, convenient, profitable, worthwhile, advisable, meet, proper, becoming, appropriate, desirable.

647 inexpedience *n* inexpediency, impropriety, unfitness, unsuitability, inappropriateness, undesirability; inconvenience, impracticality.

v be inexpedient, be inconvenient, hinder.

adj inexpedient, inopportune, unfit, unsuitable, disadvantageous, discommodious, unadvisable, unseemly, improper, unworkable, impractical, inconvenient, unprofitable, useless, worthless.

648 [good qualities] goodness *n* virtue, excellence, merit, value, worth; perfection, eminence, superiority, masterpiece, *chef d'oeuvre*, prime, flower, cream, elite, pick, pick of the litter, salt of the earth, (*informal*) A-1, (*informal*) tops, second to none; gem, jewel, treasure, one in a million; beneficence.

v be good, excel, transcend, stand the test, pass muster, challenge comparison, vie, emulate, rival, (*informal*) dwarf the competition; be beneficial, do good, profit, benefit, improve, be the making of, do a world of good, produce a good effect, do a good turn.

adj good, excellent, better, superior, above par, fine, genuine, true; best, choice, select, rare, invaluable, priceless, inestimable, superlative, perfect, inimitable, first-class, first-rate, very best, crack, prime, tip-top, capital, (*informal*) tops; beneficial, valuable, advantageous, profitable, edifying, salutary, serviceable; favorable, propitious.

649 [bad qualities] **badness** *n* harmfulness, hurtfulness, virulence, painfulness, abomination, pestilence, guilt, depravity, vice, evil, malignity, malevolence; bane, plague, evil star, ill wind, bad omen, (*informal*) jinx, (*informal*) whammy; snake in the grass, skeleton in the closet, (*informal*) ghosts, (*informal*) demons; ill-treatment, annoyance, molestation, abuse, oppression, persecution, outrage, misusage, injury, damage.

v hurt, harm, injure, damage, pain; wrong, aggrieve, oppress, persecute, trample upon, tread upon, walk over, overburden, weigh down, run down; victimize, maltreat, molest, abuse, ill-use, bruise, scratch, maul, smite, do violence, do harm, stab, pierce.

adj hurtful, harmful, baleful, injurious, deleterious, detrimental, noxious, pernicious, mischievous; oppressive, burdensome, onerous, malign, malevolent; virulent, venomous, corrosive, poisonous, deadly, destructive; bad, ill, dreadful, horrid, horrible, dire, rank, foul, rotten, as low as one can go, (*informal*) the pits; evil, wrong, reprehensible, hateful, abominable, detestable, execrable, damnable, infernal, diabolical; vile, base, villainous, cruel, mean, low; deplorable, wretched, sad, grievous, lamentable, pitiable, pitiful, woeful, painful.

650 perfection *n* ideal, summit, paragon, model, standard, pattern, mirror; impeccability, faultlessness, excellence; masterpiece, master stroke; transcendence, superiority.

v perfect, bring to perfection, ripen, mature, complete, finish; be perfect, transcend.

adj perfect, faultless, immaculate, spotless, unblemished, impeccable, exquisite, consummate; in perfect condition, sound, intact; best, model, standard, inimitable, beyond all praise.

651 imperfection *n* deficiency, inadequacy, insufficiency, immaturity; fault, defect, weak point, weak spot, flaw, taint, blemish, weakness, shortcoming, drawback.

v be imperfect, have a defect, not pass muster, fall short.

adj imperfect, deficient, inadequate, insufficient, immature, defective, faulty, unsound, out of order, out of tune, warped, lame, frail, weak, crude, incomplete, below par, found wanting; indifferent, middling, ordinary, mediocre, average, so-so, tolerable, fair, passable, decent, not bad, bearable, better than nothing; inferior, secondary, second-rate, poor substitute.

652 cleanness *n* purity, purification, purgation, cleanliness; ablution, lavation; neatness, tidiness, orderliness; cathartic, purgative, laxative; detergent, disinfectant.

v clean, cleanse, purify, purge, expurgate, clarify, refine; wash, launder, scour, scrub, disinfect, fumigate, deodorize, ventilate; rout out, clear out, sweep out, make a clean sweep of, start fresh; neaten, tidy up, order, put things in order.

adj clean, pure, immaculate, spotless, stainless, unsullied, sweet; neat, spruce, tidy, trim, kempt.

653 uncleanness *n* impurity, defilement, contamination, taint; decay, putrefaction, corruption, mold, mildew, rot, dry rot; squalor, slovenliness, filth, dirt, smut, grime, mud, mire, muck, quagmire, slime.

v be unclean, rot, putrefy, fester, rankle, reek, stink, mold, go bad; dirty, soil, tarnish, spot, smear, blot, blur, smudge, smirch; besmear, be-foul, splash, stain, sully, pollute, defile, debase, contaminate, taint, corrupt.

adj unclean, dirty, filthy, grimy, soiled; dusty, smutty, sooty, slimy; slovenly, untidy, sluttish, dowdy, unkempt, unscoured, squalid; nasty, coarse, foul, impure, offensive, abominable, beastly, reeky, fetid; moldy, musty, moth-eaten, bad, gone bad, rancid, rotten, corrupt, putrid, carious, fecal; gory, bloody; gross.

654 health *n* soundness, well-being, vigor, good health, bloom, color, vitality, robust health.

v be in health, be healthy, bloom, flourish, feel fine, feel good.

adj healthy, healthful, in health, well, sound, hearty, hale, strong, hardy, robust, vigorous, fit as a fiddle, in top shape, chipper, (*informal*) all together.

655 disease *n* illness, sickness, ill health, ailment, infirmity, indisposition, complaint, disorder, malady; delicacy, delicate condition, decline, deterioration, decay.

v ail, suffer, be affected with, droop, flag, languish, sicken, pine, gasp, waste away, fail; take sick, take ill, come down with, contract a disease, catch a bug.

adj ill, sick, indisposed, not well, unwell, in poor health, in bad health, ailing, poorly, laid up, bed-ridden, out of sorts, under the weather, (*informal*) in bad shape; sickly, infirm, unsound, unhealthy, (*informal*) falling apart, weak, lame, decrepit; disease, morbid, mangy, corrupt, contaminated, leprous.

656 salubrity *n* healthiness, healthfulness, wholesomeness.

v be salubrious, be good for, agree with.

adj salubrious, healthy, healthful, salutary, wholesome, sanitary, bracing, invigorating, benign, nutritious, tonic, hygienic.

657 insalubrity *n* unhealthiness, unsoundness.

v be unhealthy, not be good for, disagree with.

adj insalubrious, unhealthy, unwholesome, noxious, noisome, deleterious, pestilential, bad, harmful, virulent, venomous, poisonous, septic, toxic, deadly.

658 improvement *n* amelioration, amendment, emendation, correction, revision, reformation, restoration, repair, betterment, gain, advancement, elevation, increase, refinement, elaboration; acculturation, cultivation, civilization.

reformer, radical.

v improve, mend, amend, get better; ameliorate, better, amend, emend, correct, right, rectify, revise, reform, restore, repair; advance, progress, ascend, increase, fructify, ripen, mature; refine, enrich, elaborate; promote, cultivate, foster, enhance.

adj better, better off, all for the better; emendatory, corrective, reformative, restorative, improving, progressive, improved.

659 deterioration *n* debasement, recession, retrogradation, degeneracy, degeneration, degradation, deprivation, depravity, retrogression; detriment, damage, loss, injury, impairment, contamination, spoilage, corruption, adulteration; decline, declension, senility, decrepitude; decadence, decay, dilapidation, falling off, wear and tear, erosion, corrosion, rottenness, blight, atrophy, collapse.

v deteriorate, degenerate, fall off, wane, ebb, decline, droop, go down, go downhill, sink, go to seed, go to waste, lapse, break down, crack, shrivel, fade, wither, molder, rot, rankle, decay, go bad, rust, crumble, shake, totter, perish, die; taint, infect, contaminate, poison, canker, corrupt, pollute, vitiate, debase, degrade, adulterate; injure, impair, damage, harm, hurt, spoil, mar, despoil, dilapidate, waste, ravage; wound, maim, cripple, scotch, mangle, mutilate, disfigure, blemish, deface, warp; blight, rot, corrode, erode, wear away, wear out, sap, mine, undermine, shake the foundations of, break up, destroy, decimate.

adj deteriorated, unimproved, injured, degenerate, imperfect; battered, weathered, weather-beaten, all the worse for wear, stale, dilapidated, faded, shabby, threadbare, worn, far gone, (*informal*) had it; decayed, moth-eaten, worm-eaten, mildewed, rusty, moldy, seedy, time-worn, wasted, crumbling, moldering, rotten, blighted, tainted; decrepit, broken down, wornout, used up, out of commission, in a bad way, past cure, past hope, (*informal*) long gone.

660 restoration *n* reestablishment, replacement, reinstatement, renewal, rehabilitation, reconstruction, reproduction, rebuilding, renovation, revival; refreshment, resuscitation, revivification; renaissance, renascence, new birth, regeneration, reconversion; redress, retrieval, reclamation, recovery, resumption; repair, reparation, restitution, relief, deliverance, rectification, cure, healing; redemption.

v restore, recover, rally, revive, come round, pull through, get well, get over; reestablish, replace, rehabilitate, reinstate; reconstruct, rebuild, reproduce, reorganize, reconstitute, renew, renovate; redeem, reclaim, recover, retrieve, rescue, deliver; redress, recure; cure, heal, remedy, doctor, bring round; resuscitate, revive, reanimate, revivify, reinvigorate, refresh; recoup, make good, square, set to rights, correct, put in order; repair, retouch, patch up, fix.

adj restorative, recuperative, curative, remedial; restorable, remediable, retrievable, curable; restored, convalescent, renascent, reborn.

661 relapse *n* lapse, falling back, retrogradation, deterioration, backsliding.

v relapse, lapse, fall back, slip back, sink back, suffer a relapse, fall again.

adj retrograde.

662 remedy *n* help, redress, solution, answer, panacea; cure, relief, medicine, treatment, restorative, specific, medication, ointment, balm; antidote, corrective, antitoxin, counteractive.

doctor, physician, surgeon.

v remedy, cure, heal, set right, put right, doctor, nurse, restore, recondition, repair, redress; counteract, remove, correct, right, solve.

adj remedial, restorative, corrective, palliative; medicinal, therapeutic, curative; soluble.

663 bane *n* curse, evil, plague, scourge, pain, nuisance, thorn in the side, pain in the neck; poison, virus, venom; fungus, mildew, dry rot, canker, cancer; sting, fang, thorn, bramble, briar, nettle.

adj baneful, bad, sinister, pernicious, evil, baleful, poisonous, venomous, ruinous, unwholesome, harmful, deadly.

664 safety *n* security, surety, impregnability, invulnerability; safeguard, safety valve, precaution, custody, safe keeping, preservation, protection.

protector, guardian, warden, preserver, custodian, watchdog, sentinel, scout.

v be safe; protect, take care of, care for, preserve, cover, screen, shelter, shroud, guard, defend, secure, house, garrison; watch, patrol, look out, take precautions.

adj safe, secure, snug, warm, sure, sound, on the safe side, out of danger; dependable, trustworthy, sure, reliable; cautious, wary, careful; defensible, tenable, invulnerable, impregnable, unassailable, safe and sound.

665 danger *n* hazard, insecurity, instability, precariousness, slipperiness, risk, peril, jeopardy, liability,

exposure; injury, evil; warning, alarm, apprehension.

v be in danger, run into trouble, lay oneself open to, hang by a thread, totter; endanger, expose to danger, imperil, jeopardize, adventure, venture, risk, hazard, threaten.

adj dangerous, hazardous, risky, perilous, precarious, unsafe, insecure, unstable, untrustworthy, unsteady, shaky, slippery, ominous, fearful, explosive, fraught with danger; defenseless, vulnerable, open, liable.

666 refuge *n* sanctuary, retreat, asylum, hiding place, stronghold, fortress, shelter, cover; anchor, mainstay, support, check, last resort, safeguard.

v seek refuge, take refuge, find refuge, take shelter, find safety.

667 pitfall *n* snare, trap, snag, ambush, snake in the grass, wolf in sheep's clothing, menace, complication, danger; slippery ground, weak foundation, rocks, reefs, sunken rocks, sand, quicksand, breakers, shoals, shallows, precipice, maelstrom.

668 warning *n* caution, notice, premonition, prediction, admonition, advice, lesson; alarm, omen, sign, signal, augury, portent, presage.

sentinel, sentry, watch, watchman, watchdog, patrol, scout, spy.

v warn, caution, admonish, forewarn; give notice, notify, appraise, inform; menace, threaten, portend.

adj premonitory, cautionary, advisory; ominous, portentous.

669 [indication of danger] **alarm** *n* alarum, alarm bell, tocsin, distress signal, siren, danger signal, hue and cry, SOS, cry, scream.

v alarm, sound the alarm, warn, cry out.

670 preservation *n* safekeeping, conservation; guarding, safeguard, shelter, protection, defense; maintenance, support, sustenance, continuance, retention, salvation.

v preserve, keep, conserve; guard, safeguard, shelter, shield, protect, defend, rescue; keep up, maintain, continue, support, uphold, sustain; retain; store, husband, save, pickle, bottle, can.

adj preserved, unimpaired, uninjured, unhurt, safe, sound, intact; conservative, preservative.

671 escape *n* flight, evasion, loophole, retreat; reprieve, release, liberation; narrow escape, close call, near miss.

v escape, flee, abscond, fly, steal away, run away, (*informal*) take off, (*informal*) split; shun, fly, elude, evade, avoid.

adj stolen away, fled, (*informal*) cut out.

672 deliverance *n* extrication, disentanglement, rescue, reprieve, respite; liberation, release, emancipation, freedom; redemption, salvation.

v deliver, extricate, disentangle, rescue, reprieve, save, redeem; set free, liberate, release, emancipate, free; come to the rescue.

673 preparation *n* provision, plan, arrangement, anticipation, precaution, forecast, rehearsal; groundwork, homework, foundation, scaffolding; training, education, dissemination; readiness, ripeness, maturity.

v prepare, get ready, make ready, prime, arrange, make preparations, plan, devise, anticipate, lay the foundations, provide, order; mature, ripen, mellow, season, nurture; equip, arm, fit out, furnish; train, teach, prepare for, rehearse, make provision for, take steps, provide against.

adj preparatory, precautionary, provident, preparative, preparatory; provisional, preliminary; prepared, ready, available, all ready, handy; ripe, mature, mellow.

674

674 nonpreparation *n* unpreparedness, unreadiness; improvidence.

v be unprepared; extemporize, improvise.

adj unprepared, incomplete, premature, rudimental, embryonic, immature, unripe, raw, green, coarse, crude, rough, unhewn, untaught, fallow, unready; out of order, nonfunctional, (*informal*) on the fritz, in disrepair, (*informal*) out of whack; shiftless, improvident, thoughtless, careless, slack, remiss, happy-go-lucky.

675 essay *n* trial, endeavor, effort, attempt, struggle, venture, adventure, speculation, experiment.

v essay, try, experiment; endeavor, strive, tempt, attempt, venture, adventure, speculate, tempt fortune, (*informal*) give it a go, (*informal*) take a shot at.

adj experimental, tentative, probationary; venturesome, adventurous, speculative.

adv experimentally, on trial.

676 undertaking *n* task, job, venture, engagement, compact, contract, enterprise; pilgrimage, quest.

v undertake, engage in, embark on, launch into, plunge into, volunteer; engage, promise, contract, take upon onself, devote onself to, determine, take up, take in hand; tackle, set about, fall to, begin, broach.

677 use *n* employ, exercise, application, appliance; disposal; consumption; agency, usefulness; benefit, recourse, resort, avail; utilization, utility, service, wear; usage.

v use, make use of, employ, put to use, put into operation, apply, set in motion, set to work; ply, work, wield, handle, manipulate; exert, exercise, practice, avail oneself of, profit by; resort to, have recourse to, recur to, take up, try; utilize, bring into play, press into service; use up, consume, expend, tax, task, wear.

adj useful, instrumental, utilitarian, subservient, employable, applicable, beneficial.

678 disuse *n* forbearance, abstinence; relinquishment, abandonment; desuetude.

v not use, do without, dispense with, let alone, forbear, abstain, spare, waive, neglect; keep back, reserve; disuse, lay up, shelve, set aside, put aside, leave off, have done with; supersede, discard, throw aside, relinquish, dismantle.

adj not in use, unemployed, unapplied; disused, unused, done with.

679 misuse *n* misusage, misemployment, misapplication, misappropriation; abuse, profanation, prostitution, desecration; waste.

v misuse, misemploy, misapply, misappropriate; abuse, profane, prostitute, desecrate; waste, squander, destroy; overwork, overtask, overtax.

680 action *n* movement, work, labor, performance, moving, working, performing, operation; deed, act, feat, exploit; conduct, behavior, procedure, execution; energetic activity, exercise, exertion, energy, effort; affair, encounter, meeting, engagement, conflict, combat, fight, battle.

actor, doer, worker.

v act, do, perform, execute, achieve, transact, enact; commit, perpetrate, inflict; exercise, prosecute, carry on, work, function, labor, operate, exert energy, be active; behave, conduct oneself, comport oneself; play, feign, fake, imitate.

adj in action, in operation, operative.

681 inaction *n* passivity, inactivity, idleness, slothfulness; waiting, mulling around, killing time; rest, repose.

v not act, not do, be inactive, abstain from doing, do nothing, let alone, let things take their course; stand aloof, refrain, pause, wait, bide one's time, cool one's heels, waste time, lie idle.

adj inactive, passive, idle, slothful; out of work.

682 activity *n* movement, hustle, bustle, stir, fuss, flurry, action, business; industry, assiduity, assiduousness, laboriousness, drudgery; diligence, perseverance, vigilance, wakefulness, restlessness, fidgetiness; briskness, liveliness, animation, life, vivacity, spirit, dash, energy; eagerness, zeal, ardor, vigor, abandon, exertion; earnestness, intentness, devotion.

v be active, busy oneself in, stir about, rouse oneself, speed, hasten, bustle, fuss, (*informal*) raise a ruckus; push, push ahead, (*informal*) step on it, (*informal*) move it, make progress; toil, plod, persist, persevere, hustle, (*informal*) hustle it, (*informal*) push; look sharp, keep moving, seize the opportunity, carpe diem, lose no time, dash off, make haste; have a hand in, trouble oneself about.

adj active, brisk, lively, busy as a bee, vivacious, alive, frisky; quick, prompt, ready, alert, spry, sharp, smart, awake, wide awake, eager, zealous; industrious, assiduous, diligent, vigilant; businesslike; restless, fussy, fidgety, busy.

683 inactivity *n* inaction, inertness, lull, quiescence; idleness, remissness, sloth, indolence, dawdling, laziness; dullness, languor, sluggishness, torpor, stupor, lethargy; procrastination.

idler, drone, dawdler, moper, lounger, loafer, sluggard, laggard, slumberer.

v be inactive, do nothing, dawdle, lag, hang back, slouch, loll, lounge, loaf, loiter, take it easy; fritter away time, idle, piddle, putter, dabble, dally, dilly-dally; languish, flag, relax; kill time, waste time.

adj inactive, motionless; indolent, lazy, slothful, idle, remiss, slack, inert, torpid, sluggish, languid, supine, heavy, dull, listless; laggard, slow, rusty, lackadaisical, irresolute; drowsy, lethargic, soporific, dreamy, dreamy-eyed.

684 haste *n* urgency, need, hurry, flurry, bustle; spurt, rush, dash, scramble, bustle, ado, precipitancy, precipitation; swiftness, celerity, alacrity, quickness, rapidity, dispatch, speed, expedition, promptitude, timeliness, promptness.

v haste, hasten, make haste, hurry, dash, push on, press on, press forward, scurry, bustle, scramble, rush, accelerate, urge, expedite, quicken, speed, precipitate, dispatch.

adj hasty, speedy, quick, hurried, swift, rapid, fast, fleet, brisk; precipitate, rash, foolhardy, reckless, indiscreet, thoughtless, headlong; testy, touchy, irascible, petulant, waspish, fretful, fiery, excitable, irritable, peevish.

685 leisure *n* spare time, free time, convenience, liberty, pause, stay, halt, lull, breather, (*informal*) letup, breathing spell, break, (*informal*) time out; interlude, vacation, holiday.

v have leisure, take one's time; rest, relax, repose.

adj leisure, spare, free; leisurely, slow, deliberate, quiet, calm, restful, peaceful, languid, easy, gradual.

686 exertion *n* effort, action, activity, endeavor, struggle, attempt, strain, trial, stress; labor, work, toil, travail; trouble, pain; energy.

v exert, exert oneself, labor, work, toil, sweat, drudge, strive, strain; work hard, rough it, buckle to, take pains, concentrate, spare no effort.

adj laborious, wearisome, burdensome, (*informal*) tough, (*informal*) rough, strenuous, herculean, Sisyphean.

687 repose *n* rest, sleep, slumber; relaxation, breathing spell; halt, pause, respite, cessation; day of rest, Sabbath; holiday, vacation, recess.

v repose, rest; relax, unbend, slacken, catch one's breath, get one's wind, take a breather, pause; recline, lie down, go to bed, take a nap, go to sleep; take a holiday, go on vacation, shut up shop.

adj reposing, resting.

adv at rest.

688 fatigue *n* weariness, lassitude, tiredness, exhaustion, faintness; ennui, boredom, tedium, languor, yawning, drowsiness.

v be fatigued, yawn, droop, sink, flag, (*informal*) give out; gasp, pant, puff, blow, drop, swoon, faint; fatigue, tire, weary, exhaust, wear out; tax, task, strain; bore, tire, irritate, annoy.

adj fatigued, weary, drowsy, haggard, faint, exhausted, spent, tired, tired to death, worn out, (*informal*) gone; breathless.

689 refreshment *n* recovery of strength, restoration, revival, repair, relief.

v refresh, brace, strengthen, reinvigorate, revive, stimulate, freshen, cheer, enliven, reanimate; restore, repair, renew.

adj refreshing, restoring.

690 agent *n* doer, actor, performer, perpetrator, operator; practitioner, executioner, executor, executrix, minister, representative, deputy, servant, worker; participant, party to.

691 workshop *n* laboratory, factory, mill, mint, forge, studio; hive, beehive, seat of activity.

692 conduct *n* behavior, demeanor, action, actions, deportment, bearing, carriage, mien, manners; process, ways, practice, procedure, method; policy, tactics, strategy, plan; direction, management, execution, guidance, leadership, administration.

v conduct, behave, deport, act, bear; transact, execute, dispatch, discharge, proceed with, enact; direct, manage, carry on, supervise, regulate, administer, guide, lead.

adj procedural, practical, methodical, tactical, strategical, businesslike; directive, managerial, administrative, executive.

693 direction *n* guidance, advice, regulation, conduct, management, disposition, supervision, auspices, steerage, stewardship, ministration, administration, control, leadership, government, rule, command; order, command, instruction.

v direct, guide, advise, regulate, conduct, manage, control, dispose, supervise, overlook, steer, steward, pilot, minister, administer, legislate, lead, rule, govern, have charge of, command; order, instruct, prescribe.

adj directing, guiding, supervisory, managing, administering.

694 director *n* manager, governor, controller, superintendent, supervisor, overseer, inspector, foreman, surveyor, taskmaster, master, leader, boss; adviser, guide, pilot, captain, helmsman, driver; head, chief, principal, president, minister, official, functionary.

695 advice *n* counsel, opinion, recommendation, guidance, suggestion, persuasion, urging, exhortation; instruction, charge, injunction; admonition, warning, caution.

adviser, council, counselor, mentor.

v advise, give counsel to, suggest, recommend, prescribe, advocate, exhort, persuade; enjoin, enforce, charge, instruct; admonish, caution, warn; take counsel, confer, deliberate, discuss, consult, refer to; give counsel, offer counsel.

adj advisory, suggestive, persuasive, suasive; admonitory.

696 council *n* committee, court, chamber, cabinet, board, board of directors, advisory board, staff, syndicate, chapter; assembly, caucus, conclave, meeting, conference, session.

697 precept *n* direction, instruction, charge, prescript, prescription; golden rule, maxim, canon, law, code, act, statute, regulation, formula, form, technicality, rubric; order, command.

698 skill *n* skillfulness, dexterity, adroitness, expertness, proficiency, competence, facility, knack, mastery; accomplishment, acquirement, attainment, ability, art; knowledge, wisdom, *savoir faire*, tact, wit, sagacity, discretion, finesse, craftiness, cunning, management; cleverness, ingenuity, capacity, talent, talents, faculty, endowment, *forte*, turn, gift, genius; intelligence, sharpness, readiness, invention, inventiveness, aptness, aptitude, proclivity, capacity for, genius for, felicity, capability, qualification.

v be skillful, excel in, be master of, have a knack for; take advantage of.

adj skillful, dextrous, adroit, adept, expert, apt, handy, quick, deft, proficient, masterly, crack, first-rate, conversant; skilled, experienced, practiced, competent, efficient, qualified, capable, fit, fit for, trained, prepared, finished; clever, able, ingenious, felicitous, inventive; shrewd, sharp, smart, intelligent, cunning, tactful, discreet, wise, knowledgeable.

adv skillfully, artistically, with consummate skill.

699 unskillfulness *n* want of skill, incompetence, inability, inexpertness, maladroitness, ineptitude, clumsiness, awkwardness, carelessness, bumbling, bungling; indiscretion.

v be unskillful, blunder, bungle, boggle, fumble, botch, stumble.

adj unskillful, unskilled, inexpert, incompetent, unable, inapt, bungling, inept, maladroit, awkward, clumsy, gawky; unfit, ill-qualified, unhandy, not conversant; raw, rusty, out of practice.

700 expert *n* specialist, authority, master, professional, connoisseur, veteran, old hand, old soldier; genius, mastermind, wizard, prodigy, (*informal*) pro.

701 bungler *n* blunderer, blunderhead, fumbler, duffer, clown (*informal*), turkey, butter-fingers, greenhorn, amateur, rookie, novice, (*informal*) Sunday driver, (*informal*) armchair quarterback.

702 cunning *n* craftiness, skillfulness, shrewdness, artfulness, wiliness, subtlety, finesse, artifice, device, stratagem, intrigue, craft, guile, chicanery, duplicity, subterfuge, deceit, deceitfulness, slyness, deception; ability, skill, adroitness, expertness.

v be cunning, maneuver, contrive, manipulate, intrigue, finesse, surprise.

adj crafty, shrewd, artful, wily, subtle, tricky, foxy, politic, insidious, stealthy, Machiavellian, deceitful, duplicitous, sly, deceptive; canny, astute; ingenious, clever, skillful, sharp.

703 artlessness *n* simplicity, innocence, naiveté, unworldliness, inexperience, inexposure, plainness, plain speaking, sincerity, honesty, openness, candor, matter of factness, bluntness.

v be artless, speak one's mind, come to the point, pull no punches.

adj artless, natural, simple, innocent, naive, childlike, unsuspicious, unworldly, unartificial, plain; sincere, frank, open, candid, honest, ingenuous, guileless, straightforward, aboveboard, point-blank, plain spoken, outspoken, blunt, direct, matter of fact.

adv in plain English, in simple words, without mincing words.

704 difficulty *n* dilemma, predicament, quandary, fix, exigency, emergency, crisis, trouble, problem, scrape, entanglement, strait, pass, pinch; reluctance, unwillingness, obstinacy, stubbornness; demur, objection, obstacle; labor, task, hard task, herculean task.

v be difficult, pose, perplex, bother, nonplus, hinder; encumber, embarrass, entangle.

adj difficult, hard, arduous, troublesome, irksome, laborious, formidable; awkward, unwieldy, unmanageable; fastidious, particular, stubborn, intractable, perverse; obscure, complex, intricate, delicate, uncertain, ticklish, critical; unfeasible, impractical, impossible, hopeless; austere, rigid.

705 facility *n* ease, easiness, capability, feasibility, practicability; flexibility, pliancy, smoothness, child's play.

v be easy, run smoothly, work well; facilitate, smooth, ease, lighten, free, clear, disencumber, disentangle, extricate, unravel.

adj easy, facile; feasible, practicable, within reach, accessible; manageable, tractable, pliant, smooth.

adv easily, readily, smoothly.

706 hindrance *n* impediment, deterrent, hitch, encumbrance, obstruction, check, stricture, restraint, hobble, obstacle, stumbling block; interruption, interference; impeding, stopping, stoppage, preventing.

v hinder, interrupt, check, impede, retard, encumber, delay, hamper, obstruct, trammel, cramp, handicap; block, thwart, frustrate, disconcert, prevent.

adj obstructive, intrusive; onerous, burdensome, cumbersome, obtrusive.

707 aid *n* help, support, succor, assistance, service, furtherance; relief, rescue, charity; assistant, helper, supporter, servant; patronage, championship, advocacy, favor, interest.

v aid, support, help, succor, assist, serve, abet, back, second; spell, relieve, rescue; sustain, uphold, prop, hold up, bolster; promote, facilitate, ease, advocate; be of help, give help, give assistance, oblige, accommodate, humor, encourage.

adj aiding, auxiliary, helpful, supportive; charitable; friendly, amicable, well-disposed, neighborly.

708 opposition *n* antagonism, hostility, resistance, counteraction; competition, enemy, foe, adversary, antagonist; opposing, resisting, combating.

v oppose, resist, combat, withstand, thwart, confront, contravene, interfere; hinder, obstruct, prevent, check; contradict, gainsay, deny, refuse, dissent.

adj adverse, antagonistic, contrary, at variance, at odds, anti, at issue, in opposition; unfavorable, unfriendly, hostile, inimical, resistant.

adv against, versus, counter to, in conflict with, at cross purposes; in spite, in defiance.

709 cooperation *n* concert, concurrence, agreement, concord, togetherness, harmony, unanimity; complicity, collusion, participation, combination, union, team-work; association, partnership, alliance, pool, coalition, confederation, fusion, fellowship, fraternity; unanimity, partisanship, spirit, party spirit, *esprit de corps.*

v cooperate, concur, combine, unite, pool, share, band together, pull together; act in concert, join forces, fraternize; conspire, be in league with; side with, go along with, join hands with, throw in one's lot with, rally round; participate, have a hand in.

adj cooperating, cooperative, participatory; in league, party to.

adv cooperatively, unanimously, shoulder to shoulder.

710 opponent *n* adversary, antagonist, competitor, rival, opposition; enemy, foe.

711 auxiliary *n* helper, aid, ally, assistant, confederate, collaborator, colleague, associate, partner, mate, friend.

712 party *n* group, gathering, assembly, assemblage, company, crew, band; clan, family, fellowship, community; body, faction, side, circle, clique, set, gang, claque, coterie, combination, ring, league, alliance, association.

v unite, join, band together, cooperate, assemble.

adj clannish, cliquish, communal, familial, fraternal.

713 discord *n* dissidence, dissonance, disagreement, clash, shock; variance, difference, dissension, misunderstanding, cross-purposes, odds, division, split, rupture, disruption, breach, schism, feud, conflict, struggle, argument, contention, quarrel, dispute, tiff, squabble, altercation, words; strife, outbreak.

v be discordant, disagree, clash, jar, conflict, differ, dissent, fall out, quarrel, dispute, squabble, wrangle, bicker, have words with; split, break, disunite, feud.

adj discordant, dissident, dissonant; divisive, disruptive; contentious, argumentative, quarrelsome, disputatious, fractious; at variance, at cross purposes.

714 concord *n* accord, harmony, sympathy, agreement, union, unison, unity, peace; amity, friendship, alliance, *detente,* understanding, togetherness, conciliation.

v agree, accord, harmonize with, fraternize, understand one another, concur, pull together; side with, sympathize with.

adj concordant, congenial, in accord; harmonious, sympathetic, friendly, fraternal, conciliatory.

adv with one voice, unanimously, in concert with.

715 defiance *n* daring, courage, courageousness, bravery, boldness; assertiveness, aggressiveness; antagonism, insubordination, recalcitrance, rebelliousness, insolence, resistance.

v defy, challenge, resist, dare, brave, flout, scorn, despise.

adj defiant, daring, courageous, brave, bold; resistant, insolent, rebellious, recalcitrant, contumacious, insubordinate, antagonistic.

adv in the face of, under one's very nose.

716 attack *n* onslaught, assault, offense, battery, onset, charge, encounter, aggression, incursion, invasion, sally, sortie, raid, foray; criticism, blame, censure, abuse.

assailant, aggressor, invader, attacker.

v assail, assault, molest, threaten, storm, charge, set upon, invade, bombard, beset, besiege, lay siege, storm; criticize, impugn, blame, censure, abuse; declare war, begin hostilities.

adj aggressive, offensive; critical, abusive.

adv on the offensive.

717 defense *n* guard, garrison, fortification, shield, shelter, screen, preservation, protection, guardianship, safeguard, security; justification, pleading, vindication.

v defend, guard, fortify, shield, shelter, screen, preserve, protect, keep safe, guard against, watch over, safeguard, secure; parry, repel, put to flight; uphold, maintain, justify, vindicate.

adj defensive, protective.

718 retaliation *n* reprisal, requital, retort, counterstroke, counterattack, retribution, reciprocation, reciprocity, recrimination, revenge, vengeance, reaction.

v retaliate, requite, retort, counterattack, revenge, repay, return, avenge.

adj retaliatory, vengeful, revengeful, retributive, reciprocal, reactive.

adv in retaliation.

719 resistance *n* opposition, withstanding, front, stand, oppugnance, reluctance, repulsion; interference, friction; insurrection, insurgence, rebellion.

v resist, withstand, stand up, stand; confront, oppose, grapple with, rise up, revolt, rebel, repel, repulse.

adj resistant, refractory, recalcitrant, repulsive, repellent; stubborn, indomitable, obstinate.

720 contention *n* struggling, struggle, strife, discord, dissention, quarrel, disagreement, squabble, feud; rupture, break, falling out; opposition, belligerency, combat, conflict, competition, rivalry, contest; disagreement, dissension, debate, wrangle, altercation, dispute, argument, controversy.

v contend, struggle, strive, fight, battle, combat, vie, compete, rival; debate, dispute, argue, wrangle; assert, maintain, claim.

adj contentious, combative, belligerent, bellicose, warlike, quarrelsome, pugnacious; competitive.

721 peace *n* treaty, truce, accord, amity, harmony, concord; calm, quiet, tranquillity, peacefulness, calmness; order, security.

v be at peace; keep the peace; make peace.

adj peaceful, tranquil, placid, serene, calm, complacent; mellow, halcyon, pacific; peaceable, amicable, friendly, amiable, mild, gentle.

722 warfare *n* fighting, hostilities, war, combat, battle, ordeal; tactics, strategy, generalship.

v war, make war, wage war, fight, give fight, battle, do battle, combat, contend, cross swords.

adj warlike, contentious, belligerent, combative, bellicose, martial, military, militant.

adv to arms.

723 pacification *n* conciliation, reconciliation, accommodation, arrangement, adjustment, compromise; amnesty, peace offering, truce, armistice, suspension of hostilities.

v pacify, reconcile, propitiate, placate, conciliate, accommodate, appease, make peace; quiet, calm, tranquilize, assuage, still, smooth, moderate, ameliorate, mollify, meliorate, soothe, bury the hatchet.

adj pacific, concilatory.

724 mediation *n* negotiation, arbitration, parley; intervention, intercession, interposition.

mediator, arbiter, arbitrator, peacemaker, go-between, negotiator, moderator, diplomat.

v mediate, intercede, intervene, interpose, interfere; step in, negotiate, arbitrate.

adj mediatory.

725 submission *n* nonresistance, obedience, compliance, acquiescence, yielding, submissiveness, pliancy; surrender, cessation, capitulation; resignation, passivity, docility.

v succumb, submit, yield, bend, acquiesce, resign, agree, obey, comply, bow, surrender, capitulate.

adj submissive, obedient, compliant, acquiescent, passive, docile, tame, humble.

726 combatant *n* fighter, contestant, disputant, battler, litigant, contender, competitor, militarist, soldier, warrior, polemic, candidate; antagonist, foe, enemy, opponent, rival, adversary, assailant, opposition, assailer, assailant, assaulter, opposer, opponent.

727 arms *n* weapons, weaponry, armaments, armor, ammunition, munitions, deadly weapons.

v arm, outfit, ready for battle, prepare for battle.

728 arena *n* battleground, battlefield, field of battle, theater, ring, lists; playhouse, amphitheater, stage, boards; Colosseum, gymnasium, playing field.

729 completion *n* culmination, finish, conclusion, close, termination, end, finale; upshot, result; final touch, crowning touch; consummation, accomplishment, achievement, fulfillment; performance, execution; perfection, thoroughness.

v complete, finish, end, conclude, close, terminate, finalize; consummate, perfect, accomplish, do, fulfill, achieve, effect, execute, enact, dispatch, discharge.

adj whole, entire, full, intact, unbroken, one, perfect; done, consummate, perfect, thorough, through-and-through.

adv completely, thoroughly; perfectly.

730 noncompletion *n* incompleteness, nonfulfillment, nonperformance; neglect, shortcoming.

v not complete, leave unfinished, leave undone; neglect, let alone, let slip; fall short of.

adj incomplete, unfinished, sketchy.

731 success *n* progress, advance; hit, stroke, trump card; good fortune, good luck, luck, break; prosperity, achievement, fulfillment, accomplishment; ascendancy, mastery, conquest, victory, triumph; proficiency, skill, mastery.

v succeed, attain an end, secure an objective; progress, advance; accomplish, achieve, effect, complete; prosper, find fulfillment, fulfill oneself; master, conquer, triumph, surmount, overcome.

adj successful, prosperous, well-to-do; victorious, triumphant; masterful, proficient.

adv successfully, with flying colors, in triumph.

732 failure *n* unsuccessfulness, miscarriage, abortion, failing; neglect, omission, dereliction, non-performance; deficiency, insufficiency, defectiveness; blunder, mistake, fault, slip, mishap, scrape, mess, fiasco, breakdown; decline, decay, deterioration, loss; bankruptcy, insolvency, bust, dud.

v fail, come short, fall short, disappoint, miss the mark, miscarry, abort, blunder, botch, make a mess of, (*informal*) blow it, founder, flounder, sink, go amiss, go wrong, go hard with; fall off, dwindle, decline, fade, weaken, wane, give out, cease; desert, forsake.

adj unsuccessful, abortive, stillborn, fruitless, bootless, ineffectual, inefficient, insufficient, useless; lost, undone, bankrupt; wide of the mark, erroneous; frustrated, thwarted, foiled, defeated; defective, faulty.

adv unsuccessfully, in vain, to little purpose.

733 trophy *n* medal, prize, palm, laurel, honor, accolade, decoration, reward, recognition, triumph, celebration.

734 prosperity *n* well-being, success, fortune, wealth, affluence.

v prosper, thrive, flourish, rise, make one's way, flower, grow, blossom, bloom, fructify, succeed, (*informal*) make it.

adj prosperous, successful, wealthy, rich, well-to-do, well-off; favorable, propitious, fortunate, lucky, auspicious, golden, bright.

735 adversity *n* calamity, distress, catastrophe, crisis, disaster, failure; bad luck, hard times, misfortune, (*informal*) downers, (*informal*) bummers, trouble, hardship, pressure, affliction, wretchedness.

v go downhill, go to the dogs, decay, sink, decline, come to grief, (*informal*) hit the pits, fall on evil days.

adj adverse, unfavorable, unlucky, unfortunate; calamitous, disastrous, critical, dire, catastrophic; unprosperous, hapless, in a bad way, under a cloud, in adverse circumstances, down in the mouth.

adv adversely; if worst comes to worst.

736 mediocrity *n* average capacity, ordinariness,

commonplaceness, insignificance, passableness, tolerableness, indifference, inferiority, paltriness, triviality; moderation, golden mean.

v jog on, get along.

adj mediocre, average, normal, ordinary, commonplace, run-of-the-mill, insignificant, tolerable, unimportant, indifferent, inferior, poor, slight, paltry; moderate, reasonable, temperate, respectable.

II. Intersocial Volition

737 authority *n* control, influence, jurisdiction, command, rule, sway, power, dominion, supremacy; expert, adjudicator, arbiter, judge, sovereign, ruler; warrant, justification, permit, permission, sanction, liberty, authorization.

v authorize, empower, commission, allow, permit, sanction, approve; warrant, justify, legalize, support, back; rule, sway, control, administer, govern.

adj authoritative, peremptory, magisterial, imperative, dogmatic, masterful; executive, administrative, sovereign, regnant, supreme, dominant, paramount, predominant, preponderant, influential, official, decisive, valid, absolute.

738 [absence of authority] **laxity** *n* laxness, looseness, slackness, lenience, toleration, relaxation, loosening, licence, freedom.

v be lax, tolerate, relax, give a free rein.

adj lax, loose, slack, remiss, lenient, negligent, careless, weak.

739 severity *n* seriousness, gravity, sternness, harshness, austerity, rigidity, rigorousness, strictness, stringency, relentlessness, abruptness, curtness; arbitrariness, absolutism, despotism, dictatorship, autocracy, tyranny, oppression; strength, force, brute force, coercion.

tyrant, disciplinarian, despot, taskmaster, oppressor, inquisitor.

v be severe, tyrannize, domineer, dominate, bully, inflict, wreak, be hard on, ill-treat, maltreat, oppress, trample on, crush, coerce.

adj severe, serious, grave, stern, harsh, austere, rigid, stiff, dour, rigorous, strict, strait-laced, stringent, relentless, hard, inexorable, abrupt, peremptory, curt, short; arbitrary, absolute, despotic, dictatorial, autocratic, tyrannical, oppressive, coercive, inquisitorial, ruthless, cruel, malevolent, arrogant.

adv severely, with a high hand, with a heavy hand.

740 lenience *n* leniency, tolerance, toleration, moderation, mildness, gentleness, favor, indulgence, forbearance, quarter, compassion, clemency, mercy.

v be lenient, tolerate, bear with, favor, indulge, allow.

adj lenient, tolerant, mild, easy, easy-going, gentle, tender, indulgent, compassionate, sympathetic, merciful.

741 command *n* order, ordinance, direction, bidding, injunction, charge, mandate, behest, ukase, commandment, requisition, requirement, instruction, dictum, act, fiat; demand, exaction, claim, request; control, mastery, disposal, rule, sway, power, domination.

v command, order, direct, bid, demand, charge, instruct, enjoin, require, impose; decree, enact, ordain, dictate, prescribe, appoint; claim, lay claim to.

adj commanding, authoritative.

742 disobedience *n* noncompliance, nonobservance, insubordination, contumacy, infraction, infringement, defiance, unruliness, rebelliousness, obstinacy, stubbornness, resistance, mutinousness, mutiny, rebellion.

insurgent, mutineer, rebel, revolutionary, rioter, traitor, (*informal*) radical.

v disobey, transgress, violate, disregard, defy, infringe, shirk, resist, mutiny, rebel, revolt.

adj disobedient, insubordinate, contumacious, defiant, refractory, unruly, fractious, rebellious, mutinous, obstinate, stubborn, unsubmissive, uncompliant, recalcitrant, insurgent, riotous.

743 obedience *n* observance, compliance, docility, tractability, deference, respect, duty, subservience, submissiveness, obsequiousness; allegiance, loyalty, fealty, homage, devotion.

v obey, comply, submit, follow, attend to, serve.

adj obedient, submissive, compliant, tractable, docile, deferential, respectful, dutiful, loyal, subservient.

adv obediently, in compliance with, in obedience to.

744 compulsion *n* coercion, constraint, duress, enforcement, conscription, force; impulse, necessity.

v compel, force, make, drive, coerce, constrain, enforce, impel, require, necessitate, oblige, motivate; subdue, subject, bend, bow, overpower.

adj compelling, compulsory, coercive, forcible, constraining; obligatory, necessary, unavoidable, inescapable, ineluctable, irresistible, inexorable.

adv by force, forcibly, on compulsion.

745 master *n* lord, commander, commandant, chief, head, leader, director, ruler, boss, authority.

746 servant *n* subject, retainer, follower, henchman, domestic, menial, help, helper, employee, worker, laborer.

v serve, function, answer, assist, help, aid, provide, cater, satisfy; wait on, attend.

747 [insignia of authority] **scepter** *n* regalia, staff, symbol, emblem, flag, badge; title.

748 freedom *n* liberty, independence, autonomy, noninterference; immunity, franchisement, franchise, privilege, latitude, scope; ease, facility; frankness, openness, familiarity, license, looseness, laxity.

v be free, have scope, do as one likes, do what one wants; free, liberate, permit, allow, set free.

adj free, independent, at large, loose, scot free; unconstrained, unconfined, unchecked, unhindered, unobstructed, unbound, uncontrolled, ungoverned, unchained, unfettered, unshackled, uncurbed, unbridled, unmuzzled; unrestricted, unlimited, unconditional; absolute; discretionary; wanton, rampant, irrepressible, unvanquished; immune, exempt, freed; autonomous.

adv freely.

749 subjection *n* dependence, subordination, thrall, thralldom, subjugation, bondage, serfdom, slavery, servitude, enslavement; service, employ, tutelage, constraint, yoke, submission, obedience.

v be subject, be at the mercy of, depend upon, fall prey to, play second fiddle to, serve, submit; subject, subjugate, master, tame, tread down, weigh down, enslave, enthrall, rule.

adj subject, dependent, subordinate; under control, in harness.

750 liberation *n* disengagement, release, enlargement, emancipation, enfranchisement, deliverance, extrication, discharge, dismissal, acquittal, absolution.

v liberate, set free, free, disengage, release, emancipate, enfranchise, deliver, extricate, discharge, dismiss, unfetter, disenthrall, set loose, loose, let out, acquit, absolve.

adj liberated, freed.

751 restraint *n* restriction, circumscription, limitation, control, confinement, curb, check, suppression, constraint, repression.

v restrain, check, keep down, repress, curb, bridle, suppress, compel, hold, keep, constrain; restrict, circumscribe, confine, hinder.

adj restrained, constrained, restrictive, suppressive, repressive; imprisoned, pent up, under restraint.

752 prison *n* jail, gaol, cage, coop, pen, penitentiary, jailhouse, cell, block, dungeon, lock-up, stir, irons, *(informal)* calaboose, *(informal)* hoosegow, *(informal)* the joint, *(informal)* the big house.

753 keeper *n* custodian, guard, *(informal)* screw, jailer, gaoler, warder; escort, body-guard; protector, guardian, governor, governess, teacher, tutor, nurse.

754 prisoner *n* captive, convict, con, jailbird.

v be imprisoned, stand convicted.

adj in prison, in custody, in chains, under wraps, in stir.

755 [vicarious authority] **commission** *n* delegation, consignment, assignment, deputation, legation, mission, embassy, agency, special committee; errand, charge, permit; appointment, nomination, charter.

v commission, delegate, consign, assign, charge, entrust, authorize; appoint, name, nominate, ordain; install, induct, invest, employ, empower.

756 abrogation *n* abolition, cancelation, annulment, repeal, retraction, revocation, remission, recision, nullification, invalidation.

v abrogate, abolish, cancel, annul, repeal, retract, revoke, rescind, nullify, void, invalidate.

adj null and void.

757 resignation *n* abjuration, renunciation, abdication, abandonment, desertion, relinquishment, retirement.

v resign, quit, give up, abjure, renounce, forgo, disclaim, abrogate, abandon, desert, relinquish, retire.

758 consignee *n* trustee, nominee, committee, delegation, delegate, commission; functionary, agent, representative, messenger.

759 deputy *n* substitute, proxy, delegate, representative, surrogate, alternate, second, assistant.

v stand for, represent, answer for.

760 permission *n* authorization, warrant, sanction, liberty, license, enfranchisement, franchise, leave, permit, liberty, freedom, allowance, consent, concession, tolerance, sufferance, indulgence, favor.

v permit, allow, let, tolerate, bear with, agree to, suffer, concede, accord, favor, humor, indulge; grant, empower, franchise, charter, confer, license, authorize, warrant, sanction.

adj permitted, permissive, indulgent, libertarian, tolerant; permissible, allowable, legal, legalized, lawful, legitimate.

761 prohibition *n* interdiction, injunction, prevention, embargo, ban, restriction, disallowance.

v prohibit, forbid, interdict, veto, disallow, bar, restrict, limit; prevent, hinder, preclude, obstruct.

adj prohibitive, proscriptive, restrictive; preventive.

762 consent *n* assent, acquiescence, acceptance, acknowledgment, permission, compliance, concurrence, agreement, approval; accord, concord, consensus, settlement, ratification, confirmation.

v consent, assent, agree, concur, permit, allow, let, yield, grant, comply, accede, acquiesce.

adj compliant, agreeable, amenable.

763 offer *n* proposal, proposition, overture, tender, bid; offering, gift.

v offer, present, proffer, tender; propose, give, move, put forward, advance, invite, hold out, make a motion; hawk, merchandise, offer for sale.

adj for sale, in the open market.

764 refusal *n* rejection, spurning, denial, rebuff, repulse, repudiation; abnegation, protest, renunciation, disclaimer.

v refuse, decline, reject, spurn, turn down, deny, rebuff, repulse, repudiate; resist, repel, repudiate, renounce, disclaim, rescind, revoke.

adj noncompliant, dissident, recalcitrant, reluctant.

765 request *n* claim, demand, application, appeal, solicitation, petition, suit, entreaty, supplication, prayer.

v request, ask, ask for, beg, sue, petition, entreat, supplicate, solicit, beseech, plead, implore, require, demand, importune, clamor for.

adj importunate, clamorous, solicitous.

766 [negative request] **deprecation** *n* expostulation, intercession, mediation, protest, disapproval, remonstrance.

v deprecate, protest, expostulate, enter a protest, disapprove, remonstrate.

adj deprecatory, expostulatory, remonstrative; unsought.

767 petitioner *n* claimant, aspirant, postulant, seeker, solicitor, suitor, applicant, suppliant, supplicant; competitor, bidder; beggar, mendicant, panhandler, *(informal)* bum, *(informal)* streetwalker.

768 promise *n* undertaking, word, covenant, commitment, pledge, assurance, profession, vow, oath, guarantee, warranty, obligation, contract.

v promise, undertake, engage, enter into, bind oneself, commit oneself, pledge, agree, assure, warrant, guarantee, covenant, swear, give one's word; secure, give security, underwrite.

adj promissory, upon one's oath, on one's honor; promised, pledged, committed, bound, sworn.

769 compact *n* covenant, pact, contract, treaty, agreement, negotiation, bargain, arrangement, *(informal)* deal.

v contract, negotiate, bargain, stipulate, make terms; agree, engage, promise; complete, settle, confirm, subscribe, endorse.

adj compactual, contractual, promissory.

770 conditions *n* terms, articles, clauses, provisions, provisos, stipulations, promises, obligations, covenants.

v condition, stipulate, insist upon, contract, provide, bind, tie, oblige.

adj conditional, provisional.

adv conditionally, provisionally, on condition.

771 security *n* guarantee, warranty, bond, tie, pledge, promise, contract; mortgage, lien, pawn; stake, deposit, collateral, *(informal)* IOU, *(informal)* mark, promissory note; deed, bill of sale, receipt, certificate, title; sponsorship, surety, bail.

v give security, post bail, pawn, mortgage; guarantee, warrant, assure, promise; accept, endorse, underwrite, sponsor, stand for.

772 observance *n* performance, compliance, obedience, execution, discharge, acquittance, fulfillment, satisfaction; adhesion, acknowledgment, fidelity, faithfulness.

v observe, comply with, respect, abide by, acknowledge, adhere to, be faithful to, obey, act up to; meet, fulfill; carry out, execute, perform, satisfy, discharge.

adj observant, compliant, faithful, obedient, true, honorable; punctilious, scrupulous, as good as one's word.

adv faithfully.

773 nonobservance *n* evasion, failure, omission, non-compliance, neglect, negligence, laxity, laxness, carelessness, irresponsibility, disobedience; infringement, infraction, violation, transgression.

v fail, neglect, evade, omit, elude, ignore, disregard, discard, set at naught; infringe, transgress, violate, break.

adj nonobservant, lax, loose, disdainful, evasive, elusive, negligent, irresponsible, disobedient.

774 compromise *n* adjustment, negotiation, concession; compensation.

v compromise, bend, give and take, split the differences, come to an agreement, opt for the mean, adjust, arrange, settle.

775 acquisition *n* procurement, appropriation, gain, attainment, purchase, gift, find; profit, earnings, wages, winnings, income, proceeds, produce, crop, harvest, benefit.

v acquire, appropriate, gain, win, earn, attain, gather, collect; take over, take possession of, procure, secure, obtain, get, come into, receive, get hold of; profit, turn to profit.

adj profitable, advantageous, gainful, remunerative.

776 loss *n* damage, injury, privation, lapse, forfeiture, deprivation.

v lose, incur a loss, miss, mislay, let slip, forfeit; waste, get rid of.

adj lost, bereft, minus, deprived of, cut off, rid of; long lost, irretrievable.

777 possession *n* ownership, occupancy, holding, proprietorship, tenure, tenancy, control, custody; belonging.

v possess, own, have, hold, occupy, control, command, have to oneself, have in hand, belong to.

adj possessing, possessed of, in possession of, master of, in hand, at one's disposal; possessive, custodial.

777a exemption *n* exception, immunity, impunity, release.

v exempt, excuse, release; not have, be without.

adj exempt from, immune from, devoid of, without.

778 [joint possession] **participation** *n* partnership, co-ownership, joint tenancy, common holding, communion, community of possessions; communism, socialism, collectivism; cooperation.

participant, sharer, partner, copartner, shareholder; communist, socialist.

v participate, partake, share, share in, go halves, split up, divide, have in common, own in common.

adj participatory, joint, common, collective, communal, communist, communistic, socialist, socialistic.

779 possessor *n* holder, occupant, tenant, lessee; proprietor, proprietress, master, mistress, owner.

780 property *n* possession, possessions, goods, effects, chattels, estate, belongings, assets, means, resources, land, real estate, acreage; ownership, right; attribute, quality, characteristic, feature.

781 retention *n* keeping, holding, detention, custody, preservation, maintenance.

v retain, keep, hold, hold fast, secure, withhold, preserve, detain, reserve, maintain.

adj retentive.

782 relinquishment *n* renunciation, surrender, resignation, yielding, waiver, abdication, desertion, abandonment, quitting.

v relinquish, renounce, surrender, give up, resign, yield, cede, waive, forswear, forgo, abdicate,

leave, forsake, desert, quit, abandon, let go, discard, cast off, dismiss, divest oneself.

adj cast off, done away with, left, forsworn, given up, left behind.

783 transfer *n* sale, lease, release, exchange, interchange; transference, transmission, changing hands.

v transfer, convey, assign, grant, consign, make over, hand over, pass, transmit, change, exchange, interchange, change hands; devolve, succeed.

adj transferable, conveyable, transmissive, exchangeable.

784 giving *n* bestowal, presentation, concession, delivery, consignment, dispensation, endowment, investiture, award; charity, almsgiving, liberality, generosity, philanthropy; gift, donation, present, boon, favor, grant, offering; allowance, contribution, donation, bequest, legacy; alms, largesse, bounty, help, gratuity; bribe, bait.

giver, granter, donor.

v give, bestow, confer, grant, accord, award, assign, entrust, consign; invest, allow, settle upon, donate, bequeath, leave; furnish, supply, help; afford, spare, favor with, lavish; deliver, hand, pass, turn over, present, give away, dispense, dispose of, give out, deal out, dole out, mete out, fork out; pay, render, impart.

adj charitable, beneficent, tributary, liberal, generous, philanthropic.

785 receiving *n* acquisition, reception, acceptance, admission, recipient, receiver, legatee, grantee, donee, beneficiary, pensioner.

v receive, take, acquire, admit, take in, accept; come into, fall to one, accrue.

adj receiving; received.

786 apportionment *n* allotment, consignment, assignment, allocation, distribution, dispensation, division, partition; portion, lot, share, measure, dose, dole, ration, ratio, proportion, quota, allowance.

v apportion, divide, distribute, dispense, allot, share, mete, portion out, parcel out, dole out, deal, carve, administer; partition, assign, appropriate, appoint.

adj distributive; respective.

787 lending *n* loan, advance, accommodation, mortgage, investment.

v lend, loan, advance, accommodate, lend on security, pawn; let, lease.

788 borrowing *n* pledging, pawning; appropriating, stealing, theft.

v borrow, pledge, pawn, borrow money; hire, rent, lease; appropriate, use, steal from, imitate.

789 taking *n* appropriation, capture, apprehension, seizure, abduction, dispossession, deprivation, expropriation, divestment, confiscation, eviction; extortion, theft; reprisal, recovery.

v take, catch, hook, nab, bag, pocket, receive, accept; reap, cull, pluck, gather; appropriate, assume, possess oneself of, help oneself to, commandeer, make free with; take away, abduct, steal, seize, snatch, snap up, capture, get hold of, take from, take away from, dispossess, expropriate, oust, eject, divest, confiscate, usurp, strip, fleece; retake, resume, recover.

adj predatory, rapacious, parasitic, greedy, ravenous.

790 restitution *n* return, restoration, reinvestment, rehabilitation, reparation, atonement, compensation, recovery.

v return, restore, give back, render, give up, let go; recoup, reimburse, compensate, reinvest, remit, rehabilitate, repair, make good, settle up; recover, get back, redeem, take back again.

adj compensatory, redemptive, recouperative.

791 stealing *n* theft, thievery, robbery, swindling, fraud, appropriation.

v steal, take, thieve, rob, pilfer, purloin, (*informal*) swipe, filch, embezzle, swindle, appropriate, fleece, defraud, (*informal*) rip off, (infomal) screw.

adj thievish, light-fingered, piratical, predatory.

792 thief *n* robber, pilferer, filcher, rifler, crook, (*informal*) rip-off artist, cheat; burglar, housebreaker, second-story man, safecracker.

793 booty *n* spoils, plunder, prize, loot, catch, pickings, stolen goods, (*informal*) haul.

794 barter *n* exchange, trade, traffic, commerce, business, bargain; dealing, transaction, negotiation.

v barter, trade, exchange, traffic, bargain, swap, buy and sell, give and take, deal, haggle, negotiate, drive a bargain, transact.

adj commercial, mercantile; interchangeable, in trade, for sale, marketable.

795 purchase *n* buying, purchasing, acquisition; bargain, buy.

buyer, purchaser, shopper, customer, client, patron, clientele.

v purchase, buy, acquire, get, obtain, procure; shop, market, go shopping.

796 sale *n* selling, vendition, commerce, mercantilism, transaction, exchange, auction, trade.

seller, vendor, merchant.

v sell, trade, barter, vend, exchange, deal in, dispose, merchandise, hawk.

adj salable, marketable, vendible, for sale.

797 merchant *n* trader, dealer, seller, salesman, saleswoman, tradesman, shopkeeper, retailer, hawker, huckster, peddler, broker.

798 merchandise *n* goods, wares, commodity, articles, stock, produce, product, staple commodity, store, cargo.

v merchandise, sell.

799 market *n* mart, marketplace, fair, bazaar, business district, mall, shopping center, store, department store, establishment, place of business, office.

800 money *n* finance, accounts, funds, assets, wealth, supplies, ways and means, wherewithal, capital, almighty dollar, cash, currency, hard cash, (*informal*) bucks, change, small change, (*informal*) green, greenbacks; sum, amount, balance.

adj monetary, pecuniary, financial, fiscal.

801 treasurer *n* bursar, banker, purser, receiver, steward, trustee, accountant, paymaster, cashier, teller, financier.

802 treasury *n* bank, exchequer, strongbox, stronghold, coffer, chest, depository, purse, moneybag, safe, vault, cash box, cash register, till; securities, stocks, bonds, notes.

803 wealth *n* riches, fortune, opulence, affluence, easy circumstance, (*informal*) silver spoon, independence, competence, sufficiency, solvency; provision, livelihood, maintenance, means, resources, substance; income, capital, money.

v be wealthy, be rich.

adj wealthy, rich, affluent, well-off, well-to-do, comfortable.

804 poverty *n* indigence, penury, pauperism, destitution, want, need, neediness, lack, privation, distress, difficulties, straits, bad straits.

v be poor, want, lack, starve, live from hand to mouth, go to the dogs.

adj poor, indigent, destitute, poverty-stricken, needy, penniless, broke, (*informal*) bust, hard up, insolvent, seedy, beggarly.

805 credit *n* trust, score, tally, account, (*informal*) tab, bill.

creditor, lender, usurer.

v credit, accredit, entrust, keep an account with.

806 debt *n* obligation, liability, debit, score, duty, due.

debtor, borrower.

adj liable, answerable for, in debt; unpaid, in arrear.

807 payment *n* discharge, settlement, clearance, liquidation, satisfaction, reckoning, arrangment; acknowledgment, release, receipt, voucher; installment, remittance.

v pay, settle, liquidate, discharge, quit, acquit oneself of, reckon up, satisfy, compensate, reimburse, remunerate, recompense, make payment, square accounts, balance accounts, pay in full.

adj out of debt, solvent; straight, clear.

808 nonpayment *n* default, protest, repudiation; insolvency, bankruptcy, failure.

v not pay, default, fail, stop payment; run up bills.

adj in debt.

809 expenditure *n* outlay, expenses, disbursement, payment, costs, fees.

v expend, spend, pay out, disburse, (*informal*) fork out, lay out.

810 receipt *n* value received, acknowledgment of payment.

v receive, take, get, bring in.

adj profitable, remunerative.

811 accounts *n* money matters. finance, budget, bill, score, reckoning, account; statement, ledger, inventory, register, book, books, sheet; balance.

accountant, auditor, bookkeeper, financier.

v keep accounts, enter, post, book, credit, debit, balance.

812 price *n* amount, cost, expense, charge, figure, demand, damage, fare, hire, wages; worth, rate, value, valuation, appraisal; market price, quotation; bill, invoice.

v price, set a price, fix a price, appraise, assess, charge, demand, ask, require, exact; fetch, sell for, bring in, yield, accord.

813 discount *n* abatement, reduction, depreciation, allowance, qualification, rebate, sale.

v discount, put on sale, reduce, take off, allow, deduct, abate, rebate.

814 dearness *n* expensiveness, costliness, high price; overcharge, extravagance, exorbitance.

v be expensive, cost a lot; overcharge, bleed, fleece, extort.

adj dear, expensive, costly, precious; extravagant, exorbitant, unreasonable; priceless.

815 cheapness *n* low price, depreciation, bargain, value, (*informal*) steal, (*informal*) great buy.

v be cheap, cost little.

adj cheap, moderate, reasonable, inexpensive, dirt cheap.

816 liberality *n* generosity, munificence, bounty, bounteousness, hospitality, charity.

v be liberal, spend freely, give, spare no expense.

adj liberal, free, generous, bountiful, hospitable, munificent, beneficient, princely, charitable.

817 economy *n* frugality, thrift, thriftiness, saving, care, husbandry, retrenchment, parsimony.

v economize, save, retrench, husband.

adj economical, frugal, careful, thrifty, chary, parsimonious.

818 prodigality *n* unthriftiness, waste, wastefulness, profusion, profuseness, extravagance, profligacy, lavishness, squandering.

prodigal, spendthrift, squanderer.

v be prodigal, squander, lavish, misspend, waste, dissipate, fritter one's money.

adj prodigal, profuse, unthrifty, improvident, wasteful, profligate, extravagant, lavish.

819 parsimony *n* stinginess, illiberality, avarice, rapidity, rapacity, venality, cupidity, selfishness.

miser, niggard, churl, skinflint, codger, scrimp, (*informal*) tightwad, usurer, Scrooge.

v be parsimonious, grudge, begrudge, stint, pinch, hold back, withhold, starve, famish.

adj parsimonious, penurious, stingy, cheap, miserly, mean, pennywise, niggardly, tight, ungenerous, churlish, mercenary, venal, covetous, usurious, avaricious, greedy, rapacious, selfish.

Class VI

Words Relating to the Sentient and Moral Powers

I. Affections in General

820 affection *n* character, qualities, disposition, nature, spirit, temper, temperament, idiosyncrasy, habit, bent, bias, predisposition, proclivity, propensity, humor, mood, sympathy; soul, heart, inner man, essence; passion, driving spirit, ruling passion.

adj affected, characterized, formed, cast, molded, tempered, predisposed, prone, inclined, imbued; inborn, ingrained, deep-rooted.

adv at heart.

821 feeling *n* consciousness, impression; emotion, passion, sentiment, sensibility; sympathy, empathy; fervor, ardor, zeal, warmth, tenderness, sensitivity, sentimentality, susceptibility, pity; sentiment, opinion.

v feel, receive an impression, respond to.

adj feeling, emotional, sensitive, tender; sympathetic; emotional, impassioned, passionate, fervent, tender, sensitive; heart-felt, thrilling, rapturous, soul-stirring; moved, touched, affected.

adv heart and soul, from the bottom of one's heart.

822 sensibility *n* responsiveness, sensitiveness, awareness, susceptibility, impressibility, tenderness, sentimentality, sentimentalism; excitability; appreciation, understanding, moral sensibility.

v be sensitive, have a soft spot in one's heart.

adj sensitive, impressionable, susceptible, tender, warm-hearted, sentimental; excitable; aware, understanding, appreciative.

823 insensibility *n* insensitiveness, impassivity, apathy, coldness, callousness; imperturbable; dullness, boorishness.

v be insensitive, not care, be unaffected, have no interest in.

adj insensitive, unconscious, unaware; inattentive, indifferent, lukewarm; apathetic, impassive, unimpressionable; cold-blooded, cold-hearted, unmoved, unaffected, callous, thick-skinned, uncaring.

adv in cold blood.

824 excitation *n* excitation of feeling; mental excitation; galvanism, stimulation, provocation, inspiration, infection; animation, agitation, perturbation; fascination, intoxication, ravishment; irritation, anger, passion, thrill.

v excite, affect, touch, move, impress, interest, animate, inspire, infect, awake; evoke, provoke;

stir up, wake up, light up; rouse, arouse, stir, fire, kindle, inflame; stimulate, quicken, sharpen, whet, whet the appetite, fan the fire, raise to a fervor; absorb, rivet, intoxicate, fascinate, enrapture; agitate, perturb, ruffle, fluster, disturb, startle, shock, stagger, astound, electrify, galvanize; irritate.

adj excited, excitable, wrought up, overwrought, upset, hysterical, hot, red-hot, flushed, feverish, boiling, ebullient, seething, fuming, raging, raving, frantic, mad, distracted, beside oneself; exciting, warm, glowing, fervid, soul-stirring, thrilling, overwhelming, overpowering, sensational.

825 [excess of sensitiveness] **excitability** *n* impetuosity, vehemence, boisterousness, impatience, intolerance, irritability, restlessness, agitation; passion, excitement, fever, tumult, ebullition, tempest, fit, paroxysm, explosion, outburst, agony; violence, rage, fury, furor, desperation, madness, distraction, delirium, frenzy, hysterics.

v be impatient, lose patience, fuss, fidget; lose one's temper, flare up, burn, boil over, foam, fume, rage, rant, run wild, go mad, go into hysterics.

adj excitable, high-strung, nervous, irritable, impatient, intolerant; feverish, hysterical, delirious, mad; hurried, restless, fidgety, fussy; vehement, violent, wild, furious, fierce, fiery, hotheaded; overzealous, enthusiastic, impassioned, fanatical; rabid, clamorous, turbulent, tumultuous, boisterous; impulsive, impetuous, passionate, uncontrolled, uncontrollable, ungovernable, irrepressible; volcanic.

826 inexcitability *n* imperturbability, even temper, dispassion, patience, impassivity; coolness, calmness, composure, placidity, serenity, quietude; self-possession, self-restraint, stoicism; resignation, submission, sufferance, endurance, forbearance, fortitude, moderation, restraint.

v bear, endure, tolerate, suffer, put up with, reconcile oneself to, resign oneself to, brook, swallow, make the best of, stomach; compose, appease, propitiate, repress, calm down, cool down.

adj inexcitable, imperturbable, unsusceptible, dispassionate, enduring, stoical, staid, sober, sedate; easygoing, peaceful, placid, calm, cool; composed, collected, unruffled, content, resigned, subdued.

II. Personal Affections

827 pleasure *n* happiness, gladness, delectation, enjoyment, delight, joy, glee, cheer, cheerfulness, well-being, satisfaction, gratification, comfort, ease; felicity, bliss, enchantment, transport, rapture, ravishment, ecstasy, luxury, sensuality, voluptuousness.

v be pleased, joy, enjoy oneself, have one's head in the clouds, fall into raptures; be pleased with, derive pleasure from, take pleasure in, (*informal*) get into, delight in, rejoice in, indulge in, luxuriate in, relish, love, enjoy, like, (*informal*) dig, take a fancy to, take a shine to.

adj happy, blissful, joyful, gladsome, cheerful; comfortable, at ease, content; ecstatic.

adv happily, with pleasure.

828 pain *n* suffering, distress, torture, misery, dolor, anguish, agony, torment, throe, pang, ache, smart, twinge, stitch; displeasure, dissatisfaction, discomfort, discomposure, disquiet, malaise, inquietude, uneasiness, vexation, discontent, dejection, weariness; annoyance, irritation, worry, affliction, bore, bother, mortification, plague; care, solicitude, trouble, trial, ordeal, burden, load, fret; prostration, desolation, despair.

v suffer, afflict, torture, torment, distress, despair; hurt, harm, injure, trouble, grieve, disquiet, discomfort, discompose, worry, irritate, vex, mortify, plague.

adj uncomfortable, uneasy, weary; unhappy, infelicitous, poor, wretched, miserable, woebegone, careworn, cheerless, sorry, sorrowful, stricken, in tears, in despair.

829 pleasurableness *n* pleasantness, agreeableness, delectability, delight, congeniality; sprightliness, cheer, cheerfulness, liveliness; attraction, attractiveness, charm, fascination, enchantment, witchery, seduction, winning ways, amenity, amiability; loveliness, beauty, brightness; goodness.

v be pleasurable, afford pleasure, offer pleasure, please, charm, delight, gladden, cheer; attract, invite, allure, stimulate, interest, captivate, fascinate, enchant, entrance, enrapture, bewitch, ravish, enravish, transport; agree with, satisfy, gratify; slake, satiate, quench; regale, refresh, treat, amuse.

adj pleasurable, pleasant, agreeable, enjoyable, delightful, congenial, amiable; comfortable, cordial, genial, gladsome, sweet, delectable, nice, dainty, delicate, delicious, luscious, luxurious, voluptuous, sensual; attractive, lovely, beautiful, seductive, rapturous, ecstatic, beatific, heavenly; fair, sunny, bright; gay, sprightly, merry, cheery, cheerful, lively, vivacious.

830 painfulness *n* trouble, care, trial, affliction, blow, burden, curse, mishap, misfortune, adversity; annoyance, nuisance, grievance, bore, bother, vexation, mortification; wound, sore, sore subject, thorn in the side, skeleton in the closet; sorry sight, heavy news, bad news; affront, insult, offense.

v pain, hurt, wound, sadden, displease, annoy, trouble, disturb, cross, perplex, irk, vex, mortify, worry, plague, bother, pester, harass, badger, bait, heckle, irritate, anger, persecute, provoke; harrow, torment, torture; affront, insult, give offense, offend, maltreat, mistreat; sicken, disgust, revolt, nauseate, repel, shock, horrify, appal.

adj painful, hurtful, dolorous; unpleasant, disagreeable, unpalatable, bitter, distasteful; unwelcome, undesirable, obnoxious; dismal, dreary, melancholy, grievous, piteous, woeful, rueful, mournful, deplorable, pitiable, lamentable, pathetic; invidious, vexatious, troublesome, irksome, wearisome, worrisome; intolerable, insufferable, unsupportable, unbearable, unendurable, grim, dreadful, fearful, frightful, dire, odious, hateful, repulsive, repellant, abhorrent, horrid, horrible, offensive, nauseous, loathsome, vile, hideous; sore, severe, grave, hard, harsh, cruel; ruinous, disastrous, calamitous, tragic; burdensome, onerous, oppressive, cumbersome.

adv painfully.

831 content *n* contentment, complacency, satisfaction, ease, serenity, comfort; conciliation, resignation.

v gratify, satisfy, set at ease, comfort, appease, conciliate, reconcile.

adj contented, complacent, satisfied, sanguine, comfortable; assenting, acceding, resigned, willing, agreeable.

adv to one's heart's content.

832 discontent *n* discontentment, dissatisfaction, uneasiness, disquietude, restlessness, displeasure.

v be discontented, repine, regret, fret, chafe, grumble; dissatisfy, disappoint, disconcert.

adj discontented, dissatisfied, displeased, uneasy, restless, dejected, malcontent, regretful, down in the dumps.

833 regret *n* sorrow, lamentation, grief; remorse, penitence, contrition, repentance.

v regret, deplore, lament, feel sorry about, grieve at, bemoan, bewail, rue, mourn for, repent.

adj regretful, sorry, lamentable, rueful; penitent, contrite.

834 relief *n* deliverance, alleviation, ease, assuagement, mitigation, comfort, solace, consolation;

help, assistance, aid.

v relieve, ease, alleviate, assuage, mitigate, allay, comfort, soothe, lessen, abate, diminish; cheer, comfort, console; aid, help, assist, succor, refresh, remedy, support.

adj soothing, consoling, assuaging, comforting, palliative, curative.

835 aggravation *n* worsening, heightening, intensification, exaggeration, (*informal*); annoyance, irritation, vexation.

v aggravate, worsen, intensify, heighten, increase, make serious, make grave.

adj worse, intensified, irritated.

adv from bad to worse, out of the frying pan and into the fire.

836 cheerfulness *n* geniality, high spirits, liveliness, vivacity, joviality, jocularity, mirth, merriment, exhilaration.

v cheer, gladden, enliven, inspirit, delight, rejoice, exhilarate, animate, encourage; shout, applaud, acclaim, salute.

adj cheery, gay, blithe, happy, lively, spirited, sprightly, joyful, joyous, mirthful, buoyant, sparkling, vivacious, gleeful, sunny, jolly; pleasant, bright, gay, winsome, gladdening, cheery, cheering, inspiring, animating, hearty, robust.

adv cheerfully.

837 dejection *n* depression, heaviness, heavy heart, melancholy, sadness, dumps, doldrums, despondency, gloom, weariness, disgust, despair, hopelessness.

v be dejected, lose heart, frown, mope, droop, despond, brood over, sink, despair.

adj unhappy, depressed, dispirited, disheartened, discouraged, despondent, (*informal*) down, downhearted, sad, melancholy, lugubrious, heartsick, dismal, gloomy, miserable, desolate; pessimistic, cynical.

adv with a long face, with tears in one's eyes.

838 rejoicing *n* exaltation, triumph, jubilation, reveling, merrymaking, celebration, paean; smile, smirk, grin, giggle, titter, laughter, guffaw, shout, peal of laughter.

v rejoice, congratulate oneself, clap one's hands, dance, skip, sing, hurrah, cry for joy, leap with joy, exalt, triumph; smile, smirk, grin, giggle, titter, chuckle, cackle, laugh, crow, burst out, shout, split, roar, shake one's sides, split one's sides.

adj jubilant, exultant, triumphant, flushed, (*informal*) high, elated, laughing, convulsed with laughter.

839 lamention *n* lament, howl, wail, wailing, complaint, moan, moaning, groan, sob, sigh; dirge, elegy, monody, threnody.

v lament, bewail, bemoan, deplore, grieve, scream, sob, cry, weep, mourn over, sorrow over.

adj lamenting, in mourning, sorrowful, mournful, lamentable, tearful, plaintive.

840 amusement *n* enjoyment, entertainment, recreation, diversion, relaxation, pastime, pleasure, playing, festivity.

v amuse, entertain, cheer, divert, enliven, interest; amuse oneself, play, sport, make merry.

adj amusing, entertaining, diverting, relaxing, pleasant, witty, jovial, jolly, playful.

841 weariness *n* ennui, lassitude, fatigue, exhaustion, boredom; tedium, monotony, dullness.

v weary, tire, fatigue, bore, exhaust.

adj wearisome, tiresome, boring, tedious, irksome, monotonous, humdrum, dull, prosaic, trying; weary, drowsy, exhausted, tired, wearied, fatigued; uninterested, impatient, dissatisfied.

842 wit *n* drollery, facetiousness, pleasantry, repartee, cleverness, humor, fun; understanding, intelligence, sagacity, wisdom, intellect, mind, sense.

v joke, jest, banter, pun.

adj witty, quick, quick-witted, nimble, sharp, clever, facetious, whimsical, pleasant, humorous, playful, sparkling, scintillating; intelligent, sagacious, wise, perceptive, insightful.

843 dullness *n* heaviness, flatness, stupidity, obtuseness, lack of originality, banality.

v be dull, blunt, deaden, benumb.

adj dull, uninteresting, unimaginative, dry, prosaic, matter-of-fact, commonplace, boring, tedious, dreary, vapid; stupid, stolid, slow, flat.

844 humorist *n* wit, wag, comedian, comedienne, joker, jester, wisecracker, epigrammatist, punster, buffoon, clown, fool, satirist, lampooner, cutup, funnyman.

845 beauty *n* loveliness, pulchritude, elegance, grace, gracefulness, comeliness, seemliness, fairness, attractiveness, brilliance, radiance, splendor, gorgeousness, magnificence, sublimity.

v beautify.

adj beautiful, handsome, comely, seemly, attractive, lovely, pretty, fair, fine, elegant, beauteous, graceful, pulchritudinous, brilliant, radiant, gorgeous, magnificent; artistic, aesthetic, picturesque.

846 ugliness *n* homeliness, inelegance, unsightliness, distortion, disfigurement, deformity, frightfulness.

v deface, disfigure, distort.

adj ugly, displeasing, hard-featured, unlovely, unsightly, unseemly, homely; hideous, gruesome, repulsive, offensive, revolting, terrible, base, vile, squalid, gross, monstrous, heinous; disagreeable, unpleasant, objectionable.

847 ornament *n* ornamentation, adornment, decoration, embellishment, frills, finery.

v ornament, embellish, adorn, decorate, beautify.

adj ornamental, decorative; ornamented, ornate, embellished, beautified.

848 blemish *n* disfigurement, deformity, defect, flaw, fault, taint, blot, spot, speck.

v stain, sully, spot, taint, tarnish, injur, mar, damage, deface, impair.

adj disfigured, injured, imperfect, discolored, freckled, pitted.

849 simplicity *n* plainness, homeliness; clarity, chasteness, restraint, severity, lack of adornment, lack of affectation.

v simplify, uncomplicate, clarify, strip to essentials, get back to basics.

adj simple, plain, homely, natural, unadorned, unaffected, unembellished, neat, unassuming, unpretentious; chaste, severe; clear, straightforward, lucid.

850 [good taste] **taste** *n* good taste, delicacy, refinement, polish, elegance, grace, discrimination, culture, cultivation.

v show taste, appreciate, judge, criticize, discriminate.

adj tasteful, in good taste, decorous, attractive, cultivated, cultured, refined, discriminative, polished, felicitous, appropriate, suitable, apt, becoming, pleasing.

adv tastefully, elegantly.

851 [bad taste] **vulgarity** *n* bad taste, barbarism, coarseness, lack of decorum, ill-breeding, boorishness; gaudiness, tawdriness, finery, frippery, tinsel.

v be vulgar; vulgarize.

adj vulgar, in bad taste, unrefined, boorish, common, coarse, ill-bred, ill-mannered, ignoble, mean, plebeian, crude, rude, shabby; gaudy, tawdry, flashy, garish, crass, showy, (*informal*) tacky.

852 fashion *n* custom, style, vogue, mode, rage, craze; conventionality, conformity; society, polite society, beau monde; manners, breeding, air, demeanor, *savoir faire*, gentility, decorum, propriety, etiquette.

v be fashionable, be the rage; fashion, adapt, suit, fit, adjust; make, shape, frame, form, mold.

adj fashionable, in vogue, á la mode, all the rage; modish, stylish, conventional, customary; well-bred, well-mannered, civil, polite, courteous, polished, refined, genteel, decorous.

853 ridiculousness *n* outrageousness, silliness, absurdity.

v be ridiculous, make a fool of oneself, play the fool.

adj absurd, preposterous, extravagant, asinine, laughable, nonsensical, silly, funny, ludicrous, droll, comical, farcical, outlandish, outrageous, fantastic.

854 fop *n* fine gentleman, dandy, (*informal*) dude, coxcomb, beau, man about town, prig, jackanapes.

855 affectation *n* affectedness, pretense, pretension, airs, mannerisms, unnaturalness, display, show, sham, feigning, simulation, foppery.

v affect, act a part, put on airs, pretend, assume, feign, counterfeit, simulate, pose, attitudinize.

adj affected, pretentious, ostentatious, feigned, artificial, stilted, mannered, stagey, theatrical, modish, unnatural.

856 ridicule *n* derision, scoffing, mockery, gibes, jeers, taunts, raillery; satire, burlesque, sneer, banter, wit, irony.

v ridicule, deride, banter, chaff, twit, mock, taunt, make fun of, sneer at, burlesque, satirize, rail at, lampoon, jeer at, scoff at, (*informal*) put down.

adj derisory, derisive, sarcastic, ironic, ironical, burlesque, mocking.

857 [object and cause of ridicule] **laughing-stock** *n* butt, game, fair game, fool, dupe, original, oddity, queer fish, square, straight, buffoon.

858 hope *n* confidence, trust, reliance, faith, assurance; expectation, expectancy, anticipation, aspiration, longing, desire, dream, wish.

v hope, trust, rely on, lean on, have faith in; hope for, expect, presume, anticipate; long for, desire.

adj hopeful, expectant, sanguine, optimistic, confident; probable, promising, propitious, reassuring, encouraging, cheering, inspiriting.

859 hopelessness *n* despair, desperation, despondency, dejection, pessimism.

v despair, give up hope, despond.

adj hopeless, despairing, desperate, despondent, forlorn, disconsolate; irremediable, remediless, unremedial, incurable.

860 fear *n* apprehension, consternation, dismay, alarm, trepidation, dread, terror, fright, horror, panic; anxiety, solicitude, suspicion, misgiving, concern; awe, reverence, veneration.

v fear, be afraid of, apprehend, distrust, dread; revere, venerate, reverence.

adj fearful, afraid, apprehensive, dismayed, alarmed, frightened, terrified, horrified, aghast, terror-stricken, horror-stricken, panic-stricken; anxious, concerned, solicitous, suspicious; fearful, awesome, awe-inspiring; awful, dreadful, terrible.

861 courage *n* fearlessness, dauntlessness, intrepidity, guts, fortitude, pluck, spirit, nerve, heroism, daring, audacity, bravery, mettle, valor, hardihood, bravado, gallantry.

v dare, venture, look danger in the face, take heart, take the bull by the horns.

adj courageous, fearless, dauntless, intrepid, (*informal*) gutsy, spirited, stout-hearted, resolute, bold, heroic, daring, audacious, brave, valorous, enterprising, adventurous, gallant.

862 cowardice n fear, poltroonery, dastardliness, faint-heartedness, yellow streak, dread, timidity, baseness, abject fear.

coward, poltroon, craven, sneak, lily-liver, (*informal*) chicken.

v be cowardly, cower, skulk, quail, hide.

adj cowardly, fearful, craven, dastardly, pusillanimous, recreant, timid, timorous, faint-hearted, lily-livered chicken-hearted, fearful, afraid, scared, spineless, (*informal*) chicken.

863 rashness n haste, impetuosity, recklessness, impulsiveness, heedlessness, thoughtlessness, imprudence, indiscretion, audacity, carelessness, foolhardiness.

v be rash, plunge.

adj rash, hasty, impetuous, reckless, headlong, precipitate, impulsive, thoughtless, heedless, imprudent, indiscreet, careless, unwary, foolhardy, presumptuous, audacious.

864 caution n prudence, discretion, circumspection, heed, care, wariness, heedfulness, vigilance, forethought; warning, admonition, advice, injunction, counsel.

v be cautious, take care; warn, admonish, advise, counsel.

adj cautious, prudent, heedful, careful, watchful, discreet, wary, vigilant, alert, provident, chary, circumspect, guarded.

865 desire n longing, fancy, craving, yearning, wish, want, need, hunger, appetite, thirst; request, wish, ambition, aspiration; love, passion, lust.

v desire, wish for, long for, crave, want, wish, covet, fancy; ask, request, solicit; lust for.

adj desirous, desiring, craving, wishful, hungry, thirsty, covetous, fervent, ardent, lustful.

866 indifference n unconcern, listlessness, apathy, insensibility, coolness, insensitiveness, inattention.

v be indifferent, take no interest in, have no heart for, spurn, disdain.

adj indifferent, unconcerned, listless, apathetic, cool, cold, lukewarm, insensitive, inattentive.

867 dislike n disinclination, disrelish, distaste, disgust, repugnance, antipathy, antagonism, aversion, hatred, horror, loathing.

v dislike, disrelish, be averse to, be disinclined, be reluctant, have no taste for; disgust, repel, nauseate, hate, loathe.

adj disliking, disinclined, averse, loath; dislikable, distasteful, disagreeable, offensive, repulsive, repugnant, repellent, abhorrent, nauseating, disgusting, loathsome.

868 fastidiousness n nicety; hypercriticism; discernment, discrimination, judiciousness, keenness, perspicacity.

v be fastidious, split hairs.

adj fastidious, nice, dainty, delicate; hard to please, finicky, hypercritical, fussy, querulous, meticulous, exacting, scrupulous, proper, priggish, prim; discerning, discriminative, judicious, keen, sharp, perspicacious, sagacious.

869 satiety n repletion, saturation, glut, surfeit; disgust, weariness.

v sate, satiate, saturate, cloy, glut, stuff, gorge, surfeit; gall, disgust, bore, tire, weary.

adj satiated, glutted, stuffed, gorged, surfeited; disgusted, bored, tired, weary.

870 wonder n surprise, marvel, astonishment, stupefaction, amazement, awe, admiration, bewilderment, puzzlement.

v wonder, think, speculate, conjecture, meditate, ponder, question; marvel, admire, be surprised, start, stare, startle, astonish, amaze, astound, stagger, stupefy, bewilder, dumfound.

adj marvelous, wonderful, extraordinary, remarkable, awesome, startling, wondrous, miraculous, astonishing, amazing, astounding, unique, curious, strange, odd, peculiar; astonished, surprised, aghast, agog, startled, breathless, awestruck, spell-bound, lost in wonder, amazed, fascinated, bewildered.

871 expectance n expectancy, expectation.

v expect, foresee, assume, not be surprised, make nothing of.

adj expecting, expectant, relied on, expected, figured on, foreseen.

872 prodigy n phenomenon, wonder, marvel, miracle; freak, monstrosity, spectacle, curiosity; genius, intellectual giant, wizard, mastermind, expert, sage, child genius, wunderkind.

873 repute n estimation, reputation, account, regard, report; name, standing, distinction, credit, respect, respectability, dignity, greatness, eminence, honor, renown.

v consider, esteem, account, hold, regard, deem, reckon; be held in high repute, be distinguished.

adj reputed, regarded, accounted; reputable, respected, respectable, esteemed, celebrated, distinguished, dignified, honored, renowned, eminent.

874 disrepute n disgrace, dishonor, disfavor, discredit, ill repute, low repute, bad name, shame, degradation, obloquy, debasement, ignominy, infamy, stain, spot, blot, tarnish, taint.

v disgrace oneself, have a bad name, shame, disgrace, dishonor, tarnish, stain, taint, blot.

adj disreputable, base, low, unsavory, shady, unworthy, disgraced, vile, ignominious, dishonorable, opprobrious, shameful, disgraceful, infamous, tainted, tarnished.

875 nobility n distinction, eminence, stateliness, majesty, grandeur, dignity, loftiness, profundity, high-mindedness; rank, condition, high birth, gentility, quality, royalty, aristocracy, lord, lady.

v be noble; ennoble.

adj noble, exalted, honorable, dignified, imposing, stately; titled, aristocratic, patrician, high-born.

876 commonalty n the common people, the lower classes, commoners, multitude, proletariat, populace, rank and file, bourgeoisie, general public, citizenry, peasantry, crowd, herd, rabble.

adj common, mean, low, base, ignoble, vulgar, homely, plebeian, proletarian, low-born, obscure, rustic, boorish, uncivilized.

877 title n honor, name, designation, decoration.

adj titled.

878 pride n self-respect, self-assurance, self-esteem, conceit, vanity, egotism, arrogance, vainglory, self-importance; insolence, haughtiness, superciliousness, presumption.

v be proud, presume, swagger, give oneself airs.

adj proud, high-minded, dignified, stately, noble, imposing, honorable, creditable; self-assured, self-satisfied, contented, egotistical, vain, conceited, arrogant, haughty, smug, overbearing, over-confident, snobbish, supercilious, presumptuous.

879 humility n modesty, humbleness, meekness, lowliness, submissiveness.

v lower, abase, debase, degrade, humiliate, mortify, shame, subdue, crush, break.

adj humble, low, lowly, unassuming, plain, common, poor, meek, modest, submissive, unpretentious; respectful, polite, courteous.

adv with downcast eyes, on bended knee.

880 vanity n pride, conceit, self-esteem, self-complacency, egotism, self-admiration, self-love, self-glorification; hollowness, emptiness, sham, triviality.

v be vain, have too high an opinion of oneself, inflate, puff up.

adj vain, conceited, egotistical, self-complacent, proud, vainglorious, arrogant, overweening, inflated; useless, hollow, trifling, trivial.

881 modesty *n* humility, diffidence, timidity, bashfulness; moderation, decency, propriety, simplicity, chastity, prudery, prudishness.

v be modest, retire, give way to, stay in the background.

adj modest, humble, diffident, timid, timorous, bashful, sheepish, shy; moderate, humble, unpretentious, decent, becoming, proper, inextravagant, unostentatious, retiring, unassuming, unobtrusive; demure, prudish, chaste, pure, virtuous.

adv modestly, humbly, quietly, privately, without ceremony.

882 ostentation *n* pretention, pretentiousness, semblance, show, showiness, pretense, display, pageantry, pomp, pompousness, flourish, splendor.

v show off, parade, display, exhibit, blazon forth, emblazon, flaunt.

adj ostentatious, pretentious, showy, flashy, grand, pompous, garish, gaudy, flaunting, high-sounding, sumptuous, theatrical, dramatic, solemn, majestic, ceremonious, punctilious, over-blown.

adv with a flourish.

883 celebration *n* ceremony, ceremonial, commemoration, solemnization, observance, memorialization, festival, festivity.

v celebrate, commemorate, observe, keep; proclaim, announce; praise, extol, laud, glorify, honor, applaud, commend; solemnize, ritualize.

adj celebrational, commemorative, honorific, commendatory; celebrated, famous, renowned, illustrious, eminent, famed.

adv in honor of, in commemoration of, in celebration of.

884 boasting *n* bragging, swaggering, braggadocio, bravado.

boaster, braggart, blusterer, (*informal*) windbag.

v exaggerate, brag, vaunt, swagger, crow, strut, talk big.

adj boasting, boastful, pretentious, vainglorious, elated, exultant, jubilant, triumphant.

885 [undue assumption of superiority] **insolence** *n* boldness, rudeness, disrespect, impertinence, impudence, haughtiness, arrogance, audacity, abusiveness, contemptuousness.

v be insolent, swagger, assume, presume, take liberties, ride roughshod over.

adj insolent, bold, rude, disrespectful, impertinent, impudent, brazen, brassy, haughty, arrogant, audacious, presumptuous, overbearing, abusive, contemptuous, insulting.

886 servility *n* submissiveness, obsequiousness, abasement, slavishness, cringing, fawning, meanness, baseness, groveling, sycophancy, slavery.

toady, sycophant, boot-licker, (*informal*) apple-polisher, (*informal*) brown-noser.

v be servile, cringe, bow, stoop, kneel, toady, fawn, lick the boots of; sneak, crawl, crouch, cower.

adj servile, obsequious, slavish, cringing, fawning, sycophantic, groveling, sniveling, mealy-mouthed, abject, base, mean.

887 blusterer *n* swaggerer, braggart, boaster, windbag, bully, ruffian, rowdy, redneck.

III. Sympathetic Affections

888 friendship *n* amity, friendliness, harmony, concord, fellow-feeling, sympathy, good will, affection; companionship, comradeship, fellowship, fraternity, intimacy.

v be friendly, have an acquaintance with, keep company with, know, sympathize with, befriend, make friends with.

adj friendly, kind, kindly, amiable, neighborly, brotherly, cordial, genial, well-disposed, benevolent, kind-hearted, affectionate; helpful, advantageous, propitious; acquainted, familiar, intimate.

adv amicably, with open arms.

889 enmity *n* unfriendliness, dislike, discord, ill will, antagonism, animosity, hostility, malevolence, hatred.

v be at odds with.

adj inimical, unfriendly, alienated, estranged, hostile.

890 friend *n* companion, acquaintance, crony, chum, pal, mate, fellow, bosom buddy, intimate, confidant; well-wisher, patron, supporter, backer, advocate, partisan, defender, sympathizer; ally, associate.

891 enemy *n* foe, adversary, opponent, antagonist, attacker.

892 sociality *n* sociableness, gregariousness, social interaction, social intercourse, comradeship, camaraderie, companionship, cordiality, good fellowship, conviviality.

v be sociable, consort with, fraternize, welcome.

adj sociable, gregarious, social, warm, genial, cordial, friendly, convivial, amicable, clubbish, chummy, neighborly, hospitable.

893 seclusion. exclusion *n* privacy, retirement, withdrawal, solitude, sequestration, retreat, isolation, hiding, secrecy. elimination, prohibition, exception, omission, preclusion, rejection, ejection, expulsion, banishment, ostracism, exile.

recluse, hermit, cenobite, outcast, castaway, pariah, wastrel, foundling.

v seclude oneself, retire, withdraw, retreat, sequester, isolate, hide, exclude, eliminate, prohibit, reject, eject, expel.

adj secluded, retired, withdrawn, sequestered, private, isolated, solitary, excluded, eliminated, prohibited, omitted, precluded, rejected, ejected, repulsed, banished, ostracized, exiled.

894 courtesy *n* civility, sociability, politeness, good manners, good behavior, affability, gentility, graciousness, courtliness, respect.

v be courteous, behave well.

adj courteous, civil, polite, well-mannered, well-bred, gentlemanly, gallant, urbane, debonair, affable, gracious, courtly, respectful, obliging.

895 discourtesy *n* disrespect, ill-breeding, bad manners, tactlessness, rudeness, impudence, vulgarity.

v be discourteous.

adj discourteous, ill-bred, ill-mannered, ill-behaved, ungentlemanly, uncivil, impolite, ungracious, vulgar, crude, disrespectful, rude.

896 congratulations *n* felicitation, compliment, salute, salutation.

v congratulate, offer congratulations, salute.

adj congratulatory; complimentary.

897 love *n* affection, liking, regard, friendliness, kindness, kindliness, tenderness, fondness, devotion, warmth, attachment, yearning, passion, rapture, adoration, idolatry.

lover, admirer, suitor, adorer, wooer; beau, sweetheart, flame, love, truelove, paramour, boyfriend, girlfriend, ladylove, idol, darling, angel, beloved.

v love, like, be fond of, have affection for, be enamored of, be in love with, cherish, adore, revere, adulate, idolize.

adj loving, smitten, affectionate, tender, fond,

attached, enamored, devoted, amorous, passionate, adoring; lovable, adorable, winning, enchanting, bewitching.

898 hate n dislike, aversion, animosity, hatred, antipathy, detestation, loathing, abhorrence, odium, horror, repugnance.

v hate, dislike, detest, abhor, loathe, despise, execrate, abominate.

adj hateful, detestable, odious, abominable, loathsome, abhorrent, repugnant, invidious, obnoxious, offensive, disgusting, nauseating, revolting, vile, repulsive; hating, averse from, set against, bitter, spiteful, malicious.

899 favorite n pet, minion, idol, jewel, spoiled child, apple of one's eye, man after one's own heart; love, dear, darling, honey, sweetheart.

900 resentment n displeasure, pique, umbrage, animosity, bitterness, envy, jealousy, anger, wrath, indignation.

v resent, take offense, bristle over, chafe, fume, frown, pout, snarl, gnash, growl, scowl, glower, grouch, bear a grudge.

adj resentful, offended, bitter, worked up, angry, wrathful, irate, indignant; envious, jealous.

901 irascibility n irritability, excitability, sensitivity.

v be irascible, quick to fly off the handle, have a temper.

adj irascible, testy, short-tempered, hot-tempered, quick-tempered, touchy, temperamental, irritable, snappish, petulant, overly sensitive, choleric.

901a sullenness n moodiness, moroseness, churlishness, sluggishness.

v be sullen, frown, scowl, sulk, pout.

adj silent, reserved, sulky, morose, moody, ill-humored, sour, vexatious, bad-tempered, surly, cross, grumpy, peevish, perverse; gloomy, dismal, cheerless, overcast, somber, mournful, dark; slow, sluggish, dull, stagnant.

902 [expression of affection or love] **endearment** n embrace, caress, hug, kiss, blandishment, dalliance, love token.

v endear, embrace, caress, blandish, flirt, dally.

adj endearing.

903 marriage n wedding, nuptials, matrimony, wedlock; union, alliance, association, confederation.

married man, married woman, husband, wife, spouse, mate, partner, consort, better half, (informal) old man, (informal) old lady.

v marry, tie the knot, take to the altar, wive, couple.

adj married, wed, united.

904 celibacy n sexual abstinence; bachelorhood.

celibate, unmarried man, bachelor, unmarried woman, spinster, old maid, virgin, maiden; priest.

adj celibate, unmarried.

905 divorce n marital separation, legal separation; separation, disunion, isolation.

v divorce, (informal) split up, separate, isolate.

adj divorced, separated, (informal) split up.

906 benevolence n kindness, kindliness, humanity, tenderness, kindheartedness, unselfishness, generosity, liberality, charity, philanthropy, altruism.

good Samaritan, sympathizer, altruist.

v wish well, take an interest in, treat well, comfort, benefit, assist, aid.

adj benevolent, kind, kindly, well-disposed, kind-hearted, humane, tender, tender-hearted, unselfish, generous, liberal, obliging, charitable, philanthropic, altruistic.

907 malevolence n ill will, enmity, rancor, resentment, malice, maliciousness, spite, spitefulness, grudge, hate, hatred, venom.

v bear ill will.

adj malevolent, malicious, resentful, spiteful, begrudging, hateful, venomous, vicious, hostile, ill-natured, evil-minded, rancorous.

908 malediction n curse, swear, imprecation, denunciation, cursing, damning, damnation, execration; slander.

v curse, swear, imprecate, denounce, damn, execrate; slander.

909 threat n menace, danger, indication, portent, foreboding, prognostication; intimidation.

v threaten, menace, endanger, indicate, presage, impend, portend, augur, forebode, foreshadow, prognosticate; frighten, denounce, intimidate, cow, badger.

adj threatening, menacing, endangering, impending, auguring, foreshadowing, foreboding, ominous, inauspicious, sinister, frightening, intimidating.

910 philanthropy n humaneness, compassion, humanitarianism, benevolence, helpfulness, munificence, public spirit, charity.

philanthropist, humanitarian, patriot.

adj philanthropic, humanitarian, benevolent, munificent, altruistic, public spirited, civic minded, charitable.

911 misanthropy n hatred of mankind, incivism.

misanthrope, man-hater; misogynist, woman-hater.

adj misanthropic, antisocial, uncivil.

912 benefactor n succorer, patron, supporter, contributor, friend.

913 evildoer n wrongdoer, troublemaker, subversive, oppressor, destroyer.

914 pity n sympathy, compassion, commiseration, condolence, mercy.

v pity, commiserate, feel sorry for, be sorry for, sympathize with, feel for.

adj pitying, compassionate, sympathetic, touched, moved, affected, feeling.

914a pitilessness n cruelty, meanness, ruthlessness, hardheartedness.

v have no pity for.

adj pitiless, merciless, cruel, mean, unmerciful, ruthless, implacable, relentless, inexorable, hard-hearted, stony.

915 condolence n lamentation, sympathy, consolation.

v condole with, console, sympathize, lament.

916 gratitude n thanks, thankfulness, appreciation, indebtedness.

v be grateful, thank, appreciate.

adj grateful, appreciative, thankful, obliged, beholding, indebted, in one's debt.

917 ingratitude n thanklessness, unthankfulness.

ingrate.

v be ungrateful.

adj ungrateful, unthankful, unmindful, thankless.

918 forgiveness n pardon, excuse, indulgence, remission, reprieve, amnesty, grace, absolution.

v forgive, pardon, excuse, absolve, reprieve, acquit.

adj forgiving.

919 revenge n vengeance, retaliation, requital, reprisal, retribution, vindictiveness, vengefulness.

avenger, vindicator, nemesis.

v revenge, avenge, retaliate, requite, vindicate.

adj revengeful, vengeful, vindictive, spiteful, malevolent, resentful, malicious, malignant, unforgiving, implacable.

920 jealousy *n* envy, resentment; suspicion; watchfulness, vigilance.

v be jealous.

adj jealous, envious, resentful; suspicious; solicitous, watchful, vigilant.

921 envy *n* jealousy, enviousness, grudge, covetousness.

v envy, covet, begrudge, resent.

adj envious, covetous, jealous, begrudging.

IV. Moral Affections

922 right *n* virtue, justice, fairness, integrity, equity, equitableness, uprightness, rectitude, morality, morals, goodness, honor, lawfulness; accuracy, truth.

v be right; do right.

adj right, just, good, equitable, moral, fair, upright, honest, lawful; correct, proper, suitable, fit; correct, true, accurate; genuine, legitimate, rightful.

adv righteously, rightfully, lawfully, rightly, justly, fairly, equitably.

923 wrong *n* evil, wickedness, misdeed, sin, vice, immorality, iniquity, inequity, injustice, unlawfulness.

v wrong, injure, harm, maltreat, abuse, oppress, cheat, defraud, dishonor.

adj wrong, bad, evil, wicked, sinful, immoral, iniquitous, reprehensible, unjust, crooked, dishonest; erroneous, inaccurate, incorrect, false, untrue, mistaken; improper, unappropriate, unfit; awry, amiss, out of order.

adv wrongly, wickedly, sinfully.

924 claim *n* due, right, privilege, prerogative, prescription, demand, sanction, warrant, license.

claimant, appellant.

v claim, deserve, have the right, be entitled.

adj claiming, having a right to, privileged, prescribed, sanctioned, allowed, licensed, authorized, due.

925 [absence of right] **unrightfulness** *n* impropriety, illegitimacy, presumption.

usurper, pretender.

v be unentitled.

adj unrightful, having no right to, unentitled, unauthorized, unwarranted, illegitimate, not licensed.

926 duty *n* obligation, function, responsibility, onus, burden, business; conscience, moral imperative, sense of duty; homage, respect, reverence.

v do one's duty, behoove, become, befit, beseem; observe, perform, fulfill, discharge.

adj obligatory, binding, imperative, incumbent, under obligation, obliged, bound, tied, duty bound; dutiful, respectful, docile, submissive, deferential, reverential, obedient.

927 dereliction of duty *n* nonobservance, nonperformance, neglect, failure, carelessness, fault, infraction, violation, transgression.

v neglect, slight, fail, violate.

adj undutiful, negligent, careless, at fault, failing, in violation.

927a exemption *n* immunity, impunity, privilege, freedom, exception, excuse, dispensation.

v exempt, excuse, release, acquit, discharge, free.

adj exempt, immune, privileged, freed, excepted, excused, unbound.

928 respect *n* esteem, deference, regard, consideration, estimation, veneration, reverence, homage, honor, admiration, approbation, approval, affection, feeling; respects, regards, duty; regard, consideration, attention, devotion.

v honor, revere, reverence, esteem, venerate, regard, consider, defer to, admire, adulate, adore, love; regard, heed, attend, notice, consider.

adj respectful, courteous, polite, well-mannered, well-bred, civil, deferential; respected, estimable, venerable, admirable; respecting, heeding, considering, regarding, attending.

929 disrespect *n* discourtesy, impoliteness, rudeness, crudeness, incivility, impudence, impertinence, irreverence, derision.

v hold in disrespect, be disrespectful, insult, deride, scoff, mock, sneer, jeer, ridicule, scorn.

adj disrespectful, discourteous, impolite, rude, crude, uncivil, impudent, impertinent, irreverent, insulting, derisive, scornful.

930 contempt *n* scorn, disdain, derision, contumely; dishonor, disgrace, shame.

v feel contempt for, contemn, scorn, disdain, deride, despise.

adj contemptible, despicable, mean, low, miserable, abject, base, vile; contemptuous, scornful, disdainful, derisive; dishonorable, disgraceful, shameful.

931 approbation *n* approval, sanction, esteem, admiration, commendation.

v approbate, approve, esteem, value, honor, admire, appreciate, sanction, endorse, commend, praise.

adj commendatory, complimentary, laudatory; approved, praised, in high esteem, in favor; praiseworthy, commendable, good, meritorious, estimable, creditable.

932 disapprobation *n* disapproval, dislike, disesteem, odium, disparagement, deprecation, denunciation, censure.

v disapprove, dislike, object to, frown upon, censure, blame, reproach, reprove, admonish, berate.

adj disapproving, disparaging, reproachful, defamatory, denunciatory, condemnatory.

933 flattery *n* adulation, charming, lip-service, (*informal*) brown-nosing, fawning, flunkeyism, sycophancy.

v flatter, curry favor, slobber over, (*informal*) lay it on thick, wheedle, fawn, court, (*informal*) brown-nose, pander to, overpraise.

adj flattering, adulatory, honey-mouthed, smooth-tongued, servile, sycophantic.

934 detraction *n* detracting, disparagement, belittling, defamation, vilification, calumny, abuse, slander, aspersion, deprecation.

v detract, run down, criticize, decry, disparage, blacken, belittle, depreciate, cast aspersions, defame, malign, abuse, slander, vilify.

adj detracting, disparaging, belittling, derogatory, depreciating, calumnious, abusive, slanderous, vilifying, scurrilous.

935 flatterer *n* adulator, toady, flunkey, (*informal*) apple-polisher, fawner, sycophant, (*informal*) brown-noser, bootlicker, opportunist, courtier.

936 detractor *n* reprover, critic, carper, slanderer, (*informal*) hatchet man, backbiter, defamer, castigator, satirist, cynic, reviler.

937 vindication *n* exoneration, exculpation, acquittal; justification, warrant, support, defense.

apologist, vindicator, defender.

v vindicate, exonerate, acquit, clear; uphold, justify, maintain, defend, support.

adj vindicating, vindicated, exonerated, exonerating, exculpatory, acquitted; justified, warranted, supported.

938 accusation *n* arraignment, indictment, charge,

incrimination, impeachment; accusal, blaming, inculpation, charging, imputation.

accuser, prosecutor, plaintiff; relator, informer; appellant.

v charge; arraign, indict, charge, incriminate, impeach; blame, inculpate, charge, involve, point to, impute.

adj accused, accusing, accusatory, accusative, incriminatory, imputative.

939 probity *n* honesty, uprightness, virtue, rectitude, integrity.

v be honorable.

adj honest, honorable, virtuous, upright, scrupulous, high-principled.

940 improbity *n* dishonesty, wickedness, immorality, evil.

v be dishonest, play false.

adj dishonest, dishonorable, unscrupulous, immoral, wicked, evil.

941 knave *n* rogue, rascal, blackguard, sneak, villain, scoundrel.

942 disinterestedness *n* impartiality, fairness, lack of bias, unselfishness, generosity, liberality.

v be disinterested.

adj disinterested, unbiased, unprejudiced, unselfish, impartial, fair, generous, liberal.

943 selfishness *n* self-interest, self-seeking, self-love, egoism, egotism, solipsism, illiberality, parsimony, stinginess, meanness.

v be selfish, cultivate one's own garden, look after oneself, feather one's own nest.

adj selfish, self-centered, self-indulgent, self-interested, self-seeking, egotistical, solipsistic, illiberal, parsimonious, stingy, cheap, mean.

944 virtue *n* virtuousness, goodness, uprightness, morality, ethics, probity, rectitude, integrity; excellence, merit, quality, asset; innocence, chastity, purity.

v be virtuous, have the virtue of.

adj virtuous, right, upright, moral, righteous, good, chaste, pure.

945 vice *n* fault, sin, depravity, iniquity, immorality, wickedness; blemish, blot, imperfection, defect.

v sin, err, transgress, trespass.

adj vicious, immoral, depraved, profligate, wicked, sinful, sinning, corrupt, bad, iniquitous; reprehensible, blameworthy, censurable, wrong, improper; spiteful, malignant, malicious, malevolent; faulty, defective; ill-tempered, bad-tempered, refractory.

946 innocence *n* purity, virtue, virtuousness, faultlessness, spotlessness; guiltlessness, blamelessness; uprightness, honesty; naiveté, simplicity, artlessness, guilelessness, ingenuousness.

v be innocent.

adj innocent, pure, untainted, sinless, virtuous, virginal, blameless, faultless, impeccable, spotless, immaculate; guiltless, blameless; upright, honest, forthright; naive, simple, unsophisticated, artless, guileless, ingenuous.

947 guilt *n* guiltiness, culpability, criminality; sinfulness.

v be guilty.

adj guilty, culpable, to blame, in fault.

948 good man *n* model, paragon, hero, soldier, saint, salt of the earth, (*informal*) ace.

949 bad man *n* wrongdoer, evildoer, sinner, scoundrel, miscreant, villain, wretch, monster, devil, demon, scum of the earth.

950 penitence *n* contrition, atonement, compunction, repentance, remorse, regret.

penitent, prodigal son.

v be penitent, repent, rue, regret.

adj penitent, sorry, contrite, repenting; repentant, atoning, amending, remorseful, regretful; penitential.

951 impenitence *n* irrepentance, obduracy, hardness of heart.

v be impenitent, show no remorse.

adj impenitent, uncontrite, not sorry, obdurate, unrepentant, remorseless; unrepenting, unrepented, unatoned; irreclaimable.

952 atonement *n* satisfaction, reparation, compensation, amends, quittance; redemption, expiation, reclamation, conciliation, propitiation.

v atone, atone for; give satisfaction, satisfy, make amends; expiate, propitiate, reclaim, redeem, repair, absolve, purge, shrive, do penance, repent.

adj atoning, propitiating, propitiatory, redemptive, expiating, expiatory.

953 temperance *n* moderation, self-restraint, self-control, continence; sobriety, even-temperedness, calmness, coolness, detachment, dispassion.

vegetarian; teetotaler; abstainer.

v be temperate, abstain, forbear, restrain.

adj temperate, moderate, self-controlled, self-restrained, frugal, sparing; sober, calm, cool, detached, dispassionate.

954 intemperance *n* excess, exorbitance, inordinateness, extravagance; indulgence, high living, self-indulgence, epicurism, epicureanism, sybaritism; inabstinence, alcoholism.

v be intemperate, indulge, wallow in.

adj intemperate, excessive, exorbitant, inordinate, extravagant; indulgent, self-indulgent, epicurean.

954a sensualist *n* sybarite, voluptuary, pleasure-seeker, epicure, epicurean, libertine, hedonist.

955 asceticism *n* puritanism, austerity, abstemiousness, self-abnegation, self-denial, total abstinence, self-mortification.

ascetic, anchorite, puritan, martyr; hermit, recluse.

v abstain, deny oneself, fast, starve.

adj ascetic, puritanical, austere, abstemious, rigorous, rigid, stern, severe, harsh, strict, self-denying, self-mortifying.

956 fasting *n* day of fasting; going hungry, starving oneself, starvation.

v fast, starve, famish.

adj fasting, starving, unfed; starved, half-starved, hungry.

957 gluttony *n* greed, greediness, voracity; epicurism, gormandizing, gulosity, crapulence, over-eating, (*informal*) piggishness.

glutton, epicure, cormorant, hog, (*informal*) pig.

v be gluttonous, hog; overeat, gorge, stuff oneself, make a pig of oneself, guzzle, bolt, devour, engorge, gobble up.

adj gluttonous, greedy, voracious; epicurean, gormandizing, crapulent, swinish, (*informal*) piggish.

958 sobriety *n* abstinence, teetotalism.

teetotaler, abstainer.

v be sober, abstain, take the pledge.

adj sober, unintoxicated, on the wagon, (*informal*) straight, (*informal*) dry, dry as a bone.

959 drunkenness *n* intemperance, drinking, inebriety, insobriety, intoxication, alcoholism.

drunkard, sot, tippler, drinker, inebriate, dipsomaniac, alcoholic, (*informal*) boozer, (*informal*) lush, (*informal*) juicer.

v be drunk, drink, imbibe, booze, guzzle, swill, soak, sot, lush, drink like a fish, hit the bottle.

adj drunk, drunken, sotted, intoxicated, inebriated, tipsy, tight, (*informal*) potted, (*informal*) stewed, (*informal*) stewed to the gills, dead drunk, (*informal*) plowed, (*informal*) plastered, (*informal*) tanked, (*informal*) wasted, (*informal*) juiced, (*informal*) blown away, (*informal*) high, (*informal*) flying, (*informal*) feeling no pain.

960 purity *n* cleanness; decency, decorum, delicacy; continence, chastity, innocence, modesty, virtue, virginity; simplicity, genuineness, faultlessness, perfection; guiltlessness, honesty, uprightness.

virgin, vestal virgin.

v be pure.

adj pure, decent, delicate; innocent, continent, chaste, virginal, modest, virtuous, undefiled, unsullied, unstained, untainted, uncorrupted, clean, spotless, immaculate; simple, genuine, faultless, perfect; honest, upright; unmixed, unadulterated, uncontaminated.

961 impurity *n* indecency, indelicacy; incontinence, immodesty, lewdness, concupiscence, prurience, lechery; grossness, obscenity, ribaldry, smut, bawdry; uncleanness, adulteration, contamination, defilement; fault, flaw, imperfection; guilt, sin, sinfulness.

v be impure.

adj impure, indecent, indelicate; incontinent, immodest, unchaste, concupiscent, lewd, prurient, lecherous; gross, obscene, ribald, dirty, smutty, bawdy; unclean, sullied, defiled, contaminated, adulterated, tainted, stained, corrupted, jaded; faulty, flawed, imperfect; guilty, sinning, sinful, wicked.

962 libertine *n* rake, *roué*, debauchee, lecher, sensualist, voluptuary, profligate, seducer, deceiver, courtesan, prostitute, strumpet, harlot, whore, street-walker, trollop, hussy, bitch, slut, minx.

963 legality *n* legitimacy, legitimateness, lawfulness; duty, obligation.

law, code, constitution, charter, statute, regulation, decree, order.

v legalize; legislate, enact, ordain, decree, codify, formulate, pass a law.

adj legal, legitimate, authorized, licit, lawful, legalized, legislated; constitutional.

964 illegality *n* illegitimacy, unlawfulness, illicitness, lawlessness.

v be illegal, offend against the law, violate the law.

adj illegal, unlawful, illegitimate, illicit, contraband, unconstitutional, unchartered, unwarranted, unauthorized, unlicensed, proscribed, prohibited, outlawed, criminal; lawless, arbitrary, despotic, unanswerable, unaccountable.

965 [executive] **jurisdiction** *n* judicature, authority, power, right, control; territory, range, magistracy.

v judge, sit in judgment; administer.

adj jurisdictive, judicial, administrative; inquisitorial.

966 tribunal *n* court, courtroom, board, bench, court of law, court of justice, bar of justice, judgment seat, dock, forum, witness-chair.

967 judge *n* justice, judiciary, magistrate, judicator, adjudicator, jurist, juror; moderator, arbiter, arbitrator, umpire, referee.

v judge, adjudge, determine, hear a cause, try a case, pass sentence.

adj judicial, judicious, juridical, legal, juristic, judicatory, jurisdictive.

968 lawyer *n* attorney, attorney-at-law, counselor, barrister, solicitor, pleader, counsel, advocate, counselor-at-law, legal adviser; prosecutor, prosecuting attorney, district attorney, public prosecutor, attorney general.

bar, legal profession.

v practice law, be called to the bar, plead, read the law.

adj learned in the law.

969 lawsuit *n* suit, action, cause, dispute, contention; case, debate, litigation, legal proceedings, legal action, legal process, trial, debate, pleadings, argument, argumentation, disputation, prosecution; writ, summons, subpoena, affidavit.

suitor, party to a suit, litigant, verdict, decision; precedent.

v go to the law, sue, file a claim, bring to trial, put on trial, serve, serve with a writ, cite, arraign, prosecute, bring an action against, indict, impeach, attach, summon.

adj litigious.

970 acquittal *n* clearance, exculpation, exoneration, absolution, discharge, pardon; impunity, immunity.

v acquit, exculpate, exonerate, clear, absolve, pardon; discharge, release, liberate, set free.

adj acquitted, cleared, exculpated, exonerated; discharged, released, set free.

971 condemnation *n* conviction, guilty verdict, proscription.

v condemn, convict, find guilty, damn, doom, proscribe; stand condemned.

adj condemned, condemnatory, convicted.

972 punishment *n* sentence, judgment, penalty, retribution, discipline, chastisement, castigation, reproof, correction.

v punish, inflict punishment, correct, discipline, penalize, reprove, castigate, chasten, administer correction, scold, berate, jail, incarcerate, execute, torture, banish, flog, whip, lash, scourge.

adj punishing, punitive, castigatory, penalized, penalizing; punished, castigated.

973 reward *n* recompense, prize, desert, compensation, pay, remuneration, requital, merit; bounty, premium, bonus; reparation, redress; retribution, reckoning, amends.

v reward, recompense, requite, compensate, pay, remunerate.

adj rewarding, remunerative, compensatory, retributive, reparatory; rewarded.

974 penalty *n* punishment, retribution, pain, pains, penance; fine, forfeit, damages, sequestration, incarceration, confiscation.

v penalize, punish; fine, confiscate, sequester; penalized, punished.

975 scourge *n* punishment, flogging; affliction, calamity, plague, bane, pest, nuisance; whip, lash, strap, thong, rod, cane, stick; prison, house of correction.

gaoler, jailer, executioner, hangman.

V. Religious Affections

976 deity *n* divinity, god, godhead, omnipotence, providence, lord, the almighty, supreme being, first cause, prime mover, author, creator, the infinite, the eternal, the all-powerful, the all-merciful, omnipresence.

adj divine, godly, almighty, holy, hallowed, sacred, heavenly, celestial, sacrosanct; superhuman, supernatural, spiritual, ghostly, unearthly.

977 angel *n* glorified spirit, beneficent spirit, ministering spirit, heavenly spirit, winged being, seraph, cherub, archangel, helper, spirit, guardian; (*informal*) friend, patron, protector, guardian angel, love.

adj angelic, seraphic, cherubic, spiritual, ethereal; pure, good, righteous, ideal, beautiful; (*informal*) adorable, entrancing, transporting, rapturous, lovely, enrapturing.

978 devil *n* Satan, Lucifer, Beelzebub; tempter, evil one, evil spirit, serpent, prince of darkness, demon, evil incarnate.

diabolism, satanism.

adj devilish, satanic, diabolic, infernal, hellish.

979 fabulous spirit *n* god, goddess, fairy, fay, sylph, faun, nymph, nereid, dryad, sea-maid, oread, naiad, mermaid, kelpie, nixie, sprite, pixie, elf.

adj fabulous, mythological, imaginary, sylphic.

980 demon *n* demonology; devil, fiend, evil spirit, incubus, monster, succubus, succuba, fury, harpy, ghoul, vampire, ogre, gnome, imp, kobold, dwarf, urchin, troll, sprite, bad fairy, leprechaun; ghost, specter, apparition, spirit, shade, shadow, vision, hobgoblin, wraith, spook, banshee, siren, satyr.

adj demonic, supernatural, weird, uncanny, unearthly, spectral, ghostly, ghostlike, elfin, fiendish, impish, haunted.

981 heaven *n* kingdom of heaven, kingdom of God, heavenly kingdom, paradise, nirvana; celestial bliss, glory.

adj heavenly, celestial, supernal, unearthly, paradisaic, paradisical, beatific, elysian, blissful, beautiful, divine, blessed, beatified, glorified.

982 hell *n* Gehenna, inferno, Hades, Erebus, pandemonium, abyss, limbo; *(informal)* torment, torture, pain, agony, suffering.

adj hellish, infernal, stygian, satanic, diabolic, devilish; *(informal)* painful, agonizing, excruciating, horrifying, unendurable.

983 theology *n* theosophy, divinity, hagiography, theologics, theism, monotheism, religion, religious persuasion, dogma, creed, credo, doctrine, tenet, articles of faith.

theologian, theologue, divine.

adj theological, religious, theosophical, hagiological.

983a orthodoxy *n* soundness; strictness, faithfulness, adherence, observance; truth, true faith, religious truth.

adj orthodox, sound, strict, faithful, catholic, doctrinal, authoritative, official, traditional; scriptural, divine, Christian; conventional, established, approved, prescriptive, prevailing, customary.

984 heterodoxy *n* unorthodoxy, nonconformity, iconoclasm, doubt, skepticism, recusancy, dissent, misbelief, error, heresy, schism, apostasy.

pagan, heathen, dissenter, nonconformist, skeptic, heretic, atheist.

adj heterodox, nonconformist, nonconforming, iconoclastic, doubting, skeptical, unscriptural, unorthodox, uncanonical, recusant, dissenting, misbelieving, heretical, schismatic.

985 revelation *n* disclosure, discovery, declaration, expression, utterance, publication, admission, confession, acknowledgment; enlightenment, proclamation, announcement; Christian Revelation, Scriptures, Word of God.

adj revelatory; instructive; confessional.

986 religious writings *n* Scriptures, *Bible*, Old Testament, New Testament, The Vedas, Upanishads, Bhagavad Gita, Koran, Alcoran, Avesta.

987 piety *n* godliness, devoutness, devotion, humility, veneration, sanctity, grace, holiness; reverence, regard, respect.

believer, devotee, pietist, righteous man.

v be pious, have faith; believe, revere, venerate, sanctify, consecrate.

adj pious, devout, godly, reverent, religious, holy, sacred, pietistic, saintly; devoted, humble, reverential.

988 impiety *n* irreverence, irreligion, scoffing, profaneness, profanity, blasphemy, desecration, sacrilege, sin, sinfulness; hypocrisy, cant, sanctimony, sanctimoniousness.

sinner, scoffer, blasphemer, sacrilegist, hypocrite.

v be impious, scoff, swear, profane, blaspheme, desecrate, revile, commit sacrilege.

989 irreligion *n* ungodliness, laxity, impiety, indifference, apathy, skepticism, doubt, disbelief, incredulity, agnosticism, freethinking, atheism, infidelity.

skeptic, doubter, nonbeliever, agnostic, cynic, freethinker, atheist, infidel, heathen.

v be irreligious, doubt, disbelieve, lack faith, question.

adj irreligious, godless, ungodly, unholy, unhallowed, undevout; skeptical, doubting, unbelieving, indifferent, apathetic, incredulous, freethinking, agnostic, atheistic, faithless; worldly, earthly, unspiritual.

990 worship *n* reverence, homage, adoration, honor; regard, idolizing, idolatry, deification; prayer, supplication, petition; service, celebration, rites.

worshiper, congregation, suppliant, communicant, celebrant.

v worship, adore, adulate, idolize, deify, love, like; pray, kneel, bow, fall on one's knees; invoke, supplicate, offer prayers, petition; praise, bless, laud, glorify, magnify, sing praises.

adj worshiping, revering, adoring, honoring; worshipful, reverential, honorific, celebrational.

991 idolatry *n* idolism, idolatrousness, idolization, fetishism, idol-worship, deification, demonology; blind adoration, extravagant love, fervor, ardency, enchantment, hero worship.

idol, image, icon, symbol, statue, false god, pagan deity.

v idolize, worship idols, idolatrize, worship, glorify, put on a pedestal, canonize, deify, apotheosize; dote upon, treasure, prize.

adj idolatrous, idol-worshiping, pagan, fetishistic; adoring, impassioned, lovesick.

992 sorcery *n* occultism, magic, witchery, enchantment, witchcraft, spell, necromancy, divination, charm, conjuration, bewitchery, spiritualism.

v practice sorcery, conjure, charm, enchant, bewitch, divine, entrance, mesmerize, cast a spell, call up spirits, raise spirits.

adj magic, magical, bewitching, enchanting, charming, incantory, weird, cabalistic, talismanic; charmed, bewitched, enchanted.

993 spell *n* charm, incantation, exorcism, voodoo, trance, rapture, suggestion, jinx, hocus-pocus, mumbo-jumbo, abracadabra.

994 sorcerer *n* magician, conjuror, necromancer, wizard, witch, exorcist, charmer, medicine man, shaman, medium, clairvoyant, mesmerist, soothsayer, guru.

995 churchdom *n* church, ministry, priesthood, sisterhood, prelacy, hierarchy.

v call, ordain, consecrate, bestow, elect.

adj ecclesiastical, clerical, priestly, pastoral, ministerial, hierarchical.

996 clergy *n* clerical, ministry, priesthood, the cloth, clergyman, divine, ecclesiastic, churchman, pastor, shepherd, minister, preacher, parson, father, reverend, priest, rabbi.

v receive the call, take orders.

adj clerical; ordained.

997 laity *n* fold, flock. congregation, assembly, brethren, people; layman, parishioner.

v secularize.

adj lay, laical, secular, civil, temporal.

998 rite *n* ceremony, observance, function, service, procedure, form, usage.

v perform a rite.

adj ritualistic, ceremonial.

999 canonicals *n* religious garments, vestments, robe, gown, surplice.

1000 temple *n* place of worship, house of God, cathedral, church, chapel, meetinghouse, synagogue, tabernacle, mosque, shrine, pantheon; monastery, priory, abbey, friary, convent, nunnery, cloister; parsonage, rectory, vicarage.

adj churchly, cloistered, monastic.

Index

animate v 382, 824, 836; adj 357
animated adj 171, 382, 515
animated nature n 357
animate matter n 357
animating adj 836
animation n 359, 515, 682, 824
animosity n 889, 898, 900
ankle-deep adj 209
annalist n 553
annal(s) n 114
annals n 551
annex n 39; v 37
annexation n 37, 43
annihilate v 2
annihilation n 2, 162
annotate v 522
annotator n 524
announce v 527, 531, 883
announcement n 527, 531,985
annoy v 688, 830
annoyance n 649, 828, 830,835
annul v 756
annulment n 756
anoint v 332
anointment n 332, 355
anomalous adj 59, 83
anomaly n 59, 83
anon adv 132
another adj 15
another time n 119
answer n 462
answer n 479, 522, 662; v 462, 746
answerable adj 177, 462
answerable for adj 806
answer for v 759
antagonism n 14, 24, 179, 708, 715, 867, 889
antagonist n 708, 710, 726, 891
antagonistic adj 14, 24, 179, 708, 715
antagonize v 14, 179
antecedence n 116
antecedence n 62
antecedent n 64, 116; adj 62, 116
antedate v 115, 116
antediluvian adj 124
antemeridian n 125
anterior adj 62, 116, 234

anteriority n 116
anthology n 596
anthracite n 388
anthropology n 368
anti adj 708
anticipate v 115, 121, 132, 451, 507, 510, 673, 858
anticipation n 121, 132, 451, 507, 510, 673, 858
anticipatory adj 132, 510
antidote n 662
antipathy n 14, 289, 867, 898
antipodal adj 237
antipodean adj 14
antipodes n 14
antiquarian n 553
antiquarianism n 124
antiquated adj 124
antique adj 124
antiquity n 122, 124
antisocial adj 911
antithesis n 14, 218, 237
antithetical adj 14, 237
antitoxin n 662
anxiety n 459, 860
anxious adj 860
any adj 25
apace adv 274
apart adj 44, 87; adv 44
apathetic adj 383, 456, 823, 866, 989
apathy n 823, 866, 989
ape v 19
aperture n 260
apex n 8, 67, 210
aphasia n 581, 583
aphorism n 496
aphoristic adj 496
apiece adv 79
aping n 19
apologist n 937
apostasy n 607, 984
apostate n 607
a posteriori n 476
apostrophe n 589
apostrophize v 589
apothegm n 496
apotheosize v 991
appal v 830
apparel n 225; v 225
apparent adj 446, 448, 525
apprently adv 448
apparition n 4, 443, 980
appeal n 411,765
appear v 446, 448, 525
appearance n 448

appearance n 220, 240, 446, 569
appease v 174, 723, 826, 831
appellant n 924, 938
appellation n 564
append v 37
appendage n 39, 65
appendix n 39
appertain to v 9, 56
appetite n 865
appetizing adj 394
applaud v 836, 883
apple adj 435
apple of one's eye n 899
apple-polisher n 886, 935
appliance n 677
applicability n 644
applicable adj 644, 677
applicant n 767
application n 677, 765
apply v 677
appoint v 741, 755, 786
appointment n 755
apportion v 44, 51, 60, 73, 786
apportionment n 786
apportionment n 60, 73
apposite adj 23
apposition n 23, 199
appraisal n 812
appraise v 466, 480, 668, 812
appraisement n 466
appreciate v 394, 480, 850, 916, 931
appreciation n 465, 822, 916
appreciative adj 822, 916
apprehend v 490, 860
apprehension n 453, 490, 665, 789, 860
apprehensive adj 860
apprentice n 541
apprenticeship n 539
apprize v 527
apprized of adj 527
approach n 286
approach n 197, 569, 627, 632; v 121, 152, 286
approaching adj 286
approbate v 931
approbation n 931
approbation n 488, 928

appropriate v 775, 786, 788, 789, 791; adj 79, 134, 646, 850
appropriateness; n 646
appropriating n 788
appropriation n 775, 789, 791
approval n 488, 762, 928, 931
approve v 535, 737, 931
approved adj 931, 983a
approximate v 17, 197; adj 17, 197, 286
approximation n 9, 17, 19, 286
apricot adj 439
a priori n 476
apt adj 23, 498, 698, 850
aptitude n 176, 498, 602, 698
aptness n 176, 698
aqua n 337
aquamarine adj 435, 438
aquatics n 267
aqueduct n 350
aqueous adj 337
arable adj 371
arbiter n 724, 737, 967
arbitrariness n 739
arbitrary adj 83, 606, 608, 739, 964
arbitrate v 174, 724
arbitration n 724
arbitrator n 724, 967
arc n 245
arcade n 245
arced adj 245
arch n 245, 250; v 245; adj 31
archaic adj 124
archaism n 124
archangel n 977
arched adj 245, 250
archetype n 22
archipelago n 346
architect n 164
architecture n 161, 329
arch over v 245
arctic adj 383
ardency n 991
ardent adj 382, 865
ardor n 382, 574, 682, 821
arduous adj 704
area n 181
arena n 728
arenose adj 330
areola n 247

argue v 24, 467, 476, 720
arguer n 476
argument n 454, 476, 516, 713, 720, 969
argumentation n 476, 969
argumentative adj 476, 713
arguments n 476
argumentum ad hominem n 476
aria n 413
arid adj 169, 340
aridity n 340
arise v 151, 305
aristocracy n 875
aristocratic adj 875
arithmetic n 85
arithmetical adj 85
arithmetic operations n 85
arm n 343; v 157, 673, 727
armaments n 727
armistice n 723
armlet n 247
armor n 727
arms n 727
army n 72
aroma n 400
aromatic adj 400
around adv 227
arouse v 175, 382, 615, 824
arraign v 938, 969
arraignment n 938
arrange v 58, 60, 626, 673, 774
arranged adj 60
arrange in a series v 69
arrange in words v 566
arrangement n 60
arrangement n 58, 673, 723, 769
arrangment n 807
array n 58, 102; v 60, 225
arrest v 142
arrival n 292
arrive v 151, 265, 292, 342
arrogance n 878, 885
arrogant adj 739, 878, 885, 880
artery n 350
artful adj 702
artfulness n 702
art gallery n 556
article n 3, 316, 590, 595
article of faith n 537
articles n 770, 798
articles of faith n 983

be affected with *v* 655

be afraid of *v* 860

be agitated *v* 315

beak *n* 250

be alive *v* 359

be all ears *v* 418

beam *n* 420; *v* 420

be an example *v* 22

bear *v* 215, 270, 692, 826

bearable *adj* 651

bear a grudge *v* 900

bear a resemblance *v* 17

bearer *n* 271

bear fruit *v* 161

bear ill will *v* 907

bearing *n* 9, 278, 692

bearings *n* 183

bear in mind *v* 451, 505

bear no resemblance *v* 18

bear off *v* 279

be artless *v* 703

bear upon *v* 9

bear with *v* 740, 760

beast *n* 366

beastly *adj* 653

beast of burden *n* 271

beasts of the field *n* 366

beat *n* 104, 138, 314, 627; *v* 138, 276, 314, 315, 330, 406, 407

beat a retreat *v* 623

beat back *v* 289

beatific *adj* 829, 981

beatified *adj* 981

beat it out *v* 623

be at odds with *v* 889

be at peace *v* 721

be attendant on *v* 281

be attentive *v* 457

be at the mercy of *v* 749

beat time *v* 114

beat up *v* 352

be at work on *v* 625

beau *n* 854, 897

beau monde *n* 852

beauteous *adj* 845

beautified *adj* 577, 847

beautiful *adj* 242, 597, 829, 845, 977, 981

beautify *v* 845, 847

beauty *n* 845

beauty *n* 242, 829

be averse to *v* 867

be aware of *v* 450, 490

be beforehand *v* 132

be behind *v* 235

be beneficial *v* 648

be blind *v* 442

be blind to *v* 491

be blunt *v* 254

bebop *n* 415

be born *v* 359

be bound for *v* 278

be brittle *v* 328

be broad *v* 202

be called to the bar *v* 968

becalm *v* 265

be capricious *v* 608

be careful *v* 459

because *adv* 153, 155

be cautious *v* 864

be central *v* 222

be certain *v* 474

be cheap *v* 815

be cheek to cheek *v* 236

becloud *v* 421, 422

be cold *v* 383

become *v* 144, 926

become a habit *v* 613

become colorless *v* 429

become insane *v* 503

become large *v* 192

become little *v* 193

become old *v* 124

become small *v* 195

becoming *adj* 646, 850, 881

be composed of *v* 54

be concise *v* 572

be contiguous *v* 199

be contrary *v* 14

be converted into *v* 144

be courteous *v* 894

be cowardly *v* 862

be credulous *v* 486

be cunning *v* 702

be curious *v* 455

be curved *v* 245

bed *n* 204

be dark *v* 421

bedazzle *v* 420

be deaf *v* 419

be deceived *v* 547

be degrees *adv* 26

be dejected *v* 837

be dense *v* 321

bedew *v* 339

be difficult *v* 704

be diffuse *v* 573

bedim *v* 422

be dimsighted *v* 443

be disappointed *v* 509

be discontented *v* 832

be discordant *v* 414, 713

be discourteous *v* 895

be dishonest *v* 940

be disinclined *v* 867

be disinterested *v* 942

be disrespectful *v* 929

be distant *v* 196

be distinguished *v* 873

bedlamite *n* 504

bed-ridden *adj* 655

be drunk *v* 959

bedtime *n* 126

be due to *v* 154

be dull *v* 843

be dumb *v* 581

be early *v* 132

be easy *v* 705

beehive *n* 691

be elastic *v* 325

bee line *n* 246

Beelzebub *n* 978

be enamored of *v* 897

be engaged in *v* 625

be entitled *v* 924

be equivocal *v* 520

be evasive *v* 528

be evident *v* 467

be expedient *v* 646

be expeditious *v* 134

be expensive *v* 814

be exterior *v* 220

be extraneous *v* 57

be faithful to *v* 772

befall *v* 151

be fashionable *v* 852

be fastidious *v* 868

be fated *v* 601

be fatigued *v* 688

be firm *v* 150

befit *v* 23, 646, 926

be fluid *v* 333

be fond of *v* 897

be foolish *v* 499

before *adj* 62; *adv* 62, 116, 234, 280

beforehand *adv* 116, 132

before long *adv* 132

before now *adv* 122

before one's eyes *adj* 446

be forgetful *v* 506

befoul *v* 653

be fragrant *v* 400

be free *v* 748

befriend *v* 888

be friendly *v* 888

beg *v* 765

be general *v* 78

beget *v* 161

beggar *n* 767

beggarly *adj* 643, 804

begin *v* 66, 676

begin at the beginning *v* 66

begin hostilities *v* 716

beginner *n* 541

beginning *n* 66

be gluttonous *v* 957

be gone *v* 449

be good *v* 648

be good for *v* 656

be grateful *v* 916

be great *v* 31

begrudge *v* 819, 921

begrudging *adj* 907, 921

beg the question *v* 277, 477

be guilty *v* 947

be habitual *v* 613

behalf *n* 618

be haphazard *v* 139

be hard on *v* 739

behave *v* 680, 692

behave well *v* 894

behavior *n* 680, 692

behead *v* 361

be healthy *v* 654

be heavy *v* 319

be held in high repute *v* 873

behemoth *n* 192

behest *n* 741

be hidden *v* 447

behind *adv* 63, 235, 281

behind closed doors *adv* 528

behind time *adv* 133

be hip *v* 490

behold *v* 441, 444

beholder *n* 444

beholding *adj* 916

be honorable *v* 939

behoove *v* 926

be horizontal *v* 213

be hot *v* 382

be identical *v* 13

beige *n* 433; *adj* 433

be ignorant *v* 491

be illegal *v* 964

be ill timed *v* 135

be imbecilic *v* 499

be impatient *v* 825

be impenitent *v* 951

be imperfect *v* 651

be impious *v* 988

be important *v* 642

be impossible *v* 471

be impotent *v* 158

be imprisoned *v* 754

be improbable *v* 473

be impure *v* 961

be inactive *v* 172, 265, 681, 683

be inarticulate *v* 583

be in a state *v* 7

be inattentive *v* 458

be incomplete *v* 53

be inconvenient *v* 647

be incredulous *v* 487

be in danger *v* 665

be indifferent *v* 866

be indiscriminate *v* 465a

be in error *v* 495

be inert *v* 172

be inexpedient *v* 647

be inferior *v* 34

be infinite *v* 104

be influential *v* 175

be infrequent *v* 137

be in front *v* 234

being *n* 1, 3, 359

be in health *v* 654

be inherent *v* 5

be in league with *v* 709

be in love with *v* 897

be innocent *v* 946

be inodorous *v* 399

be insane *v* 503

be insensible *v* 376

be insensitive *v* 823

be inside *v* 221

be insolent *v* 885

be instantaneous *v* 113

be instrumental *v* 631

be insufficient *v* 640

be intelligent *v* 498

be intelligible *v* 518

be intemperate *v* 954

be interior *v* 221

be intrinsic *v* 5

be in trouble *v* 619

be inverted *v* 218

be invisible *v* 447

be in want *v* 640

be irascible *v* 901

be irregular *v* 139

be irreligious *v* 989

be irresolute *v* 605

be jealous *v* 920

be large *v* 192

belate *v* 133

belated *adj* 133

be latent *v* 526

be lax *v* 738

belch out *v* 297

be left *v* 40

be left over *v* 40

be lenient *v* 740

be liable *v* 177

be liberal *v* 816

belief *n* 484

butter *n* 356
butter-fingers *n* 701
butt in *v* 135
buttocks *n* 235
button *n* 250; *v* 43
button up *v* 261
buttress *n* 215
buy *n* 795; *v* 795
buy and sell *v* 794
buyer *n* 795
buying *n* 795
buzz *v* 409, 412
buzzing *n* 409
by *adv* 631
by accident *adv* 156
by and by *adv* 132
by an indirect
  course *adv* 629
by chance *adv* 156
by design *adv* 620
by dint of *adv* 631;
  prep 157
by fits and starts
  adv 70, 139, 315
by force *adv* 159,
  173, 744
bygone *adj* 122
by installments *adv*
  51
by intuition *adv* 477
by means of *adv*
  170, 631, 632
by no means *adv* 32
by rule *adv* 82
bystander *n* 444
by storm *adv* 173
by the agency of
  adv 631
by the by *adv* 10,
  134
by the way *adv* 10,
  134
by turns *adv* 138
by virtue of *prep*
  157

C

cabal *n* 626
cabalistic *adj* 992
cabinet *n* 696
cackle *v* 412, 838
cacophonous *adj*
  410, 414
cadaver *n* 362
cadaverous *adj* 362
cadence *n* 402
caesura *n* 70, 198
cage *n* 752; *v* 370
calamitous *adj* 735,
  830
calamity *n* 619, 735,
  975
calcination *n* 384
calculable *adj* 85
calculate *v* 85, 611,
  620
calculation *n* 85,
  507

calculus *n* 85
calefaction *n* 384
calendar *n* 86, 114
caliber *n* 26
call *v* 564, 995
call attention to *v*
  550
call for *v* 630
calligraphy *n* 590
calling *n* 625
call it quits *v* 67, 624
callous *adj* 823
callousness *n* 823
callow *adj* 127
call to mind *v* 505
call up *v* 505
call up spirits *v* 992
calm *n* 174, 265,
  721; *v* 174, 723;
  adj 174, 265, 403,
  685, 721, 826, 953
calm down *v* 826
calmness *n* 174,
  265, 721, 826, 953
caloric *n* 382
caloricity *n* 382
calorimeter *n* 389
calumnious *adj* 934
calumny *n* 934
camaraderie *n* 892
camouflage *v* 528
camouflaging *n* 528
can *v* 670
canal *n* 350
cancel *v* 536, 552,
  756
cancelation *n* 552,
  756
cancel out *v* 179
cancer *n* 663
candid *adj* 246, 543,
  703
candidate *n* 726
candied *adj* 396
candle *n* 423
candor *n* 525, 543,
  703
candy *v* 396
cane *n* 975
canker *n* 663; *v* 659
cankerworm *n* 165
canny *adj* 498, 702
canon *n* 697
canonicals *n* 999
canonize *v* 991
canopy *n* 223
cant *n* 988; *adj* 563
canticle *n* 413
cap *n* 261, 263; *v* 33,
  206
capability *n* 157,
  175, 698, 705
capable *adj* 157, 698
capacious *adj* 180,
  192
capacity *n* 157, 159,
  180, 192, 498,
  625, 698
capacity for *n* 698

cape *n* 250
caper *n* 309; *v* 309
capillary *adj* 205
capital *n* 632, 800,
  803; *adj* 210, 642,
  648
capitulate *v* 725
capitulation *n* 725
caprice *n* 608
caprice *n* 615a
capricious *adj* 139,
  149, 475, 605,
  608, 615a
capriciously *adv*
  139, 615a
capriciousness *n*
  139, 149, 475
capsule *n* 273
captain *n* 269, 694
captious *adj* 608
captivate *v* 829
captive *n* 754
capture *n* 789; *v* 789
car *n* 272
caravan *n* 266
carbon *n* 21, 90, 388
carbonaceous *adj*
  388
carbonization *n* 384
carcass *n* 362
cardinal points *n*
  278
care *n* 459
care *n* 451, 457,
  817, 828, 830, 864
careen *v* 217
care for *v* 642, 664
careful *adj* 451, 457,
  459, 664, 817, 864
carefulness *n* 459
careless *adj* 460,
  575, 674, 738,
  863, 927
carelessness *n* 460,
  699, 773, 863, 927
caress *n* 902; *v* 902
careworn *adj* 828
cargo *n* 190, 798
caricature *n* 21,
  555; *v* 19, 555
caricaturist *n* 559
carious *adj* 653
carmine *adj* 434
carnage *n* 361
carpe diem v 134,
  682
carper *n* 936
carriage *n* 271, 272,
  448, 692
carrier *n* 271
carrion *n* 362
carry *v* 215, 270
carry on *v* 143, 680,
  692
carry on a conver-
  sation *v* 588
carry out *v* 772

carry weight *v* 175,
  642
cart *n* 272
cartoonist *n* 559
carve *v* 44, 240,
  557, 558, 786
carving *n* 557
cascade *n* 348
case *n* 7, 232, 476,
  567, 969; *v* 223
case in point *n* 82
cash *n* 800
cash box *n* 802
cashier *n* 801
cash register *n* 802
cast *n* 21, 75, 176,
  240, 428, 448,
  550, 557; *v* 73,
  240, 284, 557,
  626; *adj* 820
cast a shadow *v* 424
cast a spell *v* 992
cast aspersions *v*
  934
castaway *n* 893
cast down v 308
cast forth *v* 73
castigate *v* 972
castigated *adj* 972
castigation *n* 972
castigator *n* 936
castigatory *adj* 972
castles in the air *n*
  515
cast light on *v* 522
cast light upon *v*
  420
cast off *v* 297, 782;
  adj 782
cast over *v* 353
casualty *n* 619
casuist *n* 476
casuistry *n* 477
cataclysm *n* 162
cataclysmic *adj* 619
catacomb *n* 363
catafalque *n* 363
catalog *n* 86; *v* 60
catalyst *n* 153
cataract *n* 442, 443
catastrophe *n* 619,
  735
catastrophic *adj*
  619, 735
catch *n* 793; *v* 789
catch a bug *v* 655
catch a glimpse of *v*
  441
catch fire *v* 384
catch on *v* 518
catch one's breath *v*
  687
catch the lay of the
  land *v* 510
catch unawares *v*
  508
category *n* 75
cater *v* 637, 746
catering *n* 637

caterwaul *v* 412
cathartic *n* 652
cathedral *n* 1000
catholic *adj* 78,
  983a
catholicity *n* 78
cattle car *n* 272
caucus *n* 696
causal *adj* 153, 156
causality *n* 153
causation *n* 153, 170
cause *n* 153
cause *n* 66, 615,
  969; *v* 153, 161
caused by *adj* 154
cause sensation *v*
  375
cauterization *n* 384
cauterize *v* 384
caution *n* 864
caution *n* 459, 487,
  668, 695; *v* 668,
  695
cautionary *adj* 668
cautious *adj* 451,
  459, 487, 498,
  664, 864
cavalcade *n* 266
cave *n* 189, 221, 252
cave in *v* 304
cavern *n* 252
cavernous *adj* 252
cavil *v* 477
cavity *n* 252
caw *v* 412
cease *v* 142, 265,
  360, 732
ceaseless *adj* 112
ceaselessness *n* 112
cede *v* 624, 782
ceiling *n* 223
celebrant *n* 990
celebrate *v* 551, 883
celebrated *adj* 873,
  883
celebration *n* 883
celebration *n* 733,
  838, 990
celebrational *adj*
  883, 990
celerity *n* 274, 684
celestial *adj* 318,
  976, 981
celestial bliss *n* 981
celestial spaces *n*
  318
celibacy *n* 904
celibate *n* 904; *adj*
  904
cell *n* 189, 357, 752
cement *v* 46, 48,
  323
cemetery *n* 363
cenobite *n* 893
censurable *adj* 945
censure *n* 716, 932;
  v 716, 932
census *n* 85
centenary *n* 98

center *n* 29, 68, 74, 221, 222; *v* 290
center of gravity *n* 222
center on *v* 74
central *adj* 68, 222
centrality *n* 222
centralization *n* 48, 222
centralize *v* 48, 222
centrally *adv* 222
central part *n* 208
centrifugal *adj* 291
century *n* 98, 108
ceramics *n* 557
cerebral *adj* 450
ceremonial *n* 883; *adj* 240, 998
ceremonious *adj* 240, 882
ceremony *n* 240, 883, 998
certain *adj* 79, 246, 474, 484
certainly *adv* 474
certainty *n* 474
certainty *n* 484
certificate *n* 771
certitude *n* 474
cessation *n* 142
cessation *n* 261, 265, 360, 687, 725
chafe *v* 378, 384, 832, 900
chaff *n* 643; *v* 856
chain *n* 69; *v* 43
chain of thought *n* 476
chaise *n* 272
chalk *n* 342
chalky *adj* 430
challenge *v* 715
challenge comparison *v* 648
chamber *n* 696
chamber group *n* 416
chamber music *n* 415
chamber orchestra *n* 416
champaign *n* 344
championship *n* 707
chance *n* 156, 621
chance *n* 152, 470, 615a; *v* 151, 156, 621; *adj* 475
chance it *v* 621
chanciness *n* 475
chancy *adj* 156, 475
change *n* 140
change *n* 20a, 144, 147, 800; *v* 15, 20a, 140, 146, 147, 605, 783
changeable *adj* 140, 144, 149, 475, 605
changeableness *n* 149

changeableness *n* 111, 140, 475, 605
changed *adj* 15, 20a, 140
change direction *v* 279
changeful *adj* 607
change hands *v* 783
changelessness *n* 150
change of mind *n* 485
change one's mind *v* 607
changeover *n* 144
change sides *v* 607
changing hands *n* 783
channel *n* 260, 302, 350, 627; *v* 259
chaos *n* 59, 162, 241
chaotic *adj* 59, 241
chap *n* 373
chapel *n* 1000
chapter *n* 696
character *n* 5, 7, 561, 569, 820
characteristic *n* 79, 550, 569, 780; *adj* 5, 15, 79, 550, 569
characterization *n* 594
characterize *v* 564, 594
characterized *adj* 820
charcoal *n* 388, 431
charge *n* 630, 695, 697, 716, 741, 755, 812, 938; *v* 52, 190, 695, 716, 741, 755, 812, 938, 938, 938
charging *n* 938
charitable *adj* 707, 784, 816, 906, 910
charity *n* 707, 784, 816, 906, 910
charm *n* 829, 992, 993; *v* 288, 615, 829, 992
charmed *adj* 992
charmer *n* 994
charming *n* 933; *adj* 992
charnel house *n* 363
chart *n* 183, 527, 626
charter *n* 755, 963; *v* 760
chary *adj* 817, 864
chase *v* 622
chase away *v* 289
chasm *n* 208, 260
chaste *adj* 242, 576, 578, 849, 881, 944, 960
chasten *v* 972
chasteness *n* 849

chastisement *n* 972
chastity *n* 881, 944, 960
chat *n* 588; *v* 588
chattels *n* 780
chatter *n* 584; *v* 584
chatterbox *n* 584
chatterer *n* 584
chattering *adj* 584
chatty *adj* 584, 588
cheap *adj* 435, 643, 815, 819, 943
cheapness *n* 815
cheat *n* 545, 548, 792; *v* 545, 923
check *n* 179, 616, 666, 706, 751; *v* 179, 233, 275, 468, 706, 708, 751
checked *adj* 440
checker *v* 440
checkered *adj* 440
checklist *n* 86
cheek *n* 236
cheek by jowl *adv* 236
cheer *n* 827, 829; *v* 411, 689, 829, 834, 836, 840
cheerful *adj* 827, 829
cheerfully *adv* 836
cheerfulness *n* 836
cheerfulness *n* 827, 829
cheering *adj* 836, 858
cheerless *adj* 828, 901a
cheery *adj* 829, 836, 836
chemistry *n* 144
cherish *v* 897
cherry-colored *adj* 434
cherub *n* 129, 977
cherubic *adj* 977
chest *n* 802
chestnut *adj* 433
chew *v* 298
chewing *n* 298
chew the fat *v* 588
chiaroscuro *n* 429
chicanery *n* 477, 702
chick *n* 129
chicken *n* 862; *adj* 862
chicken-hearted *adj* 862
chief *n* 694, 745
chiefly *adv* 31
child *n* 129, 167
childbirth *n* 163
child genius *n* 872
childhood *n* 127
childish *adj* 129, 486, 499, 575

childlike *adj* 499, 703
children *n* 167
child's play *n* 705
chill *v* 383, 385, 616; *adj* 383
chilled *adj* 385
chilliness *n* 383
chilly *adj* 383
chime *n* 408; *v* 407, 413
chimera *n* 515
chimerical *adj* 515
chimney *n* 351
chink *n* 198; *v* 408
chip *n* 32; *v* 44, 195
chip off the old block *n* 17, 167
chipper *adj* 654
chirography *n* 590
chirp *v* 412
chirrup *v* 412
chisel *v* 240, 557, 558
chiseling *n* 558
chit *n* 588
chit-chat *n* 588; *v* 588
chock-full *adj* 52
chocolate *adj* 433
choice *n* 609
choice *n* 600; *adj* 648
choice of words *n* 569
choir *n* 416
choke *v* 261, 361, 641
choleric *adj* 901
chomp *v* 298
choose *v* 609
choosing *n* 609
choosy *adj* 465
chop *v* 44
choppy seas *n* 348
chop up *v* 201
choral *adj* 415, 416
choral music *n* 415
chorus *n* 411, 416
christen *v* 564
Christian *adj* 983a
Christian Revelation *n* 985
chromatic *adj* 428
chronicle *n* 114; *v* 114, 551
chronicler *n* 553
chronicles *n* 551
chronological *adj* 114
chronological error *n* 115
chronology *n* 114
chronometer *n* 114
chronometry *n* 114
chubby *adj* 194
chuck *v* 284, 412
chuckle *v* 838

chug *v* 298
chum *n* 890
chummy *adj* 892
church *n* 995, 1000
churchdom *n* 995
churchman *n* 996
churl *n* 819
churlish *adj* 819
churlishness *n* 901a
churn *v* 315, 352
cilia *n* 205
cinder *n* 388
cinerary *adj* 363
cinnamon *adj* 433
cipher *n* 84, 550, 561
circle *n* 181, 247, 712; *v* 227, 247, 311
circle around *v* 312, 629
circling *n* 311; *adj* 248
circuit *n* 629
circuit *n* 181, 230, 247, 279, 311; *v* 311
circuitous *adj* 279, 311, 629
circuitously *adv* 279
circular *n* 592; *adj* 245, 247, 249, 311
circularity *n* 247
circularity *n* 311
circular motion *n* 311
circulate *v* 531
circulation *n* 311, 312
circumference *n* 230
circumjacent *adj* 227
circumnavigate *v* 311
circumnavigation *n* 311
circumscribe *v* 76, 195, 221, 229, 232, 233, 751
circumscribed *adj* 229
circumscription *n* 229
circumscription *n* 751
circumspect *adj* 451, 459, 864
circumspectful *adj* 457
circumspection *n* 459, 864
circumstance *n* 8
circumstance *n* 151
circumstances *n* 7, 527
circumstantial *adj* 8
circumvention *n* 311

compress v 195, 201, 321, 572, 596
compressed adj 201
compressible adj 322
compression n 195, 572
comprise v 76
compromise n 774
compromise n 29, 30, 68, 628, 723; v 628, 774
compulsion n 744
compulsion n 601
compulsory adj 601, 744
compunction n 950
computable adj 85
computation n 85
compute v 85
comradeship n 888, 892
con n 754; v 545
concatenation n 43
concave adj 252
concavity n 252
concavity n 308
conceal v 223, 447, 519, 528
concealed adj 447, 528, 533
concealment n 528
concealment n 447, 526
concede v 529, 760
conceit n 515, 878, 880
conceited adj 878, 880
conceivable adj 470, 515
conceive v 66, 168, 484, 515
concentrate v 72, 222, 290, 686
concentric adj 222
concept n 451
conception n 451, 453, 515
conceptual adj 2
concern n 9, 625, 642, 860; v 9
concerned adj 459, 860
concerning adv 9
concert n 178, 709
concert artist n 416
concertize v 416
concession n 760, 774, 784
concilatory adj 723
conciliate v 723, 831
conciliation n 714, 723, 831, 952
conciliatory adj 714
concise adj 201, 572
concisely adv 572
conciseness n 572
conciseness n 201

conclave n 72, 696
conclude v 67, 480, 604, 729
concluded adj 67
concluding adj 67
conclusion n 65, 67, 154, 480, 729
conclusive adj 67, 478, 480
conclusiveness n 478
concoct v 626
concomitance n 120
concomitant n 88; adj 88, 120
concomitants n 154
concord n 413, 714
concord n 23, 413, 488, 709, 721, 762, 888
concordance n 413
concordant adj 413, 714
concourse n 72, 290
concrete adj 3
concretion n 321
concupiscence n 961
concupiscent adj 961
concur v 120, 178, 290, 488, 709, 714, 762
concurrence n 178
concurrence n 23, 120, 290, 488, 709, 762
concurrent adj 120, 178, 290
concurrently adv 120
concurring adj 488
condemn v 971
condemnation n 971
condemnatory adj 932, 971
condemned adj 971
condensation n 195, 201, 321, 339, 596
condense v 195, 201, 321, 572, 596
condensed adj 201
condiment n 393
condition n 7, 8, 469, 514, 875; v 770
conditional adj 8, 469, 770
conditionally adv 8, 770
conditions n 770
condolence n 915
condolence n 914
condole with v 915
conduce v 176, 178
conduce to v 153
conducive adj 176
conduct n 692

conduct n 680, 693; v 270, 692, 693
conduct oneself v 680
conductor n 271
conduct to v 278
conduit n 350
conduit n 302
confabulate v 588
confabulation n 588
confederate n 711
confederation n 709, 903
confer v 695, 760, 784
conference n 588, 696
confer power v 157
confer with v 588
confess v 488, 529
confession n 529, 985
confessional adj 985
confidant n 890
confidence n 474, 484, 507, 533, 858
confidence man n 548
confident adj 474, 484, 858
confidential adj 221, 528
confidentially adv 528
confiding adj 484
configuration n 240
confine n 233; v 195, 229, 233, 751
confined adj 203, 229
confinement n 229, 751
confirm v 535, 769
confirmation n 467, 535, 762
confirmative adj 535
confirmatory adj 467
confiscate v 789, 974
confiscation n 789, 974
conflict n 24, 680, 713, 720; v 713
conflicting adj 14, 24, 179, 468
conflicting evidence n 468
conflict with v 179
confluence n 43, 290
confluent adj 290, 413
conflux n 72, 290
conform v 82
conformable to rule adj 82
conformity n 82

conformity n 16, 23, 80, 240, 613, 852
conform to v 16, 82
confound v 61, 465a, 475
confront v 234, 464, 708, 719
confuse v 41, 59, 61, 185, 465a, 475, 519, 538
confused adj 59, 447, 571
confusion n 59, 519, 571
confutable adj 479
confutation n 479
confutation n 536
confute v 479
congeal v 321, 385
congelation n 385
congenial adj 23, 413, 714, 829
congeniality n 829
congenital adj 5
congestion n 641
conglomerate n 72, 321
conglomeration n 41, 46, 72
congratulate v 896
congratulate oneself v 838
congratulations n 896
congratulatory adj 896
congregate v 72
congregation n 72, 990, 997
congress n 72, 290, 588
congruity n 23
congruous adj 23
conical adj 253
conjectural adj 514
conjecture n 514; v 514, 870
conjoin v 41, 45
conjoined adj 413
conjugation n 567
conjunction n 8, 43
conjuration n 992
conjure v 992
conjuror n 994
con man n 548
connect v 9, 43, 45, 216
connected adj 9, 11
connection n 9, 11, 43, 45, 46
connective n 45
connoisseur n 480, 700
connotative adj 550
conotation n 516
conote v 516
conquer v 731
conquest n 731

consanguineous adj 11
consanguinity n 11
conscience n 926
conscientious adj 246, 459
conscious adj 375
consciousness n 375, 821
conscription n 744
consecrate v 987, 995
consecutive adj 63, 69
consecutively adv 69
consecutiveness n 69
consensus n 762
consent n 762
consent n 23, 178, 488, 760; v 762
consenting adj 488
consequence n 62, 63, 65, 154, 642
consequent adj 63
consequential adj 642
consequently adv 154
conservation n 141, 670
conservative adj 670
conserve v 670
consider v 451, 461, 469, 480, 484, 873, 928
considerable adj 31, 192, 642
considerate adj 451
consideration n 451, 457, 469, 615, 642, 928
considering adj 928
consign v 270, 755, 783, 784
consignee n 758
consignment n 755, 784, 786
consign to oblivion v 506
consign to the grave v 363
consistency n 16, 23
consistent adj 16, 23, 413
consistent with adv 82
consist in v 1
consist of v 54
consolation n 834, 915
console v 834, 915
consolidate v 46, 48, 321
consolidation n 46, 321
consoling adj 834

correspondence

declamatory

disorder *n* 61, 173, 241, 315, 503, 655; *v* 59, 61, 185
disordered *adj* 241
disorderly *adj* 59, 173
disorganization *n* 61
disorganize *v* 61, 162
disorganized *adj* 59
disown *v* 536
disparage *v* 483, 934
disparagement *n* 932, 934
disparaging *adj* 932, 934
disparate *adj* 18, 24, 28
disparity *n* 15, 18, 24, 28, 291
dispassion *n* 826, 953
dispassionate *adj* 826, 953
dispatch *n* 592, 684; *v* 361, 684, 692, 729
dispel *v* 73, 162
dispensation *n* 784, 786, 927a
dispense *v* 73, 784, 786
dispense with *v* 678
disperse *v* 44, 49, 73, 291
dispersed *adj* 73
dispersion *n* 73
dispersion *n* 44, 186
dispirited *adj* 837
dispiriting *adj* 383
displace *v* 61, 185, 270
displaced *adj* 185
displacement *n* 185
displacement *n* 140
display *n* 448, 525, 855, 882; *v* 525, 882
displease *v* 289, 830
displeased *adj* 832
displeasing *adj* 846
displeasure *n* 828, 832, 900
disposal *n* 60, 677, 741
dispose *v* 60, 176, 615, 693, 796
dispose of *v* 784
disposition *n* 58, 60, 176, 600, 602, 613, 693, 820
dispossess *v* 789
dispossession *n* 789
disproof *n* 468, 479
disproportion *n* 24
disproportionate *adj* 24
disprove *v* 479

disputable *adj* 485
disputant *n* 476, 726
disputation *n* 476, 536, 969
disputatious *adj* 476, 713
dispute *n* 536, 713, 720, 969; *v* 24, 476, 713, 720
disputing *adj* 24
disqualify *v* 158
disquiet *n* 149, 315, 828; *v* 828
disquietude *n* 149, 832
disquisition *n* 537, 595
disregard *n* 458, 460; *v* 458, 460, 483, 742, 773
disregardful *adj* 460
disregard of time *n* 115
disrelish *n* 867; *v* 867
disreputable *adj* 874
disrepute *n* 874
disrespect *n* 929
disrespect *n* 885, 895
disrespectful *adj* 885, 895, 929
disrobe *v* 226
disrobed *adj* 226
disruption *n* 162, 713
disruptive *adj* 713
dissatisfaction *n* 489, 828, 832
dissatisfied *adj* 832, 841
dissatisfy *v* 832
dissect *v* 44, 49
dissection *n* 49
dissemble *v* 528, 544
dissembler *n* 548
dissembling *n* 528, 544
disseminate *v* 73, 531
dissemination *n* 73, 673
dissension *n* 24, 489, 713, 720
dissent *n* 489
dissent *n* 485, 603, 984; *v* 291, 485, 489, 603, 708, 713
dissenter *n* 489, 984
dissenting *adj* 24, 489, 984
dissention *n* 720
dissertation *n* 595
dissever *v* 44
dissidence *n* 24, 713
dissident *n* 489; *adj* 489, 713, 764

dissimilar *adj* 18
dissimilarity *n* 18
dissimilarity *n* 15, 28
dissimilitude *n* 18
dissipate *v* 162, 638, 818
dissipation *n* 73, 638
dissociate *v* 44
dissociation *n* 10, 44
dissolution *n* 49, 162, 335, 360
dissolvable *adj* 335
dissolve *v* 2, 4, 49, 162, 335, 360, 449
dissonance *n* 24, 410, 414, 713
dissonant *adj* 24, 410, 414, 713
dissuade *v* 616
dissuasion *n* 616
dissuasive *adj* 616
dissyllable *n* 561
distance *n* 196
distance *n* 198, 200, 235
distanced *adj* 10
distant *adj* 196
distaste *n* 867
distasteful *adj* 830, 867
distend *v* 194
distention *n* 194
distill *v* 336
distillation *n* 336
distinct *adj* 402, 446, 518, 525, 570, 580
distinction *n* 15, 31, 465, 873, 875
distinctive *adj* 15
distinctive feature *n* 79
distinctness *n* 446, 570, 580
distinguish *v* 15, 441, 465
distinguished *adj* 206, 873
distinguishing *adj* 465
distort *v* 217, 243, 523, 555, 846
distorted *adj* 243
distortion *n* 243
distortion *n* 443, 544, 555, 846
distracted *adj* 503, 824
distraction *n* 825
distress *n* 735, 804, 828; *v* 828
distress signal *n* 669
distribute *v* 60, 73, 531, 786
distribution *n* 60, 73, 531, 786
'distributive *adj* 786

district attorney *n* 968
distrust *n* 485; *v* 485, 487, 860
disturb *v* 61, 185, 315, 824, 830
disturbance *n* 59, 61, 315
disunion *n* 24, 44, 59, 905
disunite *v* 44, 713
disusage *n* 614
disuse *n* 614, 678
disuse *v* 614, 678
disused *adj* 678
ditch *n* 198, 259, 350
ditto *n* 21; *adv* 104
dive *n* 208, 310; *v* 310
diverge *v* 20a, 291
divergence *n* 291
divergence *n* 15, 18, 24, 73, 279
divergency *n* 20a
divergent *adj* 15, 24, 291
divers *adj* 15
diverse *adj* 15, 81
diversified *adj* 15, 16a, 18, 20a, 81, 440
diversify *v* 15, 18, 140, 440
diversion *n* 140, 279, 840
diversity *n* 15, 16a, 18, 81
divert *v* 279, 840
diverting *adj* 840
divest *v* 226, 789
divestment *n* 789
divest oneself *v* 782
divide *v* 44, 44, 51, 60, 73, 85, 91, 291, 778, 786
divided *adj* 51
divide into four parts *v* 97
divide into three parts *v* 94
divide in two *v* 91
divination *n* 511, 992
divine *n* 996; *v* 511, 514, 992; *adj* 976, 981, 983a
divinity *n* 976, 983
division *n* 44, 51, 60, 73, 75, 198, 291, 713, 786
divisive *adj* 713
divorce *n* 905
divorce *n* 44; *v* 44, 905
divorced *adj* 905
divulge *v* 529, 531
divulgence *n* 529, 531

do *v* 161, 170, 622, 639, 680, 729
do a good turn *v* 648
do as one likes *v* 748
do away with *v* 162, 297, 361
do a world of good *v* 648
do battle *v* 722
docile *adj* 725, 743, 926
docility *n* 725, 743
dock *n* 966
doctor *n* 662; *v* 544, 660, 662
doctrinal *adj* 983a
doctrine *n* 484, 537, 983
document *n* 551
dodge *v* 264, 279, 623
doe *n* 374
doer *n* 680, 690
doff *v* 226
dog *n* 373
dogged *adj* 150, 604a, 606
doggedness *n* 150, 604a, 606
doggerel *n* 597
dogma *n* 484, 537, 983
dogmatic *adj* 535, 606, 737
dogmatism *n* 535, 606
dogmatist *n* 606
do good *v* 648
do harm *v* 649
doing *adj* 151
doings *n* 151
doldrums *n* 837
dole *n* 32, 640, 786
dole out *v* 60, 73, 784, 786
dolor *n* 378, 828
dolorous *adj* 378, 830
dolt *n* 493, 501
doltish *adj* 499
domain *n* 75, 181
dome *n* 250
domestic *n* 746; *adj* 188, 221, 370
domestic animals *n* 366
domesticate *v* 184, 370
domesticated *adj* 370
domestication *n* 370
domicile *n* 189
dominance *n* 175
dominant *adj* 175, 737
dominate *v* 175, 739
domination *n* 741
domineer *v* 739

dominion *n* 157, 737

don *n* 540

donate *v* 784

donation *n* 784

done *adj* 729

done away with *adj* 782

donee *n* 785

done with *adj* 678

donor *n* 784

do nothing *v* 169, 681, 683

doom *n* 152, 360, 421; *v* 152, 971

doomsday *n* 121

do one's duty *v* 926

door *n* 231, 232, 260, 627

doorway *n* 232, 260

do over *v* 144

do penance *v* 952

do right *v* 922

dormancy *n* 526

dormant *adj* 172, 265, 526

dose *n* 25, 786

dot *n* 32; *v* 440

dote *v* 499

dote upon *v* 991

double *n* 17, 90, 147; *v* 90, 258; *adj* 90, 147

double-cross *v* 545

doubled *adj* 90

double dealing *n* 544

double-edged *adj* 520

double entendre *n* 520

double-meaning *n* 520

doubleness *n* 89

doubling *n* 90

doubt *n* 485

doubt *n* 475, 487, 984, 989; *v* 475, 485, 487, 989

doubter *n* 989

doubtful *adj* 473, 475, 485, 487, 520

doubtfulness *n* 473, 475

doubting *adj* 485, 984, 989

doubtless *adv* 474

dough *n* 354

doughy *adj* 324, 354

dour *adj* 739

douse *v* 310, 337

dove color *n* 432

dove-colored *adj* 432

dovetail *v* 23, 219

do violence *v* 649

dowdy *adj* 653

do what one wants *v* 748

do without *v* 678

down *v* 298; *adj* 837; *adv* 207

downfall *n* 162, 306

downhearted *adj* 837

downhill *n* 217; *adj* 217

down in the dumps *adj* 438, 832

down in the mouth *adj* 735

downright *adj* 525; *adv* 31

downstairs *adv* 207

downward *adv* 207

downy *adj* 255, 256

dozen *n* 98

drab *adj* 432

draft *n* 208, 349, 596, 626

draftsman *n* 559

drafty *adj* 349

drag *n* 285; *v* 109, 275, 285, 288, 307

drag on *v* 110

drag out *v* 110, 133

drag up *v* 307

drain *n* 295, 350; *v* 295, 297, 340

drainage *n* 295, 340

drain into *v* 348

drake *n* 373

drama *n* 599

dramatic *adj* 599, 882

dramatist *n* 599

dramatize *v* 599

dramaturgy *n* 599

drape *v* 225

drapery *n* 225

draught *n* 298

draw *n* 27; *v* 153, 230, 285, 288, 301, 556

draw a curtain *v* 424

draw aside *v* 279

drawback *n* 177, 619, 651

drawer *n* 559

draw forth *v* 301

draw in *v* 195

drawing *n* 285, 556, 626

drawing and quartering *n* 361

drawl *v* 275

drawn *adj* 27

draw near *v* 121, 286

drawn game *n* 27

draw out *v* 110, 133, 200, 301, 590

draw to a close *v* 67

draw together *v* 72

dread *n* 860, 862; *v* 860

dreadful *adj* 649, 830, 860

dreadfully *adv* 31

dream *n* 4, 515, 515, 858; *v* 515

dreamer *n* 504

dreaming *n* 515

dreamlike *adj* 515

dreamy *adj* 4, 515, 683

dreamy-eyed *adj* 683

dreary *adj* 16, 830, 843

dredge *v* 307

dregs *n* 40

drench *v* 337, 339, 348, 641

dress *n* 225

dress *v* 225

dressed *adj* 225

dribble *v* 295, 348

drift *n* 176, 278, 349; *v* 176, 264, 267, 279, 287

drift away *v* 287

drill *n* 262; *v* 260, 537

drink *n* 298; *v* 298, 959

drinkable *adj* 299

drinker *n* 959

drinking *n* 296, 298, 959

drink like a fish *v* 959

drink one's fill *v* 298

drink up *v* 298

drip *v* 295, 348

dripping *n* 356

drive *n* 266, 284; *v* 276, 284, 744

drive a bargain *v* 794

drive at *v* 516

drive away *v* 289

drive in *v* 300

drivel *n* 499

driveling *n* 499; *adj* 499

driver *n* 268, 694

driving *n* 266

driving spirit *n* 820

drizzle *n* 32, 348; *v* 348

drizzly *adj* 348

droll *n* 501; *adj* 853

drollery *n* 842

drone *n* 683

droning *n* 407

droop *v* 306, 655, 659, 688, 837

drooping *adj* 160

drop *n* 32, 306; *v* 158, 160, 306, 310, 348, 688

drop by drop *adv* 26

drop dead *v* 360

drop down *v* 306

drop down dead *v* 360

drop from the clouds *v* 508

drop in the ocean *n* 32

droplet *n* 32

drop off *v* 283, 360

drop out *v* 283

dropsical *adj* 194

dropsy *n* 194

drought *n* 340

droves *n* 102

drown *v* 337, 361, 376

drowsiness *n* 688

drowsy *adj* 683, 688, 841

drudge *v* 686

drudgery *n* 682

drug *v* 381

drugged *adj* 381

drum *n* 249; *v* 407

drumming *n* 407

drunk *adj* 959

drunkard *n* 959

drunken *adj* 959

drunkenness *n* 959

dry *v* 340; *adj* 340, 575, 579, 843, 958

dry as a bone *adj* 340, 958

dry land *n* 342

dryness *n* 340

dry rot *n* 653, 663

dry up *v* 340, 435

dual *adj* 89

dualism *n* 89

duality *n* 89

dub *v* 564

dubious *adj* 475, 485, 487, 520

dubiousness *n* 475, 520

ducking *n* 310

duct *n* 350, 351

ductile *adj* 324

ductility *n* 324

dud *n* 732

dude *n* 854

due *n* 806, 924; *adj* 924

duet *n* 415

due to *adj* 154, 155

duffer *n* 493, 701

dulcet *adj* 413

dull *v* 254, 381, 422; *adj* 160, 172, 254, 275, 337, 376, 381, 422, 428, 429, 491, 499, 575, 598, 683, 841, 843, 901a

dullard *n* 493, 501

dulled *adj* 381

dullness *n* 843

dullness *n* 172, 254, 683, 823, 841

dull understanding *n* 499

dull-witted *adj* 499

dumb *adj* 491, 581

dumb animal *n* 366

dumbness *n* 581

dumfound *v* 509, 581, 870

dumps *n* 837

dumpy *adj* 193, 201, 202

dun *adj* 429, 432

dunce *n* 493, 501

dunderhead *n* 501

dunderpate *n* 501

dungeon *n* 752

dunk *v* 310, 337

dunking *n* 310

duo *n* 415

dupe *n* 547

dupe *n* 486, 857; *v* 545

duplex *adj* 89

duplexity *n* 89

duplicate *n* 13, 21, 90; *v* 19, 90, 104; *adj* 19, 90, 641

duplicated *adj* 90

duplication *n* 90

duplication *n* 19, 104

duplicitous *adj* 520, 702

duplicity *n* 520, 544, 702

durability *n* 110

durability *n* 112, 141, 150

durable *adj* 106, 110, 141, 150

duration *n* 106, 200

duress *n* 744

during *adv* 106

dusk *n* 126, 421

duskiness *n* 421, 422

dusky *adj* 431

dust *n* 330, 362

dusty *adj* 330, 653

dutiful *adj* 743, 926

duty *n* 926

duty *n* 625, 743, 806, 928, 963

duty bound *adj* 926

dwarf *n* 980; *adj* 193

dwarfish *adj* 193

dwell *v* 186, 188, 265

dweller *n* 188

dwelling *n* 189

dwindle *v* 36, 195, 732

dwindling *n* 36

dye *n* 428; *v* 428

dyed *adj* 428

dying *n* 360

dying day *n* 360

dynamic *adj* 171

expedition *n* 132, 266, 684

expeditious *adj* 132, 274

expel *v* 185, 284, 297, 893

expend *v* 638, 677, 809

expenditure *n* 809

expenditure *n* 638

expense *n* 812

expenses *n* 809

expensive *adj* 814

expensiveness *n* 814

experience *v* 151

experienced *adj* 698

experiment *n* 463

experiment *n* 675; *v* 463, 675

experimental *adj* 463, 675

experimentally *adv* 675

experimentation *n* 463

experimenter *n* 463

experiment with *v* 140

expert *n* 700

expert *n* 500, 737, 872; *adj* 698

expertness *n* 698, 702

expiate *v* 952

expiating *adj* 952

expiation *n* 952

expiatory *adj* 952

expiration *n* 67, 360

expire *v* 67, 109, 360

expired *adj* 122

explain *v* 462, 478, 518, 522, 595

explainer *n* 524

explanation *n* 155, 478, 522, 537

explanatory *adj* 522

explicable *adj* 522

explicate *v* 522

explication *n* 522

explicit *adj* 518, 525, 570

explicitness *n* 518, 570

explode *v* 173

exploit *n* 680

exploration *n* 461

exploratory *adj* 461

exploring *adj* 461

explosion *n* 173, 404, 406, 825

explosive *adj* 173, 665

exposé *n* 529; *v* 226, 260, 529

exposed *adj* 177, 226, 260, 338

expose oneself to *v* 177

expose the error *v* 479

expose to danger *v* 665

exposition *n* 522, 525, 529, 595

expositor *n* 524

expository *adj* 522, 527

expostulate *v* 616, 766

expostulation *n* 616, 766

expostulatory *adj* 766

exposure *n* 448, 479, 529, 665

expound *v* 522, 537

expounder *n* 524

express *v* 516, 525, 527, 560, 566; *adj* 620

express by words *v* 560, 569

expression *n* 521, 525, 554, 560, 566, 985, 985

expressive *adj* 516, 518, 521, 569

expropriate *v* 789

expropriation *n* 789

expulsion *n* 185, 297, 893

expunge *n* 162, 552

expurgate *v* 652

exquisite *adj* 394, 650

exquisitely *adv* 31

extant *adj* 1

extemporaneous *adj* 612

extemporaneously *adv* 612

extempore *adv* 612

extemporize *v* 612, 674

extend *v* 35, 194, 200

extended *adj* 200, 202

extend to *v* 196, 200

extension *n* 35, 65, 180, 194

extensive *adj* 31, 76, 180

extensively *adv* 180

extent *n* 26, 106, 180, 200, 202, 233

extenuate *v* 469

extenuating *adj* 469

extenuating circumstances *n* 469

extenuation *n* 469

exterior *n* 220; *adj* 220

exteriority *n* 220

exterminate *v* 162

extermination *n* 301

external *adj* 6, 57, 220

externality *n* 57

externally *adv* 220

externals *n* 6

extinct *adj* 2, 122, 162, 360

extinction *n* 2, 162, 360, 421, 552

extinguish *v* 162, 385, 421

extirpate *v* 301

extirpation *n* 301

extol *v* 883

extort *v* 814

extortion *n* 789

extra *adj* 37

extract *v* 301

extraction *n* 301

extracts *n* 596

extradite *v* 270

extradition *n* 270

extraneous *adj* 6, 10, 57, 220

extraneousness *n* 57

extraneousness *n* 6

extraordinary *adj* 31, 83, 870

extravagance *n* 497, 499, 549, 814, 818, 954

extravagant *adj* 31, 497, 499, 549, 641, 814, 818, 853, 954

extravagant love *n* 991

extravagantly *adv* 31

extreme *n* 67; *adj* 31

extremely *adv* 31

extremity *n* 67

extricate *v* 301, 672, 705, 750

extrication *n* 301, 672, 750

extrinsic *adj* 6, 57, 220

extrinsicality *n* 6

extrinsicality *n* 57

extrinsically *adv* 6

exuberance *n* 573, 641

exuberant *adj* 573, 641

exude *v* 295

exultant *adj* 838, 884

eye *n* 247; *v* 441

eye for an eye *n* 30

eyeglasses *n* 445

eyeless *adj* 442

eyesight *n* 441

eyewitness *n* 444

eyot *n* 346

F

fable *n* 546

fabric *n* 7

fabricate *v* 161, 515, 544

fabrication *n* 161, 544, 546

fabulous *adj* 2, 515, 546, 549, 979

fabulous spirit *n* 979

facade *n* 220, 234

face *n* 220, 234, 448; *v* 223, 224, 234

facet *n* 220

facetious *adj* 842

facetiousness *n* 842

face to face *adv* 237

facile *adj* 705

facilitate *v* 705, 707

facility *n* 705

facility *n* 157, 698, 748

facing *n* 223; *adj* 237

facsimile *n* 13, 21, 90

fact *n* 1, 151, 474, 494

faction *n* 712

factious *adj* 24

factory *n* 691

facts *n* 467, 527

factual *adj* 494

faculties *n* 450

faculty *n* 698

fad *n* 608

faddish *adj* 123

faddishness *n* 123

fade *v* 4, 111, 124, 160, 287, 360, 422, 429, 449, 659, 732

faded *adj* 659

fail *v* 160, 304, 360, 655, 732, 773, 808, 927

failing *n* 732; *adj* 53, 128, 927

failure *n* 732

failure *n* 304, 460, 509, 735, 773, 808, 927

fain *adj* 602

faint *v* 158, 688; *adj* 32, 160, 203, 405, 422, 429, 430, 447, 688

faint-hearted *adj* 862

faint-heartedness *n* 862

faintly *adv* 32

faintness *n* 405

faintness *n* 575, 688

faint sound *n* 405

fair *n* 799; *adj* 174, 246, 429, 430, 651, 829, 845, 922, 942

fair game *n* 857

fairly *adv* 922

fairness *n* 174, 845, 922, 942

fairy *n* 979

faith *n* 484, 858

faithful *adj* 17, 21, 494, 772, 983a

faithfully *adv* 772

faithfulness *n* 772, 983a

faithless *adj* 544, 989

fake *n* 556; *v* 680; *adj* 19

fake god *n* 991

faker *n* 548

fall *n* 126, 162, 217, 283, 306, 348, 360; *v* 162, 306, 310, 360

fallacious *adj* 4, 477, 495, 544, 545

fallacy *n* 4, 477, 495

fall again *v* 661

fall away *v* 195

fall back *v* 145, 283, 287, 661

fall behind *v* 281, 283

fallibility *n* 475

fallible *adj* 475

fall in *v* 488

falling *n* 306; *adj* 217

falling back *n* 145, 287, 661

falling-off *n* 36, 659

falling out *n* 720

falling short *n* 304

fall into a rut *v* 613

fall into a trap *v* 547

fall into raptures *v* 827

fall off *v* 36, 659, 732

fall on evil days *v* 735

fall on one's knees *v* 990

fall out *v* 151, 713

fallow *adj* 674

fall prey to *v* 749

fall short *v* 304, 651, 732

fall short of *v* 28, 34, 53, 640, 730

fall through *v* 304

fall to *v* 151, 298, 676

fall to one *v* 785

fall to one's lot *v* 156

fall to pieces *v* 162

fall under *v* 76

false *adj* 19, 477, 495, 544, 545, 546, 923

false coloration *n* 523

103

heedlessness

immune *adj* 748, 927a

immune from *adj* 777a

immunity *n* 748, 777a, 927a, 970

immutability *n* 141, 150

immutable *adj* 110, 150

imp *n* 980

impact *n* 276, 379

impair *v* 659, 848

impairment *n* 638, 659

impale *v* 260

impart *v* 784

impartial *adj* 246, 628, 942

impartiality *n* 942

impart to *v* 527

impassable *adj* 261

impasse *n* 151

impassionate *adj* 383

impassioned *adj* 574, 821, 825, 991

impassive *adj* 456, 823

impassivity *n* 823, 826

impatience *n* 825

impatient *adj* 825, 841

impeach *v* 938, 969

impeachment *n* 938

impeccability *n* 650

impeccable *adj* 650, 946

impede *v* 179, 275, 706

impediment *n* 177, 706

impeding *n* 706

impel *v* 175, 264, 276, 284, 744

impend *v* 121, 152, 909

impending *adj* 121, 152, 286, 507, 909

impenetrability *n* 321, 571

impenetrable *adj* 261, 321, 323, 519, 571

impenetrable to light *adj* 426

impenitence *n* 951

impenitent *adj* 951

imperative *adj* 737, 926

imperceptibility *n* 447

imperceptible *adj* 193, 447

imperceptibly *adv* 32

imperfect *adj* 34, 53, 304, 640, 651, 659, 848, 961

imperfection *n* 651

imperfection *n* 28, 34, 53, 304, 640, 945, 961

imperfectly *adv* 32

imperil *v* 665

imperishable *adj* 112

impermanence *n* 111

impermanent *adj* 111

impermeability *n* 321

impermeable *adj* 261, 321

impersonate *v* 19

impersonation *n* 19, 599

impertinence *n* 885, 929

impertinent *adj* 885, 929

imperturbability *n* 826

imperturbable *n* 823; *adj* 383, 826

impervious *adj* 261

impervious to light *adj* 426

impetuosity *n* 173, 825, 863

impetuous *adj* 173, 825, 863

impetus *n* 276, 284

impiety *n* 988

impiety *n* 989

impish *adj* 980

implacable *adj* 914a, 919

implant *v* 300

implantation *n* 300

implanted *adj* 5

implausibility *n* 473

implausible *adj* 473

implement *n* 633

implicit *adj* 526

implied *adj* 526

implore *v* 765

implosion *n* 276

imply *v* 467, 472, 516

impolite *adj* 895, 929

impoliteness *n* 929

import *n* 516, 642; *v* 296, 516, 642

importance *n* 642

importance *n* 31, 62, 175

important *adj* 31, 33, 175, 642

importation *n* 296, 300

importunate *adj* 765

importune *v* 765

impose *v* 741

imposing *adj* 642, 875, 878

impossibility *n* 471

impossible *adj* 471, 704

imposter *n* 548

imposture *n* 545

impotence *n* 158

impotence *n* 160, 169, 175a

impotent *adj* 158, 160, 175a

impractical *adj* 471, 647, 704

impracticality *n* 471, 647

imprecate *v* 908

imprecation *n* 908

impregnability *n* 664

impregnable *adj* 159, 664

impregnate *v* 168, 300

impress *v* 175, 375, 824

impressibility *n* 375, 822

impressible *adj* 324

impression *n* 375, 453, 591, 821

impressionable *adj* 822

impressive *adj* 574, 642

imprint *n* 569

imprison *v* 229

imprisoned *adj* 229, 751

improbability *n* 473

improbable *adj* 473

improbity *n* 940

impromptu *adj* 612; *adv* 612

improper *adj* 499, 568, 647, 923, 945

improper time *n* 135

impropriety *n* 568, 579, 647, 925

improve *v* 282, 648, 658

improved *adj* 658

improvement *n* 658

improvement *n* 282, 618

improvidence *n* 674

improvident *adj* 674, 818

improving *adj* 658

improvisation *n* 612

improvise *v* 416, 612, 674

imprudence *n* 863

imprudent *adj* 452, 460, 863

impudence *n* 885, 895, 929

impudent *adj* 885, 929

impugn *v* 716

impulse *n* 276, 612

impulse *n* 284, 601, 615, 744

impulsion *n* 284

impulsive *adj* 149, 612, 825, 863

impulsively *adv* 612

impulsiveness *n* 863

impunity *n* 777a, 927a, 970

impure *adj* 653, 961

impurity *n* 961

impurity *n* 653

imputation *n* 155, 938

imputative *adj* 938

impute *v* 938

impute to *v* 155

in a bad way *adj* 659, 735

in abeyance *adv* 172

inability *n* 158, 699

in a body *adv* 50

inabstinence *n* 954

inaccessible *adj* 196

in accord *adj* 714

in accordance with *adj* 23; *adv* 82

inaccuracy *n* 544

inaccurate *adj* 495, 568, 923

in a column *adv* 69

inaction *n* 681

inaction *n* 623, 683; *adj* 170, 680

inactive *adj* 172, 265, 681, 683

inactivity *n* 683

inactivity *n* 172, 681

in addition *adv* 37

inadequacy *n* 28, 34, 640, 645, 651

inadequate *adj* 28, 158, 640, 651

inadmissible *adj* 55

in advance *adv* 62, 234, 280

in adverse circumstances *adj* 735

in a fair way to *adj* 176

in a great measure *adv* 31

in a jiffy *adv* 113

in a line *adj* 69

in all aspects *adv* 52

in all creation *adv* 318

in all likelihood *adv* 472

in all probability *adv* 472

in a moment *adv* 113

in and out *adv* 248, 314

inane *adj* 497

inanimate *adj* 358

inanimate matter *n* 358

inanity *n* 4, 450a, 497, 517

in anticipation *adv* 132

inapplicable *adj* 10

inappreciable *adj* 32

inappropriateness *n* 647

inapt *adj* 699

inaptitude *n* 645

in a roundabout way *adv* 629

in arrear *adj* 806

inarticulate *adj* 583

inarticulateness *n* 583

inattention *n* 458

inattention *n* 452, 460, 866

inattentive *adj* 419, 452, 458, 460, 823, 866

inattentiveness *n* 458

inaudibility *n* 405, 419

inaudible *adj* 405

inaugural *adj* 66

inaugurate *v* 66

inauguration *n* 66

inauspicious *adj* 135, 909

in bad health *adj* 655

in bad taste *adj* 851

inbeing *n* 5

in black and white *adj* 531, 590

inborn *adj* 5, 221, 820

inbound *adj* 294

inbred *adj* 5

in broad daylight *adv* 525

incalculable *adj* 104

incalculably *adv* 31

incandescent *adj* 382

incantation *n* 993

incantory *adj* 992

incapability *n* 158

incapable *adj* 158

incapacitate *v* 158

incapacitated *adj* 158

incapacity *n* 158, 499

incarcerate *v* 972

incarceration *n* 974

incase *v* 229; *adv* 8

in celebration of *adv* 883

in plain English *adv* 576, 703

in plain sight *adv* 525

in plain terms *adv* 576

in play *adj* 170

in poor health *adj* 655

in possession of *adj* 777

in preparation *adj* 53

in presence of *adv* 186

in print *adj* 531, 532

in prison *adj* 754

in private *adv* 528

in progress *adj* 53

in prospect *adj* 121, 152, 620

in proximity *adj* 186

in pursuit of *adj* 622

input *n* 175

in question *adv* 454

in quest of *adj* 622

inquietude *n* 828

inquire *v* 461

inquirer *n* 461

inquiring *n* 461; *adj* 455, 461

inquiring mind *n* 455

inquiry *n* 461

inquiry *n* 539

inquisitive *adj* 455, 461

inquisitiveness *n* 455

inquisitor *n* 461, 739

inquisitorial *adj* 461, 739, 965

in rapport *adj* 413

in readiness *adj* 507

in reality *adv* 1

in relief *adj* 250

in reserve *adj* 636

in retaliation *adv* 718

inroad *n* 294

in rotation *adv* 138

insalubrious *adj* 657

insalubrity *n* 657

insane *adj* 173, 503

insanity *n* 503

inscrutable *adj* 519

in secret *adj* 528; *adv* 528

insect *n* 366

insecure *adj* 475, 665

insecurity *n* 475, 665

insensate *adj* 499

insensibility *n* 376, 823

insensibility *n* 866

insensible *adj* 376, 381, 506

insensitive *adj* 376, 823, 866

insensitiveness *n* 823, 866

inseparability *n* 46

inseparable *adj* 43, 46

insert *v* 221, 228, 300

insertion *n* 300

insertion *n* 37, 228, 294, 296

in short *adv* 572

inside *n* 221; *adj* 221

inside out *adj* 218

insidious *adj* 545, 702

insight *n* 477, 498; *adj* 507

insightful *adj* 842

insigne *n* 550

insignificance *n* 32, 643, 736

insignificant *adj* 4, 32, 517, 643, 736

in simple words *adv* 703

insincere *adj* 544

insincerity *n* 544

insinuate *v* 527

insinuate oneself *v* 294

insinuation *n* 228, 294, 300, 527

insipid *adj* 337, 391, 575

insipidity *n* 391

insist upon *v* 604, 770

in snatches *adv* 70

insobriety *n* 959

insolence *n* 885

insolence *n* 715, 878

insolent *adj* 715, 885

insoluble *adj* 321, 519

insolvency *n* 732, 808

insolvent *adj* 804

in some degree *adv* 26

in some place *adv* 182

inspect *v* 441

inspector *n* 461, 694

inspiration *n* 477, 515, 612, 824

inspire *v* 615, 824

inspiring *adj* 836

inspirit *v* 836

inspiriting *adj* 858

in spite *adv* 708

in spite of *prep* 179

instability *n* 149, 475, 605, 665

install *v* 184, 755

installation *n* 184

installment *n* 807

instance *n* 82

instant *n* 113; *adj* 113, 118, 630

instantaneous *adj* 111, 113, 132

instantaneously *adv* 113, 132

instantaneousness *n* 113

instead *adv* 147

instigate *v* 615

instigation *n* 170, 615

instill *v* 41, 300, 537

instinct *n* 477, 601

instinctive *adj* 5, 477, 601

instinctual *adj* 5, 477

in stir *adj* 754

institute *n* 542; *v* 153, 161

in store *adj* 152, 636

instruct *v* 537, 693, 695, 741

instructed *adj* 490

instruction *n* 537, 693, 695, 697, 741

instructive *adj* 537, 985

instructor *n* 540

instrument *n* 633

instrument *adj* 415

instrumental *adj* 176, 416, 631, 632, 633, 677

instrumentalist *n* 416

instrumentality *n* 631

instrumentality *n* 170

instrumental music *n* 415

insubordinate *adj* 715, 742

insubordination *n* 715, 742

insubstantiality *n* 2, 317

in succession *adv* 69

in such and such a place *adv* 183

in such wise *adv* 8

insufferable *adj* 830

insufficiency *n* 640

insufficiency *n* 53, 304, 651, 732

insufficient *adj* 28, 32, 304, 640, 651, 732

insufficiently *adv* 32

insular *adj* 10, 44, 87, 346

insularity *n* 44

insulate *v* 44, 87

insulation *n* 44

insult *n* 830; *v* 830, 929

insulting *adj* 885, 929

insurgence *n* 719

insurgent *n* 742; *adj* 742

insurrection *n* 719

insusceptibility *n* 376

in suspense *adv* 172

intact *adj* 50, 52, 141, 650, 670, 729

intactness *n* 52

intaglio *n* 22

intangible *adj* 2, 4, 317

in tears *adj* 828

integer *n* 84

integral *adj* 50

integral part *n* 56

integrate *v* 50

integrity *n* 50, 922, 939, 944

intellect *n* 450

intellect *n* 498, 842

intellectual *n* 492; *adj* 450, 498

intellectual giant *n* 872

intellectualize *v* 450

intelligence *n* 498

intelligence *n* 480, 498, 527, 532, 698, 842

intelligencer *n* 527, 534

intelligent *adj* 498, 698, 842

intelligibility *n* 518

intelligibility *n* 570

intelligible *adj* 518, 522, 570

intemperance *n* 954

intemperance *n* 959

intemperate *adj* 954

intend *v* 451, 516, 620

intense *adj* 31, 171, 382, 428

intensely *adv* 31

intensification *n* 835

intensified *adj* 835

intensify *v* 35, 171, 835

intensity *n* 26, 31, 171, 173, 382

intent *n* 451, 516, 600, 620

intention *n* 620

intention *n* 278, 451, 516, 611, 615

intentional *adj* 600, 620

intentionally *adv* 600, 611, 620

intentiveness *n* 457

intentness *n* 682

inter *v* 363

interact *v* 12

intercalation *n* 228

intercede *v* 724

intercession *n* 724, 766

interchange *n* 148

interchange *n* 12, 219, 783; *v* 12, 147, 148, 783

interchangeability *n* 148

interchangeable *adj* 12, 148, 794

intercourse *n* 148

interdepend *v* 12

interdependence *n* 12

interdict *v* 761

interdiction *n* 761

interest *n* 455, 618, 642, 707; *v* 288, 824, 829, 840

interested *adj* 455

interfere *v* 228, 708, 724

interference *n* 179, 228, 706, 719

interfere with *v* 179

interim *n* 106, 198

interior *n* 221, 342; *adj* 221

interiority *n* 221

interjacence *n* 228

interjacent *adj* 228

interject *v* 228

interjection *n* 228

interlace *v* 41, 43, 219

interlaced *adj* 219

interlard *v* 41

interlarding *n* 41

interlineation *n* 228

interlink *v* 219

interlocation *n* 228

interlocution *n* 588

interlude *n* 106, 198, 685

intermediary *n* 534, 631; *adj* 631

intermediate *adj* 29, 68, 631

intermedium *n* 631

interment *n* 363

interminable *adj* 104, 112, 200

intermission *n* 70, 106

intermittence *n* 138

intermittent *adj* 70, 138

intermittently *adv* 138

intern *v* 221

internal *adj* 5, 221

internally *adv* 221

interpenetrate *v* 228

interpenetration *n* 228

interpolate *v* 41, 228

interpolation *n* 41, 228, 300

interpose *v* 70, 228, 724

interposition *n* 37, 228, 724

interpret *v* 462, 522, 537

interpretable *adj* 522

interpretation *n* 522

interpretation *n* 155, 516

interpretative *adj* 522

interpreter *n* 524

interpreter *n* 513

interpretive *adj* 522

interregnum *n* 106, 142, 198

interrogate *v* 461

interrogation *n* 461

interrogative *adj* 461

interrupt *v* 70, 142, 198, 706

interrupted *adj* 70

interruption *n* 61, 70, 142, 198, 706

intersect *v* 219

intersection *n* 219

interspace *n* 198, 221

intersperse *v* 228

interspersion *n* 228

interstice *n* 198

intertwine *v* 41, 43, 219

intertwined *adj* 219

interval *n* 198

interval *n* 53, 70, 106, 196

intervene *v* 70, 198, 228, 631, 724

intervening *adj* 228

intervention *n* 228, 631, 724

interview *n* 588

interweave *v* 41, 43, 219

in the altogether *adj* 226

in the background *adv* 235

in the blood *adj* 5

in the bud *adv* 66

in the buff *adj* 226

in the cards *adj* 152

in the course of *adv* 106

in the course of things *adv* 151

in the event of *adv* 8

in the face of *adv* 715

in the first place *adv* 66

in the foreground *adv* 234

in the fourth place *adv* 96

in the genes *adj* 5

in the headlines *adj* 532

in the interim *adv* 106

in the lead *adv* 234

in the long run *adv* 29, 152

in the main *adv* 50

in the matter of *adv* 9

in the meantime *adv* 106

in the middle *adv* 68

in the midst of *adv* 41

in the news *adj* 532

in the nick of time *adv* 134

in the open air *adv* 338

in the open market *adj* 763

in the rear *adv* 235, 281

in the same category *adj* 9

in the thick of *adv* 228

in the third place *adv* 93

in the vanguard *adv* 280

in the wide open spaces *adv* 338

in the wind *adj* 152

intimacy *n* 888

intimate *n* 890; *v* 527; *adj* 197, 221, 888

intimately *adv* 43

in time *adv* 109, 152

intimidate *v* 909

intimidating *adj* 909

intimidation *n* 909

intolerable *adj* 830

intolerance *n* 606, 825

intolerant *adj* 606, 825

intonation *n* 402, 580

intone *v* 580

in top shape *adj* 654

in touch with *adj* 592

in tow *adj* 285

intoxicate *v* 824

intoxicated *adj* 959

intoxication *n* 824, 959

intractable *adj* 606, 704

intractability *n* 606

in trade *adj* 794

intrepid *adj* 861

intrepidity *n* 861

intricate *adj* 248, 704

intrigue *n* 626, 702; *v* 702

intriguer 626

intrinsic *adj* 5, 221

intrinsicality *n* 5

intrinsically *adv* 5

in triumph *adv* 731

introduce *v* 62, 228, 280, 296, 300

introduction *n* 64, 66, 296, 300

introductory *adj* 62, 64, 66, 116

intrude *v* 135, 228, 294

intrusion *n* 57, 135, 228, 294

intrusive *adj* 228, 706

intuit *v* 477

intuition *n* 477

intuition *n* 477

intuitive *adj* 477

intuitively *adv* 477

in turn *adv* 58, 138

intwine *v* 219

in two shakes (of a lamb's tail) *adv* 113

inundate *v* 337, 348, 641

inundation *n* 348

in unison *adj* 413

inure *v* 613

inutile *adj* 645

inutility *n* 645

invade *v* 294, 716

invader *n* 716

in vain *adv* 732

invalidate *v* 158, 479, 536, 756

invalidation *n* 479, 536, 756

invaluable *adj* 648

invariability *n* 16, 141

invariable *adj* 5, 16, 110, 141, 150

invariably *adv* 16, 82

in various places *adv* 182

invasion *n* 294, 716

invent *v* 515, 626

invented *adj* 546

inventive *n* 515, 546, 698

inventive *adj* 515, 698

inventiveness *n* 168, 698

inventor *n* 164

inventory *n* 86, 596, 811; *v* 596

inverse *n* 237; *adj* 218, 237

inversely *adv* 218

inversion *n* 218

inversion *n* 14, 140, 145

invert *v* 14, 61, 218

inverted *adj* 59, 218

invest *v* 157, 755, 784

invested *adj* 225

investigate *v* 461

investigation *n* 461, 463, 595

investigator *n* 461

investiture *n* 784

investment *n* 787

inveterate *adj* 124

invidious *adj* 830, 898

in view *adj* 507, 620

invigorate *v* 159, 171

invigorating *adj* 171, 656

invigoration *n* 159

invincible *adj* 159

inviolate *adj* 141

in violation *adj* 927

invisibility *n* 447

invisible *adj* 193, 447

invisibleness *n* 447

invite *v* 288, 615, 763, 829

invocation *n* 586

in vogue *adj* 852

invoice *n* 812

invoke *v* 72, 586, 990

involuntary *adj* 601

involution *n* 248, 571

involve *v* 516, 938

involved *adj* 59, 248, 571

invulnerability *n* 664

invulnerable *adj* 664

inward *adj* 221; *adv* 221

in what manner *adv* 627

in what way *adv* 627

in writing *adj* 590

iota *n* 32

irascibility *n* 901

irascible *adj* 382, 684, 901

irate *adj* 900

iridescence *n* 440

iridescent *adj* 420, 440

irk *v* 830

irksome *adj* 704, 830, 841

iron *v* 255

iron-gray *adj* 432

ironic *adj* 856

ironical *adj* 856

irons *n* 752

irony *n* 856

irradiate *v* 420

irrational *adj* 497, 499

irrationality *n* 499

irreclaimable *adj* 951

irreconcilability *n* 10

irreconcilable *adj* 24

irrecoverable *adj* 122

irrefutable *adj* 246, 474

irregular *adj* 16a, 59, 70, 81, 83, 139, 243, 256, 475

irregularity *n* 139

irregularity *n* 16a, 59, 83, 256, 475

irregularly *adv* 59, 139

irrelation *n* 10

irrelevancy *n* 175a

irrelevant *adj* 10

irreligion *n* 989

irreligion *n* 988

irreligious *adj* 989

irremediable *adj* 859

irrepentance *n* 951

irrepressible *adj* 173, 748, 825

irresistibility *n* 601

irresistible *adj* 159, 601, 744

irresolute *adj* 149, 485, 605, 607, 609a, 683

irresolution *n* 605

irresolution *n* 149, 172, 314, 485, 609a

irrespective *adj* 10

irresponsibility *n* 773

irresponsible *adj* 773

irretrievable *adj* 776

irreverence *n* 929, 988

irreverent *adj* 929

irrevocable *adj* 604

irrigate *v* 348

irrigation *n* 348

irritability *n* 825, 901

irritable *adj* 684, 825, 901

irritate *v* 173, 289, 688, 824, 828, 830

irritated *adj* 835

irritation *n* 824, 828, 835
irruption *n* 294
island *n* 346
isle *n* 346
islet *n* 346
isolate *v* 44, 79, 87, 893, 905
isolated *adj* 10, 44, 87, 893
isolation *n* 44, 893, 905
issuance *n* 531
issue *n* 154, 167, 295; *v* 73, 151, 295, 531, 591
issue from *v* 154
issues *n* 151
itch *v* 380
itching *n* 380; *adj* 380
itchy *adj* 380
items *n* 79
iterate *v* 104
iteration *n* 90, 104, 136
iterative *adj* 104
itinerant *n* 268; *adj* 266

J

jabber *n* 517, 584; *v* 517, 584
jackanapes *n* 854
jaded *adj* 961
jag *v* 257
jagged *adj* 244
jail *n* 752; *v* 972
jailbird *n* 754
jailer *n* 753, 975
jailhouse *n* 752
jangle *v* 410
jar *n* 315; *v* 24, 410, 414, 713
jargon *n* 497, 517, 560
jarring *adj* 410, 414
jaundice *n* 435, 436
jaundiced *adj* 435
jaunt *n* 266
jaw *v* 584
jazz *n* 415
jealous *adj* 435, 900, 920, 921
jealousy *n* 920
jealousy *n* 900, 921
jeer *v* 929
jeer at *v* 856
jeers *n* 856
jeopardize *v* 665
jeopardy *n* 665
jerk *n* 285, 315, 493; *v* 285, 315
jerky *adj* 315
jest *v* 842
jester *n* 501, 844
jesuitry *n* 477

jet *n* 273, 348; *v* 267, 348
jet-black *adj* 431
jet-setter *n* 268
jetting *adj* 267
jettison *v* 610
jetty *n* 250
jewel *n* 648, 899
jibe *v* 23
jilt *v* 509
jingle *v* 408
jinx *n* 621; *n* 993
job *n* 676
jocularity *n* 836
jog *n* 315; *v* 276
joggle *v* 315
jog on *v* 736
join *v* 37, 41, 43, 45, 72, 87, 88, 199, 290, 712
joined *adj* 43
join forces *v* 709
join hands with *v* 709
joining *n* 37, 43, 290
joint *n* 43; *adj* 43, 88, 178, 778
jointly *adv* 43
joint tenancy *n* 778
joke *v* 842
joker *n* 844
jolly *adj* 836, 840
jolt *n* 315; *v* 276, 315
jostle *v* 179, 276, 315
jot *n* 32
jounce *v* 315
journal *n* 114, 551
journalist *n* 553
journey *n* 266
journey *n* 302; *v* 266
journeyer *n* 268
journeying *adj* 266
jovial *adj* 840
joviality *n* 836
jowl *n* 236
joy *n* 377, 827; *v* 827
joyful *adj* 377, 827, 836
joyous *adj* 836
jubilant *adj* 838, 884
jubilation *n* 838
judge *n* 967
judge *n* 480, 737, 965; *v* 451, 480, 850, 965, 967
judgment *n* 480
judgment *n* 450, 451, 453, 465, 490, 498, 972
judgmental *adj* 480
judgment seat *n* 966
judicator *n* 965, 967
judicatory *adj* 967
judicature *n* 965
judicial *adj* 480, 965, 967
judiciary *n* 967

judicious *adj* 174, 480, 498, 868, 967
judiciousness *n* 174, 868
juice *v* 354
juiced *adj* 959
juiceless *adj* 340
juicer *n* 959
juicy *adj* 333, 337, 339
jumble *n* 41, 59; *v* 41, 59, 61
jumbo jet *n* 273
jump *n* 305, 309; *v* 309, 310
junction *n* 43
junction *n* 41, 45, 48
juncture *n* 8, 43, 134
jungle *n* 59
junior *adj* 127
juridical *adj* 967
jurisdiction *n* 965
jurisdiction *n* 737
jurisdictive *adj* 965, 967
jurist *n* 967
juristic *adj* 967
juror *n* 967
just *adj* 246, 922
just as *adv* 17
just do *v* 639
justice *n* 922, 967
justification *n* 717, 737, 937
justified *adj* 937
justify *v* 717, 737, 937
just in time *adv* 134
justly *adv* 922
just now *adv* 123
jut out *v* 250
juvenile *adj* 127
juvenility *n* 123, 127
juxtapose *v* 464

K

kaleidoscope *n* 445
kaleidoscopic *adj* 440
kaput *adj* 503
karma *n* 152
keen *adj* 171, 253, 375, 868
keen blast *n* 349
keenness *n* 868
keep *n* 298; *v* 141, 143, 670, 751, 781, 883
keep accounts *v* 811
keep alive *v* 359
keep an account with *v* 805
keep apart *v* 44
keep away *v* 187
keep back *v* 678
keep clear of *v* 623

keep cold *v* 385
keep company with *v* 888
keep down *v* 751
keeper *n* 753
keep going *v* 143
keep hold *v* 150
keeping *n* 781
keeping out *n* 55
keeping secret *n* 528
keep in mind *v* 505
keep moving *v* 264, 682
keep on *v* 136, 143, 604a
keep on one's toes *v* 264
keep out *v* 55
keep out of sight *v* 528
keep pace with *v* 27, 120, 178
keep quiet *v* 265, 403, 585
keep safe *v* 717
keepsake *n* 505
keep secret *v* 528
keep silence *v* 585
keep the memory alive *v* 505
keep the peace *v* 721
keep up *v* 141, 143, 670
Kelly green *adj* 435
kelpie *n* 979
kempt *adj* 652
ken *n* 441
kernel *n* 68, 222
kerosene *n* 356, 388
kerosene lamp *n* 423
ketch *n* 273
key *n* 346, 428
keyhole *n* 260
khaki *n* 433; *adj* 433
kick *n* 276
kick up a row *v* 173
kid *n* 129
kill *v* 361
killer *n* 165
killing *n* 361
killing time *n* 681
kill time *v* 106, 683
kiln *n* 386
kind *n* 75, 569; *adj* 888, 906
kind-hearted *adj* 888, 906
kindheartedness *n* 906
kindle *v* 153, 171, 173, 384, 420, 824
kindliness *n* 897, 906
kindling *n* 388
kindly *adj* 888, 906
kindness *n* 897, 906

kindred *n* 11; *adj* 11
kinfolk *n* 11
kingdom of God *n* 981
kingdom of heaven *n* 981
kinsman *n* 11
kiss *n* 902
kith and kin *n* 11
knack *n* 698
knave *n* 941
knead *v* 324, 379
kneading *n* 379
knee *n* 244
knee-deep *adj* 209
kneel *v* 308, 886, 990
knell *n* 363
knife *n* 262
knife edge *n* 253
knit *v* 43, 259
knob *n* 249, 250
knock *n* 276; *v* 276, 406
knock down *v* 213
knot *n* 219, 321; *v* 219
knotted *adj* 59, 256
know *v* 474, 484, 490, 527, 888
know how *n* 632
knowing *adj* 490
knowingly *adv* 620
knowledge *n* 490
knowledge *n* 498, 527, 698
knowledgeable *adj* 490, 698
known *adj* 490
know no bounds *v* 104
know-nothing *n* 493; *v* 491
knuckle *n* 244
kobold *n* 980
kohl-black *adj* 431
Koran *n* 986

L

label *n* 564; *v* 550, 564
labor *n* 680, 686, 704; *v* 680, 686
laboratory *n* 691
labored *adj* 579
laborer *n* 746
laborious *adj* 686, 704
laboriousness *n* 682
labyrinth *n* 59, 248
labyrinthine *adj* 248
lace *n* 219; *v* 43
lack *n* 804; *v* 34, 53, 304, 640, 804
lackadaisical *adj* 683
lack faith *v* 989

lacking

lacking *adj* 53, 187, 304
lackluster *adj* 422, 429, 430
lack of adornment *n* 849
lack of affectation *n* 849
lack of bias *n* 942
lack of connection *n* 10
lack of decorum *n* 851
lack of discernment *n* 465a
lack of feeling *n* 376, 381
lack of interest *n* 456
lack of originality *n* 843
lack of practice *n* 614
lack of readiness *n* 603
lack of uniformity *n* 16a
laconic *adj* 572
lacquer *n* 356a; *v* 356a
lad *n* 129
lade *v* 190
lading *n* 190
ladle *v* 270
lady *n* 374, 875
ladylove *n* 897
lag *v* 275, 281, 683
laggard *n* 683; *adj* 603, 683
lagoon *n* 343
laical *adj* 997
laid low *adj* 160
laid up *adj* 655
laim *v* 158
lair *n* 189
laity *n* 997
lake *n* 343
lake *n* 343
lamb *n* 129
lame *adj* 53, 160, 651, 655
lame excuse *n* 617
lament *n* 411, 839; *v* 411, 833, 839, 915
lamentable *adj* 649, 830, 833, 839
lamentably *adv* 31
lamentation *n* 839
lamentation *n* 833, 915
lamenting *adj* 839
lamp *n* 423
lampoon *v* 856
lampooner *n* 844
lance *v* 260
lancet *n* 262
land *n* 342
land *n* 780; *v* 292, 342

landed *adj* 342
landing *n* 292
lands *n* 342
landscape *n* 448; *v* 371
landscaping *n* 371
language *n* 560
languid *adj* 160, 172, 275, 405, 575, 683, 685
languish *v* 36, 160, 655, 683
languor *n* 160, 172, 275, 683, 688
lankness *n* 203
lanky *adj* 200, 203
lantern *n* 423
lap *n* 221, 311
lap of luxury *n* 377
lapse *n* 661, 776; *v* 109, 122, 144, 659, 661
lapsed *adj* 122
lard *n* 356
large *adj* 31, 192, 202
largeness *n* 192
larger *adj* 194
largesse *n* 784
lash *n* 975; *v* 43, 173, 972
lass *n* 129
lassitude *n* 688, 841
last *v* 1, 106, 110, 141, 604a; *adj* 67, 122
last breath *n* 360
last forever *v* 112
lasting *adj* 106, 110, 141, 150
lastingness *n* 110
last resort *n* 666
last stage *n* 67
last word *n* 67
late *adj* 122, 123, 133, 275, 360; *adv* 133
lately *adv* 122, 123
latency *n* 526
latency *n* 172, 447
lateness *n* 133
latent *adj* 172, 526
latentness *n* 526
later *adj* 117; *adv* 117
lateral *adj* 236
laterality *n* 236
laterally *adv* 236
lather *n* 353; *v* 332, 353
lathering *n* 332
latitude *n* 180, 181, 202, 748
latitude and longitude *n* 183
latter *adj* 122
lattice *n* 219
laud *v* 883, 990
laudatory *adj* 931

laugh *v* 838
laughable *adj* 853
laughing *adj* 838
laughingstock *n* 857
laughingstock *n* 547
laughter *n* 838
launch *n* 273; *v* 66, 284
launch into *v* 676
launder *v* 652
laundry *n* 652
laureate *n* 597
laurel *n* 733
lavation *n* 652
lavender *adj* 437
lavish *v* 641, 784, 818; *adj* 641, 818
lavishness *n* 818
law *n* 80, 697, 963
lawful *adj* 246, 760, 922, 963
lawfully *adv* 922
lawfulness *n* 922, 963
lawless *adj* 964
lawlessness *n* 964
lawsuit *n* 969
lawyer *n* 968
lax *adj* 47, 738, 773
laxative *n* 652
laxity *n* 738
laxity *n* 47, 495, 748, 773, 989
laxness *n* 738, 773
lay *n* 413; *v* 184; *adj* 997
lay aside *v* 55
lay away *v* 636
lay bare *v* 260
lay claim to *v* 741
layer *n* 204
layer *v* 204
layered *adj* 204
lay groundwork *v* 626
lay in *v* 637
lay in a stock *v* 637
lay in a store *v* 637
lay in the grave *v* 363
lay in the ground *v* 363
lay it on thick *v* 933
layman *n* 997
lay oneself open to *v* 177, 665
lay on thick *v* 641
lay open *v* 226, 260, 529
lay out *v* 363, 809
lay over *v* 133
lay siege *v* 716
lay stress on *v* 642
lay the foundations *v* 673
lay the groundwork *v* 60
lay to rest *v* 363
layup *v* 678

lay waste *v* 162
laziness *n* 683
lazy *adj* 275, 683
lazy eye *n* 443
lead *n* 234; *v* 116, 176, 615, 692, 693
lead astray *v* 545
leaden *adj* 422
leader *n* 64, 694, 745
leadership *n* 692, 693
leading *n* 280; *adj* 66
lead the way *v* 62, 66, 280
leaf *n* 204
leafage *n* 367
league *n* 712
leak *n* 198; *v* 295
leakage *n* 295
lean *v* 176, 217; *adj* 203
leaning *n* 176, 217, 602; *adj* 176
leanness *n* 203
lean on *v* 858
lean to *v* 602
leap *n* 309
leap *n* 305, 310; *v* 309, 310
leaping *adj* 309
leap with joy *v* 838
learn *v* 490, 527, 539
learn by heart *v* 505
learned *adj* 490, 498, 539
learned in the law *adj* 968
learner *n* 541
learner *n* 492
learning *n* 539
learning *n* 490, 498, 537
learn of *v* 480a
lease *n* 783; *v* 787, 788
leash *v* 43
leave *n* 760; *v* 44, 185, 293, 302, 624, 782, 784
leave alone *v* 623
leaven *n* 320; *v* 320
leave no trace *v* 449, 552
leave off *v* 142, 678
leave out *v* 55
leaves *n* 367
leave-taking *n* 287, 293
leave undone *v* 730
leave unfinished *v* 730
leaving *n* 624
leavings *n* 40
lecher *n* 962
lecherous *adj* 961
lechery *n* 961

lecture *n* 537, 582; *v* 537, 582, 586
lecturer *n* 540
ledge *n* 215, 250
ledger *n* 86, 551, 811
lee *n* 236
leer *n* 441; *v* 441
lee side *n* 236
leeway *n* 180
left *n* 239
left *adj* 40, 449, 782
left behind *adj* 782
left hand *n* 239
left-handed *adj* 239
leftover *n* 40; *adj* 40
left side *n* 239
legacy *n* 784
legal *adj* 760, 963, 967
legal action *n* 969
legal adviser *n* 968
legality *n* 963
legalize *v* 737, 963
legalized *adj* 760, 963
legal proceedings *n* 969
legal process *n* 969
legal profession *n* 968
legal separation *n* 905
legatee *n* 785
legation *n* 755
legislate *v* 693, 963
legislated *adj* 963
legitimacy *n* 963
legitimate *adj* 494, 760, 922, 963
legitimateness *n* 963
leguminous *adj* 367
leisure *n* 685
leisure *adj* 685
leisureliness *n* 275
leisurely *adj* 275, 685; *adv* 133, 275
lemon *adj* 435
lend *v* 787
lend an ear *v* 418
lender *n* 805
lending *n* 787
lend on security *v* 787
length *n* 200
lengthen *v* 110, 133, 200
lengthened *adj* 200
lengthiness *n* 200
lengthwise *adv* 200
lengthy *adj* 200, 573
lenience *n* 740
lenience *n* 174, 738
leniency *n* 740
lenient *adj* 174, 738, 740
lenity *n* 174
lens *n* 443, 445

loop

malcontent adj 832
male n 373; adj 373
male animal n 373, 374
malediction n 908
malevolence n 907
malevolence n 649, 889
malevolent adj 649, 739, 907, 919, 945
malformation n 243
malformed adj 243
malice n 907
malicious adj 898, 907, 919, 945
maliciousness n 907
malign v 934; adj 649
malignant adj 919, 945
malignity n 649
mall n 799
malleability n 149, 324
malleable adj 82, 149, 324
maltreat v 649, 739, 830, 923
mamma n 166
mammal n 366
mammoth n 192; adj 31
man n 373
man n 372
man about town n 854
man after one's own heart n 899
manage v 58, 692, 693
manageable adj 705
management n 692, 693, 698
manager n 694
managerial adj 692
managing adj 693
mandate n 630, 741
maneuver v 702
manfully adv 604
mangle v 659
mangy adj 655
man-hater n 911
manhood n 131, 373
mania n 503
maniac n 504
maniacal adj 503
manifest adj 446, 525
manifestation n 525
manifestation n 446, 448
manifested adj 525
manifestly adv 525
manifold adj 15, 81, 102
manipulate v 379, 677, 702
manipulation n 379
mankind n 372

mankind n 372
manliness n 604
manly adj 131, 373
manner n 569, 613, 627
mannered adj 579, 855
mannerism n 79, 83, 579
mannerisms n 855
manner of speaking n 521
manners n 692, 852
man of learning n 500
mantle n 424
manual n 527
manufacture n 161; v 161
manuscript n 590
many adj 100, 102
many-colored adj 440
many-sided adj 81
map n 183, 527, 626
mar v 659, 848
marble n 249
marbled adj 440
march n 266
marches n 233
marching band n 417
march of time n 109
mare n 374
margin n 231
marine adj 341
marine blue adj 438
mariner n 269
mariner n 269
marital separation n 905
maritime adj 267, 341
mark n 26, 71, 550, 569, 590, 620; v 450, 550, 642
marked adj 79
market n 799
market v 795
marketable adj 794, 796
marketplace n 799
market price n 812
mark the time v 114
mark time v 114, 265
maroon adj 434
marquee n 223
marriage n 903
marriage n 43
marriageable adj 131
married adj 903
married man n 903
married woman n 903
marrow n 5, 221
marry v 43, 48, 903
marsh n 345

marshal v 60
marshy adj 339, 345
mart n 799
martial adj 722
martyr n 955
marvel n 870, 872; v 870
marvelous adj 31, 870
marvelously adv 31
masculine adj 373
masculinity n 373
mash v 324, 352, 354
mask n 223, 424, 530; v 442, 528
masquerade n 530
mass n 25, 31, 50, 72, 102, 192, 321
massacre n 361; v 361
massage v 379
massaging n 379
massive adj 192, 319, 321
massy adj 192
master n 745
master n 129, 540, 694, 700, 779; v 518, 539, 731, 749
masterful adj 731, 737
masterly adj 698
master mind n 500, 700, 872
master of adj 777
masterpiece n 648, 650
master stroke n 650
mastery n 698, 731, 741
mastic n 356a
masticate v 298
mastication n 298
mat n 219; v 219
match n 17, 27; v 17, 23, 27
matchless adj 33
mate n 17, 27, 711, 890, 903; v 89
material n 316; adj 3, 316
material existence n 3
materialism n 316
materialist n 316
materialistic adj 3, 316
materiality n 316
materiality n 3
materialization n 525
materialize v 316, 525
materials n 635
materials n 316
maternal adj 166
maternity n 11, 166
mates n 269

matins n 125
matriarch n 130
matriarchal adj 166
matricide n 361
matriculation n 539
matrimony n 903
matrix n 22
matted adj 219
matter n 3, 316, 516, 591, 625; v 642
matter little v 643
matter of fact n 1; adj 598, 703, 843
matter of factness n 703
matters n 151
matting n 219
mature v 144, 650, 658, 673; adj 673
mature years n 128
maturity n 124, 128, 131, 673
maul v 649
mausoleum n 363
mauve adj 437
maxim n 496
maxim n 537, 697
maximum n 210
maybe adv 470
maze n 248
mazy adj 248
meadow n 344
meager adj 32, 53, 103, 203, 575, 640, 643
meagerness n 203
mealy adj 330
mealy-mouthed adj 886
mean n 29
mean n 68, 628; v 451, 516, 620; adj 29, 32, 34, 68, 207, 435, 643, 649, 819, 851, 876, 886, 914a, 930, 943
meander v 248, 264, 266, 279, 573
meandering n 248
mélange n 41
meaning n 516
meaning n 522, 620; adj 516
meaningful adj 516
meaningless adj 497, 517
meaninglessness n 517
meanness n 32, 34, 499, 886, 914a, 943
mean nothing v 517
means n 632
means n 627, 780, 803
means of access n 627
meantime adv 106

meanwhile adv 106
measurable adj 466
measure n 25, 26, 174, 413, 466, 786; v 106, 466
measured adj 174
measure for measure n 30
measureless adj 104
measurement n 466
measurement n 25
measure time v 114
meaty adj 354
mechanical adj 601, 633
medal n 733
meddlesome adj 455
meddlesomeness n 455
medial adj 68
median n 29; adj 68
mediate v 620, 631, 724
mediation n 724
mediation n 631, 766
mediator n 724
mediatory adj 724
medication n 662
medicinal adj 662
medicine n 662
medicine man n 994
mediocre adj 28, 29, 34, 598, 651, 736
mediocrity n 736
mediocrity n 28, 34
meditate v 451, 870
meditation n 451
meditative adj 451
medium n 29, 631, 994
medley n 41
meek adj 879
meekness n 879
meet v 23, 72, 199, 290, 772; adj 646
meeting n 43, 72, 199, 290, 680, 696
meetinghouse n 1000
meet up with v 151
meet with v 151
melancholy n 837; adj 830, 837
melee n 59
meliorate v 174, 723
mellifluence n 413
mellifluous adj 413, 578
mellow v 144, 673; adj 128, 413, 428, 673, 721
melodic adj 413
melodious adj 377, 413, 580
melodiousness n 413

patronage *n* 175, 707
patronize *v* 136
patter *v* 407
pattern *n* 22, 240, 650
pattern after *v* 19
paucity *n* 32, 103, 640
pauperism *n* 804
pause *n* 70, 142, 198, 265, 685, 687; *v* 70, 142, 265, 681, 687
paw *v* 379
pawn *n* 771; *v* 771, 787, 788
pawning *n* 788
pay *n* 973; *v* 784, 807, 973
pay attention *v* 457
pay in full *v* 807
paymaster *n* 801
payment *n* 807
payment *n* 809
pay no attention to *v* 458
pay out *v* 809
pea *n* 249
peace *n* 721
peace *n* 265, 403, 714
peaceable *adj* 721
peaceful *adj* 174, 265, 685, 721, 826
peacefulness *n* 174, 721
peacemaker *n* 724
peace offering *n* 723
pea-green *adj* 435
peak *n* 206, 210
peaked *adj* 253
peal *n* 404; *v* 404, 407
peal of bells *n* 407
peal of laughter *n* 838
pearliness *n* 427, 430
pearly *adj* 427, 428, 430, 440
pear-shaped *adj* 249
peasantry *n* 876
peat *n* 388
peck at *v* 298
peculiar *adj* 5, 79, 83, 870
peculiarities *n* 5
peculiarity *n* 83, 550
peculiarly *adv* 31, 33
pecuniary *adj* 800
pedagogic *adj* 537
pedagogical *adj* 537
pedagogics *n* 537
pedagogy *n* 537
pedant *n* 492
pedantic *adj* 577
peddler *n* 797

pedestal *n* 211
pedestrian *n* 268; *adj* 598
pedigree *n* 69
peek *n* 441; *v* 441
peel *n* 204, 223; *v* 204, 226
peep *n* 441; *v* 441
peephole *n* 260
peeping *adj* 455
peep of day *n* 125
peep up *v* 446
peer *n* 27; *v* 441
peevish *adj* 684, 901a
peg *n* 250
pellet *n* 249
pellucid *adj* 425, 570
pelt *v* 276
pen *n* 232, 752; *v* 590
penalize *v* 972, 974
penalized *v* 974; *adj* 972
penalizing *adj* 972
penalty *n* 974
penalty *n* 972
penance *n* 974
penchant *n* 177, 602
pencil *v* 556
pendant *n* 214
pendent *adj* 214
pendulous *adj* 214
pendulum *n* 214
penetrate *v* 294, 302
penetrating *adj* 480, 498
penetration *n* 294, 302, 441, 480, 498
penitence *n* 950
penitence *n* 833
penitent *n* 950; *adj* 833, 950
penitential *adj* 950
penitentiary *n* 752
penmanship *n* 590
pen name *n* 565
penniless *adj* 804
pennywise *adj* 819
pensioner *n* 785
pensive *adj* 451
pent up *adj* 751
penumbra *n* 421
penurious *adj* 819
penury *n* 804
people *n* 188, 372, 997; *v* 102
people the world *v* 163
pep *n* 171
pepper *n* 393; *v* 392
peppery *adj* 392
peradventure *adv* 470
perambulate *v* 264
perambulation *n* 266

perceivability *n* 446
perceivable *adj* 446
perceive *v* 375, 441, 490
perceptibility *n* 446
perceptible *adj* 446
perception *n* 418, 441, 453, 490
perceptive *adj* 375, 465, 490, 842
perch *n* 189; *v* 184, 186
perchance *adv* 156, 470
percolation *n* 295
percussion *n* 417
perdition *n* 162
peregrination *n* 266
peremptory *adj* 737, 739
perennial *adj* 69
perfect *v* 650, 729; *adj* 31, 52, 104, 648, 650, 729, 960
perfection *n* 650
perfection *n* 52, 648, 729, 960
perfectly *adv* 729
perfidious *adj* 544
perforate *v* 260
perforated *adj* 260
perforation *n* 260
perforator *n* 262
perform *v* 161, 170, 415, 416, 599, 644, 680, 772, 926
performable *adj* 470
performance *n* 161, 599, 680, 729, 772
perform a rite *v* 998
performer *n* 416, 599, 690
performing *n* 680
perfume *n* 400; *v* 400
perfumed *adj* 400
perfunctory *adj* 53, 640
perhaps *adv* 470
peril *n* 665
perilous *adj* 475, 665
perimeter *n* 230
period *n* 108
period *n* 71, 106, 138, 198, 200
periodic *adj* 70, 138
periodical *adj* 138
periodically *adv* 138
periodicity *n* 138
peripatetic *adj* 266
periphery *n* 230
perish *v* 2, 162, 360, 659
perishable *adj* 111
permanence *n* 141
permanence *n* 16, 110, 150

permanent *adj* 106, 110, 141, 150, 613
permanently *adv* 141
permeable *adj* 260
permeate *v* 186, 228, 302
permeation *n* 186, 228, 302
permissible *adj* 760
permission *n* 760
permission *n* 737, 762
permissive *adj* 760
permit *n* 737, 755, 760; *v* 737, 748, 760, 762
permitted *adj* 760
permutation *n* 140, 148
pernicious *adj* 649, 663
perpendicular *adj* 212, 246
perpendicularity *n* 212
perpetrate *v* 680
perpetrator *n* 690
perpetual *adj* 104, 110, 112, 136, 143, 150
perpetually *adv* 112, 136
perpetuate *v* 112, 143
perpetuation *n* 143
perpetuity *n* 112
perpetuity *n* 105
perplex *v* 475, 519, 704, 830
perplexed *adj* 59
perplexity *n* 59
persecute *v* 649, 830
persecution *n* 649
perseverance *n* 604a
perseverance *n* 143, 150, 604, 682
persevere *v* 604a, 682
persevering *adj* 604a
persicuity *n* 518
persist *v* 106, 110, 141, 143, 604a, 606, 682
persistence *n* 110, 141, 143, 604a, 606
persistent *adj* 141, 143, 604a, 606
person *n* 3, 372
personage *n* 372
personal *adj* 5, 79, 372
personality *n* 5, 13, 79
personate *v* 19, 554, 599
personify *v* 554

personnel *n* 56
persons *n* 372
perspective *n* 183, 441, 448
perspicacious *adj* 480, 498, 868
perspicacity *n* 441, 480, 868
perspicuity *n* 570
perspicuous *adj* 570
perspiration *n* 299, 339
perspire *v* 299, 339
persuade *v* 175, 615, 695
persuasion *n* 175, 484, 695
persuasive *adj* 615, 695
pertain to *v* 9
pertinacious *adj* 150, 606
pertinacity *n* 150, 606
pertinent *adj* 23
perturb *v* 61, 824
perturbation *n* 61, 315, 824
peruse *v* 539
pervade *v* 186
pervasion *n* 186
pervasive *adj* 186
pervasiveness *n* 186
perverse *adj* 606, 704, 901a
perversion *n* 477, 523, 538
perversity *n* 606
pervert *v* 477, 523, 538
pessimism *n* 483, 859
pessimist *n* 165
pessimistic *adj* 483, 837
pest *n* 975
pester *v* 830
pestilence *n* 649
pestilential *adj* 657
pet *n* 899
petite *adj* 32
petition *n* 765, 990; *v* 765, 990
petitioner *n* 767
petrification *n* 321, 323
petrify *v* 321, 323
petroleum *n* 356, 388
pettifogging *adj* 477
pettiness *n* 32
petty *adj* 32, 643
petulant *adj* 684, 901
phantasm *n* 443, 515
phantom *n* 4
phase *n* 7, 8, 71, 448

phenomenon *n* 151, 448, 872
philanthropic *adj* 784, 906, 910
philanthropist *n* 910
philanthropy *n* 910
philanthropy *n* 784, 906
philology *n* 562
philosopher *n* 500
phonetic *adj* 561
phonetics *n* 402, 561
phonology *n* 402
phony *n* 548; *adj* 19, 544
phosphorescence *n* 423
phosphorescent *adj* 420, 423
photoengraving *n* 558
photography *n* 420
phrase *n* 566
phrase *n* 521; *v* 566
phraseology *n* 560, 566, 569
physical *adj* 3, 173, 316
physical elements *n* 316
physical gratification *n* 377
physical insensibility *n* 381
physicality *n* 316
physical science *n* 316
physician *n* 662
physicist *n* 316
physics *n* 316
physiognomy *n* 448
physiology *n* 357
physique *n* 364
phytology *n* 369
pick *n* 609, 648; *v* 609
picket *v* 43
pickings *n* 793
pickle *n* 7; *v* 392, 670
pick of the litter *n* 648
pickup *n* 274
picky *adj* 465
pictorial *adj* 556
pictorialization *n* 556
picture *n* 448, 556; *v* 554, 594
picture gallery *n* 556
picturesque *adj* 556, 845
piddle *v* 683
piddling *adj* 643
piebald *adj* 440
piece *n* 51
piecemeal *adv* 51

pieces *n* 596
piece together *v* 43
pied *adj* 440
pierce *v* 260, 378, 385, 649
piercer *n* 262
pierce the ears *v* 404
piercing *adj* 404, 410, 498
pietist *n* 987
pietistic *adj* 987
piety *n* 987
pig *n* 957
pigeon *n* 547
pigeonhole *n* 182
piggish *adj* 957
piggishness *n* 957
pig-headed *adj* 606
pigment *n* 428
pigmy *adj* 193
pile *n* 72, 256
pile on *v* 641
pile up *v* 37
pilfer *v* 791
pilferer *n* 792
pilgrim *n* 268
pilgrimage *n* 266, 676
pill *n* 249
pilot *n* 269, 694; *v* 693
pimple *n* 250
pin *n* 253, 262, 263; *v* 43, 45
pince-nez *n* 445
pinch *n* 8, 704; *v* 195, 378, 385, 819
pinched *adj* 203
pinch hit *v* 147
pine *v* 655
pinhole *n* 260
pink *adj* 434
pinnacle *n* 206, 210
pioneer *n* 64
pious *adj* 987
pipe *n* 350
piquancy *n* 392, 394
piquant *adj* 392
pique *n* 900
piratical *adj* 791
pirouette *n* 312
pit *n* 208, 252, 363
pitapat *n* 407
pitch *n* 26, 210, 356a, 402, 413, 431; *v* 284, 306, 314
pitch black *adj* 421, 431
pitchy *adj* 431
piteous *adj* 830
piteously *adv* 31
pitfall *n* 667
pitfall *n* 530
pith *n* 5, 221
pithiness *n* 572
pithy *adj* 572, 574
pitiable *adj* 649, 830

pitiful *adj* 643, 649
pitiless *adj* 914a
pitilessness *n* 914a
pit one against another *v* 464
pittance *n* 640
pitted *adj* 848
pity *n* 914
pity *n* 821; *v* 914
pitying *adj* 914
pivot *n* 43, 153, 222; *v* 312
pivotal *adj* 222
pixie *n* 979
placate *v* 723
place *n* 182
place *n* 8, 58, 71, 183, 184; *v* 60, 184
place a bet *v* 621
place before *v* 62
placed *adj* 184
place in the record *v* 551
place of business *n* 799
place of departure *n* 293
place of learning *n* 542
place of worship *n* 1000
place side by side *v* 464
place together *v* 72
placid *adj* 721, 826
placidity *n* 826
plagiarism *n* 19
plague *n* 649, 663, 828, 975; *v* 828, 830
plaid *adj* 440
plain *n* 344
plain *adj* 16, 246, 446, 474, 518, 525, 570, 576, 703, 849, 879
plainly *adv* 525
plainness *n* 576
plainness *n* 570, 703, 849
plainsong *n* 413
plain-speaking *n* 518, 570, 703
plain spoken *adj* 525, 703
plaint *n* 411
plaintiff *n* 938
plaintive *adj* 839
plait *n* 219, 258; *v* 219, 258
plan *n* 626
plan *n* 60, 453, 673, 692; *v* 60, 620, 626, 673
plane *n* 213, 251; *v* 255, 267, 273; *adj* 213, 251
planets *n* 318

planning *n* 60
plant *v* 184, 300, 371
plant life *n* 357, 365, 367
plastered *adj* 959
plastic *adj* 324
plasticity *n* 324
plat *v* 219
plate *n* 22, 251; *v* 204
plateau *n* 344
plate engraving *n* 558
platitude *n* 517
platter *n* 204, 251
plausibility *n* 472
plausible *adj* 472
play *n* 170, 175, 180, 599; *v* 170, 416, 554, 599, 680, 840
played out *adj* 67
player *n* 416, 599
play false *v* 544, 940
play for *v* 621
playful *adj* 840, 842
playhouse *n* 599, 728
playing *n* 840
playing field *n* 728
play of colors *n* 440
play on words *n* 520
play second fiddle to *v* 749
play the fool *v* 497, 853
play the notes *v* 416
play truant *v* 187
play with *v* 140
playwright *n* 599
playwriter *n* 599
playwriting *n* 599
plea *n* 617
plea *n* 411
plead *v* 617, 765, 968
pleader *n* 968
pleading *n* 717
pleadings *n* 969
pleasant *adj* 829, 836, 840, 842
pleasantness *n* 829
pleasantry *n* 842
please *v* 829
pleasing *adj* 413, 850
pleasing combination *n* 413
pleasing sounds *n* 415
pleasurable *adj* 377, 829
pleasurableness *n* 829
pleasure *n* 377
pleasure *n* 827
pleasure *n* 377, 600, 840

pleasure-seeker *n* 954a
pleat *n* 258; *v* 258
plebeian *adj* 851, 876
pledge *n* 177, 768, 771; *v* 768, 788
pledged *adj* 768
pledging *n* 788
plenty *n* 641
plethora *n* 641
pliability *n* 324
pliable *adj* 324
pliancy *n* 324, 705, 725
pliant *adj* 324, 705
plight *n* 7, 8
plod *v* 275, 682
plot *n* 626; *v* 626
plough *v* 371
plow *v* 259, 371
plowed *adj* 959
pluck *n* 150, 604, 604a, 861; *v* 789
plucked instruments *n* 417
pluck out *v* 301
plug *n* 261, 263; *v* 261
plugging *n* 261
plug up one's ears *v* 419
plumb *adj* 212
plum-colored *adj* 437
plump *adj* 192
plumpness *n* 192
plunder *n* 793
plunge *n* 310
plunge *n* 300; *v* 208, 300, 310, 337, 863
plunge into *v* 676
plural *adj* 100
plurality *n* 100
plus *adv* 37
ply *n* 258; *v* 677
pock *n* 250
pocket *v* 789
poesy *n* 597
poet *n* 597
poetaster *n* 597
poetic *adj* 521, 597
poetical *adj* 597
poetic device *n* 521
poeticize *v* 597
poetics *n* 521, 597
poetry *n* 597
poetry *n* 590
poignancy *n* 392
poignant *adj* 516
point *n* 8, 26, 32, 71, 180a, 182, 253, 620; *v* 253, 278
point-blank *adj* 703; *adv* 278, 576
pointed *adj* 201, 253, 516, 518

pointedly *adv* 31, 620
pointedness *n* 253
pointer *n* 550
point of departure *n* 293
point of view *n* 441
point out *v* 525
points of the compass *n* 278
point to *v* 155, 472, 516, 938
point toward *v* 278
poison *v* 659, 663
poisonous *adj* 649, 657, 663
polar *adj* 210, 383
polarity *n* 89, 179, 218, 237
pole *n* 222
polemic *n* 726
polemicist *n* 476
poles apart *adv* 237
policy *n* 626, 692
polish *n* 255, 578, 850; *v* 255, 331
polished *adj* 255, 578, 850, 852
polite *adj* 383, 457, 852, 879, 894, 928
politeness *n* 457, 894
polite society *n* 852
politic *adj* 498, 702
poll *n* 85; *v* 85
pollute *v* 653, 659
poltroon *n* 862
poltroonery *n* 862
polyglot *adj* 560
polyp *n* 250
polyphony *n* 413
polysyllable *n* 561
pommel *n* 249
pomp *n* 882
pompous *adj* 482, 577, 882
pompousness *n* 882
pond *n* 343
ponder *v* 451, 870
pondering *n* 451
ponderous *adj* 319, 579
pool *n* 343, 709; *v* 709
poor *adj* 34, 477, 575, 640, 643, 736, 804, 828, 879
poorer *adj* 34
poorly *adj* 655
poorly timed *adj* 135
poorness *n* 34, 640
poor substitute *adj* 651
pop *n* 166, 406
pop music *n* 415
pop off *v* 360
populace *n* 72, 876
popular music *n* 415

populate *v* 102
population *n* 188, 372
populous *adj* 72, 102
pop up *v* 446
porch *n* 231, 260
pore over *v* 539
porous *adj* 260
port *n* 239
portable *adj* 270
portal *n* 231, 260
portend *v* 511, 668, 909
portent *n* 511, 512, 668, 909
portentous *adj* 511, 668
porter *n* 271; 532
portion *n* 51, 100a, 786
portion out *v* 786
portly *adj* 192
portrait *n* 21
portraiture *n* 554
portray *v* 554, 594
portrayal *n* 594
pose *n* 183; *v* 475, 704, 855
position *n* 8, 71, 183, 625
positive *adj* 1, 31, 84, 246, 474, 484, 535
possess *v* 777
possessed *adj* 503
possessed of *adj* 777
possessing *adj* 777
possession *n* 777
possession *n* 780
possessions *n* 780
possessive *adj* 777
possess oneself of *v* 789
possessor *n* 779
possess the means *v* 632
possibility *n* 470
possibility *n* 2, 156
possible *adj* 2, 177, 470, 515
possibly *adv* 470
post *n* 183; *v* 184, 274, 811
post bail *v* 771
post card *n* 592
postdate *v* 115
posterior *n* 235; *adj* 117, 235
posteriority *n* 117
posteriority *n* 63
posterity *n* 167
posterity *n* 121
posthaste *adv* 274
posthumous *adj* 117
postman *n* 271
post meridian *n* 126
post mortem examination *n* 363

postpone *v* 133
postponement *n* 133
postscript *n* 65
postulant *n* 767
postulate *n* 476, 514; *v* 476
posture *n* 8, 183, 240
potable *adj* 298
pot-bellied *adj* 194
potency *n* 157, 159
potent *adj* 157, 159, 171, 175
potential *n* 2; *adj* 2, 470, 526
potentiality *n* 470, 526
potion *n* 298
potpourri *n* 41
potted *adj* 959
potting *n* 557
pound *n* 232; *v* 330
pour *v* 333, 348
pour forth *v* 584
pour in *v* 294
pour out *v* 295, 348
pour out of *v* 295
pout *v* 900, 901a
poverty *n* 804
poverty-stricken *adj* 804
powder *n* 330
powdery *adj* 330
power *n* 157
power *n* 159, 171, 175, 404, 574, 737, 741, 965; *v* 388
powerful *adj* 157, 159, 171, 175, 404, 574
powerfully *adv* 31, 157
powerless *adj* 158, 160
powerlessness *n* 158, 175a
practicability *n* 705
practicable *adj* 644, 705
practical *adj* 170, 470, 644, 692
practicality *n* 470
practically *adv* 5
practice *n* 613, 692; *v* 677
practiced *adj* 698
practice law *v* 968
practice sorcery *v* 992
practitioner *n* 690
pragmatism *n* 646
prairie *n* 344
praise *v* 883, 931, 990
praised *adj* 931
praiseworthy *adj* 931

prance *v* 315
prank *n* 608
prate *v* 584, 588
prattle *n* 582, 584, 588
pray *v* 990
prayer *n* 411, 765, 990
preacher *n* 540, 996
preamble *n* 64
precarious *adj* 111, 475, 665
precariousness *n* 665
precaution *n* 510, 664, 673
precautionary *adj* 673
precede *v* 62, 116, 280
precedence *n* 62, 280
precedence *n* 116
precedent *n* 22, 64, 80, 613, 969; *adj* 62
preceding *adj* 62, 116
precept *n* 697
precept *n* 630
precincts *n* 227
precious *adj* 31, 814
precipice *n* 212, 306, 667
precipitancy *n* 684
precipitate *v* 684; *adj* 132, 684, 863
precipitately *adv* 132
precipitation *n* 132, 684
precipitous *adj* 217, 306
précis *n* 596; *v* 596
precise *adj* 494, 518
precision *n* 80, 494, 518
preclude *v* 761
precluded *adj* 893
preclusion *n* 893
precocious *adj* 132
precocity *n* 132
precursor *n* 64
precursor *n* 62, 116, 280, 534
precursory *adj* 64, 116
predatory *adj* 789, 791
predecessor *n* 64, 116
predeliberation *n* 611
predestination *n* 611
predestine *v* 152, 611
predetermination *n* 611

predetermine *v* 611
predicament *n* 8, 183, 704
predicate *v* 514
predict *v* 507, 510, 511
prediction *n* 511
prediction *n* 668
predilection *n* 177, 609
predisposed *adj* 820
predisposition *n* 176, 820
predominance *n* 33, 175
predominant *adj* 175, 737
predominate *v* 33, 175
pre-eminence *n* 33, 206
pre-eminent *adj* 33, 206
pre-eminently *adv* 31, 33
pre-engage *v* 132
pre-existence *n* 116
pre-existent *adj* 116
preface *n* 64; *v* 62
prefatory *adj* 62, 64
prefer *v* 609
preference *n* 62, 609
preferential *adj* 609
prefix *n* 64; *v* 62
prehistoric *adj* 124
prelacy *n* 995
preliminary *adj* 62, 64, 673
prelude *n* 64, 66
premature *adj* 132, 135, 674
prematurely *adv* 132
prematurity *n* 132
premeditate *v* 611
premeditation *n* 611
premises *n* 476
premium *n* 973
premonition *n* 668
premonitory *adj* 511, 668
preordain *v* 152
preparation *n* 673
preparation *n* 60, 64, 537
preparative *adj* 673
preparatory *adj* 62, 673
prepare *v* 60, 537, 673
prepared *adj* 507, 673, 698
prepare for *v* 507, 673
prepare for battle *v* 727
prepatory *adj* 673

preponderance *n* 33, 175

preponderant *adj* 737

preposterous *adj* 497, 549, 853

preposterously *adv* 31

prepubescence *n* 131

prerequisite *n* 630

prerogative *n* 924

presage *n* 511, 668; *v* 116, 511, 909

presbyopia *n* 443

prescience *n* 510

prescient *adj* 510

prescribe *v* 693, 695, 741

prescribed *adj* 474, 924

prescript *n* 697

prescription *n* 613, 697, 924

prescriptive *adj* 124, 613, 983a

presence *n* 186

presence *n* 1, 448

present *n* 784; *v* 448, 763, 784; *adj* 118, 186

presentation *n* 784

present events *n* 151

presentiment *n* 477

present itself *v* 446

presently *adv* 132

present the music *v* 416

present time *n* 118

present to the view *v* 448

preservation *n* 670

preservation *n* 141, 664, 717, 781

preservative *adj* 670

preserve *v* 141, 143, 664, 670, 717, 781

preserved *adj* 670

preserver *n* 664

president *n* 694

press *n* 72; *v* 255, 319

press forward *v* 684

press in *v* 300

pressing *adj* 642

press into service *v* 677

press on *v* 622, 684

press onward *v* 282

pressure *n* 175, 319, 642, 735

presto *adv* 113

presumable *adj* 472

presumably *adv* 472

presume *v* 484, 514, 858, 878, 885

presumption *n* 507, 514, 878, 925

presumptive *adj* 514

presumptuous *adj* 863, 878, 885

presuppose *v* 514

pretend *v* 544, 546, 617, 855

pretender *n* 548, 925

pretense *n* 617, 855, 882

pretention *n* 577, 855, 882

pretentious *adj* 482, 855, 882, 884

pretentiousness *n* 882

pretext *n* 617

pretty *adj* 845; *adv* 31

pretty well *adv* 31, 32

prevail *v* 33, 78, 175

prevailing *adj* 78, 983a

prevail upon *v* 615

prevalence *n* 33, 78, 175, 613

prevalent *adj* 1, 78, 175, 613

prevaricate *v* 520, 544

prevarication *n* 520, 544

prevent *v* 706, 708, 761

preventing *n* 706

prevention *n* 761

preventive *adj* 761

previous *adj* 116

previously *adv* 116

prevision *n* 510

prey *n* 620

price *n* 812

price *v* 812

priceless *adj* 33, 648, 814

prick *n* 253; *v* 260, 378, 380

pricking *n* 380

prickle *n* 253

prickly *adj* 253, 256

prick up one's ears *v* 418

pride *n* 878

pride *n* 880

priest *n* 904, 996

priesthood *n* 995, 996

priestly *adj* 995

prig *n* 854

priggish *adj* 868

prim *adj* 868

primal *adj* 66, 153

primary *adj* 153, 642

primary color *n* 428

prime *n* 125, 648; *v* 537, 673; *adj* 84, 642, 648

prime mover *n* 153, 976

prime of day *n* 125

primer *n* 542, 567

primeval *adj* 124

primitive *adj* 124

primordial *adj* 124

princely *adj* 816

prince of darkness *n* 978

principal *n* 694; *adj* 642

principally *adv* 33

principle *n* 5, 80, 153, 211, 537, 615

print *n* 591; *v* 531, 558, 590, 591

printed *adj* 591

printer *n* 591

printing *n* 591

prior *adj* 62, 116

priority *n* 62, 116, 280

prior to *adv* 116

prism *n* 428, 445

prismatic *adj* 428, 440

prison *n* 752

prison *n* 975

prisoner *n* 754

pristine *adj* 122

privacy *n* 893

private *adj* 79, 221, 528, 533, 893

privately *adv* 881

privation *n* 776, 804

privilege *n* 748, 924, 927a

privileged *adj* 924, 927a

privy *adj* 528

privy to *adj* 490

prize *n* 618, 733, 793, 973; *v* 991

probability *n* 472

probability *n* 156

probable *adj* 472, 858

probably *adv* 472

probationary *adj* 675

probative *adj* 463, 478

probe *n* 262

probity *n* 939

probity *n* 543, 944

problem *n* 533, 704

problematical *adj* 59, 475

procedural *adj* 80, 626, 692

procedure *n* 80, 463, 626, 627, 680, 692, 998

proceed *v* 109, 282, 302

proceed from *v* 154

proceeding *n* 151, 282; *adj* 53

proceeds *n* 775

proceed with *v* 692

process *n* 627, 692

procession *n* 69, 266

proclaim *v* 531, 883

proclamation *n* 531, 985

proclivity *n* 176, 698, 820

procrastinate *v* 133

procrastination *n* 133, 683

procreate *v* 161, 168

procreation *n* 161, 168

procreative *adj* 168

procreator *n* 166

procure *v* 775, 795

procurement *n* 775

prod *v* 276

prodigal *n* 818; *adj* 638, 818

prodigality *n* 818

prodigality *n* 638

prodigal son *n* 950

prodigious *adj* 31

prodigy *n* 872

prodigy *n* 700

produce *n* 775, 798; *v* 153, 161, 168

produce a good effect *v* 648

produce nothing *v* 169

producer *n* 164

producer *n* 153

product *n* 84, 154, 161, 798

production *n* 161

production *n* 153

productive *adj* 153, 161, 168, 644

productiveness *n* 168

productiveness *n* 644

productivity *n* 168

proem *n* 64

profanation *n* 679

profane *v* 679, 988

profaneness *n* 988

profanity *n* 988

profession *n* 535, 625, 768

professional *n* 700; *adj* 625

professor *n* 540

proffer *v* 763

proficiency *n* 698, 731

proficient *adj* 698, 731

profile *n* 230, 236, 448; *v* 230

profit *n* 618, 775; *v* 618, 648, 775

profitability *n* 646

profitable *adj* 644, 646, 648, 775, 810

profit by *v* 677

profitless *adj* 645

profligacy *n* 818

profligate *n* 962; *adj* 818, 945

profound *adj* 31, 208, 498

profundity *n* 208, 875

profuse *adj* 102, 573, 641, 818

profuseness *n* 573, 641, 818

profusion *n* 102, 641, 818

progenitor *n* 166

progeny *n* 167

prognosticate *v* 507, 511, 909

prognostication *n* 511, 909

progress *n* 144, 264, 282, 731; *v* 282, 658, 731

progression *n* 282

progression *n* 58, 69

progressive *adj* 69, 282, 658

prohibit *v* 761, 893

prohibited *adj* 893, 964

prohibition *n* 761

prohibition *n* 55, 893

prohibitive *adj* 761

project *n* 620, 626; *v* 250, 284, 620, 626

projection *n* 250, 284

proletarian *adj* 876

proletariat *n* 876

prolific *adj* 161, 168

prolix *adj* 573

prolog *n* 64

prolong *v* 35, 110, 133, 143, 200

prolongation *n* 110, 133, 143

prolonged *adj* 110

promenade *n* 266

prominence *n* 206, 250, 307, 642

prominent *adj* 206, 250, 642

prominently *adv* 31, 33

promiscuous *adj* 41

promise *n* 768

promise *n* 771; *v* 676, 768, 769, 771

promised *adj* 768

promises *n* 770

promising *adj* 858

promissory *adj* 768, 769

promissory note *n* 771

promontory *n* 250

promote *v* 176, 658, 707

prompt *v* 505, 615; *adj* 132, 682

promptitude *n* 132, 684

promptness *n* 684

promulgate *v* 531

promulgation *n* 531

prone *adj* 207, 213, 820

proneness *n* 176, 207, 213

pronounce *v* 535, 580, 582, 586

pronouncement *n* 531, 535

proof *n* 463, 467, 478, 591

proofreader *n* 591

prop *n* 215; *v* 707

propagandist *n* 540

propagate *v* 161, 531

propagation *n* 168, 531

propane *n* 356, 388

propel *v* 264, 284

propensity *n* 176, 177, 602, 820

proper *adj* 79, 494, 578, 646, 868, 881, 922

proper name *n* 564

proper time *n* 134

property *n* 780

prophecy *n* 511

prophesy *v* 511

prophet *n* 513

prophetess *n* 513

prophetic *adj* 511

propinquity *n* 197

propitiate *v* 723, 826, 952

propitiating *adj* 952

propitiation *n* 952

propitiatory *adj* 952

propitious *adj* 134, 648, 734, 858, 888

proportion *n* 9, 242, 786

proportionate *adj* 413

proportions *n* 180, 192

proposal *n* 620, 763

propose *v* 476, 514, 620, 763

proposition *n* 476, 514, 763

propound *v* 514

proprietor *n* 779

proprietorship *n* 777

proprietress *n* 779

propriety *n* 578, 646, 852, 881

propulsion *n* 284

propulsion *n* 276

propulsive *adj* 284

propulsive force *n* 284

prop up *v* 215

prosaic *adj* 575, 598, 841, 843

pros and cons *n* 476

proscenium *n* 234

proscribe *v* 971

proscribed *adj* 964

proscription *n* 971

proscriptive *adj* 761

prose *n* 598

prosecute *v* 622, 680, 969

prosecuting attorney *n* 968

prosecution *n* 969

prosecutor *n* 938, 968

prospect *n* 121, 448, 472, 507, 510

prospective *adj* 507, 510

prospectively *adv* 121

prospects *n* 152

prospectus *n* 596

prosper *v* 731, 734

prosperity *n* 734

prosperity *n* 618, 731

prosperous *adj* 731, 734

prostitute *n* 962; *v* 679

prostitution *n* 679

prostrate *v* 213, 308; *adj* 207, 213, 308

prostration *n* 158, 207, 213, 308, 828

prosy *adj* 575, 598

protect *v* 664, 670, 717

protected *adj* 223

protection *n* 175, 664, 670, 717

protective *adj* 717

protector *n* 664, 753, 977

protest *n* 489, 764, 766, 808; *v* 489, 766

protester *n* 489

protoplasm *n* 357

prototype *n* 22

prototype *n* 80

protract *v* 110, 133, 200

protracted *adj* 110, 200, 573

protraction *n* 110, 133, 143

protrude *v* 250

protrusion *n* 250

protuberance *n* 250

protuberant *adj* 250

proud *adj* 878, 880

prove *v* 151, 463, 478

proved *adj* 478

proven *adj* 478

provender *n* 298, 637

proverb *n* 496

proverbial *adj* 496

provide *v* 637, 673, 746, 770

provide against *v* 673

provided *adj* 469; *adv* 8

provided that *adj* 469

providence *n* 976

provident *adj* 510, 673, 864

providential *adj* 134

providing *n* 637

province *n* 75, 181

provincial *adj* 181, 246

provision *n* 637

provision *n* 673, 803; *v* 637

provisional *adj* 8, 111, 673, 770

provisionally *adv* 8, 770

provisions *n* 298, 632, 770

proviso *n* 469

provisos *n* 770

provocation *n* 824

provocative *adj* 615

provoke *v* 153, 824, 830

prowl *v* 266

proximate *adj* 63, 197

proximation *n* 197

proximity *n* 186, 197, 199

proxy *n* 634, 759

prudence *n* 459, 480, 498, 510, 864

prudent *adj* 451, 459, 498, 510, 864

prudery *n* 881

prudish *adj* 881

prudishness *n* 881

prune *v* 38, 201

prurience *n* 961

prurient *adj* 961

pry *v* 441, 455

prying *n* 455; *adj* 455

pseudo *adj* 17

pseudonym *n* 565

psychical *adj* 317

puberty *n* 127, 131

pubescence *n* 131

pubescent *adj* 131

public *n* 372; *adj* 260, 372, 531

public address *n* 586

publication *n* 531

publication *n* 161, 590, 593, 985

publicity *n* 531

publicize *v* 531

public prosecutor *n* 968

public spirit *n* 910

public spirited *adj* 910

publish *v* 531, 591

published *adj* 527, 531

publisher *n* 593

pucker *n* 258; *v* 258, 259

puerile *adj* 129, 499, 575

puerility *n* 499

puff *n* 349; *v* 349, 688

puffery *n* 549

puffiness *n* 194

puff up *v* 194, 549, 880

pugnacious *adj* 720

puissance *n* 157

puissant *adj* 159

puke *v* 297

pulchritude *n* 845

pulchritudinous *adj* 845

pull *n* 288, 319; *v* 267, 285, 288, 301, 319

pull an all-nighter *v* 539

pulling *n* 285, 301

pull no punches *v* 703

pull out *v* 301

pull out of a hat *v* 612

pull out of the air *v* 612

pull the shade *v* 424

pull through *v* 660

pull together *v* 178, 709, 714

pull to pieces *v* 162

pull up *v* 142, 301

pulp *n* 354; *v* 354

pulpiness *n* 354

pulpy *adj* 354

pulsate *v* 138, 314, 315

pulsating *adj* 314, 315

pulsation *n* 138, 314

pulse *n* 138, 314

pulverization *n* 330

pulverize *v* 330

pulverulence *n* 330

pump *n* 348; *v* 349

pun *n* 520; *v* 842

punch *n* 22, 276; *v* 276

puncher *n* 262

punctilious *adj* 543, 772, 882

punctual *adj* 132, 138

punctuality *n* 132, 138

punctually *adv* 132

puncture *v* 260

pungency *n* 392

pungent *adj* 392, 394, 398, 574

punish *v* 972, 974

punished *v* 974; *adj* 972

punishing *adj* 972

punishment *n* 972

punishment *n* 974, 975

punitive *adj* 972

punster *n* 844

punt *v* 267

puny *adj* 193

pupil *n* 492, 541

puppet *n* 547

purblind *adj* 442, 443

purblindness *n* 443

purchase *n* 795

purchase *n* 775; *v* 795

purchaser *n* 795

purchasing *n* 795

pure *adj* 42, 494, 576, 578, 652, 881, 944, 946, 960, 977

purely *adv* 32

purgation *n* 652

purgative *n* 652

purge *v* 297, 652, 952

purification *n* 42, 652

purify *v* 42, 652

purist *n* 578

puritan *n* 955

puritanical *adj* 955

puritanism *n* 955

purity *n* 960

purity *n* 42, 578, 652, 944, 946

purlieus *n* 227

purloin *v* 791

purple *n* 437

purple *adj* 437

purplish *adj* 437

purport *n* 516; *v* 516

purpose *n* 451, 516, 600, 615, 620; *v* 451, 516, 620

purposeful *adj* 604

purposely *adv* 620

purr *v* 412

purring *n* 412

purse *n* 802

purser *n* 801

refraction *n* 279, 291, 420; 443
refractory *adj* 606, 719, 742, 945
refrain *v* 623, 681
refresh *v* 159, 338, 385, 660, 689, 829, 834
refreshing *adj* 689
refreshment *n* 689
refreshment *n* 159, 660
refrigerate *v* 383, 385
refrigeration *n* 385
refrigerator *n* 387
refuge *n* 666
refugee *n* 268, 623
refusal *n* 764
refusal *n* 603, 610
refuse *n* 40; *v* 536, 603, 610, 708, 764
refutable *adj* 479
refutation *n* 468, 479
refute *v* 468; 479
regale *v* 829
regalia *n* 747
regard *n* 441, 451, 457, 459, 873, 897, 928, 987, 990; *v* 9, 418, 451, 457, 480, 873, 928
regarded *adj* 873
regardful *adj* 451
regarding *n* 418; *adj* 928
regards *n* 928
regenerate *v* 163
regeneration *n* 163, 660
regenerative *adj* 163
reggae *n* 415
regicide *n* 361
regiment *n* 72
regimentals *n* 225
region *n* 181
regional *adj* 181
register *n* 86, 114, 551, 553, 811; *v* 60, 114, 551
registrar *n* 553
regnant *adj* 737
regress *n* 287; *v* 145, 283, 287
regression *n* 283
regression *n* 287
regressive *adj* 283
regret *n* 833
regret *n* 950; *v* 832, 833, 950
regretful *adj* 832, 833, 950
regular *adj* 16, 58, 60, 80, 138, 240, 242, 613
regular as clock-work *adj* 138

regularity *n* 138
regularity *n* 16, 58, 80, 138, 242
regularly *adv* 138
regulate *v* 58, 60, 174, 692, 693
regulation *n* 80
regulation *n* 693, 697, 963
regurgitate *v* 297, 348
regurgitation *n* 297
rehabilitate *v* 660, 790
rehabilitation *n* 660, 790
rehash *v* 104
rehearsal *n* 673
rehearse *v* 104, 594, 673
reign *n* 175
reimburse *v* 790, 807
reinforce *v* 37, 159
reinforcement *n* 39
reinstate *v* 660
reinstatement *n* 660
reinvest *v* 790
reinvestment *n* 790
reinvigorate *v* 660, 689
reiterate *v* 104, 136
reiteration *n* 104, 136
reject *v* 55, 297, 536, 610, 764, 893
rejected *adj* 893
rejection *n* 610
rejection *n* 55, 297, 536, 764, 893
rejoice *v* 836, 838
rejoice in *v* 827
rejoicing *n* 838
rejoin *v* 72, 462
rejoinder *n* 462
rekindle *v* 384
relapse *n* 661
relapse *v* 145, 287, 661
relate *v* 12, 216, 464, 594
related *adj* 9, 11
relate to *v* 9
relating *n* 464
relating to *adj* 9
relation *n* 9
relation *n* 11, 594
relationship *n* 9, 11
relative *n* 11; *adj* 9
relative to *adj* 9
relator *n* 938
relax *v* 47, 160, 275, 324, 683, 685, 687, 738
relaxation *n* 47, 160, 174, 687, 738, 840
relaxed *adj* 47, 160, 174

relaxing *adj* 840
release *n* 360, 671, 672, 750, 777a, 783, 807; *v* 672, 750, 777a, 927a, 970
released *adj* 970
relegate *v* 55, 270
relegation *n* 270
relent *v* 324
relentless *adj* 604, 739, 914a
relentlessness *n* 739
relevant *adj* 9
reliability *n* 150, 474
reliable *adj* 150, 246, 474, 664
reliance *n* 484, 507, 858
relic *n* 40, 124, 551
relics *n* 362
relied on *adj* 871
relief *n* 834
relief *n* 250, 660, 662, 689, 707
relieve *v* 707, 834
religion *n* 983
religious *adj* 983, 987
religious garments *n* 999
religious persuasion *n* 983
religious truth *n* 983a
religious writings *n* 986
relinquish *v* 624, 678, 757, 782
relinquishment *n* 624, 782
relinquishment *n* 678, 757
relish *n* 377, 390, 393, 394; *v* 377, 394, 827
relocate *v* 184
reluctance *n* 603, 704, 719
reluctant *adj* 603, 764
rely on *v* 484, 507, 858
remain *v* 1, 40, 106, 110, 141, 186, 265
remainder *n* 40
remaining *adj* 40
remains *n* 40, 362, 551
remake *v* 144
remark *v* 457
remarkable *adj* 31, 870
remarkably *adv* 31
remediable *adj* 660
remedial *adj* 660, 662
remediless *adj* 859

remedy *n* 662
remedy *v* 660, 662, 834
remember *v* 451, 505
remembrance *n* 505
remind *v* 505
reminder *n* 505
reminisce *v* 505
reminiscence *n* 505
reminiscent (of) *adj* 505
remiss *adj* 460, 674, 683, 738
remission *n* 756, 918
remissness *n* 460, 683
remit *v* 790
remittance *n* 807
remnant *n* 40
remodel *v* 140, 144, 146
remonstrance *n* 616, 766
remonstrate *v* 616, 766
remonstrative *adj* 766
remorse *n* 833, 950
remorseful *adj* 950
remorseless *adj* 951
remote *adj* 10, 196
remote cause *n* 153
remoteness *n* 196
remote past *n* 122
removable *adj* 38
removal *n* 38, 185, 270, 287, 293, 301
remove *n* 196; *v* 2, 38, 185, 270, 301, 662
removed *adj* 196
remunerate *v* 30, 807, 973
remuneration *n* 973
remunerative *adj* 775, 810, 973
renaissance *n* 660
renascence *n* 660
renascent *adj* 163, 660
rend *v* 44
render *v* 144, 784, 790
render blunt *v* 254
render certain *v* 474
render concave *v* 252
render curved *v* 245
render few *v* 103
render general *v* 78
render horizontal *v* 213
render insensible *v* 376
render intelligible *v* 518

render invisible *v* 447
render oblique *v* 217
render powerless *v* 158
render sensible *v* 375
render straight *v* 246
render uncertain *v* 475
render unintelligible *v* 519
render violent *v* 173
rendezvous *n* 74
renegade *n* 607
renew *v* 90, 123, 163, 660, 689
renewal *n* 90, 163, 660,
renounce *v* 536, 607, 610, 624, 757, 764, 782
renovate *v* 123, 163, 660
renovated *adj* 123
renovation *n* 123, 163, 660
renown *n* 31, 873
renowned *adj* 873, 883
rent *n* 44, 198, 260; *v* 788
renunciation *n* 607, 610, 624, 757, 764, 782
reorganize *v* 144, 660
repair *n* 658, 660, 689; *v* 658, 660, 662, 689, 790, 952
reparation *n* 30, 660, 790, 952, 973
reparatory *adj* 973
repartee *n* 842
repay *v* 718
repeal *n* 756; *v* 756
repeat *v* 90, 104, 136
repeated *adj* 104
repeatedly *adv* 104, 136
repel *v* 289, 610, 616, 717, 719, 764, 830, 867
repellant *adj* 830
repellent *adj* 289, 719, 867
repelling *adj* 289
repent *v* 833, 950, 952
repentance *n* 833, 950
repentant *adj* 950
repenting *adj* 950
repercussion *n* 145
repetition *n* 104

scope *n* 26, 180, 748
scorch *v* 384
scorched *adj* 384
score *n* 98, 259, 805, 806, 811; *v* 259
scores *n* 102
scorn *n* 930; *v* 715, 929, 930
scornful *adj* 929, 930
scotch *v* 659
scot free *adj* 748
scoundrel *n* 941, 949
scour *v* 331, 652
scourge *n* 975
scourge *v* 663, 972
scour the country *v* 266
scout *n* 664, 668
scowl *v* 900, 901a
scraggly *adj* 256
scramble *n* 59, 684; *v* 684
scrap *n* 32
scrape *n* 704, 732; *v* 38, 195, 255, 330, 331
scratch *n* 257, 259; *v* 257, 331, 380, 590, 649
scratching *n* 380; *adj* 410
scratchy *adj* 380
scrawl *v* 590
scrawny *adj* 203
scream *n* 411, 669; *v* 404, 410, 411, 839
screech *v* 411, 412
screeching *n* 412; *adj* 414
screen *n* 223, 424, 530, 717; *v* 424, 442, 528, 664, 717
screening *n* 528
screw *n* 243; *v* 43, 243
screw up the eyes *v* 443
scribble *v* 590
scribe *n* 553, 590
scrimp *v* 819
script *n* 590, 593
scriptural *adj* 983a
Sriptures *n* 985, 986
scrivener *n* 590
Scrooge *n* 819
scrub *v* 331, 652
scruple *n* 485
scrupulous *adj* 246, 459, 543, 603, 772, 868, 939
srupulousness *n* 603
scrutinize *v* 457
scrutinizing *adj* 461
scrutiny *n* 457, 461
scull *v* 267
sculpt *v* 557

sculptor *n* 559
sculpture *n* 557
scum of the earth *n* 949
scurrilous *adj* 934
scurry *v* 684
scuttle *v* 162
scuttlebutt *n* 532
sea *n* 341
sea dog *n* 269
seafaring *adj* 267
seafaring man *n* 269
sea-girt *adj* 346
seagoing *adj* 267, 341
sea-green *adj* 435
seal *n* 22; *v* 261, 550
sealing *n* 261
sealing wax *n* 356a
seam *n* 43; *v* 259
sea-maid *n* 979
seaman *n* 269
sear *v* 384
search *n* 461, 539, 622; *v* 461
season *n* 106, 106 *v* 41, 392, 393, 613, 673
seasonable *adj* 134
seasoned *adj* 392
seasoning *n* 41, 393
seat *v* 184
seat of activity *n* 691
secession *n* 624
seclude *v* 55, 87
secluded *adj* 893
seclude oneself *v* 893
seclusion *n* 893
seclusion *n* 55
second *n* 113, 759; *v* 707; *adj* 90
secondary *adj* 32, 34, 651
secondary color *n* 428
second hand *adj* 19
second-rate *adj* 34, 651
second-story man *n* 792
second thoughts *n* 65
second to none *n* 648
secrecy *n* 528, 893
secret *n* 533
secret *adj* 221, 526, 528, 533
secretary *n* 553, 590
secrete *v* 299, 528
secretion *n* 299, 528
secretive *adj* 528, 533
secretiveness *n* 528
secretly *adv* 528
secret place *n* 530
sect *n* 75

section *n* 51, 75
sectional *adj* 51
secular *adj* 997
secularize *v* 997
secure *v* 43, 132, 664, 717, 768, 775, 781; *adj* 43, 150, 484, 664
secure an objective *v* 731
securities *n* 802
security *n* 771
security *n* 664, 717, 721
sedate *adj* 826
seducer *n* 962
seduction *n* 829
seductive *adj* 288, 615, 829
see *v* 441, 457, 480a, 484
seed *n* 32, 153; *v* 371
see double *v* 443
seedy *adj* 160, 659, 804
see fit *v* 600
seeing that *adv* 8
seek *v* 461, 622
seeker *n* 268, 767
seek refuge *v* 666
seem *v* 448
seeming *n* 448; *adj* 448
seemingly *adv* 448
seemliness *n* 845
seemly *adj* 845
see one's future *v* 510
seer *n* 130, 504, 513
seesaw *adv* 314
seethe *v* 382
see the light *v* 359
seething *adj* 824
see-through *adj* 425
segment *n* 51, 100a
segregate *v* 44, 55
segregated *adj* 47
segregation *n* 44, 55
seize *v* 789
seize the day *v* 134
seize the opportunity *v* 134, 682
seize the time *v* 134
seizure *n* 789
seldom *adv* 137
select *v* 609; *adj* 648
selection *n* 609
self *n* 13; *adj* 13
self-abnegation *n* 955
self-admiration *n* 880
self-assurance *n* 878
self-assured *adj* 878
self-centered *adj* 943
self-command *n* 604

self-complacency *n* 880
self-complacent *adj* 880
self-contradictory *adj* 497
self-control *n* 600, 604, 953
self-controlled *adj* 953
self-deception *n* 486
self-delusion *n* 486
self-denial *n* 604, 955
self-denying *adj* 955
self-depreciation *n* 483
self-esteem *n* 878, 880
self-glorification *n* 880
self-importance *n* 878
self-indulgence *n* 954
self-indulgent *adj* 943, 954
self-interest *n* 943
self-interested *adj* 943
selfish *adj* 32, 819, 943
selfishness *n* 943
selfishness *n* 32, 819
self-love *n* 880, 943
self-luminous *adj* 423
self-mortifying *adj* 955
self-motification *n* 955
self-possessed *adj* 502
self-possession *n* 604, 826
self-reliance *n* 604
self-respect *n* 878
self-restrained *adj* 953
self-restraint *n* 604, 826, 953
selfsame *adj* 13
self-satisfied *adj* 878
self-seeking *n* 943; *adj* 943
self-styled *adj* 565
sell *v* 796, 798
seller *n* 796, 797
sell for *v* 812
selling *n* 796
semblance *n* 17, 19, 21, 216, 882
semi- *adj* 91
semi-circular *adj* 245
semifluid *adj* 352
semiliquid *adj* 352

semiliquidity *n* 352
seminary *n* 542
semiology *n* 550
semiopaque *adj* 427
semipellucid *adj* 427
semitransparency *n* 427
semitransparent *adj* 427
send *v* 270
send a letter *v* 592
send off *v* 284
senile *adj* 124, 128, 158
senility *n* 124, 128, 158, 160, 659
seniority *n* 128
sensation *n* 375, 379, 390
sensational *adj* 824
sensations of touch *n* 380
sense *n* 450, 498, 502, 516, 842
senseless *adj* 376, 497, 499, 517
senselessness *n* 517
sense of duty *n* 926
sensibility *n* 375, 822
sensibility *n* 821
sensible *adj* 316, 375, 498, 502
sensical *adj* 450
sensitive *adj* 375, 597, 821, 822
sensitiveness *n* 375, 822
sensitivity *n* 821, 901
sensitize *v* 375
sensual *adj* 377, 829
sensual delight *n* 377
sensualist *n* 954a
sensualist *n* 962
sensuality *n* 377, 827
sensuous *adj* 375, 377
sensuousness *n* 377
sentence *n* 972
sententious *adj* 577
sentient *adj* 375
sentiment *n* 453, 821
sentimental *adj* 822
sentimentalism *n* 822
sentimentality *n* 821, 822
sentinel *n* 444, 664, 668
sentry *n* 668
separate *v* 44, 55, 291, 905; *adj* 44
separated *adj* 905
separately *adv* 44

speak one's mind *v* 703

speak plainly *v* 576

speak prettily *v* 521

speak softly *v* 405

speak the truth *v* 543

speak to *v* 586

spear *n* 262; *v* 260, 361

special *n* 79; *adj* 20, 79, 474

special committee *n* 755

specialist *n* 700

speciality *n* 79

specialize *v* 79

specially *adv* 79

specialty *n* 79

species *n* 75

specific *n* 662; *adj* 79

specify *v* 79, 564

specimen *n* 82

specious *adj* 477, 545

speciousness *n* 477

speck *n* 32, 848

speckle *v* 440

speckled *adj* 440

spectacle *n* 448, 872

spectacles *n* 445

spectator *n* 444

specter *n* 980; 443

spectral *adj* 2, 4, 980

spectroscope *n* 428

spectrum *n* 428

speculate *v* 155, 514, 621, 675, 870

speculation *n* 156, 451, 514, 621, 675

speculative *adj* 514, 621, 675

speech *n* 582

speech *n* 560, 586

speech impediment *n* 583

speechless *adj* 403, 581, 583

speechlessness *n* 403, 590

speed *n* 264, 274, 684; *v* 274, 682, 684

speedily *adv* 132

speediness *n* 132

speed up *v* 274

speedy *adj* 274, 684

spell *n* 993

spell *n* 106, 198, 992; *v* 561, 707

spell-bound *adj* 870

spelling *n* 561

spend *v* 638, 809

spend freely *v* 816

spendthrift *adj* 638, 818

spend time *v* 106

spent *adj* 158, 160, 688

spew *v* 297

sphere *n* 26, 181, 249, 318; *v* 249

spherical *adj* 249

sphericity *n* 249

spheroid *n* 249

spice *n* 41, 393; *v* 392

spiced *adj* 392

spick and span *adj* 123

spicy *adj* 392, 400

spigot *n* 263

spike *n* 253, 263; *v* 260

spiked *adj* 253

spiky *adj* 253

spill *v* 348

spin *n* 266; *v* 312

spin a melody *v* 416

spin around *v* 312

spindly *adj* 203

spine *n* 253

spineless *adj* 862

spinelessness *n* 172

spinning *n* 312

spin out *v* 200

spinster *n* 904

spiny *adj* 253

spiral *n* 248, 311; *adj* 248

spirit *n* 5, 171, 359, 516, 574, 682, 709, 820, 861, 977, 980

spirited *adj* 171, 574, 836, 861

spiritual *adj* 2, 317, 976, 977

spiritualism *n* 992

spirituality *n* 317

spit *v* 260

spite *n* 907

spiteful *adj* 898, 907, 919, 945

spitefulness *n* 907

splash *n* 348; *v* 337, 348, 653

splendid *adj* 420

splendor *n* 420, 845, 882

splice *v* 43, 219

splint *n* 215

splinter *n* 32; *v* 44, 328

splintery *adj* 328

split *n* 44, 713; *v* 44, 91, 293, 328, 713, 838

split down the middle *v* 91

split hairs *v* 868

split one's sides *v* 838

split the difference *v* 29

split the differences *v* 774

split the eardrums *v* 404, 419

split up *v* 778, 905; *adj* 51, 905

spoil *v* 397, 659

spoilage *n* 659

spoilation *n* 638

spoiled *adj* 397

spoiled child *n* 899

spoiler *n* 165

spoils *n* 793

spokesman *n* 524, 534, 582

sponge *v* 339, 340

sponginess *n* 354

sponsor *v* 771

sponsorship *n* 771

spontaneous *adj* 612

spook *n* 980

spoonful *n* 25, 32

sporadic *adj* 103, 137, 139

sport *v* 840

spot *n* 182, 848, 874; *v* 653, 848

spotless *adj* 650, 652, 946, 960

spotlessness *n* 946

spotted *adj* 440

spottiness *n* 440

spotty *adj* 440

spouse *n* 903

spout *n* 348, 350; *v* 295, 348, 582

sprawl *v* 200, 213, 306

spray *n* 353

spread *n* 180, 291; *v* 73, 194, 291, 531; *adj* 73

spreading *n* 73, 194

spread out *v* 35, 194

spread the sails *v* 267

spread to *v* 196

sprightliness *n* 829

sprightly *adj* 829, 836

spring *n* 153, 159, 309, 325, 348; *v* 274, 309, 325

spring back *v* 277, 325

spring from *v* 154

springiness *n* 325

springtime *n* 125

spring up *v* 367

springy *adj* 309, 325

sprinkle *v* 73, 337

sprinkling *n* 32, 41

sprite *n* 979, 980

sprout *v* 35, 194, 367

spruce *adj* 652

spry *adj* 682

spun-out *adj* 110

spur *n* 250, 253, 615; *v* 615

spurious *adj* 544

spurn *v* 764, 866

spurning *n* 764

spurt *n* 274, 348, 612, 684; *v* 348

sputter *v* 348, 583

spy *n* 444, 455; *v* 441, 455

spyglass *n* 445

spying *n* 455; *adj* 455

squabble *n* 713, 720; *v* 713

squad *n* 72

squadron *n* 72

squalid *adj* 653, 846

squall *n* 349

squalor *n* 653

squander *v* 162, 638, 679, 818

squanderer *n* 818

squandering *n* 818

square *n* 857; *v* 30, 95, 660; *adj* 246

square accounts *v* 807

square one *n* 66

square-rigger *n* 273

square with *v* 23

squash *v* 162, 195, 352, 354, 409

squashy *adj* 345

squat *v* 184; *adj* 193, 201, 202, 207

squawking *adj* 410

squeak *v* 411, 412

squeal *v* 411

squeeze *v* 195, 348, 354

squeeze out *v* 301

squeezing *n* 195, 301

squelch *v* 162

squint *n* 443; *v* 443

squirt *n* 348

squishy *adj* 324

stab *v* 260, 361, 649

stability *n* 150

stability *n* 16, 110, 141

stabilization *n* 150

stabilize *v* 150

stable *adj* 110, 141, 150, 265

staff *n* 215, 696, 747

staff of life *n* 359

stag *n* 373

stage *n* 26, 71, 106, 204, 728

stage business *n* 599

stage name *n* 565

stage-play *n* 599

stagey *adj* 855

stagger *v* 275, 314, 315, 508, 824, 870

stagnant *adj* 265, 901a

stagnate *v* 265

stagnation *n* 265

stagy *adj* 599

staid *adj* 826

stain *n* 428, 874; *v* 428, 653, 848, 874

stained *adj* 961

stainless *adj* 652

stake *n* 621, 771; *v* 621

stale *adj* 124, 659

stalk *n* 215

stall *v* 133

stallion *n* 373

stalwart *adj* 192

stamina *n* 159, 604a

stammer *v* 583

stammering *n* 583

stamp *n* 7, 22; *v* 240, 550

stamp out *v* 162, 385

stand *n* 71, 211, 719; *v* 106, 110, 141, 719

stand a chance *v* 177, 470

stand aloof *v* 681

standard *n* 22, 26, 80, 466, 650; *adj* 29, 82, 650

standardization *n* 16

standardize *v* 58

stand as an example *v* 82

stand as opposites *v* 237

stand at the head *v* 66

stand by *v* 186

stand condemned *v* 971

stand convicted *v* 754

stand erect *v* 212

stand fast *v* 141, 265

stand firm *v* 150, 265, 604

stand for *v* 147, 550, 759, 771

stand immobile *v* 265

stand-in *n* 634

stand in front *v* 234

standing *n* 8, 26, 71, 110, 183, 873

stand next to *v* 197

stand one in good stead *v* 644

stand out *v* 250

standpoint *n* 183, 441

stand still *v* 265

stand straight and tall *v* 212

stand the test *v* 648

stand to reason *v* 474

stand up v 719
stand upright v 212
stand up straight v 212
staple commodity n 798
staples n 635
starboard n 238
starchy adj 352
stare n 441; v 455, 870
stark adj 31
stark-naked adj 226
stars n 423
start n 66, 293; v 66, 151, 276, 284, 293, 309, 870
start again v 66
start fresh v 652
starting point n 66, 293
startle v 508, 824, 870
startled adj 870
startling adj 508, 870
start over v 66
start up v 250, 446
starvation n 956
starve v 385, 804, 819, 955, 956
starved adj 956
starving adj 956
starving oneself n 956
stash n 636; v 636
state n 7
state n 188; v 516, 535
stated adj 474
stateliness n 875
stately adj 875, 878
statement n 535, 594, 811
station n 26, 71, 183; v 184
stationary adj 265
statistical adj 85
statistics n 85
statuary n 557
statue n 557, 963, 991
statuette n 557
stature n 206
status n 7, 8, 71
statute n 697; 963
staunch adj 150, 604a
stave in v 252
stay n 133, 215, 685; v 1, 133, 141, 142, 186, 265
stay away v 187
stay in the background v 881
stay together v 46
stead n 644
steadfast adj 150, 604, 604a

steadfastness n 150, 604a
steadiness n 138, 150
steady adj 80, 138, 150, 604a
steal v 275, 789, 791
steal a march on v 132
steal away v 623, 671
steal from v 788
stealing n 791
stealing n 788
stealthily adv 528
stealthy adj 528, 702
steam n 353; v 267, 336, 353
steamer n 273
steaming n 336
steam press v 255
steam up v 353
steamy adj 353
steel v 159
steep v 337; adj 217, 306
steepness n 217
steer n 373; v 693
steerage n 693
steer a middle course v 628
steer clear of v 279, 623
steer for v 278
steersman n 269
stench n 401
stencil n 21
stenography n 590
stentorian adj 404, 411
step n 71, 264
step by step adv 26, 58, 69, 275
step in v 724
steppe n 344
stereoscope n 445
sterile adj 158, 169
sterility n 169
stern adj 604, 739, 955
sternness n 739
stew v 382, 384
steward n 801; v 693
stewardship n 693
stewed adj 959
stewed to the gills adj 959
stick n 215, 975; v 46, 260
stick fast v 150, 265
stick in v 300
stickiness n 46, 352, 396
stick it out v 604a
stick out v 250
stick to v 143
stick to an idea v 606

stick up v 250
sticky adj 46, 327, 352, 396
stiff adj 240, 579, 739
stiff breeze n 349
stiffen v 323
stiffness n 246, 579
stifle v 361, 403
stifled adj 405
stifling adj 382
stiletto n 262
still v 174, 403, 723; adj 174, 265, 403; adv 30
still-born adj 732
stillness n 265, 403
stilted adj 307, 577, 855
stilts n 215
stimulate v 171, 173, 382, 615, 689, 824, 829
stimulating adj 171
stimulation n 824
stimulus n 615
sting v 378, 380, 663
stinginess n 819, 943
stinging n 380; adj 392
stingy adj 819, 943
stink n 401; v 401, 653
stinking adj 401
stinky adj 401
stint v 819
stipple v 558
stipulate v 769, 770
stipulations n 770
stir n 264, 315, 682, 752; v 264, 315, 375, 382, 824
stir about v 682
stirring adj 151, 505
stir up v 173, 824
stitch n 43, 378, 828; v 43
stock n 11, 25, 635, 636, 637, 798; v 637; adj 598, 613
stocks n 802
stock-still adj 265
stockyard n 232
stoical adj 383, 826
stoicism n 826
stoke v 388
stolen away adj 671
stolen goods n 793
stolid adj 499, 843
stolidity n 499
stomach v 826
stone-blind adj 442
stone-deaf adj 419
stone's throw n 197
stony adj 914a
stoop v 217, 306, 886

stop n 133, 142, 360; v 67, 70, 142, 261, 265, 403
stopcock n 263
stopgap n 147
stoppage n 142, 261, 706
stop payment v 808
stopper n 263
stopper n 261
stopping n 142, 263, 706
stop short v 142, 265
stop up v 261
stopwatch n 114
storage n 636
storage areas n 191
store n 636
store n 31, 637, 798, 799; v 72, 636, 637, 670
store up v 636
storing n 636
storm n 173, 315, 348, 349; v 173, 349, 716
stormy adj 173, 349
story n 204, 546, 593
storyteller n 548
stout adj 159, 192
stout-hearted adj 861
stoutness n 159
stove n 386
stow away v 528
strabismus n 443
straggle v 279
straggler n 268
straggling adj 59
straight n 857; adj 212, 246, 278, 807, 958; adv 132, 278
straighten v 246
straighten out v 60
straightforward adj 543, 703, 849; adv 278
straight line n 246
straightness n 246
straightway adv 132
strain n 402, 413, 415, 686; v 42, 686, 688
strait n 704
strait-laced adj 739
straitness n 203
straits n 343, 804
strand n 205, 205
strange adj 10, 83, 519, 870
strangely adv 31
strangle v 158, 361
strangulation n 361
strap n 975; v 43
strapper n 192
strapping adj 159

stratagem n 545, 626, 702
strategic adj 626
strategical adj 692
strategist n 626
strategy n 692, 722
stratified adj 204
stratosphere n 338
stratum n 204, 213
straw-colored adj 435
stray v 279; adj 73, 279
streak n 259, 420; v 440
streaked adj 440
streakiness n 440
stream n 347
stream n 264, 347, 348, 420; v 72, 264, 333, 348, 349
streamy adj 348
street-walker n 962
strength n 159
strength n 25, 26, 31, 157, 171, 327, 364, 739
strengthen v 157, 159, 171, 689
strengthening n 159
strength of mind n 604
strenuous adj 686
stress n 580, 642, 686
stretch n 180; v 194, 200, 325
stretch out v 200
stretch the meaning v 523
stretch to v 196, 200
strew v 73
strewn adj 73
striate v 440; adj 440
striated adj 259
striation n 440
stricken adj 828
strict adj 82, 739, 955, 983a
strictness n 739, 983a
stricture n 706
stride n 264
stride forward v 282
stridency n 410
strident adj 410
strife n 713, 720
strike v 170, 276
strike a balance v 27
strike dumb v 581
strike out v 552
strike up v 416
strike while the iron is hot v 134
strikingly adv 31
string n 69; v 43
stringency n 739
stringent adj 739

strings

unanswerable